The Catholic Encyclopedia

VOLUME TWO

Assize—Brownr

THE CATHOLIC ENCYCLOPEDIA

AN INTERNATIONAL WORK OF REFERENCE
ON THE CONSTITUTION, DOCTRINE,
DISCIPLINE, AND HISTORY OF THE
CATHOLIC CHURCH

EDITED BY

CHARLES G. HERBERMANN, Ph.D., LL.D.

EDWARD A. PACE, Ph.D., D.D.   CONDÉ B. PALLEN, Ph.D., LL.D.

THOMAS J. SHAHAN, D.D.   JOHN J. WYNNE, S.J.

ASSISTED BY NUMEROUS COLLABORATORS

IN FIFTEEN VOLUMES
VOLUME II

New York
ROBERT APPLETON COMPANY

List of Contributors to the Second Volume

A'BECKET, JOHN J., Ph.D, New York.

AIKEN, CHARLES F., S.T.D., Professor of Apologetics, Catholic University of America, Washington.

ALBERT, F. X. E., Ph.D., St. Joseph's Seminary, Dunwoodie, New York.

ALSTON, G. CYPRIAN, O.S.B., Downside Abbey, Bath, England.

ARBEZ, EDWARD PHILIP, M.A., Professor of Sacred Scripture, St. Patrick's Seminary, Menlo Park, California.

ARENDZEN, J. P., Ph.D., S.T.D., B.A., Professor of Holy Scripture, St. Edmund's College, Ware, England.

AVELING, FRANCIS, S.T.D., Westminster, London.

BANDELIER, AD. F., Hispanic Society of America, New York.

BARRET, T. B., S.J., Professor of Moral Theology, Woodstock College, Maryland.

BATTANDIER, ALBERT, S.T.D., J.C.D., Rome.

BECCARI, CAMILLO, S.J., Postulator General of the Society of Jesus, Rome.

BECHTEL, F., S.J., Professor of Hebrew and Sacred Scripture, St. Louis University, St. Louis.

BENIGNI, U., Professor of Ecclesiastical History, Pont. Collegio Urbano di Propaganda, Rome.

BESSE, J. M., O.S.B., Director, "Revue Mabillon", Chevetogne, Belgium.

BIRKHÆUSER, J. A., Racine, Wisconsin.

BIRT, HENRY NORBERT, O.S.B., London.

BOLLING, GEORGE MELVILLE, A.B., Ph.D., Professor of Greek and Sanskrit, Catholic University of America, Washington.

BOOTHMAN, C. T., Kingstown, Ireland.

BREEN, A. E., S.T.D., Ph.D., Professor of Holy Scripture, St. Bernard's Seminary, Rochester, New York.

BROCK, H. M., S.J., Professor of Physics, Holy Cross College, Worcester, Massachusetts.

BROM, GISBERT, S.T.D., Ph.D., Litt.D., Head of the Dutch Historical Institute at Rome, Utrecht, Holland.

BRUCHESI, PAUL, S.T.D., Archbishop of Montreal.

†BRUNETIERE, FERDINAND, Member of the French Academy, Director, "Revue des Deux Mondes", Paris.

BUONAIUTI, ERNESTO, Ph.D., S.T.D., Rome.

BURKE, EDMUND, A.B., Instructor in Latin, College of the City of New York.

BURTON, EDWIN, S.T.D., F. R. Hist. Soc., St. Edmund's College, Ware, England.

BURTSELL, R. L., Ph.D., S.T.D., Rondout, New York.

BUTIN, R., S.M., S.T.L., Ph.D., Marist College, Washington.

CABROL, FERNAND, O.S.B., Abbot of St. Michael's, Farnborough, England.

CAMM, BEDE, O.S.B., B.A. (Oxon.), Birmingham, England.

CAMPBELL, T. J., S.J., Associate Editor, "The Messenger", New York.

CANDIDE, F., O.M.Cap., Lector in Philosophy, Capuchin Monastery, Limoilou, Province of Quebec.

CASARTELLI, L. C., S.T.D., Bishop of Salford, England.

CASTLE, HAROLD, C.SS.R., M.A. (Oxon.) Lector in Theology and Church History, St. Mary's, Kinnoul, Perth, Scotland.

CASWELL, JOHN, Kenilworth, England.

CHAPMAN, JOHN, O.S.B., B.A. (Oxon.), Prior of St. Thomas's Abbey, Erdington, Birmingham, England.

CHRYSOSTOM, BROTHER, F.S.C., A.M., Manhattan College, New York.

CLEARY, HENRY W., Editor, "New Zealand Tablet", Dunedin, New Zealand.

†CLERKE, AGNES M., Hon. Member of the Royal Astronomical Society, London.

CLIFFORD, CORNELIUS, Seton Hall College, South Orange, New Jersey.

† Deceased.

v

COLEMAN, CARYL, B.A., Pelham Manor, New York.

CONDON, PETER, New York.

CONNELLAN, P. L., F.R.S.A. of Ireland, Knight of St. Gregory the Great, Rome.

CORBETT, JOHN, S.J., Professor of Holy Scripture, Woodstock College, Maryland.

COTTER, JAMES M., S.J., Woodstock College, Maryland.

CREAGH, JOHN T., J.U.D., Professor of Canon Law, Catholic University of America, Washington.

CROWNE, J. VINCENT, A.M., Ph.D., Instructor in English, College of the City of New York.

D'ALTON, E. A., M.R.I.A., Athenry, Ireland.

DE LAAK, H., S.J., Professor of Physics and Mathematics, St. Louis University, St. Louis.

DELAMARRE, LOUIS N., Ph.D., Instructor in French, College of the City of New York.

DELANEY, JOSEPH F., New York.

de MOREIRA, M., A.M., Litt.D., New York.

DE SMEDT, CH., S.J., Brussels.

DEVINE, E. J., S.J., Woodstock College, Maryland.

DEVITT, E. J., S.J., Professor of Psychology, Georgetown University, Washington.

DEVLIN, WILLIAM, S.J., Woodstock College, Maryland.

DIERINGER, BARNABAS, Professor of Languages and Music, St. Francis Seminary, St. Francis, Wisconsin.

DIONNE, N. E., S.B., M.D., Librarian to the Legislature of Quebec.

DISSEZ, P., Professor of Pastoral Theology, St. Mary's Seminary, Baltimore.

DONNELLY, F. P., S.J., St. Andrew-on-Hudson, Poughkeepsie, New York.

DONOVAN, STEPHEN M., O.F.M., Franciscan Monastery, Washington.

DOUMIC, RENE, Literary and Dramatic Critic, "Revue des Deux Mondes", Paris.

DRISCOLL, JAMES F., D.D., President of St. Joseph's Seminary, Dunwoodie, New York.

DRURY, EDWIN, Nerinx, Kentucky.

DUBRAY, C. A., S.T.B., Ph.D., Professor of Philosophy, Marist College, Washington.

DUMONT, F. M. L., President of Divinity College, Catholic University of America, Washington.

DUNN, JOSEPH, Ph.D., Assistant Professor of Celtic Languages and Literature, Catholic University of America, Washington.

EGAN, ANDREW, O.F.M., Professor of Theology, The Friary, Forest Gate, London.

FANNING, WILLIAM H. W., S.J., Professor of Church History and Canon Law, St. Louis University, St. Louis.

FENLON, JOHN F., S.S., S.T.D., President St. Austin's College, Brookland, D. C., Professor of Sacred Scripture, St. Mary's Seminary, Baltimore.

FERNANDES, P. A., Bassein, India.

FLAHERTY, M. J., A.M., Professor of the History of Philosophy and English, St. John's Seminary, Brighton, Massachusetts.

FORD, HUGH EDMUND, O.S.B., Abbot of Glastonbury, Downside Abbey, Bath, England.

FOURNET, A., S.S., Professor of Belles-Lettres, Collège de Montréal, Montreal.

FOX, JAMES J., S.T.D., B.A., Professor of Philosophy, St. Thomas's College, Washington.

FOX, WILLIAM, B.S., M.E., Associate Professor of Physics, College of the City of New York.

†FRISBEE, S. H., S.J., Woodstock College, Maryland.

FUENTES, VENTURA, A.B., M.D., Instructor, College of the City of New York.

FUREY, JOHN, Pay Inspector U. S. N. (Retired), Brooklyn, New York.

GANS, LEO, J.C.D., Professor of Canon Law, The St. Paul Seminary, St. Paul, Minnesota.

GANSS, HENRY G., Mus. D., Carlisle, Pennsylvania.

GAUDET, LOUIS, Scorton, Yorkshire, England.

GEOGHAN, J. J., S.J., Woodstock College, Maryland.

GERARD, JOHN, S.J., F.L.S., London.

GEUDENS, FRANCIS MARTIN, O.Præm., Abbot Titular of Barlings, Corpus Christi Priory, Manchester, England.

GIETMANN, G., S.J., St. Ignatius College, Valkenburg, Holland.

GIGNAC, JOS. N., S.T.D., J.C.D., Professor of Canon Law, University of Laval, Quebec.

† Deceased.

GIGOT, FRANCIS E., S.T.D., Professor of Sacred Scripture, St. Joseph's Seminary, Dunwoodie, New York.

GILDAS, M., O.C.R., La Trappe, Quebec.

GILLIAT-SMITH, FREDERICK ERNEST, Bruges.

GILLIGAN, EDWARD A., S.S., A.M., Washington.

GILLIS, JAMES M., C.S.P., S.T.L., St. Thomas's College, Washington.

GOGGIN, J. F., S.T.D., Ph.D., St. Bernard's Seminary, Rochester, New York.

GOODWIN, ENEAS B., A.M., B.D., La Grange, Illinois.

GOYAU, GEORGES, Associate Editor, "Revue des Deux Mondes", Paris.

GRATTAN FLOOD, W. H., M.R.I.A., Mus.D., Rosemount, Enniscorthy, Ireland.

GULDNER, B., S.J., St. Joseph's College, Philadelphia.

HAGEN, JOHN G., S.J., Vatican Observatory, Rome.

HANDLEY, M. L., Madison, New Jersey.

HANNA, EDWARD J., S.T.D., Professor of Theology, St. Bernard's Seminary, Rochester, New York.

HARTIG, OTTO, Assistant Librarian of the Royal and City Library, Munich.

HASSETT, MAURICE M., S.T.D., Harrisburg, Pennsylvania.

HAVEY, FRANCIS P., S.S., S.T.D., Professor of Homiletics and Pastoral Theology, St. John's Seminary, Brighton, Massachusetts.

HEALY, PATRICK J., S.T.D., Assistant Professor of Church History, Catholic University of America, Washington.

HENRY, H. T., Litt.D., Rector of Roman Catholic High School for Boys, Professor of English Literature and of Gregorian Chant, St. Charles's Seminary, Overbrook, Pennsylvania.

HERRICK, JOS. C., Ph.D., Professor of Experimental Psychology and Biology, St. Joseph's Seminary, Dunwoodie, New York.

HOFFMANN, ALEXIUS, O.S.B., St. John's College, Collegeville, Minnesota.

HOLWECK, FREDERICK G., St. Louis.

HOWLETT, J. A., O.S.B., M.A., Suffolk, England.

HULL, ERNEST R., S.J., Editor, "The Examiner", Bombay, India.

HUNT, LEIGH, Professor of Art, College of the City of New York.

HUNTER-BLAIR, D. O., Bart., O.S.B., M.A., Oxford, England.

HYDE, DOUGLAS, LL.D., Litt.D., M.R.I.A., French Park, Roscommon, Ireland.

INGOLD, A. M. P., Director, "Revue d'Alsace", Colmar, Germany.

JACOBI, MAX, Ph.D., Munich.

JUNGNITZ, JOSEPH, S.T.D., Diocesan Archivist, Breslau, Germany.

KAVANAGH, D. J., S.J., Woodstock College, Maryland.

KELLY, G. E., S.J., Woodstock College, Maryland.

KELLY, PATRICK H., S.J., St. Peter's College, Jersey City, New Jersey.

KENT, W. H., O.S.C., Bayswater, London.

KERBY, WILLIAM J., S.T.L., Ph.D., Doctor of Social and Political Sciences, Professor of Sociology, Catholic University of America, Washington.

KIMBALL, CHARLES L., S.J., Professor of Latin and Greek, Holy Cross College, Worcester, Massachusetts.

KIRSCH, Mgr. J. P., Professor of Patrology and Christian Archæology, University of Fribourg, Switzerland.

KLAAR, KARL, Government Archivist, Innsbruck.

KURTH, GODEFROI, Director, Belgian Historical Institute, Liège.

LADEUZE, P., S.T.D., Professor of Sacred Scripture and of Ancient Christian Literature, University of Louvain, President Collège du Saint Esprit, Louvain.

LANGAN, J. T., S.J., Woodstock College, Maryland.

LANGOUET, A., O.M.I., Kimberley, South Africa.

†LE BARS, JEAN, B.A., Litt.D., Member of the Asiatic Society, Paris.

LEGAL, EMILE J., S.T.D., Bishop of St. Albert, Alberta, Canada.

LEIMKUHLER, MATTHIAS, S.M., Washington.

LEJAY, PAUL, Fellow of the University of France, Professor at the Catholic Institute of Paris.

LENHART, JOHN M., O.M.Cap., Lector of Philosophy, St. Fidelis Monastery, Victoria, Kansas.

† Deceased.

LINDSAY, LIONEL ST. G., B.Sc., S.T.D., Ph.D., EDITOR IN CHIEF, "LA NOUVELLE FRANCE", QUEBEC.

LINEHAN, PAUL H., B.A., INSTRUCTOR COLLEGE OF THE CITY OF NEW YORK.

LINS, JOSEPH, FREIBURG, GERMANY.

LOPEZ, TIRSO, O.S.A., COLEGIO DE LOS AGUSTINOS, VALLADOLID, SPAIN.

LORTIE, STANISLAS A., A.M., S.T.D., PROFESSOR OF THEOLOGY, UNIVERSITY OF LAVAL, QUEBEC.

LOUGHLIN, MGR. JAMES F., S.T.D., PHILADELPHIA.

MAAS, A. J., S.J., RECTOR OF WOODSTOCK COLLEGE, MARYLAND.

MAES, CAMILLUS P., BISHOP OF COVINGTON, KENTUCKY.

MacCAFFREY, JAMES, S.T.L., ST. PATRICK'S COLLEGE, MAYNOOTH, DUBLIN.

McCAFFRAY, ARTHUR J., S.J., WOODSTOCK COLLEGE, MARYLAND.

McMAHON, ARTHUR L., O.P., LECTOR OF SACRED THEOLOGY, PROFESSOR OF MORAL THEOLOGY AND SACRED SCRIPTURE, DOMINICAN HOUSE OF STUDIES, WASHINGTON.

McMAHON, JOSEPH H., A.M., Ph.D., NEW YORK.

McNEAL, MARK J., S.J., WOODSTOCK COLLEGE, MARYLAND.

McNICHOLAS, JOHN T., O.P., S.T.L., LECTOR, WASHINGTON.

MACPHERSON, EWAN, NEW YORK.

McSORLEY, JOSEPH, C.S.P., A.M., S.T.L., ST. PAUL'S CHURCH, NEW YORK.

MANN, HORACE K., HEADMASTER ST. CUTHBERT'S GRAMMAR SCHOOL, NEWCASTLE-ON-TYNE, ENGLAND.

MEEHAN, ANDREW B., Ph.D., S.T.D., PROFESSOR OF CANON LAW AND LITURGY, ST. BERNARD'S SEMINARY, ROCHESTER, NEW YORK.

MEEHAN, THOMAS F., NEW YORK.

MELODY, JOHN WEBSTER, A.M., S.T.D., ASSOCIATE PROFESSOR OF MORAL THEOLOGY, CATHOLIC UNIVERSITY OF AMERICA, WASHINGTON.

MERCEDES, SISTER, ST. ELIZABETH'S CONVENT, CORNWELLS, PENNSYLVANIA.

MERSHMANN, FRANCIS, O.S.B., S.T.D., PROFESSOR OF MORAL THEOLOGY, CANON LAW AND LITURGY, ST. JOHN'S UNIVERSITY, COLLEGEVILLE, MINNESOTA.

MOELLER, CH., PROFESSOR OF GENERAL HISTORY, UNIVERSITY OF LOUVAIN.

MOLLAT, G., Ph.D., PARIS.

MOONEY, JAS., UNITED STATES ETHNOLOGIST, WASHINGTON.

MORICE, A. G., KAMLOOPS CITY, BRITISH COLUMBIA.

MORRISROE, PATRICK, DEAN AND PROFESSOR OF LITURGY, ST. PATRICK'S COLLEGE, MAYNOOTH, DUBLIN.

MUCKERMANN, H., S.J., PROFESSOR OF MATHEMATICS AND NATURAL SCIENCES, ST. IGNATIUS COLLEGE, VALKENBURG, HOLLAND.

MUELLER, ADOLF, S.J., DIRECTOR OF THE PRIVATE ASTRONOMICAL OBSERVATORY ON THE JANICULUM, PROFESSOR OF ASTRONOMY AT THE GREGORIAN UNIVERSITY, ROME.

MURPHY, JOHN F. X., S.J., WOODSTOCK COLLEGE, MARYLAND.

NUGENT, F. V., C.M., ST. LOUIS.

O'DANIEL, VICTOR F., O.P., S.T.L., PROFESSOR OF DOGMATIC THEOLOGY, DOMINICAN HOUSE OF STUDIES, WASHINGTON.

O'DONOGHUE, D. J., DUBLIN.

OESTREICH, THOMAS, O.S.B., PROFESSOR OF CHURCH HISTORY AND SACRED SCRIPTURE, MARYHELP ABBEY, BELMONT, NORTH CAROLINA.

O'LAUGHLIN, FRANCIS D., S.J., WOODSTOCK COLLEGE, MARYLAND.

O'MALIA, M. J., FORDHAM UNIVERSITY, NEW YORK.

O'NEIL, LEO F., A.B., S.T.L., BOSTON.

O'NEILL, J. D., A.M., S.T.D., LAKE FOREST, ILLINOIS.

O'RIORDAN, MGR. M., Ph.D., S.T.D., D.C.L., RECTOR OF THE IRISH COLLEGE, ROME.

OTT, MICHAEL, O.S.B., Ph.D., PROFESSOR OF THE HISTORY OF PHILOSOPHY, ST. JOHN'S UNIVERSITY, COLLEGEVILLE, MINNESOTA.

OTTEN, JOSEPH, PITTSBURG, PENNSYLVANIA.

OUSSANI, GABRIEL, Ph.D., PROFESSOR OF HEBREW AND THE SEMITIC LANGUAGES, ORIENTAL HISTORY AND BIBLICAL ARCHÆOLOGY, ST. JOSEPH'S SEMINARY, DUNWOODIE, NEW YORK.

†PARGOIRE, JULES, A.A., CONSTANTINOPLE.

PETERSON, JOHN B., PROFESSOR OF ECCLESIASTICAL HISTORY AND LITURGY, ST. JOHN'S SEMINARY, BRIGHTON, MASSACHUSETTS.

PETIT, L., A.A., CONSTANTINOPLE.

PETRIDES, S., A.A., CONSTANTINOPLE.

† Deceased.

PHILLIPS, G. E., Professor of Philosophy and Church History, St. Cuthbert's College, Ushaw, Durham, England.

PIAT, CLODIUS, Litt.D., Professor of Philosophy, Institut Catholique, Paris.

PLASSMAN, THOMAS, O.F.M., M.A., Ph.D., Rome.

PLOMER, J. C., C.S.B., Assumption College, Sandwich, Ontario, Canada.

POLLEN, JOHN HUNGERFORD, S.J., London.

POOLE, THOMAS H., New York.

PORTALIE, EUGENE, S.J., Professor of Theology at the Catholic Institute of Toulouse, France.

POWER, ALICE, R.S.H., Convent of the Sacred Heart, Kenwood, Albany, New York.

QUINN, DANIEL, Ph.D., Yellow Springs, Ohio.

REILLY, L. W., A.M., Washington.

REILLY, W. S., S.T.D., S.S., Professor of Scripture, St. John's Seminary, Brighton, Massachusetts.

REINHOLD, GREGOR, Freiburg, Germany.

REMY, ARTHUR F. J., A.M., Ph.D., Instructor in Germanic Languages, Columbia University, New York.

RICKABY, JOSEPH, S.J., Pope's Hall, Oxford.

ROBERGE, L. D., Vice-Chancellor, Diocese of St. Hyacinth, Canada.

ROBINSON, PASCHAL, O.F.M., Professor of Theology, Franciscan Monastery, Washington.

ROCK, P M. J., Louisville, Kentucky

ROY, J. EDMOND, Litt.D., F.R.S.C., Officer of the French Academy, Director, "Notarial Review", Lévis, Quebec.

RUDGE, F. M., M.A., Youngstown, Ohio.

RUSSELL, WILLIAM T., S.T.D., Baltimore.

RYAN, EDWIN, Catholic University of America, Washington.

RYAN, J. A., S.T.D., Professor of Moral Theology, The St. Paul Seminary, St. Paul, Minnesota.

RYAN, PATRICK, S.J., London.

SAN GIOVANNI, EDOARDO, Litt.B., A.M., Instructor in the Latin Language and Literature, College of the City of New York.

SAUER, JOSEPH, S.T.D., Editor, "Rundschau", Professor of Theology at the University of Freiburg, Germany.

SAUVAGE, G. M., C.S.C., S.T.D., Ph.D., Professor of Dogmatic Theology, Holy Cross College, Washington.

SAXTON, E. F., Baltimore.

SCANNELL, T. B., S.T.D., Editor, "Catholic Dictionary", Folkestone, England.

SCHAEFER, FRANCIS J., S.T.D., Ph.D., Professor of Church History, The St. Paul Seminary, St. Paul, Minnesota.

SCHEID, N., S.J., Stella Matutina College, Feldkirch, Austria.

SCHLAGER, HEINRICH PATRICIUS, Harreveld bei Lichtenvoorde, Holland.

SCHRANTZ, CHARLES B., S.S., A.M., Catholic University of America, Washington.

SCHREINER, CHRYSOSTOM, O.S.B., Nassau, Bahama Islands.

SCHWERTNER, THOS. M., O.P., Washington.

SELINGER, JOS., S.T.D., Jefferson City, Missouri.

SHIPMAN, ANDREW J., A.M., LL.M., New York.

SIEGFRIED, FRANCIS PATRICK, Professor of Philosophy, St. Charles's Seminary, Overbrook, Pennsylvania.

SINKMAJER, JOS., East Islip, New York.

SLATER, T., S.J., St. Beuno's College, St. Asaph, Wales.

SLOANE, CHARLES WILLIAM, New York.

SLOANE, THOMAS O'CONOR, A.M., E.M., Ph.D., New York.

SMITH, MICHAEL PAUL, C.S.P., New York.

SMITH, SYDNEY F., S.J., London.

SMOLINSKI, JOSEPH, Washington.

SMYTH, P. G., Chicago.

SOLLIER, J. F., S.M., S.T.D., Rector and Professor of Moral Theology, Marist College, Washington.

SOUVAY, CHARLES L., C.M., LL.B., S.T.D., Ph.D., Professor of Holy Scripture and Hebrew, Kenrick Seminary, St. Louis.

SPILLANE, EDWARD P., S.J., Associate Editor, "The Messenger", New York.

STEELE, FRANCESCA M., Stroud, Gloucestershire, England.

STONE, J. M., London.

SULLIVAN, JAMES J., S.J., Professor of Dogmatic Theology, St. Louis University, St. Louis.

TAAFFE, THOMAS GAFFNEY, Ph.D., Instructor in English Literature, College of the City of New York.

TAYLOR, HANNIS, Spanish Claims Commission, Washington.

THURSTON, HERBERT, S.J., London.

TIERNEY, JOHN J., A.M., S.T.D., Professor of Scripture and Semitic Studies, Mt. St. Mary's College, Emmitsburg, Maryland.

TIERNEY, R. H., S.J., Woodstock College, Maryland.

TONDINI DI QUARENGHI, CES., C.R., C.P., Rome.

TURNER, WILLIAM, B.A., S.T.D., Professor of Logic and the History of Philosophy, Catholic University of America, Washington.

UA CLERIGH, ARTHUR, M.A., K.C., London.

URQUHART, F. F., M.A., Lecturer in Modern History, Balliol College, Oxford.

VAILHE, S., A.A., Constantinople.

VAN CLEEF, AUGUSTUS, New York.

van den BIESEN, C., S.T.D., Professor of Hebrew and Old Testament Exegesis, St. Joseph's College, Mill Hill, London.

VAN DER DONCKT, C., Pocatello, Idaho.

VAN HOVE, A., D.C.L., Professor of Church History, University of Louvain.

VAN KASTEREN, JOHN P., S.J., Maastricht, Holland.

VERWYST, CHRYSOSTOM, O.F.M., Ashland, Wisconsin.

VŒLKER, J. A., Ossining, New York.

VOLZ, JOHN R., O.P., Washington.

VUIBERT, A. J. B., S.S., A.M., Professor of History, St. Patrick's Seminary, Menlo Park, California.

WALDRON, M. A., O.P., Washington.

WALSH, JAS. J., M.D., Ph.D., LL.D., Professor of the History of Medicine, Fordham University, New York.

WALSH, REGINALD, O.P., S.T.D., Rome.

WANG, E. A., Bergen, Norway.

WARD, Mgr. BERNARD, President of St. Edmund's College, Ware, England.

WEBER, N. A., S.M., S.T.L., Professor of Apologetics and Church History, Marist College, Washington.

WILHELM, J., S.T.D., Ph.D., Battle, Sussex, England.

WILLIAMSON, GEORGE CHARLES, Litt.D., London.

WIRTH, EDMUND J., S.T.D., Ph.D., Professor of Philosophy, St. Bernard's Seminary, Rochester, New York.

WITTMAN, PIUS, Ph.D., Reichsarchivrath, Munich.

WOLFSGRUBER, CŒLESTIN, O.S.B., Vienna.

WOODS, JOSEPH M., S.J., Professor of Ecclesiastical History, Woodstock College, Maryland.

YANES, FRANCISCO J., Bureau of American Republics, Washington.

YOUNG, T. J., S.J., Woodstock College, Maryland.

ZIMMERMAN, B., O.D.C., St. Luke's Priory, Wincanton, Somerset, England.

Tables of Abbreviations

The following tables and notes are intended to guide readers of THE CATHOLIC ENCYCLOPEDIA in interpreting those abbreviations, signs, or technical phrases which, for economy of space, will be most frequently used in the work. For more general information see the article ABBREVIATIONS, ECCLESIASTICAL.

I.—GENERAL ABBREVIATIONS.

a.............article.

ad an..........at the year (Lat. *ad annum*).

an., ann........the year, the years (Lat. *annus, anni*).

ap............in (Lat. *apud*).

art............article.

Assyr..........Assyrian.

A. S. ....Anglo-Saxon.

A. V. ....Authorized Version (i.e. tr. of the Bible authorized for use in the Anglican Church—the so-called "King James", *or* "Protestant" Bible.

b.............born.

Bk.............Book.

Bl. ....Blessed.

C., c...........about (Lat. *circa*); canon; chapter; *compagnie*.

can............canon.

cap............chapter (Lat. *caput*—used only in Latin context).

cf.............compare (Lat. *confer*).

cod...........codex.

col...........column.

concl..........conclusion.

const., constit. . . .Lat. *constitutio*.

curâ..........by the industry of.

d.............died.

dict...........dictionary (Fr. *dictionnaire*).

disp...........Lat. *disputatio*.

diss...........Lat. *dissertatio*.

dist...........Lat. *distinctio*.

D. V..........Douay Version.

ed., edit........edited, edition, editor.

Ep., Epp........letter, letters (Lat. *epistola*).

Fr............French.

gen...........genus.

Gr............Greek.

H. E., Hist. Eccl. .Ecclesiastical History.

Heb., Hebr......Hebrew.

ib., ibid.........in the same place (Lat. *ibidem*).

Id............the same person, *or* author (Lat. *idem*).

inf............below (Lat. *infra*).

It............Italian.

l. c., loc. cit......at the place quoted (Lat. *loco citato*).

Lat............Latin.

lat............latitude.

lib............book (Lat. *liber*).

long...........longitude.

Mon...........Lat. *Monumenta*.

MS., MSS. ......manuscript, manuscripts.

n., no..........number.

N. T..........New Testament.

Nat............National.

Old Fr., O. Fr.....Old French.

op. cit..........in the work quoted (Lat. *opere citato*).

Ord............Order.

O. T..........Old Testament.

p., pp..........page, pages, *or* (in Latin references) *pars* (part).

par...........paragraph.

passim..........in various places.

pt............part.

Q............Quarterly (a periodical), e.g. "Church Quarterly".

Q., QQ., quæst. ...question, questions (Lat. *quæstio*).

q. v...........which [title] see (Lat. *quod vide*).

Rev...........Review (a periodical).

R. S..........Rolls Series.

R. V..........Revised Version.

S., SS..........Lat. *Sanctus, Sancti*, "Saint", "Saints"—used in this Encyclopedia only in Latin context.

Sept...........Septuagint.

Sess...........Session.

Skt............Sanskrit.

Sp............Spanish.

sq., sqq.........following page, *or* pages (Lat. *sequens*).

St., Sts.........Saint, Saints.

sup...........Above (Lat. *supra*).

s. v...........Under the corresponding title (Lat. *sub voce*).

tom...........volume (Lat. *tomus*).

tr. . . . . .translation *or* translated. By itself it means "English transla-
tion", *or* "translated into English by". Where a translation
is into any other language, the
language is stated.

tr., tract . . . . .tractate.

v. . . . . .see (Lat. *vide*).

Ven. . . . . .Venerable.

Vol. . . . . .Volume.

II.—Abbreviations of Titles.

Acta SS. . . . .*Acta Sanctorum* (Bollandists).

Ann. pont. cath. . . . .Battandier, *Annuaire pontifical
catholique.*

Bibl. Dict. Eng. Cath.Gillow, Bibliographical Dictionary of the English Catholics.

Dict. Christ. Antiq. . .Smith and Cheetham (ed.),
Dictionary of Christian An-
tiquities.

Dict. Christ. Biog. . . Smith and Wace (ed.), Dictionary of Christian Biography.

Dict. d'arch. chrét. . .Cabrol (ed.), *Dictionnaire d'archéologie chrétienne et de litur-
gie.*

Dict. de théol. cath. . Vacant and Mangenot (ed.),
*Dictionnaire de théologie
catholique.*

Dict. Nat. Biog. . . . .Stephen (ed.), Dictionary of
National Biography.

Hast., Dict. of the
Bible . . . . .Hastings (ed.), A Dictionary of
the Bible.

Kirchenlex. . . . . . . .Wetzer and Welte, *Kirchenlexicon.*

P. G. . . . . .Migne (ed.), *Patres Græci.*

P. L. . . . . .Migne (ed.), *Patres Latini.*

Vig., Dict. de la Bible.Vigouroux (ed.), *Dictionnaire de
la Bible.*

Note I.—Large Roman numerals standing alone indicate volumes. Small Roman numerals standing alone indicate chapters. Arabic numerals standing alone indicate pages. In other cases the divisions are explicitly stated. Thus " Rashdall, Universities of Europe, I, ix" refers the reader to the ninth chapter of the first volume of that work; "I, p. ix" would indicate the ninth page of the preface of the same volume.

Note II.—Where St. Thomas (Aquinas) is cited without the name of any particular work the reference is always to "Summa Theologica" (not to "Summa Philosophiæ"). The divisions of the "Summa Theol." are indicated by a system which may best be understood by the following example: "I-II, Q. vi, a. 7, ad 2 am" refers the reader to the *seventh* article of the *sixth* question in the *first* part of the *second* part, in the response to the *second* objection.

Note III.—The abbreviations employed for the various books of the Bible are obvious. Ecclesiasticus is indicated by *Ecclus.*, to distinguish it from Ecclesiastes (*Eccles.*). It should also be noted that I and II Kings in D. V. correspond to I and II Samuel in A. V.; and I and II Par. to I and II Chronicles. Where, in the spelling of a proper name, there is a marked difference between the D. V. and the A. V., the form found in the latter is added, in parenthesis.

Full Page Illustrations in Volume II

Coloured Plates

Maps

THE
CATHOLIC ENCYCLOPEDIA

A

Assizes of Jerusalem.—The signification of the word assizes in this connexion is derived from the French verb *asseoir*, whose past participle is *assis*. *Asseoir* means "to seat", "to place one on a seat". Hence the idea of putting something into its place, determining it to something. Thus *assise* came to mean an enactment, a statute. Assize is the English form of the word, and used in the plural, assizes, it denotes a court. The "Assizes of Jerusalem" (*les assises de Jérusalem*) are the code of laws enacted by the Crusaders for the government of the Kingdom of Jerusalem. They are a collection of legal regulations for the courts of the Latin Kingdom of Jerusalem and Cyprus. Thus we have the "Assizes of Antioch", the "Assizes of Rumania", legal regulations for the Latin principality of Antioch and for the Latin Empire of Constantinople. It is erroneous to ascribe the "Assizes of Jerusalem" to Godfrey de Bouillon on the presumption that as he was King of Jerusalem he enacted its laws. The "Assizes of Jerusalem" were compiled in the thirteenth century, not in the eleventh; not in Jerusalem, but after its fall; not by any ruler, but by several jurists. Not even the names of these are all known, though two of them were the well-known John of Ibelin, who composed, before 1266, the "Livre des Assises de la Cour des Barons", and Philippe de Navarre, who, about the middle of the thirteenth century, compiled the "Livre de forme de plait en la Haute Cour".

There are nine treatises in the "Assizes of Jerusalem", and they concern themselves with two kinds of law: Feudal Law, to which the Upper Court of Barons was amenable; and Common Law, which was applied to the Court of the Burgesses. The latter is the older of the two and was drawn up before the fall of Jerusalem. It deals with questions of civil law, such as contracts, marriage, and property, and touches on some which fall within the province of special courts, such as the "Ecclesiastical Court" for canonical points, the "Cour de la Fonde" for commerce, and the "Cour de la Mer" for admiralty cases. It deals rather with what the law enjoins in these several fields than with determining penalties for transgressions. The celebrated "Livre de la Haute Cour" of Ibelin was adopted, after revision (1359), as the official code of the Court of Cyprus, which kingdom succeeded to the title and regulations of Jerusalem. We possess only the official text of this, which is not much older than the works of French lawyers of Rouen and Orléans. But the superiority of the "Assizes of Jerusalem" is that it reflects the genuine character of feudal law, whereas the works of the French feudalists betray something of the royal influence which affected those sections after the revival of the Roman law. No other work dwells so insistently on the rights of the vassal towards his lord, no other throws such a light on the resolution of a disputed point by an appeal to arms, its challenge, its champions, its value as evidence. In brief, the "Assizes of Jerusalem" give us a faithful and vivid picture of the part played by the law in the Latin Kingdom of Jerusalem.

BEUGNOT, *Recueil des historiens des Croisades: Lois*, 2 vols. in fol. (Paris, 1841–43), an edition which supersedes the older ones of THAUMAPRIÈRE (1690), KANSLER (1839), FOUCHER (1840); PAULIN PARIS, review of Beugnot's edition, in the *Journal des Savants* (Paris, 1841); MONNIER, *Godefroy de Bouillon et les Assises de Jérusalem* (Académie des Sciences morales, Paris, 1873–74). Consult also any work on feudal or medieval law.

CH. MOELLER.

Assmayer, IGNAZ, an Austrian musician, b. at Salzburg, 11 February, 1790; d. in Vienna, 31 August, 1862. He studied under Brunmayr and Michael Haydn, and later, when he went to Vienna, he received further instruction from Eybler. In 1808 he was organist at St. Peter's in his native town, and here he wrote his oratorio "Die Sündfluth" (The Deluge) and his cantata "Worte der Weihe". Some time after his removal to Vienna, in 1815, he became choirmaster at the Schotten kirche, and in 1825 was appointed imperial organist. After having served eight years as vice-choirmaster, he received in 1846 the appointment of second choirmaster to the Court, as successor to Weigl. His principal oratorios, "Das Gelübde", "Saul und David", and "Sauls Tod", were repeatedly performed by the *Tonkünstler-Societät*, of which he was conductor for fifteen years. He also wrote fifteen masses, two requiems, a Te Deum, and various smaller church pieces. Of these two oratorios, one mass, the requiems, and Te Deum, and furthermore sixty secular compositions, comprising symphonies, overtures, pastorales, etc., were published. As to his style Grove calls it correct and fluent, but wanting in both invention and force.

BAKER, *Biogr. Dict. of Musicians;* RIEMANN, *Dict. of Music;* GROVE, *Dict. of Music and Musicians.*

J. A. VÖLKER.

Association, RIGHT OF VOLUNTARY.—I. THE LEGAL RIGHT. A voluntary association means any group of individuals freely united for the pursuit of a common end. It differs, therefore, from a necessary association inasmuch as its members are not under legal compulsion to become associated. The principal instances of a necessary association are a conscript military body and civil society, or the State; the concept of voluntary association covers organizations as diverse as a manufacturing corporation and a religious sodality. The legal right of voluntary association—the attitude of civil authority toward bodies of this nature—has varied in different ages and still varies in different countries. Under the rule of Solon the Athenians seem to have been free to institute such societies as they pleased, so long as their action did not conflict with the public law. The multitude of societies and public gatherings for the celebration of religious festivals and the carrying on of games, or other forms of public recreation and pleasure, which flourished for so many centuries throughout ancient Greece, indicates that a considerable measure of freedom of association was quite general in that country.

The Roman authorities were less liberal. No private association could be formed without a special decree of the senate or of the emperor. And yet voluntary societies or corporations were numerous from the earliest days of the Republic. There existed *collegia* for the proper performance of religious rites, *collegia* to provide public amusements, *collegia* of a political nature, *collegia* in charge of cemeteries, and *collegia* made up of workers in the various trades and occupations. In Judea the Pharisees and Sadducees—though these were schools, or sects, rather than organized associations—and the Essenes were not seriously interfered with by the Roman governors. With the union of Church and State in 325 there came naturally an era of freedom and prosperity for associations of a religious nature, especially for the religious orders. During the period of political chaos that followed the fall of the Empire, liberty of association was as extensive as could be expected among populations whose civil rulers were not sufficiently powerful either to repress or to protect the formation of voluntary unions. Indeed, the "minor, obscure, isolated, and incoherent societies", to use the words of Guizot, that erected themselves on the ruins of the old political organization and became in time the feudal system, were essentially private associations.

As the needs, culture, and outlook of men extended, there sprang into being a great number and variety of associations, religious, charitable, educational, and industrial. Instances are the great religious orders, the societies for the relief of poverty and sickness, the universities, and the guilds which arose and flourished between the tenth and the fourteenth centuries. All of these associations were instituted either under the active direction of the Church, or with her warm encouragement, and as a rule without any serious opposition on the part of the civil power. Some of them, in fact, performed important political functions; others secured a measure of social peace that the civil authorities were unable to enforce; while as a whole they constituted a considerable check to the exercise of arbitrary power by sovereigns. Thus, the merchant and craft guilds governed trade and industry with a series of regulations that had all the force and authority of legal statutes; the associations instituted to enforce the "Truce of God", helped greatly to lessen petty warfare between different lords and different sections of the same country; while "the monarch was . . . hemmed in on all sides . . . by universities, corporations, brotherhoods, monastic orders; by franchises and privileges of all kinds, which in greater or less degree existed all over Europe".

With the rise and extension of political absolutism in most of the countries of Europe in the seventeenth century, freedom of association became everywhere greatly restricted. It was frequently subjected to unreasonable conditions in the last century, and it is still withheld by some governments. From 1820 to 1824 labour unions were absolutely prohibited in Great Britain. Up to the year 1901 non-industrial associations consisting of more than twenty persons could not be formed in France without authorization by a public official whose power in the matter was almost arbitrary. At present, authorization is required in the case of associations composed of Frenchmen and foreigners; associations whose supreme head resides outside of France; and associations whose members live in common. Owing partly to the terms of the law and partly to the course pursued by the officials charged with its enforcement, almost all the religious congregations have been driven out of France. In Prussia and in most of the other German states political associations are subject to close inspection, and can be dissolved by the public authorities in case they go outside of certain well-defined limits. Most other societies pursuing reasonable ends can obtain existence and recognition by becoming registered according to a general law of the empire. The law of Austria empowers magistrates to forbid the formation of any association that either in aim or personnel seems contrary to law, and to dissolve any society that is no longer conducted in accordance with the legal conditions to which it is subject. In Russia participation in any association not expressly authorized by the Government is a penal offence. Speaking generally, it may be said that with the exception of France, Russia, and Turkey, European governments exhibit to-day a liberal attitude toward associations pursuing reasonable ends.

In the United States associations whose purpose is pecuniary gain, and all other societies that desire a corporate existence and civil personality, must, of course, comply with the appropriate laws of incorporation. Unincorporated societies may be instituted without legal authorization, and may pursue any aim whatever, so long as their members do not engage in actions that constitute conspiracy or some other violation of public order. Even in these contingencies the members will not be liable to legal prosecution for the mere act of forming the associations. Under the present fairly liberal attitude of governments, and owing to the great increase in the number and complexity of human interests, the number and variety of associations in the Western world have grown with great rapidity. We may enumerate at least nine distinct types, namely: religious, charitable, intellectual, moral, political, mutual-benevolent, labour, industrial, and purely social. The largest increase has taken place in the three classes devoted to social intercourse and enjoyment, such as clubs and "secret" societies; to industry and commerce, such as manufacturing and mercantile corporations, and to the interests of the wage earner, such as trade unions. Probably the great majority of the male adults in the cities of the United States have some kind of membership in one or other of these three forms of association.

II. THE MORAL RIGHT.—Like all other moral rights, that of voluntary association is determined by the ends that it promotes, the human needs that it supplies. The dictum of Aristotle that man is a "political" animal, expresses more than the fact that man naturally and necessarily becomes a participant in that form of association known as the State. It means that man cannot effectively pursue happiness nor attain to a reasonable degree of self-perfection unless he unites his energies with those of his fellows. This is particularly true of modern life, and for two reasons. First, because the needs of men have greatly increased, and second, because the division of labour has made the individual more and more dependent upon other individuals and groups of individuals. The primitive, isolated family that knows only a few wants, and is able in rude fashion to supply all these, may enjoy a certain measure of contentment, if not of culture, without the aid of any other association than that inherent in its own constitution. For the family of to-day such conditions are unsatisfying and insufficient. Its members are constrained to pursue many lines of activity and to satisfy many wants that demand organized and associated effort.

Since the individual is dependent upon so many other individuals for many of those material goods that are indispensable to him, he must frequently combine with those of his neighbours who are similarly placed if he would successfully resist the tendency of modern forces to overlook and override the mere individual. A large proportion of the members of every industrial community cannot make adequate provision for the needs that follow in the train of misfortune and old age unless they utilize such agencies as the mutual benefit society, the insurance company, or the savings bank. Workingmen find it impossible to obtain just wages or reasonable conditions of employment without the trade union. On the other hand, goods could not be produced or distributed in sufficient quantities except through the medium of associations. Manufacturing, trade, transportation, and finance necessarily fall more and more under the control of partnerships and stock companies.

Turning now from the consideration of these material needs, we find that association plays a no less important part in the religious, moral, intellectual, political, and purely social departments of life. Men cannot give God due worship except in a public, social way. This implies at least the universal Church and the parish, and ordinarily it supposes devotional and other associations, such as sodalities, altar societies, church-fund societies, etc. Select souls who wish to embrace the life of perfection described by the evangelical counsels must become organized in such a way that they can lead a common life. In every community there are persons who wish to do effective work on behalf of good morals, charity, and social reform of various kinds. Hence we have purity leagues, associated charities, temperance societies, ethical culture societies, social settlements. Since large numbers of parents prefer private and religious schools for the education of their children, the need arises for associations whose purpose is educational. Literary and scientific associations are necessary to promote original research, deeper study, and wider culture. Good government, especially in a republic, is impossible without political associations which strive vigilantly and constantly for the removal of abuses and the enactment of just laws.

In the purely social order men desire to enroll themselves in clubs, "secret" societies, amusement associations, etc., all of which may be made to promote human contentment and human happiness. Many of the forms of association just enumerated are absolutely necessary to right human life; none of them is entirely useless. Finally, voluntary associations are capable of discharging many of the tasks that otherwise would devolve upon the State. This was an important feature of their activity in the Middle Ages, and it is very desirable to-day when the functions of government are constantly increasing. Chief among the organizations capable of limiting State activity are those concerned with education, charitable work, industry, and commerce, and the improvement of the working classes. In so far as these can perform their several tasks on reasonable terms and without injury to the State or to any class of its citizens, the public welfare is better served by them than it would be if they were supplanted by the Government. Individual liberty and individual opportunity have a larger scope, individual initiative is more readily called into play, and the danger of Government despotism is greatly lessened.

The right of voluntary association is, therefore, a natural right. It is an endowment of man's nature, not a privilege conferred by civil society. It arises out of his deepest needs, is an indispensable means to reasonable life and normal self-development.

And it extends even to those associations that are not in themselves necessary for these ends—that is, so long as the associations do not contravene good morals or the public weal. For the State has no right to prohibit any individual action, be it ever so unnecessary, which is, from the public point of view, harmless. Although it is not essential to his personal development that the citizen should become a member of an association that can do him neither good nor harm, it is essential to his happiness and his self-respect that he should not be prevented from doing so by the State. The moment that the State begins to practise coercion of this kind it violates individual rights. The general right of voluntary association is well stated by Pope Leo XIII in the encyclical, "Rerum Novarum": "To enter into private societies is a natural right of man, and the State must protect natural rights, not destroy them. If it forbids its citizens to form associations, it contradicts the very principle of its own existence; for both they and it exist in virtue of the same principle, namely, the natural propensity of man to live in society."

Nor is the State justified in prohibiting voluntary associations on the ground that they may become inimical to public welfare. An institution should not be utterly condemned because it is liable to abuse; otherwise an end must be made of all institutions that are erected and conducted by human beings. The State has ample power to protect itself against all the abuses to which liberty of association is liable. It can forbid societies that aim at objects contrary to good morals or the public welfare, lay down such reasonable restrictions as are required to define the proper spheres of the various associations, punish those societies that go beyond their legitimate fields, and, in extreme cases, dissolve any particular organization that proves itself to be incorrigible. Through these measures the State can provide itself with all the security that is worth having; any further interference with individual liberty would be a greater social evil than the one that is sought to be remedied. The formality of legal authorization, or registration, is not in itself unreasonable, but it ought not to be accompanied by unreasonable conditions. The procedure ought to be such that any society formed in accordance with the appropriate law of association could demand authorization, or registration, as a civil right, instead of being compelled to seek it as a privilege at the hands of an official clothed with the power to grant or refuse it at his own discretion.

The difference between these two methods is the difference between the reign of law and the reign of official caprice; between constitutional liberty and bureaucratic despotism. Precisely this sort of arbitrary power is at present exercised by French officials over religious congregations. The result is that Frenchmen and Frenchwomen who wish to live in associations of this nature are denied the right to do so. Speaking generally of religious congregations, we may justly say in the words of Pope Leo XIII, that they have "the sanction of the law of nature", that is, the same natural right to exist on reasonable conditions as any other morally lawful association, and, "on the religious side they rightly claim to be responsible to the Church alone". When the State refuses them the right to exist it violates not merely the natural moral law but the supernatural Divine law. For these associations are an integral part of the life of the Church, and as such, lie within her proper sphere. Within this sphere she is independent of the State, as independent as one sovereign civil power is of another. Abuses that may grow out of religious associations can be met by the State in the ways outlined above. Treasonable acts can be punished; excessive accumulation of property can be prevented; in fact, every action, circumstance, or tendency that constitutes a real danger to the public welfare can be successfully dealt with by other methods than that of denying these associations the right of existence.

TANQUEREY, *Synopsis Theologiæ Moralis, de Justitiâ* (New York, 1904), 76–80; ANTOINE, *Course d'économie sociale* (Paris, 1899), 384–388; *Kirchenlex.*, s. v. *Vereinswesen;* LALOR, *Cyclopedia of Political Science and Political Economy* (New York, 1888–90), s. v. *Associations;* SAY-CHAILLEY, *Dictionnaire d'économie politique*, s. v. *Association;* KENT, *Commentaries*, Lect. xxxiii, *Of Corporations;* LEVASSEUR, *Histoire des classes ouvrières avant 1789*, I, i.

JOHN A. RYAN.

Association of Ideas, (1) a principle in psychology to account for the succession of mental states, (2) the basis of a philosophy known as Associationism. The fact of the association of ideas was noted by some of the earliest philosophers; Aristotle (De mem. et rem., 2) indicates the three laws of association which have been the basis of nearly all later enumerations. St. Thomas, in his commentary on Aristotle, accepts and illustrates them at some length. Hamilton (Notes on Reid) gives considerable credit to the Spanish Humanist, Vives (1492–1540), for his treatment of the subject. Association of ideas is not, therefore, a discovery of English psychology, as has often been asserted.

It is true, however, that the principle of association of ideas received in English psychology an interpretation never given to it before. The name is derived from Locke who placed it at the head of one of the chapters of his "Essay", but used it only to explain peculiarities of character. Applied to mental states in general, the name is too restricted, since ideas, even in the English sense, are only cognitive processes. The association theory was held by Hobbes, Berkeley, Hume, and Hamilton; but it received its widest interpretation at the hands of the Associationists, Hartley, Priestley, James Mill, John Stuart Mill, Bain, and Spencer. They regarded it as a principle capable of explaining all mental phenomena. For them it is in the subjective world what the principle of gravitation is in the physical world. Association of ideas, though variously explained, is accepted by all modern psychologists. Sully, Maudsley, James, Höffding, Münsterberg, Ebbinghaus, Ziehen, Taine, Ribot, Luys, and many others accept it more or less in the spirit of the Associationists.

The traditional laws of association, based on Aristotle, are: 1. Similarity; 2. Contrast; 3. Contiguity in time or space. In the course of time efforts were made to reduce them to more fundamental laws. Contrast has been resolved into similarity and contiguity. Contrasts, to recall each other, suppose generic similarity, as white recalls black. Yet this alone will not suffice, since this gives us no reason for the fact that white recalls black in preference to green or blue; hence experience, based on the fact that nature works in contrasts, is called into aid. Spencer, Höffding, and others try to reduce all the laws of association to that of similarity, while Wundt and his school believe that all can be reduced to experience and hence to contiguity. Bain, who has analyzed the laws of association most thoroughly, holds both similarity and contiguity to be elementary principles. To these he adds certain laws of compound association. Mental states easily recall one another when they have several points of contact. And in fact, considering the complexity of mental life, it would seem probable that simple associations, by similarity or contiguity alone, never occur. Besides these primary laws of association, various secondary laws are enumerated, such as the laws of frequency, vividness, recentness, emotional congruity, etc. These determine the firmness of the association, and consequently the preference given to one state over another, in the recall. Association

of ideas is a fact of everyday experience which furnishes an important basis for the science of psychology; yet it must be remembered that the laws of association offer no ultimate explanation of the facts observed. In accounting for the facts of association we must, in the first place, reject as insufficient the purely physical theory proposed by Ribot, Richet, Maudsley, Carpenter, and others, who seek an explanation exclusively in the association of brain-processes. Psychology thus becomes a chapter of physiology and mechanics. Aside from the fact that this theory can give no satisfactory explanation of association by similarity which implies a distinctly mental factor, it neglects evident facts of consciousness. Consciousness tells us that in reminiscence we can voluntarily direct the sequence of our mental states, and it is in this that voluntary recall differs from the succession of images and feelings in dream and delirium. Besides, one brain-process may excite another, but this is not yet a state of consciousness.

Equally unsatisfactory is the theory of the ultra-spiritualists, who would have us believe that association of ideas has nothing to do with the bodily organism, but is wholly mental. Thus Hamilton says that all physiological theories are too contemptible for serious criticism. Reid and Bowne reject all traces of perception left in the brain substance. Lotze admits a concomitant oscillation of the brain elements, but considers them quite secondary and as exercising no influence on memory and recall. Like the purely physical theory, this also fails to explain the facts of consciousness and experience. The localization of activities in the various brain-centres, the facts of mental disease in consequence of injury to the brain, the dependence of memory on the healthy condition of the central organ, etc. have in this theory no rational meaning. We must, then, seek an explanation in a theory that does justice to both the mental and the physical side of the phenomena. A mere psychophysical parallelism, proposed by some, will not, however, suffice, as it offers no explanation, but is a mere restatement of the problem. The Scholastic doctrine, that the subject of sensory activity is neither the body alone nor the soul alone, but the unitary being compounded of body and soul, offers the best solution. As sense perception is not purely physiological nor purely mental, but proceeds from a faculty of the soul intrinsically united to an organ, so the association of these perceptions proceeds from a principle which is at the same time mental and physical. No doubt purely spiritual ideas also associate; but, as St. Thomas teaches, the most spiritual idea is not devoid of its physiological basis, and even in making use of the spiritual ideas which it has already acquired, the intellect has need of images stored in the brain. It requires these organic processes in the production of its abstract ideas. In its basis, the association of ideas is physiological, but it is more than this, as it does not follow the necessary laws of matter. The higher faculties of the mind can command and direct the process. The Scholastic theory does justice to the fact of the dependence of mental activities upon the organism, and yet leaves room for the freedom of the will attested by consciousness and experience.

English Associationism, while claiming to be neither idealistic nor materialistic, and disavowing metaphysics, has erected the principle of association of ideas into a metaphysical principle to explain all mental activity. James Mill enunciated the principle of indissoluble associations: Sensations or ideas occurring together frequently, and never apart, suggest one another with irresistible force, so that we combine them necessarily. This principle is employed to explain necessary judgments and metaphysical concepts. Bain applied the principles of association to logic and ethics. Spencer interpreted them in an evolutionistic sense. Certain beliefs and moral principles are such that the associations of the individual are not sufficient to explain them; they are the associations of successive generations handed down by heredity. The whole process is governed by necessary laws. Mental states associate passively, and mental life is but a process of "mental chemistry". Later Associationists, like Sully, have come to recognize that the mind exerts activity in attention, discrimination, judgment, reasoning. With this admission there should logically come also the admission of a soul-substance that attends, discriminates, judges, and reasons; but as they have not come to this conclusion, the soul is for them a "train of thoughts", a "stream of consciousness", or some other series veiled in metaphorical language. Association of ideas can never explain necessary judgments, conclusions drawn from premises, moral ideas and laws; these have their causes deeper in the nature of things.

MAHER, *Psychology* (London, 1900); MERCIER, *Psychologie* (Louvain, 1899); GUTBERLET, *Die Psychologie* (Münster, 1896); BAIN, *The Senses and the Intellect* (4th ed., London, 1855, 1894); *Association Controversies* in *Mind*, 1886; JAMES WARD, *Psychological Principles* in *Mind*, 1883–87; *Assimilation and Association* in *Mind*, 1893–94; BRADLEY, *Logic* (London, 1883); GOBLOT, *Théorie physiologique de l'association*, in *Revue philosophique*, 1898. SPENCER, *Principles of Psychology* (New York, 1903); JAMES, *Principles of Psychology* (New York, 1890); WUNDT, *Lectures on Human and Animal Psychology* (tr. by CREIGHTON AND TITCHENER, New York); RIBOT, *La psychologie anglaise contemporaine* (Paris, 1901).

EDMUND J. WIRTH.

Association of Priestly Perseverance, a sacerdotal association founded in 1868 at Vienna, and at first confined to that archdiocese. In 1879, chiefly through the influence of its periodical organ, "La Correspondance", it spread into other dioceses and countries, and in 1903 counted 14,919 living members, belonging to 150 dioceses in Austria, Germany, Switzerland, and other countries. This organization is very similar to that of the Apostolic Union of Secular Priests (q. v.).

JOSEPH H. McMAHON.

Association of the Holy Family. See HOLY FAMILY.

Associations, PIOUS.—Under this term are comprehended all those organizations, approved and indulgenced by Church authority, which have been instituted, especially in recent times, for the advancement of various works of piety and charity. Other terms used with the same meaning are: pious union, pious work, league, society, etc. Pious associations are distinguished, on the one hand, from ordinary societies composed of Catholics by having an explicitly religious purpose, by enjoying indulgences and other spiritual benefits, and by possessing ecclesiastical approbation. They are distinguished, on the other hand, from confraternities and sodalities. The latter distinction is not determined by the name and is not always apparent. In general, pious associations have simpler rules than confraternities; they do not require canonical erection, and though they have the approbation of authority, they are not subject to as strict legislation as confraternities; they have no fixed term of probation for new members, no elaborate ritual, no special costumes; they are not obliged to meet for common religious practices, and, as a rule, they make the help of others more prominent than the improvement of self. Of all these differences, only that of canonical erection seems essential. Some authorities, however, declare that practices in common constitute the trait which distinguishes a confraternity from a pious association.

Some well-known pious associations are: Society of St. Vincent de Paul; Society of the Propagation of the Faith; Apostleship of Prayer, known also as the League of the Sacred Heart of Jesus; Holy Childhood League; Priests' Eucharistic League; Cäcilienverein, an association especially developed in Germany for the advancement of religious music.

BÉRINGER, *Les indulgences* (Paris, 1906); MOCCHEGIANI, *Collectio Indulgentiarum* (Quaracchi, 1897).

F. P. DONNELLY.

Assuerus, the name of two different persons in the Bible:—1. In I Esdr., iv, 6, and Esth., i, 17, it corresponds to the Hebrew *'Acháshwērôsh*, and the Sept. 'Ασσούηρος (in Esth. 'Αρταξέρξης), and denotes Xerxes I, the King of Persia. It was to him that the Samaritans addressed their complaints against the inhabitants of Jerusalem soon after 485 B. C., i. e. in the beginning of his reign. Intent upon his pleasures and a war with Egypt, the king seems to have disregarded these charges. The report of Herodotus (VII, viii) that Xerxes convoked a council of his nobles, in the third year of his reign, to deliberate about the war against Greece agrees with Esth., i, 3, telling of the great feast given by the king to his nobles in the third year of his reign. In the seventh year of his reign, after the return of Xerxes from his war against Greece, Esther was declared queen. In the twelfth year of the king's reign, Esther saved the Jews from the national ruin contemplated by Aman. II. Another Assuerus occurs in the Greek text of Tob., xiv, 15 ('Ασύηρος), in conjunction with Nabuchodonosor; the taking of Ninive is ascribed to these two. In point of fact, Assyria was conquered by Cyaxares I, the King of Media, and Nabopolassar, the King of Babylonia, and father of Nabuchodonosor. Hence the Assuerus of Tob., xiv, 15, is Cyaxares I; his name is coupled with Nabuchodonosor because the latter must have led the troops of his father in the war against Assyria. The same Cyaxares I is probably the Assuerus ('Acháshwērôsh) mentioned in Dan., ix, 1, as the father of Darius the Mede. Most probably Darius the Mede is Cyaxares II, the son of Astyages, the King of Media. The inspired writer of Dan., ix, 1, represents him as a son of Cyaxares I, or Assuerus, instead of Astyages, on account of the glorious name of the former. This could be done without difficulty, since, in genealogies, the name of the grandson was often introduced instead of that of the son.

HAGEN, *Lexicon Biblicum* (Paris, 1905); LESÊTRE in VIG., *Dict. de la Bible* (Paris, 1895).

A. J. MAAS.

Assumption, LITTLE SISTERS OF THE, a congregation whose work is the nursing of the sick poor in their own homes. This labour they perform gratuitously and without distinction of creed. The congregation was founded in Paris in 1865, by the Rev. Etienne Pernet, A.A. (b. 23 July, 1824; d. 3 April, 1899), and Marie Antoinette Tage, known in religion as Mother Marie de Jésus (b. 7 Nov., 1824; d. 18 Sept., 1883). Both had long been engaged in charitable work, Father Pernet while a professor in the College of the Assumption at Nîmes, and Mlle. Tage as a member of the Association of Our Lady of Good Council in Paris. They met in Paris and Father Pernet placed her in charge of the work of nursing the sick poor which he had inaugurated. Out of this movement the sisterhood grew, Mother Marie de Jésus being the first superior. The nursing of the sick poor is not the only or even the chief purpose of the Little Sisters. They endeavour to bring about conversions, to regularize illicit unions, to have children baptized, sent to school, and prepared for First Communion and Confirmation. They form societies among their clients and enlist the aid of laymen and laywomen of education and means to further the work of regeneration. The congregation has established houses in Italy, Spain, Belgium, England Ireland, and the United States of America. The papal Brief approving the congregation was issued in 1897. The sisters take simple vows and are governed by a mother-general, who resides in Paris. Thomas Gaffney Taaffe.

Assumption, Sisters of the, a congregation of French nuns devoted to the teaching of young girls. It was founded in 1839 by Eugénie Milleret de Bron, in religion Mère Marie-Eugénie de Jésus (b. 1817; d. 1898), under the direction of the Abbé Combalot, a well-known orator of the time, who had been inspired to establish the institute during a pilgrimage to the shrine of Sainte-Anne d'Auray in 1825. The foundress, who had previously made a short novitiate with the Sisters of the Visitation at Côte Saint-André, was admirably adapted for the undertaking, and had the co-operation of three companions, each especially fitted to undertake the direction of some one of the activities of the order. Much of the initial success was due to the stanch friendship of Monseigneur Affre, Archbishop of Paris. The motto of the congregation is "Thy Kingdom Come", and the aim to combine with a thorough secular education a moral and religious training which will bear fruit in generations to come. The habit of the sisters is violet, with a white cross on the breast and a violet cincture. The veil is white. On certain occasions a mantle of white with a violet cross on the shoulder is worn in the chapel. Since its foundation the congregation has spread beyond France to England, Italy, Spain, and Nicaragua. Several communities devote themselves to the work of Perpetual Adoration and the instruction of poor children. The mother-house is situated at Auteuil, a suburb of Paris, in a former château, rich in historical associations. The daughters of many distinguished European families have studied at Auteuil, as well as many English and Americans, who receive a special training in the French language.

·Les origines de l'Assomption; Sisters of the Assumption in The Messenger (New York, Nov., 1899); Steele, The Convents of Great Britain (St. Louis, 1902), 241.

F. M. Rudge.

Assumption of the Blessed Virgin Mary, Feast of the, 15 Aug.; also called in old liturgical books Pausatio, Nativitas (for heaven), Mors, Depositio, Dormitio S. Mariæ. This feast has a double object: (1) the happy departure of Mary from this life; (2) the assumption of her body into heaven. It is the principal feast of the Blessed Virgin. Regarding the day, year, and manner of Our Lady's death, nothing certain is known. Epiphanius (d. 403) acknowledged that he knew nothing definite about it (Hær., lxxix, 11). The dates assigned for it vary between three and fifteen years after Christ's Ascension. Two cities claim to be the place of her departure: Jerusalem and Ephesus; common consent favours Jerusalem, where her tomb is shown [Nirschl, Haus und Grab der allerh. Jungfrau (Mainz, 1900); Mommert, Die Dormitio (Leipzig, 1900)]; but in 1906, J. Niesen brought forth new arguments in favour of Ephesus (Panagia Kapuli, Dülmen, 1906). The first six centuries did not know of the tomb of Mary at Jerusalem. The belief in the corporeal assumption of Mary is founded on the apocryphical treatise "De Obitu S. Dominæ", bearing the name of St. John, which belongs however to the fourth or fifth century. It is also found in the book "De Transitu Virginis", falsely ascribed to St. Melito of Sardis, and in a spurious letter attributed to St. Denis the Areopagite. If we consult genuine writings in the East, it is mentioned in the sermons of St. Andrew of Crete, St. John Damascene, St. Modestus of Jerusalem and others. In the West, St. Gregory of Tours (De gloria mart., I, iv) mentions it first. The sermons of St. Jerome and St. Augustine for this feast, however, are spurious. St. John of Damascus (P. G., I, 96) thus formulates the tradition of the Church of Jeru-

salem: "St. Juvenal, Bishop of Jerusalem, at the Council of Chalcedon (451), made known to the Emperor Marcian and Pulcheria, who wished to possess the body of the Mother of God, that Mary died in the presence of all the Apostles, but that her tomb, when opened, upon the request of St. Thomas, was found empty; wherefrom the Apostles concluded that the body was taken up to heaven."

To-day, the belief in the corporeal assumption of Mary is universal in the East and in the West; according to Benedict XIV (De Festis B. V. M., I, viii, 18) it is a probable opinion, which to deny were impious and blasphemous. Regarding the origin of the feast we are also uncertain. It is more probably the anniversary of the dedication of some church than the actual anniversary of Our Lady's death. That it originated at the time of the Council of Ephesus, or that St. Damasus introduced it in Rome, is only a hypothesis. According to the life of St. Theodosius (d. 529) it was celebrated in Palestine before the year 500, probably in August (Bæumer, Brevier, 185). In Egypt and Arabia, however, it was kept in January, and since the monks of Gaul adopted many usages from the Egyptian monks (Bæumer, Brev., 163), we find this feast in Gaul in the sixth century, in January [mediante mense undecimo (Greg. Turon., De gloria mart., I, ix)]. The Gallican Liturgy has it on the 18th of January, under the title: Depositio, Assumptio, or Festivitas S. Mariæ (cf. the notes of Mabillon on the Gallican Liturgy, P. L., LXXII, 180). This custom was kept up in the Gallican Church to the time of the introduction of the Roman Rite. In the Greek Church, it seems, some kept this feast in January, with the monks of Egypt; others in August, with those of Palestine; wherefore the Emperor Maurice (d. 602), if the account of the "Liber Pontificalis" (II, 508) be correct, set the feast for the Greek Empire on 15 August. In Rome (Batiffol, Brev. Rom., 134) the oldest and only feast of Our Lady was 1 January, the octave of Christ's birth. It was celebrated first at Santa Maria Maggiore, later at Santa Maria ad Martyres. The other feasts are of Byzantine origin. Duchesne thinks (Origines du culte chr., 262) that before the seventh century no other feast was kept at Rome, and that consequently the feast of the Assumption, found in the Sacramentaries of Gelasius and Gregory, is a spurious addition made in the eighth or seventh century. Probst, however (Sacramentarien, 264 sqq.), brings forth good arguments to prove that the Mass of the Blessed Virgin Mary, found on the 15th of August in the Gelasianum, is genuine, since it does not mention the corporeal assumption of Mary; that, consequently, the feast was celebrated in the church of Santa Maria Maggiore at Rome at least in the sixth century. He proves, furthermore, that the Mass of the Gregorian Sacramentary, such as we have it, is of Gallican origin (since the belief in the bodily assumption of Mary, under the influence of the apocryphal writings, is older in Gaul than in Rome), and that it supplanted the old Gelasian Mass. At the time of Sergius I (700) this feast was one of the principal festivities in Rome; the procession started from the church of St. Hadrian. It was always a double of the first class and a Holy Day of obligation. The octave was added in 847 by Leo IV; in Germany this octave was not observed in several dioceses up to the time of the Reformation. The Church of Milan has not accepted it up to this day (Ordo Ambros., 1906). The octave is privileged in the dioceses of the provinces of Sienna, at Fermo, Michoacan, etc. The Greek Church continues this feast to 23 August, inclusive, and in some monasteries of Mount Athos it is protracted to 29 August (Menæa Græca, Venice, 1880), or was, at least, formerly. In the dioceses of Bavaria a thirtieth day (a species of month's mind) of the Assumption was celebrated during the Middle Ages, 13 Sept., with the Office of the Assumption (double); to-day, only the Diocese of Augsburg has retained this old custom. Some of the Bavarian dioceses and those of Brandenburg, Mainz, Frankfort, etc., on 23 Sept. kept the feast of the "Second Assumption", or the "Fortieth Day of the Assumption" (double) believing, according to the revelations of St. Elizabeth of Schönau (d. 1165) and of St. Bertrand, O.C. (d. 1170), that the B. V. Mary was taken up to heaven on the fourteenth day after her death (Grotefend, Calendaria 2, 136). The Birgittines kept the feast of the "Glorification of Mary" (double) 30 Aug., since St. Birgitta of Sweden says (Revel., VI, lxii) that Mary was taken into heaven fifteen days after her departure (Colvenerius, Cal. Mar., 30 Aug.). In Central America a special feast of the Coronation of Mary in heaven (double major) is celebrated 18 Aug. The city of Gerace in Calabria keeps three successive days with the rite of a double first class, commemorating: 15th of August, the death of Mary; 16th of August, her Assumption, and 17th of August, her Coronation. At Piazza, in Sicily, there is a commemoration of the Assumption of Mary (double second class) the 20th of February, the anniversary of the earthquake in 1743. A similar feast (double major with octave) is kept at Martano, Diocese of Otranto, in Apulia, 19th of November.

HOLWECK, *Fasti Mariani* (Freiburg, 1892); KELLNER, *Heortologie* (Freiburg, 1901), 171.

FREDERICK G. HOLWECK.

Assur, or ASSURÆ, a titular see of Proconsular Africa, now Henchir-Zenfour. Its episcopal list (251–484) is given in Gams (p. 464). Ruins of its temples and theatres and other public buildings are still visible.

MORCELLI, *Africa Christiana* (1816), I, 85–87.

Assur (Hebrew, אשור; Sept., Ἀσσούρ). (1) The name used in the Old Testament to designate the Assyrian land and nation. (See ASSYRIA.) (2) The name of one of the sons of Sem, mentioned in Gen., x, 22. In verse 11 of the same chapter, the Douay version has: "Out of that land came forth Assur". Here the name in the original refers not to a person, but to the country, as above, and the reading: " . . . he (Nimrod) went forth into Assyria (Assur)" is preferable. Another Assur, or Ashur, "father of Thecua", is mentioned in I Paral., ii, 24, and iv, 5. (3) The national god of the Assyrians (in the cuneiform inscriptions Asshur and Ashur). The religion of the Assyrians, like their language and their arts, was in all essential particulars derived from the Babylonians. But together with the preponderance of the Assyrian power over the southern provinces came a corresponding exaltation of the local tutelary deity. Asshur, who was originally the eponymic god of the capital of Assyria (also called Asshur), thus became a national god, and was placed at the head of the Assyrian pantheon. In his name, and to promote his interests, the Assyrian monarchs claim to undertake their various military expeditions. He is styled King among the gods; the god who created himself. Differently from the other deities, Asshur is not represented as having a consort or posterity. His symbolic representation is ordinarily a winged disc, sometimes accompanied by the figure of a human bust. (See ASSYRIA.)

GABRIEL OUSSANI.

Assurbanipal. See ASSYRIA.

Assyria.—In treating of Assyria it is extremely difficult not to speak at the same time of its sister, or rather mother, country, Babylonia, as the peoples of these two countries, the Semitic Babylonians and the Assyrians, are both ethnographically and linguistically the same race, with identical religion, language, literature, and civilization. Hence Assyro-Babylonian religion, mythology, and religious literature, especially in their relation to the Old Testament, will be treated in the article BABYLONIA, while the history of the modern explorations and discoveries in these two countries will be given in the present article.

GEOGRAPHY.—Geographically, Assyria occupies the northern and middle part of Mesopotamia, situated between the rivers Euphrates and Tigris; while the southern half, extending as far south as the Persian Gulf, constitutes the countries of Babylonia and Chaldea. Assyria originally occupied but a scant geographical area, comprising the small triangular-shaped land lying between the Tigris and Zab Rivers, but in later times, owing to its wonderful conquests, its boundaries extended as far north as Armenia; to Media on the east; to northern Syria, and to the country of the Hittites, on the west; and to Babylonia and Elam on the south and south-east, occupying almost the entire Mesopotamian valley. By the Hebrews it was known under the name of *Aram-Naharaim*, i. e. "Aram [or Syria] of the two rivers", to distinguish it from Syria proper, although it is doubtful whether the Hebrew name should be read as dual, or rather as a plural; i. e. *Aram-Naharîm*, "Aram of the many rivers", or "of the great river" —the Euphrates. In later Old Testament times, it was known under the name of *Asshur*. By the Greeks and Romans it was called Mesopotamia, and Assyria; by the Aramæans, *Beth-naharin*, "the country of the rivers"; by the Egyptians, *Nahrina;* by the Arabs, *Athûr*, or *Al-Gezirah*, "the island", or *Bain-al-nahrain*, "the country between the two rivers" —*Mesopotamia*. Whether the name *Assyria* is derived from that of the god Asshur, or vice versa, or whether *Asshur* was originally the name of a particular city and afterwards applied to the whole country, cannot be determined.

The area of Assyria is about fifty thousand square miles. In physical character it is mountainous and well watered, especially in the northern part. Limestone and, in some places, volcanic rock form the basis of its fertile soil. Its southern part is more level, alluvial, and fertile. Its principal rivers are the Tigris and the Euphrates, which have their source in the Armenian mountains and run almost parallel as far south as Babylonia and Chaldea, flowing into the Persian Gulf. There are other, minor rivers and tributaries, such as the Khabur, the Balikh, the Upper and Lower Zab, the Khoser, the Turnat, the Radanu, and the Subnat. Assyria owes to these rivers, and especially to the Tigris and Euphrates, somewhat as Egypt owes to the Nile, its existence, life, and prosperity.

The principal cities of Assyria are: (1) Asshur, whose site is now marked by the mound of Kalah-Shergat, on the right bank of the Tigris. (2) Calah, on the eastern bank of the Tigris and at its junction with the Upper Zab, a city built (c. 1280 B. C.) by Shalmaneser I, who made it the capital of Assyria, in place of Asshur. Its site is nowadays marked by the ruins of Nimroud. (3) Nineveh (in the Douay Version, Ninive), represented by the villages and ruins of the modern Kujunjik and Nebi-Yunus, on the eastern bank of the Tigris, opposite Mosul. Nineveh was undoubtedly one of the most ancient cities of Assyria, and in the time of Sennacherib (7th cent. B. C.) it became the capital of the empire, and the centre of the worship of Ishtar, the Assyro-Babylonian Venus, who was called Ishtar of Nineveh, to distinguish her from Ishtar of Arbela. In the Old Testament the city of Nineveh is well known in connexion with the prophets, and especially as the theatre of Jonah's mission. (4) Dur-Sharrukin, or Dur-Sargon (i. e. Sargonsburg), built by Sargon II (8th cent. B. C.), the founder of the famous Sargonid dynasty. It was made first the royal residence of Sargon, and afterwards became the rival of Nineveh. Its site is represented by the modern Khorsabad. (5) Arbailu, or Arbela, famous in Greek and Persian annals for the decisive victory won by Alexander the Great over the formidable army of Darius, King of Persia and Babylon (331 B. C.). (6) Nasibina, or Nisibis, famous in the annals of Nestorian Christianity. (7) Harran, well known for the worship of Sin, the moon-god. (8) Ingur-Bel, corresponding to the modern Tell-Balawât. (9) Tarbis, corresponding to the modern Sherif-Khan. The sites and ruins of all these cities have been explored.

SOURCES OF ASSYRO-BABYLONIAN HISTORY.— These may be grouped as: (1) the Old Testament; (2) the Greek, Latin, and Oriental writers; and (3) the monumental records and remains of the Assyrians and Babylonians themselves.

In the first division belong the Fourth (in Authorized Version, Second) Book of Kings, Paralipomenon (Chronicles), the writings of the prophets Isaias, Nahum, Jeremias, Jonas, Ezechiel, and Daniel, as well as the laconic but extremely valuable fragments of information contained in Genesis, x, xi, and xiv. To the second group of sources belong the Chaldeo-Babylonian priest and historian Berosus, who lived in the days of Alexander the Great (356–323 B. C.) and continued to live at least as late as Antiochus I, Soter (280–261 B. C.). He wrote in Greek a great work on Babylonian history, under the title of "Babyloniaca", or "Chaldaica". This valuable work, which was based on contemporary Babylonian monuments and inscriptions, has unfortunately perished, and only a few excerpts from it have been preserved in later Greek and Latin writers. Then we have the writings of Polyhistor, Ctesias, Herodotus, Abydenus, Apollodorus, Alexander of Miletus, Josephus, Georgius Syncellus, Diodorus Siculus, Eusebius, and others. With the exception of Berosus, the information derived from all the abovementioned historians is mostly legendary and unreliable, and even their quotations from Berosus are to be used with caution. This is especially true in the case of Ctesias, who lived at the Persian court in Babylonia. To the third category belong the numerous contemporary monuments and inscriptions discovered during the last fifty years in Babylonia, Assyria, Elam, and Egypt, which form an excellent and a most authoritative collection of historical documents.

For the chronology of Assyria we have some very valuable means of information. These are (1) The "Eponym List", which covers the entire period from the reign of Ramman-nirari II (911–890 B. C.) down to that of Asshurbanipal (669–625 B. C.). The eponyms, or *limmu*, were like the eponymous archons at Athens and the consuls at Rome. They were officers, or governors, whose term of office lasted but one year, to which year they gave their name; so that if any event was to be recorded, or a contract drawn in the year, e. g. 763 B. C., the number of the year would not be mentioned, but instead we are told that such and such an event took place in the year of Pur-Shagli, who was the *limmu*, or governor, in that year. (2) Another source is found in the chronological notices scattered throughout the historical inscriptions, such as Sennacherib's inscription engraved on the rock at Bavian, in which he tells us that one of his predecessors, Tiglath-pileser (Douay Version, Theglathphalasar) reigned about 418 years before him, i. e. about 1107 B. C.; or that of Tiglath-pileser himself, who tells us that he rebuilt the temple of Anu and Ramman, which sixty years previously had been pulled down by King Asshurdan because it had fallen into decay in the course of the 641 years since its foundation by King Shamshi-Ramman. This notice, therefore, proves that

Asshur-dan must have reigned about the years 1170 or 1180 B. C. So also Sennacherib tells us that a seal of King Tukulti-Ninib I had been brought from Assyria to Babylon, where after 600 years he found it on his conquest of that city. As Sennacherib conquered Babylon twice, once in 702 and again in 689 B. C., it follows that Tukulti-Ninib I must have reigned over Assyria in any case before 1289 B. C., and possibly a few years before 1302 B. C. (3) Another chronological source is to be found in the genealogies of the kings, which they give of themselves and of their ancestors and predecessors. (4) Further valuable help may be obtained from the so-called "Synchronous History" of Babylonia and Assyria, which consists of a brief summary of the relations between the two countries from the earliest times in regard to their respective boundary lines. The usefulness of this document consists mainly in the fact that it gives the list of many Babylonian and Assyrian kings who ruled over their respective countries contemporaneously.

ASSYRO-BABYLONIAN EXPLORATION.—As late as 1849, Sir Henry Layard, the foremost pioneer of Assyro-Babylonian explorations, in the preface to his classical work entitled "Nineveh and Its Remains", remarked how, previously, with the exception of a few cylinders and gems preserved elsewhere, a case, hardly three feet square, in the British Museum, enclosed all that remained not only of the great city, Nineveh, but of Babylon itself. At that time few indeed would have had the presumption even to imagine that within fifty years the exploration of Assyria and Babylonia would have given us the most primitive literature of the ancient world. What fifty years ago belonged to the world of dreams is at the present time a striking reality; for we are now in possession of the priceless libraries of the ancient Assyrians and Babylonians, of their historical annals, civil and military records, State archives, diplomatic correspondences, textbooks and school exercises, grammars and dictionaries, hymns, bank accounts and business transactions, laws and contracts, and an extensive collection of geographical, astronomical, mythological, magical, and astrological texts and inscriptions. These precious monuments are actually scattered in all the public and private museums and art collections of Europe, America, and Turkey. The total number of tablets, cylinders, and cuneiform inscriptions so far discovered is approximately estimated at more than three hundred thousand, which, if published, would easily cover 400 octavo volumes of 400 pages each. Unfortunately, only about one-fifth of all the inscriptions discovered have been published so far; but even this contains more than eight times as much literature as is contained in the Old Testament. The British Museum alone has published 440 folio, and over 700 quarto, pages, and about one-half as much more has appeared in various archæological publications. The British Museum has more than 40,000 cuneiform tablets, the Louvre more than 10,000, the Imperial Museum of Berlin more than 7,000, that of the University of Pennsylvania more than 20,000, and that of Constantinople many thousands more, awaiting the patient toil of our Assyriologists. The period of time covered by these documents is more surprising than their number. They occur from prehistoric times, or about 5000 B. C., down to the first century before the Christian Era. But this is not all, for, according to the unanimous opinion of all modern Assyriologists, by far the largest part of the Assyro-Babylonian literature and inscriptions are still buried under the fertile soil of these wonderful regions, which have ever been the land of surprises, awaiting further explorers and decipherers.

As has already been remarked, the meagre and often unreliable information concerning Assyria and

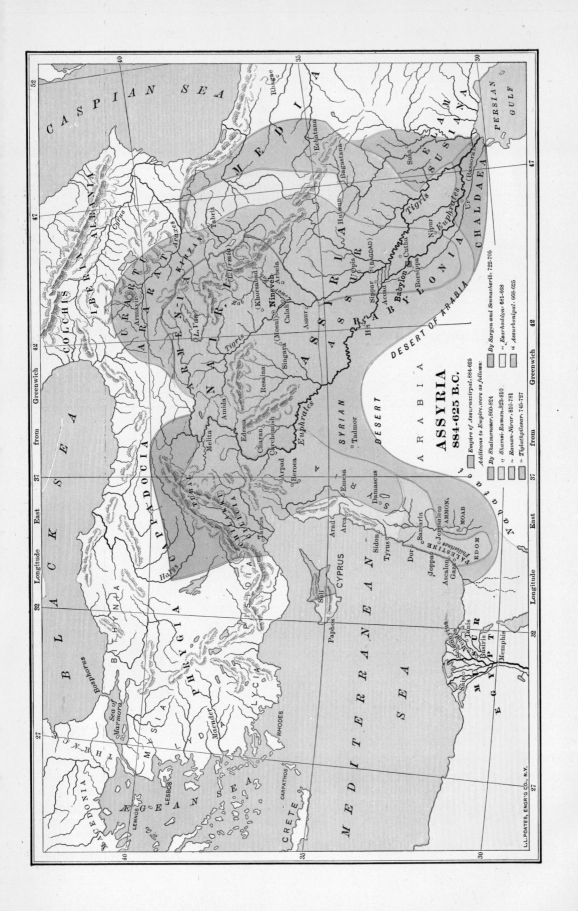

CASPIAN SEA

BLACK SEA

MEDITERRANEAN SEA

ÆGEAN SEA

PERSIAN GULF

DESERT OF ARABIA

ARABIA

SYRIAN DESERT

MEDIA

SUSIANA

ELAM

CHALDAEA

BABYLONIA

ASSYRIA

ARMENIA

URARTU

CAPPADOCIA

PHRYGIA

COLCHIS

IBERIA

ALBANIA

ASSYRIA
884-625 B.C.

Empire of Assurnazirpal, 884-625

Additions to Empire, were as follows:

By Shalmaneser, 860-824	By Sargon and Sennacherib, 722-705
Shamsi-Ramen, 823-810	Esarhaddon, 681-668
Raman-Nirar, 810-781	Assurbanipal, 668-625
Tiglathpileser, 745-727	

L.L. POATES, ENGR'G CO., N.Y.

Babylonia which has come down to us through the Persian, Greek, Latin, and Arabic writers—historians and geographers—has contributed little or nothing to the advancement of our knowledge of these wonderful countries. The early European travellers in the region of the Tigris and Euphrates valley, such as Benjamin of Tudela (1160), John Eldred (1583), Anthony Shirley (1599), Pietro della Valle (1614–26), John Cartwright (1610), Gasparo Balbi (1590), John Otter (1734), Niebuhr (1765), Beauchamp, Olivier, Hagers, and others at the end of the eighteenth century, have left us a rather vague and superficial account of their personal visits and impressions. Later travellers, however, such as Claudius James Rich (1811, 1821–22), J. S. Buckingham (1816), Sir Robert Ker Porter (1817–20), Captain Robert Mignan (1826–28), G. Baillie-Fraser (1834–35), the Euphrates Expedition under Colonel Chesney (1835–37), James Felix Jones, Lynch, Selby, Collingwood, Bewsher, and others of the first half of the nineteenth century made a far more searching and scientific study of the Mesopotamian region. But the real founders and pioneers of Assyro-Babylonian explorations are Emile Botta (1842–45), Sir Henry Austen Layard (1840–52), Victor Place (1851–55), H. Rassam (1850, 1878–82), Loftus (1850), Jules Oppert, Fresnel and Thomas (1851–52), Taylor (1851), Sir Henry Rawlinson, G. Smith, and others who have not only opened, but paved, the way for future researches and explorations. The first methodical and scientific explorations in Babylonia, however, were inaugurated and most successfully carried out by the intrepid French consul at Bassora and Bagdad, M. de Sarzec, who, from about 1877 until 1899, discovered at Tellô some of the earliest and most precious remains and inscriptions of the pre-Semitic and Semitic dynasties of Southern Babylonia. Contemporaneously with de Sarzec there came other explorers, such as Rassam, already mentioned above, who was to continue George Smith's excavations; the American Wolf expedition, under the direction of Dr. Ward, of New York (1884–85); and, above all, the various expeditions to Nippur, under Peters, Haynes, and Hilprecht, respectively, sent by the University of Pennsylvania (1888–1900). The Turkish Government itself has not altogether stood aloof from this praiseworthy emulation, sending an expedition to Abu Habba, or Sippar, under the direction of the well-known Dominican scholar, Father F. Scheil of Paris, in 1894 and the following years. Several German, French, and American expeditions have later been busily engaged in excavating important mounds and ruins in Babylonia. One of these is the German expedition under Moritz and Koldewey, with the assistance of Dr. Meissner, Delitzsch, and others, at Shurgul, El-Hibba, Al-Kasr, Tell-ibrahim, etc. The expedition of the University of Chicago, under the direction of Dr. Banks, at Bismaya, in South Babylonia, came unfortunately to an early termination.

THE LANGUAGE AND CUNEIFORM WRITING.—All these wonderful archæological researches and discoveries would have been useless and destitute of interest, had not the language of Assyro-Babylonian inscriptions been deciphered and studied. These inscriptions were all written in a language, and by means of characters, which seemed for a while to defy all human skill and ingenuity. The very existence of such a language had been forgotten, and its writing seemed so capricious and bewildering that the earlier European travellers mistook the characters for fantastic and bizarre ornamental decorations; their dagger- or arrow-headed shape (from which their name of cuneiform) presenting a difficult puzzle. However, the discovery, and tentative decipherment, of the old Persian inscrip-

tions (especially those of Persepolis and of the Behistun rock, not far from Hamadan, in Persia), by Grotefend, Heeren, the Abbé Saint Martin, Rask, Bournouf, Lassen, Westergaard, de Saulcy, and Rawlinson, all taking place at about the end of the first half of the nineteenth century, opened the way for the decipherment of the Assyro-Babylonian inscriptions. The principal credit unquestionably belongs to Rawlinson, Norris, J. Oppert, Fox Talbot, and especially to Dr. Hinks of Dublin. The acute and original researches of these scholars were successfully carried out by other Semitic scholars and linguists no less competent, such as E. Schrader and Fred. Delitzsch, in Germany; Ménant, Halévy, and Lenormant, in France; Sayce and G. Smith, in England.

The Assyro-Babylonian language belongs to the so-called Semitic family of languages, and in respect to grammar and lexicography offers no more difficulty to the interpreter than either Hebrew, or Aramaic, or Arabic. It is more closely allied to Hebrew and Aramaic than to Arabic and the other dialects of the South-Semitic group. The principal difficulty of Assyrian consists in its extremely complicated system of writing. For, unlike all other Semitic dialects, Assyrian is written not alphabetically, but either syllabically or ideographically, which means that Assyrian characters represent not consonants, but syllables, open or closed, simple or compound, and ideas or words, such as *ka, bar, ilu, zikaru,* etc. These same characters may also have both a syllabic and an ideographic value, and nearly always more than one syllabic value and as many as five or six; so that a sign like the following may be read syllabic-ally as *ud, ut, u, tu, tam, bir, par, pir, lah, lih, hish,* and *his;* and ideographically as *âmu,* "day"; *piṣu,* "white"; *Shamash,* the Sungod; etc. The shape of these signs is that of a wedge, hence the name *cuneiform* (from the Latin *cuneus,* "a wedge"). The wedges, arranged singly or in groups, either are called "ideograms" and stand for complete ideas, or they stand for syllables. In course of time the same ideographic signs came to have also the phonetic value of syllables, without losing, however, their primitive ideographic value, as can be seen from the example quoted above. This naturally caused a great difficulty and embarrassment even to the Assyro-Babylonians themselves, and is still the principal obstacle to the correct and final reading of many cuneiform words and inscriptions. To remedy this great inconvenience, the Assyro-Babylonians themselves placed other characters (called determinatives) before many of these signs in order to determine their use and value in certain particular cases and sentences. Before all names of gods, for example, either a sign meaning "divine being" was prefixed, or a syllabic character (phonetic complement), which indicated the proper phonetic value with which the word in question should end, was added after it. In spite of these and other devices, many signs and collocations of signs have so many possible syllabic values as to render exactness in the reading very difficult. There are about five hundred of these different signs used to represent words or syllables. Their origin is still a subject of discussion among scholars. The prevailing theory is that they were originally picture-signs, representing the ideas to be conveyed; but at present only about sixty of these 500 signs can be with certainty traced back to their original picture-meanings.

According to the majority of Assyriologists, the cuneiform system of writing originated with the Sumerians, the primitive non-Semitic inhabitants of Babylonia, from whom it was borrowed by the Semitic Babylonians and Assyrians, and applied to their own language. In the same way the Greeks adopted the Semitic Phœnician alphabet, and the Germans adopted the Latin. The Semitic language of Babylonia and Assyria was, therefore, written in Sumerian characters, just as Hebrew can be written in English letters, or Turkish in Armenian, or Arabic in Syriac (*Karshûni*). This same cuneiform system of writing was afterwards adopted by the Medians, Persians, Mitannians, Cappadocians, ancient Armenians, and others. Hence five or six different styles of cuneiform writings may be distinguished. The "Persian" style, which is a direct, but simplified, derivative of the Babylonian, was introduced in the times of the Achæmenians. "Instead of a combination of as many as ten and fifteen wedges to make one sign, we have in the Persian style never more than five, and frequently only three; and instead of writing words by syllables, sounds alone were employed, and the syllabary of several hundred signs reduced to forty-two, while the ideographic style was fractionally abolished." The second style of cuneiform, generally known as "Median", or "Susian", is, again, a slight modification of the "Persian". "Besides these two, there is a third language (spoken in the north-western district of Mesopotamia between the Euphrates and the Orontes), known as 'Mitanni', the exact status of which has not been clearly ascertained, but which has been adapted to cuneiform characters. A fourth variety, found on tablets from Cappadocia, represents again a modification of the ordinary writing met with in Babylonia. In the inscriptions of Mitanni, the writing is a mixture of ideographs and syllables, just as in Mesopotamia, while the so-called 'Cappadocian' tablets are written in a corrupt Babylonian, corresponding in degree to the 'corrupt' forms that the signs take on. In Mesopotamia itself quite a number of signs exist, some due to local influences, others the result of changes that took place in the course of time. In the oldest period known, that is, from 4000 to 3000 B. C., the writing is linear rather than wedge-shaped. The linear writing is the modification that the original pictures underwent in being adapted for engraving on stone; the wedges are the modification natural to the use of clay, though when once the wedges became the standard method, the greater frequency with which clay, as against stone, came to be used led to an imitation of the wedges by those who cut out the characters on stone. In consequence, there developed two varieties of wedge-writing: the one that may be termed lapidary, used for the stone inscriptions, the official historical records, and such legal documents as were prepared with especial care; the other cursive, occurring only on legal and commercial clay tablets, and becoming more frequent as we approach the latest period of Babylonian writing, which extends to within a few decades of our era. In Assyria, finally, a special variety of cuneiform developed that is easily distinguished from the Babylonian by its greater neatness and the more vertical position of its wedges" (Jastrow, The Religion of Babylonia and Assyria, Boston, 1898, p. 20).

The material on which the Assyro-Babylonians wrote their inscriptions was sometimes stone or metal, but usually clay of a fine quality most abundant in Babylonia, whence the use spread all over Western Asia. "The clay was very carefully prepared, sometimes ground to an exceeding fineness, moistened, and moulded into various forms, ordinarily into a tablet whose average size is about six by two and one-half inches in superficial area by one inch in thickness, its sides curving slightly outwards. On the surface thus prepared, and while still soft, the characters were impressed with a stylus, the writing often standing in columns, and carried over upon the back and sides of the tablet. The clay was quite frequently moulded also into cones and barrel-shaped cylinders,

having from six to ten sides on which writing could be inscribed. These tablets were then dried in the sun, or baked in a furnace—a process which rendered the writing practically indestructible, unless the tablet itself was shattered" (G. S. Goodspeed, History of the Babylonians and Assyrians, p. 28).

Unlike all other Semitic systems of writing (except the Ethiopic, which is an adaptation of the Greek), that of the Assyro-Babylonians generally runs from left to right in horizontal lines, although in some very early inscriptions the lines run vertically from top to bottom like the Chinese. These two facts evidence the non-Semitic origin of the cuneiform system of writing.

VALUE OF ASSYRIOLOGY FOR STUDY OF THE OLD TESTAMENT.—The part played by these Assyro-Babylonian discoveries in the exegesis and interpretation of the Old Testament has been important in direct proportion to the immense and hitherto unsuspected influence exercised by the Assyro-Babylonian religion, civilization, and literature upon the origin and gradual development of the literature and the religious and social institutions of the ancient Hebrews. This Babylonian influence, indeed, can be equally traced in its different forms and manifestations through all Western Asia, many centuries before that conquest of Palestine by the twelve Israelitish tribes which put an end to the Canaanitish dominion and supremacy. The triumph of Assyriology, consequently, must be regarded as a triumph for Biblical exegesis and criticism, not in the sense that it has strikingly confirmed the strict veracity of the Biblical narratives, or that it has demonstrated the fallacies of the "higher criticism", as Sayce, Hommel, and others have contended, but in the sense that it has opened a new and certain path whereby we can study the writings of the Old Testament with their correct historical background, and trace them through their successive evolutions and transformations. Assyriology, in fact, has given us such excellent and unexpected results as to completely revolutionize our former exegetical methods and conclusions. The study, it is true, has been often abused by ultra-radical and enthusiastic Assyriologists and critics. These have sought to build up groundless theories and illogical conclusions; they have forced the texts to say what they do not say, and to support conclusions which they do not support; but such an abuse, which is due to a perfectly natural enthusiasm and scientific ardour, can never vitiate the permanent value of sober Assyriological researches, which have demonstrably provided sources of the first importance for the study of the Old Testament. These few abuses can be discerned and in due time corrected by a more temperate and judicious criticism. If the value of Assyriology in its bearing upon the Old Testament has been too often exaggerated, the exaggeration is at least partly excusable, considering the comparatively recent date of these researches and their startling results in the way of discovery. On the other hand, that school of critics and theologians which disregards the genuine merits and the great value of Assyriological researches for the interpretation of the Old Testament is open to the double charge of unfairness and ignorance.

HISTORY OF ASSYRIA TO THE FALL OF NINEVEH (NINIVE.—c. 2000–606 B. C.)—The origin of the Assyrian nation is involved in great obscurity. According to the author of the tenth chapter of Genesis, the Assyrians are the descendants of Assur (Asshur) one of the sons of Sem (Shem—Gen., x, 22). According to Gen., x, 11, "Out of that land [Sennaar] came forth Assur, and built Ninive, and the streets of the city, and Chale. Resen also between Ninive and Chale ", where the Authorized Version reads: "builded Nineveh, and the city of Rehoboth, and

Calah, and Resen between Nineveh and Calah". Till quite recently the most commonly accepted interpretation of this passage was that Assur left Babylonia, where Nemrod (Nimrod) the terrible was reigning, and settled in Assyria, where he built the cities of Nineveh, Rehoboth, Chale (Calah), and Resen. Nowadays, however, this interpretation, which is mainly based on the Vulgate version, is abandoned in favour of the more probable one, according to which Nemrod himself, the beginning of whose kingdom was Babylon (Babel), Arach (Erech), Achad (Accad), and Chalanne (Calneh), in Southern Babylonia (Gen., x, 10), went up to Assyria (Assur in this case being a geographical name, i. e. Assyria, and not ethnographical or personal), and there he built the four above-mentioned cities and founded the Assyrian colony. Whichever of these two interpretations be held as correct, one thing is certain: that the Assyrians are not only Semites, but in all probability an offshoot of the Semitic Babylonians, or a Babylonian colony; although, on account of their apparently purer Semitic blood, they have been looked upon by some scholars as an independent Semitic offshoot, which, at the time of the great Semitic migration from Arabia (c. 3000–2500 B. C.), migrated and settled in Assyria. The first Assyrian rulers known to us bore the title of *Ishshaku* (probably "priest-prince", or "governor") and were certainly subject to some outside power, presumably that of Babylonia. Some of the earliest of these Ishshaki known to us are Ishmi-Dagan and his son Shamshi-Adad I (or Shamshi-Ramman). The exact date of these two princes is uncertain, although we may with reasonable certainty place them about 1840–1800 B. C. Other Ishshaki are Igur-Kapkapu, Shamshi-Adad II, Khallu, and Irishum. The two cities of Nineveh and Assur were certainly in existence at the time of Hammurabi (c. 2250 B. C.), for in one of his letters he makes mention of them. It is significant, however, that in the long inscription (300 lines) of Agumkakrime, one of the Kassite rulers of Babylonia (c. 1650 B. C.), in which he enumerates the various countries over which his rule extended, no mention is made of Assyria. Hence, it is probable that the beginning of an independent Assyrian kingdom may be placed towards the seventeenth century B. C. According to an inscription of King Esarhaddon (681–668 B. C.), the first Assyrian Ishshaku to assume the title of King was a certain Bel-bani, an inscription of whom, written in archaic Babylonian, was found by Father Scheil. His date, however, cannot be determined.

Towards the fifteenth century B. C. we find Egyptian supremacy extended over Syria and the Mesopotamian valley; and in one of the royal inscriptions of Thothmes III of Egypt (1480–27 B. C.), we find Assyria among his tributary nations. From the Tel-el-Amarna letters also we know that diplomatic negotiations and correspondences were frequent among the rulers of Assyria, Babylonia, Syria, Mitanni, and the Egyptian Pharaohs, especially Amenhotep IV. Towards this same period we find also the Kings of Assyria standing on an equal footing with those of Babylonia, and successfully contesting with the latter for the boundary-lines of their kingdom. About 1450 B. C. Asshur-bel-nishe-shu was King of Assyria. He settled the boundary-lines of his kingdom with his contemporary Kara-indash, King of Babylonia. The same treaty was concluded again between his successor, Puzur-Asshur, and Burnaburiash I, King of Babylon. Puzur-Asshur was succeeded by Asshur-nadin-Aḫḫe, who is mentioned by his successor, Asshur-uballit, in one of his letters to Amenhotep IV, King of Egypt, as his father and predecessor. During most of the long reign of Asshur-uballit, the relations between Assyria and Babylonia continued friendly, but towards the end of that reign the first open conflict between the two sister-countries broke out. The cause of the conflict was as follows: Asshur-uballit, in sign of friendship, had given his daughter, Muballitat-sherua, for wife to the King of Babylonia. The son born of this royal union, Kadashman-Charbe by name, succeeded his father on the throne, but was soon slain by a certain Nazi-bugash (or Suzigash), the head of the discontented Kassite party, who ascended the throne in his stead. To avenge the death of his grandson the aged and valiant monarch, Asshur-uballit, invaded Babylonia, slew Nazi-bugash, and set the son of Kadashman-Charbe, who was still very young, on the throne of Babylonia, as Kurigalzu II. However, towards the latter part of his reign (c. 1380 B. C.), Kurigalzu II became hostile to Assyria; in consequence of which, Belnirari, Asshur-uballit's successor on the throne of Assyria, made war against him and defeated him at the city of Sugagu, annexing the northern part of Babylonia to Assyria. Belnirari was succeeded by his son, Pudi-ilu (c. 1360 B. C.), who undertook several successful military expeditions to the east and south-east of Assyria and built various temples, and of whom we possess few, but important, inscriptions. His successor was Ramman-nirari, who not only strengthened the newly-conquered territories of his two predecessors, but also made war and defeated Nazi-Maruttash, King of Babylonia, the successor of Kurigalzu II, adding a considerable Babylonian territory to the newly arisen, but powerful, Assyrian Empire.

Towards the end of the fourteenth century B. C. (about 1330–20 B. C.) Ramman-nirari was succeeded by his son Shalmaneser I. During, or about the time of this ruler, the once powerful Egyptian supremacy over Syria and Mesopotamia, thanks to the brilliant military raids and resistance of the Hittites, a powerful horde of tribes in Northern Syria and Asia Minor, was successfully withstood and confined to the Nile Valley. With the Egyptian pressure thus removed from Mesopotamia, and the accession of Shalmaneser I, an ambitious and energetic monarch, to the throne of Assyria, the Assyrian Empire began to extend its power westwards. Following the course of the Tigris, Shalmaneser I marched northwards and subjugated many northern tribes; then, turning westwards, invaded part of north-eastern Syria and conquered the Arami, or Aramæans, of Western Mesopotamia. From there he marched against the land of Muṣri, in Northern Arabia, adding a considerable territory to his empire. For strategic reasons he transferred the seat of his kingdom from the city of Asshur to that of Kalkhi (the Chale, or Calah, of Genesis), forty miles to the north, on the eastern bank of the Tigris, and eighteen miles south of Nineveh. Shalmaneser I was succeeded by his son Tukulti-Ninib (c. 1290 B. C.), whose records and inscriptions have been collected and edited by L. W. King of the British Museum. He was a valiant warrior and conqueror, for he not only preserved the integrity of the empire but also extended it towards the north and north-west. He invaded and conquered Babylonia, where he established the seat of his government for fully seven years, during which he became obnoxious to the Babylonians, who plotted and rebelled against him, proclaiming a certain Ramman-shur-usur king in his stead. The Assyrians themselves also became dissatisfied on account of his long absence from Assyria, and he was slain by his own nobles, who proclaimed his son, Asshur-nâsir-pal, king in his stead. After the death of this prince, two kings, Asshur-narrara and Nabu-dayan by name, reigned over Assyria, of whom, however, we know nothing. Towards 1210–1200 B. C. we find Bel-Kudur-usur and his successor,

Ninib-pal-Eshara, reigning over Assyria. These, however, were attacked and defeated by the Babylonians, who thus regained possession of a considerable part of their former territory. The next Assyrian monarch was Asshur-dan, Ninib-pal-Eshara's son. He avenged his father's defeat by invading Babylonia and capturing the cities of Zaban, Irria, and Akarsallu. In 1150 B. C., Asshur-dan was succeeded by his son, Mutakkil-Nusku; and in 1140 B. C., by the latter's son Asshur-resh-ishi, who subjugated the peoples of Ahlami, Lullumi, Kuti (or Guti), and other countries, and administered a crushing defeat to his rival and contemporary, Nabuchodonosor (Nebuchadnezzar) I, King of Babylonia.

About 1120–10 B. C. Asshur-resh-ishi was succeeded by his son, Tiglath-pileser I, one of the greatest Assyrian monarchs, under whose reign of only ten years duration Assyria rose to the apex of its military success and glory. He has left us a very detailed and circumstantial account of his military achievements, written on four octagonal cylinders which he placed at the four corners of the temple built by him to the god Ramman. According to these, he undertook, in the first five years of his reign, several successful military expeditions against Mushku, against the Shubari, against the Hittites, and into the mountains of Zagros, against the people of Nairi and their twenty-three kings, who were chased by him as far north as Lake Van in Armenia; against the people of Muṣri in Northern Arabia, and against the Aramæans, or Syrians. "In all", he tells us, "forty-two countries and their kings, from beyond the Lower Zab, from the border of the distant mountains as far as the farther side of the Euphrates, up to the land of Hatti [Hittites] and as far as the upper sea of the setting sun [i. e. Lake Van], from the beginning of my sovereignty until my fifth year, has my hand conquered. I carried away their possessions, burned their cities with fire, demanded from their hostages tribute and contributions, and laid on them the heavy yoke of my rule." He crossed the Euphrates several times, and even reached the Mediterranean, upon the waters of which he embarked. He also invaded Babylonia, inflicting a heavy blow on the Babylonian king, Marduk-nadin-aḫḫe and his army, and capturing several important cities, such as Dur-Kurigalzu, Sippar, Babylon, and Opis. He pushed his triumphal march even as far as Elam. Tiglath-pileser I was also a daring hunter, for in one of his campaigns, he tells us, he killed no fewer than one hundred and twenty lions on foot, and eight hundred with spears while in his chariot, caught four elephants alive, and killed ten in his chariot. He kept at the city of Asshur a park of animals suitable for the chase. At Nineveh he had a botanical garden, in which he planted specimens of foreign trees gathered during his campaigns. He built also many temples, palaces, and canals. It may be of interest to add that his reign coincides with that of Heli (Eli), one of the ten judges who ruled over Israel prior to the establishment of the monarchy. At the time of Tiglath-pileser's death, Assyria was enjoying a period of tranquillity, which did not last, however, very long; for we find his two sons and successors, Asshur-bel-Kala and Shamshi-Ramman, seeking offensive and defensive alliances with the Kings of Babylonia.

From about 1070 to 950 B. C., a gap of more than one hundred years presents itself in the history of Assyria. But from 950 B. C. down to the fall of Nineveh and the overthrow of the Assyrian Empire (606 B. C.) the history of Assyria is very completely represented in documents. Towards 950 B. C., Tiglath-pileser II was king over Assyria. In 930 B. C. he was succeeded by his son, Asshur-dan II, and about 910 B. C. by the latter's son, Ramman-nirari II,

who, in 890, was succeeded by his son, Tukulti-Ninib II. The last two monarchs appear to have undertaken several successful expeditions against Babylonia and the regions north of Assyria. Tukulti-Ninib's successor was his son Asshur-nasir-pal (885–860 B. C.), with whose accession to the throne began a long career of victory that placed Assyria at the head of the great powers of that age. He was a great conqueror, soldier, organizer, hunter, and builder, but fierce and cruel. In his eleven military campaigns he invaded, subdued, and conquered, after a series of devastations and raids, all the regions north, south, east, and west of Assyria, from the mountains of Armenia down to Babylon, and from the mountains of Kurdistan and Lake Urmi (Urumyah) to the Mediterranean. He crossed the Euphrates and the Orontes, penetrated into the Lebanon region, attacked Karkemish, the capital of the Hittites, invaded Syria, and compelled the cities of the Mediterranean coast (such as Tyre, Sidon, Byblos, and Armad) to pay tribute. But the chief interest in the history of Asshur-nasir-pal lies in the fact that it was in his reign that Assyria first came into touch with Israel. In his expedition against Karkemish and Syria, which took place in 878 B. C., he undoubtedly exacted tribute from Amri (Omri), King of Israel; although the latter's name is not explicitly mentioned in this sense, either in Asshur-nasir-pal's inscriptions, or in the Old Testament. The fact, however, seems certain, for in the Assyrian inscriptions from about this time down to the time of Sargon—nearly 150 years—the land of Israel is frequently mentioned as the "land of Omri"; and Jehu, a later King of Israel, but not of the dynasty of Amri, is also called the "son of Omri". This seems to show that the land of Israel was known to the Assyrians as the land of that king who happened to be reigning when they were first brought into political relations with it, and we know that this king was Amri, for in 878, the year of Asshur-nasir-pal's expedition to Syria, he had been king over Israel for some nine years.

Asshur-nasir-pal was succeeded by his son, Shalmaneser II, who in the sixth year of his reign (854 B. C.) made an expedition to the West with the object of subduing Damascus. In this memorable campaign he came into direct touch with Israel and their king Achab (Ahab), who happened to be one of the allies of Benhadad, King of Damascus. In describing this expedition the Assyrian monarch goes on to say that he approached Karkar, a town to the south-west of Karkemish, and the royal residence of Irhulini.—"I desolated and destroyed, I burnt it: 1,200 chariots, 1,200 horsemen, 20,000 men of Biridri of Damascus; 700 chariots, 700 horsemen, 10,000 men of Irhulini of Hamath; 2,000 chariots, 10,000 men *of Ahab of Israel* . . . these twelve kings he [i. e. Irhulini] took to his assistance. To offer battle they marched against me. With the noble might which Asshur, the Lord, granted, with the powerful weapons which Nergal, who walks before me, gave, I fought with them, from Karkar into Gilzan I smote them. Of their soldiers I slew 14,000."—The Old Testament is silent on the presence of Achab in the battle of Karkar, which took place in the same year in which Achab died fighting in the battle of Ramoth Galaad (III Kings, xxii).

Eleven years after this event Jehu was proclaimed king over Israel, and one of his first acts was to pay tribute to Shalmaneser II. This incident is commemorated in the latter's well-known "black obelisk", in the British Museum, in which Jehu himself, "the son of Omri", is sculptured as paying tribute to the king. In another inscription the same king records the same fact, saying: "At that time I received the tribute of the Tyrians, Sidonians, and Jehu the son of Omri." This act of homage took place in 842 B. C., in the eighteenth year of Shalmaneser's reign.

After Shalmaneser II came his son Shamshi-Ramman II (824 B. C.), who, in order to quell the rebellion caused by his elder son, Asshur-danin-pal, undertook four campaigns. He also fought and defeated the Babylonian King, Marduk-balatsu-iqbi, and his powerful army. Shamshi-Ramman II was succeeded by his son, Ramman-nirari III (812 B. C.). This king undertook several expeditions against Media, Armenia, the land of Nairi, and the region around Lake Urmi, and subjugated all the coastlands of the West, including Tyre, Sidon, Edom, Philistia, and the "land of Omri", i. e. Israel. The chief object of this expedition was again to subdue Damascus, which he did by compelling Mari', its king, to pay a heavy tribute in silver, gold, copper, and iron, besides quantities of cloth and furniture. Joachaz (Jehoahaz) was then king over Israel, and he welcomed with open arms Ramman-nirari's advance, inasmuch as this monarch's conquest of Damascus relieved Israel from the heavy yoke of the Syrians. Ramman-nirari III also claimed sovereignty over Babylonia. His name is often given as that of Adad-nirari, and he reigned from 812 to 783 B. C. In one of his inscriptions, which are unfortunately scarce and laconic, he mentions the name of his wife, Sammuramat, which is the only Assyrian or Babylonian name discovered so far having any phonetic resemblance to that of the famous legendary queen, Semiramis. The personal identity of the two queens, however, is not admissible. Ramman-nirari III was succeeded by Shalmaneser III (783-773 B. C.), and the latter by Asshurdan III (773-755 B. C.), who in turn was followed by Asshur-nirari II (755-745 B. C.). Of these three kings we know little, as no adequate inscriptions of their reigns have come down to us.

In the year 745 B. C. Tiglath-pileser III (in the Douay Version, Theglathphalasar) seized the throne of Assyria, at Nineveh. He is said to have begun life as a gardener, to have distinguished himself as a soldier, and to have been elevated to the throne by the army. He was a most capable monarch, enterprising, energetic, wise, and daring. His military ability saved the Assyrian Empire from the utter ruin and decay which had begun to threaten its existence, and for this he is fitly spoken of as the founder of the Second Assyrian Empire. Tiglath-pileser's methods differed from those of his predecessors, who had been mere raiders and plunderers. He organized the empire and divided it into provinces, each of which had to pay a fixed tribute to the exchequer. He was thus able to extend Assyrian supremacy over almost all of Western Asia, from Armenia to Egypt, and from Persia to the Mediterranean. During his reign Assyria came into close contact with the Hebrews, as is shown by his own inscriptions, as well as by the Old Testament records, where he is mentioned under the name of Phul (Pul). In the Assyrian inscriptions his name occurs only as that of Tiglath-pileser, but in the "List of Babylonian Kings" he is also called Pul, which settles his identity with the Phul, or Pul, of the Bible. He reigned for eighteen years (745-727 B. C.). In his annals he mentions the payment of tribute by several kings, amongst whom is "Menahem of Samaria", a fact confirmed by IV Kings, xv, 19, 20. During his reign, Achaz was King of Juda. This prince, having been hard pressed and harassed by Rasin (Rezin) of Damascus, and Phacee (Pekah) of Israel, entreated protection from (Tiglath-pileser) Theglathphalasar, who, nothing loath, marched westward and attacked Rasin, whom he overthrew and shut up in Damascus. Two years later, the city surrendered, Rasin was slain, and the inhabitants were carried away captives (IV Kings, xvi, 7, 8, 9). Meanwhile

Israel also was overrun by the Assyrian monarch, the country reduced to the condition of a desert, and the trans-Jordanic tribes carried into captivity. At the same time the Philistines, the Edomites, the Arabians, and many other tribes were subdued; and after the fall of Damascus, Tiglath-pileser held a durbar which was attended by many princes, amongst whom was Achaz himself. His next expedition to Palestine was in 734, the objective this time being Gaza, an important town on the sea-coast. Achaz hastened to make, or, rather, to renew, his submission to the Assyrian monarch; as we find his name mentioned again with several other tributary kings on one of Tiglath-pileser's inscriptions. In 733 the Assyrian monarch carried off the population from large portions of the Kingdom of Israel, sparing, however, the capital, Samaria. Tiglath-pileser was the first Assyrian king to come into contact with the Kingdom of Juda, and also the first Assyrian monarch to begin on a large scale the system of transplanting peoples from one country to another, with the object of breaking down their national spirit, unity, and independence. According to many scholars, it was during Tiglath-pileser's reign that Jonas (Jonah) preached in Nineveh, although others prefer to locate the date of this Hebrew prophet a century later, i. e. in the reign of Asshurbanipal (see below).

Tiglath-pileser III was succeeded by his son (?), Shalmaneser IV, who reigned but five years (727-722 B. C.). No historical inscriptions relating to this king have as yet been found. Nevertheless, the "Babylonian Chronicle" (which gives a list of the principal events occurring in Babylonia and Assyria between 744 and 688 B. C.) has the following statement: "On the 25th of Thebet [December-January] Shalmaneser [in D. V. Salmanasar] ascended the throne of Assyria, and the city of Shamara'in [Samaria] was destroyed. In the fifth year of his reign he died in the month of Thebet." The Assyrian "Eponym Canon" (see above) also informs us that the first two years of Shalmaneser's reign passed without an expedition, but in the remaining three his armies were engaged. In what direction the armies of Shalmaneser (Salmanasar) were engaged, the "Canon" does not say, but the "Babylonian Chronicle" (quoted above) and the Old Testament (IV Kings, xviii) explicitly point to Palestine, and particularly to Samaria, the capital of the Israelitish Kingdom. In the second or third year of Shalmaneser's reign, Osee (Hoshea) King of Israel, together with the King of Tyre, rebelled against Assyria; and in order to crush the rebellion the Assyrian monarch marched against both kings and laid siege to their capitals. The Biblical account (Douay Version, IV Kings, xvii, 3 sqq.) of this expedition is as follows: "Against him came up Salmanasar king of the Assyrians, and Osee became his servant, and paid him tribute. And when the king of the Assyrians found that Osee endeavouring to rebel had sent messengers to Sua the king of Egypt, that he might not pay tribute to the king of the Assyrians, as he had done every year, he besieged him, bound him, and cast him into prison. And he went through all the land: and going up to Samaria, he besieged it three years. And in the ninth year of Osee, the king of the Assyrians took Samaria, and carried Israel away to Assyria; and he placed them in Hala and Habor by the river of Gozan, in the cities of the Medes."— See also the parallel account in IV Kings, xviii, 9-11, which is one and the same as that here given. The two Biblical accounts, however, leave undecided the question, whether Shalmaneser himself or his successor conquered Samaria; while, from the Assyrian inscriptions, it appears that Shalmaneser died, or was murdered, before he could personally carry his victory to an end. He was succeeded by Sargon II.

Sargon, a man of commanding ability, was, notwithstanding his claim to royal ancestry, in all probability a usurper. He is one of the greatest figures in Assyrian history, and the founder of the famous Sargonid dynasty, which held sway in Assyria for more than a century, i. e. until the fall of Nineveh and the overthrow of the Assyrian Empire. He himself reigned for seventeen years (722–705 B. C.) and proved a most successful warrior and organizer. In every battle he was victor, and in every difficulty a man of resource. He was also a great builder and patron of the arts. His greatest work was the building of Dur-Sharrukin, or the Castle of Sargon, the modern Khorsabad, which was thoroughly explored in 1844–55 by Botta, Flandin, and Place. It was a large city, situated about ten miles from Nineveh, and capable of accommodating 80,000 inhabitants. His palace there was a wonder of architecture, panelled in alabaster, adorned with sculpture, and inscribed with the records of his exploits. In the same year in which he ascended the throne, Samaria fell (722 B. C.), and the Kingdom of Israel was brought to an end. "In the beginning of my reign", he tells us in his annals, "and in the first year of my reign . . . Samaria I besieged and conquered . . . 27,290 inhabitants I carried off . . . I restored it again and made it as before. People from all lands, my prisoners, I settled there. My officials I set over them as governors. Tribute and tax I laid on them, as on the Assyrians." Sargon's second campaign was against the Elamites, whom he subdued. From Elam he marched westward, laid Hamath in ruins, and afterwards utterly defeated the combined forces of the Philistines and the Egyptians, at Raphia. He made Hanum, King of Gaza, prisoner, and carried several thousand captives, with very rich booty, into Assyria. Two years later, he attacked Karkemish, the capital of the Hittites, and conquered it, capturing its king, officers, and treasures, and deporting them into Assyria. He then for fully six years harassed, and finally subdued, all the northern and north-western tribes of Kurdistan of Armenia (Urartu, or Ararat), and of Cilicia: the Mannai, the Mushki, the Kummukhi, the Milidi, the Kammani, the Gamgumi, the Samali, and many others who lived in those wild and inaccessible regions. Soon after this he subdued several Arabian tribes and, afterwards, the Medians, with their forty-two chiefs, or princes.

During the first eleven years of Sargon's reign, the Kingdom of Juda remained peacefully subject to Assyria, paying the stipulated annual tribute. In 1711 B. C., however, Ezechias (Hezekiah), King of Juda, partly influenced by Merodach-baladan, of Babylonia, and partly by promises of help from Egypt, rebelled against the Assyrian monarch, and in this revolt he was heartily joined by the Phœnicians, the Philistines, the Moabites, and the Ammonites. Sargon was ever quick to act; he collected a powerful army, marched against the rebels, and dealt them a crushing blow. The fact is recorded in Isaias, xx, 1, where the name of Sargon is expressly mentioned as that of the invader and conqueror. With Palestine and the West pacified and subdued, Sargon, ever energetic and prompt, turned his attention to Babylonia, where Merodach-baladan was ruling. The Babylonian army was easily routed, and Merodach-baladan himself abandoned Babylon and fled in terror to Beth-Yakin, his ancestral stronghold. Sargon entered Babylonia in triumph, and in the following year he pursued the fleeing king, stormed the city of Beth-Yakin, deported its people, and compelled all the Babylonians and Elamites to pay him tribute, homage, and obedience. In 705, in the flower of his age and at the zenith of his glory, Sargon was assassinated. He was succeeded by his son, Sennacherib (705 to 681 B. C.), whose

name is so well known to Bible students. He was an exceptionally cruel, arrogant, revengeful, and despotic ruler, but, at the same time, a monarch of wonderful power and ability. His first military expedition was directed against Merodach-baladan, of Babylonia, who, at the news of Sargon's death, had returned to Babylonia, assuming the title of king, and murdering Merodach-zakir-shumi, the viceroy appointed by Sargon. Merodach-baladan was, however, easily routed by Sennacherib; fleeing again to Elam and hiding himself in the marshes, but always ready to take advantage of Sennacherib's absence to return to Babylon. In 701, Sennacherib marched eastward over the Zagros mountains and towards the Caspian Sea. There he attacked, defeated, and subdued the Medians and all the neighbouring tribes. In the same year he marched on the Mediterranean coast and received the submission of the Phœnicians, the Ammonites, the Moabites, and the Edomites. He conquered Sidon, but was unable to lay hands on Tyre, on account of its impregnable position. Thence he hurried down the coast road, captured Askalon and its king, Sidqa; turning to the north, he struck Ekron and Lachish, and dispersed the Ethiopian-Egyptian forces, which had assembled to oppose his march. Ezechias (Hezekiah), King of Juda, who together with the above-mentioned kings had rebelled against Sennacherib, was thus completely isolated, and Sennacherib, finding his way clear, marched against Juda, dealing a terrific blow at the little kingdom. Here is Sennacherib's own account of the event: "But as for Hezekiah of Judah, who had not submitted to my yoke, forty-six of his strong walled cities and the smaller cities round about them without number, by the battering of rams, and the attack of war-engines [?], by making breaches, by cutting through, and the use of axes, I besieged and captured. Two hundred thousand one hundred and fifty people, small and great, male and female, horses, mules, asses, camels, and sheep without number I brought forth from their midst and reckoned as spoil. Himself [Hezekiah] I shut up like a caged bird in Jerusalem, his royal city. I threw up fortifications against him, and whosoever came out of the gates of his city I punished. His cities, which I had plundered, I cut off from his land and gave to Mitinti, King of Ashdod, to Padi, King of Ekron, and to Cil-Bel, King of Gaza, and [thus] made his territory smaller. To the former taxes, paid yearly, tribute, a present for my lordship, I added and imposed on him. Hezekiah himself was overwhelmed by the fear of the brilliancy of my lordship, and the Arabians and faithful soldiers whom he had brought in to strengthen Jerusalem, his royal city, deserted him. Thirty talents of gold, eight hundred talents of silver, precious stones, *guhli daggassi*, large lapis lazuli, couches of ivory, thrones of elephant skin and ivory, ivory, *ushu* and *urkarinu* woods of every kind, a heavy treasure, and his daughters, his palace women, male and female singers, to Nineveh, my lordship's city, I caused to be brought after me, and he sent his ambassador to give tribute and to pay homage."

The same event is also recorded in IV Kings, xviii and xix, and in Isaias, xxxvi and xxxvii, but in somewhat different manner. According to the Biblical account, Sennacherib, not satisfied with the payment of tribute, demanded from Ezechias the unconditional surrender of Jerusalem, which the Judean king refused. Terrified and bewildered, Ezechias called the prophet Isaias and laid the matter before him, asking him for advice and counsel. The prophet strongly advised the vacillating king to oppose the outrageous demands of the Assyrian, promising him Yahweh's help and protection. Accordingly, Ezechias refused to surrender, and

Sennacherib, enraged and revengeful, resolved to storm and destroy the city. But in that same night the whole Assyrian army, gathered under the walls of Jerusalem, was stricken by the angel of the Lord, who slew one hundred and eighty-five thousand Assyrian soldiers. At the sight of this terrible calamity, Sennacherib, in terror and confusion, departed and returned to Assyria. The Assyrian and the Biblical accounts are *primâ facie* conflicting, but many more or less plausible solutions have been suggested. In the first place we must not expect to find in Sennacherib's own annals mention of, or allusion to, any reverse he may have suffered; such allusions would be clearly incompatible with the monarch's pride, as well as with the purpose of annals inscribed only to glorify his exploits and victories. In the second place, it is not improbable that Sennacherib undertook two different campaigns against Juda: in the first, to which his annals refer, he contented himself with exacting and receiving submission and tribute from Ezechias (Hezekiah); but in a later expedition, which he does not mention, he insisted on the surrender of Jerusalem, and in this latter expedition he met with the awful disaster. It is to this expedition that the Biblical account refers. Hence, there is no real contradiction between the two narratives, as they speak of two different events. Furthermore, the disaster which overtook the Assyrian army may have been, after all, quite a natural one. It may have been a sudden attack of the plague, a disease to which Oriental armies, from their utter neglect of sanitation, are extremely subject, and before which they quickly succumb. Josephus explicitly affirms that it was a *flagellum prodigiosum* (Antiq. Jud., X, i, n. 5); while, according to an Egyptian tradition preserved to us by Herodotus (Lib. II, cxli), Sennacherib's army was attacked and destroyed by a kind of poisonous wild mice, which suddenly broke into the Assyrian camp, completely demoralizing the army. At any rate Sennacherib's campaign came to an abrupt end, and he was forced to retreat to Nineveh. It is noteworthy, however, that for the rest of his life Sennacherib undertook no more military expeditions to the West, or to Palestine. This fact, interpreted in the light of the Assyrian monuments, would be the result of the complete submission of Syria and Palestine; while in the light of the Biblical narrative it would signify that Sennacherib, after his disastrous defeat, dared not attack Palestine again.

While laying siege to Jerusalem, Sennacherib received the disquieting news of Merodach-baladan's sudden appearance in Babylonia. A portion of the Assyrian army was detached and hurriedly sent to Babylonia against the restless and indomitable foe of Assyria. In a fierce battle, Merodach-baladan was for the third time defeated and compelled to flee to Elam, where, worn and broken down by old age and misfortunes, he ended his troubled life, and Asshur-nadin-shum, the eldest son of Sennacherib, was appointed king over Babylonia. After his return from the West, and after the final defeat of Merodach-baladan, Sennacherib began lengthy and active preparations for an effective expedition against Babylonia, which was ever rebellious and restless.— "The expedition was as unique in its methods as it was audacious in its conception."—With a powerful army and navy, he moved southward and, in a terrific battle near Khalulu, utterly routed the rebellious Chaldeans, Babylonians, and Elamites, and executed their two chiefs, Nergal-usezib and Musezib-Merodach. Elam was ravaged, "the smoke of burning towns obscuring the heavens". He next attacked Babylon, which was stormed, sacked, burnt, flooded, and so mercilessly punished that it was reduced to a mass of ruins, and almost obliterated. On his return to Assyria, Sennacherib

appears to have spent the last years of his reign in building his magnificent palace at Nineveh, and in embellishing the city with temples, palaces, gardens, arsenals, and fortifications. After a long, stormy, and glorious reign, he died by the hand of one of his own sons (681 B. C.). The Bible tells us that "as he [Sennacherib] was worshipping in the temple of Nesroch his god, Adramelech and Sarasar his sons slew him with the sword, and they fled into the land of the Armenians, and Asarhaddon [Esarhaddon] his son reigned in his stead" (IV Kings, xix, 37). The "Babylonian Chronicle", however, has "On 20 Thebet [December–January] Sennacherib, King of Assyria, was slain by his son in a rebellion . . . years reigned Sennacherib in Assyria. From 20 Thebet to 2 Adar [March–April] was the rebellion in Assyria maintained. On 18 Adar his son, Esarhaddon, ascended the throne of Assyria." If the murderer of Sennacherib was, as the "Babylonian Chronicle" tells us, one of his own sons, no son of Sennacherib by the name of Adrammelech or Sharezer has as yet been found in the Assyrian monuments; and while the Biblical narrative seems to indicate that the murder took place in Nineveh, on the other hand an inscription of Asshurbanipal, Sennacherib's grandson, clearly affirms that the tragedy took place in Babylon, in the temple of Marduk (of which Nesroch, or Nisroch, is probably a corruption).

Sennacherib was succeeded by his younger son, Esarhaddon, who reigned from 681 to 668 B. C. At the time of his father's death, Esarhaddon was in Armenia with the Assyrian army, but on hearing the sad news he promptly set out for Nineveh, first to avenge his father's death by punishing the perpetrators of the crime, and then to ascend the throne. On his way home he met the assassins and their army near Cappadocia, and in a decisive battle routed them with tremendous loss, thus becoming the sole and undisputed lord of Assyria. Esarhaddon's first campaign was against Babylonia, where a fresh revolt, caused by the son of the late Merodach-baladan, had broken out. The pretender was easily defeated and compelled to flee to Elam. Esarhaddon, unlike his father, determined to build up Babylon and to restore its ruined temples, palaces, and walls. He gave back to the people their property, which had been taken away from them as spoils of war during Sennacherib's destructive campaign, and succeeded in restoring peace and harmony among the people. He determined, furthermore, to make Babylon his residence for part of the year, thus restoring its ancient splendour and religious supremacy. Esarhaddon's second campaign was directed against the West, i. e. Syria, where a fresh rebellion, having for its centre the great maritime city of Sidon, had broken out. He captured the city and completely destroyed it, ordering a new city, with the name of Kar-Esarhaddon, to be built on its ruins. The King of Sidon was caught and beheaded, and the surrounding country devastated. Twenty-two Syrian princes, among them Manasses, King of Juda, surrendered and submitted to Esarhaddon. Scarcely, however, had he retired when these same princes, including Manasses, revolted. But the great Esarhaddon utterly crushed the rebellion, taking numerous cities, captives, and treasures, and ordering Manasses to be carried to Babylon, where the king was then residing. A few years later Esarhaddon had mercy on Manasses and allowed him to return to his own kingdom. In a third campaign, Esarhaddon blockaded the impregnable Tyre, and set out to conquer Egypt, which he successfully accomplished by defeating its king, Tirhakah. In order to effectively establish Assyrian supremacy over Egypt, he divided the country into twenty provinces, and over each of these he appointed a governor; sometimes a native, sometimes an

Assyrian. He exacted heavy annual tribute from every one of these twenty provinces, and returned in triumph to Assyria. "As for Tarqu [Tirhakah], King of Egypt and Cush, who was under the curse of their great divinity, from Ishupri as far as Memphis, his royal city—a march of fifteen days—every day without exception I killed his warriors in great number, and as for him, five times with the point of the spear I struck him with a deadly stroke. Memphis, his royal city, in half a day, by cutting through and scaling, I besieged, I conquered, I tore down, I destroyed, I burned with fire, and the wife of his palace, his palace women, Ushanahuru, his own son, and the rest of his sons, his daughters, his property and possessions, his horses, his oxen, his sheep without number, I carried away as spoil to Assyria. I tore up the root of Cush from Egypt, a single one—even to the suppliant—I did not leave behind. Over all Egypt I appointed kings, prefects, governors, grain-inspectors, mayors, and secretaries. I instituted regular offerings to Asshur and the great gods, my lords, for all time. I placed on them the tribute and taxes of my lordship, regularly and without fail." Esarhaddon also invaded Arabia, penetrating to its very centre, through hundreds of miles of sandy lands which no other Assyrian monarch had penetrated before. Another important campaign was that directed against the Cimmerians, near the Caucasus, and against many other tribes, in Armenia, Cappadocia, Cilicia, Asia Minor, and Media. The monarch's last expedition was a second campaign against Egypt. Before leaving Assyria, however, i. e. in the month of Iyyar (April–May), 668 B. C., as if forecasting future events, he constituted his son Asshurbanipal co-regent and successor to the throne, leaving to his other son, Shamash-shum-ukin, Babylonia. But, while on his way to Egypt, he fell sick, and on the 10th of Marsheshwan (October), in the year 668, he died.

Esarhaddon was a truly remarkable ruler. Unlike his father, he was religious, generous, forgiving, less harsh and cruel, and very diplomatic. He ruled the various conquered countries with wisdom and toleration, while he established a rigorous system of administration. A great temple-builder and lover of art, he has left us many records and inscriptions. At Nineveh he rebuilt the temple of Asshur, and in Babylonia, the temples at Ukuk, Sippar, Dur-Ilu, Borsippa, and others, in all about thirty. In Nineveh he erected for himself a magnificent palace and arsenal, and at Kalkhi (Calah; Douay, Chale) another of smaller dimensions, which was still unfinished at the time of his death. Asshurbanipal, Esarhaddon's successor, was undoubtedly the greatest of all Assyrian monarchs. For generalship, military conquests, diplomacy, love of splendour and luxury, and passion for the arts and letters, he has neither superior nor equal in the annals of that empire. To him we owe the greatest part of our knowledge of Assyro-Babylonian history, religion, literature, art, and civilization. Endowed with a rare taste for letters, he caused all the most important historical, religious, mythological, legal, astronomical, mathematical, grammatical, and lexicographical texts and inscriptions known to his day to be copied and placed in a magnificent library which he built in his own palace. "Tens of thousands of clay tablets systematically arranged on shelves for easy consultation contained, besides official dispatches and other archives, the choicest religious, historical, and scientific literature of the Babylonio-Assyrian world. Under the inspiration of the king's literary zeal, scribes copied and translated the ancient sacred classics of primitive Babylonia for this library, so that, from its remains, can be reconstructed, not merely the details of the government and administration of the Assyria of his time, but the life and

thought of the far distant Babylonian world." (G. H. Goodspeed, Hist. of the Babylonians and Assyrians, pp. 315, 316.) Of this library, which must have contained over forty thousand clay tablets, a part was discovered by G. Smith and H. Rassam, part has been destroyed, and part yet remains to be explored. Here G. Smith first discovered the famous Babylonian accounts of the Creation and of the Deluge in which we find so many striking similarities with the parallel Biblical accounts. Asshurbanipal was also a great temple-builder—in Nineveh, Arbela, Tarbish, Babylon, Borsippa, Sippar, Nippur, and Uruk. He fortified Nineveh, repaired, enlarged, and embellished Sennacherib's palace, and built next to it another palace of remarkable beauty. This he adorned with numerous magnificent statues, sculptures, bas-reliefs, inscriptions, and treasures. Assyrian art, especially sculpture and architecture, reached during his reign its golden age and its classical perfection, while Assyrian power and supremacy touched the extreme zenith of its height; for with Asshurbanipal's death Assyrian power and glory sank into the deepest gloom, and perished, presumably, to rise no more.

Asshurbanipal's military campaigns were very numerous. He ascended the throne in 668 B. C., and his first move was against Egypt, which he subdued, penetrating as far as Memphis and Thebes. On his way back, he exacted tribute from the Syrian and Phœnician kings, among whom was Manasses of Juda, who is expressly mentioned in one of the king's inscriptions. He forced Tyre to surrender, and subdued the Kings of Arvad, of Tabal, and of Cilicia. In 655, he marched against Babylonia and drove away from it a newly organized, but powerful coalition of Elamites, Chaldeans, and Arameans. He afterwards marched into the very heart of Elam, as far as Susa, and in a decisive battle he shattered the Elamite forces. In 625, Shamash-shum-ukin, Asshurbanipal's brother, who had been appointed by his father King of Babylonia, and who had till then worked in complete harmony with his brother, rebelled against Asshurbanipal. To this he was openly and secretly incited by many Babylonian, Elamite, and Arabian chiefs. Asshurbanipal, however, was quick to act. He marched against Babylonia, shut off all the rebels in their own fortresses, and forced them to a complete surrender. His brother set fire to his own palace and threw himself into the flames. The cities and fortresses were captured, the rebels slain, and Elam completely devastated. Temples, palaces, royal tombs, and shrines were destroyed. Treasures and booty were taken and carried away to Assyria, and several thousands of people, as well as all the princes of the royal family, were executed, so that, a few years later, Elam disappeared for ever from history. In another campaign, Asshurbanipal advanced against Arabia and subdued the Kedarenes, the Nabatæans, and a dozen other Arabian tribes, as far as Damascus. His attention was next attracted to Armenia, Cappadocia, Media, and the north-western and north-eastern regions. In all these he established his supremacy, so that from 640 till 626, the year of Asshurbanipal's death, Assyria was at peace. However, most scholars incline to believe that during the last years of the monarch's reign the Assyrian Empire began to decay.

Asshurbanipal is probably mentioned once in the Old Testament (I Esdras, iv, 10) under the name of Asenaphar, or, better, Ashenappar (Ashenappal) in connexion with his deportation of many troublesome populations into Samaria. He is probably alluded to by the Second Isaias and Nahum, in connexion with his campaigns against Egypt and Arabia. According to G. Brunengo, S.J. (Nabuchodnossor di Giuditta, Rome, 1886) and other scholars,

Asshurbanipal is the Nabuchodonosor (Nebuchadnezzar) of the Book of Judith; others identify him with the Sardanapalus of Greek historians. In view, however, of the conflicting characters of the legendary Sardanapalus and the Asshurbanipal of the cuneiform inscriptions, this last identification seems impossible. Besides, Asshurbanipal was not the last king of Assyria, as Sardanapalus is supposed to have been.

Asshurbanipal was succeeded by his two sons, Asshur-etil-elani and Sin-shar-ishkun. Of their respective reigns and their exploits we know nothing, except that in their days Assyria began rapidly to lose its prestige and power. All the foreign provinces—Egypt, Phœnicia, Chanaan, Syria, Arabia, Armenia, Media, Babylonia, and Elam—broke away from Assyria, when the degenerate and feeble successors of the valiant Asshurbanipal proved unable to cope with the situation. They had probably abandoned themselves to effeminate luxury and debaucheries, caring little or nothing for military glory. In the meanwhile Nabopolassar, King of Babylon, and Cyaxares, King of Media, formed a family and political alliance, the latter giving his daughter in marriage to the former's son, Nabuchodonosor (Nebuchadnezzar). At the head of a powerful army, these two kings together marched against Nineveh and laid siege to it for fully two years, after which the city surrendered and was completely destroyed and demolished (606 B. C.), and Assyria became a province of Babylonia and Media.

RELIGION AND CIVILIZATION.—The religion and civilization of Assyria were almost identical with those of Babylonia, the former having been derived from the latter and developed along the same lines. For, although the Assyrians made notable contributions to architecture, art, science, and literature, these were with them essentially a Babylonian importation. Assyrian temples and palaces were modelled upon those of Babylonia, although in the building-material stone was far more liberally employed. In sculptural decorations and in statuary more richness and originality were displayed by the Assyrians than by the Babylonians. It seems to have been a hobby of Assyrian monarchs to build colossal palaces, adorned with gigantic statues and an infinite variety of bas-reliefs and inscriptions showing their warlike exploits. Asshurbanipal's library shows that Assyrian religious literature was not only an imitation of that of Babylonia, but absolutely identical therewith. An examination of the religions of the two countries proves that the Assyrians adopted Babylonian doctrines, cults, and rites, with such slight modifications as were called for by the conditions prevailing in the northern country. The chief difference in the Assyrian pantheon, compared with that of Babylonia, is that, while in Semitic times the principal god of the latter was Marduk, that of the former was Asshur. The principal deities of both countries are: the three chief deities, Anu, the god of the heavenly expanse; Bel, the earth god and creator of mankind; and Ea, the god of humanity *par excellence*, and of the water. Next comes Ishtar, the mother of mankind and the consort of Bel; Sin, first-born son of Bel, the father of wisdom, personified in the moon; Shamash, the sun-god; Ninib, the hero of the heavenly and earthly spirits; Nergal, chief of the netherworld and of the subterranean demons, and god of pestilence and fevers; Marduk, originally a solar deity, conqueror of storms, and afterwards creator of mankind and the supreme god of Semitic Babylonia; Adad, or Ramman, the god of storms, thunders, and lightning; Nebo, the god of wisdom, to whom the art of writing and the sciences are ascribed; Girru-Nusku, or, simply, Nusku, the god of fire, as

driving away demons and evil spirits; Asshur, the consort of Belit, and the supreme god of Assyria. Besides these there were other minor deities.

I. *Excavations and Decipherment*: KAULEN, *Geschichte Assyriens und Babyloniens nach den neuesten Entdeckungen* (Freiburg, 1899); HOMMEL, *Geschichte Babyloniens und Assyriens* (Berlin, 1885), 30–134; EVETTS, *New Light on the Holy Land* (London, 1891), 79–129; VIGOUROUX, *La Bible et les découvertes modernes en Palestine, en Égypte et en Assyrie* (Paris, 1896), I, 133–204; ROGERS, *A History of Babylonia and Assyria* (New York, 1901), I, 1–253; HILPRECHT, *Explorations in Bible Lands During the 19th Century* (Philadelphia, 1903), 1–577; BOOTH, *The Discovery and Decipherment of the Trilingual Cuneiform Inscriptions* (London, 1902); FOSSEY, *Manuel d'Assyriologie* (Paris, 1904), I.

II. *History of Assyria*: HOMMEL, *op. cit. supra*; TIELE, *Babylonisch-Assyrische Geschichte* (Gotha, 1886); MUERDTER-DELITZSCH, *Kurzgefasste Geschichte Babyloniens und Assyriens* (Stuttgart, 1891); MASPERO, *The Struggle of the Nations*, and *The Passing of the Empires*, vols. II and III of the tr. of the same author's classical work, *Histoire ancienne des peuples de l'Orient classique*; WINCKLER, *Geschichte Babyloniens und Assyriens* (Leipzig, 1902); ROGERS, *op. cit. supra* in 2 vols.; GOODSPEED, *History of the Babylonians and Assyrians* (New York, 1902); as well as PANNIER in VIG., *Dict. de la Bible* and HOMMEL in HASTINGS, *Dict. of the Bible*.

III. *Collections of Assyrian Texts and Translations*: RAWLINSON, *The Cuneiform Inscriptions of Western Asia* (London, 1861–84); IDEM, *Cuneiform Texts in the British Museum* (London; 26 parts having already appeared); SCHRADER, *Keilinschriftliche Bibliothek* (Leipzig, 1889–1901); *Records of the Past—being English Translations of the Assyrian and Egyptian Monuments*, two series (London, 1888–92); HARPER, *Assyrian and Babylonian Literature* in *The World's Great Books* (New York, 1901).

IV. *Assyrian Arts and Civilization*: PERROT ET CHIPIEZ, *Histoire de l'art dans l'antiquité* (Paris, 1884), II, *Chaldée et Assyrie*, Eng. tr., ARMSTRONG (New York); the older works of BOTTA AND FLANDIN, *Monuments de Ninive* (Paris, 1849–50); works of LAYARD, OPPERT, PLACE, etc.

V. *Religion of Assyria*: JASTROW, *The Religion of Babylonia and Assyria* (Boston, 1898), German ed., much improved, and entirely rewritten; bibliography in art. BABYLONIA.

VI. *Comparative Study of Assyrian Monuments and Inscriptions and the Bible*: SCHRADER, *The Cuneiform Inscriptions and the Old Testament* (London, 1884–88), also 3d German ed., entirely rewritten by WINCKLER AND ZIMMERMAN, under the original title *Die Keilinschriften und das Alte Testament* (Berlin, 1902); VIGOUROUX, *op. cit.*; BALL, *Light from the East, or the Witness of the Monuments* (London, 1899); SAYCE, *The Higher Criticism and the Verdict of the Monuments* (London, 1894); HOMMEL, *The Ancient Hebrew Tradition as Illustrated by the Monuments* (London, 1897); PRICE, *The Monuments and the Old Testament* (Chicago, 1900); PINCHES, *The Old Testament in the Light of the Historical Records and Legends of Assyria and Babylonia* (London, 1903); JEREMIAS, *Das Alte Testament im Lichte des alten Orients* (Leipzig, 1904).

GABRIEL OUSSANI.

Astaroth (ASTARTE). See PHŒNICIA.

Asterisk (Gr., ἀστήρ, a star).—This is a utensil for the Mass according to the Greek Rite, which is not used in the Roman Rite at all. It consists of two curved bands, or slips, made of silver or gold which cross each other at right angles and thus form a double arch. It is used to place over the *amnos*, or particles of blessed bread, when spread out upon the paten during the *proskomide* and earlier part of the Greek Mass, so as to prevent the veil from coming in contact with or disturbing these blessed but unconsecrated particles of bread in carrying the paten from the *prothesis* to the altar, or while it is standing at either place. It is laid aside after the Creed and is not ordinarily used again during the Mass. The *asterisk* is usually surmounted by a cross, and often has a tiny star suspended from the central junction, and in the Greek Orthodox is somewhat larger in size than in the Greek Catholic Church. When the priest in the *proskomide* service is through incensing the blessed bread lying upon the paten, he takes up the *asterisk* and incensing it says, "And the star came forth and stood over where the child was". Then he puts it over the particles of bread upon the paten, and proceeds to cover it with the various veils and at conclusion of the *proskomide*, begins the celebration of the Mass.

KRAUS, *Real-Encyk.* s. v.; PÉTRIDÈS in *Dict. d'arch. chrét.*, s. v.; CLUGNET, *Dict. des noms liturgiques*, 22.

ANDREW J. SHIPMAN.

II.—2

Asterius, name of several prominent persons in early Christian history.—(1) Asterius of Petra, a bishop of Arabia, ill-treated by the Arian faction at the Council of Sardica (343) for withdrawing from them his support, and exiled to Upper Libya in Egypt, whence he was recalled in 362 by the edict of Julian that restored all the banished bishops. He took part in the Council of Alexandria (362), called, among other reasons, for the purpose of healing the Meletian schism that was rending the Church of Antioch. He was one of the bearers of the letter addressed by the council to the stubborn Lucifer of Cagliari and the other bishops then at Antioch. These peaceful measures were, however, rendered useless by Lucifer's precipitancy in consecrating Paulinus as successor to Melétius of Antioch, whereby the schism gained a new lease of life.—(2) Asterius of Amasea in Pontus (c. 400). The only fact in his life that is known is related by himself, viz. his education by a Scythian or Goth who had been sent in his youth to a schoolmaster of Antioch and thus acquired an excellent education and great fame among both Greeks and Romans. The extant writings of Asterius are twenty-one homilies, scriptural and panegyrical in content. The two on penance and "on the beginning of the fasts" were formerly ascribed to St. Gregory of Nyssa (Bardenhewer, Patrologie, 1901, 267). A life of his predecessor, St. Basil, is ascribed to Asterius (Acta SS., 26 April). His works (P. G., XL) are described by Tillemont (Mém., X, 409). He was a student of Demosthenes and an orator of repute. Lightfoot says (Dict. of Christ. Biogr., I, 178) that his best sermons display "no inconsiderable skill in rhetoric, great power of expression, and great earnestness of moral conviction; some passages are even strikingly eloquent." The homilies of Asterius, like those of Zeno of Verona, offer no little valuable material to the Christian archæologist. [De Buck in Acta SS., 30 Oct. (Paris, 1883), XIII, 330–334.]—(3) Asterius of Cappadocia, a Greek sophist, a friend of Arius, and also his fellow student in the school of Lucian of Antioch. St. Athanasius quotes more than once from a pro-Arian work of this writer. He wrote commentaries on the Epistle to the Romans, the Gospels, the Psalms, and "many other works" (Jerome, De Vir. Ill., c. xciv), all of which have perished (Zahn, Marcellus von Ancyra, Gotha, 1867, 68 sqq.).—(4) Asterius, a Roman senator mentioned by Eusebius (Hist. Eccl., VII, 16) as a Christian distinguished for faith and charity. Rufinus says that he suffered martyrdom at Cæsarea in Palestine in 262 (Baronius, An. Eccl. ad an. 262, §§ 81, 82).—(5) Asterius Urbanus, a Montanist writer of the latter part of the second century, referred to in Eusebius (Hist. Eccl., V, 16, 17); his work was probably a compilation of the pseudo-prophetic utterances of Montanus and his female companions Priscilla and Maximilla. THOMAS J. SHAHAN.

Asti, DIOCESE OF, one of the divisions of the province of Alexandria, and suffragan of Turin. Asti is a very old town. It became Christian at an early period of the Christian Era. The first known bishop was Pastor in 451. After him, were Majoranus in 465, Benenatus in 680, and St. Evasius in 730. From 800 begins the regular list of bishops, though the see was vacant from 1857 to 1867. There has been some controversy as to the beginning of the Diocese of Asti and the episcopate of St. Evasius, once placed by some at much earlier dates. Asti has 182,600 Catholics, 107 parishes, 300 secular priests, 12 regulars, 92 seminarists, 525 churches or chapels.
GAMS, Series episcop. Eccles. cathol. (Ratisbon, 1873), 812; UGHELLI, Italia Sacra (Venice, 1722), IV, 332; CAPPELLETTI, Le chiese d'Italia (Venice, 1866), XIV, 179; SAVIO, Gli antichi vescovi d'Italia: Premonte (Turin, 1897), I, 109–157.

Aston, name of several English Catholics of prominence.—SIR ARTHUR, member of an ancient and knightly family, an able military officer in the army of Charles I, governor of Oxford for the king, and made governor of Drogheda (Ireland) in 1649. He was killed 10 September, 1649, at the siege of that town by the forces of Oliver Cromwell; his brains were dashed out with his wooden leg during the massacre that followed the capture (D. Murphy, Cromwell in Ireland, Dublin, 1897, p. 99).—HERBERT, an English poet, b. at Chelsea, 1614, third son of Walter, first Lord Aston of Forfar, whom he accompanied to Madrid on his second embassy in 1635, author of "Tixall Poetry, Collected by the Hon. Herbert Aston, 1658" (ed. with notes and illustrations by Arthur Clifford, Esq., Edinburgh, 1813, 4to).—WALTER, father of the preceding and son of Sir Edward Aston, of Tixall in Staffordshire, educated under the direction of Sir Edward Coke, sent as one of the two ambassadors to Spain (1619) to negotiate a marriage treaty between Charles (I), Prince of Wales, and the Infanta, daughter of Philip III. He became a convert to the Catholic Faith on this occasion, and on his return to England was made Lord of Forfar (Scotland). He had a decided taste for literature, and was the patron of Drayton, who dedicated to him (1598) his "Black Prince", and in his "Polyolbion" praises the Aston's "ancient seat" of Tixall.—WILLIAM, b. 22 April, 1735, educated at St.-Omer, entered the Society of Jesus in 1751, and taught for several years in the Society's colleges of St.-Omer, Watten, and Bruges, until the suppression in 1773; d. at Liège, 15 March, 1800, as canon of the cathedral. Among his writings are "Lettres Ultramontaines" and "Le Cosmopolite".
GILLOW, Bibl. Dict. of Engl. Catholics, I, 76–82; FOLEY, Records of Engl. Province, S. J.
THOMAS J. SHAHAN.

Astorga (ASTURIGA AUGUSTA), DIOCESE OF, suffragan of Valladolid in Spain, dates, it is said, from the third century. It was the principal church of the Asturias in 344, after a long eclipse was again an episcopal see in 747, and exhibits since 841 a regular succession of bishops. It was at different times a suffragan of Braga and of Santiago. It includes the whole province of Leon, and counts 300,115 Catholics, 990 parishes, and as many parish churches, 431 chapels, and 1,183 priests.
BATTANDIER, Ann. pont. cath. (Paris, 1905), 215; WERNER, Orbis Terr. Cath. (Freiburg, 1890), 47; GAMS, Series ep. (1873) 6–9; FLOREZ, España Sagrada (1762), XVI, 77, 519; MUÑOZ, Bibl. Hist. Esp. (1858) 40.
THOMAS J. SHAHAN.

Astrolatry. See SABAISM.

Astrology, the supposed science which determines the influence of the stars, especially of the five older planets, on the fate of man (astrologia judiciaria; mundane, or judicial astrology) or on the changes of the weather (astrologia naturalis; natural astrology) according to certain fixed rules dependent upon the controlling position of the stars (constellations and aspects) at the time under consideration. Judicial astrology—the more important branch of this occult art—depended for its predictions upon the position of the planets in the "twelve houses" at the moment of the birth of a human being. The calculations necessary to settle these positions were called casting the horoscope or the diagram of the heavens (thema cœli) at the nativity. Starting with the point that was rising just at the moment of birth, the celestial equator was divided into twelve equal parts, six above and six below the horizon, and circles were drawn through these points and the intersecting points of the horizon and the meridian. Thus the heavens were divided into twelve houses. The first house (horoscopus) begins with the point of the ecliptic that is just rising (ascendens). The twelve houses are divided into cardinal houses, also called *anguli*, succeeding houses (*succedentes*, *anaphora*) and declining or cadent houses (*cadentes*, *cataphora*). The houses symbolize respectively: life, personal property, consanguinity, riches, children and jewels, health, marriage and course of life, manner of death and inheritance, intellect and disposition (also long journeys), position in life and dignities, friends and success, enemies and misfortune. In the horoscope all these symbolic meanings are considered in their relation to the newly born. A Latin hexameter thus sums up the meaning of the twelve houses:

Vita, lucrum, fratres, genitor, nati, valetudo,

Uxor, mors, sapiens, regnans, benefactaque, dæmon. The position of the planets and the sun and moon in the twelve houses at the moment of birth is decisive. The planets vary as to meaning. They are divided into day-stars (Saturn, Jupiter, and also the sun) and night-stars (the moon, Mars, and Venus); Mercury belongs both to day and night. The sun, Jupiter, and Mars are masculine; the moon and Venus are feminine, Mercury belonging again to both classes. Jupiter (*fortuna major*) and Venus (*fortuna minor*) are good planets; Saturn (*infortuna major*) and Mars (*infortuna minor*) are malignant planets. The sun, moon, and Mercury have a mixed character. Each of the planets known to antiquity, including sun and moon, ruled a day of the week; hence the names still used to designate the various days. Judicial astrology also took into consideration the position of the sun in the zodiac at the moment of birth; the signs of the zodiac also had a special astrological significance in respect to the weal and woe of the new-born, particularly his bodily health. In medical astrology every sign of the zodiac ruled some special part of the body, as for example: Aries, the Ram (♈), the head and its diseases; Libra, the Balance (♎), the intestines. Judicial astrology postulates the acceptance of the earth as the centre of the solar system. Natural astrology predicts the weather from the positions of the planets, especially the moon. Many of its theories are not to be rejected *a priori*, since the question of the moon's meteorological influence still awaits a solution which must depend upon the progress of human knowledge as to ether waves and cognate matters.

HISTORY.—The history of astrology is an important part of the history of the development of civilization; it goes back to the early days of the human race. The unchangeable, harmonious course of the heavenly bodies, the profound impression made on the soul of man by the power of such heavenly phenomena as eclipses, the feeling of dependence on the sun, the giver of daylight—all these probably suggested, in the early ages of the human race, the question whether the fate of man was not dependent on these majestic manifestations of Divine power. Astrology was, therefore, the foster-sister of astronomy, the science of the investigation of the heavens. From the start astrology was employed for the needs and benefit of daily life; the astrologers were astronomers only incidentally and in so far as astronomy assisted astrology in the functions which the latter had to perform in connexion with religious worship. According to the belief of the early civilized races of the East, the stars were the source and at the same time the heralds of everything that happened, and the right to study the "godlike science" of astrology was a privilege of the priesthood. This was the case in Mesopotamia and Egypt, the oldest centres of civilization known to us in the East. The most ancient dwellers on the Euphrates the Akkado-Sumerians were believers in judicial astrology, which was closely interwoven with their worship of the stars. The same is true of their successors, the Babylonians and Assyrians, who were the chief exponents of astrology in antiquity. The Babylonians

and Assyrians developed astrology, especially judicial, to the status of a science, and thus advanced in pure astronomical knowledge by a circuitous course through the labyrinth of astrological predictions. The Assyro-Babylonian priests (Chaldeans) were the professional astrologers of classic antiquity. In its origin Chaldaic astrology also goes back to the worship of the stars; this is proved by the religious symbolism of the most ancient cuneiform texts of the zodiac. The oldest astrological document extant is the work called "Namar-Beli" (Illumination of Bel) composed for King Sargon I (end of the third millennium B. C.) and contained in the cuneiform library of King Asurbanipal (668–626 B. C.). It includes astronomical observations and calculations of solar and lunar eclipses combined with astrological predictions, to which the interpretation of dreams already belonged. Even in the time of Chaldean, which should be called Assyrian, astrology, the five planets, together with the sun and moon, were divided according to their character and their position in the zodiac as well as according to their position in the twelve houses. As star of the sun, Saturn was the great planet and ruler of the heavens. The weather, as far back as this time, was predicted from the colour of the planets and from their rising and setting. Classical antiquity looked upon Berosus, priest of the temple of Bel at Babylon, as the oldest writer on astrology; and according to Vitruvius Berosus founded a school of astrology at Cos. Seneca says that a Greek translation, made by Berosus, of the "Namar-Beli" from the library of Asurbanipal was known to classical antiquity.

The Egyptians and Hindus were as zealous astrologers as the nations on the Euphrates and Tigris. The dependence of the early Egyptian star (sun) worship (the basis of the worship of Osiris) upon early Chaldaic influences belongs to the still unsettled question of the origin of early Egyptian civilization. But undoubtedly the priests of the Pharaohs were the docile pupils in astrology of the old Chaldean priests. The mysterious Taauth (Thoth), the Hermes Trismegistus of antiquity, was regarded as the earliest teacher of astrology in Egypt. He is reputed to have laid the foundation of astrology in the "Hermetic Books"; the division of the zodiac into the twelve signs is also due to him. In classic antiquity many works on astrology or on occult sciences in general were ascribed to this mythical founder of Egyptian astrology. The astrological rule of reckoning named after him "Trutina Hermetis" made it possible to calculate the position of the stars at the time of conception from the diagram of the heavens at the time of birth. The Egyptians developed astrology to a condition from which it varies but little to-day. The hours of the day and night received special planets as their rulers, and high and low stood under the determinative influence of the stars which proclaimed through the priestly caste the coming fate of the land and its inhabitants. It is significant that in ancient Egypt astronomy, as well as astrology, was brought to an undoubtedly high state of cultivation. The astoundingly daring theories of the world found in the Egyptian texts, which permit us to infer that their authors were even acquainted with the heliocentric conception of the universe, are based entirely on astrologico-theosophic views. The astrology of the ancient inhabitants of India was similar, though hardly so completely developed; they also regarded the planets as the rulers of the different hours. Their division of the zodiac into twenty-eight houses of the moon is worthy of notice; this conception, like all the rest of the fundamental beliefs of Hindu astrology, is to be found in the Rig-Veda. In India both astrology and the worship of the gods go back to the worship of the stars. Even to-day, the Hindus, especially the Brahmins, are considered the best authorities on astrology and the most skilful casters of horoscopes.

India influenced and aided the development of astrology in ancient China; both India and Mesopotamia that of the Medes and Persians. The Assyro-Babylonian and Egyptian priests were the teachers of the Greek astrologers. Both of these priestly castes were called Chaldeans, and this name remained the designation of all astrologers and astronomers in classic antiquity and in the period following. It speaks well for the sound sense of the early Grecian philosophers that they separated the genuine astronomic hypotheses and facts from the confused mass of erroneous astrological teaching which the Egyptian priests had confided to them. At the same time it was through the old Hellenic philosophers that the astrological secrets of the Oriental priestly castes reached the profane world. The earliest mention of the art of astrological prediction in early classical literature is found in the "Prometheus Vinctus" of Æschylus (line 486 sqq.)—a comparatively late date. The often quoted lines of the Odyssey (Bk. XVIII, 136 sqq.) have nothing to do with astrology. Astrology was probably cultivated as an occult science by the Pythagorean school which maintained the exclusiveness of a caste. The teaching of Pythagoras on the "harmony of the spheres" points to certain astrological hypotheses of the Egyptian priests. It is a striking fact that Greek astrology began to flourish when the glory of the early classical civilization had begun to wane. It was in the age of Euripides, who refers to astrological predictions in a little comedy, that the belief in astrology began to grow popular in Greece. After the overthrow of the Assyro-Babylonian Empire, the priests of those regions found refuge in Greece and spread their astrological teachings by word of mouth and writing. In this way astrology lost the character of occult science. Astronomy and astrology remained closely united, and both sciences were represented by the so-called Chaldeans, Mathematici, and Genethliacs. Astrology proper, from the time of Posidonius, was called ἀποτελεσματικά (rendered into English, "apotelesmatics" in order to indicate more clearly the influence of the stars upon man's final destiny; ἀπο, "from", and τέλος, "end"). Astrology soon permeated the entire philosophical conception of nature among the Greeks, and rapidly attained a commanding position in religious worship. Plato was obliged to take astrology into consideration as a "philosophical doctrine", and his greatest disciple, Aristotle, was the first to separate the science of astrology from that of meteorology, which was reserved for the phenomena of the atmosphere. The Stoics who encouraged all forms of divination were active promoters of astrology. The more plainly the influence of Oriental teaching manifested itself in Greek civilization, and the more confused the political conditions and religious ideas of the Greek States became, the greater was the influence of astrologers in public, and the more mischievous their activity in private, life. Every professional astronomer was at the same time an astrologer. Eudoxus of Cnidus, the author of the theory of concentric spheres, was perhaps the first to write in Greek on purely astrological topics, being led to select this subject by his studies in Egypt. Most of the Greek astronomers known to us followed in his footsteps, as, for instance, Geminus of Rhodes whose most important work treating of astronomy and astrology Εἰσαγωγὴ εἰς τὰ Φαινόμενα (Introduction to Phænomena) was commented on even by Hipparchus. About 270 B. C. the poet Aratus of Soli in his didactic poem, "Phænomena", explained the system of Eudoxus, and in a poem called "Diosemeia", which was appended to the former, he interprets the rules of judicial and natural astrology that refer to the various changes of the

stars. The poem of Aratus was greatly admired by both the Greeks and the Romans; Cicero translated it into Latin, and Hyginus, Ovid's friend, wrote a commentary on it. In this age astrology was as highly developed as in its second period of prosperity, at the Renaissance. Medical astrology had also at this date secured a definite position. Hippocrates of Cos in his work "De Aere, Aqua et Locis", which shows the influence of the Pythagoreans, discusses at length the value of astrology and its prognostications for the whole domain of medicine. In the Alexandrine school of medicine, astrological prognosis, diagnosis, and hygiene soon covered with their rank growths the inherited scientific teachings that had been tested by practice. In this way "astrological" cures grew in favour. These forms of the art of healing are not without interest both for the history of suggestion and for that of human error. The diseases of the more important bodily organs were diagnosed according to the influence of the sign of the zodiac at the time, and a medicine applied which either acted by suggestion, or was wholly inoperative. In the division of the zodiac according to its medical effect on the different parts of the body the first sign taken was the Ram (*Aries*), which ruled the head, and the last of the series was the Fishes (*Pisces*), which controlled the health or ailments of the feet. As the appetite of the Greeks for the mysterious wisdom of astrology grew keener, the Egyptian and Chaldean astrologers continually drew out still more mystical, but, at the same time, more dubious treasures from their inexhaustible store-house. The newly founded city of Alexandria, where the later Hellenic culture flourished, was a centre for all astrologers and practitioners of the occult arts. From time to time books appeared here, professing to have had their origin in the early days of Egyptian civilization, which contained the secret knowledge pertaining to astrological and mystical subjects. These writings seemed to meet the aspirations of ordinary men for the ideal, but all they offered was a chaotic mass of theories concerning astrology and divination, and the less they were understood the more they were applauded. In the Renaissance these pseudo-scientific works of antiquity were eagerly studied. It suffices here to mention the books of Nechepso-Petosiris which were believed by the neo-Platonists to be most the ancient Egyptian authority on astrology but which, probably, were written in Alexandria about 150 B. C. About this same time, in all probability, Manetho, an Egyptian priest and traveller repeatedly mentioned by Ptolemy, wrote on astrology. In order to meet the exigencies which arose, each degree of the heavens in late Egyptian astrology was assigned to some special human activity and some one disease. Besides this, the "heavenly spheres", which play so important a part in the history of astronomy, were increased to 54, and even a higher number, and from astrological calculations made from the complicated movements of these spheres the fate both of men and nations was predicted. Thus arose in late classic times the *sphæra barbarica* (foreign sphere) which in the Middle Ages also had a controlling influence over astrology.

It was to be expected that the sober-minded, practical Romans would soon be dissatisfied with the mystical and enigmatical doctrines of Alexandrian astrology. Cato uttered warnings against the mischievous activity of the Chaldeans who had entered Italy along with Greek culture. In the year 139 B. C. the Prætor Cneius Cornelius Hispallus drove all astrologers out of Italy; but they returned, for even the Roman people could not begin an important undertaking without the aid and advice of augurs and auspices. It is only necessary to recall the greatest man of ancient Rome, Julius Cæsar. Cicero, who in his younger days had busied himself with astrology, protested vigorously, but without success, against it in his work "De Divinatione". The Emperor Augustus, on the other hand, believed in astrology and protected it. The first Roman work on astrology was dedicated to him; it was the "Astronomica" written about 45 B. C. by Marcus Manilius, who was probably a Chaldean by birth. In five books this poem gives an outline of the astrology of the zodiac and constellations. The fifth book is devoted to the *sphæra barbarica*. It is a curious fact that the poem does not take up the astrology of the planets. In spite of repeated attempts to suppress it, as in the reigns of Claudius and Vespasian, astrology maintained itself in the Roman Empire as one of the leading forms of culture. The lower the Romans sank in religion and morals the more astrology became entwined with all action and belief. Under Tiberius and Nero the two astrologers named Thrasyllus, who were father and son, held high political positions. The most distinguished astronomer of antiquity, Claudius Ptolemæus, was also a zealous astrologer. His "Opus Quadripartitum, seu de apotelesmatibus et judiciis astrorum, libri IV" is one of the chief treatises on astrology of earlier times and is a detailed account of astrological teachings. This work occupied in astrology as important a position as that which the same author's Μεγάλη Σύνταξις (also called "Almagest"), held in the science of astronomy before the appearance of the Copernican theory. It is a striking fact that Ptolemy sought, in the second book of the "Opus Quadripartitum", to bring the psychical and bodily differences of the various nations into relation with the physical conditions of their native lands, and to make these conditions, in their turn, depend on the positions of the stars. The Roman astrologers wrote their manuals in imitation of Ptolemy, but with the addition of mystic phantasies and predictions. After the death of Marcus Aurelius, the Chaldeans were always important personages at the imperial court. As late as the time of Constantine the Great the imperial notary Julius Firmicus Maternus, who later became a Christian, wrote on "Mathematics, or the power and the influence of the stars" eight books which were the chief authority in astrology until the Renaissance. With the overthrow of the old Roman Empire and the victory of Christianity, astrology lost its importance in the centres of Christian civilization in the West. The last known astrologer of the old world was Johannes Laurentius (sometimes called Lydus), of Philadelphia in Lydia, who lived A. D. 490–565.

ASTROLOGY UNDER CHRISTIANITY.—From the start the Christian Church strongly opposed the false teachings of astrology. The Fathers energetically demanded the expulsion of the Chaldeans who did so much harm to the State and the citizens by employing a fantastic mysticism to play upon the ineradicable impulses of the common people, keeping their heathen conceptions alive, and fostering a soul-perplexing cult which, with its fatalistic tendencies, created difficulties in the discernment of right and wrong and weakened the moral foundations of all human conduct. There was no room in the early Christian Church for followers of this pseudo-science. The noted mathematician Aquila Ponticus was expelled from the Christian communion, about the year 120, on account of his astrological heresies. The early Christians of Rome, therefore, regarded the astrologers as their bitterest and, unfortunately, their too powerful enemies; and the astrologers probably did their part in stirring up the cruel persecutions of the Christians. As Christianity spread, the astrologers lost their influence and reputation, and gradually sank to the position of mere quacks. The conversion of Constantine the Great put an end to the importance of this so-called science, which for

five hundred years had ruled the public life of Rome. In 321 Constantine issued an edict threatening all Chaldeans, Magi, and their followers with death. Astrology now disappeared for centuries from the Christian parts of Western Europe. Only the Arabic schools of learning, especially those in Spain after the Moors had conquered the Iberian peninsula, accepted this dubious inheritance from the wisdom of classic times, and among the Arabs it became an incentive to pure astronomical research. Arabian and Jewish scholars were the representatives of astrology in the Middle Ages, while both Church and State in Christian countries rejected and persecuted this false doctrine and its heathen tendencies. Unfortunately, at the same time the development of astronomy was checked, excepting so far as it was needed to establish certain necessary astronomic principles and to calculate the date of Easter. Yet early Christian legend distinguished between astronomy and astrology by ascribing the introduction of the former to the good angels and to Abraham, while the latter was ascribed to Cham. In particular, St. Augustine ("De civitate Dei", VIII, xix, and in other places) fought against astrology and sought to prevent its amalgamation with pure natural science. Once more the East prepared a second period of prosperity for astrology. The Jews, very soon after they were driven into Western Europe, busied themselves with astrological questions, being stimulated thereto by the Talmud. Jewish scholars had, moreover, a knowledge of the most important works of classic times on astrology and they became the teachers of the Arabs. These latter, after the rapid spread of Mohammedanism in Western Asia and North Africa, and their defeat in Western Europe by Charles Martel, began to develop a civilization of their own. The mystical books which appeared in Jewish literature after the time of the Talmud, that is, the books called the "Sefer Zohar" and the "Sefer Yezirah" (Book of Creation), are full of rules of divination dealing especially with astrological meanings and calculations. The high reputation of the Talmud and the Cabbala among the Jews in the Middle Ages explains their fondness for astrological speculations; but at a very early date, it should be noted, they distinguished between astronomy, "the science of reading the stars", and astrology, "the science of divination".

Caliph Al-Mansur, the builder of Bagdad, was, like his son, the famous Harun-al-Rashid, a promoter of learning. He was the first caliph to call Jewish scholars around him in order to develop the study of the mathematical sciences, especially astronomy, in his empire. In the year 777 the learned Jew Jacob ben Tarik founded at Bagdad a school for the study of astronomy and astrology which soon had a high reputation; among those trained here was Alchindi (Alkendi), a noted astronomer. It was one of Alchindi's pupils, Abumassar (Abu Mashar), from Bath in Chorassan, born about the year 805, whom the Middle Ages regarded as the greatest of Arabian astrologers. Astrology being regarded by the caliphs as the practical application of astronomy, all the more important Arabic and Jewish astronomers who were attached to that court, or who taught in the Moorish schools were also astrologers. Among the noteworthy Jewish astrologers may be mentioned Sahl ben Bishr al-Israel (about 820); Rabban al-Taban, the well-known cabbalist and Talmudic scholar; Shabbethai Donalo (913–970), who wrote a commentary on the astrology of the "Sefer Yezirah" which Western Europe later regarded as a standard work; and, lastly, the Jewish lyric poet and mathematician Abraham ibn Ezrah. Among the noted Arabic astronomers were Massah Allah Albategnius, Alpetragius, and others. The Arabo-Judaic astrology of the Middle Ages pursued the path indicated by Ptolemy, and his teachings were apparently the immovable foundation of all astronomical and astrological activity. At the same time the "Opus Quadripartitum" of the great Alexandrian was corrupted with Talmudic subtleties and overlaid with mystical and allegorical meanings, which were taken chiefly from the Jewish post-Talmudic belief concerning demons. This deterioration of astrology is not surprising if we bear in mind the strong tendency of all Semitic races to fatalism and their blind belief in an inevitable destiny, a belief which entails spiritual demoralization. The result was that every conceivable pursuit of mankind, every disease, and indeed every nation had a special "heavenly regent", a constellation of definitely assigned position from the course of which the most daring prophecies were deduced.

Up to the time of the Crusades, Christian countries in general were spared any trouble from a degenerate astrology. Only natural astrology, the correctness of which the peasant thought he had recognized by experience, secured a firm footing in spite of the prohibition of Church and State. But the gradually increasing influence of Arabic learning upon the civilization of the West, which reached its highest point at the time of the crusades, was unavoidably followed by the spread of the false theories of astrology. This was a natural result of the amalgamation of the teachings of pure astronomy with astrology at the Mohammedan seats of learning. The spread of astrology was also furthered by the Jewish scholars living in Christian lands, for they considered astrology as a necessary part of their cabalistic and Talmudic studies. The celebrated didactic poem, "Imago Mundi", written by Gautier of Metz in 1245, has a whole chapter on astrology. Pierre d'Ailly, the noted French theologian and astronomer, wrote several treatises on the subject. The public importance of astrology grew as the internal disorders of the Church increased and the papal and imperial power declined. Towards the close of the Middle Ages nearly every petty prince, as well as every ruler of importance, had his court astrologer, upon whose ambiguous utterances the weal and woe of the whole country often depended. Such a person was Angelo Catto, the astrologer of Louis XI of France. The revival of classical learning brought with it a second period of prosperity for astrology. Among the civilized peoples of the Renaissance period, so profoundly stirred by the all-prevailing religious, social, and political ferment, the astrological teachings which had come to light with other treasures of ancient Hellenic learning found many ardent disciples. The romantic trend of the age and its highly cultivated sensuality were conditions which contributed to place this art in a position far higher than any it had attained in its former period of prosperity. The forerunners of Humanism busied themselves with astrology, and but few of them perceived the dangerous psychical effect of its teachings upon the masses. Towards the end of the thirteenth century the Florentines employed Guido Bonatti as their official astrologer, and, although Florence then stood alone in this respect, it was scarcely a hundred years later when astrology had entered in earnest upon its triumphant course, and a Cecco d'Ascoli was already its devoted adherent. In Petrarch's day the questionable activity of the astrologers at the Italian courts had made such progress that this clear-sighted Humanist (De remed. utr. fortun. I, iii, sqq; Epist. rer. famil., III, 8, etc.) again and again attacked astrology and its representatives with the keenest weapons of his wit, though without success, and even without any following except the weak objections of Villani and the still more ineffectual polemics of Salutato in his didactic poem "De fato et fortunâ". Emperors and popes became votaries of astrology—the Emperors Charles IV and V, and Popes Sixtus IV, Julius II,

Leo X, and Paul III. When these rulers lived astrology was, so to say, the regulator of official life; it is a fact characteristic of the age, that at the papal and imperial courts ambassadors were not received in audience until the court astrologer had been consulted. Regiomontanus, the distinguished Bavarian mathematician, practised astrology, which from that time on assumed the character of a bread-winning profession, and as such was not beneath the dignity of so lofty an intellect as Kepler. Thus had astrology once more become the foster-mother of all astronomers. In the judgment of the men of the Renaissance—and this was the age of a Nicholas Copernicus—the most profound astronomical researches and theories were only profitable in so far as they aided in the development of astrology. Among the zealous patrons of the art were the Medici. Catharine de' Medici made astrology popular in France. She erected an astrological observatory for herself near Paris, and her court astrologer was the celebrated "magician" Michel de Notredame (Nostradamus) who in 1555 published his principal work on astrology—a work still regarded as authoritative among the followers of his art. Another well-known man was Lucas Gauricus, the court astrologer of Popes Leo X and Clement VII, who published a large number of astrological treatises. In Germany Johann Stöffler, professor of mathematics at Tübingen, Matthias Landenberg, and, above all, Philip Melanchthon were zealous and distinguished defenders of astrology. In Pico della Mirandola (Adversus Astrologos libri XII) and Paolo Toscanelli astrology encountered its first successful antagonists; later in the Renaissance Johann Fischart and the Franciscan Nas were among its opponents. (Cf. Philognesius, Practica Practicarum, Ingolstadt, 1571.)

Gabotto's charming essay, "L'astrologia nel quattrocento", in "Rivista di filosofia scientifica", VIII, 378, sq., gives much information concerning astrology in the fifteenth century. A. Graf's "La fatalità nelle credenze del medio evo" (in "Nuovo Antologia", 3d series, XXVIII, 201, sqq.) is also of value for astrology at the turning point of the Middle Ages. Some of the late Roman astrologers, among whom was probably Firmicus Maternus, thought to reform astrology by idealizing it and raising its moral tone. The same purpose animated Paolo Toscanelli, called Maistro Pagollo, a physician greatly respected for the piety of his life, who belonged to the learned and artistic circle which gathered around Brother Ambrosius Camaldulensis in the Monastery of The Angels. There were special professors of astrology, besides those for astronomy, at the Universities of Pavia, Bologna, and even at the Sapienza during the pontificate of Leo X, while at times these astrologers outranked the astronomers. The three intellectual centres of astrology in the most brilliant period of the Renaissance were Bologna, Milan, and Mantua. The work of J. A. Campanus, published at Rome in 1495, and often commented on, namely, "Oratio initio studii Perugiæ habita", throws a clear light on the lack of comprehension shown by the Church Fathers in their attitude towards pagan fatalism. Among other things it is here said: "Quanquam Augustinus, sanctissimus ille vir quidem ac doctissimus, sed fortassis ad fidem religionemque propensior, negat quicquam vel boni vel mali astrorum necessitate contingere".

In the Renaissance, religion, also, was subordinated to the dictation of astrology. The hypothesis of an astrological epoch of the world for each religion was widely believed by Italian astrologers of the time, who obtained the theory from Arabo-Judaic sources. Thus it was said that the conjunction of Jupiter with Saturn permitted the rise of the Hebrew faith; that of Jupiter with Mars, the appearance of the Chaldaic religion; of Jupiter with the sun, the Egyptian religion; of Jupiter with Venus, Mohammedanism; and of Jupiter with Mercury, Christianity. At some future day the religion of Antichrist was to appear upon the conjunction of Jupiter with the moon. Extraordinary examples of the glorification of astrology in Italy during the Renaissance are the frescoes painted by Miretto in the Sala della Ragione at Pavia, and the frescoes in Borso's summer palace at Florence. Petrarch, as well, notwithstanding his public antagonism to astrology, was not, until his prime, entirely free from its taint. In this connection his relations with the famous astrologer, Mayno de Mayneri, are significant. (Cf. Rajna, Giorn. stor., X, 101, sq.)

Even the victorious progress of the Copernican system could not at once destroy confidence in astrology. The greatest astronomers were still obliged to devote their time to making astrological predictions at princely courts for the sake of gain; Tycho Brahe made such calculations for the Emperor Rudolph II, and Kepler himself, the most distinguished astronomer of the age, was the imperial court astrologer. Kepler was also obliged to cast horoscopes for Wallenstein, who later came completely under the influence of the alchemist and astrologer Giambattista Zenno of Genoa, the Seni of Schiller's "Wallenstein". The influence of the Copernican theory, the war of enlightened minds against pseudo-prophetic wisdom, and the increasing perception of the moral and psychical damage wrought by astrological humbug at last brought about a decline in the fortunes of astrology, and that precisely in Wallenstein's time. At the same period astrological tracts were still being written by the most celebrated of English astrologers, William Lilly of Diseworth, Leicestershire, who received a pension of £100 from Cromwell's council of state, and who, in spite of some awkward incidents, had no little political influence with Charles II. Among his works was a frequently republished "Christian Astrology". Shakespeare (in King Lear) and Milton were acquainted with and advocated astrological theories, and Robert Fludd was a representative of the art at the royal court. Francis Bacon, it is true, sought to win adherents for a purified and reformed astrology in order to destroy the existing form of the art. It was Jonathan Swift who in his clever satire, "Prediction for the Year 1708 by Isaac Bickerstaff, Esq.", which deserves to be read even at the present day, gave the deathblow to the belief of English society in astrology. The last astrologer of importance on the Continent was Jean-Baptiste Marin, who issued "Astrologia Gallica" (1661). The greatly misunderstood Swiss naturalist Theophrastus Paracelsus was an opponent of astrology, and not its advocate, as was formerly inferred from writings erroneously attributed to him. The rapid growth of experimental investigation in the natural sciences in those countries which had been almost ruined, socially and politically, by the Thirty Years War completely banished the astrological parasites from society. Once more astrology fell to the level of a vulgar superstition, cutting a sorry figure among the classes that still had faith in the occult arts. The peasant held fast to his belief in natural astrology, and to this belief the progress of the art of printing and the spread of popular education contributed largely. For not only were there disseminated among the rural poor "farmer's almanacs", which contained information substantiated by the peasant's own experience, but the printing-presses also supplied the peasant with a great mass of cheap and easily understood books containing much fantastic astrological nonsense.

The remarkable physical discoveries of recent decades, in combination with the growing desire for an elevated philosophico-religious conception of the world and the intensified sensitiveness of the modern cultured man—all these together have caused astrology to emerge from its hiding place among paltry superstitions. The growth of occultistic ideas, which should, perhaps, not be entirely rejected, is reintroducing astrology into society. This is especially true of judicial astrology, which, however, by its constant encouragement of fatalistic views unsettles the belief in a Divine Providence. At present judicial astrology is not justified by any scientific facts. To put forward the theory of ether waves as an argument for astrological assertions is not in accord with the methods of sober science. Judicial astrology, therefore, can claim a place only in the history of human error, while, however, as an historical fact, it reflects much light upon the shadowy labyrinth of the human soul.

ASTROLOGY AMONG THE ANCIENT JEWS.—The Bible is free from any base admixture of astrological delusions. There is no reason for dragging the passage Josue x, 12, into historico-astrological discussions ; the facts there related—the standing still of the sun in the valley of Gabaon and of the moon in the valley of Ajalon—are of purely astronomical interest. Only a few indications in the Old Testament suggest that, notwithstanding the Divine prohibition (Ex., xxii, 18; Deut., xviii, 10, etc.), the Jews, especially after they were exposed to the influence of Egyptian and Babylonian errors, may have practised astrology in secret, along with other superstitions. The Prophets warned the people against the pernicious ascendancy of soothsayers and diviners of dreams (Jer., xxix, 8; Zach., x, 1–2), among whom astrologers were included. Thus in the Book of Wisdom (xiii, 1–2) it is said: "All men are vain . . . who . . . have imagined either . . . the swift air, or the circle of the stars, or the great water, or the sun and moon, to be the gods that rule the world." The Book of Job, a writing of importance in the history of astronomy and star nomenclature, is also free from astrological fatalism. But to this fatalism the Jews had a natural predisposition, and when Hellenism gained a footing in the Holy Land it was accompanied by the spread of astrology, largely among the learned, the "philosophers", at whom even in an earlier age the passage in Wisdom had probably been aimed. Again, Isaias (xlvii, 13–14) derides the Babylonian astrologers ("Let now the astrologers stand and save thee, they that gazed at the stars . . . . Behold they are as stubble, fire hath burnt them"), and Jeremias exclaims (x, 2): "Be not afraid of the signs of heaven, which the heathen fear".

After the Exile, however, astrology spread so rapidly, above all among the educated classes of Israel, that as early as the Hellenistic era a Jewish astrological literature existed, which showed a strong Persico-Chaldean influence. The prophets had been keen opponents of astrology and of a relapse into fatalism. If, when they were prophesying of the great events to come, the contemplation of nature, and especially of the stars, filled them with sympathetic enthusiasm, by reason of their poetic inspiration and power of divination, this had nothing to do with astrology. On the other hand it does not appear impossible that in Daniel's time some exiled Jews practised astrology. Judging from Daniel, v, 7, 11, it is possible that the prophet himself held a high rank among the astrologers of the Babylonian court. After the Exile an attempt was made to separate astrology from sorcery and forbidden magical arts, by denying a direct Biblical prohibition of astrology and by pretending to find encouragement for such speculations in Genesis, i, 14. It is a characteristic fact that in ancient Israel astrology received no direct encouragement, but that its spread was associated with the relapse of many Jews into the old Semitic star-worship which was aided by Persico-Chaldean influence. For this Jeremias is a witness (vii, 18; xix, 13; xliv, 17-19, 25). Co-incident with the spread of astrology in old Israel and the decline of the nation was the diffusion of demonology. The Jewish prayers to the planets, in the form in which they are preserved with others in Codex Paris, 2419 (folio 277r), came into existence at the time when Hellenism first flourished in the East, namely, the third and second centuries B. C. In these prayers special angels and demons are assigned to the different planets; the greatest and most powerful planet Saturn having only one angel, Kte-toel, and one demon, Beelzebub. These planetary demons regulated the destiny of men.

The most notable witness for astrological superstitions in the era of the decadence of Israel is the apocryphal "Book of the Secrets of Henoch", which, notwithstanding its perplexing phantasies, is a rich treasure-house of information concerning cosmological and purely astronomical problems in the Hellenic East. The author of "Henoch" is said by a Samaritan writer to be the discoverer of astronomy, and the book contains valuable explanations in regard to astronomy and astrology at the time of the Machabean dynasty. The evidences for astrologic demonology in ancient Israel, when the nation was affected by Hellenism and Babylonian decadence, are found in the latter part of the "Book of the Secrets of Henoch"—the "Book of the Course of the Lights of Heaven"—as also previously in the fourth section which treats of Henoch's wanderings "through the secret places of the world". This latter is perhaps the archetype of Dante's "Divine Comedy". According to the "Book of Henoch" the human race derived its knowledge of astrology and "lunar sorceries", together with all other forms of magic, from the seven or eight spirits from whom come the chief sins of mankind (Henoch, i, 8). It is, moreover, worthy of note that the "Book of Henoch" must be regarded as a witness to Jewish national prophecy. It does not betray the ascendancy of Hellenism in any such degree as do the verses of the "Sibylline Oracles", which were recorded in the old Ionic dialect during the reign of Ptolemy Physcon (145-112 B. C.) by Jewish scholars in Egypt, and probably at a later date in the Holy Land itself.

The astrological demonology of the Jews was continually fed from Egyptian and Babylonian sources, and formed in its turn the basis for the astrology of certain neo-Platonic sects. Together with the Parsee astrology, it was the foundation of the astrological demonology of the Gnostics and Priscillianists. The influence of Hellenistic Judaism is also plainly visible in the philosophic system of the Harranites, or Sabeans. It is only necessary to mention here the high honour paid by the Sabeans to the seven planetary gods who regulate the fate of man. According to the belief of the Sabeans every planet is inhabited by a spirit as star-soul, and the deciphering of the figures of the conjunction and opposition of the planets made the prediction of future destiny possible. Other elements of late Judaic astrology were adopted by the earliest known Christian writer on astrology, the Byzantine court-astrologer, Hephæstion of Thebes. The didactic astrological poem of Johannes Kamateros (about the middle of the twelfth century), which was dedicated to the Byzantine Emperor Manuel I, appears to have been drawn from Judæo-Gnostic sources. It is a striking fact that as "demonized astrology" gained ground in ancient Israel—and this was a branch of astrology in great favour among the Jewish scholars of the age of the Ptolemies, and much practised by them—the worship of the stars ventured once more to show itself openly. It was not until the appearance of Christianity that the preposterous, and, in part, pathologically degener-

ate, teachings of late Judaic astrology were swept away.

The lower the Jewish nation sank in the scale of religion and civilization the greater was the power gained by the erratic doctrines of astrology and the accompanying belief in demonology. The earthly labours of the Saviour purified this noxious atmosphere. The New Testament is the opponent of astrology, which, by encouraging an apathetic fatalism, prevents the development of an elevating and strengthening trust in a Divine Providence. The "Star of the Wise Men" (Matt., ii, 2, 7, 9, sq.) cannot be identified by astronomy; perhaps, according to Ideler (Handbuch der mathemat. und techn. Chron.), the conjunction of the planets Jupiter and Saturn is meant. But this hypothesis, which would be of decisive importance in settling the year of the birth of Christ, still lacks convincing proof. It finds a curious support in Abrabanel's comment that, according to Jewish astrologers, a conjunction of Jupiter and Saturn was a sign of the Messias. It must, however, remain questionable whether and to what extent a prediction of Jewish astrologers, or *Kere schamajim*, is to be considered as realized in the "Star of the Wise Men" (Matt., ii, 2, etc.). The first heralds of Christianity, the Twelve Apostles, at once began a bold war against the rank growths of superstition. They also battled with the propensity of the people for astrology and in its stead planted in the hearts of men a belief in the power and goodness of God. Supported by the teachings of the Scriptures, the Church Fathers became powerful opponents of astrology and attacked with determination the bewildering and demoralizing ascendancy of its devotees. The assertion is therefore justified that the Book of Books remained free from the taint of astrological delusion. The passion for astrology evinced by decadent Judaism, and preserved in the Bible, is only one more proof of the propensity of Semitic nations for fatalistic superstitions and of the purifying and victorious power of the ethics of Christianity.

Campbell Thompson's monumental work, "The Reports of the Magicians and Astrologers of Nineveh and Babylon" (London, 1902), may be consulted for the valuable facts which throw light upon the dependence of the astrology of the ancient Jews on that of Babylon. "A special branch of astrology which was zealously cultivated in Babylon was medical astrology, or the astrological prognosis of disease." Medical astrology is important in regard to the question of astrology in the Bible. It was greatly favoured by the spread of empirical treatment of disease among the astrologers. The Bible itself gives very little information concerning this form of the science, but subordinate Jewish sources, above all the Talmud, allow conclusions to be drawn as to its importance. Medical astrology, derived from Arabo-Judaic sources, flourished again at the time of the Renaissance. Its professional representatives were then called "Iatromathematicians", after the mathematical mode of arriving at conclusions in their "art of healing". [Cf. Karl Sudhoff, Jatromathematiker, vornehml. des XV. und XVI. Jahrhund., in Abhand. zur Gesch. der Medizin (Breslau, 1902), pt. II; Wilh. Ebstein, Die Medizin im Alten Testament (Stuttgart, 1901); Gideon Precher, Das Tranzendentale, Magie im Talmud (Vienna, 1850); Trasen, Sitten der alten Hebraer (Breslau, 1853).]

The Babylonians, chiefly in relation to medical astrology, distinguished between a spherical method of calculation (from the point of view of the observer to the stars, i. e. subjectively), and a cosmical method (from the relative position of the stars, i. e. objectively). The former was used in the prognosis deduced from the observation of the twelve houses of the heavens; the latter in that drawn from the twelve signs of the Zodiac.

Grässe, *Lehrb. einer Literärgesch.* (Leipzig, 1839), II, contains a list of the earlier literature of the subject; Löw, *Astrologie in der Bibel* in *Ben Chananja* (1863); Reitzenstein, *Poimandres* (Leipzig, 1904); Maass, *Die Tagesgötter* (Berlin, 1902); Chwolson, *Ssabier und Ssabismus* (1856); Kroll in *Neue Jahrb. für Phil. und Päd.*, VII, 559, sqq.; Schiaparelli, *L'astronomia nell' Antico Testamento* (Milan, 1904); Boll, *Sphæra* (Leipzig, 1905); Reitzenstein, *Zwei religionsgesch. Fragen* (Strasburg, 1901); Bousset, *Religion des Judentums im neutestam. Zeitalter* (Berlin, 1906). See also the literature quoted for ancient astrology. In discussing the "Star of the Wise Men", spoken of in Matthew, use may be made (although caution should be observed) of the works of Felix von Oefele, *Die Angaben der Berliner Planetentafel P. 8279 verglichen mit der Geburtsgeschichte Christi*, in *Mitteilungen der Vorderasiat. Gesellsch.* (1903), VIII, Pt. II; Idem, *Das Horoskop der Empfängnis Christi*, in the same proceedings, Pt. VI.

Zimmermann, *Die Wunder der Planeten* (Berlin, s. d.); Mayer, *Handbuch der Astrologie* (Berlin, 1891); Förster, *Himmelskunde und Weissagungen* (Berlin, 1901); Mensinga, *Ueber alte und neue Astrologie* (Berlin, 1872); Lebrun, *Hist. crit. des prat. superstit.*; Maury, *La magie et l'astrol.* (Paris, 1857); Kiesewetter, *Gesch. des Okkultismus* (Leipzig, 1895), II; Bouché-Leclercq, *Hist. de la divin.* (Paris, 1879); Lenormant, *La divination chez les Chaldéens* (Paris, 1875); Häbler, *Astrol. im Altertum* (Zwickau, 1881); Hommel, *Aufsätze und Abhandlungen* (Leipzig, 1892–1901); Winkler, *Gesch. Babylon und Assyr.* (Leipzig, 1892); Id., *Altorient. Forschungen* (Leipzig, 1902), III, ii; Brugsch, *Ægyptologie*; Jensen, *Kosmologie* (1893); Epping-Strassmaier, *Astron. aus Alt-Babylon* in *Stimmen aus Maria-Laach*, II; Boll, *Sphæra* (Leipzig, 1903); Bouché-Leclercq, *L'astrol. grecque* (Paris, 1899); Kroll in *Neue Jahrbh. für Phil. und Päd.*, VII, 559; Dieterich, *Abraxas* (Leipzig, 1904); Weber, *Indien Studien*, I; Reitzenstein, *Poimandres* (Leipzig, 1904); Usenir, *Religionsgesch. Untersuch.*, I; Maass, *Die Tagesgötter* (Berlin, 1902); Steinschneider, *Hebr. Uebersetz.* (Berlin, 1893); Löwin, *Ben Chananja* (1863), 401; Burckhardt, *Kultur der Renaissance* (Leipzig, 1898), tr.; Voigt, *Wiederbelebung des klass. Altertums* (Leipzig, 1898); collection of ancient astrological writings in Fabricius, *Bibl. græc* (1790), III; Lilly, *Christian Astrology Modestly Treated* (London, 1647); Christmas, *Astrology, Cradle of the Twin Giants, Science and History* (London, 1849); Schindler, *Der Aberglaube des Mittelalters* (Breslau, 1858); *Star of Bethlehem*, see Searles in *Catholic World*, XLVII, 59.

Max Jacobi.

Astronomy (from Gr. ἄστρον, star; νέμειν, to distribute), a science of prehistoric antiquity, originating in the elementary needs of mankind. It is divided into two main branches, distinguished as astrometry and astrophysics; the former concerned with determining the places of the heavenly bodies, the latter, with the investigation of their chemical and physical nature. But the division is of quite recent date. The possibilities of antique science stopped short at fixing the apparent positions of objects on the sphere. Nor was any attempt made to rationalize the observed facts until the Greeks laboriously built up a speculative system, which was finally displaced by the vast fabric of gravitational theory. Descriptive astronomy, meanwhile, took its rise from the invention of the telescope, and the facilities thus afforded for the close scrutiny of the denizens of the sky; while practical astronomy gained continually in refinement with the improvement of optical and mechanical arts. At the present time, astrophysics may be said to have absorbed descriptive astronomy, and astrometry necessarily includes practical research. But mathematical astronomy, grounded on the law of gravitation, keeps its place apart, though depending for the perfecting of its theories and the widening of its scope upon advances along the old, and explorations in new, directions.

Prehistoric Astronomy.—Formal systems of astronomical knowledge were early established by the Chinese, Indians, Egyptians, and Babylonians. The Chinese were acquainted, probably in the third millennium B. C., with the cycle of nineteen years (rediscovered in 632 B. C. by Meton at Athens), by which, since it comprised just 235 lunations, the solar and lunar years were harmonized; they recorded cometary apparitions, observed eclipses, and employed effective measuring apparatus. European methods were introduced at Pekin by Jesuit mis-

sionaries in the seventeenth century. Indian astronomy contained few original elements. It assigned particular prominence to the lunar zodiac, called the *nakshatras*, or mansions of the moon, variously reckoned at twenty-seven or twenty-eight; and these, which were probably a loan from Chaldea, served mainly for superstitious purposes. In Egypt, on the other hand, considerable technical skill was attained, and a peculiar constellational system of obscure derivation, came into use. The Babylonians alone, among the nations of the fore-time, succeeded in laying the foundations of a progressive science. Through the medium of the Greeks, they transmitted to the West their entire scheme of uranography, our familiar constellations having been substantially designed on the plain of Shinar about 2800 B. C. Here, too, at a remote epoch, the "Saros" became known. This is a cycle of eighteen years and ten or eleven days, which affords the means of predicting the recurrence of eclipses. The changing situations of the planets among the stars were, moreover, diligently recorded, and accurate acquaintance was secured with the movements of the sun and moon. The interpretation in 1889, by Fathers Epping and Strassmaier, of a collection of inscribed tablets preserved in the British Museum vividly illuminated the methods of official Babylonian astronomy in the second century B. C. They were perfectly effectual for the purpose chiefly in view, which was the preparation of yearly ephemerides announcing expected celestial events, and tracing in advance the paths of the heavenly bodies. Further analysis in 1899 by Father Kugler, S.J., of the tabulated data employed in computing the moon's place, disclosed the striking fact that the four lunar periods—the synodic, sidereal, anomalistic, and draconitic months—were substantially adopted by Hipparchus from his Chaldean predecessors.

Greek Astronomy.—Astronomy, however, no sooner became a distinctively Greek science than it underwent a memorable transformation. Attempts began to be made to render the appearances of the sky intelligible. They were, indeed, greatly hampered by the assumption that movement in space must be conducted uniformly in circles, round an immobile earth; yet the problem was ostensibly solved by Apollonius of Perga (250–220 B. C.), and his solution, applied by Hipparchus to explain the movements of the sun and moon, was extended by Claudius Ptolemæus (Ptolemy) to the planets. This was the celebrated theory of eccentrics and epicycles, which, by the ingenuity of its elaboration, held its own among civilized men during fourteen centuries. Hipparchus, the greatest of ancient astronomers, observed at Rhodes (146–126 B. C.), but is considered as belonging to the Alexandrian school. He invented trigonometry, and constructed a catalogue of 1080 stars, incited, according to Pliny's statement, by a temporary stellar outburst in Scorpio (134 B. C.). Comparing, as the work progressed, his own results with those obtained 150 years earlier by Timocharis and Aristyllus, he detected the slow retrogression among the stars of the point of intersection of the celestial equator with the ecliptic, which constitutes the phenomenon of the precession of the equinoxes. The circuit is completed in 25,800 years; hence the tropical year, by which the seasons are regulated, is shorter than the sidereal year by just twenty-one minutes, the equinox shifting backward to meet the sun by the annual amount of $50\frac{1}{4}'$. Greek astronomy was embodied in Ptolemy's "Almagest" (the name is of mixed Greek and Arabic derivation), composed at Alexandria about the middle of the second century A. D. It was based upon the geocentric principle. The starry sphere, with its contents, was supposed to revolve, once in twenty-four hours, about the fixed terrestrial globe, while the sun and moon, and the five planets, besides sharing the common movement, described variously conditioned orbits round the same centre. The body of doctrine it inculcated made part of the universal stock of knowledge until the sixteenth century. The formidable task of demonstrating its falsity, and of replacing it with a system corresponding to the true relations of the world, was undertaken by an active and exemplary ecclesiastic, Nicholas Copernicus, Canon of Frauenburg (1473–1543). The treatise in which it was accomplished, entitled "De Revolutionibus Orbium Cœlestium", saw the light only when its author lay dying; but a dedication to Pope Paul III bespoke the protection of the Holy See for the new and philosophically subversive views which it propounded. Denounced as impious by Luther and Melanchthon, they were, in fact, favourably received at Rome until theological discredit was brought upon them by the wild speculations of Giordano Bruno (1548–1600), and the imprudent utterances of Galileo Galilei (1564–1642).

DESCRIPTIVE ASTRONOMY.—Descriptive astronomy may be said to have originated with the invention of the telescope by Hans Lippershey in 1608. Its application to the scrutiny of the heavenly bodies, by Galileo and others, led at once to a crowd of striking discoveries. Jupiter's satellites, the phases of Venus, the mountains of the moon, the spots on the sun, Saturn's unique appendages, all descried with a little instrument resembling a uniocular opera-glass, formed, each in its way, a significant and surprising revelation; and the perception of the stellar composition of the Milky Way represented the first step in sidereal exploration. Johann Kepler (1571–1630) invented in 1611, and Father Scheiner of Ingolstadt (1575–1650) first employed, the modern refracting telescope; and the farther course of discovery corresponded closely to the development of its powers. Christian Huygens (1629–95) resolved, in 1656, the *ansæ* of Saturn into a ring, divided into two by Giovanni Domenico Cassini (1625–1712) in 1675. Titan, the largest of Saturn's moons, was detected by Huygens in 1655, and four additional members of the family by Cassini before 1684. The Andromeda nebula was brought to notice by Simon Marius in 1612, the Orion nebula by J. B. Cysatus, a Swiss Jesuit, in 1618; and some few variable and multiple stars were recognized.

THEORETICAL ASTRONOMY.—The theoretical, however, far outweighed the practical achievements of the seventeenth century. Kepler published the first two of his "Three Laws" in 1609, the third in 1619. The import of these great generalizations is: (1) that the planets describe ellipses of which the sun occupies one focus; (2) that the straight line joining each planet with the sun (its *radius vector*) sweeps out equal areas in equal times; (3) that the squares of the planetary periods are severally proportional to the cubes of their mean distances from the sun. The geometrical plan of movement in the solar system was thus laid down with marvellous intuition. But it was reserved for Sir Isaac Newton (1643–1727) to expound its significance by showing that the same uniformly acting force regulates celestial revolutions, and compels heavy bodies to fall towards the earth's surface. The law of gravity, published in 1687 in "Philosophiæ Naturalis Principia Mathematica" is to the following effect: every particle of matter attracts every other with a force directly proportional to their masses, and inversely proportional to the squares of their distances apart. Its validity was tested by comparing the amount of the moon's orbital deflection in a second with the rate at which an apple (say) drops in an orchard. Allowance being made for the distance of the moon, the two velocities proved to tally perfectly; and the identity of terrestrial gravity with the force control-

ling the revolutions of the heavenly bodies was definitively established. But this was only a beginning. The colossal work remained to be accomplished of calculating the consequences of the law, in the minute details of its working, and of comparing them with the heavens. It was carried forward, first by Newton himself, and in the ensuing century, by Euler, Clairaut, d'Alembert, Lagrange, and Laplace. Urbain Leverrier (1811–77) inherited from these men of genius a task never likely to be completed; and the intricacies of lunar theory have been shown, by the researches of John Couch Adams (1819–92), of Hansen and Delaunay, of Professors Hill and Newcomb, and many more, to be fraught with issues of unexpected and varied interest.

DISCOVERIES IN THE SOLAR SYSTEM.—The extraordinary improvement of reflecting telescopes by Sir William Herschel (1738–1822) opened a fresh epoch of discovery. His recognition of the planet Uranus (13 March, 1781) as a non-stellar object marked the first enlargement of the bounds assigned of old to the solar system; two Uranian moons, Oberon and Titania, were detected by him 11 January, 1787, and the innermost Saturnian pair, Enceladus and Mimas, 28 August and 17 September of the same year. Saturn was, in 1906, known to possess ten satellites. Hyperion was descried by W. C. Bond at the observatory of Harvard College 16 September, 1848, and Professor W. H. Pickering, of the same establishment, discovered by laborious photographic researches, Phœbe in 1898, and Themis in 1905. In point of fact, an indefinite number of satellites are agglomerated in the rings of Saturn. Their constitution by separately revolving, small bodies, theoretically demonstrated by J. Clerk Maxwell in 1857, was spectroscopically confirmed by the late Professor Keeler in 1895. The system includes a dusky inner member, detected by Bond, 15 November, 1850. The discovery of the planet Neptune, 23 September, 1846, was a mathematical, not an observational feat. Leverrier and Adams independently divined the existence of a massive body, revolving outside Uranus, and exercising over its movements disturbances the analysis of which led to its capture. Its solitary moon was noted by William Lassell of Liverpool in October, 1846; and he added, in 1851, two inner satellites to the remarkable system of Uranus. With the great Washington refractor, 26 inches in aperture, Professor Asaph Hall discerned, 16 and 17 August, 1877, Deimos and Phobos, the swiftly circling moonlets of Mars; the Lick 36-inch enabled Professor Barnard to perceive, 9 September, 1892, the evasive inner satellite of Jupiter; and two exterior attendants on the same planet were photographically detected by Professor Perrine in 1904–05. The distances of the planets are visibly regulated by a method. They increase by an ordered progression, announced by Titius of Wittenberg in 1772, and since designated as "Bode's Law". But their succession was quickly seen to be interrupted by a huge gap between the orbits of Mars and Jupiter; and the conjecture was hazarded that here a new planet might be found to revolve. It was verified by the discovery of an army of asteroids. Ceres, their leader, was captured at Palermo, 1 January, 1801, by Giuseppe Piazzi, a Theatine monk (1746–1826); Pallas, in 1802 by Olbers (1758–1840), and Juno and Vesta in 1804 and 1807, by Harding and Olbers respectively. The original quartette of minor planets began in 1845 to be reinforced with companions, the known number of which now approximates to 600, and may be indefinitely increased. Their discovery has been immensely facilitated by Professor Max Wolf's introduction, in 1891, of the photographic method of discriminating them from stars through the effects of their motion on sensitive plates.

The solar system, as at present known, consists of four interior planets, Mercury, Venus, the Earth, and Mars; four exterior, and relatively colossal planets, Jupiter, Saturn, Uranus, and Neptune, the diffuse crowd of pygmy globes called asteroids, or minor planets, and an outlying array of comets with their attendant meteor-systems. All the planets rotate on their axes, though in very different periods. That of Mercury was determined by Signor Schiaparelli of Milan in 1889 to be 88 days, the identical time of his revolution round the sun, and Venus was, in the following year, shown by him to be, in all likelihood, similarly conditioned, the common period of rotation and circulation being, in her case, 225 days. This implies that both planets keep the same hemisphere always turned towards the sun, as the moon does towards the earth; nor can we doubt that the friction of tidal waves was, on the three bodies, the agency by which the observed synchronism was brought about. All the planets travel round the sun from west to east, or counter clockwise, and most of the satellites move in the same direction round their primaries. But there are exceptions. Phœbe, Saturn's remotest moon, circulates oppositely to the other members of the system; the four moons of Uranus are retrograde, their plane of movement being inclined at more than a right angle to the ecliptic; and the satellite of Neptune travels quite definitely backward. These anomalies are of profound import to theories of planetary origin. The "canals" of Mars were recognized by Schiaparelli in August, 1877, and he caught sight of some of them duplicated two years later. Their photographic registration at the Lowell observatory in 1905 proves them to be no optical illusion, but their nature remains enigmatical.

COMETS AND METEORS.—The predicted return of Halley's comet in 1759 afforded the first proof that bodies of the kind are permanently attached to the sun. They accompany its march through space, traversing, in either direction indifferently, highly eccentric orbits inclined at all possible angles to the ecliptic. They are accordingly subject to violent, even subversive disturbances from the great planets. Jupiter, in particular, sways the movements of a group of over thirty "captured" comets, which have had their periods curtailed, and their primitive velocities reduced by his influence. Schiaparelli announced in 1866 that the August shooting-stars, or Perseids, pursue the same orbit with a bright comet visible in 1862; and equally striking accordances of movement between three other comets and the Leonid, Lyraid, and Andromede meteor-swarms were soon afterwards established by Leverrier and Weiss. The obvious inference is that meteors are the disintegration-products of their cometary fellow-travellers. A theory of comets' tails, based upon the varying efficacy of electrical repulsion upon chemically different kinds of matter, was announced by Theodor Brédikhine of Moscow in 1882, and gave a satisfactory account of the appearances it was invented to explain. Latterly, however, the authority of Arrhenius of Stockholm has lent vogue to a "light-pressure" hypothesis, according to which, cometary appendages are formed of particles driven from the sun by the mechanical stress of his radiations. But the singular and rapid changes photographically disclosed as taking place in the tails of comets, remain unassociated with any known cause.

SIDEREAL ASTRONOMY.—Sir William Herschel's discovery, in 1802, of binary stars, imperfectly anticipated by Father Christian Mayer in 1778, was one of far-reaching scope. It virtually proved the realm of gravity to include sidereal regions; and the relations it intimated have since proved to be much more widely prevalent than could have been imagined beforehand. Mutually circling stars exist in such profusion as probably to amount to one in three or four of those unaccompanied. They are of limitless variety, some of the systems formed by them being exceedingly close and rapid, while others describe, in millennial periods, vastly extended orbits. Many, too, comprise three or more members; and the multiple stars thus constituted merge, by progressive increments of complexity, into actual clusters, globular and irregular. The latter class is exemplified by the Pleiades and the Hyades, by the Beehive cluster in Cancer, just visible to the naked eye, and by the double cluster in Perseus, which makes a splendid show with an opera-glass. Globular clusters are compressed "balls" of minute stars, of which more than one hundred have been catalogued. The scale on which these marvellous systems are constructed remains conjectural, since their distances from the earth are entirely unknown. Variable stars are met with in the utmost diversity. Some are temporary apparitions, which spring up from invisibility often to an astonishing pitch of splendour, then sink back more slowly to quasi-extinction. Nova Persei, which blazed 22 February, 1901, and was photographically studied by Father Sidgreaves at Stonyhurst, is the most noteworthy recent instance of the phenomenon. Stars, the vicissitudes of which are comprised in cycles of seven to twenty months, or more, are called "long-period variables". About 400 had been recorded down to 1906. They not uncommonly attain, at maximum, to 1,000 times their minimum brightness. Mira, the "wonderful" star in the Whale, discovered by David Fabricius in 1596, is the exemplar of the class. The fluctuations of "short-period variables" take place in a few days or hours, and with far more punctuality. A certain proportion of them are "eclipsing stars" (about 35 have so far been recognized as such), which owe their regularly recurring failures of light to the interposition of large satellites. Algol in Perseus, the variations of which were perceived by Montanari in 1669, is the best-known specimen. Hundreds of rapid variables have been recently detected among the components of globular clusters; but their course of change is of a totally different nature from that of eclipsing stars. Edmund Halley (1656–1742), the second Astronomer Royal, announced in 1718 that the stars, far from being fixed, move onward, each on its own account, across the sky. He arrived at this conclusion by comparing modern with antique observations; and stellar "proper motions" now constitute a wide and expansive field of research. A preliminary attempt to regularize them was made by Herschel's determination, in 1783, of the sun's line of travel. His success depended upon the fact that the apparent displacements of the stars include a common element, transferred by perspective from the solar advance. Their individual, or "peculiar" movements, however, show no certain trace of method. A good many stars, too, have been ascertained to travel at rates probably uncontrollable by the gravitational power of the entire sidereal system. Arcturus, with its portentous velocity of 250 miles a second, is one of these "runaway" stars. The sun's pace of about 12 miles a second, seems, by comparison, extremely sedate; and it is probably only half the average stellar speed. The apex of the sun's way, or the point towards which its movement at present tends, is located by the best recent investigations near the bright star Vega.

DISTANCES OF THE SUN AND STARS.—The distances of the heavenly bodies can only be determined (speaking generally) by measuring their parallaxes, in other words, their apparent changes of position when seen from different points of view. That of the sun is simply the angle subtended at his distance by the earth's semi-diameter. Efforts were made with indifferent success to fix its value by the aid of the transits of Venus in the eighteenth and nineteenth centuries. The asteroids have proved more efficient auxiliaries; and through the mediation of Iris, Sappho, and Victoria, in 1888–89, Sir David Gill assigned to the great unit of space a length of 92,800,000 miles, which the photographic measures of Eros, in 1900–01, bid fair to ratify. The stars, however, are so vastly remote that the only chance of detecting their perspective displacements is by observing them at intervals of six months, from opposite extremities of a base-line nearly 186,000 miles in extent. Thus, the annual parallax of a star means the angle under which the semi-diameter of the earth's orbit would be seen if viewed from its situation. This angle is in all cases, extremely minute, and in most cases, altogether evanescent; so that, from only about eighty stars (as at present known), the terrestrial orbit would appear to have sensible dimensions. Our nearest stellar neighbour is the splendid southern binary, α Centauri; yet its distance is such that light needs four and one-third years to perform the journey thence. Thomas Henderson (1798–1844) announced his detection of its parallax in 1839, just after Bessel of Königsberg (1784–1846) had obtained a similar, but smaller result for an insignificant double star designated 61 Cygni.

CELESTIAL PHOTOGRAPHY.—The second half of the nineteenth century was signalized by a revolutionary change in the methods and purposes of astronomy. Experiments in lunar photography, begun in 1840 by J. W. Draper of New York, were continued in the fifties by W. C. Bond, Warren de la Rue, and Lewis M. Rutherfurd. The first daguerreotype of the sun was secured at Paris in 1845, and traces of the solar corona appeared on a sensitized plate exposed at Königsberg during the total eclipse of 28 July, 1851. But the epoch of effective solar photography opened with the Spanish eclipse of 18 July, 1860, when the pictures successively obtained by Father Angelo Secchi, S.J., and Warren de la Rue demonstrated the solar status of the crimson protuberances by rendering manifest the advance of the moon in front of them. At subsequent eclipses, the leading task of the camera has been the portrayal of the corona; and its importance was enhanced when A. C. Ranyard pointed out, in 1879, the correspondence of changes in its form with the alternations of solar disturbance. The eleven-year periodicity of sunspots was published in 1851 by Schwabe of Dessau; and among the numerous associated phenomena of change, none are better ascertained than those affecting the shape of the silvery aureola seen to encompass the sun when the moon cuts off the glare of direct sunlight. At spot maxima the aureola spreads its beamy radiance round the disc. But at times of minimum, it consists mainly of two great wings, extended in the sun's equatorial plane. A multitude of photographs, taken during the eclipses of 1898, 1900, 1901, and 1905, attest with certainty the punctual recurrence of these unexplained vicissitudes. The fundamental condition for the progress of sidereal photography is the use of long exposures; since most of the objects to be delineated emit light so feebly that its chemical effects must accumulate before they become sensible. But long exposures were impracticable until Sir William Huggins, in 1876, adopted the dry-plate process; and this date, accordingly, marks the beginning of the wide-spreading serviceableness of the camera to astronomy. In nebular investigations above all, it far outranges the telescope. Halley described in 1716 six nebulæ, which he held to be composed of a lucid medium collected from space. The Abbé Lacaille (1713–62) brought back with him from the Cape, in 1754, a list

of forty-two such objects; and Charles Messier (1730–1817) enumerated, in 1781, 103 nebulæ and clusters. But this harvest was scanty indeed compared with the lavish yield of Herschel's explorations. Between 1786 and 1802 he communicated to the Royal Society catalogues of 2,500 nebulæ; he distinguished their special forms, classified them in order of brightness, and elaborated a theory of stellar development from nebulæ, illustrated by selected instances of progressive condensation. The next considerable step towards a closer acquaintance with nebulæ was made by Lord Rosse in 1845, when the prodigious light-grasp of his six-foot reflector afforded him the discovery of the great "Whirlpool" structure in Canes Venatici. It proved to be typical of the entire class of spiral nebulæ, the large prevalence of which has been one of the revelations of photography. The superiority in nebula-portraiture of the chemical to the eye-and-hand method was strikingly manifested in a photograph of the Orion nebula taken by Dr. A. A. Common, 30 January, 1883. Its efficacy for discovery became evident through the disclosure, on plates exposed by Paul and Prosper Henry, and by Isaac Roberts in 1885–86, of complex nebulous formations in the Pleiades, almost wholly invisible optically. Professor Keeler (1857–1900) estimated at 120,000 the number of nebulæ which the Crossley reflector of the Lick observatory would be capable of recording in both hemispheres with an hour's exposure, while telescopically constructed catalogues include less than 10,000. But it is through the combination of photography with spectroscopy, constituting the spectrographic mode of research, that astrophysics has achieved its most signal triumphs.

ASTROPHYSICS.—The fundamental principle of spectrum analysis, enunciated by Gustav Kirchhoff (1824–87) in 1859, depends upon the equivalence of emission and absorption. This means that, if white light be transmitted through glowing vapours, they arrest just those minute sections of it with which they themselves shine. And if the source of the white light be hotter than the arresting vapour, there results a prismatic spectrum, interrupted by dark lines, distinctive of the chemical nature of the substance originating them. Now this is exactly the case of the sun and stars. The white radiance emanating from their photospheres is found, when dispersed into a spectrum, to be crossed by numerous dusky rays indicating absorption by gaseous strata, to the composition of which Kirchhoff's principle supplies the clue. Kirchhoff himself identified in 1861, as prominent solar constituents, sodium, iron magnesium, calcium, and chromium; hydrogen was recognized by A. J. Angström (1814–74); helium by Sir Norman Lockyer in 1868; and about forty elementary substances are now known with approximate certainty to be common to the earth and sun. The chemistry of the stars is strictly analogous to that of the sun, although their spectra exhibit diversities symptomatic of a considerable variety in physical state. Father Angelo Secchi, S.J. (1818–78), based on these diversities in 1863–67 a classification of the stars into four orders, still regarded as fundamental, and supplied by Dr. Vogel in 1874 with an evolutionary interpretation, according to which, differences of spectral type are associated with various stages of progress from a tenuous and inchoate towards a compact condition. Since 1879, when Sir William Huggins secured impressions of an extended range of ultra-violet white star light, stellar spectra have been mostly studied photographically, the results being, not only precise and permanent, but also more complete than those obtainable by visual means. The same eminent investigator discovered, in 1864, the bright-line spectra of certain classes of nebulæ, by which they were known to be of gaseous composition, and recognized, as of carbonaceous origin, the typical coloured bands of the cometary spectrum, noted four years previously, though without specific identification, by G. B. Donati (1827-73) at Florence.

Doppler's principle, by which light alters in refrangibility through the end-on motion of its source, was first made effective for astronomical research by Huggins in 1868. The criterion of velocity, whether of recession or approach, is afforded by the shifting of spectral lines from their standard places; and the method was raised to a high grade of accuracy through Dr. Vogel's adaptation, in 1888, of photography to its requirements. It has since proved extraordinarily fruitful. Its employment enabled Dr. Vogel to demonstrate the reality of Algol's eclipses, by showing that the star revolved round an obscure companion in the identical period of light-change; and the first discoveries of non-eclipsing spectroscopic binaries were made at Harvard College in 1889. These interesting systems cannot be sharply distinguished from telescopic double stars, which are, indeed, believed to have developed from them under the influence of tidal friction; their periods vary from a few hours to several months; and their components are often of such unequal luminosity that only one leaves any legible impression on the sensitive plate. Their known number amounted, in 1905, to 140; and it may be indefinitely augmented. It probably includes all short-period variables, even those that escape eclipses; though the connection between their duplicity and luminous variations remains unexplained. The photography in daylight of solar prominences was attempted by Professor Young of Princeton in 1870, and the subject was prosecuted by Dr. Braun, S.J., in 1872. No genuine success was, however, achieved until 1891, when Professor Hale of Chicago and M. Deslandres at Paris independently built up pictures of those objects out of the calcium-ray in their dispersed light, sifted through a double slit onto moving photographic plates. Professor Hale's invention of the "spectroheliograph" enables him, moreover, to delineate the sun's disc in any selected quality of its light, with the result of disclosing vast masses of calcium and hydrogen *flocculi*, piled up at various heights above the solar surface.

SIDEREAL CONSTRUCTION.—The investigation of the structure of the sidereal heavens was the leading object of William Herschel's career. The magnitude of the task, however, which he attempted single-handed grows more apparent with every fresh attempt to grapple with it; and it now engages the combined efforts of many astronomers, using methods refined and comprehensive to a degree unimagined by Herschel. An immense stock of materials for the purpose will be provided by the international photographic survey, at present advancing towards completion at eighteen observatories in both hemispheres. About thirty million stars will, it is estimated, appear on the chart-plates; and those precisely catalogued are unlikely to fall short of four millions. The labour of discussing these multitudinous data must be severe, but will be animated by the hope of laying bare some hidden springs of the sidereal mechanism. The prospect is indeed remote that the whole of its intricacies will ever be penetrated by science. We only perceive that the stars form a collection of prodigious, but limited, extent, showing strongly concentrative tendencies towards the plane of the Milky Way. Nor can the nebulæ be supposed to form a separate scheme. The closeness of their relations, physical and geometrical, with stars excludes that supposition. Stars and nebulæ belong to the same system, if such the sidereal world may properly be called in the absence of any

sufficient evidence of its being in a state of dynamical equilibrium. We cannot be sure that it has yet reached the definitive term appointed for it by its Creator. Suggestive hints, on the contrary, of instability and evanescence help us to realize that the heavens are, in very truth, the changing vesture of Him whose "years cannot fail."

NEWCOMB, *Popular Astronomy* (London, 1883); YOUNG, *General Astronomy* (Boston, 1898); YOUNG, *Manual of Astronomy* (Boston, 1902); BALL, *The Story of the Heavens* (London, 1900); GRANT, *History of Physical Astronomy* (London, 1852); CLERKE, *Hist. of Astr. during the 19th Century* (London, 1903); BERRY, *Hist. of Astronomy* (London, 1898); DREYER, *Hist. of the Planetary Systems* (London, 1906); EPPING AND STRASSMAIER, *Astronomisches aus Babylon* (Freiburg, 1889); KUGLER, *Die babylonische Mondrechnung* (Freiburg, 1900); TANNERY, *Recherches sur l'hist. de l'astr. ancienne* (Paris, 1893); JENSEN, *Kosmologie der Babylonier* (Strasburg, 1890); YOUNG, *The Sun* (New York, 1897); NEWCOMB, *The Stars* (London, 1901); CLERKE, *The System of the Stars* (London, 1905); CLERKE, *Problems in Astrophysics* (London, 1903); PICKERING, *The Moon* (New York, 1903); NASMYTH AND CARPENTER, *The Moon* (London, 1903); SCHEINER, *Die Spectralanalyse der Gestirne* (Leipzig, 1890; tr. Boston, 1894); SCHEINER, *Die Photographie der Gestirne* (Leipzig, 1897); MÜLLER, *Die Photometrie der Gestirne* (Leipzig, 1897); SECCHI, *Le soleil* (Paris, 1875-77); MOREUX, *Le problème solaire* (Paris, 1900); TURNER, *Modern Astronomy* (London, 1901); MOULTON, *An Introduction to Astronomy* (New York, 1906).

AGNES M. CLERKE.

ASTRONOMY IN THE BIBLE.—No systematic observations of the heavenly bodies were made by the Jews. Astral worship was rife in Palestine, and they could hardly have attended closely to its objects without yielding to its seductions. Astronomy was, under these circumstances, inseparable from astrolatry, and the anathemas of the prophets were not carelessly uttered. As the most glorious works of the Almighty, the celestial luminaries were indeed celebrated in the Scriptures in passages thrilling with rapture; but the appeal to them for practical purposes was reduced to a minimum. Even the regulation of times and seasons was largely empirical. The Jews used a lunar year. It began, for religious purposes, with the new moon next after the spring equinox, and consisted normally of twelve months, or 354 days. The Jewish calendar, however, depended upon the course of the sun, since the festivals it appointed were in part agricultural celebrations. Some process of adjustment had then to be resorted to, and the obvious one was chosen of adding a thirteenth, or intercalary, month whenever the discrepancy between the ripening of the crops and the fixed dates of the commemorative feasts became glaringly apparent. Before the time of Solomon, the Jews appear to have begun their year in the autumn; and the custom, revived for civil purposes about the fifth century B. C., was adopted in the systematized religious calendar of the fourth century of our era.

Both the ritual and the civil day commenced in the evening, about half an hour after sunset. Its subdivisions were left indeterminate. The Old Testament makes no mention of what we call hours; and it refers to the measurement of time, if at all, only in the narrative of the miracle wrought by Isaias in connection with the sundial of Achaz (IV Kings, xx, 9-11). In the New Testament, the Roman practice of counting four night-watches has superseded the antique triple division, and the day, as among the Greeks, consists of twelve equal parts. These are the "temporary hours" which still survive in the liturgy of the Church. Since they spanned the interval from sunrise to sunset, their length varied with the season of the year, from 49 to 71 minutes. Corresponding nocturnal hours, too, seem to have been partially used in the time of the Apostles (Acts, xxiii, 23).

As might have been expected, the Sacred Books convey no theory of celestial appearances. The descriptive phrases used in them are conformed to the elementary ideas naturally presenting themselves to a primitive people. Thus, the earth figures as an indefinitely extended circular disk, lying between the realm of light above and the abyss of darkness beneath. The word *firmamentum*, by which the Hebrew *rakia* (רקיע) is translated in the Vulgate, expressed the notion of a solid, transparent vault, dividing the "upper waters" from the seas, springs, and rivers far below. Through the agency of the flood-gates, however, the waters sustained by the firmament were, in due measure, distributed over the earth. The first visibility after sunset of the crescent moon determined the beginning of each month; and this was the only appeal to the skies made for the purposes of the Jewish ritual. Eclipses of the sun and moon are perhaps vaguely referred to among the signs of doom enumerated by the Prophets Joel and Amos, who may easily have enhanced their imagery from personal experience, since modern calculations show solar totalities to have been visible in Palestine in the years 831, 824, and 763 B. C., and the moon reddened by immersion in the earth's shadow is not an uncommon sight in any part of the world. But the passages in question cannot be literally associated with mere passing phenomena. The prophets aimed at something higher than intimidation. An express warning against ignoble panic was indeed uttered by Jeremias in the words: "Be not afraid of the signs of heaven, which the heathens fear" (x, 2). The stellar vault, conceived to be situated above the firmament, is compared by Isaias to a tent stretched out by the Most High. The "host of heaven", a frequently recurring Scriptural expression, has both a general and a specific meaning. It designates, in some passages, the entire array of stars; in others it particularly applies to the sun, moon, planets, and certain selected stars, the worship of which was introduced from Babylonia under the later kings of Israel. Venus and Saturn are the only planets expressly mentioned in the Old Testament. Isaias (xiv, 12) apostrophizes the Babylonian Empire under the unmistakable type of *Helal* (Lucifer in the Vulgate), "son of the morning"; and Saturn is no less certainly represented by the star *Kaiwan*, adored by the reprobate Israelites in the desert (Amos, v, 26). The same word (interpreted to mean "steadfast") frequently designates, in the Babylonian inscriptions, the slowest-moving planet; while *Sakkuth*, the divinity associated with the star by the prophet, is an alternative appellation for *Ninib*, who, as a Babylonian planet-god, was merged with Saturn. The ancient Syrians and Arabs, too, called Saturn *Kaiwan*, the corresponding term in the Zoroastrian *Bundahish* being *Kevan*. The other planets are individualized in the Bible only by implication. The worship of gods connected with them is denounced, but without any manifest intention of referring to the heavenly bodies. Thus, *Gad* and *Meni* (Isaias, lxv, 11) are, no doubt, the "greater and the lesser Fortune" typified throughout the East by Jupiter and Venus; *Neba*, the tutelary deity of Borsippa (Isaias, xlvi, 1), shone in the sky as Mercury, and *Nergal*, transplanted from Assyria to Kutha (IV Kings, xvii, 30), as Mars.

The uranography of the Jews is fraught with perplexity. Some half-dozen star-groups are named in the Scriptures, but authorities differ widely as to their identity. In a striking passage the Prophet Amos (v, 8) glorifies the Creator as "Him that made *Kimah* and *Kesil*", rendered in the Vulgate as Arcturus and Orion. Now *Kimah* certainly does not mean Arcturus. The word, which occurs twice in the Book of Job (ix, 9; xxxviii, 31), is treated in the Septuagint version as equivalent to Pleiades. This, also, is the meaning given to it in the Talmud and throughout Syrian literature; it is supported by etymological evidences, the Hebrew term being ob-

viously related to the Arabic root *kum* (accumulate), and to the Assyrian *kamu* (to bind); while the "chains of *Kimah*", referred to in the sacred text, not inaptly figure the coercive power imparting unity to a multiple object. The associated constellation *Kesil* is doubtless no other than our Orion. Yet, in the first of the passages in Job where it figures, the Septuagint gives *Hesper;* in the second, the Vulgate quite irrelevantly inserts Arcturus; Karstens Niebuhr (1733–1815) understood *Kesil* to mean Sirius; Thomas Hyde (1636–1703) held that it indicated Canopus. Now *kesil* signifies in Hebrew "foolish", or "impious", adjectives expressive of the stupid criminality which belongs to the legendary character of giants; and the stars of Orion irresistibly suggest a huge figure striding across the sky. The Arabs accordingly named the constellation *Al-gebbar*, "the giant", the Syriac equivalent being *Gabbara*, "a strong man"; and *Kesil* is actually translated *Gabbara* in the old Syriac version of the Bible known as the *Peshitta*. We may then safely admit that *Kimah* and *Kesil* did actually designate the Pleiades and Orion. But further interpretations are considerably more obscure. In the Book of Job—the most distinctively astronomical part of the Bible—mention is made, with other stars, of *Ash* and *Ayish*, almost certainly divergent forms of the same word. Its signification remains an enigma. The Vulgate and Septuagint inconsistently render it "Arcturus" and "Hesperus". Abenezra (1092–1167), however, the learned Rabbi of Toledo, gave such strong reasons for holding *Ash*, or *Ayish*, to mean the Great Bear, that the opinion, though probably erroneous, is still prevalent. It was chiefly grounded on the phonetic resemblance between *ash* and the Arabic *na'ash*, "a bier", applied to the four stars of the Wain, the three in front figuring as mourners, under the title of *Benât na'ash*, "daughters of the bier". But Job, too, speaks of the "children of Ayish", and the inference seems irresistible that the same star-group was similarly referred to in both cases. Yet there is large room for doubt. Modern philologists do not admit the alleged connection of *Ayish* with *na'ash*, nor is any funereal association apparent in the Book of Job. On the other hand, Professor Schiaparelli draws attention to the fact that *ash* denotes "moth" in the Old Testament, and that the folded wings of the insect are closely imitated in their triangular shape by the doubly aligned stars of the Hyades. Now *Ayish* in the Peshitta is translated *Iyutha*, a constellation mentioned by St. Ephrem and other Syriac writers, and Schiaparelli's learned consideration of the various indications afforded by Arabic and Syriac literature makes it reasonably certain that *Iyutha* authentically signifies Aldebaran, the great red star in the head of the Bull, with its children, the rainy Hyades. It is true that Hyde, Ewald, and other scholars have adopted Capella and the Kids as representative of *Iyutha*, and therefore of "*Ayish* and her children"; but the view involves many incongruities. The glories of the sky adverted to in the Book of Job include a sidereal landscape vaguely described as "the chambers [i. e. *penetralia*] of the south". The phrase, according to Schiaparelli, refers to some assemblage of brilliant stars, rising 20 degrees at most above the southern horizon in Palestine about the year 750 B. C. (assumed as the date of the Patriarch Job), and, taking account of the changes due to precession, he points out that the stellar pageant formed by the Ship, the Cross, and the Centaur meets the required conditions. Sirius, although at the date in question it culminated at an altitude of 41 degrees, may possibly have been thought of as belonging to the "chambers of the south"; otherwise, this splendid object would appear to be ignored in the Bible. Job opposes to the "chambers of the south", as the source of cold, an asterism named Mezarim (xxxvii, 9). Both the Vulgate and the Septuagint render this word by *Arcturus*, evidently in mistake (the blunder is not uncommon) for Arctos. The Great Bear circled in those days much more closely round the pole than it now does; its typical northern character survives in the Latin word *septentrio* (from *septem triones*, the seven stars of the Wain); and Schiaparelli concludes, from the dual form of *mezarim*, that the Jews, like the Phœnicians, were acquainted with the Little, as well as with the Great, Bear. He identifies the word as the plural, or dual, of *mizreh*, "a winnowing-fan", an instrument figured by the seven stars of the Wain, quite as accurately as the Ladle of the Chinese or the Dipper of popular American parlance.

Perhaps the most baffling riddle in Biblical star-nomenclature is that presented by the word *Mazzaroth*, or *Mazzaloth* (Job, xxxviii, 31, 32; IV Kings, xxiii, 5), usually, though not unanimously, admitted to be phonetic variants. As to their signification, opinions are hopelessly divergent. The authors of the Septuagint transcribed, without translating, the ambiguous expression; the Vulgate gives for its equivalent Lucifer in Job, the Signs of the Zodiac in the Book of Kings. St. John Chrysostom adopted the latter meaning, noting, however, that many of his contemporaries interpreted *Mazzaroth* as Sirius. But this idea soon lost vogue, while the zodiacal explanation gained wide currency. It is, indeed, at first sight, extremely plausible. Long before the Exodus the Twelve Signs were established in Euphratean regions much as we know them now. Although never worshipped in a primary sense, they may well have been held sacred as the abodes of deities. The Assyrian *manzaltu* (sometimes written *manzazu*), "station", occurs in the Babylonian Creation tablets with the import "mansions of the gods"; and the word appears to be etymologically akin to *Mazzaloth*, which in rabbinical Hebrew signifies primarily the Signs of the Zodiac, secondarily the planets. The lunar Zodiac, too, suggests itself in this connection. The twenty-eight "mansions of the moon" (*menazil al-kamar*) were the leading feature of Arabic sky-lore, and they subserved astrological purposes among many Oriental peoples. They might, accordingly, have belonged to the apparatus of superstition used by the soothsayers who were extirpated in Judah, together with the worship of the *Mazzaroth*, by King Josias, about 621 B. C. Yet no such explanation can be made to fit in with the form of expression met with in the Book of Job (xxxviii, 32). Speaking in the person of the Almighty, the Patriarch asks, "Canst thou bring forth Mazzaroth in its time?"—clearly in allusion to a periodical phenomenon, such as the brilliant visibility of Lucifer, or Hesperus. Professor Schiaparelli then recurs to the Vulgate rendering of this passage. He recognizes in *Mazzaroth* the planet Venus in her double aspect of morning and evening star, pointing out that the luminary designated in the Book of Kings, with the sun and moon, and the "host of heaven", must evidently be next in brightness to the chief light-givers. Further, the sun, moon, and Venus constitute the great astronomical triad of Babylonia, the sculptured representations of which frequently include the "host of heaven" typified by a crowd of fantastic animal-divinities. And since the astral worship anathematized by the prophets of Israel was unquestionably of Euphratean origin, the designation of *Mazzaroth* as the third member of the Babylonian triad is a valuable link in the evidence. Still, the case remains one of extreme difficulty. Notwithstanding the scepticism of recent commentators, it appears fairly certain that the "fugitive serpent" of Job, xxvi, 13 (*coluber tortuosus* in the Vulgate) does really stand for the circumpolar reptile. The Euphratean con-

stellation Draco is of hoary antiquity, and would quite probably have been familiar to Job. On the other hand, *Rahab* (Job, ix, 13; xxvi, 12), translated "whale" in the Septuagint, is probably of legendary or symbolical import.

The subjoined list gives (largely on Schiaparelli's authority) the best-warranted interpretations of biblical star-names: *Kimah*, the Pleiades; *Kesil*, Orion; *Ash*, or *Ayish*, the Hyades; *Mezarim*, the Bears (Great and Little); *Mazzaroth*, Venus (Lucifer and Hesperus); *Hadre theman*—"the chambers of the south"—Canopus, the Southern Cross, and α Centauri; *Nachash*, Draco.

The New Testament is virtually devoid of astronomical allusions. The "Star of the Magi" can scarcely be regarded as an objective phenomenon; it was, at least, inconspicuous to ordinary notice. Kepler, however, advanced, in 1606, the hypothesis that a remarkable conjunction of Jupiter and Saturn, which occurred in May of the year 7 B. C., was the celestial sign followed by the Wise Men. Revived in 1821 by Dr. Münter, the Lutheran Bishop of Zealand, this opinion was strongly advocated in 1826 by C. L. Ideler (Handbuch der Chronologie, II, 399). But the late Dr. Pritchard's investigation (Smith's Dict. of the Bible, Memoirs Roy. Astr. Society, XXV, 119) demonstrated its inadequacy to fulfil the requirements of the Gospel narrative.

SCHIAPARELLI, *L'Astronomia nell' antico Testamento* (Milan, 1903, tr. Oxford, 1905); STOPPANI, *La Cosmogonia Mosaica* (Milan, 1887); RIEHM, *Handwörterbuch des biblischen Altertums* (Leipzig, 1893); MAHLER, *Biblische Chronologie* (Vienna 1887); SCHRADER, *Die Keilinschriften und das alte Testament* (Berlin, 1903); JENSEN, *Kosmologie der Babylonier* (Berlin, 1890——); DELITZSCH, *Commentary on Job* (Leipzig, 1864, tr. Edinburgh, 1866); GESENIUS, *Thesaurus Linguæ Hebrææ* (Leipzig, 1829); STERN, *Die Sternbilder in Hiob* in *Jüdische Zeitschrift* (1864), III, 258; IDELER, *Untersuchungen über den Ursprung der Sternnamen* (Berlin, 1809); DELITZSCH, *Das Buch Hiob* (Leipzig, 1902).

AGNES M. CLERKE.

Astros, PAUL-THÉRÈSE-DAVID D', a French cardinal, b. at Tourves (Var) in 1772; d. 29 September, 1851. He was a nephew of Portalis, a minister of Napoleon, and as such was engaged in the formulation of the Concordat of 1804. On its conclusion he was made vicar general of Archbishop (later, Cardinal) Belloy, of Paris, and after the latter's death (1808) administered the diocese until the nomination of Cardinal Maury. He received, and was accused of promulgating, the bull of Pius VII (3 May, 1808), excommunicating Napoleon. For this act he was imprisoned at Vincennes until 1814, After the Restoration he became Bishop of Bayonne. and in 1830 Archbishop of Toulouse. At the request of Louis Napoleon, Pius IX created him cardinal, in 1850. He wrote "La vérité catholique démontrée; ou, Lettre aux Protestants d'Orthez" (2 v. 8°, Toulouse, 1833). He was one of the earliest opponents of Lamennais, against whom he wrote "Censure de divers écrits de La Mennais et de ses disciples par plusieurs évêques de France, et Lettres des mêmes évêques au souverain pontife, Grégoire XVI", etc. (Toulouse, 1835).

HERGENRÖTHER, *Kardinal Maury* (1878), 82, 132 sq.; VACANT, *Dict. de théol. cath.*, I, 2142.

THOMAS J. SHAHAN.

Astruc, JEAN, b. at Sauves, 19 March, 1684; d. at Paris, 5 May, 1766. He was the son of a converted Protestant minister. After he had taught medicine at Montpellier, he became a member of the Medical Faculty at Paris. His medical writings, however numerous, are now forgotten, but a work published by him anonymously has secured for him a permanent reputation. This book was entitled: "Conjectures sur les mémoires originaux dont il paroit que Moyse s'est servi pour composer le livre de la Génèse. Avec des remarques qui appuient ou qui éclaircissent ses conjectures" (Brussels).

Astruc himself did not intend to deny the Mosaic authorship of Genesis; but his work created an era in Biblical inquiry, occasioning the modern critical theories.

KAULEN in *Kirchenlexicon*, 2d ed. (Freiburg, 1882); GUILLEREAU in VIGOUROUX, *Dict. de la Bible* (Paris, 1895); KITTO, *Cycl. of Bibl. Lit.* 3d ed. (Philadelphia, 1886); OSGOOD, in *Presbyt. and Ref. Review* (Jan. 1892), 83 sq.

A. J. MAAS.

Asuncion. See PARAGUAY.

Asylum, RIGHT OF. See RIGHT OF ASYLUM; BUILDINGS, ECCLESIASTICAL.

Atahuallpa, properly ATAU-HUALLPA (etymology usually given as from *huallpa*, the name of some indigenous bird), son of the Inca war chief Huayna Capac and an Indian woman from Quito hence (descent being in the female line) not an Inca, but an Indian of Ecuador. The protracted wars, during which the Incas overpowered the Ecuadorian tribes, having brought about the permanent lodgment of Inca war parties in Ecuador, led to intermarriages with women of that country, and the formation of a new tribe composed of Inca men with women and children from Quito. Collisions ensued between this tribe and the descendants of Inca women, and in the strife, Atau-huallpa figured as the leader of the former, whilst the latter recognized Huascar, duly elected war chief at Cuzco. Atau-huallpa acted with great cruelty, nearly exterminating such Ecuadorian tribes as resisted. He finally prevailed, and sent his warriors southward along the backbone of the mountains, against Cuzco. When Pizarro landed at Tumbez (northern Peruvian coast) in 1532, the Quito people had already overthrown the Inca tribe at Cuzco, taken the settlement, and committed the most horrible cruelties, chiefly against the keepers of ancient traditions whom they attempted to exterminate, so as to wipe out the remembrance of the past of Cuzco and begin a new era. Atau-huallpa himself remained with a numerous war party at Caxamarca. There he awaited the whites, whom he despised. The Spaniards found Caxamarca deserted, and the warriors of Atau-huallpa camping three miles from the place. Pizarro recognized that a trap had been set for him, and prepared for the worst.

On the evening of the 16th of November, 1532, Atau-huallpa entered the square of Caxamarca with a great retinue of men carrying their weapons concealed. They packed the court densely. Pizarro had placed on the roof of the building his artillery (two *pedereros*) that could not be pointed except horizontally. When the Indians thronged into the square, a Dominican friar, Fray Vicente Valverde, was sent by Pizarro to inform Atau-huallpa, through an interpreter, of the motives of the Spaniards' appearance in the country. This embassy was received with scorn, and the friar, seeing the Indians ready to begin hostilities, warned Pizarro. His action has been unjustly criticised; Valverde did what was his imperative duty under the circumstances. Then, not waiting for the Indians to attack, the Spaniards took the offensive. The sound of cannon and musketry, and the sight of the horses frightened the Indians so that they fled in dismay, leaving Atau-huallpa a prisoner in the hands of Pizarro, who treated him with proper regard. The stories of a terrible slaughter of the Indians are inordinate exaggerations. While a prisoner, Atau-huallpa caused the greater portion of the gold and silver at Cuzco to be turned over to the Spaniards, at the same time he had Huascar murdered, and laid plans for surprising the Spaniards and having them massacred. When this was discovered Pizarro had him executed, on the 29th of August, 1633. The execution was not unjustifiable. Atau-huallpa, at the time of his death, was about thirty years of age.

Modern works, like those of PRESCOTT, ROBERTSON, HELPS, MARKHAM, and others, are mostly inspired by bitter prejudice against the Catholic Church and Spain, and written without adequate knowledge of the sources, of Indian character, and of the localities. But the reports of eyewitnesses deserve particular attention. See especially FRANCISCO DE XEREZ, *Verdadera Relación de la Conquista del Perú* (1534), of which there is a good English translation by MARKHAM in *Publications of the Hackluyt Society;* ANON., *La Conquista del Perú llamada la nueva Castilla* (Seville, April, 1534); PEDRO SANCHO *Relazione per sua Mæsta,* (14 July, 1534), RAMUSIO, III, 1565; HERNANDO PIZARRO, *Carta á la Audiencia de Santo Domingo,* in OVIEDO, *Historia natural y general de las Indias;* PEDRO PIZARRO, *Relación del Descubrimiento y Conquista del Perú,* published in vol. V of the *Doc. para la Historia de España;* CRISTÓBAL MOLINA, *Conquista y Población del Perú;* ANON. MS., *Relación del Primer Descubrimiento de la Costa y Mar del Sur.* On the events at Cuzco preceding the arrival of the Spaniards, *Discurso sobre la Descendencia y Gobierno de los Incas* (1542), published in 1892 by JIMÉNEZ DE LA ESPADA under the title of *Una Antigualla Peruana.* Later authorities, like CIEZA, GARCILASO DE LA VEGA, GUTIÉRREZ DE SANTA CLARA, and others, have not the merit of the above-mentioned eyewitnesses, although indispensable for the study of the subject.

AD. F. BANDELIER.

Atahualpa, JUAN SANTOS, an Indian from Cuzco who, being in the service of a Jesuit, went to Spain with his master. Upon his return, having committed a murder at Guamanga (Ayacucho in Peru), he fled to the forests on the eastern slopes of the Andes. There, in 1742, he persuaded the Indians that he was a descendant of the Inca head-chiefs and assumed the title of "Atahualpa Apu-Inca". He claimed to have been sent by God to drive the Spaniards from western South America. As he was able to read and write Latin, as well as Spanish, he readily made the forest tribes believe him to be a powerful wizard and induced them to follow him, abandoning the towns which the Franciscans had established successfully at Ocopa and further east. To his influence was due the ruin of the prosperous missions throughout the Pampa del Sacramento in eastern Peru. Under his direction the forest tribes became very aggressive, and the missions were partly destroyed. Efforts against him proved a failure, owing partly to the natural obstacles presented by the impenetrable forests, partly to the inefficiency of the officers to whom the suppression of his revolt was entrusted. The uprising caused by his appeal to Indian superstition, was the severest blow dealt to the Christianization of the forest Indians in Peru, and it took decades of sacrifice and toil to recover the territory lost. To this day, according to reliable testimony, the Indians included under the generic name of Chunchos (properly Campas) claim to preserve the corpse of Santos Atahualpa, hidden from the whites, in a wooden, or willow, casket, as their most precious fetish.

FRAY JOSÉ AMICH, *Compendio Histórico,* etc. (Paris, 1854); von TSCHUDI, Peru, *Reiseskizzen* (St. Gall, 1846); MENDIBURÚ, *Diccionario* (Lima, 1874), I.

AD. F. BANDELIER.

Atargatis. See PHŒNICIA.

Atavism [Lat., *atavus*, a great-grandfather's grandfather, an ancestor].—Duchesne introduced the word to designate those cases in which species revert spontaneously to what are presumably long-lost characters. Atavism and reversion are used by most authors in the same sense.

I. The term *atavism* is employed to express the reappearance of characters, physical or psychical, in the individual, or in the race, which are supposed to have been possessed at one time by remote ancestors. Very often these suddenly reappearing characters are of the monstrous type, e. g. the three-toed horse. The appearance of such a monster is looked upon as a harking back to Tertiary times, when the ancestor of the modern horse possessed three toes. The three-toed condition of the monstrous horse is spoken of as atavistic. The employment of the term in connection with teratology is often abused; for many cases of so-called atavistic monstrosities have little to do with lost characters, e. g. the possession by man of supernumerary fingers and toes.

II. Atavism is also used to express the tendency to revert to one of the parent varieties or species in the case of a hybrid; this is the atavism of breeders. Crossed breeds of sheep, for example, show a constant tendency to reversion to either one of the original breeds from which the cross was formed. De Vries distinguishes this kind of atavism as *vicinism* (Lat. *vicinus*, neighbour), and says that it "indicates the sporting of a variety under the influence of others in the vicinity."

III. Atavism is employed by a certain school of evolutionistic psychologists to express traits in the individual, especially the child, that are assumed to be, as it were, reminiscences of past conditions of the human race or its progenitors. A child by its untruthfulness simply gives expression to a state that long since was normal to mankind. Also in the child's fondness for splashing about in water is exhibited a recrudescence of a habit that was quite natural to its aquatic ancestors; this latter is called water-atavism. Many such atavisms are distinguished, but it hardly needs to be said that they are in many instances highly fantastic. Atavism is commonly supposed to be a proof of the evolution of plants and animals, including man. Characters that were normal to some remote ancestor, after having been latent for thousands of generations suddenly reappear, and thus give a clue to those sources to which the present living forms are to be traced back. That a character may lie dormant for several generations and then reappear, admits of no doubt; even ordinary observation tells us that a grandchild may resemble its grandparent more than either of its immediate parents. But the sudden appearance of a tailed man, for instance, cannot be said to prove the descent of man from tailed forms. Granting that man has really descended from such ancestors, the phenomenon is more intelligible than it would be were no such connexion admitted. But the proving force of atavism is not direct, because teratological phenomena are so difficult to interpret, and admit of several explanations. Darwin, pointing to the large canine teeth possessed by some men as a case of atavism, remarks: "He who rejects with scorn the belief that the shape of his own canines, and their occasional great development in other men, are due to our early forefathers having been provided with these formidable weapons, will probably reveal, by sneering, the line of his own descent".

Atavism is appealed to by modern criminologists to explain certain moral aberrations, that are looked upon as having been at one time normal to the race. Accepting the doctrine that man has, by slow progress, come up to his present civilized state from brute conditions, all that is brutish in the conduct of criminals (also of the insane), is explained by atavism. According to this theory degeneracy is a case of atavism. The explanation offered for the sudden reappearance of remote ancestral characters is so intimately connected with the whole question of heredity that it is impossible to do more than indicate that most writers on heredity seek this explanation in the transmission from generation to generation of unmodified heredity-bearing parts, gemmules (Darwin); pangenes (De Vries); determinants (Weismann). (See HEREDITY.)

CHAMBERLAIN, *The Child* (London, 1900); DE VRIES, *Species and Varieties* (Chicago, 1906); WEISMANN, *Vorträge über Descendenztheorie* (Jena, 1904); tr. by J. A. and M. R. THOMPSON (London, 1904); DELAGE, *La structure du protoplasme et les théories sur l'hérédité et les grands problèmes de la biologie générale* (Paris, 1895); LOMBROSO, *L'homme criminel* (Paris, 1895).

JOS. C. HERRICK.

Athabasca, VICARIATE APOSTOLIC OF (North-west Territories).—Suffragan of Saint Boniface; erected

II.—3

8 April, 1862, by Pius IX. Bounded on the north by the Vicariate of Mackenzie; on the east and southeast by the Vicariate of Saskatchewan; on the south by 55° N. lat.; on the west by the Rocky Mountains. The first vicar Apostolic was Bishop Henri Faraud, O.M.I., b. at Gigondas, France, 17 March, 1828; d. at Saint Boniface, 26 Sept., 1890; ordained priest at Saint Boniface, 8 March, 1847; elected 8 May, 1862; consecrated at Tours, France, 30 Nov., 1864, titular Bishop of Anamur. He was succeeded by Bishop Emile Grouard, O.M.I., titular Bishop of Ibora; b. at Brulon, Mans, 2 Feb., 1840; ordained priest at Boucherville, 3 May, 1862, elected Bishop of Ibora, 18 Oct., 1890; consecrated at Saint Boniface, 1 Aug., 1891, and appointed vicar Apostolic. The Oblates of Mary Immaculate serve all the missions of Athabasca. There are 11 stations, 23 priests, 28 Sœurs de la Providence, 6 Sœurs Grises. Catholics, about 5,000. (See SAINT BONIFACE.)

Le Canada Ecclésiastique (1907); BATTANDIER, *Ann. pont. cath.*, 1907.

JOHN J. A'BECKET.

Athanasian Creed, THE, one of the symbols of the Faith approved by the Church and given a place in her liturgy, is a short, clear exposition of the doctrines of the Trinity and the Incarnation, with a passing reference to several other dogmas. Unlike most of the other creeds, or symbols, it deals almost exclusively with these two fundamental truths, which it states and restates in terse and varied forms so as to bring out unmistakably the trinity of Persons in God, and the twofold nature in the one Divine Person of Jesus Christ. At various points the author calls attention to the penalty incurred by those who refuse to accept any of the articles therein set down. The following is the Marquess of Bute's English translation of the text of the Creed:—

Whosoever will be saved, before all things it is necessary that he hold the Catholic Faith. Which Faith except everyone do keep whole and undefiled, without doubt he shall perish everlastingly. And the Catholic Faith is this, that we worship one God in Trinity and Trinity in Unity. Neither confounding the Persons, nor dividing the Substance. For there is one Person of the Father, another of the Son, and another of the Holy Ghost. But the Godhead of the Father, of the Son and of the Holy Ghost is all One, the Glory Equal, the Majesty Co-Eternal. Such as the Father is, such is the Son, and such is the Holy Ghost. The Father Uncreate, the Son Uncreate, and the Holy Ghost Uncreate. The Father Incomprehensible, the Son Incomprehensible, and the Holy Ghost Incomprehensible. The Father Eternal, the Son Eternal, and the Holy Ghost Eternal and yet they are not Three Eternals but One Eternal. As also there are not Three Uncreated, nor Three Incomprehensibles, but One Uncreated, and One Incomprehensible. So likewise the Father is Almighty, the Son Almighty, and the Holy Ghost Almighty. And yet they are not Three Almighties but One Almighty.

So the Father is God, the Son is God, and the Holy Ghost is God. And yet they are not Three Gods, but One God. So likewise the Father is Lord, the Son Lord, and the Holy Ghost Lord. And yet not Three Lords but One Lord. For, like as we are compelled by the Christian verity to acknowledge every Person by Himself to be God and Lord, so are we forbidden by the Catholic Religion to say, there be Three Gods or Three Lords. The Father is made of none, neither created, nor begotten. The Son is of the Father alone; not made, nor created, but begotten. The Holy Ghost is of the Father, and of the Son:

neither made, nor created, nor begotten, but proceeding.

So there is One Father, not Three Fathers; one Son, not Three Sons; One Holy Ghost, not Three Holy Ghosts. And in this Trinity none is afore or after Other, None is greater or less than Another, but the whole Three Persons are Co-eternal together, and Co-equal. So that in all things, as is aforesaid, the Unity in Trinity, and the Trinity in Unity is to be worshipped. He therefore that will be saved, must thus think of the Trinity.

Furthermore, it is necessary to everlasting Salvation, that he also believe rightly the Incarnation of our Lord Jesus Christ. For the right Faith is, that we believe and confess, that our Lord Jesus Christ, the Son of God, is God and Man.

God, of the substance of the Father, begotten before the worlds; and Man, of the substance of His mother, born into the world. Perfect God and Perfect Man, of a reasonable Soul and human Flesh subsisting. Equal to the Father as touching His Godhead, and inferior to the Father as touching His Manhood. Who, although He be God and Man, yet He is not two, but One Christ. One, not by conversion of the Godhead into Flesh, but by taking of the Manhood into God. One altogether, not by confusion of substance, but by Unity of Person. For as the reasonable soul and flesh is one Man, so God and Man is one Christ. Who suffered for our salvation, descended into Hell, rose again the third day from the dead. He ascended into Heaven, He sitteth on the right hand of the Father, God Almighty, from whence he shall come to judge the quick and the dead. At whose coming all men shall rise again with their bodies, and shall give account for their own works. And they that have done good shall go into life everlasting, and they that have done evil into everlasting fire. This is the Catholic Faith, which except a man believe faithfully and firmly, he cannot be saved.

For the past two hundred years the authorship of this summary of Catholic Faith and the time of its appearance have furnished an interesting problem to ecclesiastical antiquarians. Until the seventeenth century, the "Quicunque vult", as it is sometimes called, from its opening words, was thought to be the composition of the great Archbishop of Alexandria whose name it bears. In the year 1644, Gerard Voss, in his "De Tribus Symbolis", gave weighty probability to the opinion that St. Athanasius was not its author. His reasons may be reduced to the two following: first, no early writer of authority speaks of it as the work of this doctor; and secondly, its language and structure point to a Western, rather than to an Alexandrian, origin. Most modern scholars agree in admitting the strength of these reasons, and hence this view is the one generally received to-day. Whether the Creed can be ascribed to St. Athanasius or not, and most probably it cannot, it undoubtedly owes its existence to Athanasian influences, for the expressions and doctrinal colouring exhibit too marked a correspondence, in subject-matter and in phraseology, with the literature of the latter half of the fourth century and especially with the writings of the saint, to be merely accidental. These internal evidences seem to justify the conclusion that it grew out of several provincial synods, chiefly that of Alexandria, held about the year 361, and presided over by St. Athanasius. It should be said, however, that these arguments have failed to shake the conviction of some Catholic authors, who refuse to give it an earlier origin than the fifth century.

An elaborate attempt was made in England, in 1871, by E. C. Ffoulkes to assign the Creed to the ninth century. From a passing remark in a letter written by Alcuin he constructed the following remarkable piece of fiction. The Emperor Charlemagne, he says, wished to consolidate the Western Empire by a religious, as well as a political, separation from the East. To this end he suppressed the Nicene Creed, dear to the Oriental Church, and substituted a formulary composed by Paulinus of Aquileia, with whose approval and that of Alcuin, a distinguished scholar of the time, he ensured its ready acceptance by the people, by affixing to it the name of St. Athanasius. This gratuitous attack upon the reputation of men whom every worthy historian regards as incapable of such a fraud, added to the undoubted proofs of the Creed's having been in use long before the ninth century, leaves this theory without any foundation.

Who, then, is the author? The results of recent inquiry make it highly probable that the Creed first saw the light in the fourth century, during the life of the great Eastern patriarch, or shortly after his death. It has been attributed by different writers variously to St. Hilary, to St. Vincent of Lérins, to Eusebius of Vercelli, to Vigilius, and to others. It is not easy to avoid the force of the objections to all of these views, however, as they were men of world-wide reputation, and hence any document, especially one of such importance as a profession of faith, coming from them would have met with almost immediate recognition. Now, no allusions to the authorship of the Creed, and few even to its existence, are to be found in the literature of the Church for over two hundred years after their time. We have referred to a like silence in proof of a non-Athanasian authorship. It seems to be similarly available in the case of any of the great names mentioned above. In the opinion of Father Sidney Smith, S.J., which the evidence just indicated renders plausible, the author of this Creed must have been some obscure bishop or theologian who composed it, in the first instance, for purely local use in some provincial diocese. Not coming from an author of wide reputation, it would have attracted little attention. As it became better known, it would have been more widely adopted, and the compactness and the lucidity of its statements would have contributed to make it highly prized wherever it was known. Then would follow speculation as to its author, and what wonder, if, from the subject-matter of the Creed, which occupied the great Athanasius so much, his name was first affixed to it and, unchallenged, remained.

The "damnatory", or "minatory clauses", are the pronouncements contained in the symbol, of the penalties which will follow the rejection of what is there proposed for our belief. It opens with one of them: "Whosoever will be saved, before all things it is necessary that he hold the Catholic Faith". The same is expressed in the verses beginning: "Furthermore, it is necessary" etc., and "For the right Faith is" etc., and finally in the concluding verse: "This is the Catholic Faith, which except a man believe faithfully and firmly, he cannot be saved". Just as the Creed states in a very plain and precise way what the Catholic Faith is concerning the important doctrines of the Trinity and the Incarnation, so it asserts with equal plainness and precision what will happen to those who do not faithfully and steadfastly believe in these revealed truths. They are but the credal equivalent of Our Lord's words: "He that believeth not shall be condemned", and apply, as is evident, only to the culpable and the wilful rejection of Christ's words and teachings. The absolute necessity of accepting the revealed word of God, under the stern penalties here threatened, is so intolerable to a powerful class in the Anglican church, that frequent attempts have been made to eliminate the Creed from the public service of that Church. The Upper House of Convocation of Canterbury has already affirmed that these clauses, in their *prima facie* meaning, go beyond what is warranted by Holy Scripture. In view of the words of Our Lord quoted above, there should be nothing startling in the statement of our duty to believe what we know is the testimony and teaching of Christ, nor in the serious sin we commit in wilfully refusing to accept it, nor, finally, in the punishments that will be inflicted on those who culpably persist in their sin. It is just this last that the damnatory clauses proclaim. From a dogmatic standpoint, the merely historical question of the authorship of the Creed, or of the time it made its appearance, is of secondary consideration. The fact alone that it is approved by the Church as expressing its mind on the fundamental truths with which it deals, is all we need to know.

Jones, *The Creed of St. Athanasius;* Jewel, *Defence of the Apology* (London, 1567); in *Works* (Cambridge, 1848), III, 254; Vossius, *Dissertationes de Tribus symbolis* (Paris, 1693); Quesnel, *De Symbolo Athanasiano* (1675); Montfaucon, *Diatribe in symbolum Quicunque* in *P. G.,* XXVIII, 1567; Muratori, *Expositio Fidei Catholicæ Fortunati* with *Disquisitio* in *Anecdota* (Milan, 1698), II; Waterland, *A Critical History of the Athanasian Creed* (Cambridge, 1724; Oxford, 1870); Harvey, *The History and Theology of the Three Creeds* (London, 1854), II; Ffoulkes, *The Athanasian Creed* (London, 1871); Lumby, *The History of the Creeds* (Cambridge, 1887); Swainson, *The Nicene Creed and the Apostles' Creed* (London, 1875); Ommanney, *The Athanasian Creed* (London, 1875); Idem, *A Critical Dissertation on the Athanasian Creed* (Oxford, 1897); Burn, *The Athanasian Creed, etc.,* in Robinson, *Texts and Studies* (Cambridge, 1896); Smith, *The Athanasian Creed* in *The Month* (1904), CIV, 366; Schaff, *History of the Christian Church* (New York, 1903), III; Idem, *The Creeds of Christendom* (New York, 1884), I, 34; Tixeront, in *Dict. de théol. cath.;* Loofs, in Hauck, *Realencyklopädie für prot. Theol.,* s. v. See also the recent discussion by Anglican writers: Welldon, Crouch, Eliot, Luckock, in *The Nineteenth Century* (1904–06).

James J. Sullivan.

Athanasius, Saint, Bishop of Alexandria; Confessor and Doctor of the Church; born c. 296; d. 2 May, 373. [No accepted emblem has been assigned to him in the history of western art; and his career, in spite of its picturesque diversity and extraordinary wealth of detail, seems to have furnished little, if any, material for distinctive illustration. Mrs. Jameson tells us that according to the Greek formula, "he ought to be represented old, baldheaded, and with a long white beard" (Sacred and Legendary Art, I, 339).] Athanasius was the greatest champion of Catholic belief on the subject of the Incarnation that the Church has ever known and in his lifetime earned the characteristic title of "Father of Orthodoxy", by which he has been distinguished ever since. While the chronology of his career still remains for the most part a hopelessly involved problem, the fullest material for an account of the main achievements of his life will be found in his collected writings and in the contemporary records of his time. He was born, it would seem, in Alexandria, most probably between the years 296 and 298. An earlier date, 293, is sometimes assigned as the more certain year of his birth; and it is supported apparently by the authority of the "Coptic Fragment" (published by Dr. O. von Lemm among the Mémoires de l'académie impériale des sciences de S. Pétersbourg, 1888) and corroborated by the undoubted maturity of judgment revealed in the two treatises "Contra Gentes" and "De Incarnatione", which were admittedly written about the year 318, before Arianism as a movement had begun to make itself felt. It must be remembered, however, that in two distinct passages of his writings (Hist. Ar., lxiv, and De Syn., xviii) Athanasius shrinks from speaking as a witness at first hand of the persecution which had broken out under Maximian in 303; for

in referring to the events of this period he makes no direct appeal to his own personal recollections, but falls back, rather, on tradition. Such reserve would scarcely be intelligible, if, on the hypothesis of the earlier date, the Saint had been then a boy fully ten years old. Besides, there must have been some semblance of a foundation in fact for the charge brought against him by his accusers in after-life (Index to the Festal Letters) that at the time of his consecration to the episcopate in 328 he had not yet attained the canonical age of thirty years. These considerations, therefore, even if they are found to be not entirely convincing, would seem to make it likely that he was born not earlier than 296 nor later than 298.

It is impossible to speak more than conjecturally of his family. Of the claim that it was both prominent and well-to-do, we can only observe that the tradition to that effect is not contradicted by such scanty details as can be gleaned from the saint's writings. Those writings undoubtedly betray evidences of the sort of education that was given, for the most part, only to children and youths of the better class. It began with grammar, went on to rhetoric, and received its final touches under some one of the more fashionable lecturers in the philosophic schools. It is possible, of course, that he owed his remarkable training in letters to his saintly predecessor's favour, if not to his personal care. But Athanasius was one of those rare personalities that derive incomparably more from their own native gifts of intellect and character than from the fortuitousness of descent or environment. His career almost personifies a crisis in the history of Christianity; and he may be said rather to have shaped the events in which he took part than to have been shaped by them. Yet it would be misleading to urge that he was in no notable sense a debtor to the time and place of his birth. The Alexandria of his boyhood was an epitome, intellectually, morally, and politically, of that ethnically many-coloured Græco-Roman world, over which the Church of the fourth and fifth centuries was beginning at last, with undismayed consciousness, after nearly three hundred years of unwearying propagandism, to realize its supremacy. It was, moreover, the most important centre of trade in the whole empire; and its primacy as an emporium of ideas was more commanding than that of Rome or Constantinople, Antioch or Marseilles. Already, in obedience to an instinct of which one can scarcely determine the full significance without studying the subsequent developments of Catholicism, its famous "Catechetical School", while sacrificing no jot or tittle of that passion for orthodoxy which it had imbibed from Pantænus, Clement, and Origen, had begun to take on an almost secular character in the comprehensiveness of its interests, and had counted pagans of influence among its serious auditors (Eusebius Hist. Eccl., VI, xix).

To have been born and brought up in such an atmosphere of philosophizing Christianity was, in spite of the dangers it involved, the timeliest and most liberal of educations; and there is, as we have intimated, abundant evidence in the saint's writings to testify to the ready response which all the better influences of the place must have found in the heart and mind of the growing boy. Athanasius seems to have been brought early in life under the immediate supervision of the ecclesiastical authorities of his native city. Whether his long intimacy with Bishop Alexander began in childhood, we have no means of judging; but a story which pretends to describe the circumstances of his first introduction to that prelate has been preserved for us by Rufinus (Hist. Eccl., I, xiv). The bishop, so the tale runs, had invited a number of brother prelates to meet him at breakfast after a great religious function on the anniversary of the martyrdom of St. Peter, a recent predecessor in the See of Alexandria. While Alexander was waiting for his guests to arrive, he stood by a window, watching a group of boys at play on the seashore below the house. He had not observed them long before he discovered that they were imitating, evidently with no thought of irreverence, the elaborate ritual of Christian baptism. (Cf. Bunsen's "Christianity and Mankind", London, 1854, VI, 465; Denzinger, "Ritus Orientalium" in verb.; Butler's "Ancient Coptic Churches", II, 268 et sqq.; "Baptême chez les Coptes", "Dict. Théol. Cath.", Col. 244, 245). He therefore sent for the children and had them brought into his presence. In the investigation that followed it was discovered that one of the boys, who was no other than the future Primate of Alexandria, had acted the part of bishop, and in that character had actually baptized several of his companions in the course of their play. Alexander, who seems to have been unaccountably puzzled over the answers he received to his inquiries, determined to recognize the make-believe baptisms as genuine; and decided that Athanasius and his playfellows should go into training in order to fit themselves for a clerical career. The Bollandists deal gravely with this story; and writers as difficult to satisfy as Archdeacon Farrar and the late Dean Stanley are ready to accept it as bearing on its face "every indication of truth" (Farrar, "Lives of the Fathers", I, 337; Stanley, "East. Ch.", 264). But whether in its present form, or in the modified version to be found in Socrates (I, xv), who omits all reference to the baptism and says that the game was "an imitation of the priesthood and the order of consecrated persons", the tale raises a number of chronological difficulties and suggests even graver questions.

Perhaps a not impossible explanation of its origin may be found in the theory that it was one of the many floating myths set in movement by popular imagination to account for the marked bias towards an ecclesiastical career which seems to have characterized the early boyhood of the future champion of the Faith. Sozomen speaks of his "fitness for the priesthood", and calls attention to the significant circumstance that he was "from his tenderest years practically self-taught". "Not long after this," adds the same authority, the Bishop Alexander "invited Athanasius to be his commensal and secretary. He had been well educated, and was versed in grammar and rhetoric, and had already, while still a young man, and before reaching the episcopate, given proof to those who dwelt with him of his wisdom and acumen" (Soz., II, xvii). That "wisdom and acumen" manifested themselves in a various environment. While still a levite under Alexander's care, he seems to have been brought for a while into close relations with some of the solitaries of the Egyptian desert, and in particular with the great St. Anthony, whose life he is said to have written. The evidence both of the intimacy and for the authorship of the life in question has been challenged, chiefly by non-Catholic writers, on the ground that the famous "Vita" shows signs of interpolation. Whatever we may think of the arguments on the subject, it is impossible to deny that the monastic idea appealed powerfully to the young cleric's temperament, and that he himself in after years was not only at home when duty or accident threw him among the solitaries, but was so monastically self-disciplined in his habits as to be spoken of as an "ascetic" (Apol. c. Arian., vi). In fourth-century usage the word would have a definiteness of connotation not easily determinable to-day. (See Asceticism.)

It is not surprising that one who was called to fill so large a place in the history of his time should have impressed the very form and feature of his personality, so to say, upon the imagination of his contemporaries. St. Gregory Nazianzen is not the only writer who has described him for us (Orat., xxi, 8). A contemptuous phrase of the Emperor Julian's (Epist., li) serves unintentionally to corroborate the picture drawn by kindlier observers. He was slightly below the middle height, spare in build, but well-knit, and intensely energetic. He had a finely shaped head, set off with a thin growth of auburn hair, a small but sensitively mobile mouth, an aquiline nose, and eyes of intense but kindly brilliancy. He had a ready wit, was quick in intuition, easy and affable in manner, pleasant in conversation, keen, and, perhaps, somewhat too unsparing in debate. (Besides the references already cited, see the detailed description given in the January Μηναῖον quoted in the Bollandist life. Julian the Apostate, in the letter alluded to above sneers at the diminutiveness of his person—μηδὲ ἀνήρ, ἀλλ' ἀνθρωπίσκος εὐτελής, he writes.) In addition to these qualities, he was conspicuous for two others to which even his enemies bore unwilling testimony. He was endowed with a sense of humour that could be as mordant—we had almost said as sardonic—as it seems to have been spontaneous and unfailing; and his courage was of the sort that never falters, even in the most disheartening hour of defeat. There is one other note in this highly gifted and many-sided personality to which everything else in his nature literally ministered, and which must be kept steadily in view, if we would possess the key to his character and writing and understand the extraordinary significance of his career in the history of the Christian Church. He was by instinct neither a liberal nor a conservative in theology. Indeed the terms have a singular inappropriateness as applied to a temperament like his. From first to last he cared greatly for one thing and one thing only; that one thing was the integrity of his Catholic creed. The religion it engendered in him was obviously—considering the traits by which we have tried to depict him—of a passionate and consuming sort. It began and ended in devotion to the Divinity of Jesus Christ. He was scarcely out of his teens, and certainly not in more than deacon's orders, when he published two treatises, in which his mind seemed to strike the key-note of all its riper after-utterances on the subject of the Catholic Faith. The "Contra Gentes" and the "Oratio de Incarnatione"—to give them the Latin appellations by which they are more commonly cited—were written some time between the years 318 and 323. St. Jerome (De Viris Illust.) refers to them under a common title, as "Adversum Gentes Duo Libri", thus leaving his readers to gather the impression, which an analysis of the contents of both books certainly seems to justify, that the two treatises are in reality one.

As a plea for the Christian position, addressed chiefly to both Gentiles and Jews, the young deacon's apology, while undoubtedly reminiscential in methods and ideas of Origen and the earlier Alexandrians, is, nevertheless, strongly individual and almost pietistic in tone. Though it deals with most of those ulterior problems in defence of which Athanasius was so soon to be summoned by the force of events and the fervour of his own faith to devote the best energies of his life. The work contains no explicit discussion of the nature of the Word's Sonship, for instance; no attempt to draw out the character of Our Lord's relation to the Father; nothing, in short, of those Christological questions upon which he was to speak with such splendid and courageous clearness in a time of shifting formularies and undetermined views. Yet those ideas must have been in the air (Soz., I, xv) for, some time between the years 318 and 320, Arius, a native of Libya (Epiph., Haer., lxix) and priest of the Alexandrian Church, who had already fallen under censure for his part in the Meletian troubles which broke out during the episcopate of St. Peter, and whose teachings had succeeded in making dangerous headway, even among "the consecrated virgins" of St. Mark's see (Epiph. Haer., lxix; Soc., Hist. Eccl., I, vi), accused Bishop Alexander of Sabellianism. Arius, who seems to have presumed on the charitable tolerance of the primate, was at length deposed (Apol. c. Ar., vi) in a synod consisting of more than one hundred bishops of Egypt and Lybia (Depositio Ar., 3). The condemned heresiarch withdrew first to Palestine and afterwards to Bithynia, where, under the protection of Eusebius of Nicomedia and his other "Collucianists", he was able to increase his already remarkable influence, while his friends were endeavouring to prepare a way for his forcible reinstatement as priest of the Alexandrian Church. Athanasius, though only in deacon's orders, must have taken no subordinate part in these events. He was the trusted secretary and adviser of Alexander, and his name appears in the list of those who signed the encyclical letter subsequently issued by the primate and his colleagues to offset the growing prestige of the new teaching, and the momentum it was beginning to acquire from the ostentatious patronage extended to the deposed Arius by the Eusebian faction. Indeed, it is to this party and to the leverage it was able to exercise at the emperor's court that the subsequent importance of Arianism as a political, rather than a religious, movement seems primarily to be due.

The heresy, of course, had its supposedly philosophic basis, which has been ascribed by authors, ancient and modern, to the most opposite sources. St. Epiphanius characterizes it as a kind of revived Aristoteleanism (Haer., lxvii and lxxvi); and the same view is practically held by Socrates (Hist. Eccl., II, xxxv), Theodoret (Haer. Fab., IV, iii), and St. Basil (Adv. Eunom., I, ix). On the other hand, a theologian as broadly read as Petavius (De Trin., I, viii, 2) has no hesitation in deriving it from Platonism; Newman in turn (Arians of the Fourth Cent., 4 ed., 109) sees in it the influence of Jewish prejudices rationalized by the aid of Aristotelean ideas; while Robertson (Sel. Writ. and Let. of Ath. Proleg., 27) observes that the "common theology", which was invariably opposed to it, "borrowed its philosophical principles and method from the Platonists." These apparently conflicting statements could, no doubt, be easily adjusted; but the truth is that the prestige of Arianism never lay in its ideas. From whatever school it may have been logically derived, the sect, as a sect, was cradled and nurtured in intrigue. Save in some few instances, which can be accounted for on quite other grounds, its prophets relied more upon curial influence than upon piety, or Scriptural knowledge, or dialectics. That must be borne constantly in mind, if we would not move distractedly through the bewildering maze of events that make up the life of Athanasius for the next half century to come. It is his peculiar merit that he not only saw the drift of things from the very beginning, but was confident of the issue down to the last (Apol. c. Ar., c.). His insight and courage proved almost as efficient a bulwark to the Christian Church in the world as did his singularly lucid grasp of traditional Catholic belief. His opportunity came in the year 325, when the Emperor Constantine, in the hope of putting an end to the scandalous debates that were disturbing the peace of the Church, met the prelates of the entire Catholic world in council at Nicæa.

The great council convoked at this juncture was something more than a pivotal event in the history of Christianity. Its sudden, and, in one sense, almost unpremeditated adoption of a quasi-philosophic and non-Scriptural term—ὁμοούσιον—to express the character of orthodox belief in the Person of the historic Christ, by defining Him to be identical in substance, or

co-essential, with the Father, together with its confident appeal to the emperor to lend the sanction of his authority to the decrees and pronouncements by which it hoped to safeguard this more explicit profession of the ancient Faith, had consequences of the gravest import, not only to the world of ideas, but to the world of politics as well. By the official promulgation of the term *homoöusion*, theological speculation received a fresh but subtle impetus which made itself felt long after Athanasius and his supporters had passed away; while the appeal to the secular arm inaugurated a policy which endured practically without change of scope down to the publication of the Vatican decrees in our own time. In one sense, and that a very deep and vital one, both the definition and the policy were inevitable. It was inevitable in the order of religious ideas that any break in logical continuity should be met by inquiry and protest. It was just as inevitable that the protest, to be effective, should receive some countenance from a power which up to that moment had affected to regulate all the graver circumstances of life (cf. Harnack, Hist. Dog., III, 146, note; Buchanan's tr.). As Newman has remarked: "The Church could not meet together in one, without entering into a sort of negotiation with the powers that be; whose jealousy it is the duty of Christians, both as individuals and as a body, if possible, to dispel" (Arians of the Fourth Cent., 4 ed., 241). Athanasius, though not yet in priest's orders, accompanied Alexander to the council in the character of secretary and theological adviser. He was not, of course, the originator of the famous *homoöusion*. The term had been proposed in a non-obvious and illegitimate sense by Paul of Samosata to the Fathers at Antioch, and had been rejected by them as savouring of materialistic conceptions of the Godhead (cf. Athan., "De Syn.," xliii; Newman, "Arians, of the Fourth Cent.," 4 ed., 184–196; Petav. "De Trin.," IV, v, § 3; Robertson, "Sel. Writ. and Let. Athan. Proleg.", 30 sqq.).

It may even be questioned whether, if left to his own logical instincts, Athanasius would have suggested an orthodox revival of the term at all ("De Decretis", 19; "Orat. c. Ar.", ii, 32; "Ad Monachos", 2). His writings, composed during the forty-six critical years of his episcopate, show a very sparing use of the word; and though, as Newman (Arians of the Fourth Cent., 4 ed., 236) reminds us, "the authentic account of the proceedings" that took place is not extant, there is nevertheless abundant evidence in support of the common view that it had been unexpectedly forced upon the notice of the bishops, Arian and orthodox, in the great synod by Constantine's proposal to accept the creed submitted by Eusebius of Cæsarea, with the addition of the *homoöusion*, as a safeguard against possible vagueness. The suggestion had in all probability come from Hosius (cf. "Epist. Eusebii.", in the appendix to the "De Decretis", § 4; Soc., "Hist. Eccl.", I, viii; III, vii; Theod. "Hist. Eccl.", I, Athan.; "Arians of the Fourth Cent.", 6, n. 42; οὗτος τὴν ἐν Νικαίᾳ πίστιν ἐξέθετο, says the saint, quoting his opponents); but Athanasius, in common with the leaders of the orthodox party, loyally accepted the term as expressive of the traditional sense in which the Church had always held Jesus Christ to be the Son of God. The conspicuous abilities displayed in the Nicæan debates and the character for courage and sincerity he won on all sides made the youthful cleric henceforth a marked man (St. Greg. Naz., Orat., 21). His life could not be lived in a corner. Five months after the close of the council the Primate of Alexandria died; and Athanasius, quite as much in recognition of his talents, it would appear, as in deference to the death-bed wishes of the deceased prelate, was chosen to succeed him. His election, in spite of his extreme youth and the opposition of a remnant of the Arian and Meletian factions in the Alexandrian Church, was welcomed by all classes among the laity ("Apol. c. Arian", vi; Soz., "Hist. Eccl.", II, xvii, xxi, xxii).

The opening years of the saint's rule were occupied with the wonted episcopal routine of a fourth-century Egyptian bishop. Episcopal visitations, synods, pastoral correspondence, preaching and the yearly round of church functions consumed the bulk of his time. The only noteworthy events of which antiquity furnishes at least probable data are connected with the successful efforts which he made to provide a hierarchy for the newly planted church in Ethiopia (Abyssinia) in the person of St. Frumentius (Rufinus I, ix; Soc., I, xix; Soz., II, xxiv), and the friendship which appears to have begun about this time between himself and the monks of St. Pachomius. But the seeds of disaster which the saint's piety had unflinchingly planted at Nicæa were beginning to bear a disquieting crop at last. Already events were happening at Constantinople which were soon to make him the most important figure of his time. Eusebius of Nicomedia, who had fallen into disgrace and been banished by the Emperor Constantine for his part in the earlier Arian controversies, had been recalled from exile. After an adroit campaign of intrigue, carried on chiefly through the instrumentality of the ladies of the imperial household, this smooth-mannered prelate so far prevailed over Constantine as to induce him to order the recall of Arius likewise from exile. He himself sent a characteristic letter to the youthful Primate of Alexandria, in which he bespoke his favour for the condemned heresiarch, who was described as a man whose opinions had been misrepresented. These events must have happened some time about the close of the year 330. Finally the emperor himself was persuaded to write to Athanasius, urging that all those who were ready to submit to the definitions of Nicæa should be re-admitted to ecclesiastical communion. This Athanasius stoutly refused to do, alleging that there could be no fellowship between the Church and one who denied the Divinity of Christ.

The Bishop of Nicomedia thereupon brought various ecclesiastical and political charges against Athanasius, which, though unmistakably refuted at their first hearing, were afterwards refurbished and made to do service at nearly every stage of his subsequent trials. Four of these were very definite, to wit: that he had not reached the canonical age at the time of his consecration; that he had imposed a linen tax upon the provinces; that his officers had, with his connivance and authority, profaned the Sacred Mysteries in the case of an alleged priest named Ischyras; and lastly that he had put one Arsenius to death and afterwards dismembered the body for purposes of magic. The nature of the charges and the method of supporting them were vividly characteristic of the age. The curious student will find them set forth in picturesque detail in the second part of the Saint's "Apologia", or "Defense against the Arians", written long after the events themselves, about the year 350, when the retractation of Ursacius and Valens made their publication triumphantly opportune. The whole unhappy story at this distance of time reads in parts more like a specimen of late Greek romance than the account of an inquisition gravely conducted by a synod of Christian prelates with the idea of getting at the truth of a series of odious accusations brought against one of their number. Summoned by the emperor's order after protracted delays extending over a period of thirty months (Soz., II, xxv), Athanasius finally consented to meet the charges brought against him by appearing before a synod of prelates at Tyre in the year 335. Fifty of his suffragans went with him to vindicate his good name; but the complexion of the ruling party in the synod made it evident that justice to the accused was the last thing that was thought of. It can hardly be wondered at, that Athanasius should have refused to be tried by such a court. He, therefore, suddenly withdrew from Tyre, escaping in a boat with some faithful friends who accompanied him to Byzantium, where he had made up his mind to present himself to the emperor.

The circumstances in which the saint and the great catechumen met were dramatic enough. Constantine was returning from a hunt, when Athanasius unexpectedly stepped into the middle of the road and demanded a hearing. The astonished emperor could hardly believe his eyes, and it needed the assurance of one of the attendants to convince him that the petitioner was not an impostor, but none other than the great Bishop of Alexandria himself. "Give me", said the prelate, "a just tribunal, or allow me to meet my accusers face to face in your presence." His request was granted. An order was peremptorily sent to the bishops, who had tried Athanasius and, of course, condemned him in his absence, to repair at once to the imperial city. The command reached them while they were on their way to the great feast of the dedication of Constantine's new church at Jerusalem. It naturally caused some consternation; but the more influential members of the Eusebian faction never lacked either courage or resourcefulness. The saint was taken at his word; and the old charges were renewed in the hearing of the emperor himself. Athanasius was condemned to go into exile at Trêves, where he was received with the utmost kindness by the saintly Bishop Maximinus and the emperor's eldest son, Constantine. He began his journey probably in the month of February, 336, and arrived on the banks of the Moselle in the late autumn of the same year. His exile lasted nearly two years and a half. Public opinion in his own diocese remained loyal to him during all that time. It was not the least eloquent testimony to the essential worth of his character that he could inspire such faith. Constantine's treatment of Athanasius at this crisis in his fortunes has always been difficult to understand. Affecting, on the one hand, a show of indignation, as if he really believed in the political charge brought against the saint, he, on the other, refused to appoint a successor to the Alexandrian See, a thing which he might in consistency have been obliged to do had he taken seriously the condemnation proceedings carried through by the Eusebians at Tyre.

Meanwhile events of the greatest importance had taken place. Arius had died amid startlingly dramatic circumstances at Constantinople in 336; and the death of Constantine himself had followed, on the 22nd of May the year after. Some three weeks later the younger Constantine invited the exiled primate to return to his see; and by the end of November of the same year Athanasius was once more established in his episcopal city. His return was the occasion of great rejoicing. The people, as he himself tells us, ran in crowds to see his face; the churches were given over to a kind of jubilee; thanksgivings were offered up everywhere; and clergy and laity accounted the day the happiest in their lives. But already trouble was brewing in a quarter from which the saint might reasonably have expected it. The Eusebian faction, who from this time forth loom large as the disturbers of his peace, managed to win over to their side the weak-minded Emperor Constantius to whom the East had been assigned in the division of the empire that followed on the death of Constantine. The old charges were refurbished with a graver ecclesiastical accusation added by way of rider. Athanasius had ignored the decision of a duly authorized synod. He had returned to his see without the summons of ecclesiastical authority (Apol. c. Ar., loc. cit.). In

the year 340, after the failure of the Eusebian malcontents to secure the appointment of an Arian
candidate of dubious reputation named Pistus, the
notorious Gregory of Cappadocia was forcibly intruded into the Alexandrian See, and Athanasius
was obliged to go into hiding. Within a very few
weeks he set out for Rome to lay his case before the
Church at large. He had made his appeal to Pope
Julius, who took up his cause with a whole-hearted-
ness that never wavered down to the day of that
holy pontiff's death. The pope summoned a synod
of bishops to meet in Rome. After a careful and
detailed examination of the entire case, the primate's
innocence was proclaimed to the Christian world.

Meanwhile the Eusebian party had met at Antioch
and passed a series of decrees framed for the sole
purpose of preventing the saint's return to his see.
Three years were passed at Rome, during which time
the idea of the cenobitical life, as Athanasius had
seen it practised in the deserts of Egypt, was preached
to the clerics of the West (St. Jerome, Epistle cxxvii,
5). Two years after the Roman synod had published its decision, Athanasius was summoned to
Milan by the Emperor Constans, who laid before him
the plan which Constantius had formed for a great
reunion of the bishops of both the Eastern and Western Churches. Now began a time of extraordinary
activity for the Saint. Early in the year 343 we
find the undaunted exile in Gaul, whither he had gone
to consult the saintly Hosius, the great champion
of orthodoxy in the West. The two together set out
for the Council of Sardica which had been summoned
in deference to the Roman pontiff's wishes. At this
great gathering of prelates the case of Athanasius
was taken up once more; and once more was his
innocence reaffirmed. Two conciliar letters were
prepared, one to the clergy and faithful of Alexandria,
the other to the bishops of Egypt and Lybia, in
which the will of the Council was made known.
Meanwhile the Eusebian party had gone to Philippopolis, where they issued an anathema against
Athanasius and his supporters. The persecution
against the orthodox party broke out with renewed
vigour, and Constantius was induced to prepare
drastic measures against Athanasius and the priests
who were devoted to him. Orders were given that
if the Saint attempted to re-enter his see, he should
be put to death. Athanasius, accordingly, withdrew
from Sardica to Naïssus in Mysia, where he celebrated the Easter festival of the year 344. After that
he set out for Aquileia in obedience to a friendly
summons from Constans, to whom Italy had fallen
in the division of the empire that followed on the
death of Constantine. Meanwhile an unexpected
event had taken place which made the return of
Athanasius to his see less difficult than it had seemed
for many months. Gregory of Cappadocia had died
(probably by violence) in June, 345. The embassy
which had been sent by the bishops of Sardica to
the Emperor Constantius, and which had at first
met with the most insulting treatment, now received
a favourable hearing. Constantius was induced to
reconsider his decision, owing to a threatening letter
from his brother Constans and the uncertain condition of affairs on the Persian border, and he accordingly made up his mind to yield. But three separate
letters were needed to overcome the natural hesitation of Athanasius. He passed rapidly from Aquileia
to Trêves, from Trêves to Rome, and from Rome by
the northern route to Adrianople and Antioch, where
he met Constantius. He was accorded a gracious
interview by the vacillating Emperor, and sent back
to his see in triumph, where he began his memorable
ten years' reign, which lasted down to the third
exile, that of 356. These were full years in the life
of the Bishop; but the intrigues of the Eusebian, or
Court, party were soon renewed. Pope Julius had

died in the month of April, 352, and Liberius had
succeeded him as Sovereign Pontiff. For two years
Liberius had been favourable to the cause of Athanasius; but driven at last into exile, he was induced
to sign an ambiguous formula, from which the great
Nicene test, the *homoöusion*, had been studiously
omitted. In 355 a council was held at Milan, where
in spite of the vigorous opposition of a handful of
loyal prelates among the Western bishops, a fourth
condemnation of Athanasius was announced to the
world. With his friends scattered, the saintly Hosius in exile, the Pope Liberius denounced as acqui-
escing in Arian formularies, Athansius could hardly
hope to escape. On the night of 8 February, 356,
while engaged in services in the Church of St. Thomas,
a band of armed men burst in to secure his arrest
(Apol. de Fugâ, 24). It was the beginning of his
third exile.

Through the influence of the Eusebian faction at
Constantinople, an Arian bishop, George of Cappadocia, was now appointed to rule the see of Alexandria. Athanasius, after remaining some days in
the neighbourhood of the city, finally withdrew into
the deserts of upper Egypt, where he remained for a
period of six years, living the life of the monks and
devoting himself in his enforced leisure to the composition of that group of writings of which we have
the result in the "Apology to Constantius", the
"Apology for his Flight", the "Letter to the Monks",
and the "History of the Arians". Legend has naturally been busy with this period of the Saint's career; and we may find in the "Life of Pachomius" a
collection of tales brimful of incidents, and enlivened
by the recital of " deathless 'scapes in the breach."
But by the close of the year 360 a change was apparent in the complexion of the anti-Nicene party. The
Arians no longer presented an unbroken front to
their orthodox opponents. The Emperor Constantius, who had been the cause of so much trouble,
died 4 November, 361, and was succeeded by Julian.
The proclamation of the new prince's accession was
the signal for a pagan outbreak against the still
dominant Arian faction in Alexandria. George, the
usurping Bishop, was flung into prison and murdered
amid circumstances of great cruelty, 24 December
(Hist. Aceph., VI). An obscure presbyter of the
name of Pistus was immediately chosen by the
Arians to succeed him, when fresh news arrived that
filled the orthodox party with hope. An edict had
been put forth by Julian (Hist. Aceph., VIII)
permitting the exiled bishops of the "Galileans" to
return to their "towns and provinces". Athanasius
received a summons from his own flock, and he accordingly re-entered his episcopal capital on 22 February, 362. With characteristic energy he set to
work to re-establish the somewhat shattered fortunes
of the orthodox party and to purge the theological
atmosphere of uncertainty. To clear up the misunderstandings that had arisen in the course of the
previous years, an attempt was made to determine
still further the significance of the Nicene formularies. In the meanwhile, Julian, who seems to have
become suddenly jealous of the influence that Athanasius was exercising at Alexandria, addressed an
order to Ecdicius, the Prefect of Egypt, peremptorily
commanding the expulsion of the restored primate,
on the ground that he had never been included in
the imperial act of clemency. The edict was communicated to the bishop by Pythicodorus Trico,
who, though described in the "Chronicon Athanasianum" (xxxv) as a "philosopher", seems to have
behaved with brutal insolence. On 23 October the
people gathered about the proscribed bishop to protest against the emperor's decree; but the saint urged
them to submit, consoling them with the promise
that his absence would be of short duration. The
prophecy was curiously fulfilled. Julian terminated

his brief career 26 June, 363; and Athanasius returned in secret to Alexandria, where he soon received a document from the new emperor, Jovian, reinstating him once more in his episcopal functions. His first act was to convene a council which reaffirmed the terms of the Nicene Creed. Early in September he set out for Antioch, bearing a synodal letter, in which the pronouncements of this council had been embodied. At Antioch he had an interview with the new emperor, who received him graciously and even asked him to prepare an exposition of the orthodox faith. But in the following February Jovian died; and in October, 364, Athanasius was once more an exile.

With the turn of circumstances that handed over to Valens the control of the East this article has nothing to do; but the accession of that emperor gave a fresh lease of life to the Arian party. He issued a decree banishing the bishops who had been deposed by Constantius, but who had been permitted by Jovian to return to their sees. The news created the greatest consternation in the city of Alexandria itself, and the prefect, in order to prevent a serious outbreak, gave public assurance that the very special case of Athanasius would be laid before the emperor. But the saint seems to have divined what was preparing in secret against him. He quietly withdrew from Alexandria, 5 October, and took up his abode in a country house outside the city. It was during this period that he is said to have spent four months in hiding in his father's tomb (Soz., "Hist. Eccl.", VI, xii; Soc., "Hist. Eccl.", IV, xii). Valens, who seems to have sincerely dreaded the possible consequences of a popular outbreak, gave orders within a very few weeks for the return of Athanasius to his see. And now began that last brief period of comparative repose which unexpectedly terminated his strenuous and extraordinary career. He spent his remaining days, characteristically enough, in re-emphasizing the view of the Incarnation which had been defined at Nicæa and which has been substantially the faith of the Christian Church from its earliest pronouncement in Scripture down to its last utterance through the lips of Pius X in our own times. "Let what was confessed by the Fathers of Nicæa prevail", he wrote to a philosopher-friend and correspondent in the closing years of his life (Epist. lxxi, ad Max.). That that confession did at last prevail in the various Trinitarian formularies that followed upon that of Nicæa was due, humanly speaking, more to his laborious witness than to that of any other champion in the long teachers' roll of Catholicism. By one of those inexplicable ironies that meet us everywhere in human history, this man, who had endured exile so often, and risked life itself in defence of what he believed to be the first and most essential truth of the Catholic creed, died not by violence or in hiding, but peacefully in his own bed, surrounded by his clergy and mourned by the faithful of the see he had served so well. His feast in the Roman Calendar is kept on the anniversary of his death.

All the essential materials for the Saint's biography are to be found in his writings, especially in those written after the year 350, when the *Apologia contra Arianos* was composed. Supplementary information will be found in St. EPIPHANIUS, *Hær.*, loc. cit.; in St. GREGORY of Nazianzus, *Orat.*, xxi; also RUFINUS, SOCRATES, SOZOMEN, and THEODORET. The *Historia Acephala*, or *Maffeian Fragment* (discovered by Maffei in 1738, and inserted by GALLANDI in *Bibliotheca Patrum*, 1769), and the *Chronicon Athanasianum*, or *Index to the Festal Letters*, give us data for the chronological problem. All the foregoing sources are included in MIGNE, *P. G.* and *P. L.* The great PAPEBROCH's *Life* is in the *Acta SS.*, May, I. The most important authorities in English are: NEWMAN, *Arians of the Fourth Century*, and *Saint Athanasius*; BRIGHT, *Dictionary of Christian Biography*; ROBERTSON, *Life*, in the *Prolegomena to the Select Writings and Letters of Saint Athanasius* (re-edited in *Library of the Nicene and post-Nicene Fathers*, New York, 1903); GWATKIN, *Studies of Arianism* (2d ed., Cambridge, 1900); MÖHLER, *Athanasius der Grosse*; HERGEN-RÖTHER and HEFELE.

CORNELIUS CLIFFORD.

Atheism (a privative, and Θεός, God, i. e. without God) is that system of thought which is formally opposed to theism. Since its first coming into use the term *atheism* has been very vaguely employed, generally as an epithet of accusation against any system that called in question the popular gods of the day. Thus, while Socrates was accused of atheism (Plato, Apol., 26 c.), and Diagoras called an atheist by Cicero (Nat. Deor., I, 23), Democritus and Epicurus were styled in the same sense impious (without respect for the gods) on account of the trend of their new atomistic philosophy. In this sense, too, the early Christians were known to the pagans as atheists, because they denied the heathen gods; while, from time to time, various religious opinions and philosophical systems have, for similar reasons, been deemed atheistic. Though atheism, historically considered, has meant no more in the past than a critical or sceptical denial of the theology of those who have employed the term as one of reproach, and has consequently no one strict philosophical meaning; though there is no one consistent system in the exposition of which it has a definite place; yet, if we consider it in its broad meaning as merely the opposite of theism, we shall be able to frame such divisions as will make possible a grouping of definite systems under this head. And in so doing we shall at once be adopting both the historical and the philosophical view. For the common basis of all systems of theism as well as the cardinal tenet of all popular religion at the present day is indubitably a belief in the existence of a personal God, and to deny this tenet is to invite the popular reproach of atheism. The need of some such definition as this was felt by Mr. Gladstone when he wrote (Contemporary Review, June, 1876): "By the Atheist I understand the man who not only holds off, like the sceptic, from the affirmative, but who drives himself, or is driven, to the negative assertion in regard to the whole unseen, or to the existence of God." Moreover, the breadth of comprehension in such a use of the term admits of divisions and cross-divisions being framed under it; and at the same time limits the number of systems of thought to which, with any propriety, it might otherwise be extended. Also, if the term is thus taken, in strict contradistinction to theism, and a plan of its possible modes of acceptance made, these systems of thought will naturally appear in clearer proportion and relationship.

Thus, defined as a doctrine, or theory, or philosophy formally opposed to theism, atheism can only signify the teaching of those schools, whether cosmological or moral, which do not include God either as a principle or as a conclusion of their reasoning. The most trenchant form which atheism could take would be the positive and dogmatic denial of the existence of any spiritual and extra-mundane First Cause. This is sometimes known as dogmatic, or positive theoretic, atheism; though it may be doubted whether such a system has ever been, or could ever possibly be seriously maintained. Certainly Bacon and Dr. Arnold voice the common judgment of thinking men when they express a doubt as to the existence of an atheist belonging to such a school. Still, there are certain advanced phases of materialistic philosophy that, perhaps, should rightly be included under this head. Materialism, which professes to find in matter its own cause and explanation, may go farther, and positively exclude the existence of any spiritual cause. That such a dogmatic assertion is both unreasonable and illogical needs no demonstration, for it is an inference not warranted by the facts nor justified by the laws of thought. But the fact that certain individuals have left the sphere of exact scientific observation for speculation, and have thus dogmatized negatively, calls for their inclusion in this specific type. Materialism is the one dogmatic explanation of the universe which could in any sense justify an atheistic position. But even materialism, however its advocates might dogmatize, could do no more than provide an inadequate theoretic basis for a negative form of atheism. Pantheism, which must not be confused with materialism, in some of its forms can be placed also in this division, as categorically denying the existence of a spiritual First Cause above or outside the world.

A second form in which atheism may be held and taught, as indeed it has been, is based either upon the lack of physical data for theism or upon the limited nature of the intelligence of man. This second form may be described as a negative theoretic atheism; and may be further viewed as cosmological or psychological, according as it is motived, on the one hand, by a consideration of the paucity of actual data available for the arguments proving the existence of a super-sensible and spiritual God, or, what amounts to the same thing, the attributing of all cosmic change and development to the self-contained potentialities of an eternal matter; or, on the other hand, by an empiric or theoretic estimate of the powers of reason working upon the data furnished by sense-perception. From whichever cause this negative form of atheism proceeds, it issues in agnosticism or materialism; although the agnostic is, perhaps, better classed under this head than the materialist. For the former, professing a state of nescience, more properly belongs to a category under which those are placed who neglect, rather than explain, nature without a God. Moreover, the agnostic may be a theist, if he admits the existence of a being behind and beyond nature, even while he asserts that such a being is both unprovable and unknowable. The materialist belongs to this type so long as he merely neglects, and does not exclude from his system, the existence of God. So, too, does the positivist, regarding theological and metaphysical speculation as mere passing stages of thought through which the human mind has been journeying towards positive, or related empirical, knowledge. Indeed any system of thought or school of philosophy that simply omits the existence of God from the sum total of natural knowledge, whether the individual as a matter of fact believes in Him or not, can be classed in this division of atheism, in which, strictly speaking, no positive assertion or denial is made as to the ultimate fact of His being.

There are two systems of practical or moral atheism which call for attention. They are based upon the theoretic systems just expounded. One system of positive moral atheism, in which human actions would neither be right nor wrong, good nor evil, with reference to God, would naturally follow from the profession of positive theoretic atheism; and it is significant of those to whom such a form of theoretic atheism is sometimes attributed, that for the sanction of moral actions they introduce such abstract ideas as those of duty, the social instinct, or humanity. There seems to be no particular reason why they should have recourse to such sanctions, since the morality of an action can hardly be derived from its performance as a duty, which in turn can be called and known as a "duty" only because it refers to an action that is morally good. Indeed an analysis of the idea of duty leads to a refutation of the principle in whose support it is invoked, and points to the necessity of a theistic interpretation of nature for its own justification. The second system of negative practical or moral atheism may be referred to the second type of theoretic atheism. It is like the first in not relating human actions to an extra-mundane, spiritual, and personal lawgiver; but that, not because such a lawgiver does not exist, but because the human intelligence is incapable of so relating them. It must not be forgotten, however, that either negative theoretic atheism or negative practical atheism is, as a system, strictly speaking

compatible with belief in a God; and much confusion is often caused by the inaccurate use of the terms, *belief, knowledge, opinion*, etc.

Lastly, a third type is generally, though perhaps wrongly, included in moral atheism. "Practical atheism is not a kind of thought or opinion, but a mode of life" (R. Flint, Anti-theistic Theories, Lect. I). This is more correctly called, as it is described, godlessness in conduct, quite irrespective of any theory of philosophy, or morals, or of religious faith. It will be noticed that, although we have included agnosticism, materialism, and pantheism, among the types of atheism, strictly speaking this latter does not necessarily include any one of the former. A man may be an agnostic simply, or an agnostic who is also an atheist. He may be a scientific materialist and no more, or he may combine atheism with his materialism. It does not necessarily follow, because the natural cognoscibility of a personal First Cause is denied, that His existence is called in question: nor, when matter is called upon to explain itself, that God is critically denied. On the other hand, pantheism, while destroying the extra-mundane character of God, does not necessarily deny the existence of a supreme entity, but rather affirms such as the sum of all existence and the cause of all phenomena whether of thought or of matter. Consequently, while it would be unjust to class agnostics, materialists, or pantheists as necessarily also atheists, it cannot be denied that atheism is clearly perceived to be implied in certain phases of all these systems. There are so many shades and gradations of thought by which one form of a philosophy merges into another, so much that is opinionative and personal woven into the various individual expositions of systems, that, to be impartially fair, each individual must be classed by himself as atheist or theist. Indeed, more upon his own assertion or direct teaching than by reason of any supposed implication in the system he advocates must this classification be made. And if it is correct to consider the subject from this point of view, it is surprising to find to what an exceedingly small number the supposed atheistic ranks dwindle. In company with Socrates, nearly all the reputed Greek atheists strenuously repudiated the charge of teaching that there were no gods. Even Bion, who, according to Diogenes Laertius (Life of Aristippus, XIII, Bohn's tr.), adopted the scandalous moral teaching of the atheist Theodorus, turned again to the gods whom he had insulted, and when he came to die demonstrated in practice what he had denied in theory. As Laertius says in his "Life of Bion", he "who never once said, 'I have sinned but spare me'—

Then did this atheist shrink and give his neck
To an old woman to hang charms upon;
And bound his arms with magic amulets;
With laurel branches blocked his doors and windows,
Ready to do and venture anything
Rather than die."

Epicurus, the founder of that school of physics which limited all causes to purely natural ones and consequently implied, if he did not actually assert, atheism, is spoken of as a man whose "piety towards the gods and (whose) affection for his country was quite unspeakable" (ib., Life of Epicurus, V). And though Lucretius Carus speaks of the downfall of popular religion which he wished to bring about (De Rerum Natura, I, 79–80), yet, in his own letter to Henaeceus (Laert., Life of Epicurus, XXVII), he states plainly a true theistic position: "For there are gods: for our knowledge of them is indistinct. But they are not of the character which people in general attribute to them." Indeed, this one citation perfectly illustrates the fundamental historic meaning of the term, atheism.

The naturalistic pantheism of the Italian Giordano Bruno (1548–1600) comes near to, if it is not actually a profession of, atheism; while Tomaso Campanella (1568–1639), on the contrary, in his nature-philosophy finds in atheism the one impossibility of thought. Spinoza (1632–77), while defending the doctrine that God certainly exists, so identifies Him with finite existence that it is difficult to see how he can be defended against the charge of atheism even of the first type. In the eighteenth century, and especially in France, the doctrines of materialism were spread broadcast by the Encyclopedists. La Mettrie, Holbach, Feuerbach, Fleurens are usually classed among the foremost materialistic atheists of the period. Voltaire, on the contrary, while undoubtedly helping on the cause of practical atheism, distinctly held its theoretic contrary. He, as well as Rousseau, was a deist. Comte, it will be remembered, refused to be called an atheist. In the last century Thomas Huxley, Charles Darwin, and Herbert Spencer, with others of the evolutionistic school of philosophy, were, quite erroneously, charged with positive atheism. It is a charge which can in no way be substantiated; and the invention and rapid coming into general use of the term agnosticism, used first by Huxley in 1859, shows the long-felt want of a word more definitely defined than atheism to designate a phase of thought either critically or sceptically concerned with the process by which the common tenet of theism is maintained. The fundamental formula is not a denial of the existence of God, but an assertion that the Absolute is unknowable. In Germany, the materialism of Karl Vogt, Jacob Moleschott, Ludwig Büchner, culminating in the monism of Ernst Häckel, goes far towards forming an atheistic system of philosophy. But even the last named admits that there may be a God, though so limited and so foreign to the deity of theists that his admission can hardly remove the system from the first category of theoretic atheism.

Among the unscientific and unphilosophical there have from time to time been found dogmatic atheists of the first type. Here again, however, many of those popularly styled atheists are more correctly described by some other title. There is a somewhat rare tract, "Atheism Refuted in a Discourse to prove the Existence of God by T. P." —British Museum Catalogue, "Tom Paine", who was at one time popularly called an atheist. And perhaps, of the few who have upheld an indubitable form of positive theoretic atheism, none has been taken seriously enough to have exerted any influence upon the trend of philosophic or scientific thought. Robert Ingersoll might be instanced, but though popular speakers and writers of this type may create a certain amount of unlearned disturbance, they are not treated seriously by thinking men, and it is extremely doubtful whether they deserve a place in any historical or philosophical exposition of atheism.

REIMMAN, Historia atheismi et atheorum . . . (Hildesheim, 1725); TOUSSAINT in Dict. de théologie, s. v. (a good bibliography); JANET AND SÉAILLES, History of the Problems of Philosophy (tr., London, 1902), II; HETTINGER, Natural Religion (tr. New York, 1890); FLINT, Anti-theistic Theories (New York, 1894); LILLY, The Great Enigma (New York, 1892); DAURELLE, L'Athéisme devant la raison humaine (Paris, 1883); WARD, Naturalism and Agnosticism (New York, 1899); LADD, Philosophy of Religion (New York, 1905), II; BOEDDER, Natural Theology (New York, 1891); BLACKIE, Natural History of Atheism (New York, 1878); The Catholic World, XXVII, 471; BARRY, The End of Atheism in The Catholic World, LX, 333; SHEA, Steps to Atheism in The Am. Cath. Quart. Rev., 1879, 305; POHLE, Lehrbuch d. Dogmatik (Paderborn, 1907), I; BAUR in Kirchliches Handlexikon (Munich, 1907), s. v. See also bibliography under AGNOSTICISM, MATERIALISM, PANTHEISM, and THEISM. For the refutation of ATHEISM see the article GOD.

FRANCIS AVELING.

Athelney, THE ABBEY OF, in the County of Somerset, England, was founded by King Alfred, A. D. 888, as a religious house for monks of the Order of St. Benedict. Originally Athelney was a small island in the midst of dangerous morasses in what is now the parish of East Ling. It possessed scarcely more than two acres of firm land; was covered with alders and infested by wild animals, and was inaccessible except by boat (William of Malmesbury). Here Alfred found a refuge from the Danes; here he built the abbey dedicated to our Blessed Saviour, St. Peter, St. Paul, and St. Egelwine. He peopled it with foreign monks, drawn chiefly from France, with John of Saxony (known as Scotus) as their abbot. The original church was a small structure consisting of four piers supporting the main fabric and surrounded by four circular chancels. Little is known of the history of the abbey from the eleventh century up to the time of its dissolution except that the monks of Glastonbury attempted to annex it or have it placed under the Glastonbury jurisdiction. It was not a rich community. An indulgence of thirty days was given in 1321 for those who should assist in the rebuilding of the church, and the monks humbly petitioned Edward I to remit " corrod " for which they were unable to find the means of payment. The last abbot was Robert Hamlyn. With eight monks of his community, he surrendered 8 February, 1540, receiving a pension of £50 per annum and retaining his prebend of Long Sutton. The revenues (26 Hen. VII) were £209. 0s. ¾d.

DUGDALE, Monasticon Anglicanum; ASSER, De Rebus Gestis Alfridi; HEARNE, Script. Hist. Angl. XXVIII (1731), 587–90.

FRANCIS AVELING.

Athenagoras, a Christian apologist of the second half of the second century of whom no more is known than that he was an Athenian philosopher and a convert to Christianity. Of his writings there have been preserved but two genuine pieces:—his "Apology" or "Embassy for the Christians" and a "Treatise on the Resurrection". The only allusions to him in early Christian literature are the accredited quotations from his "Apology" in a fragment of Methodius of Olympus (d. 312) and the untrustworthy biographical details in the fragments of the "Christian History" of Philip of Side (c. 425). It may be that his treatises, circulating anonymously, were for a time considered as the work of another apologist. His writings bear witness to his erudition and culture, his power as a philosopher and rhetorician, his keen appreciation of the intellectual temper of his age, and his tact and delicacy in dealing with the powerful opponents of his religion. The "Apology", the date of which is fixed by internal evidence as late in 176 or 177, was not, as the title "Embassy" (πρεσβεία) has suggested, an oral defence of Christianity, but a carefully written plea for justice to the Christians made by a philosopher, on philosophical grounds, to the Emperors Marcus Aurelius and his son Commodus, conquerors, "but above all, philosophers". He first complains of the illogical and unjust discrimination against the Christians and of the calumnies they suffer (i–iii), and then meets the charge of atheism (iv). He establishes the principle of monotheism, citing pagan poets and philosophers in support of the very doctrines for which Christians are condemned (v–vi), and demonstrates the superiority of the Christian belief in God to that of pagans (vii–viii). This first strongly reasoned demonstration of the unity of God in Christian literature is supplemented by an able exposition of the Trinity (x). Assuming then the defensive, the apologist justifies the Christian abstention from worship of the national deities (xiii–xiv) on grounds of its absurdity and indecency, quoting at length the pagan poets and philosophers in support of his contention (xv–xxx). Finally, he meets the charges of immorality by exposing the Christian ideal of purity, even in thought, and the inviolable sanctity of the marriage bond. The charge of cannibalism is refuted by showing the high regard for human life which leads the Christian to detest the crime of abortion (xxxi–xxxvi). The treatise on the "Resurrection of the Body", the first complete exposition of the doctrine in Christian literature, was written later than the "Apology", to which it may be considered as an appendix. Athenagoras brings to the defence of the doctrine the best that contemporary philosophy could adduce. After meeting the objections common to his time (i), he demonstrates the possibility of a resurrection in view either of the power of the Creator (ii–iii), or of the nature of our bodies (iv–viii). To exercise such powers is neither unworthy of God nor unjust to other creatures (ix–xi). He shows that the nature and end of man demand a perpetuation of the life of body and soul.

MARCH and OWEN, *Douglass' Series of Christian, Greek and Latin Writers* (New York, 1876), IV; HARNACK *History of Dogma*, tr. BUCHANAN (Boston, 1903), II, 188–190. An English translation is found in *Ante-Nicene Fathers* (New York, 1903), II, 129–162; in vol. X (ibid.) pp. 36–38, is an extensive bibliography (to 1890). The best editions are those of OTTO, *Corpus Apologetarum* (Jena, 1857), VII, and the Benedictine MARANUS in P. G. (Paris, 1857), VI, 889–1024. See also SCHWARTZ in GEBHARDT AND HARNACK, *Texte und Untersuchungen* (Leipzig, 1891), IV, 2; HARNACK, *Geschichte d. altchristlichen Literatur* (Leipzig, 1893–97), I, 256–258; II, 317–319; BARDENHEWER, *Geschichte der altkirchlichen Literatur* (Freiburg, 1902), I, 267–277; IDEM, *Patrologie* (ibid., 1901) 57–58.

JOHN B. PETERSON.

Athenry, a small inland town in the county Galway, Ireland, anciently called Athnere, from *Ath-na-Riagh*, the king's ford, or the abode of the king. It was the first town established by the Anglo-Norman invaders of Connaught, and at a remote period became a place of importance. A Dominican monastery was completed there in 1261 on a site granted by Meyler de Bermingham. In time it became extensive and wealthy and was used as the chief burial place of the Earls of Ulster and the principal families of the adjoining territory. Indulgences for the benefit of the monastery were granted by the pope in 1400. The church was burned in 1423, and in 1427 two subordinate houses were established. In 1445 Pope Eugenius IV renewed the decree of Pope Martin V to encourage the repairing of the church, at which time there were thirty inmates in the monastery. A Franciscan friary was also founded there in 1464 by Thomas, Earl of Kildare, and chapels erected by his wife and the Earls of Desmond and O'Tully. The place was sacked in 1577 during the Elizabethan wars, but repaired in 1585. The northern Irish burned the town in 1596 but the abbey escaped. The Dominican establishment was revived in 1644 as a university, the town, however, never regained its ancient prestige. The Cromwellian period ruined the ecclesiastical buildings, of which the tower and east window remained in good condition to tell of the ancient extent and beauty of the foundation. The Board of Works in 1893 made extensive repairs to the ruins to preserve them.

LEWIS, *Topographical Dictionary of Ireland* (Dublin, 1839).

THOMAS F. MEEHAN.

Athens, CHRISTIAN.—Christianity was first preached in Athens by St. Paul. He came to Athens from Berœa of Macedonia, coming probably by water and landing in the Peiræevs, the harbour of Athens. This was about the year 53. Having arrived at Athens, he at once sent for Silas and Timotheos who had remained behind in Berœa. While awaiting the coming of these he tarried in Athens, viewing the idolatrous city, and frequenting the synagogue; for there were already Jews in Athens. He also frequented the *agora*, and there met and conversed with the men of Athens, telling them of the new truths which he was promulgating. Finally, at the Areopagos, he spoke to them the sermon which is preserved in the seventeenth chapter of the Acts. The Athenians did not enthusiastically accept this first preaching of Christianity. The Acts mention,

however, that a few believed in Paul's teaching. Amongst these were Dionysios, a member of the Areopagite court, and Damaris, or Thamar possibly, who may have been a Jewess. A tradition asserts that St. Paul wrote from Athens his two letters to the Christians of Thessalonika. Even if this be so, his stay in Athens was not a protracted one. He departed by sea, and went to Korinth by way of Kenchreæ, its eastern harbour. It seems that a Christian community was rapidly formed, although for a considerable time it did not possess a numerous membership. The commoner tradition names the Areopagite as the first head and bishop of the Christian Athenians. Another tradition, however, gives this honour to Hierotheos the Thesmothete. The successors of the first bishop were not all Athenians by lineage. They are catalogued as Narkissos, Publius, and Quadratus. Narkissos is stated to have come from Palestine, and Publius from Malta. In some lists Narkissos is omitted. Quadratus is revered for having contributed to early Christian literature by writing an apology, which he addressed to the Emperor Hadrian. This was on the occasion of Hadrian's visit to Athens. Another Athenian who defended Christianity in writing at a somewhat later time was Aristeides. His apology was directed to the Emperor Marcus Aurelius. Athenagoras also wrote an apology. In the second century there must have been a considerable community of Christians in Athens, for Hygeinos, Bishop of Rome, is said to have written a letter to the community in the year 139. It is probable that the early Church of Athens did not have many martyrs, although Dionysios himself graces the martyrs' list. Under Decius, we find recorded in the catalogue of martyrs the names of Herakleios, Benedimos, Pavlinos, and Leonides with his followers, the holy woman Charissa, and her companions. One reason why the martyrs were few is that the Christians were also few. Besides, the spirit of the Athenian pagans and philosophers was not one of blood; and it is probable that the persecutions in Athens were rather of the social and scholastic kind. This would account for the writings of the apologists who thus would defend themselves by weapons similar to those which their opponents used. The philosophers of the Athenian schools did not indeed admire Christianity, as they understood it; nevertheless there is some ground for believing that amongst the teachers who occupied the official and historic chairs of philosophy at Athens there later was at least one who was a Christian, Prohæresios, the sophist. Be this as it may, it is certain that the teaching of the philosophers was not rudely anti-Christian. Otherwise the presence of Christians amongst the students could not be understood. Sixtus II, or Xystos, who suffered martyrdom in Rome about A. D. 258, also may have studied in Athens and is called "the son of an Athenian philosopher". But the most noted men who frequented the schools here were Basil from Kæsareia, and Gregory from Nazianzos, about the middle of the fourth century. These schools of philosophy kept paganism alive for four centuries, but by the fifth century the ancient religion of Elevsis and Athens had practically succumbed. In the Council of Nikæa there was present a bishop from Athens. In 529 the schools of philosophy were closed. From that date Christianity had no rival in Athens.

Down to the time of Constantine, and later, there were no large Christian temples in Athens. Like the Jews, whose synagogues in pagan towns were small and unpretentious, the first Christians did not erect sumptuous temples. With their worship they did not associate splendour of temple and sanctuary as indispensable. In the time of Basil and Gregory, there were surely numerous church edifices in Athens, but they were not spacious temples. They are called ἱεροὶ οἶκοι, and probably were not much larger than the ordinary dwelling-houses of the inhabitants. The first magnificent churches in Athens were, therefore, the Greek temples which, after the disappearance of paganism, were transferred to the use of the Christian rites. It must have been about Justinian's time when the most of the ancient temples were converted into churches. Churches or ruins of churches have been frequently found on the sites where pagan shrines or temples originally stood. This is in part due to the fact that the sites were first sanctified for Christian tradition by these pagan temples or sanctuaries being made into churches. It is also to some extent true that sometimes the saint whose aid was to be invoked at the Christian shrine bore some outward analogy to the deity previously hallowed in that place. Thus in Athens the shrine of the healer Asklepios, situated between the two theatres on the south side of the Akropolis, when it became a church, was made sacred to the two saints whom the Christian Athenians invoked as miraculous healers, Kosmas and Damian. Amongst the temples converted into churches were the Parthenon and the Erechtheion on the Akropolis, and the yet well-preserved Hephæsteion (or "temple of Theseus", as it is incorrectly called) near the ancient *agora*. The Hephæsteion was, in later times, sacred to St. George. Pittakis, a noted epigraphist of Athens in the early half of the last century, published an inscription which purports to state that in the year 630 the Parthenon was consecrated under the title of "the church of Divine Wisdom" (τῆς Ἁγίας Σοφίας). But Pittakis was very careless or credulous at times in the copying of inscriptions. So we do not know with certainty what was the original title of this church. Possibly, from its first conversion the Parthenon had been dedicated to the Panagia. At least we learn from Michael Akominatos that in the twelfth century it was sacred to the Mother of God. On the columns of this church, and on its marble walls, especially around the doors, are numerous *graffiti* inscriptions which record various events, many of them important for sacred and profane history, such as the names and deaths of bishops, and public calamities. In these *graffiti* inscriptions, this church is called "the great church", "the church of Athens", and the cathedral church, or καθολικὴ ἐκκλησία. All these appellations show that it was the metropolitan church of the city. In Greek usage, the name καθολικόν or καθολικὴ ἐκκλησία, was a title applied to churches which were the sees of bishops or archbishops.

That the Parthenon was a church as far back as the sixth century is proven by the cemetery which lay along its south side. This region was filled with Christian graves, in some of which were found coins of a date as early as the reign of Justinian. In order to fit the Parthenon for a church, changes had to be made in it; an apse was built at the east end, and a great entrance door was placed in the west end. The interior walls were covered with fresco paintings of saints. After the conversion of these Greek temples into churches, perhaps two or three centuries elapsed before the Athenians found it necessary to lavishly add to the number of large church edifices by erecting many new ones. Then they followed the styles of ecclesiastical architecture which had been developed elsewhere, and had become prevalent throughout so much of the empire. From about the end of the eighth century they erected new churches more frequently. Perhaps the Empress Eirene, who was an Athenian, gave some impulse to this tendency. As years went on, Athens and the surrounding villages of Attika, and the fields were filled with churches, many of them veritable gems of Byzantine comeliness. The churches which were built in Athens and vicinity during the Middle Ages numbered hundreds.

Likewise many monasteries were founded, both in Athens itself and in the country of Attika, especially on the slopes of the surrounding mountains of Hymettos, and Pentelikos, and Parnes. A complete list of the Bishops of Athens could not be made. But as time goes on, and seals and manuscripts and inscriptions are deciphered, the list of names will grow. Pistos, Bishop of Athens, was present at the Council of Nikæa in 325. Bishop Modestus was at the Council of Ephesos in 431. John, Bishop of Athens, was amongst the Fathers who signed the Acts of the Sixth Œcumenical Council. He was present as "Legate of the Apostolic See of ancient Rome". From the *graffiti* on the Parthenon a number of other names and dates are already known. In these *graffiti* we read names of bishops prior to the exaltation of Athens to the rank of an archbishopric, then the names of archbishops, and finally those of metropolitans. The time of the elevation of this see to an archbishopric cannot yet be fixed. Gregory II, who was pastor of the Athenians during the first patriarchate of Photios, bore the title of archbishop. But it is not known whether or not he was the first who had that title. This was about 857–867. Shortly afterwards the archbishops received the higher title of metropolitan. Niketas who took part in the Eighth Œcumenical Council under Basil the Makedonian, which closed 28 February, 870, and who signed the acts of that council as "Niketas by the grace of God, Metropolitan of Athens", on his seals, or leaden bulls, simply places the inscription "Niketas, Bishop of Athens". Amongst the signatures to the acts of this council, that of Niketas stands twenty-second in order. But in a full assembly of metropolitans he would not rank so high. According to the list made by Emperor Leon the Wise (886–911), a list intended to show the relative rank of each ecclesiastical dignitary under the Patriarch of Constantinople, the Metropolitan of Athens is relegated to the twenty-eighth place. Just what sees were under the Archbishop of Athens prior to Photios is not easy to discover. After the changes brought about by Photios and his successors, the sees that were suffragan to Athens varied in number from time to time. But in general it may be stated that all of Attika belonged directly to the Archbishop of Athens, after the abolishing of the See of Marathon, about the middle of the ninth century. And under Athens were, besides other bishoprics, the Sees of Evripos, Oreos, Karystos, and Porthmos in Evbœa; Avlon; Diavleia in Phokis, and Koroneia in Bœotia; Andros, Skyros, Syros, and Seriphos of the islands; and, later, Keos and Ægina.

From Photios down to the Franks the Metropolitans of Athens were all of the Greek rite, naturally. Likewise their sympathies were rather with Constantinople than with older Rome. Their metropolitan church continued to be the ancient Parthenon. It seems that the residence of the bishops was on the Akropolis, in the great Portals, or Propylæa, and that in these Propylæa they had a private episcopal chapel. In these days education was not held in very general esteem in Athens. No special erudition characterized the clergy. Even the inscriptions which decorated the seals and bulls of bishops and abbots were often most childishly misspelled. From the time of Photios to the Franks the most noted ecclesiastic was probably the last bishop, Michael Akominatos. He, however, was Athenian neither by birth nor by education. He came to Athens expecting great things in the city of ancient wisdom, but was disappointed. Still it is wrong to say that Athens of the Middle Ages produced no scholars and noted personages. Athenaïs, who became queen to Theodosios in 421, and Eirene, who became empress in 780, were Athenians. From the sixth to the thirteenth century Athens was out and out a provincial town, exercising no influence on the world at large, and almost unheard of in the politics of the day. Nevertheless, the Emperor Konstas on his way to Sicily in 662 spent the winter in Athens; and after his victories over the Bulgarians in 1018, Basil II visited this city to celebrate his triumphs. When, under Constantine, the Empire was divided into governmental dioceses, the close relations which then were created between the Church and the State caused the ecclesiastical divisions to be often identical with the civil. By this system all of Achaia, wherein was Athens, was included within the Diocese of Eastern Illyria, of which Thessalonika was the capital. All of this Diocese of Eastern Illyria was under the direct jurisdiction of the Bishop of Rome. And so it remained until the reign of Leo the Isavrian. This emperor, incensed at Pope Gregory III, because of his strong opposition to Leo's iconoclastic passion, retorted against the pope by transferring these countries of the Illyrian diocese from the jurisdiction of the Bishop of Rome to that of the See of Constantinople. This occurred in the year 732. In this great struggle between the iconoclasts and the adherents to the use of the icons, the Athenians placed themselves on the side of iconolatry. While accepting without any recorded protest their transference to the jurisdiction of the Eastern patriarch, they retained the images in their churches and continued to venerate them. All the inhabitants of Greece north of the Korinthiac Gulf, who then were called Helladikoi, or Helladians, were opposed to the iconoclasts. And their opposition was so determined that they fitted out an expedition and manned a fleet, intending to attack Constantinople, depose Leo, and place their leader, Kosmas, on the throne. In this expedition, in which the Athenians doubtlessly had an important part, assistance was given by the inhabitants of the Kyklad islands, who probably furnished most of the ships. The attempt, however, was futile. The fleet was easily destroyed by the imperial ships in April, 727. The mutual bitterness which was evinced in Constantinople by the contending parties of Photians and Anti-Photians was reflected here in Athens. Gregory II was archbishop when Ignatios was restored to his throne as Patriarch of Constantinople. Ignatios deposed him as being an adherent of Photios. His successor, Kosmas, was also later deposed. Then Niketas, a Byzantine, came to Athens as archbishop with the title of metropolitan. This Niketas was a supporter of Ignatios. His successor, Anastasios, was a follower of Photios. Sabbas, who succeeded Anastasios, was likewise a Photian and was one of those who signed the acts of the synod which closed in May, 880, by which Photios was again recognized as patriarch. A bull of his still exists, whereon he designates himself as "Metropolitan of Athens".

Throughout the East there was a peculiar type of *Panagia-icon*, copies of which might be seen in monasteries and churches in many places. This was the *Panagia Gorgoepekoos*. This *Panagia Gorgoepekoos* seems to have been originally an Athenian icon, and was probably identical with an icon which was called the *Panagia Athenæotissa*. The *Athenæotissa* was the Madonna of the church in the Parthenon. This icon is mentioned by Michael Akominatos.

After the conquest of the Byzantine Empire by the Europeans of the Fourth Crusade, in the partitionment which followed, Athens and the rest of Greece were given to Boniface, King of Thessalonika. Boniface gave Athens to one of his followers, Otho de la Roche. At their coming to Athens the Franks found it small and insignificant. They chose Thebes to be the seat of civil power rather than Athens. Thebes was a more important

trade centre than was Athens. Athens, however, was considered important enough to be continued as an archbishopric. It thus was ranked in equal dignity with the other larger cities of Greece, such as Thebes, within de la Roche's dominion, and Patræ and Korinth in the Morea. The conquest of Greece was accomplished in 1204 and 1205. The first Latin archbishop introduced the Latin ritual into the cathedral, the Parthenon, in the year 1206. This was Archbishop Berard. Thus after a lapse of centuries from the time of Leo the Isavrian, Greece and Athens were again placed under the jurisdiction of the Bishop of Rome. During the Frankish rule the archbishops of Athens were without exception of the Latin Rite, and were of Western lineage. Likewise the canons of the cathedral, in the Parthenon, were of Latin Rite, and were Franks. Their number was fixed by Cardinal Benedict, papal legate in Thessalonika, by order of Pope Innocent III. But the ritual of the common priests was not disturbed. The people continued to enjoy their own rites, celebrated by Greek priests in the Greek language. These Greek priests had, however, at least outwardly, to acknowledge the jurisdiction of the Latin archbishop. Amongst the sees which were suffragan to the Archbishop of Athens were those of Chalkis, Thermopylæ (or Bodonitsa) Davleia, Avlon, Zorkon, Karystos, Koroneia, Andros, Skyros, Kea, and Megara. The last bishop of the Greek Rite was the learned Michael Akominatos, who, when the Franks came, retired to the Island of Keos, after first visiting the cardinal legate of the pope in Thessalonika to impetrate certain favours for those formerly under his charge who wished to adhere to the Greek form of worship. In Keos he lived as a monk in the monastery of St. John the Baptist. To support the Latin archbishop, and the canons, and the cathedral church, a number of possessions were given to him. Amongst these was the monastic property of Kæsariane, and the island of Belbina, which Pope Innocent III gave to the Archbishop of Athens in 1208. The Frankish cavaliers lived in splendour in Thebes and Athens. The dignitaries of the Church lived in ease. Along with the coming of the Franks and the Latin Church there came also Latin monks. The Cistercians established themselves near Athens in 1208 in the beautiful monastery of Daphne, which previously was in the possession of Greek Basilian Fathers. The Franciscans were the most active religious order in Greece during this period. There were also Dominican convents.

In the year 1311 another great change came over Athens. The Franks were defeated by the Catalans in the swamps of the Kephisos in Bœotia. Athens, with Thebes, became their possession. Under their sway, which lasted more than seventy-five years, the higher dignitaries of the Church continued naturally to be Latins. In these days there were fourteen suffragan sees under the Archbishopric of Athens, and at the cathedral there were eleven or twelve canons. In 1387 another change overtook Athens. The Catalonian possessions came under the ownership of the Acciajoli, Florentines who had risen to eminence as bankers. The Acciajoli retained possession of Athens until driven out by Omær Pasha, who in June of 1456 entered the city and, in 1458, took possession of the Akropolis for his Sultan, Mohammed II. The only notable change in ecclesiastical matters under the Acciajoli was that they permitted two archbishops to reside in Athens, a Greek dignitary for the Catholics of the Greek Rite, and a Latin for the Franks. In this way the defection of the Greeks of Athens from Roman jurisdiction was again a fact. The Latin archbishop lived in the *Castro*, that is, on the Akropolis, and the Greek prelate had his residence in the lower city. Franco Acciajoli was the last Duke of Athens. The last

Latin archbishop was Nicholas Protimus. He died in 1483. After his death Rome continued to appoint titular Latin archbishops to the See of Athens. Under Turkish domination the Church and all its property again became Greek. All the suffragan sees were again filled by Greek bishops, and the monasteries were again occupied by Greek monks. The Parthenon, however, was appropriated by the conquerors, who converted it into a mosque. The Greek bishops continued to live in the lower town, and during the latter half of the Turkish supremacy they usually resided near the church of the Panagia Gorgoepekoos, which they used as a private chapel. They lived elsewhere at times, however, for Father Babin mentions Archbishop Anthimos as living near the church of St. Dionysios, which was at the foot of the Areopagos Hill. In Turkish times, as previously, the sees under Athens were not always the same in number. Nor were they all identical with those that had been under the Latin archbishops. Some of them were Koroneia, Salona, Bodonitsa, Davleia, Evripos, Oreos, Karystos, Porthmos, Andros, Syra, and Skyros.

Amongst the religious orders that lived in Athens under Turkish rule were the Franciscans. They were there as early as 1658. But they had already been in Greece under the Franks. The Franciscans are to be mentioned with the Dominicans as being the first Western Europeans who sent students to Athens and other places in the East for the purpose of studying the language and literature of the Greeks. Another fact to the credit of the Franciscans of Athens is that, although not primarily interested in antiquities, they fruitfully contributed to the awakening of our interest in such studies. There appeared in Paris in the second half of the seventeenth century, a book by Guillet or "de la Guilletière", which is entirely based on information received from the Franciscans of Athens. Franciscans sketched the first plan of modern Athens. Considering how suspicious the Turks were of any kind of description of their possessions and castles, it was quite a feat for the Franciscans to have made so good a plan as they did. It was published by Guillet in his book, "Athènes, anciennes et nouvelles", 1675. In those days the Capuchins had a comfortable monastery in Athens, which they built on ground bought from the Turks in 1658, behind the choragic monument of Lysikrates. The monument itself served them as their little library. In this monastery many a traveller found hospitality. It was destroyed by fire in 1821, and the site is now owned by the French Government. The Jesuits were also active in Athens. They came in 1645. It must be noted that it was Father Babin, a Jesuit, who wrote the first careful account of the modern condition of the ruins of ancient Athens. This he did in a letter to the Abbé Pécoil, canon of Lyons. This letter was written 8 October, 1672. It was published with a commentary by Spon in 1674 under the title of "Relation de l'état présent de la ville d'Athènes". The Jesuits finally withdrew from Athens, leaving the entire field to the Franciscans. The Franciscans remained until the beginning of the war of the revolution. In the time of Babin and Spon there were about two hundred churches in Athens, all of the Greek Rite, except the chapels in the monasteries of the western monks. With the war of the insurrection, in 1821, ends the history of the older Church of Athens. A new Latin archbishopric has again its residence in Athens. (See ATHENS, MODERN DIOCESE OF.) Since 1833 the Church of the Greek Rite has undergone serious changes of jurisdiction, for it no longer recognizes the leadership of the Patriarch of Constantinople, but is a national autocephalous church.

GREGOROVIUS, Geschichte der Stadt Athen im Mittelalter (Stuttgart, 1889), Greek tr. by LAMPROS, with additional notes and an appendix (Athens, 1904–06); HOPF, Geschichte Griechenlands vom Beginn des Mittelalters bis auf unsere Zeit (Leipzig, 1870); GEORGIADES, Ἱστορία τῶν Ἀθηνῶν (Athens); NEROUTSOS, Χριστιανικαὶ Ἀθῆναι (Athens, 1889 sqq.); LEQUIEN, Oriens Christianus; MOMMSEN, Athenæ Christianæ (Leipzig, 1868); ANTONIO RUBIO Y LLUCH, La Expedición y la Dominación de los Catalanos en Oriente (Barcelona, 1883); GULDENCRONE, L'Achaïe féodale (Paris, 1886); KAMPOUROGLOS, Ἱστορία τῶν Ἀθηνῶν. Τουρκοκρατία (Athens, 1889–93); PHILADELPHEVS, Ἱστορία τῶν Ἀθηνῶν ἐπὶ Τουρκοκρατίας (Athens, 1904).

DANIEL QUINN.

Athens, MODERN DIOCESE OF.—The Greeks have long regarded their religion as a national affair. This notion is so deep-rooted that they cannot understand how a citizen can well be a true Greek if he gives his allegiance to any religion which is not that of the Greek Church. At the present time the majority of Catholics who live within the Diocese of Athens are therefore foreigners, or of foreign descent. Of the foreigners who are Catholics, the greater part are of Italian nationality. Most of those who are of foreign descent have come into Athens and other portions of this diocese from the islands of the Ægean and Ionian seas. The Catholics of these islands are largely descendants of the Western conquerors who held possession of the islands for two or three centuries, or even longer, beginning with the Fourth Crusade. As a rule, they are of Venetian and Genoese descent. In these islands some of the native Greeks, on account of the higher social and political standing of the foreign element, accepted the Catholic Faith and obedience. From these converted Greeks some Catholics in the Diocese of Athens are now descended. On three or four of the islands, outside of the Diocese of Athens, there are many such Catholics who are pure Greeks, being descended from converts to Catholicism in the time of the foreign feudal governments. These Catholics from the islands are the nucleus of the future prosperity of Catholicism in Greece, for gradually they are identifying themselves with the good of the country and its worthier ideals. Although they are still conscious of their foreign extraction, or former foreign sympathies, they now feel that their residence of centuries in Greek territory has made them Greeks. The real foreign element is made up of those Catholics who have migrated into Greece since it has become a free country. These are chiefly Italians and Maltese. Most of them are labourers who came to find employment on the railroads and other public works, or to live as fishermen or boatmen in the larger seaport towns. The exact number of Catholics cannot easily be estimated. Possibly in the entire Diocese of Athens there are about 10,000, of whom about one-fourth attend church regularly. From amongst the members of the Greek Church no converts are made to Catholicity. At least, they are extremely rare. It is against the positive and explicit law of the State for any other church to make proselytes from the established Greek or Orthodox Church. In the first National Assembly, which was held at Epidavros in 1822, it was declared that the Orthodox Church is the State Church. This declaration was repeated in the Assembly at Trœzen in 1827. Such has been the strict law ever since. But, except that propagandism is severely prohibited, the Catholic Church is perfectly free, is fairly treated, and highly respected.

Otho of Bavaria, the first king of regenerated Greece, was a Catholic. In his reign the Catholics were few. But arrangements were made that the Catholics could have a place of worship wherever they existed in sufficient numbers. After Athens became the seat of government, in 1834, an abandoned Turkish mosque was given to the Catholics as a place of worship. It is still used as a church, and is attended chiefly by Maltese and Italians who live in and around the Old Market, near the Tower of the Winds. Mass is said there on Sundays and Holy Days by a priest from the cathedral. After the lapse of some years, in 1876, an archbishopric was established in Athens. Those who have occupied this see are Archbishops Marangos, Zaffino, De Angelis, and Delendas. De Angelis was an Italian; Zaffino a native of Corfu; all the other archbishops were born in the Ægean Islands. Within the Diocese of Athens there are now eight churches. Of these two are in Athens, and there is one in each of the towns of Peiræevs (the harbour of Athens); Patræ, the chief town of the Peloponnesos; Volos, the seaport of Thessaly; Lavrion (Ergasteria), in the silver mines of Attica; Herakleion, a Bavarian settlement in Attika; and Navplion in the Argolid. Most of the Catholics, however, are concentrated at Athens, Peiræevs, and Patræ. Of the two churches in Athens, one is the ancient mosque which Otho donated to the Catholics, and the other is the cathedral of St. Dionysios. It is a stone structure in basilica style, with a portico in front supported by marble columns. The interior is divided into three naves separated from each other by rows of columns of Tenian marble. The apse has been frescoed. This cathedral was built with money sent from abroad, especially from Rome. Besides the regular parishes there are missions here and there. Some years ago there were missions at Kalamata, Pyrgos, and Kalamaki. The only considerable one at present is at Lamia. Within the Diocese of Athens there are at present eleven priests engaged in parochial work: four at the cathedral in Athens, two at Patræ, and one at each of the churches of Peiræevs, Lavrion, Volos, Herakleion, and Navplion. All of them are secular priests.

French sisters conduct schools for girls in Athens and at the Peiræevs, and Italian sisters have schools for girls at Patræ. They have boarders as well as day scholars. In the town of the Peiræevs there is a good school for boys conducted by French Salesian Fathers. Boarders and day scholars are accommodated, and both classical and commercial courses are given. But the most important school of the diocese is the Leonteion at Athens, founded by Pope Leo XIII, to supply ordinary and theological education for all Greek-speaking Catholics. It embraces a preparatory department, an intermediate or "hellenic" school, a gymnasium or college, and an ecclesiastical seminary. The average number of pupils and students for the past five years is about 175. The faculty consists of both priests and laymen. In its character as seminary, the Leonteion receives students from other dioceses as well as from that of Athens. Previous to the establishment of the Leonteion, candidates for the priesthood were educated chiefly in the Propaganda, at Rome, and in a diocesan seminary which existed in the Ægean town of Syra. The seminary at Syra has been closed, and it is now intended that all clerical training be given in the Leonteion and the Propaganda.

The only publication of note for the Catholics of this diocese is the "Harmonia", a periodical devoted to Catholic interests. The "Harmonia" is supported chiefly by a subsidy from Rome. One does not expect to find a large number of noted scholars in so small a Catholic community. But all the clergy are men of wide education. Every one of them, with other accomplishments, speaks two or three other languages as well as the vernacular Greek of the country. Amongst the laymen special mention should be made of the brothers Kyparissos Stephanos and Klon Stephanos. Kyparissos, a mathematician whose fame extended far beyond the confines of Greece, was made a professor in the National University. His brother Klon, an anthropologist of repute, engaged in special historical, archæological, and anthropological researches, became director of the Anthropological Museum of Athens. There are in Greece no Uniat Greek Catholics. All are of the Latin Rite. This is because most of these Catholics are from the West, either by descent or by birth, and they have kept their own Western rite. It might be better for Catholicism in Greece if the Catholics were to adopt the native rite, and to have their liturgy in the liturgical language of the country. But many of the Catholics of Athens would never willingly accept such a change, which they would regard rather from a national than from a religious point of view, and would consider a denial of their Italian, or other Western, origin.

DANIEL QUINN.

Athias, JOSEPH, b. in Spain, probably in Cordova, at the beginning of the seventeenth century; d. at Amsterdam, 12 May, 1700. In 1661 and 1667 he issued two editions of the Hebrew Bible. Though carefully printed, they contain a number of mistakes in the vowel points and the accents. But as they were based on the earlier editions compared with the best manuscripts, they were the foundation of all the subsequent editions. The copious marginal notes added by Jean de Leusden, professor at Utrecht, are of little value. The 1667 edition was bitterly attacked by the Protestant savant, Samuel Desmarets; Athias answered the charges in a work whose title begins: "Cæcus de coloribus". He published, also, some other works of importance, such as the "Tikkun Sepher Torah", or the "Order of the Book of the Law", and a Judæo-German translation of the Bible. The latter involved Athias in a competition with Uri Phœbus, a question that has been discussed but cannot be fully cleared up at this late date.

HEURTEBIZE in VIG., *Dict. de la Bible* (Paris, 1895); *The Jewish Encyclopedia* (New York and London, 1903), II.

A. J. MAAS.

Athos, MOUNT.—Athos is a small tongue of land that projects into the Ægean Sea, being the easternmost of the three strips in which the great mountainous peninsula of Chalcidice ends. It is almost cut off from the mainland, to which it is bound only by a narrow isthmus dotted with lakes and swamps

MONASTERY OF ESPHIGMENON, MOUNT ATHOS

interspersed with alluvial plains. It has been well called "a Greece in miniature", because of the varied contour of its coasts, deep bays and inlets, bold cliffs and promontories, steep wooded slopes, and valleys winding inland. Several cities existed here in pre-Christian antiquity, and a sanctuary of Zeus (Jupiter) is said to have stood on the mountain. The isthmus was famous for the canal (3,950 feet in length) which Xerxes had dug across it, in order to avoid the perilous turning of the limestone peak immemorially known as Mount Athos, in which the small peninsula ends, and which rises to a height of some 6,000 feet. From the summit of this peak on a clear day are visible the coasts of Macedonia and Thrace, even the entire Ægean from Mount Olympus in Thessaly to Mount Ida in Asia Minor. It is the mountain that the architect Dinocrates offered to turn into a statue of Alexander the Great with a city in one hand and in the other a perennially flowing spring. Medieval Greek tradition designated it as the "high mountain" from which Satan tempted Our Lord. Its chief modern interest lies in the fact that at least from the beginning of the Middle Ages it has been the home of a little monastic republic that still retains almost the same autonomy granted a thousand years ago by the Christian emperors of Constantinople. In 1905 the many fortified monasteries and hermitages of Athos contained 7,553 monks (including their numerous male dependents), members of the Orthodox Greek Church: Greeks, 3,207; Russians, 3,615; Bulgarians, 340; Rumanians, 288; Georgians, 53; Servians, 18; other nationalities 32. The principal monasteries bear the following names: Laura, Iviron, Vatopedi, Chilandarion, St. Dionysius, Coutloumousi, Pantocrator, Xiropotamos, Zographu, Docheiarion, Caracalla, Philotheos, Simopetra, St. Paul, Stauroniceta, Xenophon, Gregorios, Esphigmenon, St. Panteleimon, St. Anna (Rossicon), and Karyaes.

HISTORY.—The origins of monastic life on Mount Athos are obscure. It is probable that individual hermits sought its lonely recesses during the fourth and fifth centuries, and were numerous in the ninth century at the time of the first certain attempts at monastic organization. The nearest episcopal see was that of Hierissus, and in conformity with ancient law and usage its bishop claimed jurisdiction over the monks of the little peninsula. In 885 Emperor Basil the Macedonian emancipated them from the jurisdiction of the monastery of St. Colobos near Hierissus, and allotted to them Mount Athos as their property. Soon after, the oldest of the principal monasteries, Xiropotamos, was built and adopted the rule of St. Basil. Saracen pirates disturbed the monks in the ninth and tenth centuries, but imperial generosity always came to the aid of this domestic "holy land" of the Greeks. About 960 a far-reaching reform was introduced by the Anatolian monk Athanasius of Trebizond, later known as Athonites. With several companions from Asia Minor he founded by the seashore the monastery since known as Laura, where he raised the monastic life to a high degree of perfection. Eventually the new settlement was accepted as a model. With the help of the imperial authority of John Tzimisces (969–976) all opposition was set aside and the cœnobitic or community life imposed on the hermits scattered in the valleys and forests. Athanasius was made abbot general or superior (*Protos*) of the fifty-eight monastic communities then on the mountain. From this period date the monasteries known as Iviron (Iberians), Vatopedi, and Esphigmenon. At this time, also, there arose a cause of internal conflict that has never been removed. Hitherto only one nationality, the Greek, was represented among the monks. Henceforth Slavic faith and generosity, and later on Slavic interests, had to be considered. The newly converted Slavs sought and obtained admission into the recently opened monasteries; before long their princes in the Balkan Peninsula began to found independent houses for Slavic monks. In this way arose during the reign of Alexius I (1081–1118) the strictly Slavic monasteries of Chilandarion and Zographu. The Byzantine emperors never ceased to manifest their interest in the little monastic republic and even profited politically by the universal esteem that the religious brotherhood enjoyed throughout the Christian world.

With the aid of the Patriarch of Constantinople, in 1046, Constantine Monomachos regulated the domestic government of the monasteries, the ad-

ministration of their temporal possessions, and their commercial activity. By the imperial document (*typicon*) which he issued, women are forbidden the peninsula, a prohibition so strictly observed since that time that even the Turkish *aga*, or official, who resides at Karyaes (Cariez) may not take his harem with him. About the year 1100 the monasteries of Mount Athos were 180 in number, and sheltered 700 monks, with their dependents. At this time there came into general use the term *Hagion Oros* (Holy Mountain, ἅγιον ὄρος, *Monte Santo*). Alexius I granted the monasteries immunity from taxation, freed them from all subjection to the Patriarch of Constantinople, and placed them under his immediate protection. They still depended, however, on the neighbouring Bishop of Hierissus for the ordination of their priests and deacons. Alexius also chose to be buried on the Holy Mountain among the brethren (1118). A century later, after the capture of Constantinople (1204), the Latin Crusaders abused the monks, who thereupon appealed to Innocent III; he took them under his protection and in his letters (xiii, 40; xvi, 168) paid a tribute to their monastic virtues. However, with the restoration of Greek political supremacy the monks returned (1313) to their old allegiance to Constantinople.

In the fourteenth century a pseudo-spiritualism akin to that of the ancient Euchites or Messalians, culminating in the famous Hesychast controversies (see HESYCHASM; PALAMAS), greatly disturbed the mutual harmony of Greek monasteries, especially those of Mount Athos, one of whose monks, Callistus, had become Patriarch of Constantinople (1350–54) and in that office exhibited great severity towards the opponents of Hesychasm. Racial and national discord between the Greeks and the Servians added fuel to the flames, and for a while the monks were again subjected to the immediate supervision of the Bishop of Hierissus. In the meantime the Palæologi emperors at Constantinople and the Slav princes and nobles of the Balkan Peninsula continued to enrich the monasteries of Mount Athos, which received the greater part of their landed wealth during this period. Occasionally a Byzantine emperor took refuge among the monks in the hope of forgetting the cares and responsibilities of his office. Amid the political disasters of the Greeks, during the fourteenth century, Mount Athos appears as a kind of Holy Land, a retreat for many men eminent in Church and State, and a place where the spirit of Greek patriotism was cherished when threatened elsewhere with ruin (Krumbacher, 1058–59). This period was also marked by the attempts of the monastery of Karyaes to secure a pre-eminence over the others, the final exclusion of the Bishop of Hierissus from the peninsula, fresh attacks from freebooters of all kinds, and the foundation of several new monasteries: Simopetra, Castamonitu, St. Paul, and St. Dionysius. The Fall of Constantinople (1453) brought no modification of the conditions on the Holy Mountain. The monks, who had stubbornly opposed all attempts at reunion with the Apostolic See, submitted at once to the domination of the Osmanli, and, with rare exceptions, have never been interfered with by the Turkish authorities. The hospodars of Wallachia remained as ever their friends and benefactors. Though the monks sympathized with the Greeks in the War of Independence (1822–30), their estates on the Greek mainland were secularized by Capo d'Istria and a similar fate has overtaken their properties in the Danubian principal cities. They still hold numerous farms and properties in certain islands of the Archipelago and on the mainland (Kaulen in Kirchenlex., I, 1557–59; Bayet in Grande Encycl., s. v. Athos).

CONSTITUTION AND GOVERNMENT.—This monastic republic is governed by an assembly of 20 members, one representative from each of the 20 principal monasteries; from among these is elected annually, and in due rotation, a committee of 4 presidents. The great seal of the united monasteries is in four pieces and is divided among the members of this committee. One of the members is chosen as chairman, or *Protos*. Meetings of the assembly are held weekly (Saturday), at Karyaes, and the assembly acts as a supreme parliament and tribunal, with appeal, however, to the patriarch at Constantinople.

MONASTERY OF HAGIOS PAVLOS, OR ST. PAUL, MOUNT ATHOS

The Turkish Government is represented by an agent at Karyaes, the diminutive capital of the peninsula and the landing-place for visitors. A detachment of Christian soldiers is usually stationed there, and no one may land without permission of the monastic authorities. The monks have also an agent at Saloniki and another at Constantinople. Almost the only source of contention among them is the rivalry between the Greeks, inheritors of old traditions and customs, and the Russians of the great monastery of Rossicon (St. Anna), representative of the wealth, power, and interests of their church and country, and generously supported from St. Petersburg. In its present form the constitution of the monasteries dates from 1783.

MONASTIC LIFE.—Each of the twenty great monasteries (twenty-one, including Karyaes) possesses its own large church and numerous chapels within and without its enclosure, which is strongly fortified, recalling the feudal burgs of the Middle Ages. The high walls and strong towers are reminders of the troubled times of the fourteenth and fifteenth centuries when corsairs abounded and self-defence was imperative. All of the great monasteries are on the Holy Mountain proper, and are most picturesquely situated from sea to summit, amid dense masses of oak, pine, and chestnut, or on inaccessible crags. To each of these monasteries is attached a certain number of minor monasteries (σκῆται, *asceteria*), small monastic settlements (καθίσματα), and hermitages (κελλία, *cellæ*). Every monastic habitation must be affiliated to one or the other of the great monasteries and is subject to its direction or supervision. All monasteries are dedicated to the Mother of God, the larger ones under some specially significant title. The ancient Greek Rule of St. Basil is still followed by all.

In the observance of the Rule, however, the greater monasteries are divided into two classes, some following strictly the cœnobitic life, while others permit a larger personal freedom. The latter are called "idiorhythmic"; in them the monks have a right of personal ownership and a certain share in the government of the monastery (Council of Elders); they take their meals apart, and are subject to less severe regulations. In the former, known as "cœno-

bitic" (κοινόβιον, *cœnobium*, common life), there is a greater monastic rigour. The superior, or hegoumenos (ἡγούμενος), has absolute authority, and all property is held in common. The chief occupation of the monks is that of solemn public prayer, by night and by day, i. e. recitation of the Divine Office, corresponding to the solemn choir-service of the Latin Church. (See GREEK RITE, BREVIARY, PSALMODY.) This leaves little time for agricultural, industrial, or intellectual labour. Some fish, or practise minor industries in aid of the common support, or administer the monastic estates located elsewhere; others go abroad occasionally to collect a part of the yearly tribute (about two dollars and a half) that each monk must pay to the Turkish Government. A portion of this is collected from the monks themselves; the rest is secured by the revenue of their farms or other possessions, and by contributions from affiliated monasteries in the Balkan Peninsula, Georgia, and Russia. The generosity of the Greek faithful is also a source of revenue, for Mount Athos is one of the most sacred pilgrimage sites of the entire Greek Church, and the feasts of the principal monasteries are always celebrated with great pomp. It may be added that the monks practise faithfully the monastic virtue of hospitality. The usual name for the individual monk here, as elsewhere in the Greek Orient, is *Kalogeros* (good old man). In their dress the monks do not differ from other communities of Greek Basilians.

ARCHITECTURE AND THE ARTS.—Most of the buildings of Mount Athos are comparatively modern. Yet, because of the well-known conservative character of the monks, these edifices represent with much fidelity the Byzantine architecture, civil and religious, of the tenth to the fourteenth century. The churches are very richly adorned with columns and pavements of marble, frescoed walls and cupolas, decorated screens, etc.; there are not many mosaics. Some of the smaller oratories are said to be the oldest extant specimens of private architecture in the West, apart from the houses of Pompeii. The ecclesiastical art of the Greek Orient is richly represented here, with all its religious respect, though also with all its immobile conservatism and its stern refusal to interpret individual feeling in any other forms than those made sacred by a long line of almost nameless monastic painters like Panselinos and confided by his disciples to the famous "Painters' Book of Mount Athos" (see Didron, Manuel d'iconographie chrétienne, Paris, 1858). Though there is not in the 935 churches of the peninsula any art-work older than the sixteenth century (Bayet) their frescoes, small paintings on boards, gilt and jewelled metal work, represent with almost unswerving accuracy the principles, spirit, and details of medieval Byzantine art as applied to religious uses.

LIBRARIES.—Each monastery possesses its own library, and the combined treasures make up a unique collection of ancient manuscripts (Montfaucon, Palæographia Græca, Paris, 1748, 441 sqq.). By far the richest in this respect is the Russian monastery of Saint Anna (Rossicon). Some of the more valuable classical Greek manuscripts have been purchased or otherwise secured by travellers (Naumann, "Serapeum", X, 252; Duchesne, "Mémoire sur une mission au Mont Athos", Paris, 1876; Lambros, "Catalogue of the Greek Manuscripts on Mount Athos", Cambridge, 1895, 1900). It was in this way that the text of Ptolemy first reached the West. Similarly, the oldest manuscript of the second-century Christian text known as "The Shepherd of Hermas" came from Mount Athos. The manuscripts now in possession of the monks have chiefly an ecclesiastical value; their number is said to be about 8,000. There are also in the library and archives of each monastery a great many documents

II.—4

(donations, privileges, deeds, charters) in Greek, Georgian, and Old-Slavonic, beginning with the ninth century, some of which are important for the historian of Byzantine law and of the medieval Greek Church (Miklosich and Müller, Zachariä von Lingenthal, Uspenskij). The monks of Mount Athos are somewhat indifferent towards these treasures; nothing has been done to make them accessible, except the unsuccessful attempt of Archbishop Bulgaris of Corfu to found at Mount Athos, towards the close of the eighteenth century, a school of the classical languages. The monasteries conduct a few elementary schools for the teaching of reading and writing; nowhere, perhaps, is the intellectual stagnation of the Greek Schism more noticeable. The monks are chiefly devoted to the splendour of their religious services; the solitaries still cherish Hesychast ideas and an apocalyptic mysticism, and the whole monastic republic represents just such an intellectual decay as must follow on a total exclusion of all outside intercourse and a complete neglect of all intellectual effort (Kaulen).

ATHELSTAN RILEY, *Athos, the Mountain of the Monks* (London, 1887); CURZON, *Monasteries of the Levant* (6th ed., London, 1881); LANGLOIS, *Le Mont Athos et ses monastères* (Paris, 1867); DE VOGÜÉ, *Syrie, Palestine et Mont Athos* (Paris, 1878); NEYRAC, *L'Athos* (Paris, 1880); KAULEN in *Kirchenlex.*, I, 1555–63; MEYER in *Zeitschr. f. Kirchengesch.* (1890), XI, 395–435; KRUMBACHER, *Gesch. der byzant. Litt.* (2d ed., Munich, 1867), 511–515, 1058–59; SCHMIDTKE, *Das Klosterland des Athos* (1903); among older works, FALLMERAYER, *Fragmente aus dem Orient* (2d ed., Stuttgart, 1877). For the art-treasures of Mount Athos see BROCKHAUS, *Die Kunst in den Athos-Klöstern* (Leipzig, 1891); and for photographs of the principal sites, besides the above quoted works, *Vom Fels zum Meer* (1892), 19–20.

THOMAS J. SHAHAN.

Atienza, JUAN DE, b. at Tordehumos, near Valladolid, in Spain, in the year 1546, eldest son of the royal Councillor of Castile, Bartolomé de Atienza, a very distinguished jurisconsult under Charles V. He studied law in the celebrated University of Salamanca, but in 1564 forsook the legal career in order to become a Jesuit. While in Spain, he already occupied distinguished positions. He was Prefect of the College of Avila, Procurator of the Province of his order, founder of the College of Villa García, its rector and master of novices, and rector of the College of Valladolid. While thus honourably placed in his mother country, he became informed of a call for fifty Jesuits, to be sent to Peru in the interests of religion and of the Indians. Father Atienza at once asked permission to become one of their number. He reached Lima in 1581 and found there his appointment as rector of the College of San Pablo. In that capacity he was surrogate to the Provincial, Father Baltasar de Piñas, and founded, under the direction of the Company of Jesus, the College of San Martín, the first school of secular learning established at Lima. The foundation of that school was confirmed by Pope Sixtus V, in 1588, and Father Atienza became its first rector. In 1585 he was made Provincial of the Jesuits in Peru. He at once began to foster and extend the missions in Ecuador, the Gran Chaco, Tucuman, and Paraguay. Out of these efforts the province of Paraguay was born in 1607. During that period a printing press was established by the Jesuits at the Indian village of Julí. Jointly with Father José de Acosta he directed the publication of catechisms and textbooks of Christian doctrine for the use of the Indians. These religious "primers" were printed between the years 1583 and 1590, at Lima. They are in Spanish, Quichua, and Aymará.

ANELLO OLIVA, *Historia del Perv y Varones ilustres de la Compañía de Jesús* (1631; Lima c. 1892); FRAY ANTONIO DE LA CALANCHA, *Corónica moralizada* (Lima, 1638), I; DIEGO DE CÓRDOVA SALINAS, *Corónica de la Religiosísima Provincia de los Doce apóstoles del Perú* (Lima, 1651); MENDIBURÚ, *Diccionario* (Lima, 1874), vol. I; TORRES SALDAMANDO, *Los Antiguos Jesuitas del Perú* (Lima, 1882); BERNABÉ COBO, *Historia de la fundación de Lima* (1639; Lima, 1882).

AD. F. BANDELIER.

Atkinson, JAMES, Catholic confessor, tortured to death in Bridewell prison in 1595. His pathetic and romantic story tells us nothing of his early life, but he is found in the Bridewell prison, one of the worst in London, and delivered over to Topcliffe, the notorious priest-hunter, who was trying to wring out from him, by torture, evidence on which he might accuse his master, Mr. Robert Barnes, who then held Mapledurham House, of having entertained priests, and in particular the future martyr, Venerable John Jones, O. S. F. Yielding to torment, Atkinson accused his master of having done so, but shortly after repented, and was lost in despair, knowing on the one hand that Topcliffe would torture him again, perhaps unto death, and on the other fearing that no priest could possibly come to confess and absolve him before his conflict. Unknown to him, however, a Jesuit Father happened to be in the same prison. This was Father William Baldwin (or Bawden), a man who afterwards filled important positions in his order. He had been arrested on suspicion while on shipboard, and had assumed the part of an Italian merchant unacquainted with the English language, and with such success that he was on the point of being exchanged for an English officer who had been captured by the Spaniards on board the Dainty. Atkinson's despair put Father Baldwin into a quandary. It was evident that he was at best a weakling, perhaps a traitor in disguise. To speak to such a one in English, and much more to own to him that he was a priest, would be to endanger his life. So he tried to comfort him, at first through a fellow-prisoner who knew Latin, and finally offered to bring him a priest. The poor sufferer's joy was so great that the missionary ventured to creep to his bedside that night and tell him that he was a priest. Then Atkinson held back, either out of suspicion or because, as he said, he was not prepared. Father Baldwin's fears were reawakened, but next night the penitent made his confession with evident contrition, was soon again tortured, and died under or shortly after the torment. Atkinson's cause has been proposed for Beatification, but evidence for his final perseverance, though very necessary, is naturally hard to find.

CHALLONER, *Missionary Priests* (1864), II, 189; DODD, *Church History* (TIERNEY ed.), III, ap. 204; FOLEY, *Records S. J.*, III, 503; RECORD OFFICE, *Treasurer of the Chamber's accounts for 1594*, roll 196b.

J. H. POLLEN.

Atkinson, NICHOLAS, priest and martyr, is probably to be identified with Venerable Thomas Atkinson. Dodd, who mentions Nicholas's death as having taken place at York in 1610, does not mention Thomas at all; yet all the facts which he relates of the one are certainly true of the other, while there is no corroboration for Dodd's date of Nicholas's martyrdom. It seems probable, however, that there was an old Marian priest named Nicholas, or "Ninny", Atkinson (Gillow, 85).

DODD, *Church History*, II, 376.

J. H. POLLEN.

Atkinson, PAUL OF ST. FRANCIS.—One of the notable confessors of the English Church during the age which succeeded the persecution of blood. Having been condemned to perpetual imprisonment for his priesthood, about the year 1699, he died in confinement after having borne its pains for more than thirty years. He was of a Yorkshire family and was called Matthew in baptism. He joined the English Franciscan Convent at Douai in 1673, and had served with distinction on the English mission for twelve years, when he was betrayed by a maid-servant for the £100 reward. One governor of his prison, Hurst Castle on the Solent, allowed him to walk outside the prison walls; but complaint was made of this and the leave was revoked.

Correspondence of BISHOP MILNER in the *Gentleman's Magazine*, LX, 234, 332, 412; OLIVER, *Collections Illustrating History of the Catholic Religion in Cornwall*, 565; COOPER in *Dict. Nat. Biog.*, II. 224; GILLOW, *Bibl. Dict. Eng. Cath.*, I, 84.

J. H. POLLEN.

Atkinson, SARAH, philanthropist and biographer, b. at Athlone, Ireland, 13 October, 1823; d. Dublin, 8 July, 1893. She was the eldest daughter of John and Anne Gaynor, who lived on the western bank of the Shannon, in that part of Athlone which is in the County Roscommon. At the age of fifteen, she removed with her family to Dublin, where her education was completed. At twenty-five, she married Dr. George Atkinson, part proprietor of the "Freeman's Journal". The loss of her only child in his fourth year so deeply affected Mrs. Atkinson that she resolved to spend the rest of her life in charitable and other good works. With her friend, Mrs. Ellen Woodlock, she interested herself in the female paupers of the South Dublin Union, and opened a home to which many were transferred and were made useful members of society. Her house in Drumcondra soon became the rendezvous for the charitably disposed. It was even more a literary salon. Here she prepared her life of Mary Aikenhead which Mr. W. E. H. Lecky has warmly commended, and here she wrote her many valuable essays. For many years she translated into English the French "Annals of the Propagation of the Faith". Much of her time was devoted to visiting the hospitals and poor people at their homes, and to other beneficent purposes. To her is largely due the success of the Childrens' Hospital, Temple Street, Dublin. The management of the Sodality of the Children of Mary, attached to the Church of St. Francis Xavier, was one of her particular pleasures. To the Hospice for the Dying, at Harold's Cross, she was a constant benefactress. Even her writings were made to serve the great objects of her life. In Duffy's "Hibernian Magazine", 1860–64, "The Month", 1864–65, "The Nation", 1869–70, the "Freeman's Journal", 1871, and in the "Irish Monthly" after its inception are to be found many important essays by her, chiefly biographical and historical. Some of her earliest and longest essays appeared in the "Irish Quarterly Review"; the best of them are included in her volume of "Essays" (Dublin, 1895). Her "Life of Mary Aikenhead", modestly published with her initial only, appeared in 1879, and is one of the best Catholic biographies in English. Her "Essays" include complete and learned dissertations on such divergent subjects as "St. Fursey's Life and Visions", "The Geraldines", "The Dittamondo", "Devorgilla", "Eugene O'Curry", "Irish Wool and Woolens", "St. Bridget", and excellent biographies of the sculptors John Henry Foley and John Hogan, the best accounts yet written of those great artists. Indeed most of these essays are the best studies we have on the various subjects. Her "Citizen Saint" (St. Catherine of Siena) occupies a hundred pages, and is a most able summary.

MULHOLLAND, in the *Freeman's Journal* files (Dublin, July, 1893), and prefatory memoir in the *Essays*; TYNAN, *Irish Independent*, files (Dublin, July, 1893); *The Irish Monthly* (Dublin, November, 1893)—a full list of her writings.

D. J. O'DONOGHUE.

Atkinson, THOMAS, VEN. martyred at York, 11 March, 1616. He was b. in the East Riding of Yorkshire, was ordained priest at Reims, and returned to his native country in 1588. We are told that he was unwearied in visiting his flock, especially the poor, and became so well known that he could not safely travel by day. He always went afoot until, having broken his leg, he had to ride a horse. At the age of seventy he was betrayed, and carried to York with his host, Mr. Vavasour of Willitoft, and some members of the family. A pair of beads, and the form of an in-dulgence were found upon him, and he was condemned to be hanged, drawn, and quartered. He suffered "with wonderful patience, courage, and constancy, and signs of great comfort".

CHALLONER, *Missionary Priests*, II, 51; GILLOW, *Bibl. Dict. of Engl. Cath.*, I, 86.

PATRICK RYAN.

Atom.—(Gr. *a* privative, and τέμνω, cut; indivisible). Primarily, the smallest particle of matter which can exist; the ultimate and smallest division of matter; in physics, sometimes the smallest particle to which a substance can theoretically be reduced; in chemistry, the smallest particle of matter that can exist in combination with other atoms building up or constituting molecules. Two opposite doctrines of the constitution of matter were held by the ancient philosophers. One was that matter was infinitely divisible without losing its distinctive and individual properties. This is the doctrine of continuity or homœomery. Anaxagoras is given as the founder of this view of the constitution of things. According to it any substance, such as wood or water, can by no process of subdivision, however far it might be carried, be made to be anything but a mass of wood or water. Infinite subdivision would not reach its limit of divisibility. Democritus and others held that there were ultimate particles of matter which were indivisible, and these were called atoms. This is the doctrine of atomicity, upheld by Epicurus, and enlarged on by Lucretius in his "De Rerum Naturâ". The early atomists held that the atoms were not in contact, but that voids existed between them, claiming that otherwise motion would be impossible. Among the moderns, Descartes and Spinoza adhered to continuity. Leibnitz upheld atomicity, and Boscovich went to the last extreme of the theory, and defined atoms as centres of force, denying them the attribute of impenetrability.

MOLECULE AND ATOM.—Modern science holds that matter is not infinitely divisible; that there is an ultimate particle of every substance. If this particle is broken up, that particular form of matter will be destroyed. This particle is the molecule. It is composed of another division of matter called the atom. Generally, probably always, a molecule consists of several atoms. The atoms unite to form molecules and cannot exist except as constituents of molecules. If a molecule of any substance were broken up, the substance would cease to exist and its constituent atoms would go to form or to enter into some other molecule or molecules. There is a tendency to consider the molecule of modern science as identical with the atom of the old philosophers; but the modern atomic theory has given the molecule a different status from that of the old-time atom. Atom, as used in natural science, has a specific meaning based upon the theory of chemistry. This meaning is modified by recent work in the field of radio-activity, but the following will serve as a definition. It is the smallest particle of an element which can exist in a compound. An atom cannot exist alone as such. Atoms combine with each other to form molecules. The molecule is the smallest particle of matter which can exist without losing its distinctive properties. It corresponds pretty closely to the old Epicurean atom. The modern atom is an entirely new conception. Chemistry teaches that the thousands of forms of matter upon the earth, almost infinite in variety, can be resolved into about eighty substances, unalterable by chemical processes and possessing definite spectra. These substances, are called elements. The metals, iron, gold, silver, and others, sulphur, and carbon are familiar examples of elements. A mass of an element is made up of a collection of molecules. Each molecule of an element as a rule is composed of two atoms. Elements combine to form compound substances of various numbers of atoms in the molecule. Water is an example of a compound substance, or chemical compound. Its molecule contains three atoms; two atoms of hydrogen, and one atom of oxygen. If a quantity of these two elements were mixed, the result would be a mechanical mixture of the molecules of the two. But if heat, or some other adequate cause were made to act, chemical action would follow, and the molecules, splitting up, would combine atom with atom. Part of a molecule of oxygen—one atom—would combine with part of two atoms of hydrogen—two atoms. The result would be the production of a quantity of molecules of water. Each water molecule contains one atom of oxygen and two atoms of hydrogen. The splitting-up of the elemental molecules into atoms is synchronous with their combining into molecules, so that an atom never exists alone. The molecules of the elements, oxygen and hydrogen, have disappeared, and in their places are molecules of water. There are about eighty kinds of atoms known, one kind for each element, and out of these the material world is made.

INVARIABILITY OF COMPOSITION.—The invariability of composition by weight of chemical compounds is a fundamental law of chemistry. Thus water under all circumstances consists of 88.88% of oxygen and 11.11% of hydrogen. This establishes a relation between the weights of the atoms of hydrogen and oxygen in the water molecule, which is 1 : 8. Oxygen and hydrogen are gaseous under ordinary conditions. If water is decomposed, and the gases are collected and measured, there will always be two volumes of hydrogen to one of oxygen. This illustrates another fundamental law—the invariability of composition by gaseous volume of chemical compounds. From the composition by volume of water its molecule is taken as composed of two atoms of hydrogen and one of oxygen, on the assumption that in a given volume of any gas there is the same number of molecules. As there are two atoms in the molecules of both of these elements, the above may be put in a more popular way thus: the atoms of hydrogen and oxygen occupy the same space. The ratio spoken of above, of 1 : 8, is therefore the ratio of two atoms of hydrogen to one of oxygen. It follows that the ratio of one atom of hydrogen to one atom of oxygen is 1 : 16. The numbers 1 and 16 thus determined, are the atomic weights of hydrogen and oxygen respectively. Strictly speaking they are not weights at all, only numbers expressing the relation of weights. Atomic weights are determined for all the elements, based on several considerations, such as those outlined for the atoms of oxygen and hydrogen. Thus the term *atom* indicates not only the constituents of molecules, but has a quantitative meaning, the proportional part of the element which enters into compounds. The sum of the weights of the atoms in a molecule is the molecular weight of the substance. Thus the molecular weight of water is the sum of the weights of two hydrogen atoms, which is two, and of one oxygen atom, which is sixteen, a total of eighteen. If we divide the molecular weight of a compound into the atomic weight of the atoms of any element in its molecule, it will give the proportion of the element in the compound. Taking water again, if we divide its molecular weight, 18, into the weight of the atoms of hydrogen in its molecule, 2, we obtain the fraction $\frac{2}{18}$, which expresses the proportion of hydrogen in water. The same process gives the proportion of oxygen in water as $\frac{16}{18}$.

Every element has its own atomic weight, and the invariability of chemical composition by weight is explained by the invariability of the atomic weights of the elements. Tables of the atomic weights of the elements are given in all chemical text-books. The relations of the atomic weights to each other are several. The atom of lowest weight is the hydrogen atom. It is usually taken as one, which is very nearly its exact value if oxygen is taken as sixteen. On this basis one quarter of the other elements will have atomic weights that are whole numbers. This indicates a remarkable simplicity of relationship of weights, which is carried out by the close approach of the rest of the elements to the same condition, as regards their atomic weights. The range of the atomic weights is a narrow one. That of hydrogen is 1.008—that of uranium 238.5. The latter is the heaviest of all. Between these all the other atomic weights lie. Many of the elements resemble each other in their chemical relations. It might appear that those nearest to each other in atomic weight should be of similar properties. This is not the case. If the elements are written down in the order of their atomic weights, beginning with the lightest and ending with the heaviest, it will be found that the position of an element in the series will indicate pretty clearly its properties. The elements will be found to be so arranged in the list that any element will be related as regards its chemical properties to the element eight places removed from it. This relationship may be thus expressed: the properties of an element are a periodic function of its atomic weight.

MENDELÉEFF'S TABLE.—This relation is called Mendeléeff's Law, from one of two chemists who independently developed it. The elements may, as before said, be written down in the order of their atomic weights, but in eight vertical columns. Along the top line the eight elements of lightest atomic weights are written in the order of their weights, followed on the second line by the next eight, also in the order of their atomic weights. This arrangement, obviously, when carried out brings the elements eight atomic weights apart, into vertical columns. It will be found that all the elements in any vertical column are of similar chemical properties. When Mendeléeff made out his table it was supposed that several elements were as yet undiscovered. The table also brought out clearly certain numerical relations of the atomic weights. These together with other factors caused him to leave blank spaces in his table, which none of the known elements could fill. For these places hypothetical elements were assumed, whose general properties and atomic weights were stated by him. One by one these elements have been discovered, so that Mendeléeff's Law predicted the existence of elements later to be discovered. These discoveries of predicted elements constitute one of the greatest triumphs of chemical science. Up to within a very recent period the atom was treated as the smallest division of matter, although the possibility of the transmutation of the elements in some way, or in some degree, has long been considered a possibility. It was conjectured that all the elements might be composed of some one substance, for which a name, protyle, meaning first material, was coined. This seemed to conflict with the accepted definition of the atom, as protyle indicated something anterior to or preceding it. The idea rested in abeyance, as there was little ground for building up a theory to include it. Recent discoveries have resuscitated this never quite abandoned theory; protyle seems to have been discovered, and the atom has ceased to hold its place as the ultimate division of matter.

CORPUSCLES.—The most recent theory holds that the atom is composite, and is built up of still minuter particles, called corpuscles. As far as the ordinary processes of chemistry are concerned the atom remains as it was. But investigations in the field of radio-activity, largely physical and partly chemical, go to prove that the atom, built up of corpuscules as said above, depends for its atomic weight upon the number of corpuscules in it, and these corpuscules are all identical in nature. In these corpuscules we have the one first material, or protyle. It follows that the only difference between atoms of different elements is in the number of corpuscules they contain. Any process which would change the number of corpuscules in the atoms of an element would change the element into another one, thus carrying out the transmutation of elements. So far, one transmutation is accepted as effected. Experiments in radio-activity go to prove that some elements, notably radium, project particles of inconceivable minuteness into space. These particles have sometimes one-half the velocity of light. They are called corpuscules. The corpuscule is sometimes defined as a particle of negative electricity, which, in the existing state of electrical knowledge, is a very imperfect definition. They are all negatively electrified, and therefore repel each other. The condition of equilibrium of groups of such particles, if held near to each other by another external force, has been investigated by Prof. J. J. Thomson, and his investigations establish a basis for a theory of the constitution of atoms. Thus, assume an atom to consist of a number of corpuscules, not touching each other, all negatively electrified so that they repel one another, and held within the limits of the atom by what may be termed a shell of attractive force. Professor Thomson shows that such particles, under the conditions outlined above, arrange themselves into groups of various arrangement, the latter depending on their number. If the number of particles in a group be progressively increased, a periodic recurrence of groupings will occur. Assume a group of five particles. These will form a group of definite shape. If more particles are added to the group, the first additions will cause the five group to disappear, other groups taking its place, until the number reaches fifteen, when the original grouping of five will reappear, surrounded by the other ten particles. On adding more particles, the five and ten group disappear, to be succeeded by others, until the number of thirty is reached. At this point the original five group and the ten group reappear, with a new group of fifteen. The same recurrence of groupings takes place with forty-seven and sixty-seven particles. This gives the outlines of an explanation of the periodic law. If any number of particles be taken they will show groupings, characteristic of the number, and subject to periodical reappearance as the number is increased. This reappearance of groupings is exactly comparable to the phenomena of the periodic law. It is the reappearance of similar properties at periodic intervals. The corpuscular theory also accounts for the variation of the elements in atomic weight. Corpuscules are supposed to be all alike, so that the weight of an atom would depend on how many corpuscules were required to form it. Thus an atom of oxygen would contain sixteen times as many corpuscules as would an atom of hydrogen, weighing only one-sixteenth as much. The weight of an atom of hydrogen has been approximately calculated as expressed by the decimal, 34 preceded by thirteen ciphers, of a gram. This means that thirty-four thousand millions of millions of atoms of hydrogen would weigh in the aggregate one gram. These calculations are based on determination of the electric charge of corpuscules. Corpuscules are calculated as being about one-thousandth of the mass of an atom of hydrogen. Professor Oliver Lodge gives the following comparison: if a church of ordinary size represent an atom, a thousand grains of sand dashing about its interior with enormous velocity would represent its constituent corpuscules. When atoms unite to form molecules, they are said to saturate each other.

Elements vary in the saturating power of their atoms. The saturating power is called atomicity or valency. Some elements have a valency of one, and are termed monads. A monad can saturate a monad. Others are termed dyads, have a valency of two, two monads being required to saturate one dyad, while one dyad can saturate another dyad. Valencies run on through triads, tetrads, pentads, hexads, heptads, and octads, designating valencies of three, four, five, six, seven, and eight respectively.

T. O'Conor Sloane.

Atomism, [a privative and τέμνειν to cut, i. e. indivisible] is the system of those who hold that all bodies are composed of minute, indivisible particles of matter called atoms. We must distinguish between (1) atomism as a philosophy and (2) atomism as a theory of science.

Atomism as a philosophy originated with Leucippus. Democritus (b. 460 B. C.), his disciple, is generally considered the father of atomism, as practically nothing is known of Leucippus. The theory of Democritus may be summed up in the following propositions: 1. All bodies are composed of atoms and spaces between the atoms. 2. Atoms are eternal, indivisible, infinite in number, and homogeneous in nature; all differences in bodies are due to a difference in the size, shape or location of the atoms. 3. There is no purpose or design in nature, and in this sense all is ruled by chance. 4. All activity is reduced to local motion. The formation of the universe is due to the fact that the larger atoms fall faster, and by striking against the smaller ones combine with them; thus the whole universe is the result of the fortuitous concourse of atoms. Countless worlds are formed simultaneously and successively. Epicurus (342–270 B. C.) adopted the theory of Democritus, but corrected the blunder, pointed out by Aristotle, that larger atoms fall faster than smaller ones *in vacuo*. He substituted a power in the atoms to decline a little from the line of fall. Atomism is defended by Lucretius Carus (95–51 B. C.) in his poem, "De Rerum Naturâ." With the exception of a few alchemists in the Middle Ages, we find no representatives of atomism until Gassendi (1592–1655) renewed the atomism of Epicurus. Gassendi tried to harmonize atomism with Christian teaching by postulating atoms finite in number and created by God. With the application of atomism to the sciences, philosophic atomism also revived, and became for a time the most popular philosophy. Present-day philosophic atomism regards matter as homogeneous and explains all physical and chemical properties of bodies by a difference in mass of matter and local motion. The atom itself is inert and devoid of all activity. The molecule, taken over from the sciences, is but an edifice of unchangeable atoms. Philosophic atomism stands entirely on the basis of materialism, and, though it invokes the necessary laws of matter, its exclusion of final causes makes it in the last analysis a philosophy of chance.

The atomic theory was first applied to chemistry by Dalton (1808), but with him it meant little more than an expression of proportions in chemical composition. The theory supplied a simple explanation of the facts observed before him: that elements combine in definite and multiple proportions. The discovery in the same year by Gay-Lussac of the law that gases under the same pressure and temperature have equal volumes was at the same time a confirmation and an aid in determining atomic weights. Avogadro's law (1811) that gases under the same conditions of pressure and temperature have an equal number of molecules, and the law of Petit and Dulong that the product of the specific heat and the atomic weight of an element gives a constant number were further confirmations and aids. The atomic theory was soon applied to physics, and is to-day the basis of most of the sciences. Its main outlines are: Matter is not continuous but atomically consti- tuted. An atom is the smallest particle of matter that can enter a chemical reaction. Atoms of like nature constitute elements, those of unlike nature constitute compounds. The elements known to-day are about 76 in number and differ from one another in weight and physical and chemical properties. Atoms combine to form molecules, which are the smallest quantities of matter that can exist in a free state, whether of an element or a compound. Some believe that the atom retains its individuality in the molecule, whilst others consider the molecule homo- geneous throughout. The theoretic formulas of struc- ture of Frankland suppose them to remain. The spaces between the atoms are filled with an impon- derable matter called ether. Upon the nature of ether the greatest differences of opinion exist. The adoption by scientists of Maxwell's theory of light seems to render the ether-hypothesis with its many contradictions superfluous. At all events it is quite independent of the atomic theory.

The results obtained by the Hungarian Lenard, the English physicist J. J. Thomson, and many others, by means of electric discharges in rarified gases, the discovery of Hertzian waves, a better un- derstanding of electrolysis, and the discovery of ra- dium by Madame Curie have made necessary a modification of the atomic theory of matter. The atom, hitherto considered solid and indivisible, is now believed to break up into ions or electrons. This new theory, however, must not be considered as op- posed to the atomic theory; it comes rather as an extension of it. In chemistry, the principal field of the atomic theory, the atom will still remain as the chemically indivisible unit. The hypothesis of sub- atoms is, moreover, not entirely new; it was pro- posed by Spencer as early as 1872 ("Contemporary Rev.", June, 1872) and defended by Crookes in 1886. The physico-chemical theory of atomism, though not a demonstrated truth, offers a satisfactory ex- planation of a great number of phenomena, and will, no doubt, remain essentially the same, no matter how it may be modified in its details. In chemistry, it does not stop arbitrarily in the division of matter, but stops at chemical division. If another science demands a further division, or if philosophy must postulate a division of the atom into essential prin- ciples, that is not the concern of chemistry. Science has no interest in defending the indivisible atom of Democritus.

Scholastic philosophy finds nothing in the scientific theory of atomism which it cannot harmonize with its principles, though it must reject the mechanical explanation, often proposed in the name of science, which looks upon the atom as an absolutely inert mass, devoid of all activities and properties. Scho- lastic philosophers find in the different physical and chemical properties of the elements an indication of specifically different natures. Chemical changes are for them substantial changes, and chemical formulas indicate the mode in which the elements react on one another in the production of the compound. They are not a representation of the molecular edi- fice built up of unchangeable atoms. Some would accept even this latter view and admit that there are no substantial changes in inanimate nature (Gut- berlet). This view can also be harmonized more easily with the facts of stereo-chemistry. As re- gards the phenomena observed in radio-activity, a generalization, either in the materialistic sense, that all matter is homogeneous, or in the scholastic sense, that all elements can be changed into one another, is in the present state of science premature.

Manuals of History of Philosophy by TURNER, UEBER- WEG-HEINTZE, STŒCKL tr. by FINLAY; LANGE, *History of* *Materialism* (Leipzig, 1898); 6th ed., tr. by THOMAS (London, 1892); *Manuals of Chemistry;* RAMSAY, *Progress of Chemis- try in the 19th Century; Report of Smithsonian Institution* (1900); WURTZ, *Atomic Theory,* tr. by CLEMINSHAW (New York, 1881). On Scholastic interpretation of Atomism see NYS, *Cosmologie* (Louvain, 1904); GUTBERLET, *Naturphi- losophie* (Münster, 1894); BREDIN AND AHERNE, *Physical Science versus Matter and Form,* in *Dublin Rev.* (1899 and 1900).

EDMUND J. WIRTH.

Atonement, DAY OF.—The rites to be observed on the Day of Atonement [Hebrew יום הכפרים *Yom Hakkippurim.* Vulgate, *Dies Expiationum,* and *Dies Propitiationis* (Leviticus, xxiii, 27, 28)] are fully set forth in the sixteenth chapter of Leviticus (cf. Exo- dus, xxx, 10; Leviticus, xxiii, 27-31, xxv, 9; Num- bers, xxix, 7-11). It was a most solemn fast, on which no food could be taken throughout the whole day, and all servile works were forbidden. It was kept on the nineteenth day of the seventh month, *Tischri,* which falls in September—October. The sac- rifices included a calf, a ram, and seven lambs (Num- bers, xxix, 8-11). But the distinctive ceremony of the day was the offering of the two goats. "He [Aaron] shall make the two buck-goats to stand be- fore the Lord, in the door of the tabernacle of the testimony: and casting lots upon them both, one to be offered to the Lord, and the other to be the emissary-goat: That whose lot fell to be offered to the Lord, he shall offer for sin: But that whose lot was to be the emissary-goat he shall present alive before the Lord, that he may pour out prayers upon him, and let him go into the wilderness. . . . After he hath cleansed the sanctuary, and the tabernacle, and the altar, let him offer the living goat: And put- ting both hands upon his head, let him confess all the iniquities of the children of Israel, and all their offences and sins, and praying that they may light on his head, he shall turn him out by a man ready for it, into the desert. And when the goat hath carried all their iniquities into an uninhabited land, and shall be let go into the desert, Aaron shall return into the tabernacle of the testimony" (Leviticus, xvi, 7-10, 20-23). The general meaning of the ceremony is sufficiently shown in the text. But the details present some difficulty. The Vulgate *caper emis- sarius,* "emissary goat", represents the obscure Hebrew word, עזאזל (*Azazel*), which occurs no- where else in the Bible. Various attempts have been made to interpret its meaning. Some have taken it for the name of a place where the man who took the goat away used to throw it over a precipice, since its return was thought to forbode evil. Others, with better reason, take it for the name of an evil spirit; and in fact a spirit of this name is mentioned in the Apocryphal "Book of Henoch", and later in Jewish literature. On this interpretation, which, though by no means new, finds favour with modern critics, the idea of the ceremony would seem to be that the sins were sent back to the evil spirit to whose influence they owed their origin. It has been noted that some- what similar rites of expiation have prevailed among heathen nations. And modern critics, who refer the above passages to the Priestly Code, and to a post- Exilic date, are disposed to regard the sending of the goat to Azazel as an adaptation of a pre-existing ceremonial. The significant ceremony observed on this solemn Day of Atonement does but give a greater prominence to that need of satisfaction and expiation which was present in all the ordinary sin- offerings. And all these sacrifices for sin, as we learn from the teaching of the Epistle to the Hebrews, were figures of the great Sacrifice to come. In like manner these Jewish rites of atonement speak to us of the Cross of Christ, and of the propitiatory Sac- rifice which is daily renewed in a bloodless manner on the Eucharistic Altar. For this reason it may be of interest to note, with Provost Maltzew, that the Jewish prayers used on the Day of Atonement foreshadow the common commemoration of the saints and the faithful departed in our liturgies (Die Liturgien der orthodox-katholischen Kirche des Morgenlandes, 252).

The subject is treated by the commentators on Leviticus, notably CALMET and A LAPIDE, who give the interpretation of the Fathers. A more exhaustive treatment will be found in SPENCER's monumental work, *De Legibus Hebræorum ritualibus*, III, diss. 8, cf. *De Hirco Emissario et præcipuis expiationis judaicæ ceremoniis* (Tübingen, 1732). For modern views on the subject, see the articles on *Day of Atonement*, and *Azazel*, by DRIVER and WHITE in *Dictionary of the Bible*. In the Talmud the treatise *Yōma* (The Day) deals with the Day of Atonement.

W. H. KENT.

Atonement, DOCTRINE OF THE.—The word *atonement*, which is almost the only theological term of English origin, has a curious history. The verb "atone", from the adverbial phrase "at one" (M. E. *at oon*), at first meant to reconcile, or make "at one"; from this it came to denote the action by which such reconciliation was effected, e. g. satisfaction for an offence or an injury. Hence, in Catholic theology, the Atonement is the Satisfaction of Christ, whereby God and the world are reconciled or made to be at one. "For God indeed was in Christ, reconciling the world to himself" (II Cor., v, 19). The Catholic doctrine on this subject is set forth in the Sixth Session of the Council of Trent, chapter ii. Having shown the insufficiency of Nature, and of the Mosaic Law, the Council continues: "Whence it came to pass, that the heavenly Father, the Father of mercies and the God of all comfort (II Cor., i, 3), when that blessed fullness of the time was come (Gal., iv, 4) sent unto men Jesus Christ, His own Son, who had been, both before the Law and during the time of the Law, to many of the holy fathers announced and promised, that He might both redeem the Jews, who were under the Law and that the Gentiles who followed not after justice might attain to justice, and that all men might receive the adoption of sons. Him God hath proposed as a propitiator, through faith in His blood (Rom., iii, 25), for our sins, and not for our sins only, but also for those of the whole world (I John, ii, 2)." More than twelve centuries before this, the same dogma was proclaimed in the words of the Nicene Creed, "who for us men and for our salvation, came down, took flesh, was made man; and suffered." And all that is thus taught in the decrees of the councils may be read in the pages of the New Testament. For instance, in the words of Our Lord, "Even as the son of man is not come to be ministered unto, but to minister, and to give His life a redemption for many" (Matt., xx, 28); or of St. Paul, "Because in him, it hath well pleased the Father that all fulness should dwell; and through him to reconcile all things unto himself, making peace through the blood of his cross, both as to the things that are on earth, and the things that are in heaven." (Coloss., i, 19, 20).

The great doctrine thus laid down in the beginning was further unfolded and brought out into clearer light by the work of the Fathers and theologians. And it may be noted that in this instance the development is chiefly due to Catholic speculation on the mystery, and not, as in the case of other doctrines, to controversy with heretics. At first we have the central fact made known in the Apostolic preaching, that mankind was fallen and was raised up and redeemed from sin by the blood of Christ. But it remained for the pious speculation of Fathers and theologians to enter into the meaning of this great truth, to inquire into the state of fallen man, and to ask how Christ accomplished His work of Redemption. By whatever names or figures it may be described, that work is the reversal of the Fall, the deliverance from bondage, the blotting out of sin, the reconciliation of mankind with God. And it is brought to pass by the Incarnation, by the life, the

sufferings, and the death of the Divine Redeemer. All this may be summed up in the word Atonement. This is, so to say, the starting point. And herein all are indeed at one. But, when it was attempted to give a more precise account of the nature of the Redemption and the manner of its accomplishment, theological speculation took different courses, some of which were suggested by the various names and figures under which this ineffable mystery is adumbrated in Holy Scripture. Without pretending to give a full history of the discussions, we may briefly indicate some of the main lines on which the doctrine was developed, and touch on the more important theories put forward in explanation of the Atonement.

(*a*) In any view, the Atonement is founded on the Divine Incarnation. By this great mystery, the Eternal Word took to Himself the nature of man and, being both God and man, became the Mediator between God and men. From this, we have one of the first and most profound forms of theological speculation on the Atonement, the theory which is sometimes described as Mystical Redemption. Instead of seeking a solution in legal figures, some of the great Greek Fathers were content to dwell on the fundamental fact of the Divine Incarnation. By the union of the Eternal Word with the nature of man all mankind was lifted up and, so to say, deified. "He was made man", says St. Athanasius, "that we might be made gods" (De Incarnatione Verbi, 54). "His flesh was saved, and made free the first of all, being made the body of the Word, then we, being concorporeal therewith, are saved by the same" (Orat., II, Contra Arianos, lxi). And again, "For the presence of the Saviour in the flesh was the price of death, and the saving of the whole creation" (Ep. ad Adelphium, vi). In like manner St. Gregory of Nazianzus proves the integrity of the Sacred Humanity by the argument, "That which was not assumed is not healed; but that which is united to God is saved" (τὸ γὰρ ἀπρόσληπτον, ἀθεράπευτον· ὃ δὲ ἥνωται τῷ θεῷ, τοῦτο καὶ σῴζεται). This speculation of the Greek Fathers undoubtedly contains a profound truth which is sometimes forgotten by later authors who are more intent on framing juridical theories of ransom and satisfaction. But it is obvious that this account of the matter is imperfect, and leaves much to be explained. It must be remembered, moreover, that the Fathers themselves do not put this forward as a full explanation. For while many of their utterances might seem to imply that the Redemption was actually accomplished by the union of a Divine Person with the human nature, it is clear from other passages that they do not lose sight of the atoning sacrifice. The Incarnation is, indeed, the source and the foundation of the Atonement, and these profound thinkers have, so to say, grasped the cause and its effects as one vast whole. Hence they look on to the result before staying to consider the means by which it was accomplished.

(*b*) But something more on this matter had already been taught in the preaching of the Apostles and in the pages of the New Testament. The restoration of fallen man was the work of the Incarnate Word. "God was in Christ reconciling the world to himself" (II Cor., v, 19). But the peace of that reconciliation was accomplished by the death of the Divine Redeemer, "making peace through the blood of His cross" (Coloss., i, 20). This redemption by death is another mystery, and some of the Fathers in the first ages are led to speculate on its meaning, and to construct a theory in explanation. Here the words and figures used in Holy Scripture help to guide the current of theological thought. Sin is represented as a state of bondage or servitude, and fallen man is delivered by being redeemed, or bought with a price. "For you are bought with a great price" (I Cor., vi, 20). "Thou art worthy, O Lord, to take the book, and to open the seals thereof; because thou wast slain, and hast redeemed us to God, in thy blood" (Apoc., v, 9). Looked at in this light, the Atonement appears as the deliverance from captivity by the payment of a ransom. This view is already developed in the second century. "The mighty Word and true Man reasonably redeeming us by His blood, gave Himself a ransom for those who had been brought into bondage. And since the Apostasy unjustly ruled over us, and, whereas we belonged by nature to God Almighty, alienated us against nature and made us his own disciples, the Word of God, being mighty in all things, and failing not in His justice, dealt justly even with the Apostasy itself, buying back from it the things which were His own" (Irenæus, Adversus Hæreses, V, i). And St. Augustine says in well-known words: "Men were held captive under the devil, and served the demons, but they were redeemed from captivity. For they could sell themselves, but they could not redeem themselves. The Redeemer came, and gave the price; He poured forth His blood and bought the whole world. Do you ask what He bought? See what He gave, and find what He bought. The blood of Christ is the price. How much is it worth? What but the whole world? What but all nations?" (Enarratio in Psalm xcv, n. 5).

It cannot be questioned that this theory also contains a true principle. For it is founded on the express words of Scripture, and is supported by many of the greatest of the early Fathers and later theologians. But unfortunately, at first, and for a long period of theological history, this truth was somewhat obscured by a strange confusion, which would seem to have arisen from the natural tendency to take a figure too literally, and to apply it in details which were not contemplated by those who first made use of it. It must not be forgotten that the account of our deliverance from sin is set forth in figures. Conquest, captivity, and ransom are familiar facts of human history. Man, having yielded to the temptations of Satan, was like to one overcome in battle. Sin, again, is fitly likened to a state of slavery. And when man was set free by the shedding of Christ's precious Blood, this deliverance would naturally recall (even if it had not been so described in Scripture) the redemption of a captive by the payment of a ransom. But, however useful and illuminating in their proper place, figures of this kind are perilous in the hands of those who press them too far, and forget that they are figures. This is what happened here. When a captive is ransomed the price is naturally paid to the conqueror by whom he is held in bondage. Hence, if this figure were taken and interpreted literally in all its details, it would seem that the price of man's ransom must be paid to Satan. The notion is certainly startling, if not revolting. Even if grave reasons pointed in this direction, we might well shrink from drawing the conclusion. And this is in fact so far from being the case that it seems hard to find any rational explanation of such a payment, or any right on which it could be founded. Yet, strange to say, the bold flight of theological speculation was not checked by these misgivings. In the above-cited passage of St. Irenæus, we read that the Word of God "dealt justly even with the Apostasy itself [i. e. Satan], buying back from it the things which were His own". This curious notion, apparently first mooted by St. Irenæus, was taken up by Origen in the next century, and for about a thousand years it played a conspicuous part in the history of theology. In the hands of some of the later Fathers and medieval writers, it takes

various forms, and some of its more repulsive features are softened or modified. But the strange notion of some right, or claim, on the part of Satan is still present. A protest was raised by St. Gregory of Nazianzus in the fourth century, as might be expected from that most accurate of the patristic theologians. But it was not till St. Anselm and Abelard had met it with unanswerable arguments that its power was finally broken. It makes a belated appearance in the pages of Peter Lombard.

(c) But it is not only in connexion with the theory of ransom that we meet with this notion of "rights" on the part of Satan. Some of the Fathers set the matter in a different aspect. Fallen man, it was said, was justly under the dominion of the devil, in punishment for sin. But when Satan brought suffering and death on the sinless Saviour, he abused his power and exceeded his right, so that he was now justly deprived of his dominion over the captives. This explanation is found especially in the sermons of St. Leo and the "Morals" of St. Gregory the Great. Closely allied to this explanation is the singular "mouse-trap" metaphor of St. Augustine. In this daring figure of speech, the Cross is regarded as the trap in which the bait is set and the enemy is caught. "The Redeemer came and the deceiver was overcome. What did our Redeemer do to our Captor? In payment for us He set the trap, His Cross, with His blood for bait. He [Satan] could indeed shed that blood; but he deserved not to drink it. By shedding the blood of One who was not his debtor, he was forced to release his debtors" (Serm. cxxx, § 2).

(d) These ideas retained their force well into the Middle Ages. But the appearance of St. Anselm's "Cur Deus Homo?" made a new epoch in the theology of the Atonement. It may be said, indeed, that this book marks an epoch in theological literature and doctrinal development. There are not many works, even among those of the greatest teachers, that can compare in this respect with the treatise of St. Anselm. And, with few exceptions, the books that have done as much to influence and guide the growth of theology are the outcome of some great struggle with heresy; while others, again, only summarize the theological learning of the age. But this little book is at once purely pacific and eminently original. Nor could any dogmatic treatise well be more simple and unpretending than this luminous dialogue between the great archbishop and his disciple Boso. There is no parade of learning, and but little in the way of appeal to authorities. The disciple asks and the master answers; and both alike face the great problem before them fearlessly, but at the same time with all due reverence and modesty. Anselm says at the outset that he will not so much show his disciple the truth he needs, as seek it along with him; and that when he says anything that is not confirmed by higher authority, it must be taken as tentative, and provisional. He adds that, though he may in some measure meet the question, one who is wiser could do it better; and that, whatever man may know or say on this subject, there will always remain deeper reasons that are beyond him. In the same spirit he concludes the whole treatise by submitting it to reasonable correction at the hands of others.

It may be safely said that this is precisely what has come to pass. For the theory put forward by Anselm has been modified by the work of later theologians, and confirmed by the testimony of truth. In contrast to some of the other views already noticed, this theory is remarkably clear and symmetrical. And it is certainly more agreeable to reason than the "mouse-trap" metaphor, or the notion of purchase money paid to Satan. Anselm's answer to the question is simply the need of satisfaction for sin. No sin, as he views the matter, can be forgiven without satisfaction. A debt to Divine justice has been incurred; and that debt must needs be paid. But man could not make this satisfaction for himself; the debt is something far greater than he can pay; and, moreover, all the service that he can offer to God is already due on other titles. The suggestion that some innocent man, or angel, might possibly pay the debt incurred by sinners is rejected, on the ground that in any case this would put the sinner under obligation to his deliverer, and he would thus become the servant of a mere creature. The only way in which the satisfaction could be made, and men could be set free from sin, was by the coming of a Redeemer who is both God and man. His death makes full satisfaction to the Divine Justice, for it is something greater than all the sins of all mankind. Many side questions are incidentally treated in the dialogue between Anselm and Boso. But this is the substance of the answer given to the great question, "Cur Deus Homo?" Some modern writers have suggested that this notion of deliverance by means of satisfaction may have a German origin. For in the old Teutonic laws, a criminal might pay the wergild instead of undergoing punishment. But this custom was not peculiar to the Germans, as we may see from the Celtic *eirig*, and, as Rivière has pointed out, there is no need to have recourse to this explanation. For the notion of satisfaction for sin was already present in the whole system of ecclesiastical penance, though it had been left for Anselm to use it in illustration of the doctrine of the Atonement. It may be added that the same idea underlies the old Jewish "sin-offerings" as well as the similar rites that are found in many ancient religions. It is specially prominent in the rites and prayers used on the Day of Atonement. And this, it may be added, is now the ordinary acceptance of the word; to "atone" is to give satisfaction, or make amends, for an offence or an injury.

(e) Whatever may be the reason, it is clear that this doctrine was attracting special attention in the age of St. Anselm. His own work bears witness that it was undertaken at the urgent request of others who wished to have some new light on this mystery. To some extent, the solution offered by Anselm seems to have satisfied these desires, though, in the course of further discussion, an important part of his theory, the absolute necessity of Redemption and of satisfaction for sin, was discarded by later theologians, and found few defenders. But meanwhile, within a few years of the appearance of the "Cur Deus Homo?" another theory on the subject had been advanced by Abelard. In common with St. Anselm, Abelard utterly rejected the old, and then still prevailing, notion that the devil had some sort of right over fallen man, who could only be justly delivered by means of a ransom paid to his captor. Against this he very rightly urges, with Anselm, that Satan was clearly guilty of injustice in the matter and could have no right to anything but punishment. But, on the other hand, Abelard was unable to accept Anselm's view that an equivalent satisfaction for sin was necessary, and that this debt could only be paid by the death of the Divine Redeemer. He insists that God could have pardoned us without requiring satisfaction. And, in his view, the reason for the Incarnation and the death of Christ was the pure love of God. By no other means could men be so effectually turned from sin and moved to love God. Abelard's teaching on this point, as on others, was vehemently attacked by St. Bernard. But it should be borne in mind that some of the arguments urged in condemnation of Abelard would affect the position of St. Anselm also, not to speak of later Catholic theology.

In St. Bernard's eyes it seemed that Abelard, in denying the rights of Satan, denied the "Sacrament of Redemption" and regarded the teaching and example of Christ as the sole benefit of the Incarnation. "But", as Mr. Oxenham observes, "he had not said so, and he distinctly asserts in his 'Apology' that 'the Son of God was incarnate to deliver us from the bondage of sin and yoke of the Devil, and to open to us by His death the gate of eternal life.' And St. Bernard himself, in this very Epistle, distinctly denies any absolute necessity for the method of redemption chosen, and suggests a reason for it not so very unlike Abelard's. 'Perhaps that method is the best, whereby in a land of forgetfulness and sloth we might be more powerfully and vividly reminded of our fall, through the so great and so manifold sufferings of Him who repaired it.' Elsewhere, when not speaking controversially, he says still more plainly: 'Could not the Creator have restored His work without that difficulty? He could; but He preferred to do it at His own cost, lest any further occasion should be given for that worst and most odious vice of ingratitude in man' (Bern., Serm. xi, in Cant.). What is this but to say, with Abelard, that 'He chose the Incarnation as the most effectual method for eliciting His creature's love'?" (The Catholic Doctrine of the Atonement, 85, 86).

(f) Although the high authority of St. Bernard was thus against them, the views of St. Anselm and Abelard, the two men who in different ways were the fathers of Scholasticism, shaped the course of later medieval theology. The strange notion of the rights of Satan, against which they had both protested, now disappears from the pages of our theologians. For the rest, the view which ultimately prevailed may be regarded as a combination of the opinions of Anselm and Abelard. In spite of the objections urged by the latter writer, Anselm's doctrine of satisfaction was adopted as the basis. But St. Thomas and the other medieval masters agree with Abelard in rejecting the notion that this full satisfaction for sin was absolutely necessary. At the most, they are willing to admit a hypothetical or conditional necessity for the Redemption by the death of Christ. The restoration of fallen man was a work of God's free mercy and benevolence. And, even on the hypothesis that the loss was to be repaired, this might have been brought about in many and various ways. The sin might have been remitted freely, without any satisfaction at all, or some lesser satisfaction, however imperfect in itself, might have been accepted as sufficient. But on the hypothesis that God had chosen to restore mankind, and at the same time, to require full satisfaction as a condition of pardon and deliverance, nothing less than the Atonement made by one who was God as well as man could suffice as satisfaction for the offence against the Divine Majesty. And in this case Anselm's argument will hold good. Mankind cannot be restored unless God becomes man to save them.

In reference to many points of detail the Schoolmen, here as elsewhere, adopted divergent views. One of the chief questions at issue was the intrinsic adequacy of the satisfaction offered by Christ. On this point the majority, with St. Thomas at their head, maintained that, by reason of the infinite dignity of the Divine Person, the least action or suffering of Christ had an infinite value, so that in itself it would suffice as an adequate satisfaction for the sins of the whole world. Scotus and his school, on the other hand, disputed this intrinsic infinitude, and ascribed the all-sufficiency of the satisfaction to the Divine acceptation. As this acceptation was grounded on the infinite dignity of the Divine Person, the difference was not so great as might appear at first sight. But, on this point at any rate, the simpler teaching of St. Thomas is more generally accepted by later theologians. Apart from this question, the divergent views of the two schools on the primary motive of the Incarnation naturally have some effect on the Thomist and Scotist theology of the Atonement. On looking back at the various theories noticed so far, it will be seen that they are not, for the most part, mutually exclusive, but may be combined and harmonized. It may be said, indeed, that they all help to bring out different aspects of that great doctrine which cannot find adequate expression in any human theory. And in point of fact it will generally be found that the chief Fathers and Schoolmen, though they may at times lay more stress on some favourite theory of their own, do not lose sight of the other explanations.

Thus the Greek Fathers, who delight in speculating on the Mystical Redemption by the Incarnation, do not omit to speak also of our salvation by the shedding of blood. Origen, who lays most stress on the deliverance by payment of a ransom, does not forget to dwell on the need of a sacrifice for sin. St. Anselm, again, in his "Meditations", supplements the teaching set forth in his "Cur Deus Homo?" Abelard, who might seem to make the Atonement consist in nothing more than the constraining example of Divine Love, has spoken also of our salvation by the Sacrifice of the Cross, in passages to which his critics do not attach sufficient importance. And, as we have seen, his great opponent, St. Bernard, teaches all that is really true and valuable in the theory which he condemned. Most, if not all, of these theories had perils of their own, if they were isolated and exaggerated. But in the Catholic Church there was ever a safeguard against these dangers of distortion. As Mr. Oxenham says very finely, "The perpetual priesthood of Christ in heaven, which occupies a prominent place in nearly all the writings we have examined, is even more emphatically insisted upon by Origen. And this deserves to be remembered, because it is a part of the doctrine which has been almost or altogether dropped out of many Protestant expositions of the Atonement, whereas those most inclining among Catholics to a merely juridical view of the subject have never been able to forget the present and living reality of a sacrifice constantly kept before their eyes, as it were, in the worship which reflects on earth the unfailing liturgy of heaven" (p. 38).

The reality of these dangers and the importance of this safeguard may be seen in the history of this doctrine since the age of the Reformation. As we have seen, its earlier development owed comparatively little to the stress of controversy with heretics. And the revolution of the sixteenth century was no exception to this rule. For the Atonement was not one of the subjects directly disputed between the Reformers and their Catholic opponents. But from its close connexion with the cardinal question of Justification, this doctrine assumed a very special prominence and importance in Protestant theology and practical preaching. Mark Pattison tells us in his "Memoirs" that he came to Oxford with his "home Puritan religion almost narrowed to two points, fear of God's wrath and faith in the doctrine of the Atonement". And his case was possibly no exception among Protestant religionists. In their general conception of the Atonement the Reformers and their followers happily preserved the Catholic doctrine, at least in its main lines. And in their explanation of the merit of Christ's sufferings and death we may see the influence of St. Thomas and the other great Schoolmen. But, as might be expected from the isolation of the doctrine and the loss of other portions of Catholic teaching, the truth thus preserved was sometimes insensibly obscured or distorted. It will be enough to note here the presence of two mistaken tendencies. (1) The first is indicated in the above words of Pattison in which

the Atonement is specially connected with the thought of the wrath of God. It is true of course that sin incurs the anger of the Just Judge, and that this is averted when the debt due to Divine Justice is paid by satisfaction. But it must not be thought that God is only moved to mercy and reconciled to us as a result of this satisfaction. This false conception of the Reconciliation is expressly rejected by St. Augustine (In Joannem, Tract. cx, § 6). God's merciful love is the cause, not the result of that satisfaction. (2) The second mistake is the tendency to treat the Passion of Christ as being literally a case of vicarious punishment. This is at best a distorted view of the truth that His Atoning Sacrifice took the place of our punishment, and that He took upon Himself the sufferings and death that were due to our sins.

This view of the Atonement naturally provoked a reaction. Thus the Socinians were led to reject the notion of vicarious suffering and satisfaction as inconsistent with God's justice and mercy. And in their eyes the work of Christ consisted simply in His teaching by word and example. Similar objections to the juridical conception of the Atonement led to like results in the later system of Swedenborg. More recently Albrecht Ritschl, who has paid special attention to this subject, has formulated a new theory on somewhat similar lines. His conception of the Atonement is moral and spiritual, rather than juridical; and his system is distinguished by the fact that he lays stress on the relation of Christ to the whole Christian community. We cannot stay to examine these new systems in detail. But it may be observed that the truth which they contain is really found in the Catholic theology of the Atonement. That great doctrine has been faintly set forth in figures taken from man's laws and customs. It is represented as the payment of a price, or a ransom; or as the offering of satisfaction for a debt. But we can never rest in these material figures as though they were literal and adequate. As both Abelard and Bernard remind us, the Atonement is the work of love. It is essentially a sacrifice, the one supreme sacrifice of which the rest were but types and figures. And, as St. Augustine teaches us, the outward rite of sacrifice is the sacrament, or sacred sign, of the invisible sacrifice of the heart. It was by this inward sacrifice of obedience unto death, by this perfect love with which He laid down His life for His friends, that Christ paid the debt to justice, and taught us by His example, and drew all things to Himself; it was by this that He wrought our Atonement and Reconciliation with God, "making peace through the blood of His Cross".

The Catholic theology of the Atonement may be studied in the works of the Fathers and Schoolmen quoted above, notably in St. Athanasius and in St. Anselm; in the Scholastic commentaries on the *Third Book of Sentences*, and on the Third Part of the *Summa* of St. Thomas; and in later treatises *De Incarnatione*, e. g. that of Cardinal Franzelin. Two modern works may be mentioned as worthy of special attention. These are Oxenham, *The Catholic Doctrine of the Atonement: An Historical Inquiry into its Development in the Church. With an Introduction on the Principle of Theological Developments* (London, 1865); and Rivière, *Le dogme de la Rédemption. Essai d'étude historique* (Paris, 1905). Taken together, these two books, each admirable in its way, give a full view of the history of the doctrine. Much use has been made of them in this article. For modern non-Catholic theology, see Ritschl's great work on Justification and Reconciliation, *Die christliche Lehre von der Rechtfertigung und Versöhnung* (Bonn, 1870–74). The first volume, containing the history of the doctrine, was translated into English in 1872; the third, in which the author's own view is found, was translated in 1900 (Clark, Edinburgh); the second volume, giving the Biblical matter, has not been done into English. Some account of recent non-Catholic literature on the Atonement will be found in Ferries, *The Growth of Christian Faith* (Edinburgh, 1905). Like the Catholic works of Oxenham and Rivière, this book is a monograph on the doctrine of the Atonement. See also Simpson in *Dict. of Christ and the Gospels* (New York, 1906) s. v.

W. H. Kent.

Atri, Diocese of. See Civita di Penne.

Atrib, a titular see of Lower Egypt (Athribites) whose episcopal list (325–479) is given in Gams (p. 461).

Lequien, *Oriens Christ.* (1740), II, 553–556.

Atrium.—I. An open place or court before a church. It consisted of a large quadrangle with colonnaded walks on its four sides forming a portico or cloister. It was situated between the porch or vestibule and the body of the church. In the center of the atrium was a fountain or well, where the worshippers washed their hands before entering the church. A remnant of this custom still survives in the use of the holy-water font, or basin, usually placed near the inner entrances of churches. In the atrium those that were not suffered to advance farther, and more particularly the first class of penitents, stood to solicit the prayers of the faithful as they went into the church. It was also used as a burying-ground, at first only for distinguished persons, but afterwards for all believers. The covered portion next the church was called the *narthex* and was the place for penitents. The basilicas at Ravenna seem usually to have had a closed *narthex;* while those of Rome were open to the West. A mosaic in S. Apollinare Nuovo, Ravenna, shows an open narthex closed by curtains. The atrium existed in some of the largest of the early Christian churches, such as old St. Peter's at Rome in the fourth century, and Sancta Sophia at Constantinople, in the sixth. In the residences (*palatia, domus*) of the Roman aristocracy, where the Roman Christians first worshipped, there was a threefold division; first, on entering, a court called the *atrium;* then, farther in, another colonnaded court called the *peristyle;* and then the *tablinum,* where the altar was probably placed, and services conducted. (See Basilica.) So large a fore-court to a church required an area of land costly and difficult to obtain in a large city. For this reason the old Roman atrium survived only occasionally in Eastern and Western churches. Typical examples may be seen in the churches of St. Clement, at Rome, and St. Ambrose, at Milan; also in the seventh-century churches of Novara and Parenzo.

II. In secular architecture the atrium was the principal entrance-hall and apartment in a Roman house, and formed the reception-room. It was lighted by an opening in the roof, called the *compluvium,* the roof sloping so as to throw the rain-water into a cistern in the floor called the *impluvium.* In large houses it was surrounded by a colonnade.

Thomas H. Poole.

Attainder.—A Bill of Attainder may be defined to be an Act of Parliament for putting a man to death or for otherwise punishing him without trial in the usual form. Thus by a legislative act a man is put in the same position as if he had been convicted after a regular trial. It is an act whereby the judicature of the entire Parliament is exercised, and may be contrasted with the procedure by impeachment in which the accusation, presented by the Commons acting as a grand jury of the whole realm, is tried by the Lords, exercising at once the functions of a high court of justice and of a jury. In a strictly technical sense it may be said that a Bill of Attainder is a legislative act inflicting the punishment of death without a trial, and that a Bill of Pains and Penalties is such an act inflicting a milder punishment. In the popular sense, however, the term "Bill of Attainder" embraces both classes of acts, and in that sense it is evidently used in the Constitution of the United States, as the Supreme Court has declared in Fletcher v. Peck, 6 Cranch, 138, that "A bill of attainder may affect the life of an individual, or may confiscate his property, or both". Such a bill deals with the merits of a particular case and inflicts penalties, more or less severe, *ex post facto,* without trial in the

usual form. While bills of attainder were used in England as early as 1321 in the procedure employed by Parliament in the banishment of the two Despensers (1 St. tr. pp. 23, 38), it was not until the period of passion engendered by the civil war that the summary power of Parliament to punish criminals by statute was for the first time perverted and abused. Then it was that this process was first freely used, not only against the living, but sometimes against the dead, the main object in the latter case being, of course, the confiscation of the estate of the attained person. In the flush of victory which followed the battle of Towton, Edward IV obtained the passage of a sweeping bill of attainder through which the crown was enriched by forfeiture of the estates of fourteen lords and more than a hundred knights and esquires. In the seventeenth year of that reign was passed the Act of Attainder of the Duke of Clarence in which, after an oratorical preface setting out at length the offences imputed to him, it is enacted "that the said George Duke of Clarence be convicted, and atteynted of high treason". Then follows the appointment of the Duke of Buckingham as lord high steward for that occasion to do execution. It is a remarkable fact that during a period of one hundred and sixty-two years (1459–1621) there is no record of a parliamentary impeachment either in the rolls of Parliament or in the Lords' journal. After the impeachment of Lord Stanley in 1459, for not sending his troops to the battle of Bloreheath, there was not another impeachment until that of Sir Giles Mompesson and Sir Francis Mitchell in 1621. During the interval, covering a little more than the reigns of the house of Tudor, enemies of the State were disposed of either by bills of attainder, by trials in the Star Chamber, or by trials for treason in the courts of common law. In the reign of Henry VIII Bills of attainder were often used instead of impeachments, as in the cases of Wolsey, Thomas Cromwell, Queen Katharine Howard, the Duke of Norfolk, and the Earl of Surrey. During that reign religious persecution was carried on rather through the legal machinery devised for the punishment of high treason as defined by the Act of Supremacy than by bills of attainder. By the Act of Supremacy, the King was declared Head of the Church with "the title and style thereof"; by the penal act which followed as a corollary thereto, it was declared that any attempt to deprive him "of the dignity, title, or name" of his royal estate should constitute high treason; under the special act providing the amended oath, it was possible to call upon anyone to declare his belief in the validity of the new title, and a failure to do so was sufficient evidence of guilt. By that legal machinery were dashed to pieces the Charterhouse monks of London, who are admitted on every hand to have been the noblest and purest of all churchmen. Even Froude admits that they were "gallant men, whose high forms, in the sunset of the old faith, stand transfigured on the horizon, tinged with the light of its dying glory". The legal proceedings through which the Bishop of Rochester and Sir Thomas More were brought to the block were but a repetition of what had been gone through with in the case of the Carthusians. After the Tudor time the most remarkable bills of attainder are those that were directed against Lord Strafford, Lord Danby, the Duke of Monmouth, and Sir John Fenwick. As instances of bills of pains and penalties, reference may be made to those against Bishop Atterbury and Queen Caroline, usually referred to as the last instances of such legislation. When Queen Caroline returned to England, in July, 1830, all the ministers, except Canning, were induced to consent to the introduction in the House of Lords of a bill of pains and penalties, providing for the dissolution of her marriage with the King, upon the ground of adultery, and for her degradation. When the charges contained in the preamble came on to be heard, Brougham and Denman, by their bold and brilliant defence of the Queen, so aroused popular sympathy in her favour, by holding her up as a deserted and persecuted woman, that the ministry deemed it wise to drop the bill after the majority in its favour in the Lords had dwindled to nine. Reference is made to this case as an illustration of the nature of the procedure upon such bills. "The proceedings of parliament in passing bills of attainder, and of pains and penalties, do not vary from those adopted in regard to other bills. They may be introduced in either house, but ordinarily commence in the House of Lords: they pass through the same stages; and when agreed to by both houses they receive the royal assent in the usual form. But the parties who are subjected to these proceedings are admitted to defend themselves by counsel and witnesses, before both houses; and the solemnity of the proceedings would cause measures to be taken to enforce the attendance of members upon their service in parliament" (May, Parl. Practice, 744). It thus appears that, in its modern form, procedure by attainder admits the right of proof and argument. Entirely apart from the judicature of Parliament, attainder is defined by the common law of England to be the stain or corruption of blood which follows as an immediate and inseparable consequence of a death sentence. Such attainder took place after judgment of death, or upon such circumstances as were equivalent to such a judgment, such as a judgment of outlawry on a capital crime, pronounced for absconding from justice. Conviction without judgment was not followed by attainder. The consequences of attainder were: first, forfeiture; second, corruption of blood. The extent of the forfeiture depended upon the nature of the crime for which the criminal was convicted; and by corruption of blood, "both upwards and downwards," the attainted person could neither inherit nor transmit lands. After it was clear beyond dispute that the criminal was no longer fit to live, he was called attaint, stained, or blackened, and before 6 and 7 Vict., c. 85, §. 1, could not be called as a witness in any court. The doctrine of attainder has, however, ceased to be of much practical importance since 33 and 34 Vict., c. 23, wherein it was provided that henceforth no confession, verdict, inquest, conviction, or judgment of or for any treason or felony, or *felo-de-se* shall cause any attainder or corruption of blood or any forfeiture or escheat.

HANNIS TAYLOR.

Attala, SAINT, b. in the sixth century in Burgundy; d. 627. He first became a monk at Lérins, but, displeased with the loose discipline prevailing there, he entered the monastery of Luxeuil which had just been founded by St. Columban. When Columban was expelled from Luxeuil by King Theodoric II, Attala was to succeed him as abbot, but preferred to follow him into exile. They settled on the banks of the river Trebbia, a little north-east of Genoa, where they founded the celebrated Abbey of Bobbio. After the death of St. Columban in 615, Attala succeeded him as Abbot of Bobbio. He and his monks suffered many hardships at the hands of the Arian King Ariowald. As abbot, Attala insisted on strict discipline and when a large number of his monks rebelled, declaring his discipline too rigorous, he permitted them to leave the monastery. When, however, some of these perished miserably, the others, considering their death a punishment from God, returned to the monastery. Attala was buried in Bobbio where his feast is celebrated on 10 March.

MONTALEMBERT, *The Monks of the West* (Boston), I, 582; LECHNER, *Martyrolog. des Benediktiner Ordens* (Augsburg, 1855); STADLER, *Heiligen-Lexikon* (Augsburg, 1858), I, 341.

MICHAEL OTT.

Attalia, also ATTALEIA, a titular metropolitan see of Pamphylia in Asia Minor. Its episcopal list (431–879) is given in Gams (450). It is probably identical with the present Adalia, the chief port and largest place on the southern coast of Asia Minor. Remains of sculptured marbles are abundant in the vicinity. It is mentioned in Acts, xiv, 24–25, as the seaport whence Paul and Barnabas set sail for Antioch, at the close of their missionary journey through Pisidia and Pamphylia. Another city of the same name existed in Lydia, Asia Minor; its episcopal list (431–879) is given in Gams (447).

LEQUIEN, *Oriens Christ.* (1740), I, 1030; SMITH, *Dict. of Greek and Roman Geogr.*, I, 320–321.

THOMAS. J. SHAHAN.

Attaliates, MICHAEL, Byzantine statesman and historian, probably a native of Attalia in Pamphylia, whence he seems to have come to Constantinople between 1130 and 1140. He acquired in the royal city both wealth and position and was rapidly advanced, under successive emperors, to the highest offices, among others to that of judge of the supreme court of the empire. He compiled (1072) for the Emperor Michael Parapinakes a compendium of Byzantine law which supplements in a useful way the "Libri Basilici". In addition to this he also drew up an "Ordinance for the Poor House and Monastery" which he founded at Constantinople in 1077. This work is of value for the history of Byzantine life and manners in the eleventh century. It contains a catalogue of the library of his monastery. About 1079 or 1080 he published an account of Byzantine history from 1034 to 1079, a vivid and reliable presentation of the palace revolutions and female domination that characterize this period of transition from the great Macedonian dynasty to the Comneni. Attaliates writes as an eyewitness and contemporary. Though his style is not free from the usual affectations of Byzantine historians, it is more flowing and compact than that of his predecessors. Krumbacher praises his accurate judgment and sense of equity; in both respects he is superior to his continuator, the panegyrist and courtier Psellos. The law-manual of Attaliates was first edited by M. Freher (Juris Græco-Romani Tomi Duo, Frankfort, 1596, II, 1–79); the "Ordinance", or Διάταξις, is found in Miklosich and Müller, "Acta et Diplomata Græca Medii Ævi" (1887), V, 293–327; the "History" was edited by I. Bekker, in the "Corpus Script. Byz." (Bonn, 1853).

KRUMBACHER, *Gesch. d. Byz. Lit.*, 2d ed., 269–271; MORTREUIL, *Hist. du droit Byzantin*, III, 218–229; W. NISSEN, *Die Diataxis des M. Attaleiates von 1077* (Jena, 1894), 23–30; BURY, *Eng. Hist. Rev.* (1889), IV, 41–64, 251–285.

THOMAS J. SHAHAN.

Attention. See CONSCIOUSNESS.

Atticus, Patriarch of Constantinople (406–425), b. at Sebaste in Armenia; d. 425. He was educated in the vicinity of his native town by Macedonian monks, whose mode of life and errors he embraced. When still young he went to Constantinople, abjured his heretical tenets, and was raised to the priesthood. He and another ambitious priest, Arsacius, were the chief accusers of St. Chrysostom in the notorious Council of the Oak, which deposed (405) the holy patriarch. On the death (406) of the intruder Arsacius, he succeeded him in the See of Constantinople, and at first strove hard, with the help of the civil power, to detach the faithful from the communion of their lawful pastor. But finding that, even after the death of St. Chrysostom, they continued to avoid his own spiritual ministrations, he re-inserted the name of his holy predecessor in the diptychs of the churches. This change of attitude and his charity to the poor gradually made him less unpopular, and he at length managed to have himself recognized as patriarch by Innocent I. Intent upon enlarging the prerogatives of his see, he obtained from Theodosius the Younger two rescripts which placed Bithynia and Illyria under his jurisdiction. Rome resisted these encroachments, and the rescripts, thanks to the intervention of Honorius, were recalled. Atticus in some measure atoned for his ambition and the irregularity of his promotion by his zeal in the cause of orthodoxy. He drove the Messalians from Pamphylia, and his opposition to the Pelagians caused him to be praised by Celestine I as "a true successor of St. Chrysostom".

VENABLES in *Dict. Christ. Biog.*, I, 207–209; VERSCHAFFEL in *Dict. de théol. cath.* (Paris, 1903), s. v.; TILLEMONT, *Mémoires*, XII, 416, 31, 672.

A. J. B. VUIBERT.

Attigny, COUNCILS OF.—In 765, St. Chrodegang of Metz and thirty-seven other bishops mutually promised in an assembly held at the royal residence of Attigny near Vouziers (Ardennes) that after the death of each the survivors would cause the psalter to be said one hundred times and would have one hundred Masses celebrated for the repose of the soul of the departed. Each one would also say thirty Masses for the same intention. In 785, Charlemagne held a council at Attigny. Widukind and Aboin, two conquered Saxon kings, presented themselves for instruction and were baptized. In 822, Pope Paschal I was present at a Council of Attigny, convened for the reconciliation of the Emperor Louis the Pious with his three younger brothers, Hugo, Drogo, and Theodoric, whom he had caused to be violently tortured and whom he had intended to put to death. In the council he confessed publicly his wrong-doing; also the violence practised by him on his nephew, Bernard, King of Italy, and his brother, the Abbot Adelard Wala, and proposed to perform public penance in imitation of the Emperor Theodosius I. He also exhibited an earnest desire to correct abuses arising from the negligence of the bishops and the nobles, and confirmed the rule (*Aquensis Regula*) that the Council of Aachen had drawn up (816) for canons and monks. In 870, thirty bishops and six archbishops met at Attigny, to pass judgment on Karlmann, the king's son, made an ecclesiastic at an early age, and accused by his father of conspiring against his life and throne. He was deprived of his abbeys and imprisoned at Senlis. In the council of 875, Hincmar, Bishop of Laon, appealed to the pope from his uncle, Hincmar, Archbishop of Reims.

MANSI, *Coll. Conc.* Sup. I, 621, XII, 674; Sup. I, 285, XIV, 403; Sup. I, 993; XV, 680, XVI, 562; HULOT, *Attigny, avec ses dépendances . . . ses conciles*, etc. (Attigny-Reims, 1826); CHEVALIER, *Topo-bibl.* (Paris, 1894–99), 247.

THOMAS J. SHAHAN.

Attila, king and general of the Huns; d. 453. Succeeding in 433 to the kingship of Scythian hordes disorganized and enfeebled by internal discords, Attila soon made of his subjects a compact and formidable people, the terror of Europe and Asia. An unsuccessful compaign in Persia was followed in 441 by an invasion of the Eastern Roman Empire, the success of which emboldened Attila to invade the West. He passed unhindered through Austria and Germany, across the Rhine into Gaul, plundering and devastating all in his path with a ferocity unparalleled in the records of barbarian invasions, and compelling those he overcame to augment his mighty army. In 451 he was met on the Plains of Châlons by the allied Romans under Aetius and the Visigoths under Theodoric and Thorismond, who overcame the Huns and averted the peril that menaced Western civilization. Turning then to Italy, Attila, in the spring of 452, laid waste Aquileia and many Lombard cities, and was approaching Rome, whither Valentinian III had fled before him, when he was met near Mantua by an embassy, the most influential member of which was Pope Leo I, which dissuaded Attila from sacking the city. Attila died shortly after. Catholic interest in Attila centers chiefly in his relations with those bishops of France and Italy who restrained the Hunnish leader in his devastating fury. The moral power of these bishops, and particularly of the pope, during the dissolution of the empire, is evidenced as well by the confidence in which the faithful looked to them for succour against the terrible invader as by the influence they sometimes exerted in staying that invader's destroying hand. St. Agnan of Orleans sustained the courage of his people and hastened the reinforcements that saved his apparently doomed city; at Troyes, St. Lupus prevailed upon Attila to spare the province of Champagne, and gave himself as a hostage while the Hunnish army remained in Gaul; when Rome seemed destined to meet the fate of the Lombard cities which Attila had pillaged, it was Pope Leo the Great who, by his eloquence and commanding personality, overawed the conqueror and saved the city. The terror which for centuries after clung to the name of Attila, "the Scourge of God", as he came to be called, and the gratitude of the people to their deliverers· combined in time to encumber medieval hagiography with legends of saints reputed to have overcome Attila by their imposing presence, or stayed his progress by their prayers. But these fictions serve to emphasize the import of the facts which inspired them. They enable us to appreciate how widespread must have been that sentiment expressed in the recently discovered appeal of Eusebius of Dorylæum to Pope Leo I: "Curavit desuper et ab exordio consuevit thronus apostolicus iniqua perferentes defensare . . . et humi jacentes erigere, secundum possibilitatem quam habetis" [see Harnack, "History of Dogma" (Boston, 1903), II, 168]. National pride, too, came in time to invest the person of Attila with a halo of fiction. Most European countries have their legends of the Hunnish leader, who is diversely depicted, according as the vanity of nations would represent Attila as a friend who had contributed to their greatness or as a foe to whose superhuman strength it had been no discredit to succumb. Of these legends the best known is the story of Etzel (Attila) in the "Niebelungen-lied".

THIERRY, *Histoire d'Attila* (Paris, 1864); GIBBON, *Roman Empire* (New York, 1902), xxxiv, xxxv, III, 518–589, contains abundant references to sources; in SMITH AND WACE, *Dict. Christ. Biog.* (London, 1877), I, the legendary and the historical elements of ecclesiastical tradition are not sufficiently distinguished. *Acta SS.*, s. v. *St. Lupus*, XXXIV, 75–90; and *St. Leo I*, XI, 18. For the legendary elements in the Attila tradition, ibid., s. v. *St. Geneviève of Paris*, I, 135 sq., 144 sq.; *St. Auctor of Metz*, XXXVI, 536; *St. Servatius of Maestricht*, XVI, 211, 212 (St. Servatius of Tongres did not exist); *St. Geminianus of Modena*, III, 714; *St. John of Ravenna*, II, 9, 10. On the St. Servatius and St. Auctor legends see PAULUS WARNEFRIDUS, *De Gestis Episcoporum Metensium*, in *P. L.*, XCV, 701–703 and 715–717; particularly the introduction, 682–88.

JOHN B. PETERSON.

Attiret, JEAN DENIS, painter, b. at Dole, France, 31 July, 1702; d. at Pekin, 8 December, 1768. He made serious artistic studies in Rome and after returning to his native country achieved considerable reputation as a portrait painter. He entered the Jesuit novitiate as a lay brother and has left some specimens of his work in the Cathedral of Avignon and the Sodality chapel which he painted while a novice. The Jesuits had many of their men in China employed as painters. Attiret joined them in 1737 and was easily the superior of all. He was honoured with the title of Painter to the Emperor, who visited his studio daily and finally made him a mandarin in spite of the brother's unwillingness to accept the honour. As all the work was done not for art but for the sake of pleasing the emperor, every suggestion he made was carefully attended to. Oil was not agreeable, so aquarelles and distemper were resorted to. The Emperor did not like shading, for he thought it was a blot, so that disappeared. It all ended in Attiret becoming altogether Chinese in his tastes and his methods, so that he no longer painted like a European. He made portraits of all the distinguished court-personages, but most of his work was done on glass or silk and represented trees, and fruits, and fishes, and animals, etc. When, however, the emperor had beaten back the Tatars, he ordered the battles to be painted. Four Jesuit brothers, among whom was Attiret, made sixteen tableaux, which were engraved in France in 1774. When the collection arrived from France, however, Attiret was dead. The emperor manifested great concern at his loss, bore the expenses of the obsequies, and sent a special representative to show his sorrow at the tomb. Attiret is credited with at least 200 portraits.

CARAYON, Biog. particulières, 1485; AMIOT, Bibliothèque Nat. (Paris); SOMMERVOGEL, Bibl. de la c. de J.; Lettres Édifiantes (ed. 1780), XXII, 490, 528; (ed. 1843), III, 786, 795; XXVII; STÖCKLEIN, Welt Bott, XXXIX, n. 679; BEAUMONT, Acct. of the Emperor of China's Garden (London, 1752); North China Herald, 3 Nov. 1860; Précis historiques, 1856, 437, 461, 485; Journal des savants, June, 1771.

T. J. CAMPBELL.

Atto, a faithful follower of Gregory VII in his conflict with the simoniac clergy, b. probably at Milan, made Cardinal of San Marco, assisted (1079) at the retractation of Berengarius in the Roman synod of that year, and signed the decrees of the synod of 1081. He may have been Bishop of Præneste. Cardinal Mai published under his name (SS. Vet. nova coll., VI, 2, 60 sqq.), from a Vatican manuscript, a "Breviarium Canonum", or miscellaneous collection of moral and canonical decrees, genuine and forged, from Pope Clement I to Gregory the Great. It deals particularly with clerical rights and duties, ecclesiastical acts, the administration of the sacraments, censures, jurisdiction, etc. Other cardinals of the name are mentioned in the anonymous (eighteenth-century) "Diatriba de Attonibus" published by Cardinal Mai (op. cit.; cf. P.L., CXXXIV, 902).

BRÜCK in Kirchenlex, I, 1566, 1567.

THOMAS J. SHAHAN.

Atto of Pistoia, b. at Badajoz in Spain, 1070; d. 22 May, 1155. He became Abbot of Vallombrosa (Tuscany) in 1105, and in 1135 was made Bishop of Pistoia. He wrote lives of St. John Gualbert and of St. Bernard of Vallombrosa, Bishop of Parma. In 1145 he transferred to Pistoia certain relics of St. James of Compostella. His correspondence on that occasion is found in Ughelli, "Italia Sacra", VII, 296.

GIRAUD, Bibl. Sacr., II, 420; POTTHAST, Bibl. Hist. Med. Ævi, II, 1185; CHEVALIER, Répertoire (Bio-Bibl.), I, 362.

THOMAS J. SHAHAN.

Atto of Vercelli, a learned theologian and canonist of the tenth century, son of the Viscount Aldegarius, and Bishop of Vercelli (924–961). In 933 he became Grand Chancellor of Lothaire II, King of France, and obtained from the royal gratitude donations and privileges for his see of Vercelli (Ughelli, Italia Sacra, IV, 769). Several of his writings were first published by the Benedictine D'Achery (1655–77) in his "Spicilegium" VIII, 1–137; 2d ed., 1723, I, 401–442, e. g. "Epistolæ, Libellus de pressuris ecclesiasticis", and "Canones rursus statutaque Vercellensis ecclesiæ". A complete edition was executed by Baronzo del Signore, in two folio volumes (Vercelli, 1768; P. L., CXXXIV, 27–834), inclusive of his lengthy commentary on the Epistles of St. Paul. In 1832 Cardinal Mai published eighteen sermons of Atto, and his curious "Polypticum", or "Perpendiculum", an abridgment of moral philosophy, "written in a mysterious and enigmatic way". In his history of early medieval literature Ebert transfers to some Spaniard the authorship of this work, but Hauck defends the traditional view (Realencyk. f. prot. Theol., II, 214). His "Can-

ones" are in great part a compilation of earlier ecclesiastical legislation, including the False Decretals. They contain, also, certain provisions of his own and are of value for the study of contemporary ecclesiastical life and manners in Northern Italy. He is sometimes known as Atto II; an earlier homonymous bishop of Vercelli flourished about the middle of the eighth century.

SCHULTZ, Atto von Vercelli (Göttingen, 1887); VERSCHAFFEL in Dict. de théol. cath., I, 2222, 2223; TIRABOSCHI, Stor. lett. Ital. (1806), III, Pt. I, 219–22; CHEVALIER, Rép. des sources hist.: Bio-bibliogr.; I, 363.

THOMAS J. SHAHAN.

Attracta (OR ARAGHT), SAINT, a contemporary of St. Patrick from whom she received the veil. She is known as the foundress of several churches in the counties of Galway and Sligo, Ireland. Colgan's account of her life is based on that written by Augustine Magraidin in the last years of the fourteenth century, and abounds in improbable statements. However, the fact of St. Attracta receiving the veil from St. Patrick is corroborated by Tirechán, in the "Book of Armagh", as is evident from the following passage in the "Documenta de S. Patricio" (ed. Edmund Hogan, S.J.): "Et ecclesiam posuit in cella Adrachtæ, filiæ Talain, et ipsa accepit pallium de manu Patricii." A native of the County Sligo, she resolved to devote herself to God, but being opposed by her parents, fled to South Connacht and made her first foundation at Drumconnell, near Boyle, County Roscommon, whence she removed to Greagraighe, or Coolavin, County Sligo. At Killaraght, St. Attracta established a hospice for travellers, which existed as late as 1539. Her fame was so great that numerous places were named after her, e. g. Killaraght (Cill Attracta), Toberaraght, Cloghan Araght, etc., and a large village which grew up around her oratory at Killaraght in Coolavin. Colgan gives an account of the Cross of St. Attracta which was famed during the Middle Ages, and of which the O'Mochain family were hereditary keepers. A striking confirmation of the existence of this relic in the early years of the fifteenth century is afforded by an entry in the "Calendar of Papal Letters" (VI, 451), from which we learn that in 1413 the cross and cup of St. Attracta (Crux ac Cuach Aracht) were then venerated in the church of Killaraght, in the Diocese of Achonry. By an Indult of 28 July, 1864, Pius IX authorized the Office and Mass of St. Attracta, which had lapsed into desuetude, to be again celebrated in the Irish Church. The feast of St. Attracta, on 11 August, is given special honour in the Diocese of Achonry, of which she is the patroness. The prayers and proper lessons for her Office were drawn up by Cardinal Moran.

GRATTAN FLOOD, Irish Saints; Acta SS. (1658), 2 Feb., 296–297; Bibl. Hagiogr. Lat. (1901), 1156; COLGAN, Acta SS. Hibern. (1645), I, 277–282; O'HANLON, Lives of Irish Saints, VIII (11 Aug.).

W. H. GRATTAN FLOOD.

Attributes, DIVINE.—In order to form a more systematic idea of God, and, as far as possible, to unfold the implications of the truth, God is All-Perfect, this infinite Perfection is viewed, successively, under various aspects, each of which is treated as a separate perfection and characteristic inherent to the Divine Substance, or Essence. A certain group of these, of paramount import, is called the Divine Attributes.

I. KNOWLEDGE OF GOD MEDIATE AND SYNTHETIC. —Our natural knowledge of God is acquired by discursive reasoning upon the data of sense and introspection, "For the invisible things of Him, from the creation of the world, are clearly seen, being understood by the things that are made; His eternal power also, and Divinity" (St. Paul, Romans, i, 20). Created things, by the properties and activities of their natures, manifest, as in a glass, darkly, the powers and perfections of the Creator. But these refracted images of Him in finite things cannot furnish grounds for any adequate idea of the Infinite Being. Hence, in constructing a synthetic idea of God, before one can apply to the Divinity any concept or term expressing a perfection found in created being, it must be subjected to rigorous correction. The profound disparity between the Divine perfection and the intimations of it presented in the world-copy may be broadly laid down under two heads. (1) Number.—The perfections of creatures are innumerable, the Divine perfection is one. (2) Diversity.—Created perfections differ endlessly in kind and degree; the Divine perfection is uniform, simple. It is not a totality of various perfections; absolutely simple, the Divine perfection answers to every idea of actual or conceivable perfection, without being determined to the particular mode of any. Hence, when any attribute expressing modes characteristic of the world of being that falls within the range of our experience is applied to God its signification ceases to be identical with that which it has in every other case. Yet it retains a real meaning in virtue of the ratio which exists between the finite being and its Infinite analogue. In philosophical phrase, this use of terms is called analogical predication, in contradistinction to univocal, in which a word is predicated of two or more subjects in precisely the same sense. (See ANALOGY.)

II. SOURCE OF OUR NATURAL KNOWLEDGE OF GOD.—To correct, as far as possible, the inadequate character of the concepts through which we must formulate our idea of God, the first step is to distinguish created perfection into two kinds, viz., mixed perfections and pure perfections. A pure perfection is one whose exact concept does not include any note formally expressive of defect or limitation; the content of the idea is entirely positive. The idea of a mixed perfection, on the contrary, formally or directly connotes, along with what is positive in the perfection, some privation or deficiency. Examples of the former are power, truthfulness, will; as an instance of the latter, materiality may be offered. For, though the reality that belongs to matter is, of course, a participation of existence and activity, yet the concept of it connotes the imperfections of that particular kind of existence which is composite and subject to disintegration. Again, personality is a pure perfection; for, as Catholic philosophy teaches, though the finite character of human personality comes into play in the awakening of self-consciousness, yet limitation is not an essential constituent of personality. All terms that stand for pure perfections are predicated analogically of God, and are designated attributes in the wide sense of the word. When terms which signify mixed perfections are predicated of God, the analogy becomes so faint that the locution is a mere metaphor.

III. INDUCTIVE DEVELOPMENT OF ATTRIBUTES.— The elaboration of the idea of God is carried out along three converging lines: (1) The positive way of causality.—In virtue of the principle that whatever excellence is contained in an effect is represented in the efficiency of the cause, reason affirms that every positive perfection of created being has its transcendental analogue in the first cause. Hence, from the existence of an intelligent being, man, in the cosmos, we rightly infer that God is intelligent, that is to say, His infinite perfection is superabundantly adequate to all the operations of intellect. (2) The negative way.—If we fix our attention precisely on the Infinity of God, then, focusing the negation not upon the positive content of any created perfection, but upon the fact that, because it is finite it is determined in kind and limited in degree, we may affirm that it is not found in God. We may say, e. g., that He is not intelligent. The

meaning of the statement is not that God lacks intelligence, but that in Him there is not intelligence exactly as we know it. Again, since there is no imperfection in God, every concept of defect, privation, and limitation must be negated of God. Many negative names, it is true, are applied to God; as when, for instance, He is said to be immutable, uncaused, infinite. It should, however, be carefully observed that some attributes, which, from the etymological point of view, are negative, convey, nevertheless, a positive meaning. Failure to perceive this obvious truth has been responsible for much empty dogmatism on the impossibility of forming any concept of the Infinite. The basic note in the idea of the Infinite is existence, actuality, perfection; the negative note is subordinate. Furthermore, since the force of the latter note is to deny any and all limitations to the actuality represented by the former, its real import is positive, like the cancellation of a minus sign in an algebraic formula; or, it discharges the function of an exponent and raises actuality to the nth power. (3) Way of eminence.— The concept of a perfection derived from created things and freed of all defects, is, in its application to God, expanded without limit. God not only possesses every excellence discoverable in creation, but He also possesses it infinitely. To emphasize the transcendence of the Divine perfection, in some cases an abstract noun is substituted for the corresponding adjective; as, God is Intelligence; or, again, some word of intensive, or exclusive, force is joined to the attribute; as, God alone is good, God is goodness itself, God is all-powerful, or supremely powerful.

IV. DEDUCTIVE DEVELOPMENT.—Having established the existence of God from metaphysical, physical, and moral arguments, the theologian selects some one of the attributes which these proofs authorize him to predicate of the Divinity and, by unfolding its implications, reaches a number of other attributes. For instance, if God is Pure Actuality, that is, free from all static potency, it follows that, since change implies a transition from an antecedent potential condition to a subsequent condition in which the potentiality is realized, God is immutable. Here we reach the point where the term Attribute is employed in its strict sense.

V. ESSENCE AND ATTRIBUTES.—Transcendentally one, absolutely free from composition, the Divine Being is not, and may not be conceived as, a fundamental substrate in which qualities or any other modal determinations inhere. The reality to which the various attributes are ascribed is one and indivisible.— "Quæ justitia," says St. Augustine, "ipsa bonitas; quæ bonitas, ipsa beatitudo."—In this respect, the relation of the attributes to the Divine nature might be illustrated by the various reflections of one and the same object from a concave, a convex, and a plane mirror. Nevertheless, to systematize the idea of God, and to draw out the rich content of the knowledge resulting from the proofs of God's existence, some primary attribute may be chosen as representing one aspect of the Divine perfection from which the others may be rigorously deduced. Then arises a logical scheme in which the derivative attributes, or perfections, stand towards one another in a relation somewhat similar to that of the essence and the various properties and qualities in a material substance. In this arrangement the primary perfection is termed the metaphysical essence, the others are called attributes. The essence, too, may be regarded as that characteristic which, above all others, distinguishes the Deity from everything else. Upon the question, which attribute is to be considered primary, opinions differ. Many eminent theologians favour the conception of pure actuality (*Actus Purus*), from which simplicity and infinity are directly deduced. Most modern authors fix on aseity (*Aseitas; a*="from" *se*="himself"), or self-existence; for the reason that, while all other existences are derived from, and depend on, God, He possesses in Himself, absolutely and independently, the entire reason of His uncaused, infinite Being. In this, the most profound and comprehensive distinction between the Divinity and everything else, all other distinctions are implicitly expressed. Whether, and in what way, the distinctions between the attributes and the metaphysical essence, and among the attributes themselves, have an ontological basis in the Divine nature itself, was a subject which divided Nominalists and Realists, Thomists and Scotists, in the age of Scholasticism (cf. Vacant, Dict. de théol. cathol., I, 2230–34).

VI. Division of Attributes.—Taking as the basis of classification the ways by which the attributes are developed, they are divided into positive and negative. Among the negative attributes are simplicity, infinity, immutability. The chief positive attributes are unity, truth, goodness, beauty, omnipotence, omnipresence, intellect and will, personality. Some authors divide them into incommunicable and communicable. The former class comprises those which belong to God alone (e. g., all-wise, self-existent, omnipotent) to the latter belong those which are predicable, analogically, of God and creatures; as good, just, intelligent. Again, the divine nature may be considered either as static, or as the source of activity; hence another division into quiescent and active. Finally, some perfections involve a relation to things distinct from God, while others do not; and from this standpoint theologians divide the attributes into absolute and relative. The various classifications adopted by modern Protestant theologians are due partly to the results of philosophical speculation and partly to new conceptions of the nature of religion. Schleiermacher, e. g., derives the attributes of God from our threefold consciousness of absolute dependence, of sin, and of grace. Others, with Lipsius, distinguish the metaphysical attributes from the psychological and the ethical. A simpler division groups omnipotence, omnipresence, eternity, omniscience, and unity as the metaphysical predicates, justice and goodness as the moral attributes. The fundamental attribute is, according to Ritschl, love; according to Professor Royce, omniscience. The main difficulty with these writers centres about the idea of God as a personal being.

VII. Revelation.—The supernatural knowledge of God given in revelation is apprehended through the medium of conceptions that belong to natural knowledge. Therefore, the same principles of attribution that govern the one hold good also for the other.

VIII. Historical Development.—In the fourth century Aetius and Eunomius maintained that, because the Divine nature is simple, excluding all composition or multiplicity, the various terms and names applied to God are to be considered synonymous. Otherwise they would erroneously imply composition in God. This opinion was combated by St. Cyril of Alexandria, St. Basil, and St. Gregory of Nyssa (In Eunom., P. G., XLV). The principle of attribution received more precise statement at the hands of St. Augustine, in his investigation of the conditions of intellectual knowledge (De Genesi ad Litteram, IV, 32). In the ninth century, John Scotus Erigena, who was largely influenced by Neo-Platonism, transmitted through the works of the Pseudo-Dionysius, contributed to bring into clearer relief the analogical character of predication (De Divinâ Naturâ, Lib. I). The Nominalists revived the views of Eunomius, and the opposition of the Realists was carried to the other extreme by Gilbert de la Porrée, who maintained a real, ontological distinction between the Divine Essence and the attributes. His opinion was condemned by the Council of Reims (1148). St. Thomas definitively expressed the doctrine which, after some controversies between Scotists and Thomists upon minor points and subtleties, and with some divergence of opinion upon unimportant details, is now the common teaching of Catholic theologians and philosophers. It may be summarized as follows: The idea of God is derived from our knowledge of finite beings. When a term is predicated of the finite and of the Infinite, it is used, not in a univocal, but in an analogical sense. The Divine Perfection, one and invisible, is, in its infinity, the transcendental analogue of all actual and possible finite perfections. By means of an accumulation of analogous predicates, methodically co-ordinated, we endeavour to form an approximate conception of the Deity who, because He is Infinite, cannot be comprehended by finite intelligence. Modern philosophy presents a remarkable gradation, from Pantheism, which finds God in everything, to Agnosticism, which declares that He is beyond the reach of knowledge. Spinoza conceives God as "a substance consisting of infinite attributes each of which expresses eternal and infinite essence". The two attributes manifested to us are thought and extension. At the other extreme we find Agnostics of the school of Herbert Spencer (see Agnosticism) and some followers of Hegel, who hold that the nature of God, or, to use their favourite term, "the Absolute", is utterly unknowable, and its existence not determined to any mode; therefore, to predicate of it various attributes, expressive of determinations, is idle and misleading. Between the finite and the Infinite there is no common ground of predication; hence, words which signify finite perfections can have no real meaning when predicated of God; they become mere empty symbols. All theological attempts to elaborate an idea of God are vain, and result in complete absurdity when they conceive God after man's image and likeness (see Anthropomorphism), and circumscribe the Infinite in terms borrowed from human psychology. Criticism of this kind indicates that its authors have never taken the trouble to understand the nature of analogical predication, or to consider fairly the rigorous logical process of refining to which terms are subjected before being predicated of God. It often happens, too, that writers, after indulging liberally in eloquent denunciation of theological anthropomorphism, proceed, on the next page, to apply to the Infinite, presumably in a strictly univocal sense, terms such as "energy", "force", and "law", which are no less anthropomorphic, in an ultimate analysis, than "will" and "intelligence". The position of the Catholic Church, declared in the Fourth Lateran Council (1215), is again clearly stated in the following pronouncement of the Vatican Council:

"The Holy Catholic Apostolic Roman Church believes and professes that there is one living and true God, Creator and Lord of heaven and earth, omnipotent, eternal, immense, incomprehensible, infinite in intellect and will and in all perfection; Who, being One, singular, absolutely simple and unchangeable spiritual substance, is to be regarded as distinct really and in essence from the world, most blessed in and from Himself, and unspeakably elevated above all things that exist, or can be conceived, except Himself."

St. Thomas, *I Sent.*, dist. ii, Q. I; *Summa Theol.*, 1ª Q. XIII, a. 12; *De Potentiâ*, Q. VII, a. 5; *C. Gent.* L. I., *c.* xxxv; Wilhelm and Scannell, *A Manual of Catholic Theology* (New York, 1892); I, v; Gratry, *La connaissance de Dieu* (Paris, 1856), Part II; tr. Alger, *Guide to the Knowledge of God* (Boston, 1892); Toussaint in *Dict. de théol. cath.* (Paris, 1903); Flint, *Theism* (Edinburgh, 1879); Iverach.

Theism in the Light of Modern Science and Philosophy (New York, 1899); LADD, *The Philosophy of Religion* (New York, 1905); ILLINGWORTH, *Personality, Human and Divine* (London and New York, 1903); FRASER, *Philosophy of Theism* (Edinburgh, 1899); ROYCE, *The Conception of God* (New York, 1898); HUNTER, *Outlines of Dogmatic Theology* (New York, 1896), II.

JAMES J. FOX.

Attrition, or IMPERFECT CONTRITION (Lat. *attero*, "to wear away by rubbing"; p. part. *attritus*).—The Council of Trent (Sess. XIV, Chap. iv) has defined contrition as "sorrow of soul, and a hatred of sin committed, with a firm purpose of not sinning in the future". This hatred of sin may arise from various motives, may be prompted by various causes. If the detestation of sin arise from the love of God, Who has been grievously offended, then contrition is termed perfect; if it arise from any other motive, such as loss of heaven, fear of hell, or the heinousness of guilt, then it is termed imperfect contrition, or attrition. That there exists such a disposition of soul as attrition, and that it is a goodly thing, an impulse of the Spirit of God, is the clear teaching of the Council of Trent (Sess. XIV, iv). "And as to that imperfect contrition which is called attrition, because it is commonly conceived either from the consideration of the turpitude of sin, or from the fear of hell and of punishment, the council declares that if with the hope of pardon, it excludes the wish to sin, it not only does not make man a hypocrite and a greater sinner, but that it is even a gift of God, and an impulse of the Holy Spirit, who does not indeed as yet dwell in the penitent, but who only moves him; whereby the penitent, being assisted, prepares a way for himself unto justice, and although this attrition cannot of itself, without the Sacrament of Penance, conduct the sinner to justification, yet does it dispose him to receive the grace of God in the Sacrament of Penance. For smitten profitably with fear, the Ninivites at the preaching of Jonas did fearful penance and obtained mercy from the Lord." Wherefore anent attrition, the council in Canon v, Sess. XIV, declares: "If any man assert that attrition . . . is not a true and a profitable sorrow; that it does not prepare the soul for grace, but that it makes a man a hypocrite, yea, even a greater sinner, let him be anathema." This doctrine of the council is in accord with the teaching of the Old and the New Testament. The Old Testament writers praise without hesitation that fear of God which is really "the beginning of wisdom" (Ps. cx). One of the commonest forms of expression found in the Hebrew scriptures is the "exhortation to the fear of the Lord" (Ecclus., i, 13; ii, 19 sqq.). We are told that "without fear there is no justification" (ibid., i, 28; ii, 1; ii, 19). In this fear there is "confidence of strength" and it is "a fountain of life" (Prov., xiv, 26, 27); and the Psalmist prays (Ps. cxviii, 120): "Pierce thou my flesh with thy fear: for I am afraid of thy judgments."

NEW TESTAMENT.—Even when the law of fear had given way to the law of love, Christ does not hesitate to inculcate that we must "fear him who can destroy both soul and body into hell" (Matt., x, 28). Certainly, too, the vivid account of the destruction of Jerusalem, typical of the final destruction of the world, was intended by Jesus to strike terror into the hearts of those who heard, and those who read; nor can one doubt that the last great judgment as portrayed by Matthew, xxv, 31 sqq., must have been described by Christ for the purpose of deterring men from sin by reason of God's awful judgments. The Apostle appears not less insistent when he exhorts us to work out "our salvation in fear and trembling" lest the anger of God come upon us (Phil., ii, 12). The Fathers of the earliest days of Christianity have spoken of fear of God's punishments as a goodly virtue that makes for salvation. Clement of Alex-

andria (Strom., VII) speaks of righteousness which comes of love and righteousness arising from fear, and in the Strom., II, ch. vii, he speaks at length on the utility of fear, and answers all objections brought forward against his position. The most striking sentence is the one wherein he says: "cautious fear is therefore shown to be reasonable, from which arises repentance of previous sins", etc. St. Basil (4th interrogatory on the Rule) speaks of the fear of God and of His judgments, and he asserts that for those who are beginning a life of piety "exhortation based on fear is of greatest utility", and he quotes the wise man asserting, "The fear of God is the beginning of wisdom" (P. G., XXXI). St. John Chrysostom may be quoted in the same sense (P. G., XLIX, 154). St. Ambrose, in the fifteenth sermon on the Psalm cxviii speaks at large on godly fear which begets charity, begets love: *Hunc timorem sequitur charitas* (P. L., xv, 1424), and his disciple, St. Augustine, treats fully the godliness of fear as a motive to repentance. In the 161st of his sermons (P. L., XXXVIII, 882 sqq.) he speaks of refraining from sin for fear of God's judgments, and he asks: "Dare I say such fear is wrong?" He replies that he dare not, for the Lord Christ urging men to refrain from wrongdoing suggested the motive of fear. "Fear not those who kill the body", etc. (Matt., x). True, what follows in St. Augustine has been subject to much dispute, but the general doctrine of the godliness of fear is here propounded, and the difficulty, if aught there be, touches the other question hereinafter treated anent "Initial Love".

The word itself, attrition, is of medieval origin. Father Palmieri (De Pœnit., 345) asserts, on the authority of Aloysius Mingarelli, that the word is thrice found in the works of Alanus of Lille, who died at an advanced age in the year 1203; but its use in the school is contemporaneous with William of Paris, Alexander of Hales, and Blessed Albert. Even with these men its meaning was not so precise as in after years; though they all agreed that of itself it did not suffice to justify the sinner in God's sight. (See the Scholastic traditions in article ABSOLUTION, and Palmieri, loc. cit.). This fear is godly, since it excludes not only the will to sin, but also the affection for sin. There would perhaps have been little difficulty on this point if the distinction were kept in mind between that fear which is termed *servilis*, which touches will and heart, and that fear known as *serviliter servilis*, which though it makes man refrain from performing the sinful act, leaves the will to sin and the affection thereto.

ATTRITION IN THE SACRAMENT OF PENANCE.—The Church not only regards the godliness of fear as a motive to repentance, but expressly defines that attrition, though it justifies not without the Sacrament of Penance, nevertheless disposes the sinner to receive grace in the sacrament itself (Sess. XIV, iv). This particular phase of the doctrine of contrition in penance is first taught with clearness by the Schoolmen of the twelfth century, and particularly by St. Thomas, who gathered into a united whole the jarring opinions of his predecessors (See the Scholastic in article ABSOLUTION). Though some still preferred to follow the Lombards who insisted on perfect contrition, after St. Thomas there was little division in the schools up to the time of the Council of Trent. At the council there was some opposition to a clear definition, some of the Fathers insisting on the necessity of perfect contrition, and it was perhaps for this reason that the decree was couched as above, leaving it still possible to doubt whether attrition was a proximate, or only a remote, disposition for justification in the sacrament. To-day the common teaching is that the council simply intended to define the sufficiency of attrition (Vacant, Dict. de théol., col. 2246-47). And this would seem reasonable.

because it is the clear teaching of the Church that perfect contrition justifies the sinner even without the Sacrament of Penance. If perfect contrition, then, were always necessary, why did Christ institute a particular sacrament, since justification would always be imparted independently of the sacramental ceremony? If attrition is sufficient for justification in the Sacrament of Penance, then there seems no reason to deny its sufficiency when there is question of remitting sin through baptism, for the reason given above will apply equally in this place. The question has also been asked apropos of attrition, when one receives a sacrament of the living in mortal sin, of which sin he is not conscious, will attrition with the sacrament suffice unto justification? The answer is generally given in the affirmative. See St. Thomas, Summa Theol., III, 2, a. 7 ad 2^{am}, 7ed., 2; Billot, De Pœnit., p. 152.

CONDITIONS.—That attrition may make for justification, it must be interior, supernatural, universal, and sovereign. (See *Conditions* in article CONTRITION.) Interior, for the Council of Trent requires that it should exclude the will to sin. Supernatural, for Innocent XI condemned the proposition, "Probabile est sufficere attritionem naturalem modo honestam". Universal, for the motives of attrition (fear of hell, loss of heaven, etc.) are of such a nature as to embrace all sins. Sovereign, for here again the ordinary motives of attrition (fear of hell, etc.) make one hate sin above all other evil. It has been questioned whether this would be true if the motive were fear of temporal punishments (Genicot, T. 11, n. 274; Billot, De Pœnit., 159 sq.). The Reformers denied the honesty and godliness of attrition, and held that it simply made man a hypocrite. (Bull of Leo X, Exurge Domine, prop. VI; Council of Trent, Sess. XIV, can. iv.) They were followed by Baius, Jansen, and his disciples, who taught that fear without charity was bad, since it proceeded not from the love of God, but love of self (see prop. 7, 14, 15, condemned by Alexander VIII, 7 December, 1690; also 44, 61, 62, condemned by Clement X, "Unigenitus", 8 September, 1717. Also Bull of Pius VI, "Auctorem Fidei", prop. 25).

Catholic writers in the seventeenth century questioned, whether attrition must of necessity be accompanied at least by the beginning of the love of God, and, that granted, whether such love was a disinterested love of God for His own sake, or whether it might not be that love termed *concupiscentiæ*, or love of God because He is our great good. Some held that in every real act of attrition there must be the beginning of love; others denied categorically this position, exacting only that sorrow which excludes affection for sin, and hope of pardon; others insisted that there must be at least a beginning of that love which has been termed above *concupiscentiæ;* while still others exact only that love which begets hope. On these opinions see Vacant, Dict. de théol., s. v. Attrition, cols. 2252, 2253, 2254, etc. On the controversy, particularly in Belgium, see Döllinger and Reusch (Dict., col. 2219). The controversy waxed so warm that Alexander VII issued a decree, 6 May, 1667, in which he declares his distress at the almost scandalously bitter disputes waged by certain scholastic theologians as to whether the act of attrition which is conceived through fear of hell, but excludes the will of sinning and counts on obtaining the mercy of recovering grace through the Sacrament of Penance, requires in addition some act of love of God, and then "enjoins on all of whatever rank, under pain of incurring the severest ecclesiastical penalties, not to presume in future when discussing the aforesaid act of attrition to brand with any mark of theological censure, or wrong, or contempt, either one or the other of the two opinions; that denying the necessity of some sort of love of God

[*negantem necessitatem aliqualis dilectionis Dei*] in the attrition conceived through fear of hell, which to-day (1667) seems the one more generally held by scholastic theologians, or that affirming the necessity of the said love, until something shall have been defined in this matter by this Holy See." The authoritative statement of Alexander VII leaves the question still open as Benedict XIV teaches in "De Synodo", Bk. VII, xiii, n. 9. Still it is clear that Alexander considered as more probable the opinion stating attrition as sufficient for justification in the Sacrament of Penance even if it included not the beginning of love. The censure *latæ sententiæ* was omitted in the "Apostolicæ Sedis". On the formula, "*Ex attrito fit contritus*", cf. Vacant, Dict. de théol., col. 2256 sqq.

EDWARD J. HANNA.

Attuda, a titular see of Phrygia in Asia Minor, whose episcopal list (431–879) is given in Gams (446).
LEQUIEN, *Oriens Christ.* (1740), I, 825–826; SMITH, *Dict. of Greek and Roman Geogr.*, I, 336.

Aubarède, JEAN-MICHEL-D'ASTORG, canon regular, and Vicar Capitular of Pamiers, b. 1639; d. 4 August, 1692. He was educated at Toulouse (France), entered the Seminary of Pamiers, and later joined the canons regular, who formed the cathedral chapter of that diocese. After the death of the bishop, François Caulet, Aubarède was chosen vicar capitular. As administrator of the diocese, he took up and carried on vigorously the resistance of Caulet to the royal demands in the matter of the Regalia. He refused to recognize royal nominations to local ecclesiastical benefices, and excommunicated the canons appointed by the king, when they attempted to exercise their office. He was arrested by royal order, and imprisoned for six years at Caen, where he died. His courageous resistance is remarkable at a time when ecclesiastical servility in France had reached its acme. B. Jungmann remarks (in Herder, K. L., I, 1567) that the well-known Jansenistic rigorism of Caulet and his clergy was partly responsible for their stubborn defiance of Louis XIV; they rightly feared that the nominees of the king would not belong to their faction.
QUÉRIN, *L'Assemblée du clergé de France de 1682*.
THOMAS J. SHAHAN.

Aubermont, JEAN-ANTOINE D', of Bois-le-Duc, theologian, d. 22 November, 1686. He joined the Dominicans in 1633, taught philosophy and theology in several convents of his order, was made doctor of theology at Louvain in 1652, and president of the local Dominican college in 1653. His theological writings are mostly in defence of papal infallibility (1682) and against the Gallican teachings of the Declaration of 1682. Shortly before his death he defended against Papebroch St. Thomas of Aquin's authorship of the Mass for Corpus Christi.
QUÉTIF-ÉCHARD, SS. O.P., II, 709; VACANT, *Dict. de Théol. Cath.*, I, 2263.
THOMAS J. SHAHAN.

Aubery, JOSEPH, Jesuit missionary in Canada, b. at Gisors in Normandy, 10 May, 1673; d. at St. François, Canada, 2 July, 1755. At the age of seventeen he entered the Society of Jesus, and for four years studied in Paris. He arrived in Canada in 1694 and completed his studies at Quebec, where he was also instructor for five years, and where he was ordained in 1700. Assigned to the Abenaki mission, he re-established in 1701 the mission at Medoctec on the St. John River, which appears to have been abandoned by the Franciscans about a year earlier. In 1708 he was given charge of the Abenaki reduction at St. François, and exercised the apostolate in that single mission for nearly half a century. Aubery is said to have been an able linguist, but unfortunately his numerous MSS., with the mission registers, were destroyed by fire in 1759. He also wrote several memorials in opposition to the claims of the English in Acadia, and sent them to the French Government, urging that the boundaries between the French and English possessions should be determined by mutual agreement. To these memorials he added a map, giving the boundaries as defined by the treaty of Utrecht. His plan, however, was not accepted. These valuable documents are still preserved in the Paris archives. Chateaubriand reproduces the life-story of Father Aubery in the character of the missionary in his "Atala".

THWAITES, *Jesuit Relations* (Cleveland, 1900), LXVI, 344; ROCHEMONTEIX, *Les Jésuites* (Paris, 1895–96); MAURAULT, *Histoire des Abénakis* (Quebec, 1866); BRUNS, *Hist. Colls.*, I, 1896.

EDWARD P. SPILLANE.

Aubignac, FRANÇOIS HÉDELIN, ABBÉ D', grammarian, poet, preacher, archæologist, philologist, b. at Paris, 4 August, 1604; d. at Nemours, 27 July, 1676. He took his name from an abbey that was granted him. After completing his classical and theological studies, he was appointed by Cardinal Richelieu instructor to the latter's nephew, the young Duc de Fronsac, to whose gratitude he owed a pension of 4,000 *livres*. This appointment, as well as his own inclination, led him to devote his time to literary studies, especially to the classics. He was drawn into the controversy between the ancients under the leadership of Boileau, and the moderns under Perrault, his philological views being used by the latter for the support of their cause. The drama had a special attraction for d'Aubignac, who wrote not only a tragedy, "Zénobie", but also a work entitled "Pratique du Théâtre".

The abbé interests modern scholars chiefly because of his attitude on what is known as the "Homeric Question". He was one of the first to doubt the existence of Homer; he even propounded the theory that the Iliad is made up of a number of independent ballads gathered and put together by a compiler not very much later than the supposed date of Homer, whom he took to be Lycurgus. This first compilation, however, was not final, as the poem continued to be handed down by the recitation of rhapsodists who again divided the work into separate songs, Pisistratus making the final redaction. These views were based partly on statements in the Greek historians, partly on reasons drawn from the poem itself. D'Aubignac dwelt on the impossibility of transmitting so long a poem without the aid of writing which he, as did Wolf, believed to be unknown to Homer. He drew arguments from the construction of the epic, its lack of unity and its multiplicity of themes, the quarrel of Achilles being treated of in only a few books. The name Iliad he considered a misnomer, since Troy is not the subject of the story. The Iliad, he contended, has no suitable ending; the reader's curiosity remains unsatisfied. It contains many cantos that might be omitted, not only without detriment but with positive advantage to the action of the story. Besides these general considerations, he adduced numerous details which constitute flaws in the poem as we possess it, but which would be entirely justified in separate ballads. In short, there are few objections made to the Iliad by modern scholars on æsthetical and rhetorical grounds which are not touched upon by the French humanist. The arguments against a single author, drawn from the character of the language, the intermixture of the dialects and the like, d'Aubignac could not present, because linguistic studies in his day had not advanced sufficiently to enable him to appreciate the "Homeric Question" from this point of view. Though the abbé had on many occasions set forth in writing his opinions on Homer, it was only shortly before his death that he wrote an extended work on the theme, entitled "Conjectures académiques, ou dissertation sur l'Iliade". He died before he was able to make the final revision, and it was not published until 1715, forty years after his death. The work was known to Wolf, and though the French scholar anticipated many of his own views he does him scant justice. A German critic declares that d'Aubignac's arguments are substantially as strong as Wolf's, in some respects stronger, and that if Wolf's "Prolegomena" produced greater and more lasting results, this is due less to the character of his arguments than to the greater skill with which they are set forth.

FINSLER, *Die Conjectures académiques des Abbé d'Aubignac* in *Neue Jahrbücher für das klassische Altertum und für Pädagogik* (Leipzig, 1905) XV.

CHARLES G. HERBERMANN.

Aubigné, JEAN-HENRI MERLE D'. See REFORMATION.

Aubusson, PIERRE D', Grand Master of the Order of St. John of Jerusalem, b. 1423; d. 1503. He made his first campaigns against the Turks, and fought next under the French Dauphin in a war against the Swiss (1444). It was on his return from this last expedition that he obtained from Charles VII permission to join the Hospitallers. The year 1460 found him Castellan of Rhodes, and he soon after became captain-general of the city, which had been the seat of the order since 1309, and was now the chief obstacle to Ottoman supremacy in the Mediterranean. Mahomet II therefore resolved to subdue it. D'Aubusson, who had been raised (1476) to the Grand Mastership, foresaw the sultan's design, and lost no time in making what preparations he could for the defence. A letter to the houses of his order brought him whatever men and money they could spare. Additional sums came from Sixtus IV and Louis XI, together with some of the bravest soldiers of Italy and France. Yet with all his exertions he was able to muster no more than 450 knights and 2,000 auxiliaries. The Turkish armament, which appeared before Rhodes 23 May, 1480, was overwhelmingly superior in numbers, and was furnished with the best artillery then obtainable. But the example of d'Aubusson's good right arm, and his omnipresence, made heroes of all the defenders. After three months of almost incessant fighting, which cost him 25,000 of his best warriors, the Turkish commander was forced to raise the siege. For this brilliant achievement d'Aubusson received a cardinal's hat, and was revered by all Christendom as "the Shield of the Church". In his subsequent efforts to form a league that would drive the Turks from Constantinople, he failed.

BOUHOURS, *Histoire de Pierre d'Aubusson* (Paris, 1676; 3d ed., Hague, 1739; tr., London, 1679); MARULLI, *Lives of the Grand-Masters . . . of St. John . . .* (Naples, 1636); FLANDRIN, *History of the Knights of Rhodes* (Paris, 1876).

A. J. B. VUIBERT.

Auch (AUGUSTA AUSCORUM), ARCHDIOCESE OF, comprises the Department of Gers in France. Before the Revolution it had ten suffragan sees: Acqs (Dax) and Aire, afterwards united as the Diocese of Aire; Lectoure, later reunited with the Archdiocese of Auch; Couserans, afterwards united with the Diocese of Pamiers; Oloron, Lescar, and Bayonne, united later as the Diocese of Bayonne; Bazas, afterwards united with the Archdiocese of Bordeaux; Comminges, united later with the Archdiocese of Toulouse; and Tarbes. Up to 1789 the Archbishops of Auch bore the title of Primate of Aquitaine, though for centuries there had been no Aquitaine. The Archdiocese of Auch, re-established in 1882, was made up of the former archdiocese of the same name and the former Dioceses of Lectoure, Condom, and Lombez. Condom was previously a suffragan of Bordeaux, and Lombez of Toulouse; thenceforth the suffragans of Auch were Aire, Tarbes, and Bayonne. A local tradition that dates back to the beginning of the twelfth century tells us that Taurinus, fifth Bishop of Eauze (Elusa), abandoned his episcopal city, which had been destroyed by the Vandals, and transferred his see to Auch. Eauze, in fact, probably remained a metropolitan see till about the middle of the ninth century, at which time, owing to the invasions of the Northmen, it was re-united to the Diocese of Auch, which had existed since the fifth century at least and then became an archdiocese. The first Bishop of Auch known to history is the poet, St. Orientius (first half of the fifth century), in honour of whom a famous abbey was founded in the seventh century. Cardinal Melchior de Polignac, author of the " Anti-Lucrèce," was Archbishop of Auch from 1725 to 1741. The cathedral of Sainte Marie, a Gothic structure with a Byzantine façade, is, in spite of this incongruity, very imposing; its fifteenth-century windows are said to be the most beautiful in France. The ancient episcopal sees of Condom and Lombez had a monastic origin. Bossuet was non-resident Bishop of Condom for two years (1668–71). At the end of the year 1905 the Archdiocese of Auch contained 238,448 inhabitants; 29 parishes, 478 succursal or mission churches, and 61 vicariates.

Gallia Christiana (ed. Nova, 1715), I, 965–1010, 1325–30, and *Documents*, 159–172 and 202; DUCHESNE, *Fastes épiscopaux de l'ancienne Gaule*, II, 89–102; MONTLEZUN, *Vie des saints évêques de la métropole d'Auch* (Auch, 1857); CHEVALIER, *Topo-bibl.* (Paris, 1894–99), 251–252.

GEORGES GOYAU.

Auch, Councils of. In 1068 a council of Auch decreed that, with a few exceptions, all churches should pay to the Cathedral of Auch one quarter of their tithes. At a council held in 1077 (near Cliovempopulania) William, Archbishop of Auch, was deposed by Gerald, legate of Gregory VII. In 1276 a council was held at Auch in defence of ecclesiastical jurisdiction and immunities. In 1851 a provincial council of Auch drew up a number of decrees concerning faith and doctrine, the hierarchy, public worship, and ecclesiastical studies.

MANSI, *Coll. Conc.*, XIX, 1063, XXV, 107, 217–281; CAZAURAN, *Conciles et synodes du diocèse d'Auch*, in *Revue de Gascogne* (1878), XIX, 70–84; 112–126; CHEVALIER, *Topo-bibl.* (Paris, 1894–99) 251.

Auckland, DIOCESE OF, comprises the Provincial District of Auckland (New Zealand), with its islets, and the Kermadec Group. Area, 21,665 square miles. On Trinity Sunday, 1835, the Vicariate Apostolic of the Western Pacific was erected by Pope Gregory XVI. The Abbé Jean Baptiste François Pompallier was chosen as its first vicar. The territory under his jurisdiction comprised all New Zealand, the present Vicariates Apostolic of Fiji, Central Oceanica, British New Guinea, Dutch New Guinea, New Pomerania, (part of) Gilbert Islands New Caledonia, Navigators' Islands, New Hebrides, and the Prefectures Apostolic of North Solomon Islands and Northern New Guinea. The new vicar was consecrated in Rome, 30 June, and sailed from Havre, 24 December, 1836, accompanied by the Marist Fathers Servant and Bataillon (Lyons), Chanel and Bret (Belley), and three lay-brothers. Father Bret died on the voyage. Father Bataillon (afterwards Vicar Apostolic of Central Oceanica) was left at Wallis Island, and Father Chanel (Blessed Peter Chanel, Protomartyr of Australasia) at Futuna. Dr. Pompallier and Father Servant reached Hokianga (Auckland Province) 10 January, 1838, and were provided for by an Irish Catholic, Thomas Poynton. At that time there were probably fewer than 100 white Catholics in all New Zealand. Other Marist Fathers arrived in 1839 and subsequent years. The missions to the aborigines (Maoris) became very successful, despite grave calumnies propagated by Wesleyan trader-missionaries. By April, 1846, about

5,000 had been baptized, "and there were about five or six times as many catechumens." In 1845 Dr. Pompallier changed his headquarters to Auckland. In 1848 Auckland and Wellington were erected into sees. The Marist Fathers were withdrawn to the Wellington diocese in 1850. The Rev. James McDonald then became the principal missionary to the Auckland Maoris. The Maori missions in New Zealand were paralyzed by the series of native wars between 1843 and 1869. They were taken up in the Auckland diocese by the Mill Hill Fathers, in 1886. The Sisters of Mercy were introduced in 1850. In 1868 Dr. Pompallier went to France, resigned, and died in 1870. He was succeeded by Dr. Thomas William Croke (1870–74), afterwards Archbishop of Cashel. After five years, Father Walter Bisschop Steins, S.J., was appointed to Auckland (1879–81). He was succeeded by Dr. John Edmund Luck, O.S.B. (1882–96). The Right Rev. George Michael Lenihan, consecrated 15 November, 1896, succeeded him.

STATISTICS.—At the census of 1901, the white population of the Auckland Provincial District was 175,938 (of whom 27,246 were Catholics); Maoris, 21,291. The population of the Kermadecs was eight, all non-Catholics. The official estimate of the total white population of the Auckland Provincial District, 31 December, 1906, was 211,233; Catholic population of Auckland Provincial District (which is coterminous with the Diocese of Auckland if the Kermadec Islands be included), 32,272; population of the Kermadec Islands, five, all non-Catholics. According to "New Zealand Statistics, 1904 ", p. 503, there were in the Auckland Provincial District, at the close of 1904, 37 Catholic schools, with 96 teachers and 2,393 pupils. The following were the ecclesiastical statistics for April, 1906: secular clergy, 26; Mill Hill Fathers, for native population, 9; for whites and natives, 7; Catholic Maoris, about 5,000; parochial districts, 29; churches, 79; Religious Brothers, Marists, 12; Sisters of Mercy, 97; Sisters of St. Joseph, 36; Sisters of the Mission, 30; Little Sisters of the Poor, 8; colleges and high schools, 13; parochial schools, 25; orphanages, 2; home for the aged poor, 1; hospital, 1; children in Catholic schools, 2,600.

POMPALLIER, *Early History of the Catholic Church in Oceania* (E. T., Auckland, 1888); CARDINAL MORAN, *History of the Catholic Church in Australasia* (Sydney, no date); MARSHALL, *Christian Missions* (New York, 1896); *New Zealand Census*, vol. 1901 (Wellington, 1902); *New Zealand Statistics* (Wellington, 1905–06).

HENRY W. CLEARY.

Auctorem Fidei, a Bull issued by Pius VI, 28 August, 1794, in condemnation of the Gallican and Jansenist acts and tendencies of the Synod of Pistoia (1786). To understand its bearing, it is well to observe that Leopold II, Grand duke of Tuscany (1765–90), pursued the ecclesiastical policy of his brother, Joseph II of Austria; i. e. he practically arrogated to himself supreme authority over all ecclesiastical matters within his dominions. In 1785 he sent fifty-seven articles to each bishop in the grand duchy, with orders to consider them in a diocesan synod, as a preliminary to a national synod, in which they were finally to be discussed. Scipio de' Ricci, Bishop of Pistoia, held his diocesan synod, and approved not only the fifty-seven articles drawn up by order of Leopold, but added a number of others of similar import. Among them were the following: All ecclesiastical authority comes directly from the members of the Church at large, whose commissioned ministers the pastors are. The pope is only ministerially head of the Church. Bishops do not depend on the pope for any jurisdiction in the government of their diocese. In diocesan synods parish priests have the same right of voting and deciding as the bishop. Reserved cases should be abolished. Excommunication has only an external effect. It is superstition to have more devotion towards one sacred image than towards another. Civil rulers have the right of making impediments diriment of matrimony and of dispensing from them. Bishops are not bound to make an oath of obedience to the pope before their consecration. All religious orders should live under the same rule and wear the same habit. Each church should have only one altar; the liturgy should be in the vernacular, and only one Mass should be celebrated on Sundays. Leopold caused a national synod to be held at Florence in 1787, but he did not find the other bishops as pliant as Scipio de' Ricci. Nevertheless he continued assuming all ecclesiastical authority, prohibited all appeals to the pope, and even appointed bishops, to whom the pope of course refused canonical institution. Finally, the Bull "Auctorem Fidei" was published, in which eighty-five articles taken from the Synod of Pistoia were catalogued and condemned. After the publication of the Bull, Scipio de' Ricci submitted. In 1805 he took occasion of the presence of Pius VII in Florence, on his way to Rome from his exile in France, to ask in person for pardon and reconciliation. He died repentant, 1810, in the Dominican convent of San Marco at Florence.

DENZINGER-STAHL, *Enchiridion Symbolorum et Definit.* (9th ed., Freiburg, 1899), 310–38; POTTER, *Vie et Mémoires de Scipion de' Ricci* (Paris, 1826, favourable to Ricci); SCADERTO, *Stato e Chiesa sotto Leopoldo I* (Florence, 1855); REUMONT, *Geschichte von Toscana,* II, 157 sqq.; GELLI, *Memorie di Scipione de' Ricci* (Florence, 1865); PICOT, *Mémoires pour servir à l'hist eccl. du XVIIIe siècle* (Paris, 1855), V, 251–62, 272–81; VI, 407–15.

M. O'RIORDAN.

Audians. See ANTHROPOMORPHISM.

Audiences, PONTIFICAL, the receptions given by the pope to cardinals, sovereigns, princes, ambassadors, and other persons, ecclesiastical or lay, having business with or interest in the Holy See. Such audiences form an important part of the pope's daily duties. Bishops of every rite in communion with the Holy See, and from every nation, come to Rome, not only to venerate the tombs of the Apostles, but also to consult the supreme pastor of the Church. The master of the chamber (*Maestro di Camera*), whose office corresponds to that of grand chamberlain in royal courts, is the personage to whom all requests for an audience with the pope are made, even those which the ambassadors and other members of the Diplomatic Corps present through the cardinal secretary of state. He is one of the four Palatine Prelates who are in frequent relations with the pope, and his office is regarded as leading to the cardinalate. The pope receives every day the cardinal prefect of one or other of the sacred congregations. At these audiences decrees are signed or counsel given by the pope, and hence, by their very nature, they are of no slight importance to the practical work of the Church. Prelates connected with other institutions either in Rome or abroad, generals and procurators of religious orders, are also received at regular intervals and on stated days. The days and hours of regular audiences are specified on a printed form which is distributed to all cardinals and persons whose duty and privilege it is to have such audience. This printed form is changed every six months, as the hours of audience vary according to the season. Audiences to sovereigns or princes travelling under their own names and titles are invested with special ceremonies. When the pope was a temporal ruler the master of the chamber, notified beforehand by the secretary of state of the proximate arrival in Rome of a sovereign, went, accompanied by the secretary of ceremonial, several miles beyond the city gates to meet him. Returning to Rome, he notified the pope of the event, and visited the sovereign to acquaint him with the day and hour of the pontifical audience. Sovereigns

of the highest rank, being considered as equal to the pope, sit near him during audience, under the same baldachin or canopy. The attendance of guards and chamberlains and court officials is always doubled when such audiences are given. In the ordinary audiences given to priests and lay persons the general practice is that they present a letter of recommendation from the bishop of their diocese, which is presented to the rector of the national college in Rome of the country from which they come. The rector procures from the master of the chamber the necessary card of admission. Amongst the instructions printed on this card are those regulating the dress to be worn on such occasion: for priests the cassock with a large black mantle (*ferraiolone*), such as Roman secular priests wear; for lay men, evening dress with white cravat; for ladies, a black dress with black lace veil on the head. On these occasions it is forbidden to present to the pope for his signature written requests for indulgences, faculties, privileges, or the like. Since the election of Pope Pius X there has been some concession in the matter of dress for the laity in public audience; apparently, in order that every "man of good-will", non-Catholic as well as Catholic, who desires to see the pope may have his wish fulfilled. This has increased the number of persons received in audience, but it has lessened occasions for the pope's utterances on various aspects of the tendencies of the time, which distinguished the audiences of Leo XIII and of the latter years of Pius IX, and which were statements that awakened profound interest.

HUMPHREY, *Urbs et Orbis, or the Pope as Bishop and Pontiff* (London, 1899); *L'Eglise catholique à la fin du XIXe siècle* (Paris, 1900).

P. L. CONNELLAN.

Audiffredi, GIOVANNI BATTISTA, b. at Saorgio, near Nice, in 1734; d. at Rome, July, 1794. He entered the Dominican Order, and soon attracted attention by his taste for books and his talent for the exact sciences. After being occupied in various houses as professor and bibliographer, he was at length transferred to the Dominican house of studies (S. Maria sopra Minerva), and was placed in charge (1765) of the great Bibliotheca Casanatensis, founded in 1700 by Cardinal Girolamo Casanate. Audiffredi published a bibliographical work in four folio volumes entitled "Catalogus bibliothecæ Casanatensis librorum typis impressorum, 1761–1788". The work remains unfinished, not proceeding beyond the letter L, and contains a list of his own publications. Similar works were the "Catalogus historico-criticus Romanarum editionum sæculi XV" (Rome, 1785, quarto), and the more extensively planned "Catalogus historico-criticus editionum Italicarum sæculi XV" (ibid., 1794,), which was to give an account of books printed in twenty-six Italian cities. Audiffredi did not live to complete the work. The first part, extending to the letter G, contains a short biography of the author introduced by the publisher. Audiffredi's position enabled him to become an expert antiquarian, and he found time to cultivate his mathematical talent and to devote himself to astronomy. He built a small observatory, and at intervals busied himself with observation. The eighteenth century was much occupied with the problem of solar parallax. In 1761 and 1769 transits of Venus were observed, and Audiffredi contributed to the work in his publication, "Phænomena cœlestia observata—investigatio parallaxis solis. Exercitatio Dadei Ruffi" (anagram for Audiffredi). The predicted reappearance in the middle of the century of Halley's comet intensified scientific interest in cometic orbits. The epoch was favoured with a number of brilliant objects of this kind, and that of 1769 distinguished itself by its great nucleus and by the tail which stretched over more than half the sky. Audiffredi took observations of the positions of the comet and published his results under the title, "Dimostrazione della stazione della cometa, 1769" (1770). A general taste and capacity for the natural sciences distinguished this learned Dominican, but, like that of many savants, Audiffredi's life was one of retirement and obscurity.

H. De Laak.

Audin, J.-M.-Vincent, b. at Lyons in 1793; d. in Paris, 21 February, 1851. He first studied theology in the seminary of Argentière, and afterwards pursued the study of law. He passed his law examination but never practised his profession, having decided to enter on a literary career. His first publications were: "La lanterne magique" (1811); "Blanc, bleu et rouge" (1814); "Tableau historique des événements qui se sont accomplis depuis le retour de Bonaparte jusqu'au rétablissement de Louis XVIII" (1815). He also contributed to the "Journal de Lyon" founded by Ballanche. He soon left his native city and settled in Paris where he opened a bookstore and at the same time was active with his pen. He first published articles of a political cast, and historical tales in the style of the time, such as "Michel Morin et la Ligue"; "Florence ou la Religieuse"; "Le Régicide", and others. He then took up historical writing, his first work of this kind being "Le Concordat entre Léon X et François Ier" (1821), which is, for the most part, a translation of that document. This was followed by his "Histoire de la St. Barthélemy" (2 vols., 1826). These two works were fairly well received although some ecclesiastical critics accused him of being too favourable to the Protestants. Audin publicly defended himself against this imputation, and asserted his firm belief in the doctrines of the Catholic Church. He now began his most important work, the history of the Protestant Reformation, which he published from 1839 to 1842 in four books, as follows: (1) "Histoire de la vie, des ouvrages et de la doctrine de Luther" (2 vols., Paris, 1839; 2d ed., 3 vols., 1850); (2) "Histoire de la vie, des ouvrages et de la doctrine de Calvin" (2 vols., 1841; 2d ed., 1851); (3) "Histoire de Léon X et de son siècle" (2 vols., 1844; 2d ed., 1851); (4) "Histoire de Henri VIII et du schisme d'Angleterre" (2 vols., 1847; 2d ed., 1862). The author claims to have based his statements upon researches which he made in the archives of various European cities, especially in the archives of the Vatican. The work shows that this assertion cannot be accepted in its entirety. The volumes are written in a romantic manner, and contain many particulars which sober criticism has long proved to be false. Döllinger says of the work on Luther: "Audin's work is written with an extraordinary, and at times almost naïve ignorance of Luther's writings and contemporary literature, and of the general condition of Germany at that period" (Kirchenlex., s. v. Luther).

La Grande Encyclopédie, IV, 611.

J. P. Kirsch.

Audisio, Guglielmo, b. at Bra, Piedmont, Italy, 1801; d. in Rome, 27 September, 1882. He was professor of sacred eloquence in the episcopal seminary of Bra, appointed presiding officer of the Academy of Superga (Turin) by King Charles Albert, but was expelled from this office because he was opposed to the irreligious politics of the Piedmontese Government. He then went to Rome, where Pius IX appointed him professor of natural and popular rights in the Roman University, and Canon of the Vatican Basilica.

Audisio was a pious and charitable priest, and spent large sums in benevolent works. He was an excellent teacher of sacred eloquence, and his manual on the subject was translated into many languages

and frequently quoted approvingly. He also devoted himself to historical studies, especially in illustration of the papacy, bringing to them absolutely good intentions, assiduous industry, and much just and acute observation, such as was not then common in the circle which surrounded him. Nevertheless these historical labours had no great intrinsic value, especially at a time when so large a number of documents were being published. For this reason they are no longer sought after by students.

Audisio had no deep insight into theology and law, and often displayed deplorable lapses on these subjects in his writings and his lectures. At the time of the Vatican Council he was accused of Gallicanism, to the great grief of his patron Pius IX, and his work on political and religious society in the nineteenth century was condemned by the Church. Audisio, however, was profoundly Catholic in feeling, and not only did he fully submit to the condemnation of his book, but he warmly protested against the accusation of heterodoxy and disobedience. He was a fervent upholder of papal and Catholic rights against the political liberalism of Piedmont. He was one of the founders of the Catholic *intransigeant* paper, the "Armonia" of Turin. It was for this reason that he fell a victim to the anti-clerical influence which had deprived him of his post at Superga.

But in Rome Audisio united himself with that clique of liberal Italian ecclesiastics (such as Monsignor Liverani) who advocated reforms and concessions not always just and often premature, and who professed doctrines of little weight, sometimes false, often inexact. In this environment Audisio compromised himself, but his figure remains that of an extremely religious and charitable priest and of an eager student devoted to the Holy See and to the Church. Some pages of his works on the popes still merit consultation.

The works of Audisio are: "Lezioni di Eloquenza Sacra" (several editions); "Juris Naturæ et Gentium et Publica Fundamenta" (Rome, 1852); "Idea storica della diplomazia ecclesiastica" (Rome, 1864); "Storia religiosa e civile dei papi" (5 vols., Rome, 1860); "Sistema politica e religiosa di Federico II e di Pietro della Vigna" (1866); "Della società politica e religiosa rispetto al secolo XIX" (Florence, 1876), condemned by decree of the Holy Office, April, 1877; "Vita di Pio IX".

Nuova Enciclopedia Italiana (Suppl., I, 1889); *Voce della Verità* (Rome, 29 September, 1882).

U. Benigni.

Auditor, the designation of certain officials of the Roman Curia, whose duty it is to hear (Lat. *audire*) and examine the causes submitted to the pope. They cannot, however, give a decision unless they receive delegated jurisdiction. They are, therefore, not judges in the strict sense of the term. These officials have been part of the Roman Curia since the Middle Ages. Amongst the principal dignitaries bearing this title are: (1) *Auditor Papæ*. This official was at first the adviser of the pope in consistorial and theological matters, but he afterwards received also judicial power in civil and criminal cases. Since 1831, however, his duties are restricted to certain ecclesiastical affairs, such as assisting at the examinations of episcopal candidates for Italy and the transaction of matters relating to favours, etc. (2) *Auditor Cameræ* or *Auditor General*. This official originally had very extended powers, such as judging appeals against the decisions of bishops, and proceeding against bishops themselves in important cases and even punishing them without a special commission from the pope. He could also take cognizance of all cases of civil, criminal, and mixed jurisdiction in the States of the Church. Nearly all these and similar powers have now been withdrawn, and the tribunal of the *Camera Apostolica* is at present limited almost entirely to expediting commissions in certain well-defined cases. (3) *Auditors of the Rota* were originally chaplains of the pope. By degrees they were constituted into a tribunal, and are said to have derived their name from the round table (Lat. *rota*) at which they sat. Important cases laid before the Holy See by sovereigns and nations were referred to the Rota for judgment, and its decisions became precedents for all other tribunals. It also served as a supreme court for civil cases in the States of the Church. At present, however, the Auditors of the Rota are restricted practically to giving deliberative opinions in processes of beatification or canonization and deciding questions of precedence between ecclesiastical dignitaries. They are generally also attached as Consultors to various Roman Congregations.

BAART, *The Roman Court* (New York, 1895); FERRARIS, *Prompta Bibl. Can.* (Rome, 1885), I; HUMPHREY, *Urbs et Orbis* (London, 1889).

WILLIAM H. W. FANNING.

Audran, the family name of four generations of distinguished French artists, natives of Paris and Lyons, which included eight prominent engravers and two painters. They flourished in the seventeenth and eighteenth centuries, and some of their productions rank among the finest examples of the art of the burin.

CHARLES, b. in Paris, 1594; d. 1674, was the elder of two brothers, some say cousins (the other being Claude the First), who attained reputation as engravers. Charles, who reached by far the greater eminence, after receiving some instruction in drawing, went as a young man to Rome to study further the engraver's art, and while there produced some plates which attracted attention. He engraved in pure line, and took the work of Cornelius Bloemart, with whom he studied, as his model. On his return from Italy the engraver lived for some years in Lyons before settling in Paris. Among his two hundred or more plates are several original portraits, including one of Henry II, Prince of Condé, and reproductions of works by Titian, the Caracci, Domenichino, Palma the Younger, Albano and Lesueur.

CLAUDE the FIRST, b. in Paris, 1597; d. at Lyons, 1677, studied with Charles, but in his portrait and allegorical plates, which were not many, adopted a somewhat different manner. He became professor of engraving in the Academy of Lyons, and left, to perpetuate his branch of the family and its artistic reputation, three sons: Germain, Claude the Second, and Gérard, the last of whom became the most famous artist among the Audrans.

GERMAIN, the eldest son of Claude the First. b. at Lyons, 1631; d. 1710, was a pupil of his uncle Charles and worked both in Paris and Lyons. Among his plates are portraits of Richelieu and Charles Emmanuel of Savoy (the latter after F. de la Monce), landscapes after Poussin, and fancies and ornamental designs, after Lebrun among others. His four sons were Claude the Third, Benoit the Elder, Jean, and Louis.

CLAUDE the SECOND, son of Claude the First, b. at Lyons, 1639; d. in Paris, 1684, was the first painter in the family. After receiving instruction in drawing from his uncle Charles, he went to study painting in Rome. On his return to Paris he entered the studio of the celebrated historical painter Charles Lebrun, on whose style he formed his own. Audran was Lebrun's assistant in the painting, among others of his works, of the "Battle of Arbela" and the "Passage of the Granicus". He painted in fresco with much skill, under the direction of his master, the grand gallery of the Tuileries, the great staircase at Versailles, and the chapel near by, at Sceaux, of the château of that enlightened patron of art, Prime Minister Colbert.

GÉRARD, third son of Claude the First, b. at Lyons,

1640; d. in Paris, 1703, went to Paris, after being taught engraving by his father and his uncle, to receive instruction from the painter Lebrun, who gave him some of his paintings to reproduce. He worked in Paris four years, and in 1665 went to Rome, where he remained three years and, it is said, became a pupil of Carlo Maratta. He etched as well as engraved, and produced in Rome some plates—notably, a portrait of Pope Clement IX which brought him much admiration. At the suggestion of Colbert, Louis XIV sent for the artist and made him engraver to, and pensioner of the king, with apartments at the factory of the Gobelins. This recognition of his great ability spurred Audran to even greater endeavours, in which he was further encouraged by his former patron, Lebrun, more of whose paintings he reproduced, notably the "Battles of Alexander". In November, 1681, he was made a member of the Council of the Royal Academy of Painting. The first productions of Gérard Audran were stiff and dry, and his subsequent original and vigorously brilliant style is credited to the counsels of Maratta, Ciro Ferri, and, notably, of his lifelong friend Lebrun. A second visit to Rome was made, where was signed the plate after "The Four Cardinal Virtues", by Domenichino, which is in the church of San Carlo ai Catinari. Among the original works of this famous engraver are the portrait of the Rospigliosi Pope, already alluded to, those of Samuele Sorbiere, Andrea Argoli of Padua, the Capuchin Benoit Langlois, the Bishop of Angers Henri Arnauld, and the sculptor François du Quesnoy, called Fiamingo, "Wisdom and Abundance above two Genii", and the vignette, "St. Paul preaching at Athens". Particularly esteemed among the plates of Gérard Audran are two after cartoons of Raphael "The death of Ananias" and "Paul and Barnabas at Lystra", "The Martyrdom of St. Agnes", after Domenichino, and "Coriolanus" after Poussin. Among the other painters whose works he reproduced are Titian, Rubens, Giulio Romano, Annibale Caracci, Pietro da Cortona, Guercino, Guido Reni, Palma the Younger, Lanfranco, Mignard, Coypel, Lesueur, Bourguignon, Lafage, and Girardon. He was at times assisted by his nephews, Benoit the Elder and Jean. In 1683 Gérard published a work called "The Proportions of the Human Body measured by the most Beautiful Figures of Antiquity", which has been translated into English.

CLAUDE the THIRD, son of Germain, and the second painter of the family, b. at Lyons, 1658; d. in Paris, 1734, was notable as being the master of the famous Watteau. He studied with his father as well as under his uncles, Germain and Claude the Second. Chosen cabinet painter to the king, he was also for nearly thirty years keeper of the palace of the Luxembourg, where he died. He executed considerable work in oil and fresco in various royal residences.

BENOIT the ELDER, third son of Germain, b. at Lyons, 1661; d. 1721, in the vicinity of Sens, was first taught the family art by his father and then by his uncle Gérard. He made an excellent reputation by his reproduction of portraits and historical works. Among his best productions are "The Seven Sacraments", after Poussin, and "The Bronze Serpent", after Lebrun. He became a Member of the Academy and engraver to the king.

JEAN, fourth son of Germain, b. at Lyons, 1667; d. 1756, became, next to his celebrated uncle Gérard, the best engraver of the family. He studied first under his father and then with his uncle. He had already distinguished himself at the early age of twenty. He was rewarded for his subsequent successes by being made (in 1707) engraver to the king, with the regular pension and the Gobelin apartments. This was followed next year by membership in the Academy. Jean Audran worked until he was eighty. His masterpiece is considered to be "The Rape of the Sabines", after Poussin. Among his plates are portraits after Gobert—those of Louis XV, Vandyke, Coypel, Largillière, Rigaud, Trevisani, and Vivien—and compositions after, among others, Raphael, Rubens, the Caracci, Guido Reni, Domenichino, Pietro da Cortona, Albano, Maratta, Philippe de Champagne, Marot, Poussin, and Nattier. His son was Benoit the Younger.

Louis, the youngest son of Germain, b. at Lyons, 1670; d. in Paris, c. 1712, studied with his father and his uncle Gérard. He assisted his brothers, and did few original plates. A work of his to be noted is "The Seven Acts of Mercy", after Bourdon.

Benoit the Younger, b. in Paris, 1698; d. in the same place, 1772, was the last of the remarkable family to have any historical importance artistically. He was a pupil of his father and did plates after, among others, Veronese, Poussin, Watteau, Lancret, and Natoire.

Prosper Gabriel, a grandson of Jean, b. in Paris, 1744; d. 1819; he studied with his uncle, Benoit the Younger, and etched some heads. He gave up art for the law and became professor of Hebrew in the Collège de France.

Duplessis, *Les Audran;* Bryan, *Dictionary of Painters and Engravers.*

AUGUSTUS VAN CLEEF.

Auenbrugger (or von Auenbrugg), Leopold, an Austrian physician, b. 19 Nov., 1722; d. 17 May, 1807. He was the inventor of percussion in physical diagnosis and is considered one of the small group of men to whose original genius modern medicine owes its present position. He was a native of Graz in Styria, an Austrian province. His father, a hotel-keeper, gave his son every opportunity for an excellent preliminary education in his native town and then sent him to Vienna to complete his studies at the university. Auenbrugger was graduated as a physician at the age of twenty-two and then entered the Spanish Military Hospital of Vienna where he spent ten years. His observations and experimental studies enabled him to discover that by tapping on the chest with the finger much important information with regard to diseased conditions within the chest might be obtained.

Ordinarily, the lungs when percussed, give a sound like a drum over which a heavy cloth has been placed. When the lung is consolidated, as in pneumonia, then the sound produced by the tapping of the finger is the same as when the fleshy part of the thigh is tapped. Auenbrugger found that the area over the heart gave a modified, dull sound, and that in this way the limits of heart-dullness could be determined. This gave the first definite information with regard to pathological changes in the heart. During his ten years of patient study, Auenbrugger confirmed these observations by comparison with post-mortem specimens, and besides made a number of experimental researches on dead bodies. He injected fluid into the pleural cavity, and showed that it was perfectly possible by percussion to tell exactly the limits of the fluid present, and thus to decide when and where efforts should be made for its removal.

His later studies during this ten-year period were devoted to tuberculosis. He pointed out how to detect cavities of the lungs, and how their location and size might be determined by percussion. He also recognized that information with regard to the contents of cavities in the lungs, and the conditions of lung tissue might be obtained by placing the hand on the chest and noting the vibration, or *fremitus,* produced by the voice and the breath. These observations were published in a little book now considered one of the most important classics of medicine. It was called "Inventum Novum", the full English

title running, "A New Discovery that Enables the Physician from the Percussion of the Human Thorax to Detect the Diseases Hidden Within the Chest".

Like most medical discoveries, Auenbrugger's method of diagnosis at first met with neglect. Before his death, however, it had aroused the attention of Laennec, who, following up the ideas suggested by it, discovered auscultation. Since then, Auenbrugger has been considered one of the great founders of modern medicine. He lived to a happy old age, especially noted for his cordial relations with the younger members of his profession, and for his kindness to the poor and to those suffering from tuberculosis. He is sometimes said to have died in the typhus epidemic of 1798, but the burial register of the parish church in Vienna, of which he had been for half a century a faithful member, shows that he did not die until 1807.

Leopold Auenbrugger, *Jahresb. d. Ver. d. Aertzte in Steiermark* (Graz, 1866); Merbach Auenbrugger, *Jahresb. der Gesellschaft für Natur und Heilkunde* (Dresden, 1863); Walsh, *Makers of Modern Medicine* (New York, 1907).

JAMES J. WALSH.

Aufsees, Jobst Bernhard von, canon of Bamberg and Würzburg, b. 28 March, 1671, on the family estate of Mengersdorf; d. 2 April, 1738. He was baptized a Lutheran, but educated (1683–90) as a Catholic through the efforts of his uncle Carl Sigmund, canon of Bamberg and Würzburg. He was soon advanced to the same dignity in both churches, was provost of Bamberg in 1723, and held other offices of distinction in both cities. After 1709 he devoted the revenues of his benefices to the establishment of a house of studies at Bamberg: in 1728 he bestowed upon it the sum of 400,000 gulden (about $200,000). This Aufsees Seminary, or Institute, was destined for the reception of poor boys from the Dioceses of Bamberg and Würzburg. They were to be supported there during the entire time of their studies at the public academies. He originally intended to place the Jesuits in charge, but by his last will (17 February, 1738) turned it over to the care of the cathedral chapters of Bamberg and Würzburg. It was opened in 1741, and continued its beneficent career until the beginning of the nineteenth century, when the secularization of the property of the ecclesiastical principalities took place. The edifice was then turned over to the hospital for incurables, and the revenues applied in part to scholarships (*Stipendien*). King Ludwig I reopened it as a house of studies (*Königliches Studienseminar*) under governmental supervision. The director and the prefects are priests, but the Government appoints holders of the 42 free places and the 20 places for youths who pay, also the officers of the institute, and administers its revenues.

Wittmann in *Kirchenlex.*, I, 1615.

THOMAS J. SHAHAN.

Auger, Edmond, b. 1530, near Troyes; d. at Como, Italy, 31 January, 1591, one of the great figures in the stormy times in France, when the Calvinists were striving to get possession of the throne. He entered the Society of Jesus while St. Ignatius was still living, and was regarded as one of the most eloquent men of his time. Mathieu calls him the "Chrysostom of France". Wherever he went, throngs flocked to hear him, and the heretics themselves were always eager to be present, captivated as they were by the charm of his wisdom and the delicacy of his courtesy in their regard. His entrance into France as a priest was in the city of Valence, where the bishop had just apostatized, and the Calvinists were then in possession. The efforts of Auger to address the people were followed by his being seized and sentenced to be burned to death. While standing on the pyre, he harangued the multitude, and so won their good will that they asked for his deliverance. Viret, especially, the chief orator of the Calvinists, wanted to have a public discussion with him to convert him. Auger was consequently sent to prison for the night, but the Catholics rescued him before the conference took place. We find him afterwards in Lyons, during a pestilence, devoting himself to the plague-stricken. When the pest had ceased, in consequence of a vow he made, the authorities, in gratitude, established a college of the Society to which Auger asked, much to their astonishment, that the children of the Calvinists might be admitted. His whole life was one of constant activity, preaching and administering the responsible offices of Provincial, Rector, etc. that were entrusted to him. He was present in at least two battles, and was remarkable for his influence over the soldiers. He was finally made confessor of King Henry III, the first Jesuit to have that troublesome charge put upon him. The difficulty of his position was increased by the fact that the League was just then being formed by the Catholic succession. Its principles and methods were thought to trench on the royal prerogative; but Sixtus V was in favour of it. Several Jesuits, notably the Provincial, Mathieu, who was deposed by Acquaviva, were its stanch upholders. Auger's position was intolerable. Loyal to the king, he was detested by the leaguers, who at Lyons, the city that he had saved, threatened to throw him into the Rhone. They compromised by expelling him from the city. The general commanded him to relinquish the post of confessor, but the king secured the pope's order for him to stay. Finally, Auger prevailed on the monarch to release him, and he withdrew to Como in Italy, where he died. Shortly afterwards Henry was assassinated. Like Canisius in Germany, Auger published a Catechism for France. It appeared at first in Latin, and later he published it in Greek. He wrote a work on the Blessed Eucharist, instructions for soldiers, translations, some literary compositions, and also drew up the statutes for congregations, especially one in which the king was interested, called the Congregation of Penitents. There is a letter by him called "Spiritual Sugar", though he did not give it that title. He had written an address to the people of Toulouse to console them in the distress brought on by the calamities of the civil war. It so took the popular fancy that the authorities of the city published it under this curious caption.

CRÉTINEAU-JOLY, *Histoire de la c. de J.*, II; SOMMERVOGEL, *Bibliothèque de la c. de J.*, I, 632: *Varones ilustres*, V.

T. J. CAMPBELL.

Augilæ, or AUGILA, a titular see of Cyrenaica in Northern Africa. It was situated in an oasis in the Libyan desert which is still one of the chief stations (Audjelah, Aoudjila) on the caravan route from Cairo to Fezzan. Its forests of date-palms were famous in the time of Herodotus (IV, 172); they still crown the three small hills that rise out of an unbroken desert of red sand which in the near vicinity is strongly impregnated with salts of soda. The Moslem population is now about 10,000 and is governed by an official of the Bey of Tripoli who draws from the oasis an annual revenue of $12,000.

LEQUIEN, *Oriens Christ.* (1740), II, 635–638; SMITH, *Dict. of Greek and Roman Geogr.*, I, 337; ST. JOHN, *Adventures in the Libyan Desert* (London, 1861), 128, 133.

THOMAS J. SHAHAN.

Augsburg, CONFESSION OF. See CONFESSIONS OF FAITH, PROTESTANT.

Augsburg, DIOCESE OF, in the Kingdom of Bavaria, Germany, suffragan of the Archdiocese of Munich-Freising, embracing the entire government district of Swabia and Neuburg, the western part

of the government district of Upper Bavaria, and a small part of the government district of Central Franconia.

I. HISTORY. (1) *Early Period.*—The present city of Augsburg appears in Strabo as Damasia, a stronghold of the Licatii; in 14 B. C. it became a Roman colony known as Augusta Vindelicorum, received the rights of a city from Hadrian and soon became of great importance as an arsenal and the point of junction of several important trade routes. The beginnings of Christianity within the limits of the present diocese are shrouded in obscurity; its teachings were probably brought thither by soldiers or merchants. According to the acts of the martyrdom of St. Afra, who with her handmaids suffered at the stake for Christ, there existed in Augsburg, early in the fourth century, a Christian community under Bishop Narcissus; St. Dionysius, uncle of St. Afra, is mentioned as his successor.

(2) *Medieval Period.*—Nothing authentic is known about the history of the Augsburg Church during the

SOUTH DOOR OF THE CATHEDRAL, AUGSBURG

centuries immediately succeeding, but it survived the collapse of Roman power in Germany and the turbulence of the great migrations. It is true that two catalogues of the Bishops of Augsburg, dating from the eleventh and twelfth centuries, mention several bishops of this primitive period, but the first whose record has received indubitable historical corroboration is St. Wikterp (or Wichpert) who was bishop about 739 or 768. He took part in several synods convened by St. Boniface in Germany; in company with St. Magnus, he founded the monastery of Füssen; and with St. Boniface he dedicated the monastery at Benediktbeuren. Under either St. Wikterp or his successor, Tazzo (or Tozzo), about whom little is known, many monasteries were established, e. g. Wessobrunn, Ellwangen, Polling, Ottobeuren. At this time, also, the see, hitherto suffragan to the Patriarchate of Aquileia, was placed among the suffragan sees of the newly founded Archdiocese of Mainz (746). St. Sintpert (c. 810), hitherto Abbot of the monastery of Murbach, and a relative of Charlemagne, renovated many churches and monasteries laid waste in the wars of the Franks and Bavarians, and during the incursions of the Avari; he built the first cathedral of Augsburg in honour of the Most Blessed Virgin; and obtained from the Emperor Charlemagne an exact definition of his diocesan limits. His jurisdiction extended at that time from the Iller eastward over the Lech, north of the Danube to the Alb, and south to the spurs of the Alps. Moreover, various estates and villages in the valley of the Danube, and in the Tyrol, belonged to the diocese. Among the bishops of the following period a certain number are especially prominent, either on account of the offices they filled in the Empire, or for their personal qualifications; thus Witgar (887-87), Chancellor and Archchaplain of Louis the German; Adalbero (887 -910), of the line of the Counts of Dillingen, confidant and friend of Emperor Arnulf, who entrusted Adalbero with the education of his son, the German King Louis the Child, distinguished for generosity to the monasteries. The See of Augsburg reached the period of its greatest splendour under St. Ulrich (923-973); he raised the standard of training and discipline among the clergy by the reformation of existing schools and the establishment of new ones, and by canonical visitations and synods; he provided for the poor, and rebuilt decayed churches and monasteries. During the incursion of the Hungarians and the siege of Augsburg (955), he sustained the courage of the citizens, compelled the Hungarians to withdraw, and contributed much to the decisive victory on the Lechfeld (955). He built churches in honour of St. Afra and St. John, founded the monastery of St. Stephen for Benedictine nuns, and undertook three pilgrimages to Rome. The diocese suffered much during the episcopate of his successor, Henry I (973-982), for he sided with the foes of Emperor Otto II, and remained for several months in prison. After his liberation he renounced his former views and bequeathed to his church his possessions at Geisenhausen. The diocese attained great splendour under Bishop Bruno (1006-29), brother of Emperor Henry II; he restored a number of ruined monasteries, founded the church and college of St. Maurice, placed Benedictine monks in the collegiate church of St. Afra, and added to the episcopal possessions by the gift of his own inheritance of Straubing. Under Bishop Henry II (1047-63), the guardian of Henry IV, the diocese secured the right of coinage and was enriched by many donations; under Embrico (or Emmerich, 1063-77) the cathedral was dedicated (1065), and the canonicate and church of St. Peter and St. Felicitas were built. During the last years of this episcopate occurred the quarrel of Emperor Henry IV with the papacy in which Embrico took the imperial side and only temporarily yielded to the papal legate. The struggle continued under his successors; four anti-bishops were set up in opposition to Siegfried II (1077-96). Hermann, Count von Vohburg (1096 or 1097-1132) supported with treachery and cunning his claim to the see he had purchased, violently persecuted the Abbot of St. Afra, and expelled him from the city. Only after the conclusion of the Concordat of Worms (1122) did Hermann obtain the confirmation of the pope and relief from excommunication. The political disturbances resulting from the dissensions between the popes and the German emperors reacted on the Church of Augsburg. There were short periods of rest, during which ecclesiastical life received a forward impulse, as, for instance, under Bishop Walther II, Count Palatine von Dillingen (1133-52), under whom the possessions of the diocese were again consolidated and increased by his own inheritance; under Udalskalk (1184-1202), who with great ceremony placed the recently discovered bones of St. Ulrich in the new church of Sts. Ulrich and Afra. These days of peace alternated with

periods of conflict into which the Bishops of Augsburg were drawn, often against their will, in their capacity as Princes of the Empire, and the life of the Church accordingly suffered decline. Under Siboto von Lechfeld (1227-47) monasteries of the newly founded mendicant orders were first established in Augsburg. A celebrated member of the Franciscans was David of Augsburg, and of the Dominicans, Albertus Magnus of Lauingen. Additional causes of conflict were the troubles that arose between the Bishops of Augsburg and the city authorities. During the struggles between the popes and emperors, Augsburg, like other large cities throughout the greater part of Germany, attained enormous wealth, owing to the industrial and commercial activity of the citizens. From time to time efforts were made to restrict as much as possible the ancient civil rights of the bishops and their stewards, and even to abrogate them entirely. From a state of discontent the citizens passed to open violence under the Bishop Hartmann von Dillingen (1248-86), and wrung from the bishops many municipal liberties and advantages. A characteristic instance is the confirmation by Emperor Rudolph of Habsburg at the Reichstag held in Augsburg (1276) of the *Stadtbuch*, or municipal register, containing the ancient customs, episcopal and municipal rights, etc., specified in detail; on the same occasion Augsburg was recognized as a Free City of the Empire. Hartmann bequeathed to the Church of Augsburg his paternal inheritance, including the town and castle of Dillingen. Peace reigned under the succeeding bishops, of whom Frederick I (1309-31) acquired for his see the castle and stronghold of Füssen; Ulrich II, von Schöneck (1331-37), and his brother Henry III (1337-48) remained faithful to Emperor Louis the Bavarian; Markward I, von Randeck (1348-65), again redeemed the mortgaged property of the diocese, and by the favour of Emperor Charles IV was made Patriarch of Aquileia (1365). New dissensions between the Bishop and the city arose under Burkhard von Ellerbach (1373-1404), whose accession was marked by grave discord growing out of the overthrow of the *Patrizier*, or aristocratic government, and the rise in municipal power of the crafts or guilds. Irritated by Burkhard's support of the nobility in their struggle with the Swabian cities, the inhabitants of Augsburg plundered the dwellings of the canons, drove some of the clergy from the city (1381), destroyed, after a short interval of respite (1388), the episcopal stronghold, the deanery, and the mint, and became almost completely independent of the bishop. Burkhard proceeded with great energy against the heresy of the Wyclifites who had gained a foothold in Augsburg, and condemned to the stake five persons who refused to abjure. After the death of Eberhard II (1404-13), a quarrel arose in 1413 because the city of Augsburg declined to recognize the lawful Bishop, Anselm von Nenningen (1413-23), and set up in opposition Friedrich von Grafeneck who had been presented by Emperor Sigismund. This trouble was settled by Pope Martin V, who compelled both bishops to resign, and on his own authority replaced them by Peter von Schauenberg, Canon of Bamberg and Würzburg (1423-69).

Peter was endowed by the Pope with extraordinary faculties, made cardinal and legate *a latere* for all Germany. He worked with zeal and energy for the reformation of his diocese, held synods and made episcopal visitations in order to raise the decadent moral and intellectual life of the clergy; he restored the discipline and renewed the fallen splendour of many monasteries, canonries, and collegiate churches. He completed the rebuilding of the cathedral in Gothic style, consecrated it in 1431, and in 1457 laid the cornerstone of the new church of Sts. Ulrich and Afra. Succeeding prelates carried on the reformation of the diocese with no less solicitude and zeal.

Among them were Johann II, Count of Werdenberg (1469–86), tutor to the emperor's son, afterwards Emperor Maximilian I, who convened a synod in Dillingen, and encouraged the recently invented art of printing; Friedrich von Zollern (1486–1505) pupil of the great preacher Geiler von Kaysersberg, and founder of a college in Dillingen, who held a synod in the same city, promoted the printing of liturgical books, and greatly enriched the possessions of the diocese; Henry IV, von Lichtenau (1505–17), a great friend and benefactor of monasteries and of the poor, and patron of the arts and sciences. During the episcopate of these bishops Augsburg acquired, through the industry of its citizens, a world-wide commerce. Some members of its families, e. g. the Fuggers and the Welsers, were the greatest merchants of their time; they lent large sums of money to the emperors and princes of Germany, conducted the financial enterprises of the papacy, and even extended their operations to the newly discovered continent of America. Among the citizens of Augsburg famous at that time in literature and art were the humanist Conrad Peutinger; the brothers Bernard and Conrad Adelmann von Adelmannsfelden; Matthias Lang, secretary to Emperor Frederick III, and later Cardinal and Archbishop of Salzburg; the distinguished painters Holbein the elder, Burgkmair and others. With wealth, however, came a spirit of worldliness and cupidity. Pride and a super-refinement of culture furnished the rank soil in which the impending religious revolution was to find abundant nourishment.

(3) *Reformation Period.*—The Reformation brought disaster on the Diocese of Augsburg. It included 1,050 parishes with more than 500,000 inhabitants. Besides the cathedral chapter it could boast eight collegiate foundations, forty-six monasteries for men, and thirty-eight convents for women. Luther, who was summoned to vindicate himself in the presence of the papal legate before the Reichstag at Augsburg (1518), found enthusiastic adherents in this diocese among both the secular and regular clergy, but especially among the Carmelites, in whose convent of St. Anne he dwelt; he also found favour among the city councillors, burgers, and tradesmen. Bishop Christopher von Stadion (1517–43) did all in his power to arrest the spread of the new teachings; he called learned men to the pulpit of the cathedral, among others Urbanus Rhegius, who, however, soon went over to Luther; he convened a synod at Dillingen, at which it was forbidden to read Luther's writings; he promulgated throughout his diocese the Bull of Leo X (1520) against Luther; he forbade the Carmelites, who were spreading the new doctrine, to preach; he warned the magistrates of Augsburg, Memmingen, and other places not to tolerate the reformers, and he adopted other similar measures. Despite all this, the followers of Luther obtained the upper hand in the city council, and by 1524, various Catholic ecclesiastical usages, notably the observance of fast days, had been abolished in Augsburg. The apostate priests, many of whom, after Luther's example, had taken wives, were supported by the city council, and the Catholics were denied the right of preaching. The Anabaptists also gained a strong following and added fuel to the fire of the Peasants' War, in which many monasteries, institutions, and castles were destroyed. At the Diet of Augsburg in 1530, at which the so-called Augsburg Confession was delivered to Emperor Charles V in the chapel of the episcopal palace, the emperor issued an edict according to which all innovations were to be abolished, and Catholics reinstated in their rights and property. The city council, however, set itself up in opposition, recalled (1531) the Protestant preachers who had been expatriated, suppressed Catholic services in all churches except the cathedral (1534), and

in 1537 joined the League of Smalkald. At the beginning of this year a decree of the council was made, forbidding everywhere the celebration of Mass, preaching, and all ecclesiastical ceremonies, and giving to the Catholic clergy the alternative of enrolling themselves anew as citizens or leaving the city. An overwhelming majority of both secular and regular clergy chose banishment; the bishop withdrew with the cathedral chapter to Dillingen, whence he addressed to the pope and the emperor an appeal for the redress of his grievances. In the city of Augsburg the Catholic churches were seized by Lutheran and Zwinglian preachers; at the command of the council pictures were removed, and at the instigation of Bucer and others a disgraceful storm of popular iconoclasm followed, resulting in the destruction of many splendid monuments of art and antiquity. The greatest intolerance was exercised towards the Catholics who had remained in the city; their schools were dissolved; parents were compelled to send their children to Lutheran institutions; it was even forbidden to hear Mass outside the city under severe penalties.

Under Otto Truchsess von Waldburg (1543–73) the first signs of improvement were noted in the attitude towards Catholics. At the outbreak of hostilities (1546) between the emperor and the League of Smalkald, Augsburg, as a member of the league, took up arms against Charles V, and Bishop Otto invested and plundered Füssen, and confiscated nearly all the remaining possessions of the diocese. After the victory at Mühlberg (1547), however, the imperial troops marched against Augsburg, and the city was forced to beg for mercy, surrender twelve pieces of artillery, pay a fine, restore the greater number of churches to the Catholics, and reimburse the diocese and the clergy for the property confiscated. In 1547 the Bishop, Otto von Truchsess, who had meanwhile been created cardinal, returned to the city with the cathedral chapter, followed shortly afterwards by the emperor. At the Diet held at Augsburg in 1548 the so-called "Augsburg Interim" was arranged. After a temporary occupation of the city and the suppression of Catholic services by the Elector, Prince Maurice of Saxony (1552), the "Religious Peace of Augsburg" was concluded at the Diet of 1555; it was followed by a long period of peace. The disturbances of the Reformation were more disastrous in their results throughout the diocese and adjoining lands than within the immediate precincts of Augsburg. Thus, after many perturbations and temporary restorations of the Catholic religion, the Protestants finally gained the upper hand in Würtemberg, Oettingen, Neuburg, the free cities of Nördlingen, Memmingen, Kaufbeuren, Dinkelsbühl, Donauwörth, Ulm, in the ecclesiastical territory of Feuchtwangen and elsewhere. Altogether during these years of religious warfare the Diocese of Augsburg lost to the Reformation about 250 parishes, 24 monasteries, and over 500 benefices. Although the religious upheaval brought with it a great loss of worldly possessions, it was not without beneficial effect on the religious life of the diocese. Bishop Christopher von Stadion, while trying to protect Catholicism from the inroads of the Reformation, had sought to strengthen and revive ecclesiastical discipline, which had sadly declined, among both the secular and the regular clergy. The work was carried on even more energetically by Bishop Otto Truchsess, who achieved a fruitful counter-reformation. By frequent visitations he sought to become familiar with existing evils, and by means of diocesan synods and a vigorous enforcement of measures against ignorant and dissolute clerics, secular and regular, he endeavoured to remedy these conditions. He advanced the cause of education by founding schools; he summoned the Jesuits to his diocese, among others Blessed

Peter Canisius, who from 1549, in the capacity of cathedral preacher, confessor, and catechist, exercised a remarkably fruitful and efficacious ministry. In 1549 Bishop Otto founded a seminary in Dillingen for the training of priests, obtained from the pope (1554) a decree raising it to the rank of a university, and in 1564 gave the direction of the new university to the Jesuits, for whom he had built a college in Dillingen. It is due to his untiring labours and those of Canisius that much larger portions of the diocese were not lost to the Church. Under the immediate successors of Otto the revival instituted by him progressed rapidly, and many excellent decrees were formulated. Under Marquard II von Berg (1575–91) a pontifical boarding school (*alumnatus*) was founded in Dillingen, colleges were established by the Jesuits in Landsberg, and, through the bounty of the Fugger family, in Augsburg (1580). Heinrich von Knöringen, made bishop at the early age of twenty-eight, took especial interest in the University and the Seminary of Dillingen, both of which he enriched with many endowments; he convened several synods, converted Duke Wolfgang of Neuburg to Catholicism, and during his long episcopate (1598–1646) reconciled many Protestant cities and parishes to the Catholic Church, being aided in a particular manner by the Jesuits, for whom he founded establishments in Neuburg, Memmingen, and Kaufbeuren. By means of the Edict of Restitution of Emperor Ferdinand II (1629), vigorously and even too forcefully executed by the bishop, the Thirty Years' War first accomplished an almost complete restoration of the former possessions of the Diocese of Augsburg. The occupation of Augsburg by Gustavus Adolphus of Sweden (1632) restored temporarily the balance of power to the Protestants. Until the relief of the city by the imperial troops (1635) the Catholics were hard pressed and were forced to give up all they had gained by the Edict of Restitution. Finally, the Treaty of Westphalia (1648) established equality between Catholics and Protestants, and was followed by a long period of internal peace. On account of the losses entailed on the diocese by the treaty, a solemn protest was laid before the imperial chancery by Bishop Sigmund Franz, Archduke of Austria (1646–65). This bishop, on account of his youth, ruled the diocese through administrators, and later resigned his office. His successor, Johann Christopher von Freiberg (1665–90), was particularly desirous of liquidating the heavy burden of debt borne by the chapter, but was nevertheless generous towards churches and monasteries. His successor, Alexander Sigmund (1690–1737), son of the Palatine Elector, guarded the purity of doctrine in liturgical books and prayerbooks. Johann Friedrich von Stauffenberg (1737–40) founded the Seminary of Meersburg and introduced missions among the people. Joseph, Landgrave of Hesse-Darmstadt (1740–68) exhumed with great ceremony the bones of St. Ulrich and instituted an investigation into the life of Crescentia Höss of Kaufbeuren, who had died in the odour of sanctity. Klemens Wenzeslaus, Prince of Saxony and Poland (1768–1812), made a great number of excellent disciplinary regulations, and took measures for their execution; after the suppression of the Society of Jesus he afforded its members protection and employment in his diocese; he made a vigorous resistance to the rapidly spreading Rationalism and infidelity, and was honoured by a visit from Pope Pius VI (1782).

(4) *French Revolution and Secularization.*—During this episcopate began the world-wide upheaval inaugurated by the French Revolution. It was destined to put an end to the temporal power of the Church in Germany, and to bring about the fall of Augsburg from the dignity of a principality of the Empire. In 1802, by act of the Delegation of the Imperial Diet (*Reichsdeputationsrezess*), the territory of the Diocese of Augsburg was given to the Elector of Bavaria, who took possession 1 December, 1802. The cathedral chapter, together with forty canonicates, forty-one benefices, nine colleges, twenty-five abbeys, thirty-four monasteries of the mendicant orders, and two convents were the victims of this act of secularization. Unfortunately, owing to the inconsiderate conduct of the commissioners appointed by the Bavarian minister, Montgelas, innumerable artistic treasures, valuable books, and documents were destroyed. For five years after the death of the last bishop of princely rank (1812) the episcopal see remained vacant; and the parts of the diocese lying outside of Bavaria were separated from it and annexed to other dioceses. It was not until 1817 that the Concordat between the Holy See and the Bavarian government reconstructed the Diocese of Augsburg, and made it subject to the Metropolitan of Munich-Freising. In 1821 the territory subject to the ecclesiastical authority of Augsburg was increased by the addition of sections of the suppressed See of Constance, and the present limits were then defined.

(5) *The Nineteenth Century.*—As the new bishop, Franz Karl von Hohenlohe-Schillingsfürst, died (1819) before assuming office, and Joseph Maria von Fraunberg was soon called to the archiepiscopal See of Bamberg, there devolved upon their successors the important task of rearranging the external conditions and reanimating religious life, which had suffered sorely. Ignatius Albert von Riegg (1824–36) was successful in his endeavours to further the interests of souls, to raise the standard of popular education through the medium of numerous ordinances and frequent visitations. He assigned the administration and direction of studies in the Lyceum to the monks of the Benedictine Abbey of St. Stephen in Augsburg, founded by King Ludwig (1834). Petrus von Richarz (1837–55) displayed energy and persistent zeal in promoting the interests of his diocese and the Catholic Church in general, and encouraged the giving of missions to the people, the establishment of many religious institutions for the care of the sick and for educational purposes, and carefully superintended the training of the clergy. The same spirit characterized the labours of the succeeding bishops: Michael von Deinlein (1856–58), who after a short episcopate was raised to the Archbishopric of Bamberg; Pankratius von Dinkel (1858–94), under whom both seminaries and the deaf and dumb asylum were established in Dillingen, and many monastic institutions were founded; Petrus von Hötzl (1895–1902) whose episcopate was marked by the attention paid to social and intellectual pursuits, and the number of missions given among the people as well as by the solemn celebration of the beatification of the pious nun Crescentia Höss. He was succeeded by Maximilian von Lingg, b. at Nesselwang, 8 March, 1842; ordained priest, 22 July, 1865; appointed bishop, 18 March, 1902, consecrated, 20 July, 1902.

II. RELIGIOUS STATISTICS.—According to the census of 1 December, 1900, the Diocese of Augsburg contained 777,958 Catholics and about 100,000 of other beliefs; at present there are about 818,074 Catholics. Socially, the population is chiefly of the middle class; recently, however, on account of the great growth of the industrial arts in the city of Augsburg, in Lechhausen, Memmingen, and other places, the working classes are increasing in numbers. Leaving out of consideration the larger cities, in which the various denominations are well represented, it may be said that the southern part of the diocese, Algäu and the adjoining parts of Altbayern (Bavaria proper), are almost entirely Catholic, while in the northern part a mixture of creeds predominates. That small portion of Mittelfranken (Central Franconia) which belongs to the diocese is overwhelmingly Protestant. The relations between the various religious denominations are in general friendly and peaceable. For the work of sacred ministry the diocese is divided into 40 deaneries (1 city deanery at Augsburg, and 39 rural deaneries), with 862 parishes, 31 parochial curacies, 16 curacies, 226 benefices, 6 preaching-offices (*Prädikaturen*), 227 chaplaincies. In general each parish is complete and independent, but in the mountainous southern section there are many parishes to which are attached from fifty to a hundred dependent churches (*Filialkirchen*). The cathedral chapter consists of the provost of the cathedral, a dean of the cathedral, 8 canons, and 6 vicars. In 1907 the clergy of the diocese numbered 1,439: 815 parish priests and parochial curates, 49 parochial vicars, 11 curates, 73 beneficed clergymen, 53 vicars of benefices, 180 chaplains and assistant priests, 49 prebendaries and clerical professors (not including the professors of the Benedictine Abbey of St. Stephen in Augsburg); 74 priests temporarily stationed in the diocese, 95 regulars, 40 priests engaged in other dioceses or on missions. Of the religious orders of men there are the following establishments: Benedictines, 3 (Augsburg, Andechs, Ottobeuren), with 33 priests, 6 clerics, 56 lay brothers; Mission Society of St. Benedict, 1 (St. Ottilien), with 36 priests (12 at present outside the diocese), 31 clerics, 117 lay brothers; Franciscans, 3, with 7 priests and 22 lay brothers; Capuchins, 5, with 28 priests, 18 clerics, and 37 lay brothers; Brothers of Mercy, 6, with 4 priests and 54 lay brothers. Altogether there are 18 establishments conducted by the male orders, with 108 priests, 55 clerics, and 286 lay brothers. Far more numerous are the female orders and religious congregations; they number 226 establishments and branches, with 2,815 members. They are: Sisters of Mercy of St. Vincent de Paul, 59 houses, with 392 sisters; Franciscans, with their mother-houses at Augsburg, Dillingen, Kaufbeuren, and Mindelheim, 71 establishments, with 735 sisters; *Arme Franziskanerinnen* with mother-house at Mallersdorf, 34 establishments, with 171 sisters; *Englische Fräulein* (English Ladies), 11 convents with 311 ladies, 160 lay sisters, and 43 novices; Dominican nuns, 11 convents with 271 choir sisters, 17 lay sisters, and 36 novices; Poor School Sisters, 21 foundations with 166 sisters, *Elisabetherinnen* (Sisters of St. Elizabeth), 4 foundations with 41 sisters and 5 novices; Sisters of the Most Holy Redeemer with their mother-house at Oberbronn in Alsace, 61 foundations with 24 sisters; Cistercian nuns, 1 convent with 29 choir nuns, 15 lay sisters, and 2 novices; Mission Sisters of St. Benedict, 1 convent with 65 sisters and 9 novices; Sisters of St. Joseph of Ursberg, 7 foundations with 231 sisters and 92 novices.

III. EDUCATION.—As the primary schools in Bavaria are the property of the local civic corporation and under State control, there are no parochial schools in the strict sense of the word. According to the Bavarian Constitution of 1818 nothing more is assured to the Church than the direction of religious instruction and the surveillance of religious life in the school. She exercises this right in 1,074 primary schools of the Diocese of Augsburg, by means of 6 ecclesiastical county (*Bezirk*) school-inspectors and 50 ecclesiastical district school-inspectors. However, in many of the girls' schools (*Mädchenschulen*) the direction of studies is confined entirely to religious societies under State inspection. Thus the Poor School Sisters have charge of the studies in 19 schools, the Franciscans in 35, the Dominican nuns in 11, the Sisters of St. Joseph of Ursberg in 3; the English Ladies are excellent teachers for the higher education of women, and conduct 11 institutes for girls. For the training of priests there are the Lyceum and the Diocesan Seminary for ecclesiastics at Dil-

lingen; the Diocesan Seminary for boys at Dillingen; St. Stephen's Catholic House of Studies at Augsburg, under the direction of the Benedictines, which includes a Lyceum, a classical Gymnasium, a royal seminary of studies and an institute for higher education; there are besides about forty students of the Diocese of Augsburg who dwell in the Georgianum at Munich and attend the courses of the University. The state, or communal, institutions of higher studies for boys number 28 in the Diocese of Augsburg; 5 gymnasia, 1 *Realgymnasium*, 1 seminary of studies, 5 *Progymnasia*, 2 Latin schools, 7 *Realschulen*, 3 agricultural winter schools, 1 *Realschule* with Latin, 1 normal school, and 2 preparatory schools. We must also mention the Cassianeum in Donauwörth, a Catholic institute of pedagogy, which includes a training-school, a publishing house for books and periodicals, a printing press, and other appurtenances. In all of these institutions Catholic instruction is given to Catholic students by Catholic clergymen.

IV. CHARITABLE INSTITUTIONS.—The charitable institutions of the diocese are for the most part the property of the civic parishes or the unions (*Vereine*), or local associations; they are administered, however, mostly by religious communities to whom is also confided the care of the sick, or children, and of the aged. There are 37 hospitals, 24 infirmaries, 12 protectories, 2 asylums for children, 8 orphanages, 3 institutions for the deaf and dumb, 12 houses for the poor and orphans, 3 poorhouses, 1 hospital for priests, 1 home for invalids, 3 institutions for servants under the patronage of the Blessed Virgin (*Marienanstalten*), 1 House of St. Anne (*Annastift*) for the factory girls in Augsburg, 1 House of St. Elizabeth for incurables, 5 institutions for various other purposes (e. g. the Kneippianum in Wörishofen). One Catholic institution of Augsburg deserves special mention: the Fuggerei, founded in 1519 by three brothers (Ulrich, Georg, and Jakob) of the Fuggers. It consists of an extensive block of 53 houses with 106 apartments; in accordance with the conditions of the foundation these must be let at a very small rent to indigent people. It is a noble and durable memorial of the spirit of Christian charity that abounded in the Catholic Middle Ages. In recent times other works of Christian charity have been inaugurated. The good priest and superintendent of studies (*Regens*), Father Wagner of Dillingen, established many institutions for the deaf, dumb, and blind; Father Ringeisen, parish priest of Ursberg, established there the Sisters of St. Joseph for the exercise of every form of charity. For aged and infirm priests there exists a fund with 1,277 subscribers and a reserve of 1,550,000 marks ($387,500). There is also an association for the support of infirm priests, with 792 members and a fund of 26,000 marks ($6,500). Prominent among the numerous social-political and religious associations of the diocese are 16 Catholic apprentices' unions (*Lehrlingsvereine*), the local union in Augsburg maintaining its own home for apprentices; 49 Catholic journeymen's unions (*Gesellenvereine*), 4 Unions of St. Joseph; 52 Catholic workingmen's unions; 19 Catholic students' clubs; 3 Catholic clubs for working women, with 504 members; 7 Catholic "Patronages" for working people; the Ulrich-union for the support of seminaries; the Men's Catholic Association, the Christian Peasants' League; the Cecilian Club; St. Mary's Protectory for girls; the Young Women's Association, and the Association of Christian Mothers. Annual pilgrimages give visible evidence of the vigorous religious life of the diocese. Such pilgrimages are those of the Holy Cross (11 May) and to the tomb of St. Ulrich at Augsburg (4 July). There are also processions to the holy mountain of Andechs during the rogation days, and to the monastery of Lechfeld since the year of the cholera (1854). Other pilgrimages are those to the relics of St. Rasso at Grafrath, to the church of the Holy Sepulchre (*Unsers Herrn Ruh*) near Friedberg, and to Maria Siebeneich.

V. ECCLESIASTICAL ART AND MONUMENTS.— Among the ecclesiastical monuments of the Diocese of Augsburg the cathedral holds first place. It was begun in the Roman style in 994, dedicated 1010, and remodeled, 1331–1431, into a Gothic church with five naves; it was then that the lofty east choir with its circle of chapels was added. The towers were increased in height in 1488–89 and 1564. Among the innumerable art treasures of the cathedral may be mentioned the vestments of St. Ulrich; the four altars with paintings by the elder Holbein illustrating the life of the Blessed Virgin; the celebrated bronze doors of the left lateral nave, adorned with remarkable reliefs, and dating from the first half of the eleventh century; the ancient stained windows, some of which go back to the eleventh and twelfth centuries; the interesting tombs and slabs of the fourteenth and succeeding centuries, both in the cathedral itself and in the adjoining cloister, and many other objects of value and interest. The church of Sts. Ulrich and Afra, built 1467–1594, in the Gothic style, contains the tomb of St. Ulrich, the stone sarcophagus of St. Afra, the Fugger chapel with the memorial to Hans Fugger, and three magnificent altars in rococo style. The Late Gothic church of the Holy Cross was renovated, early in the eighteenth century, in florid Roman rococo style, and is a favourite place of pilgrimage. Among the chief ecclesiastical edifices outside the city of Augsburg are the Romanesque basilicas of Altenstadt, Ursberg, Thierhaupten; the Gothic churches of Kaisheim, Dinkelsbühl, Donauwörth, Landsberg; the ancient abbey-churches of Andechs (very rich in relics and costly reliquaries), Benediktbeuren, Diessen, Füssen, Kempten, Ottobeuren, and Wessobrunn, all restored and ornamented in sumptuous barocco or rococo style.

KHAMM, *Hierarchia Augustana chronologice tripartita* (Augsburg, 1709–19); STEINER, *Synodi Diœcesis Augustanæ* (Mindelheim, 1766); STEINER, *Acta selecta ecclesiæ Augustanæ* (Augsburg, 1785); VEITH, *Bibliotheca Augustana* (Augsburg, 1785–96); BRAUN, *Geschichte der Bischöfe von Augsburg* (Augsburg, 1813–15); Id., *Historisch-topographische Beschreibung der Diözese Augsburg* (Augsburg, 1823); Id., *Die Domkirche zu Augsburg* (Augsburg, 1829); *Monumenta episcopatus Augustani*, in *Monumenta Boica* (Munich, 1841–47) XXXIII–XXXV; STEICHELE, *Beiträge zur Geschichte des Bistums Augsburgs* (Augsburg, 1849–53); Id., *Archiv für die Geschichte des Bistums Augsburg* (Augsburg, 1856–60); Id., *Das Bistum Augsburg historisch und statistisch beschrieben* (vol. II–VI, Augsburg, 1864–1906; vols. V and VI by SCHRÖDER; vol. I has not yet appeared in print); HOPP, *Pfründestatistik des Bistums Augsburg* (Augsburg, 1906); BAUMANN, *Geschichte des Algäu* (Kempten, 1880–95); many original manuscripts in *Zeitschrift des Historischen Vereins für Schwaben und Neuburg* (Augsburg, 1874 sqq.; 1903); *Jahresbericht des Historischen Vereins Dillingen* (Dillingen, 1888 sqq.). For the history of the city of Augsburg see: STETTEN (Augsburg, 1745–58); MEYER, *Urkundenbuch der Stadt Augsburg* (Augsburg, 1874–78); ROTH, *Augsburger Reformationsgeschichte 1517–27* (Munich, 1881); WERNER (Augsburg, 1900, with details on earlier literature). For the history of the fine arts in Augsburg see MERZ, *Die Bildwerke an den Erztüren des Augsburger Doms* (Stuttgart, 1885); BUFF, *Augsburg in der Renaissancezeit* (Bamberg, 1893); KEMPF, *Alt-Augsburg* (100 plates, Berlin, 1898); SCHRÖDER, *Die Domkirche zu Augsburg* (Augsburg, 1900); FRIESENEGGER, *Die Sankt-Ulrichskirche in Augsburg* (Augsburg, 1900); WEIS-LIEBERSDORF, *Das Jubeljahr 1500 in der Augsburger Kunst* (Munich, 1901); RIEHL, *Augsburg* (Leipzig, 1903).

JOSEPH LINS.

Augsburg, RELIGIOUS PEACE OF. See REFORMATION.

Augsburg, SYNODS OF.—From the time of St. Boniface (d. 754), especially during periods of earnest revival of religious and ecclesiastical life, synods were frequently convened by the bishops of Germany, and sometimes by those of individual ecclesiastical provinces. As the German bishops were, on the one hand, princes of the empire, and the emperor was, on the other, the superior protector of the Roman Church, these synods came to have no little im-

portance in the general ecclesiastical and political development of Western Christendom. Two general imperial synods were held in Augsburg. The first, convened in August, 952, through the efforts of Emperor Otto the Great, provided for the reform of abuses in civil and ecclesiastical life. Frederick, Archbishop of Mainz, presided, and three archbishops and twenty bishops of Germany and northern Italy took part. Eleven canons were promulgated concerning ecclesiastical life and other matters of church discipline. A similar synod, convened by Anno, Archbishop of Cologne (27 October, 1062), was occupied with the internal conditions of the empire and the attitude of the Church of Germany towards the schism of Cadalus, anti-pope during the reign of Alexander II. The diocesan synods of Augsburg correspond as a rule with the synodal system as carried out in other parts of Germany. We find in this diocese, as elsewhere in Germany, the *synodi per villas*, convened under the influence of the Carlovingian capitularies. They were visitation-synods, held by the bishop assisted by the archdeacon and the local lord or baron (*Gaugraf*). Their purpose was inquisitorial and judicial. After the time of St. Ulrich (923–973), and in close relation to the system of provincial councils, diocesan synods were held at stated times, chiefly in connection with matters of ecclesiastical administration (legalizing of important grants and privileges, etc.), and the settlement of disputes. After the thirteenth century these diocesan synods assumed more of a legislative character; decrees were issued regulating the lives of both ecclesiastics and laymen, and church discipline was secured by the publication of diocesan statutes. The earliest extant are of Bishop Friedrich (1309–31). These diocesan synods fell into decay during the course of the fourteenth century.

In consequence of decrees of the Council of Basle the synods of the Diocese of Augsburg rose again to importance, so that after the middle of the fifteenth century they were once more frequently held, as for example: by the able Bishop Peter von Schauenburg (1424–69) and his successor, Johann von Werdenburg, also by Friedrich von Zollern (1486) and Heinrich von Liechtenau (1506). The two Bishops Christopher von Stadion (1517–43) and Otto Truchsess von Waldburg (1543–73) made use of diocesan synods (1517, 1520, 1543 in Dillingen, and 1536 in Augsburg) for the purpose of checking the progress of the Reformation through the improvement of ecclesiastical life. At a later period there were but few ecclesiastical assemblies of this kind; as early as 1567, the synod of that year, convened for the purpose of carrying out the reforms instituted by the Council of Trent, shows signs of the decline of the synod as a diocesan institution. The Bishops of Augsburg were, moreover, not only the ecclesiastical superiors of their diocese, but after the tenth century possessed the *Regalia*, the right of holding and administering royal fiefs with concomitant jurisdiction. The right of coinage was obtained by St. Ulrich. At a later period disputes were frequent between the bishops and the civic authorities, which culminated in an agreement (1389) by which the city was made practically independent of the episcopal authority. (See AUGSBURG.)

HARTZHEIM, *Concilia Germaniæ* (Cologne, 1749); HEFELE, *Conciliengesch.* (2d ed. Freiburg, 1873); STEINER, *Synodi diœc. Augustanæ* (1766); STEICHELE, *Das Bistum Augsburg historisch und statistisch beschrieben* (Augsburg, 1864); SCHMID in *Kirchenlex.*, I, 1651–55.

J. P. KIRSCH.

Augury. See DIVINATION.

Augusta, a titular see of Cilicia in Asia Minor, whose episcopal list (363–434) is given in Gams (435). Several cities bore the same name in Roman antiquity, some of which are yet flourishing, e. g. Augusta

Auscorum (Auch in Southern France); Augusta Batavorum (Leyden in Holland); Augusta Asturica (Astorga in Spain); Augusta Prætoria (Aosta in Northern Italy); Augusta Emerita (Mérida in Spain); Augusta Rauracorum (Augst in Switzerland); Augusta Suessonum (Soissons in France); Augusta Taurinorum (Turin in Italy); Augusta Trevirorum (Trier in Germany); Augusta Trinobantum (London); Augusta Vindelicorum (Augsburg in Germany).

LEQUIEN, *Oriens Christ.* (1740), II, 879–880; SMITH, *Dict. of Greek and Roman Geogr.*, I, 338.

THOMAS J. SHAHAN.

Augustin von Alfeld (ALVELDT, or ALVELDIANUS), one of the earliest and most aggressive opponents of Luther, b. in the village of Alfeld, near Hildesheim, from which he took his surname; d. probably in 1532. Nothing is known of his parentage, youth, and early training. He first comes into prominence as a Franciscan of the Regular Observance, belonging to the Saxon Province of the Holy Cross. The absence of his name on the matriculation rosters of the philosophical and theological universities of Erfurt, Rostock, Leipzig, and Wittenberg, usually frequented by the members of the above-named province, leaves the presumption that he made his studies in one of the monastic schools. At the solicitation of Adolf of Anhalt, Bishop of Merseburg, in 1520, being already Lector of Holy Writ at Leipzig, he entered the theological arena to controvert the Lutheran heresy (Mencken, Scriptores rer. Ger., II, 56). On 20 January, 1521, he presided at the public theological disputation held at Weimar, between Lange, Mechler, and the Franciscans, on the merit of monastic vows and life (Kapp, Kleinere Nachlese nützlicher Urkunden zur Erläuterung der Reformationsgeschichte, II, 514, Leipzig, 1727), the result of which has not been handed down, though it called forth a satirical poem at the time (ib., 520). In 1523 he became Guardian of the monastery at Halle, in which position he is still found in 1528. In 1529 he was elected Provincial of the Saxon Province of the Holy Cross.

Alfeld was a man of fine linguistic attainments, a fluent Latinist, familiar with the ancient classics, conversant with Greek and Hebrew, and well acquainted with the humanistic writings of his day. His theology was that of medieval scholasticism, in which he proved "that the old theological training did not leave the antagonists of Luther helpless and unprepared in combating the novel, and to the theologically disciplined mind contradictory, assertions" (Otto, Johannes Cochlæus, 132, Breslau, 1874). As Lector of Holy Writ, he devoted much attention and thought to the Bible, so that he can state that "from my childhood I have devoted my time and life to it" (Super Apostolicâ Sede, etc., iii a). In the textual studies of the Greek and Hebrew versions, the translation of Erasmus, the exegetical writings of Faber Stapulensis (Lefèvre d'Etaples) and the Complutensians, he shows a keen, analytical mind and sound judgment. His memory and reputation, however, rest on his polemical activity and writings. The latter are marred at times by a tone of bitterness and sarcasm that detract from their intrinsic worth and gave his opponents, notably Lonicer, Luther's amanuensis (Biblia nova Alveldensis Wittenbergæ Anno MDXX) opportunity to censure the catalogued epithets flung at Luther (Cyprian, Nützliche Urkunden zur Erläuterung der Reformationsgeschichte, II, 158). If it be remembered that Luther calls him *bos Lipsicus* (De Wette, Briefe, Sendschreiben, etc., I, 446); *asinus* (op. cit., 451, 453, 533); *Lipsiensis onager* (op. cit., 446); *Lipsiensis asinus* (op. cit., 471, 475, 542), merely to single out a few controversial amenities, his literary style may be measurably condoned.

LEMMENS, *Pater Augustin von Alfeld* (Freiburg, 1899); FLOSS in *Kirchenlex.*, I, 1682. The former gives a comprehensive résumé of Alfeld's writings.

HENRY A. GANSS.

Augustine, Rule of Saint.—The title, Rule of St. Augustine, has been applied to each of the following documents: (1) Letter ccxi addressed to a community of women; (2) Sermons ccclv and ccclvi, entitled "De vitâ et moribus clericorum suorum."; (3) a portion of the Rule drawn up for clerks or *Consortia monachorum;* (4) a Rule known as *Regula secunda;* and (5) another Rule called: "De vitâ eremiticâ ad sororem liber." The last is a treatise on eremitical life by Blessed Ælred, Abbot of Rievaulx, England, who died in 1166 and, as the two preceding rules are of unknown authorship, it follows that none but Letter ccxi and Sermons ccclv and ccclvi were written by St. Augustine. Letter ccxi is addressed to nuns in a monastery that had been governed by the sister of St. Augustine, and in which his cousin and niece lived. His object in writing it was merely to quiet troubles incident to the nomination of a new superior, and meanwhile he took occasion to expatiate upon some of the virtues and practices essential to the religious life. He dwells upon chastity, poverty, obedience, detachment from the world, the apportionment of labour, the mutual duties of superiors and inferiors, fraternal charity, prayer in common, fasting and abstinence proportionate to the strength of the individual, care of the sick, silence, reading during meals, etc. In his two sermons "De vitâ et moribus clericorum suorum" Augustine seeks to dispel the suspicions harboured by the faithful of Hippo against the clergy leading a monastic life with him in his episcopal residence. The perusal of these sermons discloses the fact that the bishop and his priests observed strict poverty and conformed to the example of the Apostles and early Christians by using their money in common. This was called the Apostolic Rule. St. Augustine, however, dilated upon the religious life and its obligations on other occasions. Aurelius, Bishop of Carthage, was greatly disturbed by the conduct of monks who indulged in idleness under pretext of contemplation, and at his request St. Augustine published a treatise entitled "De opere monachorum" wherein he proves by the authority of the Bible, the example of the Apostles, and even the exigencies of life, that the monk is obliged to devote himself to serious labour. In several of his letters and sermons is to be found a useful complement to his teaching on the monastic life and the duties it imposes. These are easy of access in the Benedictine edition, where the accompanying table may be consulted under the words: *monachi, monachæ, monasterium, monastica vita, sanctimoniales.*

The letter written by St. Augustine to the nuns at Hippo (423), for the purpose of restoring harmony in their community, deals with the reform of certain phases of monasticism as it is understood by him. This document, to be sure, contains no such clear, minute prescriptions as are found in the Benedictine Rule, because no complete rule was ever written prior to the time of St. Benedict; nevertheless, the Bishop of Hippo is a law-giver and his letter is to be read weekly, that the nuns may guard against or repent any infringement of it. He considers poverty the foundation of the religious life, but attaches no less importance to fraternal charity, which consists in living in peace and concord. The superior, in particular, is recommended to practise this virtue although not, of course, to the extreme of omitting to chastise the guilty. However, St. Augustine leaves her free to determine the nature and duration of the punishment imposed, in some cases it being her privilege even to expel nuns that have become incorrigible. The superior shares the duties of her office with certain members of her community, one of whom has charge of the sick, another of the cellar, another of the wardrobe, while still another is custodian of the books which she is authorized to distribute among the sisters. The nuns make their own habits, which consist of a dress, a cincture and a veil. Prayer, in common, occupies an important place in their life, being said in the chapel at stated hours and according to prescribed forms, and comprising hymns, psalms, and readings. Certain prayers are simply recited while others, especially indicated, are chanted; but as St. Augustine enters into no minute details, it is to be supposed that each monastery conformed to the liturgy of the diocese in which it is situated. Those sisters desiring to lead a more contemplative life are allowed to follow special devotions in private. The section of the Rule that applies to eating, although severe in some respects, is by no means strict beyond observance and the Bishop of Hippo tempers it most discreetly. Fasting and abstinence are recommended only in proportion to the physical strength of the individual, and when the saint speaks of obligatory fasting he specifies that such as are unable to wait for the evening or ninth hour meal may eat at noon. The nuns partake of very frugal fare and, in all probability, abstain from meat. However, the sick and infirm are objects of the most tender care and solicitude, and certain concessions are made in favour of those who, before entering religion, led lives of luxury. During meals some instructive matter is to be read aloud to the nuns. Although the Rule of St. Augustine contains but few precepts, it dwells at great length upon religious virtues and the ascetic life, this being characteristic of all primitive rules. In his sermons ccclv and ccclvi the saint discourses on the monastic observance of the vow of poverty. Before making their profession the nuns divest themselves of all their goods, their monastery being responsible for supplying their wants, and whatever they may earn or receive is turned over to a common fund, the monasteries having the right of possession. In his treatise, "De opere monachorum", he inculcates the necessity of labour, without, however, subjecting it to any rule, the gaining of one's livelihood rendering it indispensable. Monks of course, devoted to the ecclesiastical ministry observe, *ipso facto*, the precept of labour, from which observance the infirm are legitimately dispensed. These, then, are the most important monastic prescriptions found in the rule and writings of St. Augustine.

MONASTIC LIFE OF ST. AUGUSTINE.—Augustine was a monk; this fact stands out unmistakably in the reading of his life and works. Although a priest and bishop, he knew how to combine the practices of the religious life with the duties of his office, and his episcopal house in Hippo was for himself and some of his clergy, a veritable monastery. Several of his friends and disciples elevated to the episcopacy imitated his example, among them Alypius at Tagaste, Possidius at Calama, Profuturus and Fortunatus at Cirta, Evodius at Uzalis, and Boniface at Carthage. There were still other monks who were priests and who exercised the ministry outside of the episcopal cities. All monks did not live in these episcopal monasteries; the majority were laymen whose communities, although under the authority of the bishops, were entirely distinct from those of the clergy, There were religious who lived in complete isolation, belonging to no community and having no legitimate superior; indeed, some wandered aimlessly about, at the risk of giving disedification by their vagabondage. The fanatics known as *Circumcelliones* were recruited from the ranks of these wandering monks, and St. Augustine often censured their way of living.

The religious life of the Bishop of Hippo was, for a long time, a matter of dispute between the Canons Regular and the Hermits of St. Augustine, each of these two families claiming him exclusively as its own. It was not so much the establishing of an historical fact as the settling of a claim of precedence that caused the trouble, and as both sides could not be in the right, the quarrel would have continued indefinitely had not Pope Sixtus IV put an end to it by his Bull "Summum silentium" (1484). The silence thus imposed, however, was not perpetual, and in the seventeenth and eighteenth centuries controversies were resumed between the Canons and the Hermits, but all to no avail. Pierre de Saint-Trond, Prior of the Canons Regular of St. Martin of Louvain, tells the story of these quarrels in the preface to his "Examen Testamenti S. Augustini" (Louvain, 1564). Gabriel Pennot, Nicolas Desnos, and Le Large uphold the thesis of the Canons; Gandolfo, Lupus, Giles of the Presentation, and Noris sustain that of the Hermits. The Bollandists withhold their opinion. St. Augustine followed the monastic or religious life as it was known to his contemporaries, and neither he nor they even thought of establishing among those who had embraced it any distinction whatever as to congregations or orders. This idea was conceived in a subsequent epoch, hence St. Augustine cannot be said to have belonged to any particular order. He made laws for the monks and nuns of Roman Africa, it is true, and he helped to increase their numbers, while they, in turn, revered him as their father, but they cannot be classed as members of any special monastic family.

ST. AUGUSTINE'S INFLUENCE ON MONACHISM.— When we consider Augustine's great prestige, it is easy to understand why his writings should have so influenced the development of Western monachism. His Letter ccxi was read and re-read by St. Benedict, who borrowed several important texts from it for insertion in his own rule. St. Benedict's chapter on the labour of monks is manifestly inspired by the treatise "De opere monachorum", that has done so much towards furnishing an accurate statement of the doctrine commonly accepted in religious orders. The teaching concerning religious poverty is clearly formulated in the sermons "De vitâ et moribus clericorum suorum" and the authorship of these two works is sufficient to earn for the Bishop of Hippo the title of Patriarch of monks and religious. The influence of Augustine, however, was nowhere stronger than in southern Gaul in the fifth and sixth centuries. Lérins and the monks of that school were familiar with Augustine's monastic writings, which, together with those of Cassianus, were the mine from which the principal elements of their rules were drawn. St. Cæsarius, Archbishop of Arles, the great organizer of religious life in that section, chose some of the most interesting articles of his rule for monks from St. Augustine, and in his rule for nuns quoted at length from Letter ccxi. Sts. Augustine and Cæsarius were animated by the same spirit which passed from the Archbishop of Arles to St. Aurelian, one of his successors, and, like him, a monastic lawgiver. Augustine's influence also extended to women's monasteries in Gaul, where the Rule of Cæsarius was adopted either wholly or in part, as, for example, at Sainte-Croix of Poitiers, Juxamontier of Besançon, and Chamalières near Clermont.

But it was not always enough merely to adopt the teachings of Augustine and to quote him; the author of the *regula Tarnatensis* (an unknown monastery in the Rhone valley) introduced into his work the entire text of the letter addressed to the nuns, having previously adapted it to a community of men by making slight modifications. This adaptation was surely made in other monasteries in the sixth or seventh centuries, and in his "Codex regularum" St. Benedict of Aniane published a text similarly modified. For want of exact information we cannot say in which monasteries this was done, and whether they were numerous. Letter ccxi, which has thus become the Rule of St. Augustine, certainly constituted a part of the collections known under the general name of "Rules of the Fathers" and used by the founders of monasteries as a basis for the practices of the religious life. It does not seem to have been adopted by the regular communities of canons or of clerks which began to be organized in the eighth and ninth centuries. The rule given them by St. Chrodegang, Bishop of Metz (742–766), is almost entirely drawn from that of St. Benedict, and no more decided traces of Augustinian influence are to be found in it than in the decisions of the Council of Aachen (817), which may be considered the real constitutions of the Canons Regular. For this influence we must await the foundation of the clerical or canonical communities established in the eleventh century for the effective counteracting of simony and clerical concubinage. The Council of Lateran (1059) and another council held at Rome four years later approved for the members of the clergy the strict community life of the Apostolic Age, such as the Bishop of Hippo had caused to be practised in his episcopal house and had taught in his two sermons heretofore cited. The first communities of canons adopted these sermons as their basis of organization. This reform movement spread rapidly throughout Latin Europe and brought about the foundation of the regular chapters so numerous and prosperous during the Middle Ages. Monasteries of women or of canonesses were formed on the same plan, but not according to the rules laid down in the sermons " De vitâ et moribus clericorum". The letter to virgins was adopted almost immediately and became the rule of the canons and canonesses; hence it was the religious code of the Premonstratensians, of the houses of Canons Regular, and of canonesses either gathered into congregations or isolated, of the Friars Preachers, of the Trinitarians and of the Order of Mercy, both for the redemption of captives, of hospitaller communities, both men and women, dedicated to the care of the sick in the hospitals of the Middle Ages, and of some military orders.

AUGUSTINIAN FOUNDATIONS.—See also under individual titles, CANONS, REGULAR OF THE LATERAN (AUSTIN), HERMITS OF ST. AUGUSTINE, MERCEDARIANS or NOLASCANS, SERVITES, PAULINES, ALEXIAN BROTHERS, HIERONYMITES, JESUATS, AMBROSIANS, BROTHERHOOD OF THE APOSTLES AND OF VOLUNTARY POVERTY, BROTHERS OF MERCY, BETHLEHEMITES, BIRGITTINES (BRIGITTINES), URSULINES, ANGELICALS. ST. AUGUSTINE, *Epist. ccxi* in *P. L.*, XXXIII, 958–965; IDEM, *Sermones ccclv, ccclvi, P. L.*, XXXIX, 1568–81; IDEM, *De opere monachorum*, op. cit., XL, 547–852; BESSE, *Le monachisme Africain* (Paris, 1898); IDEM, *Les moines de l'ancienne France, Période galloromaine et mérovingienne* (Paris, 1906); HELYOT, *Histoire des ordres religieux et militaires* (Paris, 1792), III, IV; HEIMBUCHER, *Die Orden und Kongregationen der katholischen Kirche* (Paderborn, 1896), I, 386–540.

HERMITS OF ST. AUGUSTINE.—EMPOLI, *Bullarium ordinis Eremitarum S. Augustini* (Rome, 1628); PAMPHILI, *Chronicon ordinis fratrum Eremitarum S. Augustini* (Rome, 1681); LUBIN, *Orbis Augustinianus, sive conventuum ordinis Eremitarum S. Augustini descriptio* (Paris, 1672); CURTIUS, *Elogia virorum illustrium ex ordine Eremitarum S. Augustini* (Antwerp, 1658); GRATIANUS, *Anastasis Augustiniana, in quâ scriptores ordinis Eremitarum S. Augustini . . . in seriem digesti sunt* (Antwerp, 1636); IDEM, *Sacra eremus Augustiniana, sive de institutione Fratrum Eremitarum excalceatorum ordinis S. Augustini* (Cambrai, 1658).

OTHER ORDERS.—EGGERER, *Fragmen panis Corvi protoeremitici, sive reliquiæ annalium ordinis eremitarum S. Pauli* (Vienna, 1663); *Historia degli uomini illustri che fuorono Giesuati Morigia* (Vienna, 1604); HERMENEGILDO DE SAN-PABLO, *Origen y continuación del instituto y religión Gieronimiana* (Madrid, 1669).

J. M. BESSE.

Augustine of Canterbury, SAINT, first Archbishop of Canterbury, Apostle of the English; date of birth unknown; d. 26 May, 604. Symbols: cope, pallium, and mitre as Bishop of Canterbury, and pastoral staff and gospels as missionary. Nothing is known of his youth except that he was probably a Roman of the better class, and that early in life he became a monk in the fa-

mous monastery of St. Andrew erected by St. Gregory out of his own patrimony on the Cælian Hill. It was thus amid the religious intimacies of the Benedictine Rule and in the bracing atmosphere of a recent foundation that the character of the future missionary was formed. Chance is said to have furnished the opportunity for the enterprise which was destined to link his name for all time with that of his friend and patron, St. Gregory, as the "true beginner" of one of the most important Churches in Christendom and the medium by which the authority of the Roman See was established over men of the English-speaking race. It is unnecessary to dwell here upon Bede's well-known version of Gregory's casual encounter with English slaves in the Roman market place (H. E., II, i), which is treated under Gregory the Great (q. v.).

Some five years after his elevation to the Roman See (590) Gregory began to look about him for ways and means to carry out the dream of his earlier days. He naturally turned to the community he had ruled more than a decade of years before in the monastery on the Cælian Hill. Out of these he selected a company of about forty and designated Augustine, at that time Prior of St. Andrew's, to be their representative and spokesman. The appointment, as will appear later on, seems to have been of a somewhat indeterminate character; but from this time forward until his death in 604 it is to Augustine as "strengthened by the confirmation of the blessed Father Gregory" (*roboratus confirmatione beati patris Gregorii*, Bede, H. E., I, xxv) that English, as distinguished from British, Christianity owes its primary inspiration.

The event which afforded Pope Gregory the opportunity he had so long desired of carrying out his great missionary plan in favour of the English happened in the year 595 or 596. A rumour had reached Rome that the pagan inhabitants of Britain were ready to embrace the Faith in great numbers, if only preachers could be found to instruct them. The first plan which seems to have occurred to the pontiff was to take measures for the purchase of English captive boys of seventeen years of age and upwards. These he would have brought up in the Catholic Faith with the idea of ordaining them and sending them back in due time as apostles to their own people. He accordingly wrote to Candidus, a presbyter entrusted with the administration of a small estate belonging to the patrimony of the Roman Church in Gaul, asking him to secure the revenues and set them aside for this purpose. (Greg., Epp., VI, vii in Migne, P. L., LXXVII.) It is possible, not only to determine approximately the dates of these events, but also to indicate the particular quarter of Britain from which the rumour had come. Æthelberht became King of Kent in 559 or 560, and in less than twenty years he succeeded in establishing an overlordship that extended from the borders of the country of the West Saxons eastward to the sea and as far north as the Humber and the Trent. The Saxons of Middlesex and of Essex, together with the men of East Anglia and of Mercia, were thus brought to acknowledge him as Bretwalda, and he acquired a political importance which began to be felt by the Frankish princes on the other side of the Channel. Charibert of Paris gave him his daughter Bertha in marriage, stipulating, as part of the nuptial agreement, that she should be allowed the free exercise of her religion. The condition was accepted (Bede, H. E., I, xxv) and Luidhard, a Frankish bishop, accompanied the princess to her new home in Canterbury, where the ruined church of St. Martin, situated a short distance beyond the walls, and dating from Roman-British times, was set apart for her use (Bede, H. E., I, xxvi). The date of this marriage, so important in its results to the future fortunes of Western Christianity, is of course largely a matter of conjecture; but from the evidence furnished by one or two scattered remarks in St. Gregory's letters (Epp., VI) and from the circumstances which attended the emergence of the kingdom of the Jutes to a position of prominence in the Britain of this period, we may safely assume that it had taken place fully twenty years before the plan of sending Augustine and his companions suggested itself to the pope.

The pope was obliged to complain of the lack of episcopal zeal among Æthelberht's Christian neighbours. Whether we are to understand the phrase *ex vicinis* (Greg., Epp., VI) as referring to Gaulish prelates or to the Celtic bishops of northern and western Britain, the fact remains that neither Bertha's piety, nor Luidhard's preaching, nor Æthelberht's toleration, nor the supposedly robust faith of British or Gaulish neighbouring peoples was found adequate to so obvious an opportunity until a Roman pontiff, distracted with the cares of a world supposed to be hastening to its eclipse, first exhorted forty Benedictines of Italian blood to the enterprise. The itinerary seem to have been speedily, if vaguely, prepared; the little company set out upon their long journey in the month of June, 596. They were armed with letters to the bishops and Christian princes of the countries through which they were likely to pass, and they were further instructed to provide themselves with Frankish interpreters before setting foot in Britain itself. Discouragement, however, appears early to have overtaken them on their way. Tales of the uncouth islanders to whom they were going chilled their enthusiasm, and some of their number actually proposed that they should draw back. Augustine so far compromised with the waverers that he agreed to return in person to Pope Gregory and lay before him plainly the difficulties which they might be compelled to encounter. The band of missionaries waited for him in the neighbourhood of Aix-en-Provence. Pope Gregory, however, raised the drooping spirits of Augustine and sent him back without delay to his faint-hearted brethren, armed with more precise, and as it appeared, more convincing authority.

Augustine was named abbot of the missionaries (Bede, H. E., I, xxiii) and was furnished with fresh letters in which the pope made kindly acknowledgment of the aid thus far offered by Protasius, Bishop of Aix-en-Provence, by Stephen, Abbot of Lérins, and by a wealthy lay official of patrician rank called Arigius [Greg., Epp., VI (indic. xiv) num. 52 sqq.; sc. 3, 4, 5 of the Benedictine series]. Augustine must have reached Aix on his return journey some time in August; for Gregory's message of encouragement to the party bears the date of July the twenty-third, 596. Whatever may have been the real source of the passing discouragement no more delays are recorded. The missionaries pushed on through Gaul, passing up through the valley of the Rhone to Arles on their way to Vienne and Autun, and thence northward, by one of several alternative routes which it is impossible now to fix with accuracy, until they came to Paris. Here, in all probability, they passed the winter months; and here, too, as is not unlikely, considering the relations that existed between the family of the reigning house and that of Kent, they secured the services of the local presbyters suggested as interpreters in the pope's letters to Theodoric and Theodebert and to Brunichilda, Queen of the Franks.

In the spring of the following year they were ready to embark. The name of the port at which they took ship has not been recorded. Boulogne was at that time a place of some mercantile importance; and it is not improbable that they directed their steps thither to find a suitable vessel in which they could complete the last and not least hazardous portion of their journey. All that we know for certain is that they landed somewhere on the Isle of Thanet (Bede, H. E., I, xxv) and that they waited there in obedience to

King Æthelberht's orders until arrangements could be made for a formal interview. The king replied to their messengers that he would come in person from Canterbury, which was less than a dozen miles away. It is not easy to decide at this date between the four rival spots, each of which has claimed the distinction of being the place upon which St. Augustine and his companions first set foot. The Boarded Groin, Stonar, Ebbsfleet, and Richborough—the last named, if the present course of the Stour has not altered in thirteen hundred years, then forming part of the mainland —each has its defenders. The curious in such matters may consult the special literature on the subject cited at the close of this article. The promised interview between the king and the missionaries took place within a few days. It was held in the open air, *sub divo*, says Bede (H. E., I, xxv), on a level spot, probably under a spreading oak in deference to the king's dread of Augustine's possible incantations. His fear, however, was dispelled by the native grace of manner and the kindly personality of his chief guest who addressed him through an interpreter. The message told "how the compassionate Jesus had redeemed a world of sin by His own agony and opened the Kingdom of Heaven to all who would believe" (Ælfric, ap. Haddan and Stubbs, III, ii). The king's answer, while gracious in its friendliness, was curiously prophetic of the religious after-temper of his race. "Your words and promises are very fair" is said to have replied, "but as they are new to us and of uncertain import, I cannot assent to them and give up what I have long held in common with the whole English nation. But since you have come as strangers from so great a distance, and, as I take it, are anxious to have us also share in what you conceive to be both excellent and true, we will not interfere with you, but receive you, rather, in kindly hospitality and take care to provide what may be necessary for your support. Moreover, we make no objection to your winning as many converts as you can to your creed". (Bede, H. E., I, xxv.)

The king more than made good his words. He invited the missionaries to take up their abode in the royal capital of Canterbury, then a barbarous and half-ruined metropolis, built by the Kentish folk upon the site of the old Roman military town of Durovernum. In spite of the squalid character of the city, the monks must have made an impressive picture as they drew near the abode "over against the King's Street facing the north", a detail preserved in William Thorne's (c. 1397) "Chronicle of the Abbots of St. Augustine's Canterbury," p. 1759, assigned them for a dwelling. The striking circumstances of their approach seem to have lingered long in popular remembrance; for Bede, writing fully a century and a third after the event, is at pains to describe how they came in characteristic Roman fashion (*more suo*) bearing "the holy cross together with a picture of the Sovereign King, Our Lord Jesus Christ and chanting in unison this litany", as they advanced: "We beseech thee, O Lord, in the fulness of thy pity that Thine anger and Thy wrath be turned away from this city and from Thy holy house, because we have sinned: Alleluia!" It was an anthem out of one of the many "Rogation" litanies then beginning to be familiar in the churches of Gaul and possibly not unknown also at Rome. (Martène, "De antiquis Ecclesiæ ritibus", 1764, III, 189; Bede, "H. E.", II, xx; Joannes Diac., "De Vita Gregorii", II, 17 in Migne, P. L., LXXV; Duchesne's ed., "Liber Pontificalis", II, 12.) The building set apart for their use must have been fairly large to afford shelter to a community numbering fully forty. It stood in the Stable Gate, not far from the ruins of an old heathen temple; and the tradition in Thorn's day was that the parish church of St. Alphage approximately marked the site (Chr. Aug. Abb., 1759). Here Augus-

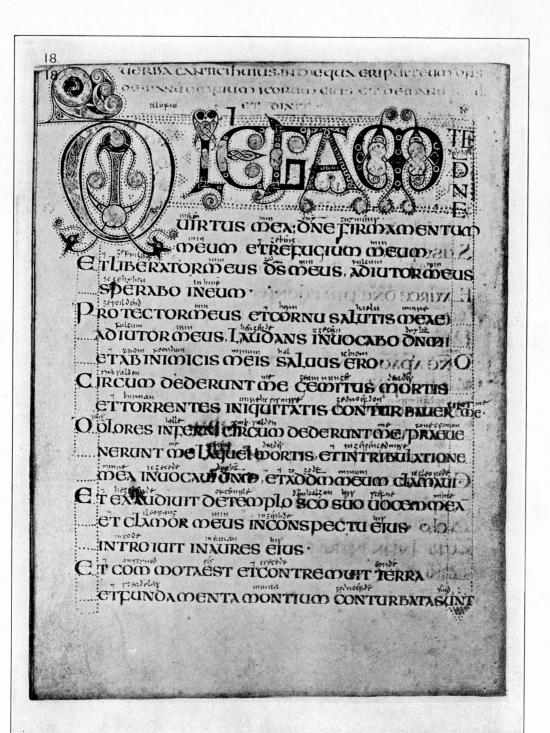

PSALTER OF ST. AUGUSTINE, CANTERBURY

ABOUT A.D. 700. BRIT. MUS. COTTON MS. VESPASIAN A. I.

tine and his companions seem to have established without delay the ordinary routine of the Benedictine rule as practised at the close of the sixth century; and to it they seem to have added in a quiet way the apostolic ministry of preaching. The church dedicated to St. Martin in the eastern part of the city which had been set apart for the convenience of Bishop Luidhard and Queen Bertha's followers many years before was also thrown open to them until the king should permit a more highly organized attempt at evangelization.

The evident sincerity of the missionaries, their single-mindedness, their courage under trial, and, above all, the disinterested character of Augustine himself and the unworldly note of his doctrine made a profound impression on the mind of the king. He asked to be instructed and his baptism was appointed to take place at Pentecost. Whether the queen and her Frankish bishop had any real hand in the process of this comparatively sudden conversion, it is impossible to say. St. Gregory's letter written to Bertha herself, when the news of the king's baptism had reached Rome, would lead us to infer, that, while little or nothing had been done before Augustine's arrival, afterwards there was an endeavour on the part of the queen to make up for past remissness. The pope writes: "Et quoniam, Deo volente, aptum nunc tempus est, agite, ut divinâ gratiâ co-operante, cum augmento possitis quod neglectum est reparare". [Greg., Epp., XI (indic., iv), 29.] The remissness does seem to have been atoned for, when we take into account the Christian activity associated with the names of this royal pair during the next few months. Æthelberht's conversion naturally gave a great impetus to the enterprise of Augustine and his companions. Augustine himself determined to act at once upon the provisional instructions he had received from Pope Gregory. He crossed over to Gaul and sought episcopal consecration at the hands of Virgilius, the Metropolitan of Arles. Returning almost immediately to Kent, he made preparations for that more active and open form of propaganda for which Æthelberht's public baptism had prepared a way. It is characteristic of the spirit which actuated Augustine and his companions that no attempt was made to secure converts on a large scale by the employment of force. Bede tells us that it was part of the king's uniform policy "to compel no man to embrace Christianity" (H. E., I, xxvi) and we know from more than one of his extant letters what the pope thought of a method so strangely at variance with the teaching of the Gospels. On Christmas Day, 597, more than ten thousand persons were baptized by the first "Archbishop of the English". The great ceremony probably took place in the waters of the Swale, not far from the mouth of the Medway. News of these extraordinary events was at once dispatched to the pope, who wrote in turn to express his joy to his friend Eulogius, Bishop of Alexandria, to Augustine himself, and to the king and queen. (Epp., VIII, xxx; XI, xxviii; ibid., lxvi; Bede, H. E., I, xxxi, xxxii.) Augustine's message to Gregory was carried by Lawrence the Presbyter, afterwards Archbishop of Canterbury, and Peter one of the original colony of missionary monks. They were instructed to ask for more Gospel labourers, and, if we may trust Bede's account in this particular and the curious group of letters embodied in his narrative, they bore with them a list of *dubia*, or questions, bearing upon several points of discipline and ritual with regard to which Augustine awaited the pope's answer.

The genuineness of the document or *libellus*, as Bede calls it (H. E., II, i), in which the pope is alleged to have answered the doubts of the new archbishop has not been seriously called in question; though scholars have felt the force of the objection which St. Boniface, writing in the second quarter of the eighth century, urges, viz. that no trace of it could be found in the official collection of St. Gregory's correspondence preserved in the registry of the Roman Church. (Haddan and Stubbs, III, 336; Dudden, "Gregory the Great", II, 130, note; Mason, "Mission of St. Augustine", preface, pp. viii and ix; Duchesne, "Origines", 3d ed., p. 99, note.) It contains nine *responsa*, the most important of which are those that touch upon local differences of ritual, the question of jurisdiction, and the perpetually recurring problem of marriage relationships. "Why", Augustine had asked "since the faith is one, should there be different usages in different churches; one way of saying Mass in the Roman Church, for instance, and another in the Church of Gaul?" The pope's reply is, that while "Augustine is not to forget the Church in which he has been brought up", he is at liberty to adopt from the usage of other Churches whatever is most likely to prove pleasing to Almighty God. "For institutions", he adds, "are not to be loved for the sake of places; but places, rather, for the sake of institutions". With regard to the delicate question of jurisdiction Augustine is informed that he is to exercise no authority over the churches of Gaul; but that "all the bishops of Britain are entrusted to him, to the end that the unlearned may be instructed, the wavering strengthened by persuasion and the perverse corrected with authority". [Greg., Epp., XI (indic., iv), 64; Bede, H. E., I, xxvii.] Augustine seized the first convenient opportunity to carry out the graver provisions of this last enactment. He had already received the pallium on the return of Peter and Lawrence from Rome in 601. The original band of missionaries had also been reinforced by fresh recruits, among whom "the first and most distinguished", as Bede notes, "were Mellitus, Justus, Paulinus, and Ruffinianus". Of these Ruffinianus was afterwards chosen abbot of the monastery established by Augustine in honour of St. Peter outside the eastern walls of the Kentish capital. Mellitus became the first English Bishop of London; Justus was appointed to the new see of Rochester, and Paulinus became Metropolitan of York.

Æthelberht, as Bretwalda, allowed his wider territory to be mapped out into dioceses, and exerted himself in Augustine's behalf to bring about a meeting with the Celtic bishops of Southern Britain. The conference took place in Malmesbury, on the borders of Wessex, not far from the Severn, at a spot long described in popular legend as Austin's Oak. (Bede, H. E., II, ii.) Nothing came of this attempt to introduce ecclesiastical uniformity. Augustine seems to have been willing enough to yield certain points; but on three important issues he would not compromise. He insisted on an unconditional surrender on the Easter controversy; on the mode of administering the Sacrament of Baptism; and on the duty of taking active measures in concert with him for the evangelization of the Saxon conquerors. The Celtic bishops refused to yield, and the meeting was broken up. A second conference was afterwards planned at which only seven of the British bishops convened. They were accompanied this time by a group of their "most learned men" headed by Dinoth, the abbot of the celebrated monastery of Bangor-is-coed. The result was, if anything, more discouraging than before. Accusations of unworthy motives were freely bandied on both sides. Augustine's Roman regard for form, together with his punctiliousness for personal precedence as Pope Gregory's representative, gave umbrage to the Celts. They denounced the Archbishop for his pride, and retired behind their mountains. As they were on the point of withdrawing, they heard the only angry threat that is recorded of the saint: "If ye will not have peace with the brethren, ye shall have war from your enemies; and if ye will not preach the way of life to the English, ye shall suffer the punishment of death at their hands".

Popular imagination, some ten years afterwards, saw a terrible fulfilment of the prophecy in the butchery of the Bangor monks at the hands of Æthelfrid the Destroyer in the great battle won by him at Chester in 613.

These efforts towards Catholic unity with the Celtic bishops and the constitution of a well-defined hierarchy for the Saxon Church are the last recorded acts of the saint's life. His death fell in the same year says a very early tradition (which can be traced back to Archbishop Theodore's time) as that of his beloved father and patron, Pope Gregory. Thorn, however, who attempts always to give the Canterbury version of these legends, asserts—somewhat inaccurately, it would appear, if his coincidences be rigorously tested —that it took place in 605. He was buried, in true Roman fashion, outside the walls of the Kentish capital in a grave dug by the side of the great Roman road which then ran from Deal to Canterbury over St. Martin's Hill and near the unfinished abbey church which he had begun in honour of Sts. Peter and Paul and which was afterwards to be dedicated to his memory. When the monastery was completed, his relics were translated to a tomb prepared for them in the north porch. A modern hospital is said to occupy the site of his last resting place. [Stanley, "Memorials of Canterbury" (1906), 38.] His feast day in the Roman Calendar is kept on 28 May; but in the proper of the English office it occurs two days earlier, the true anniversary of his death.

BEDE, *Hist. Eccl.*, I and II; PAULUS DIACONUS, JOHANNES DIACONUS, and *St. Gall MSS., Lives of St. Gregory* in *P. L.*, LXXV; *Epistolæ Gregorii*, ibid.; GREGORY OF TOURS, *Historia Francorum*, ibid., LXXI; GOSCELIN, *Life of St. Gregory* in *Acta SS.*, May, VI, 370 sqq.; WM. THORNE, *Chron. Abbat. S. Aug.* in Twysden's *Decem Scriptores* (London, 1652), pp. 1758–2202; HADDAN AND STUBBS, *Councils and Ecclesiastical Documents relating to Great Britain and Ireland* (Oxford, 1869–1873, 3 vols.); MASON (ed.), *The Mission of St. Augustine according to the Original Documents* (Cambridge, 1897); DUDDEN, *Gregory the Great, His Place in the History of Thought* (London, New York, Bombay, 1905); *St. Gallen MS.*, ed. GASQUET (1904); STANLEY, *Memorials of Canterbury* (London, 1855, 1906); BASSENGE. *Die Sendung Augustins zur Bekehrung d. Angelsachsen* (Leipzig, 1890); BROU, *St. Augustin de Canterbury et ses Compagnons* (Paris, 1897); LÉVÊQUE, *St. Augustin de Canterbury, in Rev. des Quest. Hist.* (1899), xxi, 353–423; MARTELLI, *Récits des fêtes célébrées à l'occ. du 13e centenaire de l'arrivée de St. Aug. en Angleterre* (Paris, 1899).

CORNELIUS CLIFFORD.

Augustine of Hippo, SAINT, Doctor of the Church, b. 13 November, 354; d. 28 August, 430;—"a philosophical and theological genius of the first order, dominating, like a pyramid, antiquity and the succeeding ages . . . . Compared with the great philosophers of past centuries and modern times, he is the equal of them all; among theologians he is undeniably the first, and such has been his influence that none of the Fathers, Scholastics, or Reformers has surpassed it".—The extraordinary part played by the great Bishop of Hippo, and thus eulogized by Philip Schaff in his "History of the Christian Church", accounts for the length of this article treating I. His Life; II. His Works; III. His Function as a Doctor of the Church; IV. His System of Grace; V. Augustinism in History.

I. HIS LIFE.—Augustine's life is unfolded to us in documents of unrivalled richness, and of no great character of ancient times have we information comparable to that contained in the "Confessions", which relate the touching story of his soul, the "Retractations", which give the history of his mind, and the "Life of Augustine", written by his friend Possidius, telling of the saint's apostolate. We will confine ourselves to sketching the three periods of this great life: (1) the young wanderer's gradual return to the Faith; (2) the doctrinal development of the Christian philosopher to the time of his episcopate; and (3) the full development of his activities upon the episcopal throne of Hippo.

(1) Augustine was born at Tagaste, now Souk-Ahras, about 60 miles from Bona (ancient Hippo-Regius), and at that time a small free city of proconsular Numidia which had recently been converted from Donatism. Although eminently respectable, his family was not rich, and his father, Patricius, one of the *curiales* of the city, was still a pagan. However, the admirable virtues that made Monica the ideal of Christian mothers at length brought her husband the grace of baptism and of a holy death, about the year 371. Augustine received a Christian education. His mother had him signed with the cross and enrolled among the catechumens. Once, when very ill, he asked for baptism, but, all danger being soon passed, he deferred receiving the sacrament, thus yielding to a deplorable custom of the times. His association with "men of prayer" left three great ideas deeply engraven upon his soul: a Divine Providence, the future life with terrible sanctions, and, above all, Christ the Saviour. "From my tenderest infancy, I had in a manner sucked with my mother's milk that name of my Saviour, Thy Son; I kept it in the recesses of my heart; and all that presented itself to me without that Divine Name, though it might be elegant, well written, and even replete with truth, did not altogether carry me away" (Confessions, I, iv).

But a great intellectual and moral crisis stifled for a time all these Christian sentiments. The heart was the first point of attack. Patricius, proud of his son's success in the schools of Tagaste and Madaura determined to send him to Carthage to prepare for a forensic career. But, unfortunately, it required several months to collect the necessary means, and Augustine had to spend his sixteenth year at Tagaste in an idleness which was fatal to his virtue; he gave himself up to pleasure with all the vehemence of an ardent nature. At first he prayed, but without the sincere desire of being heard, and when he reached Carthage, towards the end of the year 370, every circumstance tended to draw him from his true course: the many seductions of the great city that was still half pagan, the licentiousness of other students, the theatres, the intoxication of his literary success, and a proud desire always to be first, even in evil. Before long he was obliged to confess to Monica that he had formed a sinful liaison with the person who bore him a son (372), "the son of his sin"—an entanglement from which he only delivered himself at Milan after fifteen years of its thraldom. Two extremes are to be avoided in the appreciation of this crisis. Some, like Mommsen, misled perhaps by the tone of grief in the "Confessions", have exaggerated it: in the "Realencyklopädie" (3d ed., II, 268) Loofs reproves Mommsen on this score, and yet he himself is too lenient towards Augustine, when he claims that in those days, the Church permitted concubinage. The "Confessions" alone prove that Loofs did not understand the 17th canon of Toledo. However, it may be said that, even in his fall, Augustine maintained a certain dignity and felt a compunction which does him honour, and that, from the age of nineteen, he had a genuine desire to break the chain. In fact, in 373, an entirely new inclination manifested itself in his life, brought about by the reading of Cicero's "Hortensius" whence he imbibed a love of the wisdom which Cicero so eloquently praises. Thenceforward Augustine looked upon rhetoric merely as a profession; his heart was in philosophy.

Unfortunately, his faith, as well as his morals, was to pass through a terrible crisis. In this same year, 373, Augustine and his friend Honoratus fell into the snares of the Manichæans. It seems strange that so great a mind should have been victimized by Oriental vapourings, synthesized by the Persian Mani (215–276) into a coarse, material dualism, and introduced into Africa scarcely fifty years previously.

Augustine himself tells us that he was enticed by the promises of a free philosophy unbridled by faith; by the boasts of the Manichæans, who claimed to have discovered contradictions in Holy Writ; and, above all, by the hope of finding in their doctrine a scientific explanation of nature and its most mysterious phenomena. Augustine's inquiring mind was enthusiastic for the natural sciences, and the Manichæans declared that nature withheld no secrets from Faustus, their doctor. Moreover, being tortured by the problem of the origin of evil, Augustine, in default of solving it, acknowledged a conflict of two principles. And then, again, there was a very powerful charm in the moral irresponsibility resulting from a doctrine which denied liberty and attributed the commission of crime to a foreign principle.

Once won over to this sect, Augustine devoted himself to it with all the ardour of his character; he read all its books, adopted and defended all its opinions. His furious proselytism drew into error his friend Alypius and Romanianus, his Mæcenas of Tagaste, the friend of his father who was defraying the expenses of Augustine's studies. It was during this Manichæan period that Augustine's literary faculties reached their full development, and he was still a student at Carthage when he embraced error. His studies ended, he should in due course have entered the *forum litigiosum*, but he preferred the career of letters, and Possidius tells us that he returned to Tagaste to "teach grammar". The young professor captivated his pupils, one of whom, Alypius, hardly younger than his master, loath to leave him, after following him into error, was afterwards baptized with him at Milan, eventually becoming Bishop of Tagaste, his native city. But Monica deeply deplored Augustine's heresy and would not have received him into her home or at her table but for the advice of a saintly bishop, who declared that "the son of so many tears could not perish". Soon afterwards Augustine went to Carthage, where he continued to teach rhetoric. His talents shone to even better advantage on this wider stage, and by an indefatigable pursuit of the liberal arts his intellect attained its full maturity. Having taken part in a poetic tournament, he carried off the prize, and the Proconsul Vindicianus publicly conferred upon him the *corona agonistica*. It was at this moment of literary intoxication, when he had just completed his first work on æsthetics, now lost, that he began to repudiate Manichæism. Even when Augustine was in his first fervour, the teachings of Mani had been far from quieting his restlessness, and although he has been accused of becoming a priest of the sect, he was never initiated or numbered among the "elect", but remained an "auditor"—the lowest degree in the hierarchy. He himself gives the reason for his disenchantment. First of all there was the fearful depravity of Manichæan philosophy—"They destroy everything and build up nothing"; then, the dreadful immorality in contrast with their affectation of virtue; the feebleness of their arguments in controversy with the Catholics, to whose Scriptural arguments their only reply was: "The Scriptures have been falsified". But, worse than all, he did not find science among them—science in the modern sense of the word—that knowledge of nature and its laws which they had promised him. When he questioned them concerning the movements of the stars, none of them could answer him. "Wait for Faustus", they said, "he will explain everything to you". Faustus of Mileve, the celebrated Manichæan bishop, at last came to Carthage; Augustine visited and questioned him, and discovered in his responses the vulgar rhetorician, the utter stranger to all scientific culture. The spell was broken, and, although Augustine did not immediately abandon

the sect, his mind rejected Manichæan doctrines. The illusion had lasted nine years.

But the religious crisis of this great soul was only to be resolved in Italy, under the influence of Ambrose. In 383 Augustine, at the age of twenty-nine, yielded to the irresistible attraction which Italy had for him, but his mother suspected his departure and was so reluctant to be separated from him that she resorted to a subterfuge and embarked under cover of the night. He had only just arrived in Rome when he was taken seriously ill; upon recovering he opened a school of rhetoric, but, disgusted by the tricks of his pupils, who shamelessly defrauded him of their tuition fees, he applied for a vacant professorship at Milan, obtained it, and was accepted by the prefect, Symmachus. Having visited Bishop Ambrose, the fascination of that saint's kindness induced him to become a regular attendant at his preachings. However, before embracing the Faith, Augustine underwent a three years' struggle during which his mind passed through several distinct phases. At first he turned towards the philosophy of the Academics, with its pessimistic scepticism; then neo-Platonic philosophy inspired him with genuine enthusiasm. At Milan he had scarcely read certain works of Plato and, more especially, of Plotinus, before the hope of finding the truth dawned upon him. Once more he began to dream that he and his friends might lead a life dedicated to the search for it, a life purged of all vulgar aspirations after honours, wealth, or pleasure, and with celibacy for its rule (Confessions, VI). But it was only a dream; his passions still enslaved him. Monica, who had joined her son at Milan, prevailed upon him to become betrothed, but his affianced bride was too young, and although Augustine dismissed the mother of Adeodatus, her place was soon filled by another. Thus did he pass through one last period of struggle and anguish. Finally, through the reading of the Holy Scriptures light penetrated his mind. Soon he possessed the certainty that Jesus Christ is the only way to truth and salvation. After that, resistance came only from the heart. An interview with Simplicianus, the future successor of St. Ambrose, who told Augustine the story of the conversion of the celebrated neo-Platonic rhetorician, Victorinus (Confessions, VIII, i, ii), prepared the way for the grand stroke of grace which, at the age of thirty-three, smote him to the ground in the garden at Milan (September, 386). A few days later Augustine, being ill, took advantage of the autumn holidays and, resigning his professorship, went with Monica, Adeodatus, and his friends to Cassisiacum, the country estate of Verecundus, there to devote himself to the pursuit of true philosophy which, for him, was now inseparable from Christianity.

(2) (*From 386 to 395*).—Augustine gradually became acquainted with Christian doctrine, and in his mind the fusion of Platonic philosophy with revealed dogmas was taking place. The law that governed this change of thought has of late years been frequently misconstrued; it is sufficiently important to be precisely defined. The solitude of Cassisiacum realized a long-cherished dream. In his books "Against the Academics", Augustine has described the ideal serenity of this existence, enlivened only by the passion for truth. He completed the education of his young friends, now by literary readings in common, now by philosophical conferences to which he sometimes invited Monica, and the accounts of which, compiled by a secretary, have supplied the foundation of the "Dialogues". Licentius, in his "Letters", would later on recall these delightful philosophical mornings and evenings, at which Augustine was wont to evolve the most elevating discussions from the most commonplace incidents. The favourite topics at their conferences

were truth, certainty (Against the Academics), true happiness in philosophy (On a Happy Life), the Providential order of the world and the problem of evil (On Order) and finally God and the soul (Soliloquies, On the Immortality of the Soul).

Here arises the curious question propounded by modern critics: Was Augustine a Christian when he wrote these "Dialogues" at Cassisiacum?—Until now no one had doubted it; historians, relying upon the "Confessions", had all believed that Augustine's retirement to the villa had for its twofold object the improvement of his health and his preparation for baptism. But certain critics nowadays claim to have discovered a radical opposition between the philosophical "Dialogues" composed in this retirement and the state of soul described in the "Confessions". According to Harnack, in writing the "Confessions" Augustine must have projected upon the recluse of 386 the sentiments of the bishop of 400. Others go farther and maintain that the recluse of the Milanese villa could not have been at heart a Christian, but a Platonist; and that the scene in the garden was a conversion not to Christianity, but to philosophy, the genuinely Christian phase beginning only in 390. But this interpretation of the "Dialogues" cannot withstand the test of facts and texts. It is admitted that Augustine received baptism at Easter, 387; and who could suppose that it was for him a meaningless ceremony? So too, how can it be admitted that the scene in the garden, the example of the recluses, the reading of St. Paul, the conversion of Victorinus, Augustine's ecstasies in reading the Psalms with Monica were all invented after the fact? Again, as it was in 388 that Augustine wrote his beautiful apology "On the Holiness of the Catholic Church", how is it conceivable that he was not yet a Christian at that date? To settle the argument, however, it is only necessary to read the "Dialogues" themselves. They are certainly a purely philosophical work—a work of youth, too, not without some pretension, as Augustine ingenuously acknowledges (Confessions, IX, iv); nevertheless, they contain the entire history of his Christian formation. As early as 386, the first work written at Cassisiacum reveals to us the great underlying motive of his researches. The object of his philosophy is to give authority the support of reason, and "for him the great authority, that which dominates all others and from which he never wished to deviate, is the authority of Christ"; and if he loves the Platonists it is because he counts on finding among them interpretations always in harmony with his faith (Against the Academics, III, c. x). To be sure such confidence was excessive, but it remains evident that in these "Dialogues" it is a Christian, and not a Platonist, that speaks. He reveals to us the intimate details of his conversion, the argument that convinced him (the life and conquests of the Apostles), his progress in the Faith at the school of St. Paul (ibid., II, ii), his delightful conferences with his friends on the Divinity of Jesus Christ, the wonderful transformations worked in his soul by faith, even to that victory of his over the intellectual pride which his Platonic studies had aroused in him (On The Happy Life, I, ii), and at last the gradual calming of his passions and the great resolution to choose wisdom for his only spouse (Soliloquies, I, x).

It is now easy to appreciate at its true value the influence of neo-Platonism upon the mind of the great African Doctor. It would be impossible for anyone who has read the works of St. Augustine to deny the existence of this influence; to be convinced, it suffices to glance at the passages from Plotinus and from Augustine arranged in parallel columns by M. Grandgeorge (Saint Augustin et le Néoplatonisme, 1896, 117–147). However, it would be a great exaggeration to pretend that it

at any time sacrificed the Gospel to Plato. The same learned critic thus wisely concludes his study: "So long, therefore, as his philosophy agrees with his religious doctrines, St. Augustine is frankly neo-Platonist; as soon as a contradiction arises, he never hesitates to subordinate his philosophy to religion, reason to faith. He was, first of all, a Christian; the philosophical questions that occupied his mind constantly found themselves more and more relegated to the background" (op. cit., 155). But the method was a dangerous one; in thus seeking harmony between the two doctrines he thought too easily to find Christianity in Plato, or Platonism in the Gospel. More than once, in his "Retractations" and elsewhere, he acknowledges that he has not always shunned this danger. Thus he had imagined that in Platonism he discovered the entire doctrine of the Word and the whole prologue of St. John. He likewise disavowed a good number of neo-Platonic theories which had at first misled him—the cosmological thesis of the universal soul, which makes the world one immense animal—the Platonic doubts upon that grave question: Is there a single soul for all or a distinct soul for each? But on the other hand, he had always reproached the Platonists, as Schaff very properly remarks (Saint Augustine, New York, 1886, p. 51), with being ignorant of, or rejecting, the fundamental points of Christianity: "first, the great mystery, the Word made flesh; and then love, resting on the basis of humility". They also ignore grace, he says, giving sublime precepts of morality without any help towards realizing them.

It was this Divine grace that Augustine sought in Christian baptism. Towards the beginning of Lent, 387, he went to Milan and, with Adeodatus and Alypius, took his place among the *competentes*, being baptized by Ambrose on Easter Day, or at least during Easter-tide. The tradition maintaining that the Te Deum was sung on that occasion by the bishop and the neophyte alternately is groundless. (See TE DEUM, THE.) Nevertheless this legend is certainly expressive of the joy of the Church upon receiving as her son him who was to be her most illustrious doctor. It was at this time that Augustine, Alypius, and Evodius resolved to retire into solitude in Africa. Augustine undoubtedly remained at Milan until towards autumn, continuing his works: "On the Immortality of the Soul" and "On Music". In the autumn of 387, he was about to embark at Ostia, when Monica was summoned from this life. In all literature there are no pages of more exquisite sentiment than the story of her saintly death and Augustine's grief (Confessions, IX). Augustine remained several months in Rome, chiefly engaged in refuting Manichæism. He sailed for Africa after the death of the tyrant Maximus (August, 388) and after a short sojourn in Carthage, returned to his native Tagaste. Immediately upon arriving there, he wished to carry out his idea of a perfect life, and began by selling all his goods and giving the proceeds to the poor. Then he and his friends withdrew to his estate, which had already been alienated, there to lead a common life in poverty, prayer, and the study of sacred letters. Book of the " LXXXIII Questions" is the fruit of conferences held in this retirement, in which he also wrote "De Genesi contra Manichæos", "De Magistro", and, "De Vera Religione".

Augustine did not think of entering the priesthood, and, through fear of the episcopacy, he even fled from cities in which an election was necessary. One day, having been summoned to Hippo by a friend whose soul's salvation was at stake, he was praying in a church when the people suddenly gathered about him, cheered him, and begged Valerius, the bishop, to raise him to the priesthood. In spite of his tears Augustine was obliged to yield to their entreaties, and was ordained in 391. The new priest looked upon his ordination as an additional reason for resuming religious life at Tagaste, and so fully did Valerius approve that he put some church property at Augustine's disposal, thus enabling him to establish a monastery—the second that he had founded. His priestly ministry of five years was admirably fruitful; Valerius had bidden him preach, in spite of the deplorable custom which in Africa reserved that ministry to bishops. Augustine combated heresy, especially Manichæism, and his success was prodigious. Fortunatus, one of their great doctors, whom Augustine had challenged in public conference, was so humiliated by his defeat that he fled from Hippo. Augustine also abolished the abuse of holding banquets in the chapels of the martyrs. He took part, 8 October, 393, in the Plenary Council of Africa, presided over by Aurelius, Bishop of Carthage, and, at the request of the bishops, was obliged to deliver a discourse which, in its completed form, afterwards became the treatise "De Fide et symbolo".

(3) (*From 396 to 430*).—Enfeebled by old age, Valerius, Bishop of Hippo, obtained the authori-

But he was above all the defender of truth and the shepherd of souls. His doctrinal activities, the influence of which was destined to last as long as the Church itself, were manifold: he preached frequently, sometimes for five days consecutively, his sermons breathing a spirit of charity that won all hearts; he wrote letters which scattered broadcast through the then known world his solutions of the problems of that day; he impressed his spirit upon divers African councils at which he assisted, for instance, those of Carthage in 398, 401, 407, 419 and of Mileve in 416 and 418; and lastly struggled indefatigably against all errors. To relate these struggles were endless; we shall, therefore, select only the chief controversies and indicate in each the doctrinal attitude of the great Bishop of Hippo.

(a) *The Manichæan Controversy and the Problem of Evil.*—After Augustine became bishop the zeal which, from the time of his baptism, he had manifested in bringing his former co-religionists into the true Church, took on a more paternal form without losing its pristine ardour—"Let those rage against us who know not at what a bitter cost truth is at-

St. Augustine on the Sea-shore (Pinturicchio)

zation of Valerius, Primate of Africa, to associate Augustine with himself as coadjutor. Augustine had to resign himself to consecration at the hands of Megalius, Primate of Numidia. He was then forty-two, and was to occupy the See of Hippo for thirty-four years. The new bishop understood well how to combine the exercise of his pastoral duties with the austerities of the religious life, and although he left his convent, his episcopal residence became a monastery where he lived a community life with his clergy, who bound themselves to observe religious poverty. Was it an order of regular clerics or of monks that he thus founded?—This is a question often asked, but we feel that Augustine gave but little thought to such distinctions. Be that as it may, the episcopal house at Hippo became a veritable nursery which supplied the founders of the monasteries that were soon spread all over Africa and the bishops who occupied the neighbouring sees. Possidius (Vita S. August., xxii) enumerates ten of the saint's friends and disciples who were promoted to the episcopacy. Thus it was that Augustine earned the title of patriarch of the religious, and renovator of the clerical life in Africa.

tained. . . . As for me, I should show you the same forbearance that my brethren had for me when I, blind, was wandering in your doctrines" (Contra Epistolam Fundamenti, iii). Among the most memorable events that occurred during this controversy was the great victory won in 404 over Felix, one of the "elect" of the Manichæans and the great doctor of the sect. He was propagating his errors in Hippo, and Augustine invited him to a public conference the issue of which would necessarily cause a great stir; Felix declared himself vanquished, embraced the Faith, and, together with Augustine, subscribed the acts of the conference. In his writings Augustine successively refuted Mani (397), the famous Faustus (400), Secundinus (405), and (about 415) the fatalistic Priscillianists whom Paulus Orosius had denounced to him. These writings contain the saint's clear, unquestionable views on the eternal problem of evil, views based on an optimism proclaiming, like the Platonists, that every work of God is good and that the only source of moral evil is the liberty of creatures (De Civitate Dei, XIX, c. xiii, n. 2). Augustine takes up the defence of free will, even in man as he is, with such ardour that his works against the Manichæans are an inexhaustible storehouse of arguments in this still living controversy.

In vain have the Jansenists maintained that Augustine was unconsciously a Pelagian and that he afterwards acknowledged the loss of liberty through the sin of Adam. Modern critics, doubtless unfamiliar with Augustine's complicated system and his peculiar terminology, have gone much farther. In the "Revue d'histoire et de littérature religieuses" (1899, p. 447), M. Margival exhibits St. Augustine as the victim of metaphysical pessimism unconsciously imbibed from Manichæan doctrines. "Never", says he, "will the Oriental idea of the necessity and the eternity of evil have a more zealous defender than this bishop". Nothing is more opposed to the facts. Augustine acknowledges that he had not yet understood how the first good inclination of the will is a gift of God (Retractations, I, xxiii, n. 3); but it should be remembered that he never retracted his leading theories on liberty, never modified his opinion upon what constitutes its essential condition, that is to say, the full power of choosing or of deciding. Who will dare to say that in revising his own writings on so important a point he lacked either clearness of perception or sincerity?

(b) *The Donatist Controversy and the Theory of the Church.*—The Donatist schism was the last episode in the Montanist and Novatian controversies which had agitated the Church from the second century. While the East was discussing under varying aspects the Divine and Christological problem of the Word, the West, doubtless because of its more practical genius, took up the moral question of sin in all its forms. The general problem was the holiness of the Church; could the sinner be pardoned, and remain in her bosom? In Africa the question especially concerned the holiness of the hierarchy. The bishops of Numidia, who, in 312, had refused to accept as valid the consecration of Cæcilian, Bishop of Carthage, by a *traditor*, had inaugurated the schism and at the same time proposed these grave questions: Do the hierarchical powers depend upon the moral worthiness of the priest? How can the holiness of the Church be compatible with the unworthiness of its ministers?

At the time of Augustine's arrival in Hippo, the schism had attained immense proportions, having become identified with political tendencies—perhaps with a national movement against Roman domination. In any event, it is easy to discover in it an undercurrent of anti-social revenge which the emperors had to combat by strict laws. The strange sect known as "Soldiers of Christ", and called by Catholics *Circumcelliones* (brigands, vagrants), resembled the revolutionary sects of the Middle Ages in point of fanatic destructiveness—a fact that must not be lost sight of, if the severe legislation of the emperors is to be properly appreciated.

The history of Augustine's struggles with the Donatists is also that of his change of opinion on the employment of rigorous measures against the heretics; and the Church in Africa, of whose councils he had been the very soul, followed him in the change. This change of views is solemnly attested by the Bishop of Hippo himself, especially in his Letters, xciii (in the year 408). In the beginning, it was by conferences and a friendly controversy that he sought to re-establish unity. He inspired various conciliatory measures of the African councils, and sent ambassadors to the Donatists to invite them to re-enter the Church, or at least to urge them to send deputies to a conference (403). The Donatists met these advances at first with silence, then with insults, and lastly with such violence that Possidius, Bishop of Calamet, Augustine's friend, escaped death only by flight, the Bishop of Bagaïa was left covered with horrible wounds, and the life of the Bishop of Hippo himself was several times attempted (Letter lxxxviii, to Januarius, the Donatist bishop). This madness of the Circumcelliones required harsh repression, and Augustine, witnessing the many conversions that resulted therefrom, thenceforth approved rigid laws. However, this important restriction must be pointed out: that St. Augustine never wished heresy to be punishable by death— *Vos rogamus ne occidatis* (Letter c, to the Proconsul Donatus). But the bishops still favoured a conference with the schismatics, and in 410 an edict issued by Honorius put an end to the refusal of the Donatists. A solemn conference took place at Carthage, in June, 411, in presence of 286 Catholic, and 279 Donatist bishops. The Donatist spokesmen were Petilian of Constantine, Primian of Carthage, and Emeritus of Cæsarea; the Catholic orators, Aurelius and Augustine. On the historic question then at issue, the Bishop of Hippo proved the innocence of Cæcilian and his consecrator Felix, and in the dogmatic debate he established the Catholic thesis that the Church, as long as it is upon earth, can, without losing its holiness, tolerate sinners within its pale for the sake of converting them. In the name of the emperor the Proconsul Marcellinus sanctioned the victory of the Catholics on all points. Little by little Donatism died out, to disappear with the coming of the Vandals.

So amply and magnificently did Augustine develop his theory on the Church that, according to Specht, "he deserves to be named the Doctor of the Church as well as the "Doctor of Grace"; and Möhler (Dogmatik, 351) is not afraid to write: "For depth of feeling and power of conception nothing written on the Church since St. Paul's time, is comparable to the works of St. Augustine". He has corrected, perfected, and even excelled the beautiful pages of St. Cyprian on the Divine institution of the Church, its authority, its essential marks, and its mission in the economy of grace and the administration of the sacraments. The Protestant critics, Dorner, Bindemann, Böhringer and especially Reuter, loudly proclaim, and sometimes even exaggerate, this rôle of the Doctor of Hippo; and while Harnack does not quite agree with them in every respect he does not hesitate to say (History of Dogma, II, c. iii): "It is one of the points upon which Augustine specially affirms and strengthens the Catholic idea. . . . He was the first [!] to transform the authority of the Church into a religious power, and to confer upon practical religion the gift of a doctrine of the Church." He was not the first, for Dorner acknowledges (Augustinus, 88) that Optatus of Mileve had expressed the basis of the same doctrines. Augustine, however, deepened, systematized, and completed the views of St. Cyprian and Optatus. But it is impossible here to go into detail. (See Specht, Die Lehre von der Kirche nach dem hl. Augustinus, Paderborn, 1892.)

(c) *The Pelagian Controversy and the Doctor of Grace.*—The close of the struggle against the Donatists almost coincided with the beginnings of a very grave theological dispute which not only was to demand Augustine's unremitting attention up to the time of his death, but was to become an eternal problem for individuals and for the Church. Farther on we shall enlarge upon Augustine's system; here we need only indicate the phases of the controversy. Africa, where Pelagius and his disciple Celestius had sought refuge after the taking of Rome by Alaric, was the principal centre of the first Pelagian disturbances; as early as 412 a council held at Carthage condemned Pelagians for their attacks upon the doctrine of original sin. Among other books directed against them by Augustine was his famous "De naturâ et gratiâ". Thanks to his activity the condemnation of these innovators, who had succeeded in deceiving a synod convened at Diospolis in Palestine, was reiterated by councils held later at Carthage and Mileve and confirmed by Pope Innocent I (417). A second period of Pelagian intrigues developed at Rome, but Pope Zosimus, whom the stratagems of Celestius had for a moment deluded, being enlightened by Augustine, pronounced the solemn condemnation of these heretics in 418. Thenceforth the combat was conducted in writing against Julian of Eclanum, who assumed the leadership of the party and violently attacked Augustine. Towards 426 there entered the lists a school which afterwards acquired the name of Semipelagian, the first members being monks of Hadrumetum in Africa, who were followed by others from Marseilles, led by Cassian, the celebrated abbot of Saint-Victor. Unable to admit the absolute gratuitousness of predestination, they sought a middle course between Augustine and Pelagius, and maintained that grace must be given to those who merit it and denied to others; hence goodwill has the precedence, it desires, it asks, and God rewards. Informed of their views by Prosper of Aquitaine, the holy Doctor once more expounded, in "De Prædestinatione Sanctorum", how even these first desires for salvation are due to the grace of God, which therefore absolutely controls our predestination.

(d) *Struggles against Arianism and Closing Years.*— In 426 the holy Bishop of Hippo, at the age of seventy-two, wishing to spare his episcopal city the turmoil of an election after his death, caused both clergy and people to acclaim the choice of the deacon Heraclius as his auxiliary and successor, and transferred to him the administration of externals. Augustine might then have enjoyed some rest had Africa not been agitated by the undeserved disgrace and the revolt of Count Boniface (427). The Goths, sent by the Empress Placidia to oppose Boniface, and the Vandals, whom the latter summoned to his assistance, were all Arians. Maximinus, an Arian bishop, entered Hippo with the imperial troops. The holy Doctor defended the Faith at a public conference (428) and in various writings. Being deeply grieved at the devastation of Africa, he laboured to effect a reconciliation between Count Boniface and the empress. Peace was indeed re-established, but not with Genseric, the Vandal king. Boniface, vanquished, sought refuge in Hippo, whither many bishops had already fled for protection and this well fortified city was to suffer the horrors of an eighteen months' siege. Endeavouring to control his anguish, Augustine continued to refute Julian of Eclanum; but early in the siege he was stricken with what he realized to be a fatal illness, and, after three months of admirable patience and fervent prayer, departed from this land of exile, in the seventy-sixth year of his age.

II. HIS WORKS.—Augustine was one of the most prolific geniuses that humanity has ever known, and is admired not only for the number of his works, but also for the variety of subjects, which traverse the whole realm of thought. The form in which he casts his work exercises a very powerful attraction on the reader. Bardenhewer praises his extraordinary suppleness of expression and his marvellous gift of describing interior things, of painting the various states of the soul and the facts of the spiritual world. His latinity bears the stamp of his age. In general, his style is noble and chaste; but, says the same author, "in his sermons and other popular writings he purposely drops to the language of the people". A detailed analysis is impossible here. We shall merely indicate his principal writings and the date (often approximative) of their composition.

(1) *Autobiography and Correspondence.*—The "Confessions" are the history of his heart; the "Retractations", of his mind; while the "Letters" show his activity in the Church.

(a) The "Confessions" (towards A. D. 400) are, in the Biblical sense of the word *confiteri*, not an avowal or an account, but the praise of a soul that admires the action of God within itself. Of all the works of the holy Doctor none has been more universally read and admired, none has caused more salutary tears to flow. Neither in respect of penetrating analysis of the most complex impressions of the soul, nor communicative feeling, nor elevation of sentiment, nor depth of philosophic views, is there any book like it in all literature. (b) The "Retractations" (towards the end of his life, 426–428) are a revision of the works of the saint in chronological order, explaining the occasion and dominant idea of each. They are a guide of inestimable price for seizing the progress of Augustine's thought. (c) The "Letters", amounting in the Benedictine collection to 270 (53 of them from Augustine's correspondents), are a treasure of the greatest value, for the knowledge of his life, influence and even his doctrine.

(2) *Philosophy.*—These writings, for the most part composed in the villa of Cassisiacum, from his conversion to his baptism (386–387), continue the autobiography of the saint by initiating us into the researches and Platonic hesitations of his mind. There is less freedom in them than in the Confessions. They are literary essays, writings whose simplicity is the acme of art and elegance. Nowhere is the style of Augustine so chastened, nowhere is his language so pure. Their dialogue form shows that they were inspired by Plato and Cicero. The chief ones are: "Contra Academicos" (the most important of all); "De Beatâ Vitâ"; "De Ordine"; the two books of "Soliloquies", which must be distinguished from the "Soliloquies" and "Meditations" which are certainly not authentic; "De Immortalitate animæ"; "De Magistro" (a dialogue between Augustine and his son Adeodatus); and six curious books (the sixth especially) on *Music*.

(3) *General Apology.*—(a) In the "City of God" (begun in 413, but the books XX–XXII are of 426) Augustine answers the pagans, who attributed the fall of Rome (410) to the abolition of pagan worship. Considering this problem of Divine Providence with regard to the Roman Empire, he widens the horizon still more and in a burst of genius he creates the philosophy of history, embracing as he does with a glance the destinies of the world grouped around the Christian religion, the only one which goes back to the beginning and leads humanity to its final term. "The City of God" is considered as the most important work of the great bishop. The other works chiefly interest theologians; but it, like the "Confessions", belongs to general literature and appeals to every soul. The "Confessions" are theology which has been lived in the soul, and the history of God's action on individuals, while "The City of God" is theology framed in the history of humanity, and explaining the action of God in the world. (b) Other apologetic writings, like the "De Verâ Religione" (a little masterpiece composed at Tagaste, 389–391), "De Utilitate Credendi" (391), "Liber de fide rerum quæ non videntur" (400), and the "Letter CXX to Consentius", constitute Augustine the great theorist of the Faith, and of its relations to reason. "He is the first of the Fathers", says Harnack (Dogmengeschichte, III, 97) "who felt the need of forcing his faith to reason". And indeed he, who so repeatedly affirms that faith precedes the intelligent apprehension of the truths of revelation— he it is who marks out with greater clearness of definition and more precisely than anyone else the function of the reason in preceding and verifying the witness's claim to credence, and in accompanying the mind's act of adhesion. (Letter to Consentius, n. 3, 8, etc.) What would not have been the stupefaction of Augustine if anyone had told him that

faith must close its eyes to the proofs of the divine testimony, under the penalty of its becoming science! —Or if one had spoken to him of faith in authority giving its assent, without examining any motive which might prove the value of the testimony!— It surely cannot be possible for the human mind to accept testimony without known motives for such acceptance, or, again, for any testimony, even when learnedly sifted out, to give the science—the inward view—of the object.

(4) *Controversies with Heretics.*—(a) Against the Manichæans; "De Moribus Ecclesiæ Catholicæ et de Moribus Manichæorum" (at Rome, 368); "De Duabus Animabus" (before 392); "Acts of the Dispute with Fortunatus the Manichæan" (392); "Acts of the Conference with Felix" (404); "De Libero Arbitrio"—very important on the origin of evil; various writings "Contra Adimantem"; against the Epistle of Mani (the foundation); against Faustus (about 400); against Secundinus (405), etc. (b) Against the Donatists: "Psalmus contra partem Donati" (about 395), a purely rhythmic song for popular use (the oldest example of its kind); "Contra epistolam Parmeniani" (400); "De Baptismo contra Donatistas" (about 400), one of the most important pieces in this controversy; "Contra litteras Parmeniani", "Contra Cresconium", etc.—a good number of letters, also, relate to this debate. (c) Against the Pelagians, in chronological order, we have: 412, "De peccatorum meritis et remissione" (On merit and forgiveness); same year, "De spiritu et litterâ" (On the spirit and the letter); 415, "De Perfectione justitiæ hominis"—important for understanding Pelagian impeccability; 417, "De Gestis Pelagii" —a history of the Council of Diospolis, whose acts it reproduces; 418, "De Gratiâ Christi et de peccato originali"; 419, "De nuptiis et concupiscentiâ"; and other writings (420–428); "Against Julian of Eclanum"—the last of this series, interrupted by the death of the saint. (d) Against the Semipelagians: "De correptione et gratiâ" (427); "De prædestinatione Sanctorum" (428); "De Dono Perseverantiæ" (429).—(e) Against Arianism: "Contra sermonem Arianorum" (418) and "Collatio cum Maximino Arianorum episcopo" (the celebrated conference of Hippo in 428).

(5) *Scriptural Exegesis.*—Augustine in the "De Doctrinâ Christianâ" (begun in 397 and ended in 426) gives us a genuine treatise of exegesis, historically the first (for St. Jerome wrote rather as a controversialist). Several times he attempted a commentary on Genesis. The great work "De Genesi ad litteram" was composed from 401 to 415. The "Enarrationes in Psalmos" are a masterpiece of popular eloquence, with a swing and a warmth to them which are inimitable. On the New Testament: the "De Sermone Dei in Monte (during his priestly ministry) is especially noteworthy; "De Consensu Evangelistarum (Harmony of the Gospels—400); "Homilies on St. John" (416), generally classed among the chief works of Augustine; the "Exposition of the Epistle to the Galatians" (324), etc. The most remarkable of his Biblical works illustrate either a theory of exegesis (one generally approved) which delights in finding mystical or allegorical interpretations, or the style of preaching which is founded on that view. His strictly exegetical work is far from equalling in scientific value that of St. Jerome. His knowledge of the Biblical languages was insufficient: he read Greek with difficulty; as for Hebrew, all that we can gather from the recent studies of Schanz and Rottmanner is that he was familiar with Punic, a language allied to Hebrew. Moreover, the two grand qualities of his genius— ardent feeling and prodigious subtlety—carried him away into interpretations that were violent or more ingenious than solid.

But the hermeneutics of Augustine merit great praise, especially for their insistence upon the stern law of extreme prudence in determining the meaning of Scripture: *We must be on our guard against giving interpretations which are hazardous or opposed to science, and so exposing the word of God to the ridicule of unbelievers* (De Genesi ad litteram, I, xix, xxi, especially n. 39). An admirable application of this well-ordered liberty appears in his thesis on the simultaneous creation of the universe, and the gradual development of the world under the action of the natural forces which were placed in it. Certainly the instantaneous act of the Creator did not produce an organized universe as we see it now. But, in the beginning, God created all the elements of the world in a confused and *nebulous* mass (the word is Augustine's—*Nebulosa species apparet;* "De Genesi ad litt.", I, n. 27), and in this mass were the mysterious germs (*rationes seminales*) of the future beings which were to develop themselves, when favourable circumstances should permit. Is Augustine, therefore, an Evolutionist?—If we mean that he had a deeper and wider mental grasp than other thinkers had of the forces of nature and the plasticity of beings, it is an incontestable fact; and from this point of view Father Zahm (Bible, Science, and Faith, pp. 58–66, French tr.) properly felicitates him on having been the precursor of modern thought. But if we mean that he admitted in matter a power of differentiation and of gradual transformation, passing from the homogeneous to the heterogeneous, the most formal texts force us to recognize that Augustine proclaimed the fixity of species, and did not admit that "from one identical primitive principle, or from one germ, different realities can issue". This judgment of the Abbé Martin in his very searching study on this subject (S. Augustin, p. 314) must correct the conclusion of Father Zahm. "The elements of this corporeal world have also their well defined force, and their proper quality, from which depends what each one of them can or cannot do, and what reality ought or ought not to issue from each one of them. Hence it is that from a grain of wheat a bean cannot issue, nor wheat from a bean, nor a man from a beast, nor a beast from a man" (De Genesi ad litt., IX, n. 32).

(6) *Dogmatic and Moral Exposition.*—(a) The fifteen books "De Trinitate", on which he worked for fifteen years, from 400 to 416, are the most elaborate and profound work of St. Augustine. The last books on the analogies which the mystery of the Trinity have with our soul are much discussed. The saintly author himself declares that they are only analogous and are far-fetched and very obscure. (b) The "Enchiridion", or handbook, on Faith, Hope, and Love, composed, in 421, at the request of a pious Roman, Laurentius, is an admirable synthesis of Augustine's theology, reduced to the three theological virtues. Father Faure has given us a learned commentary of it, and Harnack a detailed analysis (Hist. of dogmas, III, 205, 221). (c) Several volumes of miscellaneous questions, among which "Ad Simplicianum" (397) has been especially noted. (d) Numberless writings of his have a practical aim: two on "Lying" (374 and 420), five on "Continence", "Marriage", and "Holy Widowhood", one on "Patience", another on "Prayer for the Dead" (421).

(7) *Pastorals and Preaching.*—The theory of preaching and religious instruction of the people is given in the "De Catechizandis Rudibus" (400) and in the fourth book "De Doctrinâ Christianâ". The oratorical work alone is of vast extent. Besides the Scriptural homilies, the Benedictines have collected 363 sermons which are certainly authentic; the brevity of these suggests that they are stenographic, often revised by Augustine himself. If

the Doctor in him predominates over the orator, if he possesses less of colour, of opulence, of actuality, and of Oriental charm than St. John Chrysostom, we find, on the other hand, a more nervous logic, bolder comparisons, greater elevation and greater profundity of thought, and sometimes, in his bursts of emotion and his daring lapses into dialogue-form, he attains the irresistible power of the Greek orator. The oratorical merit of Augustine has recently been placed in strong relief by Rottmanner in "Historisches Jahrbuch", 1898, p. 894; and H. Pope, O. P., in "The Ecclesiastical Review", September, 1906.

Editions of St. Augustine's works.—The best edition of his complete works is that of the Benedictines, eleven tomes in eight folio volumes (Paris, 1679–1700). It has been often reprinted, e. g. by Gaume (Paris, 1836–39), in eleven octavo volumes, and by Migne, P. L., XXXII–XLVII. The last volume of the Migne reprint contains a number of important earlier studies on St. Augustine—Vivès, Noris, Merlin, particularly the literary history of the editions of Augustine from Schönemann's "Bibl. hist. lit. patrum Lat." (Leipzig, 1794). For critical remarks on the Benedictine, or Maurist, edition, see R. Kukula and O. Rottmanner in the reports of the Vienna Academy of Science for 1890, 93, 98. Since 1887 a new edition of St. Augustine has been appearing in the "Corpus Scriptorum Eccl. Latinorum" of the Vienna Academy —the "Confessions" by P. Knöll (XXXIII), the "De Civitate Dei", by E. Hoffmann (XL), etc. The principal tractates of St. Augustine are also found in the collection of H. Hurter, "SS. PP. Opuscula selecta" (Innsbruck, 1868 sqq.).—*English translations.*—Dr. Pusey's "Library of the Fathers" (Oxford, 1839–55) contains translations of many works of St. Augustine—the "Confessions", sermons, treatises, expositions on the Psalms, and "Homilies on John". It is well supplemented by the "Augustinian Library" of Marcus Dods (Edinburgh, 1872–76, 15 vols., 8vo), which contains a great number of translations, from the pens of Cunningham, Findlay, Salmond, Holmes, Wallis, and others—the "City of God", the "Confessions", the Anti-Donatist, Anti-Pelagian, and Anti-Manichæan works, "On the Trinity", "Sermon on the Mount", "Harmony of the Gospels", "On Christian Doctrine", the "Enchiridion", "On the Faith and the Creed", "On Catechizing the Ignorant". These volumes, enriched with other translations and introductory discourses, were reprinted under the editorial direction of Dr. Philip Schaff (New York, 1886–88, 8 vols.). Dr. Pusey's translation of the "Confessions", he says himself, is a revision of the version of W. Watts (London, 1650), with addition of a lengthy preface and notes; the same translation, reprinted at Boston (1843), and then reputed anonymous, furnished Dr. W. G. T. Shedd (Andover, 1860) with the text for his "excellent original introduction in which he clearly and vigorously characterizes the Confessions and draws a comparison between them and the Confessions of Rousseau" (Schaff, Hist. of the Christian Church, 5th ed., New York, 1903, p. 1005). The earliest English translation of the "De Civitate Dei" bears the title: "Of the Citie of God with the learned comments of Jo. L. Vivès, Englished first by J. H(ealey), London, 1610". There is a German (Catholic) translation of several works of St. Augustine in the "Kempten Bibliothek der Kirchenväter" (1871–79, 8 vols.).

III. His FUNCTION AS A DOCTOR OF THE CHURCH.—When the critics endeavour to determine Augustine's place in the history of the Church and of civilization, there can be no question of exterior or political influence, such as was exercised by St. Leo, St. Gregory, or St. Bernard. As Reuter justly observes, Augustine was bishop of a third-rate city and had scarcely any direct control over politics, and Harnack adds that perhaps he had not the qualifications of a statesman. If Augustine occupies a place apart in the history of humanity, Eucken and men of his calibre agree that it is as a thinker, his influence being felt even outside the realm of theology, and playing a most potent part in the orientation of Western thought. It is now universally conceded that, in the intellectual field, this influence is unrivalled even by that of Thomas Aquinas, and Augustine's teaching marks a distinct epoch in the history of Christian thought. The better to emphasize this important fact we shall try to determine: (1) the rank and degree of influence that must be ascribed to Augustine; (2) the nature, or the elements, of his doctrinal influence; (3) the general qualities of his doctrine; and (4) the character of his genius.

(1) *The greatest of the Doctors.*—It is first of all a remarkable fact that the great critics, Protestant as well as Catholic, are almost unanimous in placing St. Augustine in the foremost rank of Doctors and proclaiming him to be the greatest of the Fathers. Such, indeed, was also the opinion of his contemporaries, judging from their expressions of enthusiasm gathered by the Bollandists. The popes attributed such exceptional authority to the Doctor of Hippo that, even of late years, it has given rise to lively theological controversies. Peter the Venerable accurately summarized the general sentiment of the Middle Ages when he ranked Augustine immediately after the Apostles; and in modern times Bossuet, whose genius was most like that of Augustine, assigns him the first place among the Doctors, nor does he simply call him "the incomparable Augustine", but "the Eagle of Doctors", "the Doctor of Doctors". If the Jansenistic abuse of his works and perhaps the exaggerations of certain Catholics, as well as the attack of Richard Simon, seem to have alarmed some minds, the general opinion has not varied. In the nineteenth century Stöckl expressed the thought of all when he said, "Augustine has justly been called the greatest Doctor of the Catholic world".

And the admiration of Protestant critics is not less enthusiastic. More than this, it would seem as if they had in these latter days been quite specially fascinated by the great figure of Augustine, so deeply and so assiduously have they studied him (Bindemann, Schaff, Dorner, Reuter, A. Harnack, Eucken, Scheel, and so on) and all of them agree more or less with Harnack when he says: "Where, in the history of the West, is there to be found a man who, in point of influence, can be compared with him?" Luther and Calvin were content to treat Augustine with a little less irreverence than they did the other Fathers, but their descendants do him full justice, although recognizing him as the Father of Roman Catholicism. According to Bindemann, "Augustine is a star of extraordinary brilliancy in the firmament of the Church. Since the Apostles he has been unsurpassed". In his "History of the Church" Dr. Kurtz calls Augustine "the greatest, the most powerful of all the Fathers, him from whom proceeds all the doctrinal and ecclesiastical development of the West, and to whom each recurring crisis, each new orientation of thought brings it back". Schaff himself (Saint Augustine, Melanchthon and Neander, p. 98) is of the same opinion: "While most of the great men in the history of the Church are claimed either by the Catholic or by the Protestant confession, and their influence is therefore confined to one or the other, he enjoys from both a respect equally profound and enduring". Rudolf Eucken is bolder still, when he says: "On the ground of Christianity proper a single philosopher has appeared and that is Augustine". The English writer, W. Cunningham, is no less appreciative of the extent and perpetuity of this extraordinary influence: "The whole life of the medieval

Church was framed on lines which he has suggested: its religious orders claimed him as their patron; its mystics found a sympathetic tone in his teaching; its polity was to some extent the actualization of his picture of the Christian Church; it was in its various parts a carrying out of ideas which he cherished and diffused. Nor does his influence end with the decline of medievalism: we shall see presently how closely his language was akin to that of Descartes, who gave the first impulse to and defined the special character of modern philosophy." And after having established that the doctrine of St. Augustine was at the bottom of all the struggles between Jansenists and Catholics in the Church of France, between Arminians and Calvinists on the side of the Reformers, he adds: "And once more in our own land when a reaction arose against rationalism and Erastianism it was to the African Doctor that men turned with enthusiasm: Dr. Pusey's edition of the *Confessions* was among the first-fruits of the Oxford Movement".

But Adolf Harnack is the one who has oftenest emphasized the unique rôle of the Doctor of Hippo. He has studied Augustine's place in the history of the world as reformer of Christian piety and his influence as Doctor of the Church. In his study of the "Confessions" he comes back to it: "No man since Paul is comparable to him"—with the exception of Luther, he adds.—"Even to-day we live by Augustine, by his thought and his spirit; it is said that we are the sons of the Renaissance and the Reformation, but both one and the other depend upon him".

(2) *Nature and different aspects of his doctrinal influence.*—This influence is so varied and so complex that it is difficult to consider under all its different aspects. First of all, in his writings the great bishop collects and condenses the intellectual treasures of the old world and transmits them to the new. Harnack goes so far as to say: "It would seem that the miserable existence of the Roman empire in the West was prolonged until then, only to permit Augustine's influence to be exercised on universal history". It was in order to fulfil this enormous task that Providence brought him into contact with the three worlds whose thought he was to transmit: with the Roman and Latin world in the midst of which he lived, with the Oriental world partially revealed to him through the study of Manichæism, and with the Greek world shown to him by the Platonists. In philosophy he was initiated into the whole content and all the subtilties of the various schools, without, however, giving his allegiance to any one of them. In theology it was he who acquainted the Latin Church with the great dogmatic work accomplished in the East during the fourth century and at the beginning of the fifth; he popularized the results of it by giving them the more exact and precise form of the Latin genius.

To synthesis of the past, Augustine adds the incomparable wealth of his own thought, and he may be said to have been the most powerful instrument of Providence in development and advance of dogma. Here the danger has been not in denying, but in exaggerating, this advance. Augustine's dogmatic mission (in a lower sphere and apart from inspiration) recalls that of Paul in the preaching of the Gospel. It has also been subject to the same attacks and occasioned the same vagaries of criticism. Just as it was sought to make of Paulinism the real source of Christianity as we know it—a system that had smothered the primitive germ of the Gospel of Jesus—so it was imagined that, under the name of Augustinianism, Augustine had installed in the Church some sort of syncretism of the ideas of Paul and of neo-Platonism which was a deviation from ancient Christianity, fortunate according to some,

but according to others utterly deplorable. These fantasies do not survive the reading of the texts, and Harnack himself shows in Augustine the heir to the tradition that preceded him. Still, on the other hand, his share of invention and originality in the development of dogma must not be ignored, although here and there, on special questions, human weaknesses crop out. He realized, better than any of the Fathers, the progress so well expressed by Vincent of Lérins, his contemporary, in a page that some have turned against him.

In general, all Christian dogmatics are indebted to him for new theories that better justify and explain revelation, new views, and greater clearness and precision. The many struggles with which he was identified, together with the speculative turn of his mind, brought almost every question within the scope of his research. Even his way of stating problems so left his impress upon them that there is no problem, one might almost say, in considering which the theologian does not feel the study of Augustine's thought to be an imperative obligation. Certain dogmas in particular he so amply developed, so skilfully unsheathing the fruitful germ of the truths from their envelope of tradition, that many of these dogmas (wrongly, in our opinion) have been set down as "Augustinism". Augustine was not their inventor, he was only the first to put them in a strong light. They are chiefly the dogmas of the Fall, the Atonement, Grace, and Predestination. Schaff (op. cit., 97) has very properly said: "His appearance in the history of dogma forms a distinct epoch, especially as regards anthropological and soteriological doctrines, which he advanced considerably further, and brought to a greater clearness and precision, than they had ever had before in the consciousness of the Church". But he is not only the Doctor of Grace, he is also the Doctor of the Church: his twenty years' conflict with Donatism led to a complete exposition of the dogmas of the Church, the great work and mystical Body of Christ, and true Kingdom of God, of its part in salvation and of the intimate efficacy of its sacraments. It is on this point, as the very centre of Augustinian theology, that Reuter has concentrated those "Augustinische Studien" which, according to Harnack, are the most learned of recent studies on St. Augustine. Manichæan controversies also led him to state clearly the great questions of the Divine Being and of the nature of evil, and he might also be called the Doctor of Good, or of good principles of all things. Lastly, the very idiosyncrasy of his genius and the practical, supernatural, and Divine imprint left upon all his intellectual speculations have made him the Doctor of Charity.

Another step forward due to the works of Augustine is in the language of theology, for, if he did not create it, he at least contributed towards its definite settlement. It is indebted to him for a great number of epigrammatic formulæ, as significant as they are terse, afterwards singled out and adopted by Scholasticism. Besides, as Latin was more cise and less fluid in its forms than Greek, it was wonderfully well suited to the work. Augustine made it the dogmatic language *par excellence*, and Anselm, Thomas Aquinas, and others followed his lead. At times he has even been credited with the pseudo-Athanasian creed which is undoubtedly of later date, but those critics were not mistaken who traced its inspiration to the formulæ in "De Trinitate". Whoever its author may have been, he was certainly familiar with Augustine and drew upon his works. It is unquestionably this gift of concise expression, as well as his charity, that has so often caused the celebrated saying to be attributed to him: "In essentials unity, in non-essentials liberty, in all things charity".

Augustine stands forth, too, as the great inspirer of religious thought in subsequent ages. A whole volume would not be sufficient to contain the full account of his influence on posterity; here we shall merely call attention to its principal manifestations. It is, in the first place, a fact of paramount importance that, with St. Augustine, the centre of dogmatic and theological development changed from East to West. Hence, from this view-point again, he makes an epoch in the history of dogma. The critics maintain that up to his time the most powerful influence was exerted by the Greek Church, the East having been the classic land of theology, the great workshop for the elaboration of dogma. From the time of Augustine, the predominating influence seems to emanate from the West, and the practical, realistic spirit of the Latin race supplants the speculative and idealistic spirit of Greece and the East. Another fact, no less salient, is that it was the Doctor of Hippo who, in the bosom of the Church, inspired the two seemingly antagonistic movements, Scholasticism and Mysticism. From Gregory the Great to the Fathers of Trent, Augustine's theological authority, indisputably the highest, dominates all thinkers and is appealed to alike by the Scholastics Anselm, Peter Lombard, and Thomas Aquinas, and by Bernard, Hugh of St. Victor, and Tauler, exponents of Mysticism, all of whom were nourished upon his writings and penetrated with his spirit. There is not one of even the most modern tendencies of thought but derives from him whatever it may have of truth or of profound religious sentiment. Learned critics, such as Harnack, have called Augustine "the first modern man", and in truth, he so moulded the Latin world that it is really he who has shaped the education of modern minds. But, without going so far, we may quote the German philosopher, Eucken: "It is perhaps not paradoxical to say that if our age wishes to take up and treat in an independent way the problem of religion, it is not so much to Schleiermacher or Kant, or even Luther or St. Thomas, that it must refer, as to Augustine. . . . And outside of religion, there are points upon which Augustine is more modern than Hegel or Schopenhauer".

(3) *The dominating qualities of his doctrine.*—The better to understand St. Augustine's influence, we must point out in his doctrine certain general characteristics which must not be lost sight of, if, in reading his works, one would avoid troublesome misapprehensions. First, the full development of the great Doctor's mind was progressive. It was by stages, often aided by the circumstances and necessities of controversy, that he arrived at the exact knowledge of each truth and a clean-cut perception of its place in the synthesis of revelation. He also requires that his readers should know how to "advance with him". It is necessary to study St. Augustine's works in historical order and, as we shall see, this applies particularly to the doctrine of grace.

Augustinian doctrine is, again, essentially theological, and has God for its centre. To be sure Augustine is a great philosopher, and Fénelon said of him: "If an enlightened man were to gather from the books of St. Augustine the sublime truths which this great man has scattered at random therein, such a compendium [*extrait*], made with discrimination, would be far superior to Descartes' Meditations". And indeed just such a collection was made by the Oratorian ontologist, André Martin. There is then a philosophy of St. Augustine, but in him philosophy is so intimately coupled with theology as to be inseparable from it. Protestant historians have remarked this characteristic of his writings. "The world", says Eucken, "interests him less than the action of God in the world and especially in ourselves. God and the soul are the only subjects the knowledge of which ought to fire us with enthusiasm. All

knowledge becomes moral, religious knowledge, or rather a moral, religious conviction, an act of faith on the part of man, who gives himself up unreservedly". And with still greater energy Böhringer has said: "The axis on which the heart, life, and theology of Augustine move is God". Oriental discussions on the Word had forced Athanasius and the Greek Fathers to set faith in the Word and in Christ, the Saviour, at the very summit of theology; Augustine, too, in his theology, places the Incarnation at the centre of the Divine plan, but he looks upon it as the great historic manifestation of God to humanity— the idea of God dominates all: of God considered in His essence (On the Trinity), in His government (The City of God), or as the last end of all Christian life (Enchiridion and On the Christian Combat).

Lastly, Augustine's doctrine bears an eminently Catholic stamp and is radically opposed to Protestantism. It is important to establish this fact, principally because of the change in the attitude of Protestant critics towards St. Augustine. Indeed, nothing is more deserving of attention than this development so highly creditable to the impartiality of modern writers. The thesis of the Protestants of olden times is well known. Attempts to monopolize Augustine and to make him an ante-Reformation reformer, were certainly not wanting. Of course Luther had to admit that he did not find in Augustine justification by faith alone, that generating principle of all Protestantism; and Schaff tells us that he consoled himself with exclaiming (op. cit., p. 100): "Augustine has often erred, he is not to be trusted. Although good and holy, he was yet lacking in true faith as well as the other Fathers." But in general, the Reformation did not so easily fall into line, and for a long time it was customary to oppose the great name of Augustine to Catholicism. Article 20 of the Confession of Augsburg dares to ascribe to him justification without works, and Melanchthon invokes his authority in his "Apologia Confessionis". In the last thirty or forty years all has been changed, and the best Protestant critics now vie with one another in proclaiming the essentially Catholic character of Augustinian doctrine. In fact they go to extremes when they claim him to be the founder of Catholicism. It is thus that H. Reuter concludes his very important studies on the Doctor of Hippo: "I consider Augustine the founder of Roman Catholicism in the West. . . . This is no new discovery, as Kattenbusch seems to believe, but a truth long since recognized by Neander, Julius Köstlin, Dorner, Schmidt, . . . etc.". Then, as to whether Evangelicalism is to be found in Augustine, he says: "Formerly this point was reasoned out very differently from what it is nowadays. . . . The phrases so much in use from 1830 to 1870: *Augustine is the Father of evangelical Protestantism and Pelagius is the Father of Catholicism*, are now rarely met with. They have since been acknowledged to be untenable, although they contain a *particula veri*". Philip Schaff reaches the same conclusion; and Dorner says, "It is erroneous to ascribe to Augustine the ideas that inspired the Reformation". No one, however, has put this idea in a stronger light than Harnack. Quite recently, in his 14th lesson on "The Essence of Christianity", he characterized the Roman Church by three elements, the third of which is Augustinism, the thought and the piety of St. Augustine. "In fact Augustine has exerted over the whole inner life of the Church, religious life and religious thought, an absolutely decisive influence." And again he says, "In the fifth century, at the hour when the Church inherited the Roman Empire, she had within her a man of extraordinarily deep and powerful genius: from him she took her ideas, and to this present hour she has been unable to break away from them". In his "History of Dogma" (English tr.,

V, 234, 235) the same critic dwells at length upon the features of what he calls the "popular Catholicism" to which Augustine belongs. These features are (a) the Church as a hierarchical institution with doctrinal authority; (b) eternal life by merits, and disregard of the Protestant thesis of "salvation by faith"—that is, salvation by that firm confidence in God which the certainty of pardon produces; (c) the forgiveness of sins in the Church and by the Church; (d) the distinction between commands and counsels—between grievous sins and venial sins—the scale of wicked men and good men—the various degrees of happiness in heaven according to one's deserts; (e) Augustine is accused of "outdoing the superstitious ideas" of this popular Catholicism—the infinite value of Christ's satisfaction—salvation considered as enjoyment of God in heaven—the mysterious efficacy of the sacraments (*ex opere operato*)—Mary's virginity even in childbirth—"the idea of her purity and her conception, unique in their kind". Harnack does not assert that Augustine taught the Immaculate Conception, but Schaff (op. cit., p. 98) says unhesitatingly: "He is responsible also for many grievous errors of the Roman Church . . . he anticipated the dogma of the immaculate conception of the Virgin Mary, and his ominous word, *Roma locuta est, causa finita est*, might almost be quoted in favour of the Vatican decree of papal infallibility".

Nevertheless, it were a mistake to suppose that modern Protestants relinquish all claim upon Augustine; they will have it that, despite his essential Catholicism, it was he who inspired Luther and Calvin. The new thesis, therefore, is that each of the two Churches may claim him in turn. Burke's expression quoted by Schaff (ibid., p. 102) is characteristic: "In Augustine ancient and modern ideas are melted and to his authority the papal Church has as much right to appeal as the Churches of the Reformation". No one notes this contradiction more clearly than Loofs. After stating that Augustine has accentuated the characteristic elements of Western (Catholic) Christianity, that in succeeding ages he became its Father, and that "the Ecclesiasticism of Roman Catholicism, Scholasticism, Mysticism, and even the claims of the papacy to temporal rule, are founded upon a tendency initiated by him", Loofs also affirms that he is the teacher of all the reformers and their bond of union, and concludes with this strange paradox: "The history of Catholicism is the history of the progressive elimination of Augustinism". The singular aptitude of these critics for supposing the existence of flagrant contradictions in a genius like Augustine is not so astonishing when we remember that, with Reuter, they justify this theory by the reflection: "In whom are to be found more frequent contradictions than in Luther?" But their theories are based upon a false interpretation of Augustine's opinion, which is frequently misconstrued by those who are not sufficiently familiar with his language and terminology.

(4) *The character of his genius.*—We have now to ascertain what is the dominating quality which accounts for his fascinating influence upon posterity. One after another the critics have considered the various aspects of this great genius. Some have been particularly impressed by the depth and originality of his conceptions, and for these Augustine is the great sower of the ideas by which future minds are to live. Others, like Jungmann and Stöckl, have praised in him the marvellous harmony of all the mind's higher qualities, or, again, the universality and the compass of his doctrine. "In the great African Doctor", says the Rev. J. A. Zahm (Bible, Science and Faith, Fr. tr., p. 56), "we seem to have found united and combined the powerful and penetrating logic of Plato, the deep scientific conceptions

of Aristotle, the knowledge and intellectual suppleness of Origen, the grace and eloquence of Basil and Chrysostom. Whether we consider him as philosopher, as theologian, or as exegetist . . . he still appears admirable . . . the unquestioned Master of all the centuries." Philip Schaff (op. cit., p. 97) admires above all "such a rare union of the speculative talent of the Greek and of the practical spirit of the Latin Church as he alone possessed". In all these opinions there is a great measure of truth; nevertheless we believe that the dominating characteristic of Augustine's genius and the true secret of his influence are to be found in his heart—a heart that penetrates the most exalted speculations of a profound mind and animates them with the most ardent feeling. It is at bottom only the traditional and general estimate of the saint that we express; for he has always been represented with a heart for his emblem, just as Thomas Aquinas with a sun. Mgr. Bougaud thus interpreted this symbol: "Never did man unite in one and the same soul such stern rigour of logic with such tenderness of heart". This is also the opinion of Harnack, Böhringer, Nourisson, Storz, and others. Great intellectuality admirably fused with an enlightened mysticism is Augustine's distinguishing characteristic. Truth is not for him only an object of contemplation; it is a good that must be possessed, that must be loved and lived by. What constitutes Augustine's genius is his marvellous gift of embracing truth with all the fibres of his soul; not with the heart alone, for the heart does not think; not with the mind alone, for the mind grasps only the abstract or, as it were, lifeless truth. Augustine seeks the living truth, and even when he is combating certain Platonic ideas he is of the family of Plato, not of Aristotle. He belongs indisputably to all ages because he is in touch with all souls, but he is pre-eminently modern because his doctrine is not the cold light of the School; he is living and penetrated with personal sentiment. Religion is not a simple theory, Christianity is not a series of dogmas; it is also a life, as they say nowadays, or, more accurately, a source of life. However, let us not be deceived. Augustine is not a sentimentalist, a pure mystic, and heart alone does not account for his power. If in him the hard, cold intellectuality of the metaphysician gives place to an impassioned vision of truth, that truth is the basis of it all. He never knew the vaporous mysticism of our day, that allows itself to be lulled by a vague, aimless sentimentalism. His emotion is deep, true, engrossing, precisely because it is born of a strong, secure, accurate dogmatism that wishes to know what it loves and why it loves. Christianity is life, but life in the eternal, unchangeable truth. And if none of the Fathers has put so much of his heart into his writings, neither has any turned upon truth the searchlight of a stronger, clearer intellect.

Augustine's passion is characterized not by violence, but by a communicative tenderness; and his exquisite delicacy experiences first one and then another of the most intimate emotions and tests them; hence the irresistible effect of the "Confessions". Feuerlein, a Protestant thinker, has brought out in relief (exaggeratedly, to be sure, and leaving the marvellous powers of his intellect in the shade) Augustine's exquisite sensibility—what he calls the "feminine elements" of his genius. He says: "It was not merely a chance or accidental part that his mother, Monica, played in his intellectual development, and therein lies what essentially distinguishes him from Luther, of whom it was said: 'Everything about him bespeaks the man'". And Schlösser, whom Feuerlein quotes, is not afraid to say that Augustine's works contain more genuine poetry than all the writings of the Greek Fathers. At least it cannot be denied that no thinker ever caused so many and such salutary tears to flow. This characteristic of Augustine's genius explains his doctrinal work. Christian dogmas are considered in relation to the soul and the great duties of Christian life, rather than to themselves and in a speculative fashion. This alone explains his division of theology in the "Enchiridion", which at first sight seems so strange. He assembles all Christian doctrine in the three theological virtues, considering in the mysteries the different activities of the soul that must live by them. Thus, in the Incarnation, he assigns the greatest part to the moral side, to the triumph of humility. For this reason, also, Augustine's work bears an imprint, until then unknown, of living personality peeping out everywhere. He inaugurates that literature in which the author's individuality reveals itself in the most abstract matters, the "Confessions" being an inimitable example of it. It is in this connexion that Harnack admires the African Doctor's gift of psychological observation and a captivating facility for portraying his penetrating observations. This talent, he says, is the secret of Augustine's originality and greatness. Again, it is this same characteristic that distinguishes him from the other Doctors and gives him his own special temperament. The practical side of a question appealed to the Roman mind of Ambrose, too, but he never rises to the same heights, nor moves the heart as deeply as does his disciple of Milan. Jerome is a more learned exegetist, better equipped in respect of Scriptural erudition; he is even purer in his style; but, despite his impetuous ardour, he is less animated, less striking, than his correspondent of Hippo. Athanasius, too, is subtile in the metaphysical analysis of dogma, but he does not appeal to the heart and take hold of the soul like the African Doctor. Origen played the part of initiator in the Eastern Church, just as Augustine did in the Western, but his influence, unfortunate in more ways than one, was exercised rather in the sphere of speculative intelligence, while that of Augustine, owing to the qualities of his heart, extended far beyond the realm of theology. Bossuet, who of all geniuses most closely resembles Augustine by his elevation and his universality, is his superior in the skilfulness and artistic finish of his works, but he has not the alluring tenderness of soul; and if Augustine fulminates less, he attracts more powerfully, subjugating the mind with gentleness.

Thus may Augustine's universal influence in all succeeding ages be explained: it is due to combined gifts of heart and mind. Speculative genius alone does not sway the multitude; the Christian world, apart from professional theologians, does not read Thomas Aquinas. On the other hand, without the clear, definite idea of dogma, mysticism founders as soon as reason awakes and discovers the emptiness of metaphors: this is always the fate of vague pietism, whether it recognize Christ or not, whether it be extolled by Schleiermacher, Sabatier, or their disciples. But to Augustine's genius, at once enlightened and ardent, the whole soul is accessible, and the whole Church, both teachers and taught, is permeated by his sentiments and ideas. A. Harnack, more than any other critic, admires and describes Augustine's influence over all the life of Christian people. If Thomas Aquinas is the Doctor of the Schools, Augustine is, according to Harnack, the inspirer and restorer of Christian piety. If Thomas inspires the canons of Trent, Augustine, besides having formed Thomas himself, inspires the inner life of the Church and is the soul of all the great reforms effected within its pale. In his "Essence of Christianity" (14th lesson, 1900, p. 161) Harnack shows how Catholics and Protestants live upon the piety of Augustine. "His living has been incessantly relived in the course of the fifteen hun-

dred years that have followed. Even to our days interior and living piety among Catholics, as well as the mode of its expression, has been essentially Augustinian: the soul is permeated by his sentiment, it feels as he felt and rethinks his thoughts. It is the same with many Protestants also, and they are by no means among the worst. And even those to whom dogma is but a relic of the past proclaim that Augustine's influence will live forever."

This genuine emotion is also the veil that hides certain faults from the reader or else makes him oblivious of them. Says Eucken: "Never could Augustine have exercised all the influence he has exercised if it had not been that, in spite of the rhetorical artifice of his utterance, absolute sincerity reigned in the inmost recesses of his soul". His frequent repetitions are excused because they are the expression of his deep feeling. Schaff says: "His books, with all the faults and repetitions of isolated parts, are a spontaneous outflow from the marvellous treasures of his highly-gifted mind and his truly pious heart". (St. Augustine, p. 96.) But we must also acknowledge that his passion is the source of exaggerations and at times of errors that are fraught with real danger for the inattentive or badly disposed reader. Out of sheer love for Augustine certain theologians have endeavoured to justify all he wrote, to admire all, and to proclaim him infallible, but nothing could be more detrimental to his glory than such excess of praise. The reaction already referred to arises partly from this. We must recognize that the passion for truth sometimes fixes its attention too much upon one side of a complex question; his too absolute formulæ, lacking qualification, false in appearance now in one sense now in another. "The oratorical temperament that was his in such a high degree", says Becker, very truly (Revue d'histoire ecclésiastique, 15 April, 1902, p. 379), "the kind of exaltation that befitted his rich imagination and his loving soul, are not the most reliable in philosophical speculations". Such is the origin of the contradictions alleged against him and of the errors ascribed to him by the predestinarians of all ages. Here we see the rôle of the more frigid minds of Scholasticism. Thomas Aquinas was a necessary corrective to Augustine. He is less great, less original, and, above all, less animated; but the calm didactics of his intellectualism enable him to castigate Augustine's exaggerations with rigorous criticism, to impart exactitude and precision to his terms—in one word, to prepare a dictionary with which the African Doctor may be read without danger.

IV. His System of Grace.—It is unquestionably in the great Doctor's solution of the eternal problem of freedom and grace—of the part taken by God and by man in the affair of salvation—that his thought stands forth as most personal, most powerful, and most disputed. *Most personal,* for he was the first of all to synthesize the great theories of the Fall, grace, and free will; and moreover it is he who, to reconcile them all, has furnished us with a profound explanation which is in very truth his, and of which we find no trace in his predecessors. Hence, the term *Augustinism* is often exclusively used to designate his system of grace. *Most powerful,* for, as all admit, it was he above all others who won the triumph of liberty against the Manichæans, and of grace against the Pelagians. His doctrine has, in the main, been solemnly accepted by the Church, and we know that the canons of the Council of Orange are borrowed from his works. *Most disputed, also.*—Like St. Paul, whose teachings he develops, he has often been quoted, often not understood. Friends and enemies have exploited his teaching in the most diverse senses. It has not been grasped, not only by the opponents of liberty, and hence by the Reformers of the sixteenth century, but even to-day, by Protestant critics the most opposed to the cruel predestinationism of Calvin and Luther, who father that doctrine on St. Augustine. A technical study would be out of place here; it will be sufficient to enunciate the most salient thoughts, to enable the reader to find his bearings.

(1) It is regarded as incontestable to-day that the system of Augustine was complete in his mind from the year 397—that is, from the beginning of his episcopate, when he wrote his answers to the "Questiones Diversæ" of Simplician. It is to this book that Augustine, in his last years, refers the Semipelagians for the explanation of his real thought. This important fact, to which for a long time no attention was paid, has been recognized by Neander and established by Gangaut, and also by recent critics, such as Loofs, Reuter, Turmel, Jules Martin (see also Cunningham, St. Austin, 1886, pp. 80 and 175). It will not, therefore, be possible to deny the authority of these texts on the pretext that Augustine in his old age adopted a system more antagonistic to liberty.

(2) The system of Pelagius can to-day be better understood than heretofore. Pelagius doubtless denied original sin, and the immortality and integrity of Adam; in a word, the whole supernatural order. But the parent idea of his system, which was of stoic origin, was nothing else than the complete "emancipation" of human liberty with regard to God, and its limitless power for good and for evil. It depended on man to attain by himself, without the grace of God, a stoic impeccability and even insensibility, or the absolute control of his passions. It was scarcely suspected, even up to our time, what frightful rigorism resulted from this exaggeration of the powers of liberty. Since perfection was possible, it was of obligation. There was no longer any distinction between precepts and counsels. Whatever was good was a duty. There was no longer any distinction between mortal and venial sin. Every useless word merited hell, and even excluded from the Church the children of God. All this has been established by hitherto unedited documents which Caspari has published (Briefe, Abhandlungen, und Predigten, Christiania, 1890).

(3) The system of St. Augustine in opposition to this rests on three fundamental principles: (a) God is absolute Master, by His grace, of all the determinations of the will; (b) man remains free, under the action of grace; (c) the reconciliation of these two truths rests on the manner of the Divine government.

(a) The first principle, viz., that of the absolute sovereignty of God over the will, in opposition to the emancipation of Pelagius, has not always been understood in its entire significance. We think that numberless texts of the holy Doctor signify that not only does every meritorious act require supernatural grace, but also that every act of virtue, even of infidels, should be ascribed to a gift of God, not indeed to a supernatural grace (as Baius and the Jansenists pretend), but to a specially efficacious providence which has prepared this good movement of the will (Retractations, I, ix, n. 6). It is not, as theologians very wisely remark, that the will *cannot* accomplish that act of natural virtue, but it is a fact that without this providential benefit it *would not*. Many misunderstandings have arisen because this principle has not been comprehended, and in particular the great medieval theology, which adopted it and made it the basis of its system of liberty, has not been justly appreciated. But many have been afraid of these affirmations which are so sweeping, because they have not grasped the nature of God's gift, which leaves freedom intact. The fact has been too much lost sight of that Augustine distinguishes very explicitly two orders of grace: the grace of natural virtues (the simple gift of Providence, which prepares efficacious motives for the will); and grace for salutary and supernatural acts, given with the first preludes of faith. The latter is the grace of the sons, *gratia filiorum*; the former is the grace of all men, a grace which even strangers and infidels (*filii concubinarum*, as St. Augustine says) can receive (De Patientiâ, xxvii, n. 28).

(b) The second principle, the affirmation of liberty even under the action of efficacious grace, has always been safeguarded, and there is not one of his anti-Pelagian works even of the latest, which does not positively proclaim a complete power of choice in man; "not but what it does not depend on the free choice of the will to embrace the faith or reject it, but in the elect this will is prepared by God" (De Prædest. SS., n. 10). The great Doctor did not reproach the Pelagians with requiring a power to choose between good and evil; in fact he proclaims with them that without that power there is no responsibility, no merit, no demerit; but he reproaches them with exaggerating this power. Julian of Eclanum, denying the sway of concupiscence, conceives free will as a balance in perfect equilibrium. Augustine protests: this absolute equilibrium existed in Adam; it was destroyed after original sin; the will has to struggle and react against an inclination to evil, but it remains mistress of its choice (*Opus imperfectum contra Julianum*, III, cxvii). Thus, when he says that we have lost freedom in consequence of the sin of Adam, he is careful to explain that this lost freedom is not the liberty of choosing between good and evil, because without it we could not help sinning, but the perfect liberty which was calm and *without struggle*, and which was enjoyed by Adam in virtue of his original integrity.

But is there not between these two principles an irremediable antinomy? On the one hand, there is affirmed an absolute and unreserved power in God of directing the choice of our will, of converting every hardened sinner, or of letting every created will harden itself; and on the other hand, it is affirmed that the rejection or acceptance of grace or of temptation depends on our free will. Is not this a contradiction? Very many modern critics, among whom are Loofs and Harnack, have considered these two affirmations as irreconcilable. But it is because, according to them, Augustinian grace is an irresistible impulse given by God, just as in the absence of it every temptation inevitably overcomes the will. But in reality all antinomy disappears if we have the key of the system; and this key is found in the third principle: the Augustinian explanation of the Divine government of wills, a theory so original, so profound, and yet absolutely unknown to the most perspicacious critics, Harnack, Loofs, and the rest.

Here are the main lines of this theory: The will never decides without a motive, without the attraction of some good which it perceives in the object. Now, although the will may be free in presence of every motive, still, as a matter of fact it takes different resolutions according to the different motives presented to it. In that is the whole secret of the influence exercised, for instance, by eloquence (the orator can do no more than present motives), by meditation, or by good reading. What a power over the will would not a man possess who could, at his own pleasure, at any moment, and in the most striking manner, present this or the other motive of action?—But such is God's privilege. St. Augustine has remarked that *man is not the master of his first thoughts;* he can exert an influence on the course of his reflexions, but he himself cannot determine the objects, the images, and, consequently, the motives which present themselves to his mind. Now, as chance is only a word, it is God who determines at His pleasure these first perceptions of men, either by the prepared providential action of exterior causes, or interiorly by a Divine illumination given to the soul.—Let us take one last step with Augustine: Not only does God send at His pleasure those attractive motives which inspire the will with its determinations, but, before choosing between these illuminations of the natural and the supernatural order, *God knows the response which the soul, with all freedom, will make to each of them.* Thus, in the Divine knowledge, there is for each created will an indefinite series of motives which *de facto* (but very freely) win the consent to what is good. God, therefore, can, at His pleasure, obtain the salvation of Judas, if He wishes, or let Peter go down to perdition. No freedom, as a matter of fact, will resist what He has planned, although it always keeps the power of going to perdition. Consequently, it is God alone, in His perfect independence, who determines, by the choice of such a motive or such an inspiration (of which he knows the future influence), whether the will is going to decide for good or for evil. Hence, the man who has acted well must thank God for having sent him an inspiration which was foreseen to be efficacious, while that favour has been denied to another. *A fortiori*, every one of the elect owes it to the Divine goodness alone that he has received a series of graces which God saw to be infallibly, though freely, bound up with final perseverance.

Assuredly we may reject this theory, for the Church, which always maintains the two principles of the absolute dependence of the will and of freedom, has not yet adopted as its own this reconciliation of the two extremes. We may ask where and how God knows the effect of these graces. Augustine has always affirmed the fact; he has never inquired about the mode; and it is here that Molinism has added to and developed his thoughts, in attempting to answer this question. But can the thinker, who created and until his dying day maintained this system which is so logically concatenated, be accused of fatalism and Manichæism?

It remains to be shown that our interpretation exactly reproduces the thought of the great Doctor. The texts (indicated in Vacant's "Dict. de théologie catholique", I, col. 2390 sqq.) are too numerous and too long to be reproduced here. But there is one work of Augustine, dating from the year 397, in which he clearly explains his thought—a work which he not only did not disavow later on, but to which in particular he referred, at the end of his career, those of his readers who were troubled by his constant affirmation of grace. For example, to the monks of Adrumetum who thought that liberty was irreconcilable with this affirmation, he addressed a copy of this book "De Diversis quæstionibus ad Simplicianum", feeling sure that their doubts would be dissipated. There, in fact, he formulates his thoughts with great clearness. Simplician had asked how he should understand the Epistle to the Romans ix, on the predestination of Jacob and Esau. Augustine first lays down the fundamental principle of St. Paul, that *every good will comes from grace*, so that no man can take glory to himself for his merits, and this grace is so sure of its results that human liberty will never in reality resist it, although it has the power to do so. Then he affirms that this *efficacious* grace is not necessary *for us to be able to act well*, but because, in fact, without it *we would not wish to act well*. From that arises the great difficulty: How does the power of resisting grace fit in with the certainty of the result? And it is here that Augustine replies: There are many ways of inviting faith. Souls being differently disposed, *God knows what invitation will be accepted*, what other will not be accepted. Only those are the elect for whom God chooses the invitation which is foreseen to be efficacious, but God could convert them all: "Cujus autem miseretur,

sic eum vocat, quomodo scit ei congruere ut vocantem non respuat" (op. cit., I, q. ii, n. 2, 12, 13).

Is there in this a vestige of an *irresistible grace* or of that impulse against which *it is impossible to fight*, forcing some to good, and others to sin and hell? It cannot be too often repeated that this is not an idea flung off in passing, but a fundamental explanation which if not understood leaves us in the impossibility of grasping anything of his doctrine; but if it is seized Augustine entertains no feelings of uneasiness on the score of freedom. In fact he supposes freedom everywhere, and reverts incessantly to that knowledge on God's part which precedes predestination, directs it, and assures its infallible result. In the "De Dono perseverantiæ" (xvii, n. 42), written at the end of his life, he explains the whole of predestination by the choice of the vocation which is foreseen as efficacious. Thus is explained the chief part attributed to that external providence which prepares, by ill health, by warnings, etc., the good thoughts which it knows will bring about good resolutions. Finally, this explanation alone harmonizes with the moral action which he attributes to victorious grace. Nowhere does Augustine represent it as an irresistible impulse impressed by the stronger on the weaker. It is always an appeal, an invitation which attracts and seeks to persuade. He describes this attraction, which is without violence, under the graceful image of dainties offered to a child, green leaves offered to a sheep (In Joannem, tract. xxvi, n. 5). And always the infallibility of the result is assured by the Divine knowledge which directs the choice of the invitation.

(4) The Augustinian predestination presents no new difficulty if one has understood the function of this Divine knowledge in the choice of graces. The problem is reduced to this: Does God in his creative decree and, before any act of human liberty, determine by an immutable choice the elect and the reprobate?—Must the elect during eternity thank God only for having rewarded their merits, or must they also thank Him for having, prior to any merit on their part, chosen them to the meriting of this reward? One system, that of the Semipelagians, decides in favour of man: God predestines to salvation all alike, and gives to all *an equal measure of grace;* human liberty alone decides whether one is lost or saved; from which we must logically conclude (and they really insinuated it) that the number of the elect is not fixed or certain. The opposite system, that of the Predestinationists (the Semipelagians falsely ascribed this view to the Doctor of Hippo), affirms not only a privileged choice of the elect by God, but at the same time (a) the predestination of the reprobate to hell and (b) the absolute powerlessness of one or the other to escape from the *irresistible impulse* which drags them either to good or to evil. This is the system of Calvin.

Between these two extreme opinions Augustine formulated (not invented) the Catholic dogma, which affirms these two truths at the same time: (a) the eternal choice of the elect by God is very real, very gratuitous, and constitutes the grace of graces; (b) but this decree does not destroy the Divine will to save all men, which, moreover, is not realized except by the human liberty that leaves to the elect full power to fall and to the non-elect full power to rise. Here is how the theory of St. Augustine, already explained, forces us to conceive of the Divine decree: Before all decision to create the world, the infinite knowledge of God presents to Him all the graces, and different series of graces, which He can prepare for each soul, along with the consent or refusal which would follow in each circumstance, and that in millions and millions of possible combinations. Thus He sees that if Peter had received such another grace, he would not have been converted; and if on the contrary such another Divine appeal had been heard in the heart of Judas, he would have done penance and been saved. Thus, for each man in particular there are in the thought of God, limitless possible histories, some histories of virtue and salvation, others of crime and damnation; and God will be free in choosing such a world, such a series of graces, and in determining the future history and final destiny of each soul. And this is precisely what He does when, among all possible worlds, by an absolutely free act, He decides to realize the actual world with all the circumstances of its historic evolutions, with all the graces which in fact have been and will be distributed until the end of the world, and consequently with all the elect and all the reprobate who God foresaw would be in it if *de facto* He created it.

Now in the Divine decree, according to Augustine, and according to the Catholic Faith on this point, which has been formulated by him, the two elements pointed out above appear: (a) The certain and gratuitous choice of the elect—God decreeing, indeed, to create the world and to give it such a series of graces with such a concatenation of circumstances as should bring about freely, but infallibly, such and such results (for example, the despair of Judas and the repentance of Peter), decides, at the same time, the name, the place, the number of the citizens of the future heavenly Jerusalem. The choice is immutable; the list closed. It is evident, indeed, that only those of whom God knows beforehand that they will wish to co-operate with the grace decreed by Him will be saved. It is a *gratuitous* choice, the gift of gifts, in virtue of which even our merits are a gratuitous benefit, a gift which precedes all our merits. No one, in fact, is able to merit this election. God could, among other possible worlds, have chosen one in which other series of graces would have brought about other results. He saw combinations in which Peter would have been impenitent and Judas converted. It is therefore *prior* to any merit of Peter, or any fault of Judas, that God decided to give them the graces which saved Peter and not Judas. God does not wish to give paradise *gratuitously* to any one; but He gives *very gratuitously* to Peter the graces with which He knows Peter will be saved.—Mysterious choice! Not that it interferes with liberty, but because to this question: Why did not God, seeing that another grace would have saved Judas, give it to him? Faith can only answer, with Augustine: O Mystery! O Altitudo! (De Spiritu et litterâ, xxxiv, n. 60).—(b) But this decree includes also the second element of the Catholic dogma: the very sincere will of God to give to all men the power of saving themselves and the power of damning themselves. According to Augustine, God, in his creative decree, has expressly excluded every order of things in which grace would deprive man of his liberty, every situation in which man would not have the power to resist sin, and thus Augustine brushes aside that predestinationism which has been attributed to him. Listen to him speaking to the Manichæans: "All can be saved if they wish"; and in his "Retractations" (I, x), far from correcting this assertion, he confirms it emphatically: "It is true, entirely true, that all men can, if they wish". But he always goes back to the providential preparation. In his sermons he says to all: "It depends on you to be elect" (In Ps. cxx, n. 11, etc.); "Who are the elect?—You, if you wish it" (In Ps. lxxiii, n. 5). But, you will say, according to Augustine, the lists of the elect and reprobate are closed. Now if the non-elect *can* gain heaven, if all the elect *can* be lost, why should not some pass from one list to the other? You forget the celebrated explanation of Augustine: When God made His plan, He knew *infallibly*, before His choice, what would be the response of the wills

of men to His graces. If, then, the lists are definitive, if no one will pass from one series to the other, it is not because *anyone cannot* (on the contrary, all can), it is because God knew with infallible knowledge that *no one would wish to*. Thus I cannot effect that God should destine me to another series of graces than that which He has fixed, but, with this grace, if I do not save myself it will not be because I am not able, but because I do not wish to.

Such are the two essential elements of Augustinian and Catholic predestination. This is the dogma common to all the schools, and formulated by all theologians: *predestination in its entirety is absolutely gratuitous* (*ante merita*). We have to insist on this, because many have seen in this immutable and gratuitous choice only a hard thesis peculiar to St. Augustine, whereas it is pure dogma (barring the mode of conciliation, which the Church still leaves free). With that established, the long debates of theologians on special predestination to glory *ante* or *post merita* are far from having the importance that some attach to them. (For a fuller treatment of this subtile problem see the "Dict. de théol. cath., I, coll. 2402 sqq.) I do not think St. Augustine entered that debate; in his time, only dogma was in question. But it does not seem historically permissible to maintain, as many writers have, that Augustine first taught the milder system (*post merita*), up to the year 416 (In Joan. evang., tract. xii, n. 12), and that afterwards, towards 418, he shifted his ground and went to the extreme of harsh assertion, amounting even to predestinationism. We repeat, the facts absolutely refute this view. The ancient texts, even of 397, are as affirmative and as categorical as those of his last years, as critics like Loofs and Reuter have shown. If, therefore, it is shown that at that time he inclined to the milder opinion, there is no reason to think that he did not persevere in that sentiment.

(5) The part which Augustine had in the doctrine of Original Sin has been brought to light and determined only recently.

In the first place, it is no longer possible to maintain seriously, as was formerly the fashion (even among certain Catholics, like Richard Simon), that Augustine invented in the Church the hitherto unknown doctrine of original sin, or at least was the first to introduce the idea of punishment and sin. Dorner himself (Augustinus, p. 146) disposed of this assertion, which lacks verisimilitude. In this doctrine of the primal fall Augustine distinguished, with greater insistency and clearness than his predecessors, the *punishment* and the *sin*—the chastisement which strips the children of Adam of all the original privileges—and the fault, which consists in this, that the crime of Adam, the cause of the fall is, without having been committed personally by his children, nevertheless in a certain measure imputed to them, in virtue of the moral union established by God between the head of the human family and his descendants.

To pretend that in this matter Augustine was an innovator, and that before him the Fathers affirmed the punishment of the sin of Adam in his sons, but did not speak of the fault, is a historical error now proved to demonstration. We may discuss the thought of this or that pre-Augustinian Father, but, taking them as a whole, there is no room for doubt. The Protestant R. Seeberg (Lehrbuch der Dogmengeschichte, I, p. 256), after the example of many others, proclaims it by referring to Tertullian, Commodian, St. Cyprian, and St. Ambrose. The expressions, *fault, sin, stain* (*culpa, peccatum, macula*) are repeated in a way to dispel all doubt. The truth is that original sin, while being sin, is of a nature essentially different from other faults, and does not exact a *personal act* of the will of the children of Adam in order to be responsible for the fault of their father, which is morally imputed to them. Consequently, the Fathers—the Greeks especially—have insisted on its penal and afflictive character, which is most in evidence, while Augustine was led by the polemics of the Pelagians (and only by them) to lay emphasis on the moral aspect of the fault of the human race in its first father.

With regard to Adam's state before the fall Augustine not only affirmed, against Pelagius, the gifts of immortality, impassibility, integrity, freedom from error, and, above all, the sanctifying grace of Divine adoption, but he emphasized its absolutely gratuitous and supernatural character. Doubtless, considering the matter historically and *de facto*, it was only the sin of Adam that inflicted death on us— Augustine repeats it again and again—because God had safeguarded us against the law of our nature. But *de jure* neither immortality nor the other graces were our due, and Augustine recognized this in affirming that God could have made the condition in which we were actually born the primitive condition of our first parents. That assertion alone is the very reverse of Jansenism. It is, moreover, formally confirmed in the "Retractations" (I, ix, n. 6).

(6) Does this mean that we must praise everything in St. Augustine's explanation of grace?—Certainly not. And we shall note the improvements made by the Church, through her doctors, in the original Augustinism. Some exaggerations have been abandoned, as, for instance, the condemnation to hell of children dying without baptism. Obscure and ambiguous formulæ have been eliminated. We must say frankly that Augustine's literary method of emphasizing his thought by exaggerated expressions, issuing in troublesome paradoxes, has often obscured his doctrine, aroused opposition in many minds, or led them into error. Also, it is above all important, in order to comprehend his doctrine, to compile an Augustinian dictionary, not *a priori*, but after an objective study of his texts. The work would be long and laborious, but how many prejudices it would dispel!

The Protestant historian Ph. Schaff (St. Augustine, p. 102) writes: "The great genius of the African Church, from whom the Middle Ages and the Reformation have received an impulse alike powerful, though in different directions, has not yet fulfilled the work marked out for him in the counsels of Divine Wisdom. He serves as a bond of union between the two antagonistic sections of Western Christendom, and encourages the hope that a time may come when the injustice and bitterness of strife will be forgiven and forgotten, and the discords of the past be drowned forever in the sweet harmonies of perfect knowledge and perfect love". May this dream be realized!

V. AUGUSTINISM IN HISTORY.—The influence of the Doctor of Hippo has been so exceptional in the Church, that, after having indicated its general characteristics (see above), it is proper to indicate the principal phases of the historical development of his doctrine. The word *Augustinism* designates at times the entire group of philosophical doctrines of Augustine, at others, it is restricted to his system of grace. Hence, (1) philosophical Augustinism; (2) theological Augustinism on grace; (3) laws which governed the mitigation of Augustinism.

(1) *Philosophical Augustinism.*—In the history of philosophical Augustinism we may distinguish three very distinct phases. First, the period of its almost exclusive triumph in the West, up to the thirteenth century. During the long ages which were darkened by the invasion of the barbarians, but which were nevertheless burdened with the responsibility of safeguarding the sciences of the future, we may say that Augustine was the Great Master of the West. He was absolutely without a rival, or if there was one,

it was one of his disciples, Gregory the Great, who, after being formed in his school, popularized his theories. The rôle of Origen, who engrafted neo-Platonism on the Christian schools of the East, was that of Augustine in the West, with the difference, however, that the Bishop of Hippo was better able to detach the truths of Platonism from the dreams of Oriental imagination. Hence, a current of Platonic ideas was started which will never cease to act upon Western thought. This influence shows itself in various ways. It is found in the compilers of this period, who are so numerous and so well deserving of recognition—such as Isidore, Bede, Alcuin—who drew abundantly from the works of Augustine, just as did the preachers of the sixth century, and notably St. Cæsarius. In the controversies, especially in the great disputes of the ninth and twelfth centuries on the validity of Simoniacal ordinations, the text of Augustine plays the principal part. Carl Mirbt has published on this point a very interesting study: "Die Stellung Augustins in der Publizistik des gregorianischen Kirchenstreits" (Leipzig, 1888). In the pre-Thomistic period of Scholasticism, then in process of formation, namely, from Anselm to Albert the Great, Augustine is the great inspirer of all the masters, such as Anselm, Abelard, Hugo of St. Victor, who is called by his contemporaries, another Augustine, or even the soul of Augustine. And it is proper to remark, with Cunningham (Saint Austin, p. 178), that from the time of Anselm the cult of Augustinian ideas exercised an enormous influence on English thought in the Middle Ages. As regards Peter Lombard, his Sentences are little else than an effort to synthesize the Augustinian theories.

While they do not form a system as rigidly bound together as Thomism, yet Father Mandonnet (in his learned study of Siger de Brabant) and M. de Wulf (on Gilles de Lessines) have been able to group these theories together. And here let us present a summary sketch of those theses regarded in the thirteenth century as Augustinian, and over which the battle was fought. First, the fusion of theology and philosophy; the preference given to Plato over Aristotle—the latter representing rationalism, which was mistrusted, whilst the idealism of Plato exerted a strong attraction—wisdom regarded rather as the philosophy of the Good than the philosophy of the True. As a consequence, the disciples of Augustine always have a pronounced tinge of mysticism, while the disciples of St. Thomas may be recognized by their very accentuated intellectualism. In psychology the illuminating and immediate action of God is the origin of our intellectual knowledge (at times it is pure ontologism); and the faculties of the soul are made substantially identical with the soul itself. They are its functions, and not distinct entities (a thesis which was to keep its own partisans in the Scholasticism of the future and to be adopted by Descartes); the soul is a substance even without the body, so that after death, it is truly a person. In cosmology, besides the celebrated thesis of *rationes seminales*, which some have recently attempted to interpret in favour of evolutionism, Augustinism admitted the multiplicity of substantial forms in compound beings, especially in man. But especially in the impossibility of creation *ab æterno*, or the essentially temporal character of every creature which is subject to change, we have one of the ideas of Augustine which his disciples defended with greater constancy and, it would appear, with greater success.

A second period of very active struggles came in the thirteenth century, and this has only lately been recognized. Renan (Averroes, p. 259) and others believed that the war against Thomism, which was just then beginning, was caused by the infatuation of the Franciscans for Averroism; but if the Franciscan Order showed itself on the whole opposed to

St. Thomas, it was simply from a certain horror at philosophical innovations and at the neglect of Augustinism. The doctrinal revolution brought about by Albert the Great and Thomas Aquinas in favour of Aristotle startled the old School of Augustinism among the Dominicans as well as among the Franciscans, but especially among the latter, who were the disciples of the eminent Augustinian doctor, St. Bonaventure. This will explain the condemnations, hitherto little understood, of many propositions of St. Thomas Aquinas three years after his death, on the 7th of March, 1277, by the Bishop of Paris, and on the 18th of March, 1277, by the Archbishop of Canterbury, Robert Kilwardby, a Dominican. The Augustinian school represented tradition; Thomism, progress. The censure of 1277 was the last victory of a too rigid Augustinism. The happy fusion of the two methods in the two orders of Franciscans and Dominicans little by little brought about an agreement on certain points without excluding differences on others which were yet obscure (as, for instance, the unity or the multiplicity of forms), at the same time that it made for progress in all the schools. We know that the canonization of St. Thomas caused the withdrawal of the condemnations of Paris (14 February, 1325). Moreover, the wisdom or the moderation of the new school contributed powerfully to its triumph. Albert the Great and St. Thomas, far from being adversaries of St. Augustine, as they were reported to be, placed themselves in his school, and while modifying certain theories, took over into their system the doctrine of the African bishop. How many articles in the "Summa" of St. Thomas have no other object than to incorporate in theology this or the other theory which was cherished by St. Augustine (to take only one example, that of exemplar ideas in God). Hence, there was no longer any school strictly Augustinian, because every school was such. They all eliminated certain special points and retained the same veneration for the master.

From the third period of the fifteenth century to our days we see less of the special progress of philosophical Augustinism than certain tendencies of an exaggerated revival of Platonism. In the fifteenth century Bessarion (1472) and Marsilio Ficino (1499) used Augustine's name for the purpose of enthroning Plato in the Church and excluding Aristotle. In the seventeenth century, it is impossible to deny certain resemblances between Cartesianism and the philosophy of St. Augustine. Malebranche was wrong in ascribing his own ontologism to the great Doctor, as were also many of his successors in the nineteenth century.

(2) *Theological Augustinism.*—The history of Augustine's system of grace seems to blend almost indistinguishably with the progressive developments of this dogma. Here it must suffice, first, to enumerate the principal phases; secondly, to trace the general laws of development which mitigated Augustinism in the Church.

After the death of Augustine, a whole century of fierce contests (430–529) ended in the triumph of moderate Augustinism. In vain had Pope St. Celestine (431) sanctioned the teachings of the Doctor of Hippo. The Semipelagians of the south of France could not understand the predilection of God for the elect, and in order to attack the works of St. Augustine they made use of the occasionally exaggerated formulæ of St. Fulgentius, or of the real errors of certain isolated predestinationists, as, for example, Lucidus, who was condemned in the Council of Arles (475). Happily, Prosper of Aquitaine, by his moderation, and also the unknown author of "De Vocatione omnium gentium", by his consoling thesis on the appeal addressed to all, opened the way to an agreement. And finally, St. Cæsarius of Arles obtained from Pope Felix IV a series of *Capitula* which were

solemnly promulgated at Orange, and gave their consecration to the triumph of Augustinism (529). In the ninth century, a new victory was gained over the predestinationism of Gottschalk in the assemblies of Savonnières and Toucy (859–860). The doctrine of the Divine will to save all men and the universality of redemption was thus consecrated by the public teaching of the Church. In the Middle Ages these two truths are developed by the great Doctors of the Church. Faithful to the principles of Augustinism, they place in especial relief his theory on Divine Providence, which prepares at its pleasure the determinations of the will by exterior events and interior inspirations.

In the fourteenth century a strong current of predestinationism is evident. To-day it is admitted that the origin of this tendency goes back to Thomas Bradwardin, a celebrated professor of Oxford, who died Archbishop of Canterbury (1349), and whom the best critics, along with Loofs and Harnack, recognize to have been the inspirer of Wyclif himself. His book "De causâ Dei contra Pelagium" gave rise in Paris to disputes on Augustinian "predetermination", a word which, it had been thought, was invented by Banes in the sixteenth century. In spite of the opposition of theologians, the idea of absolute determinism in the name of St. Augustine was adopted by Wyclif (1324–87), who formulated his universal fatalism, the necessity of good for the elect and of evil for the rest. He fancied that he found in the Augustinian doctrine the strange conception which became for him a central doctrine that overthrew all morality and all ecclesiastical, and even civil, government. According as one is predestined or not, everything changes its nature. The same sins are mortal in the non-elect which are venial in the predestined. The same acts of virtue are meritorious in the predestined, even if he be actually a wicked man which are of no value in the non-elect. The sacraments administered by one who is not predestined are always invalid; more than that, no jurisdiction exists in a prelate, even a pope, if he be not predestined. In the same way, there is no power, even civil or political, in a prince who is not one of the elect, and no right of property in the sinner or the non-elect. Such is the basis on which Wyclif established the communism which aroused the socialist mobs in England. It is incontestable that he was fond of quoting Augustine as his authority; and his disciples, as we are assured by Thomas Netter Waldensis (Doctrinale, I, xxxiv, § 5), were continually boasting of the profound knowledge of their great Doctor, whom they called with emphasis "John of Augustine". Shirley, in his introduction to "Zizaniorum Fasciculi", has even pretended that the theories of Wyclif on God, on the Incarnation, and even on property, were the purest Augustinian inspiration, but even a superficial comparison, if this were the place to make it, would show how baseless such an assertion is. In the sixteenth century the heritage of Wyclif and Hus, his disciple, was always accepted in the name of Augustinism by the leaders of the Reformation. Divine predestination from all eternity separating the elect, who were to be snatched out of the mass of perdition, from the reprobate who were destined to hell, as well as the *irresistible* impulse of God drawing some to salvation and others to sin—such was the fundamental doctrine of the Reformation. Calvinism even adopted a system which was "logically more consistent, but practically more revolting", as Schaff puts it (St. Augustine, p. 104), by which the decree of reprobation of the non-elect would be independent of the fall of Adam and of original sin (Supralapsarianism). It was certain that these harsh doctrines would bring their reaction, and in spite of the severities of the Synod of Dordrecht, which it would be interesting

1. ST. AUGUSTINE (Pinturicchio)   2. DEATH OF ST. AUGUSTINE (Benozzo Gozzoli)   3. ST. AUGUSTINE IN MEDITATION (Botticelli)
4. ST. AUGUSTINE TEACHING (B. Gozzoli)   5. DEATH OF ST. MONICA (B. Gozzoli)

to compare with the Council of Trent in the matter of moderation, Arminianism triumphed over the Calvinistic thesis.

We must note here that even Protestant critics, with a loyalty which does them honour, have in these latter times vindicated Augustine from the false interpretations of Calvin. Dorner, in his "Gesch. der prot. Théologie", had already shown the instinctive repugnance of Anglican theologians to the horrible theories of Calvin. W. Cunningham (Saint Austin, p. 82 sqq.) has very frankly called attention to the complete doctrinal opposition on fundamental points which exists between the Doctor of Hippo and the French Reformers. In the first place, as regards the state of human nature, which is, according to Calvin, totally depraved, for Catholics it is very difficult to grasp the Protestant conception of original sin which, for Calvin and Luther, is not, as for us, the moral degradation and the stain imprinted on the soul of every son of Adam by the fault of the father which is imputable to each member of the family. It is not the deprivation of grace and of all other supernatural gifts; it is not even concupiscence, understood in the ordinary sense of the word, as the struggle of base and selfish instincts against the virtuous tendencies of the soul; it is a profound and complete subversion of human nature; it is the physical alteration of the very substance of our soul. Our faculties, understanding, and will, if not entirely destroyed, are at least mutilated, powerless, and chained to evil. For the Reformers, original sin is not *a* sin, it is *the* sin, and the permanent sin, living in us and causing a continual stream of new sins to spring from our nature, which is radically corrupt and evil. For, as our being is evil, every act of ours is equally evil. Thus, the Protestant theologians do not ordinarily speak of *the sins* of mankind, but only of *the sin*, which makes us what we are and defiles everything. Hence arose the paradox of Luther: that even in an act of perfect charity a man sins mortally, because he acts with a vitiated nature. Hence that other paradox: that this sin can never be effaced, but remains entire, even after justification, although it will not be any longer imputed; to efface it, it would be necessary to modify physically this human being which is sin. Calvin, without going so far as Luther, has nevertheless insisted on this total corruption. "Let it stand, therefore, as an indubitable truth which no engines can shake", says he (Institution II, v, § 19), "that the mind of man is so entirely alienated from the righteousness of God that he cannot conceive, desire, or design anything but what is weak, distorted, foul, impure, or iniquitous, that his heart is so thoroughly environed by sin that it can breathe out nothing but corruption and rottenness; that if some men occasionally make a show of goodness, their mind is ever interwoven with hypocrisy and deceit, their soul inwardly bound with the fetters of wickedness". "Now", says Cunningham, "this doctrine, whatever there may be to be said for it, is not the doctrine of Saint Austin. He held that sin is the defect of a good nature which retains elements of goodness, even in its most diseased and corrupted state, and he gives no countenance, whatever to this modern opinion of total depravity". It is the same with Calvin's affirmation of the irresistible action of God on the will. Cunningham shows that these doctrines are irreconcilable with liberty and responsibility, whereas, on the contrary, "St. Austin is careful to attempt to harmonize the belief in God's omnipotence with human responsibility" (St. Austin, p. 86). The Council of Trent was therefore faithful to the true spirit of the African Doctor, and maintained pure Augustinism in the bosom of the Church, by its definitions against the two opposite excesses. Against Pelagianism it reaffirmed original sin and the absolute necessity of grace (Sess. VI, can. 2); against Protestant predestination-ism it proclaimed the freedom of man, with his double power of resisting grace (*posse dissentire si velit*—Sess. VI, can. 4) and of doing good or evil, even before embracing the Faith (can. 6 and 7).

In the seventeenth century Jansenism adopted, while modifying it, the Protestant conception of original sin and the state of fallen man. No more than Luther did the Jansenists admit the two orders, natural and supernatural. All the gifts which Adam had received—immortality, knowledge, integrity, sanctifying grace—are absolutely required by the nature of man. Original sin is, therefore, again regarded as a profound alteration of human nature. From which the Jansenists conclude that *the key to St. Augustine's system is to be found in the essential difference of the Divine government and of grace, before and after the Fall of Adam.* Before the Fall Adam enjoyed complete liberty, and grace gave him the power of resisting or obeying; after the Fall there was no longer in man liberty properly so called; there was only spontaneity (*libertas a coactione*, and not *libertas a necessitate*). Grace, or delectation in the good, is essentially efficacious, and necessarily victorious once it is superior in degree to the opposite concupiscence. The struggle, which was prolonged for two centuries, led to a more profound study of the Doctor of Hippo and prepared the way for the definite triumph of Augustinism, but of an Augustinism mitigated in accordance with laws which we must now indicate.

(3) *Laws which governed the mitigation of Augustinism.*—In spite of what Protestant critics may have said, the Church has always been faithful to the fundamental principles defended by Augustine against the Pelagians and Semipelagians, on original sin, the necessity and gratuity of grace, the absolute dependence on God for salvation. Nevertheless, great progress was made along the line of gradual mitigation. For it cannot be denied that the doctrine formulated at Trent, and taught by all our theologians, produces an impression of greater suavity and greater clarity than this or that passage in the works of St. Augustine. The causes of this softening down, and the successive phases of this progress were as follows:—

First, theologians began to distinguish more clearly between the natural order and the supernatural, and hence the Fall of Adam no longer appeared as a corruption of human nature in its constituent parts; it is the loss of the whole order of supernatural elevation. St. Thomas (Summa, I, Q. lxxxv, a. 1) formulates the great law of the preservation, in guilty Adam's children, of all the faculties in their essential integrity: "Sin (even original) neither takes away nor diminishes the natural endowments". Thus the most rigorist Thomists, Alvarez, Lemos, Contenson, agree with the great Doctor that the sin of Adam has not enfeebled (*intrinsece*) the natural moral forces of humanity.

Secondly, such consoling and fundamental truths as God's desire to save all men, and the redeeming death of Christ which was really offered and accepted for all peoples and all individuals—these truths, which Augustine never denied, but which he left too much in the background and as it were hidden under the terrible formulas of the doctrine of predestination, have been placed in the full light, have been developed, and applied to infidel nations, and have at last entered into the ordinary teaching of theology. Thus our Doctors, without detracting in the least from the sovereignty and justice of God, have risen to the highest idea of His goodness: that God so sincerely desires the salvation of all as to give absolutely to all, immediately or mediately, the means necessary for salvation, and always with the desire that man should consent to employ those means. No one falls into hell except by his own fault. Even infidels will be accountable for their infidelity. St. Thomas expresses the thought of all when he says: "It is the common teaching that if a man born among the barbarous and infidel nations really does what lies in his power, God will reveal to him what is necessary for salvation, either by interior inspirations or by sending him a preacher of the Faith (In Lib. II Sententiarum, dist. 23, Q. viii, a. 4, ad 4ᵃᵐ). We must not dissemble the fact that this law changes the whole aspect of Divine Providence, and that St. Augustine had left it too much in the shade, insisting only upon the other aspect of the problem: namely, that God, while making a sufficing appeal to all, is nevertheless not bound to choose always that appeal which shall in fact be efficacious and shall be accepted, provided that the refusal of consent be due to the obstinacy of the sinner's will and not to its lack of power. Thus the Doctors most eagerly approved the axiom, *Facienti quod in se est Deus non denegat gratiam*— God does not refuse grace to one who does what he can.

Thirdly, from principles taught by Augustine consequences have been drawn which are clearly derived from them, but which he had not pointed out. Thus it is incontestably a principle of St. Augustine that no one sins in an act which he cannot avoid— "Quis enim peccat in eo quod caveri non potest?" This passage from "De libero arbitrio" (III, xviii, n. 50) is anterior to the year 395; but far from retracting it he approves and explains it, in 415, in the "De naturâ et gratiâ", lxvii, n. 80. From that pregnant principle theologians have concluded, first, that grace sufficient to conquer temptations never fails anyone, even an infidel; then, against the Jansenists, they have added that, to deserve its name of *sufficient grace*, it ought to give a real power which is complete, even relatively to the actual difficulties. No doubt theologians have groped about, hesitated, even denied; but to-day there are very few who would dare not to recognize in St. Augustine the affirmation of the possibility of not sinning.

Fourthly, certain secondary assertions, which encumbered, but did not make part of the dogma, have been lopped off from the doctrine of Augustine. Thus the Church, which, with Augustine, has always denied entrance into Heaven to unbaptized children, has not adopted the severity of the great Doctor in condemning such children to bodily pains, however slight. And little by little the milder teaching of St. Thomas was to prevail in theology and was even to be vindicated against unjust censure when Pius VI condemned the pseudo-synod of Pistoja. At last Augustine's obscure formulæ were abandoned or corrected, so as to avoid regrettable confusions. Thus the expressions which seemed to identify original sin with concupiscence have given way to clearer formulæ without departing from the real meaning which Augustine sought to express.

Discussion, however, is not yet ended within the Church. On most of those points which concern especially the manner of the Divine action Thomists and Molinists disagree, the former holding out for an irresistible predetermination, the latter maintaining, with Augustine, a grace whose infallible efficacy is revealed by the Divine knowledge. But both of these views affirm the grace of God and the liberty of man. The lively controversies aroused by the "Concordia" of Molina (1588) and the long conferences *de auxiliis* held at Rome, before Popes Clement VIII and Pius V, are well known. There is no doubt that a majority of the theologian-consultors thought they discovered an opposition between Molina and St. Augustine. But their verdict was not approved, and (what is of great importance in the history of Augustinism) it is certain that they asked for the con-

demnation of doctrines which are to-day universally taught in all the schools. Thus, in the project of censure reproduced by Serry (" Historia Congregationis de Auxiliis", append., p. 166) the first proposition is this: "In statu naturæ lapsæ potest homo, cum solo concursu generali Dei, efficere opus bonum morale, quod in ordine ad finem hominis naturalem sit veræ virtutis opus, referendo illud in Deum, sicut referri potest ac deberet in statu naturali" (In the state of fallen nature man can with only the general *concursus* of God do a good moral work which may be a work of true virtue with regard to the natural end of man by referring it to God, as it can and ought to be referred in the natural state). Thus they sought to condemn the doctrine held by all the Scholastics (with the exception of Gregory of Rimini), and sanctioned since then by the condemnation of Proposition lvii of Baius. For a long time it was said that the pope had prepared a Bull to condemn Molina; but to-day we learn from an autograph document of Paul V that liberty was left to the two schools until a new Apostolic decision was given (Schneeman "Controversiarum de Div. grat.", 1881, p. 289). Soon after, a third interpretation of Augustinism was offered in the Church, that of Noris, Belleli, and other partisans of moral predetermination. This system has been called *Augustinianism*. To this school belong a number of theologians who, with Thomassin, essayed to explain the infallible action of grace without admitting either the *scientia media* of the Molinists or the physical predetermination of the Thomists. A detailed study of this interpretation of St. Augustine may be found in Vacant's "Dictionnaire de théologie catholique", I, cols. 2485–2501; here I can only mention one very important document, the last in which the Holy See has expressed its mind on the various theories of theologians for reconciling grace and liberty. This is the Brief of Benedict XIV (13 July, 1748) which declares that the three schools—Thomist, Augustinian (Noris), and Molinist—have full right to defend their theories. The Brief concludes with these words: "This Apostolic See favours the liberty of the schools; none of the systems proposed to reconcile the liberty of man with the omnipotence of God has been thus far condemned (op. cit., col. 2555).

In conclusion we must indicate briefly *the official authority which the Church attributes to St. Augustine in the questions of grace.* Numerous and solemn are the eulogies of St. Augustine's doctrine pronounced by the popes. For instance, St. Gelasius I (1 November, 493), St. Hormisdas (13 August, 520) Boniface II and the Fathers of Orange (529), John II (534), and many others. But the most important document, that which ought to serve to interpret all the others, because it precedes and inspires them, is the celebrated letter of St. Celestine I (431), in which the pope guarantees not only the orthodoxy of Augustine against his detractors, but also the great merit of his doctrine: "So great was his knowledge that my predecessors have always placed him in the rank of the masters", etc. This letter is accompanied by a series of ten dogmatic *capitula* the origin of which is uncertain, but which have always been regarded, at least since Pope Hormisdas, as expressing the faith of the Church. Now these extracts from African councils and pontifical decisions end with this restriction: "As to the questions which are more profound and difficult, and which have given rise to these controversies, we do not think it necessary to impose the solution of them".—In presence of these documents emanating from so high a source, ought we to say that the Church has adopted all the teaching of St. Augustine on grace so that it is never permissible to depart from that teaching? Three answers have been given: (a) For some, the authority of St. Augustine is absolute and irrefragable. The

Jansenists went so far as to formulate, with Havermans, this proposition, condemned by Alexander VIII (7 December, 1690): "Ubi quis invenerit doctrinam in Augustino clare fundatam, illam absolute potest tenere et docere, non respiciendo ad ullam pontificis bullam" (Where one has found a doctrine clearly based on St. Augustine, he can hold and teach it absolutely, without referring to any pontifical Bull). This is inadmissible. None of the pontifical approbations has a meaning so absolute, and the *capitula* make an express reservation for the profound and difficult questions. The popes themselves have permitted a departure from the thought of St. Augustine in the matter of the lot of children dying without baptism (Bull "Auctorem Fidei", 28 August, 1794). (b) Others again have concluded that the eulogies in question are merely vague formulæ leaving full liberty to withdraw from St. Augustine and to blame him on every point. Thus Launoy, Richard Simon, and others have maintained that Augustine had been in error on the very gist of the problem, and had really taught predestinationism. But that would imply that for fifteen centuries the Church took as its guide an adversary of its faith. (c) We must conclude, with the greater number of theologians, that Augustine has a real *normative* authority, hedged about, however, with reserves and wise limitations. In the capital questions which constitute the faith of the Church in those matters the Doctor of Hippo is truly the authoritative witness of tradition; for example, on the existence of original sin, the necessity of grace, at least for every salutary act; the gratuitousness of the gift of God which precedes all merit of man because it is the cause of it; the predilection for the elect and, on the other hand, the liberty of man and his responsibility for his transgressions. But the secondary problems, concerning the mode rather than the fact, are left by the Church to the prudent study of theologians. Thus all schools unite in a great respect for the assertions of St. Augustine.

At present this attitude of fidelity and respect is all the more remarkable as Protestants, who were formerly so bitter in defending the predestination of Calvin, are to-day almost unanimous in rejecting what they themselves call "the boldest defiance ever given to reason and conscience" (Grétillat, "Dogmatique", III, p. 329). Schleiermacher, it is true, maintains it, but he adds to it the Origenist theory of universal salvation by the final restoration of all creatures, and he is followed in this by Farrar, Lobstein, Pfister, and others. The Calvinist dogma is to-day, especially in England, altogether abandoned, and often replaced by pure Pelagianism (Beyschlag). But among Protestant critics the best are drawing near to the Catholic interpretation of St. Augustine, as, for example, Grétillat, in Switzerland, and Stevens, Bruce, and Mozley (On the Augustinian Doctrine of Predestination), in England. Sanday (Romans, p. 50) also declares the mystery to be unfathomable for man yet solved by God—"And so our solution of the problem of Free-will, and of the problems of history and of individual salvation, must finally lie in the full acceptance and realization of what is implied by the infinity and the *omniscience* of God". These concluding words recall the true system of Augustine and permit us to hope that at least on this question there may be a union of the two Churches in a wise Augustinism.

WORKS ON THE LIFE OF ST. AUGUSTINE.—The chief original sources are his own *Confessions* and his life (*Vita S. Aurelii Augustini*) by his friend POSSIDIUS, in Vol. XI of the Benedictine edition (*P. L.*, XXXII); for learned illustration of the text of Possidius see the Bollandists CUPER and STILTING in *Acta SS.* (1743), August, VI.—Among the principal modern biographies of the saint the following are worthy of mention: *Vita. S Aug. ex ejus potissimum scriptis concinnata* (by his Benedictine editors, very accurate, based on the notes of TILLEMONT; *P. L.*, XXXII); KLOTH, *Der hl. Kirchenlehrer, S. Augustin* (Aachen, 1840); POUJOULAT, *Histoire de S. Augustin, sa vie, ses œuvres, son siècle* (Paris, 1845–46); BINDEMANN,

Der hl. Augustin (Berlin, Leipzig, Greifswald, 1844–69); MORIARTY, *The Life of St. Augustine, Bishop, Confessor, and Doctor of the Church* (Philadelphia, 1879); BOURKE, *Life and Labours of St. Augustine* (Dublin and London, 1880); COLLETTE, *St. Augustine, a Sketch of his Life and Writings as Affecting his Controversy with Rome* (London, 1852); SCHAFF, *Saint Augustine, Melanchthon, Neander* (New York, 1886); SPALDING, *The Influence of St. Augustine's Teaching* (New York, 1886); CUNNINGHAM, *St. Austin and His Place in the History of Christian Thought* (London, 1886); BURTON, *St. Augustine: an Historical Study* (Dublin, 1888); CUTTS, *St. Augustine* (London, 1880); SHEEHAN, *Recent Writings on St. Augustine* in *Dubl. Rev.* (1888), XX, 88–107; WOLFSGRUBER, *Augustinus* (Paderborn, 1898), from the notes of RAUSCHER, an excellent study, see ROTTMANNER, *Hist. Jahrb.* (1898), 892–898; VON HERTLING, *Augustin* (Mainz, 1902); HERGENRÖTHER in *Kirchenlex.*, I, 1669–78; LOOFS in *Realencyclopädie* (3d. ed., Leipzig, 1897), II; DORNER in SCHAFF'S *Encyclop. of Relig. Knowledge* (Edinburgh, 1883); FARRAR, *Lives of the Fathers* (London, 1889), II, 298–460; DE PRESSENSÉ in *Dict. of Christian Biogr.*, I, 216–225; HERGENRÖTHER-KIRSCH, *Kircheng.* (4th ed., 1902), I, 531 sqq.

PATROLOGIES AND HISTORIES OF DOGMA.—FESSLER-JUNGMANN, *Institut. Patrol.* (Innsbruck, 1890–96), II; BARDENHEWER, *Patrologie* (Freiburg, 1901), 416–447; SCHWANE, *Dogmengesch.* (ibid., 1894), II; HARNACK, *Dogmengeschichte* (ibid., 1897).

HISTORIES OF PHILOSOPHY.—STÖCKL, RITTER, PRANTL, and among the histories of Latin literature. EBERT, *Gesch. der Litteratur des Mittelalters* (Leipzig, 1889); VILLEMAIN, *Tableau de l'éloquence chrétienne au quatrième siècle* (Paris, 1849).—The conversion of St. Augustine is the subject of several works, e. g. NAVILLE, *St. Augustin, Etude sur le développement de sa pensée, jusqu'à son ordination* (Geneva, 1872); WÖRTER, *Die Geistesentwickelung des hl. Augustinus bis zu seiner Taufe* (Paderborn, 1892); HARNACK, *Augustins Confessionen* (Giessen, 1895); BOISSIER, *La Conversion de St. Augustin* in *Revue des Deux Mondes* (1888), 43–69.—There is a very exhaustive bibliography of St. Augustine in CHEVALIER, *Rép. des sources hist. du moyen âge, Bio-bibliographie* (2nd ed., Paris, 1905), col. 371–381; see the bibliography in McCABE, *St. Augustine* (London, 1902); SCHAFF, *Hist. of the Christian Church* (New York, 5th ed., 1903), 1038–39 sqq.; also the present writer's bibliography in *Dict. de théol. cath.*, I, 2284, 2471, and *passim*. On the *Confessions of St. Augustine* see more particularly *Dub. Rev.* (1839), VII, 430; DOUAIS, *Les Confessions de St. Augustin* (Paris, 1893).

SPECIAL WORKS ON HIS DOCTRINE.—The best general works on St. Augustine are the extensive studies of TILLEMONT, *Mémoires*, etc. (Paris, 1710), XIII 1–1079 and CEILLIER, *Hist. des auteurs ecclésiastiques* (Paris, 1774), XI, and in the second edition (1861), IX. See also ALTICOZZI, *Summa Augustiniana ex collectis disputatis explicatisque sententiis D. A. Augustini* (Rome, 1775), a very profound study on the teachings of St. Augustine concerning grace, the Church, the pope; GANGAUF, *Des hl. Augustinus speculative Lehre von Gott dem dreieinigen* (Augsburg, 1866), and *Die metaphysische Psychologie des hl. Augustinus* (ibid., 1882); HEWITT, *Studies in St. Augustine* (New York, 1868).—Among Protestant writers, apart from the already quoted works of BINDEMANN, LOOFS, and HARNACK, we may mention: REUTER, *Augustinische Studien* (Gotha, 1887); DORNER, *Augustinus, sein theologisches System und seine religionsphilosophische Anschauung* (Gotha, 1888); EUCKEN, *Die Lebensanschauungen der grossen Denker* (Leipzig, 1902), 210–245.—For the philosophy of Augustine see NOURRISSON, *La Philosophie de S. Augustin* (2nd ed. Paris, 1866); VERCELLONE, *Philosophy of St. Augustine and Modern Philosophy* in *Catholic World* (1870), X, 481; RICKABY, *St. Augustine and Scientific Unbelief* in *The Month* (1876), XXVIII, 195; STORZ, *Die Philosophie des hl. Augustinus* (Freiburg, 1882); FERRAZ, *De la philosophie de S. Augustin* (Paris, 1862); MARTIN, *S. Augustin* (Paris, 1901); TURNER, *History of Philosophy* (Boston, 1903), 223–233.—For his teaching on the Church see RIBBECK, *Donatus und Augustinus* (Elberfeld, 1858); SPECHT, *Die Lehre von der Kirche nach dem hl. Augustinus* (Paderborn, 1892), an excellent work; BURTON, *St. Augustine and the Donatists* in *Dub. Rev.* (1893), 379–419; see also ibid. (1890), XXIV, 89–109.—On the Scriptural exegesis of St. Augustine see CLAUSEN, *Augustinus sacræ Scripturæ interpres* (Copenhagen, 1827); LENFANT, *Biblia Augustiniana* (Paris, 1816, 2 vols., folio), a useful concordance of the Scriptural commentaries of St. Augustine according to the order of the Biblical books; IDEM, *Concordantia Augustinianæ, sive collectio omnium sententiarum quæ sparsim reperiuntur in S. Aug. operibus* (Paris, 1656, 2 vols., folio); MOIRAN, *Notion Augustinienne de l'herméneutique* (Clermont-Ferrand, 1906); DOUAIS, *St. Augustin et la Bible* in *Revue Biblique* for 1893–94.—On grace and on Pelagianism: see the seven erudite dissertations of GARNIER, added to his edition of MARIUS MERCATOR (Paris, 1673; *P. L.* XLVIII); PETAVIUS, *De Pelagianorum et Semipelagianorum hæresi* (Paris, 1643); NORIS, *Historia Pelagiana, ... additis Vindiciis Augustinianis* (Padua, 1673); MERLIN, *Véritable clef des ouvrages de S. Augustin contre les Pélagiens* in *Refutation des critiques, etc.*, de M. Bayle *sur S. Augustin* (Paris, 1732), *P. L.*, XLVII; WIGGERS, *Pragmatische Darstellung des Augustinismus und Pelagianismus* (in two parts; Berlin, 1821, and Hamburg, 1833), the first part tr. by EMERSON (Andover, 1840); WARFIELD, *Two Studies in the History of Doctrine: Augustine and the Pelagian Controversy, The Development of the Doctrine of Infant Salvation* (New York, 1898); ROTTMANNER, *Der Augustinismus* (Munich, 1892); PORTALIÉ in *Dict. de théol. cath.*, I, 2268–2472, especially

2375–2408; Chevalier, *Répertoire des sources hist. du moyen âge* (*Bio-bibliographie*, Paris, 1905), col. 371–381.

On Augustinism in History.—For *philosophical* Augustinism see, besides the above quoted works of Mandonnet and De Wulf, Werner, *Die Augustinische Psychologie in ihrer mittelalterlichen Einkleidung und Gestaltung* (Vienna, 1882); Idem, *Der Augustinismus in der Scholastik des späteren Mittelalters* (Vienna, 1883), also other studies of the same author on *Bede, Alcuin, Guillaume d'Auvergne, St. Thomas Aquinas, Suarez*; Ehrle, *Der Augustinismus und der Aristotelismus in der Scholastik gegen Ende des XIII. Jahrhunderts*, in *Archiv für Litteratur und Kircheng. des Mittelalters* (1889). For *theological* Augustinism see all doctrine-histories. Modern theologians usually exhibit the history of errors concerning Divine grace, e. g. the Thomists Lemos and Billuart, the Molinist Suarez, the Sorbonnist Tourney, particularly Scipione Maffei, *Istoria teologica delle dottrine e delle opinioni corse ne' cinque primi secoli della Chiesa in proposito della divina grazia, del libero arbitrio, e della predestinazione* (Trent, 1742; Latin, Frankfort, 1756). Cf. also Gaillard, *Etude sur l'histoire de la doctrine de la grâce depuis S. Augustin* (Lyons-Paris, 1897); Thomassin, *Mémoires sur la grâce, où l'on représente les sentiments de S. Augustin, de S. Thomas, et de presque tous les théologiens jusqu'au concile de Trente, et depuis ce concile des plus célèbres docteurs des universités de l'Europe* (Louvain, 1668), in Latin, *Consensus scholarum de gratiâ* in his *Dogmata Theologica* (Paris, 1680), III, or (1870), VI; Duchesne, *Le Prédestinatianisme* (Paris, 1724); Mozley, *St. Augustine's Doctrine of Predestination* (London, 1855), see *Dub. Rev.* (1856), XL, 67 sqq.; Burton, *The Augustinian System, Dub. Rev.* (1891), XXVI, 48–68; Koch, *Die Autorität des hl. Augustin in der Lehre von der Gnade und Prädestination* in *Tüb. theol. Quartalschrift* (1891); Idem, *Der heilige Faustus von Riez* (Stuttgart, 1895).

Eugène Portalié.

Augustinian Canons and Canonesses. See Canons and Canonesses, Regular.

Augustinians of the Assumption, or Assumptionists.—This congregation had its origin in the College of the Assumption, established in Nîmes, France, in 1843, by the Rev. Emmanuel d'Alzon vicar-general of that diocese, some account of whose life and work is given at the end of this article. Although it was organized in 1847, the members did not take their first vows until 1850; they took their public vows at Christmas of the next year. A second house was established in Paris, and they continued their work there, encouraged by the Holy See. The congregation was formally approved by a Brief of 26 November, 1864. The chief objects of the congregation are to combat the spirit of irreligion in Europe and the spread of schism in the East. To this end the Assumptionists have devoted themselves to the work of Catholic higher and secondary education, to the spread of truth by means of the Press, to the conduct of pilgrimages, and to missionary work in the East. In addition to their college at Nîmes they established Apostolic schools where poor students were educated for the priesthood without expense to themselves. They established "La Bonne Presse", which issued periodicals, pamphlets, and books in great numbers, the chief publication, "La Croix", appearing simultaneously in several different cities. Their activities provoked the resentment of the French Government, and in 1900 the congregation was suppressed within French territory, this action being based on the charge that they were accumulating a fund to be used in a royalist movement to overthrow the Republic. Many of the Assumptionists left France after this, but some remained as secular priests under the authority of various bishops.

At the time of their suppression the Assumptionists maintained twenty Apostolic schools which in twenty-five years gave more than 500 priests to the secular clergy. These schools have all been closed, but the congregation has taken up the work in other quarters. Similar schools have been established in Italy, Belgium, England, and the United States. "La Bonne Presse" was purchased at the time of the suppression by Paul Feron-Vrau, a wealthy manufacturer of Lisle, and all its publications have been continued without any change of policy. Much of the good accomplished by the Assumptionists was effected through this medium. They entered into competition with the irreligious press in

family circles, in workshops, and places where workmen congregate, with excellent results. The Catholic papers established by them have a greater circulation than many famous non-Christian papers. Until recently no popular Catholic paper has reached a degree of circulation equal to that of "La Croix" or of "Le Pèlerin". These two papers are issued at the rate of three million per week; Saturdays this is increased to four million copies. To this must be added the circulation of 600,000 copies of "The Lives of the Saints", 70,000 of the "Les Contemporains", besides the many copies of the "Revue scientifique"; "Cosmos"; "Questions actuelles"; "Les Echos de l'Orient"; the "Petit Bleu", and many others. In Chile, where these Fathers have been for thirteen years, they publish in Spanish "Echoes from the Sanctuary of Lourdes". In their journalistic work they were aided by the Oblate Sisters of the Assumption, an order established by them to assist in their Oriental missions, but whose activities are not confined to that field. Until the suppression they directed the women's section in the publishing rooms of the "Christian Press" as well as the hospitals, orphan asylums, and schools.

Among other works carried on by the Assumptionists in France prior to their suppression was that of the "Association of Our Lady of Salvation", a society devoted to prayer, almsgiving, and setting a good example for the reformation of the working class. This society was established in eighty dioceses, and it succeeded in drawing the higher classes of society more closely to the workingmen. It encouraged everywhere social prayer, and social and national expiation, and discouraged human respect, social apostasy, and isolation in piety. It raised funds to convey workmen, pilgrims, paupers, and sick poor to Lourdes, to the number of a thousand each year; it was zealous in the cause of workmen's clubs, and of Catholic schools, and was active in the movement in favour of the keeping of Sunday as a day of rest. Another field of missionary labour was found among the Newfoundland fishermen. Every year 12,000 or 15,000 fishermen leave the coasts of France, Belgium, and Ireland, to go to the Banks of Newfoundland for codfish. The Protestants have long maintained a flotilla of hospital ships, with which they go to the aid of these unfortunate men and, while ministering to their material needs, draw their souls to heresy. The Assumptionists found here a field for their activity and zeal. They have organized the most prominent Catholic sailors into a committee and have been encouraged to equip two Catholic hospital ships, which now succour the unfortunate fishermen. The vessels have already been wrecked twice, but have been replaced, and the Assumptionists have continued their labours.

The Assumptionists have been active missionaries in the Orient, where at the present time 300 of the congregation, Fathers and Brothers, and nearly 400 Sisters are engaged. Their labours take them from the Balkans to the Dead Sea. They have established there twenty-two permanent residences, thirty regular missionary stations, and fifteen institutions entrusted to the Oblates of the Assumption. In the schools in Turkey in Europe and Turkey in Asia the Assumptionists have 2,500 scholars. Here the Oblates have opened a hospital, an orphanage, and nine gratuitous dispensaries, where they care for about 30,000 sick every year. Of the twenty-two public churches of the congregation in the East twelve are parishes, and in four of them the Offices are held in the rites of the Orient (Greek, or Slav). These rites the Assumptionists have embraced to render the teaching of the Gospel more fruitful. The Orientals, whether from love of their legitimate traditions, or from ignorance, make of the exterior form of the rites a question of supreme importance. Called in 1862 to work for the conversion of the Bulgarians to Catholic unity, the Assumptionists founded in the Turkish quarter of Adrianople, and in Karagatch the European quarter, a residence with a Slav church and a Latin church, a hospital, three schools and a Bulgarian seminary of the Greek and Slav Rites, in which forty young men receive their maintenance and are prepared for the office of the sacred ministry. A similar work is being done at Philippopoli, the cradle of the Oriental missions of the Assumptionists. There is also a primary school, attended by 200 scholars, and an educational institute, many of the former pupils of which occupy important official positions in Eastern Rumelia. The Assumptionists have also churches and schools of different rites at Yamboli and Varna.

At the instance of Cardinal Vincenzo Vannutelli, when he was Apostolic delegate, the Assumptionists went to Constantinople and established themselves in the Turkish quarter at Koum-Kapou. The animosity of the Turks and the jealousy of the Greeks and Armenians caused the new missionaries to be very badly received. To escape persecution they worked on their building at night, doing their masonry, carpentry and painting themselves. By this stratagem they constructed their church of Anastasia, the first church consecrated to Catholic worship in this quarter since 1453. This church, to favour the conversion of the schismatics, was consecrated to the Greek Rite and dedicated by the Apostolic delegate himself. The congregation possesses other Greek churches at Kadikoi (Chalcedon), on the Asiatic bank of the Bosporus, and at Gallipoli. In order to prepare a native clergy, the Assumptionists have opened at Stamboul (Constantinople) a *petit séminaire*, where sixty young men are instructed in the Greek Rite. At Kadikoi, in the great Leonine seminary, they follow with the ordinary theological course special lessons in preparation for the pastoral ministry. They are also given instructions in liturgy, history, canon law and in the Greek, Turkish, and Slav languages. At the day of its opening this seminary had thirty scholars and eight professors. At Stamboul, as at Kadikoi, there are flourishing schools for boys and girls, with more than 700 scholars in attendance. They do not suffice for receiving all the scholars who present themselves. To the labours of teaching are united those of the apostleship, in behalf of the natives as well as foreigners. At Stamboul and at Kadikoi, the priests preach and hear confessions in Italian, French, German, Greek, and Turkish. In the various houses established throughout the empire at least ten living languages are spoken. Greeks, Latins, and Orientals unite for the conferences of St. Vincent de Paul, and the Sisters visit and care for the sick to the number of 10,000 annually.

Their knowledge of the Oriental languages has been of great service to the Assumptionist Fathers in their journalistic labours. Twelve of the Fathers who are the most skilled in these studies write in the Oriental Review. They have their special bulletin, "Les Echos de l'Orient", which circulates among Greeks and Orientals. Because of the Oriental love of splendour in external worship the feasts of the Blessed Sacrament are celebrated with great pomp. With the consent of the authorities, and under the protection of a corps of soldiers, the processions of the Blessed Sacrament are conducted through all the streets around Santa Sophia. The Catholic funerals solemnized with reverential pomp produce also a great effect upon the impressionable natives. In 1890 the Congregation of the Propaganda confided to the Assumptionists the territory in Asia Minor extending from Broussa to Angora. It practically embraces the ancient Bithynia. Already six residences have been established there;

in the city of Broussa, with its population of 100,000, they have established a large college and two churches, one of which is the Latin parish. The towns of Eski-Chehir, Ismid, Sultan Eschoir, Koniah (Iconium), Fanaraki have each a residence for the priests with a public church; the Oblate Sisters are also established in these places. At Jerusalem the Assumptionists have erected the Hostelry of Our Lady of France for the reception of pilgrims, annexed to which is a scholasticate of forty religious. They have established there also the Society of the Croisés of Purgatory, and they have a church in which to receive the Latin pilgrims. The Eucharistic Congress at Jerusalem in 1893 was held in the Hostelry of Our Lady of France.

Emmanuel-Joseph-Marie-Maurice d'Alzon, founder and first Superior General of the Augustinians of the Assumption was born at Le Vigan, France, 30 August, 1810, and died at Nîmes, 21 November, 1880. He was a member of a noble family, and, being an only son, encountered strong opposition when he decided to enter the clerical state. He studied at the seminary of Montpellier and later at Rome, where he was ordained priest 26 December, 1834. On his return to France the next year he was appointed Vicar-General of the Diocese of Nîmes, which position he held for forty-five years, serving under four bishops. Among his earliest notable works was the establishment at Nîmes in 1843 of the College of the Assumption, for the education of the children of the aristocracy. This college later became the cradle of his congregation. He was associated with Guéranger, Louis Veuillot, and other champions of the Catholic cause. With the "Revue de l'enseignement chrétien", which he founded and directed, he restored the Christian spirit in classical studies. To combat Protestantism in southern France he established the Association of St. Francis de Sales. He also suggested the idea of the ecclesiastical caravan, formed by the priests at Nîmes, who by request of Mgr. Plantier came to Rome to visit the sovereign pontiff. This was the beginning of the great French pilgrimages called the national pilgrimages, the directors of which were for many years the religious of the order founded by Père d'Alzon. By his "alumnats", or Apostolic schools, he supplied the education of the poor children called to the priesthood, who, owing to lack of means, could not be admitted to the seminaries. The Fathers of the Assumption opened fifteen of these houses which in twenty-five years gave more than 500 priests to the secular clergy. To sustain this work of charity, Père d'Alzon founded the Association of Our Lady of Vocations, enriched with numerous indulgences, by Pius IX and Leo XIII. The brotherhood, by a decree of the Holy See, has been canonically established in the chapel of the College of Nîmes, and has received the approbation of many bishops. Père d'Alzon was much esteemed by the Popes Gregory XVI and Pius IX. The latter in 1863 sent him to Constantinople to found in the East the missions of the Congregation of the Assumption. More than once he was proposed for the episcopate, but he always declined the honour, preferring to devote himself to the work of his congregation.   Thomas Gaffney Taaffe.

Augustinus, Antonius, historian of canon law and Archbishop of Tarragona in Spain, b. at Saragossa 26 Feb., 1517, of a distinguished family; d. at Tarragona, 31 May, 1586. After finishing his studies at Alcalá and Salamanca, he went to Bologna (1536), to Padua (1537), and to Florence (1538) in which latter place he examined the famous "Codex Florentinus" of the Pandects and made the acquaintance of such learned men of the new historical school as Andrea Alciati, to whom he owed a confirmation of his pronounced bent towards a positive and critical treatment of the ancient materials of canonical jurisprudence. In 1541 he took his degree of Doctor of Civil and Canon Law and in 1544, at the request of the Emperor Charles V, he was made Auditor of the Rota by Paul III. In 1555 he was sent by Paul IV to England, with a message of congratulation for Queen Mary and as Counsellor to Cardinal Pole. In 1556 he was made Bishop of Alife, in the Kingdom of Naples, and in 1561 was transferred to Lerida in his native Spain. He assisted during three years at the Council of Trent and urged ardently the reformation of the clergy. "It is our fault", he said in the council, "that so great an agitation has arisen in France and Germany. We must begin with the reformation of the clergy. It is your business, O Fathers, to save by your decrees the common weal of the Church that is now threatened." In 1576 he was promoted by Gregory XIII to the archiepiscopal See of Tarragona.

Augustinus is one of the foremost figures of the Catholic Counter-Reformation that set in with so much vigour and success in the latter half of the sixteenth century. His chosen field was the *fontes*, or original sources of ecclesiastical law both papal and conciliar. The basis of the medieval canon law was the "Decretum" of Gratian, a useful codification of the middle of the twelfth century, the ecclesiastical law-book of the schools and the universities, of great academic authority, but never formally approved by the popes as church legislation. Its materials, never hitherto critically illustrated as to their prominence and form, and often badly corrupted as to their text, stood in need of judicious sifting and elucidation. It was to this task that the young Augustinus addressed himself from 1538 to 1543. In the latter year he published at Venice the first critical study on Gratian, "Emendationum et Opinionum libri IV", the result of four years' labour at the text of the old medieval Benedictine of Bologna. This text remained his life-long study; towards the close of his career, after important services rendered during ten years to the "Correctores Romani" in their edition of Gratian (Rome, 1582), he finished his own magisterial examination of the work; it was not, however, published until after his death, "De Emendatione Gratiani dialogi (30) libri II" (Tarragona, 1587).

Other important publications of the sources of civil and ecclesiastical law occupied his pen. Thus he published in 1567 an edition of the Byzantine imperial constitutions, in 1576 his "IV Antiquæ Collectiones Decretalium", in 1582 a treatise on the "Penitential Canons" together with a "Pœnitentiale Romanum" discovered by him. From 1557 he sought earnestly for the necessary patronage, papal or regal, to enable him to publish the hitherto unedited Greek text of the ancient ecclesiastical councils, and for that purpose examined many archives in Italy and Germany; the fruits of his labours were reaped at a later date by others. Among the more valuable of his posthumous publications, and appealing strongly to modern historical tastes, is a critical examination of several early medieval collections of canon law that served as original material for the "Decretum" of Gratian. This work, that Maassen and von Scherer speak of with respect, is entitled "De quibusdam veteribus Canonum Ecclesiasticorum Collectionibus Judicium et censura", and was published at Rome (1611) with the second and third parts of his "Juris Pontificii Veteris Epitome" (to Innocent III, 1198–1216), the first part of which appeared at Tarragona in 1587. It contains biographical and text-critical notes on a number of collectors of ecclesiastical laws, from the sixth to the twelfth century. In this work he treats progressively of the pseudo-Isidorian Decretals, and while he did not dispose of sufficient material to demonstrate thoroughly their spurious character or to attempt to fix

the time and place of their compilation, it is clear that he did not believe them earlier than the time of Pope Damasus (366–384) or even of the seventh century "Collectio Hispana". His notes on the correlated "Capitula Hadriani" (Angilramni) were published at Cologne in 1618. His powerful genius was truly universal. Classical philology, epigraphy, numismatics, above all the history of civil and ecclesiastical law found in him an investigator whose boldness and insight were extraordinary for that period of incipient historico-critical research. Death surprised him at the patriotic task of an edition of the works of the Spanish writer, St. Isidore of Seville. The works of Augustinus were printed in eight volumes at Lucca (1775–74); his life by Siscarius is in the second volume 1–121.

MAASSEN, *Gesch. d. Quellen und Litt. des. can. Rechts im Abendlande, etc.* (Gratz, 1870), I, xix–xxxiv; VON SCHERER in *Kirchenlex.*; SCHOTT, *Laud. Funebr. cl. viri. Ant. Augustini*, in *Gallandi, De vet. Canonum collect. dissertationum sylloge* (Mainz, 1790); PANSIROLUS, *De cl. leg. interpreta.* (Leipzig, 1721); NICÉRON, *Mémoires*, IX, 58–76; ANDRESIUS, *Ant. Aug. Epistolæ lat. et ital.* (Parma, 1804).

THOMAS J. SHAHAN.

Augustinus Maria, O. D. C. See COHEN, HERMANN.

Augustinus Novellus, O. S. A. See AGOSTINO NOVELL.

Augustinus Triumphus. See HERMITS OF ST. AUGUSTINE.

Augustinus-Verein, THE, an association organized in 1878 to promote the interests of the Catholic press, particularly the daily press, of Germany. The society proposes to attain its end (1) by giving its moral support to the establishment of Catholic papers; (2) by furnishing trustworthy information and authentic news to the daily papers; (3) by training Catholic journalists, and giving assistance to the members of the profession in need of it; (4) by representing the interests of the profession; (5) by securing positions and giving information and assistance in all matters connected with journalism, free of charge; and finally (6) by endeavouring to bring about the harmonious co-operation of Catholic publishers, as well as uniformity in treating the questions of the day. The lack of organization on the part of the Catholic Press first became obvious at an early stage of the *Kulturkampf;* several unsuccessful attempts were made to supply the deficiency, among others the formation of a society of publishers. The first feasible steps were taken at the Catholic Convention at Würzburg; at subsequent gatherings plans were matured, and at Düsseldorf, 15 May, 1878, a programme was drawn up which is substantially followed out in the present Augustinus-Verein. Düsseldorf became the centre of the Verein, which, now that it has spread throughout Germany, is divided into ten groups, corresponding to geographical divisions, each, to a large extent autonomous. A general assembly is held annually. The Verein has its own organ, the "Augustinusblatt", published at Krefeld. It also conducts a literary bureau, a beneficial society, a parliamentary correspondence association of the Centre Party, in Berlin, and an employment agency. In 1904 the society had a regular membership of 850, in addition to the associate membership.

KÖCK in BUCHBERGER, *Kirchlich. Handlex.*; MEIER in *Kirchenlex.*

F. M. RUDGE.

Augustopolis, a titular see of Palestine, suffragan of Petra. Its episcopal list (431–536) is given in Gams (p. 454). There were two other sees of the same name, one in Cilicia, a suffragan of Tarsus, the other in Phrygia (Asia Minor), suffragan of Synnada. Its episcopal list (Gams, p. 446) extends from 359 to 869.

LEQUIEN, *Oriens Christ.* (1740), II, 727–728; I, 845–886.

Augustow, DIOCESE OF. See SENJY.

Augustus.—The name by which CAIUS JULIUS CÆSAR OCTAVIANUS, the first Roman Emperor, in whose reign Jesus Christ was born, is usually known; b. at Rome, 62 B. C.; d. A. D. 14; It is the title which he received from the Senate 27 B. C., in gratitude for the restoration of some privileges of which that body had been deprived. The name was afterwards assumed by all his successors. Augustus belonged to the *gens Octavia* and was the son of Caius Octavius, a prætor. He was the grand-nephew of (Caius) Julius Cæsar, and was named in the latter's will as his principal heir. After the murder of Julius Cæsar, the young Octavianus proceeded to Rome to gain possession of his inheritance. Though originally in league with the republican party, he eventually allied himself with Mark Antony. Through his own popularity, and in opposition to the will of the senate he succeeded (43 B. C.) in obtaining the consulate. In the same year he entered into a pact with Antony and Lepidus by which it was agreed that for five years they would control the affairs of Rome. This (second) Triumvirate (*tresviri reipublicæ constituendæ*) so apportioned the Roman dominions that Lepidus received Spain; Antony, Gaul; and Augustus, Africa, Sicily, and Sardinia. The first concerted move of the Triumvirate was to proceed against the murderers of Cæsar and the party of the Senate under the leadership of Brutus and Cassius. A crushing defeat was inflicted on the latter at the battle of Philippi (42 B. C.), after which the fate of Rome rested practically in the hands of two men. Lepidus, always treated with neglect, sought to obtain Sicily for himself, but Augustus soon won over his troops, and, on his submission, sent him to Rome where he spent the rest of his life as *pontifex maximus*.

A new division of the territory of the Republic between Antony and Augustus resulted, by which the former took the East and the latter the West. When Antony put away his wife Octavia, the sister of Augustus, through infatuation for Cleopatra, civil war again ensued, whose real cause is doubtless to be sought in the conflicting interests of both, and the long-standing antagonism between the East and the West. The followers of Antony were routed in the naval battle of Actium (31 B. C.), and Augustus was left, to all intents and purposes, the master of the Roman world. He succeeded in bringing peace to the long-distracted Republic, and by his moderation in dealing with the senate, his munificence to the army, and his generosity to the people, he strengthened his position and became in fact, if not in name, the first Emperor of Rome. His policy of preserving intact the republican forms of administration and of avoiding all semblance of absolute power or monarchy did not diminish his authority or weaken his control. Whatever may be said in regard to the general character of his administration and his policy of centralization, it cannot be denied that he succeeded effectually in strengthening and consolidating the loosely organized Roman state into a close and well-knit whole. He was a patron of art, letters, and science, and devoted large sums of money to the embellishment and enlargement of Rome. It was his well-known boast that he "found it of brick and left it of marble". Under his management, industry and commerce increased. Security and rapidity of intercourse were obtained by means of many new highways. He undertook to remove by legislation the disorder and confusion in life and morals brought about, in great measure, by the civil wars. His court life was simple and unostentatious. Severe laws were made for the purpose of encouraging marriages and increasing the birth-rate. The immorality of the games and the theatres was curbed, and new laws introduced to regulate the status of freedmen and slaves. The changes wrought

by Augustus in the administration of Rome, and his policy in the Orient are of especial significance to the historian of Christianity. The most important event of his reign was the birth of Our Lord (Luke, ii, 1) in Palestine. The details of Christ's life on earth, from His birth to His death, were very closely interwoven with the purposes and methods pursued by Augustus. The Emperor died in the seventy-sixth year of his age (A. D. 14). After the battle of Actium, he received into his favour Herod the Great, confirmed him in his title of King of the Jews, and granted him the territory between Galilee and the Trachonitis, thereby winning the gratitude and devotion of Herod and his house. After the death of Herod (750, A. U. C.), Augustus divided his kingdom between his sons. One of them, Archelaus, was eventually banished, and his territory, together with Idumæa and Samaria, were added to the province of Syria (759, A. U. C.). On this occasion, Augustus caused a census of the province to be taken by the legate, Sulpicius Quirinius, the circumstances of which are of great importance for the right calculation of the birth of Christ. See ROMAN EMPIRE; LUKE, GOSPEL OF.

The chief sources for the life of Augustus are the Latin writers, SUETONIUS, TACITUS, VELLEIUS PATERCULUS, and CICERO (in his *Epistles* and *Philippics*); the Greek writers, NICHOLAS OF DAMASCUS, DIO CASSIUS, and PLUTARCH. See also his official autobiography, the famous *Monumentum Ancyranum*, ed. by MOMMSEN (Berlin, 1883), and by FAIRLEY (Philadelphia, 1898), with tr.; TILLEMONT, *Histoire des empereurs, etc.* (Brussels, 1732); MERIVALE, *History of the Romans under the Empire* (London, 1850–52); SMITH, *Dict. of Greek and Roman Biography* (London, 1890), I, 424–431; TAYLOR, *A Constitutional and Political History of Rome* (London, 1899); xvi–xviii; RAMSAY, *Was Christ born at Bethlehem?* (New York and London, 1898); *The Church under the Roman Empire* (ibid., 1893); GARDTHAUSEN, *Augustus und seine Zeit* (Leipzig, 1891), the standard work on the subject. For the origin and character of the legends that, at an early date, made Augustus one of the "prophets of Christ", see GRAF, *Roma nella memoria e nelle immaginazioni del Medio Evo* (Turin, 1882), I, ix, 308, 331. Cf. also GRAY in HASTINGS, *Dict. of Christ and the Gospels* (New York, 1906) s. v. *Augustus*, I, 143–46.

PATRICK J. HEALY.

Aumbry, variously written AMBRY, or AUMBRYE, is a derivative through the French of the classical *armarium*, or medieval Latin *almarium*. Its original meaning was a cupboard and it has never lost this more general sense, but even in classical Latin it had acquired in addition the special signification of a cupboard for holding books. This limited meaning was widely prevalent in the Middle Ages. Thus in the tenth-century rule of Cluny the library is called *armarium* and the official who had charge of it *armarius*, while by an arrangement which was long and widely observed both in Benedictine and in other monastic houses, this *armarius*, or librarian, was usually identical with the precentor. In Ælfric's Anglo-Saxon glossary, compiled at the beginning of the eleventh century, the Anglo-Saxon word *bochord* (book-hoard, i. e. library), is interpreted *bibliotheca vel armarium vel archivum*. Similarly it was a common proverb in religious houses, which meets us as early as 1170, that *claustrum sine armario est quasi castrum sine armamentario* (a monastery without a library is like a fortress without an arsenal). Besides this, owing to the number of cupboards and presses needed for storing vestments, church plate, etc., the word *armarium* was also not unfrequently used for the sacristy, though this may also be due to the fact that the books were themselves in many cases kept in the sacristy. In German the word *Almerei*, a derivative of *armarium*, has the meaning of sacristy.

CLARK, *The Care of Books* (Cambridge, 1902), 57–88; MICHAEL, *Geschichte des deutschen Volkes* (Freiburg, 1903), 42–62; GASQUET, *English Monastic Life* (London, 1904), 51–55; OTTE, *Handbuch d. kirchlichen Archäologie* (Leipzig, 1886), I, 105; VIOLLET-LE-DUC, *Dict. de Mobilier* (Paris, 1856), I.

HERBERT THURSTON.

Aunarius (OR AUNACHARIUS), SAINT, Bishop of

Auxerre in France, b. 573, d. 603. Being of noble birth, he was brought up in the royal court, but evinced a desire to enter the clerical state, was ordained priest by St. Syagrius of Autun, and eventually was made Bishop of Auxerre. His administration is noted for certain important disciplinary measures that throw light on the religious and moral life of the Merovingian times. He caused solemn litanies to be said daily in the chief centres of population, by rotation, and on the first day of each month in the larger towns and monasteries. He enforced a regular daily attendance at the Divine Office on the part both of regular and secular clergy. He held (581 or 585) an important synod of four bishops, seven abbots, thirty-five priests, and four deacons, for the restoration of ecclesiastical discipline and the suppression of popular pagan superstitions, and caused the lives of his predecessors Amator and Germanus to be written. He was buried at Auxerre, where he has always been held in veneration. His remains were later enclosed in a golden chest, but were partially dispersed by the Huguenots in 1567. A portion, however, was placed in the hollow pillar of a crypt, and saved. His feast is celebrated 25 September.

BUTLER, *Lives of the Saints*, 25 September; PÉNER, in *Acta SS.*, VII, September, 79–97; COCHARD, *Les Saints de l'église d'Orléans* (1879), 272–277; MANSI, V, 967–980.

THOMAS J. SHAHAN.

Aurea (Golden), a title given to certain works and documents: *Bulla*, the charter of Emperor Charles IV, establishing (10 January, 1356), in union with the estates of the empire, the law of future imperial elections. *Catena*, a collection of Scriptural commentaries made by St. Thomas Aquinas. *Legenda*, a collection of lives of saints (*legendæ*) by Jacopo da Voragine, Archbishop of Genoa in the thirteenth century. *Summa Hostiensis*, also *Summa Archiepiscopi*, a famous exposition of the principal parts of the Decretals of Gregory IX, by Henricus de Segusio, Cardinal of Ostia (d. 1271). *Tabula*, an index to the "Summa Theologica" of St. Thomas Aquinas prepared by Pietro da Bergamo.

Aurelian (LUCIUS DOMITIUS AURELIANUS), Roman Emperor, 270–275, b. of humble parents, near Sirmium in Pannonia, 9 September, 214; d. 275. At the age of twenty he entered the military service, in which, because of exceptional ability and remarkable bodily strength, his advancement was rapid. On the death of Claudius he was proclaimed Emperor by the army at Sirmium, and became sole master of the Roman dominions on the suicide of his rival Quintillus, the candidate of the Senate. When Aurelian assumed the reins of government the Roman world was divided into three sections: the Gallo-Roman Empire, established by Postumus, comprising Gaul and Britain; the kingdom of Palmyra, which held sway over the entire Orient, including Egypt and the greater part of Asia Minor, and the Roman Empire, restricted to Italy, Africa, the Danubian Provinces, Greece, and Bithynia. On the upper Danube, Rhætia and Northern Italy were overrun by the Juthungi, while the Vandals were preparing to invade Pannonia. The internal affairs of Rome were equally deplorable. The anarchy of the legions and the frequent revolutions in preceding reigns had shattered the imperial authority; the treasury was empty and the monetary system ruined. With no support but that afforded by the army of the Danube, Aurelian undertook to restore the material and moral unity of the Empire, and to introduce whatever reforms were necessary to give it stability. Enormous as this project was, in the face of so many obstacles, he succeeded in accomplishing it in less than five years. When he died, the frontiers were all restored and strongly defended, the unity of the Empire was established, the administration was reorganized, the finances of the Empire placed on a sound footing, and

the monetary system thoroughly revised. His scheme for the complete unification of the Empire led him to attempt to establish the worship of the sun as the supreme god of Rome. During the early years of his reign Aurelian exhibited remarkable justice and tolerance towards the Christians. In 272, when he had gained possession of Antioch, after defeating Zenobia in several battles, he was appealed to by the Christians to decide whether the "Church building" in Antioch belonged to the orthodox bishop Domnus, or to the party represented by the favourite of Zenobia, Paul of Samosata, who had been deposed for heresy by a synod held three or four years before. His decision, based probably on the Edict of Gallienus, was that the property belonged to those who were in union with the bishops of Italy and of the city of Rome (Eus., Hist. Eccl., VII, xxvii–xxx). As this act was based on political motives, it cannot be construed into one of friendliness for the Christians. As soon as he was at liberty to carry out his schemes for internal reform Aurelian revived the policy of his predecessor Valerian, threatened to rescind the Edict of Gallienus, and commenced a systematic persecution of the followers of Christ. The exact date of the inauguration of this policy is not known. It is likely, however, that an edict was issued in the summer of 275 and despatched to the governors of the provinces, but Aurelian was slain before he could put it into execution. Tradition refers to his reign a large number of *Acta Martyrum*, none of which is considered to be authentic (Dom Butler, "Journal of Theological Studies", 1906, VII, 306). His biographer, Vopiscus, says (c. xx) that he once reproached the Roman Senate for neglecting to consult the Sibylline Books in an hour of imminent peril. "It would seem", he said, "as if you were holding your meetings in a church of the Christians instead of in a temple of all the gods"; from which statement it has been rightly inferred that "the decline of the old faith was caused by the progress of the new, and that the buildings then used for the worship of the Christians were becoming more and more conspicuous".

HOMO, *Essai sur le règne de l'empereur Aurélien* (Paris, 1904); GÖRRES, *Die Religionspolitik der römischen Kaiser (Gallienus, Claudius II, Gothicus, Aurelian und Probus)* in *Zeitschr. für wissenschaftliche Theol.*, XLVIII (new series, XIII), Oct., 1905; *Dict. Christ. Biogr. s. v. Aurelian*, I, 229; DUCHESNE, *Hist. ancienne de l'église* (Paris, 1906), I, 465–474; ALLARD, *Hist. des persécutions* (Paris, 1885–90), III.

PATRICK J. HEALY.

Aureliopolis, a titular see of Lydia in Asia Minor, whose episcopal list (325–787) is given in Gams (p. 447).

LEQUIEN, *Oriens Christ.* (1740), I, 895–896; III, 959–962.

Aurelius, Archbishop of Carthage from 388 to 423. From the time of St. Cyprian, Carthage was one of the foremost sees in Christendom. Its bishop, though not formally bearing the title of Primate, confirmed the episcopal nominations in all the provinces of Africa, convoked and presided at the plenary councils, which were held almost yearly, and signed the synodal letters in the name of all the participants. Such a post Aurelius occupied with distinction at a time when Africa held the intellectual leadership in the Church. His episcopate coincided with the last great effort made by the Donatists to uphold a losing cause, and with the first appearance of Pelagianism. Both these crises Aurelius met with equal decision and wisdom. A man of conciliating disposition, and a great lover of peace, his tendency to an indulgent treatment of repentant Donatists was conspicuous in the synodal acts of his own church, and in the plenary councils over which he presided he upheld the same moderate policy. But when the Donatists resorted to rebellion and wholesale murder, he joined his colleagues in appealing to the secular power. He was the first to unmask and denounce Pelagianism. In 412 he excommunicated and drove from Carthage Cælestius, the disciple of Pelagius. In 416 he condemned them both, in a synod of sixty-eight bishops of the Proconsulate, and induced Innocent I to brand their two principal errors by defining the necessity of grace and of infant baptism. When Pope Zosimus allowed himself to be deceived by Pelagius's lying professions, he held (417) a plenary council of his African brethren, and in their names warned the pontiff, who in turn (418) condemned the heresiarchs. Aurelius is mentioned in the African martyrology on 20 July.

LECLERCQ, L'Afrique chrétienne (Paris, 1904), I; PARSONS, Studies in Church Hist. (New York, 1896), I; Acts of the Councils of Carthage; BARONIUS, Ann. Eccl. ad ann. 416–418; PORTALIÉ in Dict. de théol. cath. s. v. Augustin.

A. J. B. VUIBERT.

Aurelius Antoninus, MARCUS, Roman Emperor, A. D. 161–180, b. at Rome, 26 April, 121; d. 17 March, 180. His father died while Marcus was yet a boy, and he was adopted by his grandfather, Annius Verus. In the first pages of his "Meditations" (I, i–xvii) he has left us an account, unique in antiquity, of his education by near relatives and by tutors of distinction; diligence, gratitude, and hardiness seem to have been its chief characteristics. From his earliest years he enjoyed the friendship and patronage of the Emperor Hadrian, who bestowed on him the honour of the equestrian order when he was only six years old, made him a member of the Salian priesthood at eight, and compelled Antoninus Pius immediately after his own adoption to adopt as sons and heirs both the young Marcus and Ceionius Commodus, known later as the Emperor Lucius Verus. In honour of his adopted father he changed his name from M. Ælius Aurelius Verus to M. Aurelius Antoninus. By the will of Hadrian he espoused Faustina, the daughter of Antoninus Pius. He was raised to the consulship in 140, and in 147 received the "tribunician power". (See ROMAN EMPEROR.) In all the later years of the life of Antoninus Pius, Marcus was his constant companion and adviser. On the death of the former (7 March, 161) Marcus was immediately acknowledged as emperor by the Senate. Acting entirely on his own initiative, he at once promoted his adopted brother Lucius Verus to the position of colleague, with equal rights as emperor. With the accession of Marcus the great *Pax Romana* that made the era of the Antonines the happiest in the annals of Rome, and perhaps of mankind, came to an end, and with his reign the glory of the old Rome vanished. Younger peoples, untainted by the vices of civilization, and knowing nothing of the inanition which comes from over-refinement and over-indulgence, were preparing to struggle for the lead in the direction of human destiny. Marcus was scarcely seated on the throne when the Picts commenced to threaten in Britain the recently erected Wall of Antoninus. The Chatti and Chauci attempted to cross the Rhine and the upper reaches of the Danube. These attacks were easily repelled. Not so with the outbreak in the Orient, which commenced in 161 and did not cease until 166. The destruction of an entire legion (XXII Deiotariana) at Elegeia aroused the emperors to the gravity of the situation. Lucius Verus took command of the troops in 162 and, through the valour and skill of his lieutenants in a war known officially as the *Bellum Armeniacum et Parthicum*, waged over the wide area of Syria, Cappadocia, Armenia, Mesopotamia, and Media, was able to celebrate a glorious triumph in 166. For a people so long accustomed to peace as the Romans were, this war was wellnigh fatal. It taxed all their resources, and the withdrawal of the legions from the Danubian frontier gave an opportunity to the Teutonic tribes to pene-

trate into a rich and tempting territory. People with strange-sounding names, the Marcomanni, Varistæ, Hermanduri, Quadi, Suevi, Jazyges, Vandals, collected along the Danube, crossed the frontiers, and became the advance-guard of the great migration known as the "Wandering of the Nations", which four centuries later culminated in the overthrow of the Western Empire. The war against these invaders commenced in 167, and in a short time had assumed such threatening proportions as to demand the presence of both emperors at the front.

Lucius Verus died in 169, and Marcus was left to carry on the war alone. His difficulties were immeasurably increased by the devastation wrought by the plague carried westward by the returning legions of Verus, by famine and earthquakes, and by inundations which destroyed the vast granaries of Rome and their contents. In the panic and terror caused by these events the people resorted to the extremes of superstition to win back the favour of the deities through whose anger it was believed these visitations were inflicted. Strange rites of expiation and sacrifice were resorted to, victims were slain by thousands, and the assistance of the gods of the Orient sought for as well as that of the gods of Rome. During the war with the Quadi in 174 there took place the famous incident of the Thundering Legion (*Legio Fulminatrix*, *Fulminea*, *Fulminata*) which has been a cause of frequent controversy between Christian and non-Christian writers. The Roman army was surrounded by enemies, with no chance of escape, when a storm burst. The rain poured down in refreshing showers on the Romans, while the enemy were scattered with lightning and hail. The parched and famishing Romans received the saving drops first on their faces and parched throats, and afterwards in their helmets and shields, to refresh their horses. Marcus obtained a glorious victory as a result of this extraordinary event, and his enemies were hopelessly overthrown. That such an event did really happen is attested both by pagan and Christian writers. The former attribute the occurrence either to magic (Dion Cassius, LXXI, 8–10) or to the prayers of the emperor (Capitolinus, "Vita Marci", XXIV; Themistius, "Orat. XV. ad Theod."; Claudian, "De Sext. Cons. Hon.", V, 340 sqq.; "Sibyl. Orac.", ed. Alexandre, XII, 196 sqq. Cf. Bellori, "La Colonne Antonine", and Eckhel, "Doctrina Nummorum", III, 64). The Christian writers attributed the fact to the prayers of the Christians who were in the army (Claudius Apollinaris in Euseb., "Hist. Eccl.", V, 5; Tertullian, "Apol.", v; ad Scap. c. iv), and soon there grew up a legend to the effect that in consequence of this miracle the emperor put a stop to the persecution of the Christians (cf. Euseb. and Tert. opp cit.). It must be conceded that the testimony of Claudius Apollinaris (see Smith and Wace, "Dict. of Christ. Biogr.", I, 132–133) is the most valuable of all that we possess, as he wrote within a few years of the event, and that all credit must be given to the prayers of the Christians, though it does not necessarily follow that we should accept the elaborate detail of the story as given by Tertullian and later writers [Allard, op. cit. infra, pp. 377, 378; Renan, "Marc-Aurèle" (6th ed., Paris, 1891), XVII, pp. 273–278; P. de Smedt, "Principes de la critique hist." (1883), p. 133]. The last years of the reign of Marcus were saddened by the appearance of a usurper, Avidius Cassius, in the Orient, and by the consciousness that the empire was to fall into unworthy hands when his son Commodus should come to the throne. Marcus died at Vindobona or Sirmium in Pannonia. The chief authorities for his life are Julius Capitolinus, "Vita Marci Antonini Philosophi" (SS. Hist. Aug. IV); Dion Cassius, "Epitome of Xiphilinos"; Herodian; Fronto, "Epistolæ" and Aulus Gellius "Noctes Atticæ".

Marcus Aurelius was one of the best men of heathen antiquity. Apropos of the Antonines the judicious Montesquieu says that, if we set aside for a moment the contemplation of the Christian verities, we cannot read the life of this emperor without a softening feeling of emotion. Niebuhr calls him the noblest character of his time, and M. Martha, the historian of the Roman moralists, says that in Marcus Aurelius "the philosophy of Heathendom grows less proud, draws nearer to a Christianity which it ignored or which it despised, and is ready to fling itself into the arms of the Unknown God". On the other hand, the warm eulogies which many writers have heaped on Marcus Aurelius as a ruler and as a man seem excessive and overdrawn. It is true that the most marked trait in his character was his devotion to philosophy and letters, but it was a curse to mankind that "he was a Stoic first and then a ruler". His dilettanteism rendered him utterly unfitted for the practical affairs of a large empire in a time of stress. He was more concerned with realizing in his own life (to say the truth, a stainless one) the Stoic ideal of perfection, than he was with the pressing duties of his office.

Philosophy became a disease in his mind, and cut him off from the truths of practical life. He was steeped in the grossest superstition; he surrounded himself with charlatans and magicians, and took with seriousness even the knavery of Alexander of Abonoteichos. The highest offices in the empire were sometimes conferred on his philosophic teachers, whose lectures he attended even after he became emperor. In the midst of the Parthian war he found time to keep a kind of private diary, his famous "Meditations", or twelve short books of detached thoughts and sentences in which he gave over to posterity the results of a rigorous self-examination. With the exception of a few letters discovered among the works of Fronto (M. Corn. Frontonis Reliquiæ, Berlin, 1816) this history of his inner life is the only work which we have from his pen. The style is utterly without merit and distinction, apparently a matter of pride, for he tells us he had learned to abstain from rhetoric, and poetry, and fine writing. Though a Stoic deeply rooted in the principles developed by Seneca and Epictetus, Aurelius cannot be said to have any consistent system of philosophy. It might be said, perhaps, in justice to this "seeker after righteousness", that his faults were the faults of his philosophy rooted in the principle that human nature naturally inclined towards evil, and needed to be constantly kept in check. Only once does he refer to Christianity (Medit., XI, iii), a spiritual regenerative force that was visibly increasing its activity, and then only to brand the Christians with the reproach of obstinacy (παράταξις), the highest social crime in the eyes of Roman authority. He seems also (ibid.) to look on Christian martyrdom as devoid of the serenity and calm that should accompany the death of the wise man. For the possible relations of the emperor with Christian bishops see Abercius of Hieropolis, and Melito of Sardes.

In his dealings with the Christians Marcus Aurelius went a step farther than any of his predecessors. Throughout the reigns of Trajan, Hadrian, and Antoninus Pius, the procedure followed by Roman authorities in their treatment of the Christians was that outlined in Trajan's rescript to Pliny, by which it was ordered that the Christians should not be sought out; if brought before the courts, legal proof of their guilt should be forthcoming. [For the much-disputed rescript "Ad conventum Asiæ" (Eus., Hist. Eccl., IV, xiii), see Antoninus Pius]. It is clear that during the reign of Aurelius the comparative leniency of the legislation of Trajan gave way to a more severe temper. In Southern Gaul, at least, an imperial rescript inaugurated an entirely new and much more violent era of persecution (Eus., Hist. Eccl., V, i, 45). In Asia Minor and in Syria the blood of Christians flowed in torrents (Allard, op. cit. infra, pp. 375. 376, 388, 389). In general the recrudescence of persecution seems to have come immediately through the local action of the provincial governors impelled by the insane outcries of terrified and demoralized city mobs. If any general imperial edict was issued, it has not survived. It seems more probable that the "new decrees" mentioned by Eusebius (Hist. Eccl., IV, xxvi, 5) were local ordinances of municipal authorities or provincial governors; as to the emperor, he maintained against the Christians the existing legislation, though it has been argued that the imperial edict (Digests, XLVIII, xxix, 30) against those who terrify by superstition "the fickle minds of men" was directed against the Christian society. Duchesne says (Hist. Ancienne de l'Eglise, Paris, 1906, p. 210) that for such obscure sects the emperor would not condescend to interfere with the laws of the empire. It is clear, however, from the scattered references in contemporary writings (Celsus, "In Origen. Contra Celsum", VIII, 169; Melito, in Eus., "Hist. Eccl.", IV, xxvi; Athenagoras, "Legatio pro Christianis", i) that throughout the empire an active pursuit of the Christians was now undertaken. In order to encourage their numerous enemies, the ban was raised from the *delatores*, or "denouncers", and they were promised rewards for all cases of successful conviction. The impulse given by this legislation to an unrelenting pursuit of the followers of Christ rendered their condition so precarious that many changes in ecclesiastical organization and discipline date, at least in embryo, from this reign.

Another significant fact, pointing to the growing numbers and influence of the Christians, and the increasing distrust on the part of the imperial authorities and the cultured classes, is that an active literary propaganda, emanating from the imperial surroundings, was commenced at this period. The Cynic philosopher Crescens (see Justin Martyr) took part in a public disputation with St. Justin in Rome. Fronto, the preceptor and bosom friend of Marcus Aurelius, denounced the followers of the new religion in a formal discourse (Min. Felix, "Octavius", cc. ix, xxxi) and the satirist Lucian of Samosata turned the shafts of his wit against them, as a party of ignorant fanatics. No better proof of the tone of the period and of the widespread knowledge of Christian beliefs and practices which prevailed among the pagans is needed than the contemporary "True Word" of Celsus (see Origen), a work in which were collected all the calumnies of pagan malice and all the arguments, set forth with the skill of the trained rhetorician, which the philosophy and experience of the pagan world could muster against the new creed. The earnestness and frequency with which the Christians replied to these assaults by the apologetic works (see Athenagoras, Minucius Felix, Theophilus of Antioch) addressed directly to the emperors themselves, or to the people at large, show how keenly alive they were to the dangers arising from these literary or academic foes.

From such and so many causes it is not surprising that Christian blood flowed freely in all parts of the empire. The excited populace saw in the misery and bloodshed of the period a proof that the gods were angered by the toleration accorded to the Christians; consequently, they threw on the latter all blame for the incredible public calamities. Whether it was famine or pestilence, drought or floods, the cry was the same (Tertull., "Apologeticum", V, xli): *Christianos ad leonem* (Throw the

Christians to the lion.) The pages of the Apologists show how frequently the Christians were condemned and what penalties they had to endure, and these vague and general references are confirmed by some contemporary "Acta" of unquestionable authority, in which the harrowing scenes are described in all their gruesome details. Among them are the "Acta" of Justin and his companions who suffered at Rome (c. 165), of Carpus, Papylus, and Agathonica, who were put to death in Asia Minor, of the Scillitan Martyrs in Numidia, and the touching Letters of the Churches of Lyons and Vienne (Eus., Hist. Eccl., V, i–iv) in which is contained the description of the tortures inflicted (177) on Blandina and her companions at Lyons. Incidentally, this document throws much light on the character and extent of the persecution of the Christians in Southern Gaul, and on the share of the emperor therein.

The Roman histories of GIBBON, DURUY, and MERIVALE deal at length with his personal history; SCHILLER, *Geschichte der römischen Kaiserzeit* (Gotha, 1883); ALLARD, *Histoire des persécutions pendant les premiers siècles* (2d ed., Paris, 1892), cc. vi–vii; RENAN, *Marc-Aurèle et la fin du monde antique* (6th ed., Paris, 1901); DILL, *Roman Society from Nero to Marcus Aurelius* (London, 1904), 506–511, and *passim*; FARRAR, *Marcus Aurelius in Seekers after God* (London, 1890.) His *Meditations* have been translated into English by GEORGE LONG (London, 1862); cf. also DE CHAMPAGNY, *Les Césars (les Antonins)* (Paris, 1863); DARTIGNE-PEYRON, *Marc-Aurèle dans ses rapports avec le Christianisme* (Paris, 1897).

PATRICK J. HEALY.

Aureola. See NIMBUS.

Aureoli (AUREOLUS, D'AURIOL, ORIOL), PETRUS, a Franciscan philosopher and theologian, called on account of his eloquence *Doctor facundus*, b. 1280 at Toulouse (or Verberie-sur-Oise); d. 10 January, 1322 (Denifle; other dates assigned are 1330 and 1345). He entered the Order of Friars Minor, studied at Toulouse, taught theology there and at Paris and became (1319) provincial of his order (Province of Aquitaine). John XXII appointed him Archbishop of Aix (1321). He defended the doctrine of the Immaculate Conception in a public disputation at Toulouse (1314), in his "De Conceptione Mariæ Virginis" and "Repercussorium" (reply to opponents of the doctrine), in his "Sermons" and in his commentary on St. Bernard's teaching. His other principal works are the commentary on the "Sentences" of Peter Lombard (Rome, 1596–1605), "Quodlibeta", and "Breviarium Bibliorum", an introduction to the Scriptures with literal commentary, which appeared in numerous editions at Venice Paris, and Louvain. A new edition by Seeboeck was published at Quaracchi in 1896. In philosophy Aureoli was a Conceptualist and a forerunner of Occam. He criticized the doctrine of St. Thomas and defended, though not in all points, the views of Scotus. His writings on the Immaculate Conception were published by Petrus de Alva in the "Monumenta Seraphica Imm. Concept".

HURTER, *Nomenclator*, II, 463; STANONIK in *Der Katholik*, (1882), I; WERNER, *Thomas von Aquin*, III, 180–244; UEBERWEG-HEINZE, *Geschichte d. Philosophie* (8th ed.), II, 306.

E. A. PACE.

Aureus Codex. See CODEX.

Auricular Confession. See CONFESSION.

Auriesville, the site of the Mohawk village, Montgomery Co., New York, U. S. A., in which Father Isaac Jogues and his companions, Goupil and Lalande, were put to death for the Faith by the Indians. It is on the south bank of the Mohawk, about forty miles west of Albany. Auries was the name of the last Mohawk who lived there, and from this the present designation was formed. It was known among the Indians as Ossernenon, also Gandawaga and Caughnawaga, the latter being also

given to the settlement on the St. Lawrence opposite Lachine which was established for the Iroquois converts who wanted to withdraw from the corruption of their pagan kinsmen. To the village on the Mohawk Jogues and Goupil were brought in 1642 as prisoners, and, in 1646, Jogues again, with Lalande. In 1644 Bressani was tortured there, and later on Poncet. In 1655–56–57 Le Moyne came as ambassador to make peace; and the year after the punitive expedition of the Marquis de Tracy a permanent mission was established (1667). There Father Boniface, James de Lamberville, Fremin Bruyas, Pierron, and others laboured until 1684, when the mission was destroyed. The famous Indian girl, Tegakwitha, was born there. From it she escaped to Canada. While the missionaries were in control of Ossernenon and the adjacent Indian towns, the Mohawk converts were remarkable for their exact Christian life, and in many instances for their exalted piety.

The exact location of this village, which is so intimately associated with the establishment of Christianity in New York, was for a time a subject of considerable dispute. The researches of John Gilmary Shea, whose knowledge of the history of the early mission was so profound, at first favoured the view that the old village was on the other side of the Mohawk at what is now Tribes Hill. More thorough investigations, however, aided by the conclusions of Gen. J. S. Clarke of Auburn, whose knowledge of Indian sites both in New York and Huronia is indisputable, have shown finally that the present Auriesville is the exact place in which Father Jogues and his companions suffered death. The basic evidence is the fact that, up to the time of their destruction by de Tracy, the villages were certainly on the south side of the Mohawk and west of the Schoharie—as is clear from contemporary maps, and from Jogues's, Bressani's, and Poncet's letters. Joliet, one of the most accurate cartographers of the time, puts the village of Ossernenon at the junction of the Schoharie and Mohawk. To further particularize it, Jogues said the village was on the top of the hill, a quarter of a league from the river. The ravine in which Goupil's body was found is also specified by Jogues, and he speaks of a watercourse and a rivulet uniting there—a feature still remaining. The distances from Andagaron and Tionontoguen given by Father Jogues also fix the exact locality.

Satisfied that the precise spot had been determined, ten acres of land on the hill were purchased in 1884 by the Rev. Joseph Loyzance, S. J., who was at that time parish priest of St. Joseph's, Troy, N. Y., and who had all his life been an ardent student of the lives of the early missionaries. Father Loyzance erected a small shrine on the hill, under the title of Our Lady of Martyrs, and he was the first to lead a number of pilgrims to the place, on the 15th of August of that year, which was the anniversary of the first arrival of Father Jogues as an Iroquois captive. Four thousand people went from Albany and Troy on that day. Other parishes subsequently adopted the practice of visiting Auriesville during the summer. Frequently there are as many as four or five thousand people present. The grounds have been since extended beyond the original limits, for the purpose of keeping the surroundings free from undesirable buildings. Many of the pilgrims come fasting and receive Holy Communion at the shrine. The entire day is passed in religious exercises, but anything which could in the least savour of any public cult of the martyrs is sedulously guarded against, as such anticipation of the Church's official action would seriously interfere with the cause of their canonization, which is now under consideration at Quebec. The present buildings on the site are only of a temporary nature. If the Church pronounces on the reality of the martyrdom of the three missionaries, more suitable edifices will be erected.

SHEA, *Life of Isaac Jogues, S.J.* (New York, 1862); *Jesuit Relations, passim; Pilgrim of Our Lady of Martyrs* (New York); *Annals of the Shrine* (New York); WYNNE, *A Shrine in the Mohawk Valley* (New York, 1905).

T. J. CAMPBELL.

Aurispa, GIOVANNI, a famous Italian humanist and collector of Greek manuscripts, b. about 1369 at Noto, in Sicily; d. at Ferrara in 1459. It is not known where he first studied. In 1418 he went to Constantinople to learn Greek and to collect codices. So industrious was he that he was accused to the Greek emperor of despoiling the city of books. He returned to Venice in 1423 with 238 volumes of classical authors, purchased at Constantinople. Among his treasures were the celebrated "Codex Laurentianus" (seven plays of Sophocles, six of Æschylus, Apollonius's "Argonautica") of the tenth century, the Iliad, Demosthenes, Plato, Xenophon, etc. The next year Aurispa went to Bologna, where he became professor of Greek at the university. As a teacher he was not very successful. Thence he was invited to Florence, where he also held the chair of Greek. Later he went to Ferrara. In 1441 he was appointed secretary to Pope Eugene IV. Six years later Pope Nicholas V reappointed him to the same post. Besides being a tireless collector of manuscripts, Aurispa was a poet of some merit. His published works include letters, epigrams, and an elegy.

VOIGT, *Die Wiederbelebung des klassischen Alterthums* (Berlin, 1893); SABBADINI, *Biografia documentata di Giovanni Aurispa* (Noto, 1890).

EDMUND BURKE.

Aurora Lucis Rutilat.—This is one of the so-called Ambrosian hymns, but its author is unknown. It has been revised and separated into three hymns for the Roman Breviary. The first sixteen lines form the hymn for Lauds from Low Sunday to the Ascension, and begin in the revised form, *Aurora Cœlum Purpurat.* There are many English versions in use among Protestants. Dr. J. M. Neale's translation begins "Dawn purples all the east with light". The hymn "Tristes Erant Apostoli" (lines 17–32 of the original text) is in the Office, Common of Apostles and Evangelists for paschal time at the first and second Vespers and Matins. This hymn has also been translated into English. The Gregorian melody is in the third mode and may be found in the "Vesperale Romanum". Lines 33 to the end of the ancient hymn form "Paschale Mundo Gaudium," the hymn at Lauds in the Common of Apostles in paschal time. Among the English versions, besides Dr. Neale's, are those of J. A. Johnston in his "English Hymnal" (1852), "With sparkling rays morn decks the sky"; E. Caswall, "Lyra Catholica" (1849), "The dawn was purpling o'er the sky"; J. D. Chambers, "Lauda Syon" (1857), "Light's very morn its beams displays".

BÄUMER, *Geschichte des Breviers* (Freiburg, 1895); JULIAN, *Dict. of Hymnology* (New York, 1893).

JOSEPH OTTEN.

Ausculta Fili, a letter addressed 5 December, 1301, by Pope Boniface VIII to Philip the Fair, King of France. Philip was at enmity with the pope. Under pretext of his royal rights, he conferred benefices, and appointed bishops to sees, regardless of papal authority. He drove from their sees those bishops who, in opposition to his will, remained faithful to the pope. This letter is couched in firm but paternal terms. It points out the evils the king has brought to his kingdom, to Church and State; invites him to do penance and to mend his ways. It was unheeded by the king, and was soon followed by the famous Bull "Unam Sanctam".

The complete text of this Bull in found in the *Bullarium Magnum* (Luxemburg, 1730), IX, 121 sqq.; cf. HEFELE-KNÖPFLER, *Conciliengeschichte* (Freiburg, 1890), VI, 324–333;

TOSTI, *Storia di Bonifacio VIII* (Monte Cassino, 1846); JUNGMANN, *Dissertat. Selectæ* in *Hist. eccl.* (Ratisbon, 1886), VI, *De notificatu Bonif. VIII;* BOUTARIC, *La France sous Philippe le Bel* (Paris, 1861); FINKE, *Aus den Tagen Bonifaz VIII* (Münster, 1902); cf. *Revue des quest. historiques* (Oct., 1903).

M. O'RIORDAN.

Ausonius, DECIMUS MAGNUS, a professor and poet b. about A. D. 310; d., probably, about A. D. 394. The son of a physician of Bordeaux, he studied first in that city, then at Toulouse, with his uncle Æmilius Magnus Arborius. The latter having gone to teach in Constantinople, Ausonius returned to Bordeaux, where he became professor of grammar, and later on of rhetoric. Between 364 and 368, Valentinian I invited him to Trier to teach his son Gratian. In 368 and 369 Ausonius accompanied the emperor on the expedition against the Alemanni, and received a young Swabian, Bissula, as his share of the booty. The emperors overwhelmed him with honours, and made him first Prefect of the Gauls, then Prefect of the West conjointly with his son Hesperius (between August, 378, and July, 379). In 379 he became consul. After the assassination of Gratian, his benefactor (383), Ausonius moved to Bordeaux, where he lived among many admiring friends, and wrote a great deal of poetry. He lived through almost the whole of the fourth century. The writings of Ausonius are generally short, and they form a miscellaneous collection which is divided into two groups:—

I. OCCASIONAL WORKS.—(1) "Epigrams": short poems on different subjects, often translated from the Greek Anthology. (2) "Parentalia": thirty eulogies on deceased relatives, with some occasional expressions of personal sentiment (about 379). (3) "Commemoratio professorum Burdigalensium": a collection like the preceding, giving an idea of a university in the fourth century (after 389). (4) "Mosella": a description of the River Moselle and the country through which it flows, written while travelling from Bingen to Trier (c. 371). This poem has a certain local and archæological interest. (5) Charming poems relating to Bissula (after 368). (6) Many brief poems, which Ausonius called eclogues or "Epyllia"; paschal-time prayers (368); "Epicedion": dirge on his father's death (d. 378); advice to his grandson (about 380); "Cupido crucifixus": description of a painting in a dining-room at Trier, which represented Cupid as tormented in hell by the women who pursued him on earth, etc. (7) "Gratiarum actio dicta domino Gratiano Augusto", in which Ausonius expresses in prose his thanks for having been made consul. This was read at Trier in 379, and is made up of flowers of rhetoric and conventional flatteries. (8) "Ephemeris": the account of daily duties, from morning to night; a fragment (379). In this work is found a morning prayer composed of Biblical expressions in which the doctrine of the Trinity is set forth in detailed formulæ directed against the heresies of the times. (9) "Letters": twenty-five epistles, mostly in verse. The most interesting are addressed to St. Paulinus of Nola (393) and in them Ausonius bewails a conversion that deprives the State and literature of the benefit of such a brilliant mind, and tries to lead the saint back to worldly life at Rome. This correspondence lays before us two ideals of life; it expresses in clear colours the views which at that time were in conflict with each other, and divided society. (10) "Præfatiunculæ": prefaces and envois to poems.

II. SCHOOL EXERCISES AND FRAGMENTS.—These are chiefly mnemonic verse: "Cæsares", on the Roman emperors; consular annals; "Ordo nobilium urbium", eulogies on cities, beginning with Rome and ending with Bordeaux (after 388); "Eclogæ", a collection of mnemonic verses, treating of trees, the months, the calendar, weights, etc.; "Periochæ" (Contents), prose headings for the Iliad and the Odyssey. It is doubtful whether Ausonius wrote these, but they were at least the work of a member of the circle to which he belonged; short poems on the labours of Hercules; on the Muses; on ethical subjects (translations of Greek originals, inspired by Pythagorean philosophy). Other writings are lectures by a professor; Epitaphs, eulogies on dead heroes of the Trojan War, modelled after the Greek, and epitaphs on Niobe, Diogenes, etc., translated from the Greek; Epyllia, various pieces, among others an enigma on the number three, a diversion of a courtier forced to go to war (368); "Cento nuptialis" (an ingenious conceit of the same origin, the result of a wager made with Valentinian), extracts from Virgil, the conclusion of which (*consummatio matrimonii*) is not very refined (368); "Technopægnion", a collection of verses in which each ends in a monosyllable; the authenticity of the Consul Ausonius's prayer, written in ropalic verse (verse composed successively of words of one, two, three, four, five syllables and so on) is doubtful; "Ludus septem sapientum"; this product of the seven sages is a kind of scholastic drama, in which, after a prologue, each sage recites a proverb; at the end, they invite the audience to applaud. It is a document interesting for the history of pedagogy and also for the medieval drama.

To appraise Ausonius justly it must be borne in mind that he represents the professor of the fourth century. Some of his works, therefore, written for the school and in the spirit of the school, frequently translations from the Greek, are unimportant. A versifier to whom any subject could appeal (the more difficult and the less poetical it was, the better), Ausonius knew by heart the works of his predecessors, but by his taste and metrical peculiarities showed himself a disciple rather of the poets of the new school (*neoterici*, poetic innovators of the time of the Severi) than of the classic poets. In this work the letters to Paulinus of Nola are an exception to the whole, which is almost void of ideas. Ausonius's attitude in regard to Christianity should be explained in the same way. The paganism of his works is the paganism of the schools, and, if one would base on that the doubt that he was a Christian, inversely, his literary manner of treating mythology should make it questionable whether he was a pagan. But the paschal prayer, and still more, the prayer of the "Ephemeris", could not have been written by a pagan. An orthodox Christian in his prayers, he was a pagan in the class-room. Hence his works, which are class-room productions, may very naturally seem pagan. It is said that after the edict of Julian (362) Ausonius had to give up teaching; but there is nothing to prove this, nor is there any proof to the contrary, as Julian died the following year. It is supposed that, like some of his contemporaries, Ausonius remained a catechumen for a long time. It is possible that he was not baptized until the time when we lose all trace of him, in the last silent and obscure days of his old age.

EDITIONS.—SCHENKL in *Monumenta Germaniæ Historica; Auctores antiquissimi* (Berlin, 1883), II; PEIPER in *Bibliotheca Teubneriana* (Leipzig, 1886); *Mosella*, separately; DE MIRMONT (Bordeaux, 1889); HOSIUS (Marburg, 1894); SCHANZ, *Geschichte der römischen Literatur* (Munich, 1904), IV, 1, 20–40, including the bibliography; GLOVER, *Life and Letters in the Fourth Century* (Cambridge, 1901) 102–124.

PAUL LEJAY.

Austin, JOHN, an English lawyer and writer, b. 1613 at Walpole, in Norfolk; d. London, 1669. He was a student of St. John's College, Cambridge, and of Lincoln's Inn, and about 1640 embraced the Catholic Faith. He was highly esteemed in his profession and was looked on as a master of English style. His time was entirely devoted to books and literary pursuits. He enjoyed the friendship of such scholars as the antiquary Blount, Christopher Davenport (Franciscus a Santa Clara), John Sergeant, and

others. Among his writings are: "The Christian Moderator; or Persecution for Religion condemned by the Light of Nature, by the Law of God, the Evidence of our own Principles, but not by the Practice of our Commissioners for Sequestrations—In Four Parts" (London, 1652, 4to.). It was published under the pseudonym of William Birchley, and in it he frequently disclaims the pope's deposing power. "In this work, Austin assuming the disguise of an independent, shows that Catholics did not really hold the odious doctrines vulgarly attributed to them, and makes an energetic appeal to the independents to extend to the adherents of the persecuted church such rights and privileges as were granted to other religious bodies" (Dict. of Nat. Biogr., II, 264). "The Catholique's Plea; or an Explanation of the Roman Catholick Belief, Concerning their Church, Manner of Worship, Justification, Civil Government, Together with a Catalogue of all the Pœnal Statutes against Popish Recusants, All which is humbly submitted to serious consideration, By a Catholick Gentleman" (London, 1659, 18mo.), also under the pseudonym of William Birchley; "Reflections upon the Oaths of Supremacy and Allegiance; or the Christian Moderator, The Fourth Part, By a Catholick Gentleman, an obedient son of the Church and loyal subject of his Majesty" (London, 1661); "A Punctual Answer to Doctor John Tillotson's book called 'The Rule of Faith'" (unfinished); "Devotions, First Part: In the Ancient Way of Offices, With Psalms, Hymns, and Prayers for every Day in the Week, and every Holiday in the Year". It is not known when and where the first edition appeared; the second, a duodecimo, is dated 1672. An edition printed at Edinburgh, 1789, contains a life of the author, presumably by Dodd. This work was adapted to the uses of the Anglican Church in Hicks's "Harmony of the Gospels", etc. (London, 1701), and has been often reprinted as a stock book under the title of Hicks's Devotions. "Devotions, Second Part, The Four Gospels in one, broken into Lessons, with Responsories, To be used with the Offices, Printed Anno Domini, 1675" (2 vols., Paris, 12mo), a posthumous work, divided into short chapters with a verse and prayer at the end of each. The prayers, says Gillow, "gave rise to offence under the impression that they favoured Blackloe's doctrine concerning the middle state of souls, and on account of this the work was not republished". A third part of the "Devotions" was never printed; it contained, according to the author's own statement "Prayers for all occasions framed by an intimate friend according to his (Austin's) directions, and overlooked by himself". He also wrote several anonymous pamphlets against the divines who sat in the Westminster Assembly.

GILLOW, *Bibl. Dict. Eng. Cath.*, I, 87–90; COOPER in *Dict. Nat. Biog.*, II, 263.

THOMAS J. SHAHAN.

Austin Canons. See CANONS AND CANONESSES, REGULAR.

Austin Friars. See CANONS AND CANONESSES, REGULAR.

Australia (also known as NEW HOLLAND till about 1817) is geographically the world's great island-continent. Politically, the mainland, with the adjoining island of Tasmania, forms the Commonwealth of Australia. This is under the British Crown and consists of the following six States, which were federated on 1 Jan., 1901, and are here named in the order in which they became separate colonies of the British Empire: New South Wales (1788); Tasmania (1803); Western Australia (1826); South Australia (1836); Victoria (1851); and Queensland (1859). The Commonwealth covers an area of 2,980,632 square miles. It is, territorially, about one-fourth smaller than Europe, one-sixth larger than the United States (excluding Alaska), over once and a half the size of the Indian Empire, more than fourteen times larger than Germany or France, and about twenty-five times larger than the British Isles. At the census of 1901 the population of the six States was as follows: New South Wales, 1,359,943; Western Australia, 182,553; Victoria, 1,201,341; Queensland, 503,266; South Australia, 362,604; Tasmania, 172,475. This gave the Commonwealth in 1901 a total population of 3,782,182. The official estimate of the total population for December, 1905, was 4,002,893.

I. THE CONVICT SYSTEM.—The north and west coasts of Australia figure in the maps of Spanish and Portuguese navigators as far back as about the year 1530. But it was the War of American Independence that led to the settling of the white man on the shores of the great lone continent. At that time, and until the nineteenth century was well advanced, the maxim of Paley and of others of his school, that crime is most effectually prevented by a dread of capital punishment, held almost complete control of the legislative mind in Great Britain. "By 1809 ", says a legal authority in the "National History of England" (IV, 309), "more than six hundred different offences had been made capital—a state of law unexampled in the worst periods of Roman or Oriental despotism". Transportation was the ordinary commutation of, or substitute for, the slip-knot of the hangman. From 1718 to 1776 British convicts had been sent in considerable numbers annually, under contractors, into servitude on the American mainland. The traffic was stopped by the War of Independence. At the close of the struggle the British prisons and, later on, the prison-hulks overflowed. The colony of New South Wales (till 1826 synonymous with the whole Australian mainland) was established as a convict settlement by an Order in Council dated 6 December, 1785. On 13 May, 1787, "the first fleet ", provisioned for two years, left England, with 1,030 souls on board, of whom 696 were convicts. They reached Botany Bay on 20 January, 1788. They abandoned it after a few days because of its shallow waters, and laid the foundations of Sydney on the shores of the noble and spacious harbour to which they gave the name of Port Jackson. The men who founded Sydney and the Commonwealth of Australia "may have been convicts ", says Davitt, "but they were not necessarily 'criminals', such as we are familiar with to-day. Some account must be taken of what constituted a crime in those transportation days, and of the hideously unjust sentences which were inflicted for comparatively trivial offences" (Life and Progress in Australasia, 193–194).

Within the next decade, the ranks of the original convict population were swelled by a goodly percentage of the 1,300 unoffending Catholic peasants from the North and West of Ireland who were seized and deported by "Satanides" Carhampton and the Ulster magistrates during the Orange reign of terror in 1795–96, "without sentence ", as Lecky says, "without trial, without even the colour of legality " (Ireland in the Eighteenth Century, III, 419 ; England in the Eighteenth Century, VIII, 250). After the insurrection of 1798, "a stream of Irish political prisoners was poured into the penal settlement of Botany Bay, and they played some part in the early history of the Australian colonies, and especially of Australian Catholicism" (Lecky, England in the Eighteenth Century, VIII, 250). In his "Catholic Mission in Australia" (1836), Dr. Ullathorne says of those early Irish political convicts: "Ignorance or violation of religious principle, the knowledge or habits of a criminal life, were scarcely to any extent recognizable features in this unhappy class of Irish political prisoners. On the contrary, the deepest and purest

sentiments of piety, a thorough comprehension of religious responsibility, and an almost impregnable simplicity of manner, were their distinctive virtues on their first consignment to the guardianship of the law. In many illustrious cases, a long and dangerous residence in the most depraved penal settlements was unable to extinguish these noble characteristics." During the first three decades of the nineteenth century the convict population was notably increased by the addition of many who had taken part in the agitations in connexion with tithes, the Charter and Reform movements, the Combination·Laws, and the Corn Laws. During the first fifty years and more of the Australian penal settlements, convictions and sentences of deportation were matters of fearful facility. For no provision was made for the defence of prisoners unable to procure it for themselves; the right of defence throughout the entire trial was not recognized till 1837; jurors were allowed to act as witnesses; and, belonging, as they generally did, to "the classes ", they were too prone to convict, and judges to transport, especially during periods of popular ferment, on weak or worthless evidence, or on the mere presumption of guilt (See National History of England, IV, 310).

Convictism endured in New South Wales from its first foundation in 1788 till 1840. Tasmania remained a penal colony till 1853. Transportation to Norfolk Island ceased in 1855. Moreton Bay (in the present State of Queensland) became a convict station in 1824 and remained one till 1839. Western Australia began as a penal settlement in 1826. It continued as such for only a very brief space. Owing to the dearth of free labour, convicts (among whom was the gifted John Boyle O'Reilly, a political prisoner) were reintroduced from 1849 till 1868, when the last shadow of "the system" was lifted from Australia. Two noted Catholic ecclesiastics (Dr. Ullathorne and Dr. Willson, first Bishop of Hobart) took a prominent and honoured part in the long, slow movement which led to the abolition of the convict system in New South Wales, Tasmania, and Norfolk Island. Almost from the dawn of the colonization of New South Wales and Tasmania, voluntary settlers went thither, at first as stragglers, but in a steady stream when the advantages of the country became known, when irresponsible military rule ceased (in 1824) and when free selection and assisted immigration were planks in the policy of the young Australian colonies. The first free settlers came to Queensland (known till its separation in 1859 as the Moreton Bay District of New South Wales) in 1824, just in advance of the convicts; to Victoria (known till its separation in 1851 as the Port Phillip District of New South Wales) in 1835, and to South Australia in 1836. The gold discoveries of the fifties brought a great inrush of population, chiefly to Victoria and New South Wales. Events have moved rapidly since then. The widened influences of religion, the influx of new blood, the development of resources, prosperity, education, and the play of free institutions have combined to rid the southern lands of the traces of a penal system which, within living memory, threatened so much permanent evil to the moral, social, and political progress of Australia. The dead past has buried its dead.

The reformation of the criminal formed no part of the convict system in Australia. "The body ", says Bonwick, "rather than the soul, absorbed the attention of the governors" (First Twenty Years of Australia, 218). "Vengeance and cruelty ", says Erskine May, "were its only principles; charity and reformation formed no part of its scheme" (Constitutional History of England, III, 401). For the convict, it was a beast-of-burden life, embittered by the lash, the iron

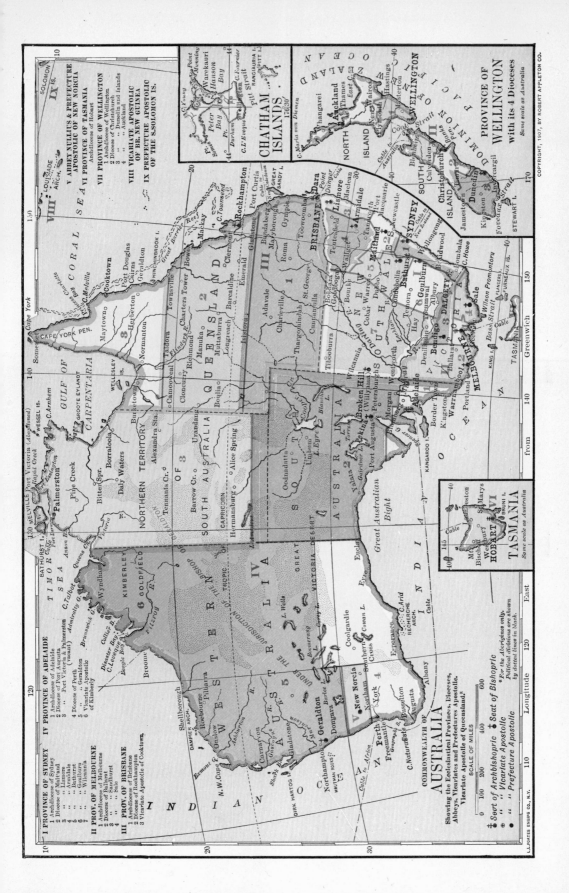

AUSTRALIA

Showing the Ecclesiastical Provinces, Dioceses, Abbeys, Vicariates and Prefectures Apostolic, Vicariate Apostolic of Queensland*

SCALE OF MILES
0 100 200 400 600

‡ Seat of Archbishopric   ✠ Seat of Bishopric
✠ " Vicariate Apostolic   *For the Aborigines only.
● " Prefecture Apostolic   Political divisions are shown
                             by dotted lines in black.

I PROVINCE OF SYDNEY
1 Archdiocese of Sydney
2 Diocese of Maitland
3   "   Lismore
4   "   Armidale
5   "   Bathurst
6   "   Goulburn
7   "   Wilcannia

II PROV. OF MELBOURNE
1 Archdiocese of Melbourne
2 Diocese of Ballarat
3   "   Sandhurst
4   "   Sale

III PROV. OF BRISBANE
1 Archdiocese of Brisbane
2 Diocese of Rockhampton
3 Vicariate Apostolic of Cooktown

IV PROVINCE OF ADELAIDE
1 Archdiocese of Adelaide
2 Diocese of Port Augusta
3   "   Port Victoria & Palmerston
4   "   Diocese of Perth
5   "   Vicariate Apostolic of Geraldton
6   "   Vicariate Apostolic of Kimberley

V ABBEY NULLIUS & PREFECTURE APOSTOLIC OF NEW NORCIA

VI PROVINCE OF TASMANIA
Archdiocese of Hobart

VII PROVINCE OF WELLINGTON
1 Archdiocese of Wellington
2 Diocese of Christchurch
3   "   Dunedin and islands
4   "   Auckland

VIII VICARIATE APOSTOLIC OF BR. NEW GUINEA

IX PREFECTURE APOSTOLIC OF THE S. SOLOMON IS.

CHATHAM ISLANDS

PROVINCE OF WELLINGTON with its 4 Dioceses
Same scale as Australia

TASMANIA
Same scale as Australia

COPYRIGHT, 1907, BY ROBERT APPLETON CO.

L.L.POATES ENG'R'G CO., N.Y.

ball, the punishment-cell, the prison-hulk, the chain-gang, and the "hell". "The 'whipping-houses' of the Mississippi", says Dilke, "had their parallel in New South Wales; a look or word would cause the hurrying of a servant to the post or the forge, as a preliminary to a month in a chain-gang on the roads" (Greater Britain, 8th ed., 373). For idleness, for disobedience, for drunkenness, for every trivial fault, the punishment was "the lash!— the lash!— the lash!" (Dr. Ullathorne, in Cardinal Moran's History of the Catholic Church in Australasia, 156). And the "cat" was made an instrument of torture (Dilke, Greater Britain, 8th ed., 374). Matters were even worse in the convict "hells" of New Norfolk (established in 1788), and of Port Arthur and Macquarie Harbour in Tasmania. In 1835 Dr. Ullathorne went to New Norfolk to prepare thirty-nine supposed conspirators for an abrupt passage into eternity. Twenty-six of the condemned men were reprieved. They wept bitterly on receiving the news, "whilst those doomed to die, without exception, dropped on their knees and with dry eyes thanked God they were to be delivered from so horrid a place". They "manifested extraordinary fervour and repentance", received their sentence on their knees "as the will of God", and on the morning of their execution "they fell down in the dust and, in the warmth of their gratitude, kissed the very feet that had brought them peace" (Ullathorne in Moran, op. cit., 164).

For a long period Australian officials and ex-officials were to all intents and purposes a great "ring" of spirit-dealers. Rum became the medium of commerce, just as tobacco, and maize, and leaden bullets were in the early days of New England (History of New South Wales from the Records, II, 271–273). The cost of building the first Protestant church in Australia (at Sydney) was, as the pastor's balance sheet shows, in part paid in rum (op. cit., II, 66). "Rum-selling and rum-distilling debauched the convicts and their guards" (José, History of Australia, 21), and the moral depravity that grew up under the system is described by Dr. Ullathorne as "too frightful even for the imagination of other lands" (Moran, op. cit., pp. 8–11, and "Historical Records of New South Wales, II and III, passim). The Irish Catholic convicts—"most of whom", says Ullathorne (in Moran, op. cit., 152–153), "were transported for the infringement of penal laws and for agrarian offences and minor delinquencies"—had generally (according to the same eyewitness) a lively dread of the depravity of the prison hells of the system. Irish Catholic female convicts were also saved to a notable extent by their robust faith from the profligacy which, almost as a matter of course, overtook their less fortunate sisters from other countries (McCarthy, History of Our Own Times, ed. 1887, I, 467; Ullathorne, in Moran, 157–158). Long before, similar testimony was given by John Thomas Bigge, after he had spent three years (1819–22) in Australia as Special Commissioner from the British Government to investigate the working of the transportation system. In his final report (dated 6 May, 1822) he said: "The convicts embarked in Ireland generally arrive in New South Wales in a very healthy state, and are found to be more obedient and more sensible of kind treatment during the passage than any other class. Their separation from their native country is observed to make a stronger impression upon their minds, both on their departure and during the voyage."

II. PERIOD OF PERSECUTION.—The influences of religion were not allowed to remedy to any great extent the hard animalism and inhumanity of the convict system. Anglicanism was de facto, although not de jure, the established religion of the Australian penal colonies. But the Anglican chaplain, frequently a farmer, run-holder, and magistrate, was more conspicuously a civil than a religious function-

ary. Methodism (then a branch of the Anglican Establishment) made a feeble beginning in Australia in 1813; Presbyterianism in 1823; other Protestant denominations at later dates (Bonwick, First Twenty Years of Australia, 240). In 1836, when Dr. Ullathorne wrote his pamphlet, "The Catholic Mission in Australia", Catholic and other dissidents were still compelled to attend the more or less perfunctory services of the Anglican Church (in Moran, op. cit., 153). The penalties for refusal, provided at various times in General Orders, consisted in reduced rations, imprisonment, confinement in prison-hulks, the stocks, and the urgent pressure of the public flagellator's "cat-o'-nine-tails"—twenty-five lashes for the first offence, fifty for the second, and for the third, the road-gangs, or transportation to the "living death" of the convict hells. (See the official and other evidence in Moran, op. cit., 11–19.) As late as 5 March, 1843, a convict named Bernard Trainer was sentenced to fourteen days' imprisonment in Brighton jail for refusing to attend the Protestant service (Therry MSS., in Moran, 19). This abuse of power continued in Tasmania till 1844 (Hogan, The Irish in Australia, 3d ed., 257–258). Both in New South Wales and Tasmania, the children of Catholic convicts and all orphans under the care of the State were brought up in the profession of the dominant creed. In 1792 there were some three hundred Catholic convicts and fifty Catholic freemen (mancipists) in New South Wales. Nine years later, in 1801, there were 5,515 inhabitants in the penal settlement (Bonwick, First Twenty Years of Australia, 175–176). About one-third of these were Catholics; but no regular statistics of religious belief were kept at the time (Kenny, The Catholic Church in Australasia to the Year 1840, 20). Among the "little flock" there were three priests who had been unjustly transported on a charge of complicity in the Irish insurrection of 1798—Fathers James Harold, James Dixon, and Peter O'Neill. The last-mentioned priest had been barbarously scourged on a suborned charge of having abetted murder—a crime of which he was afterwards proved to be wholly innocent. Father Harold was the uncle of the Rev. Dr. William Vincent Harold, O.P., famous in the Hogan Schism in Philadelphia, and en route to Ireland in 1810, from Australia, he visited Philadelphia (Moran, op. cit., 33).

These priests were strictly forbidden the exercise of their sacred ministry. After repeated representations, Father Dixon was at length, by order of the Home Government, conditionally emancipated, and permitted to celebrate Mass once a month, under galling restrictions (see Historical Records of New South Wales, V, 110). He offered the Holy Sacrifice for the first time in New South Wales, 15 May, 1803. There was no altar-stone; the chalice, the work of a convict, was of tin; the vestments were made of parti-coloured old damask curtains sacrificed for the occasion, and the whole surroundings of this memorable event in the history of the Church in Australia bespoke the poverty of Bethlehem and the desolation of Calvary. After little more than a year, Father Dixon's precious privilege was withdrawn, and the last state of the Catholic convicts became worse than the first. Father O'Neill had in the meantime (1803) been restored to Ireland, with his character completely vindicated. In 1808 Father Dixon, broken down in health, was permitted to return to his native diocese. Two years later he was followed to Ireland by Father Harold, and till 1817 a deep spiritual desolation brooded over the infant Church in Australia. In the last-mentioned year there were some 6,000 Catholics in and about Sydney alone. The representations of the returned priestly exiles resulted at length in the appointment of Father Jeremiah Flynn, an Irish Cistercian, as Prefect Apostolic of New Holland. Obstacles were thrown in his way by the Colonial Office. He placed the matter in the hands of the Rt. Rev. Dr. Poynter, and, relying on the known influence of his English friend, set sail in good faith for his distant field. On his arrival in Sydney, Governor Macquarie bluntly informed him that no "Popish missionary" would be allowed to intrude within the settlement, and that every person in the penal colony must be a Protestant.

Father Flynn ministered secretly to his flock wherever he could evade the watchful eyes of hostile officials. A few months after his arrival he was suddenly arrested without warrant or accusation, placed under lock and key in prison, and, without trial, shipped back to London as a prisoner by the first vessel homeward bound. Before his arrest he used secretly to celebrate the Sacred Mysteries in the house of a pious Catholic named Davis. There the Sacred Species were reserved for the sick and dying, in a cedar press, or tabernacle. Father Flynn vainly besought permission to return to the house. And there, for two years after his departure, the taper or lamp was ever kept alight, and, with pathetic devotion, the children of sorrow gathered in adoration around the Bread of Life. The "Holy House of Australia", with its small adjoining grounds and the sum of £1,000, was devoted to religion by Davis, and on its site now stands a fine church dedicated to God under the invocation of the national apostle of Ireland. Governor Macquarie's harsh and illegal treatment of Father Flynn created a stir in the British House of Commons. It opened up the whole scandalous story of the persecution of the Catholic convicts and settlers in Australia, created a healthy reaction, and led to the appointment of two Irish chaplains, Father Philip Connolly (who went to Hobart) and Father John Joseph Therry (who remained in Sydney), each with a slender yearly salary of £100. That was in May, 1821. With that day, to use the words of Archbishop Carr of Melbourne "what may be termed the period of the Church suffering ends, and that of the Church militant begins".

III. Period of Partial Toleration.—The new era inaugurated by Fathers Connolly and Therry was, however, one of only partial toleration of the Catholic Faith. It extended from their arrival in Australia, and was marked by long and successful struggles against religious ascendancy, the partial cessation of convictism, and the beginnings of the present hierarchical organization. In 1821 New South Wales and Tasmania (the only places then colonized) contained a white population of 35,610 souls. Some 30 per cent of these were Catholics. At a census taken in 1828 there were in eastern Australia 36,598 whites, of whom 11,236 were Catholics. Serious restrictions were still placed upon the marriage of Catholic convicts. The chaplains were strictly forbidden to receive converts from any Protestant denomination, or to interfere with the old-standing abuse of bringing up all the children in State-aided institutions in the creed of the Church of England (Hogan, The Irish in Australia, 3d ed., 236–237). And through and over it all ran the constant effort to set up the Protestant Reformed Religion as the Established Church of the new south lands. A great stride in the direction of such an establishment was made when, on 17 July, 1825, Royal Letters set apart for the ruling creed one-seventh of the whole territory of New South Wales, without prejudice to previous grants bestowed upon it. It was in a great measure to Father Therry's energy and ardour that this crowning act of ascendancy owed its partial defeat. The Royal Grant was revoked in 1834, but in the meantime, 435,000 acres of the public domain had been alienated for the benefit of the Anglican Church. Father Therry's frequent collisions with abuses created a deadlock

with the Sydney officials. This, in turn, led to the appointment of Dr. Ullathorne, a distinguished English Benedictine, as Vicar-General of the Bishop of Mauritius, who exercised jurisdiction over Australia till 1834.

Dr. Ullathorne arrived in his new field of labour in 1833. In that year the white population of New South Wales (i. e. of the whole island continent except Western Australia) had risen to 60,794. Of these, some 36,000 were free. The Catholic body, numbering 17,179, and scattered over a vast area, was ministered to by four priests. There were on the Australian mainland four Catholic schools, and four churches under construction (one of them Old St. Mary's, Sydney). Tasmania (as we still call it by anticipation) had only one Catholic priest, no school, and its one church (at Hobart) was described by Dr. Ullathorne as "a mere temporary shed". Sir Richard Bourke, a broad-minded Irish Protestant, was at that time Governor of New South Wales. Through his exertions was passed the Church Act of 1836, which broke up the quasi-monopoly of State appropriations for the clergy and the denominational schools that had hitherto been enjoyed by the Church of England (Therry, New South Wales and Victoria, ed. 1863, 17; Flanagan, History of New South Wales, I, 512, 513). Despite its admitted shortcomings, this was, in the circumstances of the time and country, a notable measure. It ended forever the dream of a Protestant ascendancy on the Australian mainland, and is justly regarded as the first Charter of the country's religious liberties. A Church Act on similar lines was passed in Tasmania in 1837. During the governorship of Sir Richard Bourke Catholics (Roger, afterwards Sir Roger, Therry, and John Hubert Plunkett) were also, for the first time in history of Australia, appointed to positions of any importance under the Crown. Under this administration the annual influx of free immigrants (some 3,000) equalled for the first time that of the convicts (Sutherland, History of Australia, 12th ed., 51, 52).

Australia was gradually rolling out of the sullen gloom of a penal settlement, and emerging into the condition of a freeman's country. The Catholic population increased rapidly. Their numbers and their distance from the immediate centre of their spiritual jurisdiction led, in 1834, to the formation of Australia, Tasmania, and the adjacent islands (including New Zealand) into a vicariate Apostolic. The Right Rev. John Bede Polding, an English Benedictine, was appointed its first bishop. In 1841 his vast diocese contained some 40,000 Catholics, ministered to by twenty-eight priests, and scattered over a territory nearly as large as Europe. The Australian mainland and Tasmania had in that year a population of 211,095 souls. At the census of that year, there were 35,690 of Bishop Polding's spiritual subjects in a total population of 130,856 in New South Wales (which then included the present States of Queensland and Victoria). Among the other scattered Catholics was a little group, poor labourers all, except one family, in a white population of some 15,000 souls in South Australia. This colony had been founded in 1836 as a free and "socially superior" Protestant settlement, from which "Papists and pagans" were to have been rigidly excluded. A few Catholics, however, crept in. They were ministered to by one priest (Father Benson) who lived among them in apostolic poverty from 1839 till the arrival of the first Bishop of Adelaide, Dr. Murphy, in 1842. In Western Australia there were 2,311 hard-pressed colonists at the census of 1840. There were very few Catholics among them, and no priest till 1845, when there arrived in the colony Dom Rudesind Salvado, a

AUSTRALIA

ST. FRANCIS XAVIER'S CATHEDRAL, ADELAIDE   ST. PATRICK'S COLLEGE, MANLY, SYDNEY
SYDNEY FROM LAVENDER BAY   MELBOURNE FROM EXHIBITION DOME
ST. PATRICK'S CATHEDRAL, MELBOURNE   ST. PAUL'S CHURCH, MT. GAMBIER

Spanish Benedictine, afterwards founder and first Abbot of New Norcia. A closer hierarchical organization was needed. At Bishop Polding's earnest solicitations new dioceses were created by the Holy See: Hobart, in 1842; Adelaide, in 1843; Perth, in 1845; Melbourne, Maitland, and Port Victoria, in 1848. Sydney also became an archiepiscopal see. Dr. Willson, the first Bishop of Hobart, will be remembered for his successful opposition to the efforts made, despite the local Church Act of 1837, to have Anglicanism placed on the same official footing as in England. It was the last serious effort to establish a religious ascendancy in any part of Australasia. In New South Wales the first synod was held in 1844. Six years later, the first sod of the first railroad in Australasia was turned in the capital of the mother-colony. At the census of 1851, the Catholic body in the mother-colony had risen to 58,899 in a total population of 190,999. In the Moreton Bay District of New South Wales (now Queensland) there were few Catholics, and no resident priest till the Passionist Fathers opened their mission to the aboriginals on Stradbroke Island, in 1843. In the Port Phillip District of New South Wales (now Victoria) there were, in 1851, 18,014 Catholics in a total population of 77,345, with six priests (in 1850) and thirteen State-aided primary schools. Dr. Gould was the first Bishop of the new see founded there in 1848.

IV. PERIOD OF COMPARATIVE CALM.—The discovery of rich gold in Victoria in 1851 had a profound and far-reaching effect on the history of Australia. There was a delirium of sudden prosperity. Population rushed into the new El Dorado. In 1851, the mainland and Tasmania had a joint population of 211,095, nearly double that of 1841. This rapid increase of inhabitants soon called for the erection of new episcopal sees. That of Brisbane was founded in 1859, the year in which Queensland became a separate colony. The Bishopric of Goulburn was established in 1864; Maitland (a titular see

since 1848) and Bathurst, in 1865; the abbacy *nullius* of New Norcia (aboriginal mission), in 1867; the See of Armidale, in 1869; and those of Ballarat and Sandhurst, in 1874. In the last-mentioned year Melbourne (since 1851 the capital of the separate colony of Victoria) became an archiepiscopal see. The Vicariate Apostolic of Cooktown was formed in 1876, and the Diocese of Rockhampton in 1882. Three years later, in 1885, Dr. Moran (successor to Dr. Vaughan in the Archiepiscopal See of Sydney) was raised to the purple as Australia's first cardinal. The Plenary Synod held in Sydney in the same year resulted in the formation, in 1887, of the Dioceses of Grafton (now called Lismore), Wilcannia, Sale, and Port Augusta, together with the Vicariates Apostolic of Kimberley (now under the jurisdiction of the Bishop of Geraldton), and of Queensland (for aborigines only), while Adelaide, Brisbane, and (in 1888) Hobart became archiepiscopal sees. The Plenary Synod of 1895 led to the formation of the Diocese of Geraldton in 1898. The occupant of that see is administrator of the Diocese of Port Victoria and Palmerston, which, founded in 1849, lost its whole European population in 1849. The latest Plenary Synod of the Church in the Commonwealth took place in 1905, and two important and highly successful Catholic Congresses were held, the first in Sydney in 1900, the second in Melbourne in 1904. In 1906, there were in the Australian Commonwealth six archbishops (one of them a cardinal, another a coadjutor), fifteen bishops (two of them coadjutors), one abbot *nullius*, and one vicar Apostolic; in all, a hierarchy of twenty-three prelates exercising episcopal jurisdiction.

V. RELIGIOUS STATISTICS.—The following table, compiled from official sources, shows the numerical strength of Catholics on the Australian mainland and in Tasmania for the years named, which have been chosen as being, in most instances, census years:—

Year	New South Wales	Victoria	Queensland	South Australia	Western Australia	Tasmania	Total Catholics	Total Population
1861	99,193	109,828	7,676	————	3,786	19,954	————	1,141,563
1871	147,627	170,620	31,822	28,271	7,282	22,657	408,279	1,650,471
1881	207,606	203,480	54,376	42,628	8,413	23,055	539,558	2,245,448
1891	286,915	248,585	92,765	47,179	12,602	25,800	713,846	3,159,085
1901	347,286	263,710	120,663	52,193	41,892	30,324	856,068	3,782,182

The Jews number 15,239 souls, and the minor Christian sects run in diminishing numbers to total memberships of mere hundreds. The following general summary of ecclesiastical statistics is from a table in the "Australasian Catholic Directory" for 1906:—

State and Ecclesiastical Provinces	Districts	Churches	Secular Priests	Regular Priests	Religious Brothers	Nuns	Ecclesiastical Seminaries	Colleges (Boys)	Boarding Schools (Girls)	Superior Day Schools	Primary Schools	Charitable Institutions	Children in Catholic Schools
State of New South Wales (Prov. of Sydney)	175	541	294	108	217	2,288	2	8	59	89	346	36	43,281
State of Victoria (Prov. of Melbourne)	107	438	204	52	74	1,190	—	9	41	27	204	15	35,398
State of Tasmania (Prov. of Tasmania)	19	63	28	—	—	135	—	—	1	4	25	2	3,280
States of South and Western Australia (Prov. of Adelaide)	65	187	95	47	113	676	—	3	14	33	92	14	11,812
State of Queensland (Prov. of Brisbane)	55	106	80	13	25	356	—	4	18	9	66	9	12,064
Commonwealth of Australia	421	1,335	701	220	429	4,645	2	24	133	162	733	76	105,835

(Certain of the figures given above are the sums of incomplete diocesan returns.)

The religious statistics of South Australia were not tabulated in 1846, 1851, and 1861. There was no enumeration of religious denominations at the Tasmania census of 1881. The figures given below for that year are an estimate by T. A. Coghlan, Statistician of New South Wales. The Catholic body in the Commonwealth is surpassed in numerical strength only by the adherents of the Church of England. The following table, compiled from the Australian Handbook for 1905, shows the numerical strength of the principal religious groups in the different States at the census of 1901:—

Religious Denominations	New South Wales	Victoria	Queensland	South Australia	Western Australia	Tasmania	Commonwealth
Church of England	623,131	423,914	184,078	106,987	75,654	83,815	1,497,579
Roman Catholic	347,286	263,708	120,405	52,193	41,893	30,314	855,799
Presbyterian	132,617	191,459	57,442	18,357	14,707	11,523	426,105
Methodist	137,638	180,263	46,574	90,125	24,540	24,999	504,139
Baptist	16,618	33,730	12,717	21,764	3,125	4,716	92,670
Congregational	24,834	17,141	8,300	13,338	4,404	5,544	73,561
Lutheran	7,387	13,934	25,170	26,140	1,703	387	74,721
Salvation Army	9,585	8,829	5,512	4,030	1,690	1,454	31,100
Total Population	1,299,096	1,132,978	460,198	332,934	167,716	162,752	3,555,674

VI. EDUCATION.—For a time all the colonies of the Australasian group followed the example initiated by New South Wales in according State aid to the clergy and the denominational schools of the principal religious bodies, Anglicans, Catholics, Presbyterians, and Methodists. These grants were withdrawn; at once or by gradually diminishing payments; by South Australia in 1851, after they had been in force only three years; by Queensland in 1860; by New South Wales in 1862; by Tasmania and Victoria, in 1875, and by Western Australia, in 1895. State grants to denominational schools ceased when the various secular systems took effect: in Victoria in 1872; in Queensland, in 1876; in South Australia, in 1878; in New South Wales, in 1879; and in Western Australia in 1896. In all the States of the Commonwealth primary education is compulsory. In Victoria, Queensland, South Australia, and Western Australia, it is also free. In New South Wales and Tasmania a small fee is charged, with free education for children whose parents cannot afford to pay for them. In Victoria fees are charged for such extra subjects as book-keeping, shorthand, Euclid, algebra, Latin, French, etc. Throughout the Commonwealth the rate of illiteracy is low. "Out of every 10,000 children between the ages of five and fifteen, there could read and write in 1861, 4,637; in 1871, 5,911; 1881, 7,058; 1891, 7,565" (Coghlan and Ewing, Progress of Australasia in the Nineteenth Century, p. 455). At the census of 1901, according to the "Victorian Year-Book" for 1903 (pp. 70–71), of the children of school age (6 to 13 years) in Victoria, 90.12 per cent were able to read and write; in Queensland, 84.42 per cent (Australian born children only); in Western Australia, 82.05 per cent; in South Australia, 82.00 per cent; in New South Wales, 80.35 per cent, and in Tasmania, 78.77 per cent. Hostility to the Catholic Church gave the chief impulse to the secularizing of public instruction in Victoria and New South Wales. In Victoria Mr. Stephen, Attorney-General, declared that the new Act was "to purge the colony of clericalism", and to lead the rising generation by sure but gradual steps to "worship in common at the shrine of one neutral-tinted deity, sanctioned by the State Department" (Moran, op. cit., 882–883). In New South Wales Henry (afterwards Sir Henry) Parkes was even more outspoken. Holding aloft his Draft Bill on Public Instruction, at a public meeting, he said: "I hold in my hand what will be death to the calling of the priesthood of the Church of Rome" (Moran, op. cit., 875). One of the first results of the withdrawal of the State grants in the various colonies was the closing of most of the Protestant primary schools. There was, on the other hand, everywhere a steady increase in the number of Catholic schools. The following figures, taken from official sources, show the growth of Catholic primary schools in Victoria from the passing of the secular Education Act till 1897:—

Year	Primary Schools	Children Attending
1881	180	20,337
1891	208	21,799
1897	226	24,066

No official returns appear in the Victorian census reports for 1901. The following extract from a table published by T. A. Coghlan (Wealth and Progress of New South Wales, 1897–98, 762) indicates the advance made by Catholic primary schools in the mother-state for twelve years after the date (1882) at which State assistance was withdrawn from denominational schools:—

Year	Schools	Teachers	Scholars on Roll	Average Attendance
1888	247	916	27,172	21,809
1891	250	1,242	30,691	23,788
1897	296	1,481	36,675	29,162

According to official returns, there were 41,112 children on the rolls of the Catholic schools in New South Wales in the December quarter, 1904, and 5,413 on the rolls of the Catholic schools of Western Australia on the last school week of 1903 (the latest Government figures available for that State). No official information appears in the census or reports of Tasmania, Queensland, or South Australia. The "Australasian Catholic Directory" for 1906 made what seems to be a somewhat conservative estimate when it set down as 105,835, the number of children attending Catholic schools throughout the Commonwealth.

VII. THE ABORIGINES.—The origin of the native tribes of Australia is one of the unsolved riddles of ethnology. An unknown number of these black-skinned people still live in their "wild" state, in small and scattered communities, over vast areas extending from Central Queensland almost to the coast of Western Australia. They have no acquaintance with metal, nor with the bow and arrow, and their weapons of war and chase are (with the exception of the boomerang) of a very rude kind, wooden spears and clubs, stone tomahawks, etc. They are extraordinarily keen and skilful hunters. They are polygamous, given at times to cannibalism and infanticide, and have no permanent dwellings, no pottery, and no idea of cultivation of the soil. They die out fast wherever they come in contact with the white man and his vices. The last Tasmanian aboriginal died in 1876. In New South Wales and Victoria, the dwindling remnants of the native tribes are mostly settled upon reserves under State control. The most permanent and successful missions to the aborigines are those in the Dioceses of Perth and Geraldton (Western Australia).

VIII. Catholic Literature.—Under the penal slavery that long prevailed over a part of Australia, intellectual and moral advancement was subordinated to the two central ideas of punishment and money-getting. For some five decades from the date of the first colonization there was scarcely such a thing as a cultured class; the struggle for existence was generally keen among the free settlers in a virgin country; and education, seldom more than primary, was mainly in the hands of convict teachers and of convict tutors assigned to private families. The literary gloom of Australian penal servitude before the days of the '48 men was lit up by two non-Catholic Irish convicts, Edward O'Shaughnessy, a gifted poet and political writer, and George Waldron (better known as George Barrington), the prince of modern pickpockets, whose romantic career has found fame even in the pages of the "Dictionary of National Biography". To Australian Catholics, however, it is especially gratifying that one of the first contributions of a writer of their faith and country dealt a severe blow at the convict system; this work was Dr. Ullathorne's heart-rending pamphlet, "The Horrors of Transportation". Time, free immigration, prosperity, higher instruction, more extended educational facilities, and the play of representative institutions have since then combined to develop in the "Land of Dawning" a rich general literature, in many respects *sui generis*, and marked, especially on its "lighter" side, by a certain weird melancholy which, according to Marcus Clarke, is the predominant feature of Australian scenery. In the literary development of the Commonwealth Catholic writers have borne an honourable part. The following list is made up exclusively of works produced by Catholic authors having at the time of writing a domicile in Australia.

History and Biography.—Ullathorne, "The Horrors of Transportation", and "The Australian Mission"; Kenny, "The Catholic Church in Australia to the Year 1840"; Therry, "Comparison of the Oratory of the House of Commons Thirty Years Ago and at the Present Day (1856)", "Reminiscences of Thirty Years' Residence in New South Wales"; Flanagan, "History of New South Wales"; Tenison Woods, "History of the Discovery and Exploration of Australia"; Finn ("Garry-Owen"), "The Chronicles of Early Melbourne"; George Collingridge (whose brother Arthur originated the real art life of the mother-state by founding the Art Society of New South Wales and the classes connected therewith), "History of Australian Discovery"; Mennell, "Dictionary of Australian Biography"; Hogan, "The Irish in Australia"; Kelsh, "Memoir of Bishop Willson". The principal work written by Cardinal Moran in Australia is his monumental "History of The Catholic Church in Australasia". Carr (Archbishop of Melbourne), "Fifty years of Progress"; Byrne, "History of the Catholic Church in South Australia" (two small vols. issued); Cleary, "The Orange Society"; Gray, "Australasia, Old and New"; Donohoe (Arthur Cayll), "History of Botany Bay".

Apologetic and Ascetic Literature.—The most noteworthy contributions to Australian Catholic apologetic literature are those of Cardinal Moran, "Letters on the Anglican Reformation", and "The Reunion of Christendom"; and of Archbishop Carr, "The Origin of the Church of England", "The Church and the Bible", "The Primacy of the Roman Pontiff", and "Letters in Reply to Dr. Rentoul", the charac-

teristic feature of which works is the frequency and effectiveness of their appeals to the writings of Protestant historians and divines; Hall, "Who translated the Bible?" A multitude of minor polemical publications on questions of history, missions, doctrine, statistics, socialism, education, medico-moral subjects, religion and science, etc., have appeared from time to time from the pens of Cardinal Moran, Archbishop Carr, Dr. Ullathorne ("Reply to Judge Barton"), Fathers W. Kelly, J. O'Malley, and E. J. Masterson, S.J., the Rev. W. Barry, D.D., the Rev. M. Watson, S.J., Benjamin Hoare, the Rev. P. O'Doherty, the Rev. M. Barrett, and others; Byrne, "True Wisdom" (translated from Thomas à Kempis); "Letters of a Mother to Her Children" and "Sketches of the Lives of Young Saints", books compiled by Loretto Nuns; Huault, "The Mother of Jesus". Devotional manuals have been published by the Fathers M. Watson and J. Ryan, S.J., and a prayerbook by the Australian Catholic Truth Society. This useful organization (established at the Second Australian Catholic Congress in 1904) is doing excellent service by its publications, which embrace nearly every department of Catholic literature. A place of honour in Australian apologetic and general literature is rightly due to the two volumes containing the Proceedings of the Australasian Catholic Congresses held at Sydney (1900) and Melbourne (1904).

Physical Science, Law, Politics, etc.—The foremost names in geological science in Australia are those of the Rev. Julian E. Tenison Woods, F.G.S., and the Rev. J. Milne Curran, F.G.S. Father Woods was author of "Geological Observations in South Australia", "Geology of Portland", and "North Australia and its Physical Geography". (Mennell says of this author: "His contributions to the pages of scientific journals and the proceedings of learned societies were numerous and valuable.") Father Curran is the author of "The Geology of Sydney and the Blue Mountains" and "Quantitative Analysis". T. A. Coghlan (Agent-General for New South Wales, Fellow of the Royal Statistical Society) is the Mulhall of Australian statistical science. The most important of his many publications while he was Statistician of New South Wales were: "The Wealth and Progress of New South Wales" and "The Seven Colonies of Australasia", both of which went through numerous editions. His successor as statistician of the mother-state is W. H. Hall, author of "The Official Year-Book of New South Wales". W. H. Archer, K.S.G.G., published sundry statistical works while Registrar-General of Victoria in its young and strenuous days, and for twenty-five years Dr. E. S. Hall compiled and published the vital statistics of Tasmania. Charles (afterwards Sir Charles) Gavan Duffy was the author of a "Guide to the Land Law of 1862", which law was passed by a coalition Ministry in which he held the portfolio of Lands. Other legal textbooks were written by Frank Gavan Duffy (son of Sir Charles), Judges Casey and Quinlan, M. Brennan, Bernard O'Dowd, N. G. Power, and J. Hood. Benjamin Hoare, author of "Preferential Trade", ranks high in political circles as an authority on protective tariffs. John D. Fitzgerald, an author of recognized ability on municipal reform, has written "Greater Sydney and Greater Newcastle". Frederick J. Bloomfield did the Australasian work in "Webster's Dictionary". Helen K. Jerome wrote a work on Japan. The Rev. Julian E. Tenison Woods compiled an "Australian Bibliography"; and useful educational works have issued from his pen and from those of Fathers P. J. O'Mara and W. Kelly, S.J., and of J. W. Foster-Rogers. Archbishop O'Reilly (Adelaide) has written pamphlets on music, a subject on which he is an authority of Australian reputation.

Fiction.—Daniel E. Deniehy, lawyer, statesman, journalist, will be best remembered for his clever skit, "How I Became Attorney-General of Barataria", which was famous in its day, and is still as readable as ever. James Francis Hogan published "An Australian Christmas Collection" of colonial stories and sketches. Ambrose Pratt is the author of "The Great Push Experiment", "Franks, Duellist", and "Three Years with Thunderbolt". Among other Australian Catholic writers of fiction whose work has appeared in book form are the following: Miss Tennyson, Roderick Quinn, Laura Archer (a collection of Queensland tales), F. M. Korner (pen name, "George Garnet"), a Loretto nun (author of "I Never Knew"), the Rev. P. Hickey ("Innisfail"). "Australian Wonderland" is a cleverly written book for children, in which two sisters (one of them a Sister of Mercy) collaborated. Newspaper and periodical literature has also been enriched with some excellent work in fiction by Australian Catholic writers.

Poetry.—Among the poets, two Irish singers, "Eva" of the Nation (Mrs. Kevin Izod O'Doherty) and "Thomasine", are now (1907) passing the evening of their lives in humble retirement in Queensland. Roderick Flanagan (the historian of New South Wales) published in his day a volume of verse. Victor J. Daley was a gifted and prolific verse-writer, but his only published work is "At Dawn and Dusk". John Farrell, for a time editor of the Sydney Daily Telegraph, was the author of "How He Died, and Other Poems". In 1897 he wrote a "Jubilee Ode" which was pronounced to be finer than Kipling's "Recessional" as a piece of national stock-taking. Roderick Quinn has written "The Higher Tide", and "The Circling Hearths"; Edwin J. Brady, a poet of the sea and wharfside, "The Way of Many Waters"; Bernard O'Dowd, "Dawnward" and "Darrawill of the Silent Land"; Cornelius Moynihan, "Feast of the Bunya, An Aboriginal Ballad", with a preface containing curious historical, legendary, and ethnological lore regarding the Queensland blacks; the Rev. W. Kelly, S.J., three convent dramas in blank verse; J. Hood, "Land of the Fern"; John B. O'Hara, "Songs of the South" (2d series), "Sonnets, Odes, and Lyrics"; the Rev. M. Watson, S.J., a series of seven handsomely illustrated Christmas booklets in verse which have gone through many editions. Volumes of verse have also been published by Marion Miller ("Songs From the Hills"), and Rena Wallace ("A Bush Girl's Songs"). Some meritorious work by Australian Catholic poetic writers (including various odes, etc., by the Rev. J. J. Malone) has not appeared in separate form.

Catholic Journalism in Australia had a long and thorny road to travel before it reached assured success. Beginning with "The Chronicle" (founded in Sydney, in 1839), the way was strewn with failures, which, however, helped to form the steps leading others to better things. The existing Catholic newspapers and periodicals of Australia, with their dates of foundation, are, *Weekly:* Sydney, N. S. W., "The Freeman's Journal" (the oldest existing newspaper in Australia, founded and first edited by Archdeacon McEncroe in 1850); and "The Catholic Press" (1895); Melbourne, Victoria, "The Advocate" (1868), "The Tribune" (1900); Brisbane, Queensland, "The Australian" (founded by Dr. O'Quinn in 1878), "The Age" (1892); Adelaide, South Australia, "The Southern Cross" (1889); Perth, W. A., "The W. A. Record" (1874); Launceston, Tasmania, "The Monitor" (founded in 1894 by amalgamating "The Catholic Standard" of Hobart, and "The Morning Star" of Launceston).—*Monthly:* Melbourne, "The Australian Messenger" (1887); "The Austral Light" (an ecclesiastical property since 1899); Sydney, "The Annals of Our Lady".—*Quarterly* and *Annual:* "The Australasian Catholic Record" (founded by Cardinal Moran, in Sydney, in 1894); "The Madonna" (Melbourne, 1897); "The Garland of St. Joseph" (1906). A useful "Catholic Almanac and Family Annual" is published for the Diocese of Maitland. Illustrated scholastic annuals are also issued by most of the Catholic colleges for boys, and by some of the secondary schools for girls.—In size, literary quality, successful management, and influence, the Catholic newspapers and magazines of Australia easily outrival the rest of the religious press in the Commonwealth. Many Catholic names of note in the political, judicial, literary, and scientific history of Australia were, for a time at least, associated with the religious or secular press of the country. Among them may be mentioned: Sir Charles Gavan Duffy; the Right Hon. William Bede Dalley, P.C., Q.C.; the Hon. John Hubert Plunkett, Q.C., M.L.C.; Sir Roger Therry; Richard Sullivan (brother of A. M. and T. D. Sullivan); Judges Therry, Real, Power, O'Connor, Casey, Heydon, and Quinlan; the Hon. Edward Butler, Q.C., M.L.C., and his brother, Thomas Butler; E. W. O'Sullivan; Sir John O'Shannassy, K.C.M.G.; the Hon. Sir Patrick Jennings, K.C.M.G., LL.D., M.L.C.; Edward Whitty, the brilliant Anglo-Irishman, who ended his days in Melbourne; William A. Duncan, C.M.G.; Roderick Flanagan; Daniel E. Deniehy; Philip Mennell, F.R.G.S.; John Farrell; Victor J. Daley; the Rev. Julian E. Tenison Woods; the Rev. J. V. O'Loghlen; the Hon. Hugh Mahon; J. F. Hogan; Benjamin Hoare; Roderick and P. E. Quinn; F. J. Bloomfield; Ambrose Pratt; Helen K. Jerome; John Hughes, K.C.S.G.; John Gavan Duffy; Frank Leverrier (noted as a scientist); Kenneth McDonall;—Nicholson; Frank and Martin Donohoe; Ernest Hoben; C. Brennan; T. Courtney; and others. Phil May first won fame as a caricaturist in the columns of an illustrated weekly published in Sydney. A number of able lay and clerical writers are associated with the Catholic newspapers and periodicals of Australia.

The Australian Handbook (various dates); the *Year-Books* of the various States; COGHLAN, *Wealth and Progress of New South Wales* (various dates), and *The Seven Colonies of Australasia* (various dates); *Acta et Decreta* of the Australian Plenary Synods of 1885 and 1895; *Historical Records of New South Wales;* BENNETT, *South Australian Almanac* (1840); KENNY, *The Catholic Church in Australia to the Year 1840;* FLANAGAN, *History of New South Wales* (1862); THERRY, *New South Wales and Victoria* (1863); *The National History of England* (1877); MAY, *Constitutional History of England* (1882); *Epitome of the Official History of New South Wales* (1883); BONWICK, *The Port Phillip Settlement* (1883), and *The First Twenty Years of Australia* (1883); FENTON, *History of Tasmania* (1884); DILKE, *Greater Britain* (1885); McCARTHY, *History of Our Own Times* (1887); HOGAN, *The Irish in Australia* (1888); SUTHERLAND, *History of Australia* (1888); LUMHOLTZ, *Among Cannibals* (1890); HUTCHINSON, *Australasian Encyclopædia* (1892); MENNELL, *Dictionary of Australian Biography* (1892); BRITTON, *History of New South Wales from the Records* (1894); MORAN, *History of the Catholic Church in Australasia;* HEATON, *Australian Dictionary of Dates* (1897); DAVITT, *Life and Progress in Australasia* (1898); COGHLAN, *Statistics of the Seven Colonies of Australasia from 1861 to 1899* (1900); JOSÉ, *History of Australia* (1901); COGHLAN AND EWING, *Progress of Australasia in the Nineteenth Century* (1903); HOWITT, *The Native Tribes of South-East Australia* (1904); SPENCER AND GILLEN, *The Native Tribes of Central Australia* (1904), and *The Northern Tribes of Central Australia* (1904); HALL, *States of Australia and New Zealand* (1905); *The Australasian Catholic Directory for 1906.*

HENRY W. CLEARY.

Austrebertha, SAINT, Virgin, born c. 630 at Therouane in the modern department of Pas-de-Calais in France; d. 10 February, 703 or 704. When her father desired to give her in marriage to a young nobleman, she fled from home and took the veil from the hands of Bishop Saint-Omer. Some time later she entered the monastery of Port on the Somme, where she was later elected prioress. Soon afterwards she was appointed first abbess of the newly erected convent of Pavilly in Lower Seine. Under her direction the nuns of Pavilly became so celebrated for sanctity that parents came from all sides to place their daughters under the guidance of Austrebertha. Her name is in the Roman martyrology and she is hon-

THE AUSTRO-HUNGARIAN MONARCHY
BOSNIA, HERZEGOVINA
(TERRITORY OF OCCUPATION)

Showing the Ecclesiastical Provinces, Prince-Archbishoprics,
and Bishoprics, Dioceses, Abbey with episcopal
jurisdiction, Abbeys, Vicariates Apostolic

AUSTRIAN DIOCESES OF THE LATIN RITE

I ECCL. PROV. OF GÖRZ-GRADISCA
1 Prince Archbishopric Görz-Gradisca
2 Prince Bishopric Laibach
3 Diocese Parenzo-Pola
4 " Triest-Capo d'Istria
5 " Veglia-Arbe

II ECCL. PROV. OF LEMBERG
1 Archdiocese of Lemberg
2 Diocese Przemyśl
3 " Tarnów

III THE EXEMPT PR-BISHOP. OF CRACOW

VI ECCL. PROVINCE OF OLMÜTZ
1 Prince Archbishopric of Olmütz
2 Diocese of Brünn

VII ECCL. PROV. OF PRAGUE
1 Prince Archbishopric Prague
2 Diocese of Budweis
3 " " Königgrätz
4 " " Leitmeritz

VIII ECCL. PROV. OF SALZBURG
1 Prince Archbishopric Salzburg
2 Prince Bishopric of Brixen and General
   Vicariate of Feldkirch
3 Prince Bishopric of Gurk
4 " " Lavant
5 " " Seckau & Diocese of Leoben
6 " " Trent

IX ECCL. PROV. OF VIENNA
1 Pr.Archbishopric of Vienna
2 Diocese of St.Pölten
3 " " Linz

X ECCL. PROV. OF ZARA
1 Archdiocese of Zara
2 Diocese of Spalato Makarska
3 " Ragusa
4 " Sebenico
5 " Lesina
6 " Cattaro

**HUNGARIAN DIOCESES OF
THE LATIN RITE**

XI ECCL. PROV. OF ESZTERGOM
1 Archdiocese of Esztergom
2 Diocese of Besztercebánya
3 " " Győr
4 " " Nyitra
5 " " Pécs
6 " " Székesfehérvár
7 " " Szombathely
8 " " Vácz
9 " " Veszprém
10 " " Eperjes |See Greek-Uniat
11 " " Munkács| Map

XII ECCL. PROV. OF KALOCSA-BÁCS
1 Archdiocese of Kalocsa-Bács
2 Diocese Magyarsand-Temesvár
3 " Transylvania (Erdély)
4 " Nagy-Várad

XIII ECCL. PROV. OF EGER
1 Archdiocese of Eger
2 Diocese of Kassa
3 " " Rozsnyó
4 " " Szatmar
5 " " Szepesvaralja

XIV ECCL. PROV. OF AGRAM
1 Archdiocese of Agram
2 Diocese of Djakovar
3 " " Zengg-Modruš
4 " Kreuz (See Greek-Uniat Map)

XVI ABBEY with episcopal jurisdiction
1 Arch-Abbey of Győr Szt-Marton

XVII ECCL. PROV. OF SARAJEVO
1 Archdiocese of Sarajevo
2 Diocese of Banjaluka
3 " " Mostar-Duvno
4 " " Marcanna-Trebinje

V THE ARCHDIOCESE OF LEMBERG (Armenian Rite)
Covers the Kingdom of Galicia, Lodomeria and Duchy of Bukovina

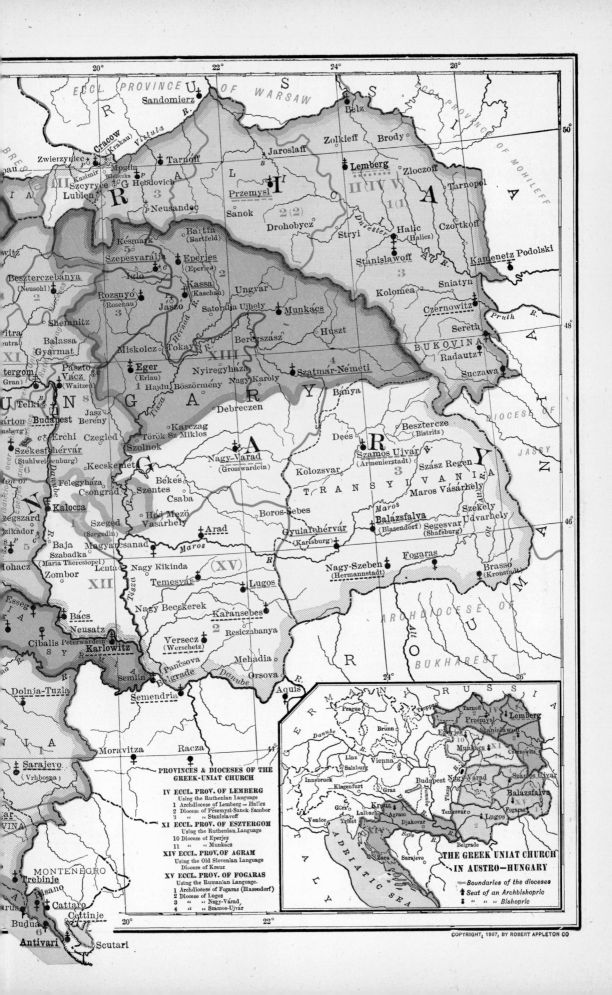

PROVINCES & DIOCESES OF THE
GREEK-UNIAT CHURCH

IV ECCL. PROV. OF LEMBERG
Using the Ruthenian Language
1 Archdiocese of Lemberg — Halicz
2 Diocese of Przemysl-Sanok Sambor
3   "   " Stanislavoff
XI ECCL. PROV. OF ESZTERGOM
Using the Ruthenian Language
10 Diocese of Eperjes
11   "   " Munkacs
XIV ECCL. PROV. OF AGRAM
Using the Old Slovenian Language
Diocese of Kreuz
XV ECCL. PROV. OF FOGARAS
Using the Rumanian Language.
1 Archdiocese of Fogaras (Blasendorf)
2 Diocese of Lugos
3   "   " Nagy-Varad
4   "   " Szamos-Ujvar

THE GREEK UNIAT CHURCH
IN AUSTRO—HUNGARY
━━ Boundaries of the dioceses
✝ Seat of an Archbishopric
✝   "   " Bishopric

COPYRIGHT, 1907, BY ROBERT APPLETON CO

oured as patron at Montreuil in the department of Pas-de-Calais.

RANBECK, *The Benedictine Calendar* (London, 1896); VACANDARD, *Vie de S. Ouen* (Paris, 1902), 208–210; STADLER, *Heiligen-Lexikon* (Augsburg, 1858), I, 363.

MICHAEL OTT.

Austremonius, SAINT, Apostle and Bishop of Auvergne (c. 314). All that is certainly known of Austremonius is deduced from a few brief sentences in the writings of St. Gregory of Tours (Hist. Franc., I, xxx, and De Gloriâ Confessorum, c. xxix). According to this authority he was one of the seven bishops sent from Rome into Gaul about the middle of the third century; he laboured in Auvergne and is said to have been the first Bishop of Clermont. But from a study of the episcopal lists as given by St. Gregory himself, St. Austremonius could hardly have antedated the commencement of the fourth century, since his third successor died in 385. It is more likely, therefore, that he was the contemporary of the three Bishops of Aquitaine who attended the Council of Arles in 314. He was not a martyr. His cult began about the middle of the sixth century, when Cantius, a deacon, saw a vision of angels about his neglected tomb at Issoire on the Couze. His body was afterwards translated to Volvic, and in 761 to the Abbey of Mauzac. Towards the middle of the ninth century, the head of the saint was brought to St.-Yvoine, near Issoire, and about 900 was returned to Issoire, the original place of burial.

Acta SS., Nov., I, 49 sq.; *Anal. Boll.*, XIII, 33–46; *Mélanges Havet.*, 36; DUCHESNE, *Bulletin critique* (1888), IX, 203–207. CHEVALIER, *Rép. des sources hist.* (*Bio-bibliog.*), 2d ed., 390, 391.

FRANCIS P. HAVEY.

Austria. See AUSTRO-HUNGARIAN MONARCHY.

Austro-Hungarian Monarchy, THE.—By this name is designated the European monarchy whose dominions have for their main life-distributing artery the River Danube, in its course from Engelhartszell, near Passau, to Orsova. South of the Danube lie the Austrian Alpine provinces and the provinces of Carinthia and Carniola; north of the Danube are the Carpathian and Sudetic provinces.

AREA AND POPULATION.—The monarchy as a whole has an area of about 262,577 square miles (680,887 square kilometres), and a population of about 48,592,000. This gives it the second place in extent of territory, and the third place in respect to population, among the political divisions of Europe. The average density of its population is, approximately, 185 to the square mile. The monarchy holds sway over: (a) the kingdoms and provinces represented in the Austrian Parliament, or Reichsrat, which have together an area of 115,695 sq. m. (300,008 sq. km.) and a population of 26,969,812; (b) the provinces of the Hungarian Crown which have a total area of 127,204 sq. m. (329,851 sq. km.) and a population of 19,885,465; (c) Bosnia and Herzegovina, with an area of 19,678 sq. m. (51,028 sq. km.) and a population of 1,737,000, occupied and administered by Austria-Hungary, though still theoretically a part of the Ottoman Empire. These populations include a great variety of races. In the Austrian territory there are: Germans, 9,171,000; Czechs, 5,955,000; Poles, 4,259,000; Ruthenians, 3,376,000; Slovenes, 1,193,000; Italians and Ladinians, 727,000. In Hungary the population is composed of: Magyars, 9,180,000; Rumanians, 2,867,000; Germans, 2,138,000; Slovaks, 2,055,000; Croats, 1,734,000; Serbs, 1,079,000; Ruthenians, 443,000. The inhabitants of Bosnia and Herzegovina are Servo-Croatians.

The capitals of the three main divisions are: Austria, Vienna, with 1,675,000 inhabitants; Hungary, Budapest, with 732,000 inhabitants; Bosnia and Herzegovina, Serajevo, with 38,000 inhabitants.

The only strip of coast land in Austria-Hungary lies on the Adriatic and has a length of 1,366 miles (2,200 km.). The countries which border on Austria-Hungary are: Italy, Switzerland, the principality of Liechtenstein, Bavaria, Saxony, Prussia, Russia, Rumania, Servia, Turkey, and Montenegro.

CHURCH HISTORY.—The Austro-Hungarian Monarchy was created by the union of the Germanic, Slavonic, and Hungarian provinces which now lie within its territory. This union took place in 1526. Upon the death of Louis II of Hungary and Bohemia at the battle of Mohács, in that year, Bohemia and Hungary were united to the Austrian possessions of Ferdinand I, of the Hapsburg family. This union was in accordance with the law of succession as well as the result of a free choice. Up to 1526 each of these three divisions of the present empire had its own separate religious history.

A. *Early Christianity.*—The Romans in the time of Augustus took possession of those provinces of the present Austria-Hungary which lie south of the Danube. In the course of time they built roads, founded cities, turned the territory into Roman provinces, and here and there converted the inhabitants to Christianity. The cities of Aquileia and Salona, episcopal sees from the middle of the first century, were centres of Christianity for Noricum and Pannonia. In the year 294 five Christian workmen were thrown from the marble bridges of Sirmium (Mitrowitz) into the Save and drowned. During the persecution of the Christians under the Emperor Diocletian, in 304, the soldier Florianus was thrown into the Enns at Lauriacum (Lorch). The house of Augustinian canons, at St. Florian, in Upper Austria, now stands on the spot where the body of this saint was buried. A tradition gives the same date for the martyrdom of the two bishops Victorinus of Petovia (Pettau in Southern Styria) and Quirinus of Siscia, who met death where the Kulpa empties into the Save. Even at this period Christianity must have had a large number of adherents in these districts, for already an established organization is found here. The bishops of Noricum were under the control of the Patriarch of Aquileia, while Pannonia was subject to the Metropolitan of Sirmium.

The last representative of Christian culture among the Roman inhabitants of the Danube district is St. Severinus. The story of his life, by his pupil Eugippius, is the only written document we have for the history of the Danubian provinces during the last years of Roman occupation. Severinus settled near the present city of Vienna, built a monastery for himself and his companions, and led so austere a life that even in winter, when the Danube was frozen, he walked up and down over the ice barefoot. His journeys upon the frozen river were errands of consolation to the despairing provincials, who saw themselves threatened on all sides by bands of marauding barbarians. In these journeys Severinus travelled as far as Castra Batava (Passau), and inland from the river up to Juvavum (Salzburg). God had granted him the gift of prophecy. When Odovakar (Odoacer), King of the Heruli, set out on his march against Rome, he came to the saint and asked for his blessing. Severinus spoke prophetically: "Go forward, my son. To-day thou art still clad in the worthless skins of animals, but soon shalt thou make gifts from the treasures of Italy." After Odovakar had overthrown the Roman Empire of the West, and had made himself master of Italy, he sent and invited Severinus to ask from him some favour. Severinus only asked the pardon of one who had been condemned to banishment. The Alamannic king, Gibold, also visited him in Castra Batava, and the saint begged as a personal grace that the king cease from ravaging the Roman territory. His usual salutation was "Sit nomen Domini benedictum", corresponding to our "Praise be to Jesus". When Severinus lay dying the sobs of his disciples prevented their praying; he himself began to recite the last psalm, and with the closing words of this psalm, "Omnis spiritus laudet Dominum", he passed away (482). Six years later the Romans withdrew from this region, taking the body of the saint with them, and returned to Italy. Here he was buried with suitable honour in the castle of Luculanum, near Naples.

B. *The Middle Ages.*—During the period of migrations which followed the fall of the Roman Empire, Austria was the fighting-ground of the barbaric hordes which poured through it. Vindobona disappeared from the face of the earth; Pannonia was entirely laid waste by the Avars, a people related to the Huns. The same fate befell Styria, Carinthia, and Carniola, desolated by the Slovenes, who now took possession of those provinces. The land lying on the upper Drave has since borne the name of "Pustertal" (from the Slovenic *pust*, "waste"). The Croats and Serbs seized the country south of the Save. The Croats are the first-born sons of the Church among the Slavs. They were converted, about the year 650, by Roman priests. The Bajuvarii (Bavarians), a people from the West, spread themselves over the whole of Upper Austria. St. Rupert, Bishop of Worms, baptized the Bavarian duke, Theodo, at Regensburg (Ratisbon) and became the Apostle of the Austrian Bajuvarii. He travelled and preached nearly as far as Lauriacum, settled in Salzburg, and there erected a see and founded the monastery of St. Peter (c. 700). St. Peter's is the oldest Benedictine monastery which has had a continuous existence down to our own times, Monte Cassino having been repeatedly destroyed and deserted. The Benedictine cloister for women, Nonnberg, founded by Rupert's niece Ehrentraut, is also still standing. The Bavarian Duke Tassilo founded the Benedictine monasteries of Mondsee (748) and Kremsmünster (777). The Bishops of Salzburg brought the Christian Faith and German customs to the Slavs. A quarrel broke out, however, between the Carinthians and the Patriarch of Aquileia. Charlemagne raised the Carinthian see of Salzburg to an archbishopric in 798, settled the dispute with Aquileia by making the Drave the dividing line of the two provinces, and in 803 established the border territories known as the Mark of Friuli and the East Mark.

Moravia was won to Christianity by two brothers, Methodius and Constantine, Greek monks from Thessalonica, known in history as the Apostles of the Slavs. Constantine invented the Glagolitic alphabet, translated the Bible into Slavic, and composed the liturgy in that language. But, as Salzburg and Passau laid claim to the region in which the brothers worked, complaint was made against them by the German ecclesiastics. Pope Hadrian II, however, authorized the liturgy in the Slavic language. Constantine remained at Rome in a monastery and took the name of Cyril, while Methodius, after many fruitful labours as Archbishop of Pannonia and Moravia, died 6 April, 885, at Vehlehrad, on the River March. The Apostles of the Slavs are now (pursuant to a decree of Leo XIII) commemorated throughout the Catholic Church on the 5th day of July. The Latin Liturgy was reintroduced in Moravia by Swatopluk, the successor of Duke Ratislaus, and soon after his death the Magyars overthrew the empire of Great Moravia (906). When Moravia is again heard of in history (founding of the bishopric of Olmütz, 1063), it is a province of Bohemia.

Christianity was introduced into Bohemia from Moravia. Of the Slavic tribes which at the end of the fifth century controlled the interior of Bohemia

and drove the Germans to the outskirts of the country, the Czechs of Prague were the most important division. In A.D. 871 their prince, Borziwoy, and his wife, Ludmilla, consented to receive baptism from St. Methodius. From this time on the history of Bohemia is an account of the struggles between two contending parties, the Christian-Germanic and the National Heathen. At the instigation of the National Heathen party the saintly Duke Wenzel (Wenceslaus) I was murdered by his brother, Boleslaw I. But even Boleslaw had to rule according to the wishes of the Christian-Germanic party, and his son Boleslaw II founded the Bishopric of Prague (973). The new see was placed under the Archbishop of Mainz, and its first bishop was the Saxon Dithmar. His successor, St. Adalbert (Wojtech), met a martyr's death (997) at the hands of the heathen Slavs of Prussia, whom he sought to bring to the truth. The Benedictine Order came into Bohemia with the founding of the monastery of Borevnov by Boleslaw II, and Boleslaw's sister, Milada, was the first abbess of St. George, the Benedictine cloister for women in Prague. Duke Bretislaw seized Gnesen and brought the body of St. Adalbert in triumph to Prague. Dabrowka, the daughter of Boleslaw I, married the Polish Duke Mieczyslaw, and the latter was baptized in 966. The son of Mieczyslaw laid the foundation of an enduring church-organization by forming the four bishoprics of Posen, Kolberg, Breslau, and Cracow, and placing them under the Archbishopric of Gnesen, which had been established in the year 1000.

The Magyars, a people from the Ural-Altai region, moved forward in 895 into the Avarian Wilderness on the Theiss. Attempts to convert them were made by the court of Byzantium as well as by St. Wolfgang, a monk of Maria Einsiedeln, by Piligrim, Bishop of Passau, who, as successor of the Bishops of Lorch, wished to be Metropolitan of all Pannonia, and by Adalbert of Prague. Thus it was brought about that the Magyar ruler Géza, great grandson of Arpad, and his wife Sarolta were favourably inclined to Christianity. The real Apostle of the Magyars, however, was Géza's great son, St. Stephen. Stephen received a Christian education and was baptized by St. Adalbert. Upon the occasion of his marriage with Gisela, sister of the future emperor, St. Henry II, Stephen vowed to give his people the blessings of Christianity. One of the most important measures taken by him for the security of the new faith was the founding at Gran of an archbishopric with ten subordinate sees. As Stephen's patron saint in battle had been St. Martin, he founded the Benedictine monastery of Martinsberg. He also founded hospices for the reception of Hungarian pilgrims at Ravenna, Rome, and Jerusalem. Astricus, the Abbot of Martinsberg, obtained for him, from the pope, the title of king. Sylvester II sent Stephen a crown of gold and, according to a tradition (which, however, is not well founded) a Bull which decreed to the Kings of Hungary the privilege of the "Apostolic Majesty" (q. v.). Having a great devotion to the Blessed Virgin, Stephen caused himself to be crowned on the festival of the Assumption, the 15th day of August, in the year 1000, and church historians have given to Hungary the title of "Mary's Realm" (*Regnum Marianum*).

The gradual advance of Christianity in Austria towards the east is shown in the shifting of the abode of the early rulers of the Babenberg (Bamberg) line from Melk, on the Kahlenberg, to Vienna. One of this family, Leopold I, the Illustrious, had already founded at Melk an establishment of secular canons. These were replaced in 1089 by twelve Benedictine monks from Lambach. At the time when Leopold's youngest son, Adalbert I, the Victorious, was margrave, three youths left this region to go to Paris to study. While on their way, they were obliged to spend a night in the open and fell to speaking of the future. Each wished to become a bishop, and each vowed that, if ever a bishop, he would found a monastery. One, Gebhard, became Archbishop of Salzburg and founded Admontund and the See of Gurk; another, Adalbero, Bishop of Würzburg, founded the monastery of Lambach; while the third, St. Altmann of Passau, founded Göttweig for twelve canons under the Rule of St. Augustine. The canons at Göttweig were replaced after the lapse of ten years by Benedictines from St. Blasien in the Black Forest. All three of these bishops remained true to Gregory VII in the controversy of investitures. The Crusades began during the reign of the Margrave Leopold II, the Saint, and many of the crusading armies traversed Austria. Leopold's mother, Ida, took part in a pilgrimage of which Thiemo, Archbishop of Salzburg, was the leader. The archbishop met the death of a martyr, and Ida was made a prisoner. Leopold erected a church on the Kahlenberg and founded the monasteries Klosterneuburg and Heiligenkreuz. His wife, Agnes, widow of the Hohenstaufen Duke Frederick, bore him eighteen children. Their third son, Otto, studied at Paris, entered the Cistercian monastery of Morimond, became Bishop of Freising, and wrote a chronicle, "De Duabus Civitatibus", and a second work, "Libri Duo De Gestis Friderici I". By reason of these two works he is the most noted German historian of the Middle Ages.

After a hard struggle, the saintly King Ladislaus (d. 1095) succeeded in regulating the ecclesiastical and civil affairs of Hungary. He founded the Bishopric of Grosswardein and summoned the dignitaries of the Church and the State to a diet at Szaboles. This diet is often called a synod, on account of the many decisions arrived at in church matters. The priests were ordered to observe celibacy strictly, the laity were commanded to keep Sunday and feast-days and to abstain from immorality. Ladislaus conquered Croatia, whose duke, Zwonimir, had received from a legate of Gregory VII at Salona (1076) a banner, sword, crown, and sceptre, with the title of king, in return for which he had sworn fealty to the pope.

Henry II, Jasomirgott, was the first Duke of Austria. He built a residence for himself at Vienna (*Am Hof*), in which was the Pancraz chapel, and founded the Schottenkloster for Benedictine monks from St. Jacob's at Regensburg. Octavian Wolzner, an architect from Cracow, erected for the new duke the church of St. Stephen, to which the parish of St. Peter was added. Leopold V, the Virtuous, son of Henry II, took part in the Third Crusade and fought so bravely that, as we are told, his armour was stained blood red, and only the part under the sword belt remained white. However, Richard the Lionhearted tore down the Austrian banner at the storming of Ascalon and the enraged duke went home at once. While on his way to England, Richard was seized at Erdberg, and held a prisoner by the duke at Dürrenstein. Crusaders being under the protection of the pope, Celestine III put Leopold V under the ban. To this the duke paid no attention; but when he fell with his horse, at Graz, broke a leg, and found himself near death, his conscience smote him; he sent for Albert III, Archbishop of Salzburg, who was in the neighbourhood, and received absolution from him. Frederick I, the eldest son of Leopold V, ruled only six years and died while on a crusade, The reign of his brother, Leopold VI, the Glorious, was a brilliant one. He too went on a crusade and endeavoured first to capture Damietta, the key to Jerusalem, but was obliged to return home without having accomplished anything. He married a Byzantine princess and formed relations with men of Greek learning and culture. The duke built a

new castle for himself (Schweizerhof) and the church of St. Michael. The church was intended for the benefit of the duke's attendants, retainers, servants, and the townspeople who settled around the castle. The scheme to form a bishopric at Vienna was not carried out, but Eberhard II of Salzburg founded bishoprics at Seckau and Lavant, for Styria and Carinthia. Leopold's son and successor, Frederick II, the last of the Babenberg line, was knighted with much religious pomp at the feast of the Purification of the Virgin, 1232, in the castle church. Bishop Gebhard of Passau celebrated Mass and gave the consecrated sword to the duke, two hundred young nobles receiving knighthood at the same time. After the ceremony the young duke rode at the head of the newly made knights to Penzing, where jousts were held.

Within a short space of time the national dynasties of the countries under discussion died out in the male lines: the Babenberg Dynasty (Austria) in 1246, the Arpadian (Hungary) in 1301, and the Premyslian (Bohemia) in 1306. In 1282 the German Emperor, Rudolph of Hapsburg, gave Austria in fief to his son Albrecht. To Austria and Styria the dukes of the Hapsburg line soon added Carinthia, Carniola, the Tyrol, and the Mark of the Wends. The rulers of this line are deserving of great praise for their aid in developing church life in these territories. Albrecht I founded the court (*Hofburg*) chapel in his castle; Duke Rudolph IV in 1359 laid the corner-stone of the Gothic reconstruction of the church of St. Stephen. A hundred and fifty years elapsed before the great tower of the church was completed. With the consent of the pope the same duke founded the University of Vienna in 1365. The university was modelled on the one at Paris and possessed great privileges (freedom from taxation, right of administering justice). When part of the Council of Basle separated from Eugenius IV and set up Felix V as antipope, the theological faculty of the university, of which at that time the celebrated Thomas Ebendorffer of Haselbach was a member, sided with the antipope. But the papal legate, John Carvajal, and Æneas Sylvius Piccolomini, the emperor's governmental secretary, prevailed upon Frederick V to espouse the cause of Eugenius and to sign the Concordat of Vienna (1448). The concordat provided that the annates and the confirmation dues should be restored to the pope, that the pope should have the right to appoint to the canonries in the uneven months, and that the filling of ecclesiastical vacancies at Rome should be reserved to him. The concordat was gradually accepted by all of the German rulers, and up to the present time the relations between the German Church and the papacy are regulated by its provisions. In 1452 Frederick was crowned emperor at Rome, being the last emperor to be crowned in that city. In his reign the Bishoprics of Laibach (1462), Vienna, and Wiener-Neustadt (both the latter in 1469) were founded. During this period a great many monastic houses were founded in Austria, especially by the more recently established orders: Carthusian houses were founded at Mauerbach, Gaming, Agsbach; Franciscan at Vienna, Klosterneuburg, St. Pölten, Maria Enzersdorf, Pupping; Dominican at Graz and Retz.

Under the Luxembourg line Bohemia attained a high degree of material and spiritual prosperity. Charles IV, before his reign began, succeeded in having Prague raised to an archbishopric (1344), and in this way made the country ecclesiastically independent of Germany. Charles had been a student at Paris, and immediately upon ascending the throne he founded the University of Prague (1348), the first university on German soil. Master Matthias of Anras and Peter Parler from Schwäbisch-Gmünd began the erection of the stately Cathedral of St.

Vitus which is now nearing completion. Parler also erected the Teynkirche (Teyn church) in Prague, and the church of St. Barbara in Kuttenberg, while Matthias of Anras built the fortress-castle of Karlstein. The crown jewels of Bohemia were preserved in the sumptuous chapel at Karlstein. But Bohemia had a sudden fall from the height it had attained. King Wenzel (Wenceslaus), son of Charles IV, had no control of his temper, and began a quarrel with the archbishop. The archbishop's vicar-general, John of Pomuk (St. John Nepomucene), refused to tell what he had heard in confession. He was first tortured and then, gagged and bound, was thrown at night into the River Moldau. At this time the first signs appeared in Bohemia of a religious agitation which was destined to bring the greatest sorrow both to Bohemia and to the adjoining countries. Jerome of Prague had become acquainted with the writings of Wyclif at Oxford. He returned home, bringing the teachings of Wyclif with him, and communicated them to his friend Hus. Hus came from Husinetz near Prachatitz. He was the child of a peasant, and had become professor of philosophy at the University of Prague, preacher in the Bohemian language at the Bethlehem chapel, and confessor to Queen Sophia. A complaint was brought in the university against Hus on account of his teaching. Of the four "Nations" (Saxons, Bavarians, Poles, and Bohemians), which had votes in the affairs of the university, only the Bohemians voted for Hus. Hus then turned a personal into a national affair. King Wenzel issued a command that henceforth the Bohemians should have three votes, and the other "Nations" only one vote. Upon this 5,000 students and the German professors withdrew and founded the University of Leipzig. The university was now simply a national one, and Hus without interference taught the following doctrines: the church consists only of the elect; no man is a temporal ruler, no man is a bishop, if he be in mortal sin; the papal dignity is an outcome of the imperial power; obedience to the church is the invention of men. Hus was suspended by Archbishop Zbinko; he appealed to the pope (Alexander V) and then to Jesus Christ. John XXIII placed Hus under the ban, Prague under an interdict, and called the Council of Constance. The Emperor Sigismund gave Hus a safe-conduct which protected him from acts of violence on the part of the indignant Germans through whose territory he must pass, but not from the verdict of the council. Hus was repeatedly examined before the council, but would not retract his opinions; the members of the council, therefore, unanimously condemned his errors and delivered him to the secular power, by which, in accordance with the law of the land at the time, he was condemned to death at the stake (1415). Jerome of Prague suffered the same death the next year. While at Constance Hus sanctioned the receiving of the sacrament in both kinds which had been introduced by Master Jacob of Miez (Calixtines). As a former monk, John of Selau, was leading a procession a stone was thrown at him from a window of the town hall. The throng, led by the knight John Zizka of Trocnov, attacked the town hall and threw the judge, the burgomaster, and several members of the town council out of the window into the street, where they were killed by the fall. This is known in history as the "First Defenestration of Prague". King Wenzel was so excited by the episode that he was struck with apoplexy and died. The Hussite wars caused fearful devastation not only in Bohemia, but in the adjacent countries as well. Fortunately, the Hussites divided into the more moderate Calixtines, under John of Rokyzana, and the "Taborites", so called from the city and mountain which they named Tabor. The Taborites were led by John Zizka and Procopius the Great,

who was also called the "Shaven" (*Iloly*) because he had been a monk. After Zizka's death the extreme radicals took the name of "Orphans" because no one was worthy to take Zizka's place. They were finally conquered, and an agreement, called the *Compactata* (Treaty of Iglau) based on the Four Articles of Prague, was made with the moderate party (1436). The Compactata provided: that in Bohemia everyone who demanded it should receive Holy Communion under both kinds; mortal sins should be punished, but only by the legal authorities; the Word of God should be freely expounded by clergy appointed for the purpose; ecclesiastics should manage their property according to the rules of the church. After this, Hussitism lived on in the "Bohemian Brethren", who elected a bishop at Lhola near Reichenau (1467), and were finally carried into the current of the Reformation.

In Hungary Christian culture flourished during the reign of the House of Anjou. Louis the Great founded universities at Altofen and Fünfkirchen, and built the fine cathedral at Kaschau. When Constantinople was captured by the Turks (29 May, 1453), a cry of horror resounded throughout Europe, and the pope sent forth John Capistran to preach a crusade. The saintly monk came with an immense following from Italy to Germany, Bohemia, and Hungary. He preached in the open, as the churches could not hold his hearers. A stone pulpit with a statue of the saintly Capistran stands on the east side of St. Stephen's Cathedral, Vienna. A hundred thousand people crowded the square and the roofs of the houses to hear him. This was the more remarkable because Capistran preached in Latin. Yet all who saw and heard him were moved to their innermost souls. The Turks, in 1456, tried to capture Belgrad, the key to Hungary. The papal legate, John Carvajal, and John Capistran raised a crusading army with which John Hunyady was able to defeat, at Belgrad, a Turkish army much more numerous. This was called the "Battle of the Three Johns". Hunyady and Capistran died shortly afterwards from camp fever. Hunyady's son had been educated by John Vitez, Bishop of Grosswardein, afterwards Archbishop of Gran. This prelate instilled such a love of learning into his pupil that when the latter ascended the throne as Matthias Corvinus, he gathered learned men about him, reestablished the decayed university at Ofen, and founded a new university at Pressburg. Thirty copyists were kept busy at Ofen transcribing the Greek and Latin classics. The volumes, which were beautifully illuminated and handsomely bound, were known as Corvinian books.

C. *Modern Times.*—If in analyzing church history Christian antiquity is taken to represent the period of the life and labours of the Church among the peoples influenced by Greek and Roman civilization, and the Middle Ages the period of the Church's life and labours among the Germans and the nations which came into contact with them, then the modern period of history must be taken as that in which the influence of the Church began to extend throughout the whole world. Modern times would, according to this theory, begin with the discovery of the New World. But if the beginning of the modern era is made, as it usually is, to coincide with the Reformation, then it is further marked by the rise of that monarchy which was formed by the union of the Austrian, Slavonian, and Hungarian provinces under the Hapsburgs in 1526.

Ferdinand of Hapsburg, the ruler of the German-Austrian crown provinces, had married, at Linz, Anna of Hungary and Bohemia. When Anna's brother, Louis II, was killed in the desperate battle of Mohács (1526), Ferdinand of Austria succeeded by right of inheritance and election as King of Bohemia and Hungary. The new doctrine taught at Wittenberg was soon brought into the Austrian provinces. Miners were the first to spread the new teaching. Noble families frequently sent their sons to German universities, and even to Wittenberg, and these students often returned with Protestant ideas, and even brought Protestant preachers with them. The constant danger from the Turks in Austria was exceedingly opportune for the new religious movement. One of the first preachers of the new doctrine in Vienna was Paul of Spretten (Speratus), a Swabian, who had been driven out of Salzburg on account of his Lutheran views. The new doctrine entered Hungary and Transylvania through merchants who brought Lutheran books with them, and it took hold, more especially, among the German population of the Zipser region and among the Saxons of Transylvania. Martin Biro, known as Devay, from the place of his origin, Deva in Transylvania, has been called "the Luther of Hungary". Most of the Hungarian bishops had fallen at the battle of Mohács, and the subsequent disputes concerning the succession to the throne distracted the monarchy. For these reasons the new doctrines spread rapidly, and Devay was able to bring over to it such noble families as the Batthyany and Bocskay. It was then that Calvinism began to be called in Hungary *Magyar hit* (Hungarian faith), Lutheranism *Nemes hit* (German faith), and Catholicism *Igaz hit* (Right faith). Equal success accompanied the preaching of John Gross of Cronstadt in Transylvania, despite the efforts of George Utyeszenich to check him. Utyeszenich (also called, after his mother, Martinuzzi) was prior of the Pauline monastery at Szenstochov near Cracow, and governed Transylvania as guardian of John Sigismund Zápolyas. Gross added *Honter* to his name in memory of his deliverance by an elder bush (in the Transylvanian dialect *hontert*) from death by drowning. In order to secure the crown for her son, John Sigismund Zápolyas, his mother, Isabella, was obliged to sanction the decisions of the diet which met at Thorenburg (Torda) near Klausenburg. These granted to adherents of the Augsburg Confession equal rights with the Catholics. In Bohemia and Moravia Lutheranism first found adherents among the Germans and especially among the sect of the Utraquists. Just as the Hapsburg Dynasty showed itself at this period to be the shield of Christianity against the advance of Islam, so also it proved itself by its constancy and zeal to be the support of the Faith against the religious innovations. Pope Pius IV conceded the cup to the laity in the Archdioceses of Gran and Prague, a concession, however, withdrawn by St. Pius V. Ferdinand I sought in many ways to be of aid: by his mandates, by the inspection of convents and parishes, by his care in selecting competent ecclesiastics, by the introduction of the newly established Society of Jesus, and by proposals which were sent to the Council of Trent in support of reforms. The mandates of Ferdinand were of little use, but the inspections and the enforcement of the decisions of the Council of Trent had effect. The Bishops of Vienna, Fabri (Heigerlein), and Frederick Nausea (a Latinization of Grau; *Nausea*, horror, disgust) were unusual men. With unflagging zeal both preached on Sundays and feast days in the Cathedral of St. Stephen and took part in the religious movement by the publication of theological pamphlets. Nausea's sermons are characterized in a rude rhyme of the day:—

Viel tausend Menschen standen da
Es predigt Bischof Nausea,
Wie er denn pflegt zu aller Zeit
Sein' Schäflein zgebn selbst die Weid.

"Many thousands gather where Bishop Nausea preaches, and himself, as his wont is, feeds his flock".
—In the Austrian provinces the Jesuits were the most important factor in the defence of the Faith and the elevation of Christian life. Ferdinand I obtained from St. Ignatius the founding of a Jesuit college in Vienna. The first two Jesuits came to Vienna in 1551. They were followed, the next year, by St. Peter Canisius, the first German member of the order, were assigned the abandoned Carmelite monastery Am Hof, obtained two chairs in the theological faculty, and founded a gymnasium with a theological seminary attached. St. Peter Canisius was named court preacher, and for a time was administrator of the Diocese of Vienna. He still influences the present day through his "Summa Doctrinæ Christianæ"; an abridgment of which, called the catechism of Canisius, is still in use. A few years later the Jesuits founded at Prague a gymnasium, a theological school, and a university for philosophical and theological studies, which in contradistinction to the "Carolinum" was called the "Clementinum". They also founded schools at Innsbruck and at Tyrnau. The tutor and court preacher of Maximilian II, Ferdinand's eldest son, was Sebastian Pfauser, a man of Protestant tendencies. It was feared that Maximilian would embrace the new creed, but the papal nuncio, Bishop Hosius of Ermland, pointed out to him those inconsistencies in Protestant doctrine which prove its falsity. Maximilian II gave permission to lords and knights to follow the Augsburg Confession in their own castles, cities, and villages. David Chyträus of Rostock drew up for the Protestants a form of church service. In Bohemia the Evangelicals united with the Bohemian and Moravian Brethren, and called the new agreement the "Bohemian Confession". They had a consistory of fifteen to which the Evangelical clergy were subordinate. Maximilian's position in the part of Hungary controlled by them was a difficult one, because rebels concealed their political schemes under the cloak of a struggle for religious freedom. His brother Charles was master of the inner Austrian provinces, Styria, Carinthia, Carniola, and Görz. He summoned the Jesuits to Graz and, in the religious pacification of Brück, granted the free exercise of religion at Graz, Klagenfurt, Laibach, and Judenburg. In return he demanded that the Protestants should leave him and his coreligionists undisturbed in their faith, rights, and estates; besides this the Lutheran preachers and teachers were obliged to leave the cities, market towns, and estates under the personal rule of the archduke. In order to counterbalance the endowed schools of the Styrian provinces the Archduke Charles founded the University of Graz (Carolina) in 1586. Charles's son Ferdinand (later the Emperor Ferdinand II) was educated at Ingolstadt, and while there he declared, "I would rather give up land and people and go away in nothing but a shirt than sanction what might be injurious to religion". When he became ruler he appointed commissioners who cleared the land of these preachers (ranters). The bishops George Stobäus of Lavant and Martin Brenner of Seckau (the Hammer of the Heretics) were at the head of these reformatory commissions. But no blood was shed in this counter-reformation. At the distribution of provinces Archduke Ferdinand, husband of Philippina Welser, had received the Tyrol. The diet of 1570 decided the religious position of that province. The governor, Jacob of Pagrsbach, declared firmly that to grant the wishes of the Protestants would be contrary to the customs and ordinances of the land and, further, that it would be folly to rend religion, the strongest tie which binds hearts together. All classes agreed with him. Rudolph II, Maximilian's eldest son and successor, lived in the Hradschin at Prague, where he carried on his studies in alchemy and art. The Archduchy of Austria was ruled by his brother Ernst. Ernst

was aided by Melchior Khlesl, who brought about the counter-reformation in Austria. Khlesl was the child of Protestant parents; his father had been a baker in Vienna. He was converted by the court preacher, George Scherer. From the time of Scherer until the suspension of the order the court preachers were chosen in unbroken succession from the Jesuits. Khlesl became Provost of St. Stephen's, Chancellor of the university, and Bishop of Vienna. During the reigns of Ernst and his brother Matthias, Khlesl was all powerful. Rudolph II having shut himself up in Prague, the members of the Hapsburg family chose the Archduke Matthias to be their head. The Bohemians held to Rudolph II, but wrung from him a rescript (*Majestätsbrief*) in 1609. This confirmed the Bohemian Confession, granted the Protestants permission to use the university, and gave them the right to choose a consistory; it also allowed the three temporal estates of lords, knights, and cities having chartered rights to build Protestant churches and schools. Contrary to the provisions of this agreement, subjects of the Archbishop of Prague built a Protestant church at Klostergrab, and subjects of the Abbot of Braunau did the same at Braunau. The bishops ordered these to be closed, and when the Emperor Matthias supported them the result was (1620) the "Second Defenestration of Prague" with which the Thirty Years War began. The Elector Palatine Frederick V, the head of the Protestant League and of the German Calvinists, was elected King of Bohemia. The cathedral was altered to suit Calvinistic church services. The altars were demolished, the pictures destroyed, and Scultetus, the court preacher, arranged a church service. No ruler ever began to reign under more distressing conditions than Ferdinand II. The insurgents under Thurn stood before the gates of Vienna; those unfriendly to Catholicism within the city made common cause with the enemy. Ferdinand, however, never lost courage. Khlesl, Bishop of Vienna, proved to be too weak and was therefore confined first in the castle of Ambras and then in the castle of Sant' Angelo at Rome. He lived to have the satisfaction of being restored in state to his diocese. He founded in Vienna the Himmelspfortkloster, which commemorates the beautiful legend of the truant nun whose place as doorkeeper was taken during her absence by the Blessed Virgin.

After the battle of the White Mountain, Ferdinand took severe measures against the disturbers of the peace; they were driven out of the country, and finally the rescript, which had been the source of so much trouble, was annulled. A new constitution was published which, among other provisions, made the clergy the highest estate of the land. The emperor was obliged to give Upper Austria in pledge to Bavaria as security for the cost of the war. The cruelties of the Bavarian troops and Ferdinand's order, requiring the people either to leave the country or to return to the old belief, led to a peasant revolt under the leadership of Stephen Fadinger, the proprietor of a farm not far from St. Agatha, which was carried on until Fadinger died of a wound at Linz. The Catholic was now again the dominant religion and the Protestants retired into the little-frequented mountain districts. In Hungary the Government could not accomplish so much. However, Peter Pázmán laboured with success against the spread of the new religious doctrines. Pázmán was born at Grosswardein (Nagy Várad) of Calvinistic parents. At sixteen he changed his creed, then entered the Society of Jesus and studied at Cracow, Vienna, and Rome. At Rome Bellarmine and Vasquez were among his teachers. When professor at Graz he published the "Imitatio Christi". He finally returned to Hungary, became Primate, and gained great influence for the Church through his eloquence, the

gentleness of his character, and his strong patriotic feeling. He brought about the return of fifty noble families to the mother church and was the author of the first Catholic polemic in the Hungarian language, a "Guide to Catholic Truth". He founded at Tyrnau a university which was later transferred to Budapest, and also the Hungarian College at Rome. Believing that the preservation of religion requires worthy servants he founded at Vienna, 1623, a college (Pazmaneum) for the training and instruction of clergy for all the dioceses of Hungary. Ferdinand II called Pázmán his friend. This emperor raised the bishops of Vienna to the rank of prince-bishops (1631). When the terrible religious war came to an end in the Peace of Westphalia, and the diplomats played with religious establishments and monasteries as boys play with nuts, and invented the term "secularization" to express the secular appropriation of the Church's estates, the Hapsburg princes were not willing to commit Austria to such a policy. At this crisis the Hapsburg Dynasty obeyed the directions of Providence. Had the house of Hapsburg then come forward as champions of the new doctrine which originated at Wittenberg, it would have been easy to renew the shattered imperial power in Germany and give to the crown of the Holy Roman Empire a lustre far exceeding that of any other European diadem. But reverence for God and Holy Church had greater weight with the emperors of this line than worldly advantage. For one hundred and twenty years they battled with the storms which the so-called Reformation had stirred up, while the armies of Islam attacked Vienna and the edge of the Ottoman Empire was pushed forward as far as Raab. Even when Louis XIV forced his way in from the West, bringing calamity in his train, and the war cry of the Osmanli was heard within the imperial citadel, the rulers of Austria still trusted in God. Innocent XI sent subsidies, and the saintly Father Marco D'Aviano aroused Christian enthusiasm by preaching a crusade. The feast of the Holy Name of Mary is a reminder that on the 12th of September, 1683, the power of Islam was forever broken before the walls of Vienna, and that the inheritance of St. Stephen was then freed from the Turkish yoke. God sent the rulers of Austria to do His work, and that they did it is an honour exceeding that of the quickly fading garlands which victory twines about the victor's chariot. During this period the Piarist and Ursuline orders were active in the work of education. New bishoprics were founded at Leitmeritz (1656) and Königgrätz (1664). Charles VI raised Vienna in 1722 to an archbishopric. While France at this time pointed with pride and reverence to its famous divines, the great preacher of Vienna was the always clever, but often eccentric, Augustinian, Father Abraham a Sanctâ Clarâ, whose family name was Ulrich Megerle. For example, preaching on the feast of the conversion of St. Paul (*Pauli*), he announced as his theme *Gauli, Mauli, and Fauli*. *Gauli* he interpreted to mean pride and sensuality (*Gaul,* "horse"); *Mauli,* gluttony, drunkenness, and wrangling (*Maul,* "mouth"); *Fauli,* indolence (*faul,* "lazy").

The fifty years preceding the French Revolution are known in history as the period of the "Enlightenment". The Rationalist writers of this period believed that by enlightenment, in their sense of the word, a cure could be found for the evils of the time, and a means of promoting the happiness of mankind. Men were led more and more away from the influence of the Church, the loftier aspirations of noble and pious souls were scorned, and only the claims of a refined sensuality deemed worthy of consideration. The new ideas made their way into Austria, and that country became the birthplace of Josephinism, so called from the Emperor Joseph II, whose policy and legislation embodied these ideas. Maria Theresa forbade the sale of the book written by Febronius, but soon its sale to the learned and discreet was permitted. Urged by her council, Maria Theresa issued the "Placitum regium", made a stole-tax ordinance and obtained from Benedict XIV a reduction of the feast days. By this last regulation all the Apostles are commemorated on the feast of Sts. Peter and Paul, and all the martyrs in the Mass and Breviary on the feast of St. Stephen. The empress also abolished the convent prisons, and ordered that passages in the Breviary lessons for the feast of St. Gregory VII which are opposed to the increase of the secular power should be covered over with paper. She also put a stop to public excommunications and public penances. The last public penance (1769) was that of a merchant at Pyrawart in Lower Austria who had struck an ecclesiastic. He stood for an hour at the church door holding a black candle. When Clement XIV suppressed the Society of Jesus, the Archbishop of Vienna, Cardinal Migazzi, sought to save that order in Austria. "If the members of the order should be scattered, it would not be easy to fill their places; it would cost much expense and time to bring conditions back to the point at which these priests had left their work if they were forced to abandon it." Just twenty years later Migazzi begged the Emperor Francis II to reestablish the order. "I can prove to Your Majesty", he said, "that even the late French ambassador, who was certainly an unprejudiced witness, did not hesitate to say that but for the suppression of the Jesuits France would never have suffered from the Revolution, which brought such terrible results in its train. Three months before the death of Your Majesty's grandmother I heard her say, 'Oh, if I had only followed your advice and had availed myself of your statements!'" After the suppression of the Jesuits their property was converted into a fund for the aid of students, and the whole system of education was remodelled from top to bottom. Rautenstrauch, Abbot of Braunau, drew up a new scheme for a theological course, in which there should be "no squabbles of schools and scholastic chaos". Father Gratian Marx, of the Congregation of the Pious Schools, planned a Realgymnasium (high school without Greek) with six classes, which proved very successful. The common schools, which Maria Theresa had called a political necessity, were reorganized by Abbot John Ignaz Felbiger of Sagen in Prussian Silesia, each parish being given a primary school, each district a high school, and the capital of each province a normal school with which an institute for training teachers was connected. Felbiger wrote the necessary school books. The school at Kaplitz in southern Bohemia, under the supervision of the parish priest, Ferdinand Kindermann, was noted as a model school.

In ten years Joseph II published 6,200 laws, court regulations, and ordinances. Even those measures which were good and appropriate in themselves generally bore the evidences of precipitancy. His very first ordinances were directed against the government of the Catholic Church and aroused discontent by their interference with the affairs of the Church. The acceptance of papal decrees without the sanction of the Government was forbidden. The bishops were forbidden to apply for, or make use of, the quinquennial faculties of the Holy See, on the ground that they had full authority to act for themselves. On the other hand, they were not allowed to issue pastoral letters or instructions without the sanction of the Government. The Government soon began to close those monasteries which were not occupied with the spiritual care of a community, teaching, or nursing, and all the brotherhoods were suspended. About 738 religious houses were closed; 13 in Vienna

alone; 51 in Lower Austria. The property of these conventual institutions was turned into a fund for church expenses, which was to be administered by the several provinces. In Lower Austria alone 231 new parishes were formed. Much discontent was caused by the appointment of an "ecclesiastical court commission" which issued a number of arbitrary regulations concerning public worship: only one Mass was to be celebrated in a church, and that at the high altar; in parish churches, during the seasons of fasting, only two fast-day sermons, on Wednesday and Friday, must be preached; afternoon devotions, the Litany of Loretto, and the Rosary were forbidden; a requiem might be celebrated in a parish church upon the occasion of a death, but not upon the anniversary; it was forbidden to expose the Blessed Sacrament in a monstrance, the ciborium must be used instead; only when the Host was displayed could more than six candles be placed on the altar. A special regulation forbade the dressing of statues of the Virgin and ordered that the bodies of the dead should be buried in sacks and covered with quicklime. Further ordinances forbade the illumination and ornamentation of sacred pictures, the exhibition of relics, and pilgrimages. The Edict of Toleration (1781) granted the private exercise of their religion to Lutherans and Calvinists. The marriage law of 1783 runs: "Marriage in itself is regarded as a purely civil contract. Both this contract and the privileges and obligations arising from it are entirely dependent for their character and force on the secular laws of the land." In 1783, also, all schools, episcopal and monastic, for the training of the clergy were abolished, and general seminaries were founded at Vienna, Budapest, Pavia, and Louvain, with branches at Graz, Olmütz, Prague, Innsbruck, Freiburg, and Pressburg. This measure was intended to check the influence of the bishops in the training of ecclesiastics, and to obtain devoted servants of the State. The Minister of State, Van Swieten, took care that the new schools were supplied with suitable teachers and superintendents.

The first lodge of Freemasons, "Zu den drei Kanonen", was formed at Vienna in 1742; a lodge called "Zu den gekrönten Sternen und zur Redlichkeit" was formed soon after at Prague. Joseph II, however, had no alliance with Freemasons. "I know little about their secrets", he said, "as I never had the curiosity to take part in their mummeries". Still, his words, "The Freemason societies increase and are now to be found in the smallest cities", show the rapid growth of the order. Although many of the representatives of the Church failed to meet the new tendencies with force and courage, the Prince-Archbishop of Vienna, Cardinal Migazzi, attacked them boldly. He wrote vigorously and defended the Church with energy. He was well supported by the Primate of Hungary, Count Joseph Batthyányi, and in the lower provinces by the Cardinal Count von Frankenberg. But their efforts were in vain; the movement continued to grow. In this condition of affairs Pius VI felt it necessary to take some action, and he resolved to visit Vienna. This visit (1782) was very opportune for the emperor and the leaders of the new tendency in the empire. Eybel issued the libellous pamphlet, "Was ist der Papst?" The value of the pamphlet literature of the Josephinist movement is not in proportion to its amount. The roads traversed by the papal cortège were lined with the faithful who were eager to obtain the blessing of the Holy Father. The emperor met the pope at Wiener-Neustadt, and on the 22d of March the two heads of the Christian world entered the imperial city. The emperor showed the pope every attention, but his chancellor of state, Prince Kaunitz, was less considerate. At Easter the pope celebrated High Mass in the church of St. Stephen and afterwards blessed, from the balcony of the church facing Am Hof, the vast throng which filled the square. But the object of the pope's visit was gained only in part, although it may be said that the Josephinist fanaticism began to give place to a more sober mood. When the Holy Father left Vienna, 22 April, after a stay of just one month, the emperor accompanied him as far as Mariabrunn. Here, after praying in the church, the two parted. The next year the emperor visited Rome, where the Spanish ambassador, Azara, and Cardinal Bernis are said to have had a moderating effect upon him. There was no break with the Curia.

One work of lasting value which this emperor undertook was in connexion with diocesan boundaries. He took from the Diocese of Passau that part which lies in Austria and formed with it the See of Linz; the episcopal residence was transferred from Wiener-Neustadt to St. Pölten, Bregenz was made the seat of a vicar-general, and a bishopric was founded at Leoben. The worst blunder committed by Joseph II in his later years was his obstinate adherence, in spite of the warnings of Cardinal Frankenberg, to the scheme of erecting a general seminary at Louvain. Van Swieten put Stöger in charge of it. Stöger was one of the few Catholic priests who had committed themselves unreservedly to the "Enlightenment" movement. Maria Theresa had dismissed him from his position as teacher of church history, and his opinions were to be found in print in his compendium of church history. The career of Aurelius Fessler is a still more distressing example of the influence of the new spirit. Fessler was born in Hungary and came to Vienna as a Capuchin monk. There he became acquainted with Eybel, and as an offset to Eybel's "Was ist der Papst?" issued "Was ist der Kaiser?" Appointed professor of theology at Lemberg, he entered the Freemason lodge "Phönix zur runden Tafel", but was soon obliged to leave Lemberg "on account of debt and frivolous demeanour unsuited to his calling". He became a Lutheran, established himself in Berlin as legal counsellor in ecclesiastical and school cases, got a divorce in order to marry again, and accepted a professorship in the academy at St. Petersburg. Obliged to leave this position in a year's time "on account of atheistical opinions", he succeeded in becoming an Evangelical bishop, and died at St. Petersburg. His "Reminiscences of My Seventy Years' Pilgrimage" presents a melancholy picture of long and weary wanderings.

Although the reforms of Joseph II were well-intentioned, yet the independence of the Church suffered detriment through them. His enactments were drafted by Austrian canonists without any previous understanding with the authorities of the Church, and in violation of her rights (*jus circa sacra*). In many instances the tender germs of religion were killed, and a careless, frivolous way of thinking resulted.

Leopold II, the successor of Joseph II, entered Vienna, 12 March, 1790, and on the 21st of the same month Cardinal Migazzi presented a memorial concerning the painful position of the Austrian Church. As a result, the bishops received an intimation that they were at liberty to point out any serious defects in the existing ecclesiastical conditions. This they did, but, more especially, Cardinal Migazzi enumerated "thirteen grievances and their remedies" in his memorandum. Among these grievances were "the lack of monastic discipline, the general seminaries, the marriage laws, and the Ecclesiastical Commission which had assumed to be the judge of the bishops and their rights". Leopold II virtually suspended the general seminaries, permitted the bishops to have seminaries under their own control, and granted to the monasteries the right to give theological courses. Religious processions were

permitted "to a point not far distant", and Saturday evening devotions were also allowed (without Benediction, however), as well as the exposition of relics.

Francis II was a devout and conscientious Christian, and a ruler who wished to be a father to his people. Nevertheless, it was during his reign that what is called the Josephinist system struck firmer roots. In the first place, the struggle with France, which lasted over twenty years, demanded all the energies of the Government, and during this reign both clergy and people grew more accustomed to the Josephinist regulations. But in addition to this Francis I clung with a childlike devotion to the memory of his uncle Joseph II, whom he called his second father. And, furthermore, whenever any concession was made to the Church, the supporters of Josephinism raised an outcry. In 1793, for instance, the Government was informed that in the church of St. Stephen Mass was celebrated simultaneously at several altars, and that in several places, at the afternoon litanies, Benediction was given with the monstrance. A priest had been the informant. After repeated conferences the cardinal obtained permission to have two Masses said at the same time in the church of St. Stephen but "the Benediction could be given only once at the close of the service". The almost insurmountable difficulty in the way of reform was the ecclesiastical court commission. It was the only means of communication between a bishop and the emperor. Migazzi wished, above everything, to eliminate this difficulty. "I am in all things", he said, "Your Majesty's most dutiful subject. But in his ecclesiastical character the chief shepherd must say boldly that the placing of such fetters upon the guardians of the Church is an offence to all Catholics, and it is a still greater offence that this power is given to men of worldly or untrustworthy reputation, and even to men known to be dangerous or of notorious character." The emperor, indeed, sought to do away with the worst features of the system which had come down to him from his predecessors. He authorized the prayer, the solemn benediction of graves, and the pilgrimages to Mariazell (the first of which, in 1792, was led by Migazzi himself), and the draping of "the poor statues of the Mother of God".

Man cannot at will be stirred to activity or lulled to sleep. However, at the beginning of the nineteenth century a number of circumstances combined to bring about an increase of the religious spirit in Austria. In 1802, the emperor issued two circulars, the first on "the means of elevating the secular clergy" and the second on "the means of improving the regular clergy". To remedy the lack of priests, the first order increased the number of gymnasia, directed the establishment of a theological training-school, with a seminary attached, for each diocese, and granted stipends to divinity students. Ecclesiastics belonging to an order were to wear the habit of their order, and must not live alone; a profession might be made in the twenty-first year, instead of the twenty-fifth. Soon after this the emperor transferred to the bishops the supervision of religious instruction (1808) and the censorship of theological works (1814). Repeated commands to officials required them to attend Sunday church-services. A university service, with a university preacher, was founded for university students. Two days before his death the emperor directed his successor to "complete the work he had begun of rectifying those laws, principles, and methods of managing church affairs which had been introduced since 1780".

The Archbishops of Vienna acted in a manner worthy of their high office. Migazzi's successor, in 1803, was Sigismund Anton Count Hohenwarth, the instructor of the emperor, and a pastor zealous for souls, who devoted himself especially to the theological schools. After him came Vincenz Eduard Milde (d. 1853) who had gained a good reputation as a theorist in pedagogics and as a practical teacher. An important part in arousing the Church was taken by the following court preachers of that period: Vincenz Darnaut, who prepared an Old Testament history; Frint, author of a compendium of religious knowledge (6 vols.), the man at whose suggestion the emperor in 1816 established the advanced school for secular clergy at St. Augustine, and the founder of the Vienna "Theologische Zeitschrift"; Vincenz Eduard Milde was the author of a textbook of the general theory of pedagogics (2 vols.); Johann Michael Leonhard, who published "Christian Doctrines" in four parts and textbooks for grammar schools; Johann Pletz, who continued Frint's periodical and published "Dogmatic Sermons"; Job, confessor to the queen mother, Caroline Augusta; Albert Schlör, who produced "Meditations upon the Entire Gospel for Ecclesiastics and Priests", a work still fruitful. The priests whom the emperor received into Austria after the secularization of the abbeys in the empire were also very active. Thirty-five monks who came from St. Blasien, in the Black Forest to St. Paul in Carinthia pursued serious studies; twenty-five from Wiblingen entered Austrian abbeys. Among these were Sebastian Zängerle, who, "praying, working, and bravely fighting", bequeathed his diocese of Seckau in excellent condition to his successor; and Gregor Thomas Ziegler, who, while professor of dogmatics at Vienna, wrote "On Theological Rationalism", "Foundation of the Catholic Faith", and a "Life of Job". Their efforts were aided by the converts Frederick von Schlegel and Zacharias Werner. Metternich was Schlegel's patron. Schlegel's lectures on modern history and on ancient and modern literature, delivered at Vienna, had a beneficial effect, and the "Konkordia", which he founded, advocated Catholic interests. Werner's conversion was finally effected by the confession of St. Peter. In reading the "Imitation of Christ" his eye happened to fall on the only words of Peter contained in the work (Im., III, liii, 1). He called the "Imitation of Christ" the "pith of all books". (*Tolle, lege.*) During the sessions of the Congress he preached at Vienna with such intense feeling that at times he wept as he recalled with remorse his youthful errors. For a while Hohenwarth entertained him in his palace and Dalberg gave him a gold pen which he presented to the shrine at Mariazell. Werner, who died eleven days after preaching a notable sermon on the feast of the Epiphany, in 1823, was buried at Maria Enzersdorf beside Blessed Clement Maria Hofbauer. Hofbauer was a man of saintly character and prayerful life who, as confessor and preacher, exercised an extraordinary influence over many and was a source of light and instruction for Vienna and Austria. He was born at Tasswitz in Moravia, entered the Redemptorist Order at Rome as its first German member, and was active in the order at Warsaw. He suffered for the Faith, being confined in the fortress of Küstrin, and after coming to Vienna was appointed assistant to the rector of the Italian church through the influence of Archbishop Hohenwarth. He was finally made confessor to the Ursulines. Without noisy effort he produced deep effects. Among his penitents were: Adam von Müller, court councillor and author, whose last words were "Only those facts are worthy of notice which the Catholic Church recognizes as true"; Schlegel; Zacharias Werner; the Princess Jablonowska and Princess Bretzenheim; Privy Councillor Francis de Paul Szeechenyi; Professors Fourerius Ackermann, Zängerle, Ziegler; Bishops Rauscher and Baraga. He converted Silbert Klinkowström and Veith. Hofbauer learned on his death-bed that the emperor had recognized

the congregation as an order, and, filled with joy, he passed away, praising God, 15 March, 1820. Tendler, who followed in Hofbauer's footsteps, was born only six days after his death. Hofbauer was beatified in 1886. Cardinal Rauscher said of him: "Father Hofbauer made the final arrangement of the Concordat possible; he gave to the spirit of the time a better direction".

There were at this time, unfortunately, priests who instead of offering to their fellow-men the pure wheat of the truth sought to give them the chaff of fantastic dreams. Among others, Martin Boos taught that "the Saviour only demands from sinners that they believe in him and make his merits their own. For this reason the formation of a particular society of believers in the living faith is necessary". Boos supported his views by referring to Professor Sailer, but was imprisoned a whole year by the consistory at Augsburg. After this he had a parish at Gallenkirchen, in Upper Austria, but was obliged to resign his position. Thomas Pöschel, a curate, at Ampfelwang, in Upper Austria, received a heavenly revelation that the millennium had begun. This was to be preceded by the arrival of Antichrist, who had just appeared in the person of Napoleon. Pöschel died at Vienna in the infirmary for priests. The "Manharter" in Tyrol took the name of the peasant Manhart, who, influenced by the assistant curate Kaspar Hagleitner, maintained that the acts of the Tyrolese ecclesiastics who had sworn fealty to Napoleon were invalid. The Archbishop of Salzburg, Augustine Gruber, and Cardinal Cappellari (Gregory XVI) quieted the peasants.

In 1848, when, as was said at the bishops' conference at Würzburg, "the judgment of God was passed on thrones and peoples", the devastating storm broke out in Austria. Even Füster, a professor of theology at the University of Vienna and a university preacher, led students astray. The Prince-Archbishop of Vienna, Vincenz Eduard Milde, issued a warning to the entire clergy "to keep within the limits of their calling". Nevertheless, the revolutionary spirit soon threatened the Church. Public demonstrations were made against Archbishop Milde and the papal nuncio, because Pius IX was said to have blessed the Italians who marched out to fight the Austrians. The Redemptorists were driven out of Vienna, and the Jesuits out of Graz. Ronge, whose followers abused the words *German* and *Catholic* by calling themselves "German-Catholic", preached in the Odeon at Vienna and in the taverns at Graz. Unfortunately, Ronge was joined by Hermann Pauli, assistant at Erdberg, and by Hirschberger, chaplain at the home for disabled soldiers. Pauli and Hirschberger came to a sad end: the former died in an insane asylum, the latter committed suicide.

With these exceptions, the clergy of Vienna behaved admirably. In May the curate, Sebastian Brunner, came to the defence of the Church against the hostile press by issuing the "Kirchenzeitung", and the bishops of various dioceses sent memorials and addresses to the ministry, the imperial diet and the emperor, such as: a statement of the bishops of the Archdiocese of Moravia drawn up by Kutschker; petition of the Prince-Bishop of Lavant to the Imperial Diet; petition of the Archbishop of Görz to the Ministry; "What are the Relations of Church and State? An Answer by the bishops of Bohemia"; memorial of the Archbishopric of Salzburg to the Imperial Diet; memorial of the Archdiocese of Vienna to the Diet; memorial of the bishops of the Archdiocese of the maritime district to the constitutional imperial diet at Kremsier. All these brochures sought the independence of the Church, the breaking of her fetters so that she might be free to raise her hand to bless.

As the appeals of individual bishops and dioceses had little effect, the minister of the interior, Count Stadion, summoned the Austrian bishops to Vienna in order to obtain a unanimous expression of their wishes. Hungary and the Lombardo-Venetian provinces were not included, as they were not yet pacified. This first conference of the Austrian bishops met, 29 April to 20 June, 1849, in the archiepiscopal palace. Sixty sittings were held. Schwarzenberg, the "German cardinal", presided, and the lately consecrated Bishop Rauscher was secretary. Hungary was represented by the Bishop of Pécs, Scitvosky. Among the theologians were Court Councillor Zenner, of Vienna; Professor Kutschker, of Olmütz; Canon Tarnoczy, of Salzburg; Canon Wiery, of Lavant; Professor Fessler, of Brixen; Canon Jablinsky, of Tarnow; and Canon Ranolder of Pécs. The voluminous memorials presented to the Government by the conference discussed marriage, the endowment funds for religion, school, and student-stipends, livings and endowments for church-services, instruction, the administration of the church, ecclesiastical offices and church services, monastic houses, ecclesiastical jurisdiction. In the resolutions, which cover 207 paragraphs, the bishops marked out for themselves a common course of action. The resolutions of this first conference of the bishops of Austria were the foundation on which the new structure of the Austrian Church has been built. Before the close of the conference an episcopal committee of five members was formed to press the settlement of the memorials, and to protect the interests of the Church. The chairman of the committee was Cardinal Schwarzenberg, the secretary was Prince-Bishop Rauscher of Seckau. Count Leo Thun, Minister of Instruction, presented the matter at last to His Majesty at two audiences, and the important imperial decrees of 18 and 23 April, 1850, were the result of these interviews. The first ordinance defined the relations of the Catholic Church to the State: Catholics "are at liberty to apply in spiritual matters to the pope"; bishops might issue regulations in matters pertaining to their office without previous permission from state officials; ecclesiastical authorities were allowed to order church punishments; careless administrators of church offices could be suspended. The ordinance of 23 April defined the relations of the Church to public instruction: teachers of religion and theological professors could not be appointed without the consent of the bishop, who could at any time withdraw his ratification; the bishop named one-half of the examining committee at theological examinations; a candidate for a theological doctorate had to subscribe to the Tridentine Confession of Faith in the presence of the bishop before obtaining his degree.

On the 14th of September, 1852, the Emperor Francis Joseph empowered Prince-Bishop Rauscher to act as his representative in drawing up a Concordat, and Pope Pius IX named as his representative, Viale Prelá, the papal nuncio in Vienna. In important questions Rauscher was to consult with the committee on the Church. This committee was composed of Thun, Minister of Instruction; Buol Schauenstein, Minister of Foreign Affairs; Bach, Minister of the Interior; R. von Salvotti, Member of the Imperial Diet; and Freiherr von Kübeck, President of the Imperial Diet. The results of the conferences were to be laid from time to time before the emperor for decision. The negotiations advanced very slowly. The Hungarian bishops presented special *desideria* (requests), the Patriarch of Venice presented *postulata et desideria* (demands and requests). In order to expedite matters, Rauscher spent seven consecutive months in Rome, busied with negotiations. The Concordat was at last signed on the emperor's birthday, 1855. It contains 36 articles. Arts. 5–8

regulate instruction: "All school instruction of Catholic children must be in accordance with the teachings of the Catholic Church; the bishops are to have charge of religious training; professors of theology are to be chosen from men whom the bishop holds to be most suited to the position: only Catholics shall be appointed professors in the gymnasia [middle schools] set aside for Catholic children; the bishops are to select the religious text-books". The bishops have the right to condemn books injurious to religion and morals, and to forbid Catholics reading them (Art. 8). The ecclesiastical judge decides matrimonial suits of an ecclesiastical character (Art. 10). The Holy See does not forbid ecclesiastics who have committed misdemeanours and crimes to be brought before the secular courts (Art. 14). The emperor, in exercising the Apostolic prerogative inherited from his ancestors, of nominating the bishops to be canonically confirmed by the Holy See, will in the future, as in the past, avail himself of the advice of the bishops, especially of the bishops of the archdiocese in which the vacant see lies (Art. 19). In all metropolitan churches the Holy Father appoints the highest dignitary. The emperor still appoints all other dignitaries and the canons of the cathedral (Art. 22). The Holy Father empowers the emperor and his successors to present to all canonries and parishes where the right of patronage is derived from the endowment fund for religious or educational foundations, but in such cases the appointee must be one of three candidates nominated by the bishop as suitable for the position (Art. 25). The bishops have the right to bring religious orders into their dioceses (Art. 28). The estates which form the endowment fund for religious and educational foundations are the property of the Church and are managed in its name, the bishops having the supervision of affairs; the emperor is to aid in making up what is lacking in the fund (Art. 31).

The Concordat was intended to be binding upon the entire monarchy, and to be carried out with uniformity in all parts. Thun, therefore, in the emperor's name, called the bishops of the entire empire to Vienna. On the 6th of April, 1856, the inhabitants of the imperial city saw 66 princes of the Church enter the Cathedral of St. Stephen in state. These ecclesiastics represented the Latin, Greek, and Oriental Rites; among them were German, Hungarian, Italian, and Polish bishops. The procession was closed by the pro-nuncio, Cardinal Viale Prelá. The assembly presented to the Government proposals, requests, and resolutions concerning schools, marriage, church estates, appointment to ecclesiastical benefices, monasteries, patronage of livings. The closing session was held 17 June. The emperor received the bishops in a farewell audience. On this occasion Cardinal Schwarzenberg said: "After God, our hope and trust rest on Your Majesty's piety, wisdom, and justice. When we have reached our dioceses we shall strive most zealously to extend the benefits of the agreement in all directions". In order to make the Concordat effectual, the bishops held synods in their dioceses: at Gran, 1858; Vienna, 1858; Prague, 1860; Kalocsa, 1863. Fresh life showed itself everywhere. It is now acknowledged that schools of all grades accomplished great things under the Concordat. The primary schools were excellently arranged, a course of study which is still in force was drawn up for the gymnasia, and the University of Vienna gained a world wide reputation under Thun, the author of the Concordat. In 1855 the Institute for Research in Austrian history was formed. Famous members of the medical faculty of the university were the professors: Skodra (percussion and auscultation); Rokitansky (pathological anatomy); Oppolzer; Hebra; Stellwag; Hyrtl; Brücke, and Billroth, the last named being the leading sur-

SALZBURG

ST. PETER'S ABBEY AND FRANCISCAN CHURCH

geon of the century. Upon Rauscher's suggestion the number of professors in the department of dogmatic theology of the University of Vienna was increased, in order to ensure a more extended course in this branch. The new men called were, Father Philip Guidi, O.P., and Father Clemens Schrader, S.J., both from Rome. The lectures were obligatory on divinity students in any one year of the four years' course, and were intended also for priests desirous of instruction. The successful development of art during this period is shown in the church of Altlerchenfeld in Vienna, which was consecrated in 1861. This fine structure was built from the designs of the architect John George Müller, and was decorated with a series of mural paintings by Joseph Führich, professor at the Academy of Fine Arts in Vienna. These paintings combine art and true dogma most admirably, and Führich is in them a veritable teacher of the Faith. He was born at Krazau in Bohemia, studied art first at the academy in Prague, afterwards for two years at Rome, and coming to Vienna passed forty-two studious and fruitful years there (d. 1876). Among the large number of his religious paintings the most famous are: The Paternoster; the Way of the Cross, in the church of St. John on the Prater, Vienna, copies of which can be found in all parts of the world; the Way to Bethlehem; illustrations of the Psalter and the Imitation of Christ; the Prodigal Son; the Book of Ruth. The manner in which Führich developed his scheme of thought in the series of pictures in the Altlerchenfeld church is extremely impressive. Pictures in churches, according to his view, were not merely decorative; through the senses they must unfold to the spirit that inner life of faith which finds its full development in the church. In the vestibule of the church, six pictures portray the work of creation, and a seventh sets forth the rest of the Creator on the Sabbath. The paintings in the two side aisles represent the Church of the Old Testament, which kept alive the longing for salvation and proclaimed its coming. The paintings of the middle aisle portray the fulfilment of the promise by scenes from the life of Christ. Between the historical pictures are placed at intervals the figure of the Saviour with appropriate historical emblems, such as Christ as a gardener, with a hoe on the shoulder. This is followed by a picture of the owner of the vineyard commanding the gardener to cut down the unfruitful tree. Then Christ as shepherd, followed by an allegorical picture of the transferring of the office of shepherd to Peter; Christ the wayfarer, followed by a representation of the man who fell among thieves; Christ the sower, followed by the approaching harvester with his sickle. These paintings, with those representing the Sermon on the Mount, decorate the church as far as the pulpit. The high altar is adorned with a picture of the Most Holy Trinity. The conception running through the whole series of paintings, from those in the vestibule to that of the high altar, is that the paradise lost by the first human beings is offered to us again by the second Adam in the new heaven.

At this moment of renewed energy in the church, Austria possessed bishops who would have excited the envy of little Cappadocia at the time of the three great Cappadocians. Among these Austrian bishops were: Cardinal Schwarzenberg (d. 1885) and Cardinal Rauscher (d. 1875; life by Wolfsgruber); Francis Joseph Rudigier, Bishop of Linz (d. 1879; life by Meindl); Vincenz Gasser, Prince-Bishop of Brixen (d. 1879; life by Zobl); Joseph Fessler, Bishop of St. Pölten (d. 1872; life by Erdinger); John B. Zwerger, Prince-Bishop of Seckau (d. 1893; life by Oer). The description of this period would not be complete without mention of the foremost German preacher and most fruitful German theologian of the nine-

teenth century, John Emanuel Veith, and of the philosopher and priest, Anton Günther. Veith was born at Kuttenplan, in Bohemia, and was of Jewish parentage. When he was nine years old his spiritual struggles began. In his twenty-first year, led by Father Hofbauer, he found peace in the Church. He faithfully kept the vow he had made: "I will devote my entire life to the only thing that is eternal, and therefore, the only thing that is important." Veith became a priest, preached for fourteen years in the Cathedral of St. Stephen at Vienna and died in 1876. At the time of his last illness he was preparing a translation, with commentary, of the Canticle of Canticles. On the day of his death he wrote down the words of Sulamit:

> Neu auch wollen wir dort oben
> Lieb und Treue ihm geloben.

—"Afresh will we there above vow to him our faith and love." Then, putting the pen aside, he said, "It is finished", and breathed his last. (Life by Löwe.) Richness of thought and a classic elegance of speech characterized Veith's sermons. Among those published are: "Die Leidenswerkzeuge Christi"; "Denkbüchlein von der göttlichen Liebe"; "Das Friedensopfer"; "Lebensbilder aus der Passionsgeschichte"; "Die heiligen Berge" (2 vols.); "Homilienkranz" (5 vols.); "Der verlorne Sohn"; "Die Samaritin"; "Die Erweckung des Lazarus"; "Mater Dolorosa"; "Festpredigten" (2 vols.); "Die Anfänge der Menschenwelt"; "Der Blindgeborne"; "Politische Passionspredigten"; "Eucharistie"; "Weltleben und Christentum"; "Charitas"; "Worte der Feinde Christi"; "Misericordia" (Psalm *Miserere*); "Das Vaterunser"; "Weg, Wahrheit, und Leben"; "Dodekatheon" (2 vols.); "Die Mächte des Unheils"; "Die Anfänge der Menschenwelt"; "Die Stufenpsalmen"; "Prophetie und Glaube"; "Homiletische Aehrenlese" (2 vols.); "Meditationen über den 118. Psalm"; "Hundert Psalmen"; "Der Leidenweg des Herrn"; "Stechpalmen"; "Dikaiosyne, Die Epistelreihe des Kirchenjahres". Karl Werner, the son of a teacher, was born at Hafnerbach in Lower Austria and died in 1888. He was first professor of moral theology at St. Pölten, then professor of higher exegesis at the University of Vienna. In Vienna he was appointed member of the advisory council of the minister of instruction, and was elected member of the Imperial Academy of Sciences. Among the many works of learned research Werner published are: "System der Ethik" (2 vols.); "Grundlinien der Philosophie"; "Der hl. Thomas von Aquino" (3 vols.); "Franz Suarez und die Scholastik der letzten Jahrhunderte" (2 vols.); "Geschichte der apologetischen und polemischen Literatur der christlichen Theologie"; "Geschichte der katholischen Theologie seit dem Trienter Konzil bis zur Gegenwart"; "Spekulative Anthropologie vom christlich-philosophischen Standpunkt"; "Beda der Ehrwürdige und seine Zeit"; "Alkuin und sein Jahrhundert"; "Gerbert von Aurillac, die Kirche und Wissenschaft seiner Zeit"; "Giambattista Vico als Philosoph und gelehrter Forscher"; "Johannes Duns Scotus"; "Geschichte der Scholastik des späteren Mittelalters" (5 vols.); "Geschichte der italienischen Philosophie des 19. Jahrh." Many of Werner's treatises are to be found in the reports of the sessions of the philosophico-historical section of the Imperial Academy of Sciences. Anton Günther, founder of the Guntherian school of philosophy, was born at Lindenau, near Leitmeritz, in Bohemia. He studied jurisprudence and philosophy at Prague, and came under the influence of the philosophical ideas of Kant, Fichte, and Jacobi. Blessed Clement Hofbauer led him back to the truth. Günther was consecrated priest, and became teacher of philosophy in noble families, especially in that to which Schwarzenberg, afterwards Cardinal, belonged. For many years he filled the modest position of sacristan of St. Ruprecht, the oldest church in Vienna. After a life spent in philosophical study he died in 1876 (life by Knoodt). Günther's chief works are: "Vorschule zur spekula- tiven Theologie des Christentums"; "Peregrins Gastmal"; "Süd- und Nordlichter am Horizont spekulativer Theologie"; "Janusköpfe für Philoso- phie und Theologie"; "Möhler der letzte Symboliker"; "Thomas a Scrupulis, zur Transfiguration der Persönlichkeits Pantheismen neuster Zeit"; "Die Justes-Milieux in der deutschen Philosophie gegen- wärtiger Zeit"; "Eurystheus und Herakles"; "Lydia" (a philosophical annual, in collaboration with Veith). Honestly intending to defend faith against the philosophical doubtings which are constantly arising in modern times, Günther fell into the mistake of making the mysteries of faith dependent on their recognition by the understanding, so that knowledge was substituted for faith. A learned war broke out in Germany, in which Günther's position was dam- aged by the vagaries of his followers, and at the end of five years' examination the Congregation of the Index condemned his writings. After the first ex- citement had subsided Günther gave a proof of the honesty of opinion which had characterized his action from the start. The verdict of the Congregation of the Index was sent to him 23 January, 1857; on 10 February he handed Cardinal Rauscher his sub- mission, to be forwarded to the Holy Father and to Cardinal Andrea, Prefect of the Congregation of the Index. The thought which consoled Günther in these days of trial was that God demanded of every man the sacrifice of his Isaac, and that this sacrifice was what he now made to God.

Goethe says that the subject of profoundest interest in the history of the world is the battle of disbelief against faith. This is still more true of the history of the Church. In 1860 Austria became a constitu- tional monarchy, and in the next year the founda- tions of a representative government were laid. The Imperial Parliament was to consist of a House of Peers, to which the archbishops and prince-bishop were to belong, and a House of Deputies. During the first session of the Parliament, Maager, a Protes- tant deputy, attacked the Concordat and demanded its revision. Upon this the members of the episco- pacy in the Upper House and some other bishops met and prepared a memorial which was sent to the emperor. "Of all the party cries", it ran, "which are put to effective use in electioneering, none has so much prominence at present as the word *toleration*. True toleration is exercised by the Catholic Church, while the harshest intolerance is practised on all sides against the Catholic Church. All its ordinances and institutions are slandered and mistrusted, and every exhibition of Catholic conviction is over- whelmed with scorn and derision." The events just noted were merely the forerunners of a terrible storm which broke after the disastrous war of 1866. In July of the next year Deputy Herbst moved the preparation of three bills concerning marriage, schools, and the mutual relations of the different religious denominations. A conference of twenty- four bishops was held at Vienna, and a second me- morial was sent to the emperor which contained the following: "A party has arisen which has chosen this time of distress for an attack on the religion to which Your Majesty, the Imperial family, and a great majority of the inhabitants of the land belong. We are in the presence of a spectacle which causes the enemies of Austria to smile derisively, and which fills Austria's sons with shame rather than with anxiety." Marriage without the blessing of the Church, schools without religion were demanded. In order to obtain suitable teachers for these schools it was proposed to found for the training of teachers institutions where contempt for all that is holy

should be instilled. It was not possible, however, to resist the liberal pressure. On the 21st of Decem- ber, 1867, the new fundamental laws received the imperial approval. The first granted full freedom of faith and conscience and freedom in scientific opinion. The second declared: "All jurisdiction in the state is exercised in the name of the emperor". Thereby the Church's exclusive jurisdiction over marriage was impugned. The third law obliged all officials to take an oath to support the constitu- tion. Two professors of dogmatics did not take the oath; these were Schrader, the Jesuit, and Hyacinth Pellegrinetti, the Dominican successor of Guidi. They were obliged to resign their professorships, and their places have not yet been filled.

During this same period the dual constitution was sanctioned, by which the Austro-Hungarian Mon- archy as it now exists, was formed "of two distinct co-ordinate States having the same constitutional, legal, and administrative rights". After a long struggle the emperor signed, 25 May, 1868, the laws concerning marriage, schools, and the status of the several denominations. The first of these laws declares marriage to be a civil contract, makes the civil marriage obligatory, and takes from the Church the judicial power *pro foro externo* in matrimonial suits. The law concerning schools takes from the bishop any control of the management as well as the right of supervision. These powers are given to an official school committee of the district and town, of which committee ecclesiastics can be chosen members. The bishops select the books used by the catechist and instructors in religious doctrine. The third law grants everyone the right to choose his own religion on attaining the age of fourteen years, but a child between seven and fourteen years of age cannot change his or her religion even at the wish of the parents. As these laws infringed the Concordat in essentials, a secret consistory was held at Rome, 22 June, at which the pope declared: "Leges auctoritate Nostrâ apostolicâ reprobamus, damnamus et decreta ipsa irrita prorsus nulliusque roboris fuisse ac fore declaramus." ("By Our Apostolic authority we reprobate and condemn these laws, and declare that their purport was, and shall be, wholly invalid and of no force.") The bishops upon this issued pastorals. The joint letter of 3 June issued by the Bohemian bishops to the clergy and their joint pastoral of 24 June were condemned by the imperial civil courts of all three instances, on the ground that they were a disturbance of the public peace, and suppressed. Penal proceed- ings were not brought against Cardinal Schwarzen- berg, but Bishop Francis Joseph Rudigier, of Linz, was prosecuted for his pastoral of 7 September. "On account of the misdemeanour committed in the pastoral letter"—of calling the law of 24 May a lie—he was brought before the Supreme Court, found guilty by the jury, and condemned to fourteen days' imprisonment with costs. The pastoral was ordered to be destroyed. Next day the emperor in a decree remitted the punishment and its legal consequences. The bishops disagreed as to whether the clergy should permit themselves to be chosen members of the school committees, but Rauscher and Schwarzenberg, who were for the permission, carried their point.

The definition of the pope's infallibility afforded von Stremayr, the Austrian Minister of Instruction, a pretext to demand the abrogation of the Concordat, on the plea that the pope, one of the contracting parties, had received from the definition a new character, which invalidated the original agreement. Beust, the Minister of Foreign Affairs, addressed to Palomba a note which declared: "The Concordat exists no longer; it is annulled." The abrogation of the Concordat produced a gap in religious legislation. To remedy this four bills were introduced, January, 1874, for regulating the legal status of the Catholic Church, the taxing of the fund for the support of religion, the legal status of monasteries, and the recognition of new religious societies. The pope expressed, on the 7th of March, his grief at the attack on the rights of the Church, implied in the assertion that the supreme power in all matters concerning the external life belonged to the State. The bishops assembled again at Vienna and sent this statement to the Ministry and the Upper House: "We repeat that we are ready to agree to the demands which the State makes on us in the bill concerning the legal status of the Catholic Church as far as these demands are in harmony with the Concordat concerning these matters. We cannot and will not acquiesce in a proposition the consummation of which would endanger the welfare of the Church."

One of the chief causes of the scarcity of priests which now began to be marked was the new law of national defence. By this law youths in their twentieth year during their course at a gymnasium were subject to military duty. The bishops again and again begged for a relaxation of the provisions of the law. But they had, for the time being, no redress except to appeal in individual cases to the indulgence of the emperor. When the bills reached the upper house the bishops defended themselves bravely. Rauscher closed his address of 10 April with these words: "So-called progress no longer considers it necessary to conceal its real aim, and has unmasked its hate against God and eternal truth. But Providence has set a natural limit to all things. The destruction of Christianity is impossible, but Austria may be destroyed if the war against religion is not checked in good time." Yet, for all this, the first two bills became law, 7 May, 1874. Among other things, the law concerning the legal status of the Church declares that: In order to obtain any ecclesiastical appointment or living, a candidate's record of past conduct must be blameless when judged by the standard of the civil law (§ 1); if the Government finds that an ecclesiastical regulation respecting a public church service is not consistent with the public interest, the Government shall then forbid it (§ 17); the total number of Catholics living in the district of a parish form the parish community (§ 35); in order to cover the expenses of a parish a tax is to be laid on its members (§ 36); the ministry of public worship and instruction is authorized to oversee the management of the funds of the churches and church institutions (§ 38); the ministry of public worship and instruction is to take care that the ecclesiastical journals do not go beyond the sphere of their proper activity (§ 60). The law concerning contributions to the fund for the support of religion declares that: Assessments shall be made on incumbents of livings and the communities of the regular orders for the fund for the support of religion in order to meet the expenses of Catholic worship and especially in order to increase the incomes of pastors which have been until now very small (§ 1); the value of the entire property of the living or of the community shall be taken as the basis (of the assessment) (§ 2); the amount of the assessments shall be fixed every ten years for the next ten years (§ 9); and they were to be "one-half of one per cent on amounts up to 10,000 florins [$4,000], one-and-a-half per cent on amounts from 10,000 florins to 20,000 florins [$4,000 to $8,000], and 10 per cent on all amounts over 90,000 florins [$36,000]". The law (signed 20 May) in regard to the legal recognition of religious societies "accepts in full" the principle of religious equality.

Since the passage of these three laws no further enactments have so far been made, with regard to the status of the various denominations in Austria. In the year following their passage Cardinal

Rauscher died (24 Nov., 1875). It was due to his wise moderation and caution that Austria escaped the evils of a *Kulturkampf* (religious conflict). In 1874, von Stremayr offered four projects for bills in the House of Deputies, one of which dealt with the legal status of monastic communities. Rauscher said that it "bore on its forehead unusual marks of mistrust, arbitrariness, and harshness. According to its provisions, the authority of the minister of worship of the time being would be sufficient to sweep from the earth a monastic house which had existed for a thousand years and to enforce the sequestration of its property." The bill reached the Upper House by the middle of January, 1876. But Cardinal Schwarzenberg succeeded, by means of a memorial of the Austrian archbishops and bishops, in inducing the emperor not to sign it, and the bill has not yet become law.

The parliamentary election of 1879 increased the number of conservative members so that the Right (*Hohenwart*) Party was in the majority. In 1882, the Karl Ferdinand University, at Prague, was divided into a German and a Czech university. Cardinal Schwarzenberg, however, would not consent to a division of the theological faculty. He wrote to the minister, Conrad von Eybesfeld: "The Church does not wish the separation of the nations, but their union in one body, the head of which is Christ. She dedicates the blessings of her activity to all nations, she recognizes the right of every people to independence, she respects and supports the demands of a people for its own language and its own form of instruction. But the Church cannot give to the claims of nationality the first place, they must always be for her a secondary interest. The theological faculty must impress this idea upon their pupils and must not, therefore, drive them apart. They should not deepen and embitter the national differences by a separation; they should strive rather to compose these differences. This duty is above all necessary among the various nationalities of Bohemia. In this country it is a special duty of the priesthood to seek to soothe and unify." The separation took place, however, directly after Schwarzenberg's death.

An amendment to the school law which somewhat improved matters was laid before the Upper House in 1883. This amendment was the result of numerous memorials from the bishops to the Government and much effort of other kinds. During the debate on the amendment Cardinal Schwarzenberg said: "The bishops for whom I speak to-day recognize the value of the amendment and are ready to work for its passage. But this does not justify the presumption that we consider the amendment as remedying all defects of the school laws, and that our votes are a corroboration of these laws. Only a denominational system of common schools can satisfy the claims of the Church and of the Christian community. The present system is unsatisfactory. While we now give our support, we reserve the right to press our just demands by way of legislation in the future." The amendment made certain concessions to children who had attended school for six years, and permitted only such persons to be made the principals of schools as were competent to give instruction in the faith to which the majority of the scholars belonged.

Cardinal Schwarzenberg had presided over every meeting of the Austrian bishops since 1849, and had always fulfilled faithfully the duties of the cardinalate. At the meeting of the bishops at Vienna in 1885 he was unable, through illness, to preside at the 8th session. The next day he appeared, although unfit to attend. He was not able to be present again and died of pneumonia 27 March.

A bill called the Prince Alfred Liechtenstein school bill was introduced in October, 1888. It was intended to give the Church greater power over the schools. But while the bishops pressed the demand of "Catholic schools for Catholic children", the social-democratic convention which met the same year at Hainburg, took its stand upon "common schools without religious teaching, the separation of Church and State, religious belief is a private matter". Gregr, of the Young Czech party, also declared in behalf of his party associates: "A Liechtenstein has come again to dig a grave for the Bohemian nation, the grave of ignorance and demoralization." This was an allusion to what had happened after the battle of the White Mountain (1620). Against such opposition the bill could not be carried.

In 1891 Leo XIII regulated the meetings of the Austrian bishops in a manner which has proved fruitful in blessings. A meeting is to be held in Vienna every year. These meetings are either special or general. At these special meetings committees prepare elaborate and exact reports which are laid before the general assembly that meets at least once every five years. These assemblies of the bishops decide the course of the Church. The Austrian bishops feel and act as a unit, as a harmonious episcopacy. Schwarzenberg's successor, Cardinal Count Schönborn, died in 1899. Cardinal Gruscha, Archbishop of Vienna, followed him at the head of the episcopacy. In reviewing the action of the bishops in their conferences since this time, it is clear that the matter which has chiefly occupied their attention has been the schools of every grade. In all their memorials to state officials, and in all their pastorals to the faithful, one thought continually appears like a vein of gold: a child should learn in school the duties of a Christian and a citizen. This end can be realized only when religion is made the central point of education from which everything radiates, to which everything returns. For this reason the bishops sought (1897, 1898) to obtain the consent of the ministry to an increase in the time given to religious instruction in the primary and secondary schools. Prizes were offered for the preparation of a Bible (1898). Two catechisms, a larger and a smaller one, were prepared after eight years' work. These were accepted by the bishops in 1897 and issued with explanatory directions. During this period religious instruction in the middle schools was rearranged, and religious exercises were again introduced. Religious societies (Sodalities of the Blessed Virgin Mary) were organized in 1897 and 1902. Religious instruction was introduced into the Sunday industrial schools (1898). Proposals were made as to the education of teachers of religion in the middle and normal schools (1901). The preparation of a correct textbook of psychology was urged (1894). Prizes were offered for textbooks on religion (1897). The bishops succeeded in obtaining a systematized course in philosophy for the theological schools (1892); they obtained, further, a rearrangement of theological studies and examinations. (Dissertations must be suitable for publication and three examinations are obligatory for a doctorate.) They complained of the spirit prevalent at the universities (1891) and of the unfair treatment of the student-societies composed of faithful Catholic students (1901).

During the reign of Maria Theresa an educational fund was created from confiscated property of the Jesuits. Under Joseph II a religious fund was created from the church property administered by the State only. But Joseph II acknowledged that the State was bound to pay the expenses of Catholic worship, for which the church revenues did not suffice. The salary of parish priests was fixed at 400 florins ($160), that of the curates at 200 florins ($80). The retiring pension was made 200 florins ($80). These sums remained unchanged for one hundred years, although the cost of living and the value of money had varied. The speech from the throne in 1871 and 1879 referred to the improvement of the material condition of the clergy as an object of solicitude on the part of the Government, and since 1872 state subventions have been granted for this purpose. In order to obtain the money for this subvention, a tax for the maintenance of the religious fund was created in 1874. But although a sum reaching ten per cent of the capital fund was demanded every ten years, few priests received from it assistance amounting to more than 100 florins ($40). As this subvention was called an "advance" to the fund for the support of religion in the different provinces, the debts of the provinces grew every year, and the entire religious fund was in danger of being used up. The bishops, therefore, sent repeated appeals to the Government, praying for a suitable increase of the salaries of the clergy. In 1903 they agreed to demand for active pastors: (a) for curates a minimum salary of 1,000 crowns ($200); for pastors of second-class parishes 1,600 crowns ($320); for parish priests without curates, 2,000 crowns ($400); for parish priests with curates, 2,200 crowns ($440); (b) four retroactive decennial allowances to be reckoned from the date of the grant; the first allowance to be 100 crowns ($20), the second, 200 crowns ($40), the third and fourth to be each 250 crowns ($50), in all 800 crowns ($160). (c) Surplus of money destined for pastoral salaries is not to be drawn upon for the pensions of retired clergymen. For retired curates the bishops suggested a minimum pension of 100 crowns for curates, and of 1,900 crowns ($380) for parish priests. In 1891 and 1894 the bishop requested from the Minister of Worship an exact list of all the debts due by the religious fund in the hands of the Government and of all pious foundations. In 1891 and 1897 they deliberated concerning the delicate question of clerical fees. After a ten years' trial (1893) the bishops pointed out the hardship of the tax on the religious fund, and pointed out where amendment should be made. The bishops repeatedly discussed (1898, 1899, 1900) the law which promised the formation of parishes. The difficult question of the patronage of livings was also taken up (1899). The Christian character of the family life, the education of the young, the duty of voting ("Vote, vote right") were repeatedly the subjects of joint pastoral letters (1891, 1901). The bishops discussed the question of founding and supporting a daily religious newspaper (1891, 1892). They assured the Holy Father of their agreement with his letter to Cardinal Guibert, Archbishop of Paris, concerning the disrespectful utterances of Catholic papers about ecclesiastical authorities. They discussed uniform action in carrying out the Apostolic constitution "Officiorum ac munerum" as applied to Catholic newspapers (1898).

As in our day large results are only obtained by association, the bishops have especially encouraged the formation of workingmen's unions, of Gesellenvereine, the St. Boniface Society (March, 1901), the Holy Childhood Society, and benevolent societies (November, 1897). In these days much that is unsound rises to the surface. The bishops issued warnings against irreligion and national embitterment (1891). They encouraged lectures on Freemasonry (1897), complained of the destructive tendencies which are undoing the strength and force of Austria, and condemned the bad press, "the dangerous foe of faith" (December, 1901).

In 1897 a movement was set on foot which ten years before would have been held to be impossible. Its name, the *Los von Rom*, is an insult to Catholics, its existence a mortal blow to Austrians. Every possible misuse of speech and writing was employed to rob Catholics of their confidence in their priests, of their attachment to the holy sacraments, and even to the Church. These ribald foes spread desolation over a good part of God's vineyard in Austria. The "Free from Rome" movement will remain a disgraceful stain, but not in the history of the Catholic Church. Filled with a sense of the sacredness of their duty as bishops and Austrians, the episcopacy warned the faithful in pastorals against the movement and its schemes (1899, 1901). They addressed an earnest memorial to the emperor on the subject (1901), as well as one to Körber, the head of the ministry (November, 1902).

In 1891 the bishops deliberated on cremation and funeral addresses by non-Catholic clergymen in Catholic cemeteries; in 1898 they drew up a form of reconciliation for duellists and their seconds. They exhorted Catholics "to observe faithfully the ordinances against duelling, whether issued by God, the Church, or the State". After due deliberations, they also adopted resolutions on the position of catechists and the admission of catechetical teachers into the ecclesiastical organization and arranged the manner in which erring ecclesiastics "should be led back to their calling and to the service of God by their fellow-clergymen". In 1891 they issued regulations concerning the social activity of the clergy, and in 1901 concerning clerical conventions and legal societies.

The bishops aided the several religious communities, and watched over the loyalty of the religious orders. In 1889 the relation of the bishops to the election and consecration of the abbots of new religious foundations was defined. In 1891, the pope granted permission to the strictly cloistered orders of women (Ursulines) to attend university lectures. The Austrian bishops celebrated the diamond jubilee of the consecration of Leo XIII to the priesthood and the golden jubilee of his consecration to the episcopacy by joint letters of veneration to the Holy Father and by joint pastorals to the faithful. In these letters they did not fail to express their regret on the subject of the so-called Roman question, of the offensive Giordano Bruno celebration, and of the 25th anniversary of the taking of Rome. In 1903 they sent a magnificent letter of congratulation to the Holy Father, Pius X.

We must go back five hundred years in the history of Austria to find another ruler who reigned fifty years. On the semi-centennial anniversary, 2 December, 1898, of the reign of the Emperor Francis Joseph, the bishops issued a joint pastoral and sent it with a dedication to the emperor. In the dedication they say: "The mysterious counsels of God have ordained that Your Majesty should spend this day in sorrow. [Empress Elizabeth was assassinated 10 September.] We all suffer with our gracious emperor and ruler. But our grief cannot silence our gratitude; our gratitude to our Lord God who has preserved Your Majesty for us, our gratitude to Your Majesty for fifty years of strong and fatherly protection, for fifty years of self-sacrificing love, for fifty years of exemplary devotion to Your Majesty's exalted but arduous calling."

Since 1851 all the provinces of the Austrian Crown have been under one uniform government. Since 1867, however, Hungary has been an independent part of the Hapsburg monarchy, enjoying equal rights with the rest. During the battle over the Concordat which raged in 1867, the Hungarian bishops did not appeal to the Concordat, for fear that the agitation might spread to Hungary. In point of fact, however, they held fast to the Concordat. John Simor, Primate of Hungary from 1866-91, preserved the peace of the Church in the kingdom. There was a conflict, however, respecting the laws concerning baptism. A law of 1868 enacted that in the case of mixed marriages the boys should be brought up in the faith of the father, the girls in that of the mother, even if this were contrary to

the desire of the parents. But, when parents so requested, Catholic priests baptized those children who according to the law should be brought up non-Catholic. This practice was called *Wegtaufen*. Even when, in 1879, the criminal code made the conferring of baptism under such circumstances punishable, the priests were not dismayed—"Go, baptize". Besides this, they were regularly acquitted by the court of last resort in the suits which were brought against them by the Protestant pastors. In 1890 "denunciation" of such baptisms was forbidden by Rome, and the excitement gradually subsided. Augustine von Roskovány, Bishop of Neutra, was the most learned man among the Hungarian bishops of this time. Von Roskovány was Doctor of Philosophy and Theology, secretary to Ladislaus Pyrker, Archbishop of Erlau, and died in 1892. His works are important authorities: "De Matrimoniis mixtis" (7 vols.); "Monumenta pro independentiâ potestatis eccles. ab imperio civili" (13 vols.); "Cœlibatus et Breviarium" (2 vols.); "Beata Virgo Maria in suo Conceptu immaculata" (9 vols.); "Romanus Pontifex Primas ecclesiæ et Princeps civilis e monumentis omnium sæculorum" (16 vols.); "Matrimonium in ecclesiâ Catholicâ potestati ecclesiasticæ subjectum" (4 vols.); "Supplementa ad Collectiones Monumentorum et Literaturæ" (10 vols.).

In 1893 the Hungarian Parliament began to meddle with religion. The head of the ministry, Wekerle, introduced three bills enacting that returns of marriages, births, and deaths should be made by a civil registrar; that the Jewish religion should be legally recognized, that permission should be given for its free exercise, and the right to enter or leave the Jewish faith should be granted. These bills were soon followed by others for the amendment of the marriage laws (civil marriage made compulsory) and concerning mixed marriages. Wekerle carried the first three bills, and they became law. Baron Desiderius Banffy was made the head of the ministry, January, 1895. In order to prevent the passage of the two remaining bills by Banffy, the papal nuncio, Agliardi, went to Hungary. But the Hungarian Parliament declared that such interference in the internal affairs of Hungary would not be permitted. Count Kalnocky, the Minister of Foreign Affairs, who had supported the nuncio, was replaced by Count Agenor Goluchowsky, and Agliardi was made a cardinal and recalled to Rome. The road was now clear. Count Ferdinand Zichy formed the Catholic people's party in opposition to Banffy's aims; but without avail. The two bills became law. The Lutz amendment on pulpits could not be passed during the lifetime of the primate, Simor, but after his death it was adopted (1899).

Article 26 of the Diet of 1790 guaranteed to the Protestants of Hungary the entire control of the affairs of their religion. The Government has hardly any power in regard to either their churches, their schools, or religious foundations. Since 1848 the Catholics have been endeavouring to obtain autonomy. The Catholic congress of 1870 prepared a bill to this end. The Catholic Autonomy Association, consisting of the bishops, the abbots, and certain elected members, clerical and lay, exists to represent the Church in regard to the faithful, on the one hand, and the Government, on the other, in all questions of schools, of church property, and especially (since the minister of public worship might happen to be a non-Catholic) to advise the king in the exercise of his prerogative of nominating bishops. It is plain that the advantage or disadvantage to the Church of autonomy would depend on the composition of the commission. For this reason a commission such as Wekerle wished to form in 1894 was rejected by the bishops, and Zichy's motion, made on occasion of the Catholic congress of 1897, did not receive government approval. In order to strengthen the claim for autonomy, the bishops, with the exception of Bishop Count Maylath, and the heads of the orders, in 1903, accepted three propositions. These are: that the right to present to bishoprics shall remain in the hands of the minister of worship; that the school system shall remain unaltered; that the fund for the support of religion shall be controlled by the minister of instruction. In 1906 the turning-point in the history of the autonomy question was probably reached in the address from the throne. The Minister of Public worship and Instruction, Count Albert Apponyi, has already requested the primate to state the position of the bishops in regard to autonomy, so that the bill may be properly prepared.

ECCLESIASTICAL ORGANIZATION.—The Catholic Church in Austria-Hungary is administered on the system of archiepiscopal provinces with suffragan dioceses, as follows:—

(a) *In the territories represented in the Imperial (Austrian) Parliament* there are seven archiepiscopal provinces of the Latin Rite and one each of the Greek and Armenian Rites. These provinces comprise in the aggregate 34 sees. *Archdiocese of Vienna* (bishopric 1468, prince-bishopric 1631, prince-archbishopric 1722), with suffragan dioceses of *St. Pölten* (or *St. Hippolytus;* transferred from Wiener-Neustadt, 1784) and *Linz* (founded 1784). *Archdiocese of Salzburg* (founded c. 700, archbishopric 800), with suffragan dioceses of *Trent* (founded in second century), *Brixen* (transferred from Säben in tenth century) with the general vicariate of Feldkirch for Vorarlberg, *Gurk* (belonging to Klagenfurt, founded 1071), *Seckau* (belonging to Graz, founded 1219), and *Lavant* (belonging to Marburg, founded 1228). *Archdiocese of Prague* (973–1344 subject to Mainz, 1344 archbishopric), with suffragan dioceses of *Budweis* (founded 1785), *Königgrätz* (or *Regina Hradecensis,* founded 1664), and *Leitmeritz* (founded 1665). *Archdiocese of Olmütz* (founded 1063, archbishopric 1777), with suffragan diocese of *Brünn* (founded 1777). *Archdiocese of Görz* (transferred from Aquileia 1751), with suffragan dioceses of *Laibach* (founded 1461), *Triest and Capo d'Istria, Parenzo and Pola* (founded sixth century), *Veglia* (founded 990). *Archdiocese of Zara* (*Jadera,* founded fourth century, archbishopric 1146), with suffragan dioceses of *Sebenico* (founded 1298), *Spalato and Macarska* (Spalato erected into an archbishopric 650), *Lesina* (*Pharus,* founded in twelfth century), *Cattaro* (founded in eleventh century), *Ragusa* (founded 990). *Archdiocese of Lemberg* (*Leopolis,* Latin Rite; transferred from Halic 1412), with suffragan dioceses of *Tarnów* (founded 1783, transferred to Tynice, then to Bochnia, 1816), and *Przemyśl* (founded 1340). The *Prince-Bishopric of Cracow* (founded about 700) is subject directly to the Holy See. The Catholics in Silesia are under the jurisdiction of the Prince-Bishop of Breslau, who has a vicar-general at Teschen and a summer residence at Johannesberg. The county of Glatz belongs to Prague. *Lemberg,* Greek-Ruthenian Rite (united in 1597, became an archbishopric in 1808), with suffragan dioceses of *Przemyśl* (subject to Lemberg since 1818) and *Stanislawow* (founded 1882). *Lemberg,* Armenian Rite, was founded 1367.

(b) *In Hungary* there are four archdioceses of the Latin Rite, with 17 suffragan dioceses; and one archdiocese of the Greek Rite, with six suffragan dioceses, making altogether 28 sees. *Archdiocese of Esztergom* (*Strigonium, Gran;* founded 1000), the incumbent of which is Primate of Hungary and ex-officio Legate (*Legatus Natus*), with suffragan dioceses of *Nyitra* (founded 1029), *Vácz* (*Vacium, Waitzen;* founded in eleventh century), *Györ* (*Jaurinum, Raab;* founded in eleventh century), *Veszprém*

(founded 1009), *Szombathly* (*Sabaria, Steinamanger;* founded 1777), *Beszterczebanya* (*Neusohl;* founded 1776), *Székes-Fehérvár* (*Alba Regalis, Stuhlweissenburg;* founded 1777), *Pécs* (*Serbinum, Quinque Ecclesiæ, Fünfkirchen;* founded 1009), *Eperjes* (Ruthenian Greek; founded 1820), *Munkács* (*Munkaczinum;* Ruthenian-Greek; founded 1771). *Archdiocese of Kalocsa and Bács* (founded 1000), with suffragan dioceses of *Nagy-Várad* (*Varadinum Majus, Grosswardein;* founded 1077), *Csanád* [*Chronadium* (*Magyarscanad-Temesvár*); founded 1035], and *Erdely* [*Transylvania* (*Karlsburg*); founded in twelfth century]. *Archdiocese of Eger* (*Agria, Erlau;* founded 1000, archbishopric 1804), with suffragan dioceses of *Rozsnyó* (*Rosnavia, Rosenau;* founded 1776), *Szatmár-Németi* (*Szathmarium;* founded 1804), *Szepes* [*Scepusia, Zips* (*Szepesváralja*); founded 1776], *Kassa* (*Cassovia, Kaschau;* founded 1804), and *Sabaria* (*Sacer Mons Pannoniæ, Martinsberg;* founded 997). *Archdiocese of Zagreb* (*Zagrabia, Agram;* founded 1093, archbishopric 1853), with suffragan dioceses of *Djakovár* (founded 1781), *Zengg-Modrus* (founded 1460), and *Kriz* (*Crisium, Kreutz,* Greek-Ruthenian Rite; founded 1777). *Archdiocese of Fogaras,* of the Greek Rite (founded 1721, archbishopric 1854), has for suffragan dioceses *Nagy-Várad* (*Varadinum Majus, Grosswardein;* founded 1777), *Lugos* (*Lugosium;* founded 1853), and *Szamos-Ujvár* (*Armenopolis;* founded 1777).

(c) *In Bosnia and Herzegovina* there is one archdiocese: *Serajevo* (founded 1881), with suffragan dioceses of *Banjaluka* (founded 1881), *Trebinje* (*Tribunium;* founded in ninth century), *Mostar* (*Mandatrium;* founded 1881). The Apostolic field-vicariate for the army and navy is directly under the control of the Holy See.

STATISTICS OF RELIGIOUS ORDERS.—The following table presents a summary of the parent and branch houses of the religious orders in Austria, together with the number of their inmates:—

Diocese	Male Orders		Female Orders	
	Houses	Inmates	Houses	Inmates
Vienna (Archd.)	41 (62)	1,611	104 (195)	4,230
St. Pölten	16	505	73 (94)	874
Linz	29	670	124 (126)	1,765
Salzburg (Archd.)	11	216	102	998
Trent	35	817	130	1.527
Brixen and Vorarlberg	43	1,171	222	2,656
Lavant	9	163	13	181
Seckau	31	825	67 (90)	1,359
Gurk	12	230	22 (26)	357
Görz (Archd.)	7	105	7	238
Laibach	12	264	19 (24)	492
Veglia	11	64	7 (8)	68
Pola	1	21	6 (8)	132
Triest	7	81	13	174
Prague (Archd.)	16	704	76	1,517
Königgrätz	12	88	48 (55)	442
Leitmeritz	21	180	61	442
Budweis	15	188	33 (36)	396
Olmütz (Archd.)	25	220	80 (87)	1,547
Brünn	13	136	28 (30)	327
Lemberg (Archd., Lat. Rite)	41 (43)	151	153	1,271
Przemyśl (Lat. Rite)	27	369	97 (99)	698
Tarnów	6	72	54 (55)	340
Lemberg (Archd., Gr. Rite)	6	27	8	86
Przemyśl (Gr. Rite)	6	134	1	19
Stanislawow (Gr. Rite)	4	25	10	44
Zara (Archd.)	5	20	4	23
Sebenico	7	83	4	23

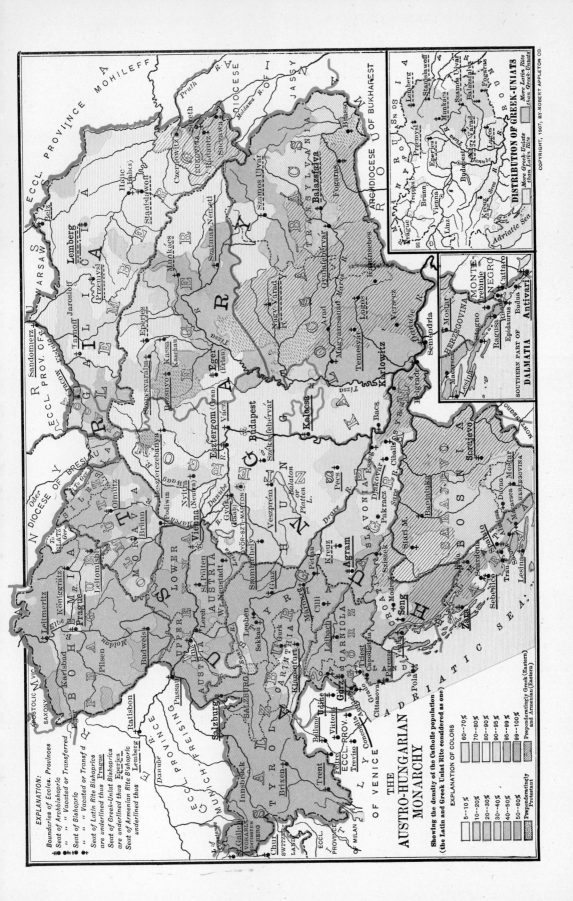

THE
AUSTRO-HUNGARIAN
MONARCHY

Showing the density of the Catholic population
(the Latin and Greek Uniat Rite considered as one)

EXPLANATION OF COLORS

5-10 %
10-20 %
20-30 %
30-40 %
40-50 %
50-60 %
60-70 %
70-80 %
80-90 %
90-95 %
95-99 %
99-100 %
Preponderatingly Greek (Eastern)
and Armenian (Eastern)
Preponderatingly
Protestant

EXPLANATION:
Boundaries of Eccles. Provinces
Seat of Archbishopric
"   " Vacated or Transferred
Seat of Bishopric
"   " Vacated or Transf'd
Seat of Latin Rite Bishoprics
are underlined thus Prague
Seat of Greek-Uniat Bishoprics
are underlined thus Eperies
Seat of Armenian Rite Bishopric
underlined thus Lemberg

DISTRIBUTION OF GREEK-UNIATS

More Latin Rite
than Greek Uniats
More Greek-Uniats
than Latin Rite

SOUTHERN PART OF
DALMATIA

COPYRIGHT, 1907, BY ROBERT APPLETON CO.

Diocese	Male Orders		Female Orders	
	Houses	Inmates	Houses	Inmates
Spalato and Macarska.	15	91	9 (14)	125
Cattaro	3	9	2	8
Ragusa	19	93	1	51
Cracow (Archd.).	30	604	58 (73)	1,166
Breslau	6	33	30	426
Lemberg (Arm. Rite).			1	16
Totals	542	9,970	1,667	24,018

DENOMINATIONAL STATISTICS.—The forty-nine million inhabitants of the Austro-Hungarian monarchy are divided, as to their religious beliefs, as follows:—

Austrian Provinces.

Catholics { Latin Rite. . . . . 20,661,000 } 23,797,000
{ Greek Rite. . . . . 3,134,000 }
{ Armenian Rite. . 2,000 }

Jews. 1,225,000
Greeks (Eastern) 607,000
Evangelicals 491,000
Old-Catholics 13,000
Of no confession. 6,000
Mohammedans. 1,000
Of other confessions. 8,000

Hungarian Provinces.

Catholics { Latin Rite. . . . . 10,299,190 } 12,207,126
{ Greek Rite. . . . . 1,907,936 }

Evangelicals 3,823,061
Greeks (Orthodox). 2,882,695
Jews. 886,466
Unitarians. \. . . 70,260
Of other confessions. 15,837

Bosnia and Herzegovina.

Greeks (Eastern) 673,000
Mohammedans. 549,000
Catholics 339,000
Jews. 8,000
Of other confessions. 4,000

KENNER, *Noricum und Pannonien* (Vienna, 1870); SAUPPE (ed.), *Eugippii Vita S. Severini* (Berlin, 1877); s. c., *Kirchen- und reichsrechtliche Verhältnisse des Salzburg Suffraganbistums Gurk* (Krems, 1872); FRIESS, *Studien über das Wirken der Benedictiner in Œsterreich*, in *Seitenlettener Gymnasialprogramme*, 1868–77; JANAUSCHEK, *Originum Cisterciensium* (Vienna, 1877), I; FRIND, *Die Kirchengeschichte Böhmens* (3 vols., Prague, 1864–66); ENDLICHER, *Rer. Hungar. Monumenta Arpadiana* (Sang, 1848); MAILATH, *Geschichte der Magyaren* (2d ed., Ratisbon, 1852); WAHRMUND, *Das Kirchenpatronat und seine Entwickelung in Œsterreich* (Vienna, 1894); SOCHER, *Historia Provinciæ Austriæ S. J.* (Vienna, 1740); GRAF VON KHEVENHILLER, *Annales Ferdinandei* (Ratisbon, 1640–46); GINDELY, *Kaiser Rudolph II und seine Zeit* (2 vols., Prague, 1863); SCHUSTER, *Fürst-Bischof Brenner* (Graz, 1898); HAMMER-PURGSTALL, *Geschichte des Kardinals Khlesl* (4 vols., 1847–51); SCHLITTER, *Die Reise des Papstes Pius VI nach Wien in Fontes Rer. Austriac.* (Vienna, 1892–94), XLVII; BRUNNER, *Mysterien der Aufklärung in Œsterreich* (Mainz, 1869); *Die theol. Dienerschaft am Hofe Josephs II* (Vienna, 1868); WOLFSGRUBER, *Kardinal Migazzi* (Saulgau, 1891); MAASSEN, *Neun Kapitel über frei Kirche und Gewissensfreiheit* (Graz, 1876), ch. viii, pp. 370–447, *Das œsterr. Konkordat*; ZSCHOKKE, *Die theologischen Studien und Anstalten der katholischen Kirche in Œsterreich* (Vienna and Leipzig, 1894); WAPPLER, *Geschichte der theol. Fakultät an der K. K. Universität Wien* (Vienna, 1884); WOLFSGRUBER, *Die Konferenzen der Bischöfe Œsterreichs* (Linz, 1905); HÜBNER-TWASCHER, *Geographisch-Statistische Tabellen* (Frankfort on the Main, 1906); VON WÜRZBACH, *Der grosse Œsterreich Hausschatz, ein nat Bibliothek biog. Lexikon* (Vienna, 1750–1850, 1857–91); LEGER, *Hist. of Austro-Hungary*, tr. HILL (London, 1889); *Statesman's Year-Book* (London, 1907); VON LÖSCHE, *Geschichte des Protestantismus in Œsterreich in Umrissen* (1902).

C. WOLFSGRUBER.

Authentic.—The term is used in two senses. It is applied first to a book or document whose contents are invested with a special authority, in virtue of which the work is called *authentic*. In its second sense it is used as a synonym for "genuine", and therefore means that a work really emanates from the author to whom it is ascribed. The article VULGATE explains the first sense of the word; the articles on the single books of Sacred Scripture illustrate the second. F. X. E. ALBERT.

Authenticity of the Bible.—The authenticity or authority of Holy Writ is twofold on account of its twofold authorship. First, the various books which make up the Bible are authentic because they enjoy all the human authority that is naturally due to their respective authors. Second, they possess a higher authenticity, because invested with a Divine, supernatural authority through the Divine authorship which makes them the inspired word of God. Biblical authenticity in its first sense must naturally be considered in the articles on the several books of Sacred Scripture; in its second sense, it springs from Biblical inspiration, for which see INSPIRATION.

VIGOUROUX, *Manuel biblique* (Paris, 1901), I, 223–225; MAZZELLA, *De Virtutibus Infusis* (Rome, 1879), 554, 555.

F. X. E. ALBERT.

Authority, CIVIL, the moral power of command, supported (when need be) by physical coercion, which the State exercises over its members. We shall consider here the nature, sources, limits, divisions, origin, and the true and false theories of authority. Authority is as great a necessity to mankind as sobriety, and as natural. By "natural" here is meant, not what accrues to man without any effort of his own (teeth, for example), but what man must secure, even with an effort, because without it he cannot well be man. It is natural to man to live in civil society; and where there is civil society, there must be authority. Anarchy is the disruption of society. Speaking generally, we may say no man loves isolation, solitude, loneliness, the life of a hermit; on the other hand, while many dislike the authority under which they live, no man wishes for anarchy. What malcontents aim at is a change of government, to get authority into their own hands and govern those who now govern them. Even the professed anarchist regards anarchy as a temporary expedient, a preparation for his own advent to power. Authority, then, in the abstract, every man loves and cherishes; and rightly so, for it is his nature to live in society, and society is kept together by authority. The model of hermits was St. Simeon Stylites, so called from his living on the top of a style, or pillar. That was his special vocation; he was no ordinary man. But the political philosopher considers man as man ordinarily and normally is. Two things would strike a stranger from Mars looking down upon this planet: how men on earth love herding together, and how they love moving about. Ordinary man can no more afford to be solitary than he can afford to be stationary, though Simeon Stylites was both. Solitary confinement is the severest of punishments, next to death. It is hard to say whether the solitude or the confinement, proves the more irksome. This simple point, that man cannot live alone, must be insisted upon, for all errors in the theory of authority are rooted in the assumption that man's living in society, and thereby coming to be governed by social authority, is something purely optional and conventional, a fashion which man could very well discard if he would, as he might discard the wearing of green clothes. Men who would make society a conventional arrangement, and authority a fashion of the hour, have appealed to the noble savage as the standard of humanity proper, forgetting that the savage is no solitary, but a member of a horde, to separate from which would be death, and to ignore the control of which would be death also. Man must live in society, and, in point of historical fact, men have always lived in society; every human development is a social progress. It is natural to man to live in society, to submit to authority, and to be governed by that custom of society which crystallizes into law.

And as it is natural to the individual, so is it natural also for the family to unite with others. Society cannot stop short at the family. As the individual is not self-sufficient, neither is the family. The family grows and then multiplies. We have a society of families; and that society grown great, and controlled as it needs to be controlled by some common authority, passes into a self-sufficient, autonomous society, otherwise called a State. Hence civil authority is defined as the moral power of command, supported (when need be) by physical coercion, which the State exercises over its constituent members. Civil authority is of God, not by any revelation or positive institution, but by the mere fact that God is the Author of Nature, and Nature imperatively requires civil authority to be set up and obeyed. Nature cannot tolerate intemperance, nor anarchy either. And what Nature absolutely requires, or absolutely refuses as incompatible with her well-being, God commands, or God forbids. God then forbids anarchy; and in forbidding anarchy He enjoins submission to authority. In this sense, God is at the back of every State, binding men in conscience to observe the behests of the State within the sphere of its competence. "Let every soul be subject to higher powers: for there is no power but from God: and those that are, are ordained of God. . . . Wherefore be subject of necessity, not only for wrath, but also for conscience' sake. . . . For they are the ministers of God, . . ." (Rom. xiii, 1, 5, 6).

Obedience, being a practical thing and not a speculation, cannot abstract from the concrete facts of the case; it is paid to the powers that be, to the authority actually in possession. Obedience is disobedience; men are never disobedient except to the government of the day. But there are limits to civil obedience, and to the competence of civil authority. As domestic obedience is not to be carried to the extent of rebellion against the civil government, so neither is the State to be obeyed as against God. It is not within the competence of the State to command anything and everything. The State cannot command what God could not command, for instance, idolatry. The authority of the State is absolute, that is to say, full and complete in its own sphere, and subordinate to no other authority within that sphere. But the authority of the State is not arbitrary; it is not available for the carrying out of every whim and caprice. Arbitrary government is irrational government; now no government is licensed to set reason aside. The government of God Himself is not arbitrary; as St. Thomas says: "God is not offended by us except at what we do against our own good" (Contra Gentiles, III, 122). The arbitrary use of authority is called tyranny. Such is the tyranny of an absolute monarch, of a council, of a class, or of a majority. The liberty of the subject is based on the doctrine that the State is not omnipotent. Legally omnipotent every State must be, but not morally. A legal enactment may be immoral, and then it cannot in conscience be obeyed; or it may be *ultra vires*, beyond the competence of the authority that enacts it, in which case compliance with the law is not a matter of obedience, but of prudence. In either case the law is tyrannical, and "a tyrannical law, not being according to reason, is not, absolutely speaking, a law, but rather a perversion of law" (St. Thomas, Summa Theol., 1ª, 2ᵃᵉ, q. 92, art. 1, ad 4). Man is not all citizen. He is a member, a part of the State, and something else besides. "Man is not subservient to the civil community to the extent of his whole self, all that he is and all that he has" (St. Thomas, Summa Theol., 1ª 2ᵃᵉ, q. 21, art. 4, ad 3). To say nothing of his eternal interests in his relations with his Maker, man has even in this life his domestic interests in the bosom of his family, his intellectual and artistic interests, none of which can be called political interests. Social and political life is not the whole of human life. Man is not the servant of the State in his every action. The State, the majority, or the despot, may demand of the individual more than he is bound to give. Were human society a conventional arrangement, were man, being perfectly well off in isolation from his fellows, to agree by way of freak to live in community with them, then we could assign no antecedent limits to civil authority. Civil authority would be simply what was bargained for and prescribed in the arbitrary compact which made civil society. As it is, civil authority is a natural means to a natural end, and is checked by that end, in accordance with the Aristotelean principle that "the end in view sets limits to the means" (Aristotle, Politics, I, 9). The immediate end of civil authority is well set forth by Suarez (De legibus, III, xi, 7) as "the natural happiness of the perfect, or self-sufficient, human community, and the happiness of individuals as they are members of such a community, that they may live therein peaceably and justly, with a sufficiency of goods for the preservation and comfort of their bodily life, and with so much moral rectitude as is necessary for this external peace and happiness". Happiness is an attribute of individuals. Individuals are not made happy by authority, but authority secures to them that tranquillity, that free hand for helping themselves, that restful enjoyment of their own just winnings, which is one of the conditions of happiness. Nor does authority make men virtuous, except according to that rough-hewn, outline virtue, which is called "social virtue", and consists mainly of justice. When the ancients spoke of "virtue" being the concern of the State, they meant justice and efficiency. Neither the virtue nor the happiness of individuals is cared for by the State except "as they are members of the civil community". In this respect, civil differs from domestic, or paternal, authority. The father cares for the members of his household one by one, singly and individually. The State cares for its members collectively, and for the individual only in his collective aspect. Hence it follows that the power of life and death is inherent in the State, not in the family. A man is hanged for the common good of the rest, never for his own good.

This, then, is one measure of authority, the end which the State has in view. Another is the stage of development at which any given particular State has arrived. For there is not one measure of authority common to all States. As the State develops, it grows in unity, and greater unity means an ampler measure of central authority. There is far more authority in the England of to-day than in the England of the Heptarchy. There was more authority in an Anglo-Saxon kingdom than in a horde of savages. In early civil societies there is no legislative authority, and no law, but only immemorial custom. There is little judicial authority, but injured men, or their families after their death, right their own wrongs, murder is restrained, not by judge, jury, and executioner, but by blood-feud. On the other hand, in highly civilized societies, especially those of a democratic character, the will of the people continually thrusts new functions upon government, such as education, the care of public health, the carrying of letters, the sending of telegrams. The recognition of this fact has been called "the principle of voluntary control". By it civil authority may be enlarged beyond its natural and essential limits. Like other principles, "the principle of voluntary control" may be pushed too far. Pushed to the limit, it would involve Socialism.

Authority, though varying in amount, is as universal as man is everywhere. Man cannot live except under authority, as he cannot live out of civil society. It is by no convention, compact, or contract, that authority takes hold of him. It is a necessity of his nature. But while civil authority, or government, is natural and universal, the distribution of authority, otherwise called the form of government, or the constitution of the State, is a human convention, varying in various countries, and in the same country at different periods of its history. It is scarcely too much to say that there are as many various distributions of civil authority, or various forms of government, as there are varieties of vertebrate animals. They are classified as monarchies, aristocracies, democracies; but no two monarchies are quite alike, nor two democracies. Thus a democracy may be direct, as in ancient Athens, or representative, as in the United States. The monarchy of Edward VII is different from that of George III.

The one point fixed by nature, and by God, is that there must be authority everywhere, and that the authority existent for the time being, under such and such a form, be under that form obeyed; for since there is no actual authority in the country except under that form, to refuse to obey that is to refuse authority simply, and to revert to anarchy, which is against nature: just as a man having nothing but bread and cheese to eat, and refusing to eat his bread and cheese, under pretence that he much prefers mutton, condemns himself to starvation, which again is unnatural. But we must beware of saying of any particular form of authority, monarchy for example, or democracy either, what is true only of authority in the abstract, namely, that all nations are bound to live under it, and that never under any pretence can it be subverted. A country, once monarchical, is not eternally bound to monarchy; and circumstances are conceivable under which a republic might pass into monarchy, as Rome did under Augustus, much to its advantage. Authority rules by Divine right under whatsoever form it is established. No one form of government is more sacred and inviolate than another. Change of persons holding office is usually provided in the constitution, sometimes by rotation, sometimes by vote of the legislative assembly. No monarchical constitution provides for the change of the person of the monarch otherwise than by death or resignation. Change of the form of government can be effected constitutionally, but, as history shows, as often as not, it is brought about unconstitutionally. When the change is complete, the new government rules by right of accomplished fact. There must be authority in the country, and theirs is the only authority available.

DIVISIONS.—The progress of civilization subdivides authority into legislative, judicial, and executive, and the latter again into civil and military. The king, or president, is chief of the executive. Authority again is subdivided into imperial and local, the latter emanating from the former and subordinate to it.

ORIGIN.—The question of the origin of authority seems first to have been raised by the Roman lawyers. In their hands it assumed the concrete form of the origin of the imperial power. This power they argued to reside primarily in the Roman people; the people, however, did not exercise nor retain it, but transferred it by some implicit *lex regia*, or king-making ordinance, as a matter of course wholly, and irrevocably to each successive emperor at his accession. With the advent of Christianity, St. Paul's doctrine came into prominence, that authority is of God; yet in no clear way was it made out how it came of God until St. Thomas Aquinas showed that it was of God inasmuch as it was an essential of the

human nature which God has created, according to the doctrine of Aristotle above exposed. Before St. Thomas arose, some churchmen had shown a disposition to cry down the civil power. They could not deny that it was of God, but they regarded it as one of the consequences of the sin of Adam, and argued that, but for the Fall, man would have lived free from coercive jurisdiction. They rehearsed the legend of Romulus, and the asylum that he opened for robbers. States, they said, usually have their origin in rapine and injustice. Others invested the pope with the plenitude of secular as well as spiritual authority, by the gift of Christ, and argued that kings reigned only as his vicegerents, even in civil matters. The Aristoteleanism of St. Thomas was opposed to all this. On the other hand, the imperial and royal party made a pope of the king or emperor; the civil ruler was as much an institution of Christ as the pope himself, and, like the pope, enjoyed a God-given authority, no portion of which could validly be taken from him. This is the doctrine of "the divine right of kings". According to it, in its rigour, in a State once monarchical, monarchy is forever the only lawful government, and all authority is vested in the monarch, to be communicated by him, to such as he may select for the time being to share his power. This "divine right of kings" (very different from the doctrine that all authority, whether of king or of republic, is from God), has never been sanctioned by the Catholic Church. At the Reformation it assumed a form exceedingly hostile to Catholicism, monarchs like Henry VIII, and James I, of England, claiming the fullness of spiritual as well as of civil authority, and this in such inalienable possession that no jot or tittle of prerogative could ever pass away from the Crown. Against these monstrous pretensions were fought the battles of Marston Moor and Naseby.

Against the same pretensions a more pacific warfare was waged by Francis Suarez, S.J. Suarez argued against James I that spiritual authority is not vested in the Crown, and that even civil authority is not the immediate gift of God to the king, but is given by God to the people collectively, and by them bestowed on the monarch, according to the theory of the Roman lawyers above mentioned, and according to Aristotle and St. Thomas. Authority, he asserted, is an attribute of a multitude assembled to form a State. By their nature they must form a State, and a State must have authority. Authority, therefore, is natural to mankind collectively; and whatever is natural, and rational, and indispensable for human progress, is an ordinance of God. Authority must be, and God will have it to be; but there is no such natural necessity of authority being all centred in one person. Authority is a Divine institution, but kings are a human invention. The saying is a platitude in our time; three centuries ago, when Suarez wrote, it was a bold and startling pronouncement. Suarez saved his loyalty by the concession that the people having bestowed the supreme power on His Majesty's ancestors ages ago, their posterity could not now resume it, but it must descend, like an heirloom, from the king to the king's son for all time. This concession was not everywhere borne in mind by posterity. Indeed it would appear a restriction on the development of a State for the distribution of authority to be thus fixed forever. In England at any rate the restriction has been broken through, and the king is not what he was in Stuart times, nor the Parliament either.

THEORIES.—There have been two great outbreaks against excess of royal prerogative; one in England, in the middle of the seventeenth century; another in France, at the end of the eighteenth. Each of these two periods was marked by the appearance of a great political writer, Thomas Hobbes in England, Jean Jacques Rousseau in France. Hobbes was a philosopher, Rousseau a rhetorician. Whoever knows Hobbes well can have little to learn from Rousseau. Hobbes is rigidly logical; such inconsistencies as appear in him come from a certain timidity in speaking out, and a humility that approaches nigh to hypocrisy. Rousseau always speaks boldly, makes no pretence to orthodoxy, and frequently contradicts himself. His brilliant style won him the ear of Europe; he popularized Hobbes. To the philosopher, Rousseau is contemptible, but Hobbes is an antagonist worthy of any man's steel. The best that can be said of Rousseau in philosophy is that he drew out of Hobbes's principles conclusions which Hobbes was afraid to formulate. Hobbes made of the king a despot; Rousseau showed that, on Hobbesian principles, a king is no better than the people's bailiff, unless indeed, by military force or otherwise, he can prevent the people from assembling and decreeing his deposition. Hobbes starts, and Rousseau after him, by contradicting Aristotle. According to Aristotle, man is "by nature a State-making animal"; the individual man, if he is to thrive at all, develops into the family man, and the family man into the citizen; and wherever there is a city, or a nation, there must be self-government, or, in other words, civil authority, whether vested in one or in many. Authority is the very breath of man's nostrils, as he is a progressive being. Isolation and anarchy are fatal to human progress. Effort, without which man cannot thrive, though it be an effort, and not an initial endowment passively received, Aristotle calls "natural". The State-making effort is "natural" to man; so is authority "natural", and, as such, of God, adds Thomas Aquinas. But Hobbes took "natural" in quite another sense. That he held to be "natural" which man is, antecedently to all effort and arrangement on his part to make himself better. Further, his philosophy was tinged with the Calvinism of his day, and he took it that man is of himself "desperately wicked". What was natural, then, was bad, bad on the whole. Reason being an original endowment of man, Hobbes allowed reason to be natural. He allowed also, with Plato, that wickedness is irrational, by which concession Hobbism is marked off from a celebrated theory stated at the beginning of the second book of Plato's Republic, to which theory in other respects it bears a strong resemblance; the theory being that right by nature is the interest of the stronger, and only by convention becomes the interest of the State.

This allowing of wickedness to be against reason is a weak point in the logic of Hobbes. But Hobbes would have it that reason is by nature utterly unable to contend with wickedness, that it is overborne by, and made subservient to, passion, and so is degraded into cunning, man becoming more wicked by his possession of reason. Of himself, in his "state of nature", Hobbesian man is a savage, solitary, sensual, and selfish. When two human beings meet, the natural impulse of each is to lord it over the other. By force, if he is strong, by stratagem, if he is weak, every man seeks to kill or enslave every other man that he meets. Man's life in this state of nature, says Hobbes, is "nasty, brutish, and short." So it would be, in an English fen, and in most other places. But Rousseau's imagination carried him to the Pacific Isles; he became enamoured of "the noble savage". He fell in with Hobbes's notion of the "natural", as being what man is and has antecedently to all human effort. But the "citizen of Geneva", as he called himself, was curiously free from Calvinistic bias, and believed enthusiastically in the primitive, unmade, natural goodness of man. In Hobbes's view, though not in Rousseau's, man had every reason for getting out of his "nasty" state of nature. This was done by a pact, or convention, of every man with all the rest of mankind, to give up solitude with its charms, its independence, and its liberty of preying upon neighbours, and to live in society, the social body thus formed having all the rights of the individuals contributing to form it. This compact of man with man to quit solitude and live in society, to abandon nature and submit to convention, was called by Rousseau, "The Social Contract". The body formed by it, commonly called the State, Hobbes termed "The Leviathan", upon the text of Job, xli, 24, "there is no power upon earth that can be compared with him. . . ."

To Hobbes and to Rousseau the State is omnipotent, containing in its one self absolutely all the rights of the citizens who compose it. The wielder of this tremendous power is the General Will, measured against which the will of the individual citizen is not only powerless, but absolutely non-existent. The individual gave up his will when he made the Social Contract. "No rights against the State", is a fundamental principle with Hobbes and Rousseau. To live in the State at all means compliance with every decree of the General Will. But there is a difficulty in locating this General Will. Hobbes, with laudable perspicacity, seeing that tyranny is better wielded by one man than by a multitude, contemplates the multitude resigning all their power into the hands of a Single Person, and denying themselves the right of meeting without his calling them together; so that, by the simple expedient of never calling them together, the Single Person may incapacitate the people from ever resuming the power which is only theirs when they are all assembled. The General Will in that case is the will of the Single Person. Hobbes's location of the General Will is not lacking in clearness. But Rousseau would have the sovereign authority to be the inalienable right of the multitude—hence called the "Sovereign People". They may, if they will, employ a king, or even an emperor; but his majesty, in Rousseau's phrase, is "Prince" not "Sovereign", and at stated times, without his calling them together, the Sovereign People must meet and decide, first, whether they will continue to support a throne at all; secondly, whether the throne shall further be filled by the present occupant. Rousseau's location is also clear, so long as it is understood that the General Will is simply the will of the numerical majority of the Sovereign People. Such a General Will is ascertained by the simple process of counting heads. If in a State of 20,000 citizens, 15,000 vote aye, aye is the General Will, not the will of the majority only, but of the whole 20,000 together; for though 5,000 persons detest the proposal, such detestation lies only in the individual will, sometimes called the "casual will", and the individual will has ceased to exist by the Compact. Personally they detest the measure, but with their "Real Will" they approve it. Thus, as Rousseau says, they remain as free as the wild man in the woods, obey none but themselves, and follow their own will everywhere.

But a canker-worm lies at the root of this, as of all ultra-democratic doctrines. All originate in a manifestly false supposition, that one man is as good as another. In any sane polity, the predominant Intelligence must guide the counsels of the State, not the predominant Will, which may be no better than caprice. But intelligence is not necessarily attached to majorities. Rousseau himself falters in presence of this awkward truth, and re-states the General Will, as the will which the people have of good in general, albeit in a particular case they are mistaken in what they take to be good. Thus they will one thing, and vote for another. The Real Will in this case is not to be gathered from the actual vote of the majority. The Real Will is of that which the majority would have voted for, had they known better. Rousseau's theory contemplates "a people of gods", so he assures us. Such a people would scarce require any government. The ideal, sylvan creatures whom his imagination brings together to form the Social Contract, if not all very intelligent, may be supposed to be all good listeners to intelligent teaching, and thus Intelligence will govern the majority, and the vote of the majority will be an ideally Real Will. Government is an easy matter on such optimistic presuppositions. The eye, however, glances back upon Hobbes's ruffian primeval, "brutish and nasty". Hobbes's view of human nature must check that of Rousseau. Both views are extreme, and the truth lies between them. The democratic rule of a numerical majority is not of universal application. One has to consider the character of the people, and peoples vary. If in one age or place the people approximate to the character of "a people of gods", or angels, in another country or another time they may be more like devils. "Force, devoid of counsel, of its own bulk comes to a crash", says Horace (Odes, III, 4). That is the danger of the General Will. Rousseau, with Hobbes to guide him, starts from a false supposition, that the natural state of man is savage solitude, not civil society; he proceeds through the false medium of the "Social Contract", false because society is not a thing of convention; false again, because out of all keeping with the evidence of history; and he is apt to end in the tyranny of a brute majority, trampling upon the rights and consciences of individuals; or again in anarchy, his disciples putting too literal a construction upon the promise that henceforth no man shall obey any other than himself.

The doctrines of Rousseau have not escaped the censure of the Church. Rousseau may be recognized in the following propositions, condemned in the Syllabus of Pius IX: "The State is the source and origin of all rights, and its rights are unlimited" (n. 39): "Authority is nothing else than numbers, and a sum of material forces" (n. 60): "It is allowable to refuse obedience to lawful princes, and even to rebel against them" (n. 63). Leo XIII, not content with condemning, teaches positive doctrine against Rousseau, to wit: the Aristotelean and Thomist doctrine already stated. Thus the Encyclical "Immortale Dei", of November, 1885: "Man's natural instinct moves him to live in civil society; for he can not, if dwelling apart, provide himself with the necessary requirements of life, nor procure the means of developing his faculties. Hence it is Divinely ordained that he should be born into the society and company of men, as well domestic as civil. Only civil society can ensure perfect self-sufficiency of life [an Aristotelean term]. But since no society can hold together unless there be some one over all, impelling individuals efficaciously and harmoniously to one common purpose, a ruling authority becomes a necessity for every civil commonwealth of men; and this authority, no less than society itself, is natural, and therefore has God for its author. Hence it follows that public power of itself cannot be otherwise than of God."

In the theory of Hobbes and Rousseau, Authority is the outcome of contract, not between people and prince, but of every man with every other man to relinquish solitude and its rights, and live in civil society. Rousseau is instant in pronouncing that between people and prince there can be no contract, but the prince is a tenant at will, who may be turned out of doors, with or without reason, any day that the Sovereign People assemble to vote upon him. But there is another theory of contract, centuries older than Hobbes, a theory greatly cherished by Locke and the English Whigs, who found in it the justification of the expulsion of James II in 1688. In this theory, the contract is said to lie between the

people and their ruler; the ruler is to be obeyed so long as he fulfils certain conditions, known as "the constitution". If he violates the constitution, he forfeits his authority and the people may cast him out. Thus ruler and subject are two "high contracting parties". The ruler has no superiority of status, but of contract only. On this it is to be observed, first, that such a contract lies not in the nature of things, and therefore is not to be taken for granted; but evidence in each particular case should be forthcoming of the contract having been made on those terms as a fact of history. Secondly, this asserted contract labours under the inconvenience that Job declared of old: " . . . in judgment. There is none that may be able to reprove both, and to put his hand between both" (Job, ix, 32, 33). The contract cannot be enforced at law, for lack of a judge; in case of dispute, each party pronounces in his own favour, and they are like to fight it out. The result is civil war, as between Charles I and his Parliament. But really ruler and subjects are not two "high contracting parties", as two nations are. The theory is prejudicial to the unity of the State, and countenances revolution. The theory was brought up to meet that delicate inquiry, "What is to be done when Government abuses its authority?" On which see "Moral Philosophy" (Stonyhurst Series), 338–343.

NEWMAN, *Aristotle, Politics*, (Clarendon Press, Oxford; there is a translation also by Weldon) I; ST. THOMAS, *De Regimine Principum*, I; LEO XIII, *Encyclicals*: Latin, five volumes (Tournai); English, *The Pope and the People, Select Letters on Social Questions* (New York); SUAREZ, *Defensio Fidei*, III, i, ii, iii; R. W. and A. T. CARLYLE, *Medieval Political Theory in the West* (London); GIERKE, *Political Theories of the Middle Age*, tr. by Maitland (Cambridge); RICKABY, *Political and Moral Essays, The Origin and Extent of Civil Authority*; HOBBES, *Leviathan* (Cambridge University Press); ROUSSEAU, *Le contrat social* (London); LOCKE, *Of Civil Government*; GREEN, *Principles of Political Obligation* (London and New York); BOSANQUET, *Philosophical Theory of the State* (London and New York).

JOSEPH RICKABY.

Authority, ECCLESIASTICAL. See CHURCH; POPE; HIERARCHY.

Authority, PATERNAL. See CHILDREN; OBEDIENCE; PARENTS.

Authorized Version, THE, name given to the English translation of the Bible produced by the Commission appointed by James I, and in consequence often spoken of as "King James's Bible". It is in general use among English-speaking non-Catholics. In order to understand its origin and history, a brief survey is necessary of the earlier English translations of the Scriptures. From very early times portions of the Bible have been translated into English. It is well known that Venerable Bede was finishing a translation of St. John's Gospel on his death-bed. But the history of the English Bible as a whole does not go back nearly so far; it dates from the so-called Wyclif Version, believed to have been completed about the year 1380. The translation was made from the Vulgate as it then existed, that is before the Sixtine and Clementine revisions, and was well and accurately done. Abbot Gasquet contends confidently (The Old English Bible, 102 sqq.) that it was in reality of Catholic origin, and not due to Wyclif at all; at any rate it seems fairly certain that he had no share in any part of it except the Gospels, even if he had in these; and there is evidence that copies of the whole were in the hands of good Catholics, and were read by them. The version, however, undoubtedly derived its chief importance from the use made of it by Wyclif and the Lollards, and it is in this connexion that it is chiefly remembered. During the progress of the Reformation a number of English versions appeared, translated for the most part not from the Vulgate, but from the original Hebrew and Greek.

Of these the most famous were Tyndale's Bible (1525); Coverdale's Bible (1535); Matthews' Bible (1537); Cromwell's, or the "Great Bible" (1539), the second and subsequent editions of which were known as Cranmer's Bible; the Geneva Bible (1557–60); and the Bishops' Bible (1568). The art of printing being by this time known, copies of all these circulated freely among the people. That there was much good and patient work in them, none will deny; but they were marred by the perversion of many passages, due to the theological bias of the translators; and they were used on all sides to serve the cause of Protestantism.

In order to counteract the evil effects of these versions, the Catholics determined to produce one of their own. Many of them were then living at various centres on the Continent, having been forced to leave England on account of the Penal Laws, and the work was undertaken by the members of Allen's College, at Douai, in Flanders, which was for a time transferred to Reims. The result was the Reims New Testament (1582) and the Douay Bible (1609–10). The translation was made from the Vulgate, and although accurate, was sadly deficient in literary form, and so full of Latinisms as to be in places hardly intelligible. Indeed, a few years later, Dr. William Fulke, a well-known Puritan controversialist, brought out a book in which the text of the Bishops' Bible and the Reims Testament were printed in parallel columns, with the sole purpose of discrediting the latter. In this he did not altogether succeed, and it is now generally conceded that the Douay Bible contained much excellent and scholarly work, its very faults being due to over-anxiety not to sacrifice accuracy. In the meantime the Protestants were becoming dissatisfied with their own versions, and soon after his accession King James I appointed a commission of revision—the only practical outcome of the celebrated Hampton Court Conference. The commissioners, who numbered forty-seven, were divided into six companies, two of which sat at Oxford, Cambridge, and Westminster, respectively; each company undertook a definite portion of the Bible, and its work was afterwards revised by a select committee chosen from the whole body. The instructions for their procedure were, to take the Bishops' Bible, which was in use in the churches, as their basis, correcting it by a comparison with the Hebrew and Greek texts. They were also given a list of other English versions which they were to consult. The commissioners set to work in 1607, and completed their labours in the short period of two years and nine months, the result being what is now known as the "Authorized Version". Although at first somewhat slow in gaining general acceptance, the Authorized Version has since become famous as a masterpiece of English literature. The first edition appeared in 1611, soon after the Douay Bible, and nearly thirty years after the Reims Testament; and although this latter was not one of the versions named in the instructions to the revisers, it is understood that it had considerable influence on them (see Preface to Revised Version, i, 2. Also, J. G. Caleton, "Rheims and the English Bible").

The Authorized Version was printed in the usual form of chapters and verses, and before each chapter a summary of its contents was prefixed. No other extraneous matter was permitted, except some marginal explanations of the meaning of certain Greek or Hebrew words, and a number of cross-references to other parts of the Scripture. At the beginning was placed a dedication to King James and a short "Address to the Reader". Books such as Ecclesiasticus, and Machabees, and Tobias, which are considered by Protestants to be apocryphal, were of course omitted. Although it was stated on the title-page that the Authorized Version was "ap-

pointed to be read in the Churches", in fact it came into use only gradually. For the Epistles and Gospels, it did not displace the Bishops' Version until the revision of the Liturgy in 1661; and for the Psalms, that version has been retained to the present day; for it was found that the people were so accustomed to singing it that any change was inadvisable, if not impossible. Considerable changes were made, from time to time, in the successive editions of the Authorized Version, in the notes and references, and some even in the text. A system of chronology based chiefly on the calculations of Archbishop Ussher was first inserted in 1701; but in many later editions both the dates and many, or even all, of the references or verbal notes have been omitted.

It is generally admitted that the Authorized Version was in almost every respect a great improvement on any of its predecessors. So much was this the case that when Bishop Challoner made his revision of the Douay Bible (1749–52), which is now commonly in use among English-speaking Catholics, he did not scruple to borrow largely from it. Indeed, Cardinal Newman gives it as his opinion (Tracts Theol. and Eccles., 373) that Challoner's revision was even nearer to the Authorized Version than to the original Douay, "not in grammatical structure, but in phraseology and diction". Nevertheless, there remained in the Authorized Version here and there traces of controversial prejudice, as for example, in the angel's salutation to the Blessed Virgin Mary, the words "highly favoured" being a very imperfect rendering of the original. In such cases, needless to say, Challoner adhered to the Douay. Moreover, while in the Authorized Version the names of persons and places were usually given in an anglicized form already in use, derived from the Hebrew spelling, Challoner nearly always kept the Vulgate names, which come originally from the Septuagint. It is partly due to this that the Authorized Version has an unfamiliar sound to Catholic ears. The Authorized Version remained in undisputed possession for the greater part of three centuries, and became part of the life of the people. In the latter half of the nineteenth century, however, it began to be considered that the progress of science called for a new version which should embrace the results of modern research. The work was set on foot by Convocation in 1870, and a Committee was formed, in which the Americans co-operated, resulting in the issue of the Revised Version (1881–84). The Revised Version has never received any definite ecclesiastical sanction, nor has it been officially introduced into church use. It has made its way simply on its merits. But although at the present day it is much used by students, for the general public (non-Catholic) the Authorized Version still holds its ground, and shows no sign of losing its popularity.

SCRIVENER, *The Authorized Edition of the English Bible* (1884); *Preface* to the *Revised Version; English Hexapla, Introduction* (s. v.); MILLIGAN, in HAST., *Dict. of the Bible,* s. v. *Versions;* GASQUET, *The Old English Bible* (London, 1897); CARLETON, *Rheims and the English Bible* (Oxford, 1902).

BERNARD WARD.

Autocephali (Gr., αὐτοκέφαλοι, independent), a designation in early Christian times of certain bishops who were subject to no patriarch or metropolitan, but depended directly on the triennial provincial synod or on the Apostolic See. In case of heresy, e. g., or other grave offences, they could only be judged by these tribunals. Such were the bishops of Cyprus (cf. Council of Ephesus, Act. VII; Trullan Council, can. 39), the Bishops of Iberia and Armenia as late as the time of Photius, those of Britain before the coming of St. Augustine, and for a while those of Ravenna. The extension of the patriarchal authority diminished their number. Quite similar were certain Oriental bishops in the Patriarchates of Constantinople, Alexandria, and Antioch, who were subject directly to the patriarch of the civil (imperial) diocese to which they belonged, and who owed no obedience to their immediate metropolitans; they were not unlike the modern "exempt" bishops immediately subject to the Apostolic See. The most ancient list of them is given in the ninth-century "Notitia" of Leo the Wise, where they are entitled archbishops and metropolitans, though they had no suffragans. Occasionally priests were called "autocephali", e. g. the clergy of a patriarchal diocese. (See Soz., Hist. Eccl., VI, 21, and Eus., Hist. Eccl., V, 23, with the note of Valesius, also BISHOP, EXEMPTION, RAVENNA.)

NEHER, in *Kirchenlex.*, I, 1733; THOMASSIN, *De Vet. et nov. ecc. discipl.*, I, 3, c. 41, n. 17; PHILLIPS, *Kirchenrecht*, VII, 440; LAURENTIUS, *Inst. Jur. Eccl.* (Freiburg, 1905), § 214.

THOMAS J. SHAHAN.

Autos Sacramentales (Sp. *auto*, act or ordinance; *sacramental*, sacramental, pertaining to a sacrament), a form of dramatic literature which is peculiar to Spain, though in some respects similar in character to the old Morality plays of England. The *auto sacramental* may be defined as a dramatic representation of the mystery of the Eucharist. At least this is the definition that would apply to the *auto* of the time of Calderón. It does not so well fit, however, those of the preceding century, many of which were sacramental in character only because they were presented during the feast of Corpus Christi. They are usually allegorical, the characters representing, for example, Faith, Hope, Air, Sin, Death, etc. There were some indeed, in which not a single human character appeared, but personifications of the Virtues, the Vices, the Elements, etc. As early as the thirteenth century religious exhibitions had been popular with the masses in Spain. These usually took the form of simple dialogue, and were presented during religious festivals, for instance, at Christmas and Easter. But it is not until the beginning of the sixteenth century that we have the first true *auto sacramental* having for its theme the mystery of the Eucharist. It was "El Auto de San Martín", by Gil Vicente. During the sixteenth and seventeenth centuries these *Autos* continued to appear, being gradually improved and elaborated until brought to their highest state of development by Calderón.

The *auto sacramental* was always presented in the streets in connexion with the celebration of the feast of Corpus Christi. It was preceded by a solemn procession through the principal streets of the city, the houses along the route being decorated in honour of the occasion. In the procession appeared the priests bearing the Host under a splendid canopy, followed by a devout throng, in which, in Madrid, often appeared the king and his court without distinction of rank, and last of all, in beautiful cars, came the actors from the public theatres who were to take part in the performance. The procession usually halted before the house of some dignitary while the priests performed certain religious ceremonies, the multitude kneeling meanwhile as if in church. At the conclusion of these, the *auto* was given. These performances, and the procession as well, were given with much splendour and at great expense, being limited only by the resources of the particular town in which they took place.

Of the better known writers of this kind of dramatic literature may be mentioned Juan de la Enzina and Gil Vicente, who wrote in the fifteenth and sixteenth centuries, while among those who wrote autos when they were at the height of their success was Lope de Vega, who composed no less than four hundred. Very few of these are now extant. Among his best are "The Harvest" and "The Wolf turned Shepherd." Then came Montalván, whose "Poly-

phemus" was his best known *auto;* Valdivielso, who wrote "The Prodigal Son"; and lastly, the most successful of all, Calderón. Although not as prolific as Lope de Vega, Calderón has left about seventy *autos*, the best known of which are "The Divine Orpheus", a work of considerable poetic merit, "The Devotion to the Mass", and "The Captivity of the Ark". These *autos sacramentales* produced a great effect on the people. From time immemorial, allegory of every kind had powerfully appealed to them, and these *autos* took a strong hold on the popular favour, coming as they did during religious festivals, with their music and their splendour, coupled with the fact that they were given at the public expense and with the sanction of the Church. In 1765, their public representation was forbidden by Charles III, but the habits of centuries could not be so easily overcome, and for many years afterward they continued to be presented in some of the smaller towns.

FITZMAURICE-KELLY, *Historia de la Literatura Española* (Madrid, 1901), *passim;* TRENCH, *Essay on the Life and Genius of Calderon* (London, 1880); SCHACK, *Geschichte der dramatischen Literatur und Kunst in Spanien* (Berlin, 1846), III.

VENTURA FUENTES.

Autpert, AMBROSE, an early medieval writer and abbot of the Benedictine Order, b. in France, early in the eighth century; d. after an abbacy of little more than a year at his monastery of St. Vincent on the Volturno, near Beneventum, in Southern Italy, 778 or 779. Autpert, if forgotten to-day, was not without a name in his own century. Charlemagne made use of his talents; Pope Stephen IV protected him; and the monastery where he spent many years, and of which he died abbot was famous among the great monasteries of Italy. He has sometimes been confounded with another Autpert who was Abbot of Monte Cassino in the next century, and who left a collection of sermons besides a spiritual treatise. His chief work is "Expositio in Apocalypsim" (P. L., XXXV, col. 2417–52).

FRANCIS P. HAVEY.

Autran, JOSEPH, a French poet, b. at Marseilles 20 June, 1813; d. in the same city, 6 March, 1877. He pursued his classical studies in the Jesuit college of Aix. His father, however, having met with reverses, Autran, obliged to earn his own living, accepted a position as teacher in a religious school. Thus engaged, he published the first work which drew attention to his merits as a poet; this was an ode written on the occasion of Lamartine's departure for the Holy Land. "Le Départ pour l'Orient" was followed (1835) by a collection of poems entitled "La mer", remarkable for descriptive power and the charms of its versification. The favour with which it was received led him to publish a second series of the same subject, "Les Poèmes de la mer", which appeared in 1852. Meantime, he had written another volume of lyrics "Ludibria ventis", which served to increase his popularity as a singer; also a prose work, "Italie et la Semaine sainte à Rome" (1841), the fruit of a voyage to the Eternal City. The French conquest of Algiers suggested the subject of an epic poem, "Milianah", published in 1842. In 1848 "La Fille d'Achille", a tragedy in five acts, shared with Emile Augier's "Gabrielle" the *Prix Monthyon* awarded by the French Academy. This was followed by: "Laboureurs et Soldats" (1845), "Vie rurale" (1856), crowned by the French Academy; "Epîtres rustiques"; "Le poème des beaux jours" (1862); "Le Cyclope", a drama after Euripides (1869); "Les Paroles de Salomon"; "Sonnets Capricieux" (1873); "La Légende des Paladins" (1875). In 1868 Autran was elected a member of the French Academy to succeed Ponsard. In his later days he was stricken with blindness. Autran, though not a poet of the first rank, is a writer whose noble sentiments, chaste imagination, and religious feeling will always endear him to lovers of pure and refreshing poetry. All his works are remarkable for their purity of expression, the music of their rhythm, and a profound feeling for the beauties of nature.

Anthologie des poètes français (Paris, 1892) 302; DE JULLEVILLE, *Hist. de la langue et de la littérature françaises* (Paris, 1899), VII, 355; DE LAPRADE, *Préface des œuvres complètes d'Autran* (1874–81).

JEAN LE BARS.

Autun (AUGUSTODONUM), DIOCESE OF, comprises the entire Department of Saône et Loire in France. It was suffragan to the Archdiocese of Lyons under the old regime. The sees of Châlons-sur-Saône and Mâcon were united to Autun after the Revolution, and it then became suffragan to Besançon (1802), afterwards to Lyons (1822). Christian teaching reached Autun at a very early period, as we know from the famous Greek inscription of Pectorius which dates from the third century. It was found in 1839 in the cemetery of St. Peter l'Estrier at Autun and bears testimony to the antiquity and efficacy of baptism and the sacramental words of the Holy Eucharist. Local recensions of the "Passion" of St. Symphorianus of Autun exhibit St. Polycarp on the eve of the persecution of Septimius Severus, assigning to St. Irenæus two priests and a deacon (Sts. Benignus, Andochius, and Thyrsus), all three of whom depart for Autun. St. Benignus goes on to Langres, while the others remain at Autun. According to this legendary cycle, which dates from about the first half of the sixth century, it was not then believed at Autun that the city was an episcopal see in the time of St. Irenæus (c. 140–c. 211). St. Amator, whom Autun tradition designates as its first bishop, probably occupied the see about 250. The first bishop known to history is St. Reticius, an ecclesiastical writer, and contemporary of the Emperor Constantine (306–337). The Bishop of Autun enjoys the right of wearing the pallium, in virtue of a privilege accorded to the see in 599 by St. Gregory the Great (590–604). In the Merovingian period two Bishops of Autun figured prominently in political affairs; St. Syagrius, bishop during the second half of the sixth century, a contemporary of St. Germanus, Bishop of Paris (a native of Autun), and St. Leodegarius (Léger), bishop from 663 to 680, celebrated on account of his conflict with Ebroïn and put to death by order of Thierry III. Charles Maurice de Talleyrand-Périgord, the future diplomat, was Bishop of Autun from 1788 to 1790, when he resigned. The last bishop of this see, appointed in 1882 (d. 1906), was Cardinal Perraud, member of the French Academy. In 670, an important council was held at Autun for the purpose of regulating the discipline of the Benedictine monasteries. The present cathedral of Autun dates from the eleventh and twelfth centuries, and was formerly the chapel of the Dukes of Burgundy; their palace was the actual episcopal residence. In the Diocese of Autun are yet to be seen the ruins of the Benedictine Abbey of Tournus and the great Abbey of Cluny, to which 2,000 monasteries were subject, and which gave to the Church the great pope, Gregory VII (1073–85). Gelasius II (1118–19) died at Cluny, and there also was held the conclave that elected Calixtus II (1119–24). The devotion to the Sacred Heart originated in the Visitation Convent at Paray-le-Monial, founded in 1644, and now the object of frequent pilgrimages. At the end of the year 1905 the Diocese of Autun contained 618,227 inhabitants, 65 parishes, 458 succursal, or auxiliary, churches, and 68 vicariates.

Gallia Christiana, ed. nova (1728), IV, 314–437 and *Documents,* 39–126; DE FONTENAY, *Autun, ses monuments* (Autun, 1889); DUCHESNE, *Fastes épiscopaux de l'ancienne Gaule,* I, 48–56, and II, 174–182 (Paris, 1894 and 1900); CHEVALIER, *Topo-bibl.* (Paris, 1894–99), 269–272.

GEORGES GOYAU.

COUNCILS OF AUTUN.—The first council, held in 663 (or 670) orders all ecclesiastics to learn by heart the Apostles' Creed and the Athanasian Creed, and this seems to be the earliest mention of the latter in France. Cardinal Pitra says in his "Histoire de St. Léger" that this canon may have been directed against Monothelitism, then seeking entrance into the Gallican churches, but condemned beforehand in the latter of these creeds. The Rule of St. Benedict was also prescribed as the normal monastic code. In the Council of 1065, Saint Hugues, Abbot of Cluny, accomplished the reconciliation of Robert, Duke of Burgundy, with the Bishop of Autun. In 1077 Hugues, Bishop of Dié, held a council at Autun, by order of St. Gregory VII; it deposed Manasses, Bishop of Reims, for simony and usurpation of the see, and reproved other bishops for absence from the council. In 1094 Hugues, Archbishop of Lyons, and thirty-three other bishops renewed at Autun the excommunication of Henry IV of Germany, the Antipope Guibert, and their partisans, also that of King Philip of France, guilty of bigamy. Simony, ecclesiastical disorders, and monastic usurpations provoked other decrees, only one of which is extant, forbidding the monks to induce the canons to enter monasteries.

MANSI, *Coll. Conc.* (1748), Supp. I, 497, XI, 126, XIX, 10 sqq.; Supp. II, 25, XX, 483; *Gallia Christiana,* ed. nova (1728), IV, 314–437, 39–126; GAGUARD, *Hist. de l'église d'Autun* (Autun, 1774); CHEVALIER, *Topo-bibl.* (Paris, 1894–99), 270.

THOMAS J. SHAHAN.

Auxentius, name of several early Christian personages. — AUXENTIUS OF MILAN, native of Cappadocia, ordained (343) to the priesthood by Gregory, the intruded Bishop of Alexandria. After the banishment of Dionysius of Milan in 355, Auxentius was made bishop of that see through Arian intrigue, though ignorant of the Latin tongue. Some of the principal Western bishops attempted, but in vain, to bring him to accept the Nicene Creed. He was publicly accused at Milan, in 364, by St. Hilary of Poitiers, and convicted of error in a disputation held in that city by order of the Emperor Valentinian. His submission was only apparent, however, and he remained powerful enough to compel the departure of St. Hilary from Milan. In 359 he forced many bishops of Illyricum to sign the creed of Rimini. Though St. Athanasius procured his condemnation by Pope Damasus at a Roman synod (369), he retained possession of his see until his death in 374, when he was succeeded by St. Ambrose.—AUXENTIUS, JUNIOR, originally Mercurinus, a Scythian, and a disciple of Ulfilas, or Wulfila, of whose life and death he wrote an account that the Arian bishop, Maximinus, included (383) in a work directed against St. Ambrose and the Synod of Aquitesa, 381. This favourite of Justina was the anti-bishop set up in Milan by the Arians, on the occasion of the election of Ambrose. He challenged the latter in 386 to a public dispute in which the judges were to be the court favourites of the Arian empress; he also demanded for the Arians the use of the Basilica Portiana. The refusal to surrender this church brought about a siege of the edifice, in which Ambrose and a multitude of his faithful Milanese had shut themselves up. The empress eventually abandoned her favourite and made peace with Ambrose. (Baunard, Saint Ambroise, Paris, 1872, 332–348; Hefele, History of the Councils, I).—AUXENTIUS OF MOPSUESTIA (360). Baronius places this bishop in the Roman martyrology, because of the story told by Philostorgius (in Suidas) that he was at one time an officer in the army of Licinius, and gave up his commission rather than obey the imperial command to lay a bunch of grapes at the feet of a statue of Bacchus. Tillemont (Mémoires, VI, 786–7) is inclined to believe that

Auxentius was an Arian; his patronage of the heretic Aetius (Philostorgius, Hist. Eccl., V, 1, 2), points to this conclusion.

VENABLES in *Dict. of Christ. Biogr.*, I, 233.

THOMAS J. SHAHAN.

Auxerre, COUNCILS OF.—In 585 (or 578) a Council of Auxerre held under St. Annacharius formulated forty-five canons, closely related in context to canons of the contemporary Councils of Lyons and Mâcon. They are important as illustrating life and manners among the newly-converted Teutonic tribes and the Gallo-Romans of the time. Many of the decrees are directed against remnants of heathen barbarism and superstitious customs; others bear witness to the persistence in the early Middle Ages in France of certain ancient Christian customs. The canons of the council of 695 or 697 are concerned chiefly with the Divine Office and ecclesiastical ceremonies.

MANSI, *Coll. Conc.*, IX, 911; XII, 107; XIV, 786; HEFELE, *Conciliengesch.*, II, 72; ZACCARIA, *Dissert. stor. eccles.* (1795), XVII, 95–105; *Chevalier, Topo-bibl.* (Paris, 1894–99), 275.

THOMAS J. SHAHAN.

Auxerre, DIOCESE AND SCHOOL OF. See SENS.

Auxiliary Bishop, a bishop deputed to a diocesan who, capable of governing and administering his diocese, is unable to perform the pontifical functions; or whose diocese is so extensive that it requires the labours of more than one; or whose episcopal see has attached to it a royal or imperial office requiring protracted presence at court. According to the present ecclesiastical discipline no bishop can be consecrated without title to a certain and distinct diocese which he governs either actually or potentially. Actual government requires residence, potential does not. Hence, there are two principal classes of bishops, the residential, or diocesan or, local, or ordinary; and the non-residential, or titular. Diocesan bishops have and exercise (*de jure*) full power of order and jurisdiction, in and over the diocese committed to their exclusive care by the pope. Titulars, as such, have not, and do not exercise, power of order and jurisdiction, in and over their titular sees. All actual jurisdiction in titular sees the pope reserves to himself, and exercises through the Sacred Congregation of Propaganda. The jurisdiction of a diocesan is ordinary. Should a titular perform a jurisdictional function, he uses delegated jurisdiction.

Titular bishops are those who have been appointed by the Holy See to a see or diocese which, in former times, had been canonically established and possessed cathedral church, clergy, and laity, but at present, on account of pagan occupation and government, has neither clergy nor people. It is essential that the titular diocese did once exist, and did cease to exist through death or defection of clergy and faithful, or pagan settlement and government. No vestige of titulars, as defined, appears until the close of the thirteenth century. Evidently the host of wandering bishops without title or see—missionary, regionary, or exiled bishops—of whom historians make mention, cannot be classed with our titulars, who did not come into existence until the greater part of the East had passed under pagan rule, and the destruction or defection of the Christian flock and the death of their shepherds ensued. The episcopal succession in those dioceses was maintained as long as a hope remained of their rehabilitation, and their bishops were hospitably received, and frequently used by the diocesans as auxiliaries or vicars, in pontificals in their respective dioceses. Ecclesiastical authority placed some of them in temporary charge of vacant Western dioceses, on condition of their immediate return to their own sees when possible. Others were given the spiritual care of dioceses by civil princes who, avaricious of the episcopal revenues, prevented the appointment of a diocesan bishop. In the fourteenth century, the great number of bishops without occupation, and their invasion of the rights and privileges of the diocesans brought about necessary legislation. Clement V (I, iii de elect. V, Clem.) prohibited the election and consecration of any cleric, without papal license, to any of those vacant sees (*sine clero populoque*).

The first mention of titular bishops occurs in the Lateran decree (sess. 9 de Cardinalibus), wherein Leo X permits the creation of titulars whom the cardinal-bishops may use as suffragans, or auxiliaries, in their respective dioceses. Afterwards, the privilege was extended for various reasons, principal among which were (a) to preserve from oblivion the memory of those once venerable and important, but now desolate, sees; (b) that the pope might have at hand efficient and capable assistants (without care of dioceses) in the discharge of the numerous and important ecclesiastical duties of the Apostolic ministry in and outside of the Roman Curia; (c) that suffragans might be given to bishops impeded by reason of infirmity, partial or entire, or of the great extent of their dioceses, or legitimate and protracted absence from performing their episcopal duties. Pius V, after the Council of Trent, decreed that suffragans were not to be given unless to cardinals, and to those bishops to whom it was customary to grant them, and who guaranteed a fixed salary to support the dignity of the auxiliary. He also decreed that such auxiliary should not, without papal permission, exercise the pontifical functions in any other diocese, save in that of the diocesan to whom he had been given. Gradually it was extended to other bishops who had solid reasons for assistance. The appointment of all titulars belongs exclusively to the Holy See (Clement, *ut supra*). Present usage requires an auxiliary, suffragan, and temporary coadjutor (used indiscriminately to mean almost the same office) to be also a titular bishop, yet the former antedate the latter by many centuries. They come down to us from Apostolic times; thus Linus and Cletus were vicars, or auxiliaries, to St. Peter at Rome; Ammianus, to St. Mark of Alexandria; Alexander, to Narcissus (aged 116 years) of Jerusalem; St. Gregory, the theologian, auxiliary in pontificals to St. Gregory, Bishop of Nazianzus; St. Augustine, coadjutor of Valerius of Hippo; so likewise those of the rural bishops (*chorepiscopi*), who had received episcopal consecration (there were many in the Orient from the third to the seventh, and, in the West, from the eighth to the tenth, centuries), and many exiled bishops, then in the West were auxiliaries to diocesan bishops even up to the Clementine law.

Though the terms auxiliary, suffragan, and coadjutor are used indiscriminately, yet there is a difference. Auxiliary bishop is as defined at the beginning of this article. Suffragan bishop is the name given to the auxiliaries of the Cardinal-Bishop of Ostia and Velletri and the Cardinal-Bishop of Sabina. Coadjutors are given to diocesans impeded from performance of their episcopal duties by old age, or bodily infirmity, or sickness, protracted and incurable, such as loss of speech, blindness, paralysis, and insanity. A coadjutor to an insane bishop has full jurisdiction and can exercise all episcopal duties, with the sole exception of disposing of ecclesiastical properties. There are coadjutors in temporals, or in spirituals, or in both temporals and spirituals. The first kind need not be a bishop; a cleric suffices. Coadjutors are also temporary and perpetual; the first has no succession, the latter has, and is called coadjutor with right of succession. Coadjutors with right of succession rarely are granted, and only when urgent necessity and an evident utility are superadded to the above reasons; and then they must be made known to, and approved as such, by the pope. It is not the practice to force a perpetual coadjutor upon an unwilling diocesan, although the pope can do so. Such perpetual coadjutor cannot mix in the ecclesiastical administration, nor do aught but as he is told or permitted by the diocesan. Some of the Fathers of the Vatican Council proposed that, in the future, auxiliary bishops should be appointed instead of perpetual coadjutors. A coadjutor is granted to aid a diocesan in order and jurisdiction as far as is needed; the auxiliary is deputed to aid only in function of order. He may be made vicar-general, and then, by virtue of that office, he has power of jurisdiction. Since auxiliarship, or temporary coadjutorship, is neither a title nor prelature, but an office, it is temporary, and ceases at the death, or suspension, or resignation, of the diocesan. The Holy See, for valid reasons, in the fifteenth century established permanent auxiliarships in Prussia, Poland, Spain, and Portugal. Pius VII (16 July, 1821, Constit. De salute animar.) confirmed such offices in Germany, etc. In these countries the office of auxiliary does not die with the diocesan, but continues under his successors. The auxiliary, *sede vacante*, however, cannot perform functions strictly episcopal. Successors to such auxiliaries are not given the same, but an entirely different, titular see. Perpetual coadjutorship is irrevocable, and its holder succeeds immediately to the vacant see; no further collation or election is necessary. Office of auxiliary, etc. is revocable at will of pope and diocesan; that of the perpetual coadjutor cannot be taken away unless for canonical causes. Auxiliaries and temporary coadjutors are appointed by the Holy Father at the request of the bishop in need of assistance. The pope (on petition of the Sacred Congregation of the Council, or of Propaganda) as a rule appoints the clergyman named by orator. The election or nomination for perpetual coadjutors is governed by the law for election or nomination (*sede vacante*) of a new diocesan. The same disposition of mind and body is required for auxiliary, etc. as for diocesan bishops. They must be thirty years complete, and have spent six months in Sacred orders prior to elevation to the episcopate, yet in the case of the auxiliaries, the most worthy has no rights over the merely worthy. For perpetual coadjutorship most worthy is demanded.

Rights and duties of auxiliaries must be considered from a twofold standpoint: i. e. titulars of a diocese, and auxiliaries of diocesan bishops. By right of consecration a titular auxiliary can validly, but not licitly, without permission of the residential, perform all the functions annexed to the episcopal order by Divine and ecclesiastical law. The Church could, but does not, require the diocesan's permission, for the validity of the latter functions. Having no actual jurisdiction, he cannot without express consent and permission of the ordinary perform pontifical functions in the city or diocese, nor can he do so, *sede vacante*, even with the permission of the chapter. Possessing only potential jurisdiction in his titular see, he cannot (a) hear, or grant faculties to hear, confession of a visiting subject from his titular see; (b) confirm or ordain him; (c) send a priest to preach, or to perform any priestly functions, in his titular see; (d) absolve, or grant faculty to a diocesan priest to absolve, a member of his own household; (e) assist at the marriage of a titular subject, a visitor where the Tridentine holds; (f) ordain his familiar of three years' standing, nor grant indulgences. Should at any time clergy or laity sufficiently numerous be found in his titular diocese, and no representative of the Holy See have supervision over it, he can immediately, without any other collation of the benefice, take possession of his titular church. He then ceases to be titular and becomes diocesan. He may, and according to some must, be invited to General Councils, and once there he has decisive vote. A few were present at the Council of Trent and quite a number at the Vatican Council. Although he has not the right to take part in Provincial Councils, he may be invited to do so, but has no decisive vote, unless by unanimous consent and permission of the Provincial Fathers. He can wear everywhere the prelatial dress and ring (the sign of his spiritual union with his titular see), and use the pontifical vestments, ornaments, and insignia, when, by permission of the ordinary, he performs pontifical functions. In general councils and every meeting of bishops where the local prelate is not present, in Rome, and outside of Rome, the titular auxiliary, etc., takes precedence of all bishops (except assistant bishops at pontifical throne) of later consecration. In provincial councils, however, all suffragans outrank all titulars without regard to date of consecration. Titular auxiliaries, as well as diocesans, are obliged to receive episcopal consecration within three months from confirmation, unless this is morally impossible; to make profession of faith and take oath of loyalty and fidelity to the Roman Pontiff, and to go to his titular diocese, if ever it is rehabilitated. By reason of the spiritual union with his see, he cannot be elected, but only postulated, for another diocese. Only the Holy Father can dissolve the spiritual union with the titular see. An auxiliary never has the title of a titular archiepiscopal see; but a perpetual coadjutor often has. The titular archbishop-coadjutor is not bound to petition for the pallium or the use of it. Titular auxiliary is not bound (a) to make visit *ad limina Apostolorum* (some say he is); (b) to residence in his titular see, or in the cathedral city of the diocese in which he holds the office of auxiliary (the place of his residence is regulated by the diocesan); (c) to say Mass for the people.

The criminal and important causes relating to auxiliary bishops are reserved to the Holy See, those of lesser moment to the Congregation of Bishops and Regulars. By virtue of the office of auxiliary he has a perpetual right to a pension suitable to maintain the episcopal dignity. This is to be paid by the diocesan from the diocesan revenues. The amount of pension and source from which it is to be obtained is generally specified in the Apostolic Letters of appointment. He can hold any benefice he had before and acquire a new one after his consecration, as the office of auxiliary is not a benefice. He enjoys the same honorific privileges (with a few exceptions, viz. throne, cappa magna, mozzetta, and rochet worn without mantelletta, and crosier); pontifical ornaments, and titles, as does the diocesan. He can and must use the prelatial dress, as in the Roman Curia, to wit: rochet over the purple soutane with purple mantelletta, in his attendance in the cathedral, where he has precedence over all other canons and dignitaries, as to choir stall and functions. When he is celebrant in pontifical functions, the canons must assist, but in the usual canonical dress, except ministers in sacred vestments. Not all the canons are bound to meet him at the church door, as he enters to celebrate pontifical Mass. During the ceremony he is assisted by a canon as assistant priest, and deacon, and sub-deacon in sacred vestments. He has no right to the usual two canon-assistant deacons, nor to the seventh candlestick, nor to the usual reverences of the canons at Kyrie, etc., nor the use of the throne or crosier unless by special permission. He uses the faldistorium. He can use the crosier with the special permission of the diocesan, and when he officiates at ordinations, consecrations, and other pontifical functions, during which the rules of the Pontifical demand its use

(Cæremon. Epis., I, xvii; Decret. Bracharen. Sept. 1607). It is proper, however, that he impart the episcopal last blessing. He cannot bless publicly the people as he wends his way through the city. It is forbidden him to make visitation of the cloister of nuns without express permission and command of the local prelate. Canons are bound to kiss the auxiliary's hand when he gives them Holy Communion on Holy Thursday, and assist him in consecrating Holy Oils, conferring Holy orders, and in all sacred functions strictly episcopal, which he performs for his diocesan. If he be a canon, he is subject, as the other cathedral canons, to diocesan law and the penalties attached to its violation. If the diocesan and the auxiliary assist simultaneously at Mass, the sub-deacon must not give the latter the pax before the canon-assistants at the throne have received it from the bishop ordinary. When the diocesan assists at Mass, or Vespers, the auxiliary must leave his stall and join the other canons in making the prescribed reverences before the Kyrie, Gloria, etc. Should the celebrant be the diocesan, assisted by the chapter in sacred vestments, the auxiliary can wear a cope and a linen mitre (with consent of the local), which latter he must take off and put on by himself. It is expedient that he substitute another in his turn for the Missa Cantata, as he cannot use a faldistorium and pontifical vestments without consent of his diocesan.

Andreucci, *Hierarachia Ecclesiastica*, I, i, *De Episcopo titulari;* Benedict XIV, *De Syn. Diœc.* II, 7, 1; 13, 6,5; XIII, 14, 15; XIII, 14, 11; XII, 6, 7; Ferraris, *Bibl. prompt.* art. VII; Wernz, *Jus Decret.* II, 994, no. 807 sqq. (*de Vicariis in Pontificalibus*); Bouix, *De Episcopo* (Paris, 1859), IV, 3, i–iii; Zitelli, I, ii, c. iii; Craisson, *Manuale Tot. Jur. Can.* (1894), I, 568 sqq.; Icard, *Prælectiones*, etc. (1893), I, 1, § 5; Riganti, *Commentaria in Regulas*, etc., I, in Reg. I, § 5, nn. 79 et seq.; Fagnanus, *Commentar.* V, *De Priv. C. Episcopalia*, no. 34 sq.; Leurenius, *De Vicariis Episcopi*, qu. 14, 15, 19; Barbosa, *Jur. Eccles. Univ.* (ed. 1677), I, xv, nos. 50, 51, 52, 53; Vecchiotti, *Instit. Canon.*, I, vii, § 72, 73, 74, 75, 76; Ferrari, *Summa Instit. Canon.* (1896), I, xvi; Aichner, *Compendium Jur. Eccles.* (1895), 418 sqq.; Aguilar, *Scientiæ Jur. Compendium*, 227 *De Epis. Auxiliaribus;* Ojetti, *Synop. Rer. Moral*, etc. (1904), s. v. *Coadjutor;* Sebastianelli, *Præl. Jur. Canon. De Personis*, Appendix *de Epis. Titularibus;* De Luca, *Prælec. Jur. Can.*, I, xviii, art. II, *De Epis. Tit.;* *Analecta Ecclesiastica*, III, 400; IV, 217; VI, 476; Taunton, *Law of the Church* (1906) s. v.

P. M. J. Rock.

Auxilius of Naples, the name (possibly fictitious, according to Hefele) of an ecclesiastic to whom we owe a series of remarkable writings (P. L., CXXIX, 1054 sqq.) that deal with the controversies concerning the succession and fate of Pope Formosus (891–896), and especially the validity of the orders conferred by him. Auxilius was a Frank, who was ordained a priest, or perhaps only a deacon, in Rome by Formosus, and lived later in lower Italy, apparently at Naples. On the death of Pope Formosus there began for the papacy a time of the deepest humiliation, such as it has never experienced before or since. After the successor of Formosus, Boniface VI, had ruled only fifteen days, Stephen VI (properly, VII), one of the adherents of the party of the Duke of Spoleto, was raised to the Papal Chair. In his blind rage, Stephen not only abused the memory of Formosus but also treated his body with indignity. Stephen was strangled in prison in the summer of 897, and the six following popes (to May, 904) owed their elevation to the struggles of the political parties. Christophorus, the last of them, was overthrown by Sergius III (May, 904–August, 911). Sergius had been a partisan of Stephen VI, and like the latter regarded the elevation of Formosus to the papacy as illegal and the orders conferred by him as null and void. Auxilius was a follower of Formosus, and in several works composed about 908–911, he made a courageous and learned defence, both of Formosus and of the validity of his orders and those of his adherents. Morinus was the first to publish two of these writings in his "De ecclesiasticis ordi-

nationibus" (Paris, 1665). They are entitled "Libellus de ordinationibus a papâ Formoso factis", and "Tractatus qui Infensor et Defensor dicitur".

A third work of Auxilius, of similar import, was found by Mabillon and published by him under the title: "Libellus super causâ et negotio Formosi papæ", in his "Vetera Analecta" (ed.1723, IV, 28–32). In his "Auxilius und Vulgarius", quoted below, Dümmler published from a Bamberg manuscript two further writings of Auxilius, one of which is known as "In defensionem sacræ ordinationis papæ Formosi libellus prior et posterior", while the other bears in the manuscript itself the title: "Libellus in defensionem Stephani episcopi et præfatæ ordinationis". (Stephen, Bishop of Naples, had been consecrated by Pope Formosus.) Still another treatise of an unknown author on behalf of Formosus, published by Bianchini in his edition of the "Liber Pontificalis" (1735, IV) is considered by Hergenröther (Photius, II, 370, 373, note 9) to be an extract from the writings of Auxilius, while Dümmler attributes it (op. cit., 42) to Eugenius Vulgarius, an Italian priest and a defender of Formosus. Two other compositions of Eugenius Vulgarius are known: "De causâ Formosianâ", and "Eugenius Vulgarius Petro Diacono fratri et amico". All these writings are very important, not only as historical sources but also from a theological point of view, because they take the position that the orders conferred by sinful and excommunicated bishops are not in themselves invalid. In a necrology of the Abbey of Monte Cassino is noted on 25 January the death of an Auxilius, deacon and monk, author of a commentary on Genesis (Mai, Spicilegium Romanum, IX, Appendix; cf. Mabillon, Ann. Ord. S. Benedicti, III, 325). This Auxilius may possibly be identical with the author of the works described above.

Dümmler, *Auxilius und Vulgarius; Quellen und Forschungen zur Gesch. des Papsttums im Anfang des 10ten Jahrh.* (Leipzig, 1866); Potthast, *Bibl. hist. medii ævi*, 2d ed. (Berlin, 1896), I, 128; Hurter, *Nomenclator*, 3d ed. (Innsbruck, 1903), I, 887 sqq.; Hefele, *Conciliengesch.*, 2d ed. (Freiburg, 1879), IV, 562 sqq.; Hergenröther-Kirsch, *Kirchengesch.*, 4th ed. (Freiburg, 1904), II, 196 sqq; Saltet, *Les Réordinations* (Paris, 1907), 156 sqq.

J. P. Kirsch.

Ava, a German poetess, the first woman known to have written in German and probably identical with a recluse of that name who died in Austria in the vicinity of Melk, A. D. 1127. Almost nothing is known of her life or personality. She herself tells us in a passage in her work that she was the mother of two sons who helped her in procuring the material for her poems. These poems are metrical versions of stories from the New Testament and consist of a "Life of Jesus", "Antichrist", "The Gifts of the Holy Ghost", "The Last Judgment", and "John the Baptist". They are preserved in two manuscripts, one at Verona, the other at Görlitz. The "John the Baptist" is found only in the latter manuscript. Ava's authorship of this poem, as well as that of the "Life of Jesus" has been questioned, but hardly on sufficient grounds. The poems are naive in tone and display deeply religious sentiments, but, except for occasional passages, they are destitute of poetic merit. Their technique is often crude, assonance taking the place of rhyme and alliteration being not infrequent. The chief source from which Ava drew her material was the New Testament, but she also made use of older German poems, and possibly other writings such as the Apocryphal Gospel of the Infancy of the Saviour by the Pseudo-Matthew.

The poems have been edited by Diemer in *Deutsche Gedichte des 11. und 12. Jahrhunderts* (Vienna, 1849), 227 sqq., and by Piper in *Zeitschrift für deutsche Philologie*, 19, 129 sq. For further information see Langguth, *Untersuchungen über die Gedichte der Ava* (Budapest, 1880); Piper, *Die geistliche Dichtung des Mittelalters*, part I, in Kürschner's *Deutsche National Litteratur*.

Arthur F. J. Remy.

Avancini, NICOLA, chiefly known as an ascetical writer, b. in the Tyrol, 1612; d. 6 December, 1686. He entered the Society of Jesus in 1677, and for some years held the chair of rhetoric and philosophy at Gratz, and subsequently that of theology at Vienna. He was rector of the Colleges of Passau, Vienna, and Gratz, Provincial of the Austrian Province, Visitor of Bohemia, and at his death Assistant for the German Provinces of the Society. In the midst of these onerous duties he found time to publish works on philosophy, theology, and sacred literature, none of which, however, have retained popularity except his "Meditations on the Life and Doctrines of Jesus Christ". This work, originally in Latin, was translated into the principal European languages and went through many editions. The meditations are considered dry by some, and the English version in use contains much additional matter drawn from the works of other authors. But these meditations, in their simple as well as their extended form, have assisted many most efficaciously in the difficult task of daily meditation. Avancini was also the author of sermons, or orations, and a large number of dramas, suitable for presentation by college students. For a complete list of his works see Sommervogel, I. In English we have the "Meditations on the Life and Doctrines of Jesus Christ. Translated from the German edition of the Rev. John E. Zollner, by T. E. Bazalgette, with a preface by the Rev. G. Porter, S.J." (London, 1875, 2 vols.). Another edition was issued in the Quarterly series by the Rev. H. J. Coleridge, S.J., in 1883. EDWARD P. SPILLANE.

Avarice (from Lat. *avarus*, "greedy"; "to crave") is the inordinate love for riches. Its special malice, broadly speaking, lies in that it makes the getting and keeping of money, possessions, and the like, a purpose in itself to live for. It does not see that these things are valuable only as instruments for the conduct of a rational and harmonious life, due regard being paid of course to the special social condition in which one is placed. It is called a capital vice because it has as its object that for the gaining or holding of which many other sins are committed. It is more to be dreaded in that it often cloaks itself as a virtue, or insinuates itself under the pretext of making a decent provision for the future. In so far as avarice is an incentive to injustice in the acquiring and retaining of wealth, it is frequently a grievous sin. In itself, however, and in so far as it implies simply an excessive desire of, or pleasure in, riches, it is commonly not a mortal sin. JOSEPH F. DELANY.

Avatār, an Anglicized form of the Sanskrit, *avatāra*, "descent", from the root *tr*, "pass" (cf. Latin *in-trare*), and the preposition *ava*, "down". The word is used, in a technical sense, in the Hindu religion to denote the descent upon earth of a portion of the essence of a god, which then assumes some coarser material form, be it animal, monster, or man. Such descents are ascribed in the mythology of Hinduism to various gods, but those ascribed to Vishnu are by far the most important. They are believed to have taken place at different ages of the world, and to have consisted of different proportions of the essence of Vishnu. Their number is variously stated, ranging from ten to twenty-eight, finally becoming indefinitely numerous. Any remarkable man is liable to be regarded as a more or less perfect avatār of Vishnu, and the consequence—one of the worst features of Hinduism—has been the offering of divine homage to men, especially the founders of religious sects and their successors.

The ten most famous avatārs are: (1) The Fish, *matsya*. The basis of this is the story told in the Satapatha Brāhmana of how Manu was saved from the Deluge by a great fish, which foretold him of the danger, commanded him to build a boat, and finally towed this boat to a mountain top. The Purānas afterwards declare that this fish was an avatār of Vishnu. (2) The Tortoise, *Kūrma*. Vishnu in this form offers his back as the pivot on which rests Mt. Mandara, while the gods and demons churn with it various valuable objects from the ocean of milk. (3) The Boar, *Varāha*. Like the first, this avatār is concerned with the rescue of the earth from a flood, the boar raising it from the water in which it had been submerged. (4) The Man-lion, *Nara-sinha*. Vishnu takes this form to deliver the world from a demon, who had obtained from Brahma the boon, that he should be slain neither by a god, a man, nor an animal. (5) The Dwarf, *Vāmana*. The world having fallen under the possession of another demon, Vishnu, in the form of a dwarf, begged for as much of it as he could cover in three steps. His request was granted, but, from the Rig-Veda on, the most prominent thing in connexion with Vishnu (originally a sun-god), was that in three strides he traverses the universe. Two strides now sufficing for the redemption of heaven and earth, compassion inspires him to leave the nether regions to the demon he has duped. (6) Rāma with the axe, *Parasu-rāma*. In the form of a hero, Rāma, armed with an axe, Vishnu destroys the Ksatriyas, or warrior caste, in the interest of the priestly caste, the Brahmins. (7) Rāma, the great hero of the Hindu Odyssey, the *Rāmā yana*, who is made into an avatār of Vishnu. (8) Krsna, the Indian Hercules, as he is styled by Megasthenes, the most popular hero of India, is the most perfect avatār of Vishnu. (9) Buddha, a curious result of the triumph of Hinduism over Buddhism. In one version it is explained that Vishnu's purpose was to destroy the wicked by leading them into a false religion. (10) Kalki. In this form Vishnu will descend when the world is wholly depraved, destroy utterly the wicked, and restore the happy conditions of the Age of Virtue.

The importance of this theory of avatārs to Hinduism is the way in which it has contributed to the wonderful adaptability of that religion. In the Buddha avatār the fact is particularly patent, but, in the Rāma and Krsna avatārs also, we clearly have the adoption into Hinduism of the cults of these heroes. It is a mere guess that similar compromises with some totemistic forms of religion are to be seen in the Fish, Boar, and Tortoise avatārs, and the same might be said of an attempt to see in the Man-lion and Dwarf avatārs, traces of the aboriginal religions. The resemblance of these avatārs to the doctrine of the Incarnation is most superficial, and, as the theory of the avatārs has a sufficient basis in Hindu philosophy, and several points of contact with the earlier mythology, it is unnecessary to suppose with Weber (Indische Studien, II, 169) that it is the result of an imitation of this dogma.

For bibliography see HINDUISM.

GEORGE MELVILLE BOLLING.

Avaugour, PIERRE DU BOIS, BARON D', d. 1664, was sixth Governor General of Canada. Born of an ancient family in Brittany, he served in the French army forty years; travelled in Persia, Russia, Poland, and Sweden, and took part in all the campaigns in Germany. This familiarity with camp life made his naturally eccentric character rough and unsociable as well. In 1661, he was chosen to succeed d'Argenson as Governor of New France, and arrived in Quebec on 31 August of that year. Utterly averse to pomp and ceremony, he refused the honours which the people of Canada wished to show him, and set out at once for Montreal, in order to familiarize himself with the state of the country. The result was embodied in a report which he sent to Colbert and the great Condé, wherein he advised the fortification of Quebec and the approaches to it by outworks at Ile d'Orléans and at Lévis. He also recommended that the colony should be freed of its useless officials, to be replaced by soldiers who could hold the Iroquois in check, and prevent the Dutch from supplying them with arms. He formed a council, at the head of which he placed the Superior of the Jesuits. The sale of drink to the Indians was forbidden under pain of death, a penalty which the governor inflicted on several who had disobeyed his orders. He became embroiled in a quarrel with the bishop and the Jesuits, because they had begged the release of a poor widow whom he had caused to be imprisoned for selling brandy. He dissolved his council, in order to surround himself with more subservient advisers, and removed the prohibition imposed on the sale of liquor. Serious disorders ensued; the priests preached against misuse of authority, and an earthquake which shook the whole valley of the St. Lawrence was looked upon by the people as a Divine chastisement. Bishop Laval found it necessary to return to France to ask for the governor's recall. D'Avaugour was relieved of his command, and a royal commissioner was charged to make enquiries as to his conduct. The governor left Quebec, 23 July, 1663. On his arrival in France he submitted two statements to the king in regard to the measures to be taken for the colonization and defence of Canada; he advised the concentration of the troops at Quebec and the building of a fort at the head of the Richelieu river, also that the Dutch should be driven out of Fort Orange (Albany), and that the French should take possession of the Hudson River, in order to gain an exit to the sea. At a later date one of his suggestions was acted on, when veteran soldiers were sent to Canada with permission to settle as colonists. D'Avaugour asked to be allowed to resume active service, and was sent to Austria, where Louis XIV was aiding the rising of the Croats. He died a soldier's death while bravely defending the fortress of Zrin against the Turks.

Papiers de Condé, series F, XXV (at the Castle of Chantilly); *New York Colonial Documents*, IX, 13–17, and 20, 21; FAILLON, *Hist. col. franç. au Canada*, III, 33–38 sqq.; 66 sqq.

J. EDMOND ROY.

Ave Maria. See HAIL MARY.

Ave Maris Stella (Hail, thou Star of Ocean), the first verse of an unrhymed, accentual hymn, of seven strophes of four lines each, assigned in the Roman Breviary to Vespers in the Common Office, the Office for Saturdays, and the Little Office (as well as for Feasts) of the Blessed Virgin. It has been ascribed wrongly to St. Bernard, but antedates him, being found in a St. Gall manuscript of the ninth century; and, also, without sufficient authority, to St. Venantius Fortunatus (d. 609). Its very frequent occurrence in the Divine Office made it most popular in the Middle Ages, many other hymns being founded upon it.

MONE, *Lateinische Hymnen*, etc., II, 216–229, for five paraphrases with notes; DANIEL, *Thesaurus Hymnol.*, I, 204–206, for text with variants, and IV, 136, for additional notes; *Analecta Hymnica*, I, 49–186; III, 40–41; IV, 49–50; VIII, 75; IX, 72; X, 103; XV, 114; XX, 142 sqq., Nos. 185–188; XXX, 282; XXXII, 33–34. An excellent study of its rhythmic features in connection with the plain-song melody of the first Mode was contributed by DOM POTHIER to the *Revue du chant grégorien* (Grenoble, 1895), 83 sqq. (reprinted with additional comment, by GIULIO BAS in his *Rhythme Grégorien*, etc. (Rome, 1906), 15–19. There are seven translations into English, that of Father Caswall appearing in his *Lyra Catholica* as "Gentle Star of Ocean," and again in his *Hymns and Poems* in an altered form, and also in many collections of Catholic hymns, sometimes modified. It is found in the Marquess of Bute's *Breviary* as "Hail, thou Star of Ocean." The other translations are by BESTE, HEWITT, CHAMBERS, and MRS. CHARLES.

H. T. HENRY.

Ave Regina, an antiphon so called from its first line, *Ave regina cælorum* (Hail, Queen of Heaven).

It is one of the four Antiphons of the Blessed Virgin sung in the Divine Office in turn throughout the year, and is assigned thus from Compline of 2 February (even when the Feast of the Purification is transferred) to Holy Thursday exclusively. It comprises two stanzas of four lines each, followed by its own versicle and response and prayer. Its date of composition is uncertain, but the conjecture of Stella (Inst. Liturg., Rome, 1895) that it antedates the fourth century seems to be without any warrant of external or internal evidence. It is found in the St. Alban's Book of the twelfth century; in a Munich MS. thought by Daniel to be of the thirteenth; in a Sarum Breviary of the fourteenth; and in York and Roman Breviaries of the fifteenth. Th. Bernard [Le Bréviaire (Paris, 1887), II, 454 sqq.] says it was introduced into the Divine Office by Clement VI in the fourteenth century. He gives a commentary, and thinks he can perceive in it elements of the "noble accents . . . aspirations of many Doctors, such as St. Athanasius, St. Ephrem, St. Ildephonsus". Said during Septuagesima, Lent, Passiontide, the time, namely, of preparation for Easter, it recalls the part Mary had in the drama of the reopening of Heaven to men, and shows her as reigning there, Queen of Angels. Its opening line was sometimes quoted as the first line of hymns and sequences in the fourteenth and fifteenth centuries (cf. Dreves and Blume, Analecta Hymnica, I, 94; X, 103; XXX, 238; XXXII, 43; XLVI, 136) which, however, had no other relation with the Antiphon, being sometimes meditations on the *Ave Maria*, sometimes distinct poetical compositions, for example:

Ave regina cœlorum,
Pia virgo tenella,
Maria (virgo), flos florum
Christi (que) clausa cella.
Gratia, quæ peccatorum
Dira tulisti bella,

and so on, throughout the whole of the Angelical Salutation down to *ventris tui*, where the poem ends (MS. of fourteenth century) (loc. cit., XLVI, 136). Or, as a distinct hymn:

Ave, regina cœlorum,
Ave, decus angelorum,
Ave, gaudium sanctorum,
Ave, solis regia,

in a MS. of the fifteenth century (loc. cit., XL, 98).

The *Ave Regina* has been translated by Caswall, "Lyra Catholica" (London, 1849, 1873, 1884; New York, 1851), whose version is used in the "Manual of Prayers" (Baltimore), 77: "Hail, O Queen of Heaven enthroned"; also by Beste, "Church Hymns" (1849): "Hail, thou mighty Queen of Heaven". The version in the Marquess of Bute's "Breviary" (Edinburgh, 1879, I, 177) begins: "Hail, O Mary, Queen of Heaven". Schlosser [Die Kirche in ihren Liedern (Freiburg, 1863), I, 251] gives a translation into German in the same metre. The plain-song melody in the 6th tone has also a simpler setting ["Manuale Missæ et Officiorum" (Rome and Tournai, 1903), 100, 103].

H. T. HENRY.

Avellano Collectio. See CANONS, COLLECTIONS of ANCIENT.

Avellino, DIOCESE OF.—An Italian diocese in the Province of Naples, suffragan to Benevento. Avellino was founded by St. Sabinus, martyr, in the beginning of the second century. The list of bishops dates from 1124. The Diocese of Frigento, whose list is from 1080 to 1455, was united with that of Avellino from 9 May, 1466, until 27 June, 1818, when it was suppressed. Avellino was vacant from 1782 to 1792. It has 118,649 Catholics; 41 parishes, 243 secular priests, 11 regulars, 80 seminarians, 90 churches and chapels.

Annuario Eccl. (Rome, 1907); CAPPELLETTI, *Chiese d'Italia* (1884), xix; ZINGARELLI, *Storia della cattedrà di Avelino e di suoi pastori, etc.* (Naples, 1856).

E. BUONAIUTI.

Avempace (IBN BADSHA, or IBN BADJA, called by the Scholastics AVEN-PACE and AVEMPACE), Arabian philosopher, physician, astronomer, mathematician, and poet, b. at Saragossa towards the end of the eleventh century; d. at Fez, 1138. In 1118 he was at Seville, where he wrote several treatises on logic. Later, he went to Granada and to Africa. He was, according to Arabian accounts, poisoned by rival physicians. He wrote treatises on mathematics, medicine, and philosophy, and commented on several of Aristotle's works, notably on the "Physics", "Meteorologica", "De Generatione et Corruptione", portions of "Historiæ Animalium" and "De Partibus Animalium". His works on philosophy included logical treatises, a work "On the Soul", "The Hermit's Guide" (Munk translates the title "Régime du Solitaire"), "On the Union of the Intellect with Man", and a "Valedictory Letter" (cited in Latin as "Epistola de Discessu" and "Epistola Expeditionis"). Avempace's logical treatises are said to exist in MSS. in the Escorial Library. His other writings are either lost or still undiscovered. Fortunately, however, a Jewish writer of the fourteenth century, Moses of Narbonne, has left us an account of "The Hermit's Guide", which supplements Averroes' unsatisfactory allusions to that work, and enables us to describe the doctrines it contains. The aim of the treatise is to show how man (the hermit) may, by the development of his own powers of mind, attain a union with the Active Intellect. (See ARABIAN SCHOOL OF PHILOSOPHY.) Avempace distinguishes two kinds of action: animal action, which is a product of the animal soul, and human action, whch is a product of the human soul, that is of free will and reflection. The man who smashes a stone because it has hurt him performs an animal action; but he who smashes the stone so that it will not injure others performs a human action. Now, the first step in the moral education of the hermit is to teach himself to be ruled by will and reason, so that his actions may all be human. That, however, is only the first step. Having attained it, the hermit must strive to higher perfection, so that his actions may become divine. He must strive to come in contact with the spiritual forms, which ascend in increasing degrees of incorporeity from the ideas of the individual soul up to the Actual Intellect itself, above which are only the forms of celestial bodies, that is to say, spiritual substances which, while they have an important cosmic function, have no relation to moral excellence in man. Through ideas, therefore, to the ideas of ideas, through these to abstract ideas of things, and through these last, to the pure form of the Active Intellect— this, according to Avempace, is the way of perfection. The mind which has come into contact with the Active Intellect becomes itself an intellect, the Acquired Intellect (*Intellectus Adeptus*). It is in reference to this last point that the Schoolmen, notably Albert the Great and St. Thomas Aquinas, mention Avempace and his teaching. Their acquaintance with the author of "The Hermit's Guide" was made, probably, through his disciple and admirer Averroes, though certain passages in the "Contra Gentiles" would justify the surmise that St. Thomas had perhaps a firsthand acquaintance with the "Epistola Expeditionis".

MUNK, *Mélanges de philosophie juive et arabe* (Paris, 1859), 410–418; MUNK, in *Dictionnaire des sciences philosophiques* (Paris, 1844–52), s. v. *Ibn-Badja*; ST. THOMAS, *Contra Gentiles*, II, 41; CASIRI, *Bibliotheca Arabo-hispana* (Madrid, 1760), I. 179; UEBERWEG-HEINZE, *Gesch. der Phil.*, II, 9th ed. 249 sqq., tr. I, 414; STÖCKL, *Gesch. der Phil. d. M. A.* (Mainz, 1865), II, 58 sqq.

WILLIAM TURNER.

Avendano, FERNANDO, priest, b. at Lima, Peru, either towards the end of the sixteenth, or in the beginning of the seventeenth, century; d. at Lima, in 1665, shortly after being appointed Bishop of Santiago de Chile. He was one of the most diligent investigators into survivals of the primitive rites and customs of the Peruvian Indians and left valuable notes on the subject, fragments of them being preserved in the work of Arriaga. Of great importance to linguistics are his "Sermones de los misterios de nuestra santa Fe católica", published in 1649 by order of the Archbishop of Lima, Pedro Villagomez. These sermons were delivered in Quichua, and are published with their translation into Spanish.

MENDIBURÚ, *Diccionario histórico-biográfico*; JIMÉNEZ DE LA ESPADA, *Tres Relaciones de Antigüedades peruanas*; ARRIAGA, *Extirpación de la Idolatría en el Perú* (1621).

AD. F. BANDELIER.

Aventinus. See TURMAIR, JOHN.

Averroes (ABUL WALID MAHOMMED IBN ACHMED, IBN MAHOMMED IBN ROSCHD), Arabian philosopher, astronomer, and writer on jurisprudence; b. at Cordova, 1126; d. at Morocco, 1198. Ibn Roschd, or Averroes, as he was called by the Latins, was educated in his native city, where his father and grandfather had held the office of cadi (judge in civil affairs) and had played an important part in the political history of Andalusia. He devoted himself to jurisprudence, medicine, and mathematics, as well as to philosophy and theology. Under the Caliphs Abu Jacub Jusuf and his son. Jacub Al Mansur, he enjoyed extraordinary favour at court and was entrusted with several important civil offices at Morocco, Seville, and Cordova. Later he fell into disfavour and was banished with other representatives of learning. Shortly before his death, the edict against philosophers was recalled. Many of his works in logic and metaphysics had, however, been consigned to the flames, so that he left no school, and the end of the dominion of the Moors in Spain, which occurred shortly afterwards, turned the current of Averroism completely into Hebrew and Latin channels, through which it influenced the thought of Christian Europe down to the dawn of the modern era. Averroes' great medical work, "Culliyyat" (of which the Latin title "Colliget" is a corruption) was published as the tenth volume in the Latin edition of Aristotle's works, Venice, 1527. His "Commentaries" on Aristotle, his original philosophical works, and his treatises on theology have come down to us either in Latin or Hebrew translations. His "Commentaries", which earned for him the title of the Commentator, were of three kinds: a short paraphrase or analysis, a brief exposition of the text, and a more extended exposition. These are known as the Minor. the Middle, and the Major Commentary, respectively. None of them is of any value for the textual criticism of Aristotle, since Averroes, being unacquainted with Greek and Syriac, based his exposition on a very imperfect Arabic translation of the Syriac version of the Greek text. They were, however, of great influence in determining the philosophical and scientific interpretation of Aristotle. His original philosophical treatises include: a work entitled "Tehafot al Tchafot", or "Destructio Destructionis" (a refutation of Algazel's "Destructio Philosophorum") published in the Latin edition, Venice, 1497 and 1527; two treatises on the union of the Active and Passive Intellects, also published in Latin in the Venice edition; logical treatises on different parts of the "Organon", published in the Venice edition under the title "Quæsita in Libros Logicæ Aristotelis"; physical treatises based on Aristotle's "Physics" (also in the Venice edition); a treatise in refutation of Avicenna and another on the agreement between philosophy and theology. Of the last two, only Hebrew and Arabic texts exist.

Averroes professed the greatest esteem for Aristotle. The word of the Stagirite was for him the highest expression of truth in matters of science and philosophy. In this exaggerated veneration for the philosopher he went farther than any of the Schoolmen. Indeed, in the later stages of Scholastic philosophy it was the Averroists and not the followers of Aquinas and Scotus who, when accused of subservience to the authority of a master, gloried in the title of "Aristotle's monkey". Averroes advocated the principle of twofold truth, maintaining that religion has one sphere and philosophy another. Religion, he said, is for the unlettered multitude; philosophy for the chosen few. Religion teaches by signs and symbols; philosophy presents the truth itself. In the mind, therefore, of the truly enlightened, philosophy supersedes religion. But, though the philosopher sees that what is true in theology is false in philosophy, he should not on that account condemn religious instruction, because he would thereby deprive the multitude of the only means which it has of attaining a (symbolical) knowledge of the truth. Averroes' philosophy, like that of all the other Arabians, is Aristoteleanism tinged with neo-Platonism. In it we find the doctrine of the eternity of matter as a positive principle of being; the concept of a multitude of spirits ranged hierarchically between God and matter and mediating between them; the denial of Providence in the commonly accepted sense; the doctrine that each of the heavenly spheres is animated; the notion of emanation or extraction, as a substitute for creation; and, finally, the glorification of (rational) mystical knowledge as the ultimate aspiration of the human soul—in a word, all the distinctively neo-Platonic elements which the Arabians added to pure Aristoteleanism.

What is peculiar in Averroes' interpretation of Aristotle is the meaning he gives to the Aristotelean doctrine of the Active and Passive Intellect. His predecessor, Avicenna, taught that, while the Active Intellect is universal and separate, the Passive Intellect is individual and inherent in the soul. Averroes holds that both the Active and the Passive Intellect are separate from the individual soul and are universal, that is, one in all men. He thinks that Alexander of Aphrodisias was wrong in reducing the Passive Intellect to a mere disposition, and that the "other Commentators" (perhaps Themistius and Theophrastus) were wrong in describing it as an individual substance endowed with a disposition; he maintains that it is, rather, a disposition in us, but belonging to an intellect outside us. The terms *Passive*, *Possible*, *Material* are successively used by Averroes to designate this species of intellect, which, in ultimate analysis, if we prescind from the dispositions of which he speaks, is the Active Intellect itself. In other words, the same intellect which, when in the act of actually abstracting intelligible species is called active, is called passive, possible, or material so far as it is acted upon, is potential, and furnishes that out of which ideas are fabricated. Besides, Averroes speaks of the Acquired Intellect (*intellectus acquisitus, adeptus*), by which he means the individual mind in communication with the Active Intellect. Thus, while the Active Intellect is numerically one, there are as many acquired intellects as there are individual souls with which the Active Intellect has come in contact. (The Scholastics speak of *continuatio* of the universal with the individual mind, translating literally the Arabic word which here means contiguity rather than union.) The sun, for instance, while it is and remains one source of light, may be said to be multiplied and to become many sources of light, in so far as it illuminates many bodies from which its light is distributed; so it is with the universal mind and the individual minds which come in contact with it.

The weakness of this doctrine, as a psychological explanation of the origin of knowledge, is its failure to take account of the facts of consciousness, which, as the Scholastics were not slow to point out, indicate that not merely an individual disposition but an active individual principle enters into the action which one expresses by the words "I think". Another weakness of the doctrine of monopsychism, or the doctrine that there is but one mind, a weakness at least in the eyes of the Scholastics, is that it leaves unanswered the question of the immortality of the individual soul. Indeed, Averroes openly admitted his inability to hold on philosophic grounds the doctrine of individual immortality, being content to maintain it as a religious tenet. Averroes' greatest influence was as a commentator. His doctrines had a varying fortune in the Christian schools; at first they secured a certain amount of adherence, then, gradually, their incompatibility with Christian teaching became apparent, and finally, owing to the revolt of the Renaissance from everything Scholastic, they secured once more a temporary hearing. His commentaries, however, had immediate and lasting success. St. Thomas Aquinas used the "Grand Commentary" of Averroes as his model, being, apparently, the first Scholastic to adopt that style of exposition; and though he refuted the errors of Averroes, and devoted special treatises to that purpose, he always spoke of the Arabian commentator as one who had, indeed, perverted the Peripatetic tradition, but whose words, nevertheless, should be treated with respect and consideration. The same may be said of Dante's references to him. It was after the time of St. Thomas and Dante that Averroes came to be represented as "the arch-enemy of the faith".

AVERROES' works in the Venice edition, 1497, 1527, and, in part, in MUNK's *Mélanges &c.* (Paris, 1859); MUNK, in *Dict. des sciences philosophiques* (Paris, 1844–52), art. *Ibn Roschd*; RENAN, *Averroés et l'Averroisme* (Paris, 9th ed., 1882); MANDONNET, *Siger de Brabant et l'Averroisme latin au XIII siècle* (Fribourg, 1899); UEBERWEG-HEINZE, *Gesch. der Phil.*, (9th ed., Berlin, 1905), VI 250 sqq. (tr. I); TURNER, *Hist. of Phil.* (Boston, 1903), 313 sqq.; STÖCKL, *Gesch. der Phil. des Mittelalters* (Mainz, 1865), II.

WILLIAM TURNER.

Aversa, DIOCESE OF, comprising twenty-one towns in the Province of Caserta and twelve in the Province of Naples, is under the immediate jurisdiction of the Holy See. This city is of relatively recent origin. It arose in the eleventh century on the ruins of Atella, a city of the Oscians, famous for their piquant raillery, which furnished the basis for the licentious interludes called *Atellanæ*. The ruins of ancient Atella, destroyed during the invasions of the barbarians, are still to be seen in the neighbourhood of Arpino. On these ruins the Norman Duke, Robert Guiscard, built a fortification which in time became a city called Aversa. The same Duke Robert, becoming a vassal of the pope and supporting him in his struggle with the emperor, obtained permission from Leo IX to have the Bishopric of Atella transferred to Aversa. The city has many fine monuments in the Norman style. It contains 54 parishes; 177 churches, chapels, and oratories; 674 secular clergy, and a population of 130,100.

VENTURI, *Storia della arte Italiana* (Milan, 1903), 502–522; UGHELLI, *Italia Sacra* (Venice, 1722), I, 485; CAPPELLETTI, *Le chiese d'Italia* (Venice, 1866), XXI, 433; GAMS, *Series episcoporum Ecclesiæ catholicæ* (Ratisbon, 1873), 855; FABOZZI, *Istoria della fondazione di Aversa* (Naples, 1770).

ERNESTO BUONAIUTI.

Avesta, THE, the sacred books of the Parsees, or Zoroastrians, and the main source of our knowledge concerning the religious and spiritual life of the ancient Persians. This collection of writings occupies the same place in the literature of Irān (ancient Persia) that the Vedas do in India. The designation Zend-Avesta, which is often employed to denote the sacred code, is not strictly correct. It owes its origin to a mistaken inversion of the Pahlavi designation *Avistāk u Zand,* a term which probably means "Text and Commentary"; for the word *Zand* (in the Avesta itself, *Zainti*) signifies "explanation", and even in the Avesta is applied to the exegetical matter in the text. It is similarly used by the Parsee priests to denote the Pahlavi version and commentary, but not the original scriptures. Whether the term *Avistāk,* which is the Pahlavi form of the word *Avesta,* has the meaning of "text", "law", is not absolutely certain. Some scholars interpret it as "wisdom", "knowledge".

Little was known concerning the religion and customs of ancient Persia before the Avesta was brought to Europe in the eighteenth century. From the allusions in Greek and Roman writers, like Herodotus, Plutarch, Pliny, and others, it had long been surmised that such a body of scriptures existed. Scattered allusions in Arabic and Syriac writers strengthened this conviction. But the information to be extracted from these references was vague and meagre. The first scholar to make the language and the contents of the sacred books of the Parsees known to Europe was a young Frenchman, Anquetil du Perron, who in 1754 went to India for this very purpose. His enthusiasm and perseverance overcame the many obstacles he encountered on his journey to Hindustan and the difficulties he met during his stay in Surat. Success at last crowned his efforts, and on his return in 1771 he was able to give to the world the first translation of the Avesta. From the moment of its publication a bitter controversy arose concerning the authenticity of the work. Some scholars, like Sir William Jones, declared that it was a clumsy forgery of modern Parsee priests, and the question was disputed for half a century until the advance made in the study of Sanskrit and comparative philology decided the matter and vindicated the genuineness of the scriptures and the value of Anquetil's work, although his translation, as a first attempt, was necessarily imperfect in many respects.

CONTENT AND DIVISIONS.—Originally, the sacred scriptures of the Parsees were of far greater extent than would appear from the Avesta in the form in which we now possess it. Only a relatively small portion of the original has in fact been preserved, and that is collected from several manuscripts, since no single codex contains all the texts now known. In its present form, therefore, the Avesta is a compilation from various sources, and its different parts date from different periods and vary widely in character. Tradition tells us that the Zoroastrian scriptures consisted originally of twenty-one *nasks* (books); but only one of these, the *Vendīdād,* had been completely preserved. The loss of the sacred books is attributed by the followers of Zoroaster to the invasion of Alexander, "the accursed Iskandar", as they call him, who burned the palace library at Persepolis, thus destroying one archetype copy of the text, and threw the other into the river near Samarkand, according to the statement of the Pahlavi records (Dīnkard, bk. III; West, "Sacred Books of the East", XXXVII, pp. xxx, xxxi; and *Shatrōīhā-ī Aīrān,* 2–5). For wellnigh five hundred years after the Macedonian invasion the Parsee scriptures remained in a scattered condition, much being preserved only by memory, until the great Zoroastrian revival under the Sassanian dynasty (A. D. 226–651), when the texts were again collected, codified, translated into Pahlavi, and interpreted. A beginning in this direction had already been made under the last of the Parthian kings, but the great final redaction took

place in Sassanian times, under Shahpuhar II (309–379). Our present Avesta is essentially the work of this redaction, although important sections of the text have been lost since then, especially after the Arabs conquered Persia. This conquest (637–651) was fatal to the Iranian religion, and caused Zoroastrianism to be supplanted by Mohammedanism and the Avesta by the Koran. As already mentioned, great portions of the scriptures have since disappeared entirely; out of the original twenty-one nasks, the nineteenth alone (the Vendīdād) has survived. Portions of other nasks are preserved, interspersed here and there among the *Yasna* and *Vīspered,* or have come down to us as scattered fragments in Pahlavi works, or have been rendered into Pahlavi, like the *Bŭndahishn* (Book of Creation) and the *Shāyast-la-Shāyast* (Treatise on the Lawful and Unlawful). In this way we are able to make good some of our losses of the old scriptures; enough has been said, however, to explain the lack of coherence noticeable in certain parts of the Avestan code.

The Avesta, as we now have it, is usually divided into five sections, relating to the ritual, hymns of praise, the liturgy, and the law. These sections are: (1) the *Yasna,* including the *Gāthās,* or hymns; (2) *Vīspered;* (3) *Yashts;* (4) minor texts, such as the *Nyāishes* (favourite prayers in daily use among the Parsees); and (5) *Vendīdād.* Besides this there are some independent fragments preserved in Pahlavi books (*Hādhōkt Nask,* etc). The main divisions, when taken together, again fall into two groups, the one liturgical, comprising Vendīdād, Vīspered and Yasna, or the Avesta proper, the other general, called *Khorda Avesta* (Abridged Avesta) and comprising the minor texts and the Yashts. A brief characterization of the five divisions will now be given.

(1) The Yasna (Skt. *yajna*), "sacrifice", "worship", the chief liturgical portions of the sacred canon. It consists principally of prayers and hymns used in the ritual, and is divided into seventy-two *hā* or *hāiti* (chapters), symbolized by the seventy-two strands of the *kushti,* or sacred girdle with which the young Zoroastrian is invested on his being received into the Church. The middle third of the Yasna (Ys., 28–53), however, is not directly connected with the ritual, but contains the Gāthās, the holy psalms, songs which preserved the metrical sayings of Zoroaster himself as used in his sermons. This is the oldest portion of the Avesta and descends directly from the prophet and his disciples. These canticles are metrical in their structure and are composed in the so-called Gāthā-dialect, a more archaic form of language than is used in the rest of the Avesta. There are seventeen of these hymns, grouped into five divisions, each group taking its name from the opening words; thus *Ahunavaiti, Ushtavaiti,* etc. Inserted in the midst of the Gāthās is the *Yasna Haptanghāiti* (the Seven-chapter Yasna) consisting of prayers and hymns in honour of the Supreme Deity, Ahura Mazda, the Angels, Fire, Water, and Earth. This selection also shows a more archaic type of language, and stands next to the Gāthās in point of antiquity. Its structure, though handed down in prose, may once have been metrical.

(2) The Vīspered (*vīspē ratavō,* "all the lords") is really a short liturgy, very similar in style and form to the Yasna, which it supplements in a briefer form. It owes its name to the fact that it contains invocations to "all the lords".

(3) The Yashts (*yeshti,* "worship by praise"), of which there are twenty-one, are hymns in honour of various divinities. These hymns are for the most part metrical in structure, and they show considerable poetic merit in certain instances,

which is not common in the Avesta. They are of especial interest historically on account of the glimpses they afford us of the great mythological and legendary material in the folklore of ancient Irān used so effectively by Firdausī in his great epic of the Persian kings, the "Shāh Nāmah". Among

MANUSCRIPT OF ONE OF THE OLDEST YASHTS (A.D. 1600)
Library of Columbia University, New York

the divinities to whom special yashts are devoted we find Ardvī Sūrā, the goddess of waters; Tishtrya, the star Sirius; Mithra, the divinity of light and truth; the Fravashis, or departed souls of the righteous, Verethragna, the genius of Victory and the Kavaya Hvarenah, "kingly glory", the divine light illuminating the ancient kings of Irān.

(4) The fourth division (minor texts) comprises brief prayers, like the five Nyāishes (to the Sun, Moon, Mithra, Water, and Fire), the Gāhs, Sīrūzas, and Afrīngāns (blessings). These selections form a manual of daily devotion.

(5) The fifth division, Vendīdād (from vī daēva dāta, "law against the demons"), is the religious law code of Zoroastrianism and comprises twenty-two fargards (chapters). It begins with an account of Creation in which Ormuzd, the god, is thwarted by Ahriman, the devil; then it describes the occurrence of a destructive winter, a sort of Iranian deluge. The remainder of the book is largely devoted to elaborate prescriptions with regard to ceremonial purification, especially the cleansing from defilement incurred by contact with the dead, and to a list of special penances imposed as a means of atoning for impurity. The Vendīdād is an ecclesiastical code, not a liturgical manual. Its different parts vary widely in character and in age. Some parts may be comparatively recent in origin, although the greater part is very old.

The Avesta does not represent the whole of the sacred scriptures of the Parsees. It is supplemented by an extensive Pahlavi literature, consisting in part of translations from the sacred canon and in part of original matter. The most notable Pahlavi works belonging here are the Dīnkard (Acts of Religion), dating from the ninth century of the Christian Era; Būndahishn, "Original Creation", finished in the eleventh or twelfth century of the Christian Era, but containing material as old as the Avesta itself, being in part a version of one of the original nasks; the Maīnōg-i-Khirad (Spirit of Wisdom), a re-

ligious conference on questions of faith, and the Arda Vīrāf Nāmak, a sort of Zoroastrian "Divina Commedia", which is especially important because of its account of the Persian ideas concerning the future life. There is also some later Zoroastrian literature in modern Persian, comprising works like the Zartushtnāmah (Book of Zoroaster), the Sad-dar (Hundred Doors, or Chapters), the Rivāyats (traditional treatises).

LANGUAGE.—The language of the Avesta is best designated simply as Avestan, not as Zend, for the reasons given in the beginning of this article. Nor is Old Bactrian a desirable term, since it is by no means proved that the language of the Avesta was spoken in ancient Bactria. The Avestan language is an Indo-Germanic tongue and belongs more specifically to the Iranian group, the other members being the Old Persian of the cuneiform inscriptions, the Pahlavi, and Pazend (or Middle Iranian), and the later dialects, New Persian, Kurdish, Afghan, etc. The Avestan speech is very closely related to Sanskrit; in fact, we are able to transpose any word from one language into the other by the application of special phonetic laws. The script employed in the Avestan texts, as we have them, is not so old as the language itself, but dates from the Sassanian period. It is read from right to left and can be traced ultimately to a Semitic source. It is not known in what script the original Avesta was recorded.

ZOROASTER.—It can no longer be doubted that Zoroaster was a real historical personage. The attempts of some scholars to represent him as a mythical being have failed, even though much that is related about his life is legendary, as in the case of Buddha. The man Zoroaster in the original texts appears as Zarathushtra, from which Zoroaster, our present form of the prophet's name, is derived through the Greek and Latin. The Avesta always writes Zarathushtra; the Pahlavi has Zartusht; the modern Persian, Zardusht. What the meaning of the name is, cannot be stated positively. All that we know is that the name is a compound, and that the second element, ushtra, means "camel"; the first part has been variously rendered as "old", "lively", "golden", "ploughing", etc. There has been much discussion as to the date when the prophet lived. The traditional date in the Pahlavi books places his era between the earlier half of the seventh and the sixth century B. C., or, more specifically, 660–583 B. C.; but many scholars assign him to a century, or even several centuries, earlier. There is also much uncertainty regarding his birthplace and the details of his life. He was undoubtedly born in Western Irān, but much of his ministry was in Eastern Irān. From Western Irān, more specifically Azerbaijan (the ancient Atropatene), he seems to have gone to Ragha (Rai) in Media, and when his mission did not meet with success in that region he turned to the East, to Bactria. There a certain king named Vishtāspa became converted to his creed, and through the generous patronage of this powerful defender of the faith the new religion soon gained a firm footing. Presumably, the faith was carried from Bactria to Media, whence it spread into Persia and was accepted in all probability by the great Achæmenian kings. In the case of Cyrus there is some doubt whether he was an adherent of Zoroastrian law, but Darius was a pronounced Mazda-worshipper and presumably, therefore, a true Zoroastrian, as we know that the last kings of the Achæmenian dynasty were genuine followers of the religion. If tradition can be believed, Zoroaster began his ministry at the age of thirty, made a convert, when he was forty-two, of King Vishtāspa, and was slain at the age of seventy-seven, when the Turanians stormed Balkh. This account of the prophet's death is given, at least, by Firdausī.

Under the kings of the Achæmenian line the religion founded by Zoroaster became one of the great religions of the ancient East. But it shared the fate of the Persian monarchy; it was shattered, though not overthrown, by the conquest of Alexander and fell consequently into neglect under the Seleucid and Parthian dynasties. With the accession of the Sassanian dynasty it met with a great revival. The kings of the house of Sassan were zealous believers and did everything in their power to spread the faith as a national creed, so that its prosperity rose again to the zenith. Sectarian movements, to be sure, were not lacking. The heresy of Mazdak for a moment imperilled the union of the Zoroastrian Church and State, and Manichæism, that menace of early Christian orthodoxy, also threatened the ascendancy of the Iranian national faith, which was really its parent. These dangers, however, were only temporary and of minor importance as compared with the Arab conquest, which followed in the seventh century (651) and dealt the fatal blow from which Zoroastrianism never recovered. The victorious followers of Mohammed carried on their proselytizing campaign with relentless vigour. The few Zoroastrians who stood firmly by their faith were oppressed and persecuted. Some remained, and were scattered throughout their native land; but the majority took refuge in India, where their descendants, the Parsees, are found even at the present day. About 10,000 are here and there throughout Persia, chiefly at Yazd and Kirman, but the bulk of the Zoroastrians, upwards of 90,000 souls, constitute a prosperous community in India, chiefly at Bombay.

The standard edition of the Avesta texts is that of GELDNER (Stuttgart, 1885–96). A French tr. by DARMESTETER appeared in the *Annales du musée Guimet* (Paris, 1892–93), XXI, XXII, XXIV, and an English tr. by DARMESTETER AND MILLS in *The Sacred Books of the East*, ed. MAX MÜLLER (Oxford, 1883–87), IV, XXIII, XXXI. Another French tr. was made by DE HARLEZ (2 ed., Paris, 1881).—The Pahlavi texts have been translated by WEST, in *The Sacred Books of the East*, V, XVIII, XXXVII, XLVII.—A good grammar for a study of the Avestan language is that of JACKSON (Stuttgart, 1892); an excellent dictionary that of BARTHOLOMÆ, *Altiranisches Wörterbuch* (Strasburg, 1904).—For information on all topics relating to the language and literature of Iran the articles in the *Grundriss der iranischen Philologie*, ed. GEIGER AND KUHN (Strasburg, 1896–1902) should be consulted; on the Avesta, the article of GELDNER. WINDISCHMANN, *Zoroastrische Studien* (ed. SPIEGEL, Berlin, 1863); JACKSON, *Zoroaster, the Prophet of Ancient Iran* (New York, 1899).

A. F. J. REMY.

Avesta, THE, THEOLOGICAL ASPECTS OF.—
I. GOD.—The name of the Supreme God of the Avestic system is *Ahura Mazda* (in the Achæmenid royal inscriptions, *Auramazda*), which probably signifies the All-Wise Lord. This divine name was later modified into the Pahlavi form *Auharmazd*, the modern Persian *Ormuzd* (Greek 'Ωρομάζης). Hence the name of *Mazdeism* commonly applied to the Avestic religion. Ahura Mazda is a pure spirit; His chief attributes are eternity, wisdom, truth, goodness, majesty, power. He is the Creator (*dātar*) of all good creatures—not, however, of Evil, or evil beings. He is the supreme Lawgiver, the Rewarder of moral good, and the Punisher of moral evil. He dwells in Eternal Light; in the later literature light is spoken of as the clothing of Ahura Mazda or even His "body", i. e. a kind of manifestation of His presence, like the Old Testament שְׁכִינָה. In this same patristic (Pahlavi) literature we find frequent enumerations of the attributes of Ahura Mazda; thus these are said to be "omniscience, omnipotence, all-sovereignty, all-goodness". Again He is styled "Supreme Sovereign, Wise Creator, Supporter, Protector, Giver of good things, Virtuous in act, Merciful, Pure Lawgiver, Lord of the good Creations".

II. DUALISM.—It has been remarked above that

Ahura Mazda is the Creator of all *good* creatures. This at once indicates the specific and characteristic feature of the Avestic theology generally known as "dualism". The great problem of the origin of evil, which has ever been the main stumbling-block of religious systems, was solved in the Zoroastrian Reform by the trenchant, if illogical, device of two separate creators and creations: one good, the other evil. Opposed to Ahura Mazda, or Ōrmuzd, is His rival, *Aṅro Mainyus* (later, *Aharman*, *Ahriman*), the Evil Spirit. He is conceived as existing quite independently of Ahura Mazda, apparently from eternity, but destined to destruction at the end of time. Evil by nature and in every detail the exact opposite of Ahura Mazda, he is the creator of all evil, both moral and physical. Zoroaster in the Gāthās says (Ys., xlv, 2, Jackson's translation):—

> Now shall I preach of the World's *two primal Spirits*,
> The Holier one of which did thus address the Evil:
> Neither do our minds, our teachings, nor our concepts,
> Nor our beliefs, nor words, nor do our deeds in sooth,
> Nor yet our consciences, nor souls agree in aught.

It is here to be remarked that the specific name of Ahura Mazda in opposition to the Evil Spirit is *Spento Mainyus*, the Holy Spirit, and Ahura Mazda and Spento Mainyus are used as synonyms throughout the Avesta. The obviously illogical doctrine of two separate and supreme creators eventually led to certain philosophical attempts to reduce the double system to uniformity. One of these consisted in throwing back the Divine Unity to an anterior stage in which *Zrvāna Akarana*, "illimitable time", becomes the single, indifferent, primordial source from which both spirits proceed. Another solution was sought in attributing two spirits (faculties or functions) to Ahura Mazda himself, his Spento Mainyus, and his Aṅro Mainyus, or his creative and destructive spirit—an idea probably borrowed from Indian philosophy. This seems the favourite doctrine of the modern Parsees of Bombay, as may be seen in Mr. Navroji Maneckji Kanga's article in the "Babylonian and Oriental Record" for May, 1900 (VIII, 224–28), and it is claimed to be strictly founded on the teaching of the Gāthās; but, although such a development of thought was inevitable in the necessary attempt to reconcile a real monotheism with the Zoroastrian dualism, these theories cannot really be called Avestic at all, except in so far as *Zrvāna Akarana* is an Avestic term. They are "patristic" or "scholastic".

The result of the dualistic conception of the universe is that of a continuous great warfare that has been going on even from the beginning between two hostile worlds or camps. All creatures belong to one or another of these camps, not only sentient and intelligent beings, like the spirits and man, but also the animal and even the vegetable worlds. All dangerous, noxious, poisonous animals and plants are evil by their very creation and nature. [We see here the primal germ of Manichæism. Māni was a heretic of the Mazdean faith (A. D. 258). This "heresy" is often reprobated in the Pahlavi religious books, together with Judaism and Christianity.] Hence—in sharp contrast to the Hindu *ahiṁsa*, a characteristic tenet of Buddhism, which prohibits the killing of any creature, even the smallest and most noxious insect—to kill as many as possible of the Khrafstras, or noxious creatures of the Evil Spirit (such as wolves, serpents, snakes, locusts, intestinal worms, ants), is one of the most meritorious of religious actions. This great warfare, both spiritual and material, will go on to the end of time. It is to end in a final triumph of the Good and the annihilation (apparently) of Evil, including Aṅro Mainyus himself. Such at least is the teaching in the later "patristic" literature.

III. ANGELOLOGY.—Dualism in its widest sense

seems to be an inherent and ineradicable tendency of the Iranian mind. Almost everything is conceived in pairs or doubles. Hence the constant reference to the "Two Worlds", the spiritual and the material. The doctrine of the Spirit World, whether belonging to the good or the evil creation, is highly developed in the Avesta and subsequent literature. Around Ahura Mazda is a whole hierarchy of spirits, corresponding very closely with our "angels". There is, however, this to be noted, that in the Zoroastrian system many of these creature-spirits are demonstrably old Aryan nature-deities who have been skilfully transformed into angels, and so fitted into a monotheistic framework, frequently enough, in hymns and other passages, by the simple interpolation of the epithet *Mazdadāta* (created by Mazda) before their names. Of the good spirits who surround Ahura, the most important are the *Amesha Spentas* ("Holy Immortals" or "Immortal Saints") generally reckoned as six (though Ahura Mazda himself is frequently included among them, and they are then called seven). These are the characteristic genii of the Gāthās, and their very names show that they are merely personified attributes of the Creator Himself. They are: *Vohu Manah* (Good Mind), *Asha Vahishta* (Best Holiness), *Khshathra Vairya* (Desirable Sovereignty), *Spenta Armaiti* (Holy Piety, a female spirit), *Haurvatāt* (Health), and *Ameretāt* (Immortality). In the Younger Avesta and later traditional literature these evident personifications, whose very names are but abstract nouns, become more and more concrete personages or genii, with varying functions; most of all Vohu Manah (Vohuman) rises to a position of unique importance. Dr. L. H. Gray, however, argues, in a very striking article, that even these are evolutions of original naturalistic deities [Archiv für Religionswissenschaft (Leipzig, 1904), VII, 345–372]. In later patristic literature Vohu Manah is conceived as the "Son of the Creator" and identified with the Alexandrine Λόγος. (See Casartelli, Philosophy of the Mazdayasnian Religion, 42–90.) Asha, also (the equivalent of the Sanskrit *Rta=Dharma*), is the Divine Law, Right, Sanctity (cf. Ps. cxviii), and occupies a most conspicuous position throughout the Avesta.

But besides the Amesha Spentas, there are a few other archangels whose rank is scarcely less, if it does not sometimes exceed theirs. Such is *Sraosha* ("Obedience"—i. e. to the Divine Law). With him are associated, in a trio, *Rashnu* (Right, Justice) and *Mithra*. This last is perhaps the most characteristic, as he is the most enigmatical figure of the Iranian angelology. Undoubtedly in origin (like the Vedic *Mitra*) a Sun-deity of the primitive Aryan nature-worship, he has been taken over into the Avesta system as the Spirit of Light and Truth—the favourite and typical virtue of the Iranian race, as testified even by the Greek historians. So important is his position that he is constantly linked with Ahura Mazda himself, apparently almost as an equal, in a manner recalling some of the divine couples of the Vedas. It is well known how in later times the Mithra cult became a regular religion and spread from Persia all over the Roman Empire, even into Britain. [See, especially, Cumont's great work, "Monuments relatifs au culte de Mithra" (Paris, 1893).] Nor must mention be omitted of Atars, the Genius of Fire, on account of the particular importance and sanctity attached to fire as a symbol of the divinity and its conspicuous use in the cult (which has given rise to the entirely erroneous conception of Zoroastrianism as "Fire-worship", and of the Parsees as "Fire-worshippers"). Water, Sun, Moon, Stars, the sacred *Haoma* plant (Skt. *Sōma*), and other natural elements all have their special spirits. But particular mention must be made of the enigmatical Fravashis, the origin and nature of whom is still uncertain. Some writers [especially Söderblom, "Les Fravashis" (Paris, 1899); "La vie future" (Paris, 1901)] have seen in them the spirits of the departed, like the *dii manes*, or the Hindu *pitris*. But, as a matter of fact, their primal conception seems to approach nearest to the pre-existent Ἰδέαι of Plato. Every living creature has its own Fravashi, existing before its creation; nay in some places inanimate beings, and, stranger still, Ahura Mazda Himself, have their Fravashis. They play an important rôle in both the psychology and the ritual cult of Mazdeism.

Face to face with the hierarchy of celestial spirits is a diabolical one, that of the *daēvas* (demons, Pahlavi and Mod. Persian *dīv*, or *dev*) and *druj's* of the Evil Spirit. They fill exactly the places of the devils in Christian and Jewish theology. Chief of them is Aka Manah (Pahlavi Akōman, "Evil Mind"), the direct opponent of Vohu Manah. Perhaps the most frequently mentioned of all is *Aēshma*, the Demon of Wrath or Violence, whose name has come down to us in the Asmodeus (*Aēshmo daēva*) of the Book of Tobias (iii, 8). The *Pairikās* are female spirits of seductive but malignant nature, who are familiar to us under the form of the Peris of later Persian poetry and legend.

IV. MAN.—In the midst of the secular warfare that has gone on from the beginning between the two hosts of Good and Evil stands Man. Man is the creature of the Good Spirit, but endowed with a free will and power of choice, able to place himself on the side of Ahura Mazda or on that of Anro Mainyus. The former has given him, through His prophet Zarathushtra (Zoroaster) His Divine revelation and law (*daēna*). According as man obeys or disobeys this Divine law his future lot will be decided; by it he will be judged at his death. The whole ethical system is built upon this great principle, as in the Christian theology. Moral good, righteousness, sanctity (*asha*) is according to the Divine will and decrees; Man by his free will conforms to, or transgresses, these. The Evil Spirit and his innumerable hosts tempt Man to deny or transgress the Divine law, as he tempted Zoroaster himself, promising him as reward the sovereignty of the whole world.—"No!" replied the Prophet, "I will not renounce it, even if body and soul and life should be severed!" (Vendîdâd, xix, 25, 26). It is well to emphasize this basis of Avestic moral theology, because it at once marks off the Avesta system from the fatalistic systems of India with their *karma* and innate pessimism. [See Casartelli, "Idée du péché chez les Indo-Eraniens" (Fribourg, 1898).] A characteristic note of Iranian religious philosophy is its essential optimism; if there is human sin, there is also repentance and expiation. In the later Pahlavi religious literature there is a proper confession of sin (*patēt*) and a developed casuistry. Asceticism, however, finds no place therein.

Divine worship, with elaborate ritual, is an essential duty of man towards his Creator. There is indeed no animal sacrifice; the leading rites are the offering of the quasi-divine *haoma* (the fermented juice of the sacred plant, a species of *Asclepias*), the exact counterpart of the Vedic *sōma*-sacrifice; the care of the Sacred Fire; the chanting of the ritual hymns and prayers, and passages of the Sacred Books (Avesta). The moral teaching is closely akin to our own. Stress is constantly laid on the necessity of goodness in thought, word, and deed (*humata, hūkhta, hvarshta*) as opposed to evil thought, word, and deed (*dushmata, duzhūkhta, duzhvarshta*). Note the emphatic recognition of sin in thought. Virtues and vices are enumerated and estimated much as in Christian ethics. Special value is attributed to the virtues of religion, truthfulness, purity, and generosity to the poor. Heresy, untruthfulness, perjury, sexual sins, violence, tyranny are specially reprobated. Zoroaster's reform being social as well as religious, agriculture and farming are raised to the rank of religious duties and regarded as spiritually meritorious. The same will account for the exaggerated importance, almost sanctity, attached to the dog. On the other hand, the one repulsive feature of Avestic morality is the glorification, as a religious meritorious act, of the *Khvaëtva-datha*, which is nothing else than intermarriage between the nearest of kin, even brothers and sisters. In later times this practice was tempered down to marriage between cousins, and now is entirely repudiated by the modern Parsees.

V. ESCHATOLOGY.—After death the disembodied soul hovers around the corpse for three days. Then it sets off across the *Cinvat* bridge to meet its judgment and final doom in the world beyond the grave. The three judges of souls are Mithra, Sraosha, and

TOWER OF SILENCE, BOMBAY

Rashnu. The soul of the just passes safely over the bridge into a happy eternity, into heaven (*Aūhu vahishta, Garo nmāna*), the abode of Ahura and His blessed angels. The wicked soul falls from the fatal bridge and is precipitated into hell (*Duzh aūhu*). Of this abode of misery a lively description occurs in the later Pahlavi "Vision of Ardā Vīrāf", whose visit to the Inferno, with the realistic description of its torments, vividly recalls that of Dante. The state called *Hamēstakān*, or Middle State, does not appear in the Avesta itself, but is a development of the later patristic theology. It is not, however, conceived exactly as our Purgatory, but rather as an indifferent state for those whose good and evil deeds are found at death to be in perfect equilibrium. They are therefore neither in suffering nor in happiness. At the end of time, the approach of which is described in the Pahlavi literature in terms strikingly like those of our Apocalypse, will come the last great Prophet, Saoshyant (Saviour) under whom will occur the Resurrection of the Dead (*Frashokereti*), the General Judgment, the ἀποκατάστασις or renewal of the whole world by the great conflagration of the earth and consequent flood of burning matter. According to the Pahlavi sources, this terrible flood will purify all creatures; even the wicked will be purified from all stains, and even hell will be cleansed and added to the "new heavens and new earth". Meanwhile a mighty combat takes place between Saoshyant and his followers and the demon hosts of the Evil Spirit, who are utterly routed and destroyed forever. (See Yasht, xix and xiii.)

VI. MAZDEISM AND THE PERSIAN KINGS.—It is frequently asserted or assumed that the Avesta religion as above sketched was the religion of Cyrus

and Darius and the other Achæmenid Kings of Persia (549–336 B. C.). From the cuneiform inscriptions of these sovereigns (in the Old Persian language, a sister dialect of the Avestic Zend) we know pretty well what their religion was. They proclaim themselves Mazdeans (*Auramazdiya*, Darius, Behistun Column, IV, 56); their Supreme God is Auramazda, greatest of gods (*Mathishta bagānām*); He is Creator of all things—heaven, earth, and man; —all things happen by His will (*vashnā*); He sees and knows all things, man must obey His precepts (*framānā*), and follow the "good way" (*pathim rāstām*); man must invoke and praise Him; He hates sin, especially falsehood, which is denounced as the chief of sins, also insubordination and despotism. Inferior spirits are associated with Him, "clan gods", and particularly Mithra and Anahita. Yet, with all these close similarities, we must hesitate to consider the two religious systems as identical. For in the Achæmenid inscriptions there is absolutely no trace of the dualism which is the characteristic and all-prevailing feature of the Avesta, and no allusion whatever to the great prophet Zoroaster, or to the revelation of which he was the mouthpiece. The exact relation between the two systems remains enigmatical.

SUMMARY.—"The highest religious result to which human reason unaided by revelation, can attain", is the deliberate verdict of a learned Jesuit theologian (Father Ernest Hull, S.J., in "Bombay Examiner", 28 March, 1903). This estimate does not appear exaggerated. The Avesta system may be best defined as monotheism modified by a physical and moral dualism, with an ethical system based on a Divinely revealed moral code and human free will. As it is now followed by the living descendants of its first votaries, the Parsees of India, it is virtually the same as it appears in the Avesta itself, except that its monotheism is more rigid and determined, and that it has shed such objectionable practices as the *Khvetûk-das* (*Khvaëtva-datha*) and seeks to explain them away. A great revival in the knowledge of the old sacred languages (Zend and Pahlavi), which had become almost forgotten, has taken place during the past half-century under the stimulus of European scholarship, whose results have been widely adopted and assimilated. The religious cult is scrupulously maintained as of old. The ancient traditional and characteristically national virtues of truth and open-handed generosity flourish exceedingly in the small, but highly intelligent, community.

WILLIAMS JACKSON, *Die iranische Religion* in *Grundriss der ir. Philologie* (Strasburg, 1896–1904), II; DE HARLEZ, *Introduction à l'étude de l'Avesta* (Paris, 1881); CASARTELLI, *Philosophie religieuse du Mazdéisme sous les Sassanides* (Louvain, 1884); IDEM, *The Philosophy of the Mazdayasnian Religion*, a tr. of the same work by FIROZ JAMASPJI (Bombay, 1889), with notes which sometimes controvert from the Parsee side the author's views; HOVELACQUE, *L'Avesta, Zoroastre et le Mazdéisme* (Paris, 1880); RASTAMJI EDULJI, *Zarathushtra and Zarathushtrianism in the Avesta* (Leipzig, 1906) giving the modern Parsee view.

L. C. CASARTELLI.

Avicebron, SALOMO BEN JEHUDA BEN GEBIROL (or GABIROL), whom the Scholastics, taking him for an Arabian, called Avicebrol (this form occurs in the oldest MSS.; the later MSS. have Avencebron, Avicembron, Avicebron, etc.); a Jewish religious poet, moralist, and philosopher, b. at Malaga in 1020 or 1021; d. at Saragossa, 1070. He was educated at Saragossa, where he spent the remainder of his life, devoting himself to moral and intellectual philosophy, and writing religious poetry. His principal philosophical work, written in Arabic, was translated into Hebrew in the thirteenth century by Falaquera, and entitled "Mekor Chajim" [this was discovered and edited with French translation by Munk, "Mélanges" etc., (Paris, 1857)], and into Latin in the twelfth century by Johannes Hispanus and Dominicus Gundissalinus (edited by Bäumker, Münster, 1895) under the title "Fons Vitæ". His poems were published by Munk (" Mélanges ", etc., Paris, 1857), and a Hebrew translation of his ethical writings (Riva, 1562, and Lunéville, 1840). Avicebron's philosophy united the traditional neo-Platonic doctrines with the religious teaching of the Old Testament. From the neo-Platonists, whom he knew chiefly through such apocryphal writings as the "Theologia Aristotelis" and the "Liber de Causis" (see ARABIAN SCHOOL OF PHILOSOPHY), he derived the doctrine of emanation, namely: that there emanated from God, in the first place, the Universal Intelligence, that from the Universal Intelligence there emanated the World-Soul, and that from the World-Soul there emanated Nature, which is the immediate principle of productivity of material things. From the same neo-Platonic sources he derived the doctrine that matter is of itself wholly inert and merely the occasion which is made use of by the Infinite Agent to produce natural effects (Occasionalism). On the other hand, he drew from Biblical sources the doctrine that the Supreme Principle in the production of the Universe was not the Thought of God, but the Divine Will, which, in Scriptural phrase, he calls the Word of God. In thus attempting to combine Jewish religious doctrine with neo-Platonism, the doctrine of creation with the notion of emanation, he introduced into his philosophy elements which are logically incompatible.

His most celebrated doctrine, however, the one by which he was best known to the Christian philosophers of the Middle Ages, was that of the universality of matter. All created things, he taught, are composed of matter and form. God alone is pure actuality. Everything else, even the highest among the angels, is made up of matter (not merely potency, but matter like that of terrestrial bodies) and form, just as man is composed of body and soul. The matter, however, of angelic bodies, while it is like terrestrial matter, is of a purer kind and is called spiritual matter. In other words, there are no created "separate substances", as the Schoolmen called them. Between the pure spirituality of God and the crude materiality of terrestrial bodies there mediate substances composed of matter and form, which range in ascending scale of spiritual-materiality from the soul of man to the highest angelic nature. This doctrine is mentioned by almost all the great scholastics, and referred by them to the "Fons Vitæ" for instance, by Albert the Great (Summa Totius Theol., I, q. xlii, art. 22), by St. Thomas (Quæst. Disp., De Animâ, art. 6; Opusculum De Subst. Separatis, passim), and Duns Scotus (De Rer. Princip. VIII, 4). But, while the first two, in common with the other Dominican teachers, refuted the author of "Fons Vitæ" on this point, the last mentioned, together with Alexander of Hales and others of the Franciscan School, adopted his doctrine as part of their theory of the angelic nature.

BÄUMKER, Avencebrolis Fons Vitæ (Münster, 1895); MUNK, Mélanges, etc., (Paris, 1857); ST. THOMAS, Opusculum De Substantiis Separatis (Op. XV of Roman ed.; ed. De Maria, Rome, 1886), III, 221 sqq.; GUTTMANN, Die Philos. des Salom. Ibn Gabirol (Göttingen, 1889); STÖCKL, Lehrb. der Gesch. der Phil. (Mainz, 1888), 555 sqq.; tr. Finlay, (Dublin, 1903), 315 sqq.; TURNER, Hist. of Phil. (Boston, 1903), 315 sqq.

WILLIAM TURNER.

Avicenna (ABN ALI AL HOSAIN IBN ABDALLAH IBN SINA, called by the Latins AVICENNA), Arabian physician and philosopher, b. at Kharmaithen, in the province of Bokhara, 980; d. at Hamadan, in Northern Persia, 1037. From an autobiographical sketch which has come down to us we learn that he was a very precocious youth; at the age of ten he knew the Koran by heart; before he was sixteen he had mastered what was to be learned of physics, mathematics, logic, and metaphysics; at the age of

sixteen he began the study and practice of medicine; and before he had completed his twenty-first year he wrote his famous "Canon" of medical science, which for several centuries, after his time, remained the principal authority in medical schools both in Europe and in Asia. He served successively several Persian potentates as physician and adviser, travelling with them from place to place, and despite the habits of conviviality for which he was well known, devoted much time to literary labours, as is testified by the hundred volumes which he wrote. Our authority for the foregoing facts is the "Life of Avicenna," based on his autobiography, written by his disciple Jorjani (Sorsanus), and published in the early Latin editions of his works. Besides the medical "Canon," he wrote voluminous commentaries on Aristotle's works and two great encyclopedias entitled "Al Schefa", or "Al Chifa" (i. e. healing) and "Al Nadja" (i. e. deliverance). The "Canon" and portions of the encyclopedias were translated into Latin as early as the twelfth century, by Gerard of Cremona, Dominicus Gundissalinus, and John Avendeath; they were published at Venice, 1493–95. The complete Arabic texts are said to be in MS. in the Bodleian Library. An Arabic text of the "Canon" and the "Nadja" was published in Rome, 1593. Avicenna's philosophy, like that of his predecessors among the Arabians, is Aristoteleanism mingled with Neo-Platonism, an exposition of Aristotle's teaching in the light of the Commentaries of Themistius, Simplicius, and other neo-Platonists. His Logic is divided into nine parts, of which the first is an introduction after the manner of Porphyry's "Isagoge"; then follow the six parts corresponding to the six treatises composing the "Organon"; the eighth and ninth parts consist respectively of treatises on rhetoric and poetry. Avicenna devoted special attention to definition, the logic of representation, as he styles it, and also to the classification of sciences. Philosophy, he says, which is the general name for scientific knowledge, includes speculative and practical philosophy. Speculative philosophy is divided into the inferior science (physics), and middle science (mathematics), and the superior science (metaphysics including theology). Practical philosophy is divided into ethics (which considers man as an individual); economics (which considers man as a member of domestic society); and politics (which considers man as a member of civil society). These divisions are important on account of their influence on the arrangement of sciences in the schools where the philosophy of Avicenna preceded the introduction of Aristotle's works. A favourite principle of Avicenna, which is quoted not only by Averroes but also by the Schoolmen, and especially by Albert the Great, was *intellectus in formis agit universalitatem*, that is, the universality of our ideas is the result of the activity of the mind itself. The principle, however, is to be understood in the realistic, not in the nominalistic sense. Avicenna's meaning is that, while there are differences and resemblances among things independently of the mind, the formal constitution of things in the category of individuality, generic universality, specific universality, and so forth, is the work of the mind. Avicenna's physical doctrines show him in the light of a faithful follower of Aristotle, who has nothing of his own to add to the teaching of his master. Similarly, in psychology, he reproduces Aristotle's doctrines, borrowing occasionally an explanation, or an illustration, from Alfarabi. On one point, however, he is at pains to set the true meaning, as he understands it, of Aristotle, above all the exposition and elaboration of the Commentators. That point is the question of the Active and Passive Intellect. (See ARABIAN SCHOOL OF PHILOSOPHY.) He teaches that the latter is the individual mind in the state of potency with regard to knowledge, and that the former is the impersonal mind in the state of actual and perennial thought. In order that the mind acquire ideas, the Passive Intellect must come into contact with the Active Intellect. Avicenna, however, insists most emphatically that a contact of that kind does not interfere with the independent substantiality of the Passive Intellect, and does not imply that it is merged with the Active Intellect. He explicitly maintains that the individual mind retains its individuality and that, because it is spiritual and immaterial, it is endowed with personal immortality. At the same time, he is enough of a mystic to maintain that certain choice souls are capable of arriving at a very special kind of union with the Universal, Active, Intellect, and of attaining thereby the gift of prophecy. Metaphysics he defines as the science of supernatural (ultra-physical) being and of God. It is, as Aristotle says, the theological science. It treats of the existence of God, which is proved from the necessity of a First Cause; it treats of the Providence of God, which, as all the Arabians taught, is restricted to the universal laws of nature, the Divine Agency being too exalted to deal with singular and contingent events; it treats of the hierarchy of mediators between God and material things, all of which emanated from God, the Source of all sources, and Principle of all principles. The first emanation from God is the world of ideas. This is made up of pure forms, free from change, composition, or imperfection; it is akin to the Intelligible world of Plato, and is, in fact, a Platonic concept. Next to the world of ideas is the world of souls, made up of forms which are, indeed, intelligible, but not entirely separated from matter. It is these souls that animate and energize the heavenly spheres. Next to the world of souls is the world of physical forces, which are more or less completely embedded in terrestrial matter and obey its laws; they are, however, to some extent amenable to the power of intelligence in so far as they may be influenced by magic art. Lastly comes the world of corporeal matter; this, according to the Neo-Platonic conception which dominates Avicenna's thought in this theory of emanation, is of itself wholly inert, not capable of acting but merely of being acted upon (Occasionalism). In this hierarchical arrangement of beings, the Active Intellect, which, as was pointed out above, plays a necessary rôle in the genesis of human knowledge, belongs to the world of Ideas, and is of the same nature as the spirits which animate the heavenly spheres. From all this it is apparent that Avicenna is no exception to the general description of the Arabian Aristoteleans as neo-Platonic interpreters of Aristotle. There remain two other doctrines of a general metaphysical nature which exhibit him in the character of an original, or rather an Arabian, and not a neo-Platonic interpreter. The first is his division of being into three classes: (a) what is merely possible, including all sublunary things; (b) what is itself merely possible but endowed by the First Cause with necessity; such are the ideas that rule the heavenly spheres; (c) what is of its own nature necessary, namely, the First Cause. This classification is mentioned and refuted by Averroes. The second doctrine, to which also Averroes alludes, is a fairly outspoken system of pantheism, which Avicenna is said to have elaborated in a work, now lost, entitled "Philosophia Orientalis". The Scholastics, apparently, know nothing of the special work on pantheism; they were, however, aware of the pantheistic tendencies of Avicenna's other works on philosophy, and were, accordingly, reluctant to trust to his exposition of Aristotle.

Avicennæ Peripatetici . . . Opera (Venice, 1495); Munk in *Dict. des sciences phil.* (Paris, 1844–52), art. *Ibn-Sina;* Carra de Vaux, *Avicenne* (Paris, 1900); Ueberweg-Heinze, *Gesch. der Phil.*, 9th ed. (Berlin, 1905), II, 247, 248; tr. Morris (New York, 1890), 412, 413; Stöckl, *Lehrb. der Gesch. der Phil.* (Mainz, 1888), I, 329 sqq., tr. Finlay (Dublin, 1903), 293 sqq.; Turner, *Hist. of Phil.* (Boston, 1903), 312, 313.

William Turner.

Avignon.— City.—Avignon, written in the form of *Avennio* in the ancient texts and inscriptions, takes its name from the House, or Clan, Avennius [d'Arbois de Jubainville, " Recherches sur l'origine de la propriété foncière et des noms des lieux habités en France" (Paris, 1890), 518]. Founded by the *Cavari*, who were of Celtic origin, it became the centre of an important Phocæan colony from Marseilles. Under the Roman occupation, it was one of the most flourishing cities of Gallia Narbonensis; later, and during the inroads of the barbarians, it belonged in turn to the Goths, the Burgundians, the Ostrogoths, and to the Frankish kings of Austrasia. In 736 it fell into the hands of the Saracens, who were driven out by Charles Martel. Boso having been proclaimed King of Provence, or of Arles, by the Synod of Mantaille, at the death of Louis the Stammerer (879), Avignon ceased to belong to the Frankish kings. In 1033, when Conrad II fell heir to the Kingdom of Arles, Avignon passed to the empire. The German rulers, however, being at a distance, Avignon took advantage of their absence to set up as a republic with a consular form of government, between 1135 and 1146. In addition to the emperor, the Counts of Forcalquier, Toulouse, and Provence exercised a purely nominal sway over the city; on two occasions, in 1125, and in 1251, the two latter divided their rights in regard to it, while the Count of Forcalquier resigned any that he possessed to the bishops and consuls in 1135. During the crusade against the Albigenses the citizens refused to open the gates of Avignon to Louis VIII and the legate, but capitulated after a three months' siege (10 June—13 September, 1226) and were forced to pull down the ramparts and fill up the moat of their city. Philip the Fair, who had inherited from his father all the rights of Alphonse de Poitiers, last Count of Toulouse, made them over to Charles II, King of Naples and Count of Provence (1290); it was on the strength of this donation that Queen Joan sold the city to Clement VI for 80,000 florins (9 June, 1348).

Avignon, which at the beginning of the fourteenth century was a town of no great importance, underwent a wonderful development during the residence there of nine popes, Clement V—Benedict XIII, inclusively. To the north and south of the rock of the Doms, partly on the site of the Bishop's Palace, which had been enlarged by John XXII, rose the Palace of the Popes, in the form of an imposing fortress made up of towers, linked one to another, and named as follows: De la Campane, de Trouillas, de la Glacière, de Saint-Jean, des Saints-Anges (Benedict XII), de la Gâche, de la Garde-Robe (Clement VI), de Saint-Laurent (Innocent VI). The Palace of the Popes belongs, by its severe architecture, to the Gothic art of the South of France; other noble examples are to be seen in the churches of St. Didier, St. Peter, and St. Agricola, in the Clock Tower, and in the fortifications built between 1349 and 1368 for a distance of some three miles, and flanked by thirty-nine towers, all of which were erected or restored by popes, cardinals, and great dignitaries of the court. On the other hand, the execution of the frescoes which adorn the interiors of the papal palace and of the churches of Avignon was entrusted almost exclusively to artists from Sienna.

The popes were followed to Avignon by agents (*factores*) of the great Italian banking-houses, who settled in the city. They acted as money-changers, as intermediaries between the Apostolic Chamber and its debtors, living in the most prosperous quarters of the city, which was known as the Exchange. A crowd of traders of all kinds brought to market the

PALACE OF THE POPES, AVIGNON

products necessary to the maintenance of a numerous court and of the visitors who flocked to it; grain and wine from Provence, from the south of France, the Roussillon, and the country round Lyons. Fish was brought from places as distant as Brittany; cloths, rich stuffs, and tapestries came from Bruges and Tournai. We need only glance at the account-books of the Apostolic Chamber, still kept in the Vatican archives, in order to judge of the trade of which Avignon became the centre. The university founded by Boniface VIII in 1303, had a good many students under the French popes, drawn thither by the generosity of the sovereign pontiffs, who rewarded them with books or with benefices.

After the restoration of the Holy See in Rome, the spiritual and temporal government of Avignon was entrusted to a legate, the cardinal-nephew, who was replaced, in his absence by a vice-legate. When, however, Innocent XII abolished nepotism, he did away with the office of legate, and handed over the government of the Pontifical States to the Congregation of Avignon (1692), which resided at Rome, with the Cardinal Secretary of State as prefect, and exercised its jurisdiction through the vice-legate. This congregation, to which appeals were made from the decisions of the vice-legate, was united to the Congregation of Loretto; in 1774 the vice-legate was made president, thus depriving it of almost all authority. It was done away with under Pius VI.

The Public Council, composed of 48 councillors chosen by the people, four members of the clergy, and four doctors of the university, met under the presidency of the *viguier*, or chief magistrate, nominated, for a year, by the legate or vice-legate. Their duty was to watch over the material and financial interests of the city; their resolutions, however, were to be submitted to the vice-legate for approval before being put in force. Three consuls, chosen annually by the Council, had charge of the administration of the streets.

From the fifteenth century onward it became the policy of the Kings of France to unite Avignon to their kingdom. In 1476, Louis XI, annoyed that Giuliano della Rovere should have been made legate, rather than Charles of Bourbon, caused the city to be occupied, and did not withdraw his troops until after his favourite had been made a cardinal. In 1536 Francis I invaded the papal territory, in order to drive out Charles V, who held Provence. In return for the reception accorded him by the people of Avignon, Francis granted them the same privileges as those enjoyed by the French, that, especially, of being eligible to offices of state. Henry III made a fruitless attempt to exchange the Marquisate of Saluces for Avignon, but Gregory XIII would not agree to it (1583). In 1663, Louis XIV, in consequence of an attack, led by the Corsican Guard, on the attendants of the Duc de Créqui, his ambassador in Rome, seized Avignon, which was declared an integral part of the Kingdom of France by the Parliament of Provence. Nor was the sequestration raised until after Cardinal Chigi had made an apology (1664). Another attempt at occupation made in 1688, without success, was followed by a long period of peace, lasting till 1768.

Louis XV, dissatisfied at Clement XIII's action in regard to the Duke of Parma, caused the Papal States to be occupied from 1768 to 1774, and substituted French institutions for those in force. These met with the approval of the people of Avignon, and a French party grew up which, after the sanguinary massacres of La Glacière, carried all before it, and induced the Constituent Assembly to decree the union of Avignon and the Comtat (district) Venaissin with France (14 September, 1791). Article 5 of the Treaty of Tolentino (19 Feb., 1797) definitely sanctioned the annexation; it stated that "The

Pope renounces, purely and simply, all the rights to which he might lay claim over the city and territory of Avignon, and the Comtat Venaissin and its dependencies, and transfers and makes over the said rights to the French Republic." Consalvi made an ineffectual protest at the Treaty of Vienna, in 1815; Avignon was not restored to the Holy See.

DUHAMEL, *Les origines du palais des papes* (Tours, 1882); CHARPENNE, *Histoire des réunions temporaires d'Avignon et du comtat Venaissin à la France* (Paris, 1886); *Histoire de la Révolution dans Avignon et le Comtat Venaissin et de leur réunion définitive à la France* (Paris, 1892); EHRLE, *Historia Bibliothecæ Romanorum Pontificum* (Rome, 1890); FANTONI CASTRUCCI, *Istoria della Città d'Avignone e del contado Venesino* (Venice, 1678); MOLLAT, *Jean XXII, fut il un avare?*, in *Revue d'Histoire Ecclésiastique* (July, 1904, and Jan., 1905); MOLLAT AND SAMARAN, *La fiscalité pontificale en France au XIVe siècle* (Paris, 1905); MÜNTZ, *Les Sources de l'histoire des arts dans la ville d'Avignon pendant le XIVe siècle*, in *Bulletin Archéologique de la Commission des travaux historiques* (1887).

G. MOLLAT.

ARCHDIOCESE OF AVIGNON exercises jurisdiction over the territory embraced by the department of Vaucluse. Before the Revolution it had as suffragan sees, Carpentras, Vaison, and Cavaillon. By the Concordat of 1801 these three dioceses were united to Avignon, together with the Diocese of Apt, a suffragan of Aix. At the same time, however, Avignon was reduced to the rank of a bishopric and was made a suffragan see of Aix. The Archdiocese of Avignon was re-established in 1822, and received as suffragan sees the Diocese of Viviers (restored in 1822); Valence (formerly under Lyon); Nîmes (restored in 1822); and Montpellier (formerly under Toulouse). There is no evidence that St. Rufus, disciple of St. Paul (according to certain traditions the son of Simon the Cyrenean) and St. Justus, likewise held in high honour throughout the territory of Avignon, were venerated in antiquity as bishops of that see. The first bishop known to history is Nectarius, who took part in several councils about the middle of the fifth century. St. Agricol (Agricolus), bishop between 650 and 700, is the patron saint of Avignon. In 1475 Sixtus IV raised the Diocese of Avignon to the rank of an archbishopric, in favour of his nephew Giuliano della Rovere, who later became Pope Julius II. The memory of St. Eucherius still clings to three vast caves near the village of Beaumont, whither, it is said, the people of Lyons had to go in search of him when they sought him to make him their archbishop. As Bishop of Cavaillon, Cardinal Philippe de Cabassoles, Seigneur of Vaucluse, was the great protector of Petrarch. (For Avignon and its religious architecture see AVIGNON, CITY OF.) At the close of 1905 the Archdiocese of Avignon had 236,949 inhabitants, 29 cures, or parishes of the first class; 144 parishes of the second class, and 47 vicariates.

Gallia Christiana, Nova (1715), I, 793–870, 1329; *Instrumenta*, 137–147; DUCHESNE, *Fastes épiscopaux de l'ancienne Gaule*, I, 258–262; GRANGET, *Histoire du diocèse d'Avignon* (Avignon, 1862).

GEORGES GOYAU.

COUNCILS OF AVIGNON.—Nothing is known of the council held here in 1060. In 1080 a council was held under the presidency of Hugues de Dié, papal legate, in which Achard, usurper of the See of Arles, was deposed, and Gibelin put in his place. Three bishops elect (Lautelin of Embrun, Hugues of Grenoble, and Didier of Cavaillon) accompanied the legate to Rome and were consecrated there by Gregory VII. In the Council of 1209 the inhabitants of Toulouse were excommunicated by a Council of Avignon (two papal legates, four archbishops, and twenty bishops) for failing to expel the Albigensian heretics from their city. The Count of Toulouse was forbidden, under threat of excommunication, to impose exorbitant burdens on his subjects and, as he persisted, was finally excommunicated. In the Council of 1270, presided over by Bertrand de Malferrat, Archbishop of Arles, the usurpers of ecclesiastical property were severely threatened; unclaimed legacies were allotted to pious uses; the bishops were urged to mutual support; the individual churches were taxed for the support of the papal legate; and ecclesiastics were forbidden to convoke the civil courts against their bishops. The Council of 1279 was concerned with the protection of the rights, privileges, and immunities of the clergy. Provision was made also for the protection of those who had promised to join the Crusade ordered by Gregory X, but had failed to go. It was also decreed that to hear confessions, besides the permission of his ordinary or bishop, a monk must also have that of his superior. In the Council of 1282 ten canons were published, among them one urging the people to frequent more regularly the parochial churches, and to be present in their own parish churches at least on Sundays and feast days. The temporalities of the Church and ecclesiastical jurisdiction occupied the attention of the Council of 1327. The seventy-nine canons of the Council of 1337 are renewed from earlier councils, and emphasize the duty of Easter Communion in one's own parish church, and of abstinence on Saturday for beneficed persons and ecclesiastics, in honour of the Blessed Virgin, a practice begun three centuries earlier on the occasion of the Truce of God, but no longer universal. The Council of 1457 was held by Cardinal de Foix, Archbishop of Arles and legate of Avignon, a Franciscan. His principal purpose was to promote the doctrine of the Immaculate Conception, in the sense of the declaration of the Council of Basle. It was forbidden to preach the contrary doctrine. Sixty-four disciplinary decrees were also published, in keeping with the legislation of other councils. A similar number of decrees were published in 1497 by a council presided over by Archbishop Francesco Tarpugi (afterwards Cardinal). The sponsors of the newly confirmed, it was decreed, were not obliged to make presents to them or to their parents. Before the relics of the saints two candles were to be kept lighted at all times. Disciplinary measures occupied the attention of the Council of 1509. The Council of 1596 was called for the purpose of furthering the observance of the decrees of the Council of Trent (1545–63), and for a similar purpose the Council of 1609. The Councils of 1664 and 1725 formulated disciplinary decrees; the latter proclaimed the duty of adhering to the Bull of Clement XI against the "Reflexions morales" of Quesnel. The Council of 1849 published, in ten chapters, a number of decrees concerning faith and discipline.

MANSI, *Coll. Conc.*, XIX, 929; XX, 533, and *passim; Coll. Lacensis Conc.*, I, 467; IV, 315; GRANJET, *Hist. du diocèse d'Avignon* (Avignon, 1862).

THOMAS J. SHAHAN.

UNIVERSITY OF AVIGNON (1303–1792), developed from the already existing schools of the city, was formally constituted in 1303, by a Bull of Boniface VIII. With Boniface, King Charles II of Naples should be considered as one of its first great protectors and benefactors. The faculty of law, both civil and ecclesiastical, existed for some time almost exclusively, and always remained the most important department of the university. Pope John XXIII erected (1413) a faculty of theology, the students of which were for a long time only few in number. The faculty of arts never acquired great importance; that of medicine developed especially only in the sixteenth and seventeenth centuries. The Bishop, since 1475 Archbishop, of Avignon was chancellor of the university. The vice-legate, generally a bishop, represented the civil power (in this case the pope) and was chiefly a judicial officer, ranking higher than the Primicerius (Rector). The latter was elected by the Doctors of Law, to whom, in 1503, were added four theologians and, in 1784, two Doctors of Medicine. The pope,

spiritual head and, after 1348, temporal ruler of Avignon, exercised in this double capacity great influence over the affairs of the university. John XXIII granted it (1413) extensive privileges, such as special university jurisdiction and exemption from taxes. Political, geographical, and educational circumstances forced the university, during the later period of its existence, to look to Paris rather than to Rome for favour and protection. It disappeared gradually during the French Revolution, and ceased to exist in 1792.

RASHDALL, *The Universities of Europe in the Middle Ages* (Oxford, 1895), II, 170–179; FOURNIER, *Les statuts et privilèges des univ. françaises* (Paris, 1890–94), II, 301–535; MARCHAND, *L'université d'Avignon aux 17e et 18e siècles* (Paris, 1900); LAVAL, *Cartulaire de l'univ. d'Avignon* (Avignon, 1884).

N. A. WEBER.

Avila (ABULA), DIOCESE OF, a suffragan of Valladolid in Spain. Its episcopal succession dates at least from the fourth century and claims an Apostolic origin. Suppressed in the course of the ninth, it was re-established early in the twelfth, century, after

CATHEDRAL OF AVILA

the expulsion of the Moors, and was a suffragan of Mérida until 1120; then of Compostella until 1857. The Catholic population is 189,926. There are 360 priests, 339 parishes, and about 500 churches and chapels. Avila is historically one of the most important cities in the medieval and modern history of Spain. In the fourth century the arch-heretic Priscillian was Bishop of Avila, and in later times many saints had Avila as their home, among them St. Teresa and John of Avila, the "Apostle of Andalusia". It was once one of the most flourishing cities of Spain, but its population has dwindled to 7,000. Its Moorish castle and ancient eleventh-century cathedral are monumental relics of the past.

BATTANDIER, *Ann. Pont. Cath.* (Paris, 1905); 216; PICATOSTE, *Tradiciones de Avila* (Madrid, 1880); GAMS, *Kirchengeschichte Spaniens*, I, 150 sqq.; FLÓREZ, *España Sagrada*, XIV, 1–36; MUÑOZ, *Bibl. Hist. España* (1858) 42–4.

THOMAS J. SHAHAN.

UNIVERSITY OF AVILA (1550–1807).—Under the patronage of Queen Isabella, the Dominicans established (1504) chairs of philosophy and theology in their College of St. Thomas at Avila, Spain. About 1550, the Papal Nuncio, Juan Poggio, raised the college to university rank. Gregory XIII, at the request of Philip II, ratified the nuncio's action by the Bull "In Apostolatus culmine", 4 April, 1576. Innocent X, in 1645, approved the statutes of the university and empowered it to grant degrees in arts, theology, medicine, and law. Its work, however, was mainly theological. Though it enjoyed the favour of the Spanish sovereigns, especially of Charles II, it never attracted a large number of students. It had no endowment, but depended upon tuition fees. As a result, it began to decline during the eighteenth century, and it was suppressed, along with several other minor universities, in 1807.

DE ZARATE, *De la Instrucción pública en España* (Madrid, 1855), II, 208; LA FUENTE, *Historia de las Universidades . . . en España* (Madrid, 1885), II, 149; *Bullarium Ord. Præd.* (Rome, 1733), V.

E. A. PACE.

Avila, FRANCISCO DE, curate or vicar in the province of Huarochiri of Peru, later curate at Huánaco, finally Canon of the Church of La Plata (now Sucre), in Bolivia. Born in Peru as a foundling (*quorum parentes ignorantur* he says himself); date of demise unknown. He was one of the most active investigators of Indian rites and customs of his time. In 1608 he wrote a treatise of the "Errors, False Gods, and Other Superstitions of the Indians of the Province of Huarochiri, Mama, and Chaclla", of which unfortunately only the first six chapters are known to exist and have been translated into English. It is, even in its incomplete form, an invaluable contribution to the knowledge of the Peruvian Indians and their primitive lore. In 1611 Avila wrote an equally important report on the Indians of Huánaco in eastern Peru, of which the unpublished MS. is extant. Such writings greatly mitigate the charges which the destruction of fetishes and other objects of primitive worship of the Indians have called forth against the Church. (See ARRIAGA, PABLO JOSÉ.)

Fables and Rites of the Incas (Hakluyt Society, 1872); MENDIBURÚ, *Diccionario histórico biográfico del Perú* (1874); ARRIAGA, *Extirpación de la Idolatría del Perú* (Lima, 1621); JIMÉNEZ DE LA ESPADA, *Tres relaciones de antigüedades peruanas* (Madrid, 1879), Introduction.

AD. F. BANDELIER.

Avila, SANCHO DE, b. at Avila of the Kings, in Old Castile, 1546, and named after the place of his birth; d. at Plasencia, in the same province, 6 or 7 December, 1625. He was of a distinguished family but was still more eminent for his saintliness, his vast knowledge, and his success as a preacher. He made his ecclesiastical studies and received his doctorate at the great University of Salamanca. He was afterwards consecrated bishop and held, at different times, the Sees of Murcia, Jaen in Andalusia, Siguenza in Old Castile, in 1615, and, seven years later, Plasencia, where he remained until his death. He had been a confessor of St. Theresa. The following works of his in Spanish are worthy of note: "The Veneration Due to the Bodies and Relics of Saints" (Madrid, 1611); "Sermons" (Baeza, 1615); "The Sighs of St. Augustine", from the Latin (Madrid, 1601, 1626); and, in manuscript, the Lives of St. Augustine and St. Thomas.

WILLIAM DEVLIN.

Avitus (ALCIMUS ECDICIUS), SAINT, a distinguished Bishop of Vienne, in Gaul, from 490 to about 518, though his death is placed by some as late as 525 or 526. He was born of a prominent Gallo-Roman family closely related to the Emperor Avitus and other illustrious persons, and in which episcopal honours were hereditary. In difficult times for the Catholic Faith and Roman culture in Southern Gaul, Avitus exercised a favourable influence. He pursued with earnestness and success the extinction of the Arian heresy in the barbarian Kingdom of Burgundy (443–532), won the confidence of King Gundobad, and converted his son, King Sigismund (516–523). He was also a zealous opponent of Semipelagianism, and of the Acacian Schism at Constantinople. Like his contemporary, Ennodius of Pavia, he was strenuous in his assertion of the authority of the Apostolic See as the chief bulwark of religious unity and the incipient Christian civilization. "If the pope", he says, "is rejected, it follows that not one bishop, but the whole episcopate threatens to fall" (*Si papa urbis vocatur in dubium, episcopatus videbitur, non episcopus, vacillare.*—Ep. xxxiv; ed. Peiper). The literary fame of Avitus rests on a poem of 2,552 hexameters, in five books, dealing with the Scriptural narrative of Original Sin, Expulsion from Paradise, the Deluge, the Crossing of the Red Sea. The first three books offer a certain dramatic unity; in them are told the preliminaries of the great disaster, the catastrophe itself, and the consequences. The fourth and fifth books deal with the Deluge and the Crossing of the Red Sea as symbols of baptism. Avitus deals freely and familiarly with the Scriptural events, and exhibits well their beauty, sequence, and significance. He is one of the last masters of the art of rhetoric as taught in the schools of Gaul in the fourth and fifth centuries. Ebert says that none of the ancient Christian poets treated more successfully the poetic elements of the Bible. His poetic diction, though abounding in archaisms and rhythmic redundancy, is pure and select, and the laws of metre are well observed. It is said that Milton made use of his paraphase of Scripture in the preparation of "Paradise Lost". He wrote also 666 hexameters "De virginitate" or "De consolatoriâ castitatis laude" for the comfort of his sister Fuscina, a nun. His prose works include "Contra Eutychianam Hæresim libri II", written in 512 or 513, and also about eighty-seven letters that are of considerable importance for the ecclesiastical and political history of the years 499–518. Among them is the famous letter to Clovis on the occasion of his baptism. There was once extant a collection of his homilies, but they have perished with the exception of two and some fragments and excerpts. In recent times Julien Havet has demonstrated (Questions mérovingiennes, Paris, 1885) that Avitus is not the author of the "Dialogi cum Gundobado Rege", a defence of the Catholic Faith against the Arians, purporting to represent the famous Colloquy of Lyons in 449, and first published by d'Achéry (1661) in his "Spicilegium" (V, 110–116). It is a forgery of the Oratorian, Jérome Viguier, who also forged the letter of Pope Symmachus (13 Oct., 501) to Avitus. The works of Avitus are found in Migne, P. L., LIX, 191–398. There are two recent editions: one by R. Peiper (in Mon. Germ. Hist.: Auct. Antiq., VI, Berlin, 1883), the other by U. Chevalier (Lyons, 1890).

Acta SS., 1 February; *Avite, sa vie, ses œuvres* (Paris, 1870); DENKINGER, *St. Avite et la déstruction de l'Arianisme en Gaule* (Geneva, 1890); GUIZOT, *Hist. de la civilisation en France* (1829), II, 198–216; GORINI, *Défense de l'Eglise* (Paris, 1866), II, 1–86; KURTH, *Hist. poétique des mérovingiens* (1893), 243 sqq.; YOUNG in *Dict. Christ. Biogr.*, I, 233; BARDENHEWER, *Patrologie* (Freiburg, 1901), 538, 539.

THOMAS J. SHAHAN.

Aviz, ORDER OF, a military body of Portuguese knights.—The Kingdom of Portugal, founded in 1128, was not only contemporaneous with the Crusades but conducted one of its own against the Moors. Some crusaders were bound only by temporary vows, and when these expired they would sometimes return to their country although the war was not ended. This accounts for the favour with which military orders were regarded beyond the Pyrenees, in Portugal as well as in Spain; for in them the vow of fighting against the infidels was perpetual, like other monastic vows. Knights Templars were found in Portugal as early as 1128, and received a grant from Queen Teresa in the year of the Council of Troyes, which confirmed their early statutes. A native order of this kind sprang up in Portugal about 1146. Affonso, the first king, gave to it the town of Evora, captured from the Moors in 1211, and the Knights were first called "Brothers of Santa Maria of Evora". Pedro Henríquez, an illegitimate son of the king's father, was the first grand master. After the conquest of Aviz the military castle erected there became the mother-house of the order, and they were then called "Knights of St. Benedict of Aviz", since they adopted the Benedictine rule in 1162, as modified by John Ziritu, one of the earliest Cistercian abbots of Portugal. Like the Knights of Calatrava in Castile, the Knights of Portugal were indebted to the Cistercians for their rule and their habit—a white mantle with a green fleur-de-lysed cross. The Knights of Calatrava also surrendered some of their places in Portugal to them on condition that the Knights of Aviz should be subject to the visitation of their grand master. Hence the Knights of Aviz were sometimes regarded as a branch of the Calatravan Order, although they never ceased to have a Portuguese grand master, dependent for temporalities on the Portuguese king. At the accession of King Ferdinand (1383) war broke out between Castile and Portugal. When João I, who had been grand master of the Knights of Aviz, ascended the throne of Portugal, he forbade the knights to submit to Castilian authority, and consequently, when Gonzalvo de Guzman came to Aviz as Visitor, the knights, while according him hospitality, refused to recognize him as a superior. Guzman protested, and the point remained a subject of contention until the Council of Basle (1431), when Portugal was declared to be in the wrong. But the right of the Calatravans was never exercised, and the next grand master of the Knights of Aviz, Rodrigo of Sequirol, continued to assert supreme authority over them.

The mission of the military orders in Portugal seemed to fail after the overthrow of Moslem domination, but the Portuguese expeditions across the sea opened up a new field for them. The first landings of Europeans in Africa, the conquest of Ceuta by King João I (1415), the attacks upon Tangier under João's son Duarte (1437), were also crusades, inspired by a religious spirit and sanctioned by similar papal Bulls. The Knights of Aviz and the Knights of Christ, scions of the Knights Templars, achieved deeds of valour, the former under the Infante Fernando, the latter under Henrique, brother of King Duarte. Fernando displayed a no less heroic forbearance during his six years of captivity among the Moslems, a long martyrdom which after his death placed him among the Blessed (Acta SS., 5 June). This splendid enthusiasm did not last. Soon the whole nation became affected by the wealth that poured in, and the Crusade in Africa degenerated into mere mercantile enterprise;

the pontifical Bulls were made a vulgar means of raising money, and after the grand mastership of the order (1551) had been vested in the king in perpetuity, he availed himself of its income to reward any kind of service in the army or the fleet. If the wealth of the Knights of Aviz was not as great as that of the Knights of Christ, it was still quite large, drawn as it was from some forty-three commanderies. The religious spirit of the knights vanished, and they withdrew from their clerical brothers who continued alone the conventual life. They were dispensed from their vow of celibacy by Alexander VI (1492), who tolerated their marriage to prevent scandalous concubinage; Julius III (1551) allowed them to dispose freely of their personal properties. Nobility of birth remained the chief requirement of aspirants to the mantle, a requirement confirmed by a decree of 1604. Queen Maria I, supported by Pope Pius VI (1 Aug., 1789), attempted a last reformation and failed. Finally, the military orders were suppressed by Dom Pedro, after the downfall of the Miguelist usurpation (1834).

For Documents: Noronha, Constituções de S. Bento de Aviz (Lisbon, 1631). For History: Jos. da Purificão, Catalogo dos Mestres de Aviz, 1722 (Acad. Real da Historia); Brito, Chronica de Cister, onde, etc. (Lisbon, 1602); cf. Almeida in Mém. acad. scient. Lisboa (1837); Hélyot, Dict. des ordres religieux (1847), I, 348–350; Schæfer, Gesch. von Portugal (Gotha, 1834–54); Herculano, History of Portugal (Lisbon, 1854–73).

CH. Moeller.

A Knight of St. Benedict of Aviz

Avranches, Diocese of. See, Coutances.

Avranches, Council of.—In 1172 (Sept., 27–28) a council was held at Avranches in France, apropos of the troubles caused in the English Church by the murder of St. Thomas Becket. Henry II, King of England, after due penance, was absolved from the censures incurred by the assassination of the holy prelate, and swore fidelity to Alexander III in the person of his legate. It was forbidden to confer on children benefices that carried with them the cure of souls, or on the children of priests the churches of their fathers. Each parish was required to have an assistant (vicarius) and the Advent fast was commended to all who could observe it, especially to ecclesiastics.

Mansi, Coll. Conc. (1778), XXII, 136; Bessin, Conc. Rotomag. (1717), 84, 263–295; Chevalier, Topo-bibl. (Paris, 1894–99), 286.

Thomas J. Shahan.

Avril, Philippe, Jesuit, b. at Angoulême, France, 16 September, 1654; d. in a shipwreck in 1698. He was professor of philosophy and mathematics at Paris when he was summoned to the missions of China. Following the instructions of Father Verbiest, then at Pekin, he attempted an overland journey, and travelled for six years through Kurdistan, Armenia, Astrakhan, Persia, and other countries of the East. Arriving at Moscow, he was refused permission to pass through Tatary, and was sent by the Government to Poland, from whence he made his way to Constantinople and from there went back to France. Though exhausted by hæmorrhages he set out again on a vessel, which was lost at sea. He has left interesting and valuable accounts of his long wanderings.

Sommervogel, Bibliothèque de la c. de J., I, 706; Michaud, Bibliog. univ.

T. J. Campbell.

Axum (Auxume), a titular metropolitan see of ancient Christian Ethiopia. Its episcopal list, from about the middle of the fourth century to 650, is found in Gams (p. 462). Modern Axum is the capital of the Abyssinian province of Tigré, and nestles in a *kloof*, or valley, beneath a lofty peak of the Adoua mountains, at 7,545 feet above the level of the sea. Beneath it is a vast plain in which arise several streams tributary to the Nile. "The features of the place", says a recent traveller, "are very marked; firstly one comes across the large sacred enclosure, nearly a mile in circumference, thickly planted with trees and reeds, in the centre of which rises the cathedral, surrounded by the monastic buildings and the residence of the *Etchigeh*, or bishop. This enclosure occupies nearly the whole of the entrance to the valley; beyond it on the hill slopes are the houses of the inhabitants, whilst running up the valley is the long line of stupendous obelisks and beyond is the ancient tank or reservoir from which the inhabitants still get their water supply" (Bent, The Sacred City of the Ethiopians).

The city is of great antiquity, and was, together with Adule (Adoua on the coast) known to the Greeks and Romans as the chief centre of trade, with the interior of Africa, for gold-dust, ivory, leather, hides, and aromatics. The population is of mixed Ethiopic (negroid) and Arab origin, and is probably descended, in great measure, from an Arab colony settled on the coast at a very remote period. The numerous Himyaritic (Arabic) inscriptions in the vicinity exhibit the influence of Arabia; similarly the stone monuments with their evidences of sun and star worship. Moreover, it is well known that in the sixth century of our era the Kings of Abyssinia, then and long after resident at Axum, extended their sway over the Sabæan and Himyarite (Homerite) tribes of Yemen on the opposite Arabian shore. Greek influences are also traceable in the architecture of Axum and from a very early date, probably from the days of the Ptolemies of Egypt. In other words, this "sacred city of the Ethiopians" has been from time immemorial an outpost of ancient civilization against the mass of African barbarism. Axum became a Christian city in the time of St. Athanasius of Alexandria, who consecrated its first bishop, St. Frumentius, still honoured as the great patron of Abyssinia; since which time (c. 330) the Abyssinian Church has remained in close dependency on the Church of Alexandria, and yet receives from Egypt its chief ecclesiastical officer, the Abouna. There is still extant (P. G., XXV, 635) a famous letter of the Emperor Constantius (337–361) to Aeizanes, the King of Axum, ordering him to send Frumentius to Alexandria to receive the Arian doctrine from the heretical successor intruded in the place of Athanasius. The other principal ecclesiastics resident at Axum are the above mentioned *Etchigeh* (*Etchagué*), or principal bishop, always a native; the *Nebrid*, a kind of archdeacon or head of the priesthood and rector of the

The Old Cathedral, Axum

cathedral; the *Lij Kaneat*, or judge in ecclesiastical matters, together with monks and priests of various grades. There are also many persons known as *defteras*, described as "lay assistants in all the services, acting as singers and performers in all the church ceremonies; the scribes, advocates, and doctors of Abyssinia and the most instructed and intelligent people of the land" (Bent, op. cit., 161).

Axum claims to hold in the innermost recesses of its cathedral the original Tables of the Law and the *tabout*, or Ark of the Covenant that the Abyssinians say was brought from Jerusalem to their ancient fortress of Ava by Menelek, the son of Solomon, and the Queen of Sheba, and transferred later to Axum. The palace of that famous Queen is also shown at Axum. Until 1538 Axum was both the civil and religious centre of Abyssinia. In that year, it was captured by Mohammed, Prince of Leïla, since which time the Negus resides at Gondar. The cathedral is a fine edifice, and was built in the sixteenth century during the period of Portuguese influence in Abyssinia, but on the substructure of a very ancient Christian church. It has a flat roof and battlements, and there is a corridor outside where the priests dance and sing. Around the cathedral are many large shade-trees beneath which are built smaller churches or treasuries, in which are stored valuables of all kinds. Its sacred enclosure is not only the centre of ecclesiastical life, but also one of the most honoured sanctuaries in Abyssinia, where any criminal can find shelter by ringing the bell in the porch and declaring three times in a loud voice his intention of claiming a refuge. Women are not allowed to enter it. Indeed, all Axum is practically a sacred, inviolable refuge, for which reason the people enjoy a condition of peace and tranquillity unknown elsewhere in Abyssinia (Bent, 163).

Very interesting are the numerous stone pedestals that once bore metal statues of the pre-Christian kings of Axum, memorials of victory, and the stone monoliths and obelisks, fallen or standing, estimated by Bent at about fifty. The latter form "a consecutive series from very rude unhewn stones up to the highly finished and decorated obelisks, and it is highly probable that we have here the origin and development of the obelisk side by side" (Bent, 132). The only standing obelisk of the decorated kind, highly carved with sham doors and beam ends, in imitation of a many-storied edifice, is nine stories high, and ends with a semi-circular finial, on which is still to be seen a representation of the solar disk. "In other words," says Mr. Bent (p. 185) "we have before us a perfect representation of the Beth-el or House of God terminating in the firmament, in which the Sabæan sun-god is supposed to reside." Altars for animal sacrifices were fitted to the bases of these obelisks; several of them are still visible. Mounds and rubbish heaps are scattered about the sacred enclosure at Axum that doubtless contain many objects of profane and ecclesiastical interest.

Near the cathedral is a square enclosure with a pillar at each of its angles, and in the centre twelve stones that Abyssinian tradition says were for the twelve judges of Prester John, but are probably the bases of ancient triumphal thrones of the Kings of Axum. Among the valuable Ethiopic manuscripts found in Abyssinia in modern times is the Book of Axum, or Abyssinian Chronicles, brought back by the traveller Bruce. In 1805 the English traveller, Salt, discovered at Axum a bilingual inscription in Greek and Gheez (the religious language of Abyssinia) of which only the Greek (thirty-one lines) remains. It refers to the exploits of King Aeizanes, already mentioned. In 1833 the German traveller, Rüppell, discovered two other Gheez inscriptions, referring to the deeds of a monarch of Axum in the sixth century. These Gheez inscriptions are valuable for the history of the Semitic alphabet. Some Greek coins, older than the fourth century have been found there, also Ethiopic coins of a somewhat later date, bearing the title, "Negush Aksum", or King of Axum.

LEQUIEN, *Oriens Christ.* (1740), II, 641–660; SMITH, *Dict. of Greek and Roman Geogr.*, I, 347; TILLEMONT, *Mémoires*, etc., VII, 284–289; BRUCE, *Travels to Discover the Source of the Nile* (Edinburgh, 1788), I, 476; SALT, *Travels in Abyssinia*, 510; BENT, *The Sacred City of the Ethiopians* (London, 1896), 152–197.

THOMAS J. SHAHAN.

Ayacucho, or GUAMANGA, DIOCESE OF.—A Peruvian diocese, suffragan to Lima. The See of Guamanga was erected by Paul V, 20 July, 1609, was vacant from 1821 to 1838, when it was transferred to Ayacucho. It has 200,610 Catholics; 96 parishes, 120 secular priests, 212 churches or chapels.

BATTANDIER, *Ann. Pont. Cath.*, 1907.

Ayeta, FRAY FRANCISCO DE, a Spanish Franciscan of the seventeenth century, and (while time and place of his birth and death are not known as yet, his memorable deeds having been overlooked and neglected until now) one of the most deserving and energetic characters of the end of that century in New Spain or Mexico. He became successively Visitor of the Province of the Holy Evangel of New Mexico, and its Procurator at Madrid; also Commissary of the Inquisition in New Spain. The decline in useful activity among the regular orders in Mexico, which began about the middle of the seventeenth century, being taken as a pretext by the secular authorities for despoiling the regulars of their missions, Ayeta became one of the most fervent defenders of the Franciscans, and he wielded a very aggressive pen. Three books are known to have been published by him, all without date and place; an "Apología del orden de San Francisco en América", which is supposed to have appeared about 1690; "Defensa de la provincia del Santo Evangelio de México sobre la retención de los curatos y doctrinas"; and "Ultimo recurso de la provincia de San José de Yucatan sobre despojo de parroquias". Ayeta investigated in person the most remote missions, especially those of New Mexico, and he was the first to warn the Spanish authorities of the storm then preparing among the Pueblo Indians. His report, from 1678, in which he exposed the defenceless condition of the New Mexican colony as against the wild Indians, and the dangerous impression which it had made upon the sedentary tribes, induced the authorities of New Spain to reinforce the garrison at Santa Fe, but it was too late. The Pueblos broke out on the tenth of August, 1680, and for fourteen years New Mexico was lost to Spain. Ayeta hurried to El Paso, and when the fugitives from the North reached that post, to the number of two thousand famished and attenuated persons, Ayeta was the first to tender them the needed relief in food and clothing. He was a man of superior mind and indomitable energy, entirely devoted to his task and to his order.

BETANCOURT, *Crónica de la provincia del Santo Evangelio de México* (2d ed., Mexico, 1871); BÉRISTAIN DE SOUZA, *Biblioteca Hispano-americana setentrional* (Mexico, 1816), I; SARINANA Y CUENCA, *Oración fúnebre . . . . en las exequias de veinte y uno religiosos de la observancia & ca. que murieron á manos de los Indios apóstatas del Nuevo México* (Mexico, 1681). This sermon is manifestly based upon the data furnished by Ayeta in a yet unpublished report on the priests who were murdered in 1680.—BANDELIER, *Histoire de la colonisation et des missions du Sonora, Chihuahua, Nouveau Mérique, et Arizona, jusq'à l'an 1700* (MSS. at the Vatican, 1888). See also *Documentos para la historia de México* (third series, very rare); and BANDELIER, *Documentary History of the Zuñi Tribe*, in *Journal Am. Arch.*, No. 1.

AD. F. BANDELIER.

Ayllón, LUCAS VÁSQUEZ DE, the Spanish discoverer of Chesapeake Bay, and the first of those daring navigators who tried to find a north-west passage from Europe to Asia, date of birth uncertain; d. 18 October, 1526. He was a member of the Superior Council in San Domingo. He sent an expedition to Florida under Francisco Gordillo, who, in June, 1521, landed in lat. 33° 30′, somewhere near Cape Fear in North Carolina. In quest of the north-west passage, Ayllón came up from Hispaniola in 1524, and tried the James River and Chesapeake Bay. He received from Charles V a grant of the land he had discovered, and, in 1526, founded the settlement of San Miguel de Guandape, not far from the site of the city of Jamestown, built by the English fully eighty years later. The employment of negro slaves in this work is perhaps the first instance of negro slave-labour within the present territory of the United States. Ayllón died of ship fever, and of the colony of 600 souls he had brought with him only 150 survivors made their way back to Hispaniola.

FISKE, *Discovery of America* (Boston, 1902), III, 321; LEE (ed.) *History of N. America* (Philadelphia, 1903), I, 338–341; WINSOR (ed.), *Narrative and Critical History of America* (Boston, 1884), IV.

EDWARD P. SPILLANE.

Aylward, JAMES AMBROSE DOMINIC, theologian and poet, b. at Leeds, 4 April, 1813; d. at Hinckley (England), 5 October, 1872. He was educated at the Dominican priory of Hinckley, entered the Order of St. Dominic, was ordained priest in 1836, became provincial in 1850, first Prior of Woodchester in 1854, and provincial a second time in 1866. He composed several pious manuals for the use of his community and "A Novena for the Holy Season of Advent" gathered from the prophecies, anthems, etc., of the Roman Missal and Breviary (Derby, 1849). He re-edited (London, 1867) a "Life of the Blessed Virgin St. Catherine of Sienna", translated from the Italian by the Dominican Father John Fen (Louvain, 1609), also an English translation of Father Chocarne's "Inner Life of Lacordaire" (Dublin, 1867). His essays "On the Mystical Elements in Religion, and on Ancient and Modern Spiritism" were edited posthumously by Cardinal Manning (London, 1874). Father Aylward's principal monument is his translation of Latin hymns, most of which he contributed to "The Catholic Weekly Instructor". In his "Annus Sanctus" (London, 1884) Orbey Shipley has reprinted many of them. He says of Father Aylward that he was "a cultured and talented priest of varied powers and gifts."

JULIAN, *Dict. of Hymnology* (New York, 1892), 105; GILLOW, *Bibl. Dict. of Eng. Cath.*, I, 90, 91.

THOMAS J. SHAHAN.

Aymará, also AYMARA (etymology unknown as yet), a numerous tribe of sedentary Indians inhabiting the northern sections of Bolivia, part of the eastern declivities of the Andes of that republic, and the sections of Peru bordering upon Lake Titicaca, except its northern extremity, which is held by Quichua-speaking Indians. It is not safe as yet to give their numbers, since white blood has been liberally introduced during three centuries, while on the eastern slopes, in the so-called Yungas, mixture with negroes has been frequent. Still there are certainly several hundred thousands of them, counting in such *mestizos* (Cholos) as live according to Indian customs. The name "Aymará" rather applies to the language, which seems allied to the Quichua, or prevailing Indian idiom of the Peruvian mountains and of the southern part of the Bolivian highlands. The Aymará are chiefly mountaineers, inhabiting the elevated table land, or *Puna*, between the eastern Cordillera and the volcanic coast chain. Limited agriculture, the raising of potatoes and kindred tubers, of *quinua* (*chenopodium quinua*), maize in the few places where it will thrive at the general altitude of over 12,000 feet of the table land. The raising of the llama and alpaca and of some cattle and donkeys, are their chief occupations, also service in the cities as journeymen, and on the lake-shore as stevedores. They live in tribal communities (*estancias*), autonomous, and with executive officers (*hilacata* and *alcalde*) whom they choose after the indications of their chief medicine-men, to be afterwards confirmed by the civil authorities of Bolivia. Duration of office is mostly one year. They pay a *per capita* tax, are not subject to military duty in theory, and are

AYMARÁ NATIVES

seldom required to perform any. Many of these Indians, while apparently indigent, possess no little wealth, chiefly in coin. Some of them are also artisans. They are nominally Catholics, but preserve a remnant of ancient idolatry, with its rituals and ceremonies, carefully hidden from outsiders. In appearance stolid and humble, they are in fact a cruel, treacherous stock, averse to every attempt at progress, hostile to the whites, particularly to foreigners. But they sometimes make good house servants. They were first visited by the Spaniards in the last days of 1533, whom they received well, owing to their hatred of the Inca tribe of Cuzco. The latter had overrun most of the Lake territory in the course of the fifteenth century and established themselves on the Islands of Titicaca and Koati (see articles) and at Copacavana on the mainland. The relations between the Kollas—as the Quichua call the Aymará to this day (see KOLLAO)—and the Incas were not friendly. The Spaniards were at first treated with hospitality, but as soon as they returned in greater numbers the western and southwestern Aymará rose in arms and had to be repressed by force. During the civil wars (1538 to 1554) the Aymará remained passive and suffered (like the rest of the Peruvian Indians) from the consequences. Uprisings of Aymará groups against the Spaniards began in 1629, and local disturbances (in many of which the Indians were at fault) continued. In 1780 a general uprising began among the Aymará of western Bolivia, but there was no concerted action, and although there were terrible massacres, and the investment of La Paz by the Aymará almost ended in the capture of that city,

the Indians were finally subdued in 1782. Since then they have remained comparatively quiet. While a necessary and important element as land-tillers and freighters, journeymen and house servants, they would be, on account of their numbers, a steady menace to Bolivia, were it not for their incapacity for united efforts, their adherence to primitive customs preventing any submission to a common leader. With the coming introduction of railways in Bolivia, the Aymará will have to submit, and modify their habits and customs.

The earliest and best description of the northern and central Aymará is found in the *Relatione per Sua Maestà*, written 15 July, 1534, by PEDRO SANCHO in the name of Pizarro and officers, and published (in Italian) by RAMUSIO in vol. III (1565).—*Relación del Sitio del Cuzco*, 1539 (Madrid, by JIMENEZ DE LA ESPADA); CIEZA, *Parte primera de la crónica del Perú* (Antwerp, 1555); *Segunda Parte* (Madrid); JUAN DE BETANZOS, *Suma y Narración de los Incas*, 1551 (recent publication at Madrid); GARCILASSO DE LA VEGA, *Comentarios reales de los Incas* (Lisbon, 1609); OVIEDO, *Historia, general y natural de las Indias* (Madrid, 1850); HERRERA, *Historia general de los Hechos de los Castellanos en las Islas y Tierra firme del Mar Océano* (1729, etc.); ANELLO OLIVA, *Historia del Perú* (Lima, without date)—this history was written in 1631—BERNABÉ COBO, *Historia del Nuevo Mundo*, 1653 (Seville, 1893). Of later works I only refer to WIENER, *Pérou et Bolivie* (Paris, 1880) and to the works of DR. MIDDENDORF.—The Aymará idiom appears first in literature in 1583. *Catecismo en la Lengua Española y Aymará del Perú, Ordenado por autoridad del Concilio Provincial de Lima* (Lima, 1583); *Tercer Catecismo y Exposición de la Doctrina Cristiana, por Sermones* (Lima, 1586); BERTONIO, *Arte de la Lengua Aymará* (Rome, 1603); IDEM, *Vocabulario de la Lengua Aymará* (Juli, southern Peru, 1612). On the uprisings of the Aymará in 1780 to 1782, BALLIVIAN, *Archivo boliviano* (Paris, 1872); also ODRIOZOLA, *Documentos históricos del Perú* (1863), I. A very rare work on the Aymará language and seldom consulted, is TORRES RUBIO, *Arte de la Lengua Aymará* (Lima, 1616).

AD. F. BANDELIER.

Aymeric of Piacenza, a learned Dominican, b. at Piacenza, Italy; d. at Bologna, 19 August, 1327. Soon after his entrance into the Lombard province of the Dominican Order, he was sent (1262) to pursue his studies at Milan, where he formed a close friendship with Niccolò Boccasini, later pope under the name of Benedict XI (1303–04). After teaching philosophy and theology for twenty-four years he was elected Provincial of Greece. In this capacity he travelled to the Chapter General of Toulouse in May, 1304, where a successor to Bernard de Jusix was to be elected, but just before the first session renounced his office and vote, with the consent of the pope. That this act of humility was the cause of his election to the master generalship of the order is the unanimous verdict of all its chroniclers. His first care was to regulate studies in those provinces where the opposition of the Fraticelli to intellectual pursuits had been most felt. He definitely determined the qualifications for degrees in the order. Oriental languages were no less encouraged by him than natural sciences. In 1309 Clement IV enjoined on Aymeric who was on his way to the chapter of Saragossa in Spain, to examine into the charges brought against the Templars. He found little to complain of. In 1310 he was summoned to the Council of Vienne to take part in the process of the Templars. In the meantime, however, he resigned his office, and thus avoided the displeasure of Clement IV, whose policy he never heartily endorsed. At the same time, as he candidly avowed, he was saved from acting against the dictates of his conscience. He is the reputed author of a treatise against the heretics of his day, and of works on moral, dogmatic, and scholastic questions, none of which are known to be extant. Montfaucon (Diarium Italicum, xxvii) speaks of a curious present given by Aymeric to the convent of Bologna. It was the Pentateuch in Hebrew and learned Jews of the time declared that the manuscript had been written by Esdras. "Although this smacks of the fabulous", cautiously remarks Montfaucon, ". . . still it cannot be denied that the codex appears to have been old when given to Aymeric". As a man of letters Aymeric was in close touch with the learned men of his time. Pietro Crescenzio of Bologna completed his "De Re Rusticâ" at the repeated solicitations of Aymeric, by whom it was corrected before the author presented it to Charles II of Sicily. The letters of Aymeric are found in "Litteræ Encyclicæ Magistrorum Generalium Ord. Præd." (ed. Reichert, Rome, 1900), which forms the fifth volume of the "Monumenta Hist. Fratr. Præd." (181–202).

TIRABOSCHI, *Storia della litt. Ital.*, V, I, 152–153; QUÉTIF AND ECHARD, *SS. Ord. Præd.*, I, 494 sqq.; MORTIER, *Histoire des Maîtres Généraux de l'ordre des Frères Prêcheurs* (Paris, 1905), II, 420–473; KAUFMANN in *Der Katholik*, Feb., 1900.

THOS. M. SCHWERTNER.

Azara, FÉLIZ DE, a Spanish naturalist, b. at Barbunales in Aragon, 18 May, 1746; d. 1811. He first embraced the military career as an engineer, distinguished himself in various expeditions, and rose to the rank of Brigadier General in the Spanish Army. He was appointed member of the Spanish commission sent to South America, in 1781, to settle the question of limits between the Portuguese and Spanish colonies. He remained in South America till 1801. While there he turned his attention to the study of mammals, less as an anatomist or physiologist than as an observer of the life and habits of quadrupeds. His observations, to which he added a large number of statements obtained by hearsay, were not always favourably criticized, but to-day the perspicacity of Azara as a student of the life of South American mammals is generally acknowledged. He also extended his investigations to birds. Before leaving South America, he sent his brother (then Spanish Ambassador at Paris) many notes and observations of a zoological nature, which Moreau de Saint-Méry published at Paris in 1801 under the title of "Essai sur l'histoire naturelle des quadrupèdes du Paraguay". In 1802 there appeared at Madrid "Apuntamientos para la Historia natural de los cuadrúpedos del Paraguay y Río de la Plata". In the same year Azara published "Apuntamientos para la Historia de los pájaros del Paraguay y Río de la Plata". In 1809 there appeared at Paris under his name "Voyage dans l'Amérique méridionale depuis 1781 jusqu'en 1801". In the latter work he criticizes the Jesuit methods of organizing and educating the Indians, showing that he completely failed to understand the nature of the American aborigines. Azara, while an efficient soldier and good engineer, as well as shrewd observer of animal life, was incapable of understanding the character of the Indian, and of grasping the only method by which the Indian could slowly but surely be civilized.

Geografía física y esférica de las provincias del Paraguay y misiones Guaranies, compuesta en el año 1790 (Montevideo, 1904, with portrait and biography by SCHULLER); TSCHUDI, *Peru Reiseskizzen* (St. Gall, 1846); IDEM, *Fauna peruana;* BREHM, *Das Thierleben* (3d ed.); and the works of Azara himself, enumerated in article.

AD. F. BANDELIER.

Azaria, ARISTACES, a Catholic Armenian abbot and archbishop, b. at Constantinople, 18 July, 1782; d. at Vienna, 6 May, 1854. He was sent at the age of fifteen to the College of the Propaganda in Rome, but his studies were interrupted (1798) by the French invasion. Having taken refuge among the Mechitarists of Triest, he entered their order in 1801, and in the same year was ordained priest. The authorities of the ephemeral Kingdom of Illyria confiscated (1810) the property of his convent, and, after vain attempts to obtain restitution, the monks settled in Vienna, where they lived by the instruction of Armenian youth and the revenue of a printing-press. Azaria was henceforth active as a missionary among his compatriots and a servant of the Holy See. In 1826 he was made general abbot of the community, and in 1827 was raised to the (titular) dignity of

Archbishop of Cæsarea. Under him the Mechitarist community in Vienna prospered, its library was increased, a bookstore added to the printing-press, and an abundant religious literature created, in Armenian and in German. He opened houses of his community in Rome, Triest, and Stamboul, founded the Armenian journal "Europa", established an academy for the literary and political improvement of his people, and obtained from the Porte (1830) the creation of an independent Catholic Armenian patriarchate. He wrote several (mostly anonymous) works, among them "De Vitâ Communi Perfectâ Religiosorum Utriusque Sexus", in which he criticizes the condition of many Austrian religious houses, and "Die Erziehung im Geiste des Christenthumes" (Vienna, 1839). After a visit to Rome (1850) in the interest of monastic reform, he returned to Vienna (1852) where he died after the celebration of his golden jubilee.

HERGENRÖTHER in *Kirchenlex.*, I, 1768.

THOMAS J. SHAHAN.

Azarias, BROTHER (PATRICK FRANCIS MULLANY), educator, essayist, littérateur, and philosopher, b. near Killenaule, County Tipperary, Ireland, 29 June, 1847. His education began at home, and after the removal of his family to Deerfield, N. Y., U. S. A., was continued in the union school of that place, and subsequently in the Christian Brothers' Academy at Utica. Believing himself called to the life of a religious teacher, he entered the novitiate of the Brothers of the Christian Schools, in New York City, on the 24th of February 1862. He taught in Albany, New York City, and Philadelphia until 1866, when he was called to the professorship of mathematics and literature in Rock

BROTHER AZARIAS

Hill College, Ellicott City, Md. Gradually his interests were diverted from mathematics and were absorbed by literature and philosophy, which, with pedagogy, continued to hold them until the end of his career. From 1879 to 1886 he was President of Rock Hill College. Then followed two years of research in European libraries, chiefly those of Paris and London. On his return to the United States, he became professor of literature in De La Salle Institute, New York City, and remained such till his death at the Catholic Summer School, Plattsburgh, 20 August, 1893. The funeral services held in St. Patrick's Cathedral, New York City, gave ample testimony to his widespread influence and to the esteem in which he was held.

The secret of his success is to be found in his deep reverence for the apostolate of teaching, a reverence which found expression beyond the walls of the class room. He was a frequent contributor to the "Catholic World", the "American Catholic Quarterly Review", and the "American Ecclesiastical Review", and his name appears in the files of the "Educational Review" and of the "International Journal of Ethics". His lectures bore the stamp of culture and scholarship. The most notable are these:— "The Psychological Aspects of Education", delivered before the Regents' Convocation, University of the

State of New York, 1877; "Literary and Scientific Habits of Thought", before the International Congress of Education, 1884; "Aristotle and the Christian Church", before the Concord School of Philosophy, 1885; "Church and State", before the Farmington School of Philosophy, 1890; "Religion in Education", before the New York State Teachers' Association, 1891; "Educational Epochs", before the Catholic Summer School, 1893. At the time of his death, he was engaged in preparing a "History of Education" for the International Education Series.

His first work as an independent author appeared in 1874, with the title, "An Essay Contributing to a Philosophy of Literature" (seventh edition, 1899). It is an excellent key both to his method of study and to the plan of presentation to which he consistently adhered in subsequent works and addresses. Renan and Emerson had attempted to make literature a substitute for religion in cultured circles; with characteristic insight and modesty, Brother Azarias proves in this essay that literature draws its life and excellence from religion. He divides the book into three parts: Facts and Principles, Theory, and Practice. In the first he discusses the nature, origin, and function of literature, examines its relation to language and architecture, and formulates the law of literary epochs. He then presents the salient features of the pre-Reformation ages, and argues that the Elizabethan era of letters was the fruit of the seeds of Catholicism that had been planted and nurtured in early Britain. After contrasting ancient and modern literature, he examines the principles of those philosophic systems that have most influenced modern thought. In the light of these results he studies the literary artist, the morality which is binding on him, and the canons that should guide him in his work. The book is of great value in giving the student correct principles of orientation.

"The Development of Old English Thought" (third edition, 1903) appeared in 1879 as the first part of a projected course in English literature, which, however, was never completed. The author begins with sketching the "continental homestead" of the English; he then contrasts the Celt and Teuton, examines the pagan traditions on which Christian literature was engrafted, and concludes with charming pen pictures of Hilda, Cædmon, Benedict Biscop, and the Venerable Bede. The period covered is the first thousand years of the Christian era.

"Aristotle and the Christian Church" (London and New York, 1888) sets forth the attitude of the Catholic Church towards Aristotelean philosophy in the thirteenth and fourteenth centuries, shows the difference in spirit between the Stagirite and the Schoolmen, and accounts in part for this by tracing the growing influence of Aristotle in the West and in the East until the two streams of thought converged to swell the tide of Scholasticism. This essay was commended by Cardinal Manning.

"Books and Reading" (seventh edition, New York, 1904) was originally a reprint of two lectures delivered before the Cathedral Library Reading Circle of New York City, 1889. The later editions of the work, while more developed and extended than the first, yet suffer from two disadvantages, the omission of an index and of suggestive courses of reading and study. The book attempts to make literature in general, and Catholic literature in particular, a living force for those even who have not received the benefits of higher education.

"Phases of Thought and Criticism" (1892) is an interesting study of the spiritual sense and its culture. In developing his thesis, Brother Azarias draws a striking contrast first between Newman and Emerson as typical thinkers, and then between the "habits of thought engendered by literary pursuits and those begotten of scientific studies." The following chapters are concerned with the spiritual sense of three great masterpieces, "The Imitation of Christ", the "Divina Commedia", and the "In Memoriam", each of which, to quote his own words, "expresses a distinct phase of thought, and is the outcome of a distinct social and intellectual force". This volume is among the most admired of his writings for thought, style, and method.

Of his minor works the most charming is "Mary, Queen of May", which was written for the "Ave Maria". It exhales the faith and trust of a devout client, and reveals those finer qualities of head and heart which bound Brother Azarias so firmly to his order and won him so many friends. After his death many of his contributions to reviews were gathered and published in three volumes, viz. "Essays Educational", "Essays Philosophical", and "Essays Miscellaneous" (1896). The first of these includes the lectures delivered at the Catholic Summer School, just before his death; the second reprints as its most notable paper the lecture on "Aristotle and the Christian Church", adding thereto the "Nature and Synthetic Principle of Philosophy", the "Symbolism of the Cosmos", "Psychological Aspects of Education", and "Ethical Aspects of the Papal Encyclical on Capital and Labor". The best papers in the third volume are "Religion in Education", "Our Catholic School System", and "Church and State"; of the remaining numbers two are literary in subject, and the third is also found in "Phases of Thought and Criticism".

SMITH, *Brother Azarias* (New York, 1897); *Addresses and Letters read at the Memorial Meeting in Honor of Brother Azarias* (Washington, 1894); HARDY, *Educational Review* (December, 1893); *The Rosary* (October, 1893); HENRY, *Brother Azarias—Threnody*, Am. Cath. Q., January, 1894; STEDMAN-HUTCHINSON, *Library of American Literature*.

BROTHER CHRYSOSTOM.

Azevedo, IGNATIUS, BLESSED. See IGNATIUS.

Azevedo, LUIZ DE, Ethiopic missionary and scholar, b., according to the more probable narration of Franco (Imogem da Vertude em o Noviciado de Coimbra, 359–61), at Carrazedo Montenegro, in the Diocese of Braga, Portugal, in 1573; d. in Ethiopia in 1634. He became a Jesuit in 1588, and sailed for the Indies in 1592. In 1605 he began his missionary labours in Ethiopia, where he remained until his death. Azevedo was called the Apostle of the Agaus, and is justly reckoned among the most illustrious of the Doctors of the Church of Ethiopia, to which he reclaimed many schismatics. He translated into Chaldaic the commentaries of Father Toletus on the Epistle of St. Paul to the Romans, and those of Francis Ribera on the Epistle of St. Paul to the Hebrews; the "Canonical Hours", the "Office of the Blessed Virgin Mary", and other works. He is the author of a grammar of the Ethiopic language, and translated into the same tongue the New Testament, a Portuguese catechism, instructions on the Apostles' Creed, and other books of the same nature.

SOMMERVOGEL, *Biblioth.*, VIII, 73; TELLEZ, *Hist. Gen. da Ethiopia;* ALTA, 266, 515, 527; VEYGA, *Relación Geral.*, 46.

JOSEPH M. WOODS.

Azor, JUAN, b. at Lorca, province of Murcia, Southern Spain, in 1535; entered the Society of Jesus, 18 March, 1559; d. in Rome, 19 February, 1603. He was professor of philosophy and later of theology, both dogmatic and moral, at Piacenza, Alcalá, and Rome, and was a member of the first committee appointed by the Father General Acquaviva to draw up the famous "Ratio Studiorum". Father Azor was a man of wide and solid learning, deeply versed in Greek, Hebrew, and history, as well as in his more special branch of theological science. His chief title to general remembrance rests on his classical work on moral theology, in three folio volumes: "Institutionum Moralium, in quibus universæ quæstiones ad conscientiam recte aut prave factorum pertinentes breviter tractantur pars 1ma'', the first volume of which appeared at Rome in 1600, the second six years later, and the last in 1611. The work met with flattering success in Rome and at all the Continental seats of learning, and was honoured by a special Brief of Clement VIII. Numerous editions were brought out at Brescia, Venice, Lyons, Cologne, Ingolstadt, Paris, Cremona, and Rome. The work continued to hold its lofty position during the succeeding centuries, was strongly recommended by Bossuet in his synodal statutes, and was held in highest regard by that master in moral theology, St. Alphonsus Liguori. Gury speaks of Father Azor as "a moderate Probabiliorist, in wisdom, in depth of learning and in gravity of judgment taking deservedly high rank among theologians". There are extant in MS. other works by Father Azor; in Rome, in the Jesuit archives, a commentary on the Canticle of Canticles; at Würzburg, an exposition of the Psalms, and at Alcalá several theological treatises on parts of the "Summa" of St. Thomas.

Sommervogel, *Bib. de la comp. de J.*; Hurter, *Nomenclator*, I, 232.

ARTHUR J. McCAFFRAY.

Azores (Portuguese *Açores*, "Falcons"), an archipelago situated in that tract of the Atlantic Ocean which is known to mariners as the Sargasso Sea. The islands lie, approximately, from S. E. to N. W., about a diagonal of the quadrilateral formed by the 37th and 40th parallels of north latitude and the 24th and 32d meridians of west longitude. Their distribution may be considered as forming three subgroups: the relatively large islands of São Miguel and Santa Maria, to the extreme south-east; Fayal, Pico, São Jorge, Terceira, and Graciosa about midway, Terceira being about 880 geographical (1012 English) miles from the Portuguese coast; Flores and Corvo on the extreme north-west. These nine islands, aggregating in area about 922 square miles, vary greatly in size, from São Miguel, with an area of 288, to Corvo, with an area of not more than 5 square miles. The Formigas and other tiny islets throughout the archipelago are of no importance except as perils to navigation. Physically, the Azores are in general characterized by the bold and irregular conformation usually found in islands of volcanic origin. The snow-capped volcano which is the predominating feature of Pico rises to a height of 8500 feet; the Vara, in São Miguel, is more than 5500 feet; but the crater of the Sete Cidades volcano, also in São Miguel, is said to be not more than 866 feet above the sea level. The volcanic character of these islands is also unmistakably shown by the recurrence in their mountain-formations of more or less extinct craters (locally called *caldeiras*— "kettles"), one of which, the Caldeira of Graciosa, forms a steaming lake of pitch. Almost all the islands contain mineral springs, the best known of which are in São Miguel, Terceira, Graciosa, and Flores. As might be expected, the Azores are specially subject to earthquakes; in 1522 the city of Villa Franca, in São Miguel, was destroyed, with, it is said, 6000 of its inhabitants, by an earthquake, and another earthquake, in June, 1811, is memorable for the birth, about two miles off the coast of São Miguel, of the little island which was named Sabrina after the British warship that was present at, and reported, the phenomenon. The climate, though mild and equable, is extremely humid, the number of rainy days in the year averaging about 163, or not far from 50 per cent, and producing a rainfall estimated at very nearly 39 inches; snow never falls, except on the highest mountains; the recorded minimum temperature is about 39 F., the maximum only 81 F. (very exceptionally as high as 86 F.), and the mean for all seasons 63 F.

HISTORY.—The existence of this archipelago was not generally known to the inhabitants of Europe before the fifteenth century of our era, although there is evidence that Phœnician, Scandinavian, and Arabian navigators visited it at different periods. In 1432 the Portuguese, Gonçalo Velho Cabral, discovered the island of Santa Maria, and by the year 1457 all the islands had been visited by either Portuguese or Flemish explorers, none of whom found any aboriginal inhabitants, wild animals, or reptiles. In 1466 Affonso V of Portugal granted to the Duchess Isabel of Burgundy, his aunt, some sort of feudal privilege in the Azores, in consequence of which the colonists for some time were mostly Flemings, and the Portuguese themselves in those days called the islands *As Ilhas Flamengas* (the Flemish Islands). The first Portuguese colonies of any importance in the Azores were those of São Miguel, and Terceira, and at the end of the fifteenth century a certain number of the Moors, driven from Granada by Ferdinand and Isabella, took refuge in the islands.

It was not until 1534 that the ecclesiastical organization of the Azores was effected. Until then they had been under the jurisdiction of the Grand Prior of the Order of Christ. The Bull of Pope Paul III, dated 5 November, 1534, immediately after that pontiff's accession to the Apostolic See, formed a diocese with its metropolis at Angra do Heroismo, in the island of Terceira, to include the whole of this archipelago. The See of Angra was made suffragan to that of Funchal, but in 1547 it was removed from this jurisdiction and placed under that of the then Archiepiscopal (now Patriarchal) See of Lisbon. From 1580 to 1640 the Azores, like the rest of the Portuguese dominions, had to submit to the rule of Spain, and during that period the neighbouring waters were the scene of many hard fights between the Spanish and the English sea-rovers. The commercial prosperity of the islands declined after the recovery of Portuguese independence and the accession of the House of Braganza in 1640. The city of Angra attained some slight historical notoriety in 1662, when Affonso VI, deposed by his brother Dom Pedro, was imprisoned there. Material prosperity began to be restored in the Azores immediately after the period of the French invasion of the Peninsula and the flight of João IV to Brazil (1807), when the former restrictions of commerce were removed. In the Portuguese revolution of 1828–33, the Azorean populations took a decided stand against the absolutist Dom Miguel, repulsed an attack upon the island of Terceira by a Miguelist fleet, and contributed largely to form the *Progressista* army which landed at Oporto in 1833, driving Dom Miguel into exile, and establishing on the throne the Queen Donna Maria da Gloria, who for two years preceding had resided at Angra.

PRESENT CONDITIONS.—The Azores are not a colony, nor a foreign dependency of Portugal, but an integral part of the kingdom. His Most Faithful Majesty is represented in the islands by a governor residing at Angra, which is regarded as the political capital; at the same time the inhabitants are on a legislative and fiscal equality with those of the Portuguese mainland, being regularly represented in the Cortes at Lisbon. The total population of the archipelago in the year 1900 was 256,291 (i. e. 277.9 to the square mile), mostly of Portuguese origin, though of course with considerable intermixture of Flemish and Moorish blood, with traces of immigration from the British Isles, and a sprinkling of negroes.

Economically, the people of the Azores depend chiefly upon agriculture, this term being taken as including the production of wine. Most of the wine produced in the archipelago comes from the island of Pico, and, under the name of Fayal wine, derived from the port whence it was shipped, used to be famous in bygone days. The area exclusively devoted to vineyards is about 9500 acres (nearly 15 square miles), producing nearly 1,000,000 gallons of wine annually. Wheat and a large variety and abundance of fruits are grown in the valleys. Some 6000 men are employed in the fisheries, and the value of their annual catch amounts to about $175,000. The populations of Terceira, São Jorge, and Graciosa, numbering about 72,000, manufacture cheese, butter, soap, linens, woolens, bricks, and tiles; in Fayal, Pico, Flores, and Corvo a population of 58,000 are chiefly engaged in basket-weaving and the fashioning of small fancy articles from the pith of the fig tree. The latest available statistics give the total of shipping annually clearing and entering all the ports of the Azores as 2,052,792 tons, with a total value of exports and imports $1,050,000.

The people are, with rare exceptions, Catholics. Werner (Orbis Terrarum Catholicus, s. v.) says that there are only about 100 Protestants and 30 Jews in the whole Diocese of Angra. This diocese contains 110 parishes and many subsidiary churches and chapels; the cathedral of Angra, under the invocation of the Saviour (São Salvador) has its full staff of dignitaries and a chapter of twelve canons, and there is a seminary which prepares 120 students for the priesthood. The secular clergy number 353 besides which there are eight religious houses in Terceira and fifteen, including four convents of female religious, in São Miguel. The population of the cathedral city is about 11,000, that of Punta Delgada, in São Miguel, exceeding it by about 6000.

WELTE in *Kirchenlex.*, I, 1776: WERNER, *Orb. Terr. Cath.*; *Grande Enc.* s. v. *Açores; Enc. Britannica*(1902), III and XXVI; MEES, *Hist. de la découverte des Iles Fortunées* (Paris, 1901).

E. MACPHERSON.

Azotus. (Heb. *Ashdodh;* in Sept. *Ἄζωτος.*) (1) One of the five great cities of the Philistines (Jos., xiii, 3), the modern Esdud, situated three miles from the Mediterranean Sea, about half-way between Gaza and Jaffa. The temple of Dagon, whither the Ark of the Covenant was carried by the Philistines, was situated here (I K., v, 1–5; I Mach., x, 83; xi, 4). Azotus, like other Philistine cities, suffered varying fortunes in the wars with Israel, Assyria, and Egypt. Ozias fought against it (II Paral., xxvi, 6), Sargon besieged and took it (Isaias, xx, 1; Schrader, "Keilinschriftliche Bibliothek", II, 66–67), and Sennacherib did likewise (Schrader, op. cit., II, 90–91). According to Herodotus, Psammetichus besieged the city for twenty years. In 163 B. C. Judas Machabeus cleared Azotus of idols (I Mach., v, 68), and in 148 B. C. Jonathan and Simon burnt the temple of Dagon (I Mach., x, 83–84). To-day Esdud is a modern village, with many ruins attesting its glorious past. In the New Testament Azotus is mentioned in connexion with Philip's return from Gaza (Acts, viii, 40). (2) The mountain to which Bacchides pursued the Jews in battle (I Mach., ix, 15).

F. X. E. ALBERT.

AZOTUS, a titular see of Palestine, near the seacoast, between Jaffa and Ascalon. Its episcopal list (325–536) is given in Gams (452). It is the Ashdod of the Book of Josue (xv, 47), was one of the five principal cities of the Philistines, and the chief seat of the worship of their god Dagon (I Sam., v, 1–7). Herodotus mentions it (II, 157) as having withstood King Psammetichus of Egypt in a siege of twenty-nine years, the longest then known.

LEQUIEN, *Oriens Christ.* (1740), III, 659–662; ROBERTSON, *Biblical Researches*, II, 368; VIGOUROUX in *Dict. de la Bible*, s. v. *Azot.*

THOMAS J. SHAHAN.

Aztecs, probably from *Aztatl* (heron), and *Tlacatl* (man), "people of the heron", in the Nahuatl, or Mexican, language of Mexico, a surname applied to the tribe of the Mexica, or Chichimeca Mexitin (whence *Mexico* and *Mexicans*), a ramification of the Nahuatl linguistic stock which occupied aboriginal Mexico, in more or less contiguous groups, at the beginning of the sixteenth century, when the Spaniards first came into contact with them. The Mexica proper held only a group of islands about the centre of Lake Tezcuco, and one or two minor settlements on the shore. In 1519 the tribe numbered about thirty thousand souls of all ages and sexes, and was able to put into the field eight thousand warriors. By far the greater part of the population was concentrated in the central settlement called Tenochtitlan (from *tetl*, "stone", *nochtli*, "prickly pear", and *tlan*, "place", or "site"), which was founded, as is generally admitted, about the year A. D. 1325. Until their settlement upon the lake, the history of the Mexican tribe is uncertain. Data, in the shape of picture-writings, are fragmentary, except such as were executed in the sixteenth century by Indians, under the impulse of the viceroys or of ecclesiastics. These documents record constant shiftings of the tribe from points which are as yet undetermined, like Aztlan (Place of the Heron) and Chicomoztoc (Seven Caves). These places are by most authorities located north of Mexico, and some colour is given to the assumption by the relationship traced between the Nahuatl language of Mexico and Nicaragua and the Shoshonian idioms of the North-west.

The Mexicans were the last of the Nahuatl-speaking Indians to reach the shore of the great Lake of Mexico. They found the valley occupied by several tribes of the same stock, and were received by these as intrusive destitutes. Thrust back and forth among these tribes for a number of years, and exposed to great sufferings, the feeble remnants of the Mexicans finally sought refuge on some sandy patches that protruded into the middle of the lake, and here they found, if not absolute, at least comparative, security. While in the beginning they had to subsist on aquatic food (fish and insects), they began to slowly increase in numbers. There being little space for tillage, they imitated a device in use among the tribe of Chalco; the construction of rafts which they covered with soil, and thus secured vegetable diet. Timber being obtainable only on the mainland, they resorted to adobe for the construction of shelters, and a settlement was gradually built up which gave promise of stability. Soon after their establishment in the lake, the Mexican tribe was composed of two groups; one of these was *Tenochtitlan*, the other bore the name of *Tlaltelolco*. Each of them having its own government, hostilities became inevitable, resulting in the defeat of the Tlaltelolco people. For some time after, the latter were held in a kind of servitude, until mutual resentment commenced to wear off. The overthrow of Tlaltelolco took place at the beginning of the fifteenth century, which is as near a date as we venture to assign, too close precision in dates previous to the conquest not being advisable as yet.

In the meantime, the other tribes speaking the Nahuatl idiom, who were established on the mainland (Tezcuco, Tlacopan, Atzcapozalco, Xochimilco, Chalco, etc.), alternately at peace and at war with each other, had not paid much attention to the Mexicans. About the time of the overthrow of Tlaltelolco, the Tecpanecas of Atzcapozalco obtained decidedly the upper hand and exacted tribute and servitude of their neighbours. They finally attempted to overrun the Aztecs also, and were successful for a short time, but the latter, directed by their warchief, Moctecuzoma Ilhuicamina, and his colleague, the Cihuacohuatl Tlacaellel, formed an alliance with the tribes of Tezcuco and defeated the Tecpanecas, reducing them to a minimum of influence in the valley. Out of this alliance arose, in the middle of the fifteenth century, a formal league between the Mexicans, the tribe of Tezcuco, and that of Tlacopan, offensive and defensive, after the manner of the "League of the Iroquois". The events preceding the formation of this league are stated in many ways, according as information has been obtained from one or the other of the tribes entering into it, each claiming, of course, the leading part; but it is certain that the Mexicans held the military leadership, and probably received the greater part of the spoils. From the formation of this league dates that extension of Mexican sway which has led to the erroneous conception of a primitive Mexican nationality and empire.

The first aggressions of the confederates were on the tribes of Xochimilco and Chalco, at the southern outlet of the valley. They seem to have been reduced to tribute and the condition of tributaries and military vassals. Then, in the second half of the fifteenth century, raids began upon Indian groups dwelling outside of the lake basin. These raids were conducted with great shrewdness. East of the valley, powerful tribes of the Nahuatl linguistic stock, such as Tlaxcala, Huexotzinco, Cholula, and Atlixco, grouped about the great volcano Popoca-tepetl, were carefully avoided at first. The war parties of the confederates circumvented their ranges, pouncing upon more distant groups, nearer the coast. The same thing took place with Indians south of the valley, where the League extended its murderous inroads to Oaxaca. The vanquished were either exterminated or dispersed, if they resisted too well or attempted to recover their independence; or else were reduced to the payment of a tribute, annually collected by special gatherers dispatched from the valley, and of whom the tributaries were mortally afraid. This tribute consisted of products of the land, and of human victims for sacrifice. Besides, the subjected tribes were bound to service in war. The social condition of the vanquished was unchanged; they kept their self-government, their autonomy. The extent of Mexican, in the sense of confederate, sway has been exaggerated; neither Yucatan nor Guatemala was affected, and what have been represented as Mexican "subjects", or "colonies", in those countries were tribes of Nahuatl language established in the South at a very early date, and having no connexion with Mexico and its Indians except the tie of common speech. Hence the so-called "Mexican Empire" was composed of a confederacy, territorially restricted to the lake basin, and outlying tribes, autonomous but tributary. All attempts of the Aztecs and their allies to overrun, in the manner above described, the more powerful tribes residing even in their immediate vicinity, failed. An attack on the Tarascans of Michuacan under the war-chief Axayacatl, about 1475, resulted in disastrous defeat. The wars with Tlaxcala, Cholula, and Huexotzinco, as well as with Atlixco, ended usually in drawn battles, with no decisive advantage for either side. Still, it is not unlikely that the confederates would ultimately have succeeded, since they had, through their raids on the coast-tribes, cut off their adversaries from the supply of salt, and also surrounded them almost completely, cutting off their resources in the direction of the sea.

This was the condition of affairs when, in 1519, Cortez landed at Vera Cruz, then an uninhabited beach. He recognized the weak points of the situation, and successively brought over to his side the enemies of the league, then one of its members, Tezcuco, and finally, with these auxiliaries, captured the lake-stronghold of the ancient Mexicans, or Aztecs, putting an end to their existence as a tribe. The degree of culture which the Mexicans, or Aztecs, had reached was not superior to that of any of the sedentary tribes of the Mexican tableland, and in some respects it was below that of the Indians

of Yucatan, Honduras, or Chiapas. Their social organization rested on the basis of localized clanship twenty clans (Calpulli), with descent in the male line, forming the autonomous units which the tribe enveloped like a shell. The representatives of these clans, one for each, constituted the supreme tribal authority, the council, or Tlatocan, and were elected for life or during good behaviour. These in turn, with the sanction of the religious chiefs, selected a head war-chief, or *Tlacatecuhtli* (Chief of Men), and an administrative head, who bore the strange title of *Cihua-Cohuatl* (Snake Woman), and probably had more religious attributes. It was the former whom the Spaniards understood to be a monarch, whereas he was properly but a chief executive, subject to removal. Moctecuzoma (Montezuma) was deposed while a captive of Cortés, and there are indications that one of the earlier chieftains (Tizoc), suffered a similar fate. The twenty clans were grouped in four principal quarters, each had its own war-chief with a special title. The four were subordinate to the Chief of Men, who was also *ex officio* the commander-in-chief of the joint forces of the confederacy. Each clan administered its own internal affairs, the tribal council only intervening in case of dissensions between clans, and managing intercourse with the two other members of the league.

The religious organization of the Mexicans had become very complex. The numerous Shamans (called priests by most authors) were grouped into four subdivisions, the medicine-men (Tlama-cazqui, probably), the hunters (Otomitl), and the warriors; above all of whom were the two Teotecuhtli as heads of worship. This organization was perpetuated, as among many Indian tribes to-day, by selection and training. The basis of the creed was a rude pantheism. Monotheism was unknown. Nor are there any traces of early Christian teachings. The so-called "cross" of Palenque is, first, not a work of the Mexicans, but of Maya tribes, and, second, it is not a cross but an imperfect *Swastika*. In consequence of the pantheistic idea of a spiritual essence pervading creation, and individualizing at will in natural or human forms, numberless fetishes, or idols, were manufactured, which entailed a very elaborate cult and a very sanguinary one, from the time that historical deities (deified men) began to assume prevalence. The chief idols of the Mexicans were historic personages, probably Shamans of very early times, surrounded by a

GOD OF WAR AND DEATH

halo of miraculous deeds, hence credited with supernatural powers and, finally, supernatural descent. These fetishes (Tezcatlipoca, Quetzalcohuatl, etc.) were sometimes of more than human size, of stone and wood, elaborately carved and bedecked with cloth and ornaments. To the idols human victims were sacrificed in various ways, and, relatively, in large numbers, although it is scarcely possible that more than hundreds—not thousands as reported—should have been slaughtered annually. The victims were obtained in warfare, and also formed part of the tribute imposed upon conquered tribes. Aside from these cruel executions, the Shamans subjected their own persons to not less cruel tortures and to severe penance.

A certain education was given to the male youth in special buildings connected with the houses of worship and called Telpuchcalli (Houses of the Youth). That education consisted in the rehearsal of ancient songs and the use of weapons. For counting, and for the preservation of historic memories, as also for tribute, pictographs, executed on a thin paste of maguey fibre spread over delicate pieces of tanned hide, were sometimes used. These paintings could indicate numbers (by dots and symbols), names (figures related to the meaning of the word), dates (dots and signs), and events (one or more human figures in action). Besides, they had two distinct calendars, the origin of which seems very ancient. Their great cycle was of fifty-two years subdivided into four periods, of thirteen years each. The years were named *Tochtli* (Rabbit), *Acatl* (Reed), *Tecpatl* (Flint), and *Calli* (House), and these four names were repeated thirteen times in the great cycle. The month consisted of twenty days, named and figured after the same method. They had also a ritual calendar, of twenty periods of thirteen days each, and for ceremonial purposes only. Their numeration went from one to twenty, from twenty to four hundred, eight thousand being the highest figure having a symbol (*Xiquipilli*, a bag, or sack). Their knowledge of heavenly bodies was limited; they knew the bissextile, and used a rude correction, but had no astronomical instruments. Neither had they any conception of the angle as a means of

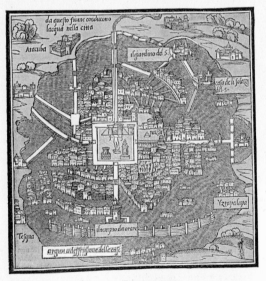

PLAN OF TENOCHTITLAN
(From "Isolano" 1528) Lenox Library, New York

measuring. Dress and adornment were elaborate, in official functions; otherwise, the costume was simple, of cotton, with sandals and without trousers. The head was bare, except in the case of chiefs and some of the Shamans. Ornaments were of gold, silver, and bright stones, mostly turquoises, the stones being esteemed for colour or brilliancy only. Gold was obtained as tribute, also silver. They knew how

to fuse the metals by means of the blowpipe. They used copper and an accidental bronze, but no iron. Obsidian played an important part, being the material for edged tools and mirrors. They had no metallic currency, gold and silver were only for ceremonial and personal decoration.

The buildings of Tenochtitlan were of adobe (sun-dried bricks). The houses were mostly low, but wide; the places of worship small and dingy chapels, erected on the tops of huge artificial mounds of earth encased in stone work. These mounds (*teo-calli*, houses of the gods, or spirits) occupied the centre of the settlement, and contained some sculptures remarkable for size and elaborateness. The *teo-calli* were also citadels to the otherwise unprotected *pueblos*. The several causeways built from Tenochtitlan to the mainland, were very creditable achievements. Tenure of lands was communal, without private ownership, each clan holding a certain area, distributed for use among its members. Agricultural implements were primitive. Land-tillage was of secondary importance to a tribe essentially lacustrine, and which relied chiefly upon warfare for its subsistence. Together with their confederates of Tezcuco and Tlacopan, the ancient Mexicans, or Aztecs, lived by preying upon other tribes, either plundering or levying tribute. They had no thought of founding a state or nationality. Commerce was carried on, even with tribes that were hostile, and it sometimes gave a welcome pretext for aggression. Of domestic quadrupeds they had only a species of indigenous dog. Like all Indian towns, Tenochtitlan had a large central market-place (*tianquiz*), the extent and resources of which have been considerably exaggerated, as well as most other features of so-called Indian civilization.

Of more recent works, ROBERTSON, *History of America*, and PRESCOTT, *History of the Conquest of Mexico*, are most widely known and have a large number of editions, but they should be consulted critically. As an accumulation of references to original sources, HUBERT H. BANCROFT, *Native Races of the Pacific States* (New York, 1875), and *History of the Pacific States* are very valuable. Eye-witnesses of the conquest like HERNANDO CORTÉS, *Cartas de Relación*, and the sources in Ramusio are of great importance, but should be treated with circumspection as interested reporters. Important also are GONZALO FERNÁNDEZ DE OVIEDO Y VALDÉS, *Historia general y moral de las Indias*, III (1853); FRANCISCO LÓPEZ DE GOMARA, *Conquista de México, Segunda Parte de la Crónica general de las Indias* (1554). Besides, for the status of the Aztecs, or Mexicans, and their degree of culture, the works of ecclesiastics and missionaries; the books of MOTOLINIA; GERÓNIMO DE MENDIETA, *Historia eclesiástica indiana*, also of JUAN DE TORQUEMADA, *Monarquía indiana* (1729), are of first rank. CAMARGO, *Historia de Tlaxcala* (Mexico, 1892); ZURITA and POMAR, *Nueva colección de Documentos para la Historia de México* (Mexico, 1891); and SAHAGUN, *Historia general de las Cosas de Nueva España* (Mexico, 1828), deserve careful attention. Lastly we refer to FATHER DIEGO DURÁN, *Historia de los indios de Nueva España* (Mexico, 1867); to TEZOZOMOC, *Crónica mexicana* (Mexico, 1878); and to the so-called *Códice Ramirez*, written by the Jesuit JUAN DE TOBAR; and printed in the same volume as the work of Tezozomoc. FERNANDO DE ALBA, *Ixtlilxochitl, Relaciones históricas* and his *Historia de los Chichimecas, antiguos Reyes de Tezcuco* (both in LORD KINGSBOROUGH'S *Antiquities of Mexico*) also belong to the same period, the sixteenth century, and were also published much later. In the eighteenth century, VETIA Y ECHEVERRIA wrote a compendious *Historia antigua de México* (Mexico, 1836), and CLAVIGERO his well-known *Storia del Messico*, of which many editions and translations have appeared. The voluminous collections entitled: *Colección de documentos inéditos del Archivo de Indias*, and *Colección de documentos para la historia de España*, contain many documents of great interest. All these sources should be treated with great critical caution and made use of from a specifically ethnological standpoint. They are all valuable, but suffer from the failings of the knowledge of their times and from the inevitable shortcomings of the personal element. Literature on the Nahuatl or Mexican (Aztec) language begins very soon after the introduction of the printing press in Mexico, that is, after 1535-36.

AD. F. BANDELIER.

Azymes (Gr. ἄζυμος, without leaven; Heb. *maççoth*), unfermented cakes used by the Jews in their various sacrifices and religious rites (Ex., xxix, 2, 23; Num., vi, 15, 17, 19; Lev., ii, 4; vi, 16–17; vii, 12; viii, 2, 26), as commanded by the Law (Ex., xxiii, 18; xxxiv, 25; Lev., ii, 11). Their use was also prescribed for the Feast of the Passover (Ex., xii, 8, 15; xiii, 3, 6, 7; Num., ix, 11; Deut., xvi, 3, 4, 8). On account of the facility with which they could be prepared, they were also made in ordinary life for unexpected guests (Gen., xviii, 6; Judges, vi, 19–21, etc.) and in times of necessity, e. g., at the time of the Exodus (Ex., xii, 34, 39), whence the name, "bread of affliction" (Deut., xvi, 3). In I Cor., v, 8, unleavened bread is the type of sincerity and truth. Unleavened cakes were especially used for the Feast of Azymes, also called the "solemn feast" (Num., xxviii, 17). This festival was instituted to commemorate Israel's deliverance from Egyptian bondage (Ex., xii, 17; xiii, 3–10). Its observance began on the fifteenth of Abib, or Nisan, "the month of new corn", and continued seven days, the first and last of which were specially solemn (Ex., xii, 15–18; xiii, 7; Lev., xxiii, 6–8, etc.). No other but unleavened bread was allowed during the whole feast. Although originally distinct, the Feast of Azymes and the Feast of the Passover are often treated as one and the same (Deut., xvi, 16; Matt., xxvi, 17; Mark, xiv, 12; Luke, xxii, 1, 7).

EDERSHEIM, *The Temple and its Services* (London, 1874); GREEN, *The Hebrew Feasts* (New York, 1885); SCHULTZ, *Old Testament Theology*, tr. (Edinburgh, 1892), I.

F. X. E. ALBERT.

Azymites (*a* privative and ζύμη, leaven), a term of reproach used by the schismatic Greeks since the eleventh century against the Latins, who, together with the Armenians and the Maronites, celebrate the Holy Eucharist with unleavened bread. Since reviling is apt to beget reviling, some few Latin controversialists have retorted by assailing the Greeks as "Fermentarians" and "Prozymites". There was, however, but little cause for bitterness on the Latin side, as the Western Church has always maintained the validity of consecration with either leavened or unleavened bread. Whether the bread which Our Lord took and blessed at the Last Supper was leavened or unleavened, is another question. Regarding the usage of the primitive Church, our knowledge is so scant, and the testimonies so apparently contradictory, that many theologians have pronounced the problem incapable of solution.

Certain it is that in the ninth century the use of unleavened bread had become universal and obligatory in the West, while the Greeks, desirous of emphasizing the distinction between the Jewish and the Christian Pasch, offered up leavened bread. Some surprise has been expressed that Photius, so alert in picking flaws in the Latin Liturgy, made no use of a point of attack which occupies so prominent a place in the polemics of the later schismatics. The obvious explanation is that Photius was shrewd and learned enough to see that the position of the Latins could not successfully be assailed. Two centuries later, the quarrel with Rome was resumed by a patriarch who was troubled with no learned scruples. As a visible symbol of Catholic unity, it had been the custom to maintain Greek churches and monasteries in Rome and some of Latin Rite in Constantinople. In 1053, Michael Cærularius ordered all the Latin churches in the Byzantine capital to be closed, and the Latin monks to be expelled. As a dogmatic justification of this violent rupture with the past, he advanced the novel tenet that the unleavened oblation of the "Franks" was not a valid Mass; and one of his chaplains, Constantine by name, with a fanaticism worthy of a Calvinist, trod the consecrated Host under his feet. The proclamation of war with the pope and the West was drawn up by his chief lieutenant, Leo of Achrida, Metropolitan of the Bulgarians. It was in the form of a letter addressed to John, Bishop of Trani, in Apulia, at the time subject to the Byzantine emperor, and by decree of Leo the Isaurian attached to the Eastern Patriarchate. John was commanded to have the letter translated into Latin and communicated to the pope and the Western bishops. This was done by the learned Benedictine, Cardinal Humbert, who happened to be present in Trani when the letter arrived. Baronius has preserved the Latin version; Cardinal Hergenröther was so fortunate as to discover the original Greek text (Cornelius Will, Acta et Scripta, 51 sqq.). It is a curious sample of Greek logic. "The love of God and a feeling of friendliness impelled the writers to admonish the Bishops, clergy, monks and laymen of the Franks, and the Most Reverend Pope himself, concerning their azyms and Sabbaths, which were unbecoming, as being Jewish observances and instituted by Moses. But our Pasch is Christ. The Lord, indeed, obeyed the law by first celebrating the legal pasch; but, as we learn from the Gospel, he subsequently instituted the new pasch. . . . He took bread, etc., that is, a thing full of life and spirit and heat. You call bread *panis*; we call it *artos* (ἄρτος). This from *airoel*(αἴρω), to raise, signifies a something elevated, lifted up, being raised and warmed by the ferment and salt; the azym, on the other hand, is as lifeless as a stone or baked clay, fit only to symbolize affliction and suffering. But our Pasch is replete with joy; it elevates us from the earth to heaven even as the leaven raises and warms the bread", etc. This etymological manipulation of *artos* from *airo* was about as valuable in deciding a theological controversy as Melanchthon's discovery that the Greek for "penance" is *metanoia*. The Latin divines found an abundance of passages in Scripture where unleavened bread is designated as *artos*. Cardinal Humbert remembered immediately the places where the unleavened loaves of proposition are called *artoi*. If the writers of the letter had been familiar with the Septuagint, they would have recalled the *artous azymous* of Ex., xxix, 2.

To Cærularius the exegetical merit of the controversy was of minor importance. He had found an effective battle-cry, well calculated to infuse into the breasts of his unreasoning partisans that hatred and defiance of the Latins which filled his own breast. The flour and water wafers of the "Franks" were not bread; their sacrifices were invalid; they were Jews, not Christians. Their lifeless bread could only symbolize a soulless Christ; therefore, they had clearly fallen into the heresy of Apollinaris. By arts like these, the unfortunate Greeks were seduced from their allegiance to the centre of Catholic unity; and a schism was precipitated which centuries have not yet healed. It is interesting to notice that this question of azyms, which brought forth a cloud of virulent pamphlets and made a deeper impression on the popular imagination than the abstruse controversy of the *Filioque*, caused little or no discussion among the theologians at the Councils of Lyons and Florence. At the latter Council the Greeks admitted the Latin contention that the consecration of the elements was equally valid with leavened and unleavened bread; it was decreed that the priests of either rite should conform to the custom of their respective Church. Modern Russians have claimed for their nation the dubious honour of having opened this crusade against azyms; but the treatises ascribed to Leontius, Bishop of Kiew, who lived a century earlier than Cærularius, and in which all the well-known arguments of the Greeks are rehearsed, are judged to have proceeded from a later pen.

HERGENRÖTHER, *Photius*, III, *passim;* and in *K. L.*, I, 1778–80; HEFELE, *Conciliengeschichte*, 2d ed., IV, 766, 772–774; PITZIPIOS, *L'Eglise Orientale;* NATALIS, *Alex. De azymorum usu, Hist. Eccl.* (1778), VII, 380–389; MABILLON, *De pane Eucharistico*, in *Vet. Ann.* (1723), 522–547; BONA, Rev. Lith. I, c. 23 (a classic text); *La question des azymes*, in *Messager des fidèles* (1889), 485–490.

JAMES F. LOUGHLIN.

B

Baader, FRANZ XAVER VON, German philosopher, b. at Munich, 1765; d. at the same place, 23 May, 1841.

I. The idealistic stream of German philosophy which started with Kant and culminated, in two divergent branches, in Hegel and Schopenhauer, encountered on the one side an opposing current of empirical realism setting back from Herbart, and on the other a partly reactionary, and yet partly concurrent movement originating in certain Catholic thinkers. Prominent among the latter was Baader. Having entered the University of Ingolstadt at sixteen and taken his doctorate at nineteen, he continued his medical studies two years longer at Vienna and then assisted his father, who was court physician. He soon gave this up, however, for mining engineering and after considerable travel in Germany he spent about five years in England (1791–96), where he became acquainted with the mysticism of Böhme and with the extremely opposite empiricism of Hume and Hartley. The work of William Godwin, "Enquiry concerning Political Justice", not only called his attention to moral and social questions but also led him to German philosophy, especially to that of Kant. Baader had a temperamental sympathy for the German Protestant mystic Böhme, but for Kant's philosophy, especially its ethical autonomism, viz.: that human reason alone and apart from God is the primary source of the supreme rule of conduct, he had nothing but disgust. This he calls "devil's morality" and fiercely declares that were Satan visibly to reappear on earth it would be in the garb of a professor of moral philosophy. For the English sceptics he had both a natural and an acquired aversion. Reared and educated as a Catholic, though holding some decidedly un-Catholic notions, he could find no satisfaction in reason divorced from faith. Passing through Hamburg on his return from England he met Jacoby, with whom he long lived in close friendship. Schelling likewise counted him as a friend and owed to him some of the mystical trend of his system. On his return to Germany Baader was made Superintendent of the Bavarian mines and was subsequently raised to the nobility for his services. He was awarded a prize of 12,000 gulden given by the Austrian Government for an important discovery relating to the use of Glauber salts instead of potash in the manufacture of glass. Retiring from business in 1820 he soon afterwards published his "Fragmenta Cognitionis" (1822–25), and at the opening of the University of Munich, in 1826, he was appointed professor of speculative theology. His philosophico-religious lectures (published as "Speculative Dogmatik", 1827–36) attracted much attention. In 1838, however, a ministerial order prohibiting laymen from lecturing on such subjects obliged him to restrict himself to anthropology. Vigorous in body and in mind he pursued his intellectual work until his final illness.

II. Baader's "Tag und Studien Bücher" (Diary), printed in the first volume of his works, affords an insight into the vicissitudes of his mind and the development of his ideals. It was primarily to his early religious training under his domestic tutor, Sailer, subsequently Bishop of Landshut, that he owed the convictions with which he combated the prevailing rationalism by appealing to innate experience and the subjective necessity of faith. Religious reading supplemented by prayer strengthened his natural tendency towards mysticism. Then, too, his eagerness to comprehend Christianity more thoroughly than the rationalistic theology succeeded in doing—the hope of finding the key, as he says, to the world of mind by putting himself in direct correspondence with the ideal—drew him, in an age poor in positive theology, towards a mystical literature which had combated, if not successfully, at least with earnestness and good intent, both the German and the French rationalism. Saint-Martin's "Philosophe inconnu", which fell into his hands in 1787, carried him back to Böhme and thence to the whole theosophic tradition which this German mystic had given to the modern world—to Paracelsus, Meister Eckart, Eriugena, the Cabbala, and the earlier Gnostics. He encountered on his way back to the past a tangible theology, notably in the works of St. Thomas upon which he comments in his Diary, but also in the Fathers and especially in the Bible.

Since, however, it was alien doctrine which had led him to the Catholic, the authority of the latter remained more or less confounded with that of the former. Moreover, his study of the English empiricists and of Kant's rationalism gave a critical cast to his thought if it did not add to his ideas. In placing theogonic speculations at the basis of his physical and moral ideas, and in seeking from mysticism an answer to the riddles of the universe, he thought to reach a solution of the fundamental problems of his time and realize the dream of his youth—a religious philosophy. Joining the contemplations of mysticism to the exactness of criticism he endeavoured to justify the appeal to both. Mysticism was to fructify criticism and criticism authorize mysticism. He aimed thus at opposing the negative with a positive rationalism. The transcendental truths (metaphysical, and especially theological concepts declared unknowable by Kant) were to find their justification and verification in the human, but at the same time Divinely impressed, consciousness. Reason and feeling separated by Kant were reunited by Baader. Jacoby's appeal to emotion for the certitude of transcendental truth Baader saw to be, at best, but a negative, an irrational, escape, while Fichte, by making such truth the creation of the Ego, failed to account for the Ego itself. The Hegelian logomachy of the Ego and the non-Ego could no more satisfy Baader than could Schelling's assertion of the absolute identity of subject and object. He had seen from the start the sterility of Schelling's principle and had confuted its pantheism.

Baader's aim was a theistic philosophy which would embrace the worlds of nature and of spirit and afford at once a metaphysical solution of the problem of knowledge (science) and an understanding of the Christian idea and the Divine activity as manifested by revelation. Whatever be thought of this ambitious endeavour, and the Catholic student must recognize its variance both with philosophy and theology, Baader's system surpasses both in depth and in breadth all the other philosophies of his time. He owes this pre-eminence not only to a deeper penetration, but likewise to a broader survey which embraced and estimated many of the facts and truths of Christianity and the science of the past. Unfortunately the false mysticism derived from Böhme led him into a fanciful interpretation of the mysteries of faith, while his attempt at rationalizing those mysteries was often hardly less bizarre. His system, therefore, if it may so be called, had the misfortune, on the one hand, of being ignored because of its purpose to synthesize Christian faith and revive the old philosophy and theology; and, on the other, of being rejected because it disfigured Christian teaching by its rationalizing spirit. It consequently may be said to have exercised an intensive and transitional, rather than an extensive and definitive, influence on the movement of thought. English sensism having resulted logically in scepticism, and Kant's critical effort to save some certainty by purely subjective scrutiny having hopelessly lost the mind in a maze of its own spinning, Baader saw that the only salvation lay in a return to the traditional line of philosophy which had been broken off by Descartes. Unfortunately in resuming that line Baader unwound some of its essential strands and inwove others of less consistent fibre wherewith the remaining threads would not cohere. But in this very harking back to a saner past Baader was influential in hastening the healthier revival which was more definitely effected by his countrymen Kleutgen and Stöckl. Moreover, in so far as Baader opposed the prevailing rationalism and defended Christian truth, his influence is declared by so unprejudiced a writer as Robert Adamson to have extended beyond the precincts of Baader's Church. Rothe's "Theologische Ethik" is thoroughly impregnated with his spirit, and among others, J. Müller's "Christl. Lehre von der Sünde" and Martinsen's "Christl. Dogmatik" show evident marks of his influence.

III. It is extremely difficult to give any satisfactory conception of Baader's system within narrow limits. Baader was a most fertile writer but threw out his thoughts in aphorisms, some of which indeed he subsequently collected, but most of which received their development in reviews and personal correspondence. Even his two principal works, "Fragmenta Cognitionis" and "Speculative Dogmatik", are really mosaics and one has to seek long before discovering any unifying principles. Moreover, he moves in leaps; his style lacks coherence and order. A suggestive expression, a Latin or French quotation gives an unlooked-for turn to a discourse. The reader is knocked about from one side to another. Now he may be driven from logic to metaphysics and again from theology to physical philosophy. The author's ideas often run into those of others leaving no line of demarcation. Add to this the uncertainty of his terminology, his equivocal and often bizarre use, or abuse, of words and the reading of Baader becomes no easy occupation. A summary of his system may be given as follows:

(1) Man's knowledge is a participation in God's knowledge. The latter necessarily compenetrates the former which is therefore always *con-scientia*. Our knowledge is a gift, something received, and in this respect is faith which is therefore a voluntary acceptance of the known object from God's knowing in us and hence proceeds from the will. This, however, is preceded by an involuntary subjection, a necessitated desire—*Nemo vult nisi videns*. We experience the Indwelling Presence soliciting us to faith. Faith however, in turn, becomes the basis of knowledge in which again faith reaches its completion. Faith is thus as necessary for knowledge as knowledge is for faith. Now the content of faith is expressed by technical formulæ in religious tradition. Hence as philosophy is necessarily connected with the subjective process of faith, so is it likewise with that of tradition. Only thus can it begin and develop. Hence all science, all philosophy, is religious. Natural theology, natural ethics, etc., strictly speaking, are impossible. Philosophy arose only when religious tradition called for explication and purification. Afterwards it divorced itself, but it thus led to its own dissolution.

(2) But faith is not simply a gift (*Gabe*); it is also a responsibility (*Aufgabe*). It must be developed by reason, penetrated, vivified, and freed from the possibility of doubt. It is not memory, nor a mere relic of the past. It must cast off the temporary but retain the abiding; be permanent but progressive. Mysteries are not impenetrable, but only concealed truths: "Deum trinum esse non creditur sed scitur" and "Deum esse non creditur sed scitur" are twin truths. The whole content of religion must be reduced to exact science. There is no closed truth just as there is no closed virtue. Science proceeds from faith, but faith is developed and recast by science.

The hopeless confusion here manifest between knowledge as a natural or purely rational process, and faith, in the Catholic sense of a supernatural virtue, finds a parallel in Baader's ethics. With him the true, i. e. religious, and hence Christian, ethics knows that God Who gives the law also fulfils it in us, so that from being a burden it ceases to be a law. Fallen man has not the power to restore himself; hereditary sin, the seed of the Serpent, hinders him in this. Still he retains the "Idea", the seed of the woman, i. e. redeemableness. This possibility is actualized by God's becoming man, and thus realizing the moral law in "the Man", the Saviour, Who by overcoming temptation has destroyed evil at its centre and from within, and Who has crushed the Serpent's head. But evil, too, must be destroyed from without by constant mortification of ego-hood. In this task man co-operating with his fellows for the attainment of happiness is neither a solitary worker, as the Kantian would say, nor completely inactive, as Luther teaches. Like hereditary sin, grace propagates itself *quasi per infectionem vitæ*. Prayer and the Eucharist place man *en rapport* with Christ, through Whom man, if he co-operate, will be restored to the spiritualized condition whence he fell by sin. This spiritualization thus becomes the final subjective end for the individual and society.

The religious idea here appears as the source and the life of Baader's sociology. The law of love for God and neighbour is the unitive principle of all social existence, liberty, and equality; as the opposite principle of self-love is the root of all disunion, slavery, and despotism. God is the binding source of all law, from Him is all social authority. Hence Baader strongly opposes the might-makes-right doctrine of Hobbes, and the social contract of Rousseau, no less than Kant's autonomism, which regards religion as an appendage of morality. Now the religious idea and the moral and juridic law being inseparably conjoined, and neither having actual existence save in Christianity which is concrete in the Catholic Church, civil society (the State), and religious society (the Church), should co-operate. Baader apparently until towards the close of his life held that the Church should have direct—not simply indirect—authority even in civil affairs, and he was enthusiastic for a reinstatement, in a form adapted to his times, of the medieval relation between the two orders. But a change seems to have come over his mind—occasioned very probably by some personal irritation which he felt at the criticism to which his theological teachings were subjected—and he taught for a short time opinions concerning the constitution of the Church and the Papacy which were utterly irreconcilable with Catholic Faith, while the language in which these opinions was conveyed was as unbecoming the philosopher as it was his subject. Before his death, however, he retracted this portion of his teaching.

While Baader's sociology maintains that religion is the very root and life of civil society, it takes account also of political and economic administration. Thus it contains his opinions favouring the organization of the classes, the revival of the medieval "corporations" or industrial associations, the political representation of the proletariat, and some well-reasoned objections to unlimited industrial competition and free trade. On the whole, his sociology is the wisest, strongest, sanest, and most practical part of his whole system, just as his technical theology is the weakest, the most bizarre, unsound, and impractical. The reason of the difference may not improbably be found in the fact that in the former the best elements of his own mind and character were free to assert themselves, while in his theology they seem almost throughout to be under the spell of Böhme whose fanciful mysticism bore him away to a region as far removed from experience—present and past—as from the world of reason and faith. Apart from theology Baader's teachings have a permanent value.

Sämmtliche Werke (Leipzig, 1851–60), XV, contains biography, XVI, an able sketch of the whole system by LUTTERBECK; HOFFMAN, *Vorhalle zur spekulativen Lehre Baaders; Philosophische Schriften*, 3 vols.; HAMBERGER, *Cardinalpunkte der Baaderschen Philosophie;* LUTTERBECK, *Philosophische Standpunkte Baaders.* See also STÖCKL, *Geschichte der modernen Philos.,* vol. II; BLANC, *Histoire de la philosophie,* vol. III; ERDMANN, *History of Philosophy* (tr.), II; HAFFNER in *Kirchenlexicon,* I, s. v.; SCHMIDT in BACHEM, *Staatslexicon,* s. v.

F. P. SIEGFRIED.

Baal, Baalim (Hebr. BÁ'ÁL; plural, BE'ALÎM), a word which belongs to the oldest stock of the Semitic vocabulary and primarily means "lord", "owner". So, in Hebrew, a man is styled "baal" of a house (Ex., xxii, 7; Judges, xix, 22), of a field (Job, xxxi, 39), of cattle (Ex., xxi, 28; Isa., i, 3), of wealth (Eccles., v, 12), even of a wife (Ex., xxi, 3; cf. Gen., iii, 16. The woman's position in the Oriental home explains why she is never called *Bá'ălah* of her husband). So also we read of a ram, "baal" of two horns (Dan., viii, 6, 20), of a "baal" of two wings (i. e. fowl: Eccles., x, 20). Joseph was scornfully termed by his brothers a "baal" of dreams (Gen., xxxvii, 19). And so on. (See IV Kings, i, 8; Isa., xli, 15; Gen., xlix, 23; Ex., xxiv, 14, etc.) Inscriptions afford scores of evidences of the word being similarly used in the other Semitic languages. In the Hebrew Bible, the plural, *be'ālîm,* is found with the various meanings of the singular; whereas in ancient and modern translations it is used only as referring to deities. It has been asserted by several commentators that by *baalim* the emblems or images of Baal (*hámmānîm, máççebhôth,* etc.) should be understood. This view is hardly supported by the texts, which regularly point out, sometimes contemptuously, the local or other special Baals.

BAAL AS A DEITY.—When applied to a deity, the word Baal retained its connotation of ownership, and was, therefore, usually qualified. The documents speak, for instance, of the Baal of Tyre, of Harran, of Tarsus, of Hermon, of Lebanon, of Tamar (a river south of Beirut), of heaven. Moreover, several Baals enjoyed special attributions: there was a Baal of the Covenant [*Bá'ál Berîth* (Judges, viii, 33; ix, 4); cf. *'El Berîth* (ibid., ix, 46)]; one of the flies (*Bá'ál Zebûb,* IV Kings, i, 2, 3, 6, 16); there was also probably one of medicine (*Bá'ál Márqôd*); perhaps one of medicine (*Bá'ál Márphê'*), and so on. Among all the Semites, the word, under one form or another (*Bá'ál* in the West and South; *Bel* in Assyria; *Bal, Bol,* or *Bel* in Palmyra) constantly recurs to express the deity's lordship over the world or some part of it. Nor were all the Baals—of different tribes, places, sanctuaries—necessarily conceived as identical; each one might have his own nature and his own name: the partly fish-shaped Baal of Arvad was probably Dagon; the Baal of Lebanon, possibly Çid, "the hunter"; the Baal of Harran, the moon-god; whereas in several Sabean and Minæan cities, and in many Chanaanite, Phœnician, or Palmyrene shrines, the sun was the Baal worshipped, although Hadad seems to have been the chief Baal among the Syrians. This diversity the Old Testament inti-

mates by speaking of *Baalim* in the plural, and specifying the singular *Baal* either by the article or by the addition of another word.

What the original conception was is most obscure. According to W. R. Smith, the Baal is a local god who, by fertilizing his own district through springs and streams, becomes its lawful owner. Good authorities, nevertheless, oppose this view, and, reversing the above argument, hold that the Baal is the genius-lord of the place and of all the elements that cause its fecundity; it is he who gives "bread, water, wool, flax, oil, and drink" (Os., ii, 5; in the Hebr. text, 7); he is the male principle of life and reproduction in nature, and as such is sometimes honoured by acts of the foulest sensuality. Whether or not this idea sprang from, and led to the monotheistic conception of a supreme deity, the "Lord of Heaven", of whom the various Baals would be so many manifestations, we shall leave to scholars to decide. Some deem that the Bible favours this view, for its language frequently seems to imply the belief in a Baal *par excellence.*

BAAL-WORSHIP AMONG THE GENTILES.—The evidence is hardly of such weight as to justify us in speaking of a worship of Baal. The Baal-worship so often alluded to and described in Holy Writ might, perhaps, be better styled Çid-worship, moon-worship, Melek (Moloch)-worship, or Hadad-worship, according to places and circumstances. Many of the practices mentioned were most probably common to the worship of all the Baals; a few others are certainly specific.

A custom common among Semitic peoples should be noticed here. Moved, most likely, by the desire to secure the protection of the local Baal for their children, the Semites always showed a preference for names compounded with that of the deity; those of Hasdrubal (*'Azrû Bá'ál*), Hannibal (*Hanni Bá'ál*), Baltasar, or Belshazzar (Bel-sar-Ushshur), have become famous in history. Scores of such names belonging to different nationalities are recorded in the Bible, in ancient writers, and in inscriptions.

The worship of Baal was performed in the sacred precincts of the high places so numerous throughout the country (Num., xxii, 41; xxxiii, 52; Deut., xii, 2, etc.) or in temples like those of Samaria (III Kings, xvi, 32; IV Kings, x, 21–27) and Jerusalem (IV Kings, xi, 18), even on the terraced roofs of the houses (IV Kings, xxiii, 12; Jer., xxxii, 29). The furniture of these sanctuaries probably varied with the Baals honoured there. Near the altar, which existed everywhere (Judges, vi, 25; III Kings, xviii, 26; IV Kings, xi, 18; Jer., xi, 13, etc.), might be found, according to the particular place, either an image of the deity (Hadad was symbolized by a calf), or the *bætylion* (i. e. sacred stone, regularly cone-shaped in Chanaan) supposed to have been originally intended to represent the world, abode of the god; of the *hámmānîm* (very possibly sun-pillars; Lev., xxvi, 30; II Par., xxxiv, 4, etc.), and the *'ăshêrah* (wrongly interpreted "grove" in our Bibles; Judges, vi, 25; III Kings, xiv, 23; IV Kings, xvii, 10; Jer., xvii, 2, etc.), a sacred pole, sometimes, possibly, a tree, the original signification of which is far from clear, together with votive or commemorative stelæ (*máççebhôth,* usually mistranslated "images"), more or less ornamented. There incense and perfumes were burned (IV Kings, xxiii, 5; Jer., vii, 9, xi, 13, and, according to the Hebrew, xxxii, 29), libations poured (Jer., xix, 13), and sacrifices of oxen and other animals offered up to the Baal; we hear even (Jer., vii, 31; xix, 5; xxxii, 35; II Par., xxviii, 3) that children of both sexes were not infrequently burned in sacrifice to Melek (D. V. Moloch, A. V. Molech), and II Par., xxviii, 3 (perhaps also IV Kings, xxi, 6) tells us that young princes were occasionally chosen as victims to this stern deity. In several shrines long trains of priests, distributed into several classes (III Kings, xviii, 19; IV Kings, x, 19; xxiii, 5; Soph., i, 4, etc.) and clad in special attire (IV Kings, x, 22) performed the sacred functions: they prayed, shouted to the Baal, led dances around the altar, and in their frenzied excitement "cut themselves with knives and lancets, till they were all covered with blood" (III Kings, xviii, 26–28). In the meantime the lay worshippers also prayed, kneeling, and paid their homage by kissing the images or symbols of the Baal (III Kings, xix, 18; Os., xiii, 2, Hebr.), or even their own hands. To this should be added the immoral practices indulged in at several shrines (III Kings, xiv, 24; IV Kings, xxiii, 7; cf. Deut., xxiii, 18) in honour of the Baal as male principle of reproduction, and of his mate Asherah (D. V. Astarthe, A. V. Ashtaroth).

BAAL-WORSHIP AMONG THE ISRAELITES.—Nothing could be more fatal to a spiritual faith than this sensual religion. In fact, no sooner had the Israelites, coming forth from the wilderness, been brought into contact with the Baal-worshippers than they were, through the guile of the Madianites, and the attractions of the licentious worship offered to the Moabitish deity (probably Chamos), easily seduced from their allegiance to Yahweh (Num., xxv, 1–9). Henceforth the name of Beelphegor remained like a dark spot on the early history of Israel [Os., ix, 10; Ps. cv (in the Hebr. cvi), 28]. The terrible punishment inflicted upon the guilty sobered for a while the minds of the Hebrews. How long the impression lasted we are hardly able to tell; but this we know, that when they had settled in the Promised Land, the Israelites, again forsaking the One True God, paid their homage to the deities of their Chanaanite neighbours (Judges, ii, 11, 13, etc.). Even the best families could not, or did not dare, resist the seduction; Gedeon's father, for instance, albeit his faith in his Baal seems to have been somewhat lukewarm (Judges, vi, 31), had erected an idolatrous altar in Ephra (Judges, vi, 25). "And the Lord, being angry against Israel, delivered them into the hands of their enemies that dwelt round about". Mesopotamians, Madianites, Amalecites, Ammonites, and, above all, Philistines, were successively the providential avengers of God's disregarded rights.

During the warlike reigns of Saul and David, the Israelites as a whole thought little of shaking off Yahweh's yoke; such also was, apparently, the situation under Solomon's rule, although the example given by this prince must have told deplorably upon his subjects. After the division of his empire, the Northern Kingdom, first led by its rulers to an unlawful worship of Yahweh, sank speedily into the grossest Chanaanite superstitions. This was the more easy because certain customs, it seems, brought about confusion in the clouded minds of the uneducated portion of the people. Names like Esbaal (I Par., viii, 33; ix, 39), Meribbaal (I Par., viii, 34; ix, 40), Baaliada (I Par., xiv, 7), given by Saul, Jonathan, and David to their sons, suggest that Yahweh was possibly spoken of as Baal. The fact has been disputed; but the existence of such a name as Baalia (i. e. "Yahweh is Baal", I Par., xii, 5) and the affirmation of Osee (ii, 16) are arguments that cannot be slighted. True, the word was used later on only in reference to idolatrous worship, and even deemed so obnoxious that *bôshéth*, "shame", was frequently substituted for it in compound proper names, thus giving, for instance, such inoffensive forms as Elioda (II Kings, v, 16), Yerúbbéshéth (II Kings, xi, 21, Hebr.), Isboseth (II Kings, ii, 10) and elsewhere, Miphiboseth (II Kings, ix, 6; xxi, 8); but these corrections were due to a spirit which did not prevail until centuries after the age with which we shall presently deal.

Achab's accession to the throne of Israel inaugurated a new era, that of the official worship. Married to a Sidonian princess, Jezebel, the king erected to the Baal of her native city (Çid, or Melkart) a temple (III Kings, xvi, 31, 32) in which a numerous body of priests officiated (III Kings, xviii, 19). To what a forlorn state the true faith in the Northern Kingdom fell Elias relates in III Kings, xix, 10, 14: "The children of Israel have forsaken thy covenant: they have thrown down thy altars, they have slain thy prophets with the sword." There remained but seven thousand men whose knees had not been bowed before Baal (III Kings, xix, 18). Ochozias, son of Achab and Jezebel, followed in his parents' footsteps (III Kings, xxii, 54), and although Joram, his brother and successor, took away the *máççebhôth* set up by his father, the Baal-worship was not stamped out of Samaria (IV Kings, iii, 2, 3) until its adherents were slaughtered, and its temple destroyed at the command of Jehu (IV Kings, x, 18–28). Violent as this repression was, it hardly survived the prince who had undertaken it. The annals of the reigns of his successors witness to the religious corruption again prevailing; and the author of IV Kings could sum up this sad history in the following few words: "They forsook all the precepts of the Lord their God: and made to themselves two molten calves, and groves [*ãshērah*], and adored all the host of heaven: and they served Baal. And consecrated their sons, and their daughters through fire: and they gave themselves to divinations, and soothsayings: and they delivered themselves up to do evil before the Lord, to provoke him. And the Lord was very angry with Israel, and removed them from his sight, . . . and Israel was carried away out of their land to Assyria, unto this day" (IV Kings, xvii, 16–18, 23).

Meanwhile the Kingdom of Juda fared no better. There, also, the princes, far from checking the drift of the people to idolatry, were their instigators and abettors. Established by Joram (IV Kings, viii, 18), probably at the suggestion of Athalia his wife, who was the daughter of Achab and Jezebel, the Phœnician worship was continued by Ochozias (IV Kings, viii, 27). We know from IV Kings, xi, 18, that a temple had been dedicated to Baal (very likely the Baal honoured in Samaria) in the Holy City, either by one of these princes or by Athalia. At the latter's death, this temple was destroyed by the faithful people, and its furniture broken to pieces (IV Kings, xi, 18; II Par., xxiii, 17). If this reaction did not crush utterly the Baal-worship in Juda, it left very little of it alive, since, for over a century, no case of idolatry is recorded by the sacred writers. In the reign of Achaz, however, we find the evil not only flourishing again, but countenanced by public authority. But a change had taken place in Juda's idolatry; instead of the Sidonian Baal, Melek (Moloch), the cruel deity of the Ammonites, had become the people's favourite (II Par., xxviii, 2; IV Kings, xvi, 3, 4). His barbarous rites, rooted out by Ezechias, appeared again with the support of Manasses, by whose influence the Assyro-Babylonian astral deities were added to the Pantheon of the Judean idolaters (IV Kings, xxi, 3). The meritorious efforts of Josias (IV Kings, xxiii, 4, 5) produced no lasting results, and after his death the various superstitions in vogue held sway until "the Lord cast out from his face Juda and Jerusalem" (IV Kings, xxiii, 32, 37; xxiv, 9, 19, and elsewhere).

The Babylonian invasions dealt to the Baal-worship in Palestine a deadly blow. At the restoration Israel shall be Yahweh's people, and He their God (Ezech., xiv, 11), and Baal will become altogether a thing of the past.

SELDEN, *De diis syris* (1617); GIGOT, *Biblical Lectures* (Baltimore, 1901), V; ID., *Outlines of Jewish History* (New

York, 1905); PEAKE in HASTINGS, *Dict. Bible*, s. v. *Baal;* THATCHER, ibid., s. v. *Phœnicia;* OTTLEY, *The Religion of Israel* (Cambridge, 1905); SAYCE, *The Gods of Canaan*, in *Contemporary Review* for Sept., 1883; W. R. SMITH, *The Religion of the Semites* (Edinburgh, 1889); BOURQUENOU ET DUTAU, *Etudes archéologiques in Etudes Religieuses* (1864–66); LAGRANGE, *Etudes sur les religions sémitiques* (Paris, 1903); MASPERO, *Histoire ancienne des peuples de l'Orient classique* (Paris, 1898); REVILLE, *La religion des Phéniciens in Revue des deux mondes*, for 15 May, 1873; TIELE, *La religion phénicienne*, in *Revue de l'histoire des religions* (1881), III; VIGOUROUX in *Dict. de la Bible*, s. v. *Baal;* ID., *La Bible et les découvertes modernes* (Paris, 1889), III; ID., *Les prêtres de Baal et leurs successeurs dans l'antiquité et dans le temps présent*, in *Revue biblique* for April, 1896; DE VOGÜÉ, *Mélanges d'archéologie orientale* (Paris, 1868); BÄTHGEN, *Beiträge zur semitischen Religionsgeschichte* (Berlin, 1888); BAUDISSIN, *Studien zur semitischen Religionsgeschichte* (1876–78); ID., in HERZOG, *Realencyklopädie*, s. v. *Baal und Bel;* MARTI, *Geschichte der israelitischen Religion* (1897); MEYER, *Ueber einige semitische Götter*, in *Zeitschrift der deutschen morgenländischen Gesellschaft* (1877); MOVERS, *Die Phönizier* (1841–56); OORT, *Dienst des Baal in Israel* (Leyden, 1864); SCHRADER, *Baal und Bel*, in *Theologische Studien und Kritiken* (1874); SMEND, *Lehrbuch der alttestamentlichen Religionsgeschichte* (Freiburg, Leipzig, 1893, 1899).

For use of the plural (Baalim), DRIVER, *Notes on the Hebrew Text of the Books of Samuel*, on I Sam., vii, 3; BURNEY, *Notes on the Hebrew Text of the Books of Kings*, on I (III) Kings, xviii, 18.

CHARLES L. SOUVAY.

Baalbek, the Heliopolis of the Greek and Latin writers, a Syrian town at the base of the western slope of the Anti-Lebanon, and the see of a Maronite and of a Melchite bishop. Nothing is known of the origin and ancient history of Baalbek, although conjectural attempts have been made to identify it with Baalgad (Jos., xi, 17; xiii, 5), Aven (A. V. Amos, i, 5), etc. Among the monuments of Baalbek were three temples: the Great Temple of Jupiter, the Temple of the Sun, and the Circular Temple of Venus; all of them date from the second century A. D. The so-called Acropolis, on the platform of which two of the temples were erected, is older. Baalbek has been destroyed almost entirely by earthquakes and wars, but even to-day its ruins are said to be the most beautiful in existence. The boldness of the architecture and the cyclopean dimensions of some of the monoliths of the Acropolis are among the many features interesting both to the scientist and the traveller. The political history of Baalbek is that of the surrounding country. (See SYRIA.)

The introduction of Christianity into Baalbek is obscure. In the life of St. Eudocia, there is mention of one Theodotus, Bishop of Heliopolis, in the reign (117–138) of Hadrian. (Acta SS., 1 March, 8 sqq.) The account is of doubtful historical value and when Constantine forbade the licentious pagan practices, there were no Christians there. Constantine, however, erected a church or perhaps simply transformed one of the temples into a Christian basilica, which he entrusted to a bishop with priests and deacons (Eusebius, Life of Const., III, lviii). During the reign of Julian (361–363) the Christians were severely persecuted (Sozomen, History, V, x). Paganism disappeared from Baalbek only after Theodosius (379–395) had destroyed the idols and probably the Great Temple. Of the former bishops of Baalbek (Heliopolis) only a few scattered names have been preserved. Baalbek is now a titular archiepiscopal see *in partibus infidelium*, with the Most Rev. Robert Seton, formerly of Newark, New Jersey, U. S. A., as incumbent, consecrated 5 July, 1903. In 1861, Baalbek was made a Maronite bishopric, with about 30,000 Catholics. The Melchite diocese was erected in 1868, and numbers some 5,000 Catholics with fifteen priests, mostly Basilian monks. The Armenians of the district are under the Armenian Archbishop of Aleppo, and the Latins under the vicar Apostolic of the same place. (See ALEPPO.) The Orthodox Greeks (schismatical) also have a resident bishop at Baalbek; further, the town is a station of the British Syrian Schools' Committee with two

missionary women, three native women, and a village school, a high school, and a dispensary.

On the ruins of Baalbek, see WOOD AND DAWKINS, *Ruins of Baalbek* (London, 1757); MURRAY, *Handbook for Travellers* (London, 1868); LEGENDRE in VIG., *Dict. de la Bib.*, s. v.

On the religious aspect of Baalbek, see LEQUIEN, *Oriens Christ.* (Paris, 1740), II, 842; WERNER, *Orb. terr. cath.* (Freiburg im Br., 1890); *Missiones catholicæ* (Rome, 1901); BATTANDIER, *Ann. pont. Cath.* (Paris, 1907).

R. BUTIN.

Baanites. See PAULICIANS.

Babel occurs in the Vulgate only in Gen., xi, 9; the form Babylonia is found in Bar., i, 1, 4; ii, 22; vi, 1–3; I Mach., vi, 4; II Mach., viii, 20; everywhere else the Vulgate uses the form Babylon. The word is derived from the Babylonian *bāb-īlu*, meaning "gate of God". Gen., xi, 9 suggests a different meaning based on the derivation of the name from the Hebrew word *bālál*, to confound. The city of Babylon had various names among its inhabitants, e. g. Ka-dingir, Babi-dingir, Tintir, Shu-an-na, etc. The prophets call it "daughter of the Chaldeans" (Is., xlvii, 1), and Sesach or Sesac (Jer., xxv, 26; li, 41), a word variously explained by commentators. It was built on the site of the modern village of Hille. According to Herodotus, a double or perhaps a triple wall, 50 cubits in width and 200 cubits in height, surrounded the town, forming a square of 120 stadia. The square of the interior wall was 90 stadia long and 360 stadia in circumference. Both the Bible and the cuneiform inscriptions assign a very great age to the city, and the Biblical data (Gen., xi, 1–9) concerning the material of the walls are confirmed by the testimony of the ruins. "Let us make brick, and bake them with fire. And they had brick instead of stones, and slime instead of mortar."

The ancient city possessed marvellous temples, splendid palaces, and curious gardens. Among the temples, two deserve special attention, E-sagila, the temple of Bel Merodach, on the eastern bank of the Euphrates, and E-zida, the temple of Nebo, west of the river. The ruins of these sanctuaries are probably identical with those of Bābil and Birs Nimrūd, though opinions differ concerning Bābil. The buildings were pyramidal in form and rose in several, usually seven, step-like sections. The storied tower of Birs Nimrūd counts seven of these quadrangular platforms painted in seven colours, black, white, yellow, blue, scarlet, silver, and gold, and in the same order sacred to the stellar gods, Adar (Saturn), Ishtar (Venus), Merodach (Jupiter), Nebo (Mercury), Nergal (Mars), Sin (the Moon), Shamash (the Sun). It has been learned in the excavations at Nippur that the pyramidal tower or *ziggurat* did not constitute the whole of the Babylonian Temple. This latter had an inner and an outer court, both nearly square and nearly of the same dimensions; the tower occupied about one-third of the area of the inner court, and near to it stood the temple proper where the sacrifices were offered. We may infer from the discoveries made in Nippur and in Sippara that a library and a school will be found to have been connected with the Babylonian temples. In the light of these discoveries the story of the Tower of Babel (Gen., xi, 4) assumes a new importance, whether we identify its remains with the ruins of Birs Nimrūd or with those of the Bel temple at Nippur, or again with those of Bābil. No doubt, it was its temples not less than its royal palaces and its hanging gardens that rendered the city of Babylon "glorious among kingdoms, the famous pride of the Chaldeans" (Is., xiii, 19). We meet with the city at the earliest dawn of history, and it flourishes, in spite of its temporary reverses, till it is finally destroyed by Seleucus Nicator; even then Jews kept on inhabiting some of the mounds of Babylon till about A. D. 1000, after which time the country was given up to the roaming tribes of Arabs, in accordance with the words of the prophet:

"wild beasts shall rest there, and their houses shall be filled with serpents, and ostriches shall dwell there, and the hairy ones shall dance there: and owls shall answer one another there, in the houses thereof, and sirens in the temples of pleasure" (Is., xiii, 21–22). (See TOWER OF BABEL, BABYLONIA.)

RAWLINSON, *The Five Great Monarchies of the Ancient Eastern World* (London, 1879); KING, *The Letters and Inscriptions of Hammurabi, King of Babylon* (London, 1898); DELATTRE, *Les Chaldéens jusqu'à la formation de l'empire de Nabuchodonosor* (Louvain, 1887); NIKEL, *Genesis und Keilschriftforschung* (Freiburg, 1903); ZIMMERN, ed., SCHRADER, *Die Keilinschriften und das Alte Testament* (Berlin, 1903); KAULEN, *Assyrien und Babylonien nach den neuesten Entdeckungen* (Freiburg, 1899); HILPRECHT, *Exploration in Bible Lands during the Nineteenth Century* (Philadelphia, 1903); PETERS, *Nippur or Explorations and Adventures on the Euphrates* (New York, 1897); BEZOLD, *Ninive und Babylon* (2d ed., Bielefeld, 1903); cf. also HAGEN, *Lex. Bibl.* (Paris, 1905); PANNIER and LEVESQUE in VIG., *Dict. de la Bible.*

A. J. MAAS.

Babenstuber, LUDWIG, a German philosopher and theologian; vice-chancellor of the University of Salzburg; b. 1660 at Teining in Bavaria; d. 5 April, 1726, at the Benedictine monastery of Ettal. Having completed his early studies he entered the novitiate of the Order of St. Benedict, at Ettal in 1681, made his religious profession in 1682, and thereafter devoted the greater part of his life to teaching. At the commencement of his studies he had given no promise of brilliancy, but by his untiring application and industry he shortly acquired so vast a store of knowledge, that he soon came to be regarded as one of the most learned men of his day—*vir consummatæ in omni genere doctrinæ et probitatis*, as he is styled in Dom Egger's "Idea ordinis Hierarchico-Benedictini", and in the "History of the University of Salzburg". Until 1690 Babenstuber was Director of the scholasticate of his order at Salzburg, taught philosophy there from 1690 to 1693, and then went to Schlehdorf to teach theology in the monastery of the canons regular.

Returning to Salzburg in 1695, he took up successively the professorships of moral theology, dogmatic theology, and exegesis, in the celebrated Benedictine university of that city. He remained at Salzburg for twenty-two years, during which period he held the office of vice-rector for three years, and that of vice-chancellor of the university for six. In 1717 he returned to his monastery at Ettal, where he spent the remainder of his days. In dogmatic theology Babenstuber was a pronounced Thomist; in moral, a vigorous defender of probabilism. He maintained, among other things, that a single author, if he were "beyond contradiction" (*omni exceptione major*), could, of his own authority, render an opinion probable, even against general opinion. In matters of faith, however, he rejected the principle of probabilism absolutely. In one of his disquisitions he had also stated that it was allowable to celebrate Mass privately on Maundy Thursday and Holy Saturday, but before his "Ethica Supernaturalis" had issued from the press, he learned that the Roman tribunals forbade it, and so he promptly corrected that assertion. Babenstuber's published works include a wide range of subjects, mainly philosophical and theological. The most important are: "Philosophia Thomistica" (4 vols., Salzburg, 1704); "Ethica Supernaturalis" (Augsburg, 1718).

EGGER, *Idea ordinis Hierarchico-Benedictini* (Constance, 1715–20), II, 560, 567; DOM FRANÇOIS, *Bibliothèque générale de tous les écrivains de l'ordre de Saint-Benoît* (Bouillon, 1777), I, 85; ZIEGELBAUER, *Hist. rei literariæ Ord. S. Benedicti* (Augsburg, 1754), II, 283; III, 444; IV, 118, 138, 182 sqq.; *Historia Univers. Salisb.*, 381; SATTLER, *Kollectaneenbl.* (1899), 248 sqq.; *Studien u. Mittheilungen aus dem Benediktiner u. d. Cistercienser-Orden*, V, 138, 359.

THOMAS OESTREICH.

Babinet, JACQUES, French physicist, b. at Lusignan, Vienne, 5 March, 1794; d. at Paris, 21 October, 1872. He began his studies at the Lycée Napoléon.

There he became a pupil of Binet, whose influence caused him to abandon the study of law, for which his family had destined him, and to devote himself to the pursuit of science. He continued at the Polytechnic School, which he left in 1812 to enter the Military School at Metz. For some time he was attached to the Fifth Regiment of Artillery, but at the Restoration he left the army and began to teach. He was professor of mathematics at Fontenay-le-Comte, then professor of physics at Poitiers, and later at the Lycée Saint-Louis. From 1825 to 1828 he delivered a course of lectures on meteorology; in 1838 he succeeded Savary at the Collège de France; and in 1840 he was elected to the Academy of Sciences.

His scientific fame rests on his work in optics, although his contributions to science include the other branches of physics and mechanics. He improved the valves of the air-pump, attaining a very high vacuum; he constructed a hygrometer and a goniometer, and invented the Babinet compensator, a double quartz wedge used in the study of elliptically polarized light. "Babinet's theorem" deals with the diffraction of light. He must, however, be chiefly remembered as a great popularizer of science, an amusing and clever lecturer, a brilliant and entertaining writer of popular scientific articles. He fully recognized the limitations of physical science, while his sincere faith showed itself especially at the end, when he passed away with touching resignation, beloved by all for his kindly and charitable nature.

Babinet's contributions to the "Revue des Deux Mondes" and to the "Journal des Débats" and his lectures on observational science before the Polytechnic Association were collected in eight volumes: "Etudes et lectures sur les sciences d'observation" (1855–65). His other serious works include: "Résumé complet de la physique" (Paris, 1825); "Expériences pour vérifier celles de M. Trevelyan" (Paris, 1835). The following four monographs are published in the Memoirs of the Société Philomathique: "Sur la masse de la planète Mercure" (1825); "Sur la couleur des réseaux" (1829); "Sur la détermination du magnétisme terrestre" (1829); "Sur la cause du retard qu'éprouve la lumière dans les milieux réfringents" (1839).

QUÉRARD, *La France littéraire; Dictionnaire de la conversation; La Grande Encyclopédie;* LAROUSSE, *Dictionnaire.*

WM. FOX.

Babington, ANTONY. See MARY QUEEN OF SCOTS.

Babylas, Bishop and Martyr.—He was the successor of Zebinus as Bishop of Antioch in the reign of the Emperor Gordianus (238–244), being the twelfth bishop of this Oriental metropolis. During the Decian persecution (250) he made an unwavering confession of faith and was thrown into prison where he died from his sufferings. He was, therefore, venerated as a martyr. St. John Chrysostom and the "Acts of the Martyrs" relate further concerning him, that Babylas once refused an emperor, on account of his wrongdoing, permission to enter the church and had ordered him to take his place among the penitents. Chrysostom does not give the name of the emperor; the Acts mention Numerianus. It is more probably Philip the Arabian (244–249) of whom Eusebius (Hist. eccl., VI, xxxiv) reports that a bishop would not let him enter the gathering of Christians at the Easter vigil. The burial-place of St. Babylas became very celebrated. The Cæsar Gallus built a new church in honour of the holy martyr at Daphne, a suburb of Antioch, and the bones of the saint were transferred to it. When after this Julian the Apostate consulted the oracle of Apollo at the temple to this god which was near by, he received no answer because of the proximity of the saint. He, therefore, had the sarcophagus of the martyr taken back to its original place of burial.

In the Middle Ages the bones of Babylas were carried to Cremona. The Latin Church keeps his feast on 24 January, the Greek Church on 4 September.

EUSEBIUS, *Hist. eccl.*, VI, xxix and xxxix; SOZOMENUS, *Hist. eccl.*, V, xviii, xxix; THEODORETUS, *Hist. eccl.*, III, xix; RUFINUS, *Hist. eccl.*, i, xxxv–xxxvi; S. JOANNES CHRYSOSTOMUS, *Sermo de S. Babyla* in, *P. G.*, IV, col. 527–534; ID., *Liber in S. Babylan contra Gentiles*, *Ibid.*, col. 533–372; *Acta SS.*, January, II, 569 sqq.; *Analecta Bollandiana* (1884), III, 140–141; XIX (1900), 5–8; TILLEMONT, *Mémoires pour servir à l'hist. ecclés.*, III, 400 sqq., 967 sqq.; HARNACK, *Gesch. der altchr. Literatur* (Leipzig, 1897), II; *Die Chronologie*, I, 214 sqq.; ALLARD, *Hist. des persécutions*, 2d ed., II, 238 sqq., 450.

J. P. KIRSCH.

Babylon, the curial title of a Latin archbishopric, also of a Chaldean patriarchate and of a Syrian archbishopric. See BAGDAD.

Babylonia.—In treating of the history, character, and influence of this ancient empire, it is difficult not to speak at the same time of its sister, or rather daughter, country, Assyria. This northern neighbour and colony of Babylon remained to the last of the same race and language and of almost the same religion and civilization as that of the country from which it emigrated. The political fortunes of both countries for more than a thousand years were closely interwoven with one another; in fact, for many centuries they formed one political unit. The reader is therefore referred to the article ASSYRIA for the sources of Assyro-Babylonian history; for the story of exploration, language, and writing; for its value in Old Testament exegesis, and for much of Babylonian history during the period of Assyrian supremacy.

GEOGRAPHY.—The country lies diagonally from north-west to south-east, between 30 and 33 N. lat. and 44 and 48 E. long., or from the present city of Bagdad to the Persian Gulf, from the slopes of Khuzistan on the east to the Arabian Desert on the west, and is substantially contained between the Rivers Euphrates and Tigris, though to the west a narrow strip of cultivation on the right bank of the Euphrates must be added. Its total length is some 300 miles, its greatest width about 125 miles; about 23,000 square miles in all, or the size of Holland and Belgium together. Like these two countries, its soil is largely formed by the alluvial deposits of two great rivers. A most remarkable feature of Babylonian geography is that the land to the south encroaches on the sea and that the Persian Gulf recedes at present at the rate of a mile in seventy years, while in the past, though still in historic times, it receded as much as a mile in thirty years. In the early period of Babylonian history the gulf must have extended some hundred and twenty miles further inland. According to historical records both the towns Ur and Eridu were once close to the gulf, from which they are now about a hundred miles distant; and from the reports of Sennacherib's campaign against Bît Yakin we gather that as late as 695 B. C., the four rivers Kerkha, Karun, Euphrates, and Tigris entered the gulf by separate mouths, which proves that the sea even then extended a considerable distance north of where the Euphrates and Tigris now join to form the Shat-el-arab. Geological observations show that a secondary formation of limestone abruptly begins at a line drawn from Hit on the Euphrates to Sâmarrâ on the Tigris, i. e. some four hundred miles from their present mouth; this must once have formed the coast line, and all the country south was only gradually gained from the sea by river deposit. In how far man was witness of this gradual formation of the Babylonian soil we cannot determine at present; as far south as Larsa and Lagash man had built cities 4,000 years before Christ. It has been suggested that the story of the Flood may be connected with man's recollection of the waters extending far north of Babylon, or of some great natural event relating to the formation of the soil; but with our present imperfect knowledge it can only be the merest suggestion. It may, however, well be observed that the astounding system of canals which existed in ancient Babylonia even from the remotest historical times, though largely due to man's careful industry and patient toil, was not entirely the work of the spade, but of nature once leading the waters of Euphrates and Tigris in a hundred rivulets to the sea, forming a delta like that of the Nile.

STATUE OF ROYAL PERSONAGE (NON-SEMITIC) WHO REIGNED AT LAGASH

The fertility of this rich alluvial plain was in ancient times proverbial; it produced a wealth of wheat, barley, sesame, dates, and other fruits and cereals. The cornfields of Babylonia were mostly in the south, where Larsa, Lagash, Erech, and Calneh were the centres of an opulent agricultural population. The palm tree was cultivated with assiduous care and, besides furnishing all sorts of food and beverage, was used for a thousand domestic needs. Birds and water-fowls, herds and flocks, and rivers teeming with fish supplied the inhabitants with a rural plenty which surprises the modern reader of the cadastral surveys and tithe-accounts of the ancient temples. The country is completely destitute of mineral wealth, and possesses no stone or metal, although stone was already being imported from the Lebanon and the Ammanus as early as 3000 B. C.; and much earlier, about 4500 B. C., Ur-Nina King of Shirpurla sent to Magan, i. e. the Sinaitic Peninsula, for hard stone and hard wood; while the copper mines of Sinai were probably being worked by Babylonians shortly after 3750, when Snefru, first king of the Fourth Egyptian dynasty, drove them away. It is remarkable that Babylonia possesses no bronze period, but passed from copper to iron; though in later ages it learnt the use of bronze from Assyria.

The towns of ancient Babylonia were the following: southernmost, (1) Eridu, Semitic corruption of the old name of *Eri-dugga*, "good city", at present the mounds of Abu-Sharain; and (2) Ur, Abraham's birthplace, about twenty-five miles north-east of Eridu, at present Mughair. Both of these towns lay west of the Euphrates. East of the Euphrates, the southernmost town was (3) Larsa, the Biblical Ellasar (Gen., xiv; in Vulg. and D. V. unfortunately rendered Pontus), at present Senkere; (4) Erech, the Biblical Arach (Gen., x, 10), fifteen miles north-west of Larsa, is at present Warka; and eight miles north-east from the modern Shatra was (5) Shirpurla otherwise Lagash, now Tellô. Shirpurla was one of Babylon's most ancient cities, though not mentioned in the Bible; probably "Raventown" (*shirpur-raven*), from the sacred emblem of its goddess and sanctuary, Nin-Girsu, or Nin-Sungir, which for a score of centuries was an important political centre, and probably gave its name to Southern Babylonia—Sungir, Shumer, or, in Gen., x, 10, Sennaar. (6) Gishban (read also *Gish-ukh*), a small city a little north of Shirpurla, at present the mounds of Iskha, is of importance only in the very earliest history of Babylonia.

(7) The site of the important city of Isin (read also *Nisin*) has not yet been determined, but it was probably situated a little north of Erech. (8) Calneh, or Nippur (in D. V., Gen., x, 10, *Calanne*), at present Nuffar, was a great religious centre, with its Bel temple, unrivalled in antiquity and sanctity, a sort of Mecca for the Semitic Babylonians. Recent American excavations have made its name as famous as French excavations made that of Tellô or Shirpurla. (9) In North Babylonia we have again, southernmost, the city of Kish, probably the Biblical Cush (Gen., x, 8); its ruins are under the present mound El-Ohêmir, eight miles east of Hilla. (10) A little distance to the north-west lay Kutha, the present Telli Ibrahim, the city whence the Babylonian colonists of Samaria were taken (IV Kings, xvii, 30), and which played a great rôle in Northern Babylonia before the Amorite dynasty. (11) The site of Agade, i. e. Akkad (Gen., x, 10), the name of whose kings was dreaded in Cyprus and in Sinai in 3800 B. C., is unfortunately unknown, but it must have been not far from (12) Sippara; it has even been suggested that this was one of the quarters of that city, which was scarcely thirty miles north of Babylon and which, as early as 1881, was identified, through British excavations, with the present Abu-Habba. (13) Lastly, Babylon, with its twin-city Borsippa, though probably founded as early as 3800 B. C., played an insignificant rôle in the country's history until, under Hammurabi, about 2300 B. C., it entered on that career of empire which it maintained for almost 2000 years, so that its name now stands for a country and a civilization which was of hoary antiquity before Babylon rose to power and even before a brick of Babylon was laid.

EARLY HISTORY.—At the dawn of history in the middle of the fifth millennium before Christ we find in the Euphrates Valley a number of city-states, or rather city-monarchies, in rivalry with one another and in such a condition of culture and progress, that this valley has been called the cradle of civilization, not only of the Semitic world, but most likely also of Egypt. The people dwelling in this valley were certainly not all of one race; they differed in type and language. The primitive inhabitants were probably of Mongolian ancestry, they are styled Sumerians, or inhabitants of Sumer, Sungir, Sennaar. They invented the cuneiform script, built the oldest cities, and brought the country to a great height of peaceful prosperity. They were gradually overcome, dispossessed, and absorbed by a new race that entered the plain between the two rivers, the Semites, who pressed on them from the north from the kingdom of Akkad. The Semitic invaders, however, eagerly adopted, improved, and widely spread the civilization of the race they had conquered. Although a number of arguments converge into an irrefragable proof that the Sumerians were the aboriginal inhabitants of Babylonia, we have no historical records of the time

HEAD OF A SUMERIAN, GUDEA EPOCH. FOUND IN TELLÔ

when they were the sole occupants of the Euphrates Valley; at the dawn of history we find both races in possession of the land and to a certain extent mixed, though the Semite was predominant in the North while the Sumerian maintained himself for centuries in the South. Whence these Sumerians came, cannot be decided, and probably all that will ever be known is that, after a nomadic existence in mountainous districts in the East, they found a plain in the lands of Sennaar and dwelt in it (Gen., xi, 2). Their first settlement was Eridu, then a seaport on the Persian Gulf, where their earliest myths represent the first man, Adapu, or Adamu (Adam?), spending his time in fishing, and where the sea-god taught them the elements of civilization. It is certain, however, that they possessed a considerable amount of culture even before entering the Babylonian plain; for, coeval with the first foundations of their oldest temples, they possessed the cuneiform script, which can be described as a cursive hand developed out of picture-signs by centuries of primeval culture. From whence the Semitic race invaded Babylonia, and what was its origin, we know not, but it must be noted that the language they spoke, though clearly and thoroughly Semitic, is yet so strikingly different from all other Semitic languages that it stands in a category apart, and the time when it formed one speech with the other Semitic tongues lies immeasurably far back beyond our calculations.

The earliest records, then, show us a state of things not unlike that of our Saxon heptarchy: petty princes, or city-monarchies successfully endeavouring to obtain lordship over a neighbouring town or a group of towns, and in turn being overcome by others. And, considering that most of these towns were but a score of miles distant from one another and changed rulers frequently, the history is somewhat confusing. The most ancient ruler at present known to us is Enshagkushanna, who is styled King of Kengi. Owing to the broken state of the sherd on which the inscription occurs, and which possibly dates soon after 5000 B. C., the name of his capital is unknown. It probably was Shirpurla, and he ruled over Southern Babylonia. He claims to have won a great victory over the City of Kish, and he dedicated the spoil, including a statue of bright silver, to Mullil, the god of Calanne (Nippur). It seems likely that Kish was the most southern city captured by Semites; of one of its kings, Manishtusu, we possess a mace-head, as a sign of his royalty, and a stele, or obelisk, in archaic cuneiforms and Semitic Babylonian. Somewhat later Mesilim, the King of Kish, retrieved the defeat of his predecessor and acted as suzerain of Shirpurla. Another probable name of a King of Kish is Urumush, or Alusharshid, though some make him King of Akkad. Whereas our information concerning the dynasty of Kish is exceedingly fragmentary, we are somewhat better informed about the rulers of Shirpurla. About 4500 B. C. we find Urkagina reigning there and, somewhat later, Lugal (*lugal*, "great man", i. e. "prince", or "king") Shuggur. Then, after an interval, we are acquainted with a succession of no fewer than seven Kings of Shirpurla: Gursar, Gunidu, Ur-Ninâ, Akur-Gal, Eannatum I, Entemena and Eannatum II—which last king must have reigned about 4000 B. C. De Sarszec found at Tellô a temple-wall some of the bricks of which bore the clear legend of Ur-Ninâ, thus leaving on record this king's building activity. Thanks to the famous stele of the vultures, now in the Louvre, to some clay steles in the British Museum, and a cone found at Shirpurla, we have an idea of the warlike propensities of Eannatum I, who subdued the people of Gishban by a crushing defeat, made them pay an almost incredible war-indemnity of corn, and appointed over that city his own viceroy, "who placed his yoke on the land of Elam", "and of Gisgal", and who is represented as braining with his club foes whose heads are protruding out of the opening of a bag in which they are bound.

That, notwithstanding these scenes of bloodshed, it was an age of art and culture can be evidently shown by such finds as that of a superb silver vase of Entemena, Eannatum's son and successor, and, as crown-prince, general of his army. After Eannatum II the history of Shirpurla is a blank, until we find the name of Lugal Ushumgal, when, however, the city has for a time lost its independence, for this ruler was the vassal of Sargon I of Akkad, about 3800 B. C.

ARCHAIC BABYLONIAN INSCRIPTION TO SUN GOD BY SARGON I, ABOUT 3800 B. C.

Yet, some six centuries afterwards, when the dynasty of Akkad had ceased to be, the *patesis*, or high-priests, of Shirpurla were still men of renown. A long inscription on the back of a statue tells us of the vast building achievements of Ur-Bau about the year 3200; and the name of his son and successor, Nammaghani. About two centuries later we find Gudea, one of the most famous rulers the city ever possessed. Excavations at Tellô have laid bare the colossal walls of his great palace and have shown us how, both by land and sea, he brought his materials from vast distances, while his architecture and sculpture show perfect art and refinement, and we incidentally learn that he conquered the district of Anshan in Elam. After Gudea, we are acquainted with the names of four more rulers of Shirpurla, but in these subsequent reigns the city seems to have quickly sunk into political insignificance. Another Sumerian dynasty was that of Erech, or Gishban. About 4000 B. C. a certain Lugal Zaggisi, son of the Patesi of Gishban, who became King of Erech, proudly styled himself King of the World, as Enshagkushanna and Alusharshid had done, claimed to rule from the Persian Gulf to the Mediterranean, and praises the supreme god Enlil, or Bel, of Nippur, who "granted him the dominion of all from the rising of the sun to the setting thereof and caused the countries to dwell in peace". Yet to us it seems but a rushlight of glory; for after his son Lugal-Kisalsi the Kingdom of Erech disappears in the night of the past. The same may be said of the dynasty of Agade. Ittibel's son, Sargon I, suddenly stands before us as a giant figure in history about 3800 B. C. He was a monarch proud of his race and language, for his inscriptions were in his Semitic mother-tongue, not in the Sumerian, like those of previous kings. He is rightly called the first founder of a Semitic empire. Under him flourished Semitic language, literature, and art, especially architecture. He established his dominion in Susa, the capital of Elam, subdued Syria and Palestine in three campaigns, set up an image of himself on the Syrian coast, as a monument of his triumphs, and welded his conquests into one empire. Naram-Sin, his son, even extended his father's conquests, invading the Sinai

Peninsula and, apparently, Cyprus, where a seal-cylinder was found on which he receives homage as a god. On inscriptions of that date first occurs mention of the city of God's Gate, or Babylon (*Bâb-ilu* sometimes *Bâb-ilani*, whence the Greek Βαβυλών), then written ideographically *Kâ-Dungir*.

After Bingani, Naram-Sin's son, Semitic successes were temporarily eclipsed; Egypt occupied Sinai, Elam became again independent, and in Babylonia itself the Sumerian element reasserted itself. We find a dynasty of Ur in prominence. This city seems at two different periods to have exercised the hegemony over the Euphrates Valley or part of it. First under Urgur and Dungi I, about 3400 B. C. This Urgur assumed the title of King of Sumer and Akkad, thus making the first attempt to unite North and South Babylonia into a political unit, and inaugurating a royal style which was borne perhaps longer than the title of any other dignity since the world was made. Ur predominates, for the second time, about 2800 B. C., under Dungi II, Gungunu, Bur-Sin, Gimil-Sin, and Ine Sin, whose buildings and fortifications are found in many cities of Babylonia. The history of Ur is as yet so obscure that some scholars (Thureau-Dangin, Hilprecht, Bezold) accept but two dynasties, others (Rogers) three, others (Hugo Radau) four. The supremacy of Ur is followed, about 2500 B. C., by that of (N) Isin, apparently an unimportant city, as its rulers style themselves Shepherds, or Gracious Lords, of Isin, and place this title after that of King of Ur, Eridu, Erech, and Nippur. Six rulers of Isin are known: Ishbigarra, Libit-Ishtar, Bur-Sin II, Ur-Ninib, Ishme-Dagan, and Enannatum. The last of the city-kingdoms was that of Larsa, about 2300 B. C., with its sovereigns Siniddinam Nur-Adad, Chedornanchundi, Chedorlaomer, Chedormabug, and Eri-Aku. The composition of these royal names with Chedor, the Elamite *Kudur*, sufficiently shows that they did not belong to a native dynasty, whether Sumerian or Semitic. One of the earliest Elamite invaders of Babylonia was Rim-Amun, who obtained such a foothold on Babylonian soil that the year of his reign was used to date contract tablets, a sure sign that he was at least king *de facto*. Chedornanchundi invaded Babylonia about the year 2285, reached Erech, plundered its temples, and captured the city-goddess; but whether he established a permanent rule, remains doubtful. Somewhat later Chedorlaomer (*Kudur-Laghamar*, "Servant of Laghamar", an Elamite deity), known to us from the Bible, seems to have been more successful. Not only does he appear as overlord of Babylonia, but he carried his conquest as far west as Palestine. Chedormabug was originally Prince of Emutbal, or western Elam, but obtained dominion over Babylonia and rebuilt the temple at Ur. His son Rim-Sin, or Eri-Aku, considered himself so well established on Babylonian territory that he affected the ancient titles, Exalter of Ur, King of Larsa, King of Sumer and Akkad. Yet he was the least of the city-kings, and a new order of things began with the rise of Babylon.

THE FIRST EMPIRE.—The dynasty which laid the foundation of Babylon's greatness is sometimes called the *Arabian*. It certainly was West-Semitic and almost certainly Amorite. The Babylonians called it the dynasty of Babylon, for, though foreign in origin, it may have had its actual home in that city, which it gratefully and proudly remembered. It lasted for 296 years and saw the greatest glory of the old empire and perhaps the Golden Age of the Semitic race in the ancient world. The names of its monarchs are: Sumu-abi (15 years), Sumu-la-ilu (35), Zabin (14), Apil-Sin (18), Sin-muballit (30); Hammurabi (35), Samsu-iluna (35), Abishua (25), Ammi-titana (25), Ammizaduga (22), Samsu-titana (31). Under the first five kings Babylon was still only the mightiest amongst several rival cities, but the sixth king, Hammurabi, who succeeded in beating down all opposition, obtained absolute rule of Northern and Southern Babylonia and drove out the Elamite invaders. Babylonia henceforward formed but one state and was welded into one empire. They were apparently stormy days before the final triumph of Hammurabi. The second ruler strengthened his capital with large fortifications; the third ruler was apparently in danger of a native pretender or foreign rival called Immeru; only the fourth ruler was definitely styled king; while Hammurabi himself in the beginning of his reign acknowledged the suzerainty of Elam. This Hammurabi is one of the most gigantic figures of the world's history, to be named with Alexander, Cæsar, or Napoleon, but best compared to a Charlemagne, a conqueror and a lawgiver, whose powerful genius formed a lasting empire out of chaos, and whose beneficent influence continued for ages throughout an area almost as large as Europe. Doubtless a dozen centuries later Assyrian kings were to make greater conquests than he, but whereas they were giant destroyers he was a giant builder. His large public and private correspondence gives us an insight into his multitudinous cares, his minute attention to details, his constitutional methods. (See "The Letters and Inscriptions of Hammurabi", by L. W. King; London, 1898, 3 vols.) His famous code of civil and criminal law throws light on his genius as legislator and judge. The stele on which these laws are inscribed was found at Susa by M. de Morgan and the Dominican friar Scheil, and first published and translated by the latter in 1902. This astounding find, giving us, in 3638 short lines, 282 laws and regulations affecting the whole range of public and private life, is unequalled even in the marvellous history of Babylonian research. From no other document can a more swift and accurate estimate of Babylonian civilization be formed than from this code. (For a complete English translation see T. G. Pinches, op. cit. infra, pp. 487-519.)

Whereas the Assyrian kings loved to fill the boastful records of their reigns with ghastly descriptions of battle and war, so that we possess the minutest details of their military campaigns, the genius of Babylon, on the contrary, was one of peace, and culture, and progress. The building of temples, the adorning of cities, the digging of canals, the making of roads, the framing of laws was their pride; their records breathe, or affect to breathe, all serene tranquillity; warlike exploits are but mentioned by the way, hence we have, even in the case of the two greatest Babylonian conquerors, Hammurabi and Nabuchodonosor II, but scanty information of their deeds of arms. "I dug the canal Hammurabi, the blessing of men, which bringeth the water of the overflow unto the land of Sumer and Akkad. Its banks on both sides I made arable land; much seed I scattered upon it. Lasting water I provided for the land of Sumer and Akkad. The land of Sumer and Akkad, its separated peoples I united, with blessings and abundance I endowed them, in peaceful dwellings I made them to live"—such is the style of Hammurabi. In what seems an ode on the king, engraved on his statue we find the words: "Hammurabi, the strong warrior, the destroyer of his foes, he is the hurricane of battle, sweeping the land of his foes, he brings opposition to naught, he puts an end to insurrection, he breaks the warrior as an image of clay." But chronological details are still in confusion. In a very fragmentary list of dates the 31st year of his reign is given as that of the land Emutbalu, which is usually taken as that of his victory over western Elam, and considered by many as that of his conquest of Larsa and its king, Rim-Sin, or Eri-Aku. If the Biblical Amraphel be Hammurabi we have in Gen., xiv, the record of an expedition of

his to the Westland previous to the 31st year of his reign. Of Hammurabi's immediate successors we know nothing except that they reigned in peaceful prosperity. That trade prospered, and temples were built, is all we can say.

The Amorite dynasty was succeeded by a series of eleven kings which may well be designated as the *Unknown Dynasty*, which has received a number of names: Ura-Azag, Uru-ku, Shish-ku. Whether it was Semite or not is not certain; the years of reign are given in the "King-List", but they are surprisingly long (60–56–55–50–28, etc.), so that not only great doubt is cast on the correctness of these dates, but the very existence of this dynasty is doubted or rejected by some scholars (as Hommel). It is indeed remarkable that the kings should be eleven in number, like those of the Amorite dynasty, and that we should nowhere find a distinct evidence of their existence; yet these premises hardly suffice to prove that so early a document as the "King-List" made the unpardonable mistake of ascribing nearly four centuries of rule to a dynasty which in reality was contemporaneous, nay identical, with the Amorite monarchs. Their names are certainly very puzzling, but it has been suggested that these were not personal names, but names of the city-quarters from which they originated. Should this dynasty have a separate existence, it is safe to say that they were native rulers, and succeeded the Amorites without any break of national and political life. Owing to the questionable reality of this dynasty, the chronology of the previous one varies greatly; hence it arises, for instance, that Hammurabi's date is given as 1772–17 in Hastings' "Dictionary of the Bible", while the majority of scholars would place him about 2100 B. C., or a little earlier; nor are indications wanting to show that, whether the "Unknown Dynasty" be fictitious or not, the latter date is approximately right.

In the third place comes the Kassite dynasty, thirty-six kings, for 576 years. The tablet with this list is unfortunately mutilated, but almost all the nineteen missing names can with some exactness be supplied from other sources, such as the Assyrian synchronistic history and the correspondence with Egypt. This dynasty was a foreign one, but its place of origin is not easy to ascertain. In their own official designation they style themselves kings of Kardunyash and the King of Egypt addresses Kadashman Bel as King of Kardunyash. This Kardunyash has been tentatively identified with South Elam. Information about the Kassite period is obtained but sparsely. We possess an Assyrian copy of an inscription of Agum-Kakrime, perhaps the seventh King of this dynasty: he styles himself: "King of Kasshu and Akkad, King of the broad land of Babylon, who caused much people to settle in the land of Ashmumak, King of Padan and Alvan, King of the land of Guti, wide extended peoples, a king who rules the four quarters of the world". The extent of territory thus under dominion of the Babylonian monarch is wider than even that under the Amorite dynasty; but in the royal title, which is altogether unusual in its form, Babylon takes but the third place; only a few generations later, however, the old style and title is resumed, and Babylon again stands first; the foreign conquerors were evidently conquered by the peaceful conquest of superior Babylonian civilization. This Agum-Kakrime with all his wide dominions had yet to send an embassy to the land of Khani to obtain the gods Marduk and Zarpanit, the most sacred national idols, which had evidently been captured by the enemy. The next king of whom we have any knowledge is Karaindash (1450 B. C.) who settled the boundary lines of his kingdom with his contemporary Asshur-bel-nisheshu of Assyria. From the Tell-el-etmarna tablets we conclude that in 1400 B. C., Babylon was no longer the one great power of Western Asia; the Kingdom of Assyria and the Kingdom of Mitanni were its rivals and wellnigh equals. Yet, in the letters which passed between Kadashman-Bel and Amenophis III, King of Egypt, it is evident that the King of Babylon could assume a more independent tone of fair equality with the great Pharao than the kings of Assyria or Mitanni. When Amenophis asks for Kadashman-Bel's sister in marriage, Kadashman-Bel promptly asks for Amenophis' sister in return; and when Amenophis demurs, Kadashman-Bel promptly answers that, unless some fair Egyptian of princely rank be sent, Amenophis shall not have his sister. When Assyria has sought Egyptian help against Babylon, Kadashman-Bel diplomatically reminds Pharao that Babylon has in times past given no assistance to Syrian vassal princes against their Egyptian suzerain, and expects Egypt now to act in the same way in not granting help to Assyria. And when a Babylonian caravan has been robbed by the people of Akko in Canaan, the Egyptian Government receives a peremptory letter from Babylon for *amende honorable* and restitution. Amenophis is held responsible, "for Canaan is thy country, and thou art its King". Kadashman-Bel was succeeded by Burnaburiash I, Kurigalzu I, Burnaburiash II. Six letters of the last-named to Amenhotep IV of Egypt suggest a period of perfect tranquillity and prosperity. For the cause and result of the first great conflict between Assyria and Babylon see ASSYRIA.

How the long Kassite dynasty came to an end we know not, but it was succeeded by the dynasty of Pashi (some read Isin), eleven kings in 132 years (about 1200–1064 B. C.). The greatest monarch of this house was Nabuchodonosor I (about 1135–25 B. C.); though twice defeated by Assyria, he was successful against the Lulubi, punished Elam, and invaded Syria, and by his brilliant achievements stayed the inevitable decline of Babylon. The next two dynasties are known as those of the Sealand, and of Bazi, of three kings each and these were followed by one Elamite king (c. 1064–900 B. C.). Upon these obscure dynasties follows the long series of Babylonian kings, who reigned mostly as vassals, sometimes quasi-independent, sometimes as rebel-kings in the period of Assyrian supremacy (for which see ASSYRIA).

THE SECOND, OR CHALDEAN, EMPIRE.—With the death, in 626 B. C., of Kandalanu (the Babylonian name of Assurbanipal), King of Assyria, Assyrian power in Babylon practically ceased. Nabopolassar, a Chaldean who had risen from the position of general in the Assyrian army, ruled Babylon as Shakkanak for some years in nominal dependence on Ninive. Then, as King of Babylon, he invaded and

INSCRIBED BOUNDARY STONE, REIGN OF MARDUK-BALATSU-IKBI, KING OF BABYLON, 830 B. C.

annexed the Mesopotamian provinces of Assyria, and when Sinsharishkun, the last King of Assyria, tried to cut off his return and threatened Babylon, Nabopolassar called in the aid of the Manda, nomadic tribes of Kurdistan, somewhat incorrectly identified with the Medes. Though Nabopolassar no doubt contributed his share to the events which led to the complete destruction of Ninive (606 B. C.) by these Manda barbarians, he apparently did not in person co-operate in the taking of the city, nor share the booty, but used the opportunity to firmly establish his throne in Babylon. Though Semites, the Chaldeans belonged to a race perfectly distinct from the Babylonians proper, and were foreigners in the Euphrates Valley. They were settlers from Arabia, who had invaded Babylonia from the South. Their stronghold was the district known as the Sealands. During the Assyrian supremacy the combined forces of Babylon and Assyria had kept them in check, but, owing probably to the fearful Assyrian atrocities in Babylon, the citizens had begun to look towards their former enemies for help, and the Chaldean power grew apace in Babylon till, in Nabopolassar, it assumed the reins of government, and thus imperceptibly a foreign race superseded the ancient inhabitants. The city remained the same, but its nationality changed. Nabopolassar must have been a strong, beneficent ruler, engaged in rebuilding temples and digging canals, like his predecessors, and yet maintaining his hold over the conquered provinces. The Egyptians, who had learnt of the weakness of Assyria, had already, three years before the fall of Ninive, crossed the frontiers with a mighty army under Necho II, in the hope of sharing in the dismemberment of the Assyrian Empire. How Josias of Juda, trying to bar his way, was slain at Megiddo is known from IV Kings, xxiii, 29. Meanwhile Ninive was taken, and Necho, resting satisfied with the conquest of the Syrian provinces, proceeded no further. A few years later, however, he marched a colossal army from Egypt to the Euphrates in hopes of annexing part of Mesopotamia. He was met by the Babylonian army at Carchemish, the ancient Hittite capital, where he wished to cross the Euphrates. Nabopolassar, being prevented by ill health and advancing age, had sent his son Nabuchodonosor, and put him in command. The Egyptians were utterly routed in this great encounter, one of the most important in history (604 B. C.). Nabuchodonosor pursued the enemy to the borders of Egypt, where he received the news of his father's death. He hastened back to Babylon, was received without opposition, and began, in 604 B. C., the forty-two years of his most glorious reign. His first difficulties arose in Juda. Against the solemn warning of Jeremias the Prophet, Jehoiakim refused tribute, i. e. rebelled against Babylon. At first Nabuchodonosor II began a small guerilla warfare against Jerusalem; then, in 597 B. C., he dispatched a considerable army, and after a while began the siege in person. Jechonias, however, son of Jehoiakim, who as a lad of eighteen had succeeded his father, surrendered; 7000 men capable of bearing arms and 1000 workers in iron were carried away and made to form a colony on a canal near Nippur (the River Chobar mentioned in Ezechiel, i, 1), and Zedekias was substituted for Jechonias as vassal King of Juda.

Some ten years later Nabuchodonosor once more found himself in Palestine. Hophra, King of Egypt, who had succeeded Necho II in 589 B. C., had by secret agents tried to combine all the Syrian States in a conspiracy against Babylon. Edom, Moab, Ammon, Tyre, and Sidon had entered into the coalition, and at last even Juda had joined, and Zedekias, against the advice of Jeremias, broke his oath of allegiance to the Chaldeans. A Babylonian army began to surround Jerusalem in 587 B. C. They were unable to take the city by storm and intended to subdue it by starvation. But Pharao Hophra entered Palestine to help the besieged. The Babylonians raised the siege to drive the Egyptians back; they then returned to Jerusalem and continued the siege in grim earnest. On July the 9th, 586 B. C., they poured in through a breach in the wall of Ezekias and took the city by storm. They captured the flying Zedekias and brought him before Nabuchodonosor at Riblah, where his children were slain before him and his eyes blinded. The city was destroyed, and the temple treasures carried to Babylon. A vast number of the population was deported to some districts in Babylonia, a miserable remnant only was allowed to remain under a Jewish governor, Godolias. When this governor was slain by a Jewish faction under Ishmael, a fraction of this remnant, fearing Nabuchodonosor's wrath, emigrated to Egypt, forcibly taking Jeremias the Prophet with them.

Babylon's expedition to Juda thus ended in leaving it a devastated, depopulated, ruined district. Nabuchodonosor now turned his arms against Tyre. After Egypt this city had probably been the mainspring of the coalition against Babylon. The punishment intended for Tyre was the same as that of Jerusalem, but Nabuchodonosor did not succeed as he did with the capital of Juda. The position of Tyre was immeasurably superior to that of Jerusalem. The Babylonians had no fleet; therefore, as long as the sea remained open, Tyre was impregnable. The Chaldeans lay before Tyre thirteen years (585–572), but did not succeed in taking it. Ethobaal II, its king, seems to have come to terms with the King of Babylon, fearing, no doubt, the slow but sure destruction of Tyrian inland trade; at least we have evidence, from a contract-tablet dated in Tyre, that Nabuchodonosor at the end of his reign was recognized as suzerain of the city. Notwithstanding the little success against Tyre, Nabuchodonosor attacked Egypt in 567. He entered the very heart of the country, ravaged and pillaged as he chose, apparently without opposition, and returned laden with booty through the Syrian Provinces. But no permanent Egyptian occupation by Babylon was the result.

Thus Nabuchodonosor the Chaldean showed himself a capable military ruler, yet as a Babylonian monarch, following the custom of his predecessors, he gloried not in the arts of war, but of peace. His boast was the vast building operations which made Babylon a city (for those days) impregnable, which adorned the capital with palaces, and the famous "procession road", and Gate of Ishtar, and which restored and beautified a great number of temples in different towns of Babylonia. Of Nabuchodonosor's

madness (Daniel, iv, 26–34) no Babylonian record has as yet been found. A number of ingenious suggestions have been made on this subject, one of the best of which is Professor Hommel's substitution of Nabuna'id for Nabu-chodonosor, but the matter had better stand over till we possess more information on this period. Of the prophet Daniel we find no certain mention in contemporary documents; the prophet's Babylonian name, Baltassar (Balatsu-usur), is unfortunately a very common one. We know of at least fourteen persons of that time called Balatu and seven called Balatsu, both of which names may be abbreviations of Baltassar, or "Protect His life". The etymology of Sidrach and Misach is unknown, but Abednego and Arioch (Abdnebo and Eriaku) are well known. Professor J. Oppert found the base of a great statue near a mound called Duair, east of Babylon, and this may have belonged to the golden image erected "in the plain of Dura of the province of Babylon" (Dan., iii, 1). In 561 B. C., Nabuchodonosor was succeeded by Evil-Merodach (IV Kings, xxv, 27), who released Joachin of Juda and raised him above the other vassal kings at Babylon, but his mild rule evidently displeased the priestly caste, and they accused him of reigning lawlessly and extravagantly. After less than three years he was assassinated by Neriglissar (Nergal-sar-usur), his brother-in-law, who is possibly the Nergalsharezer present at the taking of Jerusalem (Jer., xxxix, 3–13). Neriglissar was after four years succeeded by his son Labasi-Marduk, no more than a child, who reigned nine months and was assassinated.

The conspirators elected Nabonidus (Nabu-nā'id) to the throne. He was the last King of Babylon (555–539 B. C.). He was a royal antiquarian rather than a ruling king. From their foundations he rebuilt the great Shamash temple in Sippar and the Sin temple in Harran, and in his reign the city walls of Babylon "were curiously built with burnt brick and bitumen". But he resided in Tema, shunned the capital, offended the provincial towns by transporting their gods to Shu-anna, and alienated the priesthood of Babylon by what they would call misdirected piety. To us his antiquarian research after first foundation-stones of the temples he rebuilt is of the greatest importance. He tells us that the foundation-stone of the Shamash temple laid by Naram Sin had not been seen for 3200 years, which, roughly speaking, gives us 3800 B. C., for Sargon of Akkad, Naram Sin's father; upon this date most of our early Babylonian chronology is based. The actual duties of government seem to have been largely in the hands of the Crown Prince Baltassar (Bêl-shar-usur), who resided in Babylon as regent. Meanwhile Cyrus, the petty King of Anshan, had begun his career of conquest. He overthrew Astyages, King of the Medes, for which victory Nabonaid praised him as the young servant of Merodach; he overthrew Crœsus of Lydia and his coalition; he assumed the title of King of the Parsu, and had begun a new Indo-Germanic world power which replaced the decrepit Semitic civilization. At last Nabonaid, realizing the situation, met the Persians at Opis. Owing to internal strife amongst the Babylonians, many of whom were dissatisfied with Nabonaid, the Persians had an easy victory, taking the city of Sippar without fighting. Nabonaid fled to Babylon. Cyrus's soldiers, under the generalship of Ugbaru (Gobryas), Governor of Gutium, entered the capital without striking a blow and captured Nabonaid. This happened in June; in October Cyrus in person entered the city, paid homage at E-sagila to Marduk. A week later the Persians entered, at night, that quarter of the city where Baltassar occupied a fortified position in apparent security, where the sacred vessels of Jehovah's temple were profaned, where the hand appeared on the wall writing *Mane*, *Tekel Phares*, and where Daniel was offered the third place in the kingdom (i. e. after Nabonaid and Baltassar). That same night Baltassar was slain and the Semitic Empire of Babylon came to an end, for the ex-King Nabonaid spent the rest of his life in Carmania.

In one sense Babylonian history ends here, and Persian history begins, yet a few words are needed on the return of the Jewish captives after their seventy years of exile. It has long been supposed that Cyrus, professing the Mazdean religion, was a strict monotheist and released the Jews out of sympathy for their faith. But this king was, apparently, only unconsciously an instrument in God's hands, and the permission for the Jews to return was merely given out of political sagacity and a wish for popularity in his new domains. At least we possess inscriptions of him in which he is most profuse in his homage to the Babylonian Pantheon. As Nabonaid had outraged the religious sentiments of his subjects by collecting all their gods in Shu-anna, Cyrus pursued an opposite policy and returned all these gods to their own worshippers; and, the Jews having no idols, he returned their sacred vessels, which Baltassar had profaned, and gave a grant for the rebuilding of their Temple. The very phraseology of the decree given in I Esdras, i, 2 sqq., referring to "the Lord God of Heaven" shows his respectful attitude, if not inclination, towards monotheism, which was professed by so many of his Indo-Germanic subjects. Darius Hystaspes, who in 521 B. C., after defeating Pseudo-Smerdis, succeeded Cambyses (King of Babylon since 530 B. C.) was a convinced monotheist and adorer of Ahuramazda; and if it was he who ordered and aided the completion of the temple at Jerusalem, after the interruption caused by Samaritan intervention, it was no doubt out of sympathy with the Jewish religion (I Esdr., vi, 1 sqq.). It is not quite certain, however, that the Darius referred to is this king; it has been suggested that Darius Nothus is meant, who mounted the throne almost a hundred years later. Zerubabel is a thoroughly Babylonian name and occurs frequently on documents of that time; but we cannot as yet trace any connexion between the Zerubabel of Scripture and any name mentioned in these documents.

Some Special Bible References.—(1) The first passage referring to Babylonia is Gen., x, 8–10: "Chus begat Nemrod, and the beginning of his kingdom was Babylon and Arach and Achad and Chalanne in the land of Sennaar." The great historical value of these genealogies in Genesis has been acknowledged by scholars of all schools; these genealogies are, however, not of persons, but of tribes, which is obvious from such a bold metaphor as: "Chanaan begat Sidon, his first born" (v, 15). But in many instances the names are those of actual persons whose personal names became designations of the tribes, just as in known instances of Scottish and Irish clans or Arab tribes. Chus begat Nemrod. Chus was not a Semite, according to the Biblical account, and it is remarkable that recent discoveries all seem to point to the fact that the original civilization of Babylonia was non-Semitic and the Semitic element only gradually displaced the aborigines and adopted their culture. It must be noted, also, that in v. 22 Assur is described as a son of Sem, though in v. 11 Assur comes out of the land of Sennaar. This exactly represents the fact that Assyria was purely Semitic where Babylonia was not. Some see in Chus a designation of the city of Kish, mentioned above amongst the cities of early Babylonia, and certainly one of its most ancient towns. Nemrod, on this supposition, would be none else than Nin-marad, or Lord of Marad, which was a daughter-city of Kish. Gilgamesh, whom mythology transformed into a Babylonian Hercules, whose fortunes are described in the Gilgamesh-epos, would then be the person designated by the Biblical Nemrod. Others

again see in Nemrod an intentional corruption of Amarudu, the Akkadian for Marduk, whom the Babylonians worshipped as the great God, and who, perhaps, was the deified ancestor of their city. This corruption would be parallel to Nisroch (IV Kings, xix, 37) for Assuraku, and Nibhaz (IV Kings, xvii, 31) for Abahazu, or Abed Nego for Abdnebo. The description of "stout hunter" or hero-entrapper would fit in well with the rôle ascribed to the god Marduk, who entrapped the monster Tiamtu in his net. Both Biblical instances, IV Kings, xvii, 31, and xix, 37, however, are very doubtful, and Nisroch has recently found a more probable explanation.

(2) "The beginning of his kingdom was Babylon and Arach and Achad and Calanne".—These cities of Northern Babylonia are probably enumerated inversely to the order of their antiquity; so that Nippur (Calanne) is the most ancient, and Babylon the most modern. Recent excavations have shown that Nippur dates far back beyond the Sargonid age (3800 B. C.) and Nippur is mentioned on the fifth tablet of the Babylonian Creation-story.

(3) The next Biblical passage which requires mention is that dealing with the Tower of Babel (Gen., xi, 1–9). This narrative, though couched in the terms of Oriental folklore, yet expresses not merely a moral lesson, but refers to some historical fact in the dim past. There was perhaps in the ancient world no spot on all the earth where such a variety of tongues and dialects was heard as in Babylonia, where Akkadians, Sumerians, and Amorites, Elamites, Kassites, Sutites, Qutites, and perhaps Hittites met and left their mark on the language; where Assyrian or Semitic Babylonian itself only very gradually displaced the older non-Semitic tongue, and where for many centuries the people were at least bilingual. It was the spot where Turanian, Semitic, and Indo-Germanic met. Yet there remained in the national consciousness the memory that the first settlers in the Babylonian plain spoke one language. "They removed from the East", as the Bible says and all recent research suggests. When we read, "The earth was of one tongue", we need not take this word in its widest sense, for the same word is often translated "the land". Philology may or may not prove the unity of all human speech, and man's descent from a single set of parents seems to postulate original unity of language; but in any case the Bible does not here seem to refer to this, and the Bible account itself suggests that a vast variety of tongues existed previous to the foundations of Babylon. We need but refer to Gen., x, 5, 21, 31: "In their kindreds and tongues and countries and nations"; and Gen., x, 10, where Babylon is represented as almost coeval with Arach, Adhad, and Calanne, and posterior to Gomer, Magog, Elam, Arphaxad, so that the original division of languages cannot first have taken place at Babel. What historical fact lies behind the account of the building of the Tower of Babel is difficult to ascertain. Of course any real attempt to reach heaven by a tower is out of the question. The mountains of Elam were too close by, to tell them that a few yards more or less were of no importance to get in touch with the sky. But the wish to have a rallying-point in the plain is only too natural. It is a striking fact that most Babylonian cities possessed a *ziggurat* (a stage, or temple-tower), and these bore very significant Sumerian names, as, for instance, at Nippur, *Dur-anki*, "Link of heaven and earth"—"the summit of which reaches unto heaven, and the foundation of which is laid in the bright deep"; or, at Babylon, *Esagila*, "House of the High Head", the more ancient designation of which was *Etemenanki*, "House of the Foundation of Heaven and Earth"; or *Ezida*, at Borsippa, by its more ancient designation *Euriminianki*, or "House of the Seven Spheres of Heaven and Earth". The remains of Ezîda, at present Birs Nimrud, are tradition-

ally pointed out as the Tower of Babel; whether rightly, is impossible to say; Esagila, in Babylon itself, has as good, if not a better, claim. We have no record of the building of the city and tower being interrupted by any such catastrophe as a confusion of languages; but that such an interruption because of diversity of speech of the townspeople took place, is not impossible. In any case it can only have been an interruption, though perhaps of many centuries, for Babylon increased and prospered for many centuries after the period referred to in Genesis. The history of the city of Babylon before the Amorite dynasty is an absolute blank, and we have no facts to fill up the fifteen centuries of its existence previous to that date. The etymology given for the name Babel in Gen., xi, 9, is not the historic meaning of the word, which, as given above is *Kadungir, Bâb-Îlu*, or "God's Gate". The derivation in Genesis rests upon the similarity of sound with a word formed from the root *balal*, "to stammer", or "be confused".

(4) Next to be mentioned is the account of the battle of the four kings against five near the Dead Sea (Gen., xiv). Sennaar mentioned in v. 1 is the Sumer of the Babylonian inscriptions, and Amraphel is identified by most scholars with the great Hammurabi, the sixth King of Babylon. The initial guttural of the king's name being a soft one, and the Babylonians being given to dropping their H's, the name actually occurs in cuneiform inscriptions as Ammurapi. The absence of the final *l* arises from the fact that the sign *pi* was misread *bil* or perhaps *ilu*, the sign of deification, or complement of the name, being omitted. There is no philological difficulty in this identification, but the chronological difficulty (viz., of Hammurabi being vassal of Chedorlaomer) has led others to identify Amraphel with Hammurabi's father Sin-muballit, whose name is ideographically written Amar-Pal. Arioch, King of Pontus (Pontus is St. Jerome's unfortunate guess to identify Ellazar) is none else but Rim-Sin, King of Larsa (Ellazar of A. V.), whose name was Eri-Aku, and who was defeated and dethroned by the King of Babylon, whether Hammurabi or Sin-muballit; and if the former, then this occurred in the thirty-first year of his reign, the year of the land of Emutbalu, Eri-Aku bearing the title of King of Larsa and Father of Emutbalu. The name Chedorlahomer has apparently, though not quite certainly, been found on two tablets together with the names Eriaku and Tudhula, which latter king is evidently "Thadal, king of the Nations". The Hebrew word *gôyim*, "nations", is a clerical error for *Gutium* or *Guti*, a neighbouring state which plays an important rôle throughout Babylonian history. Of Kudur-lahgumal, King of the Land of Elam, it is said that he "descended on", and "exercised sovereignty in Babylon the city of Kar-Duniash". We have documentary evidence that Eriaku's father Kudurmabug, King of Elam, and after him Hammurabi of Babylon, claimed authority over Palestine the land of Martu. This Biblical passage, therefore, which was once described as bristling with impossibilities, has so far only received confirmation from Babylonian documents.

(5) According to Gen., xi, 28 and 31, Abraham was a Babylonian from the city of Ur. It is remarkable that the name *Abu ramu* (Honoured Father) occurs in the eponym lists for 677 B. C., and *Abê ramu*, a similar name, on a contract-tablet in the reign of Apil-Sin, thus showing that Abram was a Babylonian name in use long before and after the date of the Patriarch. His father removed from Ur to Harran, from the old centre of the Moon-cult to the new. Talmudic tradition makes Terah an idolater, and his religion may have had to do with his emigration. No excavations have as yet taken place at Harran, and Abraham's ancestry remains obscure. Aberamu of Apil-Sin's reign had a son Sha-Amūrri, which fact

shows the early intercourse between Babylonia and the Amorite land, or Palestine. In Chanaan Abraham remained within the sphere of Babylonian language and influence, or perhaps even authority. Several centuries later, when Palestine was no longer part of the Babylonian Empire, Abd-Hîba, the King of Jerusalem, in his intercourse with his over-lord of Egypt, wrote neither his own language nor that of Pharao, but Babylonian, the universal language of the day. Even when passing into Egypt, Abraham remained under Semitic rule, for the Hyksos reigned there.

(6) Considering that the progenitor of the Hebrew race was a Babylonian, and that Babylonian culture remained paramount in Western Asia for more than 1000 years, the most astounding feature of the Hebrew Scriptures is the almost complete absence of Babylonian religious ideas, the more so as Babylonian religion, though Oriental polytheism, possessed a refinement, a nobility of thought, and a piety, which are often admirable. The Babylonian account of creation, though often compared with the Biblical one, differs from it on main and essential points for (a) it contains no direct statement of the *Creation* of the world: Tiamtu and Apsu, the watery waste and the abyss wedded together, *beget* the universe; Marduk, the conqueror of chaos, shapes and orders all things; but this is the mythological garb of evolution as opposed to creation. (b) It does not make the Deity the first and only cause of the existence of all things; the gods themselves are but the outcome of pre-existent, apparently eternal, forces; they are not cause, but effect. (c) It makes the present world the outcome of a great war; it is the story of Resistance and Struggle, which is the exact opposite of the Biblical account. (d) It does not arrange the things created into groups or classes, which is one of the main features of the story in Genesis. (e) The work of creation is not divided into a number of days—the principal literary characteristic of the Biblical account. The Babylonian mythology possesses something analogous to the Biblical Garden of Eden. But though they apparently possessed the word *Edina*, not only as meaning "the Plain", but as a geographical name, their garden of delight is placed in Eridu, where "a dark vine grew; it was made a glorious place, planted beside the abyss. In the glorious house, which is like a forest, its shadow extends; no man enters its midst. In its interior is the Sun-god Tammuz. Between the mouths of the rivers, which are on both sides". This passage bears a striking analogy to Gen., ii, 8–17. The Babylonians, however, seem to have possessed no account of the Fall. It seems likely that the name of Ea, or Ya, or Aa, the oldest god of the Babylonian Pantheon, is connected with the name Jahve, Jahu, or Ja, of the Old Testament. Professor Delitzsch recently claimed to have found the name Jahve-ilu on a Babylonian tablet, but the reading has been strongly disputed by other scholars. The greatest similarity between Hebrew and Babylonian records is in their accounts of the Flood. Pirnapistum, the Babylonian Noe, commanded by Ae, builds a ship and transfers hither his family, the beasts of the field, and the sons of the artificers, and he shuts the door. Six days and nights the wind blew, the flood overwhelmed the land. The seventh day the storm ceased; quieted, the sea shrank back; all mankind had turned to corruption. The ship stopped at the land of Nisir. Pir-napistum sends out first a dove, which returns; then a swallow, and it returns; then a raven, and it does not return. He leaves the ship, pours out a libation, makes an offering on the peak of the mountain. "The gods smelled a savour, the gods smelled a sweet savour, the gods gathered like flies over the sacrificer." No one reading the Babylonian account of the Flood can deny its intimate connexion with the narrative in Genesis, yet

the former is so intimately bound up with Babylonian mythology, that the inspired character of the Hebrew account is the better appreciated by the contrast.

RELIGION.—The Babylonian Pantheon arose out of a gradual amalgamation of the local deities of the early city states of Sumer and Akkad. And Babylonian mythology is mainly the projection into the heavenly sphere of the earthly fortunes of the early centres of civilization in the Euphrates valley. Babylonian religion, therefore, is largely a Sumerian, i. e. Mongolian product, no doubt modified by Semitic influence, yet to the last bearing the mark of its

BRICK OF KURIGALZU KING OF BABYLON (ABOUT 1400 B. C.), BRITISH MUSEUM

Mongolian origin in the very names of its gods and in the sacred dead languages in which they were addressed. The tutelary spirit of a locality extended his power with the political power of his adherents; when the citizens of one city entered into political relations with the citizens of another, popular imagination soon created the relation of father and son, brother and sister, or man and wife, between their respective gods. The Babylonian Trinity of Anu, Bel, and Ea is the result of later speculation, dividing the divine power into that which rules in heaven, that which rules on earth, and that which rules under the earth. Ea was originally the god of Eridu on the Persian Gulf and therefore the god of the ocean and the waters below. Bel was originally the chief spirit (in Sumerian En-lil, the older designation of Bel, which is Semitic for "chief" or "lord") of Nippur, one of the oldest, possibly the oldest, centre of civilization after Eridu. Anu's local cult is as yet uncertain; Erech has been suggested; we know that Gudea erected a temple to him; he always remained a shadowy personality. Although nominal head of the Pantheon, he had in later days no temple dedicated to him except one, and that he shared with Hadad. Sin, the moon, was the god of Ur; Shamash, the sun, was the god of Larsa and Sippar; when the two towns of Girsu and Uruazaga were united into the one city of Lagash, the two respective local deities, Nin-Girsu and Bau, became man and wife, to whom Gudea brought wedding presents. With the rise of Babylon and the political unification of the

whole country under this metropolis, the city-god Marduk, whose name does not occur on any inscription previous to Hammurabi, leaps to the foreground. The Babylonian theologians not only gave him a place in the Pantheon, but in the Epos "Enuma Elish" it is related how, as reward for overcoming the Dragon of Chaos, the great gods, his fathers, bestowed upon Marduk their own names and titles. Marduk gradually so outshone the other deities that these were looked upon as mere manifestations of Marduk, whose name became almost a synonym for God. And though Babylonians never quite reached monotheism, their ideas sometimes seem to come near it. Unlike the Assyrians, the Babylonians never possessed a female deity of such standing in the Pantheon as Ishtar of Ninive or Arbela. In the Second Empire, Nebo, the city-god of Borsippa, over against Babylon, rises into prominence and wins honours almost equal to those of Marduk, and the twin cities have two almost inseparable gods. Judging from the continual invocation of the gods in every conceivable detail of life, and the continual acknowledgment of dependence on them, and the anxious humble prayers that are still extant, the Babylonians were as a nation pre-eminent in piety.

CIVILIZATION.—It is impossible in this article to give an idea of the astounding culture which had developed in the Euphrates Valley, the cradle of civilization, even as early as 2300 B. C. A perusal of the article HAMMURABI, and a careful reading of his code of laws will give us a clear insight in the Babylonian world of four thousand years ago. The ethical litany of the Shurpu tablets contains an examination of conscience more detailed than the so-called "Negative" confessions in the Egyptian Book of the Dead and fills us with admiration for the moral level of the Babylonian world. Though polygamists, the Babylonians raised but one woman to the legal status of wife, and women possessed considerable rights and freedom of action. Marriage settlements protected the married, and the unmarried managed their own estates. On the other hand, they possessed an institution analogous to vestal virgins at Rome. These female votaries had a privileged position in Babylonian society; we know, however, of no such dire penalty for their unfaithfulness as the Roman law inflicted. A votary could even enter into nominal marriage, if she gave her husband a maid as Sarah gave Abraham. According to Law 110 of Hammurabi, however, "if a votary who dwells not in a cloister open a wine-house or enter a wine-house for drink, that female they shall burn". On the other hand (Law 127), "if a man has caused the finger to be pointed against a votary and has not justified it, they shall set that man before the judges and mark his forehead". The dark side of Babylonian society is seen in the strange enactment: "If the child of a courtesan or of a public woman come to know his father's house and despise his foster-parents and go to his father's house, they shall tear out his eyes". The repeated coupling of the words "votary or public woman" and the minute and indulgent legislation of which they are the objects make us fear that the virtue of chastity was not prized in Babylon. Although originally only a provident, prosperous agricultural people, the Babylonians seem to have developed a great commercial talent; and well might some Assyrian Napoleon have referred to his Southern neighbours as "that nation of shopkeepers". In 1893 Dr. Hilprecht found 730 tablets twenty feet underground in a ruined building at Nippur, which proved to be the banking archives of the firm Nurashu and Sons, signed, sealed, and dated about 400 B. C. We also possess a deed of purchase by Manishtusu, King of Kish, some 4000 B. C., in archaic Babylonian, which in accuracy and minuteness of detail in moneys and values would compare well with a modern balance sheet that has passed the chartered accountants. Proofs are not lacking of the commercial talents of the Babylonians during the thirty-five centuries between these dates.

LITERATURE.—Vast as is the material of Babylonian inscriptions, equally varied are their contents. The great majority no doubt of the 300,000 tablets hitherto unearthed deal with business matters rather than with matters literary; contracts, marriage settlements, cadastral surveys, commercial letters, orders for goods or acknowledgments of their receipt, official communications between magistrates and civil or military governors, names, titles, and dates on foundation stones, private correspondence, and so on. Still a fair percentage has a right to be strictly classed as "literature" or "belles-lettres". We must moreover constantly keep in mind that only about one-fifth of the total number of these tablets have been published and that any description of their literature must as yet be fragmentary and tentative. It is convenient to classify as follows: (1) the Epos; (2) the Psalm; (3) the Historical Narrative.

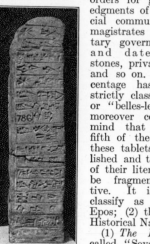

ONE OF THE SEVEN TABLETS OF CREATION

(1) *The Epos.*—(a) The so-called "Seven Tablets of Creation", because written on a series of seven very mutilated tablets in the Kouyunshik Library. Happily the lacunæ can here and there be filled up by fragments of duplicates found elsewhere. Borrowing an expression from the early Teuton literature, this might be called the "saga of the primeval chaos". Assyrian scribes called it by its first words "Enuma Elish" (When on high) as the Jews called Genesis "Bereshith" (in the beginning). Although it contains an account of the world's origin, as above contrasted with the account given in the Bible, it is not so much a cosmogony as the story of the heroic deeds of the god Marduk, in his struggle with the Dragon of Chaos. Though the youngest of the gods, Marduk is charged by them to fight Tiamtu and the gods on her side. He wins a glorious victory; he takes the tablets of fate from Kimgu, her husband; he splits open her skull, hews asunder the channels of her blood and makes the north wind carry it away to hidden places. He divides the corpse of the great Dragon and with one half makes a covering for the heavens and thus fixes the waters above the firmament. He then sets about fashioning the universe, and the stars, and the moon; he forms man. "Let me gather my blood and let me set up a man, let me make then men dwelling on the earth." When Marduk has finished his work, he is acclaimed by all the gods with joy and given fifty names. The gods are apparently eager to bestow their own titles upon him. The aim of the poem clearly is to explain how Marduk, the local god of as modern a city as Babylon, had displaced the deities of the older Babylonian cities, "the gods his fathers".

(b) The great national epos of Gilgamesh, which probably had in Babylonian literature some such place as the Odyssey or the Æneid amongst the Greeks and Romans. It consists of twelve chapters or cantos. It opens with the words *Sha nagba imûru* (He who saw everything). The number of extant tablets is considerable, but unfortunately they are all very fragmentary and with exception of the eleventh chapter the text is very imperfect and shows as yet

huge lacunæ. Gilgamesh was King of Erech the Walled. When the story begins, the city and its temples are in a ruinous state. Some great calamity has fallen upon them. Erech has been besieged for three years, till Bel and Ishtar interest themselves in its behalf. Gilgamesh has yearned for a companion, and the goddess Arurn makes Ea-bani, the warrior; "covered with hair was all his body and he had tresses like a woman, his hair grew thick as corn; though a man, he lives amongst the beasts of the field". They entice him into the city of Erech by the charms of a woman called Samuhat; he lives there and becomes a fast friend of Gilgamesh. Gilgamesh and Ea-bani set out in quest of adventure, travel through forests, and arrive at the palace of a great queen. Gilgamesh cuts off the head of Humbabe, the Elamite king. Ishtar the goddess falls in love with him and asks him in marriage. But Gilgamesh scornfully reminds her of her treatment of former lovers. Ishtar in anger returns to heaven and revenges herself by sending a divine bull against Gilgamesh and Ea-bani. This animal is overcome and slain to the great joy of the city of Erech. Warning dreams are sent to Gilgamesh and his friend Ea-bani dies, and Gilgamesh sets out on a far journey, to bring his friend back from the underworld. After endless adventures our hero reaches in a ship the waters of death and converses with Pir-napistum, the Babylonian Noe, who tells him the story of the flood, which fills up the eleventh chapter of some 330 lines, referred to above. Pir-napistum gives to Gilgamesh the plant of rejuvenescence but he loses it again on his way back to Erech. In the last chapter Gilgamesh succeeds in calling up the spirit of Ea-bani, who gives a vivid portrayal of life after death "where the worm devoureth those who had sinned in their heart, but where the blessed lying upon a couch, drink pure water". Though weird in the extreme and to our eyes a mixture of the grotesque with the sublime, this epos contains descriptive passages of unmistakable power. A few lines as example: "At the break of dawn in the morning there arose from the foundation of heaven a dark cloud. The Storm god thundered within it and Nebo and Marduk went before it. Then went the heralds over mountain and plain. Uragala dragged the anchors loose, the Annunak raised their torches, with their flashing they lighted the earth. The roar of the Storm god reached to the heavens and everything bright turned into darkness."

(c) The Adapa-Legend, a sort of "Paradise Lost", probably a standard work of Babylonian literature, as it is found not only in the Ninive library, but even among the Amarna tablets in Egypt. It relates how Adapa, the wise man or *Atrachasis*, the purveyor to the sanctuary of Ea, is deceived, through the envy of Ea. Anu, the Supreme God, invites him to Paradise, offers him the food and drink of immortality, but Adapa, mistakenly thinking it poison, refuses, and loses life everlasting. Anu scornfully says: "Take him and bring him back to his earth."

(d) Ishtar's descent into Hades, here and there bearing a surprising resemblance to well-known lines of Dante's Inferno. The goddess of Erech goes:

To the land whence no one ever returneth,
To the house of gloom where dwelleth Irkalla,
To the house which one enters but nevermore leaveth,
On the way where there is no retracing of footsteps,
To the house which one enters, and daylight all ceases.

On an Amarna tablet we find a description ghostly and graphic of a feast, a fight, and a wedding in hell.

(e) Likewise fragments of legendary stories about the earliest Babylonian kings have come down to us. One of the most remarkable is that in which Sargon of Akkad, born of a vestal maiden of high degree, is exposed by his mother in a basket of bulrushes and pitch floating on the waters of the Euphrates; he is found by a water carrier and brought up as a gardener. This story cannot but remind us of Moses' birth.

(2) *The Psalm.*—This species of literature, which formerly seemed almost limited to the Hebrew race, had a luxurious growth on Babylonian soil. These songs to the gods or to some one god are indeed often either weird incantations or dreary litanies; and when after perusal of a good number of them one turns to the Hebrew Psalter, no fair-minded person will deny the almost immeasurable superiority of the latter. On the other hand, naught but unreasoning prejudice would trouble to deny the often touching beauty and nobility of thought in some of these productions of the instinctive piety of a noble race. It is natural moreover that the tone of some Babylonian psalms should strongly remind us of some songs of Israel, where every psalmist boasted that he had as fore-father a Babylonian: Abraham from Ur of the Chaldees. Some of these psalms are written in Sumerian with Semitic Babylonian interlinear translations; others in Semitic Babylonian only. They show all sorts of technicalities in versification, parallelism, alliteration, and rhythm. There are acrostics and even double acrostics, the initial and final syllable of each line being the same. These psalms contain praise and supplication of the great gods, but, what is most remarkable, some of them are penitential psalms, the sinner mourning his sin and begging restoration to favour. Moreover, there are a great number of "lamentations" not over personal but over national calamities; and a Babylonian "prophet" wept over the fall of Nippur many centuries before Jeremias wrote his inspired songs of sorrow over the destruction of Jerusalem. Besides these there are numberless omen tablets, magical recipes for all sorts of ills, and rituals of temple service, but they belong to the history of religion and astrology rather than to that of literature.

(3) *The Historical Narrative.*—The Babylonians seemed to have possessed no *ex professo* historians, who, like a Herodotus, endeavoured to give a connected narrative of the past. We have to gather their history from the royal inscriptions on monuments and palace walls and state-cylinders, in which each sovereign records his great deeds *in perpetuam rei memoriam*. Whereas we fortunately possess an abundance of historical texts of the Assyrian kings, thanks to the discovery of Assurbanipal's library, we are as yet not so fortunate in the case of Babylonian kings; of the early Babylonian city-kings we have a number of shorter inscriptions on steles and boundary stones in true lapidary style and longer historical records in the great cylinder inscriptions of Gudea of Lagash. Whereas we possess considerable historical texts of Hammurabi, we possess but very little of his many successors on the Babylonian throne until the Second Babylonian Empire, when long historical texts tell us the doings of Nabopolassar, Nabuchodonosor, and Nabonidus. They are all of a pompous grandeur that palls a little on a Western mind, and their self-adulation comes strange to us. They are in the style which popular imagination is wont to attribute to the utterances of His Celestial Majesty, the Emperor of China. They invariably begin with a long homage to the gods, giving lengthy lists of deities, protectors of the sovereign and state, and end with imprecations on those who destroy, mutilate, or disregard the inscription. The Babylonian royal inscriptions, as far as at present known, are almost without exception peaceful in tone and matter. Their ever recurring themes are the erection, restoration, or adornment of temples and palaces, and the digging of canals. Even when at war, the Babylonian king thought it bad taste to

refer to it in his monumental proclamations. No doubt the Babylonians must have despised Assyrian inscriptions as bloodthirsty screeds. Because the genius of Babylon was one of culture and peace; therefore, though a world-centre a thousand years before Ninive, it lasted more than a thousand years after Ninive was destroyed.

In addition to literature given after article ASSYRIA: BOS-CAWEN, *The First of Empires* (2d ed., London, 1905); BEZOLD, *Ninive und Babylon* (Leipzig, 1903); PINCHES, *The Old Testament in the Light of the Historical Records and Legends of Assyria and Babylonia* (London, 1903); SAYCE, *The Archæology of the Cuneiform Inscriptions* (London, 1907); JASTROW, *Die Religion Babyloniens und Assyriens* (Giessen, I, 1905; II, 1907); RADAU, *Early Babylonian History* (New York, 1900); LA-GRANGE, *Historical Criticism and O. T.* (London, 1906); JERE-MIAS, *Das Alte Testament in Lichte des alten Orients* (Leipzig, 1906); DELITZSCH, *Babel und Bibel* (Leipzig and Stuttgart, 1905) for a collection of texts with immediate bearing on O. T.; WINCKLER, *Keilinschriftliches Textbuch zum Alten Testament* (Leipzig, 1903).

J. P. ARENDZEN.

Baccanceld (BAPCHILD, near Sittingbourne, Kent), SYNOD OF (694). This meeting was rather a *witena-gemot*, or Parliament, than an ecclesiastical synod, presided over by Wihtred, King of Kent. There were present at its deliberations Brihtwald, Archbishop of Canterbury, Tobias, Bishop of Rochester, besides abbots, abbesses, priests, deacons, and lay lords. The chief enactments are embodied in a charter whose terms secured to the Church forever the donations and privileges bestowed on it by the laity, since "what had once been given to God might never be resumed to man's use". Moreover, on the death of prelates fitting successors were to be appointed with the advice and approval of the archbishop, without any royal intervention; such action would nullify the election; and lay interference was expressly disclaimed as being outside the limits of the laity's rights. The cathedral churches of Canterbury and Rochester were granted in perpetuity immunity from royal requisitions or tribute otherwise than voluntary, and these were never to create precedent; all these privileges being secured under severe spiritual penalties for infringement. The interest and importance of this document rest on the fact that Spelman and others regard it as the most ancient English charter. Its authenticity has been called in question; but though different versions of it exist, there can be little doubt of the general genuineness of the terms common to all, as here summarized.

Cotton. MS. Domit. A., VIII; *Anglo-Saxon Chronicle;* SPEL-MAN, *Conc.*, I; WAKE, *State of the Church;* WILKINS, *Concilia;* HADDAN AND STUBBS, *Eccl. Docts.*

HENRY NORBERT BIRT.

Bacchylus, Bishop of Corinth, whom Eusebius mentions among the prominent second-century churchmen (H. E., V, xxii), is known only by the part he took in sustaining Pope Victor I in the Quartodeciman controversy. When that pope, determining to have the Roman paschal computation universally accepted, wrote to secure the co-operation of influential churches, many synods were held and their presiding bishops wrote to Victor, all, with the exception of the Asiatics, in support of his design. Among them was Bacchylus. According to a ninth-century witness (c. xiii in Hardouin, Acta Concil., V, 1495) he had held a provincial synod, about 195, with eighteen other bishops; and St. Jerome attests that his letter, qualified as *elegantem librum*, was written in the name of the bishops of Achaia (De vir. ill., c. xliv). Eusebius, however, who had perhaps seen the letter, distinguishes it from the synodical epistles by saying that it was written in Bacchylus's own name (loc. cit., xxiii). It might be that Bacchylus held a synod, but in writing gave his letter a personal rather than a collective form. No text of the letter is extant, the sources above referred to containing the only available data.

TILLEMONT, *Mémoires* (Venice, 1732), III, 106–107, 633; HARNACK, *Geschichte der altchrist. Lit.* (Leipzig, 1893), I, 261; VENABLES in *Dict. Christ. Biog.*, I, 236.

JOHN B. PETERSON.

Bachiarius, an early fifth-century writer, known only through two treatises which warrant the conjecture that he was a monk, possibly an abbot, and a Spaniard. The first of these writings, entitled by Gennadius "Liber de Fide" is an apologetical letter to the pope in which Bachiarius, like many another monk coming to Rome from Spain at the time, vindicates his faith against the suspicions of a heterodoxy akin to Priscillianism which were based on his residence in heretical lands. He points out that he left his country because of its errors (whence some conclude that he was exiled) and makes a profession of faith that witnesses to his thorough orthodoxy. The second, entitled "Ad Januariam liber de reparatione lapsi", is an appeal to an abbot, Januarius, to mitigate his severity towards an incontinent monk who though repentant was excluded from the monastery. The letter breathes a beautiful spirit of prudently tempered charity and like the first is replete with scriptural texts and allusions. The theory of Bachiarius's identity with the Spanish bishop Peregrinus seems untenable.

Texts of letters with GALLARD's introduction and GENNADIUS's references in *P. L.*, XX, 1015–62; MURATORI, *Opere* (Arezzo, 1770), XI, 248–275; TILLEMONT, *Mémoires* (Venice, 1732), XVI, 473–476; VENABLES in *Dict. Christ. Biog.*, I, 236; MANGENOT in *Dict. de théol. cath.*, II, 6.

JOHN B. PETERSON.

Bachmann (AMNICOLA), PAUL, Catholic theological controversialist, b. at Chemnitz, Saxony, about 1466. His biographical data are very meagre. Nothing is known of his youth, and very little of his life, before his appearance as an opponent of the Lutheran movement. He entered the Order of Cîteaux at the convent of Altenzelle on the Mulde. He seems to have been employed as professor in the Cistercian house of studies newly founded at Leipzig. Here he won the degree of Master of Arts. He was made procurator and finally, in 1522, Abbot of Altenzelle, in succession to Abbot Martin (1493–1522). At the outbreak of Lutheranism, Bachmann sprang into prominence as one of its most energetic opponents. He was one of that distinguished group of scholars composed of Cochlæus, Emser, Peter Forst, and Augustin von Alveldt, who, under the direction of John of Schleinitz, Bishop of Meissen, fought the movement in Saxony. Bachmann gave special attention to the reformation of monastic life and to a defence of the veneration of the Saints. While he was not wholly successful in preventing defection from the ranks of his own order, he at least hindered the secularization of his own monastery of Altenzelle during his lifetime. His vigorous defence of orthodoxy engaged him in a war of pamphlets with the reformers, in which his own contributions yield little in bitterness of tone and coarseness of language to those of his antagonists. In a contemporaneous satire entitled "Mors et sepultura doctrinæ Lutheranæ" (Strobel, Opuscula quædam satirica et ludicra tempore Reform. scripta, Fasc. 1, 1784, 49 sqq.) written in the style of the "Epistolæ obscurorum virorum", Bachmann is very severely handled. A letter is there ascribed to him over the signature "Humilis frater Paulus Hamnicolus, indignus Abatissa Monstri Cellensis in Misnia". Besides his controversial pamphlets Bachmann's writings comprise hymns and devotional works in prose and verse.

STREBER in *Kirchenlexicon*, I, 1829.

MATTHIAS LEIMKUHLER.

Backer, AUGUSTIN DE, bibliographer, b. at Antwerp, Belgium, 18 July, 1809; d. at Liège, 1 Dec., 1873. He was educated at the Jesuit Colleges of Saint-Nicholas, Beauregard, Saint-Acheul, and Fribourg. In 1835 he was received into the Society of Jesus by the General, Father Roothaan, who sent him to Nivelles, in Belgium, for his novitiate. He taught three years in the College of Namur, and in 1840 began in Louvain his studies for the priesthood. At an early age his vocation as a bibliographer began to manifest itself. While yet a student he made a collection of Elzevirs and planned a work that would give the history of the early printing presses in Europe. In order to acquire the necessary information for this compilation, he visited from 1831 to 1834 the principal libraries in Belgium and twice those of Paris, thus unwittingly preparing himself for his future labours. While at Louvain he came across the incomplete "Bibliotheca Scriptorum Societatis Jesu" published in 1676 by Father Nathaniel Southwell (Bacon), and he resolved to undertake the work that will ever remain the monument of his laborious life, "La bibliothèque des écrivains de la compagnie de Jésus". This colossal work Father de Backer, with the assistance of his brother Aloysius, published in a series of seven quarto volumes in the years 1853–61, and followed this up in 1869–76 with a new edition in three large folios containing the names of 11,000 Jesuit authors. The changes and improvements of this edition are so marked as to make it practically a new work. Besides an introductory sketch of the author, there are recorded under each title the editions, translations, and critiques as well as the works which were published in refutation. Father de Backer died while engaged on the third volume of the new edition, but the work was completed by his brother. Another collaborator in the second edition was Charles Sommervogel, whose own magnificent "Bibliography of the Society of Jesus" in eleven folio volumes was made possible by the gigantic labours of the two de Backers.

VAN TRICHT, *La Bibliothèque des écrivains de la c. de J. et le P. Augustin de Backer* (Louvain, 1876); SOMMERVOGEL, I; HUGHES, *Loyola and the Educational System of the Jesuits* (New York, 1892).

EDWARD P. SPILLANE.

Backx, PETER HUBERT EVERMODE, b. 10 December, 1805, at Tilburg, Holland; d. 28 October, 1868. Ordained priest 17 March, 1832, he may be considered the second founder of the Norbertine Abbey of Tongerloo (Province of Antwerp, Belgium), which was established in 1128, or eight years after the foundation of the Premonstratensian Order by St. Norbert. It had to suffer much from the Protestants during the second half of the sixteenth century, but the fatal blow was struck by the French Republic, which, on 6 December, 1796, expelled the religious, confiscated the abbey, and sold it to the highest bidder. At that time Tongerloo was at the height of its prosperity. After the suppression of the Jesuits, the abbot and community of Tongerloo had made all arrangements for the continuation of the "Acta Sanctorum" and the "Analecta Belgica" of the Bollandists, and four of its canons were co-operating with two of the former Bollandists in this gigantic publication. The catalogue of the Abbey of Tongerloo, made in 1796, gives the names of one hundred and nineteen priests and professed scholastics and of six novices. A large number of these lived in the abbey, others were attached to parishes belonging to it. Some were completing their theological studies in Rome or at the University of Louvain, one was President of St. Norbert's College in Rome, another was president of the college of the same name at Louvain. Under the French Republic and again, after the battle of Waterloo, during the reign of William I, King of the Netherlands, the expelled and dispersed religious were not allowed to form a new community, but better times came with the creation of Belgium as a separate kingdom, in 1830. Only sixteen of the one hundred and twenty-five religious were living at that time and nearly all were well advanced in years. The castle of Halmale near Antwerp was rented, and the first novice, Peter Hubert Backx, received the white habit and with it the name in religion of Evermode. Three more young priests and others who had finished their classical studies followed his example. In 1839 Evermode Backx was chosen superior of the revived community.

At the death of one of the proprietors one-half of the dilapidated Abbey of Tongerloo was bought at a public auction and Abbot Backx led, amidst the rejoicings of the villagers, the young community to Tongerloo, 1 July, 1840. That very afternoon, the Divine Office was resumed with the first Vespers of the Feast of Our Lady's Visitation. On the following day, the venerable Chrysostom Raemakers, who had celebrated the last Mass on the day of the suppression, 6 December, 1796, sang a solemn Mass in one of the rooms improvised as a temporary oratory, the abbey church and other buildings having been pulled down.

Evermode Backx's first work was to repair what was left of the former abbey and to erect new buildings for the growing community. In 1849 the second part of the confiscated abbey was bought and in 1852 the first stone of a large church was solemnly laid by the papal nuncio, so that the abbey began to have the appearance of a large and well-ordained monastery. After a strenuous government of twenty-eight years Evermode Backx died, regretted by his spiritual children. The work was carried on with equal zeal by his successors, the Right Rev. Abbot Chrysostom De Swert (d. 1887) who sent some of his religious to found the priories of Crowle and Spalding, England; the Right Rev. Thomas Heylen, afterwards Bishop of Namur, Belgium, the founder of Corpus Christi Priory, Manchester, and of the Norbertine missions in the Independent State of Congo, Africa; and the Right Rev. Adrian Deckers, formerly Prefect Apostolic in the Congo. The catalogue of the Abbey of Tongerloo for 1907 gives the names of 78 priests, 8 professed scholastics, 4 novices, and 23 lay brothers, or a total of 113 religious, several of whom are engaged in parish work, 14 working in England, and 16 in the Congo missions.

Van Spilbeeck, *De Abdy van Tongerloo* in *Annales Præm.; Notices* from various sources.

MARTIN GEUDENS.

Bacon, David William, first Bishop of Portland, Maine, U. S. A., b. in New York City, 15 Sept., 1813; d. in New York, 5 Nov., 1874. He made his classical studies at the Sulpician College at Montreal and his theological course at Mount St. Mary's Seminary, Emmitsburg, Maryland, and was ordained a priest in Baltimore, 13 December, 1838. Returning to New York he served on the mission at Utica and Ogdensburg, and then in New York City and at Belleville, New Jersey. In 1841 he was sent to establish the third parish in Brooklyn, and for this bought the unfinished building begun in November, 1831, as the "Independent Catholic Church" by the Rev. John Farnan, who had been suspended by Bishop Dubois. It was completed and dedicated, 10 June, 1842, under the patronage of the Assumption of the Blessed Virgin. Here he remained until 1855, when he was named first Bishop of Portland, and consecrated in St. Patrick's Cathedral, New York, on the 22d of April of that year. There were only six priests and eight churches in his diocese, which at that time included the entire State of Maine. His zeal, tact, and energy overcame the many obstacles which Know-Nothing bigotry, the Civil War, and the great fire that destroyed most of the city of Portland on the 4th of July, 1866, put in the way of the progress of the Faith in that section. He had the consolation, at his death, of leaving to his successor the care of 63

churches, 52 priests, 23 parish schools, and a Catholic population of about 80,000. In the summer of 1874 he started for Rome with Archbishop McCloskey, but having fallen ill on ship-board was forced to remain in the Naval Hospital at Brest until the Archbishop returned, on his way home. Bishop Bacon was carried on board the steamer and barely reached New York alive. He was taken to a hospital on shore, where he died a few hours later. The bronze altar of the Sacred Heart, in St. Patrick's Cathedral, New York, was erected by Archbishop McCloskey in thanksgiving because the life of his old friend was spared until he got back to his native land.

U. S. Cath. Hist. Soc. Records and Studies (New York, 1900), II, pts. I–II; Mitchell, *Golden Jubilee of Bishop Loughlin* (Brooklyn, 1891); Mulrenan, *A Brief Historical Sketch of the Catholic Church on Long Island* (New York, 1871); Reuss, *Biog. Cycl. of the Cath. Hierarchy* (Milwaukee, Wis., 1898); Shea, *Hist. Cath. Ch. in U. S.* (New York, 1904).

THOMAS F. MEEHAN.

Bacon, John (Johannes Anglicus, Johannes de Baconthorpe), an English Carmelite and theologian, b. towards the end of the thirteenth century at the place in the county of Norfolk whence he derives his name; d. in London, 1346. He is not to be confounded with Francis de Bachone, the Spanish Carmelite, reader of divinity in Paris from 1362, Procurator General, 1366, doctor, 1369, Provincial of Catalonia (d. circa 1390), *doctor sublimis*. John Bacon, surnamed *doctor resolutus*, entered the order at Snitterley, Norfolk, studied at Oxford and Paris, was bachelor previous to 1321, and master in 1325. From 1329 till 1333 he was Provincial of England; the remainder of his life was consecrated to study. He possessed a penetrating mind, and wrote on all the subjects belonging to the ordinary course of studies. His writings comprised more than one hundred and twenty volumes, but are for the greater part lost. The most celebrated among them were those on the Gospels, especially St. Matthew, on St. Paul, and the commentary on the "Sentences", which was printed in 1510 at Milan, and for a time became the textbook in the Carmelite Order. Bacon follows Averroes in preference to St. Thomas with whom he disagrees on many points. He adopted a system of Realism according to which the universals do not follow but precede the act of the intellect. Truth is materially and causally in the external object, formally in the intellect; in the order of generation and perfection the first subject is the individual substance; although the external object is in itself intelligible, the active intellect is required to render it *ultimately* intelligible; the conformity of the thing thought with the external object constitutes truth. The final cause of all things is God; but although the first object of our knowledge be the Divine essence Bacon does not admit that this knowledge comes to us by the light of our natural reason; it is, in his opinion, a supernatural gift of grace.

Crassous, *Prolusiones theologicæ* (Rome, 1710); Zagaglia, *Cursus theologici* (Parma and Ferrara, 1671–92), 6 vols; Zimmerman, *Monumenta hist. Carm.* (Lérins, 1907), I, 379; Hauréau, *Hist. de la philos. scol.* s. v.; Stöckl, *Gesch. der Phil. des Mittelalters*, II, 1044.

B. ZIMMERMAN.

Bacon, Nathaniel, better known under the assumed name of Southwell, a Jesuit priest and bibliographer, b. in the county of Norfolk, England, in 1598; d. at Rome, 2 Dec., 1676. He received his early training at St. Omers, entered the English College at Rome in 1617, and after his ordination to the priesthood in 1622 was sent to labour on the English mission. Two years later he entered the Jesuit novitiate, but shortly after was transferred to the Roman Province, where he discharged the duties of procurator and minister of the English College. Appointed in 1647 Secretary to the General of the Society of Jesus, Father Vincent Caraffa, he displayed such talent for business that he was retained as Secretary by the four succeeding Generals of the Order. Upon his retirement from this office in 1668 he began the well-known "Bibliotheca Scriptorum Societatis Jesu" in folio, published in Rome in 1676. This compilation was based on an earlier work of Father Ribadeneira, issued in 1602 and brought down to 1641 by Father Alegambe. Father Southwell revised the original works, adding copious notes of his own. Dr. Oliver praises this volume as "a compilation truly admirable for research, accuracy, elegance of language, piety, and charity of sentiment". Father Southwell was also the author of "A Journal of Meditations for Every Day in the Year", published in London in 1669. On the same authority we learn that he was accounted by his religious brethren a model of virtue and sanctity. He died in the professed house of the Gesu, at Rome.

OLIVER, *Collections etc.* (London, 1845), 193; FOLEY, *Records of the Eng. Prov. S. J.*, V, 521; VII, 26; SOMMERVOGEL, *Bibliothèque etc.* VII, 1408; MICHAUD, *Biographie Universelle*, XXXIX.

EDWARD P. SPILLANE.

Bacon, ROGER. See ROGER BACON.

Baconian System of Philosophy, THE, takes its name from its founder, Francis Bacon, Lord Verulam, Viscount St. Albans, statesman and philosopher, b. 22 January, 1561; d. 9 April, 1626. He was the second son of Lord Keeper Bacon and Anne, his second wife, daughter of Sir Anthony Cooke and sister-in-law of Lord Burghley. In his thirteenth year (1573) he entered Trinity College, Cambridge, where he studied under Whitgift. Before he left (1575) he had already acquired a considerable reputation for his ability and learning. It was at Cambridge, as he later confessed to Rawley, that he first had fallen into a dislike of the Aristotelean philosophy—"not for the worthlessness of the author, to whom he would ever ascribe all high attributes, but for the unfruitfulness of the way; being a philosophy, as his Lordship used to say, only strong for disputations and contentions but barren of the production of works for the benefit of the life of man. In which mind he continued until his dying day."

In June, 1576, he was admitted to Gray's Inn, being destined for the profession of law; but shortly afterwards was attached to the French embassy of Sir Amyas Paulet. His father died in 1579, leaving him small provision. He thereupon returned to England to continue his legal studies and was admitted barrister 27 June, 1582. Two years later he was elected to Parliament for the Borough of Melcombe Regis. In the following year he penned his "Letter of Advice to Queen Elizabeth", a document of considerable interest to Catholics, as expressing Bacon's views upon their treatment. Mary Stuart was yet alive, and there were plots and rumours of plots against the queen. There were still many adherents of the old faith; and conformity might be secured either by severe measures or by insidious ones. The young member had Catholics for the queen's enemies. It was impossible, he thought, to satisfy them; dangerous to irritate by too great severity. He recommended changes in the Oath of Supremacy and even went so far as to urge a circumspect toleration of the sectaries because their teaching led to an issue "which your most excellent Majesty is to wish and desire" viz., the diminution and weakening of Papists. His political life and advancement, notwithstanding his intrigue and incessant suit for office, were slow; his extraordinary ambition doomed for years to infruition. He had the misfortune to incur the queen's displeasure by opposing a grant of subsidies in such form as to infringe upon the privileges of the Commons. The patronage he found in Essex led to a friendship as remarkable as its end was dramatic and disastrous.

Until 1607, when James I had reigned nearly four years, he had advanced no further in office than to be given the reversion of the post of Registrar of the Star Chamber. But in 1607, he became Solicitor-General. Then, until his fall, he advanced rapidly. The Attorney-Generalship was given to him in 1613. He became successively a member of the Privy Council (1616), Lord Keeper of the Great Seal (1617), Lord Chancellor (1618). He was raised to the peerage with the title of Baron Verulam (1618) and made Viscount St. Albans (1621). Suddenly he fell. He was accused, as Chancellor, of taking bribes. To this charge he pleaded guilty, was deprived, and declared incapable of holding any office, place, or employment in the State. He was excluded from both Parliament and Court, fined £40,000, and sentenced to imprisonment in the Tower during the king's pleasure. In time, all his sentence was remitted.

His death occurred five years later. On his way to dine at Highgate, he alighted from his carriage, purchased, killed, and stuffed a hen with snow in order to observe the retarding effects of cold upon putrefaction. He caught a chill which set up bronchitis. A week later he died in the house of the Earl of Arundel; and was buried, according to his wish, at St. Alban's in the church of St. Michael.

The philosophy of Lord Bacon is too fragmentary to lend itself to criticism other than discursive, too largely conceived to be brushed aside with a mere line of comment, too full of symbolic expression to be exactly and briefly set down. It is rather of the nature of a method than a system and it is a method that is incomplete. Few attempts at giving a new direction to the pursuit of truth have been more overrated; few the butt of such vigorous criticism. It might be said that Bacon suffered most in it from falling into the very pitfalls that he indicated as dangerous to others. His confidence in his own powers was colossal. Few men could have written as he did in the "Novum Organum": "The die is cast, the book is written, to be read either now or by posterity—I care not which; it may wait a century for a reader, as God has waited 6000 years for an observer." His misconstruction and minimizing of the work of the old philosophers—except, perhaps, Democritus—is as startling as his ignorance of the contemporary science of his day, or as the application he makes of his own principles; for the incipient rules of induction (their use already exemplified in Aristotle's "Analytica Posteriora"), that find their more exact expression in Mill's Canons, should have prevented some, at least, of his cruder scientific views. With all his signalling of the insidious dangers of the *Idola*, he could not altogether rid his understanding of the preoccupations caused by them, even in the presentation of his Inductive Method. These celebrated phantoms of the mind, of which we must be at pains to rid ourselves, are four in number: the *Idola Tribus* (preoccupations common to mankind); the *Idola Specus* (belonging to the individual); the *Idola Fori* (resulting from a confusion of *words* and *things* in the common speech of the market-place); the *Idola Theatri* (consisting of the received dogmata of philosophers that take possession of the mind by reason of a presumed authority). Still, the fact that he pointed them out and laid stress upon the danger is an advance. His lists, too, of facts, his confused congeries of instances, point the way to a scientific examination of Nature. Their contents are to be treated by (1) agreement, (2) disagreement, and (3) comparison. Roughly speaking, this would be tantamount to the use of the Method of Agreement and Difference, taken together with that of Concomitant Variations. What is not brought into sufficient prominence is the extremely useful part played by guesswork and hypotheses in the generalization and grouping of facts and instances; but this is scarcely to be wondered at, since Bacon, though he does allow a grudging value to it, proposed to inaugurate a certain process by which inductions might be readily produced from facts by an almost mechanical or mathematical process.

Interesting to the scholastic philosopher is his treatment of causes—and particularly of the formal cause. There are the usual four causes, the formal and final belonging, in Bacon's scheme, to metaphysical investigation; the efficient and material to physical. The aim of the author of the "Novum Organum" was to banish final causes from the scope of physical science. His limiting of the efficient cause to physical science throws light upon his abrupt separation of philosophy and theology (*vide infra*). With regard to the formal cause of being, our author is peculiarly inconsistent. He uses the term in a succession of different suppositions, so that his true meaning is effectually obscured in the varying uses of the word. But, from a passage in the "De Augmentis", it may be inferred that he treated of what is known to the scholastic as *forma accidentalis*. The "forms" of colour, gravity, density, heat, etc. "of which the essences, upheld by matter, of all creatures do consist", are proposed for investigation —not the "forms" of substances. It will be noted that he makes the essences consist of these "forms" sustained by matter—a view that, with slight modifications, is to be found in several more modern systems.

Bacon's object was avowedly a practical one. Given the inductive knowledge of the "form", we ought to be able to produce the logically consequent quality in matter. He conceived it a possibility to juggle with the "forms" in much the same sense as the alchemist of earlier days hoped to transmute essences. His own positive contributions to the advancement of science were meagre in the extreme. No philosopher goes to his works for guidance, no scientist for information. Indeed, Dr. Whewell says that no scientific discovery has ever been made by Bacon's method. The gaps in his system were never bridged by those promised processes that were to render it complete. But it would be a mark of superficial consideration and historical inaccuracy to label the method that he advanced wholly jejune or useless. As a matter of fact, he called attention to the dangerous neglect of accurate observation that was the reproach of the later scholastics; and he gave an undoubted incentive to the prosecution of positive science. If he did little himself to raise science to the position of dignity it now occupies, he at least indicated the path upon which it should proceed. But in creating the method of induction he abased that of deduction; and without a single general principle as a basis, any philosophy, systematic or mathematical, is open to the charge of inconsequence.

Bacon's position in regard to revelation is well known. Reason can attain no positive knowledge of God. This must come by faith alone. Religion is above reason, but is not opposed by it. On the contrary, it is the office of reason to meet the objections and refute the arguments that are urged against the truths of revelation. Whether Bacon was really a rationalist or a believer has been disputed. As a statesman, he was an Anglican and Erastian. As a philosopher, religion does not come within his purview. But there are passages in his writings that show a decidedly reverent and religious spirit, especially in some of the "Essays".

Lord Bacon's chief works are contained in the following list. The dates given are those of publication. (1) "Advancement of Learning", 1605. (This was expanded and translated into Latin and edited by Rawley as "Opera F. Baronis de Verulamio . . . Tomus primus qui continet de Dignitate et Augmen-

tis Scientiarum libros IX", 1623.) (2) "De Sapientiâ Veterum", 1609 (done into English by Sir A. Gorges, Knight, as "The Wisdom of the Ancients", 1619); (3) "Essays; Religious Meditations (in Latin); Places of perswasion and disswasion; of the Colours of Good and Evil" (a fragment), 1579. In the second edition (1598) the Meditations are in English. In this first English edition there were 10 Essays; in the second (1612) 38; in the third (1625) 58. (4) "Historia Ventorum" (Part III of the "Instauratio Magna"), 1622; (5) "Historia Vitæ et Mortis" (2nd Title of Part III, I. M.), 1623; (6) "New Atlantis" (published by Rawley), 1627; (7) "Novum Organum"; "Distributio Operis"; "Parasceve"; "Catalogues", 1620. (The plan of the whole "Instauratio Magna" is laid down in the preface.) (8) "Sylva Sylvarum" (published by Rawley), 1627. The chief editions of Bacon's works were made by Rawley (1627–57); Tenison (1679); Stephens (1734). "Complete editions" by Blackbourne (1730); Mallet (1740); Birch (1763); Montague (1834); Spedding, Ellis, and Heath (1857–83).

ABBOT, *Bacon and Essex* (London, 1877); DIXON in *British Authors*, vol. CXLIX; *Personal History of Lord Bacon* (Leipzig, 1841); SPEDDING, *An Account of the Life and Times of Francis Bacon* (Boston, 1878); FOWLER, in *English Philosophers;* BACON (London, 1881); NICOL in *Philosophical Classics for English Readers; Francis Bacon* (Edinburgh, London, 1901); DE MAISTRE, *Examen de la Philosophie de Bacon* (Paris, Lyon, 1836); DOHERTY in MANNING, *Essays on Religion and Literature*, 3d Series, *Flaws in the Philosophy of Bacon;* MACAULAY, *Essay on Bacon* (London, 1865–74); WHEWELL, *Philosophy of Discovery* (London, Cambridge, 1860); for Bacon's classification of the sciences, FLINT, *Philosophy as Scientia Scientiarum* (Edinburgh, London, 1904); FISCHER, *Franz Baco von Verulam, Die Realphilosophie und ihr Zeitalter; Franz Baco und seine Nachfolger.*—The British Museum catalogue has some pages devoted to works on the Bacon-Shakespeare controversy.

FRANCIS AVELING.

Bacs, DIOCESE OF. See KALOCZA.

Badajoz, DIOCESE OF (PACENSIS).—The Latin name *Pax*, or *Civitas Pacensis*, was given to this district because it was thought to be the *Pax Julia* or *Pax Augusta* of the Romans. But it is now certain that the *Pax* of the Roman period is the city of Beja, in Portugal, not far from Badajoz, and that the latter name is of Arabic origin. The bishopric was erected in 1225, shortly after it was reconquered from the Moors by King Alfonso IX of Leon. Its first bishop was Don Pedro Perez, appointed by Alfonso X, the Wise, and from that time it has had an uninterrupted succession of bishops. The diocese, which is suffragan to Seville, is bounded on the north by the Dioceses of Coria, Plasencia, and Toledo, on the east by those of Toledo, Ciudad Real, and Cordova, on the south by the Archdiocese of Seville, and on the west by Portugal. It is composed of 136 parishes, divided into 13 vicariates, which in ancient times numbered 18, with approximately half a million souls. The cathedral has a chapter composed of 5 prelates, 13 canons, 16 beneficed clerics (formerly called *medioracioneros*), besides the chaplains and other personnel necessary for the proper carrying out of Divine worship. There is a diocesan seminary, under good instructors, for the education of aspirants to the priesthood, also colleges in the city of Badajoz and in Zafra, conducted by the Regular Priests of the Heart of Mary, and several religious communities in other cities. The Poor Clares have an establishment at Almendrales; the discalced Franciscans, Carmelites, and Sisters of St. Anne at Badajoz, and the Augustinians, Carmelites, and Poor Clares elsewhere, making in all 19 communities of cloistered nuns, besides 3 communities of Sisters of Charity who attend the sick at Badajoz, Zafra, and Frenegal de la Sierra. There are schools for primary and religious instruction in all the parishes.

The diocesan territory of Badajoz comprises almost all of the civil province of the same name, which lies between the meridians 4° 36′ 12″ and 7° 9′ west of

Greenwich, and between 37° 90' and 39° 30' north latitude, with an area of 7,143 square miles. Several rivers, among them the famous Guadiana (the *Flumen Anas* of the ancients), flow through this province, and the Madrid-Caceres-Lisbon railroad traverses it. All of this district is very fertile, and yields all kinds of cereals, wine, and oil, also cork, the manufacture of which is practically the only industry of this section. The climate is hot and unhealthy, intermittent and infectious fevers being very prevalent. This part of Spain was first inhabited by the Vettones and Veturi, descendants of the Celts, and was called Vettonia. When the Romans divided Farther Spain (*Hispania Ulterior*) into various provinces, Badajoz was made a part of the province of Lusitania, whose capital, Mérida (*Emerita Augusta*), became at the same time the metropolitan see. When the Arabs obtained possession of this territory, Mérida was annexed to the Emirate of Cordova, and ceased to be a bishopric. The city of Mérida is now included in the Diocese of Badajoz. The Kings of Leon and Castile reconquered this section and gave to the part which is now Badajoz and Caceres the name of Estremadura (*Extrema Durii*), meaning, the region on the opposite side of the River Douro, which had for a long time been the dividing line between Moors and Christians.

Hernán Cortés, the conqueror of Mexico, was a native of Medellin in the province and Bishopric of Badajoz. Massona, Archbishop of Mérida, and Paul the Deacon (Paulus Diaconus Emeritensis) may also be mentioned among the distinguished natives of this district; of whom the former took part in the Councils of Toledo, and the latter is known as the author of "De vitâ et Miraculis Patrum Emeritensium".

FLOREZ, *España Sagrada*. See also *Histories*, *Year-books*, and *Ecclesiastical Guides of Spain*.

TIRSO LÓPEZ.

Baden, GRAND DUCHY OF, is situated in the southwestern part of the German Empire, bounded by Switzerland, Alsace, the Palatinate, Hesse, Bavaria, and Würtemberg, covering an area of 5,821 square miles. According to the census of 1 December, 1905, the population numbered 2,010,728, including 1,198,511 Catholics, 762,826 Evangelicals, 8,096 Old Catholics, 2,060 Lutherans, 2,823 Reformed, 2,157 of various Evangelical denominations, 7,449 of other Christian beliefs, 25,893 Jews, and 600 others of various religious persuasions.

I. HISTORY. (a) *The Middle Ages.*—The present Grand duchy has been formed from the territories of various ecclesiastical and secular rulers. At the beginning of the Christian Era the Baden of to-day was a part of the so-called tithe lands (*agri decumates*) which were protected by a wall against the barbarian Germans. From this point the Alemanni made repeated incursions into the Roman territory, and after the death of the Emperor Aurelius Probus (282) they took possession of the southern part of the tithe lands. The victories of 496 and 536 made the Franks masters of this region, and Pepin the Short set aside the old form of government by tribal dukedoms in 748, introducing the form of organization of the Frankish Empire. The rise of the Frankish power brought Christianity into the province. The southern part of the country received the Faith about 610 from St. Columbanus and his pupil St. Gall, who were followed a hundred years later by St. Pirminius. St. Trudpert laboured in the Breisgau, and St. Kilian in the north-eastern part of the territory. The valley of the Rhine was evangelized from Mainz. Much of the credit for having converted the land belongs to the many monasteries that were founded in the course of these centuries: Reichenau, Honau near Kehl, St. Trudpert, Ettenheimmünster, Gengenbach, Schwarzach, St. Michael near Heidel-

berg, Petershausen near Constance, and St. Blasien; also monasteries for women, as Säckingen, Waldkirch, Sulzburg, and others.

Under the weak rule of the last Carlovingians and after the extinction of the dynasty, the old form of government by tribal dukedoms again prevailed, and only powerful kings like Otto I, Henry II, and Henry III were able to maintain their authority. The natural allies of the kings against the dukes of the different tribes were the ecclesiastical authorities, the bishops and abbots, who thereby obtained great influence and large possessions. Ecclesiastically the territory of the present Baden was divided into six dioceses: Constance, Speyer, Strasburg, Worms, Mainz, and Würzburg; moreover the Bishops of Bamberg were wealthy landed proprietors, Henry II having bestowed on them Crown-lands in the Ortenau, as well as placing the abbeys of Ettenheimmünster, Gengenbach, and Schuttern under their jurisdiction. The monasteries of Reichenau and St. Blasien, in particular, became possessed of large temporalities. Among secular rulers great prominence was attained by Count Berthold (d. 1078), who claimed descent from the old Allemannian dukes and in 1061 became Duke of Carinthia and Margrave of Verona. In the struggle between the papacy and Emperor Henry IV, Berthold remained faithful to the Church. The youngest of his three sons, Salomon, was Bishop of Constance (1084–1110), and the other two, Berthold II (d. 1111) and Hermann I (d. 1074), were the ancestors of the dukes and margraves of the Zähringen line. The ducal line of descendants received in fief from the Empire a part of Burgundy and central and western Switzerland, with Zürich as capital. Of these rulers Berthold II founded Freiburg in the Breisgau, Berthold IV, Fribourg in Switzerland; and Berthold V, Berne. At the death of Berthold V in 1218 this branch of the family became extinct, and its freehold estates passed on to the margraves of the other branch, whose descendants are still the reigning family of Baden. The first of the line of margraves of this branch was Hermann I, who died a monk in the Abbey of Cluny. Many of his descendants distinguished themselves in the affairs of the Empire, as, for instance, Hermann V (1190–1242), who fought against the Mongols, Rudolf I (1243–88), who was first the enemy and then the friend of Rudolph of Hapsburg; Bernhard I (1372–1431), a generous patron of the monasteries of Gottesaue and Schwarzach; and James I (1431–53), who endowed the collegiate foundation in the city of Baden-Baden. Others, however, lessened the family influence by the repeated partitions of their estates, thus contributing to the territorial subdivisions of what is now Baden.

Among the neighbouring rulers those with the largest landed possessions were the Counts of the Rhine Palatinate (Heidelberg etc.), the Hapsburg dynasty, which in the fourteenth century obtained the whole of the Breisgau, together with the cities of Freiburg, Breisach, Waldkirch, and other places; the Counts of Fürstenberg, whose domains lay chiefly in the region of the Baar (such as the town of Donaueschingen); and the Counts of Wertheim. There were, besides, numerous rulers of smaller secular principalities, knights of the Empire, and free cities. To all these must be added the ecclesiastical rulers, the six bishops, some 160 monasteries, and a few estates held in commendation by Knights of St. John and the German Knights Templars. The intellectual, spiritual, and economic life which flourished at this time on the Upper Rhine was as varied as the territorial divisions of the land. Evidences of the zeal with which the arts and learning were cultivated not only in the monasteries, but also in the cities, are to be found in the many buildings dating from that period, as, for instance, those at Constance, Freiburg, Ueberlingen, etc., in monastic libraries, in the large attendance at the Universities of Heidelberg, and Freiburg, in the intermediate schools, among which the one at Pforzheim won a high reputation, in the diffusion of the art of printing, etc. On account of the undeniable abuses which had crept into ecclesiastical life, many fell under the influence of certain intellectual movements which prepared the way for the Reformation, such as secret religious associations, and the Pseudo-mystics, the Hussites, the Flagellants, and especially Humanism, which was in great favour at the court of the Electors Palatine.

(b) *From the Reformation to the formation of the present State.*—The first impulse to revolutionary religious ideas in Baden came from Luther himself, who in 1518 spent some time in Heidelberg, where he appeared as a public speaker and soon gained adherents. The Reformation first took firm root in the Countship of Wertheim, in Constance (1530), in the Countship of Hanau-Lichtenberg (1545), and in the electoral palatinate (1546). The territories under ecclesiastical rulers and the House of Hapsburg remained true to the Catholic Faith. The progress of the Reformation in the Margravate of Baden was far from being uniform. Margrave Christopher I of Baden (1475–1527) had in 1503 united all the family territory, but the division in 1533 between his two sons Bernhard III and Ernest separated the margravate into two parts which were not re-united until 1771. Bernhard received the Margravate of Baden-Baden, and his brother the Margravate of Baden-Durlach. A part of the population of Baden-Baden had already adopted the new teachings, but at the death of Bernhard III (1536), Duke Albert V of Bavaria, the guardian of Bernhard's son, Philip II, brought the country back to the Catholic Faith. Philip himself (1569–88), who had been educated by the Jesuits at Ingolstadt, was a vigorous opponent of the new teaching.

The Baden-Durlach branch of the family laid claim to Baden-Baden during the reign of Philip's successor, Edward Fortunatus (1588–1600), occupied a part of the country until 1622, and introduced the Reformation. Margrave William (1622–77), however, after many reverses, succeeded with the aid of the Catholic party in the Empire in gaining the undisputed mastery of the margravate. Aided in an especial manner by the Jesuits and Capuchins, for whom he established houses, he brought the Protestant part of the country back to the Catholic Faith. His successor, Louis William (1677–1707), rendered many services to the Church and the Empire in fighting against the Turks (1683) and the French. Louis William, his wife, Augusta Sibylla, as regent for their son Louis George (1707–61), and the last named in his turn notably furthered the interests of the Church of Baden. With the death of Augustus George (1761–71), who by papal dispensation had left the ecclesiastical state, and who founded many religious institutions, the line of Baden-Baden became extinct, and the succession fell to the Baden-Durlach branch. Margrave Ernest (1527–53) of Baden-Durlach had favoured the Reformation, and his son Charles II (1553–77) soon established the Reformation in his domains. After this time the Protestant religion remained dominant in the land of Baden-Durlach and its supremacy was not affected even by the reconciliation to the Church of James III, third son of Charles II, as James's death followed soon upon his conversion (1690). The most noted of the Baden-Durlach rulers were: Frederick V (1622–59), who founded many schools; Frederick VI (1659–77), who distinguished himself by his devotion to the emperor and the Empire; Charles William (1709–38), who in 1715 established the present capital of Karlsruhe, greatly improved the finances and the administration of justice, and zealously promoted the interests of the schools. His grandson, Charles Frederick (1738–1811), during his long reign introduced salutary reforms in all parts of his territory, thus raising his country from the level of a petty principality to the rank of one of the greater central states of the German Empire. The extinction of the Baden-Baden branch greatly increased his possessions, which were still further enlarged by the political changes resulting from the French Revolution. In 1796 Charles Frederick was forced to surrender to France his possessions on the left bank of the Rhine, but was amply compensated by the Imperial Delegates' Enactment (1803). He received the Diocese of Constance, that part of the Rhine Palatinate lying on the right bank of the river, including the cities of Heidelberg, Mannheim, etc., parts of the Dioceses of Strasburg and Speyer, eleven religious houses and abbeys, and seven cities of the empire. By the Peace of Pressburg (1805), and the accession of Baden to the Confederation of the Rhine (1806), Baden was still further enlarged by the former possessions of Austria in the Breisgau, the city of Constance, and other territories, whereby substantially the present boundaries were established. On 13 August, 1806, Baden was proclaimed a Grand duchy. The enforced participation of the duchy in the campaigns of Napoleon resulted in heavy loss of life and property.

(c) *Recent History.*—In 1818 Grand Duke Charles (1811–18), the successor of Charles Frederick, gave the country a fairly liberal constitution. The first Landtag, however, came into conflict with the government of Grand Duke Louis (1818–30), who had been trained in the ideas of absolutism, and was able at times to rule almost despotically. Despite the introduction of many timely reforms during the reign of Grand Duke Leopold (1830–52), there were often bitter contentions between the Government and the representatives of the people. In the course of these difficulties, the opponents of the Government became constantly more inflamed until a leading party of opposition was formed, which, influenced by the prevailing political tendencies, gave evidence of a strong inclination towards radical principles. Radicalism obtained a strong footing not only in the Landtag, but also throughout the country. The revolutionary movement of 1848, which began in France, found, therefore, in Baden a most favourable soil. Although the Government granted many of the demands of the people for more liberal administration, outbreaks occurred. In the beginning these were suppressed, but a mutiny of the troops in Rastatt and Karlsruhe brought victory to the Revolutionists. In May, 1849, the insurgents took possession of Karlsruhe, proclaimed a republic, and established a provisional government. It was only through the aid of Prussia and the German Confederation that the revolution in Baden was repressed, and the Grand duke could re-establish his authority. Severe punishment was meted out to the guilty, especially to the mutinous soldiers.

II. Ecclesiastical Conflicts.—During the reign of Grand Duke Louis II (1852–56), whose brother Frederick held the regency until 1856, when he himself succeeded to the title, the Government and the representatives of the Catholic Church, who had been at odds for a long time, came into open conflict. The revolutions of the Napoleonic period had shaken the organization of the Church in Germany to its very foundations. In the modern Grand duchy of Baden, as it existed at the beginning of the nineteenth century, two-thirds of the population professed the Catholic religion. They constituted 728 parishes divided among six different dioceses (Constance, Strasburg, Speyer, Worms, Mainz, and Würzburg). A reconstruction of ecclesiastical affairs was manifestly necessary and was made, so far as the State was concerned, by the organization decrees of 1803 and the constitutional decrees of 1807, regulating the position of the State with regard to the Church. Although the first of these decrees guaranteed to Catholics a continuance of their diocesan system, the free exercise of their religion, and the possession and use of church property, shortly after their promulgation a large number of monasteries and charitable institutions were entirely abolished, others confiscated, and still others converted into secular educational institutions. In place of being organized into dioceses as formerly, Catholics were placed under two vicariates (Bruchsal and Constance). A special board was appointed for the administration of the temporal affairs of the Church, first known as the Catholic *Kirchensektion* (Church Section), and later as the Catholic *Oberkirchenrat* (Supreme Ecclesiastical Council). Despite the personal good will of Grand Duke Charles Frederick, the spirit of these decrees was unfavourable to the Catholic Church; the rights of the State were unduly extended, to the prejudice of the Church. Worse than the ordinances themselves was the way in which they were put into execution by the Liberal officials of Old Baden, who viewed the Catholic Church with open hostility. The unjust treatment of Catholics in the new Grand duchy and the indignities put upon them were so pronounced that even Napoleon, as Protector of the Confederation of the Rhine, in two notes to the Government of Baden (February and March, 1810) protested against it. Unfortunately a large part of the Catholic clergy, who had either been reared in the tenets of Josephinism, or had fallen into the religious indifferentism of the times, failed to rally to the necessary defence of the rights of the Church. Even the highest ecclesiastical dignitaries of the land, as, for example, Vicar-General Wessenberg, favoured the tenets of Febronianism and warmly encouraged the project of a German National Church independent of Rome. This state of affairs prolonged for years the negotiations which had been begun with the Holy See for the reorganization of the Church in Baden. Finally the Bull "Provida solersque" (16 August, 1821) established the province of the Upper Rhine (*Oberrheinische Kirchenprovinz*), defined the boundaries of the five dioceses therein comprised (Freiburg, Fulda, Limburg, Mainz, and Rottenburg), and assigned Freiburg as the seat of the metropolitan. In Baden, by the order of the Grand duke, the candidate for the archiepiscopal see was elected by free vote of the assembled deans (1822), but their choice of Wanker, a professor of theology in Freiburg, was condemned by the pope as canonically invalid. It was only after lengthy negotiations that an agreement was reached; and on 11 April, 1827, Leo XII promulgated the Bull of erection "Ad Dominici gregis custodiam"; on 16 October, 1827, the deed of foundation was signed; and on 21 October the first archbishop, Bernhard Boll, was consecrated and installed.

Nevertheless a satisfactory adjustment of affairs had not yet been found. The deed of foundation contained many provisions contrary to the spirit of the papal Bull. In marked contrast to the agreement made with Rome was the church law passed by the Government 30 January, 1830. True, it ensures to Catholics the free profession of faith and public exercise of religion, but, on the other hand, to the State is given an undue amount of power over the Church; all orders and enactments of any importance proceeding from spiritual authorities must, according to this law, be submitted to the approval of the civil powers; it requires that even decrees and dispensations of a general nature issued by the Church, although concerning matters purely spiritual, must be first inspected by the public authorities. It subjects papal Bulls, Briefs, and dispensations to the *placet* of the sovereign, does away with the canonical court of appeal, grants to clergy and laity, by a usurpation

of spiritual authority, recourse to the civil courts, instead of the higher ecclesiastical courts, etc. The pope as well as the archbishop entered a protest against the provisions of this law, so permeated with the spirit of a national church, but without success. Although the first archbishops, Bernhard Boll (1827–36) and his successor, Ignaz Demeter (1836–42), acceded to the wishes of the Government as far as their position as Catholic prelates permitted, all their remonstrances against the interference of the State and their appeals for a more liberal treatment of the Church were useless. On the contrary, the Government openly favoured movements of a rationalistic and irreligious nature, even on the part of professors of theology in the University of Freiburg; it allowed the just demands of the archbishop for adequate disciplinary powers to pass unnoticed, gave protection to unworthy clerics and those who had been insubordinate to their ecclesiastical superiors, almost entirely excluded the co-operation of the Church in the management of Catholic schools and in the administration of Catholic church property, permitted insults to be levelled against the Church by the Radicals in the Landtag, favoured Rongeanism, etc. In spite of this unjust treatment, however, when, in 1848, the flames of the revolution broke out, the Archbishop, Hermann von Vicari (1842–68), and the majority of the Catholic clergy remained loyal to the rightful sovereign and refused to take the oath required by the revolutionary regime. In consideration of this attitude, the Government, after the victory over the revolutionary forces, seemed disposed to change its policy; it permitted the Jesuits to hold missions among the people and allowed the archbishop greater freedom in the administration of church discipline. The change, however, was not of long duration; soon the old system of state guardianship was again in force.

The four suffragan bishops of the province of the Upper Rhine also came into conflict with their respective governments in securing freedom for the Catholic Church. To obtain unity of action Archbishop Vicari, in compliance with the regulations of the plenary council of the German Catholic episcopate held at Würzburg (1848) summoned his suffragans to Freiburg in the spring of 1851. In a memorial addressed to their respective sovereigns, they demanded the privilege of training their priests and appointing them without outside interference, the free exercise of ecclesiastical discipline among priests and laymen, and the privilege of conducting Catholic schools, of establishing religious societies and associations, and of administering church property without hindrance. Having waited in vain for a reply from the Government, the bishops addressed a reminder to the authorities (February, 1852), renewing the demand for the abolition of the state supremacy. Not until 5 March, 1853, did they receive a decision; this contained trivial concessions, but was adverse on the principal points. The old system of state tutelage was to remain unconditionally in force. Thereupon the five bishops reconvened (April, 1853) in Freiburg and embodied their demands in a second memorial dated 18 June, setting forth the inadequacy of the concessions granted 5 March, and reserving to themselves the right of taking further measures. While four of the bishops received from their respective authorities more or less far-reaching concessions, a bitter struggle was precipitated in Baden.

Meanwhile, an occurrence in Baden had increased the estrangement to an open rupture between the civil authorities and the archbishop. After the death of Grand Duke Leopold (24 April, 1852), the Government, i. e. the *Oberkirchenrat*, which in 1845 had taken the place of the *Kirchensektion*, ordered the archbishop to have services held for the deceased sovereign. In conformity with the laws of the Church, the archbishop prohibited the celebration of requiem Masses for Protestant princes and ordered other appropriate services instead. The authorities, however, persisted in their demand, declared the services ordered by the archbishop inadequate, and attempted to induce pastors to celebrate requiem Masses in defiance of the archiepiscopal mandate. Only about sixty out of the 800 priests complied, whereupon the archbishop decreed that the clergy who had disregarded his command should, in expiation, attend certain exercises of five days conducted by the Jesuit Father Roh, at the theological seminary of St. Peter. Although the civil authorities promised their protection to those priests who should resist this sentence, the clergy to a man obeyed the order of the archbishop, ensuring him a victory so complete as to give him the power of resistance in further conflicts.

In response to the second memorial from the bishops of the province of the Upper Rhine, the representatives of the State of Baden refused to make a single concession to the Catholic Church. The archbishop then informed the Government that he would take steps to secure the rights that were his, but were unjustly withheld by the civil authorities. He held competitive examinations for parish appointments and for admittance into the theological seminary, without the presence of a government commissioner; he filled parishes to which the Government could not establish a canonical right of patronage, demanded from the Oberkirchenrat an administration of church property strictly in accordance with canon law, threatening excommunication in case of disobedience. Thereupon the Government placed the official actions of the archbishop under police surveillance, banished the Jesuits from Freiburg, and threatened the clergy who submitted to the Church with the loss of their incomes, and with civil punishment. Two priests of Karlsruhe and Freiburg, who had proclaimed the sentence of excommunication pronounced upon the Oberkirchenrat by the archbishop, were actually placed under arrest. On still more unwarrantable interference by the Government, the archbishop issued a circular letter to be read from the pulpits, ordering an independent administration of ecclesiastical institutions without regard for civil mandates, and prohibiting the clergy from having any connexion with state officials. The Government, seeing in this enactment an instigation against civil authority, forbade its promulgation in the churches and attempted to seize all copies of the letter, in some cases succeeding by force. A judicial inquiry was instituted against the archbishop (18 May, 1854), charging him with disturbing and endangering the public peace. On 22 May he was placed under arrest, and confined to his room under a guard of gendarmes until 31 May. At the command of the archbishop the diocesan court continued to transact all business, and sent a dispatch to Rome asking the pope to make provisions for the administration of the diocese. All churches were to be draped in mourning, church bells were silent, altars were stripped of their adornments, and everywhere the faithful assembled for public prayer. The pope, in a note dated 8 June, addressed to the civil authorities of Baden, took the archbishop under his protection. The Government then proposed to enter into negotiations with the Holy See, and a peaceful arrangement was made, which created a tolerable *modus vivendi*. The proceedings against the archbishop and clergy were stopped, and gradually the way was opened for amicable relations between the civil authorities and the archbishop.

The lengthy negotiations with Rome were brought to a close by the signing of the Concordat of 8 June, 1859, which went far towards meeting the just claims of the Church and accorded practically all the demands of the archbishop, in particular the right of appointment to parishes, the supervision of religious instruction, participation in the management of church property, the right of decision in questions concerning marriage, etc. Thereupon the Liberals and Democrats rose in opposition to the Concordat; everywhere meetings of protest were held, resulting in 1861 in the dismissal of the Conservative and the formation of a Liberal ministry. The latter, on 29 October, without consulting the Holy See, arbitrarily declared the Concordat null and void and substituted a law quite inimical to the Church, which received the approbation of the Landtag. On 20 November, 1861, the Government and the archbishop came to an agreement concerning the filling of benefices and the administration of church property.

After a short respite, new conflicts arose between the two authorities with reference to the school system (1864). The Government, now entirely under the control of the Liberals, proposed a bill for a school law which almost entirely nullified the influence of the Church on education, conceding to the Church only the supervision of religious instruction. Although Catholic clergy exerted every effort to bring about the failure of this scheme, and the archbishop in a pastoral letter opposed it, the bill in a somewhat aggravated form became a law, and the opposition of the Catholic population expressed in numerous mass-meetings and addresses to the duke was completely disregarded. The Liberals, who were in the majority in the Landtag, and had control of the Government, hesitated at nothing to make still more practically effective their principles of hostility to the Church. In 1867 the Government instituted state examinations for theological students, to be held before a civil commissioner on the completion of the university course. The Curia protested, and forbade the theological students to submit to this examination. As a result the clergy in the parishes subject to the appointment of the Grand duke received, instead of their stipends and appointments as pastors, only those of parish administrators. After the death of the archbishop (15 April, 1868), the Government, by refusing to consider seven out of eight candidates, made the choice of an archbishop practically impossible, and the see remained vacant for eighteen years. In 1869 civil marriage was made obligatory. In 1870 all Catholic institutions not purely ecclesiastical, but devoted to education or to charity, were secularized, withdrawn from the control of the Church, and large endowments left for Catholic purposes were thus alienated from their appointed use. In 1872 the members of religious orders and congregations were forbidden to give elementary instruction, to assist in the work of the ministry, or to conduct missions. In 1873 the Old Catholics were placed on an equal footing with the Catholic Church; several Catholic churches were turned over to them, and their Bishop Reinkens was recognized by the Government as a Catholic national bishop (*Landesbischof*). In 1874 admission to any ecclesiastical office was made to depend on proof of a general scientific training, meaning thereby a three years' course at a German university, excluding all Jesuit institutions. The archiepiscopal seminaries and boarding schools for boys were closed. In 1875 undenominational schools were introduced and made obligatory, the Catholic corporation schools were made unsectarian, and several monastic educational institutions were suppressed. Not until after the retirement of the Liberal minister, Jolly, the soul of the anti-Catholic legislation, i. e. since 1876, were measures taken for the re-establishment of peace with the Catholic Church. In 1880 state examinations for theological students were dispensed with;

in 1882 the archiepiscopal see was filled by the appointment of Johann Baptist Orbin, who ruled until 1886; his successors were Johann Christian Roos, until 1896; George Ignaz Komp, who died as archbishop elect on the journey to his see (1896), and Thomas Nörber from 1896. In 1888 the boarding schools for boys and the seminaries were reopened, and members of religious orders were once more allowed to preach.

Meanwhile the political development of Baden had been undisturbed. In 1866, it is true, the Grand duke had been forced against his will to fight on the side of Austria and the German Confederation against Prussia; but as early as 28 July he arranged a truce and proclaimed his withdrawal from the German Confederation. On 17 August he concluded peace, and an offensive and defensive alliance with Prussia. The military forces of Baden were organized on Prussian lines, and when, in 1870, Baden openly took sides with Prussia, they fought with distinction in many battles. On 25 November Baden entered the North German Confederation, which was strengthened by the accession of the other South German States to the new German Empire (1871). The internal administration was now conducted along Liberal lines. The Liberal majority of the Chamber was not disturbed until 1893. In 1904 a more impartial election law was introduced. The Government, however, still holds to its Liberal tendencies, and refuses the just demands of Catholics for the admission of religious orders of men. Unfriendliness towards the Catholic Church seems again to be gaining ground, as is shown by ordinances requiring an investigation among the whole body of the Catholic clergy on account of alleged abuses of electoral influence and other charges.

III. STATE AND CHURCH IN BADEN.—The relations between the Catholic Church and the Government are not entirely satisfactory, as is evident from the historical account, the State often exercising an excessive control. According to the legislation now in force, the Roman Catholic Church in Baden possesses the right of a public corporation, with the privilege of public worship and the formation of religious societies. The Church conducts its affairs freely and independently. The clergy are not restricted in their communication with ecclesiastical superiors. The highest spiritual authority of Catholic Baden is the Archbishop of Freiburg, who is also Metropolitan of the province of the Upper Rhine; he is a member of the First Chamber of Baden, ranks immediately after the ministers of state, and enjoys the title of Excellency. Ecclesiastical offices are filled by the church authorities, but are granted only to those who are citizens of Baden and can give proof of having had a general scientific training. No exemption from a regular three years' course at a German university is granted to anyone who has completed the same course at a Jesuit institution. Every priest on entering the work of the ministry in Baden must take the constitutional oath. The public exercise of church functions is permitted to priests coming from outside of Baden only under certain conditions. Without government authorization no religious order may be brought into Baden, nor may a new foundation be made by an order already established. Moreover, this authorization is subject to revocation. The holding of missions and the work of the ministry by members of religious orders are in general forbidden, unless in case of extreme necessity. By legislation of the German Empire, the obligation of a civil marriage ceremony was introduced, the duty of military service on the part of Catholic theological students abolished, and the Society of Jesus and what the laws call "cognate" orders and congregations excluded from the German Empire.

Church Property.—The property of the archiepiscopal board, the cathedral chapter, the metropolitan church, and the seminary, as well as the funds under the immediate control of the archbishop or the chapter, are managed by the archbishop and the chapter without interference; that under rural chapters by the chapters themselves under the supervision of the ordinary; local property, i. e. the definite property of a separate parish, is administered by a parish council under the presidency of the clergy, the members being chosen for a period of six years from the Catholics of the parish. The property of the ecclesiastical institutions of a district is managed by a commission, half the members being chosen by the Government, and half by the archbishop from the Catholics of the district. The intercalary fund (that is to say, the fiscal department for the collection, management, and lawful expenditure of the incomes of vacant benefices in the Grand Duchy of Baden) is administered by a council known as the Catholic *Oberstiftungsrat*, consisting of a president and six members, under the joint supervision of the archbishop and the Government. The members are Catholics, half being appointed by the Government, and half by the archbishop. All must meet the approval of both. The president must also be selected and named with the consent of both. The Oberstiftungsrat also supervises the administration of the local and diocesan institutions and of all benefices, occupied or vacant.

Local associations of the members belonging to the churches recognized in Baden have, as parishes, the rights of public corporations. For the defrayal of expenses incident to public worship, as, for example, the maintenance and repair of parish churches and rectories, the purchase and care of the necessary church furniture, and the salaries of the under employés of the church, the parish can assess certain taxes on its members. There is, in addition, a general church assessment for the common needs of the Catholic Church of Baden, e. g. the expenses of the highest ecclesiastical authorities, the establishment of new church offices, etc. The execution of parochial rights and duties is vested in the parish meeting; in those parishes numbering eighty or more members, the parish is represented by an elective council. The resolution of the parish meeting or parochial council determining the church assessment is subject to the approval of the State. To become legally effective, any change in the formation of a parish, by reorganization, dissolution, partition, or reunion, needs the sanction of the civil authorities. The administration of ecclesiastical foundations (*Stiftungen*) is also entirely subject to state supervision. All gifts and bequests in favour of existing foundations, likewise the establishment of new and independent ones, require the approbation of the State. Churches, chapels, hospitals, and other public foundations devoted to the care of the poor and orphans, and to similar charitable purposes, are exempt from the house tax. Homes for the care of the sick and the support of the poor, as well as public educational institutions, are exempt from the income tax on the capital invested. The taxable values of rectories are exempt from any parish assessment.

Church and School.—The public educational system is under the direction of the State, the highest authority being the *Oberschulrat* (Supreme Educational Council), which is directly subject to the Minister of the Interior. The highest ecclesiastical superiors may designate a representative to attend the deliberations of the Oberschulrat whenever there is question of religious instruction and its place in the plan of studies. In the public schools instruction is given simultaneously to all children of school age, regardless of creed, with the exception of religious instruction. The local supervision over the public schools, as well as the supervision of all local school funds, including those of each religious confession, is entrusted to the town council; at the same time each of the creeds represented in the community is represented by its pastor. In the appointment of teachers to public schools all possible respect is had for the religious belief of the children; in schools attended by children of only one creed the teachers are to be of that creed. Religious instruction is provided and supervised by the respective churches and congregations. They may be assisted in this by teachers. The general plan of religious instruction is laid out by the higher spiritual authorities and supervised by their deputies. The establishment of private educational institutions is permitted, but only under certain conditions; these establishments are under state supervision; from time to time the school authorities visit them and hold examinations. Ecclesiastical corporations and institutions may found educational establishments only on the passage of a special law. Members of religious orders or of religious congregations that resemble orders are forbidden to teach in any educational institution in the Grand Duchy of Baden. The Government may grant exemption to individuals, but such exemption is revocable at will. Churches are authorized to maintain institutions for the theological and practical training of young men for the priesthood, and to conduct boarding houses (*Konvikte*) for students who frequent the gymnasia or the university with the intention of preparing themselves for the ecclesiastical state.

IV. Statistics.—Baden, with the Hohenzollern territories belonging to Prussia, forms the Archdiocese of Freiburg. The strong intermixture of creeds throughout Baden is a result of the earlier territorial dismemberment described above. According to the census of 1905, in 34 of the 53 judicial districts, the Catholics are in the majority. They are especially strong in the north-east (the Tauber valley), the farther Odenwald, and the southern half of Baden. Even here, however, predominantly Protestant districts are to be found, e. g. Kehl, Lahr, Emmendingen, the Margravate of Sulzburg as far as Basle, and the valley of the Wiese as far up as Lörrach; in addition to the districts just mentioned, the country on both sides of the Neckar and the Lower Rhine are overwhelmingly Protestant. Ecclesiastically, Baden is divided into 3 city chapters and 36 rural chapters, with about 814 parishes and curacies, 114 chaplaincies, and 259 assistants. The cathedral parish of Freiburg and the parish of St. Peter are exempted from the above-mentioned chapter system. Besides this, there are 3 military and 3 institutional chaplaincies. At the beginning of 1907 Baden had 1,260 Catholic priests, i. e. pastors, assistants, and chaplains. Of the 1187 ecclesiastical benefices of Baden, 295 are in the gift of the Grand duke as patron; 264 are left to the free collation of the archbishop; 145 are filled through presentations by noblemen, landowners, and others; 168 are disposed of by the so-called *terna*, i. e. the archbishop proposes to the Grand duke three candidates for a benefice, and the latter selects one for canonical institution. In the case of 9 benefices, the right of presentation is alternate; in 47 cases it is disputed or unknown. The salary of pastors and beneficed clergy is derived from the temporalities of the living; the income of poorly equipped parishes is supplemented by an annual state appropriation which sometimes amounts to $50,000.

Orders and Congregations.—Male orders and congregations are prohibited from making any foundations in the Grand Duchy of Baden. In proportion to the population, the number of orders and congregations of women is small, and new foundations are vigorously opposed by the Government. The following teaching orders are represented: the Sisters of the Holy Sepulchre in Baden-Baden, the Dominican Sisters in Constance, Cistercian Sisters in Lichtenthal near Baden-Baden, in Offenburg the Choir Sisters of St. Augustine from the congregation of Notre Dame (with a branch in Rheinberg), the Ursulines in Villingen (with a branch in Breisach); there are in all 5 orders for the education of girls. The following congregations for the care of the sick are represented in Baden: the Sisters of St. Vincent de Paul, with mother-house at Freiburg, the Sisters of St. Francis, with mother-house at Gengenbach, the Sisters of the Holy Cross from Ingenbohl in Switzerland, with mother-house at Hegne, near Constance. In addition there are in Baden the Vincentian Sisters from the mother-house at Strasburg, Sisters of the Most Holy Saviour (the so-called Niederbronn Sisters), from the. mother-house at Oberbronn, Alsace, Franciscan Sisters from the mother-house at Mallersdorf, Bavaria, Josephite Sisters from St. Marx (Alsace), also Sisters of the Holy Cross from the mother-house at Strasburg.

Education.—As explained above, the school system is entirely under the direction of the State; consequently there are but few purely Catholic educational institutions. For the training of the Catholic clergy there are the archiepiscopal seminary (*Priesterseminar*) at St. Peter, the home (*Konvikt*) for theological students at Freiburg, and 4 gymnasial boarding schools at Constance, Freiburg, Rastatt, and Tauberbischofsheim. At the state university (Freiburg) there is a faculty of Catholic theology numbering 11 professors; the number of theological students during the summer semester of 1907 was 226. The 62 Government intermediate schools of Baden (17 classical gymnasia, 3 "real", 4 preparatory, 7 higher gymnasia; 23 *Realschulen*, 8 high schools) recorded an attendance in 1905 of 5,157 Catholic students. In 17 of the Government intermediate schools religious instruction is given by 26 specially appointed priests (*Religionslehrer*); in the others religious instruction is cared for by the local clergy. Of the 11 private intermediate schools for boys, the Institute and School of Monsignor Lender in Sasbach (*Progymnasium* and *Realschule*) is Catholic in character; in 1905 it had 483 Catholic students, and 8 priests as religious instructors. The 7 government high schools for girls had in 1905 an attendance of 964 Catholic students. Of the 33 private intermediate schools for girls, attended by 1,437 Catholic girls, 5 are distinctly Catholic in character, and have an attendance of 1,132. The Catholic periodicals now published in Baden number 25.

Charitable Institutions.—In Baden there are 254 institutions for the care of the sick, with 13,800 beds; about 100 of these hospitals, infirmaries, etc. are directed, or are actually served, by Catholic orders and congregations. The Diocese of Freiburg contains 3 orphanages (Riegel, Gurtweil, and Walldürn); in the village of Herthen there is a large institution for the care of imbeciles, with about 400 inmates, under the direction of the Sisters of the Holy Cross; in Heitersheim there is a large institution for the reclamation of girls, directed by a Catholic sisterhood. The Baden non-sectarian Red Cross Society, to which many Catholics belong, has 34 relief-centres for men, with about 5,500 members, and 333 unions for women, with 57,600 members; the association maintains 75 stations with about 470 employés. There are in Baden 13 Catholic homes for servant girls.

Catholic Societies.—Concerning these societies there are no adequate statistics. We may mention, however, the People's Union (*Volksverein*) for Catholic Germany, with 27,100 members, Catholic workingmen's unions (150), Catholic journeymen's unions (53), apprentices' unions and clubs for young men (35), and St. Joseph's unions (2). Freiburg is the centre of the associated charities (*Charitasverband*) of Catholic Germany. The chief religious societies and confraternities are: the Archconfraternity of the Most Holy Sacrament of the Altar, the Most Pure Heart of Mary, and of Christian Mothers, the League of Prayer for Germany, the Association of the Holy Family, the Association of the Holy Childhood of Jesus, the Boniface Society, the Ludwig Mission Society, St. Michael's Society, the Societies of St. Vincent de Paul for men and women, and others.

The most important Catholic church edifices are the cathedrals of Freiburg and Constance, the churches of Ueberlingen and Breisach, and those of Baden-Baden, Salem, St. Blasien, Reichenau, Gengenbach, Bronnbach, Schwarzach, Ladenburg, Neustadt, Karlsruhe.

A complete bibliography is to be found in KIENITZ AND WAGNER, *Badische Bibliothek* (Karlsruhe, 1897 and 1900). The more important works, especially those treating of ecclesiastical history, are: SCHÖPFLIN, *Historia Zaringo-Badensis* (7 vols., Karlsruhe, 1763–66); DÜMGE, *Regesta Badensia* (Karlsruhe, 1836); MONE, *Quellensammlung der badischen Landesgesch.* (4 vols., Karlsruhe, 1836); PREUSCHEN, *Badische Geschichte* (Karlsruhe, 1842); MONE, *Die katholischen Zustände in Baden* (Ratisbon, 1841 and 1843); BADER, *Die katholische Kirche in Baden* (Freiburg, 1860); LONGNER, *Beiträge zur Geschichte der oberrheinischen Kirchenprovinz* (Tübingen, 1863); *Offizielle Aktenstücke über die Kirchen und Schulfrage in Baden* (7 numbers, Freiburg, 1864–75); VIERORDT, *Badische Geschichte bis zum Ende des Mittelalters* (Tübingen, 1865); BRÜCK, *Die oberrheinische Kirchenprovinz* (Mainz, 1868); SPOHN, *Badisches Staatskirchenrecht* (Karlsruhe, 1868); FRIEDBERG, *Der Staat und die katholische Kirche im Grossherzogtum Baden* (2d ed., Leipzig, 1874); KÖRBER, *Die Ausbreitung des Christentums im südlichen Baden* (Heidelberg, 1878); *Das Grossherzogtum Baden* (Karlsruhe, 1885); BAUMSTARK, *Die kirchenpolitischen Gesetze und Verordnungen für die römisch-katholische Kirche im Grossherzogtum Baden* (Karlsruhe, 1888); WEECH, *Badische Geschichte* (Karlsruhe, 1890); HEINER, *Gesetze die katholische Kirche (in Baden) betreffend* (Freiburg, 1890); MAAS, *Geschichte der katholischen Kirche im Grossherzogtum Baden* (Freiburg, 1891); HEINER, *Die kirchlichen Erlasse, Verordnungen und Bekanntmachungen der Erzdiözese Freiburg* (2d ed., Freiburg, 1898); MÜLLER, *Badische Landtagsgesch.* (Berlin, 1899–1902), I–IV; FESTER AND WITTE, *Regesten der Markgrafen von Baden und Hachberg* (2 vols., Innsbruck, 1900); KRIEGER, *Topographisches Wörterbuch des Grossherzogtums Baden* (2d ed., 2 vols., Heidelberg, 1903–05); GÖNNER AND SESTER, *Das Kirchenpatronatsrecht im Grossherzogtum Baden* (Stuttgart, 1904); *Zeitschrift für Geschichte des Oberrheins* (Karlsruhe, 1850–85), I–XXXIX; *Id.*, new series (Freiburg, 1886–92, Karlsruhe, 1893–1904, Heidelberg, 1902, sqq.), I–XXII.

The most important historical periodicals are: *Zeitschrift für Geschichte des Oberrheins* (Karlsruhe since 1850); *Freiburger Diözesanarchiv* (Freiburg, since 1865); ALEMANNIA (Bonn, 1873 sqq.; since 1900 in Freiburg).

JOSEPH LINS.

Badia, TOMMASO, Cardinal, author, papal legate, b. at Modena, 1483; d. at Rome, 6 September, 1547. He entered the Dominican Order in his native city, soon excelled all his brethren in learning, and taught theology successively at Ferrara, Venice, and Rome. When Sylvester de Prierias was sent on a mission to the princes of Italy, Badia was chosen to fill, temporarily, the office of Master of the Sacred Palace, to which he succeeded permanently, probably in 1523. He was put on the commission which drew up the list of abuses to be reformed in the Council of Trent. He took part in the Diet of Worms (1540), not only as disputant, but also as theologian of Cardinal Contarini. On his return to Italy Paul III created him cardinal, and though selected as one of the legates to preside at Trent he was retained at Rome to examine the doctrinal and disciplinary memoranda drawn up in the sessions of the council. It was on his favourable recommendation and approval of its constitutions that Paul III confirmed the Society of Jesus. At his own desire he was buried in the Minerva beside Cardinal Cajetan. He is the author of several philosophical treatises, as well as works on Divine Providence, the immortality of the soul and several treatises against Luther, none of which have been published.

QUÉTIF AND ECHARD, SS. O. P., II, 132; TOURON, *Hommes illust.*, IV, 116–121; HEFELE–HERGENRÖTHER, *Conciliengesch.*, IX, 944; DITTRICH, *Gasparo Contarini* (Braunsberg, 1885); L. PASTOR, *Die Correspondenz des Kardinals Contarini* in *Hist. Jahrbuch*, I, 321–392; 473–500, *passim.*

THOS. M. SCHWERTNER.

Badin, STEPHEN THEODORE, the first Catholic priest ordained within the limits of the original thirteen States of the Union, pioneer missionary of Kentucky, b. at Orléans, France, 17 July, 1768; d. at Cincinnati, Ohio, 21 April, 1853. Educated at Montaigu College, Paris, he entered the Sulpician Seminary of his native city in 1789. He was subdeacon when the seminary was closed by the revolutionary government, in 1791, and sailed from Bordeaux for the American mission in November of the same year, with the Revs. B. J. Flaget and J. B. David, both destined in God's providence to wear the mitre in Kentucky. They arrived in Philadelphia on the 26th of March, 1792, and were welcomed at Baltimore by Bishop Carroll on the 28th. Stephen T. Badin pursued his theological studies with the Sulpicians and was ordained a priest by Bishop Carroll, 25 May, 1793. His was the first ordination in the United States. After a few months spent at Georgetown to perfect himself in English, Father Badin was appointed to the Mission of Kentucky. He left for that scene of his apostolic labours with Father Barrières, 3 September, 1793, travelled on foot as far as Pittsburgh, and by flat boat down the Ohio, landing at Limestone (Maysville), Ky., where they found twenty Catholic families. They walked sixty-five miles to Lexington, and on the first Sunday of Advent, 1793, Father Badin said his first Mass in Kentucky at the house of Denis McCarthy.

He settled at White Sulphur, Scott County, sixteen miles from Lexington, and for about eighteen months attended this church and neighbouring missions. In April, 1794, his companion, who resided in Bardstown, left for New Orleans, and Father Badin was now alone in the Kentucky mission. For fourteen years he attended to the spiritual wants of the various Catholic settlements, scattered over an extent of more than 120 miles, forming new congregations, building churches, never missing an appointment. To visit his missions regularly he had to live in the saddle, and it is estimated that he rode more than 100,000 miles during his ministry in Kentucky. For many years he was unaided and alone; it was only in July, 1806, that he received permanent help, when the Rev. Charles Nerinckx came to take the larger part of the burden from his shoulders. They lived together at St. Stephen's, on Pottingers Creek, which was still their headquarters on the arrival, in 1811, of Bishop Flaget, whom Father Badin had suggested and urged as first Bishop of Bardstown. Difficulties about the holding of church property soon arose between the bishop and Father Badin, without, however, interfering with the reverence of the latter for the bishop and the bishop's friendship for him. Together they went to Baltimore in 1812 to submit the controversy to Archbishop Carroll. It was not settled. They returned to Kentucky in April, 1813, and Father Badin resumed his missionary duties and accompanied his bishop on many pastoral journeys, until 1819. The Rev. J. B. David had been appointed coadjutor in 1817, but persistently refused to accept the honour. Father Badin, believing that this selection would put an end to the controversy about church property, and be for the good of the diocese of which he was the founder, left for France in the spring of 1819. The consecration of Bishop David in September of that year, and unjust suspicions about his disposition of church properties caused him to remain abroad. In 1820 he accepted the parish of Millaney and Marreilly-en-Gault, about forty miles from Orléans. He continued, however, to take the greatest interest in the Kentucky missions, insisted on his loyalty to Bishop Flaget, and helped constantly and generously to secure gifts in money and valuable church-furniture for the missionaries. In 1822 he published in Paris a "Statement of the Missions in Kentucky", with the same purpose in view.

Father Badin returned to America in 1828. After a year on the Michigan mission, he went back to Kentucky in 1829. The next year he offered his services to Bishop Fenwick of Cincinnati, and took charge of the Pottawottomie Indians at St. Joseph's River. Miss Campau of Detroit, an expert Indian linguist, acted as interpreter and teacher, until Father Badin left the place in 1836. Having returned to Cincinnati in that year, he wrote for the "Catholic Telegraph" a series of controversial "Letters to an Episcopalian Friend". In 1837 he went to Bardstown, Ky., was appointed vicar-general, and continued to visit the various missions. In 1841 he removed to Louisville with the bishop's household. In that year he conveyed a great deal of church property (notably that of Portland, near Louisville) to the bishop, and a farm to the Very Rev. E. Sorin of Notre Dame, Indiana.

On the 25th of May, 1843, Father Badin celebrated the golden jubilee of his priesthood, at Lexington, where he had offered up the Holy Sacrifice of the Mass for the first time in Kentucky. In September, 1846, he accepted from Bishop Quarter of Chicago the pastorship of the French settlement at Bourbonnais Grove, Kankakee County, Illinois. In the winter of 1848 he was again in Kentucky, and Bishop-Coadjutor Spalding welcomed him to the episcopal household. About two years later he became the guest of Archbishop Purcell at Cincinnati, and eventually died at the archbishop's residence. His body lay undisturbed in the cathedral crypt for over fifty years. In 1904 Archbishop Elder permitted its removal to the University of Notre Dame, Indiana.

Father Badin's writings are: "Etat des missions du Kentucky" (Paris, 1822), tr. in the "U. S. Cath. Miscellany" for December, 1824, and in the "Catholic World", September, 1875; "Carmen Sacrum", a Latin poem composed on the arrival of Bishop Flaget in Kentucky, June, 1811, translated into English by Colonel Theodore O'Hara of Frankfort, Ky., author of the "Bivouac of the Dead"; "Epicedium", Latin poem composed on the occasion of the death of Col. Joe Davis at the Battle of Tippecanoe, 7 November, 1811, translated by Doctor Michell of New York (Louisville, 1844); "Sanctissimæ Trinitatis Laudes et Invocatio" (Louisville, 1843), also the original text and tr. in Webb's "The Centenary of Catholicity in Kentucky" (Louisville, 1844); "Letters to an Episcopalian Friend"—three controversial articles on the Church and the Eucharist (published in the "Catholic Telegraph" of Cincinnati, 1836).

SPALDING, *Sketches of the Early Catholic Missions of Kentucky* (Louisville, 1844); IDEM, *Life of Bishop Flaget* (Louisville, 1852); *Life of Rev. Chas. Nerinckx* (Cincinnati, 1880); WEBB, *Centenary of Catholicity in Kentucky* (Louisville, 1884).

CAMILLUS P. MAES.

Badius Ascensius. See PRINTING, ART OF.

Badius, RAPHAEL, a Florentine Dominican of the seventeenth century. He was deeply versed in Tuscan and Florentine antiquities, and his researches made him particularly conversant with quaint and curious matters of history and hagiography. He rendered valuable assistance to the Jesuit Fathers, Henschen and Papebroch, in their labours on the "Acta Sanctorum", as they themselves acknowledge (T. II, Junii, ad diem X, de Joanne Dominici, p. 395, n. 6). As Chronicler of the Convent of Santa Maria Novella, Florence, he was also known to the historian and bibliographer Cinellus, who makes frequent and grateful mention of the learned Dominican's helpful

knowledge of the literature and writers of Florence (Bib. Volante, Scanzia VI, 88; IV, 87; XII, 106). In 1681, he was Dean of the University of Florence.

QUÉTIF-ECHARD, *Scriptores Ord. Præd.* (Paris, 1721), II, 741.

JOHN R. VOLZ.

Baegert, JOHN JACOB, missionary and ethnographer, b. at Schlettstadt in Alsace, 23 December, 1717; d. at Neustadt-on-the-Haardt in the Rhenish Palatinate, 29 September (or December), 1777. Baegert belonged to an Alsatian family from which had come several members of religious orders. He studied philosophy two years, entered the Society of Jesus at Aschaffenburg, 27 September, 1736, taught the humanities at Mannheim in 1740, studied theology at Molsheim, and after ordination, 14 February, 1749, went to America as a missionary. Lower California was given to him as his field of labour. Here he founded the mission of San Ignacio and worked for seventeen years until the expulsion of the Society in 1767. He embarked at Loretto on the return journey, 3 February, 1768, and after a short stay in a Spanish monastery of the Minorites retired to the Jesuit college at Neustadt-on-the-Haardt, where he ended his days. In 1773 Baegert published anonymously at Mannheim "Nachrichten von der amerikanischen Halbinsel Californien . . . mit einem zweifachen Anhang falscher Nachrichten". The publication is distinguished by truthfulness of statement and corrects the over-favourable description of conditions in California which had been given by Father Venegas in his account issued at Madrid in 1751. Father Baegert describes the physical character of Lower California, the customs and language of the natives and narrates the history of the mission. Owing to the numerous ethnographical observations the work was of value up to the middle of the nineteenth century and an edited translation was issued by the Smithsonian Institution in 1863–64; Vivien de Saint-Martin also wrote a detailed account of the work. The contemporaries of Baegert spoke highly of his talent for poetry and of his fine personal qualities.

Reports of the Smithsonian Institution (Washington, 1863), 352 sqq.; (1864), 378 sqq.; (1865), 41 sqq.; DE SAINT-MARTIN, *L'Année géographique*, V, 1866 (Paris, 1867), 233–39; BACKER-SOMMERVOGEL, *Bibliothèque* (1890), I, 760 sqq., and (1898), VIII, 1724; HUONDER, *Deutsche Jesuitenmissionäre des XVII. und XVIII. Jahrhunderts* in *Stimmen aus Maria-Laach*, sup. to vol. LXXIV (Freiburg im Br., 1899), 106; GÉNY ed., *Historia, 1631–1765* in *Die Jahrbücher der Jesuiten zu Schlettstadt und Rufach, 1615–1765* (Strasburg, 1896), II, 699 sqq. (contains the most reliable personal data).

OTTO HARTIG.

Baert, FRANÇOIS, Bollandist, b. at Ypres, 25 August, 1651; d. at Antwerp, 27 October, 1719. He entered the Society of Jesus at Mechlin, 28 September, 1667. After passing through the novitiate he was regent of several colleges in the province of Belgian Flanders, studied theology and philosophy, and was finally ordained priest in 1680. The following year, 1681, he was made assistant to Father Daniel Papebroch, the last survivor of the first generation of Bollandists. The name of Baertius is on the title-pages of nine volumes of the Acta Sanctorum; the last four of May and of the first five of June; but to judge from the articles published in these volumes his collaboration is by no means so large as these figures would indicate. There are no articles bearing his signature either in the volumes for May nor in the fifth volume for June. The other four volumes for June contain some fifteen articles by him, all very short excepting the commentaries on St. Columba and St. Basil the Great, of the date of 9 June. In 1688, in company with Father Conrad Janninck, he made a trip to Austria and Hungary in search of literary material; the journey lasted eight months and the two returned with a large number of documents.

CUPER, *Elogium R. P. Francisci Baertii hagiographi* in *Acta SS.*, July, II.

CH. DE SMEDT.

Bæumer, SUITBERT, historian of the Breviary and one of the most scholarly patrologists of the nineteenth century, b. 28 March, 1845 at Leuchtenberg near Kaiserswerth (Rhine); d. at Freiburg 12 August, 1894. He made his university studies at Bonn and Tübingen; in 1865 he entered the Benedictine Abbey of Beuron, then newly founded, and was ordained priest in 1869. The years 1875–90 were spent at Maredsous Abbey in Belgium and at Erdington in England; in the latter year he returned to Beuron. Dom Bæumer was long the critical adviser of the printing house of Desclée, Lefebvre and associates at Tournai, for their editions of the Missal, Breviary, Ritual, Pontifical, and other liturgical works. He contributed to leading reviews a number of valuable essays, e. g. on the Stowe Missal (the oldest liturgical record of the Irish Church) in the "Zeitschrift f. kath. Theologie" (1892), on the author of the "Micrologus" (an important medieval liturgical treatise) in "Neues Archiv" (1893), on the "Sacramentarium Gelasianum" in the "Historisches Jahrbuch" (1893). He also wrote a life of Mabillon (1892) and a treatise on the history and content of the Apostles' Creed (1893). His most important work is the classical history of the Roman Breviary "Geschichte des Breviers" (Freiburg, 1895; French tr., R. Biron, Paris, 1905). In this work he condensed the labours of several generations of erudite students of the Breviary and the best critical results of the modern school of historical liturgists.

Allg. deutsche Biographie, XLVI, 257, and the biographical account prefixed to the German and French texts of his history of the Breviary.

THOMAS J. SHAHAN.

Bagamoyo, VICARIATE APOSTOLIC OF, in German East Africa, separated by a pontifical Decree of 11 May, 1906, from the Vicariate Apostolic of Northern Zanzibar. The Catholics number 14,728 (in all German East Africa there are about 6,700,000 natives, most of whom belong to mixed tribes of the Bantu race). The mission is cared for by the Congregation of the Holy Ghost and the Immaculate Heart of Mary (52) and by the Trappists (8), aided by two congregations of women: Filles de Marie (7), and Sisters of the Precious Blood, formerly Trappistines (28). The first vicar Apostolic, Rt. Rev. Franz Xaver Vogt, of the Congregation of the Holy Ghost, was elected 25 July, 1906. There are 15 churches and chapels, 15 stations with medical service, 15 orphanages, 6 industrial, or trade, and agricultural, schools, 71 schools with 7,574 native pupils, 2 leper stations, and 2 hospitals. The vicar Apostolic resides at Bagamoyo, a small seaport town near the mouth of Kingani, opposite the Island of Zanzibar, and the centre of the telegraph and cable systems of the colony. (See AFRICA.)

Missiones Catholicæ (Propaganda, Rome, 1907), 427; *Statesmen's Year-Book* (London, 1907), 1021–22, 225–226; *Heilprin's Gazetteer* (Philadelphia, 1906), 146, 711, 2047.

THOMAS J. SHAHAN.

Bagdad.—This city was founded on the Tigris by the second Abbaside Caliph Abou Giafar al Mansur (762 or 764) and named by him Medinet es-Selam, or City of Salvation; Bagdad is a popular name said to mean "Garden of Dat", a Mussulman dervish. During five centuries it was the rich and brilliant capital of the famous Arabian Empire. Houlagou, a grandson of Genghis Khan, entered it in 1262; it afterwards became a possession of the Kara Koyouli Turks, was taken by Tamerlane, and, in 1517, fell into the hands of the Persians who, except for a short interval in the sixteenth century, ruled over it until 1638, when Sultan Murad made it definitively a city of the Ottoman Empire. It is now the chief town of a vilayet, or district, of the same name, and has lost much of its former importance, though it

still remains the most important city of Asiatic Turkey, after Damascus and Smyrna, and a great emporium of international trade. It exports textile fabrics, gold and silverware, horses, dates, etc. There are many beautiful mosques in the city, and the ruins of its ancient walls are still visible. The climate is hot; fevers are frequent, and the plague sometimes appears. Its population, taken as including the neighbouring villages, is said to be about 145,000; of these 86,000 are Mussulmans, mostly Arab Sunnites and Persian Shiites; 52,000 are Jews, and 7,000 Christians. Turkish statistics, however, are usually very uncertain. The Christians are divided as follows: 3,300 Armenians (including about 1,000 Catholics and 100 Protestants), 100 Greeks (50 Catholics); 1,600 (3,000?) Chaldeans; 1,200 Syrians; and 500 Latins.

In 1638, some days after the Turkish conquest, owing to the kindness of Abbas the Great, Urban VIII created, at the expense of a pious French lady, a Latin bishopric for the Catholics in Persia, under the title of Babylon, the old city being then (though erroneously) identified with Bagdad. For a long time the bishops of this title, when they came to the East, resided at Hamadân, in Persia, and for various reasons there were often no bishops, but only vicars Apostolic. It was only in 1742 that Père Joseph-Marie de Jésus, a Carmelite, was allowed to enter this Mussulman town. In 1848 the see became an archbishopric, with Ispahan as a suffragan see, till 1874; the archbishop, Monsignor Trioche, was appointed Apostolic Delegate for the Catholics of Oriental rites. He resigned this office in 1850, and until his death, in 1887, there were special delegates, the last of whom, Monsignor Altmayer, succeeded him and reunited both titles, as did his successor, Monsignor Jean Drure. We must here, moreover, notice that the Latin Archbishop of Bagdad, according to the decree of Urban VIII, must always be of French nationality.

The limits of the ecclesiastical province extend as far as Assyria, Mesopotamia, and the territories of Bassorah and Amida, with about 2,000 Latin faithful, mostly foreigners. It includes three Apostolic prefectures: Bagdad, Mardin, and Mossul. The Prefecture of Bagdad is governed by French Discalced Carmelites, who have at Bagdad a large and beautiful college, an elementary school, a dispensary, and stations at Bassorah, Amarah, and Bushire, with primary schools and some ten churches or little chapels. French Sisters of the Presentation of Tours conduct at Bagdad an important school for girls and an orphans' institute. For the Prefectures of Mardin (French Capuchins) and Mossul (French Dominicans), see articles under those titles.

The Apostolic Delegation of Bagdad, for Mesopotamia, Kurdistan, and Armenia Minor, is, as appears from its official appellation, more extensive than the Latin archbishopric. It embraces 5 Armenian dioceses, with 40 priests and about 12,000 faithful; 5 Syrian dioceses, with 80 priests and about 12,000 faithful; 9 Chaldean dioceses, with 160 priests and about 40,000 faithful.

Since the foundation of the Chaldean patriarchate by Innocent XI in 1681, after the conversion of a great many Nestorians, the Chaldean patriarch bears the title of Babylon, i. e. Bagdad. His residence was first at Diarbekir, then at Bagdad (since about 1838), and is now at Mossul. A Syrian archbishopric was also erected in 1862, with the same title of Babylon, or Bagdad; and the titular resides, or is authorized to reside, at Bagdad.

According to Bar-Hebræus ("Chronicon Eccl.", ed. Lamy, II, 236), Elias, the Greek Patriarch of Antioch, in 910 re-established at Bagdad the ancient residence of the Orthodox Catholicos which had been unoccupied since the Nestorian Schism (432). The

Greek name for Bagdad was Eirenopolis, the equivalent of Medinet es-Selam. Eirenopolis is now considered among the Greeks a metropolitan title, and is held by a prelate who assists the Patriarch of Antioch as his vicar.

CUINET, *La Turquie d'Asie*, III, 3–212; PIOLET, *Les missions catholiques françaises au XIXe siècle*, I, 222–271; *Missiones Catholicæ* (Propaganda, Rome, 1907.)

S. PÉTRIDÈS.

Bageis, a titular see of Lydia in Asia Minor. This name is found on coins, but becomes *Bagis* in the Synecdemos of Hierocles and *Bage* in later "Notitiæ graecæ episcopatuum". Bageis takes the epithet *Cæsarea* and names the River Hermos on its coins. It has been placed by Keppel's inscriptions near Sirghe on the Hermos (Guediztchai); but the site of the city is said to be on the north bank, while Sirghe is on the south side of the river. Harnack (*Mission und Ausbreitung des Christentums in den ersten drei Jahrhunderten*, 486) maintains that its bishop was present at Nicæa, but this is an error caused by a confusion with Baris, another Lydian city; the lists edited by H. Gelzer and C. H. Turner are silent about Bageis. We know really only three bishops of Bageis: Chrysaphius, or Chrysanthus, at Ephesus (431), placed wrongly by Lequien in a non-existent see, Balcea or Balicia; Leonides, who subscribed the letter of the Lydian bishops to the Emperor Leo I (458); Basilius, at the council under Photius (879). The city still figures in a list about 1170–79. The Lydian Bageis, Bagis, or Bage, is not to be confounded with Bagæ in Numidia.

LEQUIEN, *Oriens Christ.*, I, 889; RAMSAY, *Hist. Geogr. of Asia Minor*, 131.

S. PÉTRIDÈS.

Baglioni, GIOVANNI, CAVALIERE, known as the "Deaf Man of the Barozzo", a painter of distinction, b. in Rome, 1571; d. there 1644. His artistic work is, however, overshadowed by his biographies of his contemporaries. The literary work which furnishes his chief claim to fame is his "Lives of the Painters, Sculptors, and Architects" living in Rome, from 1573 to 1642—from the pontificate of Gregory XIII to that of Urban VIII. He was a pupil of Francesco Morelli and during his life did a number of works of importance at Rome under Popes Sixtus V, Clement VIII, and Paul V, notably in the Vatican, in Saint Peter's, and in Saint John Lateran. Pope Paul V created him a Knight of the Order of Christ for his painting of Saint Peter raising Tabitha from the dead. This was in St. Peter's but is not now extant. For the church of Santa Maria dell' Orto he painted in the chapel of Our Lady with the Zuccheri scenes from the life of the Blessed Virgin. Among other works which he executed for this church is a "Saint Sebastian". An excellent example of Baglioni's work is "The Last Supper" at San Nicolò in Carcere. From his brush also there is a "Saint Stephen" in the Cathedral at Perugia, and in that of Loretto a "Saint Catherine".

BRYAN, *Dictionary of Painters and Engravers* (London, and New York, 1903–05).

AUGUSTUS VAN CLEEF.

Bagnorea (anciently NOVEMPAGI, BALNEUM REGIUM), DIOCESE OF, is situated in the district of Viterbo, Italy, and immediately subject to the Holy See. The Diocese of Bagnorea has a population of about 20,000; the city contains about 4,500 inhabitants. According to tradition, St. Ansanus preached the Gospel here in the third century, and the church of Santa Maria delle Carceri outside the Alban Gate was said to have been built above the prison in which he was confined. There are no records as to the date of the erection of this diocese; St. Gregory the Great, however, is authority for the statement that about the year 600 the Deacon John was appointed bishop of this see. Up to the time of Urban V, Montefiascone was part of the Diocese of Bagnorea, but was made by this pontiff the seat of a new diocese. Ughelli, without, however, adducing any documentary proof, says that the Diocese of Bagnorea was joined to the Diocese of Viterbo, 4 February, 1449, but neglects to mention when they were re-established as separate dioceses. Among the sacred edifices worthy of note are: the ancient Gothic cathedral and the new cathedral built by Bishop Ulderico Nardi (1698), and restored in 1764 by Bishop Giuseppe Aliuffi. Here is preserved an arm of St. Bonaventure, a citizen of Bagnorea, as well as some of his writings. Among the most celebrated bishops, besides those already mentioned, are St. Aldualdus (861), Corrado Manili (1521), a celebrated professor of law in the Universities of Padua and Pavia, Tommaso Sperandio (1574), Pietro Paolo Febei (1635), who founded the seminary, Martino Cordella, banished to France in 1789 because he would not take the oath of allegiance to the French Republic. During the barbarian invasions, between the sixth and ninth centuries, the city was taken several times by the Goths and the Lombards. In 822 the Emperor Louis I added it to the Papal States.

The Diocese of Bagnorea contains 6 rural deaneries, 24 parishes, 106 churches, chapels, and oratories, 54 secular priests, 45 seminaries, 10 priests, secular and regular, 38 lay brothers, 63 members of female religious orders, 2 schools for girls, and a population of 26,380.

CAPPELLETTI, *Le chiese d'Italia* (Venice, 1844), V, 505; *Annuario eccl.* (Rome, 1906).

U. BENIGNI.

Bagot, JEAN, theologian, b. at Rennes, in France, 9 July, 1591, d. at Paris, 23 August, 1664. He entered the Society of Jesus 1 July, 1611, taught belles-lettres for many years in various colleges of France, philosophy for five years, theology for thirteen years, and became theologian to the general of the society. In 1647 he published the first part of his work "Apologeticus Fidei" entitled "Institutio Theologica de verâ Religione". In 1645 the second part, "Demonstratio dogmatum Christianorum", appeared, and in 1646 "Dissertationes theologicæ" on the Sacrament of Penance. In his "Avis aux Catholiques", Bagot attacked the new doctrine on grace, directing against it also his "Lettre sur la conformité de S. Augustin". In 1653 his "Libertatis et gratiæ defensio" was published.

In 1655 Rousse, Curé of Saint Roch (or Masure, the Curé of St. Paul's), published a little work entitled "De l'obligation des fidèles de se confesser à leur curé, suivant le chapitre 21 du concile general de Latran". Père Bagot answered this in his "Défense du droit épiscopal et de la liberté des fidèles", which he afterwards translated into Latin. A controversy arose, in which various ecclesiastics, including Mgr. de Marca, Archbishop of Toulouse, took sides against Bagot. The work was referred to the faculty of theology at Paris, which censured some of the propositions. Bagot, however, defended his doctrine before this assembly with the result that the censure was removed. He answered his opponents in the "Réponse du P. Bagot". On his return from Rome he devoted the remaining years of his life to the congregation of the Blessed Virgin, and died superior of the professed house at Paris.

HURTER, *Nomenclator*, II, 67; DE BACKER, *Bibl. des écriv. de la c. de J.*, I, 32; SOMMERVOGEL, *Bibl. de la c. de J.*, I, 774; IDEM in *Dict. de théol. cath.*

G. E. KELLY.

Bagshaw, CHRISTOPHER, convert, priest, prisoner for the Faith, and a prominent figure in the controversies between Catholic priests in the reign of Elizabeth. He came of a Derbyshire family, but the year of his birth is unknown. He died in Paris sometime after 1625. Bagshaw was at St. John's College, Cambridge, in 1566, was graduated B. A. at Balliol, Oxford, 1572, and probably became a Fellow of that college in the same year. As a Fellow he was a party to the expulsion from the college of the afterwards famous Jesuit, Father Parsons.

At proceeding M. A. in 1575, Bagshaw was still a zealous Protestant. His administration as Principal of Gloucester Hall (1579) was unpopular and brief. In 1582, in France, he became a Catholic and was ordained a priest. Going to Rome with the permission of Cardinal Allen, he entered the English College. It is said by Bullen, that he was expelled by Cardinal Boncompagni for his quarrelsome temper and unpopularity. Foley's list of students of the English College does not contain his name. Later, at Paris he proceeded doctor of divinity and doctor of the Sorbonne, though afterwards he was dubbed by his Jesuit opponents *doctor erraticus, doctor per saltum.* On his return to England he was imprisoned (1587) in the Tower of London, under the statute of 27th of Elizabeth, an act against Jesuits and Seminarists. (The text of this law is in Hardy and Gee.) With a number of other priests out of the more than 400 labouring in England, he was imprisoned in Wisbeach Castle, 1593.

There now came to a head a factional division among the labourers on the English mission. There were two original sources of difference: the existence of a Spanish faction, headed by the Jesuits, and the Jesuits' control of the English College at Rome (Cf. Dodd and Tierney; Lingard). The partisan feelings aroused found vent in two controversies in which Bagshaw was prominent, if not first, on the side opposed to the Jesuits and their friends. The earlier dispute, arbitrated after nine months, arose from the vigorous opposition of Bagshaw and the elder clergy to the introduction of a religious rule among the thirty-three priests in Wisbeach Castle. Later, when, partly for the purpose of consolidating English Catholic sentiment in favour of a Catholic successor to Elizabeth, Cardinal Cajetan placed at the head of the English Mission, as archpriest, Father George Blackwell, with instructions to consult the Jesuit provincial on matters of importance (Lingard VIII, vii), Bagshaw headed a party of protest, which, on being disciplined, appealed, with the secret aid of Elizabeth's government, to Rome. Their appeal was in part successful, though the appointment was confirmed.

Bagshaw, after his liberation, resided abroad, and is described in Daniel Featley's "Transubstantiation Exploded" as having been Rector of Ave Maria College. This work was published in 1638, and contained notes of a public disputation with Bagshaw. His death and burial, at Paris, occurred after 1625. He may have written in part "A true Relation of the Faction begun at Wisbich by Father Edmonds, alias Weston, a Jesuit, 1595, and continued since by Father Walley, alias Garnet, the Provincial of the Jesuits in England, and by Father Parsons in Rome" (1601); "Relatio Compendiosa Turbarum quas Jesuitæ Angli unâ cum D. Georgio Blackwello, Archipresbytero, Sacerdotibus Seminariorum, Populoque Catholico concivere", etc. (Rouen, 1601).

BULLEN in *Dict. of Nat. Biog.*, II, 400; GILLOW, *Bibl. Dict. Eng. Cath.*, I, 100; LINGARD, *History of England;* FOLEY, *Records of the English Province of the Society of Jesus*, I, 42, 481; II, 239, 244; VI, 724, 725; DODD, ed. TIERNEY, *Church History of England*, III, 40 and appendix.

J. V. CROWNE.

Bahama Islands, THE, OR LUCAYOS, the most northerly group of the West Indies, are a chain of coral islands lying between 21° 42' and 27° 34' N. lat., and 72° 40' and 79° 5' W. long., composed of twenty-five permanently inhabited islands and an immense number of cays and rocks. The group lies to the east of Southern Florida, and is separated from it by the Gulf Stream; and to the north of Cuba, from which it is separated by the Old Bahama Channel. As to the name, nothing definite seems to be known of the origin of Bahama. It is undoubtably of aboriginal origin, while Lucayos is evidently the Spanish *Los Cayos*, the Cays. The following are the principal islands and their area, and their population according to the census of 1901:—

Name	Area: Sq. Miles	Pop. Census 1901
Abaco and Cays	776	3,314
Andros	1,600	5,347
Berry Islands	4	215
Bimini	8	566
Cat Island	160	4,658
Eleuthera	164	8,733
Exuma and Cays	110	3,086
Grand Bahama	430	1,780
Inagua	530	1,453
Long Cay, Acklins, and Crooked Island	204	1,565
Long Island	130	3,562
Mayaguana	96	335
New Providence	85	12,534
Rum Cay	29	529
Ragged Island	5	348
Watlings Island	60	667
Total	4,500	55,000

Of the total population, about 80 per cent are of African negro descent; less than ten per cent are whites, mostly of English and Scotch descent through Loyalists from the American Colonies; and the rest are coloured or mixed. Slavery was abolished, 1 August, 1834; the number of slaves was 10,086 and the owners received compensation at the rate of £12.14.4 per head. New Providence, on which Nassau, the capital, is situated, the only island having a safe harbour, with eighteen feet of water, is the principal island. Owing to its salubrious climate, Nassau is a favourite winter resort for American tourists. The average temperature for the four winter months is 71° F.

GOVERNMENT BUILDINGS, NASSAU

Political Status and Exports.—Politically the Bahamas are a British Colony, being governed by a Governor and an Executive Council of eight members, a Legislative Council of nine members appointed by the Crown, and an elective legislative assembly of twenty-nine members. The islands are of coral formation, thus differing completely in their geological structure from the other West India Islands as well as from the adjacent mainland of Florida. Soil and vegetation are sparse. The chief exports are sponge, tortoise shell, ambergris, pink pearls, and shells gathered in the shallow waters of the Bahama Banks. Sisal fibre, pine-apples, grapefruit, oranges, and various other tropical fruits, as well as precious woods, form the chief land products of export. The large bulk of the trade, both import and export, is with the United States.

History.—Historically the islands are of interest, because one of them, San Salvador (see SAN SALVADOR, THE LANDFALL OF COLUMBUS), was the first land of the New World discovered by Columbus, 12 October, 1492. The Spanish never made a permanent settlement in the Bahamas, but shortly after the discovery they carried off many aborigines to the mines of San Domingo, and ere long the whole population, never perhaps very large, seems to have disappeared. The statement made in some of the recent guide books, that 40,000 souls were supposed to have been carried to the mines of Hispaniola by the Spaniards, is evidently overdrawn. Had the Bahamas ever been so thickly populated, there would remain the evidence of ruins of buildings or of soil cultivation. There are few if any fruit trees whose introduction cannot be traced, and there are no food-animals on the islands. Whatever population there was, must, therefore, have subsisted on fish, corn, yams, and on a very few small wild fruits. There is nothing to warrant the supposition that the Bahamas ever had more than a very sparse aboriginal population. So little is known of the original inhabitants that they cannot be definitely classified. They may have been of Carib stock or of the race that inhabited the adjoining mainland of Florida. The brief description which Columbus gives of them, and the formation of the few skulls discovered, seem to favour the theory that they were either one with the aborigines of Florida, or a mixture of the latter with the Caribs of the West Indies. The fact that they were very mild-mannered, and not cannibalistic, favours the opinion that they were kin to the Seminoles of Florida. Excepting a few skulls, stone idols, and implements, a few of which are to be seen in the public library at Nassau, there are no aboriginal remains, and there are no ruins of any description, a fact which points to a North American, rather than to a West Indian, or Central American, origin.

In 1578 Queen Elizabeth conferred upon Sir Gilbert Humphrey all lands not already occupied by some Christian power, and finding the Bahamas neglected, he annexed them; but no settlement was established. The enmity existing between England and Spain afforded adventurers, chiefly English and French, an excuse to make them a vantage ground from which to make depredations on Spanish shipping to and from the New World, and the natural formation of the Bahamas furnished them an excellent hiding place. During the seventeenth century the islands were the rendezvous of the famous buccaneers. When, at the treaty of Riswick, in 1697, comparative peace was restored among the European nations, England withdrew her protection of the buccaneers, and some returned to more peaceful avocations (thus Morgan, a chief among them, retired to Jamaica, and subsequently was appointed governor of that island), while many others raised the black flag of piracy against all nations, and made the Bahamas a by-word for lawlessness and crime. In 1718, England began the extermination of piracy, and soon established law and order. Since then England has been in almost undisturbed possession. On 2 March, 1776, Captain Hopkins, in command of the first American Navy, took possession of Nassau, in quest of ammunition, and on 17 March departed, carrying with him Governor Brown. In 1781 the Spaniards took possession and organized a government. At the treaty of Paris, in 1783, the Bahamas reverted to England. During the early Spanish possession and depopulation nothing was done for religion, and the periods of buccaneer and pirate rule precluded religious activity. With English rule came gradually the Church of England, and in the

first years of the nineteenth century, the Methodists, Baptists, and Presbyterians made foundations in Nassau. In 1861 the Bahamas were made a bishopric of the Church of England. The inhabitants of the Bahamas are all nominally Christians, and claim allegiance to some one of the denominations named. The Baptists, served almost exclusively by native coloured preachers, are numerically the strongest. There are no reliable religious statistics.

Catholic Church in the Bahamas.—Though there existed a tradition of ruins of "religious" buildings being still visible in 1803 on Cat Island (probably dating from the temporary Spanish occupation of 1781–83), there is no evidence of any Catholic priest ever having visited the Bahamas until 1845, when a Father Duquesney, on a voyage from Jamaica to Charleston, S. C., U. S. A. made a stay of six weeks at Nassau, and held services in a private house with perhaps a few Catholic Cubans or Haitians present. In 1863 Rev. J. W. Cummings of New York, and in 1865 a Rev. T. Byrne spent each a few weeks in Nassau, and conducted services. Beginning with 1866, the Rev. Dr. Nelligan of Charleston made several visits, and the Bahamas were recognized in the public prints as belonging ecclesiastically to Charleston, S. C. In 1883 Bishop H. P. Northrop of that diocese paid a short visit. At his request the Propaganda, in a letter dated 28 July, 1885, requested the Archbishop of New York to look after the spiritual interests of the Bahamas, and since that date they have been under the jurisdiction of the Archbishop of New York.

In February, 1885, the Rev. C. G. O'Keeffe of New York, while visiting Nassau, organized the few Catholics, with the result that on 25 August, 1885, the cornerstone of the first Catholic Church in the Bahamas was laid by Georgina Ayde-Curran, wife of Surgeon Major Ayde-Curran of the British Army. On 13 February, 1887, it was dedicated under the patronage of St. Francis Xavier, by Archbishop M. A. Corrigan

HOUSE IN GRANTSTOWN

of New York. Father O'Keeffe, to whom belongs the honour of establishing the first Catholic Church in the Bahamas, remained in charge till 1889. In October, 1889, Rev. D. P. O'Flynn came to Nassau with four Sisters of Charity from Mount St. Vincent, New York, who at once opened a free school for coloured children, and a select school. In June, 1890, Rev. D. P. O'Flynn was succeeded by Rev. B. J. Reilly. In February, 1891, the Rev. Chrysostom Schreiner, O. S. B., of St. John's Abbey, Minnesota, took charge of the mission, and since 1894, two other Benedictine Fathers have been associated with him in the work. In 1893 a new mission was opened at Salvador Point, Andros Island, and in 1897, the Sacred Heart mission was opened in the eastern portion of the city of Nassau. There are, therefore, at present St. Francis Xavier's Church, and Sacred Heart Chapel in Nassau, with each of which is connected a free school, taught by the Sisters of Charity, and an Academy by the same sisters. At St. Saviour's Mission, Andros Island, there is a free school taught by a lay teacher. The statistics of the mission for 1906 are as follows: 1 church and 2 chapels; 3 Benedictine Fathers, the superior of the mission bearing the title of Vicar Forane of the Bahamas; 9 Sisters of Charity; 1

academy; 3 free schools with an attendance of 470 pupils. Total Catholic population 360.

Turks and Caicos Islands, situated to the north of Haiti, belonging geographically to the Bahama group, were separated from the other Bahamas in 1848, and made a political dependency of Jamaica. There is no Catholic population. Grand Turk, whose one industry is salt-raking, is the seat of the commissioner. It is occasionally visited by priests from Jamaica.

Colonial Office List; Memoirs of Peter H. Bruce (London, 1782); CATESBY, *Natural History of Carolina, Florida, and the Bahamas* (London, 1770); McKINNON, *Tour in the West Indies* (London, 1804); IVES, *The Isles of Summer* (New Haven, Conn., 1880); POWLES, *The Land of the Pink Pearl* (London, 1888); STARK, *History and Guide to the Bahamas* (Boston, 1891); NORTHCROFT, *Sketches of Summerland* (Nassau, 1906). The last named is the most complete and reliable; LESTER, *In Sunny Isles* (1897).

CHRYSOSTOM SCHREINER.

Bahia di tutti i Santi. See SAN SALVADOR DE BAHIA.

Bahrein Islands. See PERSIA.

Baianism. See BAIUS, MICHEL.

Bailey, THOMAS, controversialist, died c. 1657. He was son of Bishop Bailey of Bangor and was educated as an Anglican at Magdalen College, Cambridge, where he graduated B.A., in 1627, and M.A., in 1631. After ordination he was appointed Sub-Dean of Wells (1638). During the civil wars he retired to Oxford where he proceeded Doctor of Divinity. He was a stanch royalist and after the battle of Naseby was for a time in the king's retinue at Raglan Castle. Subsequently through the help of the Marquess of Worcester, who was a Catholic, he travelled abroad and thus became acquainted with Catholic life, which led to his conversion. On his return he published a work of strong royalist tendencies to prove the divine right of Episcopacy; this book gave offence to Cromwell's government and resulted in his arrest and imprisonment in Newgate. While a prisoner he wrote another book called "Herba parietis" (The Wall-flower), in allusion to his captive state. After his release he retired to Italy, where he obtained employment in the household of Cardinal Ottoboni at Ferrara. He died shortly before the Restoration, probably in the cardinal's employ, although Anthony à Wood repeats a rumour that he died at Bologna as a common soldier. Among the works published in his name is a life of Blessed John Fisher, which has given rise to some difficulty, for it was written by Dr. Richard Hall in 1559, nearly a century before. Bailey published it with additions which the martyr's latest biographer, Rev. T. Bridgett, describes as "nothing but verbiage and blunders". He adds that some of the additions "are palpably false and have brought discredit upon Hall". It was suggested by Dodd that Bailey's name was added without his knowledge by the bookseller, but if the preface signed T. B. be genuine he certainly claimed authorship, a fact which does not enhance his reputation. His authentic works are: "Certamen Religiosum" (London, 1649), an account of the conference concerning religion between Charles I and the Marquess of Worcester; answered by L'Estrange, Cartwright, and Heylyn; "The Royal Charter granted unto Kings by God Himself" (London, 1649, 1656, 1680); "Herba parietis" (London, 1650); "The End to Controversie" (Douai, 1654); "Golden Apothegms of Charles I and Henry, Marquess of Worcester" (London, 1660). Bailey also completed and published Bishop Lindsell's edition of Theophylact. The book mentioned in Walton's "Life of Bishop Sanderson" as "Dr. Bailey's Challenge" may be a separate work but more probably is merely a reference to one of the above.

COOPER in *Dict. Nat. Biog.*, III, s. v. *Bayly;* GILLOW, *Bibl. Dict. Eng. Cath.;* DODD, *Church History* (1737–42), III, 64; WOOD, *Athen. Oxon.*, ed. BLISS, II, 526; BRIDGETT, *Life of Fisher* (1890), preface.

EDWIN BURTON.

Baillargeon, CHARLES-FRANÇOIS, a French-Canadian bishop, b. 26 April, 1798, at Ile-aux-Grues, P. Q.; d. 13 October, 1870. He studied theology at the Seminary of Quebec, where he taught rhetoric. Ordained in 1822, he was successively chaplain at St. Roch, pastor of St. François, Isle of Orleans, of the joint parishes of L'Ange-Gardien and Chateau-Richer. While rector of Notre Dame de Québec, he displayed apostolic zeal and charity during three visitations of cholera (1832, 1834, 1849), and the horrors of typhus (1847), assisting many Irish orphans. He was made Bishop of Tloa and coadjutor to Archbishop Turgeon of Quebec, 23 February, 1851, being the first Canadian bishop since the conquest appointed without the intervention of the British Crown. He became administrator in 1855 and succeeded as Archbishop of Quebec, 26 August, 1867. He attended the Vatican Council. He published a French translation, with commentary, of the New Testament (2d ed., 1865), lauded by Pius IX, "Recueil d'Ordonnances" (1859), and over thirty important Pastoral Letters, besides many other official documents.

PAQUET, *Mgr. Baillargeon* (Quebec, 1870); LEGARÉ, *Eloge de Mgr. C.-F. Baillargeon* (ibid., 1871); TETU, *Les Evêques de Québec* (ibid., 1889).

LIONEL LINDSAY.

Baillet, ADRIEN, French author, b. 1649 at Neuville en Hez, near Beauvais, France; d. at Paris, 1706. His parents were poor, but the Cordeliers of La Garde, struck by the boy's piety and alertness of mind, took him into their monastery and then had him admitted to the College of Beauvais, where, at the close of his studies, he became teacher of humanities. Ordained priest in 1676, he served for a time as curate of Lardieu and was then made canon of Beaumont, but neither pastoral nor canonical functions satisfied him. At the end of four years his love of learning took him to Paris, where he secured the place of librarian to the celebrated de Lamoignon. An insatiable reader and a rigid ascetic, he spent his life in the seclusion of study and austerity. In a comparatively short time he had made an analytical catalogue, in thirty-two folios, of Lamoignon's library. The great mass of erudition thus acquired soon passed into innumerable books. His writings may be divided into three groups: (1) Erudition, (2) History, (3) Religion. To the first group belong: "Jugements des savants sur les principaux ouvrages des auteurs" (1685); "Des auteurs déguisés" (1690); "Des enfants célèbres" (1688). With the exception of the last, which still attracts by its curiousness, these books are now almost forgotten, both because they are incomplete and because they have been more than replaced by the works of such writers as Brunet, Quérard, Barbier, etc. Baillet's criticisms were not accepted by all. Ménage, who thought himself ill-treated, wrote the "Anti-Baillet" to which Baillet replied by "Des satires personnelles" (1682). La Monnoie published a revised edition of all the foregoing books, to which he joined by way of introduction an "Abrégé de la vie de M. Baillet" (Paris, 1722; Amsterdam, 1725).

To the second group belong: "Histoire de Hollande" (1690); "Vie de Descartes" (1692); "Vie de Godefroy Hermant"; "Vie de Richer" (1693); "Histoire des démêlés du Pape Boniface VIII avec Philippe le Bel" (1718), etc. The author shows too much sympathy for the Jansenist Hermant and the Gallican Richer. His life of Descartes is replete with interesting but rather garbled information. Lelong thought so well of the "History of the Conflict between Boniface VIII and Philippe le Bel" that he edited it (Paris, 1718).

To the third and by far the most important group belong: "Dévotion à la Vierge et le culte qui lui est dû" (Paris, 1694; Tournai, 1712). The avowed purpose of this book is to clear Mariology from indiscreet devotions, but Baillet clearly overreaches himself by bluntly denying the Immaculate Conception and the Assumption of Mary, and by attacking devotions sanctioned by the Church. The book was put on the "Index Expurgatorius" *donec corrigatur* in 1694 and 1701. The erudition displayed in "Les vies des saints, composées sur ce qui nous est resté de plus authentique et de plus assuré dans leur histoire" (Paris 1701 and 1794) is prodigious, yet the greater part of it (from January to August) was put on the Index in 1707 and 1711. The cause of that condemnation is the hypercritical spirit evinced throughout in the "Vie des Saints". While aiming at doing away with unauthenticated miracles, Baillet comes very near casting doubt on all miraculous manifestations. Benedict XIV (De festis, II, xvi, 8) calls him a man with an intemperate mind and an ever-ready disposition to impeach even the best attested facts. The Bollandist Stilting (Acta SS., V, 458, 488) says of him, apropos of Bl. Louis Allemand: "I deem it unnecessary to refute a man who, I find, stumbles at nearly every step". Other Bollandists reproach him for not keeping the rules he had so well laid down in his "Jugements", and find him frequently at fault, now by excess of criticism, now by excess of credulity. Eusebius is almost the only ancient historian who finds favour with Baillet. All the other writers of hagiology are held by him in suspicion and almost in contempt. That frame of mind could not yield good results. "Some French critics in sacred biography", says Alban Butler, in the introduction to his "Lives of the Saints", "have tinctured their works with a false and pernicious leaven, and, under the name of criticism, established scepticism". That sentence applies in a measure to Baillet. His contemporaries were not mistaken as to the origin of that pernicious leaven. The Bishop of Gap, Berger de Malissoles, in prohibiting the work in his diocese, wrote: "That book on a great many points of dogma and discipline savours the sentiments not only of Jansenism but also of the so-called reformers".

La Monnoie, *Abrégé de la vie de M. Baillet* (Amsterdam, 1725); Hurter, *Nomenclator* (Innsbruck, 1892); Migne, *Diction. de biographie chrétienne* (Paris, 1851).

J. F. Sollier.

Bailloquet, Pierre, missionary among the Indians of Canada, b. in 1612, at Saintes, France; d. in the Ottawa missions, 7 June, 1692. He entered the Society of Jesus at Bordeaux, 20 November, 1631, and after ordination was sent as a missionary to Canada. He arrived at Quebec in the summer of 1647, and for forty-five years laboured and suffered among the savage tribes that roamed the vast territory extending from Acadia in the east to the lands of the Illinois in the far west. The hardships and privations he endured are well nigh incredible. According to the "Relations" he frequently had "the earth for bed and mattress, and strips of bark for a palace, which was filled less with air than with smoke"; and owing to his zeal he was often in danger of being tomahawked or burned at the stake by the savages. When almost eighty years of age and stricken with grievous infirmity, he dragged himself across the snow for leagues to go to the huts of those who were unable to come to him. He died in his eightieth year, having been sixty-one years in the religious life.

De Guilhermy, *Ménologe de la c. de J., Assistance de France*, 1, 711; Thwaites, *Jesuit Relations*, LXXII, 70.

E. P. Spillane.

Baily, Thomas, a Catholic clergyman, b. in Yorkshire, England; d. at Douai, France, 7 October, 1591. He was a student at Clare Hall, Cambridge, where he obtained the degree of Bachelor of Arts in 1546. Soon after he became a Fellow of that house, receiving the degree of Master of Arts in 1549. In 1554 he was appointed Proctor and in the following year he subscribed to the Roman Catholic Articles. About November, 1557, he was appointed Master of Clare Hall and was given the degree of Bachelor of Divinity in 1558. In the same year Queen Elizabeth ascended the throne and efforts were made by the Protestant party to gain recruits to its ranks, but Baily refused to conform to the new religion. As a consequence he was deprived of his Mastership. He next visited Louvain, where he remained until 30 January, 1576, during the interval receiving the degree of Doctor of Divinity. From Louvain he went to Douai at the invitation of Doctor Allen (afterwards Cardinal), during whose absence he usually filled the position of President of the English College both at Douai and Reims. He finally left Reims, 27 January, 1589, returning to Douai, where he remained until his death. He was associated with Cardinal Allen in the management of the College, the distribution of the labour being that Cardinal Allen had charge of the discipline, Dr. Baily the temporal affairs, and Dr. Bristow, another of Cardinal Allen's co-labourers, the studies. He was buried in the Chapel of St. Nicholas in the parish church of St. James, Douai.

Cooper in *Dict. Nat. Biog.*, II, 432; Gillow, *Bibl. Dict. Eng. Cath.*, I, 105.

Thomas Gaffney Taaffe.

Bainbridge, Christopher, Archbishop of York, and Cardinal, b. at Hilton, near Appleby, in Westmoreland, probably 1464; d. at Rome, 14 July, 1514. He proceeded to Oxford, entering Queen's College, of which he became provost in or before 1495, being about that time admitted LL.D.; he became later a liberal benefactor to his college. He held a number of benefices, including the treasurership of the Diocese of London, on Henry VII's presentation, and Master of the Rolls, a post he held till his elevation to the See of Durham, which took place in 1507, nominated thereto by the king, who restored the temporalities of the see to him. He was consecrated on 12 December. This see he held but a short while, being translated to York the next year by a papal Bull dated 20 September, 1508. In 1509 he was sent by Henry VIII as his ambassador to Rome. Julius II created him a cardinal on 10 March, 1511, giving him the title of St. Praxedis, in reward for negotiating Henry's adherence to the pope as against France, for which country he felt a strong antipathy all his life. As cardinal he was commissioned by Julius to lead a military expedition against Ferrara, which he successfully besieged. He endeavoured to secure from Pope Leo X the bestowal on Henry of the title of "Most Christian King" which Louis of France had forfeited by waging war against the pope; but the peace of 1514 made this project abortive. Bainbridge was poisoned by an Italian priest named Rinaldo de Modena, who acted as his steward or bursar, in revenge for a blow which the cardinal, a man of violent temper, had given him. It was hinted that the crime was perpetrated at the instigation of Sylvester de Giglis, Bishop of Worcester, the resident English ambassador at Rome, but de Giglis exonerated himself. Bainbridge was buried in the English Hospice, now known as the English College, Rome. He was a stout upholder of Henry's interests at the Curia.

Gairdner in *Dict. Nat. Biogr.*; Wood, *Athenæ Oxon.*; Godwin, *De Præsul.*; Le Neve, *Fasti*; Stubbs, *Episc. Succession*; Weaver, *Somerset Incumbents*.

Henry N. Birt.

Baines, Peter Augustine, titular Bishop of Siga, one of the most striking figures among English Catholics at the period of Emancipation, was born at Kirkby, in Lancashire, 25 January, 1787; d. 6 July, 1843. For his early education he was sent to the English monastery at Lampspring, in Hanover, where he arrived in 1798. Four years later the monastery was suppressed by the Prussian Government, and the monks and their pupils returned to England. Some of them, Baines among the number, took refuge at the recently founded monastery at Ampleforth, in Yorkshire. It was not long before his talents and force of character brought him into prominence in the small community there. He joined the Benedictine Order, and held in succession every post of authority in the monastery, the priorship alone excepted.

In 1817 Baines left Ampleforth and was appointed to Bath, one of the most important Benedictine missions in the country. There he became a well-known figure, his sermons attracting great attention not only among Catholics, but also among Protestants. His printed letters in answer to Archdeacon Moysey created quite a stir, being commonly known as "Baines's Defence". His reputation continuing to increase, Bishop Collingridge, O. S. F., Vicar Apostolic of the Western District, chose him for his coadjutor. He received episcopal consecration as titular Bishop of Siga at the hands of Archbishop Murray, at Dublin, 1 May, 1823.

Bishop Baines soon began to formulate schemes for the future of the district, on that large scale so congenial to his mind. Realizing that, alone among the four, it was without a regular seminary for the education of its clergy, he set himself to work to supply the want. The Western District differed from the other three in that the bishop had always been chosen from among the regular clergy—Benedictines or Franciscans—and a large proportion of the missions were in their hands. Dr. Baines thought that he saw the solution of his difficulty in utilizing the new school which had been recently opened at Downside, near Bath. The fact that it was under Benedictine management appeared to him no disadvantage, and he has assured us that he meant his whole scheme to benefit his order. But he considered that a bishop should be supreme in his own seminary, and boldly proposed that the whole community of monks at Downside should be transferred from the Anglo-Benedictine Congregation, and placed under the Bishop of the Western District. The idea was not favourably received at Downside, so the bishop put forward the alternative proposition that they should exchange their property for that at Ampleforth, hoping that the members of his own monastery might take more kindly to his scheme. This proposal, however, was also refused, and there matters rested for some years.

In 1826 Bishop Baines's health gave way, and he was ordered a long tour on the Continent. He spent the greater part of the time in Rome, and Wiseman tells us (Last Four Popes, p. 323) that Leo XII, wishing to create a Benedictine Cardinal, fixed upon Bishop Baines for that dignity, and was only prevented by death from carrying out his intention. Bishop Collingridge died 3 March, 1829, the same year in which Catholic Emancipation was passed, and Bishop Baines returned to England, in restored health, to succeed as vicar Apostolic. He at once revived his scheme for the seminary at Downside, and, having failed to secure the consent of the monks, he put forward the contention that the monasteries at Downside and Ampleforth had never been canonically erected, for, owing to the unsettled condition of the English mission, the formality of obtaining the written consent of the ordinary had been overlooked. He drew the drastic conclusion that all the monastic vows had been invalid, and that the property belonged to the bishops. The case was argued out in Rome, but it was considered that, even if the strict law was on

Bishop Baines's side, equity demanded that the rights of the Benedictines should be maintained, and a *sanatio* was issued by papal authority, making good any possible defects in the past. Leave was given, however, for four of the Ampleforth monks, including the prior, to be secularized. They left, together with thirty of the boys, to join Bishop Baines, who had himself been secularized, in founding a new college. The site chosen was Prior Park, a large mansion outside Bath, which Bishop Baines bought, and he set to work to build two colleges at either end of the "mansion house", which he dedicated to St. Peter and St. Paul respectively, the former being intended as a lay college, the latter as a seminary. He seems to have had visions of a Catholic University as a sequel to Emancipation, and Prior Park was intended to be its centre.

The new college thus opened under most favourable auspices; but it never became really prosperous. The buildings were on too vast a scale for the number of students, and the older clergy viewed askance an undertaking which they feared would absorb all the resources of the diocese. To add to the difficulties, in the year 1836 a destructive fire almost completely consumed the interior of the mansion, involving fresh outlay in making good the damage. In 1840 the number of vicariates in England was raised from four to eight, Wales being separated off into a district of its own. Bishop Baines continued over the Western District for three years more, when his sudden death took place. On the 4th of July, 1843, he distributed the prizes at Prior Park; the following day he preached at the opening of the new church of St. Mary on the Quay, Bristol, returning to Prior Park in the evening, apparently in his usual health; but the following morning he was found dead in his bed. His funeral at Prior Park was conducted with the solemnity due to his position and his personality; but when, some years later, the college was sold, his body was removed to Downside, where it rests to-day.

Many of Bishop Baines's sermons, pastorals, etc., were published, and some ran to several editions. An oil painting of him, formerly at Prior Park, is now at the Bishop's House (St. Ambrose), Clifton. There is an engraving in the Catholic Directory for 1844.

GILLOW, *Bibl. Dict. Eng. Cath.*; KENT in *Dict. Nat. Biog.*; BRADY, *Episcopal Succession*; OLIVER, *Collections*; WISEMAN, *Last Four Popes*; BIRT, *Downside*; ALMOND, *Hist. of Ampleforth*; *Memoir* in *Cath. Directory*, 1844.

BERNARD WARD.

Baines, RALPH, Bishop of Lichfield and Coventry, England, b. at Knowsthorp, Yorks, date of birth uncertain; d. 18 November, 1559. Educated at St. John's College, Cambridge, he was ordained priest at Ely, 1519. Rector of Hardwicke in Cambridgeshire until 1544 when he went to Paris where he became Professor of Hebrew. In 1553 he returned to England and was consecrated Bishop of Lichfield and Coventry, 18 November, 1554. He vigorously opposed the Reformers and was one of the eight defenders of Catholic doctrine at the Westminster Conference 1558–59. On the accession of Elizabeth he was deprived of his bishopric (21 June, 1559) and committed to the care of Grindal, Protestant Bishop of London, thus becoming one of the eleven imprisoned bishops. The recent researches of the Rev. G. Philips (op. cit., inf.), who has exhaustively treated the question of the imprisonment of these bishops, prove that, though nominally a guest, he was in fact a strict prisoner. His captivity lasted until 18 November, 1559, when, as Pitts writes, he "died an illustrious Confessor of the Lord". He wrote "Prima Rudimenta in linguam Hebraicam" (Paris, 1550); "Compendium Michol, hoc est absolutissimæ grammatices Davidis Chimhi" (Paris, 1554); "In Proverbia Salomonis" (Paris, 1555).

Sanders, *Report to Cardinal Moroni, 1561* (Cath. Record Soc. Pubs., 1905), I; Pitts, *De Angl. Script.* (1623); Dodd, *Church History* (1688), Pt. III, ii, art. 3; Cooper, *Athenæ Cantabrigienses*, I, 202; Gillow, *Bibl. Dict. Eng. Cath.* (London, 1885); Bridgett and Knox, *Q. Eliz. and the Cath. Hierarchy* (London, 1889); Phillips, *Extinction of the Ancient Hierarchy* (London, 1905).

EDWIN BURTON.

Baini, ABBATE GIUSEPPE, b. in Rome, 21 October, 1775; d. there 21 May, 1844. Baini made his first musical studies under the direction of his uncle Lorenzo Baini, a distinguished disciple of the Roman School, who introduced him into the spirit and traditions of the Palestrina style. Later Baini became the pupil and friend of Jannaconi, choirmaster of the Vatican Basilica, through whom he was admitted into the choir of the Sistine Chapel as a bass singer. In 1818 Baini was unanimously elected director of the famous choir, a position which he held till his death.

While Baini has left a considerable number of compositions (notably a ten-voiced "Miserere" which is still performed, alternately with those of Allegri and Bai, during Holy Week, by the Sistine Chapel choir), all of which are written in the style of the great period of classic polyphony, his great life-work was his "Memorie storico-critiche della vita e delle opere di Giovanni Pierluigi da Palestrina" (1828). Through the translation into German of this work by Francis de Sales Kandler (Vienna, 1834), the life and labours of Palestrina's school and period became more accessible and were a powerful influence in the revival and restoration of liturgical music which was about to take its beginning. The publication of Palestrina's complete works was one of the results of Baini's biography of the master. Baini lived so completely in the great musical past that he had but scant sympathy with, or understanding for, modern developments of the art. Besides the biography of Palestrina he has left a study on the theory of rhythm of the ancients under the title: "Saggio sopra l'identità di ritmi musicali e poetici"; an unfinished history of the Sistine Chapel choir; and other essays of a critical or theoretic character.

Ambros, *Geschichte der Musik* (Leipzig, 1881); Riemann, *Musik Lex.* (Leipzig, 1905).

JOSEPH OTTEN.

Baithen, SAINT, of Iona, an Irish monk, specially selected by St. Columba as one of the band of missionaries who set sail for Britain in 563. Born in 536, the son of Brenaron, he was an ardent disciple of St. Columba, and was appointed Abbot of Tiree Island, a monastery founded by St. Comgall of Bangor. St. Adamnan, in recording the death of St. Columba, tells us that the dying words of the Apostle of Iona, as he was transcribing the fifty-third Psalm, were: "I must stop here, let Baithen write what follows". Baithen had been looked on as the most likely successor to St. Columba, and so it happened that on the death of that great apostle, in 596, the monks unanimously confirmed the choice of their founder. St. Baithen was in high esteem as a wise counsellor, and his advice was sought by many Irish saints, including St. Fintan Munnu of Taghmon.

St. Adamnan (Eunan), the biographer of St. Columba, tells many interesting incidents in the life of St. Baithen, but the mere fact of being the immediate successor of St. Columba, by the express wish of that apostle, is almost sufficient to attest his worth. The "Martyrology of Donegal" records the two following anecdotes. When St. Baithen partook of food, before each morsel he invariably recited "Deus in adjutorium meum intende". Also, "when he worked in the fields, gathering in the corn along with the monks, he used to hold up one hand towards Heaven, beseeching God, while with the other hand he gathered the corn". St. Baithen of Iona is generally known as Baithen Mor,

to distinguish him from eight other saints of the same name—the affix *mor* meaning "the Great". He wrote a life of his master, and some Irish poems, which are now lost, but which were seen by St. Adamnan. He only ruled Iona three years, as his death took place in the year 600, though the "Annals of Ulster" give the date as 598. Perhaps the true year may be 599. His feast is celebrated on October 6th. Some writers assert that St. Baithen of Iona is the patron of Ennisboyne, County Wicklow, but this is owing to a confusion with St. Baoithin, or Baithin mac Findech, whose feast is commemorated on 22 May. Another St. Baoithin, son of Cuana, whose feast is on 19 February, is patron of Tibohin, in Elphin.

Colgan, *Acta Sanctorum*; Sherman, *Loca Patriciana*; O'Hanlon, *Lives of the Irish Saints*; Reeves, *Adamnan* (Dublin, 1857); Fowler, *Vita S. Columbæ* (Oxford, 1894); *Annals of Ulster* (Rolls Series); Healy, *Insula Sanctorum et Doctorum*, 4th ed. (Dublin, 1902); Moran, *Irish Saints in Great Britain* (1903); *Acta Sanctorum Hiberniæ ex Codice Salamanticensi* (Edinburgh and London, 1888); Stokes, *Irish Lives of the Saints* (Oxford, 1890); Hyde, *Literary History of Ireland* (London, 1900).

W. H. GRATTAN FLOOD.

Baius (or DE BAY), MICHEL, theologian and author of a system known as Baianism, was b. at Melun in Hainaut, 1513, and d. at Louvain 16 September, 1589. Though poor, he succeeded in procuring, in the various colleges of the Louvain University, a complete course of studies, including humanities, philosophy, and theology. His first appointment, immediately after his ordination, was as principal of the Standonk College, 1541. Three years later he was given the chair of philosophy which he retained till 1550. In that year he took the degree of Doctor of Theology, was made President of the Collège Adrien and also substitute to the professor of Holy Scripture, then absent at the Council of Trent, the full professorship following two years later at the titular's death. Baius had very early formed a close friendship with John Hessels. While the three leaders of the university: Tapper, Chancellor; Ravestein, Professor of Theology; and Hasselius, Professor of Holy Scripture, were at the Council of Trent, Baius and Hessels profited by their absence to give vent to long cherished ideas and introduce new methods and new doctrines. On his return from Trent, in 1552, Chancellor Tapper found that evil influences had been at work and asked Cardinal de Granvelle, Archbishop of Mechlin, to interfere. Granvelle succeeded in quieting the innovators for awhile, but Tapper's death, in 1559, became the signal of fresh disturbances. At the request of the Franciscans, the Sorbonne of Paris had censured eighteen propositions embodying the main innovations of Baius and Hessels. Baius answered the censure in a memoir now lost, and the controversy only increased in acridity. Pope Pius IV, through Cardinal Granvelle, imposed silence upon both Baius and the Franciscans, without, however, rendering any doctrinal decision. When the sessions of the Council of Trent were resumed, in 1561, Baius and Hessels were selected to represent the university at Trent. The papal legate, Commendone, objected to the choice of the university, but Cardinal de Granvelle thought that the two innovators' presence at Trent would be good both for them and for the university. In 1563 he sent them to Trent, not, however, as delegates of the university, but as theologians of the King of Spain. Just before leaving Trent Baius had published his first tracts. Unfortunately, the contents of those tracts were not within the programme of the last three sessions of the Council of Trent, and no public discussion of the disputed points took place. It is known, however, that Baius' and Hessels' views were distasteful to the Fathers, and that the Catholic king's prestige alone saved them from formal condemnation.

Baius returned to Louvain in 1564 and the same year published new tracts which, with the addition of another series, were collected in "Opuscula omnia", in 1566, the year of Hessels' death. It is likely that Hessels collaborated with Baius in these "Opuscula". Their defence rested now on Baius alone, and it was no small task. Ravestein, who had succeeded Tapper as chancellor, thought it was high time to call a halt, and informed Rome, requesting decisive action; 1 October, 1567, Pope Pius V signed the Bull, "Ex omnibus afflictionibus", in which were to be found a number of condemned propositions, but without mention of Baius' name. According to the usage of the Roman Chancery, the papal document was without punctuation, divisions, or numbers. Again, as had been done before in several instances, the objectionable propositions were not censured severally, but to the whole series were applied various "notes", from "heretical" down to "offensive". Moreover, not only was Baius' name not mentioned, but for obvious reasons of prudence in those days, so near the Reformation, the text itself was not to be made public. These facts gave occasion to many quibbles on the part of the Baianists: What was the exact number of propositions?—76, 79, or 80?—Were they, or were they not, Baius' propositions?—Why had not a copy of the Bull been given to those on whose honour it was supposed to reflect? In the famous sentence, "quas quidem sententias stricto coram nobis examine ponderatas quamquam nonnullæ aliquo pacto sustineri possent in rigore et proprio verborum sensu ab assertoribus intento hæreticas, erroneas . . . damnamus", was the *comma Pianum* to be placed after *intento* or after *possent*, the meaning being reversed according as the comma came after the one or the other word? Nevertheless, Baius did not stoop to these evasions at first, but when the papal Bull (1567) was brought to the university and read to the faculty, he subscribed with the other professors. Meanwhile, the text of the Bull having been divulged by some indiscreet person, Baius began to find fault with it and wrote to, or for, the pope two lengthy apologies, in vindication, he said, not so much of himself as of St. Augustine. The tone of the apologies was respectful in appearance rather than in reality. By a Brief, dated 1569, Pius V answered that the case had been maturely examined and finally adjudged, and demanded submission. After much tergiversation, wherein he stooped to the ridiculous evasion of the *comma Pianum* and the practical stultification of a papal act, Baius abjured to Morillon, de Granvelle's vicar-general, all the errors condemned in the Bull, but was not then and there required to sign his recantation. The absence of that formality contributed later to revive the discusions. In 1570, at Ravestein's death, Baius became dean of the faculty. Then rumors went abroad that the new dean was by no means in accord with orthodox teaching. Followers and adversaries suggested a clear pronouncement. It came under the title of the "Explicatio articulorum", in which Baius averred that, of the many condemned propositions, some were false and justly censured, some only ill expressed, while still others, if at variance with the terminology of the Scholastics, were yet the genuine sayings of the Fathers; at any rate, with more than forty of the seventy-nine articles he claimed to have nothing whatever to do. Baius, after two recantations, was simply reverting to his original position. The Bull was then solemnly published at Louvain, and subscribed by the whole faculty. Baius accepted it again. His apparent magnanimity even won him sympathy and preferments; he was in quick succession made Chancellor of Louvain, Dean of St. Peter's Collegiate Church, and "conservator" of the university's privileges. Thus was peace restored, but only for a while.

Certain inconsiderate views of the master regarding the authority of the Holy See, and even of the Council of Trent, and, on the part of his disciples, the ill disguised hope that Gregory XIII might declare void all that had been done by his predecessor, bade fair to reopen the whole question. Pope Gregory XIII would not permit this. The Bull, "Provisionis nostræ" (1579), confirmed the preceding papal acts and the Jesuit Toletus was commissioned to receive and bring to the pope the final abjuration of Baius. We have it under the name of "Confessio Michaelis Baii". It reads, in part: "I am convinced that the condemnation of all those propositions is just and lawful. I confess that very many (*plurimas*) of these propositions are in my books, and in the sense in which they are condemned. I renounce them all and resolve never more to teach or defend any of them." Despite this recantation, Baius' errors had sunk too deep into his mind not to occasionally crop up in rash tenets. Up to the last few years of his life sad contests were raised by, or around, him, and nothing short of the official admission by the university of a compact body of doctrine could quell those contests. Baius died in the Church, to which his studiousness, attainments, and piety did honour, but whose doctrinal unity his rashness came near to infringing. The evil seed he had sown bore fruits of bitterness later on in the errors of Jansenism.

His System.—Baius' system has been conveniently called Baianism, as a more objective name for it would be difficult to find. It is contained in a series of *opuscula*, or pamphlets: "On Free Will"; "Justice and Justification"; "Sacrifice"; "Meritorious Works"; "Man's Original Integrity and the Merits of the Wicked"; "The Sacraments"; "The Form of Baptism"; "Original Sin"; "Charity"; "Indulgences"; "Prayers for the Dead". Baius himself collected all those pamphlets in "M. Baii opuscula theologica" (Louvain, 1566). The Maurist Gerberon gave a more complete edition: "M. Baii opera cum bullis pontificum et aliis ad ipsius causam spectantibus" (Cologne, 1696). This edition was put on the Index in 1697 on account of its second part, or "Baiana", in which the editor gives useful information about, but shows too much sympathy for, Baius. The gist of Baianism is also found in the 79 propositions censured by Pius V (Denzinger, Enchiridion, 881–959). All cavil apart, the first 60 are easily identified in Baius' printed works, and the remaining 19—"tales quae vulgo circumferrentur", says an old manuscript copy of the Bull "Ex omnibus"—represent the oral teaching of the Baianist wing. In the preface to "Man's Original Integrity" Baius says: "What was in the beginning the integrity natural to man? Without that question one can understand neither the first corruption of nature (by original sin) nor its reparation by the grace of Christ." Those words give us the sequence of Baianism: (1) the state of innocent nature; (2) the state of fallen nature; (3) the state of redeemed nature.

(1) *State of Innocent Nature.*—From the fact, so strongly asserted by the Fathers, of the actual conjunction of nature and grace in the first man, Baius infers their necessary connexion or even practical identity. In his view, primitive innocence was not supernatural, at least in the ordinary acceptation of that word, but due to, and demanded by, the normal condition of humanity (which cannot, without it, remain in the state of salvation). And that primitive state, natural to man, included among its necessary requirements destination to heaven, immunity from ignorance, suffering, and death, and the inherent power of meriting. None of these was, nor could rightly be called, a gratuitous gift of grace.

(2) *State of Fallen Nature.*—The downfall of man

is not, and cannot be, according to Baius, the mere forfeiting of gratuitous or supernatural gifts, but some positive evil reaching deep into our very nature. That evil is original sin. By original sin Baius understands, instead of a simple privation of grace, habitual concupiscence itself, transmitted according to the laws of heredity and developed according to the laws of physical and psychical growth. It is a sin or moral evil by itself, even in irresponsible children, and that outside of all relation to a will, be it original or personal. What, then, becomes of human liberty as a source of moral responsibility? Baius does not think it necessary that, in order to be moral agents, we should be free from internal determinism, but only from external compulsion. From so tainted a source, Redemption apart, only tainted actions can flow. They may sometimes appear virtuous, but it is only an appearance (*vitia virtutes imitantia*). In truth all human actions, not purified by Redemption, are vices pure and simple and damning vices at that (*vitia sunt et damnant*).

(3) *State of Redeemed Nature.*—The gifts of primitive innocence, forfeited by original sin, are restored by Jesus Christ. Then and then only do they become graces, not, indeed, on account of their supernatural character, but because of fallen man's positive unworthiness. Aided by grace, the redeemed can perform virtuous actions and acquire merits for heaven. Does that entail a higher status, an inner renovation or sanctifying grace?—Baius does not consider it necessary. Moral action, whether called justice, or charity, or obedience to the law, is the sole instrument of justification and virtue and merit. The rôle of grace consists exclusively in keeping concupiscence under control, and in thus enabling us to perform moral actions and fulfil the law. True, Baius speaks of the remission of sin as necessary for justification, but this is only a *fictio iuris*; in fact, a catechumen before baptism, or a penitent before absolution may, by simply keeping the precepts, have more charity than certain so-called just men. If the catechumen and penitent are not styled just, it is only in deference to Holy Scripture, which requires for complete justice both newness of life (i. e. moral action) and pardon of sin (i. e. of the *reatus*, or liability to punishment). To grant that kind of pardon is the only object and efficacy of the sacraments of the dead, baptism and penance. With regard to the sacraments of the living, the Eucharist—the only one on which Baius expressed his views—has no other sacrificial value than that of being a good moral action drawing us close to God.

A mere glance at the above sketch cannot fail to reveal a strange mixture of Pelagianism, Calvinism, and even Socinianism. Baius is a Pelagian in his concept of the primitive state of man. He is a Calvinist in his presentation of the downfall. He is more than a Lutheran and little short of the Socinian in his theory of Redemption. Critics know that all these errors were in a manner harmonized in Baius' mind, but they are not agreed as to what may have been the genetic principle of that theological formation. Some find it in the 38th proposition: "Omnis amor creaturæ rationalis aut vitiosa est cupiditas, quâ mundus diligitur, quæ a Joanne prohibetur, aut laudabilis illa charitas, quâ per spiritum sanctum in corde diffusâ Deus amatur" (The rational creature's love is either vicious desire, with its attachment to the world, which St. John forbids, or that praiseworthy charity which is poured forth in our hearts by the Holy Spirit, and through which God is loved). Others see it in a wrong analysis of man, the higher faculties, appertaining to the moral and religious life, being violently torn apart from the lower powers, and so magnified as to become

identical with grace and the indwelling of the Holy Ghost. Others, again, think it is optimism in appraising man's native condition, or pessimism in gauging his condition after sin, the result being the same with regard to the value of Redemption. Taking the question from an historical standpoint, we find that Baius was from the beginning a humanist with a perfect enthusiasm for Christian antiquity in general, St. Paul and St. Augustine in particular, and a dislike almost amounting to abhorrence for the thoughts and methods of medieval schoolmen. The self-assumed task of interpreting the Apostle of the Gentiles and the great African Doctor apart from the traditional current of Scholastic thought was perhaps an impossibility in itself, but certainly one for Baius' limited erudition and paradoxical mind. To this all-absorbing mania, much more than to a lack of sincere loyalty to the Church, must we trace Baius' blindness to the already defined dogmas and his half-revolts against the living *magisterium*. A partial explanation of, if not excuse for, that monomania is, however, found in the fact that at the very outset of his theological career Baius came under the influence of men who, like the Dominican Peter de Soto, believed the Catholic reaction against the Reformers had gone somewhat too far, and suggested that more stress be laid on Scripture and Patrology and less on Thomism. That, in his intention at least, Baius only wanted to take the most advantageous position in order the better to defend the Faith against heretics, we know from a letter he wrote (1569) to Cardinal Simonetta: "After reading Peter the Lombard and some other Scholastic Doctor, I endeavoured to bring theology back to Holy Scripture and the writings of the Fathers, those at least who still enjoy some credit with the heretics: Cyprian, Ambrose, Jerome, Augustine, Leo, Prosper, Gregory, and the like." Such are the various causes which may in a measure account for the position taken by Baius. The chronology of his writings teaches us little more. It fails to give us a true insight into the logical development of his thought. It may be, after all, that each of the above-mentioned genetic principles held priority in his mind at different times and in different needs.

DOCTRINE OF THE CHURCH.—The Catholic teaching, already outlined against the Pelagians by various councils and popes from the fifth century, is fully presented against the Reformers by the Council of Trent, especially Session V, Decree on Original Sin, and Session VI, Decree on Justification. In those two sessions, both anterior to Baius' writings, we find three statements which are obviously irreconcilable with Baius' three main positions described above: (1) Man's original justice is represented as a supernatural gift; (2) Original Sin is described not as a deep deterioration of our nature, but as the forfeiture of purely gratuitous privileges; (3) Justification is depicted as an interior renovation of the soul by inherent grace. The condemnation by Pius V of the 79 Baianist tenets is an act of the supreme *magisterium* of the Church, an *ex cathedrâ* pronouncement. To say, with the Baianists, that the papal act condemns not the real and concrete tenets of the Louvain professor, but only certain hypothetical or imaginary propositions; to pretend that the censure is aimed not at the underlying teaching, but only at the vehemence or harshness of the outward expressions, is to practically stultify the pontifical document. From the tenor of the Bull, "Ex Omnibus", we know that to each of the 79 propositions one or several or all of the following censures will apply: *hæretica, erronea, suspecta, temeraria, scandalosa, in pias aures offendens*. For a more precise determination of the Catholic doctrine, we have to consult, besides the Council of Trent, the *consensus Catholicorum theologorum*. That consensus was voiced with no uncertainty by such universities as Paris, Salamanca, Alcalá, and Louvain itself, and by such theologians as Cunerus Petri (d. 1580—"De Gratiâ", Cologne, 1583); Suarez (d. 1617—"De gratiâ Dei" in Op. Omn., VII, Paris, 1857); Bellarmine (d. 1623—"De gratiâ et libero arbitrio", in Controversiæ, IV, Milan, 1621); Ripalda (d. 1648—"Adversus Baium et Baianos", Paris, 1872); Stayaert (d. 1701—"In propositiones damnatas assertiones", Louvain, 1753); Tournely (d. 1729—"De Gratiâ Christi", Paris, 1726); Casini (d. 1755—"Quid est homo?" ed. Scheeben, Mainz, 1862). It should not, however, be omitted here that, even apart from Jansenism, which is a direct offshoot of Baianism, some traces of Baius' confused ideas about the natural and the supernatural are to be found here and there in the history of theology. The Augustinian School, represented by such able men as Noris, Bellelli, and Berti, adopted, though with qualifications, the idea of man's natural aspiration to the possession of God and beatific vision in Heaven. The standard work of that school, "Vindiciæ Augustinianæ", was even once denounced to the Holy See, but no censure ensued. More recently Stattler, Hermes, Günther, Hirscher, and Kuhn evolved a notion of the supernatural which is akin to that of Baius. While admitting relatively supernatural gifts, they denied that the partaking of Divine nature and the adoption to eternal life differ essentially from our natural moral life. That theory was successfully opposed by Kleutgen and seems now to have died out. The new French theory of "immanence", according to which man postulates the supernatural, may also have some kinship with Baianism, but it can only be mentioned here as it is yet the centre of rather fervid discussions. Matulewicz, "Doctrina Russorum de Statu iustitiæ originalis" (Cracow, 1903), says that modern Russian theology embodies in great measure the condemned views of Baius.

Besides works mentioned in article, DUCHESNE, *Histoire du Baianisme* (Douai, 1731); DE LA CHAMBRE, *Traité historique et dogmatique sur la doctrine de Baius* (s. l., 1739); LIGUORI, *Trionfo della chiesa* (Naples, 1772); LINSENMAN, *Michel Baius* (Tübingen, 1867); SCHEEBEN in *Kirchenlex.*, s. v., and in *Der Katholik* (Mainz, 1868); SCHWANE-DEGERT, *Histoire des dogmes* (Paris, 1904), VI; LE BACHELET in *Dict. de théol. cath.*, s. v.; WILHELM AND SCANNELL, *Manual of Catholic Theology* (New York, 1906); KROLL, *The Causes of the Jansenist Heresy* in *Am. Cath. Quart.* (1885), 577.

J. F. SOLLIER.

Baker, CHARLES, VENERABLE (*recté*, according to his own entry in the English College Diary, DAVID HENRY LEWIS), an English Jesuit martyr, b. in Monmouthshire in 1616; d. at Usk, 27 August, 1679. His father, Morgan Lewis, was a lax Catholic, afterwards converted; his mother, Margaret Pritchard, was a very devout Catholic. David was brought up as a Protestant, and educated at the Royal Grammar School at Abergavenny, of which his father was the head master. In his sixteenth year, he spent three months in Paris as companion to a son of Earl Rivers, and there was received into the Church by a Father Talbot, S. J. On returning to England, he remained with his parents till their death and then, having a desire for the priesthood, went to Rome, where he was admitted as an *alumnus* to the English College, 3 November, 1638. He was ordained priest in 1642, and entered the novitiate of the Society at Sant' Andrea, 16 April, 1644. In 1647 he was sent to the English mission, but was quickly recalled and made Spiritual Father at the Roman College. In 1648 he returned to England finally, and was assigned to the South Wales District, where he laboured zealously for twenty-eight years. It is told of him that to avoid the persecutors, he used to take long and dangerous journeys at night that he might be able to visit the faithful under cover of darkness, and that his devotedness gained for him the title of Father of the Poor.

In the summer of 1678, Titus Oates came forward with his pretended revelations, and Parliament in a frenzy of bigotry offered fresh rewards for the discovery and arrest of priests and Jesuits. Father David was one of the victims. A bigoted Calvinist magistrate named Arnold, who had hitherto professed friendship for him, caused him to be arrested at Llantarnam in Monmouthshire, 17 November, 1678. He was carried in a sort of triumphal procession to Abergavenny, where, in allusion to one article of Oates's fabrications, he was shown to the people as "the pretended Bishop of Llandaff". He was then committed for trial, and meanwhile imprisoned, first at Monmouth and then at Usk. The trial came off at Monmouth 28 March, 1679. It was impossible to connect Father David with the pretended Popish Plot, so he was charged under the Statute of 27 Elizabeth, which made it high treason to take orders abroad in the Church of Rome and afterwards to return to England and say Mass. The trial was not too fairly conducted, and the witnesses were of a worthless class. Still the breach of the law was undeniable, and he was condemned to undergo the barbarous penalties which the law prescribed. For the moment, indeed, he was reprieved, and was taken up to London to be confronted with Oates and his associates. It was hoped that he might be induced to save his life either by apostasy or by inculpating some others in the Plot. But this hope proving vain, he was sent back to Monmouthshire, and his sentence was carried out at Usk. The cause of his beatification was introduced, under the name of "David Lewis *alias* Charles Baker" by the Decree of 4 December, 1886.

COBBETT, *State Trials*, VII; *Florus Anglo-Bavaricus* (1685); CHALLONER, *Memoirs of Missionary Priests*; FOLEY, *Records of the English Province, S.J.*; GILLOW, *Bibl. Dict. Eng. Cath.*, s. v.

SYDNEY F. SMITH.

Baker, DAVID AUGUSTINE, a well-known Benedictine mystic and an ascetic writer, b. at Abergavenny, England, 9 December, 1575; d. of the plague in London, 9 August, 1641. His father was William Baker, steward to Lord Abergavenny, his mother, a daughter of Lewis ap John (*alias* Wallis), Vicar of Abergavenny. He was educated at Christ's Hospital and at Broadgate's Hall, now Pembroke College Oxford, afterwards becoming a member of Clifford's Inn, and later of the Middle Temple. At Oxford he lost his faith in the existence of God, but after some years, being in extreme peril of death, he escaped by what appeared to him a miracle. Following up the light thus given him, he was led to the threshold of the Catholic Church, and was received into its fold. In 1605 he joined the Benedictine Order at Padua, but ill-health obliged him to postpone his religious profession, and he returned home to find his father on the point of death. Having reconciled him to the Church and assisted him in his last moments, Father Baker hastened to settle his own worldly affairs and to return to the cloister. He was professed by

FATHER DAVID AUGUSTINE BAKER, O.S.B.

the Italian Fathers in England as a member of the Cassinese Congregation, but subsequently aggregated to the English Congregation. At the desire of his superiors he now devoted his time and the ample means which he had inherited, to investigating and refuting the recently started error that the ancient Benedictine congregation in England was dependent on that of Cluny, founded in 910. He was immensely helped in his studies and researches for this purpose by the Cottonian Library which contained so many of the spoils of the old Benedictine monasteries in England, and which its generous founder placed entirely at his disposal. In collaboration with Father Jones and Father Clement Reyner he embodied the fruit of these researches in the volume entitled "Apostolatus Benedictinorum in Angliâ". At Sir Robert Cotton's Father Baker came in contact with the antiquary, William Camden, and with other learned men of his day. In 1624 he was sent to the newly established convent of Benedictine nuns at Cambrai, not as chaplain, but to aid in forming the spiritual character of the religious. Here he remained for about nine years, during which time he wrote many of his ascetical treatises, an abstract of which is contained in the valuable work "Sancta Sophia" compiled by Father Serenus Cressy. In 1633 he removed to Douai, where he wrote his long treatise on the English mission, but he was nearly worn out with his austerities before the order came for him to proceed to the battle-field. During his short sojourn in London, Father Baker was forced frequently to change his abode in order to avoid the pursuivants who were on his track. It was not, however, as a martyr that he was to end his days, but as a victim of the plague to which he succumbed in the sixty-sixth year of his age. Of upwards of thirty treatises chiefly on spiritual matters written by Father Baker, many are to be found in manuscript at Downside, Ampleforth, Stanbrook, and other Benedictine monasteries in England. An adequate biography of this master of the ascetic life is still a desideratum.

Sweeney, *Life and Spirit of Father Baker* (London, 1861); Dodd, *Church History*, III, 112; Wood, *Athenæ Oxon*, ed. Bliss, III, 7; *Cotton. MS., Julius C.*, III, f. 12; Evans, *Portraits*, 12,348 –12,349; *Dublin Review*, New Series, XXVII, 337; *The Rambler*, March, 1851, p. 214; Coxe, *Cat. Codd. MSS. Collegii Jesu, Oxon.*, 25–30; Weldon, *Chronological Notes; Catalogue of Rawlinson MSS.*; Cooper in *Dict. of Nat. Biog.*

J. M. Stone.

Baker, Francis Asbury, priest of the Congregation of St. Paul the Apostle, b. Baltimore, Md., U. S. A., 30 March, 1820; d. 4 April, 1865. Father Baker was a son of Dr. Samuel Baker, a physician of note in Baltimore. He was graduated from Princeton College in 1839. His parents, whom he lost early in life, had been Methodists, but their surviving children joined the Episcopal Church. He took orders in that communion, and was ordained a presbyter in September, 1846. His career promised to be not only successful but brilliant. Possessed of many mental gifts, he had, moreover, refinement, wealth, and an engaging personality; he was deeply pious, thoroughly consecrated to his chosen work. He was assigned at first as an assistant at St. Paul's Episcopal Church, Baltimore, and six years later was named rector of St. Luke's Church in the same city. He took rank at once as an eloquent preacher.

The Oxford Movement coincided with the years of his preparation and early ministry, and its influence in the United States resulted in the conversion of many distinguished men. It was not possible that an intelligent and sincere man like Baker could remain unmoved amid the awakening and the return to Catholic principles which the study of primitive and patristic history and theology caused. The severance of intimate ties cost him much, but he obeyed the call and in April, 1853, made his profession of faith. Attracted to the religious state, he entered the Redemptorist Order, was ordained priest in the Cathedral of Baltimore, 21 September, 1856, and began forthwith a laborious but most fruitful career as a missionary. The Redemptorists had inaugurated in 1851 the work of giving missions to the English-speaking Catholics of the United States, and the flood of immigration, then at its height, made the work exhausting and continuous. The missionary band included Fathers Hecker, Walworth, Hewit, and Deshon, all converts and all Americans, an unusually strong and varied combination, and to them Father Baker proved a welcome acquisition. He brought to his work the zeal of an apostle, a matured and persuasive eloquence, and the attraction of a character at once magnetic and saintly. Nor are these the words of mere eulogy. The recollections of the generation which listened to him, the judgment of competent critics, the numerous conversions, the abiding impressions he effected, the evidences which his printed sermons display of oratorical gifts—all entitle Father Baker to a high place among Catholic preachers.

In his sermons we find a blending of argumentation with appeal, a diction at once forceful and finished, and an apt and abundant use of Holy Scripture, which, combining with his earnest and dignified delivery, gave to his message a powerful effect. Leaving the Redemptorists with Fathers Hecker, Walworth, Hewitt, and Deshon, for the purpose of organizing a special missionary community for English parishes, he shared with them the labour of founding the Paulist Institute. It was he who gave the impulse and established the tradition of rubrical exactitude and ceremonial splendour which have continued to be a characteristic of that community. He died of typhoid pneumonia contracted in ministering to the sick.

Hewit, *Memoir of the Life of the Rev. Francis A. Baker* (New York, 1865); *Sermons of the Rev. Francis A. Baker* (New York, 1896); Walworth, *The Oxford Movement in the U. S.* (New York, 1895).

Michael Paul Smith.

Baker City, Diocese of, comprises Wasco, Klamath, Lake, Sherman, Gilliam, Wheeler, Morrow, Grant, Union, Crook, Umatilla, Wallowa, Baker, Harney, and Malheur counties in the State of Oregon, U. S. A., an area of 65,683 square miles. It was established in 1903. The Rev. Charles J. O'Reilly, rector of the Church of the Immaculate Heart of Mary, Portland, Oregon, and editor of the "Catholic Sentinel" was named its first bishop and consecrated 25 August of that year. The diocese has a Catholic population estimated at about 4,000, whose spiritual needs are cared for by ten diocesan and seven Franciscan and Jesuit priests. The Sisters of St. Francis, St. Dominic, and the Most Holy Name of Jesus and Mary conduct five schools and academies. At the Umatilla Indian reservation there are more than 500 Catholic Indians attended by the Jesuit fathers of the Rocky Mountain Mission, two Brothers of Christian Instruction, and eight Sisters of St. Francis. There are 13 churches and 36 mission stations in the diocese.

Bishop O'Reilly was born 4 January, 1862, at St. John, New Brunswick, Canada, and educated at the Christian Brothers' school of St. John and at St. Joseph's College, Memramcook. He made his theological studies at the Grand Seminary, Montreal, and was ordained priest at Portland 29 June, 1890. He was then appointed to the mission of Oswego and Tegardville, and in February, 1894, was made rector of the Church of the Immaculate Heart of Mary, Portland.

Catholic Sentinel (Portland, August, 1903) files; *The Catholic Directory* (Milwaukee, 1907).

Thomas F. Meehan.

Bakócz, Thomas, Cardinal and statesman, b. about 1442, in the village of Erdoed, county Szatmár, Northeastern Hungary; d. 15 June, 1521. His family belonged to the lower class, but was raised to the rank of nobility by his older brother Valentine. Through the generosity of this same brother he was enabled to pursue a thorough course of studies first in the town of Szatmár-Németi, then in Cracow, Poland, and finally in the Italian cities of Ferrara and Padua. He returned to his native country about the year 1470, with the doctor's degree, and soon after made the acquaintance of a distinguished ecclesiastic from Italy, Gabriel Rangoni, who enjoyed the confidence of King Matthias (1458–90) and held high positions in Hungary. By this prelate Bakócz was introduced to the king about the year 1474; and through a fortunate incident he attracted the attention of his sovereign. He was retained at court, employed in the chancery, and soon became secretary to the king and substitute of the royal chancellor. In 1480 he received a provostship in the town of Titel, Southern Hungary; and in 1486 he was promoted to the Bishopric of Raab. After the death of King Matthias in 1490 Bakócz took an active part in the selection of a new ruler; and when his candidate, Ladislaus II (1490–1516), a Polish prince and King of Bohemia, was chosen, Bakócz was made chancellor of the realm. As such he became the real ruler of his country, whose destinies he directed with firmness and skill. He concluded advantageous treaties with other powers, and made the alliance with Venice the pivot of his foreign policy. On that account he kept Hungary out of the League of Cambrai formed in 1508 between Pope Julius II (1503–13), France, Spain, and the Emperor Maximilian (1493–1519) against Venice. No wonder that the authorities of Venice vied with King Ladislaus in securing honours and riches for the powerful and ambitious prelate.

When the Bishopric of Erlau became vacant in 1491, Bakócz was appointed to it by the king. Pope Alexander VI (1492–1503) at first opposed, but later ratified, the appointment in 1497; and shortly afterwards, in December of the same year, transferred Bakócz to the primatial See of Gran. In addition to this Bakócz was created cardinal in 1500, and made Patriarch of Constantinople in 1507. The republic of Venice gladly assigned to him the revenues which were found within its own territory and attached to the patriarchal title. Not satisfied with all this Bakócz aspired to the papal throne, and received assurances of support from the Emperor Maximilian and from Venice; however, adverse circumstances prevented the realization of these hopes. A man of such prominence had necessarily his part in the ecclesiastical events of a general character. When in 1510 several cardinals rebelled against Pope Julius II, both sides tried to win him for their plans. Bakócz maintained a waiting attitude, until the pope, in 1511, condemned the schismatic Council of Pisa and announced that a general synod would be held in the Lateran in 1512. Bakócz was invited to this council, and without further hesitation he sailed on a Venetian ship to Ancona, and arrived in Rome in January, 1512, where he was received by the pope with much pomp and splendour. In the council, which opened the following May, Bakócz took an active part; he was on the committee for the reform of the Church and the Roman Curia. After the death of Pope Julius II, early in 1513, and during the conclave, it became evident that he had little prospect of winning the papal tiara; in fact on the 10th of March Cardinal Medici was chosen as Leo X (1513–21).

The new pope secured at once the service of the influential Bakócz for a crusade against the Turks. He appointed the primate a legate *a latere* not only for Hungary but also for the neighbouring countries, and granted to him most ample faculties. After his return to Hungary in 1514 Bakócz made preparations at once for the expedition, and soon an army of about 100,000 soldiers was gathered under the leadership of George Dózsa. Unfortunately the nobles were opposed to the enterprise, and the whole matter ended in a civil war between them and the Crusaders, in which the nobility remained victorious. After the death of King Ladislaus II in 1516 the influence of Bakócz ceased almost completely; the last years of his life were spent more in retirement. He was a man of the world, very ambitious, and not always tender in the choice of the means to an end. Out of his large fortune, and through his influential position, he provided in a princely manner for the members of his family. Owing to the great power so long wielded by him, he made many enemies among his own countrymen, whose opposition triumphed in the end. With all that his personal conduct was blameless; not even a shadow of suspicion was cast upon his character by his enemies. He was deeply religious, and had a special devotion to the Blessed Virgin, in whose honour he fitted out a chapel in the Cathedral of Erlau, and built one near that of Gran. In the latter, a magnificent structure of the Renaissance, his remains found their last resting place.

Fraknói, *Erdödi Bakócz Tamás* (Budapest, 1889); Dankó, in *Kirchenlex* s. v. *Bakácz* (Freiburg, 1886), I.

Francis J. Schaefer.

Bakunin, Michael. See Socialism.

Balaam.—The derivation of the name is uncertain. Dr. Neubauer would connect it with the god Ammo or Ammi, as though Balaam belonged to a people whose god or lord was Ammo or Ammi. It is certainly remarkable that Balaam is said (Num., xxii, 5) to come from "the land of the children of Ammo" (D. V. reads "Ammon").

The Narrative.—The story of Balaam is contained in Numbers, chapters xxii–xxiv; xxxi, 8–16; Deut., xxiii, 4; Josue, xiii, 22; and xxiv, 9–10. There are also references to him in Nehemias, xiii, 2; Micheas, vi, 5; II Peter, ii, 15; Jude, 11; and Apoc., ii, 14. Balac, King of Moab, alarmed at Israel's victories over the Amorrhites, sent messengers with presents to Balaam, son of Beor, who dwelt in Pethor (the Pitru of the cuneiform texts) to induce him to come and curse Israel. For in those early times, men attached great importance to a curse, as, for instance, that of a father on his child; and Balaam had a special reputation in this matter. "I know", said Balac to him through his messengers, "that he whom thou shalt bless is blessed, and he whom thou shalt curse is cursed." When the messengers had delivered their message, Balaam consulted the Lord as to whether he should go or stay, and being refused permission to go, in the morning he gave a negative answer to the ambassadors. Nothing daunted, Balac sent another embassy, composed of men of higher rank, princes, with directions to offer Balaam anything he liked, provided only he would come and curse Israel. Again Balaam consulted the Lord and obtained permission to go, on condition that he undertook to do what God commanded. In view of what follows, some commentators think that this leave was extorted by importunity, and that Balaam was actuated in making his request by mercenary motives, and had fully made up his mind to curse Israel.

The next morning Balaam saddled his ass and set out with the princes of Moab. On the way, the ass manifested every sign of alarm; it swerved suddenly from the path, crushed Balaam's leg against a wall and finally sank to the ground under him, so that

Balaam cruelly beat it and even threatened it with death. Then the ass was endowed by God with the power of speech, and upbraided its master with his cruelty towards it. At the same time Balaam's eyes were opened and he saw the cause of the ass's strange conduct, viz. an angel of the Lord standing in the way with drawn sword to bar his passage. The angel upbraided Balaam with his cruel conduct towards the ass and told him that it was the action of the ass which had saved his life. Finally, he permitted Balaam to continue his journey, but only on condition that he would speak nothing but what he commanded. Balac met Balaam on the borders of Arnon, and they went together to Kiriath-huzoth, where sacrifices were duly offered. The following day, Balac took Balaam to Bamoth-Baal, whence he could see the outskirts of the host of Israel. Seven bullocks and seven rams having been sacrificed, and Balaam having gone apart to consult the Lord, the prophet returned to Balac and refused to curse Israel. On the contrary, he eulogized them: "Who", he said, "can count the dust of Jacob or number the fourth part of Israel? Let me die the death of the righteous, and my last end be like his."

Then Balac took Balaam to the top of Mount Phasga, to see if from there he would not curse Israel. But, after the same rites and formalities had been gone through, Balaam again pronounced a blessing on the Israelites, more emphatic than the former: "Behold, I have received commandment to bless. And he hath blessed, and I cannot reverse it."

"Neither bless nor curse", exclaimed Balac. But he resolved to try the prophet once more, and accordingly took him to the top of Mount Phogor which looks towards the wilderness. Here sacrifices were offered, but without further formality, Balaam, under the influence of "the spirit of God", broke forth into the beautiful eulogy of Israel which begins with the words: "How beautiful are thy tabernacles, O Jacob, and thy tents, O Israel!" Filled with anger, Balac dismissed Balaam to his home. But before departing, the prophet delivered his fourth pronouncement on the glorious future of Israel and the fate of its enemies. His vision, too, piercing beyond the earthly Kingdom of Israel, seems to have dimly seen the Messianic reign to come. "I see him", he said, "but not now; I behold him, but not nigh: there shall come forth a star out of Jacob, and a sceptre shall rise out of Israel", etc. Balac and Balaam separated, but before returning to his own country, Balaam sojourned with the Madianites. There he seems to have instigated his hosts to send Madianite and Moabite women among the Israelites to seduce them from their allegiance to Jehovah (Num., xxxi, 16). This was while the children of Israel were dwelling at Settim, and no doubt is closely connected with the troubles and disorder over Beel-phegor, told of in the twenty-fifth chapter of Numbers. The punishment inflicted by God on the Israelites was signal. A plague fell upon them, and carried off 24,000 (xxv, 9). Nor did Balaam escape. He was slain, together with the five kings of Madian, in the war waged by Israel against that nation related in the thirty-first chapter of Numbers.

CONSERVATIVE VIEW.—The usual traditional, or conservative, view of the episode of Balaam is that it is an historical narrative in the ordinary sense. The supernatural plays an important part in it, but it is contended that the credibility of the narrative requires only a belief in the miraculous, and that the acceptance of many of the most important parts of the Bible requires such a belief. The episode of the speaking ass is strange; but no stranger than the story of the speaking serpent in Paradise.

The future is foretold by Balaam; but so it is by the great prophets of Israel. A question is discussed as to what Balaam was. Was he a prophet in the true sense of the word, or a soothsayer? It does not seem possible to say that he was a prophet in the same sense as Isaias or any of the great prophets of Israel. On the other hand, in Numbers, xxiv, 2, he is said to have spoken under the influence of "the spirit of God". Indeed, throughout his connexion with Balac, he seems to have acted under the influence of God's spirit. But when his state of life is looked at as such, he cannot be regarded as having belonged to the order of the prophets. St. Thomas calls him "a prophet of the devil". Scripture does not call him a prophet, but a diviner, and Balac approached him with the price of divination. Moreover, the way in which he joined Balac in idolatrous worship seems to preclude the idea of his being a genuine servant of Jehovah. Prophecy is a gift given for the good of others. Balaam was used for the good of Israel.

CRITICAL VIEW.—Modern critics take a different view of the episode, in conformity with their general conclusions as to the Hexateuch. For them the narrative of Numbers, chapters xxii, xxiii, and xxiv, is part of the prophetical history. That is, in these chapters there is no trace of the priestly writer P, though to him is assigned the passage xxv, 6–18, which contains an account of the crime and punishment of Zambri and Cozbi. Though critics are unanimous that chapters xxii, xxiii, and xxiv are the work of the two writers called the Jahvist and the Elohist, they do not find it easy to apportion that part of Numbers between the two authors. Indeed, the only point on which they are agreed is that chapter xxii belongs to the Elohist, with the exception of verses 22–35, which they assign to the Jahvist. This section contains the episode of the ass, and critics say that it destroys the sequence of the narrative. Thus in verse 20 Balaam gets leave from God to go with the princes of Moab; but in verse 22 God is angry with him, apparently because of his going. Though this apparent inconsistency has been variously explained by conservative commentators, critics argue from it and other similar instances, that the episode of the ass (verses 22–35) has been skilfully fitted into the rest of the chapter, but is really the work of another writer; and that the original narrative which is broken off at verse 21 continues at verse 36. Further proofs of dual authorship are often far from clear. Thus, there is said to be a duplication in xxii, 3: "And the Moabites were in great fear of him, and were not able to sustain his assault". Surely this is weak in the extreme. Does not the natural tendency of the Jewish writer to parallelisms sufficiently explain it?

The reference to historical events in Balaam's fourth prophecy leads most critical writers to fix the date of its composition not earlier than David's reign. David's Moabitic war is said to be the war referred to in Num., xxiv, 17. But, putting aside the gift of prophecy, we know that writings of this kind, like the Psalms, are often retouched in ages later than that of their original composition. At most, therefore, it seems legitimate to conclude that this passage shows signs of having been expanded and re-edited at that period.

HUMMELAUER, *Genesis* (Paris, 1895); SAYCE, *Early History of the Hebrews* (London, 1897); WOODS in HAST., *Dict. of the Bible* (London, 1898); DRIVER, *Genesis* (London, 1904); RENAN, *Histoire du peuple d'Israël* (Paris, 1887); PALIS in VIG., *Dict. de la Bible* (Paris, 1893).

J. A. HOWLETT.

Balanæa, a titular see of Syria. The city of this name, a colony of Aradus (Strabo, XVI, 753), is placed by Stephanus Byzantius in Phœnicia, though it belongs rather to Syria. Its first known bishop was present at the Council of Nicæa in 325

(Lequien, Oriens Christ., II, 923). From that time to the sixth century the names of three others are known. At the latter date it was a suffragan of Apamea, the metropolis of Syria Secunda. When Justinian established a new civil province, Theodorias, with Laodicea as metropolis, Balanæa was incorporated with it, but continued to depend ecclesiastically on Apamea, till it obtained the status of an exempt bishopric. This was its condition in the tenth century, when it was directly subject to the Patriarch of Antioch. The Crusaders created there a Latin see, of which a bishop is known about 1200 (Lequien, III, 1189); the river near by it served as a boundary between the Kingdom of Jerusalem and the principality of Antioch. The Franks called it *Valania* according to the Greek pronunciation, the Mussulmans *Būlūnvoās*. Owing to the unsafe conditions of the country the Latin bishop lived at Margat, a neighbouring castle of the Hospitallers. Balanæa, to-day called Banias, is a little village at the foot of the hill of Qalcat el-Marqab, between Tartous (Tortosa) and Latakia (Laodicea); it is the residence of the *kaïmakam* of the district. It numbers about 1,550 inhabitants, 1,200 Maronites, and 230 non-Catholic Christians; they cultivate chiefly onions, olive-trees, and very good tobacco. The roadstead is excellent, but is visited only by small boats.

S. VAILHÉ.

Balbina, SAINT.—Memorials of a St. Balbina are to be found at Rome in three different spots which are connected with the early Christian antiquities of that city. In the purely legendary account of the martyrdom of St. Alexander (Acta SS., Maii, I, 367 sqq.) mention is made of a tribune Quirinus who died a martyr and was buried in the catacomb of Prætextatus on the Via Appia. His grave was regarded with great veneration and is referred to in the old itineraries (guides for pilgrims) of the Roman catacombs. Tradition said that his daughter Balbina, who had been baptized by St. Alexander and had passed her life unmarried, was buried after death near her father in the same catacomb. The feast of St. Balbina is celebrated 31 March. Usuardus speaks of her in his martyrology; his account of St. Balbina rests on the record of the martyrdom of St. Alexander. There is another Balbina whose name was given to a catacomb (cœm. Balbinæ) which lay between the Via Appia and the Via Ardeatina not far from the little church called Domine quo vadis. Over this cemetery a basilica was erected in the fourth century by Pope Mark. There still exists on the little Aventine in the city itself the old title of St. Balbina, first mentioned in an epitaph of the sixth century and in the signatures to a Roman council (595) of the time of Pope Gregory I. This church was erected in a large ancient hall. Its titular saint is supposed to be identical with the St. Balbina who was buried in the catacomb of Prætextatus and whose bones together with those of her father were brought here at a later date. It is not certain, however, that the two names refer to the same person.

Acta SS., Martii, III, 900 sqq.; ALLARD, Hist. des persécut. (Paris, 1892), I, 213 sqq.; WAGNER, Bekehrung und Martyrtod des hl. Quirinus und dessen Tochter Balbina (Nanzig, 1848); UGONIO, Historia delle stationi di Roma (Rome, 1588), 126 sqq.; MARUCCHI, Les basiliques et églises de Rome (Rome, 1902), 173 sqq.; DE ROSSI, Bull. di arch. crist. (1867), 1 sqq.

J. P. KIRSCH.

Balbinus, BOLESLAUS, a Jesuit historian of Bohemia, b. 4 December, 1621, at Königgrätz, of an ancient noble family; d. 29 November, 1688, at Prague. His entire life was devoted to collecting and editing the materials of Bohemian history, and his researches have often been utilized by the Bollandists. He wrote over thirty works, the most important of which is a "Miscellanea Historica regni Bohemiæ" or

"Miscellany of Bohemian history" (6 vols., Prague, 1679–87) in which he described the chief historical events of his native land, its natural history, the genealogies of its nobles, lives of prominent Bohemians, etc. He wrote also in Latin an "Apology for the Slavic and especially the Bohemian tongue". Balbinus was the first to edit the ancient vernacular chronicle known as the "Life of St. Ludmilla and Martyrdom of St. Wenceslas", a new edition of which was published in 1902 by Dr. Pekár and is by him held to be a text of the tenth century, and therefore "the oldest historical work written in Bohemia and by a Bohemian". Balbinus wrote also "De archiepiscopis Bohemiæ" (Prague, 1682) and "Bohemia Sancta, sive de sanctis Bohemiæ, Moraviæ, Silesiæ, Lusatiæ" (ibid., 1682).

SOMMERVOGEL, Bibl. des écriv. de la c. de J., s. v.; LÜTZOW, The Historians of Bohemia (London, 1905).

THOMAS J. SHAHAN.

Balboa, VASCO NUÑEZ DE, discoverer of the Pacific Ocean from the west coast of Central America, b. in Spain, 1475, either at Badajoz or at Jerez de los Caballeros; d. at Darien, 1517. He went to Central America in 1500 with Rodrigo de Bastidas and thence, in secret, with Martín Fernández de Enciso to Cartagena. The story that he got aboard either in an empty barrel or wrapped up in a sail may be true. He soon assumed an important rôle among the participants of the expedition, and settled Darien in 1509. Then he proclaimed himself governor, and sent both Enciso and Nicuesa away. From Darien he undertook, with a few followers, the hazardous journey across the Isthmus that led to the discovery of the Pacific Ocean, 25 September, 1513, and established beyond all doubt the continental nature of America. The appointment in 1514 of Pedrarias Dávila (see ARIAS DE AVILA) as governor of the regions discovered and partly occupied by Balboa, and his appearance on the coast of Darien with a large armament, at once gave rise to trouble. Arias was an aged man of mediocre attainments, jealous, deceitful, and vindictive. Balboa was generous, careless, and over-confident in the merits of his achievements, and was no match for the intrigues that forthwith began against him. To mask his sinister designs Arias gave one of his daughters to Balboa in marriage. The latter was allowed to continue his explorations while Arias and the Licentiate Gaspar de Espinosa were slowly tightening a net of true and false testimony around him, under cover of the inevitable *Residencia*. The Crown gave Balboa the title of *Adelantado* of the South Sea, Governor of Coyba and of what subsequently became the district of Panama, but Arias and his agents understood how to reduce these titles to empty honours. Quevedo, Bishop of Castilla del Oro, was Balboa's sincere friend and assisted him, but with Quevedo's departure for Spain the case was lost. Fearful lest the bishop's appeal for his friend might result against Arias and his party, the *Residencia* was at once converted into criminal proceedings, death sentence hastily pronounced, and Balboa beheaded for high treason in 1517 at Darien. One of the main pretexts for the sentence was Balboa's action towards Enciso and Nicuesa. Balboa has been credited by most authors with having been first to hear of Peru. This is incorrect. In his few attempts at exploring the coast of southern Panama he heard only of Indian tribes of northern or northwestern Colombia.

OVIEDO Y VALDEZ, Historia general y natural de las Indias (Madrid, 1850); Documentos inéditos de Indias (various letters and reports); GOMARA, Historia general de las Indias (Medina del Campo, 1553, Zaragoza, 1555); PASCUAL DE ANDAGOYA, Relación de los sucesos de Pedrarias Dávila, in NAVARRETE, Colección de los viajes y descubrimientos (Madrid, 1829), III, tr. MARKHAM in the Hakluyt Society's publications (1865); IRVING, Voyages and Discoveries of the Companions of Columbus (London, 1831); QUINTANA, Vidas de españoles

BALDACHINA

S. LORENZO, ROME
CHURCH OF S. PRASSEDE

ST. PAUL OUTSIDE THE WALLS, ROME
CHURCH OF SANTA MARIA IN TRASTEVERE, ROME

célebres (Madrid, 1830), II; *Diccionario de Historia y Geografía* (Mexico, 1853), I; MENDIBURÚ, *Diccionario Histórico* (Lima, 1876), II; HERRERA, *Historia General* (2d ed., Madrid, 1726–30); PRESCOTT, *History of the Conquest of Peru;* ROBERTSON, *History of America.*

AD. F. BANDELIER.

Balbuena, BERNARDO DE, a Spanish poet, b. in Val de Peñas, 1568; d. in Porto Rico, 1627. At a very early age he was taken by his parents to Mexico, where he received his education. Later he spent twelve years in Jamaica, and then passed the remainder of his days as Bishop of Porto Rico, to which see he was appointed in 1620. He published "La Grandeza Mejicana" in 1604, and in 1608, in Madrid, "Siglo de Oro en las Selvas de Eriphile", a very learned pastoral romance abounding in beautiful poetic passages. The book, however, contained no description of the scenery or manners of the New World and nothing connected with the history of the times. Possibly for this reason it was not in great demand among Balbuena's contemporaries. But in 1821 it had the honour of being republished by the Spanish Academy. Another work "El Bernardo ó Victoria de Roncesvalles" was published in Madrid in 1624 (new edition, 1808). It is an epic poem on the subject of Spain's resistance to the invasion of Charlemagne.

VENTURA FUENTES.

Balbus, HIERONYMUS (ACCELLINI), humanist, poet, diplomatist, and Bishop of Gurk in Carinthia, b. about 1450 at Venice; d. there, probably 1535. He was a pupil of Pomponius Lætus, the founder of the Roman Academy. As a young man, by his manner and bearing alike, Balbus gave great offence; he was of a quarrelsome disposition, and, for a time, led a very loose life. But in later years he was highly respected and came to be regarded as one of the most accomplished men of his day. In 1485 he was professor at the University of Paris. His overbearing manner here soon brought him into conflict with various scholars, and in consequence of the attack which these men made on his character, he was obliged to leave Paris in 1491. A few years later (1494), at the invitation of Emperor Maximilian I, he went to the University of Vienna, where he lectured on poetry, the Roman classics, and jurisprudence. He was again in Paris, for a short period, in 1495, and visited London in 1496, but resumed his professorship at Vienna in 1497. Here he became a member of the Danube Society, and lived on terms of intimate friendship with its learned founder, Conrad Celtes the Humanist, at that time professor and librarian at the University of Vienna. In little less than a year, renewed contentions with his colleagues forced him to quit Vienna. Balbus next went to Prague (1498), where he accepted a professorship which had been obtained for him by his Viennese friends. But his irregular conduct, scandalous writings, and disputatious temper soon drove him from the city. On leaving Prague he withdrew to Hungary (Fünfkirchen), and remained in retirement for a period of fifteen years, during which time he changed his manner of life completely, and even took orders. His subsequent career as an ecclesiastic was one of considerable distinction. He became provost of the Cathedral Chapter at Waizen, 1515, later also of that at Pressburg, and, for some years, held an important position at the Court of Hungary, where he was tutor of the royal princes, and private secretary to the king, Ladislaus VI. In 1521 Balbus appeared in the Diet of Worms as the ambassador of Louis II of Hungary, and attracted considerable attention by an eloquent discourse in which he protested against the innovations of Luther, and urged upon the assembled princes the necessity of a joint undertaking against the Turks. Shortly afterwards he was in the service of Arch-

duke Ferdinand of Austria, who, in 1522, designated him Bishop of Gurk, and sent him to Rome on a congratulatory embassy to the newly elected pontiff, Adrian VI. It was a part of his mission also to induce the pope to proclaim a crusade against the Turk. The address which he made on being received by the pope in a public audience, 9 February, 1523, abounded in extravagant rhetoric, but in humanistic circles it was considered a marvel of eloquence. Balbus remained in Rome for some time, and was there consecrated Bishop of Gurk, 25 March, 1523. As a bishop, he enacted many wholesome and timely ordinances, and had the preservation of church discipline sincerely at heart, but he was frequently absent from his diocese. From one of his letters we learn that in the time of Clement VII he lived at Rome for some years in the papal palace and was much in the confidence of that pontiff. In 1530, though quite an old man, he accompanied Charles V to Bologna to attend the emperor's coronation. At Bologna he wrote his best known work, "De coronatione principum", which, on account of the views it contains on the relation of Church and State, was placed on the Index, 23 July, 1611. Balbus was the author of many other works. Of these, the poetical, oratorical, and politico-moral writings were edited by Joseph von Retzer (Vienna, 1791–92, 2 vols.). His poems, in part coarse and indelicate, are of no particular merit.

VON RETZER, *Nachrichten von dem Leben und den Schriften des ehemaligen Bischofs von Gurk Hieronymus Balbi* (Vienna, 1790); ALLEN in *English Hist. Review*, XVII, 417; PASTOR, *Kirchenlex.*, s. v.; IDEM, *Gesch. der Päpste* (1907), IV, 730, 732; ASCHBACH, *Gesch. der Univ. Wien* (1877), II, 161 sqq.; HÖFLER, *Papst Adrian VI* (Vienna, 1880), 370 sqq.; BAUCH, *Die Rezeption des Humanismus in Wien* (1903), 40 sqq.

THOMAS OESTREICH.

Baldachinum of the Altar, a dome-like canopy in wood, stone, or metal, erected over the high altar of larger churches, generally supported on four columns, though sometimes suspended by chains from the roof. Other forms will be noted in tracing the cause of its history. The name is late medieval, *baldacchino*, from *Baldocco*, Italian form of Bagdad whence came the precious cloths of which in their later development these canopies were made. It was called earlier ciborium, from the Greek κιβώριον (the globular seed-pod of the lotus, used as a drinking-cup) because of the similarity of its dome top to an inverted cup. The early history of the baldachinum is obscure, but it probably originated in the desire to give to the primitive altar table a more dignified and beautiful architectural setting. The arcosolium altars of the catacombs perhaps foreshadow this tendency. With the construction or adaptation of the larger church edifices of the fourth century, the baldachinum became their architectural centre, emphasizing the importance of the sacrificial table as the centre of Christian worship. Thus, while the altar retained its primitive simplicity of form and proportions, the baldachinum gave it the architectural importance which its surroundings demanded. By its dais-like effect, it designated the altar as a throne of honour. It served also the practical purpose of supporting, between its columns, the altar-curtains, while from its roof were suspended lamps, vases, richly ornamented crowns, and other altar decorations. The summit was surmounted by the altar-cross. The earliest reference to the baldachinum is found in the "Liber Pontificalis" (ed. Duchesne, I, 172, 191, 233, 235) which described the *Fastidium argenteum* given by Constantine to the Lateran basilica during the pontificate of Sylvester I (314–335) and replaced, after the ravages of Alaric's Gothic hordes, by another erected during the pontificate of Sixtus III (432–440). The oldest representation in art is the early sixth-century mosaic in the church of St. George in Thessalonica; while the oldest actual specimen is that in the church of St. Apollinare in Classe at Ravenna (c. 810). The use of the baldachinum was general up to the twelfth century, when it yielded to the growing importance of the reliquary as an adjunct to the altar, sometimes disappearing altogether, sometimes

BALDACHINUM IN ST. PETER'S, ROME

taking the form of a canopy over the relic-casket. With the placing of the altar against the wall, the baldachinum took the form of a projecting dais canopy (v. *Altar-Canopy* under ALTAR: IN LITURGY) or became the ciborium-like superstructure of the tabernacle or central tower of the altar. Italy was less affected by this evolution than were the centres of Gothic art, and the use of the older form is common there to-day. The most magnificent baldachinum in the world is that in St. Peter's in Rome designed by Bernini for Pope Urban VIII.

BISHOP, *History of the Christian Altar* (Downside, 1906); ID. in *Downside Review* (July, 1905); NESBITT in *Dict. Christ. Antiq.* s. v. *Altar*; ROCK-WEALE, *Hierurgia* (London, 1900), II, 316–320. For descriptions of many early baldachina, see *Index of Liber Pontificalis*, ed. DUCHESNE (Paris, 1892), s. vv. *Cyburia, Fastidium, Tiburium.* See also bibliography to article ALTAR, HISTORY OF THE CHRISTIAN.

JOHN B. PETERSON.

Balde, JACOB, a German poet, b. 4 January, 1604, in the Imperial free town of Ensisheim in Upper Alsace; d. at Neuburg, 9 August, 1668. He studied the classics and rhetoric in the Jesuit college of his native town, philosophy and law at the University of Ingolstadt, where on 1 July, 1624, he was admitted into the Society of Jesus. Having undergone the usual ascetical and literary training he taught classics and rhetoric in the colleges of Munich and Innsbruck, and in his leisure hours composed the Latin mock-heroic poem "Batrachomyomachia" (The Battle of the Frogs and the Mice). After completing his theological studies at Ingolstadt, where he was ordained priest in 1633, he was appointed professor of eloquence in the university. Called to Munich a few years later to educate the sons of Duke Albert, he soon after received the office of court preacher to the elector Maximilian. Owing to failing health he

was, in 1654, sent to Neuburg on the Danube, where he became the intimate friend and adviser of the Count Palatine Philipp Wilhelm. Here he died. The poetical works of Balde are marked by a brilliant imagination, noble thoughts, wit and humour, strength and tenderness of feeling, great learning, love of nature, and knowledge of the human heart. His mastery of classical Latin was such that he wielded it with astonishing power and originality, and he used the ancient metres and poetical forms with consummate ease and skill. His poetical themes are the world and religion, friendship and fatherland, art and letters. His patriotic accents, says Herder, have made him a German poet for all time. He witnessed the horrors of the Thirty Years War, and the devastation and disruption of his country, and while lamenting the fate of Germany, sought to re-awaken in the hearts of the people the old national spirit.

Balde was above all a lyric poet, many of his odes to the Virgin Mother of God being of surpassing beauty, but he has also written epic and pastoral poems, satires, elegies, and dramas. During his lifetime he was acclaimed "the German Horace", but soon after his death he fell into neglect, until Herder, towards the end of the eighteenth century, by his translation of many of Balde's lyrics, published in the periodical "Terpsichore", revived the poet's memory and the fame of his genius among scholars. Balde, however, could never have become a popular poet in the wider sense of the word, as nearly all his works were written in Latin, which was in his time the international language of the cultured classes, whereas German was too unwieldy and crude a vehicle of poetical expression. Balde's poetry is not faultless; he occasionally offends against good taste, burdens his verses with mythological lore, and does not always keep his luxuriant imagination under control. The only complete edition of his works was published in eight volumes at Munich in 1729.

SOMMERVOGEL, *Bibliothèque de la c. de J.*, s. v.; WESTERMEYER, *Jacobus Balde, sein Leben und seine Werke* (Munich, 1868); BAUMGARTNER, *Geschichte der Weltlitteratur*, IV, 644–656; MURY-SOMMERVOGEL, *Jacques Balde, notice et bibliographie* (Strasburg, Roux, 1901).

B. GULDNER.

Balderic (BAUDRY), a monk of Liège, a writer and teacher of the twelfth century, b. date unknown, at Florennes in Belgium; d. about 1157. He was proctor at the court of Pope Eugene III, and accompanied him to France when the machinations of Arnold of Brescia compelled the pontiff to leave Rome. At a synod held in Paris in 1147, Balderic became acquainted with Albero, the Archbishop of Trier, who induced him to become head of the cathedral school in Trier. As long as Albero lived, Balderic remained his friend and adviser, and, after his death, wrote his biography, which is remarkable for its classical Latin. It is published in Mon. Germ: Script., VIII, 243 sqq., and in P. L., CLIV, 1307 sqq.

WATTENBACH, *Deutschlands Geschichtsquellen* (Berlin, 1894), II, 3; HAUCK, *Kirchengeschichte Deutschlands* (Leipzig, 1903), IV, 476.

MICHAEL OTT.

Balderic, or BAUDRY, Bishop of Dol, in France, chronicler, b. about 1050; d. 7 January, 1130. After a brilliant course of studies at the famous school at Angers, he entered the Abbey of Bourgueil in Anjou, where he became abbot in 1079. In 1107 he received from Pascal II the pallium of Bishop of Dol. He assisted at all the councils held in his day, went several times to Rome, and left an account of a journey to England. He exercised considerable activity in reforming monastic discipline. The last years of his life were spent in retirement. He is remembered as the author of important or interesting contributions to history, poetry, and hagiography.

Balderic's most valuable work is his "Historiæ Hierosolymitanæ libri IV", an account of the First Crusade, based in part on the testimony of eye-witnesses, and submitted for correction to the Abbot Peter of Maillesais, who had accompanied the Crusaders. Among his other works are poems on the conquest of England and on the reign of Philip I; lives, in Latin, of his friend Robertus de Arbrissello (published by the Bollandists under 25 Feb.), of St. Valerian (published by Bouquet, Hist. Eccl. de France), and of St. Hugh of Rouen (published by Du Monstier, "Neustria Pia"); finally a letter to the monks of Fécamp which contains some valuable material relating to Breton manners, and to English and Norman monasteries (Duchesne and Bouquet, Historiens de France).

Histoire littéraire de la France, VIII, 400; MOLINIER, *Sources de l'hist. de France.*

J. V. CROWNE.

Baldi, BERNARDINO, an Italian poet and savant, b. at Urbino, 5 June, 1553; d. at the same place, 10 October, 1617. After being initiated into higher mathematics by his fellow-townsman Commandino, he went to Padua (1573) and Rome (1576), where he managed to acquire a wide erudition, scientific, classical, and Oriental; Chaldaic, Arabic, and Persian were among the languages he learned. Having subsequently taken orders, he was made Abbot of Guastalla (Mantua) by Prince Ferrante Gonzaga. In spite of many wanderings, entailing long-protracted absences, he retained the abbacy until 1609, when his native city claimed him for the rest of his life. Cardinal Cinzio Aldobrandini, the nephew of Clement VIII, and Francesco Maria della Rovere, Duke of Urbino, were proud of his friendship. The latter entrusted him with an embassy to Venice in 1612.

Baldi's poetic laurels were mainly earned by "La Nautica", a didactic poem closely following the "Georgics" in finely polished blank verse (1576). To this were added nineteen "Egloghe miste" (1583), "L'invenzione del bossolo de navigare", miscellaneous short poems (1590), and the "Epigrammi" (1614). An attempt at introducing fourteen and eighteen syllable lines in "Lauro" (1600) and "Il Diluvio Universale" (1604), met with utter failure. In addition to his Latin poems and several polyglot compilations, we have: "Cento Apologhi" (1583), some dialogues, a well-known "Descrizione del palazzo ducale d'Urbino" (1587), the biographies of Federico, second Duke, and Guidobaldo I, of Urbino, a curious biographical work on Italian and foreign mathematicians (Urbino, 1707), two Latin treatises on Vitruvius, numerous letters and translations from the Targum Onkelos, the Arabic Psalms, Aratus, Musæus, Hero of Alexandria, Aristotle, etc. The unconstrained elegance of his diction gives him a foremost rank as a prose-writer. A standard edition of his best writings is that of Ugolini and Polidori (Florence, 1859).

P. IRENEO AFFÒ, *Vita di Bernardino Baldi* (Parma, 1783); ZACCAGNINI, *La Vita e le opere edite ed inedite di Bernardino Baldi* (Parma, 1903). As to the sources of *La Nautica*, see ZACCAGNINI, *Giornale storico della letteratura Italiana* (1902), XL, 366–396; as to the *Egloghe*, RUBERTO, *Propugnatore*, XX.

EDOARDO SAN GIOVANNI.

Baldi, BERNARDO. See BERNARD of PAVIA.

Baldinucci, ANTHONY, BLESSED, b. 19 June, 1665, at Florence; d. 6 November, 1717. He entered the Society of Jesus 21 April, 1681, and was ordained priest 28 October, 1695. After his third year of probation he began his missionary career at Monte Santo. The field of his labours were the towns of Frascati and Viterbo, in which, with the exception of some more distant places, he laboured for the rest of his life. His methods of preaching were of the most unusual and startling character. Splendid processions were organized which proceeded from various parts of the country to the place where the mission was being given. Many of the people wore crowns of thorns and scourged themselves as they went along. When Baldinucci preached he frequently carried a cross, and was loaded down with heavy chains. He often walked up and down among the people scourging himself to blood. The exercises were usually brought to a close by the burning in the public square of cards, dice, musical instruments, etc. He always carried with him a miraculous picture of the Madonna which was borne before him as he proceeded from place to place. The propagation of devotion to the Blessed Virgin was one of his special aims. To keep order among the vast throngs who flocked to hear him, he always employed a number of laymen whom he called *deputati*. They were not unfrequently men of very bad lives whom he chose purposely in order to conciliate and convert them. His work among the clergy was marked by great prudence and success. Though his preaching was incessant, he found time to write two courses of Lenten Sermons, to gather materials for many more, compose hundreds of discourses, and carry on an immense correspondence. The effect of his apostolic work on the excitable people among whom he laboured was stupendous. At times, when approaching a city, he found crowds covering the walls awaiting his arrival. His peculiar methods are explainable as those best adapted to his surroundings and times. After twenty years of labour he died at the age of fifty-two. He was already canonized in public estimation, but, although the official ecclesiastical process was begun in 1753, the decree of his beatification was issued only on 23 April, 1893.

GOLDIE, *Life of B. Anthony Baldinucci* (London, 1894); VANUCCI, *Vita del Beato A. Baldinucci* (Rome, 1893); GALUZZI, *Life of Baldinucci* (Rome, 1720); BUDRIOLI, *Summarium* (Florence); BARTHOLOMEW PACE, S.J. (Baldinucci's companion), *Evidence, Sermon*, p. 116.

T. J. CAMPBELL.

Baldovinetti, ALESSO, a notable Florentine painter, b. in Florence, 14 October, 1427; d. there, 29 August, 1499. His father was a wealthy merchant, but leaving the paternal business he registered himself, at the age of twenty-one, as a member of the Academy of Saint Luke. He called himself a pupil of Paolo Uccelli, and, according to Vasari, was the master of the famous Ghirlandajo. He experimented much with colours in fresco and oil, but his remaining works are badly preserved. He had the reputation of being the ablest worker in mosaic of his day.

Baldovinetti assisted Andrea del Castagno and Domenico Veneziano in the frescoes, since destroyed, of Santa Maria Nuova in Florence. Among his works which remain is a large fresco of "The Adoration of the Shepherds" in the cloisters of Santa Annunziata. His was the design for the portrait of Dante by Domenico del Michelino in the duomo. The large panel painting of "The Holy Trinity Adored by Saints Gualberto and Benedetto", now in the Academy at Florence, was executed for the church of Santa Trinità in that city. He painted on the walls of the choir of that edifice scenes, not now extant, from the Old Testament, containing numerous portraits of his contemporaries. In the chapel of San Miniato, Florence, are frescoes of angels, prophets, and evangelists. The same edifice also contains an "Annunciation". In the galleries of the Uffizi are an "Enthroned Virgin and Child with Saints", and a most decorative and quaintly graceful "Annunciation". His portrait by himself is in the gallery at Bergamo and Ghirlandajo painted it near his own in his frescoes in Santa Maria Novella, Florence.

PIEROTTI, *Ricordi di A. Baldovinetti* (Lucca, 1868); BRYAN, *Dictionary of Painters and Engravers* (London and New York, 1903–05).

AUGUSTUS VAN CLEEF.

Baldred, Saint, (1) a Celtic Bishop of Strathclyde, b. about 643; d. at Aldhame, Haddingtonshire, about 607. He is said to have been the immediate successor of the great St. Kentigern, or Mungo, the founder of the See of Glasgow, Scotland. Like St. Kentigern, he was of Irish ancestry, but is reckoned as a British saint, inasmuch as Strathclyde was part of Britain. The chronology of the period when he flourished is somewhat obscure, but the best authorities on Scottish history agree that St. Baldred was born towards the middle of the sixth century. Previous to his consecration, St. Baldred had laboured for many years in Strathclyde, and had founded numerous houses for monks as also for holy virgins in addition to the churches of Aldhame, Tyinguham and Preston Kirk. Owing to the disturbed state of the kingdom, he was forced after a short rule to retire from the spiritual government of the Strathclyde Britons as also happened to his predecessor. His feast is observed on 6 March. (2) Baldred, or Baltherus, a holy hermit-priest of the eighth century, who has been confounded with the preceding Scottish saint. According to Simeon of Durham and Hovendeus the date of his death is given as 756. Turgot of Durham is more explicit, and he tells us that Baldred, or Baltherus, the priest, died "in the seventeenth year of the episcopate of Cynulf", that is 756, or on the 6 March, 757. This Baldred is associated with the See of Lindisfarne, and was an Englishman. Numerous miracles are ascribed to him, and his feast is given as 6 March.

To add to the confusion, some writers have imagined that this Baldred is identical with Bilfritt, or Bilfrid, a hermit goldsmith, whose exquisite work may yet be seen in the British Museum on the cover of a Book of Gospels, generally known as the Gospels of St. Cuthbert. This cover was made during the rule of Bishops Eadfrid and Ethelwold of Lindisfarne, 698 to 740. The relics of St. Bilfrid were discovered by Aelfrid, and were placed, with those of St. Baldred, in St. Cuthbert's shrine at Durham, but were subsequently transferred to the shrine of St. Bede in 1104.

Comerarius, quoted in Forbe, *Kalendar of Scottish Saints;* Boetius, *Hist. Scot.; Reg. Ep. Glas.,* II; Chalmer, *Caledonia;* Lesley, *De Orig. Mor., et Rebus Gest. Scot.;* Butler, *Lives of the Saints* (March 6).
Acta SS. (March 6), I; Baring Gould, *Lives of the Saints,* III; Turgot, *Hist. of Dunelon;* O'Hanlon, *Lives of the Irish Saints* (March), III.

W. H. Grattan Flood.

Baldung, Hans, known as Grien or Grün, from his fondness for brilliant green, both in his own costume and in his pictures, a vigorous and distinguished painter, engraver, and draughtsman on wood, b. at Gmünd, Swabia, about 1476; d. at Strasburg, 1545. Baldung was a lifelong friend of Dürer and received a lock of the latter's hair when he died. Dürer influenced Baldung's, work, as did Matthæus Grünewald and Martin Schongauer. His portraits, when unsigned, have at times passed as the work of that greater master, Dürer. An exceptional draughtsman and a good colourist, Baldung's work is marked by an original and fertile imagination. He is thought to have worked with Dürer at Nuremberg for two years, assisting him and painting under his eye the copies of "Adam and Eve" now in the Pitti Gallery at Florence. He became a citizen of Strasburg in 1509, and was made senator the year of his death.

Baldung spent seven years at Freiburg in the Breisgau, where, in a monastery, is found his most famous work, an altar piece, the central portion showing "The Coronation of the Virgin", the wings bearing on the inside the Apostles and on the outside four scenes from the life of Our Lady. Two altar pieces in the Convent of Lichenthal, near Baden-Baden, are assumed to be his earliest works. Baldung's paint-

ings are chiefly in public galleries at Berlin, Vienna, Munich, Stuttgart, Prague, Darmstadt, Basle, Karlsruhe, Aschaffenburg, and Frankfort. In the Berlin Museum are "Christ on the Cross" (two pictures), a triptych "Adoration of the Kings", with saints on the interior and exterior of the wings, and "The Stoning of Saint Stephen"; in the Munich Pinakothek, the portrait of his friend, Margrave Phillipp Christoph of Baden; at Vienna in the Museum, the "Portrait of a Young Man", and a portrait of himself in green; in the Academy, a "Holy Family"; in the Liechtenstein Gallery, "The Ages of Man in Six Female Figures", and a "Madonna"; in the Schönborn Gallery, "Adam and Eve".

Champlin and Perkins, *Cyclopedia of Painters and Painting* (New York, 1886–87); Bryan, *Dictionary of Painters and Engravers* (London and New York, 1903–05).

Augustus Van Cleef.

Baldwin I–II. See Constantinople.

Baldwin I–V. See Jerusalem, Kingdom of.

Baldwin, Archbishop of Trier and Elector of the Holy Roman Empire, b. 1285; d. 1354; he belonged to the noble family of the Counts of Luxemburg, or Lützelburg, and was a brother of the Emperor Henry VII. When he was only three years of age, his father, Count Henry III, was killed in battle. The charge of Baldwin's education, therefore, devolved on his mother, Beatrix of Avesnes, and his brother, the future emperor. Being exceptionally talented, he was sent at the early age of thirteen to the University of Paris, where, under the direction of two private tutors, he received a thorough education. In 1305, when the Archbishop of Mainz died, Henry wished to procure this archiepiscopal see and electorate for his brother, and sent his former physician, Peter Aichspalter, then Bishop of Basle, to Pope Clement V, at Avignon, with instructions to use his influence in behalf of Baldwin. The pope, however, refused to entrust the most important archiepiscopal see of Germany to a youth who was then only nineteen years old. When Aichspalter, shortly after, cured the pope of a severe sickness, he was himself made Archbishop of Mainz, with the understanding, it seems, that Baldwin was to succeed the aged Archbishop Diether of Trier. Accordingly, when Diether died in 1307, Baldwin became Archbishop and Elector of Trier. He was consecrated, 11 March, 1308, at Poitiers by the pope himself and took possession of his archbishopric on the 2d of June, in the same year.

Though only twenty-two years old, Baldwin had many qualities which fitted him for the triple office of bishop, prince, and elector. Without levying special taxes he paid off within a short time the many debts incurred by his predecessor, and he fearlessly asserted his rights of sovereignty over the refractory municipal authorities of Trier. Shortly after the new archbishop's consecration the Emperor Albert was murdered (May, 1308), and Baldwin, acting with Archbishop Aichspalter of Mainz, prevailed upon the other electors to award the imperial crown to Henry of Luxemburg. During the short reign of Henry VII (1309–13) Baldwin was his brother's most influential adviser and accompanied him in his expeditions through the empire and to Rome. After Henry's death he desired as emperor his nephew, King John of Bohemia, then only eighteen years old. However, seeing the futility of his efforts to win the other electors for King John, and fearing the election of Frederick of Austria, who was hostile to the house of Luxemburg, Baldwin urged the election of Louis of Bavaria. But all his attempts to gain over the opposing electors were unsuccessful, and a double election resulted. During the civil war of eight years which ensued he fought on the side of Louis the Bavarian, and contributed largely to his final success. In the conflict between Louis and Pope John XXII, which was equally disastrous to Church and Empire, Baldwin also sided with Louis, and for this reason did not receive the papal approbation when the Cathedral Chapter of Mainz postulated him as successor to Aichspalter (who d. 5 June, 1320). Upon the death, in 1328, of Matthias, whom the pope had appointed Archbishop of Mainz, to succeed Aichspalter, Baldwin was again postulated as archbishop by the Cathedral Chapter of Mainz, took possession of the archdiocese, and administered it nearly nine years (1328–37), despite the protests of the pope, who had appointed Henry Virneburg to the position. On the 16th of July, 1338, he took an important part in the meeting of the imperial electors at Rense, near Coblenz, where they protested against all papal interference in the election of the emperors and decided that the emperor elected by them could exercise his imperial authority without the approbation of the pope. When Clement VI renewed the excommunication of Louis the Bavarian, and there was hope that Charles IV, a grandnephew of Baldwin, would receive the imperial crown, Baldwin finally abandoned the Bavarian and at a meeting at Rense (11 July, 1346) prevailed upon the other electors to declare Louis deposed and elect Charles IV emperor. Baldwin crowned the new emperor at Aachen, 26 July, 1349.

Within his own diocese Baldwin successfully fought against the many robber-barons who at that time infested Europe. He destroyed their strongholds and forced the barons to submit to the laws or leave his domain. He promoted commerce by erecting the bridge which still spans the River Moselle at Coblenz. Numerous churches in various parts of the diocese were built by him, and many wholesome decrees were passed at the synods which he convoked. But Baldwin, the bishop, dwindles beside Baldwin, the soldier and statesman. During the forty-six years of his reign (1308–54) the destinies of the German Empire were largely guided by the powerful hands of this prelate-prince. He was a shrewd diplomat and a brave soldier, but above all he was a member of the house of Luxemburg, and its aggrandizement was the mainspring of his political activities. The Avignonese popes, John XXII and Clement VI, may have set up unjust claims in regard to the imperial office, but there is no justification for Baldwin's siding with Louis the Bavarian even after that emperor was deservedly excommunicated. There may have been palliating circumstances as to his administration of the Archdiocese of Mainz in opposition to the pope's command, but, as a subject of the pope, he should have submitted. He was the author of the so-called "Balduineum", a collection of documents relating to the possessions and privileges of Trier, together with a series of pictures bearing on Henry's expedition to Rome, which was republished at Berlin in 1881. His remains lie in the Cathedral of Trier.

DAMBERGER, *Synchronistische Geschichte der Kirche und der Welt im Mittelalter* (Regensburg, 1860), XII–XIV, passim, XV, 213; DOMINICUS, *Baldwin von Lützelburg* (Koblenz, 1862); MÜLLER, *Der Kampf Ludwigs des Bayern mit der römischen Kurie* (Tübingen, 1879, 1880); DE LORENZI in *Kirchenlex.*, s. v.; BROWER-MASEN, *Antiq. et Annal. Trev.* (Liège, 1670), II; PRIESACK, *Reichspolitik des Erzbischofs Baldwin von Trier, 1314–1328* (Göttingen, 1894); VOGT, *Reichspolitik des Erzbischofs Baldwin in den Jahren 1328–1334* (Gotha, 1901).

MICHAEL OTT.

Baldwin (also BAUDOIN), FRANCIS, a celebrated jurist, b. 1 January, 1520 at Arras, then part of the German Empire; d. 24 October, 1573, at Paris. He was sent in his early youth to Louvain, where he studied jurisprudence with great success. At the end of his studies he came to the court of the Emperor

Charles V (1519–56) at Brussels. He subsequently travelled extensively, appearing at Paris and Geneva several times and teaching successively at Bourges (1549–56), Strasburg, Heidelberg, Douai, Paris, and Angers. The assertion of his sevenfold change of religion from Catholicism to Calvinism and from Calvinism to Catholicism cannot be substantiated. But it is certain that, in the earlier part of his life, he exhibited toward the Calvinistic system a friendliness incompatible with sound Catholic convictions. This attitude for some time recommended him to princes for the settlement of religious questions interesting both Catholics and Protestants. His attachment to the Faith gradually grew stronger, however, and beginning with the year 1560, he made a serious study of ecclesiastical questions, successfully defending the Catholic religion against Calvin. He died a devout Catholic in the arms of the celebrated Spanish Jesuit, Maldonatus.

Baldwin was a very prolific writer on juridical and ecclesiastical topics. Among his works are: "Constantinus Magnus" (Basle, 1556; Strasburg, 1612); "Minucii Felicis Octavius" (Heidelberg, 1560). He is the first to ascribe the "Octavius" to Minucius Felix; " S. Optati Libri Sex de Schismate Donatistarum" (Paris, 1563); "Discours sur le fait de la Réforme" (Paris, 1564).

NICÉRON, *Hommes Illustr.* (Paris, 1734), XXVIII, 255–277; RÄSS, *Convertiten* (Freiburg, 1866), II, 176–187; SCHAUMKELL, *Der Rechtsgelehrte F. Balduinus* (1894).

N. A. WEBER.

Baldwin of Canterbury, thirty-ninth Archbishop, a native of Exeter, date of birth unknown; d. 19 Nov., 1190. He was ordained priest and made archdeacon by Bartholomew, Bishop of Exeter. He subsequently became a Cistercian monk at the Abbey of Ford, in Devonshire, and within a year was made Abbot of Ford. In 1180 he was promoted to the Bishopric of Worcester and in the same year was elected to the primatial see by the bishops of the province. The election was disputed by the monks of Canterbury, who chose first the Abbot of Battle, then Theobald, Cardinal-Bishop of Ostia. King Henry II interfered. Baldwin, who, according to Gervase, refused to accept the archbishopric unless he was elected by the monks, was installed, and an arrangement was entered into by which, in the future, the bishops' elections were to be disallowed. He was several times engaged in disputes with the Canterbury monks, necessitating the further interference of King Richard and of the Holy See. The prior, Norreys, whom he had nominated, was deposed; but his right to appoint the priors was acknowledged.

Baldwin acted as legate in Wales, where he held a visitation in 1187, and in 1188 preached the Crusade, after having himself taken the cross on hearing the news of the loss of Jerusalem. In 1190 he set out for the Holy Land, in company with Hubert, Bishop of Salisbury, and others, providing at his own costs two hundred knights and three hundred retainers. While there he acted as vicegerent of the patriarch. Giraldus Cambrensis describes him as gentle, kindly disposed, learned, and religious. He died during the siege of Acre, leaving all he possessed for the relief of the Holy Land and naming Bishop Hubert as his executor. His works (to be found in the "Bibliotheca Patrum Cisterciensium", V) are "De Commendatione Fidei "; "De Sacramento Altaris". There are also some discourses and a penitential in MS. preserved in the Lambeth Library.

GERVASE OF CANTERBURY, *Chronicle*, I; GIRALDUS CAMBRENSIS, *De Sex Episcop. Vit.*; IDEM, *Itin. Kambriæ Epp. Cantuar.*; *Gesta Regis Henrici*; *Introduction to Memorials of Richard I* (all in Rolls Series).

FRANCIS AVELING.

Balearic Isles, a group in the western part of the Mediterranean belonging to Spain and consisting of four larger islands, Majorca, Minorca, Iviza, and Formentera, and eleven smaller islands of rocky formation. Politically they form the Balearic province, and on 31 December, 1900, had an area of 1936 square miles and a population of 311,649, almost exclusively Catholic. The capital is Palma. The original inhabitants of these islands were of Iberian stock, and were famous in antiquity as slingers. In the seventh century B. C. they were subjugated by the Carthaginians; in 206 B. C., the city of Mahon was built by Hannibal's brother Mago and called after his name. In 123–122 B. C., the Roman consul Quintus Cæcilius Metellus conquered the islands and founded the cities of Palma and Pollentia. The Romans were succeeded in the sovereignty of the islands by the Vandals (426) under Genseric as leader; during the reign of Justinian they were subject to Byzantine authority. Charlemagne incorporated them for a while with the Frankish empire, but in 798 they fell into the hands of the Arabs. About 1230 James I (Jaime) of Aragon gained possession of the islands and conferred the sovereignty on his third son, who transmitted it to his descendants; from 1276 to 1343 they formed the independent kingdom of Majorca, a secundo geniture of Aragon, at the latter date being reunited to the Crown. In the war of the Spanish Succession Minorca was occupied by the English (1708) and remained, with the exception of a brief interval (1756–63), in their possession until by the Peace of Versailles (1783) the islands were ceded back to Spain.

Christianity reached the Balearic Isles almost as soon as the Spanish mainland. As early as the fourth century mention is made of Bishops of Minorca and in the fifth century of Bishops of Majorca and Iviza. During the period of Arabian rule these sees were suppressed, and the islands were placed under the Bishop of Barcelona. After the expulsion of the Moors a see was re-established on the island of Majorca (1237), in direct dependence on the Holy See, and in 1238 Raymund de Torella was made first bishop. The diocese, which has been ruled by fifty-two bishops up to the present time, was made subject to the Archbishop of Valencia in 1492; in 1782 Iviza, and in 1795 Minorca were erected into separate sees. In 1851 Iviza was reunited with Majorca. The Balearic Isles are at present divided into two dioceses subject to the ecclesiastical province of Valencia: Majorca and Iviza (*Diœcesis Majoricensis et Ibusensis*), with Palma as the see, and Minorca (*Diocesis Minoricensis*), with Ciudadela as the see.

The Diocese of Majorca, exclusive of Iviza, embraces the islands of Majorca, Cabrera, and Colubraria; in 1906 it contained a population of 262,000, divided into 8 archipresbyterates, 39 parishes and (at the beginning of 1907) 47 mission churches; 704 priests, including 60 who are not residing in the diocese; 318 churches and oratories. The cathedral chapter consists of 5 prebendaries, 4 officials, and 7 canons. The training of young men for the priesthood is provided for in the *seminario conciliar* in Palma which has 12 professors and 145 students. In 1907 the diocese contained 33 houses of religious orders conducted by 13 religious congregations of men: Jesuits 1; Capuchins 1; Hermits of St. Augustine 1; Mercedarians 1; Tertiaries regular of St. Francis 3; Mission Priests of St. Vincent de Paul 1; Oratorians of St. Philip Neri 2; Brothers of the Christian Schools 4; Redemptorists 5; Missionaries of the Most Sacred Hearts 4; Carmelites 2; Hermits of Sts. Paul and Anthony 4; Brothers of Mercy 4; and 149 foundations conducted by twenty-five orders and congregations of women: Poor Clares, Dominicans, Hieronymites, Carmelites, Augustinians, Sisters of Mercy, Little Sisters of the Poor, Sorores de Patrocinio, etc. Among the churches the most important is the cathedral at Palma called La Leo, an enormous edifice built in

Gothic style, begun during the reign of James I and not completed until 1601; in 1905 the cathedral was raised to the rank of a minor basilica. The most frequented places of pilgrimage are the shrines of San Salvador, Nostra Señora de Lluch, and the Santuario del Puig de Pollenza.

The Diocese of Iviza nominally united with Majorca, but in reality ruled by its own vicar-capitular, contains 26,000 Catholics, 22 parishes, 26 churches and chapels, about 50 priests, and 1 seminary.

The Diocese of Minorca embraces the island of that name and contains 40,000 Catholics, 23 parishes, 80 churches and chapels, about 102 secular and 6 regular priests, an episcopal seminary, at Ciudadela, an Insituto de segunda enseñanza at Mahon, 35 primary schools, 3 benevolent institutions conducted by the Sisters of Mercy, viz: a hospital and a foundling asylum at Mahon, and a foundling asylum at Ciudadela. The cathedral was built in 1287 on the site of a mosque, and having been partially destroyed in 1628, was restored in 1719. In 1795 it was raised to the rank of a cathedral.

BIDWELL, *The Balearic Islands* (London, 1876); CARTAILHAC, *Monuments primitifs des îles Baléares* (Paris, 1892); VUILLIER, *Les îles oubliées* (Paris, 1893); SALVATOR, *Die Balearen* (2 vols., Würzburg and Leipzig, 1897); FRAISSE, *Skizzen von den Balearischen Inseln* (Leipzig, 1898); *Recensio Ecclesiæ Maioricensis, 1906* (Palma, 1906, *additiones et variationes*, 1907); SAMPOL Y RIPOLI, *Anuario bibliog.* (1897), *Apunt. para una Biblioteca mallorquina* (Palma, 1898.)

JOSEPH LINS.

Bales (or BAYLES, *alias* EVERS), CHRISTOPHER, VENERABLE, priest and martyr, b. at Coniscliffe near Darlington, County Durham, England, about 1564; executed 4 March, 1590. He entered the English College at Rome, 1 October, 1583, but owing to ill-health was sent to the College at Reims, where he was ordained 28 March, 1587. Sent to England 2 November, 1588, he was soon arrested, racked, and tortured by Topcliffe, and hung up by the hands for twenty-four hours at a time; he bore all most patiently. At length he was tried and condemned for high treason, on the charge of having been ordained beyond seas and coming to England to exercise his office. He asked Judge Anderson whether St. Augustine, Apostle of the English, was also a traitor. The judge said no, but that the act had since been made treason by law. He suffered 4 March, 1590, "about Easter", in Fleet Street opposite Fetter Lane. On the gibbet was set a placard: "For treason and favouring foreign invasion". He spoke to the people from the ladder, showing them that his only "treason" was his priesthood. On the same day Venerable Nicholas Horner suffered in Smithfield for having made Bales a jerkin, and Venerable Alexander Blake in Gray's Inn Lane for lodging him in his house.

BRIDGEWATER, *Concertatio Ecclesiæ Catholicæ in Anglia* (Trier, 1589); CHALLONER, *Memoirs*; POLLEN, *Acts of English Martyrs* (London, 1891); *Northern Catholic Calendar*; KNOX, *Douay Diaries* (London, 1878); MORRIS, *Catholics of York under Elizabeth* (London, 1891); FOLEY, *Records S. J.; Roman Diary* (London, 1880).

BEDE CAMM.

Ball, MOTHER FRANCES MARY TERESA, b. in Dublin 9 January, 1794; d. 19 May, 1861; foundress of the Irish Branch of the Institute of the Blessed Virgin Mary. (See LORETO, SISTERS OF.) She was a daughter of John Ball and Mabel Clare Bennet. At the age of nine years, Frances was sent to the convent school at the Bar, York, England, conducted by the English Ladies of the Institute of the Blessed Virgin Mary. She remained here until the death of her father, in 1808, and then spent some time with her mother at home. In 1814, under the direction of Dr. Daniel Murray, Archbishop of Dublin, Frances returned to York and entered the novitiate of the Institute of the Blessed Virgin Mary. There she received her religious training, and made her profession in 1816, taking, in religion, the name of Mary Teresa. Recalled by Archbishop Murray, she returned to Dublin with two novices, in 1821, to establish the Irish Branch of the Institute of the Blessed Virgin Mary for the instruction of children. In 1822 she opened the first institution of the order in Ireland, in Rathfarnam House, four miles from Dublin. Mother Frances was a woman of great piety and administrative ability. Her energies were devoted to the establishment of schools and to the development of the sisterhood which now has members in many countries.

COLERIDGE, *The Life of Mother Frances Mary Teresa Ball* (London, 1881).

EDWIN DRURY.

Ballarat, DIOCESE OF, one of the three suffragan dioceses of the ecclesiastical province of Melbourne, Australia. It comprises that part of the State of Victoria which is bounded on the east by the 144th meridian E. longitude, thence by the Loddon to the River Murray; on the north by the River Murray; on the west by South Australia; and on the south by the Southern Ocean.

HISTORY.—Victoria (known till 1851 as the Port Phillip District of New South Wales) was first permanently colonized in 1835. The rich pastures of the Ballarat district were occupied in 1838. For thirteen years thereafter the site of Ballarat was a picturesque pastoral scene. In 1851 the Port Phillip District was formed into a separate colony under the name of Victoria. It was a period of severe commercial depression, and many of the colonists prepared to set out for the newly discovered goldfields of Ophir, in New South Wales. On 29 June, 1851, the first profitable goldfield in Victoria was discovered at Clunes by James W. Esmond, an Irish Catholic miner, who had been on the Sacramento in '49. The hopes of the colonists rose; ebbed again as Clunes proved a passing disappointment; then came in with a rush when, in August, rich gold was struck at Ballarat. Many of the little eight-feet-square claims were marvellously rich, lined with "jewelers' shops" and "pockets" of gold. Ballarat became at a bound the richest goldfield in the world, and forty thousand people were soon encamped upon it. Rich fields were discovered in quick succession at Mount Alexander, Bendigo, and other places. Victoria became the modern Transylvania; there ensued a great rush of population to her shores; and she became, and long remained, the most populous of the Australian colonies. At Ballarat, through the lost battle of the Eureka Stockade the insurgent miners of 1854 ultimately won a victory over the exasperating old system of mining licences and "digger hunts".

Bishop Goold of Melbourne made strenuous efforts to cope with the conditions created by the sudden expansion of population. The first priest appointed to Ballarat was the Rev. Patrick Dunne, most of whose flock in Coburg had stampeded to the goldfields. Father Dunne lived in a calico hut, slept on a slab of gumtree bark, and had for his first church a canvas tent. For some years afterwards a few priests attended to the spiritual wants of what now comprises the Diocese of Ballarat. It was formed in 1874 out of the See of Melbourne. Its first bishop was the Right Rev. Michael O'Connor, a Dublin priest. He was consecrated in Rome on the 7th May, 1874, and was enthroned in his cathedral at Ballarat on the 20th December of the same year. He introduced the Christian Brothers, the Sisters of Mercy, and the Loreto nuns, and after a fruitful episcopate died on the 14th February, 1883. His successor was the Right Rev. James Moore, consecrated 27 April, 1884. Dr. Moore opened the successful boys' college at Ballarat, and introduced the Redemptorist Fathers and the Sisters of Nazareth, of St. Joseph, and of St. Brigid. He was skilled in finance, was a builder with big ideas, and at his death, 26th June, 1904, left Ballarat one of the best equipped dioceses in Aus-

tralasia. He was succeeded by the Right Rev. Joseph Higgins, who was translated from the See of Rockhampton on the 3rd of March, 1905. He made mission- and school-extension the chief work of his episcopate. The Sisters of St. Joseph of Cluny were introduced; convents, primary and high schools, and churches (over twenty in two years to March, 1907) erected; and many new missions organized. Much of the work summarized here has been carried out in the once drought-scourged, but now prosperous, Mallee country; and remote Mildura, the Ultima Thule of the diocese, has now a resident priest, a convent of the Sisters of Mercy, and a parish school with a daily attendance of 130 pupils.

RELIGIOUS STATISTICS.—In March, 1907, there were: parochial districts, 29; churches, 145; secular priests, 62; regular priests, 10; religious brothers, 17; nuns, 230; convents, 18; college (boys), 1; superior day schools (boys) 2; boarding schools (girls), 10; superior day schools (girls), 9; primary schools, 57; home for aged poor, 1; orphanage, 1; children in Catholic schools, 4,900; Catholic population, 59,488.

MORAN, *History of the Catholic Church in Australasia* (Sydney, s. d.); JOSE, *History of Australasia* (Sydney, 1901); WITHERS, *History of Ballarat* (2d ed., Ballarat, 1887); *Missiones Catholicæ* (Propaganda, Rome, 1907) 688.

HENRY W. CLEARY.

Ballerini, GIROLAMO and PIETRO, celebrated theologians and canonists, the sons of a distinguished surgeon of Verona. A rare intellectual sympathy bound these brothers together and led them to assist each other in the preparation and composition of their many works. GIROLAMO was born at Verona 29 January, 1702, and died 23 April, 1781. After finishing his course in the Jesuit college of his native city he entered the seminary and was ordained a secular priest. In the pursuit of his favourite historical studies he soon came to appreciate the valuable labours of the learned Cardinal Noris, also of Verona, and brought out (1729–33) a complete edition of his works. The scholarship of the editors is best seen in the fourth volume, especially in their dissertations against Garnerius, and in their study of the early days of the Patriarchate of Aquileia. They also published (1733) an edition of the writings of Matteo Giberti Bishop of Verona, and in 1739 a critical edition of the sermons of St. Zeno of Verona.

PIETRO, b. 7 September, 1698; d. 28 March, 1769, after completing his studies both at college and the seminary was chosen principal of a classical school in Verona. Here he began his long and notable literary career in 1724, when he prepared for his pupils a treatise on the method of study taught and followed by St. Augustine. Some passages in this work gave serious offence to the school of absolute Probabilists, and for some years Pietro was engaged in a lively dispute with them, defending his principles of Probabiliorism in three volumes. Shortly afterwards he turned his attention to the much debated question of usury, and threw his influence against the claims of the Laxists. To sustain his argument in this controversy he prepared (1740) an edition of the "Summa" of St. Antoninus which he sent to Pope Benedict XIV, and also (1774) one of the "Summa" of St. Raymond of Pennafort. During this same year he published "La Dottrina della Chiesa Cattolica circa l'usura", in which he condemned all forms of usury. This exceptional literary activity made the name of the Ballerini brothers famous throughout Italy, and in 1748 Peter was chosen by the senate of Venice to serve as its canonist in Rome in a dispute over the Patriarchate of Aquileia. His conspicuous talent on this mission attracted the attention of Pope Benedict XIV, who commissioned him to prepare an edition of St. Leo's works in refutation of the defective one published by Quesnel.

After almost nine years of labour in which he enjoyed free access to all the libraries of Rome, Pietro brought out his monumental work in three volumes (Rome, 1753–57) reproducing the entire edition of Quesnel together with elaborate refutations and additions (Migne, P. L., LIV–LVI). The third volume is a profound study of the sources of canon law. Quesnel had published a collection of canons from a codex which he believed to have been in use under Popes Innocent I, Zozimus, and Leo the Great. Besides disproving this, Pietro brought out in an improved form earlier Latin editions of the canons, together with some very old unknown versions of Greek canons. He also published two valuable works (against Febronius) on papal power, "De vi ac ratione Primatus Romanorum Pontificum" (Verona, 1766), and "De potestate ecclesiasticâ Summorum Pontificum et Conciliorum generalium" (Verona, 1765).

MAZZUCHELLI, *Gli scrittori d'Italia* (Brescia, 1753–63), II, part I, 178; FABRONI, *Vitæ Italorum doctrina excellentium* (Pisa, 1778–1805), XVIII, 109.

LEO F. O'NEIL.

Ballina, DIOCESE OF. See KILLALA.

Balliol, JOHN. See OXFORD.

Ballon, LOUISE BLANCHE. See SISTERS OF PROVIDENCE AND REFORMED BERNARDINES.

Balme (BALMA), HENRY (also called HUGH) a Franciscan theologian, born at Geneva, date uncertain; d. 23 February, 1439. He entered the Order of Friars Minor in the province of Burgundy. He was a man of exceptional worth according to the testimony of St. Colette, whose confessor he was. Possessing an intimate knowledge of his penitent's life, he wrote a brief account of her marvellous gifts. The saint, however, on hearing of its existence, caused it to be destroyed. Among his other writings is one on "Theologia Mystica" which was attributed to St. Bonaventure and is to be found in many editions of the latter's works, but the editors of the latest edition (Quaracchi, 1898, Vol. VIII, p. cxi), following Sbaralea, have restored it to its rightful owner.

ANDREW EGAN.

Balmes, JAIME LUCIANO, philosopher and publicist, b. at Vich, Spain, 28 August, 1810; d. there, 9 July, 1848. His parents enriched him with no material wealth, but he owed to them a firm, well-balanced temperament, a thorough education, and, probably to his father, a marvellous memory. If to these endowments we add a penetrating intellect, an instinctive sense of right method, an absorbing passion for knowledge, an unflinching though noble ambition, an indomitable determination, a pure life—wherein no unruly sensuousness seems to have ever beclouded the spirit—and abundant opportunities for mental development, we may be prepared to accept even what looks so much like an extravagance on the part of his biographers, that with his sixteenth year, having passed through the schools of Vich, he had completed the seminary course, including philosophy and elementary theology. The next stage of his education was completed at the University of Cervera, where after seven years he received his licentiate in 1833. Later on, he

JAIME LUCIANO BALMES

stood for the dignity of *Magistral* of Vich, contesting for the position with his former teacher, Dr. Soler. Returning to Cervera after his ordination to the priesthood he held a position as an assistant professor and pursued the study of civil and canon law. He shortly afterwards received the doctorate *in pompa*. In 1834 he went back to his native place where he devoted himself with his wonted ardour to physics and mathematics, and accepting a position as professor in the latter branch, varied the onerous duties of this position by cultivating the classics and writing poems. The latter, though not of a very high order of merit, served to extend his reputation to the capital. He wrote for the "Madrileno Católico" a prize essay on "Clerical Celibacy" which was so favourably received by the public that he was encouraged to send forth a small book, entitled "Observaciones sociales, políticas, y económicas sobre las buenes del clero" (1840), which won for him national distinction, the essay arousing special interest in the Cortes. Soon afterwards he wrote "Consideraciones sobre la situación en España", directed mainly against Espartero, then at the zenith of his power. It was a bold deed and might easily have been fatal to Balmes.

This was followed by a translation, with Spanish introduction, of the maxims of St. Francis de Sales (1840). He was now far advanced in his "Protestantism Compared with Catholicism" but suspended the work for fifteen days to compose "La Religión demonstrado al alcance de los niños" a work of advanced instruction for children which rapidly spread throughout Spain and Spanish America and was translated into English. Elected a member of the Academy of Barcelona (1841), he wrote his inaugural dissertation on "Originality", an essay which exemplifies the predominant trait of its author's mind. Having completed his reply to Guizot's "Civilization in Europe", he published it at Barcelona (1844) under the title "El Protestantismo comparado con el Catolicismo en sus relaciones con la civilización Europea". The work was at once translated into French and subsequently into Italian, German, and English, and extended the fame of Balmes throughout the world. This work, which for its wealth of fact and critical insight would alone have taxed the resources of a longer life than that which was allotted to Balmes, left to its author time and energy adequate to accomplish tasks of hardly less magnitude and significance. During the bombardment of Barcelona by Espartero, Balmes, going away unwillingly with his friends, took refuge in a country house with no other books than his breviary, "The Imitation", and the Bible, and while the cannon roared in his ears the philosopher, repeating the experience of Archimedes at the siege of Syracuse, composed the "El Criterio" (The Criterion, New York, 1875; The Art of Thinking, Dublin, 1882), a thoroughly practical guide on method in the pursuit of knowledge. It seems incredible that the work could have been produced as it was within a month. Shortly after Balmes became associated with two friends, Roca y Cornet and Ferrer y Subirana, in editing "La Civilización", a widely influential review wherein appeared one of his most powerful, because sympathetic, papers—that on O'Connell. In 1843 Balmes withdrew from the editorship to found in Barcelona a review of his own, "La Sociedad". It contained a mass of important papers meeting the social, political, and religious exigencies of the time. "La Sociedad" was reprinted at Barcelona in 1851. It was through its pages that the greater part of a notable work, subsequently completed by the author, was issued—"Cartas á un eséptico (Letters to a Sceptic, Dublin, 1875).

About the date of the appearance of "El Protestantismo" (1844) Balmes was called to Madrid where he established a newspaper "El Pensamiento de la Nación" in the interests of politics and religion. Its special purpose was the advocacy of the marriage of Isabella II with the eldest son of Don Carlos, a union which appeared to Balmes to offer the most effectual solution of the existing political problems of Spain. He even accepted a mission to Don Carlos and succeeded in persuading the latter to renounce his title of king in favour of the Count of Montemolin. Unfortunately, the plan which might have spared his country many misfortunes failed through French interference. Balmes, seeing his cherished design come to naught when Isabella married her cousin Don Francisco de Assisi, suspended the publication of "El Pensamiento" notwithstanding the remonstrance of friend and foe, for the journal had, through the impress of his mind and character and literary power, come to mark an epoch in the history of the Spanish press. Balmes now retired from the political arena to devote the closing years of a life all too short to the publication of his philosophical writings. In May, 1845, he visited France, Belgium, and England, a journey of which there are few details recorded save that he was fêted in Paris, where he also met Chateaubriand, and in Brussels, and Mechlin. Returning to Madrid, he repaired thence to Barcelona where he issued in 1846 his "Filosofía fundamental" (this was translated into English by Henry F. Brownson, with an introduction by his father Dr. Orestes A. Brownson (New York, 1864). It is an exposition of the philosophy of St. Thomas in view of the intellectual conditions of the nineteenth century. His biographer, Dr. Soler, speaks of this work as one "which, from the stupendous variety of knowledge which it manifests and the richness of its mental treasures, appears a collection of libraries, a mine of science, for there is no faculty foreign to the vast comprehension of its author". Allowing for some extravagance in this fervid eulogy, no reader competent to judge can fail to recognize the breadth, depth, and practical timeliness of the "Fundamental Philosophy".

From Barcelona he returned to his native place, where he composed his "Filosofía elemental" (Madrid, 1847), a compendium that became widely used in the schools and which was also translated into English. In 1847 he wrote his pamphlet "Pio Nono" wherein he defends the liberal policy of Pius IX, at the opening of his pontificate, when that pope gave a universal amnesty and adopted constitutional government. Though perhaps the best written of all Balmes's works, it was unfavourably received, was bitterly attacked by his enemies, and regretted by most of his friends. The pain inflicted on his sensitive spirit by the unjust aspersions and insidious innuendoes of his opponents preyed upon his constitution which, never robust, had been severely taxed by incessant labours. He retired once more to Barcelona dividing there his time between linguistic studies, his inaugural discourse for the Royal Spanish Academy, to which he had been admitted, and the Latin translation of his "Elementary Philosophy", undertaken at the request of Archbishop Affre of Paris. He returned to his native Vich, May, 1848, where his health steadily declined till the end came on the 9th of July following. Balmes is described as of more than medium stature, slight of frame though well-developed; his face was pale but delicately tinged; his eye penetrating; his aspect agreeable and naturally majestic. His temperament combined the better elements of the traditional four. He was moderate in all lines of conduct, except probably in study and intellectual work, which he seems to have carried at times to a passionate excess. His thoughts and expression were so copious and so close to his call that he could

easily dictate to two secretaries on any subject he might take in hand. Exact and methodical in his relations to God, he was no less conscientious in his duties towards his neighbour. Unostentatiously charitable to the poor, he was unaffectedly kind and affable, though somewhat reserved, in all social converse. A strong soul in a sensitive organism, his intellectual life absorbed and spiritualized the physical.

Balmes has a universally admitted place of honour amongst the greatest philosophers of modern times. He knew the reflective thought of his day and of the past. The systems of Germany, from Kant to Hegel, he studied carefully and criticized judiciously. The scholastics, especially St. Thomas, were familiar to him. He meditated on them profoundly and adopted most of their teaching, but passed it through his own mental processes and turned it out cast in the mould of his own genius. Descartes, Leibnitz, and especially the Scottish school, notably Jouffroy, had considerable influence on the method and matter of his thought, which is characterized consequently by a just eclecticism. He deemed it a danger to take lightly the opinions of any great mind, since, as he said, even if they did not reflect complete reality, they rarely were devoid of strong grounds and at least some measure of truth. Balmes was, therefore, one of the most influential causes in reviving sound philosophy in Spain and indeed throughout Europe generally during the second quarter of the nineteenth century—an influence that continues still through his permanent works. Certain indeed of his theories are open to criticism. He perhaps accords too much to an intellectual instinct, a theory of the Scottish school, and too little to objective evidence in the perception of truth. In psychology he rejects the *intellectus agens* (the abstractive intellect) and the *species intelligibilis* (intermediary presentations), and he holds the principle of life in brutes to be naturally imperishable.

These, however, are but accidental and relatively unimportant divergencies from the permanent body of the traditional philosophy—the system which receives in his "Filosofía fundamental" a fresh interpretation and a further development in answer to the intellectual conditions of his day; for it was an habitual conviction with Balmes that the philosopher's business is not merely to rethink and restate but to reshape and develop. While the book just mentioned reflects the speculative aspect of its author's mind, the work that most fully manifests his personality, his mental, moral, and religious character, and his social and political ideals, together with the range and accuracy of his learning—the work, therefore, that is likeliest to endure—is "El Protestantismo comparado". Though conceived originally as a reply to Guizot's "History of Civilization", it is much more than a critique or a polemic. It is really a philosophy of history—or rather of Christianity—combining profound insight and critical analysis with wide erudition. It searches for the basal principles of Catholicism and of Protestantism, and summons the evidence of history concerning the comparative influence exercised by the former and the latter in the various spheres of human life—intellectual, moral, social, and political. The side on which the author's sympathies lie is frankly indicated by him, while he appeals to the historical data in justification. It should be read in the Spanish to be fully estimated; for the English translation, done through a French medium, though accurate and scholarly, can hardly be expected to reflect all the light of the original.

For the rest, the general position of Balmes among his countrymen may be summed up in the words of one of the leading Spanish journals, "El Heraldo", at the time of his death. "Balmes appeared, like Chateaubriand, on the last day of the revolution of his country to demand from it an account of its excesses, and to claim for ancient institutions their forgotten rights. Both mounted on the wings of genius to a height so elevated above the passions of party that all entertained respect and veneration for them. One and the other brought such glory to their country that, though they combated generally prevailing opinions and prejudices, all good citizens wove for them well-earned crowns and loved them with enthusiasm." Besides the works mentioned above, a collection of fragments and unpublished pieces were issued after his death under the title "Escritos póstumos" (Barcelona, 1850); also "Poesías póstumas" (ib.), and "Escritos políticos" (ib.).

SOLER, *Biografía del D. J. Balmes* (Barcelona, 1850); GARCÍA DE LOS SANTOS, *Vida de Balmes* (Madrid, 1848); RAFFIN, *J. Balmès, sa vie et ses ouvrages* (Paris, 1849; Ger. tr. Ratisbon, 1852); *Art of Thinking* (Dublin, 1882, Biog. Introd.); *Protestantism and Catholicism Compared* (Baltimore, 1850, Biog. Introd.); GONZÁLEZ HERRERO, *Estudio histórico crítico sobre las doctrinas de Balmes* (Oviedo, 1905); MENÉNDEZ Y PELAYO, *Historia de los heterodoxos españoles* (Madrid, 1881) III, lib. VIII, iii; BARANERA, *Balmes* (Vich, 1905).

F. P. SIEGFRIED.

Balsam, an oily, resinous, and odorous substance, which flows spontaneously or by incision from certain plants, and which the Church mixes with olive oil for use as chrism. Balsams are very widely distributed throughout the plant kingdom, being particularly abundant in the pine family, but the name is generally restricted in the present day to resins which in addition to a volatile oil contain benzoic and cinnamic acid. Among the true balsams are the Balm of Gilead, or Mecca, which is cultivated in Arabia, Egypt, Syria, etc., and is extremely costly; the copaiva balsam, and those of Peru and Tolu—all three found chiefly in South America. The term *balsam*, however, is also applied to many pharmaceutical preparations and resinous substances which possess a balsamic odour.

The practice of the Church of using balsam, as mentioned above, is very ancient, going back possibly to Apostolic times. (See CHRISM.) The scarcity and high price of other perfumes has obliged the Latin Church to be content with balm alone in the mixture of holy chrism; but in the East, where the climate is more favourable than ours to the growth of these plants, the Church uses no less than thirty-six species of precious perfumes, according to the Euchologion, in the oil, which makes it an ointment of exquisite fragrance. The Latin Church does not insist on the quantity or the quality of the balsam to be used; any substance commonly known as a balsam may be utilized, and such a quantity as will give its odour to the oil is sufficient. This mingling of the balsam with the oil is intended to convey, by outward sign, the good odour of Christ, of whom it is written (Cantic., i, 3): " We will run after thee to the odour of thy ointments." It typifies also the odour of good works, the thought which ought to inspire those who worthily receive the sacraments; and it symbolizes an innocent life and the gifts of the Holy Spirit.

The balsam is blessed by the bishop at the Mass which he solemnly celebrates on Holy Thursday and is poured into the oil after he has administered Holy Communion to the faithful. The cruet of balsam is brought by a subdeacon to the assistant priest, who in turn places it on a table in the sanctuary before the bishop. The latter blesses the balsam, reciting over it the three prayers found in the Roman Pontifical: he calls it the fragrant tear of dry bark—the oozing of a favoured branch that gives us the priestly unction. Later he mixes the balsam with a little oil on a paten and pours it into the chrism with a suitable invocation: " May this mixture of liquors be to those who shall be anointed with it, a propitiation and a salutary protection for ever and ever. Amen."

In the early ages the pope, without using any form, as appears from the Roman *Ordines*, poured the balsam into the oil, while still in the sacristy before Mass (Ordo Romanus, X, n. 3; P. L., LXXVIII, 1010), but the blessing took place after the Communion of the pope, and before that of the clergy and the faithful (Duchesne, Christian Worship, 2d Eng. ed., 305, 306, 467). According to the Gregorian Sacramentary (Muratori, ed., P. L., LXXVIII, 330), however, the pope mixes the balsam and oil during the Mass. In the Church of Soissons in France, at one time, the " Veni Creator " was sung before the mingling of the balsam and oil.

MÖHLER in *Kirchenlex.*

ANDREW B. MEEHAN.

Balsamon, THEODORE, a canonist of the Greek Church, b. in the second half of the twelfth century at Constantinople; d. there, after 1195 (Petit). He was a deacon, nomophylax, or guardian of the Laws, and from 1178 to 1183, under the Patriarch Theodosius, he had charge of all ecclesiastical trials or cases. In 1193 he became Greek Patriarch of Antioch. Balsamon's best work is his "Scholia", or commentary on the "Nomocanon" of Photius, published first in Latin at Paris (1561), at Basle (1562); in Greek and Latin at Paris (1615), and again at Basle (1620). It is also found in Beveridge's "Pandecta Canonum", Oxford, 1672 (P. G., cxxxvii-viii). From 1852 to 1860, Rhalli and Potli published at Athens a collection of the sources of Greek canon law which contains Balsamon's commentary. In his "Scholia" Balsamon insists on existing laws, and dwells on the relation between canons and laws—ecclesiastical and civil constitutions—giving precedence to the former. Balsamon also compiled a collection of ecclesiastical constitutions and wrote other works, in all of which is apparent his animosity towards the Roman Church. Two of his letters were published: one treating of fasting, the other on the admission of novices into monasteries.

KREUTZWALD in *Kirchenlex.*, s. v.; BEVERIDGE, *Praef.* in *Pandecta Can.*, *P. G.*, LXX, 11 sqq.; MORTREUIL, *Hist. du droit byzantin* (Paris, 1846), III, 1432–45; KRUMBACHER, *Gesch. des byzant. litt.* (Munich, 1897).

ANDREW B. MEEHAN.

Baltasar, or as found in the Septuagint Βαλτασάρ, is the Greek and Latin name for Belshazzar, בלשאצר, which is the Hebrew equivalent for *Bel-sarra-usur*, i. e. "May Bel protect the king". Bel was the chief and titular god of Babylon. In Daniel, v, Baltasar is described as the son of Nabuchodonosor (A. V., Nebuchadnezzar) and the last King of Babylon. It is there narrated how the town was invaded—by the Medes under Darius, as would seem from Dan., v, 28, 29—whilst the king was giving a sumptuous feast to his nobles. The king himself was slain. The narrator further informs us that the sacred vessels which Nabuchodonosor had carried with him from Jerusalem were defiled on that occasion. By order of King Baltasar they were used during the banquet, and his wives and concubines drank out of them. In the midst of the revelry a hand is seen writing on the wall the mysterious words *Mane, Thecel, Phares* (A. V., *Mene, Tekel, Peres*). The king's counsellors and magicians are summoned to explain the writing, but they fail to do so. The Queen then enters the banquet hall and suggests that Daniel should be called for. Daniel reads and explains the words: the days of the kingdom had been numbered; the king had been weighed in the balance and had been found wanting; his kingdom would be given to the Medes and the Persians.

In the account given by Herodotus of the capture of Babylon by the Persians under Cyrus, Labynitus II, son of Labynitus I and Nicotris, is named as the last King of Babylon. Labynitus is commonly held to be a corruption of Nabonidus. Herodotus further mentions that Cyrus, after laying siege to the town, entered it by the bed of the Euphrates, having drained off its waters, and that the capture took place whilst the Babylonians were feasting (Herod., I, 188–191). Xenophon also mentions the siege, the draining of the Euphrates, and the feast. He does not state the name of the king, but fastens on him the epithet "impious", ἀνόσιος. According to him, the king made a brave stand, defending himself with his sword, but was overpowered and slain by Gobryas and Gadatas, the two generals of Cyrus (Cyrop., vii, 5). The Chaldean priest Berosus names Nabonidus as the last King of Babylon and says that the city was taken in the seventeenth year of his reign. We are further informed by him that Nabonidus went forth at the head of an army to oppose Cyrus, that he gave battle, lost, and fled to Borsippa. In this town he was besieged and forced to surrender. His life was spared, and an abode assigned to him in Karmania. (Prof. C. P. Tiele, Babylonisch-Assyrische Gesch., 479; Euseb., Præp. Ev., ix, 41; Idem, Chron., i, 10, 3.) Josephus follows the Biblical account. He remarks that Baltasar was called by the Babylonians Naboandelus, evidently a corruption of Nabonidus, and calls the queen, grandmother (ἡ μάμμη) of the king. He adheres to the Septuagint rendering in making the reward held out to Daniel to have been a third portion of the kingdom instead of the title, third ruler in the kingdom. Rabbinical tradition has preserved nothing of historical value.

The cuneiform inscriptions have thrown a new light on the person of Baltasar and the capture of Babylon. There is in the first place the inscription of Nabonidus containing a prayer for his son: "And as for Bel-sarra-usur my eldest son, the offspring of my body, the awe of thy great divinity fix thou firmly in his heart that he may never fall into sin" (Records of the Past, V, 148). It is commonly admitted that Bel-sarra-usur is the same as Belshazzar, or Baltasar. Dr. Strassmaier has published three inscriptions which mention certain business transactions of Bel-sarra-usur. They are the leasing of a house, the purchase of wool, and the loan of a sum of money. They are dated respectively the fifth, eleventh, and twelfth year of Nabonidus. Of greater importance is the analytical tablet on which is engraved an inscription by Cyrus summarizing the more memorable events of the reign of Nabonidus and the causes leading up to the conquest of Babylon. The first portion of the tablet states that in the sixth year of Nabonidus, Astyages (Istuvegu) was defeated by Cyrus, and that from the seventh till the eleventh year Nabonidus resided in Tema (a western suburb of Babylon) whilst the king's son was with the army in Accad, or Northern Babylonia. After this a lacuna occurs, owing to the tablet being broken. In the second portion of the inscription we find Nabonidus himself at the head of his army in Accad near Sippar. The events narrated occur in the seventeenth, or last, year of the king's reign.—"In the month of Tammuz [June] Cyrus gave battle to the army of Accad. The men of Accad broke into revolt. On the 14th day the garrison of Sippar was taken without fighting. Nabonidus flies. On the 16th day Gobryas the governor of Gutium [Kurdistan] and the army of Cyrus entered Babylon without a battle. Afterwards he takes Nabonidus and puts him into fetters in Babylon. On the 3rd day of Marchesvan [October] Cyrus entered Babylon" (Sayce, Fresh Light from the Ancient Monuments; Pinches, Capture of Babylon). In addition to this tablet we have the Cyrus cylinder published by Sir Henry Rawlinson in 1880. Cyrus pronounces a eulogy upon his military exploits and assigns his triumph to the intervention of the gods. Nabonidus had incurred their wrath by removing their images from the local shrines and bringing them to Babylon.

On comparing the inscriptions with the other accounts we find that they substantially agree with the statement by Berosus, but that they considerably differ from what is recorded by Herodotus, Xenophon, and in the Book of Daniel. (1) The inscriptions do not mention the siege of Babylon recorded by Herodotus and Xenophon. Cyrus says Gobryas his general took the town "without fighting". (2) Nabonidus (555–538 B. c.), and not Baltasar, as is stated in Daniel, was the last King of Babylon. Baltasar, or Bel-sarra-usur, was the son of Nabonidus. Nor was Nabonidus or Baltasar a son or descendant of Nabuchodonosor. Nabonidus was the son of Nebobaladhsu-ik-bi, and was a usurper of the throne. The family of Nabuchodonosor had come to an end in the person of Evil-Merodach, who had been murdered by Nergal-sharezer, his sister's husband. The controversy occasioned by these differences between the conservative and modern schools of thought has not yet reached a conclusion. Scholars of the former school still maintain the historical accuracy of the Book of Daniel, and explain the alleged discrepancies with great ingenuity. They assume that Baltasar had been associated with his father in the government, and that as prince-regent, or co-regent, he could be described in authority and rank as king. For this conjecture they seek support in the promise of Baltasar to make Daniel "third ruler" (D. V., "third prince") in the kingdom, from which they infer that he himself was the second. Professor R. D. Wilson, of Princeton, claims that the bearing of the title "King" by Baltasar was in harmony with the usage of the time (Princeton Theol. Rev., 1904, April, July; 1905, January, April). The other discrepancy, namely, that Nabuchodonosor is called the father of Baltasar (Dan., v, 2, 11, 18) they account for either by taking the word "father" in the wider sense of predecessor, or by the conjecture that Baltasar was his descendant on the mother's side.

On the other hand, the school of critics declines to accept these explanations. They argue that Baltasar not less than Nabuchodonosor appears in Daniel as sole and supreme ruler of the State. While fully admitting the possibility that Baltasar acted as prince-regent, they can find no proof for this either in the classical authors or in the inscriptions. The inference drawn from the promise of Baltasar to raise Daniel to the rank of a "third ruler" in the kingdom they regard as doubtful and uncertain. The Hebrew phrase may be rendered "ruler of a third part of the kingdom". Thus the phrase would be parallel to the Greek term "tetrarch", i. e. ruler of a fourth part, or of a small portion of territory. For this rendering they have the authority of the Septuagint, Josephus, and, as Dr. Adler informs us, of Jewish commentators of repute (see Daniel in the Critics' Den, p. 26). Furthermore, they argue that the emphatic way in which Nabuchodonosor is designated as father of the king leads the reader to infer that the writer meant his words to be understood in the literal and obvious sense. Thus the queen, addressing Baltasar, thrice repeats the designation "the king thy father", meaning Nabuchodonosor: "And in the days of thy father light, knowledge and wisdom were found in him [Daniel]: for King Nabuchodonosor thy father appointed him prince of the wise men, enchanters, Chaldeans, soothsayers, thy father, O King."

SAYCE, The Higher Criticism and the Monuments (London, 1894); KENNEDY, The Book of Daniel from the Christian Standpoint (London, 1898); FARRAR, Daniel (London); ANDERSON, Daniel in the Critics' Den (London); ORR, The Problem of the O. T. (London, 1906); GIGOT, Special Introduction to the Study of the O. T., pt. II, 366, 367, 369; ROGERS, A History of Babylonia and Assyria (New York, 1902); TIELE, Babylonisch-Assyrische Gesch. (Gotha, 1886).

C. VAN DEN BIESEN.

Balthazar. See MAGI.

Baltimore, ARCHDIOCESE OF, senior see of the United States of America, established a diocese 6 April, 1789; as an archdiocese 8 April, 1808; embraces all that part of the State of Maryland west of the Chesapeake Bay (6,442 square miles) including also the District of Columbia (64 square miles), making in all 6,502 square miles. The entire population of this area is about 1,273,000. The Catholics, numbering 255,000, are principally of English, Irish, and German descent. There are also Polish, Lithuanian, Bohemian, and Italian congregations, and six churches exclusively for coloured people, four in Baltimore, two in Washington. (See WASHINGTON and DISTRICT OF COLUMBIA.)

I. COLONIAL PERIOD.—(a) *Politico-Religious Beginnings.*—Catholic Maryland, the first colony in the New World where religious toleration was established, was planned by George Calvert (first Lord Baltimore), a Catholic convert; founded by his son Cecilius Calvert (second Lord Baltimore), and named for a Catholic queen, Henrietta Maria, wife of Charles I of England. Except for the period of Ingle's Rebellion (1645–47) its government was controlled by Catholics from the landing of the first colony under Leonard Calvert (25 March, 1634) until after 1649, when the Assembly passed the famous act of religious toleration. The first three Lords Baltimore, George, Cecilius, and Charles, were Catholics. The last three, Benedict Leonard, Charles, and Frederick, were Protestants. Puritans who had been given an asylum in Maryland rebelled and seized the government (1652–58) and Catholics were excluded from the administration of the province and restrained in the exercise of their faith. When Lord Baltimore again obtained control (1658), religious liberty was restored until 1692.

Taking advantage of Protestant disturbance in the colony, William of Orange, King of England, declared the Proprietary's claim forfeited, made Maryland a royal province, and sent over Copley, the first royal governor (1692). The Anglican Church was then made the established church of Maryland, every colonist being taxed for its support. In 1702, religious liberty was extended to all Christians except Catholics. Catholics were forbidden (1704) to instruct their children in their religion or to send them out of the colony for such instruction (1715). Priests were forbidden to exercise their functions and Catholic children could be taken from a Catholic parent. Appealed to by Catholics, Queen Anne intervened and the clergy were permitted to perform their duties in the chapels of private families (9 December, 1704). Thus originated the manor chapels, and the so-called "Priests' Mass-Houses". The apostasy of Benedict Leonard Calvert (1713) was a cruel blow to the persecuted Catholics. In 1716 an oath was exacted of office-holders renouncing their belief in Transubstantiation. An act disfranchising Catholics followed (1718). Charles Carroll, father of the Signer, went to France (1752) for the purpose of obtaining a grant of land on the Arkansas River for his persecuted brethren. This plan, however, failed. To exterminate Catholicity an attempt was made to pass a bill confiscating the property of the clergy (3 May, 1754, Lower House Journal in MSS., Maryland Archives). The missionaries, having received land from the Proprietaries upon the same conditions as the other colonists, divided their time between the care of souls and the cultivation of their mission-supporting farms. The cutting off of these revenues, would therefore have been disastrous to the Church. Fortunately this attempt did not succeed. Such were the political conditions until the time of the Revolution (Archives Maryland Hist. Soc. Baltimore; Johnson, Foundations of Maryland, Baltimore, 1883; Johnston, Religious Liberty in Maryland and Rhode Island, Catholic Truth Society Publications; Browne,

George and Cecilius Calvert, New York, 1890; Hall, The Lords of Baltimore, ibid., 1902).

(b) *The First Missionaries.*—In the first colony brought over by the Ark and the Dove (25 March, 1634) were three Jesuits, Fathers Andrew White and John Althan, and a lay brother, Thomas Gervase (White, Relatio Itineris in Marylandiam, Baltimore ed., 1874; cf. Am. Hist. Review, April, 1907, p. 584; Treacy, Old Catholic Maryland, Swedesboro, N. J., 1889; Hughes, Hist. of S. J. in N. America, 1907). The following year another priest and lay brother arrived. Fathers Philip Fisher (real name Thomas Copley) and John Knolles landed in 1637. In 1642, the Roman Congregation of the Propaganda, at Lord Baltimore's request, sent to Maryland two secular priests, Fathers Gilmett and Territt. Two Franciscans arrived in 1673, one of whom was Father Massæus Massey a Santa Barbara, a truly apostolic man. There were not more than six Franciscans at any time on the missions in Maryland. Their missions ceased with the death of Father Haddock in 1720. In 1716 two Scotch Recollects (Franciscans) came to the Eastern Shore of Maryland. The title "Apostle of Maryland" belongs unquestionably to Father Andrew White, S. J., whose zeal was boundless. During Ingle's Rebellion (1645–47) Fathers White and Fisher were taken in chains to England where the former died. Father Fisher returned to Maryland in 1648, dying in 1653, leaving the Rev. Lawrence Starkey alone on the mission. Fourteen years after the first colony landed nearly all the natives south of what is now Washington had embraced the Faith, living in peaceful happy intercourse with the settlers. Father White said Mass and baptized the princess of the tribe in his wigwam on the Port Tobacco River. A chapel farther down the stream replaced the wigwam which was in turn succeeded by St. Thomas's Manor church built in 1798 by the Rev. Charles Sewell, S. J. Such was the glorious result of the wisdom and zeal of the first Jesuit missionaries of Maryland (B. U. Campbell, in U. S. Cath. Hist. Magazine, Baltimore; Calvert Papers, Maryland Hist. Society, 1889–94; Treacy, op. cit.; The Catholic Cabinet, St. Louis, 1843–45; The Religious Cabinet, Baltimore, 1842).

In accordance with Lord Baltimore's instructions, a church was built in the early days at St. Mary's, the capital of the province. William Bretton and his wife, Temperance, in 1661 deeded the ground for the chapel of St. Ignatius and the cemetery at Newtown. Newtown Manor was afterwards purchased by the Jesuits. In 1677 a Catholic college was opened by Father Foster, S.J., and Mr. Thomas Hothersall, a scholastic. In 1697 we find a brick chapel at St. Mary's; frame chapels at St. Inigoes, Newtown, Port Tobacco, Newport, Father Hobart's chapel (Franciscan) near Newport; one on the Boarman estate, and one at Doncaster in Talbot County. During this period (1634–1700) there were about thirty-five Jesuits in the missions of Maryland, all of whom with two or three exceptions were English. They were men of apostolic zeal and disinterestedness. The mission at Bohemia, in Cecil County was founded by Father Mansell (1706), the priests of this mission carrying the Faith into Delaware. St. Inigoes house was established in 1708 and later a chapel was added. Hickory Mission, from which Baltimore was afterwards attended, was established in 1720, and St. Joseph's Chapel, Deer Creek (the Rev. John Digges, Jr.), in 1742. We find the Rev. Benedict Neale at Priest's Ford, Harford County, in 1747. St. Ignatius's Church, Hickory, was established (1792) by the Rev. Sylvester Boarman. About 1755, 900 Catholic Acadian refugees settled in Maryland, but the Catholics were forbidden to give them hospitality. Many of them lost the Faith, but some of their descendants still preserve the Faith for which their fathers suffered. An unfinished house in Baltimore (north-west corner of Calvert and Fayette

BALTIMORE'S FIRST CHURCH.

BALTIMORE

1. OLD ST. PATRICK'S   2. CORPUS CHRISTI CHURCH (JENKINS MEMORIAL)   3. ST. MARY'S SEMINARY

Streets) was used by them as a chapel. A Catholic school was established in Baltimore (1757) by Mary Ann March, but was closed on account of the violent persecution of Protestant clergymen. The historic Whitemarsh mission was founded in 1760 by the Rev. John Lewis. Frederick Chapel (St. John's) was built by Father Williams, S.J.; the church was built in 1800 by the Rev. John Dubois, at that time the only priest between Baltimore and St. Louis. The present church was consecrated in 1837. In 1903 the Jesuits gave up the church and novitiate. The Jesuit novitiate was opened at Georgetown, D. C., 1806. During the War of 1812, it was at St. Inigoes and Frederick for a few years, then returned to Georgetown, was removed to Whitemarsh about 1820, and to Frederick in 1833, whence in 1903 it was finally removed to St. Andrews-on-the-Hudson, near Poughkeepsie, New York.

In 1669, the Catholic population numbered 2,000; in 1708 it was 2,979 in a population of 40,000; in 1755 about 7,000. In 1766, the following missions were attended by Jesuits: St. Inigoes, Newtown, Port Tobacco, Whitemarsh, Deer Creek, Fredericktown, Queenstown, Bohemia, and Baltimore. The twenty Jesuits on the Maryland mission at the time of their order's suppression (1773) remained at their posts. The first priest born in Maryland was the Rev. Robert Brooks (1663). His four brothers also became priests. Conspicuous for unselfish zeal at this period was Rev. William Hunter; whilst for over forty years Father George Thorold laboured in Maryland (1700–42). The clergy was, in general, self-supporting. (Treacy, op. cit.; Extracts from Letters of Missionaries, Baltimore, 1877; Shea, Life and Times of Archbishop Carroll, New York, 1888.)

(c) *The Catholic Colonists.*—The Catholic population, mostly rural, was generous to the Church and hospitable to the priests. We find many deeds and bequests for ecclesiastical purposes in the early records. Enduring one hundred years of persecution from the Protestants to whom they had offered asylum, proscribed, disfranchised, offered peace and emolument in exchange for apostasy, the Catholics generally continued faithful, and it is inspiring to read the list of Catholic names that survived the dark days, and that are still in evidence on the Catholic roll of honour—Brent, Lee, Fenwick, Boarman, Sewell, Lowe, Gardiner, Carroll, Neale, Jenkins, Digges, Bowling, Edelin, Matthews, Lancaster, Stonestreet, Boone, Mattingly, Brooks, Hunter, Coombes, Spalding, Semmes, Dyer, Jamison, Queen, Hill, Gwynn, Wheeler, Elder, McAtee, Pye, Miles, Abell, Camalier, Smith, Plowden, Freeman, Maddox, Greenwell, Floyd, Drury, Mudd, Hamilton, Clark, Payne, Brock, Walton, Doyne, Darnall. During the American Revolution, Catholics, with very rare exceptions, sided with the patriots; Maryland's best Catholic names are to be found on the rolls of the Continental army, both as officers and privates. The most prominent and influential citizen of Maryland during this epoch was Charles Carroll of Carrollton, one of the signers of the Declaration of Independence. At this time only Maryland, Pennsylvania, Virginia, and Delaware had removed the disabilities against Catholics. The National Convention (Philadelphia, 1787) granted religious liberty to all. (McSherry, Hist. of Maryland, Baltimore, 1882; Scharf, Hist. of Maryland, Baltimore, 1879.)

II. AMERICAN PERIOD.—Such were the conditions in Maryland when the first bishop was appointed. Speaking of this period in 1790 Bishop Carroll said "it is surprising that there remained even so much as there was of true religion. In general Catholics were regular and unoffensive in their conduct, such, I mean, as were natives of the country"—but he complains bitterly of the injury to the Faith caused by those Catholics who came to the colony about this

time (Shea, Life of Archbishop Carroll, 49). In fact the Church began to recover from this scandal only forty years after. Catholic Americans were subject spiritually to English Catholic superiors (the archpriests), until 6 September, 1665, when Innocent XI appointed Dr. John Leyburn, Vicar-Apostolic of all England. The British Colonies in America remained under the jurisdiction of Dr. Leyburn and his successors, Bishops Gifford, Petre, Challoner, and Talbot, until the appointment of Dr. Carroll. After the Revolution it was plain that the United States could not conveniently remain subject in spirituals to a superior in England. A meeting was called at Whitemarsh (27 June, 1783) by the Rev. John Lewis, Vicar-General of the Vicar Apostolic of London. This meeting was attended by the Revs. John Carroll, John Ashton, Charles Sewell, Bernard Diderick, Sylvester Boarman, and Leonard Neale. It resulted in a petition asking for the appointment of the Rev. John Lewis as Superior, with quasi-episcopal faculties. At this time the French Minister to the United States schemed to make the missions of the United States subject to France. Benjamin Franklin, United States representative to France, ignorant of the true state of affairs, at first supported this intrigue. Congress, however, informed Franklin that the project was one "without the jurisdiction and power of Congress, who have no authority to permit or refuse it". The American priests then presented a memorial to Pius VI. As a result the appointment of the Rev. John Carroll as Superior of the missions of the United States, with power to administer confirmation, was ratified (9 June, 1784). He received the decree appointing him Prefect Apostolic 26 November, 1784. At this time, there were, according to Dr. Carroll, 15,800 Catholics in Maryland (of whom 3,000 were negroes); 7,000 Catholics in Pennsylvania; 200 in Virginia; 1,500 in New York. In 1782 the total population of Maryland was 254,000. There were nineteen priests in Maryland and five in Pennsylvania. Dr. Carroll made his first visitation in Maryland in 1785, and administered confirmation. About this time he took up his residence in Baltimore, where the Rev. Charles Sewell was pastor. In 1788, the clergy petitioned Pius VI for the appointment of a bishop. Their request was granted. They were permitted to determine whether the bishop should be merely titular, or should have a see in the United States—and to choose the place for, as well as to elect the occupant of the see.

Election of Bishop Carroll.—Twenty-four priests assembled at Whitemarsh. Twenty-three voted for Dr. Carroll, who was, accordingly, appointed first Bishop of Baltimore, subject to the Roman Congregation of the Propaganda. Dr. Carroll was consecrated in the chapel of Lulworth Castle, England, 15 August, 1790, the consecration being the Right Rev. Charles Walmesley, Senior Vicar Apostolic of England. Before leaving England, Dr. Carroll arranged with the Sulpician Fathers to establish an ecclesiastical seminary in Baltimore at their own expense. Accordingly, the superior, the Rev. Francis Nagot with three priests and five seminarians arrived at Baltimore in July, 1791. The "One Mile Tavern" and four acres of land were purchased and on 18 July, St. Mary's Seminary was opened.

(a) *Progress of Catholicism.*—The next year the Revs. J. B. David and B. J. Flaget, afterwards Bishops of Bardstown (Louisville), Kentucky, with Mr. Stephen Badin who was the first priest ordained in Baltimore (1793), arrived. In 1787, the Rev. Joseph Mosley died leaving about 600 communicants on the Eastern Shore, where he had laboured twenty-two years. At this time there was only one other priest stationed there. The next year the veteran John Lewis died, being the last of the Superiors of the original Maryland missions. In 1789 Georgetown College was founded. A frame church was erected at Westminster (1789), succeeded by Christ Church (1805), under the Rev. Joseph Zucchi. In 1791 the Diocese of Baltimore included all the territory east of the Mississippi, except Florida; in this vast territory there were churches at Baltimore, New York (1785), Boston (1788), Charleston (1788); in Maryland at St. Inigoes, Newtown, Newport, Port Tobacco, Rock Creek, Annapolis, Whitemarsh, Bohemia, Tuckahoe, Deer Creek, Frederick, Westminster; in Pennsylvania, at Philadelphia, Lancaster, Conewago, Goshenhoppen; in Delaware, at Coffee Run, also at Vincennes, Kaskaskia, Cahokia, and Prairie du Rocher. In 1790, a Carmelite community was established at Port Tobacco under Mother Frances Dickinson. The nuns remained there until 1831, when twenty-four sisters under Mother Angela Mudd removed to Baltimore. In 1791, the first diocesan synod in the United States was opened at the bishop's house in Baltimore. Twenty-two priests and the bishop were present. At this synod the offertory collections were inaugurated. Between 1791 and 1798 seventeen French priests arrived, some of whom became famous in the history of the United States—the Revs. John Dubois (1791), Benedict Flaget, J. B. David, Ambrose Maréchal (1792), William DuBourg, and John Moranvillé (1794), and John Lefevre Cheverus (1796). Until this time the burden of the missions of Maryland had been borne by the Jesuits. From 1700 to 1805 about ninety Jesuits had laboured on the mission, of whom about sixty were English, sixteen Americans, and the rest German, Irish, Welsh, Belgian, and French. They were apostolic men who devoted their lives without earthly reward to the service of others.

In 1792, Catholics in the eastern section of Baltimore, finding it inconvenient to attend the pro-cathedral, asked for a priest and rented a room in the third story of a house, corner of Fleet and Bond Streets, where the first Mass was said by Bishop Carroll. This congregation numbered about twelve persons. The Rev. Antoine Garnier, from St. Mary's Seminary, visited them twice weekly until 17 December, 1795, when the Rev. John Floyd took charge. The first church was erected on Apple Alley near Wilks Street. Father Floyd dying in 1797, Father Garnier was again made pastor until 1803, when the Rev. Michael Coddy succeeded him. Dying within the year, his place was taken by the Rev. John Moranvillé, through whose zeal the corner-stone of St. Patrick's Church (Broadway and Bank Streets) was laid 10 July, 1804. It was dedicated 29 November, 1807, being then the most imposing church in the diocese. Father Moranvillé died in 1824, and was succeeded by the Rev. Nicholas Kearney (d. 1840), the Rev. John Dolan (d. 1870), and the Rev. John T. Gaitley (d. 1892). In 1898 the old church was replaced by the present handsome Gothic edifice. St. Patrick's School, begun by Father Moranvillé, preceded all public schools in Baltimore. The earliest German Catholic congregation was established 17 February, 1702, assembling for the first time for Divine service in a house near Centre Market. About 1800 Father Reuter, a priest in charge of the German Catholics, fomented a schism amongst them. They built a church where St. Alphonsus's now stands, called it St. John the Evangelist's, and defied the bishop, who carried the case to the courts, which decided in his favour (1805). Archbishop Eccleston confided the church to the Redemptorists in 1840. The corner-stone of the new church was laid in 1841, the name being changed to St. Alphonsus's. This church is distinguished for two pastors whose repute for sanctity entitles them to special mention, the Venerable John N. Neumann (Bishop of Philadelphia, 1852–60), the process of whose beatification is still pending in Rome (Berger,

Life of Right Rev. John N. Neumann, D.D., New York, 1884); and the Rev. Francis X. Seelos who died in 1867, the first steps towards whose canonization were taken in 1901 (Zimmer, Life of Rev. F. X. Seelos, New York, 1887). St. Joseph's, Emmitsburg, was founded in 1793, by the Rev. Matthew Ryan. The Revs. John Dubois and Simon Bruté were afterwards pastors of this church. The first baptismal record of St. Mary's Church, Bryantown, was entered in 1793. Father David, the first pastor, was transferred to Georgetown in 1804. In 1794, the first church was built in Hagerstown, attended by the Rev. D. Cahill. About 1795, a log church (St. Mary's) was built at Cumberland; a brick church was substituted in 1838. It was replaced by the present church (St. Patrick's) begun in 1849 by the Rev. O. L. Obermeyer, and consecrated in 1883. St. Joseph's, Taneytown, was built by Mr. Brookes (1796). Its first pastor was the well-known Russian nobleman and convert, Father Demetrius A. Gallitzin.

It was soon seen that a coadjutor for the diocese was desirable in case of the bishop's death, and the Rev. Lawrence Græssel, a German priest of Philadelphia, was appointed to that office. This zealous priest dying soon after, the Rev. Leonard Neale, a native of Maryland, was selected, and was consecrated 7 December, 1800, at the Baltimore pro-cathedral. A notable event at this time was the marriage of Jerome Bonaparte, brother of Napoleon, to Miss Patterson of Baltimore, Bishop Carroll officiating (24 December, 1803).

(b) *Educational Institutions.*—As already stated Georgetown College was opened by the Jesuit Fathers in 1791. (Centennial Hist. of Georgetown College, Washington, 1891.) In 1803 the faculty of St. Mary's Seminary instituted an undenominational college course which continued until 1852, when Loyola College was opened. During this period it numbered among its students many who afterwards became prominent; among others Robert Walsh, A. B. Roman, the Latrobes, the Carrolls, the Jenkins, the Foleys, S. Eccleston, J. Chanche, F. E. Chatard, C. I. White, S. T. Wallis, Robert McLane, C. C. Biddle, Reverdy Johnson, Oden Bowie, Leo Knott, Christopher Johnson. At one time (1839–40) it had 207 students. In the meantime an attempt was made to separate the college from the seminary, and in 1807 Father Nagot established a college at Pigeon Hills, Pennsylvania, but in 1808, the sixteen students were transferred to a new institution begun at Emmitsburg by the Rev. John Dubois, a Sulpician. Such was the beginning of Mt. St. Mary's College. It gave to the Church one cardinal (McCloskey), five archbishops, twenty-one bishops, and five hundred priests. To carry out a design long entertained by the Sulpicians, St. Charles College, a *petit séminaire*, was begun and built on land donated by Charles Carroll of Carrollton. The corner-stone was laid in 1831, but owing to the lack of funds the college was not opened until 1848. The Rev. O. L. Jenkins was its first president, with one instructor and four students, but at his death (1869) there were thirteen instructors, 140 students, and one hundred priests among its alumni. Since 1853, St. Mary's Seminary has been exclusively a *grand séminaire*, with philosophy and theology courses. The memories of the devoted priests who during more than a century have composed its faculties, men of great learning and deep piety, are cherished with loving reverence by the numerous clergy they have taught. The alumni roll of St. Mary's contains the names of one cardinal, 30 bishops, 1,400 priests (Centennial History of St. Mary's Seminary, Baltimore, 1891). The Society of Jesus was re-established in Maryland (1805) with the Rev. Robert Molyneux as superior.

In 1808, Mrs. Elizabeth Ann Seton, a convert from Episcopalianism, went from New York to Baltimore and lived with some companions next to St. Mary's

Seminary. A convert, the Rev. Samuel S. Cooper, having given Mrs. Seton and her nine companions a lot at Emmitsburg, they founded there (1810) the Academy of St. Joseph. In 1812, the community was established under the rules of the Sisters of Charity and Mrs. Seton was elected mother superior. She died in 1821, leaving a flourishing community of fifty sisters (White, "Life of Eliza A. Seton", New York, 1853; Seton, "Memoir Letters and Journal of Elizabeth Seton", New York, 1869; De Barbarry, "Elizabeth Seton", 2 vols., Paris, 1881; Sadlier, New York, s. d.). The community remained independent until 1850, when the sisters allied themselves with the Sisters of Charity of France, adopting the French costume. Thirty-one sisters in the Diocese of New York preferred to continue under the old rule and organized a separate body. During the Civil War (1862–63), 140 Sisters of Charity gave their services on the field and in the hospitals. The following notable institutions have been founded in the diocese from the mother house at Emmitsburg: St. Mary's Orphan Asylum (1817); Mt. Hope Retreat (1840); St. Vincent's Infant Asylum (1856); St. Joseph's House of Industry (1863); St. Agnes's Hospital (1863).

(c) *The Baltimore Cathedral*.—The acquisition of Louisiana by the United States increased the labours of Bishop Carroll. In 1805, the Holy See made him Administrator Apostolic of Louisiana and the Floridas. Until this time the bishop had officiated in St. Peter's Church, built about 1770, at the corner of Northeast and Forrest Streets. The Rev. Bernard Diderick, a Belgian priest, attended the church monthly from 1775–82. The Rev. Charles Sewell of St. Mary's County was the first resident pastor. Persuaded by Dr. DuBourg, the bishop and trustees decided (1806) to erect the new cathedral on the present site. The corner-stone was laid 7 July, 1806, by Bishop Carroll. The first rector of the cathedral was the Rev. Francis Beeston. He died (1809) before the church was finished. His successor was the Rev. Enoch Fenwick (d. 1827), to whose untiring zeal was due the completion of the church in 1821. During the building of the church the congregation had grown so large that the Sulpicians opened to the public the chapel of St. Mary's Seminary, then newly dedicated (1808). For half a century it continued to be the succursal church of the cathedral. On 31 May, 1821, the cathedral was dedicated by Archbishop Maréchal. The architect who had generously given his services gratis, and faithfully watched over the erection of the edifice was Benjamin H. Latrobe, a Protestant gentleman, and a devoted friend of Archbishop Carroll. He was engaged at the same time in building the National Capitol. The high altar of the cathedral was a gift to Archbishop Maréchal from his pupils in Marseilles. The imposing portico of the building was added in 1863, under the direction of the architect, Eben Faxon. The cathedral was consecrated 25 May, 1876, by Archbishop Bayley. During Cardinal Gibbons's administration a commodious sacristy was erected (1879); the sanctuary was extended (1888); two altars, gifts of Mrs. Michael Jenkins and James Sloan, were added, and the altar rail in memory of William Boggs donated (1906). There are few edifices in the United States as rich in historical memories as the Baltimore Cathedral. Within its walls have been held three plenary councils (1852, 1866, 1884), ten provincial councils, and nine diocesan synods; three cardinals have been invested, Gibbons, 1886; Satolli, 1890; Martinelli, 1901; six archbishops have received the pallium, twenty-five bishops have been consecrated, and 644 priests have been ordained by Cardinal Gibbons alone. The bishops consecrated in the cathedral were: B. J. Fenwick (1825), Dubois (1826), Whitfield (1828), Purcell (1833), Eccleston (1834), Chanche (1841), Whelan (1841), Tyler (1844),

Elder (1844), Barry (1857), Verot (1858), Becker (1868), Gibbons (1868), Thomas Foley (1870), Gross (1873), Northrop (1882), Glorieux (1885), Curtis (1886), Haid (1888), John Foley (1888), Chapelle (1891), Donahue (1894), Allen (1897), Granjon (1900), Conaty (1901). In the chapel built by Cardinal Gibbons under the high altar repose the ashes of Carroll, Maréchal, Whitfield, Eccleston, Kenrick, and Spalding. Besides those already mentioned many distinguished clergymen have been associated with the cathedral; Revs. Roger Smith, Charles C. Pise, Charles I. White, first editor of "The Catholic Mirror", John Hickey, S.S., H.B. Coskery, Thomas Becker, Thomas Foley, Thomas S. Lee, A. A. Curtis, P. J. Donahue, and C. F. Thomas. The cathedral parish has always counted among its members a great number of distinguished persons. Among its pewholders have been Charles Carroll of Carrollton, Chief Justice Taney, David Williamson, Luke Tiernan, Thomas Sim Lee, Thomas C. Jenkins, E. Austin Jenkins, Alfred Jenkins, William George Read, John Hillen, Patrick Bennett, Basil Elder, John Walsh, Solomon Hillen, John and Richard Caton, Dr. Peter Chatard, Abraham White, Jerome Bonaparte, Courtney Jenkins, Mark Jenkins, Basil Spalding, Judge Parkin Scott, Philip Laurenson, M. Benzinger, Charles M. Dougherty, Col. J. N. Bonaparte, William Kennedy, Robert Barry, Columbus O'Donnell, John Murphy. In recent times and at present we find the Attorney-General of the United States, Hon. Charles J. Bonaparte, Michael Jenkins, Joseph Jenkins, Dr. Felix Jenkins, George Jenkins, the Misses Jenkins, Mr. and the Misses Andrews, the Misses Gardner, William Boggs, Daniel Foley, Mrs. and the Misses Mactavish, W. R. Cromwell, Mrs. John S. Gittings, Major N. S. Hill, Richard and Allen MacSherry, Charles G. Nicholson, Miss Emily Harper, C. D. Kenny, A. Leo Knott, J. M. Littig, the Drs. Milholland, Robert Rennert, Robert Jenkins, Henry Bogue, the Messrs. Abell, the Misses Abell, Mrs. Alice Caughy, Messrs. Shriver, Joseph Turner, Mrs. Van Bibber, Owen Daly, Alexander Yearley, Harry Benzinger, James R. Wheeler, Charles Tiernan, Judge Charles Heuisler, Drs. Chatard, Drs. O'Donovan, Dr. Charles Grindall, Messrs. and the Misses Boone, Edgar Gans, Captain Billups, Messrs. Key, F. Dammann, Mrs. J. I. Griffiss, and Victor Baughman. Indeed the roll-call of the cathedral parishioners contains the names of the most distinguished Catholics of their times. It is worthy of remark that although the trustee system has been continued at the cathedral for over one hundred years, there has never been any serious disagreement between the clergy and laity. The archiepiscopal residence was built during Dr. Whitfield's administration, and the two wings were added in 1865 by Captain William Kennedy.

(d) *Division of the Diocese*.—In compliance with Bishop Carroll's request for a division of his diocese, Pius VII (8 April, 1808) issued the Bulls creating four new sees, naming the Rev. Richard L. Concannen, a Dominican for New York; the Rev. Michael Egan, a Franciscan for Philadelphia; the Rev. John Cheverus for Boston, and the Rev. Benedict Joseph Flaget, Sulpician, for Bardstown. At the same time Baltimore was made the metropolitan see with Dr. Carroll as the first archbishop. Dr. Concannen, consecrated in Rome (1808), died at Naples (1810) when about to sail. Dr. Egan and Dr. Cheverus were consecrated at Baltimore in the pro-cathedral (1810) and Dr. Flaget at St. Patrick's the same year. The pallium was conferred on Archbishop Carroll in St. Peter's, Baltimore, 18 August, 1811. At this time there were in the United States about seventy priests and eighty churches. Maryland, Virginia, the District of Columbia, the Carolinas, what is now Alabama, Mississippi, Louisiana, and Florida were still under the jurisdiction of Baltimore, and in 1811 the

Holy See added some of the Danish and Dutch West Indies. At this period occurred the interference of Archbishop Troy and other Irish bishops in American affairs (Shea, Life and Times of Abp. Carroll, pp. 664–668). Dr. Carroll's protest at Rome was rendered ineffectual, owing to the representations of the Dominican Fathers Harold, who had hastened the death of Bishop Egan of Philadelphia, and afterwards, in Europe, enlisted against the Archbishop the support of the Irish prelates. Worn out with the struggle, he died 3 December, 1815.

III. SUCCESSORS OF ARCHBISHOP CARROLL.—(a) *Leonard Neale.*—Archbishop Carroll was succeeded by Leonard Neale, a native of Maryland. The Poor Clares (Mother Mary de la Marché and two others) had already opened an academy in 1801 at Georgetown, with Miss Alice Lalor as assistant teacher. These nuns returned to Europe after the death of the abbess; Miss Lalor continued the academy. Archbishop Neale erected the community of teachers into a house of the Order of the Visitation 28 December, 1817. Archbishop Neale died 17 June, at Georgetown, and was buried in the convent chapel.

(b) *Ambrose Maréchal.*—Archbishop Maréchal was born in France, and joined the Company of St. Sulpice. He had already refused the See of Philadelphia (1816), but finally consented to become Archbishop Neale's coadjutor. He was consecrated at St. Peter's, Baltimore, 4 December, 1817, by Bishop Cheverus. In his first visitation he confirmed 2,506 persons. In his diocese, which comprised Maryland, Virginia, the Carolinas, Georgia, and the territory west of Georgia to the Mississippi, there were then, according to his estimate, 100,000 Catholics. About 10,000 were in Baltimore, having increased to that figure from 800 in 1792. In one year there were 10,000 communions in the seminary chapel alone. There were fifty-two priests, principally French and American born. The Diocese of Baltimore at this time (1819) mourned the loss of Thomas Sim Lee, twice governor, and Maryland's representative in the Convention which ratified the Constitution. In 1820, two schismatic priests, aided by intriguing Irish prelates, succeeded in having Patrick Kelly secretly appointed to the See of Richmond and John England to that of Charleston. Thus, without the archbishop's knowledge or consent, New York, Philadelphia, Richmond, and Charleston were given for bishops utter strangers, bound by oath of allegiance to England, then at variance with the United States. The Diocese of Baltimore was thus divided into two parts, Maryland and the District of Columbia on the Atlantic, and a thousand miles off Alabama and Mississippi, with Richmond and Charleston between. Archbishop Maréchal, while at Rome, (1821) obtained for the provincial bishops the right to recommend candidates for vacant sees. Mississippi was erected into a Vicariate Apostolic with Dr. DuBourg as Vicar Apostolic; Alabama and Florida were attached to the Vicariate Apostolic of Mobile (1825). In 1822, Bishop Kelly returned to Ireland, and Archbishop Maréchal was appointed Administrator of the Diocese of Richmond. The archbishop died 28 January, 1828.

(c) *James Whitfield.*—He was succeeded by James Whitfield, an Englishman by birth. His consecration by Bishop Flaget took place 25 May, 1828, in the cathedral. October 4, 1829, the First Provincial Council of Baltimore was opened, and the same day the archbishop received the pallium. The Fathers of this council were Archbishop Whitfield, Bishops Flaget, the two Fenwicks (Boston and Cincinnati), England, Rosati, and Rev. William Matthews, representing Philadelphia. (See BALTIMORE, THE PROVINCIAL COUNCILS OF.) To carry out the council's decrees, a synod, attended by thirty-five priests, was held 31 October, 1831. There were at this time in Maryland about 80,000 Catholics in a population of 407,000;

in the District of Columbia about 7,000 in a population of 33,000. There were fifty-two priests in the diocese. Out of his private fortune, Archbishop Whitfield built St. James's Church, Baltimore (1833). It was first used by English-speaking Catholics, who, finding it too small for their increasing numbers, commenced the erection of St. Vincent's Church (1841). About the same time the German congregation of St. John's (Saratoga Street) began the building of their new church, St. Alphonsus; needing in the meantime a place for worship, they were granted the use of St. James's, after the opening of St. Vincent's (of which Father Gildea was the first pastor). The Redemptorists from St. Alphonsus took charge henceforth of St. James's and built there the first convent of their order in the United States. Several other churches were established by the Redemptorists. In 1845, they founded St. Michael's, a small church on the corner of Pratt and Regester Streets; the present church on the corner of Lombard and Wolfe Streets was commenced in 1857. Its congregation is now one of the largest in the city. The Redemptorists also founded Holy Cross parish, the corner-stone of the church being laid in 1858. Since 1869, the secular clergy have been in charge. The church of the Fourteen Holy Martyrs was begun (1870) by the Redemptorists; in 1874, they transferred it to the Benedictines. Rev. Meinrad Jeggle, O.S.B., was rector from 1878 to 1896. The new church was commenced in 1902. St. Wenceslaus's, dedicated in 1872, formed the nucleus of the Slav congregations in Baltimore. The Redemptorists took charge of it in 1882. A new church and school were commenced in 1903. In 1873 they began the Sacred Heart Church (Canton).

The Maryland Province of the Society of Jesus was formally established in 1833, with Father William McSherry, a Virginian, as first provincial. The Second Provincial Council met at the cathedral, Baltimore, 20 October, 1833. Besides Archbishop Whitfield, there were present Bishops David, England, Rosati, Fenwick (Boston), Dubois, Portier, F. P. Kenrick, Rese, Purcell. Bishop Flaget was absent; the Jesuits, Sulpicians, and Dominicans were represented. A Roman Ritual adapted to the wants of this country was ordered to be prepared. Rev. Samuel Eccleston elected coadjutor, was consecrated in the cathedral 14 September, 1834, by Archbishop Whitfield, who died the following October.

(d) *Samuel Eccleston.*—Archbishop Eccleston, a native of Maryland, a convert and a Sulpician, was thirty-three years old when he succeeded to the See of Baltimore. During his administration the anti-Catholic sentiment began to lose its violence and the tide of conversions set in. In 1834 there were within the jurisdiction of Baltimore (Maryland, Virginia, and District of Columbia) 70 churches and 69 priests. There were only 327 priests in the whole United States. The Visitation Nuns from Georgetown established a house in Baltimore (1837) with Mother Juliana Matthews as first superioress. Mother Anastasia Coombes established another Visitation monastery at Frederick in 1846. In 1852 another house was established (Mt. de Sales) at Catonsville, under Mother Cecilia Brooks.

The Third Provincial Council was held in the cathedral, 1837. It was attended by the archbishop, and Bishops Rosati, Fenwick (Boston), F. P. Kenrick, Purcell, Chabrat, Clancy, Bruté, Blanc. Bishop Dubois declined to assist. The Fourth Provincial Council was opened at the cathedral, 16 May, 1840. Ten bishops accepted the invitation of Archbishop Eccleston to attend the council, Flaget, Rosati, Fenwick (Boston), Portier, F. P. Kenrick, Purcell, Blanc, Loras, Miles, De la Hailandière. The Sulpicians, Dominicans, and Redemptorists were also represented. Rev. Richard Whelan and Rev. John Chanche were recommended by this council, respectively for the

CATHEDRAL OF THE ASSUMPTION, BALTIMORE

Dioceses of Richmond and Natchez, thus freeing the archbishop from the administration of Richmond. The St. Vincent de Paul Society was established in the diocese (1840) and the Young Catholic Friends' Society in 1848. In 1842, the corner-stone of Calvert Hall was laid on the site of the pro-cathedral (Saratoga Street). The present imposing building was opened 1891. Rock Hill Academy was purchased by the Christian Brothers (1857) and Rock Hill College incorporated 1865.

The Fifth Provincial Council was held in the cathedral, May, 1843. It was attended by seventeen bishops. At this time there were 90,000 Catholics, 58 churches, 70 priests, two seminaries, three colleges, two academies for boys, six for girls, five orphan asylums, and ten free schools. The total population of Maryland in 1840 was 469,232. The Sixth Provincial Council met at the cathedral, 10 May, 1846. Twenty-three bishops were present and four religious orders were represented. "The Blessed Virgin Mary Conceived Without Sin" was chosen as patroness of the Province. Sisters of Notre Dame (mother-house of Eastern Province on Aisquith Street) came to Baltimore, 5 August, 1847. "Notre Dame of Maryland" was established 22 September, 1873. The Seventh Provincial Council met at the cathedral, May, 1849. Archbishop Eccleston, in pursuance of the council's decision, issued a pastoral letter reviving the custom of Peter's-pence, and inviting Pius IX, then in exile at Gaeta, to attend. The Archbishops of Baltimore and St. Louis and twenty-three bishops were present; seven religious orders were represented. This council recommended New Orleans, Cincinnati, and New York as metropolitan sees, also the creation of the Sees of Savannah, Wheeling, and St. Paul. The fathers petitioned for the definition of the Immaculate Conception. One of their decrees forbade priests officiating at marriages where a minister had officiated or intended to do so. The Province of Baltimore now comprised the Dioceses of Philadelphia, Pittsburg, Richmond, Wheeling, Charleston, and Savannah.

About this time Rev. John Hickey established a precedent by refusing to testify in court concerning stolen property restored through a penitent. The court sustained him. During Archbishop Eccleston's time, besides those mentioned above, several other churches were erected. The corner-stone of St. Joseph's was laid in 1839. In 1849, it was given to the Jesuits, but returned to the diocesan clergy in 1860. The new church was begun in 1899. St. Peter's, begun in 1843, was consecrated in 1879 under Rev. Edward McColgan, V.G., its first pastor. The Sisters of Mercy came to St. Peter's from Pittsburg in 1855; Mother Catherine Wynne was first superioress. They afterwards opened Mt. St. Agnes (1867) of which Mother de Chantal Digges was first superioress; they also have charge of the City Hospital. St. Augustine's (Elkridge) was founded 1845. Its first pastor was Rev. B. Piot; the present beautiful church is the gift of Mr. C. D. Kenny (1902). St. Charles Borromeo (Pikesville) was commenced 16 July, 1848, by Father White. The present imposing Romanesque edifice was dedicated 12 March, 1899. The Immaculate Conception parish was organized in 1850 with Rev. Mark Anthony, C. M., as its first pastor; the present church was dedicated in 1858, during the pastorate of Rev. Joseph Giustiniani, C.M. Archbishop Eccleston died at Georgetown, 22 April, 1851, and was buried in Baltimore. At this time there were in the diocese (Maryland and District of Columbia) 83 churches and chapels; 103 priests; 6 ecclesiastical seminaries; 12 free schools, and 23 charitable institutions; Catholic population 100,000. Rev. H. B. Coskery was administrator until the following August, when Dr. Francis P. Kenrick, Coadjutor-Bishop of Philadelphia, was elevated to the See of Baltimore.

(e) *Francis Patrick Kenrick.*—Archbishop Kenrick convoked the First Plenary Council of Baltimore, 9 May, 1852. (See BALTIMORE, PLENARY COUNCILS OF.) To carry out the council's decrees a synod was called (June, 1853), attended by 35 diocesan and 17 regular priests. At this synod parochial rights and limits were defined. The Eighth Provincial Council met in the Baltimore Cathedral, 5 May, 1855. Eight sees were represented. It regulated pew rents and collections, and established a rule for the cathedraticum. Col. B. U. Campbell, a Maryland Catholic, who by his contributions laid the foundation for the history of the Church in the United States, died about this time (1855). In 1856 the Catholics of the city of Baltimore numbered 81,000, and had 13 churches, while in the entire diocese (Maryland and the District of Columbia) there were 99 churches and chapels, 130 priests, and a population of 120,000. The Forty Hours' Devotion was established in the diocese (1858). In 1858 the Ninth Provincial Council was held in the cathedral; 8 bishops were present and 6 religious orders were represented. At the Council's request the Holy See granted to the Archbishop of Baltimore the precedence in councils and meetings, held by the prelates of the United States, even though he were not senior archbishop. The petition of the Fathers of this Council for a perpetual dispensation from the Saturday abstinence was granted. In 1862, the Baltimore Province comprised Philadelphia, Pittsburg, Charleston, Savannah, Richmond, Wheeling, Erie, and the Vicariate Apostolic of Florida. In the Diocese of Baltimore there were 124 churches and chapels; 170 priests, 36 free schools, 35 charitable institutions; Catholic population 150,000.

A synod was convened (1863) at which the version of the Bible revised by the archbishop was adopted as the one to be used in the diocese. Under Archbishop Kenrick, the following churches were built in Baltimore: St. John's in 1853, with Rev. J. B. McManus as first pastor. The present church was opened in 1856. The church of St. Ignatius Loyola was consecrated 15 August, 1856. Rev. John Early, S.J., was its first pastor and founder of Loyola College on Holliday Street (1852); in 1855 the present college was opened on Calvert Street (Hist. Sketch of Loyola College, Baltimore, 1902). Many distinguished citizens claim it as their Alma Mater. St. Bridget's Church (Canton) was dedicated 1854 and was built by Rev. James Dolan out of his private means, as were also St. Mary's, Govanstown, and the Dolan Orphans' Home. Rev. John Constance was first pastor of St. Bridget's. New churches were begun in Kent County, Long Green, and Clarkesville during 1855. Archbishop Kenrick died 7 July, 1863, and Very Rev. H. B. Coskery, a native of Maryland, again became administrator. He had been appointed Bishop of Portland in 1854, but had returned the Bulls.

Coloured Catholics.—During his administration St. Francis Xavier's Church for negroes was dedicated (1864). Its first pastor was Father Michael O'Connor. It was put in charge of the Josephites (1871) from Mill Hill College, England, brought to Baltimore by Rev. Herbert Vaughan. These missionaries came to minister to the Catholic negroes of Maryland, there being—greatly to the honour of their Catholic masters—16,000 of them in the State at the time of the emancipation. From St. Francis sprung St. Monica's, St. Peter Claver's (1889), and St. Barnabas's (1907), all churches for coloured people. As early as 1828 the Sulpician Father Jacques Joubert founded at Baltimore a house of Coloured Oblate Sisters of Providence. They conduct at present St. Frances's Academy and Orphanage, and in Washington St. Cyprian's Parochial School and Academy. St. Joseph's Seminary was opened in Baltimore by the Josephites (1888) with three white and one coloured student.

Epiphany Apostolic College, its preparatory seminary, was opened in 1889 by Rev. Dominic Manley. In 1881 St. Elizabeth's Home for coloured children was established in Baltimore by Mother Winifred and three English Sisters of St. Francis. Their convent on Maryland Avenue was opened in 1889, the house being a gift to the order from Mrs. E. Austin Jenkins.

(f) *Martin John Spalding.*—At Archbishop Kenrick's death the United States Government attempted to interfere in the selection of an archbishop, but failed (Cathedral Records, Baltimore, 1906, p. 46; Shea, Hist. of Cath. Ch. in U. S., 1844–66, New York, 1889–92, p. 393), and the Rt. Rev. Martin John Spalding, Bishop of Louisville, was elected 23 May, 1864. Archbishop Spalding invited the Sisters of the Good Shepherd from Louisville (1864) to come to Baltimore, and established them in a home given by Mrs. Emily Mactavish. Their work is the reformation of fallen women and the preservation of young girls. At this time (1864) the Church lost one of its foremost members, Roger B. Taney, Chief Justice of the United States. The Tenth Provincial Council was opened in the cathedral, 25 April, 1869; 14 prelates were present. The Second Plenary Council of Baltimore met 7 October, 1866, in the cathedral. It recommended the establishment of the Apostolic Vicariate of North Carolina. St. Mary's Industrial School for Boys, erected on land donated by Mrs. Emily Mactavish, was opened in 1866, and placed in charge of the Xaverian Brothers from Belgium. Mt. St. Joseph's College, begun (1876) as an aid to the Xaverian Novitiate, has now 40 novices and 150 students. St. James's Home (Baltimore) furthers the work of the Industrial School by securing positions for, and boarding, older boys. It has about 70 boarders. A somewhat unusual event took place 8 August, 1868, when Revs. James Gibbons and Thomas Becker were consecrated together in the cathedral by Archbishop Spalding. Woodstock College, the seminary of the Jesuit Fathers, was opened in 1869; Father Angelo Barasci was its first rector. Since then many standard treatises on theology, philosophy, and science have been published by its professors, the best known being the works of Mazzella, De Augustinis, Sabetti, Maas, Piccirelli, and Sestini. In 1865 John T. Stephanini and Charles Long, Passionist Fathers, were appointed to St. Agnes's Church, Catonsville. The Passionist monastery of St. Joseph was completed in 1868; Father Long was elected its first rector. It was destroyed by fire in 1883 and a new monastery was built in 1886. The Little Sisters of the Poor were established in Baltimore, 6 April, 1869. Since then 3,082 old people have been cared for by them. Rev. Thomas Foley, who had been at the cathedral for twenty-two years, was consecrated Administrator of Chicago in 1870. Archbishop Spalding died 7 February, 1872. During his administration the churches built in Baltimore were: St. Martin's (Fulton Avenue) corner-stone laid in 1865, Rev. John Foley, first pastor; St. Mary's Star of the Sea founded in 1869, by Rev. Peter McCoy. The Sisters of St. Joseph came to this parish in 1875. After Archbishop Spalding's death, Very Rev. John Dougherty administered the diocese until the installation of Archbishop Bayley (October, 1872).

(g) *James Roosevelt Bayley.*—Archbishop Bayley had been an Episcopalian minister in New York, became a Catholic, a priest, and at the time of his elevation to Baltimore, was Bishop of Newark. Philadelphia was made a metropolitan see in 1875. The Province of Baltimore was thus limited to the Sees of Baltimore, Charleston, Richmond, Wheeling, Savannah, Wilmington, St. Augustine (created 1870), and the Vicariate of North Carolina. There were in the diocese in 1870, 160 churches and chapels; 230 priests; 18 charitable, and six educational, institutions. In one year the archbishop confirmed two hundred times. Of the 6,405 persons confirmed, 847

were converts. The Eighth Provincial Synod opened in Baltimore, 27 August, 1875; 93 priests and representatives of 8 religious communities were present. St. Ann's (York Road) built by Capt. William Kennedy and his wife, was dedicated in 1874, Rev. William E. Bartlett being its first pastor. The Capuchin Fathers established themselves in the diocese (1875) in the Monastery of St. Peter and Paul, Cumberland. In 1882, it was made the seminary of the order; 59 priests have been ordained there. Previous to this, the Redemptorist, Rev. John N. Neumann, had built the church of St. Peter and Paul on the site of Fort Cumberland (1848). In 1866, the Carmelites succeeded the Redemptorists and remained until 1875, when the Capuchin Fathers took charge. When the Redemptorists left Cumberland, they established (1867) their house of studies at Ilchester (Hist. of the Redemptorists at Annapolis, Ilchester, 1904). St. Catherine's Normal Institute for training Catholic teachers was established in Baltimore (1875) by Sisters of the Holy Cross. They have schools also attached to the churches of St. Patrick and St. Pius. The latter church was begun by Archbishop Bayley, its erection being made possible by a generous donation of Mr. Columbus O'Donnell. It was dedicated in 1879, with Rev. L. S. Malloy first pastor. The Right Rev. James Gibbons, Bishop of Richmond, was made coadjutor with right of succession 20 May, 1877. Archbishop Bayley died the following October.

(h) *James Gibbons.*—Archbishop Gibbons is the only Archbishop of Baltimore born in that city. The Third Plenary Council met in the cathedral 9 November, 1884—being the largest council held outside of Rome since the Council of Trent. The zuchetta was conferred upon Cardinal Gibbons 7 June, 1886, and the following March he was invested in Rome and took possession of his titular church, Santa Maria in Trastevere. The Ninth Provincial Synod was convened in Baltimore September, 1886, 115 priests attending; 8 religious orders were represented. The Catholic University of America was instituted in 1887, and the Archbishop of Baltimore was named, ex officio, the Chancellor. (See CATHOLIC UNIVERSITY OF AMERICA.) The centenary of the diocese was celebrated November, 1889. There were present Cardinals Gibbons and Taschereau; Mgr. Satolli, representative of the pope, 8 archbishops, 75 bishops, 18 monsignori, and 400 priests. Canada, Mexico, England, and Ireland were represented. On that occasion leading Catholic laymen took part in a Catholic Congress (Hughes, Proceedings of Catholic Congress, Detroit, 1890) and there was a procession of 30,000 men with Mr. James R. Wheeler as marshal. In 1893, the cardinal's Silver Jubilee was celebrated. Nearly every see in the United States was represented; there were also present representatives of the Holy Father, and of the episcopate of England, Ireland, Canada, and Oceania. Bishop A. A. Curtis was consecrated in the cathedral November, 1886, and Bishop P. J. Donahue in 1894. 29 April, 1906, the centenary of the laying of the corner-stone of the cathedral was celebrated. There were present the cardinal, the apostolic delegate, Most Rev. Diomede Falconio, 9 archbishops, 56 bishops, 4 abbots, and about 800 priests.

Among the late additions to the diocese are the Mission Helpers and the Sisters of Divine Providence. The Mission Helpers opened a house in Baltimore in 1890; it was canonically organized, 5 November, 1906. The Sisters of Divine Providence (of Kentucky) were established in the diocese in 1892, having charge of the household interests of the Catholic University, St. Mary's Seminary, and the cardinal's residence. The churches built during Cardinal Gibbons's administration, in addition to those already mentioned are: St. Andrew's, dedicated 6 October, 1878; St. Paul's founded in 1899 (the present imposing church was erected in 1903); St. Gregory's by

means of a donation of Mr. Patrick McKenna (1884);
St. Stanislaus's (Polish), founded in 1880 and taken
over in 1906 by the Franciscans; Corpus Christi, built
through the munificence of the sons and daughters of
Mr. Thomas C. Jenkins, in memory of their parents,
and dedicated 1 January, 1891; St. Leo's (Italian),
begun in 1880, by Rev. J. L. Andreis. During the
administration of Cardinal Gibbons 86 new churches
have been erected in the diocese. At present there
are 211 priests of the diocese and 273 of religious
orders. There are 128 churches with resident pastors
and 136 chapels. In Baltimore there are 44 (24 built
during the administration of Cardinal Gibbons) and
18 in Washington (10 built in the same period).
There are three universities, 11 seminaries, 13 colleges
and academies, 95 parochial schools with 21,711 pupils, and 7 industrial schools. The Catholic population is at present about 255,000. The increase (1906)
was 10,611, of whom 800 were converts.

Owing to the disinterested spirit of its archbishops,
the Archdiocese of Baltimore, the Mother Church of
the United States, has been subdivided until, in extent
of territory, it is one of the smallest. Yet it yields to
none in its spirit of faith and in the generosity of its
people. Whenever called upon by the voice of religion its children have responded in a manner beyond
their proportionate share. In support of the Catholic
University, it is surpassed by none in proportion to
its population. In the gatherings of the prelates of
the United States the Catholic homes of Baltimore
have welcomed the visitors to their hospitality. Probably no diocese has been so enriched by private donations for churches and institutions. The growth
of the Catholic population is due first to natural
increase, secondly to immigration, and thirdly to
conversion. The large proportion of conversions
must be attributed in a great measure to the personal
popularity of its present archbishop, Cardinal Gibbons, and to the influence of his convert-making
book, "The Faith of Our Fathers".

Shea, *History of the Catholic Church in Colonial Days* (New
York, 1886); Id., *Life and Times of Archbishop Carroll* (New
York, 1888); Id., *Hist. of the Cath. Church in the United States,
1844–68* (2 vols., New York, 1892); Catholic Almanacs and
Directories, 1834–1907; O'Gorman, *The Roman Catholic
Church in the United States* (New York, 1895); Davis, *Day-
Star of American Freedom;* Scharf, *Hist. of Maryland* (Baltimore, 1879); McSherry, *History of Maryland* (Baltimore,
1852); Scharf, *History of Baltimore City and County* (Philadelphia, 1881); Treacy, *Old Catholic Maryland* (Swedesboro, N. J.,
1879); Knott, *History of Maryland* (Baltimore, s. d.); Stanton, *History of the Church in Western Maryland* (Baltimore,
1900); Riordan, ed., *Cathedral Records* (Baltimore, 1906);
Archives of Maryland Hist. Society (Baltimore); Diocesan
Archives (ibid.); Hughes, *Hist. of S. J. in N. Am.* (Cleveland,
1907).   William T. Russell.

Baltimore, Lords. See Calvert.

Baltimore, Plenary Councils of.—While the
ecclesiastical province of Baltimore comprised the
whole territory of the American Republic, the provincial councils held in that city sufficed for the
church government of the country. When, however,
several ecclesiastical provinces had been formed,
plenary councils became a necessity for the fostering
of common discipline. As a consequence, the Fathers
of the Seventh Provincial Council of Baltimore requested the Holy See to sanction the holding of a
plenary synod. The petition was granted and the
pope appointed Archbishop Kenrick of Baltimore
as Apostolic Delegate to convene and preside over
the council.

I. The First Plenary Council of Baltimore was
solemnly opened on 9 May, 1852. Its sessions were
attended by six archbishops and thirty-five suffragan bishops. The Bishop of Monterey, California,
was also present, although his diocese, lately separated from Mexico, had not yet been incorporated
with any American province. Another prelate in
attendance was the Bishop of Toronto, Canada.
The religious orders and congregations were repre-

sented by the mitred Abbot of St. Mary of La Trappe
and by the superiors of the Augustinians, Dominicans,
Benedictines, Franciscans, Jesuits, Redemptorists,
Vincentians, and Sulpicians. The last solemn session
was held on the 20th of May. The decrees were as
follows: (No. i) The Fathers profess their allegiance
to the pope as the divinely constituted head of the
Church, whose office it is to confirm his brethren
in the Faith. They also declare their belief in the
entire Catholic Faith as explained by the œcumenical
councils and the constitutions of the Roman pontiffs.
(No. ii) The enactments of the seven provincial councils of Baltimore are obligatory for all the dioceses of the United States. (No. iii) The Roman
Ritual, adopted by the First Council of Baltimore,
is to be observed in all dioceses, and all are forbidden
to introduce customs or rites foreign to the Roman
usage. Sacred ceremonies are not to be employed
in the burial of Catholics whose bodies are deposited
in sectarian cemeteries; or even in public cemeteries,
if there be Catholic cemeteries at hand. (No. iv)
The Baltimore "Ceremonial" is to be used all through
the country. (No. v) Bishops are to observe the
canons concerning ecclesiastical residence. (No. vi)
Bishops are exhorted to choose consultors from
among their clergy and to ask their advice in the
government of the diocese. A monthly meeting of
these consultors to discuss diocesan affairs is praiseworthy. (No. vii) A chancellor should be constituted in every diocese, for the easier and more
orderly transaction of business. (No. viii) Bishops
should appoint censors for books relating to religion.
(No. ix) European priests desiring to be received
into an American diocese must have written testimonials from their former bishops and the consent of
the ordinary here. (No. x) Our quasi-parishes
should have well-defined limits, and the jurisdiction
and privileges of pastors should be indicated by the
bishops. The ordinary can change these limits and
it is his right to appoint the incumbents. (No. xi) After next Easter, matrimonial banns must be published, and bishops should dispense with this only
for grave reasons. (No. xii) Pastors themselves
should teach Christian doctrine to the young and
ignorant. (No. xiii) Bishops are exhorted to have a
Catholic school in every parish and the teachers
should be paid from the parochial funds. (No. xiv)
An ecclesiastical seminary should be erected in each
province. (No. xv) The bishops or their delegates
should demand every year an account of the administration of church funds from those who administer
them, whether laymen or clerics. (No. xvi) Laymen
are not to take any part in the administration of
church affairs without the free consent of the bishop.
If they usurp any such authority and divert church
goods to their own use or in any way frustrate the
will of the donors; or if they, even under cover of the
civil law, endeavour to wrest from the bishop's hands
what has been confided to his care, then such laymen
by that very fact fall under the censures constituted
by the Council of Trent against usurpers of ecclesiastical goods. (No. xvii) When the title to a church is
in the bishop's name, pastors are warned not to appoint trustees or permit them to be elected without
the bishop's authority. (No. xviii) Benediction of
the Blessed Sacrament must be performed in all dioceses in the manner prescribed by the Baltimore
"Ceremonial". (No. xix) Bishops should use their
influence with the civil authorities to prevent anyone
in the army or navy from being obliged to attend a religious service repugnant to his conscience. (No. xx)
A Society for the Propagation of the Faith, similar to
that in France, should be fostered and extended.
(No. xxi) The faithful are exhorted to enter into a
society of prayer for the conversion of non-Catholics.
(No. xxii) A petition should be addressed to the Holy
See asking for extraordinary faculties concerning

matrimonial cases and the power, also, of delegating such faculties. (No. xxiii) Permission to use the short formula in the baptism of adults is to be requested of the Holy See, either for perpetuity or for twenty years. (No. xxiv) The sixth decree of the Seventh Provincial Council of Baltimore is to be understood as applying to those who rashly (*temere*) marry before a Protestant minister. Priests should give no benediction to those whom they know to intend to remarry before a preacher, or who, having done so, show no signs of penitence. (No. xxv) These decrees are binding as soon as they are published by the Archbishop of Baltimore after their revision and approval by the Holy See.

In sending the pope's approval of these decrees, the prefect of the Propaganda exhorted the bishops to add the feasts of the Circumcision of Our Lord and the Immaculate Conception B. V. M. to the festivals already observed. He added that although some diversity as to fasts and feasts is found in the American dioceses, still it is not desirable to lessen the number in those places where they are in accord with the discipline of the universal Church, because fewer feasts are observed in other American dioceses. The bishops are not to labour for conformity among the dioceses in customs that are foreign to the discipline of the universal Church, for thus the appearance of a national Church would be introduced. The cardinal prefect added that the Holy See tolerated relaxations of the common law of the Church for grave reasons, but such derogations were not to be confirmed and extended, but rather every effort was to be made to bring about the observance of the universal discipline. As to the method of adult baptism, the Holy See extended the dispensations to use the short formula for another five years. A letter from Cardinal-Prefect Franzoni, added to the acts of the council, treats of the question of how the bishops are to be supported by their dioceses. It likewise insists that priests ordained *titulo missionis* are not to enter religious orders without the consent of their ordinaries, as they are required to make oath that they will serve perpetually in the diocese for which they were ordained. In the acts of this council is found a statement of the Bishop of Monterey concerning the California Missions. He informed the Fathers that a large sum of money had formerly been placed in the hands of the Mexican Government to be used under the sanction of Spanish law for the support of the Californian missionaries. For years they had received none of this money and the late revolutions made any hope of reparation unlikely. However, as it is reported that the civil power in California intends to demand this money from the Mexican treasury for public purposes, he desired to know what effort the American bishops thought it desirable to make in the premises. The outcome of the whole discussion was the sending of a letter on the subject to the Archbishop of Mexico. We may add here that this money was later recovered and employed for the Church in California. (See CALIFORNIA, *Pious Fund*.)

II. THE SECOND PLENARY COUNCIL was presided over by Archbishop Spalding of Baltimore as Delegate Apostolic. It was opened on the 7th of October and closed on 21 October, 1866. The acts note that, at the last solemn session, Andrew Johnson, President of the United States, was among the auditors. The decrees of this council were signed by seven archbishops, thirty-nine bishops or their procurators, and two abbots. The decrees are divided into fourteen titles and subdivided into chapters.

Title i, *Concerning the Orthodox Faith and Present Errors*, declares the Catholic doctrine (cap. i) on Divine revelation and the one Church of Christ; (ii) the nature and necessity of faith; (iii) the Holy Scripture; (iv) the Holy Trinity; (v) the future life; (vi) the

pious invocation and veneration of the B. V. Mary and the saints. (vii) The seventh chapter in which the present errors are discussed treats of (a) the dissensions among the Protestant sects and of zeal for their conversion. (b) Indifferentism. The Fathers warn their flock against the teaching that one religion is as good as another provided one be honest and just to his neighbour. They call this a plague, spreading under the guise of charity and benevolence. (c) Unitarianism and Universalism. These theories, the first denying the divinity of Christ and the other eternal punishment, tend to the rejection of the supernatural in religion. (d) Transcendentalism and Pantheism. These are the systems of men, who having dethroned God, make a deity of man. (e) Abuse of magnetism. The faithful are warned that magnetism is often employed for superstitious and illicit purposes, namely, to forecast the future by means of female "mediums". (f) The hallucinations and dangers of spiritism. There is little reason to doubt that some of the phenomena of spiritism are the work of Satan. It is noteworthy that the leaders of this system deny either implicitly or explicitly the divinity of Christ and the supernatural in religion.

Title ii, *Concerning the Hierarchy and the Government of the Church*, treats (cap. i) of the Roman pontiff; (ii) of the hierarchy teaching and ruling; (iii) of provincial councils, which ought to be held every three years; (iv) of diocesan synods, in which the bishop alone is legislator and judge. This chapter also treats of quarterly conferences for the discussion of theological questions by the clergy. (v) The officials of the bishop are considered in this chapter. Besides the diocesan consultors and the vicar-general, the bishop should appoint vicars forane or rural deans who are to preside at clerical conferences, to watch over ecclesiastical property, to counsel the junior clergy and report annually to the bishop on the state of their districts. Other officials mentioned are the secretary, chancellor, notary, and procurator for temporal affairs. Synodal examiners and judges for the criminal cases of clerics are also to be constituted. The latter, by delegation of the bishops, hold courts of the first instance and they should follow a judicial method closely approximating that prescribed by the Council of Trent.

Title iii, *Concerning Ecclesiastical Persons*, is divided into seven chapters. (cap. i) Of metropolitans. (ii) Of bishops; they are to make a visitation of their dioceses frequently; they should provide support for aged and infirm priests; before death they should appoint an administrator *sede vacante* for their dioceses. If this has not been done, the metropolitan is to make the appointment, or if it be a question of the metropolitan church itself, then the senior suffragan bishop constitutes an administrator until the Holy See can provide. The administrator cannot make innovations in the administration of the diocese. (iii) Of the election of bishops. A method for episcopal nominations to American sees is given, as also the requisite qualifications for candidates. (iv) Of priests exercising the sacred ministry. When several priests serve a church, one only must be designated as pastor. Priests should often preach to their people; they must not marry or baptize the faithful of other dioceses. Although our missions are not canonical parishes, yet it is the desire of the bishops to conform as much as possible to the discipline of the universal church in this matter. In cities containing more than one church, accurate limits for their districts should be assigned. When in these decrees the terms "parish" or "parochial rights" are used, the bishops have no intention of thereby indicating that the rector of a church is irremovable. No priest should be appointed to a parish unless he has made an examination before the bishop and two priests, and has been five years in the diocese. This does not apply to regulars. (v) Of preaching. While explaining the Church's doctrine, preachers should also treat fully of points denied by heretics or unbelievers. Their style, however, is not to be controversial but explanatory. In their method they should follow the Roman Catechism and make a careful study of the writings of the Fathers of the Church. Let them accommodate themselves to the capacity of their auditors. In reprehending vices, let them never become personal; neither should they be influenced in their preaching by human motives but declare the truth fearlessly. They are not to mingle political and civil matters with religious doctrines in their sermons or attack public magistrates. While the custom of delivering funeral orations is to be retained, yet care must be taken not to bestow undue praise. In all sermons let prolixity be avoided. (vi) Of clerical life and manners. Clerics are to avoid a dress and personal appearance not becoming their station. They should abstain from all improper spectacles and games. Let them avoid having recourse to civil tribunals when possible. They must not engage in trade forbidden by the canons. Let them not be importunate in speaking of money matters to their flocks. The custom of priests taking money on deposit, for which interest is to be paid, is condemned. Let bishops as well as priests observe the prescriptions of the Council of Trent concerning their households. All clerics should avoid idleness as a pest. (vii) Of ecclesiastical seminaries. The erection of preparatory as well as greater seminaries is recommended. Theology and philosophy, Scripture and Hebrew are to be taught in the latter. No student is to pass from one seminary to another without testimonial letters. In those dioceses where Germans are found who cannot speak English, it is expedient that the seminarians learn enough German to hear confessions.

Title iv, *Of Ecclesiastical Property.*—The decrees of the first seven councils of Baltimore concerning the abuses of lay trustees and of the best method of securing church property by civil sanction are repeated and re-enacted. As to lay trustees, they must not be members of secret societies nor men who have not fulfilled the paschal duty. They cannot expend a sum of money above three hundred dollars without written consent of the bishop. The pastor, not the trustees, appoints organist, singers, sacristan, school-teachers, and others employed about the parish. When difference of opinion exists between pastor and trustees, all must abide by the decision of the bishop. All misunderstanding between the ordinary and regulars concerning temporal affairs will be averted if, at the founding of a new house, a document be drawn up expressing clearly all that relates to the foundation itself, to the rights thence flowing and to the duties connected with it.

Title v, *Of the Sacraments.*—(i) The Roman Ritual and the Baltimore "Ceremonial" are to be followed. Pastors should keep registers of baptisms, confirmations, marriages, and funerals. All of these, except the last, should be written in Latin. (ii) Of baptism. It must always be conferred in the church except in case of imminent death. Whether for infants or adults, all rites omitted at baptism must be afterwards supplied. As a rule converts are to be baptized; but care must be taken to inquire if they had been previously validly baptized, lest the sacrament be repeated. The same is to be said of those baptized in danger of death by laymen. Churching after child-birth, which has been generally neglected in this country, is to be insisted upon. (iii) Of confirmation. Sponsors of the same sex as the recipient are to be employed. (iv) Of the Holy Eucharist. Frequent Communion is to be encouraged. Children should as a rule be admitted to First Communion

between ten and fourteen years of age. (v) Of penance. (vi) Of indulgences. Preachers must be careful not to recommend doubtful or fictitious indulgences. Let them propose such as the faithful can gain most frequently, easily, and with greatest fruit. (vii) Of extreme unction. Olive oil is required for this sacrament. The Fathers commend the proposition of the Bishop of Savannah to establish a community of Trappists on lands near St. Augustine, Florida, who would supply genuine olive oil, wine, and beeswax candles for the use of the churches. (viii) Of Holy orders. Clerics cannot be ordained without a canonical title. By Apostolic dispensation, our priests have thus far been ordained *titulo missionis* for the most part. The Holy See is to be petitioned for a continuation of this privilege. (ix) Of Matrimony. Rules are laid down for determining doubts concerning the probable death of soldiers in the late civil war. Mixed marriages are to be discouraged. (x) Of the sacramentals.

Title vi, *Of Divine Worship.*—(i) Of the Sacrifice of the Mass. Priests are never to leave the altar to collect alms from the faithful. Our quasi-parish-priests are not obliged to apply their Mass for their flock on festival days. (ii) Of Benediction and the Forty Hours' Exposition. The latter is to be performed according to the manner sanctioned by the Holy See for the Diocese of Baltimore. (iii) Of Vespers. The rudiments of the Gregorian chant should be taught in the parish schools.

Title vii, *Of Promoting Uniformity of Discipline.*— (i) Of fasts and feasts. Those now in use in each province are to be retained. The Patronal Feast of the Immaculate Conception is, however, to be celebrated in every diocese as of obligation. (ii) Of uniformity in other matters. Bishops should endeavour to use a uniform method of acting in granting matrimonial dispensations. Catholics may be buried with sacred rites in non-Catholic cemeteries if they possess a lot in them, provided it was not acquired in contempt of church law. The poor must be buried gratuitously. Entrance money should not be collected at churches. Orphans are to be cared for. Faculties for blessing cemeteries and church bells may be delegated to priests.

Title viii, *Of Regulars and Nuns.*—(i) When a religious community has accepted a diocesan work, strictly so called, it should not relinquish it without giving the bishop notice six months beforehand. A clear distinction is to be made as to what property belongs to a religious community and what to the diocese. (ii) Nuns are not to make solemn vows until ten years after the taking of simple vows. Bishops are not to permit religious women to travel around soliciting alms.

Title ix, *Of the Education of Youth.*—(i) Of parish schools. Teachers belonging to religious congregations should be employed when possible in our schools. The latter should be erected in every parish. For children who attend the public schools, catechism classes should be instituted in the churches. (ii) Industrial schools or reformatories should be founded, especially in large cities. (iii) A desire is expressed to have a Catholic university in the United States.

Title x, *Of Procuring the Salvation of Souls.*—(i) Of zeal for souls. (ii) Missions in parishes are to be encouraged; missionaries must not, however, interfere in the administration of the parish. (iii) Various confraternities and sodalities are named and recommended and regulations are given for their institution. (iv) Priests, both secular and regular, are exhorted to endeavour to further the conversion of the negroes in our midst.

Title xi, *Of Books and Newspapers.*—(i) Parents should guard their children against bad books. The bishops desire that textbooks in Catholic schools and colleges should be purged of everything contrary to faith. (ii) Of the dissemination of good books. (iii) Prayer books should not be published until officially revised. (iv) Newspapers are frequently injurious to good morals. When a Catholic newspaper has a bishop's approbation, this means only that he judges that nothing will be published against faith or morals in its pages. He does not make himself responsible, however, for all that the paper contains.

Title xii, *Of Secret Societies.*—The Freemasons were long ago condemned by the Church. The Odd Fellows and Sons of Temperance are also forbidden societies. In general, the faithful may not enter any society which, having designs against Church or State, binds its members by an oath of secrecy. Title xiii, *Concerning the Creation of New Bishoprics.* Title xiv, *Of the Execution of the Conciliar Decrees.*— A number of important instructions and decrees of the Holy See are appended to the Acts of this council.

III. THE THIRD PLENARY COUNCIL was presided over by the Apostolic Delegate, Archbishop Gibbons of Baltimore. Its decrees were signed by fourteen archbishops, sixty-one bishops or their representatives, six abbots, and one general of a religious congregation. The first solemn session was held 9 November, and the last 7 December, 1884. Its decrees are divided into twelve titles. *Preliminary Title.* All the decrees of the Second Plenary Council remain in force except such as are abrogated or changed by the present council. Title i, *Of the Catholic Faith.* Title ii, *Of Ecclesiastical Persons.*—(i) Of bishops. When a see becomes vacant, the archbishop will call together the consultors and irremovable rectors of the diocese and they shall choose three names which are to be forwarded to Rome and to the other bishops of the province. The latter shall meet together and discuss the candidates. If they wish, they may reject all the names proposed by the clergy and substitute others, but they must give their reasons for this action when sending their recommendation to Rome. (ii) Of diocesan consultors. They should be six or at least four in number. If this be impossible, however, two will suffice. The bishop chooses the consultors, half at his own option, the other half after nomination by the clergy. The bishop should ask the advice of his consultors as to holding and promulgating a diocesan synod; dividing parishes; committing a parish to religious; constituting a committee for diocesan seminaries; choosing new consultors or examiners non-synodically; concerning transactions about church-property where the sum involved exceeds five thousand dollars; exacting new episcopal taxes beyond the limits designated by the canons. Consultors hold office for three years and they may not be removed except for grave reasons. They are to vote collectively. When the episcopal see is vacant, the administrator must ask their counsel in all the above-mentioned cases. (iii) Of examiners of the diocesan clergy. They are to be six in number. Their duties are principally to examine the junior clergy, and the candidates for irremovable rectorships. (iv) Of deans and vicars forane. The institution of these district officials is recommended to the bishops. It is advisable to bestow on them some faculties beyond what other rectors have and some honorary preeminence. (v) Of irremovable rectors. Parishes to have such rectors must have a proper church, a school for boys and girls, and revenues sufficiently stable for the support of the priest, church, and school. In all dioceses every tenth rector should be irremovable if the requisite conditions are obtainable. The candidate for such rectorship must have been in the ministry ten years and shown himself a satisfactory administrator in spirituals and temporals. He must also make a prescribed examination (*concursus*). An irremovable rector cannot be removed

from his office except for a canonical cause and according to the mode of procedure contained in the Instruction "Cum Magnopere". (vi) Of the concursus. The examination for irremovable rectorships must take place before the bishop or vicar-general and three examiners. Candidates must reply to questions in dogmatic and moral theology, liturgy, and canon law. They are also to give a specimen of catechetical exposition and of preaching. The qualities of the candidates are also to be weighed in forming a judgment. The bishop is to give the vacant rectorship only to a candidate who has received the approving votes of the examiners. (vii) Of the diocesan clergy. 1. Priests ordained for a diocese are bound by oath to remain in it. 2. Alien priests bringing satisfactory testimonials from former bishops may be incardinated in a diocese only after a probation of three or five years, and formal adscription by the ordinary. We may note that this council speaks of presumptive incardination also, but by a later Roman decree (20 July, 1898) that form of adscription is abrogated. 3. Infirm priests should be cared for. 4. Unworthy priests have no just claims to support, yet if they wish to amend, a house governed by regulars should be provided for them. (viii) Of clerical life and manners. Priests should make a spiritual retreat once every year, or at least every two years. They are exhorted to give themselves to solid reading and study. They are to avoid conduct that can afford even the least suspicion of evil. They are not to bring an action against another cleric before a civil tribunal about temporal matters without written permission of the bishop. As to ecclesiastical affairs, they are to remember that judgment pertains only to the church authorities. (ix) Of regulars. The provisions of the papal constitution "Romanos Pontifices" are extended to the United States. This constitution treats of the exemption of regulars from episcopal jurisdiction; of what concerns their ministry in a diocese; and of their temporal possessions. All controversies on these subjects are to be referred to the prefect of the Propaganda. Bishops are to recur to him also in matters concerning institutes of simple vows that are not diocesan but have their own superior-general. Diocesan Institutes, even having a rule approved by the Holy See, are entirely subject to the jurisdiction of the ordinary. Bishops are to see that the laws of enclosure (*clausura*) are observed. Regulations are laid down for the ordinary and extraordinary confessors of nuns. Those who belong to religious brotherhoods, whose members are forbidden to aspire to the priesthood, may not, after leaving such congregation, be ordained for any diocese without a dispensation from Rome.

Title iii, *Of Divine Worship.*—(i) Of celebrating Mass twice on the same day. (ii) Of uniformity in feasts and fasts. In future in all dioceses of this country there are to be the following six feasts of obligation and no others: The Immaculate Conception, Christmas, Circumcision of Our Lord (New Year's Day), Ascension, Assumption, and All Saints' Day. No new dispositions are made as to fast days. (iii) Of the Lord's Day. The faithful are to be exhorted to observe it properly. (iv) Of sacred music. Profane melodies are forbidden. The music should accord with the sacredness of time and place. Psalms are not to be curtailed at Vespers. The Mass must not be interrupted by the length of the choir-singing.

Title iv, *Of the Sacraments.*—(i) Of the baptism of converts. The ritual prescribed for their reception into the Church is to be observed. (ii) Of matrimony. Catholics who marry before a sectarian minister are excommunicated. Mixed marriages are not to be contracted unless promises are given that the Catholic party is in no danger of perversion, and will strive to convert the non-Catholic party. Also that all the children born of the union are to be brought up Catholics. No dispensation from these promises can be given.

Title v, *Of the Education of Clerics.*—(i) Preparatory seminaries should be instituted. The pupils should be taught Christian Doctrine, English, and at least one other language according to the necessities of the diocese. They must learn to speak and write Latin. Greek is also to be taught. The usual branches of profane learning, not omitting the natural sciences, as well as music and the Gregorian chant are to be part of the curriculum. (ii) Of the greater seminaries. Judgment must be exercised in admitting aspirants to the priesthood and they must be zealously formed to virtue and learning. Two years are to be devoted to a philosophical and four to a theological course. The faculty of theology is to embrace dogmatic and moral theology, Biblical exegesis, church history, canon law, liturgy and sacred eloquence. Great care must be taken in the selection of spiritual directors and professors for the students. Examinations are to be held semi-annually or annually in the presence of the bishop or vicar-general and the examiners of the clergy. Students are to be warned to spend their vacations in a manner becoming the clerical profession. The temporal and spiritual administration of the seminary belongs principally to the bishop; he is to be aided by two commissions, one for spirituals and one for temporals. (iii) Of the principal seminary or university. The Fathers consider the times ripe for creating a Catholic university, and for this purpose they appoint a commission. The university is to be entirely under the management of the episcopate. The bishops should, however, continue to send some of their subjects to Rome, Louvain, and Innsbruck, as the new university is intended for postgraduate theological studies. (iv) Of the examinations of the junior clergy. For five years after ordination, priests must make an annual examination in Scripture, dogmatic and moral theology, canon law, church history, and liturgy. (v) Of theological conferences. All priests having cure of souls must attend ecclesiastical meetings for the discussion of questions of doctrine and discipline. These conferences are to be held four times a year in urban and twice a year in rural districts.

Title vi, *Of the Education of Catholic Youth*, treats of (i) Catholic schools, especially parochial, viz., of their absolute necessity and the obligation of pastors to establish them. Parents must send their children to such schools unless the bishop should judge the reason for sending them elsewhere to be sufficient. Ways and means are also considered for making the parochial schools more efficient. It is desirable that these schools be free. (ii) Every effort must be made to have suitable schools of higher education for Catholic youth.

Title vii, *Of Christian Doctrine.*—(i) Of the office of preaching. (ii) A commission is appointed to prepare a catechism for general use. When published it is to be obligatory. (iii) Of prayer books. (iv) Of books and newspapers. While objectionable writings are to be condemned, Catholics should oppose them also by orthodox newspapers and books.

Title viii, *Of Zeal for Souls.*—(i) Immigrants should be instructed by priests of their own language. (ii) A commission is appointed to aid the missions among Indians and Negroes. (iii) Censures against secret societies are to be made known to the faithful. If Rome has not condemned a particular society by name, it will belong only to a commission consisting of the archbishops of the country to decide whether it falls under the laws of forbidden organizations or not. If they cannot agree, the matter is to be referred to Rome. On the other hand, Catholic

societies, especially those of temperance, are to be encouraged.

Title ix, *Of Church Property.*—(i) The Church's right to hold property. (ii) The bishop is the guardian and supreme administrator of all diocesan property. (iii) Priests are diligently to guard parochial property under the direction of the bishop. If they do not request their salary at the proper time, they are supposed to have renounced their right to it. (iv) In choosing lay trustees only those members of the congregation have a voice, who, being twenty-one years of age, have fulfilled the paschal precept, have paid for a seat in the church during the past year, have sent their children to Catholic schools and belong to no prohibited society. The pastor is ex officio president of the board of trustees. (v) In all churches some seats must be set aside for the poor. Abuses incident to picnics, excursions, and fairs are to be guarded against. Balls are not to be given for religious purposes. It is a detestable abuse to refuse the sacraments to those who will not contribute to collections. Bishops are to determine the stipend proper for ecclesiastical ministries. Foreign priests or religious cannot solicit alms in a diocese without the consent of the ordinary.

Title x, *Of Ecclesiastical Trials.*—(i) Every diocese is to have an episcopal tribunal. (ii) Its officials for disciplinary cases are to be a judge, fiscal procurator or diocesan attorney, attorney for the accused, and a chancellor. To those may be added an auditor, a notary, and apparitors. For matrimonial cases the officials are to be an auditor, defender of the marriage tie, and a notary. The interested parties may also employ advocates. (iii) In criminal causes, the bishop, according as the law and case demand, may proceed either extra-judicially or judicially. This chapter describes the method to be employed in both instances.

Title xi, *Of Ecclesiastical Sepulture.*—Cemeteries should be properly cared for.

Title xii. The decrees of this council are binding as soon as they are promulgated by the Delegate Apostolic. At the request of the Fathers, the Holy See permitted the celebration in the United States of the feasts of St. Philip of Jesus, St. Turibius, and St. Francis Solano. It also granted to the bishops, under certain conditions, the power of alienating church goods without previously referring each case to Rome. The Fathers of this council signed the postulation for the introduction of the cause of beatification of Isaac Jogues and René Goupil, martyrs of the Society of Jesus, and of Catherine Tegakwita, an Iroquois virgin. This Third Plenary Council exhibits the actual canon law of the Church in the United States.

Acta et Decreta Conc. Plen. I (Baltimore, 1853); *Acta et Decreta Conc. Plen. II* (Baltimore, 1868); SMITH, *Notes on Second Plenary Council* (New York, 1874); *Acta et Decreta Conc. Plen. III* (Baltimore, 1886); NILLES, *Commentaria in Conc. Plen. III* (Innsbruck, 1888);

WILLIAM H. W. FANNING.

Baltimore, PROVINCIAL COUNCILS OF.—These councils have a unique importance for the Church in the United States, inasmuch as the earlier ones legislated for practically the whole territory of the Republic, and furnished moreover a norm for all the later provincial councils of the country. This article touches on only those parts of the legislation which may seem in any way to individualize the discipline of the Church in the United States or depict the peculiar needs and difficulties of its nascent period.

I. The First Provincial Council was held in 1829 and was attended by one archbishop and four bishops. Its decrees refer to the enactments of two previous conventions which may be summarized briefly. Bishop Carroll's Diocesan Synod of 1791 decreed: (No. 3) The ceremonies of baptism need not be supplied for converted heretics who had been previously validly baptized. (No. 4) As a rule children are not to be confirmed before the age of reason. (No. 5) The offerings of the faithful are to be divided into three parts: for the support of the pastor, the relief of the poor, and the sustentation of the church. (No. 11) The faithful are to be warned that the absolution of priests not approved by the bishop is invalid. (No. 15) None are to be married until they know the Christian Doctrine. Slaves, however, need know only the principal truths, if more cannot be acquired. (No. 16) In mixed marriages the non-Catholic must promise before witnesses to bring up the offspring of the union as Catholics. (No. 17) Hymns and prayers in the vernacular are to be encouraged at evening services. (No. 20) Catholics may work on days of obligation owing to the circumstances of place, but they must hear Mass if possible. (No. 23) The rich are to be warned that they sin grievously if, through their parsimony, pastors cannot be sustained and multiplied. (No. 24) When there is question of refusing Christian burial, the bishop must be consulted beforehand when possible.

The second series of enactments referred to are the articles concerning ecclesiastical discipline sanctioned by the common consent of the Archbishop of Baltimore and the other American bishops in 1810. The main articles are: (No. 2) Regulars should not be withdrawn from pastoral work without the consent of the bishops, if their assistance be deemed a necessity to the existence or prosperity of their missions. (No. 3) The Douay version of the Bible is to be used. (No. 5) Baptism must be conferred in the church where possible. (No. 6) If no sponsor can be obtained, private baptism only is to be administered. (No. 9) The faithful are to be warned against improper theatres, dances, and novels. (No. 10) Freemasons cannot be admitted to the sacraments.

Besides ordering the publication of these decrees along with their own synodical enactments, the fathers of the First Provincial Council decreed: (No. 1) Priests should labour in any mission assigned to them by the bishops. (No. 5) Owing to the abuses of lay trustees all future churches should be consigned to the bishop when possible. (No. 6) Trustees cannot institute or dismiss a pastor. No ecclesiastical patronage exists in this country. (No. 10) Infants of non-Catholics may be baptized if their parents promise to give them a Catholic education, but the sponsor must be a Catholic. (No. 20) In administering the sacraments and in the burial service, Latin and not English must be employed. (No. 31) A ceremonial written in English is to be drawn up. (No. 34) Catholic schools should be erected.

At one of the sessions of this council several lawyers (among them R. B. Taney, afterwards Chief Justice of the Supreme Court of the United States) gave advice to the bishops on points of American law concerning property rights and ecclesiastical courts. In addition to their decrees, the bishops asked and obtained from Rome permission to use for adults the formula of infant baptism; to consecrate baptismal water with the form approved for the missionaries of Peru, and to extend the time for fulfilling the paschal precept, i. e. from the first Sunday of Lent to Trinity Sunday.

II. The Second Council, held in 1833, was attended by one archbishop and nine bishops. The main decrees were: (No. 3) A delimitation of the American dioceses. (No. 4) A method of selecting bishops, which a later Council (Prov. VII) modified. (No. 5) Recommending the entrusting to the Jesuits of the Indian missions in the West, as also (No. 6) the missions among former American slaves, repatriated in Liberia, Africa, to the same fathers. (No. 8)

Bishops are exhorted to erect ecclesiastical seminaries.

III. The Third Council in 1837 was composed of one archbishop and eight bishops. Its decrees enacted: (No. 4) Ecclesiastical property is to be secured by the best means the civil law affords. (No. 6) Ecclesiastics should not bring ecclesiastical cases before the civil tribunals. (No. 7) Priests are prohibited from soliciting money outside their own parishes. (No. 8) Pastors are warned against permitting unsuitable music at Divine worship. (No. 9) The two days following Easter and Pentecost are to be days of obligation no longer. (No. 10) Wednesdays in Advent are not to be days of fast and abstinence.

IV. The Fourth Council in 1840 issued decrees signed by one archbishop and twelve bishops as follows: (No. 1) In mixed marriages no sacred rites or vestments are to be used. (No. 5) Temperance societies are recommended to the faithful. (No. 6) Pastors are to see that those frequenting public schools do not use the Protestant version of the Bible or sing sectarian hymns. They must also employ their influence against the introduction of such practices into the public schools. (No. 8) Bishops are to control ecclesiastical property and not permit priests to hold it in their own name. Among those attending this council was the Bishop of Nancy and Toul, France, to whom the fathers granted a right to a decisive vote. A letter of consolation was sent by the council to the persecuted bishops of Poland, and another of thanks to the moderators of the Leopold Institute of Vienna, Austria.

V. In 1843, the Fifth Council was attended by one archbishop and sixteen bishops. Among its enactments were: (No. 2) Laymen may not deliver orations in churches. (No. 4) It is not expedient that the Tridentine decrees concerning clandestine matrimony be extended to places where they have not been already promulgated. (No. 5) Pastors are to be obliged to observe the law of residence. (No. 6) Priests may not borrow money for church uses without written permission of the bishop.

VI. The Sixth Council (one archbishop and twenty-two bishops attending) in 1846, decreed: (No. 1) that the Blessed Virgin Mary conceived without sin is chosen as the patron of the United States. (No. 2) Priests ordained *titulo missionis* may not enter a religious order without permission of their ordinaries. (No. 3) The canons concerning the proclaiming of the banns of matrimony are to be observed. At the request of the fathers, the Holy See sanctioned a formula to be used by the bishops in taking the oath at their consecration.

VII. In 1849 two archbishops and twenty-three bishops held the Seventh Council. The main decrees were: (No. 2) The Holy See is to be informed that the fathers think it opportune to define as a dogma the Immaculate Conception of the Blessed Virgin Mary. (No. 3) A change in the election of bishops is introduced. (No. 5) Bishops are not to give an *exeat* at the request of a priest unless it be certain that another bishop will receive him. (No. 6) Priests are forbidden to assist at the marriages of those who have already had a ceremony performed by a Protestant minister, or who intend to have such ceremony performed. (No. 7) A national council should be held in Baltimore in 1850, by Apostolic Authority. The fathers moreover petitioned the Holy See to raise New Orleans, Cincinnati, and New York to metropolitan dignity and to make a new limitation of the Provinces of Baltimore and St. Louis. They desired likewise that Baltimore should be declared the primatial see of the Republic. The pope granted the first part of the petition, but deferred acting on the question of the primacy.

VIII. The Eighth Council was assembled in 1855. One archbishop and seven bishops or their representatives attended it. This council enacted: (No. 1) The fathers joyfully receive the dogmatic decision of the pope defining the Immaculate Conception of the Blessed Virgin Mary. (No. 2) Priests are warned that after August, 1857, adults must be baptized according to the regular formula for that service in the Roman Ritual and not according to that for infant baptism. (No. 4) No tax is to be demanded for dispensations from matrimonial impediments. (No. 6) Bishops are exhorted to increase the number of their diocesan consultors to ten or twelve. It will not be necessary, however, to obtain the opinion of all of them, even on important matters. For this, the counsel of three or four will suffice. On the death of the bishop, however, all the consultors shall send to the archbishop their written opinions as to an eligible successor for the vacant see. (No. 7) The various diocesan synods should determine on the best mode of providing for the proper support of the bishop. (No. 8) The fathers desire to see an American College erected in Rome. To the Acts of this council is appended a decree of the Holy See, sanctioning a mode of procedure in judicial causes of clerics.

IX. The Ninth Council in 1858 was attended by one archbishop and seven bishops. The main work of this synod consisted in drawing up petitions to the Holy See concerning a dispensation from abstinence on Saturdays; the conceding of certain honorary privileges to the Archbishop of Baltimore; the granting to the bishops the permission to allow the Blessed Sacrament to be kept in chapels of religious communities not subject to the law of enclosure. All of these petitions were granted by the Holy See. That concerning the Archbishop of Baltimore granted to him, as ruler of the mother-church of the United States, an honorary pre-eminence, to consist in his taking precedence of any other archbishop in the country, without regard to promotion or consecration, and in his having the place of honour in all councils and conventions. The fathers also sent to Rome an inquiry as to the nature of the vows (solemn or simple) of religious women, especially of Visitation Nuns in the United States, an answer to which was deferred to a later time (1864). The question was also discussed as to whether Archbishop Kenrick's version of the Bible should be approved for general use. It was finally decided to wait for Dr. John Henry Newman's expected version, and then to determine along with the bishops of other English-speaking countries on one common version.

X. In 1869, the Tenth Council enacted decrees that were signed by one archbishop, twelve bishops, and one abbot. Among these decrees we note: (No. 5) Bishops are exhorted to establish missions and schools for the negroes of their dioceses. (No. 7) Priests are to be appointed to aid the bishops in administering the temporal concerns of the diocese. They are also to supervise the spiritual and material affairs of religious women. At the request of the fathers, the Holy See extended for five years the privilege of using the short formula in the baptism of adults.

It should be remarked that the first seven provincial councils of Baltimore were practically, though not formally, plenary councils of the United States.

The numbers of decrees indicated in the text will be found conformable to any authorized edition of these councils; *Acta et Decreta S. Conc. Recentiorum. Collectio Lacensis. Auctoribus Presbyt.*, S. J. (Freiburg, 1875), contains in vol. III, the full text of the decrees of these ten councils; *Concilia Provincialia Baltimori Habita ab Anno, 1829 ad 1849* (Baltimore, 1851), gives the acts of only the first seven provincial councils.

WILLIAM H. W. FANNING.

Baltus, JEAN FRANÇOIS, theologian, b. at Metz, 8 June, 1667; d. at Reims, 9 March, 1743. He entered the Society of Jesus, 21 November, 1682, taught humanities at Dijon, rhetoric at Pont-à-Mousson, Scripture, Hebrew, and theology at Strasburg, where

II.—16

he was also rector of the university. In 1717, he was general censor of books at Rome, and later rector of Châlon, Dijon, Metz, Pont-à-Mousson, and Châlons. He left several works of some value to the Christian apologist, notably: (1) "Réponse à l'histoire des oracles de M. de Fontenelle", a critical treatise on the oracles of paganism, in refutation of Van Dale's theory and in defence of the Fathers of the Church (Strasburg, 1707), followed in 1708 by "Suite de la réponse à l'histoire des oracles". (2) "Défense des S. Pères accusés de platonisme" (Paris, 1711); this is a refutation of "Platonisme dévoilé", a work of the Protestant minister Souverain of Poitiers. (3) "Jugement des SS. Pères sur la morale de la philosophie païenne" (Strasburg, 1719). (4) "La religion chrétienne prouvée par l'accomplissement des prophéties de l'Ancien et du Nouveau Testament suivant la méthode des SS. Pères" (Paris, 1728). (5) "Défense des prophéties de la religion chrétienne" (Paris, 1737). To these may be added a funeral oration on the Most Rev. Peter Creagh, Archbishop of Dublin (Strasburg, 1705), the "Acts of St. Balaam, Martyr", and the "Life of St. Febronia, Virgin and Martyr" (Dijon, 1720 and 1721 respectively).

SOMMERVOGEL in *Dict. de théol. cath.*, s. v.; ID., *Bibl. de la c. de J.*, I, 856–860; VIII, 1736.

MARK J. McNEAL.

Balue, JEAN, a French cardinal, b. probably c. 1421, in Poitou; d. 5 October, 1491, at Ripatransone (March of Ancona). He has been frequently, but erroneously, called "de la Balue". He was graduated as licentiate in law about 1457, and at an early date entered the ecclesiastical state. He became so intimate with Jacques Juvénal des Ursins, Bishop of Poitiers (1449–57), that the latter named him executor of his will. The charge that in this capacity he misappropriated funds destined for the poor must be received with reserve. After the death of Des Ursins, Balue entered the service of John de Beauvau, Bishop of Angers (1451–67), who made him vicar-general (1461). In 1462, he accompanied his bishop to Rome, and thenceforth his career was marked by clever and unscrupulous intrigue. On his return, he was introduced by Charles de Melun to King Louis XI (1461–83), and, owing to the royal favour, his rise both in ecclesiastical and civil affairs was rapid. In 1464, Louis XI made him his almoner; the same year, Balue received the Abbeys of Fécamp and Saint-Thierri (Reims) and in 1465, that of Saint-Jean-d'Angély, two priories, and the Bishopric of Evreux. Having obtained the deposition of his benefactor, Beauvau, from the See of Angers, he secured the see for himself (1467). His intrigues in the affair of the Pragmatic Sanction procured him, at the request of Louis XI, the cardinalate, to which Paul II (1464–71) reluctantly raised him (1467). Guilty of high treason, he was arrested two years later (1469) with his accomplice William d'Harau-court, Bishop of Verdun (1456–1500). As a cardinal, he could not be judged by a civil tribunal, but the negotiations between the pope and the king, regarding his trial, remaining fruitless, he was held captive by Louis XI for eleven years (1469–80). The baseless story of his detention in an iron cage originated in Italy in the sixteenth century. After many fruitless attempts, the pope in 1480 obtained Balue's freedom through Cardinal Julian de la Rovère, later Pope Julius II (1503–13). Balue went to Rome with the cardinal, was restored to all his rights and dignities (1482) and was named Bishop of Albano (1483). At the death of Louis XI (1483) he came, at the request of Charles VIII, as papal legate to France and left it as French ambassador to Rome (1485). Balue succeeded, moreover, in securing, besides several benefices, the nomination as Protector of the Order of St. John of Jerusalem and Guardian to Prince Djem, brother of the Sultan of Turkey.

But his end was near; he died in 1491 and was buried at Rome. He had attained numerous dignities and amassed wealth, but dishonoured the Church.

Forgeot, *Jean Balue* (Paris, 1895); Pastor, *Gesch. der Päpste* (Freiburg, 1904), 4th ed., II, 372-375; tr. IV, 102-105 (London, 1894).

N. A. Weber.

Baluze, Etienne, a French scholar and historian, b. at Tulle, 24 December, 1630; d. in Paris, 28 July, 1718. His education was commenced at the Jesuit college of his native town, where he distinguished himself by his intelligence, his constant devotion to study, and his prodigious memory. Obtaining a scholarship on the recommendation of his professors, he completed his classical courses at the College of St. Martial, which had been founded at Toulouse, in the fourteenth century, by Pope Innocent VI for twenty Limousin students. Resolved to devote himself to the study of literature and history, Baluze set to work with great zeal, perseverance, and success. Critical and painstaking in the investigation of facts, he undertook to study the origins of the French nation, its customs, laws, and institutions, using for this purpose only genuine documents and original records instead of fanciful legends and fabulous stories, thus introducing a scientific spirit into historical research, philology, and chronology.

At the age of twenty-two he wrote a remarkable work of historical criticism. A Jesuit, Father Frizon, had just published a book, "Gallia purpurata", containing the lives of the French cardinals, which met with great success until Baluze gave out (1652) his "Anti-Frizonius" in which he pointed out and corrected many errors made by Father Frizon. In 1654, Pierre de Marca, Archbishop of Toulouse, one of the greatest French scholars in the seventeenth century, appointed Baluze his secretary. Upon the death of his patron, in June, 1662, Baluze published the "Marca Hispanica", a remarkable historical and geographical description of Catalonia. This work made him known to Colbert, who appointed him his librarian, a position he held for thirty years, many years, that is, after Colbert's death. The excellent collection of manuscripts and books which was found in the latter's library was the fruit of his care and advice. His own collection was also very important; it comprised about 1100 printed books, 957 manuscripts, more than 500 charters, and seven cases full of various documents. Baluze is to be ranked among those benefactors of literature who have employed their time and knowledge in collecting from all sources ancient manuscripts, valuable books, and state papers. He annotated them with valuable comments, being very well acquainted with profane and ecclesiastical history as well as with canon law, both ancient and modern.

The number of works Baluze published is considerable; we shall mention the most important among them: (1) "Marii Mercatoris opera" (1684), collated with manuscripts and enriched with notes illustrative of the history of the Middle Ages. (2) "Regum Francorum capitularia" (1677). This collection contains several capitularies never published before. Baluze corrected them with great accuracy and in his preface gave an account of the original documents and of the authority of the several collections of the capitularies. (3) "Epistolæ Innocentii Papæ III" (1682); not a complete collection, as Baluze was refused the use of the letters preserved in the Vatican. (4) "Conciliorum nova collectio" (1683), containing such pieces as are wanting in Labbe's collection. (5) "Les vies des papes d'Avignon" (1693), in which he gave a preference to Avignon over Rome as the seat of the Popes. (6) "Miscellanea" (1680), of which Mansi published a new edition in 1761. (7) "Historia Tutelensis" (1717), or the history of Tulle. This was Baluze's favourite work. He wrote it out of love for his native place, "ne in nostrâ patriâ peregrini atque hospites esse videamur". It embraces a period of eight centuries, from the founding of the city (900), to the episcopate of Daniel de Saint-Aulaire (1702). The history of Tulle is divided into three books, the first dealing with the counts, the second with the abbots, and the third with the bishops.

In 1670, Baluze was appointed professor of canon law at the Collège de France, of which he became director in 1707, with a pension awarded by the king. But he soon felt the uncertainty of courtly favours. Having attached himself to Cardinal de Bouillon, who had engaged him to write the history of his family, he became involved in the cardinal's disgrace. Baluze was accused of having used spurious papers in his patron's interest. Consequently he received a *lettre de cachet* ordering him to retire to Lyons. Being expelled from the university and deprived of his personal fortune, he wandered from Rouen to Blois, from Blois to Tours, and later to Orléans, where he lived until 1713. After the peace of Utrecht, the family of Cardinal de Bouillon recovered the favour of the king, and Baluze was recalled, but never again employed as a professor or as a Director of the Collège de France. He lived far from Paris and was engaged in publishing St. Cyprian's works at the time of his death. Baluze, together with Luc d'Achéry, Mabillon, Sainte-Marthe, Ducange, Montfaucon, and others, gathered an immense quantity of rich materials which the historians of the nineteenth century, such as Sismondi, Guizot, Augustin and Amédée Thierry, Michelet, Henri Martin, Fustel de Coulanges, were to use with the greatest skill.

Page, *Etienne Baluze, sa vie, ses ouvrages, son exil, sa défense* in *Bulletin de la société des lettres, sciences, et arts de la Corrèze* (Tulle, 1898), V, 20; Michaud, *Biographie universelle*, II, s. v.; Fage, *Les œuvres de Baluze cataloguées et décrites; Mémoire de l'Académie des Inscriptions*, XVIII; Delisle, *Le cabinet des manuscrits, Baluze, Colbert*, I.

Jean Le Bars.

Bamber (*alias* Reading), Edward, Venerable, priest and martyr, b. at the Moor, Poulton-le-Fylde, Lancashire; executed at Lancaster 7 August, 1646. Educated at the English College, Valladolid, he was ordained and sent to England. On landing at Dover, he knelt down to thank God, which act, observed by the Governor of the Castle, was the cause of his apprehension and banishment. He returned again, and was soon afterwards apprehended near Standish, Lancashire; he had probably been chaplain at Standish Hall. On his way to Lancaster Castle he was lodged at the Old-Green-Man Inn near Claughton-on-Brock, and thence managed to escape, his keepers being drunk. He was found wandering in the fields by one Mr. Singleton of Broughton Tower (who had been warned in a dream to help him), and was assisted and sheltered by him. Arrested the third time, he was committed to Lancaster Castle, where he remained in close confinement for three years, once escaping, but recaptured. At his trial with two other priests, Whitaker and Woodcock, two apostates witnessed against him that he had administered the sacraments, and he was condemned to die. He suffered with great constancy, reconciling to the Church a felon executed with him, and encouraging his fellow-martyrs to die bravely. His conduct so enraged the persecutors that they urged the executioner to butcher him in a more than usually cruel and savage manner. An ode composed on his death is still extant.

Challoner, *Memoirs* (1750); Watson, *Decacordon of ten Quodlibet Questions* (1602); Gillow, *Bibl. Dict. Eng. Cath.* (London, 1885).

Bede Camm.

Bamberg, Archdiocese of, in the kingdom of Bavaria, embraces almost the whole of the presidency of Upper Franconia, the northern part of

Middle Franconia (in particular the cities of Nuremberg, Fürth, Ansbach, and Erlangen), parts of Lower Franconia, of the Upper Palatinate, and of the Duchy of Saxe-Coburg. According to the census of 1 December, 1900, the archdiocese then contained 379,442 Catholics; in 1907 the Catholics numbered 410,000, and members of other denominations 720,000. Bamberg as an ecclesiastical province includes, besides the Archdiocese of Bamberg, the suffragan dioceses of Würzburg, Eichstätt, and Speyer, all of Bavaria.

History.—In the early centuries the region afterwards included in the Diocese of Bamberg was inhabited for the most part by Slavs; the knowledge of Christianity was brought to these people chiefly by the monks of the Benedictine Abbey of Fulda, and the land was under the spiritual authority of the Diocese of Würzburg. The Emperor Henry II and his pious wife Kunigunde decided to erect a separate bishopric at Bamberg, which was a family inheritance. The emperor's purpose in this was to make the Diocese of Würzburg less unwieldy in size and to give Christianity a firmer footing in the districts of Franconia. In 1008, after long negotiations with the Bishops of Würzburg and Eichstätt, who were to cede portions of their dioceses, the boundaries of the new diocese were defined, and John XVIII granted the papal confirmation in the same year. The new cathedral was consecrated 6 May, 1012, and in 1017 Henry II founded on Mount St. Michael, near Bamberg, a Benedictine abbey for the training of the clergy. The emperor and his wife gave large temporal possessions to the new diocese, and it received many privileges out of which grew the secular power of the bishops (cf. Weber in "Historisches Jahrbuch der Görresgesellschaft" for 1899, 326–345 and 617–639). Pope Benedict VIII during his visit to Bamberg (1020) placed the diocese in direct dependence on the Holy See. In 1248 and 1260 the see obtained large portions of the estates of the Counts of Meran, partly through purchase and partly through the appropriation of extinguished fiefs. The old Bishopric of Bamberg was composed of an unbroken territory extending from Schlüsselfeld in a north-easterly direction to the Franconian Forest, and possessed in addition estates in the Duchies of Carinthia and Salzburg, in the Nordgau (the present Upper Palatinate), in Thuringia, and on the Danube. By the changes resulting from the Reformation the territory of this see was reduced nearly one half in extent; in 1759 the possessions and jurisdictions situated in Austria were sold to that State. When the secularization of church lands took place (1802) the diocese covered 1276 square miles and had a population of 207,000 souls.

Up to this period the Diocese of Bamberg had been ruled by 63 bishops. The first eight were appointed by the German emperors; after this they were chosen by the clergy and people jointly; still later they were elected by the cathedral chapter. On several occasions, when the election was disputed, the appointment was made by the pope. The first bishop, Eberhard I (1007–40), chancellor to Henry II, greatly increased the possessions of the diocese; Suidger (1040–46) became pope under the name of Clement II; Hartwig (1047–53) defended the rights of his see against the Bishop of Würzburg and received the pallium from the pope in 1053; Adalbero (1053–57) was followed by Günther (1057–65) who held the first synod of Bamberg (1058). Günther died at Ödenburg (Sopron) in Hungary, while on a crusade. Hermann (1065–75) acquired the Principality of Banz; in the struggle between the empire and the papacy he took the side of the empire. He was charged with obtaining his election by simony and deposed. Rupert (1075–1102), as partisan of Henry IV, was a member of the pseudo-Synod of Brixen which declared Pope Gregory VII to be deposed; on this account the bishop was excommunicated. During his episcopate Rupert did much for the encouragement of classical learning in the diocese. St. Otto I (1102–39), the Apostle of the Prussians and Pomeranians, had a large share in the reconciliation of the pope and the emperor by the Concordat of Worms; he founded numerous churches and monasteries and during a famine showed large-hearted generosity to his subjects. Otto's immediate successors were men of less distinction: Egilbert (1139–46), who had been Patriarch of Aquileia; Eberhard II of Otelingen (1146–70) who with great pomp celebrated, in 1147, the canonization of Henry II. Eberhard increased the territory of the diocese, but, being a partisan of Frederick I, he was for a time under sentence of excommunication. He was succeeded by Hermann II, of Aurach (1170–77). Otto II, of Andechs (1177–96), rebuilt in 1181 the cathedral, which had been burned. Otto II understood how to remain loyal both to the emperor and the pope. Thiemo (1196–1202) obtained in 1200 the canonization of the Empress Kunigunde, joint foundress with the emperor Henry II of the see; Conrad, Duke of Silesia (1201–03), died soon after his election; Eckbert, Count of Meran and Andechs (1203–37), was suspected of being privy to the murder of King Philip of Germany in 1208; the ban of the empire was proclaimed against him, and he was removed from his see, but in 1212 he was restored, and in 1217 took part in an unsuccessful crusade to Palestine. In spite of his warlike disposition he was zealous in promoting the spiritual life of his clergy. Poppo I, Count of Andechs (1237–42), soon retired from his office; Henry I of Bilberstein (1242–51) received from the emperor the title of Prince-Bishop for himself and his successors, as well as numerous rights of sovereignty. Thenceforth the Bishops of Bamberg had ecclesiastical precedence directly after the archbishops.

Their power was encroached on, however, from two directions; on the one side by the cathedral canons, the so-called Brothers of St. George, who abandoned the *vita communis* during the episcopate of Bishop Berthold of Leiningen (1257 –85) and developed gradually into a cathedral chapter. In time the cathedral chapter of Bamberg was chosen, as in other German dioceses, exclusively from the nobility; the chapter, by so-called election pacts (*Wahlkapitulationen*) forced the bishops to abandon numerous privileges and many of the church livings under their control in favour of the chapter, limited the bishop's disciplinary authority over the clergy as well as his right to levy taxes, and abridged other powers. The episcopal authority was also limited, as in other parts of Germany, by the growing power of the towns which rebelled against the secular jurisdiction of the ecclesiastical princes. Thus the city of Bamberg revolted (1291) against Arnold of Solms (1286–96), a quarrel which was settled in 1291 by arbitration in favour of the bishop. During this episcopate the finances of the diocese became much involved, and the indebtedness increased under Leopold I of Gründlach (1297–1303). A Dominican appointed by the pope, Wulfing of Stubenberg (1304–18), founded in Bamberg a Dominican monastery and a convent of Dominican nuns. Several of the succeeding bishops ruled for brief periods: John of Güttingen (1322–23), afterwards Bishop of Freising; Henry II of Sternberg (1324–28), a Dominican; John, Count of Nassau (1328–29), who died before consecration; WMentho Schenk of Reicheneck (1329–35); Leopold II of Egloffstein (1335–43), who maintained ecclesiastical discipline in his diocese and shrewdly kept out of the quarrels between pope and emperor. Frederick I of Hohenlohe (1344–52) did much to establish peace between the imperial and ecclesiastical authorities; in 1348 he had a register (*urbarium*) drawn up of all the estates and rights belonging to the see. Leopold III of Bebenburg (1353–63) was granted the right of coinage and re-established the disordered finances of the see. Frederick II of Truhendingen (1364–66) was followed by Louis, Margrave of Meissen (1366–74), who soon became Elector of Mainz. Lamprecht of Brunn (1374–98), formerly Bishop of Strasburg, imposed new taxes in order to reduce the indebtedness of the see. This led to a revolt of the citizens of Bamberg, and the bishop was put to flight in 1379; in 1380 he conquered the city and imposed heavy penalties upon it. Albert, Count of Wertheim (1399–1421), settled a quarrel of many years' standing with the Burgrave of Nuremberg and protected the Jews living in the diocese. Frederick III of Aufsess (1421–31), one of the most religious princes of his age, convened a synod in order to restore ecclesiastical discipline and to check the avarice and immorality of the clergy; the opposition to these reforms, especially that of the cathedral canons, forced him to resign the see (d. 1440). Anthony of Rotenhan (1432–59) was unable to improve the bad condition of the episcopal finances of the bishopric; in 1440 the citizens of Bamberg forced him to flee, but he soon afterwards took the city by storm and executed a number of the citizens. The diocese was several times devastated by the Hussites. More peaceful times now followed: George I of Schaumberg (1459–75), an able ruler, restored ecclesiastical discipline among the people, clergy, and monasteries, and encouraged the newly discovered art of printing (the printer Pfister had a press at Bamberg as early as 1460). Philip of Henneberg (1475–87) continued the labours of his predecessor, redeemed a large number of the estates mortgaged by Anthony of Rotenhan to the Jews, and in 1478 drove the Jews out of the diocese. Henry III Gross of Trockau (1487–1501) was an energetic organizer and issued a number of laws; in 1491 he held a synod. Veit I Truchsess of Pommersfelden (1501–03) and George II Marschalk of Ebnet (1503–05) had very brief reigns.

The period of the Reformation was an unfortunate one for the diocese. Luther's doctrines very soon found entrance into its territory. The fortieth bishop, George III Schenk of Limburg (1502–22), did much to encourage art and the erection of churches, but he showed himself weak in his opposition to the religious innovations and allowed the writings of the Reformers to be printed and spread in the diocese. Luther's doctrines also found friends and well-wishers in the cathedral chapter. Weigand of Redwitz (1522–56) desired to make a stand against the progress of the Reformation, but was prevented by political and social conflicts. In 1524 the peasants, excited by the preaching of evangelical freedom by the adherents of the new teachings, revolted in several places and refused to pay tithes. The city of Bamberg also rebelled against the bishop; the citizens called on the peasants for aid, plundered the episcopal palace, the houses of the canons and clergy, the monasteries, and a large number of estates in the open country which belonged to the nobles and clergy. George von Truchsess, commander of the army of the Swabian Confederation, restored order; a number of the revolutionary leaders were executed, a heavy punishment was inflicted on the city of Bamberg, and the nobles who had suffered loss received unnecessarily large compensation. In spite of the bishop's zeal for souls, the Reformation spread through the diocese, and Protestantism gained a footing, especially in Nuremberg and in the Franconian possessions of the Electors of Brandenburg. This period was followed by an era of calm during the episcopates of George IV Fuchs von Rugheim (1556–61), Veit II of Würzburg (1561–77), John

George I Zobel of Giebelstadt (1577–80), Martin von Eyb (1580–83); none of these men, however, were able to correct abuses and reduce the debts of the see. The cathedral chapter was chiefly responsible for the troubles under which the diocese suffered; their nepotism, simony, avoidance of ordination to the priesthood, and, in many cases, their evil lives (concubinage was common) prevented reform. Ernst von Mengersdorf (1583–91) took energetic measures against the moral decay of clergy and people; in 1585 he founded a seminary in Bamberg for the training of priests; he also did much to improve the material welfare of the people. Neithart von Thüngen (1591–98) laboured with great success in behalf of the counter-Reformation; he provided for the education of the clergy, enlarged the ecclesiastical seminary, and re-established the Catholic religion in his territory in accordance with the then accepted principles of law. A less successful episcopate was that of John Philip von Gebsattel (1599–1609), during whose reign the pest desolated the diocese. John Gottfried von Aschhausen (1609–22), who, after 1617, was also Bishop of Würzburg, took energetic measures against concubinage among the clergy. In 1612 he called in the Jesuits, to whom he gave the house and church of the Carmelites; he put the Jesuits in charge of the ecclesiastical seminary and made them the cathedral preachers. In this way the bishop insured the reform of his clergy and the spiritual renewal of Catholicism. There is one stain on his memory which also rests on that of his successor: the toleration and encouragement of trials for witchcraft.

Many misfortunes befell the diocese during the Thirty Years War; among these were heavy war imposts, spoliation, and devastation. In 1632 Bamberg was conquered by the Swedes, and in 1633 was obliged to recognize Bernard of Weimar as its ruler. Bishop John George II Fuchs von Dornheim (1623–33) died in Carinthia far away from his see. Franz von Hatzfeld (1633–42) was not able to enter his diocese until 1635. Melchior Otto Voit of Salzburg (1642–53) changed the gymnasium into a university in 1647; his successors, Philip Valentine Voit von Reineck (1655–72), Philip von Dernbach (1672–83), Marquard Sebastian Schenk von Stauffenberg (1683–93), followed his example in encouraging the spiritual activity of the Jesuits and other orders, in the improvement of schools, and in reducing the indebtedness of the diocese. A time of great prosperity was the period of the two Counts von Schönborn, Lothair Franz (1693–1729), and Frederick Charles (1729–46). After 1695 the former of these two bishops, Lothair Franz, was also Elector of Mainz; he built the prince-bishop's palace (now a royal residence), a large college for the Jesuits, as well as several castles, and was a great patron of art and learning; the latter, Frederick Charles, added faculties of law and medicine to the university and adorned the city with numerous public buildings. On account of his pulpit eloquence his contemporaries gave him the name of the German Fleury. The reigns of the next bishops, John Philip Anthony von Frankenstein (1746–53) and Franz Conrad, Count von Stadion (1753–57), were also peaceful. During the administration of Adam Frederick, Count von Seinsheim (1757–79), the diocese suffered greatly from the Seven Years War; during its progress the Prussians ravaged and plundered the region, levied contributions on the inhabitants, and carried off the church treasures. When pestilence and famine followed the other miseries of war the bishop showed great liberality in providing for his starving subjects. Franz Ludwig von Erthal (1779–95), who was at the same time Bishop of Würzburg, was another prelate who aimed to promote the welfare of the diocese; he issued wise laws, tried to equalize the burdens of taxation, founded charitable institutions (the general hospital at Bamberg among them), and raised the standard of the clergy. But although personally religious, in the political relations of the Church he yielded in a measure to the prevailing tendencies of the *Aufklärung* (illumination) movement of his day. Christoph Franz von Buseck (1745–1802) was the last Prince-Bishop of Bamberg. In 1796 he took refuge at Prague from the French invasion, and in 1799 at Saalfeld. He had only just returned, in 1802, when Bavaria seized its prince-bishopric; and in 1803 the delegates of the empire formally enacted the secularization of Bamberg, and allotted it to be a possession of the Elector of Bavaria. All the provostships and monasteries were then suppressed, the university was changed into the still extant lyceum, and the prince-bishop was pensioned.

Upon the death of von Buseck (1805) George Charles von Fechenbach, Bishop of Würzburg, administered the affairs of the diocese until 1808. After this the see remained vacant for ten years; the ecclesiastical government was carried on by a vicariate-general, consisting of a president and eight counsellors. The Concordat agreed upon between Bavaria and Rome in 1817 brought in a new era. Bamberg was made an archbishopric with boundaries as given at the beginning of this article. The first archbishop, Count Joseph von Stubenberg, previously Prince-Bishop of Eichstätt, took possession of the archiepiscopal see of Bamberg in 1818 and administered both dioceses until his death in 1824. Bishop von Stubenberg deserves great credit for the manner in which he protected the property of the Catholic Church. He was followed by (1824–42) Joseph Maria, Freiherr von Fraunberg, who had been Bishop of Augsburg, (1842–58) Boniface Caspar von Urban, (1858–75) Michael von Deinlein, who founded a seminary for boys and encouraged Catholic associations and missions among the people, (1875–90) Frederick von Schreiber, and (1890–1904) Joseph von Schork, a noted pulpit orator. Archbishop von Schork promoted missions (*Volksmissionen*) among the people, as well as charitable and social organizations among clergy and laity. Frederick Philip von Abert (b. at Münnerstadt, 1 May, 1852) was appointed Archbishop, 30 January, 1905.

ECCLESIASTICAL STATISTICS.—The Archdiocese of Bamberg is divided into the archiepiscopal commissariat of the city of Bamberg and 20 rural deaneries. The diocesan year-book for 1906 gives: 194 parishes and dependent stations; 35 curacies; 113 chaplaincies; 58 benefices; 583 churches and chapels; 406 secular clergy; 29 regular clergy; 788 Catholic parish schools; 23 Catholic district school inspectors; 202 local school inspectors. The cathedral chapter is composed of 1 provost, 6 deans, 10 canons, 1 honorary canon, and six curates. The secular priests have a clerical association (*Fœdus Ottonianum*) with 320 members and a home for invalid priests; the association has also a retiring fund (*Emeritenfonds*) of $92,500. There are 7 houses of male orders, with 90 members, namely: 4 Franciscan with 17 priests and 29 brothers; 1 of Calced Carmelites with 5 priests, 3 clerics, and 7 brothers; 1 of Conventual Minorites, with 5 priests, 5 brothers, and 3 novices; 1 of Brothers of Charity, with 2 priests, 11 brothers, and three novices. The archdiocese contains a large number of houses of the female orders and congregations: 17 houses, in 8 localities, of the English Ladies (*Englische Fräulein*) with 223 inmates; 13 houses of the Poor School-Sisters, with 123 inmates; 3 houses of the Franciscan Sisters, with 11 inmates, from the mother-house of Maria-Stern at Augsburg; 8 houses of the Tertiary Sisters of St. Francis, from Mallersdorf, with 35 inmates; 8 houses of the Franciscan Sisters, from the convent of Dillingen with 43 inmates; 5 houses of Sisters of Charity of St. Vincent de Paul with 55 inmates; 17 houses in 10 localities containing 107 inmates, of the Sisters of the Most Holy Saviour from the mother-house at Oberbronn, with 107 inmates; 12 houses, with 32 inmates, of the Daughters of the Holy Redeemer from the mother-house at Würzburg; 2 convents, with 11 inmates, of the Sisters of Oberzell; making a total of 85 houses with 640 female religious. For the training of the clergy there are an archiepiscopal seminary for priests (50 students) and an archiepiscopal seminary for boys (75 pupils). The students of the seminary (*Priesterseminar*) are educated at the Royal Lyceum, which has philosophical and theological faculties and 9 clerical professors; the pupils of the seminary for boys' school (*Knabenseminar*) attend the two gymnasia of Bamberg in each of which an ecclesiastic acts as religious instructor (*Religionslehrer*). The clergy have also charge of the von Aufsess seminary and home for Catholic students. The Franciscans have at Bamberg a seminary for students at the gymnasia who wish to enter the order after completing their studies. Of the female congregations, the English Ladies conduct 3 Academies and boarding-schools for girls, and 7 primary girls' schools; the other congregations conduct common schools, housekeeping and industrial schools, and crèches. The orders and congregations in the diocese have some 90 charitable institutions under their care, among these are: 15 alms-houses and infirmaries; 12 hospitals; 22 crèches; 15 centres for obtaining visiting nurses; 1 insane asylum; 4 homes for unemployed servants; 5 poor-houses, etc. Among the Catholic societies in the diocese may be mentioned: 50 Associations for Workingmen and Mechanics; 14 Journeymen's Associations (*Gesellenvereine*); 7 Apprentices' Societies; 1 Workingwomen's and 1 Shopgirls' Association; the Ludwig-Mission Association; the St. Boniface Association; the Christian Family Association; the Society of Christian Mothers; the Catholic Men's Society, the People's Union for Catholic Germany, etc.

The most important ecclesiastical building of the diocese is the cathedral. The edifice erected by the Emperor Henry II, the Saint, was destroyed by fire in 1081; the new cathedral, built by St. Otto of Bamberg, was consecrated in 1111, and in the thirteenth century received its present late-Romanesque form. It is about 309 feet long, 92 feet broad, 85 feet high, and the four towers are each about 266 feet high. Among the finest of its monuments is that to the Emperor Henry II and his Empress Kunigunde, considered the masterpiece of the sculptor Tilman Riemenschneider. Among other noteworthy churches of the city are the twelfth-century church of the former Benedictine abbey of St. Michael and the upper parish church, a Gothic building dating from 1387. Among the noted churches of the diocese are those of the Fourteen Martyrs, Gössweinstein, and Mariaweiher—all places of pilgrimage; the Gothic church of Our Lady at Nuremberg, and the churches of the former abbeys of Banz and Ebrach.

LUDEWIG, *Scriptores rerum episcopatus Bambergensis* (Frankfort and Leipzig, 1718); SCHNEIDAWIND, *Statistische Beschreibung des Hochstifts Bamberg* (Bamberg, 1797); USSERMANN, *Episcopatus Bambergensis* (St. Blasien, 1802); ROPPELT, *Historisch-topographische Beschreibung des Hochstifts Bamberg* (Nuremberg, 1805); JÄCK, *Geschichte der Provinz Bamberg, 1006–1803* (Bamberg, 1809–10); IDEM, *Beschreibung der Bibliothek zu Bamberg* (Nuremberg, 1831–35); IDEM, *Bambergische Jahrbücher von 741 bis 1833* (Bamberg, 1829–34); VON STRAUSS, *Das Bistum Bamberg in seinen drei wichtigsten Epochen* (Bamberg, 1823); EISENMANN, *Geographische Beschreibung des Erzbistums Bamberg* (Bamberg, 1833); JAFFÉ, *Monumenta Bambergensia* (Berlin, 1869); WEBER, *Geschichte der gelehrten Schulen im Hochstift Bamberg 1007–1803* (Bamberg, 1880–81); IDEM, *Der Kirchengesang im Fürstbistum Bamberg* (Cologne, 1893); IDEM, *Das Bistum und Erzbistum Bamberg* (Bamberg, 1895); LOOSHORN, *Die Geschichte des Bistums Bamberg*—brought down to 1729 (1886–1906, vols. I–III, Munich, vols. IV–VI, Bamberg); LEIST, *Bamberg* (Bamberg, 1889); RÖSEL, *Unter dem Krummstab. 2 Jahrhunderte Bamberger Geschichte* (Bamberg, 1895); PFISTER, *Der Dom zu Bamberg* (Bamberg, 1896); WROSKY, *Die Bamberger Domskulpturen* (Strasburg,

1897); WILD, *Staat und Wirtschaft in den Bistümern Bamberg und Würzburg* (Heidelberg, 1904); *Schematismus der Geistlichkeit des Erzbistums Bamberg 1906* (Bamberg, 1906); *Jahresbericht über Bestand und Wirken des Historischen Vereins Bamberg* (Bamberg, 18— to 1905), 64 vols.

JOSEPH LINS.

Banaias (A. V. Benaiah; Kenrick, Banaiah; Heb. בניהו, also בניה, "Jehovah hath built up"—Gesenius; Gr. Βαναίας, Βαναία; Lat. Banaias, Banaia), the name of several men mentioned in the Bible. The orthography varies, but the component elements of the various forms are the same.

The most famous of all who bore the name was "the son of Joiada, the priest"—"the most valiant among the thirty"—"captain of the third company for the third month" (I Par., xxvii, 5, 6). The meaning of the text is not clear; he seems to have been a priest and one of the principal officers at court. "Joiada, the son of Banaias" (I Par., xxvii, 34) may be a false reading, in which the names have been interchanged. Banaias is credited with three notable exploits that required strength and courage: (a) He killed two lions, or perhaps brave warriors of Moab ("two lion-like champions of Moab"—Gesenius, s. v. אריאל; in Gr. and Lat. the Heb. word is merely transliterated, leaving the meaning doubtful); (b) he descended into a pit and there killed a lion; (c) he also vanquished and put to death an Egyptian hero of extraordinary size and great strength (II K., xxiii, 20, 21 = I Par., xi, 22, 23). He commanded the "Cerethi and Phelethi", or "the king's guards"— D. V. footnote (II K., viii, 18; I Par., xviii, 17), or "Cerethites" and "Phelethites" (II K., xx, 23). The D. V. describes him as "the first among the thirty, but yet to the first three he attained not: and David made him of his council" (I Par., xi, 25). In II K., xxiii, 23, the Heb. text gives the same history, but the Gr. and the Lat. versions cause confusion by notable variations. The A. V. reads: "Behold, he was honourable among the thirty, but attained not to the *first* three: and David set him over his guard" (I Chron., xi, 25). This is from the Heb., but "guard" may be questioned (Gesenius renders the word by "a hearing, audience"). "The first among the thirty" (D. V.) is far from being exact (Jos., Ant., vii, 12).

Banaias supported Solomon's title to the throne against the ambitious intrigues of Adonias (III K., i, 32–38, 44), whom, by Solomon's command, he afterwards put to death (III K., ii, 25). He also executed Joab and succeeded him as generalissimo (III K., ii, 34, 35); likewise Semei for having disobeyed Solomon (III K., ii, 46). For some Rabbinic literature, see *Jew. Encyc.* s. v.

JOHN J. TIERNEY.

Bancel, LOUIS, b. at Valence, 1628; d. at Avignon, 1685. When very young he entered the Dominican Order at Avignon. Even before his ordination to the priesthood he was appointed lector of philosophy. He afterwards taught theology at Avignon. He was remarkable for his subtle intellect and prodigious memory. He was the first to receive the appointment to the chair of theology in the University of Avignon (1654). This chair he held till his death. He was elected several times Dean of the Theological Faculty and always presided at the public defence of the theses of the candidates for academical degrees. He was also Synodal Examiner of the Diocese of Avignon, and Prefect of the Avignon legation. He wrote: "Moralis D. Thomæ, Doctoris Angelici ex omnibus ipsius operibus deprompta" (Avignon, 1677; Venice, 1723, 1757, 1758, 1780); and "Brevis universæ theologiæ cursus" (Avignon, 1684–92). As the author died while the third volume was in press, the editing of the work was finished by Joseph Patin, O. P. From the last tome was expunged a thesis maintaining

as probable the salvation of unbaptized infants by the faith of their parents. The unpublished manuscripts of "Opus integrum de Castitate" and "Opus de veritate solius religionis Christianæ" were left with the Dominicans at Avignon.

QUÉTIF AND ECHARD, *Script. Ord. Præd.*, II, 705; HURTER, *Nomenclator*, II, 585; MARCHAND, *L'université d'Avignon aux XVII et XVIII siècles* (Paris, 1900), 19.

M. A. WALDRON.

Bandello, MATTEO, b. at Castelnuovo di Scrivia in Piedmont, Italy, in 1480; d. Bishop of Agen, France, in 1565. He entered the Order of St. Dominic; but his life and writings bear slight trace of a religious character (3 Vols. Lyons, 1554 *passim;* Vol. IV appeared in 1573). He is best known by his *Novelle*, 214 in number. These tales show very considerable literary skill. But they are of no credit to the churchman. In many cases they are perverse descriptions of horrors and wickedness. Many of them were translated into English by Painter, and furnished themes to the dramatists of the Elizabethan period. It is by this means, most likely, that Shakespeare learned the story of Romeo and Juliet. The story of "Parisina" told by Bandello was later taken up by Byron. The best edition of the *Novelle* is that of Silvestri, Milan, 1813–14, in nine volumes. Some of them are contained in the second volume of the "Tesoro dei Novellieri Italiani", Paris, 1847. Some were translated by Roscoe, in "Italian Novelists", III, (London, 1825).

QUÉTIF AND ECHARD, *Script. Ord. Præd.*, II, 155; LANDALE, *Beiträge zur Gesch. der ital. Novelle* (1875); SYMONDS, *Renaissance in Italy;* DUNLOCK, *Hist. of Prose Fiction;* MASI in *Nuova Antologia*, 1892; SPAMPINATO, *Matteo Bandello e le sue novelle* (Nola, 1896).

W. S. REILLY.

Bandinelli. See ALEXANDER III.

Banduri, ANSELMO, archæologist and numismatologist, b. 1671 at Ragusa, off the coast of Dalmatia; d. at Paris, 4 January, 1743. He joined the Benedictines at an early age, studied at Naples, and was eventually sent to Florence, then a flourishing centre of higher studies. Here he made the acquaintance of the famous Benedictine scholar Montfaucon, then travelling in Italy, in search of manuscripts for his edition of the works of St. John Chrysostom. Banduri rendered him valuable services and in return was recommended to Duke Cosmo III as a proper titular for the chair of ecclesiastical history in the University of Pavia. It was also suggested that the young Benedictine be sent to Paris for a period of preparation, and especially to acquire a sound critical sense. After a short sojourn at Rome, Banduri arrived at Paris in 1702 and entered the Abbey of Saint Germain des Prés, as a pensioner of the Grand Duke of Tuscany. He soon became an apt disciple of the French Maurists and began an edition of the anti-iconoclastic writings of Nicephorus of Constantinople, of the writings of Theodore of Mopsuestia, and of other Greek ecclesiastical authors. Banduri never published these works, though as late as 1722 he announced, as near at hand, their appearance in four folio volumes. In the meantime, he was attracted by the rich treasures of Byzantine manuscript and other material in the Bibliothèque Royale and the Bibliothèque Colbert. In 1711 he published at Paris his "Imperium Orientale, sive Antiquitates Constantinopolitanæ", etc., a documentary illustrated work on the Byzantine Empire, based on medieval Greek manuscripts, some of which were then first made known. He also defended himself successfully against Casimir Oudin, an ex-Premonstratensian, whose attacks were made on a second-hand knowledge of Banduri's work. In 1718 he published, also at Paris, two folio volumes on the imperial coinage from Trajan to the last of the Palæologi (98–1453), "Numismata Imperatorum Romanorum a Trajano Decio usque ad Palæologos Augustos" (supplement by Tanini, Rome, 1791). Of this work Father Eckhel, S.J., prince of numismatologists, says (Doctrina Nummorum I, cviii) that it contains few important contributions. At the same time he praises the remarkable bibliography of the subject that Banduri prefixed to this work under the title of "Bibliotheca nummaria sive auctorum qui de re nummaria scripserunt", reprinted by Fabricius (Hamburg, 1719). In 1715 Banduri was made an honorary foreign member of the Academy of Inscriptions, and in 1724 was appointed librarian to the Duke of Orleans; he had in vain solicited a similar office at Florence on the death of the famous Magliabecchi.

FRÉRET in *Mém. de l'acad. des inscr. et belles lettres*, XVI, 348.

MAURICE M. HASSETT.

Bañez (originally and more properly VAÑEZ and sometimes, but erroneously, IBAÑEZ), DOMINGO, a Spanish Dominican theologian, b. 29 February, 1528, at Medina del Campo, Old Castile; d. there 22 October, 1604. The qualifying *Mondragonensis*, attached to his name, seems to be a patronymic after his father, John Bañez of Mondragon, Guipuzcoa. At fifteen he began to study philosophy at the University of Salamanca. Three years later he took the Dominican habit at St. Stephen's Convent, and made his profession 3 May, 1547. During a year's review of the liberal arts and later, he had the afterwards distinguished Bartolomé Medina as a fellow student. Under such professors as Melchior Cano (1548–51), Diego de Chaves (1551), and Pedro Sotomayor (1550–51) he studied theology, laying the foundations of the erudition and acquiring the acumen which later made him eminent as a theologian and an exponent and defender of Thomistic doctrine. He next began teaching, and under Domingo Soto, as prior and regent, he held various professorships for ten years. He was made master of students, explaining the "Summa" to the younger brethren for five years, and incidentally taking the place, with marked success, of professors who were sick, or who for other reasons were absent from their chairs at the university. In the customary, sometimes competitive, examinations before advancement, he is said easily to have carried off all honours. He taught at the Dominican University of Avila from 1561 to 1566. About 1567 he was assigned to a chair of theology at Alcalá, the ancient Complutum. It appears that he was at Salamanca again in 1572 and 1573, but during the four scholastic years 1573–77 he was regent of St. Gregory's Dominican College at Valladolid, a house of higher studies where the best students of the Castilian province were prepared for a scholastic career. Elected Prior of Toro, he went instead to Salamanca to compete for the chair of Durandus, left vacant by Medina's promotion to the chief professorship. He occupied this position from 1577 to 1580. After Medina's death (30 December, 1580) he appeared again as competitor for the first chair of the university. The outcome was an academic triumph for Bañez, and he was duly installed in his new position amid the acclamations of professors and students. There he laboured for nearly twenty years. His name acquired extraordinary authority, and the leading schools of orthodox Spain referred to him as the *præclarissimum jubar*—"the brightest light"—of their country.

In another way, Bañez in his prime was rendering memorable service to the Church as director and confessor of St. Teresa (1515–82). Her own words mark him as the spiritual adviser who was most relied upon as a guide and helper, both in her interior life and in her heroic work of the Carmelite reform. "To the Father Master Fra Dominic Bañez, who is now in Valladolid as Rector of the College of St. Gregory, I confessed for six years, and, whenever I had occasion to do so, communicated with him by letter. . . . All that is written and told, she communicated to him,

who is the person with whom she has had, and still has, the most frequent communications." (See "Life of St. Teresa of Jesus, by herself", tr. by David Lewis, 3d ed., London, 1904, Relation VII, 448, 450.) Of the first foundation of the reform, St. Joseph's Monastery at Avila, she wrote that Bañez alone saved it from the destruction resolved upon in an assembly of civil and religious authorities (op. cit., ch. xxxvi, 336 sqq.). He did not then know the saint, but "from that time forth he was one of her most faithful friends, strict and even severe, as became a wise director who had a great saint for his penitent." He testifies, in the process of her beatification, that he was firm and sharp with her, while she herself was the more desirous of his counsel the more he humbled her, and the less he seemed to esteem her (op. cit., p. xxxvi). He looked for the proof of her love of God in her truthfulness, obedience, mortification, patience, and charity towards her persecutors, while he avowed that no one was more incredulous than himself as to her visions and revelations. In this his mastery of the spiritual life was shown to be as scientific as it was wholesome and practical. "It was easy enough to praise the writings of St. Teresa and to admit her sanctity after her death. Fra Bañez had no external help in the applause of the many, and he had to judge her book as a theologian and the saint as one of his ordinary penitents. When he wrote, he wrote like a man whose whole life was spent, as he himself tells us, in lecturing and disputing" (ibid.).

As the schoolman, the lecturer, and academic disputant, Bañez stands forth as a figure of unprecedented distinction in scholastic Spain. In his time discussion was rife, and disquieting tendencies counter to the beaten paths of Augustine and Thomas manifested themselves. The great controversy, with whose beginnings his name is prominently associated, goes back to a public disputation held early in 1582. Francisco Zumel, of the Order of Mercy, was moderator. Prudentius Montemayor, a Jesuit, argued that Christ did not die freely, and consequently suffered death without merit, if the Father had given him a command to die. Bañez asked what the consequences would have been if the Father had given command not only as to the substance of the act of death, but also as to its circumstances. Prudentius responded that in that case there remained neither liberty nor merit. Louis de Leon, an Augustinian, sided with Prudentius and presently the discussion was taken up by the masters in attendance and carried to the kindred subjects of predestination and justification. Other formal disputations ensued, and strong feeling was manifested. Juan de Santa Cruz, a Hieronymite, felt constrained to refer the matter to the Inquisition (5 February), and to his deposition he appended sixteen propositions covering the doctrines in controversy. Leon declared that he had only defended the theses for the sake of argument. His chief thought was to prevent them from being qualified as heretical. Notwithstanding these and further admissions, he was forbidden to teach, publicly or privately, the sixteen propositions as reviewed and proscribed.

In 1588, Luis Molina, a Jesuit, brought out, at Lisbon, his celebrated "Concordia liberi arbitrii cum gratiæ donis", bearing the *censura*, or sanction, of a Dominican, Bartolomeu Ferreiro, and dedicated to the Inquisitor General of Portugal, Cardinal Albert of Austria; but a sentiment against its appearance in Spain was aroused on the ground of its favouring some of the interdicted propositions. The cardinal, advised of this, stopped its sale, and requested Bañez and probably some others to examine it. Three months later, Bañez gave his opinion that six of the forbidden propositions appeared in the "Concordia". Molina was asked to defend himself, and his answers to the objections and to some other observations were added as an appendix, with which, sanctioned anew (25 and 30 August, 1589), the work was permitted to circulate. It was regarded as an epoch-making study, and many Fathers of the Society of Jesus rallied to its defence. From Valladolid, where the Jesuit and Dominican schools in 1594 held alternate public disputations for and against its teaching on grace, the contention spread over all Spain. The intervention of the Inquisition was again sought, and by the authority of this high tribunal the litigants were required to present their respective positions and claims, and a number of universities, prelates, and theologians were consulted as to the merits of the strife. The matter was referred however, by the papal nuncio to Rome, 15 August, 1594, and all dispute was to cease until a decision was rendered. In the meantime, to offset his Dominican and other critics, Molina brought counter accusations against Bañez and Zumel. The latter submitted his defence in three parts, all fully endorsed by Bañez, 7 July, 1595. The Dominican position was set forth about the same time by Bañez and seven of his brethren, each of whom presented a separate answer to the charges. But the presiding officer of the Inquisition desired these eight books to be reduced to one, and Bañez, together with Pedro Herrera and Didacus Alvarez, was instructed to do the work. About four months later, Alvarez presented their joint product under the title: "Apologia fratrum prædicatorum in provinciâ Hispaniæ sacræ theologiæ professorum, adversus novas quasdam assertiones cujusdam doctoris Ludovici Molinæ nuncupati", published at Madrid, 20 November, 1595. It is noteworthy that this work was signed and ratified by twenty-two masters and professors of theology. To it was added a tract on the intrinsic efficacy of Divine grace. Nearly two years later, 28 October, 1597, Bañez resumed the case in a new summary and petitioned the pope to permit the Dominican schools to take up their teaching again on the disputed questions. This was the "Libellus supplex Clementi VIII oblatus pro impetrandâ immunitate a lege silentii utrique litigantium parti impositâ", published at Salamanca. An answer to the "Libellus" was conveyed in a letter of Cardinal Madruzzi, 25 February, 1598, written in the name of the pope, to the nuncio in Spain: "Inform the Fathers of the Order of Preachers that His Holiness, moderating the prohibition that was made, grants them the faculty freely to teach and discuss, as they did in the past, the subject-matter *de auxiliis divinæ gratiæ et eorum efficaciâ*, conformably to the doctrine of St. Thomas; and likewise the Fathers of the Society, that they also may teach and discuss the same subject-matter, always holding, however, to sound Catholic doctrine". (Serry, Hist. Cong. de Aux., I, XXVI.) This pronouncement practically ended whatever personal participation Bañez had in the famous controversy.

It has been contended that Bañez was at least virtually the founder of present-day Thomism, especially in so far as it includes the theories of physical premotion, the intrinsic efficacy of grace, and predestination irrespective of foreseen merit. To any reader of Bañez it is evident that he would have met such a declaration with a strenuous denial. Fidelity to St. Thomas was his strongest characteristic. "By not so much as a finger-nail's breadth, even in lesser things", he was wont to say, "have I ever departed from the teaching of St. Thomas". He singles out for special animadversion the views in which his professors and associates dissent even lightly from the opinions of the Angelic Doctor. "In and throughout all things, I determined to follow St. Thomas, as he followed the Fathers", was another of his favourite assurances. His zeal for the integrity of Thomistic teaching could brook no doctrinal novelty, partic-

ularly if it claimed the sanction of St. Thomas's name. In the voluminous literature on the De Auxiliis and related controversies, the cardinal tenets of Thomism are ascribed by its opponents to a varied origin. The Rev. G. Schneeman, S. J., (Controversiarum de divinæ gratiæ liberique arbitrii Concordiâ initia et progressus, Freiburg im Br., 1881), the Rev. Father De Regnon, S. J. (Bañez et Molina, Paris, 1883) and the Rev. Father Baudier, S. J. (in the Revue des Sciences Ecclésiastiques, Amiens, 1887, p. 153) are probably the foremost modern writers who designate the Thomists as Bannesians. But against them appears a formidable list of Jesuits of repute who were either Thomists themselves or authorities for other opinions. Suarez, for instance (Op. omn., XI, ed. Vives, Paris, 1886; Opusc., I, Lib. III, De Auxiliis, vii), credits Medina with the first intimations of physical premotion and elsewhere (Op. omn., XI, 50; Opusc. I, Lib. I, De Conc. Dei, xi, n° 6) admits that St. Thomas himself once taught it. Toletus (Comment. in 8 Lib. Aristotelis, Venice, 1573, Lib. II, c. iii, q. 8) and Pererius (Pref. to Disquisit. Magicarum, Lib. VI, I Ed.) considered as Thomistic the Catechism of the Council of Trent, which was the work (1566) of three Dominican theologians. [For Delrio see Goudin, Philosophia (Civita Vecchia, 1860), IV, pt. IV, 392, Disp. 2, q. 3, § 2.] The Rev. Victor Frins, S. J., gives it as his opinion (S. Thomæ Aq., O. P. doctrina de Cooperatione Dei cum omni naturâ creatâ præsertim liberâ; Responsio ad R. P. Dummermuth, O. P., Paris, 1893) that whilst Medina and Pedro Soto (1551) taught physical predetermination, the originator of the theory was Francis Victoria, O. P. (d. 1546). The Dominicans Ferrariensis (1576), Cajetan (1507), and Giovanni Capreolus (d. 1436) are also accredited Thomists in the estimation of such authorities as the Jesuits Becanus [Summa Theol. Schol. (Mainz, 1612), De Deo, xviii, no 14] and Azorius [Institut. Moral. (Rome, 1600–11), Lib. I, xxi, § 7], and the theologians of Coimbra (Comment. in 8 libros Phys., Lib. II, q. 13, a. 1). Molina, strangely enough, cites the doctrine of a "certain disciple of St. Thomas"—supposedly Bañez—as differing only in words from the teaching of Scotus, instead of agreeing with that of Aquinas [Concordia (Paris, 1876), q. 14, a. 13, Disp. 50]. These striking divergences of opinion of which only a few have been cited would seem to indicate that the attempt to father the Thomistic system on Bañez has failed. [Cf. Defensio Doctrinæ S. Thomæ, A. M. Dummermuth, O.P., Louvain and Paris, 1895, also Card. Zigliara, Summa Phil. (Paris, 1898), II, 525.]

The development of Thomistic terminology in the Dominican school was mainly due to the exigencies not only of the stand taken against Molina and the forbidden propositions already mentioned, but of the more important defence against the attacks and aberrations of the Reformers. The "predetermination" and "predefinition" of Bañez and his contemporaries, who included others besides Dominicans, emphasized, on the part of God's knowledge and providence, a priority to, and independence of, future free acts, which, in the Catharino-Molinistic theories, seemed to them less clearly to fall under God's causal action. These terms, however, are used by St. Thomas himself. (Comment. de divinis nominibus, Lect. iii.) The words "physical premotion" were meant to exclude, first a merely moral impulse and, secondly, a concurrence of the Divine causality and free will, without the latter's subordination to the First Cause. That such terms, far from doing violence to the teachings of their great leader, are their true expression, has, of course, been an unvaried tenet of the Thomistic school. One of the presiding officers of the Congregation De Auxiliis, Cardinal Madruzzi, speaking of Bañez in this connexion, said: "His teaching seems to be deduced from the principles of St. Thomas and to flow wholly from St. Thomas's doctrine, although he differs somewhat in his mode of speaking" (Serry, Hist. Cong. de Aux., appendix, col. 89). It seems but fair to the memory of Bañez that this opinion should ultimately prevail.

As a writer, Bañez is clear, direct and vigorous. Occasionally prolix, he is never dull or inane. He treats a subject lengthily only when it is highly important or manifestly useful. His thought is generally lucidity itself in his pithiest scholastic condensations, nor is it less perspicuous when he adopts a freer and more elegant style in behalf of a wider range of readers. Of copious erudition, he was also keen in logic and profoundly versed in metaphysics, surpassing, in this respect, the ablest of his contemporaries. He evidenced a broad-minded and progressive spirit in placing, at no little expense, a fully equipped printing establishment in the convent of St. Stephen, and in employing for its successful operation the best craftsmen that were then to be had. The list of his works is completed as follows: (1) "Scholastica commentaria in I^{am} partem angelici doctoris D. Thomæ usque ad 64 qu.", fol. Salamanca, 1584; Venice, 1585, 1602; Douai, 1614; (2) "Scholastica commentaria super cæteras I^{ae} partis quæstiones", fol. Salamanca, 1588; (3) "Scholastica commentaria in II^{am} II^{ae}, quibus quæ ad fidem, spem et charitatem spectant, clarissime explicantur usque ad quæst. XLVI", fol. Salamanca, 1584; Venice, 1586; (4) "Scholastica commentaria in II^{am} II^{ae} a quæst. LVII ad LXXVII de jure et justitia decisiones", fol. Salamanca, 1594; 1604, Venice, 1595; Cologne and Douai, 1615; (5) "Relectio de merito et augmento charitatis anno MDLXXXIX Salamanticæ in vigilia pentecostes solemniter pronunciata", Salamanca, 1590, 1627; (6) "Commentaria in quæstiones Aristotelis de generatione et corruptione", fol. Salamanca, 1585; Venice, 1596; Cologne, 1614; (7) "Institutiones minoris dialecticæ and In Aristotelis dialecticam", Cologne, 1618; (8) "Responsio ad quinque quæstiones de efficaciâ divinæ gratiæ", Angelica Library, Rome, MS. R. l. 9. fol. 272; (9) "Respuesta contra una relación compuesta por los padres de la compañia de Jesus de Valladolid", Medina del Campo, 1602, MS., Dominican Library, Avila.

BAÑEZ, *autobiography* in preface to *Comment. in I^{am} P.*, D. Thomæ.; QUÉTIF-ECHARD, *Scriptores Ord. Præd.* ⟨Paris, 1721⟩, II, 352; TOURON, *Hist. des hommes illustres de l'ordre de S. Dominique* (Paris, 1743), IV, 750; MANDONNET in *Dict. de théol. cath.* (Paris, 1903), Fasc. X, col. 140; MORGOTT in *Kirchenlex.* (2d ed., Freiburg, 1882), I, s. v. *Bañez*; SERRY, *Hist. congregationum de auxiliis* (Venice, 1740); MEYER, *Hist. congregationum de divinæ gratiæ auxiliis* (Venice, 1740); DUMMERMUTH, *S. Thomas et Doctrina Præmotionis Physicæ* (Paris, 1886); GAYRAUD, *Thomisme et Molinisme* (Toulouse, 1889); BERTHIER in *Revue Thomiste* for 1893, 87; REGNON, *Bannésianisme et Molinisme* (Paris, 1890); GAYRAUD, *Réplique au R. P. Th. de Regnon* (Toulouse, 1890).

JOHN R. VOLZ.

Bangalore. See MYSORE.

Bangor, ANTIPHONARY OF, an ancient Latin manuscript, supposed to have been originally written at Bangor (Ireland).

The codex, found by Muratori in the Ambrosian Library at Milan, and named by him the "Antiphonary of Bangor" ("Antiphonarium Benchorense"), was brought to Milan from Bobbio with many other books by Cardinal Federigo Borromeo when he founded the Ambrosian Library in 1609. Bobbio, which is situated in a gorge of the Apennines thirty-seven miles north-east of Genoa, was founded by St. Columbanus, a disciple of St. Comgal, founder of the great monastery at Bangor on the south side of Belfast Lough in the county of Down. St. Columbanus died at Bobbio and was buried there in 615. This establishes at once a connexion between Bobbio and Bangor, and an examination of the contents of the codex placed it beyond all doubt that it was originally compiled in Bangor and brought

thence to Bobbio, not, however, in the time of St. Columbanus. There is in the codex a hymn entitled "*ymnum sancti Congilli abbatis nostri*", and he is referred to in it as "*nostri patroni Comgilli sancti*". Again there is a list of fifteen abbots, beginning with Comgal and ending with Cronanus who died in 691; the date of the compilation, therefore, may be referred to 680–691. Muratori, however, is careful to state in his preface that the codex, though very old, and in part mutilated, may have been a copy made at Bobbio, by some of the local monks there, from the original service book. It is written, as regards the orthography, the form of the letters, and the dotted ornamentation of the capital letters, in "the Scottic style", but this, of course, may have been done by Gaelic monks at Bobbio. The actual bearer of the codex from Bangor is generally supposed and stated to have been St. Dungal, who left Ireland early in the ninth century, acquired great celebrity on the Continent, and probably retired to Bobbio towards the close of his life. He bequeathed his books to "the blessed Columbanus", i. e., to his monastery at Bobbio. The antiphonary, however, cannot be identified with any of the books named in the catalogue of the books bequeathed by Dungal, as given by Muratori (Antiquitatis Italicæ Medii Ævi, Milan, 1740, III, 817–824). Here only a summary can be given of the contents of the codex to which the name of "Antiphonary" will be found to be not very applicable: (1) six canticles; (2) twelve metrical hymns; (3) sixty-nine collects for use at the canonical hours; (4) special collects; (5) seventy anthems, or versicles; (6) the Creed; (7) the Pater Noster. The most famous item in the contents is the venerable Eucharistic hymn "Sancti venite Christi corpus sumite", which is not found in any other ancient text. It was sung at the Communion of the clergy and is headed, "Ymnum quando comonicarent sacerdotes". A text of the hymn from the old MS. of Bobbio, with a literal translation, is given in "Essays on the Discipline and Constitution of the Early Irish Church," (p. 166) by Cardinal Moran, who refers to it as that "golden fragment of our ancient Irish Liturgy". The Creed in this codex differs in its wording from all other forms known to exist. It is in substance the original Creed of Nicæa. It does not contain the *ex Patre Filioque procedit*, but merely states the *homoousia* of the three Persons of the Holy Trinity.

WARREN, *The Antiphonary of Bangor: an Early Irish MS.* (a complete facsimile in collotype, with a transcription, London, 1893); IDEM, *Liturgy and Ritual of the Keltic Church* (Oxford, 1881), pp. 187–194; MURATORI, *Anecdota Ambrosiana*, in *Opera Omnia* (Arezzo, 1770), II, part iii, 217; P. L., LXXII, 579; REEVES, *Ulst. Journ. Archeol.*, I, 168.

ARTHUR UA CLERIGH.

Bangor (BANGORIUM, BANGORIENSIS), DIOCESE OF, anciently known as Bangor Vawr, situated in Carnarvonshire on the Menai Straits, must be distinguished from Bangor Iscoed also in Wales, and the celebrated Irish monastery of Bangor in County Down. The foundation of the see is traditionally ascribed to St. Daniel or Deiniol (d. 584?) who is stated to have been consecrated by St. Dubricius, or, according to others, St. David. Some writers place his death in 544, others in 554, while the tenth century "Annales Cambriæ" assign it to 584. Yet even this date is regarded by recent research as too early. We may, perhaps, safely ascribe the foundation of the see to the close of the sixth century. The history of the diocese before the Norman Conquest is so obscure that Godwin (De præsulibus Angliæ, 1743) does not allow that there were any bishops at all before the coming of the Normans.

In 1092 Hervey, a cleric in the court of William Rufus, was consecrated Bishop of Bangor and in the same year was present in that capacity at the council held by St. Anselm at Westminster, being the first Welsh bishop to attend an English council. His rule was not successful, for difficulties arose owing to his people resenting the coming of a stranger ignorant of their language, customs, and character. He, on the other hand, adopted violent measures

CATHEDRAL OF BANGOR

in the assertion of his rights, with the result that bloodshed ensued, and he finally had to take refuge in England, where he was translated to the See of Ely in 1108. The cathedral had been destroyed by the Normans in 1071, but was subsequently rebuilt, though no trace of Norman work remains in the present structure. Anian (1267–1305), who, as Bishop of Bangor, baptized Edward II took the chief part in rebuilding the cathedral. He also drew up the "Missale in usum Ecclesiæ Banchorensis" and the "Pontifical" which represent the liturgical books of "the use of Bangor". It again suffered severely in the wars between the English and Welsh during the reign of Henry III, and in 1402 was entirely burnt down by Owen Glendower. There could hardly have been a vigorous diocesan life, for the cathedral and episcopal residence lay in ruins for nearly a century. At length in 1496, a vigorous administrator became bishop in the person of Henry Deane, prior of the Austin canons at Llanthony near Gloucester. He immediately began to rebuild the ruined choir and his work still exists. Besides restoring his cathedral, he was active in regaining the possessions of the see which had been annexed by the more powerful men in the neighbourhood. Unfortunately for Bangor after four years' rule he was in 1500 translated first to Salisbury, and afterwards to Canterbury. He is said to have left his crosier and mitre, both of great value, to his successor, on condition that he should proceed with the rebuilding.

But neither of the next two bishops, Thomas Pigot, Abbot of Chertsey (1500–03), and John Penny (1504–08), did anything for the fabric. On the translation of Bishop Penny to Carlisle, Bangor was entrusted to Thomas Skevington, or Pace (1509–33), who of all its bishops did most for it. He was Abbot of Beaulieu in Hampshire, and though he did not reside in his see, he showed practical interest in his diocese by completing the cathedral. He rebuilt the entire nave and tower, and presented four bells which were afterwards sold by the first "reforming" bishop. He also rebuilt the episcopal residence. He died in 1533, and after the short episcopates of John Capon (1534–39) and John Bird (1539–41), was followed by Arthur Bulkeley, who resided in the diocese indeed, but who is accused of having neglected it in his own interests. According to the Anglican historian, Godwin, he was struck blind while watching the cathedral bells, which he had sold, being shipped off. But this story is questioned by Brown Willis, the

historian of the Welsh cathedrals. Bulkeley died in 1553, and was succeeded by William Glynn (1553–58) the last Catholic bishop.

Since the Reformation the cathedral has continued to serve the Anglican bishops in its old capacity, while also doing duty as the parish church of the town. It is the smallest and humblest of all the cathedrals in England or Wales, being an embattled cruciform structure resembling a good-sized parish church. The diocese consisted of the whole of Anglesea and Carnarvonshire, with the greater part of Merionethshire and some parishes in the counties Denbigh and Montgomery. There were three archdeaconries, Bangor, Anglesea, and Merioneth. The arms of the see were gules, a bend, or gutty de poix between two mullets, argent.

WALCOTT, *Memorials of Bangor* (1860); WILLIS, *Survey of Bangor* (1721); GODWIN, *De præsulibus Angliæ* (1743); WINKLE, *Cathedral Churches of England and Wales* (London, 1860), III, 153; *Dict. Nat. Biog.*, s. v. *Daniel, Hervey, Deane, Skevington, Bulkeley.*

EDWIN BURTON.

Bangor, HERMITS OF. See COMGALL, ST.

Bangor Abbey.—The name of two famous monastic establishments in Ireland and England.

(1) The Irish Abbey of Bangor was situated in the County Down, on the southern shore of Belfast Lough. Sometimes the name was written "Beannchor", from the Irish word *beann*, a horn. According to Keating, a king of Leinster once had cattle killed there, the horns being scattered round, hence the name. The place was also called the Vale of Angels, because, says Jocelin, St. Patrick once rested there and saw the valley filled with angels. The founder of the abbey was St. Comgall, born in Antrim in 517, and educated at Clooneenagh and Clonmacnoise. The spirit of monasticism was then strong in Ireland. Many sought solitude the better to serve God, and with this object Comgall retired to a lonely island. The persuasions of his friends drew him from his retreat; later on he founded the monastery of Bangor, in 559. Under his rule, which was rigid, prayer and fasting were incessant. But these austerities attracted rather than repelled; crowds came to share his penances and his vigils; they also came for learning, for Bangor soon became the greatest monastic school in Ulster. Within the extensive rampart which encircled its monastic buildings, the Scriptures were expounded, theology and logic taught, and geometry, and arithmetic, and music; the beauties of the pagan classics were appreciated, and two at least of its students wrote good Latin verse. Such was its rapid rise that its pupils soon went forth to found new monasteries, and when, in 601, St. Comgall died, 3,000 monks looked up for light and guidance to the Abbot of Bangor.

With the Danes came a disastrous change. Easily accessible from the sea, Bangor invited attack, and in 824 these pirates plundered it, killed 900 of its monks, treated with indignity the relics of St. Comgall, and then carried away his shrine. A succession of abbots continued, but they were abbots only in name. The lands passed into the hands of laymen, the buildings crumbled, and when St. Malachy, in the twelfth century, became Abbot of Bangor he had to build everything anew. The impress of his zeal might have had lasting results had he continued in this position. But he was promoted to the See of Down, and Bangor again decayed. By the Statute of Kilkenny the "mere Irish" were excluded from it, though it did not prosper thereby. In 1469, the Franciscans had possession of it, and a century later the Augustinians, after which, at the dissolution of the monasteries in that part of Ireland, it was given by James I to James Hamilton, created Viscount Clandeboye. An irregular succession of Catholic abbots was still kept up, the last being Abbot MacCormack, who lived in France, but, returning to Ireland during the Reign of Terror, found a refuge at Maynooth College and died there in the early years of the nineteenth century.

Among the Abbots of Bangor few acquired fame, but many of the students did. Findchua has his life written in the Book of Lismore; Luanus founded 100 monasteries and St. Carthage founded the great School of Lismore. From Bangor Columbanus and Gall crossed the sea, the former to found Luxeuil and Bobbio, the latter to evangelize Switzerland. In the ninth century a Bangor student, Dungal, defended orthodoxy against the Western iconoclasts. The present town of Bangor is a thriving little place, popular as a seaside resort. Local tradition has it that some ruined walls near the Protestant church mark the site of the ancient abbey; nothing else is left of the place hallowed by the prayers and penances of St. Malachy and St. Comgall.

(2) The Welsh Abbey of Bangor was situated in Flintshire, not far from Chester, and in the Middle Ages was often confounded with Bangor in Carnarvonshire, which was an episcopal see. The date of its foundation and its founder's name are equally uncertain. With great confidence and evident conviction, Montalembert declares that its founder was St. Iltud, or Iltyde. But some allowance must be made for French partiality, for Iltud was an Armoric Gaul. His life and acts are narrated in the "Lives of the Cambro-British Saints"; they have been carefully edited by Mr. Rees; and though it is stated that he was an Armorican, and had been a soldier, and married, before he became a monk, it is not said that he was connected with Bangor. It is more probable that the abbey was founded by Dunawd, a Welshman, whence it was often called Bangor Dunawd. And if St. Deiniol was the son of Dunawd, as it is said, this would fix the foundation of the Flintshire abbey at about the beginning of the sixth century, for Bangor in Carnarvonshire was founded by St. Deiniol in 514. It would also dispose of the assertion that Pelagius, the heretic, was at one time its abbot, for he died long before. It is certain that Bangor was the greatest monastic establishment in Wales, having at one time 2,000 monks. The Angles and Saxons had then conquered Britain and had treated the Britons with great severity. A remnant of these latter found refuge in Wales, where they brooded over their wrongs, and, being Christians themselves, refused to preach the Gospel to their conquerors. When St. Augustine came to England, in the last years of the sixth century, he visited the Britons in Wales. Their moral condition was then bad; they clung to the old mode of celebrating Easter, and some errors of doctrine had also crept into their creed. He had a conference with delegates from Bangor, but they refused to co-operate with him in the work of converting the still unconverted English. In punishment, he predicted that, as they refused to preach the way of life to the English, they would at the hands of these same English suffer death. And this came to pass in 603 when Ethelfrid of Northumbria defeated the Britons near Chester. Hearing that the monks of Bangor were praying for his enemies, he turned aside from the battle and put 1,200 of them to death. Extensive ruins of this abbey still remained in the twelfth century, but in Ussher's time, in the seventeenth century, these ruins had all but disappeared. On the site of the abbey now stands the small town of Bangor-on-the-Dee.

WARREN, ed., *The Antiphonary of Bangor* (London, 1893); STOKES, *Lives of the Saints from the Book of Lismore* (Oxford, 1890); ARCHDALL, *Monasticon Hibernicum* (Dublin, 1893); O'HANLON, *Life of St. Malachy* (Dublin, 1859); LANIGAN, *Ecclesiastical History* (Dublin, 1822); USSHER, *Works* (Dublin, 1847); *Annals of the Four Masters* (Dublin, 1854); HEALY, *Ancient Schools and Scholars of Ireland* (Dublin, 1896); REEVE, *Adamnan* (Dublin, 1857); *Wars of the Gael and Gall* (London, 1867); REES, *Lives of the Cambro-British Saints* (Llandovery, 1853); LINGARD, *Anglo-Saxon Church* (London, 1845); BEDE, *Ecclesiastical History* (in Bohn's Series); *William of Malmesbury* (in Bohn's series); *Giraldus Cambrensis* (in Bohn's series); MONTALEMBERT, *Monks of the West* (New ed. London, 1898).

E. A. D'ALTON.

Banias. See CÆSARIA PHILIPPI.

Banim, JOHN and MICHAEL.—JOHN, poet, dramatist, novelist, b. 3 April, 1798, at Kilkenny, Ireland; d. 31 August, 1842. His father, following the double occupation of farmer and storekeeper, was in easy circumstances. John's literary efforts began very early; at ten he wrote some verses and a tale of considerable length. After a preparatory training in private schools he entered Kilkenny College in 1810. Having a taste for painting and drawing he went to Dublin in 1813 to study art. In two years he was back in Kilkenny, became a drawing teacher, and fell desperately in love with one of his pupils, a girl two years his junior. The girl's father refused his consent, with the result that in two months she died of a broken heart. Her lover almost followed her example. An entire disregard of self at the time of the funeral caused paralysis and left him a victim of spinal disease, which afflicted him almost incessantly and finally caused his death. At the end of a year he set out for Dublin with a literary career in view. It was not long before he made his reputation. In 1821, when only twenty-three years old, he wrote the tragedy "Damon and Pythias", which was played at Covent Garden with Macready and Charles Kemble in the principal parts. After his marriage, which took place during a visit to his parents, he planned with his brother Michael, "The Tales of the O'Hara Family". These were to be written in collaboration, each brother to submit his work to the other for revision. As a result, it is impossible to distinguish from internal evidence the work of each. Their ambition was to do for Ireland what Scott, by his Waverley Novels, had done for Scotland—to make their countrymen known with their national traits and national customs and to give a true picture of the Irish character with its bright lights and deep shadows. To London, a wider field for literary work, Banim went in 1822 "without friends and with little money to seek his fortune". The next ten years were a fruitful season, during which he contributed frequently to various periodicals, and produced a considerable number of operatic pieces, dramas, essays, and novels, but always at the expense of "wringing, agonizing, burning pain". Writing of this period to his brother, he says: "Of more than twenty known volumes I have written, and treble their quantity in periodicals, no three pages have been penned free from bodily pain". The little crumbs of comfort he received he generously shared with his countryman, Gerald Griffin, who wrote of his early struggles in London: "What would I have done if I had not found Banim?" In 1829 John Banim was ordered to France in the hope that he might repair his shattered health, but the journey was of no avail. In a few years a stroke of paralysis "deprived him of the use of his limbs and brains". In 1835 he returned to Kilkenny by slow stages. Dublin and his native city showed him signal honour by demonstrations that moved him deeply. A public appeal for assistance met with such generous response that his financial troubles were ended. The Government, in recognition of his literary work, granted him a pension of £150, and an additional sum of £40 a year for the education of his daughter. His last work was the revision of a story which he had inspired and encouraged his brother to write, "Father Connell", the picture of his beloved parish priest of Kilkenny. He died in his own Windgap Cottage, just outside

Kilkenny, at the early age of forty-four. His principal works are: the poems, "Soggarth Aroon", "Ailleen", "The Celt's Paradise"; the dramas, "Damon and Pythias" and "The Prodigal"; and the novels, "John Doe", "The Fetches", "Peter of the Castle", "The Mayor of Windgap", and "The Boyne Water", the last a political novel.

MICHAEL, novelist, and co-worker with his brother John, b. at Kilkenny, Ireland, 5 August, 1796; d. 30 August, 1874. At sixteen he began the study of law, but soon abandoned it because of business reverses which befell his father. He took upon himself his father's burden and re-established his parents in comfortable circumstances. The little leisure his business cares allowed him he made the most of by gathering material for "The Tales of the O'Hara Family". At the urgent request of John, he contributed several of the stories, his first, "Crohoore of the Billhook", being perhaps the most popular of all. But Michael generously kept himself in the background in order to let his younger brother have all the honour of their joint production. Out of twenty-four volumes he wrote thirteen. Unlike John, however, he was a man of action, and threw himself earnestly into various movements for the uplifting of his countrymen, educationally and economically. After serving for many years as postmaster of Kilkenny, he died at the age of seventy-eight at Booterstown, not far from Dublin. The principal works of Michael Banim are: "Crohoore of the Billhook", "The Ghost Hunter", "Father Connell", and "The Croppy", a tale of 1798.

The Banims may be justly called the first national novelists of Ireland. They knew their countrymen not as the strange, grotesque caricatures too often portrayed in fiction, but as members of the great human family with noble impulses and generous traits. Their work, however, is notably free from patriotic bias. Their Irishmen have their faults. Though naturally sympathetic, tender-hearted, and forgiving, these typical Celts could become stern, bitter, and revengeful. Ignorance, poverty, and cruelty are shown to exist among the peasantry. But the reader cannot fail to see the cause of all this— the natural working out of religious persecution and political oppression. Criticism has been directed against some of their writings as "harrowing", and "impure". The latter criticism is unfortunately justified; John admitted and regretted it, and Michael acted on it by preventing one of the stories, "The Nowlans", from being reprinted. As to the "harrowing" elements, which are certainly conspicuous, the brothers answered: "We paint from a people of a land among whom, for the last six centuries, national provocations have never ceased to keep alive the strongest and often the worst passions of our nature". It may be added that, besides their desire to give a true picture of their country, still crippled and prostrate from the effects of the Penal Laws, they were undoubtedly influenced by the Romantic movement, then at its height. A recent edition of the works of the Banims, in ten volumes, which gives a life of John Banim, appeared in New York, 1896.

MURRAY, *Life of John Banim* (London, 1857); READ, *Cabinet of Irish Literature* (London, 1891); *The Nation* and *The Freeman's Journal*, (Dublin) files; KRANS, *Irish Life and Irish Fiction* (New York, 1903); *Dict. of Nat. Biogr.*

M. J. FLAHERTY.

Banjaluka, DIOCESE OF, in Western Bosnia, includes some of the most beautiful portions of the province. Banjaluka is the ancient Roman *Ad Ladios*. By the Bull "Ex hâc augustâ", 5 July, 1881, restoring the Catholic hierarchy in Bosnia, Leo XIII created one archiepiscopal and three episcopal sees, Banjaluka being the first in precedence among the latter. It includes 4 deaneries, 32 parishes, and more than 80,000 faithful. Its first bishop, Marian Mar-

ković, O. S. F., was consecrated 4 May, 1884, but only as Apostolic administrator. His first cathedral was a half-ruined shed, but he afterwards acquired a little church near his residence . At present (1907) most of the parishes are held by Franciscans. In the year 1869 was founded at Mariastern an abbey of Trappists which has already sent out two monastic colonies, to Josephsburg and to Marienburg in Bosnia, and another to Zara in Dalmatia. There are hospitals and schools conducted by Sisters of Charity and Sisters of the Precious Blood. In 1900 Banjaluka and Bihatch also became a diocese for the so-called Orthodox population, the Metropolitan residing at Banjaluka.

Leonis XIII Acta (Rome, 1882), 288–312; *Missiones Catholicæ* (Rome, 1897), 92–103; *Missiones Catholicæ* (Propaganda, Rome, 1907), 109.

L. PETIT.

Bankruptcy, CIVIL ASPECT OF.—Bankruptcy (*La banqueroute;* earlier English terms, *bankruptship, bankrupture*) in civil jurisprudence as well as in popular signification is the fact of becoming, or the state of being, a bankrupt. In the statute of 1705, 4 Anne, c. XVII, as printed in the Cambridge edition of the English Statutes, the word is spelled *bankrupcy*, but the statute of 1711, 10 Anne, c. XV, as printed in the same edition, and in the London edition, adopts the present spelling. Being derived from *bankrupt*, as insolvency is derived from insolvent, the retaining of the letter *t* has been suggested to be an instance of erroneous spelling (Murray, Dict., s. v. "Bankruptcy"). Etymologically, *bankrupt* has been said to be made up of the Latin words *bancus*, "table", and *ruptus*, "broken", denoting "the wreck or breakup of a trader's business" (Murray, Dict., loc. cit.), "whose shop or place of trade is broken up or gone" (Wharton, Law Lexicon, s. v. "Bankrupt").

Statutory mention of the word *bankrupt* seems to be earlier than that of the word *bankrupcy*, and is first to be found in the title of the English statute of 1542, "against such persons as do make bankrupt", a translation, perhaps, of the French "*qui font banque route*". (Blackstone, Commentaries, Bk. II, c. xxxi, p. 472, Note e). This statute recites that some "persons craftily obtaining into their hands great substance of other men's goods" either flee to parts unknown or keep their houses, not paying "their debts and duties", but consuming "the substance obtained by credit of other men for their own pleasure and delicate living". For distribution rateably of such persons' assets among their creditors this statute provides a summary method which, to quote Blackstone, is "extra judicial", "allowed merely for the benefit of commerce" (II Commentaries, 477). We learn, however, from the recitals of a statute of 1570 that, notwithstanding the law of 1542 "made against bankrupts", "those kind of persons have and do still increase". And therefore a new definition is made of a debtor who "shall be reputed, deemed and taken for a bankrupt", and subjected to an "extra-judicial" method. Such a debtor, it is enacted, must be a native-born subject or denizen who, being a "merchant or other person using or exercising the trade of merchandise", "or seeking his or her trade or living by buying and selling", shall have been guilty of certain specified fraud and concealment. The assets of such a debtor may, pursuant to this statute, be divided rateably among those of the creditors who are native-born subjects. Thus the limitation of meaning suggested by the explanation cited of its Latin etymology was placed upon the word bankrupt, and thereafter a trader only could be adjudged a bankrupt in England. Debtors who were not traders, and whose means were inadequate to payment of their debts in ordinary course of business, were known as insolvents. But statutory definitions of persons to be deemed occupied in trade became very comprehensive. Yet with special regard, apparently, for "noblemen, gentlemen and persons of quality" investing in the "East India Company or Guiney Company" and certain other enterprises, the imputation of being merchants or traders within any "statutes for bankrupts" is, by a statute of 1662, expressly spared to persons putting in money in these stocks. The circumstance of occupation is, under the present English Bankruptcy Act, immaterial. Aliens and denizens had been brought within the law by a statute of the year 1623.

By the law of Scotland bankruptcy is not limited to any particular occupation. But according to Scotch law insolvency, that is, inability to pay debts or fulfil obligations, does not become bankruptcy until, in manner determined by statute, this inability is publicly acknowledged, and is thus, as expressed in the statute, "notour". The purpose of the English Statutes of 1542 and 1570 did not extend beyond distribution of the bankrupt's property among his creditors. Right of recourse against the debtor by ordinary process of law for any remaining indebtedness these statutes expressly preserved. But by the statute of 1705 a bankrupt, duly surrendering all his effects and conforming to the law, might obtain his discharge from liability for debts theretofore contracted. And more modern statutes permit a debtor himself to institute proceedings in bankruptcy. The Scotch law now permits a "notour bankrupt" to apply for what is termed a decree of *cessio bonorum*, by which he may be discharged from his debts.

The Constitution of the United States (Art. I, § 8) confers upon Congress power to "establish uniform laws on the subject of bankruptcies throughout the United States". Under this provision Congress may disregard any distinction between bankruptcy and insolvency laws, of which laws Chief Justice Marshall remarks (Wheaton's Reports, IV, 194) that the line of partition between them is not so distinctly marked as to enable any person to say with positive precision what belongs exclusively to the one and not to the other class of laws. Originally, however, insolvency laws and bankruptcy laws were prompted by opposite motives and were clearly distinguishable. The motive of insolvency laws was the relief of insolvent debtors, by affording them a remedy against imprisonment and, in ancient Rome, other penalties. On the contrary, the motive of bankruptcy laws was, as already seen, the relief of creditors by affording a remedy against dishonest debtors who might possibly not be insolvent, but whose conduct while indebted was deemed to be such as to entitle their creditors to the summary relief which the law "made against bankrupts" afforded. English as well as Roman insolvency laws contemplated the cases of debtors whom ordinary process of law could reach, but the operation of the English statute of 1542 is limited to debtors who "make bankrupt" and against whom such process was ineffectual, and the statute of 1570 is further limited to traders. The court afterwards established, in the reign of George III, for cases of insolvency was "the Court for relief of insolvent debtors"; but bankrupt laws, remarks Sir Edward Coke, are to be construed "for the aid, help, and relief of the creditors". And under certain circumstances a solvent debtor may by the United States law be pronounced a bankrupt.

Congress has passed four bankruptcy laws; the Act passed 4 April, 1800, which was repealed by Act of 19 December, 1803; the Act passed 19 August, 1841, repealed by Act of 3 March, 1843; the Act passed 2 March, 1867, and repealed 7 June, 1878, and the Act of 1 July, 1898, yet (1907) in force.

At the time of the adoption of the United States Constitution a suggestion was rejected that the power of Congress concerning bankruptcy should be confined to merchants and traders. Yet by the Act of 1800 only a merchant or other person resident in the United States and "actually using the trade of merchandise by buying and selling in gross, or by retail, or dealing in exchange or as a banker, broker, factor, underwriter, or marine insurer" could be adjudged a bankrupt. Voluntary bankruptcy is not mentioned in the Act of 1800, but by the Act of 1841 "all persons" residing in any State, District, or Territory of the United States owing debts not incurred through defalcation as a public officer or in a fiduciary capacity might apply to become voluntary bankrupts. Involuntary bankruptcy was still restricted to merchants and certain other classes of business men. The Act of 1867 provided for both voluntary and involuntary bankruptcy without regard to the debtor's occupation. By the Act of 1898, the several District Courts of the United States, the Supreme Court of the District of Columbia, the District Courts of the several Territories, and the United States Courts in the Indian Territory and the District of Alaska are made courts of bankruptcy. A person is within this Act insolvent whose property (exclusive of property wrongfully conveyed, transferred, concealed, or removed) is at a fair valuation insufficient to pay his debts. Any natural person or unincorporated company or business corporation as defined in the Act, and owing at least one thousand dollars (except certain natural persons specified), may be adjudged an involuntary bankrupt. Proceedings in involuntary bankruptcy are to be instituted by petition filed within four months after an act of bankruptcy. Such an act consists in conveying, transferring, concealing, or removing, or permitting to be concealed or removed, any of the debtor's property with intent to hinder, delay, or defraud his creditors or any of them; or in transferring while insolvent any property with intent to prefer a creditor or creditors; or in suffering or permitting, while insolvent, any creditor to obtain a preference through legal proceedings or in not having such preference vacated or discharged. So a general assignment for benefit of creditors and certain proceedings under Insolvent Laws, or application by an insolvent for a receiver or trustee are acts of bankruptcy. On the other hand, "any qualified person", namely, any person who owes debts provable in bankruptcy (except a corporation) "may file a petition to be adjudged a voluntary bankrupt". The assets of the bankrupt are to be divided among his creditors, and the court of bankruptcy is empowered to grant him a discharge, that is, a "release . . . from all of his debts which are provable in bankruptcy, except such as are excepted by this Act".

The power conferred on Congress by the Constitution does not wholly preclude the several States of the Union from passing bankruptcy laws. A State may enact such laws conclusive as to the rights of its own citizens, provided such laws do not impair the obligation of contracts within the meaning of the Constitution, nor conflict with any existing Act of Congress establishing a uniform system of bankruptcy.

So far we have considered our subject from a legal point of view. From the point of view of the political economist, bankruptcy and insolvency laws are of great importance. For cost of production of goods includes risk of bad debts, and therefore laws lessening this risk decrease the cost of production. John Stuart Mill concludes that most individual insolvencies are the result of misconduct. But the occurrence of many business failures in a community at any period is a warning or symptom of "the politico-economical disease" which economists denominate a commercial crisis, and for this deeper causes are sought than mere individual misconduct. By fortuitous causes which could not have been foreseen the most skilful calculations may fail; demand for particular kinds of goods may lag behind a supply which has become excessive because of mistakes of the "captains of industry" as to extent of future demand. And there results a disarrangement of the relation between production and consumption, a disturbance of equilibrium, so that commercial settlements become impossible and a crisis ensues. Notable crises of modern times were: the crisis of Hamburg in 1799, when 82 failures occurred; the English crisis of 1814, when 240 banks suspended; in the United States, the "wild-cat" crisis of 1837, when all the banks closed, the crisis of 1857, when there occurred 7,200 failures, and the crisis of 1873. To economists, conditions of this kind, resulting from the causes just mentioned, have seemed to denote the necessity for the establishment of a new equilibrium. And it has been suggested that the Jewish jubilee was a means to that end, and an ordinance somewhat in the character of an insolvency or bankruptcy law.

A political community may fail, as may an individual, in meeting financial engagements. There may thus occur what has been termed state, or public, bankruptcy. Of this an ancient instance was the action of the Roman Senate in reducing the weight of the As after the first Punic War. And similar instances of governmental dishonesty occurred during the Middle Ages. In later times State bankruptcy has often taken the form of enforced conversion, involving partial repudiation, of the State debt. At the close of the reign of Louis XIV of France, the State was bankrupt, and to the celebrated John Law was vainly entrusted its financial rescue. The government set up by the French Revolution became not only bankrupt itself, but by its contest with Austria drove the latter empire into the bankruptcy of 1811. And the bankruptcy of Austria has even been said to have become permanent. Turkey, Spain, and some Spanish-American republics may be mentioned as States becoming bankrupt through repudiation. The same remark may be made concerning some of the States of the United States.

MURRAY, *New English Dictionary* (Oxford and New York, 1888); WHARTON, *Law Lexicon* (10th ed., London, 1902); STEPHEN, *New Commentaries on the Laws of England* (14th ed., London, 1903), II, 190, 215, 220; LAROUSSE, *Grand Dictionnaire universel du XIXe siècle* (Paris, 1867), s. v. *Banqueroute; La Grande Encycl.* (Paris), s. v. *Banqueroute; The Statutes at Large* (Cambridge, 1763–64), V, 132; VI, 271; VII, 288; VIII, 128; XI, 162; XII, 308; XVI, 340; *The Statutes at Large* (London, 1769), IV, 525; *Statutes of the United Kingdom* (London, 1813), 375; COKE, *The Fourth Part of the Institutes of the Laws of England* (London, 1797), 277; PARSONS, *The Law of Contracts* (8th ed.), III, 379, 383, 384, 385; STORY, *Commentaries on the Constitution of the United States* (4th ed., Boston, 1873), II, § 1113; *ibid.*, note 2, § 1106; WHEATON, *Reports: Supreme Court of the United States* (New York, 1819), IV, 208, and (New York, 1827), XII, 213; KENT, *Commentaries on American Law*, II, 389; *United States Statutes at Large* (Boston, 1848), II, 19 and 248; *ibid.*, V, 440 and 614; *ibid.* (Boston, 1868), XIV, 517, and (Washington, 1879) XX, 99; *United States Compiled Statutes, 1901* (St. Paul, 1902), III, 3418; *ibid.* (St. Paul, 1905, Supplement, 1905), 683; BRANDENBURG, *The Law of Bankruptcy* (2d ed., Chicago, 1901), 66; BELL, *Dictionary and Digest of the Law of Scotland* (7th ed., Edinburgh, 1890), s. vv. *Bankruptcy, Cessio bonorum;* BRODIE-INNES, *Comparative Principles of the Laws of England and Scotland* (Edinburgh, 1903), 25, 26; WILLIAMS, *The Law and Practice of Bankruptcy* (8th ed., London, 1904); MILL, *Principles of Political Economy* (New York, 1881), Bk. V, ix, § 8; ROSCHER, tr. LALOR, *Principles of Political Economy* (New York, 1878), Bk. IV, i, § 215; MULHALL, *The Dictionary of Statistics* (London, 1899), s. v. *Bankruptcy;* GIBBINS, *Industry in England* (2d ed., New York, 1898) §§ 259–260; CRABB, *English Synonyms* (New York, 1879), s. v. *Insolvency,* etc.

CHARLES W. SLOANE.

Bankruptcy, MORAL ASPECT OF.—Bankruptcy must be considered not only from the legal but also from the moral point of view; for sound mo-rality prescribes that debts must be paid. But a man who becomes bankrupt proclaims his inability to pay his debts in full as they become due. Such an acknowledgment does not now entail the penalty of slavery or of imprisonment as of old; the law takes possession of his property and divides it among his creditors. If it suffices after all to pay his creditors in full, there is an end of the matter, justice and conscience are satisfied. If, however, as is usually the case, the creditors only receive a portion of what is due to them, they have suffered loss through the action of the bankrupt, and if he is the voluntary cause of that loss, he is morally to blame as the cause of injustice to his neighbour. There is no moral blame attributable to a man who through misfortune and by no fault of his own has become bankrupt and unable to pay his debts. But if bankruptcy has been brought about by the debtor's own fault, he must be condemned in the court of morals, even if he escape without punishment in a court of law. Bankruptcy may be the result of one's own fault in a great variety of ways. Living beyond one's means, negligence or imprudence in the conduct of business, spending in betting and gambling money which is due to creditors are frequent causes of debtors appearing in the bankruptcy court. All such causes are accompanied with more or less of moral guilt, in proportion to the bankrupt's advertence to their probable consequences, and the voluntariness of his action.

Breaches of the moral law are also committed in a great variety of ways in connexion with bankruptcy itself. The benefit of the law is extended to the bankrupt debtor if he faithfully complies with all its just requirements. To do this then is a matter of conscience. He is bound to make a full disclosure of all his property, and to surrender it all for the benefit of his creditors. He may indeed retain what the law allows him to retain, but nothing else, unless the law makes no provision at all for him, and the result of surrendering everything would be to reduce himself and those dependent on him to destitution. Such a result, however, must not be readily presumed in the case of modern bankruptcy law which is humane in its treatment of the unfortunate debtor and makes what provision is necessary for him. It is obvious that it is against the rights of creditors and against justice for an insolvent debtor to transfer some of his property to his wife or to a friend, who will keep it for him till the storm blows over, so that the creditors cannot get at it. In the same way a debtor is guilty of dishonesty and fraud if he hide or remove some of his property, or if he allow a fictitious debt to be proved against the estate.

Loss is caused the creditors and injustice is committed by an insolvent debtor who continues to trade after the time when he fully recognizes that he is insolvent, and that there is no reasonable hope of recovering himself. He may continue to pay what debts he can as they become due if payment is demanded by his creditors, and he may make current payments for value received. But if in contemplation of bankruptcy he pays some creditor in full with a view to giving that creditor a preference over the others, he becomes guilty of a fraudulent preference. Bankruptcy law indeed prescribes that certain privileged debts should be paid in full, but it lays down that the rest must be paid rateably among the creditors without favour to any. If a bankrupt through favour pays a creditor in full, while the others have in consequence to be satisfied with less than their just share, he is guilty of fraud. This is not only the case if such payment is made after the petition in bankruptcy has been presented, but also if it is done within a certain period, fixed by law, before the presentation of the petition. In Great Britain this period is three months, in the United States it is four months previous to the adjudication. Laws forbidding such preferential payments are just, and they should be observed. If they have been violated, and the fact becomes known, the payments may be recovered by the trustee in bankruptcy or the official receiver. However, although fraudulent preferences are contrary to positive law, it is not clear that they are against natural justice so as to impose on the guilty parties an obligation in conscience apart from any order of the court to make restitution. The question is disputed among theologians, and some maintain that no obligation to make restitution can be imposed, apart from a positive order of the court, inasmuch as after all the preferred creditor has only got what belonged to him.

If the conduct of the bankrupt with reference to his bankruptcy has been such as the law requires, the court grants him a discharge; otherwise he will be subject to certain disabilities as an undischarged bankrupt. Some special debts and obligations are not affected by the discharge, and even with regard to those which it does affect, the question arises whether an absolute discharge extinguishes the debt, or merely releases the bankrupt from legal liability. The effect of such a judicial act depends on the law of the country. If that law expressly provides that a bankrupt who has obtained his discharge is not thereby freed from his former obligations, but merely protected against legal proceedings for debt, there is an end of the question. On the other hand, it cannot be denied that the law of a country may release an honest and unfortunate debtor from his load of indebtedness, and make him free to start business afresh. In commercial societies especially such an enactment might conduce to the public good, since it is not granted to fraudulent debtors but only to such as are honest and fulfil the rigorous requirements of the law. It is merely a question of fact as to what is the effect of the law of any particular country. Lawyers and theologians are agreed that in most countries the effect of a discharge is merely to bar legal proceedings for debt against the bankrupt. His moral obligation to pay all his debts in full when he is able still remains; he may put off payment till such time as he can conveniently fulfil his obligations, and in the meanwhile he is guaranteed freedom from molestation. This seems to be the effect of the National Bankruptcy Law of the United States. "Since the discharge is personal to the bankrupt, he may waive it, and since it does not destroy the debt but merely releases him from liability, that is, removes the legal obligation to pay the debt, leaving the moral obligation unaffected, such moral obligation is a sufficient consideration to support a new promise" (Brandenburg, The Law of Bankruptcy, 391).

On the contrary, an absolute discharge, when granted to the honest bankrupt according to English law, frees the bankrupt from his debts, with certain exceptions, and makes him a clear man again. This is admitted by English lawyers and by theologians who treat of the effect of the English law of bankruptcy. When, therefore, an honest bankrupt has obtained his absolute discharge in an English court, he is under no strict obligation, legal or moral, to pay his past debts in full, though if he choose to do so, his scrupulous rectitude will be much appreciated. What has been said about bankruptcy applies also to compositions or schemes of arrangement with one's creditors when they have received the sanction of the court.

Lugo, *De Justitia et Jure* (Paris, 1869), disp. xx; Lehmkuhl, *Theologia Moralis* (Freiburg, 1898), I, nn. 1026, 1035; Crolly, *De Justitia et Jure* (Dublin, 1870–77), III, n. 1232; *Am. Eccl. Review* (Philadelphia) xxxi, 348.

T. Slater.

Banns of Marriage (Lat. *bannum*, pl. *bann-a, -i* from an Old English verb, *bannan*, to summon), in general the ecclesiastical announcement of the names of persons contemplating marriage. Its object is to discover any impediments to a proposed marriage; incidentally, it makes known to all duly interested in the latter the fact of its near celebration. The subject will be treated under the following heads: I. History; II. Tridentine Legislation; III. Mode of Publication; IV. Denunciation of Impediments; V. Sanctions; VI. Dispensation from Banns; VII. Non-Catholic Usage; VIII. Civil Law.

I. History.—From the beginning of Christian society the marriage of its members was looked on as a public religious act, subject to ecclesiastical control (Tertull., "De monog.", c. xi; "De pudicitia", c. iv). The obligation of making known to the bishop all proposed marriages dates as far back as the beginning of the second century (Ignat. ad Polyc., c. v), and ceased only when, in the fifth and succeeding centuries, owing to the development of the parochial system, it became the duty of the parish priest to prevent invalid or illicit marriages, in which duty he could and did avail himself of the aid of reputable parishioners (Capitula Caroli imp., *ad an.* 802, ed. Boretius in Mon. Germ. Hist.: Leges, I, 98). The publication in the church of the names of persons intending marriage seems to have originated in France about the end of the twelfth century; it was already a custom of the Gallican Church in 1215, when Innocent III mentions it in a letter to the Bishop of Beauvais (c. 27, x, iv, 1). In the same year the Fourth Lateran Council made it a general ecclesiastical law (c. 3, x, De clandest. desponsat., iv, 3). The Council of Trent confirmed this law, and specified to a certain extent the manner of its execution. It must be noted that by the council's own special act its marriage decree "Tametsi", with its provision for the banns (see Clandestinity), is binding only in those parishes in which it has been severally promulgated; hence, when such formal promulgation is lacking the obligation of proclaiming the banns rests not on the Tridentine law, but on the earlier Lateran canon, also on local or particular ecclesiastical legislation and custom. (See Marriage.) In England the First Council of Westminster provided (xxii, 2) that the law of publishing in the church the banns of marriage must be observed, but made no provision for the manner and time of introducing the practice (Taunton). In the United States the Sixth Provincial Council of Baltimore recommended the bishops of the province to introduce the law of the banns as laid down by the Councils of Lateran and Trent (*juxta mentem concilii Lateranensis et Tridentini*). The First Plenary Council of Baltimore (1852) decreed (no. 88) that after Easter of 1853 the banns should everywhere be published, and dispensation given only for very grave reasons. The Second Plenary Council (1866) confirmed the above (nos. 331–333) and declared the law a very useful and already received by custom (*saluberrima disciplina jam usu recepta*). According to Zitelli (Apparatus juris eccl., 403), at least one publication should be made in those regions and parishes in which the marriage decree of the Council of Trent has not been published; Von Scherer remarks (p. 146, n. 14) that the pre-Tridentine or Lateran law demanded no more than one publication. It is of some interest to note that by a decree of the Sacred Congregation of the Inquisition (14 June, 1703) the French missionaries in Canada were obliged to publish the banns for their savage converts.

II. TRIDENTINE LEGISLATION.—In order to check the increase of clandestine marriages, the Council of Trent decreed (Sess. XXIV, De ref. matr., c. i) that before the celebration of any marriage the names of the contracting parties should be announced publicly three times in the church during the solemnization of Mass, by their own parish priest on three consecutive Holy Days (Waterworth, The Canons and Decrees of the Sacred and Œcumenical Council of Trent, London, 1848, 196 sqq.). Such publication, of course, can be made only at the request of the parties themselves, and after the parish priest is aware of their mutual free consent. Moreover, the parish priest cannot refuse to publish the banns except for reasons stated in the canon law. If the contracting parties refuse to consent to the publication of the banns, the parish priest cannot assist at their marriage, and where the Tridentine legislation does not obtain he is bound to warn them not to attempt marriage elsewhere. In course of time this Tridentine decree has given occasion to more specific interpretation, regularly and primarily applicable where the decree has been promulgated. Among the more important authentic decisions are the following: The proper (own) parish priest of persons intending marriage is he in whose parish both (or one of) the contracting parties have a true domicile or quasi-domicile, i. e. a fixed residence or one that can be legally construed as such. When both parties permanently reside in the same parish no difficulty can arise as to the parish priest whose right and duty it is to publish the banns. But it may happen that one party resides in another parish, or that both parties have each more than one domicile or quasi-domicile, in which case the publication of the banns should occur, regularly speaking, in every parish where at the time of the marriage the parties retain such domicile or quasi-domicile. (See DOMICILE, PARISH PRIEST, MARRIAGE.) It may be noted here that while in general a quasi-domicile is acquired by actual residence in a place with the intention of remaining there the greater part of the year, in England and in the United States the law presumes a quasi-domicile from one month's residence of either party in the place of the marriage. (S. Congr. Inq. to the bishops of England and the United States, 7 June, 1867; see also its decree of 6 May, 1886). A decree of the same congregation (9 November, 1898) provides that anywhere a mere residence of six months shall constitute a quasi-domicile. In the case of unsettled persons possessed of no domicile (vagi) the banns are published (with episcopal permission) where the marriage takes place, and in the place or places of their birth. The banns of minors must also be published in the place of residence of their parents or guardians. The law of quasi-domicile is also frequently applicable to servants, apprentices, soldiers, and students in institutions of learning. In the case of mixed marriages, publication of the banns is forbidden (Greg. XVI to the bishops of Bavaria, 12 September, 1834), but is tolerated in the United States by a decree of the Congregation of Propaganda (3 July, 1847), provided there be no mention of the religious persuasion (confessio acatholica) of the non-Catholic party (see also S. Congr. Inq., 4 July, 1874, in Collectanea S. Congr. de Prop. Fide, Rome, 1893, no. 1223). In Germany and Austria this is also customary in some places (Heiner). The three consecutive Holy Days (dies festivi) may be Sundays or other feasts of obligation. Custom has in many places exempted Christmas, Easter, and Pentecost. It is also customary in some places to proclaim the banns on suppressed feast days, also at Vespers, provided there be on such occasions a considerable attendance of people in the church (S. Congr. Inq., 25 October, 1586; 29 April, 1823). The banns are published regularly at the parish or principal Mass, though the publication may occur at any other Mass on the prescribed days, nor is it required that such publication be repeated at more than one Mass on the aforesaid days. By a rescript of the Congregation of Propaganda the Vicars Apostolic of India were permitted to publish the banns on weekdays. In some places it is provided that the banns shall not be published on two immediately consecutive feast days; similarly that the marriage shall not take place on the day of the last publication (particularly if it be the only one). It may be noted that the general ecclesiastical law does not forbid the marriage on the day of the third publication. The period for which the publication of the banns is valid depends on local ecclesiastical authority and custom. The Roman Ritual (Tit. vii, c. i, n. 11) fixes a limit of two months, but leaves the bishop free to act as prudence dictates. The Second Provincial Council of Quebec (1863) established a period of two months. In practice the period varies from six weeks to six months. It may be added that the marriages of members of royal houses (matrimonia principum) are by custom exempted from publication of the banns.

III. MODE OF PUBLICATION.—The parish priest or his representative (vicar, curate) announces in an audible voice, usually before or after the sermon, for each of the contracting parties the baptismal and family name, names of parents, place of birth or residence, age, condition (single or previously married, and according to the Roman Ritual, loc. cit., n. 13, the name of the woman's former husband). It should also be stated whether the actual proclamation is the first, second, or third, and whether there will be a dispensation from further publications. The priest adds that a serious obligation rests on every one to reveal to him any known impediment to the proposed marriage. The parish priest is expected to keep a record or register of all publications of banns made by him, also the certificates of publications made at his request in other parishes, the fact and consequences of which he is entitled to know.

IV. DENUNCIATION OF IMPEDIMENTS.—Whoever is morally certain either by his own knowledge or through reliable persons, of an impediment (e. g. consanguinity, affinity, previous marriage) to an intended marriage, is in conscience bound to reveal it to the parish priest of the contracting parties; it then becomes the duty of such parish priest to investigate the statement made to him (usually under oath) and decide as to the character of the evidence; if a grave suspicion be aroused in him, he must refer the case to the bishop, who decides as to whether a dispensation can or cannot be granted. Confessors, lawyers, physicians, midwives, are not bound to reveal impediments known to them through the discharge of their official or professional duties, nor does an obligation rest on those who fear that to make known an impediment would cause grave detriment to themselves or their families, or who are aware that no good can result from their action, or know that the contracting parties have already made known the impediment. Once aware of the impediment, the parish priest must defer the marriage, refer the matter to the bishop, and, where the Tridentine marriage decree is not valid he ought to warn the parties not to attempt marriage elsewhere. For further details as to the obligation of revealing known impediments, see the moral theologians generally, especially the third book of Sanchez, "De Matrimonio", and the sixth volume of Ballerini-Palmieri, "Theologia Moralis" (Prato, 1894), also the "Bibliotheca Prompta" of Ferraris, s. v.

V. SANCTIONS.—Omission of the banns, even partial, makes a marriage illicit, but not invalid. The bishop may inflict on the contracting parties such ecclesiastical penance as he sees fit to impose, and he may also punish similarly the witnesses to the marriage. Should later on an impediment be discovered that renders the marriage null and void, they cannot hope, by the strict letter of the law, to obtain a dispensation, nor can they hope to have their marriage considered a putative or apparent one, entailing the legitimation of their children. The bishop is empowered by the law to inflict on the offending parish priest, besides other punishment, three years' suspension from his office; it is worth noting that a similar sanction was enjoined by the fifteenth century canon law of England (Lindwood's Provinciale, Oxford ed., 1679, p. 271).

VI. DISPENSATION FROM BANNS.—The Council of Trent allows the bishop to dispense with the publication of the banns, provided there be a sufficient reason; one such is indicated by the Council itself, i. e. fear of a malicious thwarting of the intended marriage. The vicar-general, vicar capitular, and administrator of a diocese may also dispense from the banns. In case the contracting parties belong to different dioceses, the permission of one bishop (usually the one in whose diocese the marriage takes place) is held sufficient by many canonists. In some countries, as in Bavaria, a mutual understanding to this effect exists. The bishop may also allow the deans or the parish priests to dispense from one or two publications. In many dioceses the parish priest is specially authorized to dispense from the banns for death-bed marriages; elsewhere this authority is delegated to the deans or the more centrally located parish priests. The parish priest may himself decide that the obligation of asking a dispensation no longer exists for him, i. e. in cases of urgent necessity when, on the one hand, he cannot reach the bishop and, on the other, the reasons are such that the latter would be bound to grant the dispensation. In all cases where the three publications are omitted, the contracting parties are regularly required to take the oath before the bishop (*juramentum de statu libero*) that they are not previously betrothed or married, and that they know of no impediment to their marriage (Clement X, Cum Alias, 21 August, 1670; Ballerini-Palmieri, VI, 716–718).

By a decision of the Congregation of the Inquisition (8 August, 1900) the bishop may delegate to the parish priest the performance of this duty. The banns are omitted in the case of revalidation of marriage (Sägmüller, 489) and secret marriages i. e. regularly performed in the church, but behind closed doors, and the record of which, together with the pertinent baptisms, is kept in a special book in the diocesan chancery (Ballerini-Palmieri, op. cit., VI, 778). Dispensation from all the banns is regularly granted only for a very urgent reason; less weighty reasons suffice for a dispensation from two publications or from one. Among the reasons recognized by the law, other than that mentioned by the Council of Trent, are: notable difference of age, or condition of life; peril of the good name of either party; the approach of Advent or Lent, when marriage cannot be solemnized; notable temporal or spiritual detriment; imminent departure of the bridegroom; etc. The diocesan chancery usually charges a fee to cover the clerical expenses, it being forbidden to make any charge for the dispensation itself (S. Cong. of Propaganda to the bishops of Ireland, 12 February, 1821; cf. its decree of 1750; also the Encyclical of 1768 to the same bishops, and Collectanea S. Cong. Prop. Fid., Rome, 1893, 1221). At times the parish priest collects a fee for the publication of banns (Von Scherer, 147); it is reckoned as one of his *jura stolæ*, or casual sources of revenue.

VII. NON-CATHOLIC USAGE.—The Orthodox Greek Church does not require publication of the banns; on the other hand, for every marriage the Greek priest requires regularly a special permission of the bishop; at Constantinople and in other archiepiscopal churches this permission is granted through the Chartophylax. As the presence of the priest is essential to the validity of a Greek marriage, clandestine unions are practically impossible. (For the Uniat Greeks in Italy the Tridentine decree is obligatory, having been published in Greek in all their parishes by order of Clement VIII and again by order of Benedict XIV; see Vering, 873). The German Lutheran churches provide for publication of the banns in a manner quite similar to the Catholic discipline (ibid., 874). In the Church of England the publication of the banns is a normal preliminary of marriage, both by ecclesiastical law and, as explained below, by civil statute. The Book of Common Prayer directs that the banns of all who are to be married shall be published on three several Sundays or Holy Days during the time of the morning service or of evening service (if there be no morning service) immediately after the second lesson. The form of publication is analogous to Catholic usage, and if the parties reside in different parishes, the banns must be published in both.

VIII. THE CIVIL LAW OF BANNS.—In several European countries the civil law insists by its own authority on the publication of banns; in Austria, for instance, all marriages performed without at least one publication of the banns, and in the parishes of both contracting parties, are declared invalid by the Civil Code (Vering, 862, note 23; Von Scherer, 161). In England, until 1753, there was no statutory publication of the banns; in that year was passed a marriage act, known as Lord Hardwicke's Act (26 Geo. II, c. xxxiii), which provided, among other essentials, that in the future the true names of all persons intending marriage should be published in the church, otherwise the marriage would be null and void. It was, however, expressly provided that the act should not apply across the seas; hence it never became a part of the English Common Law as received in the United States. The actual civil legislation in England dates mostly from the reign of George IV and Willian IV, and relieves Catholics and Dissenters from the obligation of having their banns published in the churches of the Establishment, as was the case after the passing of Lord Hardwicke's Act, though in other respects, and with considerable modifications, that act still governs the marriage contract in England; in substance it is the Tridentine decree. According to actual English statute legislation, a marriage in the Church of England is invalid without a previous due publication of the banns or a license from the proper ecclesiastical authority granted only within the church of the parish in which one of the parties shall have resided for fifteen days before the marriage. The true names of the parties must be published in an audible voice on three successive Sundays at the morning service after the second lesson, in the church of the parish in which the parties dwell, or with the bishop's consent, in a public chapel. The officiating clergyman is entitled to demand seven days' notice of the intended publication, with the names of the parties, place of abode, and the time they have lived there. The dissent of parents or guardians renders null and void the publication of the banns of minors. The banns or license are valid for a period of three months only. It is to be noted that the omission of the banns invalidates the marriage only when the omission is known and wilful. Non-Anglicans (Jews and Quakers excepted, as otherwise provided for) are freed from the obligations of banns or ecclesiastical license, but they must give notice to the registrar of the district within which the parties have lived for seven days previous. This notice is inscribed in a marriage notice book open to public inspection at all seasonable times, and thereafter suspended for twenty-one days in some conspicuous place in the registrar's office, and accompanied by a declaration as to absence of impediments, necessary consent of parents or guardians, etc. ("Encyclopedia of the Laws of England", London, 1897, II, 1–3; "American and English Encyclopedia of Law", 2d ed., 1901, XIX, 1190–93; Phillimore, "Ecclesiastical Law of the Church of England", 2d ed., London, 1895, II, 580 sqq.). For the publication of banns in the (Protestant) churches of Ireland and Scotland see W. P. Eversley, "The Law of the Domestic Relations" (2d ed., London, 1890). In most of the United States a license to marry must be obtained by the contracting parties; in Delaware and Ohio publication of the banns is equivalent to a license (H. J. Desmond, The Church and the Law, Chicago, 1898, 66). In all the provinces of the Dominion of Canada publication of the banns is required in default of a license to marry. In the Province of Quebec, in default of a license issued to non-Catholics, the publication of the banns is required on three Sundays or Holy Days with reasonable intervals, at morning service, or if none, at an evening service. If the parties belong to different churches, these publications must take place in each church. They must contain the names, surnames, qualities or occupation and domicile of the parties to be married, and whether they are of age or minors, also the names, surnames, occupations, and domicile of their fathers and mothers, and the name of the former husband or wife. A certificate of due publication of the banns is also required before the marriage, and mention is made of it in the Act of Marriage; this certificate must be signed by the person who published the banns, and must contain all the above details stated in the banns themselves. Such certificate is not required if the banns were published by the same person who performed the marriage. Unless the parties have an actual domicile of six months in the place of publication, the latter must occur in the place of last domicile in Lower Canada, or if out of Canada the officer must ascertain that no legal impediment exists. If the parties are under the authority of others the publication must take place in the domicile of such authority (R. S. Weir, The Civil Code of Lower Canada, Montreal, 1898, Nos. 57, 58, 130–134). In France the civil code prescribes the publication on two distinct Sundays of the names, occupations, domiciles, and names of parents of persons intending to marry. The marriage cannot take place until three days after the second publication; if a year is allowed to elapse there must be a fresh publication of the banns. Marriages contracted abroad between French subjects or between a French subject and a foreigner, but according to foreign law, are recognized in France. The publication of the banns, however, cannot be omitted under pain of invalidating the marriage.

For the history of banns see ESMEIN, *Le mariage en droit canonique* (Paris, 1891), I, 78; SCHULTE, *Handbuch des kath. Eherechts* (1855), 40; BINDER, *Vom kirchl. Aufgebot der Ehe* (1857); SCHINDLER, *Die Notwendigkeit und die Umstände des Eheaufgebots* (Warnsdorf, 1884); *Archiv f. kath. Kirchenrecht*, I, 129, 275; II, 546; IV, 391. All manuals of canon law and moral theology deal at more or less length with this subject, e. g. LAURENTIUS, *Instit. Jur. Eccl.* (Freiburg, 1903), Nos. 567–569; HEINER, *Grundriss des kath. Eherechts* (4th ed., 1900); SÄGMÜLLER, *Lehrb. des kan. Rechts* (Freiburg, 1900 sq.), 485–490; VERING, *Lehrbuch des kath. . . . Kirchenrechts* (Freiburg, 1893), 859–863; VON SCHERER, *Handbuch des Kirchenrechts* (Graz, 1898), II, 143–161. Cf. also FERRARIS, *Prompta bibliotheca can.*, s. v.; FEIJE, *De impedimentis et dispensat. matr.* (Louvain, 1874), 151–177; TAUNTON, *The Law of the Church* (London and St. Louis, 1906), s. v.; BALLERINI-PALMIERI, *Theologia Moralis* (Prato, 1894), VI, 427–447; GASPARRI, *Tractatus canon. de matrimonio* (2d ed., Rome, 1892).

THOMAS J. SHAHAN.

Banquet, EUCHARISTIC. See EUCHARIST, SYMBOLISM OF.

Bapst, JOHN, Jesuit missionary and educator, b. at La Roche, Fribourg, Switzerland, 17 December, 1815; d. at Mount Hope, Maryland, U. S. A., 2 November, 1887. At twelve he began his studies at the college of Fribourg, and on 30 September, 1835, entered the novitiate of the Society of Jesus. He was ordained priest, 31 December, 1846, after the usual course of studies and teaching. He arrived in New York in 1848 and, though ignorant of both English and Indian, was sent to minister to the Indians at Old Town, Maine. The inhabitants received him with every demonstration of joy, but he found them in a very degraded moral condition. They had been without a priest for twenty years, and he laboured zealously for their reformation. He founded several temperance societies in Maine. In 1850 he left Old Town for Eastport. His work immediately began to attract attention, both for its results among Catholics and the number of converts who were brought into the Church. As his missions covered a large extent of territory, he became generally known through the State. When the Know-Nothing excitement broke out he was at Ellsworth. Besides being disliked as a Catholic priest, he was particularly obnoxious because of his efforts to establish a Catholic school there. On 3 June his house was attacked, and on 5 June, 1854, in pursuance of an order of the Town Council, which was directed to be published in the papers, he was dragged out of the residence of one of his people, was tarred and feathered, and ridden on a rail to the woods outside the town, and ordered to leave the neighbourhood. Some accounts have it that there was an attempt to burn him to death, which, for some reason or other, was prevented. He recovered from his injuries and continued his work. The outrage at Ellsworth met with general condemnation. Father Bapst built the first church at Bangor, which was dedicated in 1856. He remained there for three years and was then sent to Boston as rector of the college which was at that time the house of higher studies for the Jesuit scholastics. He was afterwards superior of all the houses of Canada and New York, and subsequently superior of a Residence in Providence, R. I. In 1879 his mind began to fail, a result, it was thought, of the Ellsworth occurrence. His remains were interred at Woodstock, Maryland.

Woodstock Letters, XVI, 324; XVII, 218, 361; XVIII, 83, 129, 304; XX, 61, 241, 406; SHEA, *Hist. of the Catholic Church in U. S.* (New York, 1904).

T. J. CAMPBELL.

Baptism, one of the Seven Sacraments of the Christian Church, frequently called the "first sacrament", the "door of the sacraments", and the "door of the Church".

I. AUTHORITATIVE STATEMENT OF DOCTRINE.—At the outset we think it advisable to give two documents which express clearly the mind of the Church on the subject of baptism. They are valuable, also, as containing a summary of the main points to be considered in the treatment of this important matter. Baptism is defined positively in the one and negatively in the other. (a) The positive document is what is commonly designated as "The Decree for the Armenians" in the Bull "Exultate Deo" of Pope Eugene IV. It is often referred to as a decree of the Council of Florence. While it is not necessary to hold this decree to be a dogmatic definition of the matter and form and minister of the sacraments, it is undoubtedly a practical instruction, emanating from the Holy See, and as such, has full authenticity in a canonical sense, that is, it is authoritative. The decree speaks thus of Baptism: "Holy Baptism holds the first place among the sacraments, because it is the door of the spiritual life; for by it we are made members of Christ and incorporated with the Church. And since through the first man death entered into all, unless we be born again of water and the Holy Ghost, we cannot enter into the kingdom of Heaven, as Truth Himself has told us. The matter of this sacrament is true and natural water; and it is indifferent whether it be cold or hot. The form is: I baptize thee in the name of the Father and of the Son and of the Holy Ghost. We do not, however, deny that the words: Let this servant of Christ be baptized in the name of the Father and of the Son and of the Holy Ghost; or: This person is baptized by my hands in the name of the Father and of the Son and of the Holy Ghost, constitute true baptism; because since the principal cause from which baptism has its efficacy is the Holy Trinity, and the instrumental cause is the minister who confers the sacrament exteriorly, then if the act exercised by the minister be expressed, together with the invocation of the Holy Trinity, the sacrament is perfected. The minister of this sacrament is the priest, to whom it belongs to baptize, by reason of his office. In case of necessity, however, not only a priest or deacon, but even a layman or woman, nay, even a pagan or heretic can baptize, provided he observes the form used by the Church, and intends to perform what the Church performs. The effect of this sacrament is the remission of all sin, original and actual; likewise of all punishment which is due for sin. As a consequence, no satisfaction for past sins is enjoined upon those who are baptized; and if they die before they commit any sin, they attain immediately to the kingdom of heaven and the vision of God."

(b) The negative document we call the canons on baptism decreed by the Council of Trent (Sess. VII, De Baptismo), in which the following doctrines are anathematized: "The baptism of John (the Precursor) had the same efficacy as the baptism of Christ. True and natural water is not necessary for baptism, and therefore the words of Our Lord Jesus Christ 'Unless a man be born again of water and the Holy Ghost' are metaphorical. The true doctrine of the sacrament of baptism is not taught by the Roman Church. Baptism given by heretics in the name of the Father and of the Son and of the Holy Ghost with the intention of performing what the Church performs, is not true baptism. Baptism is free, that is, not necessary for salvation. A baptized person, even if he wishes it, cannot lose grace, no matter how much he sins, unless he refuses to believe. Those who are baptized are obliged only to have faith, but not to observe the whole law of Christ. Baptized persons are not obliged to observe all the precepts of the Church, written and traditional, unless of their own accord they wish to submit to them. All vows made after baptism are void by reason of the promises made in baptism itself; because by these vows injury is done to the faith which has been professed in baptism and to the sacrament itself. All sins committed after baptism are either forgiven or rendered venial by the sole remembrance and faith of the baptism that has been received. Baptism although truly and properly administered, must be repeated in the case of a person who has denied the faith of Christ before infidels and has been brought again to repentance. No one is to be baptized except at the age at which Christ was baptized or at the moment of death. Infants, not being able to make an act of faith, are not to be reckoned among the faithful after their baptism, and therefore when they come to the age of discretion they are to be rebaptized; or it is better to omit their baptism entirely than to baptize them as believing on the sole faith of the Church, when they themselves cannot make a proper act of faith. Those baptized as infants are to be asked when they have grown up, whether they wish to ratify what their sponsors had promised for them at their baptism; and if they reply that they do not wish to do so, they are to be left to their own will in the matter and not to be forced by penalties to lead a Christian life, except to be deprived of the reception of the Eucharist and of the other sacraments, until they reform." The doctrines here condemned by the Council of Trent, are those of various leaders among the early reformers. The contradictory of all these statements is to be held as the dogmatic teaching of the Church.

II. ETYMOLOGY.—The word *Baptism* is derived from the Greek word, βάπτω, or βαπτίζω, to wash or to immerse. It signifies, therefore, that laving is of the essential idea of the sacrament. Scripture uses the term *baptize* both literally and figuratively. It is employed in a metaphorical sense in Acts, i, 5, where the abundance of the grace of the Holy Ghost is signified, and also in Luke, xii, 50, where the term is referred to the sufferings of Christ in His Passion. Otherwise in the New Testament, the root word from which baptism is derived is used to designate the laving with water, and it is employed when speaking of Jewish lustrations, and of the baptism of John, as well as of the Christian Sacrament of Baptism (cf. Heb., vi, 2; Mark, vii, 4). In ecclesiastical usage, however, when the terms *Baptize*, *Baptism* are employed without a qualifying word, they are intended to signify the sacramental washing by which the soul is cleansed from sin at the same time that water is poured upon the body. Many other terms have been used as descriptive synonyms for baptism both in the Bible and Christian antiquity, as the laver of regeneration, illumination, the seal of God, the water of eternal life, the sacrament of the Trinity, etc. (cf. Bingham, Antiq. Eccl., IV). In English, the term *christen* is familiarly used for *baptize*. As, however, the former word signifies only the effect of baptism, that is, to make one a Christian, but not the manner and the act, moralists hold that "I christen" could probably not be substituted validly for "I baptize" in conferring the sacrament (Sabetti, n. 657; Lehmkuhl, n. 63; Amer. Eccl. Rev., V, I).

III. DEFINITION.—The Roman Catechism (Ad parochos, De bapt., 2, 2, 5) defines baptism thus: Baptism is the sacrament of regeneration by water in the word (*per aquam in verbo*). St. Thomas Aquinas (III, Q. lxvi, a. 1) gives this definition: "Baptism is the external ablution of the body, performed with the prescribed form of words." Later theologians generally distinguish formally between the physical and the metaphysical defining of this sacrament. By the former they understand the formula expressing the action of ablution and the utterance of the invocation of the Trinity; by the latter, the definition: "Sacrament of regeneration" or that institution of Christ by which we are reborn to spiritual life. The term "regeneration" distinguishes baptism from every other sacrament, for although penance revivifies men spiritually, yet this is rather a resuscitation, a bringing back from the dead, than a rebirth. Penance does not make us Christians; on the contrary, it presupposes that we have already been born of water and the Holy Ghost to the life of grace, while baptism on the other hand was instituted to confer upon men the very beginnings of the spiritual life, to transfer them from the state of enemies of God to the state of adoption, as sons of God. The definition of the Roman Catechism combines the physical and metaphysical definitions of baptism. "The sacrament of regeneration" is the metaphysical essence of the sacrament, while the physical essence is expressed by the second part of the definition, i. e. the washing with water (matter), accompanied by the invocation of the Holy Trinity (form). Baptism is, therefore, the sacrament by which we are born again of water and the Holy Ghost, that is, by which we receive in a new and spiritual life, the dignity of adoption as sons of God and heirs of God's kingdom.

IV. TYPES.—Having considered the Christian

meaning of the term "baptism", we now turn our attention to the various rites which were its fore-runners before the New Dispensation. Types of this sacrament are to be found among the Jews and Gentiles. Its place in the sacramental system of the Old Law was taken by circumcision, which is called by some of the Fathers "the laver of blood" to distinguish it from "the laver of water". By the rite of circumcision, the recipient was incorporated into the people of God and made a partaker in the Messianic promises; a name was bestowed upon him and he was reckoned among the children of Abraham, the father of all believers. Other forerunners of baptism were the numerous purifications prescribed in the Mosaic dispensation for legal uncleannesses. The symbolism of an outward washing to cleanse an invisible blemish was made very familiar to the Jews by their sacred ceremonies. But in addition to these more direct types, both the New Testament writers and the Fathers of the Church find many mysterious fore-shadowings of baptism. Thus St. Paul (I Cor., x) adduces the passage of Israel through the Red Sea, and St. Peter (I Pet., iii) the Deluge, as types of the purification to be found in Christian baptism. Other foreshadowings of the sacrament are found by the Fathers in the bathing of Naaman in the Jordan, in the brooding of the Spirit of God over the waters, in the rivers of Paradise, in the blood of the Paschal Lamb, during Old Testament times, and in the pool of Bethsaida, and in the healing of the dumb and blind in the New Testament.

How natural and expressive the symbolism of ex-terior washing to indicate interior purification was recognized to be, is plain from the practice also of the heathen systems of religion. The use of lustral water is found among the Babylonians, Assyrians, Egyptians, Greeks, Romans, Hindus, and others. A closer resemblance to Christian baptism is found in a form of Jewish baptism, to be bestowed on prose-lytes, given in the Babylonian Talmud (Döllinger, First Age of the Church). But above all must be considered the baptism of St. John the Precursor. John baptized with water (Mark, i) and it was a bap-tism of penance for the remission of sins (Luke, iii). While, then, the symbolism of the sacrament insti-tuted by Christ was not new, the efficacy which He joined to the rite is that which differentiates it from all its types. John's baptism did not produce grace, as he himself testifies (Matt., iii) when he declares that he is not the Messias whose baptism is to confer the Holy Ghost. Moreover, it was not John's baptism that remitted sin, but the penance that accompanied it; and hence St. Augustine calls it (De Bapt. contra Donat., V) "a remission of sins in hope". As to the nature of the Precursor's baptism, St. Thomas (III, Q. xxxviii, a. 1) declares: "The baptism of John was not a sacrament of itself, but a certain sacramen-tal as it were, preparing the way (*disponens*) for the baptism of Christ." Durandus calls it a sacrament, indeed, but of the Old Law, and St. Bonaventure places it as a medium between the Old and New Dis-pensations. It is of Catholic faith that the Pre-cursor's baptism was essentially different in its ef-fects from the baptism of Christ. It is also to be noted that those who had previously received John's baptism had to receive later the Christian baptism (Acts, xix).

V. INSTITUTION OF THE SACRAMENT.—That Christ instituted the Sacrament of Baptism is unquestion-able. Rationalists, like Harnack (Dogmengeschichte, I, 68), dispute it, only by arbitrarily ruling out the texts which prove it. Christ not only commands His Disciples (Matt., xxviii, 19) to baptize and gives them the form to be used, but He also declares explicitly the absolute necessity of baptism (John, iii): "Unless a man be born again of water and the Holy Ghost, he can not enter into the Kingdom of God." More-over, from the general doctrine of the Church on the sacraments, we know that the efficacy attached to them is derivable only from the institution of the Redeemer. When, however, we come to the question as to when precisely Christ instituted baptism, we find that ecclesiastical writers are not agreed. The Scriptures themselves are silent upon the subject. Various occasions have been pointed out as the prob-able time of institution, as when Christ was Himself baptized in the Jordan, when He declared the neces-sity of the rebirth to Nicodemus, when He sent His Apostles and Disciples to preach and baptize. The first opinion was quite a favourite with many of the Fathers and Schoolmen, and they are fond of referring to the sanctification of the baptismal water by con-tact with the flesh of the God-man. Others, as St. Jerome and St. Maximus, appear to assume that Christ baptized John on this occasion and thus in-stituted the sacrament. There is nothing, however, in the Gospels to indicate that Christ baptized the Pre-cursor at the time of His own baptism. As to the opinion that it was in the colloquy with Nicodemus that the sacrament was instituted, it is not sur-prising that it has found few adherents. Christ's words indeed declare the necessity of such an insti-tution, but no more. It seems also very unlikely that Christ would have instituted the sacrament in a secret conference with one who was not to be a herald of its institution.

The more probable opinion seems to be that bap-tism, as a sacrament, had its origin when Christ com-missioned His Apostles to baptize, as narrated in John, iii and iv. There is nothing directly in the text as to the institution, but as the Disciples acted evi-dently under the instruction of Christ, He must have taught them at the very outset the matter and form of the sacrament which they were to dispense. It is true that St. John Chrysostom (Hom., xxviii in Joan.), Theophylactus (in cap. iii, Joan.), and Ter-tullian (De Bapt., c. ii) declare that the baptism given by the Disciples of Christ as narrated in these chap-ters of St. John was a baptism of water only and not of the Holy Ghost; but their reason is that the Holy Ghost was not given until after the Resurrection As theologians have pointed out, this is a confusion between the visible and the invisible manifestation of the Holy Spirit. The authority of St. Leo (Ep. xvi ad Episc. Sicil.) is also invoked for the same opinion, inasmuch as he seems to hold that Christ instituted the sacrament when, after His rising from the dead, He gave the command (Matt., xxviii): "Go and teach . . . baptizing"; but St. Leo's words can easily be explained otherwise, and in another part of the same epistle he refers to the sanction of re-generation given by Christ when the water of baptism flowed from His side on the Cross; consequently, before the Resurrection. All authorities agree that Matt., xxviii, contains the solemn promulgation of this sacrament, and St. Leo does not seem to intend more than this. We need not delay on the arguments of those who declare baptism to have been necessarily established after Christ's death, because the efficacy of the sacraments is derived from His Passion. This would prove also that the Holy Eucharist was not instituted before His death, which is untenable. As to the frequent statement of the Fathers that the sacraments flowed from the side of Christ upon the Cross, it is enough to say that beyond the symbolism found therein, their words can be explained as re-ferring to the death of Christ, as the meritorious cause or perfection of the sacraments, but not necessarily as their time of institution.

All things considered, we can safely state, therefore, that Christ most probably instituted baptism before His Passion. For in the first place, as is evident from John, iii and iv, Christ certainly conferred baptism, at least by the hands of His Disciples, before His

Passion. That this was an essentially different rite from John the Precursor's baptism seems plain, because the baptism of Christ is always preferred to that of John, and the latter himself states the reason: "I baptize with water . . . [Christ] baptizeth with the Holy Ghost" (John, i). In the baptism given by the Disciples as narrated in these chapters we seem to have all the requisites of a sacrament of the New Law: (1) the external rite, (2) the institution of Christ, for they baptized by His command and mission, and (3) the conferring of grace, for they bestowed the Holy Ghost (John, i). In the second place, the Apostles received other sacraments from Christ, before His Passion, as the Holy Eucharist at the Last Supper, and Holy orders (Conc. Trid., Sess. XXVI, c. i). Now as baptism has always been held as the door of the Church and the necessary condition for the reception of any other sacrament, it follows that the Apostles must have received Christian baptism before the Last Supper. This argument is used by St. Augustine (Ep. clxiii, al. xliv) and certainly seems valid. To suppose that the first pastors of the Church received the other sacraments by dispensation, before they had received baptism, is an opinion with no foundation in Scripture or tradition and devoid of verisimilitude. The Scriptures nowhere state that Christ Himself conferred baptism, but an ancient tradition (Niceph., Hist. eccl., II, iii; Clem. Alex. Strom., III) declares that He baptized the Apostle Peter only, and that the latter baptized Andrew, James, and John, and they the other Apostles.

VI. MATTER AND FORM OF THE SACRAMENT.—(1) *Matter*. In all sacraments we treat of the matter and the form. It is also usual to distinguish the remote matter and the proximate matter. In the case of baptism, the remote matter is natural and true water. We shall consider this aspect of the question first. (a) It is of faith that true and natural water is the remote matter of baptism. In addition to the authorities already cited, we may also mention the Fourth Council of the Lateran (c. i). Some of the early Fathers, as Tertullian (De Bapt., i) and St. Augustine (Adv. Hær., xlvi and lix) enumerate heretics who rejected water entirely as a constituent of baptism. Such were the Gaians, Manichæans, Seleucians, and Hermians. In the Middle Ages, the Waldensians are said to have held the same tenet (Ewald, Contra Walden., vi). Some of the sixteenth century reformers, while accepting water as the ordinary matter of this sacrament, declared that when water could not be had, any liquid could be used in its place. So Luther (Tischr., xvii) and Beza (Ep., ii, ad Till.). It was in consequence of this teaching that certain of the Tridentine canons were framed. Calvin held that the water used in baptism was simply symbolic of the Blood of Christ (Instit., IV, xv). As a rule, however, those sects which believe in baptism at the present time, recognize water as the necessary matter of the sacrament. Scripture is so positive in its statements as to the use of true and natural water for baptism that it is difficult to see why it should ever be called in question. Not only have we the explicit words of Christ (John, iii, v), "Unless a man be born again of water", etc., but also in the Acts of the Apostles and the Epistles of St. Paul there are passages that preclude any metaphorical interpretation. Thus (Acts, x, 47) St. Peter says, "Can any man forbid water, that these should not be baptized?" In the eighth chapter of the Acts is narrated the episode of Philip and the eunuch of Ethiopia, and in verse 36 we read: "They came to a certain water; and the eunuch said: See, here is water: what doth hinder me from being baptized?" Equally positive is the testimony of Christian tradition. Tertullian (op. cit.) begins his treatise: "The happy sacrament of our water". Justin Martyr (Apol., I) describes the ceremony of baptism and declares: "Then they

are led by us to where there is water . . . and then they are laved in the water". St. Augustine positively declares that there is no baptism without water (Tr. xv in Joan.).

The remote matter of baptism, then, is water, and this taken in its usual meaning. Theologians tell us consequently that what men would ordinarily declare water is valid baptismal material, whether it be water of the sea, or fountain, or well, or marsh; whether it be clear or turbid; fresh or salty; hot or cold; coloured or uncoloured. Water derived from melted ice, snow, or hail is also valid. If, however, ice, snow, or hail be not melted, they do not come under the designation water. Dew, sulphur or mineral water, and that which is derived from steam are also valid matter for this sacrament. As to a mixture of water and some other material, it is held as proper matter, provided the water certainly predominates and the mixture would still be called water. Invalid matter is every liquid that is not usually designated true water. Such are oil, saliva, wine, tears, milk, sweat, beer, soup, the juice of fruits, and any mixture containing water which men would no longer call water. When it is doubtful whether a liquid could really be called water, it is not permissible to use it for baptism except in case of absolute necessity when no certainly valid matter can be obtained. On the other hand, it is never allowable to baptize with an invalid liquid. There is a response of Pope Gregory IX to the Archbishop of Trondhjem in Norway where beer (or mead) had been employed for baptism. The pontiff says: "Since according to the Gospel teaching, a man must be born again of water and the Holy Ghost, those are not to be considered validly baptized who have been baptized with beer" (*cervisia*). It is true that a statement declaring wine to be valid matter of baptism is attributed to Pope Stephen II, but the document is void of all authority (Labbe, Conc., VI). Those who have held that "water" in the Gospel text is to be taken metaphorically, appeal to the words of the Precursor (Matt., iii), "He shall baptize you in the Holy Ghost and fire". As "fire" must certainly be only a figure of speech here, so must "water" in the other texts. To this objection, it may be replied that the Christian Church, or at least the Apostles themselves, must have understood what was prescribed to be taken literally and what figuratively. The New Testament and church history prove that they never looked on fire as a material for baptism, while they certainly did require water. Outside of the insignificant sects of Seleucians and Hermians, not even heretics took the word "fire" in this text in its literal meaning. We may remark, however, that some of the Fathers, as St. John Damascene (Orth. Fid., IV, ix), concede this statement of the Baptist to have a literal fulfilment in the Pentecostal fiery tongues. They do not refer it, however, literally to baptism. That water alone is the necessary matter of this sacrament depends of course on the will of Him Who instituted it, although theologians discover many reasons why it should have been chosen in preference to other liquids. The most obvious of these is that water cleanses and purifies more perfectly than the others, and hence the symbolism is more natural.

(b) The proximate matter of baptism is the ablution performed with water. The very word "baptize", as we have seen, means a washing. Three forms of ablution have prevailed among Christians, and the Church holds them all to be valid because they fulfil the requisite signification of the baptismal laving. These forms are immersion, infusion, and aspersion. The most ancient form usually employed was unquestionably immersion. This is not only evident from the writings of the Fathers and the early rituals of both the Latin and Oriental Churches, but it can also be gathered from the Epistles of St. Paul, who speaks of baptism as a bath (Ephes., v, 26; Rom., vi, 4; Tit., iii, 5). In the Latin Church, immersion seems to have prevailed until the twelfth century. After that time it is found in some places even as late as the sixteenth century. Infusion and aspersion, however, were growing common in the thirteenth century and gradually prevailed in the Western Church. The Oriental Churches have retained immersion, though not always in the sense of plunging the candidate's entire body below the water. Billuart (De Bapt., I, iii) says that commonly the catechumen is placed in the font, and then water is poured upon the head. He cites the authority of Goar for this statement. Although, as we have said, immersion was the form of baptism that generally prevailed in the early ages, it must not thereby be inferred that the other forms of infusion and aspersion were not also employed and held to be valid. In the case of the sick or dying, immersion was impossible and the sacrament was then conferred by one of the other forms. This was so well recognized that infusion or aspersion received the name of the baptism of the sick (*baptismus clinicorum*). St. Cyprian (Ep. lxxvi) declares this form to be valid. From the canons of various early councils we know that candidates for Holy orders who had been baptized by this method seem to have been regarded as irregular, but this was on account of the culpable negligence supposed to be manifested in delaying baptism until sick or dying. That such persons, however, were not to be rebaptized is an evidence that the Church held their baptism to be valid. It is also pointed out that the circumstances under which St. Paul (Acts, xvi) baptized his jailor and all his household seem to preclude the use of immersion. Moreover, the acts of the early martyrs frequently refer to baptizing in prisons where infusion or aspersion was certainly employed.

By the present authorized ritual of the Latin Church, baptism must be performed by a laving of the head of the candidate. Moralists, however, state that in case of necessity, the baptism would probably be valid if the water were applied to any other principal part of the body, as the breast or shoulder. In this case, however, conditional baptism would have to be administered if the person survived (St. Alph., no. 107). In like manner they consider as probably valid the baptism of an infant in its mother's womb, provided the water, by means of an instrument, would actually flow upon the child. Such baptism is, however, later to be repeated conditionally, if the child survives its birth (Lehmkuhl, n. 61). It is to be noted that it is not sufficient for the water to merely touch the candidate; it must also flow, otherwise there would seem to be no real ablution. At best, such a baptism would be considered doubtful. If the water touches only the hair, the sacrament has probably been validly conferred, though in practice the safer course must be followed. If only the clothes of the person have received the aspersion, the baptism is undoubtedly void. The water to be employed in solemn baptism should also be consecrated for the purpose, but of this we shall treat in another section of this article. It is necessary in baptizing to make use of a threefold ablution in conferring this sacrament, by reason of the prescription of the Roman ritual. This necessarily refers, however, to the liceity, not to the validity of the ceremony, as St. Thomas (III, Q. lxvi, a. 8) and other theologians expressly state. The threefold immersion is unquestionably very ancient in the Church and apparently of Apostolic origin. It is mentioned by Tertullian (De cor. milit., iii), St. Basil (De Sp. S., xxvii), St. Jerome (Dial. Contra Luc., viii), and many other early writers. Its object is, of course, to honour the three Persons of the Holy Trinity in whose name it is conferred. That this threefold ablution was not considered necessary to

the validity of the sacrament, however, is plain. In the seventh century the Fourth Council of Toledo (633) approved the use of a single ablution in baptism, as a protest against the false trinitarian theories of the Arians, who seem to have given to the threefold immersion a significance which made it imply three natures in the Holy Trinity. To insist on the unity and consubstantiality of the three Divine Persons, the Spanish Catholics adopted the single ablution and this method had the approval of Pope Gregory the Great (I, Ep. xliii). The Eunomian heretics used only one immersion and their baptism was held invalid by the First Council of Constantinople (can. vii); but this was not on account of the single ablution, but apparently because they baptized in the death of Christ. The authority of this canon is, moreover, doubtful at best.

(2) *Form.*—The requisite and sole valid form of baptism is: "I baptize thee (or This person is baptized) in the name of the Father and of the Son and of the Holy Ghost." This was the form given by Christ to His Disciples in the twenty-eighth chapter of St. Matthew's Gospel, as far, at least, as there is question of the invocation of the separate Persons of the Trinity and the expression of the nature of the action performed. For the Latin usage: "I baptize thee", etc., we have the authority of the Council of Trent (Sess. VII, can. iv) and of the Council of Florence in the Decree of Union. In addition we have the constant practice of the whole Western Church. The Latins also recognize as valid the form used by the Greeks: "This servant of Christ is baptized", etc. The Florentine decree acknowledges the validity of this form and it is moreover recognized by the Bull of Leo X, "Accepimus nuper", and of Clement VII, "Provisionis nostræ". Substantially, the Latin and Greek forms are the same, and the Latin Church has never rebaptized Orientals on their return to unity. At one time some Western theologians disputed the Greek form, because they doubted the validity of the imperative or deprecatory formula: "Let this person be baptized" (*baptizetur*). As a matter of fact, however, the Greeks use the indicative, or enuntiative, formula: "This person is baptized" (βαπτίζεται, *baptizatur*). This is unquestionable from their Euchologies, and from the testimony of Arcudius (apud Cat., tit. ii, cap. i), of Goar (Rit. Græc. Illust.), of Martène (De Ant. Eccl. Rit., I) and of the theological compendium of the schismatical Russians (St. Petersburg, 1799). It is true that in the decree for the Armenians, Pope Eugene IV uses *baptizetur*, according to the ordinary version of this decree, but Labbe, in his edition of the Council of Florence seems to consider it a corrupt reading, for in the margin he prints *baptizatur*. It has been suggested by Goar that the resemblance between βαπτίζεται and *baptizetur* is responsible for the mistake. The correct translation is, of course, *baptizatur*.

In administering this sacrament it is absolutely necessary to use the word "baptize" or its equivalent (Alex. VIII, Prop. damn., xxvii), otherwise the ceremony is invalid. This had already been decreed by Alexander III (Cap. Si quis, I, x, De Bapt.), and it is confirmed by the Florentine decree. It has been the constant practice of both the Latin and Greek Churches to make use of words expressing the act performed. St. Thomas (III, Q. lxvi, a. 5) says that since an ablution may be employed for many purposes, it is necessary that in baptism the meaning of the ablution be determined by the words of the form. However, the words: "In the name of the Father", etc., would not be sufficient by themselves to determine the sacramental nature of the ablution. St. Paul (Coloss., iii) exhorts us to do all things in the name of God, and consequently an ablution could be performed in the name of the Trinity to obtain restoration of health. Therefore it is that in the form of this sacrament, the act of baptism must be expressed, and the matter and form be united to leave no doubt of the meaning of the ceremony. In addition to the necessary word "baptize", or its equivalent, it is also obligatory to mention the separate persons of the Holy Trinity. This is the command of Christ to His Disciples, and as the sacrament has its efficacy from Him Who instituted it, we can not omit anything that He has prescribed. Nothing is more certain than that this has been the general understanding and practice of the Church. Tertullian tells us (De Bapt., xiii): "The law of baptism (*tingendi*) has been imposed and the form prescribed: Go, teach the nations, baptizing them in the name of the Father and of the Son and of the Holy Ghost." St. Justin Martyr (Apol., I) testifies to the practice in his time. St. Ambrose (De Myst., IV) declares: "Unless a person has been baptized in the name of the Father and of the Son and of the Holy Ghost, he can not obtain the remission of his sins." St. Cyprian (Ad Jubaian.), rejecting the validity of baptism given in the name of Christ only, affirms that the naming of all the persons of the Trinity was commanded by the Lord (*in plenâ et adunatâ Trinitate*). The same is declared by many other primitive writers, as St. Jerome (IV, in Matt.), Origen (De Princ., i, ii), St. Athanasius (Or. iv, Contr. Ar.), St. Augustine (De Bapt., vi, 25). It is not, of course, absolutely necessary that the common names Father, Son, and Holy Ghost be used, provided the persons be expressed by words that are equivalent or synonymous. But a distinct naming of the Divine persons is required and the form: "I baptize thee in the name of the Holy Trinity", would be of more than doubtful validity. The singular form "In the name", not "names", is also to be employed, as it expresses the unity of the Divine nature. When, through ignorance, an accidental, not substantial, change has been made in the form (as *In nomine patriâ* for *Patris*), the baptism is to be held valid.

The mind of the Church as to the necessity of observing the trinitarian formula in this sacrament has been clearly shown by her treatment of baptism conferred by heretics. Any ceremony that did not observe this form has been declared invalid. The Montanists baptized in the name of the Father and the Son and Montanus and Priscilla (St. Basil, Ep. i Ad Amphil.). As a consequence, the Council of Laodicea ordered their rebaptism. The Arians at the time of the Council of Nicæa do not seem to have tampered with the baptismal formula, for that Council does not order their rebaptism. When, then, St. Athanasius (Or. ii, Contr. Ar.) and St. Jerome (Contra Lucif.) declare the Arians to have baptized in the name of the Creator and creatures, they must either refer to their doctrine or to a later changing of the sacramental form. It is well known that the latter was the case with the Spanish Arians and that consequently converts from the sect were rebaptized. The Anomæans, a branch of the Arians, baptized with the formula: "In the name of the uncreated God and in the name of the created Son, and in the name of the Sanctifying Spirit, procreated by the created Son" (Epiphanius, Hær., lxxvii). Other Arian sects, such as the Eunomians and Aetians, baptized "in the death of Christ". Converts from Sabellianism were ordered by the First Council of Constantinople (can. vii) to be rebaptized because the doctrine of Sabellius that there was but one person in the Trinity had infected their baptismal form. The two sects sprung from Paul of Samosata, who denied Christ's Divinity, likewise conferred invalid baptism. They were the Paulianists and Photinians. Pope Innocent I (Ad. Episc. Maced., vi) declares that these sectaries did not distinguish the Persons of the Trinity when baptizing. The Council of Nicæa (can. xix) ordered the rebaptism of Paulianists, and

the Council of Arles (can. xvi and xvii) decreed the same for both Paulianists and Photinians.

There has been a theological controversy over the question as to whether baptism in the name of Christ only was ever held valid. Certain texts in the New Testament have given rise to this difficulty. Thus St. Paul (Acts, xix) commands some disciples at Ephesus to be baptized in Christ's name: "They were baptized in the name of the Lord Jesus." In Acts, x, we read that St. Peter ordered others to be baptized "in the name of the Lord Jesus Christ". Those who were converted by Philip (Acts, viii) "were baptized in the name of Jesus Christ", and above all we have the explicit command of the Prince of the Apostles: "Be baptized every one of you in the name of Jesus Christ, for the remission of your sins" (Acts, ii). Owing to these texts some theologians have held that the Apostles baptized in the name of Christ only. St. Thomas, St. Bonaventure, and Albertus Magnus are invoked as authorities for this opinion, they declaring that the Apostles so acted by special dispensation. Other writers, as Peter Lombard and Hugh of St. Victor, hold also that such baptism would be valid, but say nothing of a dispensation for the Apostles. The most probable opinion, however, seems to be that the terms "in the name of Jesus", "in the name of Christ", either refer to baptism in the faith taught by Christ, or are employed to distinguish Christian baptism from that of John the Precursor. It seems altogether unlikely that immediately after Christ had solemnly promulgated the trinitarian formula of baptism, the Apostles themselves would have substituted another. In fact, the words of St. Paul (Acts, xix) imply quite plainly that they did not. For, when some Christians at Ephesus declared that they had never heard of the Holy Ghost, the Apostle asks: "In whom then were you baptized?" This text certainly seems to declare that St. Paul took it for granted that the Ephesians must have heard the name of the Holy Ghost when the sacramental formula of baptism was pronounced over them. The authority of Pope Stephen I has been alleged for the validity of baptism given in the name of Christ only. St. Cyprian says (Ep. ad Jubaian.) that this pontiff declared all baptism valid provided it was given in the name of Jesus Christ. It must be noted that the same explanation applies to Stephen's words as to the Scriptural texts above given. Moreover, Firmilian, in his letter to St. Cyprian, implies that Pope Stephen required an explicit mention of the Trinity in baptism, for he quotes the pontiff as declaring that the sacramental grace is conferred because a person has been baptized "with the invocation of the names of the Trinity, Father and Son and Holy Ghost". A passage that is very difficult of explanation is found in the works of St. Ambrose (Lib. I, De Sp. S., iii), where he declares that if a person names one of the Trinity, he names all of them: "If you say Christ, you have designated God the Father, by whom the Son was anointed, and Him Who was anointed Son, and the Holy Ghost in whom He was anointed." This passage has been generally interpreted as referring to the faith of the catechumen, but not to the baptismal form. More difficult is the explanation of the response of Pope Nicholas I to the Bulgarians (cap. civ; Labbe, VIII), in which he states that a person is not to be rebaptized who has already been baptized "in the name of the Holy Trinity or in the name of Christ only, as we read in the Acts of the Apostles (for it is one and the same thing, as St. Ambrose has explained)". As in the passage to which the pope alludes, St. Ambrose was speaking of the faith of the recipient of baptism, as we have already stated, it has been held probable that this is also the meaning that Pope Nicholas intended his words to convey (see another explanation in Pesch, Prælect. Dogm., VI, no. 389). What seems to confirm this is the same pontiff's reply to the Bulgarians (Resp. 15) on another occasion when they consulted him on a practical case. They inquired whether certain persons are to be rebaptized on whom a man, pretending to be a Greek priest, had conferred baptism? Pope Nicholas replies that the baptism is to be held valid "if they were baptized in the name of the supreme and undivided Trinity". Here the pope does not give baptism in the name of Christ only as an alternative. Moralists raise the question of the validity of a baptism in whose administration something else had been added to the prescribed form, as "and in the name of the Blessed Virgin Mary". They reply that such baptism would be invalid, if the minister intended thereby to attribute the same efficacy to the added name as to the names of the Three Divine Persons. If, however, it was done through a mistaken piety only, it would not interfere with the validity (S. Alph., n. 111).

VII. CONDITIONAL BAPTISM.—From the foregoing it is evident that not all baptism administered by heretics or schismatics is invalid. On the contrary, if the proper matter and form be used and the one conferring the sacrament really "intends to perform what the Church performs", the baptism is undoubtedly valid. This is also authoritatively stated in the decree for the Armenians and the canons of the Council of Trent already given. The question becomes a practical one when converts to the Faith have to be dealt with. If there were one authorized mode of baptizing among the sects, and if the necessity and true significance of the sacrament were uniformly taught and put in practice among them, there would be little difficulty as to the status of converts from the sects. But there is no such unity of teaching and practice among them, and consequently the particular case of each convert must be examined into when there is question of his reception into the Church. For not only are there religious denominations in which baptism is in all probability not validly administered, but there are those also which have a ritual sufficient indeed for validity, but in practice the likelihood of their members having received baptism validly is more than doubtful. As a consequence converts must be dealt with differently. If it be certain that a convert was validly baptized in heresy, the sacrament is not repeated, but the ceremonies which had been omitted in such baptism are to be supplied, unless the bishop, for sufficient reasons, judges that they can be dispensed with. (For the United States, see Conc. Prov. Balt., I.) If it be uncertain whether the convert's baptism was valid or not, then he is to be baptized conditionally. In such cases the ritual is: "If thou art not yet baptized, then I baptize thee in the name", etc. The First Synod of Westminster, England, directs that adult converts are to be baptized not publicly but privately with holy water (i. e. not the consecrated baptismal water) and without the usual ceremonies (Decr. xvi). Practically, converts in the United States are almost invariably baptized either absolutely or conditionally, not because the baptism administered by heretics is held to be invalid, but because it is generally impossible to discover whether they had ever been properly baptized. Even in cases where a ceremony had certainly been performed, reasonable doubt of validity will generally remain, on account of either the intention of the administrator or the mode of administration. Still each case must be examined into (S. C. Inquis., 20 Nov., 1878) lest the sacrament be sacrilegiously repeated.

As to the baptism of the various sects, Sabetti (no. 662) states that the Oriental Churches and the "Old Catholics" generally administer baptism accurately; the Socinians and Quakers do not baptize at all; the Baptists use the rite only for adults, and the efficacy of their baptism has been called in question owing to the separation of the matter and the form, for the latter is pronounced before the immersion takes place; the Congregationalists, Unitarians, and Universalists deny the necessity of baptism, and hence the presumption is that they do not administer it accurately; the Methodists and Presbyterians baptize by aspersion or sprinkling, and it may be reasonably doubted whether the water has touched the body and flowed upon it; among the Episcopalians many consider baptism to have no true efficacy and to be merely an empty ceremony, and consequently there is a well-grounded fear that they are not sufficiently careful in its administration. To this may be added, that Episcopalians often baptize by aspersion, and though such a method is undoubtedly valid if properly employed, yet in practice it is quite possible that the sprinkled water may not touch the skin. Sabetti also notes that ministers of the same sect do not everywhere follow a uniform method of baptizing. The practical method of reconciling heretics with the Church is as follows:—If baptism be conferred absolutely, the convert is to make no abjuration or profession of faith, nor is he to make a confession of his sins and receive absolution, because the sacrament of regeneration washes away his past offences. If his baptism is to be conditional, he must first make an abjuration of his errors, or a profession of faith, then receive the conditional baptism, and lastly make a sacramental confession followed by conditional absolution. If the convert's former baptism was judged to be certainly valid, he is only to make the abjuration or the profession of faith and receive absolution from the censures he may have incurred (Excerpta Rit. Rom., 1878). The abjuration or profession of faith here prescribed is the Creed of Pius IV, translated into the vernacular. In the case of conditional baptism, the confession may precede the administration of the rite and the conditional absolution be imparted after the baptism. This is often done as a matter of fact, as the confession is an excellent preparation for the reception of the sacrament (De Herdt, VI, viii; Sabetti, no. 725).

VIII. REBAPTISM.—To complete the consideration of the validity of baptism conferred by heretics, we must give some account of the celebrated controversy that raged around this point in the ancient Church. In Africa and Asia Minor the custom had been introduced in the early part of the third century of rebaptizing all converts from heresy. As far as can be now ascertained, the practice of rebaptism arose in Africa owing to decrees of a Synod of Carthage held probably between 218 and 222; while in Asia Minor it seems to have had its origin at the Synod of Iconium, celebrated between 230 and 235. The controversy on rebaptism is especially connected with the names of Pope St. Stephen and of St. Cyprian of Carthage. The latter was the main champion of the practice of rebaptizing. The pope, however, absolutely condemned the practice, and commanded that heretics on entering the Church should receive only the imposition of hands *in pœnitentiam*. In this celebrated controversy it is to be noted that Pope Stephen declares that he is upholding the primitive custom when he declares for the validity of baptism conferred by heretics. Cyprian, on the contrary, implicitly admits that antiquity is against his own practice, but stoutly maintains that it is more in accordance with an enlightened study of the subject. The tradition against him he declares to be "a human and unlawful tradition". Neither Cyprian, however, nor his zealous abettor, Firmilian, could show that rebaptism was older than the century in which they were living. The contemporaneous but anonymous author of the book "De Rebaptismate" says that the ordinances of

Pope Stephen, forbidding the rebaptism of converts, are in accordance with antiquity and ecclesiastical tradition, and are consecrated as an ancient, memorable, and solemn observance of all the saints and of all the faithful. St. Augustine believes that the custom of not rebaptizing is an Apostolic tradition, and St. Vincent of Lérins declares that the Synod of Carthage introduced rebaptism against the Divine law (*canonem*), against the rule of the universal Church, and against the customs and institutions of the ancients. By Pope Stephen's decision, he continues, antiquity was retained and novelty was destroyed (*retenta est antiquitas, explosa novitas*). It is true that the so-called Apostolic Canons (xlv and xlvi) speak of the non-validity of baptism conferred by heretics, but Döllinger says that these canons are comparatively recent, and De Marca points out that St. Cyprian would have appealed to them had they been in existence before the controversy. Pope St. Stephen, therefore, upheld a doctrine already ancient in the third century when he declared against the rebaptism of heretics, and decided that the sacrament was not to be repeated because its first administration had been valid. This has been the law of the Church ever since. The whole controversy on rebaptism is exhaustively treated by Hefele in the first volume of his history of church councils.

IX. NECESSITY OF BAPTISM.—Theologians distinguish a twofold necessity, which they call a necessity of means (*medii*) and a necessity of precept (*præcepti*). The first (*medii*) indicates a thing to be so necessary that, if wanting (though inculpably), salvation cannot be attained. The second (*præcepti*) is had when a thing is indeed so necessary that it may not be omitted voluntarily without sin; yet, ignorance of the precept or inability to fulfil it, excuses one from its observance. Baptism is held to be necessary both *necessitate medii* and *præcepti*. This doctrine is founded on the words of Christ. In John, iii, He declares: "Unless a man be born again of water and the Holy Ghost, he can not enter into the kingdom of God." Christ makes no exception to this law and it is therefore general in its application, embracing both adults and infants. It is consequently not merely a necessity of precept but also a necessity of means. This is the sense in which it has always been understood by the Church, and the Council of Trent (Sess. IV, cap. vi) teaches that justification cannot be obtained, since the promulgation of the Gospel, without the laver of regeneration or the desire thereof (*in voto*). In the seventh session, it declares (can. v) anathema upon anyone who says that baptism is not necessary for salvation. We have rendered *votum* by "desire" for want of a better word. The council does not mean by *votum* a simple desire of receiving baptism or even a resolution to do so. It means by *votum* an act of perfect charity or contrition, including, at least implicitly, the will to do all things necessary for salvation and thus especially to receive baptism. The absolute necessity of this sacrament is often insisted on by the Fathers of the Church, especially when they speak of infant baptism. Thus St. Irenæus (II, xxii): "Christ came to save all who are reborn through Him to God, infants, children, and youths" (*infantes et parvulos et pueros*). St. Augustine (III, De Animâ) says: "If you wish to be a Catholic, do not believe, nor say, nor teach, that infants who die before baptism can obtain the remission of original sin." A still stronger passage from the same doctor (Ep. xxviii, Ad Hieron.) reads: "Whoever says that even infants are vivified in Christ when they depart this life without the participation of His Sacrament (Baptism), both opposes the Apostolic preaching and condemns the whole Church which hastens to baptize infants, because it unhesitatingly believes that otherwise they can not possibly be vivified in Christ." St.

Ambrose (II De Abraham., c. xi) speaking of the necessity of baptism, says: "No one is excepted, not the infant, not the one hindered by any necessity." In the Pelagian controversy we find similarly strong pronouncements on the part of the Councils of Carthage and Milevis, and of Pope Innocent I. It is owing to the Church's belief in this necessity of baptism as a means to salvation that, as was already noted by St. Augustine, she committed the power of baptism in certain contingencies even to laymen and women. When it is said that baptism is also necessary, by the necessity of precept (*præcepti*), it is of course understood that this applies only to such as are capable of receiving a precept, viz. adults. The necessity in this case is shown by the command of Christ to His Apostles (Matt., xxviii): "Go and teach all nations, baptizing them", etc. Since the Apostles are commanded to baptize, the nations are commanded to receive baptism.

The necessity of baptism has been called in question by some of the Reformers or their immediate forerunners. It was denied by Wyclif, Bucer, and Zwingli. According to Calvin it is necessary for adults as a precept but not as a means. Hence he contends that the infants of believing parents are sanctified in the womb and thus freed from original sin without baptism. The Socinians teach that baptism is merely an external profession of the Christian faith and a rite which each one is free to receive or neglect. An argument against the absolute necessity of baptism has been sought in the text of Scripture: "Except you eat the flesh of the Son of man and drink his blood, you shall not have life in you" (John, vi). Here, they say, is a parallel to the text: "Unless a man be born again of water". Yet everyone admits that the Eucharist is not necessary as a means but only as a precept. The reply to this is obvious. In the first instance, Christ addresses His words in the second person to adults; in the second, He speaks in the third person and without any distinction whatever. Another favourite text is that of St. Paul (I Cor., vii): "The unbelieving husband is sanctified by the believing wife; and the unbelieving wife is sanctified by the believing husband; otherwise your children should be unclean; but now they are holy." Unfortunately for the strength of this argument, the context shows that the Apostle in this passage is not treating of regenerating or sanctifying grace at all, but answering certain questions proposed to him by the Corinthians concerning the validity of marriages between heathens and believers. The validity of such marriages is proved from the fact that children born of them are legitimate, not spurious. As far as the term "sanctified" is concerned, it can, at most, mean that the believing husband or wife may convert the unbelieving party and thus become an occasion of their sanctification. A certain statement in the funeral oration of St. Ambrose over the Emperor Valentinian II has been brought forward as a proof that the Church offered sacrifices and prayers for catechumens who died before baptism. There is not a vestige of such a custom to be found anywhere. St. Ambrose may have done so for the soul of the catechumen Valentinian, but this would be a solitary instance, and it was done apparently because he believed that the emperor had had the baptism of desire. The practice of the Church is more correctly shown in the canon (xvii) of the Second Council of Braga: "Neither the commemoration of Sacrifice [*oblationis*] nor the service of chanting [*psallendi*] is to be employed for catechumens who have died without the redemption of baptism." The arguments for a contrary usage sought in the Second Council of Arles (c. xii) and the Fourth Council of Carthage (c. lxxix) are not to the point, for these councils speak, not of catechumens, but of penitents who had died suddenly before their expiation was completed. It is true that some Catholic writers (as Cajetan, Durandus, Biel, Gerson, Toletus, Klee) have held that infants may be saved by an act of desire on the part of their parents, which is applied to them by some external sign, such as prayer or the invocation of the Holy Trinity; but Pius V, by expunging this opinion, as expressed by Cajetan, from that author's commentary on St. Thomas, manifested his judgment that such a theory was not agreeable to the Church's belief.

X. SUBSTITUTES FOR THE SACRAMENT.—The Fathers and theologians frequently divide baptism into three kinds: the baptism of water (aquæ or fluminis), the baptism of desire (flaminis), and the baptism of blood (sanguinis). However, only the first is a real sacrament. The latter two are denominated baptism only analogically, inasmuch as they supply the principal effect of baptism, namely, the grace which remits sins. It is the teaching of the Catholic Church that when the baptism of water becomes a physical or moral impossibility, eternal life may be obtained by the baptism of desire or the baptism of blood. (1) The baptism of desire (baptismus flaminis) is a perfect contrition of heart, and every act of perfect charity or pure love of God which contains, at least implicitly, a desire (votum) of baptism. The Latin word flamen is used because Flamen is a name for the Holy Ghost, Whose special office it is to move the heart to love God and to conceive penitence for sin. The "baptism of the Holy Ghost" is a term employed in the third century by the anonymous author of the book "De Rebaptismate". The efficacy of this baptism of desire to supply the place of the baptism of water, as to its principal effect, is proved from the words of Christ. After He had declared the necessity of baptism (John, iii), He promised justifying grace for acts of charity or perfect contrition (John, xiv): "He that loveth Me, shall be loved of my Father: and I will love him and will manifest myself to him." And again: "If any one love me, he will keep my word, and my Father will love him, and we will come to him, and will make our abode with him." Since these texts declare that justifying grace is bestowed on account of acts of perfect charity or contrition, it is evident that these acts supply the place of baptism as to its principal effect, the remission of sins. This doctrine is set forth clearly by the Council of Trent. In the fourteentn session (cap. iv) the council teaches that contrition is sometimes perfected by charity, and reconciles man to God, before the Sacrament of Penance is received. In the fourth chapter of the sixth session, in speaking of the necessity of baptism, it says that men cannot obtain original justice "except by the laver of regeneration or its desire" (voto). The same doctrine is taught by Pope Innocent III (cap. Debitum, iv, De Bapt.), and the contrary propositions are condemned by Popes Pius V and Gregory XII, in proscribing the 31st and 33rd propositions of Baius.

We have already alluded to the funeral oration pronounced by St. Ambrose over the Emperor Valentinian II, a catechumen. The doctrine of the baptism of desire is here clearly set forth. St. Ambrose asks: "Did he not obtain the grace which he desired? Did he not obtain what he asked for? Certainly he obtained it because he asked for it." St. Augustine (IV, De Bapt., xxii) and St. Bernard (Ep. lxxvii, ad H. de S. Victore) likewise discourse in the same sense concerning the baptism of desire. If it be said that this doctrine contradicts the universal law of baptism made by Christ (John, iii), the answer is that the lawgiver has made an exception (John, xiv) in favour of those who have the baptism of desire. Neither would it be a consequence of this doctrine that a person justified by the baptism of desire would thereby be dispensed from seeking after the baptism of water when the latter became a

possibility. For, as has already been explained the baptismus flaminis contains the votum of receiving the baptismus aquæ. It is true that some of the Fathers of the Church arraign severely those who content themselves with the desire of receiving the sacrament of regeneration, but they are speaking of catechumens who of their own accord delay the reception of baptism from unpraiseworthy motives. Finally, it is to be noted that only adults are capable of receiving the baptism of desire.

(2) The baptism of blood (baptismus sanguinis) is the obtaining of the grace of justification by suffering martyrdom for the faith of Christ. The term "laver of blood" (lavacrum sanguinis) is used by Tertullian (De Bapt., xvi) to distinguish this species of regeneration from the "laver of water" (lavacrum aquæ). "We have a second laver", he says "which is one and the same [with the first], namely the laver of blood." St. Cyprian (Ep. lxxiii) speaks of "the most glorious and greatest baptism of blood" (sanguinis baptismus). St. Augustine (De Civ. Dei, XIII, vii) says: "When any die for the confession of Christ without having received the laver of regeneration, it avails as much for the remission of their sins as if they had been washed in the sacred font of baptism." The Church grounds her belief in the efficacy of the baptism of blood on the fact that Christ makes a general statement of the saving power of martyrdom in the tenth chapter of St. Matthew: "Every one therefore that shall confess me before men, I will also confess him before my Father who is in heaven" (v. 32); and: "He that shall lose his life for me shall find it" (v. 39). It is pointed out that these texts are so broadly worded as to include even infants, especially the latter text. That the former text also applies to them, has been constantly maintained by the Fathers, who declare that if infants cannot confess Christ with the mouth, they can by act. Tertullian (Adv. Valent., ii) speaks of the infants slaughtered by Herod as martyrs, and this has been the constant teaching of the Church. Another evidence of the mind of the Church as to the efficacy of the baptism of blood is found in the fact that she never prays for martyrs. Her opinion is well voiced by St. Augustine (Tr. lxxiv in Joan.): "He does an injury to a martyr who prays for him." This shows that martyrdom is believed to remit all sin and all punishment due to sin. Later theologians commonly maintain that the baptism of blood justifies adult martyrs independently of an act of charity or perfect contrition, and, as it were, ex opere operato, though, of course, they must have attrition for past sins. The reason is that if perfect charity, or contrition, were required in martyrdom, the distinction between the baptism of blood and the baptism of desire would be a useless one. Moreover, as it must be conceded that infant martyrs are justified without an act of charity, of which they are incapable, there is no solid reason for denying the same privilege to adults. (Cf. Suarez, De Bapt., disp. xxxix.)

XI. UNBAPTIZED INFANTS.—The fate of infants who die without baptism must be briefly considered here. The Catholic teaching is uncompromising on this point, that all who depart this life without baptism, be it of water, or blood, or desire, are perpetually excluded from the vision of God. This teaching is grounded, as we have seen, on Scripture and tradition, and the decrees of the Church. Moreover, that those who die in original sin, without ever having contracted any actual sin, are deprived of the happiness of heaven is stated explicitly in the Confession of Faith of the Eastern Emperor Michael Palæologus, which had been proposed to him by Pope Clement IV in 1267, and which he accepted in the presence of Gregory X at the Second Council of Lyons in 1274. The same doctrine is found also in the Decree of Union of the Greeks, in the Bull "Lætentur Cœli" of Pope

Eugene IV, in the Profession of Faith prescribed for the Greeks by Pope Gregory XIII, and in that authorized for the Orientals by Urban VIII and Benedict XIV. Catholic theologians are unanimous, consequently, in declaring that infants dying without baptism, are excluded from the beatific vision; but as to the exact state of these souls in the next world they are not agreed. In speaking of souls who have failed to attain salvation, theologians distinguish the pain of loss (*pœna damni*), or privation of the beatific vision, and the pain of sense (*pœna sensus*). While it is certain that unbaptized infants must endure the pain of loss, it is not at all certain that they are subject to the pain of sense. St. Augustine (De Pecc. et Mer., I, xvi) held that they would not be exempt from the pain of sense, but at the same time he thought it would be of the mildest form. On the other hand, St. Gregory Nazianzen (Or. in S. Bapt.) expresses the belief that such infants would suffer only the pain of loss. Sfrondati (Nod. Prædest., I, i) declares that while they are certainly excluded from heaven, yet they are not deprived of natural happiness. This opinion seemed so objectionable to some French bishops that they asked the judgment of the Holy See upon the matter. Pope Innocent XI replied that he would have the opinion examined into by a commission of theologians, but no sentence seems ever to have been passed upon it.

Since the twelfth century, the opinion of the majority of theologians has been that unbaptized infants are immune from all pain of sense. This was taught by St. Thomas Aquinas, Scotus, St. Bonaventure, Peter Lombard, and others, and is now the common teaching in the schools. It accords with the wording of a decree of Pope Innocent III (III Decr., xlii, 3): "The punishment of original sin is the deprivation of the vision of God; of actual sin, the eternal pains of hell." Infants, of course, cannot be guilty of actual sin. As to the theory of some writers that infants may be saved also from the pain of loss by the faith of their parents, it is sufficiently evident that it is not in accord with the mind of the Church. It has been urged that, under the law of nature and the Mosaic dispensation, children could be saved by the act of their parents and that consequently the same should be even more easy of attainment under the law of grace, because the power of faith has not been diminished but increased. But this ignores the fact that infants are not said to be deprived of justification in the New Law through any decrease in the power of faith, but because of the promulgation by Christ of the precept of baptism which did not exist before the New Dispensation. Nor does this make the case of infants worse than it was before the Christian Church was instituted. While it works a hardship for some, it has undoubtedly improved the condition of most. Supernatural faith is now much more diffused than it was before the coming of Christ, and more infants are now saved by baptism than were justified formerly by the active faith of their parents. Moreover, baptism can more readily be applied to infants than the rite of circumcision, and by the ancient law this ceremony had to be deferred till the eighth day after birth, while baptism can be bestowed upon infants immediately after they are born, and in case of necessity even in their mother's womb. Finally it must be borne in mind that unbaptized infants are not unjustly deprived of heaven. The vision of God is not something to which human beings have a natural claim. It is a free gift of the Creator who can make what conditions He chooses for imparting it or withholding it. No injustice is involved when an undue privilege is not conferred upon a person. Original sin deprived the human race of an unearned right to heaven. Through the Divine mercy this bar to the enjoyment of God is removed by baptism; but if baptism be not conferred, original sin remains, and the unregenerated soul, having no claim on heaven, is not unjustly excluded from it.

As to the question, whether in addition to freedom from the pain of sense, unbaptized infants enjoy any positive happiness in the next world, theologians are not agreed, nor is there any pronouncement of the Church on the subject. Many, following St. Thomas (De Malo, Q. v, a. 3), declare that these infants are not saddened by the loss of the beatific vision, either because they have no knowledge of it, and hence are not sensible of their privation; or because, knowing it, their will is entirely conformed to God's will, and they are conscious that they have missed an undue privilege through no fault of their own. In addition to this freedom from regret at the loss of heaven, these infants may also enjoy some positive happiness. St. Thomas (In II Sent., dist. XXXIII, Q. ii, a. 5) says: "Although unbaptized infants are separated from God as far as glory is concerned, yet they are not separated from Him entirely. Rather are they joined to Him by a participation of natural goods; and so they may even rejoice in Him by natural consideration and love." Again (a. 2) he says: "They will rejoice in this, that they will share largely in the divine goodness and in natural perfections." While the opinion, then, that unbaptized infants may enjoy a natural knowledge and love of God and rejoice in it, is perfectly tenable, and indeed the more common opinion of the schools at present, yet it has not the certainty that would arise from a unanimous consent of the Fathers of the Church, or from a favourable pronouncement of ecclesiastical authority.

We may add here some brief remarks on the discipline of the Church in regard to unbaptized persons. As baptism is the door of the Church, the unbaptized are entirely without its pale. As a consequence: (1) Such persons, by the ordinary law of the Church, may not be buried in consecrated ground. This includes the infants of even Catholic parents. The reason of this regulation is given by Pope Innocent III (Decr., III, XXVIII, xii): "It has been decreed by the sacred canons that we are to have no communion with those who are dead, if we have not communicated with them while alive." By a decree, however, of the Second Plenary Council of Baltimore (No. 390), catechumens may receive ecclesiastical sepulture. This council also decrees (No. 389) that the custom of burying the unbaptized relatives of Catholics in the family sepulchres may be tolerated. (2) A Catholic may not marry an unbaptized person without dispensation, under pain of nullity. This impediment, as far as illicity is concerned, is derived from the natural law, because in such unions the Catholic party and the offspring of the marriage would, in most cases, be exposed to the loss of faith. The invalidity of such marriage, however, is a consequence only of positive law. For, in the beginning of Christianity, unions between the baptized and unbaptized were frequent, and they were certainly held valid. When, then, circumstances arise where the danger of perversion for the Catholic party is removed, the Church dispenses in her law of prohibition, but always requires guarantees from the non-Catholic party that there will be no interference with the spiritual rights of the partner of the union. (See IMPEDIMENTS OF MATRIMONY.) In general, we may state that the Church claims no authority over unbaptized persons, as they are entirely without her pale. She makes laws concerning them only in so far as they hold relations with the subjects of the Church.

XII. EFFECTS OF BAPTISM.—This sacrament is the door of the Church of Christ and the entrance into a new life. We are reborn from the state of slaves of sin into the freedom of the Sons of God. Baptism incorporates us with Christ's mystical body and makes us partakers of all the privileges flowing from the redemptive act of the Church's Divine Founder.

The principal effects of baptism are:

(1) The remission of all sin, original and actual. This is clearly contained in Holy Writ. Thus we read (Acts, ii, 2): "Be baptized every one of you in the name of Jesus Christ, for the remission of your sins; and you shall receive the Holy Ghost. For the promise is to you and to your children and to all that are far off, whomsoever the Lord our God shall call." We read also in the twenty-second chapter of the Acts of the Apostles (v. 16): "Be baptized, and wash away thy sins." St. Paul in the fifth chapter of his Epistle to the Ephesians beautifully represents the whole Church as being baptized and purified (v. 25 sq.): "Christ loved the Church, and delivered Himself up for it: that he might sanctify it, cleansing it by the laver of water in the word of life: that he might present it to Himself a glorious Church, not having spot or wrinkle, or any such thing; but that it should be holy and without blemish." The prophecy of Ezechiel (xxxvi, 25) has also been understood of baptism: "I will pour upon you clean water, and you shall be cleansed from all your filthiness" (*inquinamentis*), where the prophet is unquestionably speaking of moral defilements. This is also the solemn teaching of the Church. In the profession of faith prescribed by Pope Innocent III for the Waldensians in 1210, we read: "We believe that all sins are remitted in baptism, both original sin and those sins which have been voluntarily committed." The Council of Trent (Sess. V., can. v) anathematizes whomsoever denies that the grace of Christ which is conferred in baptism does not remit the guilt of original sin; or asserts that everything which can truly and properly be called sin is not thereby taken away. The same is taught by the Fathers. St. Justin Martyr (Apol., I, lxvi) declares that in baptism we are created anew, that is, consequently, free from all stain of sin. St. Ambrose (De Myst., iii) says of baptism: "This is the water in which the flesh is submerged that all carnal sin may be washed away. Every transgression is there buried." Tertullian (De Bapt., vii) writes: "Baptism is a carnal act in as much as we are submerged in the water; but the effect is spiritual, for we are freed from our sins." The words of Origen (In Gen., xiii) are classic: "If you transgress, you write unto yourself the handwriting [*chirographum*] of sin. But, behold, when you have once approached to the cross of Christ and to the grace of baptism, your handwriting is affixed to the cross and blotted out in the font of baptism." It is needless to multiply testimonies in the early ages of the Church. It is a point on which the Fathers are unanimous, and telling quotations might also be made from St. Cyprian, Clement of Alexandria, St. Hilary, St. Cyril of Jerusalem, St. Basil, St. Gregory Nazianzen, and others.

(2) But baptism not only washes away sin, it also remits the punishment of sin. This was the plain teaching of the primitive Church. We read in Clement of Alexandria (Pædagog., i) of baptism: "It is called a laver because we are washed from our sins: it is called grace, because by it the punishments which are due to sin are remitted." St. Jerome (Ep. lxix) writes: "After the pardon (*indulgentiam*) of baptism, the severity of the Judge is not to be feared." And St. Augustine (De Pecc. et Mer., II, xxviii) says plainly: "If immediately [after baptism] there follows the departure from this life, there will be absolutely nothing that a man must answer for [*quod obnoxium hominem teneat*], for he will have been freed from everything that bound him." In perfect accord with the early doctrine, the Florentine decree states: "No satisfaction is to be enjoined upon the baptized for past sins; and if they die before any sin, they will immediately attain to the kingdom of heaven and to the vision of God." In like manner the Council of Trent (Sess. V) teaches: "There is no cause of damnation in those who have been truly buried with Christ by baptism. . . . Nothing whatever will delay their entrance into heaven."

(3) Another effect of baptism is the infusion of sanctifying grace and supernatural gifts and virtues. It is this sanctifying grace which renders men the adopted sons of God and confers the right to heavenly glory. The doctrine on this subject is found in the seventh chapter on justification in the sixth session of the Council of Trent. Many of the Fathers of the Church also enlarge upon this subject (as St. Cyprian, St. Jerome, Clement of Alexandria, and others), though not in the technical language of later ecclesiastical decrees.

(4) Theologians likewise teach that baptism gives man the right to those special graces which are necessary for attaining the end for which the sacrament was instituted and for enabling him to fulfil the baptismal promises. This doctrine of the schools, which claims for every sacrament those graces which are peculiar and diverse according to the end and object of the sacrament, was already enunciated by Tertullian (De Resurrect., viii). It is treated and developed by St. Thomas Aquinas (III, Q. lxii, a. 2). Pope Eugene IV repeats this doctrine in the decree for the Armenians. In treating of the grace bestowed by baptism, we presume that the recipient of the sacrament puts no obstacle (*obex*) in the way of sacramental grace. In an infant, of course, this would be impossible, and as a consequence, the infant receives at once all the baptismal grace. It is otherwise in the case of an adult, for in such a one it is necessary that the requisite dispositions of the soul be present. The Council of Trent (Sess. VI, c. vii) states that each one receives grace according to his disposition and co-operation. We are not to confound an obstacle (*obex*) to the sacrament itself with an obstacle to the sacramental grace. In the first case, there is implied a defect in the matter or form, or a lack of the requisite intention on the part of minister or recipient, and then the sacrament would be simply null. But even if all these essential requisites for constituting the sacrament be present, there can still be an obstacle put in the way of the sacramental grace, inasmuch as an adult might receive baptism with improper motives or without real detestation for sin. In that case the person would indeed be validly baptized, but he would not participate in the sacramental grace. If, however, at a later time he made amends for the past, the obstacle would be removed and he would obtain the grace which he had failed to receive when the sacrament was conferred upon him. In such a case the sacrament is said to revive and there could be no question of rebaptism.

(5) Finally, baptism, once validly conferred, can never be repeated. The Fathers (St. Ambrose, Chrysostom, and others) so understand the words of St. Paul (Heb., vi, 4), and this has been the constant teaching of the Church both Eastern and Western from the earliest times. On this account, baptism is said to impress an ineffaceable character on the soul, which the Tridentine Fathers call a spiritual and indelible mark. That baptism (as well as Confirmation and Holy orders) really does imprint such a character, is defined explicitly by the Council of Trent (Sess. VII, can. ix). St. Cyril (Præp. in Cat.) calls baptism a "holy and indelible seal", and Clement of Alexandria (De Div. Serv., xlii), "the seal of the Lord". St. Augustine compares this character or mark imprinted upon the Christian soul with the *character militaris* impressed upon soldiers in the imperial service. St. Thomas treats of the nature of this indelible seal, or character, in the Summa (III, Q. lxiii, a. 2).

The early leaders of the so-called Reformation held very different doctrines from those of Christian antiquity on the effects of baptism. Luther (De Captiv. Bab.) and Calvin (Antid. C. Trid.) held that this sacrament made the baptized certain of the perpetual grace of adoption. Others declared that the calling to mind of one's baptism would free him from sins committed after it; others again, that transgressions of the Divine law, although sins in themselves, would not be imputed as sins to the baptized person provided he had faith. The decrees of the Council of Trent, drawn up in opposition to the then prevailing errors, bear witness to the many strange and novel theories broached by various exponents of the nascent Protestant theology.

XIII. MINISTER OF THE SACRAMENT.—The Church distinguishes between the ordinary and the extraordinary minister of baptism. A distinction is also made as to the mode of administration. Solemn baptism is that which is conferred with all the rites and ceremonies prescribed by the Church, and private baptism is that which may be administered at any time or place according to the exigencies of necessity. At one time solemn and public baptism was conferred in the Latin Church only during the paschal season and Whitsuntide. The Orientals administered it likewise at the Epiphany.

(a) The ordinary minister of solemn baptism is first the bishop and second the priest. By delegation, a deacon may confer the sacrament solemnly as an extraordinary minister. Bishops are said to be ordinary ministers because they are the successors of the Apostles who received directly the Divine command: "Go and teach all nations, baptizing them in the name of the Father and of the Son and of the Holy Ghost." Priests are also ordinary ministers because by their office and sacred orders they are pastors of souls and administrators of the sacraments, and hence the Florentine decree declares: "The minister of this Sacrament is the priest, to whom it belongs to administer baptism by reason of his office." As, however, bishops are superior to priests by the Divine law, the solemn administration of this sacrament was at one time reserved to the bishops, and a priest never administered this sacrament in the presence of a bishop unless commanded to do so. How ancient this discipline was, may be seen from Tertullian (De Bapt., xvii): "The right to confer baptism belongs to the chief priest who is the bishop, then to priests and deacons, but not without the authorization of the bishop." Ignatius (Ep. ad Smyr., viii): "It is not lawful to baptize or celebrate the agape without the bishop." St. Jerome (Contra Lucif., ix) witnesses to the same usage in his days: "Without chrism and the command of the bishop, neither priest nor deacon has the right of conferring baptism." Deacons are only extraordinary ministers of solemn baptism, as by their office they are assistants to the priestly order. St. Isidore of Seville (De Eccl. Off., ii, 25) says: "It is plain that baptism is to be conferred by priests only, and it is not lawful even for deacons to administer it without permission of the bishop or priest." That deacons were, however, ministers of this sacrament by delegation is evident from the quotations adduced. In the service of ordination of a deacon, the bishop says to the candidate: "It behooves a deacon to minister at the altar, to baptize and to preach." Philip the deacon is mentioned in Holy Writ (Acts, viii) as conferring baptism, presumably by delegation of the Apostles. It is to be noted that though every priest, in virtue of his ordination is the ordinary minister of baptism, yet by ecclesiastical decrees he cannot use this power licitly unless he has jurisdiction. Hence the Roman Ritual declares: "The legitimate minister of baptism is the parish priest, or any other priest delegated by the parish priest or the bishop of the place." The

Second Plenary Council of Baltimore adds: "Priests are deserving of grave reprehension who rashly baptize infants of another parish or of another diocese." St. Alphonsus (n. 114) says that parents who bring their children for baptism without necessity to a priest other than their own pastor, are guilty of sin because they violate the rights of the parish priest. He adds, however, that other priests may baptize such children, if they have the permission, whether express, or tacit, or even reasonably presumed, of the proper pastor. Those who have no settled place of abode may be baptized by the pastor of any church they choose.

(b) In case of necessity, baptism can be administered lawfully and validly by any person whatsoever who observes the essential conditions, whether this person be a Catholic layman or any other man or woman, heretic or schismatic, infidel or Jew. The essential conditions are that the person pour water upon the one to be baptized, at the same time pronouncing the words: "I baptize thee in the name of the Father and of the Son and of the Holy Ghost." Moreover, he must thereby intend really to baptize the person, or technically, he must intend to perform what the Church performs when administering this sacrament. The Roman Ritual adds that, even in conferring baptism in cases of necessity, there is an order of preference to be followed as to the minister. This order is: if a priest be present, he is to be preferred to a deacon, a deacon to a subdeacon, a cleric to a layman, and a man to a woman, unless modesty should require (as in cases of childbirth) that no other than the female be the minister, or again, unless the female should understand better the method of baptizing. The Ritual also says that the father or mother should not baptize their own child, except in danger of death when no one else is at hand who could administer the sacrament. Pastors are also directed by the Ritual to teach the faithful, and especially midwives, the proper method of baptizing. When such private baptism is administered, the other ceremonies of the rite are supplied later by a priest, if the recipient of the sacrament survives.

This right of any person whatsoever to baptize in case of necessity is in accord with the constant tradition and practice of the Church. Tertullian (De Bapt., vii) says, speaking of laymen who have an opportunity to administer baptism: "He will be guilty of the loss of a soul, if he neglects to confer what he freely can." St. Jerome (Adv. Lucif., ix): "In case of necessity, we know that it is also allowable for a layman [to baptize]; for as a person receives, so may he give." The Fourth Council of the Lateran (cap. Firmiter) decrees: "The Sacrament of Baptism . . . no matter by whom conferred is available to salvation." St. Isidore of Seville (can. Romanus de cons., iv) declares: "The Spirit of God administers the grace of baptism, although it be a pagan who does the baptizing." Pope Nicholas I teaches the Bulgarians (Resp. 104) that baptism by a Jew or a pagan is valid. Owing to the fact that women are barred from enjoying any species of ecclesiastical jurisdiction, the question necessarily arose concerning their ability to bestow valid baptism. Tertullian (De Bapt., xvii) strongly opposes the administration of this sacrament by women, but he does not declare it void. In like manner, St. Epiphanius (Hær., lxxix) says of females: "Not even the power of baptizing has been granted to them", but he is speaking of solemn baptism, which is a function of the priesthood. Similar expressions may be found in the writings of other Fathers, but only when they are opposing the grotesque doctrine of some heretics, like the Marcionites, Pepuzians, and Cataphrygians, who wished to make Christian priestesses of women. The authoritative decision of the Church, however, is plain. Pope Urban II (c. Super quibus, xxx, 4) writes: "It is true baptism if a woman in case of necessity baptizes a child in the name of the Trinity." The Florentine decree for the Armenians says explicitly: "In case of necessity, not only a priest or a deacon, but even a layman or woman, nay even a pagan or heretic may confer baptism." The main reason for this extension of power as to the administration of baptism is of course that the Church has understood from the beginning that this was the will of Christ. St. Thomas (III, Q. lxvii, a. 3) says that owing to the absolute necessity of baptism for the salvation of souls, it is in accordance with the mercy of God, who wishes all to be saved, that the means of obtaining this sacrament should be put, as far as possible, within the reach of all; and as for that reason the matter of the sacrament was made of common water, which can most easily be had, so in like manner it was only proper that every man should be made its minister. Finally, it is to be noted that, by the law of the Church, the person administering baptism, even in cases of necessity, contracts a spiritual relationship with the child and its parents. This relationship constitutes an impediment that would make a subsequent marriage with any of them null and void unless a dispensation were obtained beforehand. See AFFINITY.

XIV. RECIPIENT OF BAPTISM.—Every living human being, not yet baptized, is the subject of this sacrament.

(1) As regards adults there is no difficulty or controversy. Christ's command excepts no one when He bids the Apostles teach all nations and baptize them.

(2) Infant baptism has, however, been the subject of much dispute. The Waldenses and Cathari, and later the Anabaptists, rejected the doctrine that infants are capable of receiving valid baptism, and some sectarians at the present day hold the same opinion. The Catholic Church, however, maintains absolutely that the law of Christ applies as well to infants as to adults. When the Redeemer declares (John, iii) that it is necessary to be born again of water and the Holy Ghost in order to enter the Kingdom of God, His words may be justly understood to mean that He includes all who are capable of having a right to this kingdom. Now, He has asserted such a right even for those who are not adults, when He says (Matt., xix, 14): "Suffer the little children, and forbid them not to come to me: for the kingdom of heaven is for such." It has been objected that this latter text does not refer to infants, inasmuch as Christ says "to come to me". In the parallel passage in St. Luke (xviii, 15), however, the text reads: "And they brought unto him also infants, that he might touch them"; and then follow the words cited from St. Matthew. In the Greek text, the words βρέφη and προσέφερον refer to infants in arms. Moreover, St. Paul (Coloss., ii) says that baptism in the New Law has taken the place of circumcision in the Old. It was especially to infants that the rite of circumcision was applied by Divine precept. If it be said that there is no example of the baptism of infants to be found in Holy Writ, we may answer that infants are included in such phrases as: "She was baptized and her household" (Acts, xvi, 15); "Himself was baptized, and all his house immediately" (Acts, xvi, 33); "I baptized the household of Stephanus" (I Cor., i, 16).

The tradition of Christian antiquity as to the necessity of infant baptism is clear from the very beginning. We have given many striking quotations on this subject already, in dealing with the necessity of baptism. A few, therefore, will suffice here. Origen (in cap. vi, Ep. ad Rom.) declares: "The Church received from the Apostles the tradition of giving baptism also to infants". St. Augustine (Serm. xi, De Verb Apost.) says of infant baptism: "This the Church always had, always held; this she received from the faith of our ancestors; this she perseveringly guards even to the end." St. Cyprian (Ep. ad Fidum) writes: "From baptism and from grace . . . must not be kept the infant who, because recently born, has committed no sin, except, inasmuch as it was born carnally from Adam, it has contracted the contagion of the ancient death in its first nativity; and it comes to receive the remission of sins more easily on this very account that not its own, but another's sins are forgiven it." St. Cyprian's letter to Fidus declares that the Council of Carthage in 253 reprobated the opinion that the baptism of infants should be delayed until the eighth day after birth. The Council of Milevis in 416 anathematizes whosoever says that infants lately born are not to be baptized. The Council of Trent solemnly defines the doctrine of infant baptism (Sess. VII, can. xiii). It also condemns (can. xiv) the opinion of Erasmus that those who had been baptized in infancy, should be left free to ratify or reject the baptismal promises after they had become adult. Theologians also call attention to the fact that as God sincerely wishes all men to be saved, He does not exclude infants, for whom baptism of either water or blood is the only means possible. The doctrines also of the universality of original sin and of the all-comprehending atonement of Christ are stated so plainly and absolutely in Scripture as to leave no solid reason for denying that infants are included as well as adults.

To the objection that baptism requires faith, theologians reply that adults must have faith, but infants receive habitual faith, which is infused into them in the sacrament of regeneration. As to actual faith, they believe on the faith of another; as St. Augustine (De Verb. Apost., xiv, xviii) beautifully says: "He believes by another, who has sinned by another." As to the obligation imposed by baptism, the infant is obliged to fulfil them in proportion to its age and capacity, as is the case with all laws. Christ, it is true, prescribed instruction and actual faith for adults as necessary for baptism (Matt., xxviii; Mark, xvi), but in His general law on the necessity of the sacrament (John, iii) He makes absolutely no restriction as to the subject of baptism; and consequently while infants are included in the law, they cannot be required to fulfil conditions that are utterly impossible at their age. While not denying the validity of infant baptism, Tertullian (De Bapt., xviii) desired that the sacrament be not conferred upon them until they have attained the use of reason, on account of the danger of profaning their baptism as youths amid the allurements of pagan vice. In like manner, St. Gregory Nazianzen (Or. xl, De Bapt.) thought that baptism, unless there was danger of death, should be deferred until the child was three years old, for then it could hear and respond at the ceremonies. Such opinions, however, were shared by few, and they contain no denial of the validity of infant baptism. It is true that the Council of Neocæsarea (can. vi) declares that an infant cannot be baptized in its mother's womb, but it was teaching only that neither the baptism of the mother nor her faith is common to her and the infant in her womb, but are acts peculiar to the mother alone.

(3) This leads to the baptism of infants in cases of difficult parturition. When the Roman Ritual declares that a child is not to be baptized while still enclosed (clausus) in its mother's womb, it supposes that the baptismal water cannot reach the body of the child. When, however, this seems possible, even with the aid of an instrument, Benedict XIV (Syn. Diœc., vii, 5) declares that midwives should be instructed to confer conditional baptism. The Ritual further says that when the water can flow upon the head of the infant the sacrament is to be administered absolutely; but if it can be poured only on some other

part of the body, baptism is indeed to be conferred, but it must be conditionally repeated in case the child survives its birth. It is to be noted that in these last two cases, the rubric of the Ritual supposes that the infant has partly emerged from the womb. For if the fœtus was entirely enclosed, baptism is to be repeated conditionally in all cases (Lehmkuhl, n. 61). In case of the death of the mother, the fœtus is to be immediately extracted and baptized, should there be any life in it. Infants have been taken alive from the womb even forty-eight hours after the mother's death (Dub. Rev., no. 87). After the Cæsarean incision has been performed, the fœtus may be conditionally baptized before extraction if possible; if the sacrament is administered after its removal from the womb the baptism is to be absolute, provided it is certain that life remains. If after extraction it is doubtful whether it be still alive, it is to be baptized under the condition: "If thou art alive". Physicians, mothers, and midwives ought to be reminded of the grave obligation of administering baptism under these circumstances (Coppens, Lect., VI). It is to be borne in mind that according to the prevailing opinion among the learned, the fœtus is animated by a human soul from the very beginning of its conception (O'Kane, III, 18, etc.). In cases of parturition where the issue is a mass that is not certainly animated by human life, it is to be baptized conditionally: "If thou art a man".

(4) The perpetually insane, who have never had the use of reason, are in the same category as infants in what relates to the conferring of baptism, and consequently the sacrament is valid if administered. If at one time they had been sane, baptism bestowed upon them during their insanity would be probably invalid unless they had shown a desire for it before losing their reason. Moralists teach that, in practice, this latter class may always be baptized conditionally, when it is uncertain whether or not they had ever asked for baptism (Sabetti, no. 661). In this connexion it is to be remarked that, according to many writers, anyone who has a wish to receive all things necessary to salvation, has at the same time an implicit desire for baptism, and that a more specific desire is not absolutely necessary.

(5) Foundlings are to be baptized conditionally, if there is no means of finding out whether they have been validly baptized or not. If a note has been left with a foundling stating that it had already received baptism, the more common opinion is that it should nevertheless be given conditional baptism, unless circumstances should make it plain that baptism had undoubtedly been conferred (Sabetti, no. 662, 4). O'Kane (no. 214) says that the same rule is to be followed when midwives or other lay persons have baptized infants in case of necessity.

(6) The question is also discussed as to whether the infant children of Jews or infidels may be baptized against the will of their parents. To the general query, the answer is a decided negative, because such a baptism would violate the natural rights of parents, and the infant would later be exposed to the danger of perversion. We say this, of course, only in regard to the liceity of such a baptism, for if it were actually administered it would undoubtedly be valid. St. Thomas (III, Q. lxviii, a. 10) is very express in denying the lawfulness of imparting such baptism, and this has been the constant judgment of the Holy See, as is evident from various decrees of the Sacred Congregations and of Pope Benedict XIV (II Bullarii). We say the answer is negative to the general question, because particular circumstances may require a different response. For it would undoubtedly be licit to impart such baptism if the children were in proximate danger of death; or if they had been removed from the parental care and there was no likelihood of their returning to it; of if they

were perpetually insane; or if one of the parents were to consent to the baptism; or finally, if, after the death of the father, the paternal grandfather would be willing, even though the mother objected. If the children were, however, not infants, but had the use of reason and were sufficiently instructed, they should be baptized when prudence dictated such a course (Sabetti, no. 662). In the celebrated case of the Jewish child, Edgar Mortara, Pius IX indeed ordered that he should be brought up as a Catholic, even against the will of his parents, but baptism had already been administered to him some years before when in danger of death.

(7) As to children of Protestants in the United States, Kenrick (no. 28) and Sabetti (no. 662, 2) declare that it is not licit to baptize them against the will of their parents; for their baptism would violate parental right, expose them to the danger of perversion, and be contrary to the practice of the Church. Kenrick also strongly condemns nurses who baptize the children of Protestants unless they are in danger of death.

(8) Should a priest baptize the child of non-Catholic parents if they themselves desire it? He certainly can do so if there is reason to hope that the child will be brought up a Catholic (Conc. Prov. Balt., I, decr. x). An even greater security for the Catholic education of such child would be the promise of one or both parents that they themselves will embrace the Faith.

(9) Concerning baptism for the dead, a curious and difficult passage in St. Paul's Epistle has given rise to some controversy. The Apostle says: "Otherwise what shall they do that are baptized for the dead, if the dead rise not again at all? Why are they then baptized for them?" (I Cor., xv, 29). There seems to be no question here of any such absurd custom as conferring baptism on corpses, as was practised later by some heretical sects. It has been conjectured that this otherwise unknown usage of the Corinthians consisted in some living person receiving a symbolic baptism as representing another who had died with the desire of becoming a Christian, but had been prevented from realizing his wish for baptism by an unforeseen death. Those who give this explanation say that St. Paul merely refers to this custom of the Corinthians as an *argumentum ad hominem*, when discussing the resurrection of the dead, without approving the usage mentioned.

Archbishop Mac Evilly in his exposition of the Epistles of St. Paul, holds a different opinion. He paraphrases St. Paul's text as follows: "Another argument in favour of the resurrection. If the dead will not arise, what means the profession of faith in the resurrection of the dead, made at baptism? Why are we all baptized with a profession of our faith in their resurrection?" The archbishop comments as follows: "It is almost impossible to glean anything like certainty as to the meaning of these very abstruse words, from the host of interpretations that have been hazarded regarding them (see Calmet's Dissertation on the matter). In the first place, every interpretation referring the words 'baptized', or 'dead' to either erroneous or evil practices, which men might have employed to express their belief in the doctrine of the resurrection, should be rejected; as it appears by no means likely that the Apostle would ground an argument, even though it were what the logicians call an *argumentum ad hominem*, on either a vicious or erroneous practice. Besides, such a system of reasoning would be quite inconclusive. Hence, the words should not be referred to either the *Clinics*, baptized at the hour of death, or to the *vicarious* baptisms in use among the Jews, for their departed friends who departed without baptism. The interpretation adopted in the paraphrase makes the words refer to the Sacrament of Baptism, which all were obliged to approach with faith in the resurrection of the dead, as a necessary condition. '*Credo in resurrectionem mortuorum*'. This interpretation—the one adopted by St. Chrysostom—has the advantage of giving the words 'baptized' and 'dead' their literal signification. The only inconvenience in it is, that the word *resurrection* is introduced. But, it is understood from the entire context, and is warranted by a reference to other passages of Scripture. For, from the Epistle of the Hebrews (vi, 2) it appears that a knowledge of the faith of the resurrection was one of the elementary points of instruction required for adult baptism; and hence the Scriptures themselves furnish the ground for the introduction of the word. There is another probable interpretation, which understands the words 'baptism' and 'dead' in a metaphorical sense, and refers them to the sufferings which the Apostles and heralds of salvation underwent to preach the Gospel to the infidels, *dead* to grace and spiritual life, with the hope of making them sharers in the glory of a happy resurrection. The word 'baptism' is employed in this sense in Scripture, even by our divine Redeemer Himself,—'I have a *baptism* wherewith to be baptized', etc. And the word 'dead' is employed in several parts of the New Testament to designate those spiritually dead to grace and justice. In the Greek, the words 'for the dead', ὑπὲρ τῶν νεκρῶν that is, *on account of*, or, *in behalf of the dead*, would serve to confirm, in some degree, this latter interpretation. These appear to be the most probable of the interpretations of this passage; each, no doubt, has its difficulties. The meaning of the words was known to the Corinthians at the time of the Apostle. All that can be known of their meaning at this remote period, cannot exceed the bounds of probable conjecture" (loc. cit., chap. xv; cf. also Cornely in Ep. I Cor.).

XV. ADJUNCTS OF BAPTISM.—(1) *Baptistery.*—According to the canons of the Church, baptism except in case of necessity is to be administered in churches (Conc. Prov. Balt., I, Decree 16). The Roman Ritual says: "Churches in which there is a baptismal font, or where there is a baptistery close to the church". The term "baptistery" is commonly used for the space set aside for the conferring of baptism. In like manner the Greeks use φωτιστήριον for the same purpose—a word derived from St. Paul's designation of baptism as an "illumination". The words of the Ritual just cited, however, mean by "baptistery", a separate building constructed for the purpose of administering baptism. Such buildings have been erected both in the East and West, as at Tyre, Padua, Pisa, Florence, and other places. In such baptisteries, besides the font, altars were also built; and here the baptism was conferred. As a rule, however, the church itself contains a railed-off space containing the baptismal font. Anciently fonts were attached only to cathedral churches, but at the present day nearly every parish church has a font. This is the sense of the Baltimore decree above cited. The Second Plenary Council of Baltimore declared, however, that if missionaries judge that the great difficulty of bringing an infant to church is a sufficient reason for baptizing in a private house, then they are to administer the sacrament with all the prescribed rites. The ordinary law of the Church is that when private baptism is conferred, the remaining ceremonies are to be supplied not in the house but in the church itself. The Ritual also directs that the font be of solid material, so that the baptismal water may be safely kept in it. A railing is to surround the font, and a representation of St. John baptizing Christ should adorn it. The cover of the font usually contains the holy oils used in baptism, and this cover must be under lock and key, according to the Ritual.

(2) *Baptismal Water.*—In speaking of the matter of

baptism, we stated that true, natural water is all that is required for its validity. In administering solemn baptism, however, the Church prescribes that the water used should have been consecrated on Holy Saturday or on the eve of Pentecost. For the liceity (not validity) of the sacrament, therefore, the priest is obliged to use consecrated water. This custom is so ancient that we cannot discover its origin. It is found in the most ancient liturgies of the Latin and Greek Churches and is mentioned in the Apostolic Constitutions (VII, 43). The ceremony of its consecration is striking and symbolic. After signing the water with the cross, the priest divides it with his hand and casts it to the four corners of the earth. This signifies the baptizing of all the nations. Then he breathes upon the water and immerses the paschal candle in it. Next he pours into the water, first the oil of catechumens and then the sacred chrism, and lastly both holy oils together, pronouncing appropriate prayers. But what if during the year, the supply of consecrated water should be insufficient? In that case, the Ritual declares that the priest may add common water to what remains, but only in less quantity. If the consecrated water appears putrid, the priest must examine whether or not it is really so, for the appearance may be caused only by the admixture of the sacred oils. If it has really become putrid, the font is to be renovated and fresh water to be blessed by a form given in the Ritual. In the United States, the Holy See has sanctioned a short formula for the consecration of baptismal water (Conc. Plen. Balt., II).

(3) *Holy Oils.*—In baptism, the priest uses the oil of catechumens, which is olive oil, and chrism, the latter being a mixture of balsam and oil. The oils are consecrated by the bishop on Maundy Thursday. The anointing in baptism is recorded by St. Justin, St. John Chrysostom, and other ancient Fathers. Pope Innocent I declares that the chrism is to be applied to the crown of the head, not to the forehead, for the latter is reserved to bishops. The same may be found in the Sacramentaries of St. Gregory and St. Gelasius (Martène, I, i). In the Greek Rite the oil of catechumens is blessed by the priest during the baptismal ceremony.

(4) *Sponsors.*—When infants are solemnly baptized, persons assist at the ceremony to make profession of the faith in the child's name. This practice comes from antiquity and is witnessed to by Tertullian, St. Basil, St. Augustine, and others. Such persons are designated *sponsores, offerentes, susceptores, fidejussores*, and *patrini*. The English term is godfather and godmother, or in Anglo-Saxon, gossip. These sponsors, in default of the child's parents, are obliged to instruct it concerning faith and morals. One sponsor is sufficient and not more than two are allowed. In the latter case, one should be male and the other female. The object of these restrictions is the fact that the sponsor contracts a spiritual relationship to the child and its parents which would be an impediment to marriage. Sponsors must themselves be baptized persons having the use of reason and they must have been designated as sponsors by the priest or parents. During the baptism they must physically touch the child either personally or by proxy. They are required, moreover, to have the intention of really assuming the obligations of godparents. It is desirable that they should have been confirmed, but this is not absolutely necessary. Certain persons are prohibited from acting as sponsors. They are: members of religious orders, married persons in respect to each other, or parents to their children, and in general those who are objectionable on such grounds as infidelity, heresy, excommunication, or who are members of condemned secret societies, or public sinners (Sabetti, no. 663). Sponsors are also used in the solemn baptism

of adults. They are never necessary in private baptism.

(5) *Baptismal Name.*—From the earliest times (Martène, De Ant. Ec. Rit., I, i) names were given in baptism. The priest is directed to see that obscene, fabulous, and ridiculous names, or those of heathen gods or of infidel men be not imposed. On the contrary the priest is to recommend the names of saints. This rubric is not a rigorous precept, but it is an instruction to the priest to do what he can in the matter. If parents are unreasonably obstinate, the priest may add a saint's name to the one insisted upon (O'Kane, III, 56).

(6) *Baptismal Robe.*—In the primitive Church, a white robe was worn by the newly baptized for a certain period after the ceremony (St. Ambrose, De Myst., c. vii). As solemn baptisms usually took place on the eves of Easter or Pentecost, the white garments became associated with those festivals. Thus *Sabbatum in Albis* and *Dominica in Albis* received their names from the custom of putting off at that time the baptismal robe which had been worn since the previous vigil of Easter. It is thought that the English name for Pentecost—Whitsunday or Whitsuntide, also derived its appellation from the white garments of the newly baptized. In our present ritual, a white veil is placed momentarily on the head of the catechumen as a substitute for the baptismal robe (O'Kane, no. 350 sqq.).

XVI. CEREMONIES OF BAPTISM.—The rites that accompany the baptismal ablution are as ancient as they are beautiful. The writings of the early Fathers and the antique liturgies show that most of them are derived from Apostolic times. The infant is brought to the door of the church by the sponsors, where it is met by the priest. After the godparents have asked faith from the Church of God in the child's name, the priest breathes upon its face and exorcises the evil spirit. St. Augustine (Ep. cxciv, Ad Sixtum) makes use of this Apostolic practice of exorcising to prove the existence of original sin. Then the infant's forehead and breast are signed with the cross, the symbol of redemption. Next follows the imposition of hands, a custom certainly as old as the Apostles. Some blessed salt is now placed in the mouth of the child. "When salt", says the Catechism of the Council of Trent, "is put into the mouth of the person to be baptized, it evidently imports that, by the doctrine of faith and the gift of grace, he should be delivered from the corruption of sin, experience a relish for good works, and be delighted with the food of divine wisdom." Placing his stole over the child, the priest introduces it into the church, and on the way to the font the sponsors make a profession of faith for the infant. The priest now touches the ears and nostrils of the child with spittle. The symbolic meaning is thus explained (Cat. C. Trid.): "His nostrils and ears are next touched with spittle and he is immediately sent to the baptismal font, that, as sight was restored to the blind man mentioned in the Gospel, whom the Lord, after having spread clay over his eyes, commanded to wash them in the waters of Siloe; so also we may understand that the efficacy of the sacred ablution is such as to bring light to the mind to discern heavenly truth." The catechumen now makes the triple renunciation of Satan, his works and his pomps, and he is anointed with the oil of catechumens on the breast and between the shoulders: "On the breast, that by the gift of the Holy Ghost, he may cast off error and ignorance and may receive the true faith, 'for the just man liveth by faith' (Galat., iii, 11); on the shoulders, that by the grace of the Holy Spirit, he may shake off negligence and torpor and engage in the performance of good works; 'for, faith without works is dead' (James, ii, 26)", says the Catechism.

The infant now, through its sponsors, makes a

II.—18

declaration of faith and asks for baptism. The priest, having meantime changed his violet stole for a white one, then administers the threefold ablution, making the sign of the cross three times with the stream of water he pours on the head of the child, saying at the same time: ". . .N..., I baptize thee in the name of the Father and of the Son and of the Holy Ghost." The sponsors during the ablution either hold the child or at least touch it. If the baptism be given by immersion, the priest dips the back part of the head three times into the water in the form of a cross, pronouncing the sacramental words. The crown of the child's head is now anointed with chrism, "to give him to understand that from that day he is united as a member to Christ, his head, and engrafted on His body; and therefore he is called a Christian from Christ, but Christ from chrism" (Catech.). A white veil is now put on the infant's head with the words: "Receive this white garment, which mayest thou carry without stain before the judgment seat of Our Lord Jesus Christ, that thou mayest have eternal life. Amen." Then a lighted candle is placed in the catechumen's hand, the priest saying: "Receive this burning light, and keep thy baptism so as to be without blame. Observe the commandments of God; that, when Our Lord shall come to His nuptials, thou mayest meet Him together with all the Saints and mayest have life everlasting, and live for ever and ever. Amen." The new Christian is then bidden to go in peace.

In the baptism of adults, all the essential ceremonies are the same as for infants. There are, however, some impressive additions. The priest wears the cope over his other vestments, and he should be attended by a number of clerics or at least by two. While the catechumen waits outside the church door, the priest recites some prayers at the altar. Then he proceeds to the place where the candidate is, and asks him the questions and performs the exorcisms almost as prescribed in the ritual for infants. Before administering the blessed salt, however, he requires the catechumen to make an explicit renunciation of the form of error to which he had formerly adhered, and he is then signed with the cross on the brow, ears, eyes, nostrils, mouth, breast, and between the shoulders. Afterwards, the candidate, on bended knees, recites three several times the Lord's Prayer, and a cross is made on his forehead, first by the godfather and then by the priest. After this, taking him by the hand, the priest leads him into the church, where he adores prostrate and then rising he recites the Apostles' Creed and the Lord's Prayer. The other ceremonies are practically the same as for infants. It is to be noted that owing to the difficulty of carrying out with proper splendour the ritual for baptizing adults, the bishops of the United States obtained permission from the Holy See to make use of the ceremonial of infant baptism instead. This general dispensation lasted until 1857, when the ordinary law of the Church went into force. (See BALTIMORE, COUNCILS OF.) Some American dioceses, however, obtained individual permissions to continue the use of the ritual for infants when administering adult baptism.

XVII. METAPHORICAL BAPTISM.—The name "baptism" is sometimes applied improperly to other ceremonies. (1) *Baptism of Bells.*—This name has been given to the blessing of bells, at least in France, since the eleventh century. It is derived from the washing of the bell with holy water by the bishop, before he anoints it with the oil of the infirm without and with chrism within. A fuming censer is then placed under it. The bishop prays that these sacramentals of the Church may, at the sound of the bell, put the demons to flight, protect from storms, and call the faithful to prayer. (2) *Baptism of Ships.*—At least since the time of the Crusades, rituals have contained a blessing for ships. The priest begs God to bless the vessel and protect those who sail in it, as He did the ark of Noe, and Peter, when the Apostle was sinking in the sea. The ship is then sprinkled with holy water.

For extended bibliographies of the subject: VACANT, *Dict. de théol. cath.*, s. v. In addition to the references given in the article, the following works deal with the various aspects of Baptism: DOGMATIC THEOLOGY: SCHANZ, *Die Lehre von den Sacramenten der katholischen Kirche* (Freiburg, 1893); WILHELM and SCANNELL, *Manual of Catholic Theology* (London, 1906), II; PESCH, *Prælectiones dogmaticæ* (Freiburg, 1900), VI. MORAL THEOLOGY: LEHMKUHL, *Theol. Moral.* (Freiburg, 1898); BALLERINI-PALMIERI, *Opus theol. mor.* (Prato, 1891); GÉNICOT, *Theol. moral.* (Louvain, 1907), II; COPPENS, *Moral Principles and Medical Practice* (New York, 1905); KENRICK, *Theol. moral.* (Mechlin, 1851), II; SABETTI, *Theol. Moral.* (New York), 1888; KONINGS, *Theol. moral.* (Boston, 1874). CANON LAW: FERRARIS, *Bibl. prompta* (Roman ed., 1886), s. v.; LAURENTIUS, *Instit. jur. eccl.* (Freiburg, 1903), nos. 502–510; VON SCHERER, *Kirchenrecht* (Graz, 1898), II, 74–84; PHILLIPS, *Lehrbuch d. Kirchenrechts*, §§ 236–237; VAN ESPEN, *Jus eccl. Univ.*, II; BENEDICT XIV, *De Syn. diæc.*, VII. LITURGY: O'KANE, *Notes on the Rubrics of the Roman Ritual* (New York, 1882); THALHOFER-EBNER, *Handbuch der kathol. Liturgik* (2d ed., Freiburg, 1894); FALISE, *Liturgiæ practicæ compendium* (Ratisbon, 1876); DE HERDT, *Sacræ Liturgiæ Praxis* (Louvain, 1899), III; MARTINUCCI, *Manuale sacr. Cæremoniorum* (Rome, 1880), index, s. v. HISTORY AND ANTIQUITIES OF BAPTISM (Catholic): PROBST, *Sakramente und Sakramentalien in den drei ersten christlichen Jahrhunderten* (Tübingen, 1872); L. BOURGEOIS, *Le baptême romain au IVe siècle* (Paris, 1902); DE PUNIET, *La liturgie baptismale en Gaule avant Charlemagne*, in *Rev. des quest. hist.* (1902), LXXII, 382; ERMONI, *L'hist. du baptême depuis l'édit de Milan (313) jusqu'au Concile in Trullo*, in *Rev. des quest. hist.* (1898), 313–324; *Analecta jur. pont.* (1861), V, 107–1147, VIII (1866), 1557–1741; WEISS and KIRSCH in KRAUS, *Real-Encykl.*, II, 823–839; VACANT, *Dict. de théol. cath.*, s. v. THE PROTESTANT CHURCHES: HÖFLING (Lutheran), *Das Sacrament der Taufe* (Erlangen, 1846–48); DARWELL-STONE, *Baptism in Oxford Library of Theology* (1899), bibliogr. 229–303; MCGIFFERT, *A Hist. of Christianity in the Apostolic Age* (New York, 1903), index, s. v.; MARCUS DODS in HAST., *Dict. of Christ. and the Gospels* (N w York, 1906), 168–171; *A Chronological catena of the ancient fathers and councils, etc., on the doctrine of spiritual regeneration in holy baptism* (Oxford, 1850); WILBERFORCE, *On Baptism in Tracts for the Times*, No. 67; E. S. FFRENCH in *Dict. Christ. Biog.*, I, 241–248; DALE, *On Baptism* (4th ed., London, 1872). THE ORIENTAL CHURCHES: STÆRCK, *Der Taufritus in den griechischen Kirchen* (Freiburg, 1903); WILLIAM PALMER, *Dissertations on subjects relating to the Orthodox and Eastern Catholic Communion* (London, 1853); ARCUDIUS, *De Concordiâ Eccl. Occid. et Orient. in septem sacram. administratione septem libri* (Paris, 1619–26); A. PALMIERI, *De la rébaptisation des Latins chez les Grecs* in *Rev. de l'Orient Chrét.* (1902), VII, 618, (1903) VIII, iii; cf. *ibid.* (1901), VI, *L'ancienne et la nouvelle théologie chez les Grecs.* LAY BAPTISM AND INFANT BAPTISM IN EARLY CHRISTIAN PERIOD: BINGHAM, *A scholastical history of the practice of the Church in regard to the administration of baptism by laymen* (London, 1712–14), reprinted in his works (Oxford, 1858); A. H. NEWMAN (Baptist), *History of Anti-pedobaptism* (Philadelphia, 1897), bibliogr. 394–406. BAPTISMAL NAMES: on the right to give baptismal names, and on suitable and unsuitable names, see *Theol.-praktische Quartalschrift* (1892), XL 381, and *Theol. prakt. Monatsschrift* (1900), X, 191, 349. HERETICAL BAPTISM: Besides standard theologians see DAVID, *Dissertation, etc., sur la réception par l'Eglise du baptême des hérétiques* (Paris, 1670); TH. BOUQUILLON, *De la réitération du baptême conféré par les hérétiques* in *Rev. des sciences eccl.* (1879), XL, 145; EINIG in *Pastor Bonus* (1898), X, 57. SPECIAL POINTS (*Curiosa*) OF BAPTISM: BARBIER DE MONTAULT, *Le baptême au moyen âge* in *Rev. de l'art chrét.* (Arras, 1874). BAPTISM IN EARLY CHRISTIAN ART: For representations of baptism on early Christian monuments see STRZYGOWSKI, *Ikonographie der Taufe Christi* (Munich, 1885). These works complete or correct the earlier but yet valuable works of DE ROSSI and GARRUCCI, also LE BLANT, *Sarcophages chrét. antiques de la ville d'Arles* (Paris, 1878); see also C. F. ROGERS, *Baptism and Christian Archæology* in *Studia Biblica et Eccl.*, V, IV.

WILLIAM H. W. FANNING.

Baptism by Heretics. See BAPTISM.

Baptismal Font, a basin or vase, serving as a receptacle for baptismal water in which the candidate for baptism is immersed, or over which he is washed, in the ceremony of Christian initiation. In the Church's present practice it is ordinarily a decorative stone basin, though metal or wood are used, supported on a pedestal or columns at a convenient height for receiving the water which is poured over the head of the person baptized, a form which marks the term of a development graphically illustrating the history of the mode of conferring baptism.

ARCHÆOLOGY.—In the Apostolic Age, as in Jewish times (John, iii, 23), baptism was administered without special fonts, at the seaside or in streams or pools of water (Acts, viii, 38); Tertullian refers to St. Peter's baptizing in the Tiber (De bapt., iv); similarly, in later periods of evangelization, missionaries baptized in rivers as is narrated of St. Paulinus in England by Bede (Hist. Eccl., II, xiv–xvi). Indoor baptism, however, was not uncommon (Acts, ix, 18; xvi, 33) and, for the sake of both privacy and solemnity, came to be the rule; while reverence for the rite itself and for the water, which came in time to receive a special consecration, gave rise to the use of a special basin or font for the baptismal ceremony and, at a later period, for the preservation of the water. With the establishment of distinctively Christian places of worship this font became one of their important adjuncts. In the East it took the form of a pool or cistern, similar to those of the baths, often larger, and deep enough to permit total immersion. Whence it was called κολυμβήθρα (swimming-bath), a name which in its Latin equivalent, *natatorium*, was also used in the West, as was the term *piscina* with its apt allusion to birth and life in the waters (Tertullian, De bapt., i; St. Augustine, De schis. Donat., III, ii). The name *fons* (a spring of water) was also in early use and came to prevail.

The oldest western fonts are found in the Roman catacombs, cisterns hewn from the tufa in the floor of baptismal chapels. (See BAPTISTERY.) Examples are to be found in the Ostrian Cemetery, where in a small shallow basin in the floor a spring wells up in the Cemetery of Pontianus, where an oblong reservoir, about eighteen square feet in surface area and three feet in depth, is yet filled with water (Marucchi, Archéologie Chrétienne, II, 63); that of St. Felicitas (ibid., 304); and of St. Priscilla, where in 1901 was found a basin of particular interest on account of its presumably high antiquity as a baptismal centre (Marucchi in Nuovo Bullettino, 1901, 73). Besides these actual specimens, the font is also depicted in the remains of early Christian art. In nearly every instance it is a shallow pool or basin in which the neophyte stands with feet immersed, while water is poured on him from an overhead stream or from a vase held by the person baptizing. That this was the ordinary mode of baptizing during the early centuries, is a view the acceptance of which is compelled by all recent study in the archæology of baptismal fonts (de Rossi, Bullettino di Archeol., 1876, 8–15; Duchesne, Les Eglises séparées, Paris, 1905, 89–96). With the church-building activity of the fourth century the font was reverently enshrined in the magnificent baptisteries which date from that period. It took the form of a basin which was either entirely below the level of the baptistery floor or was partially raised above it by a low curb of masonry, over which the neophytes passed by steps, in going down into the water; to the ascent and descent, as well as to the number of steps this involved, there was often attached a mystical significance (Isidore of Seville, De divin. off., II, xxv). These fonts were either circular or octagonal in form and rarely hexagonal or square; a few were in the form of a cross (Gregory of Tours, Mirac., I, xxiv), a type more common in the East than in the West, while an occasional sarcophagus-shaped font was suggested, perhaps by the allusion to baptism in Romans, vi, 4.

In size fonts varied, but as a rule they were large enough for the simultaneous baptism of a few catechumens. Their average depth of less than three feet points to the continued prevalence of but partial immersion down to the eighth century. Water was provided either by natural springs or by pipes leading into the basins, though there are many examples of its being poured in from above the font, over the heads of the neophytes. Drain pipes conducted the water into the earth or into a nearby stream after

BAPTISMAL FONTS

NORMAN. STOKE CANNON,
DEVONSHIRE

NORMAN. HOLT,
WORCESTERSHIRE

NORMAN (transition). BELAUGH,
NORFOLK

NORMAN (transition). STONESBY,
LEICESTERSHIRE

EARLY ENGLISH. KING'S CLIFF,
NORTHAMPTONSHIRE

EARLY ENGLISH. ALL SAINTS,
LEICESTER

DECORATED. MALTBY LE
MARSH, LINCOLNSHIRE

DECORATED. KING'S WORTHY,
HAMPSHIRE

DECORATED (transition). PENTON,
HAMPSHIRE

PERPENDICULAR. NORTH
SOMERCOTES, LINCOLNSHIRE

PERPENDICULAR. LEVERINGTON,
CAMBRIDGESHIRE

PERPENDICULAR. WESTON,
SUFFOLK

the ceremony. These early fonts were lined and paved with marble or other decorative stone and were often highly ornamented, features more common in the West than in the East where simpler fonts, sometimes even of wood, were used. The "Liber Pontificalis" (ed. Duchesne, I, 174) describes in detail the Constantian font in the Lateran baptistery as a porphyry basin heavily ornamented with silver; on its rim were a golden lamb and seven silver stags from whose mouths gushed water from the Claudian aqueduct; the golden lamb was flanked by statues of the Saviour and of St. John the Baptist. From the centre of the font arose a porphyry column bearing a golden lamp in which, during the ceremonies of baptism, was burned an oil of fragrant odour. This font was despoiled by the barbarian invaders, but its general design may be seen in the present day structure. The passing of the period of adult conversion to Christianity and the growing prevalence of infant baptism with a consequent frequency of administration determined a change in the structure of the fonts. Instead of a basin below the floor level, walls of masonry were built up to a height of three or four feet, to facilitate the ministers holding a child over its opening; or a font hewn from solid stone rested on the chapel floor. Immersion of children had come to be the rule, and as the practice was adopted too in the case of adults, the fonts were sometimes large enough to admit of their being immersed. With the thirteenth century, however, simple infusion came by degrees to be adopted, and with its general use, the font became smaller and more shallow, and was raised from the floor on piers or columns. The older type of font continued to find favour in Italy, but in the Northern countries the winter chill of the waters hastened the general use of infusion, and as this rite required for each person baptized but a small quantity of water, the font generally took the simple form and small dimensions it has to-day.

CANON LAW AND LITURGY.—The Church's legislation kept pace with this development. Early enactments urged stone as the regular material, though metal was permitted. With the erection of fonts for the continual preservation of the water, reverence and cleanliness became the Church's chief concern; the font, if not of impermeable stone, must be lined with metal; it must be used exclusively for baptism, and to guard it against profanation, securely covered and locked. Frequency of thirteenth-century legislation on this point throughout Northern Europe reveals the prevalence of a passing superstitious belief in the magical efficacy of the font and its waters. The constitutions of Bishop Poore of Sarum (Salisbury, c. 1217) and of St. Edmund of Canterbury (1236) combated the abuse in England as did the Councils of Tours (1236), Trier (1238), Fritzlar (1243), and Breslau (1248), on the Continent. The cover was enacted in the name of cleanliness and decoration as well, and, besides a close-fitting, cloth-lined lid, there was demanded in many dioceses an outer dome-like cover, sometimes highly ornamented and draped with a canopy or veil. The repugnance to continued repetition of baptism over a font whose water was to last for ten months, was overcome by providing two compartments, one to contain the baptismal water, the other, always empty and clean to receive the drippings and drain them into the *sacrarium*, a provision embodied by Benedict XIII in his still authoritative "Memoriale Rituum" (Tit. vi, cap. ii, § 5, 9). The Roman Ritual (Tit. ii, cap. i, 28–30) epitomizes the present law providing that the font should be in the church or in a nearby baptistery, within a railed enclosure and secured by lock and key; of a substantial material fit to hold water; of becoming shape and ornamentation and so covered as to exclude anything unclean (cf. Council II Balt., § 234–237). As models of diocesan legislation concerning

fonts are cited the synodal acts of St. Charles Borromeo (Acta Eccl. Mediolan., Paris, 1643, 58–63) and those of Benedict XIII when Archbishop of Benevento (Collectio Lacensis, I, 69 sq.).

Two important liturgical functions centre at the font, the baptismal rite itself, and the blessing of the font. The earliest allusion to such a blessing is by Tertullian who refers to the sanctification of the water by the invocation of God (De bapt., iv). St. Cyprian speaks of its being purified and sanctified by the priest (Ep. lxx, Ad Jan.); St. Basil considered the blessing, already of long-standing practice in his day, as of Apostolic institution (De Spiritu Sancto, xxvii); St. Ambrose first refers to an extended ritual including blessings, exorcism, and invocations (De myst., iii, 14–20). The oldest extant rite is that of the Apostolic Constitutions (VII, xliii), an extended prayer in Eucharistic form. The blessing of the font is henceforward an important feature of the sacramentaries and *ordines*, which contain nearly all the features of the present rite. It served as the preliminary to baptism, which was solemnized on the vigils of Easter and Pentecost; and notwithstanding the increasing frequency of solemn baptism, the blessing was reserved for those two days on which it should now be carried out in all churches having fonts (Decreta S. R. C., 3331–4005). This blessing is in the form of a long Eucharistic prayer the burden of which is an appeal that the Holy Spirit descend on the water and endow it with regenerative virtue, during which the celebrant performs a series of expressive ceremonies of high antiquity. He divides the water in the form of a cross; signs it with the cross; divides the water and casts a portion of it toward the four cardinal points; breathes on it in exorcism, and dips in it the Paschal candle. After the prayer he pours into the water first the oil of catechumens, then the Holy chrism, a rite alluded to by St. Gregory of Tours (loc. cit.), and finally the two oils simultaneously.

ROGERS, *Baptism and Christian Archeology* (Oxford, 1903); IDEM in *Studia Biblica*, V, 239–361; COTE, *The Archeology of Baptism* (London, 1876); CORBLET, *Histoire du Sacrement de Baptême* (Paris, 1881); VENABLES in *Dict. Christ. Antiq.*, s. v.; CHARDON, *Histoire des sacrements* (Paris, 1745), I, 174–223; HEUSER in *Eccl. Rev.*, XX, 449–454; ENLART, *Etude sur quelques fonts baptismaux du nord de la France* (Paris, 1890); VAN DER STAPPEN, *Sacra Liturgia* (Mechlin, 1900), IV, 32–36; PIGHI, *Liturgia Sacramentorum* (Verona, 1902), 36–39; FERRARIS, *Bibl. prompt.* (Paris, 1852), 991–992; 1003–08.

JOHN B. PETERSON.

Baptismal Names. See NAMES, CHRISTIAN.

Baptismal Register. See REGISTER, PAROCHIAL.

Baptismal Robe. See BAPTISM.

Baptismal Vows, the name popularly given to the renunciations required of an adult candidate for baptism just before the sacrament is conferred. In the case of infant baptism they are made in the name of the child by the sponsors. It is obvious that these promises have not the theological import of vows properly so called. According to the Roman Ritual, at present in use, three questions are to be addressed to the person to be baptized, as follows: "Dost thou renounce Satan? and all his works? and all his pomps?" To each of these interrogations the person, or the sponsor in his name, replies: "I do renounce". The practice of demanding and making this formal renunciation seems to go back to the very beginnings of organized Christian worship. Tertullian among the Latins and St. Basil among the Greeks are at one in reckoning it as a usage which, although not explicitly warranted in the Scriptures, is nevertheless consecrated by a venerable tradition. St. Basil says this tradition descends from the Apostles. Tertullian, in his "De Coronâ", appears to hint at a twofold renunciation as common in his time, one which was made at the moment of baptism and another made sometime before, and publicly in the church, in the presence of the bishop. The form of this renunciation as found in the Apostolic Constitutions (VII, 4) has a quaint interest. It is as follows: "Let therefore the candidate for baptism declare thus in his renunciation: 'I renounce Satan and his works and his pomps and his worship and his angels and his inventions and all things that are under him'. And after his renunciation let him in his consociation say: 'And I associate myself to Christ and believe and am baptized into one unbegotten being' ", etc.

Where there was a baptistery the renunciations were made in the προαύλιον οἶκον, the vestibule or ante-room, as distinguished from the ἐσώτερον οἶκον, the inner room where the baptism itself was administered. The catechumen, standing with his face to the West, which symbolized the abode of darkness, and stretching out his hand, or sometimes spitting out in defiance and abhorrence of the devil, was wont to make this abjuration. It was also customary after this for the candidate for baptism to make an explicit promise of obedience to Christ. This was called by the Greeks συντάσσεσθαι Χρίστω, the giving of oneself over to the control of Christ. St. Justin Martyr testifies that baptism was only administered to those who, together with their profession of faith, made a promise or vow that they would live in conformity with the Christian code. Hence the generally employed formula: συντάσσομαι σοί, Χρίστε, "I surrender myself to thee, O Christ, to be ruled by thy precepts". This took place directly after the ἀποτάξις, or renunciation of the devil, and was variously described by the Latins as *promissum*, *pactum*, and *votum*. During this declaration of attachment to Jesus Christ the person to be baptized turned towards the East as towards the region of light.

The practice of renewing the baptismal promises is more or less widespread. This is done under circumstances of special solemnity such as at the closing exercises of a mission, after the administration of First Communion to children, or the conferring of the Sacrament of Confirmation. It is thus intended as a way of reaffirming one's loyalty to the obligations taken over by membership in the Christian Church.

BINGHAM, *Antiquities of the Christian Church* (London, 1838); DUCHESNE, *Origines du culte chrétien* (Paris, 1898).

JOSEPH F. DELANY.

Baptismal Water. See WATER; HOLY SATURDAY.

Baptist, SAINT JOHN THE. See JOHN THE BAPTIST, SAINT.

Baptista Mantuanus (or SPAGNOLI), BLESSED, Carmelite and Renaissance poet, b. at Mantua, 17 April, 1447, where he also died, 22 March, 1516. The eldest son of Peter Spagnoli, a Spanish nobleman at the court of Mantua, Baptista studied grammar under Gregorio Tifernate, and philosophy at Pavia under Polo Bagelardi. The bad example of his schoolfellows led him into irregularities. He fell into the hands of usurers and, returning home, was turned out of his father's house owing to some calumny. He went to Venice and later on to Ferrara where he carried out his resolution of entering the Carmelite convent which belonged to the then flourishing Reform of Mantua. In a letter addressed to his father (1 April, 1464), and in his first publication, "De Vitâ beatâ", he gave an account of his previous life and of the motives which led him to the cloister.

Baptista pursued his studies at Ferrara and Bologna where he was ordained priest, received his degrees, and delivered lectures in philosophy and divinity. The Duke of Mantua entrusted him with the education of his children, and the connexion with the ducal family resulted in a number of poetical works, the "Trophæum Gonzagæ" and the "Fortuna Gonzagæ", on the various misfortunes of the young duke; "Contra amorem" containing good advice to Sigismondo Gonzaga, and other poems celebrating the latter's elevation to dignities, even to the Roman purple. Six times (each for two years with four years interval) Baptista was nominated vicar-general of his congregation, and, in 1513, general of the whole order through the exertions of his former disciples, the duke and the cardinal. The chapter, however, resenting the intervention, restricted his powers. He held the office until his death, but, broken in health and energy, he exercised but little influence beyond consolidating the congregation of Albi, a French imitation of the Mantuan Reform. Baptista Mantuanus was beatified in 1890, his feast being assigned to 23 March.

Chiefly known as one of the most prolific Renaissance poets he excelled in almost every form of Latin verse; Virgil, however, was his favourite model. A monument represents the two poets of Mantua with Poetry hesitating to whom she is to offer the crown: "*Cui dabo?*" Baptista exercised too little self-restraint, however, to deserve it. He was bitterly attacked concerning the good taste of his earlier works printed without his knowledge, and also, but groundlessly, with reference to the legitimacy of his birth. To the end he made too free use of pagan mythology.

Opera omnia (Bologna, 1502); *Historia domus Lauretanæ. s. d.* (c. 1489), reprinted in CHEVALIER, *Notre Dame de Lorette* (Paris, 1906, 241 sqq.; Paris, 1513; Antwerp, 1576). His correspondence, chiefly with the two Pico de Mirandola, uncle and nephew, is in ZIMMERMAN, *Monumenta hist. Carmelitana* (Lerins, 1907), I; AMBROSIO, *De rebus gestis* (Turin, 1784); P.F. in *Chroniques du Carmel* (Soignies, 1902), 272 sqq.

BENEDICT ZIMMERMAN.

Baptistery, the separate building in which the Sacrament of Baptism was once solemnly administered, or that portion of the church-edifice later set apart for the same purpose. In ancient times the term was applied to a basin, pool, or other place for bathing. The Latin term *baptisterium* was also applied to the vessel or tank which contained the water for baptism, and in the Early Church denoted indifferently the baptismal font and the building or chapel in which it was enshrined. There is no means of knowing when the first baptisteries were built; but both their name and form seem borrowed from pagan sources. They remind one of the bathing apartments in the *thermæ*, and the fact that Pliny, in speaking of the latter, twice uses the word *baptisteria* seems to point to this derivation. The term was also applied to the bath in the circular chamber of the baths at Pompeii and to the tank in the triangular court of suburban villas. The earliest extant type of baptistery is found in the catacomb chambers in which were the baptismal-pools. (See BAPTISMAL FONT.) These rooms were sometimes spacious; that in the Roman catacomb of Priscilla adjoins other larger cubicula used perhaps for the adjuncts of the baptismal rite; that of the Pontian cemetery bears traces of sixth-century mural decoration, a beautiful *crux gemmata* with other Christian symbols being yet visible. With the construction of edifices for Christian worship a special building was erected for the ceremonies of initiation. Ordinarily circular or polygonal, it contained in the centre the font; a circular ambulatory gave room for the ministers and witnesses who, with the neophytes, were numerous at the Easter and Pentecost solemnities; radiating from the structure were rooms for the preparation of the candidates, and sometimes a chapel with altar for the Eucharistic service following baptism (cf. BAPTISM), as may be seen in the Lateran baptistery. The building sometimes joined, but was generally adjacent to, the cathedral or church to which it belonged, and was usually situated near the atrium or

BAPTISTERY, PISA, DESIGNED BY ALESSANDRO DIOTISALVI, A.D. 1153

forecourt. Immersion gradually gave way to infusion, though in the South the custom of immersing children in the baptisteries persisted long after the North had commenced infusion in the small baptismal chapels. When separate baptisteries were no longer needed, the term was then applied to that part of the church which was set apart for and contained the baptismal font. The font was sometimes placed in a separate chapel or compartment, sometimes in an inclosure formed by a railing or open screen work; and often the font stands alone, either in the vestibule of the church, or in an arm of the transept, or at the western extremity of one of the aisles, and occasionally in the floor chamber of the western tower.

The modern baptistery is merely that part of the church set apart for baptism. According to the Roman Ritual, it should be railed off; it should have a gate fastened by a lock; and should be adorned, if possible, with a picture of the baptism of Christ by St. John. It is convenient that it should contain a chest with two compartments, one for the holy oils, the other for the salt, candle, etc. used in baptism. The form of the early baptisteries seems to have been derived from the Roman circular temples of tombs. And in adopting the plans, the early Christians modified them to some extent, for the internal columns, which in Roman examples were generally used in a decorative way, were now used to support the walls carrying the domes. To cover a large area with one roof was difficult; but by the addition of an aisle in one story, round a moderate-sized circular tomb, the inner walls could be replaced by columns in the lower half, which gave such buildings as these early baptisteries.

The earliest existing baptistery is that of the Lateran, said to have been erected in its original form under Constantine. Throughout the Roman world round or polygonal baptisteries seem to have been constantly employed from the fourth century onwards. In many places the Italians have preserved the separate building for baptism, while north of the Alps the practice generally prevailed of administering the rite in the churches. The construction of the baptistery of the Lateran is interesting because of a direct adaptation of the columnar system of the basilica to a concentric plan. The inner octagon is upheld by eight simple shafts, upon the straight entablature of which a second story of columns is superimposed. The original character of the ceiling and the roof cannot now be determined, but the weak supports were hardly adapted to bear a vault of masonry. Although baptisteries and mortuary chapels were generally built as simple cylindrical halls, without surrounding passages, other examples of the two modes of extension are not lacking.

The arrangement of the baptistery requires but brief notice. A flight of steps descended into the round or polygonal font (*piscina* or *fons*), which was sunk beneath the level of the floor, and sometimes raised a little above it by a breastwork of stone. The font was surrounded by a row of columns which supported curtains to insure the most perfect privacy and decency during the immersion. The columns were united occasionally by archivolts, more frequently by architraves adorned by metrical inscriptions; the eight distichs in the Lateran baptistery are ascribed to Sixtus III.

The baptistery of Pisa, designed by Dioti Salvi in 1153, is circular, 129 feet in diameter, with encircling aisle in two stories. Built of marble, it is surrounded externally on the lower story by half columns, connected by semicircular arches, above which is an open arcade in two heights, supported by small detached shafts. It was not completed till A. D. 1278, and has Gothic additions of the fourteenth century, in consequence of which it is not easy to ascertain what the original external design really was. The structure is crowned by an outer hemispherical dome, through which penetrates a conical dome 60 feet in diameter over the central space, and supported on four piers and eight columns. Thus, if there were another internal hemispherical cupola, it would resemble the constructive dome of St. Paul, London. This baptistery bears remarkable similarity to the church of San Donato (ninth century) at Zara, in Dalmatia, which, however, has a space only 30 feet in diameter. The baptistery at Asti, if examined with those of San Antonio, will give a very complete idea of Lombardic architecture in the beginning of the eleventh century. More or less interesting examples of baptisteries ex'st at Biella, Brindisi, Cremona, Galliano, near Milan, Gravedona, Monte Sant' Angelo, Padua, Parma, Pinara, Pistoia, Spalato, Verona, and Volterra. There are very few examples in Italy of circular or polygonal buildings of any class belonging to the Gothic age. Baptisteries had passed out of fashion. One such building, at Parma, commenced in 1196, deserves to be quoted, not certainly for its beauty, but as illustrating those false principles of design shown in buildings of this age in Italy. In later Romanesque and Gothic periods, in Italy, where the churches were not derived from a combination of a circular Eastern church with a Western rectangular nave, as in France, but were correct copies of the Roman basilica, the baptistery always stands alone. In Germany, the earlier baptistery was joined to the square church and formed a western apse. The only examples in England are at Cranbrook and Canterbury; the latter, however, is supposed to have been originally part of the Treasury. It is not known at what time the baptistery became absorbed into the basilica. The change was made earlier in Rome than elsewhere. A late example of a separate baptistery, which, although small, is very beautiful in design, is in a court alongside the cathedral at Bergamo. This may be regarded as a connecting link between large buildings and fonts.

Kössing in *Kirchenlex.*, I, 1975–78; Kraus, *Real-Encyk.*, II, 839–843; Kuhn, *Kunstgeschichte*, passim; Lowrie, *Early Christian Monuments*.

Thomas H. Poole.

Baptistines.—I. Hermits of St. John the Baptist. II. Missionaries of St. John the Baptist. III. Sisterhood of St. John the Baptist.

I. The Congregation of the Hermits of St. John the Baptist of France was founded about 1630 by Brother Michel de Saint-Sabine who reformed and united the hermits of various dioceses. He established for each diocese a visitor who was aided by four majors and a secretary. The bishop received the religious when they took the habit and made their profession, and the brothers in a diocese met together once a year. The pious reformer gave the congregation a collection of statutes which regulated their mode of life. The first bishops to make these statutes obligatory in their dioceses were the Bishop of Metz (1633), and the Bishop of Cambrai (1634). Brother Jean-Baptiste who had a great reputation for virtue carried this reform into the Dioceses of Vienne, Lyons, Geneva, Le Puy, and Langres. The Bishop of Langres, Louis-Armand de Simiane de Gardes, added in 1680, for the hermits in his diocese, several ordinances to those of Brother Michel. He established four visitors, one for each division of the diocese and the brothers wore a white habit to distinguish them from vagrant and lax hermits. Brother Jean-Baptiste went to the Diocese of Angers to found the hermitage of Gardelles; and died there in the odour of sanctity, 24 December, 1691.

II. The congregation of missionary priests of St. John the Baptist, called Baptistines, was founded by a

Genoese, Domenico Olivieri. He began by uniting several zealous priests with himself for the evangelization of the people of the cities and country. His plan of forming from this company an association the members of which should devote their time especially to missions was encouraged by Cardinal Spinola and the scheme afterwards received the approbation of Benedict XIV. The pope confirmed the new congregation in his Brief of 23 September, 1755, and placed it under the control of the Cardinal Prefect of the Propaganda. The institute had a house and an oratory at Rome near the church of St. Isidoro, and the members held missions in the different churches of the city and in the surrounding country. The Propaganda, realizing their zeal and virtue, wished to employ them in distant missions. A number of them were, therefore, sent to Bulgaria, Macedonia, and China; some became bishops. Foreign missions did not absorb all their activity, for a number were employed in the service of the Church in Italy, two, Father Imperiali and Father Spinelli becoming cardinals. The only vows imposed by the pious founder were those of continuance in the congregation and readiness to go to missions to which the members should be sent by the Propaganda. Olivieri died at Genoa in the odour of sanctity, 13 June, 1766. His society disappeared during the troubles which overwhelmed Italy at the end of the eighteenth century.

III. The Baptistines, or hermit sisters of St. John the Baptist, had as their founder Giovanna Maria Baptista Solimani. In 1730, when she was forty-two years old, she gathered her first companions together at Moneglia, not far from Genoa. The congregation intended to lead a life of penitence in imitation of the precursor of Christ and under his patronage. All the choir sisters, therefore, added to their names in religion that of Baptista in honour of their illustrious model. The Capuchin, Father Athanasius, aided them by his advice during the drawing up of their constitutions. Soon after, Providence gave them the direction of the saintly priest Olivieri, the cause of whose canonization has been introduced. Shortly after taking Olivieri as their director the congregation settled in the city of Genoa. Their founder now went to Rome to obtain the confirmation of the Holy See; through the aid of the Barnabite, Mario Maccabei, the approbation of Benedict XI was obtained in 1744. Two years later, 20 April, 1746, the Archbishop of Genoa received the religious profession of Giovanna Solimani and her twelve companions. Soon after this, Mother Solimani was elected abbess and governed the house until her death, 8 April, 1758. In 1755 the congregation had sent a colony to Rome which founded a convent near the church of San Nicolà da Tolentino. Houses were also founded in some of the other cities of Italy. The congregation drew its members from among the young girls and widows who were admitted into their houses as lay-sisters. Tertiaries took care of their churches and gathered the alms of which they had need. A rigorous cloister was observed. The sisters rose at midnight for Matins, slept in their clothes, went bare-footed, and observed a continual abstinence. The whole life was one of extreme austerity. Several convents of this congregation still exist in Italy.

HÉLYOT, *Histoire des ordres religieux*, VIII, 112–116; GRANDET, *La vie d'un solitaire inconnu mort en Anjou, en odeur de sainteté* (Paris, 1699); HEIMBUCHER, *Die Orden und Kongregationen*, II, 307–308, 375.

JEAN M. BESSE.

Baptists (Greek, βαπτίζειν, to baptize), a Protestant denomination, which exists chiefly in English-speaking countries and owes its name to its characteristic doctrine and practice regarding baptism.

I. DISTINCTIVE PRINCIPLES.—The Baptists consider the Scriptures to be the sufficient and exclusive rule of faith and practice. In the interpretation of them, every individual enjoys unrestricted freedom. No non-Scriptural scheme of doctrine and duty is recognized as authoritative. General creeds are mere declarations of prevalent doctrinal views, to which no assent beyond one's personal conviction need be given. The two principal Baptist confessions of faith are the Confession of 1688, or Philadelphia Confession, and the New Hampshire Confession. The Philadelphia Confession is the Westminster (Presbyterian) Confession (1646) revised in a Baptist sense. It first appeared in 1677, was reprinted in 1688, approved by the English Baptist Assembly of 1689, and adopted by the Baptist Association at Philadelphia in 1742, a circumstance which accounts for its usual name. It is generally accepted by the Baptists in England and the Southern States of the Union, whereas the Northern States are more attached to the New Hampshire Confession. The latter was adopted by the New Hampshire State Convention in 1833. Its slight doctrinal difference from the Philadelphia Confession consists in a milder presentation of the Calvinistic system. Baptists hold that those only are members of the Church of Christ who have been baptized upon making a personal profession of faith. They agree in the rejection of infant baptism as contrary to the Scriptures, and in the acceptance of immersion as the sole valid mode of baptism. All children who die before the age of responsibility will nevertheless be saved. Baptism and the Eucharist, the only two sacraments, or ordinances as they call them, which Baptists generally admit, are not productive of grace, but are mere symbols. Baptism does not bestow, but symbolizes, regeneration, which has already taken place. In the Eucharist Jesus Christ is not really present; the Lord's Supper merely sets forth the death of Christ as the sustaining power of the believer's life. It was instituted for the followers of Christ alone; hence Baptists, in theory, commonly admit to it only their own church members and exclude outsiders (close communion). Open communion, however, has been practised extensively in England and is gaining ground to-day among American Baptists. In church polity, the Baptists are congregational, i. e. each church enjoys absolute autonomy. Its only officers are the elders or bishops and the deacons. The elder exercises the different pastoral functions and the deacon is his assistant in both spiritual and temporal concerns. These officers are chosen by common suffrage and ordained by "councils" consisting of ministers and representatives of neighbouring churches. A church may, in case of need, appeal for help to another church; it may, in difficulty, consult other churches; but never, even in such cases, can members of one congregation acquire authority over another congregation. Much less can a secular power interfere in spiritual affairs; a state church is an absurdity.

II. HISTORY.—(1) *The Baptists in the British Isles.* Persons rejecting infant baptism are frequently mentioned in English history in the sixteenth century. We learn of their presence in the island through the persecutions they endured. As early as 1535 ten Anabaptists were put to death, and the persecution continued throughout that century. The victims seem to have been mostly Dutch and German refugees. What influence they exerted in spreading their views is not known; but, as a necessary result, Baptist principles became, through them, less of an unacceptable novelty in the eyes of Englishmen. The first Baptist congregations were organized in the beginning of the seventeenth century. Almost at the very start, the denomination was divided into "Arminian", or "General" Baptists, so named because of their belief in the universal character of Christ's redemption, and "Calvinistic" or "Particular" Baptists, who maintained that Christ's redemption was intended for the elect alone. The origin of the General Baptists is connected with the name of John Smyth (d. 1612), pastor of a church at Gainsborough, Lincolnshire, which had separated from the Church of England. About 1606, pastor and flock, to escape persecution, emigrated to Amsterdam, where they formed the second English congregation. In 1609, Smyth, owing possibly in some measure to Mennonite influence, rejected infant baptism, although he retained affusion. In this he was supported by his church. Some members of the congregation returned to England (1611 or 1612) under the leadership of Helwys (c. 1550–1616) and formed in London the nucleus of the first Baptist community. Persecution had abated, and they do not seem to have been molested. By 1626 there were in different parts of England five General Baptist churches; by 1644, they had increased, it is said, to forty-seven; and by 1660 the membership of the body had reached about 20,000. It was between 1640 and 1660 that the General Baptists began to claim that immersion was the only valid mode of baptism. They were persecuted by Charles II (1660–85); but the Act of Toleration (1689) brought relief and recognized the Baptists as the third dissenting denomination (Presbyterians, Independents, and Baptists). In the eighteenth century, Anti-Trinitarian ideas spread among the General Baptists, and by 1750, many, perhaps the majority of them, had become Unitarians. As a result of the great Wesleyan revival of the second half of the eighteenth century, new religious activity manifested itself among the General Baptists.

Dan Taylor (1738–1816) organized the orthodox portion of them into the New Connexion of the General Baptists. The latter appellative soon disappeared, as the "Old Connexion", or unorthodox party, gradually merged into the Unitarian denomination. In 1816, the General Baptists established a missionary society. Their doctrinal differences with the Particular Baptists gradually disappeared in the course of the nineteenth century, and the two bodies united in 1891.

The Particular Baptists originated shortly after the General Baptists. Their first congregation was organized in 1633 by former members of a London "Separatist Church", who seceded and were rebaptized. Mr. John Spillsbury became their minister. In 1638 a second secession from the original church occurred, and in 1640 another Particular Baptist Congregation was formed. The opinion now began to be held that immersion alone was real baptism. Richard Blunt was sent to the Netherlands to be duly immersed. On his return he baptized the others, and thus the first Baptist church in the full meaning of the term was constituted in 1641. In 1644 there were seven Particular Baptist churches in London. They drew up a confession of faith (1644), which was republished in 1646. The Particular Baptists now rapidly increased in numbers and influence. Some of them held prominent positions under Cromwell. With the latter's army Baptists came to Ireland, where the denomination never flourished, and to Scotland, where it took firm root only after 1750 and adopted some peculiar practices. Wales proved a more fruitful soil. A church was founded at or near Swansea in 1649. In the time of the Commonwealth (1649–60), churches multiplied owing to the successful preaching of Vavasour Powell (1617–70); and the number of Baptists, all Calvinistic, is to-day comparatively large in Wales and Monmouthshire. One of the prominent men who suffered persecution for the Baptist cause under Charles II was John Bunyan (1628–88), the author of "The Pilgrim's Progress". In the first part of the eighteenth century the Particular Baptists injured their own cause by their excessive emphasis of the Calvinistic element in their teaching, which made them condemn missionary activity and bordered on fatalism. The Wesleyan revival brought about a reaction against the deadening influence of ultra-Calvinism. Andrew Fuller (1754–1815) and Robert Hall (1764–1831) propounded milder theological views. The Baptist Home Mission Society was formed in 1779. In 1792 the foundation of the Baptist Missionary Society at Kettering, Northamptonshire, inaugurated the work of missions to the heathen. In this undertaking William Carey (1761–1834) was the prime mover. Perhaps the most eminent Baptist preacher of the nineteenth century in England was C. H. Spurgeon (1834–92), whose sermons were published weekly and had a large circulation. In recent years, the Baptists created a "Twentieth Century Fund," to be expended in furthering the interests of the denomination.

(2) *The Baptists in the United States.*—The first Baptist Church in the United States did not spring historically from the English Baptist churches, but had an independent origin. It was established by Roger Williams (c. 1600–83). Williams was a minister of the Church of England, who, owing to his separatist views, fled to America in search of religious freedom. He landed at Boston (February, 1631), and shortly after his arrival was called to be minister at Salem. Certain opinions, e. g. his denial of the right of the secular power to punish purely religious offences and his denunciation of the charter of the Massachusetts Colony as worthless, brought him into conflict with the civil authorities. He was summoned before the General Court in Boston and, refusing to retract, was banished (October, 1635). He left the colony and purchased from the Narrangansett Indians a tract of land. Other colonists soon joined him, and the settlement, which was one of the first in the United States to be established on the principle of complete religious liberty, became the city of Providence. In 1639 Williams repudiated the value of the baptism he had received in infancy, and was baptized by Ezekiel Holliman, a former member of the Salem church. Williams then baptized Holliman with ten others, thus constituting the first Baptist church in the New World. A second church was founded shortly after (c. 1644) at Newport, Rhode Island, of which John Clarke (1609–76) became the pastor. In the Massachusetts Colony, from 1642 onward, Baptists, because of their religious views, came into conflict with the local authorities. A law was passed against them in 1644. In spite of this, we find at Rehoboth, in 1649, Baptists who began to hold regular meetings. In 1663 John Myles, who had emigrated with his Baptist church from Swansea, Wales, settled in the same place and most writers date the establishment of the first Baptist church in Massachusetts from the time of his arrival. The community removed in 1667 to a new site near the Rhode Island frontier, which they called Swansea. The first Baptist church in Boston was established in 1665, and the organization of the first one in Maine, then part of Massachusetts, was completed in 1682. The members of the latter, on account of the persecution to which they were still subjected, removed in 1684 to Charleston, South Carolina, and founded the first Baptist church in the South. The church of Groton (1705) was the first in Connecticut, where there were four in existence at the beginning of the religious revival known as the Great Awakening (1740).

During the period of these foundations in New England, Baptists appeared also in New York State, at least as early as 1656. The exact date of the establishment of the first church there is not ascertainable, but it was very probably at the beginning of the eighteenth century. From 1684 on, churches also appeared in Pennsylvania, New Jersey, and Delaware. Cold Spring, Bucks Co., had the first one in Pennsylvania (1684); and Middletown heads the list in New Jersey (1688). A congregation was organized also in 1688 at Pennepek, or Lower Dublin, now part of Philadelphia. The latter churches were to exert very considerable influence in shaping the doctrinal system of the largest part of American Baptists. Philadelphia became a centre of Baptist activity and organization. Down to about the year 1700 it seemed as if the majority of American Baptists would belong to the General or Arminian branch. Many of the earliest churches were of that type. But only Particular Baptist congregations were established in and about Philadelphia, and these, through the foundation of the Philadelphia Association in 1707, which fostered mutual intercourse among them, became a strong central organization about which other Baptist churches rallied. As a result, we see to-day the large number of Particular (Regular) Baptists. Until the Great Awakening, however, which gave new impetus to their activity, they increased but slowly. Since that time their progress has not been seriously checked, not even by the Revolution. True, the academy of Hopewell, New Jersey, their first educational institution, established in 1756, disappeared during the war; but Rhode Island College, chartered in 1764, survived it and became Brown University in 1804. Other educational institutions, to mention only the earlier ones, were founded at the beginning of the nineteenth century: Waterville (now Colby) College, Maine, in 1818; Colgate University, Hamilton, New York, in 1820; and in 1821, Columbian College at Washington (now the undenominational George Washington University).

Organized mission work was also undertaken at about the same time. In 1814 "The General Missionary Convention of the Baptist Denomination in the United States of America for Foreign Missions" was established at Philadelphia. It split in 1845 and formed the "American Baptist Missionary Union" for the North, with present head-quarters at Boston, and the "Southern Baptist Convention", with headquarters at Richmond (Virginia), and Atlanta (Georgia), for foreign and home missions respectively. In 1832, the "American Baptist Home Mission Society", intended primarily for the Western States, was organized in New York where it still has its headquarters. In 1824, the "Baptist General Tract Society" was formed at Washington, removed to Philadelphia in 1826, and in 1840 became the "American Baptist Publication Society". The Regular Baptists divided in 1845, not indeed doctrinally, but organically, on the question of slavery. Since that time, attempts at reunion having remained fruitless; they exist in three bodies: Northern, Southern, and Coloured. The Northern Baptists constituted, 17 May, 1907, at Washington, a representative body, called the "Northern Baptist Convention", whose object is "to give expression to the sentiment of its constituency upon matters of denominational importance and of general religious and moral interest." Governor Hughes of New York was elected president of the new organization.

(3) *The Baptists in Other Countries.*—(a) America. The earliest Baptist church in the Dominion of Canada was organized at Horton, Nova Scotia, in 1763, by the Rev. Ebenezer Moulton of New England. This church, like many of the earlier ones, was composed of Baptists and Congregationalists. The influx of settlers from New England and Scotland and the work of zealous evangelists, such as Theodore Seth Harding, who laboured in the Maritime Provinces from 1795 to 1855, soon increased the number of Baptists in the country. The end of the eighteenth century was marked by a period of revivals, which prepared the formation of the "Association of the Baptist churches of Nova Scotia and New Brunswick" in 1800. In 1815, a missionary society was formed, and the work of organization in every line was continued throughout the nineteenth century, growing apace with Baptist influence and numbers. In 1889 some previously existing societies were consolidated in the "Baptist Convention of Ontario and Quebec", whose various departments of work are: home missions, foreign missions, publications, church edifices, etc. Among the educational institutions of the Canadian Baptists may be mentioned Acadia College (founded 1838), Woodstock College (founded 1860), and McMaster University at Toronto (chartered 1887). Moulton College for women (opened 1888) is affiliated to the last mentioned institution. In other parts of America the Baptists are chiefly represented in the countries colonized by England. Thus we find a Baptist church in Jamaica as early as 1816. In Latin America the Baptist churches are not numerous and are of missionary origin. Recently, the Northern Baptists have taken Porto Rico as their special field, while the Southern Baptist Convention has chosen Cuba.

(b) European Continent. The founder of the Baptist churches in Germany was Johann Gerhard Oncken, whose independent study of the Scriptures led him to adopt Baptist views several years before he had an opportunity of receiving "believers' baptism". Having incidentally heard that an American Baptist, B. Sears, was pursuing his studies at Berlin, he communicated with him and was with six others baptized by him at Hamburg in 1834. His activity as an evangelist drew new adherents to the movement. The number of the Baptists increased, in spite of the opposition of the German state churches. In Prussia alone relative toleration was extended to them until the foundation of the Empire brought to them almost everywhere freedom in the exercise of their religion. A Baptist theological school was founded in 1881 at Hamburg-Horn. From Germany the Baptists spread to the neighbouring countries, Denmark, Sweden, Switzerland, Austria, Russia. Nowhere on the Continent of Europe has the success of the Baptists been so marked as in Sweden, where their number is larger to-day than even in Germany. The Swedish Baptists date from the year 1848, when five persons were baptized near Gothenburg by a Baptist minister from Denmark. Andreas Wiberg became their great leader (1855–87). They have had a seminary at Stockholm since 1866. Among the Latin nations the Baptists never gained a firm foothold, although a Particular Baptist church seems to have existed in France by 1646, and a theological school was established in that country in 1879.

(c) Asia, Australasia, and Africa. William Carey first preached the Baptist doctrine in India in 1793. India and the neighbouring countries have ever since remained a favourite field for Baptist missionary work and have flourishing missions. Missions exist also in China, Japan, and several other Asiatic countries. The first Baptist churches in Australasia were organized between 1830 and 1840 in different places. Immigration from England, whence the leading Baptist ministers were until very recently drawn, increased, though not rapidly, the numbers of the denomination. During the period which elapsed between 1860 and 1870, a new impulse was given to Baptist activity. Churches were organized in rapid succession in Australia, and missionary work was taken up in India. The two chief hindrances complained of by Baptists in that part of the world, are State Socialism, i. e. excessive concentration of power in the executive, and want of loyalty to strictly denominational principles and practices. The Baptist churches of the African continent are, if we except

South Africa, of missionary origin. The Negro Baptists of the United States had at an early date missionaries in this field. Two coloured men, Lott Carey, a former slave, and Colin Teague, set sail in 1820 for Liberia, where the first church was organized in 1821. To-day we find Baptist missions in various parts of Africa.

III. MINOR BAPTIST BODIES.—Side by side with the larger body of Baptists, several sects exist. They are found chiefly in the United States.

(1) *The Baptist Church of Christ* originated in Tennessee, about 1808, and spread to several other Southern States. Its doctrine is a mild form of Calvinism, with belief in a general atonement and admission of feet-washing as religious ordinance. [Communicants, 8,254 according to Dr. H. K. Carroll, the acknowledged authority, whose statistics, published in "The Christian Advocate" (New York, 17 January, 1907, p. 98), we shall quote for these sects.]

(2) *The Campbellites, Disciples of Christ*, or *Christians*, date back as a distinct religious body to the early part of the nineteenth century. They are the outgrowth of that movement which manifested itself simultaneously in some of the religious denominations in the United States in favour of the Bible alone without creeds. Thomas Campbell (1763-1854) and Alexander Campbell (1788-1866), father and son, became the leaders of the movement. (Communicants, 1,264,758.)

(3) *The Dunkards* (from the German *tunken*, to dip), *German Baptists*, or *Brethren*, were founded about 1708 in Germany by Alexander Mack. Between 1719 and 1729 they all emigrated to the United States and settled mostly in Pennsylvania. They are found to-day in many parts of the Union, but divisions have taken place among them. They practise threefold immersion, hold their communion service, which is preceded by the *agape*, in the evening, and seek to be excessively simple and unostentatious in their social intercourse, dress, etc. (Membership, 121,194.)

(4) *The Freewill Baptists* correspond in doctrine and practice to the English General Baptists, but originated in the United States. They exist in two distinct bodies. The older was founded in North Carolina and constituted an association in 1729. Many of its members subsequently joined the Regular Baptists. Those who did not unite became known as the "Free Willers" and later as the "Original Freewill Baptists", and are found in the two Carolinas. The larger body of the "Freewill Baptists" was founded in New Hampshire. Benjamin Randall organized the first church at New Durham in 1780. The denomination spread throughout New England and the West, and was joined in 1841 by the "Free-Communion Baptists" of New York (increase, 55 churches and 2,500 members). It maintains several colleges and academies, and has changed its official name to "Free Baptists". The American General Baptists are in substantial doctrinal agreement with the Freewill Baptists. (Membership: Original Freewill Baptists, 12,000; Freewill Baptists, 82,303; General Baptists, 29,347.)

(5) *The Old Two-Seed-in-the-Spirit Predestinarian Baptists* are Manichæan in doctrine, holding that there are two seeds, one of good and one of evil. The doctrine is credited to Daniel Parker, who laboured in different parts of the Union in the first half of the nineteenth century (12,851 communicants).

(6) *The Primitive Baptists*, also called *Old-School, Anti-Mission*, and *Hard-Shell, Baptists* constitute a sect which is opposed to missions, Sunday schools, and in general to human religious institutions. They arose about 1835 (126,000 communicants).

(7) The foundation of the *Separate* and of the *United Baptists* was the result, either immediate or mediate, of the attitude taken by some Baptists toward the Whitefield revival movement of the eighteenth century (Separate Baptist, 6,479; United Baptists, 13,209).

(8) *The Seventh-Day Baptists* differ from the tenets of the Baptists generally only in their observance of the seventh day of the week as the Sabbath of the Lord. They appeared in England in the latter part of the sixteenth century under the name of "Sabbatarian Baptists". Their first church in this country was organized at Newport, R. I., in 1671. In 1818 the name Seventh Day Baptists was adopted (Communicants, 8,493).

(9) The *Six-principle Baptists* are a small body and date from the seventeenth century. They are so called from the six doctrines of their creed, contained in Heb., vi, 1–2: (a) Repentance from dead works; (b) Faith toward God; (c) The doctrine of Baptism; (d) The imposition of hands; (e) The resurrection of the dead; (f) Eternal judgment. (858 communicants.)

(10) The *Winebrennerians* or *Church of God* were founded by John Winebrenner (1797–1860) in Pennsylvania, where their chief strength still lies. The first congregation was established in 1829. The Winebrennerians admit three Divine ordinances: baptism, feet-washing, and the Lord's Supper (41,475 communicants).

IV. STATISTICS.—According to the American Baptist Year-Book, published annually at Philadelphia, there were in 1907, not including the minor Baptist sects, 5,736,263 Baptists in the world. They had 55,505 churches and 38,216 ordained ministers. The denomination counted 4,974,014 members in North America; 4,812,653 in the United States, with church property worth $109,960,610; and 117,842 in Canada. South America has but 4,465 Baptists; Europe 564,670 (434,751 in Great Britain, 44,656 in Sweden, 33,790 in Germany, 24,132 in Russia); Asia, 155,969; Australasia, 24,402; and Africa, 12,743. The statistic statement of Dr. H. K. Carroll, already referred to above, credits the Regular Baptists together with eleven branch denominations in the United States for 1906 with a membership of 5,140,770, 54,566 churches and 38,010 ministers; Regular Baptists, North, 1,113,222; South, 1,939,563; Coloured, 1,779,69.

The divisions in the bibliography correspond to the divisions of the article.

I. STRONG, *Systematic Theology* (3d ed., New York, 1890); SCHAFF, *The Creeds of Christendom* (New York, 1877), I, 845–859; III, 738–756; MCCLINTOCK AND STRONG, *Cyclopedia of Bibl., Theol., and Eccl. Lit.* (New York, 1871), I, 653–660; CATHCART, *The Baptist Encyclopedia* (Philadelphia, 1881).

II.—(1) CROSBY, *The History of the English Baptists* (London, 1738–40); IVIMEY, *A History of the English Baptists* (London, 1811–30); TAYLOR, *The History of the English General Baptists* (London, 1818); ARMITAGE, *A History of the Baptists* (New York, 1887); VEDDER, *The Baptists* (New York, 1903) in the *Story of the Churches* Series.

(2) NEWMAN, *A History of the Baptist Churches in the United States* (4th ed., New York, 1902) in *Am. Church Hist. Ser.*, II, bibliog., xi–xv; BURRAGE, *A History of the Baptists in New England* (Philadelphia, 1894); VEDDER, *History of the Baptists in the Middle States* (Philadelphia, 1898); SMITH, *A History of the Baptists in the Western States* (Philadelphia, 1900); RILEY, *A History of the Baptists in the Southern States* (Philadelphia, 1899).

(3) NEWMAN, *A Century of Baptist Achievement* (Philadelphia, 1901); LEHMANN, *Geschichte der deutsch. Baptisten* (Hamburg, 1896); SCHROEDER, *History of the Swedish Baptists* (New York, 1898).

III. CARROLL, *The Religious Forces of the United States* (New York, 1893) in *Amer. Church Hist. Series*, I; TYLER, *The Disciples of Christ* (New York, 1894) in same *Series*, XII, 1–162; STEWART, *History of the Freewill Baptists* (Dover, New Hampshire, 1862).

N. A. WEBER.

Bar, CONFEDERATION OF. See POLAND.

Barac (Heb. *Bārāq*, lightning), the deliverer of the Israelites from the power of the Chanaanites under the judgeship of Debbora. He was the son of Abinoem of Cedes in Nephtali (Judges, iv, 6) and probably belonged to the tribe of Issachar (v, 15). When, after the death of the Judge Aod, "the children of Israel again did evil in the sight of the Lord', (iv, 1), they were delivered into the hands of the Chanaanite King Jabin of Asor who grievously oppressed them for twenty years (iv, 3). Thereupon the prophetess Debbora of Mount Ephraim, between Rama and Bethel, instigates Barac, manifestly a leading captain of the time, to assemble 10,000 men of the tribes of Nephtali and Zabulon (iv, 6; cf. v, 14) and to take the field against Sisara, the general of Jabin's army. Barac assembles his warriors at Cedes, moves to Mount Thabor, and by a rush down the mountain surprises the Chanaanites (iv, 10, 12, 14; cf. v, 15, 19, 21). The panic-stricken army of Sisara is attacked, routed, pursued, and finally cut to pieces (iv, 16). Sisara, having taken to flight, seeks refuge in the tent of Jahel, the wife of Haber, the Cinite, where he meets with a treacherous end (iv, 21; cf. v, 26). This signal victory of Barac, which put an end to the power and oppression of Jabin, and which was followed by a period of forty years' rest, is commemorated in the triumphal ode of Debbora and Barac (v). For the various accounts of Barac's exploits which critics detect in Judges, iv, and v, see JUDGES, BOOK OF.

F. X. E. ALBERT.

Baradæus, JACOB, a Syrian Monophysite bishop, born at Tella, towards the end of the fifth or the beginning of the sixth century, died in 578. He was the son of Theophilus bar Mânû, a priest of Tella, and hence his real name was Jacob bar Theophilus; the surname Búrde'ânâ, corrupted into Baradæus, was derived from the coarse horse-cloth *bárdá'thân* which he usually wore. After receiving a good education he became a monk in the monastery of Pesîltâ, and a disciple of Severus, the head of the Monophysites. In the first half of the sixth century, Monophysitism, weakened by internal dissensions and by the opposition of the Emperor Justinian, was on the verge of disappearing, especially when its leader Severus died, 538. Probably through the influence of the Empress Theodora, Baradæus was made Bishop of Edessa in 543, and henceforth devoted all his energies to the defence of Monophysitism. Through his untiring activity he breathed a new life into what seemed a mere expiring faction. At the cost of great hardships, he went around ordaining priests and deacons and strengthening his coreligionists. There exists a profession of faith addressed to him by the abbots of the province of Arabia, with 137 signatures (see Lamy, in "Actes du XIᵉ Congrès des Orientalistes", § 4, Paris, 1897) showing that he was the undisputed leader in Monophysite circles. It is because of his prominence that the Monophysites were, and still are, called after his name, Jacobites. Baradæus has left very little in writing: a liturgy, and a few letters.

The main source for the life of Baradæus is JOHN OF EPHESUS, *Ecclesiastical History*, the third part of which has been published by CURETON (Oxford, 1853), and *Lives of the Oriental Saints*, LAND ed. in his *Anecdota Syriaca*, II, 249–257; DUVAL, *Littérature Syriaque* (2d ed., Paris, 1900); KLEYN, *Jacobus Baradäus* (Leyden, 1882).

R. BUTIN.

Baraga, FREDERIC, first Bishop of Marquette, Michigan, U. S. A., b. 29 June, 1797, at Malavas, in the parish of Dobernice in the Austrian Dukedom of Carniola; d. at Marquette, Mich., 19 January, 1868. He was baptized on the very day of his birth, in the parish church of Dobernice, by the names of Irenæus Frederic, the first of which, however, he never used, retaining only the second. His parents, Johann Nepomuc Baraga and Maria Katharine Josefa (*née* de Jenčič), had five children, of whom Frederic was the fourth. His father was not rich, but his mother inherited after her father's death the estate of Malavas, besides a vast fortune. They were God-fearing and pious, and strove, while they survived, to give a good education to their children. His mother died in 1808, and his father in 1812,

and Frederic spent his boyhood in the house of Dr. George Dolinar, a layman, professor in the diocesan clerical seminary at Laibach.

In 1816 young Frederic Baraga entered the University of Vienna, studied law, and graduated in 1821, but soon turned his thoughts to the clerical state, and entered the seminary of Laibach that same year. He was ordained priest 21 September, 1823, at Laibach, and laboured with great zeal and spiritual success as assistant in St. Martin's parish, near Krainberg, and at Metlika, in Lower Carniola. On the 29th of October, 1830, he left his native land for the United States to spend the rest of his life in the Indian missionary field. After a journey of two months, he landed in New York on the 31st of December, 1830. He then proceeded to Cincinnati, Ohio, where he arrived 18 January, 1831. He was most kindly received by the Rt. Rev. Edward Fenwick, Bishop of Cincinnati, and during the winter and spring months laboured among the German Catholics of that city and elsewhere. On the 28th of May, 1831, he arrived at Arbre Croche, now Harbor Springs, his first Indian mission. There he laboured with apostolic zeal at the conversion of the Ottawas during two years and four months, during which time he baptized 547 Indian adults and children. He was succeeded in 1833 by Rev. F. Saenderl, Superior of the Redemptorists in the United States. On or about the 8th of September, 1833, Baraga left Arbre Croche to found a new Indian mission at Grand River, Mich. He arrived at his destination (now Grand Rapids, Mich.) on the 23d of September. He immediately began the building of a combination church, school, and pastoral residence, which was very poor, owing to the deficiency of funds. There he laboured most earnestly, though not as successfully as at Arbre Croche, until February, 1835, when he was succeeded by Father Andrew Viszoczky, a Hungarian priest. Baraga himself estimated the number of his converts at about two hundred, but Bishop Rese estimated the number of Indian converts in his diocese in 1834 at three thousand, with twelve churches or chapels.

Baraga's next Indian mission was among the Chippewas at La Pointe, Wisconsin, where he arrived 27 July, 1835. There he laboured successfully for about eight years, baptizing 981 Indians and whites. In 1843 he founded the L'Anse Indian mission in Michigan, arriving there on the 24th of October. For ten years he laboured in this vast mission, being for many years the only Catholic priest in Upper Michigan. He attended not only to the Indians, but also to the whites of the vast territory, as the discovery of iron and copper drew many German, French, and English-speaking Catholics to the Northern Peninsula of Michigan. Truly incredible are the hardships and labours of Baraga at this period of his life. On the 29th of July, 1853, the Northern Peninsula of Michigan was detached from the Diocese of Detroit and erected into a vicariate Apostolic, and Baraga was appointed its first bishop. He was consecrated in the cathedral

THE RIGHT REV. FREDERIC BARAGA

of Cincinnati by Archbishop Purcell, Bishop Le-Fevre of Detroit and Bishop Henni of Milwaukee officiating as assistant consecrators. Shortly after his elevation to the episcopal dignity Bishop Baraga issued two circulars to his people, one in Chippewa and the other in English. His jurisdiction extended not only to the whole Northern Peninsula of Michigan, but also to a large part of the Lower Peninsula, to Northern Wisconsin, and to the North Shore of Lake Superior. He laboured in this vast extent of territory for fifteen years, travelling almost incessantly, from the opening to the close of navigation year after year. On the 23d of October, 1865, by Apostolic authority he transferred his See from Sault Ste. Marie to Marquette, where he died at the age of seventy years.

Bishop Baraga will always rank with the foremost authors in American Indian literature. He composed the first known Chippewa grammar. This was a truly Herculean task, for he had to establish after long and close observation and deep study all the rules of the Chippewa grammar. This grammar has gone through three editions. In his preface to his Chippewa dictionary, printed in Cincinnati, O., in 1853, by Jos. A. Hermann, he says: "This is, to the best of my knowledge, the first Dictionary of the Otchipwe language ever published. The compilation of it has cost me several years of assiduous labour." This dictionary has also passed through several editions. Both grammar and dictionary are most highly prized and constantly used by Indian missionaries and others. His Indian prayer book and works of instruction are much read by both Indians and their pastors. Baraga always wrote in a very simple and clear style. His writings are admirably adapted to the limited capacity of his Indian readers, and can be understood even by ignorant Indian children. His "Dušna Taša", a prayer book in Slovenian, his own native language, passed through ten editions, the last, in 1905, with 84,000 copies. This alone is a proof of its great popularity and usefulness.

In addition to the "Theoretical and Practical Grammar of the Otchipwe [Chippewa] Language" (Detroit, 1850), the Chippewa dictionary, and the "Dušna Taša" mentioned above, the published works of Bishop Baraga include: "Veneration and Imitation of the Blessed Mother of God", in Slovenian (1830); "Animie-Misinaigan", an Ottawa prayer book; "Jesus o Bimadisiwim" (The Life of Jesus), in Ottawa (Paris, 1837); "On the manners and customs of the Indians" in Slovenian (Laibach, 1837); "Gagikwe-Masiniagan", a sermon-book, in Chippewa (1839 and 1859); "Zlata Jabelka"—"Golden Apples" (Laibach, 1844); "Kagige Debwewinan"—"Eternal Truths"; "Nanagatawendamo-Masinaigan"—Instructions on the Commandments and sacraments.

No Indian missionary of modern times was more beloved and revered by both Indians and whites than Baraga. He loved his Indians with a warmhearted devotion which they reciprocated. Men of all positions in society, Catholics and non-Catholics, revered him as an ideal man, Christian, and bishop. Michigan has named after him one of her counties, several towns, and post offices, and his name has been given to one of the principal streets of Marquette. In his native country he is, if possible, even more popular than in America. His life, published in Slovenian, in 1906, has already (1907) reached a sale of 85,000 copies. That life might be summed up in the one phrase: Saintliness in action.

VERWYST, *Life and Labours of Rt. Rev. Frederic Baraga* (Milwaukee, 1900); RAZEN, *History of the Diocese of Sault Ste. Marie and Marquette*; ELLIOTT, *Baraga among the Indians* in *Am. Cath. Q. Rev.* (1896) 106 sqq.

CHRYSOSTOM VERWYST.

Barat, MADELEINE-SOPHIE, VENERABLE, foundress of the Society of the Sacred Heart, b. at Joigny, Burgundy, 12 December, 1779; d. in Paris, 24 May, 1865. She was the youngest child of Jacques Barat, a vine-dresser and cooper, and his wife, Madeleine Foufé, and received baptism the morning after her birth, her brother Louis, aged eleven, being chosen godfather. It was to this brother that she owed the exceptional education which fitted her for her life-work. Whilst her mother found her an apt pupil in practical matters, Louis saw her singular endowments of mind and heart; and when, at the age of twenty-two, he returned as professor to the seminary at Joigny, he taught his sister Latin, Greek, history, natural science, Spanish, and Italian. Soon she took delight in reading the classics in the original, and surpassed her brother's pupils at the seminary.

After the Reign of Terror, Louis called Sophie to Paris, to train her for the religious life, for which she longed. When he had joined the Fathers of the Faith, a band of fervent priests, united in the hope of becoming members of the Society of Jesus on its restoration, he one day spoke of his sister to Father Varin, to whom had been bequeathed by the saintly Léonor de Tournély the plan of founding a society of women wholly devoted to the worship of the Sacred Heart of Jesus, to prayer and sacrifice, and destined to do for girls what the restored Society of Jesus would do for boys. Father Varin had vainly sought a fitting instrument to begin this work; he now found one in this modest, retiring girl of twenty. He unfolded the project, which seemed to satisfy all her aspirations, and she bowed before his authoritative declaration that this was for her the will of God. With three companions she made her first consecration, 21 November, 1800, the date which marks the foundation of the Society of the Sacred Heart. In September, 1801, the first convent was opened at Amiens, and thither Sophie went to help in the work of teaching. It was impossible yet to assume the name "Society of the Sacred Heart", lest a political significance be attached to it; its members were known as *Dames de la Foi* or *de l'Instruction Chrétienne*. Father Varin allowed Sophie to make her vows, 7 June, 1802, with Geneviève Deshayes.

The community and school were increasing, and a poor school had just been added, when it became evident to Father Varin that Mademoiselle Loquet, who had hitherto acted as superior, lacked the qualities requisite for the office, and Sophie, although the youngest, was named superior (1802). Her first act was to kneel and kiss the feet of each of her sisters. Such was ever the spirit of her government. November, 1804, found her at Sainte-Marie-d'en-Haut, near Grenoble, receiving a community of Visitation nuns into her institute. One of them, Philippine Duchesne, was later to introduce the society into America. Grenoble was the first of some eighty foundations which Mother Barat was to make, not only in France, but in North America (1818), Italy (1828), Switzerland (1830), Belgium (1834), Algiers (1841). England (1842), Ireland (1842), Spain (1846), Holland (1848), Germany (1851), South America (1853) Austria (1853), Poland (1857).

Mother Barat was elected superior-general in January, 1806, by a majority of one vote only, for the influence of an ambitious priest, chaplain at Amiens, wellnigh wrecked the nascent institute. Prolonged prayer, silent suffering, tact, respect, charity, were the only means she used to oppose his designs. With Father Varin, now a Jesuit, she elaborated constitutions and rules grafted on the stock of the Institute of St. Ignatius. These rules were received with joy in all the houses, Amiens alone excepted; but Mother Barat's wisdom and humility soon won submission even here. In 1818 she sent Mother Duchesne, with four companions, to the New World; her strong and holy hand was ever ready to support and guide this first missioner of the Society. She called all the superiors together in council at Paris in 1820, to provide a uniform course of studies for their schools. These studies were to be solid and serious, to fit the pupils to become intelligent wives and devoted mothers; to give that cultivation of mind, that formation of character, which go to make up a true woman; all was to be stamped and sealed with strong religious principles and devotion to the Sacred Heart.

Foundations multiplied, and Mother Barat, seeing the necessity of a stronger guarantee of unity, sought it in union with Rome. The solemn approbation was obtained much sooner than usual, owing to a memoir drawn up by the foundress and presented to Leo XII in May, 1826. The decree of approbation was promulgated in December. The society being now fully organized and sealed by Rome's approval, for forty years Mother Barat journeyed from convent to convent, wrote many thousand letters, and assembled general congregations, so as to preserve its original spirit. The Paris school gained European repute; Rome counted three establishments, asked for and blessed by three successive pontiffs. At Lyons Mother Barat founded the Congregation of the Children of Mary for former pupils and other ladies. In the same year (1832), she began at Turin the work of retreats for ladies of the world, an apostleship since widely and profitably imitated. Numerous foundations brought Mother Barat into personal contact with all classes. We find her crossing and re-crossing France, Switzerland, Italy, often on the eve of revolutions; now the centre of a society of *émigrés* whose intellectual gifts, high social position, and moral worth are seldom found united; now sought out by cardinals and Roman princesses during her visits to her Roman houses; at another time, speaking on matters educational with Madame de Genlis; or again, exercising that supernatural ascendency which aroused the admiration of such men as Bishop Frayssinous, Doctor Récamier, and Duc de Rohan.

These exterior labours were far from absorbing all Mother Barat's time or energies; they coexisted with a life of ever-increasing holiness and continual prayer; for the real secret of her influence lay in her habitual seclusion from the outside world, in the strong religious formation of her daughters which this seclusion made possible, and in the enlightened, profound, and supernatural views on education which she communicated to the religious engaged in her schools. She worked by and through them all, and thus reached out to the ends of the earth. In spite of herself she attracted and charmed all who approached her. New foundations she always entrusted to other hands; for, like all great rulers, she had the twofold gift of intuition in the choice of persons fitted for office, and trust of those in responsible posts, allowing them much freedom of action in details, guiding them only by her counsels and usually from afar. Prelates who now and then ventured to attribute to her the successes of the Society, saw that instead of pleasing, they distressed her exceedingly.

Beloved by her daughters, venerated by princes and pontiffs, yet ever lowly of heart, Mother Barat died at the mother-house in Paris, on Ascension Day, 1865, as she had foretold, after four days' illness. She was buried at Conflans, the house of novitiate, where her body was found intact in 1893. In 1879 she was declared Venerable, and the process of beatification introduced.

Life of Venerable Madeleine Louise Sophie Barat (Roehampton, 1900); BAUNARD, *Histoire de la Vénérable Mère Barat* (Paris, 1876, 1900), tr. FULLERTON (Roehampton, 1876; abr., 1893); UNE RELIGIEUSE DU SACRÉ CŒUR, *Vie de la Vénérable Mère Barat. Une Religieuse du Sacré Cœur* (Paris, 1884, 1900).

ALICE POWER.

Barat, NICOLAS, a French Orientalist, b. at

Bourges during the first quarter of the seventeenth century; d. in 1706 at Paris. He began his studies at Sens, and continued them in Paris, where he was instructor in the Mazarin College. There he came under the influence of Richard Simon, the famous Orientalist and Biblical scholar. The greater part of his published work was done in collaboration with other scholars. With Père Bordes he edited the posthumous work of Thomassin, "Glossarium universale hebraicum" (Paris, 1697), and aided J. B. Duhamel in the publication of his Bible (Paris, 1706). At the time of his death he was engaged on a French translation of Schabtai's "Rabbinical Library". His critical opinions, and much curious literary information that he had acquired, were published posthumously under the title, "Nouvelle bibliothèque choisie" (Amsterdam, 1714, 2 vols.).

TALLEMANT, *Eloge de M. Barat* in *Mémoires de l'académie des inscrip. et belles lettres*, I, 345; BOZE, *Histoire de l'acad. des inscrip.*, I, 41.

ENEAS B. GOODWIN.

Barba, ALVARO ALONZO, a secular priest of whom Nicolas Antonio (Bibliotheca hispana nova, 1786) says: "Bæticus ex oppido Lepe, apud Potosi "; hence of Andalusian origin. By Lepe and Potosi, Lipes in western Bolivia might be indicated. He lived at Potosi during the period when its silver-mines were most productive and luxury and revelry among the Spanish residents and mine-owners had nearly reached the climax. Father Barba, in the midst of a turmoil of sensuality, divided his time between his sacerdotal duties and a close study of the ores of this region and their treatment. There had been, since 1570, a complete revolution in the treatment of silver-ores, through the application of quicksilver, and a number of improvements followed, of which Barba had knowledge. In 1640 he published, at Madrid, a book entitled "Arte de los Metales", which, though properly metallurgic and out of date, is still of value as the earliest work on South American ores and minerals. Many of its indications are well worthy the attention of miners and prospectors. This is especially the case in regard to mineral localities in Bolivia. The book was republished in Spanish in 1729, in 1770 and, recently, in Chile. There is a French translation from 1751 and one also in English.

PINELO, *Epitome, etc.*, (1738), II; NICOLAS ANTONIO, *Bibliotheca hispana nova* (Madrid, 1786); MENDIBURÚ, *Dicc. Hist.-biog., etc.*, (Lima, 1876), II; *Relaciones geográficas de Indias* (Madrid, 1885), II, Appendix iv.

AD. F. BANDELIER.

Barbadoes. See DEMERARA.

Barbalissos, a titular see of Mesopotamia. It was a city in *Provincia Augusta Euphratensis*, where the *Equites Dalmatae Illyriciani* kept garrison (Notit. Dignitat. Orientis, ed. Boecking, 88, 389). Justinian raised anew its walls (Procop., De ædific., II, 19; Malalas, Chronograph., XVIII, in Migne, P. G., XCVII, 676). At an early date it was a suffragan of Hierapolis, a metropolis in the Patriarchate of Antioch. Its bishop Antonius was present at the Council of Nicæa (325); two other bishops, Aquilinus and Marinianus, are known between 431 and 451 (Lequien, II, 949). The see is still mentioned in the sixth century. From 793 to 1042 five Jacobite bishops are known bearing this title (Revue de l'Orient chrétien, VI, 192). Its site is marked by the ruins at Qala' at Balis, which partly retains the old name, south of Meskene, on the road from Aleppo to Soura, where the Euphrates turns suddenly to the east. The spellings Barbarissos and Barbairissos in later "Notitiæ" are wrong; so is *Barbaricus campus* in Procopius (De bello Persico, II, 99). Lequien (I, 407) wrongly gives Barbalissus as synonymous with Balbisse, another bishopric in Cappadocia, known only in 1143.

S. VAILHÉ.

Barbara, SAINT, Virgin and Martyr.—There is no

reference to St. Barbara contained in the authentic early historical authorities for Christian antiquity, neither does her name appear in the original recension of St. Jerome's martyrology. Veneration of the saint was common, however, from the seventh century. At about this date there were in existence legendary Acts of her martyrdom which were inserted in the collection of Symeon Metaphrastes and were used as well by the authors (Ado, Usuard, etc.) of the enlarged martyrologies composed during the ninth century in Western Europe. According to these narratives, which are essentially the same, Barbara was the daughter of a rich heathen named Dioscorus. She was carefully guarded by her father who kept her shut up in a tower in order to preserve her from the outside world. An offer of marriage which was received through him she rejected. Before going on a journey her father commanded that a bath-house be erected for her use near her dwelling, and during his absence Barbara had three windows put in it, as a symbol of the Holy Trinity, instead of the two originally intended. When her father returned she acknowledged herself to be a Christian; upon this she was ill-treated by him and dragged before the prefect of the province, Martinianus, who had her cruelly tortured and finally condemned her to death by beheading. The father himself carried out the death-sentence, but in punishment for this he was struck by lightning on the way home and his body consumed. Another Christian named Juliana suffered the death of a martyr along with Barbara. A pious man called Valentinus buried the bodies of the saints; at this grave the sick were healed and the pilgrims who came to pray received aid and consolation. The emperor in whose reign the martyrdom is placed is sometimes called Maximinus and sometimes Maximianus; owing to the purely legendary character of the accounts of the martyrdom, there is no good basis for the investigations made at an earlier date in order to ascertain whether Maximinus Thrax (235–238), or Maximianus or Maximinus Daza (of the Diocletian persecutions), is meant.

The traditions vary as to the place of martyrdom, two different opinions being expressed: Symeon Metaphrastes and the Latin legend given by Mombritius make Heliopolis in Egypt the site of the martyrdom, while other accounts, to which Baronius ascribes more weight, give Nicomedia. In the "Martyrologium Romanum parvum" (about 700), the oldest martyrology of the Latin Church in which her name occurs, it is said: "In Tuscia Barbaræ virginis et martyris", a statement repeated by Ado and others, while later additions to the martyrologies of St. Jerome and Bede say: "Romæ Barbaræ virginis" or "apud Antiochiam passio S. Barbaræ virg." These various statements prove, however, only the local adaptation of the veneration of the saintly martyr concerning whom there is no genuine historical tradition. It is certain that before the ninth century she was publicly venerated both in the East and in the West, and that she was very popular with the Christian populace. The legend that her father was struck by lightning caused her, probably, to be regarded by the common people as the patron saint in time of danger from thunder-storms and fire, and later, by analogy, as the protector of artillery-men and miners. She was also called upon as intercessor to assure the receiving of the Sacraments of Penance and Holy Eucharist at the hour of death. An occurrence of the year 1448 did much to further the spread of the veneration of the saint. A man named Henry Kock was nearly burnt to death in a fire at Gorkum; he called on St. Barbara, to whom he had always shown great devotion. She aided him to escape from the burning house and kept him alive until he could receive the last sacraments. A similar circumstance is related in an addition to the "Legenda

aurea". In the Greek and present Roman calendars the feast of St. Barbara falls on 4 December, while the martyrologies of the ninth century, with exception of Rabanus Maurus, place it on 16 December. St. Barbara has often been depicted in art; she is represented standing by a tower with three windows, carrying the palm of a martyr in her hand; often also she holds a chalice and sacramental wafer; sometimes cannon are displayed near her.

Passio, in SYMEON METAPHRASTES (Migne, *P. G.*, CXVI, col. 301 sqq.); MOMBRITIUS, *Vitæ sanctorum* (Venice, 1474), I, fol. 74; SURIUS, *De probatis sanctorum historiis* (Cologne, 1575), VI, 690, a work relating the incident at Gorkum; WIRTH, *Danae in christlichen Legenden* (Vienna, 1892); VITEAU, *Passions des saints Ecaterine, Pierre d'Alexandrie, Barbara et Anysia* (Paris, 1897); *Legenda aurea des Jacobus à Voragine*, ed. GRÄSSE (Leipzig, 1846), 901; *Martyrologies of* BEDE (Migne, *P. L.*, XCIV, col. 1134), ADO (Migne, op. cit., CXXIII, col. 415), USUARDUS (ibid., CXXIV, col. 765 and 807), RABANUS MAURUS (ibid., CX, col. 1183); GALESINO, *S. Barbaræ virg. et mart.*, ed. SURIUS, loc. cit., 690–692; CÉLESTIN, *Histoire de S. Barbe* (Paris, 1853); VILLEMOT, *Histoire de S. Barbe, vierge et martyre* (Paris, 1865); PEINE, *St. Barbara, die Schutzheilige der Bergleute und der Artillerie, und ihre Darstellung in der Kunst* (Freiberg, 1896).

J. P. KIRSCH.

Barbarigo, GIOVANNI FRANCESCO, Italian Cardinal, nephew of Blessed Gregorio Barbarigo (1625–97), b. in 1658 at Venice; d. in 1730. He first entered the diplomatic service and was twice sent as representative of the Venetian Republic to the court of King Louis XIV of France. Later he entered the ecclesiastical state and became *primicerius* of the church of St. Mark at Venice. In 1697 he was named by Innocent XII Bishop of Verona, was transferred to Brescia in 1714, created cardinal 1720, and in 1723 became a successor of his uncle in the See of Padua. He was a zealous prelate, promoted the cause of beatification of Gregorio Barbarigo, and lent his encouragement to the production of literary works. To his suggestion was due the inception of the ecclesiastical history of Verona, and the works of St. Zeno, Bishop of Verona (362–380), were reprinted at his expense (Padua, 1710).

FELLER, *Biog. Univ., supplément* (Paris, 1850), 9.

N. A. WEBER.

Barbarossa. See FREDERICK I.

Barbastro (BARBASTRUM and CIVITAS BARBASTRENSIS), DIOCESE OF, suffragan of the Spanish province of Huesca. The city (originally, perhaps, Bergidum or Bergiduna) is at the junction of the rivers Cinca and Vero. In the time of the Romans it was a part of Hither Spain (Hispania Citerior), afterwards called Tarraconensis. It was taken by the Arabs, under the leadership of Muza (711), and the name Barbaschter given to it, from which the name Barbastrum, according to the generally accepted opinion, is derived. It was held by the Saracens until about the year 1063, when it was retaken by Don Sancho Ramirez, King of Aragon. The Arabs once more obtained possession, but Aremengol IV, Count of Urgel, reconquered it, and after a third Arab conquest it was restored to Spain, in 1101, by Pedro I, King of Aragon, who, with the pope's consent, constituted it an episcopal see, transferring the see from the ancient city of Roda to Barbastro. The first bishop, Poncio, went to Rome to obtain the pope's permission for this transfer. Many provincial and diocesan councils have been held in the city; the Cortes of Spain has met there occasionally, and during one of its sessions, King Ramiro, called the Monk, abdicated the crown (1134).

The diocese is bounded on the north by the Pyrenees, on the east and south by the Diocese of Lérida, and on the west by those of Huesca and Yaca. It is a suffragan of Saragossa and is composed of 154 parishes under the supervision of ten archpriests, or vicars. The population is about 240,000. The clergy number about 220, and there are 231 churches and

177 chapels. The diocese was annexed to Huesca in the sixteenth century, but was afterwards made independent and remained so until the Concordat of 1851, which annexed it once more to Huesca, preserving its name and administration. It is administered at present by the titular Bishop of Claudiopolis, Don Juan Antonio Ruano, preconized Bishop of Lérida. Among its bishops, Ramón II, who is venerated as a saint, and the above-mentioned Ramiro, called the Monk, a prince of the royal house of Aragon, deserve special mention.

Bartolomé and Lupercio Argensola, historians and classical Spanish writers, were born in Barbastro. Bartolomé is the author of the "Historia de las Molucas", "Anales de Aragón", and "Regla de Perfección"; Lupercio wrote three tragedies, "Isabel", "Jebé", and "Alejandro", and some poems published with others written by his brother Bartolomé. The cathedral, the episcopal palace, the seminary, and the college of the Clerks Regular of the Pious Schools, or Piarists, are among the most noted buildings in the city. Besides the seminary for the education of young ecclesiastics, there are, in the diocese, various communities of both sexes devoted to a contemplative life and the education of the young. The Piarists, the Sons of the Immaculate Heart of Mary, the Poor Clares, and the Capuchin nuns have foundations in the capital, the Benedictines in the town of Pueyo, and the Discalced Carmelites in Graus and Salas-Altas. There are schools in all the towns of the diocese.

Flórez, *España Sagrada*, and its continuation by Father José de la Canal (1836), XLVI, 148–70; XLVIII, 225–28; Roman de Huesca, *Teatro de las Iglesias de Aragón* (1870), IX; Muñoz, *Bibl. hist. Esp.* (1858), 47–8.

Tirso López.

Barbelin, Felix-Joseph, styled the "Apostle of Philadelphia", b. at Lunéville, Province of Alsace, France, 30 May, 1808; d. in Philadelphia, 8 June, 1869. He was the oldest of six children, of whom five became religious, his youngest brother Ignace-Xavier being the founder of the Apostolic School at Amiens. He received his early training at the home of a reverend grand-uncle, and made his philosophical and theological studies in a seminary of which another grand-uncle was president. He entered the Society of Jesus, 7 January, 1831, at Whitemarsh, Maryland, U. S. A., and for some years was stationed at Georgetown College, D. C., as disciplinarian and teacher of French. In 1836 he became assistant pastor of Holy Trinity Church at Georgetown, and in 1838 was transferred to Philadelphia, thereafter the scene of his apostolic labours. For more than a quarter of a century he was pastor of Old St. Joseph's, Willing's Alley, which became, mainly during his term of office, the centre from which radiated Catholic influences throughout the city and diocese. His zeal was untiring. He founded St. Joseph's Hospital in his adopted city, and was the first to establish sodalities for men and women and for the young who were always the objects of his fatherly solicitude. In 1852 he was appointed the first President of St. Joseph's College. His many good works brought him into contact with most of the Catholics of the city, while his charity towards all and particularly his love of children and devotion to their interests made him an object of veneration to Catholics and Protestants alike. His memory is still held in benediction.

His life was written by Eleanor C. Donnelly (Philadelphia, 1886); *Woodstock Letters*, IV, 108; V, 81.

Edward P. Spillane.

Barbelo and Barbelites. See Gnostics.

Barber Family, The.—Daniel Barber, soldier of the Revolution, Episcopalian minister and convert, b. at Simsbury, Connecticut, U. S. A., 2 October, 1756; d. at Saint Inigoes, Maryland, 1834. The conversion of the Barber family, despite the prejudices of a Puritan education and environment, was one of the most notable and far-reaching in its results of any recorded in the early annals of the Church in New England. Daniel Barber has left a "History of My Own Times" (Washington, 1827), in which he states that his father and mother were Congregational Dissenters of strict Puritanic rule and he continued in that sect until his twenty-seventh year, when he joined the Episcopalians. Previous to this he had served two terms as a soldier in the Continental army. In his thirtieth year he was ordained a minister of the Episcopalian Church at Schenectady, New York. He married Chloe Case, daughter of Judge Owen of Simsbury, Connecticut, and about 1787, with his wife, his three sons, and a daughter, moved to Claremont, New Hampshire. He exercised the duties of the ministry for thirty years without doubt concerning the soundness of his ordination, when one day the chance reading of a Catholic book opened up for him the whole issue of the validity of Anglican orders, by impugning Parker's consecration. This doubt was further increased by a visit for conference to the famous Bishop Cheverus, then a priest in Boston, and the inability of his Episcopalian associates to offer any satisfactory refutation of the arguments advanced by the Catholic priest. Father Cheverus also gave him a number of Catholic books, which he and the other members of his family read eagerly.

In 1807, at the instance of her parents, he baptized Fanny, daughter of General Ethan Allen, who subsequently became a convert and died a nun in the convent of the Hôtel-Dieu, Montreal. A visit he made there greatly impressed him, and Miss Allen's change of faith indirectly had much to do with his own conversion. The books Father Cheverus gave him he not only studied carefully himself, but gave them to his wife and children. His son, Virgil Horace, who was a minister in charge of an Episcopalian academy at Fairfield, near Utica, New York, was specially attracted by these books when with his wife he visited his father, and he took Milner's "End of Controversy" back to New York. This visit resulted in the conversion of both husband and wife in 1817. The following year Virgil returned to Claremont from New York, taking with him Father Charles Ffrench, a Dominican who was officiating there at St. Peter's church. The priest remained a week in Daniel Barber's house preaching and saying Mass, with the result that he had seven converts, including Mrs. Daniel Barber and her children, Mrs. Noah Tyler, who was Daniel Barber's sister, and her eldest daughter Rosetta. Mrs. Tyler was the mother of William Tyler, first Bishop of Hartford, Connecticut. Her husband and six other children were subsequently converted, and four of the daughters became Sisters of Charity.

Mrs. Daniel Barber was a woman of great strength of mind and resolution. She died in her seventy-ninth year, 8 February, 1825. Her husband was not baptized with her, but on the fifteenth of November, 1818, gave up his place as minister of the Episcopalian parish of Claremont. He then went to visit friends in Maryland and Washington, where he took the final step and entered the Church. He spent the rest of his life, after the death of his wife, in Maryland and Pennsylvania, near his son Virgil, and he died in 1834 at the house of the Society of Jesus at Saint Inigoes, Maryland. Two pamphlets, printed at Washington, "Catholic Worships and Piety Explained and Recommended in Sundry Letters to a Very Dear Friend and Others" (1821), and "History of My Own Times", give interesting details of his life and show him to have been honest in his convictions and earnestly desirous of knowing the truth and disposed to embrace it when found.

VIRGIL HORACE BARBER, son of Daniel, b. at Claremont, New Hampshire, 9 May, 1782; d. at Georgetown, D. C., 25 March, 1847. He himself said that the first step leading to his conversion was the reading through curiosity of a little book "A Novena to St. Francis Xavier" belonging to a pious Irish servant girl who was employed in his house while he was principal of the Episcopalian Academy at Fairfield, New York. This raised doubts concerning his Protestant faith, which his bishop, Dr. Hobart, and other Episcopalian ministers could not solve for him. During a visit to New York City, in 1816, he called on Father Benedict J. Fenwick, S.J., with the result that he resigned his Episcopalian charge at Fairfield, and went to New York, where he and his wife Jerusha (b. New Town, Connecticut, 20 July, 1789) were received into the Church with their five children, Mary (b. 1810); Abigail (b. 1811); Susan (b. 1813); Samuel (b. 1814); and Josephine (b. 1816). At first he opened a school in New York, but this lasted only seven months, for both he and his wife determined to enter religious life, he the Society of Jesus, and she the Visitation Order. Under the direction of their friend, Father Fenwick, in June, 1817, they set out for Georgetown, D. C., where Mr. Barber and his son Samuel went to the college of the Jesuit Fathers, and his wife and the three oldest girls were received into the Visitation convent. The youngest child, Josephine, then ten months old, was taken care of by Father Fenwick's mother. The superior at Georgetown, Father John Grassi, S.J., shortly after sailed for Rome and took Mr. Barber with him as a novice. Mr. Barber remained there a year and then returned to Georgetown, where he continued his studies until December, 1822, when he was ordained a priest at Boston. After his ordination he was sent to his old home, Claremont, New Hampshire, where he built a church and laboured for two years. He then spent some time on the Indian missions in Maine, and was after recalled to Georgetown College, where he passed the remainder of his days.

Nearly three years after their separation, 23 February, 1820, husband and wife met in the chapel of Georgetown convent to make their vows in religion. She first went through the formula of the profession of a Visitation nun, and he the vows of a member of the Society of Jesus. Their five children, the eldest being ten and the youngest three and a half years old, were present. Mrs. Barber had been admitted into the Visitation convent on the twenty-sixth of July, 1817, taking the name of Sister Mary Augustine. Her novitiate was one of severe trials, as well on account of her affection for her husband as on account of her children, who were a heavy burden to the community then in a state of extreme poverty. Her pious perseverance triumphed, and she became one of the most useful members of the order, serving in the convents of Georgetown, Kaskaskia, St. Louis, and Mobile, where she died 1 January, 1860. She had the happiness of seeing all her children embrace a religious life. Mary, the eldest, entered the Ursuline convent, Mt. Benedict, near Charlestown, Massachusetts, as Sister Mary Benedicta, 15 August, 1826, and died in the convent of the order in Quebec, 9 May, 1844. Abigail, Susan, and Josephine also became Ursulines. The first died in Quebec, 8 December, 1879, and Susan in the convent at Three Rivers, Canada, 24 January, 1837. Samuel, the son, graduated at Georgetown College in 1831 and immediately entered the Society of Jesus. After his novitiate he was sent to Rome, where he was ordained. He returned to Georgetown in 1840, and died, aged fifty years, at St. Thomas's Manor, Maryland, 23 February, 1864.

DE GOESBRIAND, *Catholic Memoirs of Vermont and New Hampshire* (Burlington, Vermont, 1886); LATHROP, *A Story of Courage* (Boston, 1894); SHEA, *The Catholic Church in the United States* (New York, 1856); IDEM, *Memorial History of Georgetown College* (Washington, 1891); *U. S. Cath. Hist. Soc. Records and Studies* (New York, October, 1900).

THOMAS F. MEEHAN.

Barbieri, GIOVANNI, called from his squinting, "Il Guercino"; a famous painter of religious subjects, b. at Cento, near Bologna, 2 February, 1591; d. at Bologna, 22 December, 1666. His parents were in very humble circumstances. It is related that he gave such early indication of his great talents that before he reached the age of ten he had painted on the front wall of his home a figure of the Virgin. His first instructor was Bartolommeo Bertozzi, and when sixteen he entered the school of Benedetto Gennari, the elder, at Cento. As a youth he had studied with great admiration a famous painting of Ludovico Carracci at the convent of the Capuchins at Cento, which had much influence on his work. Father Mirandola, head of the convent, took Barbieri under his protection, had him taught, and secured him commissions.

After spending some time in Bologna, where he studied with Cremonini and Gennari, the young painter went to Venice, where he received the counsels of Palma. At Ferrara he painted the portrait of the legate, Cardinal Jacopo Serra, who made him a chevalier. On the invitation of Cardinal Ludovisi, later Pope Gregory XV, he went to Rome. There he did the "Aurora" at the Villa Ludovisi, and his celebrated painting of St. Petronilla in the Capitol. After the death of his papal patron, Barbieri, refusing the invitations of James I to go to England and of Louis XIII to visit France, returned to Cento and established there an academy which was much frequented by foreign as well as native painters. He painted the portraits of the Duke of Modena, and after the death of Guido, whose style he imitated, he settled at Bologna, where he died, leaving much wealth.

CALVI, *Life of Giovanni Barbieri* (Bologna, 1808); BRYAN, *Dictionary of Painters and Engravers* (London and New York, 1903–05).

AUGUSTUS VAN CLEEF.

Barbieri, REMIGIO. See GIBRALTAR, DIOCESE OF.

Barbo, PETER. See PAUL II.

Barbosa, AGOSTINO, a noted canonist, b. at Guimaraens, Portugal, in 1589; consecrated in Rome, 22 March, 1649, Bishop of Ugento in Otranto, Italy, he died seven months later. Having studied canon law in his native land, he went to Rome. Being without books, his astounding memory served him instead. Sanctity and affability won for him entrance into the libraries of the city, where he passed long hours reading sedulously and memorizing without effort, so that returning to his room he was able to put in writing the fruits of the day's labour. About 1632 he went to Madrid, where he applied himself to writing and fulfilled various duties confided to him till 1648.

Among Barbosa's many writings, all of which evidence intimate acquaintance with authors, sources, and controverted questions, we mention the following: "Pastoralis Sollicitudinis, sive de Officio et Potestate Episcopi Tripartita Descriptio" (Rome, 1621; Lyons, 1629; in folio, 1641, 1650, etc.). A similar work relating to parish priests was published in Rome in 1632, Lyons, 1634, Geneva, 1662, Venice, 1705, in quarto. "Variæ Juris Tractationes" (in folio, Lyons, 1631 and 1644; Strasburg, 1652). "Juris Ecclesiastici Universi Libri III" (Lyons, 1633, 1645, 1718). All the canonical works of Barbosa were published at Lyons, 1657–75, in 19 vols. in quinto, 16 vols. in folio, and again, 1698–1716, 20 vols. in quinto, 18 vols. in folio.

HURTER in *Kirchenlex.*, s. v.; WERNZ, *Jus Decretalium* (Rome, 1898), I, 408.

ANDREW B. MEEHAN.

Barbosa-Machado, IGNACIO, a Portuguese historian, b. at Lisbon in 1686; d. in 1734. He pursued his studies at the University of Coimbra, was later sent to Brazil as a magistrate, and after the death of his wife entered the ecclesiastical state. He has left a number of historical works, the most important of which is "Fastos Politicos e Militares de Antiqua e Nova Lusitania" (Lisbon, 1745), dealing with the history of Portugal and Brazil. He was a brother of the more famous Diego Machado Barbosa (1682–1772), also a priest and writer, and author of a notable monument of Portuguese literature "Bibliotheca Lusitana, Historica, Critica e Chronologica" (Lisbon, 1741–59). V. FUENTES.

Barbour, JOHN, Scottish ecclesiastic and author of "The Bruce", a historical poem in the early Scottish or Northern English dialect, b. about 1320; d. 1395. He was already Archdeacon of Aberdeen in 1357, an honour not likely to have been attained much before his fortieth year. At various times, 1357, 1364, 1365, 1368, he obtained, originally at the request of King David of Scotland, passports from the King of England for travel to Oxford or to France, presumably for the purpose of special study or research, or for the renewal of old college associations. In 1357 he was appointed by the Bishop of Aberdeen one of the commissioners to meet at Edinburgh and confer about the ransom from England of David II, captured at Neville's Cross, 1346. In 1373, and occasionally in later years, he was one of the auditors of the exchequer. In 1378, as a reward for his patriotic poem, he was assigned, from the royal rents payable by the city, a perpetual pension of twenty shillings, and in 1388, an additional royal pension for life of £10 Scots from the customs of Aberdeen. He received also from the king £10 in 1377, and £5 in 1386. Innes has pointed out that in addition to these pensions and gifts, and perquisites incidental to the wardship of a minor, Barbour enjoyed the revenue of a prebend and a considerable income as archdeacon. His pension of twenty shillings he left as a foundation for Masses for himself and his parents, to be said by all the priests at the cathedral on the Wednesday after Low Sunday. As Jamieson shows, the pension was not bequeathed to a hospital, but probably reverted to the Crown at the Reformation. The copy of the document assigning his pension to the dean and chapter of Aberdeen may be found in Skeat, along with the forty-eight other documents which establish the facts of Barbour's life.

Barbour, "the earliest poet and the first detailed historian of Scotland", writing in that northern dialect of Middle English which afterward came to be specifically called Scotch, composed, besides "The Brut" and "The Stewart's Original", which are lost, the long patriotic narrative poem called "The Bruce". This work, upon which Barbour was engaged in 1375, exists in two manuscripts, dated 1487 and 1489, written by John Ramsay, who has been identified with a later prior of the Carthusian monastery at Perth. The second of these copies was made at the request of Simon Lochmalony, vicar of Auchter Monsey, near Perth. An earlier, incomplete manuscript, written by Fenton, a monk of Melrose, in 1369, is not extant. "The Bruce", extending through 6,000 octosyllabic couplets, variously divided into fourteen or twenty books, told to a generation of Scotchmen flushed with victory and the sense of dearly-bought independence the story of the struggles of their grandfathers, sang the glories of freedom, and pictured the civic and knightly virtues of Bruce and Douglas. The narrative runs from the dispute for the crown of Scotland between Balliol and the first Robert, whom Barbour poetically identifies with his grandson, to the death of the Black Douglas in Spain while on his way to the Holy Land with the heart of Bruce. It pictures such events as Bannockburn, the siege of Berwick, the expedition to Ireland, and the wanderings of the king, and sketches the characters of Stewart, Randolph, Bruce, and Douglas. The author finds a place, too, for descriptions of nature, for touches showing the tenderness of the true soldier, for snatches of grim humour or sharp dialogue, for digressions on necromancy and astrology, and for learned allusions to the favourite classic authors of the day. This narrative, which Barbour called a romance, is regarded as being in essential points a faithful history, and was so received by generations of readers. Scott used some of its material in "Castle Dangerous", "The Lord of the Isles", and "Tales of a Grandfather". The principal editions of "The Bruce" are those of Pinkerton (Edinburgh, 1790); Jamieson (Edinburgh, 1820); Cosmo Innes (Edinburgh), and, according to more modern requirements of scholarship, that of Professor Skeat for the "Early English Text Society", and the "Early Scottish Text Society". Some fragments on the tale of Troy, and a long poem on the lives of the saints formerly attributed to Barbour are no longer thought to be his work.

MACKAY in *Dict. Nat. Biog.*; VEITCH, *Feeling for Nature in Scottish Poetry*; LANIER, *Music and Poetry*.

J. VINCENT CROWNE.

Barbus, PAULUS, Italian philosopher and theologian, b. at Soncino, Lombardy, and hence known also by the name of Soncinas which appears at the head of his books; d. at Cremona, 4 August, 1494. When a mere youth he entered the Dominican Order and made his philosophical and theological studies in its schools. He afterwards taught philosophy and theology with great success at Milan, Ferrara, and Bologna. At the time of his death he was prior of the Cremona Convent. Exhibiting extraordinary intellectual powers, and expressing his deep thoughts in eloquent speech and finished writing, he merited and received the esteem of his learned contemporaries, notably of Pico della Mirandola. Many of his writings were lost at an early date. The following have been printed frequently: (1) "Quæstiones super divinâ sapientiâ Aristotelis" (principal edition, Lyons, 1579); (2) "Divinum Epitoma quæstionum in IV libros sententiarum a principe Thomistarum Joanne Capreolo Tolesano disputatarum" (principal edition, Pavia, 1522). The place and date of (3) "In libros prædicabilium et prædicamentorum expositio" are unknown.

QUÉTIF AND ECHARD, *Scriptores Ordinis Prædicatorum*, I, 279.

ARTHUR L. McMAHON.

Barca, a titular see of Cyrenaica in Northern Africa. According to most archæologists it was situated at Medinet el Merdja, but according to Graham (Roman Africa) at Tolometa, or Tolmeita. After being often destroyed and restored, it became, during the Roman period, a mere borough (Marquardt, Staatsverwaltung, I, 459), but was, nevertheless, the site of a bishopric. Its bishop, Zopyros (Zephyrius is a mistake), was present at the Council of Nicæa in 325 (Gelzer, Patrum Nicænorum nomina, 231). The subscriptions at Ephesus (431) and Chalcedon (451) give the names of two other bishops, Zenobius and Theodorus. The see must have disappeared when the Arabs conquered the Pentapolis in 643 (Butler, The Arab Conquest of Egypt, 430).

LEQUIEN, *Oriens Christ.*, II, 625; GAMS, *Series episcop.*, 462.

L. PETIT.

Barcelona (BARCINO), DIOCESE OF, one of the suffragans of the Archdiocese of Tarragona. The city of this name is the capital of Catalonia and of the province of Barcelona. It is situated on the coast of north-eastern Spain, and is familiarly known as the "Queen of the Mediterranean".

History.—Barcelona is one of the most ancient cities of Spain, and the most important after the capital. Founded by Hamilcar in the ancient region of Laletana, it was in the possession of the Carthaginians until they were driven out of Spain, when it passed under the power of the Romans, who favoured it in many ways. Julius Cæsar bestowed on it the name of *Julia Augusta Faventia* in recognition of the support given him in his struggle with Pompey; later he made it a Roman colony and gave it the *jus Latii*, which conferred on the inhabitants, although still belonging to *Hispania Tarraconensis*, the full privileges of Roman citizenship. The city remained unimportant until Ataulf, King of the Visigoths, chose it for his residence (415). Later it passed successively into the hands of the Arabs (713) and the Franks (801). Finally, Wilfrid the Hairy declared his independence and gave the Spanish March, or the *Marca Hispanica*, as the Franks had called it, the name of the County of Barcelona. It remained under the independent government of its own counts until the marriage of Petronilla, daughter of Ramiro the Monk, with the Count of Barcelona (1137) united Aragon and Catalonia. After 1164, when Petronilla resigned in favour of her son Alfonso, the two states formed but one kingdom.

Barcelona, being situated on the shores of the Mediterranean and on the military road between Spain and France, was comparatively easy of access, and the Gospel was preached there by the immediate disciples of the Apostles. The See of Barcelona, unlike most very ancient sees, whose origins are obscure, has preserved catalogues of its bishops from Apostolic times, and although all the names given cannot be admitted as authentic, the greater number are handed down in all the catalogues. In the twelfth century the diocese was restored by Ramon Berengar, Count of Barcelona, since which time the succession of bishops has been uninterrupted.

In the long line of bishops we find many illustrious names. St. Severus, a native of the city, was martyred by Dacianus in the reign of Diocletian. St. Pacianus (360–390) is famous for the clearness and spirituality of his doctrinal writings; in chapter cvi of his "De Scriptoribus Ecclesiasticis", St. Jerome praises the chaste life of Pacianus, his eloquence, and his writings on baptism and penance, also those against heretics, particularly the Novatians. St. Oligarius, noted for the great purity of his life, was the first metropolitan of this province. Bishop Urquinaona was revered for his great charity, one of the handsomest plazas of Barcelona is still called by his name. Among the saints of this diocese are: the famous virgin, St. Eulalia, a martyr of the third century, whose relics are preserved in a rich shrine in the crypt of the cathedral; Sts. Juliana and Sempronia, virgins and martyrs; the African saints, Cucuphas and Felix, martyred in the city of Barcelona; St. Raymund of Pennafort, founder of the Order of Mercy for the Redemption of Captives, confessor of Gregory IX (1227–41), and compiler of the famous "Decretals", in which he collected the scattered decrees of popes and councils.

Councils of Barcelona.—Many councils and assemblies of Spanish bishops were held in Barcelona, two provincial councils in the Visigothic period. The first (c. 540), at which the metropolitan and six bishops assisted, promulgated ten canons, ordaining that the *Miserere* should be said before the Canticle; that in the Vespers and Matins the benediction should be given to the people; that clerics should not wear the hair long or shave their beards; that penitents should wear the hair short, put on a religious garb, and devote their time to prayer; that the "beatific benediction" should be given to the sick so that they could receive Holy Communion, and that the decrees of the Council of Chalcedon (451) with regard

to monks should be observed. At the Second Provincial Council (c. 599), attended by the metropolitan and twelve bishops, four canons were promulgated, the first and second prohibiting any fee for Holy orders and for the chrism used for Confirmation; the third and fourth commanding the observation of the canons referring to those awaiting Holy orders, and excommunicating those who, after having made a vow of chastity and changed their secular dress for the religious garb, should contract a carnal marriage, even if a woman had been forced by violence, unless she immediately separated from the one who had violated her; a similar excommunication was also pronounced on those who married after they had received the "blessing of penance" (*benedictio pœnitentiæ*), i. e. penitents who had taken an additional vow of continency. Other councils were also held there: that of 1125, presided over by St. Ole-

MONASTERY OF ST. CUGAT DEL VALLE, CLOISTER AND LANTERN

garius, the Metropolitan and Bishop of Barcelona; that of 1339 to decide in the matter of the subsidies asked from the clergy; that of 1377, a quasi-plenary council; that of 1387, on the occasion of the Western Schism, which proclaimed legitimate the election of Clement VII; those of 1417, 1517, and 1564 which are of no special importance. In 1904 the *Congreso Hispano-Americano de las Congregaciones Marianas* was held at Barcelona and was attended by thousands of persons for the purpose of making uniform laws for this congregation and that of the *Luises*.

Monuments.—Among the many monuments of the city, the most important is the cathedral, built in the early days of the Church in honour of the Holy Cross. It was rebuilt by order of Berengar I, the Old, Count of Barcelona, and his wife, Doña Almodis, and consecrated in 1058. In the thirteenth century it was enlarged, and was finally completed in 1338. It is Gothic in style, one of its most notable features being the "door of the Inquisition", a beautiful piece of work composed of small columns and pointed arches on a diminishing scale, which conceals the jasper steps that lead to the sanctuary. The façade La Piedad, composed of graceful pointed arches, is one of the purest examples of Spanish Gothic. The church of St. Severus unites in its façade all the architectural charms of the fifteenth century in which it was built; its main tabernacle is noted for the rich carving of its pointed arches; its chapel of St. Eulalia is exceedingly delicate and beautiful. The church of Santa Ana has two pictures by Juncosa. The ancient church of Santa María del Mar is also a beautiful specimen of Gothic architecture. Santa María del Pino has the most spacious and lofty nave of all the Gothic churches in Barcelona. The church of Sts. Justo and Pastor was the first dedicated to the worship of the true God in Barcelona. Judging from its present appearance, the unfinished Templo Expiatorio de la Sagrada Familia, built from the alms of the faithful, will be the finest ecclesiastical edifice in Barcelona. The famous sanctuary of Monserrat is outside the city. Apart from its antiquity and religious interest, it is remarkable for its wealth of precious stones, and for the beautiful chapels representing the mysteries of the Rosary; all these are modern and are an evidence of the piety of the faithful. The Diocese of Barcelona also possesses archives of great value in which many precious documents, saved from the Almohad conquest under Almanzor (1184–98), are preserved, as well as the priceless books called *Exemplaria*, wherein are chronicled ecclesiastical functions, oaths of kings, and other notable events, which make them the best source of information for the history of Catalonia.

Charity and Education.—It would be difficult to find in Spain another city where Christian charity is manifested in more ways than in Barcelona. Besides many general and private hospitals in the city, there exist a multitude of asylums for all classes of persons maintained by religious congregations and pious associations. Notable among them is the girls' orphan asylum of San José de la Montaña. The asylum and maternity home (*casa de lactancia*) of Bressol, for the children of labourers, takes care annually of 1,200 healthy and 2,300 sick children. The asylum of La Sagrada Familia cares for about 300 children of working mothers. The asylum of La Madre de Dios del Carmen of Hostafranchs, besides sheltering about 600 children and old persons, has a pious association especially for arranging marriages between persons who have been living together illegally, and legitimizing the children; in one year it procured 120 such marriages. The asylum of St. Raphael is for scrofulous children, and the asylum Del Parque relieves annually 94,234 poor, and provides sleeping accommodations for 20,000 poor annually. The house of the Good Shepherd shelters about 300 young women rescued from houses of ill fame. The asylum of the Visitation assists young women who are in want, and in the nineteen years of its existence has preserved the purity and virtue of more than 3,000 young women. There are between forty and fifty other institutions for charitable purposes, among them the Durán asylum for incorrigible boys. Two have for their object the distribution of food and the serving of meals to working-men; one distributed 117,125 free rations in one year, and the other fed about 300 working-men daily. The *Montes Píos* of Nuestra Señora de la Esperanza, of Barcelona, of Santa Madrona, and of Nuestra Señora de Monserrat. are societies for the aid of female domestics and working-men. An association of fathers of families has in one year prevented the publication of 45,000 obscene books and photographs.

In addition to the diocesan seminary, there are Christian Doctrine classes attended by 6,000 children, and Sunday Schools, supervised by 161 young ladies,

where over 2,000 women receive instruction, and are thus prevented from attending public dance-halls. Connected with each of the asylums before mentioned is one or more schools; the religious orders conduct free schools attended by 12,000 boys and girls. There are 8 colleges, under the Jesuits, the Piarists, and other religious orders.

A number of Catholic periodicals are published in the diocese: the "Boletín Eclesiástico de la Diócesis", the "Revista Popular", founded and directed by Dr. Sarda y Salvany, author of the famous book "Liberalismo es Pecado", which has been translated into many languages; the "Comentarius Scholaris", published by the diocesan seminary students; "Anales del culto á San José"; the "Mensajero del Niño Jesús de Praga"; "Anales de Nuestra Señora del Sagrado Corazón"; "La Montaña de San José", official organ of the association; "El Boletín Salesiano"; "Las Misiones Católicas"; "La Hormiga de Oro"; "La Revista Social"; and "Los Estudios Franciscanos". "El Correo Catalán" is the only strictly Catholic newspaper. It has the blessing of the sovereign pontiff, and counts many of the clergy among its contributors.

Statistics.—There are 231 parishes, 13 archipresbyterates, 1,180 secular priests, 360 regular clergy, and 89 religious communities. In 1906 the population, nearly all Catholic, was 1,054,531.

V. DE LA FUENTE, *Hist. Ecca. de España* (Madrid, 1875); VILLANUEVA, *Viage literario á las iglesias de España* (Madrid, 1803–52), XVII, 128–226; XVIII, 1–83, and *passim;* FLÓREZ, *España Sagrada* (Madrid, 1754 sqq.), XXVIII–XXIX; AYMERICH, *Nomina et Acta ep. Barc.* (ibid., 1760); GAMS, *Kircheng. Spaniens* (Ratisbon, 1874), II, ii; *España Ecca.* (Madrid, 1902), IV; *Colección de documentos hist.* (Barcelona, 1893–95); ALBÓ Y MARTI, *The Charities of Barcelona* (Spanish, ibid., 1901).

TIRSO LÓPEZ.

Barcelona, UNIVERSITY OF.—This was an outgrowth of the ecclesiastical schools founded in the eleventh century. To these were added gradually the chairs held by the Dominicans in their convent and those established in the *Academia* by the Kings of Aragon. In 1430, the town council of Barcelona took measures for the founding of a *Studium Generale* in order to prevent the migration of their young men to Lerida and to the foreign universities of Paris, Toulouse, and Bologna. But the university as such dates from 1450, the year in which its charter was granted by Alfonso V of Aragon and confirmed by the Bull "Constitutus in Speculo" of Pope Nicholas V. The pope conferred upon the new university all the privileges enjoyed by the University of Toulouse and authorized the erection of chairs in theology, canon and civil law, arts, and medicine. The young institution had to struggle with all sorts of difficulties. For nearly a century it had no buildings adapted to its purposes. In 1544, however, it entered upon a new era, with suitable structures and equipment, and in 1567 it received the richly endowed priory of St. Ann, formerly held by the Order of St. John. The teaching of grammar and rhetoric was entrusted to the Jesuits (1576) and the diocesan seminary was affiliated to the university (1568). In 1714 the Faculties, with the exception of that of medicine, were transferred to Cervera. By royal decree of Charles III, a college of surgery was established at Barcelona in 1764. The Faculties returned from Cervera to Barcelona in 1823, and in 1837 the new university was formally inaugurated. It withstood the disturbances that occurred in 1840 and 1856, passed under State control in 1857, and was provided with additional buildings (1863–73). At present it has five Faculties: philosophy and letters, law, science, medicine, and pharmacy, with 56 instructors and 1,900 students. The Archives of the Crown of Aragon, founded in 1346, contain 3,759,314 documents, and the library about 2,000 manuscripts.

La Fuente, *Historia de las Universidades* (Madrid, 1884), I; Zarate, *De la Instrucción Pública en España* (Madrid, 1855); Rashdall, *Universities of Europe in the M. A.* (Oxford, 1895), II, Pt. 1, 94.

E. A. Pace.

Barcena (also Barzana), Alonzo de, a native of Baeza in Andalusia, Spain, b. 1528; d. at Cuzco, Peru, 15 January, 1598. He became a Jesuit in 1565, and went to Peru in 1569. He was first destined for the missions of Huarochiri, whence he was ordered (1577) to Juli, on the shores of Lake Titicaca in Southern Peru. He became one of the founders of this important mission. Barcena remained in Central Bolivia for eleven years, when the Provincial Atienza sent him to Tucuman in Argentina. His work among the various tribes of that region and of Paraguay continued until 1593, when he was made Commissary of the Inquisition in those provinces. Exhausted physically by his long and arduous labours, Barcena died at Cuzco in Peru. He is credited with having had a practical knowledge of eleven Indian languages and with having written grammars, vocabularies, catechisms in most of them. These manuscripts are possibly still in the archives of Lima. Only one of his writings is known to have been published: a letter full of important ethnographic and linguistic detail, on the Indians of Tucuman, on the Calchaquis, and others. The letter (see below), published in 1885, is dated 8 September, 1594, at Asunción in Paraguay, and is addressed to the Provincial Juan Sebastian.

Calancha, *Corónica moralizada* (Lima, 1638), I; Lozano, *Historia de la Compañía de Jesús de la provincia del Paraguay* (Madrid, 1755); Idem, *Descripción del Gran Chaco* (Cordova, 1733); Lorenzo Hervas, *Catalogo delle Lingue conosciuti e notizia della loro affinità e diversità* (Foligno, 1784); Charlevoix, *Histoire du Paraguay* (Paris, 1757); Saldamando, *Antiguos Jesuitas del Perú* (Lima, 1882); *Relaciones geográficas de Indias* (Madrid, 1885), II, contains the *Carta de P. Alonso de Barzana, de la Compañía de Jesús, al P. Juan Sebastian, su Provincial*, the letter mentioned above (Appendix 30, III). Ludewig, *The Literature of American Aboriginal Indians* (London, 1858), 76, mentions a work of Father Barcena under the title of *Lexica et præcepta grammatica, item liber confessionis et precum in quinque Indorum Linguis* (Peru, 1590); it is probably one of the manuscripts alluded to above. The title is taken from Sotwell, *Bibliotheca Societatis Jesu* (Rome, 1676).

Ad. F. Bandelier.

Barclay, John, author of the political novel "Argenis" and other Latin works in prose and verse, was b. 28 January, 1582, at Pont-à-Mousson; d. in Rome, August, 1621. His father was William Barclay (q. v. infra). John Barclay received his early schooling from the Jesuits, and at the age of nineteen he published a commentary on the "Thebais" of Statius. In 1603 father and son, perhaps attracted by the union of the Scotch and English crowns, tried their fortunes in France. The son dedicated to James his "Euphormionis Lusinini Satyricon". After a brief stay in France, John returned to England in 1605.

He married a brilliant and clever Frenchwoman, and was again in London in 1606. He published, in Paris, 1607, the second part of his "Satyricon" and about the same time his poems, under the title "Sylvæ", and a narrative of the Gunpowder Plot (English translation, Oxford, 1634). His publication in 1609 of his father's work, "De Potestate Papæ", which denied the temporal jurisdiction of the pope over princes, and his declaration therewith that he would defend his father's memory, led to a prolonged controversy, in which his known opponents were Bellarmine and a Jesuit, Andreas Eudæmon Joannes. A further series of polemics was occasioned by his "Apology" (1611) for the "Satyricon", in which he attacked the Jesuits and his father's former patron, the Duke of Lorraine. In his "Icon Animorum", a fourth part of the "Satyricon" (London, 1614), he described the character and manners of the European nations, mentioning Scot-

land with special affection. In 1615 a volume of his poems appeared in London.

In England Barclay received occasional help from the king and the Earl of Salisbury, and won the friendship of Isaac Casaubon, Ralph Thorie, and especially, in 1606, of du Peiresc, an attaché of the French Embassy and a patron of learning. In 1616 Barclay, at the invitation of Paul V, went to Rome, where he was welcomed by Bellarmine and pensioned by the pope. Perhaps to prove his Catholic loyalty he published in 1617 his "Parænesis ad Sectarios". Completing in July, 1621, his Latin novel "Argenis", he died in the following month. The facts as to the removal of his monument and inscription from St. Onofrio have been perhaps permanently obscured by partisan dispute. His friend Ralph Thorie published an elegy in 1621. Barclay was admired by his contemporaries for his honesty, his rare courtesy, and a conversational charm that owed something to grave irony. His varied learning and talents made him a formidable opponent.

The most important of Barclay's writings, the "Argenis", published by du Peiresc at Paris, 1621, has been admired by Richelieu, Leibnitz, Jonson, Grotius, Pope, Cowper, Disraeli, and Coleridge. This work is a long romance which introduces the leading personages of international importance. To it were indebted, in whole or in part, Fénelon's "Télémaque", du Ryer's tragi-comedy "Argénis et Poliarque", Calderon's "Argenis y Poliarco", an Italian play "Argenide", by de Cruylles, and a German play by Christian Weysen, 1684. The "Argenis" was soon translated into French, Spanish, and German. English translations appeared as follows: by Kingsmill Long, London, 1626; by Sir Robert Le Grys and Thomas May, London, 1629, and in 1772, under the title of "The Phœnix", by Clara Reeve. Ben Jonson in 1623 entered a translation at Stationers' Hall. There have been translations into Italian, Dutch, Greek, Hungarian, Polish, Swedish, and Icelandic. An English translation, by Thomas May, of the fourth part of the "Satyricon", under the title, "The Mirror for Minds", was printed in London, 1633.

Portraits of Barclay may be found in the first edition of the "Argenis", in the volume of 1629 of Le Grys and May, and in the later work of Collignon.

Garnett in *Dict. Nat. Biog.*, s. v.; Gillow, *Bibl. Dict. Eng. Cath.*, s. v.; Hailes, *Life of John Barclay* (Edinburgh, 1786); Barclay, poems in *Delitiæ Poetarum Scotorum*; Boucher, *Latin Dissertation on Argenis* (Paris, 1874); Dupond, *L'Argénis de Jean Barclay* (Paris, 1875); Dukas, *Bibliographie du Satyricon de J. B.* (Paris, 1880); Collignon, *Notes sur l'Euphormion de J. B.* (Paris, 1901); Idem, *Notes Hist., Litt., et Bibliographiques sur l'Argénis de J. B.* (Paris, 1902); Schmid, *Barclay's Argenis*—with bibliography and key (Munich, 1903).

J. V. Crowne.

Barclay, William, Scottish Jurist, b. 1546; d. at Angers, France, 3 July, 1608. He was of a good Aberdeenshire family, and studied first at Aberdeen University and later, having emigrated to France like so many of the Catholic youth of Scotland at that time, under eminent teachers at Paris and Bourges. In 1578, on the recommendation of his uncle, Edmund Hay, first rector of the newly founded University of Pont-à-Mousson, he was appointed to the chair of civil law there by the Duke of Lorraine, who made him also dean of the faculty of law and a counciller of state. Three years later he married Anne de Malleviller, a lady of an honourable Lorraine family. Barclay published in 1600 his largest work, "De Regno et Regali potestate", in defence of the rights of kings, against Buchanan and other writers. The doctrines laid down in this book, which was dedicated to Henry IV, are discussed at length by Locke in his "Civil Government". After twenty-five years' tenure of his professorship, Barclay resigned his chair in 1603 and returned to England, where the new monarch, James I, was inclined to welcome with favour one who had so learnedly asserted the views on the Divine right of kings which he himself held. Barclay's fidelity, however, to the Catholic religion stood in the way of his advancement, and, rejecting the king's offer of a lucrative appointment on condition that he renounced his faith, he returned to France. An offer was immediately made to the renowned jurist to accept the professorship of law in the University of Angers, which had been vacant for some years. In 1605 he published at Paris an elaborate work on the Pandects, dedicated to King James. Barclay mentions in this work his intention to write a book about the king, but he never lived to publish it. He was buried at the Cordeliers Church at Angers. His most famous work, "De Potestate Papæ", directed against the pope's authority over kings in temporal matters, appeared in 1609, with a preface written by his son. Cardinal Bellarmine published a rejoinder to it. (See BARCLAY, JOHN.)

IRVING, *Lives of Scottish Writers*, I, 210–233; MENAGE, *Remarques sur la vie de Pierre Ayvault* (1675), 228–230; MACKENZIE, *Writers of the Scots Nation* (1722), III, 468, 478; OTTO, *Thesaurus Juris Romani*, III.

D. O. HUNTER-BLAIR.

Barco Centenera, MARTIN DEL, b. 1535, at Logroño, in the Diocese of Plasencia of Estremadura (Spain); died c. 1602. He became a secular priest and in 1572 accompanied, as chaplain, the expedition of Juan Ortiz de Zárate to the Rio de La Plata. For twenty-four years he followed the vicissitudes of Spanish exploration in the Argentine with undaunted courage, and was made archdeacon of the church of Paraguay. In 1582 he went to Lima and acted as secretary to the third council held in that city. He returned to Europe, where he finished his poetical work, known as "La Argentina", which he dedicated to the Viceroy of Portugal (for Philip III of Spain). It appeared in 1602. Soon after, del Barco died. The poetic merit of the "Argentina" is slender, like that of all the epics composed about his time on American subjects. It is a work of ponderous rhyme. But its historical value is considerable. He describes nearly a quarter of a century of Spanish efforts in the Argentine and adjacent countries, of which he was mostly an eyewitness, and thus fills a considerable blank in our knowledge of the history of that period, otherwise but little known. He also alludes to the English piracies committed by Drake and Cavendish, and to events of importance in Peru during the administration of the Viceroy Toledo. Several of the violent earthquakes of the time are also mentioned and described, though not always with correctness in regard to dates.

LEÓN Y PINELO, *Epítome* (1629–1738); NICOLAS ANTONIO, *Bib. Hisp. nova* (Madrid, 1786); BARCIA, *Historiadores primitivos de Indias*, 1749 (reprint of the *Argentina*; a later reprint appeared in DE ANGELIS's collection); *La Argentina, Conquista del Río de la Plata y Tucuman* (in 28 Cantos, Lisbon, 1602); MENDIBURÚ, *Diccionario histórico biográfico* (Lima, 1876), II.

AD. F. BANDELIER.

Barcos, MARTIN DE, a French theologian of the Jansenist School, b. at Bayonne, 1600; d. at St. Cyran, 1678. He was a nephew of du Vergier de Hauranne, Abbot of St. Cyran, who sent him to Belgium to be taught by Jansen. When he returned to France he served for a time as tutor to the son of Arnauld d'Andilly and later, 1644, succeeded his uncle at the Abbey of St. Cyran. He did much to improve the abbey; new buildings were erected, the library much increased, and the strictest rule enforced. Unlike many commendators of his day who scarcely ever saw the abbeys over which they held authority, Barcos became an active member of St. Cyran, was ordained priest 1647, and gave himself up to the rigid asceticism preached by his sect. His

friendship with du Vergier and Arnauld and, through them, with Port-Royal soon brought him to the front in the debates of Jansenism. He collaborated with du Vergier in the "Petrus Aurelius" and with Arnauld in the book on "Frequent Communion".

Of his own treatises, some bear on authority in the Church and some on the then much-mooted questions of grace and predestination. To the first class belong (1) "De l'autorité de St. Pierre et de St. Paul" (1645). (2) "Grandeur de l'Eglise de Rome qui repose sur l'autorité de St. Pierre et de St. Paul" (1645). (3) "Eclaircissements sur quelques objections que l'on a formées contre la grandeur de l'Eglise de Rome" (1646). These three books were written in support of an assertion contained in the book "On Frequent Communion", namely: "St. Peter and St. Paul are the two heads of the Roman Church and the two are one". This theory of dual church authority, implying an equality of the two Apostles, was condemned as heretical by Pope Innocent X, in 1674 (Denzinger, Enchiridion, 965).

To the second class belong (1) A censure of Sirmond's "Prædestinatus" (1644). (2) "Quæ sit Sancti Augustini et doctrinæ eius auctoritas in ecclesiâ?" (1650). Barcos holds that a proposition clearly founded on St. Augustine can be absolutely accepted and taught, regardless of a papal Bull. That exaggeration of the African Doctor's authority was, from the beginning of the controversy, the main prop of the Jansenists who read in St. Augustine what they pleased and then claimed immunity from the authority of the Church. This new error was condemned by Pope Alexander VIII, 1690 (Cf. Denzinger, no. 1187). (3) "Exposition de la foy de Eglise romaine touchant la grâce et la prédestination" (1696). This book was written at the request of the Jansenist Bishop of Aleth, Pavillon, and may be looked upon as the official exposé of Jansenism. It was condemned by the Holy Office, 1697, and again 1704, when it was published with the "Instructions sur la grâce" of Antoine Arnauld.

HURTER, *Nomenclator*, II (Innsbruck, 1893); MIGNE, *Dict. de biog. chrét.* (Paris, 1851); JUNGMANN in *Kirchenlex.*, I, 1994; BEARD, *Port-Royal* (London, 1861); FUZET, *Les Jansenistes* (Paris, 1876); SAINTE-BEUVE, *Port-Royal* (Paris, 1878).

J. F. SOLLIER.

Bard, HENRY, BARON BROMLEY and VISCOUNT BELLAMONT, an English soldier and diplomat, b. 1604; d. 1660. He was the son of the Reverend George Bard, Vicar of Staines, Middlesex, England, a representative of an old Norfolk family. He was educated at Eton, and in 1632 entered King's College, Cambridge, where he took the Master's degree and a fellowship. Before this date he had travelled considerably, having visited Paris, and journeyed on foot through France, Italy, Turkey, Palestine, and Egypt. It is alleged that during his sojourn in the last country he surreptitiously got possession of a copy of the Koran which was the property of one of the mosques, and which he appropriated and afterwards presented to his college.

Bard's habits of life were expensive, the liberality and generosity of his wealthy brother, Maximilian, enabling him to indulge them. His accomplishments included the knowledge of several languages and, coupled with his experience as a traveller and a wide knowledge of men and events, served to commend him to Charles I, with whom he became a favourite, and whose policy throughout the Civil War he sustained as a strong partisan. He was one of the earliest to take up arms in the king's behalf, obtaining through the queen a colonel's commission. He distinguished himself at York, and at the battle of Cheriton Down, was severely wounded, lost an arm, and was taken prisoner. In May of 1646 he received his discharge and on again joining the king received the reversionary grant of the office of Governor of the

Island of Guernsey and Captain of Cornet Castle. Later he was appointed to the command of a brigade and was made governor of Camden House, Gloucestershire. Failing to hold this post against the assaults of the Parliamentarians, he burned the house to the ground.

Bard was also Governor of Worcester about 1643, and in October, 1646, he distinguished himself by being among the first to scale the ramparts, a feat which he is said to have performed at Naseby also. On 8 July, 1646, he was created Baron Bard and Viscount Bellamont in the Kingdom of Ireland. In the following December Bard was again taken prisoner, when on his way to Ireland, but was finally liberated on his promising to go beyond the sea and never to return without permission. The court of Charles II at The Hague furnished the needed resting-place. In May of 1649 he was arrested, charged with murdering Dr. Dorislaus. The charge came to naught, and in 1656 Bard was sent from Bruges as special ambassador by Charles II to the Shah of Persia, to obtain financial help to recover the throne of England. The mission failed, as the Persian monarch was under obligations to England for aid rendered him at Ormuz and was therefore unable to comply with the request of Charles. Bard, who had been a Catholic for several years, lost his life in a windstorm in the desert of Arabia about 1660.

HENDERSON in *Dict. Nat. Biog.*, III, 175; GILLOW, *Bibl. Dict. Eng. Cath.*, I, 128.

THOMAS GAFFNEY TAAFFE.

Bardesanes and Bardesanites.—Bardesanes (*Bar-Daisan*), a Syrian Gnostic or, more correctly, a Syrian poet, astrologer, and philosopher, b. 11 July, 154 (164?), at Edessa, of wealthy Persian, or Parthian, parents; d. 222, at Edessa. To indicate the city of his birth his parents called him "Son of the Daisan", the river on which Edessa is situated. On account of his foreign extraction he is sometimes referred to as "the Parthian" (by Julius Africanus), or "the Babylonian" (by Porphyrius); and, on account of his later important activity in Armenia, "the Armenian" (by Hippolytus). His pagan parents, Nuḥama' and Naḥ'siram, must have been people of rank, for their son was educated with the crown-prince of the Osrhoenic kingdom, at the court of Abgar Manu VIII. Julius Africanus says that he saw Bardesanes, with bow and arrow, mark the outline of a boy's face with his arrows on a shield which the boy held. Owing to political disturbances in Edessa, Bardesanes and his parents moved for a while to Hierapolis (Mabûg), a strong centre of paganism. Here the boy was brought up in the house of a heathen priest Anûdûzbar. In this school, no doubt, he learnt all the intricacies of Babylonian astrology, a training which permanently influenced his mind and proved the bane of his later life. At the age of twenty-five he happened to hear the homilies of Hystaspes, the Bishop of Edessa; he received instruction, was baptized, and even admitted to the diaconate or the priesthood. "Priesthood", however, may merely imply that he ranked as one of the college of presbyters, for he remained in the world, had a son called Harmonius, and when Abgar IX, the friend of his youth, ascended the throne (179) he took his place at court. He was clearly no ascetic, but dressed in Oriental finery, "with berylls and caftan", according to St. Ephrem.

His acceptance of Christianity was perfectly sincere; nor do later stories, that he left the Catholic Church and joined the Valentinian Gnostics out of disappointed ambition, deserve much credit. His royal friend became (probably after 202, i. e. after his visit and honourable reception at Rome) the first Christian king; and both king and philosopher laboured to create the first Christian State. Bardesanes showed great literary activity against Marcion and Valentinus, the Gnostics of the day. But unfortunately, with the zeal of a convert anxious to use his previous acquirements in the service of the newly found truth, Bardesanes mixed his Babylonian pseudo-astronomy with Christian dogma and thus originated a Christian sect, which was vigorously combated by St. Ephrem. The Romans under Caracalla, taking advantage of the anti-Christian faction in Edessa, captured Abgar IX and sent him in chains to Rome. Thus the Osrhoenic kingdom, after 353 years' existence, came to an end. Though he was urged by a friend of Caracalla to apostatize, Bardesanes stood firm, saying that he feared not death, as he would in any event have to undergo it, even though he should now submit to the emperor. At the age of sixty-three he was forced to take refuge in the fortress of Ani in Armenia and tried to spread the Gospel there, but with little success. He died at the age of sixty-eight, probably at Edessa. According to Michael the Syrian, Bardesanes had besides Harmonius two other sons called Abgarun and Hasdû.

WRITINGS.—Bardesanes apparently was a voluminous author. Though nearly all his works have perished, we find notices of the following: (a) Dialogues against Marcion and Valentinus (Theodoretus, Hær. fab., I, xxii; Eusebius, Hist. Eccl., IV, xxx, 3). (b) Dialogue "Against Fate" addressed to Antoninus. Whether this Antoninus is merely a friend of Bardesanes or a Roman emperor and, in the latter case, which of the Antonini is meant, is a matter of controversy. It is also uncertain whether this dialogue is identical with "The Book of the Laws of the Countries", of which later on (Eusebius, Hist. Eccl., IV, xxx, 2; Epiphanius, Hær., LVI, i; Theodoretus, I, xxii). (c) A "Book of Psalms", 150 in number, in imitation of David's Psalter (St. Ephrem, Serm. adv. hær., liii). These psalms became famous in the history of Edessa; their words and melodies lived for generations on the lips of the people. Only when St. Ephrem composed hymns in the same pentasyllabic metre and had them sung to the same tunes as the psalms of Bardesanes, these latter gradually lost favour. We probably possess a few of Bardesanes' hymns in the Gnostic "Acts of Thomas"; the "Hymn on the Soul"; the "Espousals of Wisdom"; the consecratory prayer at Baptism and at Holy Communion. Of these, however, only the "Hymn on the Soul" is generally acknowledged to be by Bardesanes, the authorship of the others is doubtful. Though marred by many obscurities, the beauty of this hymn on the soul is very striking. The soul is sent from its heavenly home to the earth, symbolized by Egypt, to obtain the pearl of great price. In Egypt it forgets for a while its royal parentage and glorious destiny. It is reminded thereof by a letter from home, succeeds in snatching the pearl from the Serpent, and, once more clothed in a raiment of light, it returns to receive its rank and glory in the kingdom of its father. (d) Astrologico-theological treatises, in which his peculiar tenets were expounded. They are referred to by St. Ephrem, and amongst them was a treatise on light and darkness. A fragment of an astronomical work by Bardesanes was preserved by George, Bishop of the Arab tribes, and republished by Nau in "Bardésane l'astrologue" etc. (Paris, 1899). (e) A "History of Armenia". Moses of Chorene (History of G. A., II, 66) states that Bardesanes, "having taken refuge in the fortress of Ani, read there the temple records in which also the deeds of kings were chronicled; to these he added the events of his own time. He wrote all in Syriac, but his book was afterwards translated into Greek." Though the correctness of this statement is not quite above suspicion, it probably has a foundation in fact. (f) "An Account of India". Bardesanes obtained his information from the Hindu ambassadors to the Emperor Eliogabalus. A few extracts are preserved by Porphyry and Stobæus (Langlois, Fragm. hist. græc., V, lxviii sqq.). "Book of the Laws of the Countries". This famous dialogue, the oldest remnant not only of Bardesanite learning, but even of Syriac literature, if we except the version of Holy Writ, is not by Bardesanes himself, but by a certain Philip, his disciple. The main speaker, however, in the dialogue is Bardesanes, and we have no reason to doubt that what is put in his mouth correctly represents his teaching. Excerpts of this work are extant in Greek in Euseb. (Præp. Ev., VI, x, 6 sqq.) and in Cæsarius (Quæstiones, xlvii, 48); in Latin in the "Recognitions" of Pseudo-Clement, IX, 19 sqq. A complete Syriac text was first published from a sixth- or seventh-century MS. in the British Museum, by Cureton, in his "Spicilegium Syriacum" (London, 1855), and recently by Nau. It is disputed whether the original was in Syriac or in Greek; Nau is decidedly and rightly in favour of the former. Against a questioning disciple called Abida, Bardesanes seeks to show that man's actions are not entirely necessitated by Fate, as the outcome of stellar combinations. From the fact that the same laws, customs, and manners often prevail amongst all persons living in a certain district, or, though locally scattered, living under the same traditions, Bardesanes endeavours to show that the position of the stars at the birth of individuals can have but little to do with their subsequent conduct. Hence the title "Book of the Laws of the Countries."

SYSTEM.—Various opinions have been formed as to the real doctrine of Bardesanes. As early as Hippolytus (Philos., VI, 50) his doctrine was described as a variety of Valentinianism, the most popular form of Gnosticism. A. Hilgenfeld in 1864 wrote an able defence of this view, based mainly on extracts from St. Ephrem, who devoted his life to combating Bardesanism in Edessa. But the strong and fervent expressions of St. Ephrem against the Bardesanites of his day are not a fair criterion of the doctrine of their master. The extraordinary veneration of his own countrymen, the very reserved and half-respectful allusion to him in the early Fathers, and above all the "Book of the Laws of the Countries" suggest a milder view of Bardesanes's aberrations. He cannot be called a Gnostic in the proper sense of the word. He believed in an Almighty God, Creator of heaven and earth, whose will is absolute, and to whom all things are subject. God endowed man with freedom of will to work out his salvation. This world He allowed to be a mixture of good and evil, light and darkness. All things, even those which we now consider inanimate, have a measure of liberty. In all of them the light has to overcome the darkness. After six thousand years this earth shall have an end, and a world without evil shall take its place. To Bardesanes the sun, moon, and planets were living beings, to whom, under God, the government of this world was largely entrusted; and though man was free, he was strongly influenced for good or for evil by the constellations. Bardesanes' catechism must have been a strange mixture of Christian doctrine and references to the signs of the Zodiac. Misled by the fact that "spirit" is feminine in Syriac, he seems to have held erroneous views on the Trinity. He apparently denied the Resurrection of the Body, but thought Our Lord's body was endowed with incorruptibility as with a special gift.

SCHOOL.—Bardesanes's son Harmonius strayed farther from the path of orthodoxy. Educated at Athens, he added to the Chaldee astrology of his father Greek errors concerning the soul, the birth and destruction of bodies, and a sort of metempsychosis. A certain Marinus, a follower of Bardesanes, is refuted in the "Dialogue of Adamantius". This Marinus, a dualist, held the doctrine of a two-fold prime-

val being; for the devil, according to him, is not created by God. He was also a Docetist, as he denied Christ's birth of a woman. According to St. Ephrem, the Bardesanites of his day were given to many puerilities and obscenities. Sun and Moon were considered male and female principles, and the ideas of heaven amongst the Bardesanites were not without an admixture of sensuality. St. Ephrem's zealous efforts to suppress this powerful heresy were not entirely successful. Rabbula, Bishop of Edessa in 431–432, found it flourishing everywhere. Its existence in the seventh century is attested by Jacob of Edessa; in the eighth by George, Bishop of the Arab tribes; in the tenth by the historian Masudi; and even in the twelfth by Shashrastâni. Bardesanism seems to have degenerated first into Valentinianism and then into common Manichæism. The last-named writer states: "The followers of Daisan believe in two elements, light and darkness. The light causes the good, deliberately and with free will; the darkness causes the evil, but by force of nature and necessity. They believe that light is a living thing, possessing knowledge, might, perception, and understanding; and from it movement and life take their source; but that darkness is dead, ignorant, feeble, rigid, and soulless, without activity and discrimination; and they hold that the evil within them is the outcome of their nature and is done without their co-operation" [Haarbrücker tr. (Halle, 1850), I, 293].

BUONAIUTI, Lo Gnosticismo (Rome, 1907); NAU, Bardésane l'astrologue, le livre des lois des pays (2d ed., Paris, 1899); IDEM, Dictionnaire de théol. cath., s. v. (Paris, 1903); BARDENHEWER, Gesch. der altk. Lit. (Freiburg, 1902), I, 337 sqq.; MERX, Bardesanes von Edessa (Halle, 1863); HILGENFELD, Bardesanes der letzte Gnostiker (Leipzig, 1864); HORT in Dict. of Christ. Biog., s. v.; SCHÖNFELDER in Kirchenlex., s. v.

J. P. ARENDZEN.

Bardstown. See LOUISVILLE.

Bar Hebræus (Abu'l Faraj), a Jacobite Syrian bishop, philosopher, poet, grammarian, physician, Biblical commentator, historian, and theologian, b. at Melitene (Malatia), Asia Minor, 1226; d. at Maragha, Persia, 1286. He was the son of a Jewish physician, Aaron, a convert to the Jacobite faith; hence his surname of Bar 'Ebrāyâ (Bar Hebræus), "Son of the Hebrew". Under the care of his father he began as a boy (a teneris unguiculis) the study of medicine and of many other branches of knowledge, which he pursued as a youth at Antioch and Tripoli, and which he never abandoned until his death. In 1246 he was consecrated Bishop of Gubos, by the Jacobite Patriarch Ignatius II, and in the following year was transferred to the See of Lacabene. He was placed over the Diocese of Aleppo by Dionysius (1252) and finally was made Primate, or Maphrian, of the East by Ignatius III (1264). His episcopal duties did not interfere with his studies; he took advantage of the numerous visitations, which he had to make throughout his vast province, to consult the libraries and converse with the learned men whom he happened to meet. Thus he gradually accumulated an immense erudition, became familiar with almost all branches of secular and religious knowledge, and in many cases thoroughly mastered the bibliography of the various subjects which he undertook to treat. How he could have devoted so much time to such a systematic study, in spite of all the vicissitudes incident to the Mongol invasion, is almost beyond comprehension. The main claim of Bar Hebræus to our gratitude is not, however, in his original productions, but rather in his having preserved and systematized the work of his predecessors, either by way of condensation or by way of direct reproduction. Both on account of his virtues and of his science, Bar Hebræus was respected by all, and his death was mourned not only by men of his own faith, but also by the Nestorians and the Armenians. He was buried at the convent of Mar

Matthew, near Mosul. He has left us an autobiography, to be found in Assemani, "Biblioth. Orient.", II, 248–263; the account of his death (ibid.) was written by his own brother, Bar Sauma. The works of Bar Hebræus are:—

I. ENCYCLOPEDIC AND PHILOSOPHICAL.—(1) His great encyclopedic work is his *Hêwáth Hékhmethâ,* "The Cream of Science", which deals with almost every branch of human knowledge, and comprises the whole Aristotelean discipline, after Avicenna and other Arabian writers. This work, so far, has not been published, with the exception of one chapter, by Margoliouth, in "Analecta Orientalia ad poeticam Aristoteleam" (London, 1887), 114–139. The rest is to be found only in MSS., preserved at Florence, Oxford, London, and elsewhere. (2) *Têghráth Têghrãthâ,* "Commerce of Commerces", a résumé of the preceding, also unpublished. (3) *Kethãbhâ dhe-Bhâbhãthâ,* "Book of the Pupils of the Eyes"; compendium of logic and dialectics. (4) *Kethãbhâ dhe-Sewãdh Sophia,* "Book of the Speech of Wisdom"; compendium of physics and metaphysics. To these should be added a few translations of Arabic works into Syriac, as well as some treatises written directly in Arabic.

II. BIBLICAL.—The most important work of Bar Hebræus is *Auçár Rãzê,* "Storehouse of Secrets", a commentary on the entire Bible, both doctrinal and critical. Before giving his doctrinal exposition of a passage, he first considers its critical state. Although he uses the Peshitto as a basis, he knows that it is not perfect, and therefore controls it by the Hebrew, the Septuagint, the Greek versions of Symmachus, Theodotion, Aquila, by the Oriental versions, Armenian and Coptic, and finally by the other Syriac translations, Heraclean, Philoxenian and especially Syro-Hexapla. The work of Bar Hebræus is of prime importance for the recovery of these versions and more specially of the Hexapla of Origen, of which the Syro-Hexapla is a translation by Paul of Tella. His exegetical and doctrinal portions are taken from the Greek Fathers and previous Syrian Jacobite theologians. No complete edition of the work has yet been issued, but many individual books have been published at different times. (See bibliography at end of article.)

III. HISTORICAL.—Bar Hebræus has left a large historical work called *Mákhtbhãnúth Zãbhnê,* "Chronicon", in which he considers the history from the Creation down to his own day. It is divided into two portions: the first deals with political and civil history and is known as the "Chronicon Syriacum"; the second, "Chronicon Ecclesiasticum", comprising the religious history, begins with Aaron and treats in a first section of the history of the Western Syrian Church and the Patriarchs of Antioch, while a second section is devoted to the Eastern Church, the Nestorian Patriarchs, and the Jacobite Maphrians. Bar Hebræus utilized almost all that had been written before him. The best edition of the "Chronicon Syriacum" is that of Bedjan, "Gregorii Barhebræi Chronicon Syriacum" (Paris, 1890). The best edition of the "Chronicon Ecclesiasticum" is that of Abbeloos and Lamy (3 vols., Louvain, 1872–77). The "Chronicon Syriacum" was rendered into Arabic by Bar Hebræus himself under the name of "History of Dynasties"; the latest and best edition of this work is that of Salhani (Beirut, 1890).

IV. THEOLOGICAL.—In theology Bar Hebræus was a Monophysite. He probably, however, thought that the differences between Catholics, Nestorians, and the rest were of a theological, but not of a dogmatical nature, and that they did not affect the common faith; hence, he did not consider others as heretics, and was not himself considered as such, at least by the Nestorians and the Armenians. In this field, we have from him *Menãrãth Qúdhshê,* "Lamp

of the Sanctuary", and the *Kethãbhâ dhe-Zálgê,* "Book of the Rays", a summary of the first. These works have not been published, and exist in manuscript in Paris, Berlin, London, Oxford, Rome. Ascetical and moral theology were also treated by Bar Hebræus, and we have from him *Kethãbhâ dhe-'Ithîqon,* "Book of Ethics", and *Kethãbhâ dhe-Yaunâ,* "Book of the Dove", an ascetical guide. Both have been edited by Bedjan in "Ethicon seu Moralia Gregorii Barhebræi" (Paris and Leipzig, 1898). The "Book of the Dove" was issued simultaneously by Cardahi (Rome, 1898). Bar Hebræus codified the juridical texts of the Jacobites, in a collection called *Kethãbhâ dhe-Húdhãyê,* "Book of Directions", edited by Bedjan, "Barhebræi Nomocanon" (Paris, 1898). A Latin translation is to be found in Mai, "Scriptorum Veter. Nova Collectio", vol. X.

Bar Hebræus has left besides many other works. On grammatical subjects we have the "Book of Splendours" and "Book of the Spark", both edited by Martin, "Œuvres grammaticales de Aboul Faradj dit Barhebræus" (2 vols., Paris, 1872); also works on mathematics, astronomy, cosmography, medicine, some of which have been published, but others exist only in manuscript.

Most editors of Bar Hebræus' works also give in their introductions some valuable biographical and bibliographical notes. ASSEMANI, *Bibliotheca Orientalis* (Rome, 1719–28), II, 248–321; WRIGHT, *A short history of Syriac Literature* (London, 1894), 265–281; DUVAL, *La littérature Syriaque* (Paris, 1900), *passim,* see index; GÖTTSBERGER, *Bar Hebræus u. seine Scholien z. Heiligen Schrift* (Freiburg im Breisgau, 1900).

For information as to works of BAR HEBRÆUS *classified above under* I: DUVAL, op. cit., 262, 432; GÖTTSBERGER, op. cit., 29–34.

For II (*Biblical*), lists of the published works are given in: KLOSTERMANN, *Syrische Grammatik* (Berlin, 1905), 138 sqq.; DUVAL, op. cit., 81, n. 2; GÖTTSBERGER, op. cit., 76; to which should be added GÖTTSBERGER in *Zeitschr. f. d. Alttest. Wissenschaft* (1901), 101–144. There exist several MSS. of the *Storehouse of Secrets,* for which see DUVAL, loc. cit.; GÖTTSBERGER, op. cit., 62–71.

III. *For the Chronicon,* see list of sources in ASSEMANI, op. cit., 313 sqq.

IV. (*Theological*) ASSEMANI, op. cit., 284 sqq.; DUVAL, op. cit., 235.

R. BUTIN.

Bari, ARCHDIOCESE OF, is situated in the province of the same name, in Apulia, Southern Italy. The city of Bari is the principal city in the province, with a population of about 65,000, and is located on a peninsula which extends into the Adriatic. Anciently called Barium, it fell into the power of the Romans after the war with Pyrrhus, retaining, however, its autonomy. Being a seaport facing the Orient, Bari must have received Christianity at a very early date. According to a local tradition, St. Peter himself preached the Gospel there and consecrated the first bishop. History, however, is silent as to the beginning of Christianity in this city.

The first known Bishop of Bari was Gervasius, who, in 347, assisted at the Council of Sardica. In 530 Bishop Peter held the title of Metropolitan under Epiphanius, Patriarch of Constantinople. In 780 Bishop Leontius was present at the Seventh Œcumenical Council, the Second of Nicæa. In the ninth century the Saracens laid waste Apulia, destroyed the city of Canosa (Canusium) and captured Bari. In 841, however, the Byzantine army reconquered Bari, and in 844 St. Angelarius, Bishop of Canosa, then in ruins, brought to Bari the relics of Sts. Rufinus, Memorus, and Sabinus, which he had rescued from the ruins. Pope Sergius II conferred on him the title of Bishop of the two dioceses of Bari and Canosa, a title which the Archbishops of Bari retain to the present time. In 933 Pope John XI granted the Bishops of Bari the use of the pallium. It seems that the Bishops were dependent on the Patriarch of Constantinople until the tenth century. Giovanni II (952) was able to withdraw from this influence, refusing to accept the prescriptions of the patriarch concerning liturgical points. All connexion was finally severed in the eleventh century, and Bari became a direct dependency of Rome. Archbishop Bisanzio (1025) obtained from the pope the privilege of consecrating his suffragans; he also began the construction of the new cathedral, which was continued by his successors, Nicolò (1035), Andrea (1062), and Elia (1089), the last-named a member of the Benedictine Order.

In 1097 some Bari sailors, on their return from the East, brought with them the relics of St. Nicholas, Bishop of Mira, for which Roger, Duke of Apulia, built a splendid church; this became the object of great veneration and of innumerable pilgrimages. About this time Urban II, being in Apulia, went to Bari to venerate the relics of the holy wonderworker and to consecrate the basilica. Here also he held a council, attended by 183 bishops, to consider the reunion of the Greeks with the Church of Rome. St. Anselm of Canterbury distinguished himself at this council by his learned defence of the procession of the Holy Ghost and the use of unleavened bread for the Holy Eucharist. Another council had been held at Bari in 1064, presided over by Arnoldo, Vicar of Alexander II. Of the later provincial councils that of 1607 is worthy of mention. In the reorganization of the dioceses of the Kingdom of Naples, at the beginning of the nineteenth century, the Diocese of Bitetto was suppressed and made a part of the Diocese of Bari. The suffragan sees under Bari are: Conversano, Rufo, and Bitonto.

The most celebrated religious edifice of Bari is the church of San Nicolò, one of the most beautiful examples of Norman architecture. It consists of an upper and a lower church, both richly adorned with precious marbles. The cathedral, dedicated to the Assumption, is likewise remarkable for the two high bell towers with which it is flanked.

The most celebrated Archbishops of Bari, in addition to those already mentioned, are: Romualdo Grisoni (1280), distinguished for his restorations of churches; Bartolomeo Prignano (1377), later Pope Urban VI, who, however, never saw this see; Ascanio Gesualdo (1613), who gave a wonderful example of charity in the earthquake of 1632; Diego Sersale (1638), who at his own expense rebuilt the cathedral, the episcopal palace, and the seminary; the Dominican Tommaso Maria, of the Dukes of Bagnara (1684), who died in the odour of sanctity.

The Diocese of Bari contains a population of 300,400. It contains 7 rural deaneries, 33 parishes, 260 churches, chapels, and oratories, 250 secular priests, 110 seminarists, 30 regular clergy, 34 lay brothers, 200 members of female congregations, 45 schools for boys, 35 for girls.

CAPPELLETTI, *Le chiese d'Italia* (Venice, 1844), XXI; *Annuario eccl.* (Rome, 1906).

U. BENIGNI.

Barillon, EMILE. See MALACCA, DIOCESE OF.

Barjesus (Gr. Βαριησοῦς), a false prophet found in the company of the Proconsul Sergius Paulus by St. Paul and Barnabas during their stay at Paphos in Cyprus (Acts, xiii, 6-12). Because of his opposition to the Proconsul's conversion to Christianity, Barjesus was struck blind by St. Paul. He was also called Elymos (Arab, '*alim*, i. e. "wise"), which St. Luke translated by "magician" (Acts, xiii, 8).

F. X. E. ALBERT.

Bar-Kepha, MOSES, one of the most celebrated Jacobite bishops and writers of the ninth century, b. at Balad, about the year 813; d. at the age of ninety, in 903. A biography of him, written by an anonymous Syriac writer, is preserved in one of the Vatican manuscripts, extracts from which are given by Assemani in his "Bibliotheca Orientalis" (II,

218 sq.). He was a monk and afterwards became bishop of three cities, Beth-Ramman, Beth-Kionaya, and Mossoul on the Tigris, assuming the name of Severus. For ten years he was the patriarchal "Periodeutes", or visitor, of the Diocese of Tagrit, where, by his wise administration and learning, he acquired a great fame and reputation. He was buried in the monastery of St. Sergius, situated on the Tigris, near his native city.

The works of Moses Bar-Kepha are very numerous, and deal with many theological, philosophical, controversial, exegetical, and liturgical subjects. The principal are: (1) A Commentary on the Old and New Testaments, often quoted by Bar Hebræus, and most of it still extant in manuscript form; (2) a treatise on predestination and free will, preserved in a MS. in the British Museum (Add. 14,731); (3) a commentary on Aristotle's "Dialectics", mentioned by Bar Hebræus; (4) a commentary on the Hexameron in five books, preserved in the Bibliothèque Nationale at Paris (Syr. 241), a passage of which is translated into French by Abbé Nau in his "Bardésane l'astrologue" (Paris, 1899), p. 59; (5) a "Tractatus de Paradiso", in three parts, dedicated to his friend Ignatius. [The Syriac original of this work is lost, but a Latin version of it was published by Masius (Antwerp, 1569) under the title "De Paradiso Commentarius".] (6) A treatise on the soul, in forty chapters, with a supplementary essay on the utility of offering prayers and sacrifices for the dead. [This treatise is preserved in the Vatican Library; a German translation of it is given by O. Braun in his "Moses Bar-Kepha und sein Buch von der Seele" (Freiburg, 1891).] (7) A "Tractatus de sectis", or, "Liber disputationum adversus hæreses" (see Assemani, B. O. II, 57); (8) a treatise on the Sacraments; (9) a commentary on the Liturgy; (10) an ecclesiastical history. His other works comprise discourses, homilies, and a commentary on the writings of St. Gregory Nazianzen.

BRAUN, *Moses Bar-Kepha*; BAR HEBRÆUS, *Chronicon Ecclesiasticum*, ed. LAMY (Louvain, 1872-77), I, 394-395; II, 217; ASSEMANI, *Bibliotheca Orientalis*, II, 218 sqq.; WRIGHT, *A Short History of Syriac Literature* (London, 1894), 207-211; *Kirchenlex.*, s. v.; DUVAL, *La Littérature Syriaque* (Paris, 1907), 391-392.

GABRIEL OUSSANI.

Barkworth (*alias* LAMBERT), MARK, VENERABLE, priest and martyr, b. about 1572, in Lincolnshire; executed at Tyburn 27 February, 1601; he was educated at Oxford, and converted to the Faith at Douai in 1594, by Father George, a Flemish Jesuit. In 1596 Barkworth went to Rome and thence to Valladolid. On his way to Spain he is said to have had a vision of St. Benedict, who told him he would die a martyr, in the Benedictine habit. Admitted to the English College, 16 December, 1596, he was ordained priest in 1599, and set out for the English Mission together with Ven. Thomas Garnet. On his way he stayed at the Benedictine Abbey of Hyrache in Navarre, where his ardent wish to join the order was granted by his being made an Oblate with the privilege of making profession at the hour of death. After having escaped great peril at the hands of the heretics of La Rochelle, he was arrested on reaching England and thrown into Newgate, where he lay six months, and was then transferred to Bridewell. Here he wrote an appeal to Cecil, signed "George Barkworth". At his examinations he behaved with extraordinary fearlessness and frank gaiety. Having been condemned he was thrown into "Limbo", the horrible underground dungeon at Newgate, where he remained "very cheerful" till his death.

Barkworth suffered at Tyburn with Ven. Roger Filcock, S.J., and Ven. Anne Lyne. It was the first Tuesday in Lent, a bitterly cold day. He sang, on the way to Tyburn, the Paschal Anthem: "Hæc dies quam fecit Dominus exultemus et lætemur in ea".

On his arrival he kissed the robe of Mrs. Lyne, who was already dead, saying: "Ah, sister, thou hast got the start of us, but we will follow thee as quickly as we may"; and told the people: "I am come here to die, being a Catholic, a priest, and a religious man, belonging to the Order of St. Benedict; it was by this same order that England was converted". He was tall and burly of figure, gay and cheerful in disposition. He suffered in the Benedictine habit, under which he wore a hair-shirt. It was noticed that his knees were, like St. James', hardened by constant kneeling, and an apprentice in the crowd picking up one of his legs, after the quartering, called out to the ministers: "Which of you Gospellers can show such a knee?"

Barkworth's devotion to the Benedictine Order led to his suffering much from the hands of the superiors of the Valladolid College. These sufferings are probably much exaggerated, however, by the anti-Jesuit writers Watson, Barneby, and Bell.

CAMM, *A Benedictine Martyr in England* (London, 1897); CHALLONER, *Memoirs* (1750); W.C., *A Reply to Father Persons' Libel* (1603); WATSON, *Decacordon of ten Quodlibet Questions* (1602); KNOX, *Douay Diaries* (London, 1878).

BEDE CAMM.

Barlaam, MONK OF GERACE. See HESYCHASM.

Barlaam and Josaphat, the principal characters of a legend of Christian antiquity, which was a favourite subject of writers in the Middle Ages. The story is substantially as follows: Many inhabitants of India had been converted by the Apostle St. Thomas and were leading Christian lives. In the third or fourth century King Abenner (Avenier) persecuted the Church. The astrologers had foretold that his son Josaphat would one day become a Christian. To prevent this the prince was kept in close confinement. But, in spite of all precautions, Barlaam, a hermit of Senaar, met him and brought him to the true Faith. Abenner tried his best to pervert Josaphat, but, not succeeding, he shared the government with him. Later Abenner himself became a Christian, and, abdicating the throne, became a hermit. Josaphat governed alone for a time, then resigned, went into the desert, found his former teacher Barlaam, and with him spent his remaining years in holiness. Years after their death, the bodies were brought to India and their grave became renowned by miracles. Barlaam and Josaphat found their way into the Roman Martyrology (27 November), and into the Greek calendar (26 August). Vincent of Beauvais, in the thirteenth century, had given the story in his "Speculum Historiale". It is also found in an abbreviated form in the "Golden Legend" of Jacobus de Voragine of the same century.

The story is a Christianized version of one of the legends of Buddha, as even the name Josaphat would seem to show. This is said to be a corruption of the original Joasaph, which is again corrupted from the middle Persian *Búdásif* (*Budsaif = Bodhisattva*). Still it is of historical value, since it contains the "Apology" presented by the Athenian philosopher Aristides to the Emperor Adrian (or Antoninus Pius). The Greek text of the legend, written probably by a monk of the Sabbas monastery near Jerusalem at the beginning of the seventh century, was first published by Boissonade in his "Anecdota Græca" (Paris, 1832), IV, and is reproduced in Migne, P. G., XCVI, among the works of St. John Damascene. The legend cannot, however, have been a work of the great Damascene, as was proved by Zotenberg in "Notices sur le livre de Barlaam et Josaphat" (Paris, 1886) and by Hammel in "Verhandl. des 7 internat. Orientalisten Congresses", Semit. Section (Vienna, 1888). Another edition of the Greek was made by Kechajoglos (Athens, 1884). From the original Greek a German

translation was made by F. Liebrecht (Münster, 1847). Latin translations (Migne, P. L., LXXIII), were made in the twelfth century and used for nearly all the European languages, in prose, verse and in miracle plays. Among them is prominent the German epic by Rudolph of Ems in the thirteenth century (Königsberg, 1818, and somewhat later at Leipzig). From the German an Icelandic and a Swedish version were made in the fifteenth century. At Manila the legend appeared in the Tagala language of the Philippines. In the East it exists in Syriac, Arabic, Ethiopic, Armenian, and Hebrew.

MÜLLER, *Migration of Fables* in *Contemp. Review* (July, 1870); IDEM, *Selected Essays* (London, 1881); LIEBRECHT in *Jahrbuch für romanische und englische Litteratur* II; BRAUNHOLZ, *Die erste nichtchristliche Parabel des Barlaam u. Josaphat, ihre Herkunft und Verbreitung* (Halle, 1884); KUHN, *B. u. J., eine bibliographisch-litteraturgeschichtliche Studie* (München, 1893); *Zeitschrift für katholische Theologie*, 1892; BARDENHEWER, *Geschichte der altkirchlichen Litteratur* (Freiburg, 1902); *The Month* (1881), XLI, 137; COSQUIN in *Revue des Quest. Hist.* (1880), XXXVIII, 579–608; KUHN in *Abhandl. d. Bayer. Akad. der Wissenschaften* (1893); *Analecta Bollandiana*, XIII, 299; JACOBS, *Barlaam and Josaphat, English Lives of Buddha* (London, 1896); VACANT, *Dict. de théol. cath.*, II, 410; KRUMBACHER, *Gesch. d. Byzant. Litteratur* (2d ed., Munich, 1897), 886; *Biblioth. Hag. Latina*, 147.

FRANCIS MERSHMAN.

Barletta, GABRIEL (sometimes called BARLETE, DE BAROLO, BAROLUS), preacher, b., according to some, in the Neapolitan territory at Barletta, whence he took his name, or, according to others, at Aquino; d. sometime after 1480. Little is known of his life other than that he was a Dominican and probably a pupil of St. Antoninus. All his contemporaries held him in high esteem as an orator. He was generally proposed, even during his lifetime, as the model orator. After his death his fame did not diminish, if the popular saying which Altamura has preserved for us be a criterion. Throughout Italy it was the common saying: *Nescit prædicare qui nescit barlettare*. His sermons appeared in two volumes at Brixen in 1497, and have been reprinted very frequently since. Echard says that no less than thirteen editions appeared in eighty years. The best edition is that of Venice (1577), in two volumes.

In form his sermons are nothing else than the ordinary homily on the virtues and vices of life. He spares none of the foibles and weaknesses of his contemporaries, and in his denunciations passages of eloquent and biting sarcasm are often met with. At times he descends to an almost burlesque mimicry, as witness his sermon on the manner in which the rich ecclesiastic says the Lord's prayer. Coarse things are also to be found, but not so frequently as in the printed sermons of some of his rivals. He has been blamed for this coarseness by Bayle and Theophilus Raynaud, but his name has been completely vindicated by Dominic Casales, O.P., in the work "Candor lilii seu Ordo Prædicatorum a calumniis Petri a Valle Clausa [i. e. Theop. Reynaldi] vindicatus". Some maintain (Tübing. Quartalschrift, 1872, II, 270) that Barletta is not the author of the sermons which bear his name. They base their contention on a sentence of Leander Alberti [Descrizzione di tutta Italia (Bologna, 1550), 200], who says that an unskilled youth whom he knew gathered together old and unknown sermons and ascribed them to Barletta. Furthermore, they must have appeared in the vernacular, whilst we know them in the Latin alone. Thus they have suffered many changes and alterations. But up to the seventeenth century there was no question of the authorship. They show sure signs of the times and are not unworthy of his fame. Hence, scholars generally accept them as authentic.

QUÉTIF AND ECHARD, *Scriptores Ord. Præd.*, I, 844, append., II, 823; TIRABOSCHI, *Storia della letteratura italiana*, VI, 1124; PAULUS in *Literarische Beilage der Kölnischen Volkszeitung* (1904), No. 10.

THOS. M. SCHWERTNER.

Barletta, DIOCESE OF. See TRANI AND BARLETTA.

Barlings, ABBEY OF, located about six miles E.N.E. of Lincoln, England, founded in 1154 in honour of Our Lady by Ralph de Haye who had given some lands to the Abbot of Newhouse (also in Lincolnshire, the first abbey of the Norbertine Order erected in England, founded in 1143) with the request to send a colony of White Canons to Barlings. The abbey was afterwards removed to Oxeney, another locality in the same township, where it was dissolved by Henry VIII in 1537. Much information concerning the Abbey of Barlings, as well as concerning other Norbertine abbeys in England, may be derived from Bishop Redman's "Register of Visitations", preserved in the Bodleian Library at Oxford, and lately published in three volumes by Abbot Gasquet under the title of "Collectanea Anglo-Premonstratensia". This register contains various documents, lists of White Canons in each abbey, notes and remarks made at the time of each visitation, during a period of about thirty-five years that Redman was visitor of all the Norbertine abbeys and priories in England for the Abbot-General of the Order of Prémontré. Richard Redman was Abbot of the Norbertine Abbey of Shap in Westmoreland when he became visitor, and he acted in the same capacity when he successively became Bishop of St. Asaph in 1472, of Exeter in 1495, and of Ely in 1501. He died 24 August, 1505.

This register records no fewer than nine visitations of Barlings Abbey made by Redman. The various lists found therein give the names of about eighteen canons at each visitation. The names of nineteen abbots are known; the first abbot was called Adam (1154), the last Matthew Mackarel (1532–37) who is said to have been one of the leaders of the Pilgrimage of Grace in Lincolnshire. The supposed complicity of Abbot Mackarel, like that of other heads of religious houses, gave Henry VIII the opportunity of laying hands upon the Abbey of Barlings and of placing it under the law of attainder. The abbey church, 300 feet in length, was defaced, the lead torn from the roofs, and melted down under the special direction of Cromwell. Abbot Mackarel, some of his religious, and many of the clergy and laity were taken to Lincoln, and some of these were afterwards sent to the Tower in London. Those in Lincoln, among whom there were four canons of Barlings, were tried 6 March, 1537, and ordered for immediate execution. Towards the end of March, Abbot Matthew Mackarel, one of his canons and some others were tried in London before Chancellor Oudeley, found guilty, and condemned to be hanged and quartered. At the time of the dissolution the abbey and its possessions were granted to Charles, Duke of Suffolk. An arch and part of a wall are the only remains. The Right Rev. Martin Geudens, of Corpus Christi Priory, Manchester, was named Titular Abbot of Barlings, 7 May, 1898, and blessed 17 September, of the same year.

Annales Præm.; Monasticon Anglic.; REDMAN, *Mss. Register in* GASQUET, *Collectanea Anglo-Premonstratensia;* GASQUET, *Henry VIII and the English Monasteries* (6th ed., London, 1895).

MARTIN GEUDENS.

Barlow, EDWARD. See BOOTH.

Barlow (*alias* RADCLIFFE and BRERETON), EDWARD AMBROSE, VENERABLE, priest and martyr, b. at Barlow Hall, 1585; d. 10 September, 1641. He was the fourth son of Sir Alexander Barlow, Knight of Barlow Hall, near Manchester, by Mary, daughter of Sir Uryan Brereton, Knight of Handforth Hall, Co. Chester, and was baptized at Didsbury Church 30 November, 1585; the entry in the register may still be seen. Educated at the Benedictine monastery of St. Gregory, Douai, he entered the English College, Valladolid, 20 September, 1610, but returned to Douai,

where his elder brother William Rudesind was a professed monk. He was himself professed in 1616 and ordained, 1617. Sent to England, he laboured in South Lancashire with apostolic zeal and fervour. He resided chiefly at Wardley Hall, the seat of the Downe family, near Manchester, and at Morley's Hall, a mansion of the Tyldesleys, in the parish of Leigh, some seven miles from Manchester. At the former, his skull is still preserved, in a little receptacle on the staircase. At the latter he was apprehended for the fifth and last time on Easter Sunday, 25 April, 1641. He was arrested by the Vicar of Eccles, who marched at the head of his parishioners, clad in his surplice, and was followed by some 400 men armed with clubs and swords. He was preaching at the time and could have escaped in the confusion, but yielded himself up to his enemies, and was carried off to Lancaster Castle. Here after four months' imprisonment he was tried, on 6 or 7 September, and sentenced next day, having confessed that he was a priest. On Friday, 10 September, he suffered the usual penalties at Lancaster.

A beautiful picture of his life is given by Challoner from two MS. relations belonging to St. Gregory's monastery, one written by his brother Dom Rudesind Barlow, President of the Anglo-Benedictine Congregation. There is another MS., entitled "The Apostolical life of Ambrose Barlow", written by one of his pupils for Dom Rudesind, which is at present in the Library of Owen's College, Manchester. It is to be printed among the publications of the Chetham Society. This contains many details hitherto unpublished. Two portraits of this martyr exist and also one of his father, Sir Alexander. Many of his relics are also preserved, a hand being at Stanbrook Abbey near Worcester. A full biography is in course of preparation.

ALLANSON, *Biographical MSS.* (preserved at Ampleforth Abbey), I; GILLOW, *Bibl. Dict. Eng. Cath.* (London, 1885); CHALLONER, *Memoirs;* FLETCHER MOSS, *Pilgrimages to Old Homes* (Didsbury, 1903); IDEM, *History of Didsbury* (Manchester); IDEM, *Chronicles of Cheadle, Cheshire* (Didsbury, 1894); DODD, *Church History of England* (Brussels, 1739).

BEDE CAMM.

Barlow, WILLIAM RUDESIND, third son of Sir Alexander Barlow of Barlow Hall, near Manchester, England, and Mary Brereton his wife, date of birth uncertain; d. at Douai, 19 Sept., 1656. The martyr, Ven. Edward Barlow, was his younger brother and was educated with him at the English College, Douai. Wishing to become a Benedictine, he joined the Spanish congregation, being professed at Cella Nueva in Gallicia in 1605. Ordained priest in 1608 he became Doctor of Divinity at Salamanca. In 1611 he went to St. Gregory's, Douai, where he was made prior in 1614, and, two years later, professor of theology at St. Vaast's College, an office which he held for forty years. Weldon says: "He formed almost all the bishops, abbots, and professors that flourished in those parts for some time after. He was esteemed the first or chief of the scholastic divines or casuists of his time, and in knowledge of the canon law inferior to no one of his time or the age before." The circle of his friends included Bellarmine and other contemporary scholars.

He more than once refused the dignity of abbot and bishop, "and it was thought he would have refused that of cardinal, which was said to have been preparing for him." From 1621 to 1629 he was President-General of the English Congregation. In 1633 he became titular Cathedral-Prior of Canterbury. Beyond a circular letter to the English Benedictines about their relations to the vicar Apostolic, none of his writings are left, although Gee, writing in 1624, attributes to him a book called "The Enemies of God". Weldon adds that after his death a bishop offered the Benedictines of Douai an establishment if they would give him Father Rudesind's writings. "But in vain they were sought for, for they were destroyed by an enemy." It is said that on the death of Dr. Bishop, the vicar Apostolic, he was consulted by the pope as to the best successor, and that he warmly recommended Dr. Smith, who was appointed, but later he opposed that prelate on the question of the extent of the vicar Apostolic's jurisdiction.

WELDON, *Chronological Notes of the Eng. Benedictines, 1709* (London, 1881), XXXI; SNOW, *Necrology of the Eng. Benedictines* (London, 1883); GILLOW, *Bibl. Dict. Eng. Cath.* (London, 1885), I, 136.

EDWIN BURTON.

Barnabas, EPISTLE ATTRIBUTED TO.—*Authorities for the Text and Editions.*—There is a triple tradition of the Greek text of this document. Up to 1843 eight manuscripts of the Epistle of Barnabas were known to be in Western libraries. These manuscripts were all derived from a common source, and no one of them contained chapters i–v, 7a. Since then two complete manuscripts of the text have been discovered that are independent of each other and of the preceding group of texts, namely: the famous Codex Sinaiticus of the Bible (fourth century), in which the Epistle of Barnabas and the "Pastor" follow the books of the New Testament, and the Jerusalem Codex (eleventh century), which includes the Didache. There is also an old Latin version of the first seventeen chapters which is, perhaps, of the end of the fourth century (St. Petersburg, Q., I, 39). This version is a very free one and can hardly serve for the restoration of the text. The same is true of the citations from the epistle in the writings of Clement of Alexandria, of Origen, and others. The best authority for the text is the Codex Sinaiticus. The Epistle of Barnabas has been edited among the works of the Apostolic Fathers. The two chief editions are: Gebhard and Harnack, "Barnabæ Epistula" in "Patrum Apostolicorum Opera" (Leipzig, 1878), I, II, and Funk, "Patres Apostolici" (Tübingen, 1901), I. Use can also be made of the edition of Sharpe, "St. Barnabas' Epistle in Greek with Translation" (London, 1880), as well as that of Lightfoot, ed. Harmer, "The Apostolic Fathers" (London, 1898), and of Vizzini, "Patres Apostolici" (Rome, 1902), III.

Contents.—The Epistle of Barnabas contains no clue to its author nor to those for whom it was intended. Its aim is to impart to its readers the perfect wisdom (*gnosis*), that is an exact knowledge of the economy of salvation. It is made up of two parts, the subject of each being announced in verses 6 and 7 of the first chapter. The first part (ch. i–v, 4) is hortatory; in the evil days that are now at hand in which the end of the world and the Judgment shall appear, the faithful, freed from the bonds of the Jewish ceremonial law, are to practise the virtues and to flee from sin. The second part (ch. v, 5–xvii) is more speculative, although it tends, owing to the nature of the argument, to establish the freedom of Christians in respect to the Mosaic regulations. The author wishes to make his readers comprehend the real nature of the Old Testament. He shows how the ordinances of the Law should be understood as referring allegorically to the Christian virtues and institutions, and he pauses to make plain by a series of symbolical explanations, that are often singular, how the Old Testament prefigures Christ, His Passion, His Church, etc. Before concluding (ch. xxi) the author repeats and enlarges the exhortations of the first part of the epistle by borrowing from another document (the Didache or its source) the description of the two ways, the way of light and that of darkness (xviii–xx).

Use of Allegory.—The epistle is characterized by the use of exaggerated allegory. In this particular the writer goes far beyond St. Paul the author of the Epistle to the Hebrews, and St. Ignatius. Not content with regarding the history and institutions of the Jews as containing types of Christianity, he casts aside completely the transitory historical character of the old religion. According to many scholars he teaches that it was never intended that the precepts of the Law should be observed in their literal sense, that the Jews never had a covenant with God, that circumcision was the work of the Devil, etc.; thus he represents a unique point of view in the struggle against Judaism. It might be said more exactly that he condemns the exercise of worship among the Jews in its entirety because, in his opinion, the Jews did not know how to rise to the spiritual and typical meaning which God had mainly had in view in giving them the Law. It is this purely material observance of the ceremonial ordinances, of which the literal fulfilment was not sufficient, that the author holds to be the work of the Devil, and, according to him, the Jews never received the Divine covenant because they never understood its nature (ch. vii, 3, 11; ix, 7; x, 10; xiv).

Intent.—The Epistle of Barnabas is not a polemic. The author takes no notice of paganism. Although he touches on different points that had relations to the doctrines of the Gnostics, still he has no knowledge of these latter. The perfectly composed manner in which he expounds the wisdom he desires to impart shows that another, heretical wisdom (*gnosis*) is not in his thoughts. Moreover, the way in which he speaks of the Old Testament would not be explicable if he had known the wrong use that a Basilides or a Marcion could make of it. Besides, there was nothing in the Judaizing theories to alarm his faith. He speaks of Judaism only in the abstract, and nothing in the letter excites the suspicion that the members of his flock had been exposed to the peril of falling again under the yoke of the Law. No clear situation is described in the letter. In short, it should be regarded rather as the peaceful speculations of a catechist and not as the cries of alarm of a pastor. Consequently, it cannot be admitted that the author may have wished to take part in the struggle against the Judaizers either at Jerusalem (Di Pauli) or at Rome (Völter).

Date.—This abstract discussion of Judaism is the sign of an epoch when the Judaizing controversies were already a thing of the past in the main body of the Church. In settling the date of the letter reference is often made to verses 3–5 of chapter four, where the writer, it is believed, finds the fulfilment of the prophecy of Daniel (Dan., vii, 7, sqq.) in the succession of the Roman Emperors of his time. Starting from this, some critics place the composition of the epistle in the reign of Vespasian (Weizsäcker, Lightfoot), others in the reign of Domitian (Wieseler), and still others in the reign of Nerva (Bardenhewer, Funk). But there is nothing to prove that the author considers the prophecy to be already accomplished. Besides, he might have taken the words of the prophecy to mean a series of kingdoms instead of a line of kings. It is necessary, therefore, to fall back, with Schürer and Harnack, on verses 3–5 of chapter xvi. Reference is here made to the command given by Adrian in A. D. 130 for the reconstruction, in honour of Jupiter, of the Temple at Jerusalem, which had been destroyed by Titus. Adrian had also forbidden the Jews to practise circumcision. The writer of the letter makes allusion to this (ch. ix, 4). The epistle must, consequently, have been written in A. D. 130–131.

General Characteristics.—In what befell Jerusalem and the Temple the author saw the refutation by events of the errors of the Jews, or rather of the Ebionites, for it is the latter that he has in mind whenever his language grows more definite (ch. iv, 4, 6; v, 5; xii, 10; xvi, 1). His flock are not in danger of falling into these errors. Therefore he never attacks them directly. He simply takes advantage of the opportunity that occurrences offer him to give his opinions as to the position and nature of Judaism and its Law. Hence the epistle, in its general character, is more like a treatise or a homily than a letter. However, the epistolary form is not entirely fictitious. The author is not writing to Christians in general, but to a particular church in which he has exercised the office of a διδάσκαλος and from which he finds himself separated (ch. i, 2, 4; xxi, 7, 9).

From a literary point of view the Epistle of Barnabas has no merit. The style is tedious, poor in expression, deficient in clearness, in elegance, and in correctness. The author's logic is weak, and his matter is not under his control; from this fact arise the numerous digressions. These digressions, however, afford no reason for doubting the integrity of the letter, or for regarding as interpolations either entire chapters (Schenkel, Heydecke, Völter), or a consecutive number of verses or parts of verses in each chapter (Weiss). Wehofer recently thought that he had discovered, in the arrangement of the epistle, an adherence to the laws of the Semitic strophe. But the phenomena noted are found in all authors who work out their thought without being able to subordinate the argument to the rules of literary style.

From the dogmatic point of view the chief importance of the epistle is in its relation to the history of the Canon of the Scriptures. It cites, in fact, the Gospel of St. Matthew as Scripture (ch. iv, 14), and even recognizes as in the Canon of the Sacred Books (γέγραπται), along with the collection of Jewish writings, a collection of Christian ones (ch. v, 2), the contents of which, however, cannot be determined. The author regards several apocryphal books as belonging to the Old Testament—probably IV Esdras (ch. xii, 1) and without doubt Henoch (ch. iv, 3; xvi, 5). In his Christology, his soteriology and his doctrine concerning justification the author develops the ideas of Paul with originality. It has been wrongly said that he regards the pre-existent Christ as only a spirit in the image of God. Without explicitly asserting the consubstantiality and the true sonship, he evidently acknowledges the Divine nature of Christ from before the Creation. The eschatological descriptions are decidedly moderate. He is a millenarian, but in speaking of the Judgment to come he simply expresses a vague belief that the end is approaching.

Nationality of the Author.—History of the Epistle.— The extremely allegorical character of the exegesis leads to the supposition that the author of the letter was an Alexandrian. His way of constantly placing himself and his readers in opposition to the Jews makes it impossible to believe that either he or the larger part of his readers were of Jewish origin. Besides, he is not always familiar with the Mosaic rites (cf. ch. vii). The history of the epistle confirms its Alexandrine origin. Up to the fourth century only the Alexandrians were acquainted with it, and in their Church the epistle attained to the honour of being publicly read. The manner in which Clement of Alexandria and Origen refer to the letter gives confirmation to the belief that, about the year A. D. 200, even in Alexandria the Epistle of Barnabas was not regarded by every one as an inspired writing.

RICHARDSON, *The Ante-Nicene Fathers* (Buffalo, 1887), I, *Bibl. Syn.*, 16–19; MILLIGAN in *Dict. Christ. Biog.* (London, 1900); FUNK, *Patres Apostolici* (Tübingen, 1901), *Proleg.*, pp. xx–xxxii; BARDENHEWER, *Gesch. der altkirchl. L t.* (Freiburg, 1902), I, 97, 98; WEHOFER, *Untersuch. zur altchristl. Epistolographie* (Vienna, 1901); VAN VELDHUYZEN, *De Brief van Barnabas* (Groningen, 1901); BARTLET, *Barnabas and His Genuine Epistle* in *Expositor* (1902); DI PAULI, *Kritisches zum Barnabasbrief* in *Historischpolitische Blätter* (1903); TURMEL, *La Lettre de Barnabas* in *Ann. de phil. chrét.* (1903); SCHWEIT-ZER, *Der Barnabasbrief über Glaube und Werke* in *Der Katholik* (1904), 3d series, XIX; VÖLTER, *Die apostolischen Väter neu untersucht* (Leyden, 1904), I; HENNECKE, *Neutestamentliche Apokryphen in Verbindung mit Fachgelehrten in deutscher Uebersetzung und mit Einleitungen herausgegeben* (Tübingen, 1904).

P. LADEUZE.

Barnabas (originally JOSEPH), SAINT, styled an Apostle in Holy Scripture, and, like St. Paul, ranked by the Church with the Twelve, though not one of them; b. of Jewish parents in the Island of Cyprus about the beginning of the Christian Era. A Levite, he naturally spent much time in Jerusalem, probably even before the Crucifixion of Our Lord, and appears also to have settled there (where his relatives, the family of Mark the Evangelist, likewise had their homes, Acts, xii, 12) and to have owned land in its vicinity (iv, 36, 37). A rather late tradition recorded by Clement of Alexandria (Strom., II, 20, P. G., VIII, col. 1060) and Eusebius (H. E., II, i, P. G., XX, col. 117) says that he was one of the seventy Disciples; but Acts (iv, 36–37) favours the opinion that he was converted to Christianity shortly after Pentecost (about A. D. 29 or 30) and immediately sold his property and devoted the proceeds to the Church. The Apostles, probably because of his success as a preacher, for he is later placed first among the prophets and doctors of Antioch (xiii, 1), surnamed him Barnabas, a name then interpreted as meaning "son of exhortation" or "consolation". (The real etymology, however, is disputed. See Encyl. Bibl., I, col. 484.) Though nothing is recorded of Barnabas for some years, he evidently acquired during this period a high position in the Church.

When Saul the persecutor, later Paul the Apostle, made his first visit (dated variously from A. D. 33 to 38) to Jerusalem after his conversion, the Church there, remembering his former fierce spirit, was slow to believe in the reality of his conversion. Barnabas stood sponsor for him and had him received by the Apostles, as the Acts relate (ix, 27), though he saw only Peter and James, the brother of the Lord, according to Paul himself (Gal., i, 18, 19). Saul went to his house at Tarsus to live in obscurity for some years, while Barnabas appears to have remained at Jerusalem. The event that brought them together again and opened to both the door to their lifework was an indirect result of Saul's own persecution. In the dispersion that followed Stephen's death, some Disciples from Cyprus and Cyrene, obscure men, inaugurated the real mission of the Christian Church by preaching to the Gentiles. They met with great success among the Greeks of Antioch in Syria, reports of which coming to the ears of the Apostles, Barnabas was sent thither by them to investigate the work of his countrymen. He saw in the conversions effected the fruit of God's grace and, though a Jew, heartily welcomed these first Gentile converts. His mind was opened at once to the possibilities of this immense field. It is a proof how deeply impressed Barnabas had been by Paul that he thought of him immediately for this work, set out without delay for distant Tarsus, and persuaded Paul to go to Antioch and begin the work of preaching. This incident, shedding light on the character of each, shows it was no mere accident that led them to the Gentile field. Together they laboured at Antioch for a whole year and "taught a great multitude". Then, on the coming of famine, by which Jerusalem was much afflicted, the offerings of the Disciples at Antioch were carried (about A. D. 45) to the mother-church by Barnabas and Saul (Acts, xi). Their mission ended, they returned to Antioch, bringing with them the cousin, or nephew of Barnabas (Col., iv, 10), John Mark, the future Evangelist (Acts, xii, 25).

The time was now ripe, it was believed, for more systematic labours, and the Church of Antioch felt inspired by the Holy Ghost to send out missionaries to the Gentile world and to designate for the work Barnabas and Paul. They accordingly departed, after the imposition of hands, with John Mark as helper. Cyprus, the native land of Barnabas, was first evangelized, and then they crossed over to Asia Minor. Here, at Perge in Pamphylia, the first stopping place, John Mark left them, for what reason his friend St. Luke does not state, though Paul looked on the act as desertion. The two Apostles, however, pushing into the interior of a rather wild country, preached at Antioch of Pisidia, Iconium, Lystra, at Derbe, and other cities. At every step they met with opposition and even violent persecution from the Jews, who also incited the Gentiles against them. The most striking incident of the journey was at Lystra, where the superstitious populace took Paul, who had just cured a lame man, for Hermes (Mercury) "because he was the chief speaker", and Barnabas for Jupiter, and were about to sacrifice a bull to them when prevented by the Apostles. Moblike, they were soon persuaded by the Jews to turn and attack the Apostles and wounded St. Paul almost fatally. Despite opposition and persecution, Paul and Barnabas made many converts on this journey and returned by the same route to Perge, organizing churches, ordaining presbyters and placing them over the faithful, so that they felt, on again reaching Antioch in Syria, that God had "opened a door of faith to the Gentiles" (Acts, xiii, 13; xiv, 27; see article PAUL, SAINT).

Barnabas and Paul had been for "no small time" at Antioch, when they were threatened with the undoing of their work and the stopping of its further progress. Preachers came from Jerusalem with the gospel that circumcision was necessary for salvation, even for the Gentiles. The Apostles of the Gentiles, perceiving at once that this doctrine would be fatal to their work, went up to Jerusalem to combat it; the older Apostles received them kindly and at what is called the Council of Jerusalem (dated variously from A. D. 47 to 51) granted a decision in their favour as well as a hearty commendation of their work (Acts, xiv, 27; xv, 30; see articles JERUSALEM, COUNCIL OF; PETER, SAINT). On their return to Antioch, they resumed their preaching for a short time. St. Peter came down and associated freely there with the Gentiles, eating with them. This displeased some disciples of James; in their opinion, Peter's act was unlawful, as against the Mosaic law. Upon their remonstrances, Peter yielded, apparently through fear of displeasing them, and refused to eat any longer with the Gentiles. Barnabas followed his example. Paul considered that they "walked not uprightly according to the truth of the gospel" and upbraided them before the whole church (Gal., ii, 11–15). Paul seems to have carried his point. Shortly afterwards, he and Barnabas decided to revisit their missions. Barnabas wished to take John Mark along once more, but on account of the previous defection Paul objected. A sharp contention ensuing, the Apostles agreed to separate. Paul was probably somewhat influenced by the attitude recently taken by Barnabas, which might prove a prejudice to their work. Barnabas sailed with John Mark to Cyprus, while Paul took Silas and revisited the churches of Asia Minor. It is believed by some that the church of Antioch, by its God-speed to Paul, showed its approval of his attitude; this inference, however, is not certain (Acts, xv, 35–41).

Little is known of the subsequent career of Barnabas. He was still living and labouring as an Apostle in 56 or 57, when Paul wrote I Cor. (ix, 5, 6), from which we learn that he, too, like Paul, earned his own living, though on an equality with the other Apostles. The reference indicates also that the friendship between the two was unimpaired. When Paul was a prisoner in Rome (61–63), John Mark was attached to him as a disciple, which is regarded as an indication that Barnabas was no longer living (Col., iv, 10). This seems probable. Various traditions represent him as the first Bishop of Milan, as preaching at Alexandria and at Rome, whose fourth (?) bishop, St. Clement, he is said to have converted, and as having suffered martyrdom in Cyprus. The traditions are all late and untrustworthy. With the exception of St. Paul and certain of the Twelve, Barnabas appears to have been the most esteemed man of the first Christian generation. St. Luke, breaking his habit of reserve, speaks of him with affection, "for he was a good man, full of the Holy Ghost and of Faith". His title to glory comes not only from his kindliness of heart, his personal sanctity, and his missionary labours, but also from his readiness to lay aside his Jewish prejudices, in this anticipating certain of the Twelve; from his largehearted welcome of the Gentiles, and from his early perception of Paul's worth, to which the Christian Church is indebted, in large part at least, for its great Apostle. His tenderness towards John Mark seems to have had its reward in the valuable services later rendered by him to the Church. The feast of St. Barnabas is celebrated on 11 June. He is credited by Tertullian (probably falsely) with the authorship of the Epistle to the Hebrews, and the so-called Epistle of Barnabas (see BARNABAS, EPISTLE ATTRIBUTED TO) is ascribed to him by many Fathers.

RAMSAY, *St. Paul, the Traveller and the Roman Citizen* (London, 1895); SCHMIEDEL in *Encyc. Bib.* (New York, 1899); FOUARD, *St. Peter* (New York, 1893); IDEM, *St. Paul and His Missions* (New York, 1894); CAVE, *Lives of the Most Eminent Fathers of the Church* (Oxford, 1840); CONYBEARE AND HOWSON, *Life and Epistles of St. Paul* (New York, 1869); LE CAMUS in VIG., *Dict. de la Bib.* (Paris, 1893).

JOHN F. FENLON.

Barnabas of Terni (*Interamna*), Friar Minor and missionary, d. 1474 (or 1477). He belonged to the noble family of the Manassei and was a man of great learning, being Doctor of Medicine and well versed in letters and philosophy. Despising the honours and vanities of the world, he entered the Order of Friars Minor in the Umbria province of the order and practised, with unusual fervour, every virtue of the religious life. After devoting himself assiduously to the study of theology, Barnabas began to preach with wonderful success, but a severe illness obliged him to abandon this work. Although gifted with the grace of prayer and contemplation in an eminent degree, he was almost continually employed in different offices of importance, for which his prudence, kindness, and affability well fitted him. By word and example he proved himself a zealous promoter of that branch of the order known as the Observance. He died at the hermitage of the Carceri on Mount Subiaco at an advanced age and his remains were deposited there in the Chapel of St. Mary Magdelene. He is commemorated in the Franciscan martyrology on 17 February. To Barnabas belongs the honour of having established the first of the celebrated *monti di pietà*, or charitable loan-institutions, designed to protect poor people against the outrageous usury of the Jews. After consulting his fellow religious Fortunatus Coppoli, who had been an eminent jurisconsult, and with the generous co-operation of the wealthy Perugians, Barnabas established the first *monte di pietà* in their city in 1462. Violent opposition ensued, but Barnabas and Fortunatus prevailed over their enemies at a public disputation. Barnabas next extended his work to other cities; it was enthusiastically taken up by several great Franciscan missionaries, and, in their day, the *monti di pietà* wonderfully improved the social conditions of Italy. (See BERNARDINE OF FELTRE.)

WADDING, *Annales Minorum* (2d ed.), XIV, 93, XV, 318; HOLZAPFEL, *Die Anfänger der Montes Pietatis* (Munich, 1903), 35 *passim*.

THOMAS PLASSMANN

Barnabites, the popular name of a religious order which is canonically known by the title, given to it by Pope Paul III in 1535, of Regular Clerics of St. Paul (*Clerici Regulares Sancti Pauli*). This institute was founded by three Italian noblemen: St. Anton Maria Zaccaria (canonized by Leo XIII, 27 March, 1897), Ven. Barthelemy Ferrari, and Ven. Jacopo Morigia, the last two of Milan. Second in seniority of the orders of regular clerics (the Theatines being first), the foundation of the Barnabites as a congregation dates from the year 1530. Clement VII, by the Brief "Vota per quæ vos", 18 February, 1533, canonically approved of the congregation; Paul III, by the Bulls "Dudum felicis recordationis", 28 July, 1535, and "Pastoralis officii cura", 29 November, 1543, exempted them from the jurisdiction of their diocesan. Lastly, the Bulls of Julius III, "Rationi congruit" and "Ad hoc nos Deus prætulit", dated respectively 22 February, and 11 August, 1550, confirmed and augmented the existing privileges of the institute, which, from being a congregation, thenceforward became a religious order in the strict canonical sense, its members, however, still adhering to the custom of calling it "the Congregation".

The popular name *Barnabites* came naturally to the Congregation through its association with the church of St. Barnabas, Milan, which came into its possession within the earliest years of the foundation of the institute, which was at first peculiarly Milanese. St. Charles Borromeo, Archbishop of Milan, presided, in 1579, as Cardinal Protector, over the commission which determined once for all the constitution of the order, and the general chapters were regularly held at Milan until the reign of Alexander VII (1655–67), who ordered them to convene in Rome. Innocent XI (1676–89), however, finally decreed that the general chapters of the Barnabites should assemble in Rome and Milan alternately. These assemblies of the provincials are held every three years for the election of a new general, whose term of office is limited to that period, only one re-election being allowed to each incumbent of the office. The members of the order make, in addition to the three regular vows of poverty, chastity, and obedience, a vow never to strive for any office or position of dignity, or to accept such otherwise than under a command of the Holy See. The scope of their special vocation, besides preaching in general, catechizing, hearing confessions, giving missions, ministrations in hospitals and prisons, and the education of youth, includes also a particular devotion to the thorough study and exposition of St. Paul's Epistles. Their habit is the black soutane (*tunica talaris*) which formed the usual garb of Milanese secular priests in the time of St. Charles Borromeo.

Spread of the Order.—The Congregation has never failed of the holy object for which it was instituted: to revive the ecclesiastical spirit and zeal for souls among the clergy. Church history records the substantial assistance which that saint received from them in his great work of reforming the Diocese of Milan; his biographies make mention of his affection for them and of the satisfaction which he took in sojourning at their house of St. Barnabas. St. Francis of Sales, who loved to call himself a Barnabite, invited the Congregation into his diocese, to establish colleges at Annecy and at Thonon; while the Barnabite Guérin was his coadjutor and later, having succeeded him in the See of Geneva, was conspicuous for the zeal with which he promoted his canonization. The Barnabites, who take a holy pride in the title of *episcoporum adjutores*, have constantly cultivated the meek and gentle spirit of St. Francis of Sales in their relations with ecclesiastical authorities, the diocesan clergy, and members of other religious orders. Though never very extensive, the spreading of the order in Europe began very soon after its founda-

tion. Their chief theatres of action were in Italy, France, Savoy, Austria, and Bohemia. In 1582, Pope Gregory XIII, at the solicitation of the Sovereign Order of St. John of Jerusalem, sent Barnabite Fathers to Malta, and in 1610 Henry IV of France obtained their services in defence of Catholicism in Béarn, whence they spread to Paris and other parts of France. The Emperor Ferdinand II invited them into Austria, in 1627, to oppose the spread of Protestantism, and gave them the court parish of St. Michael, where a house was built for their accommodation. The order also possesses at Vienna the parish church of Maria-Hilf, a famous sanctuary erected in thanksgiving for Sobieski's deliverance of the city from the Turks in 1683. Belgium has recently proved a providential refuge for the order, those expelled from France by the Government of that country having established themselves at Brussels and in other parts of the neighbouring kingdom.

Foreign Missions.—In 1718, when Clement XI sent Monsignor Mezzabarba to the Emperor of China to attempt a settlement of the famous question of the Chinese Rites, His Holiness attached five Barnabites to the special mission. No substantial result was obtained, but when the rest of the party left the country, one member of the order, Father Ferrari, remained in China, taking up his residence first at Peking and then at Canton, where he sowed the first seed of that work of the Holy Infancy with which the name of the French Bishop Forbin-Janson is justly associated. From that time until 1738 the companions of Father Ferrari preached the Gospel in Cochin China, where Father Alessandro degli Alessandri was for sixteen years vicar Apostolic. The Holy See meanwhile desiring a regular Barnabite mission in Ava and Pegu, the order willingly assumed that duty, and the mission was maintained until 1832, when the inability to supply labourers for this field, the consequence of Napoleon's suppression of the religious orders, necessitated its transfer to the Paris Society of Foreign Missions. An account of what the Barnabites accomplished in Ava and Pegu may be found in Cardinal Wiseman's translation (published by the Asiatic Society) of Sauzerman's "Religione del regno Birmano". The Regular Clerics of St. Paul also kept missionaries, for some time, in Scandinavia. Their missions are now established in Brazil.

Saints and other distinguished members of the Congregation.—Besides its canonized Saints Anton Maria Zaccaria and Alexander Sauli, and Blessed Xavier M. Bianchi (d. 1815) who was known as the Thaumaturgus of Naples, the Barnabite Order glories in a number of Venerables, among whom have been several religious distinguished for their austere purity and taken to their reward while yet young. Upon the extraordinary graces, such as miracles and visions, undeniably vouchsafed to members of the order, it is not expedient here to insist; Alfonso Paleotti, however, who in 1591 succeeded his cousin, Cardinal Gabriel Paleotti, in the Archbishopric of Bologna, relates in his autobiography that when he was praying for light and help in the government of his archdiocese, a holy man who was commonly called *il Vidente*, on account of his gift of visions, told him, as a message from the Blessed Virgin, that he ought to send for the Barnabites and make them *penitenzieri*, because they had a great devotion for her, were her faithful servants, and she would assist them in drawing souls to the practice of daily Communion.

Learning, the pursuit of which the Barnabites regard as a great preservative of religious observance has always been cultivated among them in all its branches. To cite only a few names, the order has been distinguished in theology by Rotarius, Pozzobonelli, and Maderni; in Biblical science by Corio and Vercellone; in ecclesiastical history by Tornielli, whose "Annales Sacri" are regarded as an introduction to those of Baronius; in liturgiology by Gavantus; in archæology by Caronni, whose work receives praise in Eckel's "Doctrina nummorum veterum"; Cortenova, who illustrated the antiquities of Friuli and Aquileia; Delle Torre, who restored the *Forum Julii* of Cividale; Ungarelli the Egyptologist, friend of Champollion and Rosellini, and interpreter of the Roman obelisk; and Benzi, who elucidated the inscription of Vercelli. Among the names of Barnabites who have been eminent in philosophy are those of Baranzano, the friend of Galileo and of Francis Bacon, who communicated to him first the theory of the "Novum Organum", of Cardinal Gerdil, and of Pini, the author of "Protologia"; among those eminent in physical and mathematical science, Frisi, Cavallezi, Denza, founder of the Italian Meteorological Society and first director of the Vatican Observatory, and Bertelli, the seismologist. To the Barnabite architect Binaghi is due the restoration of the Escorial towards the close of the sixteenth century, whilst the Barnabite Mazenta was the architect both of the Cathedral of Bologna and of the fortifications of Leghorn. To these names might be added those of many Barnabites who have become famous in literature, and the order has given to the Catholic Church more than fifty bishops and these six members of the Sacred College: Caddini, Fontana, Gerdil, Lambruschini, Bilio, and Graziello.

In 1856 Count Schouvaloff, a distinguished Russian convert, joined the Barnabite Congregation, and died in 1859. It was his ardent desire that his brethren might do something for the reunion of Christendom. With this object the order has founded an Association of Masses, and by the Brief "Apositum super Nobis", dated 30 April, 1872, Pius IX granted a plenary indulgence to all who should assist at the Mass for the reunion of Christendom to be celebrated once a month in the Chapel of the Barnabites at Paris. His Holiness, moreover, granted to the general of the order faculties for extending the like privilege to any other church in which a monthly Mass for the same intention should be said upon the day appointed by the ordinary. This privilege is freely extended by the general to all bishops who may desire it.

Sicco and Mosio, *De Cleric. Reg. S. Pauli Cong. et Parentibus Syonpsis* (Milan, 1682); Barelli, *Memorie dell' origine . . . della Congregazione dei Chierici Reg. . . . Barnabiti* (Bologna, 1703–07); *Constitutiones Cleric. Reg. S. Pauli Decollati* (Milan, 1579; Milan, 1617; Naples, 1829); Grazioli, *Præstantium virorum qui in Congregatione S. Pauli vulgo Barnabitarum memoriâ nostrâ floruerunt* (Bologna, 1751); Ungarelli, *Bibliotheca Script. e Cong. Cleric. Reg. S. Pauli* (Rome, 1836); Gabuzio, *Hist. Cong. Cleric. Reg. S. Pauli* (Rome, 1852); Colombo, *Profili biografici di insigni Barnabiti* (Lodi, 1871).

Ces. Tondini di Quarenghi.

Baroccio (Barocci), Federigo, called Fiore d'Urbino, a distinguished painter and engraver, b. at Urbino, 1528; d. at the same place, 30 September, 1612. His father, who was Ambrogio Baroccio, a sculptor, of a Milanese family, gave him his first art lessons. He then studied drawing with Francesco Manzocchi of Forli. His uncle, the architect Bartolommeo Genga, deciding that Federigo must become an artist, placed him with the eminent Venetian painter, Battista Franco, then in the service of Duke Guidobaldo II at Urbino. On Franco's departure Baroccio went to his uncle's house at Pesaro, and while studying perspective with him, copied some pictures of Titian in the ducal gallery. When twenty he went to Rome and spent his time chiefly in the study of the works of his great townsman, Raphael. On his return to Urbino, Baroccio copied the pastels of Correggio, and painted some pictures which brought him much reputation. His subjects were chiefly religious, and included some large altarpieces. Of these he etched two masterpieces, "The Pardon of San Francesco d'Assisi", which is

at Urbino, and "The Annunciation", which is at Loretto.

Returning to Rome, where Guido della Rovere was one of his patrons, the artist, together with Federigo Zuccaro, received from Pope Pius IV the commission to decorate the little palace of the Bosco di Belvedere in the Vatican. At this time it is said that he was poisoned at a banquet given him by some painters jealous of his success. From this he never recovered, for four years was unable to work at all, and for the rest of his life but a few hours a day. After three years at Perugia, and a short visit to Florence, Baroccio returned to end his long life of eighty-four years at Urbino, dying of apoplexy. In the Louvre are his "Circumcision", "The Virgin and Child Jesus adored by St. Anthony and St. Lucy", and "St. Catherine"; in the London National Gallery a "Holy Family"; at Urbino a "Last Supper" and "St. Sebastian"; at the cathedral in Perugia a "Descent from the Cross"; at Ravenna "The Martyrdom of St. Vitalis"; at Naples a "Holy Family"; and at Rome a "Last Supper" and "Christ and Magdalen".

Bryan, *Dictionary of Painters and Engravers* (London and New York, 1903–05).

Augustus van Cleef.

Barocco style (Fr. *baroque*), a debased application to architecture of Renaissance features. The term is also employed to denote a bad taste in design and ornament generally. Carlo Maderna (1556–1639), Bernini (1589–1680), and Borromini (1599–1667), were among the more famous who practised this form of art. Among the most prominent examples are the churches of Santa Maria della Vittoria by Maderna, and Santa Agnese, by Borromini, both at Rome. Naples particularly is full of baroque churches, a few of which, like the Gesû Nuovo, are dignified and creditable designs. The domical church of Santa Maria della Salute, at Venice, by Longhena, is a majestic edifice in excellent style, and here and there other churches offer exceptions to the then prevalent baseness of architecture. The three Venetian churches, San Barnaba (1749), San Basso (1670), and San Moise, are examples of three different types of the baroque. This style prevailed in church architecture for nearly two centuries. See Renaissance. Thomas H. Poole.

Baron, Bonaventura, a distinguished Irish Franciscan theologian, philosopher, and writer of Latin prose and verse, b. at Clonmel, County Tipperary, Ireland, 1610; d. at Rome, 18 March, 1696. His mother was a sister of the well-known Franciscan, Luke Wadding, and his brother Geoffrey was a trusted ambassador of the Irish Confederates in their negotiations with the continental rulers. He himself joined the Franciscan community of Clonmel, pursued his studies in philosophy at Louvain, and afterwards proceeded to Rome, where he took up his residence in the Irish College of St. Isidore founded by his uncle, Father Wadding. Here, on the completion of his theological course, he was appointed professor, and devoted himself specially to a defence of the Scotist system then generally assailed. During his stay in Rome he published numerous works on theology, philosophy, and history, a full list of which is appended below. About the year 1651 he left Rome, owing, it is said, to some difficulty with the master of the sacred palace, and went first to a house of his order at Schwaz in the Tyrol, and then to Salzburg, where he was kindly received by Archbishop Guidobald. He was sent as provincial commissary into Hungary (about 1656), was again in Schwaz (1661), went to Paris, taught for some time at Würzburg, where he published a volume of his "Opuscula" (1668), taught theology at Lyons, and finally returned to Italy. It is said that representations were made to secure his appointment to the

Archbishopric of Cashel, but that he declined the office. He was appointed historiographer (1676) by Cosmo de' Medici, Grand-duke of Tuscany, and was elected a member of the Academy of Florence. While under the patronage of the grand-duke he published the "Trias Tuscia", in honour of three remarkable religious of the country, and, in the same year. the "Orbes Medicei". His last work was a history of the Order for Redemption of Captives, from 1198 till 1297. He died 18 March, 1696, and was buried at St. Isidore's in Rome, where his tomb with the inscription, written by John De Burgo, a rector of the college, still exists. Two contemporary oil paintings of him have come down to us, one preserved in St. Isidore's, the other in the Franciscan house, Dublin. His principal works are: "Panegyrici Sacroprophani" (Rome, 1643; Lyons, 1656); "Obsidio et expugnatio Arcis Duncannon sub Thomâ Preston"; "Prælusiones Philosophicæ" (Rome, 1651; Lyons, 1661); "Boetius Absolutus" (Rome, 1653); "Scotus defensus et amplificatus" (3 vols., Cologne, 1664); "Cursus Theologicus" (6 vols., 1670); "Opuscula" (4 vols., 1666–71); "Annales Ordinis Sanctæ Trinitatis pro redemptione captivorum ab anno 1198 usque ad annum 1297" (Rome, 1864).

Annales Minorum (Fonseca, 1731); WARE, *Irish Writers*, ed. HARRIS, 253; GILBERT ed., *History of Irish Confederation and War in Ireland, 1641–43* (Dublin, 1882); *Franciscan MSS.* (Dublin); MEEHAN, *Rise and Fall of the Irish Franciscan Monasteries* (Dublin, 1872), 89–93, 217.

JAMES MACCAFFREY.

Baron, VINCENT, a Dominican theologian and preacher b. at Martres, in the department of the Haute-Garonne, France, 17 May, 1604; d. in Paris, 21 January 1674. At the age of seventeen he passed from the college of the Jesuits in Toulouse to the Dominican convent of St. Thomas in the same city. There he made his religious profession, 16 May, 1622, completed his course in philosophy and theology, and taught these branches. As early as 1634 he was first professor in his convent and conventual doctor in the University of Toulouse. Rare erudition, depth of thought, and clearness of exposition earned for him the reputation of being one of the leading theologians of France. While discharging his professorial duties he delivered courses of Lenten sermons in the principal churches of Toulouse, Avignon, Bordeaux, and other cities of Southern France. Upon the invitation of the bishops of Languedoc he preached throughout their dioceses for ten years, reviving the faith of Catholics, elevating their morals, and combating the errors of the Calvinists, with whose ministers he frequently joined in open debate, sometimes in their public synods. He published an abridgment of these controversies under the title "L'hérésie convaincue" (Paris, 1668). Of his sermons to Catholic congregations we have only those preached at Paris in 1658 and 1659 (Paris, 1660), doctrinal discourses and panegyrics possessing much intellectual merit, composed in the forced style and manner of his age. In the pulpit Father Baron was always a teacher; but while intent upon forming the minds of his hearers he won their hearts by his disinterestedness, sincerity, and charity. From 1630 to 1659 he filled the office of prior in the convents of Toulouse (twice), Rhodez, Castres, Albi. Avignon, and in the general novitiate in Paris, always promoting the reforms in study and religious observance inaugurated by Sebastian Michaelis in the first years of the century. In 1660, having declined the office of provincial in the Province of Toulouse, he was sent by the master-general of his order to make a canonical visitation of the Portuguese convents. On his return to Paris he devoted himself during the remaining fourteen years of his life to the composition of theological works.

His most important productions were written to satisfy the desire expressed by Pope Alexander VII to the Dominicans assembled in a general chapter at Rome in 1656, that they should publish a course in moral theology conformable to the doctrine of St. Thomas, and thus correct the laxity of morals encouraged by certain casuists. These works were: (1) "Theologiæ Moralis adv. laxiores probabilistas pars prior" (Paris, 1665); (2) "Manuductionis ad Moralem Theologiam pars altera" (Paris, 1665); (3) "Theologiæ moralis Summa bipartita" (Paris, 1667). In these works, while condemning opinions that seemed too lax, and censuring others that appeared to be too rigorous, he ably defended the system of Probabiliorism. With the famous critic Jean de Launoy he was long in controversy as to the "Summa Theologica" of St. Thomas Aquinas the authenticity of which he ably defended, although he did not demonstrate it, as later writers have done. The manuscript of a work entitled "Apologia pro sacrâ congregatione Indicis" having been published with alterations made by a stranger, which brought upon it the condemnation of the Sacred Congregation, he promised a new edition, which was embodied in his "SS. Augustini et Thomæ vera et una mens de libertate humanâ" (Paris, 1666). Another valuable work is his "Libri V apologetici pro religione, utrâque theologiâ, moribus ac juribus Ord. Præd." (Paris, 1666). At the time of his death he was engaged on a complete course in theology to be entitled "D. Thomas sui Interpres". From this work, but half completed and never published, the one bearing the same title by Antoninus Massoulié, O.P., is entirely distinct.

QUÉTIF ET ECHARD, *Script. Ord. Præd.*, II, 655; TOURON, *Hist. des hommes illust. de l'ordre de St. Dominique*, V, 489–498.

ARTHUR L. MCMAHON.

Baronius, CESARE, VENERABLE, Cardinal and ecclesiastical historian, b. at Sora in the Kingdom of Naples, 30 August, 1538; d. at Rome, 30 June, 1607; author of "Annales Ecclesiastici", a work which marked an epoch in historiography and merited for its author, after Eusebius, the title of a Father of Ecclesiastical History.

Baronius was descended from the Neapolitan branch of a once powerful family, whose name, *de Barono*, was changed by Cesare himself to the Roman form, *Baronius*. His parents, humble citizens of Sora in the Sabines, some sixty miles east of Rome, could bestow no ancestral wealth and power upon their only son. He was, however, to possess qualities which better proclaim nobility—a deeply religious spirit, a charity to which selfishness was painfully repugnant, a firmness of will tempered in humble obedience, and a keenness and vigour of mind scrupulously dedicated to the cause of truth. These qualities distinguished Baronius as a peer in sanctity and scholarship among many saintly and learned contemporaries. He inherited his more vigorous traits of character from his father, Camillo, a worldly and ambitious man, whose strong will and tenacity of purpose were one day to clash with like qualities

CARDINAL CESARE BARONIUS

in his equally determined son. To the influence of his pious and charitable mother, Portia Phaebonia, whose devotion to Cesare's religious interests was intensified by what she considered his miraculous deliverance from death in infancy, he owed his conspicuous tender qualities and childlike simplicity of faith. To this latter was due his vivid realization of God's guidance, vouchsafed often in visions and dreams. Baronius received his early education from his intelligent parents and in the schools of nearby Veroli. His intense love of study and intellectual maturity encouraged his father to send him, at the age of eighteen, to the school of law at Naples. There, after a few months, the confusion due to the Franco-Spanish war for Italian dominion compelled him to remove to Rome, where, in 1557, he became a pupil of Cesare Costa, a master in civil and canon law.

He was there but a short time when he met one who was potently to influence his destiny and determine, even to details, his career and occupations. It was Philip Neri, a priest remarkable for his sanctity and for the spirit of piety and charity with which he inspired a little group of priests and laymen whom he had formed into a confraternity of good works at the church of San Girolamo della Carità. The importance of this meeting cannot be overestimated; a Baronius the world might have had, but the Baronius of history is the creature of St. Philip Neri. He was impressed by the serious law student of such transparent innocence of life and finding in him a responsive subject, enrolled him in his little band. This did not prevent Baronius from continuing the studies for which he came to Rome, but in all else his surrender of self to Philip's guidance was spontaneous and complete. It was not without its sacrifices. In token of renunciation he burned a volume of his own Italian verses in the composition of which he had shown marked proficiency; the same fate later befell his doctorate diploma. For three years, in his zeal, he yearned to become a Capuchin friar, but Philip restrained him. More distressing still was the bitter antagonism of his father, who saw in all this but folly and the frustration of his paternal ambition. He feared, too, the extinction of his family, whose hope for a brilliant revival was centred alone in Cesare. Father and son were firm. Camillo cut off his scanty allowance and Cesare was compelled to live on the hospitality of one of Philip's friends. For six years Baronius led a semi-religious life with the community of San Girolamo, the nucleus of the Congregation of the Oratory. From Philip he received direction in study and spiritual guidance, and at his bidding gave all his spare time to charitable work among the sick and poor. During the year 1558 Philip assigned to him the important work of preaching at the conferences given often during the week in the church of San Girolamo. In 1564 he received priestly ordination and resolved to cast his lot with Philip's little band, but so intense was his ardour for the religious life that he had already taken vows of poverty, chastity, humility, and obedience to Philip as to a superior. Of his will he was to be the yielding instrument for yet twenty-five years. That time was to be given to the preparation for his work on ecclesiastical history, about which Baronius' life-interest henceforth centres.

The credit of its conception belongs to Philip, as Baronius testifies with filial devotion in the "Annals". The saint shared keenly in the distress and dismay caused in Catholic circles by the publication of the "Centuries of Magdeburg" (Ecclesiastica Historia: integram ecclesiæ Christi ideam complectens, congesta per aliquot studiosos et pios viros in urbe Magdeburgicâ, 13 vols., Basle, 1559–74). The purpose of this work was to commit history to the cause of Protestantism by showing how far the Catholic Church had departed from primitive teaching and practices, in contrast to the consonance therewith of the Reformed Church. It was conceived in 1552 by Mathias Flach Francowiez (Flacius Illyricus) and, with the collaboration of several Lutheran scholars and the co-operation of evangelical princes and other wealthy Protestants, was hurriedly completed. Its thirteen volumes dealt each with a century of the Christian Era, whence the name "Centuriators" applied to the authors. Though the work had the great merit of being the pioneer in the field of modernized church history, and displayed considerable critical spirit, its unscrupulously partisan colouring of Lutheran claims and its misrepresentations of Catholicity predestined it to but ephemeral honour. It is of interest only as a sunken landmark in the field of historical literature, and as the stimulus of Baronius's genius. The publication of its initial volumes, however, at a time when its polemical value made it acceptable to Protestants, provided the Reformers with a most formidable weapon of attack on the Catholic Church. It did much harm. The feasibility of a counter attack appealed to Catholic scholars, but nothing adequate was provided, for the science of history was still a thing of the future. Its founder was as yet but twenty-one years of age and knew very little of history. It was in that youth that St. Philip Neri discerned a possible David who would rout the Philistines of Magdeburg. He forthwith directed Baronius to devote his conferences at San Girolamo exclusively to the history of the Church. Baronius was disconcerted. History had no attraction for him. His youthful zeal would rather vent itself in the fiery moral conferences which he had creditably given during the preceding year. But he obeyed, and within three years summarily covered the field of church history in his conferences and developed a keen interest in historical studies. Twice he gave the course before his ordination to the priesthood, and five times again did he repeat it during the following twenty-three years, perfecting his work with each succeeding series. The early historians and the Fathers became his familiars. The libraries of Rome yielded to his diligent quest a host of unpublished documents. Monuments, coins, and inscriptions told to him unsuspected stories. What he did in and about Rome willing correspondents did for him elsewhere, and the name of Baronius came to be known over Europe as a synonym for unprecedented historical penetration, power of research, and zeal for verification. Philip's plan for arranging in lasting form the material thus garnered must have been made known to Baronius before 1569, but despite the importance of the work, he was compelled by his master to share in all the exercises of the now growing Oratory. At the church of San Giovanni dei Fiorentini, which he served from 1564 to 1575, he had his part in the parish ministrations and took his turn in the menial domestic services. "Baronius coquus perpetuus" was the legend he playfully inscribed in the Oratory kitchen, where he often received distinguished visitors. To the many mortifications imposed by Philip he added generously, and thereby provoked the digestive disorders that often racked his body in life and ultimately precipitated his death. Despite all obstacles, his prodigious capacity for work and contentment with but four to five hours sleep a night made possible an amazing progress in his researches. After the canonical foundation of the Oratory (15 July, 1575) he took up his residence at Santa Maria in Vallicella, definitive home of the new congregation, and led the same busy life. In the early eighties plans were matured for the publication of the new church history, and by 1584, a quarter of a century since he began his preparation, Baronius had the work well under way, when his patience suffered a new trial. Gregory XIII confided to him the revision of the Roman Martyrology. The work was necessary because of confusion in feast-days due to the Gregorian calendar-reform (1582); besides, it was an opportune time to correct the many errors of copyists long accumulating in the Martyrology. Baronius gave two years to the wide research and keen criticism the work demanded. His annotations and corrections were published in 1586, and in a second edition he corrected several errors which he was chagrined to have overlooked in the first (Martyrologium Romanum, cum Notationibus Cæsaris Baronii, Rome, 1589).

The difficulties which beset Baronius in the publication of the "Annals" were many and annoying. He prepared his manuscript unaided, writing and rewriting every page with his own hand. His brother Oratorians at Rome could lend him no assistance. Those at Naples, who helped him in revising his copy, were scarcely competent and almost exasperated him by their dilatoriness and uncritical judgment. The proofs he read himself. His printers, in the infancy of their art, were neither prompt nor painstaking. In the spring of 1588 the first volume appeared and was universally acclaimed for its surprising wealth of information, its splendid erudition, and its timely vindication of papal claims. The "Centuries" were eclipsed. Those highest in ecclesiastical and civil authority complimented the author; but more gratifying still was the truly phenomenal sale the book secured and the immediate demand for its translation into the principal European languages. It was Baronius' intention to produce a volume every year; but the second was not ready until early in 1590. The next four appeared yearly, the seventh late in 1596, the other five at still longer intervals, up to 1607, when, just before his death, he completed the twelfth volume, which he had foreseen in a vision would be the term of his work. It brought the history down to 1198, the year of the accession of Innocent III.

Baronius' student life during the twenty years of publication was even more disturbed than formerly. His growing repute brought heavy penalties to one of his humility. Three successive popes would have made him a bishop. In 1593 he became superior of the Oratory, succeeding the aged Philip, on whose death, in 1596, he was re-elected for another triennial term. In 1595 Clement VIII, whose confessor he was, made him protonotary Apostolic and, on 5 June, 1596, created him cardinal. Baronius bitterly regretted his removal from the Oratory to reside at the Vatican, or even away from Rome when the papal court was absent from the city, a circumstance doubly distressing as it prevented active work on the "Annals". In 1597 Clement paid the highest possible tribute to his erudition by naming him Librarian of the Vatican. This office, together with the charge of the newly founded Vatican press and his duties in the Congregations, left him still less time for his "Annals". Troubles he had of another order. His zeal for the liberties of the Church had early invited the disfavour of Philip II of Spain, who, because he was the strongest Catholic sovereign in Europe, was striving to exercise undue influence on the papacy. He incurred Philip's further displeasure by supporting the cause of his enemy, the excommunicate Henry IV of France, whose absolution Baronius warmly advocated. The "Annals" were condemned by the Spanish Inquisition. Later on, when he published his treatise on the Sicilian Monarchy, proving the prior claim of the papacy to that of Spain in the suzerainty of Sicily and Naples, he provoked the bitter hostility of both Philip II and Philip III. He found solace, however, in the thought that the enmity of Spain would prevent the growing possibility of his being made pope. This hope was

severely tried in the two conclaves of 1605. Baronius was the choice of a majority of the cardinals and, despite Spanish opposition, might have been elected had he not turned his diplomacy to encompass his own defeat. Thirty-seven votes out of a necessary forty in the first conclave and a violent attempt to precipitate his "adoration" in the second attest the esteem in which he was held.

In the spring of 1607 Baronius returned to the Oratory, for a vision had warned him that his sixtyninth year would be his last, and he had reached the portended last volume of the "Annals". Soon, critically ill, he was removed to Frascati, but, discerning the end, he returned to Rome, where he died 30 June, 1607. His tomb is at the left of the high altar in the church of Santa Maria in Vallicella (Chiesa Nuova).

Cardinal Baronius left a reputation for profound sanctity which led Benedict XIV to proclaim him "Venerable" (12 January, 1745). The restorations which he made in his titular church of Sts. Nereus and Achilleus and in St. Gregory's on the Cœlian still feebly bespeak his zeal for decorous worship. But the "Annals" constitute the most conspicuous and enduring monument of his genius and devotion to the Church. For three centuries they have been the inspiration of students of history and an inexhaustible storehouse for research. No one work has treated so completely the epoch with which they deal. Nowhere are there to be found collected so many important documents. Unbiassed scholars recognize in them the foundation-stone of true historical science, and in their author the qualities of the model historian: indefatigable diligence in research, passion for verification, accuracy of judgment, and unswerving loyalty to truth. Even in the bitter controversies which the early volumes aroused, Baronius' most scholarly critics acknowledged his thoroughness and honesty. But this does not imply that his work was faultless or final. Master though he was, Baronius was a pioneer. Gifted with a critical spirit which was, to say the least, much keener than that of his contemporaries, his exercise of it was tentative and timid. Yet he stimulated a spirit of criticism which would infallibly advance the science of history far beyond the reaches attainable by himself. With this wider vision his successors have been enabled to subject the "Annals" to no little corrective criticism. His scanty knowledge of Greek and Hebrew limited his resources in dealing with Oriental questions. Despite his care, he cited many documents as authentic which a more enlightened criticism has rejected as apocryphal. His most serious defects were incident to the very accuracy he essayed in casting his history in the strictly annalistic form. The attempt to assign to each successive year its own events involved him in numerous chronological errors. Baronius himself recognized the possibility of this and made many corrections in his second edition (Mainz, 1601–05); and later it was by his allies, and not by enemies, that the most thorough efforts at chronological revision were made, a point seemingly lost on those who refer to Pagi's "refutation" of Baronius' errors. One has but to recall the diversity of opinion in matters of chronology among the chief exponents of historical science to-day to find palliation for the mistakes of that science's founder. Whatever must be said in justice to Baronius, it remains true that the present-day value of his work is to be measured in the light of these defects, and it is to the critical editions of the "Annals" that the student will profitably refer, bearing always in mind that the mistakes of Baronius affect but little the value of the precious legacy his industry and genius handed down to later historians. The most extensive work of emendation is that of the Pagi: "Critica historico-chronologica in Annales", etc.

(3d ed., Antwerp, 1727, 4 vols.). Its preface contains a good study of the early criticism of the "Annals". To the original twelve volumes of the "Annals" there have been added continuations in the style of Baronius. The most worthy are those of the three Oratorians: Raynaldus, ablest of the continuators, who with material accumulated by Baronius carried the history to the year 1565 (Rome, 1646–77, 9 vols.); Laderchi, who continued it thence to 1571 (Rome, 1728–37, 3 vols.); and August Theiner, to 1583 (Rome, 1856). Less notable are the continuations of the Polish Dominican, Bzovius, 1198 to 1571 (Cologne, 1621–30, 9 vols.), and the French bishop, Spondé, 1198 to 1647 (Paris, 1659). There is a good study of the work of the continuators by Mansi in the Bar-le-Duc edition of Baronius, XX, pp. iii–xi. Many epitomes of the work have been made, the best being that of Spondé (Cologne, 1690, 2 vols.). As an exemplar of recent scientific working of a small portion of the field covered by Baronius may be cited, Rauschen, "Jahrbücher der Christlichen Kirche unter dem Kaiser Theodosius dem Grossen. Versuch einer Erneuerung der Annales Ecclesiastici des Baronius für die Jahre 378–395" (Freiburg im Br., 1897). The best editions of Baronius are those of Lucca (1738–59, 38 vols.) and Bar-le-Duc (1864–83, 37 vols.); the former contains the continuations of Raynald and Laderchi, the critique of Pagi and others, and is enriched by the notes of Archbishop Mansi; the latter contains what is best in the former and the editorial additions of Father Theiner, whose continuation was to be included. Publication was suspended with the history of the year 1571. Baronius published many lesser works, most of which found place in the "Annals". His life of St. Gregory Nazianzen is in Acta SS., XV, 371–427.

Materials for the life of Baronius are found in an unfinished *Life* in Buccio's MS. preserved in the Roman Oratory; the extant correspondence etc. has been gathered by Alberi-cius, *Ven. Cæsaris Baronii . . . Epistolæ, Opuscula . . . Vita* (Rome, 1759–70, 3 vols.); recent discoveries by Laemmer, *De Cæsaris Baronii Litterarum Commercio Diatriba* (Freiburg im Br., 1903). The older *Lives*, based largely on Buccio, and the references Baronius makes to his work in the *Annals* are by Spondé in his *Epitome ;* Barnabeo (Vienna, 1718); and Ricci (Rome, 1745); Sarra, *Vita del Venerabile Card. Ces. Baronio* (Rome, 1862); Le Febvre, *Vie de Card. Baronius* (Douai, 1868); Kerr, *Life of Cesare Card. Baronius* (London, 1898); Capecelatro-Pope, *Life of St. Philip Neri* (London, 1882), I, 316–321; II, 1–31, 529–530.
Adverse criticism of Baronius: Casaubon, *Exercitationes* (Geneva, 1654), cf. Pattison, *Isaac Casaubon* (Oxford, 1892), 315–341—shallow and extreme; Cave, *Historia Literaria Scriptor. Eccl.* (London, 1868), XXV–XXVI; Dowling, *Introduction to Critical Study of Eccl. History* (London, 1838), 105–128.

JOHN B. PETERSON.

Baronius, Justus. See Calvin, Justus.

Barquisimeto (de Barquisimeto), Diocese of, in Venezuela, South America. The city is the capital of the State of Lara, is about 161 miles southwest of Caracas, and contains about 30,000 inhabitants, though some authorities give a lower figure. Founded in 1552 by the Spaniards, under the name of Nueva Segovia, Barquisimeto is one of the oldest Spanish possessions in South America. In 1812 it was almost entirely destroyed by an earthquake. The Diocese of Barquisimeto was erected in 1847, comprising the three States of Lara, Carabobo, and Falcon. By a decree of the Congregation of the Consistory, 12 February, 1907, the episcopal residence was transferred to Valencia (38,654), in the State of Carabobo, and the boundaries of the diocese rearranged. It is now bounded on the north and west by the Caribbean Sea, on the south by the Diocese of Merida (or the State of Trujillo), on the east by the State of Calabozo and the two dioceses of Zamora, and Guiana. The diocese contains 528,215 Catholics, 68 priests, and 110 churches and chapels.

Battandier, *Ann. pont. cath.* (Paris, 1906), 198; *Missiones Catholicæ* (Propaganda, Rome, 1907).

U. BENIGNI.

Barradas, Sebastião, a Portuguese exegete and preacher, b. at Lisbon in 1543; d. at Coimbra in 1615. In 1558 he entered the Society of Jesus. He was professor of Scripture for many years at Coimbra and Evora and preached with such zeal that he was styled the Apostle of Portugal. He published two works: (1) "Commentaria in concordiam et historiam evangelicam" (4 vols., Coimbra, 1599–1611). This work, which is a treasure house for preachers on the Gospels, was frequently reprinted in Germany, Italy, and France. The last edition was printed at Augsburg, 1642. (2) "Itinerarium filiorum Israel ex Ægypto in terram repromissiones" (Lyons, 1620). It is a useful commentary on the Book of Exodus.

Sommervogel, *Bibl. de la c. de J.,* I, 911; Idem in Vig., *Dict. de la Bible.*

JOHN CORBETT.

Barral, Louis Mathias, Count de, Archbishop of Tours, France, b. 26 April, 1746, at Grenoble; d. 7 June, 1816, at Paris. He was educated for the priesthood at the seminary of St. Sulpice, in Paris, and after ordination was made secretary, then coadjutor, and in 1790, successor, to his uncle, the Bishop of Troyes. In 1791, he refused to take the oath to the civil constitution of the clergy, and withdrew from France to Constance in Switzerland and later to England. In 1801 he returned home, and was appointed, under the new concordat between France and the Holy See, to govern the Diocese of Meaux, and in 1805 was promoted to the Archbishopric of Tours. During the long and harassing negotiations which Napoleon carried on with Pope Pius VII, while the latter was virtually a prisoner at Savona and Fontainebleau, Archbishop de Barral acted frequently as the emperor's intermediary. He was afterwards appointed almoner to the Empress Josephine, and he pronounced her funeral oration. Later still he was named a senator and a count of the Empire. On the downfall of Napoleon, the archbishop took his seat in the Chamber of Peers under Louis XVIII, and in the government of the "Hundred Days", which followed on the return of Napoleon from Elba, he still retained his political position. On the second restoration of the Bourbons, however, he was obliged to resign, and from this time till his death, which occurred in the following year, he confined himself entirely to the administration of his archdiocese. He has left among other works:—"Fragments relatifs à l'histoire ecclésiastique des premières années du XIXe siècle" (Paris, 1814); and a posthumous work, published by his brother: "Défense des libertés de l'église gallicane et de l'assemblée du clergé de France tenue en 1682, ou refutation de plusieurs ouvrages publiés récemment en Angleterre sur l'infaillibilité du Pape" (Paris, 1817).

Rohrbacher, *Histoire universelle de l'église catholique* (Paris, 1883); Debidour, *Histoire des rapports de l'église et de l'état en France de 1789 à 1870* (Paris, 1898); Baudrillart, *Quatre cents ans de concordat* (Paris, 1905); Sevestre, *L'histoire du concordat de 1801* (Paris, 1905); Sicard, *L'Ancien clergé de France, les évêques pendant la révolution* (Paris, 1903).

EDWARD A. GILLIGAN.

Barrande, Joachim, French palæontologist, b. at Sangues (Haute-Loire), 11 August, 1799; d. at Frohsdorff, near Vienna, 5 October, 1883. He was educated at the Ecole Polytechnique in Paris and was selected by Charles X to be the tutor of his grandson, the Duc de Bordeaux, also known as the Count de Chambord. When the king abdicated in 1830 he accompanied the royal family to England and Scotland and finally to Prague. He continued throughout his life on terms of intimate friendship with the duke, who, after the death of the king, took up his residence at Frohsdorff, and he acted also as the administrator of his property. Barrande's interest was early awakened in the fossil remains of his adopted country and their distribution in the various strata. The field was a new one for until the date of his first publication scarcely any attention had been paid to stratigraphical geology and palæontology in Bohemia. During the summers of 1840–50 he made preliminary surveys on foot of the Silurian district, an area of about 140 sq. miles. This was the beginning of his extensive investigations on the Silurian system of Bohemia. Quarries were opened and workmen engaged to search for fossils, and for forty-three years he devoted his time and resources to the vast undertaking and especially to describing, naming, and figuring the numerous specimens which were discovered. The results of his labours are contained in his great work—"Système silurien du centre de la Bohême—which stands almost unrivalled in palæontological literature" (von Zittel). The first volume was published in 1852 and at the time of his death twenty-two large quarto volumes with 1160 plates had appeared. Barrande was also the author of "Colonie dans le bassin silurien de la Bohême" (1860); "Documents sur la faune primordiale et le système taconique en Amérique" (1861); "Représentation de colonies de la Bohême dans le bassin silurien du nord-ouest de la France" (1863); "Cephalopodes—Etudes générales". His private life was simple and uneventful. He carried on a correspondence with the leading geologists of other countries, some of whom visited him at Prague. At his death he provided means for the completion of his "Système silurien" and bequeathed his library and valuable collection of fossils to the Natural History Museum at Prague.

Geological Magazine (Dec., 1883; new series, Decade II. Vol. X, No. xii); von Zittel, *History of Geology and Palæontology* (London, 1901).

H. M. Brock.

Barrasa (or Barraza), Jacinto, b. at Lima, Peru, early in the seventeenth century; d. there, 22 Nov., 1704. When, in the seventeenth century, the different religious orders appointed historiographers or official chroniclers of the work done in their several American provinces, the Jesuits selected Father Ignacio Arbieto for their Peruvian missions, but as his account was not accepted Father Jacinto Barrasa was appointed in his stead. His fame was principally as a preacher, and two volumes of his "Sermones" were published, one at Madrid in 1678, the other at Lima in 1679. In the latter year he finished his voluminous history of the Society of Jesus in Peru, which is still at Lima in private hands, and comprises 1,350 pages of manuscript. Its title is: "Historia de las fundaciones de los colegios y casas de la Compañía de Jesús, con la noticia de las vidas y virtudes religiosas de algunos varones ilustres que en ella trabajaron." No allusions are made in that chronicle to any other events than those of a religious or ecclesiastical nature. In addition to the "Sermones", a "Panegírico", pronounced by him in 1669 on the beatification of St. Rose of Lima, was also printed.

Torres Saldamando, *Los antiguos Jesuitas del Perú* (Lima, 1882); Cobo, *Historia de la fundación de Lima* (published at Lima, 1882, but written in the year 1639).

Ad. F. Bandelier.

Barre, Antoine-Lefebvre, Sieur de la, tenth French Governor-General of Canada, b. at Paris in 1622; d. in 1690. De la Barre was made a counsellor of the Parlement (High Court) in 1646, master of requests in 1653, and was Intendant of Paris during the civil war. After this he successively held other offices until he became Intendant of Bourbonnais in 1663. There he formed a company called "Compagnie de la France équinoxiale" to colonize Guiana, and was appointed lieutenant-general and governor of that part of America. He sailed from Rochelle in 1664 with the Marquis de Tracy, who had been appointed viceroy of the French possessions in America. After establishing himself at Cayenne,

which de Tracy had taken from the Dutch, de la Barre returned to France in the autumn of the same year, and while there published an account of his mission and his hopes for the future of Guiana, under the title of "La Description de la France équinoxiale". Soon after, he was appointed commander of Guiana and the French Antilles. In 1671 he was made captain of a man-of-war; in the same year he published the "Journal du voyage du sieur de la Barre en la terre ferme et île de Cayenne".

De la Barre was appointed Governor-General of Canada to replace Frontenac, and reached Quebec early in October, 1682. He received wise and detailed instructions for his guidance in the government of the colony and was especially directed to prevent the disorders caused by the traders and to keep them from fraudulent practices. De la Barre was already old and was animated more by the love of money than by the desire to advance the interests of the colony. He was induced by some of the traders to join in various enterprises. Instead of devoting himself to the organization of the internal affairs of the colony he allowed his advisers to dispatch a trading expedition to Hudson Bay and aided them in sending clandestine trading parties to Albany, to the region of the Mississippi, and the West. In 1684, under pretext of overawing the Iroquois, he took a body of ill-equipped troops as far as Fort Frontenac at the head of Lake Ontario. The troops were in reality intended to be an escort to a trading expedition in which he was interested. Sickness broke out among his soldiers, and he was obliged to make a disgraceful treaty with the Iroquois. De la Barre gave the Iroquois unrestricted rights in the region extending towards the country of the Illinois Indians, which de la Salle at that time was on the point of winning for France in spite of all the obstacles that the governor put in his way. Louis XIV heard of the disastrous expedition to Fort Frontenac and recalled de la Barre (10 March, 1685), who did not leave Quebec, however, until the arrival of his successor, the Marquis de Denonville, in October, 1685. In 1687 de la Barre was again appointed Governor of Cayenne and died three years later.

Hozier Manuscripts; Collection Moreau Saint-Méry, IV; *Archives coloniales de France*, Series B, IX, X; C, VI, VII; *New York Colonial Documents*, IX; Parkman, *Frontenac and New France under Louis XIV*, 72–115.

J. Edmond Roy.

Barreira, Balthasar, a Portuguese Jesuit missionary, b. at Lisbon, 1531; d. 1612, on the mission of Angola, south-west coast of Africa, the scene of his life's labours. His literary works consist chiefly of "Relations" written to the superiors of the Society of Jesus, describing the condition of the province with regard to both its political and spiritual aspects. He has recounted in detail the victory of the Spaniards, led by Paul de Morales, over an army of native negroes in the year 1583. Accounts of the conversion of pagan tribes and the baptisms of native kings as well as treatises on the manners and customs of the people are the principal subjects of his writings.

Sommervogel, *Bibl. de la c. de J.*, I, 918.

James M. Cotter.

Barrientos, Lopez de, a Spanish Dominican bishop, patriot, and diplomat, b. at Medina del Campo, Kingdom of Leon 1382; d. at Cuenca, 21 May, 1469. He was of noble parentage, and after receiving a liberal education in the University of Salamanca, entered the Dominican Order, in his native town, when about eighteen years of age. After his religious profession, he was again sent to Salamanca for a course of divinity. In this he showed extraordinary talent and love for study. He soon became known as one of the greatest theologians of Spain, and was appointed to the first chair of theology in that famous university. In 1433,

John II of Castile and Leon called him to his court, to be his confessor and tutor to the heir presumptive, afterwards Henry IV. Because of his ability and prudence, he was then made Grand Chancellor of State and Inquisitor General. He became successively Bishop of Segovia, 1439; of Avila, 1442; of Cuenca, 1444. Later he refused the Archbishopric of Compostella. John II, in his last will and testament, 1454, also named him tutor to Prince Alphonsus, a younger son. By his wise counsel and eminent statesmanship, he rendered his king and country conspicuous service. He also did much in the way of religious reformation and works of charity, and was a liberal patron of learning. His name frequently appears in the Spanish history of those troublous times. His writings comprise a treatise on the sacraments, a compendium of moral theology, a commentary on a part of the "Book of Decretals" (all in Latin), and several Spanish manuscripts on ecclesiastical matters and doctrinal subjects.

Touron, *Hist. des hommes ill. de l'ordre de Saint Dominique* (Paris, 1743–49), III; Echard, *Script. Ord. Præd.* (Paris, 1719–21), I; Mariana, *Historia de rebus Hispaniæ* (Toledo, 1592).

VICTOR F. O'DANIEL.

Barrière, JEAN DE LA. See FEUILLANTS.

Barros, JOÃO DE, historian, b. in Portugal, 1496; d. 20 October, 1570. Of his early youth little is known. In 1522, he went to Mina in Portuguese Africa, and was made treasurer of the Casa da India, Mina, and Ceuta (African possessions) in 1525, and again in 1532. Here he cultivated his literary inclinations and attached himself to the Crown of Portugal by other ties than those of a faithful subordinate and accountant. At the age of twenty-four, he published a chronicle of the Emperor Clarimundo, which at once gave him a reputation as an historian. In 1539, when Brazil had begun to be looked upon as an important accession to Portuguese colonial possessions, he obtained a grant of fifty leagues along the coast at the mouth of the Amazon and forthwith equipped an expedition to occupy it. Ten vessels with nine hundred men, under command of Aires da Cunha, set sail for Brazil, but were wrecked at the bar of the Maranhão, and nearly everybody perished. Two sons of Barros were in the expedition, but their fate is not given. This brought Barros almost to the verge of poverty. He thereafter clung to historic studies, protected and favoured by the king, at whose instigation he wrote his classical work, "Asia", considered of value as a fine piece of Portuguese literature and for the information it affords. Besides giving an account of discovery and conquest, it touches frequently upon the earliest attempts at Christianization by the Portuguese in their African and Asiatic possessions, the founding of churches, etc. The first decade appeared in 1552. Only three have been fully published. A fourth, of somewhat questionable authenticity, has been partly printed.

On the life of Barros, see DE FERIA, *Vida de João de Barros* (Lisbon, 1778); SILVA, *Diccionario bibliográfico portuguez* (Lisbon, 1859), III; *Biographie universelle* (Paris, 1854), I.

AD. F. BANDELIER.

Barrow, JOHN, priest, descended from a family of stanch Catholic yeomen, b. 13 May, 1735, at Westby-in-the-Fylde, Lancashire; d. 12 February, 1811, at Claughton, Lancashire. His uncle, Father Edward Barrow, S.J., had been serving the mission at Westby Hall in 1717 when he was outlawed as a popish priest and his goods forfeited. John Barrow, after a course of seven years at the English College in Rome, was impressed at Portsmouth and served five years in the navy. Deserting at Dunkirk, he was acquitted by the court-martial through pretending successfully to understand no language but Italian. In 1761, after escorting two young women from London to the Convent of the Poor Clares at Gravelines, where his sister was a nun, he resumed his studies at Douai, and was ordained there 27 June, 1766. After a short stay in London at the house in Red Lion Square occupied by the parents of Bishop Milner, he set out on horseback for Claughton in Lancashire. At this mission, which had been formerly attached to the Hall, the seat of the ancient family of Brockholes, he remained from the time of his arrival, in July, 1766, until his death. He was buried at the adjoining mission of New House.

Father Barrow was a man of notable courage, will, and industry. He was a master of French and Italian, wrote elegant Latin and forceful English. "He may sometimes have shown but scant courtesy to the wishes or commands of his own bishop, but he insisted that everybody else should be obedient and deferential to ecclesiastical authority" (Gillow). He enlarged the parish church of Claughton, in 1794, improved the roads as township overseer, made wise reinvestments of the fund for the secular clergy, and negotiated with Sir Edward Smythe for the acquirement by exchange of the land for Ushaw College. Though his name is on the list of Douai writers, no description of his writings is recorded. It is likely that he contributed to the Catholic Committee controversy. Gillow's quotations from unpublished letters would imply that Barrow was no gentle opponent. In a letter preserved at Claughton the Cardinal Secretary of State praises warmly Father Barrow's Catholic loyalty and his zeal for the cause of the Holy See.

Gillow, *Bibl. Dict. Eng. Cath.*, I, 145; Gradwell, *Historical Sketch of the Mission of Claughton* in the *Liverpool Catholic Almanac*, 1885.

J. V. CROWNE.

Barrow, WILLIAM, VENERABLE (*alias* WARING, *alias* HARCOURT), an English Jesuit martyr, b. in Lancashire, in 1609; d. 30 June, 1679. He made his studies at the Jesuit College, St. Omers, and entered the Society at Watten in 1632. He was sent to the English mission in 1644 and worked on the London District for thirty-five years, becoming, in the beginning of 1678, its superior. In May of that year he was arrested and committed to Newgate on the charge of complicity in the Oates Plot. The trial, in which he had as fellow-prisoners his colleagues, Fathers Thomas Whitbread, John Fenwick, John Gavan, and Anthony Turner, commenced 13 June, 1679, and is famous, or rather infamous, in history. Lord Chief Justice Scroggs presided, and Oates, Bedloe, and Dugdale were the principal witnesses for the Crown. The prisoners were charged with having conspired to kill the king and subvert the Protestant religion. They made a brave defence, and by the testimony of their own witnesses and their cross-examinations of their accusers proved clearly that the latter were guilty of wholesale perjury. But Scroggs laid down the two monstrous principles that (1) as the witnesses against them had recently received the royal pardon, none of their undeniable previous misdemeanours could be legally admitted as impairing the value of their testimony; and (2) that no Catholic witness was to be believed, as it was presumable that he had received a dispensation to lie. Moreover, he obstructed the defence in every way by his brutal and constant interruptions. Accordingly, Father Barrow and the others, though manifestly innocent, were found guilty, and condemned to undergo the punishment of high treason. They suffered together at Tyburn, 20 June, 1679. By the papal decree of 4 December, 1886, this martyr's cause was introduced under the name of "William Harcourt".

Cobbett, *State Trials*, VII; Tanner, *Brevis Relatio* (Prague, 1683); *Florus Anglo-Bavaricus* (Liège, 1685); Foley, *Records of the English Province, S.J.*, V; Gillow, *Bibl. Dict. Eng. Cath.*, s. v. *Barrow*; Idem, *Lancashire Recusants*.

SYDNEY F. SMITH.

Barruel, AUGUSTIN, controversialist and publicist, b. at Villeneuve de Berg (Ardèche), 2 October, 1741; d. at Paris, 5 October, 1820. He entered the Society of Jesus in 1756 and taught grammar at Toulouse in 1762. The storm against the Jesuits in France drove him from his country and he was occupied in college work in Moravia and Bohemia until the suppression of the order in 1773. He then returned to France and his first literary work appeared in 1774: "Ode sur le glorieux avènement de Louis Auguste au trône". That same year he became a collaborator of the "Année littéraire", edited by Fréron. His first important work was "Les Helviennes, ou Lettres Provinciales philosophiques" (Amsterdam, 1781). The seventh edition of the work (Paris, 1839) contains a sketch of the author. Of these letters, the seventy-sixth is considered the most brilliant. His book provoked a controversy with M. Giraud-Soulavie, and the replies and counter-replies were many.

In the meantime, national affairs in France were growing more and more turbulent, but Barruel continued his literary activity, which from now on occupied itself specially with public questions. In 1789 appeared "Lettres sur le Divorce", a refutation of a book by Hennet. From 1788 to 1792 he edited the famous "Journal Ecclésiastique" founded by Dinouart in 1760. In this periodical was published Barruel's "La Conduite du S. Siège envers la France", a vigorous defence of Pope Pius VI. He likewise wrote a number of pamphlets against the civil oath demanded from ecclesiastics and against the new civil constitution during 1790 and 1791. He afterwards gathered into one "Collection Ecclésiastique" all the works relative to the clergy and civil constitution. The ninth volume of this collection was published in 1793.

The storm of the French Revolution had in the meantime (1792) forced Barruel to seek refuge in England, where he became almoner to the refugee Prince de Conti. Here he wrote in 1793 his well-known "Histoire du Clergé pendant la Révolution Française". He dedicated the work to the English nation in recognition of the hospitality it had shown towards the unfortunate French ecclesiastics. It has been translated into German, Italian, Spanish, Polish, and English. The English version went through several editions and did much to strengthen the British nation in its opposition to French revolutionary principles. An American edition of the work appeared at Burlington in 1824. While in London, Barruel published an English work: "A Dissertation on Ecclesiastical Jurisdiction in the Catholic Church" (1794). But none of his works attracted so much attention as his "Mémoires pour servir à l'histoire du Jacobinisme" (London, 1797–98). It appeared in an English dress: "Memoirs of the History of Jacobinism and Freemasonry of Barruel, translated into English by the Hon. Robert Clifford" (London, 1798) in four volumes. This important work is an endeavour to account for the French Revolution by a study of the anti-Christian and anti-social principles of the secret societies and encyclopedic philosophers. Owing to its translation into every modern language it was everywhere read and commented upon. A sharp criticism in the "Monthly Review", brought forth a reply from Barruel, who greatly increased the circulation of his book by issuing an abridgment of it in 1798. The Freemasons of France, Germany, and England angrily contested his assertions and a voluminous literature was the consequence. While some are of the opinion that Barruel's work attributes to the secret societies many evil deeds for which they are not responsible, all admit that his exposition of their principles and the logical consequences flowing from them is the work of a powerful mind. Barruel, indeed, seems to have

been the first to portray clearly the necessary consequences to civil governments, to the Church, and to social order that must result from the atheistic oathbound associations which had acquired such tremendous power on the continent of Europe.

On the fall of the Directory in 1802, Barruel was enabled to return to France. He fully accepted and persuaded many other clergymen to accept the new political order of things in his native country and he wrote several books to defend his opinions. When the Concordat was made in 1803 between Pius VII and Napoleon, Barruel wrote: "Du Pape et de ses Droits Religieux". His last important controversy was a defence of the Holy See in its deposition of the French bishops, which had been necessitated by the new order of things in France, established by the Concordat. His book appeared also in English: "The Papal Power, or an historical essay on the temporal power of the Pope" (London, 1803). Many attacked the work, but as usual the author did not suffer an antagonist to go unanswered. His new book involved him in a very extended controversy, for his work was translated into all the principal European languages. His friends and foes alike became involved in a wordy war. Blanchard published in London no less than three refutations. Two works are erroneously attributed to Barruel: "L'Histoire civile, politique et religieuse de Pie VI" and "Découverte importante sur le système de la Constitution du Clergé, décrété par l'Assemblée nationale". The many articles Barruel contributed to journals and his many published letters are not touched on here. He had promised to compose two works which never appeared, viz: "Histoire des Sociétés Secrètes au Moyen-Age" and "Dissertation sur la Croisade contre les Albigeois". In regard to the latter work, Barruel stated that his object would be to defend the Church against the reproach of having deposed kings and having freed their subjects from the oath of allegiance. He contended that objections on this score arose only from an ignorance of history. During the whole course of a life of multiplied activity, Barruel was ever the wakeful apologist and unwearied defender of Christian truth and of the rights of the Church. At the time of his death, he was engaged on a refutation of the philosophical system of Kant, but never completed his work.

SOMMERVOGEL, *Bibl. de la c. de J.* (Brussels, 1890); DUSSAULT, *Notice sur la vie de Barruel* (Paris, 1825); HURTER, *Nomen. Lit.*, III (Innsbruck, 1895); DE BACKER, *Bibl. des écrivains, S. J.* (Liège, 1853); QUÉRARD, *La France littéraire* (Paris, 1827), I, 196, 97.

WILLIAM H. W. FANNING.

Barry. See GIRALDUS CAMBRENSIS.

Barry, JOHN, captain in the United States navy, b. at Tacumshane, County Wexford, Ireland, in 1745; d. at Philadelphia, 13 September, 1803. At an early age Barry was sent to sea. He arrived at Philadelphia when he was fifteen years old, and made that city his home to the time of his death. He was employed in the West Indian trade and commanded several vessels until December, 1774, when he sailed from Philadelphia, as captain of a fine large ship "The Black Prince", bound for Bristol, England, returning to Philadelphia 13 October, 1775, the day the Continental Congress, then in session there, authorized the purchase of two armed vessels for the beginning of the Continental Navy. Barry immediately volunteered his services, and he was assigned to the command of the first vessel purchased, the "Lexington". His commission was dated 7 December, 1775, the first issued by the Marine Committee of the Continental Congress. On 22 December, 1775, Esek Hopkins was appointed Commander-in-chief of the Navy—but was dropped from its roll in March, 1777. Barry was in command of the "Lexington" from his appointment until October, 1776, when he was assigned to the "Effingham", 28 guns, then building in Philadelphia. During that time he performed efficient service in lower Delaware Bay; on 31 March, 1776, he put to sea, eluding the British man-of-war "Roebuck" on guard in Delaware Bay, and on 7 April fell in with the "Edward", a tender of the British man-of-war "Liverpool", and after a sharp engagement captured her; Barry brought his prize to Philadelphia, arriving 11 April, 1776. This was the first war-vessel captured by a commissioned Continental naval officer that was brought to that city. He was officially connected with the "Effingham" until her destruction, 7 May, 1778, by the British forces then in control of Philadelphia. She had been sunk, by order of Washington and the Naval Board, in the Delaware for some time previously and then raised only to be destroyed by the enemy. In December, 1776, Barry, owing to the blockade of his ship in the Delaware by the English, with a company of volunteers joined the army under Washington and took part in the battles of Trenton and Princeton. He was aid to General Cadwallader and special aid to General Washington, who held him in high esteem. Returning to his command, he carried out many gallant and daring boat expeditions on the Delaware, successfully annoying and capturing vessels laden with supplies for the British army. In 1778 he was ordered to command the "Raleigh", 32 guns, and sailed from Boston 25th September, 1778. On the 27th he fell in with two British frigates, the "Experiment", 50 guns, and "Unicorn", 22 guns, and after a gallant and unequal engagement Barry ran his ship ashore and set her on fire, escaping with most of his crew. Being without a Continental command Barry accepted, 18 February, 1779, command of the privateer "Delaware", 12 guns, and during the cruise captured the British sloop of war "Harlem", 14 guns. In November, 1780, he was ordered to command the "Alliance", 36 guns, at Boston, in which he sailed to France, 11th February, 1781, with Col. John Laurens, special commissioner to the French Government. On the return trip he captured the brig "Mars", 22 guns, and the brig "Minerva", 10 guns. On 28th May, he fell in with the "Atalanta", 16 guns, and the "Trepassey", 14 guns, and after a very sharp fight of three hours they struck their colours. In this fight Barry was severely wounded in the shoulder by a grape shot. On 23 December, 1781, he sailed from Boston for France with the Marquis de Lafayette as passenger, and returning arrived at New London 13 May, 1782. He sailed, 4 August, 1782, on the most successful cruise of the war; the prizes he captured sold for more than £600,000. Returning by way of the West Indies and Havana, on 10 March, 1783, he fell in with the British frigate "Sybille", 38 guns, and after a sharp fight of forty-five minutes she hauled off apparently much injured and joined two other ships with which she had been in company. This was the

JOHN BARRY, U.S.N.

last encounter of the Revolutionary war at sea. Peace was declared 11 April, 1783, the "Alliance" was sold, and the country was without a navy. The United States navy was permanently organized by Act of Congress, 27 March, 1794. Six captains were appointed by President Washington, "by and with the consent of the Senate", and Barry headed the list. His commission, signed by George Washington, President, was dated 22 February 1797 and appointed him captain in the navy "to take rank from the 4th day of June, 1794"—"Registered No. I". He was thus made officially the ranking officer of the United States navy. He superintended the building of the frigate "United States", 44 guns, and made several cruises in her with other vessels under his command. In 1801 the navy was reduced to a peace basis; nine captains were retained Barry being at the head of the list. His sea service was ended, and being in poor health he remained at his home in Philadelphia until his death. Barry has often been referred to as "Commodore"; there was no such grade in the United States navy until 17 July, 1862. Captain was the highest grade before that date, although the non-official title of commodore was generally applied to a captain while in command of two or more vessels. Barry was married twice, both times to Protestants who subsequently became converts to the Catholic faith. His first wife died in 1771, and on 7 July 1777 he married Sarah Austin who survived him. She died 13 November, 1831. Both his wives were buried with him in the graveyard of St. Mary's Church, Philadelphia. There was no issue from either marriage. His epitaph was written by Dr. Benjamin Rush, a signer of the Declaration of Independence. A statue and fountain were erected to his memory in 1876, in Fairmount Park, Philadelphia, by the Catholic Total Abstinence Union of America. A portrait (copy of original by Gilbert Stuart) was presented to the city of Philadelphia by the Friendly Sons of St. Patrick, 18 March, 1895, to be placed in Independence Hall. In 1906 Congress passed a bill appropriating $50,000 for the erection of a monument in Washington to the memory of Captain John Barry; and 16 March, 1907, a bronze statue of him was erected in Independence Square, Philadelphia, by the Friendly Sons of St. Patrick.

DRAKE, *Dictionary of American Biography* (Boston, 1872); ALLEN, *American Biog. Dict.* (3d ed., Boston, 1857); ABBOT, *The Naval History of the U. S.* (New York, 1896); MACLAY, *History of the Navy* (New York, 1895); SPEARS, *The History of Our Navy* (New York, 1897); LOSSING, *History of the U. S. Navy* (Hartford, 1870); PAULLIN, *The Navy in the American Revolution* (Cleveland, Ohio, 1906); GRIFFIN, *History of Commodore John Barry* (Centennial ed., Philadelphia, 1903); PREBLE, *The Flag of the U. S.* (Boston, 1880); COOPER, *Naval History* (1856).

JOHN FUREY.

Barry, JOHN, second Bishop of Savannah, Georgia, U. S. A.; b. 1799 in the parish of Oylegate, Co. Wexford, Ireland; d. in Paris, 19 November, 1859. He was accepted as an ecclesiastical student by

Bishop England, and was ordained priest at Charleston, S. C., 24 September, 1825. After ministering for several years in Georgia, in which State he opened the first Catholic day school at Savannah, he was made Vicar-General of the Diocese of Charleston and superior of the seminary in 1844, while still retaining charge of the parish at Augusta, Georgia. In 1853 he was appointed Vicar-General of Savannah, under Bishop Gartland, and when, in 1854, that prelate died of yellow fever, he was named administrator of the diocese, and as such attended the Eighth Provincial Council of Baltimore, in May, 1855. He was then appointed to the vacant see and consecrated at Baltimore, 2 August, 1857. He governed the diocese with energy and was especially notable during his missionary labours for his charity and zeal in several yellow-fever epidemics. Ill health forcing him to make a visit (July, 1859) to Europe, he died at the house of the Brothers of St. John of God, in Paris, 19 November, 1859, having lost his reason some time before his death. His body was brought back to Savannah for burial, in September, 1865.

SHEA, *Hist. Cath. Ch. in U. S.* (New York, 1904); REUSS, *Biog. Cycl. of the Cath. Hierarchy* (Milwaukee, Wis., 1898); CLARKE, *Lives of the Deceased Bishops* (New York, 1872); *Catholic Almanac*, 1833 to 1860.

THOMAS F. MEEHAN.

Barry, PATRICK, horticulturist, b. near Belfast, Ireland, May, 1816; d. at Rochester, New York, U. S. A., 23 June, 1890. After teaching for a while in his native land, he emigrated to America in 1836 and was employed by a nurseryman at Flushing, Long Island. In 1849 he became a partner in the same business with George Ellwanger at Rochester, New York. The firm took the lead in importing from abroad or developing by culture improved varieties of flowering plants and fruits, hardy exotics, and introducing to cultivation wild species of shade trees. Their nurseries developed into the largest in the country. Barry wrote extensively on subjects connected with pomology and flower-gardening, and edited "The Genesee Farmer" from 1844 to 1852, and "The Horticulturalist" from 1852 to 1854. His published works include a "Treatise on the Fruit Garden" (New York, 1851; new ed. 1872) and a "Catalogue of the American Pomological Society".

Cycl. of Am. Biog. (New York, 1900).

THOMAS F. MEEHAN.

Barry, PAUL DE, b. at Leucate in 1587; d. at Avignon, 28 July, 1661. He was a member of the Society of Jesus, rector of the Jesuit colleges at Aix, Nîmes, and Avignon, and Provincial of Lyons. He composed a number of devotional works on the Blessed Virgin, St. Joseph, and the saints, and a "Pensez-y-bien", which latter had a large circulation and has been translated into several languages. The only ones of his works translated into English are "Pious Remarks upon the Life of St. Joseph", published in 1600; the "Glories of St. Joseph" (Dublin, 1835); "Devotions to St. Joseph", edited by the Rev. G. Tickell, S.J. (London, 187–).

Bibliothèque de la compagnie de Jésus, I, 945.

S. H. FRISBEE.

Barry, THOMAS FRANCIS. See CHATHAM, DIOCESE OF.

Barsanians. See MONOPHYSITES.

Barthe, JOHN MARY. See TRICHINOPOLY, DIOCESE OF.

Barthel, JOHANN CASPAR, a German canonist, b. 10 June, 1697, at Kitzingen, Bavaria; d. 8 April, 1771. He was the son of a fisherman, attended the schools of his native place, and from 1709 to 1715 studied at the Jesuit College at Würzburg. In 1715 he entered the seminary of the latter city and in 1721 was ordained priest. Christopher von Hutten, Prince-Bishop of Würzburg, sent him, in 1725, to Rome to study ecclesiastical law under Prosper Lambertini, later Pope Benedict XIV. Barthel returned as *Doctor Utriusque Juris*, in 1727, to Würzburg, where he became president of the seminary and (1728) professor of canon law at the university. Other ecclesiastical and academical honours, among them the vice-chancellorship of the university (1754), were conferred upon him. He took an active part in settling the controversy occasioned by the erection of the new Diocese of Fulda (1752). His chief importance, however, lies in his career as a teacher. His work in that line was appreciated by both Catholics and Protestants, and his lectures were circulated at various schools. He broke with the traditional method in canonical science, being one of the first to adopt the historico-critical treatment in Germany. His efforts to distinguish between the essentials and nonessentials in Catholic doctrines, and his attribution of excessive power to the State in its relations with the Church caused his opinions to be denounced at Rome as unorthodox. In his "Promemoriâ" (1751) he submitted his views and method to his former teacher, Benedict XIV, and obtained a favourable decision. His works, apart from what was written in the Fulda controversy, as "De Pallio" (1753), deal principally with the relations between Church and State, especially in Germany. Several of them are found in the "Opuscula juridica varii argumenti" (Würzburg, 1765, 1771).

STAMMINGER in *Kirchenlex.*, I, 2051, 2052; SCHULTE, *Die Geschichte d. Quellen* in *Lit. des kan. Rechts* (Stuttgart, 1875–80), III, i, 183–185; IDEM, *Allg. deutsch. Biograph.* (Leipzig, 1875—), II, 103.

N. A. WEBER.

Barthélemy, JEAN-JACQUES, a celebrated French numismatologist and writer, b. at Cassis (Provence), 1716; d. in Paris, 1795. He began his classical studies at the College of the Oratory in Marseilles, took up philosophy and theology at the Jesuits' college, and finally attended the seminary of the Lazarists, where he devoted most of his time to Oriental languages. He soon became renowned for his scholarship and earnestness in learned researches, in which he rivalled the Humanists of the Renaissance. Having completed his course, he received the tonsure and wore the ecclesiastical habit without taking Holy orders. For several years he lived in his lonely residence at Aubagne, near Marseilles, devoting himself entirely to numismatics, under the direction of his friend, M. Cary of Marseilles. In 1744, he went to Paris and became secretary to M. de Boze, keeper of the medals at the King's Library, and three years later he was elected to the Academy of Inscriptions and Belles-Lettres. In 1753, he succeeded M. de Boze and remained in this position until the Revolution, during his term nearly doubling the collection.

In 1754, he was sent to Italy on a scientific mission. On his way, he gathered a large number of medals, and conceived the idea of the book which made his name famous, "Voyage du Jeune Anacharsis en Grèce vers le milieu du IVe siècle avant l'ère vulgaire". This book, begun in 1756, was not finished until 1788, and was a description of ancient Greece, of Hellenic civilization, institutions, arts, history philosophy, and literature, appealing to every class by reason of its charming narratives and vivid pictures. In successive reprints and English translations (London, 1790, 1800), it still finds readers. Recent archæological discoveries have shown some of the statements to be erroneous, but on the whole the book remains a very successful attempt to diffuse a correct knowledge of Greek manners and customs. From the time of Barthélemy's journey through Italy, the Duke of Choiseul had been his patron and had given him many pensions and benefices. After the fall of his friend (1770), Barthélemy followed him into exile at Chanteloup, near Amboise, where unlike the *abbés de cour* he was busily engaged in polishing his elaborate literary productions. He was elected to the French Academy in 1789. During the Revolution, he was arrested (September, 1793) and confined in a prison for a few days. On his release, he declined to resume his functions as keeper of the medals, and having been despoiled of his fortune by the Revolution died in poverty. Besides the "Voyage du jeune Anacharsis", Barthélemy has left a number of essays on Oriental languages and archæology, originally read before the Academy of Inscriptions and Belles-Lettres; "Les amours de Caryte et de Polydore", a novel illustrating ancient manners; "Un voyage en Italie"; and "Mémoires" of his life. His works were edited by Villenave (1821).

BARTHÉLEMY, *Mémoires* (works, 1821), I; MANCINI-NIVERNAIS, *Essai sur la vie de J. J. Barthélemy* (Paris, 1795); SAINTE-BEUVE, *Causeries du Lundi*, VII; VILLEMAIN, *Tableau de la littérature française au XVIIIe siècle* (Paris, 1828), xlii; VILLENAVE in Barthélemy's works (1821), I.

LOUIS N. DELAMARRE.

Bartholi, FRANCESCO DELLA ROSSA, Friar Minor and chronicler, died c. 1272. Little is known of his life save what may be gathered from his own writings. A native of Assisi, he is found in 1312 as a student in Perugia, and in 1316 at Cologne, whence he returned to Umbria bearing many relics, including those of St. Louis, King of France, given him by the latter's daughter, Princess Blanche, who had become a Poor Clare. In 1320 and in 1326, he was lector of theology at the Porziuncula, in 1332 guardian at S. Damiano and in 1334 he was at the Sacro Convento. He appears to have lived to a great age. He was acquainted with Marinus of Assisi, Blessed John of La Verna, Alvarus Pelagius and other well-known Franciscans. Whether he is to be identified with the Francesco Rubea who is mentioned among the partisans of Michael de Cesena or with the Franciscus de Assisio who was long imprisoned at Florence on a charge of heresy is a matter of conjecture. Although Bartholi wrote several works including a history of the Passion, he is best known for his "Tractatus de Indulgentiâ Sanctæ Mariæ de Portiunculâ" composed about 1335. He spent many of his later years in retouching and completing this treatise, which is of great importance for the history of the origin and evolution of the Indulgence, in so far as it comprises a complete collection of the ecclesiastical information and popular legends then obtainable on the subject. It was first published by Paul Sabatier with a wealth of critical apparatus in the "Collection d'Etudes" (Paris, 1900, Vol. II). (See PORTIUNCULA.)

WADDING, *Script. Ord. Min.* (1650), 114; SBARALEA, *Supplementum* (1806), 245; MAZZUCHELLI, *Scrittori d'Italia* (1758), II, 1, 441–442; NARDUCCI, *Giunte al Mazzuchelli* (1884), 60; FALOCI in *Miscell. Francescana* (1887), II, 149–153; VAN ORTROY in *Analect. Bolland.* (1902), XXI, 372–380.

PASCHAL ROBINSON.

Bartholomæus a Martyribus. See BARTHOLOMEW OF BRAGA.

Bartholomæus Anglicus, Franciscan encyclopedist of the thirteenth century. An Englishman by birth he had been professor of theology at the University of Paris, when, in 1224 or 1225, he entered the newly established Order of St. Francis in company with his countryman and fellow-professor of theology, Haymo of Faversham, and two other professors of the same faculty. He continued his lectures in the claustral school till 1231, when he was sent to Magdeburg in Germany. He was succeeded by his illustrious countryman Alexander of Hales (q. v.) who, by being a member of the university, raised the private school of the Franciscans to the dignity of a school of

the university. The date of Bartholomæus's death is unknown. He was formerly identified with a later Franciscan and Englishman, Bartholomæus de Glanvilla, or Glaunvilla, who died about 1360, and to him the famous work "De proprietatibus rerum" was ascribed. Recent researches place beyond doubt that the two men must be distinguished and that the authorship of the work in question must be attributed to the Magdeburg professor of 1231

"De proprietatibus rerum" is an encyclopedia of all the sciences of that time: theology, philosophy, medicine, astronomy, chronology, zoology, botany, geography, mineralogy, are the subjects treated in the nineteen books of this work. We have in it the first important encyclopedia of the Middle Ages and the first in which the works of Greek, Arabian, and Jewish naturalists and medical writers, which had been translated into Latin shortly before, were laid under contribution. Aristotle, Hippocrates, Theophrastus, the Jew Isaac Medicus, the Arabian Haly, and other celebrities are quoted. To Bartholomæus must be given that honour which has been accorded until recently to the Dominican, Vincent of Beauvais, whose work exceeds by ten times the 400-page folio volume of Bartholomæus. Like the later "Speculum universale" of Vincent, the "De proprietatibus rerum" enjoyed unbounded popularity. Witness to this are the many manuscripts and editions. There is hardly a large library in Europe which has not manuscript copies of it, the National Library at Paris possessing as many as eighteen. Very many editions appeared in print, at least fourteen before the year 1500, and one as late as 1601 at Frankfort. By being translated and thus made accessible to the laity, the encyclopedia of Bartholomæus exercised a greater influence on medieval thought than that of Vincent. Of the latter's work only the "Speculum historiale" was translated, but Bartholomæus's work went through eight editions in French, two in Belgian, one in English, and one in Spanish prior to 1500. The work of Bartholomæus, though not fulfilling modern requirements of natural sciences, remains a valuable source of information to the student of medieval times.

DELISLE in *Histoire litt. de la France* (Paris, 1888), XXX, 352 sqq.; FELDER, *Geschichte der Studien im Franziskanerorden* (Freiburg, 1904), 248, 395 sqq.

JOHN M. LENHART.

Bartholomew, SAINT, one of the Twelve Apostles, mentioned sixth in the three Gospels lists (Matt., x, 3; Mark, iii, 18; Luke, vi, 14), and seventh in the list of Acts (i, 13). The name (Βαρθολομαῖος) means "son of Talmai" (or Tholmai), which was an ancient Hebrew name, borne, e. g. by the King of Gessur whose daughter was a wife of David (II Kings, iii, 3). It shows, at least, that Bartholomew was of Hebrew descent; it may have been his genuine proper name or simply added to distinguish him as the son of Talmai. Outside the instances referred to, no other mention of the name occurs in the New Testament. Nothing further is known of him for certain. Many scholars, however, identify him with Nathanael (John, i, 45–51; xxi, 2). The reasons for this are that Bartholomew is not the proper name of the Apostle; that the name never occurs in the Fourth Gospel, while Nathanael is not mentioned in the synoptics; that Bartholomew's name is coupled with Philip's in the lists of Matthew and Luke, and found next to it in Mark, which agrees well with the fact shown by St. John that Philip was an old friend of Nathanael's and brought him to Jesus; that the call of Nathanael, mentioned with the call of several Apostles, seems to mark him for the apostolate, especially since the rather full and beautiful narrative leads one to expect some important development; that Nathanael was of Galilee where Jesus found most, if not all, of the Twelve; finally, that on the occasion of the appearance of the risen Saviour on the shore of the Sea of Tiberias, Nathanael is found present, together with several Apostles who are named and two unnamed Disciples who were, almost certainly, likewise Apostles (the word "apostle" not occurring in the Fourth Gospel and "disciple" of Jesus ordinarily meaning Apostle) and so, presumably, was one of the Twelve. This chain of circumstantial evidence is ingenious and pretty strong; the weak link is that, after all, Nathanael may have been another personage in whom, for some reason, the author of the Fourth Gospel may have been particularly interested, as he was in Nicodemus, who is likewise not named in the synoptists. (See NATHANAEL.)

No mention of St. Bartholomew occurs in ecclesiastical literature before Eusebius, who mentions that Pantænus, the master of Origen, while evangelizing India, was told that the Apostle had preached there before him and had given to his converts the Gospel of St. Matthew written in Hebrew, which was still treasured by the Church. "India" was a name covering a very wide area, including even Arabia Felix. Other traditions represent St. Bartholomew as preaching in Mesopotamia, Persia, Egypt, Armenia, Lycaonia, Phrygia, and on the shores of the Black Sea; one legend, it is interesting to note, identifies him with Nathanael. The manner of his death, said to have occurred at Albanopolis in Armenia, is equally uncertain; according to some, he was beheaded, according to others, flayed alive and crucified, head downward, by order of Astyages, for having converted his brother, Polymius, King of Armenia. On account of this latter legend, he is often represented in art (e. g. in Michelangelo's Last Judgment) as flayed and holding in his hand his own skin. His relics are thought by some to be preserved in the church of St. Bartholomew-in-the-Island, at Rome. His feast is celebrated on 24 August. An apocryphal gospel of Bartholomew existed in the early ages.

LE CAMUS, *Vie de Notre-Seigneur* (tr. New York, 1906), I; IDEM in VIG., *Dict. de la Bible*, where references are given for the sources of the traditions; FOUARD, *Life of Christ* (New York, 1891). JOHN F. FENLON.

Bartholomew, Apostle of Armenia, also called Bartholomæus Parvus (the Little), b. at Bologna, year not known; d. 15 August, 1333. Nothing certain has been preserved as to his family. At the end of the thirteenth century, while still young, he entered the Dominican Order, made his studies in the monastery of his native town, and soon became noted as a capable theologian and a preacher zealous for souls. Pope John XXII cherished a great desire not only to keep the Catholic Armenians in connexion with the Roman See, but also to lead the schismatic part of this people into unity with the Church; for this reason he supported and encouraged the Dominican missions in the regions inhabited by Armenians. Bartholomew was selected to be the head and leader of a little band of Dominican missionaries whom John XXII sent to Armenia. He was consecrated bishop and received as his see the city of Maragha, lying east of Lake Urumiah. Accompanied by several companions the new missionary bishop arrived (1318–20) in the territory assigned to him. He studied the Armenian language, built a monastery for his brethren of the order, and with the aid of these began his apostolic labours. He met with such success that large numbers of heathen and Mohammedans were converted and many schismatic Armenians were brought into Catholic unity. The zealous bishop gave great care to this latter part of his missionary labours, as he found many Armenians favourably disposed to union. Bartholomew's reputation for saintliness and learning spread rapidly into distant regions and came to the knowledge of a group of Armenian monks who were striving after a higher degree of perfection and the attainment of Church unity. The leader of these monks was the learned John of Kherna (Kherni), the head of a monastery near Kherna in the district of Erentschag (now Alenja), not far from Nachidjewan. John was a pupil of the celebrated theologian Isaias, whose school had produced 370 doctors of theology (*Vartabed*). In 1328 John of Kherna sought out Bishop Bartholomew, remained with him a year and a half and became a warm advocate of union with the Roman Church. He sent an invitation to a conference, drawn up by the zealous missionary, to his former fellow-students, and Bartholomew went with him to Kherna, where the conference was held. The result was that a large number of learned monks joined John of Kherna in submitting to the authority of the Holy See. In order to promote union and raise religious life John founded in 1330, with the consent of Bartholomew, a religious congregation called the "Uniats (Unitores) of St. Gregory the Illuminator", which was later incorporated with the Dominicans. About this time Bartholomew seems to have substituted Nachidjewan for Maragha as his see. This brought him nearer to the centre of Armenia, so that he was able to work more efficiently for the development of the union. He translated a number of works into the Armenian language, as: the Psalter, treatises of St. Augustine, the "Summa contra Gentiles" of St. Thomas, and a part of the Summa theologica; he also wrote several original works, especially a work on casuistry and a treatise on the sacraments.

Conciliationes ecclesiæ Armenæ cum Romanâ, ed. CLEM. GALANO, Armenian and Latin (Rome, 1650), Pt. I, 598 sqq.; MELLONI, *Atti e memorie degli uomini illustri in santità nati o morti in Bologna* (Bologna, 1779), cl. II, vol. II, 110–142; TOURON, *Hist. des hommes illustres de l'ordre de S. Dominique* (Paris, 1743—), II, 110 sqq.; TOURNEBIZE, *Histoire politique et religieuse de l'Arménie; Les Frères-Unis de S. Grégoire l'Illuminateur* in *Revue de l'Orient chrétien* (1906), 74 sqq.; BRÉHIER, *L'Eglise et l'Orient au moyen âge* (Paris, 1907), 280–281. J. P. KIRSCH.

Bartholomew, GOSPEL OF. See APOCRYPHA.

Bartholomew of Braga, VENERABLE, b. at Verdela, near Lisbon, May, 1514; d. at Viana, 16 July, 1590. Bartholomew Fernandez, later known as a Martyribus, out of veneration for the church in which he was baptized, came of humble parentage. He entered the Dominican Order, 11 November, 1527, and was professed 20 November, 1529. On the completion of his studies, he taught philosophy in the monastery at Lisbon, and then for about twenty years theology in various houses of his order. In 1551 he received the Master's degree at the provincial chapter of Salamanca. While teaching theology in the monastery of Batalha, he was summoned to Evora by the Infante Dom Luis to undertake the religious education of his son, Dom Antonio, who was entering the ecclesiastical state. He devoted two years to this task. In 1558, against his own desires, and only out of obedience to his provincial, Luis of Granada, he accepted the appointment to the archiepiscopal See of Braga, for which he had been chosen by Queen Catherine, and in 1559 received episcopal consecration. With true apostolic zeal he devoted himself to the duties of his new office.

On the resumption of the General Council of Trent in 1561, Bartholomew repaired to the council and took part in the last sessions. He was highly esteemed among the Fathers of the council both on account of his theological learning and the holiness of his life, and he exercised great influence in the discussions, particularly those with regard to the decrees on the reform of ecclesiastical life. On the conclusion of the council he returned, in February, 1564, to his see, and in 1566 held an important provincial synod in which excellent decrees were passed for the restoration of ecclesiastical discipline and the elevation of the moral life of clergy and people (Concilium provinciale Bracarense quartum,

Braga, 1567). The archbishop now devoted himself most zealously to the task of carrying out the reforms of the Council of Trent as well as the decrees of his own provincial synod. A great famine and a visitation of the plague revealed the depths of his charity. After repeated requests, having received, on 20 February, 1582, permission to resign his see, he withdrew to the monastery of his order at Viana, to prepare in solitude for the end.

In 1845 Gregory XVI declared him Venerable. In the interests of a truly Christian life and the promotion of ecclesiastical discipline, he wrote: "Compendium spiritualis doctrinæ ex variis sanct. Patrum sententiis magna ex parte collectum" (Lisbon, 1582); "Stimulus pastorum ex gravissimis sanct. Patrum sententiis concinnatus, in quo agitur de vitâ et moribus episcoporum aliorumque prælatorum" (Rome, 1564; published at the instance of St. Charles Borromeo); "Catechismo ou Doutrina christiana" (Lisbon, 1562). All these writings have been frequently republished and translated into several languages. A collective edition is: "Opera omnia curâ et studio Malachiæ d'Inguinbert, archiep. Theodos." (1 vol. fol. in 2 parts, Rome, 1734–35).

QUÉTIF-ECHARD, Script. ord. Præd. (Paris, 1721), II, 296; MUÑOZ, Vida de Fra Bartolomé de los Martyres (Madrid, 1645); DE SACY, La vie de Dom Barthélémy des Martyrs (Paris, 1663). There is a detailed biography in the introduction to the above-mentioned collective edition of his works. For his beatification, Romana seu Bracharen. beatificationis et canonizationis Barth. de Martyribus positio super virtutibus (3 vols. fol., Rome, 1819–44).

J. P. KIRSCH.

Bartholomew of Bragança, b. about 1200; d. 1 July, 1271. He made his studies at Padua, receiving there the habit of the Dominican Order from the hands of St. Dominic. According to Leander, author of the oldest life of Bartholomew, he was made master of the sacred palace in 1235, during the pontificate of Gregory IX; but there is no mention of this event in his last testament, where he expressly states the important positions held by him. He was appointed to the See of Nemonicum, in Cyprus, 1248; what city this was is not now known. While King Louis of France was engaged upon his expedition against the Infidel, Bartholomew joined the king and queen at Joppa, Sidon, and Acre, in the character of Apostolic legate, according to some writers, his own account merely stating that he visited the king and queen at these places. King Louis desired him to make a visit to France, promising rich relics for his church, should he comply with the request. To ensure the presence of so distinguished a prelate at his own court, Alexander IV made him Bishop of Vicenza, in 1256, and during his tenure of that see he was subject to the tyranny of Ezzelino, a notorious enemy of religion. This persecution, however, served to bring out the true qualities of pastor which Bartholomew possessed in a high degree. It has been said that he was named Patriarch of Jerusalem, but this is doubtful, his testament being silent on this point also. In 1254, he was sent as legate to the courts of England and France and as Henry III was, at this time, in Aquitaine, thither Bartholomew betook himself, towards the close of that year, accompanying the English king and queen to Paris. He was, on this occasion, presented by the King of France with a relic of the true Cross and a thorn from Our Saviour's Crown. These he afterwards placed in the beautiful Dominican Church, built by him, at Vicenza and known as the Church of the Crown. He was venerated by the people and, according to the Bollandists, has always been honoured with the title of Blessed. He wrote commentaries on Scripture, was the reputed author of a commentary on the "Hierarchy" of St. Dionysius the Areopagite, of two volumes of sermons, and some smaller works.

Acta SS., July, I, 246 sqq.; also May, VII, 692.

WILLIAM DEVLIN.

Bartholomew of Brescia, an Italian canonist, b. probably in the second half of the twelfth century at Brescia; d. 1258. He studied Roman and ecclesiastical law at Bologna, where he himself became a teacher. It is believed that he was murdered, when Ezzelino, the leader of the Ghibellines, captured Brescia (1258). His literary work consisted almost entirely in the revision of the productions of other writers. His "Brocarda", or Canonical Rules (Lyons, 1519), were a working-over of those of Damasus (twelfth and thirteenth centuries); his "Casus decretorum" were a revision of the "Casus" of Benencasa (d. c. 1206); the "Historiæ super libro Decretorum" reproduced the work of an unknown author. Both his "Casus" and "Historiæ" derive their importance from their incorporation into the Paris edition (1505) of Gratian's "Decretum". The "Ordo Judiciarius" of Tancred (d. c. 1235) was also revised by Bartholomew. More important than the preceding works was his "Glossa Ordinaria" to the "Decretum" of Gratian, a correction of the "Glossa", or "Apparatus", of Johannes Teutonicus (thirteenth century). His only certain independent work was the "Quæstiones dominicales et veneriales", lectures delivered on Sundays and Fridays.

SCHULTE, Gesch. der Quellen u. Literatur des kan. Rechts (Stuttgart, 1875–80), II, 83–88; SCHERER in Kirchenlex. (2d ed., Freiburg, 1882), I, 2055, 2056; HURTER, Nomenclator.

N. A. WEBER.

Bartholomew of Carranza. See CARRANZA, BARTOLOMEO.

Bartholomew of Edessa, Syrian apologist and polemical writer. The place of his birth is not known, it was probably Edessa or some neighbouring town, for he was certainly a monk of that city, and in his refutation of Agarenus, he calls himself several times "the monk of Edessa". The time in which he flourished is also doubtful; it is certain, however, that it was after the Mohammedan conquest of Syria, and the controversy concerning the sacred images which began in 725. There is a work of his written in Greek, which he directed against one Agarenus, a Mohammedan. The beginning of the refutation is lost; the title as given by Le Moyne (Varia Sacra, Leyden, 1685), is "Elenchus et Confutatio Agareni". This work may be read in the Migne collection, P. G., CVI, 1381–1448. This treatise, as it now stands, opens with a statement of the objections of Mohammedans against Christianity, among which are the dogmas of the Blessed Trinity, of the Incarnation, and of Confession. Bartholomew then gives his answers, and makes many counter-charges against Mohammed and his so-called Revelation.

The main lines of argumentation are taken from the life of the prophet himself. Bartholomew shows that nothing either in his parentage, education, or life betrays any God-given mission. From this he concludes that Mohammed was an impostor, preaching without any Divine credentials. Bartholomew is well acquainted not only with the Christian position which he defends, but also with the position of his adversaries; he knows the customs, practices, and beliefs of the Arabs, and he boasts that he has read all of their books. A second treatise "Contra Muhammedum" is also printed in Migne (loc. cit., 1448–58) under the name of Bartholomew of Edessa; but, in spite of the numerous resemblances, explainable otherwise than by identity of authorship, the differences are of such a nature as to make the ascription of it to Bartholomew unjustified. Such are e. g. the names and the number of Mohammed's wives and children; the editor of the Koran; the Nestorian monk who taught Mohammed Christianity, etc.

CAVE, *Dissertatio de scriptoribus incertæ ætatis* in *Scriptorum Ecclesiasticorum Historia Literaria* (Oxford, 1740–43), II; CEILLIER, *Histoire générale des auteurs sacrés et ecclésiastiques* (Paris, 1860–68), XII, 103.

R. BUTIN.

Bartholomew of Lucca (or DE FIADONIBUS, sometimes abbreviated PTOLOMEO or TOLOMEO), historian, b. about 1227 at Lucca; d. about 1327. At an early age he entered the Dominican Order. He was distinguished for piety, and his intense application to study, for which reasons he won the respect and warm friendship of St. Thomas Aquinas. He was not only his disciple, but also his confidant and confessor (Ptolom., H. E., XXIII, viii). In 1272 he accompanied St. Thomas from Rome to Naples where he still was in 1274, when the news of his master's death at Fossa Nuova reached him. He was elected prior of the convent of his native city in 1288. At Naples (1294), he took an active part in the public demonstration which was made to prevent Pope Celestine V from resigning. In 1301 he was elected Prior of Santa Maria Novella at Florence. Later he removed to Avignon where he was chaplain for nine years (1309–18) to Cardinal Patrasso, Bishop of Albano, and after the Cardinal's death in 1311 to his fellow-religious Cardinal William of Bayonne. Echard affirms that he was the close friend and often the confessor of John XXII, who appointed him Bishop of Torcello, March 15, 1318. A conflict with the Patriarch of Grado concerning the appointment of an abbess of St. Anthony's at Torcello led to his excommunication in 1321, and exile. In 1323 he made peace with the patriarch, returned to his see, and died there in 1327.

The best-known work of Bartholomew is his "Annales" (1061–1303), finished about 1307, wherein are recorded in terse sentences the chief events of this period. (Muratori, Rer. Ital. Script., XI, 1249 sqq.; or in the better edition of C. Minutoli, "Documenti di Storia Italiana", Florence, 1876, VI, 35 sqq.). His "Historia Ecclesiastica Nova" in twenty-four books relates the history of the Church from the birth of Christ till 1294; considering as appendixes the lives of Boniface VIII, Benedict XI, and Clement V, it reaches to 1314 (Muratori, loc. cit., XI, 751 sqq.; the life of Clement V is in Baluze, "Vitæ pap. Aven.", 23 sqq.). He also wrote a "Historia Tripartita" known only from his own references and citations. The "Extracta de chronico Fr. Ptolomæi de Luca" and the "Excerpta ex chronicis Fr. Ptolomæi" are no longer considered original works by separate authors, but are extracts from the "Historia Ecclesiastica Nova" by some unknown compiler who lived after the death of Bartholomew. He is also well known for his completion of the "De Regimine Principum", which St. Thomas Aquinas had been unable to finish before his death. This was no small task, for the share of Bartholomew begins with the sixth chapter of the second book and includes the third and fourth books (vol. XVI, in the Parma, 1865, edition of St. Thomas). Though he does not follow the order of the saint, yet his treatment is clear and logical. A work on the "Hexæmeron" by him was published by Masetti in 1880. With a few exceptions, the writings of Bartholomew have always been held in high esteem. He showed great care in verifying his statements. The lives of the Avignon popes were written from original documents under his hands and were controlled by the statements of eye-witnesses. His acceptance of fables now exploded, e. g. the Popess Joan, must be attributed to the uncritical temper of his time.

KRÜGER, *Des Ptolomæus Lucencis Leben und Werke* (Göttingen, 1874); KÖNIG, *Tolomeo v. Lucca, ein biographischer Versuch* (Harburg, 1878); QUÉTIF AND ECHARD, *SS. O.P.*, I, 541; POTTHAST, *Bibl. hist. med. ævii* (Berlin, 1896), 945.

THOS. M. SCHWERTNER.

Bartholomew of Pisa, Friar Minor and chronicler. The fact that there were two Friars Minor named Bartholomew living in Pisa at the same time has caused considerable confusion, and most recent writers, following Marianus of Florence, Mark of Lisbon, and Wadding, have fallen into the error of attributing to Bartholomew Albisi the famous "Book of Conformities", which was really written by Bartholomew Rinonico. The latter, with whom we are here concerned, was a Pisan of noble family. In 1352 he was a student at Bologna and later filled the office of Lector there as well as at Padua, Pisa, Sienna, and Florence. He also preached for many years with great success in different Italian cities. He died about 1401, renowned no less for sanctity than for learning, and is commemorated in the Franciscan Martyrology on 4 November.

Bartholomew's chief title to fame rests upon his remarkable book, "De Conformitate Vitæ B. P. Francisci ad Vitam Domini Nostri Jesu Christi", begun in 1385 and formally approved by the general chapter held at Assisi in 1399. Enthusiastically received on its appearance and long held in high esteem, this work became the object of bitter and stupid attacks on the part of Lutherans and Jansenists. Against it Erasmus Alber wrote the "Alcoranus Franciscanus" (Der Barfüsser Mönche Eulenspiegel und Alcoran mit einer Vorrede D. M. Luthers, 1531) in reply to which Henry Sedulius, O. F. M., published his "Apologeticus adversus Alcoranum Franciscanorum pro libro Conformitatum" (Antwerp, 1607). Subsequent writers on Franciscan history treated the Pisan's work with most unmerited ostracism; more recently it has come to be lauded in certain circles in terms which savour of exaggeration. Between these extreme views, the patient and discerning student will find the "Conformities" a book of very uneven value. The parallels between the lives of Our Lord and St. Francis which form its basis are sometimes forced, but nowhere does it make St. Francis the equal of Christ. Side by side with fantastic legends, ridiculous visions, and other absurdities, it contains much really credible and precious historical information, revealing besides a deep knowledge of Scripture and theology and a critical temper not usual at the time it was written. It is rightly considered a source of great importance for students of Franciscan history. It was first printed at Milan in 1510 and in 1513. The new edition published at Bologna in 1590 is mutilated and corrupted, especially in the historical parts, at almost every page. A sorely needed critical edition of the text has lately been published in tom. IV of the "Analecta Franciscana" (Quaracchi, 1906).

In addition to the "Conformities", Bartholomew left some thirty other works, including an exposition of the Rule of the Friars Minor found in the "Speculum" Morin (Rouen, 1509) and a book "De Vitâ B. Mariæ Virginis", published at Venice in 1596; his Lenten sermons were printed at Milan in 1498, Venice, 1503, and Lyons, 1519. Sbaralea and others have erroneously attributed to him the "Summa Casuum Conscientiæ", which is really the work of Bartholomew a S. Concordio of Pisa, O. P., and the "Vita B. Gerardi", which was written by Bartholomew Albisi mentioned above.

WADDING, *Annales*, ad. ann. 1399, IX, vii, viii, and *Scriptores* (1650), 48; SBARALEA, *Supplementum*, 109; TIRABOSCHI, *Stor. lett. Ital.* (1805), V, 144; DA CIVEZZA, *Bibl. San Francescana* (1879), 463–464, 470–471; SABATIER, *Vie de S. François* (Paris, 1894), *Etude*, pp. cxv sqq.; FELDER, *Gesch. der Wissenschaftl. Studien im Franziskanerord.* (Freiburg, 1904), 104 and *passim*; GOUBOVICH, *Biblioteca Bio-Bibliografica* (Quaracchi, 1906), 71 and *passim*; FALOCI in *Miscell. Francesc.* (1901), VIII, fasc. V, 148 sqq.

PASCHAL ROBINSON.

Bartholomew of San Concordio (also OF PISA), canonist, and man of letters, b. at San Concordia, near Pisa about 1260; d. at Pisa, 11 June, 1347. He entered the Dominican Order in 1277, studied at Pisa, Bologna, and Paris, and taught at Lucca,

Florence, and Pisa. A preacher of renown, he was as learned as he was devout, as skilled in Latin and Tuscan poetry as he was versed in canon and civil law. His fame rests chiefly on his alphabetically arranged "Summa de Casibus Conscientiæ", variously called "Pisana", "Pisanella", "Bartholomæa", and "Magistruccia". The idea if not the basis of this work was a "Summa Confessorum" by John Rumsik, O. P., Lector of Freiburg (d. 1314). Bartholomew's treatise was clear and concise, and it conformed to the newer laws and canons of his time. Evidently a highly useful digest, it was very popular and much used during the fourteenth and fifteenth centuries, and was among the first books undertaken by some of the earliest printers of Germany, France, and Italy. Nicholas of Osimo, O. M., added a supplement in 1444, which also appeared in many editions. Others likewise incorporated the work in later handbooks, notably James of Ascoli, O. M., 1464, and Ange de Clavasio, O. M., in his "Summa Angelica". Apart from several MSS. on moral and literary subjects, his works include "De documentis antiquorum", edited by Albertus Clarius, O. P. (Tarvisi, 1601) in 8vo. The same treatise in the vernacular, "Ammæstramenti degli antichi" (Florence, 1662), came to be regarded as a Tuscan classic.

QUÉTIF-ECHARD, *Scriptores Ord. Præd.* (Paris, 1719), I, 623; MANDONNET in *Dict. de théol. cath.*, 436; PANZER, *Aelteste Buchdruckergeschichte Nürnbergs* (Nuremberg, 1789), p. 18, n. 22; HURTER, *Nomenclator* (Innsbruck, 1906), II, 612.

JOHN R. VOLZ.

Bartholomew's Day, MASSACRE OF. See SAINT BARTHOLOMEW'S DAY.

Bartholomites, the name given to Armenian monks who sought refuge in Italy after the invasion of their country by the Sultan of Egypt in 1296. The first of their number landed at Genoa, where a church of St. Bartholomew was built for them, hence their name Bartholomites. Others soon followed this first band and were established in various Italian cities, in Parma, Sienna, Pisa, Florence, Città-Vecchia, Rome, and Ancona. To these early foundations were afterwards added others at Milan, Naples, Perugia, Gubbio, Ferrara, Bologna, Padua, Rimini, Viterbo, etc.; in fact the Bartholomites were both numerous and prosperous. In the beginning they observed the Rule of St. Basil and the Armenian Liturgy, Clement V acknowledging their right thereto. But in time they abandoned their national traditions for the Roman Liturgy, adopted a habit resembling that of the Dominicans and finally replaced the Rule of St. Basil by that of St. Augustine. Innocent VI, who approved this change (1356), also confirmed the union of their monasteries into one congregation governed by a superior-general and a general chapter. The superiors-general were at first elected for life, but in 1474 Pope Sixtus IV caused them to be voted for every three years.

Boniface IX granted the congregation the privileges of the Order of St. Dominic and Innocent VIII and Paul III ratified the same; nevertheless the Bartholomites were prohibited from joining any other religious order except that of the Carthusians. Durazzo, their first cardinal protector, was appointed by Urban VIII in 1640, but they did not long enjoy this signal advantage. Their regular observance began to decline, their ranks were but meagerly recruited and most of their houses had to be closed till at length only four or five were left, in which about forty monks lived as best they could. There seemed to be no way of averting this decadence. Innocent X authorized the Bartholomites to enter other religious orders or else to secularize themselves, assuring each of them a pension. He suppressed their congregation and its houses and revenues were put to new uses. Among the most noted Bartholomites were: Father Martin, who conducted the first Armenian monks to

Genoa and was their superior; Father Anthony of Pisa, who was the first superior-general of their congregation; Estaban Palma, who four times held the office of general and laboured zealously for the reform of the congregation; Cherubini Cerbelloni of Genoa and Paul Costa of Milan, who were celebrated preachers and Scoti, Pori, Girolamo Cavalieri, J. B. Ladriani, and Gregorio Bitio who left literary works which were, however, soon forgotten. In their church at Genoa is still preserved the celebrated portrait of Christ known as the Holy Face of Edessa.

BITIO, *Relazione del principio e statto della Religione de' Fr. di S. Basili degli armeni in Italia;* HÉLYOT, *Histoire des ordres monastiques,* I, 243-248.

J. M. BESSE.

Bartoli, DANIELLO. a historian and *littérateur,* b. at Ferrara, 12 February, 1608; d. in Rome, 12 January, 1685. After a brilliant course of studies under the Jesuits, he entered the novitiate of San Andrea, Rome, in 1623, before the completion of his sixteenth year. The story of the labours and sufferings of the members of the Society of Jesus in the Indies and Japan awakened in the youthful religious an ardent desire to emulate the zeal and devotion of the missionaries. He asked to be sent on the foreign missions, but Father Mutius Vitelleschi. the General of the order, kept him in Italy. After some years of teaching, Father Bartoli began his apostolic career as a preacher, his sermons meeting with extraordinary success in Ferrara, his native place, Genoa Lucca, Florence, and Rome. He was engaged in this fruitful ministry when the contemplation of the evils to youth, caused by the reading of romances, suggested one of his first books, "The Learned Man". This work was received with great applause and is said to have gone through eight editions in the first year of its publication; it was translated into French, German. and English.

The success of this venture decided the vocation of Father Bartoli as a writer. He was called to Rome by his superiors in 1650, and from that time until his death he published many works in history as well as in other departments of literature, all of them written in Italian. The best known and the most important is a history of the Society of Jesus, which appeared in Rome from 1650 to 1673. in six volumes folio, and was translated into Latin by Father Janin, S.J. Bartoli's works were collected and published in Florence in 1826, in 50 vols., 16mo. He is universally esteemed for his erudition, as well as for the purity and elegance of his style. His fellow-countrymen have honoured him with a place among the classical writers of the Italian language.

BARTOLI, *Opere Varie* (Venice, 1716). A sketch of the author is prefixed to the first volume. See also edition of MARIETTI (Turin, 1825-56); PATRIGNANI, *Menologio* for 13 Jan., p. 119; SOUTHWELL, *Biblioth. Script. S. J.,* 164; BOERO, *Comm. della vita e delle opere del P. Dan. Bartoli* (Bologn ., 1865); SOMMERVOGEL, *Biblioth.,* I, 965 sq.; FELLER, *Dict. Histor;* CRÉTINEAU-JOLY, *Hist. de la c. de J.* (Brussels, 1851), IV 261; DREWS, *Fasti Soc. Jes.* for 13 Jan., p. 17; DE GUILHERMY, *Menol. de la c. de J., Assistance d'Italie,* Part I.

EDWARD P. SPILLANE.

Bartoli di Sassiferato. See ROMAN LAW.

Bartolocci, GIULIO, a Cistercian monk and learned Hebrew scholar, b. at Celleno in the old kingdom of Naples, 1 April, 1613; d. at Rome, 19 October, 1687. He began his Hebrew studies under Giovanni Battista, a converted Jew, and in 1651 was appointed professor of Hebrew and rabbinical literature at the Collegium Neophytorum at Rome and Scriptor Hebraicus at the Vatican Library. It was here that he, with the assistance of Battista, collated the materials for his famous work "Bibliotheca Magna Rabbinica" which appeared in four volumes during the years 1675–93. The last volume was published by his disciple, Carlo Giuseppi Imbonati, who also published a supplementary volume in 1694. This monumental work contains an account of Jewish literature and embodies, besides its numerous bibliographical and biographical data, a number of dissertations on Jewish customs, etc. Although it has been adjudged uncritical by Richard Simon, Bartolocci's work was adopted by Wolf as the basis of his own "Bibliotheca Hebraica". Bartolocci died as Abbot of the monastery of St. Sebastiani ad Catacumbas in Rome.

WOLF, *Bibl. Hebr.*, i, 6–9; FÜRST, *Bibl. jud.*, i, 89, iii, lxxiv; *Nouvelle Biographie Universelle*, s. v.; *Jewish Encyclopedia*, s. v.; KAULEN in *Kirchenlexicon*, s. v.

F. X. E. ALBERT.

Bartolommeo, FRA, an Italian painter and a member of the Dominican Order, b. in 1475 in the territory belonging to Florence; d. at Florence in 1517. He bore the worldly name of Bartolommeo di Pagholo del Fattorino and was called, more familiarly, Baccio della Porta, the nickname being a reference to the circumstances of his family. His work as a painter characterizes the transition of the Renaissance from its early period to the time of its greatest splendour. In 1484 he entered the studio of Cosimo Rosselli, one of whose pupils at the same time was a lad of about Bartolommeo's age, Mariotto Albertinelli. The friendship between Bartolommeo and the somewhat more worldly Albertinelli caused the two to form a business partnership in 1490 which lasted until 1512. At times the two friends were estranged on account of Bartolommeo's admiration for Savonarola.

Bartolommeo adopted Savonarola's theories concerning art, painted the reformer's picture a number of times and after Savonarola's tragic end (1498) entered the same order to which the reformer had belonged. Before this, though, he had painted the

THE DESCENT FROM THE CROSS (Pitti Gallery, Florence)

fresco of the Last Judgment, which is in the Church of Santa Maria Nuova, Florence. The upper part of the fresco depicts the Saviour, the Virgin Mary, and the Apostles; the figures while preserving their traditional dignity exhibit a striking freedom in the pose. The work also shows an entirely new perception of perspective. The lower half of the fresco, painted by Albertinelli, is also skilfully composed. At times, perhaps, a little more action would be preferable. Besides this work all that we have of Bartolommeo's first period are numerous carefully executed drawings which are in various collections. Savonarola made the same deep impression on Bartolommeo that he made on many other Florentine painters. According to Vasari, the artist, influenced by Savonarola's preach-

ing, threw his secular and mythological designs into the bonfire.

For a number of years after his entrance (1500) into the Convent of San Marco he gave up his art, although he did not become a priest. However, he resumed his work, painting in the style of Angelico, which was in agreement with the spirit of Savonarola, and also in part in the style of Masaccio and Filippino. He had previously studied the Florentine art of the time with great care and painted, above all, in the manner of this school. The influence of Leonardo da Vinci, who worked at Florence, or near by, from 1501 to 1508, is also evident. The "Last Judgment" drew the attention of Raphael, who was eight years the younger of the two, to Bartolommeo. Bartolommeo had charge of the studio of San Marco when Raphael came to Florence. Raphael visited Bartolommeo and the acquaintance was productive of benefit to both. In 1508 Raphael went to Rome. In the same year a visit to Venice gave Bartolommeo a new stimulus. The influence of the rich colouring used by Bellini and Titian showed itself in the altar-piece (in the Museum at Lucca), which represents God the Father, with St. Catherine and Mary Magdalen in ecstasy. Some years later Bartolommeo went for a short time to Rome. Here he studied the works of Michelangelo in addition to those of Raphael. For a while he was in Lucca, but generally he worked at San Marco, where he finally died.

Fra Bartolommeo developed his undoubted talent for painting by the most diligent study. In his work depth of religious feeling and the dignity suitable to sacred subjects are happily united with the advance in the technic of art of his time. In perspective, characterization of his subject, drapery, colour, grouping, and rhythm of pose and movement Bartolommeo holds to the Cinquecento, while the impression made by his devotional pictures is in no way lowered by realism or by seeking after external effect. The works which he painted to sell are not so naive and unconscious as the Fiesole pictures, for Bartolommeo came more in contact with the world. The "Vision of St. Bernard" exhibits a shy, tender grace; the "Marriage of St. Catherine" (in the Pitti Palace, Florence) has more animation although filled with the mystic depths of religious feeling. Bartolommeo loved symmetry in the grouping, but he understood how to avoid monotony by varying the position of the body, the turn of the head, and by the use of other signs of movement as, for example, in the "Mother of Mercy" in the museum at Lucca. In an unfinished altar-piece a beauty of form expressive of the character of the personages is united to skilful variety and strict adherence to the subject. This altar-piece (in the Uffizi Palace, Florence) represents the patron saints of Florence with the Madonna and Child. St. Anna who is also portrayed is somewhat higher in position, while two angels sit at the foot of the altar and others are poised over the whole group.

The art with which Bartolommeo expressed the individuality of his subjects is still greatly admired in small frescoes which he produced, such as the "Ecce Homo" and representations of the Madonna with various saints. The heroic figure of St. Mark in the Pitti Palace, Florence, an imitation of the style of Michelangelo, is less striking in expression and pose than in the treatment of the drapery. A delightful simplicity and dignity characterize the painting of a Risen Christ blessing the world. The evangelists are with him and the world is seen as a landscape in a mirror held by two angels. Still more unassuming but yet more beautiful is a Madonna with St. Stephen and John the Baptist. Another canvas which is greatly admired is a "Descent from the Cross"; or, "Lamentation over Christ", in which the expression of suffering on the faces is most finely graded and so subdued that a heavenly peace illumines the group. Bartolommeo's masterpieces are to be found chiefly in Florence and Lucca.

Scott, *Fra Bartolommeo* (London, 1881); Lübke, *Geschichte der italienischen Malerei* (Stuttgart, 1878), II; Frantz, *Fra Bartolommeo della Porta* (Ratisbon, 1879); Idem, *Geschichte der christlichen Malerei* (Freiburg, 1894), II.

G. Gietmann.

Bartolozzi, Francesco, an engraver, etcher, and painter, b. at Florence, 1727; d. at Lisbon, 1815. His father was a goldsmith of excellent family and early taught the use of the burin to his boy who, when ten years of age, engraved two heads which gave promise of his future powers. In the Florentine Academy he learned to work in oil, chalks, and aquarelle. Unsurpassed by any artist of his day in his knowledge of anatomy, and with a passion for the antique, young Bartolozzi became a master in depicting beauty of expression, movement, and form.

From 1745 until 1751 he studied with Wagner, the Venetian historical engraver. This apprenticeship ended, he married Lucia Ferro and the young pair, on Cardinal Bottari's invitation, went to Rome. Returning to Venice, his fame grew very rapidly, and in 1764, Dalton, King George III's librarian, took him to England, where he was appointed Engraver to the King, and, four years later, Royal Academician. In London he engraved over two thousand plates, nearly all in stipple or the "red-chalk style", a method recently invented by the French, but brought into vogue and elevated into a distinct art by Bartolozzi. He devoted himself to the human figure, and his engravings abound in sweet and tender types of beauty, graceful in form and outline. Everywhere are found delicate modulations of light and shade with a roundness, finish, and suggestion of flesh never before seen in engraved work.

Bartolozzi's drawing was superb; and although he was a reproductive artist he improved the work he copied, especially the drawing, even Sir Joshua Reynolds thanking him for such a service. His pupils called him the "god of drawing". His splendid line work was obscured by the great popularity attained by his stippled prints, and his few etchings show a free, bold, and unfettered sweep of line. They, too, were reproduced from pictures by others, but the translation always improved on the original. In 1802 Bartolozzi went to Lisbon, where he was knighted, and where he worked and taught until his death. He was buried in the church of Saint Isabella. Among Bartolozzi's best productions are the "Royal Academy Diploma", "The Marlborough Gems", the "Illustrations to Shakespeare", and some of his small "Tickets", all in stipple; and "The Silence" and "Clytie", engraved in pure line.

Tuer, *Bartolozzi and His Works* (London, 1881), 2 vols.

Leigh Hunt.

Barton, Elizabeth, b. probably in 1506; executed at Tyburn, 20 April, 1534; called the "Nun of Kent". The career of this visionary, whose prophecies led to her execution under Henry VIII, has been the source of a historical controversy which resolves itself into the question: Was she gifted with supernatural knowledge or was she an impostor? In 1525, when nineteen years of age, being then employed as a domestic servant at Aldington, Kent, she had an illness, during which she fell into frequent trances and told "wondrously things done in other places whilst she was neither herself present nor yet heard no report thereof". From the first her utterances assumed a religious character and were "of marvellous holiness in rebuke of sin and vice". Her parish priest, Richard Masters, convinced of her sincerity, reported the matter to the Archbishop of Canterbury, who sent a commission of three Canterbury Benedictines, Bocking, Hadleigh, and Barnes, two Franciscans, Hugh Rich and Richard Risby, a diocesan official, and the parish priest to examine her again. Shortly after this commission pronounced in her favour, her prediction that the Blessed Virgin would cure her at a certain chapel was fulfilled, when in presence of a large crowd she was restored to health. She then became a Benedictine nun, living near Canterbury, with a great reputation for holiness. Her fame gradually spread until she came into wide public notice. She protested "in the name and by the authority of God" against the king's projected divorce. To further her opposition, besides writing to the pope she had interviews with Fisher, Wolsey, and the king himself. Owing to her reputation for sanctity she proved one of the most formidable opponents of the royal divorce, so that in 1533 Cromwell took steps against her, and after examination by Cranmer she was in November, with Dr. Bocking, her confessor, and others, committed to the Tower. Subsequently all the prisoners were made to do public penance at St. Paul's and at Canterbury and to publish confessions of deception and fraud.

In January, 1534, a bill of attainder was framed against her and thirteen of her sympathizers, among whom were Fisher and More. Except the latter, whose name was withdrawn, all were condemned under this bill; seven including Bocking, Masters, Rich, Risby, and Elizabeth herself being sentenced to death, while Fisher and five others were condemned to imprisonment and forfeiture of goods. Elizabeth and her companions were executed at Tyburn on 20 April, 1534, when she is said to have repeated her confession. Protestant authors allege that these confessions alone are conclusive of her imposture, but Catholic writers, though they have felt free to hold divergent opinions about the nun, have pointed out the suggestive fact that all that is known as to these confessions emanates from Cromwell or his agents; that all available documents are on his side; that the confession issued as hers is on the face of it not her own composition; that she and her companions were never brought to trial, but were condemned and executed unheard; that there is contemporary evidence that the alleged confession was even then believed to be a forgery. For these reasons the matter cannot be considered as settled, and unfortunately the difficulty of arriving at any satisfactory and final decision now seems insuperable.

Act of Attainder, 25 *Henry VIII*, cap. *xii*; Wright, *Suppression of the Monasteries*; Gairdner, *Letters and Papers of Henry VIII* for 1533–4; Lee in *Dict. Nat. Biog.*, III, 343; Gasquet, *Henry VIII and the Eng. Monasteries* (1889), I, iii; Bridgett, *Life of Fisher* (1890), xi; Idem, *Life of More* (1892), xvii.

Edwin Burton.

Baruch (Heb. ברוך, *Bārûkh*, blessed, Benedict; Sept. Βαρούχ), I. Baruch, the disciple of Jeremias, and the traditional author of the deutero-canonical book, which bears his name. He was the son of Nerias (Jer., xxxii, 12, 16; xxxvi, 4, 8, 32; Bar., i, 1), and most probably the brother of Saraias, chief chamberlain to King Sedecias (Jer., xxxii, 12; li, 59; Bar., i, 1). After the Temple of Jerusalem had been plundered by Nabuchodonosor (599 B. C.), he wrote under the dictation of Jeremias the oracles of that great prophet, foretelling the return of the Babylonians, and read them at the risk of his life in the hearing of the Jewish people. He wrote also the second and enlarged edition of the prophecies of Jeremias after the first had been burned by the infuriated king, Joakim (Jer., xxxvi). Throughout his life he remained true to the teachings and ideals of the great prophet, although he seems at times to have given way to feelings of despondency, and perhaps even of personal ambition (cf. Jer., xlv). He was with Jeremias during the last siege of Jerusalem, and witnessed the purchase by the prophet of his ancestral estate in Anathoth (Jer., xxxii). After the fall of the Holy City and the ruin of the Temple (588 B. c.) Baruch lived probably for some time with Jeremias at Masphath. His enemies accused him of having prompted the prophet to advise the Jews to remain in Juda, instead of going down into Egypt, as they were contemplating. In consequence, he was carried, together with his master, to Egypt (Jer., xliii), where, according to a Hebrew tradition preserved by St. Jerome (In Isai., xxx, 6, 7), both died before Nabuchodonosor invaded that country. This tradition, however, conflicts with the data found in the opening chapter of the Prophecy of Baruch, wherein we are told of Baruch writing his book in Babylonia, reading it publicly in the fifth year after the burning of the Holy City, and apparently being sent to Jerusalem by the Jewish captives with sacred vessels and gifts destined to the sacrificial service in Yahweh's Temple. It conflicts likewise with various traditions, both Jewish and Christian, which perhaps contain some particles of truth, but which do not allow us to determine the date, place, or manner of Baruch's death, with anything like probability.

In the Catholic Bible "the Prophecy of Baruch" is made up of six chapters, the last of which bears the special title of an "Epistle of Jeremias", and does not belong to the book proper. The Prophecy opens with an historical introduction (i, 1–14), stating first (1–2) that the book was written by Baruch at Babylon in the fifth year after Jerusalem had been burned by the Chaldeans, and next (vv. 3–14) that it was read in an assembly of King Jechonias and other Babylonian exiles upon whom it produced the most beneficial effects. The first section in the body of the book (i, 15; iii, 8) contains a twofold confession of the sins which led to the exile (i, 15—ii, 5; ii, 6–13), together with a prayer that God may at length forgive His people (ii, 14; iii, 8). While the foregoing section has much in common with the Book of Daniel (Dan., ix, 4–19), Baruch's second section (iii, 9; iv, 4) closely resembles passages in Job, xxviii, xxxviii. It is a beautiful panegyric of that Divine Wisdom which is nowhere found except in the Law given to Israel; only in the guise of the Law has Wisdom appeared on the earth and become accessible to man; let, therefore, Israel prove faithful again to the Law. The last section of the Book of Baruch extends from iv, 5 to v, 9. It is made up of four odes, each beginning with the expression, "Take courage" (iv, 5, 21, 27, 30), and of a psalm closely connected with the eleventh of the apocryphal Psalms of Solomon (iv, 36; v, 9). Chapter vi contains as an appendix to the whole book "The Epistle of Jeremias", sent by that prophet "to them that were to be led away captives into Babylon" by Nabuchodonosor. Because of their sins they were to be removed to Babylon and to remain there "for a long time, even to seven generations". In that heathen city they would witness the gorgeous worship paid to "gods of gold, and of silver, and of stone, and of wood", but should not conform to it. All such gods, it is argued in various ways, are powerless and perishable works of man's hand; they can do neither harm nor good; so that they are not gods at all.

It is certain that this sixth chapter of Baruch is truly distinct from the rest of the work. Not only its special title, "The Epistle of Jeremias", but also its style and contents clearly prove that it is a writing wholly independent of the Prophecy of Baruch. Again, while some Greek MSS. that have Baruch have not the "Epistle", others, among the best, have it separate from the Book of Baruch and immediately before the Lamentations of Jeremias. The fact that the sixth chapter of Baruch bears the title, "The Epistle of Jeremias", has been, and is still in the eyes of many, a decisive reason for holding the

time-honoured view that that great prophet is its author. It is also urged that the vivid and accurate description of the splendid, but infamous, worship of the Babylonian gods in Baruch, vi, makes for the traditional authorship, since Jer., xiii, 5, 6, probably speaks of the twofold journey of Jeremias to the Euphrates. Finally it is affirmed that a certain number of Hebraisms can be traced back to a Hebrew original point in the same direction. Over against this traditional view, most contemporary critics argue that the Greek style of Baruch, vi, proves that it was originally written not in Hebrew, but in Greek, and that consequently Jeremias is not the author of the Epistle ascribed to him. For this and for other reasons suggested by the study of the contents of Baruch, vi, they think that St. Jerome was decidedly correct when he called this writing Ψευδεπί-γραφος, that is, inscribed with a false name. However this may be, an impartial study of the Canon of Holy Writ proves that, despite the assertions of Protestants to the contrary, Baruch, vi, has always been recognized by the Church as an inspired work.

With regard to the original language of the Book of Baruch proper (chaps. i–v), a variety of opinions prevail among contemporary scholars. Naturally enough, those who simply abide by the title which ascribes the Book to Baruch, admit that the whole work was originally written in Hebrew. On the contrary, most of those who question or reject the correctness of that title think that this writing was totally, or at least partially, composed in Greek. It is indeed true that the Greek literary features of the various sections do not point back with equal force to a Hebrew original. Yet, it can hardly be doubted that the whole of Baruch proper in its extant Greek form looks like a translation. The linguistic evidence is also confirmed by the following considerations: (1) It is highly probable that Theodotion (end of the second century of our era) translated the Book of Baruch from a Hebrew original. (2) There are some marginal notes of the Syro-Hexaplar text stating that a few words in the Greek "are not found in the Hebrew". (3) Baruch, i, 14, says that the book was meant to be read publicly in the Temple; hence it must have been composed in Hebrew for that purpose. Besides this unity as regards its original language, Baruch presents a certain unity in point of subject-matter, so that most of those who maintain that the whole work was primitively written in Hebrew admit also its unity of composition. There are, however, in the Book of Baruch many traces of the compilatory process whereby its various parts were apparently brought together. The difference in literary form between i–iii, 8, on the one hand and iii, 9–5, is very great indeed, and, taken together with the abrupt manner in which the panegyric on Wisdom is introduced at iii, 9, suggests a difference with respect to origin. The two confessions of the sins which led to the exile in i, 15; iii, 8, are put side by side without any natural transition. The literary differences between iii, 9—iv, 4, and iv, 5—v, 9, are considerable, and the beginning of the third section at iv, 5, is no less abrupt than that of the second at iii, 9. Again, the historical introduction seems to have been composed as a preface to only i, 15—ii, 5. In view of these and other such facts, contemporary critics generally think that the work is the outcome of a compilatory process, and that its unity is due to the final editor, who put together the various documents which obviously bore upon the exile. Such a literary method of composition does not necessarily conflict with the traditional authorship of the Book of Baruch. Many of the sacred writers of the Bible were compilers, and Baruch may, and, according to the Catholic scholars who admit the compilatory character of the work inscribed to him, must, be numbered among them. The grounds of Catholics for this view are chiefly three: (1) The book is ascribed to Baruch by its title; (2) it has always been regarded as Baruch's work by tradition; (3) its contents present nothing that would be later than Baruch's time, or that should be regarded as foreign to the style and manner of that faithful disciple and secretary of Jeremias. Over against this view, non-Catholics argue: (1) That its ultimate basis is simply the title of the book; (2) that this title itself is not in harmony with the historical and literary contents of the work; and (3) that those contents, when impartially examined, point to a much later compiler than Baruch; in fact some of them go so far as to ascribe the composition of the book to a writer living after A. D. 70. Catholics easily disprove this last date for the Book of Baruch; but they do not so easily dispose of the serious difficulties that have been raised against their own ascription of the whole work to Baruch. Their answers are considered as sufficient by Catholic scholars generally. Should any one, however, judge them inadequate, and therefore consider the Book of Baruch as the work of a later editor, the inspired character of the book would still remain, provided this later editor himself be regarded as inspired in his work of compilation. That the Book of Baruch is "a sacred and canonical" writing has been defined by the Council of Trent; that it has just as much right to be held "inspired of God" as any other book of Holy Writ can readily be shown by a close study of the Canon of the Bible. Its Latin rendering in our Vulgate goes back to the old Latin version anterior to St. Jerome, and is tolerably literal from the Greek text.

II. BARUCH, the son of Zachai, who helped to rebuild the wall of Jerusalem (II Esd., iii, 20).

III. BARUCH, a priest who signed the renewed Covenant after the Exile; perhaps the same as the foregoing (II Esd., x, 6).

IV. BARUCH, one of the children of Juda who settled in Jerusalem after the Captivity (II Esd., xi, 5).

Commentaries by FRITZSCHE (1851); REUSCH (1853); REUSS AND LOCH (1870); TROCHON (1878); KNEUCKER (1879); BISSEL (1885); KNABENBAUER (1891); REUSS (1894); ZÖCKLER (1891).

Introductions of S. DAVIDSON (1863); VIGOUROUX (1880); KAULEN (1890); TROCHON (1890); CORNELY (1897); GIGOT (1906).

FRANCIS E. GIGOT.

Baruch, APOCALYPSE OF. See APOCRYPHA.

Basedow, JOHANN BERNHARD. See PHILANTHROPINISM.

Basil, CONFESSION OF. See CREEDS.

Basil, LITURGY OF SAINT.—Several Oriental liturgies, or at least several anaphoras, have been attributed to the great St. Basil, Bishop of Cæsarea in Cappadocia from 370 to 379. That St. Basil composed a liturgy, or rather reformed an existing liturgy, is beyond doubt, since besides the constant tradition of the Byzantine Church there are many testimonies in ancient writings to establish the fact. In a treatise on the tradition of the Divine liturgy attributed to St. Proclus, Patriarch of Constantinople (434–466), it is stated that when St. Basil noticed the slothfulness and degeneracy of men, how they were wearied by the length of the liturgy, he shortened it in order to cure their sloth (P. G., LXV, 849). More certain testimony to the existence of a liturgical text which went under the name of St. Basil is given in a letter of Peter the Deacon, one of the Scythian monks sent to Rome to settle certain dogmatic questions. Writing about the year 520 to the African bishops in exile in Sardinia, Peter, an Oriental, mentions a Liturgy of St. Basil, which was known and used throughout the entire East, and even quotes a passage from it: "Hence, also, Blessed Basil, Bishop of Cæsaria, in a prayer of the holy altar, with which almost the entire East is familiar, says

among other things: Grant us, O Lord, Thy strength and protection; make the evil good and preserve the just in their righteousness. For Thou canst do all things and there is no one who may oppose Thee; for when Thou desirest, Thou savest, and no one resists Thy will." (P. L., LXV, 449.)

Leontius of Byzantium, writing about the middle of the sixth century, censures Theodore of Mopsuestia because he was not content with the liturgies handed down by the Fathers to the churches, but composed a Mass of his own, showing, thereby, no reverence either for that of the Apostles, or for that composed in the same spirit by the great St. Basil (P. G., LXXXVI, 1368). The Quinisext, or Trullan Council (692), in its thirty-second canon draws an argument from the written liturgy of the archbishop of the church of the Cæsareans, St. Basil, whose glory has spread through the whole world (Mansi, Coll. Conc., XI, 958). Finally, in the Barberini library there is a manuscript of the latter part of the eighth, or the early part of the ninth, century which contains a Greek liturgy entitled the "Liturgy of St. Basil".

It is not known precisely just what the nature of the Basilian reform was, nor what liturgy served as the basis of the saint's work. Very probably he shortened and changed somewhat the liturgy of his own diocese, which was akin to the Liturgy of St. James. In later times it underwent some development, so that with our present knowledge of its history it would be almost impossible to reconstruct it as it came from the pen of the Bishop of Cæsarea. According to the tradition of the Greek Orthodox Church, their liturgy is practically the work of St. Basil, due allowance being made for changes and amelioration in the course of time. This is older than either of the other two Byzantine liturgies, and is mentioned under the name of St. Basil in ancient times as if it were then the normal liturgy. Of the anaphoras attributed to St. Basil the Syriac and Armenian are probably derived from the Byzantine Greek with some modifications. The Abyssinian is a translation of the Coptic, while the Coptic, Arabic, and Greek Egyptian liturgies are substantially the same. These Egyptian anaphoras of St. Basil are different from the Cæsarean or Byzantine liturgy, and do not possess all the characteristics of the Alexandrian Rite, but appear rather to be modelled on the Syrian type, so they are probably an importation into Egypt. The Greek Egyptian contains several prayers (identical with those in the Byzantine liturgy) expressly ascribed to St. Basil, and from these it may derive its title.

The Cæsarean or Byzantine Liturgy is used in the countries which were evangelized from Constantinople, or which came under its influence for any considerable period. It is used, for example, by the Orthodox and Uniat Greek churches in the Orient, as well as by the Greek communities in Italy and Sicily. Translated into the Old Slavonic it is used by Orthodox and Uniat Catholics in Russia and in some parts of the Austrian Empire; translated into Georgian and Rumanian it is used respectively in Georgia and Rumania. It has also been translated into several other languages and dialects for use in the Russian dependencies and where the Russian Church has missions, as well as into Arabic for use in Syria. Since the Liturgy of St. John Chrysostom has become the normal liturgy of the Greek Church, that of St. Basil is now used only on the Sundays of Lent with the exception of Palm Sunday, on Holy Thursday and Holy Saturday, on the vigils of Christmas and of the Epiphany, and on the feast of St. Basil, which in the Greek calendar occurs on the first day of January.

The liturgy may be divided into the Mass of the catechumens and the Mass of the faithful. The first contains the prayers of the prothesis, of the antiphons, of the little entrance, and of the trisagion, the lessons, and the prayers of the ectenes and of the catechumens. The Mass of the faithful begins with the two prayers of the faithful, and contains the prayer of the great entrance, the prayer of the Offertory, which is expressly ascribed to St. Basil, the kiss of peace, the Creed, and the Anaphora. The Anaphora proper, starting with the Eucharistic Preface followed by the Sanctus, embraces the preparatory prayers for the Consecration, the Consecration itself, the Epiclesis or invocation of the Holy Ghost, the Great Intercession for the living and the dead, the Lord's Prayer, the inclination, Elevation, Communion, thanksgiving, and dismissal.

GOAR, Εὐχολόγιον sive rituale græcorum (Venice, 1730); BRIGHTMAN, Liturgies Eastern and Western (Oxford, 1906) I, prints the Barberini MS., p. 309, the prayers of the modern liturgy, p. 400. Tr. will be found in: BRETT, A Collection of the Principal Liturgies (London, 1838), and SWAINSON, The Greek Liturgies (Cambridge, 1884); NEALE, History of the Holy Eastern Church (London, 1850); PROBST, Liturgie des vierten Jahrhunderts und deren Reform (Münster, 1893); RENAUDOT, Liturgiarum orientalium collectio (Frankfort, 1847).

J. F. GOGGIN.

Basil, RULE OF SAINT,—I. Under the name of Basilians are included all the religious who follow the Rule of St. Basil. The monasteries of such religious have never possessed the hierarchical organization which ordinarily exists in the houses of an order properly so called. Only a few houses were formerly grouped into congregations or are to-day so combined. St. Basil drew up his Rule for the members of the monastery he founded about 356 on the banks of the Iris in Cappadocia. Before forming this community St. Basil visited Egypt, Palestine, Cœlesyria, and Mesopotamia in order to see for himself the manner of life led by the monks in these countries. St. Gregory of Nazianzus, who shared the retreat, aided Basil by his advice and experience. The Rule of Basil is divided into two parts: the "Greater Monastic Rules" (Regulæ fusius tractatæ, Migne, P. G., XXXI, 889–1052), and the "Lesser Rules" (Regulæ brevius tractatæ, ibid, 1051–1306). Rufinus who translated them into Latin united the two into a single Rule under the name of "Regulæ sancti Basilii episcopi Cappadociæ ad monachos" (P. L., CIII, 483–554); this Rule was followed by some western monasteries. For a long time the Bishop of Cæsarea was wrongly held to be the author of a work on monasticism called "Constitutiones monasticæ" (P. G., XXXI, 1315–1428). In his Rule St. Basil follows a catechetical method; the disciple asks a question to which the master replies. He limits himself to laying down indisputable principles which will guide the superiors and monks in their conduct. He sends his monks to the Sacred Scriptures; in his eyes the Bible is the basis of all monastic legislation, the true Rule. The questions refer generally to the virtues which the monks should practise and the vices they should avoid. The greater number of the replies contain a verse or several verses of the Bible accompanied by a comment which defines the meaning. The most striking qualities of the Basilian Rule are its prudence and its wisdom. It leaves to the superiors the care of settling the many details of local, individual, and daily life; it does not determine the material exercise of the observance or the administrative regulations of the monastery. Poverty, obedience, renunciation, and self-abnegation are the virtues which St. Basil makes the foundation of the monastic life.

As he gave it, the Rule could not suffice for anyone who wished to organize a monastery, for it takes this work as an accomplished fact. The life of the Cappadocian monks could not be reconstructed from his references to the nature and number of the meals and to the garb of the inmates. The superiors

had for guide a tradition accepted by all the monks. This tradition was enriched as time went on by the decisions of councils, by the ordinances of the Emperors of Constantinople, and by the regulations of a number of revered abbots. Thus there arose a body of law by which the monasteries were regulated. Some of these laws were accepted by all, others were observed only by the houses of some one country, while there were regulations which applied only to certain communities. In this regard Oriental monasticism bears much resemblance to that of the West; a great variety of observances is noticeable. The existence of the Rule of St. Basil formed a principle of unity.

II. THE MONASTERIES OF THE EAST.—The monasteries of Cappadocia were the first to accept the Rule of St. Basil; it afterwards spread gradually to all the monasteries of the East. Those of Armenia, Chaldea, and of the Syrian countries in general preferred instead of the Rule of St. Basil those observances which were known among them as the Rule of St. Anthony. Neither the ecclesiastical nor the imperial authority was exerted to make conformity to the Basilian Rule universal. It is therefore impossible to tell the epoch at which it acquired the supremacy in the religious communities of the Greek world; but the date is probably an early one. The development of monasticism was, in short, the cause of its diffusion. Protected by the emperors and patriarchs the monasteries increased rapidly in number. In 536 the Diocese of Constantinople contained no less than sixty-eight, that of Chalcedon forty, and these numbers continually increased. Although monasticism was not able to spread in all parts of the empire with equal rapidity, yet what it probably must have been may be inferred from these figures. These monks took an active part in the ecclesiastical life of their time; they had a share in all the quarrels, both theological and other, and were associated with all the works of charity. Their monasteries were places of refuge for studious men. Many of the bishops and patriarchs were chosen from their ranks. Their history is interwoven, therefore, with that of the Oriental Churches. They gave to the preaching of the Gospel its greatest apostles. As a result monastic life gained a footing at the same time as Christianity among all the races won to the Faith. The position of the monks in the empire was one of great power, and their wealth helped to increase their influence. Thus their development ran a course parallel to that of their Western brethren. The monks, as a rule, followed the theological vicissitudes of the emperors and patriarchs, and they showed no notable independence except during the iconoclastic persecution; the stand they took in this aroused the anger of the imperial controversialists. The Faith had its martyrs among them; many of them were condemned to exile, and some took advantage of this condemnation to reorganize their religious life in Italy.

Of all the monasteries of this period the most celebrated was that of St. John the Baptist of Studium, founded at Constantinople in the fifth century. It acquired its fame in the time of the iconoclastic persecution while it was under the government of the saintly *Hegumenos* (abbot) Theodore, called the Studite. Nowhere did the heretical emperors meet with more courageous resistance. At the same time the monastery was an active centre of intellectual and artistic life and a model which exercised considerable influence on monastic observances in the East. Further details may be found in "Prescriptio constitutionis monasterii Studii" (Migne, P. G., XCIX, 1703–20), and the monastery's "Canones de confessione et pro peccatis satisfactione" (ibid, 1721–30). Theodore attributed the observances followed by his monks to his uncle, the saintly Abbot Plato, who first introduced them in his monastery of Saccudium. The other monasteries, one after another, adopted them, and they are still followed by the monks of Mount Athos. The monastery of Mount Athos was founded towards the close of the tenth century through the aid of the Emperor Basil the Macedonian and became the largest and most celebrated of all the monasteries of the Orient; it is in reality a monastic province. The monastery of Mount Olympus in Bithynia should also be mentioned, although it was never as important as the other. The monastery of St. Catherine on Mount Sinai, which goes back to the early days of monasticism, had a great fame and is still occupied by monks. Reference to Oriental monks must here be limited to those who have left a mark upon ecclesiastical literature: Leontius of Byzantium (d. 543), author of a treatise against the Nestorians and Eutychians; St. Sophronius, Patriarch of Jerusalem, one of the most vigorous adversaries of the Monothelite heresy (P. G., LXXXVII, 3147-4014); St. Maximus the Confessor, Abbot of Chrysopolis (d. 662), the most brilliant representative of Byzantine monasticism in the seventh century; in his writings and letters St. Maximus steadily combated the partisans of the erroneous doctrines of Monothelitism (ibid, XC and XCI); St. John Damascene, who may perhaps be included among the Basilians; St. Theodore the Studite (d. 829), the defender of the veneration of sacred images; his works include theological, ascetic, hagiographical, liturgical, and historical writings (P. G., XCIX). The Byzantine monasteries furnish a long line of historians who were also monks: John Malalas, whose "Chronographia" (P. G., XCVII, 9–190) served as a model for Eastern chroniclers; Georgius Syncellus, who wrote a "Selected Chronographia"; his friend and disciple Theophanes (d. 817), Abbot of the "Great Field" near Cyzicus, the author of another "Chronographia" (P. G., CVIII); the Patriarch Nicephorus, who wrote (815–829) an historical "Breviarium" (a Byzantine history), and an "Abridged Chronographia" (P. G., C, 879–991); George the Monk, whose Chronicle stops at A. D. 842 (P. G., CX). There were, besides, a large number of monks, hagiographers, hymnologists, and poets who had a large share in the development of the Greek Liturgy. Among the authors of hymns may be mentioned: St. Maximus the Confessor; St. Theodore the Studite; St. Romanus the Melodist; St. Andrew of Crete; St. John Damascene; Cosmas of Jerusalem, and St. Joseph the Hymnographer. Fine penmanship and the copying of manuscripts were held in honour among the Basilians. Among the monasteries which excelled in the art of copying were the Studium, Mount Athos, the monastery of the Isle of Patmos and that of Rossano in Sicily; the tradition was continued later by the monastery of Grotta Ferrara near Rome. These monasteries, and others as well, were studios of religious art where the monks toiled to produce miniatures in the manuscripts, paintings, and goldsmith work. The triumph of orthodoxy over the iconoclastic heresy infused an extraordinary enthusiasm into this branch of their labours.

From the beginning the Oriental Churches often took their patriarchs and bishops from the monasteries. Later, when the secular clergy was recruited largely from among married men, this custom became almost universal, for, as the episcopal office could not be conferred upon men who were married, it developed, in a way, into a privilege of the religious who had taken the vow of celibacy. Owing to this the monks formed a class apart, corresponding to the upper clergy of the Western Churches; this gave and still gives a preponderating influence to the monasteries themselves. In some of them theological instruction is given both to clerics and to laymen. As long as the spirit of proselytism existed in the East the monasteries furnished the Church with all its missionaries. The names of two have been inscribed by Rome in its calendar of annual feasts, namely, St. Cyril and St. Methodius, the Apostles of the Slavs. The Byzantine schism did not change sensibly the position of the Basilian monks and monasteries. Their sufferings arose through the Mohammedan conquest. To a large number of them this conquest brought complete ruin, especially to those monasteries in what is now Turkey in Asia and the region around Constantinople. In the East the convents for women adopted the Rule of St. Basil and had constitutions copied from those of the Basilian monks.

III. Schismatic Basilians.—The two best known monasteries of the schismatic Basilians are those of Mount Athos and of Mount Sinai. Besides these there are still many monasteries in Turkey in Asia, of which 10 are in Jerusalem alone, 1 at Bethlehem, and 4 at Jericho. They are also numerous on the islands of the Ægean Sea: Chios 3, Samos 6, Crete about 50, Cyprus 11. In Old Cairo is the monastery of St. George. In Greece where there were formerly 400 monasteries, there were, in 1832, only 82, which by 1904 had increased to 169; 9 Basilian convents for women are now in existence in Greece. In Rumania there are 22 monasteries; in Servia 44, with only about 118 monks; in Bulgaria 78, with 193 inmates. Montenegro has 11 monasteries and about 15 monks; Bosnia 3 and Herzegovina 11. In Dalmatia are 11 monasteries and in Bukowina 3. Hungary has 25 monasteries and 5 branch houses. The schismatic monks are much more numerous in Russia; in this country, besides, they have the most influence and possess the richest monasteries. Nowhere else has the monastic life been so closely interwoven with the national existence. The most celebrated monasteries are Pescherskoi at Kieff and Troïtsa at Moscow; mention may also be made of the monasteries of Solovesk, Novgorod, Pskof, Tver, and Vladimir. Russia has about 9,000 monks and 429 monasteries. There is no diocese which has not at least one religious house. The monasteries are divided into those having state subventions and monasteries which do not receive such aid.

IV. Catholic Basilians.—A certain number of Basilian monasteries were always in communion with the Holy See. Among these were the houses founded in Sicily and Italy. The monastery of Rossano, founded by St. Nilus the Younger, remained for a long time faithful to the best literary traditions of Constantinople. The monasteries of San Salvatore of Messina and San Salvatore of Otranto may be mentioned; the monastery of Grotta Ferrata was also celebrated. The emigration of the Greeks to the West after the fall of Constantinople and the union with Rome, concluded at the Council of Florence, gave a certain prestige to these communities. Cardinal Bessarion, who was Abbot of Grotta Ferrata, sought to stimulate the intellectual life of the Basilians by means of the literary treasures which their libraries contained.

A number of Catholic communities continued to exist in the East. The Holy See caused them to be united into congregations, namely: St. Saviour, founded in 1715, which includes 8 monasteries and 21 hospices with about 250 monks; the congregation of Aleppo with 4 monasteries and 2 hospices; that of the Baladites (Valadites) with 4 monasteries and 3 hospices. These last two congregations have their houses in the district of Mount Lebanon. St. Josaphat and Father Rutski, who laboured to bring back the Ruthenian Churches into Catholic unity, reformed the Basilians of Lithuania. They began with the monastery of the Holy Trinity at Vilna (1607). The monastery of Byten, founded in 1613, was the citadel of the union in Lithuania. Other houses adopted the reform or were founded by the reformed monks. On 19 July, 1617, the reformed monasteries were organized into a congregation under a proto-archimandrite, and known as the congregation of the Holy Trinity, or of Lithuania. The congregation increased with the growth of the union itself. The number of houses had risen to thirty at the time of the general chapter of 1636. After the Council of Zamosc the monasteries outside of Lithuania which had not joined the congregation of the Holy Trinity formed themselves into a congregation bearing the title of "Patrocinium [Protection] B. M. V." (1739). Benedict XIV desired (1744) to form one congregation out of these two, giving the new organization the name of the Ruthenian Order of St. Basil and dividing it into the two provinces of Lithuania and Courland. After the suppression of the Society of Jesus these religious took charge of the Jesuit colleges. The overthrow of Poland and the persecution instituted by the Russians against the Uniat Greeks was very unfavourable to the growth of the congregation, and the number of these Basilian monasteries greatly diminished. Leo XIII, by his Encyclical "Singulare præsidium" of 12 May, 1881, ordained a reform of the Ruthenian Basilians of Galicia. This reform began in the monastery of Dabromil; its members have gradually replaced the non-reformed in the monasteries of the region. They devote themselves, in connexion with the Uniat clergy, to the various labours of the apostolate which the moral condition of the different races in this district demands.

V. LATIN BASILIANS.—In the sixteenth century the Italian monasteries of this order were in the last stages of decay. Urged by Cardinal Sirlet Pope Gregory XIII ordained (1573) their union in a congregation under the control of a superior general. Use was made of the opportunity to separate the revenues of the abbeys from those of the monasteries. The houses of the Italian Basilians were divided into the three provinces of Sicily, Calabria, and Rome. Although the monks remained faithful in principle to the Greek Liturgy they showed an inclination towards the use of the Latin Liturgy; some monasteries have adopted the latter altogether. In Spain there was a Basilian congregation which had no traditional connexion with Oriental Basilians; the members followed the Latin Liturgy. Father Bernardo de la Cruz and the hermits of Santa María de Oviedo in the Diocese of Jaen formed the nucleus of the congregation. Pope Pius VI added them to the followers of St. Basil, and they were affiliated with the monastery of Grotta Ferrata (1561). The monasteries of Turdon and of Valle de Guillos, founded by Father Mateo de la Fuente, were for a time united with this congregation but they withdrew later in order to form a separate congregation (1603) which increased very little, having only four monasteries and a hospice at Seville. The other Basilians, who followed a less rigorous observance, showed more growth; their monasteries were formed into the two provinces of Castile and Andalusia. They were governed by a vicar general and were under the control, at least nominally, of a superior general of the order. Each of their provinces had its college or scholasticate at Salamanca and Seville. They did not abstain from wine. Like their brethren in Italy they wore a cowl similar to that of the Benedictines; this led to recriminations and processes, but they were authorized by Rome to continue the use of this attire. Several writers are to be found among them, as: Alfonso Clavel, the historiographer of the order; Diego Niceno, who has left sermons and ascetic writings; Luis de los Angelos, who issued a work on "Instructions for Novices" (Seville, 1615), and also translated into Spanish Cardinal Bessarion's exposition of the Rule of St. Basil; Felipe de la Cruz, who wrote a treatise

on money loaned at interest, that was published at Madrid in 1637, and one on tithes, published at Madrid in 1634. The Spanish Basilians were suppressed with the other orders in 1833 and have not been re-established. At Annonay in France a religious community of men was formed (1822) under the Rule of St. Basil, which has a branch at Toronto, Canada. (See BASILIANS, PRIESTS OF THE COMMUNITY OF ST. BASIL.)

BESSE, *Les moines d'Orient* (Paris, 1900); MARTIN, *Les moines de Constantinople* (Paris, 1897); GUÉPIN, *Un apôtre de l'union des églises au XVIIᵉ siècle, St. Josaphat* (Paris, 1897), LEROY-BEAULIEU *La religion* in *L'empire des Tsars et les Russes* (Paris, 1889) III; CLAVEL, *Antigüedad de la religión y regla de san Basilio* (Madrid, 1645); HÉLYOT, *Histoire des ordres monastiques*, I; HEIMBUCHER, *Die Orden und Kongregationen*, I, 44–47; MINIASI, *San Nilo* (Naples, 1892); RODOTÀ; *Origine, progresso e stato attuale del rito greco in Italia* (Rome, 1755); SILBERNAGL-SCHNITZER, *Verfassung*, etc., in *Kirchen des Orients* (Munich, 1905); MILASCH-PESSIĆ, *Kirchenrecht d. morgene. Kirche* (2nd ed., Mostar, 1905).

J. M. BESSE.

Basilians (PRIESTS OF THE COMMUNITY OF ST. BASIL).—During the French Revolution, Mgr. d'Aviau, the last Archbishop of Vienne, saw his clergy diminish so rapidly through persecution, that only about one-third of them remained, with no recruits to replace them. It was impossible to maintain a college or a seminary, so in 1800 he founded a school in the almost inaccessible little village of St. Symphorien de Mahun, in the mountains of the Vivarais. This institution was placed in the charge of Father Lapierre, who had managed to take care of the parish of St. Symphorien during this period of persecution. His assistant was Father Marie Joseph Actorie, who had been professor of philosophy in the seminary of Die before the Revolution. In spite of its humble beginning and the many dangers to which it was exposed, the school prospered. In 1802, the state of the country had improved to such an extent that concealment was no longer necessary, and Father Picansel, parish priest of Annonay, and vicar general of the diocese, succeeded in obtaining from the municipal authorities of that town the lease of a former Franciscan monastery, to which the school was transferred. For many years the school performed the work which the bishop had expected from it, but the long fight against poverty and the persecution of so-called liberals threatened at last to be too much for those in charge. Some other method had to be tried, and in 1822, the professors asked to be permitted to found a religious community, with the college at Annonay for its mother-house. The Bishop of Viviers, in whose diocese the town of Annonay was included, granted the necessary permission, and appointed a commission to draw up a rule for the new society. On 21 November, 1822, the ten members who were at the time the teaching staff of the college, made the promise which bound them temporarily to the work. They were, Fathers Lapierre, Duret, Vallon, Polly, Tourvieille, Tracol, Martinèche, Fayolle, Payan, and Pages.

In 1837 a constitution was drawn up and sent to Rome for approval. By this the members of the society were to be bound by the simple vows of poverty, obedience, chastity, and stability. The vow of poverty, however, was limited. Each member of the community could retain all his own property and his Mass intentions, and was to receive a small salary from the community. By his vow he could not accumulate and increase his possessions, but had to spend all his salary and the annual income from his property, and this included the prohibition of speculation or any other worldly moneymaking. The community was to be under the direction of a superior general, residing at Annonay, in the Diocese of Viviers, France. The aim of the society was to be the education of Catholic youth, especially of such as intended to become priests. This constitution was signed by several French bishops, all of whom had been able to appreciate the work done by the community, and to testify to the piety and zeal of its members. The Holy See was pleased to declare the society worthy of praise, and in 1863 Pius IX confirmed this decree, granting at the same time certain privileges and imposing certain restrictions on the possessions of the community. A few years ago, the constitutions were again sent to Rome, but the Holy See wished to make some changes in the administration of the community, and these are now being tested with a view to their final approval. When the recent decree banishing religious orders from France was put in force, the Basilians had colleges in Annonay, Périgueux, Aubenas, Privas, and Vernoux, in France; Blidah and Bone in Algiers; and Plymouth in England. All these, with the exception of the last, were transferred to seculars or confiscated,

the commercial, the classical, and the philosophical. Among the more prominent of those who made their studies, either partially or entirely, at St. Michael's were the Archbishop of Toronto and the Bishops of Hamilton, Peterborough, London, and Sault Ste. Marie in Canada, and Albany and Columbus in the United States.

The American Province includes four other colleges and numerous parishes. The colleges are Assumption College, Sandwich, Canada; St. Basil's College, Waco; St. Thomas's College, Houston, and St. Mary's Seminary, La Porte, in Texas. Of the parishes in charge of the Basilians, the most important are, St. Basil's and the Holy Rosary, Toronto, Sandwich, Amherstburg, and Owen Sound in Canada, and St. Anne's, Detroit. The novitiate of the community and the scholasticate are in Toronto. The novitiate lasts for one year, after which the members remain under

INTERIOR OF SANT' APOLLINARE NUOVO, RAVENNA

and the religious obliged to scatter until more favourable times.

In 1852, Mgr. de Charbonnel, Bishop of Toronto, Canada, requested the Basilians to found a college in his diocese. Accordingly, a small number were sent there, and opened a school which has developed into the present St. Michael's College, the headquarters of the Basilians in America. It was opened in a small house, but was soon moved to a wing of the bishop's palace which had been built for the purpose. In September, 1855, the cornerstone of the present building was laid. Since then various additions have been made, and the college is now able to accommodate a large number of students. The first superior was Father Soulerin, who managed the college from 1852 to 1865, when he was elected superior general of his community. St. Michael's is federated with the University of Toronto, its president is ex officio a member of the Senate of the university and of the university council, and it also appoints two other representatives to the senate. There are three courses of study open to its students,

temporal vows for three years. As no one can enter the society who does not intend to become a priest, the final vows are not taken until the subdiaconate, so that, if at the end of three years the scholastic is not ready for Holy orders, he renews his temporal vows. St. Basil's College, Waco, Texas, was founded in 1889. The course of studies includes both the commercial and classical departments. St. Thomas's College, Houston, Texas, was founded in 1900. It is a day school. St. Mary's Seminary, La Porte, Texas, was opened in October, 1901, by the Rt. Rev. N. A. Gallagher, Bishop of Galveston. Its primary object is the education of young men for the priesthood, but there is also maintained in connexion with the seminary a college in which boys and young men are prepared for any of the learned professions. It is under the direct supervision of the Bishop of Galveston.

J. C. PLOMER.

Basilica (στοὰ βασιλική, or βασίλειος) signifies a kingly, and secondarily a beautiful, hall. The name indicates the Eastern origin of the building, but it is in the West, above all in Rome, that the finest examples of the basilica are found. Between 184 and 121 B. C. there were built in the Forum at Rome the basilicas of Porcia, Fulvia, Sempronia, and Opimia; after 46 B. C. the great Basilica Julia of Cæsar and Augustus was erected. These buildings were designed to beautify the Forum and to be of use both for market purposes and for the administration of justice. They were open to the public and were well lighted. According to Vitruvius, who in this certainly agrees with Greek authorities, the usual construction of a basilica was the following:—

The ground plan was a parallelogram in which the width was not greater than one-half of the length and not less than one-third of it. When there was more space in the length, porticoes were built on the short sides. The middle space was separated by columns from a lower ambulatory or portico; the width of the ambulatory equalled the height of the columns and measured one-third of the width of the central space. Above the columns just mentioned stood others, giving entrance to light, which were shorter and slighter, in order that, as in organic structures, a tapering effect upwards should be given (De architecturâ, V, i, or ii). A basilica erected by Vitruvius himself showed a decided variation from this plan. It had two ambulatories, one above the other. Part of the columns of the middle space was left free so that light might enter. These columns rose up to the rafters. Pilasters leaning against the columns served to carry the flat roof of the ambulatories. The length of the middle nave was double its breadth and six times the breadth of the ambulatory. One of the long sides of the parallelogram spread out into an apse where legal cases were tried, but it was separated by the width of the ambulatory from the space for merchants (the ancient exchange).

The same writer speaks (VI, viii or v) of half-public basilicas in the houses of distinguished statesmen which served as council-chambers and for the settlement of disputes by arbitration. Vitruvius compares these (VI, v or iii) with the Egyptian halls because the latter had also covered ambulatories around a middle space supported by columns and openings for light between columns above. These are the distinctive features of a basilica which we may venture to define as an oblong structure with columns, having an ambulatory of lower height, receiving light from above, and possessing a projecting addition designed to serve a particular purpose.

The form of the basilica of the early Christian Church corresponds so exactly to the shape of the basilica of the Forum or of the house that it does not seem necessary to seek another model, as for instance, the *atrium* or the cemetery cells. The dark, narrow temple was entirely unsuited for the holding of the Christian church services. These services, which began with the Last Supper, were often held in large rooms in the dwellings of prosperous Christians. When these facts are considered it cannot be a matter of surprise that as early as the time of Constantine the style and name of the basilica seem to have been in common use for the Christian place of worship. Moreover, the chief deviations from the general type of the ancient basilica, such as five aisles, pillars, angular form of the apse, omission of the portico, etc., have been used as well in the Christian basilica to which the original meaning of the word *basilica*, "the hall of the king", could now again be applied.

As a rule, the building at this time was divided into three parts by columns, the well-lighted central part rose higher than the other divisions, and there was an apse. Only, in place of the former surrounding portico, or ambulatory, there was a side aisle to the right and left. There were also basilicas with five and seven aisles. The old construction of the basilica with an apse was well suited to the service of the altar. A transept extending more or less towards both sides was often placed between the nave and the apse both to serve practical needs and on account of its symbolism. The roofing of the

BASILICA OF CONSTANTINE, ROME

transept together with the apse and portico produced variety in the exterior of the basilica. Vaulting, in the West, was used only at times in the side aisles; nothing beyond a flat roof was ventured upon for the very broad middle nave, and often, at the beginning, the rafters of the roof were left uncovered.

It was only after the fifth century that round or square side-towers came into use. These towers were first incorporated in the main building in Syria. The early Christian basilica showed a high, yet light construction, and was roomy and well lighted. The arcades with slender columns which led up to the altar were a particularly beautiful feature. The round form of the arches, of the window-heads, and the ground plan of the basilica were the first indications of the Romanesque style. The idea of a room in which the King of Kings gave audience naturally led to rich ornamentation. The back wall of the apse and the "arch of triumph", which opened into the transept, were decorated with mosaics. The altar stood in or before, the apse under a decorated baldacchino (ciborium). The walls were often adorned with pictures, and the floor was made of mosaic. Much use was made in the rich churches of beautiful woven stuffs and of fine goldsmith-work. If the employment of these symbols had a tendency to inspire pride, other observances produced humility of mind, as, for example, the symbolic washing at the fountain. G. GIETMANN.

Basilici Libri. See ROMAN LAW.

Basilides, the earliest of the Alexandrian Gnostics; he was a native of Alexandria and flourished under the Emperors Adrian and Antoninus Pius, about 120–140. St. Epiphanius's assertion that he was a disciple of Menander at Antioch and only later moved to Alexandria is unlikely in face of the statement of Eusebius and Theodoret that he was an Alexandrian by birth. Of his life we know nothing except that he had a son called Isidore, who followed in his footsteps. The remark in the Acts of Archelaus (lv) that Basilides was "a preacher amongst the Persians" is almost certainly the result of some confusion. Basilides invented prophets for himself named Barcabbas and Barcoph, and claimed to have received verbal instructions from St. Matthias the Apostle and to be a disciple of Glaucias, a disciple of St. Peter.

BASILICAS

ST. PAUL OUTSIDE THE WALLS, ROME
BUILT A.D. 380.   BURNT 1823.   REBUILT UNDER
PIUS IX AND LEO XIII

SAN LORENZO, ROME
BUILT ABOUT A.D. 330.   ENLARGED IN THE 6TH
CENTURY AND COMPLETED BY HONORIUS III 1216

His System.—As practically nothing of Basilides' writing is extant and as we have no contemporaneous Gnostic witnesses, we must gather the teaching of this patriarch of Gnosticism from the following early sources: (a) St. Irenæus, "Contra Hæreses", I, xxiv, written about 170; (b) Clement of Alexandria, "Stromata", I, xxi, II, vi, viii, xx, IV, xi, xii, xxv, V, i, etc., written between 208–210, and the so-called "Excerpta ex Theodoto" perhaps from the same hand; (c) Hippolytus of Rome, "Philosophumena", VII, written about 225; (d) Pseudo-Tertullian, "Against All Heresies", a little treatise usually attached to Tertullian's "De Præscriptionibus", but really by another hand, perhaps by Victorinus of Pettau, written about 240 and based upon a non-extant "Compendium" of Hippolytus; (e) Artistic remains of Gnosticism such as Abrasax gems, and literary remains like the Pistis Sophia, the latter part of which probably dates back to the end of the second century and, though not strictly Basilidian, yet illustrates early Alexandrian Gnosticism. Later sources are Epiphanius, "Adv. Hær.", xxiv, and Theodoret, "Hær. Fab. Comp.", I, iv. Unfortunately, the descriptions of the Basilidian system given by our chief informants, St. Irenæus and Hippolytus, are so strongly divergent that they seem to many quite irreconcilable. According to Irenæus, Basilides was apparently a dualist and an emanationist, and according to Hippolytus a pantheistic evolutionist.

Seen from the viewpoint of Irenæus, Basilides taught that Nous (Mind) was the first to be born from the Unborn Father; from Nous was born Logos (Reason); from Logos, Phronesis (Prudence); from Phronesis, Sophia (Wisdom) and Dynamis (Strength) and from Phronesis and Dynamis the Virtues, Principalities, and Archangels. By these angelic hosts the highest heaven was made, by their descendants the second heaven, and by the descendants again of these the third, and so on till they reached the number 365. Hence the year has as many days as there are heavens. The angels, who hold the last or visible heaven, brought about all things that are in the world and shared amongst themselves the earth and the nations upon it. The highest of these angels is the one who is thought to be the God of the Jews. And as he wished to make the other nations subject to that which was especially his own, the other angelic principalities withstood him to the utmost. Hence the aversion of all other peoples for this race. The Unborn and Nameless Father seeing their miserable plight, sent his First-born, Nous (and this is the one who is called Christ) to deliver those who should believe in him from the power of the angelic agencies who had built the world. And to men Christ seemed to be a man and to have performed miracles. It was not, however, Christ who suffered, but rather Simon of Cyrene, who was constrained to carry the cross for him, and mistakenly crucified in Christ's stead. Simon having received Jesus' form, Jesus assumed Simon's and thus stood by and laughed at them. Simon was crucified and Jesus returned to His Father. Through the Gnosis (Knowledge) of Christ the souls of men are saved, but their bodies perish.—Out of Epiphanius and Pseudo-Tertullian we can complete the description thus: the highest god, i. e. the Unborn Father, bears the mystical name Abrasax (q. v.), as origin of the 365 heavens. The Angels that made the world formed it out of Eternal Matter; but matter is the principle of all evil and hence both the contempt of the Gnostics for it and their docetic Christology. To undergo martyrdom in order to confess the Crucified is useless, for it is to die for Simon of Cyrene, not for Christ.

Hippolytus sets forth the doctrine of Basilides as follows: "There was a time when nothing existed, neither matter nor form, nor accident; neither the simple nor the compound, neither the unknowable nor the invisible, neither man nor angel nor god nor any of those things, which are called by names or perceived by the mind or the senses. The Not-Being God (οὐκ ὢν θεός), whom Aristotle calls Thought of thought (νόησις τῆς νοήσεως), without consciousness, without perception, without purpose, without aim, without passion, without desire, had the will to create the world. I say 'had the will' ", continues Hippolytus, "only by way of speaking, because in reality he had neither will, nor ideas nor perceptions; and by the word 'world' I do not mean this actual world, which is the outcome of extension and division, but rather the Seed of the world. The seed of the world contained in itself, as a mustard seed, all things which are eventually evolved, as the roots, the branches, the leaves arise out of the seedcorn of the plant." Strange to say this World-seed or All-seed (Panspermia) is still described as Not-Being. It is a phrase of Basilides: "God is Not-Being, even He, who made the world out of what was not; Not-Being made Not-Being."—Basilides distinctly rejected both emanation and the eternity of matter. "What need is there", he said, "of emanation or why accept 'Hyle' [ὕλη, Matter]; as if God had created the world as the spider spins its thread or as mortal man fashions metal or wood. God spoke and it was; this Moses expresses thus: 'Let there be light and there was light'." This sentence has a Christian ring, but we must not forget that to Basilides God was Absolute Negation. He cannot find words enough to bring out the utter non-existence of God; God is not even "unspeakable" (ἄρρητον), He simply is Not. Hence the popular designation of Oukontiani for people who always spoke of Oukôn, Not-Being. The difficulty lies in placing the actual transition from Not-Being into Being. This was probably supposed to consist in the Sperma or Seed, which in one respect was Not-Being, and in the other, the All-seed of the manifold world. The Panspermia contained in itself a threefold Filiation, Hyiŏtês (υἱότης): one composed of refined elements, Leptomeres (λεπτομερές), a second of grosser elments, Pachymeres (παχυμερές), and a third needing purification, Apokatharseos deomenon (ἀποκαθάρσεως δεόμενον). These three Filiations ultimately reach the Not-Being God, but each reaches him in a different way. The first Filiation rose at once and flew with the swiftness of thought to the Not-Being God. The second, remaining as yet in the Panspermia, wished to imitate the first Filiation and rise upwards; but, being too gross and heavy, it failed. Whereupon the second Filation takes to itself wings, which are the Holy Ghost, and with this aid almost reaches the Not-Being God. But when it has come near, the Holy Ghost, of different substance from the Second Filiation, can go no further, but conducts the Second Filiation near to the First Filiation and leaves. Yet he does not return empty but, as a vessel full of ointment, he retains the sweet odour of Filiation; and he becomes the "Boundary Spirit" (Methorion Pneuma, μεθόριον πνεῦμα), between the Supermundane and the Mundane where the third Filiation is still contained in the Panspermia. Now there arose out of the Panspermia the Great Archon, or Ruler; he sped upwards until he reached the firmament, and thinking there was nothing above and beyond, and not knowing of the Third Filiation, still contained in the Panspermia, he fancied himself Lord and Master of all things. He created to himself a Son out of the heap of Panspermia; this was the Christ and being himself amazed at the beauty of his Son, who was greater than his Father, he made him sit at his right hand; and with him he created the ethereal heavens, which reach unto the Moon. The sphere where the Great Archon rules, i. e. the higher heavens, the lower boundary of which is the plane where the moon revolves, is called the Ogdoad.

The same process is repeated and we have a second Archon and his Son and the sphere where they rule is the Hebdomad, beneath the Ogdoad. Lastly, the third Filiation must be raised to the Not-Being God. This took place through the Gospel. From Adam to Moses the Archon of the Ogdoad had reigned (Rom., v, 14); in Moses and the Prophets the Archon of the Hebdomad had reigned, or God of the Jews. Now in the third period the Gospel must reign. This Gospel was first made known from the First Filiation through the Holy Ghost to the Son of the Archon of the Ogdoad; the Son told his Father, who was astounded and trembled and acknowledged his pride in thinking himself the Supreme Deity. The Son of the Archon of the Ogdoad tells the Son of the Archon of the Hebdomad, and he again tells his father. Thus both spheres, including the 365 heavens and their chief Archon, Abrasax, know the truth. This knowledge is now conveyed through the Hebdomad to Jesus, the Son of Mary, who through his life and death redeemed the third Filiation, that is: what is material must return to the Chaos, what is psychic to the Hebdomad, what is spiritual to the Not-Being God. When the third Filiation is thus redeemed, the Supreme God pours out a blissful Ignorance over all that is and that shall so remain forever. This is called "The Restoration of all things".

From Clement of Alexandria we get a few glimpses into the ethical side of the system. Nominally, faith was made the beginning of the spiritual life; it was not, however, a free submission of the intellect, but a mere natural gift of understanding (Gnosis) bestowed upon the soul before its union with the body and which some possessed and others did not. But if faith is only a natural quality of some minds, what need of a Saviour, asks Clement, and Basilides would reply that faith is a latent force which only manifests its energy through the coming of the Saviour, as a ray of light will set naphtha on fire. Sin was not the result of the abuse of free will but merely the outcome of an inborn evil principle. All suffering is punishment for sin; even when a child suffers, this is the punishment of its own sin, i. e. the latent evil principle within; that this indwelling principle has had no opportunity to manifest itself, is immaterial. The persecutions Christians underwent had therefore as sole object the punishment of their sin. All human nature was thus vitiated by the sinful; when hard pressed Basilides would call even Christ a sinful man, for God alone was righteous. Viewed in another way evil was a sort of excrescence on the rational soul, the result of an original disturbance and confusion. "Their whole system", says Clement, "is a confusion of the Panspermia (All-seed) with the Phylokrinesis (Difference-in-kind) and the return of things thus confused to their own places." St. Irenæus and St. Epiphanius reproach Basilides with the immorality of his system, and St. Jerome calls Basilides a master and teacher of debaucheries. It is likely, however, that Basilides was personally free from immorality and that this accusation was true neither of the master nor of some of his followers. That Basilidianism, together with the other forms of Gnosticism, eventually led to gross immorality, there can be no doubt. Clement of Alexandria and St. Epiphanius have preserved for us a passage of the writings of Basilides' son and successor, which counsels the free satisfaction of sensual desires in order that the soul may find peace in prayer. And it is remarkable that Justin the Martyr in his first Apology (xxvi), that is, as early as 150–155, suggests to the Roman emperors that possibly the Gnostics are guilty of those immoralities of which Christians are falsely accused. It is true that in this passage he mentions only Simon, Menander, and Marcion by name; but the passage is general

in tone, and elsewhere Valentinus, Basilides, and Saturninus follow in the list.

WRITINGS.—Nearly all the writings of Basilides have perished, but the names of three of his works and some fragments have come down to us. (a) *A Gospel*. Origen in his Homily on Luke, i, states that Basilides had dared to write a Gospel according to Basilides. St. Jerome and St. Ambrose adopt this statement of Origen; and St. Jerome, in the Prologue of his Commentary on St. Matthew, again speaks of an "Evangelium Basilidis". In all likelihood this "Gospel" was compiled out of our canonical Gospels, the text being curtailed and altered to suit his Gnostic tenets, a diatessaron on Gnostic lines. (b) *A Gospel Commentary* in twenty-four books. (Clement of Alexandria calls it "Exegetica"; the Acta Archelai et Manetis, "Tractatus".) Fragments of this Commentary have come down to us (in Stromata, IV, 12–81, sqq.; Acta Arch., lv; probably also in Origen, Commentary on Romans V, i). (c) *Hymns*. Origen in a note on Job, xxi, 1 sqq., speaks of "Odes" of Basilides; and the so-called Muratorian Fragment, containing a list of canonical and non-canonical books (170 or thereabouts) ends with the words: "etiam novu psalmorum librum marcioni conscripserunt una cum Basilide assianum catafrycum constitutorem". This sentence, notwithstanding its obscurity, supports Origen's statement. For a collection of Basilidian fragments see Hilgenfeld, "Ketzergeschichte des Urchrist" (Leipzig, 1884), 207, 213.

SCHOOL.—Basilides never formed a school of disciples, who modified or added to the doctrines of their leader. Isidore, his son, is the only one who elaborated his father's system, especially on the anthropological side. He wrote a work on the "Psyche Prosphyes" (περὶ προσφυοῦς ψυχῆς), or Appendage-Soul; another work, called "Ethics" by Clement and "Parænetics" by Epiphanius; and at least two books of "Commentaries on the Prophet Parchor. Basilidianism survived until the end of the fourth century as Epiphanius knew of Basilidians living in the Nile Delta. It was however almost exclusively limited to Egypt, though according to Sulpicius Severus it seems to have found an entrance into Spain through a certain Mark from Memphis. St. Jerome states that the Priscillianists were infected with it. Of the customs of the Basilidians, we know no more than that Basilides enjoined on his followers, like Pythagoras, a silence of five years; that they kept the anniversary of the Baptism of Jesus as a feast day and spent the eve of it in reading; that their master told them not to scruple eating things offered to idols; that they wore amulets with the word Abrasax and symbolic figures engraved on them, and, amongst other things, believed them to possess healing properties.

Although Basilides is mentioned by all the Fathers as one of the chiefs of Gnosticism, the system of Valentinus seems to have been much more popular and wider spread, as was also Marcionism. Hence, though anti-Gnostic literature is abundant, we know of only one patristic work, which had for its express purpose the refutation of Basilides, and this work is no longer extant. Eusebius (Hist. Eccl., IV, vii, 6–8) says: "There has come down to us a most powerful refutation of Basilides by Agrippa Castor, one of the most renowned writers of that day, which shows the terrible imposture of the man." With the exception of a few phrases given by Eusebius we know nothing of this Agrippa and his work. (See GNOSTICISM.)

BUONAIUTI, *Lo Gnosticismo* (Rome, 1907); DUCHESNE, *Hist. ancienne de l'Eglise* (3d ed., Paris, 1907), I, xi, s. v. *La Gnose et le Marcionisme*; BAREILLE in *Dict. de théol. cath.*, s. vv. *Abrasax, Basilide*; LECLERCQ, *Dict. d'arch. chrét.*, s. v. *Abrasax*; BARDENHEWER, *Gesch. der altkirch. Lit.* (Freiburg, 1902), I; KING, *The Gnostics and Their Remains* (2d ed., London, 1887);

MEAD, *Fragments of a Faith Forgotten* (London and Benares, 1900); HORT in *Dict. Christ. Biog.*, I, 268–281; MANSEL, *Gnostic Heresies;* DE GROOT, *Basilides als erster Zeuge für das N. T.* (Leipzig, 1868); UHLHORN, *Das Basilidianische System* (Göttingen, 1855).

J. P. ARENDZEN.

Basilides.—Martyrs bearing the name of Basilides are mentioned in the old martyrologies on three different days, namely, on 10, 12, and 28 June. Under the last date is placed the long list of Alexandrian martyrs who suffered during the persecution of Septimius Severus, and among these occurs the name of a Basilides. Eusebius gives an entire chapter of his church history (VI, v) to Basilides and Potamiana. After Potamiana had been sentenced to death Basilides, an officer of the court, led her to execution. He showed himself compassionate to Potamiana and kept back the heathen rabble who would have mocked her. Potamiana thanked him and exhorted him to be consoled, for after her death she would entreat the Lord concerning him and would reward his kindness. Shortly after this Basilides was called on to take an oath. He replied that he could not swear, and openly acknowledged himself to be a Christian. When taken before the judge he made an unwavering confession and was thrown into prison. He was visited by several Christians to whom he related that, three days after her martyrdom, Potamiana had appeared to him and had set a crown on his head with the assurance that the Lord would soon take Basilides to Himself. Basilides was then baptized and the next day he was beheaded. In the present Roman martyrology his name appears on 30 June. In the so-called martyrology of St. Jerome and in the present list of Roman martyrs the name of a Basilides appears on 10 and 12 June. On each occasion the name is accompanied by a statement of the locality of the martyrdom at Rome on the Via Aurelia. The names of the companions in martyrdom of Basilides vary on the two different days. The list for 12 June is very involved; apparently the same martyr is referred to on both days and for some reason his name is repeated on 12 June. The Acts of the martyrdom of a Roman Basilides are still in existence; they have, however, no historical existence and belong to a date considerably later.

EUSEBIUS, *Hist. eccl.* (Turin, 1746), VI, v, ed. VALESIUS, I, 228; *Martyrol. Hieronym.*, ed. DE ROSSI and DUCHESNE in *Acta SS.*, November, II, 77; MOMBRITIUS, *Sanctuarium* (Venice, 1474); *Acta SS.*, Junii, II, 508 sqq., 355 sqq.; ALLARD, *Hist. des persécutions* (Paris, 1866), II, 76 sqq.

J. P. KIRSCH.

Basilides, GOSPEL ACCORDING TO. See APOCRYPHA.

Basilinopolis, a titular see of Asia Minor. Originally a small village in Bithynia Prima, it obtained the rank of a city under, or perhaps shortly before, Julian the Apostate (Mansi, VII, 305). The first known bishop, Alexander, was consecrated by St. John Chrysostom about 400. Other bishops are Gerontius (451), Cyriacus (518), Sisinnius (680), Georgius (787), and Anthimus in 878 (Lequien, Or. Chr., I, 623–625). At Chalcedon (451) the see had been the object of a sharp contest between the metropolitans of Nicomedia and Nicæa about jurisdiction. Basilinopolis was finally made by the council a suffragan of Nicomedia (Mansi, ibid., 301–314); and it remained so until about 1170 under Manuel Comnenus (Hierocles, Synecdemos, ed. Parthey, 169). The see does not figure in a "Notitia episcopatuum" of the fifteenth century, the city doubtless having been destroyed by the Osmanli. Its exact site is not known. According to W. M. Ramsay (Hist. Geogr. of Asia Minor, 179), it was probably situated on the western side of the Lake of Nicæa (Isnik-Ghueul), near Bazar-Keui, between Kios (Ghemlek) and Nicæa (Isnik).

LEQUIEN, *Oriens Christ.*, I, 623–626.   S. VAILHÉ.

Basilissa.—Various female martyrs, attributed to different localities yet bearing the common name of Basilissa, are referred to in all the catalogues of martyrs both of early Christianity and of the Middle Ages; their names also appear in the calendars and liturgical books of the Greek and Roman Churches. Nothing is known positively as to any one of these sufferers for the Christian Faith; the Acts of their martyrdoms, so far as such exist, are purely legendary and originated at a later date. The fact, however, that the name occurs several times in the so-called martyrology of St. Jerome and in old Greek catalogues is certain proof that a number of female martyrs named Basilissa were actually venerated in the ancient Church. At the same time it is not impossible that the same martyr is recorded on different days. Among these saints should be mentioned: Julian and Basilissa of Antioch; in the martyrology of St. Jerome (ed. Rossi-Duchesne, 6) they are given as martyrs under 6 January. A later legend makes Basilissa the virgin wife of Julian and narrates that she died a natural death together with other virgins, while Julian suffered martyrdom in company with many other Christians during the Diocletian persecution. The same martyrology makes mention, under 12 March, of a female martyr Basilissa, wife of Felicio, and states the locality "in Asia". On the next day, 13 March, occurs the name of another martyr called Basilissa, wife of the presbyter Eustacius of Nicomedia. Later legends, which were accepted by the Greek menologies and synaxaria, speak of a virgin and martyr, Basilissa of Nicomedia, whose feast was celebrated on 3 September; this Basilissa is probably identical with the one just mentioned. On 22 March the names of two martyrs, Basilissa and Callinice, are given with the statement "in Galatia". Under 16 April the old catalogues contain the names of a number of martyrs of Corinth, among whom appears a Basilissa; according to later accounts these sufferers for the Faith were all thrown into the sea. Under the previous day, 15 April, two Roman matrons, Basilissa and Anastasia, are recorded; they apparently died in the persecution of Nero. Another female martyr of Rome, whose name is sometimes written Basilla and sometimes Basilissa, was venerated on 20 May. She was buried, it is stated, on the Via Salaria. The celebrated Roman martyr Basilla, who died in 304 and whose feast is entered from the year 354 under 22 September in the oldest known Roman catalogue of feasts (Depositio martyrum), was buried in the catacomb of Hermes on the Via Salaria Vetus. It is, therefore, a question whether the saint given under 20 May and this latter Basilla are not one and the same person; but the identity of the two cannot be positively affirmed. The present martyrology includes several of these saints; 9 January, Basilissa of Antioch; 22 March, Basilissa and Callinice; 15 April, Basilissa and Anastasia; 3 September, Basilissa of Nicomedia.

For Basilissa of Antioch and her companions, *Acta SS.*, January, I, 570 sqq., and MOMBRITIUS, *Sanctuarium*, I, 216 sqq.; II, 45 sqq. For Basilissa and Anastasia, *Acta SS.*, April, II, 372. For Basilissa and Callinice, *Ibid.*, March, III, 277. For Basilissa of Nicomedia, *Ibid.*, September, I, 609 sqq.

J. P. KIRSCH.

Basilissa (WIFE OF JULIAN). See JULIAN AND BASILISSA.

Basil of Amasea (BASILEUS or BASILIUS), Bishop and Martyr. In St. Jerome's Latin version of the Chronicle of Eusebius the statement occurs under the 275th Olympiad (A. D. 321–324) that Basileus, Bishop of Amasea in Pontus, suffered martyrdom in the reign of Licinius [ed. Schöne (Berlin, 1875), 191]. There is no reason for doubting the trustworthiness of this information. Among the signatures of the bishops who attended the Councils of Ancyra and Neo-Cæsarea (314) is to be found the name of Basileus of Amasea (Mansi, Coll. conc., II, 534, 548). Eusebius also relates (Hist. eccl., X, viii) that in the time of Licinius Christians were treated with great cruelty, especially in Amasea and the other cities of Pontus, and that, in particular, the governor inflicted upon several bishops the ordinary punishments of evildoers. St. Athanasius mentions the great Basileus of Pontus among the bishops of the early part of the fourth century who held firmly to the like substance of the Son with the Father; the reference is evidently to the martyr-bishop of Amasea (Athan. Opera, ed. Mannius, I, 122). The statement of Philostorgius [ed. Valesius; Eusebius, Hist. eccl. (Turin, 1748), III, 433], that Basileus attended the Council of Nicæa, cannot be quoted against this proof of the martyrdom of Basileus under Licinius, as there is evidently a mistake in what Philostorgius says; among the signatures at the Council of Nicæa appears that of Eutychianus as Bishop of Amasea. The Acts of the martyrdom of Basileus, supposedly written by an eye-witness, a presbyter named Johannes, are not authentic and the narrative is entirely legendary. The feast of Basileus falls on 26 April, on which date it occurs both in the Greek synaxaria and menæa and in the Roman martyrology.

Acta SS., April, III, 416–422; SURIUS, *De prob. vitis Sanctor.* (Cologne, 1571), II, 857–864; TILLEMONT, *Mémoires* (Brussels, 1732), V, 219 sqq., 352 sqq.

J. P. KIRSCH.

Basil of Seleucia, Bishop and ecclesiastical writer, date of birth uncertain; d., probably, between 458 and 460; was distinguished during the period when the Eastern Church was convulsed by the Monophysite struggles, and was necessarily obliged to take sides in all those controversies. Those of his writings which have come down to us, though somewhat too rhetorical and involved, prove clearly that he was a man of great literary ability.

He was appointed Bishop of Seleucia in Isauria, between the years 432 and 447, and was one of those who took part in the Synod of Constantinople, which was summoned (448) by the Patriarch Flavian for the condemnation of the Eutychian errors and the deposition of their great champion, Dioscurus of Alexandria. Curiously enough, though Basil seems to have agreed to these measures, he attended the Latrocinium, or Robber Synod, of Ephesus, held in the next year (449), and, induced probably more by the threats and violence of the Monophysite party than by their arguments, he voted for the rehabilitation of Eutyches and for the deposition of the Patriarch of Constantinople, and was thus regarded for a time as a supporter of Monophysite opinions. Like the other prominent supporters of Dioscurus, he should have been removed from his see had he not in the meantime accepted the doctrine contained in the Dogmatic Epistle of Pope Leo to Flavian, and joined in the condemnation of Eutyches and Dioscurus. After this period he seems to have continued a zealous opponent of the Monophysite party, for we find that in the year 458 he joined with his fellow-bishops of Isauria, in an appeal to the Emperor Leo I, requesting him to use his influence in forwarding the Decrees of Chalcedon, and in securing the deposition of Timotheus Ælurus, who had intruded himself (457) into the Patriarchate of Alexandria. This is the last reference we find to Basil, and it is commonly supposed that he died shortly afterwards.

Forty-one sermons (λόγοι) on different portions of the Old Testament have come down to us under his name, and are found in Migne (P. G., LXXXV, 27–474), where is also his history of the protomartyr Thecla and of the miracles wrought at her grave (ibid., 477–618). Most of these sermons may be regarded as genuine, though some of them are now generally assigned to Nestorius. According to

Photius, Basil also dealt in verse with the life and miracles of Thecla.

HEFELE, *Conciliengeschichte* (2d ed.), II, 331, 375, 430; *Fabricius-Harles, Bibl. Gr.*, IX, 90, 97; LIPSIUS, *Die apok. Apostelgesch.* (1887), II, i, 426, 432; BATIFFOL, *Revue Bib.* (1900), IX, 329–353; BARDENHEWER, *Patrologie* (Freiburg, 1901), 468, 469.

JAMES McCAFFREY.

Basil the Elder, SAINT. See BASIL THE GREAT, SAINT.

Basil the Great, SAINT, Bishop of Cæsarea, one of the most distinguished Doctors of the Church, b. probably 329; d. 1 January, 379. He ranks after Athanasius as a defender of the Oriental Church against the heresies of the fourth century. With his friend Gregory of Nazianzus and his brother, Gregory of Nyssa, he makes up the trio known as "The Three Cappadocians", far outclassing the other two in practical genius and actual achievement.

LIFE.—St. Basil the Elder, father of St. Basil the Great, was the son of a Christian of good birth and his wife, Macrina (Acta SS., January, II), both of whom suffered for the Faith during the persecution of Maximinus Galerius (305–314), spending several years of hardship in the wild mountains of Pontus. St. Basil the Elder was noted for his virtue (Acta SS. May, VII) and also won considerable reputation as a teacher in Cæsarea. He was not a priest (Cf. Cave, Hist. Lit., I, 239). He married Emmelia, the daughter of a martyr, and became the father of ten children. Three of these, Macrina, Basil, and Gregory are honoured as saints; and of the sons, Peter, Gregory, and Basil attained the dignity of the episcopate.

Under the care of his father and his grandmother, the elder Macrina, who preserved the traditions of their countryman, St. Gregory Thaumaturgus (c. 213–275) Basil was formed in habits of piety and study. He was still young when his father died and the family moved to the estate of the elder Macrina at Annesi in Pontus, on the banks of the Iris. As a boy, he was sent to school at Cæsarea, then "a metropolis of letters", and conceived a fervent admiration for the local bishop, Dianius. Later, he went to Constantinople, at that time "distinguished for its teachers of philosophy and rhetoric", and thence to Athens. Here he became the inseparable companion of Gregory of Nazianzus, who, in his famous panegyric on Basil (Or. xliii), gives a most interesting description of their academic experiences. According to him, Basil was already distinguished for brilliancy of mind and seriousness of character and associated only with the most earnest students. He was able, grave, industrious, and well advanced in rhetoric, grammar, philosophy, astronomy, geometry, and medicine. (As to his not knowing Latin, see Fialon, Etude historique et littéraire sur St. Basile, Paris, 1869.) We know the names of two of Basil's teachers at Athens, Prohæresius, possibly a Christian, and Himerius, a pagan. It has been affirmed, though probably incorrectly, that Basil spent some time under Libanius. He tells us himself that he endeavoured without success to attach himself as a pupil to Eustathius (Ep., I). At the end of his sojourn at Athens, Basil being laden, says St. Gregory of Nazianzus, "with all the learning attainable by the nature of man", was well equipped to be a teacher. Cæsarea took possession of him gladly "as a founder and second patron" (Or. xliii), and as he tells us (ccx), he refused the splendid offers of the citizens of Neo-Cæsarea, who wished him to undertake the education of the youth of their city.

To the successful student and distinguished professor, "there now remained", says Gregory (Or. xliii), "no other need than that of spiritual perfection". Gregory of Nyssa, in his life of Macrina, gives us to understand that Basil's brilliant success both as a university student and a professor had left traces of worldliness and self-sufficiency on the soul of the young man. Fortunately, Basil came again in contact with Dianius, Bishop of Cæsarea, the object of his boyish affection, and Dianius seems to have baptized him, and ordained him Reader soon after his return to Cæsarea. It was at this time also that he fell under the influence of that very remarkable woman, his sister Macrina, who had meanwhile founded a religious community on the family estate at Annesi. Basil himself tells us how, like a man roused from deep sleep, he turned his eyes to the marvellous truth of the Gospel, wept many tears over his miserable life, and prayed for guidance from God: "Then I read the Gospel, and saw there that a great means of reaching perfection was the selling of one's goods, the sharing of them with the poor, the giving up of all care for this life, and the refusal to allow the soul to be turned by any sympathy towards things of earth" (Ep. ccxxiii). To learn the ways of perfection, Basil now visited the monasteries of Egypt, Palestine, Cœle-Syria, and Mesopotamia. He returned, filled with admiration for the austerity and piety of the monks, and founded a monastery in his native Pontus, on the banks of the Iris, nearly opposite Annesi. (Cf. Ramsay, Hist. Geog. of Asia Minor, London, 1890, p. 326.) Eustathius of Sebaste had already introduced the eremitical life into Asia Minor; Basil added the cenobitic or community form, and the new feature was imitated by many companies of men and women. (Cf. Sozomen, Hist. Eccl., VI, xxvii; Epiphanius, Hær., lxxv, 1; Basil, Ep. ccxxiii; Tillemont, Mém., IX, Art. XXI, and note XXVI.) Basil became known as the Father of Oriental monasticism, the forerunner of St. Benedict. How well he deserved the title, how seriously and in what spirit he undertook the systematizing of the religious life, may be seen by the study of his Rule. He seems to have read Origen's writings very systematically about this time, for in union with Gregory of Nazianzus, he published a selection of them called the "Philocalia".

Basil was drawn from his retreat into the arena of theological controversy in 360 when he accompanied two delegates from Seleucia to the emperor at Constantinople, and supported his namesake of Ancyra. There is some dispute as to his courage and his perfect orthodoxy on this occasion (cf. Philostorgius. Hist. Eccl., IV, xii; answered by Gregory of Nyssa, In Eunom., I, and Maran, Proleg., vii; Tillemont, Mém., note XVIII). A little later, however, both qualities seem to have been sufficiently in evidence, as Basil forsook Dianius for having signed the heretical creed of Rimini. To this time (c. 361) may be referred the "Moralia"; and a little later came the books against Eunomius (363) and some correspondence with Athanasius. It is possible, also, that Basil wrote his monastic rules in the briefer form while in Pontus, and enlarged them later at Cæsarea (Baert). There is an account of an invitation from Julian for Basil to present himself at court and of Basil's refusal, coupled with an admonition that angered the emperor and endangered Basil's safety. Both incident and correspondence however are questioned by some critics (e. g. Maran; cf. Tillemont, De Broglie, Fialon).

Basil still retained considerable influence in Cæsarea, and it is regarded as fairly probable that he had a hand in the election of the successor of Dianius who died in 362, after having been reconciled to Basil. In any case the new bishop, Eusebius, was practically placed in his office by the elder Gregory of Nazianzus. Eusebius having persuaded the reluctant Basil to be ordained priest, gave him a prominent place in the administration of the diocese (363). In ability for the management of affairs Basil so far eclipsed the bishop that ill-feeling arose between the two. "All the more eminent and wiser portion of the church was roused against the bishop" (Greg. Naz., Or. xliii; Ep. x), and to avoid trouble Basil

again withdrew into the solitude of Pontus. A little later (365) when the attempt of Valens to impose Arianism on the clergy and the people necessitated the presence of a strong personality, Basil was restored to his former position, being reconciled to the bishop by St. Gregory of Nazianzus. There seems to have been no further disagreement between Eusebius and Basil and the latter soon became the real head of the diocese. "The one", says Gregory of Nazianzus (Or. xliii), "led the people the other led their leader". During the five years spent in this most important office, Basil gave evidence of being a man of very unusual powers. He laid down the law to the leading citizens and the imperial governors, settled disputes with wisdom and finality, assisted the spiritually needy, looked after "the support of the poor, the entertainment of strangers, the care of maidens, legislation written and unwritten for the monastic life, arrangements of prayers, (liturgy?), adornment of the sanctuary" (op. cit.). In time of famine, he was the saviour of the poor.

In 370 Basil succeeded to the See of Cæsarea, being consecrated according to tradition on 14 June. Cæsarea was then a powerful and wealthy city (Soz., Hist. Eccl., V, v). Its bishop was Metropolitan of Cappadocia and Exarch of Pontus which embraced more than half of Asia Minor and comprised eleven provinces. The See of Cæsarea ranked with Ephesus immediately after the patriarchal sees in the councils, and the bishop was the superior of fifty *chorepiscopi* (Baert). Basil's actual influence, says Jackson (Prolegomena, XXXII) covered the whole stretch of country "from the Balkans to the Mediterranean and from the Ægean to the Euphrates". The need of a man like Basil in such a see as Cæsarea was most pressing, and he must have known this well. Some (e. g. Allard, De Broglie, Venables, Fialon) think that he set about procuring his own election; others (e. g. Maran, Baronius, Ceillier) say that he made no attempt in his own behalf. In any event, he became Bishop of Cæsarea largely by the influence of the elder Gregory of Nazianzus. His election, says the younger Gregory (loc. cit.), was followed by disaffection on the part of several suffragan bishops "on whose side were found the greatest scoundrels in the city". During his previous administration of the diocese Basil had so clearly defined his ideas of discipline and orthodoxy, that no one could doubt the direction and the vigour of his policy. St. Athanasius was greatly pleased at Basil's election (Ad Pallad., 953; Ad Joann. et Ant., 951); but the Arianizing Emperor Valens, displayed considerable annoyance and the defeated minority of bishops became consistently hostile to the new metropolitan. By years of tactful conduct, however, "blending his correction with consideration and his gentleness with firmness" (Greg. Naz., Or. xliii), he finally overcame most of his opponents.

Basil's letters tell the story of his tremendous and varied activity; how he worked for the exclusion of unfit candidates from the sacred ministry and the deliverance of the bishops from the temptation of simony; how he required exact discipline and the faithful observance of the canons from both laymen and clerics; how he rebuked the sinful, followed up the offending, and held out hope of pardon to the penitent. (Cf. Epp. xliv, xlv, and xlvi, the beautiful letter to a fallen virgin, as well as Epp. liii, liv, lv, clxxxviii, cxcix, ccxvii, and Ep. clxix, on the strange incident of Glycerius, whose story is well filled out by Ramsay, The Church in the Roman Empire, New York, 1893, p. 443 sqq.) If on the one hand he strenuously defended clerical rights and immunities (Ep. civ), on the other he trained his clergy so strictly that they grew famous as the type of all that a priest should be (Epp. cii, ciii). Basil did not confine his activity to diocesan affairs, but threw himself vigorously into the troublesome theological disputes then rending the unity of Christendom. He drew up a summary of the orthodox faith; he attacked by word of mouth the heretics near at hand and wrote tellingly against those afar. His correspondence shows that he paid visits sent messages, gave interviews, instructed, reproved, rebuked, threatened, reproached, undertook the protection of nations, cities, individuals great and small. There was very little chance of opposing him successfully, for he was a cool, persistent, fearless fighter in defence both of doctrines and of principles. His bold stand against Valens parallels the meeting of Ambrose with Theodosius. The emperor was dumbfounded at the archbishop's calm indifference to his presence and his wishes. The incident, as narrated by Gregory of Nazianzus, not only tells much concerning Basil's character but throws a clear light on the type of Christian bishop with which the emperors had to deal and goes far to explain why Arianism, with the court behind it, could make so little impression on the ultimate history of Catholicism.

While assisting Eusebius in the care of his diocese, Basil had shown a marked interest in the poor and afflicted; that interest now displayed itself in the erection of a magnificent institution, the Ptochotropheion, or Basileiad, a house for the care of friendless strangers, the medical treatment of the sick poor, and the industrial training of the unskilled. Built in the suburbs, it attained such importance as to become practically the centre of a new city with the name of ἡ καινὴ πόλις or "Newtown". It was the mother-house of like institutions erected in other dioceses and stood as a constant reminder to the rich of their privilege of spending wealth in a truly Christian way. It may be mentioned here that the social obligations of the wealthy were so plainly and forcibly preached by St. Basil that modern socialists have ventured to claim him as one of their own, though with no more foundation than would exist in the case of any other consistent teacher of the principles of Catholic ethics. The truth is that St. Basil was a practical lover of Christian poverty, and even in his exalted position preserved that simplicity in food and clothing and that austerity of life for which he had been remarked at his first renunciation of the world (Nitti, Catholic Socialism, New York, 1895, iii; Villemain, Tableau d'éloq. Chrét., Paris, 1891, 116 sqq.).

In the midst of his labours, Basil underwent suffering of many kinds. Athanasius died in 373 and the elder Gregory in 374, both of them leaving gaps never to be filled. In 372 began the painful estrangement from Gregory of Nazianzus. Anthimus, Bishop of Tyana, became an open enemy, Apollinaris "a cause of sorrow to the churches" (Ep. cclxiii), Eustathius of Sebaste a traitor to the Faith and a personal foe as well. Eusebius of Samosata was banished, Gregory of Nyssa condemned and deposed. When Emperor Valentinian died and the Arians recovered their influence, all Basil's efforts must have seemed in vain. His health was breaking, the Goths were at the door of the empire, Antioch was in schism, Rome doubted his sincerity, the bishops refused to be brought together as he wished. (Duchesne, L'Eglise d'Orient, Paris, 1881.) "The notes of the church were obscured in his part of Christendom, and he had to fare on as best he might,—admiring, courting, yet coldly treated by the Latin world, desiring the friendship of Rome, yet wounded by her reserve,—suspected of heresy by Damasus, and accused by Jerome of pride" (Newman, The Church of the Fathers). Had he lived a little longer and attended the Council of Constantinople (381), he would have seen the death of its first president, his friend Meletius, and the forced resignation of its second, Gregory of Nazianzus. Basil died 1 January,

379. His death was regarded as a public bereavement; Jews, pagans, and foreigners vied with his own flock in doing him honour. The earlier Latin martyrologies (Hieronymian and Bede) make no mention of a feast of St. Basil. The first mention is by Usuard and Ado who place it on 14 June, the supposed date of Basil's consecration to the episcopate. In the Greek "Menæa" he is commemorated on 1 January, the day of his death. In 1081, John, Patriarch of Constantinople, in consequence of a vision, established a feast in common honour of St. Basil, Gregory of Nazianzus, and John Chrysostom, to be celebrated on 30 January. The Bollandists give an account of the origin of this feast; they also record as worthy of note that no relics of St. Basil are mentioned before the twelfth century, at which time parts of his body, together with some other very extraordinary relics were reputed to have been brought to Bruges by a returning Crusader. Baronius (c. 1599) gave to the Naples Oratory a relic of St. Basil sent from Constantinople to the pope. The Bollandists and Baronius print descriptions of Basil's personal appearance and the former reproduce two icons, the older copied from a codex presented to Basil, Emperor of the East (877–886).

By common consent, Basil ranks among the greatest figures in church history and the rather extravagant panegyric by Gregory of Nazianzus has been all but equalled by a host of other eulogists. Physically delicate and occupying his exalted position but a few years, Basil did magnificent and enduring work in an age of more violent world convulsions than Christianity has since experienced. (Cf. Newman, The Church of the Fathers.) By p sonal virtue he attained distinction in an age of saints; and his purity, his monastic fervour, his stern simplicity, his friendship for the poor became traditional in the history of Christian asceticism. In fact, the impress of his genius was stamped indelibly on the Oriental conception of religious life. In his hands the great metropolitan See of Cæsarea took shape as a sort of model of the Christian diocese; there was hardly any detail of episcopal activity in which he failed to mark out guiding lines and to give splendid example. Not the least of his glories is the fact that toward the officials of the State he maintained that fearless dignity and independence which later history has shown to be an indispensable condition of healthy life in the Catholic episcopate.

Some difficulty has arisen out of the correspondence of St. Basil with the Roman See. (Bossuet, "Gallia Orthodoxa", c. lxv; Puller, "Primitive Saints and the See of Rome", London, 1900.) That he was in communion with the Western bishops and that he wrote repeatedly to Rome asking that steps be taken to assist the Eastern Church in her struggle with schismatics and heretics is undoubted; but the disappointing result of his appeals drew from him certain words which require explanation. Evidently he was deeply chagrined that Pope Damasus on the one hand hesitated to condemn Marcellus and the Eustathians, and on the other preferred Paulinus to Meletius in whose right to the See of Antioch St. Basil most firmly believed. At the best it must be admitted that St. Basil criticized the pope freely in a private letter to Eusebius of Samosata (Ep. ccxxxix) and that he was indignant as well as hurt at the failure of his attempt to obtain help from the West. Later on, however, he must have recognized that in some respects he had been hasty; in any event, his strong emphasis of the influence which the Roman See could exercise over the Eastern bishops, and his abstaining from a charge of anything like usurpation are great facts that stand out obviously in the story of the disagreement. With regard to the question of his association with the Semi-Arians, Philostorgius speaks of him as championing the Semi-Arian cause.

and Newman says he seems unavoidably to have Arianized the first thirty years of his life. The explanation of this, as well as of the disagreement with the Holy See, must be sought in a careful study of the times, with due reference to the unsettled and changeable condition of theological distinctions, the lack of anything like a final pronouncement by the Church's defining power, the "lingering imperfections of the Saints" (Newman), the substantial orthodoxy of many of the so-called Semi-Arians, and above all the great plan which Basil was steadily pursuing of effecting unity in a disturbed and divided Christendom. (Cf. De Broglie, "L'Eglise et l'Empire Romain", Paris, 1866, V, ii; Rivington, "The Primitive Church and the See of Peter", London, 1894; Newman, "The Church of the Fathers", Idem, "The Arians of the Fourth Century"; Jungmann, "Dissertationes select. in hist. eccl.", II, 13; De Smedt, "Dissertationes select. in primam ætatem hist. eccl.", p. 276.)

WRITINGS.—*Dogmatic.*—Of the five books against Eunomius (c. 364) the last two are classed as spurious by some critics, The work assails the equivalent Arianism of Eunomius and defends the Divinity of the Three Persons of the Trinity; it is well summarized by Jackson (Nicene and Post Nicene Fathers, Series II, VIII). The work "De Spiritu Sancto", or treatise on the Holy Spirit (c. 375) was evoked in part by the Macedonian denial of the Divinity of the Third Person and in part by charges that Basil himself had "slurred over the Spirit" (Gregory Naz., Ep. lviii), that he had advocated communion with all such as should admit simply that the Holy Ghost was not a creature (Basil, Ep. cxiii), and that he had sanctioned the use of a novel doxology, namely, "Glory be to the Father with the Son together with the Holy Ghost" (De Sp. S., I, i). The treatise teaches the doctrine of the Divinity of the Holy Ghost, while avoiding the phrase "God, the Holy Ghost" for prudential reasons (Greg. Naz., Or. xliii. Wuilcknis and Swete affirm the necessity of some such reticence on Basil's part. (Cf. Jackson, op. cit., p. XXIII, note.) With regard to Basil's teaching on the Third Person, as expressed in his work against Eunomius (III, i), a controversy arose at the Council of Florence between the Latins and the Greeks; but strong arguments, both external and internal, availed to place Basil on the side of the "Filioque". The dogmatic writings were edited separately by Goldhorn, in his "S. Basilii Opera Dogmatica Selecta" (Leipzig, 1854). The "De Spiritu Sancto", was translated into English by Johnston (Oxford, 1892); by Lewis in the Christian Classic Series (1888); and by Jackson (op. cit.). *Exegetical.*—These include nine homilies "On the Hexæmeron" and thirteen (Maran) genuine homilies on particular Psalms. A lengthy commentary on the first sixteen chapters of Isaias is of doubtful authenticity (Jackson), though by a contemporary hand. A commentary on Job has disappeared. "The Hexæmeron" was highly admired by Gregory of Nazianzus (Or. xliii, n. 67). It is translated entire by Jackson (op. cit.). The homilies on the Psalms are moral and hortatory rather than strictly exegetical. In interpreting the Scripture, Basil uses both the literal and the allegorical methods, but favours the literal system of Antioch. His second homily contains a denunciation of usury which has become famous. *Homiletical.*—Twenty-four sermons, doctrinal, moral, and panegyrical in character, are looked upon as generally genuine, certain critical difficulties, however, remaining still unsolved. Eight of these sermons were translated into Latin by Rufinus. The discourses place Basil among the very greatest of Christian preachers and evince his special gift for preaching upon the responsibilities of wealth. The most noteworthy in the collection are the homilies on the rich (vi and vii) copied by St. Ambrose

(De Nabuthe Jez., v, 21–24), and the homily (xxii) on the study of pagan literature. The latter was edited by Fremion (Paris, 1819, with French translation), Sommer (Paris, 1894), Bach (Münster, 1900), and Maloney (New York, 1901). With regard to Basil's style and his success as a preacher much has been written. (Cf. Villemain, "Tableau d'éloq. chrét. au IVe siècle", Paris, 1891; Fialon, "Etude Litt. sur St. B.", Paris, 1861; Roux, "Etude sur la prédication de B. le Grand", Strasburg, 1867; Croiset, "Hist. de la litt. Grecque", Paris, 1899.) *Moral and Ascetical.*—This group contains much of spurious or doubtful origin. Probably authentic are the latter two of the three prefatory treatises, and the five treatises: "Morals", "On the Judgment of God", "On Faith", "The Longer Monastic Rules", "The Shorter Monastic Rules". The twenty-four sermons on morals are a cento of extracts from the writings of Basil made by Simeon Metaphrastes. Concerning the authenticity of the Rules there has been a good deal of discussion. As is plain from these treatises and from the homilies that touch upon ascetical or moral subjects, St. Basil was particularly felicitous in the field of spiritual instruction. *Correspondence.*—The extant letters of Basil are 366 in number, two-thirds of them belonging to the period of his episcopate. The so-called "Canonical Epistles" have been assailed as spurious, but are almost surely genuine. The correspondence with Julian and with Libanius is probably apocryphal; the correspondence with Apollinaris is uncertain. All of the 366 letters are translated in the "Nicene and Post-Nicene Fathers". Some of the letters are really dogmatic treatises, and others are apologetic replies to personal attacks. In general they are very useful for their revelation of the saint's character and for the pictures of his age which they offer. *Liturgical.*—A so-called "Liturgy of St. Basil" exists in Greek and in Coptic. (See LITURGY, GREEK.) It goes back at least to the sixth century, but its connexion with Basil has been a matter of critical discussion (Brightman, "Liturgies, Eastern and Western", Oxford, 1896, I; Probst, "Die Liturgie des vierten Jahrhunderts und deren Reform", Münster, 1893, 377–412).

EDITIONS OF ST. BASIL.—The *editio princeps* of the original text of the extant works of Basil appeared at Basle, 1551, and the first complete Latin translation at Rome, 1515 (autograph manuscript in the British Museum). The best edition is that of the Maurist Benedictines, Garnier and Maran (Paris, 1721–30), republished with appendixes by Migne (P. G., XXIX–XXXII). For fragments attributed to Basil with more or less certainty, and edited by Matthæi, Mai, Pitra, and others, see Bardenhewer, "Patrologie" (Freiburg, 1901), 247. Portions of letters recently discovered in Egyptian papyri were published by H. Landwehr, "Griechische Handschriften aus Fayûm", in "Philologus", XLIII (1884).

BIBLIOGRAPHIES.—CHEVALIER, *Répertoire, Biobibliographie*, s. v.; BARDENHEWER, *Gesch. der altkirch. Lit.* (Freiburg, 1902). CONTEMPORARY AUTHORITIES.—GREG. NAZ., *Orationes*, especially xliii; IDEM, *Epistolæ*; IDEM, *Carm. de vitâ suâ*; GREG. NYSS., *Vita Macrinæ*; IDEM, *Or. in laudem fratris Basilii*; IDEM, *In Eunom.*, I; SOCRATES, *Hist. Eccl.*, IV, xxvi; VI, iii; SOZOMEN, *Hist. Eccl.*, VI, xv, xvi, xvii, xxii; RUFINUS, *Hist. Eccl.*, II, ix; THEODORET, *Hist. Eccl.*, IV, xix; PHILOSTORGIUS, *Hist. Eccl.*, VIII, xi–xiii; EPHRÆM SYRUS, *Encomium in Bas.*, ap. COTELIER, *Mon. Eccl. Gr.*, II; JEROME, *De Vir. Illust.*, cxvi. The *Vita Basilii* by AMPHILOCHIUS is a forgery of about the ninth century.

STUDIES ON BASIL.—BÆRT in *Acta SS.*, June, III; MARAN AND GARNIER in *P. G.*, XXIX; TILLEMONT, *Mémoires*, IX; BARONIUS, *Annales*, 354, 378; CEILLIER, *Hist. Gen. des aut. sac.*, IV, ch. xvii; TRICALET, *Bibl. Port. des Pères* (Paris, 1759), II; ALLARD, *Saint Basile* (Paris, 1903); ALLARD in *Dict. de théol. cath.*, s. v. *Basile*; JACKSON, *A Select Library of the Nicene and Post-Nicene Fathers*, 2nd Series (New York, 1895), VII, *Prolegomena*, XI–LXXVI; VENABLES in *Dict. Christ. Biog.*, s. v.; BUTLER, *Lives of the Saints*, 14 June; NEWMAN, *Church of the Fathers*, I–III; SWETE, *Doctrine of the Holy Spirit* (Cambridge, 1874); BAYLE, *St. Basile* (Paris, 1898); JAHN, *Basilius Platonizans* (Berne, 1838); MARTIN, *Essai sur les lettres de St. Basile le grand* (Rennes, 1865); SCHOLL, *Die Lehre des heil. B. von der*

Gnade (Freiburg, 1881); FUNK in *Theolog. Quartalschrift*, LXX; RAMSAY in *The Expositor*, 1896; EGAR in *American Church Review*, 1878–79; *The North American Review*, XC, 356; CHASE in *Christian Review*, XXIII, XXIV.

JOSEPH MCSORLEY.

Basin, ECCLESIASTICAL USE OF.—Basins were extensively used in the Jewish Ritual and were in early use in Christian churches for ablutions and to receive lamp-drippings etc. The Missal prescribes its use at the "Lavabo" of the Mass (Rit. Cel. vii, 10); the "Cæremoniale Episcoporum" provides a basin for bearing the cruets (Lib. I, xi, 10) and for the preparatory ablutions of bishops (ibid., 12). They are ordinarily of ornamented metal.

CATALANI, *Cæremoniale Episcoporum comment.* (Paris, 1860), I, 225–229; VAN DER STAPPEN, *Sacra Liturgia* (Mechlin, 1902), III, 111–112; WALCOTT, *Sacred Archeology* (London, 1868), 62–63; KENNEDY in HAST., *Dict. of Bible*, s. v.

JOHN B. PETERSON.

Baslé, AUGUSTINE FRANCIS. See MYSORE, DIOCESE OF.

Basle, COUNCIL OF, convoked by Pope Martin V in 1431, closed at Lausanne in 1449. The position of the pope as the common Father of the Christian world had been seriously compromised by the transfer of the papal court to Avignon, and by the subsequent identification of the interests of the Church with those of a particular race. Men began to regard the papacy more as a national than a universal institution, and their feeling of religious loyalty was often nearly balanced by the promptings of national jealousy. Nor was the papacy likely to be strengthened by the events of the Great Western Schism (1378–1417), when rival claimants were seen contending for the throne of St. Peter and for the allegiance of the Christian nations. Such a spectacle was well calculated to shake men's belief in the monarchical form of government and to drive them to seek elsewhere a remedy for the evils which then afflicted the Church. It was not strange that the advocates of a general council as the final arbitrator, the ultimate court of appeal to which all, even the pope, must yield, should have secured a ready attention. The success of the Council of Constance (1414–18) in securing the withdrawal or deposition of the three rival popes had supplied a strong argument in favour of the conciliar theory. It is clear both from the speeches of some of the Fathers of Constance as well as from its decrees that such a feeling was rapidly gaining ground, and that many people had come to regard the government of the Church by general councils, convoked at regular intervals, as the one most in harmony with the needs of the time. As a result, in the 39th session of the Council of Constance (9 October, 1417) we find it decreed: that general councils should be held frequently; that the next should be convoked within five years; the following seven years later, and after this, a council should be held every ten years; that the place of convocation should be determined by the council itself, and could not be changed even by the pope unless in case of war or pestilence, and then only with the consent of at least two-thirds of the cardinals. It was in accordance with this decree that Martin V convoked the Council of Basle, and it is only by understanding the feeling underlying this decree that we can grasp the significance of the dispute waged between Eugene IV and the council. Which was to govern the Church? Was it to be the pope or the council? That was the issue really at stake.

Whether Basle is to be regarded as a general council, and if so, in what sense, has been often warmly discussed. The extreme Gallicans (e. g. Edmund Richer, Hist. Concil. Gen., III, vii) contend that it should be reckoned as œcumenical from its beginning (1431) till its end in Lausanne (1449); while the moderate writers of the Gallican school

(e. g. Nat. Alexander, IX, pp. 433–599) admit that after the appearance of the Bull of Eugene IV (18 September, 1437) transferring the council to Ferrara, the proceedings at Basle can be regarded only as the work of a schismatical conventicle. On the other hand, writers like Bellarmine (De Concil., I, vii), Roncaglia, and Holstein absolutely refuse to number Basle among the general councils of the Church on account of the small number of bishops in attendance at the beginning, and the subsequent rebellious attitude in face of the papal decrees of dissolution. The true opinion seems to be that put forward by Hefele (Conciliengesch., 2d ed., I, 63–99) that the assembly at Basle may be regarded as œcumenical from the beginning until the Bull "Doctoris Gentium" (18 September, 1437) transferred its sessions to Ferrara, and that the decrees passed during that period regarding the extirpation of heresy, the establishment of peace among Christian nations, and the reform of the Church, if they are not prejudicial to the Apostolic See, may be considered as the decrees of a general council. In accordance with the above-mentioned decree of Constance, the Council of Pavia had been convoked by Martin V (1423), and on the appearance of the plague in that city its sessions were transferred to Sienna. Very little was done except to determine the place where the next council should be held. An Italian city was looked upon with disfavour, as likely to be too friendly to the papacy; the French bishops and the Paris University were anxious that some place in France should be selected; but finally, owing mainly to the representations of Emperor Sigismund, Basle was agreed upon by all, and this choice having been made, the council was dissolved (7 March, 1424). As the time approached for the assembling of the council Martin V was urged from all sides to place no obstacle in the way, and though knowing the tendency at the time, and fearing that the council would lead to revolution rather than reform, he finally gave his consent and appointed Cardinal Giuliano Cæsarini as president (1 February, 1431).

The principal purpose of the council was to be the reformation of the Church in its "head and members", the settlement of the Hussite wars, the establishment of peace among the nations of Europe, and finally the reunion of the Western and Eastern Churches. The demands of the Roman Curia, its constant interference in the bestowal of benefices, the right of appeal on all matters to the prejudice of the local authorities, the financial burdens involved in such institutions as annates, expectancies, and reservations, not to speak of the direct papal taxation, only too common since the thirteenth century, had given just grounds for complaint to the clergy and secular powers of the different nations. These papal taxes and encroachments on the rights of the local authorities, both ecclesiastical and civil, had long been bitterly resented, especially in England and Germany, and it was because a remedy for these abuses was hoped for only from a general council that people regarded sympathetically the assembly at Basle, even at times when they did not agree with its methods. In addition to these, the question of simony, of concubinage among the clergy, of reorganization of diocesan and provincial synods, of the abuse of censures, especially of interdict, called for some reform in the discipline of the Church. But besides these disciplinary matters the teaching of Wyclif and Hus had found sympathetic supporters in England and Bohemia, and notwithstanding the condemnation at Constance the Hussites were still a powerful party in the latter country. Though the death of their leader Ziska (1424) had proved a serious loss, the different sections still continued the struggle, and Emperor

Sigismund was naturally anxious that an end should be put to the war which had already taxed his resources to the uttermost. Furthermore, the growing power of the Turks was a menace not alone to the existence of the Eastern Empire but to the whole of Europe, and made it imperative upon the Christian princes to abandon their internecine strife and unite with the Greeks in defence of their common Christianity against the power of Islam. The movement in favour of reunion had been specially favoured by Martin V and by the Emperor John VII Palæologus (1425–48).

The president of the council, Cardinal Giuliano Cæsarini, appointed by Martin V and confirmed by Eugene IV, presided at the first public session, but retired immediately upon the receipt of the papal Bull dissolving the council (December, 1431). The members then nominated Bishop Philibert of Constance as president. Later on, probably at the seventh general session (6 November, 1432), Cæsarini resumed the presidency and continued the guiding spirit in opposition to the pope till the extreme element under Cardinal d'Allemand of Arles began to gain the upper hand. In the general assembly (6 December, 1436) he refused to agree to the wishes of the majority that Basle, Avignon, or some city of Savoy should be selected as the meeting place of the council to be held for the reunion of the Greeks with the Western Church, but he continued to act as president till the 31st of July, 1437, when a decree was passed summoning Pope Eugene IV to appear at Basle within sixty days to answer for his disobedience. Cæsarini finally left Basle after the appearance of the Bull, "Doctoris Gentium" (18 September, 1437) transferring the council to Ferrara, and joined the adherents of the pope. After his withdrawal, Cardinal d'Allemand played the leading part and on the election of the antipope, Felix V, was nominated by him as president of the assembly. The nomination however, was disregarded by the members who thereupon elected the Archbishop of Tarentaise. The other members of the council who took a prominent part in the proceedings were Capranica who had been appointed cardinal by Martin, but who as his appointment had not been published was not admitted to the conclave on the death of Martin nor recognized by Eugene; Æneas Sylvius Piccolomini, afterwards Pope Pius II; the renowned scholar Nicholas of Cusa; Cardinal Louis d'Allemand; John of Antioch; John of Ragusa, and the two canonists, Nicholas, Archbishop of Palermo, and Louis Pontanus.

Eugene IV confirmed his predecessor's appointment of Cæsarini as president on the very day of his coronation (12 March), but with certain reservations which were dictated by Eugene's desire of holding a council in some city more convenient for the representatives of the Greeks. There was present at Basle on the day on which the council should have been opened (4 March) only one delegate, but by the beginning of April, three representatives arrived from the University of Paris, together with the Bishop of Chalons and the Abbot of Cîteaux. These six came together (11 April) and issued pressing letters of invitation to the cardinals, bishops, and princes of Europe. Cæsarini, who. up to this time had been engaged in the crusade organized against the Hussites, endeavoured to reassure the delegates and to restrain their eagerness, while the influence of Sigismund was employed in the same direction. The pope wrote to Cæsarini (31 May) requesting him to settle the affair of the Hussites as quickly as possible and then to proceed to Basle for the opening of the council. On the reception of this letter the legate determined, after consultation with Sigismund, to remain with the military

forces, but at the same time to dispatch two of his companions, John of Palomar and John of Ragusa, to act as his representatives at Basle. These arrived there on 19 July and held an assembly (23 July) in the Cathedral of Basle at which the documents of authorization were read, and the council declared formally opened. Though there were not a dozen members present the assembly immediately arrogated to itself the title of a general council, and began to act as if its authority were secured.

Cæsarini, after the failure of his crusade against the Hussites, arrived in Basle on the 11th of September and a few days later (17 September), in accordance with instructions received from Eugene, dispatched John Beaupère to Rome, in the capacity of delegate, to inform the pope of the proceedings. The delegate who was unfavourable to the continuance of the council represented to the pope that very few prelates had attended, that there was little hope of an increased number owing to the war between Burgundy and Austria and the general unsafety of the roads, and that even the city of Basle itself was in danger and its people unfriendly to the clergy. On the receipt of this news Eugene issued (12 November) a commission to Cæsarini, signed by twelve cardinals, empowering him to dissolve the council, if he should deem it advisable, and to convoke another to meet at Bologna eighteen months after the dissolution. Meanwhile the assembly at Basle had entered into communication with the Hussites, requesting them to send representatives to the council, and, in case they complied, granting letters of safe-conduct. This was understood at Rome as indicating a desire to reopen for discussion questions of doctrine already settled at Constance and at Sienna, and as a result Eugene IV issued (18 December) a Bull dissolving the council and convoking another to meet at Bologna.

Before the arrival of this Bull Cæsarini had already (14 December) held the first public session, at which were present three bishops, fourteen abbots, and a considerable body of doctors and priests. Naturally enough, the Bull of dissolution, though not entirely unexpected, gave great offence to those present, and on the 3d of January, 1432, when it was to have been read, the members absented themselves from the sitting to prevent its publication. Cæsarini forwarded to Rome a strongly worded protest against the dissolution, in which he pointed out the evil consequences which would result from such a step, but at the same time in obedience to the papal Bull he resigned his position as president of the council. Sigismund, who had already appointed Duke William of Bavaria protector of the council, was also opposed to the action of Eugene IV, as he had great hopes that through this council the Hussite controversy might be terminated; on the other hand, he wished to stand well with the pope, from whom he expected the imperial crown. Hence it is that while sympathizing generally with the council, he played the rôle of mediator rather than that of defender. Delegates were dispatched from Basle to secure the withdrawal of the Bull.

Many of the princes of Europe who had hoped for useful reforms from the labours of the council expressed their disapproval of the papal action, and more especially the Duke of Milan who was personally hostile to Eugene IV. Relying on this support the second public session was held (15 February, 1432) at which were renewed the decrees of Constance declaring that a general council had its authority directly from Christ and that all, even the pope, are bound to obey it. Besides, it was decreed that the "General Council" now in session could not be transferred, prorogued, or dissolved without its own consent. Everything seemed just then to favour the council. Sigismund had a powerful army in Northern Italy; an Assembly of the French Clergy at Bourges (February, 1432) declared for the continuation of the council at Basle and resolved to send representatives; the Duke of Burgundy wrote that he would send the bishops of his own nation and would use his influence with the King of England to induce him to do likewise; the Dukes of Milan and Savoy were equally sympathetic, while the Paris University declared that the devil alone could have inspired the pope to adopt such a course. Thus encouraged the council held its third public session (29 April, 1432) in which the pope was commanded to withdraw the Bull of dissolution and to appear at Basle either personally or by proxy within three months. A similar summons was addressed to the cardinals, and both pope and cardinals were threatened with judicial proceedings unless they complied. In the fourth public session (20 June, 1432) it was decreed that in case the papal throne should become vacant during the time of the council, the conclave could be held only at its place of session; that in the meantime Eugene IV should appoint no cardinals except at the council, nor should he hinder any person from attending, and that all censures pronounced against it by him were null and void. They even went so far as to appoint a governor for the territory of Avignon and to forbid any papal embassy to approach Basle unless letters of safe-conduct had been previously requested and granted.

Sigismund was in constant communication with the pope and urged him to make some concessions. In the beginning Eugene IV agreed to allow a national council to be held in some German city for the reform of abuses in the Church of Germany and for the settlement of the Hussite controversy. Later on, he was willing to permit the council at Basle to continue its discussions on church reform, the Hussite controversy, and the establishment of peace among Christian nations, provided that its decisions were subject to the papal confirmation, and provided, too, that a council should be held in Bologna, or some Italian city for the reunion of the Eastern Church. Sigismund forwarded this letter to Basle (27 July) and exhorted the delegates to moderation. On the 22d of August, the plenipotentiaries of the pope were received at Basle and addressed the council at length, pointing out that the monarchical form of government was the one established by Christ, that the pope was the supreme judge in ecclesiastical affairs, and that the Bull of dissolution was not due to the pope's jealousy of a general council as such. They ended by declaring that the assembly at Basle, if it persisted in its opposition to Eugene, could be regarded only as a schismatical conventicle and was certain to lead, not to reform, but to still greater abuses. In the name of the pope they made an offer of Bologna or some city in the Papal States as the place for the future council, the pope to resign his sovereign rights over the city selected, so long as the assembly should be in session. The council replied to this communication (3 September) by reasserting the superiority of a general council over the pope in all matters appertaining to faith, discipline, or the extirpation of schism, and by an absolute rejection of the offers made by the plenipotentiaries.

In the sixth public session (6 September), at which were present four cardinals (Cæsarini, Branda, Castiglione, and Albergati) and thirty-two bishops, it was proposed to declare Eugene and his eighteen cardinals contumacious, but this proposal was postponed, owing, mainly, to the representations of Sigismund. In October, the standing orders for the transaction of the business of the council were drawn up. Without reference to their ecclesi-

astical rank the members were divided into four committees, on which the four nations attending the council should be equally represented. The votes of the cardinals or bishops were of no more importance than those of the professors, canons, or parish priests; in this way it was secured that the inferior clergy should have the controlling voice in the decisions of the council. Each committee was to carry on its sittings in a separate hall and to communicate its decisions to the others, and it was only when practical unanimity had been secured among the committees that the matter was introduced at a public session of the whole body. This arrangement, whereby the irresponsible members had gained the upper hand, tended to bring affairs to a crisis. In the seventh public session (6 November) it was arranged that in case of Eugene's death the cardinals should appear at the council within 60 days for the holding of the conclave. Shortly afterwards, at the eighth public session (18 December), the pope was allowed a further term of sixty days to withdraw the Bull of dissolution, under threat of canonical proceedings in case he failed to comply, and, finally, at the tenth public session (19 February, 1433) this threat was enforced, and in the presence of five cardinals and forty-six bishops the pope was declared contumacious and canonical proceedings were instituted against him.

Eugene IV, afflicted with bodily suffering, deserted by many of his cardinals, and hard pressed by Italian rebels, endeavoured by every means in his power, together with the support of Philip, Duke of Milan, to bring about a settlement. He proposed (14 December, 1432) an Italian town as the place for the council, allowing the assembly at Basle four months to settle up the Hussite controversy; on the rejection of this, he agreed that it should be held in a German city provided twelve impartial bishops and the ambassadors of the different countries so wished it. Later still (1 February, 1433) he accepted a German town unconditionally, and even went so far as to agree to accept (14 February, 1433) Basle itself in case the decrees against the papal power were withdrawn, his own legate allowed to preside, and the number of bishops present at least seventy-five. These offers were rejected by the council (March, 1433), the decree about the superiority of a general council renewed (27 April), and it was with difficulty that Duke William of Bavaria prevented the opening of the process against the pope in the twelfth general session (13 July). Meanwhile Sigismund had made peace with Eugene and had received the imperial crown in Rome (31 May, 1433). He requested the council not to proceed further against the pope until he himself should be present, and on the other hand he pressed the pope to make some further concession. In response to this appeal Eugene issued (1 August, 1433) a Bull in which he declared that he was willing and content that the council should be recognized as lawfully constituted from the beginning and continued as if nothing had happened, and that he himself would assist its deliberations by every means in his power, provided, however, that his legates were admitted as real presidents, and that all decrees against himself or his cardinals were withdrawn. This declaration coincided exactly with the formula sent by Cæsarini to the emperor (18 June) except that the pope had inserted "we are willing and content" (*volumus et contentamur*) in place of the words "we decree and declare" (*decernimus et declaramus*). This change was displeasing to the council, implying, as it did, mere toleration and not the approbation which they desired; so relying upon Eugene's troubles in Italy with the Colonnas, the Duke of Milan, and others, they refused to accept even this concession. Finally, on the 15th of December, 1433,

Eugene issued a Bull in which he accepted the formula "we decree and declare" by which he withdrew all his previous manifestoes against the Council of Basle.

Thus peace was established between the two parties, but the reconciliation was more apparent than real. The papal legates were indeed admitted as presidents, but their jurisdiction was denied, their powers limited by the will of the council, they were even forced to accept the decrees of Constance which they did in their own name but not in the name of the pope (24 April, 1434), and finally, when in the eighteenth public session (26 June) the Constance decrees were solemnly renewed they refused to attend. In spite of their efforts the council continued in its opposition to the pope, claiming jurisdiction in all affairs, political and religious, and entering into negotiations with the Greeks about the reunion of the Churches. At the twentieth public session (22 January, 1435) the reform of church discipline was begun. Decrees were passed against concubinage of the clergy and the abuse of excommunications and interdicts. On the 9th of June, 1435, annates and all the customary papal taxes were abolished, although no steps were taken to provide for the financial status of the papacy. Later still the papal collectors were ordered to appear in Basle to render an account of their work, and all outstanding debts due to the pope were to be paid at Basle. The papal delegates, especially Traversari and Anton de Vito, defended the rights of Eugene, but the moderate element was gradually losing control in the assembly, and the extreme party, gathered around Cardinal Louis d'Allemand, could no longer be restrained. No legislation had any chance of being passed unless directed against the Holy See. At last, after the papal deputies, Cardinals Albergati and Cervantes, had been received very badly at Basle (25 March, 1436), and after decrees had been passed regarding the future conclave, the papal oath, the number of cardinals, etc., Eugene IV realized that conciliation was no longer possible, and addressed a Note to the princes of Europe in which he summed up the injuries inflicted on the papacy by the council and requested the different rulers to withdraw their bishops from Basle and assist in the preparation for another general council from the deliberations of which something better might be awaited.

The council had previously opened communication with the Greeks (September, 1434) to determine where the assembly for reunion should be held. In December, 1436, it was proposed that the council should be held either at Basle itself, at Avignon, or in Savoy. Cardinal Cæsarini refused to put this proposal to the meeting, but on the motion of Cardinal d'Allemand it was passed. The pope refused to consent, and the deputies of the Greek Emperor protested against it (23 February, 1437), whereupon a new embassy was dispatched to Constantinople. The Greeks refused to come either to Basle or Savoy, and the people of Avignon had shown no desire that the council should be held there. A strong minority, including the papal legates, and most of the bishops present, wished that some Italian city should be selected; the majority, led by Cardinal d'Allemand and composed mainly of the inferior clergy, were opposed to this proposal, and after a disorderly session (7 May, 1437), at which both parties published their decrees, Eugene IV confirmed that of the minority, and the Greek ambassador declared it to be the one acceptable to the emperor. The revolutionary party now completely controlled the council. Against the wishes of Cæsarini, Cervantes, and Sigismund, the pope was commanded (31 July, 1437) to appear before the council to answer for his disobedience, and

on the 1st of October he was declared contumacious. Eugene IV replied to these excesses by the publication of the Bull "Doctoris gentium" (18 September), in which it was stated that unless the delegates abandoned their methods and confined themselves for a limited number of days only to the Bohemian affair the council would be transferred to Ferrara. The reply was a reassertion of the superiority of a general council (19 October). Cardinal Cæsarini made one final effort to effect a reconciliation, but failed, and then, accompanied by all the cardinals except d'Allemand and by most of the bishops, he left Basle and joined the pope at Ferrara, to which place the council had been definitely transferred by a Bull of Eugene IV (30 December).

Henceforth the assembly at Basle could be regarded only as schismatical. Most of the Christian world stood loyal to the pope and to the Council of Ferrara. England, Castile and Aragon, Milan, and Bavaria disavowed the assembly at Basle, while, on the other hand, France and Germany, though recognizing Eugene IV, endeavoured to maintain a neutral position. In a meeting of the French Clergy at Bourges (May, 1438), at which were present delegates from the pope and from Basle, it was determined to remain loyal to Eugene, while at the same time many of the reforms of Basle were accepted with certain modifications. It was on this basis that the twenty-three articles of the Pragmatic Sanction of Bourges were drawn up (7 July, 1438). In Germany, after the death of Sigismund (9 December, 1437), delegates of both parties attended at Frankfort (1438) to seek the assistance of the princes, but they declared for neutrality until a king had been elected, and even after the election of Albrecht II the attitude of neutrality was maintained till at last, in Mainz (March, 1439), they followed the example of France and declared for Eugene IV as lawful pope while they accepted many of the reforms of Basle.

In Basle itself it was resolved to depose the pope and in order to prepare the way for deposition three articles were drawn up, namely: (1) that a general council is superior to a pope; (2) that the pope cannot prorogue, or dissolve such an assembly; (3) that whoever denies these is a heretic. Cardinal d'Allemand was the leading spirit in this undertaking. Against the wishes of the bishops and most of the ambassadors present, these decrees were passed (16 May, 1439), and Eugene IV was deposed as a heretic and schismatic (25 June). Immediately steps were taken to elect his successor. Cardinal Louis d'Allemand, eleven bishops, five theologians, and nine jurists and canonists formed the conclave, and on the 30th of October, 1439, Amadeus, ex-Duke of Savoy, was elected and took the name of Felix V. Since his retirement he had been living with a body of knights, which he organized as the Order of St. Maurice, on the banks of the Lake of Geneva. He was closely connected with many of the princes of Europe, and the council stood in bad need of the wealth which he was reputed to possess. He named Cardinal d'Allemand president, but the conventicle resented this act of authority and elected instead the Bishop of Tarentaise (26 February, 1440). Steps were also taken to levy taxes on ecclesiastical benefices to provide revenue for Felix V (4 August, 1440). But the election of an antipope alienated the sympathy of the world from Basle. Henceforth they could rely only upon Switzerland and Savoy.

Disputes soon broke out between Felix V and the conventicle at Basle. It refused to allow his name to precede that of the council in the promulgation of its decrees, and he was unwilling to undergo the expense of supporting nuncios in the different countries. The sessions became less frequent, the relations between Felix V and the council were strained until, at last, in defiance of its wishes, he left Basle and took up his residence at Lausanne (December, 1442). Disappointed in the hope of securing the support of Sforza, Aragon, or Milan, the council held its last session at Basle (16 May, 1443), and decreed that a general council should be held in Lyons after three years; that until the opening of this the Council of Basle should continue its work, and in case the city of Basle should become unsafe that it should be transferred to Lausanne. No decrees of general interest were passed after this session. But it was some time before the princes of Germany could be induced to abandon the attitude of neutrality. At different diets, Nuremberg (1438), Mainz (1441), Frankfort (1442), Nuremberg (1443, 1444), Frankfort (1445), it was proposed that a new general council should be held to settle the disputes between Basle and Eugene IV. A sentence of deposition issued by Eugene IV against the Prince-Electors of Cologne and Trier who favoured Basle roused all the princes of Germany against him, and at the Diet of Frankfort (1446) it was resolved to send an embassy to Rome to demand the convocation of a new council, and, in the meantime, the recognition of the reforms effected in Basle; else they would withdraw from their allegiance. The Emperor Frederick III dissented from this decision and sent his secretary, Æneas Sylvius, to confer with the pope. At last, after long negotiation in Rome and Frankfort, an agreement was arrived at (February, 1447) known as the Concordat of the Princes. On their side they agreed to abandon the attitude of neutrality, while the pope restored the deposed princes and accepted with modifications certain of the reforms of Basle. In accordance with this agreement the Vienna Concordat was drawn up between the successor of Eugene IV and the Emperor Frederick III. The pope's rights in the appointment to benefices were clearly defined, and the sources of revenue to take the place of the annates, then abolished, were agreed upon. Once this had been concluded, Frederick III forbade the city of Basle to harbour any longer the schismatical assembly, and in June, 1448, they were obliged to retire to Lausanne. Finally, after a few sessions at Lausanne, Felix V resigned and submitted to the lawful pope, Nicholas V. The members of the assembly also elected Nicholas as pope and then decreed the dissolution of the council (25 April, 1449).

It only remains to deal with the negotiations between the Council of Basle and the Hussites. The latter were invited, as we have seen, at the very beginning of the council, but it was only in the fourth session (20 June, 1432) that the conditions proposed by the Hussites were accepted, and prayers ordered for their return to the Church. About the beginning of January, 1433, nearly three hundred of the Calixtine party arrived, and after repeated negotiations in Prague and Basle, the four articles demanded by the Hussites were agreed upon with certain modifications. These were Communion under both kinds, though their priests were to teach that Communion under one kind was equally valid; free preaching of the word of God, but subject to ecclesiastical authority; the punishment of mortal sin, but only by a lawful tribunal; the retention of their temporalities by the clerics, who were however, bound to bestow their superfluous wealth according to the canons. These formed the Compact of Prague, agreed upon the 30th of November, 1433. Many of the more extreme sects, such as the Taborites, refused to accept this treaty, but after their defeat (Lippau, 1434) a better feeling set in, and a similar compact was proclaimed at Iglau in July, 1436, and enforced by the Council of Basle (15 January, 1437).

The Council of Basle might have done much to secure reforms, then so badly needed, and to restore confidence in ecclesiastical authority. From all sides it was assured of sympathy and support as the one remedy for the abuses which existed. But under the influence of extreme theories and theorists it allowed itself to be hurried into an inglorious struggle with the pope, and the valuable time and energy which should have been given up to useful legislation were spent in useless discussions. It succeeded in fixing the eyes of the world upon the abuses, but without the pope it had not sufficient authority to carry through the necessary reforms, and as a consequence the secular rulers undertook what the ecclesiastical authority had shamefully failed to set right. It struck a terrible blow at the rights of the Holy See and shook men's faith in the pope's spiritual power at a time when his temporal sovereignty was in imminent danger. In this way it led directly in France, through the Pragmatic Sanction of Bourges, to the establishment of Gallicanism as a definite formula, while in Germany, through the long intervals of neutrality, people were prepared for the complete severance from the Holy See which was afterwards effected in the Reformation.

MANSI, *Concil. Coll.*, XXIX–XXXI; HARDOUIN, *Concil.*, VIII, IX; *Monumenta Concil. General. sæc. XV*, ed. Acad. Scient. (Vienna, 1857–96), I–III; *Deutsche Reichstagsakten* VII–XI; MARTÈNE AND DURAND, *Veterum script. et monument. collectio*, VIII; ÆNEAS SYLVIUS, *De rebus Basileæ gestis*, ed FEA, in *Pius II Pont. Max. a calumniis vindicatus* (Rome, 1823); AUGUSTINUS PATRICIUS, *Summa Conciliorum Basil. et Floren.*, ed. HARDOUIN, *Concilia*, IX; HALLER, *Studien und Quellen zur Geschichte des Konzils von Basel* (Basle, 1895, 1903), I, IV; CECCONI, *Studii storici sul concilio di Firenze* (Florence, 1869); HEFELE, *Conciliengeschichte*, VII; PASTOR, *History of the Popes*, tr. ANTROBUS (London, 1891), I, 280–350; CREIGHTON, *A History of the Papacy* (London, 1892), II, 92–194.

JAMES MACCAFFREY.

Basle-Lugano, DIOCESE OF, is the largest Catholic diocese of Switzerland. It is composed of the two Dioceses of Basle and Lugano which are united only by having a bishop in common.

I. THE DIOCESE OF BASLE.—This has taken the place of the old Diocese of Augst (Augusta Rauracorum), the origin of which is obscure; a Bishop of Augst was a member of a council held at Cologne in 346. When Augusta Rauracorum sank into decay during the disorders of the migrations the seat of the diocese was transferred to the present Basle (Basilea), founded in 374 by the Emperor Valentinian I. No definite information has been preserved concerning the first bishops. The most important bishop in the early period of the history of the diocese is Hatto, a Benedictine from the monastery of Reichenau, who was a friend of Charlemagne; he was Bishop of Basle from the year 805. He issued a capitulary of great importance for his diocese, resigned his position in 822, and retired to Reichenau where he died in 836. During the episcopate of Adalbert (999–1025) the foundation of the secular jurisdiction of the Bishops of Basle was laid by the grants made by King Rudolph III of Burgundy; the king appointed the bishop administrator and protector of several religious foundations, bestowed a number of towns and territories on him, and conferred various rights, such as the right of coinage, hunting-rights, etc. Adalbert rebuilt the cathedral which had been pillaged by the Magyars and consecrated it with much pomp in 1019 in the presence of the Emperor Henry II and his wife. Adalbert's immediate successors Ulrich II (1025–40) and Dietrich (1041–53) were included among the spiritual princes of the Holy Roman Empire. In the period following Adalbert's administration the territory of the diocese was greatly increased, especially through gifts made by the Emperors Henry II, Henry III, and Conrad II. As princes of the empire the Bishops of Basle were drawn into the struggle between the papacy and the empire; most of the bishops took sides with the emperors against the popes. Berengar (1057–72) promoted, in opposition to Alexander II, the nomination of the Antipope Honorius at a synod held at Basle in 1061; Burkhard of Hasenburg (1071–1107) was one of the most resolute champions of the imperial claims and a faithful partisan of Henry IV whom he accompanied to Canossa. Ortlieb of Froburg (1137–64) went with the Emperor Conrad III on a crusade to Palestine and took part in the Italian campaigns of Frederick Barbarossa; Ludwig of Ortlieb was also a partisan of the emperor and of the Antipope Paschal; Alexander III, therefore, deposed him in 1179. Among the succeeding bishops the most noteworthy were: Henry II of Thun (1238–49), who built the oldest bridge across the Rhine near Basle (replaced in 1904–06 by a new one); Henry of Isny (1275–86), a Franciscan, who after 1286 was Archbishop of Mainz, as was also his successor Peter Rich of Richenstein (1286–96), a devoted partisan of Rudolph of

Hapsburg; Peter of Aspelt (1296–1306), later Archbishop of Mainz, who laboured to restore church discipline in his diocese. During the fourteenth century the prestige of the See of Basle declined; many of the bishops involved the diocese in debt in various ways; by taking part in the political quarrels, by feuds with the nobles living in Basle, and by quarrels with the city, which was rapidly growing in strength. The city of Basle bought nearly the whole of the jurisdiction over itself from the impecunious bishops and made itself almost entirely independent of episcopal secular rule. When John II of Münsingen (1335–65) was placed under the ban, along with the city of Basle, as a partisan of Louis the Bavarian, the citizens of the town threw the papal nuncio into the Rhine and forced the clergy to continue the church services or to leave the place. The earthquake of 1356 destroyed a large part of the city and also did much damage to the cathedral. John III of Vienne (1366–82) became involved in a dispute with Bern which led to a quarrel with Basle and the siege of this city by the bishop. The increased burden of debt thus caused was a source of great anxiety to the succeeding bishops, several of whom resigned their office. It was not until the episcopate of John IV of Fleckenstein (1423–36), who held two reform synods, that the see rose again to high reputation. The Council of Basle (1431–49) was held in the city of the same name during this episcopate and that of the following bishop, Frederick of the Rhine (1436–51). (See BASLE, COUNCIL OF.) The diocese suffered greatly at the time of the struggle of the Swiss confederation with Charles of Burgundy; many towns and castles were ravaged and burned during these troubles.

The Diocese of Basle attained its greatest extent in the course of the fifteenth century. The spiritual

power of the bishops, but not their secular jurisdiction, extended over the entire northwestern part of present Switzerland lying between the Rivers Aare, Rhine, and Doubs, over the southern part of the present Alsace as far as Rappoltsweiler and Schlettstadt, as well as over some small districts in Baden and France. The Reformation was to rob the bishops of a large part of their flock. At the beginning of the religious agitation the diocese was under the rule of Christopher of Utenheim (1502–27), one of the most distinguished of the Prince-Bishops of Basle. He was a friend of the arts and sciences and a promoter of the new art of printing, then flourishing at Basle. In order to train and reform his clergy Bishop Christopher held in 1503 a synod at which excellent statutes were issued; he also called learned men as professors and preachers for the university that had been founded in 1460. This last measure, however, promoted the entry of the new doctrine. A number of the scholars who had been appointed, as Capito, Pellicanus, Œcolampadius, and for a time also, Erasmus and Glareanus, took sides with the Reformers and worked for the spread of the Reformation. Basle became a centre for the printing and dispatch in all directions of the writings of the Reformers. Before long the Great Council and the citizens were split into two religious parties and internal disputes were common. Bent from extreme age, Bishop Christopher, in 1527, resigned his see. Before his successor Philip of Gundelsheim (1527–53) was able to enter the city, the party advocating the new doctrine obtained control, the Catholic members of the Great Council were driven from office, the Catholic religion was declared to be abolished, the monasteries were closed, and the churches were plundered. The bishop changed his place of residence to Pruntrut (Porrentruy); the cathedral chapter went to Freiburg-in-the-Breisgau and did not return into the territory of the diocese until 1678 when it established itself at Arlesheim.

Succeeding bishops devoted themselves to repairing the severe losses which the diocese had suffered during the Reformation. The bishop who deserves the greatest credit for the restoration of the prosperity of the bishopric was Jacob Christopher Blarer von Wartensee (1575–1608). He made an alliance offensive and defensive with the Catholic cantons of Switzerland in 1580, proclaimed the decisions of the Council of Trent, held in 1581 a diocesan synod which bore good fruit, and brought back to the Church numerous subjects who had been estranged from the Catholic religion. He was ably seconded in his labours by the Jesuits whom he called in 1591 to Pruntrut and put in charge of the newly founded college. His successors followed in his footsteps, especially Joseph William Rink von Baldenstein (1608–28). In the course of the Thirty Years War the diocese suffered from invasions by the troops of Bernard of Weimar. During the episcopate of Bishop John Conrad von Roggenbach (1656–93) the cathedral chapter established itself once more in the diocese, at Arlesheim, as has been mentioned above. Bishop Conrad von Reinach (1705–37), who founded the seminary for priests and built Castle Delsberg, a residence of the prince-bishops, issued a series of ordinances in 1726 which curtailed the rights and privileges of the land. This caused a revolt that lasted into the episcopate of his successor Jacob Sigmund von Reinach (1737–43) and was only suppressed with the aid of French troops. The three leaders of the revolt were executed in 1740. An estrangement resulted that was not overcome in spite of all the efforts of the succeeding bishops, Joseph William Rink von Baldenstein (1744–62), Simon Nicholas von Froberg (1762–75), and Frederick Ludwig von Wangen-Geroldseck (1775–82).

The French Revolution put an end to the secular

jurisdiction of the bishops. The prince-bishopric was occupied by French troops in 1792 and Bishop John Sigmund von Roggenbach (1782–94) fled to Constance. His territory was turned into the Rauracian Republic which after four months was incorporated, 1793, in the French Republic. Besides the loss of secular jurisdiction the bishop had also to forego a large part of his ecclesiastical diocese, for, according to the Concordat made in 1801 between Pius VII and Napoleon, a large part of the Bishopric of Basle was given to the Diocese of Strasburg. The next bishop, Francis Xavier von Neveu (1794–1828), resided first at Constance and then at Offenburg; he ruled only a small territory in the present Cantons of Solothurn, Aargau, and Bern. It was not until 1814 that the bishop obtained again the right to ecclesiastical supervision over the larger part of the former prince-bishopric; but his efforts to bring about the restoration of the secular power were unavailing. In 1815 the Congress of Vienna gave the territory of the diocese to the Cantons of Bern and Basle, with the exception of the portion already belonging to Germany. Not long after this, however, the Diocese of Basle was enlarged. After the disorders of the Napoleonic era the Swiss confederation had been reorganized; in order to make it equally independent in Church matters the Swiss part of the Diocese of Constance was separated in 1814 from that bishopric and placed provisionally under a vicar Apostolic. Long negotiations were entered into between the cantons in the territory of which these portions of the diocese lay, and it was finally resolved to carry out the plan that had been steadily urged by the Canton of Solothurn; this was, to revive the Bishopric of Basle and to define anew its boundaries. The negotiations with Rome were concluded in 1828; the Bull of Leo XII, "Inter præcipuâ Nostri Apostolatus munerâ", issued 7 May, 1828, settled the boundaries of the new Diocese of Basle, and the Bull of 13 July, 1828, was solemnly read at Solothurn in the collegiate church of Sts. Ursus and Victor which had been elevated to a cathedral. Bishop Francis Xavier von Neveu died a few days later. The new cathedral chapter, which had been appointed, in order to bring it into existence by the pope, nominated as bishop the dean of the cathedral who had formerly been the administrator Apostolic, Anthony Salzmann (1828–54). The new Diocese of Basle, which is directly dependent on the Apostolic See, embraced at first the Cantons of Lucerne, Bern, Solothurn, and Zug; in 1829 Aargau and Thurgau were added; somewhat later Basle, for the Catholic district of Birseck; in 1841 Schaffhausen, first provisionally, and then, in 1858, definitely although without confirmation from Rome.

The germs of many conflicts lay hid in this merely provisional new arrangement and in the uncertainty as to the legal relations of the new see. However, during the episcopate of Bishop Salzmann and that of his immediate successor Charles Arnold (1854–62), the founder of a seminary for priests at Solothurn, peace was fairly well preserved. During the episcopate of Eugene Lachat (1863–85) a struggle broke out, caused by the Old-Catholic movement which won many adherents in Switzerland. The liberal cantons of the Diocese of Basle (all except Lucerne and Zug) closed the seminary for priests in April, 1870, and forbade the promulgation of the decrees of the Council of the Vatican. When in 1871 the bishop, nevertheless, proclaimed these decrees, the majority of the cantons belonging to the diocese voted his deposition, 29 January, 1873, and dissolved the cathedral chapter, 21 December, 1874, which had refused to elect a new bishop. The bishop, being forced to leave his residence, went to Lucerne which, like the canton of Zug, had protested against the action of the other cantons and had remained faith-

ful to the bishop. Here in Lucerne he continued to administer the diocese. His appeals to the federal authorities of Switzerland were rejected and the Catholic community was forbidden to have communication with him. It was not until the pontificate of Leo XIII that this unfortunate state of affairs was brought to an end and peace re-established. Bishop Lachat resigned his office in 1885 and was made titular Archbishop of Damietta and Administrator Apostolic of the newly formed Bishopric of Lugano (see below). He died in 1886. On 19 January, 1885, the Holy See appointed Frederick Fiala Bishop of Basle (1885–88). The new bishop sought to efface the traces of the late struggle and re-establish the cathedral chapter; he died 4 May, 1888. Leonard Haas (1888–1906) was appointed to the see 11 July, 1888. Bishop Haas was an eloquent preacher; he encouraged the use of congregational singing and held a diocesan synod in 1896. He was followed in 1906 by Dr. Jacob Stammler, born 2 January, 1840, and ordained to the priesthood in 1863.

STATISTICS.—The present Diocese of Basle (excluding Lugano) embraces the Cantons of Basle, Bern, Lucerne, Solothurn, Aargau, Thurgau, and Schaffhausen; in 1900 it contained 444,471 Catholics and 903,400 Protestants. The majority of the inhabitants are Germans, although in the Canton of Bern some 6,000 Catholics speak French. For the spiritual direction of the Catholic community the diocese is divided into 8 deaneries, 14 rural chapters, 406 parishes, and 149 curacies and chaplaincies. The parishes in the Cantons of Zug and Schaffhausen are not united in a rural chapter. The secular priests number 660; the regular clergy (O.S.B. and O.M.C.) 85. The cathedral senate, which has the right to elect the bishop, consists of five resident canons (*canonici residentiales*) and six non-resident canons (*canonici forenses*); besides these there are seven cathedral capitulars, who do not belong to the cathedral senate. In 1907 the office of capitular was vacant. There is a collegiate church at Lucerne having an independent provost and 9 canons (in 1907 the canonries were not filled), and a collegiate church at Beromünster with 1 provost and 20 regular canons (the number of canons in 1907 was 17).

The schools for the education of the clergy are: a cantonal theological school at Lucerne with a seminary for priests, and at Zug St. Michael's boarding-school for boys. The private seminary for teachers at Zug is entirely Catholic in character. In accordance with the Swiss constitution the public schools are open to members of all denominations, consequently there are no genuine Catholic parish schools. In the Cantons of Lucerne and Zug, which are almost entirely Catholic, instruction is given in many of the schools by Catholic teaching-sisters, who are obliged to pass a state examination. The male orders and their houses in the Diocese of Basle are as follows: Capuchins, 7 houses with 73 priests, 19 clerics, and 24 lay brothers; the Hermit-Brothers of Luthern, 1 house; the Benedictines of Mariastein, who were included in the Swiss congregation of the Benedictines, were driven in 1874 from Mariastein and have gone to Dürrenberg near Salzburg; the Benedictines of Muri have gone for the same reason to Gries near Bozen, and the Cistercians of Wittengen to Meherau near Bregenz. The female orders and congregations are more largely represented in the diocese than the male orders. These institutes and their houses are as follows: Benedictine nuns, 1 house; Ursulines, 4 houses; Capuchin nuns, 4; Franciscan Sisters, 1; Cistercians, 2; Clares, 1; Sisters of St. Francis de Sales, 1 house with a boarding-school for girls attached; Sisters of Charity, 5; Sisters of the Divine Providence, 1. There are large numbers of the Sisters of the Cross of Ingenbohl, who have charge chiefly of orphan asylums and hospitals and who act as attendants on the sick; also of the teaching Sisters of the Holy Cross of Menzingen, who carry on large institutes for girls at Menzingen, Baldegg, and Cham, and conduct, besides, 250 elementary schools, and 45 institutions for the poor, orphans, and sick in different parts of Switzerland. In addition to the three Catholic schools for girls mentioned above, there are similar institutions at Solothurn and Lucerne. The most important Catholic church of the diocese is the Cathedral of Solothurn, which was built, 1762–63, in the style of the Italian Renaissance; others worthy of mention are: the collegiate church of St. Leodegar at Lucerne (built 1633–35); the church of St. Oswald at Zug; the churches of the former monasteries of Fischingen, Kreuzlingen, and Beromünster; the church of the institute at Menzingen, etc. The most frequented pilgrimages are: Mariastein near Basle, and Vorburg near Delsberg. (See SWITZERLAND.)

NEUGART, Episcopatus Constantiensis Alemannicus (St. Blasien, 1803, Freiburg, 1862, 2 vols.); SCHNELLER, Die Bischöfe von Basel (Zug, 1830); TROUILLAT, Monuments de l'histoire de l'ancien évêché de Bâle (Porrentruy, 1852–66, 5 vols.); MERIAN, Geschichte der Bischöfe von Basel (Basle, 1860–62), 2 parts extending to 1330; ATTENHOFER, Die rechtliche Stellung der katholischen Kirche gegenüber der Staatsgewalt in der Diözese Basel (Lucerne, 1869); VAUTREY, Histoire des évêques de Bâle (Einsiedeln, 1884–86, 2 vols.); SCHMIDLIN, Die katholisch-theologische und kirchliche Litteratur des Bistums Basel vom Jahre 1750 bis zum Jahre 1893 (Bern, 1894–95); FLEINER, Staat und Bischofswahl im Bistum Basel (Leipzig, 1897); DAUCOURT, Les évêchés suisses (Freiburg, 1901); IDEM, Dictionnaire historique des paroisses de l'évêché de Bâle (Porrentruy, 1893–1905, 5 vols.); BÜCHI, Die katholische Kirche der Schweiz (Munich, 1902); Status cleri omnium Helvetiæ diæcesium (Solothurn, 1905).

II. THE DIOCESE OF LUGANO.—The Diocese of Lugano was erected by a Bull of Leo XIII (7 September, 1888). It includes the Swiss Canton of Ticino, where the population is almost entirely Catholic and Italian is the common language. Before the Diocese of Lugano was founded the Canton of Ticino was under the jurisdiction, in ecclesiastical matters, of bishops who were not Swiss. The smaller, northern part belonged to the Archdiocese of Milan, and, consequently, still uses the Ambrosian Rite; the other, and much larger part of the canton, belonged to the Diocese of Como. Soon after the formation of the Canton of Ticino, in 1803, efforts were made to separate it in its church relations as well as from foreign powers and to unite it in these with the rest of Switzerland. But it was several decades before the Great Council, in 1855, went thoroughly into the matter. Without consultation with the Holy See the Federal Council in 1859 declared the jurisdiction of the Bishops of Como and Milan to be abolished in the territory of Switzerland; after this negotiations were begun with Rome. No settlement of the question was reached until the pontificate of Leo XIII. By the convention of 1 September, 1884, made between the Curia and the Federal Council, Ticino was canonically separated from its former diocesan connexions and was placed, provisionally, under an administrator Apostolic, the pope appointing as administrator, Bishop Lachat of Basle (see above). After Bishop Lachat's death (1886) the new Bishopric of Ticino was formed by the Bull of circumscription "Ad universam" of Leo XIII (7 September, 1888), and united with the Diocese of Basle under the title of the Diocese of Basle-Lugano. The same year the Church of San Lorenzo was elevated to a cathedral. The union is merely a nominal one, for, although the Bishop of Basle is called the Bishop of Lugano he exercises no rights of jurisdiction in this diocese. It is, in reality, under the independent rule of an administrator Apostolic who has the rank and power of a bishop. He is appointed by the pope with the concurrence of the Bishop of Basle from among the members of the clergy of the Canton of Ticino. The first administrator Apostolic was Eugene Lachat; he was followed by Mgr. Vincent Molo (1887–1904),

and Mgr. Alfred Peri-Morosini. The latter was born 12 March, 1862, and was consecrated 17 April, 1904.

STATISTICS.—According to the Swiss census of 1900 the Diocese of Lugano includes 135,200 Catholics in a total population of 142,800 for the Canton of Ticino. For purposes of religious administration the diocese is divided into 14 episcopal vicariates, 5 rural chapters, and 248 parishes and chaplaincies; 54 parishes use the Ambrosian Rite; the other 194 parishes belong to the Latin Rite. The care of souls is exercised by 330 secular priests and 22 regular clergy. The cathedral chapter consists of an archpriest and 16 canons (10 resident and 6 non-resident). The collegiate churches are: Bellinzona, a provost and 14 canons; Agno, a provost and 7 canons; Locarno, a provost and 8 canons; Balerna, a provost and 8 canons, and Mendrisio, a provost and 8 canons. Catholic institutions of learning are: the seminary for priests at Lugano; the episcopal seminary for boys, Santa Maria near Pollegio; the papal academy at Ascona; the College Don Bosco at Bellinzona; the Institute Dante Allighieri, conducted by the Somaschi, at Bellinzona, and the institute at Olivone. The orders and congregations in the diocese and the number of their houses are as follows: Capuchins, 4 houses; the Somaschi, 1; Benedictine nuns, 1; Augustinian nuns, 1 house, which has an academy in connection with it; Capuchin nuns, 1; Sisters of Mercy of St. Vincent de Paul, 2 (hospitals at Lugano and Locarno); School-Sisters of Menzingen, 2 (college at Bellinzona); Sisters of the Holy Cross, 3 (they also conduct an asylum for the deaf and dumb at Locarno); Sisters of St. Vincent de Paul, 1; Sisters of the Childhood of Jesus, 1; and the Sisters of the Divine Providence, 1. The most noted church of the diocese is the cathedral of San Lorenzo at Lugano, which was built in the fifteenth and sixteenth centuries and has a celebrated Renaissance façade; the most frequented place of pilgrimage is the shrine Madonna del Sasso not far from Locarno, which is the national shrine of the Canton of Ticino.

FRANSCINI, Der Kanton Tessin, historisch, geographisch und statistisch geschildert (St. Gall and Bern, 1835); PERI-MOROSINI, La questione diocesana ticinese, ovvero origine della diocesi di Lugano (Einsiedeln, 1892); RAHN, Die mittelalterlichen Kunstdenkmäler des Kantons Tessin (Zurich, 1893); BORRANI, Il Ticino sacro (Lugano, 1899); CANTÙ, Storia della città e della diocesi di Como (Milan, 1829–32, 3d ed., Como, 1899–1900); MOTTA, Bolletino storico di Ticino (since 1879), and the works by BÜCHI and DAUCOURT quoted in the bibliography above.

JOSEPH LINS.

Bas-relief, a sculpture executed upon and attached to a flat surface. The usual impression produced by an artistic relief is that about one-half of the actual proportions of the object are being seen in their third dimension of depth. Strictly speaking, however, relief sculpture is subdivided into various kinds. In alto-rilievo (It. for high relief) the figures are sculptured partly or wholly in the round, that is, they project entirely, or almost entirely, from the surface of the block in which they are cut. The metopes from the Parthenon (Elgin Marbles) now in the British Museum, are among the best examples of alto-rilievo. Mezzo-rilievo (It. for semi-relief; Fr., demi-relief) presents figures that are rounded to half their natural proportions, but without detached parts. Basso-rilievo (It. for low-relief; Fr., bas-relief) is a form of surface-ornamentation in which the projection is very slight. The finest known specimen of low relief is the frieze around the cella of the Parthenon; large portions of it are to be seen in the British Museum. The lowest kind of relief is that described by the Tuscan term rilievo-stiacciato (depressed or flattened relief). This scarcely rises from the surface upon which it is carved, and is mostly an art of fine lines and delicate indications. Donatello's Florentine Madonnas and saints are among the best examples. Finally cavo-rilievo

(It. for hollow relief; Fr., *relief-en-creux*) is a method of concave sculpture in which the highest part or outline is on a level with the surface, while the roundness is considerably below it. Cavo-rilievo was practised chiefly by the Egyptians whose hollow reliefs are known by the Greek term *Koilanaglyphs*.

Relief is the form of sculpture that comes nearest to painting, both having composition, perspective, and the play of light and shadow. Relief would seem to have much in common with drawing, though in reality less importance attaches to line than to the modelling of contour and to the true and effective rendering of chiaroscuro. The human form is undoubtedly the proper object of relief, which appears to be particularly suited to the representation of numerous figures in action. In the Greek and Roman classic reliefs these figures are usually in processional order, engaged in historic or military events, or in the ceremonial of worship. Relief is

existed before the introduction of sculpture in the round, or when only rude figures of the deities had been attempted. The Babylonians, Assyrians, and Hittites practised it contemporaneously with sculpture in the round. The Egyptians, though they employed a kind of low relief, especially on the interiors of buildings, made a still greater use of Koilanaglyphs. The Greeks, conceiving relief sculpture in its purely plastic sense, achieved the greatest mastery of the art. With them it was used both as an ornament and as an integral part of the plan when allied with architecture. Distinguishing strictly between high and low relief, they used the former between the triglyphs, and in the tympana of the temples, and the latter in friezes, tombstones, etc. Certain fixed principles governed the Greek relief: the spaces were adequately filled, the backgrounds never carved, and it was a rule that all heads should be at the same height from the base, whether the figures sat, rode, or stood (*Iso-*

The Annunciation, Andrea Della Robbia, Hospital of the Innocents, Florence

well suited, also, to the portrayal of series of scenes, as in the bronze doors of various Italian baptisteries illustrating the Old and the New Testament. Figures and objects in relief are generally worked out in the same material as the background, though there are exceptions to this rule in Greek art, and in the decorative work of the Chinese and Japanese. In the larger reliefs marble, bronze, and terra-cotta are used exclusively; while in smaller works the precious metals and stones, ivory, stucco, enamel, wood, etc., predominate. The reliefs of the Egyptians and Assyrians, not highly plastic, were made more effective by the introduction of strong colours. The early Greeks also made use of polychromy, as instanced in the metope relief in the Museum of Palermo. In Gothic art and in the Renaissance it was the custom to tint wood, terra-cotta, and stucco, but not marble or stone. Relief is one of the earliest forms of sculpture practised, and probably originated with the stone-cutters of prehistoric days, though clay and wood are supposed to have been the earliest materials employed, owing to greater facility in moulding and carving them.

There is reason to believe that relief sculpture

kephaleia). In the Hellenistic period a more picturesque and dramatic form of composition prevailed, and the backgrounds were carved in pictorial style. With the Etruscans relief was applied mainly in the artistic handicrafts. In Rome it frequently degenerated into a pictorial mode in which several planes were employed, but examples are still extant that are highly classic, e. g. the groups of the Arch of Titus, the continuous winding reliefs of the Column of Trajan, imperial sarcophagi (in the Vatican), and reliefs of the Capitol Museum, Rome. The Romans no doubt owed their finest reliefs to the Greek artists they harboured and employed upon themes taken from the history of Rome.

The Christian Era inaugurated what might be mistaken for a new art, but the change was in subject more than in mode, for all the early examples show a great similarity to antique models in form, pose, and drapery. Christian relief appears mainly in the sarcophagi with their Biblical, Apostolic, or symbolic subjects: Daniel in the lions' den, Moses striking water from the rock, the adoration of the Magi, the raising of Lazarus, the Good Shepherd. Heathen myths are also used, invested with a new significance: Orpheus is Christ, drawing the creatures of the wild by the sweet strains of his music; Ulysses attached to the mast is believed to typify the Crucifixion (O. Marucchi). Occasionally a carving on a Catacomb tombstone shows real merit, and the lamps adorned with Christian symbols are frequently artistic. As they depart from the classic tradition, however, Christian reliefs grow ruder and more imperfect. Those of the latter part of the second and the third century have little merit. The fourth century, in spite of the decline, bequeathes some specimens, now in the Lateran Museum; the sarcophagus of Junius Bassus in the vaults of St. Peter's is highly esteemed as a work of art. When the Christian basilica replaced the cubiculum the influence of imperial Constantinople had substituted mosaics for both sculpture and painting. The few reliefs of that period that have survived bear a strongly Byzantine character, which is also apparent in all early Frankish workmanship, reliefs, ivory diptychs, etc. The reliefs of Ravenna, from the time of Theodoric, show the same influence in combina-

HEAD OF ST. JOHN PRESENTED TO HEROD, DONATELLO

tion with the Teutonic spirit, as in the sixth-century sculptures of San Vitale. In figure-carving, however, there is a distinct tending from symbolism to realism. The rude Lombardic bas-reliefs of Milan and Brescia frequently border on the grotesque, but the authors went to nature for their hunting scenes and forms of animals. The bronze reliefs of the church of St. Michael, Hildesheim, Germany, are one of the legacies of the eleventh century; those of the Golden Gate, Freiburg, are considered the finest work of the late Romanesque period.

With the merging of the Romanesque into the Gothic, relief sculpture assumes a new character and a peculiar importance in its close association with architecture, and in the many uses it is put to in tympana, spandrels, etc. As a purely Christian and beautiful form of art it ranks high; numerous examples are extant, especially in the northern countries of Europe. In Italy it had small hold, for as early as 1300 Andrea Pisano, who is called a Gothic, was inaugurating a renaissance. Picturesque relief reached its fullest development in Florence, as in the baptistery doors of Ghiberti and the marble pulpit of Santa Croce by Benedetto da Majano. Donatello in his admirable high and low reliefs and the Della Robbias in their enamels return to a more plastic

conception. During the entire baroque period (Michelangelo being the last Italian sculptor of the late Renaissance) works of a low order of inspiration prevailed. The Danish sculptor Thorwaldsen, influenced by the study of Attic models, produced reliefs of great beauty and plasticism. The works of Canova were likewise classics, though frequently cold and feeble. Rauch in Germany and Rude in France modelled spirited reliefs. In our day at the head of the admirable French school of sculpture stands Rodin, an impressionist and psychologist, producing unfin-

BAS-RELIEF, ANDREA DELLA ROBBIA HOSPITAL OF THE INNOCENTS, FLORENCE.

ished reliefs which nevertheless are almost Greek in their imprint of life. In Germany, Austria, and England, fine reliefs, especially decorative works, are being modelled. In Spain and Italy the younger men are forming new schools of plastic work. In America, though good work in relief is done, sculpture in the round prevails. Everywhere the tendency is to neglect the distinction between the different kinds of relief, to be independent in method and treatment, and principles sway as of old between the pictorial and the plastic.

LÜBKE, *History of Art* (tr. New York, 1877); GARDNER, *A Handbook of Greek Sculpture* (London, 1897); MARUCCHI, *Les catacombes romaines* (Rome, 1890); PERKINS, *Historical Handbook of Italian Sculpture* (London, 1883); MÜNTZ, *Les précurseurs de la Renaissance* (Paris, London, 1882).

M. L. HANDLEY.

Basse Terre, DIOCESE OF. See GUADELOUPE.

Bassein, a town situated twenty-nine miles north of Bombay in British India, and now of much historic interest as an old settlement of the Portuguese. It is the birthplace of St. Gonsalo Garcia, the only Indian saint, who was a companion of St. Philip de las Casas, the first native of America to be canonized. These two missionaries were in the group of the first martyrs of Japan, crucified on the hill of Nagasaki, 5 February, 1597. Bassein was the most important settlement of the Portuguese in the north of India, Goa lying farther to the south. In many respects Bassein was Goa's rival in the sixteenth and seventeenth centuries, as Bombay is of Calcutta now. The city of Bassein, in the island of the same name, was founded in 1536 by Nunho de Cunha, one of those intrepid Portuguese soldiers who distinguished themselves in India as warriors, administrators, and zealous workers for the spread of the Gospel. He conquered the island from its Mohammedan ruler, Bahadur Shah, King of Gujerat, and soon had a strong fort built in the south-western corner. The island is rich in timber, which was regarded in the sixteenth century as the best material for shipbuilding. Its fertility and position, together with its healthy climate, made it a commercial centre of some importance, and the home of many Portuguese noblemen.

Side by side with this early conquest and colonization the Gospel was spread by the zeal of the Franciscan missionary, Antonio do Porto, to whom is attributed the conversion of 10,156 pagans, and who is known as the "Apostle of Bassein". Father Antonio do Porto built at Agasshi in the northern

Bassein district, as early as 1535, an orphanage for the education and maintenance of forty boys, all converts from paganism, under the invocation of Nossa Senhora da Luz. This orphanage gave to the Church the first Indian martyrs known to history. In April, 1540, a Mohammedan force from Gujerat approached the orphanage, on the return from a fruitless attack on the Bassein fort. Nearly all the inmates of the orphanage had fled for shelter to the fort, but five of them had remained. These were at first urged to renounce their faith; failing in this, the Mohammedans cruelly tortured them, and locking them in a room set fire to it.

In 1542 the Jesuits came to Bassein. St. Francis Xavier visited the city of Bassein three times, once in 1544, and twice in 1548. During his last visit, in December, 1548, he founded the College of the Holy Name of God. The Jesuits on their advent divided both the missionary and educational work with the Franciscans, the latter labouring among the lower, and the former among the higher, classes. Other religious orders also found their way to Bassein, which became the centre of their missionary activity. In the college of the Jesuits in the Bassein fort St. Gonsalo Garcia was brought up from his early youth. He was born about the year 1564. At the age of sixteen he voluntarily accompanied some of the Jesuit fathers of the college, who were ordered to join the mission of Japan. He laboured with singular zeal as a catechist for eight years, having acquired the Japanese language marvellously within a short time. During that time he petitioned to join the order, but as his reception was delayed he left the Jesuits on the best of terms and became a merchant. He was blessed with an abundance of riches which he distributed largely among the poor.

Business interests often took Gonsalo to Manila, where he used to visit the Franciscan fathers and assist them as an interpreter in hearing the confessions of some Japanese Christians. On one occasion, when deep in prayer, he was inspired to seek admission into the Franciscan Order. He did so, and became an exemplary lay brother. On 21 May, 1593, he was sent back to Japan with a body of Franciscans to aid them in preaching the Gospel. The many conversions made by them caused a persecution which gave to the Church the first martyrs of Japan. They were twenty-six in number and were crucified on a hill at Nagasaki 5 February, 1597. They were beatified in 1627, and canonized in 1862.

Bassein was taken from the Portuguese by the Mahrattas in 1739, from the Mahrattas by the English in 1802, and is now a ruined town of much historic interest which no one who goes to Bombay fails to visit. The fort is perhaps the best of the ruined Portuguese fortifications in India. Bassein is a Christian oasis in the midst of the pagan and Mohammedan population of India. It has nine churches, twelve priests, and 16,119 Christians, all Catholics; a Protestant mission was opened in 1904 by the Ritualists but did not flourish and is now practically abandoned.

D'CUNHA, *History and Antiquities of Bassein; The Bombay Gazetteer*, XIII, XIV; FERNANDES, *Life of St. Gonsalo Garcia.*

P. A. FERNANDES.

Bassett, JOSHUA, convert and controversialist, Master of Sidney Sussex College, Cambridge, England, under James II, b. about 1641, at Lynn Regis, where his father was a merchant; d. in London, in 1720. In 1657, after preliminary instruction by a Mr. Bell, he was admitted sizar of Gonville and Caius College, Cambridge, in care of a Mr. Bolt. He proceeded B. A. in 1661, M. A. in 1665, and B. D. in 1671. In 1664 he became junior fellow, and in 1673 senior fellow of his college. On the death of Dr. Richard Minshull in December, 1686, he was, by mandate of James II, elected Master of Sidney Sussex College.

He was installed without the usual oaths, and in January declared himself a Catholic. He had Mass celebrated in his private rooms, and altered some of the college statutes which stood in the way of his co-religionists. He was concerned in the famous dispute which arose when the king demanded that the university confer the degree of M. A. upon the Benedictine, Alban Francis. After the Revolution, when Bassett, having left the college in haste, desired to take away his personal belongings, he was threatened with arrest as a priest. It is thought, however, that Bassett had not been ordained. He died in extreme poverty.

The critics of Bassett admitted that he possessed learning and ability, but objected to his pride and to his interference, for religious reasons, with college regulations and routine. He forbade a chapel service on the 5th of November, disciplined a speaker who had satirized Rome, and threatened to take over the chapel for Catholic services. Craven, who was Master of Sidney Sussex College, declared in 1725 that Bassett "had so many nostrums in his religion that no part of the Roman Church could own him". Gillow believes that Bassett acted in his conversion from a thorough conviction. His known or supposed writings are: (1) "Ecclesiæ Theoria Nova Dodwelliana Exposita" (1713), the only work containing his name on the title page; (2) "Reason and Authority" (1687); (3) "Essay towards a proposal for a Catholic communion . . . by a minister of the Church of England" (1704); this was reprinted in 1879, with an introduction, in "An Eirenicon of the Eighteenth Century" by H. N. Oxenham; (4) Occasional verses in the University collections.

COOPER in *Dict. Nat. Biog.*, III, 381; GILLOW, *Bibl. Dict. Eng. Cath.*, I, 153; MACAULAY, *History of England.*

J. V. CROWNE.

Bassi, MATTHEW OF, founder and first Superior-General of the Order of Friars Minor Capuchins, the principal branch issued from the Reform of the Observance, b. in 1495, at Bascio, Diocese of Montefeltro, in the Duchy of Urbino; d. at Venice in 1552. At the age of seventeen he entered the Order of the Observants at Montefiorentino. In 1525 he was a priest and missionary, being a member of the Reformed Province of Ancona. Moved by the need of reform which was felt almost all through the Franciscan family, he resolved, in 1525, the year of the Jubilee, to begin a more austere life, choosing a form of garb more resembling that of St. Francis. Clement VII granted his request and also permitted him to preach everywhere and to have a companion. Some other members of the Observance asked and obtained permission to join him, and on the 3d of July, 1528, the pope issued the Bull "Religionis zelus", by which the new Reform was canonically approved and placed under the nominal jurisdiction of the Conventuals. The name "Capuchin", at first given by the people to the new Franciscan monks, was afterwards officially adopted. In the pontifical decrees Bassi's followers are variously styled "Capucini", "Capuciati", "Capulati", and "Fratres de Observantiâ Capucinorum".

In April, 1529, the new order held its first chapter at Albacina, where Matthew of Bassi was elected vicar-general by acclamation. A code of constitutions which was to serve as a basis to the Reform was elaborated. But the humble founder did not hold his charge very long. After visiting his brethren, wishing to resume his apostolic career, and perhaps feeling powerless against the difficulties which menaced his disciples, he resigned his office. Thenceforward he took no part in the government of the order. He even decided, about 1537, to return to the obedience of the Observants, through fear of incurring some ecclesiastical censure. As it was, these last had obtained, at different times,

Bulls or Decrees against the new Reform. Bassi preached through the whole of Italy and part of Germany. He died at Venice, in the midst of his labours, and was buried in the Church of the Observants of that city in the presence of a vast concourse of people attracted by his reputation as a saint. The following eulogy by Arthur du Monstier is read in the Franciscan Martyrologium under the 3d of August: "There died at Venice, Blessed Matthew, confessor, founder of the congregation of Capuchins. His continual fastings, vigils and prayers, his most high poverty and ardent zeal for souls, lastly his extraordinary holiness and the gift of miracles made his memory glorious".

JOAN. DE TERRANOVA, *Chronica de origine fratrum capucinorum s. Francisci*. in *Acta SS*., VIII, 4 Maii, 281–289; DE LISBONNE, *Chronica dos Menores* (Lisbon, 1615); BOVERIUS, *Annales Capucinorum* (Lyons, 1632); WADDING, *Annales Minorum* (Lyons, 1647); *Bullarium Capucinorum* (Rome); *Chronica historico-legalis seraphici Ordinis FF. Min*. (Naples, 1650), I, 258; DA CESINALE, *Storia delle Missione dei Cappuccini* (Paris, 1867); PATREM, *Tableau synoptique de l'histoire de tout l'Ordre séraphique* (Paris, 1879); *Analecta Ord. Min. Capuc.;* PALOMÈS, *Des Frères mineurs et de leurs dénominations* (Palermo, 1901); DE PAVIE, *L'Aquitaine séraphique* (Vanves, 1905), III, xi, 183.

F. CANDIDE.

Bassianus, Bishop of Ephesus (444–448). As a priest of Ephesus the charities of Bassianus so won the affection of the people that his bishop, Mennon, aroused to jealousy, sought his removal by promoting him to the Bishopric of Evaza. Bassianus repudiated the consecration to which he was violently forced to submit, an attitude approved by Mennon's successor, Basil. On the latter's death (444) Bassianus succeeded him and though popular enthusiasm disregarded canonical procedure his election was confirmed by Theodosius II and reluctantly by Proclus, Patriarch of Constantinople. Bassianus reigned undisturbed for four years. At the Easter celebration in 448 he was seized by a mob and imprisoned. The emperor was importuned to remove him, and the case was referred to Pope Leo I and the Bishops of Constantinople, Alexandria, and Antioch, who declared the election invalid. Stephen, whom Bassianus called the ringleader of his opponents, was elected in his stead. The Council of Chalcedon on 29 October, 451, considered the plea of Bassianus for reinstatement and was disposed to favour him, but owing to the complex irregularities of the case it was deemed advisable to declare the see vacant. Bassianus and Stephen were retired on a pension with episcopal dignity. During the process Stephen cited Pope Leo's letter deposing Bassianus, a document unfortunately lost.

HARDOUIN, *Acta Concil*. (Paris, 1714), II, 546–558; TILLEMONT, *Mémoires* (Venice, 1722), XV, 460–465, 690–692, 895–896; HEFELE, *Conciliengesch*. (Freiburg, 1875), II, 491–497; tr. (Edinburgh, 1883), III, 370–376; VENABLES in *Dict. Christ. Biog*., I, 298.

JOHN B. PETERSON.

Bastiat, CLAUDE-FRÉDÉRIC, a French economist, b. at Mugron, a small city in the Department of Landes, 29 June, 1801; d. at Rome, 24 December, 1850. He was the son of Pierre Bastiat, whose father had founded at Bayonne a business house that prospered in consequence of the franchise granted this port by the Treaty of Versailles, but ceased to flourish under the prohibitory regime of the Empire. The widely different effects of these two economic systems upon the fortunes of his family undoubtedly gave rise to Bastiat's free-trade opinions. Left an orphan at the age of nine, he was brought up by his paternal grandfather and, after pursuing his studies at St. Sever and Sorèze, entered the business founded by his grandfather and then conducted by his uncle at Bayonne. Returning to Mugron in 1825, he inherited an extensive estate through the death of his grandfather, and subsequently devoted himself to farming. After the Revolution of 1830 he was appointed justice of the peace at Mugron and, being deeply interested in political economy, gave himself up to it with great earnestness and constituted himself the champion of commercial liberty. In 1841 he published his first essay "Le fisc et la vigne" and, apprised of the free-trade movement that Cobden was then directing in England, joined forces with him. In 1844, his article, "L'influence des tarifs anglais et français" in the "Journal des Economistes" opened his way to fame. Then appeared successively: "Sophismes économiques", "Cobden et la ligue", and several pamphlets, one of which, "Pétition des marchands de chandelles", against the sun that interferes with the candle merchants' trade, is a little masterpiece of verve and delicate irony. Elected to the Constituent Assembly in 1848, and then to the Legislative Assembly, he became the implacable enemy of socialism, against which he wrote: "Propriété et loi", "Capital et rente", "Justice et fraternité", "Protectionisme et communisme", and other treatises. In 1849 he published "Harmonies économiques", which the illness that had already undermined his health prevented him from finishing.

Bastiat belonged to the Liberal school and enunciated its principles on the following lines: "Let men work, trade, learn, form partnerships, act and react upon one another, since according to the decrees of Providence, naught save order, harmony, and progress can spring from their intelligent spontaneity". (Harmonies, p. 12.) Of a sincere and generous nature he was fitted to understand and defend Catholic truth; but the prejudices in the midst of which he lived kept him aloof from the Faith until the very eve of his death. It was in Rome that his eyes were opened to the light of Catholicism, and Proudhon, his enemy, says that in his last hour Bastiat cried out with Polyeucte: "I see, I know, I believe; I am a Christian". Some time before his death he declared that if God would but grant him a new lease of life he would devote his energy to the development of Christian harmony and political economy, but he did not live to fulfil this vow. Bastiat's complete works were published by Guillaumin (Paris, 1854, 1872).

BAUNARD, *La Foi et ses victoires* (Paris, 1884–1902), II, 107; PERRIN, *Les doctrines économiques depuis un siècle* (Paris, 1880), IX, 125; GARDELLE, *Frédéric Bastiat* (discourse at the reopening of the Court of Appeals at Pau, 1879); PASSY, *Notice biographique sur Frédéric Bastiat* (Paris, 1855); DE FONTENAY, *Notice sur la vie et les écrits de Frédéric Bastiat* (introduction to his works); DE MOLINARI, *F. Bastiat*, in *Journal des économistes*, XXVII, 15 Feb., 1851; MACLEOD in *Dict. of Political Economy*.

STANISLAS A. LORTIE.

Baston, GUILLAUME-ANDRÉ-RENÉ, a French theologian, b. at Rouen, 29 November, 1741; d. at Saint-Laurent, 26 September, 1825. He studied theology at St. Sulpice in Paris and finished his studies at Angers. He was then appointed professor of theology at Rouen. During the Revolution he wrote against the Civil Constitution of the Clergy. Having refused to take the oath, he was obliged to go into exile (1792), first to London, then to Holland, and finally to Kösfeld in Westphalia. In 1803 he returned to Rouen, where he was appointed vicar-general and dean of the chapter by Archbishop Cambacérès. As a Gallican, he won the favour of Napoleon, who appointed him Bishop of Séez (1813) and the chapter of the cathedral accepted him as capitular vicar. Pope Pius VII failing to approve of this nomination, the cathedral chapter revoked the nomination (1814), and Baston went into retirement at Saint-Laurent near Pont-Audemer, where he died. Baston was the author of numerous works on theology, the most important being "Lectiones theologicæ", written while he was professor of theology, in collaboration with Abbé Tuvache (10 vols., Rouen, 1818), and he published several polemical works on the subject of theology: "Réponse au mémoire et à la consultation de M. Linguet, touchant l'indissolubilité du mariage" (Paris, 1772); "Les entretiens du pape Ganganelli" (Clement XIV) (Antwerp, 1777); "Voltairimeros, ou première journée de M. de Voltaire dans l'autre monde" (Brussels, 1779). During the Revolution he wrote many pamphlets against the Civil Constitution of the Clergy and his book "Doctrine catholique sur le mariage" (1791) was published about the same time. During his exile in Kösfeld he began his "Mémoires", edited lately by the Société d'histoire contemporaine (3 vols., Paris, 1897–99). In his last years he wrote "Réclamation pour l'Eglise de France et pour la vérité contre l'ouvrage de M. le comte de Maistre [Du Pape]" (Rouen, 1821); "Antidote contre les erreurs et la réputation de l'Essai sur l'indifférence en matière de religion" (Paris, 1823); "Concordance des lois civiles et des lois ecclésiastiques touchant le mariage" (Paris, 1824).

Mémoires de l'Abbé Baston, ed. LOTH AND VERGER (Paris, 1897); HURTER, *Nomenclator* (Innsbruck, 1895), III; BELLAMY in *Dict. de théol. cath.*, s. v.

G. M. SAUVAGE.

Basutoland, PREFECTURE APOSTOLIC OF.—Basutoland, a mountainous district of South Africa, is bounded on the north and west by the Orange River Colony, on the east by Natal, and on the south by Cape Colony. It has an area of 10,293 square miles. The white population is about 700 and natives number about 309,000. The chief town is Maseru. The county is administered by native chiefs under an acting British Resident Commissioner who meets the National Assembly or "Pitso" in council once a year. Whites require special permission to settle in the country. The climate is healthful, though cold in winter, while the summer is characterized by heavy rains. The country has no railway nor roads properly so called. Basutoland was annexed to Cape Colony in 1871, and became a British Crown Colony in 1884. The inhabitants, till about 1820, were Bushmen of a low type but they have been replaced by highly intelligent Kafirs. The principal articles of export are wheat, mealies, and wool, Kafir corn, mohair, and cattle.

Basutoland, first a part of the Vicariate Apostolic of Natal, and later of the Vicariate of Kimberley, was made an independent prefecture by the Holy See on 8 May, 1894. It comprises the whole of the territory known as Basutoland. The first prefect Apostolic of the new ecclesiastical territory was the Rev. Father Monginoux, O.M.I.; he was succeeded by the Rev. Father Baudry, O.M.I., and the latter by the Rev. Father Cenez, O.M.I. The Oblates of Mary Immaculate established themselves in that portion of South Africa about 1862. Roma, the first Catholic mission in Basutoland, was founded by the Right Rev. Dr. Allard, O.M.I., in 1862. The first church was built in the same year. The second mission situated about six miles from Roma was founded in 1867 and received the name of St. Michael. Since then, several new missions have been established in different parts of the territory. The prefecture possesses at present 19 churches, chapels, and stations, 5 convents, and 9 schools. The missionary work is carried on by the Oblates of Mary Immaculate assisted by the Sisters of the Holy Family. The total number of Oblate Fathers in Basutoland is at present 19; lay brothers, 6; European Sisters, 34; native Sisters, 12; total number of Catholics, about 8,900; catechumens, 700; children attending school, about 1,200.

Undoubtedly Christianity has progressed immensely during recent years in Basutoland, and it would have spread still more speedily had the resources been more abundant. Unfortunately, there, as elsewhere in South Africa, everything seems to be precarious. Agriculture is too often compromised by long droughts, and crops are sometimes destroyed by locusts, all of which bring on misery and famines. In addition to this the limited number of priests does not allow the evangelization of the country to be carried out on a very large scale. The population, however, is well settled, which greatly facilitates the work of the missionary, who can remain always in touch with his flock.

BARKLEY, *Among Boers and Basutos* (London, 1900); WIDDICOMBE, *Fourteen Years in Basutoland* (London, 1892); *Missiones Catholicæ* (Propaganda, Rome, 1907), 431.

A. LANGAUET.

Batavia, VICARIATE APOSTOLIC OF.—When the Portuguese took possession of the island of Java, of which Batavia is the capital, they brought the Christian religion with them; but the Dutch, having conquered Java in 1596, set about the destruction of Catholicism. Nevertheless, the memory has been preserved of a Friar Minor who was expelled from Batavia in 1721, and attempted to continue his apostolic labours in China. It was with difficulty that a priest could enter Java, and, if recognized, he was hunted out. When in 1807 Louis Napoleon became King of Holland, Pius VII divided all the Dutch territory outside of Europe into three prefectures, two in the West Indies and the third, with Batavia for its seat, in the East Indies. At this period the Dutch missionaries James Nelissen and Lambert Preffen set out for the Sunda Islands, and reached Batavia, 4 April, 1808. The Government gave them at first a ruinous Calvinist place of worship, and then added to this act of generosity sufficiently to enable them to erect a church, which was blessed, under the title of Our Lady of the Assumption, 6 November, 1829. Nelissen died 6 December, 1817, and Preffen succeeded him in this practice.

On the 20th of September, 1842, Gregory XVI raised the Prefecture of Batavia to a vicariate Apostolic, and Monsignor Groof, titular Bishop of Canea, and previously prefect Apostolic of Surinam, became the first vicar Apostolic. A coadjutor was given him, 4 June, 1847, in Monseigneur Pierre-Marie Vrancken, titular Bishop of Colophon, who succeeded him in 1852. The Dutch Government, however, did not leave the first missionaries in peace, and Monsignor Groof, together with Father Van den Brand, a missionary priest, was expelled. Monsignor Vrancken died in 1874, and Pius IX then entrusted the mission of Batavia to the Dutch Jesuits. The first Jesuit vicar Apostolic was Monsignor Claessens (1874–93), who was succeeded by Monsignor Staal (1894–97) and Monsignor Luypen, the present (1907) incumbent of the office. The Jesuits energetically set about the development of the mission, which then comprised the islands of Java, Sumatra, Borneo, the Sunda group, Timor, the Celebes, and the Moluccas.

In 1851 the Catholics in the vicariate numbered between 5000 and 6000; in 1879 there were 23,527, not including the Catholic members of the garrison, and 27 missionaries were labouring in different parts of the Sunda Islands. Although the whole island of Borneo and Dutch New Guinea have since been separated from the vicariate, Streit's "Atlas des missions" now gives the following statistics: Total population of the vicariate, 37,325,000; native Christians, 27,313 (in addition to 25,000 European Catholics); 720 catechumens; 54 religious in priest's orders; 40 male religious not priests; 250 Sisters of different orders; 94 catechists; 22 principal stations; 78 secondary stations; 40 churches, and 59 schools with 2482 pupils.

Pius IX had separated the British portions of the islands of Borneo and Labuan from the vicariate in 1855; in 1903 Leo XIII erected Dutch New Guinea into a new prefecture; and Pius X, in 1905, formed a prefecture out of the remainder of the island of

Borneo, again taken from the territory of the vicariate. There still remains of its territory: the island of Sumatra, 181,250 sq. m.; Java, 50,715 sq. m.; the small islands of the Sunda group (Bali, Lombok, Sumbawa, Sumba, Flores, and Timor) aggregating 36,507 sq. m.; and Celebes, 73,270 sq. m. The Moluccas have been attached to the Prefecture of Dutch New Guinea. The Vicariate of Batavia, therefore, now comprises an area of more than 340,000 sq. m., or more than the combined areas of the German Empire and Great Britain and Ireland. The principal stations are: in Sumatra, Medan, in the north-east and Padang, in the west; in Java, Batavia (residence of the vicar Apostolic), Samerang, and Surabaya; in Timor, Fialarang; in Flores, Maumeri and Larantuk; in Celebes, Macassar and Menado. The natives speak their own dialects, but in the coast towns Dutch and Malay are the languages current. The Ursulines, established at Batavia and Surabaya, furnish the largest contingent of religious women in the vicariate, amounting to 170.

Analecta ord. min. capuc. for September, 1905; STREIT, *Atlas des missions; Missiones Catholicæ* (Propaganda, Rome, 1907), 263.

ALBERT BATTANDIER.

Bath Abbey.—The first religious house in Bath was a monastery of nuns founded by King Osric, A. D. 676. This was followed by a community of Benedictine monks, who were visited and reformed by St. Dunstan. King Edgar was solemnly crowned

BATH ABBEY

in the abbey church of St. Peter in 973, and a few years later the abbot was St. Elphege, afterwards Bishop of Winchester and Archbishop of Canterbury, who was killed by the Danes in 1012. Ælfsige, who died in 1087, was the last Abbot of Bath; for in 1088 William Rufus granted the abbey and its lands to John de Villula, Bishop of Wells, and the resident superior was henceforth a cathedral prior instead of an abbot. This bishop later restored its lands to the monastery, which was endowed also by other benefactors. A great fire, in 1137, destroyed nearly the whole city, greatly damaging the abbey buildings, which were promptly rebuilt. In the following century there was a warm dispute between the monks of Bath and the canons of Wells as to their

respective rights in electing the bishop. Innocent IV decreed, in 1245, that the election should be held alternately in either city, that the bishop should have a throne in both churches and should be styled Bishop "of Bath and Wells". This arrangement continued until the Reformation, and the subsequent occupants of the see have retained the double title. Henry VIII's Commission visited Bath in August, 1535, and a report of the usual type followed. In 1539 Prior Hollewell surrendered the house and revenues (valued at £617) to the king, and the monastic life of the abbey came to an end.

The present church of St. Peter, occupying only the nave of the great Norman fabric, was begun by Prior Birde, about 1500, to replace John de Villula's church, which had fallen into decay. The new church was not finished until 1572, and is thus one of the latest specimens of Perpendicular work in England. The latest so-called restoration took place in 1874. No trace remains of the monastery, of which the last portion (probably the prior's lodgings) disappeared in 1755. Since 1679 the Catholic mission of Bath has been served by the English Benedictines.

HUNT (ed.), *Chartularies of the Priory of St. Peter at Bath* (1893); FOWLER, *The Benedictines in Bath* (1895); BRITTON, ed. PEACH, *Bath Abbey Church* (1887); *Somerset Record Society*, VII; CARTER, *Account of the Abbey of Bath* (1798); MORRIS (ed.), *British Association Handbook to Bath* (1888).

D. O. HUNTER-BLAIR.

Bath and Wells (BADONIENSIS ET WELLENSIS) ANCIENT DIOCESE OF (Bath, *Aquæ Solis, Bathonia, Bathensis, Bathoniensis;* Wells, *Theoradunum, Velliæ, Ecclesia Fontanensis, Vellensis, Wellensis*), coextensive with the County of Somerset, England. The first Bishop of Bath and Wells, properly so described, was appointed by the pope in 1244, but the diocese has a much longer history, though its bishops used different titles; Somerset, Wells, Bath, or Bath and Glastonbury, being at different times employed. Æthelhelm (909–914), afterwards Archbishop of Canterbury, first exercised episcopal jurisdiction there, choosing the secular church of Wells as his cathedral. Henceforth, there was a certain rivalry between the secular canons of Wells and the monks of the two great abbeys, Glastonbury and Bath. The advantage, however, lay with the latter and the cathedral church at Wells maintained but a struggling existence. During the time of Edward the Confessor (1042–66), the energetic Bishop Gisa (1060–88), who on his appointment found the church small and poor, and the few canons who served it forced to beg their bread, succeeded in putting matters on a firmer foundation. He not only erected buildings in which they could live a community life, but obtained grants of lands for their support from St. Edward the Confessor, Harold, and William the Conqueror. This good work was partly undone by his successor, John de Villula (1088–1122), who removed the see to Bath, using the abbey there as his cathedral. It was not until the appointment of Bishop Robert of Lewes (1136–66), who rebuilt the cathedral at Wells and in other ways proved himself a wise and liberal administrator, that an arrangement was made by which Bath should take precedence of Wells, but that future bishops should have a throne in both churches and should be elected by the two chapters conjointly. This arrangement lasted through the administrations of Reginald de Bohun (1174–91), who brought St. Hugh of Lincoln to England; the turbulent Savaric (1192–1205), who annexed Glastonbury by force, and lastly Jocelin Troteman de Welles (1206–42), who though a native of Wells was known as Bishop of Bath and Glastonbury until 1219, when he gave up all claim to Glastonbury and styled himself Bishop of Bath. But though he omitted Wells from his title, he did more than any other bishop for the town, for he restored and enlarged the cathedral, adding the beautiful west front, increased the number of canons from thirty-five to fifty, and founded a grammar school. On his death, the monks of Bath ignoring the chapter of Wells, elected as his successor Roger, one of their own community, for whom they obtained royal and papal confirmation, but the consequent appeal by the Wells chapter brought about the final settlement of the difficulty. The pope decided that Roger should remain bishop with the style "Bishop of Bath and Wells", and that the old arrangement as to joint election should in future be observed.

The history of the see was thenceforth tranquil, only three bishops during the next two centuries calling for special mention, Ralph of Shrewsbury (1329–63), who completed the buildings; Thomas Bekynton (1443–65), another liberal benefactor of the city; and Oliver King (1495–1503), who rebuilt Bath Abbey in the Perpendicular style. One bishop, William Bytton (1267–74), died with a reputation for sanctity and his tomb became a place of pilgrimage. In the fifteenth century there were two absentee bishops, Adrian de Castello (1504–18), during whose tenure the see was administered by the historian Polydore Vergil; and Cardinal Wolsey (1518–23), who held the see simultaneously with that of York. After the dissolution of Bath Abbey in 1538, the bishop, though retaining the old style, had his seat at Wells alone, but final ruin was impending. In 1549 the notorious William Barlow was intruded into the see, and alienated much of its property. On the accession of Mary he fled, and was succeeded by the last Catholic Bishop, Gilbert Bourne (1554–59), who held the see till he was deprived of it by Elizabeth and imprisoned in the Tower, thus becoming one of the eleven Confessor-Bishops who died in bonds. He died in 1569. Of the twin cathedrals of the diocese, Bath Abbey was rebuilt (1499–1539) in late Perpendicular style and is the last complete monastic building erected before the Reformation, while the cathedral at Wells, though small, is the most perfect example of a secular cathedral and one of the most beautiful Gothic buildings in England. Dating in the main from the early thirteenth, it was practically complete by the middle of the fourteenth century. The diocese contained three archdeaconries, Bath, Wells, and Taunton. The arms of the see were:—Azure, a saltier quarterly quartered, or and az.

HUNTER, *A brief History of the bishoprick of Somerset to 1174* (Camden Society, 1840), 8; FREEMAN, *History of the Cathedral Church of Wells* (London, 1870); REYNOLDS, *Wells Cathedral, its Foundation, Constitution, History and Statutes* (1880); *Registers of Bishops Giffard, Bowett and Fox* (Somerset Record Society, 1889–99); CHURCH, *Chapters in the Early History of the Church of Wells, 1136–1333* (London, 1894); DEARMER, *The Cathedral Church of Wells and a History of the Episcopal See* (London, 1898, 3d ed., 1903); *Somerset Archæological Society Transactions.*

EDWIN BURTON.

Bathe, WILLIAM, writer on music and education, b. at Dublin, Ireland, 2 April, 1564; d. at Madrid, 17 June, 1614. His parents, John Bathe and Eleanor Preston, were distinguished both by their lineage and by their loyalty to the Catholic Faith. He went to Oxford about 1583 and while a student there wrote "A Brief Introduction to the Art of Music" (London, 1584). Another treatise from his pen, "A Brief Introduction to the Skill of Song", was published at London in 1600. These writings and his skill as master of various instruments, especially the Irish harp, won him the favour of Queen Elizabeth to whom he was related through the Kildare family. His own inclinations, however, were towards the religious life. From the English court he went to Louvain where he studied theology. On 6 August, 1595 (1596) he entered the novitiate of the Society of Jesus at Tournai. His later studies were pursued at St. Omer and completed at Padua. In 1601 Bathe was selected by the father general to accompany

Father Mansoni, the Apostolic Nuncio, to Ireland. This mission led them first to the Court of Spain and while there they learned that peace had been concluded between Spain and England and that the journey to Ireland was no longer necessary. Bathe remained in Spain, living at Valladolid and later at the Irish College in Salamanca. It was here that he wrote his principal work "Janua Linguarum" (Salamanca, 1611). It was designed to facilitate the study of languages and thus to aid missionaries, confessors, and students both young and old. For this purpose, 1330 short sentences were grouped under certain headings, the Latin and Spanish on opposite pages, with an index giving the translation of the Latin words—in all about 5300. The work went through many editions in which its method was applied, by various combinations, to eleven languages, including Greek and Hebrew. It was printed at London (1615), Leipzig (1626), Milan (1628), Venice (1655), and by 1637 it had been published in Bohemian, Illyrian, and Hungarian. An English edition (London, 1617) bore the title, "The Messe of Tongues (Latin, French, English, Hispanish)". It naturally found imitators, and among these the great work by John Amos Comenius holds first rank. In the preface to his "Janua Linguarum Reserata" (1631), Comenius acknowledges his indebtedness to Bathe, while in the work itself he adopts and develops the plan which the Jesuit had originated. Bathe is also credited by some of his biographers (Alegambe, Sherlock) with a treatise on "The Mysteries of Faith" and another on the "Sacrament of Penance". Sommervogel, however, takes a different view. To his industry as a writer Bathe added an unflagging zeal for the spiritual welfare of his fellowmen, the relief of suffering, and the instruction of the poorer classes. He had just been invited by the King of Spain to give the spiritual exercises to the members of the Court when death ended his labours.

SOMMERVOGEL, *Bibl. de c. de J.;* MACDONALD in *The Irish Eccl. Record*, X, 527; HOGAN, *Distinguished Irishmen of the Sixteenth Century* (London, 1894); COOPER in *Dict. of Nat. Biog.;* PACE, *Bathe and Comenius*, in *Cath. Univ. Bull.* (Washington, 1907), XIII.

E. A. PACE.

Bathilde (or BATILDE), SAINT, wife of Clovis II, King of France, time and place of birth unknown; d. January, 680. According to some chronicles she came from England and was a descendant of the Anglo-Saxon kings, but this is a doubtful statement. It is certain that she was a slave in the service of the wife of Erchinoald, mayor of the palace of Neustria. Her unusual qualities of mind and her virtues inspired the confidence of her master who gave many of the affairs of the household into her charge and, after the death of his wife, wished to marry her. At this the young girl fled and did not return until Erchinoald had married again. About this time Clovis II met her at the house of the mayor of the palace, and was impressed by her beauty, grace, and the good report he had of her. He freed and married her, 649. This sudden elevation did not diminish the virtues of Bathilde but gave them a new lustre. Her humility, spirit of prayer, and large-hearted generosity to the poor were particularly noticeable.

Seven years after their marriage Clovis II died, 656, leaving Bathilde with three sons, Clothaire, Childeric, and Thierry. An assembly of the leading nobles proclaimed Clothaire III, aged five, king under the regency of his mother, Bathilde. Aided by the authority and advice of Erchinoald and the saintly bishops, Eloi (Eligius) of Noyon, Ouen of Rouen, Léger of Autun, and Chrodebert of Paris, the queen was able to carry out useful reforms. She abolished the disgraceful trade in Christian slaves, and firmly repressed simony among the clergy. She also led the way in founding charitable and religious institutions, such as hospitals and monasteries. Through her generosity the Abbey of Corbie was founded for men, and the Abbey of Chelles near Paris for women. At about this date the famous Abbeys of Jumièges, Jouarre, and Luxeuil were established, most probably in large part through Bathilde's generosity. Berthilde, the first Abbess of Chelles, who is honoured as a saint, came from Jouarre. The queen wished to renounce her position and enter the religious life, but her duties kept her at court. Erchinoald died in 659 and was succeeded by Ebroin. Notwithstanding the ambition of the new mayor of the palace, the queen was able to maintain her authority and to use it for the benefit of the kingdom. After her children were well established in their respective territories, Childeric IV in Austrasia and Thierry in Burgundy, she returned to her wish for a secluded life and withdrew to her favourite Abbey of Chelles near Paris.

On entering the abbey she laid down the insignia of royalty and desired to be the lowest in rank among the inmates. It was her pleasure to take her position after the novices and to serve the poor and infirm with her own hands. Prayer and manual toil occupied her time, nor did she wish any allusion made to the grandeur of her past position. In this manner she passed fifteen years of retirement. At the beginning of the year 680 she had a presentiment of the approach of death and made religious preparation for it. Before her own end, that of Radegonde occurred, a child whom she had held at the baptismal font and had trained in Christian virtue. She was buried in the Abbey of Chelles and was canonized by Pope Nicholas I. The Roman martyrology places her feast on 26 January; in France it is celebrated 30 January.

Acta SS., II; Dubois, *Histoire ecclésiastique de Paris*, 198; Binet, *La vie excellente de Sainte Bathilde* (Paris, 1624); Corblet, *Hagiographie du diocèse d'Amiens* (1874); Des Essarts, *Sainte Bathilde* in *Correspondant* (1873), XXXII, 227–246; Driou, *La reine Bathilde* (Limoges, 1865); Grécy in *Revue archéologique* (1865), XII, 603–610.

A. Fournet.

Bathurst, Diocese of, situated in New South Wales, Australia, in the ecclesiastical Province of Sydney, comprises the territory immediately west of the Dividing Range; it extends north to the Barwon River, is bounded on the west by the Macquarie River as far up as Warren and thence by a line to the Lachlan River twenty miles below Eauabolong.

History.—Bathurst (population in 1901, 9,223) was founded in 1824. Owing to the hostility of the aboriginals and other causes, population filtered slowly into the rich Bathurst plains till the first paying goldfield was discovered in the district, in 1851. The first church in Bathurst, says Cardinal Moran, "was nothing better than a bark hut". It was superseded in 1861 by a fine new edifice (now the cathedral), which was erected at a cost of £12,000 by Dean Grant, pastor of Bathurst for nearly twenty years till his death in 1864. In 1865 Bathurst, then part of the Diocese of Sydney, was made the cathedral centre of a new diocese, which extended from the River Murray to Queensland, and from the Blue Mountains to the border of South Australia. That vast and sparsely populated territory was divided at the time into five missions, ministered to by six priests, with seven small churches and six state-aided Catholic schools, attended by 492 pupils. Its first bishop was the Right Rev. Matthew Quinn, who had taken an active part in organizing the Irish Brigade that fought for the defence of the Papal States in 1860. He was consecrated in Dublin, 14 November, 1865, and reached Bathurst 1 November, 1866, accompanied by five priests and seven pioneer Sisters of Mercy. Years of toilsome organization followed— laborious visitations; opening new missions and supplying them with clergy; church, school, and convent extension; the introduction of the (Australian) Sis-

ters of St. Joseph and the Patrician Brothers; the founding of a Catholic newspaper, the "Record"; the erection of St. Stanislaus' College, in 1873, at a cost of £15,000, and of St. Charles' Ecclesiastical Seminary eight years later. Dr. Quinn was a man of great energy, deep piety, cultivated intellect, and, says Cardinal Moran, was one of the "foremost champions of religious education in Australia". At his death, 16 January, 1885, there were in the diocese 28 priests, 56 Catholic schools, 21 convents, 192 nuns, and 5 religious brothers. Dr. Quinn was succeeded by the Right Rev. Joseph Patrick Byrne (consecrated 9 August, 1885). In 1887 the new Diocese of Wilcannia was formed out of the Bathurst Diocese. At the same time some districts from the Maitland diocese were added to the Bathurst jurisdiction. Dr. Byrne, says Cardinal Moran, "strenuously and successfully carried on the great work of education and religion begun by his predecessor", and, like him, was "a model to his clergy in his unwearying and self-sacrificing toil". St. Stanislaus' College, which from its foundation had been under the control of secular priests, was in 1888 entrusted to the Vincentian Fathers. It is now (1907) one of the foremost educational institutions in Australia, and noted for the work done in its well-equipped physical and chemical laboratories. When pronounced to be stricken by an incurable malady, Dr. Byrne received from his priests and people, on the Epiphany, 1901, a pathetic demonstration of affection, accompanied by a money gift of £2,530. He passed away on the 12th of January, 1901. To him succeeded the Right Rev. John Dunne—builder, missioner, organizer— who was consecrated 8 September, 1901. He is to complete the architecturally fine college of St. Stanislaus, and under his administration the missionary and scholastic traditions of the diocese are well sustained. The efficiency of the Catholic schools is in no small measure due to the system of inspection inaugurated by the Rev. J. J. Brophy, D. D., LL. B. The principal lay benefactors of the diocese are Mr. James Dalton, K.S.G., and Mr. John Meagher, K.S.G.

Religious Statistics.—In the diocese there are: 18 parochial districts; 89 churches; 29 secular priests; 7 regular priests; 7 religious brothers; 242 nuns; 1 college; 8 boarding schools for girls; 11 day high schools; 39 primary schools (with 3,496 pupils); 1 orphanage; 4,298 children in Catholic schools; and a Catholic population of about 27,000.

Moran, *History of the Catholic Church in Australasia* (Sydney, s. d.); Hutchinson, *Australasian Encyclopædia* (London, 1892); *The Australian Handbook* (Sydney, 1906); *Australasian Catholic Directory for 1907* (Sydney, 1907); *Report of the Catholic Schools in the Diocese of Bathurst for the Year 1906* (Dubbo, 1907); *Missiones Catholicæ* (Propaganda, Rome, 1907), 694.

Henry W. Cleary.

Batrun, Diocese of. See Gibail and Batrun.

Battaglini, Marco, a historian of the councils, b. at Rimini, Italy, 25 March, 1645; d. at Cesena, 19 September, 1717. He studied law at Cesena, both civil and ecclesiastical, and at the age of sixteen he obtained the degree of doctor in both branches. After some years of service in the civil administration of the Papal States, he entered the priesthood, was appointed Bishop of Nocera in Umbria, 1690, and in 1716 was transferred to Cesena. He was greatly esteemed for his learning, and for his generous and frank character. His principal works are: (1) "Il legista filosofo" (Rome, 1680), or the man of law as a philosopher; (2) "Istoria universale di tutti i concilii" (Venice, 1686, 1689, 1696, 1714). The first edition contained the history of only 475 councils; in subsequent editions that of 403 more was added. A valuable supplement was the catalogue of all the ancient and contemporary episcopal sees; (3) "Annali del sacerdozio e dell' imperio intorno all' intero secolo decimo settimo" (Venice, 1701–

11; Ancona, 1742), or a history of the world during the seventeenth century in the form of annals.

HURTER, *Nomenclator*, II; BAUER in *Kirchenlex.*, II.

FRANCIS J. SCHÆFER.

Batteux, CHARLES, abbé and writer on philosophy and æsthetics, b. near Vouziers, France, 6 May, 1713; d. at Paris, 14 July, 1780. He was professor at Paris of the humanities and rhetoric, then of Greek and Roman philosophy, and was made a member of the Academy of Inscriptions and of the Académie Française. His works on Epicurus and other Greek philosophers attracted much attention. At the time of his death he was issuing a large collection of memoirs on China; the series was continued by Bréquigny and de Guignes. Of Batteux's writings those that received at once the most praise and blame were the following three works: "Beaux-arts réduits à un même principe", "Cours de belles-lettres", and "Traité de la construction oratoire". These were issued later in five volumes under the common title: "Cours des belles-lettres", and in a new edition of six volumes, in 1824, as "Principes abrégés de la littérature".

Following Aristotle, but taking at the same time a somewhat one-sided and superficial view of the philosopher's meaning, Batteux deduced art from the free imitation of nature, that is, from the free copying of nature in its beautiful forms. Utility is the aim of the mechanical arts; beauty, the end of the fine arts, and both utility and beauty the aim of the beautifying arts. Architecture and oratory belong to the last category. The arts aim to influence either sight or hearing and are divided, therefore, into two classes. Besides these the rhythmical arts, music and dancing, and, in addition, painting and poetry are closely related to one another. In these writings there is a lack of comprehensive definitions of the different arts; those given are often inexact and uncertain. Nevertheless, Batteux may be regarded as the real founder of æsthetics in France. Of his works devoted exclusively to rhetoric and poetry mention should be made of "Les quatres poétiques d'Aristote, d'Horace, de Vida, et de Boileau" in two volumes.

Critical mention of Batteux may be found in: *Nécrologe des hommes célèbres de France*, XVI; *Année littéraire, 1780*; SCHASLER, *Gesch. der Æsthetik*; ZIMMERMANN, *Gesch. der Æsthetik*.

G. GIETMANN.

Battista, GIOVANNI GIUDA GIONA (his original name was JEHUDA JONA BEN-ISAAC), b. of Jewish parents at Safed in Galilee, on the 28th of October, 1588; d. at Rome, 26 May, 1668. As a Jewish rabbi he undertook an extensive journey through Europe, and it was during his stay in Poland that he was converted to Catholicism. After his conversion he was sent by the King of Poland on a mission to Constantinople, where he was arrested as a spy, and narrowly escaped with his life through the intervention of the ambassador of Venice. Later he went to Italy, where he taught Hebrew and Aramaic at the Academy of Pisa and then at the Propaganda at Rome. Among his pupils was Giulio Bartolocci, who is indebted to his learned master for the idea and plan of his famous work "Bibliotheca Magna Rabbinica". Battista's principal work was the translation of the Gospels from Latin into Hebrew, published, with a preface by Clement IX, at Rome, 1668.

REY in VIG., *Dict. de la Bible*, s. v.; *Jewish Encyclopedia*, s. v. *Bartolocci*.

F. X. E. ALBERT.

Battle Abbey, founded by William the Conqueror on the site of the Battle of Senlac or Hastings (1066), nearly seven miles from the town of Hastings, in the County of Sussex, England. The building was begun in the following year, but was erected on such a great scale that it was not finished till the reign of William

Rufus. It was designed for one hundred and forty monks, though there were never more than sixty in residence at any one time. The first monks were from the Benedictine Abbey of Marmoutier in Normandy; the new foundation was dedicated to the Holy Trinity, St. Mary, and St. Martin, and was consecrated on 11 February, 1094. The king offered there his father's sword and coronation robes, and the abbey was enriched by many privileges, including the right of sanctuary, of treasure trove, of free warren, and of inquest, and the inmates and tenants were exempt from all episcopal and secular jurisdiction. It was ruled by a mitred abbot who afterwards had a seat in Parliament and who had the curious privilege of pardoning any criminal he might meet being led to execution. The monastic buildings were about a mile in circuit and formed a large quadrangle, the high altar of the church being on the spot where Harold fell. At the Abbey was kept the famous "Roll of Battle Abbey" which was a list of all those who accompanied William from Normandy. As time went on and the honour of descent from one of these Norman families was more highly thought of, unauthentic additions seem to have been made, and the present state of the text of the Roll is unsatisfactory from a critical point of view. At the time of the suppression of the Abbey (May, 1538), there were seventeen monks in residence and the income was returned as £987 which would be more than £10,000 in present value. Abbot Hammond, the last of the line of thirty-two abbots, was pensioned off and the buildings were given to Sir Antony Browne, a royal favourite, who pulled down the abbey, and built a mansion on its site. The entrance gate and considerable ruins now alone remain of the original buildings. In 1719, Lord Montague sold Battle Abbey to Sir Thomas Webster whose descendants held it until 1858, when it was bought by Lord Harry Vane, afterwards Duke of Cleveland. On the death of the Duchess of Cleveland in 1901 it was purchased by Sir Augustus Webster, a descendant of its former owners. Through the eighteenth century a small Catholic congregation continued to exist at Battle, and now there is a Catholic church and a resident priest in the town.

The Chronicle of Battle Abbey, 1066–1176, ed. LOWER (London, 1851); *Chronicon Monast. de Bello* in *Anglia Christiana* (London, 1846); DUGDALE, *Monasticon* (London, 1821), III, 233–259; *Custumals of Battle Abbey 1283–1312* (Camden Society, 1887), New Series, XLI; DUCHESS OF CLEVELAND, *The Battle Abbey Roll* (London, 1889), 3 vols.; CLARKE, *Catalogue of Muniments of Battle Abbey* (London, 1835), in 97 folio volumes.

EDWIN BURTON.

Bauberger, WILHELM, German physician, novelist, and poet, b. at Thannhausen in Swabian Bavaria, 3 March, 1809; d. at the same place, 8 February, 1883. As a physician he was greatly esteemed for his skill, but more so for his kindliness of manner. His fame rests chiefly, however, on his tales. The earliest of these, "Die Beatushöhle", written at the age of nineteen, while the author was still a medical student, met with such extraordinary success among all classes of readers that Bauberger published all his subsequent tales as by the author of "Die Beatushöhle". He drew his most successful themes from history and legend. His recognized model for the spirit and tone of his stories was Christoph Schmid.

Bauberger also essayed lyrical and dramatic compositions, but with indifferent success, for, along with much that is strong and beautiful, his verse contains more that is feeble and commonplace. His fame as a writer suffered no permanent eclipse from the inferiority of his poetry, for new tales, exhibiting all the charm of his early work, constantly appeared to redeem his dramatic failures or half-successes. Bauberger's literary activity continued

BATTLE ABBEY; ENTRANCE GATE

unabated until his death. A list of his works printed during his lifetime is found in Kehrein's "Lexicon der kath. Dichter, Volks- und Jugendschriftsteller im 19ten Jahrhundert" (1872), I, 13, and a complete list of his posthumous works in the "Allgemeine deutsche Biographie", XLVI, 232 sqq.

HEINDLE, *Repertorium der Pädagogik*, I, 34.

MATTHIAS LEIMKUHLER.

Baudeau, NICOLAS, Regular Canon and economist, b. at Amboise, France, 25 April, 1730; d. in 1792. He became a religious of the Abbey of Chancelade, near Périgueux, and taught theology there for some time. It was there that he wrote his "Analyse de l'ouvrage du pape Benoît XIV sur les béatifications et canonisations" (Paris, 1759), which was examined and approved by the pope himself. It is found in Migne's "Theologiæ Cursus Completus" (tom. III). He was called to Paris by the Archbishop de Beaumont and there he gave all his time to the study of economics. In 1765 he founded a periodical "Les Ephémérides du citoyen" in which he attacked the principles of Quesnay and of the physiocratical school. Soon after, he accepted and defended these principles and became one of their most notable supporters. In 1771 he published his most important work, "Première introduction à la philosophie économique", in which he expounds the doctrines of the physiocratical school. There are two great economic factors, nature and art; and there are three kinds of art, fecund or productive, which consists in helping nature to give the most abundant production possible (hunting, fishing, breeding, agriculture, etc.); sterile or non-productive, which gives to these productions a more useful or pleasing form (industry, commerce, etc.); social art, which gives the knowledge, protection, and means necessary for the exercise of the productive and non-productive arts (instruction, religious worship, protection, administration). Productive art is the most important.

When he died he had lost the use of his faculties. Besides the works already mentioned, he wrote "Idées d'un citoyen sur l'administration des finances du roi" (1763); "Idées d'un citoyen sur les besoins, les droits, et les devoirs des vrais pauvres" (1765); "Lettres sur les émeutes populaires" (1768); "Lettres d'un citoyen sur les vingtièmes et autres impôts" (1768); "Principes économiques de Louis XII et du Cardinal d'Amboise, de Henri IV, et du duc de Sully sur l'administration des finances" (1775); "Charles V, Louis XII, et Henri IV aux Français" (1787).

MIGNE, *Theologiæ Cursus Completus*, III; ESPINAS, *Histoire des doctrines économiques*; DAIRE, *Collection des principaux économistes*.

G. M. SAUVAGE.

Baudouin, MICHEL, Indian missionary, b. in Quebec, Canada, 8 March, 1692, entered the Society of Jesus in France at the age of twenty-one, arrived in Louisiana (on his return to America) in 1728; d. at New Orleans in, or after, 1768. Shortly after his arrival in Louisiana, he was sent to the Choctaw Mission, where he laboured for eighteen years. When he was on the eve of deriving some fruit from his labours, he was recalled by his superior to New Orleans, owing to the disturbances excited by the English among the Indians and the dangers to which he was exposed. He was Superior-General of the Louisiana Mission from 1749 until the expulsion of the Jesuits from that colony in 1763. When that untoward event took place, Father Baudouin was not banished from the country as his fellow Jesuits were, but with a pension of three or four hundred francs was allowed to remain in the colony, a planter having offered the aged priest a home on his estate.

THWAITES, *Jesuit Relations*, Index Vol. LXXII, 78, where full references are given; KIP, *Early Jesuit Missions in North America* (London, 1847), II.

EDWARD P. SPILLANE.

Baumgartner, GALLUS JACOB, a Swiss statesman, b. 18 October, 1797, at Altstätten, Switzerland; d. 12 July, 1869, at St. Gallen. After attending the gymnasium at St. Gallen he studied law at Fribourg, Switzerland, and at Vienna. From 1817 to 1819 he was a tutor in Hungary. Returning to Vienna in 1819, he was arrested there after the murder of Kotzebue by Sand on the false suspicion of belonging to a Swiss political society and was expelled from the city in 1820. He began his political career as keeper of the archives of his native canton, St. Gallen. This position gave him the opportunity of learning the topography, history, laws, and legal relations of the canton. In 1822 he was made official secretary; in 1825 he became a member of the great council of the canton and was appointed chancellor.

On account of his knowledge of business he was selected, in 1831, for the position of *Landammann*, or chief magistrate of the canton, and held the office until 1846. During his administration he bent all his energies to making a closely united republic out of the loosely connected cantons, and to improving the Swiss roads and water-ways. Appointed a delegate, at this time, to the diet at Lucerne he endeavoured at the diet to bring about a reorganization of the confederation. He wished to create a vigorous, organically united republic similar to that of the United States, retaining at the same time a large amount of independence for the individual cantons. Baumgartner's chief opponents in carrying out this project were the Catholic clergy, for he aimed to separate the Church entirely from Rome and to place it under the control of the State. He was largely influenced by "Josephinism" and by the ideas of Wessenberg.

In 1832, at his suggestion, the Bishopric of Chur was dissolved. In 1834, at the so-called Assembly of Baden, he gave expression to his views in the motions he introduced. These were, that ecclesiastical administration of law be placed under the control of the State, that he should have direction of the education of the clergy, that the ecclesiastical right of patronage should be limited and that the privileges of the religious orders should be revoked. When his political friends in 1841 dissolved the monastic houses of Aargau by force, plundered them, and drove their inmates away, he saw to what his Church policy would lead. Soon after this he changed his opinions and came over to the side of his former opponents. On this account he had to retire from his position as *Landammann*. In 1845 he again entered the diet as representative of the Catholic Peoples' party, but after two years was forced out by the victory of the Liberals. He now urged the views of the Catholic Church in the press and in popular assemblies. He was once more a member of the Swiss federal assembly, 1857–60, and became again *Landammann* but was overthrown in 1864.

The present political organization, well-ordered administration, and material prosperity of the canton of St. Gallen are due to Baumgartner's public labours; the Catholic Church owes to him especially the founding of the Bishopric of St. Gallen. Besides all this he prepared the way for the later development of Switzerland in the outline of a new constitution for the confederation which he drew up. After his defeat in 1864, Baumgartner withdrew altogether from public life and devoted himself to the study of the history of his native canton. The results of his researches appeared in two works issued by him: "Die Schweiz in ihren Kämpfen und Umgestaltungen von 1830–1850" (4 vols., Zurich, 1853, 1866), and "Geschichte des schweizerischen Freistaats und Kantons St. Gallen" (2 vols., Zurich, 1868). A third volume of the history was prepared by his son, Alexander, from the papers Baumgartner left at his death, and issued at Einsiedeln in 1890. A biography of Baumgartner giving full detail of his life has been published by his son under the title: "Gallus Jakob Baumgartner und die neuere Staatsentwicklung der Schweiz" (Freiburg, Baden, 1892).

PATRICIUS SCHLAGER.

Baunard, LOUIS, educator, b. at Bellegarde (Loiret), France, in 1828. He was one of the clergy of Orléans, until 1877, after which he was attached to the Catholic University of Lille, first as professor, and later as rector. No Catholic university profited more by the Law of 1875 that granted freedom of higher education. The transfer of the State University from Douai to Lille did not retard the progress of the Catholic institution. Guided by its zealous rector, and supported by the active charity of the manufacturers of Northern France, the University of Lille has graduated a great number of Catholic physicians, lawyers, and business men. Many young priests also have been prepared at Lille for the career of teaching, which they have since followed as professors in the *petits séminaires* and boarding schools. Technical courses exist for those who intend to devote themselves to manufacturing industries; a department of economics and the social sciences was established through the efforts of M. Duthoit for the development of the social principles of Catholicism; finally the "university extension", a sort of popular circulating university, provides for lectures by the university professors in all the industrial centres of Northern France.

Mgr. Baunard received the degree of Doctor of Letters, in 1860; in the two theses which he wrote he treated of the pedagogy of Plato and of Theodulphus, Bishop of Orléans in the time of Charlemagne; both works which marked the beginning of a literary activity surpassed by few. As hagiographer he wrote on St. John the Apostle (1869) and St. Ambrose (1871). He wrote the biographies of Louise de Marillac, the foundress of the Daughters of Charity (1898); of Madame Barat (1876), foundress of the Ladies of the Sacred Heart; of Vicomte Armand de Melun (1880), Cardinal Pie, Bishop of Poitiers (1886), General de Sonis (1890, his most successful work), Cardinal Lavigerie (1896), M. Ernest Lelièvre, founder of the Little Sisters of the Poor (1905), and M. Vrau, the great Christian manufacturer (1906). The French religious history of the nineteenth century was summarized by him in "Un siècle de l'Eglise de France" (1901). He contributed notable works of religious psychology in his celebrated books, "Le doute et ses victimes" (1865), in which the pages on Jouffroy were both new and surprising, and "La foi et ses victoires" (1881–83). Whatever his subject, Mgr. Baunard was always an "awakener of souls" by reason of his delicate literary conscientiousness and his admirable fecundity. His "Espérance" (1892) throws much light on the beginnings of the contemporary religious revival among intelligent Frenchmen; his "L'évangile du pauvre" (1905) appeared opportunely during a period of social unrest. As university rector, Mgr. Baunard occupies a foremost place in the history of the Catholic university movement; as author, he collected much important material for the religious history of modern France.

GEORGES GOYAU.

Bauny, ETIENNE, theologian, b. in 1564 at Mouzon, Ardennes, France; d. 3 December, 1649, at Saint Pol de Léon. He was admitted into the Society of Jesus, 20 July, 1593, and after teaching humanities and rhetoric he was promoted to the chair of moral theology which he occupied for sixteen years. He was for a time superior of the Jesuit residence at Pontoise. So high was his reputation for learning and holiness, that he had the confidence of the most distinguished prelates of his age, especially of François Cardinal de la Rochefoucauld, who chose him as his spiritual director, and of René de Rieux, Bishop of Léon, who entrusted to him the settlement of the most delicate affairs of his episcopate. Bauny's knowledge of moral theology was singularly profound, but he was in many points too lenient. His undue indulgence excited the pharisaical indignation of the Jansenists, and it was to him that Pascal, Arnauld, and others turned, when they accused the Society of Jesus of teaching lax morality. He was a man of extraordinary severity towards himself, a skilful guide of souls, full of charity towards sinners, prudent in the management of affairs; hence we are not surprised to read that he died in the odour of sanctity, almost in the very exercise of his apostolic ministry, at the advanced age of eighty-five.

His published works are: (1) "Constitutiones Synodales diœcesis Leonensis, a Renato de Rieux Episcopo Leonensi promulgatæ Paulipoli in Leoniâ" (Paris, 1630); (2) "Pratique du droit canonique au gouvernement de l'Eglise, correction des mœurs, et distribution des bénéfices, le tout au style et usage de France" (Paris, 1634); (3) "De Sacramentis ac Personis Sacris, earumque dignitate, obligationibus ac jure, juxta sacrarum litterarum testimonia, SS. Patrum sententias Canonum ac Conciliorum sanctiones, cum summariis, indice duplice, uno tractatuum et quæstionum, rerum altero. Theologiæ moralis pars prima" (Paris, 1640) in fol.; (4) "Tractatus de censuris ecclesiasticis" (Paris, 1642), in fol.; (5) "Nova beneficiorum praxis . . ." (Paris, 1649). The second and third of these works are on the Index.

GUILHERMY, *Ménologe de la c. de J.*, *Assistance de France*, II, 559; HURTER, *Nomenclator*, I, 494; SOMMERVOGEL, *Bibliothèque de la c. de J.*, I, col. 1058.

T. B. BARRETT.

Bausset, LOUIS-FRANÇOIS DE, a French cardinal, writer, and statesman, b. in 1748 at Pondichéry, where his father held an administrative position; d. in Paris, 1824. He studied in France at the Jesuit "Collège de la Flèche" and at St. Sulpice. Ordained priest, he became vicar-general at Aix in 1772; administrator of Digne, 1778; Bishop of Alais, in Languedoc, 1784. Although a prominent member of the Assembly of Notables of Languedoc in 1786 and in 1788, he was not delegated to the Etats Généraux of 1789. In 1791, Bausset was one of the first bishops who endorsed the "Exposition of Principles on the Civil Constitution of the Clergy". He declined to take the oath and passed to Switzerland. Returning to France in 1792, he was incarcerated, but set free when Robespierre fell (9 Thermidor). He then retired to Villemoison, where he began his literary career. After the Concordat of 1801 Bausset cheerfully resigned his see into the hands of Pius VII. Ill health prevented his appointment to one of the newly-formed sees, but Napoleon made him a canon of St. Denis (1806) and a member of the Council of the University of France (1808). Under the Restoration, he became president of the University Council and peer of the realm (1815); Member of the French Academy (1816); Cardinal (1817), and Minister of State (1821). The valuable library and manuscripts of Bausset were bequeathed to St. Sulpice.

The career of Bausset as educator and statesman deserves no special notice; he was guided by, more than he guided, the policy of the two regimes under which he served. From his pen we have, besides several minor writings, "Exposé des principes sur le serment", with a long introduction by Emery (Paris, 1796); "Notices historiques" on Cardinal Boisgelin (Paris, 1804), on Legris-Duval (Paris, 1820), and on Talleyrand (Paris, 1821); two considerable biographies: "Histoire de Fénelon" (Versailles, 1809; Paris, 1823; ed. Migne, 1826) and "Histoire de J.-B. Bossuet, évêque de Meaux" (Paris, 1814, 1819; Versailles, 1821; Besançon, 1847). The original documents concerning Fénelon he had from the Abbé Emery, Superior of Saint-Sulpice. Bossuet's manuscripts, not yet purchased by the National Library, he borrowed from Lamy, a bookseller into whose hands they had fallen. The purity of his style won for Bausset the decennial prize awarded by the Institute of France to the best biography. Still, that very purity often passes into a tiresome sameness which fails to suggest either the winning qualities of Fénelon's character or the elevation of the Eagle of Meaux. As a historian, Bausset fails in critical acumen and judicial impartiality. His "Histoire de Fénelon" is so much of a panegyric that, especially in the delicate and intricate question of the Quietist movement, it needs to be supplemented and corrected by such works as those of Griveau and of Crouslé. It is said that the "Histoire de Bossuet" was written as an offset against the partiality which Bausset had shown to Fénelon; if so, Bausset had a strange way of rehabilitating the subject of his second biography, praising Bossuet's Gallicanism as Bossuet himself, tormented in his last years by the "Defensio cleri gallicani", would not have wished it praised. Brunetière calls Bausset's "Histoire of Bossuet" "la plus franchement gallicane de toutes".

VILLENEUVE-BARGEMONT, *Notice historique sur le Cardinal Bausset* (Marseilles, 1824); DUSSAULT, *Annales littéraires*, (Paris, 1818), t. IV.

J. F. SOLLIER.

Bautain, LOUIS-EUGÈNE-MARIE, philosopher and theologian, b. at Paris, 17 February, 1796; d. there, 15 October, 1867. After a course at the Ecole Normale, where he was influenced by Cousin and Jouffroy, he became (1819) professor of philosophy at Strasburg. Three years later he took up the study of medicine and finally that of theology and was ordained priest (1828). As director of the seminary at Strasburg, he at first won distinction by his work in apologetics, especially against atheism and materialism. He was chiefly interested, however, in the problem of the relations between faith and reason, concerning which he accepted the views of Fideism and Traditionalism, and reduced to a minimum the function of reason. Divine revelation, he claimed, is the only source of knowledge and certitude. He was consequently obliged to sign (18 November, 1835) six propositions containing the Catholic doctrine on faith and reason. After the examination at Rome of his work, "Philosophie du christianisme" (Paris, 1835), Bautain signed (8 September, 1840) six other propositions differing but slightly from those of 1835. Finally, in obedience to the Congregation of Bishops and Regulars, he promised (26 April, 1844) not to teach that the existence of God, the spirituality and immortality of the soul, the principles of metaphysics, and the motives which make revelation credible are beyond the reach of unaided reason. Bautain was appointed Vicar-General of Paris (1850) and taught at the Sorbonne (1853–62). His works include: "De l'enseignement de la philosophie au 19me siècle" (Strasburg, 1833); "Psychologie expérimentale" (ib., 1839); "Philosophie morale" (ib., 1842); "La religion et la liberté" (Paris, 1848); "La morale de l'Evangile" (ib., 1855); "La philosophie des lois" (ib., 1860); "La Conscience" (ib., 1868).

DE RÉGNY, *L'abbé Bautain, sa vie et ses œuvres* (Paris, 1884); BELLAMY in *Dict. de théol. cath.*, s. v.; INGOLD, *Lettres inédites du P. Rozaven* in *Bulletin Critique*, 5 April, 25 June, 1902. (These letters refer to Bautain's visit to Rome in 1840.) HURTER, *Nomenclator*, III, 999.

E. A. PACE.

Bautista, FRAY JUAN, b. at Mexico, 1555; date of death unknown, but probably between 1606 and 1615. He joined the Franciscans in his native city, and taught theology and metaphysics at the convent of St. Francis of Mexico. He was also a definitor of the province, and became Guardian of Tezcuco twice (1595 and 1606), of Tlatelolco (1600), and of Tacuba in 1605. Although born at Mexico, he did not at first care to familiarize himself with the language of the Mexican Indians who formed the main part of the population among which he had been born and raised. He looked with indifference on the Nahuatl, the language of the so-called Aztecs. But after joining the Franciscans and becoming acquainted with the educational work going on through the Church among the Indians he willingly listened to the representations of older members of the order, and soon acquired a thorough knowledge of the idiom. A number of his works are known by title only. Ten of these were written in the Nahuatl language, previous to 1607; several were printed at Mexico.

MENDIETA, *Historia eclesiástica Indiana* (finished in 1599 but first published by Ycazbalceta, Mexico, 1870); JUAN DE TORQUEMADA, *Los veinte y uno Libros Rituales y Monarchia Indiana con el origen y guerras de los Indios occidentales* (first ed., Madrid, 1613; 2d ed., ibid., 1725); PINELO, *Epítome* (2d ed., Madrid, 1737–58); NICOLÁS ANTONIO, *Biblioteca Hispana nova* (Madrid, 1766), II; JOAQUÍN GARCÍA YCAZBALCETA, *Bibliografía mexicana del Siglo XVI* (Mexico, 1886).

AD. F. BANDELIER.

Bavaria, THE KINGDOM OF.—I. *Political Constitution, Area, Population, etc.*—The present Kingdom of Bavaria—named after the German tribe called Boiarii—has formed, since 1871, a constituent part of the German Empire. It is an independent State of the confederation with special rights; its rulers belong to the Wittelsbach dynasty, the head of the Government in 1907 being Prince-Regent Luitpold. In time of peace the king or his representative is the head of the army; in time of war the emperor, as head of all the forces, has, by agreement, the control. As the second state (in size) of the empire Bavaria has six representatives in the Federal Council and forty-eight in the Imperial Parliament (Reichstag), the latter deputies being chosen by direct vote. In its present form Bavaria consists of two parts of unequal size, geographically some distance from each other, on either side of the Rhine. It has an area of 29,283 square miles, and a population (census of 1 December, 1905) of 6,254,372 persons. According to individual declaration of belief 4,608,469 persons, or 70 per cent of the population, belong to the Catholic Church; 1,843,123 persons, or 28.3 per cent of the population, are adherents of the Lutheran and Calvinist confessions; while other religious bodies (Old-Catholics, Irvingites, Mennonites, Methodists, etc.) have but a small following. There are in Bavaria 56,000 Jews, living chiefly at Munich, Nuremberg, and Fürth, who are engaged principally in commercial and industrial pursuits; they form a large proportion of the physicians, lawyers, and judges of the country. The German population of Bavaria is made up as follows: descendants of the Boiarii, living in Upper and Lower Bavaria and in the greater part of the Upper Palatinate; Franconians, a mixture of Rhine Franks, Thuringians, and Slavs, found in the region of the Main and the Redwitz; Swabians, living in the province bearing their name; and the inhabitants of the Palatinate, a mixed race of Roman and German blood having their home on the left bank of the Rhine. The difference of stock is evidenced by the variety of dialects and provincial characteristics. Naturally these distinctions are not so marked in the cities.

Outside the Rhenish Palatinate Bavaria is an elevated, hilly country. It is bounded on the south by the Alps, on the east by the mountains called the Bohemian Forest (Böhmerwald), and on the north by the range called the Franconian Forest (Frankenwald), while the various ranges called Fichtelgebirge, Spessart, and Rhöngebirge represent isolated districts of larger or smaller extent. The Rhine Palatinate is divided by spurs of the Vosges into an easterly and a westerly half, both parts having a fruitful soil. The chief rivers are the Danube and the Rhine. The former enters the country at Ulm and leaves it at Passau. Under ordinary conditions it is navigable for large craft below Ratisbon. Its tributaries in Bavaria from the south are the Iller, a stream rich in fish, the Lech, the Isar, and the Inn; from the north its tributaries are the Wörnitz, the Altmühl, the Regen, and the Vils. For a distance of about fifty-three miles the Rhine forms the boundary between the Rhenish Palatinate and Baden. The three Franconian provinces lie in the valley of the Main, a stream bordered by vineyards and much used for commerce beyond Bamberg. Three flourishing Bavarian cities are situated on its banks: Schweinfurt, Würzburg, and Aschaffenburg. The southern tributaries of the Main, which leave Bavarian territory near Ostheim, are the Regnitz and the Tauber; the northern are the Rodach and the Saale. Only a small part of Lake Constance belongs to Bavaria, but there are numerous lakes in Swabia and a still larger number in Upper Bavaria. Many of these bodies of water are noted for their picturesque scenery, such as the Ammersee, Alpsee, Würmsee, Tegernsee, Königssee, and especially Chiemsee, known as the "Lake of Bavaria". It also contains much mineral wealth: iron, coal, granite, basalt, and salt, of which last there is a large yield of excellent quality. There are numbers of mineral springs, some of which are known throughout the world. Farming in lower Bavaria and cattle-breeding in Swabia, Upper Bavaria, and Middle Franconia are the chief occupations, while the wines of Franconia and the Palatinate and the fruit and vegetables of Bamberg have a high reputation. Industrial life centres in Nuremberg, Fürth, Augsburg, and Ludwigshafen. As a centre of art Munich holds, without question, the highest rank in Germany. The railway lines have a length of about 3,700 miles, to which additions are constantly being made.

No expense is spared in advancing education. In 1903–04 the common schools cost over $7,500,000. The Bavarian troops are equipped with the same arms as the other divisions of the Imperial German army but wear a different uniform. They are commanded by native generals and consist of three army corps which are divided as follows: 23 infantry regiments, 11 cavalry regiments, 14 artillery regiments, 2 *chasseur* regiments, 3 battalions of pioneers, 3 transportation battalions, and 1 railway battalion. Including all the reserves the Bavarian army numbers over 200,000 men. The annual cost of the army is $20,000,000.

II. *Early History.*—The early history of Bavaria varies according to the province in question; the races that now live peacefully together under the rule of the Wittelsbach dynasty were once constantly engaged in bloody feuds. A thousand years ago the Bavarian domain included what is now Upper and Lower Austria and the Alpine provinces of the Tyrol and Styria. (See AUSTRO-HUNGARIAN MONARCHY.) The Palatinate was united with Bavaria proper through its rulers; on the extinction (1778) of the younger (Bavarian) branch of the Wittelsbach line the elder (Palatinate) branch became the reigning house of electoral Bavaria. Before the changes caused by the French Revolution and the disappearance of the Holy Roman Empire (1803 and 1819) those parts of Franconia and Swabia which now belong to Bavaria enjoyed a more or less independent existence, such as Ansbach-Bayreuth, the Archbishoprics of Würzburg, Bamberg, Eichstätt, Augsburg, etc., the free cities of Augsburg, Nuremberg, Schweinfurt, Kempten, etc., the principalities of Castell and Oettingen, the possessions of the Counts of Orttenburg, Giech, etc. Only the most important

periods in the history of the Duchy and, later, Electorate of Bavaria can be touched on in this article.

The Boiarii, apparently, were either related to the Marcomanni or else identical with that people who, after the Romans had been driven out of the region in the fifth century, began to spread from the right bank of the Danube and gradually extended their control as far as the River Lech and deep into the Alpine region. The chiefs of the Boiarii belonged to the family of the Agilolfings who chose Ratisbon at an early date as their capital. Duke Garibald I, who lived in the middle of the sixth century, seems to have had the power of a sovereign. His daughter, Theodelinda, became Queen of the Langobardi. Her brother, Tassilo I, was, however, obliged to acknowledge the supremacy of the Franks which his son, Garibald II, was able to throw off for a time (about 630). But this independence was of short duration. The Franks under Charles Martel again subdued his descendants. When Tassilo II, who had done much to further the spread of Christianity and civilization in the direction of Eastern Europe, sought to regain his lost independence he was deposed and sent to a monastery.

Bavaria now became a Frankish province ruled by representatives of the Frankish king (794). It came into greater prominence when Louis the German, who had received the eastern part of the Frankish kingdom by the Treaty of Verdun (843), made his residence in Bavaria. His grandson Arnulf, Duke of Carinthia, was crowned emperor in 896. One of his relatives, Margrave Leopold, who fell in a battle (906) against the Magyars, is regarded as the first of the line of Scheyren-Wittelsbach. Upon the extinction of the Carlovingian dynasty Arnulf, son of Leopold, claimed the position of a sovereign prince. This involved him in war with Henry I the Saxon, King of Germany, whose partly successful attempt to conquer Arnulf was completed by Otto I. After the deposition of Eberhard I, the elder son of Duke Arnulf (939), Bavaria no longer had native-born rulers but Saxons, Franconians, and members of the Welf family who ruled as vassals of the king with the title of duke. Not until Emperor Frederick I, in 1180, rewarded Otto of Wittelsbach for his courage by granting him Bavaria did a genuine Bavarian ascend the throne of his fathers. Otto and his energetic successors laid the foundation of the future importance of Bavaria.

In 1214 the Rhine Palatinate was united to Bavaria. Louis II (1253–94) was succeeded by his son Louis III (known as Emperor Louis IV of the Holy Roman Empire) who, by an agreement in 1329 at Pavia, took Bavaria proper, leaving to Rudolph, his brother, the Rhine Palatinate. The large possessions which Louis III secured for his family (Holland, Brandenburg, the Tyrol, etc.) were lost to his successors by discord and successive partitions. Albert IV, however, reunited the country into one domain and secured it against further division by his law of 1506. His son William IV (1508–50) and his grandson Albert V (1550–79) prevented Lutheran and Anabaptist doctrines from entering Bavarian territory. During the reign of William V (1579–98) and still more during the reign of Maximilian I (1598–1651), Bavaria stood at the head of the counter-Reformation and the Catholic League. To these two rulers it was due that the progress of the Reformation was checked, and that some of the territory which had been affected by it was restored to the Church. The Emperor Ferdinand II granted Duke Maximilian of Bavaria for his loyalty the electoral dignity (1623). Bavaria paid a bitter price for its new position in the devastations of the Thirty Years' War. Ferdinand Maria (1651–79) sought to restore the prosperity of the country, but affairs were thrown into confusion during the reigns of his son, Maximilian Emanuel (1679–1726), conqueror of the Turks, and of his grandson Charles Albert (1726–45) by the wars of the Spanish and Austrian successions. It was not until the reign of the Elector Maximilian (Joseph) III (1745–77) that order was again restored. During this reign the Jesuits were suppressed (1773).

Maximilian was the last of the younger branch of the Wittelsbach line. After his death the elder (Palatinate) branch of the family succeeded to the throne in the person of the art-loving Charles Theodore (1778–99), under whom a papal nunciature was established at Munich (1785). The last years of Charles Theodore were embittered by many misfortunes. The young French Republic took from him the territory on the other side of the Rhine and he had to endure many humiliations from his subjects. Up to this time Bavaria had been entirely a Catholic country. New conditions arose when Maximilian IV (Joseph) ascended the throne (1799). This ruler was twice married to Protestants; non-Catholics were granted the same political rights as Catholics, and Lutheran services allowed at the capital. The Government proceeded with severity against all forms of Catholic religious life. The number of churches which were dismantled or profaned at this time is hardly credible; treasures of art of earlier days were sold for a mere pittance or shamefully treated; whole wagonloads of books and documents were burned or thrown into the river; professorial positions filled by avowed opponents of all religions; and an extravagant and frivolous luxury became the fashion at Court. In 1805 Bavaria entered into an alliance with Napoleon against Austria and Russia. In return for this the victorious Corsican made Bavaria a kingdom (1 January, 1806). As a member of the Rhenish Confederation Maximilian (Joseph) IV fought against Prussia in 1806, against Austria in 1809, and against Russia in 1812. Thirty thousand Bavarian troops died in Russia, victims of the climate or of encounters with the Cossacks. After the battle of Leipzig Bavaria joined the Allies at the right moment, so that it was able to retain the greater part of its territory. After the chancellor, Count von Montgelas, had retired from office (2 February, 1817) efforts were made to restore former conditions and that same year a Concordat, which is still operative, was made with the Roman Curia; the next year the king granted a constitution which has produced good results in every respect.

During the reign of the King Louis I (1825–48) the Church prospered greatly; old cathedrals were restored; new churches and monasteries founded; and painters and sculptors came in large numbers to Munich where they found profitable employment. The colossal figure of Bavaria, the Hall of Fame, the Walhalla, the Hall of Freedom, and the basilica of St. Boniface keep alive the memory of Louis I, the greatest ruler in the history of Bavaria. The revolutionary movement of 1848 compelled Louis to abdicate. His son, Maximilian II (1848–64), a well-meaning but weak ruler, did much to further learning, especially in the domain of history; he was not fortunate, however, in the men he selected to fill professorships and on this account lost popularity with his Catholic subjects. His successor, the visionary Louis II (1864–86), ascended the throne at the age of eighteen. The civil war of 1866 obliged Bavaria to make great sacrifices. Four years later the Bavarian army took an honourable part in the Franco-German war, and in 1871 Bavaria became a member of the new German Empire. During the reign of Louis II special encouragement was given to architecture and industrial art. The growing insanity of the king necessitated the appointment of Prince Leopold as "regent of the kingdom", and not long after Louis met his death, in a manner

never clearly explained, in the Starnbergersee. As his brother Otto was mentally incapable of ruling, Leopold (b. 12 March, 1821) continued in his office of regent. Bavaria has prospered greatly under his wise rule; his grandson Leopold, assures the succession in his line.

III. *Introduction of Christianity.*—The Christian faith was probably first introduced into Bavaria, both on the Danube and on the Rhine, by Roman soldiers and merchants. [Cf. Huber, "Geschichte der Einführung und Verbreitung des Christenthums in Südosten Deutschlands" (Salzburg, 1874–75), 4 vols.; Hefele, "Geschichte der Einführung des Christenthums im südwestlichen Deutschland" (Tübingen, 1837).] In the earliest ages of the Church Augusta Vindelicorum (Augsburg) was famous on account of the martyrdom of St. Afra and her companions; Ratisbon had also its confessors and the same may be said of Speyer. But it was not until the end of the German migrations and the establishment of more orderly conditions in the Merovingian-Carlovingian Empire that Christianity took firm root. As is well known, at first Irish, and later Frankish and Anglo-Saxon missionaries sowed the seed of the Gospel in the hearts of the rude warriors whose life until then had been given to fighting, hunting, gambling, and drinking. Among these missionaries were: St. Kilian and his pupils Colonat (Coloman) and Totnan at Würzburg; in the Alpgau region St. Magnus; at Ratisbon and Freising St. Rupert, St. Emmeram, and St. Corbinian. Stricter regulations were introduced by Winfrid (St. Boniface) who is in truth entitled to the name of the "Apostle of the Germans". The Dioceses of Freising, Ratisbon, Passau, Würzburg, and Eichstätt were either established or reorganized, while the founding of monasteries made it possible to train the priesthood properly and to raise the spiritual and moral level of the laity. When Boniface was created Archbishop of Mainz (747) Augsburg and Constance became his suffragans, having previously belonged, respectively, to Aquileia and Besançon. After Charlemagne had overthrown the native ruling family, the Agilolfings, Pope Leo III erected (798) the new province of Salzburg to which Ratisbon, Freising, Passau, and Seben (Brixen) in what is now the Tyrol, were attached. But the first mentioned dioceses together with Neuburg, which in a short time disappeared, were left dependent on Mainz. With some changes of names and boundaries these are still in existence. The Diocese of Bamberg, later formed from the existing provinces, was not a suffragan of Mainz but was directly dependent on the Apostolic See. The small Diocese of Chiemsee, founded in 1206, was always dependent on Salzburg; it was suppressed at the beginning of the nineteenth century.

IV. *Ecclesiastical Divisions.*—The present ecclesiastical divisions of Bavaria rest upon the Bull of Circumscription issued by Pope Pius VII, 1 April, 1818, and made public, 23 September, 1821. According to this Bavaria is divided into the two church provinces of Munich-Freising and Bamberg; the first archdiocese has for suffragans Augsburg, Passau, and Ratisbon; the suffragans of the second are Würzburg, Speyer, and Eichstätt. The Ministry of the Interior for Worship and Education has charge of the interests of the Crown and State in their relations to the Catholic Church of the country; this ministry is the chief State guardian of the various religious and charitable endowments and is aided therein by the civil authorities of the governmental districts. A court of administration has been in existence since 1878 which has control over various matters relating to religious societies (among others, the religious training of children). Cf. Silbernagl, "Verfassung und Verwaltung sämmtlicher Religionsgenossenschaften in Bayern" (4th ed. Ratisbon, 1900); Schecht,

"Bayerns Kirchenprovinzen, ein Ueberblick über Geschichte und gegenwärtigen Bestand der katholischen Kirche im Königreich Bayern" (Munich, 1902).

The boundaries of the dioceses do not agree with the boundaries of the political divisions except in the case of Würzburg (Lower Franconia) and of Speyer (Rhine Palatinate). The Archdiocese of Bamberg extends across Bavaria from Würtemberg to Bohemia and Saxony; the territory of the suffragan Diocese of Würzburg stretches beyond the boundaries of the country. Eichstätt includes parts of Middle Franconia, the Upper Palatinate, Upper Bavaria, and Swabia. Ratisbon is the largest diocese; it includes not only the greater part of the Upper Palatinate but also parts of Upper and Lower Bavaria, as well as Upper Franconia. The Archdiocese of Munich-Freising embraces besides the greater part of Upper Bavaria a part of Lower Bavaria, chiefly included in the suffragan Diocese of Passau. The Diocese of Augsburg includes the whole of Swabia and the western judicial districts of Upper Bavaria; in the north it extends well into Middle Franconia.

V. *Church Statistics.*—According to the "Zeitschrift des königlichen bayerischen statistischen Bureau" (1906, nos. 2 and 3) the Catholic population of the various districts was as follows:—

Upper Bavaria	1,299,372
Lower Bavaria	700,118
Rhine Palatinate	391,200
Upper Palatinate and Ratisbon	525,933
Upper Franconia	316,545
Middle Franconia	227,119
Lower Franconia	546,962
Swabia and Neuburg	646,220
	4,653,469

In the Rhine Palatinate, Upper Franconia, and especially in Middle Franconia the non-Catholic population is decidedly in the majority, namely: Rhine Palatinate, 479,694; Upper Franconia, 362,519; Middle Franconia, 623,546. In Upper Bavaria, Lower Franconia, and Swabia the Protestants number over 100,000 persons, while in the Upper Palatinate the figures are hardly half as large. In Lower Bavaria there are not over 10,000 non-Catholics. Rapid growth is reported in the Catholic parishes of Nuremberg (90,000), Augsburg (70,000), Erlangen, Schweinfurt, and Memmingen; the Protestant parishes have increased in population in Munich (80,000), Würzburg (15,000), Aschaffenburg, Ingolstadt, and Forchheim; while in the Catholic provinces Protestant churches and chapels are rapidly springing up. The same can hardly be said of Catholic churches in the Protestant districts, although more has been done in this direction lately than in former years and a few parishes like Wunsiedel, Hof, and Weissenburg here and there possess creditable churches. The establishment of the Boniface Verein might have proved very helpful in this respect and would have counteracted the efforts of the Gustavus-Adolphus Verein; but a false respect for King Louis I (founder of the Ludwig-Mission Verein, which is exclusively Bavarian) has, in spite of all efforts, prevented its establishment in the kingdom.

Every diocese has a cathedral chapter which, according to the Concordat, besides choir-service acts as a council for the bishop. These chapters include a provost, dean, a number of canons, and curates. In Munich, besides the chapter there is a collegiate foundation of court preachers (St. Cajetan) similarly organized. At the close of 1904 there were 3,022 parishes served by 3,144 parish priests or curates, and 2,578 vicars and chaplains; there were also 1,985 regular clergy (Benedictines, Franciscans, Carmelites, Capuchins) living in 86 monasteries and hospices. The orders for women had at that date 12,586 members in 79 houses and 1,087 dependencies. With a few exceptions the female religious devote themselves to teaching and nursing. There are in Bavaria over 1,000 Protestant parishes with 1,400 pastors and assistant preachers. In 1903 the Catholic Church funds, including real estate, amounted to about $42,500,000; the funds of the Protestant denominations to $5,000,000. As the revenues from the church funds are often not sufficient to keep the church buildings, etc., in repair, a number of cities have decided to impose a church tax, which so far has been moderate. [Cf. Geiger, "Taschenkalender für den katholischen Klerus" (Ratisbon, 1907), as to the salaries, pensions, and ranking of the clergy.]

VI. *Education and Charitable Institutions.*—The school system consists of public schools, continuation and technical schools, gymnasia with classical courses, *Realgymnasia* (no Greek), *Realschulen* (high-schools without Latin and Greek), *Oberrealschulen* (gymnasia with no Latin or Greek, which prepare for the technical schools), commercial schools, seminaries for teachers, lyceums, 3 universities, a technical high-school, etc. Except in rare cases the primary schools are chiefly denominational. The middle and high-schools are used by all denominations. Religious instruction is provided for these schools as well as for the primary ones. The universities at Munich and Würzburg have Catholic theological faculties. There is at Munich a seminary for the training of priests called the Georgianum and the the provinces have similar institutions, generally in connexion with lyceums. Following the directions of the Council of Trent there are in all the dioceses seminaries for boys (*petits séminaires*) which are intended to prepare youths without means to study in the gymnasia. In Munich the total number of university instructors is 250; in Würzburg, 158; in Erlangen, 100; in the technical high-school, 100. In the other institutions the number of teachers is correspondingly smaller.

The attendance of students at Munich is between 5,000 and 6,000; at Würzburg, 1,400. The students at the technical high-school number about 3,000; the academy of fine arts and the academy of music have each 300 students. In 1904 the lyceums had about 1,000 matriculated students. Some of the gymnasia, such as that of St. Stephen at Augsburg and those at Metten and Münnerstadt, are in charge of members of the regular orders (Benedictines and Augustinians). The majority of the professors are, however, laymen. In Bavaria for various reasons relatively more Protestants than Catholics study the higher branches, consequently the non-Catholic professors nearly everywhere equal in number those of the Catholic Faith. This condition of affairs has been somewhat changed by the labours of the Albertus-Magnus Verein as well as by the work of the associations and leagues of Catholic students. Efforts have also been made to increase the number of *progymnasia* (without higher classes) in certain Catholic districts; the Protestant districts are better equipped with such schools.

Bavaria is well supplied with institutions for the care of the sick, the crippled, children, and old people. Many of these foundations are largely endowed and date back to the earlier centuries. In the Catholic benevolent institutions members of the religious orders of both sexes are active; the Protestant institutions are served by deaconesses. There are also institutions in which both faiths are represented, as the hospital at Augsburg, where patients of both denominations are cared for by Catholic and Protestant sisters. At Munich there are only sisters of the Society of St. Vincent de Paul, and at Nuremberg deaconesses, although in both places the percentage of patients of other faiths is large. The clergy of the different faiths exercise their office undisturbed in the hospitals of both cities. Of the other humanitarian associations mention should be made of the Gesellenverein which gives travelling journeymen-mechanics an opportunity for further education. In nearly all the larger towns it has lodging-houses and in a few places large, well-equipped homes. Workingmen's Unions endeavour to counteract the tendencies of the Social Democrats; citizens' and voters' associations strive to send to the Bavarian as well as to the Imperial Parliament representatives of pronouncedly Christian principles.

Civil Status of the Church.—The relations of Church and State are settled in all important points by the Concordat and the Constitution [cf. Silbernagl, op. cit.; Idem, "Lehrbuch des katholischen Kirchenrechts" (Ratisbon, 1903), 4 vols.; Girón y Arcas, "La situación jurídica de la Iglesia en los diversos estados de Europa y de América" (Madrid, 1905)]. Although the promises made the Holy See were not kept in all particulars, for instance in the early seventies of the nineteenth century, yet, taken altogether, conditions are satisfactory; this is owing largely to the strong religious feeling of the reigning dynasty, once more thoroughly Catholic. The Catholic Church has, however, no special privileges. It is on the same footing as the Lutheran, the Reformed, and the Greek schismatics.

Parishes under the jurisdiction of monasteries, as in Austria, are not known in Bavaria. Where members of the religious orders assume pastoral functions, it is only by way of substitution; in these cases they receive the same governmental support as do the secular clergy. The funds of the Church are liable to taxation as other funds. No concession or mitigation is granted. Priests are not obliged to sit as lay assessors, nor to act as jurors, nor to be guardians of minors. Military service is not obligatory on theological students, at least, if when the army is mobilized, they have been ordained subdeacons. In this case they are employed as nurses. The civil code has limited ecclesiastical jurisdiction in matters of marriage, but Catholics still respect the teaching of the Church, especially that death alone can dissolve marriage. A serious question is the great increase of mixed marriages, especially in the large cities, and the consequent Protestant education of children. Owing to various considerations, the evil has not been combated as vigorously as it should be. Prisons and reformatories are, as a rule, visited by clergymen of all faiths, but full provision is made for the pastoral supervision of Catholic prisoners. Prisoners condemned to death are accompanied by priests to the scaffold. Gifts and testamentary bequests for religious and benevolent objects are frequent. They are made under the regulations of the civil code by which any association that has given proper notification to the authorities is regarded as a person in the sense of the law. In the cities the cemeteries belong, as a rule, to the civil community, but nearly everywhere in the country they are part of the parish and are used in common by the Christian confessions. Cremation is not permitted in Bavaria although there is an agitation in its favour.

Those desiring more detailed information are referred to the following authorities: Hopf, "Bayerische Geschichte in Zeittafeln" (Nuremberg, 1865); Denk and Weiss, "Unser Bayerland" (Munich, 1906); Riezler, "Geschichte Bayerns" (Gotha, 1878, 1903), 6 vols.; Döberl, "Entwickelungsgeschichte Bayerns" (Munich, 1906), 1 vol., extending to 1648. A reliable authority on the Wittelsbach dynasty is: Häutle, "Genealogie des erlauchten Stammhauses Wittelsbach" (Munich, 1870). Among the authorities for the Rhine Palatinate are: Häusser, "Geschichte der rheinischen Pfalz" (Heidelberg, 1845), 2 vols.; Remling, "Geschichte der Bischöfe zu Speyer" (Mainz, 1852), 4 vols.; Hilgard, "Urkundenbuch zur

Geschichte der Stadt Speyer" (Strasburg, 1885); Molitor "Urkundebuch bezüglich zur Geschichte der Stadt Zweibrücken" (Zweibrücken, 1888). For the history of Franconia: Stein, "Geschichte Frankens" (Schweinfurt, 1883–86), 2 vols. For the history of Swabia: Braun, "Geschichte der Bischöfe von Augsburg" (Augsburg, 1813), 4 vols.; Steichele, "Das Bisthum Augsburg, historisch und statistisch beschrieben" (Augsburg, 1864–94), 6 vols., continuation by Schröder; Baumann, "Geschichte des Algäu" (Kempten, 1880–94), 3 vols.

PIUS WITTMANN.

Bawden (or BALDWIN), WILLIAM, an English Jesuit, b. at Cornwall, 1563; d. at St.-Omer, 28 September, 1632. Father Bawden studied for five years at Oxford and later spent some time at Douay College, from whence he went to Reims, arriving at the latter institution 31 December, 1582. Leaving Reims, he went, 13 August, 1583, to Rome and in the English College at that city he completed his studies for the priesthood and was ordained priest 16 April, 1586. After his ordination he served one year as English penitentiary at St. Peter's, when his health failed. He next went to Belgium and in 1590, on joining the Jesuits, be became professor of theology at Louvain. His health failing again, he went to Brussels, where he resided for eleven years. His next change was to Germany, where he was arrested and sent to England for an alleged connexion with the Gunpowder Plot. He was incarcerated in the Tower for eight years and was tortured in the hope of extracting a confession from him. His innocence being established, he was liberated, but at the same time banished. In 1621 he was appointed rector of Louvain and the next year was transferred to the rectorship of St.-Omer's College, where he remained until his death.

COOPER in *Dict. Nat. Biog.*, III, 39; GILLOW, *Bibl. Dict. Eng. Cath.*, I, 156.

THOMAS GAFFNEY TAAFFE.

Bayer, ADÈLE, *née* Parmentier, eldest daughter of Andrew Parmentier, b. in Belgium, 4 July, 1814, and d. in Brooklyn, New York, 22 January, 1892. Andrew Parmentier, a horticulturist and civil engineer, was b. at Enghien, Belgium, 3 July, 1780, and d. in Brooklyn, New York, 26 November, 1830. His father, Andrew Joseph Parmentier, was a wealthy linen merchant, and his eldest brother Joseph had a European repute as a horticulturist and landscape gardener. Trained by the latter, Andrew emigrated to New York in 1824, on his way to the West Indies, taking with him his share of the family estate. He was persuaded by friends to remain in New York as a place where his abilities and scientific training would meet with recognition. He purchased a tract of land near Brooklyn which he laid out as a horticultural park. It became famous in a short time and his services as an expert in designing pleasure grounds were sought for in many places North and South. He is said to have exercised a more potent influence in landscape gardening in the United States than any other person of his profession up to that time. He was the first to introduce into the United States the black beech tree and several varieties of shrubs, vegetables, and vines. He was one of the founders and trustees of St. James's, the first Catholic church in the present Diocese of Brooklyn, and was at the height of his influence and repute when he died in Brooklyn, 26 November, 1830. After his death his daughter Adèle and her mother (Sylvia M., b. at Louvain, Belgium, 1793; d. in Brooklyn, New York, 27 April, 1882), carried on his Botanical and Horticultural Gardens until 1832, when they were sold. Thereafter they devoted most of their time and income to works of charity, aided substantially the Indian missions of Father De Smet, S.J., the establishment in Indiana of the Sisters of Providence from Brittany, the Little Sisters of the Poor in Brooklyn, and other good works. Adèle was married, 8 Sept., 1841, to Edward Bayer, a German Catholic merchant (d. 3 Feb., 1894), at the first nuptial Mass celebrated in Brooklyn. During the Civil War Madame Bayer began caring for the spiritual and temporal wants of the sailors at the Brooklyn Navy Yard, a work to which she devoted the remainder of her life. For thirty years she toiled unostentatiously at this voluntary task and was known and revered as a guardian and friend by seamen all over the world.

STILES, *History of the City of Brooklyn* (Brooklyn, 1870); *U. S. Cath. Hist. Soc. Records and Studies* (New York, 1900), II, pt. I; *Ibid.* (New York, 1904), III, pt. II.

THOMAS F. MEEHAN.

Bayeu y Subias, FRANCISCO, b. at Saragossa, 9 March, 1734; d. Madrid, 4 August, 1795, a distinguished religious and historical painter. He first studied at Tarragona with José Luzán Martinez, and gaining the first prize at the Academy there, he received a pension to go to Madrid, where he entered the San Fernando Academy and had for his master Antonio Gonzales Velasquez. While there he attracted the attention of Raphael Mengs, then court painter to Carlos III. After returning to Saragossa, he was recalled, on the suggestion of Mengs, by that monarch, who put him to work on the country palaces of El Pardo and Aranjuez and on the new Royal Palace at Madrid. He also painted pictures for several churches in Madrid. Painting with, and presumably partly under the direction of, Mengs he became devoted to his style and is classed with his school. Don Pedro de Madrazo in the Prado catalogue speaks of him as a mannered painter only to be appreciated as a frescoist. In 1765 Bayeu y Subias was chosen a member of the San Fernando Academy, and became, twenty-three years later, its director and painter to the court. In the palace at Madrid are his frescoes, "The Fall of the Giants", "The Apotheosis of Hercules", and "The Conquest of Granada". He decorated the royal chapel at Aranjuez, and pictured scenes from the life of St. Bruno at the convent of the Carthusians in Madrid. He painted many frescoes in the churches of Toledo and Saragossa, being assisted on the latter by his brother and pupil, Ramón, b. Saragossa, 1746; d. Aranjuez, 1793. His subjects at the Toledo cathedral are scenes from the life of St. Eugenio. There are fifteen works by the painter in the Museum of the Prado at Madrid. Among them are "The Coronation of the Virgin", "The Ascension", "The Evangelist St. Matthew", "The Evangelist St. Mark", "The Evangelist St. Luke", "The Evangelist St. John", "Olympus"—all studies for more important works—"St. Francis de Sales Founding the Order of the Visitation", the last being attributed by some to Ramón Bayeu y Subias, "View of the Canal of Manzanares", "View of the Paseo de las Delicias in Madrid", "Luncheon in the Country", a scene in a Manzanares orchard, and four sketches of sacred allegories for arch panels at the college of San Ildefonso. Don Francisco was an etcher as well as a painter, and executed a small number of plates.

CHAMPLIN AND PERKINS, *Cyclopedia of Painters and Painting* (New York, 1886–88); BRYAN, *Dictionary of Painters and Engravers* (London and New York, 1903–05).

AUGUSTUS VAN CLEEF.

Bayeux (BAJOCÆ), DIOCESE OF, coextensive with the Department of Calvados, is suffragan to the Archbishopric of Rouen. At the time of the Concordat (1802) the ancient Diocese of Lisieux was united to that of Bayeux. A pontifical Brief, in 1854, authorized the Bishop of Bayeux to call himself Bishop of Bayeux and Lisieux.

THE SEE OF BAYEUX.—A local legend, found in the breviaries of the fifteenth century, makes St. Exuperius, first Bishop of Bayeux, an immediate disciple of St. Clement, and his see a foundation of the first century. St. Regnobertus, the same legend tells us, was the successor of St. Exuperius. But the Bollandists and M. Jules Lair have shown how little ground there is for this legend; it was only towards the middle of the fourth century that St. Exuperius founded the See of Bayeux; after him the priest St. Reverendus did much for the propagation of the Faith in these parts. A certain number of the successors of St. Exuperius were saints: Rufinianus; Lupus (about 465); Vigor (beginning of the sixth century), who destroyed a pagan temple, then still frequented; Regnobertus (about 629), who founded many churches, and whom the legend, owing to an anachronism, made first successor to Exuperius; and Hugues (d. 730), simultaneously bishop of two other sees, Paris and Rouen. We may also mention Odon de Conteville (1050–97), brother of William the Conqueror, who built the cathedral, was present at the Battle of Hastings, intrigued for the tiara on the death of Gregory VII (1085), and died a crusader in Sicily; Cardinal Trivulce (1531–48), papal legate in the Roman Campagna during the siege and pillage of Rome by the Constable de Bourbon; Cardinal d'Ossat (1602–04), an illustrious diplomatist prominently identified with the conversion of Henry IV. Claude Fauchet, who after being court preacher to Louis XVI, became one of the "conquerors" of the Bastille, was chosen Constitutional Bishop of Bayeux in 1791, and was beheaded 31 October, 1793. Mgr. Amette, coadjutor, with right of succession to the Cardinal Archbishop of Paris was, until 1905, Bishop of Bayeux. In the municipal Musée Archéologique is preserved the famous "Bayeux Tapestry", one of the most remarkable relics of medieval textile art. Its contemporary embroideries reproduce scenes from the Norman Conquest of England (1066) and are valuable as illustrations of eleventh-century costume and life.

THE SEE OF LISIEUX.—The first known Bishop of Lisieux is Theudibaudes, mentioned in connexion with a council held in 538. The most celebrated among his successors were Freculfus (d. 850), a pupil of the palace school founded by Charlemagne, and author of a universal history; Arnoul (1141–81), statesman and writer; Nicole Oresme (1378–82), philosopher, mathematician, and tutor to Charles V; Pierre Cauchon (1432–42), concerned in the condemnation of Joan of Arc; Thomas Basin (1447–74), the historian of Charles VII, and one of the promoters of the rehabilitation of Joan of Arc; Guillaume du Vair (1618–21), the well-known philosopher who left the bench for the Church.

In the Middle Ages both sees were very important. The Bishop of Bayeux was senior among the Norman bishops, and the chapter was one of the richest in France. The See of Lisieux maintained the Collège de Lisieux at Paris for poor students of the diocese. Important councils were held within this diocese, at Caen, in 1042 and 1061; in the latter was proclaimed "the Truce of God". The statutes of a synod held at Bayeux about 1300, furnish a very fair idea of the discipline of the time.

Among the abbeys of the Diocese of Bayeux should be mentioned those of St. Stephen (Abbaye-aux-Hommes) and of the Trinity (Abbaye-aux-Dames), both founded at Caen by William the Conqueror (1029–87) and his wife Matilda, in expiation of their unlawful marriage. The former of these abbeys was governed by the celebrated Lanfranc, afterwards Archbishop of Canterbury. Other abbeys were those of Troarn of which Durand, the successful opponent of Berengarius, was abbot in the eleventh century, and the Abbaye du Val, of which Rancé was abbot in 1661, prior to his reform of La Trappe. The Abbey

CATHEDRAL OF NOTRE DAME, BAYEUX

of St. Evroul (Ebrulphus) in the Diocese of Lisieux, founded about 560 by St. Evroul, a native of Bayeux, is famous as the home of Ordericus Vitalis, the chronicler (1075–1141). Venerable Jean Etudes founded in 1641 in Caen the congregation of Notre Dame de Charité du Refuge, which is devoted to the protection of girls and includes 33 monasteries in France and elsewhere. At Tilly, in the Diocese of Bayeux, Michel Vingtras established, in 1839, the politico-religious society known as *La Miséricorde*, in connexion with the survivors of *La Petite Eglise*, which was condemned in 1843 by Gregory XVI. Daniel Huet, the famous savant (1630–1721) and Bishop of Avranches, was a native of Caen.

The cathedral of Bayeux (twelfth to fourteenth centuries) and of Lisieux (twelfth and thirteenth centuries) are inferior in point of interest to the church of St. Etienne at Caen, which is one of the most beautiful architectural monuments of Normandy (eleventh and twelfth centuries). The church of Notre-Dame de la Délivrande (the devotion to Our Lady of Deliverance dates back to the seventh century) is visited by the Bishops of Bayeux even before they enter their own cathedral.

At the close of the year 1905 the Diocese of Bayeux included a population of 410,178, 73 pastorates, 640 mission churches, and 120 curacies remunerated by the State. According to the latest statistics (1907) obtainable, the Diocese of Bayeux has 2 infant asylums, 16 infant schools, 1 deaf-mute institute, 1 orphanage where farming is taught, 9 girls' orphanages, 4 industrial schools, 2 trades schools, 1 refuge for young women, 6 hospitals and hospices, 1 dispensary, 4 communities for the care of the sick in their homes, 3 private hospitals, 1 private insane asylum, 9 homes for the aged, all conducted by sisters; and 1 orphanage where farming is taught, conducted by brothers.

In 1900 the following congregations were represented in the diocese: the Franciscans at Caen and the Premonstratensians, who have an abbey at Juaye-Mondaye. Among the local congregations are the diocesan missionaries, stationed at the basilica of Notre Dame de la Délivrande, directors of several educational institutions throughout the diocese. In this diocese also was founded the congregation of Our Lady of Charity and Refuge established at Caen in 1641 by Venerable Jean Eudes for the preservation of young girls. This congregation has 33 monasteries in France and other countries.

Gallia christiana (nova) (1759), XI, 346–405, 762–814, *Instrumenta*, 59–106, 199–218; *Acta SS.* XVI, May; Lair, *Etudes sur les origines de l'évéché de Bayeux* in *Bibliothèque des Ecoles des Chartes* (1861–63); Farcy, *Abbayes du diocèse de Bayeux* (Laval, 1886–88); Chevalier, *Topo-bibl.*, 327–331, 1707–08; Comte, *Tapestry of Bayeux* (Paris, 1878).

Georges Goyau.

Bayle, Pierre. See Rationalism.

Bayley, James Roosevelt, first Bishop of Newark, New Jersey, U. S. A.; eighth Archbishop of Baltimore, Maryland; b. at Rye, New York, 23 August, 1814; d. at Newark, 3 October, 1877. His Dutch and English non-Catholic ancestors were locally notable. His father was the son of Dr. Richard Bayley, professor of anatomy in Columbia College, New York, and inaugurated the New York quarantine system. Mother Seton, foundress of the Sisters of Charity in the United States, was his aunt. He was named after his maternal grandfather, James Roosevelt, a merchant of large fortune, who made him his heir, but altered the will when Bayley became a Catholic priest, under the mistaken idea that priests could not possess property. A large part of the money went to build the Roosevelt Hospital in New York. Bayley's early school days were spent at Amherst College, where he once thought of going to sea and obtained a commission of midshipman in the navy. He abandoned the plan, however, and continuing his studies, entered Trinity College, Hartford, Connecticut, to prepare for the Episcopalian ministry. He graduated here in 1835 and after receiving orders was appointed rector of St. Peter's church, Harlem, New York. He resigned this charge in 1841 and went to Rome, where on 28 April, 1842, he was baptized and received into the Catholic church in the room of St. Ignatius by Father Esmond, S.J. He then entered the seminary of St. Sulpice at Paris for his theological studies. Returning to New York, he was ordained priest by Bishop Hughes, 2 March, 1844, and made a professor and the vice-president of the seminary at Fordham. He was acting president there in 1846 and was next given charge of the parish at the Quarantine Station on Staten Island, so long the residence of his grandfather, Dr. Bayley. Bishop Hughes then appointed him his private secretary, an office he held for several years and in which his administrative ability was specially manifested. He devoted some of his leisure to the collection and preservation of local historical data, much of which would otherwise have been lost. Part of this material he published in a small volume "A Brief Sketch of the Early History of the Catholic Church on the Island of New York" (New York, 1853; 2nd ed., 1870).

When the Diocese of Newark was established he was named its first bishop and consecrated 30 October, 1853, in St. Patrick's Cathedral, New York, by Archbishop Bedini, the Apostolic Nuncio to Brazil, who was then *en route* to Rome. The Bishops of Brooklyn and Burlington were consecrated at the same time, the first occurrence of such an elaborate ceremony in the United States. Bishop Bayley's work of organizing the new diocese was not easy. He had more than 40,000 Catholics, mainly of Irish and German extraction, with only twenty-five priests to minister to them. There was not a single diocesan institution, no funds, and poverty on all sides. He therefore applied for help to the Association of the Propagation of the Faith of Lyons, France, and to the Leopoldine Association of Vienna and from both received material assistance. In a letter he wrote 10 April, 1865, reviewing the condition of the diocese after his first ten years there he says: "I find that while the Catholic population has increased a third, the churches and priests have doubled in number. In 1854 there was no religious community. Now we have a monastery of Benedictines, another of Passionists, a mother-house of Sisters of Charity, conducting seventeen different establishments; two convents of Benedictine nuns, two others of German Sisters of Notre Dame and two others of the Sisters of the Poor of St. Francis. In 1854 there was no institution of learning; to-day we have a flourishing college and a diocesan seminary, an academy for young ladies, a boarding school for boys, and parish schools attached to almost all the parishes." In addition to these he introduced the Jesuits and the Sisters of St. Joseph and of St. Dominic into the diocese, and was one of the strongest upholders of the temperance movement of the seventies. He made several journeys to Rome and the Holy Land, attending the canonization of the Japanese martyrs at Rome in 1862; the centenary of the Apostles in 1867; and the Œcumenical Council in 1869.

At the death of Archbishop Spalding of Baltimore he was promoted, on 30 July, 1872, to succeed that prelate. He left Newark with much reluctance. In 1875 as Apostolic Delegate he imposed the cardinal's biretta on Archbishop McCloskey of New York. In May, 1876, he consecrated the Baltimore cathedral, having freed it from debt. Convening the Eighth Provincial Synod of the clergy, August, 1875, he enacted many salutary regulations, particularly with regard to clerical dress, mixed marriages, and church music. Illness obliged him to ask for a coadjutor and Bishop Gibbons of Richmond was appointed to that position 29 May, 1877. The archbishop then went abroad to seek for relief, but in vain. He returned to his former home in Newark in August, 1877, and after lingering for two months, died in his old room, where he had laboured so long. At his own request he was buried beside his aunt, Mother Seton, at the convent at Emmitsburg, Maryland. He was a noble model of a Christian bishop. He seemed animated with the spirit of St. Francis de Sales, full of zeal in the episcopal office and of kindness and charity to all mankind. In conversation he once told Bishop Corrigan that before his conversion he thought of becoming a Jesuit, and before his consecration a Redemptorist, but from both intentions his director dissuaded him. In addition to the volume on the Church in New York he wrote the "Memoirs of Simon Gabriel Bruté, First Bishop of Vincennes" (New York, 1855).

FLYNN, *The Catholic Church in New Jersey* (Morristown, 1904); SHEA, *History of the Cath. Ch. in the U. S.* (New York, 1889–92); *Cathedral Records* (Baltimore, 1906); REUSS, *Biog. Cycl. of the Cath. Hierarchy of the U. S.* (Milwaukee, 1898).

THOMAS F. MEEHAN.

Bayma, JOSEPH, a Jesuit mathematician and scientist, b. in Piedmont, Italy, 9 November, 1816; d. at Santa Clara, California, U. S. A., 7 February, 1892. He entered the Society of Jesus, 5 February, 1832, and distinguished himself in literature, mathematics, and physics. He was in charge of the episcopal seminary of Bertinoro when the troubles of 1860 forced him and many of his brethren to seek shelter in England. Hitherto he had given no special attention to philosophy, but at Stonyhurst he took it up and taught it for some seven years. His powerful and original mind soon produced three volumes of "Realis Philosophia", which were printed for private circulation. No sooner were they out than he introduced numerous corrections; thus the printed volumes cannot be relied upon as evidence of his mature opinions. In 1868 Father Bayma left for California, where he was Rector of Saint Ignatius' College, San Francisco, for three years, but afterwards resided at Santa Clara, teaching elementary mathematics there till his death. At his death he left behind, in manuscript, an elaborate new edition of the "Realis Philosophia" which never saw the light. His published works are "Molecular Mechanics" (Cambridge, 1866); "The Love of Religious Perfection", originally written in Italian, in the style of "The Imitation of Christ" (published in English, Dublin, 1863); articles in "The Catholic World", XVII–XXI (1873–75), the best printed account of his philosophy; two articles in the "Am. Cath. Q. Rev.", II (1877); and "A Discussion with an Infidel", being a review of Büchner's "Force and Matter" (New York, London, and Leamington, 1901). His elementary works on mathematics, all published at San Francisco, are: "Algebra" (1890), "Geometry" (1895), "Analytical Geometry" (1887), "Plane and Spherical Trigonometry" (1886), "Infinitesimal Calculus" (1889).

Father Bayma took the Venerable Bede for his model, and loved to refer to the old Breviary Lesson, which used to be read in England on St. Bede's day. It ran: "Bede [and Bayma too] was handsome of stature, grave of gait, rich and sonorous of voice, eloquent of speech, noble of countenance, a blend of affability with severity. He was affable to the good and devout, formidable to the proud and negligent. He was always reading, always writing, always teaching, always praying." Only the young men who sat under him could know his fascination as a teacher. To posterity he must be known by his "Molecular Mechanics", a metaphysical and mathematical work treating of the constitution of matter. With Roger Boscovich, Bayma reduces all matter to unextended points, centres of force acting in the inverse square of the distance. Thus acting upon one another, but of course not touching, for Bayma abhorred continuous matter and upheld *actio in distans*, these points were bound up into molecules, and molecules into bodies. Boscovich made his points, or elements, attractive at molar distances, repulsive at molecular. Bayma divides elements into attractive and repulsive, the former always attracting, the latter always repelling; the attractive elements preponderating in the nucleus of the molecule, the repulsive in the envelope. The work drew attention at Cambridge, and at Trinity College, Dublin. The author was advised to test his theories by ten years of experiments in chemistry and electricity. Unhappily, this was never done. One of his proofs certainly lies open to grave objection, but Bayma's main theory does not stand or fall with that proposition. The gravest objection against the theory is its alleged failure to account for inertia. Father Bayma ever professed the utmost reverence for St. Thomas. His saying was: "the metaphysics of St. Thomas, with modern physics".

JOSEPH RICKABY.

Bayonne (LAPURDUM), DIOCESE OF, comprises the Department of Basses-Pyrénées. Reorganized in 1802, it included, besides certain parishes of the Dioceses of Dax and Tarbes, the Dioceses of Oloron and Lescar. It was suffragan to the Archiepiscopal See of Toulouse from 1802 to 1822, thereafter to that of Auch.

Diocese of Bayonne.—Local tradition maintains that St. Leo, the martyr, with whose memory is associated a miraculous fountain, was the first Bishop of Bayonne. No bishop is historically known prior to the sixth century, although some think that Bayonne, designated as *civitas* in the Treaty of Andelot (587), must have had a bishop at that time, whilst others couple the foundation of the See of Bayonne with the establishment of the Kingdom of Aquitaine (778). Until 1566, the Diocese of Bayonne included much Spanish territory, i. e. the four Archpresbyteries of Bastan, Lérin, Cinco Villas in Navarre, and Fontarabia in Guipuzcoa, a remnant of Charlemagne's conquests beyond the Pyrenees. Christophe de Beaumont, afterwards Archbishop of Paris, occupied the See of Bayonne from 1741 to 1745 and Astros occupied it from 1820 to 1830.

Sees of Lescar and Oloron—A local legend recorded in the great "Bréviaire de Lescar" of 1541, and patterned after the Limousin legend of St. Martial, holds that St. Julian, sent from Bordeaux by St. Leontius, was the first Bishop of Lescar; but according to history, St. Galactorius, martyred perhaps by the Visigoths after their defeat at Vouillé, and St. Gratus, both mentioned in the Council of Agde (506), were respectively the first incumbents of the See of Lescar and the See of Oloron known to history. Until 1789 the Bishops of Lescar presided by right over the Assembly of the States of Béarn. Amongst those who occupied the See of Oloron was Roussel, the Dominican (1536–50), protégé of Margaret of Navarre and a convert to Calvinism. Sponde (Spondanus, 1568–1643), Bishop of Pamiers, who carried on the work of Baronius; Duvergier de Hauranne (1581–1643), Abbé de St. Cyran, the second founder of Jansenism, and Cardinal Lavigerie were born in territory now included in the Diocese of Bayonne. Bétharram is celebrated as a place of pilgrimage as also are Notre Dame de Piétat, at Paradies, and Notre Dame de Sarrance, visited by King Louis XI. In 1899 the following institutions were to be found in the diocese: 1 infant asylum, 38 infant schools, 2 orphanages where farming is taught, 10 girls' orphanages, 5 gratuitous industrial schools, 2 houses of refuge for young girls, 2 *patronages*, 1 temporary home for servants, 4 hospitals or hospices,

1 insane asylum, 6 homes for the aged, and 1 private hospital, all conducted by Sisters, and 2 orphanages where farming is taught, conducted by Brothers, and 4 *patronages* for young people conducted either by priests or brothers. At the close of 1905 the Diocese of Bayonne contained 426,347 inhabitants, 43 pastorates, 449 *succursales* or mission churches, and 91 curacies.

In 1900 the following religious orders were represented in the diocese: the Jesuits and Franciscans at Pau, and the Capuchins at Bayonne. Among the local congregations are: the Auxiliary Priests of the Sacred Heart of Jesus, devoted to teaching and missionary work, founded at Bétharram in 1841. They have missions at Bethlehem, Buenos Ayres, and Montevideo. The Servants of Mary, who teach and serve in hospitals; their mother-house is at Anglet. The Bernardines, with mother-house also at Anglet, were founded in 1846; they keep perpetual silence and divide their time between prayer and the work of sewing and embroidery.

Gallia christiana (nova) (1715), I, 1261–1324; *instrumenta*, 197–202; Dubarat, *Etudes de l'histoire locale et religieuse* (Pau, 1889–92); Idem, *Le bréviaire de Lescar de 1541* (Pau, 1891); Dubarat and Haristoy, *Etudes historiques et religieuses du diocèse de Bayonne* (1892); Duchesne, *Fastes épiscopaux*, II; Chevalier, *Topobibliographie*, s. v.

Georges Goyau.

Baysio (Baisio), Guido de, an Italian canonist, b. about the middle of the thirteenth century of a noble Ghibelline family; d. at Avignon, 10 August, 1313. The probable place of his birth is Reggio, where he also studied law under Guido de Suzaria. Here he became, successively, doctor and professor of canon law and also obtained an ecclesiastical benefice as canon. Gerhard, Bishop of Parma, attached him to himself and remained his patron also as Cardinal-Archbishop of Sabina (d. 1302). To this patron Baysio dedicated his chief work, a commentary on the "Decretum" of Gratian, which he wrote about the year 1300 and entitled "Rosarium". It is an excellent collection of older glossaries, not contained in the "Glossa Ordinaria", and principally compiled from Huguccio. Many additions to the glossary which are found in the editions published since 1505 (Paris), are taken from the "Rosarium" of Baysio and appear over his name.

In 1296 Pope Boniface VIII appointed Baysio Archdeacon of Bologna and chancellor of the celebrated university in that city. Here he at first taught canon law privately and later on became a public professor, which position he held for three years. Called to Avignon in 1304 he retained the dignity of archdeacon, held the office of papal chaplain, and also served in the Apostolic chancery until his death. His stay at Avignon was marked by several literary productions. Here he wrote an accurate and complete, but rather diffuse, commentary on the Liber Sextus and also a "Tractatus super hæresi et aliis criminibus in causâ Templariorum et D. Bonifacii". This latter work was written in connexion with the condemnation of the Templars at the Council of Vienne. The second part of the work constitutes a defence of the orthodoxy of Boniface VIII, and is published in Mansi, "Coll. Sacr. Concil.", XXV (Venice, 1782), 415–426. Having held the position of archdeacon, Baysio is often known by the name of Archidiaconus and thus quoted (see Ferraris, Bibliotheca, Rome, 1892), VIII, 271. His chief work, the "Rosarium", has gone through many editions: Strasburg, 1472; Rome, 1477; Venice, 1480; 1513; 1601, etc. The "Apparatus ad Sextum", Milan, 1480; Venice, 1577.

Schulte, *Geschichte der Quellen u. Litteratur des kan. Rechts* (Stuttgart, 1875), II, 186–190; Hurter, *Nomenclator* (Innsbruck, 1899), IV, 413; Scherer in *Kirchenlex.*, II, s. v.

Leo Gans.

Bazin, John Stephen, third Bishop of Vincennes (now the Diocese of Indianapolis), b. at Duerne, near Lyons, France, 15 Oct., 1796; d. at Vincennes, Indiana, U. S. A., 23 April, 1848. He was educated in his native country and ordained in the Cathedral of Lyons, 22 July, 1822. In 1830 he came to America and began his labours among the Catholics of Mobile, Alabama, where for seventeen years he toiled zealously for the religious instruction of the young, organizing the Sunday schools and establishing the Catholic Orphan Asylum Society. He was also the vicar-general of the diocese. In 1846 at the request of Bishop Portier, Father Bazin went to France to secure the services of the Society of Jesus for the College of Spring Hill, Alabama, and of the Brothers of the Christian Schools for the Boys' Orphan Asylum. In both efforts he was successful. When the Right Rev. Célestine de la Hailandière, Bishop of Vincennes, resigned his see in 1847, Father Bazin was consecrated his successor on the 24th of October of that year. His episcopal career, which promised to be one of great usefulness to the Church, was cut short by his untimely death.

Clarke, *Lives of the Deceased Bishops* (New York, 1888), II, 370; Shea, *History of the Catholic Church in U. S.* (New York, 1889), IV, 200 sqq.; Reuss, *Biographical Cyclopædia of the Catholic Hierarchy* (Milwaukee, Wis., 1898).

Edward P. Spillane.

Beads, Use of, at Prayers.—Beads variously strung together, according to the kind, order, and number of prayers in certain forms of devotion, are in common use among Catholics as an expedient to ensure a right count of the parts occurring in more or less frequent repetition. Made of materials ranging from common wood or natural berries to costly metals and precious stones, they may be blessed, as they are in most cases, with prayer and holy water, thereby becoming sacramentals. In this character they are prescribed by the rules of most religious orders, both of men and women, to be kept for personal use or to be worn as part of the religious garb. They are now mostly found in the form of the Dominican Rosary, or Marian Psalter (see Rosary); but Catholics are also familiar with the Brigittine beads, the Dolour beads, the Immaculate Conception beads, the Crown of Our Saviour, the Chaplet of the Five Wounds, the Crosier beads, and others. In all these devotions, due to individual zeal or fostered by particular religious bodies, the beads serve one and the same purpose of distinguishing and numbering the constituent prayers.

Rationalistic criticism generally ascribes an Oriental origin to prayer beads; but man's natural tendency to iteration, especially of prayers, and the spirit and training of the early Christians may still safely be assumed to have spontaneously suggested fingers, pebbles, knotted cords, and strings of beads or berries as a means of counting, when it was desired to say a specific number of prayers. The earliest historical indications of the use of beads at prayer by Christians show, in this as in other things, a natural growth and development. Beads strung together or ranged on chains are an obvious improvement over the well-known primitive method instanced, for example, in the life of the Egyptian Abbot Paul (d. a. d. 341), who used to take three hundred pebbles into his lap as counters and to drop one as he finished each of the corresponding number of prayers it was his wont to say daily. In the eighth century the penitentials, or rule books relating to penitents, prescribed various penances of twenty, fifty, or more, paters. The strings of beads, with the aid of which such penances were accurately said, gradually came to be known as paternosters. Archæological records mention fragments of prayer beads found in the tomb of the holy abbess Gertrude of Nivelles (d. 659); also similar devices discovered in the tombs of St. Norbert and of St. Rosalia, both of the twelfth century. The Bollandists quote William of Malmesbury (De Gest. Pont. Angl., IV, 4) as stating that the Countess Godiva, who founded a religious house at Coventry in 1040, donated, when she was about to die, a circlet or string of costly precious stones on which she used to say her prayers, to be placed on a statue of the Blessed Virgin. In the course of the eleventh, twelfth, and thirteenth centuries, such paternosters came into extensive use especially in the religious orders. At certain times corresponding to the canonical hours, lay brothers and lay sisters were obliged to say a certain number of Our Fathers as an equivalent of the clerical obligation of the Divine Office. The military orders likewise, notably the Knights of St. John, adopted the paternoster beads as a part of the equipment of lay members. In the fifteenth century, wearing the beads at one's girdle was a distinctive sign of membership in a religious confraternity or third order. If a certain worldliness in the use of beads as ornaments in those days had to be checked, as it was by various capitulary ordinances prohibiting monks and friars, for instance, from having beads of coral, crystal, amber, etc., and nuns from wearing beads around the neck, evidence is not wanting that paternosters were also openly carried as a sign of penance, especially by bands of pilgrims processionally visiting the shrines, churches, and other holy places of Rome. From their purpose, too, it is natural that prayer beads were prized as gifts of friendship. They were especially valued if they had been worn by a person of known sanctity or if they had touched the relics of any saint, in which cases they were often piously believed to be the instruments of miraculous power and healing virtue.

Beads were generally strung either on a straight thread, or cord, or so as to form a circlet, or loop. At the present time chained beads have almost entirely taken the place of the corded ones. To facilitate the counting or to mark off certain divisions of a devotion, sets of beads, usually decades, are separated from each other by a larger bead or sometimes by a medal or metal cross. The number of beads on a chaplet, or Rosary, depends on the number of prayers making up each particular form of devotion. A full Rosary consists of one hundred and fifty Hail Marys, fifteen Our Fathers, and three or four beads corresponding to introductory versicles and the "Glory be to the Father", etc. Such a "pair of beads" is generally worn by religious. Lay people commonly have beads representing a third part of the Rosary. The Brigittine beads number seven paters in honour of the sorrows and joys of the Blessed Virgin, and sixty-three aves to commemorate the years of her life. Another Crown of Our Lady, in use among the Franciscans, has seventy-two aves, based on another tradition of the Blessed Virgin's age. The devotion of the Crown of Our Lord consists of thirty-three paters in honour of the years of Our Lord on earth and five aves in honour of His sacred wounds. In the church Latin of the Middle Ages, many names were applied to prayer beads as: *devotiones, signacula, oracula, precaria, patriloquium, serta, preculæ, numeralia, computum, calculi,* and others. An old English form, *bedes,* or *bedys,* meant primarily prayers. From the end of the fifteenth century and in the beginning of the sixteenth, the name paternoster beads fell into disuse and was replaced by the names ave beads and Rosary, chaplet, or crown.

The use of beads among pagans is undoubtedly of greater antiquity than their Christian use; but there is no evidence to show that the latter is derived from the former, any more than there is to establish a relation between Christian devotions and pagan forms of prayer. One sect in India used a chaplet consisting generally of one hundred and eight beads made of the wood of the sacred Tulsi shrub, to tell the names of Vishnu; another accomplished its invocations of Siva by means of a string of thirty-two or sixty-four berries of the Rudrāksha tree. These or other species of seeds and berries were chosen as the material for these chaplets on account of some traditional association with the deities, as recorded in sacred legends. Some of the ascetics had their beads made of the teeth of dead bodies. Among some sects, especially the votaries of Vishnu, a string of beads is placed on the neck of children when, at the age of six or seven, they are about to be initiated and to be instructed in the use of the sacred formularies. Most Hindus continue to wear the beads both for ornament and for use at prayers. Among the Buddhists, whose religion is of Brahminic origin, various prayer-formulas are said or repeated with the aid of beads made of wood, berries, coral, amber, or precious metals and stones. A string of beads cut from the bones of some holy lama is especially valued. The number of beads is usually one hundred and eight; but strings of thirty or forty are in use among the poorer classes. Buddhism in Burma, Tibet, China, and Japan alike employs a number of more or less complicated forms of devotion, but the frequently recurring conclusion, a form of salutation, is mostly the same, and contains the mystic word *OM,* supposed to have reference to the Buddhistic trinity. It is not uncommon to find keys and trinkets attached to a Buddhist's prayer beads, and generally each string is provided with two little cords of special counters, ten in number, in the form of beads or metal disks. At the end of one of these cords is found a miniature thunderbolt; the other terminates in a tiny bell. With the aid of this device the devotee can count a hundred repetitions of his beads or 108x10x10 formulas in all. Among the Japanese, especially elaborate systems of counting exist. One apparatus is described as capable of registering 36,736 prayers or repetitions.

The Mohammedans use a string of ninety-nine (or one hundred) beads called the *subha* or *tasbih,* on which they recite the "beautiful" names or attributes of Allah. It is divided into three equal parts either by a bead of special shape or size, or by a tassel of gold or silk thread. The use of these Islamic beads appears to have been established as early as the ninth century independently of Buddhistic influences. Some critics have thought the Mohammedan chaplet is kindred to a Jewish form of one hundred blessings. The beads in general use are said to be often made of the sacred clay of Mecca or Medina. Among travellers' records of prayer beads is the famous instance, by Marco Polo, of the King of Malabar, who wore a fine silk thread strung with one hundred and four large pearls and rubies, on which he was wont to pray to his idols. Alexander Von Humboldt is also quoted as finding prayer beads, called Quipos, among the native Peruvians.

Esser, *Zur Archæologie der Paternoster Schnur* in *Compte rendu du IV congrès scien. Internat.,* etc. (Fribourg, 1898), *Sciences Religieuses,* § 1; Thurston, *Archæology of the Rosary Beads* in *The Month,* No. 442, April, 1901; Esser, *Unserer lieben Frauen Rosenkranz* (Paderborn, 1889).

John R. Volz.

Beard.—Among the Jews, as among most Oriental peoples, the beard was especially cherished as a symbol of virility; to cut off another man's beard was an outrage (II Kings, x, 4); to shave or to pluck one's own beard was a sign of mourning (Jer., xli, 5; xlviii, 37); to allow the beard to be defiled constituted a presumption of madness (I Kings, xxi, 13). Certain ceremonial cuttings of the beard which probably imitated pagan superstition were strictly forbidden (Lev., xix, 27; xxi, 5). On the other hand, the leper was commanded to shave (Lev., xiv, 9). These usages which we learn from the Bible are confirmed by the testimony of the monuments, both Egyptian and Assyrian, in which the Jews are invariably depicted as bearded. The Egyptians themselves commonly shaved, and we are told that Joseph, on being taken from his prison, was made to shave before appearing in the presence of the king (Gen., xli, 14).

Similarly in Greece and in Rome, shortly before the time of Christ, it was the fashion to shave, but from the accession of Hadrian onwards, as we may see from the existing statues of the Roman emperors, beards once more became the order of the day. With regard to the Christian clergy, no clear evidence is available for the early centuries. The Apostles, in our most ancient monuments, are for the most part represented as bearded, but not uniformly so. (See Weiss-Liebersdorff, Christus- und Apostelbilder, Freiburg, 1902.) St. Jerome seems to censure the practice of wearing long beards, but no very definite conclusion can be drawn from his allusions or from those of his contemporary, St. Augustine. The earliest positive legislation on the subject for clerics appears to be Canon xliv of the so-called Fourth Council of Carthage, which in reality represents the synodal decrees of some council in Southern Gaul in the time of St. Cæsarius of Arles (c. 503). There it is enjoined that a cleric is to allow neither hair nor beard to grow freely (*Clericus nec comam nutriat nec barbam*), though this prohibition is very probably directed only against beards of excessive length. Still this canon, which was widely quoted and is included in the "Corpus juris", had great influence in creating a precedent. (See for example the "Penitential" of Halitgar and the so-called "Excerptions" attributed to Egbert of York.) So far as concerns England in particular it was certainly regarded throughout the Middle Ages as uncanonical to allow the beard to grow. A cleric was known as a shorn man (*bescoren man*, Laws of Wihtred, A. D. 696), and if it should seem that this might refer to the tonsure, we have a law of King Alfred: "If a man shave off another's beard let him make amends with xx shillings. If he bind him first and then shave him like a priest (*hine to preoste bescire*) let him make amends with lx shillings." And under King Edgar we find the canon: "Let no man in holy orders conceal his tonsure, nor let himself be misshaven nor keep his beard for any time, if he will have God's blessing and St. Peter's and ours." A similar practice obtained generally throughout the West and it was one of the great subjects of reproach on the part of the Greek Church, from the time of Photius onwards, that the Roman clergy systematically cut off their beards. But as Ratramnus of Corbie protested, it was foolish to make an outcry about a matter which concerned salvation so little as this *barbæ detonsio aut conservatio*.

The legislation requiring the beard to be shaved seems to have remained in force throughout the Middle Ages. Thus an ordinance of the Council of Toulouse, in 1119, threatened with excommunication the cleric who "like a layman allowed hair and beard to grow", and Pope Alexander III ordained that clerics who nourished their hair and beard were to be shorn by their archdeacon, by force if necessary. This last decree was incorporated in the text of the canon law (Decretals of Gregory IX, III, tit. i, cap. vii). Durandus, finding mystical reasons for everything, according to his wont, tells us that "length of hair is symbolical of the multitude of sins. Hence clerics are directed to shave their beards; for the cutting of the hair of the beard, which is said to be nourished by the superfluous humours of the stomach, denotes that we ought to cut away the vices and sins which are a superfluous growth in us. Hence we shave our beards that we may seem purified by innocence and humility and that we may

be like the angels who remain always in the bloom of youth." (Rationale, II, lib. XXXII.)

In spite of this, the phrase *barbam nutrire* which was classical in the matter, and was still used by the Fifth Council of Lateran (1512), always remained somewhat ambiguous. Consequently usage in the sixteenth century began to interpret the prohibition as not inconsistent with a short beard. There are still many ordinances of episcopal synods which deal with the subject, but the point upon which stress is laid is that the clergy "should not seem to be aping the fashions of military folk" or wearing flowing beards like goats (*hircorum et caprarum more*), or allowing the hair on their upper lip to impede their drinking of the chalice. This last has always been accounted a solid reason in favour of the practice of shaving. To judge by the portraits of the popes, it was with Clement VII (1523) that a distinct beard began to be worn, and many among his successors, for example Paul III, allowed the beard to grow to considerable length. St. Charles Borromeo attempted to check the spread of the new fashion, and in 1576 he addressed to his clergy a pastoral "De barbâ radendâ" exhorting them to observe the canons. Still, though the length of clerical beards decreased during the seventeenth century, it was not until its close that the example of the French court and the influence of Cardinal Orsini, Archbishop of Beneventum, contributed to bring about a return to the earlier usage. For the last 200 years there has been no change, and an attempt made by some of the clergy of Bavaria in 1865 to introduce the wearing of beards was rebuked by the Holy See.

As already noted, in Eastern lands a smooth face carries with it the suggestion of effeminacy. For this reason the clergy, whether Uniat or Schismatic, of the Oriental churches have always worn their beards. The same consideration, together with a regard for practical difficulties, has influenced the Roman authorities in according a similar privilege to missionaries, not only in the East but in other barbarous countries where the conveniences of civilization cannot be found. In the case of religious orders like the Capuchins and the Camaldolese Hermits the wearing of a beard is prescribed in their constitutions as a mark of austerity and penance. Individual priests who for medical or other reasons desire to exempt themselves from the law require the permission of their bishop.

Barbier de Montault, *Le costume et les usages ecclésiastiques* (Paris, 1901), I, 185, 196; Thalhofer in *Archiv f. kath. Kirchenrecht* (Innsbruck, 1863), X, 93 sqq.; Id. in *Kirchenlex.*, I, 2049–51; Seghers, *The Practice of Shaving in the Latin Church* in *Am. Cath. Quart. Rev.* (1882), 278; Wernz, *Jus Decretalium* (Rome, 1904), II, n. 178. For pre-Christian times see: Vigouroux in *Dict. de la Bible*, s. v. *Barbe*; Ewing in Hast., *Dict. of the Bible*, s. v. *Beard*.

Herbert Thurston.

Beardsley, Aubrey, English artist, b. at Brighton, 1872; d. at Mentone, France, 16 March, 1898. It has been cleverly said that Beardsley was "a boy who never grew up", and the statement has a considerable amount of truth in it. He was a wonderfully precocious boy all his life, with the frank merriment, enthusiasm, and exuberance of a lad. He was unable to withstand the desire to do clever, mischievous things and to shock people of narrow opinions, and his ignoble and vicious works were more the result of his Puck-like mischief and eccentricity of habit than of any evil disposition. His earliest published work was a programme for an entertainment in 1888 at Brighton Grammar School, where he was a pupil, and his next in the "Bee Magazine", Blackburn, 1891.

Young Beardsley commenced work as a clerk in the Guardian Fire Office, but at the earnest persuasions of Aymer Vallance and Pennell he entered Fred Brown's studio at Westminster and devoted his attention to illustration. While still a lad he attracted the attention of Sir E. Burne-Jones and Puvis de Chavannes, and it said much for his genius that it received encouragement from men so different in their aims and practice. When nineteen he accepted the tremendous task of illustrating the "Morte D'Arthur", and carried it through. The famous article upon him in the "Studio" appeared in April, 1893, and from that moment his work was in great demand. In April, 1894, he became art editor of the "Yellow Book", the first numbers of which caused a great sensation. He was responsible for the first four volumes and then, with Arthur Symons, started the "Savoy", to which he contributed a series of drawings. During his short life he carried the art of black and white further than any man since Albrecht Dürer. His special qualities were described by Hammerton as of "extreme economy of means the perfection of discipline, of self-control, and of thoughtful deliberation at the very moment of invention".

Beardsley had a marvellous knowledge of the quality of line, a real and powerful sense of beauty, coupled with a constant desire to be quaint, fanciful, or bizarre. He possessed a vigour, inventiveness, and daintiness almost unapproachable in the work of any other man. Hammerton speaks of the "serene surety of his drawing", of his "superb sense of style"; but Beardsley's love of mischief, which he deeply regretted, led him into serious faults and caused him to be often misunderstood. By those who knew him he was regarded as the most original, brilliant, witty, and lovable man they ever met. His illustrations of "Salome", "The Rape of the Lock", "Mademoiselle de Maupin" and "Volpone" are amongst his greatest works. From boyhood he had bad health and suffered from frequent attacks of hæmorrhage. He was always a man of deep religious feeling and became a Catholic at the close of his life (31 March, 1895).

SYMONS, *Life of Beardsley* (London, 1898); *The Studio* (1893); *The Magazine of Art* (1893–94); Ross, *Eulogy of Beardsley* in *Volpone* (London, 1898); GALLATIN, Bibliog. of his drawings and of magazine articles (New York, 1900).

GEORGE CHARLES WILLIAMSON.

Beatific Vision, the immediate knowledge of God which the angelic spirits and the souls of the just enjoy in Heaven. It is called "vision" to distinguish it from the mediate knowledge of God which the human mind may attain in the present life. And since in beholding God face to face the created intelligence finds perfect happiness, the vision is termed "beatific". For further explanation of the subject, see HEAVEN.

E. A. PACE.

Beatification and Canonization.—1. HISTORY.— According to some writers the origin of beatification and canonization in the Catholic Church is to be traced back to the ancient pagan apotheosis. (See APOTHEOSIS.) In his classic work on the subject (De Servorum Dei Beatificatione et Beatorum Canonizatione) Benedict XIV examines at the very outset and refutes this view. He shows so well the substantial differences between them that no rightthinking person need henceforth confound the two institutions or derive one from the other. It is a matter of history who were elevated to the honour of apotheosis, on what grounds, and by whose authority; no less clear is the meaning that was attached to it. Often the decree was due to the statement of a single person (possibly bribed or enticed by promises, and with a view to fix the fraud more securely in the minds of an already superstitious people) that while the body of the new god was being burned, an eagle, in the case of the emperors, or a peacock (Juno's sacred bird), in the case of their consorts, was seen to carry heavenward the spirit of the departed (Livy, Hist. Rome, I, xvi; Herodian, Hist. Rome, IV, ii, iii). Apotheosis was awarded to most

members of the imperial family, of which family it was the exclusive privilege. No regard was had to virtues or remarkable achievements. Recourse was frequently had to this form of deification to escape popular hatred by distracting attention from the cruelty of imperial rulers. It is said that Romulus was deified by the senators who slew him; Poppæa owed her apotheosis to her imperial paramour, Nero, after he had kicked her to death; Geta had the honour from his brother Caracalla, who had got rid of him through jealousy. Canonization in the Catholic Church is quite another thing. The Catholic Church canonizes or beatifies only those whose lives have been marked by the exercise of heroic virtue, and only after this has been proved by common repute for sanctity and by conclusive arguments. The chief difference, however, lies in the meaning of the term *canonization*, the Church seeing in the saints nothing more than friends and servants of God whose holy lives have made them worthy of His special love. She does not pretend to make gods (cf. Eusebius Emisenus, Serm. de S. Rom. M.; Augustine, De Civitate Dei, XXII, x; Cyrill. Alexandr., Contra Jul., lib. VI; Cyprian, De Exhortat. martyr.; Conc. Nic., II, act. 3).

The true origin of canonization and beatification must be sought in the Catholic doctrine of the worship (*cultus*), invocation, and intercession of the saints. As was taught by St. Augustine (Quæst. in Heptateuch., lib. II, n. 94; contra Faustum, lib. XX, xxi), Catholics, while giving to God alone adoration strictly so-called, honour the saints because of the Divine supernatural gifts which have earned them eternal life, and through which they reign with God in the heavenly fatherland as His chosen friends and faithful servants. In other words, Catholics honour God in His saints as the loving distributor of supernatural gifts. The worship of *latria* ($\lambda \alpha \tau \rho \epsilon i \alpha$), or strict adoration, is given to God alone; the worship of *dulia* ($\delta o \nu \lambda \epsilon i \alpha$), or honour and humble reverence, is paid the saints; the worship of hyperdulia ($\dot{\nu} \pi \epsilon \rho \delta o \nu \lambda \epsilon i \alpha$), a higher form of *dulia*, belongs, on account of her greater excellence, to the Blessed Virgin Mary. The Church (Aug., Contr. Faustum, XX, xxi 21; cf. De Civit. Dei, XXII, x) erects her altars to God alone, though in honour and memory of the saints and martyrs. There is Scriptural warrant for such worship in the passages where we are bidden to venerate angels (Ex., xxiii, 20 sqq.; Jos., v, 13 sqq.; Dan., viii, 15 sqq.; x, 4 sqq.; Luke, ii, 9 sqq.; Acts, xii, 7 sqq.; Apoc., v, 11 sqq.; vii, 1 sqq.; Matt., xviii, 10; etc.), whom holy men are not unlike, as sharers of the friendship of God. And if St. Paul beseeches the brethren (Rom., xv, 30; II Cor., i, 11; Col., iv, 3; Ephes., vi, 18, 19) to help him by their prayers for him to God, we must with even greater reason maintain that we can be helped by the prayers of the saints, and ask their intercession with humility. If we may beseech those who still live on earth, why not those who live in heaven? It it objected that the invocation of saints is opposed to the unique mediatorship of Christ Jesus. There is indeed "one mediator of God and man, the man Christ Jesus". But He is our mediator in His quality of our common Redeemer; He is not our sole intercessor nor advocate, nor our sole mediator by way of supplication. In the eleventh session of the Council of Chalcedon (451) we find the Fathers exclaiming, "Flavianus lives after death! May the Martyr pray for us!" If we accept this doctrine of the worship of the saints, of which there are innumerable evidences in the writings of the Fathers and the liturgies of the Eastern and Western Churches, we shall not wonder at the loving care with which the Church committed to writing the sufferings of the early martyrs, sent these accounts from one gathering of the faithful to another, and promoted the veneration of the martyrs. Let one instance suffice. In the circular epistle of the Church of Smyrna (Eus., Hist. Eccl., IV, xxiii) we find mention of the religious celebration of the day on which St. Polycarp suffered martyrdom (23 February, 155); and the words of the passage exactly express the main purpose which the Church has in the celebration of such anniversaries: "We have at last gathered his bones, which are dearer to us than priceless gems and purer than gold, and laid them to rest where it was befitting they should lie. And if it be possible for us to assemble again, may God grant us to celebrate the birthday of his martyrdom with gladness, thus to recall the memory of those who fought in the glorious combat, and to teach and strengthen, by his example, those who shall come after us." This anniversary celebration and veneration of the martyrs was a service of thanksgiving and congratulation, a token and an evidence of the joy of those who engaged in it (Muratori, de Paradiso, x), and its general diffusion explains why Tertullian, though asserting with the Chiliasts that the departed just would obtain eternal glory only after the general resurrection of the body, admitted an exception for the martyrs (de Resurrectione Carnis, xliii).

It must be obvious, however, that, while private moral certainty of their sanctity and possession of heavenly glory may suffice for private veneration of the saints, it cannot suffice for public and common acts of that kind. No member of a social body may, independently of its authority, perform an act proper to that body. It follows naturally that for the public veneration of the saints the ecclesiastical authority of the pastors and rulers of the Church was constantly required. The Church had at heart, indeed, the honour of the martyrs, but she did not therefore grant liturgical honours indiscriminately to all those who had died for the Faith. St. Optatus of Mileve, writing at the end of the fourth century, tells us (De Schism. Donat., I, xvi, in P. L., XI, 916–917) of a certain noble lady, Lucilla, who was reprehended by Cæcilianus, Archdeacon of Carthage, for having kissed before Holy Communion the bones of one who either was not a martyr or whose right to the title was unproved. The decision as to the martyr having died for his faith in Christ, and the consequent permission of worship, lay originally with the bishop of the place in which he had borne his testimony. The bishop inquired into the motive of his death and, finding he had died a martyr, sent his name with an account of his martyrdom to other churches, especially neighbouring ones, so that, in the event of approval by their respective bishops, the cultus of the martyr might extend to their churches also, and that the faithful, as we read of St. Ignatius in the "Acts" of his martyrdom (Ruinart, Acta Sincera Martyrum, 19), "might hold communion with the generous martyr of Christ" (*generoso Christi martyri communicarent*). Martyrs whose cause, so to speak, had been discussed, and the fame of whose martyrdom had been confirmed, were known as proved (*vindicati*) martyrs. As far as the word is concerned it may probably not antedate the fourth century, when it was introduced in the Church of Carthage; but the fact is certainly older. In the earlier ages, therefore, this worship of the saints was entirely local and passed from one church to another with the permission of their bishops. This is clear from the fact that in none of the ancient Christian cemeteries are there found paintings of martyrs other than those who had suffered in that neighbourhood. It explains, also, the almost universal veneration very quickly paid to some martyrs, e. g. St. Lawrence, St. Cyprian of Carthage, Pope St. Sixtus of Rome [Duchesne, Origines du culte chrétien (Paris, 1903), 284].

The worship of confessors—of those, that is, who

died peacefully after a life of heroic virtue—is not as ancient as that of the martyrs. The word itself takes on a different meaning after the early Christian periods. In the beginning it was given to those who confessed Christ when examined in the presence of enemies of the Faith (Baronius, in his notes to Ro. Mart., 2 January, D), or, as Benedict XIV explains (op. cit., II, c. ii, n. 6), to those who died peacefully after having confessed the Faith before tyrants or other enemies of the Christian religion, and undergone tortures or suffered other punishments of whatever nature. Later on, confessors were those who had a holy life and closed it by a holy death in Christian peace. It is in this sense that we now treat of the worship paid to confessors.

It was in the fourth century, as is commonly held, that confessors were first given public ecclesiastical honour, though occasionally praised in ardent terms by earlier Fathers, and though an abundant reward (*multiplex corona*) is declared by St. Cyprian to be theirs (De Zelo et Livore, col. 509; cf. Innoc. III, De Myst. Miss., III, x; Benedict XIV, op. cit., I, v, n° 3 sqq; Bellarmine, De Missâ, II, xx, n° 5). Still Bellarmine thinks it uncertain when confessors began to be objects of cultus, and asserts that it was not before 800, when the feasts of Sts. Martin and Remigius are found in the catalogue of feasts drawn up by the Council of Mainz. This opinion of Innocent III and Benedict XIV is confirmed by the implicit approval of St. Gregory the Great (Dial., I, xiv, and III, xv) and by well attested facts: in the East, for example, Hilarion (Sozomen, III, xiv, and VIII, xix), Ephrem (Greg. Nyss., Orat. in laud. S. Ephrem), and other confessors were publicly honoured in the fourth century; and, in the West, St. Martin of Tours, as is gathered plainly from the oldest Breviaries and the Mozarabic Missal (Bona, Rer. Lit., II, xii, n° 3), and St. Hilary of Poitiers, as can be shown from the very ancient Mass-book known as "Missale Francorum" (Thomassin, "Traité des fêtes de l'église", in the second volume of his "Traités historiques et dogmatiques", Paris, 1683), were objects of a like cultus in the same century (Martigny, Dictionnaire des antiquités chrétiennes, s. v. Confesseurs). The reason of this veneration lies, doubtless, in the resemblance of the confessors' self-denying and heroically virtuous lives to the sufferings of the martyrs; such lives could truly be called prolonged martyrdoms. Naturally, therefore, such honour was first paid to ascetics (Duchesne, op. cit., 284) and only afterwards to those who resembled in their lives the very penitential and extraordinary existence of the ascetics. So true is this that the confessors themselves are frequently called martyrs. St. Gregory Nazianzen calls St. Basil a martyr (Orat. de laud., P. L., XXXVI, 602); St. Chrysostom applies the same title to Eustachius of Antioch (Opp. II, 606); St. Paulinus of Nola writes of St. Felix of Nola that he won heavenly honours, *sine sanguine martyr* ("a bloodless martyr"—Poem., XIV, Carm. III, v, 4); St. Gregory the Great styles Zeno of Verona a martyr (Dial. III, xix), and Metronius gives to St. Roterius (Acta SS., II, May 11, 306) the same title. Later on, the names of confessors were inserted in the diptychs, and due reverence was paid them. Their tombs were honoured (Martigny, loc. cit.) with the same title (*martyria*) as those of the martyrs. It remained true, however, at all times that it was unlawful to venerate confessors without permission of the ecclesiastical authority as it had been so to venerate martyrs (Bened. XIV, loc. cit., vi).

We have seen that for several centuries the bishops, in some places only the primates and patriarchs (August., Brevic. Collat. cum Donatistis, III, xiii, n° 25 in P. L., XLIII, 628), could grant to martyrs and confessors public ecclesiastical honour; such honour, however, was always decreed only for the local territory over which the grantors held jurisdiction. Still, it was only the Bishop of Rome's acceptance of the cultus that made it universal, since he alone could permit or command in the Universal Church [Gonzalez Tellez, Comm. Perpet. in singulos textus libr. Decr. (III, xlv), in cap. i, De reliquiis et vener. Sanct.]. Abuses, however, crept into this form of discipline, due as well to indiscretions of popular fervour as to the carelessness of some bishops in inquiring into the lives of those whom they permitted to be honoured as saints. Towards the close of the eleventh century the popes found it necessary to restrict episcopal authority on this point, and decreed that the virtues and miracles of persons proposed for public veneration should be examined in councils, more particularly in general councils. Urban II, Calixtus II, and Eugenius III followed this line of action. It happened, even after these decrees, that "some, following the ways of the pagans and deceived by the fraud of the evil one, venerated as a saint a man who had been killed while intoxicated". Alexander III (1159–81) took occasion to prohibit his veneration in these words: "For the future you will not presume to pay him reverence, as, even though miracles were worked through him, it would not allow you to revere him as a saint unless with the authority of the Roman Church" (c. i, tit. cit., X, III, xlv). Theologians do not agree as to the full import of this decretal. Either a new law was made (Bellarmine, De Eccles. Triumph., I, viii), in which case the pope then for the first time reserved the right of beatification, or a pre-existing law was confirmed. As the decretal did not put an end to all controversy, and some bishops did not obey it in as far as it regarded beatification (which right they had certainly possessed hitherto), Urban VII published, in 1634, a Bull which put an end to all discussion by reserving to the Holy See exclusively not only its immemorial right of canonization, but also that of beatification.

NATURE OF BEATIFICATION AND CANONIZATION.— Before dealing with the actual procedure in causes of beatification and canonization, it is proper to define these terms precisely and briefly in view of the preceding considerations. Canonization, generally speaking, is a decree regarding the public ecclesiastical veneration of an individual. Such veneration, however, may be permissive or preceptive, may be universal or local. If the decree contains a precept, and is universal in the sense that it binds the whole Church, it is a decree of canonization; if it only permits such worship, or if it binds under precept, but not with regard to the whole Church, it is a decree of beatification. In the ancient discipline of the Church, probably even as late as Alexander III, bishops could in their several dioceses allow public veneration to be paid to saints, and such episcopal decrees were not merely permissive, but, in my opinion, preceptive. Such decrees, however, could not prescribe universal honour; the effect of an episcopal act of this kind, was equivalent to our modern beatification. In such cases there was, properly speaking, no canonization, unless with the consent of the pope extending the cultus in question, implicitly or explicitly, and imposing it by way of precept upon the Church at large, In the more recent discipline beatification is a permission to venerate, granted by the Roman Pontiffs with restriction to certain places and to certain liturgical exercises. Thus it is unlawful to pay to the person known as Blessed (i. e. the *Beatus*, Beatified), public reverence outside of the place for which the permission is granted, or to recite an office in his honour, or to celebrate Mass with prayers referring to him, unless special indult be had; similarly, other methods of honour have been interdicted. Canonization is a precept of the Roman pontiff commanding public

veneration to be paid an individual by the Universal Church. To sum up, beatification, in the present discipline, differs from canonization in this: that the former implies (1) a locally restricted, not a universal, permission to venerate, which is (2) a mere permission, and no precept; while canonization implies a universal precept. In exceptional cases one or other element of this distinction may be lacking: thus, Alexander III not only allowed but ordered the public cultus of Bl. William of Malavalle in the Diocese of Grosseto, and his action was confirmed by Innocent III; Leo X acted similarly with regard to Bl. Hosanna for the city and district of Mantua; Clement IX with regard to Bl. Rose of Lima, when he selected her as principal patron of Lima and of Peru; and Clement X, by making her patron of all America, the Philippines, and the Indies. Clement X also chose Bl. Stanislaus Kostka as patron of Poland, Lithuania, and the allied provinces. Again, in respect to universality, Sixtus IV permitted the cultus of Bl. John Boni for the Universal Church. In all these instances there was only beatification. The cultus of Bl. Rose of Lima, it is true, was general and obligatory for America, but, lacking complete preceptive universality, was not strictly speaking canonization (Benedict XIV, op. cit., I, xxxix).

Canonization, therefore, creates a cultus which is universal and obligatory. But in imposing this obligation the pope may, and does, use one of two methods, each constituting a new species of canonization, i. e. formal canonization and equivalent canonization. Formal canonization occurs when the cultus is prescribed in an explicit and definitive decision, after due judicial process and the ceremonies usual in such cases. Equivalent canonization occurs when the pope, omitting the judicial process and the ceremonies, orders some servant of God to be venerated in the Universal Church; this happens when such a saint has been from a remote period the object of veneration, when his heroic virtues (or martyrdom) and miracles are related by reliable historians, and the fame of his miraculous intercession is uninterrupted. Many examples of such canonization are to be found in Benedict XIV: e. g. Saints Romuald, Norbert, Bruno, Peter Nolasco, Raymond Nonnatus, John of Matha, Felix of Valois, Queen Margaret of Scotland, King Stephen of Hungary, Wenceslaus Duke of Bohemia, and Gregory VII. Such instances afford a good proof of the caution with which the Roman Church proceeds in these equivalent canonizations. St. Romuald was not canonized until 439 years after his death, and the honour came to him sooner than to any of the others mentioned. We may add that this equivalent canonization consists usually in the ordering of an Office and Mass by the pope in honour of the saint, and that mere enrolment in the Roman Martyrology does not by any means imply this honour (Bened. XIV, l. c., xliii, n° 14).

PAPAL INFALLIBILITY AND CANONIZATION.—Is the pope infallible in issuing a decree of canonization? Most theologians answer in the affirmative. It is the opinion of St. Antoninus, Melchior Cano, Suarez, Bellarmine, Bañez, Vasquez, and, among the canonists, of Gonzales Tellez, Fagnanus, Schmalzgrüber, Barbosa, Reiffenstül, Covarruvias (Variar. resol., I, x, n° 13), Albitius (De Inconstantiâ in fide, xl, n° 205), Petra (Comm. in Const. Apost., I, in notes to Const. I, Alex., III, n° 17 sqq.), Joannes a S. Thomâ (on II–II, Q. I, disp. 9, a. 2), Silvester (Summa, s. v. Canonizatio), Del Bene (De Officio Inquisit. II, dub. 253), and many others. In Quodlib. IX, a. 16, St. Thomas says: "Since the honour we pay the saints is in a certain sense a profession of faith, i. e. a belief in the glory of the Saints [*quâ sanctorum gloriam credimus*] we must piously believe that in this matter also the judgment of the Church is not liable to error".

These words of St. Thomas, as is evident from the authorities just cited, all favouring a positive infallibility, have been interpreted by his school in favour of papal infallibility in the matter of canonization, and this interpretation is supported by several other passages in the same Quodlibet. This infallibility, however, according to the holy doctor, is only a point of pious belief. Theologians generally agree as to the fact of papal infallibilty in this matter of canonization, but disagree as to the quality of certitude due to a papal decree in such matter. In the opinion of some it is of faith (Arriaga, De fide, disp. 9, § 5, n° 27); others hold that to refuse assent to such a judgment of the Holy See would be both impious and rash, as Suarez (De fide, disp. 5, § 8, n° 8); many more (and this is the general view) hold such a pronouncement to be theologically certain, not being of Divine Faith as its purport has not been immediately revealed, nor of ecclesiastical Faith as having thus far not been defined by the Church.

What is the object of this infallible judgment of the pope? Does he define that the person canonized is in heaven or only that he has practised Christian virtues in an heroic degree? I have never seen this question discussed; my own opinion is that nothing else is defined than that the person canonized is in heaven. The formula used in the act of canonization has nothing more than this: "In honour of . . . we decree and define that Blessed N. is a Saint, and we inscribe his name in the catalogue of saints, and order that his memory be devoutly and piously celebrated yearly on the . . . day of . . . his feast." (Ad honorem . . . beatum N. Sanctum esse decernimus et definimus ac sanctorum catalogo adscribimus statuentes ab ecclesiâ universali illius memoriam quolibet anno, die ejus natali . . . piâ devotione recoli debere.) There is no question of heroic virtue in this formula; on the other hand, sanctity does not necessarily imply the exercise of heroic virtue, since one who had not hitherto practised heroic virtue would, by the one transient heroic act in which he yielded up his life for Christ, have justly deserved to be considered a saint. This view seems all the more certain if we reflect that all the arguments of theologians for papal infallibility in the canonization of saints are based on the fact that on such occasions the popes believe and assert that the decision which they publish is infallible (Pesch, Præl. Dogm., I, 552).

This general agreement of theologians as to papal infallibility in canonization must not be extended to beatification, notwithstanding the contrary teaching of the canonical commentary known as "Glossa" [in cap. un. de reliquiis et venerat. SS. (III, 22) in 6; Innocent., Comm. in quinque Decretalium libros, tit. de reliquiis, etc., n° 4; Ostiensis in eumd. tit. n° 10; Felini, cap. lii, De testibus, etc., X (II, 20); Caietani, tract. De indulgentiis adversus Lutherum ad Julium Mediceum; Augustini de Ancona, seu Triumphi, De potestate eccl., Q. xiv, a. 4]. Canonists and theologians generally deny the infallible character of decrees of beatification, whether formal or equivalent, since it is always a permission, not a command; while it leads to canonization, it is not the last step. Moreover, in most cases, the cultus permitted by beatification is restricted to a determined province, city, or religious body (Benedict XIV, op. cit., I, xlii). Some, however, have thought otherwise (Arriaga, Theol., V, disp. 7, § 6; Amicus, Theol., IV, disp. 7, § 4, n° 98; Turrianus on II–II, V, disp. 17, n° 6; Del Bene, De S. Inquisit. II, dub. 254).

PRESENT PROCEDURE IN CAUSES OF BEATIFICATION AND CANONIZATION.—We must first distinguish causes of martyrs from those of confessors or virgins, since the method followed is not entirely identical in both cases.

(a) *The Beatification of Confessors.*—In order to secure beatification (the most important and difficult step in the process of canonization) the regular procedure is as follows:

(1) Choosing of a vice-postulator by the postulator-general of the cause, to promote all the judicial inquiries necessary in places outside of Rome. Such inquiries are instituted by the local episcopal authority.

(2) The preparation of the inquiries (*processus*), all of which are carried on by the ordinary episcopal authority. They are of three kinds: *Informative* inquiries regard the reputation for sanctity and miracles of the servants of God, not only in general, but also in particular instances; there may be several such inquiries if the witnesses to be examined belong to different dioceses. Processes *de non cultu* are instituted to prove that the decrees of Urban VIII regarding the prohibition of public worship of servants of God before their beatification have been obeyed; they are generally conducted by the bishop of the place where the relics of the servant of God are preserved. Other inquiries are known as *Processiculi diligentiarum* and have for their object the writings attributed to the person whose beatification is in question; they vary in number according to the dioceses where such writings are found, or are thought likely to be found, and may not be judicially executed before an "Instruction" is obtained from the promotor of the Faith by the postulator-general and by him sent to the bishop in question.

(3) The results of all these inquiries are sent to Rome, to the Congregation of Rites, in charge of a messenger (*portitor*) chosen by the judges, or by some other secure way, in case a rescript of the congregation dispenses from the obligation of sending a messenger.

(4) They are opened, translated if necessary into Italian, a public copy is made; and a cardinal is deputed by the pope as *relator* or *ponens* of the cause, for all which steps rescripts of the congregation, confirmed by the pope, must be obtained.

(5) The writings of the servant of God are next revised by theologians appointed by the cardinal relator himself, authorized to so act by a special rescript. Meantime, the advocate and the procurator of the cause, chosen by the postulator-general, have prepared all the documents that concern the introduction of the cause (*positio super introductione causæ*). These consist of (α) a summary of the informative processes, (β) an information, (γ) answers to the observations or difficulties of the promoter of the Faith sent by him to the postulator.

(6) This collection of documents (*positio*) is printed and distributed to the cardinals of the Congregation of Rites forty days before the date assigned for their discussion.

(7) If nothing contrary to faith and morals is found in the writings of the servant of God, a decree is published authorizing further action (*quod in causâ procedi possit ad ulteriora*), i. e. the discussion of the matter (*dubium*) of appointment or non-appointment of a commission for the introduction of the cause.

(8) At the time fixed by the Congregation of Rites an ordinary meeting (*congregatio*) is held in which this appointment is debated by the cardinals of the aforesaid congregation and its officials, but without the vote or participation of the consultors, though this privilege is always granted them by rescript.

(9) If in this meeting the cardinals favour the appointment of the aforesaid commission, a decree to that effect is promulgated, and the pope signs it, but, according to custom, with his baptismal name, not with that of his pontificate. Thenceforward the servant of God is judicially given the title of Venerable.

(10) A petition is then presented asking remissorial letters for bishops *in partibus* (outside of Rome),

authorizing them to set on foot by Apostolic authority, the inquiry (*processus*) with regard to the fame of sanctity and miracles in general. This permission is granted by rescript, and such remissorial letters are prepared and sent to the bishops by the postulator-general. In case the eyewitnesses be of advanced age, other remissorial letters are usually granted for the purpose of opening a process known as "inchoative" concerning the particular virtues and miracles of the person in question. This is done in order that the proofs may not be lost (*ne pereant probationes*), and such inchoative process precedes that upon the miracles and virtues in general.

(11) While the Apostolic process concerning the reputation of sanctity is under way outside of Rome, documents are being prepared by the procurator of the cause for the discussion *de non cultu*, or absence of cultus, and at the appointed time an ordinary meeting (*congregatio*) is held in which the matter is investigated; if it be found that the decree of Urban VIII has been complied with, another decree provides that further steps may be taken.

(12) When the inquiry concerning the reputation of sanctity (*super famâ*) has arrived in Rome, it is opened (as already described in speaking of the ordinary processes, and with the same formalities in regard to rescripts), then translated into Italian, summarized, and declared valid. The documents *super famâ* in general are prepared by the advocate, and at the proper time, in an ordinary meeting of the cardinals of the Congregation of Rites, the question is discussed: whether there is evidence of a general repute for sanctity and miracles of this servant of God. If the answer is favourable, a decree embodying this result is published.

(13) New remissorial letters are then sent to the bishops *in partibus* for Apostolical processes with regard to the reputation for sanctity and miracles in particular. These processes must be finished within eighteen months and when they are received in Rome are opened, as above described, and by virtue of an equal number of rescripts, by the cardinal prefect, translated into Italian, and their summary authenticated by the Chancellor of the Congregation of Rites.

(14) The advocate of the cause next prepares the documents (*positio*) which have reference to the discussion of the validity of all the preceding processes, informative and Apostolic.

(15) This discussion is held in the meeting called *congregatio rotalis* from the fact that it is only judges of the Rota who vote. If the difficulties of the promotor of the Faith are satisfactorily answered, the decree establishing the validity of the inquiries or processes is published.

(16) Meanwhile all necessary preparation is made for the discussion of the question (*dubium*): Is there evidence that the venerable servant of God practised virtues both theological and cardinal, and in an heroic degree? (*An constet de virtutibus Ven. servi Dei, tam theologicis quam cardinalibus, in heroico gradu?*) In the causes of confessors this step is of primary importance. The point is discussed in three meetings or congregations called respectively, ante-preparatory, preparatory, and general. The first of these meetings is held in the palace of the cardinal relator (reporter) of the cause, and in it only consultors of the Congregation of Sacred Rites are allowed to vote; the second takes place in the Vatican, and again only the aforesaid consultors vote, though on this occasion in presence of the Cardinals of the Congregation of Rites, and with their chairman, or prefect, presiding; the third is also held in the Vatican, and at it the pope presides, and both cardinals and consultors vote. For each of these congregations the advocate of the cause prepares and prints official reports (*positiones*), called respectively *report*, *new report*,

final report, concerning the virtues, etc.,—*positio, positio nova, positio novissima, super virtutibus*. In each case, before proceeding to the subsequent meeting, a majority of the consultors must decide that the difficulties of the promotor of the Faith have been satisfactorily solved.

(17) When the Congregation of Rites in the above described general meeting has decided favourably, the pope is asked to sign the solemn decree which asserts that there exists evidence of the heroic virtues of the servant of God. This decree is not published until after the pope, having commended the matter to God in prayer, gives a final consent and confirms by his supreme sentence the decision of the congregation.

(18) The miracles now remain to be proved, of which two of the first class are required in case the practice of virtues in the heroic degree has been proved, in both ordinary and Apostolic inquiries or processes, by eyewitnesses—three, if the eyewitnesses were found only in the ordinary processes; four, if the virtues were proven only by hearsay (*de auditu*) witnesses. If the miracles have been sufficiently proven in the Apostolic processes (*super virtutibus*) already declared valid, steps are taken at once to prepare the documents with regard to miracles (*super miraculis*). If in the Apostolic processes only general mention has been made of the miracles, new Apostolic processes must be opened, and conducted after the manner already described for proving the practice of virtues in an heroic degree.

(19) The discussion of the particular miracles proceeds in exactly the same way and in the same order as that of the virtues. If the decisions be favourable, the general meeting of the congregation is followed by a decree, confirmed by the pope, in which it is announced that there is proof of miracles. It must be noted here that in the *positio* for the ante-preparatory congregation there are required, and are printed, opinions of two physicians, one of whom has been chosen by the postulator, the other by the Congregation of Rites. Of the three reports (*positiones*) above mentioned, and which are now also required, the first is prepared in the usual way; the second consists of an exposition of the heroic virtues of the servant of God, an information, and a reply to later observations of the promotor of the Faith; the last consists only of an answer to his final observations.

(20) When the miracles have been proved, another meeting of the Congregation of Rites is held in which it is debated once, and only once, whether or not, given the approbation of the virtues and miracles, it be safe to proceed with the solemnities of beatification. If a majority of the consultors be favourable, a decree to this effect is issued by the pope, and at the time appointed by him the solemn beatification of the servant of God takes place in the Vatican Basilica, on which occasion a pontifical Brief is issued permitting the public cultus and veneration of the beatified person now known as Blessed (*Beatus*).

(b) *The Beatification of Martyrs.*

(1) The causes of martyrs are conducted in the same way as those of confessors as far as the informative processes and those *de non cultu* and *ad introductionem causæ* are concerned. But when once the commission of introduction has been appointed they advance much more rapidly.

(2) No remissorial letters are granted for Apostolic processes concerning the general reputation for martyrdom and miracles; the letters sent call for an immediate investigation into the fact of martyrdom, its motive, and the particular miracles alleged. There is no longer a discussion of the general reputation for martyrdom or miracles.

(3) The miracles are not discussed, as formerly, in separate meetings, but in the same meetings that deal with the fact and the motive of the martyrdom.

(4) The miracles (*signa*) required are not those of the first class; those of the second class suffice, nor is their number determined. On some occasions the decision as to miracles has been entirely dispensed with.

(5) The discussion as to martyrdom and miracles, formerly held in three meetings or congregations, viz. the ante-preparatory, preparatory, and general, is now usually conducted, through a dispensation to be had in each instance from the sovereign pontiff, in a single congregation known as *particularis*, or special. It consists of six or seven cardinals of the Congregation of Rites and four or five prelates especially deputed by the pope. There is but one *positio* prepared in the usual way; if there be an affirmative majority a decree is issued concerning the proof of martyrdom, the cause of martyrdom, and miracles. (*Constare de Martyrio, causâ Martyrii et signis.*)

(6) The final stage is a discussion of the security (*super tuto*) with which advance to beatification may be made, as in the case of confessors; the solemn beatification then follows. This procedure is followed in all cases of formal beatification in causes of both confessors and martyrs proposed in the ordinary way (*per viam non cultus*). Those proposed as coming under the definition of cases excepted (*casus excepti*) by Urban VIII are treated in another way. In such cases it must be proved that an immemorial public veneration (at least for 100 years before the promulgation, in 1640, of the decrees of Urban VIII) has been paid the servant of God, whether confessor or martyr. Such cause is proposed under the title of "confirmation of veneration" (*de confirmatione cultus*); it is dealt with in an ordinary meeting of the Congregation of Rites. When the difficulties of the promotor of the Faith have been satisfied, a pontifical decree confirming the cultus is promulgated. Beatification of this kind is called equivalent or virtual.

(c) *The Canonization of Confessors or Martyrs.*— The canonization of confessors or martyrs may be taken up as soon as two miracles are reported to have been worked at their intercession, after the pontifical permission of public veneration as described above. At this stage it is only required that the two miracles worked after the permission awarding a public cultus be discussed in three meetings of the congregation. The discussion proceeds in the ordinary way; if the miracles be confirmed another meeting (*super tuto*) is held. The pope then issues a Bull of Canonization in which he not only permits, but commands, the public cultus, or veneration, of the saint.

It is with the utmost possible brevity that I have described the elements of a process of beatification or canonization. It may be easily conjectured that considerable time must elapse before any cause of beatification or canonization can be conducted, from the first steps of the information, inquiry, or process, to the issuing of the decree *super tuto*. This is especially true at present, when a great number of causes, new and old, are proposed for discussion before the Sacred Congregation of Rites (see "Catalogus ac Status Causarum Beatificationis", Rome, 1901). According to the constitution of this Congregation, more than one important discussion (*dubia majora*) cannot be proposed at the same time. It must be remembered (a) that the same cardinals and consultors must vote in all discussions; (b) that there is but one promotor of the Faith and one sub-promotor, who alone have charge of all observations to be made with regard to the *dubia;* (c) that these cardinals and consultors have to treat questions of ritual as well as processes of canonization and beatification. To execute all this business there is but one weekly meeting (*congressus*), a kind of minor

congregation in which only the cardinal prefect and the major officials vote; in it less important and practical questions are settled regarding rites as well as causes, and answers are given, and rescripts which the pope afterwards verbally approves. The other meetings of the congregation (ordinary, rotal, and "upon virtues and miracles") may be as few as sixteen in the course of the year. Some other cause must therefore be found for the slow progress of causes of beatification or canonization than a lack of good will or activity on the part of the Congregation of Rites.

EXPENSES.—It will not be out of place to give succinctly the ordinary actual expenses of canonization and beatification. Of these expenses some are necessary others merely discretionary, i. e. some are specified (e. g. the expenses incurred in obtaining the different rescripts) others, though necessary, are not specified. Such are the expenses of the solemnity in the Vatican Basilica, and for paintings representing the newly beatified which are afterwards presented to the pope, the cardinals, officials, and consultors of the Congregation of Rites. The limits of this class of expenses depend on the postulator of the cause. If he chooses to spend a moderate sum the entire cause from the first process to the solemn beatification will not cost him less than $20,000. The expenses of the process from beatification to canonization will easily exceed $30,000. In illustration of this we subjoin the final account of the expenses of the public solemnities in the Vatican Basilica for the canonization, by Leo XIII, of Saints Anthony Maria Zaccaria and Peter Fourier, as published by the Most Rev. Diomede Panici, titular Archbishop of Laodicea, then Secretary of the Congregation of Rites.

To decoration of the Basilica, lights, architectural designs, labour, and superintendence,......................*Lire*	152,840.58
Procession, Pontifical Mass, preparation of altars in Basilica,................	8,114.58
Cost of gifts presented to Holy Father,..	1,438.87
Hangings, Sacred Vestments, etc,.......	12,990.60
Services rendered and different offerings,	3,525.07
Recompense for services and money loaned,..........................	3,535.00
To the Vatican Chapter as perquisites for decorations and candles,.............	18,000.00
Propine and Competenza,..............	16,936.00
Incidental and unforeseen expenses,.....	4,468.40

Lire 221,849.10

—or (taking the *lira* as equivalent to $.193 in United States money) $42,816.87. (See also BLESSED.)

BENEDICT XIV, *De servorum Dei beatificatione et beatorum canonizatione* (the classic text on this subject); SCHMALZGRÜBER, *Jus Ecclesiasticum Universum*, III, tit. 45; FERRARIS, *Bibliotheca Canonica*, s. v. *Veneratio Sanctorum;* FORNARI, *Codex pro postulatoribus;* GARDELLINI, *Decreta authentica S. C. Congr. Rituum;* REIFFENSTÜL, *Jus Canonicum Universum*, III, tit. 45; VON MOY, s. v. in *Kirchenlex.*—Other writers of importance have been quoted in the text.

CAMILLUS BECCARI.

Beatitudes, MOUNT OF.—This name is given to the place where Our Saviour delivered the "Sermon on the Mount", beginning with the Beatitudes, The scene of this discourse is traditionally located on Karn Hattin (or Kurun Ḥattîn), the *Horns* of Hattin, a mountain which receives its name from the little village at its northern base and from the two cones or horns which crown its summit. Karn Hattin is in Galilee, within easy distance of Nazareth, Cana, and Mt. Tabor to the south-west, of Tiberias and Lake Gennesaret (the Sea of Galilee) to the east, and of Capharnaum to the north-east, in the centre, therefore, of much of the ministry of Jesus. It lies 1,816 feet above the lake and 1,135 feet above the sea level (according to Bædeker, Palestine and Syria, Leipzig, 1898, pp. 285, 288, which has the high authority of Socin and Benzinger). This mountain, rising above the hills that skirt the lake, is the only height to the west that can be seen from its shores. It consists of a low ridge about one-quarter of a mile long, extending east and west, and rising at each extremity into a cone or horn. The eastern horn, which is the taller, is only sixty feet above the ridge. Between the horns lies an uneven platform which could easily accommodate the crowd that followed Jesus; but it is believed that the spot on which the discourse was given is lower down, on a level place on the southern side of the mountain, corresponding with St. Luke's description (τοπόν πεδινοῦ), vi, 17, which may mean a level place, as well as a "plain". From the eastern slope of the hill there is a beautiful view, to the east, of the lake with the Jôlan (Gaulanitis) mountains beyond, to the south the plateau of Ard el-Hamma and Mt. Tabor, and to the north the snowy height of Mt. Hermon. The tradition that there was a village on the mountain top, if true (the only proof being the remains of a wall which served as defence to a camp), might lend point to the reference in the sermon to the city which was seated on a hill and could not be hid (Matt., v, 14); and the beautiful flowers that abound there might include the unidentified "lilies of the field" (vi, 28). Bishop Le Camus (Notre Voyage aux Pays Bibliques, II, pp. 220–222) thought he never saw elsewhere and never imagined so lovely a variety and harmony in the beauty of flowers; other travellers are scarcely so enthusiastic, but all agree the spot has a charm of its own. The Horns of Hattin are mentioned by a feeble and late tradition as the site of the second multiplication of loaves. The Jews of the locality point out here also the tomb of Jethro, father-in-law of Moses. During the Crusades the plain below was the scene of the battle in which Saladin dealt the death-blow to French power in Palestine (3–4 July, 1187).

The tradition regarding the scene of the Sermon on the Mount, though usually received with a certain degree of favour by Scriptural scholars, apparently does not go back beyond the crusaders. St. Jerome, the best informed man of his day on points of this nature, knew of no such tradition and merely conjectured that the scene was on Mt. Tabor or some other high mountain of Galilee (Comm. in Ev. S. Matt. in Cap. v). The Gospels, in fact, afford but little help in determining the site. Matt., v, 1, locates the sermon on *the* mountain (τὸ ὄρος), and Luke, vi, 12, uses the same expression for the spot from which Our Lord descended before He preached on the "level place", vi, 17. The expression most naturally "suggests that the sermon had long been traditionally connected with a mountain and seems to mean *the* mountain on which the sermon was delivered" (Allen, St. Matthew, New York, 1907). Some scholars even see in the definite article the indication of a particular mountain which the Evangelists suppose known to the reader; but popular curiosity concerning the scene of particular Gospel events is a growth of later date. Some interpret it as "the mountain that was at hand". Others refuse to see in *the* mountain a reference to any particular mountain at all, but interpret the word as meaning "the tableland, the mountainous district". Τὸ ὄρος is used in this sense in the Septuagint translation of Gen., xix, 17, 19, 30, xxxi, 23, 25, xxxvi, 8, 9. and appears to have the same meaning in Matt., xiv, 23, xv, 29, Mark, vi, 46, Luke, ix, 28, John, vi, 3. Possibly the word is to be thus interpreted here also, but St. Luke more probably refers (vi, 12) to a particular mountain on which Our Lord spent the night in prayer and from which He descended to the level place or tableland to preach the discourse.

According to another opinion recently put forth by certain critics, the mountain is purely ideal in Matthew, while in Luke a plain is the place on which the Beatitudes were spoken. The author of the First Gospel, in the opinion of Loisy (Le Discours sur la Montagne) "desires to have for the publication of the New Law, a setting analogous to that which is described in Exodus (xx, 18–22) for the Old Law. The mountain of Matthew is the Sinai of the Gospel where Jesus speaks as prince of the kingdom of God and shows Himself greater than Moses. . . . To seek an exact geographical determination here is no more expedient than in the case of the mountain of the temptation", which was purely ideal, being represented as high enough to afford a view of all the kingdoms of the world. There is most probably an element of truth in this opinion; nearly all the Fathers seek a symbolic meaning in the mountain (v. St. Thomas Aquinas, Catena Aurea, loc. cit.) and are probably right in attributing it to Matthew. But his account and that of St. Luke have too matter-of-fact an air to allow us to believe that either intended the mountain to be regarded as purely ideal. Matthew believed, then, that the New Law, just as the Old, was really given on a mountain. We are assuming here, of course, that the Sermon on the Mount was a genuine discourse by Our Lord, not a mere rearrangement of His sayings made by Matthew.

If we seek to determine the particular mountain to which the Evangelists allude, we cannot advance with anything like certainty beyond the ancient opinion of St. Jerome (Comm. in Ev. Matt.) that the events before and after the discourse show that it was given on some mountain of Galilee. It is not unlikely that the locality was not far distant from Capharnaum, into which Our Lord entered after finishing His discourse (Matt., viii, 5; Luke, vii, 1); but the Evangelists do not say how soon after the discourse He entered Capharnaum. We know from their literary methods that it may have been a day, a week, or even more, for they had little interest in the chronological sequence of events, and the attempt to press details of this sort only results in interminable contradictions. Besides, the site of Capharnaum itself is uncertain. Neither Evangelist gives us a hint as to what vicinity Jesus set out from to ascend the mountain, except that it was somewhere in Galilee; how then can the mountain be determined? It is true many (e. g. Stanley) assume it must have been from the lakeside or its neighbourhood; but no word in the Gospels warrants the assumption, though it is the most likely one.

In favour of Karn Hattin, it is said, is the fact that it is accessible from all sides, which is thought to be demanded by the narratives of Matthew (iv, 25, v, 1) and Luke (vi, 17). But this argument, although it is accepted by Dean Stanley (Sinai and Palestine, London, 1883, p. 369) who is usually quite rigorous in requiring proof, has little force, since the multitude did not flock to the mountain from all sides, but, according to Matthew, at least, first gathered together and followed Jesus up the mountainside. (Cf. iv, 25, v, 1, with vii, 28, where the multitude, not merely the disciples, are found on the spot where the sermon was delivered.) There is little but negative evidence in favour of Karn Hattin; Edersheim (Life and Times of Jesus, New York, 1896) says there are several reasons which make it unsuitable, but gives none. It is near the scenes of Our Lord's greatest activity and fulfils all the requirements of the narrative. We must add, however, that so great an authority as Robinson (Biblical Researches in Palestine, III, 487) says there are a number of hills to the west of the lake equally as suitable as Karn Hattin; but this hardly gives its proper force to the word, *the* mountain, which seems to mark the place as distinct from the hills of almost uniform height in the vicinity.

Legendre in Vig., *Dict. de la Bible, 1528*, s. v. *Béatitudes, Mont des;* Fouard, *The Christ* (New York, 1891); Andrews, *The Life of Our Lord* (New York, 1901); Tholuck, *Die Bergrede*, tr. *The Sermon on the Mount* (Philadelphia, 1860); Votaw in Hast., *Dict. of the Bible*, Extra Volume, s. v. *Sermon on the Mount;* Le Camus, *The Life of Christ* (tr. New York), II; Maas, *The Gospel according to St. Matthew* (St. Louis, 1898), 57, 58.

John F. Fenlon.

Beatitudes, The Eight, the solemn blessings (*beatitudines, benedictiones*) which mark the opening of the Sermon on the Mount, the very first of Our Lord's sermons in the Gospel of St. Matthew (v, 3–10). Four of them occur again in a slightly different form in the Gospel of St. Luke (vi, 22), likewise at the beginning of a sermon, and running parallel to Matthew, 5–7, if not another version of the same. And here they are illustrated by the opposition of the four curses (24–26). The fuller account and the more prominent place given the Beatitudes in St. Matthew are quite in accordance with the scope and the tendency of the First Gospel, in which the spiritual character of the Messianic kingdom—the paramount idea of the Beatitudes—is consistently put forward, in sharp contrast with Jewish prejudices. The very peculiar form in which Our Lord proposed His blessings makes them, perhaps, the only example of His sayings that may be styled poetical—the parallelism of thought and expression, which is the most striking feature of Biblical poetry, being unmistakably clear.

The text of St. Matthew runs as follows:—

3. Blessed are the poor in spirit: for theirs is the kingdom of heaven.
4. Blessed are the meek: for they shall possess the land.
5. Blessed are they that mourn: for they shall be comforted.
6. Blessed are they that hunger and thirst after justice: for they shall have their fill.
7. Blessed are the merciful: for they shall obtain mercy.
8. Blessed are the clean of heart: for they shall see God.
9. Blessed are the peacemakers: for they shall be called the children of God.
10. Blessed are they that suffer persecution for justice' sake, for theirs is the kingdom of heaven.

Textual Criticism.—As regards textual criticism, the passage offers no serious difficulty. Only in verse 9, the Vulgate and many other ancient authorities omit the pronoun αὐτοί, *ipsi;* probably a merely accidental omission. There is room, too, for serious critical doubt, whether verse 5 should not be placed before verse 4. Only the etymological connexion, which in the original is supposed to have existed between the "poor" and the "meek", makes us prefer the order of the Vulgate.

First Beatitude.—The word "poor" seems to represent an Aramaic '*ányâ* (Hebr. '*ānî*), bent down, afflicted, miserable, poor; while "meek" is rather a synonym from the same root, '*ánwān* (Hebr. '*ánāw*), bending oneself down, humble, meek, gentle. Some scholars would attach to the former word also the sense of humility; others think of "beggars before God" humbly acknowledging their need of Divine help. But the opposition of "rich" (Luke, vi, 24) points especially to the common and obvious meaning, which, however, ought not to be confined to economical need and distress, but may comprehend the whole of the painful condition of the poor: their low estate, their social dependence, their defenceless exposure to injustice from the rich and the mighty. Besides the Lord's blessing, the promise of the heavenly kingdom is not bestowed on the actual

external condition of such poverty. The blessed ones are the poor "in spirit", who by their free will are ready to bear for God's sake this painful and humble condition, even though at present they be actually rich and happy; while on the other hand, the really poor man may fall short of this poverty "in spirit".

Second Beatitude.—Inasmuch as poverty is a state of humble subjection, the "poor in spirit" come near to the "meek", the subject of the second blessing. The '*ănăwîm*, they who humbly and meekly bend themselves down before God and man, shall "inherit the land" and possess their inheritance in peace. This is a phrase taken from Ps., xxxvi (Hebr., xxxvii), 11, where it refers to the Promised Land of Israel, but here, in the words of Christ, it is of course but a symbol of the Kingdom of Heaven, the spiritual realm of the Messiah. Not a few interpreters, however, understand "the earth". But they overlook the original meaning of Ps., xxxvi, 11, and unless, by a far-fetched expedient, they take the earth also to be a symbol of the Messianic kingdom, it will be hard to explain the possession of the earth in a satisfactory way.

Third Beatitude.—The "mourning" in the Third Beatitude is in Luke (vi, 25) opposed to laughter and similar frivolous worldly joy. Motives of mourning are not to be drawn from the miseries of a life of poverty, abjection, and subjection, which are the very blessings of verse 3, but rather from those miseries from which the pious man is suffering in himself and in others, and most of all the tremendous might of evil throughout the world. To such mourners the Lord Jesus carries the comfort of the heavenly kingdom, "the consolation of Israel" (Luke, ii, 25) foretold by the prophets, and especially by the Book of Consolation of Isaias (xl–lxvi). Even the later Jews knew the Messiah by the name of *Menáhhēm,* Consoler. These three blessings, poverty, abjection, and subjection, are a commendation of what nowadays are called the passive virtues: abstinence and endurance, and the Eighth Beatitude (verse 10) leads us back again to the same teaching.

Fourth Beatitude.—The others, however, demand a more active behaviour. First of all, "hunger and thirst" after justice; a strong and continuous desire of progress in religious and moral perfection, the reward of which will be the very fulfilment of the desire, the continuous growth in holiness.

Fifth Beatitude.—From this interior desire a further step should be taken to acting; to the works of "mercy", corporal and spiritual. Through these the merciful will obtain the Divine mercy of the Messianic kingdom, in this life and in the final judgment. The wonderful fertility of the Church in works and institutions of corporal and spiritual mercy of every kind shows the prophetical sense, not to say the creative power, of this simple word of the Divine Teacher.

Sixth Beatitude.—According to Biblical terminology "cleanness of heart" (verse 8) cannot exclusively be found in interior chastity, nor even, as many scholars propose, in a general purity of conscience, as opposed to the Levitical, or legal, purity required by the Scribes and Pharisees. At least the proper place of such a blessing does not seem to be between mercy (verse 7) and peacemaking (verse 9), nor after the apparently more far-reaching virtue of hunger and thirst after justice. But frequently in the Old and New Testaments [Gen., xx, 5; Job, xxxiii, 3; Pss., xxiii (Hebr., xxiv), 4; lxxii (Hebr., lxxiii), 1; I Tim., i, 5; II Tim., ii, 22] the "pure heart" is the simple and sincere good intention, the "single eye" of Matt., vi, 22, and thus opposed to the unavowed by-ends of the Pharisees (Matt., vi, 1–6, 16–18; vii, 15; xxiii, 5–7, 14). This "single eye" or "pure heart" is most of all required in the works of mercy (verse 7)

II.—24

and zeal (verse 9) in behalf of one's neighbour. And it stands to reason that the blessing, promised to this continuous looking for God's glory, should consist of the supernatural "seeing" of God Himself, the last aim and end of the heavenly kingdom in its completion.

Seventh Beatitude.—The "peacemakers" (verse 9) are those who not only live in peace with others but moreover do their best to preserve peace and friendship among mankind and between God and man, and to restore it when it has been disturbed. It is on account of this godly work, "an imitating of God's love of man" as St. Gregory of Nyssa styles it, that they shall be called the sons of God, "children of your Father who is in heaven" (Matt., v, 45).

Eighth Beatitude.—When after all this the pious disciples of Christ are repaid with ingratitude and even "persecution" (verse 10) it will be but a new blessing, "for theirs is the kingdom of heaven".

So by an inclusion, not uncommon in Biblical poetry, the last blessing goes back to the first and the second. The pious, whose sentiments and desires, whose works and sufferings are held up before us, shall be blessed and happy by their share in the Messianic kingdom, here and hereafter. And viewed in this light the different kinds of blessing enumerated in the intermediate verses seem to express, in partial images of the one endless beatitude, the same possession of the Messianic salvation. The eight conditions required constitute the fundamental law of the kingdom, the very pith and marrow of Christian perfection. For its depth and breadth of thought, and its practical bearing on Christian life, the passage may be put on a level with the Decalogue in the Old, and the Lord's Prayer in the New, Testament, and it surpasses both in its poetical beauty of structure.

Besides the commentaries on St. Matthew and St. Luke, and the monographs on the Sermon on the Mount, the Beatitudes are treated in eight homilies of ST. GREGORY OF NYSSA, *P. G.*, XLIV, 1193–1302, and in one other of ST. CHROMATIUS, *P. L.*, XX, 323–328. Different patristical sermons on single beatitudes are noticed in *P. L.*, CXXXI (Index IV), 23 sqq.

JOHN P. VAN KASTEREN.

Beaton (or BETHUNE), DAVID, Cardinal, Archbishop of St. Andrews, b. 1494; d. 29 May, 1546. He was of an honourable Scottish family on both sides, being a younger son of John Beaton of Balfour, Fife, by Isabel, daughter of David Monypenny of Pitmilly, also in Fife. Educated first at St. Andrews, he went in his seventeenth year to Glasgow, where his uncle, James Beaton, was then archbishop, and where his name appears in the list of students of the university, in 1511. He completed his education in Paris, and in 1519 was appointed by James V Scottish resident at the French court. His first ecclesiastical preferment was to the rectories of Campsie and Cambuslang, to which he was presented by his uncle, the Archbishop of Glasgow, and when the latter was translated to the primatial see in 1522, he resigned to his nephew the commendatory Abbacy of Arbroath, obtaining for him from Pope Adrian IV a dispensation from wearing the monastic habit. Beaton returned from France in 1525, took his seat in Parliament as Abbot of Arbroath, and was soon created by the young king Lord Privy Seal, in succession to Bishop Crichton of Dunkeld. James dispatched him to Paris in 1533, with Sir Thomas Erskine, in order to renew the Scottish alliance with Francis I, and to negotiate for the marriage of James with Magdalen, only daughter of the French king. Beaton was present at the marriage of the royal pair at Notre-Dame on 1 January, 1537, and returned with them to Scotland in May; but the young queen died of consumption two months later. We next find Beaton on a mission in England, negotiating about certain difficulties which had arisen on the Border. The Queen-Mother (Margaret) wrote specially commending the Abbot of Arbroath

to her brother, Henry VIII, mentioning that he was "gret wyth the Kyng" (of Scots). A few months later he was again in Paris, arranging for the marriage of his widowed king with Mary of Guise. After the ceremony (by proxy) in the French capital, Beaton conducted the bride to Scotland, assisted at the solemnization of the marriage in St. Andrews Cathedral, and was afterwards sponsor (together with the Archbishop of Glasgow) to the first child that was born of the union. His elevation to the episcopate took place during this second embassy to the French court. King Francis nominated him to the Bishopric of Mirepoix (a suffragan see of Toulouse, with an

DAVID CARDINAL BEATON
(Original in Holyrood Palace)

annual revenue of 10,000 livres), and he received the papal confirmation on 5 December, 1537. Two months later he assisted at the coronation of James and Mary at Holyrood, himself crowning the queen. In 1538 the Kings of France and Scotland showed their appreciation of Beaton's services by petitioning Pope Paul III to advance him to the cardinalate. James in making this request (15 August, 1538) protested his own firm attachment to the Holy See, and urged the necessity of some ecclesiastic being invested with a dignity which would enable him to represent the majesty of the Church in Scotland, and better withstand the "insane errors" of the time. The king repeated his request a month later, and on 20 December, 1538, Beaton was created Cardinal-Priest of the Title of St. Stephen on the Cœlian Hill. This had been the title of Cardinal John de Salerno, who had presided at the meeting of Scottish bishops at Perth in the reign of William the Lion; but the only Scottish cardinal before Beaton had been William Wardlaw, Bishop of Glasgow, who died in 1387. Early in 1539 Archbishop James Beaton of St. Andrews died, and his nephew the cardinal (who had six months before been appointed his coadjutor with right of succession) was promoted to the primacy of Scotland. A year later, at his request, William Gibson, Titular Bishop of Libaria, was nominated his coadjutor, with an annual income of £200, paid out of the revenues of the archiepiscopal see.

Beaton, whose commanding ability had now raised him to the highest position attainable in Scotland by a subject, was to have that ability fully tested in the growing unrest of the times, and in the relations, becoming rapidly more and more strained, between James V and his uncle, Henry VIII of England. The latter, in his designs to detach Scotland from its allegiance to the Holy See and bring it into subjection to himself, was supported by the Douglases and other powerful nobles, and by the sympathy of his sister, the Queen-Mother Margaret. James, on the other hand, was backed by the zeal, wealth, influence, and talent of the whole clergy of the realm, and by many loyal Scottish lords; he had the sympathy of France and of the Emperor of Germany, the strong support of the Holy See, and the warm adherence of the great mass of his subjects. Henry in vain tried to shake his nephew's confidence in Beaton by sending two successive embassies to

Scotland, in order to urge James to follow his example in usurping the supremacy of the Church in his dominions. The King of Scots refused to be drawn into Henry's net, maintained his unshaken trust in Beaton's statesmanship and patriotism, and declined to leave his kingdom for a personal interview with his uncle. His intrigues being baffled, Henry had recourse to force; and hostilities broke out between the two kingdoms in 1542. The Scotch, successful in the first engagement, were hopelessly defeated by the English forces on Solway Moss, and James died broken-hearted at Falkland soon afterwards, leaving a daughter (Mary) a week old, to inherit the crown. Beaton produced a document in which he, with three nobles, was appointed regent by the late monarch's will; but the nobles assembled in Edinburgh refused to act on this, declared the Earl of Arran (heir-presumptive to the throne) regent during the queen's minority, and imprisoned the cardinal on a false charge of conspiring with the Duke of Guise against Arran's authority. Henry now commenced negotiations with the Scottish regent and Parliament with the object of arranging a marriage between the infant queen and his own heir (afterwards Edward VI), of getting the Scottish fortresses and the government of the country committed into his hands, and the person of Mary entrusted to his custody. Arran and the Parliament agreed to the project of marriage, but were resolute against the rest of Henry's schemes. Meanwhile the unjust imprisonment of the cardinal-primate had been followed by the proclamation of an interdict throughout the kingdom; and so deep was the feeling aroused among the still Catholic people by the closing of the churches and the suspension of the sacraments that it was thought prudent at once to release Beaton. The undaunted primate instantly summoned the bishops and clergy to St. Andrews; and the assembly, fully alive to the imminent danger (menacing both Church and State) of Henry's insolent demands, spontaneously voted a large sum, taxed on their own benefices, in defence of the national rights. Beaton by his patriotic ardour awakened similar sentiments in the people at large; the person of the baby queen was safeguarded, and a number of the nobles, including the regent himself (who about this time abjured the new doctrines and submitted to the Catholic Church), abandoned their unnatural alliance with the enemies of Scotland, and ranged themselves on the cardinal's side.

In October, 1543, Marco Grimani, Patriarch of Aquileia, came from Rome as nuncio to the Scottish court; and it was during his sojourn in Scotland that the high dignity of legate *a latere* was (in January, 1544) bestowed on Beaton by the pope. About the same time the cardinal was invested with the office of chancellor of the kingdom; the Parliament annulled the treaty of marriage between the queen and Prince Edward, on the ground of the duplicity and bad faith of Henry VIII; vigorous measures were taken against the "English party" among the Scottish nobles; and the bishops were desired to take equally stern measures for the suppression of heretical doctrines. Furious at the frustration of his schemes, Henry now connived at, and indeed openly encouraged, a plot for the removal from his path of the able and patriotic man who had been the chief instrument in foiling his ambitious plans. George Wishart (whose identity, long disputed, with the Wishart afterwards put to death as a heretic has been conclusively proved by the published State Papers of the time) was employed to negotiate between Crichton of Brunston and Beaton's English enemies, on the subject of the assassination of the cardinal. Nearly three years were devoted to the intrigues and correspondence connected with this dark scheme; and, meanwhile, the primate never relaxed his zeal

and diligence in the performance of his high functions. He summoned another convention of the clergy in Edinburgh in January, 1546, when further large sums were voted in support of the defence of the realm against the invading armies of England; and two months later he convoked a provincial council at St. Andrews. The great general council was already sitting at Trent, but no Scottish prelate was able to attend it, the cardinal himself seeking dispensation from Pope Paul III, on the ground of the overwhelming nature of his duties in Scotland. The council at St. Andrews was interrupted by the apprehension and trial, for preaching heretical doctrines, of George Wishart. The trial took place in St. Andrews Cathedral, in presence of the two archbishops and other prelates; the articles of accusation were read and duly proved; and Wishart, remaining obdurate in his errors, was condemned to death, and suffered (being first strangled and afterwards burned) at St. Andrews on 28 March, 1546.

The profound impression caused throughout Scotland by Wishart's execution induced Beaton's enemies to hurry on their murderous designs; and two months later a pretext was found for the consummation of the long-cherished plot in a dispute which had arisen, on a question of property, between the cardinal and Norman Leslie, Master of Rothes. The latter, with his uncle John Leslie, Kirkaldy of Grange, and James Melville, undertook the work of butchery; and at daybreak on 29 May, 1546, they obtained admission into the castle of St. Andrews, and dispatched the cardinal with repeated blows of their swords. Thus perished, in the forty-fifth year of his age, one to whom (as his most recent, and far from partial, biographer, Professor Herkless, declares) "historic truth must give a place among Scotland's greatest statesmen and patriots". No student of his life and of the history of his times can deny the justice of this tribute; and it may fairly be added that he proved himself not less vigilant in the discharge of the spiritual functions of his office, in watching over the interests of the Scottish Church, and protecting her by every means at his command from the inroads of heresy and schism. As to the charge of persecution brought against him, account must be taken of the age in which he lived, and the prevailing sentiments of the time. Seven persons in all are said to have suffered death under him; and Hosack, comparing this number with the hundreds of lives sacrificed under some of his contemporaries, concludes that Beaton deserves rather to be commended for his moderation than denounced for his barbarity. With regard to his moral character, it has been violently attacked by his enemies, and no less warmly defended by his friends. The charges of immorality against him, never raised until after his death, are in many cases absurd and contradictory; and Leslie, Winzet, and others who strenuously denied them, are fully as worthy of credit as those who maintained them. The evidence from contemporary history is indeed insufficient to decide the truth or falsity of these charges; and Lyon, the historian of St. Andrews, prudently concludes that the accusations and the denials may be considered as neutralizing one another.

There are two well-known portraits of Beaton, one (formerly in the Scots College at Rome, now at Blairs College, Aberdeenshire), depicting him in his doctor's cap, with slightly silvered brown hair, clear-cut features, and a noble and commanding air. In the other portrait, which hangs in Holyrood Palace, he is represented in a black dress, with white bands, and wearing the red skull-cap of a cardinal.

LESLEY, *Hist. of Scotland* (Bannatyne Club, 1830), 149, 155, 158; *State Papers, Henry VIII* (Foreign and Domestic), V, VI; THEINER, *Monumenta*, 609, 611, 613; LYON, *Hist. of St. Andrews, Ancient and Modern* (Edinburgh, 1838); HERKLESS, *Cardinal Beaton, Priest and Politician* (Edinburgh, 1891);

Diurnal of Occurrents in Scotland to the year 1575; KEITH, *Catalogue of the Bishops of Scotland* (1755), 23, 24; LYNDSAYE, *Tragedy of David Cardinall and archbishoppe of Sainct Andrewes* (London, 1546); *Epistolæ Reg. Scot.,* I, 339–341; HAY, *Ad Cardinalem D. Betoun Gratulatorius Panegyricus.*

D. O. HUNTER-BLAIR.

Beaton (or BETHUNE), JAMES, a Scottish Archbishop; b. c. 1473; d. at St. Andrews, 1539, was the sixth and youngest son of John Beaton of Balfour, in Fife. He graduated as Master of Arts at St. Andrews University in 1493, four years later was Precentor of Dornoch Cathedral (Diocese of Caithness), and in 1503 Provost of the Collegiate Church of Bothwell. Next year he became Prior of Whithorn and Abbot of Dunfermline, and in 1505 was made Treasurer of the Kingdom. In 1508 he was elected to the See of Galloway, in succession to George Vaus, but before his consecration he was chosen to succeed Robert Blackader (who had died, whilst on a pilgrimage to the Holy Land, in July, 1508) as Archbishop of Glasgow, and was consecrated at Stirling, 15 April, 1509. With the archbishopric he held the commendatory Abbeys of Arbroath and Kilwinning, and in 1515 he became Chancellor of Scotland. King James V, whose father had fallen at Flodden in 1513, was at this time a child of three, and Beaton, as one of the Council of Regency, without whose consent the queen-mother could not act, was one of the most important personages in the realm during the minority of the young king. The country was at this time distracted by the feuds between two of the regents, Angus and Arran, and Beaton, who was connected with the latter (for Arran had married as his third wife a daughter of Sir James Beaton of Creich), naturally espoused his kinsman's side. A well-known story tells how Bishop Gavin Douglas of Dunkeld came to Glasgow to urge the archbishop to allay the strife within the council, and how Beaton, striking his breast as he declared upon his conscience that he was powerless in the matter, caused the coat of mail which he wore under his ecclesiastical habit to rattle. "Alas, my Lord", said his brother bishop at this strange sound, "I fear your conscience clatters!" In 1522 Beaton was translated to St. Andrews, vacant by the death of Archbishop Foreman. As primate he threw all his powerful influence into the scale against the intrigues of Henry VIII to obtain predominance in Scotland; and it was greatly owing to his statesmanship that the old league with France was maintained, and that the young king chose for his bride Magdalen of France instead of Mary of England. Albany's jealousy had deprived Beaton of the chancellorship some years previously, and he was never reappointed, though he enjoyed the full favour of the king. A few months after the second marriage of James (to Mary of Guise) the primate got his nephew, David Cardinal Beaton, appointed his coadjutor with right of succession and he died in the autumn of 1539 in his castle at St. Andrews.

The stormy period in which Beaton's public life was cast, with France and England both intriguing for the alliance of Scotland, and the independence of the kingdom trembling in the balance, has made him, perhaps inevitably, appear to posterity more prominent as a statesman (in which quality there is no room for doubt as to his ability or his patriotism) than as a churchman and a prelate. There is, however, evidence that during both his thirteen years' tenure of the See of Glasgow and the seventeen years during which he held the primacy, he concerned himself closely with both the material and spiritual interests of the two dioceses, and in particular with the advancement of learning. In Glasgow he added and endowed altars in his cathedral, made additions also to the episcopal palace, which he encircled with a wall, and he erected stone bridges in various parts of the diocese. He was, moreover, as sedulous as his predecessors had been in safeguarding the ancient privileges of the archiepiscopal see. On his translation to St. Andrews he proved himself a constant benefactor to the university of that city, and he founded there a new college (St. Mary's) for the study of divinity, civil and canon law, medicine, and other subjects. The new college was confirmed by Pope Paul III in February, 1538, and was extended and completed by Beaton's successor, Archbishop Hamilton, sixteen years later. It still exists as the divinity college of the university. Finally, Beaton showed himself ever zealous for the preservation of the unity of the Faith in Scotland. Under the direct orders of the pope (Clement VII) and unhesitatingly supported by the king, he caused many of those engaged in propagating the new doctrines to be arrested, prosecuted, and in some cases put to death. Modern humanity condemns the cruel manner of their execution; but such severities were the result of the spirit of the age, for which Archbishop Beaton cannot be held responsible. There is no reason to doubt that his motive in sanctioning the capital punishment of notorious heretics was simply to avert the miseries which religious schism could not but entail on a hitherto united people.

Regist. Episcop. Glasg., II, 547 sqq.; THEINER, *Monumenta,* 553, 594, 597; *Acts Parl. Scotl.,* II; KEITH, *Hist. Cat. of Scott. Bishops* (1755); WALCOTT, *Ancient Church of Scotland,* 190, 191; TEULET, *Papiers d'état,* III.

D. O. HUNTER-BLAIR.

Beaton (or BETHUNE), JAMES, Archbishop of Glasgow, b. 1517; d. 24 April, 1603; the son of James Beaton of Balfarg (a younger son of John Beaton of Balfour) and nephew to Cardinal David Beaton. He was elected to the archbishopric in 1551, on the resignation of the archbishop-elect Andrew Gordon, and not being yet in priest's orders was ordained in Rome, and consecrated there on the 28th of August, 1552. For eight troublous years he administered the affairs of his diocese and stood faithfully by the queen-regent, Mary of Guise, in her dealings with the disaffected Scottish nobles, who were plotting the destruction of the ancient Church in order to enrich themselves with the spoils. In March, 1539, we find him assisting at the provincial council at Edinburgh summoned by the primate, Archbishop Hamilton—the last assembly of the kind which was to meet in Scotland for three hundred and twenty-six years. The events of 1560, the treaty of alliance with England against France, the commencement of the work of destruction of cathedrals and monasteries, and, finally, the death of the queen-regent, no doubt actuated Beaton in his resolve to quit the distracted kingdom. He repaired to Paris, taking with him a great mass of the muniments and registers of his diocese, and much church plate and other treasures, which he deposited in the Scots College.

Queen Mary immediately appointed him her ambassador at the French Court, and he remained, both up to her forced abdication in 1567, and during the rest of her life, her most faithful friend and adviser. He did not hesitate, after the murder of Darnley, to inform her frankly of the dark suspicions attaching to her, and the necessity of the assassins being punished. On the 15th of February, 1574, Beaton's name appears at the head of the list of the Catholic prelates and clergy declared outlaws and rebels by the Scottish Privy Council; but he nevertheless continued to enjoy in his exile the favour of the young king (James VI) who, about 1586, appointed him, as the late sovereign had done, ambassador at Paris. Beaton held several benefices in France, including the income of the Abbey De la Sie, in Poitou, and the treasurership of St. Hilary of Poitiers. His intimate association with the House of Guise had naturally led him to join with the League against Henry IV, and on its dissolution he was threatened with banishment; but by the intervention of Cardinals Bourbon and Sully and of the king himself, he was allowed to remain in France, where he was regarded with the greatest esteem. Perhaps the most remarkable testimony to the respect felt for his character in Scotland is to be found in the fact that in 1598, nearly forty years after the overthrow of the ancient Church, the archbishop was formally restored, by an act of the Scottish Parliament, to all his "heritages, honours, dignities, and benefices, notwithstanding that he has never acknowledged the religion professed within the realm". He survived to witness, a month before his death, the union of the English and Scottish crowns under King James. On the 24th of April, 1603, when James was actually on his way to London to take possession of his new kingdom, the archbishop died in Paris, in the eighty-sixth year of his age, and half a century after his episcopal consecration.

Beaton had lived in Paris for forty-three years, and had been Scottish ambassador to five successive kings of France. He was buried in the church of St. John Lateran at Paris, his funeral being attended by a great gathering of prelates, nobles, and common people. The poetical inscription on his tomb eulogizes him, in the exaggerated language of the times, as the greatest bishop and preacher of his age in the whole world. A sounder estimate of his worth is that of his Protestant successor in the See of Glasgow, Spottiswoode, who describes him as "a man honourably disposed, faithful to his queen while she lived and to the king her son; a lover of his country, and liberal to all his countrymen". No breath of scandal, in a scandalous age, ever attached to the honour of his name or the purity of his private life. Beaton left his property, including the archives of the Diocese of Glasgow, and a great mass of important correspondence, to the Scots College in Paris. Some of these documents had already been deposited by him in the Carthusian monastery in the same city. In the stress of the French Revolution many of these valuable manuscripts were packed in barrels and sent to St. Omers. These have unfortunately disappeared, but the papers left in the college were afterwards brought safely to Scotland, and are now preserved at Blairs College, the Catholic seminary near Aberdeen.

Regist. Episc. Glasg., pp. i–ix, liii; GRUB, *Eccles. Hist. of Scotl.*, II, 31, 155, 279; CHAMBERS, *Biogr. Dict. of Eminent Scotsmen*, I, 108, 109; *Acts of Parl. of Scotl.*, IV, 169, 170; *Reg. Priv. Coun. Scotl.*, II, 334; KEITH, *Cat. of Scott. Bishops*, 153, 154.

D. O. HUNTER-BLAIR.

Beatrix (or BEATRICE).—The name Beatrix has been borne by a certain number of holy persons, but no one of them has attained to any very eminent renown of sanctity.

I. BEATRIX, SAINT, a Roman virgin and martyr, inscribed in the Roman Martyrologium on 29 July. She is believed to have been the sister of the martyrs Simplicius and Faustinus whom she buried in the Via Portuensi. The legend says that she was then denounced as a Christian by Lucretius to whom she was betrothed, and was strangled by her own servants. Lucretius shortly afterwards died suddenly by the visitation of God.

II. BEATRIX D'ESTE, SAINT, d. 1262. Custom seems to warrant the giving the title Saint to one of the two holy nuns named Beatrix d'Este. She belonged to the family of the Norman Dukes of Apulia and was herself the daughter of the Marquess of Ferrara. She was betrothed to Galeazzo Manfredi of Vicenza, but he died of his wounds, after a battle, just before the wedding day, and his bride refused to return home, but attended by some of her maidens, devoted herself to the service of God, following the

Benedictine Rule, at San Lazzaro just outside Ferrara. Her cultus was approved by Clement XIV, and Pius VI allowed her festival to be kept on 19 January.

III. BEATRIX seems also to have been accepted as the Latin name of a noble lady of Bohemia, called in Bohemian Bozena, who lived at the end of the twelfth century and became a nun. Her brother was the famous St. Hrosnata, one of the patrons of the Kingdom of Bohemia. From the Bollandist life of Hrosnata (Acta SS., 4 July) it would seem that his sister Beatrix was honoured on 13 November.

IV. BEATRIX D'ESTE, aunt of the saint of that name, who is generally known as Blessed Beatrix, seems to have died in 1226 or perhaps in 1246. She was born in the castle of Este, became a nun in the convent of Santa Margherita at Solarolo, but not finding herself sufficiently secluded from the world, she founded another religious house in a deserted monastery at Gemmola. Her body after death was translated to the church of Santa Sophia at Padua and it was a tradition that when anything important was about to befall the family of Este she turned in her grave so that the noise was audible throughout the church. An account of her is given in the Acta SS. under 10 May.

V. BEATRIX, BLESSED, a Cistercian nun, first prioress of the convent called Nazareth near Lier in Brabant; d. 1269. She came of a wealthy family, but wishing to consecrate herself to God, at the age of seven she went to live with the Béguines. She afterwards joined the Cistercian nuns at Vallis Florida whence she was sent to commence the new foundation at Nazareth. She practised very severe austerities, wearing a girdle of thorns and compressing her body with cords. Our Lord is said to have appeared to her and to have pierced her heart with a fiery dart. After Nazareth was abandoned in a time of disturbance, the body of Blessed Beatrix is believed to have been translated by angels to Lier. Her day is 29 July, and a short life of her is included by Henriquez in his "Lilia".

VI. BEATRIX OF ORNACIEUX, BLESSED, d. about 1306, a Carthusian nun who founded a settlement of the order at Eymieux in the department of Drome. She was specially devout to the Passion of Christ and is said to have driven a nail through her left hand to help herself to realize the sufferings of the Crucifixion. Her cultus was confirmed by Pius IX in 1869. (See "Anal. jur. pont.", 1869, XI, 264.) There are modern lives by Bellanger and Chapuis and a full account in Lecoulteux, "Ann. Ord. Cath." (V, 5). Her feast is on 13 February.

VII. BEATRIX DA SILVA, BLESSED, a Portuguese nun, d. 1 September, 1490. In Portuguese she is known as Blessed Brites. She was a member of the house of Portalegre and descended from the royal family of Portugal. She accompanied the Portuguese Princess Isabel to Spain, when she married John II of Castile. There Beatrix seems to have aroused the jealousy of her royal mistress and was imprisoned for three days without food. After a vision of Our Blessed Lady, whom she saw attired in the blue mantle and white dress of the Conception Order which she was afterwards to found, Beatrix was allowed to retire to Toledo where she entered the Dominican Order. There she lived forty years, being specially honoured and frequently visited by Queen Isabel the Catholic. The latter aided her to found an order in honour of the Immaculate Conception, which adopted the Franciscan Rule. It was approved by Innocent VIII in 1489 and with some modifications by Julius II in 1511. Beatrix died ten days before the solemn inauguration of her new order. She is much honoured in Spain, and there is a life of her by Bivar. (See also the "Anal. jur. pont.", III, 549.)

A fuller notice of all the above will be found in Dunbar, *Dictionary of Saintly Women* (London, 1904), I, 107–110. Several of them also are noticed with more or less fullness in the *Acta SS.* on their respective days. Cf..Chevalier, *Rép. des sources hist.*, Bio-Bibl. (2d ed., 1905).

HERBERT THURSTON.

Beaufort, LADY MARGARET, Countess of Richmond and Derby, b. 1441; d. 1509, daughter and heiress of John Beaufort, first Duke of Somerset. Her father, the grandson of John of Gaunt, Duke of Lancaster, and great-grandson of Edward III, having died when she was three years old, she was brought up by her mother with the greatest care and devotion. Married while a mere child to John de la Pole, son of the Duke of Suffolk, whose ward she was, she refused to ratify the union on attaining the years of discretion and was then given in marriage to Edmund ap Meredith ap Tudor, Earl of Richmond and brother of Henry VI, of whom, with his brother Jasper, she became the ward on Suffolk's attainder. Edmund died (1456) a few months after the marriage, his posthumous son Henry, Earl of Richmond (afterwards Henry VII), being born 28 January, 1456. In 1459 Margaret married Lord Henry Stafford, her cousin on both her father's and mother's side, who traced his descent from Henry III. He died in 1482. Her third husband was Thomas, Lord Stanley, afterwards created Earl of Derby. She was instrumental in bringing to an end the disastrous Wars of the Roses; her son, the head of the Lancastrian party, who, as a result of the victory of Bosworth (1485) became King Henry VII, took in marriage Elizabeth of York, daughter of Edward IV.

Lady Margaret Beaufort was an exceedingly religious woman—"to God and to the Churche full obedient and tractable sechyng his honour and plesure full besyly" (Mornynge Remembraunce),— and a model of piety and devotion. Blessed John Fisher, who became her chaplain in 1502 and who had singular opportunities of understanding the nobleness of her character both as her spiritual director and as the instrument of her princely benefactions, bears testimony to her virtues and good works in the funeral oration preached at her Month's Mind. All England, he says, had cause to mourn her death. The poor would miss her bounteous alms: the students of both universities, "to whom she was as a moder", and the learned her patronage. The virtuous and devout lost in her a loving sister; religious and priests and clerks a powerful defender. Divine service "dayly was kept in her chappel with grate nombre of preests clerckes and children to her grate charge and cost". She was used to recite the Divine Office, as well as the Office of Our Lady, and to assist at many Masses daily. She made a public vow of chastity before Fisher and was enrolled as a "sister" in many monastic houses, among others in those of the Charterhouse, Croyland, Durham, and Westminster. In her own establishment she provided for the education of numbers of young men at her own cost, for many of whom she used her influence with great wisdom and discernment in the matter of ecclesiastical preferment.

Besides her private works of charity and of benevolence, and her benefactions to religious houses, she was a munificent patron of learning, establishing Readerships (now Professorships) in Divinity at Oxford and Cambridge (Royal Licenses, 1496, 1497: Charters, 8 September, 1503); and, in 1504, she made provision for a preacher to deliver six yearly sermons "to the praise and honour of the Holy Name of Jesus and the Annunciation of the Blessed Virgin Mary". By her liberality God's House at Cambridge was refounded as Christ's College (Royal License, 1505) for a master, twelve fellows, and forty-seven scholars. St. John's College, Cambridge, was also established, in the place of the ancient founda-

tion of St. John's Hospital, by provision made in her will, in a codicil to which she states her intention of founding and suitably endowing a college for a master and fifty scholars. She had a tender devotion to the Real Presence and translated into English and caused to be printed the fourth book of the "Imitation of Christ", which treats of the Blessed Sacrament. The "Mornynge Remembraunce" refers to the burning faith with which she received the Body of the Lord upon her death-bed. She also herself translated "The Mirroure of Golde for the sinful soule". Historians agree in extolling her many signal qualities and virtues, criticizing, if anything the "devotion those days afforded", the "errors of the age she lived in". The Catholic sees the important part she played in the civil and political history of her time, but perceives in her as well a singularly high example of a Christian life, in which a robust and sturdy faith bore its natural and wholesome fruits in deeds of liberality and benevolence.

FISHER, *The Funeral Sermon of Margaret, Countess of Richmond and Derby* (ed. T. BAKER; 2d ed. HYMERS, London, 1840); COOPER, *Memoir of Margaret, Countess of Richmond and Derby* (London, 1874); HALSTED, *Life of Margaret Beaufort, Countess of Richmond and Derby* (London, 1839); *Dublin Review*, VIII, p. 134; BRIDGETT, *Life of Blessed John Fisher* (London); BAKER, *History of the College of St. John the Evangelist*; LODGE, *Illustrious personages of Great Britain*.

FRANCIS AVELING.

Beaulieu Abbey (*abbatia quæ vocitatur Bellus Locus*) was a Cistercian house in Hampshire, one of the three monasteries founded by King John (c. 1204) and peopled by thirty monks from Cîteaux. The founder granted it a rich, if miscellaneous, endowment, including land in the New Forest, corn, money, one hundred and twenty cows, twelve bulls, a golden chalice, and an annual tun of wine. The buildings were dedicated in 1246, in the presence of Henry III and his queen, Richard Earl of Cornwall, and many prelates and nobles. Pope Innocent III constituted Beaulieu an "exempt abbey", with the right of sanctuary; and this was sought in 1471 by Ann Neville, wife of Warwick the King-maker, the day before the battle of Barnet. Twenty-six years later Perkin Warbeck fled to Beaulieu from the pursuing armies of Henry VII. Shortly before the suppression of the monastery in 1539, the Visitors' report mentioned that "thirty-two sanctuary-men, who were here for debt, felony, or murder", were living within the monastic precincts with their wives and families.

The first Abbot of Beaulieu was Hugh, and the last Thomas Stephens, elected in 1535. In the following year the abbey, with its annual revenue of £326, was granted to Thomas Wriothesley, afterwards Earl of Southampton. It passed later through the Dukes of Montagu to the Dukes of Buccleuch; and Lord Montagu of Beaulieu, the Duke of Buccleuch's nephew, now (1907) owns it. He resides in the old gatehouse of the abbey, which has been carefully restored. Little else remains of the domestic buildings, except the fine early English refectory, used as the parish church. The cloisters are in ruins, but the guest-house dormitory still exists, and has been restored. Not a stone is left of the beautiful church, 335 feet long, with a nave of nine bays, transepts, tower, and double-aisled choir with circular apse, of a purely Continental type most unusual in England. The late Duke of Buccleuch had the foundations of the church, with every column and buttress, carefully traced out and marked in sand. Netley Abbey, on the other side of Southampton Water, was founded from Beaulieu in 1239, by Henry III.

DUGDALE, *Monast. Anglic.*, V, 680 sqq.; *Registr. Cart. Mon. de Bello Loco* (Cott. MSS., Brit. Mus., Nero, A, xii, 1); TANNER, *Notitia Monastica* (Hampshire, vi); *Hampshire and the Isle of Wight* (Victoria County Histories), II, 140–146.

D. O. HUNTER-BLAIR.

Beaune, RENAUD DE, a French Bishop, b. in 1527,

at Tours; d. 1606 in Paris. Before entering the ecclesiastical state he held secular positions such as Councillor of Parliament and Chancellor of Francis of Valois, Duke of Touraine. The royal court greatly favoured him and appointed him to numerous ecclesiastical offices. In 1568, he became Bishop of Mende and in 1581, Archbishop of Bourges. King Henry IV of France named him his grand almoner in 1591 and appointed him to the Archbishopric of Sens in 1595; but the pope did not confirm the appointment until 1602. He was a member of the commission instituted by Henry IV in 1600 to reform the University of Paris. By his contemporaries, Renaud de Beaune was considered one of the greatest orators of the time. Posterity rated his work for the pacification of France higher than his oratorical talent. It was his influence that led to the successful issue of the conference of Suresnes, near Paris, in 1593. He promised the conversion of Henry IV and brought about peace between the latter and the "League". He received the abjuration of the king, and, although the absolution of an excommunicated prince was reserved to the pope, absolved him, July, 1593, on condition, however, that the approval of the Roman authorities should be obtained. In spite of this condition the absolution was invalid, and the action of the archbishop caused, at least partly, the delay in obtaining the papal confirmation of his nomination to the See of Sens. The principal works of de Beaune are: (1) Some discourses, among them funeral orations on Mary, Queen of Scots (1587), and on Queen Catharine de Medici (1589); (2) translation of the Psalms of David into French (Paris, 1575, 1637); (3) "La réformation de l'université de Paris (1605, 1667).

CHALMEL, *Histoire de Touraine* (Paris, 1828), IV, 29–32; GAUTIER in *Grande Encyc.*, V, 1054.

N. A. WEBER.

Beauregard, JEAN-NICOLAS, celebrated French pulpit orator, b. at Metz in Lorraine, 4 Dec., 1733; d. at the castle of Gröningen in Southern Germany, 27 July, 1804. He entered the Society of Jesus at Nancy, 30 Sept., 1749. After his noviceship and higher studies, he taught classics and rhetoric with distinction for six years at the colleges of the Society in Nancy, Verdun, Strasburg, and Pont-à-Mousson. His theological studies, which followed, were made in Strasburg, and after the year of third probation Father Beauregard was back at Nancy for the year 1766–67 as perfect of studies. The next year he was assigned to the task of preaching, which thenceforth became the work of his life. Having gained a wonderful reputation in the lesser towns of France, he was summoned to Paris, where his success was even more phenomenal. Especially noteworthy was the course of sermons preached before the Court during the Lent of 1789, in which Father Beauregard is said to have clearly foretold the evils that were about to engulf France. Father Beauregard escaped the first terrors of the Revolution, but was forced to flee to London in 1794. Later on he established himself at Mæstricht, then at Cologne, while his declining years were spent at the castle of the Princess Sophie of Hohenlohe-Bartenstein. His works, which for the most part are still only in manuscript, consist of sermons and letters. A collection of his sermons, made by one of his hearers, was first printed at Paris in 1820, often reprinted, and later embodied in Migne's "Orateurs Sacrés", vol. LXXI.

DANIEL, *Le P. Beauregard, sa vie et ses travaux;* SOMMERVOGEL, *Bibl. de la c. de J.*, I; HAMY, *Galerie illustrée de la c. de J.*, I.

JOHN F. X. MURPHY.

Beauregard, PIERRE GUSTAVE TOUTANT, soldier, b. near New Orleans, Louisiana, U. S. A., 28 May, 1818; d. there 20 February, 1893. He was appointed to the U. S. Military Academy at West Point and graduated in 1838. Assigned first to an artillery regiment, he passed to the engineers and served thereafter in that corps. During the war with Mexico he was engaged in the siege operations at Vera Cruz, Cerro Gordo, Contreras, Chapultepec, and the city of Mexico, being wounded twice in the last-mentioned battle (13, 14 September, 1847), and was brevetted major. After fourteen years of continuous service he was made Captain of Engineers, 3 March, 1853. The war over, he was given supervision of the construction work along the Gulf coast, and on 23 January, 1861, was detailed as superintendent of the Military Academy at West Point. He almost immediately resigned, however, on 20 February, 1861, and threw in his lot with the seceding States of the Southern Confederacy. He was placed in command at Charleston, South Carolina, and began the Civil War by the attack on Fort Sumter. When the fort was evacuated he was sent to Virginia and was in charge of the Confederate forces in the battle of Bull Run, 21 July. He was then sent to Tennessee, was second in command to A. S. Johnson at the battle of Shiloh; succeeding Johnson, when the latter was killed, he nearly routed the Union army in the first day's fight. Reinforcements arriving for his adversary, Gen. Grant, he was forced to retreat on the next day. Beauregard's failing health compelled him to take a leave of absence for three months, when, with a promotion to a general's rank, he was again placed in command at Charleston, where he successfully resisted for a year and a half the siege operations of Gen. Gilmore and his naval assistants. In May, 1864, he joined Lee in Virginia and held Petersburg against the Union advance. In October of the same year he was made commander of the military division of the West and sent to Georgia, and then to North Carolina where he united with Gen. J. E. Johnson to resist the march of Gen. Sherman. The attempt was futile and they surrendered, April, 1865. After the war he became president of the New Orleans, Jackson and Mississippi Railroad, and Adjutant-General of the State of Louisiana. In 1866 he refused the offer of the chief command of the Rumanian army, and in 1869 that of the army of the Khedive of Egypt. He lent his name to the Louisiana Lottery and as its salaried manager was for several years one of its chief supporters. He was the author of "Principles and Maxims of the Art of War" (Charleston, 1863) and "Report of the Defence of Charleston" (Richmond, 1864).

ROMAN, *Military Operations of Gen. Beauregard in the War between the States, 1861–65* (New York, 1884); *Cycl. of Am. Biog.* (New York, 1900).

THOMAS F. MEEHAN.

Beauvais (BELLOVACUM), DIOCESE OF, a suffragan of the archiepiscopal See of Reims. The Dioceses of Beauvais, Noyon, and Senlis having been suppressed by the Concordat of 1802 for the benefit of Amiens, a see was re-established at Beauvais in 1822, having within its jurisdiction the former Diocese of Beauvais and a large portion of the ancient Dioceses of Noyon and Senlis. A pontifical Brief of 1851 authorizes the incumbents of the See of Beauvais to call themselves Bishops of Beauvais, Noyon, and Senlis.

Diocese of Beauvais.—Tradition looks upon St. Lucianus, sent to Beauvais by Pope Fabianus and martyred, about 275, with his companions Maxianus and Julianus, as the founder of Christianity in that place. The martyrdom of St. Romana under Diocletian, of St. Just during the atrocious persecution by the legendary Rictiovarus (about 410), of St. Maxentia, daughter of the King of Scotland, who, about 450, preferred to die rather than follow her fiancé, render the primitive Church of Beauvais illustrious. The exact date of the foundation of the episcopal see is obscure, but we know that the bishop who occupied it from 632 to 660 was the thirteenth incumbent. Among its bishops Beauvais counts Odo (860–881), charged by Nicholas I in 867 to answer with Hincmar the grievances of Photius; Gui (1063–85), who founded St. Quentin of Beauvais, the great school of theology; Pierre Cauchon (1420–32), identified with the condemnation of Joan of Arc; Jean Juvenal des Ursins (1433–44), author of the Chronicle of Charles VI; Cardinal Odet de Châtillon (1535–62), nephew of Coligny, who turned Protestant at

MAIN ENTRANCE, CATHEDRAL OF BEAUVAIS

the Reformation; François-Joseph de la Rochefoucauld (1772–92), martyred in the Carmelite prison in 1792; and Feutrier (1825–30), minister of ecclesiastical affairs in the Martignac cabinet.

Diocese of Senlis.—The Church founded at Senlis by St. Rieul (Regulus) about 300, had its ninth bishop, St. Levangius, in 511. Saints Sanctinus, Agmarus, and Autbertus were bishops in the sixth and seventh centuries.

Diocese of Noyon.—The headquarters of the city of the Veromandui, who undoubtedly had a bishop from the beginning of the fourth century, having been destroyed by the barbarians, the bishops were without a residence until St. Médard (530–545), fourteenth bishop, installed himself at Noyon. This city counted among its bishops the goldsmith St. Eloi (Eligius, 640–659), Dagobert's prime minister; St. Mummolenus (second half of seventh century), and St. Eunutius (eighth century). The Belgian See of Tournai was cut off from Noyon in 1146.

These sees played an important part in the history of France during the Carlovingian, and at the beginning of the Capetian, period. A council convoked at Beauvais by Charles the Bald, in 845, elected Hincmar Archbishop of Reims. At Compiègne where, next to his hunting-lodge, Charles the Bald had built the great Abbey of Notre Dame, placing therein the bodies of Sts. Cornelius and Cyprian, and where Kings Louis the Stammerer and Eudes were crowned and buried, there were held, in the course of the ninth century, numerous councils which regulated the political and religious questions of the time. A council at Compiègne in 1092 forced

the heretic Roscelin to retire, and one at Senlis in 1310, condemned nine Templars. Being Count of Beauvais from 1013, and Peer of France from the twelfth century, the Bishop of Beauvais wore the royal mantle at the coronation of the Kings of France; it was he, who, with the Bishop of Langres, was wont to raise the king from his throne to present him to his people. The Bishop of Noyon was both duke and peer. The monastic life was established in this region by St. Evrost in the sixth, and St. Germer in the seventh, century.

The medieval Cathedrals of Beauvais and Senlis are inferior in point of interest to that of Noyon, which is one of the most beautiful monuments of the twelfth century. During the Middle Ages, on each recurring 14th of January, the Feast of Asses was celebrated in the Beauvais Cathedral, in commemoration of the flight of the Virgin into Egypt (see ASSES, FEAST OF), and every year, on 27 June, there is a religious procession through the streets of Beauvais to perpetuate Jeanne Hachette's opposition to Charles the Bold in 1472. John Calvin was a native of Noyon, and Cardinal Pierre d'Ailly was born in Compiègne. The places of pilgrimage are: Notre Dame de Bon Secours at Compiègne, a shrine erected in 1637 as an expression of gratitude for the raising of the siege of the city by the Spaniards; Notre Dame de Bon Secours at Gannes; Notre Dame de Bon Secours at Feuquières; Notre Dame du Hamel at L'Hamel Notre-Dame; Notre Dame de Bon Secours at Montmélian; Notre Dame de Senlis at Senlis; Notre Dame des Fleurs at Ville-en-Braye.

In 1899 the following institutions were found in the diocese: 6 infant asylums, 44 infant schools, 14 girls' orphanages, 1 free industrial school, 2 *patronages*, 2 charity kitchens, 9 hospitals and hospices, 1 house of retreat, 12 homes for the aged, 9 communities devoted to care for the sick in their homes, all conducted by nuns; and 2 *patronages* under the care of the Brothers of the Christian Schools. In 1900 there were the following religious orders for men: Marists at Senlis, Redemptorists at Thury in Valois, and Fathers of the Holy Ghost at Beauvais. Among the orders for women there were no congregations belonging exclusively to the diocese. At the close of 1905 the Diocese of Beauvais had 407,808 inhabitants, 39 pastorates, 501 succursal parishes (mission churches), and 10 curacies.

Gallia christiana (1751), IX, 691–773; *Instrumenta*, 239–280; X, 1378–1465; *Instrumenta*, 423–520; IX, 918–1036; *Instrumenta*, 359–394; DELETTRE, *Histoire du diocèse de Beauvais depuis son établissement au troisième siècle* (Beauvais, 1842–1843); VITET, *Monographie de Notre Dame de Noyon* (Paris, 1854); DUCHESNE, *Fastes épiscopaux*, I, 13–14; CHEVALIER, *Topobibl.*, 342–344.

GEORGES GOYAU.

Beauvais, GILLES-FRANÇOIS-DE, Jesuit writer and preacher, b. at Mans, France, 7 July, 1693; d. probably at Paris about 1773. He entered the Society of Jesus 16 August, 1709, and taught belles-lettres, rhetoric, and philosophy. After ordination he was assigned to preach and gave the Advent course at Court in 1774, during which year he published his "Life of the Ven. Ignatius Azevedo, S. J.", and in 1746 that of Ven. John de Britto, S. J., the latter of which has been translated into English by Father Faber of the Oratory (Richardson, London, 1851). He wrote a number of other works of devotion and for spiritual reading.

SOMMERVOGEL, *Bibl. de la c. de J.*, IX, 1080–82.

MARK J. MCNEAL.

Beauvais, JEAN-BAPTISTE-CHARLES-MARIE DE, a French bishop, b. at Cherbourg, 17 October, 1731; d. at Paris, 4 April, 1790. The sermons he preached before the court during Advent, 1768, and Lent, 1773, raised his reputation as a pulpit orator to such a height that he was promoted to the See of Senez. He distinguished himself on all occasions by his devotion to the Church and is considered one of the best preachers of the eighteenth century. In 1783 he resigned his bishopric and settled at Paris. In 1789 he was made a member of the States-General. His sermons were printed at Paris in 1806, prefaced by an interesting account, written by the Abbé Boulogne, of the preacher and his discourses. The most celebrated of his funeral orations is the one on Louis XV; this discourse, however, failed to please the courtiers. The best of his panegyrics are one on St. Augustine, delivered before the Assembly of the Clergy of France, and one on St. Louis, before the Académie Française.

De Feller, *Biographie universelle* (Paris, 1847); Bernard, *La chaire française au dix-huitième siècle* (Paris, 1901).

Jos. N. Gignac.

Beauvan, René-François de. See Toulouse.

Beaven, Thomas. See Springfield, Diocese of.

Bébian, Roch-Amboise-Auguste, b. 4 August, 1789 at Pointe-à-Pitre, Guadeloupe; d. there 24 February, 1839. His father sent him to France, where he was committed to the care of his godfather, the Abbé Sicard, the well-known educator of the deaf and dumb. The latter put him under the direction of Abbé Jauffret then exhibiting a great interest in the education of deaf-mutes. After a brilliant course at the Lycée Charlemagne in Paris, Bébian devoted himself to the study of the system of education of the deaf and dumb. He followed the courses of instruction given by Abbé Sicard and gave special attention to Laurent Clerc, a deaf-mute who afterwards became president of an institution for the deaf and dumb at Hartford, Connecticut, U. S. A. As prefect of studies in the institution for the deaf and dumb at Paris, he directed all his efforts to finding the signs best adapted, in precision and extension of meaning, to the expression of the ideas of the deaf and dumb.

Bébian published the result of his studies in his first book, "Essai sur les sourds-muets et sur le langage naturel" (1817). His principal works, under the titles "Mimographie" (1822) and "Manuel d'enseignement pratique des sourds-muets" (1822), laid down the principles used in the institution for the deaf and dumb in Paris. After leaving this school, he published several other works, the most important being "L'éducation des sourds-muets mise à la portée des instituteurs primaires et de tous les parents". Having refused the direction of the schools for the deaf and dumb of St. Petersburg and New York he founded a similar institution at Paris on the boulevard Montparnasse; later he became director of the school of Rouen and finally went back to Guadeloupe, where he founded a school for the negroes. He had already written, in 1819, "Eloge historique de l'abbé de l'Epée", which was awarded the prize offered by the Academy of Sciences.

G. M. Sauvage.

Bec, Abbey of.—The Benedictine Abbey of Bec, or Le Bec, in Normandy, was founded in the earlier part of the eleventh century by Herluin, a Norman knight, who about 1031 left the court of Count Gilbert of Brionne to devote himself to a life of religion. The abbey itself is now in ruins, but the modern name of the place, Bec-Helloin, preserves the memory of its founder. There is some difference in reckoning the date of the foundation, for Herluin's religious family was twice moved to new quarters, and any one of the three dates may be regarded as the beginning of the famous abbey. Herluin's first foundation was at Bonneville, or Burneville, where a monastery was built in 1034, and here in 1037, Herluin was consecrated abbot. But in a few years it was decided to move to a more suitable site, two miles away, by the banks of the Bec (Danish, *Bæk*, a brook) which gave its name to the abbey. This removal took place about 1040. About two years after this, Lanfranc,

who had already become famous for his lectures at Avranches, left the scene of his triumphs and came to bury himself in this humble home of piety. At first his retreat was unknown to the world without, while his new brethren seem to have been unaware of his worth. But within a few years from his arrival at Bec, he had opened a new school, and scholars were flocking from all parts to listen to his lectures. The abbey grew and prospered, and the good work begun by the simple piety of Herluin was crowned by the learning of Lanfranc. Before long it was necessary to build a larger and more lasting monastery. As the site first chosen had proved to be unsatisfactory, the new foundations were laid in another spot, higher up the valley of the Bec and further away from the water. This important change was really the work of Lanfranc, who was now the prior and the right hand of the aged abbot. As the first change of site was closely followed by the arrival of one great teacher, this second foundation was almost coincident with the coming of a yet greater glory of the abbey, St. Anselm of Canterbury.

The future archbishop and Doctor of the Church first came to Bec in 1060 while the work of building was in progress, and the year before the monks were able to move into their new home. In 1062, Lanfranc was appointed Abbot of Caen, and Anselm, in spite of the fact that he had been such a short time at Bec, was chosen to take his place as prior. In the school also the famous master was succeeded by his yet more illustrious disciple. When the new abbey church at Bec, which had taken some fifteen years to build, was finished in 1077, it was appropriately consecrated by Lanfranc, who was now Archbishop of Canterbury. Abbot Herluin, the founder, died in the following year, and Anselm succeeded him as second Abbot of Bec. Only six years later Abbot Anselm was called to take the place of his old master, Lanfranc, as Archbishop of Canterbury. The abbey continued in existence down to the French Revolution. The long list of abbots from the eleventh to the eighteenth century, given in "Gallia Christiana" (XI, 222–239), contains many of the most illustrious French names, and shows that even in its later years Bec was a place of some importance. It had suffered much in the Hundred Years War with England, and still more in the Huguenot troubles. But after these days of desolation it was restored to something of its former state by the Congregation of St. Maur. Thus the chief house of medieval learning was renewed by the fathers of modern historical scholarship. This restoration was too soon undone by the forces of revolution; but the Maurists rendered a more enduring service to the abbey by their admirable editions of Lanfranc, Anselm, and the "Chronicon Beccense". Of the old abbey whose erection is recorded in that chronicle, some ruins still remain. The later buildings now serve as a military station. This transformation is a curious counterpart to the happier change effected at Fort Augustus.

In its later years the Abbey of Bec was but one among many religious houses doing good work for learning and religion, but in the golden age of Lanfranc and Anselm it held a unique position, and exerted a far-reaching influence on the course of church history and the advancement of theological learning. In its early days the abbey gave three archbishops to the See of Canterbury: Lanfranc, Anselm, and Theobald the fifth abbot. Among other prelates who came from this famous school, it will be enough to mention Pope Alexander II, William, Archbishop of Rouen, Arnost, Gundulf, and Ernulf, Bishops of Rochester, Ivo of Chartres, Fulk of Beauvais, and Gilbert Crispin, Abbot of Westminster. Of the influence of Lanfranc's work at Bec John Richard Green says very truly: "His teaching raised Bec in a few years into the most famous school of

Christendom. It was in fact the first wave of the intellectual movement which was spreading from Italy to the ruder countries of the West. The whole mental activity of the time seemed concentrated in the group of scholars who gathered around him; the fabric of the canon law and of medieval scholasticism with the philosophical scepticism which first awoke under its influence, all trace their origin to Bec" (A Short History of the English People, I, ii, 3). When we remember how deep and far-reaching has been the influence of its greatest scholar, Anselm, on later theology, we cannot but feel that though the old Abbey may be in ruins the school of Bec still lives on, and all may sit at the feet of its famous masters.

Chronicon Beccensis (1034–1468), ed. D'ACHÉRY in *Lanfranci Cant. Op.* (Paris, 1648), app. 1–32 (an excerpt from an old history of the abbey carrying the story to 1591); also in *P. L.*, CL; GILBERT CRISPIN, *Life of Herluin* in *P. L.*, CL, 695 sqq.; MILO CRISPIN, *Vitæ Lanfr. et al. abb.* in *d'Achéry*, op. cit., 1 sqq.; 311 sqq. (containing lives of the next four abbots). Cf. also lives and letters of Anselm and Lanfranc; RULE, *The Life and Times of St. Anselm* (London, 1883); RAGEY, *Histoire de Saint Anselme* (Paris, 1889), the last two containing full and graphic accounts of the foundation and early history of Bec; PORÉE, *L'Abbaye du Bec au dix-huitième siècle* (Evreux, 1901).

W. H. KENT.

Becan (VERBRECK, VAN DER BRECK), MARTIN, controversialist, b. at Hilvarenbeek, Brabant, Holland, 6 January, 1563; d. at Vienna, 24 January, 1624. He entered the Society of Jesus, 22 March, 1583, taught theology for twenty-two years at Würzburg, Mainz, and Vienna, and was confessor to Emperor Ferdinand II from 1620 until the time of his death. He possessed a style clear and dignified, and noticeably free from the bitterness which marked the polemical literature of the day. His writings were directed principally against Calvin, Luther, and the Anabaptists; of these his "Manuale Controversiarum", Mainz, 1623, treating of predestination, free will, the Eucharist, and the infallibility of the Church, passed through several editions. For a complete list see Sommervogel, "Bibliothèque de la compagnie de Jésus" (I, col. 1091–1111), wherein are mentioned by title forty-six volumes. His chief theological work, "Summa Theologiæ Scholasticæ (4 vols. 4to, Mainz, 1612) is in great part a compendium of Suarez's Commentary on St. Thomas Aquinas. By a decree of the Congregation of the Index, 3 January, 1613, his book "Controversia Anglicana de potestate regis et pontificis" was put on the Index *donec corrigatur*, not so much to condemn certain exaggerations it contained as to prevent the faculty of theology of Paris from condemning it and at the same time adding some declarations against papal authority. The "Controversia" was corrected and published somewhat later with a dedication to Pope Paul V. Becan, in 1608, published at Mainz, "Aphorismi doctrinæ Calvinistarum ex eorum libris, dictis et factis collecti", in reply to Calvin's "Aphorismi doctrinæ Jesuitarum". Aphorismus XV, "Jesuitæ vero qui se maxime nobis opponunt, aut necandi aut si id commode fieri non potest, ejiciendi, aut certe mendaciis ac calumniis opprimendi sunt" (The Jesuits, our chief adversaries, ought to be put to death, or, if that cannot be easily done, they ought to be banished, or, at any rate, overwhelmed with lies and calumnies), has been misconstrued so as to make it appear that Becan wished to say that Aphorismus XV contained the very words of Calvin. That such was not Becan's intention is clear from the title of the book "Aphorismi ex eorum libris dictis et factis collecti" and the development shows that the author was only drawing what he considered a logical conclusion from the action of the Calvinists of the time. A lengthy discussion about this aphorism was carried on by A. Sabatier in the "Journal de Genève" (26 January, 1896; 10 May, 1896) and the "Revue Chrétienne"

(1 March, 1896; 1 June, 1896), and by J. Brucker in the "Etudes" (15 April, and 15 July, 1896).

SOMMERVOGEL, *Bibliothèque de la c. de J.*, I, 1091–1111; DE BACKER, *Bibl. des écriv. de la c. de J.*, I, 56; BRUCKER in *Dict. de théol. cath.*, s. v.; HURTER, *Nomenclator*, I, 293.

FRANCIS D. O'LAUGHLIN.

Beccarelli, GIUSEPPE. See QUIETISM.

Beccus (Gr. Βεκκος), JOHN, Patriarch of Constantinople in the second half of the thirteenth century, one of the few Greek ecclesiastics who were sincerely in favour of reunion with the Church of Rome. He was born in the early part of the thirteenth century in Constantinople, where he joined the ranks of the clergy. His ability, learning, and moral qualities marked him for advancement, and he was soon promoted to the office of *chartophylax*. The Patriarch Arsenius (1255–66) held him in high esteem, and defended him against the emperor's displeasure which he had incurred by suspending a priest who blessed a marriage in the church of an imperial palace without permission. Beccus, however, recovered the imperial favour, and gradually gained the confidence of Michael Palæologus (1259–82). He was selected repeatedly to conduct delicate or difficult negotiations with foreign potentates. His sentiments towards the Christians of Western Europe, or the Latins, were not at all friendly at the beginning. When, after the destruction of the Latin Empire in Constantinople, the Emperor Michael Palæologus conceived the plan of reuniting the Greek and the Latin Churches, the Patriarch Joseph (1268–75) and his *chartophylax*, John Beccus, were strongly opposed to it. In a meeting of the ecclesiastics of Constantinople held about the year 1273, Beccus declared in the presence of the emperor that the Latins were in reality heretics, although they were not called thus. His audacity was punished with imprisonment. In his enforced retirement Beccus found leisure to study the points of difference between the Greeks and Latins. The emperor, anxious to win him over, sent such writings to him as were favourable to the views of the Latin Church, among them the works of Nicephorus Blemmida or Blemmydes. From the works of Athanasius, Cyril of Alexandria, Maximus the Confessor, and others he learned that the Greek and the Latin Fathers substantially agreed on matters of Christian faith. The only difference was, that while the Latin writers considered the Holy Ghost to proceed from Father and Son, the Greeks preferred to state that He proceeds from the Father through the Son. Once satisfied on this subject, he became actively interested in the work of reunion, and retained these sentiments to the end. Meanwhile the union was happily concluded in the council held at Lyons (1274) and proclaimed at Constantinople (January, 1275). The Patriarch Joseph could not be induced to accept it, and was removed from his office according to a previous understanding. John Beccus was elected in his place. On the 2d of June, Pentecost Sunday, 1275, he received the episcopal consecration.

After his elevation to the patriarchal see one of his main objects was to convince of the lawfulness of the union those of the Greeks who were either partisans of the schism or else had renounced it only in a half-hearted way. In April, 1277, a synod was held in Constantinople, where the union was again approved; a letter was also written to Pope John XXI (1276–77), which acknowledged the papal primacy and the orthodoxy of the Latin doctrine on the Procession of the Holy Ghost. When a faction of the schismatics rebelled against the emperor, John Beccus excommunicated them (July, 1277), while Michael Palæologus defeated their armies. In 1279, Beccus assured the legates of Pope Nicholas III (1277–80), then in Constantinople, that the Greek Church entirely agreed with Rome in matters of doctrine. Several synods were held shortly afterwards, all with the same object in view; and in one of them it was discovered that a certain Penteclesiota had tampered with a passage of St. Gregory of Nyssa, where testimony was rendered to the procession of the Holy Ghost from Father and Son. Finally, he tried also to defend in writing the doctrines of the Latin Church, although at first he had resolved not to notice the many pamphlets of the schismatics, lest he should make the dissensions even greater.

The intercourse of Beccus with the emperor was not always pleasant. The patriarch pleaded much with his imperial master for the needy and for those unjustly condemned by the officers of the law. But the emperor grew weary of these importunities and restricted the patriarch's liberty of access to him. Matters were aggravated by the enemies of the union, who purposely calumniated Beccus, as if his conduct were immoral, as if he misused the treasures of the Church, and insulted or even cursed the emperor. Such accusations were not altogether unwelcome; and the emperor, to show his indignation, curtailed the patriarch's jurisdiction over all the sacred places that were outside of Constantinople. Thereupon Beccus grew tired of his office, resigned, and withdrew to a monastery in March, 1279. But as the papal legates arrived soon after, he was induced to resume his duties and to treat with the representatives of the pope, which he did as related before. After the death of Michael Palæologus, which occurred 11 December, 1282, the union with Rome was at once denounced by the new Emperor Andronicus (1282–1328); and Beccus was forced to resign. In a synod held in 1283, he was forced to sign his name to a creed prepared by his enemies, and to abdicate the patriarchal office, after which he was banished to the city of Prusa in Bithynia. In 1284, he was again summoned to a synod in Constantinople; but he defended energetically the doctrines of the Western Church, for which he was confined to the fortress of St. Gregory on the Black Sea, where he underwent many privations. Nothing, however, could induce him to sacrifice his convictions. He still continued to write in favour of the Latin Church. Death brought an end to his sufferings about the year 1298.

The principal works of John Beccus (in P. G., CXLI) are the following: "Concerning the Union and Peace of the Churches of Ancient and New Rome"; "The Epigraphæ", a collection of passages from the Fathers; "On the Procession of the Holy Ghost"; the polemical works against Photius, Andronicus Camateros, and Gregory of Cyprus; the works addressed to his friends Theodore, Bishop of Sugdæa in Moesia, and a certain Constantine; a letter to Agallianos Alexios, a deacon of Constantinople; several orations and an "Apologia"; his "Testamentum" written while in prison. In all of these writings there is a sincere conviction of the truth defended by him, and great enthusiasm for the peace of the Church through union with Rome, among whose Greek adherents Beccus holds easily the first place.

GEORGIUS PACHYMERES, MICHAEL PALÆOLOGUS, and ANDRONICUS PALÆOLOGUS in P. G., CXLIII, CXLIV; NICEPHORUS GREGORAS, Historia Byzantina, ibid., CXLVIII; RAYNALDUS, Annales eccl. (Lucca, 1748), III; HEFELE, Conciliengeschichte (Freiburg, 1890), VI; KRUMBACHER, Geschichte der byzant. Litteratur (Munich, 1897); HERGENRÖTHER in Kirchenlex., s. v.; HURTER, Nomenclator (Innsbruck, 1899) IV.

FRANCIS J. SCHAEFER.

Beche, JOHN (alias THOMAS MARSHALL), BLESSED, English Benedictine abbot and martyr; date of birth unknown; d. at Colchester, England, 1 December, 1539. Educated at Oxford (probably at Gloucester Hall, now Worcester College), he took his degree of Doctor of Divinity in 1515, and within the next

fifteen years ruled the Abbey of St. Werburgh, Chester, his name appearing as twenty-sixth on the roll of abbots of that foundation. He was elected Abbot of St. John's, Colchester, 10 June, 1530, and, with sixteen of his monks, took Henry VIII's Oath of Supremacy, 7 July, 1534. The year 1535 brought the martyrdoms of the three Carthusian priors (4 May), of Bl. John Fisher (22 June), and of St. Thomas More (6 July), all five for the Divine right of the Roman Church to universal supremacy in spirituals. Beche was so deeply affected by these examples that his unguarded expressions of reverence and veneration for the martyrs, reported by spies, drew down upon him the resentment of the schismatical king. In November, 1538, the Abbot of St. John's further exasperated Henry and his ministers by denying the legal right of a royal commission to confiscate his abbey. Within a year of this he was committed to the Tower on a charge of treason, was discharged from custody, and rearrested some time before the 1st of November, 1539. Witnesses were found to testify how the abbot had said that God would "take vengeance for the putting down of these houses of religion", that Fisher and More "died like good men and it was pity of their deaths", and that the reason for the king's revolt from Catholic unity was the king's desire to marry Anne Boleyn. In his own examination the abbot yielded to human weakness and tried to explain away his former assertions of Catholic truth. In spite of these lapses he eventually received the crown of martyrdom. Tried at Colchester, by a special commission, in November, 1539, he no longer pleaded against the charge of contumacy to the newly established order of things. He was convicted and executed. An anonymous contemporary partisan of Henry's schism, quoted by Dom Bede Camm in "Engl. Martyrs", I, 400, says of Abbot Beche and others who died at that time for the same offences, "It is not to be as these trusty traitors have so valiantly jeopardized a joint for the Bishop of Rome's sake . . . his Holiness will look upon their pains as upon Thomas Becket's, seeing it is for like matter". The decree of Pope Leo XIII by which Abbot John Beche received beatification bears date 13 May, 1895.

CAMM, Lives of the Eng. Martyrs (London, 1904), I; GASQUET, Henry VIII and the English Monasteries (London, 1899), I, 398 and II, 373; GAIRDNER, Preface to Calendar of Papers and Domestic (London, 1895); MOORE ed. Cartularium Monasterii S. Joannis de Colecestria (London, 1897); Record Office: Crumwell Correspondence, VI, 145.

E. MACPHERSON.

Beckedorff, GEORG PHILIPP LUDOLF VON, b. at Hanover, 14 April, 1778; d. at Grünhof, 27 February, 1858. He first studied theology at Jena, then medicine at Göttingen, where he obtained the degree of doctor in 1799. In 1810 he gave up the medical profession and accepted the office of tutor to the crown-prince of Anhalt-Bernburg. For seven years he lived at Ballenstedt. In the movement for the reunion of the churches, then agitating the various religious sects, he took an active part by able and timely publications. An appeal "To Young Men of Germany over the body of the murdered Kotzebue" brought him into a wider field of action. The Prussian Government secured his services, and he became a member, first of the High Privy Council, then of the Ministry of Public Worship, and later on, supervisor of the public school system. In this capacity he contributed largely, in co-operation with Nicolovius, to the uplifting of popular education and published in nine volumes the "Year Book of the Prussian Schools". The State recognized his efficiency by appointing him attorney-general for the University of Berlin. His official duties and inclinations kept Beckedorff in close touch with the religious union movement and while studying the history and claims of the various sects, his conviction became stronger that the Catholic Church was the true Apostolic Church. It was not an easy step for one in his position to follow up his conviction; but the death of a beloved child decided him and he informed the king of his resolve. The kindly crown-prince advised a consultation with Bishop Sailer of Ratisbon, and a few days' intercourse with this prelate sufficed to prepare Beckedorff for abjuration, Holy Communion, and Confirmation in June, 1827. His dismissal from public office quickly followed and he withdrew with his family from the capital to Grünhof in Pomerania.

Beckedorff now devoted himself to the management of his estate and the education of his children, but his abilities were too marked to suffer this retirement for long. In spite of repeated refusals of the Government to ratify his election, his admiring countrymen chose him again as their deputy. It was not until the accession of King Frederick William, however, that his rights and merits were recognized. In reparation for the injustice done, the king raised him to the nobility and made him president of the state agricultural department. Two volumes on agricultural economy attest his competence in an entirely new office and his zeal in the service of his country. With the still higher aim of furthering religious union and peace he published several works on the mutual relations of family, school, State, and Church. His work, "The Catholic Truth, Words of Peace", went through three editions and still ranks as an excellent popular manual of apologetics. Nowhere was Beckedorff's influence felt more than at Grünhof and in its neighbourhood. Having learned that some Catholics were scattered throughout the district, he built a church for them and maintained the resident priest in his own house. He founded also a school and home for poor children and entrusted them to the Sisters of Charity; both of these institutions began to flourish during his lifetime.

ROSENTHAL, *Convertitenbilder aus dem XIX. Jahrhundert* (Ratisbon, 1889), I, i, 481 sqq.

CHARLES B. SCHRANTZ.

Becker, THOMAS ANDREW, sixth Bishop of Savannah, Georgia, U. S. A., b. at Pittsburg, Pennsylvania, 20 December, 1832; d. at Washington, Georgia, 29 July, 1889. His parents were German Protestants and he became a convert in early manhood. He made his theological course at the College of Propaganda, Rome, where he was ordained 18 July, 1859. Returning to the United States, he was given charge of a mission at Martinsburg, West Virginia, whence he went to Mount St. Mary's College, Emmitsburg, to act as one of the professors. Archbishop Spalding then made him his secretary. Later he was sent to St. Peter's Church, Richmond, Virginia, and while there was appointed, 3 March, 1868, first Bishop of the new Diocese of Wilmington, Delaware, for which he was consecrated by Archbishop Spalding at Baltimore, 16 August, 1868. He ruled this diocese until, on the promotion (1 February, 1885) of Bishop William H. Gross from Savannah to the Archbishopric of Oregon City, Bishop Becker was transferred to the See of Savannah, 26 March, 1886. He was regarded as one of the most accomplished bishops of his day, and was noted for his ability as a linguist. He was one of the secretaries of the Fourth Plenary Council of Baltimore, and contributed frequently to current reviews and periodicals. A series of articles in the "American Catholic Quarterly Review" on the idea of a true university attracted wide attention. He was devoted always to the cause of temperance, and by a clause in his will left $15,000 in trust for twenty-five years for the education of worthy and deserving young men, on condition that they be American born, total abstainers, and willing to devote their energies to the service of the Diocese of Savannah.

Catholic News, files (New York, 5 August, 1889); REUSS, *Biographical Cyclopædia of the Catholic Hierarchy* (Milwaukee, 1898); SHEA, *History of the Cath. Ch. in U. S.* (New York, 1894); *Catholic Directory* (New York, 1868–90).

THOMAS F. MEEHAN.

Becket, THOMAS À. See THOMAS À BECKET, ST.

Beckx, PIERRE-JEAN, twenty-second General of the Society of Jesus, b. at Sichem, Belgium, 8 February, 1795; d. at Rome, 4 March, 1887. Father Beckx was ordained priest, 7 March, 1819, and appointed to a little parish near Brussels; eight months afterwards he resigned this office and entered the Society of Jesus at Hildesheim, Germany. Having learned the German language, he was soon able to preach, hear confessions, and give retreats in German. The Duke and Duchess of Anhalt-Köthen were converted to the Catholic Faith in 1825 and asked for a Jesuit chaplain; Father Beckx was appointed to this duty and went to live in Köthen. He found only twenty Catholics there; in four years he had 200 converts. In 1830 he went to live in Vienna, where he was the only Jesuit for many years. From time to time he was called to Rome and sent on important missions to Lombardy, Hungary, and Bavaria. In 1852, he was made Provincial of Austria and brought back the Fathers of the Society to Innsbruck, Linz, and Lemberg. The next year, on the death of Father Roothaan, he was chosen General of the Society by the unanimous vote of delegates from all parts of the world. The new father-general brought to his office a deep spirit of faith; a profound knowledge of the human heart; firmness and dignity; serenity of mind in extreme trial; faultless manners; and a remarkable soundness of judgment.

During the thirty-four years that Father Beckx governed the society its membership was doubled, new provinces were established in Ireland, France, Spain, Portugal, and America; new missions were begun in different parts of the world; the education of youth was continued with success; new colleges were opened in every province. During his term of office eighty Jesuits were raised to the honours of the altar; all but three of these were missionaries or martyrs. The society was expelled from Italy in 1860, from Spain in 1868, from Germany in 1873, from France and the French colonies in 1880. In 1873 Father Beckx went to live at Fiesole near Florence, where he remained until the election of Father Anderledy as Vicar-General, in 1883; then he went back to Rome, abdicating his charge entirely. There, four years later, he died at the advanced age of ninety-two years. Father Beckx was the author of "Der Monat Maria", Vienna, 1838, which passed through thirty editions in German, and was translated into English, French, Italian, Dutch, Polish, Armenian, and Arabic.

SOMMERVOGEL, *Bibl. de la c. de J.*; *Woodstock Letters*, XV; *Messenger of the Sacred Heart* (New York, 1887); *Précis Historique* (April, 1887).

PATRICK H. KELLY.

Becquerel, ANTOINE-CÉSAR, French physicist, b. at Châtillon-sur-Loing (Loiret), 7 March, 1788; d. at Paris, 18 January, 1878. In 1806 he entered the Polytechnic School after having studied at the Central School of Fontainebleau under Billy, and later at the Collège Henri IV with Cauchy. In 1808 he was sent to the military school (*d'application*) at Metz, which he left the following year with the rank of second lieutenant. During two and a half years, he fought under General Suchet in the Spanish campaign, distinguishing himself at several of the important sieges. Ill health obliged him to ask for a leave of absence. He was raised to the rank of captain, made Chevalier of the Legion of Honour, and nominated to the new position of assistant inspector of studies at the Polytechnic School. During the invasion of 1814 he resumed military service for a time, but was soon retired with the rank of *chef de bataillon*.

A change of career then became necessary. After some hesitation, he settled down to the real work of his life, the study and advancement of the science of electricity. Becquerel's achievements are numerous and important. He combated Volta's contact theory of the electromotive force in a cell and showed that the real source of voltaic electricity is to be found in chemical action. That in fact, the generation of electricity in any case is possible only where there is chemical action, frictional work, or difference of temperature. He observed the diamagnetic properties of the metal antimony

ANTOINE-CÉSAR BECQUEREL

before Faraday, and constructed a constant cell with two liquids which was the forerunner of the well-known "Daniell cell". His differential galvanometer increased the accuracy to be attained in the measurement of electrical resistances. He applied the results of his study of thermo-electricity to the construction of an electric thermometer and measured with it the temperature of the interior of animals, of the soil at different depths, of the atmosphere at different heights. He was also very much interested in questions of meteorology, climate, and agriculture.

Becquerel's work in electro-chemistry brought him, in 1837, the award of the Copley medal of the Royal Society of London. He was a member of the Academy of Sciences (1829), professor-administrator of the Museum of Natural History, and Commander of the Legion of Honour. His character seems best described by the chemist Dumas: "Becquerel loved his country, his science, his family." Fizeau ends his funeral oration with these words: "He died with the serenity of a sage and the tranquillity of a good man, with confidence in God and the immortal hopes of a Christian".

More than 500 papers were published in the "Comptes Rendus" in Vols. I–LXXXV, and in the "Annales de Chimie et Physique", series II–V. The following are some of his more important works: (1) Traité expérimental de l'électricité et du magnétisme et de leurs phénomènes naturels (Paris, 1834–40, 7 vols.; 1855, 2 vols.); (2) La physique considérée dans ses rapports avec la chimie et les sciences naturelles (1844, 2 vols.); (3) Eléments de physique terrestre et de météorologie (1847, with his son Edmond); (4) Résumé de l'histoire de l'électricité et du magnétisme (1858); (5) Des forces physico-chimiques, de leur intervention dans la production des phénomènes naturels (with plates, Paris, 1873). The title of this book "On the Physico-chemical forces and their intervention in the production of natural phenomena" would appear to indicate a materialistic philosophy. This impression is entirely removed by his explicit statement that "we must admit the existence of a creative Power which manifests itself at certain times", especially in order to explain the appearance of organic life.

BARRAL, *Eloge historique d'A.C.B.* (Paris), 1879.

WILLIAM FOX.

Bédard, PIERRE, a French-Canadian lawyer and member of the Assembly of Lower Canada, b. at Charlesbourg near Quebec, 13 November, 1762; d. at Three Rivers, 26 April, 1829. He was the son of Pierre-Stanislas Bédard and Marie-Josephine Thibault. After he had completed the course of studies at the seminary of Quebec, where he proved himself an excellent pupil, he studied law and was admitted to the bar. In 1792 Bédard was elected member of the Assembly for Northumberland and continued a member of the Assembly until 1812. During these years he represented successively Northumberland, the lower town of Quebec, and Surrey, and gave proof of his sterling qualities. He devoted himself, however, chiefly to the study of constitutional questions of which many of the government officials seemed to have but an imperfect conception. When the newspaper, "Le Canadien" was founded in 1806, he became a regular contributor and expressed his views concerning the constitutional government of the province of Quebec with such warmth that the governor, Sir James Craig, in the spring of 1810 suppressed "Le Canadien" and threw Bédard into prison. Here Bédard remained some twelve months, although the governor offered him his freedom several times, so that he could take the seat in the Assembly to which he had been elected during his imprisonment. Bédard, however, demanded a regular trial, which the authorities were not willing to grant. Finally for the sake of peace Bédard left the prison. After Craig had resigned his position and gone to England, the new governor, Sir George Prevost, appointed Bédard a judge of the superior court at Three Rivers as compensation for what he had endured. Bédard filled this position from 11 December, 1813, until March, 1827, when illness obliged him to absent himself from his duties for some months. After this his health failed steadily until his death. He was buried in the parish church at Three Rivers. Bédard had four children one of whom, Elzevir, became a distinguished judge.

N. E. DIONNE.

Bede (or BEAD, whence *Bedehouse, Bedesman, Bederoll*).—The old English word *bede* (Anglo-Saxon *béd*) means a prayer, though the derivative form, *gebéd*, was more common in this sense in Anglo-Saxon literature. When, in the course of the twelfth and thirteenth centuries, the use of little perforated globes of bone, wood, or amber, threaded upon a string, came into fashion for the purpose of counting the repetitions of the Our Father or Hail Mary, these objects themselves became known as bedes (i. e. prayers), and our modern word *bead*, as applied to small globular ornaments of glass, coral, etc., has no other derivation. In middle English the word *bedes* was used both in the sense of prayer and rosary. Thus Shakespeare could still write (Rich. III, iii, 7)

When holy and devout religious men
  Are at their beads [prayers], 'tis much to draw
    them thence,
So sweet is zealous contemplation.

While of Chaucer's Prioress we are told
  Of smal coral aboute hire arm she bar
    A peire of bedes, gauded al with grene.

The gauds, or gaudys, were the ornaments or larger beads used to divide the decades. The phrase *pair of beads* (i. e. set of beads—cf. pair of stairs), which may still be heard on the lips of old-fashioned English and Irish Catholics, is consequently of venerable antiquity. With such speakers a pair of beads means the round of the beads, i. e. the chaplet of five decades, as opposed to the whole rosary of fifteen. Again, to "bid beads" originally meant only to say prayers, but the phrase "bidding the beads", by a series of misconceptions explained in the "Historical English Dictionary", came to be attached to certain public devotions analogous to the prayers which precede the kissing of the Cross in the Good Friday Service. The prayers referred to used to be recited in the vernacular at the Sunday Mass in medieval England, and the distinctive feature of them was that the subject of each was announced in a formula read to the congregation beforehand. This was called "bidding the bedes". From this the idea was derived that the word "bidding" meant commanding or giving out, and hence a certain survival of these prayers, still retained in the Anglican "Book of Canons", and recited before the sermon, is known as the "bidding prayer".

The words *bedesman* and *bedeswoman*, which date back to Anglo-Saxon times, also recall the original meaning of the word. *Bedesman* was at first the term applied to one whose duty it was to pray for others, and thus it sometimes denoted the chaplain of a guild. But in later English a bedesman is simply the recipient of any form of bounty; for example, a poor man who obtains free quarters in an almshouse, and who is supposed to be bound in gratitude to pray for his benefactors. Similarly, *bedehouse*, which originally meant a place of prayer or an oratory, came at a later date to be used of any charitable institution like an almshouse. It has now practically disappeared from literary English, but survives provincially and in a number of Welsh place-names in the form *bettws*, e. g. Bettws y Coed. Finally, *bede-roll*, as its etymology suggests, meant the roll of those to be prayed for, and in some sense corresponded to the diptychs of the early Church. The word is of tolerably frequent occurrence in connexion with the early English guilds. In these associations a list was invariably kept of departed members who had a claim on their prayers. This was the bede-roll.

For beads in the sense of rosary, see ROSARY.

MURRAY AND BRADLEY, eds., *The English Historical Dictionary* (Oxford, 1884), I; ROCK, *Church of our Fathers* (2d ed., London, 1904), II, 330; III, 107; SIMMONS, *The Lay Folks' Mass-Book* (Early Eng. Text Soc., London, 1879) 315, 345.

HERBERT THURSTON.

Bede, THE VENERABLE, historian and Doctor of the Church, b. 672 or 673; d. 735. In the last chapter of his great work on the "Ecclesiastical History of the English People" Bede has told us something of his own life, and it is, practically speaking, all that we know. His words, written in 731, when death was not far off, not only show a simplicity and piety characteristic of the man, but they throw a light upon the composition of the work through which he is best remembered by the world at large.

"Thus much", he says, "concerning the ecclesiastical history of Britain, and especially of the race of the English, I, Bæda, a servant of Christ and priest of the monastery of the blessed apostles St. Peter and St. Paul, which is at Wearmouth and at Jarrow (in Northumberland), have with the Lord's help composed so far as I could gather it either from ancient documents or from the traditions of the elders, or from my own knowledge. I was born in the territory of the said monastery, and at the age of seven I was, by the care of my relations, given to the most reverend Abbot Benedict [St. Benedict Biscop], and afterwards to Ceolfrid, to be educated. From that time I have spent the whole of my life within that monastery, devoting all my pains to the study of the Scriptures, and amid the observance of monastic discipline and the daily charge of singing in the Church, it has been ever my delight to learn or teach or write. In my nineteenth year I was admitted to the diac-

onate, in my thirtieth to the priesthood, both by the hands of the most reverend Bishop John [St. John of Beverley], and at the bidding of Abbot Ceolfrid. From the time of my admission to the priesthood to my present fifty-ninth year, I have endeavoured for my own use and that of my brethren, to make brief notes upon the holy Scripture, either out of the works of the venerable Fathers or in conformity with their meaning and interpretation." After this Bede inserts a list or *Indiculus*, of his previous writings and finally concludes his great work with the following words: "And I pray thee, loving Jesus, that as Thou hast graciously given me to drink in with delight the words of Thy knowledge, so Thou wouldst mercifully grant me to attain one day to Thee, the fountain of all wisdom and to appear for ever before Thy face."

It is plain from Bede's letter to Bishop Egbert that the historian occasionally visited his friends for a few days, away from his own monastery of Jarrow, but with such rare exceptions his life seems to have been one peaceful round of study and prayer passed in the midst of his own community. How much he was beloved by them is made manifest by the touch-

PAGE FROM BEDE'S ECCLESIASTICAL HISTORY
(VIII Century)

ing account of the saint's last sickness and death left us by Cuthbert, one of his disciples. Their studious pursuits were not given up on account of his illness and they read aloud by his bedside, but constantly the reading was interrupted by their tears. "I can with truth declare", writes Cuthbert of his beloved master, "that I never saw with my eyes or heard with my ears anyone return thanks so unceasingly to the living God." Even on the day of his death (the vigil of the Ascension, 735) the saint was still busy dictating a translation of the Gospel of St. John. In the evening the boy Wilbert, who was writing it, said to him: "There is still one sentence, dear master, which is not written down." And when this had been supplied, and the boy had told him it was finished, "'Thou hast spoken truth', Bede answered, 'it is finished. Take my head in thy hands for it much delights me to sit opposite any holy place where I used to pray, that so sitting I may call upon my Father.' And thus upon the floor of his cell singing, 'Glory be to the Father and to the Son and to the Holy Ghost' and the rest, he peacefully breathed his last breath.''

The title *Venerabilis* seems to have been associated with the name of Bede within two generations after his death. There is of course no early authority for the legend repeated by Fuller of the "dunce monk" who in composing an epitaph on Bede was at a loss to complete the line: *Hac sunt in fossâ Bedæ . . . . ossa* and who next morning found that the angels had filled the gap with the word *venerabilis*. The title is used by Alcuin, Amalarius, and seemingly Paul the Deacon, and the important Council of Aachen in 835 describes him as *venerabilis et modernis temporibus doctor admirabilis Beda*. This decree was specially referred to in the petition which Cardinal Wiseman and the English bishops addressed to the Holy See in 1859 praying that Bede might be declared a Doctor of the Church. The question had already been debated even before the time of Benedict XIV, but it was only on 13 November, 1899, that Leo XIII decreed that the feast of Venerable Bede with the title of *Doctor Ecclesiæ* should be celebrated throughout the Church each year on 27 May. A local cultus of St. Bede had been maintained at York and in the North of England throughout the Middle Ages, but his feast was not so generally observed in the South, where the Sarum Rite was followed.

Bede's influence both upon English and foreign scholarship was very great, and it would probably have been greater still but for the devastation inflicted upon the northern monasteries by the inroads of the Danes less than a century after his death. In numberless ways, but especially in his moderation, gentleness, and breadth of view, Bede stands out from his contemporaries. In point of scholarship he was undoubtedly the most learned man of his time. A very remarkable trait, noticed by Plummer (I, p. xxiii), is his sense of literary property, an extraordinary thing in that age. He himself scrupulously noted in his writings the passages he had borrowed from others and he even begs the copyists of his works to preserve the references, a recommendation to which they, alas, have paid but little attention. High, however, as was the general level of Bede's culture, he repeatedly makes it clear that all his studies were subordinated to the interpretation of Scripture. In his "De Schematibus" he says in so many words: "Holy Scripture is above all other books not only by its authority because it is Divine, or by its utility because it leads to eternal life, but also by its antiquity and by its literary form" (*positione dicendi*). It is perhaps the highest tribute to Bede's genius that with so uncompromising and evidently sincere a conviction of the inferiority of human learning, he should have acquired so much real culture. Though Latin was to him a still living tongue, and though he does not seem to have consciously looked back to the Augustan Age of Roman Literature as preserving purer models of style than the time of Fortunatus or St. Augustine, still whether through native genius or through contact with the classics, he is remarkable for the relative purity of his language, as also for his lucidity and his sobriety, more especially in matters of historical criticism. In all these respects he presents a marked contrast to St. Aldhelm who approaches more nearly to the Celtic type.

WRITINGS AND EDITIONS.—No adequate edition founded upon a careful collation of manuscripts has ever been published of Bede's works as a whole. The text printed by Giles in 1844 and reproduced in

Migne (XC–XCIV) shows little if any advance on the Basle edition of 1563 or the Cologne edition of 1688. It is of course as an historian that Bede is chiefly remembered. His great work, the "Historia Ecclesiastica Gentis Anglorum", giving an account of Christianity in England from the beginning until his own day, is the foundation of all our knowledge of early British history and a masterpiece eulogized by the scholars of every age. Of this work, together with the "Historia Abbatum", and the "Letter to Egbert", Plummer has produced an edition which may fairly be called final (2 vols., Oxford, 1896). Bede's remarkable industry in collecting materials and his critical use of them have been admirably illustrated in Plummer's Introduction (pp. xliii–xlvii). The "History of the Abbots" (of the twin monasteries of Wearmouth and Jarrow), the "Letter to Egbert", the metrical and prose lives of St. Cuthbert, and the other smaller pieces are also of great value for the light they shed upon the state of Christianity in Northumbria in Bede's own day. The "Ecclesiastical History" was translated into Anglo-Saxon at the instance of King Alfred. It has often been translated since, notably by T. Stapleton who printed it (1565) at Antwerp as a controversial weapon against the Reformation divines in the reign of Elizabeth. The Latin text first appeared in Germany in 1475; it is noteworthy that no edition even of the Latin was printed in England before 1643. Smith's more accurate text saw the light in 1742.

Bede's chronological treatises "De temporibus liber" and "De temporum ratione" also contain summaries of the general history of the world from the Creation to 725 and 703, respectively. These historical portions have been satisfactorily edited by Mommsen in the "Monumenta Germaniæ historica" (4to series, 1898). They may be counted among the earliest specimens of this type of general chronicle and were largely copied and imitated. The topographical work "De locis sanctis" is a description of Jerusalem and the holy places based upon Adamnan and Arculfus. Bede's work was edited in 1898 by Geyer in the "Itinera Hierosolymitana" for the Vienna "Corpus Scriptorum". That Bede compiled a Martyrologium we know from his own statement. But the work attributed to him in extant manuscripts has been so much interpolated and supplemented that his share in it is quite uncertain.

Bede's exegetical writings both in his own idea and in that of his contemporaries stood supreme in importance amongst his works, but the list is long and cannot be fully given here. They included a commentary upon the Pentateuch as a whole as well as on selected portions, and there are also commentaries on the Books of Kings, Esdras, Tobias, the Canticles, etc. In the New Testament he has certainly interpreted St. Mark, St. Luke, the Acts, the Canonical Epistles, and the Apocalypse. But the authenticity of the commentary on St. Matthew printed under his name is more than doubtful. (Plaine in "Revue Anglo-Romaine", 1896, III, 61.) The homilies of Bede take the form of commentaries upon the Gospel. The collection of fifty, divided into two books, which are attributed to him by Giles (and in Migne) are for the most part authentic, but the genuineness of a few is open to suspicion. (Morin in "Revue Bénédictine", IX, 1892, 316.)

Various didactic works are mentioned by Bede in the list which he has left us of his own writings. Most of these are still preserved and there is no reason to doubt that the texts we possess are authentic. The grammatical treatises "De arte metricâ" and "De orthographiâ" have been adequately edited in modern times by Keil in his "Grammatici Latini" (Leipzig, 1880), VII, and the "De Schematibus et Tropis" by Halm in his "Rhetores Latini minores" (Leipzig, 1863). But the larger works "De naturâ rerum", "De temporibus", "De temporum ratione", dealing with science as it was then understood and especially with chronology, are only accessible in the unsatisfactory texts of the earlier editors and Giles. Beyond the metrical life of St. Cuthbert and some verses incorporated in the "Ecclesiastical History" we do not possess much poetry that can be assigned to Bede with confidence, but, like other scholars of his age, he certainly wrote a good deal of verse. He himself mentions his "book of hymns" composed in different metres or rhythms. So Alcuin says of him: *Plurima versifico cecinit quoque carmina plectro*. It is possible that the shorter of the two metrical calendars printed among his works is genuine. The Penitential ascribed to Bede, though accepted as genuine by Haddan and Stubbs and Wasserschleben, is probably not his (Plummer, I, 157).

Venerable Bede is the earliest witness of pure Gregorian tradition in England. His works "Musica theoretica" and "De arte Metricâ" (Migne, XC) are found especially valuable by present-day scholars engaged in the study of the primitive form of the chant.

GODET in *Dict. de théol. cath.*; PLAINE in *Dict. de la Bible*, I; WERNER in *Kirchenlex.*, II; HUNT in *Dict. Nat. Biog.*; STUBBS in *Dict. Christ. Biog.*; PLUMMER, *Bede's Eccles. Hist.* (Oxford, 1896), Introd.; GEHLE, *De V. Bedæ vitâ et scriptis* (Leyden, 1838); WERNER, *Beda d. Ehrwürdige u. s. Zeit* (Vienna, 1881); PLAINE in *Revue Anglo-Romaine* (1896), III, 49–96; EBERT, *Gesch. der Litt. des Mittelalters* (Leipzig, 1889), I; MAYOR AND LUMBY, *Bede's Eccles. Hist.* (Cambridge, 1879); LINGARD, *Anglo-Saxon Church* (London, 1848); MORIN in *Revue Bénédictine*, IX, 121; XI, 472; ROGER, *L'enseignement des lettres classiques* (Paris, 1905), 304–310; SANDYS, *History of Classical Scholarship* (Cambridge, 1903), 451–454; RAWNSLEY, *The Venerable Bede* (Sunderland, 1903). For further bibl. cf., CHEVALIER, *Répertoire, Bio-bibl.* (Paris, 1905); PETER WAGNER, *Einführung in die gregorianischen Melodien* (Fribourg, Switzerland, 1900); GIETMANN, *Kirchenmusikalisches Jahrbuch* (Ratisbon, 1905).

HERBERT THURSTON.

Bedford, GUNNING S., medical writer and teacher, b. at Baltimore, Maryland, U. S. A., of a distinguished family in 1806; d. in New York, 5 September, 1870. He was a nephew and namesake of Gunning Bedford, first Attorney-General of Delaware and one of the framers of the Constitution of the United States, who was aide-de-camp to General Washington and was appointed by him U. S. Judge for the District of Delaware. Dr. Bedford graduated in 1825 at Mount St. Mary's College, Emmitsburg, Maryland, and took his degree in medicine from Rutgers College, New York. He spent two years in foreign study and in 1833, when only twenty-six years of age, became professor of obstetrics in Charleston Medical College. From here he accepted a professorship in the Albany Medical College. He went to New York in 1836 and four years later founded the University Medical College, which became a great success. In connexion with it he established an obstetrical clinic for those too poor to pay a doctor's fee. This was the first of its kind in the country and was of great service to the poor and to medical science. Dr. Bedford continued to teach until his health broke down in 1862 and he died in 1870. His funeral panegyric was preached by Archbishop McCloskey who had been his fellow student at Mount St. Mary's. Two books written by him, "Diseases of Women" and "Practice of Obstetrics" went through many editions, were translated into French and German, and were adopted as textbooks in American schools.

Medical Record, files (New York, 1870), p. 330; *Cyclopædia of American Biography*, s. v.

JAMES J. WALSH.

Bedford, HENRY, writer, educator, b. in London 1 October, 1816; d. in Dublin, Ireland, 21 May, 1903. With the intention of becoming a clergyman of the Church of England, to which his family belonged, he entered Cambridge University in 1835 and after a distinguished course received the degree of M. A.

He made his theological studies and after ordination was given charge of a church in London where he became noted in High Church circles as a popular writer and preacher. A very advanced "Puseyite" sermon during the Tractarian excitement brought him in conflict with the Bishop of London and led to his conversion to Catholicism in 1851. He wished to take Holy orders, but a natural defect in his right hand was a canonical obstacle to ordination. In 1852 he accepted an invitation to join the staff of All Hallows Missionary College, Drumcondra, near Dublin, Ireland, and there lived a long life of active, effective work as professor of natural science, treasurer, and one of the college directors. He also did much in furtherance of the Catholic movement then at its height in England and was a constant contributor to Catholic periodicals and a public lecturer on Catholic topics. His writings on a variety of subjects, embracing travels, archæology, art, science, music and the general treatment of past periods of English literature were frequent features of "The Month", "The Irish Monthly", and "The Irish Ecclesiastical Record". Some of them were later reprinted for private circulation in pamphlet form, notably his "Vacation Rambles", which were issued in a series (1874–75–76–78–79) subsequent to their appearance in "The Month".

All Hallows Annual (Dublin, 1906); *The Freeman's Journal* files (Dublin); *The Irish Monthly* files (Dublin).

THOMAS F. MEEHAN.

Bedingfeld, FRANCES (*alias* LONG) superioress of the English Institute of Mary, b. 1616 of a gentle family of Norfolk, England; d. at Munich, Germany, 1704. She and her eleven sisters entered religious life. Sent abroad to finish her education, she entered the English Institute of Mary at Munich and was professed in 1633. This society, founded at St. Omer in 1603, had been transferred in 1629 to Liège and then to Munich. Frances's sister Winefrid, the first superioress, died 26th December, 1666. In 1669, Frances, who had become head of the Munich house, was induced by Catherine of Braganza, wife of Charles II, to establish a house in London. With a group of the English members she set up a school for young women, first at St. Martin's Lane, then at Hammersmith. In England, she wore a secular garb, and was known as Mrs. Long. Summoned before a magistrate, she was liberated through family influence, but warned against harbouring priests or instructing youth. Though disregarding this injunction, she was not again molested. In 1677, with the aid of Sir Thomas Gascoigne, she established a community in the north, in a house on the site of the present convent, outside Micklegate Bar, York. From 1677 to 1686 she divided her time between her two English communities, but after 1686, having transferred the care of the Hammersmith house to Mrs. Cicely Cornwallis, she remained at York. In her seventy-eighth year, after her house had been repeatedly searched and threatened with destruction, she, with her niece, Mother Dorothy Paston Bedingfeld, was summoned before the Mayor of York and committed to Ousebridge Gaol. Released soon afterwards, she was again attacked, and in 1695 her house barely escaped destruction. In 1699, resigning in favour of her niece, Mother Bedingfeld returned to Munich and died there, one year after the rule of her institute had been approved by Clement XI.

GILLOW, *Bibl. Dict. of Eng. Cath.*; FOLEY, *Rec. Eng. Prov. S.J.*, V; PETRE, *Notices of English Colleges and Convents Abroad*.

J. VINCENT CROWNE.

Bedingfeld, SIR HENRY, Knight, b. 1509; d. 1583. He was the grandson of Sir Edmund Bedingfeld who had served in the Wars of the Roses, and to whom were granted by Edward IV for his faithful service letters patent authorizing him "to build towers, walls, and such other fortifications as he pleased in his manors of Oxburgh, together with a market there weekly and a court of pye-powder". Sir Henry was mainly instrumental, together with Sir Henry Jerningham, in placing Mary Tudor on the throne. He proclaimed her at Norwich, and for his loyalty received an annual pension of £100 out of the forfeited estates of Sir Thomas Wyatt. Ultimately he became Lieutenant of the Tower of London and Captain of the Yeomen of the Guard. As "jailer" of the Princess Elizabeth, who was suspected of complicity in Wyatt's rebellion, he has been persistently misrepresented by Foxe and others, but the whole history of his custodianship of Elizabeth is contained in a series of letters addressed to the Queen and the Privy Council, and in their replies. This correspondence, which has been published by the Norfolk and Norwich Archæological Society, completely exonerates Sir Henry from either cruelty or want of courtesy in his treatment of the royal captive. On Elizabeth's accession he retired to Oxburgh and was called upon in a letter, in which the Queen addressed him as "trusty and well-beloved", to furnish a horse and man armed, as his contribution to the defence of the country against an expected invasion of the French.

When, however, the penal laws against Catholics were enforced with extreme severity, Sir Henry Bedingfeld was not spared. He was required to pay heavy monthly fines for non-attendance at the parish church, while his house was searched for priests and church-furniture, and his servants dismissed for refusing to conform to the new state religion. Together with his fellow-Catholics, he was a prisoner within five miles of his own house and might pass that boundary only by a written authorization of the Privy Council. He was buried in the Bedingfeld chantry at Oxburgh. He married Katharine, daughter of Sir Roger Townshend, ancestor of the present Marquess Townshend, by whom he had numerous issue.

State Papers relating to the custody of the Princess Elizabeth at Woodstock (Norfolk and Norwich Archæological Society); BLOMEFIELD, *History of Norfolk;* MASON, *History of Norfolk; Calendar of State Papers. Dom. Eliz., 1581–90;* original letters in the *Oxburgh archives.*

J. M. STONE.

Bedingfield, THOMAS. See DOWNES, THOMAS.

Bedini, CAJETAN, Italian Cardinal and diplomat, b. at Sinigaglia, Italy, 15 May, 1806; d. at Viterbo, 6 Sept., 1864. He was appointed in 1849, by Pope Pius IX, Commissary Extraordinary at Bologna, one of the four Papal Provinces then recently in revolt and in which the Government of the Holy See was being maintained with the aid of the military power of Austria. He retired from this office in 1852 and after serving in various diplomatic posts was promoted to be titular Archbishop of Thebes. In 1853, upon his appointment as Apostolic Nuncio to the Court of Brazil, he was commissioned by the Holy Father to visit the United States to examine into the state of ecclesiastical affairs and, incidentally, to call on the President and present to him the compliments and good wishes of the pope. Arriving in New York in June, 1853, he at once visited Washington and called upon President Franklin Pierce, by whom he was received with great courtesy and to whom he presented an autograph letter of the Holy Father. This visit, purely one of courtesy, was afterwards distorted into an attempt to gain official recognition of himself as the diplomatic representative of the pope in the United States. His arrival in this country was the signal for a series of anti-Catholic demonstrations against him lasting throughout his tour. In New York the colony of Italian revolutionists who had fled to this country, urged on by the apostate priest Gavazzi, and aided by the Know-nothing element, held a mass meeting and denounced the nuncio. A plot to assassinate him was formed, but was defeated through a warning given by one of the conspirators, Sassi, who himself was stabbed to death by one of his associates in New York City a day or two after.

Monsignor Bedini travelled extensively throughout the country and participated in many public religious ceremonies. In many of the larger cities, notably Pittsburg, Louisville, and Cincinnati, his visit excited hostile comment and demonstration, chiefly by the adherents of Know-nothingism, which was then rampant. In Cincinnati, particularly, this element, co-operating with some German infidel revolutionary exiles, plotted to do violence to him and to attack the cathedral where he was to officiate, but this design was frustrated by the vigilance of the city authorities, not, however, without bloodshed and rioting in which a number of the rioters lost their lives. He remained in this country until January, 1854, when he returned to Rome. So apprehensive of personal violence had he become, that when about to depart from New York, he left the city secretly and journeyed to Staten Island, twenty miles distant, where a tug carried him to the outgoing steamer. Later, he was elevated to the rank of cardinal and received the appointment to the See of Viterbo and Toscanella.

SHEA, *Hist. of Cath. Ch. in U. S.* (New York, 1892), IV; HASSARD, *Life of Archbishop Hughes* (New York, 1866); *U. S. Cath. Hist. Soc.; Hist. Records and Studies* (New York, 1903).

PETER CONDON.

Bedlam (an English abbreviation of BETHLEHEM), a London hospital originally intended for the poor suffering from any ailment and for such as might have no other lodging, hence its name, *Bethlehem,* in Hebrew, the "house of bread." During the fourteenth century it began to be used partly as an asylum for the insane, for there is a report of a Royal Commission, in 1405, as to the state of lunatics confined there. The word *Bethlehem* became shortened to *Bedlam* in popular speech, and the confinement of lunatics there gave rise to the use of this word to mean a house of confusion. Bedlam was founded in 1247 as a priory in Bishopsgate Street, for the order of St. Mary of Bethlehem, by Simon Fitz Mary, an Alderman and Sheriff of London. This site is now occupied by the Liverpool Saint railway station. In the next century it is mentioned as a hospital in a license granted (1330) to collect alms in England, Ireland, and Wales. In 1375 Bedlam became a royal hospital, taken by the crown on the pretext that it was an alien priory. It seems afterwards to have reverted to the city. At the beginning of the sixteenth century the word Bedlam was used by Tyndale to mean a madman, so that it would seem as though the hospital were now used as a lunatic asylum exclusively. In January, 1547, King Henry VIII formally granted St. Bartholomew's hospital and Bedlam, or Bethlehem, to the city of London, on condition that the city spend a certain amount on new buildings in connexion with St. Bartholomew's. In 1674, the old premises having become untenable, it was decided to build another hospital, and this was erected in what is now Finsbury Circus. This came to be known as old Bedlam, after the erection of a new building in St. George's Fields, which was opened August, 1815, on the site of the notorious tavern called the Dog and the Duck.

The attitude of successive generations of Englishmen towards the insane can be traced interestingly at Bedlam. Originally, it was founded and kept by religious. Every effort seems to have been made to bring patients to such a state of mental health as would enable them to leave the asylum. An old English word, "a Bedlam" signifies one discharged and licensed to beg. Such persons wore a tin plate on their arm as a badge and were known as Bedlamers, Bedlamites, or Bedlam Beggars. Whenever outside inspection was not regularly maintained, abuses crept into the management of Bedlam, and in every century there were several commissions of investigation. Evelyn in his Diary, 21 April, 1656, notes that he saw several poor creatures in Bedlam in chains. In the next century it became the custom for the idle classes to visit Bedlam and observe the antics of the insane patients as a novel form of amusement. This was done even by the nobility and their friends. One penny was charged for admission into the hospital, and there is a tradition that an annual income of four hundred pounds was thus realized. This would mean that nearly 100,000 persons visited the hospital in the course of a year. Hogarth's famous picture represents two fashionable ladies visiting the hospital as a show place, while his "Rake", at the end of the "Progress", is being fettered by a keeper. After an investigation in 1851, the hospital came under regular government inspection and has since been noted for its model care of the insane. It accommodates about three hundred, with over sixty attendants. Its convalescent home at Witley is an important feature.

Tuke, *Bethlehem Royal Hospital* in *British Journal of Mental Science*, 1876; Burdette, *British Hospitals and Charities Annual*, 1905.

JAMES J. WALSH.

Bee, Saint. See Begha.

Beelen, Ian Theodor, exegete and Orientalist, b. at Amsterdam, 12 January, 1807; d. at Louvain, 31 March, 1884. After a brilliant course of studies at Rome, crowned by the Doctorate of Theology, he was in 1836 appointed Professor of Sacred Scripture and Oriental languages in the recently reorganized Catholic University of Louvain. This position he held till 1876, when he resigned his place to his pupil, Prof. T. J. Lamy. He was the author of the following Biblical works, among which his commentary on the Epistle to the Romans is especially esteemed: "Dissertatio theologica quâ sententiam . . . esse S. Scripturæ multiplicem interdum sensum litteralem, nullo fundamento satis firmo niti demonstrare conatur" (Louvain, 1845); "Interpretatio ep. S. Pauli ad Philip." (ib., 1849; 2nd ed., ib., 1852, entitled: Commentarius in ep. S. Pauli ad Philip.); "Commentarius in Acta Apost.", with Greek and Latin text (2 vols., ib., 1850–55; 2nd ed., without Greek and Latin texts, ib., 1864); "Commentarius in ep. S. Pauli ad Rom." (ib., 1854); "Grammatica græcitatis N. T." (ib., 1857); and in Dutch, "Rules for a new Translation of the N. T." (Louvain, 1858); a translation of the N. T. made in accordance with these rules (3 vols., ib., 1859–69); "The Epistles and Gospels of the Ecclesiastical Year", with annotations (ib., 1870); translation of the Psalms, with annotations (2 vols., ib., 1877–78); translation of Proverbs and of Ecclesiasticus (ib., 1879). He also published two works in the field of Oriental scholarship: "Chrestomathia rabbinica et chaldaïca (3 vols., Louvain, 1841–43); and "Clementis Rom. epistolæ binæ de Virginitate, syriace" (ib., 1856), in which he defends the genuineness of these two letters. Beelen also deserves the credit of reviving Oriental studies in Belgium, and of introducing into that country Oriental printing by means of a complete font of Hebrew, Syriac, Arabic, and Ethiopic type, which he purchased. In recognition of his merits as a scholar he was made domestic prelate of the pope, consultor of the Congregation of the Index, honorary canon of Liège, and Knight of the Order of Leopold.

Hurter, *Nomenclator*, III, 1290; Rey in Vig., *Dict. de la Bible; The Tablet* (London, 1884), LXIII, 541.

F. BECHTEL.

Beelphegor (בעל פעור, βεελφεγώρ), or BAALPEOR, was the *baal* of Mt. Phogor, or Peor, a mountain of Moab. The exact idea of *baal* seems to be "the possessor", the one who holds the real domination (Lagrange, Religions Sémitiques, 83, 84); so Beelphegor was the Moabite divinity who ruled over Phogor. Some identify him with Chamos (Chemosh), the national god of Moab, but this is not at all certain, as many localities had their local deities, apparently distinct to the popular mind. To the *baal* was generally ascribed the fertility of the soil and the increase of flocks; he was worshipped by offerings of the products he gave and often by unchaste practices done in his honour at his sanctuary. One of the great works of the prophets was to stamp out this immoral cult on the soil of Palestine.

Israel came in contact with Beelphegor at Settim, on the plains of Moab, their last station before entering the land of Canaan. Here many men of Israel, as a sequel to their immoral intercourse with the women of Moab, took part in the sacrificial banquets in honour of Beelphegor, for which crimes they were punished by death (Num., xxv). It is commonly held, in view of the occurrences at Settim and of the general nature of baal-worship, that immoral rites were part of the worship of this god; while the text does not make this certain, the large number of persons involved and the fact that "the affair of Phogor" is ascribed to the instigation of the seer Balaam, seem to indicate that it had relation to the cult of Beelphegor (xxxi, 16). Marucchi believes the survival of the cult till the middle of the second century is attested by an inscription dedicated by some soldiers from Arabia (?) to Jupiter Beellepharus, whom he identifies with Beelphegor. The proof is slight, nothing more than the resemblance in name. The terrible chastisement inflicted on Israel for the sin at Settim is mentioned several times in the Bible, and St. Paul (I Cor., x, 8) uses it to point a moral.

Gray, *Comm. on Numbers* (New York, 1903); Marucchi in Vig., *Dict. de la Bible* (Paris, 1894); Lagrange, *Religions Sémitiques* (Paris, 1905), 83 sqq.; Smith, *Religion of the Semites* (London, 1894); Article *Baal* in *Encyc. Biblica* and in Hastings, *Dict. of the Bible*.

JOHN F. FENLON.

Beelzebub (בעל זבוב), or BAALZEBUB, (1) the Philistine god of Accaron (Ekron), scarcely 25 miles west of Jerusalem, whose oracle King Ochozias (Ahaziah) attempted to consult in his last illness, IV (II) Kings, i, 2. It is only as an oracle that the god is known to us; no other mention of him occurs in the Old Testament. The name is commonly translated "the lord of the flies", and the god is supposed to be so called either because as a sun god he brings the flies, though the Ba'al was probably not a sun god, or more likely because he is invoked to drive away the flies from the sacrifice, like the Zeus Apomuios, who drove them from Olympia, or the hero Myiagros in Arcadia. Halévy and Winckler interpret the name, according to the analogy of very many names compounded with *baal*, as "the lord of Zebûb", supposed to be a locality in Accaron; there is no proof, however, for the existence of such a locality, and besides Beelzebub is called the god of Accaron. Cheyne thinks the original form of the name is Ba'al Zebûl, "the lord of the mansion", or high house, which would refer to the god's temple or to the mountain on which the gods dwelt, or rather, in his opinion, to both. But the textual evidence, as Lagrange objects, is entirely in favour of *Zebub*. Cheyne, admitting this, holds that the title "lord of the high house", which would suggest to the writer of Kings a reference to Jehovah's temple or to His heavenly dwelling place, would be considered offensive, and would induce him, in contempt, to change it to *Ba'al Zebub*, the lord of flies. The tradition of the true name, lingering on, accounts for its presence in the Gospels (Zeboul). This conjecture, which has a certain plausibility, leaves unexplained why the contempt should lead to the particular form, *Baal Zebub*, a name without parallel in Semitic religions. It seems more reasonable, then, to regard

Baalzebub as the original form and to interpret it as "lord of the flies".

(2) In the New Testament, there is question of an evil spirit, Beelzeboul. On account of the great similarity of names, he is usually identified with Baalzebub, *beel* being the Aramaic form of *baal*, and the change from the final *b* to *l* such as might easily occur. But there were numberless names for demons at that time, and this one may have been newly invented, having no relation to the other; the fact that one element of the compound is Aramaic and the other Hebrew would not disprove this. The meaning of the term is "lord of the mansion" or dwelling, and it would be supposed by the Jews of this time to refer to the nether regions, and so be an appropriate name for the prince of that realm. Beelzeboul (Beelzebub) is used, then, merely as another name for Satan (Matt., xii, 24–29; Luke, xi, 15–22), by whom the enemies of Our Lord accused Him of being possessed and by whom they claimed He cast out demons. Their charge seems to have been that the good Our Lord did was wrought by the Evil One in order to deceive, which Jesus showed to be absurd and a wilful blindness. If the New Testament name be considered a transformation of the old, the question arises as to how the god of the little town of Accaron came to give a name to the Prince of Darkness. The mission on which Ochozias sent his followers seems to show that Beelzebub already had a wide renown in Palestine. The narrative (IV Kings, i) was a very striking one, well known to the contemporaries of Our Lord (Luke, ix, 54); from it might easily be derived the idea of Beelzebub as the special adversary of God, and the change in the final letter of the name which took place (*ex hypothesi*) would lead the Jews to regard it as designating the prince of the lower regions. With him was naturally connected the idea of demoniacal possession; and there is no need of Cheyne's conjecture that Beelzebub's "name naturally rose to Jewish lips when demoniacal possession was spoken of, because of the demoniacal origin assumed for heathen oracles". How can we account for the idea of Beelzeboul exorcizing the demons? On the assumption that he is to be identified with the Philistine god, Lagrange thinks the idea is derived from the special prerogative of Beelzebub as fly-chaser (*chasse-mouche*). In the Babylonian epic of the deluge, "the gods gather over the sacrificer like flies" (see Driver, Genesis, 105). It was easy for the heathen Semites, according to Lagrange, to come to conceive of the flies troubling the sacrifice as images of spirits hovering around with no right to be there; and so Beelzebub, the god who drove away the flies, became the prince of demons in whose name the devils were exorcized from the bodies of the possessed. Others think the idea naturally arose that the lord of the demons had power to command them to leave the possessed. It seems much more reasonable, however, to regard this faculty of Beelzebub not as a tradition, but simply as a charge invented by Our Lord's enemies to throw discredit on His exorcisms. His other miracles were probably accounted for by ascribing them to Beelzebub and so these likewise. Allen (Comm. on Matt., 107, 134) has endeavoured to simplify the problem by the use of higher criticism. According to him, the rôle of Beelzebub as arch-demon and exorcist was not a Palestinian belief; in Mark's Gospel, Beelzebub is simply the demon said to possess Our Lord. Matthew and Luke by mistake fuse together two independent clauses of Mark, iii, 22 and identify Beelzebub with Satan, to whom the faculty of exorcism is ascribed. The fusion, however, seems to be justified by the next verse of Mark, which is more naturally interpreted in the sense of Matthew and Luke, though Allen's interpretation may be admitted as possible. Beelzebub does not appear in the Jewish literature of the period; there we usually find Beliar (Belial) as an alternative name for Satan.

Lagrange, *Religions Sémitiques* (Paris, 1905); Cheyne in *Encyc. Bibl.* (New York, 1899), s. v. *Baalzebub, Beelzebul;* Allen, *Commentary on St. Matthew* (New York, 1907); Lesêtre in Vig., *Dict. de la Bible* (Paris, 1895), s. v. *Béelzébub;* Holtzmann, *Life of Jesus* (London, 1904).

John F. Fenlon.

Beesley (or Bisley), George, Venerable, martyr, b. at The Hill in Goosnargh parish, Lancaster, England, of an ancient Catholic family; d. 2 July, 1591. He was ordained priest at the English College at Reims, 14 March, 1587, and left for England, 2 November, 1588. A man of singular courage, young, strong, and robust, he was captured by Topcliffe late in 1590, and was by his tortures reduced to a skeleton. He endured all with invincible courage and could not be induced to betray his fellow Catholics. He suffered by the statute of 27 Eliz., merely for being a priest, in Fleet Street, London. His last words were "Absit mihi gloriari nisi in Cruce Domini Nostri Jesu Christi" and, after a pause, "Good people, I beseech God to send all felicity".

Gillow, *Bibl. Dict.* (London, 1885); Challoner, *Memoirs;* Pollen, *Acts of English Martyrs* (London, 1891).

Bede Camm.

Begging Friars. See Mendicant Friars.

Begin, Louis Nazaire. See Quebec, Archdiocese of.

Begnudelli-Basso, Francesco Antonio, a canonist who lived at the end of the seventeenth century; d. at Freising, 9 October, 1713. From 1675 he was Vicar-General of Trent, his native place. In 1679, however, he held a canonry in the Cathedral of Freising, where also he became in 1696 vicar-general of the diocese, and where he died. His "Bibliotheca juris canonico-civilis practica seu repertorium quæstionum magis practicarum in utroque foro" ranked him among the best canonists of his day. His canonical acumen is especially noteworthy, while he speaks in the clearest terms of papal infallibility. The work was published in Freising in 1712, four vols. in folio; Geneva, 1747; Modena and Venice, 1758. It has, however, lost its practical usefulness owing to the later editions of Lucius Ferraris's "Bibliotheca", which is vastly superior to the work of Begnudelli.

Krautzwald in *Kirchenlex;* Wernz, *Jus Decretalium* (Rome, 1898), I, no. 324, p. 418; Hurter, *Nomenclator*, II, 857.

Andrew B. Meehan.

Beguines; Beghards.—The etymology of the names *Beghard* and *Beguine* can only be conjectured. Most likely they are derived from the old Flemish word *beghen*, in the sense of "to pray", not "to beg", for neither of these communities were at any time mendicant orders; maybe from Bega, the patron saint of Nivelles, where, according to a doubtful tradition the first Beguinage was established; maybe, again, from Lambert le Bègue, a priest of Liège who died in 1180, after having expended a fortune in founding in his native town a cloister and church for the widows and orphans of crusaders.

As early as the commencement of the twelfth century there were women in the Netherlands who lived alone, and without taking vows devoted themselves to prayer and good works. At first there were not many of them, but as the century grew older their numbers increased; it was the age of the Crusades, and the land teemed with desolate women—the raw material for a host of neophytes. These solitaries made their homes not in the forest, where the true hermit loves to dwell, but on the fringe of the town, where their work lay, for they served Christ in His poor. About the beginning of the thirteenth century some of them grouped their cabins together, and the community thus formed was the first Beguinage.

The Beguine could hardly be called a nun; she took no vows, could return to the world and wed if she would, and did not renounce her property. If she was without means she neither asked nor accepted alms, but supported herself by manual labour, or by teaching the children of burghers. During the time of her novitiate she lived with "the Grand Mistress" of her cloister, but afterwards she had her own dwelling, and, if she could afford it, was attended by her own servants. The same aim in life, kindred pursuits, and community of worship were the ties which bound her to her companions. There was no mother-house, nor common rule, nor common general of the order; every community was complete in itself and fixed its own order of living, though later on many adopted the rule of the Third Order of Saint Francis. These communities were no less varied as to the social status of their members; some of them only admitted ladies of high degree; others were exclusively reserved for persons in humble circumstances; others again opened their doors wide to women of every condition, and these were the most densely peopled. Several, like the Great Beguinage of Ghent, numbered their inhabitants by thousands. Such was this semi-monastic institution. Admirably adapted to the spiritual and social needs of the age which produced it, it spread rapidly throughout the land and soon began to exercise a profound influence on the religious life of the people. Each of these institutions was an ardent centre of mysticism, and it was not the monks, who mostly dwelt on the country side, nor even the secular clergy, but the Beguines, the Beghards, and the sons of Saint Francis who moulded the thought of the urban population of the Netherlands. There was a Beguinage at Mechlin as early as 1207, at Brussels in 1245, at Louvain in 1234, at Bruges in 1244, and by the close of the century there was hardly a commune in the Netherlands without its Beguinage, whilst several of the great cities had two or three or even more. Most of these institutions were suppressed during the religious troubles of the fifteen-hundreds or during the stormy years which closed the eighteenth century, but a few convents of Beguines still exist in various parts of Belgium. The most notable are those of Bruges, Mechlin, Louvain, and Ghent, which last numbers nearly a thousand members.

The widespread religious revival of which the Beguinage was the outcome brought forth also about the same time several kindred societies for men. Of these the Beghards were the most widespread and the most important. The Beghards were all of them laymen, and, like the Beguines, they were not bound by vows, the rule of life which they observed was not uniform, and the members of each community were subject only to their own local superiors; but, unlike them, they had no private property; the brethren of each cloister had a common purse, dwelt together under one roof, and ate at the same board. They were for the most part, though not always, men of humble origin—weavers, dyers, fullers, and so forth—and thus they were intimately connected with the city craft-guilds. Indeed, no man could be admitted to the Beghards' convent at Brussels unless he were a member of the Weavers' Company, and this was in all probability not a unique case. The Beghards were often men to whom fortune had not been kind—men who had outlived their friends, or whose family ties had been broken by some untoward event, and who, by reason of failing health or advancing years, or perhaps on acount of some accident, were unable to stand alone. If, as a recent writer has it, "the medieval towns of the Netherlands found in the Beguinage a solution of their feminine question", the establishment of these communities afforded them at least a partial solution of another problem which pressed for an answer: the difficult problem of how to deal with the worn-out workingman. Albeit the main object of all these institutions was not a temporal but a spiritual one:

they had banded together in the first place to build up the inner man. Nor whilst working out their own salvation were they unmindful of their neighbours in the world, and thanks to their intimate connexion with the craft-guilds, they were able to largely influence the religious life, and to a great extent to mould the religious opinion of the cities and towns of the Netherlands, at all events in the case of the proletariat, during more than two hundred years.

Bearing in mind the wretched and down-trodden class from which the Beghards were generally recruited, and the fact that they were so little trammelled by ecclesiastical control, it is not surprising that the mysticism of some of them presently became a sort of mystical pantheism, or that some of them gradually developed opinions not in harmony with the Catholic Faith, opinions, indeed, if we may trust John Ruysbroek, which seem to have differed little from the religious and political opinions professed by anarchists to-day. The heretical tendencies of the Beghards and Beguines necessitated disciplinary measures, sometimes severe, on the part of ecclesiastical authority. Various restrictions were placed upon them by the Synods of Fritzlar (1259), Mainz (1261), Eichstätt (1282); and they were forbidden as "having no approbation" by the Synod of Béziers (1299). They were condemned by the Council of Vienne (1312), but this sentence was mitigated by John XXII (1321), who permitted the Beguines, as they had mended their ways, to resume their mode of life. The Beghards were more obstinate. During the fourteenth century they were repeatedly condemned by the Holy See, the bishops (notably in Germany), and the Inquisition. It should be noted, on the other hand, that in spite of widespread abuses, men of faith and piety were found among the Beghards. In their behalf Gregory XI (1374–77) and Boniface IX (1394) addressed Bulls to the bishops of Germany and the Netherlands. An echo of the theological errors into which the Beghards fell is found in the doctrine of Quietism.

Nor did the Beghard communities of the Netherlands escape the fate which sooner or later overtakes all human institutions: before the close of the Middle Ages most of them were in full decadence. Not, as so often happens, that their life was crushed out by the weight of gold; though, as time went on, they acquired endowments, they were never rich; they waned with the waning of the cloth trade, and, when that industry died, gradually dwindled away. Their crazy ships were sorely tried by the storm of the fifteen-hundreds; some of them went to the bottom, some weathered its fury, but were so battered that they afterwards sank in still water; a few, somehow or other, managed to keep afloat till the hurricane of the French Revolution at last dashed them to pieces. The highest number of these medieval foundations in Belgium was 94. They were reduced (1734) to 34 and (1856) to 20. Their membership in 1631 was 2,487; in 1828, 1,010; in 1856, about 1,600.

Geldulphus a Ryckel, *Vita S. Beggæ et Historia Begginariorum Belgii* (Louvain, 1630); Hélyot, *Histoire des ordres monastiques* (Paris, 1719), VIII; Thomas de Cantimpré, *De Apibus* (Douai, 1627); Thomassin, *Discip. Ecc. Vet.*, II, IV; Coens, *Disquis. Histor. de orig. Begh.* (Liège, 1629); Doutreman, *Hist. de Valenciennes* (referred to by Hélyot); Mosheim, *De Begh. et Begu. Commentarium* (Leipzig, 1790); Wauters, *Histoire des environs de Bruxelles* (Brussels, 1855), contains much curious information about the numerous Beguine convents in the neighbourhood of Brussels. See *Table Alphab.* in I and II, 500–508; Pirenne, *Hist. de Belgique* (Brussels, 1903), I, 337–340; Mohler, *Kirchengesch.*; Von Gruse, *Gerhart Groot u. seine Stiftungen* (Bonn, 1883); Delprat, *Verhandl. over de Broederschap van G. G.* (Utrecht, 1822); *Gerardi Magni Epistolæ XIV* (Amsterdam, 1857); Buschicos, *Chronicon Canon. Reg.* (1621); *The Chronicles of the Canons regular of Mount Agnes* (London, 1906); Kettlewell, *Thomas à Kempis and the Brothers of the Common Life* (London, 1886); Heimbucher, *Die Orden u. Kongregationen;* Bauer in *Kirchenlex.* s. v.

Ernest Gilliat-Smith.

Behaim, ALBERT VON (known also as ALBERTUS BOHEMUS); b. c. 1180, probably at Böheiming, in the Diocese of Passau; d. at Passau, 1260; a partisan of the popes in their struggle with the Emperor Frederick II (1215–50). In 1205 he went to Rome, where he was employed at the papal court as an expert in law. In 1237 he went to Germany, and through his efforts a league was formed against Frederick II between Otto of Bavaria, Wenceslaus of Bohemia, and came to an end in 1253. From that time he lived in Passau, where he had been dean of the chapter since 1246. He laboured with zeal and credit to himself, but not without many conflicts, until his death. He left two diaries, known as the first and second *Missivbuch*. Fragments of the first were edited by Oefele, in "Rerum Boicarum Scriptores", vol. I; the second by Höfler in "Bibliothek des litterarischen Vereins" (Stuttgart, 1847).

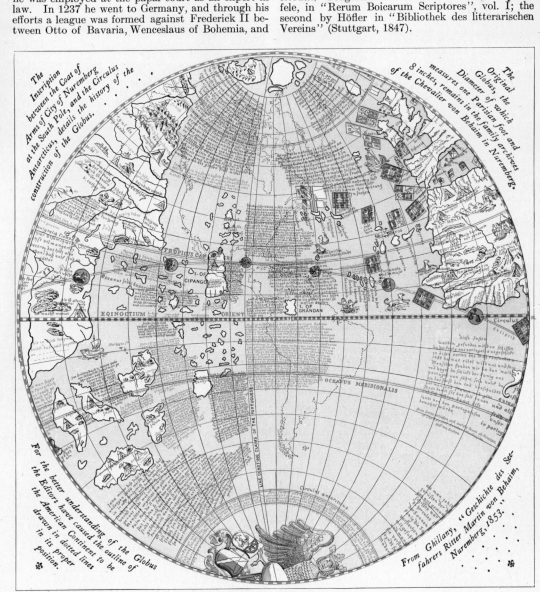

MARTIN BEHAIM'S GLOBE

Frederick of Austria. When excommunication was pronounced against the emperor in 1239, Behaim was made a permanent delegate and commissioned to make the sentence effective. For that purpose he appealed to the bishops of Germany (1240), and when they proved themselves negligent he excommunicated a number of ecclesiastics and laymen of prominence. At the same time, he worked for the election of a new king. However, his excessive severity had no effect, and he was forced to leave the country. In 1245 he was at the Council of Lyons, where Frederick was again excommunicated, and he worked as before against the emperor. His office of papal delegate

LERCHENFELD-AHAM, *Albert Behaim* (Munich, 1874); RATZINGER, *Albertus Bohemus* in *Historisch-politische Blätter* (Munich, 1869, 1879, 1880); HEFELE, *Conciliengesch.* (Freiburg, 1886), V; HAUCK, *Kirchengesch. Deutschl.* (Leipzig, 1903), IV; SEIDL in *Kirchenlex.* (Freiburg, 1886), I, 411; HURTER, *Nomenclator*, IV.

FRANCIS J. SCHAEFER.

Behaim, MARTIN (MARTINUS DE BOHEMIA), a German cartographer and navigator, b. at Nuremberg in 1459; d. at the German hospice of St. Bartholomew in Lisbon, Portugal, 29 July, 1507. Behaim came from a wealthy merchant family which settled in Nuremberg about 1300 and which is still in existence. He received the usual education but, according to his own statement, had among his teachers the celebrated mathematician and astronomer Regiomontanus. Behaim entered business life at an early age and became an agent at Antwerp. In 1481 or 1482 he went to Lisbon on business. Here his reputation as a pupil of Regiomontanus led to his appointment by King John (João) II as a member of a commission, the "junta dos mathematicos", which was to find some improved method for determining latitude. Behaim furnished them with the so-called Jacob's-staff, or cross-staff, and the astronomical tables necessary for ascertaining the declination of the sun. Having in this way become favourably known, Behaim was offered the opportunity of accompanying Diego Cam (Cão) on a voyage of discovery along the west coast of Africa. In the course of his explorations Cam discovered the mouth of the Congo and went as far as Walfisch Bay. After his return Behaim was made a Knight of the Portuguese Order of Christ in 1486, and married a daughter of Jobst von Hurter, hereditary governor of the islands of Fayal and Pico of the Azores group. In 1492, while he was at Nuremberg, Behaim made the well-known globe, probably with the scientific help of Hartmann Schedel, the Nuremberg humanist.

His influence on the great discoverers of his time was formerly much overestimated; at present it is questioned whether he had any such influence at all. It cannot be proved either that Columbus was stimulated by him or that Magellan (Magalhães) in his search for a southern passage made use of a chart of the world drawn by Behaim, as was once believed. It has even been questioned of late years whether Behaim had any right to call himself a pupil of Regiomontanus or whether he had taken part in the discoveries of Cam. Nevertheless his "apple", the oldest of all existing globes, ensures his lasting fame. The globe is about twenty-one inches in diameter and has no network to mark longitudes and latitudes. It is provided merely with the equator, one meridian, the tropics and the constellations of the zodiac, and is a unique example of miniature painting. There is an unmistakable connexion between Behaim's manner of representing the world and the geographical views of Toscanelli whose chart is usually reconstructed with the aid of Behaim's globe. Unfortunately the reproductions of Behaim's globe, so far made, are not satisfactory. The first copy was published by Doppelmayr in his "Historie von den Nürnberger Mathematicis" (1730) and was reproduced by Nordenskjöld in his "Facsimile Atlas to the Early History of Cartography" (1889). Another was drawn in 1847 for Jomard by Jean Müller who gave Dr. Ghillany a copy which the latter used in his biography of Behaim. This drawing is also to be found in Ruge, "Geschichte des Zeitalters der Entdeckungen" (1881), in Günther's biography of Behaim, and in Kretschmer, "Die Entdeckung Amerikas" (1892).

VON MURR, *Diplomatische Geschichte des portugiesischen berühmten Ritters Martin Behaim* (Nuremberg, 1778; GHILLANY, *Der Erdglobus des Martin Behaim vom Jahre 1492 und der des Johann Schöner vom Jahre 1520* (Nuremberg, 1842); IDEM, *Geschichte des Seefahrers Ritter Martin Behaim* (Nuremberg, 1853); REICHENBACH, *Martin Behaim, ein deutscher Seefahrer aus dem XV. Jahrhundert* (Wurzen-Leipzig, 1889); GÜNTERH, *Martin Behaim*, vol. XIII of the *Bayerische Bibliothek* (Bamberg, 1890); WAGNER, *Die Rekonstruktion der Toscanelli-Karte vom J. 1474 und die Pseudo-Facsimilie des Behaim-Globus vom J. 1492*, in the *Nachrichten von der k. Gesellsch. der Wissensch. zu Göttingen*, philol.-histor. division, 1894 (Göttingen, 1895), 208 sqq.; RAVENSTEIN, *Martin de Bohemia* in *Bibliotheca da Ravista Portugueza colonial e maritima* (Lisbon, 1900); STAUBER, *Die Schedelsche Bibliothek* in *Stud. u. Darstell. aus dem Gebiete der Gesch.* (Freiburg im Br., 1907), VI.

OTTO HARTIG.

Beiderlinden, BERNARD. See POONA, DIOCESE OF.

Beirut, in Phœnicia, a titular Latin see, and the residential see of several prelates of Oriental rites. The earliest form was likely *Beeroth* "springs", not Beroth (II Kings, viii, 8) or Berotha (Ezech., xlvii, 16), probably situated near Baalbek in Cœle-Syria. It is difficult to explain the more usual form, *Berytos*, but it probably comes from *Berûti*, the Phœnician name of a fish-goddess related to the god of Gebal or Byblos, two towns of the Giblites, a Chanaanite tribe. Berytos was the birthplace of Sanchoniathon, an early Phœnician author, and seems to have been unimportant in remote times. It is mentioned by the Greeks before Alexander, but is not spoken of in connexion with the expeditions of this conqueror. After the time of Antiochus IV, Epiphanes (175–164 B. C.), Berytos was known as Laodicea of Chanaan, a name which it kept until the reign of Alexander II, Zabinas (129–123 B. C.); see J. Rouvier, in "Revue de numismatique" (1896), and "Revue biblique", VII, 272–275. According to Strabo (XVI, ii, 9) it was destroyed by King Tryphon (137–134 B. C.). If this be true, it must have been rebuilt after a short time, for there are records for the complete series of the coins of Berytos from 123 to 14 B. C. It is certain that the Romans enlarged and embellished it; that it was garrisoned by two legions, the Leg. V Macedonica and Leg. VIII Augusta, and that in the year 14 B. C. it became a Roman colony with the name *Colonia Julia Augusta Felix Berytus*, so called after Julia, the daughter of Augustus (Mommsen, Res gestæ divi Augusti, II, 119). The Jewish kings Herod the Great, Herod Agrippa I, and Herod Agrippa II built sumptuous monuments at Berytos and gave gladiatorial combats there (Josephus, Bell. Jud., I, xxi, 11; Antiq., XVI, xi, 2; XVII, x, 9; XIX, vii, 5; XX, ix, 4); Titus also, after the siege of Jerusalem, gave gladiatorial games at Berytos, in which the combatants were Jews. (Josephus, Bell. Jud., VII, iii, 1.) From that time dates the magnificent aqueduct, the remains of which are yet visible, which carried to the city the waters of the River Magoras, now Nahr Beiruth. About the middle of the third century Berytos became the seat of the most renowned law school in the Eastern Roman Empire. Many celebrated jurisconsults were among its teachers (Montreuil, Hist. du droit byzantin, I, 264–273, 279–283). This school was spared by Justinian when he closed all similar schools in favour of Constantinople. The town had suffered much from an earthquake in 529, and when taken by the Arabs about 635 it had fallen into decay.

Berytos became a Christian see at an early date, and was a suffragan of Tyre in Phœnicia Prima, a province of the Patriarchate of Antioch. In antiquity its most famous bishop was Eusebius, afterwards Bishop of Nicomedia, the courtier-prelate and strong supporter of Arianism in the fourth century. Lequien (II, 815–820) gives a list of thirteen Greek bishops reaching to 1673, rectified and completed by Cyril Charon, a Greek Catholic priest (in Al-Mashriq, Beirut, 1 March, 1905). In 450 Beirut obtained from Theodosius II the title of metropolis, with jurisdiction over six sees taken from Tyre; but in 451 the Council of Chalcedon restored these to Tyre, leaving, however, to Beirut its rank of metropolis (Mansi, VII, 85–98). Thus, from 451 Beirut was an exempt metropolis depending directly on the Patriarch of Antioch. The city was captured on 27 April, 1111, by Baldwin I, King of Jerusalem, and with the exception of short intervals was held by the Franks till 1241. At an early date they established there a Latin see subject to Tyre and, with the provinces of Arabia and Phœnicia Prima, erroneously comprised in the Patriarchate of Jerusalem. Lists of its Latin bishops are available (Lequien, III, 1325–27; Gams, 434; Eubel, I, 137; II, 117; Revue bénédictine, 1904, 133–34).

Owing to the fertility of the soil and the security of the harbour, Beirut soon became one of the most active commercial cities in the East. The Druse

Ameer Fakhr ed-Din (1595–1634) improved the city and made it better known in Europe. He was a ruler of genius, and succeeded in creating a principality all but independent of the Porte. Beirut was his residence, and the environs his gardens. He planted near the city the beautiful pine wood which is still its finest walk. He had relations with the Venetians and with the Medici at Florence; in 1633 he embraced Catholicism, and in the following year suffered martyrdom for his faith. The fact is undeniable, for the letters of the Capuchin who was the means of his conversion have just been published (de Barenton, O. M. C., "La France catholique en Orient", 158–164). In the course of the seventeenth and eighteenth centuries the Turkish Government succeeded in reducing the power of several native families that had forced themselves upon Beirut; at the present time Turkish authority is supreme. The city was shelled in 1840 by the English and in 1860 occupied by the French after the frightful slaughter of Christians in Syria; since that date it has been steadily thriving. Ships of the heaviest tonnage visit its harbour; railroads connect it with Damascus by way of Lebanon, and with Tripoli; carriage-roads connect it with the inland and seaboard towns. The country is well watered and cultivated, and the view from the city is beautiful. Beirut is the capital of a homonymous vilayet. The population, which is about 150,000, shows a steady increase. There are 40,000 Mussulmans, besides the small garrison; 40,000 Maronites, 35,000 Greeks, 12,000 Catholic or Melchite Greeks, 2,000 Latins, 2,000 Protestants, 2,000 Jews, Druses, and Gregorian Armenians, 1,000 Catholic Syrians and Armenians.

Apart from its interest as a Latin titular bishopric, it may be noted that Beirut is: (1) a Greek metropolitan see with about 70,000 believers and many elementary schools; in the city of Beirut are 5 schools for girls conducted by 23 teachers in the pay of the Russian Government; (2) a metropolitan see for Catholic Greeks or Melchites, who number about 15,000 and have a large college at Beirut; (3) a Maronite see, with 50,000 subjects; 50 churches and chapels, 30 priests, and a seminary and college located in the city; (4) a Syrian Catholic see, with about 1,000 faithful, the residence of the Syrian patriarch having been transferred from Mardin to Beirut. The Latin Vicar-Apostolic of Syria, who is also the Apostolic delegate for Oriental rites, has been stationed since 1890 at Beirut (previously at Aleppo), with about 6,000 under his spiritual rule.

In Beirut are many Maronite and Greek Catholic monasteries of Baladites, Aleppines, and Salvatorians, who unaided would be unable to compete with the Protestant propaganda which has taken Beirut as a centre whence it spreads over the whole of Syria. Since 1866 the German mission has had charge of the Hospital of the Knights of St. John, an orphan asylum, and a school for girls conducted by deaconesses. The Jewish mission of the Church of Scotland since 1864 has conducted two schools for boys and girls. Miss Taylor's "St. George's Institute" has charge of Mussulman or Druse girls. Since 1860 the British Syrian Mission has had a parish, 10 schools, and a normal school for women. Since 1825 the Presbyterian Church of New York has maintained at Beirut a church, a printing-house, its Bible agency, and a school for girls. At a later period it built there the American university, which includes an intermediate college, a medical school, and a theological school for the training of native preachers and clergymen. It also publishes a newspaper and a review; and maintains outside of Beirut 130 primary schools with 109 teachers and 8,000 pupils. In spite of so much effort and expense the Protestant missions have gained in the last 80 years only about 5,000 adherents in all Syria.

The Catholic opposition to their propaganda is supported chiefly by French missionaries. The Capuchins, Franciscans, and Lazarists each have a monastery and a school; the Christian Brothers, schools and a college; the Sisters of Charity, priory schools, a boarding-school, an orphan asylum, and an industrial school for orphan girls; they also have charge of the hospital at the Catholic University. The Sisters of St. Joseph and the Dames de Nazareth have a boarding-school; the Sisters of the Holy Family, a school; the Mariamets, native nuns, their principal house. The most imposing institutions are those of the Jesuits. They maintain and direct outside of Beirut 192 schools for boys and girls, with 294 teachers and 12,000 pupils. There is in the city a faculty of medicine (120 students) founded in 1881 with the help of the French Government; its examinations are conducted before French and Ottoman physicians, and its diplomas are recognized by both France and Turkey. They conduct, moreover, St. Joseph's Catholic University, the title of which was granted by Leo XIII, 25 February, 1881. This university includes: (1) a seminary (60 students) for natives of all rites, which up to 1902 had sent out 228 students, including 3 patriarchs, 15 bishops, 115 priests, and 83 friars; (2) a faculty of philosophy and theology (30 students), which grants the same degrees as the Gregorian University in Rome; (3) a faculty of Oriental languages and sciences, founded in 1902, which teaches the literary and conversational use of Arabic, Hebrew, Syriac, Coptic, and Ethiopic; the comparative grammar of Semitic languages; the history and geography of the Orient; Oriental archæology; Græco-Roman epigraphy and antiquities; (4) a classical and modern tuition college (400 pupils); (5) 3 primary schools (600 pupils). A printing-house, inaugurated in 1853, is now famous as the foremost Arabic printing-house. Since 1871 the Jesuits have published "Al-Bashir", a weekly Arabic newspaper, and since 1898 a fortnightly Arabic review, "Al-Mashriq", the editors of which took rank at once among the best Orientalists. In 1906 they began a collection of philological papers, "Mélanges de la Faculté orientale de l'Université Saint-Joseph". Finally, they contribute to many scientific periodicals and publish, chiefly in Arabic, works of great value. We may mention here another precious collection: "Documents inédits pour servir à l'histoire du christianisme en Orient", the first volume of which appeared at Paris in 1905. These missionaries are the strongest bulwark of Catholicism in Syria.

Robinson, *Palästina*, III, 725 sqq.; Renan, *Mission de Phénicie* (Paris, 1864), 342–353; Pietschmann, *Geschichte der Phönicier*, 50; Schürer, *Geschichte des jüdischen Volkes*, I, 340; de Barenton, *La France catholique en Orient* (Paris, 1902), passim; Jullien, *La nouvelle mission de la c. de J. en Syrie* (Paris, 1899); *L'imprimerie catholique de Beyrouth et son œuvre en Orient, 1853–1903* (Brussels, 1903); Gressien, *Réponse à M. Charlot in Études . . . de la c. de J.* (Paris, 5 December, 1906), 577–590; *Mélanges de l'Université de St. Joseph* (Beirut, 1906).

S. Vailhé.

Beja (Beiensis), Diocese of, in Portugal, suffragan of Evora. It was created 10 June, 1770, and numbers 175,000 Catholics, with 115 parishes, 120 priests, and 197 churches. It is the capital of the district of Baixo Alemtejo. The city is supposed to be the *Pax Julia*, or *Paca*, of the Romans, and is still surrounded by remains of old Roman walls, which, however, were partly restored during the Middle Ages. Beja was taken from the Moors in 1162 by Affonso Henriques. It stands on the summit of a high hill surrounded by beautiful and fertile valleys under cultivation, as the district is rich in agricultural products, mainly cereals, olive oil, and wine. The best example of medieval architecture still extant in Portugal is the castle built in Beja by King Dom Diniz. It is a square, massive structure 120 feet high, from the top of which the whole of the Alemtejo country and the Cintra mountains may be seen. The walls of the castle are covered with hieroglyphics. Beja was in its early days an episcopal city, but at the time of the invasion by the Moors lost its dignity. The Cathedral of Beja is an old temple, though so much modernized as to make it impossible to determine with any degree of certainty its original date. Other famous churches are those of Our Lady of the Conception, St. Iago, or Santiago, and Santa Maria de la Feira, said to have been an old Moorish mosque. The College of St. Sissenando, which belonged to the Jesuits, and was built principally at the expense of Donna Maria Sophia, in 1695, stands in the street where the saint was born. Part of this building is now occupied by the episcopal palace. The city has about 8,000 inhabitants, modern improvements, schools, banks, libraries, etc. It is said to be the richest in Roman remains of all the cities in Portugal, except Evora, which now possesses a large collection of Roman antiquities collected in Beja.

Gerarchia Cattolica (Rome, 1907); FLÓREZ, España Sagrada (1786), XIV, 230–276; Coll. de livres inédits sur l'hist. du Portugal (1824), V, 486–545. FRANCISCO J. YANES.

Bejarno, FERNANDO. See MIJES.

Belasyse, JOHN, BARON BELASYSE, b. about 1614; d. 1689, a loyal Catholic English nobleman, second son of Thomas first Lord Fauconberg. His mother was Barbara, daughter of Sir Henry Cholmondeley of Roxby, Yorkshire. John Belasyse, who represented Thirsk in both the Short and Long Parliaments, but was "disabled" as a Royalist to sit, played a conspicuous part in the civil war, commanding a "Tertia" on the Royalist side. He raised six regiments of horse and foot at his own expense, took part in the battles of Edgehill, Newbury, and Naseby, as well as the sieges of Reading and Bristol, and was subsequently made Lieutenant-General of the King's forces in the North of England and Governor of York. He was wounded several times and in January, 1645, was raised to the peerage by the King at Oxford under the title of Baron Belasyse of Worlaby, Lincolnshire. During the Commonwealth Lord Belasyse acted as a sort of Royalist agent in England and was in frequent communication with Charles II and his supporters in the Netherlands. After the Restoration he was made Lord-Lieutenant of the East Riding of Yorkshire (1661–73) and Governor of Hull, while from 1664 to 1666 he held the post of Captain-General of the forces in Africa and Governor of Tangier. Somewhat later, however, upon the passing of the Test Act (1673) he found himself as a Catholic unable to take the necessary oath and resigned all his appointments. At the time of the Oates plot, Belasyse, along with four other Catholic peers, the Lords Arundell of Wardour, Stafford, Powys, and Petre, was denounced as a conspirator and formally impeached in Parliament. Belasyse in particular was said to have been designated Commander-in-Chief of the Popish army, but Charles II, according to Von Ranke, ridiculed the idea on the ground that the man could then hardly stand on his feet with gout. Nevertheless, Lord Belasyse lived on for another ten years. The impeached Catholic peers, though they endured a long imprisonment in the Tower, were never brought to trial, and at the accession of James II Belasyse was again received into high favour. His appointment in 1687 as First Lord Commissioner of the Treasury was a step which roused strong religious feeling against James's government. Lord Belasyse died in 1689, the year of the accession of William of Orange. He was three times married, and left five children, but the title became extinct upon the death of his grandson Henry, third Baron Belasyse of Worlaby.

DODD, Church History of England (Brussels, 1742), III; GILLOW, Bibl. Dict. of Eng. Cath., I; KEARY in Dict. Nat. Biog., IV, 142; CLARENDON, History of the Great Rebellion, and the Clarendon State Papers in the Bodleian Library.
HERBERT THURSTON.

Belchiam, THOMAS, VENERABLE, a Franciscan martyr in the reign of Henry VIII, date of birth uncertain; d. 3 August, 1537. He boldly opposed the king's first divorce, and denounced the tyrant as a heretic. He wrote a book addressed to his brethren, beginning with the text: "They that wear soft clothing are in kings' houses", in which he rebuked the faithless bishops, who were afraid to tell the king the truth. The book seems to be lost, but one copy got into Henry's hands, and he is said to have been moved to tears by reading it, though he soon repented of this weakness. Belchiam and some thirty of the Observant Franciscans were thrown into prison, where they perished of hunger.

DODD, Church History (Brussels, 1739); BOURCHIER, Historia Ecclesiastica de Martyrio Fratrum Ord. D. Francisci (Paris, 1581); WADDING, Annales Minorum (Ancona, 1736), tom. XVI; STONE, Faithful unto Death (London, 1892).
BEDE CAMM.

Belem do Pará, ARCHDIOCESE OF, in South America, formerly (after 4 March, 1719) a suffragan diocese of Bahia (San Salvador), but raised to metropolitan rank 3 May, 1906. The city of Belem is the capital of the Brazilian State of Pará, and is situated on the Bay of Guajara, in the richest rubber and coffee section of the Republic. Santa Maria de Nazareth do Pará, to give the city its full name, was founded in 1615, but has reached its present importance as one of the largest shipping ports of northern Brazil only during the last twenty years. Not only is it the most northerly port of any importance in South America, and as such the nearest to the great shipping centres of North America and Europe, but it is also the great outlet for the natural products of the State of Pará. It has a population of 100,000, an export trade of about $25,000,000, and an import trade of about $12,000,000 annually. The mean temperature is about 80° Fahrenheit.

Among the churches of this cathedral city is that of Santa Maria de Nazareth in the pretty suburb of Nazareth. The old convent and chapel of the Carmelite Order have been converted into a seminary, while the old Jesuit College is now occupied by the episcopal palace and another seminary. The city has all modern improvements, and what are considered the best museum and botanical gardens in Brazil. The Amparo Orphan Asylum is ranked among the leading charitable institutions of the State and the city.

In 1903 the Prælatura Nullius of Santarem was made from the Diocese of Belem; and again, in 1904, a new delimitation of the same quasi-episcopal territory took place. The Catholic population of the Archdiocese of Belem is now about 480,000. There are about 500 Protestants. In this vast territory, which before the above-mentioned division included 1,176,100 square miles, the parishes are 77 in number, with 29 filial churches. There are 47 secular, and 13 religious, priests, and 21 Brothers.

Gerarchia Cattolica (Rome, 1907); WERNER, Orbis Terr. Cath. (Freiburg, 1890); SODRÉ, The State of Pará (London, 1893); BUREAU OF AMERICAN REPUBLICS, Handbook of Brazil (Washington, 1901); GROSSI, Storia della Colonizzazione Europea al Brasile (Rome, 1905).
FRANCISCO J. YANES.

Belfast. See DOWN AND CONNOR.

Belfry.—The upper part of the tower or steeple of a church, for the reception of the bells; or a detached tower containing bells, as the campanile of the Italians. The term is sometimes applied to the timber frame by which the bells are supported; also to the room or loft in the tower of a church, from which the bells are rung. Originally it denoted a tower in which sentinels were placed to ring bells, and thus give notice of the approach of the enemy, or a tower used in besieging a fortified place; it was of wood and movable. In England the bell-tower usually forms a part of the church, but it is sometimes detached from it, as at Evesham, Worcestershire, and Berkeley, Gloucestershire; Chichester cathedral, Sussex, etc. At Pembridge, in Herefordshire, there is a detached belfry built entirely of wood, the frame in which the bells are hung arising from the ground, with merely a casing of boards.

In Belgium, one of the earliest architectural expressions of the newly acquired independence (12th century) was the erection of a belfry. The right of possessing a bell was one of the first privileges in all old charters, not only as a symbol of power, but as a means of calling the community together. The tower, too, in which the bell was hung was a symbol of power in the Middle Ages; the first care of every enfranchised community was to erect a "tower of pride" proportionate to its importance. The tower was generally the record-office of the city. All these uses have passed away, and most of the belfries have either fallen into neglect or been appropriated to other purposes. Of those remaining the oldest seems to be that of Tournay, a fine tower, though it is a good deal altered and its effect destroyed by modern additions. The belfry at Ghent was commenced in 1183, but the stone-work was only completed in 1337. In 1376 a wooden spire was placed upon it, making the height 237 feet. This spire was recently taken down in order to complete the tower according to the original design, which, like that of most of the unfinished buildings of Belgium, has been carefully preserved. When finished it will be about 300 feet in height, and one of the finest belfries in the country.

Fergusson, *History of Architecture*, I, 600, 601; II, 101; Parker, *Glossary of Architecture*, I, 53; Nicholson, *Glossary of Architecture*, I, 35; Britton, *Dictionary of Architecture and Archæology*, 82; *Dictionary of Architecture, Architectural Publication Society*, I, 57; Sturgis, *Dictionary of Architecture*, I, 268, 272.

Thomas H. Poole.

Belgium.—I. The Napoleonic Era.—The victory of Fleurus, gained by the French army over the Austrian forces, 26 June, 1794, gave to revolutionary France all the territories which constitute Belgium of to-day: the Austrian Netherlands, the ecclesiastical principality of Liège, the little monastic principality of Stavelot-Malmedy, and the Duchy of Bouillon. The French, who professed to have entered the country to deliver the Belgians from the yoke of tyranny and to liberate them, in reality gave themselves up to such pillaging and extortion that, as a Brussels magistrate said, they left the inhabitants nothing but their eyes to weep with. After this, in alleged compliance with the express wish of the Belgians, who as a matter of fact had not been consulted, a decree of the Convention, dated 1 October, 1795, proclaimed the annexation of the Belgian provinces to France.

At the beginning of the French rule, which was to last twenty years (1794–1814), religious conditions were not identical in the annexed countries. Religion was deeply rooted in what had formerly been the Austrian Netherlands. They had revolted in 1789 against the reforms of Joseph II, which were inspired by the spirit of sophistry. Jansenism, Febronianism, and Josephinism had gained but few partisans there; the University of Louvain was a bulwark of Catholic orthodoxy; even the Vonckist party, which in 1789 had been clamouring for political reforms, showed great respect for religion and had taken as its motto *Pro aris et focis*. On the other hand, in the ancient principality of Liège, which, since the fourteenth century had shown the deepest sympathy with France, public sentiment was gallophile, revolutionary, and even somewhat Voltairean; the predominant desire was to throw off the yoke of

the priests, and the principality had literally cast itself into the arms of France through hatred of the theocracy. But the French Government soon caused these local differences to be lost sight of in the common hatred of the foreign oppressor.

The Directory began by enforcing, one after another, the French revolutionary laws concerning monastic orders and public worship in Belgium. Religious houses, except those devoted to teaching or to the care of the sick, were suppressed; it was forbidden to wear an ecclesiastical garb; the clergy were forced to publish a declaration recognizing the people of France as the sovereign authority, and promising submission and obedience to the laws of the Republic; the communes were forbidden to contribute to the expenses of public worship and every external symbol of religion was prohibited. The Belgians stood firm, and the elections of the fifth year having shown an undeniable reaction of public opinion against the revolutionary spirit, the clergy appealed to the Five Hundred (*Cinq Cents*) to demand a suspension of the declaration until a papal decision should be received settling the question of its licitness. In the meanwhile, the priests who had not made the declaration continued to exercise their priestly functions in the Belgian provinces, and the tribunal of La Dyle acquitted those who were brought before it. At this juncture, Camille Jordan made a favourable report to the *Cinq Cents* on the clergy's request, and thus the Belgians had the honour of changing the current of French legislation for the better.

The *coup d'état* of the fifth Fructidor, however, carried out by the revolutionary members of the Directory, destroyed all hope. The victorious conspirators dismissed many Belgians who had been elected, and the elections of the sixth year, conducted under the violent pressure of republican deputies, gave the Government the wished-for results. Then persecution began again. The observance of the *decadi*, or the last day of the republican decade (week of ten days), was made obligatory and the Sunday rest was forbidden; for the second time, the wearing of any ecclesiastical garb was prohibited; in the suppression of religious orders no exception was made for nursing and teaching orders; seminaries and secular chapters were likewise abolished. The University of Louvain was closed on the ground of not having "the kind of public instruction conformable to Republican principles". As if the "declaration" had not sufficiently overtaxed consciences, priests were compelled to take an oath of hatred for royalty. On the refusal of the great majority, they were banished *en masse* and a decree issued, closing all churches served by recalcitrant priests. The officials of many communes ignored this order, and in more than one respect, it became a source of trouble. The interdicted priests continued to exercise their functions in the woods, or in private houses which afforded them places of retreat; in many places the faithful, deprived of the clergy, assembled in churches or in barns, to celebrate "blind Masses", as they were called, viz. Masses without consecration, or any services at the altar. The French deputies daily devised new methods of persecution in revenge for the opposition of public opinion, all the more unconquerable by reason of its silence and its tranquillity.

Things did not rest here. The spark that started the conflagration was the enforcing (1798) in the Belgian provinces of the French conscription laws requiring the enlistment of young men in the armies of the Republic. Rather than shed their blood for masters whom they hated, they rose in revolt, first in Waesland and in Campine, then in Flanders and in German Luxemburg. The Walloon provinces took part in the movement, but with much less energy. This was "the peasants' war" called in Luxemburg, "the war of the cudgels" (*Klöppelkrieg*). There was no lack of courage and devotion among the combatants, and some among them afforded admirable examples of heroism. However, they were poorly armed, had inefficient commanders, and were totally lacking in discipline and military organization; they were deprived of the support of the nobility and of the middle class, who remained absolutely inactive, and they were abandoned even by the Austrian Government which had every reason to stir up a Belgian insurrection. Consequently they could offer no serious resistance to the French troops. They fell back every time they met the enemy in open field; those who did not die in battle were later shot.

After this rising had been quelled, the persecution of the clergy was resumed; 7,500 priests were illegally condemned to be deported. The great majority escaped, only four or five hundred being arrested. Of this number, the oldest and those who were ill were detained in Belgium and in France; about three hundred were sent to Rochefort with Guiana as their ultimate destination, and, in the interval, were held at the Ile de Ré and the Ile d'Oléron where they had much to undergo from ill treatment. It was the darkest hour during the French domination, and was terminated by the *coup d'état* of 18 Brumaire, 1799. The new Government did not persecute on principle, but only in so far as it was believed necessary to enforce the revolutionary laws, to maintain the interests of the party in power. A solution of difficulties was supposed to have been discovered when the clergy were required to take merely an oath of "fidelity to the Republic as resting on the sovereignty of the people". The Belgian bishops who were refugees in England condemned this oath because the doctrine of the sovereignty of the people seemed to them heretical. They also refused to sanction the promise of fidelity to the Constitution of the seventh year, which the Government exacted of the clergy before permitting them to exercise the duties of their ministry, because the Constitution rested on false bases and contained articles deserving of condemnation. The leader of this opposition was a priest named Corneille Stevens (1747–1828), who, appointed administrator of the Diocese of Namur (1799) by Cardinal Frankenberg, Archbishop of Mechlin, forbade the clergy to promise fidelity to the Constitution, and who, in a series of pamphlets appearing under the pseudonym of Lemaigre, continued to advocate resistance. Finally, the Concordat of 15 August, 1801, brought, if not final peace, at least a truce. At the pope's request, the four Belgian bishops who had survived the persecutions tendered their resignations and of the nine episcopal sees into which Belgium had been divided since 1559, five only were retained: Mechlin Tournai, Ghent, Namur, and Liège. The bishoprics of Antwerp, Bruges, Ypres, and Ruremonde were suppressed. This organization of 1801 is still effective with this difference, however, that the See of Bruges was re-established in 1834, and that of Ruremonde in 1840.

Great was the rejoicing in the Belgian provinces when, on Pentecost day, 1802 (6 June), Catholic worship was solemnly re-established throughout the country. For some years, the name of Bonaparte, the First Consul, was most popular, and it even seemed as if the "new Cyrus", by the great boon which he had granted Belgium, had gained the support of the Belgians for a foreign government. The bishops appointed by Napoleon fostered in the people sentiments of personal devotion to him, and to such an extent that to-day they cannot be acquitted of the charge of exceeding all bounds in their adulation and servility. There were, it is true, protests against the new regime. The "non-communicants", as they were styled, refused to recognize the Concordat, contending that it had been forced upon the pope, and they formed a schismatical group, termed

the "little church" (*la petite église*), which, though continually falling off in numbers, has preserved its existence, until very recent times. The members have often been erroneously designated as Stevenists. Stevens did not oppose the Concordat. The champion of a rigorous and uncompromising orthodoxy, he recognized the authority of the bishops of the Concordat, but mercilessly condemned their cringing attitude towards the civil authorities, against whose religious policy he never ceased protesting. From the recesses of his retreat he sent forth brochures, training his guns upon "Saint Napoleon", whose feast day had been fixed by the Government as the 15th of August. He also attacked bitterly the imperial catechism of 1806 already adopted by the greater part of the French clergy, which contained a special chapter upon the duties of the faithful toward the emperor. This uninterrupted propaganda struck a responsive chord in the national consciousness and was doubtless responsible for the courage displayed by the Belgian episcopacy in refusing to accept the imperial catechism, which was adopted only in the Diocese of Mechlin. Stevens was perhaps the most unbending adversary Napoleon ever encountered, and their contest was extremely interesting. Although the emperor offered thirty thousand francs to anyone who would deliver Father Stevens into his hands, the priest was never seized; nor was he silenced as long as the Empire lasted. When Napoleon fell (1814) he came out of his retreat, entered the jurisdiction of the Bishop of Namur, and submitted all his writings to the judgment of the Holy See, which, however, never pronounced upon them.

The Belgian bishops were wearied with the exactions of the Government, which went so far as to require every year special pastoral letters impressing upon the people their military duty on the occasion of each call for conscripts, and they, as well as the body of the people, had already lost confidence in Napoleon, when, in 1809, he made the tremendous mistake of suppressing the temporal power of the pope and of annexing the States of the Church to the Empire. From that day, he was regarded by the Belgians as a persecutor. Count de Mérode-Westerloo, a Belgian, and Prince Corsini, an Italian, alone dared to express publicly in the Senate their disapproval of this usurpation, and thus prevented it from receiving a unanimous ratification. The more anti-religious the policy of the emperor, the more energetic became the resistance of the Belgians, and the more spirited the conduct of their bishops, who discarded the language of the courtier for that of the pastor. While the Bishops of Mechlin and Liège, recently appointed by the emperor, denounced their own clergy, at Ghent, Tournai, and Namur, Bishops de Broglie, Hirn, and Pisani de la Gaude, respectively gave examples of noble firmness. Named Chevalier of the Legion of Honour, Bishop de Broglie declined on the plea of being unable in conscience to take the oath to maintain the territorial integrity of the Empire which thenceforth would comprise the States of the Church. "Your conscience is a fool", said the Emperor, turning his back. At the famous council of 1811, convoked by Napoleon without the authorization of the imprisoned pope, the attitude of de Broglie and of Hirn was no less courageous; they, together with the Bishop of Troyes, succeeded in inducing the council to defeat the imperial decree limiting the pope's right of institution. The very next day, the council was dissolved by imperial command, and the three bishops were arrested and thrown into prison, not to be released until they had been forced to tender their resignations. Their successors appointed by Napoleon were not recognized in their respective dioceses, in which the clergy and the faithful were a unit in their resistance. More and more incensed, the emperor fell to striking blindly; numbers of priests were

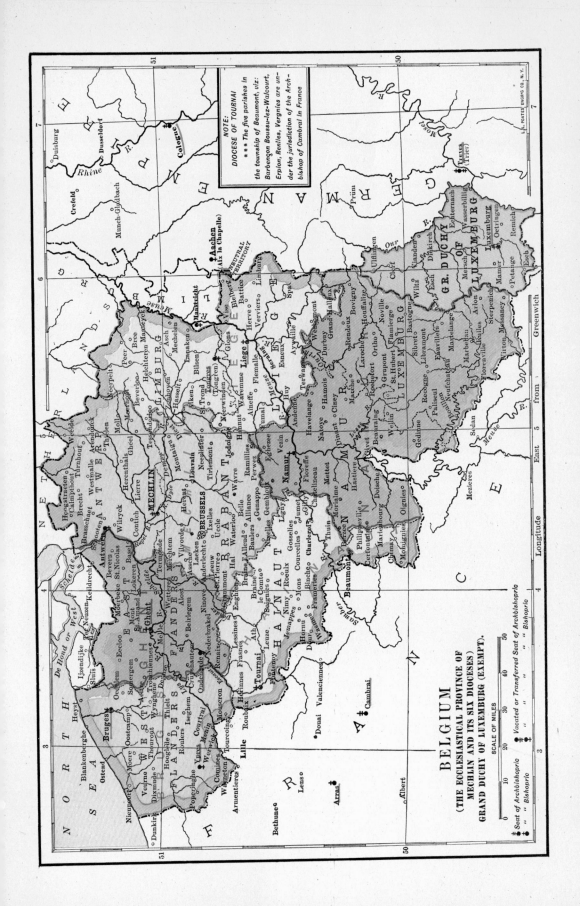

BELGIUM

(THE ECCLESIASTICAL PROVINCE OF
MECHLIN AND ITS SIX DIOCESES)
GRAND DUCHY OF LUXEMBURG (EXEMPT).

SCALE OF MILES

NOTE:
DIOCESE OF TOURNAI
*** The five parishes in
the township of Beaumont, viz:
Barbençon Boussu-lez-Walcourt,
Erpion, Renlies, Vergnies are un-
der the jurisdiction of the Arch-
bishop of Cambrai in France

imprisoned, and all the seminarists of Ghent were drafted into the army and dispatched to Wesel on the Rhine, where forty-nine of them succumbed to contagious diseases (1813). Such was the end of a regime which had been acclaimed by the Belgians with universal joy. The fall of Napoleon was greeted with no less satisfaction, and many Belgian volunteers took up arms against him in the campaigns of 1814 and 1815. In this nation of loyal Catholics, it was Napoleon's blundering religious policy which alienated his subjects.

II. THE KINGDOM OF THE NETHERLANDS (1814–30).—Soon after the victory of the Allied Powers, who became masters of Belgium, they established there a provisional government under the Duke of Beaufort (11 June, 1814). The new governing powers promptly proclaimed to the Belgians that, in conformity with the intentions of the Allied Powers, "they would maintain inviolable the spiritual and the civil authority in their respective spheres, as determined by the canonical laws of the Church and by the old constitutional laws of the country". These declarations roused hopes which, however, were destined to be disappointed; for by the secret treaty of Chaumont (1 March, 1814), confirmed by Article 6 of the Treaty of Paris (30 May, 1814), it had even then been decided that Holland should receive an addition of territory, and that this addition should be Belgium. The secret Treaty of London (23 June, 1814) furthermore provided that the union of the two countries was to be internal and thorough, so that they "would form one and the same State governed by the constitution already established in Holland, which would be modified by mutual consent to accord with new conditions". The new State took the name of the Kingdom of the Netherlands, and was placed under the sovereignty of William I of Orange-Nassau.

The object of the Powers in creating the Kingdom of the Netherlands was to give France on her northern frontier a neighbour strong enough to serve as a barrier against her, and with this aim in view they disposed of the Belgian provinces without consulting them. The State resulting from this union seemed to offer numerous guarantees of prosperity from the standpoint of economics. Unfortunately, however, the two peoples, after being separated for more than two centuries, had conflicting temperaments; the Dutch were Calvinists, the Belgians Catholics, and the former, although greatly in the minority, 2,000,000 as against 3,500,000 Belgians, expected to rule the Belgians and to treat them as subjects. These differences could have been lessened by a sovereign who would take the duty on himself; they were, however, aggravated by the policy adopted by William I. Arbitrary, narrow-minded, obstinate, and moreover an intolerant Calvinist, he surrounded himself almost exclusively with Dutchmen, who were totally ignorant of Catholic matters and of the Belgian character. In addition, he was imbued with the principles of "enlightened despotism" which made him regard his absolutism as the form of government best suited to the needs of his kingdom, and thus he was unequal to his task from the very outset. While still Prince of Fulda, he had persecuted his Catholic subjects until the Diet was forced to check him. As King of the Netherlands, he showed that he had learned nothing by experience, and imagined that he could effect the fusion of the two peoples by transforming Belgium into Holland as far as possible.

On the other hand, the Belgians, passionately attached to their national traditions, and even more to their religious unity, did not take sufficiently into account the profound changes which had taken place in the conditions of the two peoples. Forgetful of the French Revolution and the consequent upheaval of Western Europe they were convinced that past conditions could be restored even in the midst of a society

that had outgrown them; nor did they grasp the fact that as the Treaty of London established freedom of worship in the Kingdom of the Netherlands they were under an international obligation which could not be put aside. They calmly demanded, first of the Allied Sovereigns, then of the Congress of Vienna, not only the restoration of the former rights of the Church, but the re-establishment of their old constitution in its entirety. Their disappointment was great when their sovereign, obeying the provisions of the Treaty of London, submitted for their acceptance the "Fundamental Law of Holland", with some modifications. Leaving out of the question the initial injustice in granting each country the same numerical representation in the States-General, despite the fact that the population of Belgium was almost twice that of Holland, it entirely overthrew the old order of things, suppressed the clergy as an order, abolished the privileges of the Catholic Church, and guaranteed the enjoyment of the same civil and political rights to every subject of the king, and equal protection to every religious creed. The Belgian bishops promptly made respectful appeals to the king. William having disregarded these, they issued a "Pastoral Instruction" for the use of the prominent Belgians summoned to present their views on the revised Fundamental Law. This condemned the Law as contrary to religion and forbade its acceptance. The high-handed course taken by the Government to hinder the effectiveness of these measures proved unavailing; of the 1,603 prominent Belgians consulted, 280 did not vote, 796 voted against the Fundamental Law, and only 527 declared themselves in favour of it. The Fundamental Law was therefore rejected by the nation; for, adding to the 527 favourable votes the 110 unanimous votes of the States of Holland, there was a total of only 637 votes. Nevertheless, the king declared the Fundamental Law adopted, because, according to him, those who did not vote were to be regarded as favouring it, while of the 796 who opposed it, 126 did so only because they misunderstood its meaning. Owing to this "Dutch arithmetic", as King William's computations were termed, Belgium found itself under a constitution which it had legally repudiated, a constitution too which proved to the Kingdom of the Netherlands a heavy burden during its brief, stormy existence.

The adoption of the Fundamental Law, by the king's decision, did not end the conflict between the civil authority and the Belgian conscience. Besieged with questions as to whether it was permissible to take the oath of fidelity to the Fundamental Law, the bishops published their "Doctrinal Decision", which condemned it (1815). In consequence, many Catholics in obedience to their religious superiors, refused to take the oath, resigned their offices and their seats in the legislature. On the other hand, the Prince de Méan, former Prince-Bishop of Liège, took the required oath, and the king immediately appointed him to the archiepiscopal See of Mechlin, then vacant. The king next attempted to gain the Holy See for his side in his struggle with the Belgian episcopacy, by practically demanding of it Bulls of canonical investiture for his candidate as well as a formal censure of the "Doctrinal Decision". The pope replied gently but firmly, condemning the words of the oath of allegiance to the Fundamental Law, sending a Brief of commendation to the bishops, and refusing investiture to the Prince de Méan until he should have publicly declared that his oath had not bound him to anything "contrary to the dogmas and laws of the Catholic Church, and that in swearing to protect all religious communions, he understood this protection only in its civil sense". The condescension of the Holy See in this matter, instead of winning the king to moderation, seemed to make him bolder. Reviving the obsolete claims of the old Gallican and Josephinist governments, and determined to overcome the opposition of the Bishop of Ghent, he had the bishop prosecuted for having published the "Doctrinal Decision"; for having corresponded with Rome without authorization; and for having published the papal Bulls without approbation. The Brussels Court of Assizes condemned the bishop to be deported for contumacy (1817), and the Government, carrying the sentence even farther, had the bishop's name written on the pillory, between two professional thieves sentenced to be pilloried and branded. The clergy of the Diocese of Ghent who remained faithful to the bishop were also persecuted by the State. The conflict would have continued indefinitely had not the prelate died in exile, in 1821, after having had twice confessed the Faith in the face of persecution. After his death, the Government conceded that the oath should be binding only from the civil point of view, which set at rest the Catholic conscience and ended the difficulties which had beset the first six years of the Kingdom of the Netherlands.

If there had been any real desire on the part of King William to respect the conscience of Catholics, who constituted the greater part of the nation, he would now have inaugurated a policy, which would have set aside religious differences, and started the kingdom along lines leading to the frank and cordial fusion of the two peoples. This was not done. On the contrary, in his obstinate determination to treat the sovereign pontiff as an outsider, and to bring the Catholic Church under the omnipotence of the State, William in his blind fury continued his policy of oppression. Before the above-mentioned conflict, the king had created a State commission for Catholic affairs and had declared in the decree that "no church ordinance coming from a foreign authority—[i. e. the pope] could be published without the approval of the Government". This was equivalent to re-establishing in the full dawn of the nineteenth century the *placet* of the despotic governments of the former regime. Going farther, he instructed this commission "to be on their guard in maintaining the liberties of the Belgian Church", an extravagant formula borrowed from defunct Gallicanism, implying that the commission should take care to withdraw the Belgian Church from the legitimate authority of the pope. The men he had chosen to help him pushed their distrust and hatred of the Catholic hierarchy farther than he did. Baron Goubau, the head of the board of Catholic worship, and his superior, Van Maanen the minister of justice, by a system of petty persecutions soon made their names the most hated in Belgium, and largely increased the unpopularity of the Government.

In 1821 the Government began to be chiefly occupied with the suppression of liberty in the matter of education. Since the foundation, in 1817, of the three State universities, Liège, Ghent, and Louvain, higher education had been entirely under the control of the State, which now assumed control of middle inferior education (20 May, 1821) by a ministerial ordinance which allowed no free school to exist without the express consent of the Government. Lastly, a decree of 14 June, 1825, suppressed free middle superior instruction by determining that no college could exist without being expressly authorized, and that no one could teach the children of more than one family without an official diploma. A second decree of the same date declared anyone who had made his studies abroad ineligible for any public office in the kingdom. The State having monopolized all lay education, there still remained the training of the clergy, which by the general canons of the Church, and those of the Council of Trent, in particular, belonged exclusively to the bishops. By a third decree, 14 June, 1825, said to be a revival of that of Joseph II,

establishing the General Seminary, a State institution was erected under the name of Philosophical College (*Collège philosophique*), in which every aspirant for the priesthood was obliged to make a course of at least two years before he could be admitted to a *grand séminaire*.

On this occasion, the Archbishop of Mechlin, whose servility toward the king had till then known no limit, did not hesitate to make some respectful remonstrances to the Government, declaring that he could not in conscience accept these decrees. Goubau, in answering, repeated in substance Napoleon's gibe to the Prince de Broglie, "Your conscience will be regarded as a mere pretext and for good reasons". The other bishops, however, the capitular vicars of vacant sees, and the rest of the clergy, unanimously took sides with the Archbishop of Mechlin and joined in his protest. The Catholic Belgian deputies to the States-General protested; the Holy See protested in its turn. Nothing availed; the Government closed the free colleges one after another, thereby ruining a flourishing educational system in which Belgian families had absolute confidence; the Philosophical College was opened with great pomp, with a corps of instructors little thought of, either from a scientific or a moral point of view; students were drawn thither by bursaries or scholarships, and by exemption from military service. The Government becoming more radical than ever, then undertook to create a schism in the Belgian Church by elaborating a plan, whereby the authority of the Holy See would be abolished and the bishops placed immediately under the Government.

But all these measures only increased the discontent of the Belgians and their passive resistance. To get the mastery, the Government conceived the idea of having recourse a second time to the sovereign pontiff, and broaching again the project of a Concordat, which had failed in 1823, on account of the king's inadmissible claims. The king counted, on the one hand, on wresting as many concessions as possible from the Holy See, and on the other, on gaining popularity among the Belgians through the arrangement he would make with the pope. These calculations failed, and once more the superiority of papal diplomacy was made manifest in the difficult negotiations which finally resulted in the Concordat of 1827. The Philosophical College ceased to be obligatory for clerics and became a matter of choice; in place of having the right of designating the bishops, the king was obliged to content himself with that of vetoing the choice made by the Chapters. The Concordat, which filled the Catholics with joy, excited the ire of the Calvinists and the Liberals, and the Government tried hard to quiet the latter by showing the worst possible will in the application of the treaty which it had just concluded with the Vatican. The Philosophical College was not declared optional until 20 June, 1829; vacant episcopal sees were provided with titulars elected according to the conditions laid down in the Concordat, but a royal decree rendered the recruiting of the clergy almost impossible save from the ranks of the old pupils of the Philosophical College. The Catholic opposition, headed by Bishop Van Bommel, the new Bishop of Liège, was so vigorous, and political complications so grave, that the king at last consented to permit the bishops to reorganize their seminaries as they wished (20 October, 1829). Then, as the crisis became more serious, he went farther, and on 9 June, 1830, entirely suppressed the Philosophical College, which had been deserted from the time attendance had become optional. On 27 May of the same year, the king even revoked his decrees regarding freedom in education; he thanked Goubau and committed to Catholic zeal the direction of matters concerning Catholic worship, and would have left no ground for grievance on the part of

Catholics had he not, at the last moment, seen fit, in the negotiations with the Holy See, to demand the right of approving appointments to canonries. But all the king's concessions, which were really extorted from him by the force of circumstances, and despite his dogged reluctance, came too late, and the negotiations in regard to the question of canons were still in progress when the Belgian Revolution broke out.

As to the causes of an event so decisive for the future of the Belgian people, it is highly improbable that if King William had given them grounds for complaint only in religious matters, the public discontent would have culminated in a revolution. The Catholics, faithful to the teachings of the Church and to the counsels of their pastors, had no wish to exceed what was lawful and knew that they should confine themselves to peaceful protests. But the Government had injured many other interests to which a great number were more sensitive than they were to the oppression of the Catholic Church, at which they would have been wholly indifferent if, indeed, they would not have rejoiced. It will suffice to recall the principal grievances. Although Holland's population was less than Belgium by almost half, each nation was allowed the same number of deputies in the States-General. Acquaintance with the Dutch language was at once made obligatory for all officials. The greater number of institutions of the central Government were located in Holland, and the majority of the offices were reserved for the Dutch. Taxes on corn and on slaughtering weighed most heavily on the southern provinces. The press was under the arbitrary control of the Government and the courts, and they vigorously prohibited any criticism of the Government and its deputies. The Government stubbornly opposed the introduction of the jury system, the verdicts of which, inspired by a saner appreciation of public feeling, would often have calmed opinion instead of inflaming it. Lastly, as if wishing to fill the measure of its blunders, the Government shamelessly hired an infamous forger condemned by the French tribunals, a certain Libri-Bagnano, whose journal, the "National", never ceased insulting and taunting every Belgian who had the misfortune of incurring the displeasure of the Government. There came a time when the Liberals, who, as late as 1825, had applauded the Government in its persecution of the Church, found themselves attacked in their turn, and began to protest with more violence than the Catholics had ever done.

Then the inevitable happened. Equally oppressed, the two parties forgot their differences, and joined forces. The fiery anti-clerical Louis de Potter, author of various historical works extremely irreligious in tone, was one of the first to advocate, from the prison in which he was confined for some violation of laws concerning the press, the union of the Catholics and the Liberals. This union was made the more easy because the greater part of the Catholics, under the influence of the teachings of Lamennais and the pressure of events, had abandoned their stand of 1815 and had rallied to the doctrine of "liberty in all and for all". Once effected, the union of Catholics and Liberals soon bore fruit. Their first step, proposed by the Catholics who wished to employ lawful means only, was the presentation of petitions by every class of society in turn. Hundreds of petitions piled up in the offices of the States-General, demanding liberty of education, freedom of the press, and the righting of other wrongs. While these petitions were being circulated the perfect order that was maintained deceived the king. On a tour which he made through the southern provinces, to convince himself personally as to the state of the public mind, he received such demonstrations of loyalty that he persuaded himself that the petitioning was a factitious movement, and went so far as to declare, at Liège,

that the conduct of the petitioners was infamous (1829).

This false step was his undoing. In the face of his refusal to initiate any reforms, the country became incensed, and the direction of the national movement passed from the hands of the peaceful Catholics into those of the impatient Liberals. The resistance soon took on a revolutionary character. The ecclesiastical authorities had foreseen this, and had for a long time opposed both the "Union", and the petitions which were its first manifestation. The Bishops of Ghent and Liège had come forward to remind the faithful of their duties to the sovereign; the Archbishop of Mechlin had assured the Government of the neutrality of the clergy; the nuncio had shown his disapproval of the "Union", and the Cardinal-Secretary of State had stigmatized it as monstrous. But the religious authorities soon found themselves powerless to control the movement. The Catholics, imitating the Liberals, had recourse to violent language; their most important periodical refused to print the conciliatory letter of the Bishop of Liège, which one of the Liberal leaders styled an episcopal-ministerial document; the lower clergy, in turn, allowed itself to be drawn into the current; the Government, wilfully blind, continued wantonly, in its imprudence, to pile up the materials for a great conflagration; at last, nothing was lacking but a fuse. This came from France. The revolution of July, 1830, lasting from the 27th to the 29th, overthrew the government of Charles X; on 25 August, of the same year, a riot broke out in Brussels and brought on the revolution which culminated in the conflicts between (24–26 September) the Dutch troops and the people of Brussels assisted by re-enforcements of volunteers from the provinces. The whole country rose up; at the end of some weeks the Dutch army had evacuated the soil of the southern provinces, and Belgium was free.

III. INDEPENDENT BELGIUM (1830–1905).—As has been shown, not only was the revolution the work of two parties but the chief rôle in it had been played by the Liberals, and for a long time, although a minority in the nation, their ranks supplied the principal leaders in national life. The Catholics did not close their eyes to this state of things. Sincerely attached to the Union of 1828, they wanted a unionist policy without laying too much stress on party names. The provisional government which assumed the direction of affairs after the revolution had but one Catholic among its ten members, and had as head and inspiration, Charles Rogier, who, in September, 1830, had come, at the head of the Liège volunteers, to lend a strong helping hand to the combatants in Brussels. The constituent Congress, convoked by the provisional government, was in great majority composed of Catholics; partisans of liberty "in all and for all", in conformity with the teachings of Lamennais. The Liberal minority was split into two groups; the stronger professed the same ideas of liberty as the Catholics; the other was made up of a small number of sectarians and of State idolaters who had dreams of bringing the Catholic Church into subjection to the civil power. The leaders of the Catholic group were Count Félix de Mérode, a member of the provisional government, and Baron de Gerlache, President of the Congress; the most prominent among the Liberals were Charles Rogier, Joseph Lebeau, Paul Devaux, J. B. Nothomb, and Sylvan Van de Weyer; the group of sectarians followed the orders of Eugene Defacqz. The Constitution which resulted from the deliberations of the Congress reflected the dispositions of the great majority of the assembly and showed at the same time a reaction against the tyrannical regime of King William. It proclaimed the absolute freedom of worship and of the press, which the Liberals put first, and also freedom of education and association, two things especially dear to the Catholics; concessions were even made to the prejudices of some, by rendering obligatory the priority of civil marriage over the religious ceremony and commanding that no one should be forced to observe the religious holidays of any denomination. The Congress showed the same broad-mindedness in the choice of a sovereign. The first selection fell on the Duke de Nemours, son of Louis Philippe, but the French king, fearing the jealousy of the European powers, dared not accept the throne for his son. Then, after having given the regency for some months to Baron Surlet de Chokier, the Congress declared in favour of Prince Leopold de Saxe-Coburg Gotha, widower of the Princess Charlotte, heir presumptive to the Crown of England. Though a Protestant prince, Leopold I (1831–65) showed himself worthy of the confidence of a Catholic people; during his entire reign he maintained an even balance between the two parties, and never lost his solicitude for the moral and religious interests of the nation. Owing largely to Leopold's wise policy, Belgium successfully inaugurated free institutions, and showed the world that a Catholic people is capable of progress in every field.

During the early years of the new kingdom both sides remained faithful to the union of 1828, the administration being divided between the Catholics and Liberals. The dominant thought was to defend against Holland the patrimony of independence and of liberty won by the revolution, patriotism inspiring unanimous opposition to the foreigner. The tendency towards mutual conciliation was evident in the organic laws perfected during these early years, especially in that of 1842 on primary education which was passed unanimously by the Chamber, save for three blank votes, and received the unanimous vote of the senate. This law, the work of J. B. Nothomb, the minister, made religious teaching obligatory, but dispensed dissidents from attendance. King Leopold expressed his gratification on signing it. For thirty-seven years this remained the fundamental charter of public education. At this time, everyone of whatever party was convinced of the necessity of religion in the education of the people. The clergy readily rallied to the support of the bill and even suffered a great number of the 2,284 private schools which they had opened to be closed that they might co-operate in the establishment of the public schools.

The law of 1842 was, in a way, the last product of Unionist principles. Since the treaty of 1839 had definitely regulated Belgium's position in regard to Holland, the fear of an outside enemy had been removed, and the Liberal party was convinced that there was no longer anything to hinder its political doctrines from prevailing in the national government. This attitude was partly justified by the state of affairs. The Catholics were weak, without organization, without a press, without consciousness of their own strength; they had no relish for partisan contests, and they counted on Unionism to maintain public life along the lines of 1830. In contrast to the Catholic masses who lacked cohesion, and consciousness of their strength, the Liberals formed a young, spirited, united party, gaining recruits from the bourgeoisie and the learned classes alike, commanding much sympathetic support from official circles, in possession of a press with twenty times the influence of the Catholic press, in a word, master of the Belgium Government since 1830. Paul Devaux, one of the most remarkable men of this party and one of the organizers of the Union in 1828, became the apostle of Liberalism in its later development, which implied the abolition of the Union and the victory of a policy exclusively Liberal in character. The articles which, beginning with 1839, he published in the "National Review", founded by him, exerted an enormous influence upon his party and even gradually won over to his ideas a large number of moderate Liberals.

While the Union of 1828 was being dissolved and some of its promoters were seeking to give a partisan predominance to mixed ministries, the dissenters, who cherished an implacable hatred for the Catholic Church, wished to profit by the new turn of affairs in Liberal ranks to avenge the defeat they had met with at the hands of the constituent Congress. The Masonic lodges entered on the scene with the avowed intention of forming the "conscience" of the Liberal party and of outlining its programme. They established a large society called "The Alliance", which soon numbered 1,000 members, and which was to serve as their agent and go-between with that part of the people in which Freemasonry awakened distrustfulness. In 1846, the Alliance called together a Liberal Congress, presided over by Eugene Defacqz, the dissenter of 1830, now Grand Master of Belgian Freemasonry. The same secrecy was preserved in the deliberations of the Congress as in the Lodges, from which it originated, and the only knowledge of its proceedings was to be gained from the programme which it published. In this document, side by side with political reforms, appeared "the real independence of the civil power", a mere formula signifying systematic war on the Church, and "the organization of public instruction under the exclusive direction of civil authority, which should be granted legal means to maintain a competition with private establishments, without the interference of the clergy, on the ground of authority. At the time that this programme was being drawn up, the Congress made plans for a general confederation of Liberalism in Belgium, which with the Alliance as centre and type, was to establish in each district an association of free Liberal electors, bound in honour to vote for the candidates chosen by the Congress. There were also to be electoral divisions in every one of the cantons to extend the influence of the association. General reunions were to be held periodically to enable the alliance to reach the members of the associations and imbue them with the Masonic spirit. The Liberal Congress of 1846 brought the session to a close with "a resolution favouring the liberation of the lower clergy", whom they hoped to incite against the bishops by suggesting possibilities of bettering their condition. This resolution brought out strongly the true character of the Congress, as a reactionary movement against the work of the National Congress of 1830. It stands to reason that the strong impulse stirred up by the Congress in the ranks of the Liberal party, and the ardent hopes based on it reacted on the legislative elections, while the Catholics remained buried in their dream of Unionism, then merely an anachronism. The elections of 1847 placed the Liberals in power.

The new Government brought together in the same ministry Charles Rogier, member of the Congress of 1830, and Frère-Orban, one of the promoters of the Congress of 1846. Under the influence of the latter, a man of great talent but extremely arbitrary, whose imperious will got the better of the Unionist scruples of his colleague, the Cabinet declared that it would inaugurate a "new policy" taking as its principle the "independence of the civil power". And as a matter of fact, from this time forth, war was made on religious influence with a bitterness destined to divide the Belgian nation into two hostile camps. De Haussy, the Minister of Justice, set about applying to charitable foundations the most unheard-of principles. According to him, only charitable (State) bureaux could receive charitable bequests, and all endowments were to be turned over to them, even though the testator had made the selection of an administrator for the endowment an indispensable condition. On the other hand, the law of 1850 on middle-superior education was inspired by a spirit diametrically opposite to that of the law concerning

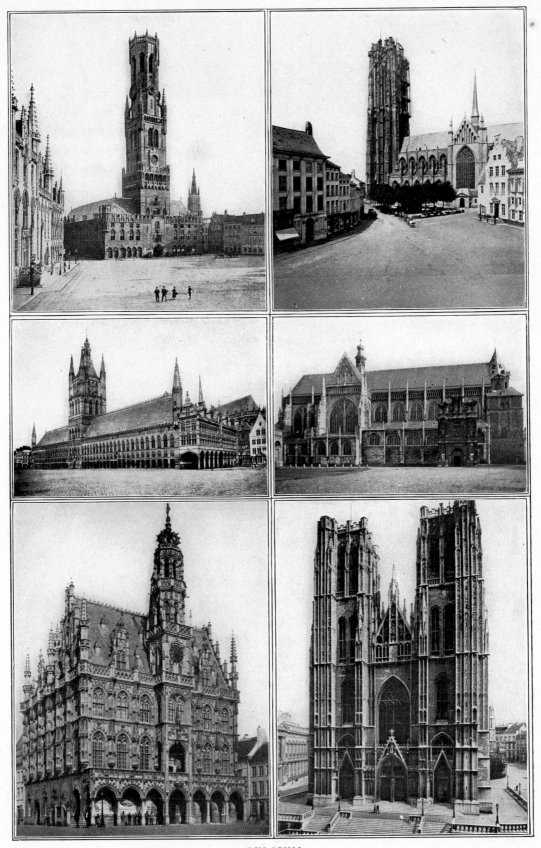

BELGIUM

THE BELFRY OF BRUGES
CITY HALL AT YPRES
CITY HALL, OUDENARDE

CATHEDRAL OF MECHLIN
CHURCH OF ST. JAMES (JACQUES) LIÈGE
CHURCH OF ST. GUDULE, BRUSSELS

primary education; it showed the Government's intention of using the taxpayers' money to start competition with free education, and if, as a matter of policy, the clergy were invited to give religious instruction in public institutions, conditions were such as to make their co-operation lack both dignity and effectiveness.

The Belgian nation was not yet ripe for the adoption of a policy so out of harmony with the spirit of its national traditions, and after five years, the cabinet was overthrown. A more moderate Liberal cabinet modified the law of 1850 by adopting the "agreement of Antwerp" made between the communal administration of that city and the bishops, giving to the clergy the guarantees required for their admission to the public institutions of secondary education. The support given to this agreement, by the Chamber, the vote being 86 to 7, showed that the necessity of religious instruction was still understood by a large number of Liberals. The elections of 1855, which returned a Catholic majority, resulted in a cabinet presided over by P. de Decker, who may be called the last of the Unionists. This cabinet, which its friends might have reproached with excessive moderation, was destined to be overthrown as reactionary. One of its members, A. Nothomb, drafted a law concerning charitable bequests intended to protect the interests of testators and repair the unfortunate effects of De Haussy's legislation. Testators were authorized to appoint special administrators for their bequests, but the powers of the latter were circumscribed and their exercise placed under the strict supervision of the State (1857). Under the leadership of Frère-Orban, who under the pseudonym of Jean Van Damme had just written a sensational pamphlet, the Liberals pretended to find in this scheme a roundabout restoration of the monastic *main-morte;* they called it the law of the convents, and when the plan was brought up for discussion, they organized riots which intimidated the head of the cabinet. He took advantage of the communal elections, which had been favourable to the Liberal party, to tender the resignation of the cabinet. This pusillanimous conduct delivered the Government again into the hands of the Liberals, who held power for thirteen years (1857–70).

During this long period the new ministry, which was merely the outcome of a riot, did nothing but emphasize the anti-religious character of its policy. The real head was Frère-Orban, who in the end forced his colleague, Rogier, to retire (1868), and carried out successively the principal features in his programme of secularization. More prominent than ever was the alleged aim of protecting civil society against the "encroachments of the clergy". The law of 1859 on charitable endowments was the counterpart of that of 1857 and the despoiling policy inaugurated in 1847 by de Haussy. A law of 1869, of the same animus, confiscated all the bursaries for free scholarships, nine-tenths of which had been established to advance the Christian education of the young, annulling the formal provisions of the testators. A law of 1870 confined exemption from military service to students of the *grands séminaires*, refusing it to novices of religious orders. In actual practice, the Government was sectarian and intolerant towards religion and the clergy. It countenanced the efforts prompted by the Masonic lodges to secularize cemeteries, notwithstanding the decree of Prairial, twelfth year, that there should be a cemetery for each denomination, which left Catholic cemeteries under the Church's jurisdiction. Appointments to public offices, especially to the magistracy, were noticeably partisan. An example of the petty prejudice of the Government was its suppression of the annual subsidy which the Bollandists (q. v.) had hitherto received for the continuation of their magnificent work, the "Acta Sanctorum".

It seemed as if the rule of the Liberal party would continue indefinitely, and that Catholics were permanently excluded from power, which their adversaries declared they were incapable of exercising. However, the Catholics made use of their long exclusion from a share in governmental affairs in at last seriously attempting to organize their forces. Jules Malou devoted himself most energetically to this task, and for the first time, the broad outlines of organization were visible, an organization such as the Liberal party had long possessed. At the same time, in imitation of the German Catholics, they held important Congresses at Mechlin, in 1863, 1864, and 1867, which awakened Catholic enthusiasm and gave courage to the pessimists. In this way, Catholics found themselves able to resume the struggle with new vigour. Dissensions in the Liberal party, the strenuous opposition to the Liberals, or Doctrinaires, of the Government, on the part of men of advanced ideas, who claimed the double title of Progressists, and of Radicals, combined to help the Catholics and in 1870, they finally succeeded in overthrowing the Liberal Government.

The Liberals then had recourse to the means which had contributed to their success in 1857. The ministry had appointed as Governor of Limburg P. de Decker, who had been the head of the ministry of 1855, and whose name had been connected with the failure of a financial association. The Liberals affected to be greatly scandalized and organized riots which so frightened Leopold II that he dismissed his ministry (1871). He replaced it, it is true, by another Catholic ministry, of which Jules Malou was president. Though formed during the disturbances of a popular outbreak in defiance of the wishes of the large cities, which were all Liberal in their sympathies, and secretly impugned before the king by Jules Van Praet, the royal secretary, who was nicknamed the "Seventh Ministry", this ministry managed to hold out until 1878 only by dint of being as unobtrusive as possible. None of the anti-religious laws made by the Liberals were revised, not even the one concerning bursaries, which had been passed by a bare majority. There was no restoration of the balance of power in public offices, which continued to be held by the Liberals. In 1875, the Burgomaster of Liège having forbidden the Jubilee processions in that city, in defiance of the Constitution, the Government dared not annul his illegal order and had the humiliation of seeing the 1,500 Liberals tender him a complimentary banquet. Catholic rule seemed in very truth what its adversaries called it, an "empty parenthesis", and, towards the end of his administration, Jules Malou in a Catholic meeting, summed it up in these words: "we have existed"—*Nous avons vécu.*

When a turn in the elections brought the Liberals back into power, after the Catholic administration had dragged out a precarious existence of eight years, they were able to continue their anti-Catholic policy from the point where they had left it. While out of office they had become more irreligious owing to the growing influence of Masonry. Not only the clergy, but the Church, and religion itself, became the objects of their attacks. They encouraged writers who, like Professor Laurent of the University of Ghent, denied the necessity of granting liberty to the Church, or who, like Professor de Laveleye of the University of Liège, asserted the superiority of Protestantism. Their Antwerp associations flooded the country with copies of a pamphlet written by the latter in this vein. Besides this, the Liberals sought to make the country Protestant by supporting de Laveleye and Goblet d'Alviella, who, taking advantage of a quarrel between the villagers of Sart-Dame-Aveline and the parish priest, introduced Protestant worship there and tried to proselytize the inhabitants. They adopted the name *Gueux* (beggars) which they found in the story of the religious troubles of the sixteenth century. Their presses daily waged war on the Catholic religion; their carnival pageants were vulgar parodies which exposed the most sacred things to popular derision. Lastly, the leaders of the movement agreed upon a revision of the law of 1842 dealing with primary instruction. Once more in power they set about their work of uprooting Christianity without delay, and framed the famous school law of 1879, which the Catholics called the "Law of Misfortune" (*Loi de malheur*), a name it still retains.

The work of drafting this law was placed in charge of Van Humbeck, the Minister of Public Instruction, a Freemason who some years before had declared in his lodge that "Catholicism was a corpse that barred the way of progress and would have to be thrown into the grave". The law did him justice, being in every respect the reverse of the law of 1842; it excluded from the schools all religious instruction, and barred from the ranks of teachers all graduates of free normal, i. e. religious schools. But for once, Freemasonry had counted too much on the apathy and good nature of the Catholic masses. The resistance was unanimous. At the call of the bishops Catholics rose in a body and entered on a campaign of petitions; committees for resistance were everywhere formed; public prayers were offered in all the churches for delivery from "teachers without faith", and "godless schools". In the Chambers, the Catholics after emphatic protests refused to take any part in the discussion of the law even of its amendment, which forced the Liberals to do their worst and to shoulder the entire responsibility. It was carried without formal opposition. The President of the Senate, Prince de Ligne, a Liberal, resigned his post, deploring the division of the nation into Guelphs and Ghibellines. The Catholics, co-operating with the bishops and the clergy, achieved wonders. In one year they erected three or four thousand Catholic schools; the rule that there should be one to each commune was obeyed with few exceptions. More than 2,000 teachers of both sexes resigned their positions, the greater number to take part in free education often at a very small salary. At the end of a year, the State schools had lost fifty-five per cent. of their pupils, and retained only thirty-eight per cent. of the entire body of school children, while the Catholic schools had sixty-one per cent. Many of the State schools were entirely deserted, and others had a ridiculously small attendance. Dumbfounded and enraged at such unexpected resistance, the Government tried every resource, however contemptible or absurd. Negotiations were begun with the Vatican, and a breach of diplomatic relations threatened, in the hope of forcing Leo XIII to condemn the action of the Belgian bishops. Nothing came of this, and in consequence the Belgian ambassador to the Holy See was recalled. To intimidate the clergy and the Catholics, a decree was passed ordering an inquiry as to the execution of the school law, and the investigators journeyed through the country like real judges, and cited people before their tribunal at random, exposing the most respectable people to the insults of the mob. This tour of investigation was scarcely finished, when the Freemasons, carrying their blindness to the limit, proposed to the Chamber another inquiry concerning the *main-morte* measure that is to say, a campaign against convents. This time, the nearness of elections dictated a more prudent policy and the motion was lost by a majority of two votes.

The country was roused to great excitement. In the face of open persecution, the Catholics showed unexpected energy. Foreseeing their triumph, they established the "Union for the Redress of Grievances", to compel their candidates in the event of their election to adopt a vigorous policy. On 10 June, 1884, the country was called on to pronounce judgment. The result was overwhelming. Half the members of the Chamber had been candidates for re-election. Only two Liberal deputies were returned, the others being defeated in the whirlwind which uprooted Liberalism. Amid great national rejoicing, the Catholics resumed the reins of power, which they have held uninterruptedly for twenty-three years. "We shall surprise the world by our moderation" said one of their leaders; and in this moderation which is not devoid of energy, lies their strength. The school law of 1879 was repealed without delay, the first time in the history of Belgium that a Catholic Government had courage to repeal a law made by the Liberals. The legislators of 1884, however, did not revive the law of 1842. Taking into consideration the change of times, they took the primary schools from State control and placed them under the communes, leaving each commune to decide whether or not religious instruction should be given; the State subsidized these schools, on condition that they would accept the State programme and would submit to State inspection; all laws subversive of liberty were repealed, and, needless to say, relations with the Vatican were resumed.

The Liberals, counting on the support of the cities, thought that by violence they could bring about a reaction against the decision of the electoral body, as they had done in 1857 and 1871. With the connivance of the Burgomaster of Brussels, they assailed and scattered a peaceful procession of 80,000 Catholics, who had come to the capital to make a demonstration in favour of the Government, and, as in 1857, appealed to false statistics of the communal elections of 1884, to prove that the voters had changed their minds. In this way, they obtained from King Leopold II the dismissal of Charles Woeste and Victor Jacobs, the two ministers whom they held in special aversion. Jules Malou, the head of the Cabinet, protested, and followed his colleagues into retirement. But the Catholic party remained in power and M. Beernaert, who succeeded Malou, inaugurated the era of prosperity which has placed Belgium in the front rank among nations.

The situation confronting the Government bore no resemblance to that of former years. Since 1830, the inner national energy had been absorbed by the struggle between the Catholics and the Liberals, both representing bourgeois voters, who were divided as to the amount of influence to be allowed to Catholicism in public affairs. By 1886 a change had come about. A third party had come into existence known as the "Workingman's Party", which, recruited entirely from the labouring classes, presented a dangerous platform, comprehending not reforms but economic and social revolutionary measures. This Socialist party had been secretly taking shape since 1867, and continued in Belgium the traditions of the "Internationale", created by Karl Marx. It proclaimed to the workingmen that they were slaves, promised to give them liberty and prosperity and, as the first means towards the necessary reforms, to secure for them the right of suffrage. In this way the great mass of the people were won over and organized while the two older parties were wholly occupied with their traditional quarrel. Not that eminent Catholics, such as Edouard Ducpétiaux, to mention one of the highest rank, had not sought for a long time a way of bettering the condition of the working classes, or that many zealous men had not made disinterested attempts to bring about such a result; but the body of the nation had not realized the political rôle soon to be played by the dense ranks of the organized proletariat, and hence had not tried to find legislative means of satisfying their demands. Moreover, the administrative classes, Liberals as well as Catholics, were under the influence of the Manchester school. The policy of non-interference was accepted as the guiding principle, and particularly when there was any question of labour legislation, the words on every tongue were: "most liberty, least government."

When, therefore, in 1886, serious uprisings, plainly revolutionary in character, took place, first at Liège (18 March), and soon afterwards in the industrial districts of Hainaut, the whole country was thrown into a state of consternation and alarm. The labour party came forward and put the social question before the country in the form of incendiarism and riots. The most enlightened Catholics grasped the significance of these events and saw that the time had come for turning their attention towards labour reform. Under the presidency of Bishop Doutreloux of Liège, three Congresses of Social Works were held at Liège, in 1886, 1887, and 1890, in which the most vital questions were studied and exhaustively discussed. Groups were formed, especially among the younger men, to introduce the most urgent reforms into the Catholic platform; Canon Pottier, professor of moral theology in the *grand séminaire* of Liège, became the apostle of the reform movement; the Catholic friends of reform established a Democratic Christian League, which, encouraged by the bishops and keeping within the bounds of the strictest orthodoxy, bent all its energies on reform. The Bishop of Liège formed among the secular priests a new order, "The Almoners of Labour", whose zeal and devotion were entirely directed to bettering the lot of the working people.

As for the Government, it proved equal to its task, new and unforeseen as it was. A thorough investigation of the labour question gave an understanding of the nature and extent of the principal grievances of the working classes, after which the necessary reforms were energetically entered upon. For several years, the entire legislative activity devoted itself to the redress of the most crying evils. Councils of Industry and of Labour were formed; legislation was passed on the following subjects: workingmen's dwellings, wages, the abolition of the truck system, the illegality of attaching or assigning wages, labour inspection, child-labour, and the labour of women. Strong encouragement was given to mutual benefit societies which had been hitherto in anything but a flourishing condition. To these important laws was added the commendable law of conditional condemnation and liberation, the work of M. Lejeune, the minister of justice; it has since been imitated by many larger countries.

This work, which extended over ten years, culminated in a revision of the Constitution, which the advanced members of the Liberal party had been demanding for a long time, and which the Socialists were now insisting on. This revision had become imperative. Belgium was a country which had very few voters; out of a population of more than six millions there never were more than 150,000, and during the last years of the Liberal Government no less than six laws had been passed to diminish this number still further by excluding entire classes of Catholic voters. In spite of this, and though it was clear to all that the Catholics would be the first to profit by a revision, through a spirit of conservatism, they shrank from taking the initiative in this matter. One of their leaders, M. Woeste, was its declared adversary. The Liberals, observing this hesitation on the part of their opponents, joined the Socialists in demanding the revision, hoping for its refusal. Under these circumstances, and with a full appreciation of the necessities of the situation, M. Beernaert proposed the revision of the Constitution, and succeeded, after many difficulties, in having the revision adopted by the party of the Right. The revision was as broad as possible: the motion for universal suffrage was passed without opposition—

a suffrage, however, modified by plural voting as proposed by M. Nyssens, a deputy of the Right. Each Belgian was to have one vote; a married man who could prove his title to some property had two; a man able to give certain proofs of education had three. The electoral body was increased tenfold, and henceforth only the worthless and the incompetent were excluded from the administration of public affairs in Belgium (1893).

In this way the Belgian Government, by exercising prudence as well as courage, succeeded in a few years in carrying out a splendid reform programme, and deserved the admirable eulogy of Fernand Payen, a French jurisconsult: "We have before us the most complete body of legislation which the history of this century can show in any country." A former liberal minister praised hardly less emphatically the wise policy of the Catholic Government, by declaring that it was difficult to combat it because it offered no grounds for complaint. For the first time in the history of Belgium Catholics showed their ability to govern, that is to say, their ability to comprehend at a glance the needs of the times and to meet them satisfactorily. Even the king, hitherto distrustful of Catholics, gradually gave up his prejudices, and at every election the voters confirmed their tenure of power. The party of the Right showed their ingratitude towards M. Beernaert, by declining, partly through motives of personal interest, to vote for the proportional representation of parties, and this the head of the Cabinet demanded as an indispensable item in the revision of the Constitution. On this refusal, M. Beernaert resigned his position at the head of the Cabinet, in 1894, depriving Belgium of her greatest statesman.

Results proved M. Beernaert's wisdom. From the time of the revision, the Liberal party, which had its exclusive support in the bourgeoisie of the cities, had been entirely shut out of Parliament, where its place had been taken by a strong group of Socialists. This group, destitute, for the most part, of culture and parliamentary training, introduced coarse and violent methods of discussion into the Chamber, seriously compromising the dignity of parliamentary debate. On the other hand, the total suppression of Liberal representation was both an injustice, since this party still retained the sympathies of the middle class in the large cities, and a danger, for the true parliamentary spirit was violated by the exclusion from public life of views which had lately been all powerful and were still very much alive. Proportional representation seemed to be the only way of restoring parliamentary balance, and it came about that those who had caused M. Beernaert's loss of power to avoid this very thing were won over to his views. Proportional representation was therefore proposed and carried, making electoral legislation in Belgium the most complete in the world. The Liberals returned to the Chambers, the Catholics sacrificing their overwhelming majority in their desire for the representation of every shade of opinion to be found in the electoral body, thus substituting the three parties for the two which had divided the power previous to 1893.

The Catholics, nevertheless, retained a permanent majority. The successors of M. Beernaert continued to conduct the Government along his lines, even if with less prestige and authority. From time to time the administration was affected by reactionary influences, occasionally compromised by mistakes in policy, but the current of social legislation has not changed its course. In 1895, a special department of Labour was created, and M. Nyssens, the first minister, filled the position with great distinction. Laws were passed regulating workshops, trade unions, pensions for workmen, insurance against accidents while working, and providing for rest on Sundays.

The number and importance of these legislative enactments was such that a Socialist deputy codified and published them in a collection, rendering thereby tacit but significant homage to the Government responsible for them.

But the very stability of the Government, which each successive election retained in power, was the despair of its enemies who saw the impossibility of overthrowing it by legal methods. The Socialists decided that their success would be greater if they obtained by threats, or, if necessary, by violence, a new revision of the Constitution, suppressing the plural vote and replacing it by universal suffrage, pure and simple: "One man, one vote." Failing to bring about this reform by intimidating the Chamber, they sent revolutionary bands into the streets. "I have always tried to dissuade you from violence", said Vandervelde, their leader, to his audience of workingmen; "but to-day, I say to you: The pear is ripe, and must be plucked." Another leader, Grimard, the Socialist senator, and a millionaire, even went so far as to declare that he would turn over his whole fortune to the workingmen and would start again with nothing. Intoxicated by these words, the workingmen of many large cities and industrial districts abandoned themselves to excesses, and blood was shed in several places, notably at Louvain. The energy with which the Government applied repressive measures, however, soon put an end to these attempts. Then the General Council of the workingmen's party declared a general strike, the last weapon of the revolutionary party. This failed after a few days, and the General Council was forced to advise the workmen to return to work. The prestige of the Socialists with the popular masses was greatly impaired by the failure of so great an effort and the Catholic Government came out of the crisis stronger than ever (1902).

There remained but one way of overcoming the Government: the alliance of the two opposition parties, the Socialists and the Liberals. This was effected at the time of the general elections of 1906. Although from the economic point of view the two parties were antipodal, they were united in their anticlerical sympathies, and there was reason to fear that their success would mean the downfall of religion. In their certainty of success they circulated the names of their future ministers, and open preparations were made for the festivities attendant on their victory. But their alliance met with a crushing defeat in the elections of 1906, which left the Catholic Government as strong as ever. The fêtes, commemorating the seventy-fifth anniversary of national independence, had been celebrated throughout the country with unrestrained enthusiasm, under the patronage of the Catholic Government, which, in 1909, will celebrate the twenty-fifth anniversary of its own existence. In the history of Belgium no government has held power so long, and the Catholic party has come to be more and more of a national party, or, to speak more correctly, the nation itself.

This summary would be incomplete if the history of the struggles in defence of religion and of social order were not supplemented by the internal history of the Catholic people of Belgium, i. e. the development of popular opinion during a quarter of a century. Generally, in the face of adversaries who attacked their most precious possession, the religion of their fathers, Catholics had proclaimed themselves "conservatives"; their political associations were thus designated and it was the name which the leaders of the party were fond of applying to themselves in Parliament. But the appearance of the workingmen on the political scene and the programme of their claims in pointed opposition to the conservatives (1886), brought home to enlightened Catholics the danger of this name. Hence the name "Conserva-

tive" was repudiated not only by the advanced members of the party, who called themselves "Democratic Christians", but even by the Catholics opposed to reforms, who really aimed at preserving the economic regime which had caused all the grievances of the working class. The latter, rejecting the term "Conservative" as a wrong done them, desire to be called simply "Catholics". Of the two groups, that of the Democratic Christians is at present numerically inferior, although more influential by reason of its enthusiasm, its activity, its faculty for taking the initiative, and its propaganda. To understand this it must be recalled that before the revision of the Constitution the Catholic, like the Liberal, party was exclusively a bourgeois party, as its members had to pay a large poll tax for the privilege of suffrage. Its leaders for the most part were drawn from the upper bourgeoisie, and those whose ability and energy called them to a share in the direction of affairs had no other ideals, or interests, than those of the bourgeoisie. When the revision heavily recruited their ranks, the new voters, though large in number, played the part of mere privates and had no active part in the management of the parties. Those of the new-comers, who were conscious of possessing the requisite ability and courage in order to carry out their ideas and programme were obliged to organize new groups, which were looked at askance by the former leaders, often even regarded with suspicion, and accused of socialistic tendencies.

In a large number of arrondissements, the rivalry of conservative and democratic tendencies among Belgian Catholics resulted in the establishment of two distinct political groups, and the Belgian bishops, and the most farsighted leaders, found it a hard task to prevent an open rupture. At Ghent, where the Democratic Christians assumed the harmless name of Anti-Socialists, there was never any real danger of a break in the ranks. At Liège, which was a centre of opposition to democratic ideas, Catholic circles being under the control of employers and financiers inimical to reform principles, a rupture was barely averted. At Alost, where the break was beyond control, the Abbé Daens organized an independent and radical body, which, taking the name of "Christene Volksparty" (Christian people's party), abandoned by the Anti-Socialists, opposed the Catholics more bitterly than the Socialists. It made common cause with the latter in carrying on a campaign against the Government in the elections of 1906. But, apart from the Daensists, a group, very small at most, which in its best days was unable to send more than two or three representatives to the Chamber, the Democratic Christians, in all their electoral battles, have always marched to the polls side by side with the conservative Catholics. They hold the controlling vote indispensable for any victory, and their leaders in Parliament have been in the front ranks in advocating the labour legislation which has produced the social laws. After opposing them for a long time, the Conservatives have gradually become accustomed to regard them as an essential factor of the Catholic army. In the meantime, the birth and progress of this group clearly marked the evolution which is taking place in the Catholic party in the direction of a new social ideal, an evolution too slow for some, and too rapid for others, but in any case, evident and undeniable.

IV. CONCLUSION.—This politico-religious history of Belgium, covering over a hundred years, contains more than one lesson. In the first place, it clearly establishes the fact that in every generation the Belgian nation has fought with vigour against every regime that was inimical to its faith. It struggled against the French Republic, against Napoleon I, against William I, against the Liberal Government, against the coalition of the Liberals and the Socialists, and has come forth victorious. In the second place it must be remarked that the war on the religion of the people has daily assumed a more threatening aspect. At the close of the eighteenth century, Belgium had no enemies except its foreign oppressors, abetted by a few handfuls of traitors. Under the Dutch Government, it was evident that the generation which developed under the French domination had been partly won over to revolutionary doctrines, and that among the bourgeoisie of the cities there was a body which no longer recognized the authority of religion in social matters. After 1846, it was manifest that this faction was under the control of the Masonic lodges, and had positively declared itself for war upon religion and the Church. In 1886, it was evident that, in the bourgeois class, the great mass of workingmen had been won over to the cause of irreligion and that the population of the industrial districts had been seriously affected. In addition to this, the four larger cities of Belgium, Brussels, Antwerp, Liège, and Ghent, and most of the cities of the Walloon provinces, had gone over to the Anti-Catholic party. The defenders of religion and its oppressors tended to become numerically equal, a state of things that would be apparent to all, were it not masked in a way by the system of plural voting. In the votes cast at the general elections there is always a Catholic majority, but it is a question whether the majority of voters are Catholics. If it is asked whether the Catholics, namely, the Belgians who submit to the teachings of the Church, still constitute the majority of the nation, the answer would be more or less doubtful. This leads to a third remark. The resistance to the enemies of religion has not been as effective as the duration and intensity of the contest might lead one to believe. Whenever the Catholics were successful, they have been satisfied with keeping the power in their hands; they have not exercised it to carry out their programme. No Catholic wrongs have been redressed; every law made by the Liberals against the Church and the clergy has remained unrepealed, and it was only in 1884 that the Government, supported by the entire nation, felt strong enough to inaugurate a bolder policy. But the revision of the School Law of 1879 is the solitary instance of this progress, and will probably continue to be so for some time to come.

The social condition of the Catholic religion in Belgium, while doubtless favourable, is not, therefore, free from danger. The School Law of 1884, amended in 1895, is inadequate to guarantee the Christian education of the people. It is evaded by the municipal government of the capital, which manages by trickery to exempt the majority of the children from religious instruction, and even in the Liberal communes, where the pupils receive religious instruction, it is neutralized by the lessons given them by their freethinking teachers. Many of the public schools are now developing generations of unbelievers. This is a matter that needs attention. It is also imperative to re-enforce the Catholic army by drawing recruits from the only source open to it, namely, the people. To do this the Government must accentuate the character of its social legislation, which is too often compromised by provisions which deprive it of a large part of its effectiveness. The law on trade unions deprives them of the means most likely to make them prosper, which is to make trade. The law on labour accidents would be excellent, if insurance against accidents was made obligatory. The law enjoining the Sunday rest, carried with the co-operation of the Socialists, contains such a large number of exceptions and is enforced with such want of earnestness that it is almost a dead letter. The Socialists declare, often with a semblance of truth, that the laws passed to benefit the workingmen are mere blinds, and it is

not always easy to convince them of the contrary. The continuation of the Catholic regime in Belgium seems to be contingent on a radical reform of school legislation, on provision for the division of State subventions among all the communal or private schools in proportion to the services that they render, and greater boldness in the solution of the labour questions. Religion has in Belgium so strong a support in popular loyalty and devotion that by judiciously taking advantage of them at the proper time, an indefinite tenure of power will be ensured.

V. STATISTICS.—According to the census of 31 December, 1905, the population of Belgium is 7,160,547. The great majority of the inhabitants are Catholic, but the lack of religious statistics makes it difficult to give the exact number of non-Catholics. There are about 30,000 Protestants, 3,000 to 4,000 Jews and several thousand persons who, not having been baptized, do not belong to any faith. The kingdom is divided into six dioceses, namely: The Archdiocese of Mechlin and the suffragan Dioceses of Bruges, Ghent, Liège, Namur, and Tournai. Each diocese has a seminary and one or several preparatory schools for the training of the clergy; there are, in addition, the Belgian College at Rome, a seminary to which all the Belgian bishops send the best of their pupils, and the College of the Saint-Esprit at Louvain, where a superior theological course is pursued. The secular clergy number 5,419; the regular clergy, 6,237; these latter are distributed in 293 houses. The religious orders in Belgium have 29,303 members living in 2,207 houses; the members of the orders, both male and female, devote their time chiefly to teaching and nursing the sick; the male orders also aid the secular clergy in parochial work.

Under the guidance of this large body of labourers for the Church, the religious life in Belgium is intense, and the works of piety and charity are very numerous. Statistics of these charities are given in Madame Charles Vloebergh's "La Belgique charitable", in the preface to which M. Beernaert states that no country has their equal. Belgium also takes a share out of all proportion to the size of its territory in international works of piety and in foreign missions. It is at the head of the work of the Eucharistic Congress, two of its bishops, Monseigneur Doutreloux, of Liège, and Monseigneur Heylen, of Namur, having been the first two presidents of the association. Five sessions of this congress have been held in Belgium; at Liège (1883), Antwerp, Brussels, Namur, and Tournai. Equally distinguished are the services of Belgium in the sphere of Catholic missions. The congregation of secular priests of the Immaculate Heart of Mary, founded at Scheutveld near Brussels in 1862, labour for the evangelization of Mongolia and the Congo; several of their members have suffered martyrdom in these countries. The Belgian Jesuits have for their mission-field Calcutta and Western Bengal. Their missionaries are trained in the Apostolic school established at Turnhout. The American seminary at Louvain (1857) aids in recruiting the secular clergy of the United States. Other religious orders also labour for the evangelization of foreign regions. The toils and heroism of a number of the Belgian missionaries have given them a world-wide renown; such are, Father Charles de Smedt, the apostle to the Indians of the Rocky Mountains, and Father Damien de Veuster, who devoted himself to the lepers of Molokai.

The great success of Catholicism in Belgium is largely explained by the freedom it enjoys under the Constitution. "The freedom of religions and their public exercise, as well as the right to the expression of opinions on all subjects are guaranteed, with the exception of misdemeanours committed in exercising this liberty" (art. 14). The sole restriction to this liberty is contained in article 16 of the Constitution which says that a civil marriage must always precede the religious ceremony, with such exceptions as may be established by law. The priest who, in fulfilling his duty, blesses a marriage *in extremis* under this article is in danger of prosecution and condemnation; the law which the Constitution provided for, and which would have protected such cases, has never been passed. With the exception of this and the law authorizing divorce, to which, however, recourse is seldom had, it may be said that the legislation of Belgium conforms to the Catholic standard of morality. Although the Church is independent in Belgium, and the country has no State religion, it does not follow that the governmental and the religious authorities have no connexion with each other. Tradition and custom have produced numerous points of contact and relations of courtesy between Church and State. The latter pays the stipends of the Catholic clergy as well as of the clergy of the Protestant and Jewish religions, very moderate salaries which have been slightly increased by a law passed in 1900. The State also assists in the expense of erecting buildings for religious purposes and of keeping them in repair. The parishes have been granted a civil existence and can hold property; each parish has a board of administration, of which the mayor of the town is a member by law, for the aid of the clergy in the management of the finances of the Church. The Liberal party, it is true, has tried a number of times to get control of the church property, but the law of 1870 (a compromise law), concerning the temporalities of the different religions, only requires the supervision of the public authorities over expenses concerning which the intervention of these authorities is requested. Students at the theological seminaries, who are to be parish priests, are exempted from military duty. Finally, the civil authorities are officially present at the "Te Deum" which is sung on the national anniversaries; and except during the period of 1880–84 (see above) the Government has maintained diplomatic relations with the Holy See.

VI. EDUCATION.—The most successful work of the Belgian Church has been done in the field of education, in spite of most violent opposition on the part of the Liberal party. Article 17 of the Constitution, says, concerning instruction: "Teaching is free; all preventive measures are forbidden; the repression of offences is reserved to the law. Public instruction given by the State is equally regulated by law." The Constitution, therefore, supposes at the same time a free instruction and an instruction by the State; it guarantees complete liberty to the first and subordinates the latter to the enactments of the law. The Catholics alone have made use of this article of the Constitution to establish a flourishing series of schools and colleges leading up to a university. The Liberals have contented themselves with founding a university (subsidized by the city of Brussels and the province of Brabant) and an insignificant number of schools, and are generally satisfied with State instruction for their children; this instruction they endeavour to make as neutral, that is, as irreligious as possible. They also favour in every way State instruction to the detriment of the free teaching. There are two State universities, Ghent and Liège, which have, respectively, 1000 and 2000 students. There are also 20 State athenæums with 6000 students, besides 7 communal colleges having about 1000 pupils; these institutions are for secondary education in its upper classes. The lower classes are taught in 112 intermediate schools, 78 of which are for boys and 34 for girls, with a total of 20,000 pupils. There are also 11 intermediate schools opened by the communes, 5 for boys and 6 for girls, with a total of 4000 pupils. The law of 1895 makes the communes responsible for primary instruction; each commune is

obliged to have at least one school, but it may be relieved of this responsibility if it is shown that private initiative has made sufficient provision for instruction. The State intervenes also in primary instruction by means of its normal schools for male and female teachers, by employing school inspectors whose business it is to see whether all the legal requirements are observed, and by the subsidies granted to communes which carry out the law.

Compared with these State institutions the schools established for free education are equal and in several respects superior. The Catholic University of Louvain, founded by the bishops, has 2200 students; it is surrounded by several institutes, one of the most famous of which is the "Institut philosophique", of which Monseigneur Mercier, now Cardinal Archbishop of Mechlin, was the founder and first president (until 1906). The Episcopal Institute of St. Louis at Brussels and the Jesuit College of Notre-Dame at Namur prepare pupils for the degrees of philosophy and letters. There are 90 free colleges for intermediate instruction, most of them diocesan, others carried on by the different religious orders, among whom the Jesuits take the lead with 12 colleges, having 5500 pupils. The free colleges have a total of 18,000 pupils, which is more than three times that of corresponding State schools. The situation in the intermediate classes of the lower grade is not so satisfactory for Catholics and may be called the dark page of their school statistics.

Since 1879 the subject of primary education has been the real battle-field; during this struggle the Catholics almost attained the ideal, having at least one school in almost every commune. But this was done at the cost of great sacrifices, so that since the suppression of the "Law of Misfortune" (*Loi de malheur*) of 1879, which had taken the Christian character from the primary schools, Catholics have accepted the communal schools in their renewed Christian form and have given up those which they had founded. The State, moreover, subsidizes the free schools when they give the guarantees necessary from a pedagogical point of view, and it authorizes the communes to adopt them as communal schools. Notwithstanding this, the legislation concerning primary teaching is far from being absolutely satisfactory; the large communes evade or even openly disregard the law, and it is only at long intervals that the Government interferes to check the most scandalous abuses. The law puts the State instruction and the free teaching on an absolute equality, and this equality is maintained by the Government; the diplomas granted by the free universities open the way to government positions just as do those granted by the State universities; the certificates given by the free institutes are equal to those of the State schools.

VII. CEMETERIES.—It is only by the greatest exertions that the Catholics of Belgium have saved the Catholic schools. In regard to the question of cemeteries they have shown less vigour. The decree of Prairial of the year XII (1804), by which the cemeteries of Belgium were regulated, stipulated that, in localities where several religions exist, each form of faith should have its own cemetery, and that where there was but one cemetery it should be divided into as many sections as there were different denominations. The Catholic cemeteries, in conformity with the Ritual, had separate sections for those who had died in communion with the Church, for infants dying without baptism, for those to whom the Church had refused religious burial, and for free-thinkers who died outside of the Catholic communion. There was no conflict until 1862 when, obedient to the order of the Freemason lodges, the Liberals declared the law of 1804 to be unconstitutional. The Government, then carried on by the Liberals, left it to the communal authorities to apply the law of 1804 or not, and for some fifteen years the law was disregarded or observed at the pleasure of the mayors of the towns. With the lapse of time the enforcement of the law declined, and a further step was taken; in 1879, the year of the *Loi de malheur*, the Court of Cassation suddenly changed its traditional method and began to convict those mayors who enforced the law of 1804. From this date the enforcement of the law became a misdemeanour, and many adverse sentences fell on the authorities who believed themselves bound in conscience to maintain this decree. Owing to the inactivity of the Catholics, there has been, since that time, no freedom with regard to cemeteries in Belgium.

CLAESSENS, *La Belgique chrétienne depuis la conquête française jusqu'à nos jours, 1794–1880* (Brussels, 1883); DE LANZAC DE LABORIE, *La domination française en Belgique, 1795–1814* (Paris, 1895); VAN CAENGHEM, *La guerre des paysans* (Grammont, 1900); DE GERLACHE, *Histoire du royaume des Pays-Bas* (Brussels, 1875); TERLINDEN, *Guillaume I, roi des Pays-Bas, et l'Eglise catholique en Belgique, 1814–1830* (Brussels, 1906); JUSTE, *La révolution belge de 1830* (Brussels, 1872); COLENBRANDER, *De Belgische omwenteling* (The Hague, 1905); THONISSEN, *La Belgique sous le règne de Léopold I* (Liège, 1855–1858); BALAU, *Soixante-dix ans d'histoire contemporaine de Belgique, 1815–1884* (Brussels, 1889); DISCAILLES, *Charles Rogier* (Brussels, 1893–95); HYMANS, *Frère-Orban* (Brussels, 1905); NYSSENS, *Eudore Pirmez* (Brussels, 1893); DE TRANNOY, *Jules Malou* (Brussels, 1893); VERHAEGEN, *La lutte scolaire en Belgique* (Ghent, 1905); VAN HOOREBEKE, *Histoire de la politique contemporaine en Belgique depuis 1830* (Brussels, 1905); BERTRAND, *Histoire de la démocratie et du socialisme en Belgique depuis 1830* (Brussels, 1906); MACDONNEL, *King Leopold II: His Rule in Belgium and the Congo* (London, 1905); BLOK, *Geschiedenis van het nederlandsche volk* (Leyden, 1907). Statistics of Belgium in the *Census* of 31 December, 1900; *Annuaire de statistique* (1906); *Annuaire du clergé belge* (1906); VLOEBERGHS, *La Belgique charitable* (Brussels, 1904).

GODEFROID KURTH.

Belgrade and Smederevo, titular (united) sees of Servia. The history of these sees is as confused as their present plight is pitiful from the Catholic standpoint. Dalmatia and Illyria claim St. Titus, the disciple of St. Paul, as their first Christian missionary; but the first Bishop of Belgrade, Theodosius, dates only from 1059. As the ancient Singidunum, however, it was an episcopal see in the fourth century, but gradually declined during the invasions of the barbarian Slavs. The medieval see was founded by the King of Croatia. The Hungarians and the Venetians disputed the possession of Belgrade (Serb *Beograd*, white city). The latter having destroyed the town (1126), the episcopal see was transferred to the neighbouring Scardona, so extensively embellished by them that it received the name of Scardona Nova. Religion had long flourished there, for one of the bishops at the Council of Salona (530) signs as *Episcopus Ecclesiæ Scardonitanæ*. On the occasion of the transfer to Scardona the title of Belgrade disappears for centuries from ecclesiastical history. The neighbouring city of Smederevo (Lat. *Semendria*) was also an episcopal see. Gams gives the names of four of its bishops from 1544 to 1605, a list, beginning 1334, of bishops whom he styles "of Belgrade and Semendria" (*Nadoralbenses et Belgradenses*). It is certain that in 1650 Innocent X re-established the title and See of Belgrade; for a Brief (4 December, 1651) is extant addressed to Matthew Benlich, *Episcopus Bellegradensis, Ecclesiæ Samadiensis Administrator*, creating him vicar Apostolic for those sees of the Church of Hungary which were under Turkish domination.

In 1729 the two Dioceses of Belgrade and Smederevo were united by Benedict XIII, and in 1733 Vincent Bagradin became the first holder of the double title. Thenceforward the list of bishops is regular and complete. The "Notizie di Roma" (the official annual of the Holy See) gives the names of all the prelates of this see. Until recent years Belgrade and Smederevo were considered residential sees; it is expressly so stated in the consistory of 1858. It

was added that these two sees (ancient Alba Græca and Singidunum respectively) were suffragans of the metropolitan See of Antivari, and that the nomination to them resided in the Emperor of Austria, "but as they are held by the infidels, their actual state is passed over in silence". For many years the title was given to the auxiliary of an Hungarian bishop (at present to the auxiliary of the Archbishop of Zagrab) who was bound to reside with his superior. The "Gerarchia" for 1906, without giving any notice of the change, has transferred this see to the list of titular bishoprics, though Bishop Krapac, who now holds the title, was named in 1904 as a residential bishop.

The present condition of this Church is most lamentable. The limits of the diocese are those of the Kingdom of Servia, which has an area of 18,630 square miles and a population (1905) of 2,676,989, belonging for the most part to the Greek schism, which is the official religion of the State. Since 1851 the Bishop of Diakovar acts as administrator Apostolic; since 1886 the territory is united to the ecclesiastical province of Scutari (Kirch. Handlex., I, 533). There are only two or three priests, who divide their activities between the three principal stations of Belgrade (4,000 Catholics), Kragujevatz (200), and Nish (1,000). There are also seven secondary stations, numbering about 1,000 Catholics all told. (It is to be noted that according to the "Statesman's Year Book" for 1907, the Servian census of 1900 gives 10,243 Catholics.) One church, two chapels, and two elementary schools (at Belgrade and Nish respectively) complete the list of the mission's resources. The statistics say nothing of Uniat Greeks, which leads us to suppose that these Latin Catholics are only western Europeans whose business obliges them to reside in Servia. Belgrade has (1905) a population of 80,747. Situated on the right bank of the Danube, just below the Save, it has always been a natural fortress, and as such is famous in military history. From 1522 to 1867 it passed alternately from Turks to Austrians; in the latter year the Turkish garrison was withdrawn, and in 1878, by the Treaty of Berlin, Belgrade became the capital of the new Christian Kingdom of Servia.

Missiones Catholicæ (1906); GAMS, *Series Episcoporum*, 396; EUBEL, I, 371, II, 219; FARLATI, *Illyr. Sacr.* (1769–1819), IV, 1–9, VIII, 144–151, 250–254; KALLAY, *Geschichte des Serben* (1878); MOLLAT, *La Serbie contemporaine* (Paris, 1902).

ALBERT BATTANDIER.

Belgrado, GIACOPO, Italian Jesuit and natural philosopher, b. at Udine, 16 November, 1704; d. in the same city, 26 March, 1789. He belonged to a noble family and received his early education at Padua. He entered the novitiate of the Society of Jesus, 16 October, 1723, and showed marked talent, studying mathematics and philosophy at Bologna under Father Luigi Marchenti, a former pupil of Varignon at Paris. After completing his philosophical studies he taught letters for several years at Venice, where he won the affection of his students as well as the esteem and friendship of the scholars of that city. He studied theology at Parma and then became professor of mathematics and physics at the university, holding this position for twelve years. While at Parma he did much experimental work in physics with apparatus specially constructed by two of his assistants. After pronouncing his solemn vows, on 2 February, 1742, Belgrado was summoned to the court, where he was appointed confessor, first to the Duchess and later to the Duke Don Philippo. The title of mathematician of the court was also bestowed on him. In 1757 he erected an observatory on one of the towers of the college of Parma and furnished it with the necessary instruments. In 1773 he became rector of the college of Bologna. He was a member of most of the academies of Italy and a corresponding member of the Académie des Sciences of Paris. He was likewise one of the founders of the Arcadian colony of Parma. He wrote on a variety of subjects, among his works being: "I Fenomeni Elettrici" (1749); "Della riflessione de' corpi dall' acqua e della diminuzione della mole de' sassi ne' torrenti e ne' fiumi" (1755); "De analyseos vulgaris usu in re physicâ" (1761–62); "Delle sensazioni del freddo e del calore" (1764); "Theoria Cochleæ Archimedis" (1767); "Dell' esistenza di Dio da' teoremi geometrici" (1777), etc.

MAZZUCHELLI, *Gli Scrittori d'Italia* (Brescia 1760), II, ii; SOMMERVOGEL, *Bibliothèque de la c. de J.* (new ed., Paris, 1890).

H. M. BROCK.

Belial, found frequently as a personal name in the Vulgate and various English translations of the Bible, is commonly used as a synonym of Satan, or the personification of evil. This sense is derived from II Cor., vi, 15, where Belial (or Beliar) as prince of darkness is contrasted with Christ, the light. It is clear in the Vulgate and Douay translations of III Kings, xxi, 10 and 13, where the same Hebrew word is rendered once as Belial and twice as "the devil". In the other instances, too, the translators understood it as a name for the prince of evil, and so it has passed into English. Milton, however, distinguishes Belial from Satan, regarding him as the demon of impurity. In the Hebrew Bible, nevertheless, the word is not a proper name, but a common noun usually signifying "wickedness" or "extreme wickedness". Thus, Moore renders "sons of Belial" as "vile scoundrels" (Judges, xix, 22); most prefer "worthless fellows". In some cases *belial* seems to mean "destruction", "ruin"; thus in Ps., xli, 9 (Heb.), the word is parallel to the thought of utter destruction and seems to mean the same. In Ps., xviii, 5, it is parallel to "death" and "Sheol"; some understand it as "destruction", Cheyne as "the abyss". The etymology of the word בליעל is doubtful; it is usually given as בלי, "not", "without", and יעל, a verb which occurs only in the Hiphil (causative active) form, "to use", "be of use", "to be profitable to"; the compound is supposed to mean worthlessness. Cheyne suggests בלי יעלה, that from which no one comes up, namely, the abyss, Sheol. St. Jerome's etymology "without yoke", which he has even inserted as a gloss in the text of Judges, xix, 22, is contrary to Hebrew philology. Belial, from meaning wickedness or Sheol, could develop into a name for the prince of evil or of darkness; and as such was widely used at the beginning of our era. Under the names Beliar, Berial, he plays a very important rôle in apocryphal literature, in the "Ascension of Isaias", the "Sibylline Oracles", and the "Testament of the Twelve Patriarchs". He is the prince of this world and will come as Antichrist; his name is sometimes given also to Nero, returning as Antichrist.

CHEYNE in *Encyc. Bib.* (New York, 1899); MOORE, *Commentary on Judges* (New York, 1900), 419; GARVIE in HAST., *Dict. of Bible* (New York, 1903); DEANE, *Pseudepigrapha* (Edinburgh, 1891); LESÊTRE in VIG., *Dict. de la Bible* (Paris, 1894); CHARLES, *Ascension of Isaiah* (London, 1900); CHARLES, *Eschatology, Hebrew, Jewish, and Christian* (London, 1899).

JOHN F. FENLON.

Belief (*be* and *lyian*, to hold dear), that state of the mind by which it assents to propositions, not by reason of their intrinsic evidence, but because of authority. Though the term is commonly used in ordinary language, as well as in much philosophical writing, to cover a great many states of mind, the quasi-definition advanced is probably the best calculated to differentiate belief from all other forms of mental assent. In framing it, respect is paid to the motive of the assent rather than to its nature; for, since intellectual assent is of its nature simple and indivisible, no *differentiæ proximæ* can be assigned by which it could be separated into various species.

As the objects of belief, also, are of a nature similar to those of knowledge, opinion, and doubt, so, again, no criterion of division can be found in them (as in the case of the objects of separate faculties) to distinguish it from other mental states. St. Thomas Aquinas qualifies his definition of faith with the addition of the note of certainty (Summa, I–II, Q. i, a. 4). Though he treats of faith as a theological virtue in the article cited, his words may well be extended to include belief as a purely natural state of the mind. It will thus be seen to cover intellectual assent to truths accepted on authority either human or Divine. In the former case belief may be designated by the synonym credence; in the latter the more usual term is faith. Often, also, belief is used in the sense of *fiducia*, or trust; and this especially in Protestant theology as a substitute for faith. By the definition given above we are enabled to distinguish belief (1) from intelligence, in that the truth of the fact or proposition believed is not seen intuitively; (2) from science or knowledge, since there is no question of resolving it into its first principles; (3) from doubt, because belief is an assent and positive; (4) from opinion and conjecture, in which the assent is not complete.

Belief, however, as has already been noted, is often indiscriminatingly used for these and for other states of mind from which for the sake of accuracy it should be as carefully distinguished as is possible. Though we may know a thing and at the same time believe it (as in the case of the existence of God, which is a natural verity as well as a revealed truth), it is in the interest of clearness that we should keep to the distinction drawn and not confound belief and knowledge, because of the fact that the same truth may simultaneously be the object of both. But there is another very general use of the term belief in which it is taken to designate assent complete enough to exclude any practical doubt and yet distinguishable from the assent of knowledge. In this use no account is taken of authority. We have many convictions resting upon evidence that is not sufficiently clearly presented to our mind to enable us to say we know, but abundantly sufficient for us to produce a practically unqualified assent. While this would seem to fall under the Scholastic head of opinion, it is the point about which has turned the controversy that has been waged since David Hume brought the question into prominence upon the philosophic issue. Briefly, to select a certain number of typical writers for examination, the issues involved are these. How far do we believe—in the sense of trusting our natural faculties in their reports and judgments; and in how far can we be said to know? Hume, in accordance with his sensistic principles, would restrict our knowledge to purely ideal truths. We are capable of knowing, according to the Scotch sceptic, such ideal principles as those of mathematics, together with the conclusions that are derived from them. But our attribution of an objective reality to what we imagine to be the causes of sensations is a belief. So also are such judgments as that of the principle of causality. We cannot be said to know, but to believe, that there is actually such a relation as that of effect to cause. We believe this, and other similar truths, because of a peculiar character of vivacity, solidity, firmness, or steadiness attaching to our conceptions of them. The division is an arbitrary one and the explanation offered as to the nature of belief unsatisfactory and insufficient. Similarly, James Mill would have the assent given to the objective reality of beings a belief. With him the occasion of the belief is the association of ideas: or, rather, as he wrongly states it, the association of ideas is the belief. If belief is a state of mind at all, it can scarcely be described as an association of ideas. Such an association could at most be considered as a cause of the belief. John Stuart Mill in his note to his father's Analysis, makes belief a primitive fact. It is impossible to analyze it. Locke, though he deals at some length with belief, does not try to analyze it or do more than assign objects to it and investigate the grounds of credibility. Alexander Bain originally held belief to be a function of the will rather than a state of the intellect. In his opinion it was the development of the will under the pursuit of immediate ends. Later, he modified this opinion, and, while retaining the essentially volitional and emotional character, or tendency, as causes, relegated the act of belief itself to the intellectual part of man's nature. Father Maher, S.J., whose admirable treatment of the whole subject ought to be consulted, advances an acute criticism of Dr. Bain's position. He points out (1) that readiness to act is a test of belief, not the belief itself; (2) that belief is generally not active but characteristically passive; (3) that primitive credulity, which Bain makes a chief factor in belief, involves a vicious circle, explaining, as it does, belief by credulity or believing.

A not inconsiderable part of the "Grammar of Assent" is concerned with this subject, though hardly dealing with the problem on the foregoing lines. In his treatment of "Simple Assent", and especially in sections 4 and 5 of Chapter iv, Par. 1, Cardinal Newman's view can be found. He calls the notional assent that we give to first principles presumption. We cannot be said to trust our powers of reasoning or memory as faculties, though we may be supposed to have a trust in any one of their particular acts. That external nature exists is a first principle and is founded upon an instinct. The use of the term is justified by the consideration that the brute creation also possesses it. Further, "the belief in causation" is one of these presumptions, and the assent to it notional. But, on the other hand, "we believe without any doubt that we exist; that we have an individuality and identity all our own; . . . that we have a present sense of good and evil, of a right and a wrong. . . ." Again: "Assent on reasonings not demonstrative is too widely recognized an act to be irrational, unless man's nature is irrational, too familiar to the prudent and clearminded to be an infirmity or an extravagance." It will be noted that Newman (1) justifies belief as an assent because based on a common use of the rational faculty. Demonstrative grounds may be lacking, but the conviction is none the less neither an infirmity nor an extravagance, but rational. (2) He groups belief and knowledge together under the heading of presumption without drawing any hard and fast line between them. And indeed, from the point of view of mere assent, there is nothing psychological by which they are to be distinguished: since assent itself, as has been noted, is a simple and ultimate fact. The difference lies elsewhere. In this broader sense of belief, it is to be found in the antecedent cause of the assent. For knowledge there will be explicit, for belief implicit, intuition or evidence.

Of German philosophers who have treated this topic, Germar, Fechner, and Ulrici may be consulted. The first limits belief to a conscious assent arising from fact; that is, an assent given without consciousness of its causes or grounds. In the case where the causes or grounds become actual factors in the consciousness, the belief rises to the dignity of knowledge. Kant's view naturally has belief as the necessitated result of the practical reason. It is to be considered epistemologically rather than psychologically. We believe in such truths as are necessitated by the exigencies of our moral nature. And these truths have necessary validity on account of the requirements of that moral nature. We need motives upon which to act. Such beliefs are practical and

lead to action. All natural truths that we accept on belief might conceivably be accepted as truths of knowledge. The implicit may unfold and become explicit. This frequently happens in ordinary experience. Evidence may be adduced to prove assertions. Similarly, any truth of knowledge may be accepted as belief. What is said to be known to one individual may be, and often is, accepted upon his testimony by another.

A great variety of factors may play their part in the genesis of belief. We are accustomed to assent to propositions that we cannot be said to know, on account of many different causes. Some of them are often inadequate and even frivolous. We frequently discover that our beliefs rest on no stable foundation, that they must be reconstructed or done away with altogether. The ordinary reasons upon which belief may be based can be reduced to two: testimony and the partial evidence of reason. A third class of causes of belief is sometimes added. Feeling, desire, and the wish to believe have been noted as antecedent causes of the act of assent. But that feeling, desire, or the wish to believe is a direct antecedent is open to discussion. It cannot be denied that many so-called beliefs, more properly described, perhaps, as trust or hope, have their immediate origin in feelings or wishes; but, as a rule, they seem not to be capable of bearing any real strain; whereas we are accustomed to consider that belief is one of the most unchangeable of mental states. Where these antecedents work indirectly through the election of the will, to which reference is made below, belief may issue as a firm and certain assent. (1) Testimony is a valid and satisfactory cause of assent provided it possess the necessary note of authority, which is the sole direct antecedent of the ensuing belief. Our ultimate witness must know his facts or truths and be veracious in his presentation of them. Intermediate witnesses must have accurately preserved the form of the original testimony. In the case of human testimony, the ordinary rules of prudence will naturally be applied before giving credence to its statements. Once, however, the question of knowledge and veracity is settled, belief may validly issue and an assent be given as to a certainty. Of course there is room also for doubt or for opinion, as the credentials of the authority itself may vary almost indefinitely. But there is a further class of truths believed upon testimony that does not fall within the scope of natural investigation and inquiry. The supersensible, supra-intellectual truths of revelation, at any rate in the present state of man's existence, cannot be said to be assented to either on account of an intuition of their nature or because of any strict process of demonstration of their validity. They are neither evident in themselves nor in their principles. The assent to such truths is of the same nature as that given to truths believed naturally. Only here the authority motiving it is not human but Divine. Acts of assent on such authority are known as acts of faith and, theologically speaking, connote the assistance of grace. They are, none the less, intellectual acts, in the eliciting of which the will has its part to play, just as are those in which assent is given to the authoritative utterances of credible human witnesses. With regard to the nature of this authority upon which such supernatural truths are assented to in faith, it is sufficient to indicate that God's knowledge is infinite and His veracity absolute. (2) The partial evidence of reason has already been touched upon. It may be noted, however, that the evidence may be relative either relatively or absolutely. In the first case we may have recourse to the authority of those who know for our belief, or base it for ourselves upon such evidence as is forthcoming. In the second, as is the case with much of the teaching of science and philosophy, the whole human race can have no more than a strictly so-called belief in it. Probable opinions, conjectures, obscured or partially recalled memories, or any truths or facts of which we have not a consciously evidential grasp, are the main objects of a belief resultant upon partial evidence. In this its distinction from knowledge lies. We are said to know intuitional truths as well as all those that are indirectly evident in their principles. We know all facts and truths of our own personal experience, whether of consciousness or of objective nature. Similarly, we know the truth of the reports of memory that come clearly and distinctly into consciousness. Nor is it necessary, with Hamilton, to have recourse to an initial belief or trust as implied in all knowledge. We cannot properly be said to trust our faculties. We do not believe evident truth. (3) With the two immediate causes of belief already noted, the action of the will must also be alluded to. Under this head emotion, feeling, and desire may conveniently be grouped, since they play an important, though indirect, part in motiving assents through the election of the will and so causing belief. The action of the will referred to is observed especially in a selection of the data to be examined and approved by the intellect. Where there are several sets of evidences or partial arguments, for and against, the will is said to cause belief in the sense of directing the intellect to examine the particular set of evidences or arguments in favour of the resultant assent and to neglect all that might be urged against it. In this case, however, the belief can easily be referred to the partial evidence of reason, in that as a rational, rather than a volitional act, it is due to the actual considerations before the mind. Whether these are voluntarily restricted or incomplete from the very nature of the case, does not alter the fact that the assent is given because of the partial evidence they furnish. In faith the meritorious nature of the act of belief is referred to this elective action of the will.

The effects of belief may be summed up generally under the head of action or movement, though all beliefs are not of their nature operative. Indeed, it would seem to depend more on the nature of the content of the belief than upon the act of believing. As with certain truths of knowledge, there are beliefs that leave us unmoved and even tend to restrict and prevent rather than instigate to action. The distinction drawn between the assents of knowledge and belief cannot be said to be observed at all closely in practice, where they are frequently confused. It is none the less undoubtedly felt to exist, and, upon analysis of the antecedents, the one can readily be distinguished from the other. It is found that most of the practical affairs of ordinary life depend entirely upon beliefs. In the vast majority of cases in which action is called for it is impossible to have strictly so-called knowledge upon which to act. In such cases belief readily supplies its place, growing stronger as it is justified by the event. Without it, as a practical incentive to action and a justification of it, social intercourse would be an impossibility. Such things as our estimates of the character of our friends, of the probity of those with whom we transact business, are examples of the beliefs that play so large and so necessary a part in our lives. In their own subject-matter they are on a par with the reasonable beliefs of science and philosophy—founded, as are hypotheses and theories, upon practically sufficient, yet indemonstrative and incomplete data.

MAHER, *Psychology* in *Stonyhurst Series* (London, 1890); NEWMAN, *An Essay in Aid of a Grammar of Assent* (London, 1870); BAIN, *Mental and Moral Science* (London, 1868–72); MILL, *Analysis of the Phenomena of the Human Mind* (London, 1829); J. S. MILL, *Notes* to new edition of *The Analysis* (London, 1869); IDEM, *Dissertations and Discussions* (London, 1859–75); SULLY, *Sensation and Intuition: Studies in Psychology and Æsthetics* (London, 1874); JAMES, *The Principles of Psychology* (New York, 1890); BALFOUR, *A Defence of Philosophic Doubt*
(London, 1879); WARD, *The Wish to Believe* (London, 1885); ULRICI, *Glauben und Wissen, Spekulation und exacte Wissenschaft* (Leipzig, 1858); FECHNER, *Die drei Motive und Gründe des Glaubens* (Leipzig, 1863); BALDWIN, *Dict. of Philosophy*, s. v.

FRANCIS AVELING.

Belin, ALBERT (JEAN) French prelate and writer, b. in Besançon early in the seventeenth century; d. 29 April, 1677. He made his profession in the Benedictine monastery of Faverney, 29 December, 1629, and spent some time at the monasteries of Charité-sur-Loire, Nevers, and Paris as prior and subsequently as abbot. He was consecrated Bishop of Belley, 14 February, 1666. His works, which were written in French, are: "Pierre philosophale" (Paris, 1653); "Talismans justifiés" (ibid., 1653); "Poudre de sympathie mystérieuse" (ibid., 1653); "Poudre de projection demontrée" (ibid., 1653); "Le voyage inconnu" (ibid., 1653); "Principes de la foi demontrés par la raison" (ibid., 1667); "Preuves convainquantes des vérités du christianisme" (ibid., 1666); "Emblèmes eucharistiques, ou octave du très S. Sacrement" (1647, 1660); "Les solides pensées de l'ame, pour la porter à son devoir" (Paris, 1668). He is probably identical with Alphonsus Belin, O.S.B., Prior of Charité-sur-Loire in the latter half of the seventeenth century, and author of "La vérité de la religion catholique et la fausseté de la religion prétendue réformée" (Nevers, 1683).

HURTER, *Nomenclator* (Innsbruck, 1893); ZIEGELBAUER, *Historia Rei Literariæ O. S. B.* (Augsburg, 1754), III; CALMET, *Bibliothèque Lorraine* (1751).

ALEXIUS HOFFMANN.

Bell, ARTHUR (*alias* FRANCIS), VENERABLE, Friar Minor and English martyr, b. at Temple-Broughton near Worcester, 13 January, 1590; d. at London, 11 December, 1643. When Arthur was eight his father died and his mother gave him in charge of her brother Francis Daniel, a man of wealth, learning, and piety, who sent him at the age of twenty-four to the English college at St.-Omer; thence he went to Spain to continue and complete his studies. Having been ordained priest, he received the habit of the Franciscan Order at Segovia, 9 August, 1618, and shortly after the completion of his novitiate was called from Spain to labour in the restoration of the English

ARTHUR BELL

province. He was one of the first members of the Franciscan community at Douai, where he subsequently fulfilled the offices of guardian and professor of Hebrew. In 1632 Bell was sent to Scotland as first provincial of the Franciscan province there; but his efforts to restore the order in Scotland were unsuccessful and in 1637 he returned to England, where he laboured until November, 1643, when he was apprehended as a spy by the parliamentary troops at Stevendege in Hertfordshire and committed to Newgate prison.

The circumstances of his trial show Bell's singular devotedness to the cause of religion and his desire to suffer for the Faith. When condemned to be drawn and quartered it is said that he broke forth into a solemn Te Deum and thanked his judges profusely for the favour they were thus conferring upon him in allowing him to die for Christ. The cause of his beatification was introduced at Rome in 1900. He wrote "The History, Life, and Miracles of Joane of the Cross" (St.-Omer, 1625). He also translated from the Spanish of Andrew a Soto "A brief Instruction how we ought to hear Mass" (Brussels, 1624).

THADDEUS, *The Franciscans in England* (London, 1898), V, 35, 36; VI, 39; VII, 47, 49, 50; IX, 62, 66–68; XV, 200–202; ANGELUS A S. FRANCISCO (RICHARD MASON), *Certamen Seraphicum* (Quaracchi, 1885), 127–157; ORTOLANI, *De causis beatorum et servorum Dei ord. min.* (Quaracchi, 1905), 14.

STEPHEN M. DONOVAN.

Bell, JAMES, priest and martyr, b. at Warrington in Lancashire, England, probably about 1520; d. 20 April, 1584. For the little known of him we depend on the account published four years after his death by Bridgewater in his "Concertatio" (1588), and derived from a manuscript which was kept at Douay when Challoner wrote his "Missionary Priests" in 1741, and is now in the Westminster Diocesan Archives. A few further details were collected by Challoner, and others are supplied by the State Papers. Having studied at Oxford he was ordained priest in Mary's reign, but unfortunately conformed to the established Church under Elizabeth, and according to the Douay MS. "ministred their bare few sacraments about 20 years in diverse places of England". Finally deterred by conscience from the cure of souls and reduced to destitution, he sought a small readership as a bare subsistence. To obtain this he approached the patron's wife, a Catholic lady, who induced him to be reconciled to the Church. After some time he was allowed to resume priestly functions, and for two years devoted himself to arduous missionary labours. He was at length apprehended (17 January, 1583–84) and, having confessed his priesthood, was arraigned at Manchester Quarter Sessions held during the same month, and sent for trial at Lancaster Assizes in March. When condemned and sentenced he said to the Judge: "I beg your Lordship would add to the sentence that my lips and the tops of my fingers may be cut off, for having sworn and subscribed to the articles of heretics contrary both to my conscience and to God's Truth". He spent that night in prayer and on the following day was hanged and quartered together with Ven. John Finch, a layman, 20 April, 1584.

BRIDGEWATER, *Concertatio ecclesiæ Catholicæ in Anglia*, 1588; YEPEZ, *Historia particular de la persecucion de Inglaterra*, 1599; CHALLONER, *Missionary Priests*, 1741; *Dict. Nat. Biog.*, IV, 163; GILLOW, *Bibl. Dict. Eng. Cath.*, I, 173, citing State Papers in Public Record Office.

EDWIN BURTON.

Bellamy, JEROME, of Uxenden Hall, near London, England, d. 1586, a member of an old Catholic family noted for its hospitality to missionaries and recusants. He was a warm sympathizer with Mary Queen of Scots. In the latter years of the sixteenth century the Babington plot to free Mary and assassinate Elizabeth was exposed, and Babington, with two of his fellow-conspirators, Barnewell and Donne, sought refuge in Bellamy's house. He concealed them and was later arrested with them and accused of complicity in the plot. All four were indicted, tried, convicted 15 September, 1586, and within six days thereafter executed.

GILLOW, *Bibl. Dict. Eng. Cath.*, I, 176.

THOMAS GAFFNEY TAAFFE.

Bellarini, JOHN, Barnabite theologian, b. at Castelnuovo, Italy, in 1552; d. at Milan, 27 August, 1630. He was Visitor and twice Assistant General of his order. He taught theology at Padua and Rome, and was highly esteemed by bishops and cardinals, particularly by Gregory XV. Best known as a moral theologian, he has left a number of solid theological treatises, the most valuable of which is a commentary on the Council of Trent and the Roman Catechism, in two parts, forming two distinct volumes. The first, for the instruction of the

faithful, is entitled "Doctrina d. Concilii Tridentini et Cathechismi Romani de Symbolo Apostolorum" (Brescia, 1603). The parts of this work relating to the decalogue have been published in French. The second work, designed for the conversion of heretics, and entitled "Doctrina Catholica ex Sacro Concilio Tridentini et Catechismo Romano" (Milan, 1620), has passed through several editions. Bellarini also composed a number of booklets in Italian for confessors and penitents, and a treatise on the doctrine of St. Thomas on physical predetermination and on the determination in general of all things and causes into active operation (Milan, 1606). He is also the author of a work on method (Milan, 1606), which was republished under a slightly different title, along with his "Mirror of Divine and Human Wisdom" (Milan, 1630).

MANGENOT in *Dict. de théol. cath.*, II, 559; *Bibliotheca Scriptorum e Cong. Cler. Regul. S. Pauli* (Rome, 1836), 140.

S. H. FRISBEE.

Bellarmine (BELLARMINO), ROBERT FRANCIS ROMULUS, VENERABLE, a distinguished Jesuit theologian, writer, and cardinal, b. at Montepulciano, 4 October, 1542; d. 17 September, 1621. His father was Vincenzo Bellarmino, his mother Cinthia Cervini, sister of Cardinal Marcello Cervini, afterwards Pope Marcellus II. He was brought up at the newly founded Jesuit college in his native town, and entered the Society of Jesus on 20 September, 1560, being admitted to his first vows on the following day. The next three years he spent in studying philosophy at the Roman College, after which he taught the humanities first at Florence, then at Mondovi. In 1567 he began his theology at Padua, but in 1569 was sent to finish it at Louvain, where he could obtain a fuller acquaintance with the prevailing heresies. Having been ordained there, he quickly obtained a reputation both as a professor and a preacher, in the latter capacity drawing to his pulpit both Catholics and Protestants, even from distant parts. In 1576 he was recalled to Italy, and entrusted with the chair of Controversies recently founded at the Roman College. He proved himself equal to the arduous task, and the lectures thus delivered grew into the work "De Controversiis" which, amidst so much else of excellence, forms the chief title to his greatness. This monumental work was the earliest attempt to systematize the various controversies of the time, and made an immense impression throughout Europe, the blow it dealt to Protestantism being so acutely felt in Germany and England that special chairs were founded in order to provide replies to it. Nor has it even yet been superseded as the classical book on its subject-matter, though, as was to be expected, the progress of criticism has impaired the value of some of its historical arguments.

VENERABLE ROBERT CARDINAL BELLARMINE

In 1588 Bellarmine was made Spiritual Father to the Roman College, but in 1590 he went with Cardinal Gaetano as theologian to the embassy Sixtus V was then sending into France to protect the interests of the Church amidst the troubles of the civil wars. Whilst he was there news reached him that Sixtus, who had warmly accepted the dedication of his "De Controversiis", was now proposing to put its first volume on the Index. This was because he had discovered that it assigned to the Holy See not a direct but only an indirect power over temporals. Bellarmine, whose loyalty to the Holy See was intense, took this greatly to heart; it was, however, averted by the death of Sixtus, and the new pope, Gregory XIV, even granted to Bellarmine's work the distinction of a special approbation. Gaetano's mission now terminating, Bellarmine resumed his work as Spiritual Father, and had the consolation of guiding the last years of St. Aloysius Gonzaga, who died in the Roman College in 1591. Many years later he had the further consolation of successfully promoting the beatification of the saintly youth. Likewise at this time he sat on the final commission for the revision of the Vulgate text. This revision had been desired by the Council of Trent, and subsequent popes had laboured over the task and had almost brought it to completion. But Sixtus V, though unskilled in this branch of criticism, had introduced alterations of his own, all for the worse. He had even gone so far as to have an impression of this vitiated edition printed and partially distributed, together with the proposed Bull enforcing its use. He died, however, before the actual promulgation, and his immediate successors at once proceeded to remove the blunders and call in the defective impression. The difficulty was how to substitute a more correct edition without affixing a stigma to the name of Sixtus, and Bellarmine proposed that the new edition should continue in the name of Sixtus, with a prefatory explanation that, on account of *aliqua vitia vel typographorum vel aliorum* which had crept in, Sixtus had himself resolved that a new impression should be undertaken. The suggestion was accepted, and Bellarmine himself wrote the preface, still prefixed to the Clementine edition ever since in use. On the other hand, he has been accused of untruthfulness in stating that Sixtus had resolved on a new impression. But his testimony, as there is no evidence to the contrary, should be accepted as decisive, seeing how conscientious a man he was in the estimation of his contemporaries; and the more so since it cannot be impugned without casting a slur on the character of his fellow-commissioners who accepted his suggestion, and of Clement VIII who with full knowledge of the facts gave his sanction to Bellarmine's preface being prefixed to the new edition. Besides, Angelo Rocca, the Secretary of the revisory commissions of Sixtus V and the succeeding pontiffs, himself wrote a draft preface for the new edition in which he makes the same statement: (Sixtus) "dum errores ex typographiâ ortos, et mutationes omnes, atque varias hominum opiniones recognoscere cœpit, ut postea de toto negotio deliberare atque Vulgatam editionem, prout debebat, publicare posset, morte præventus quod cœperat perficere non potuit". This draft preface, to which Bellarmine's was preferred, is still extant, attached to the copy of the Sixtine edition in which the Clementine corrections are marked, and may be seen in the Biblioteca Angelica at Rome (see this question well discussed by Père Prat in the "Etudes religieuses" for September, 1890).

In 1592 Bellarmine was made Rector of the Roman College, and in 1595 Provincial of Naples. In 1597 Clement VIII recalled him to Rome and made him his own theologian and likewise Examiner of Bishops and Consultor of the Holy Office. Further, in 1599 he made him Cardinal-Priest of the title of Santa Maria *in viâ*, alleging as his reason for this promotion that "the Church of God had not his equal in learning". He was now appointed, along with the

Dominican Cardinal d'Ascoli, an assessor to Cardinal Madruzzi, the President of the Congregation *de Auxiliis*, which had been instituted shortly before to settle the controversy which had recently arisen between the Thomists and the Molinists concerning the nature of the concord between efficacious grace and human liberty. Bellarmine's advice was from the first that the doctrinal question should not be decided authoritatively, but left over for further discussion in the schools, the disputants on either side being strictly forbidden to indulge in censures or condemnations of their adversaries. Clement VIII at first inclined to this view, but afterwards changed completely and determined on a doctrinal definition. Bellarmine's presence then became embarrassing, and he appointed him to the Archbishopric of Capua just then vacant. This is sometimes spoken of as the cardinal's disgrace, but Clement consecrated him with his own hands—an honour which the popes usually accord as a mark of special regard. The new archbishop departed at once for his see, and during the next three years set a bright example of pastoral zeal in its administration.

In 1605 Clement VIII died, and was succeeded by Leo XI, who reigned only twenty-six days, and then by Paul V. In both conclaves, especially the latter, the name of Bellarmine was much before the electors, greatly to his own distress, but his quality as a Jesuit stood against him in the judgment of many of the cardinals. The new pope insisted on keeping him at Rome, and the cardinal, obediently complying, demanded that at least he should be released from an episcopal charge the duties of which he could no longer fulfil. He was now made a member of the Holy Office and of other congregations, and thenceforth was the chief adviser of the Holy See in the theological department of its administration. Of the particular transactions with which his name is most generally associated the following were the most important: The inquiry *de Auxiliis*, which after all Clement had not seen his way to decide, was now terminated with a settlement on the lines of Bellarmine's original suggestion. 1606 marked the beginning of the quarrel between the Holy See and the Republic of Venice which, without even consulting the pope, had presumed to abrogate the law of clerical exemption from civil jurisdiction and to withdraw the Church's right to hold real property. The quarrel led to a war of pamphlets in which the part of the Republic was sustained by John Marsiglio and an apostate monk named Paolo Sarpi, and that of the Holy See by Bellarmine and Baronius. Contemporaneous with this Venetian episode was that of the English Oath of Allegiance. In 1606, in addition to the grave disabilities which already weighed them down, the English Catholics were required under pain of *præmunire* to take an oath of allegiance craftily worded in such wise that a Catholic in refusing to take it might appear to be disavowing an undoubted civil obligation, whilst if he should take it he would be not merely rejecting but even condemning as "impious and heretical" the doctrine of the deposing power, that is to say, of a power, which, whether rightly or wrongly, the Holy See had claimed and exercised for centuries with the full approval of Christendom, and which even in that age the mass of the theologians of Europe defended. The Holy See having forbidden Catholics to take this oath, King James himself came forward as its defender, in a book entitled "Triplici nodo triplex cuneus", to which Bellarmine replied in his "Responsio Matthæi Torti". Other treatises followed on either side, and the result of one, written in denial of the deposing power by William Barclay, an English jurist resident in France, was that Bellarmine's reply to it was branded by the Regalist *Parlement* of Paris. Thus it came to pass that, for following the *via media* of the indirect power, he was condemned in 1590 as too much of a Regalist and in 1605 as too much of a Papalist.

Bellarmine did not live to deal with the later and more serious stage of the Galileo case, but in 1615 he took part in its earlier stage. He had always shown great interest in the discoveries of that investigator, and was on terms of friendly correspondence with him. He took up too—as is witnessed by his letter to Galileo's friend Foscarini—exactly the right attitude towards scientific theories in seeming contradiction with Scripture. If, as was undoubtedly the case then with Galileo's heliocentric theory, a scientific theory is insufficiently proved, it should be advanced only as an hypothesis; but if, as is the case with this theory now, it is solidly demonstrated, care must be taken to interpret Scripture only in accordance with it. When the Holy Office condemned the heliocentric theory, by an excess in the opposite direction, it became Bellarmine's official duty to signify the condemnation to Galileo, and receive his submission. Bellarmine lived to see one more conclave, that which elected Gregory XV (February, 1621). His health was now failing, and in the summer of the same year he was permitted to retire to Sant' Andrea and prepare for the end. His death was most edifying and was a fitting termination to a life which had been no less remarkable for its virtues than for its achievements.

His spirit of prayer, his singular delicacy of conscience and freedom from sin, his spirit of humility and poverty, together with the disinterestedness which he displayed as much under the cardinal's robes as under the Jesuit's gown, his lavish charity to the poor, and his devotedness to work, had combined to impress those who knew him intimately with the feeling that he was of the number of the saints. Accordingly, when he died there was a general expectation that his cause would be promptly introduced. And so it was, under Urban VIII in 1627, when he became entitled to the appellation of Venerable. But a technical obstacle, arising out of Urban VIII's own general legislation in regard to beatifications, required its prorogation at that time. Though it was reintroduced on several occasions (1675, 1714, 1752, and 1832), and though on each occasion the great preponderance of votes was in favour of the beatification, a successful issue has never yet been reached. This was partly because of the influential character of some of those who recorded adverse votes, Barbarigo, Casanate, and Azzolino in 1675, and Passionei in 1752, but still more for reasons of political expediency, Bellarmine's name being closely associated with a doctrine of papal authority most obnoxious to the Regalist politicians of the French Court. "We have said", wrote Benedict XIV to Cardinal de Tencin, "in confidence to the General of the Jesuits that the delay of the Cause has come not from the petty matters laid to his charge by Cardinal Passionei, but from the sad circumstances of the times" (Etudes Religieuses, 15 April, 1896).

A full list of Bellarmine's writings, and of those directed against him, may be seen in Sommervogel's "Bibliothèque de la compagnie de Jésus". The following are the principal: *Controversial works.* "Disputationes de Controversiis Christianæ Fidei adversus hujus temporis hæreticos", of the innumerable editions of which the chief are those of Ingolstadt (1586–89), Venice (1596), revised personally by the author, but abounding in printer's errors, Paris or "Triadelphi" (1608), Prague (1721), Rome (1832); "De Exemptione clericorum", and "De Indulgentiis et Jubilæo", published as monographs in 1599, but afterwards incorporated in the "De Controversiis"; "De Transitu Romani Imperii a Græcis ad Francos" (1584); "Responsio ad præcipua capita Apologiæ . . . pro successione Henrici Navarreni" (1586);

"Judicium de Libro quem Lutherani vocant Concordiæ" (1585); four *Risposte* to the writings on behalf of the Venetian Republic of John Marsiglio and Paolo Sarpi (1606); "Responsio Matthæi Torti ad librum inscriptum Triplici nodo triplex cuneus" 1608); "Apologia Bellarmini pro responsione suâ ad librum Jacobi Magnæ Britanniæ Regis" (1609); 'Tractatus de potestate Summi Pontificis in rebus temporalibus, adversus Gulielmum Barclay" (1610). *Catechetical and Spiritual Works.* "Dottrina Cristiana breve", and "Dichiarazione più copiosa della dottrina cristiana" (1598), two catechetical works which have more than once received papal approbation, and have been translated into various languages; "Dichiarazione del Simbolo" (1604), for the use of priests; "Admonitio ad Episcopum Theanensem nepotem suum quæ sint necessaria episcopo" (1612); "Exhortationes domesticæ", published only in 1899, by Père van Ortroy; "Conciones habitæ Lovanii", the more correct edition (1615); "De Ascensione mentis in Deum" (1615); "De Æternâ felicitate sanctorum" (1616); "De gemitu columbæ" (1617); "De septem verbis Christi" (1618); "De arte bene moriendi" (1620). The last five are spiritual works written during his annual retreats. *Exegetical and other works.* "De Scriptoribus ecclesiast." (1615); "De Editione Latinâ Vulgatâ, quo sensu a Concilio Tridentino definitum sit ut ea pro authenticâ habeatur", not published till 1749; "In omnes Psalmos dilucida expositio" (1611). Complete editions of Bellarmine's *Opera omnia* have been published at Cologne (1617); Venice (1721); Naples (1856); Paris (1870).

Ven. R. Bellarmini, S.R.E. Cardinalis, vita quam ipse scripsit (with an Appendix), written in 1613, at the request of Fathers Eudæmon Joannis and Mutius Vitelleschi, first published among the *acta* of the Process of Beatification, 1675; republished in 1887 by DÖLLINGER AND REUSCH, with notes many of which are useful but the general tone of which is unfair and spiteful; a multitude of unpublished documents in the archives of the Vatican, Simancas, Salamanca, the Society of Jesus, etc.; *Epistolæ familiares* (1650); EUDÆMON JOANNIS, *De pio obitu Card. Bellarmini* (1621); FINALI, *Esame fatto per me,* that is, by the lay brother who attended him in his last sickness, MS.; lives by FULIGATI (1624; translated into Latin with additions by PETRA SANCTA, 1626) and BARTOLI, (1678); CERVINI, *Imago virtutum* (1625). These form the chief original material. Of derived lives the best are those by FRIZON (1708), and COUDERC (1893). See also LE BACHELET in VACANT, *Dict. de théol. cath.*; and for Bellarmine's doctrine on papal authority, DE LA SERVIÈRE, *De Jacobo Angl. Rege cum Card. R. Bellarmine . . . disputante* (1900).

SYDNEY F. SMITH.

Bellasis, EDWARD, Serjeant-at-Law, b. 14 October, 1800; d. 24 January, 1873; was one of the most able and respected of that little band of English converts who in the later years of the Tractarian movement joined the Catholic Church from the ranks of the legal profession. The distinguished advocate, J. R. Hope-Scott, who married Sir Walter Scott's granddaughter, and the conveyancer, Edward Badeley, to whom Cardinal (then Doctor) Newman in 1867 dedicated his volume of "Verses on Various Occasions", were the Serjeant's lifelong friends, and all three became Catholics about the same time. Edward Bellasis was the son of the Rev. George Bellasis, D.D., a scion of a younger branch of the Belasyse family (see BELASYSE, JOHN), and of his second wife, Leah Cooper Viall, the daughter and heiress of Emery Viall of Walsingham, Norfolk. His uncle, General John Bellasis, and his half-brothers, Joseph and George, won high military honours in India towards the close of the eighteenth century. Edward was educated at Christ's Hospital, and after making his legal studies at the Inner Temple he contrived at a relatively early age to form an excellent practice at the Chancery bar. It was, however, the period of great railway developments in the United Kingdom, and Bellasis, turning his attention to the Parliamentary Committees, was constantly retained as counsel for the various companies in the proceedings to which the opening up of the new lines gave rise. In 1844 he received the coif of Serjeant-at-Law, a dignity now abolished, and amongst other *causes célèbres* took part in the famous libel action, Achilli *v.* Newman, in 1852, and in the litigation connected with the title and estates of the last Catholic Earl of Shrewsbury. In this, as in all his legal work, Bellasis set an example of great disinterestedness. He retired from the profession in 1867, leaving behind him the reputation of an excellent lawyer and a careful and finished speaker.

Although brought up amid rather evangelical surroundings, Serjeant Bellasis had followed with great interest the developments of the Oxford movement. His Catholic tendencies were stimulated partly by the narrowness of anti-Roman prejudice which he recognized in the attitude of his fellow-religionists, and partly by his intercourse with Catholics whom he met on his travels abroad. His approach towards the Church was slow and characteristically prudent, but the friendships he formed with many advanced Anglicans like Oakley, W. G. Ward, and J. B. Morris, who before long passed over to the Roman side, could not fail to produce an effect. Eventually he was received into the Church by Father Brownbill, S.J., 27 December, 1850. His wife and children followed soon after. From that time until his death Serjeant Bellasis was amongst the most devoted and edifying of Catholic laymen. His interest in all Catholic projects was keen, his social and intellectual position was such as commanded respect, and his charity was inexhaustible. From the founding of the new school of the Oratorians under the direction of Dr. Newman, at Edgbaston, to the providing of scientific apparatus for the Observatory at Stonyhurst; from the collection of relics for churches to the encouragement of the Nazareth House Sisters who tended the aged poor, the Serjeant was foremost in every good work. His personal holiness, fostered by constant private retreats, and his kindliness towards all won him universal respect and lent additional effectiveness to the conciliatory pamphlets which he occasionally published in explanation of Catholic truth. His first wife had died as early as 1832. By his second marriage, in 1835, with Miss Eliza Garnett, he left ten children, of whom two sons, the eldest and the youngest, are priests, and three daughters became nuns. In nothing is the beauty of the Serjeant's character more plainly seen than in those fragments of his intercourse with his children which have been reproduced by his biographer. After his death on the 24th of January, 1873, Cardinal Newman wrote: "He was one of the best men I ever knew". Newman's "Grammar of Assent", published in 1870, bears a dedication to Bellasis. Of the Serjeant's own publications the best remembered is a volume of short dialogues collected under the title "Philotheus and Eugenia".

BELLASIS, *Memorial of Mr. Serjeant Bellasis* (2d ed., London, 1895), a charming biography written by his son, Mr. Edward Bellasis, Lancaster Herald, and partly based on some autobiographical notes. It includes two excellent portraits. *Dict. of Nat. Biog.*, IV, 180; GILLOW, *Bibl. Dict. of Eng. Cath.*, I.

HERBERT THURSTON.

Bellecius, ALOYSIUS, Jesuit ascetic author, b. at Freiburg im Breisgau, 15 February, 1704; d. at Augsburg, 27 April, 1757. He taught philosophy one year and theology seven, and spent four years as a missionary in South America among the Indians living along the Amazon. Recalled to Europe, he was charged with the spiritual care of his religious brethren and later with the direction of the seminary of Porrentruy in the Diocese of Basle. He is the author of a number of ascetic works in Latin, most of which have been translated into different languages

and often reprinted. The most noteworthy of these are: "Christianus pie moriens" (1749); "Virtutis Solidæ præcipua impedimenta, subsidia, et incitamenta" (1755); "Medulla Asceseos seu Exercitia S. P. Ignatii" (1757); "Triduum Sacrum præcipue Religiosorum usui accomodatum" (1757). English translations of the last three have been made and are still in print. The first, entitled "Solid Virtue", is translated from the French (London, 1887); the second appeared under the title "Spiritual Exercises according to the method of St. Ignatius", translated from the Italian version of Father Bresciani, S. J., by William Hutch, D.D. (London, 1876). In this translation Father Bresciani slightly modified some of the opinions of Bellecius which he considered too rigid. The third translation was made by Father John Holzer, S. J., and was published in New York in 1882. It is entitled "Solid Virtue: A Triduum and Spiritual Conferences". The Triduum is an abridgment of Bellecius's larger work on "Solid Virtue"—an abridgment made by himself. The three Spiritual Conferences show practically in what solid virtue consists.

Bibliothèque de la compagnie de Jésus, I, 1260; WATRIGANT in *Dict. de théol. cath.*, II, 599.

S. H. FRISBEE.

Bellenden (BALLENDEN, or BALLANTYNE), JOHN, a Scotch poet, b. at Haddington or Berwick in the latter part of the fifteenth century; d. at Rome, c. 1587. He was a Catholic and at an early age matriculated at the University of St. Andrews. Later he went to Paris, where he took the degree of Doctor of Divinity at the Sorbonne. Returning to Scotland, he brought with him from Paris the great work by Hector Boece, the "Historia Scotorum", and was received with great favour at the court of James V. He was subsequently appointed by the king to undertake the work of translating the "Historia" into the Scotch vernacular, which, together with some poems that he wrote at this period, occupied him about three years. He was also commissioned by the king to translate Livy into English, a work which hitherto had not been attempted. Bellenden was appointed Archdeacon of Moray, and in the succeeding reign he was vigorous in his opposition to Protestantism. This opposition subsequently led to his flight to escape persecution. He is supposed to be identical with one of the same name who was at one time secretary to Archibald, Earl of Angus.

Dict. Nat. Biog., IV, 186.

THOMAS GAFFNEY TAAFFE.

Belleville, DIOCESE OF, comprises that part of southern Illinois, U. S. A., which lies south of the northern limits of St. Clair, Clinton, Marion, Clay, Richland, and Lawrence counties, an area of 11,678 square miles. This territory was formerly a part of the Diocese of Alton, but upon the demise of Bishop Baltes, of that see, a new diocese was erected, 7 January, 1887, with the episcopal see at Belleville, St. Clair Co. The Rev. John Janssen, who had held the office of vicar-general successively under Bishop Juncker and Bishop Baltes of Alton, was appointed first bishop of the newly erected diocese on 28 February, 1888, and consecrated on 25 April, 1888. The standing of the new diocese at that time is shown by the following statistics: secular priests fifty-six; regular four; churches with resident priests fifty-three; missions with churches twenty-nine; academies three; parochial schools fifty-three; children attending 5,395; orphan asylum 1; orphans 30; hospitals 3. The Catholic population was about 50,000 and remained almost stationary for a number of years. The mining industries in the southern part of the diocese are fast developing, so that, with immigration, the population has increased to 56,200, with bright prospects for the future. The diocese has 100 secular and two regular priests; eighty-two churches with resident priests; thirty-two missions with churches; eighteen chapels; twenty-four ecclesiastical students; a high school for boys; two academies for young ladies; sixty-seven parochial schools with 5,033 pupils; an orphan asylum with 112 orphans; eight hospitals; and a house for the aged. The following religious communities are represented in the diocese: Brothers of Mary, Sisters of Christian Charity, Sisters of St. Dominic, Franciscan Sisters, Hospital Sisters of St. Francis, School Sisters of St. Francis, Sisters of the Poor Handmaids of Christ, Sisters of the Holy Cross, Sisters of St. Joseph, Polish Sisters of St. Joseph, Sisters of Loretto, School Sisters of Notre Dame, Sisters of the Precious Blood, Servants of Mary, Ursuline Sisters, and White Benedictine Sisters of Mt. Olive.

To this diocese belong some of the oldest missions of the West. The records of the church of Kaskaskia date from the year 1695 and give the name of the Rev. Jac. Gravier, S.J., as the missionary priest. The Jesuits continued to attend to the wants of the Indian tribe of the Kaskaskias and of the French, and alternately the Jesuit Fathers De Beaubois, Le Boullenger, Tartarin, Aubert, and Meurin had this territory as the field of their apostolic labours. Father Meurin was the last Jesuit doing missionary work at Kaskaskia; the order was suppressed in his time. He died at Prairie du Rocher and is buried at Florissant, Missouri. The Rev. P. Gibault who in 1768 came from Quebec was the first secular priest, who as resident pastor of Kaskaskia had charge also of the large surrounding territory, and who became vicar-general of the territory of Illinois. He continued his arduous labours until 1791, the time of his death. Until 1820 the Lazarist Fathers were in this field; after that the work was continued by secular priests. The old town of Kaskaskia, with its statehouse and church, has been swallowed up by the Mississippi River and about two miles farther inland a new town and a new church have been built up.

The organization of the congregation of Prairie du Rocher coincides with the building of the first Fort Chartres on the banks of the Mississippi in 1720. The Rev. J. Le Boullenger, chaplain of the militia stationed at the Fort, was placed in charge of the congregation. The church, built by the people, was placed under the protection of St. Anne. In 1743 the Rev. J. Gagnon, S.J., took charge of the mission and laboured there until his death in 1755. His remains were interred by the side of the altar in the chapel in the cemetery. This chapel was built in 1734, and placed under the patronage of St. Joseph. When the river inundated one corner of the newly built stone structure at Fort Chartres and threatened the village and St. Anne's church, the Fort was evacuated, the village deserted; its inhabitants sought the high ground at the foot of the bluffs, and the cemetery chapel became the parish church and served as such until 1858, when a brick church was erected. Among the missionaries who worked there, the names of Gabriel Richard (later Delegate to Congress from Michigan); Doutien Olivier (who lived to be ninety-five years of age); Xavier Dahmen, and John Timon (later Bishop of Buffalo, New York) deserve special mention. The early records of the old church of Cahokia have been lost, and accurate data can be found from the year 1783 only. At that time the religious wants of the Catholics of Cahokia and the surrounding territory, including St. Louis across the river, were attended to by Father De Saintpierre. When in 1843 the Diocese of Chicago was erected, Cahokia, Prairie du Long, Belleville, Shoal Creek (now Germantown), Kaskaskia, Prairie du Rocher, and Shaw-

neetown were the only parishes in the territory now comprised by the Diocese of Belleville.

SHEA, *Hist. of Cath. Ch. in U. S.* (New York, 1904); *Missiones Catholicæ* (Propaganda, Rome, 1907), 539.

H. J. HAGEN.

Belley (BELLICIUM), DIOCESE OF, coextensive with the civil department of Ain and a suffragan of the Archbishopric of Besançon. Although suppressed at the time of the Concordat, the Diocese of Belley was re-established in 1822 and took from the Archdiocese of Lyons the arrondissements of Belley, Bourg, Nantua, and Trévoux, and from the Archdiocese of Chambéry the arrondissement of Gex.

Local tradition maintains that Belley was evangelized in the second century by the martyrs Marcellus and Valerian, companions of St. Pothinus. The first bishop of historic certainty is Vincentius, mentioned in 552. Others who occupied the see were St. Hippolytus, Abbot of Condat (eighth century); St. Anthelm (1163–78), seventh General of the Carthusian Order; St. Arthaud (1179–90), founder of the Carthusians at Arvières; Camus (1609–29), a noted preacher and romancist; and Monseigneur François M. Richard (1872–75), later Cardinal and Archbishop of Paris. Belley honours in a special manner St. Amandus, Bishop of Maastricht, who founded the Abbey of Nantua about 660; St. Vulbas, a patrician of Bourgogne and a war companion of King Dagobert, treacherously assassinated in 642; St. Rambert, killed by order of Ebroin in the seventh century, whose name has been given to a city of the diocese; St. Trivier, the solitary, who died about 650; St. Barnard (ninth century), who founded the great Benedictine Abbey of Ambronay and died Archbishop of Vienna; St. Lambert (twelfth century), founder of the Cistercian Abbey at Chezery; St. Roland (twelfth century), Abbot of Chezery; St. Stephen of Châtillon, who founded the Carthusian monastery at Portes, in 1115, and died Bishop of Die; St. Stephen of Bourg, who founded the Carthusian monastery at Meyria in 1116; and St. Jean-Baptiste Vianney (1786–1857), parish priest at Ars.

The Diocese of Belley which, in the Middle Ages, had no less than eight Carthusian monasteries, was the birthplace of the Joséphistes, a congregation founded by Jacques Crétenet (1606–67), a layman and surgeon who became a priest after the death of his wife; of the teaching order of the Sisters of St. Charles, founded by Charles Démia of Bourg (1636–89); and of three teaching orders founded in the first half of the nineteenth century: the Brothers of the Society of the Cross of Jesus; the Brothers of the Holy Family of Belley, and the Sisters of St. Joseph of Bourg. In 1858 a Trappist monastery was established in the unhealthy Dombes district. Cardinal Louis Aleman (1390–1450) and Sœur Rosalie (1787–1856), noted in the history of modern Parisian charities, were both natives of the Diocese of Belley. Blessed Pierre-Louis-Marie Chanel was born at Cuet near Bourg. For thirty years of its existence (1701–31), "Le Journal de Trévoux", a valuable repertory of the literary and religious history of the period, was published by the Jesuits at Trévoux, in this diocese. The church at Brou, near Bourg, is a marvel of architecture and contains some wonderful pieces of sculpture. It was built between 1511 and 1536 under the direction of Margaret of Austria, widow of Philibert (II) the Fair, Duke of Savoy.

The latest statistics for the diocese give the following institutions: 1 maternity hospital, 66 infant schools, 1 deaf-mute institute, 3 boys' orphanages, 10 girls' orphanages, 21 hospitals, or hospices, 2 dispensaries, 21 communities for the care of the sick in their homes, 1 home for incurables, and 5 homes for the aged, all conducted by sisters; and 1 deaf-mute institute, and 2 insane asylums conducted by brothers.

In 1900 the following religious orders were represented in the Diocese of Belley: Carthusians, at Portes and Sélignac; Trappists at Notre Dame des Dombes; Marists at Belley; Lazarists at Musiniens; and Fathers of the Blessed Sacrament at Trévoux. Congregations local to the diocese are: two teaching orders; the Brothers of the Society of the Cross of Jesus founded by M. Bochard in 1824, and the Brothers of the Holy Family, founded by Brother Taborin in 1835; and the Sisters of St. Joseph, with motherhouse at Bourg, very numerous throughout the department. At the close of the year 1905 the Diocese of Belley contained 350,416 inhabitants, 36 parishes, 404 mission churches, and 75 curacies.

Gallia christiana (1860), XV, 601–644; *Instrumenta*, 305–358; Depéry, *Histoire hagiologique de Belley* (Bourg, 1834, 1835); Nyd, *Etudes sur les origines du siège épiscopal de Belley* and *Recherches historiques sur les origines et les temps anciens du diocèse de Belley* in the *Revue de la société littéraire de l'Ain* (1878, 1879, 1884, 1885); Duchesne, *Fastes épiscopaux*, I, 16; Chevalier, *Topobibl.*, 362.

GEORGES GOYAU.

Bellings (or Belling), Sir Richard, Irish historian, b. near Dublin early in the seventeenth century; d. in 1677. He was the son of Sir Henry Bellings, a Catholic landowner in Leinster. He was trained to the law and entered Lincoln's Inn, London, and while there wrote a supplementary book (the sixth) to Sir Philip Sydney's "Arcadia", which has been generally printed with that work. He returned to Ireland, became a member of the Irish Parliament, and married a daughter of Viscount Mountgarret. In 1642, when the Irish Confederation was formed, Bellings joined, his father-in-law being president, and became secretary to the Supreme Council. He was sent to the continent in 1644 as a representative of this body. In the following year he returned to Ireland and was active as a royalist till 1649, when he withdrew to France, most of his property having been confiscated by the Cromwellians. His estate was restored to him after the accession of Charles II, who, with Ormonde, held him in high regard. He died in 1677 and was buried near Dublin. Perhaps his chief work is his defence of the Catholics of Ireland, "Vindiciarum Catholicorum Hiberniæ libri duo", which, under the pseudonym of "Philopater Irenæus", was published at Paris in 1650. During his later years he also wrote an account of Irish affairs (1641–48), an imperfect copy of which was printed in 1772. The complete work was, however, recovered, and was published under the editorship of John T. Gilbert, with the following title: "History of the Irish Confederation and the War in Ireland, 1641–48". This edition (Dublin, 1882–85) is enriched with many valuable documents and many illustrative notes, and was published from the original MSS. The above-mentioned "Vindication" is regarded as one of the most trustworthy of the many works written on that period. However, the Irish Franciscan, Father John Ponce, controverted many of its statements in his "Richardi Bellingi Vindiciæ Eversæ" (Paris, 1653). A "Letter from Richard Bellings to M. Callaghan" on Irish affairs (Paris, c. 1652) is to be found in a French translation of the same date in the Gilbert Library, Dublin.

Harris, *Writers of Ireland* (Dublin, 1764), I, 165.

D. J. O'DONOGHUE.

Bellini, Giacomo (Jacopo), father of Gentile and Giovanni Bellini, b. about 1400; d. 1471. Interest in him arises mainly from the fact that he was the teacher of his sons who were the chief founders of the Venetian school of painting. The paintings produced by Giacomo Bellini which are still in existence are unimportant and few in number. His interesting sketch-book proves, however, his industry and power of observation. It contains copies of antique statues and re-

liefs, drawings portraying Biblical stories and Christian legends, and sketches from nature and life which are executed with animation and show a sense of perspective in the composition. He was a competitor in art of the painters of the Vivarini family who came from the neighbouring island of Murano; Antonio and Bartolommeo Vivarini opened a studio in Venice but they were excelled by the Bellinis. Giacomo Bellini had worked under Gentile da Fabriano in his native city and at Florence. He had also been employed at other places, especially at Padua, where he came under the influence of the classic and plastic tendencies of Squarcione. His sons at an early age became his assistants at Venice.

Gentile Bellini, (b. about 1427; d. 1507). He was the elder of the brothers. He also had been in Padua and painted at first in the style of Squarcione, Donatello, and Mantegna; this style was good in conveying individuality, but it was weak in composition and somewhat clumsy. The painting containing the four heroic-sized figures of Saints Mark, Theodore, Jerome, and Francis, the picture of the patriarchs surrounded by ecclesiastics and angels, a Madonna with the benefactors of a religious foundation, and a bust-portrait of the doge belong to this period. At first Gentile worked mainly in partnership with his father and brother, as at Padua in the Cappella di Gattamelata. But after the father retired, Gentile's fame soon exceeded that of the elder Bellini. He painted eight pictures in the Scuola di San Giovanni Evangelista at Venice in continuation of his father's work "The Miracle of the Holy Cross". Three of these pictures, painted between 1490–1500, are preserved in a damaged condition at the Academy of Venice. These pictures bear throughout the characteristic peculiarities of the Venetian school of painting. They are filled with figures from real life, which are clearly modelled, each figure having its own individuality; the religious processions are stately, the architecture which appears is of great splendour, and skill is shown in the perspective of lines and atmosphere.

The "Sermon of St. Mark at Alexandria", now at Milan, which Giovanni completed after the death of his brother, equals those just mentioned in worth. It also shows a large number of figures skilfully grouped, an over-elaborate architectural background, much pomp in the scene depicted, brilliant light, and great richness of colour. The Oriental costumes added a new grace to the painting. In 1479 Gentile had gone to Constantinople on the recommendation of the Signory, who had been requested by the Sultan Mohammed II to send him a portrait-painter. Gentile painted the Sultan and other important personages. He brought home a great many sketches, including one of the Sultan and the Dowager Sultana in sitting posture. The journey to Constantinople was not only instructive but greatly increased the fame of the painter. Among the fruits of this trip are a portrait (in the Layard collection at Venice) giving the head and shoulders of Mohammed, and the canvas "Reception of the Venetian Ambassadors by the Grand Vizier", now in the Louvre. The visit to Constantinople had, however, interrupted another large undertaking. In 1474 Gentile had been honoured with the commission to restore the paintings in the Great Council Chamber of the doge's palace and to add to their number. Earlier artists had painted for the hall a series of pictures on a large scale representing scenes from the history of Venice. Gentile after his return from Constantinople, in company with his brother, went on with the work. The seven pictures they produced were destroyed in the fire of 1577. In his middle and later period Gentile abandoned tempera and painted in oil.

Giovanni Bellini (b. about 1428; d. 1516) carried the new form of art to its greatest height. He was greatly influenced by the tendencies which have been mentioned; of these the style of his father and of the Paduan school had the most effect upon him. Mantegna was his brother-in-law. Another painter who strongly affected him was Antonello da Messina. Messina was the first person in Italy to understand the Flemish method of painting in oil, and towards the end of his life he spent several years (1474–76) in Milan and Venice. The surroundings of Venetian life and the realistic direction which Venetian art had taken gave the Venetian painters a keen perception of the charm of colour, so that even the short time during which Messina was with them sufficed to lead them into a new path. The genius of Giovanni Bellini enabled him to obtain the full benefit of the new stimulus; at the same time other painters, Bartolommeo and Luigi Vivarini, Gentile Bellini, and other men, also took up the new technic. The use of the new medium produced a softness of outline and an improvement in the modelling which tempered the hardness of the Paduan style and obtained beautiful effects in colour. Giovanni had more feeling and a keener spiritual insight than his brother, and his style gradually developed until he attained a perfect har-

which represent Mary Magdalen and St. Catherine, or St. Paul and St. George, in company with the Madonna. Similar to these is the fine picture "The Presentation of Jesus in the Temple". Mary offers the Child to the high-priest over a table while the aged Simeon and Joseph worship. Giovanni did not attempt to solve, even in his larger works, such difficult problems of perspective and of the gradation of light and shade as his brother undertook. He had, however, learned from his brother the entire art of the distribution of light and shade and applied it with more skill to bringing out the inner feeling of a composition. Unfortunately we are not able to judge of his style in historical work as we are in the case of his brother. His historical compositions, seven in all, were painted for the Great Council Chamber of the doge's palace. He worked on these from 1479 until his death; at times the work was done in conjunction with his brother, at times he had the aid of other men. The paintings were all destroyed by fire in 1577. Two duplicates remain of the portraits of the doges, painted in the same place, and these show his skill in portrait-painting. His master-

THE DOGE LOREDANO   GIOVANNI BELLINI   MADONNA

mony of drawing, perspective, drapery, light, and colour.

His two Pietàs, in Venice, produce a deep effect on the mind, yet they betray a striking harshness which becomes at times even ugliness, showing that the characteristic qualities of his style had not yet developed into a harmonious beauty. The painting at Berlin of the "Angels Mourning over Christ" although in the relief style, is noble, tender, and rich in colour. The feeling of devotion loses nothing here through the realistic portrayal of all the details. A peculiarity of these pictures is the upright position of the dead body of Christ. The smaller pictures of the Madonna appear at all stages in the development of the artist. Notwithstanding their large number they show no real repetition; at times the expression of Mother and Child is very earnest, at times strange, then again it is lovely and perfectly natural. In one of them the Child listens in a most winning way to the song of the angels and looks upward with open mouth in childlike astonishment, while the Mother is absorbed in her Infant.

The carefully worked out details of these pictures are not too obtrusive. Giovanni preferred half-length figures even when a number of saints were grouped together; as, for example, in the pictures

pieces, however, are his great devotional and altar pictures.

Giovanni's artistic powers entered their period of highest development in 1479. In this year he completed the first large oil painting produced at Venice. In a niche which rises in arched form over pilasters is enthroned the Madonna holding with a solemn, earnest expression the Divine Child. The Child stretches out its little hands towards the worshipping sufferer, Job, who is thus honoured as a patron of the Church. Near Job stands St. Francis, farther back is John the Baptist, to the right are St. Sebastian, St. Dominic, and Bishop Leo. At the foot of the throne are angels playing musical instruments, above in the curve of the arch are cherubim and the inscription, "Ave virginei flos intemerate pudoris". The Virgin herself seems to be thrilled by the solemn inspiration of the moment and raises her left hand as if in warning not to disturb the music of the angels. Deep devotion is expressed on all the faces. A large picture of the year 1488 at Murano in which St. Martin presents the Doge Barbarigo to the enthroned Madonna suffers somewhat from a mechanical symmetry. Nevertheless the same musical tone prevails in it, together with great richness of colouring and costume. On each side is seen a beautiful landscape in the distance. By means of the action represented a greater unity is obtained in this canvas than in the one just mentioned, and much more still than in the Madonna of San Zaccaria, Venice (1505). In the latter the enthroned Madonna holding the Child is surrounded by Saints Catherine, Peter, Jerome, and Lucia. Each one of the saints is separately absorbed in devotion while an angel at the foot of the throne softly touches the strings of his instrument in accompaniment to the spirit of adoration. Here also the feeling produced by the music creates the unity of the whole composition and the painting is a wonderful expression of adoring worship. The scene is laid in a beautiful renaissance structure the arches of which are adorned with mosaics.

One can perceive the unity of composition attained by means of this spirit of devotion and music of the angels even in those canvases where the surrounding saints stand in separate niches. Such, for example, is the picture where four saints are represented on the wings of an altar-piece in the church of Santa Maria dei Frari at Venice (1488). The Mother and Child are enthroned in the middle space; at their feet two boy-angels are playing cheerfully on the lute and flute. A lighter, although by no means a jarring impression, is made by this triptych. The separated positions of the saints, to whom an altar and a church had been consecrated, recalls the practice of the older painters. By uniting the saints in the same space and giving them an outer as well as an inner relation to one another Bellini created the so-called "Sacre Conversazioni", or "the Societies of Saints". It was not necessary that the personages should belong to the same historical time, as they receive in the altar-piece a new, ideal life. The spirit of devotion inspired by the Madonna and her Divine Child unites them sufficiently but the more so when a new bond of union arises from the action indicated in the composition, such as, in many cases, the beautiful music or even the effect produced by light and shade.

A couple of pictures should be mentioned in which Giovanni, whom time never robbed of the freshness of his imagination, set for himself problems in landscape-painting. In 1501 he painted a "Baptism of Christ" in which the art of Giorgione and Titian seems to be apparent. The scene is laid in a romantic mountain-valley lighted by the evening sunshine. Three kneeling angels are the witnesses. The influence of younger painters is very evident in a picture having the same tone as the one just mentioned, the picture of St. Jerome. Giovanni continued to learn even when he was old, although he was properly more often the teacher and never obscured his own individuality of style. St. Jerome, in this picture, is seated on a great rock in front of a mountain landscape and is absorbed in the study of the Scriptures. In the foreground, on an eminence, stands St. Augustine absorbed in thought, and on the other side is St. Christopher holding the Child Jesus. These three mighty men of Christianity may also be considered as bound together by an inner spiritual unity. In the "Death of Peter the Martyr" there is a prospect to right and left from the forest out over a city and mountains. Such vistas are always important features in the genre pictures for which Giovanni had a strong liking. Giovanni had little taste for mythological scenes and his few canvases of this kind do not need mention.

BERENSON, The Venetian Painters (New York and London, 1897); WOLTMANN AND WOERMANN, Geschichte der Malerei (Leipzig, 1879); RIEHL, Kunstcharaktere (Frankfort, 1893); WOERMANN, Geschichte der Kunst (Leipzig, 1900).

G. GIETMANN.

Belloy, JEAN-BAPTISTE DE, Cardinal-Archbishop of Paris, b. 9 October, 1709, at Morangles in the Diocese of Beauvais; d. in Paris, 10 June, 1808. Although of an ancient family of no mean military fame, young Belloy preferred an ecclesiastical career, made his classical and theological studies at Paris, where he was ordained priest, and received the degree of Doctor in Theology in 1737. In the ministry he shone more by his virtue than by his learning. Sweetness of character, enlightened and moderate zeal, unswerving fidelity to the principles and traditions of the Church, characterized him through life, and rendered even his early ministry remarkably fruitful. His bishop, Cardinal de Gèvres, appointed him vicar-general and archdeacon of his cathedral. In 1751 he was consecrated Bishop of Glandèves. At the famous Assembly of the French Clergy of 1755, he took sides with the moderate party and contributed to the restoration of tranquillity in the Church of France. Dissensions occasioned by the Bull "Unigenitus" had become so great in the Diocese of Marseilles that, at the death of the saintly Bishop de Belsunce, there was imminent danger of schism. In this emergency a chief pastor of consummate prudence and tact was needed, and Bishop de Belloy was accordingly transferred to that see. Without sacrifice of principle or duty, by gentleness, tact, and justice, he gained the confidence of both parties and restored peace. In July, 1790, the National Assembly decreed the suppression of the Diocese of Marseilles. The bishop withdrew, but sent to the assembly a letter of protest against the suppression of one of the oldest episcopal sees of France. He retired to Chambly, a little town near his native place, where he remained during the most critical period of the Revolution. When, in 1801, the sovereign pontiff decided that the French bishops should tender their resignation in order to facilitate the conclusion of the Concordat, he was the first to comply, setting an example which exercised great influence over the other bishops. Napoleon, highly pleased with this act of devotion to Church and State, appointed the nonagenarian bishop to the See of Paris. Notwithstanding his extreme age he governed his new diocese with astonishing vigour and intelligence, reorganized the parishes, provided them with good pastors, and visited his flock in person. He restored the Crown of Thorns (10 August, 1806) to its place of honour in the Sainte Chapelle. Napoleon was so well satisfied that he asked and readily obtained for him the cardinal's hat, which Pius VII placed on the prelate's venerable head in a consistory held in Paris, 1 February, 1805. At his death Cardinal de Belloy had spent seventy-five years in the holy ministry to the edification of all and the evident satisfaction of both Napoleon and Pius VII, then engaged in deadly conflict. He is buried in Notre Dame, Paris, where the monument erected by Napoleon in his honour is one of the finest in the cathedral.

FISQUET, La France pontificale (Paris), I, 542–556; FELLER Biog. univ., II, 199.

CHARLES B. SCHRANTZ.

Bells.—The subject will be treated under the following heads: I. Origin; II. Benediction; III. Uses; IV. Archæology and Inscriptions; V. Points of Law.

I. ORIGIN.—That bells, at any rate hand-bells of relatively small size, were familiar to all the chief nations of antiquity is a fact beyond dispute. The archæological evidence for this conclusion has been collected in the monograph of Abbé Morillot and is quite overwhelming. Specimens are still preserved of the bells used in ancient Babylonia and in Egypt, as well as by the Romans and Greeks, while the bell undoubtedly figured no less prominently in such independent civilizations as those of China and Hindustan. There is consequently no reason why the bells upon the high priest's ephod (Ex., xxxiii, 33) should not have been tiny bells of normal shape. Further, it may be inferred from the purposes for which they were used that the *tintinnabula* of which we read in

THE MIGUELETE, VALENCIA

BELL TOWERS

THE LEANING TOWER, SARAGOSSA

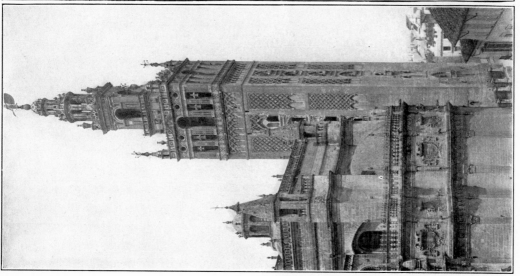

THE GIRALDA, SEVILLE

the classics, must at least in some instances have betokened hand-bells of larger size. See for example Martial, "Epig.", xiv, 161, where the signal for the opening of the baths is made with a *tintinnabulum* also described as *æs thermarum*. None the less, the question whether anything corresponding in size to a church bell was known in pre-Christian times does not readily admit of an answer. We are not only ignorant of the dimensions but also of the shape of the κώδων which was used for example to announce the opening of the public markets (Cf. Strabo, Geogr., IV, xxi). We translate the word as bell, but it is possible that it would be more correctly rendered gong or cymbals. The officer who made the round of the sentries at night carried a κώδων (Thucyd., IV, cxxxv; Aristoph., Aves, 842 sqq.), and it is difficult to believe that anything resembling an ordinary bell could have been used for a duty in which the avoidance of accidental noise must often have been of the highest importance.

In coming to the Christian period the same difficulty is encountered. A new set of terms is introduced, *signum, campana, clocca, nola,* which are all commonly translated "bell", and it is certain that at a later period these were all used to denote what were in the strictest sense "church bells" of large size. The first Christian writer who frequently speaks of bells (*signa*) is Gregory of Tours (c. 585). We learn that they were struck or shaken, and we even find mention of a cord being used for this purpose (*funem illum de quo signum commovetur,* "De Vitâ Martini", I, xxviii), while as regards the use of these *signa* it appears that they rung before church services and that they roused the monks from their beds. Again, the word *signum* appears in the almost

BELL TOWER OF PISA

contemporary "Life of St. Columban" (615), for when one of his monks was dying Columban is said to have assembled the community by ringing the bell (*signo tacto omnes adesse imperavit,* Krusch, "Scrip. Merov.", IV, 85). Similar expressions, *signo tacto,* or *cum exauditum fuerit signum,* are used in Constitutions attributed to St. Cæsarius of Arles (c. 513) and in the Rule of St. Benedict (c. 540). Moreover, if Dom Ferotin's view of the very early date of the Spanish ordinals which he has published (Monumenta Liturgica, V) could be safely accepted, it is possible that large bells were in common use in Spain at the same period. Still it must be remembered that *signum* primarily meant a signal and we must not be too hasty in attributing to it a specific instead of a generic meaning when first employed by Merovingian writers.

Again, the word *campana,* which even in the early Middle Ages undoubtedly meant a church bell and nothing else, occurs first, if Reifferscheid's "Anecdota Cassinensia" (p. 6) may be trusted, in Southern Italy (c. 515) in a letter of the deacon Ferrandus

to Abbot Eugippius. It has been suggested from a Latin inscription connected with the Arval Brethren (C. I., L. VI, no. 2067) that it was previously used to mean some kind of brazen vessel. However no quite satisfactory examples of *campana* in church Latin seem to be forthcoming before the latter part of the seventh century, and it is then found in the North. It is used by Cummian at Iona (c. 665) and by Bede in Northumbria (c. 710), and frequently elsewhere after that date. In Rome the "Liber Pontificalis" tells us that Pope Stephen II (752–757) erected a belfry with three bells (*campanæ*) at St. Peter's. It was probably this name which led Walafrid Strabo in the first half of the ninth century to make the assertion that bells were of Italian origin and that they came from Campania and more particularly from the town of Nola. Later writers went further and attributed the invention to St. Paulinus of Nola, but as St. Paulinus himself in the minute description which he has left of his own church makes no mention of bells, this is extremely improbable.

The word *clocca* (Fr. *cloche;* Ger. *Glocke;* Eng. clock) is interesting because in this case it is definitely known what was meant by it. It was certainly Irish in origin and it occurs at an early date both in Latin and in the Irish form *clog.* Thus it is found in the Book of Armagh and is used by Adamnan in his life of St. Columbkill written c. 685. The Irish and English missionaries no doubt imported it into Germany where it appears more than once in the Sacramentary of Gellone. It is plain that in primitive Celtic lands an extraordinary importance was attached to bells. A very large number of these ancient bells, more than sixty in all—the immense majority being Irish —are still in existence. Many of them are reputed to have belonged to Irish saints and partake of the character of relics. The most famous is that of St. Patrick, the *clog-an-edachta* or "bell-of-the-will" now preserved in the Museum of the Royal Irish Academy, Dublin. There seems no serious reason to doubt that this was the bell which lay upon St. Patrick's breast and was taken from his tomb in the year 552. Like most of these bells it had an official and hereditary custodian (in this case named Mulholland) in whose possession it remained, being handed down for centuries from father to son. Other similar early bells are those of St. Senan (c. 540) and St. Mura; there are several in Scotland and Wales, one at St. Gall in Switzerland, one known as the Saufang at Cologne, and another at Noyon in France. The evidence for the extraordinary veneration with which these bells were regarded in Celtic lands is overwhelming. Even Giraldus Cambrensis notes in the twelfth century that upon them was taken the most solemn form of oath. They were also carried into battle, and though the earlier specimens are nothing but rude cow-bells, wedge-shape in form and made of iron plate bent and roughly rivetted, still they were often enclosed at a later date in cases or "shrines" of the richest workmanship. The shrine of St. Patrick's bell bears an inscription of some length from which we learn that this beautiful specimen of the jeweller's craft must have been wrought about the year 1005. History tends to repeat itself, and if we remember the important part played in the missionary work of St. Francis Xavier by the hand-bell with which he gathered round him the children, the idle, or the curious, we have probably a clue to the intimate association of these early Celtic bells with the work of Christianity. When in 1683 Father Maunoir, the great Breton missionary, had at last to relinquish further expeditions, the bell which he handed on to his successor was regarded as a sort of investiture. It may be noted that the famous round towers of Ireland, which are now generally recognized to have been places of refuge against the inroads of the

Danes and other marauders, were commonly called *cloc teach*. The bells occasionally stored there for the sake of safety seem to have been regarded as the most precious of their treasures and from this circumstance the towers probably derived their name, though it is of course possible that they in some cases served as belfries in the more ordinary sense.

The great development in the use of bells may be identified with the eighth century. It was then, seemingly, that they began to be regarded as an essential part of the equipment of every church, and also that the practice of blessing them by a special form of consecration became generally prevalent. If we interpreted literally a well-known passage in Bede (Hist. Eccl., IV, xxi) we should have to believe that already in the year 680, the bell (*campana*) that was rung at Whitby at the passing away of St. Hilda was heard at Hackness thirteen miles off. But the whole setting of the story implies that Bede regarded the occurrence as miraculous and that the distance might as well have been thirty miles as thirteen. On the other hand, it is clear that in the eighth century church towers began to be built for the express purpose of hanging bells in them, which implies that the bells must have been increasing in size. The case of St. Peter's at Rome has already been noticed. So in the annals of St. Vandrille (cap. x, p. 33) we read that in the time of Ermharius who died in 738, that abbot had a bell made, to be hung in the little tower (*turricula*) "as is the custom of such churches"; while the "Monachus Sangallensis" (De Carolo Magno, I, xxxi) tells the story of a monastic bell-founder who asked Charlemagne to give him a hundred pounds of silver with a proportionate amount of copper to provide materials for a single great bell. In any case it is certain from Charlemagne's "Capitularies", as well as from Alcuin, Amalarius, and other writers of the early ninth century, that by that time in the Frankish dominions every parish church was expected to have at least one bell. In the next century Regino of Prüm, providing a programme of questions to be asked at an episcopal visitation, puts in the very first place a question about the church bells. Seeing that the clearest evidence of the popularity of church bells in Carlovingian times is encountered in regions where the influence of Irish or English missionaries had prevailed, it may perhaps be concluded that this development should be traced to Celtic influence. The missionary's hand-bell, with which he gathered his congregation together in the open air, would soon become sacred as a thing immediately associated with him and his work. Moreover, the idea would grow up that no religious service could take place without some preliminary ringing of a bell. Although we have traces of the use of *signa* and *campanæ* in monasteries before the Irish became missionaries, there is no evidence to show that these were bells rather than gongs. On the other hand, the σήμαντρον, used to announce the beginning of service in Greek monasteries was a flat plate of metal and its name (from σημαίνειν, "to make a signal") is obviously the counterpart of *signum*. Further we also find in an old glossary of the tenth century that the Greek word τύμπανον (drum) is given as the equivalent of *campanum* (Corpus Glossariorum Latinorum, III, 24). At the same time we can trace in Ireland itself a gradual evolution of the shape of the bell, passing from the small cow-bell of rivetted iron to the cast bronze instrument of considerable size, nearly approximating the bell with which we are now familiar.

II. BENEDICTION.—Since the beginning of the sixteenth century there has been much purposeless controversy over the question of the so-called "baptism" of bells. Protestant critics, following the lead of Luther himself, have professed to find in the rite not only superstition but a profanation of the sacra-ment. But one might as well be scandalized at the ceremonial usually followed in the launching and christening of a ship. The phrase "baptism of bells" is merely popular and metaphorical. It has been tolerated, but has never been formally recognized by the Church (Benedict, XIV, Instit., 47, n. 33). Every Catholic child is aware that the essence of the Sacrament of Baptism consists in the form: "I baptize thee", etc., but no properly authorized ritual for the blessing of bells is known to have contained any phrase which can be regarded as an equivalent or parody of these words. Certain local "agenda" in which something of the sort is found, for example at Cologne (see Schönfelder, Liturgische Bibliothek, I, 99–100) appear never to have received any official recognition (cf. The Month, September, 1907). On the other hand, the ceremonial of the Church is often imitative. The rite for the blessing of palms closely follows the arrangement of the variable portions of the Mass. The order for the coronation of a king copies so nearly that for the consecration of a bishop that Anglican writers have recently contended that the king is a "spiritual person" invested with episcopal powers. Hence it would not be surprising that in the "Benedictio Signi vel Campanæ" a certain resemblance should be traced to details in the ritual of baptism. Exorcisms are used, and water and salt and unctions with the holy oils; the bell receives a name, and formerly, at least, the name was suggested by a "godfather". But for all the controversy the resemblances are really very superficial. The following is a summary of the ceremony now in use from which the medieval pontificals differ but slightly. The bishop in white vestments first recites seven psalms with his attendant clergy to implore the Divine assistance. Then he mixes salt with water, reciting prayers of exorcism analogous to those always used in the preparation of holy water, but making special reference to the bell and to the evil influences of the air—the phantoms, the storms, the lightning—which threaten the peace of devout Christians who come to the church to sing the praises of God. Then the bishop and his attendants "wash" (*lavant*) the bell inside and out with the water thus prepared and dry it with towels, the Psalm "Laudate Dominum de cœlis" and five others of similar import being sung meanwhile. These are followed by various unctions, those on the outside of the bell being made with the oil of the sick in seven places, and those on the inside with chrism in four places. In the accompanying prayers mention is made of the silver trumpets of the Old Law and of the fall of the walls of Jericho, while protection is asked once more against the powers of the air, and the faithful are encouraged to take refuge under the sign of the Holy Cross. In this respect the prologue of Longfellow's "Golden Legend" leaves a generally correct impression, despite the inaccurate statement:

> For these bells have been anointed
> And baptized with holy water.

In making the unctions, and not, be it noticed, in washing the bell, a form is used introducing the patron saint: "May this bell be + hallowed, O Lord, and + consecrated in the name of the + Father, and of the + Son and of the + Holy Ghost. In honour of St. N. Peace be to thee". Finally the thurible with incense (*thymiama*) and myrrh are placed under the bell so that the smoke arising may fill its concavity. Then another prayer is said of similar purport to the last, and the ceremony ends with the reading of the passage in the Gospel concerning Martha and Mary.

In all essentials this ritual agrees with that in use in Carlovingian times, found in many manuscripts, and dating probably as far back as the pontificate of

Egbert of York in the middle of the eighth century. The washing and the unctions were prescribed as at present, but of old we find no trace of the form of words or of the name-giving which now accompany the unctions. That the ritual for the blessing of bells, which has thus been in use in the Church for nearly twelve hundred years, was framed with any design of imitating the ceremonies of baptism seems highly improbable for many reasons. First there is no triple immersion nor even strictly speaking any pouring of water. The bell is "washed" by the bishop and his assistants, just as the altars are washed on Maundy Thursday. Further there is nothing whatever to recall the *ephpheta* ceremony, yet this is the one detail in the rite of baptism which would seem in place if the ritual were transferred to a bell. Against the argument used by the Reformers that Charlemagne in his capitularies decreed *ut cloccas non baptizent*, it may be urged as a quite natural explanation of this ordinance that some practice may have begun to grow up which seemed too closely to parody the rite of baptism and that the prevalence of our existing less objectionable ceremonial was precisely the result of Charlemagne's intervention. It is probable that a rubric found in one or two, but no more, of the extant pontificals, "Tunc sub trinâ infusione aquæ sanctæ impone ei [i. e. campanæ] nomen, si velis", preserves the trace of the practice which Charlemagne condemns. Certain Spanish ordinals, the original of which must date from the seventh century or earlier, contain a quite different rite for the blessing of bells (Ferotin, Monumenta Liturgica, V, 160). Here there is no mention of unctions or of any washing with holy water, but there are exorcisms and prayers of the same general purport as those found in the Roman Pontifical. Indirectly this Spanish ritual, by speaking of "hoc vas concretum generibus metallorum", proves that from an early date a combination of metals was used in founding bells.

III. Uses.—The first ecclesiastical use of bells was to announce the hour of church services. It is plain that in the days before watches and clocks some such signal must have been a necessity, more especially in religious communities which assembled many times a day to sing the Divine praises. Among the Egyptian cenobites we read that a trumpet was used for the purpose; among the Greeks a wooden board or sheet of metal was struck with a hammer; in the West the use of bells eventually prevailed. In the Merovingian period there is no trustworthy evidence for the existence of large bells capable of being heard at a distance, but, as it became needful to call to church the inhabitants of town or hamlet, bell turrets were built, and bells increased in size, and as early as the eighth century we hear of two or more bells in the same church. Perhaps these were at first intended to reinforce each other and add to the volume of sound. But in any case it became in time a recognized principle that the *classicum*, the clash of several bells ringing at once, constituted an element of joy and solemnity befitting great feasts (Rupert of Deutz, De Div. Offic., I, 16). Medieval consuetudinaries show that where there were many bells, different bells were used for different purposes. Even in ordinary parish churches it was customary to ring not only for Mass but before both Matins and Vespers (Hartzheim, IV, 247; V, 327) while differences in the manner of ringing and the number of bells employed indicated the grade of the feast, the nature of the service, the fact that a sermon would be preached, and many other details. The custom of making such announcements by bell still survives here and there. Thus in Rome on the evening before a fast day the bells are rung for a quarter of an hour in all the parish churches to remind people of their obligations on the morrow.

Some rude lines quoted in the gloss of the "Corpus Juris", and often found in inscriptions, describe the principal functions of a bell (cf. Longfellow, The Golden Legend):

Laudo Deum verum plebem voco congrego clerum
Defunctos ploro, nimbum fugo, festa decoro.

(I praise the true God, I call the people, I assemble the clergy;
I bewail the dead, I disperse storm clouds, I do honour to feasts.)

Or otherwise:

Funera plango fulmina frango sabbata pango
Excito lentos dissipo ventos paco cruentos

(At obsequies I mourn, the thunderbolts I scatter, I ring in the sabbaths;
I hustle the sluggards, I drive away storms, I proclaim peace after bloodshed.)

Under *defunctos ploro* we may reckon the "passing bell", which in its strict meaning is a usage of very early date. In all monastic orders when any one of the community seemed to be at the point of death a signal was given by ringing a bell or striking a wooden board (*tabula*) either to summon the monks to his bedside or to admonish them to pray (see Eddius, Vita Wilfridi, 64). This was extended later to parish churches, and a bell was rung to announce that a parishioner was in his agony, which seemingly also developed further into a bell tolled after his decease to solicit prayers for his soul. So deeply rooted were these practices in England that it was found impossible at the Reformation to abolish them altogether. Hence the "Canons" of the Church of England prescribe (Can. lxvii): "When any is passing out of this life a bell shall be tolled and the minister shall not then slack to do his last duty. And after the party's death, if it so fall out, there shall be rung no more than one short peal, and one other before the burial and one other after the burial". "Though the tolling of this bell", says Ellacombe, "has been prescribed for four distinct occasions, modern custom has limited it to two: first, after the death of the parishioner, to which the term passing-bell has been incorrectly transferred; and the second time during the procession of the funeral from the house of the deceased to the church-gate or entrance". In many places it was formerly customary by some variation in the manner of ringing to indicate the sex, quality, or age of the deceased. Thus Durandus in the fourteenth century directed that when anyone was *in extremis* the passing-bell should be tolled twice for a woman, thrice for a man, and for a cleric a greater number of times according to the orders which he had received. Among Celtic peoples the ancient hand-bells which, as already noted, were so deeply venerated partly as objects immediately connected with God's worship, partly as relics of holy men, were usually carried and rung at funerals. To this day St. Finnan's little bell lies exposed upon the altar of a ruined chapel in one of the Catholic dis-

Byzantine Hand-Bell of Bronze in the Collection of the Abp. of Reims

tricts of the Highlands of Scotland. It is used at funerals, but is otherwise left unprotected, being regarded with such deep veneration by all that no one dares to interfere with it (see Macdonald, Moidart, Oban, 1889, 120). In many parts of France there were formerly confraternities of hand-bell-ringers who regularly attended funerals, walking at the head of the procession. They also paraded the streets at night and rang to remind people to pray for the holy souls. This happened especially on the eve of All Saints and on Christmas Eve (Morillot, Clochettes, 160 sqq.).

In Rome the "De Profundis" is rung every evening by the parish churches one hour after the Ave Maria. Clement XII in 1736 granted an indulgence for this practice and endeavoured to extend it. This custom is observed in many other places, particularly in North America.

The Curfew (*ignitegium*), a warning to extinguish fires and lights, after which all respectable characters went home to bed, was possibly of ecclesiastical origin but seems to have been rung as a rule by the town bell (*campana communiæ, bancloche*). Still in many cases one of the church bells was used for this and similar purposes. In England this was particularly frequent, and in many small towns and parishes the curfew is rung to this day at hours varying from 8 p. m. to 10.

The Angelus or Ave Maria may or may not have developed out of the curfew. There seems good reason to believe that a special bell, often called the Gabriel bell, was devoted to this purpose. In the Middle Ages the Angelus seems commonly to have been rung with three equal peals, and this arrangement still obtains in many places. In Rome, where the Ave Maria is sung half an hour after sunset this method obtains: three strokes and a pause, four strokes and a pause, five strokes and a pause, a final stroke.

From the introduction of the Elevation of the Host in the Mass at the beginning of the thirteenth century it seems to have been customary to ring one of the great bells of the church, at any rate during the principal Mass, at the moment when the Sacred Host was raised on high. This was to give warning to the people at work in the fields in order that they might momentarily kneel down and make an act of adoration. It seems, however, not improbable that in England the big bell was not commonly rung but that a small hand-bell was used for the purpose. This was taken to a small window (low side window) ordinarily closed by a shutter, thrust through the aperture and rung outside the church. Whether this was distinct from the little bell which the rubrics of the Mass now order to be rung by the server is not quite clear. It may be noted here that in regard to this same *tintinnabulum* usage varies very much in different countries. In Belgium, France, and some other places, this little bell is rung also at the "little elevation" before the Pater Noster. In Rome it is never rung at the Domine non sum dignus and is not used at all at Masses said by the pope or by cardinals.

In the rite of the blessing of bells the verse is applied to them *vox Domini in virtute, vox Domini in magnificentiâ* (The voice of the Lord is in power; the voice of the Lord in magnificence, Ps., xxviii, 4). It is no doubt in virtue of the solemnity which they lend to worship that the "Ceremoniale Episcoporum" directs that they are to be rung in honour of the bishop when he visits the parish. The same mark of respect is observed in the case of secular princes, while such occasions as processions of the Blessed Sacrament, solemn Te Deums, marriages, and days of national rejoicing are similarly distinguished. On the other hand, in token of mourning the bells are silent from the Gloria of the Mass on Maundy Thursday until the Gloria on Holy Saturday. This rule

goes back to the eighth century and Amalarius is authority for the statement that then as now a wooden rattle was used in their place. Again the idea of *vox Domini in Virtute* in remembrance of their special consecration has led to the bells being rung at times of storm and apprehended danger. The inscription *Salva Terra* often found in the old bells of the South of France seems to bear special reference to this virtue of the bells as sacramentals.

IV. ARCHÆOLOGY AND INSCRIPTIONS.—Unquestionably the oldest existing Christian bells are those of Irish, or at least Celtic, origin, of which, as already stated, a surprisingly large number are preserved. The earliest, made of iron plate, bent and rivetted, seem to have been dipped in melted bronze, a process which probably much improved their sonority. Somewhat later hand-bells began to be cast in bronze, and one such specimen (eight inches in diameter and nearly a foot high) can be dated by the aid of the inscription which it bears ŌR AR CHUMASCACH M̄C AILILLA [A prayer upon (i. e. for) Chumascach son of Aillil]. Now as Chumascach, steward of the Church of Armagh, died in 904, this bell probably belongs to the closing years of the ninth century. Another bell of early date, but of small size (five and one-half inches high and seven inches in diameter), is preserved in the Museum of Cordova. It bears the inscription: "Offert hoc munus Sanson abbatis [*sic*] in domum sancti Sebastiani martyris Christi era DCCCCLXIII". This is the Spanish Era and corresponds with A. D. 925. Of church bells properly so called, the earliest existing specimens seem to belong to the eleventh, twelfth, and thirteenth centuries. They are for the most part of a sort of beehive, thimble or barrel shape, sometimes disproportionately broad, sometimes narrower, while the sides are commonly straight or even in some few instances converge a little toward the bottom. They are also often perforated with three or four small triangular apertures in the upper part of the bell. The inscriptions, when they occur, are engraved and not as a rule cast in relief. Most of them are very short, but this is probably due to the accident that so very few early bells have survived, for we have record of much longer inscriptions engraved on bells as far back as the ninth century. Thus Folcuin who was Abbot of Lobbes from 965 to 990, tells us in his chronicle of one of his predecessors Harbert (835–864) who had a bell made with this inscription:—

Harberti imperio componor ab arte Paterni
Nec musis docta en cantus modulabor amœnos
Nocte dieque vigil depromam carmina Christi.

Folcuin himself set up bells which bore the words: "Jussu Fulcuini me condidit artificis manus Danielis, ad laudem triadis"; and "Fulcuinus Deo et patrono suo S. Ursmaro."

This last instance, perhaps the earliest example of a bell with a name, throws an interesting light on the origin of the practice of assigning bells to a particular patron. Again we know that the Cistercians of Waverley about 1239 had a bell made with the legend:

Dicor nomine quo tu Virgo domestica Christi
Sum Domini præco cuius tutela fuisti

And an even longer inscription consisting of four hexameter lines was to be read upon the bell called Edmund at Bury, which dated from about 1105. The oldest church bell now in existence is probably that known as the Lullus bell at Hersfeld which may belong to the middle of the eleventh century, but the oldest which bears a certain date (i. e. 1164) is said to be one at Iggensbach in Bavaria. It may be doubted, however, whether certain ancient Italian bells at Siena and elsewhere have yet been adequately studied (see Ellacombe, 405, 530). In England many medieval bells still survive, but no dated bell is older than that of Claughton in Lancashire, 1296. As regards the lettering of the inscriptions, it suffices to say that while the earlier bells often show a very ornate style of character, known as "crowned Lombardic", those of the fifteenth and late fourteenth century approximate to the ordinary Gothic or "black letter" type.

As regards the inscriptions themselves, both purport and wording are infinitely varied. Some are barbarous in syntax and metre, others have evidently been submitted to some sort of scholarly revision. That the practice of naming bells began, as stated by Baronius, with the dedication of a bell to St. John the Baptist by Pope John XIII in 969 rests on unsatisfactory evidence, but most existing medieval bells preserve some indication of the name by which they were called. A very large number were in one way or other dedicated to the Blessed Virgin, and most of these were probably used either for the Angelus or at the Mary Mass. The inscriptions vary indefinitely. One of the commonest was

Protege prece piâ quos convoco sancta Maria

or what is metrically a little more correct:

Ora mente piâ pro nobis Virgo Maria.

In Germany a very favourite inscription for Mary bells was:

Maria vocor. O rex gloriæ veni cum pace.

This almost certainly was meant as a reference to the Incarnation, for in many cases this legend was joined with the words: "Et homo factus est". Such

bells were probably used for the Angelus. Bells in honour of St. Peter were also very common. In England we find many such inscriptions as

Petrus ad æternæ ducat nos pascua vitæ

or again:

Nomen Petri fero qui claviger exstat in ævo.

Inscriptions to the saints, notably to St. Gabriel for the Angelus, were numerous. Thus, to take an English example, we have at Shapwick, Dorset,

I Kateryne, Goddes derlyng, to thee Mari shal I synge.

Among French bells allusion to protection against the powers of darkness was frequent, and many bells were called *Sauveterre*. Thus we have: "Jhs autem transiens per medium illorum ibat. Salva

terre m'étais nommée". Or again we often find only: "Xtus vincit; Xtus regnat; Xtus imperat". Later inscriptions were often chronographic. Thus in a bell of 1659 we have:

Rupta bis ante fui nunc integra reddita cantem
Magno IgnI LIqVefaCta Deo reparata benIgno
—capitals in second line giving date MDCLVIIII.

The following inscriptions are on the principal bell of St. Peter's Basilica, Rome (shown in illustration): On the upper part:

+In nomine Domini Matris, Petrique Paulique,
Accipe devotum, parvum licet, accipe munus
Quod tibi Christe datum Petri Paulique triumphum
+Explicat, et nostram petit populique salutem
Ipsorum pietate dari meritisque refundi.
  Et Verbum caro factum est.

+Anno milleno trecenteno cum quinquageno
Additis et tribus, Septembris mense, colatur.
Ponderat et mille decies septiesque librarum.

+Campanam hanc longo usu confractam non plus quam quatuordecim mille libras pendere compertum est; Benedictus XIV addito usque ad viginti mille libras metallo, conflari et denuo refici iussit, anno reparatae salutis MDCCXLVII.

+Eandem septimo vix exacto lustro, rimis actis inutilem, uno plus et viginti millibus pondo metalli repertam, Pius Sextus, Pont. Max. non mediocri metallo superaddito ad idem ponderis conflari fundique mandavit, anno Domini MDCCLXXXV, Pont. XI.

  Aloysius eques Valadier construxit.

For the credit of eighteenth century scholarship, it seems desirable to explain that only the latter part of this inscription belongs to the pontificate of Pius VI. The earlier portion with its metrical irregularities is simply a copy of what was read upon the great bell of St. Peter's at the beginning of the fourteenth century. Probably the metal came from the bell originally cast by Leo IV in 850, or even earlier, under Pope Stephen II. Then, when the campanile was burned down in 1303, Boniface VIII had a new bell made with the inscription which stands first in the above series. Only fifty years afterwards the tower was struck by lightning, and a new great bell was founded (*colatur*, cf. the French *couler*) in September, 1353. Then Benedict XIV had the bell recast in larger size in 1747, and when this cracked (*rimis actis*), the metal was once more used by Aloysius Valadier to make the present beautiful bell under Pius VI in 1785. (See Cancellieri, De Secretariis, Rome, 1786, III, 1357, and IV, 1995 sqq.)

In point of size any very great development of medieval bells was probably checked by the mechanical difficulty of ringing them. At Canterbury, for example, we hear of as many as twenty-four men being required to ring one bell, while sixty-three men were needed for the whole peal of five (Ellacombe, 443). In the eleventh century a bell given by King Robert to the church at Orleans was thought to be of remarkable size, but it weighed little over a ton. The "Cantabona" bell of Blessed Azelin at Hildesheim (eleventh century) is said to have weighed about four tons, a Rouen bell of 1501 sixteen tons, and the still existing "Maria Gloriosa" of Erfurt Cathedral, cast in 1497, weighs thirteen tons. Of modern bells consecrated with the rites of the Catholic Church, the largest is that of Cologne Cathedral, which was made out of captured French cannon, and weighs nearly twenty-seven tons. That in the church of the Sacred Heart at Montmartre weighs over eighteen, and others at Vienna and Rouen about seventeen. In the Catholic cathedral of Montreal is a bell of thirteen and one-half tons. The very beautiful bell of St. Peter's, Rome, weighs about nine tons. The gigantic bells cast in Russia, China,

Japan, and Burma seem only to be struck with a hammer and never properly "rung". The largest bell in England is that of St. Paul's Cathedral, London, which weighs seventeen and one-half tons.

V. POINTS OF LAW.—In medieval England it was distinctly laid down that the church bells and ropes had to be provided at the cost of the parishioners. The canon law assumed that a cathedral had five or more bells, a parish church two or three, while the churches of the mendicant orders, like public oratories, were originally limited to one. The solemn ceremony of benediction provided in the Pontifical can only be carried out by a bisdop or by a priest specially empowered, and it is only to be employed in the case of bells intended for church use. For other bells a simpler blessing is provided in the "Rituale". Numerous prohibitions exist against the church bells being used for "profane" purposes, e. g. for summoning meetings or for merely secular festivities and in particular for executions. In Catholic ecclesiastical legislation the principle is maintained that the control of the bells rests absolutely with the clergy. In cathedral churches according to the "Ceremoniale Episcoporum" this jurisdiction is vested in the *Sacrista.* Theoretically, the actual ringing of the bells should be performed by the *ostiarius* and in the conferring of this minor order the cleric is given a bell to ring, but for centuries past his functions have everywhere become obsolete, and lay bell-ringers have been almost exclusively employed. Finally, we may note a decision of the secular courts given in an action brought against the Redemptorists of Clapham, England, in 1851, whereby an injunction was granted to restrain these Fathers from ringing their bells at certain hours, at which, as it was complained, such ringing caused unreasonable annoyance to residents in the neighbourhood.

STREBER in *Kirchenlex.,* V, 697; THALHOFER, *Liturgik,* (Freiburg, 1883), I, 830–839; ELLACOMBE, *The Church Bells of Devon* and *Suppl.* (Exeter, 1872); RAVEN, *The Church Bells of England* (London, 1906); OTTE, *Glockenkunde* (Leipzig, 1884); IDEM, *Zur Glockenkunde* (1891); BARBIER DE MONTAULT, *Traité Pratique de l'Ameublement des Eglises* (Paris, 1878), I, 345–358; BERTHELÉ, *Enquêtes campanaires* (Montpellier, 1903); VACANDARD in *Rev. du Clergé Français* (Paris, 1902), XXIX, 337; BERGNER, *Handbuch des kirchlichen Kunstalterthümer* (Leipzig, 1905); CATALANI, *Commentarii in Pontificale Romanum* (Rome, 1738), II, 335; BONA, *De Campanis in Rerum Liturgicarum Libri Duo* (Rome, 1671); KRAUS, *Real-Encyk.,* I, 622; STOKES, *Early Christian Art in Ireland* (London, 1887), 59 sqq.; REEVES in *Transactions of Royal Irish Academy* (Dublin, 1877), XXVII, 1–30; MILLIGAN, *Ancient Ecclesiastical Bells in Ulster* in *Journal of Royal Society of Antiquaries, Ireland* (Dublin, 1903), XXXIII, 46–58; MORILLOT, *Les clochettes dans l'antiquité* (Dijon, 1887); CANCELLIERI, *Le due nuove Campane in campidoglio* (Rome, 1806); GERMAIN, *Les Cloches de Sangues* (Nancy, 1890); STAHLSCHMIDT, *Surrey Bells* (London, 1884); IDEM, *Church Bells of Kent* (London, 1887); NORTH, *Church Bells of Bedfordshire* (London, 1883); RAVEN, *Church Bells of Suffolk* (London, 1889); ELLACOMBE, *Church Bells of Somerset* (London, 1875); BERGNER, *Zur Glockenkunde Thuringiens* (Leipzig, 1896); LIEBESKIND, *Die Glocken des Neustadter Kreises* (Leipzig, 1905); EFFMAN, *Die Glocken der Stadt Freiburg in der Schweiz* (1899); SAMSON, *Zur Geschichte und Symbolik der Glocken* (Leipzig, 1897); SAUVETERRE, *Essai sur le symbolisme de la cloche* (Paris, 1883); STEFFENS, *Kirchweihe und Glockensegnung* (Freiburg, 1893); SCHNABEL, *Weihe der Glocken* (Mainz, 1905); WERNZ, *Jus Decretalium* (Rome, 1904), III, 509. For further references cf. CHEVALIER, *Topobibl.,* s. v. *Cloches.*

HERBERT THURSTON.

Belluno-Feltre, DIOCESE OF.—Belluno, which was anciently called Bellunum, the metropolis of the province of that name in Venetia, Italy, is situated on a hill between the torrent of Ardo and the River Piave, and has a population of 10,000. At the end of the tenth century Belluno was affected by the political disturbances then agitating the Venetian provinces. Bishop Joannes II (959) obtained from Emperor Otto I for himself and his successors the title of count and temporal sovereignty over this city and the surrounding territory. He also fortified the city. In the course of time there were many disputes over the civil mastery of Belluno, but in 1420 the inhabitants of their own accord acknowledged the authority of Venice. Belluno is the seat of a bishopric suffragan to the Patriarchate of Venice, and is united with the See of Feltre. Christianity is said to have been first preached there by St. Hermagoras, a disciple of St. Mark and first Bishop of Aquileia, and next by Prosdocimus, first Bishop of Padua. Ughelli places the first bishop, Theodorus, in the reign of Emperor Commodus and the second, St. Salvator, as succeeding under Pertinax. About 300 another Theodorus is thought to have brought from Egypt the remains of St. Giovata, patron of the city. The first bishop known to history is a certain Laurentius, who, in 587, attended the schismatic assembly convened by Severus, Patriarch of Aquileia, in connexion with the dispute of the Three Chapters. The twelfth century was a stormy period for Belluno, in both civil and ecclesiastical respects. In 1197 Bishop Gerardo de Taccoli was murdered by the inhabitants of Treviso, after which Innocent III united the Diocese of Belluno with that of Feltre.

Feltre, the ancient Feltria, is situated in the province of Belluno in Venetia, on the River Colmeda, and contains 13,000 inhabitants. From the year 80 B. C. it enjoyed the rights of Roman citizenship. It was besieged during the invasion of Attila. Emperor Henry III created the Bishops of Feltre counts of the city and vicinity, but their authority was almost constantly assailed by the Counts of Camino, by Ezzelino da Romano, the Scaligeri, the Carrara, and finally by the Visconti themselves. At last, in 1404, the city fell into the power of the Venetians. Feltre also claims to have received the Gospel from St. Prosdocimus. St. Victor, a martyr, is said to have lived there about A. D. 170. The first Bishop of Feltre whose date can be fixed is Fonteius, who in 579 took part in a council in Aquileia and in 591 dedicated a book to Emperor Mauritius. Drudo of Camino (1174) was the first bishop of the united sees of Belluno and Feltre, the latter being the residence of the bishop. The twelfth, thirteenth, and fourteenth centuries were filled with civil strife.

In 1462, at the request of the Venetian Republic, the two dioceses were separated. The first Bishop of Belluno was Ludovico Donato. Bishops Pietro Barozzi, Mosè Buffarello, and Bernardo Rossi (1499) rebuilt the cathedral. One of the most illustrious bishops was Luigi Lollin (1595) who did much to promote the love of learning among the clergy and left large bequests to perpetually provide for a number of priests at the University of Padua. Giulio Berlendis (1655) completed the work of enforcing the Tridentine reforms, and Gianfrancesco Bembo, a member of the Somaschi (1695), was very zealous in the cause of popular education. In 1818 the diocese was reunited with that of Feltre. Among the Bishops of Feltre after the separation mention should be made of Angelo Faseolo (1464), who was appointed on many legations in connexion with the Crusade against the Turks; Lorenzo Campeggio (1512), famous as the nuncio to England during the time of Henry VIII, later made cardinal and transferred (1520) to Bologna. He was succeeded by his nephew Tommaso Campeggio, who was nuncio several times. Agostino Gradenigo (1610) restored the cathedral; Zerbino Lugo (1640) built the seminary; Giovanni Bortoli (1748) was a distinguished professor of canon law at Padua.

The most remarkable sacred edifices in Belluno are, in addition to the cathedral, the church of San Pietro, and that of San Stephano, the latter in Gothic style; all three contain paintings by the most distinguished Venetian artists. In Feltre there are the cathedral, dedicated to St. Laurence, the oratory of San Giacomo, the churches of San Giorgio in Villabruna, and San Rocco; in the last named the painting over the high altar is the work of Palma il Vecchio.

Outside the city, on the slopes of Mount Misnea is the church of SS. Vittore e Corona, erected by the Crusaders of Feltre after the First Crusade.

The Diocese of Belluno contains 72 parishes, 280 churches, chapels, and oratories, 137 secular priests, 22 regulars, 22 seminarists, 5 lay brothers, 29 sisters, and a population of 127,500. Feltre has 17 parishes, 100 churches, chapels, and oratories, 48 secular priests, 25 regulars, 56 seminarists, 2 schools for boys and 2 for girls, and a population of 48,000.

CAPPELLETTI, *Le chiese d'Italia* (Venice, 1844); *Annuario eccl.* (1906).

U. BENIGNI.

Belmont, FRANÇOIS VACHON DE, fifth superior of the Sulpicians at Montreal, b. at Grenoble, France, 1645; d. 1732. He went to Canada in 1680 and was appointed a missionary among the Indians of La Montagne; he filled this position until 1700, when he succeeded Dollier de Casson as superior of the order. He erected at his own expense Fort de La Montagne on the site of the present Grand Séminaire, built the old seminary which still exists in the street of Notre Dame, and began the construction of the Lachine canal. Among his writings are: "Histoire du Canada", printed in the "Collection de mémoires et de relations sur l'histoire ancienne du Canada", published by the Historical Society of Quebec; "Histoire de l'eau-de-vie en Canada", printed in the above-mentioned "Collection"; "Oraison funèbre de la Mère Bourgeoys", quoted by Faillon in "Vie de la Sœur Bourgeoys", II, 88–98; "Eloges de quelques personnes mortes en odeur de sainteté à Montréal", and a number of memoirs still in manuscript. Mention should also be made of the funeral oration of Bishop Montmorency-Laval, first Bishop of Quebec, delivered at Montreal, June, 1708.

BERTRAND, *Bibliothèque Sulpicienne ou hist. litt. de la c. de Saint-Sulpice* (Paris, 1900).

A. FOURNET.

Belson, THOMAS, VENERABLE, martyr, b. at Brill in Oxfordshire, England, date uncertain; d. 5 July, 1589. He was at the college at Reims in 1584, and in 1589 was arrested at the Catherine Wheel Inn, near Balliol College, Oxford, with his confessor George Nicols, Richard Yaxley, a priest, and Prichard, a servant. They were sent to London, whence, after examination before Walsingham and repeated tortures in Bridewell and the Tower, they were sent back to Oxford to be tried. Belson was found guilty of felony for assisting the priests, and was executed with his companions at Oxford, He suffered after the priests and, kissing the dead bodies of his pastors, begged the intercession of their happy souls that he might have the grace to imitate their courage and constancy.

YEPES, *Historia Particular de la persecución de Inglaterra* (Madrid, 1599); CHALLONER, *Memoirs*; KNOX, *Douay Diaries*; STAPLETON, *Post-Reformation Catholic Missions in Oxfordshire* (London, 1906).

BEDE CAMM.

Belsunce de Castelmoron, HENRI FRANÇOIS XAVIER DE, Bishop of Marseilles, b. 1671 at the Château de la Force, in Périgord; d. 1755 at Marseilles. His father was Armand de Belsunce, Marquis de Castelmoron and his mother Anne de Caumont de Lausun. He studied classics in Paris at the Collège de Clermont or Louis-le-grand and then entered the Society of Jesus. In 1699 he left the Society to become Vicar-General of Agen. The "Vie de Suzanne de Foix", his aunt, was written by him and published while at Agen, 1709. That same year he was made Bishop of Marseilles. The heroic charity he displayed during the plague of 1720 and 1721 has made his name a household word and won for him the title of "Good Bishop". When the plague broke out a large fleet was taking the Princess of Orléans to Italy where she was to marry the Duke of Modena. The suite of the princess took to flight, and with them all the notables of the city, but Bishop Bel-

sunce remained with a few heroic friends, and together they battled against the plague with heroic self-sacrifice and devotion, till they conquered it. In his address to the Assembly of the Clergy in 1725, Belsunce stated that more than 250 priests and religious perished in their mission of Christian charity. But he was the soul of the rescuers and the praises bestowed on him by Pope and Millevoye ("Essay on Man" and "Belsunce ou la peste de Marseille") are not above his real merits. The King of France offered him, by way of recognition, the See of Laon to which was attached the first ecclesiastical peerage of the realm and afterwards the metropolitan See of Bordeaux. Belsunce refused both and contented himself with accepting the pallium sent him by Clement XII. During his incumbency Belsunce fought against another plague called Jansenism. He attended, 1727, the Synod of Embrun where Soanen was condemned. He opposed with all his power Colbert of Pamiers. In spite of the protest of the Parliament of Provence, he instructed his priests to refuse absolution to the appellants against the Bull "Unigenitus". Nearly all his pastoral instructions are against Jansenism. Belsunce was a writer of no mean power. Besides the "Vie de Suzanne de Foix" (Agen, 1709), and his pastoral instructions, we have from his pen "Le combat chrétien" translated from St. Augustin's "De Agone Christiano" and "L'art de bien mourir" translated from Bellarmine's "De Arte Bene Moriendi", also "Antiquités de l'Eglise de Marseille" (Marseilles, 1747–51). All these writings have been published by Jauffret under the title of "Œuvres de Belsunce" (Metz, 1822).

BARBET, *Eloge de Belsunce* (Paris, 1821); ROHRBACHER, *Histoire universelle* (Paris, 1885), XI; BERENGIER, *Vie de Mgr. de Belsunce* (Paris, 1887).

J. F. SOLLIER.

Belz. See CHELM.

Belzoni, GIAMBATTISTA, an Egyptian explorer, b. at Padua, Italy, in 1778; d. at Gato, Africa, 3 Dec., 1823. His father was a barber, and intended his son to follow that trade, but the boy, who was a born traveller, left home at the age of fifteen, and after some wanderings settled down at Rome, where he began the study of hydraulics. Whether or not he became a monk is uncertain, but, at any rate, he quitted Rome in 1798 and travelled as far as Holland. Having returned to Italy, he again departed in 1803 and travelled through the British Isles, being finally obliged, by reduced circumstances, to secure an engagement in pantomime. Leaving England, he went to Egypt, where, at the request of the pasha, he undertook a scheme for raising the waters of the Nile at Zubra, but the work was later abandoned by the authorities, and he turned his attention to unearthing the colossal bust of Memnon now in the British Museum. Having accomplished this difficult task, he ascended the Nile, and besides many other important Egyptological investigations, made his famous discovery of the mummy of Psammethis. Again setting out from Cairo, he explored the pyramid of Chephren, travelled through Fayûm, visited Lake Mœris and the ruins of Arsinoe, penetrated into Libya, and reached the oasis of El-Cassar. In 1819 he went to England, whence, after a stay of a few years, he set out for further travels in Africa, intending to explore Timbuktu and the sources of the Niger, and to visit Benin and Abyssinia; but having landed, he was attacked by a fever, and died. He printed a narrative of his journeys at London, in 1821, and his original drawings of "The Tombs of the Kings" were published by his widow, at London, in 1829.

EDWIN RYAN.

Bema. See AMBO.

Bembo, PIETRO, a famous Italian scholar and Cardinal, b. of a noble family at Venice, 20 May,

1470; d. at Rome, 18 January, 1547. He was the son of Bernardo Bembo, whose enthusiasm for Italian literature led him to raise a monument to Dante at Ravenna. His early education was received at Florence. He afterwards studied Greek under Lascaris at Messina and philosophy under Pomponazzo at Padua. After spending some time at the court of Ferrara, where he met Lucrezia Borgia, with whom he maintained a Platonic friendship for many years, he went in 1506 to Urbino, where he became the leading figure among the brilliant group of men of wit and culture gathered about the court. In 1512 he accompanied

CARDINAL BEMBO
Medal attributed to Benvenuto Cellini

his intimate friend, Giuliano de' Medici, to Rome, where a short time afterwards he was appointed secretary to Pope Leo X. He remained at Rome for eight years, enjoying the society of many distinguished men and loved and admired by all who knew him. There he became enamoured of the beautiful Morosina. It was at her urgent solicitation that Bembo, in 1520, on the death of Leo X, withdrew from public affairs and retired with his health impaired by severe sickness to Padua, where he lived in ease and elegance, devoting himself to literary pursuits and the society of his learned friends. Here he collected an extensive library and formed a rich museum of medals and antiquities. His Paduan retreat became the gathering-place of all the most cultured and most scholarly men in Italy. In 1529 he accepted the office of historiographer of the Republic of Venice, and shortly afterwards was appointed librarian of St. Mark's. In 1539 Pope Paul III recalled him to Rome and conferred on him the cardinal's hat. From the time of Bembo's ecclesiastical preferment there was a marked change in his conduct. Heretofore his life had been anything but edifying—in fact it had been more pagan than Christian. But now he renounced the study of the classics and applied himself chiefly to the study of the Fathers and the Holy Scriptures. Two years after he was raised to the cardinalate, he was made Bishop of Gubbio, and still later he received the Bishopric of Bergamo. He died more admired and lamented than any man of letters of his time and was buried not far from Pope Leo in the Church of the Minerva.

Bembo was a thorough master of elegant diction. He possessed beyond any contemporary the formal perfection of style, both in Latin and Italian, demanded by the age in which he lived. In his Latin writings it was his aim to imitate as closely as possible the style of Cicero. His letters were masterpieces of Latin style and of the art of letter-writing. He is said to have passed his compositions through numerous portfolios, revising them in each one of them. Bembo's works include a history of Venice, poems, dialogues, criticisms, and letters. The most important are: "Rerum Veneticarum Libri XII" (1551), a history of Venice covering the period from 1487 to 1513, originally published in Latin, but afterwards translated by the author into Italian; "Gli Asolani" (Venice, 1505), a dialogue in Italian on Platonic love, composed in imitation of Cicero's Tusculan Disputations, and dedicated to Lucrezia Borgia; "Le Prose", a short treatise on the Italian language; "Le Rime" (Venice, 1530); "Carmina" (Venice, 1533), a collection of Latin poems; and several volumes of letters, written in Latin. Besides these original works he edited the Italian poems of Petrarch, printed by Aldus (1501), and the "Terze rime" of Dante (1502). His collected works were published at Venice in four volumes in 1729.

SYMONDS, *Renaissance in Italy* (New York, 1900), II; *The Revival of Learning;* GARNETT, *A History of Italian Literature* (New York, 1898); VON REUMONT, *Gesch. der Stadt Rom.;* TIRABOSCHI, *Stor. lett. Ital.* (1809), VII, 1, 110–111, 235–251; III, 926–931, 1120; IV, 1560; BATTAGLIA, *Elogio del Cardinale P. Bembo* (Venice, 1827); BECCATELLI, *Vita di Pietro Bembo, cardinale,* in *Istor. case Venez.* (1718), II, xxxii–li.

EDMUND BURKE.

Benadir, PREFECTURE APOSTOLIC OF, in Africa, lies between 8° and 12° N. lat., and between 42° and 51° 16′ E. long. It comprises the whole territory of Italian Somaliland, the area of which is a little more than 192,800 square miles, or nearly twice that of Italy; and its boundaries are identical with those of the Italian possessions in East Africa, namely: on the east, the Indian Ocean; on the north, the Gulf of Aden from Cape Guardafui to the boundary of British Somaliland; on the west, the same British boundary as far south as the Juba River; and on the south, the course of that river from Lugh to the Indian Ocean. The longest meridian within this territory measures 776 miles, while the greatest width is 559 miles.

The commercial company which had been formed for the exploitation of El Benadir (i. e. "The Ports", now the littoral region of Italian Somaliland) found it to its own interest to call the Church to its aid, and asked for missionaries, to whom it assigned a subsidy of 10,000 lire ($2,000) per annum. Propaganda, by a decree of 21 January, 1904, entrusted the mission to the Discalced Trinitarians, for which order the redemption of captives is a special tradition, and the first prefect Apostolic, Father Leander of the Seven Dolours, embarked within the same year. However, the presence of a religious who would jealously watch the slave trade, and denounce infractions of the treaties, might become inconvenient; the governor, therefore, forbade Father Leander to enter his territory, and the prefect Apostolic, excluded from his mission, was obliged to take refuge in the British territory to the south. The governor's order was rescinded in May, 1906, and Father Leander then entered upon his prefecture; but on the 10th of July, 1906, he died at Gelib, nearly 250 miles from the coast. Towards the end of that year Father Guglielmo da San Felice was sent as successor to Father Leander, taking with him five religious of his own order. At the present writing (1907) too short a time has, of course, elapsed to permit of obtaining any information as to the actual progress of missionary work in Italian Somaliland.

The residence of the prefect Apostolic is at Brava, while the headquarters of the colonial government are at Mogadishu (Mogadoxo, or Mukdishu). The population of the whole territory is estimated at 3,000,000, almost all Mohammedans. Slavery is practised, and the efforts of the Anti-Slavery Society to suppress the slave trade, by representations to the Italian Government, have so far had no result.

Missiones Catholicæ (Propaganda, Rome, 1907), 355; *Statesman's Year Book* (London, 1907).

ALBERT BATTANDIER.

Bénard, LAURENT, chief founder of the Maurist Congregation of the Benedictine Order, b. at Nevers, 1573; d. at Paris, 1620. He joined the Cluniac Benedictines at Nevers, became a Doctor of the Sorbonne and later Prior of the Cluny College, Paris, which he reformed with the help of two monks of the recently established Congregation of St.-Vannes. Refusing the abbacy of St. Etienne, Caen, and the grand-priorship of Cluny, he passed through a second novitiate at St.-Vannes, and renewed his profession there in 1615. At his suggestion the Congregation of St.-Maur was formed, to be for France what that of St.-Vannes was for Lorraine. Royal letters patent were obtained for it in 1618 and the project was warmly supported by Cardinal de Retz and others. Bénard's works include "Parénèses", "De l'esprit des ordres religieux", "Instructions Monastiques", "L'éloge Bénédictin", and "Police régulière", all published in Paris between 1616 and 1619.

TASSIN, *Hist. Lit. Cong. S. Maur* (Brussels, 1770); SAINTE-MARTHE, *Gallia Christiana* (Paris, 1744), VII, 474.

G. CYPRIAN ALSTON.

Benavides (BENAVIDEZ), FRAY ALONZO, Archbishop of Goa in the Portuguese Indies. Although a prelate of high rank, the life of Fray Alonzo de Benavides is very imperfectly known. He was born on the Island of San Miguel, professed in the Franciscan convent of Mexico in 1603, and, after acting as master of novices at the convent of Puebla, became Custos of the Missions of New Mexico, returned to Spain in 1630 and there was in communication with the Venerable María de Agreda. Upon his return to America he was made Archbishop of Goa. The date and place of his death are as yet unknown. Fray Alonzo de Benavides was indefatigable in his efforts to promote the welfare, temporal and spiritual, of New Mexico. He it was who, through the agency of Fray Esteban de Peréa, secured a reinforcement of missionaries for the utterly neglected province. In order to excite interest in those remote regions, he wrote and published two booklets, full of exaggerations in regard to the number of Indians, but otherwise of the highest value for the ethnography and ethnology of New Mexico. They must be judged as "encouraging guides", embodying at the same time much accurate and valuable information gathered from personal knowledge. His account of the numbers of people and villages may have been influenced by data taken from Espejo but such mistakes do not affect the value of his writings in general. He published "Relación de los grandes Tesoros espirituales y temporales descubiertos con el auxilio de Dios en el Nuevo Mexico", in 1630, and is best known through the "Memorial que Fray Juan de Santander de la orden de San Francisco &c. presenta á la Majestad Católica del Rey" (Madrid, 1630; translated into various languages and republished).

Memorial (Madrid, 1630); PINELO, *Epítome* (Madrid, 1738), II; BÉRISTAIN, *Biblioteca, etc.* (Mexico, 1816), II; VETANCOURT, *Teatro mexicano* (Mexico, 1698); especially *Crónica de la Provincia del Santo Evangelio de México;* BANDELIER, *Final Report, etc.,* I and II.

AD. F. BANDELIER.

Benda, a titular see of Albania. Its history is closely connected with that of the Sees of Narenta and Mostar. Narenta, or in Italian Narona, represents the ancient Chelmium, or Chulmia, and its bishop, a suffragan of Dyrrhachium (Durazzo), took the title of *episcopus Stephanensis*, or *Stephaniacensis*, the cathedral being dedicated to St. Stephen; this is the title of Cosmas at the council under Photius in 879. But as these bishops resided at Spalato, the title shortly became *Spalatensis*. About the middle of the fourteenth century, Narenta became the seat of a Latin bishopric, to which was united the See of Benda, the chief town in a district of this name, near Croia, in the pashalik of Scutari. Its bishop thus obtained a double title, *episcopus Bendensis et Stephanensis*, to which, about 1400, was added the title *Priscensis*, or *Prisnensis*, from Prisca, or Prisna, probably identical with the village Presa, or Press, in Albania. Be that as it may, these three titles were borne from the first by only one titular; Gams separates them wrongly (Series episcop., 422). The first titular was not, as is commonly said, the Dominican Petrus de Anagnia, but Demetrius, probably identical with the Franciscan Demetrius de Scutaro who is

mentioned in the Bullar. Franciscan. (VI, n. 662). From the seventeenth century the see became titular, probably because the bishops had transferred their residence to Mostar, on the left bank of the River Narenta, a see known as *Mandatriensis et Dumnensis*.

FARLATI, *Illyricum sacrum*, VII, 401–405; EUBEL, *Hierarchia Catholica medii ævi*, I, 488; II, 266 and 327.

L. PETIT.

Benedetti, PIETRO. See AMBARACH, PETER.

Benedict I-X, POPES.—Of the first Pontiff who bore the name of Benedict practically nothing is known. The date of his birth is unknown; he d. 30 July, 579. He was a Roman and the son of Boniface, and was called Bonosus by the Greeks (Evagrius, Hist., V, 16). The ravages of the Lombards rendered it very difficult to communicate with the emperor at Constantinople, who claimed the privilege of confirming the election of the popes. Hence there was a vacancy of nearly eleven months between the death of John III and the arrival of the imperial confirmation of Benedict's election, 2 June, 575. He reigned four years, one month, and twenty-eight days. Almost the only act recorded of him is that he granted an estate, the *Massa Veneris*, in the territory of Minturnæ, to Abbot Stephen of St Mark's "near the walls of Spoleto" (St. Gregory I, Ep. ix, 87, l. al. 30). Famine followed the devastating Lombards, and from the few words the Liber Pontificalis has about Benedict, we gather that he died in the midst of his efforts to cope with these difficulties. He was buried in the vestibule of the sacristy of the old basilica of St. Peter. In an ordination which he held in December he made fifteen priests and three deacons, and consecrated twenty-one bishops.

BENEDICT II, SAINT, POPE, date of birth unknown; d. 8 May, 685; was a Roman, and the son of John. Sent when young to the *schola cantorum*, he distinguished himself by his knowledge of the Scriptures and by his singing, and as a priest was remarkable for his humility, love of the poor, and generosity. He became pope 26 June, 684, after an interval of over eleven months. To abridge the vacancies of the Holy See which followed the deaths of the popes, he obtained from the Emperor Constantine Pogonatus a decree which either abolished imperial confirmations altogether or made them obtainable from the exarch in Italy [cf. "Liber Diurnus RR. PP., ed. Sickel (Vienna, 1889), and Duchesne's criticism, "Le Liber Diurnus" (Paris, 1891)]. He adopted Constantine's two sons by receiving locks of their hair sent him by the emperor. To help to suppress Monothelism, he endeavoured to secure the subscriptions of the Spanish bishops to the decrees of the Sixth General Council (see ep. in P. L., XCVI, 423), and to bring about the submission to them of Macarius, ex-Bishop of Antioch. He was one of the popes who favoured the cause of St. Wilfred of York (Eddius, "Vita Wilfridi", ed. Raine in "Historians of York", I, 62 sqq. Cf. Raine, "Lives of the Archbishops of York", I, 55 sqq.). Many of the churches of Rome were restored by him; and its clergy, its deaconries for the care of the poor, and its lay sacristans all benefited by his liberality. He was buried in St. Peter's.

BENEDICT III, POPE, date of birth unknown; d. 17 April, 858. The election of the learned and ascetic Roman, Benedict, the son of Peter, was a troubled one. On the death of Leo IV (17 July, 855) Benedict was chosen to succeed him, and envoys were despatched to secure the ratification of the decree of election by the Emperors Lothaire and Louis II. But the legates betrayed their trust and allowed themselves to be influenced in favour of the ambitious and excommunicated Cardinal Anastasius. The imperial *missi*, gained over in turn by them, endeavoured to force Anastasius on the Roman

Church. Benedict was insulted and imprisoned. Most of the clergy and people, however, remained true to him, and the *missi* had to yield. Benedict was accordingly consecrated on the 29th of September, or 6th of October, 855, and though his rival was condemned by a synod, he admitted him to lay communion. Owing to dissensions and attacks from without, the kingdom of the Franks was in disorder, and the Church within its borders was oppressed. Benedict wrote to the Frankish bishops, attributing much of the misery in the empire to their silence (cf. "Capitularia regum Francorum", ed. Boretius, II, 424); and to lessen its internal evils endeavoured to curb the powerful subdeacon Hubert (Ep. Bened., in Mon. Germ. Epp., V, 612), who was the brother-in-law of Lothaire II, King of Lorraine, and defied the laws of God and man till he was slain, in 864. In an appeal made to Benedict from the East, he held the balance fair between St. Ignatius, Patriarch of Constantinople, and Gregory, Bishop of Syracuse. He was visited by the Anglo-Saxon King Ethelwulf with his famous son Alfred, and completed the restoration of the *Schola Anglorum*, destroyed by fire in 847. He continued the work of repairing the damage done to the churches in Rome by the Saracen raid of 846. He was buried near the principal gate of St. Peter's. One of his coins proves there was no Pope Joan between Leo IV and himself [Garampi, "De nummo argenteo Bened. III" (Rome, 1749)].

BENEDICT IV, POPE, date of birth unknown; d. in the summer of 903. The Popes Benedict from the fourth to the ninth inclusive belong to the darkest period of papal history. The reigns of several of them were very short, and very little is known about their deeds. The dates of their accession to the See of Peter and of their deaths are largely uncertain. Benedict IV, a Roman and the son of Mammalus, became pope in the first half of 900. His high birth, his generosity, his zeal for the public good are loudly commended by the contemporary historian Frodoard, who gives him the title of "Great". The principal historic act of his reign was his crowning Louis the Blind as emperor. He supported the decision of Pope Formosus, who had ordained him priest, in favour of Argrim's claim to the See of Langres (Jaffé, "Regesta", 3527, 3528), upheld the cause of Stephen, Bishop of Naples (Auxilius ap. Dümmler, "Auxilius und Vulgarius", 96 sqq.), excommunicated the assassin of Fulk, Archbishop of Reims (Frodoard, Hist. Remensis, IV, 10), and offered practical sympathy to Malacenus, Bishop of Amasia, who had been driven from his see by the advances of the Saracens (Jaffé, loc. cit., 3530). Fulda and other monasteries received privileges from him. He was buried in front of St. Peter's near the gate of Guido.

BENEDICT V, POPE, date of birth unknown; d. 4 July, 965; was elected pope (May, 964) in very critical circumstances. The powerful emperor, Otho I, had forcibly deposed the unworthy John XII, and had replaced him by a nominee of his own who took the title of Leo VIII. But at the first opportunity the Romans expelled Leo, and on the death (14 May, 964) of the lawful pope, John XII, elected the Cardinal-Deacon Benedict (known from his learning as Grammaticus—see Benedict of Soracte, xxxvii). Otho was furious, marched on Rome, seized Benedict, and put an end to his pontificate (23 June, 964.—Liutprand, Hist. Ottonis, xxi; Thietmar, Chron., II, 18). It is more probable that Benedict was degraded by force than that he voluntarily declared himself an intruder. After reinstating Leo, Otho left Rome and carried Benedict with him to Germany. Placed under the care of Adaldag, Archbishop of Hamburg-Bremen, who treated him with great consideration, he was even

then acknowledged as pope by some of the German clergy. His remains, first laid to rest in the cathedral at Hamburg, were afterwards translated to Rome (Adam of Bremen, Gesta, II, 10; IV, 39, 40; VI, 53).

BENEDICT VI, POPE, date of birth unknown; d. August, 974 (see Ricobaldi of Ferrara, Compil. Chron., in Rer. Ital. SS. IX). Benedict, Cardinal-Deacon of St. Theodore, a Roman and the son of Hildebrand, was elected as the successor of John XIII, who died 6 September, 972; but the necessity of waiting for the ratification of the Emperor Otho delayed his consecration till 19 January, 973. Nothing is known of his deeds, except that he confirmed the privileges of some churches and monasteries. The most striking event of his pontificate is its tragic close. He was seized and thrown into the Castle of Sant' Angelo by a faction of the nobility headed by Crescentius and the Deacon Boniface Franco, who afterwards become the antipope Boniface VII. There, after a confinement of less than two months, he was strangled by their orders, to prevent his release by Sicco, an imperial envoy, sent to Rome by Otho II.

BENEDICT VII, POPE, date of birth unknown; d. c. October, 983. Acting under the influence of Sicco (see BENEDICT VI), the Roman clergy and people elected to succeed Benedict VI another Benedict, Bishop of Sutri, a Roman and the son of David (October, 974). His authority was opposed by Boniface VII, and, though the antipope himself was forced to fly, his party followed fiercely in his footsteps and compelled Benedict to call upon Otho II for help. Firmly established on his throne by the emperor, he showed himself both desirous of checking the tide of simony which was rising high in the Church, and of advancing the cause of monasticism, which then meant that of civilization. In response to a request of the people of Carthage "to help the wretched province of Africa", he consecrated the priest James, who had been sent to him for the purpose (see the letter of the papal legate, the Abbot Leo, to the Kings Hugh Capet and Robert). Though he did not die till about October, 983, our knowledge of his undertakings is not in proportion to the length of his pontificate.

BENEDICT VIII, POPE, date of birth unknown; d. 9 April, 1024. The first of the Tusculan popes, being the son of Gregory, Count of Tusculum, and Maria, and brother of John XIX, he was, though a layman, imposed on the chair of Peter by force (18 May, 1012). Nevertheless, dislodging a rival, he became a good and strong ruler. On the 14th of February, 1014, he crowned the German king, Henry II, emperor (Thietmar, Chron., VI, 61), and ever kept friendly with him. The peace of Italy was promoted by his subjugating the Crescentii, defeating the Saracens, and allying himself with the Normans, who appeared in its southern parts in his time. Going to Germany, he consecrated the cathedral of Bamberg (Ann. Altahen. Majores, 1020; Chron. Cass., II, 47), visited the monastery of Fulda, and obtained from Henry a charter confirmatory of the donations of Charlemagne and Otho. To restrain the vices of clerical incontinence and simony, he held, with the emperor, an important synod at Pavia (1022—Labbe, Concilia, IX, 819), and supported the reformation which was being effected by the great monastery of Cluny. To further the interest of peace, he encouraged the "Truce of God" and countenanced the ecclesiastical advancement of Gauzlin, the natural brother of Robert the Pious, King of France. This he did because, though illegitimate, Gauzlin was a good man, and his royal brother was very desirous of his promotion (cf. life of Gauzlin, in "Neues Archiv.", III). Benedict VIII was one of the many popes who were called upon to intervene in the interminable strife for precedence between the Patriarchs of Grado and of Aquileia (Dandolo, Chron., IX, 2, n. 2). In 1022 he received Ethelnoth of Canterbury "with great worship and very honourably hallowed him archbishop", and reinstated in his position Leofwine, Abbot of Ely (A. S. Chron., 125, 6, R. S.). A friend of St. Odilo, Abbot of Cluny, and one of the few popes of the Middle Ages who was at once powerful at home and great abroad, Benedict VIII has, on seemingly insufficient grounds, been accused of avarice.

BENEDICT IX, POPE.—The nephew of his two immediate predecessors, Benedict IX was a man of very different character to either of them. He was a disgrace to the Chair of Peter. Regarding it as a sort of heirloom, his father Alberic placed him upon it when a mere youth, not, however, apparently of only twelve years of age (according to Raoul Glaber, Hist., IV, 5, n. 17. Cf. V, 5, n. 26), but of about twenty (October, 1032). Of his pontifical acts little is known, except that he held two or three synods in Rome and granted a number of privileges to various churches and monasteries. He insisted that Bretislav, Duke of Bohemia, should found a monastery, for having carried off the body of St. Adalbert from Poland. In 1037 he went north to meet the Emperor Conrad and excommunicated Heribert, Archbishop of Milan, who was at enmity with him (Ann. Hildesheimenses, 1038). Taking advantage of the dissolute life he was leading, one of the factions in the city drove him from it (1044) amid the greatest disorder, and elected an antipope (Sylvester III) in the person of John, Bishop of Sabina (1045—Ann. Romani, init. Victor, Dialogi, III, init.). Benedict, however, succeeded in expelling Sylvester the same year; but, as some say, that he might marry, he resigned his office into the hands of the Archpriest John Gratian for a large sum. John was then elected pope and became Gregory VI (May, 1045). Repenting of his bargain, Benedict endeavoured to depose Gregory. This resulted in the intervention of King Henry III. Benedict, Sylvester, and Gregory were deposed at the Council of Sutri (1046) and a German bishop (Suidger) became Pope Clement II. After his speedy demise, Benedict again seized Rome (November, 1047), but was driven from it to make way for a second German pope, Damasus II (November, 1048). Of the end of Benedict it is impossible to speak with certainty. Some authors suppose him to have been still alive when St. Leo IX died, and never to have ceased endeavouring to seize the papacy. But it is more probable that the truth lies with the tradition of the Abbey of Grottaferrata, first set down by Abbot Luke, who died about 1085, and corroborated by sepulchral and other monuments within its walls. Writing of Bartholomew, its fourth abbot (1065), Luke tells of the youthful pontiff turning from his sin and coming to Bartholomew for a remedy for his disorders. On the saint's advice, Benedict definitely resigned the pontificate and died in penitence at Grottaferrata. [See "St Benedict and Grottaferrata" (Rome, 1895), a work founded on the more important "De Sepulcro Benedicti IX", by Dom Greg. Piacentini (Rome, 1747).]

BENEDICT X, POPE.—The bearer of this name was an antipope in the days of Nicholas II, 1056-61.

The most important source for the history of the first nine popes who bore the name of Benedict is the biographies in the *Liber Pontificalis*, of which the most useful edition is that of DUCHESNE, *Le Liber Pontificalis* (Paris, 1886–92), and the latest that of MOMMSEN, *Gesta Pontif. Roman.* (to the end of the reign of Constantine only, Berlin, 1898). JAFFÉ, *Regesta Pont. Rom.* (2d ed., Leipzig, 1885), gives a summary of the letters of each pope and tells where they may be read at length. Modern accounts of these popes will be found in any large Church History, or history of the City of Rome. The fullest account in English of most of them is to be read in MANN, *Lives of the Popes in the Early Middle Ages* (London, 1902, passim).

HORACE K. MANN.

Benedict XI, POPE (NICHOLAS BOCCASINI), b. at Treviso, Italy, 1240; d. at Perugia, 7 July, 1304. He entered the Dominican Order at the age of fourteen. After fourteen years of study, he became lector of theology, which office he filled for several years. In 1296 he was elected Master General of the Order. As at this time hostility to Boniface VIII was becoming more pronounced, the new general issued an ordinance forbidding his subjects to favour in any way the opponents of the reigning pontiff; he also enjoined on them to defend in their sermons, when opportune, the legitimacy of the election of Boniface. This loyalty of Boccasini, which remained unshaken to the end,

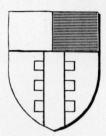

ARMS OF BENEDICT XI

was recognized by Boniface, who showed him many marks of favour and confidence. Thus with the two cardinal-legates, the Dominican General formed the important embassy, the purpose of which was the concluding of an armistice between Edward I of England and Philip IV of France, then at war with each other. In the year 1298 Boccasini was elevated to the cardinalate; he was afterwards appointed Bishop of Ostia and Dean of the Sacred College. As at that time Hungary was rent by civil war, the cardinal-bishop was sent thither by the Holy See as legate *a latere* to labour for the restoration of peace. At the time of the return of the legate to Rome, the famous contest of Boniface VIII with Philip the Fair had reached its height. When, in 1303, the enemies of the pope had made themselves masters of the sacred palace, of all the cardinals and prelates only the two Cardinal-Bishops of Ostia and Sabina remained at the side of the venerable Pontiff to defend him from the violence of William of Nogaret and Sciarra Colonna.

A month after this scene of violence, Boniface having died, Boccasini was unanimously elected Pope, 22 October, taking the name of Benedict XI. The principal event of his pontificate was the restoration of peace with the French court. Immediately after his election Philip sent three ambassadors to the pope bearing the royal letter of congratulation. The king, while professing his obedience and devotion, recommended to the benevolence of the pope the Kingdom and Church of France. Benedict, judging a policy of indulgence to be necessary for the restoration of peace with the French court, absolved Philip and his subjects from the censures they had incurred and restored the king and kingdom to the rights and privileges of which they had been deprived by Boniface. The Colonna cardinals were also absolved from their censures, but not reinstated in their former dignities. This policy of leniency Benedict carried out without compromising the dignity of the Holy See or the memory of Boniface VIII. Nogaret and Sciarra Colonna and those implicated in the outrage of Anagni were declared excommunicated and summoned to appear before the pontifical tribunal. After a brief pontificate of eight months, Benedict died suddenly at Perugia. It was suspected, not altogether without reason, that his sudden death was caused by poisoning, through the agency of William of Nogaret. Benedict XI was beatified in the year 1773. His feast is celebrated at Rome and throughout the Dominican Order on the 7th of July. He is the author of a volume of sermons and commentaries on a part of the Gospel of St. Matthew, on the Psalms, the Book of Job, and the Apocalypse.

PTOL. LUC., *Hist. Eccl.*, III, 672; BERNARDUS GUIDONIS, *Vit. pont. rom.*, IX, 1010; *Script. Ord. Præd.*, I, 444; GRANDJEAN, *Les registres de Benoît XI* (Paris, 1883); FUNKE, *Papst Benedikt*

XI (Münster, 1891); Artaud de Montor, *History of the Popes* (New York, 1867), I, 481–484; *Année Dominicaine*, vii, 125–54; 874–77, and the monograph of Ferreton (Treviso, 1904).

M. A. Waldron.

Benedict XII (Jacques Fournier), third of the Avignon popes, b. at Saverdun in the province of Toulouse, France, elected 20 December, 1334; d. at Avignon 24 April, 1342. Nothing is known of his parentage or boyhood. In youth he became a Cistercian monk in the monastery of Boulbonne, whence he moved to that of Fontfroide, whose abbot was his natural uncle, Arnold Novelli, by whose name Fournier was also known. He studied at the University of Paris, where he received the doctorate in theology. Meantime he was made Abbot of Fontfroide, succeeding his uncle who was created cardinal 19 December, 1310. In December

Arms of Benedict XII

1317, he became Bishop of his native Diocese of Palmiers, was translated to Mirepoix 26 January, 1327, and was made cardinal by Pope John XXII, 18 December, 1327. On the latter's death, 4 December, 1334, the cardinals in conclave, most of whom opposed a return to Rome, demanded of Cardinal de Comminges whose election seemed assured, the promise to remain at Avignon. His refusal precipitated an unexpected canvass for candidates. On the first ballot, 20 December, 1334, many electors, intending to sound the mind of the conclave, voted for the unlikely Cardinal Fournier, who, though he was one of the few men of real merit in the college, was but lightly regarded because of his obscure origin and lack of wealth and following. He amazed the conclave by receiving the necessary two-thirds vote. On 8 January, 1335, he was enthroned as Benedict XII.

Resolved to re-establish the papacy at Rome, Benedict signalized his accession by providing for the restoration of St. Peter's basilica and the Lateran. He was prepared to acquiesce in the petition of a Roman deputation soliciting his return, but his cardinals pictured the impossibility of living in faction-rent Italy. They were right, whatever were their motives, and Benedict yielded. Conscience-stricken during a critical illness, he proposed as a compromise a transfer of his court to Bologna. The cardinals urged the slender hope of securing obedience, and Benedict decided to remain at Avignon, where in 1339 he commenced to build the massive papal castle which still exists. Mindful always of distracted Italy, he often sent money to succour the famine-stricken people and to restore churches. Reform of abuse was Benedict's chief concern. Immediately after his elevation he remanded to their benefices clerics not needed at Avignon, and menaced with summary chastisement violators of the law of residence. He revoked the scandalous "expectancies" granted by his predecessors and forbade conferring benefices *in commendam*. (See Commendatory Abbot.) He condemned unseemly "pluralities" and conferred benefices with such conscientious discrimination that several were left long vacant, and so gave colour to the calumny that he was himself harvesting their revenues. He inveighed vigorously against greed for gain among ecclesiastics; regulated the taxes on documents issued by papal bureaux; made episcopal visitation less of a financial burden to the clergy; abolished the practice of countersigning requests for papal favours, which was extremely lucrative to venal officials; and established the Registry of Supplications for the control of such petitions. Abhorring nepotism, he granted preferment to but one relative, naming the eminent John Bauzian Archbishop of Arles in deference to the insistence of the cardinals; he compelled his only niece to discourage noble suitors and marry one of her own humble rank. A legend, vouched for by Ægidius of Viterbo (d. 1532), accredits him with saying, "a pope should be like Melchisedech, without father, mother, or genealogy". Monastic reform particularly engaged his zeal. Himself a Cistercian, he sought to revive pristine monastic fervour and devotion to study. Pertinent papal constitutions and visitations of monasteries attest his solicitude for a monastic renaissance.

Being a learned theologian, he was as bishop, cardinal, and pope, keenly interested in scholastic discussions. He terminated the controversy on the vexed question as to whether the Beatific Vision was enjoyed before or only after the General Judgment. John XXII had advocated the latter view and stirred up vigorous discussion. Eager to solve the question, Benedict heard the opinions of those maintaining the theory of deferred vision, and, with a commission of theologians, gave four months to patristic research. Their labours terminated in the proclamation (29 January, 1336) of the Bull "Benedictus Deus" defining the immediate intuitive vision of God by the souls of the just having no faults to expiate. Zealous too for the preservation of the Faith, he stimulated the bishops of infected districts to vigilance in the repression of heresy and urged the use of the preventive remedies of the Inquisition. He combatted energetically the anti-papal doctrines which the ecclesiastico-political theorists of the disturbed Avignon period had spread, and which were unfortunately sustained by a school of misguided Franciscans. (See Fraticelli, Marsilius of Padua, William of Occam; Michael of Cesena.) Distressed by disloyalty in Ireland, he tried to persuade Edward III to establish the Inquisition in his realm and urged him to assist the Irish bishops to extirpate heresy. But, though the most ardent foe of heresy, Benedict was remarkably patient and loving in dealing with heretics. He looked also to the interests of the Faith in the East; negotiated for the union of the Eastern Church with Rome through a delegate of the Emperor Andronicus, whose sincerity, however, Benedict was forced to question; manifested his solicitude for the Church in Armenia which, in the early fourteenth century, suffered from Mohammedan invasions, succouring the unfortunates in temporal matters and healing doctrinal differences which had long rent Armenia with schism.

In purely ecclesiastical affairs Benedict's pontificate was creditable to himself and productive of good to the Church. Pious, prudent, and firm, he strove conscientiously to meet the Church's needs at a critical period. In political relations, however, he was not so successful. Inexperienced in politics, he had little taste for diplomacy and an imperfect knowledge of men and affairs of the world. Conflicting political motives confused him, and hesitancy and vacillation contrasted painfully with his firmness and decision in ecclesiastical matters. Though determined to act independently of Philip VI of France, the latter generally succeeded in committing the pope to his policy. He helped to prevent his return to Rome. He frustrated his desire to make peace with the Emperor Louis of Bavaria whom John XXII had excommunicated for fomenting sedition in Italy, proclaiming himself King of the Romans, and intruding an anti-pope. Willing to absolve him should he but submit to the Church, Benedict exposed to Louis's delegates his generous terms of peace (July, 1335). But Philip, aided by the cardinals, persuaded the pope that his generosity encouraged heresy and rebellion. Benedict yielded. Thrice the imperial envoys came to Avignon, but French influence prevailed, and, on 11 April, 1337, Benedict declared it impossible to absolve Louis. The latter, as Benedict feared, allied himself with Edward III of England against France. In vain the pope tried to avert war, but he was no match for the kings and their allies. His good offices were spurned; and he was humiliated by Philip's later alliance with Louis, who had also allied to himself the pope's political and ecclesiastical enemies, and by the emperor's denial of the pope's authority over him, and, worst insult of all, by his usurpation of papal power in declaring the nullity of the marriage of John Henry of Bohemia and Margaret Maultasch, that the latter might marry his son, Louis of Brandenburg. The French king hindered Benedict's projected crusade against the infidels, making the war with England an excuse to forego his promise to lead the armies, and even diverting the money subscribed for it to financing his own wars, despite the protests of the conscientious pope. Benedict's crusading ardour found solace in Spain, where he encouraged the campaign against the Mohammedans who in 1339 invaded the peninsula.

Benedict XII has not escaped calumny. Reformer, foe of heresy, builder of the Avignon papal palace, unwilling ally of France and enemy of Germany, he made many enemies whose misrepresentations have inspired most non-Catholic appreciations of his character. Much harm was done to his memory by the satires of Petrarch, who, though befriended and honoured by Benedict, yet bitterly resented his failure to return to Rome. His natural obesity, too, stimulated caricature and undeserved criticism. But history offers a vindication and testifies that, though he failed to cope successfully with the political difficulties to which he fell heir, his piety, virtue, and pacific spirit, his justice, rectitude, and firmness in ruling, his zeal for doctrinal and moral reform, and his integrity of character were above reproach.

RAYNALDUS, in BARONIUS, *Annales* (Bar-le-Duc, 1872), XXV, 20–274; CHRISTOPHE, *Hist. de la papauté pendant le XIVe siècle* (Paris, 1853), II, 36–79; ROCQUAIN, *La Cour de Rome* (Paris, 1895), II, 437–463; PASTOR-ANTROBUS, *History of the Popes* (St. Louis, 1898), I, 83–86; VIDAL, *Benoît XII: Lettres* (Paris, 1902); DAUMET, *Benoît XII: Lettres* (Paris, 1889); *Acta SS.*, XIII, 83–86; *Liber Pontificalis*, ed. DUCHESNE (Paris, 1886), II, 486, 527; MURATORI, *Rerum Italicarum Scriptores* (Milan, 1734), III–XIII; LE BACHELET in *Dict. théol. cath.*, II, 653–704, an exhaustive theological study with a good bibliography.

JOHN B. PETERSON.

Benedict XIII, POPE (PIETRO FRANCESCO ORSINI), b. 2 February, 1649; d. 23 February, 1730. Being a son of Ferdinando Orsini and Giovanna Frangipani of Tolpha, he belonged to the archducal family Orsini-Gravina. From early youth he exhibited a decided liking for the Order of St. Dominic, and at the age of sixteen during a visit to Venice he entered the Dominican novitiate against the will of his parents, though he was the eldest son and heir to the title and estates of his childless uncle the Duke of Bracciano. Their appeal to Clement IX was fruitless; the pope not only approved the purpose of the young novice, but even shortened his novitiate by half in order to free him from the importunities of his relatives. As student and novice, the young prince was a model of humility and zeal, and devoted himself to the acquisition of ecclesiastical learning. At the age of twenty-one he was promoted to a professorship. On 22 February, 1672, he was elevated to the cardinalate by his relative Clement X. He protested strenuously against this honour, but was compelled to accept it under the vow of obedience by the General of the Dominicans, at the instance of the pope. As cardinal he adhered

ARMS OF BENEDICT XIII

strictly to the observance of the rule of his order, and never laid aside its habit. In 1675 having the choice between the Archbishopric of Salerno and that of Manfredonia (Siponto) he chose the latter because it was a poor diocese and required great exercise of pastoral zeal. His virtuous life not only overcame the opposition made by his relatives when he became a monk, but exercised such a salutary influence that in time his mother, his sister, and two of his nieces embraced the religious life in the Third Order of St. Dominic. During the conclave that followed the death of Clement X (1676), he was one of the band of cardinals known as the *zelanti* who had agreed that no considerations of worldly prudence would influence them in the choice of a new pope. In the government of his diocese, Cardinal Orsini was unremitting in his labours and zeal. He visited even the most remote hamlets and was not less watchful over temporal than over spiritual things. He provided for the needs of the people, repaired churches and held a diocesan synod, the decrees of which he published. In 1680, when Innocent XI transferred him to Cesena, he left to the people of Siponto a memorial of his apostolic activity in a pastoral letter on the rules of Christian life which he had always inculcated. At Cesena his frugality, modesty, and activity, his devotion to the poor and his constant preaching brought about a thorroughgoing reformation among both clergy and people. Seeing on his frequent journeys the condition of the churches in even the poorest parishes, he neglected none and by the promulgation of strict rules, he abolished all known abuses.

In 1686, a serious illness, attributed by his physicians to the climate, caused his transfer to Benevento, where he remained for thirty-eight years or until he was elected pope. During this long period he seldom left his diocese. Each year he made an episcopal visitation to every parish. Whenever necessary, he built or renovated churches. He built hospitals and strove incessantly for the alleviation of the sufferings of the poor. Twice during his episcopate (5 June, 1688, and 14 March, 1702) Benevento was visited by earthquakes and on these occasions his courage, his active charity in behalf of the stricken inhabitants, and his energy in the reconstruction of the city, won for him the title of the "Second Founder" of Benevento. He held two provincial synods, the first in 1693 attended by eighteen bishops, the second in 1698, with an attendance of twenty, the acts of which were approved at Rome. The only reproach made against his administration is that his simplicity and childlike confidence exposed him to the wiles of some unscrupulous persons who abused his confidence.

Cardinal Orsini had already taken part in four conclaves, when Innocent XIII died in March, 1724; and in all he had acted in the spirit of the *zelanti*. The conclave at which he was himself chosen assembled on 20 March; two months afterwards (25 May) no choice had been made. This long delay weighed heavily on the soul of Orsini, who commenced a novena of prayers to his patron, St. Philip Neri, that the election of a new pope might be no longer delayed. Before the novena was finished he saw with terror that he himself would be chosen, and, reluctant to accept a position which filled him with dread, he sought by all means in his power to prevent his election. Against his oft repeated protestations he was chosen 29 May, 1724, and even after the final vote was taken he refused to yield, arguing that his age, his physical weakness, his incapacity, and a resolution which he made never to become pope, should exempt him from such a grave responsibility. He yielded only when it was made clear to him that grave dangers were to be feared if the conclave should be reopened. So with tears, and obeying the command of the general of his order, he allowed himself to be proclaimed pope. In honour of Benedict XI, a member of the Dominican Order, he took the name of Benedict XIV, which he shortly changed to Benedict XIII as Peter de Luna who had previously borne the name (1394–1423) was a schismatic.

His first concern as pope was to enforce rigidly ecclesiastical discipline. He issued several decrees on ecclesiastical dress and was unsparing in his efforts to aDolisH any semblance of luxury or worldly pomp among the cardinals. During the Jubilee of 1725, he discharged personally the duties of Grand Penitentiary, and is said to have seriously considered the revival of public penances for certain grave offences. In order to encourage the foundation of diocesan seminaries, he organized a special commission (*Congregatio Seminariorum*). At a provincial Roman Lateran synod held in 1725, he required an unqualified acceptance of the Bull "Unigenitus" and through his efforts Cardinal de Noailles, Archbishop of Paris, was led to accept it in 1728. During his pontificate Benedict retained the Archbishopric of Benevento which he administered by a vicar-general and which he twice visited (1727, 1729).

In diplomatic matters and in his relations with foreign powers Benedict did not exhibit the vigour and conservatism which marked his administration in religious matters. His love of peace led him to attempt a settlement of the dispute in regard to the ecclesiastical privileges of the Kings of Naples (*Monarchia Sicula*) by a revocation of the constitution of Clement XI (1715) and by granting to the King of Naples (and Sicily) and his successors the right to appoint a spiritual judge in ecclesiastical affairs, reserving, however, the most important cases to the Holy See. The quarrel with Victor Amadeus of Savoy was compounded by giving to the king the right of patronage over the churches and monasteries in his dominions, without, however, conceding any claim to the incomes from vacant benefices. Towards John V, King of Portugal, the pope exhibited extraordinary firmness in refusing a claim based on the privilege held by other courts to propose candidates for the cardinalate. This was in consequence of the protests made by the cardinals against the elevation of Vincenzo Biechi, Nuncio to Lisbon. In retaliation John recalled all Portuguese residents in Rome, forbade all communication with the Roman Curia, and attempted to prevent the sending of the customary alms from Portugal to Rome; he also interfered with applications for dispensations from matrimonial impediments. At many courts of Europe grave offence was taken by the extension (1728) to the Universal Church of the Office of Gregory VII containing an account of the excommunication and deposition of Henry IV, which to Gallicans and Protestants seemed offensive.

Although full justice can scarcely be done to the virtuous life and the fatherly zeal for the interests of religion of Benedict, his pontificate lost much of its lustre because of his misplaced confidence in Cardinal Nicolò Coscia, who had been his coadjutor at Benevento. The pope was ignorant of the peculations and venality of his favourite, whose greed did much to diminish the prestige of the Holy See, and against whom a popular uprising took place on the pope's death, resulting in a ten years' imprisonment for this unworthy cardinal. Benedict's theological writings were published in three volumes (Ravenna, 1728).

QUÉTIF-ECHARD, *Script. Ord. Præd.*, I, 814; CAVALIERI, *Galleria de' sommi pontefici, Patriarchi . . . dell' O. P.* (Benevento, 1696), I, 668; PITTONI, *Vita del sommo pontefice Benedetto XIII* (Venice, 1730); BORGIA, *Benedicti XIII vita* (Rome, 1752); GUARNACCI, *Hist. pontif. roman.*, I, 39, II, 409 sqq.; SANDINI, *Vitæ pontif. roman.* (Rome, 1763); GRONE, *Papstgeschichte* (Ratisbon, 1875); SENTIS, *Die Monarchia Sicula* (Freiburg, 1869), 159 sqq.; ARTAUD DE MONTOR, *History of the Roman Pontiffs* (New York, 1867), II.

PATRICK J. HEALY.

Benedict XIV (PROSPERO LORENZO LAMBERTINI), son of Marcello Lambertini and Lucretia Bulgarini, b. at Bologna 31 March, 1675; d. 3 May, 1758. His early education was received from tutors. At the age of thirteen he went to the Collegium Clementinum in Rome where he studied rhetoric, philosophy, and theology. St. Thomas Aquinas was his favourite author, but the bent of his own mind was towards historical and legal studies in which latter he excelled, as well in civil as in ecclesiastical law. In 1694, though only nineteen, he received the degree of Doctor of Theology and *Doctor Utriusque Juris* (canon and civil law). On the death of Innocent XII he was made consistorial advocate by Clement XI, and shortly afterwards Consultor of the Holy Office. In 1708 he was appointed Promoter of the Faith; in 1712 canon theologian at the Vatican and assessor of the Congregation of Rites; in 1713 he was named domestic prelate; in 1718 secretary of the Congregation of the Council; and in 1725 titular Bishop of Theodosia. He was made Bishop of Ancona in 1727 and cardinal 30 April, 1728. He was transferred to the Archbishopric of Bologna in April, 1731, in succession to Lorenzo Corsini who had become pope as Clement XII.

ARMS OF BENEDICT XIV

Benedict XIV is best known to history as a student and a scholar. Though by no means a genius, his enormous application coupled with more than ordinary cleverness of mind made him one of the most erudite men of his time and gave him the distinction of being perhaps the greatest scholar among the popes. His character was many-sided, and his range of interests large. His devotion to science and the serious investigation of historical problems did not interfere with his purely literary studies. "I have been reproached", he once said, "because of my familiarity with Tasso and Dante and Ariosto, but they are a necessity to me in order to give energy to my thought and life to my style." This devotion to the arts and sciences brought Lambertini throughout his whole life into close and friendly contact with the most famous authors and scholars of his time. Montfaucon, whom he knew in Rome, said of him: "Young as he is, he has two souls: one for science, the other for society." This last characterization did not interfere with his restless activity in any of the many important positions which he was called on to fill, nor did it diminish his marvellous capacity for the most arduous work.

The zeal and energy which Lambertini carried to this office infused new life into all his subjects. He himself explained his assiduity by saying that he looked on the episcopate not as an honour, but as an opportunity to do good. His administration was exemplary: he visited all parts of his diocese, held synods, incited the people to piety by word and example, and supervised the affairs of his diocese so thoroughly that nothing needing change or correction escaped him. His humility and vast learning were a source of inspiration and strength to his clergy, and his broad firm grasp of public affairs and public questions gave him a position of unique influence among rulers and people. In his opinion the foundation of success in episcopal administration was thorough harmony between bishop and clergy, and this he succeeded in obtaining. Because of his wonderful gifts and his extraordinary success as Bishop of Ancona, Pope Benedict XIII wished to transfer him to some position of greater responsibility affording a wider field for the display of his powers and activity, but he replied in his usual jocose vein that no change of place could make him other than he was, cheerful, joyous, and the friend of the pope. When he was transferred to Bologna in 1731 his energies and activities seemed to redouble. He became all things to all men and is said to have never allowed anyone to leave his presence dissatisfied or in anger, and without being strengthened and refreshed by his wisdom, advice, or admonitions. His efforts were largely directed to the improvement of clerical education in his diocese. He reformed the programme of studies in his seminary and drew up a new curriculum in which special stress was laid on the study of Sacred Scripture and patrology.

POPE BENEDICT XIV

When Clement XII died (6 February, 1740) the fame of Lambertini was at its highest. Through intrigues of various kinds the conclave which commenced on 17 February lasted for six months. It was composed of fifty-four cardinals of whom forty-six were Italians, three French, four Spanish, and one German. These were split into several parties. One was composed of those who had been appointed by Clement XI, Innocent XIII, and Benedict XIII; another of those appointed by Clement XII who were known as the new college. The long, tedious session and the intense heat did not improve the temper of the cardinals; after six months of fruitless effort and constant intrigue, the election seemed no nearer than in the beginning. Various expedients were suggested, such as the withdrawal of the names of the leading candidates and the substitution of others, but without avail. After several plans had been tried to end the deadlock, Lambertini, whose name had been proposed as a compromise, addressed the conclave, saying: "If you wish to elect a saint, choose Gotti; a statesman, Aldobrandini; an honest man, elect me." These words spoken as much perhaps in jest as in earnest helped to end the difficulty. Lambertini was chosen and took the name of Benedict XIV in honour of his friend and patron Benedict XIII. As pope, Lambertini was no less energetic, brave, and unassuming than before his election. His great learning placed him in a position to deal successfully with ecclesiastical situations that needed reformation, and the broad Christian spirit which animated his dealings with foreign powers removed the pressure and hostility of even Protestant courts and rulers. He was undoubtedly liberal in his political dealings, though he never lost sight of the essential interests of the Church and religion.

PUBLIC POLICY.—To go to the extreme limit of concession and conciliation seems to have been the principle that dominated all Benedict's actions in his negotiations with governments and rulers, so much so, indeed, that he has not escaped criticism even from those within the Church as being too prone to settle difficulties by making concessions or compromises. However his actions may be judged, and whatever may be thought of his motives, it cannot be denied that he aimed constantly at peace and that few causes of friction remained after the close of his administration. Moreover, in estimating the value and effect of his concessions, it is seen that in nearly every case he strengthened the moral influence of the papacy even though some rights of patronage or other material interests were abandoned. Nor was his influence less potent among Protestant than Catholic rulers; the universal esteem in which he was held throughout the world meant much in an epoch, the close of which was to witness the disruption of many time-honoured institutions, social and political as well as religious. An enumeration of his principal dealings with the heads of states will show that Benedict wisely abandoned, in most cases, the shadow of temporal authority to maintain the substance of spiritual supremacy.

The King of Portugal received the right of patronage over all the sees and abbeys in his kingdom (1740) and was further favoured with the title of *Rex Fidelissimus* (1748). In the matter of church revenues and the allotment of ecclesiastical benefices Spain was also treated very generously. In 1741 permission was granted to tax the income of the clergy, and in 1753 the Government received the right of nomination to nearly all the Spanish benefices; in 1754 an agreement was ratified by which the revenues from all the benefices in Spain and in the American colonies were paid into the government treasury to carry on the war against the African pirates. The King of Sardinia received the title of Vicar of the Holy See which carried with it the right of nomination to all ecclesiastical benefices in his dominions and the income of the pontifical fiefs in lieu of which a yearly indemnity of one thousand ducats was to be paid. Through the mediation of the pope a tribunal was established in Naples consisting of an equal number of clerical and lay members presided over by an ecclesiastic, which formed the final court for the trial of ecclesiastical cases. As mediator between the Knights of Malta and the King of Naples the pope brought a long standing controversy to a happy termination. By the Encyclical "Ex omnibus christiani orbis" (16 October, 1756), the bitter controversy regarding the question of admitting to the sacraments persons who would not accept the Bull "Unigenitus" was brought to a close. While insisting on the authority of the "Unigenitus" and pointing out that it was the duty of all the faithful to accept it with veneration, the pope decrees that only those persons should be excluded from the sacraments whose opposition to the pontifical constitution was public and notorious, and who therefore should be regarded as public enemies. The title of King of Prussia, taken in 1701 by the Elector of Brandenburg, was recognized by Benedict against the vigorous opposition of many members of the Curia. He was referred to as the *sage par excellence* by Maria Theresa, and received many encomiums from the sultan to whom he playfully referred in his writings as the "Good Turk". At the close of his pontificate the only question of importance in the foreign relations of the Holy See which had not been successfully settled was that concerning the Patriarchate of Aquileia over which the Republic of Venice and the emperor claimed control. Benedict decided that the rights of the patriarchate should be divided between the Archbishopric of Görz, in Austria, and that of Udine in the Venetian States. This decision was regarded as unjust by Venice, which in retaliation decreed that no Bull, Brief, or communication of the Holy See should be promulgated within the jurisdiction of the Republic without the supervision and approval of the Government.

TEMPORAL AND SPIRITUAL RULER.—As temporal sovereign Benedict governed the States of the Church with wisdom and moderation and introduced many reforms for the purpose of diminishing abuses and promoting the happiness and prosperity of the people. With a view to replenishing the treasury which had been exhausted by the extravagance of some of his predecessors, especially that of Benedict XIII under the influence of Cardinal Coscia, and because of the enormous outlay for public buildings under Clement XII, he made no promotions to the Sacred College for four years. Measures were set on foot to reform the nobility, a new regional division of the city was introduced for the purpose of greater administrative efficiency, agriculture was fostered and encouraged by the introduction of new and improved methods, commerce was promoted, and luxury restrained, while the practice of usury, against which he published the Encyclical "Vix Pervenit" (1745), was almost entirely suppressed. (See USURY.) Benedict abandoned none of the claims of his predecessors, but the liberal use of his powers had no other aim than the promotion of the arts of peace and industry. How serious the problem was is best seen from his own words: "The pope orders, the cardinals do not obey, and the people do as they please."

In purely spiritual and religious matters the influence of Benedict left a lasting impress on the entire Church and its administration. His Bulls and Encyclicals, which have played such an important part in defining and clarifying obscure and difficult points of ecclesiastical law, were learned treatises full of wisdom and scholarship. The vexed question of mixed marriages, unions between Catholics and Protestants, demanded settlement in consequence of the increasing frequency with which they occurred. Much of the bitterness of the Reformation time had passed away and Protestants sought to have their marriages with Catholics solemnized with ceremonies equal to those when both parties were Catholics. Though the doctrine prevailed in Rome that the contracting parties were the real ministers of the Sacrament of Matrimony, no general unanimity prevailed among theologians on this point. Without derogating in the least from this theory, Benedict in reply to the questions from bishops in many places, especially in Holland and Poland, decreed by the Bull "Magnæ nobis admirationis" (29 June, 1748) that mixed marriages were allowable only under certain well-defined conditions, the principal of which was that children born of those marriages should be brought up in the Catholic Faith, but that such marriages while tolerated, should never be performed with the ceremonies that imply formal ecclesiastical approval.

RELATIONS WITH EASTERN CHURCHES.—Under the skilful hand of Benedict a formal union was consummated with some of the Eastern Churches. The frequent attempts of the Greek Melchite Patriarchs of Alexandria, Antioch, and Jerusalem to obtain recognition from the Holy See did not for a long time result in any definite union, because of dissatisfaction on the part of the popes with the formulation of the Oriental creeds. In 1744, Benedict XIV sent the pallium to Seraphin Tanas whom he acknowledged as Patriarch of the Greek Melchites of Antioch. The conflicts in the Maronite Church, after the deposition of Jacob II, which seriously threatened its unity were settled in a national council (1736), the decrees of which were approved by Benedict. On 18 March, 1751, he renewed the prohibitions of Clement XII against the Freemasons, and though very few governments regarded the suppression of this society as demanding decisive action on their part, laws were at once passed by Spain and Naples, and in 1757 by Milan. The controversy in regard to Chinese and Malabar customs, or the system of accommodation to heathenism which some missionaries had permitted their converts to practice, and by which it was said

that pagan ideas and pagan practices had been grafted on Christianity, was terminated by Benedict XIV who issued two Bulls on the subject, and required the missionaries to take an oath that such abuses would not be tolerated in the future. The Bull "Ex quo singulari", in regard to the abuses in China, was published 11 July, 1742; that in regard to Malabar, "Omnium sollicitudinum", 12 September, 1744. (See CHINA, INDIA.) Because of the manner in which church festivals had been multiplied, Benedict strove to diminish them. This he did in Spain in 1742, in Sicily and Tuscany in 1748, and later in Sardinia, Austria, and the Papal States. Such a move met with much opposition from many cardinals. Benedict silenced their reproaches by saying that fewer feasts observed in a more Christian manner would contribute more to the glory of religion.

LITURGICAL REFORMS.—In liturgical matters Benedict XIV was extremely conservative. He viewed with grief the profound changes which had been introduced into the Roman Calendar since the time of Pius V. The increase in the number of Feasts of Saints and the multiplication of offices with the rank of *Duplex* had superseded the old ferial and dominical offices, and throughout his entire pontificate he set himself determinedly against the introduction of any new offices in the Breviary, a policy which he adhered to so strictly that the only change it underwent during his administration was that Leo the Great received the title of Doctor. So profoundly impressed was he with the necessity of a thorough revision of the Breviary which would eliminate those portions with which the critical sense of the eighteenth century found fault that he commissioned the Jesuit, Fabio Danzetto, to prepare a report on the subject. This report in four volumes of notes was of such a sweeping character that it is said to have caused Benedict to desist from his project. The plan of reforming the Roman Martyrology was, however, carried to a successful issue, and a new edition was published by his authority in Rome in 1748. The same is true of the "Cæremoniale Episcoporum", which Benedict XIII undertook to reform and which Benedict XIV published (1752) in the now usual form. The classical work of Benedict on liturgical matters is his "De Servorum Dei Beatificatione et de Beatorum Canonizatione" which still regulates the process of beatification and canonization. Other important liturgical writings of Benedict deal with the sacrifice of the Mass and the feasts of Our Lord, the Blessed Virgin, and some saints. Besides these he published numerous works on the rites of the Greeks and Orientals; Bulls and Briefs on the celebration of the octave of the Holy Apostles, against the use of superstitious images, on the blessing of the pallium, against profane music in churches, on the golden rose, etc.

In order that the clergy should not be deficient in ecclesiastical and historical science, and that they might not lack opportunity to profit by the intellectual progress of the period, he founded at Rome four academies for the study of Roman antiquities, Christian antiquities, the history of the Church and the councils, and the history of canon law and liturgy. He also established a Christian museum, and commissioned Joseph Assemani to prepare a catalogue of the manuscripts in the Vatican Library which he enriched by the purchase of the Ottobonian Library containing 3,300 MSS. of unique value and importance. He founded chairs of chemistry and mathematics in the Roman university known as the Sapienza, and many others for painting, sculpture, etc., at other schools. Over all these foundations he exercised the closest supervision; he also found time to carry out many schemes for the building and adornment of churches in Rome. The fact that Benedict never raised a Jesuit to the cardinalate is attributed to his hostility to the Society; on the other hand, it must be noted that it was to a Jesuit, Emmanuel Azevedo, that he committed the complete edition of his works (1747–51). He had been long urged by his friends Cardinals Passionei and Archinto to order a thorough reformation of that body, but it was not until the last year of his life that any decisive action was taken. On 1 April, 1758, he issued a Brief by which Cardinal Saldanha was commissioned to inspect all the colleges and houses of the Society in Portugal, and to undertake a reform of the same, but this authority was withdrawn by his successor, Clement XIII.

Benedict XIV sought recreation in the society of learned men and artists, among whom he shone as a wit and a scholar. Gay, lively, and talkative, his conversation at times amazed, if it did not shock, the staid sensibilities of some of the dignified courtiers who came in contact with him. Mild and gracious in

TOMB OF BENEDICT XIV

his demeanour to all who approached him, the pope was at times lacking neither in energy nor spirit. On one occasion a violent scene took place in which the pope expressed in a most decided manner his disapproval of the tactics of the French court. Choiseul, the French ambassador, called at the Vatican to request that the appointment of Cardinal Archinto to succeed Cardinal Valenti as Secretary of State be deferred until after some matters in which the French king was interested were decided. Choiseul himself gives an account of this scene (Letters, p. 169), without, however, relating all the details. The conversation was more lively than Choiseul reported, and from the "Mémoires" of the Baron de Besonval (p. 106) we learn that when the pope had grown tired of the importunities of Choiseul he seized him by the arm and pushing him into his own seat said: "Be pope yourself" (*Fa el Papa*). Choiseul replied: "No, Holy Father, let us each do his part. You

continue to be pope and I shall be ambassador." This brusqueness, however, was not usual with Benedict. He could be gay as well as serious. The Abbate Galiani once presented him with a collection of minerals saying: *Dic ut lapides isti panes fiant* (Command that these stones be made bread), and the hint was not lost. The miracle requested was performed and the abbé received a pension.

To his subjects Benedict was an idol. If they complained at times that he wrote too much and governed them too little, they all agreed that he spoke well and wittily, and his jokes and bon mots were the delight of Rome. Cares of state, after his elevation to the pontificate prevented him from devoting himself as much as he would have wished to his studies of former days; but he never lacked intellectual stimulus. He surrounded himself with such men as Quirini, Garampi, Borgia, Muratori, and carried on an active correspondence with scholars of many shades of opinion. His intellectual pre-eminence was not only a source of pride to Catholics, but formed a strong bond with many not of the Faith. Voltaire dedicated to him his "Mahomet" with the words: "Au chef de la véritable religion un écrit contre le fondateur d'une religion fausse et barbare". On another occasion he composed for a portrait of the pope the following distich:

Lambertinus hic est, Romæ decus, et pater orbis,
Qui mundum scriptis docuit, virtutibus ornat.

(This is Lambertini, the pride of Rome, the father of the world, who teaches that world by his writings and honours by his virtues.) The distich caused discussion regarding the quantity of "hic", but the pope defended the prosody of Voltaire who confirmed his opinion by a quotation from Virgil which he said ought to be the epitaph of Benedict.

Great as a man, a scholar, an administrator, and a priest, Benedict's claim to immortality rests principally on his admirable ecclesiastical writings. The most important of them, besides those already mentioned, are: "Institutiones Ecclesiasticæ", written in Italian, but translated into Latin by P. Ildephonsus a S. Carolo; it is a collection of 107 documents, principally pastoral letters, letters to bishops and others, independent treatises, instructions, etc., all of which are really scientific dissertations on subjects connected with church law or the care of souls; the classical work "De Synodo Diœcesanâ", published after his elevation to the papacy, an adaptation to diocesan administration of the general ecclesiastical law; this book is called by Schulte, because of its influence, one of the most important, if not the most important, modern work in canon law; "Casus Conscientiæ de mandato Prosp. Lambertini Archiep. Bonon proposition et resoluti", valuable for the lawyer as well as the confessor; "Bullarium Benedicti XIV", which contains the legislation of his pontificate, many of its documents being scientific treatises. He also compiled a "Thesaurus Resolutionum Sacræ Congregationis Concilii", the first attempt at a scientific presentation of the "Praxis" of the Roman Congregations. A complete edition of his works appeared at Rome (1747–51) in twelve folio volumes, by Emmanuel Azevedo, S.J., who also translated into Latin the Italian documents. A better and more complete edition is that of Venice, 1788. The latest and most serviceable (Prato, 1844) is in seventeen volumes. Some letters of Benedict were published by Kraus: "Briefe Benedicts XIV an den Canonicus Pier Francesco Peggi in Bologna (1729–1758) nebst Benedicts Diarium des Conclaves von 1740" (2d ed., Freiburg, 1888). Cf. Batiffol, "Inventaire des lettres inédites du Pape Bénoît XIV" (Paris, 1894); R. De Martinis, "Acta Benedicti XIV" (Naples, 1884, *passim*). In 1904 Heiner edited three hitherto unpublished treatises of Benedict XIV on rites, the feasts of the Apostles, and the Sacraments.

The best account of the writings of Benedict and the sources for his life are contained in the above-mentioned work of KRAUS. See also GUARNACCI, *Vitæ et res gestæ Romanor. Pontif. et Card. a Clem. X usque ad Clem. XI* (Rome, 1857); NOVAES, *Storia de' Sommi Pontefici* (Rome, 1822); RANKE, *Die röm. Päpste in den letzten vier Jahrh.* (Leipzig, ed. 1900); *Vie du Pape Bened. XIV* (Paris, 1783); GRÖNE, *Papst-Geschichte* (Ratisbon, 1875), II. For a long account of the Curia and the character of the cardinals in the time of Benedict XIV, see CHOISEUL, *Lettres et Mémoires inédites, publiées par Maurice Boutry* (Paris, 1895). On Benedict as a canonist see SCHULTE, *Gesch. der Quellen und Litt. des can. Rechts* (Stuttgart, 1880), III. 503 sqq.

PATRICK J. HEALY.

Benedict, RULE OF SAINT.—This work holds the first place among monastic legislative codes, and was by far the most important factor in the organization and spread of monasticism in the West. For its general character and also its illustration of St. Benedict's own life, see the article BENEDICT, SAINT. Here, however, it is treated more in detail, under the following heads: I. The Text of the Rule; II. Analysis of the Rule; III. Practical Working of the Rule.

I. THE TEXT OF THE RULE.—The exact time and place at which St. Benedict wrote his Rule are not known, nor can it be determined whether the Rule, as we now possess it, was composed as a single whole or whether it gradually took shape in response to the needs of his monks. Somewhere about 530, however, may be taken as a likely date, and Monte Cassino as a more probable place than Subiaco, for the Rule certainly reflects St. Benedict's matured monastic and spiritual wisdom. The earliest chronicler says that when Monte Cassino was destroyed by the Lombards in

RULE OF ST. BENEDICT, MS. A.D. 1129
(British Museum)

581, the monks fled to Rome, carrying with them, among other treasures, a copy of the Rule "which the holy Father had composed"; and in the middle of the eighth century there was in the pope's library a copy believed to be St. Benedict's autograph. It has been assumed by many scholars that this was the copy brought from Monte Cassino; but though the supposition is likely enough, it is not a certainty. Be that as it may, this MS. of the Rule was presented by Pope Zachary to Monte Cassino in the middle of the eighth century, a short time after the restoration of that monastery. Charlemagne found it there when he visited Monte Cassino

towards the end of the century, and at his request a most careful transcript of it was made for him, as an exemplar of the text to be disseminated throughout the monasteries of his empire. Several copies of the Rule were made from it, one of which survives to this day; for there can be no doubt that the present Codex 914 of the St. Gall Library was copied directly from Charlemagne's copy for the Abbey of Reichenau. An exact diplomatic reprint (not in facsimile) of this codex was published at Monte Cassino in 1900, so that the text of this MS., certainly the best individual text of the Rule in existence, can be studied without difficulty. Various other MSS. go back to Charlemagne's MS., or to its original at Monte Cassino, which was destroyed by fire in 896, and thus the text of the so-called autograph may be restored by approved critical methods with quite unusual certainty, and could we be certain that it really was the autograph, there would be no more to say.

But as already pointed out, it is not quite certain that it was St. Benedict's autograph, and the case is complicated by the circumstance that there is in the field another type of text, represented by the oldest known MS., the Oxford Hatton MS. 42, and by other very early authorities, which certainly was the text most widely diffused in the seventh and eighth centuries. Whether this text was St. Benedict's first recension and the "autograph" his later revision, or whether the former is but a corrupted form of the latter, is a question which is still under debate, though the majority of critics lean towards the second alternative. In either case, however, the text of the "autograph" is the one to be adopted. The MSS., from the tenth century onwards, and the ordinary printed editions, give mixed texts, made up out of the two earliest types. Thus the text in current use is critically a bad one, but very few of the readings make any substantial difference.

The Rule was written in the *Lingua Vulgaris* or Low Latin vernacular of the time, and contains much syntax and orthography not in conformance with classical models. There is as yet no edition of the Rule that satisfies the requirements of modern criticism, though one is in process of preparation for the Vienna "Corpus" of Latin Ecclesiastical writers.

A sufficiently good manual edition was published by Dom Edmund Schmidt, of Metten, at Ratisbon in 1892, presenting in substance the text of the St. Gall MS., with the Low Latin element eliminated.

The number of commentators on the Rule is legion. Calmet gives a list of over one hundred and thirty such writers, and Ziegelbauer gives a similar list. The earliest commentary, in point of date, is that which has been variously ascribed to Paul Warnefrid (a monk of Monte Cassino about 780–799), Hildemar, Ruthard of Hirsau, and others. Hildemar, a Gallic monk, brought to Italy by Angelbert, Archbishop of Milan, reformed the monastery of Sts. Faustinus and Jovita at Brescia and died in 840. Martène, who considered this commentary to be the best ever produced, maintained that Hildemar was its real author, but modern critics attribute it to Paul Warnefrid. Amongst other commentators the following deserve mention: St. Hildegarde (d. 1178), the foundress and first Abbess of Mount St. Rupert, near Bingen on the Rhine, who held that St. Benedict's prohibition of flesh-meat did not include that of birds; Bernard, Abbot of Monte Cassino, formerly of Lérins and afterwards a cardinal (d. 1282); Turrecremata (Torquemada) a Dominican (1468); Trithemius, Abbot of Sponheim (1516); Perez, Archbishop of Tarragona and Superior-General of the congregation of Valladolid; Haeften, Prior of Afflighem (1648); Stengel, Abbot of Anhausen (1663); Mège (1691) and Martène (1739), Maurists; Calmet, Abbot of Senones (1757); and Mabillon (1707), who discusses at length several portions of the Rule in his Prefaces to the different volumes of the "Acta Sanctorum O. S. B."

It is impossible to gauge the comparative value of these and other commentaries, because the different authors treat the Rule from different points of view. That of Calmet is perhaps the most literal and is exhaustive on many important points; those of Martène and Haeften are mines of information regarding monastic tradition; Perez and Mège are practical and pious, though the latter has been considered lax in many of the views maintained; that of Turrecremata is useful as treating the Rule from the standpoint of moral theology; and others give mystical interpretations of its contents. It may here be pointed out that in studying the Rule as a practical code of monastic legislation, it is necessary to remember that in order to facilitate uniformity of observance, each congregation of the order has also its own Constitutions, approved by the Holy See, by which are regulated many matters of detail not touched upon in the Rule itself.

Before proceeding to analyze St. Benedict's Rule and to discuss its leading characteristics, something must be said about the monasticism that preceded his times, and out of which his system grew, in order that some idea may be gained as to how much of the Rule was borrowed from his precursors and how much was due to his own initiative. Such considerations are important because there is no doubt whatever that the introduction and propagation of St. Benedict's Rule was the turning-point which changed the whole trend of monasticism in the West.

The earliest forms of Christian monachism were characterized by their extreme austerity and by their more or less eremitical nature. In Egypt the followers of St. Anthony were purely eremitical, whilst those who followed the Rule of St. Pachomius, though they more nearly approached the cenobitical ideal, were yet without that element of stability insisted upon by St. Benedict, viz: the "common life" and family spirit. Under the Antonian system the austerities of the monks were left entirely to their own discretion; under the Pachomian, though there was an obligatory rule of limited severity, the monks were free to add to it

what other ascetical practices they chose. And, in both, the prevailing idea was that they were spiritual athletes, and as such they rivalled each other in austerity. Syrian and strictly Oriental monasticism need not be considered here, as it had no direct influence on that of Europe. When St. Basil (fourth century) organized Greek monasticism, he set himself against the eremitical life and insisted upon a community life, with meals, work, and prayer, all in common. With him the practice of austerity, unlike that of the Egyptians, was to be subject to the control of the superior, for he considered that to wear out the body by austerities so as to make it unfit for work, was a misconception of the Scriptural precept of penance and mortification. His idea of the monastic life was the result of the contact of primitive ideas, as existing in Egypt and the East, with European culture and modes of thought.

Monasticism came into Western Europe from Egypt. In Italy, as also in Gaul, it was chiefly Antonian in character, though both the rules of St. Basil and St. Pachomius were translated into Latin and doubtless made their influence felt. As far as we know, each monastery had practically its own rule, and we have examples of this irresponsible form of monastic life in the community which St. Benedict was called from his cave to govern, and in the *Gyrovagi* and *Sarabaitæ* whom he mentions in terms of condemnation in the first chapter of his Rule. A proof that the pervading spirit of Italian monachism was Egyptian lies in the fact that when St. Benedict determined to forsake the world and become a monk, he adopted, almost as a matter of course, the life of a solitary in a cave. His familiarity with the rules and other documents bearing upon the life of the Egyptian monks is shown by his legislating for the daily reading of the "Conferences" of Cassian, and by his recommendation (c. lxxiii) of the "Institutes" and "Lives" of the Fathers and the Rule of St. Basil.

When, therefore, St. Benedict came to write his own Rule for the monasteries he had founded, he embodied in it the result of his own mature experience and observation. He had himself lived the life of a solitary after the most extreme Egyptian pattern, and in his first communities he had no doubt thoroughly tested the prevailing type of monastic rule. Being fully cognizant, therefore, of the unsuitability of much in the Egyptian systems to the times and circumstances in which he lived, he now struck out on a new line, and instead of attempting to revivify the old forms of asceticism, he consolidated the cenobitical life, emphasized the family spirit, and discouraged all private venture in austerities. His Rule thus consists of a carefully considered combination of old and new ideas; rivalry in austerity was eliminated, and there was to be henceforth a sinking of the individual in the community. In adapting a system essentially Eastern, to Western conditions, St. Benedict gave it coherence, stability, and organization, and the verdict of history is unanimous in applauding the results of such adaptation.

II. Analysis of the Rule.—Of the seventy-three chapters comprising the Rule, nine treat of the duties of the abbot, thirteen regulate the worship of God, twenty-nine are concerned with discipline and the penal code, ten refer to the internal administration of the monastery, and the remaining twelve consist of miscellaneous regulations.

The Rule opens with a prologue or hortatory preface, in which St. Benedict sets forth the main principles of the religious life, viz.: the renunciation of one's own will and the taking up of arms under the banner of Christ. He proposes to establish a "school" in which the science of salvation shall be taught, so that by persevering in the monastery till death his disciples may "deserve to become partakers of Christ's kingdom". In chapter i are defined the four principal kinds of monks: (1) Cenobites, those living in a monastery under an abbot; (2) Anchorites, or hermits, living a solitary life after long probation in the monastery; (3) Sarabaites, living by twos and threes together, without any fixed rule or lawfully constituted superior; and (4) Gyrovagi, a species of monastic vagrants, whose lives, spent in wandering from one monastery to another, only served to bring discredit on the monastic profession. It is for the first of these classes, as the most stable kind, that this Rule is written. Ch. ii describes the necessary qualifications for an abbot and forbids him to make distinction of persons in the monastery except for particular merit, warning him at the same time that he will be answerable for the salvation of the souls committed to his care. Ch. iii ordains the calling of the brethren to council upon all affairs of importance to the community. Ch. iv summarizes the duties of the Christian life under seventy-two precepts, which are called the "Instruments of good works" and are mainly Scriptural either in letter or spirit. Ch. v prescribes prompt, cheerful, and absolute obedience to the superior in all things lawful, which obedience is called the first degree of humility. Ch. vi deals with silence, recommending moderation in the use of speech, but by no means prohibiting profitable or necessary conversation. Ch. vii treats of humility, which virtue is divided into twelve degrees or steps in the ladder that leads to heaven. They are: (1) fear of God; (2) repression of self-will; (3) submission of the will to superiors; (4) obedience in hard and difficult matters; (5) confession of faults; (6) acknowledgment of one's own worthlessness; (7) preference of others to self; (8) avoidance of singularity; (9) speaking only in due season; (10) stifling of unseemly laughter; (11) repression of pride; (12) exterior humility. Ch. ix–xix are occupied with the regulation of the Divine Office, the *opus Dei* to which "nothing is to be preferred", or Canonical Hours, seven of the day and one of the night. Detailed arrangements are made as to the number of Psalms, etc., to be recited in winter and summer, on Sundays, weekdays, Holy Days, and at other times. Ch. xix emphasizes the reverence due to the presence of God. Ch. xx directs that prayer in common is to be short. Ch. xxi provides for the appointment of deans over every ten monks, and prescribes the manner in which they are to be chosen. Ch. xxii regulates all matters relating to the dormitory, as, for example, that each monk is to have a separate bed and is to sleep in his habit, so as to be ready to rise without delay, and that a light shall burn in the dormitory throughout the night. Ch. xxiii–xxx deal with offences against the Rule and a graduated scale of penalties is provided: first, private admonition; next, public reproof; then separation from the brethren at meals and elsewhere; then scourging; and finally expulsion; though this last is not to be resorted to until every effort to reclaim the offender has failed. And even in this last case, the outcast must be received again, should he so desire, but after the third expulsion all return is finally barred. Ch. xxxi and xxxii order the appointment of a cellarer and other officials, to take charge of the various goods of the monastery, which are to be treated with as much care as the consecrated vessels of the altar. Ch. xxxiii forbids the private possession of anything without the leave of the abbot, who is, however, bound to supply all necessaries. Ch. xxxiv prescribes a just distribution of such things. Ch. xxxv arranges for the service in the kitchen by all the monks in turn. Ch. xxxvi and xxxvii order due care for the sick, the old, and the young. They are to have certain dispensations from the strict Rule, chiefly in the matter of food.

Ch. xxxviii prescribes reading aloud during meals, which duty is to be performed by such of the brethren, week by week, as can do so with edification to the rest. Signs are to be used for whatever may be wanted at meals, so that no voice shall interrupt that of the reader. The reader is to have his meal with the servers after the rest have finished, but he is allowed a little food beforehand in order to lessen the fatigue of reading. Ch. xxxix and xl regulate the quantity and quality of the food. Two meals a day are allowed and two dishes of cooked food at each. A pound of bread also and a *hemina* (probably about half a pint) of wine for each monk. Fleshmeat is prohibited except for the sick and the weak, and it is to be always within the abbot's power to increase the daily allowance when he sees fit. Ch. xli prescribes the hours of the meals, which are to vary according to the time of year. Ch. xlii enjoins the reading of the "Conferences" of Cassian or some other edifying book in the evening before Compline and orders that after Compline the strictest silence shall be observed until the following morning. Ch. xliii–xlvi relate to minor faults, such as coming late to prayer or meals, and impose various penalties for such transgressions. Ch. xlvii enjoins on the abbot the duty of calling the brethren to the "work of God" in choir, and of appointing those who are to chant or read. Ch. xlviii emphasizes the importance of manual labour and arranges the time to be devoted to it daily. This varies according to the season, but is apparently to be never less than about five hours a day. The times at which the lesser of the "day-hours" (Prime, Terce, Sext, and None) are to be recited control the hours of labour somewhat, and the abbot is instructed not only to see that all work, but also that the employments of each are suited to their respective capacities. Ch. xlix treats of the observance of Lent, and recommends some voluntary self-denial for that season, with the abbot's sanction. Ch. l and li contain rules for monks who are working in the fields or travelling. They are directed to join in spirit, as far as possible, with their brethren in the monastery at the regular hours of prayers. Ch. lii commands that the oratory be used for purposes of devotion only. Ch. liii is concerned with the treatment of guests, who are "never wanting in a monastery" and who are to be received "as Christ Himself". This Benedictine hospitality is a feature which has in all ages been characteristic of the order. The guests are to be met with due courtesy by the abbot or his deputy, and during their stay they are to be under the special care of a monk appointed for the purpose, but they are not to associate with the rest of the community except by special permission. Ch. liv forbids the monks to receive letters or gifts without the abbot's leave. Ch. lv regulates the clothing of the monks. It is to be sufficient in both quantity and quality and to be suited to the climate and locality, according to the discretion of the abbot, but at the same time it must be as plain and cheap as is consistent with due economy. Each monk is to have a change of garments, to allow for washing, and when travelling shall be supplied with clothes of rather better quality. The old habits are to be put aside for the poor. Ch. lvi directs that the abbot shall take his meals with the guests. Ch. lvii enjoins humility on the craftsmen of the monastery, and if their work is for sale, it shall be rather below than above the current trade price. Ch. lviii lays down rules for the admission of new members, which is not to be made too easy. These matters have since been regulated by the Church, but in the main St. Benedict's outline is adhered to. The postulant first spends a short time as a guest; then he is admitted to the novitiate, where, under the care of the novice-master, his vocation is severely tested; during this time he is always free to depart. If, after twelve months' probation, he still persevere, he may be admitted to the vows of Stability, Conversion of Life, and Obedience, by which he binds himself for life to the monastery of his profession. Ch. lix allows the admission of boys to the monastery under certain conditions. Ch. lx regulates the position of priests who may desire to join the community. They are charged with setting an example of humility to all, and can only exercise their priestly functions by permission of the abbot. Ch. lxi provides for the reception of strange monks as guests, and for their admission if desirous of joining the community. Ch. lxii empowers the abbot to choose certain of his monks for ordination, which, however, shall not give them any higher rank in the community, unless perchance they be promoted for special merit. Ch. lxiii lays down that precedence in the community shall be determined by the date of admission, merit of life, or the appointment of the abbot. Ch. lxiv orders that the abbot be elected by his monks and that he be chosen for his charity, zeal, and discretion. Ch. lxv allows the appointment of a provost, or prior, if need be, but warns such a one that he is to be entirely subject to the abbot and may be admonished, deposed, or expelled for misconduct. Ch. lxvi provides for the appointment of a porter, and recommends that each monastery should be, if possible, self-contained, so as to avoid the need of intercourse with the outer world. Ch. lxvii gives instructions as to the behaviour of a monk who is sent on a journey. Ch. lxviii orders that all shall cheerfully attempt to do whatever is commanded them, however hard it may seem. Ch. lxix forbids the monks to defend one another. Ch. lxx prohibits them from striking one another. Ch. lxxi encourages the brethren to be obedient not only to the abbot and his officials, but also to one another. Ch. lxxii is a brief exhortation to zeal and fraternal charity; and Ch. lxxiii is an epilogue declaring that this Rule is not offered as an ideal of perfection, but merely as a means towards godliness and is intended chiefly for beginners in the spiritual life.

Characteristics of the Rule.—In considering the leading characteristics of this Holy Rule, the first that must strike the reader is its wonderful discretion and moderation, its extreme reasonableness, and its keen insight into the capabilities as well as the weaknesses of human nature. Here are no excesses, no extraordinary asceticism, no narrow-mindedness, but rather a series of sober regulations based upon sound common-sense. We see these qualities displayed in the deliberate elimination of austerities and in concessions made with regard to what the monks of Egypt would have looked upon as luxuries. A few comparisons between the customs of these latter and the prescriptions of St. Benedict's Rule will serve to bring out more clearly the extent of his changes in this direction.

With regard to food, the Egyptian ascetics reduced it to a minimum, many of them eating only twice or thrice in the week, whilst Cassian describes a meal consisting of parched vetches with salt and oil, three olives, two prunes, and a fig, as a "sumptuous repast" (Coll. viii, 1). St. Benedict, on the other hand, though he restricts the use of flesh-meat to the sick, orders a pound of bread daily and two dishes of cooked food at each meal, of which there were two in summer and one in winter. And he concedes also an allowance of wine, though admitting that it should not properly be the drink of monks (Ch. xl). As to clothing, St. Benedict's provision that habits were to fit, to be sufficiently warm, and not too old, was in great contrast to the poverty of the Egyptian monks, whose clothes, Abbot Pambo laid down, should be so poor that if left on the road no one would be tempted to take them (Apophthegmata,

in P. G., LXV, 369). In the matter of sleep, whereas the solitaries of Egypt regarded its diminution as one of their most valued forms of austerity, St. Benedict ordered from six to eight hours of unbroken sleep a day, with the addition of a siesta in summer. The Egyptian monks, moreover, frequently slept on the bare ground, with stones or mats for pillows, and often even sitting or merely reclining, as directed in the Pachomian Rule, whilst Abbot John was unable to mention without shame the finding of a blanket in a hermit's cell (Cassian, Coll. xix, 6). St. Benedict, however, allowed not only a blanket but also a coverlet, a mattress, and a pillow to each monk. This comparative liberality with regard to the necessaries of life, though plain and meagre perhaps, if tested by modern notions of comfort, was far greater than amongst the Italian poor of the sixth century or even amongst many of the European peasantry at the present day. St. Benedict's aim seems to have been to keep the bodies of his monks in a healthy condition by means of proper clothing, sufficient food, and ample sleep, so that they might thereby be more fit for the due performance of the Divine Office and be freed from all that distracting rivalry in asceticism which has already been mentioned. There was, however, no desire to lower the ideal or to minimize the self-sacrifice that the adoption of the monastic life entailed, but rather the intention of bringing it into line with the altered circumstances of Western environment, which necessarily differed much from those of Egypt and the East. The wisdom and skill with which he did this is evident in every page of the Rule, so much so that Bossuet was able to call it "an epitome of Christianity, a learned and mysterious abridgment of all the doctrines of the Gospel, all the institutions of the Fathers, and all the Counsels of Perfection".

St. Benedict perceived the necessity for a permanent and uniform rule of government in place of the arbitrary and variable choice of models furnished by the lives and maxims of the Fathers of the Desert. And so we have the characteristic of collectivism, exhibited in his insistence on the common life, as opposed to the individualism of the Egyptian monks. One of the objects he had in view in writing his Rule was the extirpation of the Sarabaites and Gyrovagi, whom he so strongly condemns in his first chapter and of whose evil lives he had probably had painful experience during his early days at Subiaco. To further this aim he introduced the vow of Stability, which became the guarantee of success and permanence. It is only another example of the family idea that pervades the entire Rule, by means of which the members of the community are bound together by a family tie, and each takes upon himself the obligation of persevering in his monastery until death, unless sent elsewhere by his superiors. It secures to the community as a whole, and to every member of it individually, a share in all the fruits that may arise from the labours of each monk, and it gives to each of them that strength and vitality which necessarily result from being one of a united family, all bound in a similar way and all pursuing the same end. Thus, whatever the monk does, he does it not as an independent individual but as part of a larger organization, and the community itself thus becomes one united whole rather than a mere agglomeration of independent members. The Vow of Conversion of Life indicates the personal striving after perfection that must be the aim of every Benedictine monk. All the legislation of the Rule, the constant repression of self, the conforming of one's every action to a definite standard, and the continuance of this form of life to the end of one's days, is directed towards "putting off the old man and putting on the new", and thereby accomplishing that *conversio morum* which is inseparable from a life-long perseverance in the maxims of the Rule. The practice of obedience is a necessary feature in St. Benedict's idea of the religious life, if not indeed its very essence. Not only is a special chapter of the Rule devoted to it, but it is repeatedly referred to as a guiding principle in the life of the monk; so essential is it that it is the subject of a special vow in every religious institute, Benedictine or otherwise. In St. Benedict's eyes it is one of the positive works to which the monk binds himself, for he calls it *labor obedientiæ* (Prologue). It is to be cheerful, unquestioning, and prompt; to the abbot chiefly, who is to be obeyed as holding the place of Christ, and also to all the brethren according to the dictates of fraternal charity, as being "the path that leads to God" (Ch. lxxi). It is likewise extended to hard and even impossible things, the latter being at least attempted in all humility. In connexion with the question of obedience there is the further question as to the system of government embodied in the Rule. The life of the community centres round the abbot as the father of the family. Much latitude with regard to details is left to his "discretion and judgment", but this power, so far from being absolute or unlimited, is safeguarded by the obligation laid upon him of consulting the brethren—either the seniors only or else the entire community—upon all matters affecting their welfare. And on the other hand, wherever there seems to be a certain amount of liberty left to the monks themselves, this, in turn, is protected against indiscretion by the repeated insistence on the necessity for the abbot's sanction and approval. The vows of Poverty and Chastity, though not explicitly mentioned by St. Benedict, as in the rules of other orders, are yet implied so clearly as to form an indisputable and essential part of the life for which he legislates. Thus by means of the vows and the practice of the various virtues necessary to their proper observance, it will be seen that St. Benedict's Rule contains not merely a series of laws regulating the external details of monastic life, but also all the principles of perfection according to the Evangelical Counsels.

With regard to the obligation or binding power of the Rule, we must distinguish between the statutes or precepts and the counsels. By the former would be meant those laws which either command or prohibit in an absolute manner, and by the latter those that are merely recommendations. It is generally held by commentators that the precepts of the Rule bind only under the penalty of venial sin, and the counsels not even under that. Really grave transgressions against the vows, on the other hand, would fall under the category of mortal sins. It must be remembered, however, that in all these matters the principles of moral theology, canon law, the decisions of the Church, and the regulations of the Constitutions of the different congregations must be taken into consideration in judging of any particular case.

III. PRACTICAL WORKING OF THE RULE.—No higher testimony as to the inherent excellencies of the Rule can be adduced than the results it has achieved in Western Europe and elsewhere; and no more striking quality is exhibited by it than its adaptability to the ever-changing requirements of time and place since St. Benedict's days. Its enduring character is the highest testimony to its wisdom. For fourteen centuries it has been the guiding light of a numerous family of religious, men and women, and it is a living code at the present day, just as it was a thousand years ago. Though modified and adapted, from time to time, to suit the peculiar necessities and conditions of various ages and countries, by reason of its wonderful elasticity its principles still remain the same, and it has formed the fundamental basis of a great variety of other religious bodies. It has merited the encomiums of councils, popes, and commentators, and its vitality is as vigorous at the present time as it was in the ages of faith. Though it was no part of St. Benedict's design that his spiritual descendants should make a figure in the world as authors or statesmen, as preservers of pagan literature, as pioneers of civilization, as revivers of agriculture, or as builders of castles and cathedrals, yet circumstances brought them into all these spheres. His sole idea was the moral and spiritual training of his disciples, and yet in carrying this out he made the cloister a school of useful workers, a real refuge for society, and a solid bulwark of the Church (Dudden, Gregory the Great, II, ix). The Rule, instead of restricting the monk to one particular form of work, makes it possible for him to do almost any kind of work, and that in a manner spiritualized and elevated above the labour of merely secular craftsmen. In this lies one of the secrets of its success.

The results of the fulfilment of the precepts of the Rule are abundantly apparent in history. That of manual labour, for instance, which St. Benedict laid down as absolutely essential for his monks, produced many of those architectural triumphs which are the glory of the Christian world. Many cathedrals (especially in England), abbeys, and churches, scattered up and down the countries of Western Europe, were the work of Benedictine builders and architects. The cultivation of the soil, encouraged by St. Benedict, was another form of labour to which his followers gave themselves without reserve and with conspicuous success, so that many regions have owed much of their agricultural prosperity to the skilful husbandry of the sons of St. Benedict. The hours ordered by the Rule to be devoted daily to systematic reading and study, have given to the world many of the foremost scholars and writers, so that the term "Benedictine erudition" has been for long centuries a byword indicative of the learning and laborious research fostered in the Benedictine cloister. The regulations regarding the reception and education of children, moreover, were the germ from which sprang up a great number of famous monastic schools and universities which flourished in the Middle Ages.

It is true that as communities became rich and consequently less dependent upon their own labours for support, the primitive fervour for the Rule diminished, and for this reason grave charges of corruption and absolute departure from monastic ideals have been made against the monks. But, although it is impossible to deny that the many reforms that were initiated seem to give colour to this view, it cannot be admitted that the Benedictine Institute, as a whole, ever became really degenerate or fell away seriously from the ideal established by its legislator. Individual failures there certainly were, as well as mitigations of rule, from time to time, but the loss of fervour in one particular monastery no more compromises all the other monasteries of the same country than the faults of one individual monk reflect necessarily upon the rest of the community to which he belongs. So, whilst admitting that the rigour of the Rule has varied at different times and in different places, we must, on the other hand, remember that modern historical research has entirely exonerated the monastic body as a whole from the charge of a general departure from the principles of the Rule and a widespread corruption of either ideal or practice. Circumstances have often rendered mitigations necessary but they have always been introduced as such and not as new or better interpretations of the Rule itself. The fact that the Benedictines still glory in their Rule, guard it with jealousy, and point to it as the exemplar according to which they are endeavouring to model their lives, is in itself the strongest proof that they are still imbued with its spirit, though recognizing its latitude of application and its adaptability to various conditions.

MONTALEMBERT, *Monks of the West* (Tr., London, 1896), IV; TOSTI, *Saint Benedict*, tr. WOODS (London, 1896); DOYLE, *The Teaching of St. Benedict* (London, 1887); DUDDEN, *Gregory the Great* (London, 1905); BUTLER *Lausiac History of Palladius*, Introd., XIX in *Cambridge Texts and Studies* (Cambridge, 1898); IDEM, *The Text of St. Benedict's Rule*, in *Downside Review*, XVIII, 223; and in *Journal of Theol. Studies*, III, 458; BESSE, *Le Moine Bénédictin* (Ligugé, 1898); HAEFTEN, *Disquisitiones Monasticæ* (Antwerp, 1644); SCHMIDT, *Regula Sti. Benedicti* (Ratisbon, 1880, 1892); WÖLFFLIN, *Benedicti Regula Monachorum* (Leipzig, 1895); TRAUBE, *Textgeschichte der Regula S. Benedicti* (Munich, 1898).

COMMENTARIES.—WARNEFRID (Monte Cassino, 1880); MÈGE (Paris, 1687); MARTÈNE (Paris, 1690), also in *P. L.*, LXVI; CALMET (Paris, 1734); MABILLON, Prefaces to *Acta Sanctorum O. S. B.* (Venice, 1733).

ENGLISH TRANSLATIONS OF RULE.—ANONYMOUS (Ramsgate, 1872; Rome, 1895); DOYLE, ed. (London, 1875); VERHEYEN (Atchison, Kansas, 1906); HUNTER-BLAIR (Fort Augustus, Scotland, 1906).

G. CYPRIAN ALSTON.

Benedictbeurn, ABBEY OF, situated in the Bavarian Alps, about thirty miles south of Munich. It was formerly in the Diocese of Augsburg, but some writers, including Mabillon, have wrongly described it as having been in that of Freising. The name has been variously spelt as Beuren, Beuern, Buron, Beweren, Baiern, Beyrn, etc., but that given above is the officially accepted spelling at the present time. Tradition, as well as manuscripts dating as far back as the tenth century, ascribe its foundation, in the year 740, to three brothers of noble birth, named Lanfrid, Wulfram, and Eliland, acting under the influence of St. Boniface, who was then preaching the Faith in Bavaria. The three founders, each in turn, ruled the monastery, which in 955 (or 973 according to some authorities) was destroyed by the Huns, who then ravaged the country. Restored in 969 by Wolfold, a secular priest, it continued as a college of regular clergy, or canons, until 1031. Through the influence of the Emperor Henry III, the Benedictine rule was revived there in 1031 by Abbot Ellinger and eleven monks from the neighbouring Abbey of Tegernsee.

Under the next abbot, Gothelm, the famous monastic school was established. The abbey also became a great place of pilgrimage and the scene of many miracles, by reason of the relics of St. Anastasia which were brought thither in 1053. Throughout the Middle Ages it continued to flourish as a home of learning and piety. Many privileges were granted by different popes, and several of the emperors honoured it with their favour and their visits. The Abbots Ortolph II (1271–84) and Henry III (1284–89) were made Princes of the Empire by Rudolph of Hapsburg. The abbey was four times burnt down, viz: in 1248, 1377, 1378, and 1490, and as often rebuilt. In 1611 its numbers were depleted by a plague which carried off many of the monks, and it also suffered during the Swedish invasion under Gustavus Adolphus and the Thirty Years' War in the seventeenth century. In 1803 the abbey was suppressed by the Government and the monks, thirty-four in number, dispersed. The conventual buildings became successively a barracks, a military hospital, and a stud-house. In 1901 Freiherr von Kramer-Klett, the restorer of several Bavarian monasteries, offered five and one-half million marks for the property, but was met by a demand for twelve millions, which he refused.

The library and archives contained many priceless manuscripts and charters. Ziegelbauer (Hist. Lit. Ord. S.B., I, 543) printed a catalogue of the library, dated 1250, in which more than one hundred and fifty books and MSS. are enumerated. Mabillon, who visited the abbey in 1683, and Bernard Pez, librarian of Melk, who was there in 1717, have both left on record their testimony as to the great value of the codices there preserved. At the suppression the library comprised 40,000 volumes. A number of these were incorporated with the Court Library and the remainder left to be disposed of by the subsequent occupants of the abbey.

Amongst the illustrious men produced by Benedictbeurn the following deserve mention: Gothelm, abbot 1032–62; founded the monastic school in 1033. Gotschalk, who translated the relics of St. Anastasia to Beurn in 1053; the first historian of the abbey ("Breviarium Gotschalki" in Mon. Germ. Hist., IX, 221). Dom Simon Speer, martyr; tortured and put to death by the Swedes for refusing to surrender the goods of the abbey, 1632. Magnus, abbot 1707–40; resuscitated the school, 1711. Dom Carolus Meichelbeck, "the Livy of Bavaria", b. 1669; took the habit, 1687 and was librarian and archivist from 1696 till his death in 1734. He taught philosophy and theology and wrote various historical works, including the "History of the Diocese of Freising", the "Chronicon Benedicto-Buranum", and the "Annals of the Bavarian Congregation".

Various charters, etc., in *Monumenta Boica* (Munich); YEPES, *Chronicon Generale O.S.B.* (Yrache, 1609), III, 87; MABILLON, *Annales O.S.B.* (Paris, 1703–39), ed. 1735, II, 114; MEICHELBECK, *Chronicon Benedicto-buranum* (Benedictbeurn, 1752); KUEN, *Collectio Scriptorum* (Ulm, 1755); PERTZ, *Mon. Germ. Hist.*: Script. (Hanover, 1851), IX, 210; VON HEFNER, *Leistungen des Klosters Benediktbeuern*, in *Oberbaierisches Archiv*, III, 337; RETTBERG, *Deutschl. Kirchengesch.*, II, 165; DAFFNER, *Gesch. des Klosters Benediktbeuren* (Munich, 1893); SCHLEGMANN, *Gesch. der Säkularisation im rechtsrheinischen Bayern* (Regensburg, 1903–05).

G. CYPRIAN ALSTON.

Benedict Biscop, SAINT, an English monastic founder, b. of a noble Anglo-Saxon family, c. 628; d. 12 January, 690. He spent his youth at the court of the Northumbrian King Oswy. When twenty-five years old, he made the first of his five pilgrimages to Rome. On his return to England, Benedict introduced, wherever he could, the religious rites as he saw them practised in Rome. Soon afterwards he made a second pilgrimage to Rome, stopping on his return at Lérins, in 666, to take the religious habit. When, two years later, he returned to Rome, Pope Vitalian sent him and the monk Adrian as advisers with Theodore, the newly appointed Archbishop of Canterbury. On their arrival in England, Theodore appointed Benedict Abbot of St. Peter's at Canterbury. After two years, in 671, he resigned this office and made another pilgrimage to Rome. During this and his two succeeding pilgrimages to the city of the Apostles he collected numerous relics, books, and paintings for the monasteries of Wearmouth and Jarrow, the former of which he founded in 674, the latter in 682. He also engaged Abbot John, Arch-cantor of St. Peter's in Rome, to teach Roman chant at these monasteries. Benedict was the first to introduce into England the building of stone churches and the art of making glass windows. His festival is observed on 12 February.

MONTALEMBERT, *Monks of the West* (Boston), II, 493; HOPE, *Conversion of the Teutonic Race* (London), I, 400; STANTON, *A Menology of England and Wales* (London, 1892); ALLIES, *Hist. of the Church in England* (London, 1892), I, 59; MABILLON, *Acta SS. O. S. B.*, sæc. II. His biography in Latin by ST. BEDE is published in *P. L.*, XCIV, 711–734.

MICHAEL OTT.

Benedicti, JEAN, a Franciscan theologian of the sixteenth century belonging to the Observantine Province of Tours and Poitiers. He became in time secretary of the order and in this capacity accompanied the minister-general, Christopher a Capite Fontium, throughout the whole of Europe in the latter's canonical visitation of Franciscan houses. Afterwards he was made commissary-general of the French and visitor of many Italian Provinces, and in order to fulfil a vow went on a pilgrimage to the Holy Land. Wadding says that he was a man of most distinguished parts and great culture, having thoroughly mastered the learning of his day and being especially conversant with the Hebrew, Greek, and Latin tongues. In 1599 the first edition of his "Somme des péchés et le remède d'iceux comprenant tous les cas de conscience" was published in Paris and was immediately in great demand among confessors, for we learn that after having been revised, corrected, and augmented by the Theological Faculty of Paris it reached its fifteenth edition. He also wrote "La triomphante victoire de la Sainte Vierge" which tells of a remarkable exorcism in the church of the Cordeliers at Lyons. His remains were interred in the Friary at Laval.

WADDING, *Annales minor. ad ann.*, 1596, IV; SBARALEA, *Supp. ad script. O. M.* (Rome, 1806).

ANDREW EGAN.

Benedict Joseph Labre, SAINT, b. 26 March, 1748, at Amettes in the Diocese of Boulogne, France; d. in Rome, 16 April, 1783. He was the eldest of fifteen children. His parents, Jean-Baptiste Labre and Anne-Barbe Grandsire, belonged to the middle class and so were able to give to their numerous offspring considerable opportunities in the way of education. His early training he received in his native village in a school conducted by the vicar of the parish. The account of this period furnished in the life written by his confessor, Marconi, and that contained in the one compiled from the official processes of his beatification are at one in emphasizing the fact that he exhibited a seriousness of thought and demeanour far beyond his years. Even at that tender age he had begun to show a marked predilection for the spirit of mortification, with an aversion for the ordinary childish amusements, and he seems from the very dawning of reason to have had the liveliest horror for even the smallest sin. All this we are told was coexistent with a frank and open demeanour and a fund of cheerfulness which remained unabated to the end of his life. At the age of twelve his education was taken over by his paternal uncle, François-Joseph Labre, curé of Erin, with whom he then went to live. During the six following years which he spent under his uncle's roof, he made considerable progress in the study of Latin, history, etc. but found himself unable to conquer a constantly growing distaste for any form of knowledge which did not make directly for union with God. A love of solitude, a generous employment of austerities, and devotedness to his religious exercises were discernible as distinguishing features of his life at this time and constitute an intelligible prelude to his subsequent career. At the age of sixteen he resolved to embrace a religious life as a Trappist, but having on the advice of his uncle returned to Amettes to submit his design to his parents for their approval he was unable to win their consent. He therefore resumed his sojourn in the rectory at Erin, redoubling his penances and exercises of piety and in every way striving to make ready for the life of complete self-annihilation to which the voice within his soul seemed to be calling him.

After the heroic death of his uncle during an epidemic in September, 1766, Benedict, who had dedicated himself during the scourge to the service of the sick and dying, returned to Amettes in November of the same year. His absorbing thought at this time was still to become a religious at La Trappe, and his parents fearing that further opposition would be resistance to the will of God fell in with his proposal to enter the cloister. It was suggested, however, by his maternal uncle, the Abbé Vincent, that application be made to the Carthusians at Val-Sainte-Aldegonde rather than to La Trappe. Benedict's petition at Val-Sainte-Aldegonde was unsuccessful, but he was directed to another monastery of the same

order at Neuville. There he was told that as he was not yet twenty there was no hurry, and that he must first learn plain-chant and logic. During the next two years he applied twice unsuccessfully to be received at La Trappe and was for six weeks as a postulant with the Carthusians at Neuville; he finally sought and obtained admission to the Cistercian Abbey of Sept-Fonts in November, 1769. After a short stay at Sept-Fonts during which his exactness in religious observance and humility endeared him to the whole community, his health gave way, and it was decided that his vocation lay elsewhere. In accordance with a resolve formed during his convalescence he then set out for Rome. From Chieri in Piedmont he wrote to his parents a letter which proved to be the last they would ever receive from him. In it he informed them of his design to enter some one of the many monasteries in Italy noted for their special rigour of life. A short time, however, after the letter was dispatched he seems to have had an internal illumination which set at rest forever any doubts he might have as to what his method of living was to be. He then understood "that it was God's will that like St. Alexis he should abandon his country, his parents, and whatever is flattering in the world to lead a new sort of life, a life most painful, most penitential, not in a wilderness nor in a cloister, but in the midst of the world, devoutly visiting as a pilgrim the famous places of Christian devotion". He repeatedly submitted this extraordinary inspiration to the judgment of experienced confessors and was told he might safely conform to it. Through the years that followed he never wavered in the conviction that this was the path appointed for him by God. He set forward on his life's journey clad in an old coat, a rosary about his neck, another between his fingers, his arms folded over a crucifix which lay upon his breast. In a small wallet he carried a Testament, a breviary, which it was his wont to recite daily, a copy of the "Imitation of Christ", and some other pious books. Clothing other than that which covered his person he had none. He slept on the ground and for the most part in the open air. For food he was satisfied with a piece of bread or some herbs, frequently taken but once a day, and either provided by charity or gotten from some refuse heap. He never asked for alms and was anxious to give away to the poor whatever he received in excess of his scanty wants.

The first seven of the thirteen remaining years of his life were spent in pilgrimages to the more famous shrines of Europe. He visited in this way Loreto, Assisi, Naples, Bari, Fabriano in Italy; Einsiedeln in Switzerland; Compostella in Spain; Paray-le-Monial in France. The last six years he spent in Rome, leaving it only once a year to visit the Holy House of Loreto. His unremitting and ruthless self-denial, his unaffected humility, unhesitating obedience and perfect spirit of union with God in prayer disarmed suspicion not unnaturally aroused as to the genuineness of a Divine call to so extraordinary a way of existence. Literally worn out by his sufferings and austerities, on the 16th of April, 1783, he sank down on the steps of the church of Santa Maria dei Monti in Rome and, utterly exhausted, was carried to a neighbouring house where he died. His death was followed by a multitude of unequivocal miracles attributed to his intercession. The life written by his confessor, Marconi, an English version of which bears the date of 1785, witnesses to 136 miraculous cures as having been certified to up to 6 July, 1783. So remarkable, indeed, was the character of the evidence for some of the miracles that they are said to have had no inconsiderable part in finally determining the conversion of the celebrated American convert, Father John Thayer, of Boston, who was in Rome at the time of the saint's death.

Benedict was proclaimed Venerable by Pius IX in 1859 and canonized by Leo XIII 8 December, 1881. His feast is kept on the 16th of April, the day of his death.

Biog. Univ. (Paris, 1811–28); *Biog. Eccles. Completa* (Madrid, 1857); *Life of Venerable Benedict Joseph Labre*, French tr., BARNARD (London, 1785); *Life of the Venerable Servant of God, Benedict Joseph Labre* (Oratorian Series, London, 1850).

JOSEPH F. DELANY.

Benedictine Order, THE, comprises monks living under the Rule of St. Benedict, and commonly known as "black monks". The order will be considered in this article under the following sections: I. History of the Order; II. Lay brothers, Oblates, Confraters, and Nuns; III. Influence and Work of the Order; IV. Present Condition of the Order; V. Benedictines of Special Distinction; VI. Other Foundations Originating from, or Based upon, the Order.

I. HISTORY OF THE ORDER.—The term *Order* as here applied to the spiritual family of St. Benedict is used in a sense differing somewhat from that in which it is applied to other religious orders. In its ordinary meaning the term implies one complete religious family, made up of a number of monasteries, all of which are subject to a common superior or "general" who usually resides either in Rome or in the mother-house of the order, if there be one. It may be divided into various provinces, according to the countries over which it is spread, each provincial head being immediately subject to the general, just as the superior of each house is subject to his own provincial. This system of centralized authority has never entered into the organization of the Benedictine Order. There is no general or common superior over the whole order other than the pope himself, and the order consists, so to speak, of what are practically a number of orders, called "congregations", each of which is autonomous; all are united, not under the obedience to one general superior, but only by the spiritual bond of allegiance to the same Rule, which may be modified according to the circumstances of each particular house or congregation. It is in this latter sense that the term *Order* is applied in this article to all monasteries professing to observe St. Benedict's Rule.

Beginnings of the Order.—St. Benedict did not, strictly speaking, found an order; we have no evidence that he ever contemplated the spread of his Rule to any monasteries besides those which he had himself established. Subiaco was his original foundation and the cradle of the institute. From St. Gregory we learn that twelve other monasteries in the vi-

THE ABBEY OF SUBIACO

cinity of Subiaco also owed their origin to him, and that when he was obliged to leave that neighbourhood he founded the celebrated Abbey of Monte Cassino, which eventually became the centre whence his Rule and institute spread. These fourteen are the only monasteries of which there is any reliable evidence of having been founded during St. Benedict's lifetime. The tradition of St. Placid's mission to Sicily in 534, which first gained general credence in the eleventh century, though accepted as genuine by such writers as Mabillon and Ruinart, is now generally admitted to be mere romance. Very little more can be said in favour of the supposed introduction of the Benedictine Rule into Gaul by St. Maurus in 543, though it also has been strenuously upheld by many responsible writers. At any rate, evidences for it are so extremely doubtful that it cannot be seriously regarded as historical. There is reason for believing that it was the third Abbot of Monte Cassino who began to spread a knowledge of the Rule beyond the circle of St. Benedict's own foundations. It is at least certain that when Monte Cassino was sacked by the Lombards about the year 580, the monks fled to Rome, where they were housed by Pope Pelagius II in a monastery adjoining the Lateran Basilica. There, in the very centre of the ecclesiastical world, they remained for upwards of a hundred and forty years, and it seems highly probable that this residence in so prominent a position constituted an important factor in the diffusion of a knowledge of Benedictine monasticism. It is generally agreed also that when Gregory the Great embraced the monastic state and converted his family palace on the Cœlian Hill into a monastery dedicated to St. Andrew the Apostle, it was the Benedictine form of monachism that he adopted there.

It was from the monastery of St. Andrew in Rome that St. Augustine, the prior, and his forty companions set forth in 595 on their mission for the evangelization of England, and with them St. Benedict's idea of the monastic life first emerged from Italy. The arguments and authorities for this statement have been admirably marshalled and estimated by Reyner in his "Apostolatus Benedictinorum in Angliâ" (Douai, 1626), and his proofs have been adjudged by Mabillon to amount to demonstration. [Cf. Butler, "Was St. Augustine a Benedictine?" in Downside Review, III (1884).] At their various stopping places during the journey through France the monks left behind them traditions concerning their rule and form of life, and probably also some copies of the Rule, for we have several evidences of its having been gradually introduced into most of the chief monasteries of Gaul during the seventh century. Lérins, for instance, one of the oldest, which had been founded by St. Honoratus in 375, probably received its first knowledge of the Benedictine Rule from the visit of St. Augustine and his companions in 596. Dismayed by the accounts they had heard of the ferocity of the English, the missionaries had sent their leader back to Rome to implore the pope to allow them to abandon the object of their journey. During his absence they remained at Lérins. Not long after their departure, Aygulph, Abbot of Fleury, was called in to restore the discipline and he probably introduced the full Benedictine observance; for when St. Benedict Biscop visited Lérins later on in the seventh century he received the Benedictine habit and tonsure from the hands of Abbot Aygulph. Lérins continued through several centuries to supply from its monks bishops for the chief churches of Southern Gaul, and to them perhaps may be traced the general diffusion of St. Benedict's Rule throughout that country. There, as also in Switzerland, it had to contend with and supplement the much stricter Irish or Celtic Rule introduced by St. Columbanus and others. In some monasteries the two rules were amalgamated, or practised side by side. Gregory of Tours says that at Ainay, in the sixth century, the monks "followed the rules of Basil, Cassian, Cæsarius, and other fathers, taking and using whatever seemed proper to the conditions of time and place", and doubtless the same liberty was taken with the Benedictine Rule when it reached them. In other monasteries it entirely displaced the earlier codes, and had by the end of the eighth century so completely superseded them throughout France that Charlemagne could gravely doubt whether monks of any kind had been possible before St. Benedict's time. The authority of Charlemagne and of his son, Louis the Pious, did much, as we shall presently see, towards propagating the principles of the Father of western monachism.

A BENEDICTINE MONK

St. Augustine and his monks established the first English Benedictine monastery at Canterbury soon after their arrival in 597. Other foundations quickly followed as the Benedictine missionaries carried the light of the Gospel with them throughout the length and breadth of the land. It was said that St. Benedict seemed to have taken possession of the country as his own, and the history of his order in England is the history of the English Church. Nowhere did the order link itself so intimately with people and institutions, secular as well as religious, as in England. Through the influence of saintly men, Wilfrid, Benedict Biscop, and Dunstan, the Benedictine Rule spread with extraordinary rapidity, and in the North, when once the Easter controversy had been settled and the Roman supremacy acknowledged (Synod of Whitby, 664), it was adopted in most of the monasteries that had been founded by the Celtic missionaries from Iona. Many of the episcopal sees of England were founded and governed by the

Benedictines, and no less than nine of the old cathedrals were served by the black monks of the priories attached to them. Even when the bishop was not himself a monk, he held the place of titular abbot, and the community formed his chapter.

Germany owed its evangelization to the English Benedictines, Sts. Willibrord and Boniface, who preached the Faith there in the seventh and eighth centuries and founded several celebrated abbeys. From thence spread, hand in hand, Christianity and Benedictine monasticism, to Denmark and Scandinavia, and from the latter even to Iceland. In Spain monasteries had been founded by the Visigothic kings as early as the latter half of the fifth century, but it was probably some two or three hundred years later that St. Benedict's Rule was adopted. Mabillon gives 640 as the date of its introduction into that country (Acta Sanctorum O. S. B., sæc. I, præf. 74), but his conclusions on this point are not now generally accepted. In Switzerland the disciples of Columbanus had founded monasteries early in the seventh century, two of the best known being St. Gall's, established by the saint of that name, and Dissentis (612), founded by St. Sigisbert. The Celtic rule was not entirely supplanted by that of St. Benedict until more than a hundred years later, when the change was effected chiefly through the influence of Pepin the Short, the father of Charlemagne. By the ninth century, however, the Benedictine had become the only form of monastic life throughout the whole of Western Europe, excepting Scotland, Wales, and Ireland, where the Celtic observance still prevailed for another century or two. At the time of the Reformation there were nine Benedictine houses in Ireland and six in Scotland, besides numerous abbeys of Cistercians.

Benedictine monasticism never took such deep root in the eastern countries of Europe as it had done in the West. The Bohemians and the Poles, nevertheless, owed their conversion respectively to the Benedictine missionaries Adalbert (d. 997) and Casimir (d. 1058), whilst Bavaria and what is now the Austrian Empire were evangelized first by monks from Gaul in the seventh century, and later on by St. Boniface and his disciples. A few of the larger abbeys founded in these countries during the ninth and tenth centuries still exist, but the number of foundations was always small in comparison with those farther west. Into Lithuania and the Eastern Empire the Benedictine Rule never penetrated in early times, and the great schism between East and West effectually prevented any possibilities of development in that direction.

Early Constitution of the Order.—During the first four or five centuries after the death of St. Benedict there existed no organic bond of union amongst the various abbeys other than the Rule itself and obedience to the Holy See. According to the holy legislator's provisions each monastery constituted an independent family, self-contained, autonomous, managing its own affairs, and subject to no external authority except that of the local diocesan bishop, whose powers of control were, however, limited to certain specific occasions. The earliest departures from this system occurred when several of the greater abbeys began sending out offshoots, under the form of daughter-houses retaining some sort of dependence upon the mother abbey from which they sprang. This mode of propagation, together with the various reforms that began to appear in the eleventh and succeeding centuries, paved the way for the system of independent congregations, still a feature peculiar to the Benedictine Order.

Reforms.—A system which comprised many hundreds of monasteries and many thousands of monks, spread over a number of different countries, without any unity of organization; which was exposed, moreover, to all the dangers and disturbances inseparable from those troublous times of kingdommaking; such a system was inevitably unable to keep worldliness, and even worse vices, wholly out of its midst. Hence it cannot be denied that the monks often failed to live up to the monastic ideal and sometimes even fell short of the Christian and moral standards. There were failures and scandals in Benedictine history, just as there were declensions from the right path outside the cloister, for monks are, after all, but men. But there does not seem ever to have been a period of widespread and general corruption in the order. Here and there the members of some particular house allowed abuses and relaxations of rule to creep in, so that they seemed to be falling away from the true spirit of their state, but whenever such did occur they soon called forth efforts for a restoration of primitive austerity; and these constantly recurring reform movements form one of the surest evidences of the vitality which has pervaded the Benedictine Institute throughout its entire history. It is important to note, moreover, that all such reforms as ever achieved any measure of success came invariably from within, and were not the result of pressure from outside the order.

The first of the reforms directed towards confederating the monastic houses of a single kingdom was set on foot early in the ninth century by Benedict of Aniane under the auspices of Charlemagne and Louis the Pious. Though a Benedictine himself, born in Aquitaine and trained at Saint-Seine near Dijon, Benedict was imbued with the rigid austerity of the East, and in his Abbey of Aniane practised a mode of life that was severe in the extreme. Over Louis he acquired an ascendancy which grew stronger as years went on. At his instigation Louis built for him a monastery adjoining his own palace at Aix-la-Chapelle, which was intended to serve as a model according to which all others were to be reformed, and to bring about this end Benedict was invested with a general authority over all the monasteries of the empire. Absolute uniformity of discipline, observance, and habit, after the pattern of the royal monastery, was then the general scheme which was launched at an assembly of all the abbots at Aachen (Aix-la-Chapelle) in 817 and embodied in a series of eighty *capitula* passed by the meeting. Though by reason of the very minuteness of these *capitula*, which made them vexatious and ultimately intolerable, this scheme of centralized authority lasted only for the lifetime of Benedict himself, the *capitula* (printed in full in Herrgott, "Vetus Disciplina Monastica", Paris, 1726) were recognized as supplying a much needed addition to St. Benedict's Rule concerning points not sufficiently provided for therein, and as filling much the same place then as the approved Constitutions of a monastery or congregation do now.

A century later, in 910, the first real reform that produced any widespread and general effect was commenced at the Abbey of Cluny in Burgundy, under St. Berno, its first abbot. The object was an elaboration of the Benedictine ideal, for the uniform preservation of which a highly centralized system of government, hitherto unknown to Benedictine monachism, except as suggested by St. Benedict of Aniane, was introduced. It was in fact the establishment of a veritable *order*, in the common acceptance of that term, within the Benedictine family, the abbot of Cluny retaining an actual headship over all dependent houses, the latter being governed only by priors as his vicars. For two centuries or more Cluny was probably the chief religious influence in the Latin Church, as it was also the first abbey to obtain exemption from episcopal oversight. Through the efforts of Berno's immediate successors the congregation grew apace, partly by

founding new houses and partly by incorporating those already existing, so that by the twelfth century Cluny had become the centre and head of an order embracing some 314 monasteries in all parts of Europe, France, Italy, the Empire, Lorraine, Spain, England, Scotland, and Poland. Although the congregation had its own constitutions and was absolutely autonomous, its members always claimed to be and were actually recognized as real Benedictines; hence it was not strictly a new order but only a reformed congregation within the order. (See CLUNY.)

A BENEDICTINE MONK, IN CHOIR DRESS

Following the example of Cluny, several other reforms were initiated from time to time in different parts during the next three centuries, which while taking the Rule of St. Benedict as a basis, aimed frequently at a greater austerity of life than was practised by the black monks or contemplated by the holy Rule. Some were even semi-eremitical in their constitution, and one—Fontevrault—consisted of double monasteries, the religious of both sexes being under the rule of the abbess. In dealing with these reformed congregations a distinction must be made between those which, like Cluny, continued to be considered as part of the main Benedictine body, and those which constituted practically new and independent orders, like Cîteaux, and have always been looked upon as outside the Benedictine confederation, though still professing the Rule of St. Benedict in some form or other. Those of the former category are treated here, since they and their successors constitute the order as we understand it at the present day. In the latter class the most important were Camaldoli (1009), Vallombrosa (1039), Grammont (1076), Cîteaux (1098), Fontevrault (1099), Savigny (1112), Monte Vergine (1119), Sylvestrines (1231), Celestines (1254), and Olivetans (1319). All of these will be described in detail under the respective titles.

The influence of Cluny, even in monasteries which did not join its congregation or adopt any of the other reforms mentioned above, was large and far-reaching. Many such abbeys, including Subiaco and Monte Cassino, adopted its customs and practices, and modelled their life and spirit according to the example it set. Monasteries such as these often became in turn the centres of revival and reform in their respective neighbourhoods, so that during the tenth and eleventh centuries there arose several free unions of monasteries based on a uniform observance derived from a central abbey. These unions, the germ of the congregational system which developed later on, deserve a somewhat detailed enumeration here. In England there had been three distinct efforts at systematic organization. The various monasteries founded by St. Augustine and his fellow-monks had preserved some sort of union, as was only natural with new foundations in a pagan country proceeding from a common source of origin. As Christianity spread through the land this necessity for mutual dependence diminished, but when St. Benedict Biscop came to England with Archbishop Theodore in 669, it fell to him to foster a spirit of uniformity amongst the various Benedictine monasteries then existing. In the tenth century St. Dunstan set himself to reform the English monastic houses on the model of Fleury and of what he had seen successfully carried out at Ghent during his exile in Flanders. With his co-operation St. Ethelwold brought out his "Concordia Regularis", which is interesting as an early attempt to procure a uniform observance in all the monasteries of a nation. A century later Lanfranc continued the same idea by issuing a series of statutes regulating the life of the English Benedictines. It should be noted here that these several attempts were directed only towards securing outward uniformity, and that as yet

A BENEDICTINE ABBOT

there was apparently no idea of a *congregation*, properly so called, with a central source of all legislative authority. In France the abbeys of Fleury, Marmoûtier, St. Benignus (Dijon), St. Denis, Chaise-Dieu (Auvergne), St. Victor (Marseilles), St. Claude, Lérins, Sauve-Majour, Tiron, and Val-des-Choux, were all centres of larger or smaller groups of houses, in each of which there was uniformity of rule as well as more or less dependence upon the chief house. Fleury adopted the Cluniac reform, as did also St. Benignus of Dijon, though without subjection to that organization; and all were eventually absorbed by the congregation of St. Maur in the seventeenth century, excepting St. Claude, which preserved its independence until the Revolution, Val-des-Choux, which became Cistercian, and Lérins, which in 1505 joined the Italian congregation of St. Justina of Padua. In Italy the chief groups had their centres at Cluse in Piedmont, at Fonte Avellana, which was united to the Camaldolese congregation in 1569, La Cava, which joined the congregation of St. Justina in the fifteenth century, and Sasso-Vivo, which was suppressed as a separate federation in the same century and its forty houses united to other congregations of the Benedictine family. The monasteries of Germany were divided chiefly between Fulda and Hirschau, both of which eventually joined the Bursfeld Union. (See BURSFELD.) In Austria there were two groups of monasteries, the abbeys of Melk (Molck or Melek) and Salzburg being the chief houses. They continued thus until well into the seventeenth century, when systematic congregations were organized in compliance with the Tridentine decrees, as will be described in due course. Other free unions, for purposes of mutual help and similarity of discipline, were to be found also in Scotland, Scandinavia, Poland, Hungary, and elsewhere, in which the same idea was carried out, viz., not so much a congregation in its later sense, with a centralized form of government, as a mere banding together of houses for the better maintenance of rule and policy.

Notwithstanding all these reform movements and unions of monasteries, a large number of Benedictine abbeys in different countries retained to the end of the twelfth century, and even later, their original independence, and this state of things was only terminated by the regulations of the Fourth Lateran Council, in 1215, which were to change materially the whole trend of Benedictine polity and history. By the twelfth canon of this council it was decreed that all the monasteries of each ecclesiastical province were to unite into a congregation. The abbots of each province or congregation were to meet in chapter every third year, with power to pass laws binding on all, and to appoint from amongst their own number "visitors" who were to make canonical visitations of the monasteries and to report upon their condition to the ensuing chapter. In each congregation one of the abbots was to be elected president, and the one so chosen presided over the triennial chapter and exercised a certain limited and well-defined authority over the houses of his congregation, in such a way as not to interfere with the independent authority of each abbot in his own monastery. England was the first and for some time the only country to give this new arrangement a fair trial. It was not until after the issue of the Bull "Benedictina" by Benedict XII, in 1336, that other countries, somewhat tardily, organized their national congregations in conformity with the designs of the Lateran Council. Some of these have continued to the present day, and this congregational system is now, with very few exceptions and some slight variations in matters of detail, the normal form of government thoughout the order.

Progress of the Order.—At the time of this important change in the constitution of the order, the black monks of St. Benedict were to be found in almost every country of Western Europe, including Iceland, where they had two abbeys, founded in the twelfth century, and from which missionaries had penetrated even into Greenland and the lands of the Eskimo. At the beginning of the fourteenth century the order is estimated to have comprised the enormous number of 37,000 monasteries. It had up to that time given to the Church no less than 24 popes, 200 cardinals, 7,000 archbishops, 15,000 bishops, and over 1,500 canonized saints. It had enrolled among its members 20 emperors, 10 empresses, 47 kings, and 50 queens. And these numbers continued to increase by reason of the additional strength which accrued to the order from its consolidation under the new system. In the sixteenth century the Reformation and the religious wars spread havoc amongst its monasteries and reduced their number to about 5,000. In Denmark, Iceland, and Sweden, where several houses had joined the German (Bursfeld) Union, the order was entirely obliterated by the Lutherans about 1551 and its property confiscated by the crown. The arbitrary rule of Joseph II of Austria (1765–90) and the French Revolution and its consequences completed the work of destruction, so that in the early part of the nineteenth century the order numbered scarcely more than fifty monasteries all told. The last seventy years, however, have witnessed a remarkable series of revivals and an accession of missionary enterprise, with the result that there are now over one hundred and fifty monasteries of black monks, or, including affiliated congregations and convents of nuns, a total of nearly seven hundred. These revivals and examples of expansion will now be treated in detail under the headings of the various congregations, which will bring the history of the order down to the present day.

(1) *The English Congregation.*—The English were the first to put into practice the decrees of the Lateran Council. Some time was necessarily spent

in preliminary preparations, and the first general chapter was held at Oxford in 1218, from which time up to the dissolution under Henry VIII the triennial chapters appear to have been held more or less regularly. (Details of these chapters will be found in Reyner, "Apostolatus Benedictinorum".) At first only the monasteries of the southern province of Canterbury were represented, but in 1338, in consequence of the Bull "Benedictina", the two provinces were united and the English congregation definitely established. This system of the union of houses and periodical chapters interfered in the least possible degree with the Benedictine tradition of mutual independence of monasteries, though the Bull "Benedictina" was intended to give some further development to it. In other countries attempts were made from time to time to effect a greater degree of organization, but in England there was never any further advance along the path of centralization. At the time of the dissolution there were in England nearly three hundred houses of black monks, and though the numbers had from one cause or another somewhat declined, the English congregation may truthfully be said to have been in a flourishing condition at the time of the attempt to suppress it in the sixteenth century. The grave charges brought against the monks by Henry VIII's Visitors, though long believed in, are not now credited by serious historians. This reversal of opinion has been brought about mainly through the researches of such writers as Gasquet (Henry VIII and the English Monasteries, London, new ed., 1899; Eve of the Reformation, London, 1890), and Gairdner (Prefaces to "Calendars of State Papers of Henry VIII").

Throughout the period of suppression the monks were the champions of the old Faith, and when turned out of their homes very few conformed to the new religion. Some sought refuge abroad, others accepted pensions and lingered on in England hoping for a restoration of the former state of things, whilst not a few preferred to suffer lifelong imprisonment rather than surrender their convictions and claims. In Queen Mary's reign there was a brief revival at Westminster, where some of the surviving monks were brought together under Abbot Feckenham in 1556. Of the monks professed there during the three years of revived existence, Dom Sigebert Buckley alone survived at the beginning of the seventeenth century; and he, after forty years of imprisonment, when nigh unto death, in 1607, invested with the English habit and affiliated to Westminster Abbey and to the English congregation two English priests, already Benedictines of the Italian congregation. By this act he became the link between the old and the new lines of English black monks, and through him the true succession was perpetuated. About the same time a number of English monks were being trained abroad, mostly in Spain, for the English mission, and these were in 1619 aggregated by papal authority to the English congregation, though the monasteries founded by them had perforce to be situated abroad. St. Gregory's at Douai was established in 1605, St. Lawrence's at Dieulouard in Lorraine in 1606, and St. Edmund's at Paris in 1611. The first two of these communities remained on the continent until driven to England by the French Revolution, but the third has only recently returned. In 1633, by the Bull "Plantata", Pope Urban VIII bestowed upon the restored English congregation "every privilege, grant, indulgence, faculty, and other prerogative which had ever belonged to the ancient English congregation" and also approved of its members taking an oath by which they bound themselves to labour for the reconversion of their country. So zealous were they in this work that during the penal times no fewer than twenty-seven suffered martyrdom for the Faith, whilst eleven died

in prison. Two other monasteries were added to the congregation, viz., Lamspring in Germany in 1643, and Saint-Malo in Brittany in 1611, the latter, however, being passed over to the French (Maurist) congregation in 1672.

In 1795 the monks of Douai were expelled from their monastery by the Revolution, and after many hardships, including imprisonment, escaped to England, where, after a temporary residence at Acton Burnell (near Shrewsbury), they settled in 1814 at Downside in Somerset. The monks of Dieulouard were also driven out at the same time and after some years of wandering established themselves in 1802 at Ampleforth in Yorkshire. The monks of St. Edmund's, Paris, not successful in making their escape from France, were dispersed for a time, but when, in 1818, the buildings of St. Gregory's at Douai were recovered by the congregation, the remnants of St. Edmund's community reassembled and resumed conventual life in 1823. For eighty years they continued undisturbed, recruited by English subjects and carrying on their school for English boys, until, in 1903, the "Association Laws" of the French government once more expelled them from their monastery; returning to England, they have established themselves at Woolhampton in Berkshire. The Abbey of Lamspring continued to flourish amongst Lutheran surroundings until it was suppressed by the Prussian Government in 1802 and the community dispersed. In 1828 a restoration of conventual life in a small way was attempted at Broadway in Worcestershire, which lasted until 1841. The monks then went to other houses of the congregation, though the community was never formally disbanded. Continuity was preserved by the last survivors of Broadway being incorporated in 1876 into the newly founded community of Fort Augustus in Scotland. In 1859 St. Michael's priory, at Belmont, near Hereford, was established, in compliance with a decree of Pius IX, as a central novitiate and house of studies for the whole congregation. It was also made the pro-cathedral of the Diocese of Newport, the bishop and canons of which are chosen from the English Benedictines, the cathedral-prior acting as provost of the chapter. Up to 1901 Belmont had no community of its own, but only members from the other houses who were resident there either as professors or students; the general chapter of that year, however, decided that novices might henceforth be received for St. Michael's monastery. In 1899 Leo XIII raised the three priories of St. Gregory's (Downside), St. Lawrence's (Ampleforth), and St. Edmund's (Douai) to the rank of abbeys, so that the congregation now consists of three abbeys and one cathedral-priory, each with its own community, but Belmont still remains the central novitiate and *tyrocinium* for all the houses. Besides its regular prelates, the English congregation is, by virtue of the Bull "Plantata" (1633), allowed to perpetuate as titular dignities the nine cathedral-priories which belonged to it before the Reformation, viz., Canterbury, Winchester, Durham, Coventry, Ely, Worcester, Rochester, Norwich, and Bath; to these have been added three more, Peterborough, Gloucester, and Chester, originally Benedictine abbeys but raised to cathedral rank by Henry VIII. Six ancient abbacies also, St. Alban's, Westminster, Glastonbury, Evesham, Bury St. Edmunds, and St. Mary's, York, are similarly perpetuated by privilege granted in 1818.

(2) *The Cassinese Congregation.*—To prevent confusion it is necessary to point out that there are two congregations of this name. The first, with Monte Cassino as its chief house, was originally known as that of St. Justina of Padua, and with one exception has always been confined to Italy. The other is of much later institution and is distinguished by the

title of "Primitive Observance". What follows relates to the former of these two.

Most of the Italian monasteries had fallen under the influence of Cluny in the tenth and eleventh centuries, and had adopted its customs, but by the end of the fourteenth century they had so greatly declined that there was then hardly one left in which the Cluniac observance was retained. The Abbey of St. Justina at Padua, which had formerly been Cluniac, was in a very corrupt and ruinous state in 1407 when Gregory XII bestowed it *in commendam* on the Cardinal of Bologna. That prelate, desirous of reform, introduced some Olivetan monks, but the three remaining Cluniac monks appealed to the Venetian Republic against this encroachment on their rights, with the result that the abbey was restored to them and the Olivetans dismissed. The cardinal resigned the abbey to the pope, who thereupon gave it to Ludovico Barbo, a canon regular of St. George in Alga. He took the Benedictine habit and received the abbatial blessing in 1409. With the help of two Camaldolese monks and two canons of Alga, he instituted a reformed observance, which was quickly adopted in other monasteries as well. Permission was obtained from the pope for these to unite and form a new congregation, the first general chapter of which was held in 1421, when Abbot Barbo was elected the first president. Amongst those that joined were the celebrated abbeys of Subiaco, Monte Cassino, St. Paul's in Rome, St. George's at Venice, La Cava, and Farfa. In 1504 its title was changed to that of the "Cassinese Congregation". It gradually came to embrace all of the chief Benedictine houses of Italy, to the number of nearly two hundred, divided into seven provinces, Rome, Naples, Sicily, Tuscany, Venice, Lombardy, and Genoa. In 1505 the Abbey of Lérins in Provence together with all its dependent houses joined it. A highly centralized system of government was developed, modelled on the Italian republics, by which the autonomy of the individual houses was almost entirely destroyed. All power was vested in a committee of "definitors", in whose hands were all appointments, from that of president down to the lowest official in the smallest monastery. But in spite of this obvious departure from the Benedictine ideal and the dangers arising from such a system, the congregation continued in considerable prosperity until the wars of the Revolution period; and the later decrees of the Italian government put a check to its reception of novices and began a series of suppressions which have reduced its numbers enormously and shorn it of much of its former greatness. The formation of the congregation of Primitive Observance from out of its midst has still further diminished the congregation, until it now consists nominally of sixteen monasteries, some entirely without communities, and only three or four with sufficient numbers to keep up full conventual observances.

(3) *The Cassinese Congregation of Primitive Observance.*—In the year 1851 Abbot Casaretto of Subiaco initiated at Genoa a return to a stricter observance than was then in vogue, and several other monasteries of the Cassinese congregation, including Subiaco itself, desiring to unite in this reforming movement, Pius IX joined all such abbeys into one federation, which was called after its chief house, the "Province of Subiaco". Before long monasteries in other countries adopted the same reformed observance and became affiliated to Subiaco. In 1872 this union of monasteries was separated altogether from the original congregation and erected as a new and independent body under the title of the "Cassinese Congregation of Primitive Observance", which was divided into provinces according to the different countries in which its houses were situated, with the Abbot of Subiaco as abbot-general of the whole

federation. (a) The Italian Province dates from the original federation in 1851, and comprises ten monasteries with over two hundred religious. One of these is the Abbey of Monte Vergine, formerly the mother-house of an independent congregation, but which was aggregated to this province in 1879.

(b) The English Province was formed in 1858, when certain English monks at Subiaco obtained permission to make a foundation in England. The Isle of Thanet, hallowed by the memory of St. Augustine's landing there twelve hundred and sixty years previously, was selected and a church which Augustus Welby Pugin had built at Ramsgate was placed at their disposal. By 1860 a monastery had been erected and full conventual life established. It became a priory in 1880 and in 1896 an abbey. In course of time, in addition to serving several neighbouring missions, the community embarked on work in New Zealand, where Dom Edmund Luck, a Ramsgate monk, was made Bishop of Auckland. They also undertook work in Bengal in 1874, but this has since been relinquished to the secular clergy.

(c) The Belgian Province began in 1858 with the affiliation to Subiaco of the eleventh-century Abbey of Termonde. Afflighem followed in 1870, and since then two new foundations have been made in Belgium, and quite recently missionary work has been undertaken in the Transvaal, South Africa.

(d) The French Province, perhaps the most numerous and flourishing in the congregation, dates from 1859. Jean-Baptiste Muard, a parish priest and founder of a society of diocesan missioners, became a monk at Subiaco. After his profession there in 1849, he returned to France with two companions and settled at Pierre-qui-Vire, a lonely spot amid the forests of Avallon, where a most austere form of Benedictine life was established. After his death in 1854, the abbey he had founded was affiliated to the Cassinese P. O. congregation and became the mother-house of the French province. New foundations were made at Béthisy (1859), Saint-Benoît-sur-Loire, the ancient Fleury (1865), Oklahoma, Indian Territory, U. S. A., with an Apostolic vicariate attached (1874), Belloc (1875), Kerbeneat (1888), Encalcat (1891), Niño-Dios, Argentina (1899), and Jerusalem (1901). In 1880 the French Government annexed Pierre-qui-Vire and expelled the community by force; some of them, however, were able to regain possession a year or two later. The remainder sought refuge in England, where in 1882 they acquired the site of the old Cistercian Abbey of Buckfast, in Devonshire. Here they are gradually rebuilding the abbey on its original foundations. The "Association Laws" of 1903 again dispersed the congregation, the monks of Pierre-qui-Vire finding a temporary home in Belgium, those of Belloc and Encalcat going to Spain, and Kerbeneat to South Wales, whilst those of Béthisy and Saint-Benoît, being engaged in parochial work, obtained authorization and have remained in France.

(e) The Spanish Province dates from 1862, the year in which the ancient Abbey of Montserrat, founded in the ninth century, was affiliated to the Cassinese P. O. congregation. The old Spanish congregation, which ceased to exist in 1835, is dealt with separately. Other old monasteries which had been restored, St. Clodio in 1880, Vilvaneira in 1883, and Samos in 1888, were, in 1893, joined with Montserrat to form the Spanish province. Since then new foundations have been made at Pueyo (1890), Los Cabos (1900), and Solsona (1901), besides one at Manila (Philippines) in 1895. This province also includes the Abbey of New Nursia in Western Australia, founded in 1846 by two exiled monks from St. Martin's Abbey, Compostella, who after the general suppression in 1835 had found a home at La Cava in Italy. Seeing no hope of a return to Spain they had volunteered for foreign mission work and were sent to Australia in 1846. Their names were Joseph Serra and Rudesind Salvado. They settled amongst the aboriginal inhabitants at a place some seventy miles north of Perth, which they called New Nursia in honour of St. Benedict's birthplace, and there worked as pioneers of civilization and Christianity amongst the natives. Their labours were crowned with success and their abbey gradually became the centre from which a number of outlying mission stations were established. Dom Serra became coadjutor to the Bishop of Perth in 1848, and Dom Salvado was made Bishop of Port Victoria in 1849, though he still remained superior of New Nursia, which was made an abbey in 1867 with a diocese attached. It had been aggregated to the Italian province of the congregation in 1864, but was transferred to the Spanish province on its formation in 1893. The monks own vast tracts of bushland around their monastery and they rear horses, sheep, and cattle on a large scale. The community includes a number of aboriginal converts amongst its lay brethren.

(4) *The Bursfeld Union.*—Although more fully dealt with in a separate article, something must be said here about this congregation. Formed in 1430, it included all the principal monasteries of Germany, and at the height of its prosperity numbered one hundred and thirty-six houses of men and sixty-four of women. It flourished until the Protestant Reformation, which with the religious wars that followed entirely obliterated it, and most of its monasteries passed into Lutheran hands. In 1628 the few remaining representatives of the congregation, having recovered a right to some of their possessions, offered seven monasteries to the newly resuscitated English congregation, on condition that the task of getting rid of the Lutheran occupants should devolve upon the English monks, whilst the monasteries should be restored to the Bursfeld congregation in the event of its ever requiring them. No advantage was taken of this offer except with regard to two houses—Rintelin, which was used as a seminary for a few years by the English Benedictines, and Lamspring, which continued as an abbey of English monks from 1644 to 1802. No other monasteries of the Bursfeld Union were ever restored to Benedictine uses. (See BURS-FELD.)

(5) *The Spanish Congregation.*—There were originally two distinct congregations in Spain, that of the "Claustrales" or of Tarragona, formed in 1336, and that of Valladolid, organized in 1489. At the time of the general suppression in 1835, the former comprised sixteen abbeys, and the latter fifty, besides one or two priories in Peru and Mexico. Belonging to the Claustrales were Our Lady's Abbey, Vilvaneira, St. Stephen's, Rivas del Sil, founded in the sixth century, and St. Peter's, Cardena, which claimed to be the oldest in Spain. The Valladolid congregation had St. Benedict's, Valladolid (founded 1390), for its mother-house, and amongst its houses were St. Martin's, Compostella (ninth century); St. Benedict's, Sahagun, the largest in Spain; St. Vincent's, Salamanca, famous for its university; Our Lady's, Montserrat; and St. Domingo at Silos. Of the sixty-six monasteries suppressed in 1835, five have been restored, viz., Montserrat (1844), St. Clodio (1880), Vilvaneira (1883), and Samos (1888) by the Cassinese P. O. congregation, and Silos (1880) by the French monks from Ligugé. Of the rest, sixteen remain as parish churches, thirteen are now occupied by other religious orders, two or three are used as barracks, two as prisons, one as a diocesan seminary, a few have been converted into municipal buildings or private residences, and the remainder have been destroyed.

(6) *The Portuguese Congregation.*—In the sixteenth

century the monasteries of Portugal were all held by commendatory abbots and consequently were in a very unsatisfactory state as regards discipline. A reform was initiated in 1558 in the Abbey of St. Thirso, monks from Spain being introduced for the purpose. After much difficulty the leaders succeeded in spreading their reform to two or three other houses, and these were formed into the Portuguese congregation by Pius V in 1566. The first general chapter was held at Tibaes in 1568 and a president elected. The congregation eventually comprised all the monasteries of Portugal and continued in a flourishing state until the wholesale suppression of religious houses in the early part of the nineteenth century, when its existence came to an abrupt end. Only one Benedictine monastery in Portugal has since been restored—that of Cucujães, originally founded in 1091. Its resuscitation in 1875 came about in this way: to evade the law forbidding their reception of novices, the Brazilian Benedictines had sent some of their subjects to Rome for study and training in the monastery of St. Paul's, where they were professed about 1870. The Brazilian government refusing them permission to return to that country, they settled in Portugal and obtained possession of the old monastery of Cucujães. After twenty years of somewhat isolated existence there, unable to re-establish the Portuguese congregation, they were, in 1895, affiliated to that of Beuron. Thus Brazil, which had received its first Benedictines from Portugal, became in turn the means of restoring the Benedictine life in that country.

(7) *The Brazilian Congregation.*—The first Benedictines to settle in Brazil came from Portugal in 1581. They established the following monasteries: St. Sebastian, Bahia (1581); Our Lady of Montserrat, Rio de Janeiro (1589); St. Benedict, Olinda (1640); the Assumption, São Paulo (1640); Our Lady's, Parahyba (1641); Our Lady's, Brotas (1650); Our Lady's, near Bahia (1658); and four priories dependent on São Paulo. All these remained subject to the Portuguese superiors until 1827, when in consequence of the separation of Brazil from the Kingdom of Portugal, an independent Brazilian congregation was erected by Leo XII, consisting of the above eleven houses, with the Abbot of Bahia as its president. A decree of the Brazilian government in 1855 forbade the further reception of novices, and the result was that when the empire came to an end in 1889, the entire congregation numbered only about twelve members, of whom eight were abbots of over seventy years of age. The abbot-general appealed for help to the pope, who applied to the Beuronese congregation for volunteers. In 1895 a small colony of Beuronese monks having spent some time in Portugal learning the language, set out for Brazil and took possession of the abandoned Abbey of Olinda. The divine office was resumed, mission work in the neighbourhood commenced, and a school of *alumni* (pupils destined for the monastic state) established. Two new abbeys have also been added to the congregation: Quixadá, founded in 1900, and St. André at Bruges (Belgium) in 1901, for the reception and training of subjects for Brazil. In 1903 Rio de Janeiro was made the mother-house of the congregation and the residence of the abbot-general.

(8) *The Swiss Congregation.*—The earliest monasteries in Switzerland were founded from Luxeuil by the disciples of Columbanus, amongst whom was St. Gall, who established the celebrated abbey afterwards known by his name. By the end of the eighth century the Benedictine Rule had been accepted in most, if not in all of them. Some of these monasteries still exist and their communities can boast of an unbroken continuity from those early days. The various monasteries of Switzerland were united to form the Swiss congregation in 1602, through

the efforts of Augustine, Abbot of Einsiedeln. The political disturbances at the end of the eighteenth century reduced the number of abbeys to six, of which five still continue and constitute the entire congregation at the present day. They are as follows: (a) Dissentis, founded in 612; plundered and destroyed by fire in 1799; restored 1880. (b) Einsiedeln, founded 934, the abbey from which the Swiss-American congregation has sprung. (c) Muri, founded 1027; suppressed 1841; but restored at Gries (Tyrol) 1845. (d) Engelberg, founded 1082. (e) Maria Stein, founded 1085; the community was disbanded in 1798, but reassembled six years later; again suppressed in 1875, when the members went to Delle in France; expelled thence in 1902, they moved to Dürnberg in Austria, and in 1906 settled at Bregenz. The sixth abbey was Rheinau, founded 778, which was suppressed in 1862; its monks, being unable to resume conventual life, were received into other monasteries of the congregation.

(9) *The Congregation of St.-Vannes.*—To counteract the evils resulting from the practice of bestowing ecclesiastical benefices upon secular persons *in commendam*, then rife throughout Western Europe, Dom Didier de la Cour, Prior of the Abbey of St.-Vannes in Lorraine, inaugurated in 1598 a strict disciplinary reform with the full approbation of the commendatory abbot, the Bishop of Verdun. Other monasteries soon followed suit and the reform was introduced into all the houses of Alsace and Lorraine, as well as many in different parts of France. A congregation, numbering about forty houses in all, under the presidency of the prior of St.-Vannes, was formed, and was approved by the pope in 1604. On account of the difficulties arising from the direction of the French monasteries by a superior residing in another kingdom, a separate congregation—that of St.-Maur—was organized in 1621 for the monasteries in France, whilst that of St.-Vannes was restricted to those situated in Lorraine. The latter continued with undiminished fervour until suppressed by the French Revolution, but its privileges were handed on by Gregory XVI in 1837 to the newly founded Gallican congregation, which was declared to be its true successor, though not enjoying actual continuity with it.

(10) *The Congregation of St.-Maur.*—The French monasteries which had embraced the reform of St.-Vannes were in 1621 formed into a separate congregation named after St. Maur, the disciple of St. Benedict, which eventually numbered one hundred and eighty houses, i. e. all in France except those of the Cluniac congregation. The reform was introduced mainly through the instrumentality of Dom Laurent Bénard and quickly spread through France. Saint-Germain-des-Prés at Paris became the motherhouse, and the superior of this abbey was always the president. The constitution was modelled on that of the congregation of St. Justina of Padua and it was a genuine return to the primitive austerity of conventual observance. It became chiefly celebrated for the literary achievements of its members, amongst whom it counted Mabillon, Montfaucon, d'Achéry, Martène, and many others equally famous for their erudition and industry. In 1790 the Revolution suppressed all its monasteries and the monks were dispersed. The superior general and two others suffered in the massacre at the Carmes, 2 September, 1792. Others sought safety in flight and were received into Lamspring, and abbeys of Switzerland, England, and North America. A few of the survivors endeavoured to restore their congregation at Solesmes in 1817, but the attempt was not successful, and the congregation died out, leaving behind it a fame unrivalled in the annals of monastic history. (See MAURISTS.)

(11) *The Congregation of St. Placid.*—This congregation was also an outcome of the reform instituted at St.-Vannes. The Abbey of St. Hubert in Ardennes, which had been founded about 706 for canons regular but had become Benedictine in 817, was the first in the Low Countries to embrace the reform. To facilitate its introduction, monks were sent from St.-Vannes in 1618 to initiate the stricter observance. In spite of some opposition from the community as well as from the diocesan, the Bishop of Liège, the revival of discipline gradually gained the supremacy and before long other monasteries, including St. Denis in Hainault, St. Adrian, Afflighem, St. Peter's at Ghent, and others followed suit. These were formed into a new congregation (c. 1630) which was approved by Pope Urban VIII, and existed until the Revolution. Two abbeys of this congregation, Termonde and Afflighem, have since been restored and affiliated to the Belgian province of the Cassinese P. O. congregation.

(12) *The Austrian Congregations.*—For many centuries the monasteries of Austria maintained their individual independence and their abbots acquired positions of much political power and dignity, which, though considerably diminished since medieval times, are still such as are enjoyed by no other Benedictine abbots. The example of reform set by the congregation of St. Justina in the fifteenth century exercised an influence upon the Austrian monasteries. Beginning (1418) in the Abbey of Melk (founded about 1089), the reform was extended to other houses, and in 1460 a union of those that had adopted it was proposed. Sixteen abbots were present at a meeting held in 1470, but for some reason this union of abbeys does not seem to have been at all lasting, for in 1623 a new Austrian congregation was projected to consist of practically the same abbeys as the former congregation: Melk, Göttweig, Lambach, Kremsmünster, Vienna, Garsten, Altenburg, Seitenstetten, Mondsee, Kleinck, and Marienberg. In 1630 it was proposed to unite this congregation, those of Bursfeld and Bavaria, and all the houses that were still independent, into one general federation, and a meeting was held at Ratisbon to discuss the scheme. The Swedish invasion, however, put an end to the plan and the only result was the formation of another small congregation of nine abbeys, with that of St. Peter's, Salzburg, at its head. These two congregations, Melk and Salzburg, lasted until towards the end of the eighteenth century, when the despotic rule of Joseph II (1765–90) gave them their death-blow. In 1803 many of the abbeys were suppressed and those that were suffered to remain were forbidden to receive fresh novices. The Emperor Francis I, however, restored several of them between the years 1809 and 1816, and in 1889 those that still survived, some twenty in number, were formed into two new congregations under the titles of the Immaculate Conception and St. Joseph, respectively. The former comprises ten houses under the presidency of the Abbot of Göttweig, and the latter seven, with the Abbot of Salzburg at its head. The congregation of the Immaculate Conception, in which are Kremsmünster, dating from 777, St. Paul's in Carinthia, and the Scots monastery at Vienna, includes none of later date than the twelfth century; whilst in the congregation of St. Joseph there are Salzburg (before 700), Michaelbeuern (785), four others of the eleventh century, and only one of recent foundation, Innsbruck (1904).

(13) *The Bavarian Congregation.*—A reform initiated amongst the monasteries of Bavaria, based upon the Tridentine decrees, caused the erection of this congregation in 1684. It then consisted of eighteen houses which flourished until the general suppression at the beginning of the nineteenth century. Beginning in 1830, the pious King Ludwig I restored the abbeys of Metten and Ottobeuern

(founded in the eighth century), Scheyern (1112), and Andechs (1455), and founded new monasteries at Augsburg (1834), Munich (1835), Meltenburg (1842), and Schäftlarn (1866). Pius IX restored the congregation (1858) comprising the above houses, of which the Abbot of Metten is president. The abbeys of Plankstetten (1189) and Ettal (1330) were restored in 1900 and 1904, respectively and added to the congregation.

(14) *The Hungarian Congregation.*—This congregation differs from all others in its constitution. It comprises the four abbeys of Zalavár (1019), Bakony-bél (1037), Tihany (1055), and Dömölk (1252), which are dependent on the Arch-Abbey of Monte Pannonia (Martinsberg), and to these are added six "residences" or educational establishments conducted by the monks. The members of this body are professed for the congregation and not for any particular monastery, and they can be moved from one house to another at the discretion of the arch-abbot and his sixteen assessors. The arch-abbey was founded by Stephen, the first king of Hungary, in 1001, and together with the other houses enjoys an unbroken succession from the date of foundation. The congregation is affiliated to the Cassinese, though it enjoys a status of comparative independence.

(15) *The Gallican Congregation.*—This, the first of the new congregations of the nineteenth century, was established in 1837 at Solesmes in France by Dom Guéranger. He had been professed at St. Paul's, Rome, and though at one time desirous of joining the community of Monte Cassino, was urged by the Bishop of Le Mans to restore the Benedictine Order in France. He acquired possession of the old Maurist priory of Solesmes, which Pope Gregory XVI made an abbey and the mother-house of the new congregation. He also declared it to be the true successor to all the privileges formerly enjoyed by the congregations of Cluny, St.-Vannes, and St.-Maur. Guéranger was soon joined by numbers of zealous monks, which enabled him to send out several offshoots. In this way Ligugé, originally founded by St. Martin of Tours in 360, was restored in 1853, Silos (Spain) in 1880, Glanfeuil in 1892, and Fontanelle (St. Wandrille), founded 649, in 1893. New foundations were likewise made at Marseilles in 1865, Farnborough (England), and Wisque in 1895, Paris 1893, Kergonan 1897, and a cell from Silos was established in Mexico in 1901. The community

MARIA LAACH ABBEY

of Solesmes have been expelled from their monastery by the French government no less than four times. In the years 1880, 1882, and 1883 they were ejected by force, and, being afforded hospitality in the neighbourhood, kept up their corporate life as far

as possible, using the parish church for the Divine Office. Each time they succeeded in re-entering their abbey, but at the final expulsion in 1903 they were, in common with all other religious of France, driven out of the country. The Solesmes monks have settled in the Isle of Wight, England, those of Fontanelle, Glanfeuil, Wisque, and Kergonan have gone to Belgium, those of Ligugé to Spain, and those

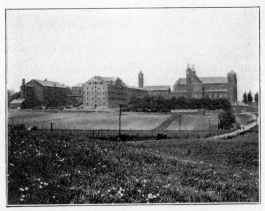

ST. VINCENT'S ARCH-ABBEY, BEATTY, PENN.

of Marseilles to Italy. The Fathers at Paris have been allowed to remain, in consideration of the important literary and historical work on which they are engaged. This congregation has endeavoured to carry on the work of the Maurists, and numbers many well-known writers amongst its members. The Abbot of Solesmes is the superior general, to which position he has been twice re-elected.

(16) *The Congregation of Beuron.*—This congregation was founded by Dom Maurus Wolter, who, whilst a seminary professor, was fired with the desire of restoring the Benedictine Order in Germany. He went to St. Paul's, Rome, where he was joined by his two brothers, and all were professed in 1856, one dying soon after. The two survivors, Maurus and Placid, set out in 1860, with a sum of £40 and the pope's blessing, to reconquer Germany for St. Benedict. In 1863, through the influence of the Princess Katharina von Hohenzollern, they obtained possession of the old Abbey of Beuron, near Sigmaringen, which had been originally founded in 777, but was destroyed in the tenth century by Hungarian invaders and later restored as a house of canons regular; it had been unoccupied since 1805. Dom Maurus became the first abbot of Beuron and superior of the congregation. In 1872 a colony was sent to Belgium to found the Abbey of Maredsous, of which Dom Placid was first abbot. The community of Beuron were banished in 1875 by the "May Laws" of the Prussian Government and found a temporary home in an old Servite monastery in the Tyrol. Whilst there their numbers increased sufficiently to make new foundations at Erdington, England, in 1876, Prague in 1880, and Seckau, Styria, in 1883. In 1887 Beuron was restored to them, and since then new houses have been established at Maria Laach, Germany (1892), Louvain, and Billerbeck, Belgium (1899 and 1901), and in 1895 the Portuguese monastery of Cucujães was added to the congregation. The founder died in 1900, and his brother, Dom Placid Wolter, succeeded him as Arch-abbot of Beuron.

(17) *The American Cassinese Congregation.*—Nothing very definite can be said with regard to the first Benedictines in North America. There were probably settlements amongst the Eskimo from Iceland, by way of Greenland, but these must have disap-

peared at an early date. In 1493 a monk from Montserrat accompanied Columbus on his voyage of discovery and became vicar-Apostolic of the West Indies, but his stay was short, and he returned to Spain. During the seventeenth and eighteenth centuries one or two English monks, and at least one of the Maurist congregation, worked on the American mission; and at the time of the French Revolution negotiations had been commenced by Bishop Carroll, first Bishop of Baltimore, for a settlement of English Benedictines in his diocese, which, however, came to nothing. The Benedictine Order was first established permanently in America by Dom Boniface Wimmer, of the Abbey of Metten, in Bavaria. A number of Bavarians had emigrated to America, and it was suggested that their spiritual wants in the new country should be attended to by Bavarian priests. Dom Wimmer and a few companions accordingly set out in 1846, and on their arrival in America they acquired the church, a house, and

Newark, New Jersey, founded 1857, with a school of 100 boys; Maryhelp Abbey, Belmont, North Carolina, founded 1885, the abbot of which is also vicar-Apostolic of North Carolina; attached to the abbey are two colleges and a school, with over 200 students; St. Procopius's Abbey, Chicago, founded 1887, with a school of 50 boys and an orphanage attached; St. Leo's Abbey, Pasco County, Florida, founded 1889; this abbey has a dependent priory in Cuba; St. Bernard's Abbey, Cullman County, Alabama, founded 1891, with a school of over 100 boys; St. Peter's Priory, established in Illinois in 1892 and transferred to Muenster, Saskatchewan, N. W. T., in 1903; St. Martin's Priory, Lacey, the State of Washington, founded 1895.

(18) *The Swiss American Congregation.*—In 1854 two monks from Einsiedeln in Switzerland came to America and founded the monastery of St. Meinrad, in Indiana, serving the mission and conducting a small school for boys. It became a priory in 1865,

MARYHELP ABBEY, BELMONT, N. C.

some land belonging to the small mission of St. Vincent, Beatty, Pennsylvania, which had been founded some time previously by a Franciscan missionary. Here they set to work, establishing conventual life, as far as was possible under the circumstances, and applying themselves assiduously to the work of the mission. Reinforced by more monks from Bavaria and their poverty relieved by some munificent donations, they accepted additional outlying missions and established a large college. In 1855 St. Vincent's, which had already founded two dependent priories, was made an abbey and the mother-house of a new congregation, Dom Wimmer being appointed first abbot and president. Besides St. Vincent's Arch-Abbey, the following foundations have been made: St. John's Abbey, Collegeville, Minnesota, founded 1856, mainly through the generosity of King Ludwig I of Bavaria; connected with the abbey is a large college for boys, with an attendance of over 300; St. Benedict's Abbey, Atchison, Kansas, founded 1857, said to possess the finest Benedictine church in America, built in the style of the Rhenish churches of the tenth and eleventh centuries; there is in connexion a school with 150 boys; St. Mary's Abbey,

and in 1870 was made an abbey and the centre of the congregation which was canonically erected at the same time. The first abbot, Dom Martin Marty, became, in 1879, first Vicar Apostolic of Dakota, where he had some years previously inaugurated mission work amongst the Indians. The following new foundations were made: Conception Abbey, Conception, Missouri (1873), the abbot of this abbey being president of the congregation; New Subiaco Abbey, Spielerville, Arkansas (1878); St. Benedict's Abbey, Mount Angel, Oregon (1882); St. Joseph's Abbey, Covington, Louisiana (1889); St. Mary's Abbey, Richardton, North Dakota (1899); St. Gall's Priory, Devil's Lake (1893), the last two communities subject to the same abbot. To all these monasteries are attached numerous missions, in which the monks exercise the cure of souls. They also have several seminaries and colleges.

(19) *The Congregation of St. Ottilien.*—This congregation, specially established for the work of foreign missions, was commenced in 1884 in the Abbey of St. Ottilien, in Bavaria, under the title of the "Congregation of the Sacred Heart". It was not then Benedictine, but in 1897 was affiliated to the Cassinese

congregation and in 1904 formally incorporated into the Benedictine Order. The Abbot of St. Ottilien is the superior general and the Beuronese Abbot of Seckau the apostolic visitor. This congregation has been largely recruited from the congregation of Beuron, to which it is bound by close ties. In 1901 it established a cell at Wipfeld, in Bavaria, and it has also ten mission stations in Central Africa, one of its members being Vicar Apostolic of Zanzibar. Its roll of honour was opened in August, 1905, by a bishop, two monks, two lay brothers, and two nuns, who suffered martyrdom for the Faith at the hands of the Central African natives.

(20) *Independent Abbeys.*—Besides the above congregations there also are two independent abbeys, which belong to no congregation, but are immediately subject to the Holy See: (a) The Abbey of Fort Augustus, Scotland. Founded in 1876, as a priory of the English congregation, mainly through the munificence of Lord Lovat, its first community was drawn from the other houses of that body. It was intended partly to continue the community of Sts. Denis and Adrian, originally of Lamspring, which had been dispersed since 1841, and of which there were only one or two surviving members; and partly to preserve continuity with the Scottish monasteries that had from time to time been founded in different parts of Germany and Austria, and of which there was, likewise, only one survivor—Father Anselm Robertson, professed at St. James's, Ratisbon, in 1845. These monks took up residence with the new community and assisted in the clothing of the first novice received for Fort Augustus. In order that its members might be exempt from the external mission work with which the English Benedictines are specially charged, the monastery was, in 1883, separated from the English congregation by the Holy See, and in 1888 was made an independent abbey, directly subject to the pope. A monk of the Beuron congregation, Dom Leo Linse, was at the same time appointed its first abbot. The Beuronese constitutions were first adopted, but these have since been replaced by new constitutions. Of late years the community has undertaken the spiritual care of three parishes in the vicinity of the abbey. (b) St. Anselm's Abbey and International Benedictine College, Rome. This was originally founded in 1687 as a college for Benedictines of the Cassinese congregation, but later on monks of other congregations were also admitted. Having ceased to exist in 1846, it was revived on a small scale by the Abbot of St. Paul's, and reconstituted in 1886 as a college and university for Benedictines from all parts of the world by Leo XIII, who at his own expense erected the present extensive buildings. In 1900 the abbey church was consecrated, in the presence of a great gathering of abbots from all over the world, by Cardinal Rampolla, acting as representative of the pope. St. Anselm's is presided over by Abbot Hildebrand de Hemptinne (who is also Abbot of Maredsous) with the title of "Abbot Primate" of the whole order. It has power to grant degrees in theology, philosophy, and canon law, and both professors and students are drawn from all congregations of the order. There is accommodation for one hundred students, but the full number in residence at one time has not yet exceeded sixty.

II. LAY BROTHERS, OBLATES, CONFRATERS, AND NUNS.—(1) *Lay Brothers.*—Up to the eleventh century in Benedictine houses no distinction of rank was made between the clerical and the lay brethren. All were on an equal footing in the community and at first comparatively few seem to have been advanced to the priesthood. St. Benedict himself was probably only a layman; at any rate it is certain that he was not a priest. A monk not in sacred orders was always considered as eligible as a priest

for any office in the community, even that of abbot, though for purposes of convenience some of the monks were usually ordained for the service of the altar; and until literary and scholastic work, which could only be undertaken by men of some education and culture, began to take the place of manual labour, all shared alike in the daily round of agricultural and domestic duties. St. John Gualbert, the founder of Vallombrosa, was the first to introduce the system of lay brethren, by drawing a line of distinction between the monks who were clerics and those who were not. The latter had no stalls in choir and no vote in chapter; neither were they bound to the daily recitation of the breviary Office as were the choir monks. Lay brothers were entrusted with the more menial work of the monastery, and all those duties that involved intercourse with the outside world, in order that the choir brethren might be free to devote themselves entirely to prayer and other occupations proper to their clerical vocation. The system spread rapidly to all branches of the order and was imitated by almost every other religious order. At the present day there is hardly a congregation, Benedictine or otherwise, that has not its lay brethren, and even amongst numerous orders of nuns a similar distinction is observed, either between the nuns that are bound to choir and those that are not, or between those that keep strict enclosure and those that are not so enclosed. The habit worn by the lay brethren is usually a modification of that of the choir monks, sometimes differing from it in colour as well as in shape; and the vows of the lay brethren are in most congregations only simple, or renewable periodically, in contrast with the solemn vows for life taken by the choir religious. In some communities at the present time the lay brothers equal and even outnumber the priests, especially in those, like Beuron or New Nursia, where farming and agriculture are carried out on a large scale.

(2) *Oblates.*—This term was formerly applied to children offered by their parents in a solemn way to a monastery, a dedication by which they were considered to have embraced the monastic state. The custom led to many abuses in the Middle Ages, because oblates sometimes abandoned the religious life and returned to the world, whilst still looked upon as professed religious. The Church, therefore, in the twelfth century, forbade the dedication of children in this way, and the term *oblate* has since been taken to mean persons, either lay or cleric, who voluntarily attach themselves to some monastery or order without taking the vows of religion. They wear the habit and share all the privileges and exercises of the community they join, but they retain dominion over their property and are free to leave at any time. They usually make a promise of obedience to the superior, which binds them as long as they remain in the monastery, but it only partakes of the nature of a mutual agreement and has none of the properties of a vow or solemn contract.

(3) *Confratres.*—A custom sprang up in the Middle Ages of uniting lay people to a religious community by formal aggregation, through which they participated in all the prayers and good works of the monks, and though living in the world, they could always feel that they were connected in a special way with some religious house or order. There seem to have been Benedictine *confratres* as early as the ninth century. The practice was widely taken up by almost every other order and was developed by the mendicants in the thirteenth century into what are now called "third orders". It was peculiar to Benedictine *confratres* that they were always aggregated to the particular monastery of their selection and not to the whole order in general, as is the case with others. The Benedictines have numbered

kings and emperors and many distinguished persons amongst their *confratres*, and there is hardly a monastery of the present day which has not some lay people connected with it by this spiritual bond of union.

(4) *Nuns.*—Nothing very definite can be said as to the first nuns living under the Rule of St. Benedict. St. Gregory the Great certainly tells us that St. Benedict's sister, Scholastica, presided over such a community of religious women who were established in a monastery situated about five miles from his Abbey of Monte Cassino; but whether that was merely an isolated instance, or whether it may be legitimately regarded as the foundation of the female department of the order, is at least an open question. We do not even know what rule these nuns followed, though we may conjecture that they were under St. Benedict's spiritual direction and that whatever rule he gave them probably differed but little, except perhaps in minor details, from that for monks which has come down to us bearing his name. It seems tolerably certain, at any rate, that as St. Benedict's Rule began to be diffused abroad, women as well as men formed themselves into communities in order to live a religious life according to its principles, and wherever the Benedictine monks went, there also we

A BENEDICTINE NUN

find monasteries being established for nuns. Nunneries were founded in Gaul by Sts. Cæsarius and Aurelian of Arles, St. Martin of Tours, and St. Columbanus of Luxeuil, and up to the sixth century the rules for nuns in most general use were those of St. Cæsarius and St. Columbanus, portions of which are still extant. These were, however, eventually supplanted by that of St. Benedict, and amongst the earliest nunneries to make the change were Poitiers, Chelles, Remiremont, and Faremoûtier. Mabillon assigns the beginning of the change to the year 620, though more probably the Benedictine Rule was not received in its entirety at so early a date, but was only combined with the other rules then in force. Remiremont became for women what Luxeuil was for men, the centre from which sprang a numerous spiritual family, and though later on it was converted into a convent of noble cannonesses, instead of nuns properly so called, a modified form of the Benedictine Rule was still observed there. St. Benedict's Rule was widely propagated by Charlemagne and his son, Louis the Pious, and the Council of Aix-la-Chapelle in 817 enforced its general observance in all the nunneries of the empire. The Abbey of Notre Dame de Ronceray, at Angers, founded in 1028 by Fulke, Count of Anjou, was one of the most influential convents in France in the Middle Ages, and had under its jurisdiction a large number of dependent priories.

The earliest convents for women in England were at Folkestone, founded 630, and St. Mildred's in Thanet, established 670, and it is probable that under the influence of the successors of St. Augustine's monks at Canterbury and elsewhere, these nunneries observed the Benedictine Rule from the first. Other important Anglo-Saxon convents were: Ely, founded by St. Etheldreda in 673, Barking (675), Wimborne

(713), Wilton (800), Ramsey, Hants (967), and Amesbury (980). In Northumbria, Whitby (657) and Coldingham (673) were the chief houses of nuns. St. Hilda was the most celebrated of the abbesses of Whitby, and it was at Whitby that the synod which decided the paschal controversy was held in 664. Most of these convents were destroyed by Danish invaders during the ninth and tenth centuries, but some were subsequently restored and many others were founded in England after the Norman conquest.

The first nuns in Germany came from England in the eighth century, having been brought over by St. Boniface to assist him in his work of conversion and to provide a means of education for their own sex amongst the newly evangelized Teutonic races. Sts. Lioba, Thecla, and Walburga were the earliest of these pioneers, and for them and their companions, who were chiefly from Wimborne, St. Boniface established many convents throughout the countries in which he preached. In other parts of Europe nunneries sprang up as rapidly as the abbeys for men, and in the Middle Ages they were almost, if not quite, as numerous. In later medieval times the names of St. Gertrude, called the "Great", and her sister St. Mechtilde, who flourished in the thirteenth century, shed a lustre on the Benedictine nuns of Germany. In Italy the convents seem to have been very numerous during the Middle Ages. In the thirteenth century several were founded in which the reform of Vallombrosa was adopted, but none of these now exist. There were also convents belonging to the reforms of Camaldoli and Mount Olivet, of which a few still survive.

Except in the Bursfeld Union, which included houses of both sexes, and in the Cistercian reform, where the nuns were always under the Abbot of Citeaux, and a few others of minor importance, the congregational system was never applied to the houses of women in an organized way. The convents were generally either under the exclusive direction of some particular abbey, through the influence of which they had been established, or else, especially when founded by lay people, they were subject to the jurisdiction of the bishop of the diocese in which they were situated. These two conditions of existence have survived to the present day; there are nine belonging to the first and over two hundred and fifty to the second category.

Early in the twelfth century France was the scene of a somewhat remarkable phase in the history of the Benedictine nuns. Robert of Arbrissel, formerly chancellor to the Duke of Brittany, embraced an eremitical life in which he had many disciples, and having founded a monastery of canons regular, carried out a new idea in 1099 when he established the double Abbey of Fontevrault in Poitou, famous in France for many centuries. The monks and nuns both kept the Benedictine Rule, to which were added some additional austerities. The law of enclosure was very strictly observed. In 1115 the founder placed the entire community, monks as well as nuns, under the rule of the abbess, and he further provided that the person elected to that office should always be chosen from the outside world, as such a one would have more practical knowledge of affairs and capacity for administration than one trained in the cloister. Many noble ladies and royal princesses of France are reckoned amongst the abbesses of Fontevrault. (See FONTEVRAULT.)

Excepting at Fontevrault the nuns seem at first not to have been strictly enclosed, as now, but were free to leave the cloister whenever some special duty or occasion might demand it, as in the case of the English nuns already mentioned, who went to Germany for active missionary work. This freedom with regard to enclosure gave rise, in course of time, to grave scandals, and the Councils of Constance (1414), Basle (1431), and Trent (1545), amongst others, regulated that all the professedly contemplative orders of nuns should observe strict enclosure, and this has continued to the present time as the normal rule of a Benedictine convent.

The Protestant Reformation in the sixteenth century affected the nuns as well as the monks. Throughout north-western Europe the Benedictine institute was practically obliterated. In England the convents were suppressed and the nuns turned adrift. In Germany, Denmark, and Scandinavia the Lutherans acquired most of the nunneries and ejected their inmates. The wars of religion in France also had a disastrous effect upon the convents of that country, already much enfeebled by the evils consequent on the practice of *commendam*. The last few centuries, however, have witnessed a widespread revival of the Benedictine life for women as well as for men. In France, especially, during the seventeenth and eighteenth centuries, there sprang up several new congregations of Benedictine nuns, or reforms were instituted among those already existing. These were not strictly congregations in the technical sense, but rather unions or groups of houses which adopted a uniform observance, though the individual convents still remained for the most part subject to their respective bishops. Mention may be made of the reforms of Montmartre, Beauvais, Val-de-Grace, and Douai, and those of the Perpetual Adoration founded at Paris in 1654 and Valdosne in 1701. The French Revolution suppressed all these convents, but many have since been restored and fresh foundations added to their number.

The first convent of English nuns since the Reformation was founded at Brussels in 1598; and another was established at Cambrai in 1623 under the direction of the English Benedictine Fathers of Douai, from which a filiation was made at Paris in 1652. At Ghent in 1624 a convent was founded under Jesuit guidance, and established daughter-houses at Boulogne in 1652, Ypres in 1665, and Dunkirk in 1662. All these communities, except that of Ypres, were expelled at the French Revolution and escaped to England. That of Cambrai is now at Stanbrook and still remains a member of the English congregation under the jurisdiction of its abbot-president. The Brussels community is now at East Bergholt, and the Paris nuns at Colwich, whence an off-shoot has been planted at Atherstone (1842). Those of Ghent are now at Oulton; Boulogne and Dunkirk, having combined, are settled at Teignmouth. The convent of Ypres alone remains at the place of its original foundation, having survived the troublous times of the Revolution. There are also small Benedictine convents of more recent foundation at Minster (Thanet), Ventnor, Dumfries, and Tenby, and one at Princethorpe, originally a French community founded at Montargis in 1630, but driven to England in 1792, and now almost exclusively English. The nuns of Stanbrook, Oulton, Princethorpe, Ventnor, and Dumfries conduct boarding-schools for the higher education of young ladies, and those of Teignmouth, Colwich, Atherstone, and Dumfries have undertaken the work of perpetual adoration.

In Austria many of the medieval convents have remained undisturbed, and likewise a few in Switzerland. In Belgium there are seven dating from the seventeenth century, and in Germany fourteen, established mostly during the last half century. In Italy, where at one time they were very numerous, there still remain, in spite of recent suppressions, eighty-five Benedictine convents dating from the Middle Ages, with over a thousand nuns. Holland has three convents of modern date, and Poland one, at Warsaw, founded in 1687. The convents of Spain numbered thirty at the time of the suppressions of 1835. The nuns were then robbed of all their possessions, but managed to preserve their corporate existence, though in great poverty and with reduced numbers. Ten of the old convents have since been restored, and eleven new ones founded. It is a peculiarity of the Spanish convents that their abbesses, who are elected triennially, receive no solemn blessing, as elsewhere, nor do they make use of any abbatial insignia.

Benedictine life in America may be said to be in a flourishing condition. There are thirty-four convents with nearly two thousand nuns, all of which have been founded within the last sixty years. The first establishment was at St. Mary's, Pennsylvania, where Abbot Wimmer settled some German nuns from Eichstätt in 1852; this is still one of the most important convents in the United States, and from it many filiations have been made. St. Benedict's convent at St. Joseph, Minnesota, founded in 1857, is the largest Benedictine convent in America. Other important houses are at Allegheny (Pennsylvania), Atchison (Kansas), Chicago (2), Covington (Kentucky), Duluth (Minnesota), Erie (Pennsylvania), Ferdinand (Indiana), Mount Angel (Oregon), Newark (New Jersey), New Orleans (Louisiana), Shoal Creek (Arkansas), and Yankton (South Dakota). The nuns are chiefly occupied with the work of education, which comprises elementary schools as well as boarding schools for secondary education. All the American convents are subject to the bishops of their respective dioceses.

III. Influence and Work of the Order.— The influence exercised by the Order of St. Benedict has manifested itself chiefly in three directions: (1) the conversion of the Teutonic races and other missionary works; (2) the civilization of north-western Europe; (3) educational work and the cultivation of literature and the arts, the forming of libraries, etc.

(1) *Missionary Work of the Order.*—At the time of St. Benedict's death (c. 543) the only countries of Western Europe which had been Christianized were Italy, Spain, Gaul, and parts of the British Isles. The remaining countries all received the Gospel during the next few centuries, either wholly or partially through the preaching of the Benedictines. Beginning with St. Augustine's arrival in England in 597, the missionary work of the order can be easily traced. The companions of St. Augustine, who is usually called the "Apostle of England", planted the Faith anew throughout the country whence it had been driven out nearly two centuries previously by the Anglo-Saxon and other heathen invaders. St. Augustine and St. Lawrence at Canterbury, St. Justus at Rochester, St. Mellitus at London, and St. Paulinus at York were Benedictine pioneers, and their labours were afterwards supplemented by other monks who, though not strictly Benedictine, were at least assisted by the black monks in establishing the Faith. Thus St. Birinus evangelized Wessex, St. Chad the Midlands, and St. Felix East Anglia,

whilst the Celtic monks from Iona settled at Lindisfarne, whence the work of St. Paulinus in Northumbria was continued by St. Aidan, St. Cuthbert, and many others. In 716 England sent forth Winfrid, afterwards called Boniface, a Benedictine monk trained at Exeter, who preached the Faith in Friesland, Alemannia, Thuringia, and Bavaria, and finally, being made Archbishop of Mentz (Mainz), became the Apostle of central Germany. At Fulda he placed a Bavarian convert named Sturm at the head of a monastery he founded there in 744, from which came many missionaries who carried the Gospel to Prussia and what is now Austria. From Corbie, in Picardy, one of the most famous monasteries in France, St. Ansgar set out in 827 for Denmark, Sweden, and Norway, in each of which countries he founded many monasteries and firmly planted the Benedictine Rule. These in turn spread the Faith and monasticism through Iceland and Greenland. For a short time Friesland was the scene of the labours of St. Wilfrid during a temporary banishment from England in 678, and the work he began there was continued and extended to Holland by the English monks Willibrord and Swithbert. Christianity was first preached in Bavaria by Eustace and Agilus, monks from Luxeuil, early in the seventh century; their work was continued by St. Rupert, who founded the monastery and see of Salzburg, and firmly established by St. Boniface about 739. So rapidly did the Faith spread in this country that between the years 740 and 780 no less than twenty-nine Benedictine abbeys were founded there.

Another phase of Benedictine influence may be found in the work of those monks who, from the sixth to the twelfth century, so frequently acted as the chosen counsellors of kings, and whose wise advice and guidance had much to do with the political history of most of the countries of Europe during that period.

In more recent times the missionary spirit has manifested itself anew amongst the Benedictines. During the penal times the Catholic Church in England was kept alive in great measure by the Benedictine missioners from abroad, not a few of whom shed their blood for the Faith. Still more recently Australia has been indebted to the order for both its Catholicity and its hierarchy. The English congregation supplied some of its earliest missionaries, as well as its first prelates, in the persons of Archbishop Polding, Archbishop Ullathorne, and others during the first half of the nineteenth century. Later on, the Spanish monks, DD. Serra and Salvado, arrived and successfully evangelized the western portion of the continent from New Nursia as a centre. Mention must also be made of the numerous missions amongst the North American Indians by the monks of the Swiss-American congregation from St. Meinrad's abbey, Indiana; and those of the American-Cassinese congregation in various parts of the United States, from St. Vincent's Arch-Abbey, Beatty, Pennsylvania. Apostolic work was also done by the English Fathers of the Cassinese P. O. congregation amongst the Hindus in Western Bengal, and amongst the Maoris in New Zealand; and French monks of the same congregation laboured in the Apostolic vicariate of the Indian Territory, U. S. A., from the headquarters at the Sacred Heart Abbey, Oklahoma. In Ceylon the Sylvestrine Benedictines have undertaken (1883) missionary work amongst the natives in the Diocese of Kandy, the bishop of which is a member of the order; and still more recently the congregation of St. Ottilien, expressly established to provide workers for the foreign mission field, has established missions amongst the native tribes of Central Africa, where the seeds of the Faith

have already been watered by the blood of its first martyrs.

(2) *Civilizing Influence of the Order*.—Christianity and civilization go hand in hand, and hence we naturally look to North-western Europe for the effects of the civilizing influences exerted by the Benedictine missionaries. St. Benedict himself began by converting and civilizing the barbarians who overran Italy in the sixth century, the best of whom came and learned the Gospel principles at Monte Cassino. Previous to the institution of monasticism labour had been regarded as the symbol of slavery and serfdom, but St. Benedict and his followers taught in the West that lesson of free labour which had first been inculcated by the fathers of the desert. Wherever the monks went, those who were not employed in preaching tilled the ground; thus whilst some sowed in pagan souls the seeds of the Christian Faith, others transformed barren wastes and virgin forests into fruitful fields and verdant meadows. This principle of labour was a powerful instrument in the hands of the monastic pioneers, for it attracted to them the common people who learned from the monasteries thus reared as from object lessons the secrets of organized work, agriculture, the arts and sciences, and the principles of true government. Neander (Eccl. Hist.) points out that the profits accruing from the labour of the monks were employed ungrudgingly for the relief of the distressed, and that in times of famine many thousands were saved from starvation by the charitable foresight of the monks. The accounts of the beginnings of abbey after abbey present the same features with recurring regularity. Not only were the marshes drained, sterile plains rendered fertile, and wild beasts tamed or driven away, but the bandits and outlaws who infested many of the great highways and forests were either put to flight or converted from their evil ways by the industrious and unselfish monks. Around many of the greater monasteries towns grew up which have since become famous in history; Monte Cassino in Italy and Peterborough and St. Alban's in England are examples. Large-hearted abbots, eager to advance the interests of their poorer neighbours, often voluntarily expended considerable annual sums on the building and repairing of bridges, the making of roads, etc., and everywhere exercised a benign influence directed only towards improving the social and material condition of the people amongst whom they found themselves. This spirit, so prevalent during the ages of faith, has been successfully emulated by the monks of later times, of which no more striking instances in our own day can be cited than the wonderful influence for good amongst the aboriginal inhabitants of Western Australia possessed by the Spanish Benedictines of New Nursia, and the great industrial and agricultural work done amongst the native tribes of South Africa by the Trappists at Mariannhill and their numerous mission stations in Natal.

(3) *Educational Work and the Cultivation of Literature*.—The work of education and the cultivation of literature have always been looked upon as belonging by right to the Benedictines. In the earliest days of the order it was the custom to receive children in the monasteries that they might be educated by the monks. At first such children were always destined for the monastic state, and St. Benedict legislated in his Rule for their solemn dedication by their parents to the service of God. St. Placid and St. Maur are examples from St. Benedict's own day and amongst others may be instanced the English saint, Bede, who entered the monastery of Jarrow in his seventh year. The education of these children was the germ out of which afterwards developed the great monastic schools. Although St. Benedict urged upon his monks the duty of systematic read-

ing, it was Cassiodorus, the quondam minister of the Gothic kings, who about the year 538 gave the first real impetus to monastic learning at Viviers (Vivarium) in Calabria. He made his monastery a Christian academy, collected a great number of manuscripts, and introduced an organized plan of study for his disciples. The liberal arts and the study of the Holy Scriptures were given great attention, and a monastic school was established which became the pattern after which many others were subsequently modelled.

In England St. Augustine and his monks opened schools wherever they settled. Up to that time the tradition of the cloister had been opposed to the study of profane literature, but St. Augustine introduced the classics into the English schools, and St. Theodore, who became Archbishop of Canterbury in 668, added still further developments. St. Benedict Biscop, who returned to England with Archbishop Theodore after some years abroad, presided over his school at Canterbury for two years and then, going north, transplanted the new educational system to Wearmouth and Jarrow, whence it spread to Archbishop Egbert's school at York, which was one of the most famous in England in the eighth century. There Alcuin taught the seven sciences of the "trivium" and "quadrivium", i. e. grammar, rhetoric, and logic, arithmetic, music, geometry, and astronomy. (See ARTS, THE SEVEN LIBERAL.) Later on King Alfred, St. Dunstan, and St. Ethelwold did much to foster learning in England, substituting monks for secular canons in several cathedrals and greatly improving the monastic schools. Ramsey Abbey, founded by St. Oswald of Worcester, long enjoyed the reputation of being the most learned of the English monasteries. Glastonbury, Abingdon, St. Alban's, and Westminster were also famous in their day and produced many illustrious scholars.

In France Charlemagne inaugurated a great revival in the world of letters and stimulated the monks of his empire to study, as an essential of their state. To further this end he brought over from England in 782 Alcuin and several of the best scholars of York, to whom he entrusted the direction of the academy established at the royal court, as well as various other schools which he caused to be started in different parts of the empire. Mabillon gives a list of twenty-seven important schools in France established under Charlemagne (Acta Sanctorum O. S. B., sæc. IV, præf., 184). Those of Paris, Tours, and Lyons eventually developed into universities. In Normandy, later on, Bec became a great scholastic centre under Lanfranc and St. Anselm, and through them gave a fresh impetus to the English schools. Cluny also took its share in the work and became in turn the custodian and fosterer of learning in France.

In Germany St. Boniface opened a school in every monastery he founded, not only for the younger monks, but also for the benefit of outside scholars. Early in the ninth century two monks of Fulda were sent to Tours by their abbot to study under Alcuin, and through them the revival of learning gradually spread to other houses. One of the two, Rabanus Maurus, returning to Fulda in 813, became *scholasticus* or head of the school there, later abbot, and finally Archbishop of Mainz. He was the author of many books, one of which, his "De Institutione Clericorum", is a valuable treatise on the faith and practice of the Church in the ninth century. This work probably exercised a beneficial influence on all the cloister-schools of the Frankish Empire. Hirschau, a colony sent out from Fulda in 830, became a celebrated seat of learning and survived till the seventeenth century, when both the monastery and its library were destroyed during the Thirty Years War. Reichenau, which suffered a similar fate at the same time, owed its early celebrity to its

school under Walafrid Strabo, who had studied at Fulda and on his return became *scholasticus* and subsequently abbot. In Saxony the monastery of New Corbie also possessed a famous school, which sent forth many learned missionaries to diffuse learning over Denmark, Sweden, and Norway. It was founded by Ansgar, the apostle of Scandinavia, who came from Old Corbie in 822, where he had been the favourite disciple of Paschasius Radbertus, a theologian, poet, musician, and author of Scriptural commentaries and an exposition of the doctrine of the Holy Eucharist.

After the death of Charlemagne the revival of secular learning which he had begun waned somewhat, except in the Benedictine abbeys where the study of letters still remained the prerogative of the monks. The Abbey of St. Gall, in particular, during the tenth century drew to its walls numerous students desirous of gaining the knowledge that was imparted there, and produced many celebrated writers. The fame of Reichenau also revived, and from it was founded Einsiedeln (934), which helped to carry on the traditions of the past. Nor was Italy behindhand, as is shown by the history of such monastic schools as Monte Cassino, Pomposia, and Bobbio.

Most of the older universities of Europe have grown out of monastic schools. Paris, Tours, and Lyons have been mentioned; amongst others were Reims and Bologna, and, in England, Cambridge, where the Benedictines of Croyland first set up a school in the twelfth century. At Oxford, the English Benedictines, though they could not claim to be the founders, took an important part in the university life and development. Monks had from time to time been sent from different abbeys to study there, but in 1283 a number of the chief monasteries combined in founding a joint college for their members, called St. Benedict's, or Gloucester, Hall, which is now Worcester College. In 1290 the cathedral-priory of Durham established for its own monks St. Cuthbert's College, which is now Trinity; and in 1362 another college, now Christ Church, was founded for the monks of Canterbury. The Cistercians had Rewley Abbey just outside the town, founded about 1280, and St. Bernard's College, now St. John's, established in 1436 by Archbishop Chichele. All these colleges flourished until the Reformation, and even after the dissolution of the monasteries many of the ejected monks retired to Oxford on their pensions, to pass the remainder of their days in peace and seclusion of their Alma Mater. Feckenham, afterwards Abbot of Westminster under Queen Mary, was the last English Benedictine to graduate at Oxford (about 1537) until, in 1897, the community of Ampleforth Abbey opened a hall and sent some of their monks there to study for degrees.

Besides being the chief educational centres during the Middle Ages, the monasteries were, moreover, the workshops where precious manuscripts were collected, preserved, and multiplied. To the monastic transcribers the world is indebted for most of its ancient literature, not only the Scriptures and the writings of the Fathers, but those of the classical authors also. (Numerous examples are cited in Newman, Essay on the Mission of St. Benedict, § 10.) The monastic *scriptoria* were the book-manufactories before the invention of printing, and rare MSS. were often circulated amongst the monasteries, each one transcribing copies before passing the original on to another house. Without doubt the copying was often merely mechanical and no sign of real scholarship, and the pride taken by a monastery in the number and beauty of its MSS. sometimes rather that of the collector than of the scholar, yet the result is the same as far as posterity is concerned. The monks preserved and perpetuated the ancient writings which, but for their industry, would undoubtedly have been lost to us. The copyists of Fontanelle, Reims, and Corbie were especially noted for the beauty of their penmanship, and the number of different MSS. transcribed by some of their monks was often very large.

Full particulars are given by Ziegelbauer (Hist. Lit. O. S. B., I) of the most important medieval Benedictine Libraries. The following are some of the chief amongst them: In England: Canterbury, founded by St. Augustine, enlarged by Lanfranc and St. Anselm, containing, according to a catalogue of the thirteenth century, 698 volumes; Durham, catalogues printed by the Surtees Society (VII, 1838); Whitby, catalogues still existing; Glastonbury, catalogues still existing; Wearmouth; Croyland, burnt in 1091, containing 700 volumes; Peterborough. In France: Fleury, MSS. deposited in the town library of Orleans, 1793; Corbie, 400 of the most valuable MSS. removed to Saint-Germain-des-Prés, Paris, 1638, the remainder, partly to the National Library, Paris (1794), and partly to the town library of Amiens; Saint-Germain-des-Prés; Cluny, MSS. dispersed by the Huguenots, except a few which were destroyed at the Revolution; Auxerre; Dijon. In Spain: Montserrat, the majority of the MSS. still existing; Valladolid; Salamanca; Silos, library still existing; Madrid. In Switzerland: Reichenau, destroyed in the seventeenth century; St. Gall, dating from 816, still existing; Einsiedeln, still existing. In Germany: Fulda, much indebted to Charlemagne and Rabanus Maurus, with 400 copyists under Abbot Sturm, and containing, in 1561, 774 volumes; New Corbie, MSS. removed to the University of Marburg in 1811; Hirschau, dating from 837; St. Blaise. In Austria and Bavaria: Salzburg, founded in the sixth century, and containing 60,000 volumes; Kremsmünster, of the eleventh century, with 50,000 volumes; Admont, the eleventh century, 80,000 volumes; Melk, the eleventh century, 60,000 volumes; Lambach, the eleventh century, 22,000 volumes; Garsten; Metten. In Italy: Monte Cassino, three times destroyed, by the Lombards in the sixth century, by the Saracens, and by fire in the ninth, but each time restored and still existing; Bobbio, famous for its palimpsests, of which a tenth-century catalogue is now in the Ambrosian Library, Milan, printed by Muratori (Antiq. Ital. Med. Aev., III); Pomposia, with an eleventh-century catalogue printed by Montfaucon (Diarium Italicum, c. xxii).

Besides preserving the writings of the ancient authors, the monks were also the chroniclers of their day, and much of the history of the Middle Ages was written in the cloister. English history is especially fortunate in this respect, the monastic chroniclers including St. Bede, Ordericus Vitalis, William of Malmesbury, Florence of Worcester, Simeon of Durham, Matthew Paris, and Eadmer of Canterbury. The rise of the scholastics, for the most part outside the Benedictine Order, in later medieval times, seems to have checked, or at any rate relegated to the background, both the literary and the educational activity of the black monks, whilst the introduction of the art of printing rendered superfluous the copying of MSS. by hand; at the same time it is worth noticing that many of the earliest printing presses were set up in Benedictine cloisters, e. g. by Caxton at Westminster, and by some authorities the invention of movable types is also ascribed to the sons of St. Benedict.

The most notable revival of learning in post-Reformation times was that effected by the congregation of St.-Maur in France in the seventeenth century. Diligent and profound study in all departments of ecclesiastical literature was one of the professed objects of this reform, and a congregation that produced such men of letters as Mabillon, Montfaucon, d'Achéry, Ménard, Lami, Garnier, Ruinart, Martène, Sainte-Marthe, and Durand needs no further eulogy than a reference to their literary achievements. Their editions of the Greek and Latin Fathers and their numerous historical, theological, archæological, and critical works are sufficient evidence of their industry. They were not less successful in the conduct of the schools they established, of which those at Sorèze, Saumur, Auxerre, Beaumont, and Saint-Jean d'Angély were the most important. (See MAURISTS.)

The arts, sciences, and utilitarian crafts also found a home in the Benedictine cloister from the earliest times. The monks of St. Gall and Monte Cassino excelled in illumination and mosaic work, and the latter community are credited with having invented the art of painting on glass. A contemporary life of St. Dunstan states that he was famous for his "writing, painting, moulding in wax, carving of wood and bone, and for work in gold, silver, iron, and brass". Richard of Wallingford at St. Alban's and Peter Lightfoot at Glastonbury were well-known fourteenth-century clockmakers; a clock by the latter, formerly in Wells cathedral, is still to be seen in the South Kensington Museum, London.

In modern times the monks of Beuron have established a school of art where painting and design, especially in the form of polychromatic decoration, have been brought to a high stage of perfection. The printing presses of Solesmes and Ligugé (both now confiscated by the French Government) have produced much excellent typographical work, whilst the study and restoration of the traditional plainchant of the Church in the same monasteries, under DD. Pothier and Mocquereau, is of world-wide reputation. Embroidery and vestment-making are crafts in which many communities of nuns excel, and others, like Stanbrook, maintain a printing office with considerable success.

IV. PRESENT CONDITION OF THE ORDER.—*Development of external organization.*—A brief sketch of the constitution and government of the order is necessary for a proper understanding of its present organization. According to St. Benedict's idea, each monastery constituted a separate, independent, autonomous family, the members of which elected their own superior. The abbots, therefore, of the different houses were equal in rank, but each was the actual head of his own community and held his office for life. The necessities of the times, however, the need for mutual support, the establishment of daughter-houses, and possibly the ambition of individual superiors, all combined in course of time to bring about a modification of this ideal. Although foreshadowed by the Aachen (Aix-la-Chapelle) *capitula* of 817 under St. Benedict of Aniane, the actual results of which died out with their originator, the first real departure from the Benedictine ideal, subjecting the superiors of different houses to one central authority, was made by Cluny in the tenth century. The plan of the Cluniac congregation was that of one grand central monastery with a number of dependencies spread over many lands. It was feudalism applied to the monastic institute. Every prior or subordinate superior was the nominee of the Abbot of Cluny and held office only during his pleasure; the autonomy of the individual communities was destroyed so far, even, that no monk could be professed in any house except by permission of the Abbot of Cluny, and all were obliged usually to spend some years at Cluny itself. But notwithstanding the extent of this departure from Benedictine tradition, the Cluniacs were never considered to have seceded from the main Benedictine body or to have instituted a new order. Hirschau, in Germany, copied Cluny, though with less conspicuous success, and Cîteaux developed the system still further and constituted a new order outside the Benedictine fold, which has ever since been regarded as such.

The example of Cluny produced imitators and many new unions of monasteries subject to a central abbey resulted. The Lateran Council of 1215, perceiving the good points of the system as well as its dangers, set itself to strike the mean between the two. The risks of an ever-widening breach between those which adhered to Benedictine tradition and those which had adopted the Cluniac ideas, were to be minimized, whilst at the same time uniformity of observance and the mutual strength resulting therefrom, were to be fostered. The council decreed that the monasteries of each country should be banded together into a congregation; periodical representative chapters were to ensure systematic government after one pattern; the appointment of definitors and visitors was to secure uniformity and cohesion; and at the same time, whilst the independence of the abbots and the autonomy of the individual monasteries were to be preserved. The plan promised well, but England alone seems to have given it a fair trial. In some of the countries it was not until the issue of the Bull "Benedictina" in 1336, or even the Tridentine decrees of two centuries later, that any serious attempt was made towards carrying out the proposals of 1215. Meanwhile certain Italian reforms had produced a number of independent congregations outside the order, differing from each other in organization and spirit, and in each of which the departure from Benedictine principles was carried a stage further. Even in the Cluniac congregation the power of the Abbot of Cluny was, after the twelfth century, somewhat curtailed by the institution of chapters and definitors. The Sylvestrines (1231) preserved the perpetuity of superiors and recognized the advantages of a representative chapter, though its chief superior was something more than a mere *primus inter pares*. The Celestines (1274) adopted a somewhat similar system of centralized authority, but differed from it in that their superior was elected triennially. The Olivetans (1319) marked the furthest point of development by instituting an abbot-general with jurisdiction over all the other abbots as well as their communities. The general chapter nominated the officials of all the houses; the monks belonged to no one monastery in particular, but to the whole congregation; and by thus destroying all community rights, and placing all power in the hands of a small committee, the Olivetan congregation approximated nearest to the later orders like the Dominicans and Jesuits, with their highly centralized systems of government. The congregation of St. Justina of Padua was modelled on similar lines, though afterwards considerably modified, and some centuries later St.-Vannes and St.-Maur followed in its wake. The Spanish congregation of Valladolid, too, with its abbot-general, and with superiors who were not perpetual and chosen by the general chapter, must be classed with those that represent the line of departure from earlier Benedictine tradition; as must also the resuscitated English congregation of the seventeenth century, which inherited its constitution from that of Spain. In these two latter congregations, however, there were some modifications, which made their dissent from the original ideal less marked than in those previously enumerated. On the other side, as representing those that preserved the traditional autonomy and family spirit in the individual houses, we have the Bursfeld Union which, in the fifteenth century, made an honest attempt to carry out the Lateran decrees and the provisions of the Bull "Benedictina". The Austrian, Bavarian, and Swiss congregations of the same period followed out the same idea, as do also almost all of the more modern congregations, and by the legislation of Leo XIII the traditional principles of government have been revived in the English congregation. In this way the true Benedictine ideal

was restored, whilst by means of general chapters, at which every monastery of the congregation was represented, and by the periodical visitations made by the presidents or others elected for that duty, uniform observance and regular discipline were preserved. The presidents were elected by the other abbots composing the chapter and their office was merely presidential, not that of a superior general or *abbas abbatum*.

Present System of Government.—All the congregations of more recent formation have been constituted, with slight variations, on the same plan, which represents the normal and traditional form of government in the order. Uniformity in the various congregations is further secured by what are called *Constitutions*. These are a series of declarations on the holy Rule, defining its interpretation and application, to which are added other regulations on points of discipline and practice not provided for by St. Benedict. The constitutions must be approved at Rome, after which they have binding force upon the congregation for which they are intended. The *capitula* of Aachen and the *Concordia Regularis* were the earliest examples of such constitutions. Amongst others may be mentioned the "Statutes" of Lanfranc, the "Discipline of Farfa", the "Ordo" of Bernard of Cluny, and the "Constitutions" of St. William of Hirschau. (The three latter are printed by Herrgott in "Vetus Disciplina Monastica", Paris, 1726.) Since the thirteenth century every congregation has had its own set of constitutions, in which the principles of the Rule are adapted to the particular work of the congregation to which they apply. Each congregation is composed of a certain number of monasteries, the abbots of which, with other officials and elected representatives, form the general chapter, which exercises legislative and executive authority over the whole body. The power possessed by it is strictly limited and defined in the constitutions. The meetings of the chapter are held usually every two, three, or four years and are presided over by one of the members elected to that office by the rest. Whilst the office of abbot is usually for life, that of the president is generally only for a term of years and the person holding it is not in all cases eligible for continuous re-election. Each president, either by himself or in conjunction with one or more specially elected visitors, holds canonical visitations of all the houses of his congregation, and by this means the chapter is kept informed of the spiritual and temporal condition of each monastery, and discipline is maintained according to the constitutions.

The Abbot Primate.—In order the better to bind together the various congregations that constitute the order at the present day, Pope Leo XIII, in 1893, appointed a nominal head over the whole federation, with the title of Abbot Primate. The traditional autonomy of each congregation, and still further of each house, is interfered with in the least possible degree by this appointment, for, as the title itself indicates, the office is in its nature different from that of the general of an order. Apart from matters explicitly defined, the abbot primate's position with regard to the other abbots is to be understood rather from the analogy of a primate in a hierarchy than from that of the general of an order like the Dominicans or Jesuits.

Methods of Recruiting.—The recruiting of the order differs according to the nature and scope of the influence exerted by each individual house. Those that have schools attached to them naturally draw their members more or less from these schools. The English congregation is recruited very largely from the schools attached to its monasteries; and other congregations are similarly recruited. Some educate and train in their monasteries a number of *alumni*, or pupils provisionally intended for the monastic state, who though not in any way bound to do so, if showing any signs of vocation, are encouraged to receive the habit on reaching the canonical age.

A candidate for admission is usually kept as a *postulant* for at least some weeks in order that the community he seeks to join may judge whether he is a suitable person to be admitted to the probationary stage. Having been accepted as such, he is "clothed" as a *novice*, receiving the religious habit and a religious name, and being placed under the care of the novice-master. According to the Rule he has to be trained and tested during his period of noviceship, and canon law requires that for the most part the novice is to be kept apart from the rest of the community. For this reason the novices' quarters are generally placed, if possible, in a different part of the monastery from those occupied by the professed monks. The canonical novitiate lasts one year, at the end of which, if satisfactory, the novice may be admitted to simple vows, and at the conclusion of another three years, unless rejected for grave reasons, he makes his solemn vows of "Stability, Conversion of manners, and Obedience". (Rule of St. Benedict.)

Habit.—With slight modifications in shape in some congregations the habit of the order consists of a tunic, confined at the waist by a girdle of leather or cloth, a scapular, the width of the shoulders and reaching to the knees or ground, and a hood to cover the head. In choir, at chapter, and at certain other ceremonial times, a long full gown with large flowing sleeves, called a "cowl", is worn over the ordinary habit. The colour is not specified in the Rule but it is conjectured that the earliest Benedictines wore white or grey, as being the natural colour of undyed wool. For many centuries, however, black has been the prevailing colour, hence the term "black monk" has come to signify a Benedictine not belonging to one of those separate congregations which has adopted a distinctive colour, e. g. the Camaldolese, Cistercians, and Olivetans, who wear white, or the Sylvestrines, whose habit is blue. The only differences in colour within the Benedictine federation are those of the monks of Monte Vergine, who though now belonging to the Cassinese congregation of Primitive Observance, still retain the white habit adopted by their founder in the twelfth century, and those of the congregation of St. Ottilien, who wear a red girdle to signify their special missionary character.

Present Work of the Order.—Parochial work is undertaken by the following congregations: Cassinese, English, Swiss, Bavarian, Gallican, American-Cassinese, Swiss-American, Beuronese, Cassinese P. O., Austrian (both), Hungarian, and the Abbey of Fort Augustus. In the majority of these congregations the missions are attached to certain abbeys and the monks serving them are under the almost exclusive control of their own monastic superiors; in others the monks only supply the place of the secular clergy and are, therefore, for the time being, under their respective diocesan bishops.

The work of education is common to all congregations of the order. It takes the form in different places of seminaries for ecclesiastical studies, schools, and gymnasia for secondary education not strictly ecclesiastical, or of colleges for a higher or university course. In Austria and Bavaria many of the government *lycées* or gymnasia are entrusted to the care of the monks. In England and America the Benedictine schools rank high amongst the educational establishments of those countries, and compete successfully with the non-Catholic schools of a similar class. Those of the American Cassinese congregation have already been enumerated; they include three seminaries, fourteen schools and colleges, and an orphanage, with a total of nearly two thousand students. The Swiss American congregation carries on scholastic work at five of its abbeys. At St. Meinrad's, besides the seminary, there is a commercial college; at Spielerville (Arkansas) and Mount Angel (Oregon) are seminaries; and at Conception, Spielerville, Covington (Louisiana), and Mount Angel are colleges. The English Benedictines have large and flourishing colleges attached to each of their abbeys, and belonging to Downside are also two other smaller schools, one a "grammar school" at Ealing, London, and the other a preparatory school recently established at Enniscorthy, Ireland.

Foreign Missionary Work.—Besides the congregation of St. Ottilien, which exists specially for the purpose of foreign missionary work, and has ten mission stations in the Apostolic Vicariate of Zanzibar, a few others are also represented in the foreign mission field. Both American congregations labour amongst the Indians, in Saskatchewan (N. W. T., Canada), Dakota, Vancouver's Island, and elsewhere. The Cassinese P. O. congregation has missions in the Apostolic Vicariate of the Indian Territory (U. S. A.) and in Argentina, under the monks of the French province, in New Zealand under the English province, in Western Australia (Diocese of New Nursia and Apostolic Vicariate of Kimberley) and in the Philippines under the Spanish province, and the Belgian province has quite lately made a foundation in the Transvaal, South Africa. The Brazilian congregation has several missions in Brazil, which are under the direction of the Abbot of Rio de Janeiro, who is also a bishop. In the island of Mauritius the Bishop of Port Louis is generally an English Benedictine. Mention has already been made of the work of the Sylvestrine Benedictines in Ceylon and of the Cistercians in Natal, South Africa.

STATISTICS OF THE ORDER

Congregation	Monasteries	Monks	Missions and Churches served	No. of souls administered to	Schools	Students
Cassinese	16	188	274	170,540	6	476
English	4	277	79	87,328	5	380
Swiss	5	355	42	34,319	7	978
Bavarian	11	383	51	78,422	10	1,719
Brazilian	13	110	6		4	770
Gallican	11	374	1	550	2	42
American Cassinese	10	753	151	110,320	18	1,702
Beuronese	9	711	14	3,812	5	141
Swiss American	7	348	103	35,605	10	675
Cassinese P. O.	36	1,092	90	115,410	17	859
Austrian:						
Imm. Conc.	11	647	367	460,832	11	1,891
St. Joseph	7	293	61	55,062	10	901
Hungarian	11	198	145	37,269	6	1,668
St. Ottilien	2	163	10	2,835	3	190
Fort Augustus	1	47	8	430		
St. Anselm's	1	1				
	155	5,940	1,402	1,192,734	114	12,392

Orders and congregations professing the Rule of St. Benedict but not included in the Benedictine Federation are as follows:—

	MONASTERIES		NO. OF RELIGIOUS
Camaldolese	19		241
Vallombrosa	3		60
Cistercians (Common Observance)	29		1,040
" (Trappists)	58		3,637
Sylvestrines	9		95
Olivetans	10		122
Mechitarists	14		152
	142		5,347

Nuns, Benedictine and others:—

Convents	No. of Religious
Benedictine Nuns:	
1. Under Benedictine Abbots........ 9	251
2. Under Bishops.... 253	7,156
Camaldolese Nuns 5	150
Cistercian Nuns 100	2,965
Olivetan Nuns........ 20	200
387	10,722

The foregoing tables, which are taken from the "Album Benedictinum" of 1906, give a grand aggregate of 684 monasteries, with 22,009 religious of both sexes. The statistics for missions and churches served include those churches and missions over which the monasteries exercise the right of patronage, as well as those actually served by monks.

V. BENEDICTINES OF SPECIAL DISTINCTION.—The following lists are not intended to be in any way exhaustive; they merely profess to include some of the more famous members of the order. The names are classified according to the particular sphere of work in which they are most celebrated, but although many of them might therefore have a just claim to be included in more than one of the different classes, when the same individual was distinguished in several different departments of work, from considerations of space and for the avoidance of unnecessary repetition, his name has been inserted only under one head. The lists are arranged more or less chronologically, except where some connecting features seem to call for special grouping. To most of the names the country to which the individual belonged is added in parenthesis.

Popes.—St. Gregory the Great (Rome); born c. 540, d. 604; one of the four Latin Doctors; celebrated for his writings and his reform of ecclesiastical chant; called the "Apostle of England" because he sent St. Augustine to that country in 596. Sylvester II or Gerbert (France), 999–1003; a monk of Fleury. St. Gregory VII or Hildebrand Aldobrandeschi (Tuscany), 1073–85; a monk of Cluny and afterwards Abbot of St. Paul's, Rome. Bl. Victor III (Benevento), 1086–87; Abbot of Monte Cassino. Paschal II (Tuscany), 1099–1118; a monk of Cluny. Gelasius II or Giovanni da Gaeta, John Cajetan (Gaeta), 1118–19; historian. St. Celestine V or Pietro di Murrhone (Apulia), b. 1221, d. 1296; founder of the order of Celestines; was elected pope 1294, but abdicated after reigning only six months. Clement VI (France), 1342–52; a monk of Chaise-Dieu. Bl. Urban V (France), 1362–70; Abbot of St. Victor, Marseilles. Pius VII or Barnaba Chiaramonti (Italy), 1800–23; was taken by force from Rome and imprisoned at Savona and Fontainebleau (1809–14) by Napoleon, whom he had crowned in 1804; returned to Rome in 1814. Gregory XVI or Maurus Cappellari (Venice), 1831–46, a Camaldolese monk and Abbot of St. Andrew's on the Cœlian Hill, Rome.

Apostles and Missionaries.—St. Augustine (Rome), d. 604; Prior of St. Andrew's on the Cœlian Hill; the Apostle of England (596); first Archbishop of Canterbury (597). St. Boniface (England), b. 680, martyred 755; Apostle of Germany and Archbishop of Mainz. St. Willibrord (England), born c. 658, d. 738; the Apostle of Friesland. St. Swithbert (England), d. 713; the Apostle of Holland. St. Rupert (France), d. 718; the Apostle of Bavaria and Bishop of Salzburg. St. Sturm (Bavaria), d. 779; first Abbot of Fulda. St. Ansgar (Germany), b. 801, d. 865; monk of Corbie and Apostle of Scandinavia. St. Adalbert, d. 997; the Apostle of Bohemia.

Founders of Abbeys and Congregations, Reformers, etc.—St. Erkenwald (England), died c. 693; Bishop of London; founder of Chertsey and Barking abbeys.

St. Benedict Biscop (England), d. 690; founder of Wearmouth and Jarrow. St. Filbert (France), d. 684; founder of Jumièges. St. Benedict of Aniane (France), d. 821; reformer of monasteries under Charlemagne; presided at council of abbots, Aachen (Aix-la-Chapelle), 817. St. Dunstan (England), d. 988; Abbot of Glastonbury (c. 945), and afterwards Archbishop of Canterbury (961); reformer of English monasteries. St. Berno (France), d. 927; founder and first Abbot of Cluny (909). St. Odo or Eudes (France), b. 879, d. 942; second Abbot of Cluny. St. Aymard (France), d. 965; third Abbot of Cluny. St. Majolus or Maïeul (France), b. 906, d. 994; fourth Abbot of Cluny; Otto II desired to make him pope in 974 but he refused. St. Odilo (France), d. 1048; fifth Abbot of Cluny. Bernard of Cluny (France), d. 1109; famous in connexion with the eleventh-century "Ordo Cluniacensis" which bears his name. Peter the Venerable (France), d. 1156; ninth Abbot of Cluny; employed by several popes in important affairs of the Church. St. Romuald (Italy), b. 956, d. 1026; founder of the Camaldolese congregation (1009). Herluin (France), d. 1078; founder of Bec (1040). St. Robert of Molesmes (France), b. 1018, d. 1110; founder and Abbot of Molesmes (1075); joint-founder and first Abbot of Cîteaux (1098). St. Alberic (France), d. 1109; joint-founder and second Abbot of Cîteaux. St. Stephen Harding (England), d. 1134; joint-founder and third Abbot of Cîteaux. St. Bernard (France), b. 1091, d. 1153; joined Cîteaux with thirty other noblemen (1113); founded Clairvaux (1115); wrote many spiritual and theological works; was a statesman and adviser of kings, and a Doctor of the Church; he preached the Second Crusade throughout France and Germany at the request of Eugenius III (1146). St. William of Hirschau (Germany), c. 1090; author of "Constitutions of Hirschau". St. John Gualbert (Italy), b. 999, d. 1073; founder of Vallombrosa (1039). St. Stephen or Etienne (France), d. 1124; founder of Grammont (1076). Bl. Robert of Arbrissel (France), d. 1116; founder of Fontevrault (1099). St. William (Italy), d. 1142; founder of Monte Vergine (1119). St. Sylvester (Italy), b. 1177, d. 1267; founder of the Sylvestrines (1231). St. Bernard Ptolemy (Italy), b. 1272, d. 1348; founder of the Olivetans (1319). Ludovico Barbo (Italy), d. 1443; first a canon regular, then Abbot of St. Justina of Padua and founder of the congregation of the same name (1409). Didier de la Cour (France), b. 1550, d. 1623; founder of the congregation of St.-Vannes (1598). Laurent Bénard (France), b. 1573, d. 1620; Prior of Cluny College, Paris, and founder of the Maurist congregation (1618). José Serra (Spain), b. 1811, died c. 1880; Coadjutor Bishop of Perth, Australia (1848); and Rudesind Salvado (Spain), b. 1814, d. 1900; Bishop of Port Victoria (1849); founders of New Nursia, Australia. Prosper Guéranger (France), b. 1805, d. 1875; founder of the Gallican congregation (1837); restored Solesmes (1837); well known as a liturgical writer. Jean-Baptiste Muard (France), b. 1809, d. 1854; founder of Pierre-qui-Vire and of the French province of the Cassinese Congregation of Primitive Observance (1850). Maurus Wolter (Germany), b. 1825, d. 1900; founder of the Beuronese congregation (1860); Abbot of Beuron (1868). Pietro Francesco Casaretto (Italy), b. 1810, d. 1878; founder and first Abbot-General of Cassinese congregation of Primitive Observance (1851). Boniface Wimmer (Bavaria), b. 1809, d. 1887; founder of American Cassinese congregation (1855). Martin Marty (Switzerland), b. 1834, d. 1896; founder of Swiss American congregation (1870); Abbot of St. Meinrad's, Indiana (1870); Vicar Apostolic of Dakota (1879). Jerome Vaughan (England), b. 1841, d. 1896; founder of Fort Augustus Abbey (1878). Gerard van Caloen

(Belgium), b. 1853; restorer of Brazilian congregation; Abbot of Bahia (1896); titular Bishop of Phocæa (1906).

Scholars, Historians, Spiritual Writers, etc.—St. Bede (England), b. 673, d. 735; monk of Jarrow, Doctor of the Church, historian, and commentator. St. Aldhelm (England), d. 709; Abbot of Malmesbury and Bishop of Sherborne. Alcuin (England), d. 804, monk of York; founder of schools in France under Charlemagne. Rabanus Maurus (Germany), d. 856; Archbishop of Mainz. St. Paschasius Radbertus (Germany), d. 860; Abbot of Corbie. Ratramnus (Germany), d. 866; a monk of Corbie, who took part in Sacramentarian controversy. Walafrid Strabo (Germany), d. 849; a monk of Fulda, and afterwards Abbot of Reichenau. Abbon of Fleury (France), tenth century; at one time a monk at Canterbury. Notker (Switzerland), d. 1022; a monk of St. Gall; theologian, mathematician, and musician. Guido d'Arezzo (Italy), died c. 1028; inventor of the gamut. Hermannus Contractus (Germany), eleventh century; a monk of St. Gall; learned in Eastern languages; author of the "Salve Regina". Paul Warnefrid, or Paul the Deacon (Italy), eighth century; historian and teacher (*scholasticus*) at Monte Cassino. Hincmar (France), d. 882; a monk of St. Denis; Archbishop of Reims (845). St. Peter Damian (Italy), b. 988, d. 1072; a monk of the Camaldolese reform at Fonte Avellano; Cardinal Bishop of Ostia (1057). Lanfranc (Italy), b. 1005 in Lombardy, d. at Canterbury, 1089; a monk at Bec (1042); founder of the school there; Archbishop of Canterbury (1070). St. Anselm (Italy), b. 1033 in Piedmont, d. 1109; a monk at Bec (1060); Abbot of Bec (1078); Archbishop of Canterbury (1093); usually considered the first scholastic. Eadmer (England), d. 1137; a monk of Canterbury and disciple of St. Anselm, whose life he wrote. The English historians: Florence of Worcester, d. 1118; Simeon of Durham, d. 1130; Jocelin de Brakelonde, d. 1200, a monk and chronicler of Bury St. Edmunds; Matthew Paris, d. 1259, a monk of St. Albans; William of Malmesbury, died c. 1143; Gervase of Canterbury, died c. 1205; Roger of Wendover, d. 1237, a monk of St. Albans. Peter the Deacon (Italy), died c. 1140; a monk of Monte Cassino. Adam Easton (England), d. 1397, a monk of Norwich; Cardinal (1380). John Lydgate (England), died c. 1450; a monk of Bury St. Edmunds; poet. John Wheathamstead (England), d. 1440; Abbot of St. Albans. Johannes Trithemius (Germany), b. 1462, d. 1516; Abbot of Spanheim, a voluminous writer and great traveller. Louis Blosius (Belgium), b. 1506, d. 1566; Abbot of Liessies (1530); author of the "Mirror for Monks". Juan de Castaniza (Spain), d. 1599; a monk of St. Saviour's, Onna. Benedict van Haeften (Belgium), b. 1588, d. 1648; Prior of Afflighem. Clement Reyner (England), b. 1589, d. 1651; a monk at Dieulouard (1610); Abbot of Lamspring (1643). Augustine Baker (England), b. 1575; d. 1641; a monk of Dieulouard and author of "Sancta Sophia". Augustine Calmet (France), b. 1672, d. 1757; Abbot of Senones-en-Vosges; best known for his "Dictionary of the Bible". Carolus Meichelbeck (Bavaria), b. 1669; d. 1734; librarian and historian of Benediktbeuern. Magnoald Ziegelbauer (Germany), 1689, d. 1750; author of a literary history of the Order of St. Benedict. Marquard Herrgott (Germany), b. 1694, d. 1762; a monk of St.-Blasien. Suitbert Bäumer (Germany), b. 1845, d. 1894; a monk of Beuron. Luigi Tosti (Italy), b. 1811, d. 1897; abbot; Vice-Archivist to the Holy See. J. B. F. Pitra (France), b. 1812, d. 1889; a monk of Solesmes; Cardinal-Bishop of Frascati (1863); librarian of the Holy Roman Church. Francis Aidan Gasquet (England), b. 1846; a monk of Downside and Abbot-President of the English Bene-

dictine congregation. Fernand Cabrol (France), b. 1855; Abbot of Farnborough (Gallican congregation). Jean Besse (France), b. 1861; a monk of Ligugé. Germain Morin, of the Beuronese congregation, b. 1861. John Chapman, of the Beuronese congregation, b. 1865. Edward Cuthbert Butler (England), b. 1858; Abbot of Downside (1906).

The Congregation of St.-Maur.—The following are some of the chief writers of this congregation: Adrien Langlois, d. 1627; one of the first Maurists. Nicolas Ménard, b. 1585, d. 1644. Grégoire Tarrisse, b. 1575, d. 1648; first Superior General of the congregation. Luc d'Achéry, b. 1609, d. 1685. Antoine-Joseph Mège, b. 1625, d. 1691. Louis Bulteau, b. 1625, d. 1693. Michel Germain, b. 1645, d. 1694; a companion of Mabillon. Claude Martin, b. 1619, d. 1696. Claude Estenniot, b. 1639, d. 1699; a companion of Mabillon. Jean Mabillon, b. 1632, d. 1707; the greatest of the Maurists. Thierry Ruinart, b. 1657, d. 1709; a companion and biographer of Mabillon. François Lamy, b. 1636, d. 1711. Pierre Coustant, b. 1654, d. 1721. Denis de Sainte-Marthe, b. 1650, d. 1725. Julien Garnier, b. 1670, d. 1725. Edmond Martène, b. 1654, d. 1739. Ursin Durand, b. 1682, d. 1773. Bernard de Montfaucon, b. 1655, d. 1741. René-Prosper Tassin, d. 1777.

Bishops, Monks, Martyrs, etc.—St. Laurence (Italy), d. 619; came to England with St. Augustine (597), whom he succeeded as Archbishop of Canterbury (604). St. Mellitus (Italy), d. 624; a Roman abbot, sent to England with other monks to assist St. Augustine (601); founder of St. Paul's, London, and first Bishop of London (604); Archbishop of Canterbury (619). St. Justus (Italy), d. 627; came to England (601); first Bishop of Rochester (604) and afterwards Archbishop of Canterbury (624). St. Paulinus of York (Italy), d. 644; came to England (601); first Bishop of York (625); Bishop of Rochester (633). St. Odo (England), d. 961; Archbishop of Canterbury. St. Elphege or Ælfheah (England), d. 1012; Archbishop of Canterbury (1006); killed by the Danes. St. Oswald (England), d. 992; nephew of St. Odo of Canterbury; Bishop of Worcester (959); Archbishop of York (972). St. Bertin (France), b. 597, d. 709; Abbot of Saint-Omer. St. Botolph (England), d. 655; abbot. St. Wilfrid, born c. 634, d. 709; Bishop of York. St. Cuthbert, d. 687; Bishop of Lindisfarne. St. John of Beverley, d. 721; Bishop of Hexham. St. Swithin, d. 862; Bishop of Winchester. St. Ethelwold, d. 984; Bishop of Winchester. St. Wulfstan, d. 1095; Bishop of Worcester. St. Ælred, b. 1109, d. 1166; Abbot of Rievaulx, Yorkshire. St. Thomas of Canterbury or Thomas Becket, born c. 1117, martyred 1170; Chancellor of England (1155); Archbishop of Canterbury (1162). St. Edmund Rich, d. 1240; Archbishop of Canterbury (1234); died in exile. Suger (France), b. 1081, d. 1151; Abbot of St. Denis and Regent of France. Bl. Richard Whiting, abbot of Glastonbury, Bl. Roger James, and Bl. John Thorn, monks of Glastonbury; Bl. Hugh Faringdon, Abbot of Reading, Bl. William Eynon, and Bl. John Rugg, monks of Reading; and Bl. John Beche, Abbot of Colchester; all executed (1539) for denying the supremacy of Henry VIII in ecclesiastical matters. John de Feckenham (or Howman), d. 1585; last Abbot of Westminster; died in prison. Sigebert Buckley, born c. 1517, d. 1610; a monk of Westminster; the link between the old and new English congregations. Ven. John Roberts, born c. 1575, martyred 1610; founder of St. Gregory's, Douai. William Gabriel Gifford, b. 1554, d. 1629; professor of theology at Reims (1582); Dean of Lille (1597); a monk at Dieulouard (1609); Archbishop of Reims (1622). Leander of St. Martin (John Jones), b. 1575, d. 1635; President of the English congregation and Prior of St. Gregory's, Douai. Philip Ellis, b. 1653, d. 1726; Vicar Apostolic of the Western District (1688); transferred to Segni, Italy (1708). Charles Walmesley, b. 1722, d. 1797; Vicar Apostolic of the Western District (1764); a Doctor of the Sorbonne and F. R. S. William Placid Morris, b. 1794, d. 1872; a monk of Downside; Vicar Apostolic of Mauritius (1832). John Bede Polding, b. 1794, d. 1877; a monk of Downside; Vicar Apostolic in Australia (1834); first Archbishop of Sydney (1851). William Bernard Ullathorne, b. 1806, d. 1889; a monk of Downside; Vicar Apostolic of the Western District (1846); transferred to Birmingham (1850); resigned (1888). Roger Bede Vaughan, b. 1834, d. 1883; a monk of Downside; Cathedral Prior of Belmont (1863); coadjutor to Archbishop Polding (1872); succeeded as Archbishop of Sydney (1877). Cardinal Sanfelice (Italy), b. 1834, d. 1897; Archbishop of Naples; formerly Abbot of La Cava. Joseph Pothier (France), b. 1835; inaugurator of the Solesmes school of plain-chant; Abbot of Fontanelle (1898). André Mocquereau (France), b. 1849; Prior of Solesmes and successor to Dom Pothier as leader of the school. John Cuthbert Hedley, b. 1837; a monk of Ampleforth; consecrated Coadjutor Bishop of Newport (1873); succeeded as Bishop (1881). Benedetto Bonazzi (Italy), b. 1840; Abbot of La Cava (1894); Archbishop of Benevento (1902). Domenico Serafini (Italy), b. 1852; Abbot General of the Cassinese Congregation of Primitive Observance (1886); Archbishop of Spoleto (1900). Hildebrand de Hemptinne (Belgium), b. 1849; Abbot Primate of the order; Abbot of Maredsous (1890); nominated Abbot Primate by Leo XIII (1893).

Nuns.—St. Scholastica, died c. 543; sister to St. Benedict. Among English Benedictine nuns, the most celebrated are: St. Etheldreda, d. 679; Abbess of Ely. St. Ethelburga, died c. 670; Abbess of Barking. St. Hilda, d. 680; Abbess of Whitby. St. Werburgh, d. 699; Abbess of Chester. St. Mildred, seventh century; Abbess in Thanet. St. Walburga, d. 779; a nun of Wimborne; sister to Sts. Willibald and Winnibald; went to Germany with Sts. Lioba and Thecla to assist St. Boniface c. 740. St. Thecla, eighth century; a nun of Wimborne; Abbess of Kitzingen; died in Germany. St. Lioba, d. 779; a nun of Wimborne; cousin to St. Boniface; Abbess of Bischofsheim; died in Germany. Among other Benedictine saints are: St. Hildegard (Germany), b. 1098, d. 1178; Abbess of Mount St. Rupert; St. Gertrude the Great (Germany), d. 1292; Abbess of Eisleben in Saxony (1251). St. Mechtilde, sister to St. Gertrude and nun at Eisleben. St. Frances of Rome, b. 1384, d. 1440; widow; founded order of Oblates (Collatines) in 1425.

VI. Foundations Originating from or Based upon the Benedictine Order.—It has already been shown in the first part of this article how the reaction which followed the many relaxations and mitigations that had crept into the Benedictine Order produced, from the tenth century onwards, a number of reforms and independent congregations, in each of which a return to the strict letter of St. Benedict's Rule was attempted, with certain variations of ideal and differences of external organization. That of Cluny was the first, and it was followed, from time to time, by others, all of which are dealt with in separate articles.

St. Chrodegang.—Besides those communities which professedly adhered to the Benedictine Rule in all its strictness, there were others founded for some special work or purpose, which, while not claiming to be Benedictine, took that Rule as the basis upon which to ground their own particular legislation. The earliest example of this was instituted by St. Chrodegang, Bishop of Metz, who in the year 760 brought together his cathedral clergy into a kind

of community life and drew up for their guidance a code of rules, based upon that of St. Benedict. These were the first "regular canons", and the idea thus started spread very rapidly to almost every cathedral of France, Germany, and Italy, as well as to some in England. In the latter country, however, it was not an entirely new idea, for we learn from Bede's "Ecclesiastical History" (I, xxvii) that even in St. Augustine's time some sort of "common life" was in vogue amongst the bishops and their clergy. St. Chrodegang's institute and its imitations prevailed almost universally in the cathedral and collegiate churches until ousted by the introduction of the Austin Canons.

Carthusians.—A word must here be said as to the Carthusian Order, which some writers have classed amongst those founded on the Benedictine Rule. This supposition is based chiefly on the fact that they have retained the name of St. Benedict in their *Confiteor*, but this was more probably done out of recognition of that saint's position as the Patriarch of Western Monasticism than from any idea that the order was a filiation from the older body. Confusion may also have arisen on account of the founder of the Carthusians, St. Bruno, being mistaken for another of the same name, who was Abbot of Monte Cassino in the twelfth century and therefore a Benedictine.

Independent Benedictine Congregations.—The various reforms, beginning with Cluny in the tenth century and extending to the Olivetans of the fourteenth, have been enumerated in the first part of this article and are described in greater detail in separate articles, under their respective titles. To these must be added the Order of the Humiliati, founded in the twelfth century by certain nobles of Lombardy who, having rebelled against the Emperor Henry V, were taken captive by him into Germany. There they commenced the practice of works of piety and penance, and were for their "humility" allowed to return to Lombardy. The order was definitely established in 1134 under the guidance of St. Bernard, who placed it under the Benedictine Rule. It flourished for some centuries and had ninety-four monasteries, but through popularity and prosperity corruption and irregularities crept in, and after an ineffectual attempt at reformation, Pope Pius V suppressed the order in 1571. Mention must also be made of the more modern Armenian Benedictine congregation (known as Mechitarists), founded by Mechitar de Petro in the eighteenth century, in communion with the Holy See; this is now reckoned amongst the non-federated congregations of the order. (See HUMILIATI, MECHITARISTS.)

Quasi-Benedictine Foundations.—1. Military Orders.—Hélyot enumerates several military orders as having been based upon that of St. Benedict or in some way originating from it. Though founded especially for military objects, as for instance the defence of the holy places at Jerusalem, when not so engaged, these knights lived a kind of a religious life in commanderies or preceptories, established on the estates belonging to their order. They were not in any sense clerics, but they usually took vows of poverty and obedience, and sometimes also of chastity. In some of the Spanish orders, permission to marry was granted in the seventeenth century. The knights practised many of the customary monastic austerities, such as fasting and silence, and they adopted a religious habit with the tunic shortened somewhat for convenience on horseback. Each order was governed by a Grand Master who had jurisdiction over the whole order, and under him were the commanders who ruled over the various houses. The following were the military orders connected with the Benedictine Order, but for fuller details the reader is referred to separate articles. (a) The Knights Templars, founded in 1118. St. Bernard of Clairvaux drew up their rule, and they always regarded the Cistercians as their brethren. For this reason they adopted a white dress, to which they added a red cross. The order was suppressed in 1312. In Spain there were: (b) The Knights of Calatrava founded in 1158 to assist in protecting Spain against the Moorish invasions. The Knights of Calatrava owed their origin to the abbot and monks of the Cistercian monastery of Fitero. The general chapter of Cîteaux drew up a rule of life and exercised a general supervision over them. The black hood and short scapular which they wore denoted their connexion with Cîteaux. The order possessed fifty-six commanderies, chiefly in Andalusia. The Nuns of Calatrava were established c. 1219. They were cloistered, observing the rule of the Cistercian nuns and wearing a similar habit, but they were under the jurisdiction of the Grand Master of the knights. (c) Knights of Alcántara, or of San Julian del Pereyro, in Castile, founded about the same time and for the same purpose as the Knights of Calatrava. They adopted a mitigated form of St. Benedict's Rule, to which certain observances borrowed from Calatrava were added. They also used the black hood and abbreviated scapular. It was at one time proposed to unite this order with that of Calatrava, but the scheme failed of execution. They possessed thirty-seven commanderies. (d) Knights of Montesa, founded 1316, an offshoot from Calatrava, instituted by ten knights of that order who placed themselves under the abbot of Cîteaux instead of their own Grand Master. (e) Knights of St. George of Alfama, founded in 1201; united to the Order of Montesa in 1399.

In Portugal there were three orders, also founded for purposes of defence against the Moors:—(f) The Knights of Aviz, founded 1147; they observed the Benedictine Rule, under the direction of the abbots of Cîteaux and Clairvaux, and had forty commanderies. (g) The Knights of St. Michael's Wing, founded 1167; the name was taken in honour of the archangel whose visible assistance secured a victory against the Moors for King Alphonso I of Portugal. The rule was drawn up by the Cistercian Abbot of Alcobaza. They were never very numerous, and the order did not long survive the king in whose reign it was founded. (h) The Order of Christ, reared upon the ruins of the Templars about 1317; it became very numerous and wealthy. It adopted the Rule of St. Benedict and the constitutions of Cîteaux, and possessed 450 commanderies. In 1550 the office of grand master of this order, as well as that of Aviz, was united to the crown. (i) The Monks of the Order of Christ. In 1567 a stricter life was instituted in the convent of Thomar, the principal house of the Order of Christ, under this title, where the full monastic life was observed, with a habit and vows similar to those of the Cistercians, though the monks were under the jurisdiction of the grand master of the Knights. This order now exists as one of the noble orders of knighthood, similar to those of the Garter, Bath, etc., in England. In Savoy there were the two orders: (k) the Knights of St. Maurice, and (l) those of St. Lazarus, which were united in 1572. They observed the Cistercian rule and the object of their existence was the defence of the Catholic Faith against the inroads of the Protestant Reformation. They had many commanderies and their two principal houses were at Turin and Nice. In Switzerland also the Abbots of St. Gall at one time supported (m) the military Order of the Bear, which Frederick II had instituted in 1213.

(2) Hospitallers.—The Order of the Brothers Hospitallers of Burgos originated in a hospital attached to a convent of Cistercian nuns in that town. There were a dozen Cistercian lay brothers who assisted the nuns in the care of the hospital, and these, in 1474, formed themselves into a new order intended to be independent of Cîteaux. They met with much opposition, and, irregularities having crept in, they were reformed in 1587 and placed under the abbess of the convent.

(3) Oblates.—The Oblates of St. Frances of Rome, called also Collatines, were a congregation of pious women, founded in 1425 and approved as an order in 1433. They first observed the rule of the Franciscan Tertiaries, but this was soon changed for that of St. Benedict. The order consisted chiefly of noble Roman ladies, who lived a semi-religious life and devoted themselves to works of piety and charity. They made no solemn vows, neither were they strictly enclosed, nor forbidden to enjoy the use of their possessions. They were at first under the direction of the Olivetan Benedictines, but after the death of their foundress, in 1440, they became independent.

(4) Orders of Canonesses.—Information is but scanty concerning the chapters of noble canonesses, which were fairly numerous in Lorraine, Flanders, and Germany in medieval times. It seems certain, however, that many of them were originally communities of Benedictine nuns, which, for one reason or another, renounced their solemn vows and assumed the state of canonesses, whilst still observing some form of the Benedictine Rule. The membership of almost all these chapters was restricted to women of noble, and in some cases of royal, descent. In many also, whilst the canonesses were merely seculars, that is, not under vows of religion, and therefore free to leave and marry, the abbesses retained the character and state of religious superiors, and as such were solemnly professed as Benedictine nuns. The following list of houses is taken from Mabillon and Hélyot, but all had ceased to exist by the end of the eighteenth century:—In Lorraine: Remiremont; founded 620; members became canonesses in 1515; Epinal, 983; Pouzay, Bouxières-aux-Dames, and Metz, of the eleventh or twelfth century. In Germany: Cologne, 689; Homburg and Strasburg, of the seventh century; Lindau, Buchau, and Andlau of the eighth century; Obermünster, Niedermünster, and Essen of the ninth century. In Flanders: Nivelles, Mons, Andenne, Maubeuge, and Belisie of the seventh century; and Denain, 764. The members of the following houses in Germany having renounced their solemn vows and become canonesses in the sixteenth century, abandoned also the Catholic Faith and accepted the Protestant religion: Gandersheim, Herford, Quedlinburg, Gernrode.

THE BENEDICTINE ORDER IN GENERAL.—MONTALEMBERT, Monks of the West (London, 1896), Eng. tr., new ed., with preface by GASQUET; NEWMAN, Mission of St. Benedict and Benedictine Schools, in Historical Sketches (London, 1873); GASQUET, Sketch of the Life and Mission of St. Benedict (London, 1895); MAITLAND, The Dark Ages (London, 1845); MABILLON, Annales O. S. B. (Paris, 1703–39); ID., Acta SS. O. S. B. (Venice, 1733); YEPEZ, Chronicon generale Ord. S. P. N. Benedicti (Cologne, 1603); HÉLYOT, Histoire des ordres religieux (Paris, 1792); ID., Dict. des ordres religieux (Paris, 1860); MÈGE, Commentaire sur la règle de S. Benoît (Paris, 1687); CALMET, Commentaire (Paris, 1734); MÉNARD, Codex regularum (Paris, 1638); BESSE, Le moine bénédictin (Ligugé, 1898); BRAUNMÜLLER in Kirchenlex., s. v.; HERZOG, Realencyclopädie (Leipzig, 1897), s. v.; HEIMBUCHER, Die Orden und Kongregationen der katholischen Kirche (Paderborn, 1896), I; ZIEGELBAUER, Hist. lit. O. S. B. (Augsburg, 1754); Album Benedictinum (St. Vincent's, Pennsylvania, 1880; Rome, 1905); TANNER, Notitia Monastica (London, 1744); DUGDALE, Monasticon Anglicanum, with Stevens's continuation (London, 1817–30); GASQUET, Henry VIII and the English Monasteries (London, 1899); ID., The Eve of the Reformation (London, 1890); GAIRDNER, Prefaces to Calendars of State Papers of Henry VIII; TAUNTON, English Black Monks of St. Benedict (London, 1897); DUDDEN, Gregory the Great (London, 1905), I; ECKENSTEIN, Woman under Monasticism (Cambridge, 1896); HOPE, St. Boniface and the Conversion of Germany (London, 1872); REYNER, Apostolatus Benedictinorum in Angliâ (Douai, 1626); HIND, Benedictines in Oxford in Ampleforth Journal, VI, 1901.

THE ASCENSION OF JESUS CHRIST

FROM THE BENEDICTIONAL OF ST. ETHELWOLD, ABOUT A.D. 975. LIBRARY OF THE DUKE OF DEVONSHIRE

Special Congregations.—Duckett, *Charters and Records of Cluni* (Lewes, England, 1890); Sackur, *Die Cluniacenser* (Halle a. S., 1892–94); Janauschek, *Origines Cisterciensium* (Vienna, 1877); Gaillardin, *Les Trappistes* (Paris, 1844); Guibert, *Destruction de Grandmont* (Paris, 1877); Salvado, *Memorie Storiche* (Rome, 1851); Berengier, *La Nouvelle-Nursie* (Paris, 1878); Brullée, *Vie de P. Muard* (Paris, 1855), tr. Robot, 1882; Thompson, *Life of P. Muard* (London, 1886); de Broglie, *Mabillon* (Paris, 1888); Id., *Montfaucon* (Paris, 1891); Houtin, *Dom Couturier* (Angers, 1899); van Caloen, *Dom Maur Wolter et les origines de la cong. de Beuron* (Bruges, 1891); Dolan, *Succisa Virescit* in *Downside Review*, I–IV.

G. Cyprian Alston.

Benediction, Nuptial. See Mass, Nuptial.

Benedictional (*Benedictionale*), a book containing a collection of benedictions or blessings in use in the Church. In the ancient sacramentaries, particularly in the Gregorian, various early forms of blessings are found. In some manuscripts these benedictions are interspersed throughout the book, while in others they are given separately. The blessings collected from the Gregorian Sacramentary constitute the so-called *Benedictionale*. From the very ancient manuscript of the Cæsarean Library, Lambecius edited this *Benedictionale*, believing that he was the first to give it to the public. In this, however, Lambecius erred, since nearly all the blessings contained in this manuscript had been previously published, though under a different order, or arrangement, by Ménard (d. 1644). Pamelius (Liturgicon Ecclesiæ Lat., II) also edited a benedictional from two manuscripts of the time of Charlemagne or a little later, formerly in the library of the Queen of Sweden, now in the Vatican. Many discrepancies, nevertheless, are to be noted between the work of Pamelius and the original manuscripts from which it is supposed to be drawn. The "Liber Sacramentorum" of Ratoldus, of the tenth century, likewise contains numerous blessings; but the most complete benedictional is that found in two manuscripts (Nos. 62, 63) of the monastery of St. Theodoric, near Reims, written about 900. From a manuscript in the Abbey of St. Eligius Ménard edited a benedictional, while Angelo Rocca has given us one from a manuscript of the Vatican Library. The pontifical of Egbert, Archbishop of York (732–766), published by the Surtees Society in 1853, contains numerous forms of blessings. The blessings in use in the present day are found for the most part in the Missal and in the Ritual.

Præf. in librum Sacram. S. Greg., in *P. L.*, LXXVIII, 601 sqq.; CXXI, 865 sqq.; Sinker in *Dict. of Christ. Antiq.*

Andrew B. Meehan.

Benediction of Abbots. See Abbot.

Benediction of the Blessed Sacrament.—One of the most generally popular of Catholic services is Benediction of the Blessed Sacrament, known in France as *Salut* and in Germany as *Segen*. It is ordinarily an afternoon or evening devotion and consists in the singing of certain hymns, or litanies, or canticles, before the Blessed Sacrament, which is exposed upon the altar in a monstrance and is surrounded with lights. At the end, the priest, his shoulders enveloped in a humeral veil, takes the monstrance into his hands and with it makes the sign of the cross (hence the name Benediction) in silence over the kneeling congregation. Benediction is often employed as a conclusion to other services, e. g. Vespers, Compline, the Stations of the Cross, etc., but it is also still more generally treated as a rite complete in itself. There is a good deal of diversity of usage in different countries with regard to details, but some of the elements are constant. The use of incense and wax candles, which even in the poorest churches must not be less than ten in number, the singing of the "Tantum ergo" with its versicle and prayer, and the blessing given with the Blessed Sacrament are obligatory everywhere.

In Rome the principle obtains that the only portion of the service which is to be regarded as strictly liturgical is the singing of the "Tantum ergo" and the giving of the Benediction which immediately follows. This idea is emphasized by the fact that in many Roman churches the celebrant, vested in cope and preceded by thurifer, acolytes, etc., only makes his entry into the sanctuary just before the "Tantum ergo" is begun. Previously to this the Blessed Sacrament is exposed, informally so to speak, by a priest in cotta and stole; and then choir and congregation are left to sing litanies and canticles, or to say prayers and devotions as the occasion may demand, the whole service being of a very popular character.

In English-speaking countries the service generally begins with the entry of the priest and his assistants in procession and with the singing of the "O Salutaris Hostia" as soon as the Blessed Sacrament is taken out of the tabernacle. Indeed in England the singing of the "O Salutaris" is enjoined in the "Ritus servandus", the code of procedure approved by a former synod of the Province of Westminster. On the other hand, the Litany of Our Lady, though usually printed after the "O Salutaris" and very generally sung at Benediction, is nowhere of obligation. It may be added that further solemnity is often given to the service by the presence of deacon and subdeacon in dalmatics. When the bishop of the diocese officiates he uses mitre and crosier in the procession to the altar, and makes the sign of the cross over the people three times in giving the benediction. On the other hand, a very informal sort of service is permitted, where the means for carrying out a more elaborate rite are not available. The priest, wearing cotta and stole, simply opens the tabernacle door. Prayers and devotions are said or sung, and then the priest blesses those present with the veiled ciborium before the tabernacle door is again closed. The permission, general or special, of the bishop of the diocese is necessary for services where Benediction is given with the monstrance.

History of the Devotion. It is easy to recognize in our ordinary Benediction service, the traces of two distinct elements. There is of course in the first place the direct veneration of the Blessed Sacrament, which appears in the exposition, blessing, "Tantum ergo", etc. But besides this we note the almost invariable presence of what at first sight seems an incongruous element, that of the litany of Loreto, or of popular hymns in honour of Our Lady. Tracing our present service back to its origin we find that these two features are derived from different sources. The idea of exposing the Blessed Sacrament for veneration in a monstrance appears to have been first evolved at the end of the thirteenth or the beginning of the fourteenth century. When the elevation of the Host at Mass was introduced in the early years of the thirteenth century, probably as a form of protest against the theological views of Peter the Chanter, the idea by degrees took firm hold of the popular mind that special virtue and merit were attached to the act of looking at the Blessed Sacrament. To such extremes did this prepossession go, that the seeing of the Host at the moment of the elevation was judged to be the most vital part of attendance at Mass. In certain churches in Spain a screen of black velvet was held up behind the altar in order that the priest's hands and the Host might be more easily seen from afar; in others strict injunctions were given to the thurifer that he should on no account allow the smoke of the thurible to obstruct the view of the Host. Futhermore, we read that when men were dying and were unable on account of vomiting or any other cause to receive Holy Viaticum, the Blessed Sacrament was brought to them and held up before them to look at. Indeed, a virtual prohibition of this practice stands to this day amongst the rubrics of the "Rituale Romanum".

Under the influence of this idea, the Blessed Sacrament in the processions which became common after the institution of the feast of Corpus Christi in 1246, came by degrees to be carried in transparent vessels, resembling our present monstrances. Moreover, a custom grew up, especially in Germany, of keeping the Blessed Sacrament continually exposed to view in churches. It was forbidden by many synods, but a sort of compromise was arrived at through the construction of the *Sakramentshäuschen* of which so many examples still exist in central Europe. These tabernacles, of great height and imposing appearance, were erected in the most conspicuous part of the church, and there the Blessed Sacrament was reserved in a monstrance behind a metal door of lattice-work which allowed a more or less free view of the interior. It was thus that the practice developed, though partly kept in check by synodal decrees, of adding solemnity to any function, even the Mass itself, by exposing the Blessed Sacrament during its continuance.

Turning now to our second element, we find that from the beginning of the thirteenth century, a custom prevailed among the confraternities and guilds which were established at that period in great numbers, of singing canticles in the evening of the day before a statue of Our Lady. These canticles were called *Laude* and were often composed in the vulgar tongue, becoming in the hands of such poets as the Franciscan Giacopone da Todi, one of the great popular influences which helped to develop a native Italian literature. Confraternities were formed for the express purpose of singing these canticles and their members were called *Laudesi*. It was such a company of *Laudesi* that brought together the seven holy founders who, in the first half of the thirteenth century, established the Order of Servites, or Servants of Mary. Although the *laude* hardly flourished outside Italy, where both the language and the character of the people lent themselves readily to the composition of innumerable canticles, the idea of an evening service of a popular character sung before the statue of Our Lady, spread throughout Europe. In particular, the "Salve Regina", a special devotion of the Servites, Dominicans, Carmelites, and other orders, was consecrated by usage to this rite, and we find traces everywhere of its being sung, often by choirs of boys, for whom a special endowment was provided, as a separate evening service. In France, this service was commonly known as a *Salut*, in the Low Countries as the *Lof*, in England and Germany, simply as the *Salve*.

Now it seems certain that our present Benediction service has resulted from the general adoption of this evening singing of canticles before the statue of Our Lady, enhanced as it often came to be in the course of the sixteenth and seventeenth centuries by the exposition of the Blessed Sacrament, which was employed at first only as an adjunct to lend it additional solemnity. The blessing at the close seems to have been added simply because the custom gained ground of making the sign of the cross over the people whenever the Blessed Sacrament was replaced in the tabernacle after a procession or after being carried to the sick or any kind of an exposition. But in the course of the seventeenth century, we find numberless bequests for *Saluts* in French wills, the items to be sung, often of a most miscellaneous character, being minutely specified, and among these the condition is frequently appended that the Blessed Sacrament should be exposed during the whole time of the *Salut*.

The development which is too intricate to be given here in further detail, may be investigated in the works mentioned below.

To the REV. V. DE BUCK, the Bollandist, belongs the merit of having first called attention to the true history of this devotion. See *Précis Historiques* (Brussels, 1872), XXI, 59–70. His conclusions have been developed by the present writer in *The Month*, June to September, 1901, October, 1905, and in the book *Corpus Domini* (in preparation, 1907). Useful material may be found in THIERS, *Traité de l'Exposition du S. Sacrement*, written in 1673. The account of Benediction given by such authorities as CORBLET, *Histoire du Sacrement de l'Eucharistie* (Paris, 1885), II, 419–431, is not satisfactory. For the rubrical aspects of the service see DE MONTAULT, *Œuvres Complètes* (Paris, 1892), VI, 503–531; *Revue Théologique* (Paris, 1857), II, 305, 464, 643; WAPELHORST, *Compendium Sacræ Liturgiæ* (New York, 1904), 6th ed., 218, sq.; LOAN, *Ceremonies of some Ecclesiastical Functions* (3d ed., Dublin, 1901), 152–163.

HERBERT THURSTON.

Benedictis, JACOBUS DE. See STABAT MATER.

Benedict Levita (of Mainz), or BENEDICT THE DEACON, is the name given to himself by the author of a forged collection of capitularies which appeared in the ninth century. The collection belongs to the group of pseudo-Isidorian forgeries that includes the pseudo-Isidorian recension of the Spanish collection of canons, the so-called "capitula Angilramni", and the collection of false decretals of the pseudo-Isidore. The name Benedict is, without doubt, an assumed one; the statement that he had been a deacon in the Church of Mainz and that the collection had been made from the archiepiscopal archives of Mainz at the command of the late Archbishop Autgar (825–847) is clearly also untrue. Nothing is known concerning the real author. On internal evidence it may be accepted that these forged capitularies were composed in the western part of the Frankish empire and not at Mainz; the grounds for this belief are, especially, the opposition shown to the institution of "chorepiscopi", and further the circumstance that the collection was first used and found readiest acceptance among the Western Franks. The close relationship between this collection and Pseudo-Isidore lends some probability to the supposition that it arose in the Archdiocese of Reims. As to the time when it appeared there is no reason to doubt the statement of the author that Archbishop Autgar of Mainz was then dead. Consequently the collection was made after 847 (Autgar died 21 April, 847). This is confirmed by a metrical panegyric, prefixed to the collection, in praise of the Carlovingian rulers, and in which Louis the German, the Emperor Lothair, and Charles the Bald are described as living, a fact which points to the years following 843. Another clue is offered by "Additamentum" IV in which the forged pseudo-Isidorian decretals have evidently been used. But the way in which these decretals are employed by Benedict shows that the Pseudo-Isidorian collection had not yet reached its completed form. The latest date for the appearance of this collection of canons may, therefore, be given as from 848 to 850. The time of composition cannot be more exactly determined; it was somewhere between the years 847–850.

The author represents his collection as the continuation and completion of the collection of genuine capitularies in four books, "Capitularia regum Francorum", produced in 827 by Ansegisus, Abbot of Fontanelle. He divides it into three books which he designates as "liber quintus", "sextus", and "septimus". Three other writings precede the first book; a prologue in verse, a preface in prose which treats of the origin and contents of the collection, and the aforesaid metrical panegyric on the rulers of the Carlovingian line; beginning with Pepin and Carloman and ending with the sons of Louis the Pious. Four supplementary writings (additamenta) are annexed to the last book; (I) The Aachen capitulary of 817 concerning the monasteries; (II) the report of the bishops (August, 829) to the Emperor Louis the Pious; (III) a few genuine capitularies and a large number of forged ones, just as in the main body of the collection; (IV) a large number (170) of extracts taken from various sources, among which are also forgeries of the Pseudo-Isidore. The work of Abbot Ansegisus was taken as a model for the collection. As to the sources of the collection, about one-fourth of it consists of genuine capitularies (a certain kind of royal decrees customary in the Frankish Empire); in fact, the genuine materials used by the author surpass sometimes those used by Ansegisus. Most of the pretended capitularies are, however, not genuine. Among the genuine sources, from which the larger portion of them are drawn, are: the Holy Scriptures; the decrees of councils; papal decrees; the collection of Irish canons; the ordinances of the Roman law, the "leges Visigothorum" and "Baiuwariorum"; the "Libri Penitentiales" or penitential books; the writings of the Church Fathers, and letters of bishops. He repeats himself frequently; a number of chapters are duplicated literally or nearly word for word. The chief aim of the forger was to enable the Church to maintain its independence in face of the assaults of the secular power. The author stands for the contemporary movement in favour of ecclesiastical reform, and in opposition to the rule of the Church by the laity. The first two editions (Tilius, Paris, 1548, and Pithœus, Paris, 1588) are incomplete; the collection is found complete in Baluze, Capitularia regum Francorum (Paris, 1677), I, col. 801–1232, and in Pertz, Monumenta Germaniæ Hist.: Leges, II (Hanover, 1837), 2, 39–158 (cf. Migne, P. L., XCVII, col. 699–912). E. Seckel is preparing a new edition for the Monum. Germ. Hist.: Capitularia, III).

HINSCHIUS, *Decretales pseudoisidorianæ et Capitula Angilramni* (Leipzig, 1863); SCHNEIDER, *Die Lehre von den Kirchenrechtsquellen* (2nd ed., Ratisbon, 1892), 75 sqq.; LOT, *Etudes sur le règne de Louis Capet* (Paris, 1903), 361 sqq.; HAUCK, *Kirchengeschichte Deutschlands* (2nd ed., Leipzig, 1900), II, 527 sqq.; SECKEL, *Studien zu Benedict Levita in Neues Archiv.* (1900), XXVI, XXIX, XXXI.

J. P. KIRSCH.

Benedict of Aniane, SAINT, b. about 745–750; d. at Cornelimünster, 11 February, 821. Benedict, originally known as Witiza, son of the Goth, Aigulf, Count of Maguelone in Southern France, was educated at the Frankish court of Pepin, and entered the royal service. He took part in the Italian campaign of Charlemagne (773), after which he left his royal master to enter the religious life, and was received into the monastery of St. Sequanus (Saint-Seine). He gave himself most zealously to practices of asceticism, and learned to value the Rule of St. Benedict as the best foundation for the monastic life. Returning home in 779, he established on his own land near the little river of Aniane a new monastic settlement, which soon developed into a great monastery, uuder the name of Aniane, and became the model and centre of the monastic reform in France, introduced by Louis the Pious. The emperor's chief adviser was Benedict, and the general adoption of the Rule of St. Benedict in the monasteries of the Empire was the most important step towards the reform. Benedict took a prominent part in the synods held in Aachen in 816 and 817, the results of which were embodied in the important prescriptions for the restoration of monastic discipline, dated 10 July, 817; he was the enthusiastic leader of these assemblies, and he himself reformed many monasteries on the lines laid down in the ordinances promulgated there. In order to have him in the vicinity of his royal residence, Louis in 814 had founded on the Inde, a stream near Aachen, the Abbey of Cornelimünster, which was to be an exemplar for all other abbeys, and to be under the guidance of Benedict. In the dogmatic controversy over Adoptianism, under the leadership of Felix of Urgel, Benedict took the part of orthodoxy. To promote the monastic reforms, he compiled a collection of monastic rules. A pupil of

his, the monk Ardo, wrote a biography of the great abbot.

For Benedict's writings see *Codex regularum monasticarum et canonicarum* in P. L., CIII, 393–702; *Concordia regularum.* loc. cit.; *Letters*, loc. cit., 703–1380. Other treatises (loc. cit., 1381 sqq.) ascribed to him are probably not authentic. ARDO SMARAGDUS, *Life*, op. cit., CIII, 353 sqq.; *Mon. Germ. Hist.: Script.*, XV, I, 200–220; *Acta SS.*, Feb., II, 606 sqq.; NICOLAI, *Der hl. Benedikt, Gründer von Aniane und Corneli-münster* (Cologne, 1865); PAULINIER, *S. Benoît d'Aniane et la fondation du monastère de ce nom* (Montpellier, 1871); FOSS, *Benedikt von Aniane* (Berlin, 1884); PÜCKERT, *Aniane und Gellone* (Leipzig, 1899); HAUCK, *Kirchengesch. Deutschlands* (2nd ed., Leipzig, 1900), II, 575 sqq.; BUTLER, *Lives of the Saints*, 12 Feb.

J. P. KIRSCH.

Benedict of Nursia, SAINT, founder of western monasticism, b. at Nursia, c. 480; d. at Monte Cassino, 543. The only authentic life of Benedict of Nursia is that contained in the second book of St. Gregory's "Dialogues". It is rather a character sketch than a biography and consists, for the most part, of a number of miraculous incidents, which, although they illustrate the life of the saint, give little help towards a chronological account of his career. St. Gregory's authorities for all that he relates were apparently trustworthy, being, as he says, four of the saint's own disciples, viz.: Constantinus, who succeeded him as Abbot of Monte Cassino; Valentinian, who for many years was head of the monastery attached to the Lateran Basilica; Simplicius, who was the third Abbot of Monte Cassino; and Honoratus, who was Abbot of Subiaco when St. Gregory wrote his "Dialogues".

Benedict was the son of a Roman noble of Nursia, a small town near Spoleto, and a tradition, which St. Bede accepts, makes him a twin with his sister Scholastica. His boyhood was spent in Rome, where he lived with his parents and attended the schools until he had reached his higher studies. Then "giving over his books, and forsaking his father's house and wealth, with a mind only to serve God, he sought for some place where he might attain to the desire of his holy purpose; and in this sort he departed [from Rome], instructed with learned ignorance and furnished with unlearned wisdom" (Dial. St. Greg., II, Introd. in Migne, P. L., LXVI). There is much difference of opinion as to Benedict's age at this time. It has been very generally stated as fourteen, but a careful examination of St. Gregory's narrative makes it impossible to suppose him younger than nineteen or twenty. He was old enough to be in the midst of his literary studies, to understand the real meaning and worth of the dissolute and licentious lives of his companions, and to have been deeply affected himself by the love of a woman (ibid., II, ii). He was capable of weighing all these things in comparison with the life taught in the Gospels, and he chose the latter. He was at the beginning of life, and had at his disposal the means to a career as a Roman noble; clearly he was not a child. As St. Gregory expresses it, "he was in the world and was free to enjoy the advantages which the world offers, but drew back his foot which he had, as it were, already set forth in the world" (ibid., Introd.). If we accept the date 480 for his birth, we may fix the date of his abandoning the schools and quitting home at about A. D. 500.

Benedict does not seem to have left Rome for the purpose of becoming a hermit, but only to find some place away from the life of the great city; moreover, he took his old nurse with him as a servant and they settled down to live at Enfide, near a church dedicated to St. Peter, in some kind of association with "a company of virtuous men" who were in sympathy with his feelings and his views of life. Enfide, which the tradition of Subiaco identifies with the modern Affile, is in the Simbrucini mountains, about forty miles from Rome and two from Subiaco. It stands on the crest of a ridge which rises rapidly from the valley to the higher range of mountains, and seen from the lower ground the village has the appearance of a fortress. As St. Gregory's account indicates, and as is confirmed by remains of the old town and by the inscriptions found in the neighbourhood, Enfide was a place of greater importance than is the present town. At Enfide Benedict worked his first miracle by restoring to perfect condition an earthenware wheat-sifter (*capisterium*) which his old servant had accidentally broken. The notoriety which this miracle brought upon Benedict drove him to escape still farther from social life, and "he fled secretly from his nurse and sought the more retired district of Subiaco". His purpose of life had also been modified. He had left Rome to escape the evils of a great city; he now determined to be poor and to live by his own work. "For God's sake he deliberately chose the hardships of life and the weariness of labour" (ibid., i).

A short distance from Enfide is the entrance to a narrow, gloomy valley, penetrating the mountains and leading directly to Subiaco. Crossing the Anio and turning to the right, the path rises along the left face of the ravine and soon reaches the site of Nero's villa and of the huge mole which formed the lower end of the middle lake; across the valley were ruins of the Roman baths, of which a few great arches and detached masses of wall still stand. Rising from the mole upon twenty-five low arches, the foundations of which can even yet be traced, was the bridge from the villa to the baths, under which the waters of the middle lake poured in a wide fall into the lake below. The ruins of these vast buildings and the wide sheet of falling water closed up the entrance of the valley to St. Benedict as he came from Enfide; to-day the narrow valley lies open before us, closed only by the far-off mountains. The path continues to ascend, and the side of the ravine, on which it runs, becomes steeper, until we reach a cave above which the mountain now rises almost perpendicularly; while on the right hand it strikes in a rapid descent down to where, in St. Benedict's day, five hundred feet below, lay the blue waters of the lake. The cave has a large triangular-shaped opening and is about ten feet deep. On his way from Enfide, Benedict had met a monk, Romanus, whose monastery was on the mountain above the cliff overhanging the cave. Romanus had discussed with Benedict the purpose which had brought him to Subiaco, and had given him the monk's habit. By his advice Benedict became a hermit and for three years, unknown to men, lived in this cave above the lake. St. Gregory tells us little of these years. He now speaks of Benedict no longer as a youth (*puer*), but as a man (*vir*) of God. Romanus, he twice tells us, served the saint in every way he could. The monk apparently visited him frequently, and on fixed days brought him food.

During these three years of solitude, broken only by occasional communications with the outer world and by the visits of Romanus, he matured both in mind and character, in knowledge of himself and of his fellow-man, and at the same time he became not merely known to, but secured the respect of, those about him; so much so that on the death of the abbot of a monastery in the neighbourhood (identified by some with Vicovaro), the community came to him and begged him to become its abbot. Benedict was acquainted with the life and discipline of the monastery, and knew that "their manners were diverse from his and therefore that they would never agree together: yet, at length, overcome with their entreaty, he gave his consent" (ibid., iii). The experiment failed; the monks tried to poison him, and he returned to his cave. From this time his miracles seem to have become frequent, and many people, attracted by his sanctity and character,

came to Subiaco to be under his guidance. For them he built in the valley twelve monasteries, in each of which he placed a superior with twelve monks. In a thirteenth he lived with "a few, such as he thought would more profit and be better instructed by his own presence" (ibid., iii). He remained, however, the father or abbot of all. With the establishment of these monasteries began the schools for children; and amongst the first to be brought were Maurus and Placid.

The remainder of Benedict's life was spent in realizing the ideal of monasticism which he has left us drawn out in his Rule, and before we follow the slight chronological story given by St. Gregory, it will be better to examine the ideal, which, as St. Gregory says, is Benedict's real biography (ibid., xxxvi). We deal here with the Rule only so far as it is an element in St. Benedict's life. For the relations which it bore to the monasticism of previous centuries, and for its influence throughout the West on civil and religious government, and upon the spiritual life of Christians, the reader is referred to the articles MONASTICISM and BENEDICT, SAINT, RULE OF.

THE BENEDICTINE RULE.—1. Before studying St. Benedict's Rule it is necessary to point out that it is written for laymen, not for clerics. The saint's purpose was not to institute an order of clerics with clerical duties and offices, but an organization and a set of rules for the domestic life of such laymen as wished to live as fully as possible the type of life presented in the Gospel. "My words", he says, "are addressed to thee, whoever thou art, that, renouncing thine own will, dost put on the strong and bright armour of obedience in order to fight for the Lord Christ, our true King." (Prol. to Rule.) Later, the Church imposed the clerical state upon Benedictines, and with the state came a preponderance of clerical and sacerdotal duties, but the impress of the lay origin of the Benedictines has remained, and is perhaps the source of some of the characteristics which mark them off from later orders.

2. Another characteristic feature of the saint's Rule is its view of work. His so-called order was not established to carry on any particular work or to meet any special crisis in the Church, as has been the case with other orders. With Benedict the work of his monks was only a means to goodness of life. The great disciplinary force for human nature is work; idleness is its ruin. The purpose of his Rule was to bring men "back to God by the labour of obedience, from whom they had departed by the idleness of disobedience". Work was the first condition of all growth in goodness. It was in order that his own life might be "wearied with labours for God's sake" that St. Benedict left Enfide for the cave at Subiaco. It is necessary, comments St. Gregory, that God's elect should at the beginning, when life and temptations are strong in them, "be wearied with labour and pains". In the regeneration of human nature in the order of discipline, even prayer comes after work, for grace meets with no co-operation in the soul and heart of an idler. When the Goth "gave over the world" and went to Subiaco, St. Benedict gave him a bill-hook and set him to clear away briars for the making of a garden. "*Ecce! labora!*" go and work. Work is not, as the civilization of the time taught, the condition peculiar to slaves; it is the universal lot of man, necessary for his well-being as a man, and essential for him as a Christian.

3. The religious life, as conceived by St. Benedict, is essentially social. Life apart from one's fellows, the life of a hermit, if it is to be wholesome and sane, is possible only for the few, and these few must have reached an advanced stage of self-discipline while living with others (Rule, i). The Rule, therefore, is entirely occupied with regulating the life of a community of men who live and work and pray and eat

together, and this not merely for a course of training, but as a permanent element of life at its best. The Rule conceives the superiors as always present and in constant touch with every member of the household. This explains its characteristic form of government, which is best described as patriarchal, or paternal (ibid., ii, iii, lxiv). The superior is the head of a family; all are the permanent members of a household. Hence, too, much of the spiritual teaching of the Rule is concealed under legislation which seems purely social and domestic organization (ibid., xxii–xxxii, xxxv–xli). So intimately connected with domestic life is the whole framework and teaching of the Rule that a Benedictine may be more truly said to enter or join a particular household than to join an order. The social character of Benedictine life has found expression in a fixed type for monasteries and in the kind of works which Benedictines undertake, and it is secured by an absolute communism in possessions (ibid., xxxiii, xxxiv, liv, lv), by the rigorous suppression of all differences of worldly rank—"no one of noble birth may [for that reason] be put before him that was formerly a slave" (ibid., ii), and by the enforced presence of everyone at the routine duties of the household.

4. Although private ownership is most strictly forbidden by the Rule, it was no part of St. Benedict's conception of monastic life that his monks, as a body, should strip themselves of all wealth and live upon the alms of the charitable; rather his purpose was to restrict the requirements of the individual to what was necessary and simple, and to secure that the use and administration of the corporate possessions should be in strict accord with the teaching of the Gospel. The Benedictine ideal of poverty is quite different from the Franciscan. The Benedictine takes no explicit vow of poverty; he only vows obedience according to the Rule. The Rule allows all that is necessary to each individual, together with sufficient and varied clothing, abundant food (excluding only the flesh of quadrupeds), wine, and ample sleep (ibid., xxxix, xl, xli, lv). Possessions could be held in common, they might be large, but they were to be administered for the furtherance of the work of the community and for the benefit of others. While the individual monk was poor, the monastery was to be in a position to give alms, not to be compelled to seek them. It was to relieve the poor, to clothe the naked, to visit the sick, to bury the dead, to help the afflicted (ibid., iv), to entertain all strangers (ibid., liii). The poor came to Benedict to get help to pay their debts (Dial. St. Greg., xxvii); they came for food (ibid., xxi, xxviii).

5. St. Benedict originated a form of government which is deserving of study. It is contained in chapters ii, iii, xxxi, lxiv, lxv of the Rule and in certain pregnant phrases scattered through other chapters. As with the Rule itself, so also his scheme of government is intended not for an order but for a single community. He presupposes that the community have bound themselves, by their promise of stability, to spend their lives together under the Rule. The superior is then elected by a free and universal suffrage. The government may be described as a monarchy, with the Rule as its constitution. Within the four corners of the Rule everything is left to the discretion of the abbot, the abuse of whose authority is checked by religion (Rule, ii), by open debate with the community on all important matters, and with its representative elders in smaller concerns (ibid., iii). The reality of these checks upon the wilfulness of the ruler can be appreciated only when it is remembered that ruler and community were bound together for life, that all were inspired by the single purpose of carrying out the conception of life taught in the Gospel, and that the relations of the members

of the community to one another and to the abbot, and of the abbot to them, were elevated and spiritualized by a mysticism which set before itself the acceptance of the teachings of the Sermon on the Mount as real and work-a-day truths.

6. (a) When a Christian household, a community, has been organized by the willing acceptance of its social duties and responsibilities, by obedience to an authority, and, further, is under the continuous discipline of work and self-denial, the next step in the regeneration of its members in their return to God is prayer. The Rule deals directly and explicitly only with public prayer. For this Benedict assigns the Psalms and Canticles, with readings from the Scriptures and Fathers. He devotes eleven chapters out of the seventy-three of his Rule to regulating this public prayer, and it is characteristic of the freedom of his Rule and of the "moderation" of the saint, that he concludes his very careful directions by saying that if any superior does not like his arrangement he is free to make another; this only he says he will insist on, that the whole Psalter shall be said in the course of a week. The practice of the holy Fathers, he adds, was resolutely "to say in a single day what I pray we tepid monks may get through in a whole week" (ibid., xviii). On the other hand, he checks indiscreet zeal by laying down the general rule "that prayer made in common must always be short" (ibid., xx). It is very difficult to reduce St. Benedict's teaching on prayer to a system, for this reason, that in his conception of the Christian character, prayer is coextensive with the whole life, and life is not complete at any point unless penetrated by prayer.

(b) The form of prayer which thus covers the whole of our waking hours, St. Benedict calls the first degree of humility. It consists in realizing the presence of God (ibid., vii). The first step begins when the spiritual is joined to the merely human, or, as the saint expresses it, it is the first step in a ladder, the rungs of which rest at one end in the body and at the other in the soul. The ability to exercise this form of prayer is fostered by that care of the "heart" on which the saint so often insists; and the heart is saved from the dissipation that would result from social intercourse by the habit of mind which sees in every one Christ Himself. "Let the sick be served in very deed as Christ Himself" (ibid., xxxvi). "Let all guests that come be received as Christ" (ibid., liii). "Whether we be slaves or freemen, we are all one in Christ and bear an equal rank in the service of Our Lord" (ibid., ii).

(c) Secondly, there is public prayer. This is short and to be said at intervals, at night and at seven distinct hours during the day, so that, when possible, there shall be no great interval without a call to formal, vocal, public prayer (ibid., xvi). The position which St. Benedict gave to public, common prayer can be best described by saying that he established it as the centre of the common life to which he bound his monks. It was the consecration, not only of the individual, but of the whole community to God by the oft-repeated daily public acts of faith, and of praise and adoration of the Creator; and this public worship of God, the *opus Dei*, was to form the chief work of his monks, and to be the source from which all other works took their inspiration, their direction, and their strength.

(d) Lastly, there is private prayer, for which the saint does not legislate. It follows individual gifts —"If anyone wishes to pray in private, let him go quietly into the oratory and pray, not with a loud voice, but with tears and fervour of heart" (ibid., lii). "Our prayer ought to be short and with purity of heart, except it be perchance prolonged by the inspiration of divine grace" (ibid., xx). But if St. Benedict gives no further directions on private prayer, it is because the whole condition and mode of life secured by the Rule, and the character formed by its observance, lead naturally to the higher states of prayer. As the saint writes: "Whoever, therefore, thou art that hastenest to thy heavenly country, fulfil by the help of Christ this little Rule which we have written for beginners; and then at length thou shalt arrive, under God's protection, at the lofty summits of doctrine and virtue of which we have spoken above" (ibid., lxxiii). For guidance in these higher states the saint refers to the Fathers, Basil and Cassian.

From this short examination of the Rule and its system of prayer, it will be obvious that to describe the Benedictine as a contemplative order is misleading, if the word is used in its modern technical sense as excluding active work; the "contemplative" is a form of life framed for different circumstances and with a different object from St. Benedict's. The

We can now take up again the story of Benedict's life. How long he remained at Subiaco we do not know. Abbot Tosti conjectures it was until the year 529. Of these years St. Gregory is content to tell no more than a few stories descriptive of the life of the monks, and of the character and government of St. Benedict. The latter was making his first attempt to realize in these twelve monasteries his conception of the monastic life. We can fill in many of the details from the Rule. By his own experiment and his knowledge of the history of monasticism the saint had learnt that the regeneration of the individual, except in abnormal cases, is not reached by the path of solitude, nor by that of austerity, but by the beaten track of man's social instinct, with its necessary conditions of obedience and work; and that neither the body nor the mind can be safely overstrained in the effort to avoid evil (ibid., lxiv). Thus at Subiaco we find no solitaries, no conventual her-

The Abbey of Monte Cassino

Rule, including its system of prayer and public psalmody, is meant for every class of mind and every degree of learning. It is framed not only for the educated and for souls advanced in perfection, but it organizes and directs a complete life which is adapted for simple folk and for sinners, for the observance of the Commandments and for the beginnings of goodness. "We have written this Rule", writes St. Benedict, "that by observing it in monasteries, we may shew ourselves to have some degree of goodness in life and a beginning of holiness. But for him who would hasten to the perfection of religion there are the teachings of the holy Fathers, the following whereof bringeth a man to the height of perfection" (ibid., lxxiii). Before leaving the subject of prayer it will be well to point out again that by ordering the public recitation and singing of the Psalter, St. Benedict was not putting upon his monks a distinctively clerical obligation. The Psalter was the common form of prayer of all Christians; we must not read into his Rule characteristics which a later age and discipline have made inseparable from the public recitation of the Divine Office.

mits, no great austerities, but men living together in organized communities for the purpose of leading good lives, doing such work as came to their hand —carrying water up the steep mountain-side, doing the other household work, raising the twelve cloisters, clearing the ground, making gardens, teaching children, preaching to the country people, reading and studying at least four hours a day, receiving strangers, accepting and training new-comers, attending the regular hours of prayer, reciting and chanting the Psalter. The life at Subiaco and the character of St. Benedict attracted many to the new monasteries, and with their increasing numbers and growing influence came the inevitable jealousy and persecution, which culminated with a vile attempt of a neighbouring priest to scandalize the monks by an exhibition of naked women, dancing in the courtyard of the saint's monastery (Dial. St. Greg., viii). To save his followers from further persecution Benedict left Subiaco and went to Monte Cassino.

Upon the crest of Monte Cassino "there was an ancient chapel in which the foolish and simple country people, according to the custom of the old

Gentiles, worshipped the god Apollo. Round about it likewise upon all sides there were woods for the service of devils, in which, even to that very time, the mad multitudes of infidels did offer most wicked sacrifice. The man of God, coming hither, beat in pieces the idol, overthrew the altar, set fire on the woods, and in the temple of Apollo built the oratory of St. Martin: and where the altar of the same Apollo was, he made an oratory of St. John: and by his continual preaching he brought the people dwelling in those parts to embrace the faith of Christ" (Rule, viii). On this spot the saint built his monastery. His experience at Subiaco had led him to alter his plans, and now, instead of building several houses with a small community in each, he kept all his monks in one monastery and provided for its government by appointing a prior and deans (Rule, lxv, xxi). We find no trace in his Rule, which was most probably written at Monte Cassino, of the view which guided him when he built the twelve small monasteries at Subiaco. The life which we have witnessed at Subiaco was renewed at Monte Cassino, but the change in the situation and local conditions brought a corresponding modification in the work undertaken by the monks. Subiaco was a retired valley away in the mountains and difficult of access; Cassino was on one of the great highways to the south of Italy, and at no great distance from Capua. This brought the new monastery into more frequent communication with the outside world. It soon became a centre of influence in a district in which there was a large population, with several dioceses and other monasteries. Abbots came to see and advise with Benedict. Men of all classes were frequent visitors, and he numbered nobles and bishops among his intimate friends. There were nuns in the neighbourhood whom the monks went to preach to and to teach. There was a village nearby in which St. Benedict preached and made many converts (Dial. St. Greg., xix). The monastery became the protector of the poor, their trustee (ibid., xxxi), their refuge in sickness, in trial, in accidents, in want.

Thus during the life of the saint we find what has ever since remained a characteristic feature of Benedictine houses, i. e. the members take up any work which is adapted to their peculiar circumstances, any work which may be dictated by their necessities. Thus we find Benedictines teaching in poor schools and in the universities, practising the arts and following agriculture, undertaking the care of souls, or devoting themselves wholly to study. No work is foreign to the Benedictine, provided only it is compatible with living in community and with the performance of the Divine Office. This freedom in the choice of work was necessary in a Rule which was to be suited to all times and places, but it was primarily the natural result of the end which St. Benedict had in view, and in which he differs from the founders of later orders. These latter had in view some special work to which they wished their disciples to devote themselves; St. Benedict's purpose was only to provide a Rule by which anyone might follow the Gospel counsels, and live, and work, and pray, and save his soul. St. Gregory's narrative of the establishment of Monte Cassino does little more for us than supply disconnected incidents which illustrate the daily life of the monastery. We gain only a few biographical facts. From Monte Cassino St. Benedict founded another monastery near Terracina, on the coast, about forty miles distant (ibid., xxii). To the wisdom of long experience and to the mature virtues of the saint, was now added the gift of prophecy, of which St. Gregory gives many examples. Celebrated among these is the story of the visit of Totila, King of the Goths, in the year 543, when the saint "rebuked him for his wicked deeds, and in few words told him all

that should befall him, saying: 'Much wickedness do you daily commit, and many great sins have you done: now at length give over your sinful life. Into the city of Rome shall you enter, and over the sea shall you pass: nine years shall you reign, and in the tenth shall you leave this mortal life.' The king, hearing these things, was wonderfully afraid, and desiring the holy man to commend him to God in his prayers he departed: and from that time forward he was nothing so cruel as before he had been. Not long after he went to Rome, sailed over into Sicily, and in the tenth year of his reign he lost his kingdom together with his life." (ibid., xv).

Totila's visit to Monte Cassino in 543 is the only certain date we have in the saint's life. It must have occurred when Benedict was advanced in age. Abbot Tosti, following others, puts the saint's death in the same year. Just before his death we hear

CENTRAL COURT, MONTE CASSINO
(Designed by Bramante)

for the first time of his sister Scholastica. "She had been dedicated from her infancy to Our Lord, and used to come once a year to visit her brother. To whom the man of God went not far from the gate to a place that did belong to the abbey, there to give her entertainment" (ibid., xxxiii). They met for the last time three days before Scholastica's death, on a day "when the sky was so clear that no cloud was to be seen". The sister begged her brother to stay the night, "but by no persuasion would he agree unto that, saying that he might not by any means tarry all night out of his abbey. . . . The nun receiving this denial of her brother, joining her hands together, laid them upon the table; and so, bowing down her head upon them, she made her prayers to Almighty God, and lifting her head from the table, there fell suddenly such a tempest of lightning and thundering, and such abundance of rain, that neither venerable Bennet nor his monks that were with him, could put their head out of door" (ibid., xxxiii). Three days later, "Benedict beheld the soul of his sister, which was departed from her body, in the likeness of a dove, to ascend into heaven: who rejoicing much to see her great glory, with hymns and lauds gave thanks to Almighty God, and did impart the news of this her death to his monks whom also he sent presently to bring her corpse to his abbey, to have it buried in that grave which he had provided for himself" (ibid., xxxiv).

It would seem to have been about this time that St. Benedict had that wonderful vision in which he came as near to seeing God as is possible for man in this life. St. Gregory and St. Bonaventure say that Benedict saw God and in that vision of God saw the whole world. St. Thomas will not allow that this could have been. Urban VIII, however, does not hesitate to say that "the saint merited, whilst still in this mortal life, to see God Himself and in God all that is below Him". If he did not see the Creator, he saw that light which is in the Creator, and in that light, as St. Gregory says, "saw the whole world gathered together as it were under one beam of the sun. At the same time he saw the soul of Germanus, Bishop of Capua, in a fiery globe carried up by angels to heaven" (ibid., xxxv). Once more the hidden things of God were shown to him, and he warned his brethren, both "those that lived daily with him and those that dwelt far off" of his approaching death. "Six days before he left this world he gave orders to have his sepulchre opened, and forthwith falling into an ague, he began with burning heat to wax faint; and when as the sickness daily increased, upon the sixth day he commanded his monks to carry him into the oratory, where he did arm himself receiving the Body and Blood of Our Saviour Christ; and having his weak body holden up betwixt the hands of his disciples, he stood with his own hands lifted up to heaven; and as he was in that manner praying, he gave up the ghost" (ibid., xxxvii). He was buried in the same grave with his sister "in the oratory of St. John the Baptist, which [he] himself had built when he overthrew the altar of Apollo" (ibid.). There is some doubt whether the relics of the saint are still at Monte Cassino, or whether they were moved in the seventh century to Fleury. Abbot Tosti, in his life of St. Benedict, discusses the question at length (chap. xi) and decides the controversy in favour of Monte Cassino.

Perhaps the most striking characteristics in St. Benedict are his deep and wide human feeling and his moderation. The former reveals itself in the many anecdotes recorded by St. Gregory. We see it in his sympathy and care for the simplest of his monks; his hastening to the help of the poor Goth who had lost his bill-hook; spending the hours of the night in prayer on the mountain to save his monks the labour of carrying water, and to remove from their lives a "just cause of grumbling"; staying three days in a monastery to help to induce one of the monks to "remain quietly at his prayers as the other monks did", instead of going forth from the chapel and wandering about "busying himself with some earthly and transitory things". He lets the crow from the neighbouring woods come daily when all are at dinner to be fed by himself. His mind is always with those who are absent; sitting in his cell he knows that Placid has fallen into the lake; he foresees the accident to the builders and sends a warning to them; in spirit and some kind of real presence he is with the monks "eating and refreshing themselves" on their journey, with his friend Valentinian on his way to the monastery, with the monk taking a present from the nuns, with the new community at Terracina. Throughout St. Gregory's narrative he is always the same quiet, gentle, dignified, strong, peace-loving man who by the subtle power of sympathy becomes the centre of the lives and interests of all about him. We see him with his monks in the church, at their reading, sometimes in the fields, but more commonly in his cell, where frequent messengers find him "weeping silently in his prayers", and in the night hours standing at "the window of his cell in the tower, offering up his prayers to God"; and often, as Totila found him, sitting outside the door of his cell, or "before the gate of the monastery reading upon a book". He has given his own portrait in his ideal picture of an abbot (Rule, lxiv):—

"It beseemeth the abbot to be ever doing some good for his brethren rather than to be presiding over them. He must, therefore, be learned in the law of God, that he may know whence to bring forth things new and old; he must be chaste, sober, and merciful, ever preferring mercy to justice, that he

himself may obtain mercy. Let him hate sin and love the brethren. And even in his corrections, let him act with prudence, and not go too far, lest while he seeketh too eagerly to scrape off the rust, the vessel be broken. Let him keep his own frailty ever before his eyes, and remember that the bruised reed must not be broken. And by this we do not mean that he should suffer vices to grow up; but that prudently and with charity he should cut them off, in the way he shall see best for each, as we have already said; and let him study rather to be loved than feared. Let him not be violent nor over anxious, not exacting nor obstinate, not jealous nor prone to suspicion, or else he will never be at rest. In all his commands, whether spiritual or temporal, let him be prudent and considerate. In the works which he imposeth, let him be discreet and moderate, bearing in mind the discretion of holy Jacob, when he said: 'If I cause my flocks to be overdriven, they will all perish in one day'. Taking, then, such testimonies as are borne by these and the like words to discretion, the mother of virtues, let him so temper all things, that the strong may have something to strive after, and the weak nothing at which to take alarm."

BIOGRAPHY:—*St. Gregory's Dialogues*, II, in P. L., LXVI, tr. ed. COLERIDGE (London, 1874); TOSTI, *Della vita di San Benedetto* (Monte Cassino, 1892), tr. WOODS (London, 1896). HISTORY OF THE PERIOD:—HODGKIN, *Italy and Her Invaders* (Oxford, 1892–99); DUDDEN, *Gregory the Great* (London, 1905); GREGOROVIUS, *History of the City of Rome*, tr. HAMILTON (London, 1900–02). RULE OF SAINT BENEDICT:—*Rule*, tr. HUNTERBLAIR (London, 1906); SCHMIDT, *Editio minor* (Ratisbon, 1891); WARNEFRID, *Commentary* in P. L., LXVI), new ed. (Monte Cassino, 1880); CALMET, *Commentary* (Paris, 1734); MARTÈNE, *Commentary* (Paris, 1690); ZÖCKLER, *Askese und Mönchtum* (1897); BUTLER in *Downside Review* (Dec., 1899); IDEM, in *Journal of Theol. Studies* (Apr., 1902).

HUGH EDMUND FORD.

Benedict of Paris (CAPUCHIN). See LANGEOIS.

Benedict of Peterborough, abbot and writer, place and date of birth unknown; d. 1193. He was educated at Oxford, and was appointed in 1174 chancellor to Richard, Archbishop of Canterbury, and in 1175 became Prior of Christ Church, Canterbury. As Abbot of Peterborough from 1177 to his death in 1193, he was a learned and able executive. He restored the abbey finances to a sound basis, and was active till his death in completing and beautifying the buildings. Through his personal favour with Richard I he secured for his abbey various rights and privileges. He has been sometimes confused with Benedict of Sansetun, later Bishop of Rochester, vice-chancellor during the absence of King Richard. He had the library enriched with transcriptions of standard works in theology, exegesis, law, science, and poetry. He wrote a history of Becket's "Passion", preserved in part in the work on Becket known as "Quadrilogus", and also, a first-hand account of Becket's "Miracles" (Robertson, "Materials for the History of Thomas Becket", Rolls Series, 1876). He was formerly regarded as the author of "Gesta Henrici II", which Stubbs would identify with the lost "Tricolumnis" of Richard Fitz-Neal, author of the "Dialogus de Scaccario".

GARDINER and MULLINGER, *Introduction to the Study of Eng. Hist.* (London, 1894); GILES, *Life and Miracles of St. Thomas of Canterbury, by Benedict*, etc. (Caxton Society, 1850).

J. V. CROWNE.

Benedict of San Philadelphio (or BENEDICT THE MOOR), SAINT, b. at San Philadelphio or San Fradello, a village of the Diocese of Messina in Sicily, in 1526; d. 4 April, 1589. The parents of St. Benedict were slaves from Ethiopia who were, nevertheless, pious Christians. On account of their faithfulness their master freed Benedict, the first-born child. From his earliest years Benedict was very religious and while still very young he joined a newly formed association of hermits. When Pope Pius IV dissolved this association, Benedict, called from his origin Æthiops or Niger, entered the Reformed Recollects of the Franciscan Order. Owing to his virtues he was made superior of the monastery of Santa Maria de Jesus at Palermo three years after his entrance, although he was only a lay brother. He reformed the monastery and ruled it with great success until his death. He was pronounced Blessed in 1743 and was canonized in 1807. His feast is celebrated 3 April.

GUÉRIN, *Le palmier séraphique ou vie des saints et des hommes et femmes illustres des ordres de St. François* (Bar-le-Duc, 1872), IV, 44–75; LÉON, *L'auréole séraphique, Vie des saints et bienheureux des trois ordres de St. François* (Paris, 1882), II, 1 sqq.

J. P. KIRSCH.

Benedictus, (CANTICLE OF ZACHARY), THE, given in Luke, i, 68–79, is one of the three great canticles in the opening chapters of this Gospel, the other two being the *Magnificat* and *Nunc dimittis*. The *Benedictus* was the song of thanksgiving uttered by Zachary on the occasion of the birth of his son, St. John Baptist. It is Jewish in form, but Christian in sentiment. The local colouring and nationalistic character of the first half are so noticeable that Loisy has conjectured that it existed previously as a simple psalm, which Zachary adapted, his additions being, he contends, easily discernible. (Revue d'hist. et de lit. relig., May–June, 1903, p. 289.) There are, however, grave objections to this view, and an opposite theory has been put forth, that the *Benedictus* was composed with special reference to the names of Elizabeth, Zachary, and John, for Elizabeth, *Jusjurandum quod juravit;* Zachary, *Memorari (testamenti sui sancti)*; and John, *Ad faciendam misericordiam.*

The whole canticle naturally falls into two parts. The first (verses 68–75) is a song of thanksgiving for the realization of the Messianic hopes of the Jewish nation; but to such realization is given a characteristically Christian tone. As of old, in the family of David, there was power to defend the nation against their enemies, now again that of which they had been so long deprived, and for which they had been yearning, was to be restored to them, but in a higher and spiritual sense. The horn is a sign of power, and the "horn of salvation" signified the power of delivering or "a mighty deliverance". While the Jews had impatiently borne the yoke of the Romans, they had continually sighed for the time when the House of David was to be their deliverer. The deliverance was now at hand, and was pointed to by Zachary as the fulfilment of God's Oath to Abraham; but the fulfilment is described as a deliverance not for the sake of worldly power, but that "we may serve him without fear, in holiness and justice all our days".

The second part of the canticle is an address by Zachary to his own son, who was to take so important a part in the scheme of the Redemption; for he was to be a prophet, and to preach the remission of sins before the coming of the Orient, or Dawn, from on high. The prophecy that he was to "go before the face of the Lord to prepare his ways" (v. 76) was of course an allusion to the well-known words of Isaias (xl, 3) which St. John himself afterwards applied to his own mission (John, i, 23); and which all the three Synoptics adopt (Matt., iii, 3; Mark, i, 2; Luke, iii, 4). It is probably due to the first part of the canticle, as a song of thanksgiving for the coming of the Redeemer, that it finds an appropriate place in the office of the Church every morning at Lauds. It is believed to have been first introduced by St. Benedict (Beaume, I, 253). According to Durandus, the allusion to Christ's coming under the figure of the rising sun had also some influence on its adoption. It is also used in various other liturgical offices, notably at a funeral, at the moment of interment, when words of thanksgiving for the Redemption are specially in place as an expression of Christian hope.

See the commentaries on Saint Luke; also HASTINGS, *Dict. of Christ and the Gospels* (New York, 1906), I, 90–91.

BERNARD WARD.

Benedictus Polonus, a medieval Friar Minor missionary and traveller (c. 1245) companion of Giovanni da Piancarpino, and author of the brief chronicle "De Itinere Fratrum Minorum ad Tartaros", concerning the first Franciscan missions to the Tatars. This work was unknown apparently to Wadding and Sbaralea, the literary historians of the order. It was first published by D'Avezac in the "Recueil de Voyages" (Paris, 1839, IV, 774–779). Cf. the "Chronicle" of Glassberger in "Analecta Franciscana" (II, 71). The report of Benedictus is important for the curious letter of the Great Khan to Innocent IV.

GOLUBOVICH, *Biblioteca bio-bibliografica della terra santa e dell' oriente Francescano* (Quaracchi, 1906), 213–215.

THOMAS J. SHAHAN.

Benefice (Lat. *Beneficium*, a benefit).—Popularly the term benefice is often understood to denote either certain property destined for the support of ministers of religion, or a spiritual office or function, such as the care of souls, but in the strict sense it signifies a right, i. e. the right given permanently by the Church to a cleric to receive ecclesiastical revenues on account of the performance of some spiritual service. Four characteristics are essential to every benefice: (a) the right to revenue from church property, the beneficed cleric being the usufructuary and not the proprietor of the source of his support; (b) a twofold perpetuity, objective and subjective, inasmuch as the source of income must be permanently established and at the same time the appointment to the benefice must be for life, and not subject to revocation, save for the causes and in the cases specified by law; (c) a formal decree of ecclesiastical authority giving to certain funds or property the character or title of a benefice; (d) an annexed office or spiritual function of some kind, such as the care of souls, the exercise of jurisdiction, the celebration of Mass or the recitation of the Divine Office. This last mentioned element is fundamental, since a benefice exists only for the sake of securing the performance of duties connected with the worship of God, and is based on the Scriptural teaching that they who serve the altar should live by the altar. In fact, as Innocent III declares, the sole purpose of the foundation of benefices was to enable the church to have at her command clerics who might devote themselves freely to works of religion.

HISTORY.—The need which benefices are intended to meet was in the earlier centuries of the life of the Church satisfied in other ways. From the beginning, the clergy was supported by the liberality of the faithful, but originally all offerings were transmitted to the bishop, who took charge of their administration and distribution. Usually the mass of donations was divided into four portions, of which one went to the support of the bishop, another to the maintenance of the clergy, a third to the repair and construction of churches, and a fourth to the relief of the needy and afflicted. Under this system even those clerics who ministered in rural parishes were obliged to send the oblations received in their churches to the bishop, to swell the common fund and to be submitted to the ordinary rule of allotment. The inconvenience attending this method, especially because the offerings were frequently in kind, increased with the growth of the Church, particularly with the multiplication of country parishes. Moreover the Church came to possess considerable real property. Hence early in the sixth century we find in some places the practice of allowing some of the clergy to retain for themselves and for their churches the gifts which they had received or even the income from property which the Church had acquired. The latter form of grant, in connexion with lands or permanent endowments, was known as *precaria*, a name which indicates its unstable tenure; on the death of the possessor the source of his revenue reverted to the common fund of church property, and could not serve for the support of a cleric unless devoted anew to this purpose by a formal act of ecclesiastical authority. Though these *precariæ* were in the beginning contrary to the canons, circumstances justified their increasing employment, and they paved the way for the recognition of the modern benefice.

All that was needed to transform the *precariæ* into benefices, was to do away with the need of a new episcopal decree assigning the income from certain lands or other property to the support of a priest on the occurrence of a vacancy, and to recognize in the source of income a perpetual foundation for this specific purpose. When this was done and the incumbent was given permanency in office, the modern benefice came into being. It was of gradual growth, its beginning dating from the sixth century and its universal adoption being delayed until the eleventh century. Since the usufruct allowed to clerics resembled the grants of land which sovereigns were accustomed to make to subjects who had distinguished themselves by military or political service, and which the Church was at times compelled to concede to powerful lay lords in order to secure necessary protection in troubled times, it was natural that the term benefice, which had been applied to these grants, should be employed to denote the similar practice in regard to ecclesiastics. Wherever the common law of the Church holds sway the establishment of benefices is the rule. In more than one country a system developed by centuries of piety has fallen before decrees of secularization, but if the usurping government makes a pretence of compensation by stipends to the clergy, such stipends are regarded by the Church as beneficiary revenue, and those who receive them retain the status of beneficed clerics. In the United States benefices are almost unknown. A solitary example in New Orleans figured as a notable exception in the decree of the Second Plenary Council. A few parochial benefices are found in the province of San Francisco, and there is good ground for the opinion which sees in permanent rectorships all the requisites of a benefice; but these instances, with the episcopates, are in marked contrast with the general organization of the Church in the United States. In England, also, benefices are the exception, but in Canada they are more common (Gignac, Compend. Jur. Eccl., Quebec, 1906). The beneficiary system plays an important part in the discipline of the evangelical churches on the continent of Europe, and of the State church of England. In 1900, out of 22,800 clergymen at work in the Anglican Church, 13,872 were beneficed. (For benefices or "livings" in the Anglican Church see Phillimore, "Ecclesiastical Law"; Idem, "Book of Church Law", London, 1899, 227; ibid. the Benefices Act of 1898. For the Evangelical Churches see Hinschius, "Kirchenrecht", Berlin, 1869 sq.; Friedberg, "Lehrbuch des Kirchenrechts", 4th ed., 1895; Real Encyk. f. Prot. Theol. und Kirche, 3d ed., 1897, II, 596.)

DIVISION.—Benefices are divided into simple and double; major and minor; elective, presentative, and collative; residential and non-residential; perpetual and manual; secular and regular. Simple benefices are those which involve only the duty of reciting the Divine Office or of celebrating Mass. Double benefices imply the care of souls or jurisdiction in the external forum or administrative functions, and, if they be episcopal or supra-episcopal in rank, are styled major benefices. A benefice is elective when the appointing authority may collate only after some electoral body has named the future incumbent; presentative when such nomination belongs to a patron; collative when the bishop or other superior appoints independently of any election or presentation. The distinction between residential and non-residential benefices is based upon the fact that in some cases the canons or articles of foundation impose the obligation of residence in the locality of the benefice while in other cases no such obligation is annexed. Manual benefices are not benefices in the strict sense, since their distinctive note is that appointments to them are revocable at the will of the collating authority. A legal presumption exists that all benefices are secular, but those which exist in churches or houses of religious orders or which by custom or by the will of the founder have been appropriated to religious are known as regular benefices. This last distinction has at times a special importance because of the rule requiring that secular benefices be conferred only on secular clerics, regular benefices only on regulars.

CREATION.—Benefices can be created only by ecclesiastical authority, since the right to revenue which they suppose is always necessarily connected with some spiritual function, and is therefore reckoned among the *jura spiritualia* controlled by the Church. The competent authority may be the pope or a bishop or one possessing quasi-episcopal authority, it being always understood that the pope has exclusive control of all major benefices. A benefice must be erected in a church or at an altar, under the title of some saint or mystery, and with the annexed obligation of rendering some spiritual service. Since the idea of compensation is always implied, a sufficient endowment must in every case be guaranteed, the amount varying with the character of the benefice, the locality of the foundation, and the nature of the services which are to be rendered. In some countries, as in Austria, the consent of the civil authorities is a necessary preliminary to the creation of a benefice.

MODIFICATION.—A benefice once erected is understood to be perpetual, but the law must and does provide for circumstances which may require an alteration of the status of a benefice by union or division, or even its entire suppression or extinction. Sometimes, owing to changed conditions, especially to a diminution of revenue, it becomes necessary to unite two or more benefices. This union may be effected in two ways, either so that an entirely new individual entity is brought into being, or so that the original titles remain, but are conferred on one cleric instead of several. In this latter case a distinction has to be made between a union in which both benefices retain their legal autonomy and a union in which one benefice is made legally dependent on the other. The pope alone can unite major benefices; minor benefices are subject in this respect to episcopal authority, with very few exceptions. A bishop is not allowed to proceed to the union of benefices unless such action be justified by reasons of necessity or of advantage, and unless a hearing be first granted to all interested persons. The patron, if there be one, and the cathedral chapter are the only parties whose consent, as distinguished from mere opinion, is required. The division of benefices, which is most frequently verified in connexion with parishes, is authorized when the incumbent is unable on account of increasing obligations to meet the requirements of his office, even with the help of such auxiliaries as the law allows. The formalities are generally the same as for a union. The term "dismembration" is frequently employed as a synonym for division, but strictly speaking it denotes an act by which a part of the goods or revenues of one benefice is given perpetually to another benefice or to some other ecclesiastical entity. In this case no new benefice is set up, and the act in question is in reality simply an alienation of church property, and is therefore governed by the rules applicable to alienation. Dismembration is also used at times to signify the separation of a certain territory with its inhabitants from one parish and its incorporation in another, which may be effected for sufficient reason. The extinction of benefices occurs when both the benefice and the church to which it is attached are utterly destroyed or cease completely to have any connexion with Catholic worship, as happened in the past when certain countries were overrun by infidels or heretics, and in more recent times on the occasion of acts of usurpation by the civil power. Suppression differs from extinction in that it simply terminates the existence of a benefice, leaving intact the church and any other benefices which may be connected with it. Suppression involves a diminution of religious service, and is consequently regarded as odious in law. Nevertheless a bishop may for good reasons and with the consent of his chapter proceed to suppression, and at times such action is rendered necessary by a considerable depreciation in the value of the beneficiary property or by the departure of the population to whose spiritual needs the benefice was intended to minister. Suppression is not infrequently requested by patrons. In such cases the practice is not to consent to absolute suppression, at least of the religious service depending on the benefice, but simply to the exoneration of the patron and his renunciation of the *jus patronatus*.

COLLATION.—The collation or granting of benefices may be ordinary or extraordinary, free or necessary. The distinction between ordinary and extraordinary collation is based upon the fact that while ordinarily major benefices are disposed of by the pope and minor benefices by bishops, it may occasionally happen that this rule suffers an exception in so far as it relates to bishops, either because of a special provision of the law in favour of the pope or of some other authority, or because, on the failure of the bishop to act, the right to appoint devolves on his superior. These exceptions are known as extraordinary collations. From the eleventh century, extraordinary collations by the pope became more and more common, usually taking the form of *mandata de providendo, literæ expectativæ*, and reservations. The *mandata de providendo* were intended to give to the cleric named therein a right to a benefice already vacant in the diocese of the bishop to whom the mandate was directed. *Literæ expectativæ* were similar papal interventions in regard to diocesan benefices, but affected benefices not yet vacant, the recipient of the letter being given a claim on a benefice as soon as it should be at the disposal of the bishop. These two methods of extraordinary collation were not productive of happy results; they proved to be prejudicial to episcopal authority; they were taken advantage of by unworthy aspirants for ecclesiastical offices; and at times they were fraudulently obtained and offered for sale. Hence their reprobation by the Council of Trent (Sess. XXIV, cap. xix De ref). This animadversion of Trent was not, it is needless to say, a limitation of any papal prerogative; its sole purpose being to forestall possible abuses on the part of petitioners for favours from the Holy See. Reservations are still in operation, and consist in this, that the pope reserves to himself in specified cases the collation of certain diocesan benefices. After serving for centuries as a cause of much controversy, they were finally regulated by laws defining accurately the instances in which collation was to be reserved to the pope. One of the most important reservations which may serve as an example is contained in the ninth rule of the Apostolic Chancery (see CHANCERY, APOSTOLIC), which provides that those diocesan benefices which fall vacant during eight months of the year are to be at the disposal of the pope, but that bishops who observe the law of residence may freely dispose of all benefices vacated during the six alternate months beginning with February. To-day reservations are in effect to some extent throughout the Church; for example, they affect the first dignities in chapters in the Province of Quebec and canonries in England; but Italy is the only country in which they are in full operation. Apart from cases provided for in reservations, the pope rarely, if ever, exercises his right of extraordinary collation. A collation, whether made by the pope or by a bishop, is said to be free when it is not conditioned by any act of an elector or of a patron; necessary when it follows election or nomination by competent persons or presentation by patrons. In many countries, concordats have secured to the representatives of civil authority an important part in appointments to benefices. Thus in Bavaria the king nominates to all archiepiscopal and episcopal sees; and a similar right has been granted to the Emperor of Austria and to the King of Portugal; in Hanover the chapter, before proceeding to the election of a bishop, must allow the Government to cancel the names of those candidates whom it judges unacceptable. Secular intervention in the collation of minor benefices varies from the royal nomination of the King of Portugal to the governmental exequatur required by Italian law. The interests of religion are safeguarded by the canonical requirement that in every case the candidate must be confirmed by ecclesiastical authority before he can lawfully begin his incumbency. (For abuses in the collation of benefices, see PATRONAGE, COMMENDATORY ABBOTS, INVESTITURES.)

CONDITION OF COLLATION.—In order that benefices may the more effectually fulfill the purposes for which they were instituted, various laws have been enacted governing the act of collation. Whether the collation be free or necessary it must always be gratuitous, to avoid simony; free, that is without coaction; unconditional; public, so that it may be readily proved; and granted within six months from the date of vacancy. Moreover no benefice can be conferred before it is vacant, nor can seculars receive the benefices of regulars, nor regulars those which are secular in character. Plurality of benefices also is forbidden. This last regulation was introduced very early in the history of benefices to assure the faithful execution of the trust attached to ecclesiastical foundations, as well as to guard against the evils which follow luxury; but in the course of time its effectiveness was considerably diminished by a distinction drawn between compatible and incompatible benefices. It was claimed that a benefice which does not require residence is perfectly compatible with one which does, and also that several simple benefices might very properly be held at the same time. This view held sway down to the time of the Council of Trent, which ordained that the possession of more than one benefice is lawful only when the first benefice obtained does not suffice for the support of the incumbent, and that in no case should both be residential. The Holy See alone can dispense from the observance of this law. The act of collation is further conditioned by canons requiring certain qualities in the appointee: (a) *The clerical state and celibacy.*—Tonsure is necessary for all benefices, and higher orders must be received by aspirants to important charges; thus cardinals are obliged to receive within the year the order corresponding to their rank in the sacred college; archbishops and bishops must have been subdeacons for at least six months; parish priests must receive the priesthood within a year. (b) *Age.*—Before the

Council of Trent a simple benefice could lawfully be conferred on a cleric as early as his seventh year, but since that council the recipient of a simple benefice must be in his fourteenth year, and for double benefices the age of twenty-four years completed is always required. A greater maturity is demanded for certain offices, e. g. thirty years completed for the episcopate, and forty years for the post of canon penitentiary. (c) *Character.*—The appointee must be of legitimate birth and of good reputation, and free from censure and irregularity. (d) *Relative worthiness.*—In the case of a choice between several candidates for a bishopric or for a parish, the collator must appoint the most worthy, i. e. the one who possesses in the highest degree the qualities necessary for a successful discharge of the duties connected with the benefice in question. The same rule applies to prelacies with quasiepiscopal jurisdiction, to the canon theologian and to the canon penitentiary. As to other benefices authorities differ, the preferable opinion maintaining that in all cases the most worthy is to be chosen. (e) *Science.*—According to a law of Trent (Sess. VII, c. xiii, De ref.) no one can be collated to a benefice unless his fitness has been demonstrated in an examination conducted by the ordinary. In the case of parochial benefices, this examination must take the form of a concursus. (See CONCURSUS.) For some appointments the possession of a degree in theology or in canon law is demanded, as evidence of requisite learning; a bishop must be a doctor or a licentiate in canon law or in theology, or have the public testimony of a university as to his fitness to teach others; an archdeacon also must be a doctor or a licentiate in canon law or in theology; and similar qualifications are demanded for other offices. The Holy See is, at the present time, insisting that the law concerning degrees be faithfully observed. (f) *Extraordinary requirements.*—These may be imposed by the articles of foundation or by secular law. Founders of benefices are given a great deal of liberty in attaching conditions to the act of collation, provided that these conditions be approved by ecclesiastical authority. In consequence, it happens at times that only members of a certain family or citizens of some town or city are eligible, or even, in some few instances, persons of noble birth. More onerous, and not always acceptable to the church, is the interference of civil authorities in the matter of collation. In many places only a person declared acceptable to the Government, or a citizen, or a native, or one who swears fidelity to the Government at the time of appointment, or who receives the royal exequatur, can hope to be collated. In Portugal and in Bavaria, the permission of the Government is necessary for ordination, and without this permission, which is given after an examination by secular authorities, a cleric is incapacitated for benefices in these two kingdoms. The Bavarian law also contains the curious provision that no subject is to enter the German College at Rome so long as it is conducted by the Fathers of the Society of Jesus, or by any similar order, and that all who contravene this ordinance are to be considered as *personæ non gratæ* to the Government and excluded from all benefices and posts at its disposal.

OBLIGATIONS.—All beneficed clerics are bound to make a profession of faith within two months from the date of taking possession, to perform faithfully the duties pertaining to their charge, to recite the canonical hours, and if the benefice held be double, to reside in the place in which their benefice is located. Violation of the law of residence is punished by loss of revenues during the time of absence, and if persisted in, by privation.

VACANCY.—The tenure of the incumbent of a benefice is perpetual, in the sense that it can be terminated only by death or for causes specified in the law. It is provided in the law that in the event of certain acts vacancy shall occur *ipso facto;* as when the incumbent marries or attempts marriage, when he takes solemn vows in a religious order, when he violates the canon forbidding plurality, when he fails to receive within the prescribed time the necessary ordination, when he obtains episcopal consecration, when he is guilty of any crime to which penalty of deprivation is expressly attached. In other cases deprivation follows a judicial process, instituted in virtue of laws authorizing the bishop to punish certain offences in this manner. Moreover a cleric has the right to resign his benefice provided the resignation be offered freely and for just reasons, and be accepted by a competent superior, and he may also, with certain conditions, exchange benefices with another incumbent.

REVENUES.—The holder of a benefice is not the owner of the foundation from which he derives his support; he occupies in reference to it the position of a tutor or guardian who must defend its interests. His chief duty is to maintain it as a perpetual means of support for ministers of religion. Its fruits or revenues, however, belong to him, but with the obligation of devoting to pious causes, and especially to the relief of the poor, all that is not needed for his own support. Formerly, this superfluous revenue could not be disposed of by will, but a universal custom has long since authorized such testamentary disposal, provided it be made in favour of pious causes or of the poor. In fact, in most places on account of the difficulty of distinguishing a cleric's patrimonial property from his beneficiary revenue, the right is recognized to dispose freely by will of all property. (See JUS SPOLII.)

DUARENE, *De Sacris Ministeriis et Beneficiis* (Paris, 1564); REBUFFI, *Praxis Beneficiorum* (Lyons, 1580); GARZIAS, *De Beneficiis* (Cologne, 1614); CORRADUS, *De Praxi Beneficiariâ* (Naples, 1656); LOTTERIUS, *De Re Beneficiariâ* (Lyons, 1659); LEURENIUS, *Forum Beneficiale* (Cologne, 1674); GOHARD, *Traité des Bénéfices* (Paris, 1765); SGUANIN, *Tractatus Beneficiarius* (Rome, 1751); THOMASSINUS, *Vetus et Nova Disciplina circa Ecclesiæ Beneficia et Beneficiarios* (Venice, 1766), the classic historical work on Benefices; GAGLIARDI, *Tractatus de Beneficiis* (Naples, 1842); ZITELLI, *Apparatus Juris Eccl.* (Rome, 1907); GROSS, *Das Recht an der Pfründe* (Graz, 1887); GALANTE, *Il Beneficio Ecclesiastico* (Milan, 1895); VERING, *Lehrbuch des kath. prot. und oriental. Kirchenrechts*, etc. (3d ed., Freiburg, 1893), 452 sqq.; ROTH, *Geschichte des Beneficialwesens* (Erlangen, 1850); STUTZ, *Geschichte des Beneficialwesens bis Alexander III* (Berlin, 1895); TAUNTON, *The Law of the Church* (London, 1906).

JOHN T. CREAGH.

Benefit of Clergy, the exemption from the jurisdiction of the secular courts, which in England, in the Middle Ages, was accorded to clergymen. This exemption included all who had been tonsured and wore the ecclesiastical dress, and was shared in by monks and nuns. In Saxon days ecclesiastical and civil cases were decided in shire and hundred courts where the bishop sat side by side with the ealdorman or sheriff. From the days of the Conqueror ecclesiastical courts were held distinct from the secular courts. Gratian (cap. xlvii, 11a pars Dec., Causa XI, ix 1) sums up the privilege of the clergy thus: "From the above it is to be understood that a clergyman is not to be brought before the public courts either in a civil or criminal case, unless perhaps the bishop should not wish to decide the civil case, or unless he should, in a criminal case, degrade him". William forbade his judges and ministers and every layman to meddle with the laws regarding the bishop. These privileges of the clergy were substantially respected by the Norman kings, though their tendency to arbitrariness caused them in special cases to seek to override them. They were at the root of the controversy between Henry II and St. Thomas Becket. Henry alleged that the old customs of the kingdom required that a criminous clerk should be accused in a lay court, whence he was to be transferred to the ecclesiastical court, and, if found guilty, to be degraded and returned for punishment to the lay court. St. Thomas objected, in the name of the Church law, to the first accusation in the lay court. Fitzstephen (Materials III, 47, quoted in Pollock and Maitland, History of English Law) says of the alleged customs: "They had never been previously written, nor were there any such customs in the Kingdom". The author of the "Leges Henrici" (ibid.) says plainly that no accusation, be it for grave crime, be it for light offence, is to be brought against any ordained clerk save before his bishop. (Leg. Hen. I, 57, § 9.) When a clerk was brought before a lay court, he proved his claim to benefit of clergy by reading, and he was turned over to the ecclesiastical court, as only the clergy were generally able to read. This gave rise to the extension of the benefit of clergy to all who could read. By statute in the reign of Edward III (25 Edw. III, c. 4) it was enacted that all manner of clerks, secular and religious, should enjoy the privilege of Holy Church for all treasons and felonies, except those immediately affecting his Majesty. This provision was applicable also to all who could read. In the reign of Henry VII a distinction was drawn between persons actually in Holy orders and those who in other respects secular, were able to read, by which the latter were allowed the benefit of the clergy only once, and on receiving it were to be branded on the left thumb with a hot iron in order to afford evidence against them on a future occasion. Henry VIII (28 Hen. VIII, c. 1, § 32, Hen. VIII, c. iii, § 8) had even the clergy branded for the first time, but Edward VI abolished this, and excepted atrocious crimes, murder, poisoning, burglary, highway robbery, and sacrilege from benefit of clergy (1 Edw. VI, c. xii § 10), but peers of the realm were to be discharged in every case for the first offence, except murder and poisoning, even though unable to read. After a layman was burnt on the hand, a clerk discharged on reading, a peer without either burning or penalty, they were delivered to the ordinary to be dealt with according to the ecclesiastical canons. The clerical authorities instituted a kind of purgation. The party was required to take an oath of innocence, twelve compurgators were called to testify to their belief in the falsehood of the charges. Afterwards he brought forward witnesses to completely establish his innocence. If found guilty, the culprit was degraded if a clerk, and all were compelled to do penance. Many escaped by perjury and leniency; hence steps were taken in the more atrocious crimes to annul the privilege. Later this privilege was allowed only after conviction for men who claimed it because able to read, and then they knelt to the court praying for their clergy and (18 Elizabeth, c. vii, § 2) the party was burnt on the hand, and discharged without any interference of the Church to annul his conviction. The judges were empowered (18 Elizabeth, c. vii) to direct the prisoner to be imprisoned for a year or a shorter period. Women in the reign of William and Mary were admitted to the privileges of men in clergyable felonies, on praying the benefit of the statute (3 and 4 Will. and M. c. ix, § 5). The idle ceremony of reading was abolished by 5 Anne c. vi, and all before entitled were now admitted to its benefit. Branding was abolished and the offenders could be committed to a house of correction for six to twenty-four months. (Geo. IV, c. xi; 6 Geo. I, c. xxiii provides for felonious thefts the transportation of offenders to America for seven years.) The privilege of benefit of clergy was entirely abolished in England in 1827, by Statutes 7 and 8 Geo. IV, c. xxviii, § 6. In the colonies it had been recognized, but by Act of Congress of 30 April, 1790, it was taken away in the federal courts of the United States.

Traces of it are found in some courts of different states, but it has been practically outlawed by statute or by adjudication. It is now universally obsolete in English and American law.

STEPHEN, *History of Criminal Law*, I, xiii; POLLOCK AND MAITLAND, *History of English Law* (Cambridge), I, s. v. *Clergy*, GREEN, *History of the English People*, II, bk. II, i; FLANAGAN, *History of Church in England, A. D. 1076* (London, 1857); CHITTY, *Criminal Law*, s. v. *Benefit of Clergy*; DESMOND, *The Church and The Law* (Chicago, 1898); BLACK, *Law Dictionary*, s. v.

R. L. BURTSELL.

Benettis, JEREMIAH, a Friar Minor Capuchin and historical writer, d. in 1774. He belonged to the Province of Piedmont in Italy, and left two valuable historical treatises. The first, entitled "Chronica et critica historiæ sacræ et profanæ" (Rome, 1766), deals with various astronomical questions and the religious rites and ceremonies of ancient peoples, and was written with a view to facilitate the study of Sacred Scripture. In the second work, entitled "Privilegiorum S. Petri vindicia" (Rome, 1756–66), he gives a history of the primacy of the Roman Pontiff.

HURTER, *Nomenclator*, III, 111.

STEPHEN M. DONOVAN.

Benevento (BENEVENTANA), ARCHDIOCESE OF.— Benevento, the ancient Beneventum, the principal city of the province of the same name in Campania, is situated on the River Calore, and contains a population of 25,000. It was founded at a very early period by the Samnites, who named it Maleventum. In 275 B. C. the Romans, having conquered Pyrrhus not far from there, took possession of the city and changed its name to the present form. In 268 B. C. a Roman colony was established at Beneventum, which was enlarged and beautified by Augustus and other emperors. The arch of Trajan (*porta aurea*), entirely of Parian marble, still bears eloquent witness to the munificence of that emperor. In 545 the city was captured and destroyed by Totila, King of the Goths, but was rebuilt in 589 by the Lombard King Autharis, and made the seat of a duchy. In 1047 it fell into the hands of the Normans, who, however, were forced to relinquish it by Emperor Henry III in 1053.

The city, with the surrounding territory, was then turned over to Pope Leo IX, a relative of the emperor, in payment of the annual tribute rendered the Holy See by the Church of Bamberg; but shortly afterwards it was reoccupied by the Normans. The pope thereupon placed himself at the head of a powerful army "ut saltem humano terrore resipiscerent, qui divina iudicia minime formidant" (that those who fear not the judgments of God may at least repent through human dread; Ep. VII ad Constantin. Monomach.). The opposing forces met at the Dragonara, and after a severe struggle the papal troops were put to flight, and the pope himself was forced to retire to Civitella. There Leo wrought more by word of mouth than the arms of all his soldiers had been able to accomplish. The Norman leaders swore fealty to the sovereign pontiff, conducted him back to Benevento with great honour, and continued from that time forward the most devoted and loyal champions of the Holy See. This warlike expedition of Leo IX called forth the severe criticism of St. Peter Damian. Thenceforward Benevento was a part of the territory of the Holy See, which was always represented there by a delegate. From 1769 to 1774 it was in the possession of Ferdinand I of Naples, and in 1806 Napoleon made Talleyrand Duke of Benevento. In 1814 it again came under the jurisdiction of the Holy See; and from 1838 to 1841 Joachim Pecci, later Leo XIII, was civil delegate to this part of the papal state in the heart of the Kingdom of Naples, and won great praise for his wise administration and his stern repression of brigandage. In 1860 Benevento was annexed to the Kingdom of Italy. Most noted among the citizens of Benevento during ancient times are: Papinianus, the jurisconsult, and Arbilius, the grammarian; Popes Felix IV, Victor III (Dauferio), and Gregory VIII (Alberto di Morra) who were natives of Benevento; Cardinal Pietro Morra, Giovanni da Castrocelo, Dionisio Lorerio, Nicolò Coscia, Camillo Domenico, Gennaro de Simone, Bartolommeo Pacca, and Carlo Maria Pedicini.

Benevento is the seat of an archdiocese, which has as suffragans the Dioceses of Alife, Ariano, Ascoli, and Cerignola, Avellino, Boiano, Bovino, Larino, Lucera, San Severo, Sant' Agata de' Goti, Telese, and Termoli. According to local tradition, the Christian Faith was first preached there by St. Potinus, at the command of St. Peter the Apostle. At a later period, during the persecution of Diocletian, we find mentioned as bishop of this city St. Januarius, who together with Proculus, his deacon, and two laymen, was imprisoned and beheaded at Pozzuoli in 305. His relics are preserved in the Cathedral of Naples, which also contains the remains of St. Agrippinus who was Bishop of Benevento. In 929 Benevento was raised to the dignity of a metropolitan see.

The cathedral, founded at a very early period, was rebuilt in 1692, after being destroyed in the earthquake of 1688. The interior, divided into five naves, has fifty-four marble columns, which furnish a magnificent perspective. Mention should also be made of the two thrones near the high altar, carved about 1311 by a sculptor named Nicola. Of special historical interest is the so-called "altar of peace", erected in memory of the peace concluded at Benevento between Clement VII and Charles V, after the famous sack of Rome (1527). The façade is entirely of a yellowish marble; the great central door is of bronze, of Byzantine workmanship, brought from Constantinople in the twelfth century. In the spacious vestibule are the tombs of the Lombard dukes. The bell tower, constructed almost entirely of the fragments of ancient monuments, was begun by Bishop Capo di Ferro (1254). The church of St. Sophia, in form a great rotunda, is also deserving of mention. It dates back to the Lombard epoch, if indeed it is not a pagan temple converted into a church. The cupola is particularly remarkable, being set upon six antique Corinthian columns. The church of Santa Maria delle Grazie is held in great veneration; adjoining it is a monastery, the abode first of Benedictines, but since 1450 of monks of the Minor Observance. The statue of the Madonna with the Child in her arms is said to have been brought from Greece by St. Artelais, niece of Narses, general of the army of Justinian.

A number of councils were held at Benevento: those of 1059, 1061, and 1087, in the last of which Victor III excommunicated Guibert, the Antipope; that of 1091, in which the excommunication was renewed, and a number of disciplinary canons formulated; that of 1108 against lay investitures; those of 1113 and 1117, the latter against the Antipope Burdinus; others in 1119, 1314, 1470, 1545, as recorded by Harduin, in the seventh volume of his collection of the Councils. In the following centuries the Archbishops of Benevento frequently held provincial synods. Gian Battista Foppa (1643) and Vincenzo Maria Orsini, O. P. (1686), later Pope Benedict XIII, did much to restore and beautify the churches of the city.

Among the bishops famous in the history of the Church of Benevento, passing over some saints of uncertain date, are: St. Marcianus (533), St. Zenoe (543), St. Barbatus (663), who had a golden serpent, an object of idolatrous worship of the Lombards, melted and made into a sacred paten which was preserved up to the time of the French invasion in 1799; Arnaldo, a Franciscan monk (1533); Gaspare Colonna, generous in the decoration of churches, who, at the time of the Colonna conspiracy against Pope Eugenius IV, was imprisoned with the others, but quickly released; Giovanni della Casa, a distinguished writer

and Italian orator (1544); Cardinal Giacomo Savelli (1560), founder of the seminary; Cardinal Pompeio Arrigoni (1607); Cardinal Sinibaldo Doria (1731) who suffered much from the intrigues of Nicolò Coscia, administrator under the above-mentioned Archbishop Orsini. Doria founded a great library, subsequently enlarged by Cardinal Francesco Maria Banditi in 1775; Cardinal Domenico Spinucci (1796); Cardinal Camillo Siciliano di Rende (1879).

The Archdiocese of Benevento has a population of 590,500 Catholics, with 138 parishes, 460 churches and chapels, 839 secular priests, 70 priests belonging to religious orders, 350 seminarists, 40 lay brothers, and 120 members of female religious orders.

Cappelletti, *Le chiese d'Italia* (Venice, 1844), III, 9; *Annuario Eccl.* (Rome, 1907), 292–297; Steffano Borgia, *Memorie Storiche della pontificia città di Benevento* (Rome, 1763–69); Meomartini, *I Monumenii e le opere d'arte della città di Benevento* (ibid., 1889–92); Barbier de Montault, *Le palais archiép. de Bénévent* in *Revue de l'art Chrétien* (1875), III, 345–385; Zigarelli, *Storie di Benevento* (Naples, 1860).

U. Benigni.

Bengtsson, Jöns Oxenstjerna (Joannes Benedicti), Archbishop of Upsala, Sweden, b. 1417; d. in 1467. He was a member of the illustrious Oxenstjerna family, various representatives of which had already become prominent in the public life of Sweden. At the time of his appointment to the archbishopric (1448) Bengtsson was archpriest of the chapter of Upsala. He asked the Council of Basle for a confirmation of his election, and he had himself consecrated (30 June, 1448) by his suffragans, the day after they had crowned Karl Knutsson Bonde as king. On 1 July, Archbishop Bengtsson crowned the queen. The confirmation of his appointment by Pope Nicholas V did not reach him until the ensuing year.

The importance of Archbishop Bengtsson is political rather than ecclesiastical, though his pastoral visitations show that he was not unmindful of the spiritual welfare of those under his care. In 1457, as Archbishop of Upsala, he received from the pope the title of Primate of Sweden; the Archbishops of Lund, however, were permitted to retain their title of Primate of the Church of Sweden. The life of Archbishop Bengtsson fell in Sweden's most troublous days. By the Union of Calmar (1397) the three kingdoms of Sweden, Denmark, and Norway, while preserving their individual independence, were to be ruled by one king, and the foreign affairs of all three were to be regulated as those of a united country. The advantages of this union were lost sight of on the death of its promoter, Queen Margaret (1412). Her successor, Erik of Pomerania, by a change of policy, aroused in Sweden a spirit of discontent, which, after successive revolutions and the election of Karl Knutsson as viceroy (1438), resulted in the deposing of Erik. His successor, Christopher of Bavaria, died in 1448. In Sweden, which was torn by the strife between the partisans of a national kingdom and those of a government in union with Denmark and Norway, the national party elected Karl Knutsson king. A few months later Christian I became King of Denmark, and two years afterwards also King of Norway. Meanwhile, dissensions increased in Sweden. As King Karl Knutsson, to escape from money troubles, increased taxes and confiscated church property, dissatisfaction spread among clergy and people, and Archbishop Bengtsson placed himself at the head of the opposition (1457). Entering his cathedral, he laid aside his pontifical insignia, took up helmet, breastplate, and sword, and announced his intention not to resume his pontifical robes until Karl Knutsson should be banished from the country. Knutsson was forced to yield and fled to Germany. Thereupon Christian I came from Denmark and was formally recognized King of Sweden, and crowned at Stockholm by Archbishop Bengtsson.

General discontent soon followed, especially when Christian I, on becoming heir to his uncle, Duke Adolph of Holstein, found himself in great financial straits. To meet his obligations, he levied enormous taxes, even in Sweden, without exempting ecclesiastics, religious foundations, or the moneys collected by papal mandate to defray the expenses of a crusade against the Turks. During a temporary absence of Christian I in Finland, the archbishop held the regency of Sweden; seeing the people in revolt against him and the heavy imposts, he took up their cause and suspended the collection of taxes. The king showed his displeasure by arresting the archbishop and sending him to Denmark. A revolution broke out afresh in Sweden, Karl Knutsson was recalled to the throne, and Christian I, to recover the country, became reconciled with his prisoner. Bengtsson went at once to Sweden, where he roused the people against King Karl Knutsson, whom he excommunicated. The archbishop succeeded finally in bringing about Knutsson's abdication, and the recognition of Christian I once more as King of Sweden. In reality, however, the archbishop held the reins of power and administered affairs as though he were the actual sovereign. He was unable to sustain this rôle. Discontented factions combined against him and, in 1466, elected Erik Axelsson Thott as regent, whereupon Archbishop Bengtsson was compelled to retire. Dissensions continued, and the king of the Swedish party, Knutsson, once more took the place of the king who represented the union of the three countries. The archbishop found an asylum with his friend Magnus Gren, on the island of Œland, where he died 15 December, 1467, "poor and exiled, regretted by no one, hated by many, and feared by all".

The key to the political activity of Bengtsson is to be found in the ambition that was a part of his character—ambition for his family and his country. There was a strong antagonism between the great Oxenstjerna family, to which the archbishop belonged, and the Bonde family, of which the king, supported by the national party, was a member. Moreover, the archbishop was aware that the nobility and the leading men of Sweden, before the Union of Calmar, had in general failed to respect the clergy and the property of the Church. In a union of Sweden with Denmark and Norway, he foresaw a limitation of the power of the Swedish nobles; in his character of archbishop, it was clear to him that such curtailment would be a safeguard to the temporalities of the Church.

REUTERDAHL, *Svenska Kyrkans historia* (Lund, 1838–66); ALLEN, *De tre nordiske rigers historie* (Copenhagen, 1870); DALIN, *Svea Rikes Historia* (Stockholm, 1747–62); GEIJER, *Svenska Folkets Historia* (Œrebro, 1832–36); STRINHOLM, *Svenska Folkets Historia fra äldsta til närvaranda Tider* (Stockholm, 1834–54); MONTELIUS, HILDEBRAND, ALIN, *Sveriges Historia* (1876–81); STYFFE, *Bidrag til Skandinaviens Historia* (Stockholm, 1870); MÜLLER, *De förste Konger of det oldenburgske hus;* OVERLAND, *Illustr. Norges historie* (Krnia, 1885–95); NISSEN, *De nordiske Kirkers historie* (Krnia, 1884); DUNHAM, *History of Denmark, Sweden and Norway* (London, 1840); CRONHOLM, *A History of Sweden* (Chicago, 1902).

E. A. WANG.

Bengy, ANATOLE DE, a martyr of the French Commune, b. at Bourges, 19 September, 1824; d. in Paris, 26 May, 1871. He spent nine years in residence at the Jesuit College of Brugelette, and in 1843 entered the Society of Jesus. During the Crimean War he served as chaplain to the French soldiery and thereafter until 1870 devoted his life to college work. When the Franco-Prussian War broke out, he again sought and obtained the post of chaplain. He rendered signal service to the sick and wounded during the siege of Paris. After the war he retired to the school of Sainte-Geneviève to resume his work as pro-

fessor, but he did not long enjoy the tranquillity of school-life. At midnight, 3 April, a battalion of National Guards surrounded the school and placed all the Jesuit inmates under arrest as hostages of the Commune. De Bengy cheered his companions during the dark days of anticipated death. On Friday, 26 May, with two Jesuit companions and some forty other victims, he was led to the court of the Cité Vincennes, Rue Haxo, where he met his death joyfully amid the frenzied shouts of the maddened Communists.

DE PONLEVOY, *Actes de la captivité et de la mort des RR. PP. Olivaint, Ducoudray, Caubert, Clerc, de Bengy* (15th ed., Paris, 1882).

D. J. KAVANAGH.

Benignus (BENEN), SAINT, date of birth unknown; d. 467, son of Sesenen, an Irish chieftain in that part of Ireland which is now County Meath. He was baptized by St. Patrick, and became his favourite disciple and his coadjutor in the See of Armagh (450). His gentle and lovable disposition suggested the name Benen, which has been Latinized as Benignus. He followed his master in all his travels, and assisted him in his missionary labours, giving most valuable assistance in the formation of choral services. From his musical acquirements he was known as "Patrick's psalm-singer", and he drew thousands of souls to Christ by his sweet voice. St. Benignus is said not only to have assisted in compiling the great Irish code of Laws, or *Senchus Mor*, but also to have contributed materials for the "Psalter of Cashel", and the "Book of Rights". He was present at the famous synod which passed the canon recognizing "the See of the Apostle Peter" as the final court of appeal in difficult cases, which canon is to be found in the Book of Armagh. St. Benignus resigned his coadjutorship in 467 and died at the close of the same year. His feast is celebrated on the 9th of November. Most authorities have identified St. Patrick's psalm-singer with the St. Benignus who founded Kilbannon, near Tuam, but it is certain, from Tirechán's collections in the Book of Armagh, that St. Benignus of Armagh and St. Benignus of Kilbannon were two distinct persons. The former is described as son of Sesenen of County Meath, whilst the latter was son of Lugni of Connaught, yet both were contemporaries. St. Benignus of Kilbannon had a famous monastery, where St. Jarlath was educated, and he also presided over Drumlease. His sister, Mathona, was Abbess of Tawney, in Tirerrill.

CAPGRAVE, *Nova Legenda Angliæ* (1516), fol. 36, for the oldest lives of the saint; see also HARDY, *Descriptive Catalogue,* etc., I, 89; WARE-HARRIS, *Antiquities of Ireland,* I, 34, II, 6; O'HANLON, *Lives of Irish Saints* (9 November), XI; WHITLEY STOKES (ed.), *Tripartite Life of St. Patrick,* Rolls Series (London, 1887), in index s. v. BENÉN, BENIGNUS; *Bibl. Hagiogr. Lat.* (1898), 172, 1324; FORBES in *Dict. of Christ. Biog.,* I, 312. The very ancient *Leabhar-na-gceart* or *Book of Rights,* said to have been compiled by BENIGNUS was edited by O'DONOVAN for the Celtic Society (Dublin, 1847). BENIGNUS is also said to have been the original compiler of the *Psalter of Cashel* (see CASHEL).

W. H. GRATTAN FLOOD.

Benignus of Dijon, SAINT, Martyr, honoured as the patron saint and first herald of Christianity of Dijon (Divio), an old city in the territory of the Gallic tribe of the Lingones (*civitas Lingonum,* Langres). It is an historical fact that Benignus suffered martyrdom in a persecution of the third century and was publicly honoured as a martyr. His feast falls on 1 November; his name stands under this date in the so-called Martyrology of St. Jerome (ed. Rossi-Duchesne; cf. Acta SS., November, II, 138). Early in the sixth century no particulars concerning the person and life of Benignus were known at Dijon. According to Gregory of Tours the common people reverenced his grave; but Bishop Gregory of Langres (507 or 507–539 or 540) wished to put an end to this veneration, because he believed the grave to belong to a heathen. Having learned in a vision at night that the burial spot was that of the holy martyr Benignus, he had the tomb in which the sarcophagus lay restored, and he built a basilica over it. About this date there was a sudden appearance of Acts of the martyrdom of the saint, which were brought to Dijon by a pilgrim on the way to Italy (Gregor. Tur., De gloriâ martyrum, I, li; Migne, P. L., LXXI, 752). These accounts have no historical basis; according to them St. Polycarp of Smyrna had sent Benignus as a missionary to Dijon, where he had laboured as a priest and had finally died a martyr. For some unknown reason his death is placed in the persecution under Aurelian (270–275). The author had not noticed that the sending by Polycarp and the martyrdom under Aurelian are chronologically irreconcilable. Duchesne has proved that these "Acts" belong to a whole group of legends which arose in the early years of the sixth century and were intended to describe the beginnings of Christianity in the cities of that region (Besançon, Autun, Langres, Valence). They are all falsifications by the same hand and possess no historical value.

Acta SS., Nov., I, 134 sqq.; DUCHESNE, *Fastes épiscopaux de l'ancienne Gaule* (Paris, 1894), I, 48 sqq.; TILLEMONT, *Mémoires* (ed. 1695), III, 38 sqq., 603 sqq.; DE BELLOGUET, *Origines Dijonnaises* (Dijon, 1852); BOUGAUD, *Etude hist. et crit. sur la mission, les actes, et le culte de S. Bénigne* (Autun, 1859); BEAUNE, *De la mission de S. Bénigne et du martyre des SS. Jumeaux à Langres* (Langres, 1861).

J. P. KIRSCH.

Benin, VICARIATE APOSTOLIC OF THE COAST OF (ORÆ BENINI), includes an extensive negro country and the former kingdom of Western Equatorial Africa, in Upper Guinea, on the Bight of Benin, or Gulf of Guinea. In 1860 a mission was founded in the former Kingdom of Dahomey, but as this name was disliked by the inhabitants the title was changed to "Vicariate of the Coast of Benin". The mission of Dahomey was separated from Benin in 1882 and made a Prefecture Apostolic, in 1901 a Vicariate Apostolic. On 10 May, 1894, the Niger mission was also cut off. Since the latter date the Vicariate of the Coast of Benin has been bounded by Dahomey, the Niger, and the Bight of Benin; it includes the British colony of Lagos (Southern Nigeria), the native Kingdom of Porto Novo (under French protection), and the native kingdoms of Yoruba, Isebou, Ibadan, etc.

The region is rich in vegetable resources. Cotton is indigenous and is woven by the women. Among the pagan blacks human sacrifices are frequent; cruelty in atrocious forms is characteristic of these natives. The coast is indented with estuaries, some of considerable breadth and studded with islands. Behind the flat shores plateaux rise to heights of 2000 and 3000 feet. There is an extensive traffic in salt, palm oil, and other staples. The area is about 55,985 square miles, about one-half of which belongs to Great Britain; the population in 1901 numbered 1,500,000, and there were in the territory about 308 Europeans. The appointment of a vicar Apostolic dates from 1891; the residence is at Lagos, which in 1901 had a population of 41,847, of whom 233 were Europeans. The vicar Apostolic is chosen from the members of the Society for African missions of Lyons to whom the mission has been entrusted. The development of this mission has been greater than that of Dahomey, as the British Government grants the missionaries greater freedom for their spiritual labours and gives subsidies to the mission schools when this course furthers British interests. The first converts among the blacks were ex-slaves returned from Brazil; for a long time they were catechized by one of their own race, known as "Padre Antonio", who kept alive the Faith till the arrival of the Fathers from Lyons (Louvet, 291). The missionaries number 26 regular clergy and 1 lay brother; they have charge of about 15,500 Catholics. The

chief stations are: Lagos, situated on an island at the mouth of the Ogun, and known as the "African Liverpool", Titolo, Tocpo, Abeokuta, Oyo, Ibadan, Ishuré, Ibowon. Less important and more irregularly served are Eboute-Meta, Bada-gri, Iboaké, Awé, Ishwo. The vicariate has a number of flourishing schools with 2,059 pupils, of whom 800 are in the school at Lagos. There are 25 catechists. Orphanages and hospitals have also been founded, and a promising agricultural school exists at Tocpo. The principal hospital is the one conducted at Abeokuta by Father Coquard, commonly called Dr. Coquard; he is consulted as a physician as far as Lagos, a town where there are English physicians. The King of Aqué, the head of the federation of Abeokuta, grants a subsidy to the hospital and, although a heathen, is present with his followers at the chief festivals of the Catholic mission. The mission territory includes three large cities: Abeokuta, Ilorin, and Ibadan. Constrained to defend themselves against raids from Dahomey, the native blacks have gathered in Abeokuta, on the left bank of the Ogun, in large numbers, variously estimated from 150,000 to 200,000, and have surrounded the city, or collection of 140 villages, with a wall twenty-four miles in circuit. Ibadan has a reputed population of 150,000 and Ilorin 60,000 to 80,000. As yet no Catholic missions have been established in them.

La société des missions africaines de Lyon et ses missions (Lyons); HEILPRIN, *Gazetteer* (Philadelphia, 1906); *Statesman's Year-Book* (London, 1907); *Missiones Catholicæ* (Rome, 1906); BINGER, *Du Niger au Golfe de Guinée* (Paris, 1892); TOUTÉE, *Dahomé, Niger et Touarez* (Paris, 1897); MIELE, *La Côte d'Ivoire* (Paris, 1900); PLANQUE in PIOLLET, *Missions franc. cath. au XIXe siècle* (Paris, 1902), *Afrique*, V, 196–200; LOUVET, *Miss. cath. au XIXe siècle* (Paris, 1898), 292.

ALBERT BATTANDIER.

Benito, MARCUS. See MIJES.

Benjamin (Heb. בנימין, *binjâmîn*, "son of the right hand"). (1) The youngest son of Jacob born of Rachel. His original name was Ben-oni (Heb. בן־אוני, "son of my sorrow"), given to him by his mother just before she died in child-birth, but was changed to Benjamin by Jacob (Gen., xxxv, 18). The Samaritan reading, *Benjamîm*, i. e. "son of days", would refer to the advanced age of Jacob at the time of Benjamin's birth. Upon the loss of Joseph, Benjamin's full-brother, Jacob's affections were bestowed upon Benjamin, and it was only with great reluctance that he permitted his beloved child to accompany his brethren to Egypt to purchase corn (Gen., xlii, 36; xliii, 15). Joseph, too, showed a marked preference of Benjamin to his other brethren and puts the latter's mind concerning him to a rather severe test (Gen., xliv–xlvi). (2) The son of Balan and grandson of Benjamin, Jacob's son (I Paralip., vii, 10). (3) One of the sons of Herem who had married a foreign wife in the days of Esdras (I Esdras, x, 32). (4) One of those who took part in the rebuilding of the walls of Jerusalem at the time of Nehemias (II Esdras, iii, 23; cf. xii, 33). (5) The name of a gate in the northern wall of Jerusalem (Jer., xxxvii, 12; Zach., xiv, 10). It is not mentioned by Nehemias in his enumeration of the gates of Jerusalem (II Esdras, iii). (6) The name of the northern gate of the Temple, where Jeremias was imprisoned (Jer., xx, 2; xxxviii, 7, 14), probably the same as "watch-gate" (II Esdras, xii, 38) and as the one spoken of in Jeremias (viii, 3, 5, 16; ix, 2). (7) Name of eastern gate of the ideal Jerusalem as drawn by Ezechiel (Ezech., xlviii, 32). (8) Name of one of the twelve tribes of Israel which during the sojourn in Egypt numbered 35,400 warriors, and according to a second census 45,600 (Num., i, 36; xxvi, 41). The territory assigned to it is defined in Josue, xviii, 11 sqq. It was about twenty-five miles in length and twelve in breadth, and was bounded on the north by Ephraim, on the east by the Jordan, on the south by Juda, and on the west by Dan. The nature of the territory was conducive to breed a race of hardy warriors such as the Benjamites who are depicted by Jacob as "a ravenous wolf, in the morning [he] shall eat the prey, and in the evening shall divide the spoil" (Gen., xlix, 27). During the period of the Judges the tribe was well nigh exterminated on account of a crime committed within its territory (Jud., xix–xxi). It was from this tribe that Saul, the first king of the monarchy, was chosen (I Sam., ix, 1, 2, 19; x, 1, 20 sqq.). After the death of Saul the tribe of Benjamin remained loyal to his son, Isboseth (II Sam., ii, 9 sqq.), until David became king of all Israel (II Sam., v, 1–5). At the time of the revolt from Rehoboam the tribes of Benjamin, Juda, and Simeon remained true and formed the Kingdom of Juda (III Kings, xii, 21), which also constituted the nucleus of the restored nation. St. Paul glories in belonging to the tribe of Benjamin (Philipp., iii, 5).   F. X. E. ALBERT.

Benkert, FRANZ GEORG, a German theologian and historical writer, b. 25 September, 1790, at Nordheim, near the mountain district of Rhön, Germany; d. 20 May, 1859, at Coburg. After finishing his studies at the gymnasium in Münnerstadt he studied theology at Würzburg and was ordained priest in 1816. He was first a curate at Gaurettersheim and, in 1821, was made vice-principal of the theological seminary at Würzburg. While holding these positions Benkert continued his studies. In 1823 he received a doctorate, having offered the dissertation: "De Duplici Missâ Catechumenorum et Fidelium". From 1823 to 1838 he had the position of principal, and in 1838 he was made a cathedral canon and cathedral dean.

At that time, in common with the ecclesiastics of other dioceses, the clergy of the Diocese of Würzburg suffered greatly from the religious disease of the age, "Josephinism", and were inclined to a sickly and enervating rationalism. The destructive effects of these rationalistic tendencies showed themselves everywhere in the life of the Church. Even when acting as vice-principal Benkert showed himself deserving of much praise in that he sought to reawaken in the younger clergy the spirit of the Church and to cultivate in them an interest in, and a knowledge of, the old theological schools. In 1822 he founded the periodical: "Der Religionsfreund für Katholiken mit Beiträgen religiös gesinnter Männer". He issued the periodical in the desire to increase the influence of his efforts and also to win over the older ecclesiastics.

The periodical appeared in six volumes, 1822–26. It attracted much attention and was copied in France in the "Ami de la Religion". In connexion with G. J. Saffenrevter he issued, 1828–40, a continuation of this, his first, periodical, entitled: "Allgemeiner Religions- und Kirchenfreund und Kirchenkorrespondent, eine theologische und kirchenhistorische Zeitschrift". At the same time he published, 1828–34, a periodical entitled: "Athanasia, eine theologische Zeitschrift, besonders für die gesamte Pastoral, für Kirchengeschichte, auch für Pädagogik". This appeared in sixteen volumes. He continued the same publication from 1835 to 1840 in connexion with J. M. Düx. As Benkert was more apt to be swayed by his zeal for the right than by prudence, he made many enemies, especially among the older clergy. He therefore severed his connexion with his periodicals in 1840, and devoted himself to the study of the history of his native district. His historical writings have only a local interest. A larger and more important work which he undertook on the Rhön was never completed.

KERZ, *Litteraturzeitung* (1824), II, 101 sqq.

PATRICIUS SCHLAGER.

Benno, SAINT, Bishop of Meissen, b., as is given in biographies written after his lifetime, about 1010; d., probably, 16 June, 1106. He is said to have been the son of a Count Frederick von Woldenberg (Bultenburg) and to have been educated by his relative St. Bernward of Hildesheim. But these statements and the date of his birth cannot be proved to be historically correct. It is, however, certain that he was a canon of Goslar about the middle of the eleventh century, and that he was made Bishop of Meissen in 1066. At that time the great struggle between the Emperor Henry IV and the papacy over investiture, which involved the independence of the Church, was raging. Benno took part in the revolt of the Saxon nobles against Henry (1073). In 1075 he was taken prisoner by the emperor, who was then victorious, and kept in prison for a year. As, later, he upheld the party of Pope Gregory VII he was deposed at the synod of Mainz, 1085, by the prelates belonging to the imperial party and Felix, a partisan of the emperor, received the bishopric. Three years later Benno recognized the Antipope Wibert (Clement III) and obtained his see again; at a later date, however, he separated himself from his schismatical party and recognized Urban II (1088–99) as the rightful pope. The authorities of the eleventh and twelfth centuries contain no further information as to his life.

The Diocese of Meissen extended towards the east as far as the River Bober and included Upper and Lower Lausitz, which were inhabited by Slavs. According to later tradition Benno devoted the last years of his life to missions among these heathen tribes. He was reputed to be the founder of the cathedral of Meissen and in after-ages was the most venerated bishop of the diocese. He was canonized by Pope Adrian VI in 1523 (Bull "Excelsus Dominus" in Bullarium Romanum, Turin ed., VI, 18 sqq.), and his relics were, with great solemnity, exposed for veneration, 16 May, 1524. Luther took this occasion to publish his lampoon "Wider den neuen Abgott und alten Teufel, der zu Meissen soll erhoben werden". After Saxony had adopted Protestantism Duke Albert V of Bavaria had the relics of the saintly bishop transferred to Munich and placed in the church of Our Lady (now the cathedral). Since this time Benno had been the patron saint of Munich; his feast is celebrated 16 June. He is represented with a fish and a key; according to a legend he gave the key of the cathedral of Meissen, when starting on his journey to Rome, to one of the canons with the command to throw it into the Elbe as soon as Henry IV should be excommunicated. This was done; after Benno's return a large fish was caught in the Elbe and the key was found hanging to one of its fins, so that the bishop received it again.

Acta SS., June, III, 148 sqq., contains the *Epitome Vetus* and the *Vita* by EMSER; the *Vita* was first published at Leipzig, 1512, and claims to be founded on an older life which has been lost, but this is disputed with good reason; LANGER, *Kritik der Quellen zur Geschichte des hl. Benno*, in the publications of the Historical Society of the city of Meissen (1884), I, 3, pp. 70–95; IDEM, *Bischof Benno von Meissen* in op. cit. (1886), I, 5, pp. 1–38; (1888), II, 2, pp. 99–144; DÖBNER, *Aktenstücke zur Gesch. der Vita Bennonis ep. Misnensis* in *Neues Archiv für sächs. Gesch.* (1886), 131 sqq.; SEYFFARTH, *Ossilegium Bennonis seu vita et acta ipsius* (Munich, 1765); CRAMMER, *Apologia Bennonis sive S. Benno vindicatus* (Munich, 1773); MACHATSCHEK, *Gesch. der Bischöfe des Hochstifts Meissen* (Dresden, 1884); WILL, *St. Benno Bischof von Meissen* (Dresden, 1887); KLEIN, *Der hl. Benno* (Munich, 1904).

J. P. KIRSCH.

Benno II, Bishop of Osnabrück, b. at Lüningen in Swabia; d. 27 July, 1088, in the Benedictine monastery of Iburg near Osnabrück. His parents sent him at an early age to the monastic school of Strasburg where the learned Herman (Contractus) of Reichenau was then teaching. Having completed his education and made a pilgrimage to the Holy Land, he taught for some time at Speyer in Rhenish Bavaria. On account of his skill in architecture he was made imperial architect by Emperor Henry III and, as such, supervised the construction of numerous castles and churches in the empire. When the Rhine, which flowed close to the Cathedral of Speyer, threatened to undermine the foundation of that building, Benno saved the majestic structure by changing the course of the river. In 1047 he became teacher at the Benedictine school of Goslar (Hanover) and, shortly after, was made head master of the cathedral school at Hildesheim. In 1051 he accompanied Azelin, bishop of that see, on the emperor's Hungarian campaign and upon his return was made provost of the Cathedral of Hildesheim and archpriest at Goslar.

In 1069 Benno was consecrated Bishop of Osnabrück, then vacant through the death of Benno I. During the conflict between Gregory VII and Henry IV, Benno for a long time sided with the emperor. When, at the Synod of Worms, in 1076, Gregory VII was deposed, Benno, like most other German bishops, signed the formula of deposition and incurred ecclesiastical excommunication. With some other well-meaning excommunicated bishops, Benno hastened to Italy, where the pope freed them from the ban at Canossa, before Henry himself arrived there to feign repentance. After the emperor's second excommunication, Benno tried to bring about a reconciliation, but, seeing the insincerity of the emperor, gave up in despair and retired to the monastery of Iburg, which he had founded in 1070. In a little house near the monastery he lived according to the rule of the monks during the week, while on Sundays and holydays he assisted at his cathedral in Osnabrück. Benno's piety and justice made him much beloved by his flock. Strunck (Westphalia Sancta, Paderborn, 1855) and Heitemeyer (Die Heiligen Deutschlands, Paderborn, 1889) include him in the list of saints. Kerler (Die Patronate der Heiligen, Ulm, 1905) says that he is invoked against grasshoppers, because he once dispersed them by his prayers.

THYEN, *Mittheil. des hist. Vereins zu Osnabrück*, IX, 1–243; WATTENBACH, *Geschichtsquellen im Mittelalter* (Berlin, 1894), II, iii. The most important source is *Vita Bennonis*, by NORBERT, a contemporary of Benno and third Abbot of Iburg (1085–1117). It is published in *Mon. Germ. Hist.: Script.*, XII, 58–84. See also BRESLAU, *Die echte und interpolierte Vita Bennonis* in *Neues Archiv der Gesellschaft für ältere deutsche Geschichtskunde* (Strasburg, 1902), 77–135.

MICHAEL OTT.

Benoît, MICHEL, b. at Autun (or Dijon), France, 8 October, 1715; d. at Peking, 23 October, 1774, a Jesuit scientist, for thirty years in the service of Kien Lung, Emperor of China. He studied at Dijon and at St. Sulpice, Paris, and entered the Jesuit Novitiate at Nancy, 18 March, 1737. After three years of renewed entreaties he was granted his desire of the Chinese mission, but before his departure completed his astronomical studies at Paris under De l'Isle, de la Caille, and Le Monnier, who attached much importance to his later correspondence. On his arrival at Peking, in 1774 (or 1775), a persecution was raging against the missionaries in the provinces; still, as their scientific ability made them indispensable to the government, Father Benoît was retained at court and entrusted with the task of designing and carrying out a great system of decorative fountains in the royal gardens. He spent many years in this work, for which he evinced rare talent. He built European houses within the enclosure of these gardens and in front of one, in the Italian style of architecture, he constructed a curious water clock. The Manchus characterize the twelve hours of their day (twenty-four hours, European time) by twelve animals of different species. On two sides of a large triangular basin of water Father Benoît placed figures of these animals, through the mouths of each of which successively, for two hours, was forced a jet of water by some ingenious mechanical device.

While applying himself to his astronomical studies he taught the emperor the use of the reflecting telescope. Among his numerous works were: (1) A large map of the world (twelve and a half by six and a half feet), to which he added valuable astronomical and geographical details.—(2) A general chart of the Empire and surrounding country, engraved on copper, though at the outset he was as little versed in this art as were his Chinese collaborators, whom he had chosen from the best wood-engravers in the country. The work was done on 104 plates (two feet two inches by one foot two inches, Chinese measure). Sixteen designs of the emperor's battles had been engraved on copper in France, at the expense of Louis XV, and when these were sent to China, with numerous prints made from them, the emperor immediately desired Father Benoît to print further copies. This required new presses for these delicately wrought French plates, new methods of wetting paper, distributing ink, etc. The result was successful, even rivalling the work done in France, but it was Father Benoît's last service. He died of apoplexy, ripe in religious and apostolic virtues. The emperor said of him, "This was a good man and generous in his service"; a missionary remarked, on hearing this, that, had the words been said of a Tatar or Chinese, they would have rendered illustrious a long line of descendants. Father Benoît was the author of many letters, preserved in the "Lettres édifiantes"; he translated into Chinese "The Imitation of Christ", while in the "Mémoires sur les Chinois" are many memoirs, descriptions, and sketches ascribed to him, but unsigned.

SOMMERVOGEL, *Bibl. de la c. de J.*; DE FELLER-PÉRENNÉS, *Biog. univ.* (Paris, 1834), II, 217.

WILLIAM DEVLIN.

Benoît de Canfield. See FYTCHE, WILLIAM BENEDICT.

Benthamism.—Jeremy Bentham, an English jurist and reformer, b. at Houndsditch, London, 15 February, 1748; d. in London 6 June, 1832, was of middle-class parentage. After passing through Westminster school he went to Oxford, where he took his Bachelor's degree in 1763 and his Master's degree in 1776. He qualified for the Bar, but soon, disgusted with what he called the "Demon of Chicane", he abandoned the practice of law and devoted himself to the study of philosophers then in favour, chiefly Locke, Hume, Montesquieu, Helvétius, Beccaria, and Barrington. Under the influence of these writers, he entered upon what proved to be a lifelong and fruitful career of speculation upon the principles of legislation and political government. Bentham's primary purpose was not the construction of theories or the establishment of abstract principles. He first attacked specific abuses in the English system of penal legislation. In tracing these abuses to their source he was led to investigate the ultimate principles of law; and subsequently he undertook to construct a complete science of legislation. In like manner, his efforts to lay bare the evils existing in the legislative machinery carried him on to assail the defects of the British Constitution itself.

He published anonymously, in 1776, his first noticeable work, "A Fragment on Government", in the preface of which he formulated his celebrated utilitarian principle, "the greatest happiness of the greatest number", which he borrowed from Beccaria or Priestly. It is the use which he makes of this principle that characterizes Bentham among philosophers. By it exclusively he would estimate the value of juridical, political, social, ethical, and religious systems and institutions; does utility justify their existence? In 1779 Bentham's chief work, "Introduction to the Principles of Morals and Legislation", appeared. It is the only important one that was published by himself alone; all the others were compiled with more or less co-operation from his followers. One of these disciples, E. Dumont, helped to secure for Bentham, at the opening of the nineteenth century, international fame as a legal and social reformer by arranging Bentham's writings and publishing them in French. About this period he was engaged in many philanthropic schemes, the chief of which was one for the reform of the convict prison system. This undertaking, though aided by the British Government, proved a failure. After the peace of 1815, when the codification of laws was occupying a large place in the attention of statesmen, Bentham's writings were studied, and he himself consulted, by jurists of Russia, Spain, Germany, and some South American countries. He also exerted an influence upon legislation in the United States, notably Pennsylvania and Louisiana. In England his ideas of political reform were taken up by the leaders of the rising radicalism, Cobbett, George Grote, the two Mills, and others. With them, in 1823, he established the "Westminster Review" as the organ of the party. He maintained a correspondence with many prominent men of his day, including Madison and Adams, Presidents of the United States.

Bentham attacked the Established Church as a factor in the general system of abuse, and from the Church he passed, characteristically, to the Catechism, then to the New Testament, and finally to Religion itself. In the "Analysis of Religion", published by George Grote under the pseudonym of Philip Beauchamp, he applies the utilitarian test to religion, and finds religion wanting. True to this same principle in ethics, Bentham maintained happiness to be the sole end of conduct; pleasure and pain, the discriminating norm of right and wrong; and he reduced moral obligation to the mere sanction inherent in the pleasant or painful results of action.

The patriarch of utilitarianism, as Bentham has been called, was of upright character and simple in his manner of life. His bent of mind was for the abstract; and he was singularly deficient in the wisdom of the practical man of the world. Nevertheless, circumstances turned him to grapple with intensely practical problems; and, with the help of his followers, he has wielded on political development and philosophic thought in England a powerful influence which is far from exhausted. The spread of his ideas contributed signally to the carrying of Catholic Emancipation in 1829 and the beneficent parliamentary reform of 1832. At the same time they helped to open the way in English ethical and theological speculation for the positivism and agnosticism of the last half of the nineteenth century. One of his principal works, "Deontology, or the Science of Morality", was published after the author's death by his disciple Sir J. Bowring, who also edited Bentham's collected works in eleven volumes (1838–43). This edition has not been superseded. A good edition of the "Fragment on Government" was issued by the Clarendon Press in 1891.

STEPHEN, *The English Utilitarians* (New York and London, 1900), I, which contains a complete list of Bentham's voluminous writings; ATKINSON, *Bentham: his life and work* (London, 1905); ALBEE, *A History of English Utilitarianism* (New York and London, 1902); HALÉVY, *La formation du radicalisme philosophique* (Paris, 1901); REEVES, *Bentham and American Jurisprudence* (London, 1906); DILLON, *Laws and Jurisprudence of England and America* (Boston, 1894); AUSTIN, *Lectures on Jurisprudence* (London, 1865, 5th ed.).

JAMES J. FOX.

Bentivoglio, FAMILY OF, originally from the castle of that name in the neighbourhood of Bologna, Italy. They claimed descent from Enzio (c. 1224–72), King of Sardinia, a natural son of Frederick II. During the fourteenth century the family belonged to one of the workingmen's guilds at Bologna, where it became all-powerful in the fifteenth century. It contracted alliances with the Kings of Aragon, the Dukes of Milan and other sovereigns; and in its later history,

became one of the prominent families of Ferrara. The following are the principal ecclesiastical members: (1) GUIDO, Cardinal, b. at Ferrara 1579; d. at Rome 1644. He studied at Padua, went to Rome and was subsequently sent by Paul V as nuncio to Flanders (1607) and France (1617). He successfully settled the differences that arose between Catholics and Huguenots, was created cardinal in 1621, and appointed by King Louis XIII protector of French interests at Rome. He held the latter position until 1641, the date of his appointment to the episcopal See of Palestrina. He was the most trusted friend of Pope Urban VIII and would undoubtedly have become his successor, had he not died during the conclave. He left several historical works, dealing chiefly with affairs in Flanders and France; they were translated into French, and published as a collection (Venice, 1668). (2) CORNELIO, Cardinal, b. at Ferrara 1668; d. at Rome 1732. He went at an early age to Rome, was appointed Archbishop of Carthage, and in 1712 nuncio to Paris. He showed more zeal than discretion in his dealings with the Jansenists and had to be recalled at the death of Louis XIV (1715). He became cardinal in 1719, and Spanish Minister Plenipotentiary at Rome in 1726, a position which he held until his death.

KAULEN in *Kirchenlex.*, II, 385, 386; MAZZUCHELLI, *Scrittori d'Italia* (Brescia, 1760) II, ii, 867–82.

N. A. WEBER.

Bentley, JOHN FRANCIS, English architect, b. at Doncaster, Yorkshire, in 1839; d. in London, February, 1902. From early days he exhibited a strong inclination towards the profession in which he was to make so great a mark. His parents were not in sympathy with him, so, at the age of sixteen, he placed himself voluntarily with the Clerk of the Works at Loversall Church. In 1855 he began his probation with Sharpe, Stewart & Co., of Manchester, going to London, in 1858, where he was associated with Holland & Hannan and then with Henry Clutton. He started for himself in 1868. He was a firm believer in the architectural principles and methods of the Middle Ages, giving to every detail in his work, from foundation to furniture, his personal attention. He was an apt modeller and had tried his hand with success at stone carving. As a draughtsman, and especially as a colourist, he was very successful, his designs for marble and metal work, jewellery, stained glass, and heraldic decorations being of great beauty.

JOHN FRANCIS BENTLEY

His first important commission was from Cardinal Manning, for the seminary at Hammersmith, and amongst his buildings should be mentioned the Church of the Holy Rood, at Watford; the convent chapel, at Braintree; the chapel of Beaumont College, Old Windsor; St. Anne's Cathedral, Leeds; and St. Mary's, Cadogan Place, Chelsea. He was also responsible for the baptistery, font, and monstrance at St. Francis, Notting Hill; the reredos and altar at St. Charles, Ogle Street, Marylebone, sedilia and Sacred

Heart chapel in the church of the Jesuit Fathers at Farm Street; and the decoration at Carlton Towers. In 1894, he received his commission to build the cathedral at Westminster, and at once started for Italy to make a careful study of the various great basilicas, and the mosaic work at Ravenna. He devoted himself with great concentration to this, his life memorial, producing the most remarkable ecclesiastical building erected in England since the Reformation, and receiving high praise all over Europe on his extraordinary success.

He was a person of brusque, reserved manner, but kind and friendly to those who really knew him. He had the strongest dislike to the preparation of show drawings and to the system of architectural competition and, being a man wholly lacking in self-assertion, and reticent in conversation, was never as well known in general circles as he deserved to be. His great characteristics as an architect were his careful attention to detail, his solicitude that all the fittings should be in perfect harmony with the building, and the sparing use he made of iron. He was awarded the gold medal of the Institute of Architects in February, 1902, but never received it, as on the 1st of March he was seized with paralysis and died the following morning. He was present at the trial of acoustic qualities made in his cathedral, but was not spared to see its formal opening. He was buried at Mortlake.

Architectural Review, XI, XII; The Builder, LXXXII; Journal of the Royal Institute of British Architects, IX; Obituary Notice in The Times (London, March, 1902).

GEORGE CHARLES WILLIAMSON.

Bentney (alias BENNET), WILLIAM, an English Jesuit priest b. in Cheshire, 1609; d. 30 October, 1692. He entered the Society of Jesus 7 September, 1630, was sent to the English mission in 1640, and laboured there with great zeal and success for forty-two years. He was then arrested, at the instigation of a nobleman to whose sisters he was administering the sacraments, and was taken to Leicester gaol. No one in those parts being willing to bear witness against him, Bentney was at once transferred to Derby, where he was tried and sentenced to death at the spring assizes of 1682. His execution was delayed for unknown reasons, and on the accession of James II he was released. He was rearrested, however, tried, and condemned after the Revolution, but the sentence remained suspended, and in 1692 he died in Leicester gaol.

FOLEY, Records, V, 490, and Collect.; GILLOW, Bibl. Dict. Eng. Cath.

SYDNEY F. SMITH.

Benziger, ALOYSIUS. See QUILON, DIOCESE OF.

Benziger, JOSEPH CHARLES, founder of the Catholic publishing house that bears his name, b. at Einsiedeln, Switzerland, 1762; d. there, 1841. In 1792 he started a small business in religious articles, but he soon felt the effects of the French Revolution. The French invasion forced him to take flight with his family, and for about a year they resided at Feldkirch, Austria, where his eldest son, Charles, was born. In 1800 they returned to Einsiedeln, which had been devastated by pillage and army requisitions. All Mr. Benziger's modest fortune was gone, but with redoubled efforts he set about repairing his losses, and started in business as a bookseller. He was made president of the county, and his credit and personal financial sacrifices proved of great help, especially during the famine of 1817. In 1833, Charles and Nicholas Benziger succeeded their father under the firm name of "Charles and Nicholas Benziger Brothers", and two years later, in addition to their book publishing business began the lithographing of religious pictures, as well as the colouring of them by hand, before the introduction of chromolithography.

Charles Benziger, son of the founder, b. 1799, d. 1873, a man of unusual strength and energy, with a good classical education, devoted himself especially to the literary end of the business. In 1840 the "Einsiedler Kalender" was founded; it is still published and furnishes an interesting illustration of the development of the art of printing. "The Pilgrim", a popular Catholic periodical established at the same time, lasted only ten years. Charles, too, took an active part in public life, and showed moderation and energy as President of the Canton of Schwyz. His health failed and in 1860 he retired from business.

Nicholas Benziger, brother of the preceding, b. 1808, d. 1864, who took charge of the technical part of the business, proved himself a pioneer, introducing to the mountain village of Einsiedeln a series of improved trades methods as they appeared from time to time in the great centres of Europe and America. Under his guidance the work of book-binding, which was formerly carried on in the family at home, was systematized. In 1844 the old hand-press was superseded by the first power press. Stereotyping was introduced in 1846; in 1856 steel and copper printing; and in 1858 electrotyping. In 1853, a house was opened in New York. By this time the two brothers had built up a business in Catholic books and prints that was known the world over. They also took an active part in charitable work, and started a fund for a hospital, which has since been erected.

On the retirement of Charles and Nicholas Benziger (1860) the business was continued by Charles, Martin, and J. N. Adelrich, sons of the former, and Nicholas, Adelrich, and Louis, sons of the latter. Under this third generation, the different branches of the house were still further developed, chromolithography and other modern printing methods being added. In 1867, the "Alte und Neue Welt", the first illustrated popular Catholic German magazine on a large scale, was begun, and then appeared a number of illustrated family books of devout reading and a series of school books, including a Bible history in twelve languages, together with prayer books by well-known authors. Between 1880 and 1895 a fourth generation succeeded to the business, and the firm name was changed to Benziger and Company.

The house of Benziger Brothers in the United States was established in New York in 1853 by the Swiss house, but its development as a publishing house did not begin until 1860 when J. N. Adelrich Benziger (d. 1878) and Louis Benziger (d. 1896) took charge. In 1860, a house was opened in Cincinnati and in 1887 one in Chicago. The publishing of English Catholic books was vigorously undertaken, and to-day the catalogue covers the field of devotional, educational, and juvenile literature, besides works of a theological character. Since 1864 the firm has manufactured sacred vessels and church furniture. The American firm of Benziger Brothers is now independent of the Swiss house. The Holy See conferred on the firm the title "Printers to the Holy Apostolic See" in 1867, and "The Pontifical Institute of Christian Art" in 1888.

THOMAS F. MEEHAN.

Benzoni, GIROLAMO, b. at Milan about 1519. He went to America in 1541 and successively visited the Antilles and the Isthmus, Guatemala, and the west coast of South America. He returned to Spain and thence to Italy, in 1556. Of his subsequent life nothing is known. Some hints in his book suggest that his main purpose in the New World was commerce, which he often had to carry on with difficulty, as trading by foreigners in the Spanish colonies was not looked upon with favour by the Spaniards. Benzoni, while not unsuccessful in what he undertook, conceived an inveterate hatred of the Spanish people and Government and in return for the protection given him and for favours which he was compelled reluctantly to acknowledge, wrote and published a book of diatribes and accusations against Spain in America. It contains interesting details about the countries he visited, but abounds in errors and often in intentional misstatements. What Benzoni states about the Antilles is a clumsy rehash of Las Casas. His reports on the conquests of Mexico, and Peru bristle with errors.

The book of Benzoni "Historia del Mondo Nuovo", was published at Venice in 1565. He dedicated it to Pope Pius IV. It was at the time when the controversy concerning the treatment of the Indians was hottest, and a work, written by one who had just returned from the New World after a stay of fifteen years, could not fail to attract attention. In writing it, no standard of criticism was applied; this was not in the spirit of the times. The ultra-philanthropists found Benzoni a welcome auxiliary, and foreign nations, all more or less leagued against Spain for the sake of supplanting its mastery of the Indies, eagerly adopted his extreme statements and sweeping accusations. Several editions were published in rapid succession; translations were made into English as well as into several other languages. Intrinsically, the book has small merit, except in as far as it presents and describes facts witnessed by the author. Even these are not always faithfully reported. It might be called a controversial document because of its violent partiality and hostility. It does not notice mitigating circumstances, and ignores what is good when it does not suit the author. Benzoni writes sometimes like a disappointed trader, and always as a man of limited education and very narrow views. His "Historia del Mondo Nuovo" (Venice, 1565) was reprinted in 1572, and translated into French by Eustace Vignon, 1579. Aside from the annotations which are often trivial and as partial as the book itself, the English translation, "History of the New World by Girolamo Benzoni" (London, 1857), by the Hakluyt Society, is certainly the best. AD. F. BANDELIER.

Beogh, ABBOT OF BANGOR. See LOUGH DEARG or ST. PATRICK'S PURGATORY.

Bequests, RELIGIOUS. See LEGACIES.

Berach, SAINT, of Termonbarry, d. 595; a disciple of St. Kevin and a celebrated Irish saint, whose memory is still fresh in County Roscommon. He was of the tribe of Cinel Dobtha, or O'Hanley of Doohey Hanley, to which also belong the MacCoilidh family. Most of his long life was spent in the Diocese of Elphin, and he built his church at Cluain Coirpthe since known as Termonbarry or Kilbarry. His sister, St. Midabaria, was abbess of a nunnery at Bumlin (Strokestown), of which she is venerated as patroness on 22 February. Her ancient conventual church and graveyard are still to be seen. Under the title of "Berach of Cluain Coirpthe" St. Berach is honoured in several martyrologies, and his holy life attracted pilgrims to Kilbarry from all parts of Ireland. The MacCoilidh family, whose name was anglicized to Cox in the early years of the seventeenth century, were hereditary custodians of St. Berach's crosier, and were *coarbs*, or lay abbots, of Kilbarry. The crosier is now in the Dublin Museum. In 1890, Dr. M. F. Cox, of Dublin, the lineal representative of the MacCoilidhs, unearthed St. Berach's boat, and had it placed beside the present Catholic church of Whitehall, near Kilbarry. St. Berach's oratory at Cluain Coirpthe was replaced by a fine *damhliag* (stone church), built by MacCoilidh and O'Hanley in 916, and acquired the name of Termon Barry, or Kilbarry, that is the church of St. Berach. Some authorities give his feast as 11 February, but most martyrologists assign him

15 February. Kilbarrack Church, County Dublin, was also called after this saint, as in his early days he spent some time there and performed many miracles, duly recorded in his life. His bell was long preserved at the Abbey of Glendalough, but has disappeared since the sixteenth century.

O'DONOVAN, *Acta Sanctorum; Annals of the Four Masters; Annals of Ulster* (Rolls Series); O'HANLON, *Lives of the Irish Saints* (15 February), II; STOKES, *Early Christian Art in Ireland* (1887); COLGAN, *Acta Sanct. Hib.* (15 February); HEALY, *Ireland's Ancient Schools and Scholars* (4th ed., 1902); COX, *MS. Meccoilidhana;* KELLY, *Patron Saints of the Diocese of Elphin* (1904).

W. H. GRATTAN FLOOD.

Berard of Carbio (or BERALDUS), SAINT, Friar Minor and martyr; d. 16 January, 1220. Of the noble family of Leopardi, and a native of Carbio in Umbria, Berard was received into the Franciscan Order by the Seraphic Patriarch himself, in 1213. He was well versed in Arabic, an eloquent preacher, and was chosen by St. Francis, together with two other priests, Peter and Otho, and two lay-brothers, Accursius and Adjutus, to evangelize the infidels of the East. On the conclusion of the Second General Chapter in 1219, St. Francis believed that the time had then come for the religious of his order to extend their apostolic labours beyond the Italian peninsula and Northern Europe; and, choosing for himself and twelve other religious the greater part of Syria and Egypt, he allotted to Berard and his companions the missions of Morocco. The five missionaries set sail from Italy, and after sojourning some time in Spain and Portugal finally arrived in the Kingdom of Morocco. Their open preaching of the Gospel there and their bold denunciation of the religion of Mahomet soon caused them to be apprehended and cast into prison. Having vainly endeavoured to persuade them to abandon the true religion, the Moorish king in a fit of rage opened their heads with his scimitar, and thus were offered to God the first fruits of the blood of the Friars Minor. Berard and his companions were canonized by Sixtus V, in 1481. The feast of the martyrs of Morocco is kept in the order on the 16th of January.

LEO, *Lives of the Saints and Blessed of the Three Orders of St. Francis* (Taunton, 1885), I, 99–111; WADDING, *Annales Minorum,* I, 155, 318, 320 *et passim; Analecta Franciscana* (Quaracchi, 1885), II, 13; *Passio Sanctorum Martyrum Fratrum Beraldi,* etc., in *Anal. Francis.* (Quaracchi, 1897), III, 579– 596; also *Anal. Francis.* (Quaracchi, 1906), IV, 322–323; *Acta SS.,* January, II, 426–435; *Catalogus SS. Frat. Min.,* ed. LEMMENS (Rome, 1903).

STEPHEN M. DONOVAN.

Berardi, CARLO SEBASTIANO, a canonist, b. at Oneglia, Italy, 26 August, 1719; d. 1768. Having studied theology at Savona under the Piarists, he was promoted to the priesthood and then began the study of law at Turin, paying particular attention to canonical jurisprudence. In 1749 he was appointed prefect of the law-faculty of the University of Turin, while from 1754 till his death he was professor of canon law in the same institution.

Berardi's works are: (1) "Gratiani canones genuini ab apocryphis discreti, corrupti ad emendatiorum codicum fidem exacti, difficiliores commodâ interpretatione illustrati" (4 vols. quarto, Turin, 1752– 57; Venice, 1777, 1783). Richter (in Proleg. ad Gratiani Decretum) says of this work that one knows not whether to admire more the knowledge or diligence evidenced in it, while all unanimously declare that, as a critical exposition of Gratian's Decretum, it is surpassed by Antonio Agostino's work alone. The great value of the work lies in this, that it sets forth the original authorities of the Decretum, though carelessness is apparent at times in the author's endeavours to distinguish genuine sources from those that are spurious. Berardi, moreover, is occasionally hypercritical. A compendium of this work by an unknown writer, published at Venice, 1778, is entitled, "Compendium

Commentariorum Caroli Sebastiani Berardi in Canones Gratiani. (2) "De Variis Sacrorum Canonum Collectionibus ante Gratianum", published together with his first work. (3) "Commentaria in Jus Ecclesiasticum Universum", four vols. quarto, Turin, 1766; two vols. octavo, Venice, 1778, 1789; 1847).—This is an excellent treatise from the viewpoint both of theory and practice. (4) "Institutiones Juris Ecclesiastici" (2 vols. Turin, 1769), a work that is to be read with caution.

WEURNZ, *Jus Decretalium* (Rome, 1898), I, n. 315, 396, 397; SCHÜLTE, *Die Geschichte d. Quellen*, III, par. 1, 524; VALLAURI, *Storia delle Università degli Studi del Piemonte*, III, 219.

A. B. MEEHAN.

Bérault-Bercastel, ANTOINE HENRI DE, a writer of church history, b. 22 November, 1720, at Briey, Lorraine; d. about 1794 at Noyon, France. At an early age he entered the Society of Jesus, but left it after his ordination to the priesthood. He was made parish priest of Omerville and later a canon of Noyon. His most important work is entitled "Histoire de l'église" and was issued at Paris, 1778–90, in twenty-four volumes. The history gives a circumstantial account of the Church from the time of its founding up to the year 1721. It is not so much intended for students and learned investigators as for educated Christians, and especially for those priests whose professional cares do not allow them time to carry on higher studies. On account of its general usefulness his work has had a large circulation; in spite of many defects, especially in the later volumes, it has often been republished, as at Maastricht (1780–91), at Toulouse (1811). It has also been translated into foreign languages; it was published in Italian at Venice (1793), and in German at Vienna (1784). Various scholars have continued the history or have issued it in a condensed form. Instances are the edition of Guillon (Besançon, and Paris, 1820–21), that of Pelier de la Croix (Ghent, 1829–33), and that of Robiano (Lyons and Paris, 1835 and 1842). The best edition, with a continuation up to 1844, was edited by Hevrion (Paris, 1844). The best condensed edition was edited by Gams (Innsbruck, 1854–60).

HURTER, *Nomenclator*, III, 347.

PATRICIUS SCHLAGER.

Bercharius (BERERUS), SAINT, Abbot of Hautvillers in Champagne, b. 636; d. 28 March, 696. Descended from a distinguished Aquitanian family, he received his instruction from St. Nivard (Nivo), Archbishop of Reims, under whose charge he advanced rapidly in virtue and learning. Believing himself called to the sacred ministry, he entered the monastery of Luxeuil under St. Walbert, and by his humble and faithful performance of duty soon excelled his fellow-novices. Upon his return to Reims he induced St. Nivard to erect the cloister of Hautvillers, of which Bercharius himself became the first abbot. Wholly given up to prayer and meditation he also instructed his brethren to lead a contemplative life. Ever zealous for the propagation of the Faith, he founded two cloisters in the Diocese of Châlons-sur-Marne, the one (Puisye or Moutier-en-Der) for men, the other (Pellmoutier, *Puellarum Monasterium*) for women. These institutions he enriched by donations of valuable relics, procured on a journey to Rome and the Holy Land.

The monk Daguin, provoked by a reprimand from Bercharius, stabbed him during the night. No word of complaint or censure did he utter when the murderer was led before him; but he gloried in exhorting the transgressor to penance and in requesting him to make a pilgrimage to Rome to obtain pardon and absolution. Daguin left the monastery never to return. After two days of severe suffering, the saint succumbed to his wound, a martyr not for the Faith, indeed, but for charity and justice. His remains were preserved at Moutier-en-Der until the suppression of religious orders at the close of the eighteenth century. The commemoration of his name occurs in the martyrology on the 16th of October.

BUTLER, XV, 252; ADSO, *Vita S. Bercharii;* SURIUS, X, 481.

BARNABAS DIERINGER.

Bercheure (BERCHOIRE, BERSUIRE), PIERRE, a learned French Benedictine, b. 1290 at St. Pierre du Chemin (Vendée); d. 1362 at Paris. He joined the Order of St. Benedict at Maillezais, later lived at Avignon for a period of twelve years with Cardinal Peter de Pratis, Bishop of Præneste, and in 1354 was made prior of St. Eligius at Paris. He was an eloquent preacher and a voluminous homiletical writer. His most important work is the "Repertorium morale", for the use of preachers, a kind of Biblico-moral dictionary, in which the principal words of Scripture are arranged alphabetically and moral reflections attached thereto. It appeared some time before 1355 and was dedicated to Cardinal de Pratis. The "Repertorium" proved to be one of the most popular books of its kind and was frequently printed—first at Cologne in 1477, and again at Nuremberg (1489), Lyons (1517), Paris (1521), Venice (1589), Antwerp (1609), etc. A French translation by Richard Leblanc appeared at Paris in 1584. Other works of Bercheure are: "Reductorium morale" to the Sacred Scriptures in thirty-four books, embracing all the books of the Bible, printed at Strasburg in 1474, Basle (1515), Lyons (1536); "Inductorium morale biblicum"; sixteen books on God and the world; and a French translation (the earliest) of Livy, made about 1350 at the request of King John the Good—published at Paris in 1514 in three volumes. His "Inductorium morale biblicum", commentaries, discourses, letters, and other treatises, have never been printed. Editions of his collected works appeared at Lyons (1520), Venice (1583, 1631), Cologne (1650, 1669), etc.

GAUTIER in *Actes acad. Bordeaux* (1844), VI, 495; PANNIER, in *Bibl. de l'éc. d. Chartes* (1872), XXXIII, 325–364; CHEVALIER, *Bio-bibliographie*, s. v. *Bersuire;* BRAUNMÜLLER in *Kirchenlex.*, II, 389; ZIEGELBAUER, *Hist. rei litt. Ord. S. Ben.*, III, 183 sqq.

THOMAS OESTREICH.

Berchmans, SAINT JOHN. See JOHN BERCHMANS, SAINT.

Berchtold (BERTHOLD), BLESSED, Abbot of the Benedictine Monastery of Engelberg in Switzerland; date of birth unknown; d. 3 November, 1197. Before becoming abbot he was a monk at Engelberg and a favourite disciple of the learned abbot, Blessed Frowin. When Frowin was on the point of dying he advised his monks to elect the pious Berchtold as his successor. Accordingly, after Frowin's death, which occurred 27 March, 1178, Berchtold was chosen abbot. Following in Frowin's footsteps, he was intent on maintaining strict monastic discipline, the importance of which he inculcated by his own example. Nor did he neglect, at the same time, to encourage his monks in the pursuit of Divine and human knowledge. By his order they reproduced many old writings, some of which are still extant in the library of Engelberg. The more learned monks were encouraged to write original works. When Abbot Burchard openly taught that the souls of the just had gone to heaven before the Resurrection of Christ, Berchtold himself wrote "Apologia contra errorem Burchardi Abbatis S. Joannis in Thurthal seu Vallis Taurinæ", in which he shows himself not only well versed in Holy Scriptures and the writings of the Fathers, but also a master in theological knowledge and dialectical skill. Abbot Burchard became convinced of his error, retracted, and died a saintly death. Though especially mindful of the spiritual and intellectual advancement of his monks, Berchtold did not omit to provide also for the temporal welfare of Engelberg. He procured for his monastery many financial privileges, among which was the right to levy tithes upon the churches of Stanz and Buochs, which were under his jurisdiction. The contemporaneous annals of Engelberg, which are published in "Mon. Germ. Hist., SS.", XVII, 280, relate that Berchtold foretold the death of Emperor Frederick Barbarossa. Later chronicles state that, through his blessing, the lake near Stanzstad was stocked with fish, and that shortly before his death he three times changed water into wine. He is generally represented in the act of blessing fish. His miracle of turning water into wine is corroborated by an epigram beneath a representation of him which was kept in the choir of Engelberg up to the seventeenth century. At Engelberg his feast is celebrated on the anniversary of his death.

Acta SS. (Paris, 1887), Nov. 1, 385; MURER, *Helvetia Sancta* (Lucerne, 1648; St. Gall, 1751); BURGENER, *Helvetia Sancta* (Einsiedeln and New York, 1860), I, 80; *Versuch einer urkundlichen Darstellung des reichsfreien Stiftes Engelberg* (Lucerne, 1846); MAYER, *Das Benediktiner Stift Engelberg* (Lucerne, 1891).

MICHAEL OTT.

Berea. See BERŒA.

Berengar, FREDOLI. See FREDOLI.

Berengarius of Tours, b. at Tours about 999; d. on the island of St. Cosme, near that city, in 1088. Having completed his elementary studies in his native city, he went to the school of Chartres in order to study arts and theology under the direction of the famous Fulbert. There he was distinguished for his curious and quick intelligence. It seems that even at this early time his bent of mind and singular opinions were a source of anxiety to his master. (M. Clerval, Les Ecoles de Chartres au Moyen Age, Chartres, 1895.) After the death of Fulbert (1029) Berengarius left Chartres and took charge, as *scholasticus*, of the school of St. Martin of Tours. His reputation spread rapidly and attracted from all parts of France numerous and distinguished disciples, who afterwards held positions of importance in the Church. Among them are mentioned, though there is some doubt about the first two, Hildebert of Lavardin who became Bishop of Le Mans and Archbishop of Tours, St. Bruno, the founder of the Carthusians, Eusebius Bruno, afterwards Bishop of Angers, Frolland, Bishop of Senlis, Paulinus, dean of Metz. In 1039 Berengarius was chosen archdeacon of Angers by Hubert, bishop of that city. Berengarius accepted this office, but continued to live at Tours and direct his school.

It was about 1047 that the teaching of Berengarius touching the Holy Eucharist began to attract attention. In the Eucharistic controversy of the ninth century, Radbert Paschasius, afterwards abbot of Corbie, in his "De Corpore et Sanguine Domini" (831), had maintained the doctrine that in the Holy Eucharist the bread is converted into the real body of Christ, into the very body which was born of Mary and crucified. Ratramnus, a monk of the same abbey, defended the opinion that in the Holy Eucharist there is no conversion of the bread; that the body of Christ is, nevertheless, present, but in a spiritual way; that it is not therefore the same as that born of Mary and crucified. John Scotus Erigena had supported the view that the sacraments of the altar are figures of the body of Christ; that they are a memorial of the true body and blood of Christ. (P. Batiffol, Etudes d'histoire et de théologie positive, 2d series, Paris, 1905.) When, therefore, Hugues, Bishop of Langres, and Adelman *écolâtre* of Liège, discussed Berengarius's teaching on this subject, the latter answered by appealing to the authority of Erigena. It was at this point that Lanfranc, abbot of the monastery of Le Bec, attacked as heretical the opinion of Erigena and defended the doctrine of Radbert Paschasius. Berengarius, in his defence, wrote a letter which Lanfranc received in Rome whither he had gone to take part in a council. The letter was read in this council (1050); Berengarius was condemned, and was ordered to appear at a council which was to be held the same year at Vercelli. King Henry I being titular Abbot of St. Martin of Tours, Berengarius applied to him for permission to go to the council. It is probable that at this time the conferences of Brionne and Chartres were held in which Berengarius unsuccessfully defended his opinions. (Cf. Durand of Troarn, Liber de Corpore et Sanguine Christi, xxxiii, in Migne, P. L., CXLIX, 1422.) The king, for reasons which are not exactly known, ordered Berengarius to be imprisoned, and at the Council of Vercelli (1050) his doctrine was examined and condemned.

The imprisonment, however, did not last long. The Bishop of Angers, Eusebius Bruno, was his disciple and supporter, and the Count of Anjou, Geoffrey Martel, his protector. The following year, by order of Henry I, a national synod was held in Paris to judge Berengarius and Eusebius Bruno; neither was present, and both were condemned. At the Council of Tours (1055), presided over by the papal legate Hildebrand, Berengarius signed a profession of faith wherein he confessed that after consecration the bread and wine are truly the body and blood of Christ. At another council held in Rome in 1059, Berengarius was present, retracted his opinions, and signed a formula of faith, drawn up by Cardinal Humbert, affirming the real and sensible presence of the true body of Christ in the Holy Eucharist. (Mansi, XIX, 900.) On his return, however, Berengarius attacked this formula. Eusebius Bruno abandoned him, and the Count of Anjou, Geoffrey the Bearded, vigorously opposed him. Berengarius appealed to Pope Alexander II, who, though he intervened in his behalf, asked him to renounce his erroneous opinions. This Berengarius contemptuously refused to do. He then wrote his "De Sacrâ Coenâ adversus Lanfrancum Liber Posterior", the first book of which—now lost—had been written against the Council of Rome held in 1059. He was again condemned in the Councils of Poitiers (1075), and of St. Maixeut (1076), and in 1078, by order of Pope Gregory VII, he came to Rome, and in a council held in St. John Lateran signed a profession of faith affirming the conversion of the bread into the body of Christ, born of the Virgin Mary. The following year, in a council held in the same place Berengarius signed a formula affirming the same doctrine in a more explicit way. Gregory VII then recommended him to the bishops of Tours and Angers, forbidding that any penalty should be inflicted on him or that anyone should call him a heretic. Berengarius, on his return, again attacked the formula he had signed, but as a consequence of the Council of Bordeaux (1080) he made a final retraction. He then retired into solitude on the island of St. Cosme, where he died, in union with the Church.

DOCTRINES AND THEIR CONDEMNATION.—According to some of his contemporaries, Berengarius held erroneous opinions about the spiritual power, marriage, the baptism of children, and other points of doctrine. (Bernold of Constance, De Berengerii hæresiarchæ damnatione multiplici in P. L., CXLVIII, 1456; Guitmond, De Corporis et Sanguinis Christi veritate in Eucharistiâ, P. L., CXLIX, 1429, 1480.) But Berengarius's fundamental doctrine concerns the Holy Eucharist.

In order to understand his opinion, we must observe that, in philosophy, Berengarius had rationalistic tendencies and was a nominalist. Even in the study of the questions of faith, he held that reason is the best guide. Reason, however, is dependent upon and is limited by sense-perception. Authority, therefore, is not conclusive; we must reason according to the data of our senses. There is no doubt that Berengarius denied transubstantiation (we mean the substantial conversion expressed by the word; the word itself was used for the first time by Hildebert of Lavardin); it is not absolutely certain that he denied the Real Presence, though he certainly held false views regarding it. Is the body of Christ present in the Eucharist, and in what manner? On this question the authorities appealed to by Berengarius are, besides Scotus Erigena, St. Jerome, St. Ambrose, and St. Augustine. These fathers taught that the Sacrament of the Altar is the figure, the sign, the token of the body and blood of the Lord. These terms, in their mind, apply directly to what is external and sensible in the Holy Eucharist and do not, in any way, imply the negation of the real presence of the true body of Christ. (St. Aug. Serm. 143, n. 3; Gerbert, Libellus De Corp. et Sang. Domini. n. 4, P. L., CXXXIX, 177.) For Berengarius the body and the blood of Christ are really present in the Holy Eucharist; but this presence is an intellectual or spiritual presence. The substance of the bread and the substance of the wine remain unchanged in their nature, but by consecration they become spiritually the very body and blood of Christ. This spiritual body and blood of Christ is the *res sacramenti;* the bread and the wine are the figure, the sign, the token, *sacramentum.*

Such is the doctrine of Berengarius in his various discussions, letters, and writings up to the Council of Rome in 1059. (Migne P. L., CXLII, 1327; CL, 66; Martène and Durand, Theasaurus Novus Anecdotorum, Paris, 1717, IV.) At this council, Berengarius signed a profession of faith affirming that the bread and wine after consecration are not only a sign, but the true body and blood of Christ which can be perceived in a sensible and real manner. (Lanfranc, De Corp. et Sang. Domini, ii, in P. L., CL, 410.) As already said, Berengarius retracted this confession. He maintained that the bread and wine, without any change in their nature, become by consecration the sacrament of the body and blood of Christ, a memorial of the body crucified and of the blood shed on the cross. It is not, however, the body of Christ as it is in heaven; for how could the body of Christ which is now in heaven, necessarily limited by space, be in another place, on several altars, and in numerous hosts? Yet the bread and wine are the sign of the actual and real presence of the body and blood of Christ. (De Sacrâ Cœnâ; Lanfranc, op. cit.)

In the two councils of Lateran (1078 and 1079) Berengarius accepts and signs this profession of faith that "after the consecration, the bread is the true body of Christ, the very body born of the Virgin";—that "the bread and wine on the altar, by the mystery of the sacred prayer and words of our Redeemer, are substantially converted into the very flesh and blood of our Lord Jesus Christ, true and life-giving", etc. (Martène et Durand, op. cit., IV, 103; Denzinger, Enchiridion, Würzburg, 1900, n. 298.) In his explanation of this profession of faith, written after the council, Berengarius again clearly denies transubstantiation. He declares that, at the Last Supper, by virtue of the Lord's blessing, the bread and wine, keeping their natural properties, received a power of sanctification and became the sacrament of His body and blood; that the bread and wine on the altar are the very body of Christ, His true and human body. (Martène et Durand, op. cit., IV, 107.) From all of which we conclude that, during his life, and before his final profession of faith, Berengarius certainly denied transubstantiation. As to the real presence, his thought is rather obscure and his

attitude hesitating. There is much divergence of opinion among historians and theologians on the interpretation of Berengarius's doctrine about this point, if it does not appear clearly that he denies the Real Presence, if perhaps the difficulty for him is in the mode rather than in the fact of the real presence; yet his exposition of it, together with his principles of philosophy, endanger the fact itself of the Real Presence and sounds very much like a negative of it.

INFLUENCES.—Outside of Eusebius Bruno who supported Berengarius, at least for a time, no theologian of importance systematically defended his doctrine. We know, however, from ecclesiastical writers of his own and the following period that the influence of his principles was widespread and caused serious disturbance. (Guitmund, op. cit. in P. L., CXLIX, 1429 sqq.; Durand of Troarn, Liber de Corp. et Sang. Christi, in P. L., CXLIX, 1421.) The writers of the following century continue their dissertations against the "New Berengarians" (cf. Gregorius Barbarigo in Hurter's Sanctorum Patrum opuscula selecta, XXXIX); they find traces of his influence in various current phrases and sometimes warn against expressions which might be understood in the Berengarian sense. The Council of Piacenza (1095) again condemned Berengarius' doctrine. His teachings favoured, at least to some extent, the diverse heresies of the Middle Ages about the Holy Eucharist, as also the views of the Sacramentarians of the sixteenth century. The great theologians of the time were unanimous in protesting against his principles, attacking his opinion as contrary to the teaching of tradition and the doctrine of the Church. Among them we may mention especially Adelman, Scholasticus of Liège; Hugues, Bishop of Langres; Lanfranc, then Abbot of Le Bec; Guitmund, a disciple of Lanfranc who became Bishop of Aversa; Durand, Abbot of St. Martin of Troarn; Bernold of Constance, and others, most of them Benedictines. (L. Biginelli, I benedittini e gli studi eucaristici nel medio evo, Turin, 1895.)

The error of Berengarius, as is the case with other heresies was the occasion which favoured and even necessitated, a more explicit presentation, and a more precise formulation of Catholic doctrine about the Holy Eucharist. Some expressions, among those used even by the adversaries of the Berengarian doctrine, were corrected. It was Hildebert of Lavardin, a contemporary of Berengarius if not his pupil, who first used the word "transubstantiation". (Sermones xciii; P. L., CLXXI, 776.) The Council of Rome in 1079 in its condemnation of Berengarius, expresses more clearly than any document before it, the nature of this substantial change; and St. Thomas, in his definition of Transubstantiation uses almost the same terms as the council. (Sum. Theol., III, Q. lxxv, a. 4.) Though the feast of Corpus Christi was officially established only in the thirteenth century, its institution was probably occasioned by these eucharistic controversies. The same may be said of the ceremony of the elevation of the Host after the consecration in the Holy Sacrifice of the Mass.

There is no complete edition of the works of Berengarius. Only one volume has been published by Visher in Berlin (1834) containing the second part of his "De Sacrâ Cœnâ", under the title: "Berengarii Turonensis opera quæ Supersunt tam inedita quam edita, I, De Sacrâ Cœnâ adversus Lanfrancum liber posterior". Others of his opinions and writings are to be found in the works quoted above and in P. L., CL, 63, 66; H. Sudendorf, "Berengarius Turonensis oder eine Sammlung ihn betreffender Briefe" (Hamburg, 1850).

DE ROYE, *Vita, Hær. et Pœnit. Berengarii Andegavensis Archidiaconi* (Angers, 1656); SCHWANE, *Dogmengesch. der mittleren Zeit* (Freiburg im. Br., 1882); DELARC, *Les orig. de l'hér. de Bérenger* in *Rev. des quest. hist.* (Paris, 1876), XX; *St. Grégoire VII et la réforme de l'Eglise au XIe Siècle* (Paris, 1889); SCHNITZER, *Bérengar von Tours, ein Beitrag zur Abendmahlslehre des beginn. M. A.* (Munich, 1890); CLERVAL, *Les Ecoles de Chartres au M. A.* (Chartres, 1895); GORE, *Dissertations on Subjects Connected with the Incarnation* (London, 1895); BIGINELLI, *La Rinascenza degli Studi Eucaristici nel Medio Evo* in *Compte Rendu du IVe cong. internat. scientif. des cath. tenu à Fribourg (Suisse), Ie sec.: Sciences Relig.* (Fribourg, 1898); RENAUDIN, *L'hérésie Euchar. de Bérenger* in *L'Université Cath., nouv. série* (Lyons, 1902), XL; VERNET in *Dict. de théol. cath., s. v. Bérenger.*

GEORGE M. SAUVAGE.

Bérenger, PIERRE (PETER OF POITIERS, PETRUS SCHOLASTICUS), a French writer who flourished about the middle of the twelfth century. From the second name we may, perhaps, infer that Poitiers was his native place. He was a disciple of Abelard, and is celebrated chiefly for his vigorous defence of his master in a letter which he addressed to St. Bernard after Abelard's condemnation at the Council of Soissons in 1141. Later on he wandered through the Cévennes Mountains, hunted, he tells us, not by wild beasts, but by the Christian faithful of the Diocese of Mende, who apparently took sides with St. Bernard. Those attacks were the occasion of a letter which he directed to the Bishop of Mende, and in which he retracted all that he had said against "the man of God" in his former epistle. There is also extant a letter of Bérenger's against the monks of the Grand Chartreux (Contra Carthusienses). Finally, we find mention of a treatise, now lost, in which he discussed the doctrine of the Incarnation. The three letters are published by Migne (P. L., CLXXVIII, 1857 sqq.). That addressed to St. Bernard, while not wanting in grace and elegance of style, is altogether too intemperate in tone to deserve serious consideration as an historical document. In it occurs the well-known description of an informal meeting of the bishops on the eve of the Council of Soissons. If we are to believe Pierre, the prelates were primed in a most disgraceful manner in St. Bernard's interests, and the condemnation of Abelard was decided before the council actually opened. Even if the author of this story had not afterwards excused it on the ground that it was the work of an inconsiderate youth, overcome by the ardour of his devotion to his teacher, the violent tone of the letter itself would be enough to condemn it. In the letter to the Bishop of Mende Pierre protests that he would recall all that he has written against St. Bernard were it possible to suppress all the copies of the letter, and begs that what he wrote be taken as a jest. He goes even farther when he says that his more mature judgment condemns the doctrines attributed by St. Bernard to Abelard—not, indeed, because they are untrue, but because they are unsafe. The invective against the Carthusians pays high tribute to the rule of the order, but finds fault with the proclivity of the members of the order to indulge in malicious gossip. Pierre exhibited many of the traits of his master. He was by nature a lover of contention, totally devoid of respect for the prestige of either person or institution. His sole merit was the undeniable vivacity and brilliancy of his style and his unusually extensive acquaintance with the poets of classical antiquity. He professed his devotion to Catholic dogma and apparently maintained that Abelard, though he had spoken of matters of faith in a manner novel and unsafe, had not been guilty of formal heresy, and had not been treated with that mercy to which his love of Catholic truth, as he saw it, entitled him.

RÉMUSAT, *Abélard* (Paris, 1855), I, 234 sqq.; COUSIN, *Petri Abælardi opera* (Paris, 1859), II, 771 sqq.; VACANDARD in *Dict. de théol. cath., s. v.*

WILLIAM TURNER.

Berenice, a titular see of Egypt which was situated at the end of Major Syrtis where Bengâzi stands to-day. Its old name was Euhesperides, or Hesperides, for which Ptolemy III Evergetes substituted Berenice in honour of his wife (Droysen, Geschichte des Hellenismus, III, 2, 331). Like the other cities of Cyrenaica, it had received a Jewish colony, so it became early an important Christian centre. Dionysius of Alexandria (264–282) wrote a letter to its bishop, Ammonas (Eusebius, H. E. VII, 26), who is also spoken of in the "Apophthegmata Patrum" (Cotelier, Monum. eccles. græc. I, 385; Migne, P. G., LXV, 119). Daces was present at the Council of Nicæa in 325 (H. Gelzer, Patrum Nicæn. nomina, 219). In 394, Probatius followed to Constantinople the Patriarch of Alexandria, Theophilus (Mansi, III, 852). The city was restored by Justinian (Procopius, De Aedif. VI, 2). It is mentioned with the wrong spelling "Beronice", by Hierocles (733, 3) and by Georgius Cyprius (n. 794) among the bishoprics of the Lybian Pentapolis, but is omitted by the later "Notitiæ". It must have disappeared, like so many other sees, at the time of the Arab invasion in the seventh century.

LEQUIEN, *Oriens Christ.*, II, 623–626; GAMS, *Series episcoporum*, 462.

L. PETIT.

Beretta. See BIRETTA.

Bergamo, DIOCESE OF.—The city, called by the ancients Bergonum, is capital of the province of that name in Lombardy, and contains 45,000 inhabitants. It is said to be of Etruscan foundation. During the anarchy that reigned in Italy in the eleventh century, Bergamo set itself up as a commune, and as such joined the various leagues of Lombard communes formed to resist the power of the German emperors. At a later period, however, a number of powerful families succeeded each other in the mastery of the city, e. g. the Turriani, the Visconti, and the Suardi. From 1797 to 1859 Bergamo passed through all the political vicissitudes of Northern Italy. It has always been a city of great industrial and commercial importance. The neighbouring territory is rich in minerals, chiefly iron; there are also extensive quarries of choice marble. Among the celebrities of Bergamo are the poet, Bernardo Tasso, father of Torquato; the Jesuit Maffei, known for his history of Italian literature; Donizetti, the musical composer; Cardinal Angelo Mai, etc.

Bergamo is the seat of a bishop, suffragan to the Archbishop of Milan; the diocese contains a population of 430,000. Legend traces the beginnings of Christianity in this city back to St. Barnabas, said to have ordained St. Narnus who became first Bishop of Bergamo. More trustworthy is the account of the martyrdom of St. Alexander, said to have been tribune of the Theban Legion. Whatever the value of the details of the legend, the fact has been proved that long before Diocletian proclaimed the great persecution in 303, both Galerius and Maximian in the West inaugurated, on their own responsibility, a crusade against Christianity and sought particularly to remove all Christians from the armies (Allard, La persécution de Dioclétien, I, 101–146). St. Alexander was one of the victims of this persecution, and his martyrdom may well have taken place in 287. To this martyr was dedicated the first cathedral of the city, richly endowed by the Lombard king, Grimoaldus, and by Charlemagne. In 1561 this was destroyed by the Venetians on account of its adaptability to the purposes of a fortress, and the church of San Vincenzo was raised to the dignity of a cathedral under the title of San Alessandro. This is a magnificent church adorned with a cupola of unusual size, rebuilt in 1689 after the designs of Carlo Fontana. It contains paintings by Previtali, Tiepolo, Ferrari, Moroni, Palma il Giovine, and Colghetti who decorated the interior of the cupola in the nineteenth century; likewise basso-rilievos of Fantoni, of exquisite workmanship. Worthy of special note is the octagonal baptistery formed of eight pieces of rosso antico (old red marble), the work of Giovanni da Campione, originally placed in the church of Santa Maria Maggiore, the most beautiful of the churches of Bergamo. The interior is decorated with wonderful frescoes by Cavagna, Procaccini, Luca Giordano, Ciro Ferri, etc. Remarkable also are the tombs of Cardinal Longo, of the Alessandri, and of Bartolommeo Colleoni, the last a work of the sculptor Amedeo. The chapel of this tomb is adorned with paintings by Tiepolo, Angelica Kaufmann, and Giuseppe Crespi. Other churches are those of San Alessandro in Colonna, with a beautiful "Last Supper" by Calligarino; San Alessandro della Croce, adorned by Palma il Vecchio, Bramantino, and others; San Andrea with paintings of Padovanino and Moretto; San Grata; San Bartolomeo; Santa Maria del Sepolcro with a wonderful picture of St. Sigismund, the masterpiece of Previtali. Among the shrines of the diocese may be mentioned that of the Blessed Virgin della Cornabusa, formed by a great natural cavern, extending between three and four hundred feet into Monte Albenza, not far from the Jura Pass. Within recent times Bergamo has become the centre of important and far-reaching Catholic movements of a popular character.

The diocese contains 350 parishes, 512 churches, chapels, and oratories, 1,157 secular and 58 regular clergy, 400 seminarists, 84 lay brothers, 478 members of female religious orders, 8 schools for boys, 34 for girls, and a population of 430,000.

CAPPELLETTI, *Le chiese d'Italia* (Venice, 1844), XI, 445; MUTIO, *Sacra istoria di Bergamo* (1616); GERRINO, *Synopsis eccl. bergomensis* (1734); LUPI, *Codex diplomaticus civitatis et ecclesiæ bergomensis* (1784).

U. BENIGNI.

Bergier, NICOLAS-SYLVESTRE, French theologian, b. 31 December, 1715 at Darney in Lorraine; d. at Versailles, 9 April, 1790. After a course of theology in the University of Besançon, he received the degree of doctor, was ordained priest, and went to Paris to finish his studies. Returning to Besançon in 1748, he was given charge of a parish and later became president of the college of the city, which had formerly been under the direction of the Jesuits. In 1769 the Archbishop of Paris, M. de Beaumont, appointed him canon of the cathedral, and thenceforth Bergier resided at Paris. A pious priest and an energetic student, he devoted a great part of his time to writing in defence of religion. He agreed to correct certain articles of the "Encyclopédie", but found himself obliged to write entirely original articles which then formed the "Dictionnaire de théologie" as a part of the "Encyclopédie".

The works of Bergier are in the fields of apologetics and theology, except "Les éléments primitifs des langues" (Besançon, 1764) and "L'origine des dieux du paganisme" (Paris, 1767). Among his apologetical and theological works, the most important are: "Le déisme refuté par lui-même" (Paris, 1765); "La certitude des preuves du christianisme" (Paris, 1767, also published in Migne's "Démonstrations évangéliques", XI); "Réponses aux Conseils raisonnables de Voltaire" (Paris, 1771, also in Migne, ibid.); "Apologie de la religion chrétienne"—against d'Holbach's "Christianisme dévoilé" (Paris, 1769); "Réfutation des principaux articles du dictionnaire philosophique"; "Examen du matérialisme" (Paris, 1771); "Traité historique et dogmatique de la vraie religion" (Paris, 1780, and 8 vols. 8vo., 1820). The "Dictionnaire théologique" has been often edited, especially by Gousset in 8 vols. (Besançon, 1838) and Migne (Paris, 1850). Some of his writings concerning divorce, the question of the mercy of God,

and the origin of evil, and one volume of sermons were published after his death. Though on certain points, as on the questions of grace and the supernatural necessity of revelation, the doctrine of Bergier lacks precision and completeness, the value of his theological and apologetical work cannot be denied.

Notice historique, as an introduction to the *Dictionnaire théologique*, ed. by MIGNE (Paris, 1850); JANNER in *Kirchenlex.*, II, 408; HURTER, *Nomenclator* (Innsbruck, 1895), III; DUBLANCHY in *Dict. de théol. cath.*, s. v.

G. M. SAUVAGE.

Bergomensis PETRUS. See PETER OF BERGAMO.

Berington, CHARLES, titular Bishop of Hiero-Cæsarea, b. at Stock, Essex, England, 1748; d. 8 June, 1798. His life is a continued story of disappointed hopes and expectations. At thirteen he was sent to the English College at Douai, where his abilities at once showed themselves; but he never applied himself to his work. His progress was so unsatisfactory that four years later he was removed and sent to St. Gregory's Seminary, Paris. According to his cousin, the Rev. Joseph Berington, he did very little better at Paris than at Douai, though he succeeded at last in taking his doctorate at the Sorbonne in 1776. On his return to England, he became chaplain at Ingatestone Hall, a few miles from his birthplace. After travelling for two years with young Mr. Giffard of Chillington, on his return, Berington was appointed coadjutor to Bishop Thomas Talbot, Vicar Apostolic of the Midland District, becoming at the same time titular Bishop of Hiero-Cæsarea.

The Midland District, one of the four into which for ecclesiastical purposes England was then divided, was at that time the stronghold of "Cisalpine" opinions. With these Charles Berington was in full sympathy, in consequence of which, in 1788, he was elected a member of the Catholic Committee, who were then agitating for the repeal of the Penal Laws, for which end they were unfortunately willing to minimize some of their Catholic principles. Two other ecclesiastics were elected at the same time, the Rev. Joseph Wilkes, O. S. B., and Bishop James Talbot, Vicar Apostolic of the London District, though the latter's appointment was merely nominal, for he never attended the meetings. Berington took a leading part in the disputes which followed between the Committee and the bishops, and though his sympathies were chiefly with the former, he exerted a restraining influence on them, and was ever trying to bring about an understanding between the two contending parties. Nevertheless, he did not scruple to sign his name to the most extreme documents which appeared in the official publications of the Committee known as the "Blue Books", and he defended the oath intended to be imposed by the legislature on Catholics, which was afterwards condemned by the Holy See. In the midst of these disputes Bishop James Talbot died, and endeavours were made by the Committee to secure the appointment of Berington in his place, so that he might reside in London and exert the influence attached to the position. These endeavours failed, and Dr. Douglass was appointed Vicar Apostolic. Some of the more extreme laymen, however, maintained that they had a right to choose their own bishop, and called upon the Catholic body to disavow the prelate appointed by Rome, and to rally round Berington; but on this occasion the latter showed his sound sense by publishing a letter in which he refused to have anything to do with these machinations, by which action he practically put an end to them.

Bishop Thomas Talbot died in 1795, and Charles Berington succeeded as Vicar Apostolic of the Midland District. Again he appeared to have a career before him. Before giving him his special faculties, however, Rome called upon him to withdraw his signature from the Blue Books. For several years he demurred, being still under "Cisalpine" influence. At length, through the intervention of Monsignor Erskine, who was living in England as an informal papal envoy, Berington was induced to sign the necessary retractation, on 11 October, 1797. After some delay due to the disturbed state of Rome, his faculties were sent, but they never reached him, for he died suddenly of apoplexy while riding home from Sedgley Park.

CHARLES BUTLER, *Hist. Memoirs of English Catholics;* MILNER, *Supplem. Memoirs;* GILLOW, *Bibl. Dict. Eng. Cath.;* AMHERST, *History of Catholic Emancipation;* HUSENBETH, *Life of Milner;* BRADY, *Episcopal Succession in England and Ireland,* etc.

BERNARD WARD.

Berington, JOSEPH, one of the best known Catholic writers of his day, b. at Winsley, in Herefordshire, 16 January, 1743; d. at Buckland, 1 December, 1827. He was educated at the English College at Douai, showing such talent and originality of mind that after his ordination to the priesthood he was promoted to the chair of philosophy in the university. In this position his inclination towards liberal opinions became apparent, and his theses, prepared for the exhibition of his pupils, created such a stir that he thought it prudent to resign. On his return to England, he occupied several positions in turn, each intended to give him leisure to pursue his studies. From 1776 to 1782 he was chaplain to Mr. Thomas Stapleton, of Carlton, Yorkshire, acting at the same time as tutor to his son, with whom he afterwards travelled around Europe. We next find him at Oscott, then a lonely country mission, where his cousin, Charles Berington, who had been appointed coadjutor bishop, joined him. Both the Beringtons were of the same caste of mind; both were favourers of the committee appointed to represent the Catholics in their struggle for emancipation, which gained for itself an unfortunate notoriety for its liberalizing principles, and the generally anti-episcopal tendency of its action. The Midland District was the chief centre of these opinions, and fifteen of the clergy of Staffordshire formed themselves into an association of which Joseph Berington was the leader, the primary object being to stand by their bishop, Thomas Talbot, who was partly on that side. Afterwards, however, they were led into other action, especially in taking up the case of Rev. Joseph Wilkes, who had been suspended by his bishop in consequence of his action on the committee, which laid them open to criticism.

Joseph Berington was by this time becoming well known as an author with an attractive style of writing, but of very advanced views. His "State and Behaviour of English Catholics" (1780) contained more than one passage of doubtful orthodoxy; his "History of Abelard" (1784) brought into prominence the same philosophical tendencies which he had before manifested at Douai; and his "Reflexions", addressed to Rev. J. Hawkins, an apostate priest (1785 and 1788), were much criticized; while perhaps more than all, the "Memoirs of Panzani", which he edited with an Introduction and Supplement (1793), gave him the reputation of being a disloyal Catholic. Under these circumstances, when Sir John Throckmorton of Buckland in Berkshire, appointed Berington his chaplain, Dr. Douglass, Bishop of the London District (in which Buckland was situated), refused to give him faculties, till in 1797 he printed a letter explaining his views, which the bishop considered satisfactory. A year or two later, Dr. Douglass again suspended him, until he signed a further declaration in 1801.

Berington passed the remainder of his life at Buckland, where he wrote the most extensive of all his works, "The Literary History of the Middle Ages" (1811). He published many other books at different times; but some of his writings remained in manuscript, lest their publication should give offence. In private life Joseph Berington was a model priest, exact in the discharge of his duties, and noted for his charity to the poor. He was respected by all who knew him, Catholic and Protestant alike, and after his death a slab was erected in his memory in the Protestant church at Buckland with an inscription written by his friend, Rev. John Bew, formerly President of Oscott. The only likeness extant is a silhouette, in the Catholic Directory for 1832. Berington's works (besides those mentioned in the text) are: "Present State of Caths." (1787); "Rights of Dissenters" (1789); "Henry II, Richard and John" (1790); "Examination of Events termed Miraculous" (1796); "Gother's Prayers" (1800); "Faith of Catholics" (1813); "Decline and Fall of Cath. Relig. in Eng." (1813, a reprint of Memoirs of Panzani); numerous letters and pamphlets and many other works in MS.

COOPER in *Dict. of Nat. Biog.;* GILLOW, *Bibl. Dict. Eng. Cath.;* WARD, *Cath. London a Century ago* (1905); HUSENBETH, *Life of Milner; Cath. Miscellany* (1828).

BERNARD WARD.

Berisford, HUMPHREY, Confessor (c. 1588) of whom the only extant account occurs in the MS. marked "F", compiled during the seventeenth century by Father Christopher Grene. This MS. which is now at the English College in Rome has been partly printed in Foley's "Records" (III). Of Humphrey Berisford it states that he was a gentleman of the county of Derby, whose father, an esquire, was a Protestant. The account continues: "He studied at Douay about two years. Returning from thence, his father employed him about his suit in law, and having once a suit against one, who fearing to be cast by his means, accused him before the judge for a recusant. When the cause should have been heard the judge examined him. He constantly professed his faith. Then the judge offered both favour to his cause and liberty if he would but only say he would go to their church; which he utterly refused. Therefore he was committed to prison where he remained seven [blank in original] then died a prisoner". Gillow conjectures that the missing word was years and states that he died in Derby Gaol about 1588. To this account nothing can with certainty be added. The "Douay Diaries" mention one "Beresfordus" among other "sons of men of position" (*nobilium filii*) as leaving the college in November, 1576. On 31 May, 1577, he is spoken of a returning from Paris and is then alluded to as *clarus adolescens.* But this young man cannot be certainly identified with Humphrey Berisford as there were at this time other Catholics of the same name, three of whom, James, Oswald, and Frederick Beresford, were prisoners in the Poultry Counter in London, in this very year.

FOLEY, *Records Eng. Prov., S.J.* III, 230; GILLOW, *Bib. Dict. Eng. Cath.* (London, 1885), I, 200; *Douay Diaries* (London, 1877), 113, 122.

EDWIN BURTON.

Berissa (BERISA or VERISSA), a titular see of Pontus Polemoniacus, in Asia Minor which Kiepert and Ramsay have rightly identified with the modern village of Baulus or Bolus, south-west of Tokat. In the time of St. Basil it was included in the Diocese of Ibora, as appears from letters LXXXVI and LXXXVII of the great bishop, but soon after became an independent bishopric in Armenia Prima, with Sebasteia as metropolis. This important change took place before 458, when its bishop, Maxentius (written wrongly Auxentius), subscribed with his colleagues of Armenia Prima the synodal letter to the Emperor Leo (Mansi, XII, 587–589). Hierocles, at the beginning of the sixth century, does not treat it as an independent city; but it is mentioned as such by Justinian in a Novella of 536, among the cities of Armenia Secunda. It must be remembered that this emperor, when creating the province of Armenia Quarta in 536, gave to Armenia Prima the name of Armenia Secunda, without altering, however, the established ecclesiastical organization, so that Berissa remained a suffragan see of Sebasteia. Among its bishops may be mentioned Thomas, who was present at the fifth œcumenical council, in 553 (Mansi, IX, 175), and another at the sixth in 680 (ibid., XI, 676). It appears still later in the "Notitiæ Episcopatuum" as suffragan to Sebasteia, and its name is written sometimes Βηρισση, sometimes Βερισση; Μερισση and Κηρισση are merely palæographical mistakes. Berissa was a Latin bishopric as late as the fifteenth century, when Paul II appointed the Franciscan Libertus de Broehun to succeed the deceased bishop, John (Wadding, Annales Minorum, VI, 708).

LEQUIEN, *Oriens Christ.*, I, 433; III, 1071; GAMS, *Series episcop.*, 440; RAMSAY, *Hist. Geogr. of Asia Minor*, 329.

L. PETIT.

Beristain y Martin de Souza, JOSÉ MARIANO, Mexican bibliographer, b. in Puebla, Mexico, 22 May, 1756; d. at Mexico, 23 March, 1817. He went to Spain and spent some time in the family of the former Bishop of Puebla, then Archbishop of Toledo. Returning to Mexico (1811) he was made Archdeacon of the Metropolitan church of Mexico (1813), and was afterwards its Dean. Beristain was a secular priest who had made thorough studies at Mexico and perfected them in Spain under the most favourable circumstances. He wrote a number of treatises, some of them on economic subjects, but hardly any were published, the manuscripts being mostly lost through carelessness in sending them to Europe. His great work is the "Biblioteca hispano-americana septentrional," the last part of which was published after his death. For this he used as a basis the "Biblioteca mexicana" of Bishop Juan José de Eguiara y Eguren of which only the first volume (as far as "J") appeared in print. Beristain at first intended to republish Eguiara, completing the alphabet by means of sketches and notes left by the author, but, as he proceeded to carry out the idea, he found that it would be preferable to compose an independent bibliography, incorporating in it the material Eguiara had collected. The "Biblioteca" of Beristain is, thus far, the most complete work on the subject that exists, but it contains many errors in names and dates. Still, if we take into account the time when he wrote, and the great obstacles he had to overcome in the shape of distances from sources and their frequent inaccessibility, it must be considered a monumental work and, up to this day, the principal source of knowledge of the bibliography of Mexico and Central America.

Autobiography in the *Biblioteca hispano-americana septentrional* (Mexico, 1816–19); *Diccionario universal de Historia y Geografía* (Mexico, 1853), I; YCAZBALCETA, *Bibliotecas de Eguiara-y de Beristain; Memorias de la academia Mexicana* (Mexico, 1878), I.

AD. F. BANDELIER.

Berlage, ANTON, dogmatic theologian, b. 21 December, 1805, at Münster, Westphalia; d. there, 6 December, 1881. He studied philosophy and theology in the same city, after completing his course at the Gymnasium, and proceeded to the University of Bonn in 1826. Esser, at Münster, and especially Hermes, at Bonn, led him to such speculations in theology as would have proved detrimental, had he not prosecuted his studies at Tübingen, during 1829 and 1830, under Drey, Hirscher, and Möhler, who influenced him by their historic method, thus saving him from the danger of philosophical systems then prevalent in Germany. He graduated as Doctor of Theology at the University of Munich while yet a

deacon, and soon after began his long career as professor in the Academy of Münster, his native town, where he taught till his death. In 1832 he was ordained priest without ever having taken a course in any ecclesiastical seminary. His first book, "Apologetik der Kirche", was published in 1835, and favourably noticed by Protestant critics. He was appointed, first, associate professor, then regular professor, lecturing on apologetics and moral theology, but he ultimately restricted himself to dogmatic theology. His influence on the theological faculty of the Academy was so marked that its spirit may be said to be his. He became dean of the faculty in 1849 and, with Bisping, Schwane, and others, established the fame of his Alma Mater, excelling less in speculation than in argument and in positive exposition of dogma. Kihn numbers him among those who discussed theological matters philosophically, while Knöpfler regards him as belonging to the Tübingen school. Brück, in his history of the Catholic Church in the nineteenth century, declares, "Berlage's writings excel in correct expression of dogmatic principles, in elegance of language, and in clearness of diction". Those who have been his pupils say that as a lecturer he was concise, direct, and refined. He garnered the fruit of his studies in seven volumes, "Katholische Dogmatik", published 1839–64.

KAULEN in *Kirchenlex.*, s. v.; BRÜCK, *Geschichte der Kathol. Kirche im XIX. Jahrhundert;* KIHN, *Encyclopädie und Methodologie der Theologie*, 404; KNÖPFLER, *Lehrbuch der Kirchengeschichte*, 727; *Litterarische Handweiser*, 1881, no. 303.

JOS. SELINGER.

Berland, PIERRE, Archbishop of Bordeaux, b. 1375 in Médoc; d. 1457 at Bordeaux. Being of humble extraction, it was only through the liberality of friends that he was able to study the humanities at Bordeaux and canon law at Toulouse. Ordained priest, he was, first, secretary to the Archbishop of Bordeaux, then canon of St. Andrew's, and afterwards pastor of Soliac. In 1430 he was made Archbishop of Bordeaux. During his incumbency, he took a great interest in educational matters, founded the University of Bordeaux, endowed St. Raphael's College with twelve scholarships for indigent students, and in general won the character of a highly cultured and saintly prelate. His position as archbishop was most delicate. During the Hundred Years' War, the province of Guyenne had showed marked preference for the English Crown. On the other hand, the conduct of the English toward Joan of Arc, martyred shortly after Berland's preferment, coupled with the ambition of Henry VI, who had himself solemnly crowned King of France at Paris, could not meet the approval of the worthy archbishop. Twice he went north in an endeavour to bring his suzerain to greater moderation. Having failed in this, he transferred his allegiance to Charles VII, King of France, and was instrumental in bringing about the submission of the whole province to the French Crown, and with it the termination of the Hundred Years' War. Berland, old and infirm, resigned his see in 1457 and died shortly afterwards, venerated by his people. His remains were laid at rest in the vault of the cathedral, and his name is yet honoured at Bordeaux. The tower he caused to be built at St. Andrew's church in 1440, is called in his honour "Pey Berland" or "Père Berland" even to this day. Louis XI had obtained from Sixtus IV the appointment of a commission with a view towards Berland's beatification, but the cause fell through at that prince's death. This fact, coupled with the veneration of the people, accounts for the appellation "Bienheureux Berland" by which he is known.

Gallia Christ. (Paris, 1720), II; MORERI, *Dict. hist.* (Amsterdam, 1740); *Comptes-rendus des travaux de la commission des monuments historiques de la Gironde* (Paris, 1852).

J. F. SOLLIER.

Berlanga, Fray Tomás de, Bishop of Panama, b. at Berlanga in Spain, date uncertain; d. there 8 August, 1551. He was professed at the convent of San Esteban of Salamanca, 10 March, 1608, in the Dominican Order, and in time was elected prior of the convent on the Island of Hispaniola (Santo Domingo). The Dominicans of Hispaniola then depended on the province of Andalusia, but Berlanga obtained at Rome, in 1528, the establishment of a separate province under the name of Santa Cruz, of which he was made provincial in 1530. From Santo Domingo he claimed the newly founded province of Santiago de México as being under his jurisdiction, but was successfully opposed by Fray Domingo de Betanzos. About the same time he was proposed for the Bishopric of Panama, and went thither. His vast and indefinite diocese embraced everything discovered, and to be discovered, on the South-American west coast, from which but a few years previous had come the news of the discovery of Peru by Pizarro. When, therefore, the Spanish crown began to notice signs of trouble between Pizarro and Almagro, about their respective territorial limits, it sent Bishop Berlanga to Peru with power to arbitrate between the two on any question at issue. At the same time the Spanish monarch, the Emperor Charles V, by a decree (*cédula*) dated 19 July, 1534, ordered Berlanga to make a report on the condition and prospects of Peru, its geographical and ethnographic peculiarities. The arbitration failed. Pizarro had (perhaps because he had been secretly informed of the bishop's mission) settled for the time being with Almagro and sent him off to Chile, so that no communication from Berlanga reached him. The latter's office as arbitrator was thereby practically vacated, and he returned to his see, refusing all advances made to him by Pizarro. The latter displayed considerable feeling, complaining that, as long as the conquest was in doubt, he had been left alone, but that now that it had been achieved "a step-father had been sent to him". Berlanga sent to the crown a description of what he saw, a brief and unvarnished report from the standpoint of a cool-headed observer. His mission was well intended, but practically impossible. Pizarro had artfully removed the other party to the proposed arbitration, and Berlanga was too honest to yield to insinuations of a one-sided investigation. Of the gifts tendered he accepted for himself a dozen silver spoons valued at twelve ducats, 600 pesos for the hospital of Panama, and 400 for the hospital of Nicaragua. After promoting the construction of the convent of Santo Domingo at Lima, Berlanga returned, in 1537, to Spain where he died in his native town.

Oviedo, *Historia general, etc.* (Madrid, 1850, etc.); Cieza, *Crónica del Perú;* Vedia, *Historiadores primitivos de Indias,* II, and especially the third part: *Guerra de las Salinas,* MSS. unpublished; *Documentos inéditos de Indias* (important letters by Berlanga); Dávila Padilla, *Historia de la fundación y discurso de la provincia de Santiago de México* (2d ed., Brussels, 1625); Herrera, *Historia general,* (2d ed., Antwerp, 1729, etc.); Anon., *Conquista y población del Perú in Historiadores primitivos de Chile;* Mendiburú, *Diccionario* (Lima, 1876), II; *Relaciones geográficas de Indias* (1885), I, Introduction. Jiménez de la Espada, in the same introduction, mentions a report by Berlanga, *Relación de la calidad de la tierra, puertos y población del Perú* (dated February 3, 1538, printed on page 41 of the Introduction); *Libro primero de Cabildos de Lima* (Lima, 1888).

Ad. F. Bandelier.

Berlin, capital of the German Empire and of the Kingdom of Prussia, and residence of the German Emperor and Prussian, King. It is situated in the heart of the Mark of Brandenburg, on both sides of the Spree above its entrance into the Havel. The city covers an area of $24\frac{1}{2}$ sq. miles and had, 1 December, 1905, 2,040,148 inhabitants, not including the population of the suburbs which are virtually parts of the city. Of the inhabitants of Berlin 223,948 are Catho-

lics; 1,695,251 are Protestants; 98,893 Jews, and 22,056 belong to other denominations.

History.—The present city of Berlin has grown out of two settlements of the Wends: Kölln, lying on an island in the Spree, and Berlin, opposite, on the right bank of the Spree. Kölln is mentioned for the first time in an official document dated 1237; Berlin, in 1244. Even at this date both places possessed the rights of Brandenburgian cities, but were not equal in importance to other cities of the Mark. A number of old churches, which are still among the most important ones of the city, testify to the active religious life prevalent at this early date, as: the church of St. Mary, erected at the end of the thirteenth century; the church of St. Nicholas; the church of the Grey Monastery (*Kirche des grauen Klosters*), a Gothic edifice built at the end of the thirteenth century. Altogether there were about eighteen church-buildings in Berlin before the Reformation. It was not until the two towns were united into one community, in 1307, that the place grew to be of some importance. In the tumultuous times which prevailed in the Mark of Brandenburg during the fourteenth century, Berlin and Frankfort-on-the-Oder became the leaders of the confederation of the cities against the nobles, and joined the Hanseatic League. When the Emperor Charles IV obtained the Mark from the house of Wittelsbach, Berlin rose against him, but was defeated and compelled to open its gates to the emperor. Berlin paid an unwilling obedience to Frederick I of Hohenzollern who made his entry into the city in 1415. When the Elector Frederick II again separated the two cities and erected a fortified castle between Berlin and Kölln, on the site of the present royal residence, the inhabitants, under the leadership of Bernd Ryke, revolted, stormed the house in which the elector was accustomed to live when in Berlin, and destroyed the public records. Frederick conquered the rebels and took from the city its jurisdiction and other privileges. In 1451 the castle was completed; Elector John Cicero chose it for his usual residence, which greatly increased the importance of Berlin. The Reformation found ready acceptance in Berlin, and after the death of the Elector Joachim I (see Brandenburg) it triumphed over the old Faith. The nobility living in the neighbourhood of Berlin accepted the new doctrine at Teltow, April, 1539, and the Elector Joachim II, in the same year, followed their example. On the 2d of November the first celebration of the Lord's Supper according to the Lutheran Rite took place at Berlin in the Dominican church, which was later transformed into a Protestant cathedral. In 1540 the new church ritual for the Mark was settled and printed at Berlin. The Reformation in a short time gained a complete ascendancy, the monasteries were suppressed, and the Franciscan Father Petrus (d. 1571) was the last Catholic priest in Berlin until the coming of the Dominicans about one hundred and fifty years later.

The city suffered greatly during the Thirty Years War, its population sinking to 4,000 in consequence of a plague. It slowly recovered from the injuries inflicted by this war during the reign of Frederick William, the Great Elector, grew in size, and was surrounded by new fortifications. Immigrants from the Low Countries and French Huguenots, who brought many branches of industry with them, raised the number of inhabitants to 20,000. Frederick I made Berlin the royal residence and adorned it with many fine buildings, the most famous architect and sculptor of the time being Schlüter. In 1709 Frederick introduced a common government for the five divisions of the city which had gradually grown up. In 1696 he founded the Academy of Fine Arts, and in 1700 the Academy of Sciences, of which Leibnitz was the first president. Berlin suffered greatly during the Seven Years War, in the course of which it was seized and plundered in 1757 by the Austrians, and in 1760 by the Russians; but under the wise rule of Frederick the Great (Frederick II) it rapidly recovered from the damage done to it and became an important centre of commerce, industry, and intellectual life. The number of inhabitants increased to 115,000. Frederick William II also spent large sums of money in beautifying the royal city. Under Frederick William III there was a temporary check to its development during the era of the Napoleonic ascendancy. In 1808 the city acquired the right of self-government to a limited degree, and in 1809 the University of Berlin was founded. During the long period of peace which followed the downfall of Napoleon a new development of the city began and its artistic embellishment by Schinkel, Rauch, Schadow, and others made rapid progress. In 1838 the first railway, from Berlin to Potsdam, was opened; the railway traffic increased the industrial importance of the city, and in 1844 the first large industrial exhibition of the German States belonging to the customs-union was held here. On the 15th of March, 1848, a revolution broke out; more than 1,000 barricades were erected, and encounters between the soldiers and the populace occurred; on the 18th of March a bloody struggle took place in the streets of Berlin in which the soldiers were victorious, but they afterwards withdrew from the city at the order of the king. In 1871 Berlin became the capital of the new German Empire. From 13 June to 13 July, 1878, were held the sessions of the Berlin Congress; since this date Berlin has developed into a great metropolis; it has become the most important industrial city of the European continent, the most important railway centre, and one of the chief commerical cities of the empire.

For about one hundred and fifty years after the Reformation Catholicism was suppressed in Berlin; public Catholic church services were forbidden; Mass could be said only in the private chapels of the Catholic embassies. As late as 1653 the elector was obliged to promise the Protestant diet that he would not allow private or public Catholic church services. In order to be able to raise troops more easily in Catholic districts Frederick William I in 1720 gave the first permission for the holding of public Catholic services in a private house in Berlin; soon after this the first Catholic chapel was fitted up. The pastoral care was exercised by Dominicans from Halberstadt; the saintly Father Bruhns being particularly successful in his labours. The conquest of Catholic Silesia by Frederick the Great drew many Catholics to Berlin, and the church of St. Hedwig was built for the Catholic community (1747–73), Frederick the Great giving the ground. He also built a small church at the home for disabled soldiers, for the Catholic pensioners. The addition of large Catholic territories in consequence of the partition of Poland, the secularization of 1802–03, and that of 1815 by the Vienna Congress likewise increased the number of Catholics in Berlin, but it was not until 1848 that they obtained more freedom. Since then the growth of the Catholic population has kept pace with the development of the municipality. Under Frederick the Great the Catholic population was about 5,000 in 107,000 inhabitants; in 1817 there were 186,570 Protestants to 6,157 Catholics; in 1843, 16,453 Catholics to 328,253 Protestants; 1853, 19,075 Catholics; 1871, 51,517; 1885, 99,579; 1900, 188,440 Catholics in Berlin proper. Church buildings did not increase in the same ratio, and the need of more edifices grew continually greater. With the aid of the whole of Catholic Germany a number of Catholic churches was erected in the decade beginning with 1890 to meet this want, but the construction of new church buildings, especially in the rapidly growing environs and suburbs of Berlin is still one of the most impera-

tive needs of Catholicism in the capital of the German Empire.

STATISTICS.—Ecclesiastically, Berlin belongs to the Delegation of the Mark of Brandenburg, which is under a delegate of the Prince-Bishop of Breslau; the delegate is the Provost of St. Hedwig's in Berlin. The Archipresbyterate of Berlin embraces the city of Berlin with the exception of a small part of Friedrichsberg (2,686 Catholics), and includes also the suburbs called Treptow, Stralau, Schöneberg, and a part of Charlottenburg (as far as the parish of St. Matthias); the Catholics in the presbyterate numbered in 1907, 239,666, of whom 221,262 lived in Berlin proper. The other suburbs, both large and small, belong to the Archipresbyterate of Charlottenburg. In 1907 the Catholic clergy of Berlin consisted of 13 clergy of higher rank (the provost, 7 parish priests, and 5 military chaplains), 31 assistant clergy, 7 priests in other positions, and 15 living in community—altogether 66 priests, of whom 26 do not come from the Diocese of Breslau. The archipresbyterate is divided for the cure of souls into 14 districts composed of 8 parishes and 6 vicariates; in 1907 another vicariate was in process of erection. The Catholic soldiers are formed into 5 church communities or parishes; Berlin is also the seat of the Catholic field-provostship for the Prussian army and the imperial navy. In 1907 Berlin had 8 Catholic parish churches and 18 chapels where public church services were held; these with the private chapels made 31 church edifices; 1 church building and 1 chapel were then in process of construction. With the exception of the church of St. Hedwig and the church in the home for invalided soldiers, all of the Catholic church buildings of Berlin were erected in more recent times. The principal churches are: St. Hedwig (1747–73—see above); in the style of the Pantheon at Rome; St. Michael, the first Catholic garrison-church of Berlin (1851–61) in early Renaissance style; St. Sebastian, the largest Catholic church of Berlin (1890–93) in Gothic style, tower 269 feet high; St. Paul, a Dominican church (1892–93) in Gothic style; St. Matthew, a Gothic building (1893–95), tower 302 feet high; St. Pius (1893–94), rather tasteless Gothic; St. John, the second Catholic garrison church and one of the largest church buildings of Berlin (1894–97), in Romanesque style; church of the Heart of Jesus (*Herz-Jesukirche*), Romanesque style (1897–98).

SCHOOLS.—There has been no public Catholic higher school for boys in Berlin since the struggle between the Catholic Church and the State (*Kulturkampf*) swept away the Catholic Progymnasium; there is, however, a private higher school for boys with about 130 pupils. The Catholic boys who attend the state and city high-schools are divided, for purposes of religious instruction, into twelve groups of four sections each. There are 3 higher Catholic schools for girls; two of these prepare teachers, and one is conducted by the Ursulines and includes a conservatory of music. There are 30 Catholic schools for primary instruction, attended by over 20,000 Catholic children, namely the parish school of St. Hedwig and 29 Catholic town-district schools.

ORDERS, CONGREGATIONS, AND CHARITABLE INSTITUTIONS.—The male orders in Berlin are: Dominicans, 1 house with 10 priests and 7 brothers; the Poor Brothers of St. Francis, 1 house with 17 brothers who carry on an orphan asylum for boys. The female orders and congregations in Berlin proper had, in 1907, 18 houses and 387 inmates: the Ursulines, a house with 37 inmates, carry on a boarding-school for girls, a higher school for girls united to a private seminary for teachers and a conservatory of music; the Sisters of St. Charles Borromeo, a house with 56 Sisters, have charge of St. Hedwig's hospital, which has an average of 530 patients and 160 convalescents; Dominican nuns, 4 houses with 95 sisters, carry on the St. Katharine Home, which includes a day-nursery and home for women servants, the St. Antonius Home, which includes a kindergarten and nursery for small children, a home for women servants, and an institution of visiting nurses for the sick and poor, the Maria-Victoria Sanatorium, a hospital and institution for visiting-nurses for the sick and poor, and the St. Vincent Ferrer Home, a dispensary and home of nurses for the sick and poor and a home for women servants; the Grey Sisters, 7 houses with 137 sisters, have in charge 4 dispensaries and homes for visiting-nurses, St. Joseph's Hospital, and the St. Afra Home, which includes a rescue and orphan asylum, a home for women servants, and a crèche; these sisters are also the nurses in 2 garrison hospitals. The Sisters of St. Mary, 58 sisters in 4 houses, 1 of which is in Berlin-Rixdorf, conduct the Hospital of St. Mary, 3 homes for visiting-nurses, and a house-keeping and needlework school combined with a kindergarten. The Sisters of St. Joseph, 13 sisters in 1 house, conduct a hospice or boarding-home for single women and young girls, a boarding-school where housekeeping is taught, and a house for retreats. St. Joseph's Orphan Asylum, housing 200 children, is conducted by ladies, not professed religious, who lead a kind of conventual life. Taking these and other Catholic institutions together, there are in Berlin proper 4 Catholic hospitals, 12 dispensaries and homes for visiting-nurses, 4 institutions for convalescents, 3 institutions for the care of small children, 9 day-nurseries, 5 homes for children of school-age, 3 hospices for young men, 6 hospices, or boarding-homes, for ladies—for self-supporting women who are bookkeepers, telephone employees, and the like—8 homes for girls who are out of employment; 7 housekeeping and needlework schools, 3 orphan asylums and institutions for first communicants, 1 rescue home for girls.

ASSOCIATIONS.—There is much activity among the Catholic societies of Berlin. In 1907 the religious associations were: 21 brotherhoods and confraternities of the Rosary; 9 societies of the Childhood of Jesus; 8 societies of Christian mothers; 7 confraternities of the Holy Family; 7 altar societies for the making of vestments; 11 St. Charles Borromeo societies; 9 societies for collecting funds, especially for the Boniface associations; 12 sodalities of the B. V. M., 10 youths' or St. Aloysius sodalities. Among the local charitable associations are: the Catholic charity organization of Berlin and its suburbs, an association of all the Catholic benevolent institutions, endowments, and societies of Berlin and its environs; Societies of St. Vincent de Paul, including 16 conferences for men and 16 conferences for women; the St. Hedwig's women's association; the society of the B. V. M. for the protection of girls; 4 societies for the care of lying-in women; the Catholic burial association; the society for the care of the Catholic deaf and dumb of Berlin, its environs, and the whole delegature. The most important associations in connexion with the various callings are: the Catholic Journeymen's Union, having a building of its own; the Catholic Apprentices' Union; the Master-Workmen's Union; 13 Catholic workmen's unions, with about 2800 working-men members, which belong to the district organization for Berlin; 11 associations, having 1500 members, which belong to the Berlin district organization, and are composed of working-women, unmarried, and married women; the unions of the organized Catholic Workingmen's associations (28); the Christian unions, 32 groups with over 4000 workingmen members; the Catholic business men's society with 400 members; 2 societies of Catholic male and female teachers; 9 associations of Catholic students; 2 *Philister* societies. Among the political associations should be named: the People's Union of Catholic Germany with about 4000 members; 13 organized groups in Berlin proper of the Centre Party; the Windthorst Union. Besides these there are some 20 singing, and church-choir, societies, and about 25 social societies. The most important of the 6 Catholic papers are: "The Germania", and the "Märkische Zeitung".

STRECKFUSS, *Berlin im 19. Jahrh.* (Berlin, 1867–69); IDEM, *500 Jahre Berliner Gesch.* (5th ed., Berlin, 1900); SCHWEBEL, *Gesch. der Stadt Berlin* (Berlin, 1888); GEIGER, *Berlin 1688–1840* (Berlin, 1893–94); HOLTZE, *Gesch. der Stadt Berlin* (Tübingen, 1906); CORTAIN, *Das kathol. Berlin* (Berlin, 1906); *Amtliche Führer durch die fürstbischöfliche Delegatur* (Berlin, 1907).

JOSEPH LINS.

Berlioz, HECTOR, French composer, b. at La Côte Saint-André, near Grenoble, 11 December, 1803; d. at Paris, 8 March, 1869. His father, a physician, wished Hector to follow his own profession, and for that purpose sent him to the Medical School in Paris. Young Berlioz soon changed the dissecting room for the library of the Conservatoire, where he sought to acquaint himself with the scores of the masters of music. Heretofore his musical studies had been confined to a rudimentary knowledge of the flute and of the guitar. After studying harmony with Lesveur for a few months, Berlioz composed a mass, which was performed in the church of St. Roch. Being admitted to the Conservatoire in 1823, be became noted not only for his great talent, but also for his rebellion against academic traditions. For the pure classicism of Cherubini, the head of the school, he had no respect, nor did he ever learn to understand and appreciate Palestrina, Händel, or Bach. Bent on giving expression to his teeming ideas in his own fashion, Berlioz, like the romanticists in literature, proceeded by violating or ignoring every established rule. As a consequence he never fully mastered the various forms of composition. With his "Fantastic Symphony", a cantata called "La mort de Sardanapale" which won for him the "Prix de Rome" (carrying with it a five years' pension), and a number of lesser works, Berlioz laid the foundation of the new school of composition which is known as the school of programme music. It is the endeavour of composers of this school to express by means of music definite ideas and moods and even to relate definite events. Although Berlioz has written a number of works on liturgical texts, hardly any of them have the liturgical character. His "Requiem", written for double chorus, an enormous orchestra, four military bands, and organ, suggests Michelangelo in its gigantic conception. While it strikes terror into the heart of the hearer, it does not inspire devotion. A "Te Deum" is built on equally large scale, and is more notable for its pomp and splendour than for its prayerfulness. Although Berlioz was a child of his time and in his music gave expression to every passion of man, he did not lose the Catholic sense, as is shown by the attraction liturgical texts had for him, and also by numerous other traits. Thus in his "Damnation de Faust" he sends Faust to eternal perdition accompanied by most gruesome music, instead of ultimately saving him in accordance with the pantheistic creed of Goethe. Berlioz is one of the most striking examples of modern subjectivism, and the numerous works he has left behind—symphonies with and without chorus, operas, an oratorio, "The Childhood of Christ", songs, choruses, etc.—give us an idea of what he might have been had he remained faithful to Catholic ideals.

BERLIOZ, *Mémoires;* AMBROS, *Bunte Blätter;* JULIEN, *Hector Berlioz* (Paris, 1888); HIPPEAU, *Berlioz, l'homme et l'artiste* (Paris, 1888).

JOSEPH OTTEN.

Bernal, AGOSTINO, Spanish theologian, b. at Magallon in Aragon in 1587; d. at Saragossa, 13 September, 1642. He entered the Society of Jesus in 1603 when sixteen years old. Being a finished classical scholar he taught humanities and rhetoric with success. The greater part of his life, however, he spent as professor of philosophy and theology at Saragossa, where he died. He was a man of rare innocence and candour of soul; so great was his love of prayer that it would be hard to say to which he devoted more time, to meditation or to study. He was looked upon by many as one of the most learned men of his age. His published works are: "Disputationes de Divini Verbi Incarnatione" (Saragossa, 1639); "Disputationes de Sacramentis in genere, Eucharistiâ et Ordine" (Lyons, 1651) a posthumous work.

SOUTHWELL, *Bibliotheca*, 93; HURTER, *Nomenclator*, 380.

TIMOTHY B. BARRETT.

Bernard (or BARNARD), SAINT, Archbishop of Vienne, France, b. in 778; d. at Vienne, 23 January, 842. His parents, who lived near Lyons and had large possessions, gave him an excellent education, and Bernard, in obedience to the paternal wish, married and became a military officer under Charlemagne. After seven years as a soldier the death of his father and mother recalled him. Dividing his property into three parts, one for the Church, one for the poor, and one for his children, he retired to the wilderness of Ambronay, where there was a poor monastery. Bernard bought the monastery, enlarged it, and become one of its inmates. Upon the death of the abbot he was elected (805) to the vacant position. In 810 he was chosen Archbishop of Vienne to succeed Volfère, but it was only upon the command of Pope Leo III and of Charlemagne that he accepted the honour. He was consecrated by Leidtrade, Archbishop of Lyons, and distinguished himself by his piety and learning. He took part in drawing up the Capitularies of Charlemagne and aided Agobard in a work upon Jewish superstitions.

Bernard was a member of the Council of Paris (824) convoked by Louis the Pious, at the request of Eugenius II, in the hope of bringing about an agreement between the Church of France and that of the East as to the devotion to be paid to images. Bernard took an unfortunate position in the quarrels between Louis the Pious and his sons over the partition of the empire between the three sons of his first marriage, to which the monarch had agreed. Like Agobard of Lyons, Bernard sided with the oldest son, Lothair, and was one of the prelates who deposed the emperor at Compiègne and condemned him to make a public penance. Louis soon regained his authority and another council of bishops annulled the action of the one of Compiègne. Agobard and Bernard were deposed, but the sentence of deposition was never carried out, owing to the intervention of Lothair, who had been reconciled to his father. From this time on, the archbishop devoted himself entirely to the duties of his pastoral office. Towards the end of his life he loved to retire to a solitary spot on the banks of the Isère where stands to-day the town of Romans which owes its origin to him. On the approach of death he had himself removed to Vienne. He is honoured in Dauphiny as the patron saint of agricultural labourers.

Acta SS. (3d ed.), January, III, 157–187; *Bibl. hag. lat.* (1898), 149–150; CHAPHUIS, *St. Bernard, Archévêque de Vienne* (Grenoble, 1898).

A. FOURNET.

Bernard, ALEXIS-XYSTE. Bishop of St. Hyacinth, P. Q., Canada. b. at Belœil, P. Q., 29 December, 1847. He made his classical and theological studies under the Sulpician Fathers in Montreal, and was ordained priest 1 October, 1871. After a year as curate he became successively President of Sorel College, Canon of the Cathedral, Archdeacon, Secre-

tary for the diocese, Vicar-General, Provost of the Chapter, and Prothonotary Apostolic. After the death of Bishop Moreau, in 1901, Mgr. Bernard was continued in the office of Vicar-General by Bishop Decelles, and, when the latter died, in 1905, was elected Vicar-Capitular. The Institute of the Sisters of St. Joseph, owe to him their organization, and formation as a teaching body. Besides "Synodal Decrees" and a summary of the "Clerical Conferences", he edited the "Pastoral Letters" of the bishops of the diocese, in nine volumes. He declined the See of St. Hyacinth on the plea of his enfeebled health, until he received from Pope Pius X a peremptory order to accept. He was consecrated 15 February, 1906.

L. O. ROBERGE.

Bernard Carvajal. See CARVAJAL.

Bernard Circa. See BERNARD OF PAVIA.

Bernard, CLAUDE, a French ecclesiastic known as "the poor priest" (le pauvre prêtre), b. at Dijon, 23 December, 1588; d. in Paris, 23 March, 1641. His father was a distinguished lawyer, and filled successively offices of honour and responsibility. Young Bernard was educated at the Jesuit college of Dôle and was remarked for his brilliant imagination and wit. Pierre Le Camus Bishop of Belley urged him to enter the priesthood, but he declined, saying that he preferred the life of a poor gentleman to that of a poor priest. Shortly afterwards he went to Paris as a protégé of M. de Bellegarde, Governor of Bourgogne. For a while the social life of the capital attracted him; gradually, however, some disappointments, together with the death of an intimate friend who was killed in a duel, brought about a decided change in his mode of life and led up to his entrance into the priesthood. He was ordained by the above-mentioned Bishop Le Camus, and invited to his first Mass the poor of the city, distributing to them all his possessions, and, later on, an inheritance of 400,000 livres, or about eighty thousand dollars.

Henceforth Bernard devoted himself to the service of the poor, and delighted in the name of "the poor priest". The poor, the sick, and the prisoners were his special care; he fed, nursed, consoled, and instructed them with more than motherly tenderness. This life of self-sacrifice seemed rather to increase his personal charms. Wealthy and distinguished persons sought his company, and for the honour of entertainment at his modest table contributed abundantly to his charities. His kindly wit never deserted him. When Cardinal Richelieu once pressed upon him the acceptance of some favours he replied that he would be pleased if stronger boards were placed in the tumbril, or cart, on which the condemned were taken to execution. "It is a pity", said he, "that the constant dread of falling through the vehicle should distract our attention from God".

Bernard's methods were characterized by some as odd and reprehensible. He continued, however, to enjoy the friendship and admiration of saintly priests like Bourdoise, Olier, and St. Vincent de Paul, an ample justification of his character and sacerdotal ministry. In the history of charity he bears a striking resemblance to St. Francis of Assisi and St. Vincent de Paul, and his beatification has often been urged by the royal court and by the clergy of France. He founded at Paris, for the education of poor candidates for the priesthood, the seminary of the Trente-Trois, which still exists. He contributed much to popularize the beautiful prayer to the Blessed Virgin known as the *Memorare*, sometimes attributed to him, but certainly of an earlier date.

The life of Bernard has been written by GAUFFRE (1680), LEMPEREUR (1708); RIOM (1834); FELLER, *Biog. univ.* (Paris; 1834), II, 244; ROHRBACHER, *Hist. de l'Eglise* (Paris, 1850), XXV, 251–261.

CHARLES B. SCHRANTZ.

Bernard, Claude.—French physiologist, b. 12 July, 1813 at Saint Julien near Villefranche, France; d. at Paris, 10 February, 1878. His father was the proprietor of a vineyard and his early education, which was begun by the village *curé*, was obtained at the Jesuit college in Villefranche. Going to Lyons to continue his studies, he became instead a pharmacist's assistant. While here, his literary ambitions led him to write a comedy, "La rose du Rhône", which was put on the stage. Encouraged by its reception, he wrote a five act drama and setting out in 1834 for Paris, submitted it to Saint Marc Girardin, the well-known critic. The latter found

CLAUDE BERNARD

evidence of literary ability in the young author's work, but advised him to study medicine as a more certain means of securing a livelihood than literature. Bernard followed this counsel, which proved the turning point in his career, and the play "Arthur de Bretagne" was not published until long after his death in 1886.

Bernard devoted himself particularly to anatomy and physiology but, being of a retiring disposition and somewhat awkward in manner, he did not impress his professors or fellow students with the power of which he was later to give proof. In 1839, he was appointed interne to Magendie, professor of medicine at the Collège de France, and one of the physicians of the Hôtel Dieu, noticing his skill in dissection, soon made him his *préparateur*, or lecture assistant. This latter appointment, in spite of many disadvantages, proved a fortunate one, and Bernard now began the researches in physiology which made him famous. His first important work was a study of the pancreas and its functions. This was followed by the discovery of the glycogenic function of the liver—perhaps his most noteworthy achievement, particularly on account of its bearing on current views in biology. It had been supposed by biologists that the animal, unlike the plant, could not build up complex compounds within itself, but could only utilize those furnished by the plant such as carbohydrates, proteids, etc., resolving them into constituents suited to its own needs. Bernard undertook the task of tracing out the various transformations of food stuffs within the animal organism, beginning with the carbohydrates; and he not only found, contrary to the accepted view, that sugar was formed in the liver, but he was also able to isolate a substance from the hepatic tissue which, though not sugar, was converted by fermentation into dextrose. He made a special study of its properties and called it "glycogen".

Bernard did not pursue his investigations in this field any farther, but took up the study of the influence of the nervous system on animal heat. This led to the discovery of the vaso-motor system. He found that severing the cervical sympathetic on one side of the neck of a rabbit caused a sensible rise in the temperature of the affected region. Further experiments on the sub-maxillary and other glands showed, as he announced to the Académie des Sciences, in 1858, that when the gland is actively secreting, the venous blood issuing from it is red. Two sets of nerves control the action of the gland, stimulation of the chorda tympani making the venous blood red, while stimulation of the sympathetic nerve makes it darker than usual. He was thus able to formulate the statement: "the sympathetic nerve is the constrictor of the blood vessels; the chorda tympani is their dilator", and it may be said with truth that all subsequent work on the vasomotor system has been based on these researches. The physiological effects of poisons, particularly of curare and carbon monoxide, also engaged Bernard's attention. He found that the former—an arrow poison employed by South American Indians—rendered the motor nerves inactive, while the sensory and central nervous system remained intact. His analysis of the action of the latter showed that it instantly replaces the oxygen of the red blood corpuscles, while it cannot of itself be subsequently replaced by oxygen.

In 1855 Bernard succeeded Magendie as professor at the Collège de France, having been appointed his deputy as early as 1847. In 1862 his health failed and it was not until 1870 that he fully recovered. In his later years he made the acquaintance of Napoleon III, who was much impressed by him and established two well-equipped laboratories for him—one at the Sorbonne, the other at the Musée d'Histoire Naturelle. In 1867 the emperor made him a member of the Senate, and in 1868 he was admitted to the Académie des Sciences. He devoted himself to scientific work and the revision of his published lectures until shortly before his death. He received a public funeral, at the expense of the State, from the Cathedral of Notre Dame, being the first Frenchman of science to be thus honoured. A statue was erected in his honour in 1886 in the court of the Collège de France, and also, in 1894, in the court of the Faculty of Medicine at Lyons. Bernard's chief contribution to physiological literature, apart from his original papers presented to various societies, are his "Leçons", in seventeen volumes, upon various topics in physiology. These comprise his lecture courses which were reported by his students and revised by himself.

FOSTER, *Claude Bernard* (New York, 1899); WALSH, *Makers of Modern Medicine* (New York, 1907).

HENRY M. BROCK.

Bernard Guidonis, Inquisitor of Toulouse against the Albigenses and Bishop of Lodève, b. at Royères (Limousin) in 1261; d. at Lauroux (Hérault), 30 December, 1331. He was one of the most prolific writers of the Middle Ages. He entered the Dominican Convent at Limoges, and made his profession in 1280. Ten years later he was made Prior of Albi, and subsequently at Carcassonne, at Castres, and at Limoges. In recompense for his services as Inquisitor he was made Bishop of Tuy in Galicia, by Pope John XXII, and a year later Bishop of Lodève. In spite of his manifold occupations he wrote numerous works of great importance such as: "Fleurs des chroniques", which is a universal chronicle from the time of Our Lord to 1331; "Chronique abrégée des empereurs", "Chronique des rois de France", "Catalogue des Évêques de Limoges", "Traité sur les saints du Limousin", "Traité sur l'histoire de l'abbaye de St. Augustin de Limoges", "Chronique des Prieurs de Grandmont" (as far as 1318), "Chronique des Prieurs d'Artige" (as far as 1313), "Chronique des évêques de Toulouse" (as far as 1327), "Sanctoral ou Miroir des saints", "Vie des saints", "Traité sur les soixante-douze disciples et sur les apôtres", "Traité sur l'époque de la célébration des conciles", "Compilation historique sur l'ordre des Dominicains", "Pratique de l'inquisition". This last is practically his most important work. It is an exposé of the prerogatives and duties of the inquisitor; its citations, its forms of condemnation, its instructions for examinations, constitute a unique document for the study of the Inquisition during the first period of its existence. This work, lost for a time, was published later *in extenso* by l'abbé Douais, "Practica Inquisitionis hæreticæ pravitatis, auctore Bernardo Guidonis (Toulouse, 1886). Bernard is also the author of a number of theological treatises; "Abrégé de la doctrine chrétienne", "Traité de la messe", "Traité sur la conception de la Vierge", and also of different sermons.

DELISLE, *Notice sur les manuscrits de Bernard-Guy* in Coll. (Paris, 1879), XXVII; MOLINIER, *L'inquisition dans le midi de la France au XIII et au XIV siècle* (Paris, 1880).

M. DE MOREIRA.

Bernard of Besse, Friar Minor and chronicler, a native of Aquitaine, date of birth uncertain; he belonged to the custody of Cahors and was secretary to St. Bonaventure. He took up the pen after the Seraphic Doctor, he tells us, to gather the ears the latter had dropped from his sheaf, lest anything of so great a memory as that of St. Francis might perish. His "Liber de Laudibus Beati Francisci" composed about 1280, besides a résumé of some of the earlier legends, contains brief and valuable information about the companions of St. Francis and the foundation of the three Franciscan Orders, and is the only thirteenth-century document which specifies the first biographies of St. Francis. About 1297–1300 he compiled a catalogue of the ministers general up to his time, which is also a source of much importance for the study of Franciscan history. Critical editions of both these works have been published by the Friars Minor of Quaracchi [In Analecta Franciscana, III (1897), 666–707] and by Father Hilarin Felder of Lucerne, O. M. Cap. "Liber de Laudibus" etc. (Rome, 1897). Bernard also wrote the life of Blessed Christopher of Cahors inserted in the "Chronica XXIV Generalium" (ed. Quaracchi, 1897, 161–173) and is very probably the author of the "Speculum Disciplinæ" and of the "Epistola ad Quendam Novitium" erroneously attributed to St. Bonaventure (See Bonav. Opera Omnia ed. Quaracchi, 1898, VIII, 583 sqq. and 663 sqq.).

WADDING, *Scriptores Ord. Minorum* (1650), 59, and SBARALEA, *Supplementum* (1806), 135; FABRICIUS, *Bib. Med. Aev.* (1734), 218; DANOU, *Hist. Litt. France* (1838), XIX, 437; EHRLE in *Zeitschr. f. kath. Theol.* (1883), VII, 767–774; DENIFLE, *Archiv. f. Litt. und Kirchengesch. des M. A.* (1885), I, 145 sqq. and 630 sqq., also *Misc. Francescana* (1886), I, L sqq.; OTHON, *L'Aquitaine Séraphique* (1900), I, passim.

PASCHAL ROBINSON.

Bernard (or BERNARDINE) **of Bologna** (FLOVIANO TOSELLI), Friar Minor Capuchin and Scotist theologian, b. at Bologna, 17 December, 1701; d. 19 February, 1768. In 1717 he entered the Capuchin Order and some years later filled successively the offices of professor of moral and dogmatic theology and several times held positions of responsibility. Perhaps the best known of Bernard of Bologna's writings is the "Bibliotheca Scriptorum O. Min. S. Francisci Cap.", a work which resembles Wadding's well-known "Scriptores Ord. Min." It was published at Venice in 1747, and an appendix appeared at Rome in 1852. Besides this work Bernard wrote an elementary treatise on philosophy according to Duns Scotus entitled "Institutio Philosophica præmittenda theologiæ" (Venice, 1766), and a treatise on dogmatic theology, "Institutio Theologica" (Venice, 1746). He is also the author of a "Phrasarium S. Scripturæ" composed for the use of preachers and authors.

HURTER, *Nomenclator*, III, 6.

STEPHEN M. DONOVAN.

Bernard of Botone, generally called PARMENSIS from his birthplace, Parma in Italy, a noted canonist of the thirteenth century; date of birth unknown; d. 1263, or, according to Hurter, 24 March, 1266.

Under Tancred he studied in Bologna, where later he accepted the chair of canon law. Here Durantis was his disciple. Bernard obtained a canonry in the Cathedral of Bologna, and was also named chaplain to Popes Innocent IV and Alexander IV, by whom he was employed in solving questions of weight. According to the inscription on his tombstone he was Chancellor of the University of Bologna. Bernard found ample scope for his literary activity in his chosen branch, canon law. From glosses, summaries, and similar works, which had appeared on the Decretals of Gregory IX and other collections, he completed, just before his death, a work on the Gregorian Decretals. This, owing to his exact knowledge of former collections and thorough grasp of his subject, won for him the admiration of his contemporaries; so that he was styled "Glossator", and his work, commonly known as "Glossa Ordinaria", became the fruitful source of later glosses, which were printed with Gregory's collection. Bernard was careful to note what he had taken from others, while his own comments were signed "Bern." The "Glossa Ordinaria" was given to the press in Mainz in 1472, 1473, and in Rome in 1474. In this Roman edition there are additions, especially from the "Novella Commentaria" of Giovanni Andrea (d. 1348). Bernard's "Casus Longi" on separate chapters of the same Gregorian Decretals is equally meritorious. It was frequently edited: Paris, 1475; Venice, 1477; Bologna, 1487; Strasburg, 1488, 1493; Lyons, 1500. Another work, entitled "Summa super Titulis Decretalium", was based on similar writings of his master, Tancred, of Bernard of Pavia and others. It is a clear, concise treatise, found in the works of Nicolaus de Tudeschis (Milan, five volumes in folio).

HURTER, *Nomenclator*, IV, coll. 290, 291; LEURIN, *Introductio in Corpus Juris Canonici* (Freiburg, 1889), 149, 150; SCHULTE, *Die Geschichte der Quellen und Lit. des kanonischen Rechts* (Stuttgart, 1875–80,) II, 114–117.

ANDREW B. MEEHAN.

Bernard of Clairvaux, SAINT, b. in 1090, at Fontaines, near Dijon, France; d. at Clairvaux, 21 August, 1153. His parents were Tescelin, Lord of Fontaines, and Aleth of Montbard, both belonging to the highest nobility of Burgundy. Bernard, the third of a family of seven children, six of whom were sons, was educated with particular care, because, while yet unborn, a devout man had foretold his great destiny. At the age of nine years, Bernard was sent to a much renowned school at Chatillon-sur-Seine, kept by the Secular Canons of Saint-Vorles. He had a great taste for literature and devoted himself for some time to poetry. His success in his studies won the admiration of his masters, and his growth in virtue was no less marked. Bernard's great desire was to excel in literature in order to take up the study of Sacred Scripture, which later on became, as it were, his own tongue. "Piety was his all", says Bossuet. He had a special devotion to the Blessed Virgin, and there is no one who speaks more sublimely of the Queen of Heaven. Bernard was scarcely nineteen years of age when his mother died. During his youth, he did not escape trying temptations, but his virtue triumphed over them, in many instances in a heroic manner, and from this time he thought of retiring from the world and living a life of solitude and prayer.

St. Robert, Abbot of Molesmes, had founded, in 1098, the monastery of Cîteaux, about four leagues from Dijon, with the purpose of restoring the Rule of St. Benedict in all its rigour. Returning to Molesmes, he left the government of the new abbey to St. Alberic, who died in the year 1109. St. Stephen had just succeeded him (1113) as third Abbot of Cîteaux, when Bernard with thirty young noblemen of Burgundy, sought admission into the order. Three

APPARITION OF THE B. VIRGIN TO ST. BERNARD—FILIPPINO LIPPI

BADIA, FLORENCE

years later, St. Stephen sent the young Bernard, at the head of a band of monks, the third to leave Cîteaux, to found a new house at Vallée d'Absinthe, or Valley of Bitterness, in the Diocese of Langres. This Bernard named Claire Vallée, or Clairvaux, on the 25th of June, 1115, and the names of Bernard and Clairvaux thence become inseparable. During the absence of the Bishop of Langres, Bernard was blessed as abbot by William of Champeaux, Bishop of Châlons-sur-Marne, who saw in him the predestined man, *servum Dei*. From that moment a strong friendship sprang up between the abbot and the bishop, who was professor of theology at Notre Dame, of Paris, and the founder of the cloister of St. Victor.

The beginnings of Clairvaux were trying and painful. The regime was so austere that Bernard's health was impaired by it, and only the influence of his friend William of Champeaux, and the authority of the General Chapter could make him mitigate his

VESTMENT OF ST. BERNARD OF CLAIRVAUX

austerities. The monastery, however, made rapid progress. Disciples flocked to it in great numbers, desirous of putting themselves under the direction of Bernard. His father, the aged Tescelin, and all his brothers entered Clairvaux as religious, leaving only Humbeline, his sister, in the world and she, with the consent of her husband, soon took the veil in the Benedictine Convent of Jully. Clairvaux becoming too small for the religious who crowded there, it was necessary to send out bands to found new houses. In 1118, the monastery of the Three Fountains was founded in the Diocese of Châlons; in 1119, that of Fontenay in the Diocese of Auton (now Dijon) and in 1121, that of Foigny, near Veirins, in the Diocese of Lain (now Soisson). Notwithstanding this prosperity, the Abbot of Clairvaux had his trials. During an absence from Clairvaux, the Grand Prior of Cluny, Bernard of Uxells, sent by the Prince of Priors, to use the expression of Bernard, went to Clairvaux and enticed away the abbot's cousin, Robert of Châtillon. This was the occasion of the longest, and most touching of Bernard's letters.

In the year 1119, Bernard was present at the first general chapter of the order convoked by Stephen of Cîteaux. Though not yet thirty years old, Bernard was listened to with the greatest attention and respect, especially when he developed his thoughts upon the revival of the primitive spirit of regularity and fervour in all the monastic orders. It was this general chapter that gave definitive form to the constitutions of the order and the regulations of the "Charter of Charity" which Pope Calixtus II confirmed 23 December, 1119. In 1120 Bernard composed his first work "De Gradibus Superbiæ et Humilitatis" and his homilies which he entitles "De Laudibus Mariæ". The monks of Cluny had not seen, with satisfaction, those of Cîteaux take the first place among the religious orders for regularity and fervour. For this reason there was a temptation on the part of the "Black Monks" to make it appear that the rules of the new order were impracticable. At the solicitation of William of St. Theirry, Bernard defended himself by publishing his "Apology" which is divided into two parts. In the first he proves himself innocent of the invectives against Cluny, which had been attributed to him, and in the second he gives the reasons for his attack upon averred abuses. He protests his profound esteem for the Benedictines of Cluny whom he declares he loves equally as well as the other religious orders. Peter the Venerable, Abbot of Cluny, answered the Abbot of Clairvaux without wounding charity in the least, and assured him of his great admiration and sincere friendship. In the meantime Cluny established a reform, and Suger himself, the minister of Louis le Gros, and Abbot of St. Denis, was converted by the apology of Bernard. He hastened to terminate his worldly life and restore discipline in his monastery. The zeal of Bernard did not stop here; it extended to the bishops, the clergy, and the faithful, and remarkable conversions of persons engaged in worldly pursuits were among the fruits of his labours. Bernard's letter to the Archbishop of Sens is a real treatise "De Officiis Episcoporum". About the same time he wrote his work on "Grace and Free Will".

In the year 1128, Bernard assisted at the Council of Troyes, which had been convoked by Pope Honorius II, and was presided over by Cardinal Matthew, Bishop of Albano. The purpose of this council was to settle certain disputes of the bishops of Paris, and regulate other matters of the Church of France. The bishops made Bernard secretary of the council, and charged him with drawing up the synodal statutes. After the council, the Bishop of Verdun was deposed. There then arose against Bernard unjust reproaches and he was denounced even in Rome, as a monk who meddled with matters that did not concern him. Cardinal Harmeric, on behalf of the pope, wrote Bernard a sharp letter of remonstrance. "It is not fitting", he said "that noisy and troublesome frogs should come out of their marshes to trouble the Holy See and the cardinals". Bernard answered the letter by saying that, if he had assisted at the council, it was because he had been dragged to it, as it were, by force. "Now illustrious Harmeric", he added, " if you so wished, who would have been more capable of freeing me from the necessity of assisting at the council than yourself? Forbid those noisy troublesome frogs to come out of their holes, to leave their marshes . . . Then your friend will no longer be exposed to the accusations of pride and presumption". This letter made a great impression upon the cardinal, and justified its author both in his eyes and before the Holy See. It was at this council that Bernard traced the outlines of the Rule of the Knights Templars who soon became the ideal of the French nobility. Bernard praises it in his "De Laudibus Novæ Militiæ".

The influence of the Abbot of Clairvaux was soon felt in provincial affairs. He defended the rights of the Church against the encroachments of kings and princes, and recalled to their duty Henry, Archbishop of Sens, and Stephen de Senlis, Bishop of Paris. On the death of Honorius II, which occurred on the 14th of February, 1130, a schism broke out in the Church by the election of two popes, Innocent II and Anacletus II. Innocent II having been banished from Rome by Anacletus took refuge in France. King Louis le Gros convened a national council of the French bishops at Etampes, and Bernard, summoned thither by consent of the bishops, was chosen to judge between the rival popes. He decided in favour of Innocent II, caused him to be recognized by all the great Catholic powers, went with him into Italy, calmed the troubles that agitated the country, reconciled Pisa with Genoa, and Milan with the pope and Lothaire. According to the desire of the latter, the pope went to Liège to consult with the emperor upon the best means to be taken for his return to Rome, for it was there that Lothaire was to receive the imperial crown from the hands of the pope. From Liège, the pope returned to France, paid a visit to the Abbey of St. Denis, and then to Clairvaux where his reception was of a simple and purely religious character. The whole pontifical court was touched by the saintly demeanour of this band of monks. In the refectory only a few common fishes were found for the pope, and instead of wine, the juice of herbs was served for drink, says an annalist of Cîteaux. It was not a table feast that was served to the pope and his followers, but a feast of virtues. The same year Bernard was again at the Council of Reims at the side of Innocent II, whose oracle he was; and then in Aquitaine where he succeeded for the time in detaching William, Count of Poitiers, from the cause of Anacletus.

In 1132, Bernard accompanied Innocent II into Italy, and at Cluny the pope abolished the dues which Clairvaux used to pay to this celebrated abbey —an action which gave rise to a quarrel between the "White Monks" and the "Black Monks" which lasted twenty years. In the month of May the pope, supported by the army of Lothaire, entered Rome. but Lothaire, feeling himself too weak to resist the partisans of Anacletus, retired beyond the Alps, and Innocent sought refuge in Pisa in September, 1133. In the meantime the abbot had returned to France in June, and was continuing the work of peacemaking which he had commenced in 1130. Towards the end of 1134, he made a second journey into Aquitaine, where William X had relapsed into schism. This would have died out of itself if William could have been detached from the cause of Gerard, who had usurped the See of Bordeaux and retained that of Angoulême. Bernard invited William to the Mass which he celebrated in the Church of La Couldre. At the moment of the Communion, placing the Sacred Host upon the paten, he went to the door of the church where William was, and pointing to the Host, he adjured the Duke not to despise God as he did His servants. William yielded and the schism ended. Bernard went again to Italy, where Roger of Sicily was endeavouring to withdraw the Pisans from their allegiance to Innocent. He recalled the city of Milan, which had been deceived and misled by the ambitious prelate Anselm, Archbishop of Milan, to obedience to the pope, refused the Archbishopric of Milan, and returned finally to Clairvaux. Believing himself at last secure in his cloister Bernard devoted himself with renewed vigour to the composition of those pious and learned works which have won for him the title of "Doctor of the Church". He wrote at this time his sermons on the "Canticle of Canticles".

In 1137 he was again forced to leave his solitude by order of the pope to put an end to the quarrel between Lothaire and Roger of Sicily. At the conference held at Palermo, Bernard succeeded in convincing Roger of the rights of Innocent II and in silencing Peter of Pisa who sustained Anacletus. The latter died of grief and disappointment in 1138, and with him the schism. Returning to Clairvaux, Bernard occupied himself in sending bands of monks from his too-crowded monastery into Germany, Sweden, England, Ireland, Portugal, Switzerland, and Italy. Some of these, at the command of Innocent II, took possession of Three Fountains Abbey, near the Salvian Waters in Rome, from which Pope Eugenius III was chosen. Bernard resumed his commentary on the "Canticle of Canticles", assisted in 1139, at the Second General Lateran Council and the Tenth Œcumenical, in which the surviving adherents of the schism were definitively condemned. About the same time, Bernard was visited at Clairvaux by St. Malachi, metropolitan of the Church in Ireland, and a very close friendship was formed between them. St. Malachi would gladly have taken the Cistercian habit, but the sovereign pontiff would not give his permission. He died, however, at Clairvaux in 1148.

In the year 1140, we find Bernard engaged in other matters which disturbed the peace of the Church. Towards the close of the eleventh century, the schools of philosophy and theology, dominated by the passion for discussion and a spirit of independence which had introduced itself into political and religious questions, became a veritable public arena, with no other motive than that of ambition. This exaltation of human reason and rationalism found an ardent and powerful adherent in Abelard, the most eloquent and learned man of the age after Bernard. "The history of the calamities and the refutation of his doctrine by St. Bernard", says Ratisbonne, "form the greatest episode of the twelfth century". Abelard's treatise on the Trinity had been condemned in 1121, and he himself had thrown his book into the fire. But in 1139 he advocated new errors. Bernard, informed of this by William of St. Thierry, wrote to Abelard who answered in an insulting manner. Bernard then denounced him to the pope who caused a general council to be held at Sens. Abelard asked for a public discussion with Bernard; the latter showed his opponent's errors with such clearness and force of logic that he was unable to make any reply, and was obliged, after being condemned, to retire. The pope confirmed the judgment of the council, Abelard submitted without resistance, and retired to Cluny to live under Peter the Venerable. where he died two years later.

Innocent II died in 1143. His two successors, Celestin II and Lucius, reigned only a short time, and then Bernard saw one of his disciples, Bernard of Pisa, Abbot of Three Fountains, and known thereafter as Eugenius III, raised to the Chair of St. Peter. Bernard sent him, at his own request, various instructions which compose the "Book of Consideration", the predominating idea of which is that the reformation of the Church ought to commence with the sanctity of its head. Temporal matters are merely accessories; the principal are piety, meditation, or consideration, which ought to precede action. The book contains a most beautiful page on the papacy, and has always been greatly esteemed by the sovereign pontiffs, many of whom used it for their ordinary reading.

Alarming news came at this time from the East. Edessa had fallen into the hands of the Turks, and Jerusalem and Antioch were threatened with similar disaster. Deputations of the bishops of Armenia solicited aid from the pope, and the King of France also sent ambassadors. The pope commissioned

Bernard to preach a new Crusade and granted the same indulgences for it which Urban II had accorded to the first. A parliament was convoked at Vezelay in Burgundy in 1134, and Bernard preached before the assembly. The King, Louis le Jeune, Queen Eleanor, and the princes and lords present prostrated themselves at the feet of the Abbot of Clairvaux to receive the cross. The saint was obliged to use portions of his habit to make crosses to satisfy the zeal and ardour of the multitude who wished to take part in the Crusade. Bernard passed into Germany, and the miracles which multiplied almost at his every step undoubtedly contributed to the success of his mission. The Emperor Conrad and his nephew Frederick Barbarossa, received the pilgrims' cross from the hand of Bernard, and Pope Eugenius, to encourage the enterprise, came in person to France. It was on the occasion of this visit, 1147, that a council was held at Paris, at which the errors of Gilbert de la Porée, Bishop of Poitiers, were examined. He advanced among other absurdities that the essence and the attributes of God are not God, that the properties of the Persons of the Trinity are not the persons themselves, in fine that the Divine Nature did not become incarnate. The discussion was warm on both sides. The decision was left for the council which was held at Reims the following year (1148), and in which Eon de l'Etoile was one of the judges. Bernard was chosen by the council to draw up a profession of faith directly opposed to that of Gilbert, who concluded by stating to the Fathers: "If you believe and assert differently than I have done I am willing to believe and speak as you do". The consequence of this declaration was that the pope condemned the assertions of Gilbert without denouncing him personally. After the council the pope paid a visit to Clairvaux, where he held a general chapter of the order and was able to realize the prosperity of which Bernard was the soul.

The last years of Bernard's life were saddened by the failure of the Crusade he had preached, the entire responsibility for which was thrown upon him. He had accredited the enterprise by miracles, but he had not guaranteed its success against the misconduct and perfidy of those who participated in it. Lack of discipline and the over-confidence of the German troops, the intrigues of the Prince of Antioch and Queen Eleanor, and finally the avarice and evident treason of the Christian nobles of Syria, who prevented the capture of Damascus, appear to have been the cause of disaster. Bernard considered it his duty to send an apology to the pope and it is inserted in the second part of his " Book of Consideration". There he explains how, with the crusaders as with the Hebrew people, in whose favour the Lord had multiplied His prodigies, their sins were the cause of their misfortunes and miseries. The death of his contemporaries served as a warning to Bernard of his own approaching end. The first to die was Suger (1152), of whom the Abbot wrote to Eugenius III: "If there is any precious vase adorning the palace of the King of Kings it is the soul of the Venerable Suger". Thibaud, Count of Champagne, Conrad, Emperor of Germany, and his son Henry died the same year. From the beginning of the year 1153, Bernard felt his death approaching. The passing of Pope Eugenius had struck the fatal blow by taking from him one whom he considered his greatest friend and consoler. Bernard died in the sixty-third year of his age, after forty years spent in the cloister. He founded one hundred and sixty-three monasteries in different parts of Europe; at his death they numbered three hundred and forty-three. He was the first Cistercian monk placed on the calendar of saints and was canonized by Alexander III, 18 January, 1174. Pope Pius VIII bestowed on him the
II.—32

title of Doctor of the Church. The Cistercians honour him as only the founders of orders are honoured, because of the wonderful and widespread activity which he gave to the Order of Cîteaux.

The works of St. Bernard are as follows: "De Gradibus Superbiæ", his first treatise; "Homilies on the Gospel 'Missus est' " (1120); "Apology to William of St. Thierry" against the claims of the monks of Cluny; "On the Conversion of Clerics", a book addressed to the young ecclesiastics of Paris (1122); "De Laudibus Novæ Militiæ", addressed to Hughes de Payns, first Grand Master and Prior of Jerusalem (1129). This is a eulogy of the military order instituted in 1118, and an exhortation to the knights to conduct themselves with courage in their several stations. "De amore Dei" wherein St. Bernard shows that the manner of loving God is to love Him without measure and gives the different degrees of this love; "Book of Precepts and Dispensations" (1131), which contains answers to questions upon certain points of the Rule of St. Benedict from which the abbot can, or cannot, dispense; "De Gratiâ et Libero Arbitrio" in which the Catholic dogma of grace and free will is proved according to the principles of St. Augustine; "Book of Consideration", addressed to Pope Eugenius III; "De Officiis Episcoporum", addressed to Henry, Archbishop of Sens.

His sermons are also numerous: "On Psalm XC, 'Qui habitat' " (about 1125); "On the Canticle of Canticles". St. Bernard explained in eighty-six sermons only the first two chapters of the Canticle of Canticles and the first verse of the third chapter. There are also eighty-six "Sermons for the Whole Year"; his "Letters" number 530. Many other letters, treatises, etc., falsely attributed to him are found among his works, such as the "l'Echelle du Cloître", which is the work of Guigues, Prior of La Grande Chartreuse, les Méditations, l'Edification de la Maison intérieure, etc.

Works of St. Bernard, ed. MABILLON, 2 vols. fol. (1667, 1690), the latter edition forming the basis of MIGNE'S ed.; EALES AND HODGES, tr. (London, 1889), in MIGNE, P. L. This contains three lives of the saint: Vita Prima by WILLIAM OF ST. THIERRY, ERNAUD DE BONNEVAL, and GEOFFROY OF AUXERRE; Vita Secunda by ALAIN OF AUXERRE; and Vita Bernardi by JOHN L'ERMIT. Besides these there are in the same edition the Liber Miraculorum of HERBERT, the Exordium Magnum Cistercience, and the Chronicon Claravallense (Paris, 1839–40, 4 vols. fol.; Milan, 1892, 3 vols. quarto); ABBÉ DE RATISBONNE, Life of St. Bernard (1842); HUFFER, Der heilige Bernard von Clairvaux (Münster, 1886); NEANDER, Der heilige Bernard (Gotha, 1889); ABBÉ VACANDARD, St. Bernard, Orator (1877), who also published a life (Paris, 1895–97).

M. GILDAS.

Bernard of Cluny (or OF MORLAIX), a Benedictine monk of the first half of the twelfth century, poet, satirist, and hymn-writer, author of the famous verses "On the Contempt of the World". His parentage, native land, and education are hidden in obscurity. The sixteenth-century writer John Pits (Scriptores Angliæ, Sæc. XII) says that he was of English birth. He is frequently called Morlanensis, which title most writers have interpreted to mean that he was a native of Morlaix in Brittany, though some credit him to Murlas near Puy in Béarn. A writer in the "Journal of Theological Studies" (1907), VIII, 354–359 contends that he belonged to the family of the Seigneurs of Montpellier in Languedoc, and was born at Murles, a possession of that distinguished family; also that he was at first a monk of St. Sauveur d'Aniane, whence he entered Cluny under Abbot Pons (1109–22). It is certain that he was a monk at Cluny in the time of Peter the Venerable (1122–56), for his famous poem is dedicated to that abbot. It may have been written about 1140. He left some sermons and is said to be the author of certain monastic regulations known as the "Consuetudines Cluniacenses" (Hergott, Vetus Discipl. Monast., Paris, 1726; Albers, Consuet. Cluniac. antiquiores, Monte Cassino, 1906), also of a dialogue (Colloquium) on the Trinity. The "De Contemptu Mundi" contains about 3,000 verses, and is for the most part a very bitter satire against the moral disorders of the monastic poet's time. He spares no one; priests, nuns, bishops, monks, and even Rome itself are mercilessly scourged for their shortcomings. For this reason it was first printed by Matthias Flaccus as one of his *testes veritatis*, or witnesses of the deep-seated corruption of the medieval Church (Varia poemata de corrupto ecclesiæ statu, Basle, 1557), and was often reprinted by Protestants in the course of the seventeenth and eighteenth centuries. Its complete Latin text is found in Thomas Wright (Anglo-Latin Satirical Poets of the Twelfth Century, London, 1872). This Christian Juvenal does not proceed in an orderly manner against the vices and follies of his age. It has been well said that he seems to eddy about two main points: the transitory character of all material pleasures and the permanency of spiritual joys. Bernard of Cluny is indeed a lyrical writer, swept from one theme to another by the intense force of ascetic meditation and by the majestic power of his own verse, in which there lingers yet a certain fierce intoxication of poetic wrath. His highly wrought pictures of heaven and hell were probably known to Dante; the roasting cold, the freezing fire, the devouring worm, the fiery floods, and again the glorious idyl of the Golden Age and the splendours of the Heavenly Kingdom are couched in a diction that rises at times to the height of Dante's genius. The enormity of sin, the charm of virtue, the torture of an evil conscience, the sweetness of a God-fearing life alternate with heaven and hell as the themes of his majestic dithyramb. Nor does he dwell in generalities; he returns again and again to the wickedness of woman (one of the fiercest arraignments of the sex), the evils of wine, money, learning, perjury, soothsaying, etc.; this master of an elegant, forceful, and abundant latinity cannot find words strong enough to convey his prophetic rage at the moral apostasy of his generation, in almost none of whom does he find spiritual soundness. Youthful and simoniacal bishops, oppressive agents of ecclesiastical corporations, the officers of the Curia, papal legates, and the pope himself are treated with no less severity than in Dante or in the sculptures of medieval cathedrals. Only those who do not know the utter frankness of certain medieval moralists could borrow scandal from his verses. It may be added that in medieval times "the more pious the chronicler the blacker his colours". The early half of the twelfth century saw the appearance of several new factors of secularism unknown to an earlier and more simply religious time: the increase of commerce and industry resultant from the Crusades, the growing independence of medieval cities, the secularization of Benedictine life, the development of pageantry and luxury in a hitherto rude feudal world, the reaction from the terrific conflict of State and Church in the latter half of the eleventh century. The song of the Cluniac is a great cry of pain wrung from a deeply religious and even mystical soul at the first dawning consciousness of a new order of human ideals and aspirations. The turbid and irregular flow of his denunciation is halted occasionally in a dramatic way by glimpses of a Divine order of things, either in the faraway past or in the near future. This poet-preacher is also a prophet; Antichrist, he says, is born in Spain; Elijah has come to life again in the Orient. The last days are at hand, and it behoves the true Christian to awake and be ready for the dissolution of an order now grown intolerable, in which religion itself is henceforth represented by cant and hypocrisy.

The metre of this poem is no less unique than its diction; it is a dactylic hexameter in three sections, devoid of cæsura, with tailed rhymes and a feminine leonine rhyme between the two first sections; the verses are technically known as *leonini cristati trilices dactylici*, and are so difficult to construct in great numbers that the writer claims Divine inspiration (the impulse and inflow of the Spirit of Wisdom and Understanding) as the chief agency in the execution of so long an effort of this kind. To Archbishop (then Dean) French, who first translated about one hundred lines (Sacred Latin Poetry, London, 1849, 1864), the metre seemed repulsive and awkward; to the famous liturgiologist Dr. Neale (The Rhythm of Bernard of Morlaix, 8th ed., London, 1868) it seems "one of the loveliest of mediæval measures". It is, indeed, a solemn and stately verse, rich and sonorous, not meant, however, to be read at one sitting, at the risk of surfeiting the appetite. Bernard of Cluny is an erudite writer, and his poem leaves an excellent impression of the Latin culture of the Benedictine monasteries of France and England in the first half of the twelfth century (Bishop Stubbs, Seventeen Lectures on Medieval History, London, 1893). The modern interest of English-speaking circles in this semi-obscure poet centres in the lovely hymns of exceptional piety, warmth, and delicacy of sentiment dispersed through his lurid satire; one of them, in particular, "Jerusalem the Golden", has been made universally famous in the translation of the above-mentioned Dr. Neale, first printed in his "Mediæval Hymns and Sequences" (London, 1851). Other translations of the brief portion made known in English by the aforesaid writers are owing to S. G. Duffeld (1867) and Charles Lawrence Ford (1898). A complete English translation (in prose) appeared from the pen of Henry Preble, in the "American Journal of Theology" (1906, 72–101, 286–308, 495–516), with a biographical note by Samuel Macauley Jackson.

LEYSER, *Poetæ med. ævi* (1721), 412–414, 427; MORIN in *Rev. des quest. hist.* (1880), XL, 603–613; OWEN in *Eng. Hist. Rev.* (1887), II, 525; *Bulletin critique* (1890), XI, 297; JULIAN, *Dict. of Hymnology*, s. v.

THOMAS J. SHAHAN.

Bernard of Compostella (1) ANTIQUUS, a canonist of the early thirteenth century, a native of Compostella in Spain. He is called Antiquus to distinguish him from another, as below. He became a professor of canon law in the University of Bologna. Bernard compiled a collection of the decrees promulgated by Innocent III during the first ten years of his pontificate (1198–1208). This work, often called by the scholars of Bologna "Compilatio Romana", because the author took his documents from the Roman archives, was not of much practical worth, since an official or authentic collection, extending to 1210, rendered Bernard's compilation superfluous. Only portions of either of these collections were printed (ed. "Ant. Augustini Opera", Lucca, 1769, IV, 600–608).—(2) JUNIOR or MODERNUS, a canonist who lived in the middle of the thirteenth century, called Compostellanus from the fact that he possessed an ecclesiastical benefice in Compostella. He was known also as Brigantius from his birthplace in Galicia, Spain; later of Monte Mirato. Bernard was chaplain to Innocent IV, a noted canonist, at whose exhortation he wrote a work entitled "Margarita", an index of Innocent's "Apparatus", or commentary on the five books of the Decretals of Gregory IX. The "Margarita" was published in Paris, 1516. Bernard was the first to write a commentary on the constitutions of Innocent IV (not published). A third work was entitled "Casus seu Notabilia" on the five books of Decretals, which was intended as a complete and practical commentary, but which owing to the author's death, did not go beyond title sixth of the first book, consequently not published.

Schulte, *Die Geschichte der Quellen*, II, 118, 119; Laurin, *Introductio in Corpus Jur. Can.* (Freiburg, 1889), III; Hurter, *Nomenclator*, IV col. 192.
ANDREW B. MEEHAN.

Bernard of Luxemburg, Dominican theologian, controversialist, and Inquisitor of the Archdioceses of Cologne, Mainz, and Trier; b. at Strassen near Cologne; d. at Cologne, 5 October, 1535. He studied at the latter place where he entered the Order of Preachers, received the baccalaureate at Louvain, 1499, and was appointed Master of Students at Cologne, 1505, 1506. In 1507 he became Regent of Studies at Louvain; fellow of the college of Doctors at Cologne, in 1516; and served twice as Prior of Cologne. As the author of the "Catalogus hæreticorum", he has been described as somewhat lacking in critical judgment; but he was otherwise a safe and indefatigable defender of the Faith against the heretics of his time. His important works are: "Catalogus hæreticorum omnium", etc. (Erfurt,

to devote himself to their conversion. For forty-two years he continued to preach the Gospel to these people and carried the light of faith even into many cantons of Lombardy, effecting numerous conversions and working many miracles.

For another reason, however, Bernard's name will forever be famous in history. Since the most ancient times there was a path across the Pennine Alps leading from the valley of Aosta to the Swiss canton of Valais, over what is now the pass of the Great St. Bernard. This pass is covered with perpetual snow from seven to eight feet deep, and drifts sometimes accumulate to the height of forty feet. Though the pass was extremely dangerous, especially in the springtime on account of avalanches, yet it was often used by French and German pilgrims on their way to Rome. For the convenience and protection of travellers St. Bernard founded a monastery and hospice at the highest point of the pass, 8,000

THE HOSPICE OF ST. BERNARD

1522; Cologne, 1523; Paris, 1524); "Concilium generale malignantium", etc. (1528); "De ordinibus militaribus", etc. (Cologne, 1527).

Quétif-Echard, *Script. Ord. Præd.* (Paris, 1721), II, 93; Paulus in *Der Katholik* (Mainz, 1897), XVI, 166–171; Mandonnet in *Dict. de théol. cath.* (Paris, 1903), 788; Hurter, *Nomenclator* (Innsbruck, 1906), II, 1251.
J. R. VOLZ.

Bernard of Menthon, SAINT, b. in 923, probably in the castle Menthon near Annecy, in Savoy; d. at Novara, 1008. He was descended from a rich, noble family and received a thorough education. He refused to enter an honourable marriage proposed by his father and decided to devote himself to the service of the Church. Placing himself under the direction of Peter, Archdeacon of Aosta, under whose guidance he rapidly progressed, Bernard was ordained priest and on account of his learning and virtue was made Archdeacon of Aosta (966), having charge of the government of the diocese under the bishop. Seeing the ignorance and idolatry still prevailing among the people of the Alps, he resolved

feet above sea-level, in the year 962. A few years later he established another hospice on the Little St. Bernard, a mountain of the Graian Alps, 7,076 feet above sea-level. Both were placed in charge of Augustinian monks after pontifical approval had been obtained by him during a visit to Rome.

These hospices are renowned for the generous hospitality extended to all travellers over the Great and Little St. Bernard, so called in honour of the founder of these charitable institutions. At all seasons of the year, but especially during heavy snow-storms, the heroic monks accompanied by their well-trained dogs, go out in search of victims who may have succumbed to the severity of the weather. They offer food, clothing, and shelter to the unfortunate travellers and take care of the dead. They depend on gifts and collections for sustenance. At present, the order consists of about forty members, the majority of whom live at the hospice while some have charge of neighbouring parishes.

St. Bernard ended his career after futile attempts

in the synod at Pavia to reconcile Henry IV with Gregory VII. He was interred in the cloister of St. Lawrence. Venerated as a saint from the twelfth century in many places of Piedmont (Aosta, Novara, Brescia), he was not canonized until 1681, by Innocent XI. His feast is celebrated on the 15th of June.

SURIUS, VI, 358; DORSAZ, *Vie d. S. Bernad de Menthon* (Paris, 1862); BUTLER, *Lives of the Saints*, VI, 577; *Miscell. Stor. Ital.* (1894) xxxi, 341 sqq.; ALDEGUIER, *Vie de St. Bernard, Apôtre des Alpes* (Toulouse, 1858).

BARNABAS DIERINGER.

Bernard of Pavia, a noted canonist, provost of the cathedral chapter of Pavia, and, in 1190, promoted to the Bishopric of Faenza, became Bishop of Pavia in 1198; d. 18 September, 1213. About 1190 he compiled a work entitled "Breviarium Extravagantium" to complete and bring down to his own day Gratian's "Decretum". Bernard quotes authorities in an abbreviated form; hence the title. With the exception of a small fragment of a letter of St. Gregory the Great, he took nothing from Gratian. Later decrees and a few fragments of Roman and German civil law are found in the work. The "Breviarium" soon found favour in the University of Bologna, and from the time of Tancred (d. about 1235) was termed "Compilatio Prima"— the first collection of canon law after Gratian's— while other collections are styled "Compilatio Secunda", "Tertia", etc.

The "Breviarium" is divided into five books, the books into 152 titles, the titles into 912 chapters, the chronological order being observed as far as possible. The first book treats of persons who exercise ecclesiastical jurisdiction, the second of civil judicial processes, the third of matters pertaining to clerics and regulars, the fourth of matrimony, the fifth of ecclesiastical crimes and criminal procedure. While no rubrics are prefixed to the books of Bernard, his titles and chapters have their own peculiar inscriptions. The "Breviarium" was published in a work entitled "Antiquæ Collectiones Decretalium, cum Ant. Augustini, Episcopi Ilerdensis, notis" (Lerida, 1576; Paris, 1609); also in the work: "Ant. Augustini Opera" (Lucca, 1765——; 4 vols.) Joseph Anthony de Riegger, a professor in the University of Prague (d. 1795) published an incomplete edition of the "Breviarium" (Freiburg, 1778) in which he attempted to harmonize Bernard's work with the Decretals of Gregory IX.

Bernard wrote a "Summa Decretalium", a compendium of his "Breviarium", which for a long time constituted the chief text-book of the schools and was edited by Laspeyres (Ratisbon, 1860). Bernard's first work was entitled: "Summa de Matrimonio", which was followed by another: "Summa de Electione". Both are short treatises (see Laspeyres, op. cit., 287–323). His last work, begun in Faenza and finished after he became Bishop of Pavia, bears the title, "Casus Decretalium", part of which Laspeyres edited. Bernard also wrote a glossary on his "Breviarium", a life of St. Lanfranc, Bishop of Ticino, and commentaries on Ecclesiasticus and the Canticle of Canticles.

LAURIN, *Introductio in Corpus Juris Can.* (Freiburg, 1888), 97 sqq.; HURTER, *Nomenclator*, IV, 191, 192; ÆMILIUS FREIBERG in *Quinque Compilationes Antiquæ* (Leipzig, 1882), pp. vi sqq.

ANDREW B. MEEHAN.

Bernard Tolomeo, SAINT, founder of the congregation of the Blessed Virgin of Monte Oliveto, b. at Siena in Tuscany in 1272; d. in 1348. He received at baptism the name of Giovanni, but took that of Bernard out of admiration for the saintly Abbot of Clairvaux. He was educated by his uncle, Christopher Tolomeo, a Dominican, and desired to enter the religious life, but his father's opposition prevented, and he continued his studies in secular surroundings. After a course in philosophy and mathematics he devoted himself to the study of civil and canon law and of theology. For a time Bernard served in the armies of Rudolph of Hapsburg. After his return to Siena he was appointed by his fellow-citizens to the highest positions in the town government. While thus occupied he was struck with blindness. Having recovered his sight through the intervention of the Blessed Virgin he retired (1313) to a solitary spot about ten miles from Siena, where he led a life of the greatest austerity.

The fame of his virtues soon attracted many visitors, and Bernard was accused of heresy. He went to Avignon and cleared himself of this charge before John XXII without difficulty. Upon his return he founded the congregation of the Blessed Virgin of Monte Oliveto, giving it the Rule of St. Benedict. The purpose of the new religious institute was a special devotion to the Blessed Virgin. Guido, Bishop of Arezzo, within whose diocese the congregation was formed, confirmed its constitutions (1319), and many favours were granted by Popes John XXII, Clement VI (1344), and Gregory XI. Upon the appearance of the pest in the district of Arezzo, Bernard and his monks devoted themselves to the care of the sick without any personal ill-effects. After having ruled the religious body he had founded for twenty-seven years Bernard died, at the age of seventy-six. His death was followed by many miracles and the congregation became a nursery of saints. In 1634 the Congregation of Rites declared that the Blessed Bernard Tolomeo was deserving of veneration among the saints. In the Roman Martyrology he is commemorated on 21 August.

CUPER, in *Acta SS* (1739) Aug. IV, 464–75; MARÉCHAUX, *Vie du bienheureux Bernard Tolomei* (Paris, 1898).

A. FOURNET.

Bernardin de Picquigny. See PICONIO (A PICONIO).

Bernardine of Feltre, BLESSED, Friar Minor and missionary, b. at Feltre, Italy, in 1439 and d. at Pavia, 28 September, 1494. He belonged to the noble family of Tomitano and was the eldest of nine children. In 1456 St. James of the Marches preached the Lenten course at Padua, and inspired to enter the Franciscan order, Bernardine was clothed with the habit of the Friars Minor in May of the same year. He completed successfully his studies at Mantua and was ordained priest in 1463. Cured miraculously of an impediment in his speech, Bernardine began the long and fruitful apostolate which has caused him to be ranked as one of the greatest Franciscan missionaries of the fifteenth century. Every city of note and every province from Lombardy in the north to Sardinia and the provinces of the south became successively the scene of his missionary labours; and the fruits of his apostolate were both marvellous and enduring. Bernardine, however, will be best remembered in history in connexion with the *monti di pietà* of which he was the reorganizer, and, in a certain sense, the founder. The word *mons* which literally means an accumulation of wealth or money, now called capital, seems to have been a generic term used in the fifteenth century to signify lending-houses in general; and hence the *montes pietatis* or *monti di pietà* were a species of charitable lending-houses not, perhaps, unlike our modern pawnbrokers' establishments, but possessing, of course, none of the sinister features of the latter. As originally instituted the *monti di pietà* were intended as a timely and effectual remedy for the evils occasioned by the usury then practiced by the Jews upon the people of Christian Italy; and Blessed Bernardine's zeal in reorganizing them and in founding them in places where they had not previously existed affords an explanation of the fact that he is generally represented carrying in his hand a *monte di pietà*, that is, a little green hill composed of three mounds and on the top either a cross or a standard with the inscription: *Curam illius habe*. As an author Bernardine has left us little if anything of importance, but it is interesting to note that the authorship of the well-known *Anima Christi* has as often as not been ascribed to Blessed Bernardine of Feltre. The fact, however, that the *Anima Christi* was composed sometime before the birth of Blessed Bernardine disproves any claim that he might have of being its author. As in the case of St. Ignatius, Bernardine also made frequent use of it and recommended it to his brethren. The feast of Blessed Bernardine is kept in the Order of Friars Minor on the 28th of September. (See MONTI di PIETÀ.)

LEO, *Lives of the Saints and Blessed of the Three Orders of St. Francis* (Taunton, 1886), III, 243–265; WADDING, *Annales Minorum*, VI, 142, XII, 442, passim; *Acta SS.*, September, VII, 814–914; ZANETTINI, *Compendio della vita del Beato Feltrese, Bernardino Tomitano* (Milan); FLORNOY, *Le Bienheureux Bernardin de Feltre* (Paris, 1898); LUDOVICE DE BESSE, *Le Bienheureux Bernardin de Feltre et son œuvre* (Tours, 1902).

STEPHEN M. DONOVAN.

Bernardine of Fossa, BLESSED, of the Order of Friars Minor, historian and ascetical writer, b. at Fossa, in the Diocese of Aquila, Italy, in 1420; d. at Aquila, 27 November, 1503. Blessed Bernardine belonged to the ancient and noble family of the Amici, and sometimes bears the name of Aquilanus on account of his long residence and death in the town of Aquila. He received his early training at Aquila and thence went to Perugia to study canon and civil law. On the 12th of March in the year 1445, he received the Seraphic habit from St. James of the Marches who was then preaching a course of lenten sermons at Perugia. From the time of his entrance into religion, Bernardine never ceased to advance in religious perfection, and the success which crowned his missionary labours throughout Italy, as well as in Dalmatia and Serigonia, bears witness to the eminent sanctity of his life. Bernardine fulfilled the office of provincial of the province of St. Bernardine and of the province of Dalmatia and Bosnia, and would have been chosen Bishop of Aquila had not his humility forbidden him to accept this dignity. His cult was approved by Leo XII, 26 March, 1828. His feast is kept in the Franciscan Order on the 7th of November. The writings of Blessed Bernardine include several sermons and divers ascetical and historical opuscules; among the latter, the "Chronica Fratrum Minorum Observantiæ" deserves special mention. This interesting chronicle was first edited by Leonard Lemmens, O. F. M., from the autograph manuscript, and is prefaced by an interesting life of Blessed Bernardine and a critical estimate of his writings. It may also be mentioned that Bernardine is the author of the first life of his patron, St. Bernardine of Siena.

LEO, *Lives of the Saints and Blessed of the three Orders of St. Francis* (Taunton, 1887), IV, 42–44; LEMMENS, *Chronica Fratrum Minorum Observantiæ B. Bernardini Aquilani* (Rome, 1905); WADDING, *Annales Minorum*, XII, 277–480; HURTER, *Nomenclator*, IV, 968; HUGH A PESCOCOSTANZA, *Vita del B. Bernardino da Fossa* (Naples, 1872).

STEPHEN M. DONOVAN.

Bernardine of Siena, SAINT, Friar Minor, missionary, and reformer, often called the "Apostle of Italy", b. of the noble family of Albizeschi at Massa, a Sienese town of which his father was then governor, 8 September, 1380; d. at Aquila in the Abruzzi, 20 May, 1444. Left an orphan at six Bernardine was brought up with great care by his pious aunts. His youth was blameless and engaging. In 1397 after a course of civil and canon law, he joined the Confraternity of Our Lady attached to the great hospital of Santa Maria della Scala. Three years later, when the pestilence revisited Siena, he came forth from the life of seclusion and prayer he had embraced, to minister to the plague-stricken, and, assisted by ten companions, took upon himself for four months entire charge of this hospital. Despite his youth Bernardine proved fully equal to this task, but the heroic and unremitting labour it involved so far shattered his health that he never completely recovered. Having distributed his patrimony in charity, Bernardine received the habit of the Friars Minor at San Francesco in Siena, 8 September, 1402, but soon withdrew to the Observantine convent of Columbaio outside the city. He was professed 8 September, 1403 and ordained 8 September, 1404. About 1406 St. Vincent Ferrer, while preaching at Alexandria in Piedmont, foretold that his mantle should descend upon one who was then listening to him, and said that he would return to France and Spain leaving to Bernardine the task of evangelizing the remaining peoples of Italy.

Nearly twelve years passed before this prediction was fulfilled. During this period, of which we have no details, Bernardine seems to have lived in retirement at Capriola. It was in 1417 that his gift of eloquence was made manifest and his missionary life really began at Milan at the close of that year. Thenceforth, various cities contended for the honour of hearing him, and he was often compelled to preach in the market places, his auditors sometimes numbering thirty thousand. Bernardine gradually gained an immense influence over the turbulent, luxurious Italian cities. Pius II, who as a youth had been a spellbound auditor of Bernardine, records that the saint was listened to as another Paul, and Vespasiano da Bisticci, a well-known Florentine biographer, says that by his sermons Bernardine "cleansed all Italy from sins of every kind in which she abounded". The penitents, we are told, flocked to confession "like ants" and in several cities the reforms urged by the saint were embodied in the laws under the name of *Riformazioni di frate Bernardino*. Indeed, the success which crowned Bernardine's labours to promote morality and regenerate society, can scarcely be exaggerated. He preached with apostolic freedom, openly censuring Visconti, Duke of Milan, and elsewhere fearlessly rebuking the evil in high places which undermined the *Quattrocento*. In each city he denounced the reigning vice so effectively that bonfires were kindled and "vanities" were cast upon them by the cartload. Usury was one of the principal objects of the saint's attacks, and he did much to prepare the way for the establishment of the beneficial loan societies, known as *Monti di Pietà*. But Bernardine's watchward, like that of St. Francis, was "Peace". On foot he traversed the length and breadth of Italy peace-making, and his eloquence was exercised with great effect towards reconciling the mutual hatred of Guelphs and Ghibellines. At Crema, as a result of his preaching, the political exiles were recalled and even reinstated in their confiscated possessions. Everywhere Bernardine persuaded the cities to take down the arms of their warring factions from the church and palace walls and to inscribe there, instead, the initials I. H. S. He thus gave a new impulse and a tangible form to the devotion to the Holy Name of Jesus which was ever a favourite topic with him and which he came to regard as a potent means of rekindling popular fervour. He used to hold a board in front of him while preaching, with the sacred monogram painted on it in the midst of rays and afterwards expose it for veneration. This custom he appears to have introduced at Volterra in 1424. At Bologna Bernardine induced a card-painter, who had been ruined by his sermons against gambling, to make a living by designing these tablets, and such was the desire to possess them that the man soon realized a small fortune.

In spite of his popularity—perhaps rather on account of it—Bernardine had to suffer both opposition and persecution. He was accused of heresy, the tablets he had used to promote devotion to the Holy Name being made the basis of a clever attack by the adherents of the Dominican, Manfred of Vercelli, whose false preaching about Antichrist Bernardine had combated. The saint was charged with having introduced a profane, new devotion which exposed the people to the danger of idolatry, and he was cited to appear before the pope. This was in 1427. Martin V received Bernardine coldly and forbade him to preach or exhibit his tablets until his conduct had been examined. The saint humbly submitted, his sermons and writings being handed over to a commission and a day set for his trial. The latter took place at St. Peter's in presence of the pope, 8 June, St. John Capistran having charge of the saint's defence. The malice and futility of the charges against Bernardine were so completely demonstrated that the pope not only justified and commended the saint's teaching, but urged him to preach in Rome. Martin V subsequently approved Bernardine's election as Bishop of Siena. The saint, however, declined this honour as well as the Sees of Ferrara and Urbino, offered to him in 1431 and 1435, respectively, saying playfully that all Italy was already his diocese. After the accession of Eugene IV Bernardine's enemies renewed their accusations against him, but the pope by a Bull, 7 January, 1432, annulled their highhanded, secret proceedings and thus reduced the saint's calumniators to silence, nor does the question seem to have been reopened during the Council of Basle as some have asserted. The vindication of Bernardine's teaching was perpetuated by the feast of the Triumph of the Holy Name, conceded to the Friars Minor in 1530 and extended to the Universal Church in 1722.

In 1433 Bernardine accompanied the Emperor Sigismund to Rome for the latter's coronation. Soon after he withdrew to Capriola to compose a series of sermons. He resumed his missionary labours in 1436, but was forced to abandon them in 1438 on his election as Vicar-General of the Observants throughout Italy. Bernardine had laboured strenuously to spread this branch of the Friars Minor from the outset of his religious life, but it is erroneous to style him its founder since the origin of the Observants may be traced back to the middle of the fourteenth century. Although not the immediate founder of this reform, Bernardine became to the Observants what St. Bernard was to the Cistercians—their principal support and indefatigable propagator. Some idea of his zeal may be gathered from the fact that, instead of the one hundred and thirty Friars constituting the Observance in Italy at Bernardine's reception into the order, it counted over four thousand before his death. In addition to the number he received into the order, Bernardine himself founded, or reformed, at least three hundred convents of Friars. Not content with extending his religious family at home, Bernardine sent missionaries to different parts of the Orient and it was largely through his efforts that so many ambassadors from different schismatical nations attended the Council of Florence in which we find the saint addressing the assembled Fathers in Greek. Having in 1442 persuaded the pope to accept his resignation as vicar-general so that he might give himself more undividedly to preaching, Bernardine resumed his missionary labours. Although a Bull was issued by Eugene IV, 26 May, 1443, charging Bernardine to preach the indulgence for the Crusade against the Turks, there is no record of his having done so. There is, moreover, no good reason to believe that the saint ever preached outside Italy, and the missionary journey to Palestine mentioned by one of his early biographers may perhaps be traced to a confusion of names.

In 1444, notwithstanding his increasing infirmities, Bernardine, desirous that there should be no part of Italy which had not heard his voice, set out to evangelize the Kingdom of Naples. Being too weak to walk, he was compelled to ride an ass. But worn out by his laborious apostolate of forty years the saint was taken down with fever and reached Aquila in a dying state. There lying on the bare ground he passed away on Ascension eve, the 20th of May, just as the Friars in choir were chanting the anthem: *Pater manifestavi nomen Tuum hominibus . . . ad Te venio*. The magistrates refused to allow Bernardine's body to be removed to Siena, and after a funeral of unprecedented splendour laid it in the church of the Conventuals. Miracles multiplied after the saint's death, and he was canonized by Nicholas V, 24 May, 1450. On 17 May, 1472, Bernardine's body was solemnly translated to the new church of the Observants at Aquila, especially erected to receive it, and enclosed in a costly shrine presented by Louis XI of France. This church having been completely destroyed by earthquake in 1703, was replaced by another edifice where the precious relics of St. Bernardine are still venerated. His feast is celebrated on 20 May.

St. Bernardine is accounted the foremost Italian missionary of the fifteenth century, the greatest preacher of his day, the Apostle of the Holy Name, and the restorer of the Order of Friars Minor. He remains one of the most popular of Italian saints, more especially in his own Siena. With both painters and sculptors he has ever been a favourite figure. He frequently finds a place in della Robbia groups; perhaps the best series of pictures of his life is that by Pinturicchio at Ara Cœli in Rome, while the carved reliefs on the façade of the Oratory of Perugia, built in 1461 by the magistrates of that faction-rent city in gratitude for Bernardine's efforts for peace among them, are considered one of the loveliest productions of Renaissance art. But the best portrait of Bernardine is to be found in his own sermons and this is especially true of those in the vernacular. That we are able to enter so thoroughly into the spirit of these *Prediche volgari* is due to the pious industry of one Benedetto, a Sienese fuller, who took down word for word, with a style on wax tablets, a complete course of Bernardine's Lenten sermons delivered in 1427, and afterwards transcribed them on parchment. Benedetto's original MS. is lost, but several very ancient copies of it are extant. All the forty-five sermons it comprises have been printed (Le Prediche Volgari di San Bernardino di Siena. Edite da Luciano Banchi, Siena, 1880–88, 3 vols.). These sermons which often lasted three or four hours, throw much light on the fifteenth-century preaching and on the customs and manners of the time. Couched in the simplest and most popular language—for Bernardine everywhere adapted himself to the local dialect and parlance—they abound in illustrations, anecdotes, digressions, and asides. The saint often resorted to mimicry and was much given to making jokes. But his native Sienese gayety and characteristic Franciscan playfulness detracted nothing from the effect of his sermons, and his exhortations to the people to avert God's wrath by penance, are as powerful as his appeals for peace and charity are pathetic. Very different from these popular Italian sermons taken down *della viva voce* are the series of Latin sermons written by Bernardine, which are in fact formal dissertations with minute divisions and subdivisions, intended to elucidate his teaching and to serve rather as a guide to himself and others than for practical delivery. Besides these Latin sermons which reveal profound theological knowledge, Bernardine left a number of other writings which enjoy a high reputation—dissertations, essays, and letters on practical, ascetical, and mystical theology, and on religious discipline, including treatises on the Blessed Virgin and St. Joseph, used in the Breviary lessons, and a commentary on the Apocalypse. Bernardine's writings were first collected and published at Lyons in 1501. De la Haye's edition, "Sti. Bernardini Senensis Ordinis Seraphici Minorum Opera Omnia", issued at Paris and Lyons in 1536, was reprinted there in 1650, and at Venice in 1745. As a result of the petition addressed to the Holy See in 1882 by the General Chapter of the Friars Minor, requesting that St. Bernardine be declared a Doctor of the Church, a careful inquiry was instituted as to the authenticity of the works attributed to the saint. Some of these are certainly spurious and others are doubtful or interpolated, while not all the saint's genuine works are contained in the editions we possess. A complete and critical edition of St. Bernardine's writings is much needed. An excellent selection from his ascetical works was recently issued by Cardinal Vives (Sti. Bernardini Senensis de Dominicâ Passione, Resurrectione et SS. Nomine Jesu Contemplationes, Rome, 1903).

We are fortunate in possessing several detailed lives of St. Bernardine written by his contemporaries. Three of these are given in full in the Acta Sanctorum Maji, V, with Comm. Præv. by Henschen. The earliest by Bernabæus Senensis, an eyewitness of much he records, was compiled in 1445 shortly after the saint's death. The second by the celebrated humanist, Maphæus Vegius, who knew the saint personally, was printed in 1453. The third by Fra Ludovicus Vincentinus of Aquila was issued after the translation of the saint's body in 1472. A fourth contemporary biography by a Friar Minor, hitherto unedited, has lately been printed both by Father Van Ortroy, S.J., in the Anal. Bolland. (XXV, 1906, pp. 304–389) and by Father Ferdinand M. d'Ardules, O.F.M. (Rome, 1906). The life of St. Bernardine written in Italian by his namesake, Bl. Bernardine of Fossa (d. 1503), and mentioned by Sbaralea and others does not appear to have come down to us. But the latter's "Chronica Fratrum Minorum Observantiæ", edited by Lemmens (Rome, 1902), contains several important references. A valuable account of Bernardine's youth is furnished by Leonardus (Benvoglienti) Senensis, Sienese ambassador to the pope. This work which was edited by Father Van Ortroy in Anal. Bolland., XXI (1902), 53–80, was compiled in 1446 at the instance of St. John Capistran. The "Life" of St. Bernardine attributed to St. John himself, and the one transcribed by Surius in his "Vita SS." (1618), V, 267–281, as well as the tributes to Bernardine of Pius II and St. Antoninus and the acts of his canonization are found in vol. I of de la Haye's edition of Bernardine's works.

WADDING, *Annales*, XII, ad ann. 1450, n. I and *Scriptores* (1650), 57–58; SBARALEA, *Supplementum* (1806), 131–134, 725; AMADIO LUZZO, *Vita di S. Bernardino* (Venice, 1744; Rome, 1826; Siena, 1854; Monza, 1873); BERTHAUMIER, *Hist. de S. Bernardin* (Paris, 1862); TOUSSAINT, *Das Leben des h. Bernardin von Siena* (Ratisbon, 1873); *Life of St. Bernardine of Siena* (London, 1873); LEO DE CLARY, *Lives of the Saints of the Three Orders of St. Francis* (Taunton, 1886), II, 220–275; LEON, *Vie de St. Bernardin* (Vanves, 1893); ALESSIO, *Storia di S. Bernardino e del suo tempo* (Mondovi, 1899); RONZONI, *L'Eloquenza di S. Bernardino* (Siena, 1899). Undoubtedly the best modern life of St. Bernardine is that by Paul Thureau-Dangin of the French Academy: *Un prédicateur populaire dans l'Italie de la Renaissance: S. Bernardin de Siène* (Paris, 1896). This brilliant monograph has been translated into Italian (1897), German (1904), and English (1906).

PASCHAL ROBINSON.

Bernardines, THE, title of certain sisters of the order of Cîteaux who at the end of the sixteenth and in the seventeenth century, made energetic efforts to restore the primitive observance of their rule. They were the Bernardine Recollects (*Bernardas Recoletas*) in Spain; the Bernardines of Divine Providence, the Bernardines of the Precious Blood; and the Bernardines of Flines and of Lille, in France and Savoy; and some isolated foundations in Belgium and in Peru. The first reform was due to the Abesses of Las Huelgas of Burgos, who towards the end of the sixteenth century, had reformed the Abbeys of Gradefes, Perales, and St. Anne of Valladolid, where Jane de Ayala introduced the true spirit of Cîteaux. In 1601 St. Anne of Valladolid became the mother-house of the new reform, and in 1606 the constitutions were approved by Paul V. This reform extended as far as the Indies and the Canary Islands.

In 1622 Louise-Theresa-Blanche de Ballon, daughter of Charles-Emmanuel de Ballon, chamberlain of the Duke of Savoy and later ambassador of this prince in France and Spain, began, under the direction of St. Francis of Sales, her near relative, the reform of the monastery of St. Catherine (Savoy). She afterwards went with five sisters to Rumilly and founded the Congregation of Bernardines of Divine Providence. This reform spread into Savoy and France. The constitutions were printed in 1631. In 1634 Mother de Ponçonnas, who with four other Cistercian sisters of Grenoble had embraced the reform, having gone to Paris to found a new house, had the constitutions reprinted with some changes. Louise de Ballon then had them again printed so as to conform to the first constitutions—an action which caused the separation of the convents of France and Savoy. The convents of France formed what is known as the congregation "of St. Bernard". Mother Baudet de Beauregard who succeeded Mother de Ponçonnas in the government of the monastery of Paris, changed the name from Bernardines of Divine Providence to Bernardines of the Precious Blood (1654). Their rules were approved by the Abbot of Prières, Vicar General of the Strict Observance of Cîteaux, and the Prior of St. Germain-des-Prés, as Vicar General of the Cardinal de Bourbon, received the vows of the new community on the 27th of August of the same year.

The monasteries of the congregation now number (I) Bernardine Recollects, 13; (II) Bernardines founded by Mother de Ballon, 2; (III) Bernardines of Flines, 2; (IV) Bernardines of Lille, 3; (V) Bernardines isolated in Belgium and Peru, 6. The houses of France have been closed by the Government. The Bernardines of to-day are engaged in teaching and follow a somewhat modified rule.

The Bernardines of Spain rise every day at three o'clock, and on days of great solemnities at two o'clock. For the office they follow the Cistercian Breviary. They fast two days a week from Pentecost to the 14th of September, four days a week from the 14th of September to Easter Sunday, and every day during Advent, Septuagesima time, and Lent. Meat is allowed three times a week except during Advent and the nine weeks before Easter Sunday. Their habit consists of a woolen robe and their bed is conformable to the regulations. They live in community in sickness as well as in health. With the Bernardines of Mother de Ballon this rule is still more mitigated. They rise at five o'clock summer and winter. Silence is kept except during the recreation which follows dinner and supper. They fast two days a week from Easter Sunday to Pentecost, and on Saturday also during Advent. They abstain from meat on the Wednesdays, Fridays, and Saturdays of the whole year. M. GILDAS.

Berne, the fourth city of Switzerland in population, capital of a canton of the same name which is the second of the Swiss cantons in size and first in population, and since 1848, capital of the Swiss Confederation, is situated at a point 1,788 feet above the sea level, in Lat. 46° 57′ N., and Long. 7° 26′ E. The larger part of the city is built on a peninsula that projects into the Aar from its left bank. In the Middle Ages Berne contained over 5,000 inhabitants; in 1764, 13,681; in 1850, 27,558; in 1900, 64,064. This last number includes 60,622 Germans, 3,087 French, 902 Italians, 762 of mixed Romance blood;

divided as to religion, there are 57,946 Protestants, 6,278 Catholics, 668 Jews, and 481 persons belonging to other creeds. As capital of the Swiss Confederation, Berne is the seat of the national, as well as of the cantonal, government, and the official residence of all representatives of foreign Powers. Being the point of junction of seven different lines of railroad, Berne is visited annually by some 200,000 tourists and is the headquarters of a number of international unions and associations, such as the International Postal Union; the International Telegraph Union; the International Patent Office; the International Express Union; the International Publishers' Congress; the International Peace Society; the Blue Cross Society. It is the residence of a "Christian-Catholic" (Old-Catholic) bishop, and a Catholic parish priest, the centre of a large trade in agricultural produce and of considerable manufactures (chiefly spun silk, machinery, and scientific and musical instruments). It is one of the best built cities in Switzerland, having broad streets and large squares, while it has preserved, more than most of the larger Swiss cities, the old national characteristics in its domestic and municipal architecture. There are six bridges across the Aar, of which the two most important are the iron Kirchenfeldbrücke, 217 yards long, built in 1882–83, and the Kornhausbrücke, 388 yards long, and 157 feet above the River Aar, built in 1896–98. The city contains 7 churches and several chapels. The Catholic church of the Holy Trinity, built in 1896–1900, with a tower 147 feet high, is in the style of an early Christian basilica. The church of Sts. Peter and Paul, originally Catholic, was turned over to the Old Catholics in 1874. The most important of the secular buildings are: the Rathaus of the Canton, built 1406–16; the old and new Federal Buildings; the Parliament Building (*Parlamentsgebäude*), erected 1895–1902; and the new University Buildings (1900–03).

The University of the Canton of Berne was founded in 1834 by the reorganization of the academy already in existence; it has a Protestant theological faculty, an Old Catholic theological faculty, and faculties of philosophy, law, medicine, and veterinary medicine; its yearly expenses are 880,000 francs ($176,000), and the endowment amounts to over a million francs ($200,000). Connected with the university are an observatory, a botanical garden, and numerous institutes and clinics; the University Library was, in 1905, united with the City Library, the joint collection amounting to some 200,000 volumes, including many valuable manuscripts. Besides these there are a public and a private gymnasium, a secondary school for boys, a public and a private secondary school for girls, a normal school (at Muristalden), an industrial art school, which is combined with the cantonal industrial art museum, students' workshops, and schools for mechanics, art, and music. Among the numerous learned societies established at Berne are the Swiss Society for the Natural Sciences, founded in 1815, and the Historical Research Society of Switzerland, founded in 1840; the Cantonal Hospital contains 360 beds and has an endowment of over eight million francs ($1,600,000); it was founded in 1354, and since 1884 has been situated on the Kreuzmatte in Holligen. Other hospitals are: a hospital for infectious diseases, founded in 1284, and containing 128 beds; a hospital for women, with maternity department, 1781; the city *Burgerspital*, founded in 1742, and having an endowment of some 7 million francs ($1,400,000); the city *Zieglerspital*, founded in 1867, and having an endowment of some 3 million francs ($600,000); the *Jennerspital* for Children; the Cantonal Insane Asylum; a town orphan asylum for boys and girls, Magdalen asylum, and numerous private institutions. Among the Catholic societies and associations are: the Catholic

Journeymen's Union (*Gesellenverein*), founded in 1868; the Association of St. Vincent de Paul for aiding the poor, 1868; Women's Society for the Encouragement of Religious Life and Aid of the Poor, 1875; Congregation of the Children of Mary, for young girls, 1881; the parish Cecilia Association (since 1878) a church-choir society; Men's Society, founded in 1872, reorganized in 1899 as the Catholic Association of the City of Berne, for the protection of Catholic interests, and united with the social union, Bernia, founded in 1887.

HISTORY.—The many remains discovered show that the territory surrounding Berne was occupied in prehistoric times. After the Romans had been driven out, the region was occupied by the Alemanni and Burgundians; in A. D. 534 it belonged to the Franks, in 888 it formed part of the second Burgundian empire, together with which it was absorbed into the Holy Roman Empire in 1032. The Dukes of Zähringen received the territory as a fief from the empire, and the last duke of this line, Berthold V, founded the city of Berne in 1191. At his death (1218) it was made a free city of the empire. With but few interruptions the city was able to preserve its independence during its long and frequent wars with the Counts of Kyburg, the Emperor Rudolph of Hapsburg, the Burgundian ruler, Charles the Bold, and so on. It was also able by a clever and consistent policy to increase the size of its territory; in 1415 it conquered Aargau, and Vaud was annexed in 1536. The Disputation of Berne, held in January, 1528, through the efforts of Berthold Haller, Valerius Anshelm, Franz Kolb, and other friends of Zwingli, resulted in the adoption of the Reformation by the city and the increase of the possessions of the State by the confiscation of church property; the land thus acquired amounted to 186 square miles. During the many religious wars which followed (1529, 1531, 1656, 1712) Berne suppressed all forms of Catholic life; in this it followed the example of, and acted in concert with, Zurich, which, with Berne, occupied the most prominent position in the Confederation. The extreme oligarchical rule of the few patrician families caused a rebellion of the peasants in 1653, and the conspiracy of Samuel Henzi in 1749, both of which uprisings were suppressed with much bloodshed, and the power of the Government became more absolute. It was not until the French Revolution that the oligarchy was swept away. After a brave struggle, Berne was taken and plundered by the French (5 March, 1798); it lost the Aargau and Vaud and became the capital of the newly founded Helvetian Republic. As compensation for the loss of the Aargau and Vaud, the Congress of Vienna (1815) gave Berne the greater part of the suppressed Bishopric of Basle and the cities of Biel and Neuenstadt. The oligarchical government, which was re-established, was obliged to abdicate at the outbreak of the Revolution of July, and a new Constitution was adopted (21 July, 1831) which granted democratic representation. This Constitution was amended in a radical direction in 1848 by the adoption of direct voting without property qualification; in 1896 a new Constitution was accepted which granted initiative by the people.

It was not until 1798 that the Catholics, in virtue of section 6 of the Constitution of the Helvetian Republic, were able to re-establish their church organization. In 1799 the Franciscan Father Girard became the first parish priest, being at the same time vicar-general to the Bishop of Lausanne; in 1804 he retired from Berne to become a teacher at Freiburg and Lucerne. Relations with the cantonal government were fairly good during the pastorates of his numerous successors, yet the Catholic community remained a private association and was not recognized by the authorities, although the Constitution of 1848 guaranteed freedom of public worship. The Catholic community made use of the French Protestant church until Father Baud (1832–67) built a Catholic church (1858–64); in 1864 the parish, together with the old part of the canton, was included in the Diocese of Basle. The Catholics refused to recognize the deposition of Bishop Lachat of Basle and rejected the laws of 1873–74, which were unfavourable to the Church; these included the laws concerning parish elections, the cantonal synod as the highest church authority, and civil marriage. In the consequent religious struggle (*Kulturkampf*) they were obliged to give up their church and all church-endowments to the Old Catholics, who were favoured in every way by the authorities, as was shown by the erection of an Old Catholic theological faculty in 1874, etc. It was not until the decade beginning with 1880 that, during the pastorate of Father Jacob Stammler, a truce was established between Church and State. Father Stammler built a new church, 1896–1900, and was raised to the See of Basle-Lugano in 1906.

The chronicles of VALERIUS ANSHELM (d. 1540) and other medieval writers have been edited (1884–1901) by the Historical Society of the Canton of Berne. See also *Fontes rerum Bernensium* (a collection of documents earlier than the year 1366—Berne, 1877–1903). WALTHARD, *Description de la ville de Berne* (Berne, 1827); FISCHER, *Geschichte der Disputation und Reformation in Bern* (Berne, 1828); VON RODT, *Bernische Stadtgeschichte* (1886); IDEM, *Berns Burgerschaft und Gesellenschaft* (Berne, 1891); IDEM, *Bern in den XIII.-XIX. Jahrhut.* (Berne, 1898–1907); SCHWAB AND DEMME, *Die Armenpflege der Stadt Bern* (1899); VON MÜLINEN, *Berns Geschichte 1191–1891* (a pamphlet—Berne, 1891); GEISER, *Die Verfassung des alten Bern 1191–1798* (Berne, 1891); IDEM, *Geschichte des Armenwesen im Kanton Bern* (Berne, 1894); STAMMLER, *Die St. Antoniuskirche in Bern* in *Katholische Schweizerblätter* (1893); IDEM, *Geschichte der Römischkatholischen Gemeinde in Bern* (Solothurn, 1901); DAGUET, *Le Père Girard et son temps* (Paris, 1896), II; TÜRLER, *Das Franziskanerkloster in Bern*, in pamphlet issued at the opening of the new high-school at Berne (Berne, 1903); *Annual Reports of the Statistical Bureau of Berne*.

GREGOR REINHOLD.

Berne, ABBEY OF. See HEESWIJK.

Berni, FRANCESCO, an Italian comic poet, b. at Lamporecchio (Florence) 1497 or 1498; d. at Florence, 26 May, 1535. The son of noble but impoverished parents, he spent his early years in the Tuscan capital fighting want. At twenty better luck awaited him in Rome, where Cardinal Bibbiena, his relative the Cardinal's nephew, Angelo Dovizi, and Giovanni Mattia Giberti, Bishop of Verona and Datary to Leo X, successively employed him. In the datary, however, he had found a hard taskmaster, who kept him at his correspondence all day long and would not countenance the buffooneries in which the young clerk took huge delight. So, in 1531 we find Berni at Padua in rapturous freedom, gaily bent on bandying insults with the notorious Aretino. Still, the autumn of the same year saw him back at his desk in the episcopal residence of Verona, penning letters with a reluctant hand. Not until 1533, when Cardinal Ippolito dei Medici, who had engaged him the year before, made him a canon of the Florentine cathedral, did he find a position that pleased him. But that long dreamed of life, with its unbridled frolic and happy idleness, was not to last, for, becoming involved in the feud then raging between Ippolito and Alessandro dei Medici, he fell a victim to poison under very mysterious circumstances two years afterwards.

Berni's most extensive work, the refashioning of Matteo Maria Boiardo's chivalric poem, "L'Orlando innamorato", was published at Milan seven years after his death and again at Venice, 1545. Leaving the original plot and detailed *dénouement* entirely unchanged, the jovial Florentine sought to enamel with a smooth diction, and colour with many a quip and prank what he thought offensive on account of its ruggedness of form and dullness of style. Thus he unwittingly made a parody of a creation strong and noble in its native simplicity. Undoubtedly Berni's fame is more deservedly due to his "Rime", embracing "Sonetti", "Sonettesse", and "Capitoli", wherein the Bernesque manner found its inception as well as highest achievement, and snivelling Petrarchists were pitilessly flouted. In spite of numberless imitators, including such men as Benedetto Varchi, Ercole Bentivoglio, Giovanni Mauro, Matteo Franzesi, and Ludovico Dolce, Berni's easy flowing tercets, fairly bubbling over with graceful raillery and capering mirth, dwarfed all his rivals. The "Rime, Poesie latine, e Lettere" were edited by A. Virgili at Florence, in 1885. Nor are the Latin poems, a rustic farce known as "Catrina" (Florence, 1567), and the "Dialogo contro i poeti" (Ferrara, 1527) unworthy productions of his facile pen. The morality of Berni's writings is far from commendable.

VIRGILI, *Francesco Berni, con documenti inediti* (Florence, 1881). About the Bernesque type of poetry see: MAZZONI, *Fra libri e carte* (Rome, 1887); GASPARY, *Geschichte der ital. Lit.* (Strasburg, 1888), II, 514.

EDOARDO SAN GIOVANNI.

Bernier, ETIENNE-ALEXANDRE, French Bishop, b. at Daon (Mayenne), 31 October, 1762; d. at Paris, 1 October, 1806. He was at first professor of theology in the higher seminary and in the University of Angers, then pastor of St. Laud's parish, in that city. During the Revolution he refused to take the Civil Oath, and succeeded by his eloquence in arousing the peasants of Anjou and Vendée into insurrection. He then became one of the most important leaders of the whole movement by his personal influence both with the chiefs and on the different military councils. He was called "L'Apôtre de la Vendée". As to what was his real conduct during this insurrection, towards the end of it especially, its various historians do not agree. At any rate, after the 18th Brumaire, Bernier played the part of negotiator between the First Consul and the insurgents. When Bonaparte had resolved, in spite of all difficulties and opposition, to unite the French nation and the Catholic Church, he chose the Abbé Bernier to represent the French Government in the preparatory negotiations. This choice was a happy one, on the part of the First Consul, for, despite how widely historians differ in their appreciations of Bernier's character, none of them denies him a deep and subtle intelligence, an untiring and resourceful activity, and a seductive influence—all qualities which made him a clever politician.

As soon as Mgr. Spina and Caselli, the pope's envoys, arrived at Paris, in November, 1800, Bernier entered into relations with them, and, at once began, with Mgr. Spina, the preparatory negotiations on the important points which were to be discussed, namely, the resignation of the bishops, the reduction of the number of dioceses, the alienation of ecclesiastical properties, nomination to the bishoprics, and the taking of the oath of fidelity to the constitution. They successively presented four projects of reduction, followed by another project drawn up by Napoleon himself. Difficulties arose, necessitating the presence in Paris of the Papal Secretary of State, Consalvi, in June, 1801. The Concordat was to be signed on 13 July, and Bernier had been appointed by a decree of the preceding day (Messidor 23, an. IX) as one of the three representatives of the French Government, to conclude the Concordat and sign it. In the meantime, the project agreed upon had been changed by Bonaparte; letters were exchanged between Consalvi and Bernier; Consalvi refused to sign the new project. Negotiations continued until the 16th of July, when an agreement was reached and the Concordat signed at 2 o'clock in the morning. (See CONCORDAT.) In 1802 Bernier was named Bishop of Orléans, by Bonaparte.

D'HAUSSONVILLE, *L'Eglise romaine et le premier empire* (1868); CRÉTINEAU-JOLY, *Histoire de la Vendée militaire;* LÉON SÈCHE, *Les origines du Concordat* (Paris, 1895); COCHARD, *Mgr. Bernier, évêque d'Orléans* (Orléans, 1901); MATHIEU, *Le Concordat de 1801* (Paris, 1903); SEVESTRE, *L'Histoire, le texte, el la destinée du concordat de 1801* (2nd ed., Paris, 1905); CONSALVI, *Mémoires* (1864); THEINER, *Documents inédits relatifs aux affaires de l'Eglise de France, 1790–1800* (1857); IDEM, *Histoire des deux concordats de la République Française* (Paris, 1875); BOULAY DE LA MEURTHE, *Documents sur la négociation du Concordat et sur les autres rapports de la France avec le S. Siège* (Paris, 1891–97), I–III; RINIERI, *La diplomatie pontificale au XIXe siècle, le concordat entre Pie VII et le Premier consul 1800–1802* (French tr., Paris, 1903).

G. M. SAUVAGE.

Bernini, DOMENICO, son of the famous artist Giovanni Lorenzo Bernini, lived in the early part of the eighteenth century. He became a prelate and canon of Santa Maria Maggiore in Rome. He devoted himself to the study of ecclesiastical history and wrote an extensive history of the heresies, "Istoria di tutte l'heresie", 4 vols. fol. (Rome, 1705–17); also, "Memorie istoriche di ciò che hanno operato i sommi pontefici nelle guerre contra i Turchi" in quarto (Rome, 1685); "Il tribunale della S. Ruota Romana (Rome, 1717).

Acta Eruditorum (Leipzig, 1708), 494; HURTER, *Nomenclator,* II.

G. M. SAUVAGE.

Bernini, GIOVANNI LORENZO, one of the most vigorous and fertile of Italian architects and sculptors, b. at Naples in 1598; d. at Rome in 1680. Bernini in his art is the most industrious of Roman artists, and his work tends largely to the baroque. In addition to his abilities as sculptor and architect he possessed those of a painter and even of a poet. His father, a painter and sculptor of moderate skill, gave him his first lessons in art. In 1608 the father was called to Rome and took Lorenzo with him. It is said that the boy even in his eighth year had carved a beautiful marble head of a child; in his fifteenth year he produced the "David with a Sling" which is now in the Villa Borghese. Paul V employed him, and under the five following popes he rose to great fame and importance. He was the favourite of Urban VIII (Barberini). In 1629 he became the architect of St. Peter's and superintendent of Public Works in Rome. He ruled in art like a second Michaelangelo, although his style bore little resemblance to that of the latter. Mazarin tried in 1664 to persuade him to come to Paris, but he did not visit that city until 1665 when he accepted an invitation from Louis XIV. A son named Paul and a numerous suite accompanied him to Paris and Versailles. Jealousy, however, prevented the carrying out of his plans for the Louvre, nor was he able to maintain himself long in Paris. His pupil, Mathias Rossi, was also forced, not long after the master's departure, to leave the city. The king, however, treated Bernini with great honour during his stay and rewarded him munificently. Bernini made a bust and an equestrian statue of Louis XIV which were in a style agreeable to the taste of that monarch. Queen Christina of Sweden visited Bernini during her stay in Rome; and on an order of King Philip IV he made a huge crucifix for the royal mortuary chapel. He also carved busts of Charles I of England and his wife Henrietta. Bernini triumphed over all his detractors and became in the end as rich as he was famous.

It is not necessary to speak here of his writings and of his comedies in verse. Nor need mention be made of his paintings which amount to some two hundred canvases. He owes his fame to his architectural work, for which he had in Rome great and inspiring examples. He never lacked imagination, inventive power, or courage in undertaking a task. He did not copy the simplicity of the antique and often deliberately departed from the canons of art in the hope of excelling them (*chi non esce talvolta della regola, non la passa mai*). The art of this period in aiming at outward effect lost all moderation and went to too great an extreme. In completing the church of St. Peter Bernini was naturally obliged to exert all his powers. As the seventh architect engaged in the work he gave the finishing touches to the great undertaking. With sound judgment he followed the plan of Maderna—to increase the effect of the façade by means of flanking towers. He wished, however, to make the towers a more important feature than in Maderna's scheme, keeping them though in such proportion that in the distance they should appear some thirty metres below the dome. As one tower was well under way it fell down on account of the weakness of the foundation laid by Maderna. One of the most brilliant works of Bernini is the colonnade before St. Peter's. It proves the truth of the axiom he laid down: "An architect proves his skill by turning the defects of a site into advantages". The slope of the ground from the doorway of the basilica to the bridge over the Tiber suggested the scheme of laying out the great stairway of twenty-two steps and the great and equally well-conceived terrace. The ground available being limited on two sides by neighbouring houses, Bernini avoided the danger of coming too close to the buildings by adopting the beautiful elliptic form of the colonnade, which encloses, nevertheless, as large a ground-surface as the Colosseum.

The avenue thus formed is perhaps the most beautiful one in the world. When the piazza is approached from the distance a fine view is at first obtained of the dome; unfortunately the dome is more and more obscured, on nearer approach, by the portico and the façade of the church. Four rows of Tuscan columns, placed to right and left and having altogether the form of an ellipse, traverse the piazza from one end to the other. Between the middle rows of columns two carriages can pass. The slope of the ground without being sharp enough to produce fatigue causes the eye to look steadily upward. In the middle of the ellipse, which is 895x741 feet, stands the obelisk, 84 feet high, which was placed here in 1586 by Sixtus V. Back of the ellipse rises the terrace. Two galleries unite the ellipse with the portico, the height of which is best realized by comparing it with these galleries. Everything here is on a great scale. When, however, the pope gives the blessing from the balcony, the convergence of the lines in the arrangement of the piazza causes the space to appear much greater than it really is. The stairway (Scala Regia), which ascends from the portico to the Sala Regia, offers a fine perspective. Limitation was here turned into a source of beauty. Bernini had a large share in the erection of the stately Barberini palace at Rome. He built the beautiful Odescalchi palace, took part in adorning the Piazza Navona with the obelisk, and designed the pleasing statues of the river-gods for the great fountain.

In speaking of Bernini's work as a sculptor it may be said that in this field the decadence of his art makes itself apparent. The skeleton representing Death on the tomb of Urban VIII, in the church of St. Peter, is placed in the midst of ideal and really beautiful figures. Weaker still, with the exception of the portrait, is the tomb of Alexander VII. "St. Theresa pierced by an Arrow" is exceedingly effective, the "Rape of Proserpine", as well as his "Apollo and Daphne", are weak and sensuous. On the other hand, the equestrian statue of Constantine in St. Peter's suffers from its size, as the heroic proportions do not appear to be united with the necessary intrinsic worth. To-day the canopy (*baldacchino*) is as universally condemned as it was then (1633) admired. Neither is approval now given to

COLONNADE OF ST. PETER'S, DESIGNED BY LORENZO BERNINI (1667)

the "Chair of St. Peter" in the tribune of the basilica. Viewed as a sculptor Bernini is at times extreme, without force, theatrical in the pose, affected in details, or over-luxuriant in physical graces. He was entirely in accord with the spirit of his time and countenanced it with all the authority of his ability and fame. He attached more importance to grace of outward form than to intrinsic merit, and aimed more at external effect than at the real artistic completeness of the work. Yet among his productions as a sculptor are many excellent works. As examples may be given the tomb of the Countess Matilda in St. Peter's, and the statues of St. Ludovica Albertoni and St. Bibiana in the niches of the colonnade of St. Peter's. In the niches of these columns are 162 statues made after designs by Bernini. In his work on the Bridge of Sant' Angelo he shows at least wonderful richness of design. He by no means failed in designs for tombs and in portrait busts; for example, the bust of his daughter and that of Innocent X.

He often spoiled the pure plastic effect of his work by two or three false conceptions. He held that the antique repose of sculpture, which, it must be acknowledged, at times nearly degenerates into stiffness, must be transformed into effective action at any cost. The naturalistic painting of the time drove the sculptors into this course. But in the plastic arts the reason for extreme action is often not clear and it appears weak, sentimental, and theatrical. When the work is executed in polished marble, for which Bernini had a strong predilection, over-action is apt to degenerate into the opposite of what is intended and to become an extreme ugliness, or a miscarried attempt at grandeur. On account of these misconceptions of art Bernini's work was often a failure. The style of sculpture which aims solely at outward effect is seen to best advantage when it is used in connexion with architecture. The statues designed by Bernini for the façade of St. Peter's and of the Lateran belong to this form of art. Action appears at its best in sculpture when used as decoration and on a small scale. The decorative architectural style is better suited, therefore, for relief work than for sculpture in the round.

DOMINICI, *Vite dei Pittori, Scultori ed Architetti Napolitani* (Naples, 1840); KUHN, *Kunstgeschichte* (Einsiedeln, 1891); IDEM, *Roma* (Einsiedeln, 1878); DOHME, *Kunst und Künstler* (Leipzig, 1879).

G. GIETMANN.

Bernini, GIUSEPPE MARIA, a Capuchin missionary and Orientalist, b. near Carignan in Piedmont; d. in Hindustan in 1753. For many years he was a missionary in the East Indies, and acquired a remarkable knowledge of the languages and dialects of India. In his travels through the country he made a special and careful study of the manners, customs, and religious beliefs and practices of the people. The results of his studies were collected in his work: "Notizie laconiche di alcuni usi, sacrifizi, ed idoli nel regno di Neipal, raccolte nel anno 1747". This work has never been published, but is preserved in manuscript in the library of the Propaganda at Rome, and in the museum of Cardinal Borgia. Bernini also wrote "Dialogues", in one of the Indian languages, also preserved in manuscript in the Propaganda; a translation of "Adhiatma Ramayana"; one of "Djana Sagara", and a collection of historical studies under the title, "Mémoires historiques" (Verona).

Dizionario Biografico Universale (Florence, 1840). A very mediocre translation of the *Notizie* into English has been published in *Asiatic Researches*, II.

ENEAS B. GOODWIN.

Bernis, FRANÇOIS-JOACHIM-PIERRE DE, a French cardinal and statesman, b. 1715 at Saint-Marcel-d'Ardèche; d. at Rome, 1794. The Bernis family possessed many titles of nobility but was almost reduced to poverty. François, the youngest son, was destined for an ecclesiastical career and sent to St.-Sulpice. He left that institution at the age of nineteen to go into the world to retrieve the family fortune. The title of Abbé, by which he was known, meant in those days little more than the tonsure and the black gown; it certainly meant only that to him. Young Bernis was a worldling in the full sense of the word, but success was slow in coming. His noble birth gave him access to the chapters of Brioude and Lyons; his ready wit and courteous manners opened to him the mansions of the wealthy, and the French Academy admitted him in recognition of certain literary essays whose principal merit was gallantry; but all this only concealed, without relieving, his poverty. It was at this time that Bernis was introduced to the future Madame de Pompadour, an acquaintance which soon meant a pension of 1500 livres and, later, the appointment as ambassador to Venice.

Once at Venice, Bernis rapidly rose. He succeeded in adjusting some differences between the Venetians and Pope Benedict XIV, and thus won the favour of the latter. The knowledge he had acquired of European diplomacy made him valuable to his Government, and partly in view of possible preferment in the Church and partly through a desire of breaking with the past, Bernis received the subdeaconship at the hands of the Patriarch of Venice. In 1756 Louis XV recalled him to make him his minister of foreign affairs, but his tenure of office was short and full of trials. The alliance of France with Austria against England and Prussia resulted in the Seven Years' War in which France was the loser, and Bernis was held responsible for both the alliance and its consequences. It is true that this new policy had been practically inaugurated by Rouillé, Bernis's predecessor in the foreign office; that the worthlessness of the French generals, all creatures of Madame de Pompadour, and not Bernis's carelessness or incompetency, was the true cause of the defeats of the French; that the treaty of Paris, which terminated the war, insured to the French some appreciable advantages; yet, despite this, Bernis lost the favour of the people and, along with it, the friendship of Madame de Pompadour. He tendered his resignation, and was, by a harsh letter of Louis XV, banished to the Abbey of Vic-sur-Aisne, near Soissons. Pope Clement XIII was the only one to remember him. Just as the fallen minister was going into exile, he received a papal *motu proprio* making him cardinal (1758).

Bernis profited by his six years of enforced retirement, receiving the diaconate and the priesthood. In 1764, after the anger of the king and Madame de Pompadour had subsided, he was sent to Albi as archbishop. His zeal there won him the esteem of all and prepared him for a still higher position, that of ambassador of France at Rome (1769). Bernis's influence in Rome was considerable. It was felt in the conclave of 1769, which elected Ganganelli, and in that of 1774, which elected Braschi. In the suppression of the Jesuits by Clement XIV, Bernis is far from deserving all the blame that is put on him. It is well known that he personally regretted the measure, and that as ambassador he tried to avert it by assisting the wavering pope in securing the delays for which he had asked. But the pressure exercised by the Bourbons of Spain, Naples, and France, and the passive attitude and tacit consent of Austria brought the negotiations to an abrupt termination. When the French Revolution broke out, Bernis held, in the national church of St. Louis des Français, a solemn funeral for the martyred Louis XVI; he also placed his palace at the disposal of the princesses of France who had sought refuge in Rome, and finally resigned his post rather than take the constitutional oath. The last three years of his life he spent in Rome in comparative poverty, devoting himself to the French exiles and fully justifying the epithet, "Protector of the Church of France", bestowed upon him by Pius Pope VI. The French colony in Rome erected a magnificent mausoleum in his honour, and the church of St. Louis received his remains.

Bernis's life has too long received but scant appreciation because of the levity of his youth, which he was the first to regret and called the *delicta iuventutis meæ*. The publication of his "Mémoires" in 1878 has put a new construction on many things and given us a truer and better opinion of him. Although the first part of his life cannot be defended, still, from the time of his ordination at Venice and Soissons, the courtier took a higher view of the sanctity of the priestly character, and was no discredit to it. Bernis was a writer of no mean talent. His "Poésies" show a bright imagination and a facile pen; his "Letters" are not inferior to Voltaire's; and the poem "Religion vengée", though lacking the calm beauty of Racine's similar production, still has inspiring passages. Didot published Bernis's "Œuvres mêlées en prose et en vers" (Paris, 1797), and Masson edited his "Mémoires" (1878).

Encyclopédie des gens du monde (Paris, 1834); MASSON, *Mémoires et lettres de François-Joachim, Cardinal de Bernis* (Paris, 1878); IDEM, *Le Cardinal de Bernis depuis son ministère* (Paris, 1884); DE LA ROCHETERIE, *Revue des questions historiques* (Paris, 1879), XXVI, 214; THEINER, *Histoire de Clément XIV* (Paris, 1852); D'ARMAILHAC, *L'église nationale de St. Louis des Français* (Rome, 1894).

J. F. SOLLIER.

Berno (ABBOT OF REICHENAU), famous as orator, poet, philosopher, and musician, born (date unknown) at Prüm near Trier; d. 7 June, 1048. He became Abbot of Reichenau in 1008. Educated in the school of St. Gall, Berno visited Rome with the Emperor Henry II, and upon his return introduced many reforms in the liturgical music of his native land. Among his books are the "Tonarium", "De variâ psalmorum atque cantuum modulatione", and "De consonâ tonorum diversitate", all of which are contained in Migne's "Patrology" and in Gerbert's "Scriptores". Another work attributed to him, but less known, is entitled "De instrumentis musicalibus".

Living and writing at a time when the traditions of Rome and St. Gall were still fresh, Berno has left, in his works on music, a fruitful source of information to those who are interested in ascertaining and restoring the rhythmical form in which the Gregorian melodies were originally sung. Berno's testimony, with that of other early writers, supports the view of those who hold that the Gregorian melodies consist of long and short note-values, as against the theory that all notes in the chant are of equal length.

WAGNER, *Neumenkunde* (Freiburg, 1905); BONVIN, *On Gregorian Rhythm* (New York, 1906); *Voix de St. Gall* (Fribourg, Switzerland, 1906).

JOSEPH OTTEN.

Berno (APOSTLE OF THE OBOTRITES), in the latter half of the twelfth century. The Obotrites were one of the Slav tribes known under the common name of Wends, and dwelt along the Baltic in Mecklenburg. Three bishoprics had been erected in their country as early as the tenth century, Oldenburg (transferred to Lübeck in the twelfth century), Ratzeburg, and Mecklenburg, but they remained vacant during the greater part of the eleventh century. Duke Henry the Lion, of Saxony, having partly subdued the Obotrites, re-established the three bishoprics, and in 1155 selected Berno as Bishop of Mecklenburg. He was a Cistercian monk of the flourishing monastery of Amelungsborn on the Weser, and was conse-

crated in Rome by Pope Adrian IV. As these sees were not only episcopal residences but also political centres and strongholds of foreign power, the Obotrites identified the Christian with the German name and detested both. No wonder that Berno at first met with small success in his missionary labours. The Obotrite Prince Niklot, the fiercest enemy both of the Germans and of the Christian religion, had not yet submitted to German ascendency and was the greatest obstacle to the conversion of the people. Berno was even obliged in 1158 to transfer his episcopal see from Mecklenburg to Schwerin, whither German colonists had already penetrated. From Schwerin as a centre, the zealous and intrepid missionary bishop began his work of preaching, destroying idols, baptizing, and building churches, and penetrated as far as Demmin in hither Pomerania. Here, in 1163, he converted the powerful Prince Pribislav, son of Niklot, who, however, fell away again the very next year, made war upon the Germans, and attacked, and nearly killed the bishop at the altar. In the end he had to acknowledge the German supremacy and remained henceforth loyal to the Christian religion.

In 1168 Berno undertook a missionary expedition to the island of Rügen and destroyed the temple and the great idol of the pagan inhabitants, whom by patience and kindness he won over to the Christian religion. In the year 1171 he consecrated the Cathedral of Schwerin, where in 1177, he held the first synod. The greatest service which this apostolic man rendered to those countries was the introduction of his religious brethren, the Cistercian monks. The monastery of Doberan, which through the bishop's efforts was founded by Pribislav in 1171, soon became a centre from which radiated Christian civilization far and wide. The monks had been brought from his own monastery of Amelungsborn. Two years later Dargun was founded and entrusted to Danish monks. This monastery, however, did not flourish until the Danish monks were replaced by monks from Doberan. During the schism caused by Frederick Barbarossa, Berno, like all the Cistercians, never wavered in his loyalty to the legitimate pope, though his metropolitan, the Archbishop of Bremen, had joined the cause of the antipope. When at last Frederick made his peace with Alexander III, Berno was enabled to make a journey to Rome (1178) to pay his homage to the pope, who confirmed the erection of his diocese. During the Lent of the following year he took part in the General Council of the Lateran. During his absence in Rome, the Wends had risen against the Germans, the great monastery of Doberan had been destroyed and its seventy-eight inmates massacred. When peace was re-established Doberan was rebuilt and again peopled by monks from Amelungsborn in 1186. Berno died in 1191 (1190?) having laboured as bishop in Mecklenburg for over thirty years.

DIEKAMP in *Kirchenlex.*, II, s. v.; *Allgemeine deutsche Biog.*, II, s. v.; HERGENRÖTHER-KIRSCH, *Kirchengesch.*, II, 536–538, a full bibliography, ibidem, 277, 278, 535, 536; CHEVALIER, *Bio-bibl.* (Paris, 1905), s. v.

B. GULDNER.

Bernold of Constance, historian and theologian, b. in Swabia about 1054; d. at Schaffhausen, 16 September, 1100. He entered the school of Constance under the renowned Bernard of Constance, and made rapid progress in study. He attended the Lenten Synod of Rome, in 1079, at which Berengarius retracted his errors. Remaining in Italy till 1084 he returned to Constance for the episcopal consecration of Gebhard, whose action in enforcing the reform decrees of Gregory VII he later on defended. In the same year he was ordained priest by the papal legate, Cardinal Otto of Ostia. In 1086 he went with Bishop Gebhard as counsellor to King Herman, to the battle of Bleichfeld. About the same time he entered the Benedictine Abbey of St. Blasien in the Black Forest near Schaffhausen, and in 1091 the Abbey of All Saints in the city itself, where he died. His name has ever been associated with the reforms of Gregory VII. The seventeen tracts that have reached us are mostly apologies for the pope's policy, or vindications of men who advocated or enforced it in Germany. Chief among these are: "De prohibendâ sacerdotum incontinentiâ", written against the married clergy; "De damnatione schismaticorum", wherein he justified the pope's condemnation of that abuse; "Apologeticus super excommunicationem Gregorii VII", a defence of the pope's excommunication of Henry IV and his partisans. Bernold is the author of a chronicle (Mon. Germ. Hist., Script., V) which is still highly esteemed. The latter part is a terse record of contemporary events by a knowing and intelligent observer. Dom Morin has shown (Revue Bénédictine, VIII, 385–395) that Bernold is the author of the "Micrologus", an important medieval liturgical treatise. Several other works are ascribed to him, but without sufficient evidence.

STRELAU, *Leben und Werke des Mönches Bernold von Sanct-Blasien* (Jena, 1889); SCHULTZEN, *De Bertholdi et Bernoldi chronicis* (Bonn, 1867); PEYRET, *Bernold de Constance; La Réforme de Saint Grégoire VII* (Saint-Etienne, 1904); PERTZ in *Mon. Germ. Hist., Script.*, V; THANER, *ibid.*, II; WATTENBACH, *Deutschlands Geschichtsquellen im Mittelalter* (Berlin, 1877), II, 43.

THOS. M. SCHWERTNER.

Bernward, SAINT, thirteenth Bishop of Hildesheim, Germany, b. about the middle of the tenth century; d. 20 November, 1022. He claimed descent from a noble Saxon family, which counted among its members men of distinction in Church and State. His grandfather was Athelbero, Count Palatine of Saxony. Having lost his parents at an early age, he came under the care of his uncle Volkmar, Bishop of Utrecht, who entrusted his education to Thangmar, the pious and learned director of the cathedral school at Heidelberg. Under this master, Bernward made rapid progress in Christian piety as well as in the sciences and in the liberal and even mechanical arts. He became very proficient in mathematics, painting, architecture, and particularly in the manufacture of ecclesiastical vessels and ornaments of silver and gold. He completed his studies at Mainz, where he was ordained priest by Archbishop Willigis, Chancellor of the Empire (975–1011). He declined a valuable preferment in the diocese of his uncle, Bishop Volkmar, and chose to remain with his grandfather, Athelbero, to comfort him in his old age. Upon the death of the latter, in 987, he became chaplain at the imperial court, and was shortly afterwards appointed by the Empress-Regent Theophano, tutor to her son Otto III, then six years of age. The youthful emperor is known to have been a learned and religious prince, for which he was indebted in no small degree to his instructor.

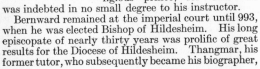

A BERNWARD CANDLESTICK

Bernward remained at the imperial court until 993, when he was elected Bishop of Hildesheim. His long episcopate of nearly thirty years was prolific of great results for the Diocese of Hildesheim. Thangmar, his former tutor, who subsequently became his biographer,

describes in eloquent terms, how the saint, after performing his episcopal functions in the cathedral, was wont to visit the various workshops connected with the cathedral school, and with his own hands manufactured gold and silver vessels for the enrichment of the altars. Under his direction arose numerous churches and other edifices, including even fortifications for the defence of his episcopal city against the invasions of the pagan Normans. As evidences of his skill in the practice of the mechanical arts there are still preserved in Hildesheim a cross of rich and exquisite workmanship, known as the "Bernward Cross", the famous Bernward column, with winding reliefs representing scenes from the life of Christ,

THE BERNWARD CROSS

two bronze doors of the Cathedral of Hildesheim, showing Scriptural scenes, and two candlesticks symbolic of Christ, the light of the world. A monument of his zeal and skill is St. Michael's abbey-church at Hildesheim—now Protestant—one of the most magnificent basilicas in Germany. His knowledge and practice of the arts were wholly employed in the service of the Church. A man of extraordinary piety, he was much given to prayer and the practice of mortification. Shortly before his death in 1022 he had himself invested with the Benedictine habit. He was canonized by Pope Celestine III in 1193. His feast occurs on 20 November.

Stimmen aus Maria Laach (1885), XXVIII; GFRÖRER, *Papst Gregor VII*, V, XXXIII, LIV; KUHN, *Allgemeine Kunst-Geschichte*, XIII.

J. A. BIRKHAEUSER.

Berœa (later, BERRHŒA, BEROIE, and BEROE), a titular see of Macedonia, at the foot of Mount Bermios, now Doxa; it still preserves its ancient name, pronounced Veria by the Greeks (Turkish *Kara-Feria*, Slav *Ber*). The Romans captured it after the battle of Pydna (168 B. C.) and from 49 to 48 Pompey took up his winter quarters there (Plutarch, Pomp. 64). In its Jewish synagogue St. Paul preached successfully (Acts, xvii, 10, 13); on withdrawing he left at Berœa his disciples Silas and Timothy. Onesimus, formerly Philemon's slave, was its first bishop according to the Apostolic Constitutions (VII, 46). At the time of the last partition of the empire, it was allotted to Macedonia Prima (Hierocles, Synecdemos, 638), and its see made suffragan to Thessalonica. Amongst its bishops, Gerontius was present at Sardica in 344, Luke at the Latrocinium of Ephesus in 449, Timothy at the Council of Constantinople under the Patriarch Menas in 536, Joseph at the Eighth Œcumenical Council in 869. Under Andronicus II (1283–1328) Berœa was made a metropolis. The actual Greek metropolitans add the title of Naoussa, a neighbouring city. It has now about 10,000 inhabitants.

Besides this Berœa, there was in Thracia a Beroe, or Augusta Trajana (Hierocles, 635), whither Pope Liberius (355–358) was exiled (Sozomen, IV, 11). It is called Berrhœa, or Beroe, in episcopal lists (Georgius Cyprius, 53; Parthey, Notit. episc., VI, 57; VII, 53; VIII, 57). Its Turkish name was *Eski-Zagra*, for which the present Bulgarian substitute is *Stara-Zagora*. For its episcopal list see Lequien, I, 1165–68; Gams, 427. Berœa is also an ancient name of Aleppo.

LEQUIEN, *Or. Christ.*, II, 71–74; GAMS, *Series episcop.*, 429; LEAKE, *Northern Greece*, III, 290 sqq.; COUSINÉRY, *Voyage en Macédoine*, I, 57 sqq.

L. PETIT.

Berosus (Βηρωσός or Βηρωσσός), the name of a native historian of Babylonia and a priest of the great god Bel (Bel-Marduk). He flourished during and after the lifetime of Alexander the Great, although the exact dates of his birth and death are unknown. It is certain, however, that he lived in the days of Alexander (356–326 B. C.) and continued to live at least as late as Antiochus I Soter (280–261 B. C.), to whom he dedicated his famous history of Babylonia. The meaning of his name is uncertain, notwithstanding the fanciful etymology of Scaliger and others who claim it is composed of *Bar* and *Hosea*, "Son of Hosea". Concerning his personality very little is known with certainty. According to Vitruvius and Pliny (whose testimony, taken as a whole, is to be accepted with caution), Berosus was profoundly versed in the science of astronomy and astrology; that much is certain. Leaving Babylonia, he settled for awhile in Greece, on the island of Cos, where he opened a school of astronomy and astrology. From there he passed to Athens where his wonderful learning and remarkable astronomical predictions brought him such fame that a statue with a gilt tongue was erected in his honour in the public gymnasium. Vitruvius attributes to him the invention of a semi-circular sundial. Justin Martyr, undoubtedly through a misunderstanding, affirms that the Babylonian Sibyl who gave oracles at Cumæ in the time of the Tarquins was a daughter of Berosus. Tatian, the disciple of Justin, and himself a Mesopotamian by birth, rightly calls Berosus the most learned historian of Western Asia. It is doubtful, however, whether the Babylonian Berosus is the same personage as the astronomer Berosus of whom many Greek and Latin historians make mention.

Berosus wrote a history of Babylonia, probably under title of "Babyloniaca", though it is referred to under the title of "Chaldaica" by Josephus and Clement of Alexandria. The work was divided into three books, or parts, of which the first dealt with human history from the beginning of the world to the Flood, the second from the Flood to Nabonassar (747 B. C.), and the third from Nabonassar to Alexander the Great and even as far down as the reign of his patron Antiochus. The materials of this history, written in Greek, he professes to have derived from ancient Babylonian chronicles and inscriptions preserved in the temple of Bel in Babylon, and there is every reason to believe in the truth of his assertion, as most of his statements, notwithstanding the manifold and unconscientious handlings which his work underwent at the hands of later Greek and

Roman writers, show a remarkable agreement with the cuneiform records and inscriptions found in the libraries and temples of Babylonia and Assyria. Unfortunately, however, by far the greater part of this priceless work has perished. What has come down is in the form of fragments preserved principally by late Greek historians and writers, such as Alexander Polyhistor, Abydenus, and Apollodorus, whose writings are quoted by Josephus, Nicholas of Damascus, Julius Africanus, Eusebius, Syncellus, and a few others. So it is apparent that the views put forth by Berosus come down in a very roundabout manner. In places his statements have been so garbled as to seem absurd, and yet, fragmentary as his work is, it is of great importance.

Of the origin of the gods and of the world, according to the cosmology and mythology of the Babylonians, Berosus has the following account, preserved by Damascius, which shows a remarkable agreement with the Babylonian Creation epic discovered recently and masterly discussed and studied by Smith, Delitzsch, Jenson, Zimmern, Jastrow, King, Dhorme, and others. "Among the barbarians, the Babylonians seem to pass over the first of all principles in silence, imagining two to begin with, Tavthe (Tiamat, the Hebrew Tehôm) and Apason (Apsu), making Apason the consort of Tavthe, whom they called the 'mother of the gods'. The issue of their union, as they said, was an only son, Myomis (Mummu), who seems to me to stand for the visible world, offspring of the first two principles, from whom are subsequently produced another generation, Dache and Dachos (should be Lachme and Lachmos = Laḥamu and Luḥmu). A third follows from the same parents, Kissare (Kishar) and Assoros (Anshar), of whom three gods are born: Anos (Anu), Illinois (Elim? = Bel) and Aos (Ea); finally the son of Aos and of Davke is Belos (Bel-Marduk), called by them the 'demiurge'" (Damascius, De primis principiis, ed. Kopp, 125, p. 184).

Berosus's account of the creation of the world and of mankind, as preserved to us by Syncellus who copied it from Alexander Polyhistor, runs as follows: "There was a time when all was darkness and water, and from the midst thereof issued spontaneously monstrous animals and the most peculiar figures: men with two wings, and others with four, with two faces or two heads, one of a man, the other of a woman, on one body, and with the two sexes together; men with goats' legs and goats' horns, or with horses' hoofs; others with the hinder parts of a horse and the foreparts of a man, like the hippocentaurs. There were, besides, human-headed bulls, dogs with four bodies and fishes' tails, horses with dogs' heads, animals with the head and body of a horse and the tail of a fish, other quadrupeds in which all sorts of animal shapes were confused together, fishes, reptiles, serpents, and every kind of marvellous monster presenting the greatest variety in their shapes, representations of which may be seen in the paintings of the temple of Belos. A woman named Omoroca (Um-Uruk, the mother of Uruk) presided over this creation; in the Chaldean language she bears the name of Thavatth (Tiamat), signifying in Greek 'the sea', and she is also identified with the moon.

"Things being in this condition, Belos (Bel-Marduk) came upon the scene and cut the woman in half; of the lower part of her body he made the earth, and of the upper half the heavens, and all the creatures that were in her disappeared. This is a figurative way of explaining the production of the universe and of animated beings from humid matter. Belos then cut off his own head, and the other gods having kneaded the blood flowing from it with the earth, formed men, who by that means were gifted with understanding, and made participants of divine thought.

"Thus it was that Belos, interpreted by the Greeks as signifying Zeus, having divided the darkness, separated the heavens and the earth, and ordered the world; and all animated beings who were not able to endure the action of light perished. Belos, seeing that the earth was a desert, though fertile, commanded one of the gods to cut off his head, and kneading the blood which flowed with earth, he produced men, as well as those animals who are able to live in contact with the air.—Then Belos also formed the stars, the sun, the moon, and the five planets." (Ap. Syncell., 29; Euseb., Chronic. Armen., I, ii, iv, ed. Mai, p. 10; ed. Lenormant, Fragment 1.)

His account of the Deluge, which shows a remarkable agreement with the eleventh tablet of the Gilgamesh epic and a striking similarity to the parallel narrative of Genesis, is of great importance, and has come down to us through Alexander Polyhistor; a short extract is also given by Abydenus. After referring to the ten antediluvian kings (cf. the ten antediluvian patriarchs of Genesis), Berosus proceeds as follows: "Obartes (Ubaratutu) being dead, his son, Xisuthros, reigned eighteen sars (64,800 years). It was in his time that the great Deluge came to pass, the history of which is related in the following manner in the sacred documents: Cronus (Ea) appeared to him in his sleep and announced to him that on the 15th of the month of Daisios (the Assyrian month Sivan, a little before the summer solstice), all mankind would perish by a deluge. He then commanded him to take the beginning, the middle and the end of all that had been consigned to writing, and to bury it in the city of the Sun, Sippara; after that to build a ship, and go on board of it with his family and dearest friends; to place in the vessel provisions for food and drink, and to introduce into it animals, both fowls and quadrupeds; lastly, to get everything ready for navigation. And when Xisuthros asked in which direction he should steer his vessel, he was told 'toward the gods', and to pray that good should come of it to men.

"Xisuthros obeyed, and built a ship five stadia long and two broad; he gathered in all that had been commanded him, and took on board his wife, his children, and his intimate friends.

"The deluge having come upon them, and soon subsiding, Xisuthros loosed some birds, who, having found neither food or place of rest, returned to the vessel. Some days later, Xisuthros again gave them their liberty, but they returned once more to the ship, their feet soiled with mud.

"At last, being loosed for a third time, the birds returned no more. Then Xisuthros understood that the earth was bare; he made an opening in the roof of the ship and found that it had gone aground upon a mountain. Then he came down with his wife, his daughter and his pilot, worshipped the Earth, raised an altar and sacrificed thereon to the gods; at this moment he disappeared with those who bore him company.

"Nevertheless, those who remained in the ship, not seeing Xisuthros return, also descended to the ground and began to look for him, calling him by name. They never saw Xisuthros again, but a voice from heaven made itself heard, bidding them be pious towards the gods; that he had received the reward of his piety in being taken up to dwell henceforth among the gods, and his wife, his daughter and the pilot of the vessel shared this great honour. The voice said, moreover, to those who were left, that they should return to Babylonia, and agreeably to the decrees of fate dig up the writings buried at Sippara, in order to transmit them to men. It added that the country where they then were was Armenia. After hearing the voice they sacrificed to the gods, and returned on foot to Babylonia. A portion of Xisuthros' ship, which finally went aground

in Armenia, is still found in the Gordyæan Mountains in Armenia, and pilgrims bring away asphaltum which they have scraped from the fragments; they use it against witchcraft. As to the companions of Xisuthros, they arrived in Babylonia, dug up the writings buried at Sippara, founded a number of cities, built temples, and restored Babylon".

The chronological history of Babylonia, according to Berosus, was as follows: The first period, reaching from the Creation to the Flood, is said to have included ten reigns of 432,000 years. Some of the names of these antediluvian kings have been found also in the cuneiform inscriptions. The second period includes eighty-six kings and a period of 34,080 years, which bring us down to about 2500 B. C. The third period includes eight Median kings who, towards 2500 B. C. must have invaded Babylonia. These are followed by eleven other monarchs, the record of the duration of whose reigns is lost. The fifth period includes forty-nine Chaldean kings and 458 years. The end of this period brings us down to about 2000 B. C. The sixth period includes nine Arabian kings with 245 years. This so-called Arabian dynasty is identical with the now historically ascertained first Semitic dynasty, to which Hammurabi belonged. The seventh period includes forty-five kings and 526 years. The succeeding parts of Berosus's chronology are lost, up to the period of Nabonassar whose era commenced in 747 B. C. The history of this period, which reaches the reign of Alexander the Great, including such illustrious kings as Nabopolassar, Nebuchadnezzar, Nabonidus, Cyrus, etc., is well known to us from the cuneiform inscriptions.

Collections of the fragments of Berosus have been made by RICHTER (Leipzig, 1825); MÜLLER, *Fragmenta Historicum Græcorum* (2 vols., Paris, 1848); CORY, *Ancient Fragments* (London, 1832). The best and most exhaustive study on Berosus and his history is that of the late Catholic Assyriologist, LENORMANT, *Essai de Commentaire de fragments cosmogoniques de Bérose* (Paris, 1871). For the best text of Berosus see EUSEBIUS, SCHÖNE ed., with GUTSCHMID's comments. See also SMITH, *Dictionary of Greek and Roman Biography and Mythology*, s. v.; ROGERS, *History of Babylonia and Assyria* (New York, 1901), I, 258 sqq., 327 sqq.; BRUNENGO, *L'impero di Babilonia e di Ninive* (1885), I, 67 sqq.

GABRIEL OUSSANI.

Beroth (BEEROTH), a city in Chanaan, one of the confederation of cities under the headship of Gabaon (Gibeon), whose territory was invaded by the Israelites under Josue (Jos., ix). Its inhabitants, together with those of three neighbouring cities, in order to save themselves from extermination, went to Josue in the disguise of travellers from afar and begged mercy; the Israelites entered into a league with them, but when the deception was discovered made them hewers of wood and drawers of water for themselves. Their city was afterwards assigned to the tribe of Benjamin (Jos., xviii, 25), but it seems to have remained Chanaanite till the monarchy, as it was only "reckoned" among the cities of Benjamin (II Kings, iv, 2). Later the Berothites fled to Gethaim (iv, 3), probably at the time Saul sought to slay the Gabaonites (Gibeonites, II Kings, xxi, 2), with whom the Berothites seem to have been reckoned (Jos., ix, 3, 17). Two descendants of these Berothites slew Isboseth, the son of Saul, claimant to his throne and rival of David; they brought his head to David, who punished the murder with death (II Kings, iv). Probably revenge on Saul for his injury to their fathers was one of their motives, for blood feud was regarded as a duty. Naharai, armour-bearer of Joab, David's great general, was a Berothite (II Kings, xxiii, 37), and we read of men of Beroth among the returned exiles (I Esd., ii, 25; II Esd., vii, 29), though these were more probably Israelites.

Beroth is usually identified with El-Bîreh, a town of 800 inhabitants, about 9 miles north of Jerusalem, near which is an abundance of water (Beroth, wells) at which tradition reports Joseph and Mary halted on their return from Jerusalem when they missed the Child Jesus (Luke, ii). It was the usual stopping place of caravans to Nâbulus and Nazareth.

LEGENDRE in VIG., *Dict. de la Bible* (Paris, 1895); ROBINSON, *Biblical Researches in Palestine* (Boston, 1874), I, 452.

JOHN F. FENLON.

Berrettini, PIETRO (called PIETRO DA CORTONA), a distinguished Italian painter, architect, and writer, b. at Cortona, in Tuscany, 1 November, 1596; d. at Rome, 16 May, 1669. He studied first under his uncle, Filippo Berrettini, and then at Florence under Andrea Commodi. At the age of fifteen he left that city for Rome, and entered the studio of Baccio Ciarpi, a Florentine painter. There he applied himself to the study of the works of Raphael, Michelangelo, and Polidoro, to that of the antique sculptures and notably of the bas-reliefs of the column of Trajan. While still very young he attracted the attention of Cardinal Sacchetti, who became his protector, and for whom were painted the first two of his works, "The Battles of Alexander" and "The Rape of the Sabines". Thereupon, Pope Urban VIII gave him the order to decorate a chapel of the church of Santa Bibiana. Such was his success there that he received the commission to paint what proved to be his most celebrated work, the ceiling of the great *salon* of the Barberini Palace, representing, in allegory, the history of that family. He then designed some mosaics for the dome of St. Peter's. After a trip through Lombardy and a sojourn at Venice, he went to Florence, where the Grand Duke Ferdinand II employed him to decorate the Pitti Palace. There he painted several important frescoes, but left without completing the series, angered by the actions of jealous rivals. The compositions included "Clemency of Alexander to the Family of Darius", "The History of Masinissa", "The Continence of Cyrus", and "The Firmness of Porsenna". The work was completed by his pupil Ciro Ferri. On his return to Rome Berrettini received many important commissions, acquiring a great reputation. He executed a number of frescoes in churches, as well as easel pictures. He became wealthy, and Pope Alexander VII created him a Chevalier of the Order of the Golden Spur. His principal pupils were Francesco Romanelli, Ferri, Testa, Giordano, and Borgognone. He is buried in the church of San Martino, of which he was architect, and to which he left a large sum of money.

BRYAN, *Dictionary of Painters and Engravers* (London and New York, 1903–05).

AUGUSTUS VAN CLEEF.

Berruguete, ALONSO, for his mastery of the arts of painting, sculpture, and architecture, sometimes called the Spanish Michelangelo, b. at Paredes de Nava, in Castile, about 1480; d. at Toledo, 1561. He was the second son of the painter, Pedro Berruguete, who was his first instructor. His family, however, chose the law for his profession and obtained for him an official position at Valladolid, the title of which he held for years, probably long after he had devoted himself to art. It is said that the fame of Michelangelo led him to Italy after his father's death and he entered the school of that great master in Florence and had among his friends Andrea del Sarto and Bandinelli. In the competition with Leonardo he made a copy of Buonarroti's great cartoon of Pisa. Accompanying his master to Rome, where he assisted him in the Vatican, he was one of the sculptors chosen by Bramante to compete in making a copy of the Laocoön to be cast in bronze, Sansovino, however, being the winner. On his return to Florence, he was engaged by the nuns of San Geronimo to finish an altarpiece left unfinished at

his death by Filippo Lippi. After a long residence in Italy, Berruguete, in 1520, went back to Spain, where he was greatly honoured by Charles V, who appointed him a chamberlain, and court painter and sculptor, and gave him much work to do at Madrid, at the Palace of El Prado, and at the Alhambra. With Philip II he continued in favour and became a rich man, married a lady of quality and bought the lordship of Ventosa near Valladolid. After his return to Spain, the artist lived for some time at Saragossa, where he made an altar and a tomb for the church of Santa Engracia. At Valladolid he executed many works for churches and monasteries, notable among which is the high altar of the Church of San Benito el Real, belonging to the convent of the Benedictines, on which he spent six years. Berruguete worked with Felipe de Vigar on the sculptures of the cathedral at Toledo. There also, in the hospital of St. John the Baptist, is one of his finest works, executed when he was nearly eighty years of age, the monument of its founder, the Cardinal Archbishop Juan de Tavera. His best work in painting is considered to be in the cathedral of Palencia and in the church of Ventosa; his best work in bronze and marble in the cathedral and other buildings of Toledo.

SIR WILLIAM STIRLING-MAXWELL, *Annals of the Artists of Spain* (London, 1891); BRYAN, *Dictionary of Painters and Engravers* (London and New York, 1903–05).

AUGUSTUS VAN CLEEF.

Berruyer, ISAAC-JOSEPH, b. at Rouen, 7 November, 1681; d. at Paris, 18 February, 1758. He entered the Society of Jesus in 1697. His great work is a "History of the People of God", published in three parts. The first of these parts bears the title "Histoire du peuple de Dieu depuis son origine jusqu'à la venue du Messie" (7 vols., Paris, 1728). A revised and augmented edition of this was published at Paris in 1733. Next followed (Paris, 1734) a supplement, containing the continuation of the prophesies of the Old Testament, the History of Job, maps necessary for understanding the sacred history, etc. By 1736 seven editions of the work had been issued. It was translated into German, Spanish, Italian, and Polish. The second part of the "History" was published, also at Paris, in 1753: "Histoire du peuple de Dieu depuis la naissance du Messie jusqu'à la fin de la Synagogue". In 1754 an *édition plus exacte* appeared at Antwerp (8 vols.), and in 1755, at Paris, still another edition (4 vols.). The latter contained five questions: (1) On Christ, the object of the Scriptures; (2) On Christ, the Son of God; (3) On Christ, the Son of Man; (4) On Christ, the founder of a new religion; (5) On the Presentation of Christ in the Temple and the Purification of the B. V. M. According to de Backer, this second part of the History was published without the knowledge, and against the will, of the superiors of the Jesuit house in Paris. Berruyer put his name to only a small number of copies of this publication. The third part of the work has the title, "Histoire du peuple de Dieu, ou paraphase des Epîtres des Apôtres" (2 vols., Lyons, 1757).

The work, as its various parts appeared, aroused a great uproar and some bitter controversy. Written in a brilliant, very rhetorical and lively style, it was, nevertheless, deservedly criticized. Serious fault was found with the author for giving to portions of the sacred narrative the air of romance rather than of sober history. The freedom with which he described certain facts was considered unbecoming in a Christian writer, and offensive to the Christian reader. Some propositions put forward by him were construed as favouring Nestorianism. But above all Berruyer was blamed for following the singular and paradoxical opinions of Hardouin. For these reasons the work was condemned by many bishops of France, by the superiors of the society, by the Sorbonne, and by the Parliament of Paris. The first part was put on the Index, 27 May, 1732; the second part, 3 December, 1754, and by a Brief of Benedict XIV, 17 February, 1758; the third part 24 April, 1758, and by a Brief of Clement XIII, 2 December, 1758. (See "Index Librorum Prohibitorum", Rome, 1900, 62). A corrected edition of the first part, approved by the Roman censors, was published at Besançon in 1828.

SOMMERVOGEL, *Bibl. de la c. de J.*, I, 1357; DE BACKER, *Bibl. des écrivains de la c. de J.*, III, 144; HURTER, *Nomenclator Literarius*, II, 1350.

JOSEPH M. WOODS.

Berryer, PIERRE-ANTOINE, French advocate, orator, and statesman, son of Pierre-Nicolas Berryer, an advocate, b. at Paris, 4 January, 1790; d. at Augerville, 29 November, 1868. A pupil of the Collège de Juilly, which the Oratorians had reopened in 1796, Berryer, after having believed himself favoured with an ecclesiastical vocation, eventually consecrated himself to the forensic career. "Leaving college to the sound of the artillery of Jena", he displayed his Bonapartist sentiments in certain verses upon Marie Louise which he wrote in 1810; but eighteen months' study of the reports of the Constituent Assembly, under the guidance of Bonnemant, a former member of that assembly, made a monarchist of Berryer, in 1812, and a monarchist he remained to the end of his days. He always maintained the principle that "the king is not the head of a party"; he took the view that France was not antagonistic to the king personally, or to the king's right, but to the monarchist party, and it was always Berryer's idiosyncrasy to be independent with respect to that party. He distinguished himself at the beginning of the Restoration by assisting his father and the elder Dupin in the defence of Marshal Ney and by his own defence of two generals, Debelle and Cambronne, compromised in the Hundred Days. Debelle, condemned to death, had his punishment commuted to ten years' imprisonment, after an application made by Berryer to the Duc d'Angoulême; Cambronne was acquitted, and Berryer, accused of having in his speech for the defence, maintained the right of insurrection, defended himself victoriously. In 1818 he defended General Canuel, and in 1820 General Donnadieu, both charged with exaggerating the importance of the Lyons and Grenoble risings, which they had suppressed. These interventions of Berryer were very displeasing to the Decazes ministry; but the young advocate, having thus combated the spirit of reprisals against the old Napoleonic army, which the Restoration was developing, next directed his energies to opposing a certain shade of liberalism which seemed to him dangerous to monarchical principles. In 1830, in order to supply the property qualification needed to legalize his election as Deputy for the Department of Haute-Loire, his friends purchased for him the estate of Angerville, in Loiret. His first parliamentary speech (9 March, 1830) was in defence of the Crown and the Polignac Ministry against the address of the two hundred and twenty-one, which he considered seditious. On hearing this speech Royer-Collard remarked, "There is a Power" (*Voilà une puissance*).

Under the July Monarchy Berryer was one of the most formidable members of the opposition. After vainly endeavouring to dissuade the Duchesse de Berri from her insurrectionary enterprise, he was himself arrested as an accomplice, but was acquitted by the jury. He then entered upon a campaign for the liberation of the duchess, and defended Chateaubriand against the charge of complicity. Returned by various constituencies in successive general elections he was the idol of both Legitimists and Republicans. His political life interfered so much

II.—33

with his law practice that in order to live he was obliged to sell his estate of Angerville; Legitimists and Republicans united, in 1836, to buy it back for him. He continued to advocate every measure calculated to limit the arbitrary power of the central government—jury trials for press offences, nomination of mayors by the communes, abolition of the property qualification. The speech was long famous with which, in 1834, he defeated the treaty according to the United States tardy compensation for vessels confiscated by Napoleon. He was of counsel for the defence in the case of Louis Bonaparte's Boulogne attempt, in 1840; defended the Republican Ledru-Rollin in 1841, in a series of four addresses to the Chamber; in 1844 gloried in the "Belgrave Square Pilgrimage" which, with four other Legitimists, he had made to the Comte de Chambord. Elected by the Department of Bouches-du-Rhône to the Constituent Assembly of 1848, and to the Legislative of 1849, Berryer voted with the Right, but without supporting any of the intrigues of Louis Bonaparte. After the 2d of December 1851, he returned to his practice at the Bar. Montalembert, prosecuted in 1858 for an article suspected of advocating for France the liberties of England, had Berryer for his advocate. Monarchist to the end, he exerted himself as a private individual to reconcile the Houses of Bourbon and Orléans. In 1863 he was chosen to represent the Bouches-du-Rhône, sat with the opposition, and sharply attacked the Mexican war policy of the Imperial Government.

The Academy received Berryer in 1855; on the 20th of December, 1861, the fiftieth anniversary of his call to the Bar, all the advocates of France united in honouring him with a splendid banquet. Only a few days before his death, he wrote to the Comte de Chambord a letter which is an admirable testament of the Monarchist faith. Berryer was a life-long defender of religious liberty. He was the first to make clear (in his articles on the Gallican Church in the "Quotidienne") the changes wrought by the Revolution in the relations between Church and State; he showed that what the State called "Gallican liberties" represented henceforth only a right to oppress the Church. In 1846 and 1847, in two letters to Bishop Fayet of Orléans, he urged Catholics to take their stand on the common ground of liberty. It was in this spirit that, in 1826, he had pleaded for Lamennais, who had accused the Gallican Church of atheism, and that, in 1828, he wrote against the Martignac ordinances on the episcopal schools (*petits séminaires*). In 1831 he spoke against the re-establishment of divorce; in 1833 against the project of Portalis tending to state recognition of marriages by priests. His reply to M. Thiers, 3 March, 1845, on the Jesuits, remains, says M. Thureau-Dangin, "a sovereign, definitive refutation of all those who, then or since, have pretended to invoke against the religious orders the old laws of proscription". Berryer defended the religious associations with all the more authority because, in that same year, pleading for three carpenters who had combined to secure a suspension of work, he formally asserted the right of labour to combine (*droit de coalition ouvrière*), which right French law was not to recognize until 1863. He gained great popularity among the labouring classes when he compared the restrictions imposed on them with the toleration accorded to "coalitions formed in other spheres of society, with the aim of securing not a wage-increase of 10 centimes, but an enormous advantage for operations involving hundreds of millions". Liberty of association for all; respect by the State for the autonomy of the Church—such was the principle from which he never wavered, and in the name of which he brought about, in 1850, the defeat of Jules Favre's project which would have compelled the Church to re-establish the non-amovability of certain members (*desservants*) of the lower clergy. The return of Berryer to the practice of his religious duties, under the influence of his friend, Père de Ravignan, S. J., was the crowning reward of his fruitful activity in behalf of the Church.

Berryer never wrote his discourses; he meditated before speaking. Even his apparent improvisations were deceptive—"The extempore speaker", he used to say, "has repeated the same thing to himself twenty or a hundred times." During the Restoration his lectures on eloquence at the "Société des Bonnes Etudes" were attended by such men as Montalembert and Lacordaire. He was admired by all for his sincerity and the absence of all oratorical artifice. There was something astounding in the suddenness with which, after a moment of apparent inattention, he was wont to crush his opponent's argument. "If I could act as M. Berryer speaks!" said the actress Rachel, moved by his natural and spontaneous eloquence. On another occasion when Berryer was speaking against Jules Favre, the latter referred to him as "my sublime adversary".

BERRYER, *Discours parlementaires*, 5 vols.; *Plaidoyers*, 4 vols. (Paris, 1872-78); CAUVIÈRE, *Berryer, sa vie judiciaire, ses discours* (Marseilles, 1871); LECANUET, *Berryer* (Paris, 1892); LACOMBE, *Berryer*, 3 vols. (Paris, 1894-95), the leading work on Berryer.

GEORGES GOYAU.

Bersabee (באר שבע‎), or BEERSHEBA, a town on the southern extremity of Palestine, one of the most familiar geographical names of Holy Writ, known on account of its position and its connexion with several incidents in Hebrew history. Throughout most of that history, it was proverbially the extreme point to the south in the country; from "Dan to Bersabee" included the entire length of the country, from north to south (Jud., xx, 1, etc.; I Par., xxi, 2 "from Bersabee to Dan"); later, after the destruction of the northern kingdom, the territory was sometimes described as extending "from Gabaa to Bersabee" (IV K., xxiii, 8), or "from Bersabee to Mount Ephraim" (II Par., xix, 4); and finally, after the exile, the place still remains as the southernmost point in the phrase "from Bersabee unto the valley of Ennom" (II Esdras, xi, 30). Milton has helped to fix the name and locality of the town in the minds of English readers by his reference

To Beërsaba, where the Holy Land
Borders on Egypt and the Arabian shore.

Still, it was not exactly on the southern border, which was considered to run "along the 'river of Egypt', the present Wady el-Arish, nearly 60 m. S. E. of Beersheba" (G. A. Smith); but there was little arable land beyond it, and it was practically the last stopping point in the country.

The name means, literally, "the well of seven", but Gen., xxi, 30, 31, and xxvi, 26-33, explain it as "the well of swearing". The former narrative, with its insistence on the "seven" (*sheba*) ewe-lambs, leads one to expect the name to be interpreted as "the well of seven", and inclines one to regard the other explanation as a gloss, or as evidence of the interweaving of another narrative; yet it may be "that the two explanations resolve themselves into one; for the Hebrew word 'to swear' (*nishba*, the reflexive of the unused *shāba*) seems to mean properly (as it were) 'to seven-oneself', i. e. to pledge oneself in some way by seven sacred things, so that if it be assumed that the 'seven lambs' were used for this purpose, only one ceremony would be described in the passage" (Driver, Genesis, 215). Seven was regarded as a sacred number. Still, Driver prefers the explanation "well of seven", that is, seven wells; but there is no evidence that there were ever seven wells in the vicinity. G. A. Smith inclines to the meaning, "well of the seven gods", but offers no proof to support it.

Each of the two narratives referred to has its own account of the occasion which gave rise to the name. In the first, it was bestowed by Abraham, when, after a conflict between his herdsmen and those of King Abimelech as to the ownership of a well, he concluded a covenant with the king, who was accompanied by his captain, Phicol. In the second, it was bestowed many years later by Isaac when, after a conflict between his herdsmen and those of King Abimelech as to the ownership of a well, he concluded a covenant with the king, who was accompanied by his captain, Phicol. Other points in the two accounts are parallel also, though there are many differences. The traditional opinion regards them as narratives of two different series of events which befell the two patriarchs, surprising in certain details, perhaps, yet not remarkable for the essential facts which are such as might easily recur. The modern critical opinion considers that the same tradition became attached to two different names and was embodied in two different documents (the Elohistic and the Jahvistic; see articles: ABRAHAM, GENESIS, PENTATEUCH). "Doubtless, history repeats itself", says Prof. Sayce (Early Hebrew History, 64); "disputes about the possession of wells in a desert-land can frequently recur, and it is possible that two kings of the same name may have followed one another on the throne of Gerar. But what does not seem very possible is that each of these kings should have had a 'chief captain of his host' called by the strange non-Semitic name of Phicol; that each of them should have taken the wife of the patriarch, believing her to be his sister; or that Beersheba should twice have received the same name from the oaths sworn over it." The differences of detail are regarded by the upholders of the traditional opinion as proofs that two distinct facts are related, and by critics as variations that "would naturally arise from the fluctuation of tradition". (Driver, Genesis, 255.)

Bersabee, the village that grew up around the wells at this spot, is identified with the present Bir es-Seba which is twenty-eight miles south-west of Hebron, on the road to Egypt. The country surrounding it, known as the desert of Bersabee, is a soil that is said to be naturally very fertile, needing only irrigation to make it productive; the few cultivated plots in the valley give "fine crops of wheat and barley". In the spring, sheep, goats, and camels find there a rich pasture land. Three wells may be seen there to-day, one of which, however, is dry. The largest is believed to have been dug by Abraham (Gen., xxi) and is at least very ancient. It is a solidly constructed piece of masonry, about thirty-eight feet deep; it still furnishes abundant sweet water. The climate of Bersabee, though very hot, is regarded as healthy. The highest altitude is 950 feet above the Mediterranean. At this day, the desert presents a picture of the same pastoral, patriarchal life that we see in Genesis (Conder, Palestine, 52-55). Bersabee, with the desert around, is the cradle of the Hebrew race and connected with memories of Agar and Ismael (Gen., xxi), of Abraham (ib.), of Isaac (xxvi), of Jacob who was born there, and his sons (xxviii, xlvi), of the sons of Samuel (I K., viii, 2), of Elias (III K., iii), and of Amos, who denounced its idolatry (v, 5, viii, 14). It formed, at first, part of the territory of Juda (Josue, xv, 28) and later fell to the lot of Simeon (xix, 2). Its site as a halting-place on the road to Egypt made it well known to all. After the Exile, it again became a centre for the Jews (II Esd., xi, 27), and in the days of the empire had a Roman garrison. It was most flourishing in the early Christian ages, when the hermits flocked there. For a time, it was an episcopal see. Extensive ruins of dwellings and public edifices, mostly of Roman days, still remain.

CONDER, *Palestine* (New York, s. d.); IDEM, *Tent Work* (London, 1880); DRIVER, *Genesis* (New York, 1904); LEGENDRE in Vig., *Dict. de la Bible;* Smith in *Encyc. Bib.* (New York, 1899); Hull in Hast., *Dict. of Bible* (New York, 1903).

JOHN F. FENLON.

Bertha.—Of the various holy women bearing the name of Bertha, five are more particularly worthy of notice. I. Bertha, Queen of Kent, d. c. 612. She was a Frankish princess, daughter of Charibert and the pious Ingoberga. In marrying the pagan King Ethelbert of Kent, she brought her chaplain Liudhard with her, and restored a Christian church in Canterbury, which dated from the Roman occupation, dedicating it to St. Martin. The present St. Martin's at Canterbury occupies the same site. St. Augustine, who was sent by Gregory the Great to preach the Gospel in England in 596, no doubt owed much of his favourable reception to the influence of Bertha. St. Gregory in 601 addressed to her a letter of thanks, which is still preserved. It is printed in Haddan and Stubbs, III, 17. Ethelbert himself was baptized on Whitsunday in 597, and Canterbury became the mother-church of England. Bertha was sometimes styled "Saint", but there is no clear evidence of cultus. (See, on this point, the poems of Reginald of Canterbury in the "Neues Archiv", xiii.) Fuller accounts of Bertha will be found in Lingard, "Anglo-Saxon Church;" "Dict. Nat. Biog.", Plummer, "Bede", and Routledge, "Church of St. Martin".

II. St. Bertha, virgin and martyr, Abbess of Val d'Or, near Avenay, Reims, d. about 690. She was wife of St. Gumbert, Lord of Champenois, a nobleman of royal blood. He built a nunnery for his wife and her maidens at Avenay, and retired himself to a monastery on the coast, where he was soon afterwards put to death by pagan marauders. When the people of Avenay suffered from lack of water, St. Peter appeared to Bertha and showed her a field where there was a good spring. This she bought for a pound of silver. It became a holy well which cured diseases and supplied both her own nuns and the hamlet of Avenay with water. Bertha was martyred by Gumbert's relatives, who were indignant at the distribution of his money to the poor. Whether the abbey founded at Avenay followed the Benedictine or the Columban Rule, does not seem certain even to Mabillon. The whole legend in fact is very late and unreliable. St. Bertha's feast is on the 1st of May. (See Acta SS. for that day.)

III. St. Bertha, Abbess of Blangy in Artois, d. about 725. She was the daughter of Rigobert, Count of the Palace under Clovis II, and married Siegfried, a relation of the king. After twenty years, when he died, she determined to found a nunnery. Two buildings which she constructed fell down, but an angel in a vision guided her to another spot, and there after many difficulties a nunnery was built, which she entered with her two elder daughters, Deotila and Gertrude. A still later legend represents this Gertrude as much persecuted by the attentions of a great noble, Roger, who wished to marry her by force, but she was saved from his violence by her mother's firm courage and trust in God. Some time before her death Bertha is said to have resigned her office of abbess and to have shut herself up in a little cell built against the church wall. But the whole story of Bertha, as Mabillon and the Bollandists agree, is of very late date and historically worthless. Her feast is kept on the 4th of July. (See Acta SS. for that day, and Décobert, "Ste. Berthe et son Abbaye de Blangy", Lille, 1892.)

IV. Blessed Bertha de Bardi, abbess, b. in Florence, date uncertain; d. 24 March, 1163. She was the daughter of Lothario di Ugo, Count of Vernio, and is ordinarily called Bertha de Bardi, but the name should probably be d'Alberti. She joined the order of Vallombrosa, a branch of the Benedictines, at Florence, but she was soon sent to govern and reform a convent of the order at Cavriglia in

Valdarno, where she lived famous for miracles until her death. (See Acta SS. for that day, and Soldani, "Vita di S. Berta", Florence, 1731.)

V. Blessed Bertha de Marbais, d. 1247. She was a Cistercian nun, who became the first abbess of a convent which was founded by Jane, Countess of Flanders, in 1227 at Marquette or Marchet, near Lille. She died on 18 July, and is briefly noticed on that day in the Acta SS. Bertha is called Blessed by the Cistercian chronicler, Henriquez, but the evidence of cultus is very slight.

Dunbar, *Dictionary of Saintly Women* (London, 1904); Chevalier, *Répertoire des sources historiques: Bio-Bibliographie* (Paris, 1905).

HERBERT THURSTON.

Berthier, Guillaume-François, a Jesuit professor and writer, b. at Issoudun, 1704; d. at Bourges, 1782. He taught philosophy at Rennes and Rouen, and theology at Paris. From 1745 to 1762 he was editor of the "Mémoires de Trévoux", and because of his powerful opposition to the infidel "encyclopédistes" was bitterly attacked, notably by Voltaire. Between 1745 and 1749 he published volumes XIII to XVIII of the history of the French Church (1320–1559). The previous volumes had been prepared by Fathers Longueval (I–VIII), Fontenai (IX, X, and part of XI), and Brumoy (end of XI and XII). In 1762, when the Society of Jesus was suppressed in France, the Dauphin appointed him tutor of his sons and librarian of the court library, but two years later his position at court became so disagreeable that he left France and spent the following ten years in Germany. On his return, in 1774, he retired to Bourges. These years of retirement were spent in study and writing. After his death several of his works were published by Father de Querbeuf: (1) A translation of the Psalms with notes (8 vols.); this was often reprinted. (2) Five volumes on Isaias. (3) Five volumes of "Réflexions Spirituelles".

De Querbeuf in *Psaumes traduits*, preface; Sommervogel, *Bibl. de la c. de J.*, I, 1377 with complete bibliography; Brucker in *Dict. de théol. cath.*, s. v.

JOHN CORBETT.

Berthold, Bishop, Apostle of the Livonians, killed 24 July, 1198, in a crusade against the pagan Livonians who threatened destruction to all Christians that lived in their territory. He was previously Abbot of the Cistercian monastery of Lockum in Hanover. At the death of Meinhard, the first Bishop of Livonia (c. 1196), Archbishop Hartwig of Bremen, to whose province belonged the newly converted countries along the eastern shores of the Baltic Sea, appointed Abbot Berthold successor. It seems very probable that, as Damberger asserts in his "Synchronistische Geschichte der Kirche und der Welt im Mittelalter", when Meinhard came to Bremen in 1186 to obtain help in his apostolic labours in Livonia, Berthold joined the band of missionaries who accompanied him thither. On this assumption, Berthold had been working ten years as a missionary among the Livonians when he became their second bishop and was, therefore, well acquainted with his field of labour.

The Livonian pagans were fanatically opposed to Christianity. Berthold's predecessor, assisted by merchants from Bremen and Lübeck and a few converted natives, had built fortifications along the River Düna, where the Christians held their religious services and could protect themselves against the fury of the pagans. Following in the footsteps of his predecessor, Berthold tried to gain their confidence and good will by kindness. At first they appeared to become less hostile, but soon their old hatred revived. When Berthold attempted to bless the Christian cemetery at Holm, their pagan fanaticism broke loose in all its fury and they decided either to burn the bishop together with his church at Holm or to drown him in the Düna. The Christians fled to their strongholds at Uxküll and Holm, while the bishop escaped in a ship to Lübeck.

Pope Celestine III, shortly before his death, was preparing to send a fleet of crusaders to protect the Christians of the Baltic Provinces, and his successor, Innocent III, continued the work. Berthold gained the financial assistance of Archbishop Hartwig and many merchants of Bremen and Lübeck. In a short time a large fleet was ready for departure well equipped and loaded with crusaders and many German peasants who were to settle permanently in Livonia. It put to sea at Lübeck and crossed the Baltic, entering the River Düna from what is now called the Gulf of Riga. Near the mouth of the Düna the German peasants landed with the purpose of making their homes in the vicinity, and laid the foundations of the city Riga, at present one of the most important commercial seaports in Russia. Berthold, accompanied by the crusaders, sailed up the river as far as Holm, where the pagan Livonians had gathered with the intention of attacking the fleet. Having vainly attempted to come to a peaceful agreement with them, Berthold and his companions sailed some distance down the river, with the Livonians in eager pursuit. Finally, the pagans agreed to a suspension of hostilities to gain time for collecting larger forces. At the first opportunity, however, they fell upon the Christians who ventured outside their fortifications, and hostilities were resumed. The crusaders were victorious, but Berthold's horse became intractable and galloped into the midst of the fleeing Livonians. A pagan by the name of Ymant thrust his lance into Berthold's back, inflicting a wound that caused speedy death. The bishop's body was buried by the crusaders at Uxküll whence it was transferred to Riga by Bishop Albert of Apeldern whom Archbishop Hartwig of Bremen had appointed Berthold's successor. Soon after the death of Berthold many of the vanquished pagans came to the crusaders, expressing their regret at the unhappy occurrence and asked to be baptized. The final conversion of Livonia was effected by Bishop Albert, who was assisted in his apostolic labours by the newly founded Order of the Brothers of the Sword which in 1237 was affiliated with the Teutonic Order.

GRUBER, *Origines Livoniæ sacræ et civiles* (Frankfort and Leipzig, 1740); DAMBERGER, *Synchronistische Geschichte der Kirche und der Welt im Mittelalter* (Ratisbon, 1856), IX, 328–336, 437–438; SEITERS, in *Kirchenlex.*, s. v.

MICHAEL OTT.

Berthold of Chiemsee, a German bishop and theological writer, b. 1465 at Salzburg, Austria; d. 19 July, 1543, at Saalfelden (duchy of Salzburg). His real name was Berthold Pürstinger, frequently called Pirstinger; but he is generally known as Berthold of Chiemsee, from his episcopal see, situated on one of the islands of the Bavarian lake of Chiemsee. We have but little information regarding his early life. He was licentiate in civil, and doctor in ecclesiastical law, and in 1495 he appears as the *Magister Cameræ* of the Archbishop of Salzburg, and in 1508 was appointed Bishop of Chiemsee. During his episcopal career (1508–25), he resided at Salzburg, in the quality of coadjutor to the archbishop of the latter place.

Berthold twice conspicuously used his influence with the Archbishop of Salzburg in behalf of the unfortunate: in 1511 in favour of the Salzburg town-councillors who had been condemned for high treason, and again in 1524 in the interest of the rebellious peasants. He was present at the Provincial Council of Salzburg (1512), and also took an active part in 1522 in that of Mühldorf (Bavaria), which

was convened to devise means of stemming the tide of Lutheran progress. Soon after, he resigned his bishopric (1526) and retired to the monastery of Raitenhaslach on the Austro-Bavarian frontier. In 1528, or 1529, he removed to Saalfelden, where he founded (1533) a hospital with a church for infirm priests. He died here and was buried in the parish church.

After his resignation of his episcopal functions Berthold devoted his time to literary pursuits. At the suggestion of Matthew Lang, the Cardinal Archbishop of Salzburg (1519–40), he wrote his "Tewtsche Theologey" (German Theology—Munich, 1528) and translated it afterwards into Latin (Augsburg, 1531). Earnestness in the suppression of abuses and mildness in his dealings with others were characteristic traits of Berthold, and they appear also in his works; his "Theology" does not bear the bitterly polemical stamp of similar contemporaneous writings. The work does not seem to have been in great demand, as neither the original nor the translation was reprinted until Reithmeier re-edited the work (1852). The book, however, was important. The German original is valuable from both a linguistic and theological point of view. Linguistically, it proves that Luther was not the only able exponent of religious doctrines in the vernacular; theologically, it exhibits the character of Catholic teaching at the time.

The other writings of Berthold were: (1) "Tewtsch Rational", a treatise on the Mass; (2) "Keligpuchel", a defence of the Catholic doctrine and practice of Communion under one kind, against the Reformers; (3) "Onus Ecclesiæ" or "Burden of the Church" (Landshut, 1524) is also generally attributed to him. It is a fearless exposition, from a Catholic point of view, of the abuses then prevalent in the Church. The book occasioned much comment and was reprinted twice in 1531, at Cologne and probably at Augsburg, and again in 1620 without indication of place.

GREINZ, *Berthold von Chiemsee* (Salzburg, 1904); REITTMEIER, *Tewtsche Theologey* (Munich, 1852); WERNER, *Die Flugschrift "Onus Ecclesiæ"* (Giessen, 1901); FICKER in *Realencyclop. für Protest. Theol.* (Leipzig, 1905), XVI, 307–315; MATTES-PUNKES in *Kirchenlex.*, II, 472–475; SCHAFF-HERZOG, *Relig.-Encyl.* (New York), I, 252.

N. A. WEBER.

Berthold of Henneberg, Archbishop and Elector of Mainz, b. 1441; d. 21 December, 1504. Having completed his education at the University of Erfurt, he became a canon of the Cathedral of Cologne in 1464. Three years later he came to the imperial court of Frederick III. He was chosen Archbishop of Mainz in 1484 and consecrated 20 May, 1485. When in 1486 Maximilian I was elected Roman King, to rule in union with his father, Frederick III, Berthold, as imperial chancellor, obtained the right of having all royal documents submitted to him for signature. Being heart and soul for a political reform of the tottering empire, he used all his influence to bring about a change in its constitution. How Berthold wished to reform the empire may be gathered from the programme submitted to the emperor at the diet of Worms in 1495. All state affairs were to be managed by an imperial council (Reichsrath) consisting of seventeen members. The councillors were to be chosen by the electors and the estates, while the emperor was to appoint the president of the council. The emperor, of course, justly rejected such a programme which would have changed the empire into an oligarchy, with the emperor a mere figurehead.

Berthold's ecclesiastical reforms, on the other hand, which were even more pressing than political changes, were accompanied with great success. He encouraged and urged the reformation of the clergy and the religious orders, which was already in progress, and was especially solicitous for a better education of the clergy. He courageously resisted the heretical tendencies of many humanists and, though friendly disposed towards the better ones, scathingly rebuked others. To guard against impure literature he established in his diocese, on 4 January, 1486, a censorship of the press, which was the first in history. Berthold had long been dissatisfied with the many pecuniary demands of Rome upon Germany and the improprieties that often accompanied the preaching of indulgences, and shortly before his death he respectfully submitted these grievances of the German nation to Pope Pius III, who had just succeeded Alexander VI. He is buried in the Cathedral of Mainz, where a magnificent monument perpetuates his memory.

WECKERLE, *De Bertholdi Hennebergensis archiep. Mog. studiis politicis* (Münster, 1868); JANSEN, *Geschichte des deutschen Volkes seit dem Ausgang des Mittelalters* (Freiburg im Breisgau, 1893) I, *passim* (tr., St. Louis); MAX JANSEN, *Kaiser Maximilian I* (Munich, 1905), 65 sq.

MICHAEL OTT.

Berthold of Ratisbon, a Franciscan of the monastery of that city and the most powerful preacher of repentance in the thirteenth century, b. about 1210; d. at Ratisbon, 14 December, 1272. He was probably a member of a well-to-do middle class family of Ratisbon named Sachs. The excellence of his literary training is proved by his sermons which show more than common acquaintance with the ancient classics. From his knowledge of the usages of secular life, it may be inferred that he was a man of mature age before he entered the monastery. The first fixed date in Berthold's life is 1246, when the papal legate appointed him and David of Augsburg inspectors of the convent of Niedermünster, a proof of the high regard in which Berthold was then held. One of his contemporaries, the Abbot of Niederaltaich, who is a reliable historian, speaks in 1250 of the great reputation that Berthold had in Bavaria as a preacher. Four years later the missionary trips of this preacher extended as far as the valley of the Rhine, Alsace, and Switzerland. During the next ten years Berthold's apostolic labours led him eastward into Austria, Moravia, Bohemia, and Silesia. In 1263 Pope Urban IV appointed him to preach the Crusade and Albert the Great was designated as his assistant.

When speaking to Slavonic audiences Berthold naturally employed an interpreter, just as St. Bernard, in his day, made use of an interpreter in Germany. Notwithstanding any difficulties that might arise as to speech, wherever he went Berthold exerted an extraordinary power of attraction over his hearers so that the churches were not able to hold the great crowds of plain people who came from all quarters to his services, and he was often obliged to preach in the open air. When this was the case, a pulpit was generally arranged under the spreading branches of a linden tree. Long after his day "Berthold's linden" was to be seen at Glatz. About 1270 he seems to have returned to Ratisbon where he remained the rest of his life. The Franciscan martyrology includes his name among the blessed of the order, and his remains form the most precious relic among the treasures of the cathedral at Ratisbon. The poets and chroniclers of his time made frequent reference to Berthold. He was called "sweet Brother Berthold", "the beloved of God and man", "a second Elias", "the teacher of the nations"; all of these expressions are proofs of the high esteem in which his activities were held. The secret of the preacher's success lay partly in the saintliness of his life and partly in his power to make use of the language of humble life. He became the great master, it may be said, the classic of homely speech, and this rank has been maintained by his sermons to the present day. One of his two popular discourses on the Last Judgment became a favourite book of the people under the title "The Valley of Josaphat".

There is no doubt that Brother Berthold preached in German. For a long time, however, scholars disagreed as to how his sermons had been preserved. It is now generally accepted that the sermons were often written down afterwards in Latin, frequently with marginal comments in German; these reports of the sermons, as they may be called, partly German, partly Latin, or at times in the language in which they were delivered, are what have been handed down to posterity. The discourses thus preserved are of the greatest importance for the history of the development of the literature of homiletics; they are of equal value as rich sources for determining the condition of education and culture in the thirteenth century. It is difficult, therefore, to understand how this greatest of German preachers to the poor could have been forgotten for centuries. It was not until some of Brother Berthold's sermons were published in 1824 that attention was called to the eloquent Franciscan. Since this date, the enthusiasm for Berthold has grown steadily so that he has become a favourite, both of Germanic scholars and of the historians of the development of German civilization. He is also regarded as the great pattern of homely pulpit eloquence.

KLING, *Bertholds, des Franziskaners, deutsche Predigten* (Berlin, 1824); PFEIFFER UND STROBL, *Berthold von Regensburg* (Vienna, 1862, 1880); GÖBEL, *Die Missionspredigten des Franziskaners Berthold von Regensburg, in jetziger Schriftsprache* (Ratisbon, 1873); HÖTZL, *Beati Fr. Bertholdi a Ratisbona sermones ad religiosos* (Munich. 1882); UNKEL, *Berthold von Regensburg* (Cologne, 1882); STROMBERGER, *Berthold von Regensburg* (Güterslob, 1877); MICHAEL, *Gesch. des deutschen Volkes vom 13. Jahrh. bis zum Ausgange des M. A.* (Freiburg im Br., 1897), II, III, 144–180.

N. SCHEID.

Berthold of Reichenau, a Benedictine monk and chronicler of the celebrated Abbey of Reichenau on the Lake of Constance; d. probably in 1088. He was a disciple and friend of the learned Hermannus Contractus. When Hermann saw death approaching, he entrusted to Berthold all the wax tablets that contained the writings which he had not yet committed to parchment and commissioned Berthold to peruse them and, after careful revision, to copy them on parchment. Berthold was also exhorted by his dying master to continue the famous world-chronicle, begun by Hermann, which in chronological order related the history of the world from the birth of Christ to 1054, the year in which Hermann died. To the continuation of this chronicle and to a biography of his master and friend, Hermannus Contractus, is due whatever fame is attached to the name of Berthold.

The chronicle, as far as it was written by Berthold, comprises a concise and impartial history of the troublesome times immediately preceding the accession of Gregory VII and probably also of the early reign of this great pontiff. It is reprinted to the year 1080, with an introduction by Pertz, in "Mon. Germ. Hist.: Script." V, 264–326, and in P. L., CXLVII, 314–442. Pertz contends that Berthold did not begin the continuation of Hermann's chronicle until 1076, and that in the execution of it he made use of another chronicle, written by Bernold who was also a monk of Reichenau; but it has been proved almost beyond doubt by Giesebrecht and Schulzen that Berthold was the first to continue Hermann's chronicle and that Bernold's chronicle is a continuation of Berthold's. It is, however, still undecided as to what year Berthold's chronicle extends. Ussermann and Schulzen hold that it extends only to the year 1066, while Pertz, Giesebrecht, and others believe that Berthold wrote the chronicle at least to the middle of the year 1080, where the manuscript suddenly ceases in the middle of a sentence.

The original text of Berthold is no longer in existence and all the existing copies have been compiled from various manuscripts found in the monasteries of St. Gall, St. Blaise, Muri, and Engelberg. The chronicle was continued by Bernold to the year 1100, and by others to the year 1175. From various passages in Berthold's chronicle it appears that, for a short time at least, he considered Cadalus, Bishop of Parma, as the legitimate occupant of the papal throne; but he soon noticed his mistake and from the year 1070, or even earlier, acknowledged Alexander II as the true pope. Bernold remarks in his chronicle under the year 1088 that Berthold, an excellent teacher who was very well versed in Holy Scripture, died at an advanced age on the 12th of March.

GIESEBRECHT, *Gesch. der deutschen Kaiserzeit* (4th ed.), III, 1032; SCHULZEN, *De Bertoldi et Bernoldi Chronicis dissertatio historica* (Bonn, 1867); WATTENBACH, *Deutschlands Geschichtsquellen* (Berlin, 1894), II, vii; HAUCK, *Kirchengeschichte Deutschlands* (Leipzig, 1906), III, 952.

MICHAEL OTT.

Berti, GIOVANNI LORENZO, an Italian theologian, b. 28 May, 1696, at Sarravezza, Tuscany; d. 26 March, 1766, at Pisa. His parents were of the lower class. At the age of fifteen he entered the Augustinian order, and preached with success before he had attained his twenty-third year. He subsequently occupied important offices in his order, i. e. those of general secretary, prefect of the Angelica (the former valuable library of the Augustinians at Rome), general assistant. He first taught philosophy, then theology, at Sienna, Florence, Bologna, Padua, Rome, and finally (1748) became professor of ecclesiastical history at Pisa. He suffered, in 1762, a stroke of apoplexy which was repeated and eventually caused his death. His literary career was an agitated one. By order of Father Schiaffinati, his Superior General, he wrote the extensive work "De Theologicis Disciplinis" (Rome, 1739–45), an exposition of the theological teaching of St. Augustine. The book, which appeared in several editions, was vehemently attacked by d'Ise de Saléon (who was successively Bishop of Agen, 1730–35, Bishop of Rodez, 1735–46, and Archbishop of Vienne, 1747–51) and by Languet de Gergy, Archbishop of Sens (1731–53). They accused Berti of Jansenism. In answer, the latter published: (1) "Augustinianum Systema de Gratiâ" (Rome, 1747; Munich, 1750); (2) "In Opusculum" (Leghorn, 1756). The accusations against Berti were submitted to the Roman authorities. Benedict XIV (1740–58) had his book examined and found its teaching sound. Besides other works published in this controversy, Berti wrote: (1) "Commentarius de Rebus gestis S. Augustini" (Venice, 1756); (2) "S. Augustini Quæstionum de Scientiâ, . . . dilucidatio" (Pisa, 1756); (3) "De Hæresibus Trium Prierum Sæculorum" (Bassano, 1769); (4) "Historia Ecclesiastica" (Florence, 1753), an ecclesiastical history, which he later published in an abridged form (Pisa, 1760), and which, thus shortened, was frequently re-edited (recently at Turin, 1892).

HURTER, *Nomenclator* (Innsbruck, 1895), III, 1–5; HEURTEBIZE in *Dict. de théol. cath.* (Paris, 1905), II, 795–796; KELLER in *Kirchenlex.* (Freiburg, 1887), II, 482, 483.

N. A. WEBER.

Bertin, SAINT, Abbot of St. Omer, b. near Constance about 615; d. about 709. At an early age he entered the monastery of Luxeuil in France where, under the austere Rule of St. Columban, he prepared himself for his future missionary career. About the year 638 he set out, in company with two confrères, Mummolin and Ebertram, for the extreme northern part of France in order to assist his friend and kinsman, Bishop St. Omer, in the evangelization of the Morini. This country, now the Department Pas-de-Calais, was then one vast marsh, studded here and there with hillocks and overgrown with seaweed and bulrushes. On one of these hillocks, Bertin and his companions built a small house whence they went out daily to preach the word of God among the natives, most of whom were still heathens. Gradually some converted heathens joined the little band of missionaries and a larger monastery had to be built. A tract of land called Sithiu had been donated to Omer by a converted nobleman named Adrowald. Omer now turned this whole tract over to the missionaries, who selected a suitable place on it for their new monastery. But the community grew so rapidly that in a short time this monastery also became too small and another was built where the city of St. Omer now stands. Shortly after Bertin's death it received the name of St. Bertin. Mummolin, perhaps because he was the oldest of the missionaries, was abbot of the two monasteries until he succeeded the deceased St. Eligius as Bishop of Noyon, about the year 659. Bertin then became abbot.

The fame of Bertin's learning and sanctity was so great that in a short time more than 150 monks lived under his rule, among them St. Winnoc and his three companions who had come from Brittany to join Bertin's community and assist in the conversion of the heathen. When nearly the whole neighbourhood was Christianized, and the marshy land transformed into a fertile plain, Bertin, knowing that his death was not far off, appointed Rigobert, a pious monk, as his successor, while he himself spent the remainder of his life preparing for a happy death. Bertin began to be venerated as a saint soon after his death. His feast is celebrated on 5 September. In medieval times the Abbey of St. Bertin was famous as a centre of sanctity and learning. The "Annales Bertiniani" (830–882; Mon. Germ. Hist.: Script., I, 419–515) are important for the contemporary history of the West Frankish Kingdom. The abbey church, now in ruins, was one of the finest fourteenth-century Gothic edifices. In later times its library, archives, and art-treasures were renowned both in and out of France. The monks were expelled in 1791 and in 1799 the abbey and its church were sold at auction. The valuable charters of the abbey are published in Guerard, "Cartulaire de l'abbaye de St. Bertin" (Paris, 1841; appendix by Morand, ibid., 1861). The list of abbots is given in "Gallia Christiana nova", III, 485 sqq. See Laplane, "Abbés de St. Bertin" (St. Omer, 1854–55).

MABILLON, *Acta SS. O. S. B., sæc. III*, I, 93–150; *Acta SS.*, 2 September, 549–630; BUTLER, *Lives of the Saints*, 5 Sept.; BARING-GOULD, *Lives of the Saints*, 5 Sept.; MONTALEMBERT, *Monks of the West* (Boston), I, 628 sqq.; GUÉRIN, *Vies des Saints* (Paris), X, 492 sqq. The earliest sources are two anonymous biographies, one of them written before the middle of the ninth century, the other somewhat later. They are published by MABILLON and by the Bollandists, loc. cit.

MICHAEL OTT.

Bertinoro, DIOCESE OF.—Bertinoro, anciently called Forum Truentinorum, and, at the time of the Gothic war, Petra Honorii, whence the present name, is a small city in Romagna, province of Forli, Italy. According to legend, about the year 303 St. Illuminata, a virgin of Ravenna, took refuge here, but did not escape martyrdom. Up to 1360 Bertinoro was subject to the Bishop of Forlimpopoli; in that year, however, Cardinal Albornoz being commander of the troops of Pope Gregory IX, the latter city was destroyed, and the episcopal seat was transferred to Bertinoro. A word will first be said of Forlimpopoli.

Forlimpopoli was founded in 173 B. C. by the Consul M. Popilius Lænas. The first bishop is supposed to have been St. Rufillus, appointed by Pope St. Sylvester, and he is supposed to have transformed a temple of Isis into a church. At all events St. Rufillus is the patron of the city, and the church in which his body is preserved is said to have been an ancient temple of Hercules. In 500 Asellus, Bishop of Forlimpopoli, was present at the Roman synod that passed on the election of Pope Simmacus, and in 649 Bishop Stephen attended the Roman council concerning the Monothelites. This city had much to suffer from the Lombards, and in 665 or 670, while the people were assembled in the cathedral for the ceremonies of Holy Saturday, it was suddenly attacked by King Grimoald, who pillaged it and butchered numbers of the people and clergy (Paul Diac., Hist. Lang., V, x). By the famous donation of Pepin, Forlimpopoli with the other cities of the exarchate and the Pentapolis was made a part of the patrimony of St. Peter. In 1073 during the episcopate of Pietro, St. Peter Damian went to Forlimpopoli to reform ecclesiastical discipline, and on this occasion is thought to have delivered a sermon on St. Rufillus, which Vecchiazzani, an historian of this city, claims to have discovered at Rimini in the Library of St. Jerome. But this is very doubtful. Among the successive bishops, Ubertello (1214) and Taddeo (1285) were noted for their beneficence and their efforts for the preservation of peace. During the fourteenth century Romagna was at the mercy of petty tyrants and Forlimpopoli was ruled by the Ordelaffi of Forli. Innocent VI first tried censures as a means of enforcing his commands as sovereign, and sent Cardinal Albornoz to Forlimpopoli (1355). Francesco II, of the Ordelaffi family, however, when the cardinal had left, burned the statue of the pope in the public square, and was guilty of great cruelty towards the clergy.

In 1360 Albornoz took the city by force, obliged the inhabitants to abandon it, and razed it to the ground. The episcopal see was then transferred to Bertinoro, and the bishop, Roberto dei Resinelli, an Augustinian, took with him the relics of St. Rufillus. Forlimpopoli was gradually rebuilt, and Leo XII restored it to the rank of a city. The bishop, however, remained at Bertinoro. In 1377 Roberto was succeeded by Bishop Teobaldo, who received from Urban VI the civil authority over Bertinoro and Cesena, and by virtue of his authority fought against the bodies of mercenaries recruited by the Antipope Clement VII, by whom he was made prisoner. Bishop Ventura degli Abati was highly praised by Martin V for his learning and piety. Tommaso Caselli, a Dominican (1544), was an able theologian; Gianandrea Caligari (1580), formerly nuncio to Poland, restored the Cathedral of Santa Caterina. Giovanni della Robbia (1624), a Dominican, established at Forlimpopoli the Accademia degli Infiammati. In 1803 Pope Pius VII was obliged to suppress the Diocese of Bertinoro which, however, was re-established in 1817. From 1824 to 1859 it was united to the Diocese of Sarsina. In the Diocese of Bertinoro is situated the celebrated church of Polenta, in Romanesque style, which inspired one of the most beautiful odes of Carducci.

The diocese contains 63 parishes, 93 churches, chapels, and oratories, 92 secular priests, 78 regulars, 32 seminary students, 5 lay brothers, 90 members of female religious orders, 1 school for boys, and 5 for girls, and a population of 32,500.

CAPPELLETTI, *Le chiese d'Italia* (Venice, 1844), II; *Annuario eccl.* (Rome, 1906).

U. BENIGNI.

Bertonio, LUDOVICO, an Italian missionary, b. 1552 at Rocca Contrada near Ancona; d. at Lima, Peru, 3 August, 1625. He entered the Society of Jesus in 1575. Sent to Peru six years later, he laboured principally among the Aymará Indians of Southern Peru and of Bolivia, and has left valuable works on the Aymará language. His earliest publications on that idiom appeared under the title "Arte breve de la lengua aymará para introducir el Arte grande de la misma lengua" (Rome, 1603), also "Arte y gramática muy copiosa de la lengua aymará" etc. The printing press having been introduced and established by the Jesuits at the Indian mission

of Juli in Southwestern Peru, Bertonio had the following works printed there, all in the year 1612:— "Arte de la lengua aymará con una selva de frases en la misma lengua y su declaración en romance"; "Vocabulario de la lengua aymará" (first and second part); "Confesionario muy copioso en dos lenguas, aymará y española" etc.; "Libro de la vida y milagros de Ntro Señor Jesuchristo en dos lenguas, aymará y romance, traducido del que recopiló el Licenciado Alonso de Villegas" etc. The publications by Father Bertonio being as rare as they are important, Platzmann has published in facsimile the "Arte y gramática" of 1603 and the Vocabularies. Manuel Vicente Ballivian in a pamphlet conclusively refutes the slur cast by Sir Clements Markham on Bertonio, that the latter invented the name "Aymará".

TORRES SALDAMANDO, *Los antiguos Jesuitas del Perú* (Lima, 1882); MENDIBURÚ, *Diccionario* (Lima, 1876), II; BALLIVIAN, *Boletín de la Sociedad geográfica de la Paz.*

AD. F. BANDELIER.

Bertrand, SAINT LOUIS. See LOUIS BERTRAND, SAINT.

Bertrand, PIERRE (1) a French Cardinal, theologian, and canonist, b. 1280 at Annonay in Vivarais; d. 1348 or 1349 at the Priory of Montaud, near Avignon. His noble parentage is known to us through the manuscript memoir of Grasset, a Celestine monk of the seventeenth century (Discours généalogique de la noble maison de Bertrand et de leur alliance avec celle de Colombier). The legal profession seems to have been the first aim of his education. He successively studied and taught law in the Universities of Avignon, Montpellier, Orléans, and Paris. Prized as one of the best lawregents of his day, he soon reached high positions in the Parliament of Paris, the King's Council, and the Queen's Chancery. His definite calling lay, however, in another direction, and he became a priest. His priestly career was no less brilliant than his legal success. We find him in rapid succession Dean of Puy-en-Valais, Bishop of Nevers, Bishop of Autun. In 1331 Pope John XXII made him a cardinal in recognition of many services rendered to the Church. Among these services are to be reckoned several charitable institutions founded at Annonay, and the Collège d'Autun, or Collège Cardinal, established in Paris on behalf of fifteen poor students, five for theology, five for law, and five for the fine arts. Bertrand's best title to recognition is, however, his defence of the rights of the Church both by word of mouth and also with his pen. Fournier, in his "Officialités du moyen-âge" (Paris, 1880), points out, at the beginning of the Valois dynasty, a strong tendency of the State towards curtailing the Church's traditional rights. In 1329 took place the famous "Conférence de Vincennes", where Pierre de Cugnières, speaking for Philippe de Valois, bitterly complained of undue extension of ecclesiastical privileges (e. g., the ordination of clerics for the sole purpose of enjoying the *privilegium fori; causes des veuves,* or widow's causes drawn to ecclesiastical courts; the free use of censures to enforce the Church's privileges; appeals to the Church from the decision of civil courts, etc.). Pierre Bertrand, then Bishop of Autun, was the principal spokesman of the clergy. He replied in a spirit of conciliation to all charges bearing on minor points, but strongly upheld what he considered the essential rights of the Church. Following on the lines of the Bull "Unam Sanctam" of Boniface VIII, he summed up his plea in four statements; (1) the secular power is from God; (2) yet, it is not by itself sufficient for the government of the people, for which spiritual jurisdiction is also required; (3) although nothing prevents the two powers from being in the same hands; (4) still, whether in the same or different hands, they stand in a certain relation of subordination, the spiritual power being the higher of the two. His views are to be found in "Libellus adversus Petrum de Cugneriis" and "De origine et usu iurisdictionum", published in Paris in 1495 and 1584 respectively, and later inserted in volume XIV of the "Magna Bibliotheca Veterum Patrum" (Cologne, 1618). Many other writings of Cardinal Bertrand (apologetical, canonical, pastoral) have not been published and are reported to be in the Vatican Library.

(2) BERTRAND, PIERRE, DE COLOMBIER (also known as BERTRAND PIERRE), a French cardinal, nephew of the foregoing, whose name he adopted, b. in 1279, at Colombier, in Vivarais; d. in 1361 at the priory of Montaud, near Avignon. Like his uncle, he studied law and occupied important positions in the Parliament of Paris. Ordained priest, he soon rose to distinction, became Bishop of Nevers, then of Autun, later of Arras, and was made cardinal by Clement VI, 1344. His career as a cardinal was a distinguished one. The popes at Avignon used him as their trusted agent in many delicate missions, notably for the termination of the war between France and England and the election of Charles of Bohemia to the imperial throne. He met little success in his endeavour to stop the Hundred Years' War, but brought about the desired election of Charles IV, and, having in the meantime become Dean of the Sacred College, was naturally chosen by Innocent VI to go to Rome and crown the new emperor. Cardinal de Colombier left no writings. The Celestine monks of Colombier and Montaud, whose benefactor he was, held his and his uncle's memory in great veneration. We are indebted to them for many biographical details on the two Cardinals Bertrand.

BARONIUS-MANSI, Annales Ecclesiastici, anno 1329 (Lucca, 1750), XXIV; Gallia Christiana (Paris, 1720–70), III, IV and XII; MAZON in Grande Encyclopédie; IDEM, Essai historique Vivarais (Tournon, 1890); CHEVALIER, Rép. des sources hist.: Bio-bibl.

J. F. SOLLIER.

Bertulf, SAINT, Abbot of Bobbio, date of birth unknown; d. 639 or 640. He was the son of a pagan nobleman in Austrasia and a near relative of St. Arnulf, Bishop of Metz, whose pious example had such an influence on Bertulf that he became a Christian and in 620 entered the monastery of Luxeuil. A few years later he became acquainted with Abbot Attala, who had come to Luxeuil on a visit, and, with permission of Abbot Eustace of Luxeuil, joined Attala's community at Bobbio in Italy. Upon the death of Attala, in 627, Bertulf was elected by the monks of Bobbio as their abbot. Like his holy predecessor, he insisted on the observance of the austere rule introduced by St. Columban, the founder of Bobbio, and preached fearlessly against Arianism, which had gained a firm foothold in Italy under the Lombard kings. When the Bishop of Tortona endeavoured to bring Bobbio under his own jurisdiction, Bertulf hastened to Rome, where Pope Honorius received him kindly and granted the monastery entire exemption from episcopal jurisdiction. Jonas, a monk of Bobbio, who accompanied Bertulf on his journey to Rome, relates that, while returning to his monastery, Bertulf was attacked by a deadly fever, and cured miraculously by St. Peter. The same author ascribes a few other miracles to the prayers of St. Bertulf. Most martyrologies give him the title of saint. His feast is celebrated on 19 August.

The first source for Bertulf's biographies is a short life written by the above-mentioned monk, JONAS OF BOBBIO; MABILLON, Acta SS. O. S. B., sæc. II, 160; and the BOLLANDISTS, Acta SS., August, III, 752, have published this biography. See also MABILLON, Annales Benedictini, ad an. 628, vii; MONTALEMBERT, Monks of the West (Boston), I, 582 sqq.; LECHNER, Martyrologium des Benediktiner-Ordens (Augsburg, 1855), 323; GUÉRIN, Vies des Saints (Paris), X, 27 sqq.

MICHAEL OTT.

Bérulle, PIERRE DE, cardinal, and founder of the French congregation of the Oratory, b. in the province of Champagne, France, at the château of Cérilly, 4 February, 1575; d. 2 October, 1629. De Bérulle came from a distinguished family of magistrates. From his youth and even before his ordination he devoted himself to the conversion of Protestants and wrote a "Discourse on Interior Abnegation". After entering the priesthood he was made chaplain to Henry IV and, in company with his friends the Cardinal du Perron and St. Francis de Sales, he continued his labours for the conversion of the Huguenots. With the co-operation of Madame Acarie (the Bl. Marie of the Incarnation) he introduced Carmelite nuns of the Reform of St. Teresa into France, a work attended with many difficulties. In 1611 de Bérulle founded the congregation of the Oratory on the model of the one formed some years before by St. Philip Neri at Rome. Owing to the differences of time and place the French congregation varied in some important respects from the Italian Oratory. (Cf. ORATORY, FRENCH CONGREGATION OF THE.) In speaking of the French Oratorians it should be remembered that from this congregation proceeded the seventeenth-century reform of the clergy of France. The celebrated Jesuit Cotton called the French Oratory "necessary to the Church", and St. Francis de Sales said also that there was "nothing more saintly and more useful to the Church and God". While filling the office of Superior-General of the Oratory Father de Bérulle was also actively employed in the public affairs of the time; for example, in the arrangements for the marriage of Charles I of England with Henrietta of France, sister of Louis XIII. Pope Urban VIII in 1627 rewarded de Bérulle's services to Church and State by creating him a cardinal. Two years later de Bérulle died while saying Mass. His disciple, St. Vincent de Paul, said of him: "He is one of the most saintly priests I have known", and his friend St. Francis de Sales declared: "He is everything which I should desire to be myself".

Cardinal de Bérulle left several works, the remarkable qualities of which led Pope Urban VIII to call him the Apostolus Verbi incarnati. "This expression", wrote Cardinal Perraud, also an Oratorian, in his work "L'Oratoire de France aux XVIIe et XVIIIe siècles", "is more than a magnificent panegyric awarded to the piety of the founder of the Oratory; in a word, it contains the essential epitome of his written works, for it may be said of them, as of the entire life of the saintly cardinal, that the one aim was to make our Saviour Jesus Christ better known and more loved." The chief works of Cardinal de Bérulle are: (1) "Traité des énergumènes" (Troyes, 1599). (2) "Discours etc." (Paris, 1609) on various subjects. (3) "Discours de l'état et des grandeurs de Jésus" (Paris, 1623). The last mentioned work was reprinted several times; the substance and often the actual expressions are to be found in the diffuse "Méditations" of Father Bourgoing and also in Bossuet's "Élévations sur les mystères". (4) "Vie de Jésus" (Paris, 1629); this was a sequel to the preceding work, which the pious author had just finished at the time of his death. (5) "Élévation à Jésus-Christ sur Sainte Madeleine" (Paris, 1627). Father Bourgoing issued a complete edition of the works of Cardinal de Bérulle (Paris, 1644), which included some writings not mentioned above, and he added to the edition a "table of the theology of this great author arranged according to the order of the 'Summa' of St. Thomas". In 1856 the Abbé Migne reprinted the third edition of the complete works. Cardinal de Bérulle's writings exhibit a robust and vigorous doctrine full of unction and piety, which is set forth at times in a somewhat diffuse style. One of his biographers, Father Cloysenet, has said: "He wrote the books at his leisure and weighed each word", and the biographer adds very justly that the reader is rewarded for his trouble, for "it is impossible to read them without feeling oneself filled with love for our Saviour Jesus Christ".

TABARAUD, *Histoire du Père de Bérulle* (Paris, 1817), II; PERRAUD, *L'Oratoire de France*, ch. iii, iv; HOUSSAYE, *M. de Bérulle et les Carmélites; Le Père de Bérulle et l'Oratoire; Le cardinal de Bérulle et Richelieu* (Paris, 1872–76), III; INGOLD, *Essai de bibliographie oratorienne* (Paris, 1882); IDEM, *Les miracles du cardinal de Bérulle* (Paris, 1881).

A. M. P. INGOLD.

Bervanger, MARTIN DE, a French priest, founder of charitable institutions; b. at Sarrelouis, 15 May, 1795; d. at Paris, 1865. After being for some time assistant pastor in his native city, he took part, in 1822, in the foundation of the Association Royale de Saint-Joseph, and later of the Œuvre de Saint-Henri. These two institutions were destined to give to workingmen free instruction and professional training. To reach this end more effectively, he founded, in 1827, a boarding-school where, besides manual training, poor boys could receive intellectual, religious, and moral education. This is the Œuvre de Saint-Nicolas. In the beginning only seven children were in the establishment, but it soon developed and was transferred from its poor quarters in the Faubourg Saint-Marceau, to a better location in the Rue Vaugirard. At the time of the Revolution of 1830, the first two institutions disappeared, but the Institution Saint-Nicolas remained. It had many difficulties to overcome; the resources were insufficient; proper instructors could not always be found; suspicions of political intrigues were entertained by the Government, which led to various vexatious inquiries. De Bervanger succeeded in overcoming all obstacles, and the institution became more and more prosperous. Soon a branch establishment was founded at Issy. In 1859 De Bervanger turned over the institution to Cardinal Morlot, Archbishop of Paris, who gave the direction of it to the Christian Brothers. It has since been enlarged. De Bervanger wrote the "Règle de l'Œuvre de Saint-Nicolas" (1853).

Dictionnaire de pédagogie (Paris, 1887), I, pt. I, 189.

C. A. DUBRAY.

Besançon (VESONTIO), ARCHDIOCESE OF, coextensive with the departments of Doubs, Haute-Saône, and the district of Belfort. Few nineteenth-century dioceses have undergone similar territorial changes. The Concordat of 1802 gave the Diocese of Besançon all those districts which, in 1822, constituted the Diocese of St.-Claude. In 1806, Besançon was given jurisdiction over the three parishes of the principality of Neufchâtel (Switzerland) which fell under the control of the See of Lausanne in 1814. In 1870, after the annexation of Alsace-Lorraine by Germany, the district of Belfort was withdrawn from the See of Strasburg and attached to that of Besançon. The metropolitan jurisdiction of Besançon also underwent singular changes. In 1802 its suffragans were the Bishoprics of Dijon, Autun, Metz, Nancy, and Strasburg. Under the Restoration, Dijon and Autun were withdrawn from Besançon, the latter becoming the metropolitan of the Sees of Saint-Dié, Verdun, and Belley. In 1874, after the German conquest, the churches of Metz and Strasburg were under the direct control of the Holy See.

Local legends attribute the evangelization of Besançon to Sts. Ferréol and Ferjeux, sent thither by St. Irenæus, Bishop of Lyons. Duchesne has proved that these legends belong to a chain of narratives forged in the first half of the sixth century and of which the "passion" of St. Benignus of Dijon was the initial link. The catalogue of the earliest bishops of Besançon is to be read with caution. The first bishop known to history is Celidonius (c. 445); other incumbents of the see were St. Rothad-

ius, a monk at Luxeuil and organizer of the monastic life; St. Donatus; St. Hugh I (1031–67), prince of the empire, the real founder of the city whose markets, commerce, and schools he established; Cardinal de Granvelle (1584–86), the famous minister of Philip II, who built the palace of Besançon; Antoine-Pierre de Grammont (1662–98), who strenuously opposed Jansenism and the Reformation, strove to uplift the clergy, and, in 1691, transferred to Besançon the University of Dôle; Le Coz (1802–15), former constitutional bishop whose personality provoked in the diocese no little opposition to the Concordat; Cardinal de Rohan-Chabot (1828–33); Cardinal Mathieu (1834–75), who distinguished himself by his defence of the temporal power, and was a member of the "Opposition" at the Vatican council. He opposed strenuously in his diocese the "simultaneous churches" which sprang up throughout the district of Montbéliard where Protestants are numerous.

The monastery of Luxeuil, founded by St. Columbanus (d. 615), gave to the Diocese of Besançon a series of saints. First came the direct successors of St. Columbanus; the Abbot St. Eustasius who founded a celebrated school in this monastery; the Abbot St. Valbert who sent monks to found the Abbeys of St.-Valéry, St.-Omer, and St.-Bertin, and died in 665; the Abbot St. Ingofroid; St. Donatus, who became Bishop of Besançon; and St. Anségisus, author of a celebrated collection of capitularies. The Abbey of Lure was founded at the beginning of the seventh century by St. Déicole (Deicolus), or Desle, disciple of St. Columbanus; later its abbots were princes of the Holy Empire. The Abbey of Baume les Dames, founded in the fifth century and in which Gontran, King of Burgundy, was buried, was the school where St. Odo, afterwards Abbot of Cluny, studied in the tenth century; at the end of the eighth century there was built near it an abbey for Benedictine nuns, members of the nobility. During the Revolution, the superb church of this abbey was laid waste. Among the other saints of the Diocese of Besançon may be mentioned the hermit St. Aldegrin (tenth century), and St. Peter Fourier (1565–1640), one of those who, in the seventeenth century, inaugurated systematic education for girls. During the Middle Ages several popes visited Besançon, among them Leo IX who consecrated the altar of the old Cathedral of St. Etienne in 1050, and Eugenius III, who, in 1148, consecrated the church of St. Jean, the new cathedral. A council was held at Besançon in 1162, presided over by Frederick Barbarossa, in the interest of the Antipope Victor against Pope Alexander III. Guido of Burgundy who was pope from 1119 to 1123 under the name of Calixtus II, and the Jesuit Nonnotte (1711–93), an adversary of Voltaire, were natives of Besançon. The miracle wrought through the Sacred Host of Faverney, during a fire in the year 1608, is annually commemorated by elaborate ceremonies. The places of pilgrimage are: Notre Dame du Chêne at Scey; Notre Dame d'Aigremont; the pilgrimage of St. Pierre of Tarentaise at Cirey-les-Bellevaux, where St. Pierre de Tarentaise died in 1174; Notre Dame des Jacobins at Besançon; and Notre Dame de la Motte at Vesoul. Parts of the Cathedral of St. Jean at Besançon were erected as early as the eleventh century.

In 1899 the following institutions were to be found in the diocese: 15 infant schools in Besançon and 35 in Vesoul; 1 deaf-mute institute in Besançon; 3 girls' orphanages in Besançon and 3 in Vesoul; 2 protectories in Besançon; 1 house of correction in Besançon and 1 in Vesoul; 2 hospitals and hospices in Besançon and 8 in Vesoul; 12 communities for the care of the sick in their homes at Besançon and 8 in Vesoul; 1 house of retreat in Besançon and 1 in

Vesoul; 3 homes for the aged in Besançon; 1 infant asylum, 1 boys' orphanage, and 4 gratuitous industrial schools in Vesoul, all conducted by nuns; 1 deaf-mute institute and 1 boys' orphanage in Besançon conducted by brothers.

In 1900 the diocese had the following religious orders, *Men:* Capuchins, Eudists, and Marianists at Besançon, and Trappists at Notre Dame de la Grâce de Dieu. *Women* (purely local orders): Sisters of Charity of Besançon, nursing and teaching, founded in 1799; Sisters of the Divine Providence of Frasne-le-Chateau, teaching, founded in 1780; the Daughters of St. James, nursing sisters with a mother-house at Besançon. At the close of 1905 the Archdiocese of Besançon had 657,773 inhabitants, 60 pastorates, 814 succursal parishes (mission churches), and 97 curacies.

Gallia christiana (1860), XV, 1, 322; *Instrumenta*, 1–124; RICHARD, *Histoire des diocèses de Besançon et de Saint-Claude* (Besançon, 1847–50); SUCHET, *Notre Dame de Besançon et du département du Doubs* (Besançon, 1892); BERGIER, *Étude sur l'hymnaire bisontin du cardinal Mathieu, archévêque de Besançon* (Besançon, 1886); DUCHESNE, *Fastes épiscopaux*, 1; CHEVALIER, *Topobibl.*, 382–384.

GEORGES GOYAU.

Besange, JEROME LAMY, O.S.B., b. at Linz, 1726; d. 1781. For twenty-four years he taught Scripture at Salzburg. He published the following works: "Introductio in Vetus Testamentum" (2 vols., Steyr, 1765); "Introductio in sancta quatuor Evangelia" (Venice, 1775); "Introductio in Acta Apostolorum" (Pavia, 1782); "Fasciculus Myrrhæ", a commentary on the Passion (Steyr, 1766); "Die sieben Busspsalmen" (Salzburg, 1776).

PARISOT in VIG., *Dict. de la Bible.*

JOHN CORBETT.

Beschefer, THEODORE, Jesuit missionary in Canada, b. at Châlons-sur-Marne, 25 May, 1630; d. at Reims, 4 February, 1711. He entered the Society of Jesus at Nancy, 24 May, 1647, studied philosophy and theology at Pont-à-Mousson, taught humanities and rhetoric for seven years in various colleges in France, and after his third year of probation came to Canada in 1665. From Quebec, where he was stationed for three years after his arrival, he set out on an embassy to the Mohawks, and to the Dutch at Albany, but a sudden outbreak of Indian hostilities compelled him to turn back. In 1670–71, however, he was a missionary among the Iroquois. In 1672, he returned to Quebec, becoming superior of the Canadian missions in 1680, and retaining that office until at least 1687. A year later he was prefect of classes in the College of Quebec and in 1689 returned to France, where he acted as procurator of the missions. During his stay in Canada he was for sixteen years the spiritual director of the Ursulines at Quebec, and their annals describe him as "a man of distinguished merit and a director of great wisdom and experience".

THWAITES, *Jesuit Relations*, LXII, 91; XLIX, 273, 274; ROCHEMONTEIX, *Les Jésuites et la Nouvelle-France au XVIIe siècle* (Paris, 1895–96), III, 371; SOMMERVOGEL, *Bibl. de la c. de J.*, I 1402; VIII, 1830.

EDWARD P. SPILLANE.

Beschi, COSTANZO GIUSEPPE, b. at Castiglione in the Venetian Republic, 1680; d. at Manapar c. 1746. He entered the Society of Jesus in 1698, and went to the Madura mission in 1710, during nearly forty years of apostolic life proving himself a worthy successor of the founder of the Madura Mission, the celebrated Roberto de' Nobili. Once he barely escaped suffering death for the Christian religion. Though primarily a missionary and always at the head of a district, he is better known as one of the classical writers of Tamil literature. No sooner had he arrived in India than he began the study of Sanskrit, Telugu, and especially of Tamil. Thanks to his genius and indefatigable industry, he mastered the Tamil grammar in five years, and for the next twenty years made so thorough a study of the whole field of Tamil literature that the native men of letters bowed to him as their master. He composed a grammar of High Tamil, and was the first to write a grammar of Low Tamil (the common dialect) which still remains the foundation of scientific Tamil philology. He is also the compiler of several Tamil dictionaries, among them the quadruple lexicon containing words, synonyms, categories of words and rhymes; a Tamil-Latin and a Tamil-Latin-Portuguese dictionary. He wrote several ascetical books in Tamil, especially doctrinal instructions for the use of the native catechists; also controversial tracts against the Danish Lutheran missionaries who sought to gain a foothold in the Madura Mission. Beschi is, however, best known as a Tamil poet. In a poem of 1100 stanzas, "Kittêri ammalle saritiram", he sings the praises of the martyr St. Quiteria (not St. Catherine, as some writers have mistakenly asserted). His greatest poetical work is the "Têmbâvani". (The Unfading Garland), one of the Tamil classics. This Tamil "Divina Commedia" is divided into thirty-six cantos, containing 3,615 stanzas. "It is", says Baumgartner, "the noblest epic poem in honour of St. Joseph written in any literature, East or West. In one of the most difficult languages of Southern India Beschi produced a poem which for richness and beauty of language, for easy elegance of metre, popular treatment, and true poetical conception and execution, is the peer of the native classics; in nobility of thought and subject-matter, it is as superior to them as the harmonious civilization of Christianity rises above the confused philosophical dreams and ridiculous fables of idolatry." Another poem "Paramartaguru Kadey" (the adventures of the Guru Paramarta), in which he delightfully satirizes the foibles and conceited ignorance of the native *gurus* (heathen teachers), is the most entertaining book in Tamil literature, bubbling over with wit and humour. Beschi himself translated it into Latin. It has also been translated into English, French, German, Italian, and Canarese. Grässe and Babington, editors respectively of the German and English translations, seem to be ignorant both of Beschi's authorship of the book and of his great importance in the literature of Southern India, for they make no mention of his name. The tradition that he was at one time prime minister to a native raja is not sufficiently authenticated. In 1744 he was rector of the Mission of Manapar, where he died. His memory lives to this day in Southern India.

SOMMERVOGEL, *Bibliothèque de la c. de J.*, I, col. 1402–09, s. v.; BERTRAND, *La Mission du Maduré*, IV, 342–375; JEAN, *Le Maduré* (Tournai, 1894), I, 152–163; in particular BAUMGARTNER, *Geschichte der Weltliteratur* (Freiburg im Br., 1897), II, 345–354.

B. GULDNER.

Beseleel, (Beçál'ēl, in the shadow of God). I. The son of Uri and grandson of Hur of the tribe of Juda (Ex., xxxi, 2; xxxv, 30; I Paral., ii, 20; II Paral., i, 5). Being naturally endowed with a certain originality of invention, he was expressly called by God to be the chief architect of the tabernacle and its many appurtenances (Ex., xxxi, 2 sqq.). To him were entrusted the preparation of the holy oils, the incense, the priestly vestments, and finally the building of the ark and of the furniture for court and tabernacle. Special Divine gifts were also given to him and his assistants, especially Ooliab, for the proper execution of their office (Ex., xxxi, 3–6; xxxv, 34–35; xxxvi, 1).

II. One of the sons of Phahath-Moab who married a foreigner in the days of Esdras (I Esdras, x, 30).

F. X. E. ALBERT.

Besoigne, JÉRÔME, a Jansenist writer, b. at Paris,

1686; d. 1763. Ordained in 1715, he received the doctorate of the Sorbonne three years later. He was also assistant principal of the College of Plessis, but his defence of Jansenism and his opposition to the Bull "Unigenitus" obliged him to resign the post. In 1729, the Sorbonne erased him from the list of Doctors and, in 1731, he was exiled from Paris. During the following year he was allowed to return. He wrote a "History of the Abbey of Port Royal" (6 vols.), and "Lives of the Four Bishops engaged in the case of Port Royal". We have also from his pen two works on Scripture: "Concorde des livres de la Sagesse" (Paris, 1737), reprinted in Migne's "Cursus Completus" (XVIII) and "Morale des Apôtres ou concorde des épîtres de saint Paul et des épîtres canoniques du N. T." (Paris, 1747).

Mémoire sur la vie et les ouvrages de Jérôme Besoigne (Paris, 1763); QUÉRARD, *La France littéraire* (Paris, 1827), I, 315–316; HEURTEBIZE in *Dict. de théol. cath.*, with a list of his Jansenistic writings; REY in *Dict. de la Bible.*

JOHN CORBETT.

Besoldus, CHRISTOPHER, a German jurist and publicist, b. of Protestant parents in 1577 at Tübingen, Würtemberg; d. 15 September, 1638 at Ingolstadt, Bavaria. He studied jurisprudence and graduated as Doctor of Law in 1598; and in 1610 became professor of law at Tübingen. He was held in high regard as a teacher, and his counsel was frequently sought in juridical questions by the civil administration. His studies extended beyond his specialty; he acquired the knowledge of nine languages; perused the Scriptures, the writings of the Fathers, and of the medieval mystics. His inclination towards the Catholic religion grew with his knowledge of it. He was publicly converted at Heilbronn in 1635. Two years later, he accepted the chair of Roman Law at the University of Ingolstadt. He was considering the offer of a professorship at the University of Bologna, tendered him by Pope Urban VIII, when he died. On his death-bed he conjured his wife to embrace the Catholic faith; three months later she was received into the Church with her eight-year old daughter. The nobleness of character and erudition of Besoldus have been recognized even by his opponents, although an attempt was made to ascribe his conversion to interested motives. His works are very numerous. His publication of three volumes of documents from the Stuttgart archives gave offence because their contents tended to prove that the immediate dependency of the Würtemberg monasteries on the Empire (*Reichsunmittelbarkeit*) implied for the local dukes the obligation of restoring the confiscated religious property. His writings are important for the history of the causes of the Thirty Years War.

RÄSS, *Convertiten* (Freiburg, 1867), V, 310–328; GÜNTER, *Religionsedikt von 1629* (Stuttgart, 1902), 294–306; STINTZING, *Gesch. d. deutschen Rechtswissensch.* (1880), I, 692 sqq.; STEMMER-BRÜCK in *Kirchenlex.*, II, 526–528.

N. A. WEBER.

Bessarion, JOHANNES (or BASILIUS), Cardinal, b. at Trebizond, 1389, or according to others, 1395, but most probably in 1403; d. at Ravenna 18 November, 1472. Some claim illustrious parentage for him, but as to this nothing certain is known. In 1413, while still very young, he was sent to Constantinople, where he devoted himself to study, achieving great success in the field of letters. In 1423 he entered the Order of St. Basil and in the same year was sent to the Peloponnesus to study philosophy under Gemistus Pletho. It is known that Pletho was a bitter opponent of Aristotle, against whom he championed with immoderate zeal the doctrines of Plato, without, however, distinguishing between genuine Platonism and neo-Platonism. The lessons of Pletho, though making Bessarion a follower of Plato, did not prevent him from perceiving the many points of contact between the two philosophers, and, during the revival of ancient learning, constantly defending the harmonizing of the two systems; he criticized the unrestrained partisanship of his master quite as much as that of Michael Apostolius. His learning and eloquence soon excited the admiration and respect of all and brought him, within a short space of time, various ecclesiastical dignities. In 1436 he was made Bishop of Nicæa, but was not destined to see his diocese, however, as the emperor, John VIII Palæologus, had him accompany him to the Council of Ferrara, which they reached 4 March, 1438. Here his dignity and touching eloquence, as well as his vast theological erudition, gave him such great authority among the Greek bishops that the happy issue of the council—the reunion with the Latin Church —may be attributed in great part to him. This was fully recognized, as on 6 July, 1439, in the cathedral of Florence, to which the council had been transferred, he was commissioned to read the Greek redaction of the Act of Union.

JOHANNES, CARDINAL BESSARION

Bessarion returned to Greece, but during the same year is found once more at Florence with Eugenius IV, who, in the consistory of 18 December, 1439 (according to others 8 January, 1440), created him cardinal of the title of the Twelve Holy Apostles. At the same time another Greek, Archbishop Isidore, received the sacred purple. The brief duration of the union of the churches is well known. Bessarion himself, having changed to the Latin Rite was cordially hated by the schismatic Greeks. This notwithstanding, Bessarion continued to work zealously for the union of the other Oriental schismatic churches, the Jacobites and Ethiopians (1442), the Syrians (1444), the Chaldeans and Maronites (1445). At this time, also, to refute the accusations of Marcus of Ephesus, against the council, he wrote the book: "De successu synode florentinæ". Nicholas V, like Eugenius IV, gave evidence of the great regard in which he held the Greek scholar. In 1449 he made him Bishop of Ulazzara and in the same year conferred on him the suburbicarian See of Sabina, for which that of Frascati was shortly after substituted. In the following year he was sent as papal legate to Bologna, a city torn by constant factional quarrels. In the Brief of appointment of 26 February, 1450, the pope says he is sending Bessarion *tamquam angelum pacis*, and expresses the hope that with his experience and prudence he may be able to govern the city in peace.

Bessarion continued as governor of Bologna for five years, achieving complete success in calming the internal discord. Not satisfied with that, he introduced wise reforms into the city government and in the administration of justice. Above all he lavished all his attention and generosity on the university, Bologna's greatest glory, restoring the building which threatened to fall into ruins. He gathered there as teachers the most famous professors of the time, supplying at his own expense the deficiencies in their honoraria, and encouraging with munificence particularly the study of the classics. Thus, he gathered about him a court of poets and men of letters. He was cordial to all, even the lowliest; by stringent legislation he sought to curb immoderate luxury; and he rebuilt and adorned many churches of the city, among them that of San Luca. By his prudent and far-seeing administration and his absolute impartiality he won the confidence of the citizens of Bologna, so that on his departure they honoured his memory in an inscription; and ever afterwards, in all their necessities and in all transactions with the Holy See, they had recourse to his intervention.

While Bessarion was legate in Bologna, Cardinal Stefano Porcaro was in banishment in that city, being assigned one hundred ducats in addition to the annual pension of three hundred granted him by the pope. Porcaro succeeded in eluding Bessarion's vigilance and escaping to Rome. Bessarion did not delay in apprising the pope of his flight. The rest is well known. In 1453 Nicholas V died; and in the conclave following his death, Bessarion was all but chosen to succeed him; however, Calixtus III was finally elected. Constantinople had just fallen into the hands of the Turks and the Byzantine Empire had been destroyed. Thereupon Bessarion used all his influence with Francesco Foscari, the Doge of Venice, as well as with the new pope to persuade them to take up the offensive against the invading barbarians. Not confining his efforts to words, at the cost of heavy pecuniary sacrifices he furthered the cause of the crusade. His zeal was still more pronounced under Pius II, whose election was due in a special manner to him. In the congress of Mantua, convened by the pope in 1459 for the purpose of forming a league of all Christian princes against the Turks, Bessarion took a most active part, not justified, however, by results. The love of his native land impelled him to accept the commission given him by the pope to attend two German diets held the following year, one on the 2nd of March at Nuremberg, the other on the 25th of the same month at Worms. Neither, however, had any practical results. At the command of the pope he went to Vienna to induce the emperor to assist with arms and supplies Matthias Corvinus, the young King of Hungary. After a long wait the German leaders, 17 September, asked for another delay, and only the express wish of Pius II kept Bessarion in Germany for a whole year, pleading the cause of the Christians of the Orient. Internal discord among the German leaders prevented them from reaching any decision concerning the crusade, and Bessarion returned to Rome disillusioned and discouraged. As a reward for his labours the pope bestowed on him the commendatory Abbey of Grotta-Ferrata of Greek Basilians, which became a centre of learned pursuits. Shortly afterwards, on the death of Cardinal Isidore, metropolitan of Kiew and Patriarch of Constantinople, Bessarion received the patriarchal title.

In 1463 Pius II once more sent him to Venice to win that republic over to the cause of the crusade which the pope, on his own initiative, wished to organize. Long, serious discussions ensued, and at last, in September of the same year, the republic signed a treaty of alliance with Matthias Corvinus, and on 20 October the crusade was solemnly proclaimed. The results hoped for, however, were not entirely achieved. During the pontificate of Paul II who continued the crusade, Bessarion withdrew from active affairs and devoted himself entirely to study, cultivating the friendship of many Greek and Italian scientists then in Rome, and engaging in learned discussions with them. Thus he won the title of *Litterarum patronus*. In his house the first *Accademia* was founded. In 1470 when Paul II desired to organize a new crusade, Bessarion wrote the letter "De Bello Turcis inferendo". Sixtus IV, who approved the plans of his predecessor, sent Bessarion once more as legate to the King of France, the Duke of Burgundy, and the King of England to settle the discords which had arisen between the first two, and to induce the last-mentioned to join in the great expedition against the enemy of Christianity. On 20 April, 1472, he left Rome—but was received in an unfriendly manner both in Burgundy and at Paris so that he was forced to return to report the complete failure of his mission. The disappointment, the discomforts of travelling, and his great age made sad havoc on his strength. At Ravenna he was obliged to interrupt his journey; there his death occurred at the Abbey of St. John the Evangelist, 18 November, 1472. His body was taken to Rome and interred in a tomb which had been erected in the portico of the convent of the Conventual Minorites, close by the Basilica of the Twelve Holy Apostles. A simple sarcophagus, on which is inscribed a Greek distich of his own composition, contains his remains.

All the aspirations of Bessarion, which, more than great, were unique, were absorbed by three ideas: the union of the Oriental Church with the Latin, the rescue of Greek lands from the Mussulman yoke, and the triumph of classic literature and philosophy, especially the Greek. If the realization of the first two was only partial or, in a way, temporary, the third was certainly fulfilled to a more complete degree than perhaps Bessarion himself had dared hope. His labours in that direction had lasting success. By his translations of Xenophon's "Memorabilia", Aristotle's "Metaphysics", etc., he paved the way for a more exact knowledge of the real thought of the Stagyrite. His part in the reconciliation of Platonism and Aristoteleanism has already been mentioned. In this contest of intelligence, he wrote the works "In calumniatorem Platonis" against George of Trebizond, who in his translation of the Laws of Plato had sharply criticized their author, exalting Aristotle instead. In the fifth book of his work, Bessarion, in turn, enumerates the faults of translation and the errors in the commentary of George. At a tremendous outlay, he gathered together a library of eight hundred codices of Greek MSS., and still at his own expense had many others copied by men of letters. After 1464 he gave these treasures to the Republic of Venice with which he had always been in the greatest sympathy. These codices formed the nucleus of the famous "Bibliotheca Sancti Marci".

The greater part of BESSARION'S works are to be found in *P. L.*, CLXI. Concerning Bessarion: AL. BLANDINIUS, *De vitâ et rebus gestis Bessarionis* (Rome, 1777); WOLFG. V. GOETHE, *Studien und Forschungen über das Leben und Zeit des Card. B.* (Jena, 1874); VAST, *Le Card. B.* (Paris, 1878); SADOV, *Bessarion de nicée son rôle au concile de Ferrara* (Florence and St. Petersburg, 1883); ROCHOLL, *Bessarion* (Leipzig, 1904).

U. BENIGNI.

Bessel, JOHANN FRANZ (in religion GOTTFRIED), Benedictine, abbot, and historian, b. 5 September, 1672, at Buchen, in the Grand-duchy of Baden; d. at Göttweig, 22 January, 1749. He made his course in the humanities at Aschaffenburg, Würzburg, and Bamberg, and in 1690 entered the University of Salzburg, conducted by the Benedictines, where he specialized in philosophy, also attending lectures on theology and jurisprudence. Attracted by the learning and piety of his teachers, he resolved to become a religious and entered the Benedictine Order at Göttweig on the Danube, Lower Austria, 15 June, 1692. After making his vows (21 June, 1693), he completed his theological course at Vienna, was ordained (21 March, 1696), and on 23 May was granted the degree of Doctor of Theology, being shortly afterwards appointed Lector in philosophy and theology in the monastery of Seligenstadt on the Main. In 1699 he was summoned to the electoral court of Mainz by Archbishop Lothar Franz von Schönborn, who immediately sent him to Rome to study the curial practice of the Rota Romana. Having completed a two years' course in law, he obtained the degree of *Doctor Juris Utriusque*, and on his return to Mainz (1703) he was appointed vicar-general and supreme judge of the whole archdiocese by his benefactor. He was also employed on various diplomatic missions, as, for instance, to the court of Brunswick-Wolfenbüttel in connexion with the conversion of Duke Anton Ulrich and his granddaughter, the Princess Elisabeth Christine, later the wife of Emperor Charles VI. He made three journeys to Rome to settle differences between the pope and the emperor concerning the limits of the province of Comacchio. On 7 February, 1714, he was elected Abbot of Göttweig, and from that time forward was commissioned by the emperor to conduct diplomatic negotiations, in addition to being made imperial theologian and serving twice as honorary rector of the University of Vienna.

Abbot Bessel was the second founder of Göttweig, which became, under his rule of thirty-five years, a centre of learning. He added to the rare Hebrew, Greek, and Roman coins and bracteates collections of copper-plate engravings (over 20,000), minerals, shells, and paintings. By the expenditure of princely sums he enriched the library with thousands of volumes, chiefly on historical subjects, as well as *incunabula* and MSS. Himself a thorough scholar, he encouraged among his religious all undertakings of a scientific or artistic nature. When the abbey was almost totally destroyed by fire, he gathered, by judicious management, means sufficient to rebuild it on a more splendid scale.

Personally, Abbot Bessel was a retiring religious, presenting to all a shining example of monastic piety and virtue. Besides several comparatively unimportant works, such as "Margarita pretiosa", "Curiæ Romanæ praxis", and "Austriæ ritus", he published (Vienna, 1732) two letters of St. Augustine to Optatus, Bishop of Mileve, which had been until then unknown. He is erroneously credited with the authorship of "Quinquaginta Romano-catholicam fidem omnibus aliis præferendi motiva" (Mainz, 1708), a controversial work written originally in Latin, but translated into almost every European tongue. The work which brought him lasting renown and a place in the records of the science of history is entitled "Chronicon Gottwicense, tomus prodromus" (Tegernsee, 1732). Not, as might be thought, a history of the abbey, this single volume is a comprehensive work on German diplomatics, treating of manuscripts found in registers and archives, original documentary evidence, diplomas of German emperors and kings, and inscriptions and seals, illustrated with maps and engravings on copper. The author also discusses medieval geography, as well as the royal palace-domains (*Pfalzen*) and the various districts of Germany. Great learning and clear critical acumen distinguish this work, which marked an epoch in the history of German diplomatics, and has served as the basis of all later works on the same subject.

ALBERT, *Gottfried Bessel und das Chronicon Gottwicense* in *Freiburger Diöcesan-Archiv.* (1899), XXVII, 217–250.

PATRICIUS SCHLAGER.

Beste, HENRY DIGBY, miscellaneous author, b. at Lincoln, England, 21 October, 1768; d. at Brighton, 28 May, 1836. He was the son of the Rev. Henry Beste, D.D., prebendary of Lincoln Cathedral. His mother, Magdalen, daughter and heiress of Kenelm Digby, Esq., of North Luffenham in Rutland, claimed to be the representative of the extinct male line of the historic Sir Everard and Sir Kenelm Digby. His father dying in 1782, Henry was sent two years later by his mother to Oxford. He became a commoner of Magdalen College, where he took his B.A. degree in 1788 and his M.A. in 1781. He was afterwards elected to a fellowship, which he resigned when the family estates came to him on the death of his mother. In September, 1791, he took deacon's

orders in the Anglican Church, and a little later retired to Lincoln, displaying great activity there as a preacher. Doubts about the spiritual authority of the Established Church sprang up in his mind, which were strengthened by intercourse with the Abbé Beaumont, then in charge of the small Catholic chapel at Lincoln. The result was that he was received into the Catholic Church by Rev. Mr. Hodgson, Vicar-General of the London district, 26 May, 1798. In 1800, he married Sarah, daughter of Edward Sealy, Esq., and was the father of the well-known author, John Richard Digby Beste. His first works were a treatise entitled "The Christian Religion briefly defended against the Philosophers and Republicans of France" (octavo, 1793), and in the same year a discourse on "Priestly Absolution" which was republished in 1874. It is interesting that this latter work anticipated some of the Tractarian arguments and met with the warm commendation of the chief members of the University of Oxford in 1794. After his conversion Beste was an occasional contributor to Catholic periodicals. He also travelled abroad and spent several years in France and Italy. Cardinal Wiseman met him at Rome in the Jubilee of 1825, and mentions him in his "Last Four Popes" (Boston, 1858, p. 245). In 1826 Beste published "Four Years in France, or Narrative of an English Family's Residence there during that period, preceded by some account of the Conversion of the Author to the Catholic Faith" (octavo). Two years later he wrote a similar book on his stay in Italy. Ten years after his death appeared his last work, called "Poverty and the Baronet's Family, a Catholic Story" (12mo, 1846).

GILLOW, *Bibl. Dict. Eng. Cath.*, s. v.; KENT in *Dict. Nat. Biog.*, IV, 416.

EDWARD P. SPILLANE.

Bestiaries, medieval books on animals, in which the real or fabulous characteristics of actually existent or imaginary animals (such as the griffin, dragon, siren, unicorn, etc.) were figuratively treated as religious symbols of Christ, the devil, the virtues and vices. The origins of a symbolism of this character, taken from nature, are to be sought in antiquity and above all in the ancient East. Eastern literature, as well as the Greco-Roman literature dependent on it, ascribed to certain animals, whether fabulous or real (the lion, the tiger, the snake, the eagles), a certain connexion with the life and actions of man and the gods, and made a corresponding religious use of them. This is exemplified in the Oriental and especially Egyptian worship of animals. Many reminiscences of this animal symbolism are encountered in the Old Testament. From the earliest period Christian fancy interpreted these animals according to the symbolism of the Old Testament, and so depicted them in Christian art. Thus, for example, in the Catacombs some are symbolic of what is good, e. g. the lamb or sheep representing the soul or the believer, the dove the soul, the phœnix Christ or immortality, and the peacock immortality; others symbolic of what is bad, e. g. the serpent representing the devil; still others, especially in later times, are to be interpreted in various senses; thus the lion may symbolize either Christ or the devil. An early compilation of such allegorical interpretations of the nature of plants and animals, made up partly from antique materials, is still extant in the "Physiologus", the much copied and much used "natural history" of the Middle Ages, and the basis of all later bestiaries. Similar compilations are the "Liber formularum" of Eucherius, some parts of the "Libri originum" of Isidore, parts of the writings of Bede and Rabanus, and the treatise long ascribed to the second-century Melito of Sardes, and known as "Clavis" or "The Key", which appeared in its present form towards the eleventh century. Later bestiaries obtained much valuable material from the "Libri moralium" of Gregory the Great. The medieval bestiaries are more or less exact translations or imitations of the "Physiologus"; e. g. the bestiary of Philippe de Thaun, about 1121, edited by Thomas Wright (London, 1841), and two bestiaries of the thirteenth century, one by Pierre of Picardy, the other by Guillaume of Normandy published by Hippeau (Caen, 1852). The bestiary appears in its complete development in Richard de Fournival's "Bestiaire d'Amour", written in the fourteenth century and published by Hippeau (Paris, 1860), in the treatise "De animalibus" attributed to Bl. Albertus Magnus, in the "Tractatus de bestiis et aliis rebus" supposed to have been written by Hugo of St. Victor, above all in the "Speculum naturale" of Vincent of Beauvais.

The influence of the symbolism of the bestiaries is plainly seen in the various forms of medieval intellectual life. It was evident in the sermon and also in the liturgy as shown by the symbolic use of the bee in the blessing of Easter candles and the blessing of wine on the feast of St. John as a preventive of poisoning from snake-bites. The metrical animal fables, particularly, exhibit the widespread taste for this form of allegory. The influence of the symbolism of the bestiaries is still more manifest in medieval sculpture, both Romanesque and Gothic. Though the use of animal subjects in the oldest Irish and Merovingian art has apparently no deeper aim than the enjoyment of grotesque forms, yet animal symbolism appears from the earliest date as an element of Romanesque art, especially in miniature and sculpture, in both of which it often exhibits a close dependence on the bestiaries. (See ANIMALS IN CHRISTIAN ART; SYMBOLISM.)

ECKL, *Die symbolische Zoologie* in *Organ für christ. Kunst* (1869), No. XII–XXII; KOLLOFF, *Die sagenhafte und symbolische Tiergesch. des Mittelalters* in RAUMER, *Taschenbuch* (1867), 177–269; KREPNER, *Ueber die Tierbücher des Mittelalters* in HERRIG, *Archiv*, Vol. LV; *Katholischer Seelsorger* (1898), 460 sqq.

JOSEPH SAUER.

Betanzos, FRAY DOMINGO, a Dominican missionary, d. at Valladolid, Sept., 1549. One of the most illustrious Dominicans of the sixteenth century in America. A native of Leon in Spain, he first studied jurisprudence at Salamanca, then became a Benedictine and lived as a hermit on the Island of Ponza for five years. He then joined the Dominicans, who had established themselves on the Island of Hispaniola (Santo Domingo) in 1510. Betanzos went there four years later. In 1516 he, with several other Dominicans, wrote a violent letter to Las Casas on the rapid disappearance of the Indians of the Antilles, indulging in the grossest exaggerations about the numbers of the aboriginal population (which they had no means of knowing, even approximately), and the excesses purported to have been committed by the Spaniards. In 1526, Betanzos went to Mexico and founded the Dominican province of Santiago de México. Hardly had it been established when Fray Tomás de Berlanga set forth a claim that it belonged to his newly founded province of Santa Cruz with the provincial seat at Santo Domingo. Betanzos went to Spain in 1531 and obtained from the Holy See the independence of his foundation. He also established the Dominican Province of Guatemala. As Provincial of Mexico in 1535, he at once organized missions among three Indian linguistic stocks: Nahuatl (Aztec, or Mexican), Mixteco, and Tzapoteco. He returned to Spain in 1549, and died in September of the same year at Valladolid. The Bishopric of Guatemala was tendered to Betanzos, but he declined it. While, in his letter of 1516, he acquiesced in the extreme views of his brethren of the order on the question of Indian policy, in the "Opinion" (*Parecer*) given by

him in 1541, and approximately repeated in 1543, just as the unfortunate "New Laws" regarding the Indies were to be promulgated under the influence of Las Casas, he assumed an entirely different attitude. Free from all controversial spirit, he quietly gave his opinion in a sense diametrically opposed to the measures Las Casas pressed upon the Government. This is significant, coming from a member of the same order and of almost equal rank. Betanzos was an intimate friend of the most distinguished Franciscans of Mexico—Archbishop Zumárraga, Motolinia, and others, who did not harmonize with Las Casas in his extreme tendencies. He is credited with the authorship of an addition to the "Doctrina" of Fray Pedro de Córdova which appeared in 1544, and possibly in 1550, but this is not yet fully established.

YCAZBALCETA, *Colección de Documentos para la Historia de México* (Mexico, 1866), I; DOMINGO DE BETANZOS, *Parecer; Documentos inéditos de Indias*, VII; *Carta á Bartolomé de las Casas;* MENDIETA, *Historia eclesiástica indiana*, 1599 (Mexico, 1870); DÁVILA PADILLA, *Historia de la fundación y discurso de la provincia de Santiago de México* (2d ed., Brussels, 1625); BÉRISTAIN, *Biblioteca hispano-americana setentrional* (Mexico, 1816), I; REMESAL, *Historia de la Provincia de San Vicente de Chyapa y Guatemala de la Orden de Santo Domingo* (Madrid, 1619); the same book is also known as, *Historia general de las Indias Occidentales y particular de la gobernación de Chiapas y Guatemala;* GIL GONZALEZ DÁVILA, *Teatro eclesiástico de la primitiva Iglesia de las Indias occidentales* (Madrid, 1649); *Diccionario de Historia y Geografía* (Madrid, 1865), I.

AD. F. BANDELIER.

Betanzos, FRAY PEDRO DE, a Franciscan missionary, b. at Betanzos in Galicia; d. at Chomez, Nicaragua, 1570. He was one of the earliest Franciscan missionaries to Guatemala, and founder of the Church in Nicaragua. He is said to have acquired, in eight years, the use of fourteen Indian languages, including the Nahuatl. It is certain that he possessed an extraordinary gift for linguistics since in one year he mastered the three principal idioms of Guatemala: Quiché, Kakchiquel, and Zutuhil, speaking them as perfectly as the Indians themselves. It was during this time, and on account of his writings, that the controversy began between the Franciscans and Dominicans over the use of the Indian term "Cabovjl" as a synonym for God. Betanzos insisted that they were not synonymous and always wrote "Dios", even in Indian idioms. The Dominicans on the other hand kept up the native term "Cabovil". The Franciscans were right, since the aborigines had no conception of monotheism, and "Cabovil" means, not a personal supreme Deity, but the spiritual essence which all Indians believe to pervade the world, localizing and individualizing at will; an animistic idea underlying Indian fetishism. Betanzos was one of the authors of a work published at Mexico and entitled, "Arte, Vocabulario y Doctrina Christiana en Lengua de Guatemala". It is probably the book printed in Mexico previous to 1553 and ascribed to the "Franciscan Fathers", and also to Bishop Marroquin of Guatemala. No copy of it, however, is known to exist. It is the earliest work printed in any of the languages of Guatemala.

Casual mention of Fray Pedro de Betanzos is found in YCAZBALCETA, *Bibliografía mexicana*, etc. (Mexico, 1886), in which an edition of the *Catecismo y Doctrina* is mentioned (Mexico, 1556), and a reimpression (Guatemala, 1724). The title of the 1556 edition is *Catecismo y Doctrina Cristiana en idioma Utlateco;* of the 1724 print, *Doctrina Cristiana en lengua Guatemalteca*, and while the former is attributed to Bishop Marroquin, the latter has for its authors FRAY JUAN DE TORRES and FRAY PEDRO DE BETANZOS. The biographic data are found in BÉRISTAIN, *Bibliot. hispano-americana set.* (Mexico, 1816), I, who in turn obtained them from VAZQUEZ, *Crónica de la Provincia del Illmo. Nombre de Jesús, del Orden de San Francisco de Guatemala* (Guatemala, 1714–16). SQUIER, *Monograph of Authors*, etc. (New York, 1861), copies BÉRISTAIN. See also LUDEWIG, *Literature of American Aboriginal Languages* (London, 1858). On the controversy over the use of the words "Dios" and "Cabovil" see REMESAL, *Historia de la provincia de San Vicente de Chyapa y Guatemala* (Madrid, 1619).

AD. F. BANDELIER.

Betanzos, JUAN DE.—Unfortunately very little is

known as yet of this official, who has left such valuable works on the Indian traditions and language of Peru. He was a Spaniard by birth and came to Peru at an early day. Whether or not he was still on the Island of Santo Domingo in 1539, as notary or scribe, is uncertain. He was at Cuzco in 1542 and officiated as quasi-interpreter at the investigation of Indian historical traditions ordered by Vaca de Castro. (See Peru.) Even then he had acquired a solid acquaintance with the Quichua idiom. He married an Indian girl of the Inca tribe and composed the first catechism known to us in the Quichua language. The manuscript is now in the National Archives at Lima. In 1551 he finished his book entitled "Suma y Narración de los Incas &c" (dedicating it to the viceroy Antonio de Mendoza), one of the most important sources for ancient Peruvian history. Unfortunately only a part of this work is still known to

of the Mount of Olives. It is not mentioned in the Old Testament; in the New Testament it comes into prominence as the Village of Mary, Martha, and Lazarus, and as the scene of the great miracle of the raising of Lazarus to life by Jesus. Here Jesus often received hospitality in the house of his friends, Mary, Martha, and Lazarus; and near this village Jesus ascended into Heaven. The most accepted etymology of the name is Beit-'Ania', "House of Misery". The Talmud derives the name from Beit-Hinê, or Bêt'uni, "House of Dates". The modern name of the village is el-'Azariye, so called from the memory of Lazarus. The initial letter of the name Lazarus is elided in Arabic after the *l* of the article.

Some believe that the present village of Bethany does not occupy the site of the ancient village; but that it grew up around the traditional cave

THE VILLAGE OF BETHANY

exist. It embodies the earliest accounts of Indian traditions from Bolivia and extreme southern Peru, and as they were gathered by Betanzos within less than fifteen years after the landing of Pizarro, they can hardly be much tainted by contact with Europeans. Of the life of Betanzos, after 1551, practically nothing is known.

Betanzos, *Suma y Narración de los Incas que los Indios Llamaron Capaccuna* (1551, published by Jiménez de la Espada, Madrid, 1880); Espada, *Tres Relaciones de Antigüedades peruanas* (Madrid, 1878, Introduction); García, *El Origen de los Indios* (Father García owned the complete manuscript of Betanzos as late as 1607); Espada, *Una Antigualla peruana* (Madrid, 1892). The report on the Incas bears the title *Discurso sobre la Descendencia y Gobierno de los Ingas*, and is dated 1542; Bandelier, *Aboriginal Myths and Traditions concerning the Island of Titicaca* (1904, *Am. Anthropologist*, VI, No. 2); Idem, *The Cross of Carabuco* (ibid., VI, No. 5); Mendiburú, *Diccionario*, etc. (Lima, 1876), II.

AD. F. BANDELIER.

Bethabara. See Bethany beyond the Jordan.

Bethany (Βηθανία), a village of Palestine, fifteen furlongs, or one mile and three-quarters, east of Jerusalem, at the base of the south-eastern slope

which they suppose to have been at some distance from the house of Martha and Mary in the village. Zanecchia (La Palestine d'aujourd'hui, 1899, I, 445 sq.) places the site of the ancient village of Bethany higher up on the south-eastern slope of the Mount of Olives, not far from the accepted site of Bethphage, and near that of the Ascension. It is quite certain that the present village formed about the traditional tomb of Lazarus, which is in a cave in the village. The identification of this cave as the tomb of Lazarus is merely possible; it has no strong intrinsic or extrinsic authority. The site of the ancient village may not precisely coincide with the present one, but there is every reason to believe that it was in this general location. St. Jerome testifies: "Bethany is a village at the second milestone from Aelia [Jerusalem], on the slope of the Mount of Olives, where the Saviour raised Lazarus to life, to which event the church now built there bears witness" (Onom. ed. Lagarde, 108, 3).

In the early ages this church was called the "Lazarium" and held in great veneration. Towards the close of the fourth century St. Silvia declares that on the Saturday before Palm Sunday the clergy of Jerusalem and the people go out to the Lazarium at Bethany, so that not only the place itself but the fields round about are full of people. In memory of this ancient custom the Franciscan Fathers of the Holy Land and the pilgrims go out and worship at the tomb of Lazarus on Friday of Passion Week. There is no Catholic chapel at Bethany. The Schismatic Greeks have a monastery and chapel there. The land about Bethany is largely a desert of stone, and from the elevated ground north of the village, the eye sweeps over an undulating desert even to the valley of the Jordan. The present village is made up of about forty wretched Moslem houses; there is not a Christian in the village. The only notable ruin at Bethany is that of a tower, a few paces south-east of the tomb of Lazarus. The massive stones yet remaining in portions of the walls indicate that it is older than the Crusades; it may date from the fourth or fifth century. In 1138 Melisenda, wife of King Fulke I, of Jerusalem, founded a cloister of nuns at Bethany; but the ruins of this cloister have not been identified. The sites of the house of Martha and Mary, and of that of Simon the leper are shown at Bethany; but it is evident that these localizations are purely imaginary.

Quarterly statements of the Palestine Exploration Fund; Palestine Pilgrims' Text Society; HEIDET in VIG., *Dict. de la Bib.;* GUÉRIN, *Samarie;* BAEDEKER-BENZIGER, *Palästina und Syrien;* MURRAY, *Handbook, Syria and Palestine;* DE HAMME, *Ancient and Modern Palestine,* tr. ROTTHIER (New York), IV; FAHRNGRUBER, *Nach Jerusalem,* II, 15 sqq.; *Survey of Western Palestina,* Mem., II, 89; MOMMERT, *Ænon und Bethania* (Leipzig, 1903), 30–56; HAGEN, *Lexicon Biblicum;* BREEN, *Diary of my Life in the Holy Land.*

A. E. BREEN.

Bethany Beyond the Jordan (βηθανία πέραν τοῦ Ἰορδάνου).—In the text of St. John's Gospel, i, 28, the author locates the event of Our Lord's baptism by St. John the Baptist at Bethany across the Jordan and there is herein a celebrated variant. The greatest number of the ancient codices, and those of greatest authority, have βηθανία, "Bethany". This reading is approved by Lachmann, Tischendorf, Westcott-Hort, and others. The uncial codices, C², K, T, U, Λ, Π, many minuscule codices, the Sinaitic Syriac, and Cureton's Syriac text have βηθαβαρά, "Bethabara". This reading was approved by Origen, Jerome, Eusebius, and Chrysostom. Origen, in his commentary on this place of St. John's Gospel, declares as follows: "We are not ignorant that in nearly all codices Bethany is the reading. But we were persuaded that not Bethany, but Bethabara should be read, when we came to the places that we might observe the footprints of the Lord, of His disciples, and of the prophets. For, as the Evangelist relates, Bethany the home of Lazarus, Mary, and Martha, is distant from Jerusalem fifteen furlongs, while the Jordan is distant one hundred and eighty furlongs. Neither is there a place along the Jordan which has anything in common with the name Bethany. But some say that among the mounds by the Jordan Bethabara is pointed out, where history relates that John baptized".

Archæological research has failed to identify either Bethany or Bethabara beyond the Jordan; the conjectures range from the ruins on the bank of the Jordan opposite Mahâdet Hadschle, less than two miles north of the mouth of the Jordan, even to Maḥadet 'Abâra, a ford of the Jordan near Bethshean. All things considered, the most probable opinion is that there was a Bethany fifteen furlongs from Jerusalem, and another across the Jordan. The name of this latter may have been a transliteration of בית אניה אניה, "the place of the ship". Bethany across the Jordan has shared the fate of many other Biblical sites which have disappeared from the earth.

The reading "Bethabara" came into the codices on the authority of Origen.   A. E. BREEN.

Betharan, a city of the Amorrhites in the valley-plain east of the Jordan, about twelve miles from Jericho (Num., xxxii, 36; Jos., xiii, 27). It was re-built by the tribe of Gad and later fortified by Herod Antipas, who named it Livias in honour of the wife of Augustus. As she was later called Julia, Josephus speaks of the city as Julias. Having been burnt at the fall of Jerusalem, it was restored by the Christians and became a bishopric. The site is identified by some with Tell el Rameh, six miles east of the Jordan, by others with Beit Harran.

HEIDET in VIG., *Dict. de la Bible;* RIESS, *Bibel-Atlas* (2nd ed., 1887); MERRILL, *East of the Jordan,* 383.

JOHN CORBETT.

Bethdagon, name of two cities in Palestine. (1) A city (Jos., xv, 41) of the tribe of Juda "in the plains", that is, the territory below Joppa between the mountains and the Mediterranean. Its site is uncertain. (2) A city (Jos., xix, 27) of Aser near Zabulon, supposed to be Tell Da'ouk, south-east of Akka.

For references and conjectures see HAGEN, *Lex. Biblicum,* s. v.

JOHN CORBETT.

Bethel (בית־אל, "house of God"), an ancient Canaanitish town, twelve miles north of Jerusalem, not far from Silo on the way to Sichem. The primitive name was Luza. Abram twice offered sacrifice east of Bethel (Gen., xii, 8; xiii, 3). In these passages the name of Bethel is used by anticipation, as it was given to the town by Jacob after his vision (Gen., xxviii, 19). When the Israelites entered the promised land, Bethel was allotted to the tribe of Benjamin, but it was taken and occupied by the Ephraimites (Judges, i, 22–26). It was a place of importance in the subsequent history. Here the Israelites in the days of the Judges were wont to consult the Lord (Judges, xx, 18, 26; xxi, 2; the phrase "in Silo" added in these texts by the Vulgate is a mistake) and the Ark of the Covenant was probably here for a time. Samuel was wont to judge in Bethel every year. After the division of the kingdoms Jeroboam desecrated the place by erecting a golden calf and introducing the Egyptian worship of Apis. This continued until Israel was led captive to Assyria (IV K., x, 29) and was frequently denounced by the prophets Osee and Amos. Shortly before his assumption, Elias visited Bethel, where there was a school of prophets (IV K., ii, 2, 3); the boys from the town mocked Eliseus on his return and were destroyed by bears (ibid., 23). One of the priests who had been carried away captive was allowed to return somewhat later and dwelt in Bethel to teach the people (IV K., xvii, 28). Great confusion of idolatrous worship sprang up, until Josias finally destroyed the altar and the high place there (IV K., xxiii, 15). After the Captivity, the Benjaminites returned to Bethel. In the time of the Macchabees, it was fortified by Bacchides. There is no mention of Bethel in the New Testament, but Josephus records that it was taken by Vespasian (Bell. Jud., IV, ix, 9). Eusebius mentions the place as a village. It is commonly identified nowadays with Beitin. The ruins of several Christian churches on the spot would indicate that in the Middle Ages it had again grown to some importance. The name "Bethel" is also read in Jos., xii, 16 and I K., xxx, 27; it is probably another name for Bethul (Jos., xix, 4), a city of the tribe of Simeon, the site of which is uncertain.

HAGEN, *Lexicon Biblicum,* s. v.; SMITH, *Hist. Geogr. of the Holy Land,* 119, 250 sqq.; 290 sqq., 352; ZANECCHIA, *La Palestine d'aujourd'hui* (1890), II, 488 sqq.; SCHENZ in *Kirchenlex.,* s. v.

JOHN CORBETT.

Bethlehem, a titular see of Palestine. The early name of the city was Ephrata; afterwards Bethlehem,

VIEW OF BETHLEHEM
INTERIOR OF THE CHURCH OF THE NATIVITY, BETHLEHEM

"House of Bread"; to-day Beith-Lahm, "House of Flesh". There died Rachel, Jacob's wife (Gen., xv, 60); David was born there (I Kings, xvi, 2), and many other Biblical personages. There was enacted the gracious idyll of Ruth and Booz. There, above all, the Saviour was born, a descendant of David, and from this fact the humble village has acquired unparalleled glory. It was at Bethlehem, also, that in the fourth century St. Jerome, St. Paul, and St. Eustochium fixed their residence. According to John Cassian, it was in a monastery of Bethlehem that the office of Prime was instituted. As early as the second century it was indicated by St. Justin Martyr, a native of Neapolis (Nâblous), as the place of the Nativity. About A. D. 330 Constantine the Great built a basilica on this site. The present church appears to date from a later time—either the fifth or the sixth century—and has been repaired at still later periods. The Frankish kings were wont to come from Jerusalem to be crowned at Bethlehem, in memory of the coronation of David by Samuel. The greater part of the church is now shared by various communions; while the choir belongs to the Greeks alone, the Grotto of the Nativity is open to the Latins, the Greeks, and the Armenians, who hold services there each in turn.

The first Bishop of Bethlehem, Arnolfo (1099–1103), was appointed by the Crusaders. The see was not canonically erected until 1109, when the title was united with that of Ascalon, till then a Greek diocese (Revue de l'Orient latin, I, 141). The Diocese of Bethlehem-Ascalon existed from 1109–1378, but since the middle of the thirteenth century its bishops resided at Clamecy in France. The Diocese of Bethlehem-Clamecy was created in 1378, and suppressed by the Concordat between Napoleon and Pius VII, in 1801. The titular Bishoprics of Bethlehem and Ascalon, however, had existed separately from 1378 to 1603, when they were suppressed. From 1801 to 1840 both residential and titular sees, either of Bethlehem or Ascalon, were extinct. In 1840, Gregory XVI reunited the title of Bethlehem *in perpetuum* to the independent Abbey of St. Maurice d'Agaune in Switzerland. In 1867 the titular See of Ascalon was also re-established.

Bethlehem is to-day a little town with about 10,000 inhabitants, exclusive of foreigners (5,000 Latins, 100 Catholic, or Melchite, Greeks, 4,000 Greeks, a few Armenians and Mussulmans). The inhabitants are very active and industrious. Besides agriculture, they are engaged in the fabrication of wooden, mother-of-pearl, and bituminous limestone objects, such as beads, crosses, etc. The women are remarkably beautiful and wear a peculiar costume which is very rich and of ancient pattern. The Franciscans govern the Latin parish, a scholasticate, a primary school, and an asylum; the Christian Brothers have a novitiate for native young men; the Fathers of the Sacred Heart, or Betharramites, have a scholasticate for their missions in South America; the Salesians conduct an industrial school with an orphanage and an elementary school; the Sisters of St. Joseph of the Apparition have two convents, a school, an orphanage, and an infant school; the Sisters of Charity have a hospital and an orphanage; the Carmelite nuns, a monastery. The Greek Catholic parish lately established has not yet a church. There are also Greek and Armenian monasteries, and schools conducted by Greeks, Armenians, and Protestants.

LEQUIEN, *Ord. Christ.*, III, 1275–1386; GAMS, 516; EUBEL, I, 138; II, 118; RIANT, *Etudes sur l'histoire de l'évêché de Bethléem* (Genoa, 1888), completed by papers in *Revue de l'Orient latin*, I, 140–160, 381–412, 475–524; II, 35–72, with an exhaustive bibliography; MAS-LATRIE, *Trésor de chronologie* (Paris, 1889), col. 1391–94; GUÉRIN, *Judée*, I, 120–207; CONDER, *Tentwork in Palestine*, I, 282.

S. VAILHÉ.

Bethlehem.—The old Hebrew name *bêth lehem*, meaning "house of bread", has survived till the present day. In its Arabic form, however, *bêt lahm*, it means "house of meat". Several scholars (Smith, Hist. Geog. of the Holy Land, 1906, 318, n. 2) hold that the name is connected with Lakhmu, one of the divinities in the Babylonian Creation myth and that Bethlehem was a sacred shrine of that god in ancient times. This is possible, but there is no actual evidence in favour of the conjecture. Two cities of the name are known from Sacred Scripture: I. BETHLEHEM is mentioned in Jos., xix, 15, as one of the twelve cities belonging to the tribe of Zabulon. It is but a small town, poorly built, and of no great importance (Buhl, Geog. des alten Palästina, 1896, 215), a little less than seven miles south-west of Sapphoris (Ṣaffūrieh) and seven miles north-west of Nazareth, the home of Our Lord. Critics do not agree among themselves whether the Bethlehem described in Judges, xii, 8, 10, as the home of Abesan (Ibzan), one of the minor judges, is the same as that of Jos., xix, 15, or Bethlehem of Juda. A large number if not the majority of modern commentators, are in favour of Bethlehem of Zabulon. But ancient tradition (Josephus, Antiq., V, vii, 13; cf. also Moore, Judges, Int. Crit. Com.) made Abesan spring from Bethlehem of Juda and the view is ably defended by Father Lagrange in his commentary (Smith, op. cit.; Hogg, Encyc. Bib., IV, 5389). In any case

GENERAL VIEW OF BETHLEHEM

the importance of that city was never great. But the efforts of some modern critics have made it more famous. Unable to accept as historical the narratives of Our Lord's birth in Bethlehem of Juda, these scholars would place the Nativity in Bethlehem of Zabulon, referred to in the Talmud (Megilla, 70, a) as Bethlehem *ṣeriyyah*, which is regarded as equivalent to *nōṣĕryyah*, i. e. Bethlehem of Nazareth (of Galilee), a certainly remarkable combination of two names so well known from the Gospels (Réville, Jésus de Nazareth, 2nd ed., Paris, 1906, I, 360).

II. BETHLEHEM OF JUDEA [so the Greek text of Matt., ii, 1, erroneously corrected by St. Jerome to Bethlehem of Juda, thinking that the Evangelist had in his original text conformed to the Old Testament usage (Judges, xvii, 7, xix, 1; I Kings (Sam.), xvii, 12)], is much more celebrated than its northern namesake as the birthplace of David, and above all, of Our Lord. The city, which numbers now about 10,000 inhabitants, almost exclusively Christians, is situated five miles south of Jerusalem at a very short distance from the highroad from Jerusalem to Hebron, in the midst of a most beautiful country (Buhl, op. cit., 19), which contrasts favourably with the neighbourhood of

Jerusalem. At an altitude of 2,350 feet it spreads out between the Wadi el Hrobbe in the North and the Wadi er-Rāhib in the south; the land of Moab is visible in the south-east, a detail to be remembered in reading the beautiful story of Ruth the Moabitess, the scene of which is Bethlehem (Smith, op. cit.). The main resources of Bethlehem are agriculture and the sale of religious articles; the city is also the market-place of the peasants and bedouins of the neighbourhood.

According to Gen., xxxv, 16, 19; xlviii, 7, Bethlehem was associated with the patriarchal history. The sepulchre of Rachel, or Qubbet Rāhîl (Rachel's dome) as it is called now, about one mile north of Bethlehem, still shown to the pilgrim and venerated by Christians, Mohammedans, and Jews, is referred to again in I Kings (Sam.), x, 2, and Matt., ii, 16–18; cf. Jer., xxxi, 15. As an examination of these passages shows, the tradition presents some obscurities, and critics question the correctness of the gloss (Gen., xxxv, 19) which identifies Ephrata with Bethlehem, supposing it the result of a confusion between Bethlehem-Ephrata [Ruth, iv, 11; Mich., v, 2 (1)], i. e. our Bethlehem, and another Ephrata in the north, otherwise unknown, or assume two different traditions regarding Rachel's sepulchre. (Cf. commentaries: Driver in Hast., "Dict. of the Bible", IV, 193, a; Buhl, op. cit., 156, 159; Bädeker-Benzinger, "Palästina und Syrien", 1904, 91.) Bethlehem is mentioned also in Judges as the home of the young Levite who went to Michas (xvii, 7 sqq.) and of the young woman (xix, 1 sqq.) whose death caused the expedition against the tribe of Benjamin. In the Old Testament, however, it is connected especially with the great King David (I Kings, xvi, 1 and *passim*), whose name is given to the three cisterns (Bi 'ār Dā 'ūd), found north-west of the town, not far from the tomb of Rachel. A tradition not older than the end of the fifteenth century, according to Bädeker-Benzinger (p. 91), sees therein the cistern referred to in II Kings, xxiii, 14 sqq. and I Par. (Chron.), xi, 16 sqq. Later the city was fortified by Roboam (II Par., xi, 6), and I Esd. (Ezrah), ii, 21 sqq. [cf. II Esd. (Nehem.), vii, 26] informs us of the return of 123 Bethlehemites from the Captivity.

In the New Testament, we have, with the exception of John, vii, 42, references to Bethlehem only in Matt., ii, and Luke, ii, whose narratives of the birth of the Saviour in the city of David have rendered it most dear to Christians. Many modern critics, however, are making Bethlehem again "little among the thousands of Judah" (Schmidt, The Prophet of Nazareth, 1905, 246) by attacking the historical value of the Gospel narratives. Some place Our Lord's birth at Nazareth, called His πατρίς in the Gospels (Mark, vi, 1, and parall.; cf. i, 9; i, 24, etc.); this is done by almost all those who deny the historicity of the Infancy, endeavouring to explain our narratives as a legend arisen from the Jewish tradition that the Messiah had to be born in Bethlehem, occasioned by Micheas, v, 2 (1). (Cf. Targum; also John, vii, 42; Strauss, Life of Christ, tr. Eliot, from the 4th Germ. edit., 1840, § 32, end, § 39; Usener in "Encyc. Bib.", III, 3346–47; Schmidt, op. cit., 243, 246; Weiss in "Die Schriften des N. T.", Göttingen, 1906, I, 1, pp. 46, 221–223, 393–395.) Others more seldom give the explanation already mentioned.

This question, which is part of the larger problems connected with cc. i–ii of Matt. and Luke, cannot be discussed here. [See besides the lives of Jesus and commentaries: Ramsay, "Was Christ born at Bethlehem?", 1898, and QUIRINIUS, CENSUS OF.] Suffice it to remark here that if the second explanation removes some difficulties, it requires us to go entirely behind the narratives of both Matt. and Luke, who most clearly mean only Bethlehem of Juda (see Knowling, "Dictionary of Christ and the Gospels",

New York, 1906, I, 204). Against the first explanation it may be noted with many critics that Matt. and Luke agree independently in placing the birth at Bethlehem without, in St. Luke's case, any sign of influence of Micheas' prophecy (Knowling, op. cit.; Nichol, "Dictionary of Christ", I, 195, a; Jacquier, "Hist. des livres du N. T.", Paris, 1905, II, 209). We must not, however, exaggerate the value of that argument. (Cf. Revue d'histoire et de littérature religieuses, Jan.–Feb., 1906, 62 sqq.) These difficulties were unknown to the ancient writers, who reproduce simply the Gospel narratives with additions, in some cases possibly historical. About 150 we find St. Justin Martyr referring (Dial., lxxviii) to the Saviour's birth as having taken place in a cave near the village of Bethlehem; such cave stables are not rare in Palestine. (Cf. Massie in Hast., Dict. of the Bible, III, 234; Expository Times, May, 1903, 384; Bonaccorsi, "Il Natale", Rome, 1903, 16–20.) The tradition of the birth in a cave was widely accepted, as we see from Origen's words about a century later: "In Bethlehem the cave is pointed out where He was born, and the manger in the cave where He was wrapped in swaddling clothes, and the rumour is in those places and among foreigners of the Faith that indeed Jesus was born in this cave". (Contra Celsum, I, li.) It is reproduced also in the apocryphal gospels (Pseudo-Matt., xiii, ap. Bonaccorsi, op. cit., 159–163; Protevang. of James, xvii sqq., Bonaccorsi, 155–159; Gospel of the Infancy, II–IV, Bonaccorsi, 163–164). Over the traditional spot of the Nativity stands a church (St. Mary of the Nativity), surrounded on the north-west and south-west by the convents of the Latins (Franciscans), Greeks, and Armenians, respectively. The building is, apart from additions and modifications made by Justinian (527–565), substantially the work of Constantine (about 330). Underneath that most ancient and venerable monument of Christianity, a favourite resort of pilgrims throughout the centuries, is the grotto of the Nativity. The Nativity chapel, running in the same general direction as the church (east to west), is situated under the choir; at the eastern end is a silver star with the inscription: *Hic de Virgine Maria Jesus Christus natus est*, and near the chapel of the Crib (see Bonaccorsi, op. cit., 77–113). Other grottoes to the north and north-west connected with that of the Nativity are associated, mostly by recent traditions (c. fifteenth century), with the narratives of Matt., ii, mainly, and with the memory of the great scholar St. Jerome and his company of pious and learned friends (Sanders, Etudes sur S. Jérôme, Paris, 1903, 29 sqq.).

EDWARD ARBEZ.

Bethlehem, an architectural term used in the Ethiopic Church for the oven or bakehouse for baking the Korbân or Eucharistic bread. It is a usual attachment to Coptic churches and is generally situated somewhere within the enclosure of the church. It is shown in the plan of Mâri Mîna and the adjoining church of Mâri Banai. The four walls of Dair Abu Makar enclose one principal and one or two smaller court-yards around which stand the cells of the monks, domestic buildings, such as the milkroom, the oven (Bethlehem), the refectory and the like.

BUTLER, *The Ancient Coptic Churches of Egypt*, I, 48.

THOMAS H. POOLE.

Bethlehem, COUNCILS OF. See JERUSALEM, SYNOD OF.

Bethlehemites.—I. Military order; II. Hospitalers. I. There were two military orders dedicated to Our Lady of Bethlehem and known under the name of Bethlehemites. Matthew Paris calls attention to the former in his "Grande Chronique" (tr. Huillard-Bréholles, Paris, 1840, 8vo, III, 300) where he mentions that Henry III of England authorized them to open a house in a suburb of Cambridge (1257); but he leaves us in complete ignorance as to their founder, where they originated, and their history. We only know that their habit was similar to that of the Dominicans and that a red star, whose five rays emanated from an azure centre, decorated the breast of their cape. This was in commemoration of the star that appeared to the Magi and led them to Bethlehem. Nothing further is known of this military order. There was an order of knights whose members wore a red star on their costume and who might have been called Bethlehemites because of having a house in Bethlehem at the time of the Crusades; this was the Military Order of Crusaders of the Red Star (*Ordo militaris crucigerorum cum rubeâ stellâ*). They came from Palestine to Bohemia in 1217, and Blessed Agnes of Bohemia confided two hospitals to their charge. They have since remained in that country where they devote themselves to the care of the sick, to education, and to the various works of the ecclesiastical ministry.

After the taking of Constantinople by the Turks (1453), Pius II founded under the patronage of Our Lady of Bethlehem an order of knights for the defence of the Island of Lemnos which Cardinal Louis, Patriarch of Aquileia, had recaptured from Mohammed II. The island was to be their headquarters whence they were to oppose the attacks of the Moslems by way of the Ægean Sea and the Hellespont. The order was composed of brother-knights and priests governed by an elective grand-master. The white costume worn by the members was decorated with a red cross and the rule prescribed for them was very similar to that of the Knights of St. John of Jerusalem. The pope installed this community 18 January, 1459, and, that their needs might be supplied, turned over to them the property and revenues of the orders of St. Lazarus, of Sainte-Marie du Château des Bretons, of Bologna, of the Holy Sepulchre, of Santo Spirito in Sassia, of St. Mary of the Crossed Friars, and of St. James of Lucca, all of which were suppressed for this purpose. Pius II alluded in a Bull to this foundation and the bravery of its knights, but the second capture of Lemnos by the Turks rendered the institution useless. Thus the order of Our Lady of Bethlehem was suppressed almost as soon as founded and those orders whose goods the pope had transmitted to it were re-established.

II. The hospitaler Bethlehemites, or Belemites, were founded by the Ven. Pedro de Betancourt. A descendant of the celebrated Juan de Betancourt, who, early in the fifteenth century, achieved the conquest of the Canary Islands for Henry III of Spain, Pedro was born at Villaflora on the Island of Teneriffe in 1619. From childhood he led a pious, austere life and in 1650 left family and country, thus carrying out his desire of going to the West Indies. During the following year he reached Guatemala, the capital of New Spain, where he intended to prepare for the priesthood that later he might go forth and evangelize Japan. However, three years of unsuccessful study at a Jesuit college led him to abandon this idea and, after holding the position of sacristan for a while in a church dedicated to the Blessed Virgin, he rented a house in a suburb of the city called Calvary, and there taught reading and catechism to poor children. But this charitable work did not furnish sufficient outlet for his zeal. The condition of the sick poor excited his compassion and he sheltered them in his home which he converted into a hospital. His zeal elicited benefactions from those around him and the bishop and governor supplied him with all the conveniences he required. Several individuals provided for the purchase of the houses surrounding the one he then occupied and on their site was erected a hospital in which this servant

of God could labour to better advantage. He himself worked with the masons. The hospital was thoroughly equipped and stocked and even offered an opportunity for the religious installment of those who tended the sick. The institution was placed under the patronage of Our Lady of Bethlehem.

Helpers soon joined Pedro de Betancourt and at length was formed a congregation of brothers generally known as Bethlehemites and so called on account of their house. But the care of the sick did not totally absorb their attention; they likewise lent their assistance in the two other hospitals of the city and Pedro continued to befriend poor children. The prisoners also excited his compassion. Every Thursday he begged for them through the city and visited them in their cells. The neglected souls in purgatory were also the objects of his solicitude and at the principal gates of the city he founded two hermitages, or chapels, wherein religious of his community begged, so that masses might be celebrated for the souls of the deceased. He himself would travel the streets at night ringing a bell and recommending these souls to be prayed for. His devotion to the Blessed Virgin was inspiring and during a novena of preparation for the feast of the Purification his religious, with arms extended in the form of a cross, recited the rosary in their chapel at midnight in the midst of a great throng. In 1654 he made a vow to defend the Immaculate Conception even at the peril of his life. He died, exhausted by labour and penance, 25 April, 1667, at the age of forty-eight. His funeral was impressive and at the request of the Capuchin Fathers he was buried in their church where, for a long time, his remains were held in veneration.

Before establishing his Guatemala hospital Pedro de Betancourt had become affiliated with the Third Order of St. Francis, adopting its religious garb which he still retained after founding his congregation. He personally trained his first disciples and had no wish to organize a community, but simply to establish his hospital. He sent Brother Anthony of the Cross to Spain to solicit the king's approbation of the work. The favour was granted, but Pedro died before the messenger's return. From that time the community prospered, beginning with the extension of the hospital and the erection of a beautiful church. Brother Anthony, who assumed the government, drew up constitutions which he submitted to the bishop of the diocese for approval and it was at this juncture that the Capuchins requested him to make some alterations in the habit worn by his religious. A free school for poor children was always connected with the Bethlehem hospital, a feature of all new foundations. One of these was soon undertaken by Brother Anthony of the Cross who sent two of his community to Peru where they were very favourably received by the viceroy to whom he had recommended them. Doctor Antoine d'Avila gave them the Hospital of Notre Dame du Carmel which he was then establishing at Lima and afterwards solicited admission among them. In 1672 Brother Roderick of the Cross obtained the confirmation of this establishment by the King of Spain and it was also through his efforts that Pope Clement X confirmed the congregation and its constitutions (1673). After his return to America this religious founded the Hospital of St. Francis Xavier in Mexico and those of Chachapoyas, Cajamarca, and Trujillo, going back to Spain in 1681 to secure the confirmation of these new institutions. The Council of the Indies assigned the hospital of Lima an income of 3,000 crowns. The Bethlehemites, because of making only simple vows, remained under diocesan jurisdiction from which they wished, however, to be freed so that their congregation might be converted into a regular religious order bound by solemn vows. The Spanish court did not approve this plan and at first the Holy See was not favourable to it, but due chiefly to the influence of Cardinal Mellini, former nuncio at Madrid, Roderick of the Cross at length overcame all difficulties and in the Bull of 26 March, 1687, Innocent XI authorized these religious to make the three solemn vows according to the rule of St. Augustine and to have a superior-general, and granted them all the privileges of the Augustinian friars and convents. Later, Clement XI renewed this authorization and these favours, adding thereunto the privileges of the mendicant orders, of the Regular Clerks, of the Ministers of the Sick, and of the Hospitallers of Charity of St. Hippolytus (1707).

Meanwhile the order was multiplying its foundations in Latin America and was established in Arequipa, Cuzco, Santiago de Cuba, Puebla, Guadalajara, Guanajuato, Dajaka, Vera Cruz, Havana, Santiago de Chile, Buenos Ayres, and Guatemala la Nueva. A school for poor children was connected with every hospital and the pious, devoted lives of these religious won them esteem and gratitude. They were especially admired during the plague of 1736, a fact unanimously acknowledged by the writers who describe the condition of Latin America in the eighteenth century. But this did not prevent their suppression, as well as that of all other religious, in 1820. At that time their superior-general resided in Mexico and the Bethlehemites were scattered throughout two provinces, that of Peru including twenty-two houses and that of New Spain, eleven. To the ordinary religious vows they added that of caring for the sick even at the risk of their own lives. In 1688 Brother Anthony of the Cross, with the help of a pious woman, Marie Anne del Gualdo, founded at Guatemala a community of Bethlehemite nuns and a hospital exclusively for women. These nuns were cloistered and observed the same rule as the men and they, too, were suppressed in 1820.

HÉLYOT, *Histoire des ordres monastiques*, III, 355–356; VIII, 371–372; BARONIUS, *Annales ecclesiastici* (Lucca, 1753), XXIX, 179–180; HEIMBUCHER, *Die Orden und Kongregationen*, I, 497–498; DE MONTALVO, *Vida del venerable Pedro de San José Betancourt* (Rome, 1718); EYZAGUIRRE, *Los intereses católicos en América* (Paris, 1859), II, 304–306, 408–410.

J. M. BESSE.

Bethsaida.—I. A CITY, or perhaps two cities, on the shore of the Lake of Genesareth, the frequent scene of Christ's preaching and miracles (Matt., xi, 21; Luke, x, 13).—II., in the Vulgate, a POOL in Jerusalem, also called Bethesda (John, v, 2).—III. A TITULAR SEE.

I. THE CITY. (Gr. βηθσαιδά; Aram. בית צידא, "house, or place, of fishing".) The old writers, up to the sixteenth century, knew of but one Bethsaida, though they do not seem to have always indicated the same site. Since then it has been a much debated question whether there were not two places of this name: one east of the Jordan; the other west, near Capharnaum. A Bethsaida, which the Tetrarch Philip enlarged into a city and named Julias, after the daughter of Augustus, existed east of the river, near where it enters the lake (Josephus, Ant., XVIII, ii, 1; Bell. Jud., II, ix, 1; III, x, 7; Vita, 72). Near this Bethsaida took place the feeding of the five thousand (Luke, ix, 10) and the healing of the blind man (Mark, viii, 22). Whether another is to be admitted, depends on two questions on which the controversy mainly turns: whether Julias, though belonging politically to Gaulonitis, was comprised within the limits of Galilee (John, xii, 21) and whether, in Mark, vi, 45, and John, vi, 17, a direct crossing from the eastern to the western shore is intended. The negative view seems to be gaining ground. In the supposition of two Bethsaidas, the western would be the home of Peter, Andrew, and Philip (John, i, 44; xii, 21), and the Bethsaida of Matt., xi, 21 and Luke, x, 13. Julias is identified by many with et-Tell; but, as this is

somewhat too far up the river to answer Josephus's description, others prefer El-Araj, close to the shore, or Mes'adîyeh farther east. The partisans of a western Bethsaida are much divided on its site. 'Ainet-Tâbigha and Khân Minyeh are most favoured.

II. THE POOL. [Gr. βηθσαιδά, βηθεσδά, βηθζαθά. —Bethesda is supported by most Gr. MSS., still Bethzatha may be the true reading and Bethesda a corruption, as Bethsaida most probably is. Bethesda probably = בית חסדא (House of Mercy). The etymology of Bethzatha is uncertain.] This pool had five porches in which the sick lay "waiting for the moving of the waters" (John, v, 3) and most likely steps led down to it. Here the Saviour cured a man "that had been eight and thirty years under his infirmity". The Vulgate and most of the Fathers call it a "sheep pool" (προβατική, probatica), but the Greek text of John, v, 2, is commonly un-

THE POOL OF BETHSAIDA

derstood to mean that it was situated near the sheep gate. This would place it north of the temple area. The early writers speak of it as a double pool, the fifth portico running between the two basins, but give no details as to its location. From the sixth to the thirteenth century, it is mentioned as being near the present church of St. Anne. Just west of this church an old double pool was discovered some years ago, which is, there is little doubt, the pool spoken of by medieval writers, and probably the old pool of Bethesda. Since the fourteenth century Birket Isrâ'în, north-east of the temple area, is pointed out as Bethesda. Others prefer the Fountain of the Virgin ('Ain Sitti Mariam, or 'Ain Umm ed-Derej) because of its intermittent flow; or the pool of Siloe, which, being fed by the preceding, shares its intermittence. Lastly, some advocate Hammâm esh-Shifâ (Bath of Health), west of the temple area, because of its name.

III. THE TITULAR SEE.—It is uncertain at what period Bethsaida, the former of the two cities (Julias) mentioned under I, became a titular see depending on Scythopolis. There was in the region of Nineveh another Bethsaida, with a Jacobite titular bishop in 1278.

I.—In favour of the hypothesis of two cities of the same name, ROBINSON, *Bibl. Researches* (London, 1856), II, 405; III, 358; RELAND, *Palästina* (Utrecht, 1714), 653, 869; GUÉRIN, *Galilee* (Paris, 1880), I, 329; EWING in HASTINGS, *Dict. of the Bible*; VAN KASTEREN in *Rev. Bibl.*, III, 65 sqq. In favour of one, SMITH, *Histor. Geogr. of the Holy Land*, 457 sqq.; MARTA in *Rev. Bibl.*, III, 445; BUHL, *Geogr. d. alt. Paläst.* (Freiburg im Br., 1896), 241 sqq.; FURRER in *Zeitschr. d. Deutsch. Pal. Ver.*, II, 66. See also: SCHÜRER, *Jewish People* (tr. New York, 1891), I, ii, 14; II, i, 135; HEIDET in VIG., *Dict. de la Bible*, I, 1713 sqq.

II.—*Survey of Western Palest., Jerusalem*, 115 sqq.; *Palest. Explor. Fund*, Quart. Stat., 1888, 115 sqq.; ROBINSON, *Bibl. Researches* (London, 1856), I, 330 sqq.; GUÉRIN, *Jérusalem* (Paris, 1889), 282 sqq.; LIÉVIN DE HAMME, *Terre Sainte* (1897), I, 338–340; TOBLER, *Denkblätter aus Jerus.*, 53–69; SCHICK in *Zeitschr. d. Deutsch. Pal. Ver.*, XI, 178–183; HEIDET in VIG., *Dict. de la Bible*, 1723 sqq.

III.—LEQUIEN, *Oriens Christ.*, II, 1577.

F. BECHTEL.

Bethsan (Heb. בֵּית־שְׁאָן, Bêth Shĕān, or בֵּית־שַׁן, Bêth Shān, "place of rest"), a city within Issachar, but assigned to Manasses (Jos., xvii, 11; I Par., vii, 29); later Scythopolis, now the village Beisân, three miles west of the Jordan. Because of its strength the Israelites could not take it at the time of the conquest (Jos., xvii, 16; Judges, i, 27), and when the Philistines hung up the bodies of Saul and his three sons on its walls after the battle of Gelboe (II Kings, xxi, 12), it was probably still in the hands of the Chanaanites. Under Solomon it was the centre of an administrative district (III Kings, iv, 12). About the beginning of the third century B. C. it was named Scythopolis, probably because Scythians had settled there. After paying tribute to the Ptolemies, it passed under Syrian rule in 198 B. C., and in 107 fell into the hands of John Hyrcanus. Pompey took it from the Jews, and thenceforth it was a free city and one of the chief towns of Decapolis. In Christian times it became an episcopal and later a metropolitan see.

ROBINSON, *Bibl. Researches* (London, 1856), III, 326–332; *Survey of Western Palest.*, Mem. II, 101–114; SCHÜRER, *Jewish People* (tr. New York, 1891), II, i, 110–113; RELAND, *Palästina* (Utrecht, 1714), 992, 998; GUÉRIN, *Samarie* (Paris, 1874, 1875), I, 284–299.

F. BECHTEL.

Bethulia (Gr., βετυλούα), the city whose deliverance by Judith, when besieged by Holofernes, forms the subject of the Book of Judith. The view that Bethulia is merely a symbolic name for Jerusalem or a fictitious town, has met with little favour, even among those who deny the historical character of the book. Bethulia is clearly distinguished from Jerusalem (iv, 6; xi, 14, 19; xv, 5, 8; the references throughout the article being to the fuller Greek text), and the topographical details leave no doubt that the story, even if it be only a pious romance, is connected with a definite place. Its site, however, is in dispute. Beside Sânûr, Mithilîyeh, or Misilîyeh, Tell Kheibar and Beit-Ilfa, which have had divided opinion for some time, Haraiq el-Mallah, Khirbet Sheikh Shibel, el-Bârid and Sichem (Bethulia being considered a pseudonym) have recently been proposed as sites of Bethulia.

The city was situated on a mountain overlooking the plain of Jezrael, or Esdrelon, and commanding narrow passes to the south (iv, 6, 7; vi, 11–13); at the foot of the mountain there was an important spring, and other springs were in the neighbourhood (vi, 11; vii, 3, 7, 12). Moreover it lay within investing lines which ran through Dothain, or Dothan, now Tell Dothân, to Belthem, or Belma, no doubt the same as the Belamon of viii, 3, and thence to Kyamon, or Chelmon, "which lies over against Esdrelon" (vii, 3). These data point to a site on the heights west of Jenîn (Engannim), between the plains of Esdrelon and Dothan, where Ḥaraiq, Kh. Sheikh Shibel, and el-Bârid lie close together. Such a site best fulfils all requirements. It lies between lines drawn from Tell Dothân to Bel'ema, probably Belma, or Belamon, and from the latter to el-Yâmûn, probably Kyamon; there are a number of springs and wells in the neighbourhood, and near by are the two passes of Kefr Adân and Burqîn, so narrow

in places that two horsemen cannot ride abreast. One of the three above-named places is in all probability the site of ancient Bethulia. The other sites are all deficient in some essential requirement.

Survey of Western Palest., Mem. II, 156; ROBINSON, *Bibl. Researches* (London, 1856), III, 337 sqq.; TORREY in *Journ. Am. Or. Soc.*, XX, 160 sqq.; GUÉRIN, *Samarie* (Paris, 1874, 1875), I, 344–350; RAUMER, *Paläst.* (4th ed., Leipzig, 1860), 151; RITTER, *Erdkunde* (Berlin, 1848–52), XV, 423 sqq.; SCHULTZ in *Zeitschr. d. deutsch. morgenl. Gesch.*, III, 48; HEIDET in VIG., *Dict. de la Bible*, I, 1751 sqq.; MARTA, *Intorno al vero sito di Betulia* (Florence, 1887); BRUNENGO in *Civiltà Catt.*, ser. 13, IX, 527; ZANECCHIA, *La Palest. d'aujourd.*, II, 581.

F. BECHTEL.

Bethune, JAMES. See BEATON, JAMES.

Betrothal (Lat. *sponsalia*), the giving of one's troth —that is, one's true faith or promise. Betrothal, in the Catholic Church, is a deliberate and free, mutual, true promise, externally expressed, of future marriage between determinate and fit persons. It is a promise, compact, or agreement—not merely an intention; and, like all contracts, it must be entered into with deliberation proportionate to the obligation which it begets; it must be free from force, substantial error, and grave fear. The promise given must be mutual; a promise on the part of one only, with acceptance by the other, does not constitute a betrothal. The consent, of course, as in all contracts, must be true, or sincere, not feigned; it must be given with the intention of binding oneself, and this intention must be expressed verbally, by writing, or by action, in person or by proxy. Lastly, this contract, like matrimony, can exist only between two definite persons whose capacity is recognized by the Church; that is, between whom there is no matrimonial impediment, either as regards the licitness or validity of the contract. The betrothal is a promise of future marriage, and hence it differs from the marriage contract itself, which deals with that state as in the present.

FORMALITIES.—Formal betrothal is not customary in the United States, or in English-speaking countries generally, as it is among certain nations, where the ceremony is sometimes solemn (before ecclesiastical witnesses) and sometimes private (made at home before the family or friends as witnesses). Among English-speaking peoples the betrothal, if it occurs, is generally without the presence of a third party. In Spain (S. C. C., 31 January, 1880; 11 April, 1891) and in Latin America (Acta et Decreta Conc. Pl. Amer. Lat., p. 259, in note 1) a betrothal compact is considered invalid by the Church unless written documents pass between the contracting parties. This practice obtains in other countries also, but its observance is not necessary to validate the agreement.

EFFECTS.—A valid betrothal begets chiefly two effects. There arises first an obligation in justice, binding the contracting parties to keep their agreement; viz. to marry at the time specified; or, when the date of marriage is not agreed upon, whenever the second party to the compact reasonably demands the fulfilment of the marriage-promise. Marriage, consequently, with a third party is forbidden, though not invalid. There arises, secondly, owing to an ecclesiastical law, a diriment impediment, known as "public decency", extending to relatives in the first degree of the parties betrothed. Hence, a marriage contracted between the male party to a betrothal and the mother, sister, or daughter of the other party; and, vice versa, between the woman and the father, brother, or son of the man, would be null and void. This impediment continues to exist in all its force, even after the betrothal has been legitimately dissolved. The first of these effects, an obligation of justice, may arise, it will be seen, from a betrothal compact which has not all the essentials of the definition given above; not so, however, of the second effect. It is sometimes stated that a betrothal does not bind in English-speaking countries. This is inexact, to say the least. There is no exception at any time, or in any country, to the binding force arising from a valid betrothal, even though it be not public (S. C. S. Off., 11 Aug., 1852), or to the impediment begotten thereby. Engagements very frequently, though not always, are rather proposals of matrimony than promises as explained above, and in them an essential element of the betrothal is wanting (Sabetti, Theol. Mor., n. 838, qu. 30; Kenrick, Theol. Mor., nos. 23, 37).

DISSOLUTION.—A betrothal may be dissolved: (1) By the mutual and free consent of the contracting parties. (2) By a diriment impediment, which subsequently arises between said parties. In this case the innocent party is released from his or her obligation, but not the one through whose fault the impediment arose. The latter may be held to the contract, if the impediment be such that the Church can dispense from it. (3) By a valid marriage entered into with a third person. (4) By protracted delay on the part of either of the contracting parties in fulfilling the agreement to marry, in which case the innocent party is released from obligation. (5) By one of the contracting parties choosing a higher state of perfection, as for example by solemn profession in a religious order, by the reception of major orders, etc. (6) By any notable change in body or soul or worldly state of one of the parties—any grave circumstance which if it had happened or been known before the betrothal would have prevented it. To these may be added the impossibility of contracting matrimony, and a dispensation granted by the pope for just causes.

PROCEDURE FOR BREACH OF PROMISE.—In case of refusal to complete the contract by marriage an action before the diocesan court is permissible. Bishops, however, are counseled not ordinarily to enforce marriage in such cases, as generally it would prove unhappy. In English-speaking countries these matters are, as a rule, taken into the civil courts, where the only remedy is a breach-of-promise suit, the penalty being a fine. In the United States, before the civil law, betrothal has only the moral force of a mutual promise. Betrothal in England was once a legal bar to matrimony with another; at present the only legal remedy for the violation of the betrothal is an action for breach of promise.

HISTORY.—Jewish and Roman laws and customs must have influenced the early practice of the Church anent betrothal. The Jewish laws of marriage, and consequently of betrothal, were based in a great measure on the supposition that it was a purchase. In the law of Moses there are certain provisions respecting the state of the virgin who is betrothed, but nothing particularly referring to the act of betrothal. Selden's "Uxor Hebraica" gives the schedule of later Hebrew contracts of betrothal. Where the contract was in writing, it was written out by the man before witnesses and delivered to the woman, who must know its import. Rome, on the other hand, at the beginning of the Christian Era, had ceased to consider marriage as a wife-purchase. Marriage, and still more betrothal, was a purely civil compact, verbally concluded. Under later Roman law, which constituted a basis for our ecclesiastical legislation, betrothal was looked upon simply as a contract of future marriage, stronger indeed than the engagement, since to enter into a second betrothal compact was held to be as infamous as bigamy itself. No legal forms were prescribed for the early Roman betrothal, but the compact was generally accompanied by the man's sending to the woman the iron betrothal ring (annulus pronubus). As the Empire grew in importance, so did the betrothal contract, while at the same time its obliga-

tions were more frequently disregarded. Hence the practice of giving earnest-money, or pledges of fidelity (arrhæ), came into prominence; another step led to gifts being bestowed by the parties, one upon the other. The kiss, the joining of hands, and the attestation of witnesses were other elements introduced. Even in England formal engagements of this kind were common down to the time of the Reformation. As barbarian influence, however, began to affect the Empire, the betrothal took on more the semblance of wife-purchase.

The Church, at the beginning of the third century at the latest, recognized betrothal as a perfectly valid and lawful contract. In the fourth century, in Africa at least, according to the testimony of St. Augustine (Sermo viii, 18; Sermo xxxvii, 7; Sermo cccxxxii, 4, etc.), espousals were contracted in writing, the instrument (tabulæ), signed by the bishop, being publicly read. At the same time the dowry, if any, was given, or nuptial gifts were exchanged. Pope Benedict I (573–577), writing to the Patriarch of Gran, declares that it is connubial intercourse that makes two one, that mere betrothal would not prevent a man from entering into wedlock with the sister of his betrothed. The question of relationship, then, arising from the betrothal contract was mooted even at that early period. Gregory the Great (590–603) allowed a woman who was betrothed to dissolve her engagement in order to enter a convent (Bk. VI, Ep. xx).

At the end of the ninth century betrothal had become a very frequent subject of Church legislation. From a reply of Pope Nicholas to the Bulgarians in 860 (Responsa ad Consulta Bulgarorum, c. iii) it is apparent that the preliminaries leading up to a marriage in the Church were: (1) The betrothal or espousal; the expression of consent by the contracting parties, and the consent also of their parents, or guardians, to the projected marriage. (2) The subarrhatio, or delivery of the ring by the man to the woman by way of an earnest, or pledge. (3) The documentary transfer, by the man to the woman, of the dowry, in the presence of witnesses. The marriage was to follow immediately, or after an interval more or less protracted. These rites are still recognized in modern uses. The ceremony of betrothal is found in a measure in the present nuptial service. There is a declaration of consent, which, since the marriage follows immediately after, is de præsenti. The placing of the ring on the finger of the bride by the bridegroom constitutes the subarrhatio, while in many places transferring of the dowry is represented by a medal or coin—a relic of Salic law and of wife-purchase. (See Martène, De Antiq. Ecc. Ritibus, I, ix, a. 3, n. 4, speaking of a ritual of the Church of Reims.)

Consult recognized authorities in canon law or moral theology for present discipline. MAGANI, L'Antica Liturgia Rom. (Milan, 1897), 360 sqq.; DUCHESNE, Christian Worship (tr. 1904), XIV; LUDLOW in Dict. Christ. Antiq., s. v.

ANDREW B. MEEHAN.

Betrothal Ring. See RING.

Bettiah, PREFECTURE APOSTOLIC OF, in northern India, includes as part of its jurisdiction the entire native state of Nepal, which has an area of more than 59,000 square miles and a population of nearly 3,000,000. The prefecture is bounded on the north by Tibet; on the east, by the Ghagra; on the south, by the Ganges; and on the west, approximately, by the Kusi.

In 1738 Father Joseph of Carignano, a Capuchin, on his way to the missions of Nepal and Tibet, arrived at Bettiah, not far from the southern boundary of the former kingdom. The Queen of Bettiah, being grievously sick, was cured by him; in return, she allowed him to preach the Gospel. The Nepal war of 1769 obliged the Christians to retire southwards.

to the neighbourhood of Bettiah. In 1883 Father Alexander of Albano opened an orphanage at Chaknee; but, as the number of Italian missionaries was falling off, this district, then a portion of the Allahabad mission, was turned over (29 October, 1889) to the Capuchins of the Province of Northern Tyrol. By a decree of 20 April, 1892, this country was made an independent prefecture, suffragan to the See of Agra; the districts of Bettiah, Champaru, Sarun, Tiroot, Mazuffarpore, Dharbanga, and part of those of Bhagalpur and Monghyr were assigned to it. Propaganda added, 19 May, 1893, the whole of Nepal, a territory wider than the whole of the original prefecture, and which extends to the borders of Tibet. Nepal thus became separated from the Diocese of Allahabad; it can scarcely be said, however, to have ever been evangelized, seeing that within its 59,000 square miles Rampur is the only station.

Generally speaking, missionary activity in this prefecture has been concentrated in the Bettiah district. According to the latest statistics of the Capuchin missions, the prefecture numbers 13,000,000 inhabitants, of whom only 3,633 are Catholics. Nearly all the Europeans (220) are Anglicans. In 1889 the mission had only three stations; there are now 12 stations and 11 churches or chapels. The principal stations are Bettiah (the residence of the Prefect Apostolic, Ilarione da Abtei), Chohoree, Chaknee, Latonah, Somastipore, Dharbanga, Somesar, Rampur (in Nepal), and Ramnagar. The minor stations are Mazuffarpore, Sonepore, Chapra, and Hipore. The mission is administered by 14 Capuchin priests, aided by 8 lay brothers. There are also 20 Sisters of the Holy Cross (*Kreuzschwestern*) from Switzerland; 35 schools, with 854 pupils; and 10 orphanages, with 403 orphans.

Status Missionum Ord. Min. Cap. (1906).

ALBERT BATTANDIER.

Betting.—A bet may be defined as the backing of an affirmation or forecast by offering to forfeit, in case of an adverse issue, a sum of money or article of value to one who, by accepting, maintains the opposite and backs his opinion by a corresponding stipulation. Although there are no Federal statutes in the United States on this matter, many of the States make it a penal offence when the bet is upon a horse-race, or an election, or a game of hazard. Betting contracts are also frequently made void. Similarly in Great Britain betting in streets and public places, and the keeping of betting houses are forbidden by law, and wagering contracts are null and void. Such laws are just and useful, inasmuch as they serve to keep within the bounds of decency the dangerous habit of gambling, and the many evils which are usually associated with it. Although betting is to be discouraged as being fraught with danger, and although it may be morally wrong, still in particular cases it is not necessarily so. As I may give the money of which I have the free disposal to another, so there is nothing in sound morals to prevent me from entering into a contract with another to hand over to him a sum of money if an assertion be found to be true, or if a certain event come to pass, with the stipulation that he is to do the same in my favour if the event be otherwise.

This may be an innocent form of recreation, or a ready way of settling a dispute. However, the practice is very liable to abuse, and that it may be morally justifiable theologians require the following conditions: The parties must have the free disposal of what they stake, and both must bind themselves to stand by the event and pay in case of loss. Welshing is wrong in morals as it is in law. Both must understand the matter of the bet in the same sense, and it must be uncertain for them both. If, however, one has absolutely certain evidence of the truth of his contention, and says so to the other party, he is not precluded from betting if the latter remains obstinate. If a bet fulfils these conditions and the object of it is honest, so that the bet is not an incentive to sin, it will be a valid contract, and therefore obligatory in conscience. Debts of honour then are also debts that we are bound in conscience to pay if they fulfil the conditions just laid down. It follows that the avocation of the professional bookmaker need not be morally wrong. It is quite possible to keep the moral law and at the same time so to arrange one's bets with different people that, though in all probability there will be some loss, still there will be gain on the whole. (See GAMBLING.)

LEHMKUHL, *Theologia Moralis* (Freiburg, 1898), I, n. 1138; BALLERINI, *Opus Morale* (Prato, 1892), III, 788.

T. SLATER.

Beugnot, AUGUSTE-ARTHUR, COUNT, French historian and statesman, b. at Bar-sur-Aube, 25 March, 1797; d. at Paris, 15 March, 1865. He was a son of Jacques-Claude Beugnot, who was a Deputy in the Legislative Body of 1791, Minister of Finance to Jerome, King of Westphalia in 1807, Minister of the Interior under the Provisional Government of 1814, and Postmaster General in 1815. At the age of twenty-one Auguste-Arthur Beugnot made known his ability as an historical writer by dividing with Mignet the prize of the Académie des Inscriptions (1818) for the best essay on the institutions of St. Louis. The competitions of 1822 and 1831 led to his work on "The Jews of the West" and his "History of the Destruction of Paganism in the West", in consequence of which he was elected to the Académie des Inscriptions. To the general public the latter of these two works was more especially known; it was placed on the Index, and has lost its vogue since the appearance of Seeck's treatise on the same subject. The learned, however, attach a higher value to the works of Beugnot on the Middle Ages; his editions of the "Assizes of Jerusalem" (1841–43), of Beaumanoir's book of the "Customs of Beauvaisis" (1842), and of the "Olim", or ancient registers of the Parliament of Paris (1839–48). These editions are of great value for the history of feudal and customary law, and of juridical procedure. The name of Beugnot, lastly, is associated with the voluminous publication of the "Historians of the Crusades", which began in a memoir written by him in 1834. Beugnot entered politics in 1841 as a Peer of France, was Deputy for Haute-Marne in the Chamber of 1849, and under the Empire went into a retirement which lasted until his death.

The Villemain educational plan of 1844, to subject the heads of independent institutions to the jurisdiction of the university, and to impose upon their pupils the obligation of making their studies in rhetoric and philosophy in certain prescribed establishments, was opposed by Beugnot on liberal principles, whilst others opposed it on religious grounds. This project was withdrawn in January, 1845, its author having become demented. Beugnot, who had destroyed the draft of a speech in support of the Villemain programme, was welcomed by the Catholics as a labourer entering the vineyard at the eleventh hour. In 1845 he advocated the claim of the bishops, as of all other citizens, to the right of petition. In his pamphlet, "L'état théologien", he made it clear that the attacks on the Jesuits were neither more nor less than attempts to destroy the liberty of association, and the Jesuits empowered him to treat with Guizot in their name at the time of the negotiations between France and the Holy See in regard to the dispersion of the Society. As drafter of the Law of 1850 on Liberty of Teaching, he vainly endeavoured to prevent the return of the bill to the Council of State, 7 November, 1849, and in the decisive debate (14 January to 15 March, 1850) he vigorously seconded the efforts of Montalembert, Parieu, and

Thiers which resulted in victory for the Church and liberty.

WALLON, *Eloges académiques* (Paris, 1882), I.

GEORGES GOYAU.

Beuno, SAINT, Abbot of Clynnog, d. 660(?), was, according to the "Bucched Beuno", born in Powis-land and, after education and ordination in the monastery of Bangor, in North Wales, became an active missioner, Cadvan, King of Gwynedd, being his generous benefactor. Cadwallon, Cadvan's son and successor, deceived Beuno about some land, and on the saint demanding justice proved obdurate. Thereupon, Cadwallon's cousin Gweddeint, in reparation, "gave to God and Beuno forever his township", where the saint (c. 616) founded the Abbey of Clynnog Fawr (Carnarvonshire).

Beuno became the guardian and restorer to life of his niece, the virgin St. Winefride, whose clients still obtain marvellous favours at Holywell (Flintshire). He was relentless with hardened sinners, but full of compassion to those in distress. Before his death "on the seventh day after Easter" he had a wondrous vision. Eleven churches bearing St. Beuno's name, with various relics and local usages, witness to his far-reaching missionary zeal. He is commemorated on the 21st of April.

REES, *Lives of Cambro-British Saints* (1853); the *Bucched Beuno* found in this work gives a secure basis of names and dedications; cf. POLLEN in *The Month*, February, 1894, 235; STUBBS, *Councils*, I, 160; *Dict. Nat. Biog.*, IV, 444.

PATRICK RYAN.

Beverley Minster, a collegiate church at Beverley, capital of the East Riding of Yorkshire, served by a chapter of secular canons until the Reformation. The foundation owes its origin to St. John of Beverley early in the eighth century, when the locality was a clearing in the forest of Deira (Indrawood), afterwards known as Beverlac (A. S. *Beoferlic*), a name possibly due to the colonies of beavers in the river Hull. St. John here founded a community of monks and another of nuns, but traditions as to the existence of an earlier church are legendary and untrustworthy. Later the saint, having resigned his See of York, retired here and died (721), his shrine being in the minster. After the destruction of the monastery by the Danes, a chapter of secular canons was founded by King Athelstan in gratitude for his victory at Brunanburh (937), as he had visited the shrine on his march north. It remained a popular place of pilgrimage throughout the vicissitudes of the Danish and Norman invasions. Few particulars about the early history of the church are known, but a fire in 1188 destroyed the greater part of it, and the present Gothic minster, rivalling the great cathedrals in beauty, dates from that time. The west front in particular is unsurpassed as a specimen of the Perpendicular style. The choir and double transepts were built early in the thirteenth century; while the present nave replaced the Norman nave a century later. Throughout the Middle Ages the shrine was frequented by pilgrims, and the charters of its liberties were renewed by successive monarchs. Its banner was placed on the standard at the "battle of the Standard" (1138), and it was further honoured after the victory of Agincourt, which was won on the feast of the translation of St. John (25 October, 1415), and was attributed by Henry V to that saint's intercession (Lyndwode, "Provinciale", II, "Anglicanae"). The minster was originally served by a chancellor, precentor, sacrist, nine canons, nine vicars-choral and seven *berefellarii* or clerks, but in time several chantry priests and minor officials were added. The temporalities were administered by a provost, who was not necessarily a member of the chapter. The former office was held by many noted Englishmen, including St. Thomas Becket and John de Thoresby, afterwards Cardinal. Blessed John

Fisher is believed to have received his first education at the grammar school attached to the minster. The chapter being secular, the minster escaped the ruin that fell on the monasteries under Henry VIII, but was dissolved in 1547 under the "Colleges and Chantries Act" of Edward VI. The seventy-seven collegiate officers thus dispossessed were replaced by a vicar and three assistants reduced, under Elizabeth, to a vicar and one curate. Gradually the minster fell into decay until, in 1713, a restoration became necessary to save it from ruin. This was successfully executed, and as a result of further work in 1866 and subsequent years it still remains one of the most remarkable Gothic churches in England.

DUGDALE, *Monasticon*; POULSON, *Beverlac* (London, 1829); OLIVER, *History and Antiquities of the Town and Minster of Beverley* (Beverley, 1829); PETIT, *Remarks on Beverley Minster*, in *Arch. Institute's York Vol.* (1848); CRICKMER, *Ecclesiastical History of Beverley Minster* (Beverley, 1890); HIATT, *Beverley Minster* (London, 1904).

EDWIN BURTON.

Beyerlinck, LAWRENCE, Belgian theologian and ecclesiastical writer, b. at Antwerp, April, 1578; d. at the same place, 22 June, 1627. The son of a noted pharmacist, he prepared at Louvain for the same profession but, deciding to enter the priesthood, he was ordained June, 1602. While a theological student he taught poetry and rhetoric at the college of Vaulx and as pastor of Herent was professor of philosophy at a nearby seminary of canons regular. In 1605 he came to the ecclesiastical seminary of Antwerp, taught philosophy and theology and later became superior. In 1608 he was canon, censor, and theologian of the church of Antwerp; in 1614 he was made protonotary. Beyerlinck was an exemplary priest, a gifted rhetorician, orator, and administrator, and an indefatigable worker. Besides seminary and diocesan work he was engaged continually in preaching and writing. Compilation was his bent. His works are mainly encyclopedic; his knowledge more extensive than profound. He wrote, e. g. a second volume (Antwerp, 1611) of the "Opus Chronographicum orbis universi a mundi exordio usque ad annum MDCXI" (first volume to year 1572 by Opmeer), a collection of lives of popes, rulers, and illustrious men; and the "Magnum Theatrum Vitæ Humanæ, hoc est Rerum Divinarum Humanarumque syntagma Catholicum Philosophicum Historicum Dogmaticum", etc. (Cologne, 1631, 7 vols.; Venice, 1707, 8 vols.), an encyclopedia of information on diverse subjects arranged in alphabetical order. Its scope ranges from profound theological dissertations to merest trivialities. Much of its vast material was gathered by others, but to Beyerlinck belongs the credit of giving the work its final form. His numerous other publications are listed in the works referred to in the appended bibliography.

Vita Auctoris in *Magnum Theatrum* (Cologne, 1631), I, preface; FOPPENS, *Bibliotheca Belgica* (Brussels, 1739), 804–805; *Biog. univ.* (Paris, 1811), IV, 426.

JOHN B. PETERSON.

Beza Codex. See CODEX.

Bianchi and Neri. See FLORENCE.

Bianchi, GIOVANNI ANTONIO, Friar Minor and theologian, b. at Lucca, 2 October, 1686; d. at Rome, 18 January, 1768. At the age of seventeen he entered the Franciscan Order. He was once elected to the office of Provincial of the Roman Province, and for a number of years was professor of philosophy and theology. During these years of professorship, he no doubt acquired much of the extensive and accurate acquaintance with ecclesiastical subjects displayed in the productions of his later life. He possessed a memory of such range and tenacity that he was considered a prodigy by the many students and scholars who came to visit him in his convent cell. Bianchi was held in high esteem by the Roman Curia and by Clement XII, whose successor, Benedict XIV, appointed him consultor of the Holy Office.

It was perhaps at the instance of Clement XII that Bianchi composed his scholarly and exhaustive defence of the rights and privileges of the Roman Pontiff, which had been attacked by the Neapolitan lawyer, Pietro Giannone, in the latter's "Storia civile del regno di Napoli". Bianchi's work which was entitled "Della podestà e della polizia della chiesa, trattati due contro le nuove opinioni di Pietro Giannone" appeared in Rome in six volumes between the years 1745 and 1751. In the first treatise (2 vols.) Bianchi defends the indirect power of the Roman Pontiff over temporal sovereigns; while he lucidly and forcibly defends the rights of the pope as regards the external laws and government of the Church, in the second treatise, which comprises the remaining four volumes. Amid the storm of controversial literature provoked by the treatise of the Dominican theologian, Daniele Concina, "De Spectaculis theatralibus", Bianchi's "Sui vizii e sui difetti del moderno teatro e sul modo di corregerli ed emendarli" appeared at Rome in 1753. In this he contends with Scipio Maffei against Concina for the lawfulness, within certain limits, of modern theatrical displays. Notwithstanding these graver preoccupations, Bianchi found time to indulge his predilection for poetry and tragic writing, and his compositions in this field, though of minor importance, show him to be an accomplished master of his own native Tuscan.

HURTER, *Nomenclator*, II, 1530–32; D'ALENÇON in *Dict. de théol. cath.* (Paris, 1900), II, 812; SCHULTE, *Geschichte der Quellen und Litteratur des Canonischen Rechts*, (Stuttgart, 1880), III, 512; FELLER, *Biographie universelle* (Paris, 1848), II. 2.

STEPHEN M. DONOVAN.

Bianchini, FRANCESCO, a student of the natural sciences, and an historian, b. at Verona, Northern Italy, 13 December, 1662; d. at Rome, 2 March, 1729. At first he devoted himself to the study of mathematics, physics, and astronomy; later he also took a course in theology. In 1699 he was advanced to deaconship, but never became a priest. In 1684 he transferred his residence to Rome, where he found at once a protector in Cardinal Pietro Ottoboni, of whose library he became custodian. When the cardinal became Pope Alexander VIII (1689–91) he still extended his favours to Bianchini; after Alexander's death, his nephew, also Cardinal Pietro Ottoboni, lodged the scholar in his own palace. Bianchini received also many honours and commissions of trust from succeeding popes. In 1703 he was elected president of the society devoted to the study of historical antiquities; he was made secretary of the commission for the reform of the calendar and he was sent to Paris with the cardinal's hat destined for Rohan Soubise. During this journey he was received everywhere with consideration by the learned. The University of Oxford furnished the expenses of his sojourn in England. Benedict XIII (1724–30) appointed him historiographer of the synod held at the Lateran, Rome (1725). He was a member of many learned academies in Italy and elsewhere. He was distinguished for "a great purity of life and an exceeding modesty of mind", as the canons of St. Mary Major expressed it in his epitaph. His chief works are: "Two Dissertations on the Calendar and the Cycle of Julius Cæsar, and the Paschal Canon of St. Hippolytus" (Rome, 1703); "A Solution of the Paschal Problem" (Rome, 1703); one volume of "A Universal History" (Rome, 1697); an edition of the "Liber Pontificalis" in four volumes, three of which were edited by himself (Rome, 1718–28), and the fourth by his nephew, Giuseppe Bianchini (Rome, 1735). Besides the text of the lives of the popes the work contains learned introductions, various readings of the manuscripts,

copious notes by himself and others, and several documents relative to the history of the popes. It was republished in Migne, P. L., CXXVII–CXXVIII.

HURTER, *Nomenclator*, II; DUCHESNE, *Etude sur le Lib. Pontif.* (Paris, 1877), 118, 119.

FRANCIS J. SCHAEFER.

Bianchini (BLANCHINI), GIUSEPPE, Italian Oratorian, Biblical, historical, and liturgical scholar, b. at Verona, 1704; d. in Rome, 1764. Clement XII and Benedict XIV, who highly appreciated his learning, entrusted him with several scientific labours. Bianchini had contemplated a large work on the texts of the Sacred Scriptures, "Vindiciæ Canonicarum Scripturarum Vulgatæ latinæ editionis", which was to comprise several volumes, but only the first, in which, among other things, are to be found fragments of the "Hexapla" (cod. Chisianus), was published (Rome, 1740). Much more important is his "Evangeliarium quadruplex latinæ versionis antiquæ", etc., 2 vols. (Rome, 1749). Among his historical labours may be mentioned the fourth volume which Bianchini added to the publication of his uncle, Francesco Bianchini, "Anastasii bibliothecarii Vitæ Rom. Pontif." (Rome, 1735); he also published the "Demonstratio historiæ ecclesiasticæ quadripartitæ" (Rome, 1752–54). The chief liturgical work of Bianchini is "Liturgia antiqua hispanica, gothica, isidoriana, mozarabica, toletana mixta" (Rome, 1746). He also undertook the edition of the works of Bl. Thomasius (Tomasi), but only one volume was issued (Rome, 1741).

VILLAROSA, *Memorie degli Scrittori Filippini* (Naples, 1837); MANGENOT, *Joseph Bianchini et les anciennes versions latines de la Bible* (Amiens, 1892); HURTER, *Nomenclator*, III, 71 sqq.

R. BUTIN.

Bianconi, CHARLES, merchant and philanthropist, b. 26 September, 1785, in the duchy of Milan; d. near Clonmel, Ireland, 22 September, 1875. At an early age he was sent to Ireland, as apprentice to an Italian printseller, became a distinguished and wealthy merchant, and was the first to establish (1815–58) throughout the island a system of rapid and cheap transportation of persons and of government mail. He was an intimate friend of O'Connell, a promoter of Catholic Emancipation, a benefactor of many Catholic charities, and a practical friend of the Catholic University at Dublin. The English postmaster general in his Report for 1857 said that "no living man has ever done more than he for the benefit of the sister kingdom". In the development of his vast transportation system he displayed extraordinary energy and ingenuity, and did much to increase the resources of his adopted country, while he promoted in a remarkable way its social relations. His residence at Longfield, near Clonmel, was a centre of hospitality, and a source of much practical activity for the general welfare of his country.

O'RYAN, *Charles Bianconi* (Dublin, 1905), and Bianconi's life by his daughter, Mrs. Morgan John O'Connell (Dublin, 1885).

THOMAS J. SHAHAN.

Biard, PIERRE, Jesuit missionary, b. at Grenoble, France, 1567; d. at Avignon, 17 November, 1622. In 1608 he was called from a chair of Scholastic theology and Hebrew at Lyons by Father Coton, the king's confessor and preacher, to take charge of the Jesuit mission in Acadia. As de Monts, the founder of Acadia, was a Calvinist, and a considerable number of the colonists were also of that religion, vehement opposition was made to the appointment of Biard and his companion, Edmond Masse, as missionaries. Through the interposition of the Marquise de Guercheville, who purchased the vessel that was bringing out supplies, the Jesuits, after three years of waiting, were enabled to obtain passage by becoming part owners of the ship and cargo. They left France, 21 January, 1611, and arrived on Pentecost Day,

22 May, at Port Royal. They met with but little success. The predecessor of the missionaries, a secular priest named Josue Flesche, had baptized indiscriminately. This the Jesuits refused to do. The colonists, moreover, remained hostile, and viewed as a business speculation, the enterprise was a failure. Madame de Guercheville, who had succeeded de Monts as proprietor, finally sent out another vessel under La Saussaye, and ordered him to stop at Port Royal, and, taking the two Jesuits, found a colony elsewhere. Obeying instructions, La Saussaye sailed over to what is now Bar Harbor. The new establishment was called Saint Sauveur. This was in 1613. It was hardly begun when Samuel Argall came up from Virginia, plundered the colony, and took Biard and another Jesuit with four colonists to Jamestown where only the authority of Argall prevented them from being hanged. Another expedition was fitted out to complete the destruction of Saint Sauveur and Port Royal, and the two Jesuits were compelled to accompany the marauders.

Everything was ruined and Biard and his companion were made to appear as if they had instigated the attack. They sailed off with the attacking party who intended to return with them to the English colony, where they would probably have been executed, but the vessel on which they were held as prisoners was driven by storms across the ocean. Frequently they were on the point of being thrown overboard, but when the ship was compelled to enter the Port of Fayal in the Azores, Biard and his companions consented to remain in the hold lest their discovery should entail the death of their captor. A second time, upon entering Milford Haven, in Wales, the captain having no papers, and being in a French ship, was on the point of being hanged as a pirate. But Father Biard saved him by explaining the situation to the authorities. The missionary was then sent to France, where he had to meet a storm of abuse because of the suspicion that he had helped in the destruction of Port Royal. Champlain, however, vindicated him. He never returned to Canada, but resumed his work as professor of theology, and afterwards became famous as a missionary in the south of France, and towards the end of his life was made military chaplain in the armies of the king. Lescarbot, who was unfriendly to the Jesuit missionaries, speaks of Biard in flattering terms.

ROCHEMONTEIX, *Les Jésuites et la Nouvelle France;* CHARLEVOIX, *Hist. de la Nouvelle France; Les Relations; Œuvres de Champlain*, V, viii; FAILLON, *Colonie Française;* PARKMAN, *Pioneers of France in the New World.*

T. J. CAMPBELL.

Bibbiena (BERNARDO DOVIZI) an Italian Cardinal and comedy-writer, known best by the name of the town Bibbiena, where he was born 4 Aug., 1470; d. at Rome, 9 Nov., 1520. His obscure parentage did not prevent him from securing a literary training at the hands of the best scholars and from associating with the most conspicuous men that Florence could boast. A jovial temper and racy Tuscan wit enhancing the charm of good looks and courtly manners soon made him the preceptor as well as the boon companion of Giovanni dei Medici's merry hours. When the Medici were banished and sorrow followed mirth (Nov., 1494) it was seen that a gay man of the world could become a brave and steadfast friend. Not long after, the protection of Julius II and many honours at the Roman court were to be his reward. In 1513 his strenuous exertions on behalf of his lifelong patron secured the election of Giovanni dei Medici to the pontifical throne. Such services Leo X repaid by bestowing on him the purple robe, appointing him his treasurer and entrusting him with many important missions, among them a legation to France (1518). Later on, the cardinal's

strong sympathies for France lost him Leo's confidence. The story, however, that he was poisoned, in spite of Giovio and Grassi's reports, has absolutely no foundation. (Pastor, Geschichte der Päpste, IV, Part I, Leo X.) As cardinal he steadily extended a generous patronage to art. From Raphael, whose devotion he won, we have his best likeness. His literary fame is mainly connected with the first good comedy written in Italian prose, "La Calandra" (also, known as "Il Calandro" and "La Calandria"), a distinctly juvenile production, probably given for the first time at Urbino,

BERNARDO CARDINAL BIBBIENA

about 1507, and very elaborately performed at Rome, seven years later, in the presence of Leo X and Isabella Gonzaga d'Este, Marchioness of Mantua. Though marred by many scenes glaringly immoral, and though built upon the plot of Plautus's "Menæchmi", it possessed the features of modern comedy and won plaudits for its sparkling wit and fine characterization. Ariosto and Machiavelli imitated him in their plays. The latest edition of "La Calandra" is in the "Teatro Italiano Antico" (Florence, 1888).

GASPARY, *Geschichte der italienischen Litteratur* (Strasburg, 1888), II, 577; ROSCOE, *Life of Leo X;* BANDINI, *Il Bibbiena il ministro di Stato* (Florence, 1760); MORETTI, *Bibbiena Dovizi e la Calandra* in the Nuova Antologia (1882), 601, 623; SOLERTI, *La rappresentazione della Calandra a Lione nel 1548* (Florence, 1901).

EDOARDO SAN GIOVANNI.

Bibiana, SAINT.—The earliest mention in an authentic historical authority of St. Bibiana (Vibiana), a Roman female martyr, occurs in the "Liber Pontificalis" where in the biography of Pope Simplicius (468–483) it is stated that this pope "consecrated a basilica of the holy martyr Bibiana, which contained her body, near the 'palatium Licinianum'" (ed. Duchesne, I, 249). This basilica still exists. In the fifth century, therefore, the bodily remains of St. Bibiana rested within the city walls. We have no further historical particulars concerning the martyr or the circumstances of her death; neither do we know why she was buried in the city itself. In later times a legend sprang up concerning her, connected with the Acts of the martyrdom of Sts. John and Paul and has no historical claim to belief. According to this legend, Bibiana was the daughter of a former prefect, Flavianus, who was banished by Julian the Apostate. Dafrosa, the wife of Flavianus, and his two daughters, Demetria and Bibiana, were also persecuted by Julian. Dafrosa and Demetria died a natural death and were buried by Bibiana in their own house; but Bibiana was tortured and died as the result of her sufferings. Two days after her death a priest named John buried Bibiana near her mother and sister in her home, the house being later turned into a church. It is evident that the legend seeks to explain in this way the origin of the church and the presence in it of the bodies of the above mentioned confessors. The account contained in the martyrologies of the ninth century is drawn from the legend.

Mombritius, *Sanctuarium*, I, 278 sqq.; *Acta SS.*, June, IV, 74 sqq.; *Catalogus codicum hagiogr. latin.* in *Bibliotheca Nationali Parisien.*, ed. Bollandists (Brussels, 1889), I, 520–523; Aringhi, *Roma subterranea* (Paris, 1659), II, 124; Dufourcq, *Etude sur les Gesta martyrum romains* (Paris, 1900), 123–126; De Rossi in *Bull. della Commiss. archeol. communale di Roma* (1890), 280–284; Armellini, *Le chiese di Roma* (Rome, 1891), 804–806; Marucchi, *Basiliques et églises de Rome* (Rome, 1902), 344 sqq.

J. P. Kirsch.

Bible, The, a collection of writings which the Church of God has solemnly recognized as inspired. The name is derived from the Greek expression τὰ βιβλία (the books), which came into use in the early centuries of Christianity to designate the whole sacred volume. In the Latin of the Middle Ages, the neuter plural form *Biblia* (gen. *bibliorum*) gradually came to be regarded as a feminine singular noun (*biblia*, gen. *bibliæ*), in which singular form the word has passed into the languages of the Western world. It means "The Book", by way of eminence, and therefore well sets forth the sacred character of our inspired literature. Its most important equivalents are: "the Divine Library" (*Bibliotheca Divina*), which was employed by St. Jerome in the fourth century; "the Scriptures", "the Holy Scriptures"—terms which are derived from expressions found in the Bible itself; and "the Old and New Testament", in which collective title, "the Old Testament" designates the sacred books written before the coming of Our Lord, and "the New Testament" denotes the inspired writings composed since the coming of Christ.

It is a fact of history that in the time of Christ the Jews possessed a collection of sacred books, which differed widely from one another in subject, style, origin and scope, and it is also a fact that they regarded all such writings as invested with a character which distinguished them from all other books. This was the Divine authority of every one of these books and of every part of each book. This belief of the Jews was confirmed by Our Lord and His Apostles; for they supposed its truth in their teaching, used it as a foundation of their doctrine, and intimately connected with it the religious system of which they were the founders. The books thus approved were handed down to the Christian Church as the written record of Divine revelation before the coming of Christ. The truths of Christian revelation were made known to the Apostles either by Christ Himself or by the Holy Ghost. They constitute what is called the Deposit of Faith, to which nothing has been added since the Apostolic Age. Some of the truths were committed to writing under the inspiration of the Holy Ghost and have been handed down to us in the books of the New Testament. Written originally to individual Churches or persons, to meet particular necessities, and accommodated as they all were to particular and existing circumstances, these books were gradually received by the universal Church as inspired, and with the sacred books of the Jews constitute the Bible.

In one respect, therefore, the Bible is a twofold literature, made up of two distinct collections which correspond with two successive and unequal periods of time in the history of man. The older of these collections, mostly written in Hebrew, corresponds with the many centuries during which the Jewish people enjoyed a national existence, and forms the Hebrew, or Old Testament, literature; the more recent collection, begun not long after Our Lord's ascension, and made up of Greek writings, is the Early Christian, or New Testament, literature. Yet, in another and deeper respect, the Biblical literature is pre-eminently one. Its two sets of writings are most closely connected with regard to doctrines revealed, facts recorded, customs described, and even expressions used. Above all, both collections have one and the same religious purpose, one and the same inspired char-

acter. They form the two parts of a great organic whole the centre of which is the person and mission of Christ. The same Spirit exercised His mysterious hidden influence on the writings of both Testaments, and made of the works of those who lived before Our Lord an active and steady preparation for the New Testament dispensation which He was to introduce, and of the works of those who wrote after Him a real continuation and striking fulfilment of the old Covenant.

The Bible, as the inspired record of revelation, contains the word of God; that is, it contains those revealed truths which the Holy Ghost wishes to be transmitted in writing. However, all revealed truths are not contained in the Bible (see Tradition); neither is every truth in the Bible revealed, if by revelation is meant the manifestation of hidden truths which could not otherwise be known. Much of the Scripture came to its writers through the channels of ordinary knowledge, but its sacred character and Divine authority are not limited to those parts which contain revelation strictly so termed. The Bible not only contains the word of God; it is the word of God. The primary author is the Holy Ghost, or, as it is commonly expressed, the human authors wrote under the influence of Divine inspiration. It was declared by the Vatican Council (Sess. III, c. ii) that the sacred and canonical character of Scripture would not be sufficiently explained by saying that the books were composed by human diligence and then approved by the Church, or that they contained revelation without error. They are sacred and canonical "because, having been written by inspiration of the Holy Ghost, they have God for their author, and as such have been handed down to the Church". The inerrancy of the Bible follows as a consequence of this Divine authorship. Wherever the sacred writer makes a statement as his own, that statement is the word of God and infallibly true, whatever be the subject-matter of the statement.

It will be seen, therefore, that though the inspiration of any writer and the sacred character of his work be antecedent to its recognition by the Church yet we are dependent upon the Church for our knowledge of the existence of this inspiration. She is the appointed witness and guardian of revelation. From her alone we know what books belong to the Bible. At the Council of Trent she enumerated the books which must be considered "as sacred and canonical". They are the seventy-two books found in Catholic editions, forty-five in the Old Testament and twenty-seven in the New. Protestant copies usually lack the seven books (viz: Tobias, Judith, Wisdom, Ecclesiasticus, Baruch, and I, II Machabees) and parts of books (viz: Esther, x, 4–xvi, 24, and Daniel iii, 24–90; xiii, 1–xiv, 42) which are not found in the Jewish editions of the Old Testament.

The Bible is plainly a literature, that is, an important collection of writings which were not composed at once and did not proceed from one hand, but rather were spread over a considerable period of time and are traceable to different authors of varying literary excellence. As a literature, too, the Bible bears throughout the distinct impress of the circumstances of place and time, methods of composition, etc., in which its various parts came into existence, and of these circumstances careful account must be taken, in the interests of accurate scriptural interpretation. As a literature, our sacred books have been transcribed during many centuries by all manner of copyists to the ignorance and carelessness of many of whom they still bear witness in the shape of numerous textual errors, which, however, but seldom interfere seriously with the primitive reading of any important dogmatic or moral passage of Holy Writ.

In respect of antiquity, the Biblical literature belongs to the same group of ancient literature as the literary collections of Greece, Rome, China, Persia, and India. Its second part, the New Testament, completed about A. D. 100, is indeed far more recent than the four last named literatures, and is somewhat posterior to the Augustan age of the Latin language, but it is older by ten centuries than our earliest modern literature. As regards the Old Testament, most of its contents were gradually written within the nine centuries which preceded the Christian era, so that its composition is generally regarded as contemporary with that of the great literary works of Greece, China, Persia, and India. The Bible resembles these various ancient literatures in another respect. Like them it is fragmentary, i. e. made up of the remains of a larger literature. Of this we have abundant proofs concerning the books of the Old Testament, since the Hebrew Scriptures themselves repeatedly refer us to more ancient and complete works as composed by Jewish annalists, prophets, wise men, poets, and so on (cf. Numbers, xxi, 14; Josue, x, 13; II Kings, i, 18; I Paralip., xxix, 29; I Mach., xvi, 24; etc.). Statements tending to prove the same fragmentary character of the early Christian literature which has come down to us are indeed much less numerous, but not altogether wanting (cf. Luke, i, 1–3; Colossians, iv, 16; I Corinthians, v, 9). But, however ancient and fragmentary, it is not to be supposed that the Biblical literature contains only few, and these rather imperfect, literary forms. In point of fact its contents exhibit nearly all the literary forms met with in our Western literatures together with others peculiarly Eastern, but none the less beautiful. It is also a well-known fact that the Bible is so replete with pieces of transcendent literary beauty that the greatest orators and writers of the last four centuries have most willingly turned to our sacred books as pre-eminently worthy of admiration, study, and imitation. Of course the widest and deepest influence that has ever been, and ever will be, exercised upon the minds and hearts of men remains due to the fact that, while all the other literatures are but man's productions, the Bible is indeed "inspired of God" and, as such, especially "profitable to teach, to reprove, to correct, to instruct in justice" (II Timothy, iii, 16).

Providentissimus Deus in the *Great Encyclicals of Pope Leo XIII* (New York, 1903); BARRY, *The Tradition of Scripture* (New York, 1906); VAUGHAN, *The Bible: Its Use and Abuse;* BREEN, *Introduction to Holy Scripture;* HUMPHREY, *The Written Word;* GIGOT, *General Introduction;* CORNELY, *Introductio Generalis;* HUNTER, *Outlines of Dogmatic Theology*, I.

FRANCIS E. GIGOT.

Bible Christians. See METHODISM; (BRYANITES).

Bible Commentary. See EXEGESIS.

Bible Communists. See ONEIDA CONGREGATIONS.

Bible Editions. See EDITIONS OF THE BIBLE.

Bible Manuscripts. See MANUSCRIPTS OF THE BIBLE.

Bible Societies.—Protestant Bible Societies, established for the purpose of publishing and propagating the Bible in all parts of the world, are the logical outcome of the principle: "The Bible, and the Bible alone is the religion of Protestants." Precisely to what extent that theological formula is held true even by the stanchest evangelicals, may be a matter of dispute, but the consistent and heroic efforts of the Bible societies to provide a version of the sacred text in every tongue and to supply the ends of the earth with Bibles, can scarcely be explained unless Chillingworth's famous formula be taken to mean literally that the possession of a copy of the Bible is an indispensable means of salvation. Nevertheless, it is remarkable that the societies for the world-wide propagation of the Bible, like the Protestant missionary societies, are a late outgrowth of Protestantism. It is well known that the sects did not seriously bestir themselves about mission work

until two hundred years after the Reformation, and historically the Bible societies are an appendage and a consequence of the missionary organizations. Some efforts were made to provide a systematic dissemination of Bibles as early as the time of Charles I of England, and before the formation of Bible societies on a scale of world-wide activity, there existed a number of organizations which made Bible distribution a feature of their work. Among them were, (1) The Society for Promoting Christian Knowledge (1698), which spread copies of Holy Writ in England, Wales, India, and Arabia; (2) The Society for the Propagation of the Gospel in Wales (1662); (3) The Society for Sending Missionaries to India, founded in 1705 by King Frederick of Denmark; (4) The Society for the Propagation of the Gospel in Foreign Parts (1701), which devoted a large share of its attention to the American Colonies; (5) The Scottish Society for Propagating Christian Knowledge among the Poor (1750); (8) The Naval and Military Bible Society (1780). The foundation of these and similar societies was but an indication of the vast work that was to come. The great reaction against the religious apathy, and, indeed, infidelity of the English people in the eighteenth century brought with it the foundation of numerous missionary societies, and this new enthusiasm for Christianity resulted in the foundation of the most famous and the most effective of all Bible societies, The British and Foreign Bible Society, 7 March, 1804. The first impulse to the formation of this organization was given by a group of Nonconformist ministers and laymen, but when completely formed, the society included an equal number of members of the Established Church and of the various sects. Its avowed purpose was "to encourage the wider circulation of the Bible without note or comment".

At present, the British and Foreign Society is governed by an executive committee of 36 laymen, 15 from the Church of England, 15 dissenters, and 6 foreign members who must reside in or near London. The growth and work of this society have been extraordinary. It controls, according to the latest statistics (1906) almost 8,000 auxiliary societies; 5,729 in Great Britain and 2,224 abroad. Its translations of the sacred text number about 380. Its operations in India have been particularly thorough, but in every country where its agencies are established, its work can only be measured in vast figures. It disposes annually of about 5,190,000 copies of the Scriptures (whole Bibles, New Testaments and other portions), and spends each year £250,000 ($1,210,000). In the hundred years of its existence, this society has distributed 186,680,000 volumes at an expenditure of £14,194,000 ($68,699,000). There have been numerous offshoots, some in the nature of developments, others schisms, but the size, wealth, and prestige of the parent society have always overshadowed those of its children and its rivals. Mention must also be made of the Hibernian Bible Society, and the National Bible Society of Scotland, the names of which sufficiently designate their field of labour.

On the Continent, Count Canstein founded a German Bible Society in 1710. Others were established at Nuremberg (1804), Berlin (1806), Saxony (1813), and Schleswick-Holstein (1826). The Berlin society was united with the Prussian Bible Society in 1814. The Danish Bible Society dates from 1814, the Russian from 1812; a Bible society was founded in Finland in 1812, one in Norway in 1815, one in the Netherlands 1813, one in Malta in 1817, and one in Paris 1818.

In America, we find the Continental Congress so impressed with the scarcity of Bibles that in 1777 it passed a resolution calling for the printing of 20,000 copies. Facilities were not at hand for the fulfilment of such a work, and it was not done. But in 1782, Congress commended the publication of the Bible which had just been made in Philadelphia. There had been local Bible societies in the Colonies, but these were not united with the American Bible Society until 1816. This society has become next in size and in importance to its counterpart, the British and Foreign Bible Society and in 1907 controlled 620 auxiliary societies in the United States and 11 agencies in the Latin-American countries and elsewhere. The Society has no established agency in Europe, but maintains correspondents in Norway, Sweden, Russian Finland, Germany, Switzerland, France, Spain, Italy, and Austria. In these countries it either co-operates with the National Bible societies, or lends assistance to the local Protestant churches. For example, the American Bible Society has been co-operating closely for the last fifty years with the Methodist Episcopal Church in Bremen, Germany, and in that time and place has assisted in the publication of over a million volumes of Scripture. The American Society has extended its efforts into the Levant, a regular agency being established in Constantinople. It works in conjunction with the Protestant missionaries in Bulgaria, Turkey, Asia Minor, Mesopotamia, Syria, Egypt, and the Sudan. In these countries alone, it has distributed over 3,000,000 volumes during the past half-century. All told, the copies of the Bible, or parts of the Bible distributed by the American Bible Society for one year, ending 31 March, 1906, were 2,236,755, and during the ninety years of its work it has disposed of 78,509,529 volumes.

After being duly impressed by these figures and those of the still more prolific British Society, the Catholic reader naturally questions whether the amount of good done is, after all, to be measured by the number of volumes distributed. A considerable number of Protestant missionaries have already answered the question negatively, and if we may judge from many letters from ministers in the mission field, there is a growing feeling among thinking Protestants that the promiscuous distribution of the Bible "without note or comment" is a doubtful means of propagating Christian doctrine. Even as a means of proselytism, the scattering of Bibles seems not to produce the expected results. A missionary on the Malay peninsula, among others, complains that although thousands of Bibles were distributed, it was, so far as he could learn, "with scarcely any perceptible benefit". He "did not hear of a single Malay convert on the whole peninsula". The natives of the missionary countries are, according to reports, eager to obtain books from the societies, but agents and missionaries and bishops have reported that in many cases the volumes were used for vulgar and profane purposes. Indeed, the reckless distribution of the Scriptures in too many cases becomes an occasion for the profanation of the written Word, rather than for the growth of religion. Instances of abuse of the Bible could be collected freely from the letters of missionaries, Catholic and non-Catholic alike.

But for deeper reasons than this, the attitude of the Church toward the Bible societies is one of unmistakable opposition. Believing herself to be the divinely appointed custodian and interpreter of Holy Writ, she cannot without turning traitor to herself, approve the distribution of Scripture "without note or comment". The fundamental fallacy of private interpretation of the Scriptures is presupposed by the Bible societies. It is the impelling motive of their work. But it would be likewise the violation of one of the first principles of the Catholic Faith—a principle arrived at through observation as well as by revelation—the insufficiency of the Scriptures alone to convey to the general reader a sure

knowledge of faith and morals. Consequently, the Council of Trent, in its fourth session, after expressly condemning all interpretations of the sacred text which contradict the past and present interpretation of the Church, orders all Catholic publishers to see to it that their editions of the Bible have the approval of the bishop. Besides this and other regulations concerning Bible-reading in general, we have several acts of the popes directed explicitly against the Bible societies. Perhaps the most notable of these are contained in the Encyclical "Ubi Primum" of Leo XII, dated 5 May, 1824, and Pius IX's Encyclical "Qui Pluribus", of 9 November, 1846. Pius VIII in 1829 and Gregory XVI in 1844, spoke to similar effect. It may be well to give the most striking words on the subject from Leo XII and Pius IX. To quote the former (loc. cit.): "You are aware, venerable brothers, that a certain Bible Society is impudently spreading throughout the world, which, despising the traditions of the holy Fathers and the decree of the Council of Trent, is endeavouring to translate, or rather to pervert the Scriptures into the vernacular of all nations. . . . It is to be feared that by false interpretation, the Gospel of Christ will become the gospel of men, or still worse, the gospel of the devil." The pope then urges the bishops to admonish their flocks that owing to human temerity, more harm than good may come from indiscriminate Bible-reading. Pius IX says (loc. cit.): "These crafty Bible Societies, which renew the ancient guile of heretics, cease not to thrust their Bibles upon all men, even the unlearned,—their Bibles, which have been translated against the laws of the Church, and often contain false explanations of the text. Thus, the divine traditions, the teaching of the fathers, and the authority of the Catholic Church are rejected, and everyone in his own way interprets the words of the Lord, and distorts their meaning, thereby falling into miserable errors".

Thus are given the chief reasons of the opposition of the Church. Furthermore, it can scarcely be denied that the Bible societies, by invading the Catholic countries and endeavouring to foist the Protestant versions upon a Catholic people, have stirred up much discord, and have laid themselves open to the charge of degrading the Sacred Book by using it as an instrument of proselytism. Still in almost all the books and pamphlets which are written to show the results of Bible propagandism, naïve complaints are made by the writers that the Catholic priests forbid the dissemination of the Scriptures among their people. The societies do not offer to supply Catholics with Catholic Bibles, fortified with the ecclesiastical Imprimatur, and supplied with the necessary notes of explanation. If such an offer were refused, there might be some pretext for the complaints of the societies, but so long as they follow their present course, it must be evident that they have small ground for wonder if the authorities of the Church oppose them. The true attitude of the Church towards the popular use of the Scriptures is shown by the establishment of the Società di San Geronimo, for the translation and diffusion of the Gospels and other parts of the Bible among the Italian peoples.

There have been many dissensions and some schisms among the members of the Bible societies themselves. At the very foundation of the British and Foreign Bible Society Bishop Marsh, consistently with the principles of the Church of England, objected to the printing of the text, "without note or comment", and recommended the addition of the Book of Common Prayer. The objection was, of course, overruled. In 1831, the British and Foreign Bible Society decided to demand belief in the Trinity as a requisite to membership. This led to a schism and the foundation of the Trinitarian Bible Society. Another schismatic society, originating from a doctrinal difference, is the Bible Translation Society, a body composed of Baptists who were dissatisfied because the original society's Bibles did not translate the texts which relate to baptism by words that would signify immersion. Again, from the American Bible Society, there has been a schism of Baptists, originating, as in England, over the translation of βαπτίζειν. This dissident body, founded in 1837, is called The American and Foreign Bible Society. This organization in turn experienced a secession, the recalcitrants forming the American Bible Union, in 1850.

After a Hundred Years (London, 1904), report of the British and Foreign Bible Society for the centenary year; CANTON, *The Story of the Bible Society* (London, 1904); *The Centenary History of the Bible Society* (1907); *The American Bible Society, Eighty-ninth Annual Report* (1905); VAUGHAN, *Concerning the Holy Bible, its Use and Abuse* (London, 1904), 160, reports from Protestant missionaries in foreign lands, concerning abuses in Bible-distribution; *Encyclopedia of Missions* (New York, 1904), s. v. *American Bible Society, British and Foreign Bible Society;* DARLOW AND MOULE, *Hist. Catalogue of the Printed Editions of Holy Scripture* (London, 1903–04).

JAMES M. GILLIS.

Bible Versions. See VERSIONS OF THE BIBLE.

Bibles, PICTURE.—In the Middle Ages the Church made use of pictures as a means of instruction, to supplement the knowledge acquired by reading or oral teaching. For books only existed in manuscript form and, being costly, were beyond the means of most people. Besides, had it been possible for the multitude to come into the possession of books, they could not have read them, since in those rude times, education was the privilege of few. In fact, hardly anyone could read, outside the ranks of the clergy and the monks. So frescoes of scenes from the Old and New Testaments, stained-glass windows, and the like were set up in the churches, because, as the Synod of Arras (1025) said: "The illiterate contemplated in the lineaments of painting what they, having never learnt to read, could not discern in writing". Especially did the Church make use of pictures to spread abroad a knowledge of the events recorded in the Bible and of the mutual connexion between the leading facts of the Old and New Testaments, whether as type and antitype, or as prophecy and fulfilment. For this purpose the picture Bibles of the Middle Ages were copied and put in circulation. The most important of the picture Bibles of the Middle Ages which have survived is that variously styled the "Bible Moralisée", the "Bible Historiée", the "Bible Allégorisée" and sometimes "Emblêmes Bibliques". It is a work of the thirteenth century, and from the copies that still survive there is no doubt that it existed in at least two editions, like to one another in the choice and order of the Biblical texts used, but differing in the allegorical and moral deductions drawn from these passages. The few remarks to be made here about the "Bible Moralisée" will be made in connexion with copies of the first and second redactions which have come down to us.

The copy of the first edition, to which reference has been made, is one of the most sumptuous illustrated MSS. preserved to us from the Middle Ages. Unfortunately, it no longer exists in the form of a single volume, nor is it kept in one place. It has been split up into three separate parts kept in three distinct libraries. The first part, consisting of 224 leaves, is in the Bodleian Library at Oxford. The second part of 222 leaves is in the National Library in Paris; and the third part, made up of 178 leaves, is kept in the library of the British Museum. Six leaves of the third part are missing, so that it ought to contain 184 leaves. When complete and bound together, therefore, the whole volume consisted of 630 leaves, written and illustrated on one side only. This Bible, as indeed all the picture Bibles of the Middle Ages, did not contain the full text of the Bible. Short passages only were cited, and these not so as to give any continuous sense or line of thought. But the object of the writer seems to have been chiefly to make the texts cited the basis of moral and allegorical teaching, in the manner so common in those days. In the Psalter he was content with copying out the first verse of each psalm; whilst when dealing with the Gospels he did not quote from each evangelist separately, but made use of a kind of confused diatessaron of all four combined. An attempt was made to establish a connexion between the events recorded in the Old Testament and those recorded in the New, even when there does not seem to be any very obvious connexion between them. Thus the sleep of Adam, recorded in the beginning of Genesis, is said to prefigure the death of Christ; and Abraham sending his servant with rich presents to seek a wife for his son is a type of the Eternal Father giving the Gospels to the Apostles to prepare the union of His Son with the Church.

The entire work contains about 5,000 illustrations. The pictures are arranged in two parallel columns on each page, each column having four medallions with pictures. Parallel to the pictures and alternating with them are two other narrower columns, with four legends each, one legend to each picture; the legends consisting alternatively of Biblical texts and moral or allegorical applications; whilst the pictures represent the subjects of the Biblical texts or of the applications of them. In the MS. copy of the "Bible Moralisée", now under consideration, the illustrations are executed with the greatest skill. The painting is said to be one of the best specimens of thirteenth-century work, and the MS. was in all probability prepared for someone in the highest rank of life. A specimen of the second edition of the "Bible Moralisée" is to be found in the National Library in Paris (MS. Français No. 167). Whilst it is identical with the copy which has just been examined in the selection and order of the Biblical passages, it differs from it in the greater simplicity and brevity of the moral and allegorical teaching based on them. Another important Bible, intended to instruct by means of pictures, was that which has been called the "Bible Historiée toute figurée". It was a work of the end of the thirteenth or the beginning of the fourteenth century. In general outline and plan it resembles the class of Bible which has gone before, but it differs from it in the selection of Bible passages and in the allegorical explanations derived from them. Coming to the life of Our Lord, the author of the "Bible Historiée toute figurée" dispensed with a written text altogether, and contented himself with writing over the pictures depicting scenes of Our Saviour's life, a brief explanatory legend. Many specimens of this Bible have come down to us, but we select part of one preserved in the National Library in Paris (MS. Français No. 9561) for a brief description. In this MS. 129 pages are taken up with the Old Testament. Of these the earlier ones are divided horizontally in the centre, and it is the upper part of the page that contains the picture illustrative of some Old Testament event. The lower part represents a corresponding scene from the New Testament. Further on in the volume, three pictures appear in the upper part of the page, and three below. Seventy-six pages at the end of the volume are devoted to depicting the lives of Jesus Christ and the Blessed Virgin.

It must not be supposed that these were the only Bibles of this class that existed in the Middle Ages. On the contrary, from the great number of copies that have survived to our own day we may guess how wide their circulation must have been. We have a MS. existing in the British Museum (addit. 1577) entitled "Figures de la Bible" consisting of

PICTURE BIBLE

PROPHECY OF ISAIAH, LIII AND LIV, REGARDING JESUS CHRIST AND THE CHURCH

pictures illustrating events in the Bible with short descriptive text. This is of the end of the thirteenth, or the beginning of the fourteenth, century. Of the same date is the "Historia Bibliæ metrice" which is preserved in the same library and, as the name implies, has a metrical text. But we have specimens of manuscript illustrated Bibles of earlier date. Such is the Bible preserved in the library of St. Paul's, outside the walls of Rome; that of the Amiens Library (MS. 108), and that of the Royal Library of The Hague (MS. 69). So numerous are the surviving relics of such Bibles, back even so far as the eleventh and twelfth centuries, that it may be safely said that the Church made a systematic effort to teach the Scriptures in those days by means of illustrated Bibles.

SINGLE ILLUSTRATED BOOKS OF THE BIBLE.—The Bibles that have come under notice so far illustrate the entire Scriptures. But what was done for the Bible in full was also done for its various parts. Numerous beautifully illustrated psalters have come down to us, some of them going as far back as the ninth century, as, for instance, the Psalter of the University of Utrecht. One thing that comes out clearly from a study of the contents and character of these psalters is that a very large proportion of them were executed by artists working in England. So, too, the book of Job and the Apocalypse were copied separately and adorned with numerous illustrations. But, as we should have expected, the Gospels were a specially favourite field for the medieval artists who devoted their time to picture-painting.

BIBLIA PAUPERUM.—A class of illustrated Bibles to which no allusion has been made, but which had a wide circulation especially in the fifteenth century was the "Biblia Pauperum". As its name indicates, it was especially intended for the poor and ignorant, and some say that it was used for purposes of preaching by the mendicant orders. It existed at first in manuscript (indeed a manuscript copy is still in existence in the library of the British Museum); but at a very early period it was reproduced by xylography, then coming into use in Europe. As a consequence the "Biblia Pauperum" was published and sold at a much cheaper rate than the older manuscript picture Bibles. The general characteristics of this Bible are the same as those of the earlier picture Bibles. The pictures are generally placed only on one side of the page, and are framed in a kind of triptych of architectural design. In the centre is a scene from the New Testament, and on either side of it typical events from the Old Testament. Above and below the central picture are busts of four noted prophets or other famous characters of the Old Testament. In the corners of the picture are the legends. The number of these pictures in the "Biblia Pauperum" was usually from forty to fifty.

Picture Bibles of the Middle Ages did not exhaust the resources of Christians in illustration of the Bible. Since the fifteenth century a host of artistic geniuses have contributed to make the events of Scripture live in colour before our eyes. Most noted amongst them were Michelangelo and Raphael; the former chiefly famous for his Pietà and the frescoes in the Sistine Chapel; the latter for the fifty-two pictures adorning the Vatican and known as "Raphael's Bible", and still more for the seven cartoons illustrating events in the New Testament. Perhaps no sacred picture has been so often copied as "The Last Supper" of Leonardo da Vinci painted in the refectory of the Dominican convent in Milan. Well known, too, are Fra Bartolomeo's "Presentation in the Temple" in Vienna, and Rubens's numerous Bible pictures, to be found in the Louvre, Brussels, Vienna, Munich, and London, but chiefly at Antwerp, where are his "Descent from the Cross", "Crucifix-

ion", and "Adoration of the Magi", the most famous of his works. These are but a few out of a number of illustrious names too numerous to mention here and including Botticelli, Carrucci, Holman Hunt, Leighton, Murillo, Veronese, Tintoretto, and Watts.

To study the works of the great Bible-illustrators is not so difficult as might be supposed. For of late years a great number of collections of Bible prints have been made, some containing engravings of the most famous paintings. In the first half of last century Julius Schnorr collected together 180 designs called his "Bible Pictures, or Scripture History"; and another series of 240 pictures was published in 1860 by George Wigand; whilst later in the century appeared Dalziel's "Bible Gallery". Hodder and Stoughton have published excellent volumes reproducing some of the pictures of the greatest masters. Such are "The Old Testament in Art" (2 parts); "The Gospels in Art", "The Apostles in Art", and "Bethlehem to Olivet", this latter being made up of modern pictures. The Society for the Promotion of Christian Knowledge has not been behindhand, but has issued amongst other publications a volume on "Art Pictures from the Old Testament" with ninety illustrations, and another on the Gospels with 350 illustrations from the works of the great masters of the fourteenth, fifteenth, and sixteenth centuries.

HORNE, *Introduction to the Holy Scriptures* (London, 1822), II, 3d ed.; HUMPHREY, *History of the Art of Printing* (London, 1868); LEVESQUE in VIG., *Dict. de la Bible* (Paris, 1894), s. v. *Bible en image;* DELISLE, *Hist. littéraire de la France* (Paris, 1893), XXXI, 213–285; BERJEAU, *Biblia Pauperum,* reproduced in facsimile from one of the copies in the British Museum, with an historical and bibliographical introduction (London, 1859).

J. A. HOWLETT.

Biblia Magna. See LA HAYE.

Biblia Maxima. See LA HAYE.

Biblia Pauperum (BIBLE OF THE POOR) a collection of pictures representing scenes from Our Lord's life with the corresponding prophetic types. The series commonly consists of forty or fifty pages. The page is divided into nine sections. The four corners are used for explanatory texts. The central pictures represent scenes from Our Lord's life, arranged chronologically. Above and below these are pictures of prophets and on each side are scenes from the Old Testament. It is thus a concordance of the Old and the New Testaments in which is gathered together the common tradition of the Church on the types and figures of the Old Testament, as taught by the liturgy and the Fathers. Hence they were called sometimes "Figuræ typicæ Veteris Testamenti atque antitypicæ Novi Testamenti" or "Historia Christi in Figuris". An interesting reproduction and description of a page on the Blessed Sacrament is given in Vigouroux, "Dictionnaire de la Bible", s. v.

The invention of these picture-books is ascribed to St. Ansgar, Bishop of Bremen. This is stated in a note added to a copy at Hanover and in the cathedral at Bremen there are remains of pictures, corresponding to this copy. The name, however, of "Biblia Pauperum" does not seem to have been primitive. It was added by a later hand to a MS. in the Wolffenbüttel library; the MS. was thus catalogued, and the name became common. It is uncertain why they were so called. Perhaps it was because of the ancient saying that pictures were the Bible of the poor, that is, of the uneducated. Some think that the name came from their use by the mendicant orders as books of instruction. Others suppose that the term means inexpensive; manuscripts had been beyond the means of most people; when the art of printing from engraved blocks was introduced these picture-books were among the first printed and gained a wide circulation. We have no definite information as to the purpose for which these books were intended. Probably it was for religious instruction; perhaps also to serve as models for artists. It is certain that they exercised a great influence in spreading a knowledge of the mysteries of Faith, affording themes for preachers and artists. At Hirschau in Swabia, the entire series of pictures is reproduced in stained glass.

Only a few manuscript copies of the "Biblia Pauperum" are extant; they come from the school of John van Eyck (1366–1466). The block-book, or xylographic process, appeared early in the fifteenth century, and Sotheby counts seven editions made from these wooden slabs. Only one side of the paper was printed, two sheets being pasted together to make a leaf. Five copies are in the Bibliothèque Nationale: four have forty plates; one copy is coloured by hand; the fifth has fifty plates. The first edition from movable types was printed by Pfister at Bamberg in 1462. The earlier editions have Latin texts; later they were printed in the vernacular. A German "Armenbibel" was published in 1470, and at Paris in 1503, A. Vérard published "Les Figures du Vieil Testament et du Nouveau". In some of the printed editions the original arrangement of pictures and texts was modified. In the latter half of the fifteenth century these books were very popular. As improved methods made it possible to issue the whole Bible with illustrations, the "Biblia" fell into disuse and disappeared. Several facsimile reproductions have appeared with historical and bibliographical introductions notably by Berjeau (1859); Camesina and Heider (Vienna, 1863); Unwin (London, 1884), with introduction by Dean Stanley; Einsle (Vienna, 1890); Laib and Schwarz (1892) and P. Heitz (1902).

SOTHEBY, *The Block-Books or Xylographic Delineations of Scripture History issued in Holland, France, and Germany* (London, 1858). See also the introductions to the facsimile editions, VIGOUROUX, *Dict. de la Bible*, s. v.; STREBER in *Kirchenlex.*, s. v.; CHEVALIER, *Rép. des sources hist. du moyen âge: Topo-bibl.*

JOHN CORBETT.

Biblical Antiquities.—This department of archæology has been variously defined and classified. Some scholars have included in it even Biblical chronology, geography, and natural history, but wrongly so, as these three branches of Biblical science belong rather to the external environment of history proper. Archæology, properly speaking, is the science of antiquities, and of those antiquities only which belong more closely to the inner life and environment of a nation, such as their monumental records, the sources of their history, their domestic, social, religious, and political life, as well as their manners and customs. Hence, history proper, geography, and natural history must be excluded from the domain of archæology. So also the study of monumental records and inscriptions and of their historical interpretation must be left either to the historian, or to the sciences of epigraphy and numismatics. Accordingly, Biblical Archæology may be appropriately defined as: the science of I. DOMESTIC, or SOCIAL, II. POLITICAL, and III. SACRED, ANTIQUITIES of the Hebrew nation.

Our principal sources of information are: (a) The Old Testament writings; (b) the archæological discoveries made in Syria and Palestine; (c) the Assyro-Babylonian, Egyptian, and Canaanitish monuments; (d) the New Testament writings; (e) the writings of the Jewish historian Josephus, and of the Babylonian and Jerusalem Talmuds; (f) comparative study of Semitic religions, customs, and institutions.

I. DOMESTIC ANTIQUITIES.—(1) *Family and clan.*— The Old Testament books present us the Hebrews as having passed through two stages of social development: the pastoral and the agricultural. The stories of the Patriarchs, Abraham, Isaac, and Jacob, picture

them as dwelling in tents and constantly moving from one pasture-ground to another. In course of time tents merged into huts, huts into houses, and these into settlements, villages, and cities, surrounded by cornfields, vineyards, oliveyards, and gardens. Flocks and herds became rarer and rarer till the time of the early monarchy and afterwards, when, with few exceptions, they gave way to commerce and trade. As among all nations of antiquity, a coalition of various members, or branches, of the same family constituted a clan which, as an organization, seems to have antedated the family. A coalition of clans formed a tribe which was governed by its own chiefs or leaders. Some of the Hebrew clans at the time of the settlement in Canaan seem to have been organized, some to have been broken up and wholly or partially incorporated with other clans. A man's standing in his clan was so important that if he was cast out he became *ipso facto* an outlaw, unless, indeed, some other clan could be found to receive him. After the settlement, the Hebrew clan-system changed somewhat and slowly degenerated till the time of the monarchy, when it fell into the background and became absorbed by the more complicated system of national and monarchical government.

(2) *Marriage and the constitution of the family.*— In ancient Hebrew times the family, as a social organization, and as compared with the clan, must have held a secondary place. Comparative Semitic analogy and Biblical evidences seem to indicate that among the early Hebrews, as among other early Semitic nations, man lived under a matriarchate system, i. e. kinship was constituted by uterine ties, and descent was reckoned through female lines; the father's relation to his children being, if not ignored, certainly of little or no importance. Hence a man's kin were the relatives of his mother, not those of his father; and consequently all hereditary property descended in the female line. The position of woman during the early Hebrew period, although inferior to what it became later, was not as low and insignificant as many are inclined to believe. Many episodes in the lives of women like Sarah, Rebeccah, Rachel, Deborah, Mary the sister of Moses, Delilah, Jephtah's daughter, and others are sufficient evidences. The duties of a woman, as such and as a wife and mother, were heavy both physically and morally. The work in and about the home devolved upon her, even to the pitching of the tent, as also the work of the field with the men at certain seasons. The position of the man as father and as the head of the household was of course superior to that of the wife; upon him devolved the duty and care of the training of the children, when they had reached a certain age, as also the offering of sacrifices, which necessarily included the slaughtering of domestic animals, and the conduct of all devotional and ritualistic services. To these must be added the duty of maintaining the family, which presupposes a multitude of physical and moral obligations and hardships.

Polygamy was an acknowledged form of marriage in the patriarchal and post-patriarchal periods, although in later times it was considerably restricted. The Mosaic law everywhere requires a distinction to be made between the first wife and those taken in addition to her. Marriage between near relatives was common, owing to a desire to preserve, as far as possible, the family bond intact. As the family was subordinate to the clan, the whole social life of the people, marriage, and even property rights were under the surveillance of the same. Hence a woman was to marry within the same clan; but if she chose to marry without the clan, she should do so only upon such terms as the clan might permit by its customs or by its action in a particular case. So, also, a woman might be allowed, where compensation was made, to marry and leave her clan, or she might contract through her father or other male relative with a man of another clan provided she remained with her people and bore children for her clan. This marriage-form, known to scholars under the term of *Sadiqa-marriage*, was undoubtedly practised by the ancient Hebrews, as positive indications of its existence are found in the Book of Judges and particularly in the cases of Jerubbaal, Samson, and others. The fact itself that Hebrew harlots who received into their tents or dwellings men of other clans, and who bore children to their own clan, were not looked upon with much disfavour is a sure indication of the existence of the *Sadiqa-marriage* type among the Hebrews. One thing is certain, however, that no matter how similar the marriage customs of the ancient Hebrews may have been to those of the early Arabs, the marriage tie among the former was much stronger than, and never as loose as, among the latter. Another form of Hebrew marriage was the so-called levirate type (from the Lat. *levir*, i. e. brother-in-law), i. e. the marriage between a widow, whose husband had died childless, and her brother-in-law. She was, in fact, not permitted to marry a stranger, unless the surviving brother-in-law formally refused to marry her. The levirate marriage was intended, first, to prevent the extinction of the name of the deceased childless brother; and secondly, to retain the property within the same tribe and family. The first-born son of such a union took the name of the deceased uncle instead of that of his father, and succeeded to his estate. If there were no brother of the deceased husband alive, then the next of kin was supposed to marry the widow, as we find in the case of Ruth's relative who yielded his right to Boaz. According to the laws of Moses, a man was forbidden to remarry a divorced wife, if she had married again and become a widow, or had been divorced from her second husband. Israelites were not forbidden to intermarry with any foreigners except the seven Canaanitish nations; hence Moses' marriage to a Midianite, and afterwards to a Cushite, woman and that of David to a princess of Geshur were not against the Mosaic law. The high-priest was to marry a virgin of his own people, and in the time of Ezechiel even an ordinary priest could not marry a widow, unless she were the widow of a priest.

Betrothal was mostly a matter of business to be transacted by the parents and near family friends. A distinction between betrothal and marriage is made even in the Mosaic law, where betrothal is looked upon as more than a promise to marry; it was in fact its initial act, and created a bond which could be dissolved only by death or by legal divorce. Faithlessness to this vow of marriage was regarded and punished as adultery. Betrothal actually took place after a dowry had been agreed upon. As a rule, it was given to the parents of the bride, though sometimes to an elder brother. Marriage contracts appear to have been mostly oral, and made in the presence of witnesses. The earliest account of a written one is found in the Book of Tobit (D. V. Tobias). The wedding festivities lasted ordinarily seven days, and on the day of the wedding the bridegroom, richly dressed and crowned, went in procession to the bride's house to take her away from her father. The bride, deeply veiled, was led away amid the blessings of her parents and friends. The bridal procession not infrequently took place at night, in the blaze of torches and with the accompaniment of songs, dancing, and the highest expressions of joy.

Adultery was punished by death, through stoning of both participants. A man suspecting his wife of unfaithfulness might subject her to a terrible ordeal which, it was thought, no guilty wife could well pass through without betraying her guilt. Divorce among the ancient Hebrews was as frequent as among any other civilized nation of antiquity. Mosaic laws attempted only to restrict and to regulate it. Any "unseemly thing" was sufficient ground for divorce, as also was barrenness. The wife, however, was not allowed to separate herself from her husband for any reason; in the case of her husband's adultery, he as well as the other guilty party, as we have seen, would be punished with death.

Concubinage, which differs widely from polygamy, was also extensively practised by the Hebrews. A concubine was less than a wife, but more than an ordinary mistress, and her rights were jealously guarded in the Mosaic Code. The children born of such a union were in no case considered as illegitimate. The principal distinction between a legal wife and a concubine consisted in the latter's social and domestic inferiority. Concubines were not infrequently either handmaids of the wife, or captives taken in war or purchased of their fathers. Canaanitish and other foreign women or slaves could in no case be taken as concubines. The seducer of an unbetrothed maiden was compelled either to marry her or to pay her father a heavy fine. In later times, ordinary harlotry was punished, and if the harlot was the daughter of a priest she was burnt. Idolatrous harlotry and sodomy were severely punished.

The domestic and social life of the Hebrews was frugal and simple. They indulged very little in public games and diversions. Hunting and fishing were looked upon as necessities of life. Slavery was extensively practised, and slaves were either Hebrews or foreigners. The Mosaic law is against any kind of involuntary slavery, and no Hebrew slave was allowed to be sold to foreigners. An Israelitish slave was to be set free after five or six years servitude and not without some compensation, unless he were willing to serve another term. As was natural, Hebrew slaves were more kindly treated by their Hebrew masters than were foreign ones, who were either captives in war or purchased.

(3) *Death and burial.*—The principal sicknesses and diseases mentioned in the Old Testament are: intermittent, bilious, and inflammatory fevers, dysentery produced by sunstroke, inflammation of the head, fits, apoplectic paralysis, blindness, inflammation of the eyes, hæmorrhages, epilepsy, diarrhœa, dropsy, various kinds of skin eruptions, scabies, and the various forms of leprosy. To these must be added some psychical diseases, such as madness, melancholy, etc., and also various forms of demoniacal possession. No explicit mention of professional physicians and surgeons is made in the Old Testament.

In case of death, the body was washed and wrapped in a linen cloth and, if financial circumstances allowed, anointed with sweet-smelling spices and ointments. Embalming was neither a general nor a common practice. Burial took place, usually, on the day of the person's death. The dead body was never burnt, but interred, unless for some particular reason, as in the case of Saul and his sons. Mourning customs were various, such as wearing sackcloths, scattering dust and ashes on the head, beating the breast, plucking and pulling out the hair and the beard, throwing oneself upon the earth; rending the garments, going about barefooted, veiling the face, and in some cases abstaining from eating and drinking for a short time. The usual period of mourning lasted seven days. With few exceptions the bodies were interred outside of the town, either in caves or in public cemeteries. Persons of high social and financial standing were publicly mourned, and their bodies placed in sepulchres hewn in rock.

(4) *Food and meals.*—The principal articles of food among the ancient Hebrews can be easily summarized from the interesting description of the land of Canaan occurring in the Book of Deuteronomy, where it is said to be "a land of wheat, and barley, and vines, and fig trees, and pomegranates; a land of oil olive, and honey; a land wherein thou shalt eat bread without scarceness, thou shalt not lack any thing in it" (Deut., viii, 8, 9). Their meals were undoubtedly of the simplest description, and their table was more rich with fish, milk, fruit, and vegetables than with meat. Animal food in general was in favour with the people at large, but the Mosaic law restricted its use to almost the minimum. Animals or parts of animals designated for sacrifice or other holy uses could only be eaten under specific conditions. In the eleventh chapter of Leviticus and the fourteenth of Deuteronomy, a list is given of a large class of animals which were looked upon as ceremonially unfit to be eaten. Animals, furthermore, were classified as pure and impure, or clean and unclean, and the complicated legislation of the Pentateuch concerning the use of these is partly based on sanitary, partly fanciful, and partly ceremonial grounds. The evening meal was the principal meal of the day, and if knives, forks, spoons, and other like instruments were used in the preparation of the meals, they were not used at the table. Hands were washed before and after meals. Neither prayer, nor grace, nor blessing seems to have been proffered before or after the repast. In other particulars the table usages and customs of the ancient Hebrews may reasonably be supposed to have been like those of modern Palestine.

(5) *Dress and ornaments.*—The materials for clothing were principally cotton, linen, and wool; silk is once, or never, mentioned in the Old Testament. The wearing of a mixed fabric of wool and linen was forbidden by the Mosaic law. So, also, either sex was forbidden to wear the garments proper to the opposite sex. The outer garment of men consisted of loose, flowing robes, which were of various types and forms. On the four corners of this outer robe a fringe, or tassel, was attached. The undergarment, which was the same for both sexes, consisted, generally, of a sleeveless tunic or frock of any material desired, and reached to the knees or ankles. That of the woman was longer and of richer material. The tunic was fastened at the waist with a girdle. The fold made by the girdle served at the same time as a pocket. A second tunic and the shawl, which was long and of fine material, were also in use. The outer garment of the Hebrew women differed slightly from that of the men, and no detailed description of it is found in the Bible. It was undoubtedly richer and more ornamented than that of the other sex. The most accepted colour for ordinary garments was white, and the art of bleaching cloth was from very early times known and practised by the Hebrews. In later times, the purple, scarlet, and vermilion colours were extensively used, as well as the black, red, yellow, and green. Girdles were worn by both sexes, and golden girdles were not unknown. Men covered the head with some kind of a turban, or cap, although it is doubtful whether its use was universal in pre-Mosaic and Mosaic times. In ancient times women did not wear veils, but probably covered their heads with kerchiefs, mufflers, or mantles. Sandals were in general use, but not among the poorer classes, or among the farmers and shepherds. Worthy of notice is the ceremony mentioned in Deut., xxv, 9, according to which if a man refuses to marry the wife of his brother, who had died childless, "Then shall his brother's wife come unto him in the presence of the elders, and *loose his shoe from off his foot*, and spit in [or before] his face, and she shall answer and say, So shall it be done unto the man that will not build up his brother's house". The drawing off of the shoe evidently indicated the surrender of the rights which the law gave the man to marry his brother's widow. Likewise the modern custom of throwing a slipper sportively after a newly wedded pair leaving the parental house appears to have a like symbolical significance; the parents and family friends thereby symbolically renounce their right to the daughter or son in favour of the husband or wife. Finger-rings, ear-rings, and bracelets were extensively used by both men and women, but more so by the latter. Prosperous men always carried a staff and a seal. All these ornamental articles, however, were more indulged in by the Egyptians, Assyrians, and other Oriental nations than by the Hebrews. Hebrew women wore also cauls, anklets, and ankle-chains, scent-bottles, and decorated purses, or satchels. Perfumery was also indulged in; and extensive use was made of pigments as applied to the eyelids and eyebrows by women. Tattooing on the face, arms, chest, and hands was in all probability practised by the Hebrews, although it was to a certain extent incompatible with certain Mosaic prescriptions.

(6) *Pastoral and agricultural life.*—According to the Biblical records, tilling the ground and the rearing of cattle and sheep were the first and earliest occupations of men. In Patriarchal times the latter was in greater favour, while in the later Hebrew period the first prevailed over the second. This transition from the pastoral, or nomadic, to the agricultural, or settled, life was a natural consequence of the settlement in Canaan, but at no time did the two occupations exclude each other. Both, in fact, were important, indispensable, and necessary. The sheep was, of course, the principal animal both as an article of food and as wool-producer, besides its constant use as a sacrificial animal. Sheep's milk was also a favourite article. Rams also, with from two to as many as eight horns, are not infrequently mentioned. Goats are frequently mentioned, and cows and oxen were utilized for milk and butter and for tilling the ground. Horses and camels were imported from Arabia. Poultry and hens are not once mentioned in the Old Testament. The ass was a common and useful animal for transportation, but the mule is not mentioned in the Bible prior to the time of the monarchy. The life of the Hebrew and Eastern shepherds in general was by no means easy or uneventful. Jacob, in fact, in reproaching his father-in-law, Laban, says: "Thus I was: in the day the drought consumed me, and the frost by night; and my sleep fled from mine eyes" (Gen., xxxi, 40); and of his own pastoral life and its perils David tells us that "there came a lion, and a bear, and took a lamb out of the flock: and I went out after him, and smote him, and delivered it out of his mouth" [I Sam. (D. V. I Kings), xvii, 34, 35]. The shepherd's duties were to lead out the flock to pasture, watch them, supply them with water, go after the straying ones, and bring them all safely back to the fold at night. These formed his riches, trade, occupation, and sustenance.

Agriculture is the natural product of settled life. Nevertheless we read of Isaac that during the prevalence of a famine in Palestine he cultivated land in the vicinity of Gerar, which produced a hundredfold (Gen., xxvi, 12). The Mosaic law recognizes land as the principal possession of the Hebrews, and its cultivation as their chief business. Hence every Hebrew family was to have its own piece of ground, which could not be alienated, except for limited periods. Such family estates were carefully surveyed; and it was regarded as one of the most flagrant of crimes to remove a neighbour's landmark. Estates were divided into so many yokes, that is, such portions as a yoke of oxen could plough in a single day. The value of the land was according to its yield in grain.

Irrigation was practised to a certain extent in Palestine, though not carried to the same extent as in Assyria, Babylonia, and Egypt. The chief dependence for moisture was on the dew and the drenching rains of the rainy season. The climate of Palestine was, as a whole, favourable to agriculture, although in modern times the valleys and the plains have greatly deteriorated in fertility. The ground was ordinarily fertilized by the ashes of burnt straw and stubble, the chaff left after threshing, and the direct application of dung. According to the Mosaic law, every tillable land should enjoy on each seventh year a *sabbath*, or a rest. The year in question is called the Sabbatic Year, in which the field was not to be tilled. The object of this prescription was to heighten the natural fertility of the soil. What grew spontaneously in that year was to be not alone for the owner, but, on equal terms, for the poor, for strangers and for cattle. It is doubtful, however, whether this law was scrupulously observed in later Hebrew times. The most widely cultivated grains were wheat and barley, as well as spelt and millet. Of plants and vegetables the principal were grape-vines, olive-trees, nuts, apples, figs, pomegranates, beans, lentils, onions, melons, cucumbers, etc. The season for ploughing and cultivating the ground extended from October to March; that of gathering the crops from April or May to September. The plough was similar to our modern one. It was ordinarily drawn by two oxen, cows or asses, never, however, by an ass and an ox together. It was also forbidden under penalty of confiscation to sow the same field with two kinds of seeds. The beginning of the harvest was signalized by bringing a sheaf of new grain (presumably barley) into the sanctuary and waving it before the Lord. The grain was generally cut with the sickle, and sometimes pulled up by the roots. Fields and fruit-orchards were not to be gleaned by their owners, as this privilege was given to the poor and strangers, as in the case of Ruth. The threshing and winnowing were performed in the open field, the first by means of cattle yoked together, the other by shovels and fans.

(7) *Commerce.*—The Hebrew people of olden times were not inclined towards commerce and did not indulge in it. This is probably due partly to the geographical position of Palestine and partly to its physical features. For although, geographically, Palestine would seem to have offered the most natural highway to connect the opulent commercial nations of Egypt, Syria, Phœnicia, Assyria, and Babylonia, nevertheless, it lacked a sea-coast. Hence the Israelites remained essentially agriculturists. The trade of the Israelites consisted chiefly in the mutual exchange of products among themselves. At the time of David and Solomon, caravans from Egypt, Arabia, and Syria were not infrequently sent to Palestine and vice versa. The ships which Solomon is said to have sent to remote lands were built and manned by the Phœnicians. But even this revival of commercial spirit among the Hebrews was short-lived, for it ended with the life of Solomon. Solomon's commercial activities have been also greatly misunderstood and exaggerated. A faint revival of the Solomonic commercial spirit was inaugurated by King Jehoshaphat, of whom we read that he made "ships of Tharshish to go to Ophir for gold: but they went not; for the ships were broken at Eziongeber" [I (D. V. III) Kings, xxii, 48]. During and after the Babylonian Captivity, the Hebrews were compelled by circumstances to resort to trade and commerce, as they had come into constant contact with their Babylonian brethren and with the numerous Syro-Phœnician and Aramæan tribes and colonies. The historian Josephus well summarizes this whole matter when, in his work against Apion, he says: "We neither inhabit a maritime country, nor do we delight in merchandise, nor in such a mixture with other men as arises from it."

Previous to the Babylonian Captivity, coined money does not seem to have circulated among the Hebrews, although a few references in Isaiah and other prophets seem to indicate its existence. Silver and gold were bought and exchanged by weight and value. The talent, the shekel, the *kesitah*, and the *maneh* (*mina*) are late Hebrew terms and of Babylonian origin. After the Exile, and especially during the Persian, Greek, and Roman dominations, coined money became quite common in Palestine, such as the *quadrans*, the *assarion*, the *denarius*, the *drachma*, the *stater*, the *didrachma*, etc.

During the time of the monarchy and afterwards, such trades and occupations as woodworking, metalworking, stoneworking, tanning, and weaving were thoroughly in evidence among the most industrious class of the Israelites, but the Chosen People cannot be said to have attained considerable skill and success in these directions.

(8) *Science, arts, etc.*—At no time can the Hebrews be said to have developed a liking for the study of history, astronomy, astrology, geometry, arithmetic, grammar, and physical science in general. The Book of Job, Proverbs, and the many parables which Solomon is said to have written contain but meagre and popular notions, mostly drawn from observations of everyday life and happenings, while others are, to a great extent, due to the Babylonian influence and civilization which, from very early times, and especially during and after the Captivity, seem to have invaded the entire literary and social life of the Hebrews. Hence the Hebrew astronomical system, their calendar, constellations, sacred numbers, names of the months, solar and lunar months, etc., are of Babylonian origin. The Book of Job no less than the early chapters of Genesis show the traces of this same Babylonian influence.

As the Tell-el-Amarna letters have conclusively shown, the art of writing must have been known in Canaan and among the ancient Hebrews as early as the Mosaic age, and even earlier. Whether, however, this art was utilized by them to any great extent, is another question. Hebrew literature is one of the most venerable and valuable literary productions of the ancient East; and, although in respect of quantity and variety far inferior to that of the Assyro-Babylonians and Egyptians, nevertheless, in loftiness of ideals, sublimity of thoughts, and standard of morals and ethics, it is infinitely superior to them.

The art of music, both vocal and instrumental, occupies a high position in the Bible. Previous to the time of David, the music of the Hebrews seems to have been of the simplest character, as direct efforts to cultivate music among them appear first in connexion with the schools of the prophets, founded by Samuel. Under David's direction not less than four thousand musicians, i. e. more than the tenth part of the tribe of Levi, praised the Lord with "instruments" in the service of the temple. A select body of two hundred and eighty-eight trained musicians led this chorus of voices, one person being placed as leader over a section consisting of twelve singers. Heman, Asaph, and Ethan were among the most famous of these leaders. Men and women were associated together in the choir. In later Hebrew times the art of music developed still further till it reached its acme under Hezekiah and Josiah. The Hebrew musical instruments were, like those of other nations of antiquity, chiefly of three kinds, viz: stringed instruments, wind instruments, and such as were beaten or shaken to produce sound. To the first class belong the harp, the psaltery (also rendered "viol", "dulcimer", etc.), the sackbut (Lat. *Sambuca*). To the second belong the flute, the pipe (Lat. *fistula*), and the trumpet. To the last belong the tabret, or timbrel, the castanets, and the cymbals.

In mechanical arts, the Israelites were far behind their Egyptian and Assyro-Babylonian neighbours. The author of I Samuel (D. V. I Kings) gives a sorry but true picture of the times preceding the activity of Samuel as follows: "Now there was no smith found throughout all the land of Israel . . . but all the Israelites went down to the Philistines, to sharpen every man his share, and his coulter, and his axe, and his mattock." In the times of Solomon, however, as it appears in connexion with the building of the temple, conditions materially improved. Of the artisan classes, those working in wood and metals were always, perhaps, the most numerous in Israel. Among the former were carpenters, cabinet-makers, wood-carvers, manufacturers of wagons, of baskets, of various household utensils, including the distaff and the loom, and of the tools used in agriculture, such as ploughs, yokes, threshing-machines, goads, and winnowing-shovels. Workers in metals mentioned in the Bible are gold- and silversmiths and workers in brass and iron. Some of the tools of which they made use were the anvil, the bellows, the smelting-furnace, the fining-pot, the hammer, and the tongs. Among the various products of these Hebrew metal-workers are settings for precious stones, gilding, axes, saws, sickles, knives, swords, spear-heads, fetters, chains, bolts, nails, hooks, penstocks, pans for cooking purposes, plough-shares, and the wheels of threshing-instruments. Copper or bronze was also used in manufacturing some of these articles. Other artisans mentioned in the Bible are: stone-masons, brick- and tile-makers, engravers, apothecaries, perfumers, bakers, tanners, fullers, spinners, weavers, and potters. Most of these trades and mechanical arts, however, came into prominence during the reign of Solomon and his successors.

II. POLITICAL ANTIQUITIES.—(1) *Civil administration.*—It has been truly said that law as law was unknown in early Israel. The customs of the clans and the conduct of the elders or of the most influential members of the tribe were looked upon as the standards of law and morality. Lawfulness was a matter of custom more or less ancient and more or less approved; and penalty was equally a matter of custom. When custom failed in a specific case, judgment could be rendered and new precedents might be made which in process of time would crystallize into customs. Hence the old tribal system among primitive Semitic clans, and especially in early Israel and Arabia, knew no legislative authority; and no single person or group of persons was ever acknowledged as having power to make laws or to render judgment. Of course prominent individuals or families within the tribe enjoyed certain privileges in acknowledgment of which they performed certain duties. In many cases they were called upon to settle differences, but they had no judicial powers and, if their decision did not satisfy the litigants, they had neither the right nor the power to enforce obedience, much less to inflict punishment. Within the tribe all men are on a footing of equality, and under a communistic system petty offences are unreasonable. Serious misdemeanour is punished by expulsion; the offender is excluded from the protection of his kinsmen, and the penalty is sufficiently severe to prevent it being a common occurrence. The man who is wronged must take the first step in gaining redress; and when it happens that the whole tribe is aroused by the perpetration of any exceptionally serious crime, the offence is fundamentally regarded as a violation of the tribe's honour, rather than as a personal injury to the family of the sufferer. This condition of

affairs, however, does not necessarily imply a condition of utter lawlessness. On the contrary, tribal customs formed practically a law of binding character, although they were not regarded as law in the proper sense of the term.

That such was the prevalent social condition of the ancient Hebrews in the patriarchal period is quite certain. The few recorded incidents in the lives of Abraham, Isaac, and Jacob furnish ample illustration of it. The long sojourn of the Hebrews in Egypt and the comparatively advanced civilization with which they there came in contact, as well as their settlement in Canaan, might be expected to have influenced their old tribal system of law and justice. Nevertheless, the authentic historical records of Israel's national formation and even the legislation of the Book of the Covenant, which is undoubtedly the oldest Hebrew code of laws, when carefully examined, utterly fail to show any such remarkable advance in the administration of law and justice over the old nomadic tribal system. It is true, that as Dr. Benzinger remarks, "before the monarchy Israel had attained a certain degree of unity in matters of law; not in the sense that it possessed a written law common to all the tribes, or as a uniform organization for the pronouncing of legal judgments, but in the sense that along with a common God it had a community of custom and of feeling in matters of law, which community of feeling can be traced back very far. 'It is not so done in Israel' and 'Folly in Israel, which ought not to be done' are proverbial expressions reaching back to quite early times". Nevertheless, law as law, with legislative power and authority, or a uniform system of legal procedure with courts and professional judges, were unknown in the earlier period of Israelitish history.

A study of the different Hebrew terms for *judge* clearly shows that a professional class of judges and, consequently, duly constituted courts did not exist in Israel till the first period of the monarchy, and even later. The *Shoterim* were primarily subordinate military officials, who were employed partly in the maintenance of civil order and military discipline. It was not until post-Exilic times that the term was applied to one with judicial power. *Mehokek* (primarily from *hakak*, "to cut in", "to inscribe", "to decide", etc., and subsequently, as in Arabic, "to be just", "right", etc.) meant originally commander or ruler. The *shophetim* (Lat. *sufetes;* Assyrian *sapatu*), from which the "Book of Judges" takes its title, were not judges, but champions and deliverers. Hence, in Hosea (D. V. Osee), vii, 7, and Ps., ii, 10, *shophetim* is a synonym of "kings" and "rulers", and the *sufetes* of the Phœnician cities and colonies were called "kings" by the Greeks. Other terms, such as *palil, quasin*, the meaning of which is rather obscure, primarily mean "umpire" in general, "chief", and "petty ruler". The only Hebrew word which, properly speaking, means "judge", in its etymology and historical significance, is *dayyan* (found in all Semitic languages: Arab. *dayyân;* Aramaic *dayyâna;* Assyrian *da-a-nu* or *da-ia-nu*, etc.). Although the stem meant originally "to requite", "to compensate", "to govern", and "to rule", we have sufficient warrant to believe that it meant, from the very earliest times, "to decide", and "to render decision". In the Old Testament, however, the word rarely occurs. In I Sam. (D. V., I Kings), xxiv, 15, it is even questionable whether it belongs to the original text, and it is only in post-Exilic times that the word meant "professional judge".

What was the polity of the Hebrew tribes prior to the time of Moses is not difficult to describe.

"Abraham, Isaac, and Jacob governed their families with an authority well nigh unlimited. Their power over their households was little short of a sovereign dominion. They were independent princes. They acknowledged no subjection, and owed no allegiance to any sovereign. They formed alliances with other princes. They treated with kings on a footing of equality. They maintained a body of servants, trained to the use of arms; were the chiefs who led them in war, and repelled force by force. They were the priests who appointed festivals, and offered sacrifices. They had the power of disinheriting their children, of sending them away from home without assigning any reason, and even of punishing them capitally.

"The twelve sons of Jacob ruled their respective families with the same authority. But when their descendants had become numerous enough to form tribes, each tribe acknowledged a prince as its ruler. This office, it is likely, was at first hereditary in the oldest son, but afterwards became elective. When the tribes increased to such an extent as to embrace a great number of separate households, the less powerful ones united with their stronger relatives, and acknowledged them as their superiors. In this way, there arose a sub-division of the tribes into collections of households. Such a collection was technically called a family, a clan, a house of fathers, or a thousand. This last appellation was not given because each of these sub-divisions contained just a thousand persons, or a thousand households; for in the nature of things, the number must have varied, and in point of fact, it is manifest from the history, that it did. As the tribes had their princes, so these clans, families, or thousands had their respective chiefs, who were called heads of houses of fathers, heads of thousands, and sometimes simply heads. Harrington denominates these two classes of officers phylarchs, or governors of tribes, and patriarchs, or governors of families. Both, while the Israelites were yet in Egypt, were comprehended under the general title of elders. Whether this name was a title of honour, like that of *sheikh* (the aged) among the Arabs, and that of *senator* among the Romans, or whether it is to be understood, according to its etymology, as denoting persons actually advanced in years, is uncertain. These princes of tribes and heads of thousands, the elders of Israel, were the rulers of the people, while they remained still subject to the power of the Pharaohs, and constituted a kind of 'imperium in imperio'. Of course they had no written constitution, nor any formal code of laws, but governed by custom, reason, and the principles of natural justice. They watched over and provided for the general good of the community, while the affairs of each individual household continued under the control of its own father. For the most part, it may be supposed, only those cases which concerned the fathers of families themselves would come under the cognizance and supervision of the elders."

During their wanderings through the Desert the Hebrew tribes had no occasion to introduce any radical change in this form of government, for they had to contend with continuous difficulties of a social, moral, and religious character. And, although numerically superior to many Canaanitish tribes, they were, nevertheless, lacking in military discipline and were constantly moving from place to place. Realizing the necessity of defending themselves against the predatory tribes and rivals for the possession of fertile lands and oases, they soon developed a military spirit, which is the strongest external principle of cohesion in nomadic life.

The administration of justice in Israel in the Mosaic age, and for a long time after, was in the hands of the elders, the local judges, and, somewhat later, the priests and the Levites, joined afterwards by the prophets. The elders, who represented the former heads of the families and clans under the tribal system, had undoubtedly ample jurisdiction concerning family affairs, disputes about conjugal relations, inheritances, the division of property, the appointment of the *goel* or upholder of the family, and the settlement of blood-revenge. The local judges, as we have remarked, were not what this technical title ordinarily means. They were merely arbitrators and advisers in settling disputes which could not be settled by the elders, and very often they had to decide cases of appeal from the ordinary bench of elders at the city gates. They were, as a rule, taken from the body of the elders of the city, and later on from the princes, chiefs, and military officers of the army. The third class consisted of priests, and later on of prophets. They were appealed to in all difficult cases, their authority and influence being undoubtedly very strong. To appeal to a priest was to appeal to God Himself, for the priest was universally acknowledged as the official representative of Yahweh. His decisions were regarded as "directions", and as such they were of an advisory character, thus constituting the "oracle" of the Hebrews. As originally each family group had its own priest, resort was naturally had to him for light on practical difficulties, not so much the settling of disputes as pointing out the safe, judicious, or righteous way for the individuals of the household in embarrassment. The prophets were also, in course of time, appealed to, not so much as official representatives of Yahweh as from the fact that they were regarded as men eminent in wisdom and spiritual authority. From the eighth century downwards the authority of the priests was greatly overshadowed by that of the prophets, who managed the destinies of the whole nation with an almost unlimited authority and assertiveness, proclaiming themselves as the messengers of Yahweh and the mouthpieces of His orders. A single judicial centre for the whole nation was never attained till the period of the monarchy. During the period of the Judges several leading judicial centres existed, such as Shiloh, Beth-el, Gilgal, Mizpah, Ramah, etc.

Whether Hebrew judges held their office for life is not altogether certain, although the presumption is that they did. It is likewise uncertain whether any salary or compensation was attached to the office. In the case of the Ten Judges, no revenues were appropriated for them, except, perhaps, a larger share of the spoils taken in war; and in case of the ordinary local judges or elders the offering of presents was quite common. This at first may have been a kind of testimonial of gratitude and respect, but it afterwards degenerated into mere bribery and corruption.

Whether the office of princes of tribes, chiefs, military officers, elders, and judges was hereditary or elective, is not easy to determine. Both systems may have been according to the different circumstances; but that in the majority of cases it was hereditary, admits of no doubt, for such was the prevailing custom in the ancient East and, to a certain extent, is so even in our own days.

No external sign of honour seems to have been attached to the dignity of judges and elders in Israel. They were without pomp, retinue, or equipage, although the passage in the Song of Deborah relating to those "who ride on white asses and sit in judgment" probably refers to the princes of the tribes, chiefs, elders, and judges in their respective capacities of military commanders, magistrates, and moral advisers and arbiters. In the East, even at the present day, the *quadis*, or chief judges and magistrates, have the distinctive privilege of riding either on mules or white asses, as against the military officers and civil governors who must ride on horses.

That the office of chief magistrate was unknown in ancient Israel is quite certain. In the whole Pentateuchal legislation allusion to such an institution is absolutely wanting. The supreme authority of the Hebrew community was in Yahweh. Moses, strictly speaking, was but the viceroy of Yahweh; and the same, to a certain extent, may also be said of Joshua. Their successors, the judges, were rather military commanders than judges or magistrates in the strict sense. With the beginning of the monarchy, the civil as well as the military power began to be concentrated, as far as possible, in the person of the king. But the Pentateuchal legislation as a whole is decidedly adverse to the idea of concentrating all power in the person of the king, or in that of any individual, and it is not improbable that the writer of Deut., xvii, was influenced by Israel's historical experience under the monarchy.

Allusions to the administration of law and justice in the old Book of the Covenant are extremely meagre and utterly fail to give us any clear (or even vague) reference to legal procedure, judges, courts, or to any system of administration of justice. It is true that the Book of the Covenant contains statutes and judgments, apparently enacted by some authoritative power; for such an authority must be assumed, otherwise there would be no meaning in the precise fixing of punishment, etc., such as the punishment of death, seven times prescribed, and the avenging on the body of the guilty person the wrong he had done. Still, as Kautzsch rightly remarks, "we are wholly in the dark as to the circle from which all the statutes and judgments proceeded, and, above all, as to the public authority by which scrupulous obedience was ensured. And, emphatically as justice and impartiality in legal cases is insisted on (xxiii, ff.), there is not a single indication as to who is authorized to pronounce sentence or to supervise the execution of the verdict." In two cases, however, viz., in Exodus, xxi, 6 and xxii, 8, in which the case is complicated and the law doubtful, the Book of the Covenant insists that the parties should present themselves "before God" (*Elohim*): in the first case probably to perform a symbolic act which will have legal effect, and in the second probably to obtain an oracle. The Septuagint seems to have understood the sense of the phrase *before God* in its most obvious meaning, rendering it "before the tribunal of God", i. e. that the matter is to be referred to the judgment of God, presumably in the sanctuary or before the priest. Rabbinical tradition, however, as early as the time of St. Jerome, took the word *Elohim* (God) as a plural, i. e. "gods", arguing that the word here means simply "judges", from the fact that, on account of the sacredness of their office, and the place where their decisions were rendered (often in the temple or at some sacred shrine) the judges were called "gods". The rabbinical interpretation which has been followed by the majority of ancient and modern commentators, ingenious though it be, is nevertheless erroneous; for, considering the fact that the two cases referred to were such as no judge could decide with any certainty or probability, and in which only a divine intervention could bring about a satisfactory solution, we may assume that the rabbinical interpretation is untenable. This conclusion has been admirably vindicated by the Code of Hammurabi, where, in several cases in which the doubt is such as to make any human wisdom of no avail, and any judicial decision untrustworthy, the decision is left to God Himself. Hence, in all such cases Hammurabi decrees that the litigants should present themselves "before God", and swear by His name, i. e. take an oath. The expression used by Hammurabi is exactly the same as that used in the two passages of Exodus referred to, and the cases in which the expression is applied are analogous. But in the Code of Hammurabi "to appear before God" is the same as "to swear by the name of God", or "to take a solemn oath"; hence, in the two passages of Exodus, to

appear before *Elohim* does not mean to appear before the judges, but to take a solemn oath at some holy place or sanctuary where the presence of the deity was more sensibly felt. By taking an oath the man in question constitutes God as the judge before whom he protests his innocence and affirms his rights. God is thereby called upon to avenge Himself upon the perjurers. And this God is neither Bel, nor Marduk, nor any other particular god, but is the Deity in its almost abstract form—He who is considered to be everywhere and to know everything. Hence the rabbinical interpretation, followed, till the discovery of the Code of Hammurabi, by the majority of commentators, may be confidently dismissed.

The legislation of Deuteronomy, on the other hand, which is in the main considerably later than that of the Book of the Covenant, furnishes us with more abundant details concerning the administration of law and justice in Israel. These are contained mainly in xvi, 18–20; xvii, 8–13, and 14–20; xix, 15–20, and xxv, 1–4. From II Chronicles (D. V. Paralipomenon) we learn that King Jehoshaphat established in Jerusalem a supreme tribunal, or court of justice, where priests and lay judges participated in the administration of justice each in their own sphere, and that he appointed judges in all cities of Judah. Details are lacking, but in its broader features the judicature thus established by Jehoshaphat agrees remarkably with the system prescribed in Deuteronomy, xvii, 8–13. Even in this case it is doubtful whether these judges and tribunals could in any satisfactory measure compare with the Babylonian legal system of the time of Hammurabi. In Ezechiel's time (and this brings us down to the sixth century B. C.) the priests seem to have absorbed all administrative power, while the author of I Chronicles, evidently influenced by Ezechiel or Deuteronomy, tells us that David had appointed 6,000 Levites as judges, which is quite inadmissible. In the post-Exilic times, and during the Greek and Roman periods, reference is made to professional judges, local courts, and tribunals in all the cities of Israel, which was undoubtedly due to Babylonian, Persian, Greek, and Roman influences.

Judicial or legal procedure was very simple in early Israel. In Exodus, xviii, 22, we are told that the elders appointed by Moses at Horeb were to judge the people "at all seasons"; and in Numbers, xxvii, 2 (cf. Exodus, xviii, 19 sqq.), we read that Moses rendered judgments before the tabernacle of Yahweh, where he sat with Aaron and the princes or elders of the congregation to teach statutes and give judgments. According to Deuteronomy, xxi, 19; xxii, 15; and xxv, 7 (cf. Prov., xxii, 22; Amos, v, 11, 15; and Ruth, iv, 1, etc.), the judges in the cities had their seat at the gate, which was the thoroughfare of the public, or in the public squares of the city, where the markets were held, or in some other open place. Even the supreme judges administered justice in public; Deborah, for instance, under a palm-tree, and the kings at the gate, or in the court, of the royal palace. Solomon is said to have erected a porch, or hall of judgment, in Jerusalem, for his own royal court of justice, and from Jeremiah we learn that in later times the princes of Judah exercised judgment in a chamber of the royal palace. Jeremiah himself, when accused by the priests and false prophets, was judged by the princes of the people, who are said to have come out of the king's house into the temple to judge at the entrance of the new gate before the assembled people. The litigants, viz., the plaintiff and the defendant, appeared personally before the elders, and presented their complaints orally. The accused, if not present, could be summoned to appear. Advocates are unknown in the Old Testament, for the plaintiff was supposed to look after his own case if he desired satisfactory judgment. Litigants were also at liberty to settle their differences personally, without appealing to the judge. The judge was held bound to hear and examine the case closely and conscientiously, his chief method of inquiry being the examination of the testimony of the witnesses. The accusations of the father against his rebellious child needed no support of witness. In other cases, however, especially criminal cases, not fewer than two or three witnesses were absolutely required. In all probability the testimony of slaves, children under age, and women was not accepted, as is expressly stated by Josephus and the Talmud, although not mentioned in the Old Testament. Witnesses were thoroughly examined, and, as in the Code of Hammurabi, false witnesses were punished according to the *lex talionis*, viz., by inflicting the precise kind of punishment the false witness had intended to bring upon his victim by his falsehood. Witnesses do not seem to have been put on oath, but when the nature of the case was such as to make it impossible to have or to produce witnesses, as in a case of theft, the oath was then administered to the accused, and the case decided. When the discovery of the crime and of the guilty party was a practical impossibility, Yahweh was looked to for the accomplishment of the task.

The Law affixes no civil punishment for perjury; it forbids it as a profanation of Yahweh's name and threatens it with divine punishment. It must be noted, however, that in all cases in which an oath was taken before a judgment-seat it consisted merely of an adjuration addressed by the judge and responded to by the person sworn with an *Amen*. "Only in common life did the person swearing himself utter the oath, either: 'So Yahweh do to me, and more also', or 'God [*Elohim*] do so to me', etc., or 'as Yahweh liveth'. But in such cases the name of Yahweh was probably avoided, and the oath was taken by the life (soul) of the man, to whom one wished to protest by oath. In later times, it became common, especially among the Pharisees, to swear by heaven, by the earth, by the temple, the holy city, and by one's own head."

The verdict, or the sentence, was pronounced orally, although from Job, xiii, 16; and Isaiah, x, 1, it appears that in some cases the sentence may have been given in written form. The sentence was to be executed without delay. Punishment was administered before the eyes of the judge, and that of stoning by the whole congregation or the people of the city, the witnesses being required to put their hands first to the execution of the guilty.

The practice of ordeals as means for ascertaining the truth, or obtaining a confession of guilt, was by no means unknown in Israel, although Josephus expressly tells us that torture and the bastinado for this purpose were first introduced into Israel by the Herodians. The most important one is the so-called "ordeal of jealousy", prescribed in Numbers, v, 11–31, in the case of a woman suspected of adultery which cannot be legally proved. For this purpose the husband of the suspected woman would bring her to the priest; he must also bring with him an offering of barley meal, which is called "a meal-offering of jealousy, a meal-offering of memorial bringing guilt to remembrance". The priest brings the woman before Yahweh, makes her take an oath of purgation, and then gives her to drink a potion described as "the water of bitterness that causeth the cure", consisting of "holy water" with which dust from the floor of the tabernacle has been mingled, and into which the written words of the oath have been washed. If the woman be guilty the potion proves harmful; if innocent,

harmless; in the latter case, moreover, the woman becomes fruitful.

The existence, at least at certain periods, of corruption and dishonesty in the administration of justice in Israel, and especially among the priests, need hardly be insisted on. The example of the two sons of Eli, notorious for their greed, is well known. Micah, Isaiah, Hosea, Zephaniah, Jeremiah, and Malachi freely and vehemently accuse the Hebrew judges of unfairness, injustice, respect of persons, bribery, and dishonesty in their legal decisions.

(2) *The army.*—While in Egypt, the Hebrews lived a peaceful pastoral life under the supreme control of the Pharaohs. During their forty-years wandering in the desert, they had no enemy to fight, and no land to conquer; but when the time of their entering Canaan approached, the situation was completely changed. Here they were face to face with old settled Canaanitish tribes and nations, such as the Philistines, the Ammonites, the Moabites, the Amorites, the Jebusites, the Hivites, the Perizzites, and many others, whom they had to attack, defeat, and exterminate. "Ye shall utterly destroy", was the command of Yahweh, "all the places, wherein the nations which ye shall possess served their gods, upon the high mountains, and upon the hills, and under every green tree: and ye shall overthrow their altars, and break their pillars, and burn their groves with fire; and ye shall hew down the graven images of their gods, and destroy the names of them out of that place" (Deut., xii, 2, 3). Hence the creation and organization of an army became a necessity, and it is morally certain that in their first wars every available Hebrew fighter took part. From the time of David down to the late monarchical period a regular army was selected and organized. From Num., i, 3, it appears that the whole male population over twenty years of age, if capable of bearing arms, were liable to military duty. At the time of the Judges, it is certain that the Israelitish army was composed wholly of infantry, as David was the first to use horses and chariots for military purposes, and it was Solomon who first established a distinct cavalry army. In the middle days of the monarchy the Hebrews could raise an army of one hundred and eighty thousand men [I Kings (D. V. III Kings), xii, 21], and on some occasions twice and even three times as many [see II Chronicles (D. V. Paralip.), xiii, 3, and xiv, 8]. These figures, however, need be greatly lowered, as they are due probably to a copyist's error. The army was divided into hundreds and thousands, with their appropriate leaders, captains of hundreds and captains of thousands, if on their arrival by septs or clans they were not thus organized. It is certain, however, that in point of armament and military organization and discipline the Hebrew army was greatly inferior to either the Egyptian or the Assyrian. Before undertaking any military operation, Yahweh was consulted through a prophet or through the Urim and Thummim, and sacrifices were offered just as in Homer's times. This custom, however, was practised by all nations of antiquity. From many Biblical passages [such as Judges, vii, 16; I Sam. (D. V. Kings), xi, 11; II Sam. (D. V. Kings), xviii, 2; I Kings (D. V. III Kings), xx, 27; and II Macc., viii, 22, etc.] it clearly appears that the attacking Israelitish army was usually divided into three divisions, one in the centre and two on the flanks. Isaiah refers even to the "wings" of the army (viii, 8). A column advancing to conflict was preceded by two ranks of spearmen; next to these was a rank of bowmen, and behind them came the slingers. Spies were often sent out in advance to learn the position and the strength of the enemy, while night-attacks, with skilfully divided forces, were not infrequent. The beginning of the battle was signalized by the blast of a trumpet,

accompanied by the shouts of the combatants. The Ark with its *ephod* was considered indispensable. It was borne before the army, who, as it was taken up, cried out, "Arise, O Yahweh, and let Thine enemies be scattered, and let them that hate Thee flee before Thee". The principal equipment for war was the helmet, shield, and other defensive armour, the bow, the sling, the sword, the spear, the javelin, and other instruments which must have been common to all Oriental nations, although not explicitly mentioned in the Bible.

III. SACRED ANTIQUITIES.—Some of the Hebrew festivals are originally of historical character, i. e. are commemorative of some great historical event in the life of the Hebrew nation; while others are primarily religious, or of ethico-religious significance. To the first category belong the Feast of Passover, the Feast of Pentecost, and the Feast of Tabernacles, and other minor ones mentioned below, such as the Feast of Purim, etc. To the second class belong the Sabbath, the New Moon, the Feast of Trumpets, the Sabbatical Year and the Year of Jubilee. The former were more properly called *festivals;* the latter, *sacred seasons.* The latter are lunar; the former are solar—based on the lunar and solar system respectively. The principal features of the three great historical festivals consisted in making a pilgrimage, or a visit, to the Temple, as prescribed in Exodus, xxiii, 14, 17: "Three times in the year shalt thou hold pilgrimage unto me, three times in the year shall all thy men appear before Yahweh, the God of Israel."

The *Passover* (whence our *Pascha*), with which the Feast of the Unleavened Bread is closely connected and almost identified, although originally distinct from it, constituted the opening festival of the Jewish ecclesiastical year, and was celebrated on the 14th of Nisan (Abib), which month approximately corresponds to our April. It was instituted in commemoration of the Exodus from Egypt, when the Angel of Death went forth to destroy the first-born of the Egyptians, passing over (whence *Passover*), however, the houses of the Hebrews, on the lintels of whose doors the blood of a lamb had been sprinkled. The Passover Festival was celebrated as follows: An unblemished male lamb a year old (called the paschal lamb) was to be selected by each family in Israel. It was to be killed on the evening of the fourteenth day and consumed the same night. The flesh was to be roasted, not eaten raw, or boiled, and not a bone of the animal was to be broken. Along with it, unleavened bread and bitter herbs might be used, but nothing more; and whatever portions were not needed for food were to be destroyed the same night by burning. Hence, on the evening of the thirteenth day of Nisan, all leaven was scrupulously removed from the Jewish homes. The fourteenth day was thus regarded as a holiday, on which all servile work was suspended. In later Hebrew times, however, the Passover Festival was somewhat modified.

The *Feast of the Pentecost*, also called the Feast of Weeks, Feast of Harvest, Day of Firstfruits, etc., was celebrated on the fiftieth day after the Passover, i. e. on or about the 8th of Siwan, the third month of the Jewish ecclesiastical year. It lasted a single day, and it marked the completion of the corn harvest. According to later Jewish traditions, the Feast of Pentecost was also instituted in commemoration of the giving of the Law to Moses. It is mentioned in the Bible for the first time in the second Book of Maccabees. With the Feast of Pentecost the New Year holiday season closed. The characteristic ritual of this feast consisted in offering and waving to Yahweh in his Temple two leavened loaves of wheaten flour, together with a sin offering, burnt offering, and peace offering, and its object

was to offer to Yahweh the firstfruits of the harvest, and to thank Him for it.

The *Feast of Tabernacles*, or *Booths*, was observed for seven days, i. e. from the 15th to the 22nd of Tisri (the seventh month of the Jewish year, approximately corresponding to our October), following closely upon the Day of Atonement. It marked the completion of the fruit-harvest (which included the oil- and wine-harvest), and, historically, it commemorated the forty-years wandering in the wilderness, when all the Hebrew tribes and families, for lack of houses and buildings, lived in tents and booths. "The sacrifices at this feast were far more numerous than at any other. On each of the seven days one kid of the goats was offered as a sin offering, and two rams and fourteen lambs as a burnt-offering. Also seventy bullocks were offered on the seven days, beginning with thirteen on the first day and diminishing by one each day, until on the seventh day seven were offered. After the seven days a solemn day of 'holy convocation' was observed which marked the conclusion, not only of the feast of Tabernacles, but of the whole cycle of the festal year. On this day one bullock, one ram, and seven lambs were offered as a burnt offering, and one goat for a sin offering." The earliest Biblical allusion to this feast is found in I (D. V. III) Kings, viii, 2, and xii, 32.

Besides these three great festivals, certain minor ones were observed by the Hebrews: The word *Purim* is probably of Persian origin (*Furdigan, Pordigân,* or *Pardiyân*), and the feast so named was instituted to commemorate the overthrow of Haman, the triumph of Mordecai, and the escape of the Jews from utter destruction in the time of Esther. It was celebrated in the 14th and 15th day of Adar (the twelfth and last month of the Jewish Year).— The *Feast of the Dedication of the Temple* was instituted in 164 B. C. by Judas Maccabæus, when the Temple, which had been desecrated by Antiochus Epiphanes, was once more purified and rededicated to the service of Yahweh. It commenced on the 25th of Chislew, the ninth month of the Jewish year (corresponding to our December), and lasted for eight days. It was a feast of universal and unbounded joy, delight, and happiness, as was that of Purim. Other minor feasts were *the Feast of the Wood Offering; The Reading of the Law; Feast of Nicanor; of the Captured Fortress; of Baskets,* etc.

The sacred seasons, or religious festivals, are primarily a development of the institution of the Sabbath and based on the lunar system of the Calendar. It has been often remarked, and with good reason, that in all the Hebrew Religious Festivals the sacred number seven is the dominating factor. "Every 7th day was a Sabbath. Every seventh month was a sacred month. Every seventh year was a Sabbatical year. Seven times seven was the year of Jubilee. The Feast of the Passover, with the Feast of the Unleavened Bread, began fourteen days (2x7) after the beginning of the month, and lasted seven days. The Feast of Pentecost was seven times seven days after the Feast of the Passover. The Feast of Tabernacles began fourteen days (2x7) after the beginning of the month and lasted seven days. The seventh month was marked by (1) the Feast of Trumpets on the first day, (2) the Fast of Atonement on the tenth day, (3) Feast of Tabernacles from the fifteenth day to the twenty-first. The days of the "Holy Convocation" were seven in number—two at the Passover, one at Pentecost, one at the Feast of Trumpets, one at the Day of Atonement, and one at the Feast of Tabernacles, and one on the day following, the eighth day."

The institution of the Hebrew Sabbath may be traced in its origin to the early Babylonians who, according to the majority of Assyriologists, seem to have been its originators, although among the Hebrews it developed on altogether different lines. It was celebrated on the 7th, 14th, 21st, and 28th day of the lunar month. It is doubtful whether it was known and observed in patriarchal and pre-Mosaic times. Moses, in instituting—or rather in modifying—the old institution of the Sabbath, connects it with the seventh day of the Creation period, on which God is said to have rested. By the ancient Babylonians it was looked upon as an unlucky day, on which it was unlucky to do any public work, and consequently was a day of rest.

The *New Moon Festival* consisted in celebrating the reappearance of the moon, and as such it was universally practised by all Semitic nations. Hence, in all probability, it was an acknowledged pre-Mosaic Hebrew institution. On this day the law enjoined only the offering of special sacrifices and the blowing of trumpets. Abstinence from work was not obligatory. On the day of the new moon of the seventh month the festival in question was more solemnly and more elaborately celebrated. After the Babylonian exile, however, the festival assumed a new character, similar to that of the New Year Celebration.

The *Feast of Trumpets* is the New Moon Festival of the seventh, or Sabbatical, month of the year.

The *Sabbatical Year* occurred every seventh year, and in it fields were not to be tilled.

The *Year of Jubilee* occurred every fifty years, i. e. at the end of seven Sabbatic years, just as Pentecost occurred on the fiftieth day after the Passover Festival. Its principal features were the emancipation of the Hebrew slaves and the return of mortgaged property to its hereditary owners.

The great Hebrew *Fast Festival* was the "Day of Atonement", or Yom Kippur. It was celebrated on the tenth day of the seventh month, on which day atoning sacrifices were offered for the sins and uncleannesses of the people of Israel as a whole, and for the purification of the temple in all its parts and appurtenances. It is significant that the earliest mention of it in the Bible occurs in such post-Exilic writings as Zech. (D. V. Zach.), iii, 9; Nehemiah, vii, 73; ix, 38; and Sirach, l, 5 sqq. A ceremony connected with the Day of Atonement is the so-called *For Azazel.* It consisted in sending into the wilderness the remaining goat (the "emissary goat"), the sins of the people of Israel having first been placed symbolically upon its head.

Treatises on *Biblical Archæology* by JAHN (Vienna, 1817); ROSENMÜLLER (Leipzig, 1823–31); DE WETTE (Leipzig, 1864); EWALD (Göttingen, 1866); HANEBERG (Munich, 1869); ROSKEFF (Vienna, 1857); KINZLER (Stuttgart, 1884); SCHEGG (Freiburg, 1886). For English readers the best and most available works are KEIL, *Manual of Biblical Archæology* (tr., 2 vols., Edinburgh, 1887); BISSELL, *Biblical Antiquities* (Philadelphia, 1888); FENTON, *Early Hebrew Life* (London, 1880); DAY, *The Social Life of the Hebrews* in the *Semitic Series* (New York, 1901); TRUMBULL, *The Blood Covenant;* ID., *The Threshold Covenant;* ID., *The Salt Covenant;* various articles in SMITH, *Dictionary of the Bible;* KITTO, *Biblical Cyclopedia;* VIGOUROUX, *Dict. de la Bible;* HASTINGS, *Dict. of the Bible;* and *Jewish Encyclopedia.* The most recent and authoritative works on the subject, however, are BENZIGER, *Hebräische Archäologie* (Freiburg im Br., 1894); NOWACK, *Lehrbuch der hebräischen Archäologie* (Freiburg im Br., 1894); BUHL, *Die socialen Verhältnisse der Israeliten* (Berlin, 1899), tr. into French by CINTRE (Paris, 1904); LEVY, *La famille dans l'antiquité Israelite* (Paris, 1905). Of great value, especially for later Old Testament times, are also the classical works of SCHÜRER, *Geschichte des jüdischen Volkes im Zeitalter Jesu Christi* (3 vols., 1898–1901), tr. from the 2nd ed. (5 vols., London and New York); EDERSHEIM, *The Rites and Worships of the Jews* (New York, 1891); ID., *The Temple, its Ministry and Service* (London, 1874); ID., *Life and Times of Jesus the Messiah* (London and New York). GABRIEL OUSSANI.

Biblical Commission, THE, a committee of cardinals at Rome who, with the assistance of consultors, have to secure the observance of the prescriptions contained in the Encyclical "Providentissimus Deus" for the proper interpretation and defence of Sacred Scripture. Its official name is "Commissio Pontificia de re biblicâ". It was formally established by the Apostolic letter of Leo XIII, "Vigilantiæ", 30 October, 1902.

Constitution.—The Commission was first appointed in August, 1901, with three cardinal members and twelve consultors. After the formal establishment two cardinals and twenty-eight consultors from various parts of the world were added to the first list. There is no limitation to the number of consultors. In June, 1907, the Commission was made up of five cardinals, Rampolla, Satolli, Merry del Val, Segna, and Vives y Tuto. The consultors were forty-three: Amelli, O.S.B. (Rome), Balestri, O.S.A. (Rome), Bardenhewer (Munich), Cereseto, Cong. Orat. (Genoa), Ceriani (Milan), Chauvin (Laval), Cornely, S.J. (Rome), Delattre, S.J. (Tronchiennes), Düsterwald (Cologne), Esser, O.P. (Rome), Fillion, P.S.S. (Paris), Fleming, O.F.M. (England), Fracassini (Perugia), Genocchi, M.S.C. (Rome), Gismondi, S.J. (Rome), Gonfalonieri (Florence), Grannan (Washington), Gutberlet (Fulda), Hoberg (Freiburg im Br.), Höpfl (Rome), van Hoonacker (Louvain), von Hummelauer, S.J. (Valkenburg), Janssens, O.S.B., Second Secretary (Rome), Jorió (Palencia), Kaulen (Bonn), Lagrange, O.P. (Jerusalem), Lamy (Louvain), Legendre (Angers), Lepicier, S.M. (Rome), Lepidi, O.P. (Rome), Lesètre (Paris), Mangenot (Paris), Méchineau, S.J. (Rome), Mercati (Rome), Molini, O.F.M. (Rome), Nikel (Breslau), Poels (Washington), Prat, S.J. (Rome), B. Schaefer (Vienna), Scheil, O.P. (Paris), Talamo (Rome), Vigouroux, P.S.S., First Secretary (Rome), and Weiss (Braunsberg).

Method of Procedure.—The Commission is constituted on the lines of an ordinary Roman Congregation. The consultors in Rome hold meetings twice a month, at which the secretaries preside. The results of their deliberations are presented by the secretaries to the cardinals, who also meet twice a month, on the second and fourth Sundays. It belongs to the cardinals to propose the questions for the study of the Commission and they alone have a vote in determining the answers. They may sanction or modify the judgments of the consultors, or send back the entire question for further study, or may commission one or other consultor to make a special report. After the meeting, the secretaries report to the Holy Father, who may ratify the decision or remand the question for further consideration. Papers sent by consultors who live at a distance from Rome are read at the meetings of the consultors, when relevant to the subject under discussion.

Scope of the Commission.—It is the duty of the Commission: (1) to protect and defend the integrity of the Catholic Faith in Biblical matters; (2) to further the progress of exposition of the Sacred Books, taking account of all recent discoveries; (3) to decide controversies on grave questions which may arise among Catholic scholars; (4) to give answers to Catholics throughout the world who may consult the Commission; (5) to see that the Vatican Library is properly furnished with codices and necessary books; (6) to publish studies on Scripture as occasion may demand. It was the wish of Leo XIII that a periodical bulletin of Biblical studies should be published at Rome, and a special Institute for higher Biblical studies established. Lack of funds has made such an establishment impossible for the present, but the idea has not been abandoned. To the Commission has been entrusted the awarding of an annual prize, founded by Lord Braye, for the best essay on a Biblical topic. In April, 1907, the Commission, with the approval of the sovereign pontiff, invited the Benedictine Order to undertake a collection of the variant readings of the Latin Vulgate as a remote preparation for a thoroughly amended edition.

Degrees in Sacred Scripture.—On 23 February, 1904, Pius X empowered the Commission to confer the degrees of Licentiate and Doctor in the faculty of

Sacred Scripture on priests who, having previously attained the doctorate in theology, should pass successful examinations, oral and written, in matter defined by the Commission. The judges must be at least five consultors. Examinations have since been held twice a year, in June and November. The official announcements of the Commission are communicated to the "Revue Biblique", which is not, however, the official organ of the Commission. (See "Revue Biblique", 1905, p. 448.)

Decisions of the Commission.—Four important decisions on disputed Biblical questions have been issued by the Commission: (1) On the occurrence in Scripture of "implicit citations", i. e. quotations from uninspired documents which the sacred writer does not vouch for, though he does not expressly acknowledge them as quotations. These may not be admitted unless proved by solid arguments (13 February, 1905). (2) On the historical character of certain narratives. It is not lawful to question the historical character of books hitherto regarded as historical, unless in a case where the sense of the Church is not opposed and where, subject to her judgment, it is proved by solid arguments that the sacred writer did not intend to write history (23 June, 1905). (3) On the Mosaic authorship of the Pentateuch. This has not been disproved by critical arguments. Mosaic authorship, however, need not imply that Moses wrote with his own hand or dictated all of it; the books may have been composed by secretaries to whom he suggested the thoughts and whose work he approved as principal and inspired author. It is consistent also with the use by Moses of documents, oral or written, and does not exclude the presence of such additions or imperfections in the present text as would leave it substantially and integrally the work of Moses (27 June, 1906). (4) On the authorship and historical character of the Fourth Gospel. It is historically certain that St. John wrote it. The Gospel is an historical document, narrating the actual facts and speeches of Our Lord's life (29 May, 1907).

Authority of its Decisions.—The Commission though formed like a Congregation is not a Congregation but seemingly of lower rank. Its decisions are approved by the pope and published by his command. Such approval, when given *in formâ communi*, does not change the nature of the decisions as emanating from a Congregation or Commission, nor does it make them specifically pontifical acts; much less does it imply an exercise of the pope's personal prerogative of infallibility. Hence they are not infallible or unchangeable, though they must be received with obedience and interior assent, by which we judge that the doctrine proposed is safe and to be accepted because of the authority by which it is presented. These decisions are not the opinions of a private assembly, but an official directive norm; to question them publicly would be lacking in respect and obedience to legitimate authority. We are not hindered from private study of the reasons on which they are based, and if some scholar should find solid arguments against a decision they should be set before the Commission.

For details about the Commission consult the Roman correspondence of *The Tablet* (London), 11 January, 15 November, 22 November, 1902; 7 February, 23 May, 1903; 12 March, 2 July, 19 November, 1904; for the documents, *Revue biblique* (1903 and later); for the English translation of the Letter *Vigilantiæ, The Great Encyclical Letters of Pope Leo XIII* (New York, 1903), 537; for the authority of decisions, *Nouvelle revue théol.* (Tournai), May, 1907; CHOUPIN, *Valeur des décisions doctrinales et disciplinaires du S.-Siège* (Paris, 1907).

JOHN CORBETT.

Bibliotheca Maxima Patrum. See FATHERS, LIBRARIES OF THE CHRISTIAN.

Bickerdike, ROBERT, VENERABLE, martyr, a Yorkshire layman, b. at Low Hall, near Knares-borough (date unknown), but residing at York; d. 5 August (or 8 October), 1585. Arrested for giving a priest, Ven. John Boste, a glass of ale, he was also accused at his trial of using treasonable words. He was acquitted, but Judge Rhodes, determined to have his blood, had him removed from the city gaol to the Castle and tried once more at the Lammas Assizes on the same charge. He was then condemned. One of his offences was that, when Ven. Francis Ingleby was being dragged on the hurdle to execution, hearing a minister's wife say, "Let us go into the Tolbooth and we shall see the traitorly thief come over on the hurdle", he said, "No; no thief, but as true as thou art". These words were supposed to be the cause of his death. He suffered at York.

BRIDGEWATER, *Concertatio* (Trier, 1589); MORRIS, *The Catholics of York under Elizabeth* (London, 1891); CHALLONER, *Memoirs.*
BEDE CAMM.

Bicknor, ALEXANDER, Archbishop of Dublin, date of birth unknown; d. 1349. As his surname suggests he came from a family of Kent, England. He was elected Archbishop of Dublin in 1310, being at that time Prebendary of Maynooth and Treasurer of Ireland. This selection was, however, set aside by Edward II in favour of Lech who soon died; after this, in May, 1314, Edward petitioned Pope Clement V to confirm Bicknor's appointment. The request was earnestly repeated in 1317, and he was finally consecrated in Rome, 22 July of this year. In 1318 he was appointed Lord Justice of Ireland. On some unrecorded ground his name appears as attending the English Parliament, and he took part on 24 September, 1318, in promulgating at St. Paul's the excommunication of Robert Bruce. Even though, as a diplomatist, he was frequently absent from his diocese, he showed his interest in it by building an episcopal residence, and he endeavoured, unsuccessfully, to attach a college to St. Patrick's Cathedral. In 1323 he was in France on an embassy, in 1324 he was engaged in negotiating peace with France and in arranging a Spanish match for Edward, Prince of Wales. In this he failed; and on his return Edward II charged him with the loss of La Rozelle. About this time he joined with Queen Isabella in concerting the overthrow of the Despensers, then the royal favourites. On 28 May, 1325, Edward II asked the pope to remove Bicknor from the kingdom, accusing him of the surrender of La Rozelle, of defaming Hugh Despenser, of improperly excommunicating Robert Pinchbeck, and of not accounting for sums received while Treasurer of Ireland. Bicknor joined Queen Isabella and others in declaring Prince Edward guardian of the kingdom, at an assembly at Bristol; later, in 1327, he swore publicly at the London Guildhall to maintain the queen's cause as against the king. In 1329 Edward seized his diocesan revenues as a set-off to the sums unaccounted for by Bicknor as Treasurer of Ireland. In 1330 Bicknor became papal collector. He quarrelled with the Bishop of Ossory, who, on appeal to Edward II, was banished for nine years, during which period Bicknor, as metropolitan, visited the See of Ossory and seized the revenues. In 1348 Bicknor held a synod at Dublin at which useful disciplinary decrees were passed. He engaged in a dispute with the Archbishop of Armagh about the right to the primacy of Ireland.

Dict. Nat. Biogr.; RYMER, *Fœdera; Chronicles of Edward I and II* in Rolls Series; *Ypodigma Neustriæ.*
HENRY NORBERT BIRT.

Bidermann, JAMES, a poet and theologian of great learning and sanctity, b. at Ehingen, Germany, in 1578; d. at Rome, 20 August, 1639. He entered the Society of Jesus at Lansberg in 1594, and after the usual preliminary training he taught rhetoric in Munich from 1606 to 1615, and later spent eight years teaching philosophy and theology at Dillingen. In

1624, he was called to Rome where he fulfilled the duties of theologian and censor of books till his death. From an early age Bidermann distinguished himself in many branches of learning. Such was his reputation for scholarship, that the famous Matthew Rader, a professor of Dillingen, celebrated his fame in a Latin poem, in which he spoke of him as another Aquinas, Aristotle, Cicero, and Maro. Besides numerous volumes of dramas, epigrams, biographical sketches, etc., Bidermann wrote many books on philosophy and theology. Amongst the best-known of these are: "Theses Theologicæ" (1620), "Sponsalia" (1621); "Pœnitentiæ, Sacramentum" (1621); "Matrimonii Impedimenta" (1621); "Censuræ" (1622); "Irregularitas" (1622); "Suffragia" (1623); "Jesu Christi Status Triplex, Mortalis, Immortalis, Sacramentalis" (1623); "Conscientia" (1624); "Prolusiones Theologicæ quibus Pontificis Rom. dignitas adversus haeresim propugnata est" (1624); "Eleemosyna" (1625); "Gratia" (1625); "Agnosticon libri tres pro miraculis" (1626).

SOMMERVOGEL, *Bibl. de la c. de J.*, I, 1443; BERNARD in *Dict. de théol. cath.*, XII, 813; HURTER, *Nomenclator*, I, 303.

R. H. TIERNEY.

Biel, GABRIEL, called "the last of the Scholastics", b. at Speyer, Germany, c. 1425; d. at Tübingen, 1495. His studies were pursued at Heidelberg and Erfurt. While still a young man, he was noted as a preacher in the cathedral of Mainz, of which he was vicar. Later he became superior of the "Clerics of the Common Life" at Bützbach, and in 1479 was appointed provost of the church in Urach. At this period he co-operated with Count Eberhard of Würtemberg in founding the University of Tübingen. Appointed in 1484 the first professor of theology in the new institution, he continued the most celebrated member of its faculty until his death. Though he was almost sixty years of age when he began to teach, Biel's work, both as professor and as writer, reflected the highest honour on the young university. His first publication, on the Canon of the Mass, is of permanent interest and value. His second and most important work is a commentary on the "Sentences" of Peter Lombard. In this he calls Occam his master, but the last three books show him more Scotist than Nominalist. Scheeben describes him as "one of the best of the Nominalists, clear, exact, and more positive as well as more loyal to the Church than any of the others" (Dogmatik, no. 1073). The historian Janssen declares that he was one of the few Nominalists who erected a theological system without incurring the charge of unorthodoxy. (Cf. Geschichte des deutschen Volkes, I, 127, 15th ed.) He was neither narrow nor excessively speculative. Though a Nominalist, he was tolerant of Realism, which also flourished at Tübingen under the leadership of Konrad Summenhart. A Scholastic, he was, to quote Janssen, "free from empty speculations and ingenious intellectual juggling, being concerned with questions and needs of actual life" (ibidem), was interested in the social movements of his time, and maintained friendly relations with the Humanists. One of the latter, Heinrich Bebel, gave him the title of "monarch among theologians". His theological writings were repeatedly brought into the discussions of the Council of Trent.

Living as he did in a transition period, Biel exhibits characteristics of two intellectual eras. According to some, he was a Scholastic who expounded Aristotle rather than the Scriptures; according to others, he defended freer theological teaching, and opposed the ancient constitution of the Church and the authority of the pope. As a matter of fact, he acknowledged the primacy and supreme power of the Roman Pontiff, but, in common with many other theologians of his time, maintained the superiority of general councils, at least to the extent that

they could compel the pope's resignation. And he displayed no more theological freedom than has been claimed and exercised by some of the strictest theologians. Among the opinions defended by Biel concerning matters controverted in his day, the following are worthy of mention: (a) That all ecclesiastical jurisdiction, even that of bishops, is derived either immediately or mediately from the pope. In this connexion it is to be noted that his defence of the episcopal claims of Diether von Ysenburg won him the thanks of Pius II. (b) That the power of absolving is inherent in sacerdotal orders, and that only the matter, i. e. the persons to be absolved, can be conceded or withheld by the ordinary. (c) That the minister of baptism need have no more specific intention than that of doing what the faithful, that is, the Church, intends. (d) That the State may not compel Jews, or heathens, or their children to receive baptism. (e) And that the *Contractus Trinus* is morally lawful. All of these opinions have since become the prevailing theological doctrine.

The subject on which Biel held the most progressive views is political economy. Roscher, who with Schmoller introduced him to modern students of economics, declares that Biel's grasp of economics enabled him not only to understand the work of his predecessors, but to advance beyond them. (Cf. Geschichte der Nationalökonomik in Deutschland, 21 sqq.) According to Biel, the just price of a commodity is determined chiefly by human needs, by its scarcity, and by the difficulty of producing it. His enumeration includes all the factors that govern market price, and is more complete and reasonable than any made by his predecessors. (Cf. Garnier, L'idée du juste prix, 77.) The same author maintains that concerning the occupation of the merchant or trader, Biel is more advanced than St. Thomas, since he attaches no stigma to it, but holds it to be good in itself, and the merchant entitled to remuneration because of his labour, risks, and expenses. Biel's discussion of these subjects is contained in book IV of his commentary on the "Sentences". He wrote a special work on currency, *ein wahrhaft goldenes Buch*, in which he stigmatizes the debasing of coinage by princes as dishonest exploitation of the people. In the same work he severely condemns those rulers who curtailed the popular rights of forest, meadow, and water, and who imposed arbitrary burdens of taxation, as well as the rich sportsmen who encroached upon the lands of the peasantry. His works are: "Sacri canonis Missæ expositio resolutissima literalis et mystica" (Brixen, 1576); an abridgment of this work, entitled "Epitome expositionis canonis Missæ" (Antwerp, 1565); "Sermones" (Brixen, 1583), on the Sundays and festivals of the Christian year, with a disquisition on the plague and a defence of the authority of the pope; "Collectorium sive epitome in magistri sententiarum libros IV" (Brixen, 1574); "Tractatus de potestate et utilitate monetarum".

MOSER, *Vitæ professorum Tubingensium ord. theolog. dec. 1* (Tübingen, 1718); WINKELMANN, *Beschreibung von Hessen und Hersfeld* (Bremen, 1711); LINSENMANN, *Gabriel Biel*, in *Theologische Quartalschrift* (Tübingen, 1865), *passim*; PLITT, *Gabriel Biel als Prediger* (Erlangen, 1879); GARNIER, *De l'idée du juste prix* (Paris, 1900), 74–83; LINSENMANN in *Kirchenlex.*, s. v.; HURTER, *Nomenclator*; SCHWANE, *Dogmengeschichte* (Freiburg, 1882), III, *passim*; TURNER, *Hist. of Philosophy* (Boston, 1903) 409; ASHLEY, *English Economic History* (New York, 1893), II, 382, 441–46.

JOHN A. RYAN.

Biella, DIOCESE OF.—The city of Biella, the see of the diocese of that name, is an important industrial centre (anciently called Bugella) of Piedmont, Italy, in the province of Novara. The diocese contains about 200,000 inhabitants, and is a suffragan of the Archdiocese of Vercelli. Until 1772 Biella had no bishop, but was under the jurisdiction of the Archdiocese of Vercelli. In that year

Clement XI, yielding to the desire of King Charles Emmanuel III of Sardinia, established the Diocese of Biella by the Bull "Præcipua". The first bishop was Giulio Cesare Viancino, formerly Archbishop of Sassari in Sardinia. In 1803 Napoleon suppressed the diocese, which again fell under the jurisdiction of Vercelli, but was re-established in 1817 by Pius VII who appointed as bishop the Minor Observantine, Bernardino Ballato. It is difficult to determine when the Gospel was first preached at Biella; certainly not before it reached Vercelli. According to the opinion of Fedele Savio, S.J., the latter city received the Faith in the second half of the third century from Milan.

In the shrine of Maria Santissima d'Oropa, situated on a lofty mountain near Biella, the diocese preserves a memorial of St. Eusebius, the great Bishop of Vercelli, who was banished to the Orient by Emperor Constantius for his courageous defence of Catholic truth against Arianism. St. Eusebius, according to tradition, upon his return from the East, is said to have brought three pictures of the Madonna painted on cedar wood, one of which, the image of Oropa, he placed in a small oratory he had built. In the tenth century the chapel was placed in charge of the Benedictines. The latter having abandoned the place, Pius II, in 1459, made over the shrine to the chapter of the collegiate church, now the Cathedral of Biella, to which it has since belonged. In the sixteenth century, the inhabitants of Biella, in thanksgiving for their deliverance from the plague, built a stately church over the chapel. Even to-day the shrine of Oropa draws many devout pilgrims.

Among the religious edifices of the city of Biella, the most notable is the Gothic cathedral, built in 1402. Its beautiful choir is by Galliari. The baptistery, in the form of a small temple, is said to be an ancient Roman edifice.

CAPPELLETTI, *Le chiese d'Italia* (Venice, 1844), XIV, 649.

U. BENIGNI.

Bielski (or WOLSKI), MARCIN, a Polish chronicler, b. of noble parentage on the patrimonial estate of Biala (whence the family name), in the province of Sieradz, Poland, in 1495; d. there, 1575; the name Wolski is derived from his estate at Wola. One of two Polish writers, of the same name, he was the first to use the Polish language, hence his designation as the father of Polish prose. He was educated in the University of Cracow, founded by Casimir the Great in 1364, and spent some time with the military governor of that city. He served in the army in the wars against the Wallachians and Tatars, and participated in the battle of Obertyn (Galicia), 1531. He ranks among Poland's most prolific writers, and the development of historical studies in that country is due to his extensive writings. He is the author of numerous works: "Żywoty Filosofów" (Lives of the Philosophers, 1535); "Kronika Swiata" (Universal Chronicle, 1550–64), from the earliest time down to his day, divided into six periods, was the first important universal history published in the national idiom, and the first attempt at a comprehensive history of Poland, from 550 to 1580; in the second edition (1554) there is a reference to America; after the author's death the work was continued, rearranged, and brought down to the year 1597, under the title of "Kronika Polska" (Chronicle of Poland) by his son Joachim (b. 1540; d. 1599), secretary to King Sigismund III; "Sprawa Rycerskiego", a treatise on military art (1569), according to the Greek science of warfare, in eight parts, contains valuable data about the Polish army, and kindred subjects. After the demise of Bielski several satirical poems were published: "Seym Majowy", (The May Diet, 1590), descriptive of the degradation of Hungary, and an appeal to his countrymen to emulate a higher standard of life:

"Seym Niewieści", (Woman's Council, 1586–95), analytical of the then existing political conditions in Poland: "Sen Maiowy" (Dream of a Hermit, 1586); "Komedia Justina y Konstanciey" (Comedy of Justinian and Constantia, 1557).

ESTREICHER, *Polish bibliography* (1800–70); BOHOMOLEC, *Collection of Histories* (Warsaw, 1764); IDEM, *Martin Bielski* (Warsaw, 1764); SOBIESZCZANSKI, *Chronicle of Poland* (Warsaw, 1851); SIBENEYCHER, *Chronicle of Poland* (Cracow, 1597); TUROWSKI, *Chronicle of Poland* (Cracow, 1855–62).

JOSEPH SMOLINSKI.

Biennium Canonicorum. See CHAPTER SCHOOLS.

Bienville, JEAN-BAPTISTE LE MOYNE, SIEUR DE, French Governor of Louisiana and founder of New Orleans, b. in Montreal, Canada, 24 February, 1680; d. in Paris, 7 March, 1767. His father, Charles le Moyne de Bienville, settled in Canada in 1640; his three brothers, Iberville, Serigny, and Châteauguay, likewise distinguished themselves in the early history of Louisiana. In 1698–1699, Bienville accompanied his brother Iberville in an expedition despatched from France to explore the territory near the mouth of the Mississippi. They founded a settlement at old Biloxi, where in 1700 Bienville became commandant, and, after Iberville's death in 1706, governor of the colony.

It was believed in France that Louisiana presented a rich field for enterprise and speculation and a grant with exclusive privileges was obtained by Antoine Crozat for fifteen years. In 1712 Crozat appointed M. la Mothe Cadillac, governor, and M. de Bienville lieutenant-governor. But Cadillac dying in 1715, Bienville once more assumed the reins of government. In 1716, he conducted an expedition against the Natchez Indians, and having brought them to terms, finished the fort "Rosalie" which had been commenced by his brother, Iberville, sixteen years before. In 1717, Epinay, a new governor, arrived in the colony, bringing with him the decoration of the Cross of St. Louis for Bienville. In the meantime, Crozat, failing to realize the great profits he had expected, abandoned the whole enterprise and surrendered his charter to the king in 1717. Another company was at once formed and Bienville received a new commission as governor of the province. He now resolved to remove the headquarters from Biloxi, Mobile, and St. Louis Bay to the more fertile region of the Mississippi River, and in 1718 he selected the site for a new settlement, which he called New Orleans. He left fifty persons there to clear the land and build some houses, but it was not till 1722 that it became the seat of government.

Experience had shown Bienville that the fertile soil of the lower Mississippi, as well as the climate, was well adapted to the cultivation of sugar, cotton, tobacco, and rice, and that Europeans were not fitted for field-work in the burning suns of Louisiana, for they sickened and died. The first plantation of any extent was therefore commenced with negroes imported from Guinea. In 1719, the province became involved in hostilities with the Spaniards in consequence of the war with France and Spain. The governor twice reduced the town of Pensacola and sent detachments to prevent the Spaniards from making inroads into upper Louisiana, and the country bordering on the Rio Grande.

When peace was restored, immigrants began to arrive in great numbers from France and Germany. In the autumn of 1726, the Government of Louisiana passed out of the hands of Bienville and he retired to France to recruit his health. In 1734, the king reappointed him Governor and Commandant-General of Louisiana, and early in the autumn he arrived at New Orleans and entered upon the duties of his office. An expedition against the Chickasaw Indians in the spring of 1736 resulted in disaster, but another expedition in 1739 met with better success. This campaign closed his military and official career in the colony. He returned to France under a cloud of censure from the Government, after having faithfully served his country for more than forty years. He was buried with military honours in the cemetery of Montmartre.

French, *Louisiana Historical Collections* (New York, 1846–53), Pt. III, 20–22; Hamilton, *Col. Mobile*, vii–xiv; Thwaites, *Jesuit Relations*, LXVI, 342; French, *Historical Memoirs of Louisiana* (New York, 1853), for portrait and valuable additional information.

E. P. Spillane.

Bigamy (in Canon Law).—According to the strict meaning, the word should signify the marrying of a second after the death of the first wife, in contradistinction to polygamy, which is having two simultaneous wives. The present usage in criminal law of applying the term *bigamy* to that which is more strictly called polygamy is, according to Blackstone (Lib. IV, n. 163), a corruption of the true meaning of bigamy. Canonically viewed, bigamy denotes (a) the condition of a man married to two real or interpretative wives in succession, and as a consequence (b) his unfitness to receive, or exercise after reception, tonsure, minor and sacred orders. This unfitness gives rise to an irregularity which is an impediment impediment and not diriment, hence orders conferred in violation of it are valid but illicit. This irregularity is not a punishment, medicinal nor punitive, as there is no sin nor fault of any kind in a man marrying a second wife after the death of his first, or a third after the death of his second; it is a bar against his receiving or exercising any ecclesiastical order or dignity.

Origin.—This irregularity is not affixed to bigamy by either the natural or Mosaic law. It has its true origin in the apostolic injunction of St. Paul: "It behoveth, therefore, a bishop to be blameless, the husband of one wife" (I Tim., iii, 2); "Let deacons be the husbands of one wife" (loc. cit., 12) and, ". . . the husband of one wife" (Tit., i, 6). By these words the Apostle does not enjoin marriage on bishops and deacons [Sts. Paul, Titus, and Timothy were celibates as were, according to Tertullian ("Monogamy", iv, in "Ante Nicene Fathers", Amer. Edit.) all the Apostles with exception of St. Peter], but he forbids bigamists to be admitted to Sacred orders. Owing to the small number of those who practised celibacy at the coming of Christ, the Apostles found it impossible to supply celibates for bishops, priests, and deacons and were forced to admit married men to Sacred orders. Blamelessness of life, however, was required, and since iteration of marriage was considered by the Apostles and the people as a strong presumption of incontinency it was decreed that should the bishop-elect (priest- or deacon-elect) be a married man, he must have had only one wife, and further, that after his ordination he should live apart from her. St. Epiphanius (Hær. lxiv, 4) and St. Jerome (Epist. Contra Vigilantium, I) assert that such was the general custom of the Church. This practice of celibacy before or after ordination was universal in all the Churches of the East as well as of the West until about the year A. D. 700 when in the Synods of Trullo concession was made to Greek priests to cohabit with the wives they had married before ordination. They were forbidden, however, to marry again under penalty of absolute deposition from the ministry. In the Pauline injunction no mention is made of sub-deacons or clerics in minor orders, for the simple reason that those orders were not then instituted. The Apostolic Canons (fourth century), which extended the Pauline prohibition to all grades of the sacrament of orders, were not universally observed. Vestiges of a lax discipline on this point are to be met with in France (I Council of Orange, c. xxv) and in Spain (Counc. of Toledo, cc. iii and iv). The Church

of Rome, on the contrary, strictly followed the Apostolic canons. This is evident from the decrees of the Sovereign Pontiffs Innocent I (401–417), Hilary (461–468), Gregory I (590–604), Celestine III (1191–98), and Innocent III (1198–1216). Gregory IX (1227–41) and Gregory X (1271–76) further decreed that bigamists should be deprived of every clerical privilege and the right to wear the clerical garb and tonsure under penalty of excommunication. The Council of Trent finally forbade bigamists to exercise functions attached to minor orders, even though these functions were, on account of the necessity of the times, allowed to be performed by laymen (Sess. XXIII, c. xvii, de Reform.). The reason for the existence of this irregularity is twofold: moral and mystical. The moral reason, which was that of the Orientals and some Latin Fathers, is the presumed incontinency on the part of the bigamist and his consequent unfitness to discharge efficiently the office of the priesthood among a people who looked with great suspicion upon a bigamist and held him in little or no esteem. The mystical reason, which was and is the primary reason of the Western Church (it admits the moral reason, but as secondary to the mystical) is the defect in the perfect resemblance of the second marriage to the great type of Christian marriage—the mystical union of Christ with the Church. This union is the union of one husband (Christ) with one spouse (the Church) without spot or blemish. Second marriages destroy the unity of one husband with one virgin wife, and cause a dividing of one flesh with two bodies, instead of cementing the union of two bodies in one, according to Genesis, ii, 24, "They shall be two [one husband, one wife] in one flesh". This division of one body with two, instead of union with one body, is the bed-rock of this irregularity. This defect in the perfect resemblance of the second marriage (real or interpretative) to the great type of marriage gives rise to the irregularity, and to the name by which it is known, "ex defectu sacramenti". It is not proper that one who has received a sacrament defective in its resemblance to its exemplar should become a dispenser of sacraments to others.

Division.—In the first centuries there was only one kind of bigamy called true, or real, or proper. A second kind, called interpretative or fictitious, was afterwards added. In the Middle Ages a third kind, called *similar*, was introduced by the scholastics (Devoti, can. univ., II, p. 206). Durandus was the first to use the term *similitudinaria* (Specul., pars. I, de dispens. Juxta. n. 6). Since then the traditional division has been and is threefold, viz. real, interpretative, and similar. Many canonists of this century and last hold that similar bigamy should not be included under the irregularity *ex bigamia*. Another division is made, but there is unanimity concerning it, i. e. bigamy *ex defectu sacramenti* (by reason of defective sacrament) and bigamy *ex delicto* (by reason of guilt). D'Annibale (Summul. Theol., Pars. I, n. 417 and 418, note 11 fourth edit.) holds that similar bigamists and not a few interpretative bigamists are irregular *ex delicto*, and not *ex defectu sacramenti*. St. Alphonsus (lib. VII, de Irregul., n. 436) and very many others, as well as the National Synods of the Syrians (an. 1888, p. 173, edit. 1899) and of the Copts (Cairo, an. 1898, p. 142), class all three kinds of bigamists as irregular *ex defectu sacramenti*. Bigamy in general is the state of a man who has really or interpretatively contracted and consummated two valid or two invalid marriages, or one valid and the other invalid, or one real, and the other a spiritual, marriage. Two things are essential to every kind of bigamy: (1) a marriage valid or invalid—adulterous connexions or concubinage do not enter into the question at all; (2) a carnal knowledge by which the parties legally married become one flesh, and without which there is neither bigamy nor irregularity.

Real bigamy demands two valid and legal and consummated marriages with virgins; therefore, two real wives one after the other. It is indifferent whether or not the marriages took place before or after baptism, or one before and the other after; the second successive marriage imperfectly symbolizes "the great Sacrament of Christ in the Church" (Ephes., v, 32), and the irregularity is present (Pope Innocent I, Decret., can. 13, dist. 34). There is, therefore, no real bigamy (a) if either or both marriages are invalid, (b) if either or both have not been consummated, (c) if either or both women have not been virgins, (d) if one of the two ceremonies was a valid, consummated marriage, and the other a mere betrothal followed by carnal union.

Interpretative bigamy is the state of a man who has not as a matter of fact had two legal wives in succession, but whose matrimonial ventures—whether one or two—are accompanied with such circumstances as to warrant the law by a legal fiction to hold him as a bigamist and irregular. It is to be remembered that the laws which govern fictitious (similar and interpretative) bigamy must be strictly construed, for two reasons: (1) because there is question of an irregularity—something odious; and (2) it is a fiction of law and therefore does not hold unless in those cases expressly mentioned in the law (Fagnanus, cap. In Præsen., n. 23, de Probat.). Pope Benedict XIV wisely remarks (Ad audientiam, 15 February, 1753, par. 15), "It is the sole right of the legislator, and beyond the power of any private author or doctor, to draw legal conclusion from a fiction of law. Many, therefore, of the ablest canonists of recent years (v. g. D'Annibale, Gaspari, Icard, Wernz, Lombardi, Ballerini-Palmieri), as also the national synods of the Copts and Syrians, restrict real and interpretative bigamies to the case where a man marries either two valid and legal wives, or a widow, or a corrupt woman, or knows his wife carnally after she has been corrupted by a third party.

Interpretative bigamy is threefold:—

(1) When a man contracts and consummates only one, and that a valid marriage, or weds one wife to whom he is united in one flesh, yet the circumstances are such that the law considers two marriages and two wives. Of this class there are three cases: (a) When a single man marries a widow already made one flesh with a former husband (Decretal Greg., Lib. I, Tit. xxi, Cap. iii). Here the woman has had two husbands and has divided her flesh with two instead of being cemented to only one. Her marriage to the second husband is defective in its resemblance to the marriage symbol—union of Christ with the Church; the second husband is not the only husband of the one wife who herself should have been the wife of only one husband. As the wife in this case has had two real husbands, so, by fiction of law, her husband is considered to have had two interpretative wives. (b) When he marries an unmarried woman, already by a third party corrupted (Pope Hilary, Synod. Rom. Cap. ii, Dist. XXXIV, c. ix, Decret.). Here again is a division of flesh with two instead of union with one, and hence the defect, and, as a consequence, the irregularity. (c) When he carnally knows his own wife after she has committed adultery or has been forcibly oppressed (Decretum, c. xi; c. xii). The husband in this case is not barred from orders unless the adultery of the wife whom he as a layman has married was conclusively proved; nevertheless, in this case, as in cases (a) and (b), ignorance on the part of the husband (*sc.* of the widowhood or corruption or adultery or rape of his wife) would not except him from bigamy and irregularity, since there is here question of an irregularity *ex defectu sacramenti* and

not *ex delicto*. The defect is present irrespective of his knowledge.

(2) When he marries once, but the marriage is invalid. (a) The one in Sacred orders who marries a widow—marriage invalid on account of diriment impediment of S. Orders—and is carnally joined to her, is an interpretative bigamist and irregular (Cap. VII, Tit. XXI, De. Big.). Pope Innocent (loc. cit.) says that although this cleric is not a real bigamist, yet with him, as with a real bigamist, it was not lawful to dispense as the husband of a widow, not because of the defect in the sacrament, but on account of the marital intention joined with carnal union. Although not expressed in the above canon, yet it is the common opinion that the cleric in major order who marries a woman corrupted by a third party is a bigamist and irregular. He would not be irregular if he married a woman seduced by himself and known by no other man (Schmalz., Tit. XXI, De Bigam., n. 6). Civil marriage will suffice in this case, even where the Tridentine law is published (S. U. I., December 22, 1880). (b) Invalid by reason of a preexisting marriage bond (*ligamen*), as, for instance, where the man marries a woman who has been divorced, repudiated, or rejected by a former husband, or who has divorced or left him. In this case the marriage is defective, the woman having shared her body with two, and hence he who married her is irregular for the above-mentioned reason (Lib. I, Tit. XXI, C. I; Dist. XXXIV, Can. xv). (c) If the marriage was invalid by reason of a diriment impediment other than order and *ligamen*, the more prominent opinion holds that the irregularity is incurred. Fagnanus (Comment., Cap. iv, De Big., n. 45) asserts that the prelates of the Rota, to whom the case was specially referred by the pope, decided that a cleric in minor orders who contracted and consummated an invalid marriage with a widow was an interpretative bigamist and irregular and stood in need of dispensation, and that Pope Urban, upon the strength of that decision, granted dispensation. Many of the best canonists of to-day (v. g. D'Annibale and Gaspari) hold the contrary. The case is not expressed in law, they say, and is a legal fiction which at all times is dangerous and is totally unwarranted if the two cases differ in every respect, as do these—the one being in major, and the other in minor orders; the one in bad faith and the other in good faith. Yet, after all is said *pro* and *con*, it still remains true that the proximate cause of the irregularity in the law cited is identical with that of the second case, to wit, marital intent with carnal consummation.

(3) When a man marries twice and either or both marriages are invalid, as (a) he who having contracted and consummated a marriage with a virgin, upon her death received Sacred orders, and afterwards, without any deception on his part, contracts and consummates a sacrilegious and invalid marriage with a virgin or widow, becomes an interpretative bigamist and irregular, not because of any defect in the sacrament in the second marriage, which is no marriage and no sacrament, but because of the marital intent followed by consummation by means of which the necessary division of his body with two has been effected (Innocent III, cap. iii, iv, De Big.). Should the cleric feign, rather than honestly intend, the second marriage, in order to accomplish the carnal union, some are of the opinion that he does not incur the irregularity, the marital intent required by the Innocentian law not being verified; others more commonly affirm that irregularity is contracted. The reason given by the affirmants is that the Innocentian marital intent is not so much the intention to contract a valid marriage, as to externally contract and consummate, an intention that is always presumed to be present in such cases. External marriages are always supposed to be free and voluntary.

Simulation is never presumed, but must, on the contrary, be demonstrated. (b) Should the first marriage before receiving Sacred orders be invalid on account of any diriment impediment (v. g., consanguinity or the like), although the case is not expressly stated in the law, the general opinion, with a few exceptions, is that he is an interpretative bigamist and irregular. In answer to their opponents, the affirmants say that the marriage mentioned (Cap. iv, De Big.) may have been invalid, as there is no certainty that it was valid, in which case the argument from one species to another would be legitimate. (c) Should both marriages be invalid, some assert there is no interpretative bigamy or irregularity. Certainly there is no law for it. Others, as St. Alphonsus (Vol. VII, n. 455; Suarez., Disp. XLIX, Sect. II, n. 11) teach as the most common and notable opinion that there is present the marital intent with the carnal consummation which alone suffices to induce the irregularity. Canonists differ in opinion as to the case where two invalid marriages were contracted and consummated in good faith. The most common and probable opinion is that irregularity is contracted, for the reason that it is not the guilt of the desire, but the intention to contract and consummate the two marriages which is the reason of the irregularity as laid down by Innocent III (Cap. 4, De Big). By almost common consent the irregularity is said to be contracted by the cleric tonsured or in minor orders or layman who, after having contracted and consummated a marriage invalid on account of a known impediment and afterwards, whether his wife be living or dead, contracts and consummates another marriage even with a virgin. There is present in the case a division of flesh and the marital intent necessary to produce irregularity.

Similar Bigamy is nowhere clearly and expressly stated in the law. It owes its existence to the almost universal and constant teaching of canonists and theologians since the time of Durandus. Similar bigamy is twofold: (1) When a religious who has been solemnly professed in a religious order approved by the Church marries a virgin and carnally knows her as such. (2) When a cleric in Sacred orders, in violation of the law of celibacy, contracts and consummates a marriage with a virgin. This form of bigamy presupposes only one carnal marriage and a spiritual marriage, which are interpretatively considered two marriages, and each putative husband is considered to have two interpretative wives. The carnal marriages are invalid by reason of the diriment impediment of solemn religious profession and of orders respectively; but because of the marital intent followed by carnal consummation, some claim that similar bigamy and irregularity are incurred by reason of the defective signification of the sacrilegious marriage by the symbol of matrimony; some admit that there is no bigamy, but an irregularity arising from the sacrilegious marriage; others again insist that there is an irregularity on account of some kind of a defect in the sacrament, but there is no law declaring it to be bigamous and irregular. Gaspari (De Sacra Ordin., nn. 393 sqq.) and others reject the first opinion altogether and very conclusively show that the canons of common law and the canons of Gratian upon which the first opinion is grounded are not to the point. Gaspari shows that the decrees (Decretales—Lib. IV, Tit. 6, Cap. i, 2 and 4) of Pope Alexander III do not refer to bigamy or irregularity, but speak of suspensions and excommunications; that the Gratian canons treat of religious men and women who have broken their vows and are to be removed from their grade, and subjected to the same penances as were at that period imposed upon bigamists. Pope Clement, in his decree (Lib. 4, Tit. Unicus de Cons. et aff. Clem.) also speaks of excom-

munication and not irregularity. The constitution of Pius IX, "Apostolicæ Sedis" imposes upon similar bigamists excommunication reserved to the ordinaries, and nothing more. It is evident, therefore, that the law affixes no note of irregularity to a so-called similar bigamist. Practically speaking, however, there is little difference, as the so-called similar bigamists are prevented, on account of the censure and the infamy of their act, from receiving higher orders or exercising those already received; and should they solemnly exercise the functions of their grade, they would become irregular on account of the violated censure. The bishop can, when they have put away the woman, done penance, and led edifying lives, absolve them from the censure and dispense them from any irregularity, if any has been incurred, and promote them to higher orders. It is certain, however, that religious, not in Sacred orders, with simple vows, who contract and consummate marriage with a virgin or with a renegade nun who has broken her solemn vows, is neither a bigamist nor irregular. No such case is found in the canon.

EFFECTS.—Bigamy begets irregularity, the principal effect of which is to entirely exclude from the reception and use and exercise of any ecclesiastical order and benefice attached to any order. Pope Gregory X (Lib. I, Tit. XII, Cap. Unic. in Sexto) further declared that bigamists should be stripped of every clerical privilege, removed from the protection of the ecclesiastical, and subjected to civil jurisdiction, deprived of the canon safeguarding their person from personal attack, and forbidden to wear the tonsure and clerical garb, under penalty of excommunication to be incurred at the moment of their attempted marriage. The Council of Trent also forbids to bigamists the exercise of any office or function of minor orders, even of such functions as are usually, by permission, allowed to married laymen on account of scarcity of celibate clerics (Sess. XXIII, C. 17, De Reform). Clerics in minor orders whose marriages were invalid are not comprehended under the Tridentine law. Clerics in Sacred orders and religious clerics, who, by virtue of the law of celibacy and religious profession, are spiritually wedded to the clerical and religious states respectively, are not comprehended under the law stripping them of every clerical privilege, and the use of tonsure and clerical garb, and this out of respect to their sacred character. Clerics on the other hand, in minor orders are not wedded to the clerical state; hence they come under the law. Bishops who knowingly and without permission confer Sacred orders on a bigamist are by the Third Council of Arles (Dist. LV, Can. 2) suspended from saying Mass for one year, and by the decretal law (Lib. 1, Tit. 21, Cap. ii) were deprived of the power of giving to others the orders they had conferred on a bigamist. Since the constitution "Apostolicæ Sedis", the only punishment is that which the Holy Father may deem fit to impose upon the bishop violating the canons.

DISPENSATION.—This irregularity is removed neither by baptism nor religious solemn profession, but by dispensation. The pope, and he alone, can dispense with this prohibition to receive orders. He can dispense with a mere ecclesiastical law, such as is the Pauline injunction, although it is of Apostolic origin. Pope Lucius III, whilst urging the unlawfulness of granting a dispensation in face of St. Paul's prohibition, did, however, grant it to Nicholas de Tudeschis, a celebrated canonist, better known as Abbas Panormitanus (Glossa, ad verb. *Fiat*, C. Lector, XVIII, Dist. XXXIV). Dispensations in cases of one who marries two real wives or a widow are exceedingly difficult to obtain (Lib. I, Tit. 9, De Renunt. Sec. Personæ). Worthy of note is the fact that the dispensation does not efface the defect in the sacrament, but the unfitness arising therefrom is removed. It is the universal opinion of to-day, whatever may have been the opinion of canonists in the past, that the pope alone can dispense all bigamists, real and interpretative, as regards minor as well as Sacred orders, and the collation and use of the simple, as of great, benefices. The reason is evident: bishops cannot dispense in the laws of their superiors, to wit, the pope or General Council. Some canonists claim that bishops, by virtue of the Council of Trent (Sess. XXIV, C. 6, De Ref) can dispense with interpretative bigamy arising from occult guilt. D'Annibale (loc. cit.) on this point well remarks that it is exceedingly difficult for such acts to be private. Sanchez asserts that it is of little moment whether or not the fact is private or public, since the irregularity is not *ex delicto*, but *ex defectu sacramenti*. It is certain that bishops, where there is a grave and positive doubt about the existence of interpretative bigamy and its consequent irregularity, can grant dispensation. Bishops can dispense with all similar bigamists as above defined after they have left their putative wives, done penance, and led edifying lives, and can admit them to the exercise of all ecclesiastical functions (Lib. IV, Tit. VI, Cap. i, Qui Clerici et Vov.; Lib. III, Tit. III, Cap. Sane 4). Regular prelates, i. e. generals, provincials, abbots, priors, guardians, having quasi-episcopal jurisdiction, cannot, in virtue of the common law and apart from special privileges, dispense their own subjects with real or interpretative bigamy, even as regards minor as well as major orders. No such power has been given them by pope or general council. By virtue of privilege of Pius V (Constit. "Rom. Pont. Circumspecta", June 21, 1571, Sec. 3), joined with that of the Council of Trent (Sess. XXIV, Cap. vi, etc.) power to dispense in irregularities on account of occult guilt, given to bishops, was extended to regular prelates. By virtue of the privilege of Sixtus IV, regular prelates cannot dispense with real, interpretative, and public similar bigamists (P. Venantius, O. F. M., Compend. Privil. Regularium, ed. 1906; Piat. Vol. II, p. 577, 2). As a matter of fact, the Sixtine constitution (Reg. Univ. Eccles., August 31, 1474) makes a special exception in the case of bigamy. The general opinion, that they cannot grant dispensation to their subjects who are real or interpretative bigamists, is evident from the fact that the decretal law (C. Altercationis in 60) has reserved that faculty to the pope; second, Tridentine law is against such faculty; third, declaration of s. c. c. (3 January, 1589) has so decided; fourth, present practice of granting privileges and faculties to religious orders as a rule makes an exception of bigamy v. g., constit. of Leo XII, 1826, "Plura Intra", directed to the Society of Jesus, withholds the faculty of dispensing with bigamists. If religious prelates do possess the faculty of dispensing in such cases, it must be by virtue of some special privilege of recent date. Bishops of the United States and of England, and vicars Apostolic subject to the Propaganda (these latter only *in foro interno*) have special faculties (Formula I, II, and IV respectively) to dispense interpretative bigamists; and in cases of paramount importance, on account of great scarcity of priests, bishops in the United States can dispense also with real bigamists. According to general opinion, the multiplication of marriages does not increase the number of irregularities contracted; so the bigamist and trigamist equally incur only one irregularity. In applications for dispensations mention of only two out of the many marriages is sufficient, and that whether they are all real or interpretative or mixed bigamies. In the opinion, however, of those who divide interpretative bigamies into *ex defectu sacramenti* and *ex delicto* bigamies, it is necessary, in the case where

a grave sin is the cause of the irregularity, to name both the irregularity *ex delicto* (with sin) and the irregularity *ex defectu sacramenti* (without sin).

FERRARIS, *Bibliotheca* (Rome, 1885), s. v.; FAGNANUS, *Comment. in Decret.* (1709), I, 497 sqq.; PIRHING (ed., 1674), I, 489–499; VAN ESPEN, *Jus. Eccles. Univ.* (ed., 1781), II, Pars. II, pp. 104 sqq.; DEVOTE, *Jus. Can. Univ.* (Rome, 1839), II, 206 sqq.; WERNZ, *Jus. Decret.*, II, 156–164; GASPARI, *De Sacrâ Ordinat.*, I, 236–254; SANTI (ed., 1898), I, 203–210; D'ANNIBALE, *Summula Theol. Mor.*, Pars. I, 428, Ed. IV; BALLERINI-PALMIERI, *Opus. Theol.*, VII, *De Censuris*, 385 sqq.; ANDRE-WAGNER, *Diction. Canonique*, s. v.

P. M. J. ROCK.

Bigamy (Fr. *bigamie*, from Lat. *bis*, twice, and Gr. γάμος, marriage) IN CIVIL JURISPRUDENCE, and especially in criminal law, is "a formal entering into of a marriage while a former one remains un-dissolved" (Bishop, Commentaries on the Law of Statutory Crimes, § 577), "the crime of having two wives or husbands at once" (Murray, New Dict., s. v.) or two or more wives or husbands (Century Dict., s. v.). Bigamy, being "a species of polygamy" (Stephen, New Commentaries, IV, 83), may be designated by the latter word (Bishop, op. cit.); for Sir Edward Coke defines "polygamus" to be one "qui duas vel plures duxit uxores" (3d Instit., XXVII). But its very general use in English statutes and authorities renders *bigamy* in many instances the word of more ready reference (Russell, A Treatise on Crimes, 659).

Bigamy as defined is classed by jurists among those acts injurious to public morality by which the State or community generally is injured, and which may therefore properly be made criminal. The crime consists, according to French law (Carpentier, Codes et lois; Code pénal, 340, note) "in the fact of the celebration of the second marriage before dissolution of the first", or, to quote an American authority, in "the prostitution of a solemn ceremony which the law allows to be applied only to a legitimate union", involving "an outrage on public decency and morals" and "a public scandal" (Bishop, op. cit.). And so Boswell quotes Dr. Samuel Johnson, commenting on Luther's allowing the Landgrave of Hesse two wives with the consent of the wife to whom he was first married, thus: "There was no harm in this, so far as she was only concerned, because *volenti non fit injuria*. But it was an offence against the general order of society, and against the law of the Gospel, by which one man and one woman are to be united."

Although among many nations plurality of wives or polygamy has been legally recognized, yet the fact has been observed "that among not a few uncivilized people polygamy is almost unknown or even prohibited" (Westermarck, The History of Human Marriage, 435), and where tolerated, bigamy is its usual form, as was the case among the Hebrews (op. cit., 430). In the earlier days of Babylon, bigamy is said to have been the exception and monogamy the prevailing practice (Johns, Babylonian and Assyrian Laws, 134). The Assyrian kings appear to have been monogamists, the kings of ancient Egypt seem to have had only one wife, and the same remark may be made of their subjects (Westermarck, 432, 442, 447). The law of China prohibits taking of a second wife during lifetime of the first (Westermarck, 445). Mohammed, when allowing his followers four wives, is said to have sought to restrict what he felt himself unable to abolish. And he is said to have been of opinion that, although an unlimited number of wives might live together in harmony, this among so few as four would be impossible. Events seem to have proved the correctness of his judgment, for "the quarrels, jealousies and expenditure of four wives vying with each other" (Colquhoun, Summary etc., § 575) are said to have brought about the monogamy usual among modern Mohammedans. Of those in India ninety-five per cent are monogamists, and it is said that in Persia two per cent only have a plurality of wives (Wester-marck, 439). "'Tis true", writes Lady Mary Wortley Montagu from Adrianople, in 1717, concerning the Turks, "their law permits them four wives; but there is no instance of a man of quality that makes use of his liberty or of a woman of rank that would suffer it" (Works, II, 190). The ancient Romans were monogamists (Westermarck, 433). And in the time of the Emperor Justinian (527–565) the illegality of bigamy was firmly established: "Duas uxores eodem tempore habere non licet" and "eadem duobus nupta esse non potest" are the expressions of the Institutes (Lib. I, tit. x, vv. 6, 7).

The law of England is thus laid down by an authority supposed to be of the time of Edward I (1272–1307), the king, "who", remarks Sir William Blackstone, "hath justly been styled our English Justinian" (Commentaries, IV, 425): "It has sometimes been that a man from wickedness has married several women, all living at the same time; but Holy Church says that of such women none but the first is his lawful wife; wherefore, the law regards the others only as false wives" (Britton, Lib. V, 11). While the first marriage continues undissolved by death, or by judgment of a court of competent jurisdiction, a subsequent marriage is, by English common law, a mere nullity and void (Kent, Commentaries on American Law, Part IV, 80; Bishop, New Commentaries on Marriage, etc., 1, § 717). No length of absence and no error as to survival of the absent can render valid the second ceremony. But in defining bigamy as a crime, statutes have been more indulgent. Notwithstanding what we have quoted from the authority of the thirteenth century, there seems to have been no English statute defining and punishing bigamy as a crime until the year 1604, English law being in this respect more backward than the law of Scotland, which so early as 1551 pronounced bigamy a crime punishable with the pains of perjury, these being confiscation of goods, imprisonment, and infamy (Bell, Dict. and Digest of the Laws of Scotland, s. v.). By an English statute of 1604, upon which later English laws and laws in the United States have been modelled, any married person who should marry within England or Wales, the former husband or wife being living, became guilty of felony. But the statute did not extend to persons whose husband or wife remained continually "beyond the seas by the space of seven years", nor to a person "whose husband or wife shall absent him or herself the one from the other by the space of seven years together in any parts within his majesty's dominions, the one of them not knowing the other to be living within that time". The statute thus established an arbitrary period of absence as exempting from criminality a second marriage. That absence within England should justify the second marriage, the one marrying was required to be ignorant of the survival of the absent husband or wife; but respecting absence "beyond the seas" we are told by Blackstone, "Where either party hath been continually abroad for seven years whether the party in England hath notice of the other's being living or no" (Commentaries, Bk. IV, 164), there can be no felony under the statute. The statute, not otherwise providing, and its violation being made a felony, men prosecuted thereunder were, according to the general law of the period, entitled to "benefit of clergy" (Coke, sup.), subject to which, conviction under the statute was punishable with death. The English statute of 1861, now in force, exempts from punishment a second marriage only where there has been continual absence of seven years, and the person marrying shall not know the absent husband or wife "to be living within that time". Those guilty under the statute are liable to penal servitude of not more

than seven nor less than three years or to imprisonment of not more than two years. Bigamy is a crime within the statute, if committed by a British subject, wherever the offence may be committed. The French "Code pénal" provides the punishment of "travaux forcés à temps" for a person who, being married, shall contract another marriage before dissolution of the former marriage.

A United States Statute declares guilty of polygamy every person, having a husband or wife living, who "in a territory or other place over which the United States have exclusive jurisdiction", marries another, unless there shall have been absence of five years, the absent husband or wife "not known to be living and believed to be dead", or unless there shall have been a divorce or judicial annulment of the previous marriage. The punishment provided is a fine of not more than five hundred dollars and not more than five years' imprisonment. The Constitution of the United States declares that "Congress shall make no law respecting an establishment of religion or prohibiting the free exercise thereof" (Constitution, Amendments, Art. 1). The question has accordingly been raised whether legislation such as has just been quoted may not violate the Constitution in the instance of an adherent to a religion of which bigamy is claimed to be a tenet. But the Supreme Court of the United States, speaking by Mr. Justice Field, held that "however free the exercise of religion may be, it must be subordinate to the criminal laws of the country, passed with reference to actions regarded by general consent as properly the subject of punitive legislation", that "bigamy and polygamy are crimes by the laws of all civilized and Christian countries", few crimes being "more pernicious to the best interests of society", and therefore that "to call their advocacy a tenet of religion is to offend the common sense of mankind". Free exercise of religion ought not, in the opinion of the Court, to be construed to mean toleration of crime (Davis v. Reason, United States Reports, CXXXIII, 333, 341, 342, 345). Alien polygamists are, by a United States Statute excluded from admission to the United States. The statute books of various States of the Union contain laws modelled upon, and with provisions more or less similar to, those of the English law of 1604, and defining bigamy, or in the statutes of some States, polygamy, as a crime. Formerly, by the Virginia law (United States Reports, XCVIII, 165) and by the law of North Carolina (Kent, Commentaries, Part IV, 79, note d), bigamy was punished by death. Now its punishment in Virginia is imprisonment of not more than eight nor less than three years (Code, § 3781), and in North Carolina of not more than ten years nor less than four months (Revisal, § 3361). In the State of New York the punishment is not more than five years' imprisonment, and the period of absence excusing second marriage is fixed at five years, the former husband or wife having been absent from the one remarrying "without being known by him or her within that time to be living and believed by him or her to be dead" (Birdseye, Revised Statutes, 306). Divorce (unless for fault of the party remarrying), due permission of Court, or annulment of the previous marriage, or sentence to life imprisonment of the former husband or wife also excuses the remarriage. Absence, therefore, not dissolving a previous marriage, on proof that a husband or wife who had been supposed to be dead is in fact living, the second marriage may be adjudged to be a nullity. The law will not sanction bigamy by recognizing the two marriages to be simultaneously valid. According to the law of New York, the earlier marriage ceases to be binding until one of the three parties to the two marriages procures a judgment pronouncing the second marriage void (New York Court

II.—36

of Appeals Reports, CXIV, 120; Birdseye, op. cit., 1042; cf. Bishop, New Commentaries).

The recently recovered Code of the Babylonian King Hammurabi (about 2250 B. C.), in its regulations respecting bigamy affords some interesting comparisons with modern legislation on the same subject. By that ancient statute a wife "has no blame" who remarries after her husband has been taken captive, "if there was not maintenance in his house" (§ 134). But "if there was maintenance in his house", the captive's wife who remarries "shall be prosecuted and shall be drowned" (§ 133). Another section resembles a provision of an existing New York statute. By this statute, if the second marriage be annulled because the former husband or wife is living, children of this marriage are deemed to be "legitimate children of the parent who at the time of the marriage was competent to contract" (Birdseye, Revised Statutes, 993). In like manner this code of four thousand years ago ordains that if, in the instance of the woman who "has no blame", there be children of her second marriage, she shall return to her first husband if "he return and regain his city", "but the children shall follow their own father". As if to rebuke want of patriotism or love of home, the wife of a man who "has left his city and fled" might remarry and "because he hated his city and fled" the fugitive returning was not allowed to reclaim his wife (§ 136).

Tennyson has made double marriage the subject of his poem "Enoch Arden". We may notice how carefully the poet causes a period to elapse longer than the seven years mentioned in the English Statute:—

> . . . . ten years
> Since Enoch left his hearth and native land
> Fled forward, and no news of Enoch came,

before his wife listens to the argument, which, however, the poet is not so unpoetical as to reinforce by quoting the statute:—

> It is beyond all hope, against all chance,
> That he who left you ten long years ago
> Should still be living.

—And, like the woman pronounced blameless by the old Babylonian Code, for whom "there was not maintenance", Enoch's wife was "poor and wanting help" when she consented to the remarriage which Enoch, returning contrary to all seeming hope and chance, after having been so long "cast away and lost", ratified in his self-effacing prayer for strength "not to tell her, never to let her know"—cf. Hammurabi, Code, § 135.

MURRAY, *New English Dictionary* (Oxford and New York 1888), s. v.; *The Century Dictionary* (New York), s. v.; BISHOP, *Commentaries on the Law of Statutory Crimes* (3d ed., Chicago, 1901); ID., *New Commentaries on Marriage, Divorce, and Separation* (Chicago, 1891); STEPHEN, *New Commentaries on the Laws of England* (14th ed., London, 1903); RUSSELL, *A Treatise on Crimes and Misdemeanours* (6th ed., London, 1896); HOLLAND, *The Elements of Jurisprudence* (10th ed., New York and London, 1906); *The Statutes at Large* (London, 1770), 111; *A Compendious Abstract of the Public General Acts* (London, 1861), XXXIX; BELL, *Dictionary and Digest of the Laws of Scotland* (Edinburgh, 1890), tit. *Bigamy;* CARPENTIER, *Codes et lois* (Paris, 1899); COKE, *The Third Part of the Institutes of the Laws of England* (London, 1680), XXVII; BIRDSEYE, *The Revised Statutes, Codes, and General Laws of the State of New York* (3d ed., New York, 1901); *Reports of Cases decided in the Court of Appeals* (Albany, 1889), CXIV, 120; POLLARD, *Code of Virginia* (St. Paul, 1904), §§ 3781, 3782; *Revisal of 1905 of North Carolina* (Raleigh, 1905), § 3361; *Compiled Statutes of the United States, 1901* (St. Paul, 1902), 3633; *Supplement* (to the same), *1905* (St. Paul, 1905), 276; BOSWELL, *Life of Johnson,* ed. HILL (Oxford, 1887), V, 217; WESTERMARCK, *The History of Human Marriage* (London, 1891); DE COLQUHOUN, *A Summary of the Roman Civil Law* (London, 1849); *Works of the Rt. Hon. Lady Mary Wortley Montagu* (6th ed., London, 1817), II, 190; BRITTON, tr. NICHOLS (Washington, 1901); JOHNS, *Babylonian and Assyrian Laws, Contracts, and Letters* (New York, 1904).

CHARLES W. SLOANE.

Bigne (BINIUS, BIGNÆUS), MARGUERIN DE LA, French theologian and patrologist, b. about 1546 at Bernières-le-Patry, Normandy; d. about 1595. He studied at the College of Caen, and at the Sorbonne in Paris where he received the doctorate. He was named canon of his native Diocese of Bayeux and, later, dean of the church of Mans. At the Provincial Council of Rouen, in 1581, he sustained the rights of his cathedral chapter against Bernadin de St. François, Bishop of Bayeux, and provoked an unfortunate conflict with the latter which ended in de la Bigne's resignation from his canonry. He resumed, then, at the Sorbonne the patristic studies in which he had been long engaged. He had early perceived that Protestant misquotation and misinterpretation of patristic texts was a menace to Catholic interests and resolved to collect and edit the available documents of the Fathers. He published in 1575 his "Sacra Bibliotheca Sanctorum Patrum" (Paris, 8 vols.; additional volume in 1579; later editions, Paris, 1589; Lyons, 27 vols., 1677; Cologne, 1694). It contains the writings, some complete, some fragmentary, of our two hundred Fathers, many published for the first time. Particular care was given to the elucidation of texts corrupted by heretics. This work was the pioneer in the field of critical patristics. He published, also, "Statuta Synodalia Parisiensium Episcoporum, Galonis Adonis et Willielmi; item Decreta Petri et Galteri, Senonensium Episcoporum" (Paris, 1578); and an edition of St. Isidore of Seville (Paris, 1580), in which for the first time the latter's works were gathered in one work.

MIGNE, *P. L.*, LXXXI, 209–212.

JOHN B. PETERSON.

Billiart, MARIE-ROSE-JULIE. See JULIE BILLIART, BLESSED.

Billick (STEINBERGER, Lat. *Latomus, Lapicida*), EBERHARD, German theologian, opponent of the Reformation, b. 1499 or 1500 at Cologne; d. there, 12 January, 1557. Of a family which gave a number of prominent men to the Carmelites of Cologne, Eberhard entered the Carmelite Order in 1513, took his vows in 1514, became priest and master of students in 1525, and reader of divinity in 1526; he matriculated at the University of Cologne in 1528, was made Prior of Cassel, 1531, Prior of Cologne, 1536–42, received his licentiate and doctorate of divinity, 1540 and in 1542 was appointed Provincial of the province of Lower Germany. He retained this dignity until his death, for, although nominated auxiliary Bishop of Cologne, he did not live to be consecrated. Billick's activity on behalf of his order was successful; he enrolled numerous candidates, improved the plan of studies, saved several monasteries from destruction, re-established others, and reformed both his own province and that of Upper Germany. His chief importance, however, lies in his dealings with the Archbishop of Cologne. If Cologne remained true to the Catholic cause the merit is principally due to the provincial of the Carmelites. As the leader of the lower clergy he protested against the heretical tendencies of Archbishop Hermann von Wied, who since 1536 had favoured the Reformers. Von Wied was excommunicated in 1546, gave up the archbishopric in 1547, and died in 1552. It was Billick's exposure of the archbishop's breach of faith that led to the latter's deposition. Writing against Bucer, Billick drew upon himself the ire of Luther and Melanchthon. He took part in the disputations of Worms, 1540, Ratisbon, 1541 and 1546, and Augsburg, 1547, and as theologian accompanied the new Archbishop of Cologne to the Council of Trent, 1551.

POSTINA, *Der Karmelit Eberhard Billick* (Freiburg im Br., 1901), contains his life, a complete bibliography, list of his writings and a calendar of his correspondence.

B. ZIMMERMAN.

Billuart, Charles-René, Dominican preacher, controversialist, and theologian, b. at Revin, a small town of the Ardennes on the Meuse, Belgium, 28 January, 1685; d. there 20 January, 1757. He completed his classics at the Jesuit college of Charleville and soon after entered the Dominican convent in his native town. He was sent to the novitiate at Lille, whence he returned a year later for profession, 7 November, 1702. He followed the regular courses, receiving ordination in 1708. The two following years he spent at Liège, pursuing higher studies, and in 1710 was appointed professor of philosophy at Douai. The next year he was transferred to Revin, but was speedily promoted to a chair of theology which he held until 1715, when he was appointed master of students at Douai. Here, in 1718, he became second regent of studies and was also designated to preach the Advent and Lenten courses at Liège. Invited to Maastricht by Count Tilly, the famous Catholic governor of the city and Commander-in-Chief of the armies in Holland, he preached on the Real Presence during the Corpus Christi celebration and later defended the doctrine at a public discussion in the town hall. All this had been arranged by the count, who had the satisfaction of seeing the ministers reduced to silence by Billuart's incisive logic and irresistible learning. After three years as Prior of Revin, Billuart was called to the regency of Douai and three years later, 15 October, 1728, he was elected provincial. The honours of the doctorate were conferred upon him in 1729. In 1732 he again preached a course at Liège, adding to his fame as a preacher. He next held the office of Prior of Revin for three successive terms until, in 1741, he was re-elected provincial. In 1746 he began and in five years completed his celebrated and monumental work, the "Summa S. Thomæ hodiernis Academiarum moribus accomodata" (19 vols. Liège, 1746–51). This work had been entrusted to him by the master general of the order nearly fourteen years before. It was a fitting response to a petition of his former colleagues at Douai, and it answered a general demand, as is evidenced by its publication in thirteen standard editions. In 1754, while serving a third term as provincial, Billuart published a compendium, also well known to the scholastic world, in six editions, the "Summa Summæ S. Thomæ, sive compendium theologiæ" (Liège, 1754).

Billuart's work is characterized by a facile style, copious treatment, and fearless exposition; by well planned logical divisions and precise, clear-cut distinctions. It ranks among the leading commentaries on St. Thomas. It is esteemed for its annexed historical essays, the materials for which are drawn largely from the ecclesiastical history of Natalis Alexander, O. P. In his moral science Billuart favours a moderate probabiliorism, in which position, however, he no longer commands a very great following outside of his own school. Generally speaking, Billuart stands forth as a theologian of authority. He is one of the foremost writers who have shed lustre on the school of the Angelic Doctor. In his polemical writings, Billuart was a devoted member of his order and a keen disciple of St. Thomas, zealous for the integrity of the saint's accepted teachings. Dignified in bearing, he was gentle to those around him. He was unremitting in his labours and a man of prayer withal, much given to devotion to the Blessed Sacrament.

His principal works, besides those mentioned, are the following: "Supplementum cursus theologiæ ' (Liège, 1759); "De mente ecclesiæ catholicæ circa accidentia eucharistiæ" (Liège, 1715); "Le thomisme vengé de sa prétendue condamnation par la constitution Unigenitus" (Brussels, 1720); "Lettre à MM. les docteurs de la faculté de théologie de l'université de Douai" (1723); "Examen critique des réflexions sur le bref de notre S. Père le pape Benoît XIII" (1725); "Le thomisme triomphant par le bref Demissas preces

de Benoît XIII"; "Réponse . . . à M. Stiévenard, Chanoine de Cambrai, au sujet de son Apologie pour feu Mgr. de Fénelon"; "Avis à M. Stiévenard sur la seconde Apologie pour Mgr. Fénelon"; "Justification de l'avis"; "Apologie du thomisme triomphant" (Liège, 1731); "Réponse à l'auteur d'un libelle" (1734); "Apologie . . . contre l'Histoire du baianisme composée par le Père Duchesne" (Avignon, 1738); "Sermons du R. P. C. R. Billuart", edited by Abbé Lelièvre (2 vols., Paris, 1846).

Labye, *Vita Auctoris* in *Supplementum Cursus Theol.* (Liège, 1759); Mandonnet in *Dict. de théol. cath.*; Lelièvre, preface to *Sermons du R. P. Billuart* (Paris, 1846), I; Hurter, *Nomenclator*, II, 1284.

J. R. Volz.

Billy, (Billi) Jacques de, a French patristic scholar, theologian, jurist, linguist, and Benedictine abbot, b. 1535 at Guise in Picardy; d. 25 December, 1581 at Paris. He began his studies at Paris, completed a course of philosophy and theology before he was eighteen years of age, and then, at the request of his parents went to Orléans and later to Poitiers to study jurisprudence. But having no inclination for law, he devoted most of his time to literature. The early death of his parents (Louis de Billy, of an old French family originally from Ile-de-France, and Marie de Brichanteau) gave him the opportunity he desired of pursuing unhampered his favourite study of letters. Quietly withdrawing to Lyons and later to Avignon, de Billy devoted himself, for a period, entirely to the study of Greek and Hebrew. He already held *in commendam* the Abbey of St.-Léonard de Ferrières in Anjou, and the Priory of Taussigny in Tourraine, when his older brother Jean, who had hitherto led a very worldly life, suddenly announced his intention of becoming a Carthusian, and resigned in favour of Jacques his two abbeys, Notre-Dame des Châtelliers and St.-Michel-en-l'Herme. After some hesitation de Billy accepted them, then entered the Order of St. Benedict, and later was made a regular abbot. Thenceforth he led a very ascetic life and governed his monasteries with great prudence. He was especially solicitous for the proper observance of monastic discipline and with that object in view renewed, in 1566, the statutes of his predecessor, Abbot Bertrand de Moussy. During the civil wars that devastated France at this period the monastery of St.-Michel-en-l'Herme was wholly destroyed. The abbot himself was frequently obliged to seek refuge from the ravages of war, and resided, for short periods, at Laon, Nantes, Paris, and in the Priory of Taussigny. The hardships he had to undergo in his journeyings, his incessant toil and study, and his ascetic observances gradually shattered his health, and while staying in Paris with his friend Gilbert Génébrard, he died at the comparatively early age of forty-six. He was buried in the choir of the church of Saint-Séverin.

From the day on which he entered the novitiate, de Billy set aside all profane studies and devoted himself exclusively to the study of the Fathers. His critical abilities and exceptional linguistic attainments (he wrote Greek and Latin with singular purity and precision) enabled him to do much for the emendation of the text and the correct interpretation of many obscure passages in the Church Fathers. His favourite among the Fathers was St. Gregory Nazianzen. His principal works are: (1) "S. Gregorii Nazianzeni opera omnia latine" (Paris, 1569; a second and better edition appeared in 1583. (2) "Consolations et instructions" (Paris, 1570). (3) "Récréations spirituelles" (Paris, 1573). (4) "S. Gregorii Nazianzeni opuscula" (Paris, 1575). (5) "Interpretatio Latina xviii priorum capitum S. Irenæi" (Paris, 1575). (6) "Anthologia sacra" (Paris, 1576). (7) "Joannis Damasceni opera"

(Paris, 1577). (8) "Locutiones Græcæ" (Paris, 1578). (9) "Opuscula aliqua S. Joannis Chrysostomi" (Paris, 1581). (10) "S. Isidori Pelusiotæ epis. libri tres" (Paris, 1585). (11) "S. Epiphanii opera" (Paris, 1612).

ZIEGELBAUER, *Hist. rei lit. O. S. B.* (Augsburg, 1754), III, 353; IV, 90, 99, 107; NICERON, *Mémoires*, XXII, 187; DOM FRANCOIS, *Bibl. gen. des écrivains de l'ordre de S. Benott*, (Bouillon. 1777), I, 126; DUPIN, *Nouv. Bibl. des auteurs eccl.* (Amsterdam, 1710), XVI, 123; HUET, *De clar. interpr.*, 261; *Gallia Christiana* (Paris, 1720), II, 1296, 1421; NATALIS ALEXANDER, *Hist. Eccl.* (Venice, 1771), XVII, 335; *P. G.*, XXV, prol.

THOMAS OESTREICH.

Bilocation (Latin *bis*, twice, and *locatio*, place). I. The question whether the same finite being (especially a body) can be at once in two (bilocation) or more (replication, multilocation) totally different places grew out of the Catholic doctrine on the Eucharist. According to this Christ is truly, really, and substantially present in every consecrated Host wheresoever located. In the endeavour to connect this fact of faith with the other conceptions of the Catholic mind theologians make the following distinctions: (1) The place of a body is the surface of the body or bodies immediately surrounding and in contact with the located body. (2) A physical body is in place commensurably (circumscriptively) inasmuch as the individual portions of its exterior surfaces answer singly to the corresponding portions of the immediately environing surfaces of the body or bodies that constitute its place. (3) A being is definitively in place when it is entire in every portion of the space it occupies. This is the mode of location proper to unembodied spirits and to the human soul in the organism whereof it is the "substantial form", i. e. the actuating and vitalizing principle. A spirit cannot, of course, be *in loco* circumscriptively since, having no integrant parts, it cannot be in extensional contact with the surrounding dimensions. It may be said, therefore, to locate itself by its spiritual activity (will) and rather to occupy than to be occupied by place, and consequently to be virtually rather than formally *in loco*. Such a mode of location cannot be natural to a physical body. Whether it can be so absolutely, supernaturally, miraculously, by an interference on the part of Omnipotence will be considered below. (4) A mixed mode of location would be that of a being which is circumscriptively in one place (as is Christ in heaven), and definitively (sacramentally) elsewhere (as is Christ in the consecrated Host).

II. That bilocation (multilocation) is physically impossible, that is, contrary to all the conditions of matter at present known to us, is the practically unanimous teaching of Catholic philosophers in accordance with universal experience and natural science. As to the absolute or metaphysical impossibility, that is, whether bilocation involves an intrinsic contradiction, so that by no exertion even of Omnipotence could the same body be at once in wholly different places—to this question the foregoing distinctions are pertinent. (1) Catholic philosophers maintain that there is no absolute impossibility in the same body being at once circumscriptively in one place and definitively elsewhere (mixed mode of location). The basis of this opinion is that local extension is not essential to material substance. The latter is and remains what it is wheresoever located. Local extension is consequent on a naturally universal, but still not essentially necessary, property of material substance. It is the immediate resultant of the "quantity" inherent in a body's material composition and consists in a contactual relation of the body with the circumambient surfaces. Being a resultant or quasi effect of quantity it may be suspended in its actualization; at least such suspension involves no absolute impossibility and may therefore be effected by Omnipotent agency. Should, therefore, God choose to deprive a body of its extensional

relation to its place and thus, so to speak, delocalize the material substance, the latter would be quasi spiritualized and would thus, besides its natural circumscriptive location, be capable of receiving definitive and consequently multiple location; for in this case the obstacle to bilocation, viz., actual local extension, would have been removed. Replication does not involve multiplication of the body's substance but only the multiplication of its local relations to other bodies. The existence of its substance in one place is contradicted only by non-existence in that same place, but says nothing *per se* about existence or non-existence elsewhere. (2) If mixed replication involves no absolute contradiction, definitive replication a fortiori does not. (3) Regarding the absolute possibility of a body being present circumscriptively in more than one place, St. Thomas, Vasquez, Silv. Maurus, and many others deny such possibility. The instances of bilocation narrated in lives of the saints can be explained, they hold, by phantasmal replications or by aerial materializations. Scotus, Bellarmine, Suarez, DeLugo, Franzelin, and many others defend the possibility of circumscriptive replication. Their arguments as well as the various subtle questions and difficulties pertinent to the whole subject will be found in works cited below.

BALMES, *Fundamental Philosophy* (New York, 1864); DALGAIRNS, *The Holy Communion* (London, 1868); FABER, *The Bl. Sacrament* (Baltimore, 1855); GUTBERLET, *Die Metaphysik* (Münster, 1880); NYS, *Cosmologie* (Louvain, 1906); LA FARGE, *L'idée de continu* (Paris, 1894); PESCH, *Philosophia Nat.* (Freiburg, 1897); URRABURU, *Cosmologia* (Valladolid, 1892).

F. P. SIEGFRIED.

Bination, the offering up of the Holy Sacrifice of the Mass twice on the same day by the same celebrant.

It is believed by some (Magani, L'Antica Liturgia Romana, Pt. I, p. 296, Pt. II, p. 187) that even from Apostolic times private Masses were celebrated whenever convenient. Be this as it may, it is certain that in the first years of Christianity public Masses were offered on Sundays only; later, on Wednesdays and Fridays also (Tertullian, De Oratione, xiv). To these three days Saturday was added, especially in the East (St. Basil, Ep., cclxxxix). St. Augustine, who died in 430, assures us (Ep. liv.) that while, in his time, Mass was celebrated only on Sundays in some places, in others on Saturdays and Sundays, it was nevertheless in many places customary to have the Holy Sacrifice daily (St. August., Sermo lviii, De Orat. Domin.), as in Africa (St. August., op. cit.), in Spain (Council of Toledo, year 400), in Northern Italy (St. Ambrose, Sermo xxv), in Constantinople (St. John Chrysos. in Ep. ad Ephesios), as well as elsewhere. The daily Mass became universal about the close of the sixth century. Nay more, it was not long before priests began to celebrate the Holy Sacrifice two, three, or more times daily, according to their own desire, till the sacred canons (Gratian, De Consecr., dist. i, can. liii) put a limit to their devotion in this regard, and Alexander II (d. 1073) decreed that a priest should be content with saying Mass once a day, unless it should be necessary to offer a second—never more—for the dead. Notwithstanding this legislation, the practice continued of celebrating oftener on some of the greater feasts: thus on the first of January one Mass was said of the Octave of the Nativity of Christ, another in honour of the Blessed Virgin; three Masses were said by bishops on Holy Thursday, in one of which sinners were reconciled to the Church, a second for the Consecration of the Oils, and a third in keeping with the feast; two Masses were said on the Vigil of the Ascension, as well as on the feast itself; three Masses were celebrated on Easter, and three also on the Nativity of St. John Baptist. On the feast of Sts. Peter and Paul the pope said one Mass in the basilica of St. Peter and a second in that of St. Paul. Finally, abolishing all these customs, Pope Innocent III (d. 1216) prescribed that a simple priest should say but one Mass daily, except on Christmas, when he might offer the Holy Sacrifice three times; while Honorius III (d. 1227) extended this legislation to all dignitaries. This then is the discipline of both the Eastern and Western Church, from which no one may recede without grave sin.

It must be noted, nevertheless, that the Church has found it advisable under certain conditions to modify her discipline in this regard. Thus moral theology permits a priest to say two Masses on Sundays and Holy Days of obligation, in case of necessity, when, namely, a number of the faithful would otherwise be deprived of the opportunity of hearing Mass. This would be verified, for example, were a priest in charge of two parishes or missions with no other celebrant available, or were the church too small to accommodate at one time all the parishioners (See Bull, "Declarasti", of Benedict XIV, Bullarium IV, 32 sqq., 16 March, 1746; Leo XIII, Litt. Apost. "Trans Oceanum", 18 April, 1897). The ordinary of the diocese, however, is to judge, in these and similar cases, of the necessity of binating. For similar causes, the gravity of which is not quite so apparent, Rome grants to priests of missionary countries the privilege of saying two Masses (three in Mexico, according to an indult of Pope Leo XIII, Acta S. Sedis, XIII, 340, XXIX, 96) on Sundays and Holy Days of obligation, under conditions practically the same as stated above (See Bull "Apostolicum ministerium", of Benedict XIV, for the Anglican Missions, 30 May, 1753, Bullarium, X, 197 sqq.; Conc. Plen. Balt. III, Tit. iii, cap. i; Acta et Decreta Conc. Plen. Americæ Latinæ, no. 348 sqq.; Putzer, "Commentarium in Facultates Apost.", no. 159 sqq.). As regards permission to binate, theologians are agreed that it should not be given unless about thirty persons would otherwise be put to notable inconvenience to avoid missing Mass. In certain extraordinary cases this number is reduced to twenty, while, if there is question of those detained in prison or bound by the laws of the papal cloister, from ten to fifteen inmates will suffice to permit bination. It must be borne in mind that even in such cases a priest is permitted to say a second (never a third) Mass only in case another celebrant may not be had; that a stipend may not be accepted for the second Mass; that the ablutions are not to be taken at the first Mass, as this would break the fast prescribed. A celebrant who is to say two Masses in the same church uses the same chalice for both, not purifying it at the first Mass. If the second Mass is to be said in a different church, the celebrant immediately after the last Gospel of the first Mass returns to the centre of the altar, consumes whatever drops of the Precious Blood may still remain in the chalice, and then purifies the chalice with water only. This water, which is poured from the chalice into a glass on the altar, is consumed together with the second ablution of a subsequent Mass, or emptied into the sacrarium. It might even be given to a lay person who is in the state of grace and fasting, as is done with the water in which the priest's fingers are cleansed, when Holy Communion is given to the sick. The chalice thus purified at the end of the first Mass may be used for the second Mass or not, as the celebrant may see fit.

Pope Benedict XIV (d. 1758) conceded to all priests, secular and regular, of the kingdoms of Spain and Portugal the privilege of saying three Masses on All Souls' Day (2 November). This privilege still holds for all places which belonged to one or other of these kingdoms at the time when it was granted. The ordinary stipend is allowed for one only of these Masses; while the other two must be offered for all the souls of purgatory.

HERGENRÖTHER in *Kirchenlex.*, s. v. *Bination*; BAMBERGER, *Pastoralblatt*, 1878, N. 46–48; NEHER, *Die Bination* (RATISBON, 1874); *Instructio S. C. de Propag. Fide*, 24, May 1870.
ANDREW B. MEEHAN.

Biner, JOSEPH, canonist, historian, and theologian, b. at Gluringen, Switzerland, 1697; d. at Rottenburg, Germany, 24 March, 1766. His fame rests principally on a truly amazing erudition. He entered the Society of Jesus in 1715, received the usual training of its members and was later professor of canon law in the universities of Ingolstadt, Dilingen, and Innsbruck. He entered zealously into all the controversies with the sectaries of his time, especially with the Swiss heretics. As a consequence, all his works have a polemical tinge.

In 1739 appeared his "Catholische Anmerkung über die neueste uncatholische Controvers-Schreiber", directed against certain opponents in Zurich. This was followed in 1744 by "Indifferentismus", a treatise on religious indifference and liberalism in dogmatic teaching. Biner published "Heiligkeit der Kirche" in 1750, discussing the marks of the true Church and giving sketches of eminent Catholics. The best of his polemical works, one of enduring merit, is "De Summâ Trinitate, Fide Catholicâ et Hierarchiâ Ecclesiasticâ". It appeared in 1765 and shows him at his best as a theologian and canonist. His last controversial treatise, which appeared the same year and was published like all the others at Vienna, is entitled: "Kurzer Begriff der heutigen Glaubenstreitigkeiten". It is an examination and refutation of various Protestant confessions of faith.

Biner's chief work of a purely canonical character is "Dissertationes juridicæ de beneficiis ecclesiasticis" (Innsbruck, 1746). His masterpiece is the "Apparatus eruditionis ad jurisprudentiam ecclesiasticum". The work, despite its title, is not restricted to canon law, but is also historical, polemical, and theological. It was published at Vienna, 1754–66 in eight quarto volumes. It is a work of vast erudition and a veritable storehouse of history and canon law. Dividing his material by centuries, Biner treats of the various species of law, of the history of the church councils, of the political and religious vicissitudes of the various nations, of treaties and concordats, etc. Interspersed in the work are many valuable excursuses on Jansenism, Probabilism, Public Penance, Origin of Imperial Electors, etc. It is to be regretted, however, that a work displaying such stupendous industry and erudition should be rendered less valuable for students by an unscientific arrangement of material and the want of an index. The vastness of the knowledge which Biner displays, however, has received its meed of praise even from his opponents. He wrote many other works besides those mentioned in the text, which may be found in De Backer and Sommervogel.

HURTER, *Nomenclator* (Innsbruck, 1895), III; DE BACKER, *Bibl. des Ecrivains, S. J.* (Liège, 1853); SOMMERVOGEL, *Bibl. de la c. de J.* (Brussels, 1890).
WILLIAM H. W. FANNING.

Binet, ETIENNE, Jesuit author, b. at Dijon, France, 1569; d. at Paris, 1639. He entered the Society of Jesus in 1590 and was rector of the colleges at Rouen and Paris, and provincial of Paris, Lyons, and Champagne. He was the author of forty-five published works, the first of which, on devotion to the Blessed Virgin, passed through eleven editions. His "Flowers from the Psalms" (Rouen, 1615) was translated into Italian and Latin; "Consolation and Joy for the Sick and the Afflicted" (Rouen, 1616) was republished fourteen times in eight years; an "Essay on Nature's Wonders" (Rouen, 1621) was one of the most popular scientific works of the century; it passed through twenty-four editions before 1658. Father Binet published a "Life of St. Ignatius" and a "Life of St. Francis Xavier", in 1622, when these saints were canonized. His "Vies des SS. Elzéar et Dauphine" was translated into English (London, 1638); "Vie de Ste. Aldegonde" was published in English at Paris (1632); "Purgatory Surveyed," a translation by Father Ashby (London, 1663), was brought out again by Father Anderdon (London, 1874); "The Rich Man Saved by the Golden Gate of Heaven; Motives and Power of Almsgiving" (Paris, 1627) is dedicated to his mother, who was still living at the age of eighty-five (Latin, Italian, and German translations of this work were published); "Mary, God's Masterpiece" (Paris, 1634) had six editions. Two years later, he published a work which was received with the greatest enthusiasm: "How Should Religious Superiors Govern?" Twelve editions of this were published in French, three in Latin, three in Italian, and one in German. "Divine Favours Granted to St. Joseph" (Paris, 1639) was translated into English (London, 1890). Father Binet's works are marked by a clear, graceful style and quite an original turn of thought; they abound in apt quotations from Scripture and the Fathers; although written 250 years ago they still furnish both pleasant and profitable spiritual reading. Father Binet was the school-fellow and life-long friend of St. Francis de Sales, whose cheerful spirituality his own so much resembles.

SOUTHWELL, *Bibl.*; PAPILLON, *Bibl. des auteurs de Bourgogne;* SOMMERVOGEL, *Bibl.*, I, 1487-1506; BUTENSCHOEN in *Archiv. litt. de l'Europe,* III, 315-325; HAMY, *Notice biographique,* prefixed to his edition of FATHER BINET'S *Des attraits . . . de l'amour de Jésus Christ* (Paris, 1900).

PATRICK H. KELLY.

Binet, JACQUES-PHILIPPE-MARIE, French mathematician and astronomer, b. at Rennes, in Brittany, 2 February, 1786; d. in Paris, 12 May, 1856. After two years of study at the Ecole Polytechnique, he was appointed, in 1806, student-engineer in the government department of bridges and roads. Teaching, however, soon attracted him. For some time, he was professor of mathematics at the Lycée Napoléon. He then became, at the Ecole Polytechnique, successively, *répétiteur* of descriptive geometry, examiner, professor of mechanics, and *inspecteur-général* of studies. In 1823, he succeeded Delambre in the chair of astronomy at the Collège de France. Because of his intense devotion to the cause of Charles X, the Government of July, 1830, removed him from the Ecole Polytechnique, although it allowed him to retain his professorship at the Collège de France. He had been made a member of the Société Philomathique, in 1812. In 1843, he was elected to succeed Lacroix in the Académie des Sciences, of which he was a most active member and had become president at the time of his death. Binet was a man of modest manner and a devout Catholic.

To mathematics, mechanics, and astronomy, Binet contributed many valuable articles on a great variety of topics. These articles were published in the "Bulletins de la Société philomathique", in the "Comptes rendus de l'Académie des sciences", in the "Journal des Mathématiques" (Liouville) and, chiefly, in the "Journal de l'Ecole polytechnique." He also rewrote, to a large extent, the second volume of the "Mécanique analytique" of Lagrange for the edition of 1816. A few of his principal articles are: "Mémoire sur la théorie des axes conjugués et des moments d'inertie des corps", enunciating the principle sometimes called Binet's Theorem (Journ. de l'Ec. pol., IX, 1813; "Mémoire sur la détermination analytique d'une sphère tangente à quatre autres sphères" (ibid., X, 1815); "Mémoire sur la détermination des orbites des planètes et des comètes" (ibid., XIII, 1831); "Mémoire sur les intégrales définies eulériennes et sur leur application à la théorie des suites ainsi qu'à l'évaluation des fonctions des grands nombres" (ibid., XVI, 1839; Paris, 1840); "Mémoire sur les inégalités séculaires du mouvement des planètes"

(Journal de Math., V, 1840); "Mémoire sur la formation d'une classe très étendue d'équations réciproques renfermant un nombre quelconque de variables" (Paris, 1843).

Comptes rendus de l'Académie de sciences; Journal de l'Ecole polytechnique.

PAUL H. LINEHAN.

Binius, SEVERIN, historian and critic, b. in 1573 in the village of Randerath, Western Germany; d. 14 February, 1641. He made his studies at the gymnasium of St. Lawrence, in Cologne, and later taught in the same school for several years. After his ordination to the priesthood he obtained the degree of Doctor of Divinity from the University of Cologne, where he taught general ecclesiastical history and ecclesiastical discipline, eventually becoming (1627-30) Rector Magnificus of the university. Binius was successively canon in two chapter-churches of Cologne and finally in the cathedral. In 1631 he was made counsellor and vicar-general of the archdiocese, a promotion due to his learning and one which was amply justified by his ability in managing the affairs of the archdiocese. Besides his many ordinary occupations he was active in the ecclesiastical ministry; he was also very charitable towards the poor, especially to needy students.

The reputation of Binius is owing chiefly to his edition of the Councils of the Church. The previous collections by Jacques Merlin, Peter Crabbe, and Lorenzo Surius appeared incomplete to him, lacking as they did explanatory notes. With the help of other scholars he prepared a new edition of the councils in four volumes (Cologne, 1606) under the title "Concilia generalia et provincialia". It gives only the Latin text, and contains the acts of the councils, the decretal letters, and the lives of the popes. Binius added copious explanatory notes, drawn largely from the "Ecclesiastical Annals" of Baronius. A second edition, considerably enlarged and containing also the Greek text, appeared at Cologne in 1618. In 1639 a third edition in nine volumes appeared at Paris, in preparation for which extensive use was made of the collection of councils published at Rome from 1608 to 1612. Binius also prepared an edition of the ecclesiastical histories of Eusebius, Socrates, Theodoret, Sozomen, and Evagrius.

KESSEL in *Kirchenlex.* (Freiburg, 1887) II; HURTER, *Nomenclator* (Innsbruck, 1892), I; HEFELE, *Conciliengesch.* (Freiburg, 1873), I; HARTZHEIM, *Bibl. Colon.* (Freiburg, 1747), 295.

FRANCIS J. SCHAEFER.

Binterim, ANTON JOSEPH, b. at Düsseldorf, 19 September, 1779; d. at Bilk, 17 May, 1855; a theologian of repute and for fifty years parish-priest of Bilk. He attended the Jesuit school in his native town, and then entered the Franciscan Order at Düsseldorf, 8 May, 1796. After his studies at Düren and Aachen (Aix-la-Chapelle), he was ordained priest at Cologne, 19 September, 1802. On the suppression (1803) of the Franciscan monastery to which he was attached, he was forced to retire from the religious life; after the usual examinations, he was appointed pastor of Bilk, 21 June, 1805, and administered the parish until his death. Father Binterim was the author of numerous theological treatises in defence of the Church against the attacks of the rationalists of the day, drawing his material from ancient ecclesiastical and literary sources. His many successes in controversy gained him numerous enemies and particularly the hatred of the partisans of Hermes who accused him of unlawful intrigue with Rome, evil transactions with the Jesuits, and treasonable practices against the Government. At one period, he suffered imprisonment for six months in the citadel of Wesel. Father Binterim wrote indefatigably against the existing evil of mixed marriages and the Prussian legislation of 17 August, 1825, on such marriages, depriving the mother of all rights in the education of her child; he advised the formation of societies to protest against such abuses, and urged on pastors the duty of warning the young of the evils following upon marriages with Protestants. Resisting all offers of preferment, he remained in his parish until his death. He left his large library to the people of his parish.

Binterim's writings are chiefly remarkable for their depth of research into the sources of ecclesiastical history and literature. In particular his principal work, "Die vorzüglichsten Denkwürdigkeiten der christkatholischen Kirche mit besonderer Berücksichtigung der Disciplin derselben in Deutschland, frei bearbeitet nach der Schrift des Neapolitaners Pelliccia (de christianâ ecclesiæ primæ mediæ et novissimæ ætatis politiâ)" (7 vols., 17 parts, Mainz, 1825–41), is illustrative of many points of Christian Archæology. In addition to this mention may be made of: "Pragmatische Geschichte der deutschen Concilien" (7 vols., Mainz, 1835–49); and "Die alte und neue Erzdiöcese Köln" (Mainz, 1828–30), a treatise on the geography, statistics, and history of the Archdiocese of Cologne. He also wrote a large number of smaller works on theological, historical, controversial, and apologetic subjects, such as matrimonial questions; the use of Latin in the church ritual; the discussion as to whether St. Peter was ever in Rome, or was Bishop of Rome; the *Monita Secreta* of the Jesuits (Düsseldorf, 1853), an old myth revamped in Northern Germany; the sale of Hosts in Germany and France (2d ed., Düsseldorf, 1852).

KESSEL in *Kirchenlex.*, II, 848.

WILLIAM DEVLIN.

Biogenesis and Abiogenesis.—According to their Greek derivation these two terms refer to the origin of life. Biogenesis is the theory that life originates only from pre-existing life; whilst the theory of abiogenesis implies that life may also spring from inorganic matter as such.

Some philosophers maintain that life existed prior to inorganic matter. Thus Fechner considers the stars and the universe as conscious organic beings of a higher order, which in the course of time differentiated themselves to organisms of an inferior kind. W. Preyer imagines the present world of organisms as a last remnant of gigantic primeval organisms, whose breath, perchance, was luminous iron-vapour, whose blood was liquid metal, and whose food meteorites—a fantastic conception which offers no solution of the problem. Others, again, as Liebig, Helmholtz, W. Thompson, E. Dubois-Reymond, assume the transference of small living germs from other cosmic globes to our cooling earth by means of meteorites—an evasion of the question at issue, with the additional difficulties arising from the nature of meteorites. Lastly, others admit that life must have originated somewhere and at some time, since our earth and all the celestial spheres were once in a state of fusion, incapable of sustaining living germs. But here opinions diverge. Those who deny a special directive principle assert that matter and energy as such are sufficient to account for the origin of life. Vitalists, on the other hand, maintain that life is generated from living beings only; its origin must ultimately be sought in a creative act of God, who endowed matter with a force *sui generis* that directed the material energies towards the formation and development of the first organisms. Hence the distinction between abiogenesis and biogenesis. Let us examine which view harmonizes best with the facts actually observed.

A most careful and universal research has proved beyond prudent doubt that all visible organisms arise only from germs of the same kind and never from inorganic matter. *Omne vivum ex vivo.* However the conditions of the experiment be varied, provided the receptacles and materials are free from living germs, results always verify Pasteur's well-known aphorism: *La génération spontanée est une chimère.* The attempts of J. B. Burke to produce small living cells from inorganic matter by means of radium were unsuccessful; the radiobes produced were merely bursting gas bubbles of microscopic size. Similarly, Pflüger's cyanic acid, which he compared to half-living molecules, is but a dead chemical compound. The formation of cells by a process of crystallization, as was assumed by the founders of the cell-theory has likewise proved unfounded. In short, Virchow's statement, *Omnis cellula ex cellulâ*, has become an axiom of biology. Now, it is a principle universally acknowledged that the laws derived from present observations of nature are applicable also to past phenomena. How, then, can the defenders of abiogenesis uphold their theory in the face of contrary facts?—Two explanations are offered. Many authors, such as Halliburton, Verworn, Rosenthal, assume that the conditions of the earth during earlier periods were perhaps more favourable for the origin of life than those which come under our experience. Others call the spontaneous origin of life from inorganic matter a logical necessity, and add as explanation that the cell must consist of more primitive units of life, which will ever remain invisible, and whose spontaneous origin from matter is thus withdrawn from observation. These units of life have received various names; Weismann, for instance, calls them "biophorids".

But these assumptions are arbitrary. Scientific research has established the cell as the simplest and lowest unit of visible independent life. No living organism has as yet been discovered that did not contain at least two essential elements of great complexity: a granule of chromatin and some amount of cytoplasmic substance. Deprived of these constituents no cell continues to live. Hence, if life ever originated from inorganic matter, it had to appear in the form of an organized cell. Invisible biophorids are no more capable of life than the visible chromatin granules, whose parts they are supposed to be. Even if such entities as biophorids could live independently, they could not have originated spontaneously; for however primitive an organism be imagined, it must at least be capable of nourishing itself, of propagating its kind, and of evolving into higher specific forms. But such a diversity of function supposes a differentiation of structure, made up of different chemical compounds of high tension and continuously unstable equilibrium. Besides, there must be in the most primitive biophorids a perfect correlation of parts and a purposeful anticipation of future ends, tending towards the gradual perfection of individual and species. But crystals, as well as all chemical combinations and physical mixtures, show clearly that inorganic matter as such tends toward stability of equilibrium and homogeneity of structure. How, then, did those complicated chemical compounds of unstable equilibrium which composed the first organisms originate, especially since, at the beginning, the crust of the earth, totally burnt, was in the desolate condition of perfect oxidation? Besides, it is hard to see how the energy of the sun could serve to reduce the ashes, since to-day that action depends on the presence of chlorophyll and similar substances, which again are products of cells. Even if some form of energy would all at once commence continually to unite the atoms to such unstable and complicated bodies as the phosphoric proteids, there is still wanting a directive to build up, by means of existing matter and energy, the chemical compounds into correlated structures, and to make them active organisms.

Matter, then, can never, not even under the most favourable circumstances, produce either living cells or living biophorids, and hence we conclude that life owes its origin to God, the Creator of matter and energy.

Von Hartmann, *Das Problem des Lebens* (Bad Sachsa, 1906), 178; Tyndall, *Fragments of Science;* Bastian, *Nature and Origin of Living Matter* (London); Wasmann, *Die Moderne Biologie und die Entwicklungstheorie* (Freiburg, 1906), 182; Rosenthal, *Allgemeine Physiologie* (Leipzig, 1901), 552; Weismann, *Vorträge über die Descendenztheorie* (Jena, 1904), II, 305; Muckermann in *The Messenger* (New York, April, 1906).

H. Muckermann.

Biology (from βίος, life, and λόγος, reason, account, reasoning) may be defined as the science on life and living organisms. It is essentially a science of observation and experiment and comprises the study of the structure, origin, development, functions, and relation to environment of plants and animals, discussing at the same time the causes of these phenomena. Biology is obviously divided into zoology (ζῷον, "animal") and botany (βοτάνη, "herb"), according as the organism is either an animal or a plant. The biology of man is called anthropology (ἄνθρωπος, "man") which, as far as it concerns man's body, is a subdivision of zoology. The science of insects is called entomology (ἔντομον, "insect"). Biology is not a science of yesterday, but is as old as the human race. Its main development, however, took place during the last centuries. As a result of this development a great number of daughter-sciences have sprung into existence, each commanding its own more or less distinct field of research, and all united again to approach more and more the nature of life and to give us a clearer and more comprehensive idea of the variety and causes of vital phenomena.

An organism, be it plant or animal, may be considered under a threefold aspect: either in its *structure,* or in its *functions,* or in its *development.* And the science of biology is divided, correspondingly.

I. Branches and Subdivisions.—The science which describes the *structure* of organisms is called *morphology* (μορφή, "shape"). This may be either external or internal, and either simply descriptive or comparative. But in every case morphology concerns itself only with structure, in so far as this is a definite arrangement of matter.

External morphology treats of the size and shape of external parts and organs. Its chief purposes are, first, the identification of plants and animals according to certain systems of classification and, secondly, to facilitate the study of the functions of the various organs which it describes. It is practically the same as systematic biology, which treats of the kingdoms, classes, orders, families, genera, species, and varieties of organisms.

Internal morphology studies the interior structure of organisms and their parts; that is, organs, tissues, and cells. Accordingly it is subdivided into *anatomy* (ἀνατέμνω, "cut up"), dealing with the gross structure of organisms, *histology* (ἱστός, "web"), with the minute structure of the tissues, and *cytology* (κύτος, "cell"), with that of the cells, which are the ultimate structural and functional units of life.

Secondly, there are two sciences which refer to the *functions,* or activities, of organisms, according as these are performed by the single parts of the organism or by the organism as a whole. The latter science is called *bionomics;* the former *physiology.* Both physiology and bionomics not only describe and compare, but also inquire into the proximate causes of the various activities, and are thus intimately related to physics and chemistry, and at the same time are of paramount importance for the philosophy of life and of plant and animal activity. *Bionomics*

(sometimes called *œcology*) observes how an organism acts with regard to its environment; that is, it describes the mode of nutrition, dwelling-place (οἶκος), propagation, care of offspring, peculiar relation to certain classes of other organisms (symbiosis), geographical and geological distribution, and so forth. *Physiology* explains in detail how the single organs, tissues, and cells discharge their manifold functions, how a muscle contracts, how a gland pours out its secretion, and whether such functions are due to physical and chemical forces, whether and how far they are subject to a special directive.

Thirdly, the several biological sciences which describe the *development* of organisms are comprised under the general name of *morphogeny* (μορφή and γενεά, "origin"), or *biogeny.* The two branches of morphogeny are *ontogeny* (ὀντ—, participial stem, "being") and *phylogeny* (φῦλον, "race", "stock"). The former traces the gradual development of a single individual from the egg to the perfect being; the latter, that of the so-called "systematic species" from its ultimate ancestor, from which it is supposed to have been derived by evolution. *Embryology* is a special branch of ontogeny, and describes the gradual differentiation of the fertilized ovum until it has attained the structure peculiar to the particular organism.

Supplementary to the biological sciences above enumerated is the science of *palæontology,* which describes the fossil forms of plants and animals buried and petrified in the strata of the earth. The sciences of pathology, teratology, and numerous others, which pertain rather to medicine, cannot be considered here.

II. The Historical Development of the biological sciences may aptly be divided into four great periods: the first centring around Aristotle, Galen, and Albertus Magnus; the second commencing with Vesalius; the third, with Linnæus; the last with the theory of the cell, established by Schwann.

First period.—Aristotle (384–322 b. c.) laid the foundations upon which the magnificent edifice of biology has been constructed. His works, "De historiâ animalium", "De partibus animalium", and "De generatione animalium", contain the first scientific attempt to classify animals and to explain their various biological and physiological functions. Aristotle enumerates in his works about 500 kinds of animals. He distinguished groups (γένη) from species (εἴδη), divided all animals into animals with blood (ἔναιμα) and animals without blood (ἄναιμα), and again into eight principal groups, and thus established a system of classification which is still maintained, at least in a corresponding form, in our own days. He also knew many physiological facts, and made several discoveries in bionomics which were rediscovered only in the nineteenth century. The influence of the great Stagirite upon posterity was very great, and for nearly 2,000 years most students of biology were more or less satisfied, like the younger Pliny, to study and commentate the works of Aristotle. In morphology and physiology, however, a considerable advancement was made by Claudius Galen, who was born in a. d. 131. Galen was a Greek by birth and later on a well-known physician in Rome. He was the first to define physiology as the science which explains the functions of the single parts (*usus partium*) of an organism.

Together with Aristotle's works Galen's morphological and physiological teachings reigned supreme in all the schools of the Middle Ages till the time of Vesalius. Only among the princes of Scholastic philosophy were there any who stepped out of the narrow circle of Aristotelean biology and commenced to study and interpret anew the living book of nature. We refer here mainly to the Dominican, Blessed Albertus Magnus (1193–1280) and to his pupils,

Thomas of Chatimpré and Vincent of Beauvais. Blessed Albertus wrote seven books on plants and twenty-six books on animals. Of the latter works, some are based on original research, while others contain many new and accurate observations which to-day are becoming more and more highly appreciated by scientists.

The second period began with the Belgian anatomist Andreas Vesalius, b. at Brussels, 1 January, 1515. Vesalius was the first who dared to oppose energetically the authority of Galen in certain anatomical questions and to insist that in such matters not the method of interpretation, but that of dissection and of personal observation alone could lead to truth and progress. In 1537 Vesalius was made Doctor of Medicine in the University of Padua, where, during the following five years he conducted the public dissections. At the end of this time he published an illustrated folio on the structure of the human body, "Fabrica humani corporis", which appeared at Basle in 1543. In this famous volume Vesalius corrected many errors of Galen, introduced his new method of dissection and experiment in the study of anatomy, and thus became the founder of modern anatomy. The attempt of Vesalius to overthrow traditional methods met with much encouragement, but much more opposition, apparently, for a year after the publication of his "Fabrica" he accepted the post of court physician offered to him by Charles V. In 1563 he made a pilgrimage to Jerusalem, and on his way back, in 1564, died on the island of Zante.

One of the greatest successors of Vesalius was William Harvey, b. at Folkestone, England, in 1578. Harvey studied medicine at Padua at the time when the Tuscan Fabricius ab Aquapendente (1537–1619) held the chair of anatomy and wrote his exposition of the Galenic doctrine concerning the circulation of the blood. In 1604 he joined the Royal College of Physicians in London. Later on he became physician to Charles I, and died 3 June, 1667. The importance of Harvey's work for biology consists in the demonstration of the true circulation of the blood through the arteries and veins. This demonstration, which he developed for the first time in his anatomical lectures at the Royal College in the year 1615, was published in 1628 under the title of "Exercitatio de cordis motu". Together with the discovery of the lymphatics by Aselli (1623), to which it gave rise, it constitutes the beginning of modern physiology whose existence and development is in no small degree due to the purely experimental method definitely introduced by Harvey.

Meanwhile Galileo Galilei had made his discoveries in physics, and it was not long before these discoveries began to exercise their influence upon biological studies. It was especially Giovanni Alphonso Borelli, b. at Naples, 28 January, 1608, who successfully attacked the mechanical problems suggested by muscular movement. When professor of mathematics at the University of Pisa he became acquainted with Marcello Malpighi, of Bologna, through whom he became interested in anatomical studies, and soon set about preparing a treatise on animal motion, "De motu animalium", which was the first of the great contributions to physical physiology. This influential work appeared in 1680, shortly after the death of its author. While Borelli was still at work on his "De motu", another anatomist, Nicolaus Stenson, or Steno (1638–86) developed in the same line, together with his friend Malpighi, the special physiology of glands and tissues. Steno, a convert from Lutheranism to Catholicism, was professor of anatomy in Copenhagen, his native city, and afterwards a priest and bishop in Hanover. He was one of the first to recognize the importance of the rising science of chemistry, although his attention was too much occupied with the new science of geology, which he had founded, to leave him much time for other investigations. The introduction of chemical methods in biological studies had already been accomplished by Jan Baptista van Helmont, b. at Brussels in 1577, who in his turn was greatly influenced by the fantastic pilgrim Paracelsus (Theophrastus Bombast von Hohenheim), and through him by the Benedictine monk Basil Valentine. The latter lived about the time of Johannes Gutenberg and is known as the last alchemist and the first chemist.

Van Helmont's important work, "Ortus medicinæ" appeared four years after his death, but it was the first of its kind and, like Borelli's book, exercised an important influence on future investigations. The most valuable idea of the "Ortus medicinæ" is the explanation of digestion by fermentative processes. Perhaps the most influential of van Helmont's intellectual descendants was Franz de la Boe, or Franciscus Sylvius, professor of medicine at Leyden from 1658 till his death in 1672. Sylvius was the teacher of such brilliant men as Steno and Regner de Graaf, to whom we owe several important biological discoveries. Without making any great discoveries himself he succeeded in directing the attention of physiologists, much more than van Helmont had done, to the importance of chemistry for the solution of biological problems. Thus he became the founder of the iatro-chemical school which, in opposition to the iatro-physical school of Borelli's followers, attempted to explain all vital processes by mere chemistry.

The work of Malpighi both closes this second period in the history of biology and reaches far out into modern times. Marcello Malpighi was born at Crevalcore near Bologna, in 1628, the year in which Harvey published his essay on the circulation of the blood. He did more for the general advancement of biology than any other scientist since the days of Vesalius. With the Englishman Nehemiah Grew, he laid the foundation of vegetable morphology. His work on the silkworm argues him a remarkable anatomist, and his description of the development of the hen's egg entitles him to be considered the first embryologist. But his most important work consists in the discovery of the capillaries and the airsacs in the lungs, and of the structure of glands and glandular organs. During the greater part of his splendid career Malpighi was professor of medicine at Bologna. In 1691 Pope Innocent XII called him to Rome to be the papal physician; Malpighi complied with the invitation, and died at Rome, 28 November, 1694. A great part of Malpighi's success was due to the fact that the microscope, one of the most important scientific instruments of modern times, had just been invented.

It is noteworthy that nearly all the great pioneers of biological progress during this second period were devoted Catholics. The Church never hampered these great scientists, so long as they proceeded by way of exact demonstration, and kept within their own province, but left them perfectly free in their investigations. The exceptional ecclesiastics who assumed an unfriendly attitude towards scientific enlightenment may well be excused when we consider, as a mere physiological fact, how deeply inherited conceptions take root in the individual mind, and, moreover, how easily any novel idea may be misinterpreted as conflicting with religious truth. But the most determined opponents of biological innovations were indeed not ecclesiastics at all, but professors of biology who found it hard to give up the ancient traditions of their lifelong study.

Third period.—Of Linnæus (Karl von Linné) it has been said that he found natural science a chaos and left it a cosmos. The son of a Protestant minister, he was b. 23 May, 1707, at Rashult in the south of Sweden; d. 1778. In 1741 he was made professor of medicine, and a little later of botany, in the University of Upsala, of which he was an alumnus. His main work, "Systema naturæ", was published for the first time in 1735. Its most complete edition is the 17th, which appeared ten years after the author's death. As its title indicates, the work is essentially a system of classification, comprising all the minerals, plants, and animals known in Linnæus' time, arranged according to classes, genera, and species. The value of this classification is mainly due to the precision of its new nomenclature. According to this "binomial" nomenclature each plant or animal received a generic and a specific name, as, for instance, *Felis catus* and *Felis leo*, indicating at once the systematic relation of the organism. Linnæus exercised a vast influence upon the biologists of his time and considerably furthered the collection of numerous morphological facts which served the great scientists of the following century as the foundation of their various theories.

To the Frenchman, Marie-François-Xavier Bichat (1771–1802), morphology owes its position as a logically co-ordinated science. Bichat was the first to introduce into biology the distinction between systems composed of heterogeneous organs and systems composed of homogeneous tissues. In a system of the former class all the organs serve some particular group of vital functions, as, for instance, the digestive system. The latter class of systems comprises all tissues which have an identical structure, as, for instance, the system of secretion. To the scientific principle established by Bichat two others were soon added which are of still greater importance in morphology. These are the laws of correlation and of homology of organs. According to the law of correlation there is a certain interdependence of all the organs of an animal, so that from the peculiar structure of one organ we may conclude as to the structure of most other organs. The law of the homology of organs maintains that all organs constructed according to the same pattern must have similar functions. But, as the same function is not necessarily bound to the same structure (e. g., the function of breathing, which may be accomplished by gills as well as by lungs), the law was complemented by the principle of the analogy of organs.

These highly suggestive laws were chiefly established by George Dagobert Cuvier—like Linnæus, a devout Protestant—who was b. in 1769 at Mömpelgardt, Würtemberg, and died, a peer of France, in 1832. His chief works were written when he was professor of comparative anatomy at the Jardin des Plantes in Paris. In Cuvier's mind originated the celebrated theory of types, which was established in the year 1812. Taking the principle for the new division of the animal kingdom from the peculiar organization of the animal, Cuvier comprises the classes of mammals, birds, and reptiles under the name of *vertebrates*, which had shortly before been introduced by Lamarck. The other classes of animals were divided into three provinces (*embranchements*), the molluscs, the articulates, and the radiates. As the doctrine of the constancy of species, Cuvier's system was opposed by Etienne-Geoffroy Saint-Hilaire (1722–1844), who emphasized the universal unity of the plan of structure pervading the animal kingdom. Cuvier also made an extensive study of the petrified organisms of prehistoric ages, and thus became the founder of the science of palæontology. Cuvier's system was further developed by C. E. von Baer (1792–1876), who discovered the mammalian ovum, and through his studies of the development of the chick laid the foundations to the science of comparative morphogeny.

During the same period of the eighteenth century the science of physiology made considerable progress through the work of Boerhaave, Stahl, and Haller. Hermann Boerhaave (1668–1738) was for a long time professor of medicine at Leyden. He was an adherent neither of the extreme chemical nor of the extreme physical school, but tried to reconcile both doctrines. His main work, "Institutiones medicæ", was published in 1708. A similar position as to the causes of physiological phenomena was assumed by George Ernest von Stahl (1660–1734), famous in the annals of chemistry for his *phlogiston* theory. Stahl's views were embraced by a pupil of Boerhaave, Albrecht von Haller (1708–77), who united in his voluminous work, "Elementa Physiologiæ corporis humani", all the theories and discoveries known to his time, and grouped them in a new manner, so that his book may be called the first modern text-book of physiology. About the time when Haller died Antoine-Laurent Lavoisier (who was guillotined by the Convention in 1794) added to the sum of physiological knowledge by solving the problem of oxidation and respiration.

Fourth period.—Meanwhile another important discovery had been made which gradually inaugurated the fourth and most splendid period of biology, the chief activities of which centre about the structure and functions of the cell, and about individual and specific evolution. During the same period immense progress has been made in bionomics, palæontology, morphology, physiology, and, indeed, all biological sciences. The fact has already been alluded to that, towards the close of the sixteenth century, a native of Holland, Zachary Janssen, had invented the microscope, which, after it had been considerably improved by Francesco Fontana, of Naples, and Cornelis van Drebbel, of Holland, was used by Malpighi, Jan Swammerdam (1627–80) of Amsterdam, the Englishmen Hooke and Grew, and by Antonius von Leeuwenhoek (1632–1723), the famous discoverer of the infusorians. Robert Hooke (1635–1702) was the first to represent in his "Micrographia" a group of cells which he had discovered with his microscope in plants; but Malpighi and Grew are generally credited with having discovered the cell. About a century later Kaspar Friedrich Wolff published his important "Theoria generationis" (1759), which clearly shows that he must have observed cells in plants as well as in animals. All this, however, was but preliminary; the new era in biology was fairly opened only when, in the years 1838 and 1839, the botanist Schleiden and, especially, the zoologist Schwann, established the first theory of the cell: that *the cell is the ultimate structural and functional unit of life.* Theodor Schwann was b. at Neuss, near Cologne, in 1810 and became professor of anatomy at Louvain in 1839, and at Liège in 1848, and died in 1882. He was a faithful Catholic throughout his life. Schwann's theory was further developed by F. Leydig (1857), by M. Schultze (1861), and by a host of such eminent scientists of the present generation, as J. Reinke, O. Hertwig, Waldeyer, Edmund B. Wilson, and many others. The name *histology* (see definitions at beginning of this article) was introduced by K. Meyer in 1819, whilst John B. Carney, who died in 1899 as a Catholic priest and professor at Louvain, is the acknowledged author and able promoter of *cytology*.

Together with cytology there came into prominence the science of ontogeny which has led many biologists of to-day back to a vitalistic conception of the phenomena of life. This science it was that suggested E. Häckel's biogenetic law, to which it also gave the deathblow. According to Häckel's theory, ontogeny is said to be a short and rapid repetition of phylogeny. The first to trace the entire development of all the tissues from the germ cells was Schwann.

The question: whether the embryo was preformed in the egg and originated by a simple evolution; or whether it had to be developed by an entirely new formation, or epigenesis; was mainly solved by the theory of epigenetic evolution established by Driesch and numerous colabourers. The science of phylogeny began when Lamarck, the founder of the modern theory of descent, controverted the immutability of species on scientific grounds.

The Chevalier de Lamarck (Jean-Baptiste-Pierre-Antoine de Monet de Lamarck) was born in 1744. At the age of forty-nine he became professor of the zoology of invertebrates in the Jardin des Plantes at Paris. His theory of evolution was fully explained for the first time in his "Philosophie zoologique" and later in his "Histoire naturelle des animaux sans vertèbres". During the last seventeen years of his life Lamarck was blind and lived in extreme poverty. The last two volumes of his "Histoire naturelle" he dictated to an affectionate daughter, who remained at her father's side till his death in 1829. During its first period of energetic development the theory of evolution, as proposed by Lamarck and, in a modified form, by Saint-Hilaire, failed to supersede the theory of the constancy of species, which was defended by such influential men as Cuvier; nor, indeed, were the facts known at that time in any way sufficient to ensure its acceptance. However, after Charles Darwin had published his "Origin of Species", in 1859, the new science progressed with the greatest rapidity, and at the present day there are but few prominent naturalists who do not contribute their share to phylogeny. At the same time it has gone through a considerable intrinsic development, mainly with respect to the rise and decline of the theory of natural selection as the chief factor in the development of species. Charles Darwin was born at Shrewsbury in 1809. He studied at the universities of Edinburgh and Cambridge, from 1831 to 1836 accompanied an English scientific expedition on board the "Beagle", and passed the rest of his life in the village of Down, Kent, where he produced the numerous works which had such an incalculable influence on his age. Among Darwin's fellow-workers Alfred Russel Wallace (b. 1822) occupies the first place, since he was the co-discoverer of the principle of natural selection. Other distinguished men who took part in the development of this branch of biology were Huxley, Lyell, Nägeli, Weismann, Asa Gray. Probably the most important discoveries were those made by Hugo De Vries and by Gregor Johann Mendel, Abbot of the Augustinian Monastery at Altbrünn, where he died in 1884. Mendel's laws of heredity, based as they are on a splendid array of facts, will be of especial influence upon future theories of heredity and development.

Together with phylogeny the science of palæontology, founded by Cuvier, developed mainly through the influence and personal activity of such men as Joachim Barrande (1799–1883), Jean-Baptiste-Julien d'Omalius d'Halloy (1783–1875), James Dwight Dana (1813–95), Oswald Heer (1809–83), and many more. These giants in the natural sciences were at the same time faithful Christians, the first two being Catholics. Still more impressive than the progress of palæontology is that of systematic biology and bionomics, branches to which a thousand modern scientists have devoted the entire energy of their lives. The result of all this scientific activity is apparent in the immense collections preserved in the museums of Washington, London, New York, and other large cities, and in the simple fact that the systematic species scientifically described amount to no fewer than 500,000 animals and 200,000 plants. The Linnæan system of classification was perfected in many ways, especially by the botanists A. L. von Jussieu (1789), A. P. Decandelle (1813), and by the

zooligists Cuvier, C. T. E. von Siebold (1848), and R. Leuckart (1847). The greatest of modern morphologists since the time of Albrecht von Haller are Richard Owen (1870–92), the comparative anatomist, Johann Müller, the father of German medicine, and Claude Bernard, the prince of physiologists. Müller was b. 14 July, 1801, at Coblenz, and d. 28 April, 1858, as professor of anatomy and physiology in the University of Berlin. He was the teacher of such well-known men as Virchow, Emil Dubois-Reymond, Helmholtz, Schwann, Lieberkühn, M. Schultze, Remak, Reichert, all of whom have done magnificent work in various departments of biology. Müller was chiefly an experimental physiologist, and established a vast number of facts which he described with great accuracy. At the same time he defended with energy the existence of a special vital force, which directs the various physical and chemical forces for the attainment of specific structures and functions. In the present generation biologists are gradually returning to Müller's views, which for a time they had more or less completely abandoned. The great physiologist lived all his life, as he died, a faithful Catholic. The same may almost be said of his contemporary in France, Claude Bernard, b. in 1813, at St.-Julien, not far from Lyons, and d. in 1880. Bernard's main discoveries refer to the phenomena of nervous inhibition and internal glandular secretion. For a time he yielded to the materialistic philosophy of his age, but he soon abandoned it, perhaps through the influence of his friend Pasteur.

Louis Pasteur (d. 28 September, 1895), the father of preventive medicine, was probably the most gifted and influential biologist of the nineteenth century. His discoveries, which are inscribed on his tomb, in the Institut Pasteur, at Paris, extend from 1848 to 1885, and relate to the nature of fermentations, to the minutest organisms and the question of abiogenesis, to the diseases of silkworms, to the propagation of diseases by microbes, and above all to the supremely important principle of experimental immunity to pathogenic bacteria. Pasteur was a model Catholic, the most ideal scientist known in the history of biology.

Many more prominent biologists, such as Ramon y Cajál, Wundt, Brooks, Strassburger, Wasmann, have done and are still doing admirable work in the interest of biological sciences.

FOSTER, Lectures on the History of Physiology during the 16th, 17th, and 18th Centuries (Cambridge, 1901); KNELLER, Das Christentum und der Vertreter der neueren Naturwissenschaft (Freiburg, 1903); WASMANN, Die moderne Biologie und die Entwicklungstheorie (Freiburg, 1906); WALSH, Makers of Modern Medicine (New York, 1907); Catholic Churchmen in Science (Philadelphia, 1906); OSBORN, From the Greeks to Darwin (New York, 1905).

H. MUCKERMANN.

Biondo, FLAVIO, a distinguished Italian archæologist and historian, b. at Forlì in 1388; d. at Rome in 1463. He was the founder of the science of archæology and of Christian and medieval topography. He studied under Ballistario of Cremona and was remarkable for learning even in his youth. He lived for some time at Milan, where he discovered and copied the only manuscript of Cicero's dialogue "Brutus". In 1432 he became secretary to Pope Eugenius IV, who was afterwards driven out of Rome. Biondo accompanied the pope in his exile, was his secretary at Ferrara and Florence, and returned to Rome with him. Later he served in the same capacity under Popes Nicholas V, Calixtus III, and Pius II. An earnest student of antiquities and a man of wonderful erudition, he applied himself with indefatigable industry to the task of collecting materials for his historical, archæological, and topographical works. He gathered his materials from original sources. Biondo was the author of three encyclopedias, which have formed the basis of all subsequent dictionaries of Roman archæology and antiquities. His works, which were edited after his death by his sons, include: "Romæ Instauratæ Libri Tres" (1482), dedicated to Pope Eugenius IV, a valuable study of the ancient monuments of Rome, the first attempt at a topographical description of the city, giving also a complete list of the principal Christian churches and chapels, when and by whom built, etc.; "Romæ Triumphantis Libri Decem" (1482), dedicated to Pius II, a study of the institutions and customs of the ancient Romans; "Italia Illustrata" (1474), a description of Italy in fourteen regions, with an accurate list of the cities, etc. Biondo's historical researches bore fruit in a great work entitled "Historiarum ab Inclinatione Romanorum Imperii, Decades III, Libri XXXI" (Venice, 1483), covering the period from the fall of the Roman Empire to the author's own time (1440). The work was divided into decades, but Biondo's death prevented him from completing the vast undertaking after he had written three decades and the first book of the fourth.

GREGOROVIUS, *Rome in the Middle Ages*, tr. HAMILTON (London, 1900), VII, Pt. II, 603 sqq.; PASTOR, *The History of the Popes*, tr. and ed. ANTROBUS (London, 1891); MASIUS, *Flavio Biondo, sein Leben und seine Werke* (Leipzig, 1879).

EDMUND BURKE.

Biot, JEAN-BAPTISTE, physicist and mathematician, b. at Paris, France, 21 April, 1774; d. there, 3 February, 1862. He studied at first at the College of Louis-le-Grand; in 1793 he joined the artillery of the Army of the North, but soon left the service to enter the École Polytechnique. After going to Beauvais as a professor in the central school of that city, he returned to Paris, in 1800, to occupy, at the age of 26, the chair of mathematical physics in the Collège de France. He had the distinction of ultimately belonging to three of the classes of the Institute; in 1803 he was admitted to the Academy of Sciences; in 1841, to the Academy of Inscriptions and Belles-Lettres; and in 1856, to the French Academy. After beginning his career as a mathematician and astronomer, he was assigned to the section of geometry in the Academy of Sciences. Among the interesting incidents in his career may be cited his ascension in a balloon with Gay-Lussac in 1804. They rose to a height of 13,000 feet for the purpose of studying the magnetic, electrical, and chemical condition of the atmosphere at various elevations.

Biot was actively engaged in the various branches of the geodetic work involved in the famous measurement of the quadrant of a meridian, for the purpose of standardizing the length of the new unit, the meter. As a member of the Bureau of Longitudes he went, in 1806, with young Arago, to Formentera, in the Balearic Islands, to resume the measurement of a degree of the meridian, interrupted by the death of Mechian. In 1808 he determined, with Mathieu, the length of the seconds pendulum at Bordeaux and Dunkirk. In 1817 he went to Scotland and the Shetland Islands to verify the geodetic operations of the English under Colonel Mudge. In 1824 he returned to Italy, Sicily, and Spain, in order to correct some of the observations of the year 1808. He contributed more than 250 memoirs to various societies and periodicals. This enormous work covers the entire field of experimental and mathematical physics, as well as ancient and modern astronomy. He was the champion of the corpuscular theory of light which he extended to some most ingenious explanations of the very complex phenomena of polarization. Biot discovered the laws of rotary polarization by crystalline bodies and applied these laws to the analysis of saccharine solutions. His fame rests chiefly on his work in polarization and double refraction of light.

Regular habits of study and recreation kept him in good health and led to a ripe old age. His mental attitude may be indicated by his opposition to the open meetings of the Academy; he feared the influence of the vulgar public upon the scientific tone of the Institute. Since he was brought up in the turbulent times of the Revolution, it is not surprising to find him among the insurgents, in 1795, attempting to overthrow the Convention. Again, in 1804, he succeeded at first in prevailing on the Institute not to vote for Bonaparte's elevation to the throne. He protested against the introduction of purely political matters into the deliberations of a scientific body. His religious views became more pronounced towards the end of his life. He is said to have received the Sacrament of Confirmation at the hands of his own grandson.

The more elaborate works of Biot are: "Traité de géometrie analytique", 1802 (8th ed., 1834); "Traité de physique expérimentale et mathématique", 4 vols., 1816; "Précis de physique", 2 vols., 1817; "Traité d'astronomie physique", 6 vols. with atlas, 1850; "Mélanges scientifiques et littéraires", 3 vols., 1858. The last is a compilation of a great many of his critiques, biographies, and accounts of voyages.

Proc., Am. Ass'n of Arts and Sciences, 1862, VI; SAINTE-BEUVE, *Nouveaux Lundis* (Paris, 1879), II.

WILLIAM FOX.

Birds (IN SYMBOLISM).—Many kinds of birds are used in Christian symbolism. The first to be so employed was the *Dove ;* it stood for the Third Person of the Blessed Trinity, for when Jesus was baptized the Holy Ghost descended in bodily shape as a dove upon Him (Luke, iii, 22). It was also used as a symbol of peace, because a dove brought to Noe a bough of an olive-tree as a sign that the deluge of wrath was at an end. In early Christian art the Apostles and the faithful were generally represented as doves, the first because they were the instruments of the Holy Ghost, carrying peace to the world; the second because in their baptism they received the gift of reconciliation, entering with the dove (the Holy Ghost) into the Ark of God, the Church. Sometimes in symbolical writing it stands for rest: Who will give me wings like a dove, and I will be at rest?—(Ps., liv, 7); often for simplicity, innocence, and love: Be ye therefore wise as serpents and simple as doves (Matt., x, 16); Open to me, my sister, my love, my dove, my undefiled; One is my dove, my perfect one. (Cant., v, 2; vi, 8.) The *Eagle* is a symbol of Christ and His Divine nature, of regeneration by baptism; it is also an emblem of St. John the Evangelist. As the eagle can gaze upon the shining orb of the sun with steadfast eyes, so can Christ gaze undazzled upon the refulgent glory of God the Father. Dante refers to the strong eye of the eagle (Parad., i, 47, 48):—

I saw Beatrice turn'd, and on the sun
Gazing, as never eagle fix'd his ken.

—It was a popular delusion among the ancients that the eagle could renew its youth by plunging three times into a spring of pure water, a belief alluded to by David: Thy youth shall be renewed like the eagle's (Ps., cii, 5), hence the primitive Christians, and later the medieval symbolizers, used the eagle as a sign of baptism, the well-spring of salvation, in whose water the neophyte was dipped three times, in the name of the Father, the Son, and the Holy Ghost, in order to wash from his soul the old man of sin and put on the youth of a child of light. This bird was used as the emblem of St. John, because in his Gospel St. John dwells particularly upon the Divinity of the Redeemer and contemplates with the unflinching eye of an eagle the highest truths.

The *Pelican* is a symbol of the atonement and the Redeemer. It was supposed to wound itself in order to feed its young with its blood and to bring to life those who were dead—the "pelicane who stricketh

blood out of its owne bodye to do others good"
(Lyly, Euphues). Allusion is made to this belief in
"Hamlet" (act iv):—

> To his good friend thus wide I'll ope my arms
> And, like the kind, life-rendering pelican,
> Repast them with my blood.

Therefore it was deemed a fitting symbol of the Saviour, the *nostro pelicano* of Dante, Who shed His
blood in order to give eternal life to the children of
men. Skelton in his "Armorie of Birds" says:—

> Then sayd the Pellycan:
> When my Byrdts be slayne
> With my bloude I them revyve.
> Scripture doth record
> The same dyd our Lord
> And rose from deth to lyve.

The *Phœnix* is a symbol of the Resurrection and of
eternity. According to legend this mythical bird
could never die; on attaining its five-hundredth year
it committed itself to the flames of a funeral pyre,
only to rise reborn from its own ashes. Dante used
it as a symbol of the souls of the damned (Inf.,
xxiv, 197–208).

The *Peacock* in Byzantine and early Romanesque
art was used to signify the Resurrection, because its
flesh was thought to be incorruptible. (St. Augustine, City of God, xxi, c, iv.) It was also a symbol
of pride. The *Raven* is a symbol of the Jews, of
confession and penance. The *Cock* is a symbol of
vigilance, and also an emblem of St. Peter. The
Vulture has always typified greed. Many other birds
were used during the Middle Ages for symbolic and
ecclesiological purposes; while the preachers of these
centuries developed the symbolism of each one of
these emblems to a degree that now seems far-fetched
and often obscure, nevertheless, they made it clear
that religious instruction can be gained from birds
and even from the common things of life.

LAUCHERT, *Geschichte des Physiologus* (Strasburg, 1889);
CAHIER, *Mélanges d'archéol.* (Paris, 1847–56); NEAL AND
WEBB, *The Symbolism of Churches and Church Ornaments*
(New York, 1896); DIDRON, *Christian Iconography* (London,
1851); EVANS, *Animal Symbolism in Ecclesiastical Architecture*
(London, 1896); VIOLLET-LE-DUC, *Dictionnaire raisonné de
l'architecture française du XIe au XVIe siècle* (Paris, 1853).

CARYL COLEMAN.

Biretta, a square cap with three ridges or peaks
on its upper surface, now commonly worn by clerics
of all grades from cardinals downwards. The use
of such a cap is prescribed by the rubrics both at
solemn Mass and in other ecclesiastical functions.
Etymologically, the word *biretta* is Italian in origin
and would more correctly be written *beretta* (cf. however the French *barette* and the Spanish *bireta*). It
probably comes from *birrus*, a rough cloak with a
hood, from the Greek πυρρός, flame-coloured, and
the *birretum* may originally have meant the hood.
We hear of the birettum in the tenth century, but,
like most other questions of costume, the history is
extremely perplexed. The wearing of any head-
covering, other than hood or cowl, on state occasions
within doors seems to have originally been a distinction reserved for the privileged few. The constitutions of Cardinal Ottoboni issued by him for
England in 1268 forbid the wearing of caps vulgarly
called "coyphæ" (cf. the coif of the serjeant-at-law)
to clerics, except when on journeys. In church and
when in the presence of their superiors their heads
are to remain uncovered. From this law the higher
graduates of the universities were excepted, thus
Giovanni d'Andrea, in his gloss on the Clementine
Decretals, declares (c. 1320) that at Bologna the
insignia of the Doctorate were the *cathedra* (chair)
and the birettum.

At first the birettum was a kind of skull cap with a
small tuft, but it developed into a soft round cap
easily indented by the fingers in putting it on and
off, and it acquired in this way the rudimentary
outline of its present three peaks. We may find
such a cap delineated in many drawings of the fifteenth century, one of which, representing university
dignitaries at the Council of Constance, who are
described in the accompanying text as *birrectati*, is
here reproduced.

MONUMENT REPRESENTING DOCTOR
OF LAWS WEARING BIRETTA, A.D.
1352

The same kind
of cap is worn by
the cardinals sit-
ting in conclave
and depicted in
the same contem-
porary series of
drawings, as also
by preachers ad-
dressing the as-
sembly. The
privilege of wear-
ing some such
head-dress was
extended in the
course of the six-
teenth century
to the lower
grades of the cler-
gy, and after a
while the chief
distinction be-
came one of col-
our, the cardinals
always wearing
red birettas, and
bishops violet.
The shape dur-
ing the sixteenth
and seventeenth centuries was everywhere considerably modified, and, though the question is
very complicated, there seems no good reason
to reject the identification, proposed by several
modern writers, of the old doctor's birettum with
the square college cap, popularly known as the
"mortar-board", of the modern English universities.

The college cap
and ecclesiasti-
cal biretta have
probably devel-
oped from the
same original,
but along dif-
ferent lines.
Even at the
present day
birettas vary
considerably in
shape. Those
worn by the
French, Ger-
man, and Span-
ish clergy as a
rule have four
peaks instead of
three; while
Roman custom
prescribes that
a cardinal's bi-
retta should
have no tassel.
As regards us-

DRAWING, A. D. 1414, DIGNITARIES AT
COUNCIL OF CONSTANCE

age in wearing the biretta, the reader must be
referred for details to some of the works mentioned
in the bibliography. It may be said in general that
the biretta is worn in processions and when seated, as
also when the priest is performing any act of jurisdiction, e. g. reconciling a convert. It was formerly
the rule that a priest should always wear it in giving absolution in confession, and it is probable that
the ancient usage which requires an English judge

to assume the "black cap" in pronouncing sentence of death is identical in origin.

BARBIER DE MONTAULT, *Le costume et les usages ecclésias-tiques* (Paris, 1901), I, 227–236; BOCK, *Liturgische Gewänder* (Munich, 1866), II, 342 sqq.; DE VERT, *Explication des céré-monies* (Paris, 1710), II, 273–277; BONANNI, *Gerarchia Eccle-siastica* (Rome, 1720), plates 17, 18, 19; STAHL in *Kirchenlex.,* II, s. v. *Biret;* CLARK in *Archæological Journal* (London, 1893 and 1904), L, 147 sqq. and LXI, 32 sqq.; ROBINSON, *The Pileus Quadratus* in *Transactions of St. Paul's Ecclesiological Society* (London, 1905), V, 1–16. The most thorough account is to be found in BRAUN *Die Liturgische Gewandung* (Freiburg, 1907), 321, 510, 514.

HERBERT THURSTON.

Birgida, Birgit, Birgitta. See BRIGID, SAINT.

Birinus (BERIN), SAINT, Confessor, first Bishop of Dorchester (in what is now the County of Oxford, not Dorchester, the capital of Dorsetshire), and Apostle of Wessex; date of birth unknown; d. 3 December, 650, at his see and was buried in his own church there. Later (680) his remains were deposited by Bishop Headda in the cathedral at Winchester, where finally (4 September, 972) Bishop Ethelwold enshrined them in silver and gold. According to Bede, Birinus came to Britain on the advice of Pope Honorius I (625–638), having been consecrated bishop by Asterius at Genoa. He promised "to sow the seed of the holy faith in the inner parts beyond the English", but on his arrival (634) found the West Saxons so pagan that he decided to devote his ministry to them. God blessed his zeal by the conversion of their king, Cynegils (635), of his son Cwichelm (636), and of Cwichelm's son Cuthred (639). Cynegils' daughter (Cyneburga?) was also baptized, and Oswald, the holy King of Northumbria, who had come to Cynegils in suit of her hand, was sponsor to her father and wedded her. Doubtless his presence helped Birinus much in his first spiritual conquests. Immediately after this, Oswald and Cynegils gave him Dorcic, or Dorchester, the capital of Wessex, for his see, where "he built and consecrated many churches and by his labours called many to the Lord".

Birinus had great devotion for the Body of Our Lord, as is shown in the account of his walking on the sea to procure the corporal given him by Pope Honorius, wherein he ever carried the Blessed Eucharist. Field strangely disposes of this miracle and others as allegorical or fabricated, after allowing, however, that their chroniclers had some common source of information lost to us now. Many miracles took place at the discovery of Birinus's relics, and Huntingdon among others speaks of "the great miracles of Birin". At present, there is a growing devotion to him in the Established Church, due probably to the connexion of the royal family with Cerdic, a side branch of whose stock was Cynegils. Field enumerates many modern Protestant memorials. The Catholics of Dorchester honoured their patron, in, 1849, with a beautiful chapel.

BEDE, *Hist. Eccl.,* III, vii; IV, xii; BUTLER, *Lives of the Saints,* II; ALLIES, *The Church in England* (London, 1892), 37; MONTALEMBERT, *Monks of the West,* XI, 2; FIELD, *Saint Berin, The Apostle of Wessex* (London and New York, 1902); HARDY, *Catalogue of Materials for English History* in R. S., XLVIII; GILES, *Six Old English Chronicles* (London, 1896); HADDAN AND STUBBS, *Councils,* III.

CHARLES L. KIMBALL.

Birkowski, FABIAN, Polish preacher, b. at Lemberg, 1566; d. at Cracow, 1636. He completed his studies at the University of Cracow, where he also began to teach philosophy in 1587. After having taught there for five years he entered the Dominican Order (1592), and devoted himself for some time to a deeper study of theology. Thereupon he began his career as a preacher in the church of the Holy Trinity at Cracow where the king attended Divine worship. During fourteen years his fame as a preacher drew immense crowds. Sigismund II was much attached to him and often consulted him on matters temporal

and spiritual. He induced Birkowski to follow the court when it was transferred to Warsaw. He also appointed him court-preacher to his son Wladislaw. In the crusades of 1617 and 1618 against Turkey, Russia, and Walachia, the friar took no small part, and some of his best sermons were delivered to the soldiers. Two years before his death he retired to his monastery and never left it save to preach on some great occasion or in behalf of charity. Birkowski is considered one of the greatest orators of Poland. His contemporaries spoke of him as the "Sarmatian Chrysologus", and posterity has not found anyone superior to him in purity of diction in the sixteenth century. He uses Scripture quotations very often, though he also refers frequently to Virgil, Horace, and Homer, and among later writers to Justus Lipsius. He has no respect for the learning and temper of Erasmus. Of his sermons only a few have been published. There are three volumes of sermons for Sundays and Holy Days, besides panegyrics on St. Josaphat, Sigismund III, his wife Constantia, and sermons on the Blessed Virgin delivered in camp.

QUÉTIF AND ECHARD, *Script. ord. Præd.,* II, 542; MECHER-ZYNSKI, *Hist. wymowy w Polasce,* II, 325–329.

THOS. M. SCHWERTNER.

Birmingham, DIOCESE OF (BIRMINGHAMIA, BIR-MINGHAMIENSIS).—One of the thirteen dioceses erected by the Apostolic Letter of Pius IX, 27 September, 1850, which restored a hierarchy to the Catholic Church in England. It comprises the counties of Oxford, Stafford, Warwick, and Worcester. It takes its name from the municipal city of Birmingh : n in Warwickshire, the largest town of the four counties. Previous to 1850, these same four counties were included, first in the Midland, then in the Central, District or Vicariate, which had been governed by vicars-Apostolic since 1688, of whom by far the most illustrious was Bishop Milner (1803–26)—a man equally learned in polemics, ecclesiastical history, and sacred archæology. To his untiring energies and undaunted front against a strongly organized schismatical opposition, the Church in England owes its present stability and its solid ecclesiastical unity. Under Milner, whose episcopal residence was at Wolverhampton (Staffordshire), this vicariate became the starting-point and then the centre of the Catholic Movement, or Revival, in the last century (1800–50). Its prominence as well as its lustre was due not merely to its central position, but chiefly to Milner's brilliant talents, his magnetic influence, and clear foresight. Its two educational establishments —Sedgley Park School, Wolverhampton, and St. Mary's College, Oscott, Birmingham—presided over and staffed by exceptionally able men, lent their aid also to this great movement by supplying a zealous body of clergy and a laity thoroughly grounded in Catholic principles. When, later on, the Oxford movement led to so many conversions, Oscott College became the rallying point for the Catholic forces, inasmuch as its then president, Bishop Wiseman (1840–17), was the acknowledged leader and interpreter. To Oscott John Henry Newman had come from Littlemore after his reception into the Church, and many other distinguished converts besides.

The last vicar-Apostolic of this henceforth historic vicariate was William Bernard Ullathorne, O.S.B., who was consecrated 21 June, 1846. After ruling the Western Vicariate for a short time he was translated to the Central District, to become the first Bishop of the newly created See of Birmingham. Next to Wiseman, he had done most to promote the restoration of the hierarchy. On 27 October, 1850, Bishop Ullathorne was enthroned in St. Chad's Cathedral, Birmingham, when Dr. Newman preached his celebrated sermon "Christ on the Waters", second only to the "Second Spring" delivered at the First Provincial Synod of Westminster at Oscott

(July, 1852). The cathedral and bishop's house had been erected in Bishop Walsh's vicariate (21 June, 1840) from designs drawn by Augustus Welby Pugin, the foremost promoter of the revival of Gothic architecture, who, through the munificence of John, 16th Earl of Shrewsbury, adorned the diocese with many ecclesiastical buildings. Over the high altar of St. Chad's Cathedral rest the relics of its patron which had been enshrined till the Reformation in Lichfield Cathedral. On 24 June, 1852, the cathedral chapter, consisting of a provost and ten canons, was duly erected, to which three honorary canons have since been added. The first and third provosts, respectively, were Mgr. Weedall, D.D., and Dr. Northcote, both presidents of Oscott. The first diocesan synod was held 9 and 10 November, 1853, since which time there have been thirteen other synods (1853–1906). In 1873, owing to refusal to renew the lease, Sedgley Park School was transferred to St. Wilfrid's, Cotton, Staffordshire, formerly the residence of Father Faber and the Oratorians. In the October of the same year St. Bernard's Diocesan Seminary was opened at Olton, Warwickshire, of which the first rector was the Rev. Edward Ilsley, successively canon and bishop-auxiliary (December 4, 1879).

In July, 1887, Bishop Ullathorne resigned, becoming Titular Archbishop of Cabasa. He retired to Oscott, where he died 21 March, 1889. Two persons stand forth conspicuous in the history of the Birmingham diocese whose relations with Bishop Ullathorne were exceptionally close, Cardinal Newman and Mother Margaret Hallahan. The former lived and died at the oratory, Edgbaston, Birmingham, and the new basilica opened 9 October, 1906, will perpetuate his memory. The latter was the foundress of the English Congregation of Nuns of the Third Order of St. Dominic, who have convents and hospitals at Stoke on Trent and Stone. The latter is the burying place both of Archbishop Ullathorne and Mother Margaret. The large number of communities of women who have found a home in this diocese attracted by the personality of Bishop Ullathorne include Benedictines (2 abbeys, 3 priories), Poor Clares, Little Sisters of the Poor, Sisters of Mercy and of St. Paul—the latter introduced from Chartres by Mother Geneviève Dupuis. Another religious force, specially characteristic of the diocese, has been the annual reunions in the Town Hall, Birmingham, which, begun in 1855, have been presided over by eminent Catholics, and have tended to keep the clergy and laity in touch with one another. Mention, too, must be made of John Hardman of Birmingham, whose firm has done so much in promoting ecclesiastical art, notably stained-glass and metal work, and whose benefactions to the cathedral choir have enabled it to reach a standard of excellence in church music which places it first among Catholic choirs. On 17 February, 1888, Dr. Ilsley became the second Bishop of Birmingham, and at once took in hand the difficult task of protecting and rescuing the destitute Catholic children of the diocese. St. Edward's Home for homeless boys was opened at Coleshill (Warwickshire), 6 November, 1906, with branch houses for boys and girls, similarly situated, in various centres, besides a Home for Working Boys and a Night Refuge, both in Birmingham. In July, 1889, Oscott College was closed to lay students and reopened as a Central Seminary for ecclesiastics only. The progress of Catholicism since 1850 is gauged by a comparison of a few statistics for the years 1851 and 1906, respectively: clergy, 124 and 297; churches, 82 and 189; religious communities, 19 and 97.

The Catholic Directory (1800–1907); *Birmingham Catholic Calendar and Directory* (1900–07); AMHERST, *History of Catholic Emancipation* (London, 1886); ULLATHORNE, *Restoration of Hierarchy* (London, 1881); *The Oscotian* (3d series); HUSENBETH, *Life of Milner* (Dublin, 1862); IDEM, *Life of Mgr. Weedall* (London, 1860); DEANE, *Letters of Abp. Ullathorne* (London,

1892); *Autobiography of Abp. Ullathorne* (London, 1891); ULLATHORNE, *Pastorals* (1850–88); HUSENBETH, *History of Sedgley Park School* (London, 1856); WARD, *Life and Times of Card. Wiseman* (London, 1897); BARRY, *Newman* (London, 1904); IDEM, *Sermon Preached at Requiem of Provost Northcote* (1907); DEVINE, *Life of Fr. Ignatius Spencer* (London, 1866); *Life of M. Margaret Hallahan* (London, 1869); *Life of M. Francis Raphael Deane, O.S.D.* (London, 1895); *History of St. Chad's Cathedral* (Birmingham, 1904); STAPLETON, *History of Post-Reformation Missions in Oxfordshire* (London, 1906); GILLOW, *History of St. Austin's, Stafford* (London, s. d.); IDEM, *Bibl. Dict. Eng. Cath.; Memorials of Bp. Amherst* (London, 1903); WILLINGTON, *Catholicism in Leamington* (1906); NORRIS, *Baddesley Clinton* (London, 1897); CHATTAWAY, *Salford Priors* (1895); FERREY, *Memoirs of Augustus Welby Pugin* (London, 1861); ILSLEY, *Pastorals* (1888–1907).

JOHN CASWELL.

Birnbaum, HEINRICH (also known as DE PIRO, the latinized form of his German name), a pious and learned Carthusian monk, b. in 1403; d. 19 February, 1473. Little is known of him before his entrance into the Carthusian monastery at Cologne on 14 March, 1435, at the age of 32 years. On account of his edifying example in the observance of the rule and his extensive scriptural and theological learning he was highly esteemed by his confrères, and as early as 1438, only three years after his entrance into the order, he became prior of the monastery of Mont Saint André at Tournai (Doornik) in Belgium. The desire for a reform of the religious orders, which animated many great men of the fifteenth century, had also penetrated the soul of Birnbaum. Being a true reformer, he soon succeeded, by the irresistible force of his own pious example, in abolishing the few abuses that had found admittance into the various monasteries over which he became prior, and in restoring the austere monastic discipline established by the founder St. Bruno. After holding the position of prior at Mont Saint André for eleven years, he was active in the same office successively at Wesel in Rhenish Prussia, until 1457; at Rettel in Lorraine, until 1459; at Trier, until 1461; and at Diest in Belgium, until 1463. In 1463 he was appointed prior at Liège, but ill health forced him to resign this position and retire to the Carthusian monastery at Cologne, where he had spent the first days of his monastic life. The remaining ten years of his life Birnbaum spent in writing several ascetic works and in preparing for a happy death. There were with him at that time in the Carthusian monastery of Cologne some of the most learned and saintly men of Germany, such as Hermann Appeldorn (d. 1472), Hermann Grefken (d. 1480), Heinrich von Dissen (d. 1484), and Werner Rolewink (d. 1502). Birnbaum wrote for the instruction and direction of the members of his order a number of works, many of which, however, have not yet been put in print, also: "Defensio pro Immaculato Conceptu B. M. V.", and "Excerpta ex malo granato cum nonnullis conjunctis". He has often been confounded with his uncle of the same name, one of the most learned jurists of the fifteenth century, who was for some time provost of St. Kunibert's at Cologne, and who died in 1439. See "Le Grand Dictionnaire Historique" (Amsterdam, 1698), III, 138; also Jöcher, "Gelehrten Lexicon", III, 1589.

KESSEL in *Kirchenlexikon*, II, 862; MARX, *Geschichte des Erzstiftes Trier*, II, ii, 331.

MICHAEL OTT.

Birth, THE DEFECT OF (ILLEGITIMACY), a canonical impediment to ordination. When used in this connexion, the word *illegitimate* has, in canon law, a well-defined meaning, which is: "born out of lawful wedlock". Illegitimate birth is an impediment to the reception of orders, and inhibits the exercise of the functions of orders already received. It is a canonical impediment, because established and laid down in the canon law as a hindrance to entering the clerical state. This prohibition does not touch the validity of orders, but makes the reception of them illicit. It extends to first tonsure. The inhibition that is set up is restricted to the functions that belong exclusively to the clergy. In the early ages of the Church no law prevented the ordination of illegitimates. They were then, sometimes, debarred from ordination, but only because of a real or supposed depravity of life. Pope Urban II (1088–99) prohibited the ordination of the illegitimate offspring of clerics, unless they became members of approved religious orders. The Council of Poitiers, under Paschal II (1099–1118), extended this prohibition to all persons of illegitimate birth. These regulations were later approved by other popes and councils.

The law as laid down in the Decretals of Gregory IX (I, X) mentions only the offspring of clerics and those begotten in fornication. But in the sixth book of the Decretals all persons of illegitimate birth are expressly included. These may be ranged in the following classes: (1) Natural illegitimates, or the offspring of parents who at the time of the birth or conception of such offspring, were capable of contracting Christian marriage. (2) Spurious illegitimates, or those born of a known mother and an unknown father—unknown because the mother had carnal relations with several men. (3) Adulterine illegitimates, those begotten of parents, one or both of whom, at the time of the conception and birth of such offspring, were lawfully married to a third person. (4) Incestuous illegitimates, or persons whose parents could not marry because of an invalidating impediment of consanguinity or affinity. (5) Sacrilegious illegitimates, or the offspring of parents who are restrained from marriage because of the impediment of Holy orders or solemn religious vows. The practice of the present day also holds as illegitimates abandoned children of unknown parentage. Legitimacy may not be presumed nor established by negative proof. Positive documentary evidence must be adduced.

The law of illegitimacy directly debars all the foregoing classes of persons from promotion to orders, and the exercise of the functions proper to the orders already received; and it indirectly prevents such persons from obtaining a benefice. Directly, also, it prevents them from obtaining certain benefices, for the Council of Trent (Sess. 25, c. 15 de ref.) decreed that the illegitimate children of clerics should be incapacitated from obtaining any kind of a benefice in the Church where their fathers held one; from rendering any service in said church; and from receiving any pensions on the revenues of the paternal benefice. This law is not established and laid down as a punishment for the person to whom it is applied. It safeguards the honour and dignity of Holy orders. The clerical state which has the dispensing of the mysteries of God must be beyond reproach. No stain should be upon it, no blame possible. Therefore the Church raises the barrier of illegitimacy before the entrance to the priesthood. Thus the crime of the parents is held up to just reprobation, and is condemned even in the lives of their offspring. The danger of the father's incontinence being continued in the life of the son is greatly lessened, for strong indications of purity of life must be given before the door of God's ministry can be opened.

The defect of illegitimate birth may be cured in four ways: (1) By the subsequent marriage of the parents; (2) By a rescript of the pope; (3) By religious profession; (4) By a dispensation. (1) The subsequent marriage of the parents of an illegitimate has, by a fiction of law, a retroactive power which carries the marriage back to the time of the birth of the offspring and covers it with lawful wedlock. In order that the fiction of law may produce this effect, the parents, at the time of the conception or, at least, at the birth of such offspring, must have been capable of contracting lawful marriage. Therefore, this mode

of legitimation is applicable only to natural illegitimates. And these, though legitimized by the subsequent marriage of the parents, or even by an Apostolic dispensation, are forever excluded from the dignity of the cardinalate. (2) A rescript of the pope confers legitimacy in so far as it is required for spiritual affairs throughout the universal Church. (3) Religious profession in an approved order cures the defect of illegitimacy. Religious profession is the taking of the solemn religious vows; but the simple vows taken after the novitiate in some orders produce a like effect. This mode of legitimation only renders illegitimates capable of ordination. It cannot be extended to dignities or even to regular prelacies. Hence, illegitimates thus legitimized are still debarred from the position of abbot; and women of illegitimate birth, for like reasons, cannot hold the position of abbess or prioress. (4) A dispensation granted by a lawful superior removes the defect of illegitimate birth, but only for some express purpose. It is not a mode of absolute legitimation. The purposes for which it is granted must be specified; as for promotion to minor orders, to major orders, to a specified benefice.

A dispensation of this kind runs counter to the common law. It is of strict interpretation, and therefore cannot be extended from like to like or from greater to less, unless the one is included in, and presupposes, the other. Such is the case when a dispensation is conceded to an illegitimate to receive Holy orders. Such orders require a title, and this title is, in canon law, a benefice. The pope is the lawful superior for the universal Church, and as such he can dispense in all cases where a dispensation is possible. Bishops and other prelates having quasi-episcopal jurisdiction can dispense their own subjects, in this matter, for first tonsure, minor orders, or a simple benefice; but not for major orders, even though the illegitimacy be occult. This episcopal, or quasi-episcopal, jurisdiction does not extend to a benefice which was immediately possessed by the father of the person seeking the dispensation, nor to a benefice which by custom or privilege requires its possessor to be in major orders.

FERRARIS, *Prompta Bibliotheca*; SCHMALZGRÜBER, *Jus Ecclesiasticum*; SANTI-LEITNER, *Prælectiones Juris Canonici* (New York, 1905); *Dizionario di Casuistica Morale* (Venice, 1841); SABETTI, *Theologia Moralis* (New York, 1889); KONINGS, *Theologia Moralis* (Boston, 1874); BŒNNINGHAUSEN, *Tractatus Juridico-canon. de irregularitatibus* (Münster, 1863).

JAMES H. DRISCOLL.

Birtha, a titular see of Osrhaene, probably identical with Birejik (Zegma) on the left bank of the Euphrates, c. 62 miles west of Orfa (Edessa), and 95 miles north of Aleppo. Birtha (Aramæan, *Bîrthâ* "castle") is spoken of as a castle by ancient authors (Hierocles, 715, 2). There was also a see called by the Greeks Macedonopolis, the foundation of the city being attributed by legend to Alexander the Great (Amm. Marcell., XX, vii, 17). That Macedonopolis and Birtha are one see is proved by the subscriptions at the Council of Nicæa, where we see that *Bjrt'* in both Syriac and Arabic lists corresponds with Macedonopolis in Greek and Latin lists (Gelzer, Patrum Nicænorum nomina, 242). The true name of the bishop present at the council is Mareas, not Marcus. Daniel, Bishop of Macedonopolis, is said to have been present at the Council of Chalcedon (451). From the sixth century only the name Birtha survives (Georgius Cyprius, n. 899). Emperor Anastasius, after his victories over the Persians in 505, entrusted Sergius, Bishop of Birtha, with the work of repairing the city (Wright, ed., The Chronicle of Joshua the Stylite, XCI, lxxi), an undertaking that was completed by Justinian (Procop., De ædific. Just., II, 4). The oldest "Tacticon" of the Patriarchate of Antioch, issued under Anastasius I (599) places Birtha first among the suffragan sees of Edessa (Kerameus, ed., 'Ανέκδοτα 'Ελληνικά, lxv); the name is written Βύρτη in a later redaction (ibid., lxix), and *Virchi* in an old Latin translation (Tobler and Molinier, Itinera Hierosolymitana, I, 322). Birtha was destroyed by Timour-Leng in the fourteenth century. Birejik is to-day the chief town of a *caza* in the vilayet of Aleppo with 10,000 inhabitants, including 1,500 Christians, all Armenians, one-half of whom are Catholics.

Ptolemy (V, xviii, xix) speaks of a fortress Birtha on the Tigris in Southern Mesopotamia and of another in Arabia on the Euphrates below Thapsacus. The site of the first is unknown, the latter is at Ed-Deir (Ritter, Erdkunde, XI, 691), but perhaps both are the same as Birtha or Macedonopolis.

LEQUIEN, *Oriens Christ.*, II, 985; CUINET, *La Turquie d'Asie*, II, 265–269; GEORGIUS CYPRIUS, ed. GELZER, 154; GAMS, *Series Episcoporum*, 437.

L. PETIT.

Bisaccia. See SANT' ANGELO DE' LOMBARDI.

Bisarchio, DIOCESE OF, situated in Sardinia, in the province of Sassari, district of Nuoro, and suffragan to the Archdiocese of Sassari. The episcopal residence, however, is at Ozieri. Nothing is known as to the early history of Christianity in either the city or Diocese of Bisarchio. The first bishop mentioned is Costantino Madrone (c. 1102), who was succeeded in 1116 by Bishop Pietro. The bishop's residence was changed several times, once to Giracle, and again to Ardera. In 1503, at the death of Fra Calcerando, bishop of this see, Bisarchio was incorporated into the Diocese of Alghero. The diocese was re-established by Pius VII in his Bull of 9 March, 1803, and bestowed upon Giannantioco Azzei, who in 1819 was promoted to the archiepiscopal See of Oristano, his native place. The episcopal residence was then definitely transferred to Ozieri. The cathedral, built in 1153, is well planned.

The Diocese of Bisarchio contains 24 parishes, 116 churches, chapels, and oratories, 78 secular priests, 25 seminarists, and a population of 40,000.

CAPPELLETTI, *Le chiese d'Italia* (Venice, 1844); *Annuario eccl.* (Rome, 1906).

U. BENIGNI.

Bisceglie. See TRANI, DIOCESE OF.

Bishop (A. S. *Biscop, Bisceop,* Ger. *Bischof;* from Gr. ἐπίσκοπος, an overseer, through Lat. *episcopus;* It. *vescovo;* O. Fr. *vesque;* Fr. *évêque.* See Murray, "New Eng. Dict.", Oxford, 1888, I, 878), the title of an ecclesiastical dignitary who possesses the fullness of the priesthood to rule a diocese as its chief pastor, in due submission to the primacy of the pope. It is of Catholic faith that bishops are of Divine institution. In the hierarchy of order they possess powers superior to those of priests and deacons; in the hierarchy of jurisdiction, by Christ's will, they are appointed for the government of one portion of the faithful of the Church, under the direction and authority of the sovereign pontiff, who can determine and restrain their powers, but not annihilate them. They are the successors of the Apostles, though they do not possess all the prerogatives of the latter. (Council of Trent, Sess. XXIII, ch. iv; can. vi, vii. See COLLEGE, APOSTOLIC.) The episcopate is monarchical. By the will of Christ, the supreme authority in a diocese does not belong to a college of priests or of bishops, but it resides in the single personality of the chief. The subject will be treated under five heads: I. Historical Origin; II. Present Legislation; III. Rights and Powers of the Bishop; IV. Obligations of the Bishop; V. Non-Catholic use.

I. HISTORICAL ORIGIN.—The historical origin of the episcopate is much controverted; very diverse hypotheses have been proposed to explain the texts of the inspired writings and of the Apostolic Fathers

relating to the primitive ecclesiastical hierarchy. They are most easily found in the work of von Dunin-Borkowski, on the latest researches concerning the origin of the episcopate (Die neueren Forschungen über die Anfänge des Episkopats, Freiburg, 1900). The Apostolic and consequently the Divine origin of the monarchical episcopate has always been contested but especially so since Protestantism put forward the doctrine of a universal Christian priesthood. At the present day, rationalistic and Protestant writers, even those who belong to the Anglican Church, reject the Apostolic institution of the episcopate; many of them relegate its origin to the second century. Löning attempts to prove that originally there were several different organizations, that some Christian communities were administered by a body of presbyters, others by a college of bishops, others again by a single bishop. It is the last named form of organization, he declares, which has prevailed (Gemeindeverfassung des Urchristentums, Halle, 1889). Holtzmann thinks that the primitive organization of the churches was that of the Jewish synagogue; that a college of presbyters or bishops (synonymous words) governed the Judæo-Christian communities; that later this organization was adopted by the Gentile churches. In the second century one of these presbyter-bishops became the ruling bishop. The cause of this lay in the need of unity, which manifested itself when in the second century heresies began to appear. (Pastoralbriefe, Leipzig, 1880.) Hatch, on the contrary, finds the origin of the episcopate in the organization of certain Greek religious associations, in which one meets with ἐπίσκοποι (superintendents) charged with the financial administration. The primitive Christian communities were administered by a college of presbyters; those of the presbyters who administered the finances were called bishops. In the large towns, the whole financial administration was centralized in the hands of one such officer, who soon became the ruling bishop (The Organization of the Early Christian Churches, Oxford, 1881). According to Harnack (whose theory has varied several times), it was those who had received the special gifts known as the *charismata* (χαρίσματα), above all the gift of public speech, who possessed all authority in the primitive community. In addition to these we find bishops and deacons who possess neither authority nor disciplinary power, who were charged solely with certain functions relative to administration and Divine worship. The members of the community itself were divided into two classes: the elders (πρεσβύτεροι) and the youths (νεώτεροι). A college of presbyters was established at an early date at Jerusalem and in Palestine, but elsewhere not before the second century; its members were chosen from among the πρεσβύτεροι, and in its hands lay all authority and disciplinary power. Once established, it was from this college of presbyters that deacons and bishops were chosen. When those officials who had been endowed with the charismatic gifts had passed away, the community delegated several bishops to replace them. At a later date, the Christians realized the advantages to be derived from entrusting the supreme direction to a single bishop. However, as late as the year 140, the organization of the various communities was still widely divergent. The monarchic episcopate owes its origin to the need of doctrinal unity, which made itself felt at the time of the crisis caused by the Gnostic heresies. (Von Dunin-Borkowski, 100–101.)

J. B. Lightfoot, who may be regarded as an authoritative representative of the Anglican Church, holds a less radical system. The Primitive Church, he says, had no organization, but was very soon conscious of the necessity of organizing. At first the apostles appointed deacons; later, in imitation of the organization of the synagogue, they appointed presbyters, sometimes called bishops in the Gentile churches. The duties of the presbyters were two-fold: they were both rulers and instructors of the congregation. In the Apostolic age, however, traces of the highest order, the episcopate properly so called, are few and indistinct. The episcopate was not formed from the Apostolic order through the localization of the universal authority of the Apostles, but from the presbyteral (by elevation). The title of bishop originally common to all came at length to be appropriated to the chief among them. Within the period compassed by the Apostolic writings, James, the brother of the Lord, can alone claim to be regarded as a bishop in the later and more special sense of the term. On the other hand, though especially prominent in the Church of Jerusalem, he appears in the Acts as a member of a body. As late as the year 70, no distinct signs of episcopal government had yet appeared in Gentile Christendom. During the last three decades of the first century, however, during the lifetime of the latest surviving Apostle, St. John, the episcopal office was established in Asia Minor. St. John was cognizant of the position of St. James at Jerusalem. When, therefore, he found in Asia Minor manifold irregularities and threatening symptoms of disruption, he not unnaturally encouraged in these Gentile churches an approach to the organization, which had been signally blessed and had proved effectual in holding together the mother-church of Jerusalem amid dangers no less serious. The existence of a council or college necessarily supposes a presidency of some kind, whether this presidency be assumed by each member in turn, or lodged in the hands of a single person. It was only necessary, therefore, to give permanence, definiteness, stability to an office the germ of which already existed. There is no reason, however, for supposing that any direct ordinance was issued to the churches by St. John. The evident utility and even pressing need of such an office, sanctioned by the most venerated name in Christendom, would be sufficient to secure its wide though gradual reception. The earliest bishops, however, did not hold the position of independent supremacy which was and is occupied by their later representatives. This development is most conveniently grasped in connexion with three great names: Ignatius, Irenæus, and Cyprian, who represent as many successive advances towards the supremacy ultimately attained. By Ignatius the bishop is regarded as the centre of unity; to Irenæus he is the depositary of primitive truth; to Cyprian, he is the absolute vicegerent of Christ in things spiritual (Lightfoot, The Christian Ministry, 181–269, in his commentary on St. Paul's Epistle to the Philippians, London, 1896).

Catholic writers agree in recognizing the Apostolic origin of the episcopate, but are much divided as to the meaning of the terms which designate the hierarchy in the New Testament writings and the Apostolic Fathers. One may even ask if originally these terms had a clearly defined significance (Bruders, Die Verfassung der Kirche bis zum Jahre 175, Mainz, 1904). Nor is there greater unanimity when an attempt is made to explain why some churches are found without presbyters, others without bishops, others again where the heads of the community are called sometimes bishops, sometimes presbyters. This disagreement increases when the question comes up as to the interpretation of the terms which designate other personages exercising a certain fixed authority in the early Christian communities. The following facts may be regarded as fully established: (1) To some extent, in this early period, the words bishop and priest ($\epsilon\pi\iota\sigma\kappa\sigma\pi\sigma s$ and $\pi\rho\epsilon\sigma\beta\acute{v}\tau\epsilon\rho\sigma s$) are synonymous. (See the principal interpretations in the article: COLLEGE, APOSTOLIC.) (2) These terms may designate either simple priests (A. Michiels, Les origines de l'épiscopat, Louvain, 1900, 218 sqq.) or bishops possessing the full powers of their order. (Batiffol, Etudes d'histoire et de théologie positive, Paris, 1902, 266 sqq.; Duchesne, Histoire ancienne de l'église, Paris, 1906, 94.) (3) In each community the authority may originally have belonged to a college of presbyter-bishops. This does not mean that the episcopate, in the actual sense of the term, may have been plural, because in each church the college of presbyter-bishops did not exercise an independent supreme power; it was subject to the Apostles or to their delegates. The latter were bishops in the actual sense of the term, but they did not possess fixed sees nor had they a special title (Batiffol, 270). Since they were essentially itinerant, they confided to the care of some of the better educated and highly respected neophytes the fixed necessary functions relating to the daily life of the community. (4) Sooner or later the missionaries had to leave the young communities to themselves, whereupon their direction fell entirely upon these local authorities who thus received the Apostolical succession. (5) This local superior authority, which was of Apostolic origin, was conferred by the Apostles upon a monarchic bishop, such as is understood by the term to-day. This is proved first by the example of Jerusalem, where James, who was not one of the Twelve Apostles, held the first place, and afterwards by those communities in Asia Minor of which Ignatius speaks, and where, at the beginning of the second century the monarchical episcopate existed, for Ignatius does not write as though the institution were a new one. (6) In other communities, it is true, no mention is made of a monarchic episcopate until the middle of the second century. We do not wish to reject the opinion of those who believe that there are in several documents of the second century traces of the monarchic episcopate, that is to say, of an authority superior to that of the college of the presbyter-bishops. The reasons which some writers allege, in order to explain why, for example, in the Epistle of Polycarp no mention is made of a bishop, are very plausible. The best evidence, however, for the existence at this early date of a monarchical episcopate is the fact that nowhere in the latter half of the second century is the least trace to be found of a change of organization. Such a change would have robbed the supposed college of presbyter-bishops of their sovereign authority, and it is almost impossible to comprehend how this body would have allowed itself to be everywhere despoiled of its supreme authority, without leaving in the contemporary documents the least trace of a protest against so important a change. If the monarchical episcopate began only in the middle of the second century, it is impossible to comprehend how at the end of the second century the episcopal lists of several important bishoprics giving the succession of monarchic bishops as far back as the first century were generally known and admitted. Such, for instance, was the case at Rome. (7) This theory, it must be carefully noted, does not contradict the historical texts. According to these documents, there was a college of presbyters or of bishops which administered several churches, but which had a president who was none other than the monarchic bishop. Although the power of the latter had existed from the beginning it became gradually more conspicuous. The part played by the *presbyterium*, or body of priests, was a very important one in the earlier days of the Christian Church; nevertheless it did not exclude the existence of a monarchic episcopate (Duchesne, 89–95).

During the first three centuries, the entire religious life of the diocese centred around the person of the bishop. The priests and deacons were his auxiliaries, but they worked under the immediate direction of the bishop. In large cities, however, like Rome, it was soon found necessary to hand over permanently to the priests and deacons certain definite functions. Moreover, as a result of the spread of Christianity outside the great centres of population, the bishop gradually left to other ecclesiastics the administration of a fixed portion of the diocesan territory. In the East, at first bishoprics were created in all districts where there was a considerable number of Christians. But this system presented great inconveniences. To distant or rural localities, therefore, the Church sent bishops, who were only the delegates of the bishop of the city, and who did not possess the right of exercising the most important powers of a bishop. Such bishops were known as *Chorepiscopi* or rural bishops. Later on, they were replaced by priests (Gillman, Das Institut der Chorbischöfe im Orient, Munich, 1903). The establishment of parishes from the fourth and the fifth century on gradually freed the bishops from many of their original charges; they reserved to themselves only the most important affairs, i. e. those which concerned the whole diocese and those which belonged to the cathedral church. However, above all other affairs the bishops retained the right of supervision and supreme direction. While this change was taking place, the Roman Empire, now Christian, granted bishops other powers. They were exclusively empowered to take cognizance of the misdemeanours of clerics, and every lawsuit entered into against the latter had to be brought before the bishop's court. The Emperor Constantine even permitted all Christians to carry their lawsuits before the bishop, but this right was withdrawn at the end of the fourth century. Nevertheless, they continued to act as arbitrators, which office the earliest Christians had committed to them. More important, perhaps, is the part which the Roman law assigns to the bishops as protectors of the weak and oppressed. The master was permitted to legally emancipate his slave in the bishop's presence; the latter had also the power to remove young girls from immoral houses where their parents or masters had placed them, and to restore them to liberty. Newly born infants abandoned by their parents were legally adjudged to those who sheltered them, but to avoid abuses it was required that the bishop should certify that the child was a foundling. The Roman law allowed the bishops the right to visit prisons at their discretion for the purpose of improving the condition of prisoners and of ascertaining whether the rules in favour of the latter were observed. The bishops possessed great influence over the Christian emperors, and though in the Eastern Church these intimate relations between Church and State led to Cæsaropapism, the bishops of the West preserved in a great measure their independence of the Empire (Löning, Geschichte des deutschen Kirchenrechts, Strasburg, 1878, I, 314–331; Troplong, De l'influence du christianisme sur le droit civil des Romains, Paris, 1842, new ed., 1902).

The authority of the bishop was even greater after the barbarian invasions; among the Germanic peoples he soon became an influential and powerful personage. He inspired confidence and commanded respect. He was beloved, for he protected the young and the weak, he was the friend of the poor, was accustomed to intercede on behalf of the victims of injustice, and especially on behalf of orphans and women. Through his influence, in many spheres, the bishop became the real master of the episcopal city. The only functionaries whose authority was comparable with that of the bishop were the dukes and counts, representatives of the king. In certain districts the pre-eminence showed itself clearly in favour of the bishop; in some cities the bishop became also count. In France, as a general rule, this state of affairs did not continue, but in Germany many bishops became temporal lords or princes. Finally, the bishop ac-

quired an extensive civil jurisdiction not only over his clergy but also over the laity of his diocese (Viollet, Histoire des institutions politiques de la France, Paris, 1890, I, 380–409). Such an exalted position was not without its difficulties. One of the gravest was the interference of the lay authority in the election of bishops. Until the sixth century, the clergy and the people elected the bishop on condition that the election should be approved by the neighbouring bishops. Undoubtedly, the Christian Roman emperors sometimes intervened in these elections, but outside the imperial cities only, and generally in the case of disagreement as to the proper person. As a rule they contented themselves with exercising an influence on the electors. But from the beginning of the sixth century, this attitude was modified. In the East, the clergy and the *primates*, or chief citizens, nominated three candidates from whom the metropolitan chose the bishop. At a later date, the bishops of the ecclesiastical province assumed the exclusive right of nominating the candidates. In the West, the kings intervened in these elections, notably in Spain and Gaul, and sometimes assumed the right of direct nomination (Funk, "Die Bischofswahl ım christlichen Altertum und im Anfang des Mittelalters" in "Kirchengeschichtliche Abhandlungen und Untersuchungen", Paderborn, 1897, I, 23–39; Imbart de la Tour, "Les élections épiscopales dans l'ancienne France", Paris, 1890). This interference of princes and emperors lasted until the quarrel about Investitures, which was especially violent in Germany, where from the ninth to the eleventh centuries abbots and bishops had become real temporal princes. (See INVESTITURE.) The Second Lateran Council (1139) handed over to the chapter of the cathedral church the sole right of choosing the bishop, and this legislation was sanctioned by the Decretals (Decretum Gratiani, P. I., Dist. lxiii, ch. xxxv; ch. iii, De causâ possessionis et proprietatis, X, II, xii; ch. liv, De electione et electi potestate, X, I, vi; Friedberg, Corpus Juris Canonici, Leipzig, 1879–81, I, 247, II, 95, 276). The bishops of the Middle Ages acquired much temporal power, but this was accompanied by a corresponding diminution of their spiritual authority. By the exercise of the prerogative of the primacy the Holy See reserved to itself all the most important affairs, the so-called *causæ majores*, as for instance the canonization of saints (ch. i, De reliquiis, X, III, xlv; Friedberg, II, 650); the permission to venerate publicly newly discovered relics, the absolution of certain grave sins, etc. Appeals to the pope against the judicial decisions of the bishops became more and more frequent. The religious orders and the chapters of cathedral and collegiate churches obtained exemption from episcopal authority. The cathedral chapter obtained a very considerable influence in the administration of the diocese. The pope reserved also to himself the nomination to many ecclesiastical benefices (C. Lux. Constitutionum apostolicarum de generali beneficiorum reservatione collectio et interpretatio, Breslau, 1904). He also claimed the right to nominate the bishops, but in the German Concordat of 1448 he granted to the chapters the right of electing them, while in that of 1516 he permitted the King of France to nominate the bishops of that nation. Subsequently the Council of Trent defined the rights of the bishop and remedied the abuses which had slipped into the administration of dioceses and the conduct of bishops. The council granted them the exclusive right of publishing indulgences; it also impressed upon them the obligation of residence in their dioceses, the duty of receiving consecration within three months after their elevation to the episcopate, of erecting seminaries, of convoking annual diocesan synods, of assisting at provincial synods, and of visiting their dioceses. It also forbade them to cumulate benefices, etc. The same council diminished exemptions from episcopal authority, and delegated to the bishops some of the rights which in the past the Holy See had reserved to itself. Subsequent pontifical acts completed the Tridentine legislation, which is still valid. Protestantism and at a later date the French Revolution destroyed all temporal power of the bishops; thenceforth they were free to consecrate themselves with greater earnestness to the duties of their spiritual ministry.

II. PRESENT LEGISLATION.—Two classes of bishops must be distinguished, not with regard to the power of order, for all bishops receive the fullness of the priesthood, but with regard to the power of jurisdiction: the diocesan bishop and the titular bishop or, as he was called before 1882 the *episcopus in partibus infidelium*. The former is here considered. Those belonging to the second class cannot perform any episcopal function without the authorization of the diocesan bishop; for as titular bishops they have no ordinary jurisdiction. They can, however, act as auxiliary bishops, i. e. they may be appointed by the pope to assist a diocesan bishop in the exercise of duties arising from the episcopal order but entailing no power of jurisdiction. (See AUXILIARY BISHOP.) Such a bishop is also called *vicarius in pontificalibus*, i. e. a representative in certain ceremonial acts proper to the diocesan bishop, sometimes suffragan bishop, *episcopus suffraganeus*. In the proper sense of the term, however, the suffragan bishop is the diocesan bishop in his relations with the metropolitan of the ecclesiastical province to which he belongs, while the bishop who is independent of any metropolitan is called an exempt bishop, *episcopus exemptus*. The titular bishop may also be coadjutor bishop when he is appointed to assist an ordinary bishop in the administration of the diocese. Sometimes he is incorrectly called auxiliary bishop. He possesses some powers of jurisdiction determined by the letters Apostolic appointing him. Often also, notably in missionary countries, the coadjutor bishop is named *cum jure successionis*, i. e. with the right of succession; on the death of the diocesan bishop he enters on the ordinary administration of the diocese (Taunton, The Law of the Church, London, 1906, 55, 204, 617).

The Council of Trent determined the conditions to be fulfilled by candidates for the episcopate, of which the following are the principal: birth in lawful wedlock, freedom from censure and irregularity or any defect in mind, purity of personal morals, and good reputation. The candidate must also be fully thirty years of age and have been not less than six months in Holy orders. He ought also to have the theological degree of Doctor or at least be a licentiate in theology or canon law or else have the testimony of a public academy or seat of learning (or, if he be a religious, of the highest authority of his order) that he is fit to teach others (c. vii, De electione et electi potestate, X, I, vi; Friedberg, II, 51. Council of Trent, Sess. XXII, De ref., ch. ii). The Holy Office is charged with the examination of persons called to the episcopate, with the exception of the territories subject to the Congregation of the Propaganda or to the Congregation of Extraordinary Ecclesiastical Affairs, or of those countries where the nomination of bishops is governed by special laws and concordats ("Motu proprio" of Pope Pius X, 17 December, 1903; "Acta sanctæ Sedis, 1904, XXXVI, 385). We have said that the Decretals recognize the right of the cathedral chapters to elect the bishop. This right has been long withdrawn and is no longer in force. In virtue of the second rule of the Papal Chancery the choice of bishops belongs exclusively to the pope (Walter, Fontes juris ecclesiastici antiqui et hodierni, Bonn, 1861, 483). Exceptions to this rule, however, are numerous. In Austria (with the exception of some episcopal sees), in Bavaria, in Spain, in Portugal and in Peru, the Government presents to the sovereign pontiff the candidates for the episcopate. It was so in France, and in several South American Republics before the rupture or denunciation of the concordats between these states and the Apostolic See. By the cessation of these concordats such states lost all right of intervention in the nomination of bishops; this does not, however, prevent the Government in several South American Republics from recommending candidates to the sovereign pontiff. The cathedral chapter is authorized to elect the bishop in several dioceses of Austria, Switzerland, Prussia, and in some States of Germany, notably in the ecclesiastical province of the Upper Rhine. The action of the electors, however, is not entirely free. For example, they may not choose persons distasteful to the Government (Letter of the Cardinal Secretary of State to the Chapters of Germany, 20 July, 1900; Canoniste Contemporain, 1901, XXIV, 727). Elsewhere the pope himself nominates bishops, but in Italy the Government insists that they obtain the royal exequatur before taking possession of the episcopal see. In missionary countries the pope generally permits the "recommendation" of candidates, but this does not juridically bind the sovereign pontiff, who has the power to choose the new bishop from persons not included in the list of recommended candidates. In England the canons of the cathedral select by a majority of votes, at three successive ballots, three candidates for the vacant episcopal see. Their names, arranged in alphabetical order, are transmitted to the Propaganda and to the archbishop of the province, or to the senior suffragan of the province, if the question is one of the election of an archbishop. The bishops of the province discuss the merits of the candidates and transmit their observations to the Propaganda. Since 1874 the bishops are empowered, if they so desire, to propose other names for the choice of the Holy See, and a decision of the Propaganda (25 April, 3 May, 1904) confirms this practice (Instruction of Propaganda, 21 April, 1852; "Collectanea S. C. de Propagandâ Fide", Rome, 1893, no. 42; Taunton, 87–88). Analogous enactments are in force in Ireland. The canons of the cathedral and all the parish priests free from censure and in actual and peaceful possession of their parish or united parishes, choose in a single ballot three ecclesiastics. The names of the three candidates who have obtained the greatest number of votes are announced and forwarded to the Propaganda and to the archbishop of the province. The archbishop and the bishops of the province give the Holy See their opinion on the candidates. If they judge that none of the candidates is capable of fulfilling the episcopal functions no second recommendation is to be made. If it is a question of the nomination of a coadjutor bishop with the right of succession the same rules are followed, but the presidency of the electoral meeting, instead of being given to the metropolitan, his delegate, or the senior bishop of the province, belongs to the bishop who asks for the coadjutor (Instruction of Propaganda, 17 September, 1829, and 25 April, 1835; "Collectanea," nos. 40 and 41). In Scotland, when there is a chapter of canons, they follow the same rules as in England; and when there is no chapter, the bishops of Scotland and the archbishops of Edinburgh and Glasgow choose by a triple ballot the three candidates. The names of these latter are communicated to the Holy See together with the votes which each candidate has obtained. At the same time is transmitted useful information about each of them according to the questions determined by the Propaganda (Instruction of the Propaganda, 25 July, 1883; "Collectanea", no. 45). In the United States of America the diocesan consultors and the irremovable rectors of the diocese assemble under the presidency of the archbishop or the senior bishop of the province, and choose three candidates, the first *dignissimus*, the second *dignior*, and the third *dignus*. Their names are sent to the Propaganda and to the archbishop of the province; the archbishop and the bishops of the province examine the merits of the candidates proposed by the clergy and in their turn, by a secret ballot propose three candidates. If they choose other candidates than those designated by the clergy, they indicate their reasons to the Propaganda. In the case of the nomination of a coadjutor with right of succession, the meeting of the clergy is presided over by the bishop who demands a coadjutor. If it concerns a newly created diocese, the consultors of all the dioceses from whose territory the new diocese was formed and all the irremovable rectors of the new diocese choose the three candidates of the clergy. Finally, if it is a matter of replacing an archbishop or of giving him a coadjutor with right of succession, all the metropolitans of the United States are consulted by the Propaganda (Decree of Propaganda, 21 January, 1861, modified by that of 21 September, 1885; Collectanea, no. 43). In Canada by a decree of 2 December, 1862, the Church still follows the rules laid down by the Propaganda on 21 January, 1861, for the United States (Collectanea, no. 43; Collectio Lacensis, Freiburg, 1875, III, 684, 688). Every three years the bishops must communicate to the Propaganda and to the metropolitan the names of the priests they think worthy of episcopal functions. In addition, each bishop must designate in a secret letter three ecclesiastics whom he believes worthy to succeed him. When a vacancy occurs, all the bishops of the province indicate to the archbishop or to the senior bishop the priests whom they consider recommendable. The bishops then discuss in a meeting the merits of each of the priests recommended, and proceed to the nomination of the candidates by secret vote. The acts of the assembly are transmitted to the Propaganda. In Australia, a method similar to that in use in the United States is followed. Two differences, however, are to be noted: first, the bishops still signify, every three years, to the metropolitan and to the Propaganda the names of the priests whom they consider worthy of the episcopal office. Second, when the nomination of a coadjutor bishop is in question, the presidency over the assembly of consultors and irremovable rectors belongs not to the bishop who demands a coadjutor, but to the metropolitan or to the bishop delegated by him (Instruction of Propaganda, 19 May, 1866, modified by the decree of 1 May, 1887; Collectanea, no. 44).

Whatever the manner of his nomination, the bishop possesses no power until his nomination has been confirmed by the Holy See, whether in consistory or by pontifical letters. Moreover, he is forbidden to enter the administration of his diocese before taking possession of his see by communicating to the cathedral chapter the letters Apostolic of his nomination (Const. "Apostolicæ Sedis", 12 October, 1869, V, i; "Collectanea", no. 1002). From this moment, even before his consecration, the new bishop is entitled in his diocese to all rights of jurisdiction. He is required to make the prescribed profession of faith in the first provincial synod held after his elevation (Council of Trent, Sess. XXV, De ref., ch. ii). Finally, he is obliged within the space of three months to receive episcopal consecration. The right of consecrating a bishop belongs to the sovereign pontiff, who generally permits the newly elected to be consecrated by three bishops of his own choice. However, if the consecration takes place in Rome, he must select a cardinal or one of the major patriarchs residing at Rome. If, however, his own metropolitan is at that time in Rome, he would be obliged to choose him. The consecration ought to take place on a

Sunday or on the feast of an Apostle, by preference in the cathedral church of the diocese or at least within the ecclesiastical province (Council of Trent, Sess., XXIII, De ref., ch. ii). Before consecration, the bishop must take an oath of fidelity to the Holy See. (For the formula of this oath for the bishops of the United States of America see "Acta et Decreta conc. Plen. Balt., III", Baltimore, 1886, Appendix, 202.) Consecration by a single bishop would not be invalid but would be illicit. However, the bishops of South America have the privilege of being consecrated by one bishop assisted by two or three priests, if it prove difficult for them to obtain three bishops (Letters Apostolic of Leo XIII, "Trans Oceanum", 18 April, 1897; "Acta Sanctæ Sedis", 1896–97, XXIX, 659). Episcopal consecration has the effect of giving to the bishop the full powers of Order. (See HOLY ORDERS.)

III. RIGHTS AND POWERS OF THE BISHOP.—The bishop possesses, as already stated, the powers of order and jurisdiction. The power of order comes to him through episcopal consecration, but the exercise of this right depends on his power of jurisdiction. The sacerdotal ordination performed by every duly consecrated bishop is undoubtedly valid, yet the bishop can ordain only in conformity with the enactments of canon law. Only the bishop can confer major orders. The question has been discussed, as to whether the pope could delegate to a priest, for example the abbot of a monastery, the power to ordain a deacon. The bishop is the only ordinary minister of the Sacrament of Confirmation (Council of Trent, Sess. XXIII, can. vii). Ecclesiastical law has reserved certain benedictions and consecrations to him, viz., those which are performed with holy oil. The following functions are reserved to the bishop: the dedication of a church, the consecration of an altar, of chalices and patens, and generally of the articles serving for the celebration of Holy Mass, the reconciliation of a desecrated church, the benediction of bells, the benediction of an abbot, the benediction of the holy oils, etc. A bishop is forbidden to exercise the *Pontificalia*, i. e. to perform episcopal functions in another diocese without the consent of the ordinary, i. e. the proper bishop (Council of Trent, Sess. VI, De ref., ch. v).

Besides the power of order, bishops possess that of jurisdiction; they have the right to prescribe for the faithful the rules which the latter must follow in order to obtain eternal salvation. The power of jurisdiction is of Divine origin, in the sense that the pope is held to establish in the Church bishops whose mission it is to direct the faithful in the way of salvation. The bishops have then in their dioceses an ordinary jurisdiction, limited, however, by the rights that the pope can reserve to himself in virtue of his primacy. But this jurisdiction is independent of the will and consent of the faithful, and even of the clergy. In certain important matters, however, the bishop must at times seek the advice, at other times the consent, of the cathedral chapter. In certain countries, where chapters are not established, the bishop is bound to consult in some specified cases the *consultores cleri diœcesani*, or diocesan consultors (Third Council of Baltimore, nos. 17–22, 33, 179). On the other hand, certain classes of persons, especially the regulars properly so called, are exempt from episcopal authority, and certain matters are removed from the bishop's jurisdiction. Moreover, he has no power against the will of a superior authority, i. e. the pope, the councils, whether general, plenary, or provincial. The bishop possesses also other important powers through "delegated" jurisdiction which is accorded to him either by law, whether written or established by custom, or by grant of the sovereign pontiff through the Roman Congregations. The last named jurisdiction he exercises in the name of the Apostolic

See (see below). Certain writers attribute to the bishop a third kind of jurisdiction which they call "quasi-ordinary" jurisdiction, but there are wide differences as to the definition of this kind of jurisdiction. Several writers (such as Wernz, II, 10; Bargilliat, "Prælect. jur. can.", Paris, 1900, I, 164; and among the older canonists, Bouix, "De princip. juris canonici", Paris, 1852, 530) think that this distinction is useless; the jurisdiction known as quasi-ordinary is nothing else than an ordinary or delegated jurisdiction granted by written law or by custom.

It is a controverted question whether the bishops hold their jurisdiction directly from God or from the sovereign pontiff. The latter opinion, however, is almost generally admitted at the present day, for it is more in conformity with the monarchical constitution of the Church, which seems to demand that there should be no power in the Church not emanating immediately from the sovereign pontiff. Authors who hold the contrary opinion say that it is during the episcopal consecration that bishops receive from God their power of jurisdiction. But habitually before their consecration the bishops have already all powers of jurisdiction over their dioceses (Bargilliat, I, 442–445). Another question also discussed is whether the *potestas magisterii*, or teaching authority, is a consequence of the power of order or of jurisdiction (Sägmüller, Lehrbuch des katholischen Kirchenrechts, Freiburg, 1900–04, 24–25). Whatever the conclusion, teaching authority will here be ranked among the powers of jurisdiction. The teaching authority of the bishop and his governing authority (*potestas regiminis*) will now be successively considered, the latter comprising the legislative, dispensative, judicial, coercive, and administrative powers.

A. *Teaching Authority.*—By Divine law bishops have the right to teach Christian doctrine (Matt., xxviii, 19; Council of Trent, Sess. XXIV, De ref., ch. iv; Encyclical of Leo XIII, "Sapientiæ christianæ", 10 January, 1890; "Acta Sanctæ Sedis", 1890, XXII, 385). At the same time, the obligation of instructing the faithful either personally or, if hindered, through other ecclesiastics is incumbent upon them. They are bound also to see that in the parish churches the parish priests fulfil the requirements of preaching and teaching which the Council of Trent imposes upon them (Sess. V, De ref., ch. ii; Sess. XXIV, De ref., ch. iv). The bishop must also supervise the teaching of Christian doctrine in the seminaries, as well as in secondary and primary schools (Conc. Balt. III, nos. 194 sqq.; Const. "Romanos pontifices", 8 May, 1881; op. cit., Appendix, 212). In virtue of this right of superintendence, and because of the intimate relations which exist between instruction and education, the bishop is empowered to forbid attendance at undenominational schools, at least in those districts where Catholic schools exist, and where attendance at the former schools is dangerous. In virtue of the same right he will very often be bound to erect Catholic schools or favour their establishment (Third Council of Baltimore, nos. 194–213). No one is allowed to preach Christian doctrine without the consent of the bishop, or at least without his knowledge if it is a question of exempt religious preaching in their own churches (Council of Trent, Sess. V, De ref., ch. ii; Sess. XXIV, De ref., ch. iv). The bishop has power to supervise writings published or read in his diocese; works regarding the sacred sciences are subject to his approbation; he may forbid the reading of dangerous books and newspapers. He exercises a special control over the publications of the secular clergy, who are bound to consult him before undertaking the direction of newspapers or of publishing works even upon profane matters (Const. of Leo XIII, "Officiorum et munerum", 25 January, 1897; Vermeersch, "De prohibitione et censurâ librorum", 4th ed., Rome, 1906). He has the right

of special supervision over the manuals used in educational establishments, and as far as possible he will encourage the publication of good books and good newspapers (Third Council of Baltimore, nos. 201, 220, 221, 225, 226). The bishop is the *Inquisitor natus* or protector of the faith for his diocese. He has not, it is true, the right to define, outside an œcumenical council, controverted questions with regard to faith and morals, but when a heated discussion arises in his diocese, he can impose silence upon the parties concerned while awaiting a decision from the Holy See. If anyone, however, denies a point of doctrine defined by the Church, even though it be an exempt religious, the bishop will have the power to punish him (Council of Trent, Sess. V, De ref., ch. ii; Sess. XXIV, De ref., ch. iii). He must likewise guard the faithful of his diocese against dangerous societies condemned by the Holy See (Third Council of Baltimore, nos. 244–255).

B. *Governing Authority.*—(1) *Legislative Power.*—The bishop can enact for his diocese those laws which he considers conducive to the general good. Though he is not bound to convoke a synod for this purpose his legislative power is not absolute. He cannot legislate *contra jus commune*, i. e. enact a law contrary to the general law of the Church, written or established by custom, or to the decisions of general, plenary, or provincial councils. This is on the principle that an inferior cannot act contrary to the will of his superiors (ch. ii, De electione et electi potestate", I, iii, in the Clementines; Friedberg, II, 1135) He can, however, enact laws *juxta jus commune*, i. e. he can urge the observance of provisions of the common ecclesiastical law by penalizing the violation of the same (ch. ii, De constitutionibus, VI, I, ii; Friedberg, II, 937). He can determine the common ecclesiastical law, i. e. he can permit or forbid that which the common law neither forbids nor permits with certitude, and can apply to the particular needs of his diocese the general enactments of the pontifical laws. Many writers say that the bishop has also the power to enact laws *praeter jus commune*, i. e. to regulate those matters concerning which the common ecclesiastical law is silent, or at least particular points unforeseen by the common law. In any case, if the bishop wishes to add to the enactments of the common law (and the same principle is valid when it is a question of applying to the needs of his own diocese a general law of the Church), he must take care to make no enactments on matters which the common law, in the intention of the supreme legislator, has completely regulated. The common law implicitly forbids any episcopal action in such matters. Thus, e. g., the bishop cannot introduce new irregularities. In his diocesan legislation the bishop must not go beyond the purpose intended by the common ecclesiastical law. Thus, the latter forbids the clergy to take part in games of chance (*ludi aleatorii*), the aim of the law being to condemn the love of lucre and to avoid scandal; at the same time the bishop cannot forbid in private houses other games, which are not games of chance. On the other hand, if it be a matter concerning which the common law is silent, the bishop may take all necessary measures to prevent and put an end to abuses and to maintain ecclesiastical discipline. He must abstain, however, from imposing on his clergy extraordinary charges and obligations, and from unusual innovations. The legislative power of the bishop *praeter jus commune*, is, therefore, far from being absolute (Claeys-Bouuaert, De canonicâ cleri sæcularis obedientiâ, Louvain, 1904, 69–77). Canonical writers discuss the right of the bishop to abrogate a local custom contrary to the enactments of the common ecclesiastical law. He probably has not the right, provided that the custom be juridical, i. e. a reasonable one and legitimately prescribed. As this custom obtains only because of pontifical consent, it does not belong to the bishop to act contrary to the will of the pope. The power of granting dispensations is correlative to the legislative power. The bishop may, therefore, dispense with regard to all diocesan laws. He may also dispense, in particular cases only, from the laws of provincial and plenary synods; any dispensation from these laws would be next to impossible, if it were necessary on all such occasions to convoke a fresh provincial or plenary synod. The bishop, however, cannot dispense from enactments that relate directly to himself, and impose obligations upon him, or from enactments that accord rights to a third party. The bishop cannot dispense from laws made by the sovereign pontiff. To this there are, however, some exceptions. In certain matters, the written law or custom has granted this right to the bishop. He may also dispense from such laws in virtue of an expressly delegated power, or even sometimes in virtue of the consent, presumed or tacit, of the sovereign pontiff. These cases in reality are determined by custom. Canonical writers also admit that a bishop may grant a dispensation, when there is a doubt whether a dispensation is required, though in such a case it may be a question whether any dispensation at all is requisite (Bargilliat, I, 483–491).

(2) *Judicial Power.*—This power is exercised in two ways: without legal apparatus (*extra judicialiter*) or in a judicial process (*judicialiter*). In his diocese the bishop is judge in the first instance in all trials, civil and criminal, that pertain to the ecclesiastic tribunal, unless the persons be exempt from his authority, or the matters reserved for other judges; such, e. g., are the process of canonization reserved to the pope or the misdemeanours of a vicar-general, which fall under the cognizance of the archbishop. (Ch. vii, De officio judicis ordinarii, VI, I, xvi; Friedberg, II, 988; Council of Trent, Sess. XXIV, De ref., ch. xx.) In ecclesiastical trials he must conform to the general or special provisions of the law. (For matrimonial trials see "Instructio de judiciis ecclesiasticis circa causas matrimoniales" in "Acta et decreta Concilii Plenarii Baltimorensis III", Appendix, 262; for trials of ecclesiastics see the Instruction of the Propaganda, "Cum Magnopere", which reproduces substantially the Instruction of the Congregation of Bishops and Regulars of 11 June, 1880, op. cit., 287; see also S. Smith, "New procedure in criminal and disciplinary causes of ecclesiastics", 3d ed., New York, 1898.) The bishop has also judicial power which he exercises *extra judicialiter* both *in foro externo* (publicly) and *in foro interno* (in conscience). He has the power to absolve his subjects from all sins and censures not reserved to the Holy See. Moreover, the absolution from a censure inflicted by an ecclesiastical judge is always reserved to the latter or to his superiors (Bull, "Sacramentum Pœnitentiæ", 1 June, 1741 in "Benedicti XIV, Bullarium", Venice, 1778, I, 22; Const. "Apostolicæ Sedis", "Collectanea S. C. P.", 1002). On the other hand, the bishop may reserve to himself absolution from certain sins (Council of Trent, Sess. XIV, "De pœnit.", ch. vii; Third Plenary Council of Baltimore, nos. 124, 127).

(3) *Coercive Power.*—The right to punish is a necessary consequence of the right to judge. Formerly the bishop could and did inflict even corporal punishments and fines. These are no longer customary, even for ecclesiastics. The usual penalties for the laity are censures; for ecclesiastics, religious exercises, confinement for a time in a monastery (Third Plenary Council of Baltimore, nos. 72–73), degradation to an office of less importance (*privatio officii ecclesiastici*), and censures, especially suspension. The bishop may inflict suspension *ex informatâ conscientiâ*, i. e. on his personal responsibility, and without observing any legal formality, but in cases foreseen by the law (Instruction of Propaganda, 20 October, 1884; Conc. Balt. III, Appendix, 298). To the coercive power of the bishop belongs also the right of issuing certain commands (*præcepta*), i. e. of imposing on a particular ecclesiastic special obligations sanctioned by certain penalties (Constitution, "Cum Magnopere" nos. 4 and 8). He has also the lawful power to remove the penalties inflicted by him. Bishops can also grant indulgences: cardinals 200, archbishops 100, and bishops, 50 days' indulgence (Decree of Congregation of Indulgences, 28 August, 1903; Acta Sanctæ Sedis, XXXVI, 318).

(4) *Administrative Power.*—The matters to which the administrative power of the bishop extends can only be briefly indicated here: (a) The foremost is the supreme direction of the clergy. At the present day, generally speaking, it might be said that the bishop has the right to retain in his diocese a priest to whom he has entrusted ecclesiastical functions and given the means of subsistence (Claeys-Bouuaert, 200–244). In case of necessity or great utility, e. g. given a scarcity of priests, the bishop may compel an ecclesiastic to accept ecclesiastical functions, but he will require a pontifical indult to impose upon him the *cura animarum*, or cure of souls. Ecclesiastics ordained *titulo missionis* (see HOLY ORDERS, MISSIONS) take upon themselves special obligations in this matter. (See Instruction of Propaganda, 27 April, 1871, and the Reply of 4 February, 1873; Conc. Plen. Balt. III, Appendix, 204–211; decree "De seminariorum alumnis", 22 December, 1905; "Acta Sanctæ Sedis", 1905, XXXVIII, 407.) The bishop may also nominate to the benefices and ecclesiastical functions of his own diocese. Certain nominations, however, are reserved to the Holy See, and in several countries the right of patronage still exists. (b) The bishop, moreover, intervenes in the administration of ecclesiastical property. No alienation whatever of ecclesiastical goods is possible without his consent, and he exercises supreme supervision over their administration. (c) He has a special right of intervention in all matters relating to Divine worship and to the sacraments; he authorizes and supervises the printing of liturgical books, regulates public worship, processions, exposition of the Blessed Sacrament, celebration of the Holy Mass, celebration of Mass twice on the same day by the same priest (see BINATION), and exorcisms; his consent is required for the erection of churches and oratories; he authorizes the public veneration of the relics of saints and of those who have been beatified; he exercises supervision over statues and images exposed for the veneration of the faithful; he publishes indulgences, etc. But in all these matters his power is not unlimited; he must conform to the enactments of the canon law.

Bishops have also a "delegated jurisdiction", which they exercise in the name of the Holy See; this power is granted to them *a jure* or *ab homine*. Ecclesiastical law frequently accords to bishops delegated powers; but it would be wrong to say, for instance, that every power of dispensation granted by a general law of the Church is a delegated one. Such power is perhaps quite as often an ordinary power. But when the law accords a power of jurisdiction to the bishop, *tanquam Sedis apostolicæ delegatus*, it is a delegated power that he receives. (See, for example, Council of Trent, Sess. V, De ref., ch. i, ii; Sess. VI, De ref., ch. iii; Sess. VII, De ref., ch. vi, viii, xiv, etc.) Writers do not agree as to the nature of the power accorded to the bishop also as delegate of the Apostolic See, *etiam tanquam sedis apostolicæ delegatus*. Some maintain that in this case the bishop has at the same time both ordinary and delegated power, but only relative to such persons as are subject to his jurisdiction (Reiffenstuel, Jus canonicum universum, Paris, 1864, tit. xxix, 37); others contend that in this case the bishop has ordinary jurisdiction with regard to his subjects, and only a delegated one with regard to those who are exempt (Hinschius, System des katholischen Kirchenrechts, Berlin, 1869, I, 178; Scherer, Handbuch des Kirchenrechtes, Graz, 1886, I, 421, note 36); others again maintain that the bishop has at the same time both an ordinary and a delegated power over his subjects, and a delegated power over those who are exempt (Wernz, II, 816); finally, others see in this formula only a means of removing any obstacles which might prevent the bishop from using the power accorded to him (Santi, Prælect. jur. can., New York, 1898, I, 259). The delegated powers *ab homine* are at the present of very great importance, especially in missionary countries. The Apostolic Penitentiary grants those which are only concerned with the forum of conscience. The others are granted by the Congregation of the Propaganda. They are called *facultates habituales*, because not granted for a determined individual case. These faculties are no longer accorded only to the bishop in his own person but to the ordinaries, that is to say, to the bishop, to his successor, to the administrator *pro tem.* of the diocese, and to the vicar-general, to vicars Apostolic, prefects, etc. (Declaration of the Holy Office, 26 November, 1897, 22 April, 1898, 25 June, 1898, 5 September, 1900; Acta Sanctæ Sedis, 1897–98, XXX, 627, 702; 1898–99, XXXI, 120; 1900–01, XXXIII, 225). As a general rule the bishop can subdelegate these powers, provided that the faculties do not forbid it (Holy Office, 16 December, 1898; Acta Sanctæ Sedis, 1898–99, XXXI, 635). For further information see Putzer-Konings, "Commentarium in facultates apostolicas" (5th ed., New York, 1898). On the other hand, the bishop can always ask the Holy See for such delegated powers as are necessary in the administration of his diocese. The bishop is also the ordinary and habitual executor of the dispensations which the Holy See grants *in foro externo*, i. e. for public use or application.

IV. OBLIGATIONS OF THE BISHOP.—In describing the rights of bishops we have already in great measure indicated what their obligations are. All their efforts must aim at preserving the true faith and a high moral tone among the people; they attain this end by good example, by preaching, by daily solicitude for the good administration of the diocese, and by prayer. Bishops, in effect, are bound by the Divine law to implore the help of God for the faithful committed to their care. Canon law has determined more fully this obligation, and imposes upon the bishops the obligation of celebrating Mass for the faithful of their dioceses (*missa pro grege*) every Sunday, on the feast days of obligation and on the abrogated feast days (Const. Leo XIII "In supremâ", 10 June, 1882; "Collectanea, S. C. P.", no. 112). The bishop is bound to take special care of the education of youth and of the training of his clergy; he must exercise continual vigilance over the latter and assist them with his counsels. The Church has imposed as special obligations upon bishops the canonical visitation of the diocese and the holding of an annual diocesan synod. The bishop is bound to visit each year the greater part of his diocese, either personally or, if prevented, through his delegates. This visit will permit him to administer the Sacrament of Confirmation (Council of Trent, Sess. XXIV, De ref., ch. iii). The Third Plenary Council of Baltimore grants the bishop three years for making this visitation (Acta et decreta, no. 14). The Council of Trent ordered that an annual diocesan synod should be held (Sess. XXIV, De ref., ch. ii). At present, the Holy See no longer urges the strict observation of this legislation (Santi, Prælect. Jur. can., I, 360). The Third Council of Baltimore decreed that the bishop should take counsel with the

diocesan consultors whenever he wished to convoke a synod (Acta et decreta, no. 20). It is then unnecessary for the synod to assemble every year. However in missionary countries the Holy See desires that these synods should be rather frequent and dispenses the bishop from the observation of the formalities difficult to fulfil, e. g. the convoking of all ecclesiastics who ought to be present at the synod (Letter of Propaganda to the Bishop of Milwaukee, 29 July, 1889, "Collectanea, S. C. P.", no. 117). It is evident, finally, that the bishop cannot fulfil the duties of his office unless he observes the law of residence. The bishop is obliged to reside in his diocese and it is proper that he should be in the episcopal city on the principal feast days of the year. He cannot be absent from his diocese for more than three months, except for grave reason approved of by the Holy See (Council of Trent, Sess. VI, De ref., ch. i; Sess. XXIII, De ref., ch. i; Benedict XIV, "Ad universæ christianæ", 3 September, 1746; Letters of Propaganda, 24 April and 24 August, 1861; "Collectanea, S. C. P.", nos. 103, 105).

The bishop has also obligations regarding the Holy See. Throughout his entire administration he must conform to the general legislation of the Church and the directions of the pope. In this respect two special obligations are incumbent upon him: he must pay the *Visitatio ad limina Apostolorum*, and present the *Relatio de statu diæcesis*, i. e. he must visit the shrines of Sts. Peter and Paul at Rome and present a report on the condition of his diocese. In the time of Paschal II (1099–1118), only metropolitans were bound to pay this visit. The Decretals imposed this obligation upon bishops whose consecration the pope reserved to himself (C. iv, "De electione et electi potestate"; X, I, vi; c. xiii, "De majoritate et obedientiâ", X, I, xxxiii; c. iv, "De jurejurando", X, II, xxiv; Friedberg, II, 49, 201, 360). It has become general since the fifteenth century, and Sixtus definitely ruled in favour of this obligation (Bull, "Romanus Pontifex", 20 December, 1585; "Bullarum amplissima collectio", ed. Cocquelines, Rome, 1747, IV, iv, 173). According to this Bull the bishops of Italy and the neighbouring islands, of Dalmatia and Greece, must make the visit *ad limina* every three years; those of Germany, France, Spain, England, Portugal, Belgium, Bohemia, Hungary, Poland, and the islands of the Mediterranean Sea every four years; those of other parts of Europe, of North Africa, and the isles of the Atlantic Ocean situated to the east of the New World, every five years; those of other parts of the world every ten years. The bishops of Ireland, in virtue of a privilege of 10 May, 1631, are bound to pay this visit only every ten years. Even in the case of more recently erected sees the years are counted from 20 December, 1585, date of the aforesaid Bull (Instruction of Propaganda, 1 June, 1877; "Collectanea, S. C. P.", no. 110). The bishops must pay this visit personally and for this purpose are allowed to absent themselves from their dioceses, the bishops of Italy for four months, other bishops for seven months. The Holy See sometimes dispenses a bishop from the obligation of paying this visit personally, and permits him to send, as his delegate, a priest of his diocese, especially one of those who have been promoted to a high office (*dignitates*), or a priest of the diocese sojourning at Rome, or even the agent of the bishop in that city, if an ecclesiastic. While this visit, as stated above, ought to be paid the third, fourth, fifth, or tenth year, the rule suffers frequent exceptions in practice (Wernz, II, 914). The *Visitatio Liminum* includes a visit to the tombs of St. Peter and St. Paul, an audience with the Holy Father, and a written report which the bishop ought to present to the Congregation of the Council (*Congregatio specialis super statu ecclesiarum* also called *Concilietto*) according to the formula of

Benedict XIII. in 1725 (A. Lucidi, De Visitatione sacrorum Liminum, 5th ed., Rome, 1883).

Bishops subject to the Propaganda present this statement to the latter congregation (the proper formula is in "Acta Sanctæ Sedis", 1891–92; XXIV, 382, "Collectanea", no. 104). In addition they ought also to send, every five years, a report to the Propaganda according to the formulary drawn up by this congregation, 24 April, 1861 (Collectanea, no. 104). This obligation had formerly been an annual one (Decrees of Propaganda, 31 October, 1838, 27 September, 1843, and 23 March, 1844; Collectanea, nos. 97–99; Third Council of Baltimore, no. 14).

Finally, mention may be made of certain privileges enjoyed by bishops. They do not fall under suspensions and interdicts, *latæ sententiæ*, i. e. incurred *ipso facto*, unless express mention of them is therein made; those who are guilty of assaults upon them are punished with an excommunication reserved *speciali modo* to the sovereign pontiff; they possess the right of having a domestic chapel and enjoy the privilege of the *altare portabile*, or portable altar, etc.

V. Non-Catholic Use.—The title of bishop is still retained in certain Protestant churches. For its use in the Anglican Church see Sir R. Phillimore, "Ecclesiastical Law in the Church of England" (new ed., 1895); F. Makower, "Verfassung der Kirche von England" (1894), and the "Encycl. Britannica" (9th ed.), III, 788–789; cf., also, O. J. Reichel, "A Short Manual of Canon Law" (The Sacraments), London, 1896, 283–298. For its use in the national Protestant Churches of Denmark and Sweden, see articles treating of those countries, and for its history and use in the Evangelical churches of Prussia and the European continent, Jacobson-Friedberg in "Real-Encycl. f. prot. Theol. und Kirche" (3d ed., 1897), III, 246–247. For its use in Protestant churches of the United States see Baptists, Methodists, Mormons. The antiquities and constitution of the Greek episcopate are treated by J. M. Heineccius in "Abbildung der alten und neuen griechischen Kirche" (Leipzig, 1711), and in Milasch-Pessič, "Das Kirchenrecht der morgenländischen Kirche" (Germ. tr. of 2nd ed., Mostar, 1905); the actual conditions of the Greek episcopate, Catholic and Orthodox (Schismatic), are described in Silbernagl-Schnitzer, Verfassung und gegenwärtiger Bestand sämtlicher "Kirchen des Orients" (2nd ed., Ratisbon, 1904), *passim*.

Paganus, *Tract. de ord., jurisdict. et resident. episc.* (Venice, 1570); Filesacus, *De sacrá episcoporum auctoritate* (Paris, 1605); Alzedo, *De præcellentiá episcopalis dignitatis deque episcopi functionibus* (Lyons, 1630); Barbosa, *Pastoralis sollicitudinis sive de officio et potestate episcopi tripartitá descriptio* (Lyons, 1628); Piacesius, *Praxis episcopalis et ecclesiastica omnia et singula officium potestatemque episcopi concernentia complectens* (Cologne, 1665); Antonelli, *De regimine ecclesiæ episcopalis* (Venice, 1705); Benedict XIV, *De synodo diœcesaná* (Louvain, 1763); Andreucci, *Hierarchia ecclesiastica in varias suas partes distributa* (Rome, 1766); Petavius, *Dissertatio de episcopis et eorum jurisdictione et auctoritate* (Vienna, 1766); Gavanti, *Enchiridion seu manuale episcoporum* (Venice, 1769); Thomassin, *Vetus ac nova Ecc. disciplina circa beneficia etc.* (Venice, 1768), Pt. I, bk. I, ch. i (2), 50–60; Helfert, *Rechten und Pflichten der Bischöfe und Pfarrer und deren Gehilfen und Stellvertreter* (Prague, 1832); Bouix, *Tractatus de episcopo ubi et de synodo diœcesaná* (Paris, 1859); Von Scherer, *Handbuch des Kirchenrechts* (Graz, 1886) I, 553 (good bibliography); Melchers, *De canonicá diœcesis visitatione cum appendice de visitatione sacrorum liminum* (Cologne, 1893); De Brabandere, *Juris canonici compendium* (7th ed., Bruges, 1903), I, 257–299; Zitelli, *Apparatus juris ecclesiastici* (3d ed., Rome, 1903), 32–60; Smith, *Elements of Ecclesiastical Law* (New York, 1881), I, 271–356; Taunton, *The Law of the Church* (London, 1906), 79–123; Vives y Tuto, *De Dignitate et Officiis Episcoporum et Prælatorum* (Rome, 1905), an encyclopedia of the episcopal office; *Cath. Univ. Bulletin* (1906), XII, 363, 364. The antiquities of the bishop's office are collected in Thomassin, op. cit.; Kraus in *Realencycl.* (1880), I, 162–168; Binterim, *Denkwürdigkeiten der christkathol. Kirche* (1825–58), I (2), 121–145; 363–377; Bingham, *Antiquities of the Christian Church* (new ed., Oxford, 1855), I, *passim* (see index in Vol X). For the bishop in medieval England see Lingard, *History and Antiquities of the Anglo-Saxon Church* (reprint, London, 1899), *passim*; Stubbs, *Constitutional History of England* (London, 1891),

passim. For the office of bishop in medieval Ireland see Adamnan, *Life of St. Columba*, Reeves, ed. (Dublin, 1857), 339–341 and *passim*; Lanigan, *Eccl. Hist. of Ireland* (Dublin, 1828); Joyce, *A Social Hist. of Ireland* (London, 1903), 320–324, 388 and *passim*; (with caution) Ware-Harris, *Antiquities of Ireland* (Dublin, 1764), I, *passim* (Bishops of Ireland); Skene, *Celtic Scotland* (Edinburgh, 1887), II, *passim*; Cardinal Moran, *Essay on the Origin, Doctrines, and Discipline of the Early Irish Church* (Dublin, 1864).

A. Van Hove.

Bishop, Auxiliary. See Auxiliary Bishop.

Bishop, Coadjutor. See Bishop.

Bishop, William, the first superior in England in episcopal orders since the old hierarchy died out in the reign of Elizabeth, born c. 1553 at Brailes, in Warwickshire, where his family continued to reside until recent times; d. 16 April, 1624. He went to Gloucester Hall, Oxford, in 1570; but retired abroad four years later, and joined Allen at the English College, Douai. From thence he went to Rome, and after completing his studies and being ordained priest, we find him once more in England, where he was called upon to endure many and great hardships. On at least two occasions, he was apprehended, imprisoned for some years, and then banished. It was during one of these periods of banishment that he went to Paris and took the degree of Doctor of Divinity at the Sorbonne. Dr. Bishop took a leading part in the unfortunate disputes between seculars and regulars at that time. The latter party, by means of their influence at Rome, had secured the appointment of an "archpriest" as superior of the English mission. The secular clergy resented this, calling out for the restoration of episcopal government in some form. They became known as "the Appellants", and were favoured by Elizabeth, who contrived to assist them secretly to prosecute their appeals. In 1598 Bishop himself went to Rome, with another priest, to lay their case before the Holy See. On their arrival, however, they found the Jesuit influence still supreme, and by order of Cardinal Cajetan, Protector of England, they were imprisoned at the English College, under Father Persons. After three months' confinement, they were dismissed, but with a strict injunction not to go back to England. It was not until there had been further representations and another deputation to Rome that four years later this injunction was removed.

Soon after his return, in 1603, Bishop drew up the famous "Protestation of Allegiance" to Queen Elizabeth, signed by twelve other priests besides himself, in which they definitely took up their stand against those who aimed at the conversion of England by political means. At least one of these priests (Roger Cadwallador) was afterwards martyred and probably also a second (Robert Drury), though there is some doubt about his identity. Elizabeth never saw the "Protestation", for on the very day on which it was signed, she was seized with what proved to be her last illness. It was violently denounced by the opposing party; but it would seem that Rome was large-minded enough not to condemn it, for when more than twenty years later the petition of the clergy was at length granted, and a vicar Apostolic of England was appointed with episcopal powers, William Bishop was chosen for the office. He became nominally Bishop of Chalcedon, *in partibus infidelium*. Dr. Bishop was only to be Vicar Apostolic for ten months; but during that short time he organized a systematic form of ecclesiastical government, consisting of five vicars-general, assisted by archdeacons and rural deans throughout the country. He also instituted a chapter of twenty-four canons, who were to assume jurisdiction whenever there should be for any reason no vicar Apostolic, which happened at one time for thirty years. His right to make such institution has often been questioned, but during the period referred to, Rome recognized their jurisdiction. On the restoration of the hierarchy in 1850, when diocesan chapters were erected, the "Old Chapter" did not dissolve, but changed its name, and as the "Old Brotherhood of the Secular Clergy" it exists to-day, a lasting memorial to the work of the first vicar Apostolic. An oil painting of Bishop hangs at Archbishop's House, Westminster, London, a print of which appeared in the "Catholic Directory" for 1810. The works of Bishop are: "A Reformation of a Catholicke Deformed, in answer to W. Perkins" (1604; Part II, 1607); "Answer to Mr. Perkins's Advertisement" (1607); "Reproof of Dr. Abbot's Defence of a Catholicke Deformed" (1608); "Disproof of Dr. Abbot's Counterproofs" (1614); "Defence of King's Title"; "Pitts, de Illustribus Angliæ Scriptoribus" (1619); "Protestation of Loyalty" (see above); pamphlets on archpriest controversy, etc.

Dodd, *Ch. Hist. of Eng.*, ed. Tierney; *Douay Diaries;* Gillow, *Bibl. Dict. of Eng. Catholics;* Butler, *Hist. Memoirs* (1819); Berington, *Memoirs of Panzani* (1794); *Catholic Directory,* 1810; Brady, *Annals of Cath. Hierarchy* (1877); Law, *Jesuits and Seculars in Reign of Elizabeth* (1889); MS. Life in Westminster Archives, London.

BERNARD WARD.

Bishopric. See DIOCESE.

Bishop's Book. See HENRY VIII; BOOK OF COMMON PRAYER.

Bishop's Crook. See PASTORAL STAFF.

Bisignano, DIOCESE OF. See SAN MARCO.

Bisomus, a tomb large enough to contain two bodies. The ordinary tombs (*loci*) in the galleries of the Roman catacombs contained one body. It sometimes happened, however, that a space large enough to contain two bodies was excavated. Such a double grave is referred to in inscriptions as *locus bisomus.* An inscription from the catacomb of St. Calixtus, for instance, informs us that a certain Boniface, who died at the age of twenty-three years and two months, was interred in a double grave which had been prepared for himself and for his father (Bonifacius, qui vixit annis XXIII et II (mens) es, positus in bisomum in pace, sibi et patr. suo). A fourth-century inscription tells of two ladies who had purchased, for their future interment, a bisomus in a "new crypt" which contained the body of a Saint:—

IN CRYPTA NOBA RETRO SAN
CTVS EMERVM VIVAS BALER
RA ET SABINA MERUM LOC
V BISOM AB APRONE ET A
BIATORE

Like so many pious but rather superstitious persons of that age "Balerra" and "Sabina" wished to be buried in the closest proximity to a martyr, *retro sanctos,* a privilege which, as we learn from another inscription, "many desire but few receive" (*quod multi cupiunt et rari accipiunt*).

Nesbitt in *Dict. Christ. Ant.,* s. v.; Northcote and Brownlow; *Roma Sott.* (London, 1878); Marucchi, *Eléments d'arch. chrét.: notions gén.* (Paris, 1899).

MAURICE M. HASSETT.

Bitonto, DIOCESE OF. See REWO.

Bkerke. See GIBIAL AND BOTRI, DIOCESE OF.

Blackburne, ROBERT, an English Catholic who suffered imprisonment in the closing years of the seventeenth, and during the earlier half of the eighteenth, centuries, d. 1748; was a son of Richard Blackburne, of Thistleton, Lancaster. The Blackburne family is one of the most ancient and respected Catholic families in Lancashire. Robert Blackburne was arrested in 1695 on suspicion of being connected with what was known as the Lancashire Plot. He was never brought to trial, although kept in prison for fifty-three years. The case was more than once brought to the attention of Parliament, but nothing was done for his relief. He was never tried or released, and finally died in prison.

Gillow, *Bibl. Dict. Eng. Cath.,* I, 223.

THOMAS GAFFNEY TAAFFE.

Black Fast, THE.—This form of fasting, the most rigorous in the history of church legislation, was marked by austerity regarding the quantity and quality of food permitted on fasting days as well as the time wherein such food might be legitimately taken.

In the first place more than one meal was strictly prohibited. At this meal flesh meat, eggs, butter, cheese, and milk were interdicted (Gregory I, Decretals IV, cap. vi; Trullan Synod, Canon lvi). Besides these restrictions abstinence from wine, especially during Lent, was enjoined (Thomassin, Traité des jeûnes de l'Eglise, II, vii). Furthermore, during Holy Week the fare consisted of bread, salt, herbs, and water (Laymann, Theologia Moralis, Tr. VIII; De observatione jejuniorum, i). Finally, this meal was not allowed until sunset. St. Ambrose (De Elia et jejunio, sermo viii, in Psalm CXVIII), St. Chrysostom (Homil. iv in Genesim), St. Basil (Oratio i, De jejunio) furnish unequivocal testimony concerning the three characteristics of the black fast. The keynote of their teaching is sounded by St. Bernard (Sermo. iii, No. 1, De Quadragesima), when he says "hitherto we have fasted only until none" (3 p. m.) "whereas, now" (during Lent) "kings and princes, clergy and laity, rich and poor will fast until evening". It is quite certain that the days of Lent (Muller, Theologia Moralis, II, Lib. II, Tr. ii, § 165, no. 11) as well as those preceding ordination were marked by the black fast. This regime continued until the tenth century when the custom of taking the only meal of the day at three o'clock was introduced (Thomassin, loc. cit.). In the fourteenth century the hour of taking this meal was changed to noon-day (Muller, loc. cit.). Shortly afterwards the practice of taking a collation in the evening began to gain ground (Thomassin, op. cit., II, xi). Finally, the custom of taking a crust of bread and some coffee in the morning was introduced in the early part of the nineteenth century. During the past fifty years, owing to ever changing circumstances of time and place, the Church has gradually relaxed the severity of penitential requirements, so that now little more than a vestige of former rigour obtains.

St. Thomas, *Summa Theol.,* II, Q. ii, 2–147; Bingham, *Antiquities of the Christian Church* (London, 1844); Gunning, *The Paschal or Lent Fast* (Oxford, 1845).

J. D. O'NEILL.

Blackfoot Indians, an important tribe of the Northern Plains, constituting the westernmost extension of the great Algonquian stock. Instead of being a compact people with a head chief and central government, they are properly a confederacy of three sub-tribes speaking the same language, namely: Siksika or Blackfoot proper; Kaina (Kæna), or Blood; Pikûni, or Piegan, each of which sub-tribes is again subdivided into bands, to the number of some fifty in all. In close alliance with them are the Atsína, or Grosventres, a branch of the more southern Arapahoe, and the Sassi, a detached band of the Beaver Indians farther to the north. As is usually the case with Indian etymologies, the origin of the name is disputed. One tradition ascribes it to the blackening of their moccasins from the ashes of prairie fires on their first arrival in their present country. It may have come, however, from the former wearing of a black moccasin, such as distinguished certain southern tribes. The name is also that of a prominent war-society among tribes of the Plains.

As indicated by linguistic affinity, the Blackfeet

are immigrants from the East. About one hundred years ago, and until gathered upon reservations, they held most of the immense territory stretching from the southern headwaters of the Missouri, in Montana, almost to the North Saskatchewan, in Canada, and from about 105° W. longitude to the base of the Rocky Mountains. They are now settled on three reservations in the Province of Alberta, Canada, and one in Montana, U. S., being about equally divided between the two governments. The Atsína are also now settled in Montana, while the Sassi are in Alberta.

Most of the early estimates of Blackfoot population are unreliable and usually exaggerated. The estimate made by Mackenzie (about the year 1790) of 2250 to 2550 warriors, or perhaps 8500 souls, is probably very near the truth for that period. In 1780, 1837, 1845, 1857, and 1869, they suffered great losses by smallpox. In 1883–84 some 600 on the Montana reservation died of starvation in consequence of a simultaneous failure of the buffalo and reduction of rations. In addition to these wholesale losses, they suffered a continual wasting from wars with the surrounding tribes—Cree, Assiniboin, Sioux, Crow, Flathead, Kutenai—for the Blackfeet were a particularly warlike and aggressive people, and, with the exception of the two small tribes living under their protection, they had no allies. The official Indian report for 1858 gives them 7300 souls, but a careful unofficial estimate made about the same time puts them at 6720. In 1906 they were officially reported to number in all 4617, as follows: Blackfoot Agency, Alberta, 842; Blood Agency, Alberta, 1204, Piegan Agency, Alberta, 499; Blackfoot Agency (Piegan), Montana, 2072.

In their culture the Blackfeet were a typical Plains tribe, living in skin tipis, roving from place to place without permanent habitation, without pottery, basketry, or canoes, having no agriculture except for the planting of a native tobacco, and depending almost entirely upon the buffalo for subsistence. Their traditions go back to a time when they had no horses, hunting the buffalo on foot by means of driveways constructed of loose stones; but as early as 1800 they had many horses taken from the southern tribes, and later became noted for their great herds. They procured guns and horses about the same time, and were thus enabled to extend their incursions successfully over wide areas. While generally friendly to the Hudson's Bay Company traders, they were, in the earlier period, usually hostile towards Americans, although never regularly at war with the government. Upon ceremonial occasions each of the three principal tribes camped in a great circle, as usual among the Plains tribes, the tipis of each band occupying a definite section of the circle, with the "medicine lodge", or ceremonial sacred structure, in the centre of the circle. The assertion that these smaller bands constituted exogamic clans seems consistent with Plains Indians custom. There was also a military society consisting of several subdivisions, or orders, of various rank, from boys in training to the retired veterans who acted as advisers and directors of the rites. Each of these orders had its distinctive uniform and equipment, songs and dance, and took charge of some special function at public gatherings. There were also the ordinary secret societies for the practice of medicine, magic, and special industrial arts, each society usually having its own sacred tradition in the keeping of a chosen priest. The industrial societies were usually composed of women. The ordinary dress in old times was of prepared deerskins; the arms were the bow, knife, club, lance, and shield, and, later, the gun. The principal deity was the sun, and a supernatural being known as *Napi*, "Old Man"— perhaps an incarnation of the same idea. The great

tribal ceremony was the Sun Dance, held annually in the summer season. The marriage tie was easily broken, and polygamy was permitted. The dead were usually deposited in trees, or sometimes in tipis erected for the purpose on prominent hills. In physique the Blackfeet are tall and finely built; in temper, aggressive, unruly, and uncertain.

The earliest missionary work among the Blackfeet was that of the French Jesuits who accompanied the explorer Verendrye in the Saskatchewan region in 1731–42. Among these may be named Fathers Nicholas Gonnor, Charles Mesaiger, and Jean Aulneau. Nothing more was done until the establishment of the Red River colony by Lord Selkirk, who, in 1816, brought out Fathers Dumoulin and Provencher from Montreal to minister to the wants of the colonists and Indians. Their Indian work, at first confined to the Crees and Ojibwa, was afterwards extended, under the auspices of the Oblates, to the Blackfeet and Assiniboin. Among the most noted of these Oblate missionaries were Father Albert Lacombe (1848–90), author of a manuscript Blackfoot dictionary, as well as of a monumental grammar and dictionary of the Cree, and Father Emile Legal (1881–90), author of several important manuscripts relating to the Blackfoot tribe and language. Protestant mission work in the tribe was begun by the Wesleyan Methodists about 1840 (though without any regular establishment until 1871), and by the Episcopalians at about the same date.

GRINNELL, *Blackfoot Lodge Tales* (1892); HAYDEN, *Ethnography and Philology of the Missouri River Valley Tribes* (1862); HODGE, *Handbook of Am. Indians*; MOONEY, *Missions, Siksika*, etc., in *Reports, Bureau of Am. Ethnology* (1907); MACKENZIE, *Voyages* (1801); PILLING, *Bibliography of the Algonquin Languages*, *s. vv. Blackfoot, Lacombe, Legal, McLean, Tims*, in *Reports, B. Am. Ethn.* (1891); WISSLER, *Blackfoot Indians* in *Ontario Archæological Report for 1905* (Toronto, 1906); *Annual Reports of the Commissioner of Indian Affairs* (U. S.) and *Superintendent of Indian Affairs* (Canada).

JAMES MOONEY.

Black Friars. See DOMINICANS; CANONS AND CANONESSES REGULAR OF ST. AUGUSTINE; HERMITS OF ST. AUGUSTINE.

Blackloe, THOMAS. See WHITE, THOMAS.

Black Monks. See BENEDICTINE ORDER; CANONS AND CANONESSES REGULAR OF ST. AUGUSTINE; HERMITS OF ST. AUGUSTINE.

Black Sisters (AUGUSTINIAN NUNS). See ALEXIAN NUNS.

Black Sunday. See PASSION SUNDAY.

Blackwood, ADAM, author, b. at Dunfermline, Scotland, 1539; d. 1613. He was a great-nephew of Robert Reid, Bishop of Orkney (1541–58), who provided for his education, both his parents being dead, at the University of Paris. On the bishop's death, Queen Mary's generosity enabled Adam to complete his studies at Paris and Toulouse. He taught philosophy at Paris and published there a funeral poem on King Charles IX (1574) and a work on the relation between religion and government (1575). Archbishop James Beaton recommended him to Mary for the office of Judge of the Parliament of Poitiers (Poitou was under her jurisdiction as Dowager of France), and here he married Catherine Courtinier. Blackwood collected a good library, and wrote several books, one an "Apology for Kings", denouncing Buchanan's views with much bitterness, and another a vigorous defence of Queen Mary, published in Paris (nominally in Edinburgh) after her death. Other works by him were a book of pious meditations in prose and verse and an ascetic commentary on the fiftieth Psalm. Blackwood died in 1613, and was buried at Poitiers. His widow married François de la Mothe le Vayer, and one of his daughters became the wife of George Crichton, Regius Professor of Greek in the University of Paris.

Adami Blacvodæi opera omnia (Paris, 1644), ed. GABRIEL; NAUDÉ (with a portrait and prefatory life); IRVING, *Scottish Writers*, I, 161–169; DEMPSTER, *Hist. Eccles: Gentis Scotorum*, 116; BLACKWOOD, *Martyre de la Royne d'Escosse* is included in JEBB, *De vitâ et rebus gestis Mariæ Scot. Reginæ* (1725), II, 175 (Maitland Club tr., 1734).

D. O. HUNTER-BLAIR.

Blais, ANDREW. See RIMOUSKI, DIOCESE OF.

Blaise (BLASIUS), Saint, bishop and martyr.— The ninth-century martyrologies of Europe in their lists, which are accompanied by historical notices, give on 15 February the name of St. Blasius, Bishop of Sebaste and martyr. The Greek synaxaria mention him under 11 February. In the oldest known recension of the so-called martyrology of St. Jerome the name of St. Blasius does not appear; it is only in the later, enlarged catalogues that he is mentioned. The historical notices concerning him in the above-mentioned martyrologies and synaxaria rest on the legendary Acts. All the statements agree that St. Blasius was Bishop of Sebaste in Armenia and most of the accounts place his martyrdom in the reign of Licinius (about 316). As these reports may rest on old traditions which are bound up with the veneration of the saint in the Church liturgy, they are not to be absolutely rejected. It can perhaps be assumed that St. Blasius was a bishop and that he suffered martyrdom at the beginning of the fourth century. All the particulars concerning his life and martyrdom which are found in the Acts are purely legendary and have no claim to historical worth. There are besides various recensions of the text of the Acts. According to the legend Blasius was a physician at Sebaste before he was raised to the episcopal see. At the time of the persecution under Licinius he was taken prisoner at the command of the governor, Agricolaus. The hunters of the governor found him in the wilderness in a cave to which he had retired and while in prison he performed a wonderful cure on a boy who had a fishbone in his throat and who was in danger of choking to death. After suffering various forms of torture St. Blasius was beheaded; the Acts relate also the martyrdom of seven women. The veneration of the Oriental saint was brought at an early date into Europe, as is shown by the recitals in the historical martyrologies of the ninth century, and the Latin recension of the legend of St. Blasius; so that Blasius became one of the most popular saints of the Middle Ages. The actual reason for the unusual veneration has not yet been made clear. Most probably one ground was that according to the legend he was a physician and wonderful cures were ascribed to him; for this reason the faithful sought his help and intercession when ill. Numberless churches and altars were dedicated to him and many localities (Taranto, Ragusa, the Abbey of St. Blasius in the Black Forest, etc.) claimed to possess some of his relics. He was also one of the Fourteen Holy Martyrs. In many places on the day of his feast the blessing of St. Blasius is given: two candles are consecrated, generally by a prayer, these are then held in a crossed position by a priest over the heads of the faithful or the people are touched on the throat with them. In other places oil is consecrated in which the wick of a small candle is dipped and the throats of those present are touched with the wick. At the same time the following blessing is given: "Per intercessionem S. Blasii liberet te Deus a malo gutteris et a quovis alio malo" (May God at the intercession of St. Blasius preserve you from throat troubles and every other evil). In some dioceses is added: "in nomine Patris et Filii et Spiritus" and the priest makes the sign of the cross over the faithful. In the Latin Church his feast falls on 3 February, in the Oriental Churches on 11 February. He is represented holding two crossed candles in his hand (the Blessing of St. Blasius), or in a cave surrounded

by wild beasts, as he was found by the hunters of the governor.

Acta SS., February, I 331–336; (*Commentarius*), 336–353 (*Acta*); MOMBRITIUS, *Sanctuarium*, I, 81–83; ed. BOLLANDISTS (Brussels, 1898–99), I, 204–205; METAPHRASTES, *Vitæ Sanctorum* in MIGNE, *P. G.*, CXVI, col. 817 sqq.; *Synaxarium Constantinopel.*, ed. DELAHAYE (Brussels, 1902), 458; UHRIG, *Die XIV heiligen Nothelfer* in *Theol. Quartalschrift* (Tübingen, 1888), 72 sqq.; NICCOLAI, *Memorie storiche di S. Biagio, vescovo e martire, protettore della republica di Ragusa* (Rome, 1752); *Vita e martirio di S. Biagio, vescovo di Sebaste* (Monza, 1889); ELLES, *The Holy Helpers, Sts. Blaise and Erasmus* in *The Dublin Review* (1889), 340 sqq.; PISTRE, *Vie de S. Blaise, évêque de Sébaste* (Toulouse, 1861).

J. P. KIRSCH.

Blanc, ANTHONY, fifth Bishop, and first Archbishop, of New Orleans, La., U. S. A., b. at Sury, near Lyons, France, 11 Oct., 1792; d. at New Orleans, 20 June, 1860. He was one of the first ecclesiastical students after the restoration of the Church in France, and was ordained priest on 22 July, 1816, by Bishop Dubourg of New Orleans, in the Seminary at Lyons, during a visit of that prelate in search of help and volunteers for the American mission. He came to America in September, 1817, landing at Annapolis, Md., with several young seminarians, and was entertained until the end of October by Charles Carroll at Carrolton. He then went with Bishop Dubourg to New Orleans and for nearly fifteen years led the arduous life of a missionary over the wide field of the Mississippi Valley. In 1831, Bishop De Neckere appointed him his vicar-general and wanted to make him his coadjutor, but he refused the promotion. When the Bishop died, in 1853, Father Blanc was named administrator, and was consecrated bishop of the diocese, 22 November, 1835. His jurisdiction extended over the States of Louisiana and Mississippi, and in 1838 Texas was added. In 1842 he came into conflict with the lay trustees of the Cathedral over his right to appoint its rector, in the course of which contest he had to interdict the church. Litigation in the courts and appeals to the State Legislature dragged out the controversy for more than a year, but all the issues were decided in favour of the Bishop. In 1838 he established a diocesan seminary and introduced into the diocese the Lazarists, the Jesuits, the Redemptorists, the Christian Brothers, the Sisters of Charity, the Sisters of Notre Dame, the Sisters of the Good Shepherd, and the Congregations of Our Lady of Mount Carmel and of the Holy Cross. He attended the First Plenary Council of Baltimore, and was one of the few American prelates present in Rome when the dogma of the Immaculate Conception was proclaimed (8 Dec., 1854). New Orleans was made an archbishopric, 19 July, 1850, and he received the pallium, 16 February, 1851. During his tenure of the see many old abuses were corrected; the number of churches was increased from 26 to 73, of priests from 27 to 92, and many schools, academies, colleges, convents, and asylums testified to his zeal and labours. He died suddenly at his residence in New Orleans, discharging with activity to the last the arduous duties of his office.

SHEA, *Hist. Cath. Ch. in U. S.* (New York, 1904); REUSS, *Biog. Cycl. of the Catholic Hierarchy* (Milwaukee, Wis., 1898); CLARKE, *Lives of the Deceased Bishops* (New York, 1872), II; *Catholic Almanac 1861; Delta* (files, New Orleans, 23 June, 1860).

THOMAS F. MEEHAN.

Blanc, Le. See LE BLANC.

Blanchard (DUCHESNE), JEAN-BAPTISTE, a French Jesuit and educator, b. 12 October, 1731, at Tourteron in the department of Ardennes; d. 15 June, 1797. In 1746 he entered the Society of Jesus, and later was professor at Metz, Verdun, and Pont-à-Mousson. At the time of the suppression of the Society he changed his name of Duchesne to that of Abbé Blanchard, under which his works were published.

He left the order, however, in 1762, before it was suppressed, retired to Belgium, and for seven years remained near Namur, occupied with pedagogical questions. He wrote "Le temple des Muses fabulistes" (Liège, 1776, 2 vols.) and "L'Ecole des mœurs" (Namur and Paris, 1775, 2 vols.). The latter work was first published without the author's name under the title, "Le poète des mœurs, ou les maximes de la sagesse . . ." (1771), and later was reprinted several times with the title "Maximes de l'honnête homme, ou le poète des mœurs". Blanchard's main work was published after his death by Bruyset: "Préceptes pour l'éducation des deux sexes à l'usage des familles chrétiennes" (Lyons, 1803, 2 vols.); a new edition in 1807 was entitled "Education chrétienne à l'usage de l'un et de l'autre sexe". Blanchard adapts to Christian education the principles found in Rousseau's "Emile". In the work there is little originality; yet, besides judiciously chosen quotations, we find very useful suggestions and good criticisms of Rousseau's views. It is divided into three parts: physical education, moral education, and education of girls. Great importance is attached to physical culture, health, hygiene of the whole organism, and of the special sense-organs. Useful rules are given for the formation of the intellect, feelings, and will. Good pronunciation and reading are insisted on. Blanchard rightly rejects the principle of negative education advocated by Rousseau. It would be very harmful to wait till reason is developed in order to make the child exercise it; on the contrary, it must be developed by proper exercise and under proper guidance. To start for a long journey, he says, the traveller does not wait till the sun is high in the sky, but rather profits by the first rays of light; so must it be with the child. As to the education of women, Blanchard's views seem rather narrow to-day. Woman is made for dependence. Her instruction must be limited to a few elementary notions; Fénelon's principles and the "Avis d'une mère à sa fille" of Madame de Lambert, which Blanchard reproduces, must form the basis of her moral education.

BOUILLOT, *Biographie ardennaise;* COMPAYRÉ in *La grande encyclopédie*, VI, 1011, and in *Dictionnaire de pédagogie* (Paris, 1887), I, 262; SOMMERVOGEL, *Bibliothèque de la c. de J.* (2d ed., Brussels and Paris, 1890), I, 1538; *Dictionnaire des ouvrages anonymes et pseudonymes* (Paris, 1884), 729.

C. A. DUBRAY.

Blanche, GUSTAVE, Eudist. See GULF OF ST. LAWRENCE, VICARIATE APOSTOLIC OF.

Blanchet, FRANÇOIS NORBERT, missionary and first Archbishop of Oregon City, U. S. A., son of Pierre Blanchet, a Canadian farmer, b. 30 September, 1795, near Saint-Pierre, Rivière du Sud, Province of Quebec; d. 18 June, 1883, at Portland, Oregon. After three years in the village school he went in 1810, with his brother Augustin Magloire, later the first Bishop of Nesqually, to the Seminary of Quebec, where he was ordained priest 18 July, 1819. He was stationed at the cathedral for a year and was then sent to Richibucto, New Brunswick, as pastor of the Micmac Indians and Acadian settlers, among whom he spent seven years of missionary apprenticeship, enduring poverty, isolation, and innumerable hardships. In 1827 he was recalled to Montreal and appointed pastor of St. Joseph de Soulanges, a parish of 2,000 souls. During the cholera epidemic of 1832 Father Blanchet attended the stricken so fearlessly that the Protestants of the place presented him with a testimonial. In 1837 he was appointed vicar-general by Archbishop Signay for the Oregon mission, a vast region never before visited by a priest, and he set out on 3 May, 1838, accompanied by the Rev. Modeste Demers with the annual express of the Hudson's Bay Company. The journey from Lachine to Fort Vancouver a distance of about 5,000 miles, was made in canoes,

by portages, in barges, on horseback, and in light boats. It took them nine days to cross the Rocky Mountains, on the summit of which, at three o'clock in the morning of 16 October Father Blanchet celebrated Mass. They arrived at Fort Vancouver on 24 November. The territory assigned to the two priests embraced about 375,000 square miles. It extended from California to Alaska and from the Rocky Mountains to the Pacific Ocean.

For four years they laboured alone, going from settlement to settlement, facing every peril of a wild country, recalling the scattered faithful to the practice of religion and instructing the aborigines. Then two other priests

MOST REV. FRANÇOIS NORBERT BLANCHET

from Canada, the Revs. A. Langlois and Z. Bolduc, came to their assistance. In 1844 they were reinforced by the great missionary, Father De Smet, with four other Jesuit priests, three lay brothers, and six Sisters of Notre Dame de Namur. The immense territory of the Oregon mission was made an Apostolic vicariate 1 December, 1843; Father Blanchet was named its first vicar Apostolic and titular Bishop of Philadelphia. The letters from Rome arrived in August, 1844. To receive episcopal consecration he started for Canada 5 December, boarded a steamer on the Columbia River, touched at Honolulu, doubled Cape Horn, landed at Dover, England, went by rail to Liverpool, took a vessel to Boston and thence proceeded by rail to Montreal, a journey of 22,000 miles. He was consecrated by Bishop Bourget in the Cathedral of Montreal 25 July, 1845. Later he returned to Europe, visiting Rome, France, Belgium, Germany, and Austria in the interests of his diocese. He gathered together six secular priests, four Jesuit priests, three lay brothers, and seven Sisters of Notre Dame. They sailed from Brest 22 February, 1847, and reached the Columbia River on 12 August. The bishop was translated to the See of Draza by letters of 4 May, 1844, to avoid the confusion of his former title with that of Philadelphia, U. S. A. The Vicariate was erected into a province 24 July, 1846. Bishop Blanchet was made Archbishop of Oregon City, his brother Magloire became Bishop of Walla Walla, and Father Demers Bishop of Vancouver's Island.

The archbishop was indefatigable. He summoned his first provincial council in 1848; attended the First Plenary Council of Baltimore in 1852; went in 1855 to South America and collected for two years in Chile, Peru, and Bolivia; returned to Canada in 1859 and took back to Oregon 31 priests, sisters, and servants. He attended the Second Plenary Council of Baltimore in 1866; celebrated, 19 July, 1869, the golden jubilee of his ordination, and in the following October set out for Rome to assist at the Vatican Council, where he voted for the definition of the dogma of Papal Infallibility. He was still in the city 26 September, 1870, when the temporal power of the papacy was overthrown. When Bishop Seghers was made his coadjutor in 1879 he retired to the hospital of the Sisters of Providence at Portland. He wrote the story of the Oregon mission (Historical sketches of

Catholicity in Oregon) in a series of papers published in the "Catholic Sentinel" of that city. In 1880 he resigned and was appointed titular Archbishop of Amida. He consecrated three bishops—Demers, D'Herbomez, and Seghers. He found on the Pacific coast a wilderness, spiritual as well as material; he left, after forty-six years of heroic work, a well-provided ecclesiastical province. His name will be forever illustrious in the history of the Church in America as the first archbishop of the North-west and the Apostle of Oregon.

BLANCHET, AUGUSTIN MAGLOIRE, brother of preceding, first Bishop of Walla Walla-Nesqually, State of Washington, U. S. A., b. 22 August, 1797, on his father's farm near the village of Saint-Pierre, Rivière du Sud, Canada; d. 25 February, 1887, at Fort Vancouver, Washington. After attending the village school for three years, he was sent to Quebec, with his brother François Norbert, to study for the priesthood. He was ordained 3 June, 1821. After a twelve-month as assistant pastor at St. Gervais, he was sent as missionary to the Isles de la Madeleine and later to Cape Breton Island. He gave four years of ministry to the Gulf provinces. Then he was recalled to the vicariate Apostolic of Montreal and was successively pastor of four parishes, in one of which he was the successor of his elder brother. In 1846 while a canon of the Montreal cathedral, he was appointed Bishop of the new Diocese of Walla Walla in what is now the State of Washington. He was consecrated 27 September, 1846. In the following spring he set out overland for his distant see with one priest, Rev. J. A. B. Brouillet, and two students. At Pittsburgh he declared his intention to become a citizen of the United States. At St. Louis the party was increased by Father Richard, two deacons and Brother Blanchet, all members of the Order of Mary Immaculate. Fort Walla Walla was reached on 5 September, 1847. The Bishop located at The Dalles and thence multiplied his apostolic labours throughout the vast territory under his care. He endured the many hardships of a pioneer country and braved all the perils of a region infested with wild beasts and still more savage men. He was full of zeal. He established missions; he built churches; he founded academies and colleges; he started schools for the Indians; he begged for priests in Canada and abroad; he obtained sisters to open hospitals and other institutions.

In 1850 the See of Walla Walla was suppressed and that of Nesqually was erected in its stead, with headquarters at Fort Vancouver. The bishop built there a cathedral of logs, and a house for himself out of the same material. In 1852 he attended the First Plenary Council of Baltimore, but, on account of infirmities, he was unable to go to Rome for the Vatican Council. In 1879, after thirty-two years of arduous service in Washington, he resigned his see and was named titular Bishop of Ibora. Worn out with labours, he spent his last eight years in prayer and suffering. His peaceful death was a fitting close for his life of sacrifice. He is revered as the Apostle of Washington.

DE SMET, *Oregon Missions and Travels in the Rocky Mountains*; MURRAY, *Popular Hist. of the Cath. Church in the U. S.* (New York, 1876); O'GORMAN, *Hist. of the R. C. Church in the United States* (New York, 1895), 421, 464; CHITTENDEN AND RICHARDSON, *Life, Letters, and Travels of Fr. Pierre Jean De Smet* (New York, 1905); SHEA, *History of the Catholic Church in the United States* (New York, 1889–92); REUSS, *Biog. Cycl. of the Cath. Hierarchy of the U. S.* (Milwaukee, 1898); CLARKE, *Lives of Deceased Bishops of the Catholic Church in the United States* (New York, 1888).

L. W. REILLY.

Blandina, SAINT, virgin and martyr.—She belongs to the band of martyrs of Lyons who, after some of their number had endured the most frightful tortures, suffered a glorious martyrdom in the reign of Marcus Aurelius (177) and concerning whose death we have the touching report sent by the Church of Lyons to the Churches of Asia Minor (Eusebius, Hist. eccl., V, 2). The fanaticism of the heathen populace in Lyons had been excited against the Christians so that the latter, when they ventured to show themselves publicly, were harassed and ill-treated. While the imperial legate was away the chiliarch, a military commander, and the duumvir, a civil magistrate, threw a number of Christians, who confessed their faith, into prison. When the legate returned, the imprisoned believers were brought to trial. Among these Christians was Blandina, a slave, who had been taken into custody along with her master, also a Christian. Her companions greatly feared that on account of her bodily frailty she might not remain steadfast under torture. But although the legate caused her to be tortured in a horrible manner, so that even the executioners became exhausted "as they did not know what more they could do to her", still she remained faithful and repeated to every question "I am a Christian and we commit no wrongdoing." Through fear of torture heathen slaves had testified against their masters that the Christians when assembled committed those scandalous acts of which they were accused by the heathen mob, and the legate desired to wring confession of this misconduct from the Christian prisoners. In his report to the emperor the legate stated that those who held to their Christian belief were to be executed and those who denied their faith were to be released; Blandina was, therefore, with a number of companions subjected to new tortures in the amphitheatre at the time of the public games. She was bound to a stake and wild beasts were set on her. They did not, however, touch her. After this for a number of days she was led into the arena to see the sufferings of her companions. Finally, as the last of the martyrs, she was scourged, placed on a red-hot grate, enclosed in a net and thrown before a wild steer who tossed her into the air with his horns, and at last killed with a dagger. Her feast is celebrated 2 June.

Acta SS., June, I, 161 sqq.; ALLARD, *Histoire des persécutions* (Paris, 1892), I, 397 sqq.

J. P. KIRSCH.

Blane (or BLAAN), SAINT, Bishop and Confessor in Scotland, b. on the island of Bute, date unknown; d. 590. His feast is kept on 10 August. He was a nephew of St. Cathan, and was educated in Ireland under Sts. Comgall and Kenneth; he became a monk, went to Scotland, and eventually was bishop among the Picts. Several miracles are related of him, among them the restoration of a dead boy to life. The Aberdeen Breviary gives these and other details of the saint's life, which are rejected, however, by the Bollandists. There can be no doubt that devotion to St. Blane was, from early times, popular in Scotland. His monastery became the site of the Cathedral of Dunblane. There was a church of St. Blane in Dumfries and another at Kilblane. The year of the saint's death is variously given as 446, 590, and 1000; 446 (Butler, Lives of the Saints) is evidently incorrect; the date 1000, found in Adam King, "Kalendar of Scottish Saints" (Paris, 1588), in Dempster, "Menologium Scotorum" (Bonn, 1622), and in the "Acta SS.", seems to have crept in by confusing St. Kenneth, whose disciple Blane was, with a Kenneth who was King of Scotland about A. D. 1000. The highest authorities say the saint died 590. The ruins of his church at Kingarth, Bute, where his remains were buried, are still standing and form an object of great interest to antiquarians; the bell of his monastery is preserved at Dunblane.

FORBES, *Kalendars of Scottish Saints* (Edinburgh, 1872); BARRETT, *A Calendar of Scottish Saints* (Fort Augustus, 1904); *Acta SS.*, 10 August, XXXVI, 560.

M. J. O'MALIA.

Blarer of Wartensee. See St. Gall, Abbey of.

Blasendorf. See Fogaras, Diocese of.

Blasphemy (Gr. βλάπτειν, "to injure", and φήμη, "reputation") signifies etymologically gross irreverence towards any person or thing worthy of exalted esteem. In this broad sense the term is used by Bacon when in his "Advancement of Learning" he speaks of "blasphemy against learning". St. Paul tells of being blasphemed (I Cor., iv, 13) and the Latin Vulgate employs the word *blasphemare* to designate abusive language directed either against a people at large (II Kings, xxi, 21; I Par., xx, 7) or against individuals (I Cor., x, 30; Tit., iii, 2).

I. Meaning.—While etymologically blasphemy may denote the derogation of the honour due to a creature as well as of that belonging to God, in its strict acceptation it is used only in the latter sense. Hence it has been defined by Suarez as "any word of malediction, reproach, or contumely pronounced against God" (De Relig., tract. iii, lib. I, cap. iv, n. 1). It is to be noted that according to the definition (1) blasphemy is set down as a word, for ordinarily it is expressed in speech, though it may be committed in thought or in act. Being primarily a sin of the tongue, it will be seen to be opposed directly to the religious act of praising God. (2) It is said to be against God, though this may be only mediately, as when the contumelious word is spoken of the saints or of sacred things, because of the relationship they sustain to God and His service. Blasphemy, by reason of the significance of the words with which it is expressed, may be of three kinds. (1) It is heretical when the insult to God involves a declaration that is against faith, as in the assertion: "God is cruel and unjust" or "The noblest work of man is God". (2) It is imprecatory when it would cry a malediction upon the Supreme Being as when one would say: "Away with God". And finally (3), it is simply contumelious when it is wholly made up of contempt of, or indignation towards, God, as in the blasphemy of Julian the Apostate: "Thou hast conquered, O Galilæan". Again blasphemy may be (1) either direct, as when the one blaspheming formally intends to dishonour the Divinity, or (2) indirect, as when without such intention blasphemous words are used with advertence to their import.

II. The Malice of Blasphemy.—Blasphemy is a sin against the virtue of religion by which we render to God the honour due to Him as our first beginning and last end. St. Thomas says that it is to be regarded as a sin against faith inasmuch as by it we attribute to God that which does not belong to Him, or deny Him that which is His (II–II, Q. xiii, art. I). De Lugo and others deny that this is an essential element in blasphemy (De just. et jure cæterisque virt. card., lib. II, c. xlv, disp. v, n. 26), but as Escobar (Theol. mor., lib. xxviii, c. xxxii, n. 716 sqq.) observes, the contention on this point concerns words only, since the followers of St. Thomas see in the contempt expressed in blasphemy the implication that God is contemptible—an implication in which all will allow there is attributed to God that which does not belong to Him. What is here said is of blasphemy in general; manifestly that form of the sin described above as heretical is not only opposed to the virtue of religion but that of faith as well. Blasphemy is of its whole nature (*ex toto genere suo*) a mortal sin, the gravest that may be committed against religion. The seriousness of an affront is proportioned to the dignity of the person towards whom it is directed. Since then the insult in blasphemy is offered to the ineffable majesty of God, the degree of its heinousness must be evident. Nevertheless because of slight or no advertence blasphemy may be either a venial sin only or no sin at all. Thus many expressions voiced in anger escape the enormity of a grave sin, except,

as is clear, when the anger is vented upon God. Again, in the case where blasphemous speech is uttered inadvertently, through force of habit, a grave sin is not committed as long as earnest resistance is made to the habit. If, however, no such effort is put forth there cannot but be grave guilt, though a mortal sin is not committed on the occasion of each and every blasphemous outburst. It has been said that heretical blasphemy besides a content directed against religion has that which is opposed to the virtue of faith. Similarly, imprecatory blasphemy is besides a violation of charity. These forms of the sin being specifically distinct from the simpler kind, it is necessary to specify their character in confession. Whether blasphemy has been direct or indirect, however, calls not for specification on the part of the penitent, since both these forms are specifically the same, though clearly differing in the degree of malice. The question has been raised whether blasphemy against the saints differs in kind from that uttered immediately against God. While De Lugo thinks that such a difference obtains (De Pœnit., disp. xvi, n. 178 sqq.) the opposite opinion of St. Alphonsus seems more tenable, for as the latter theologian observes, the saints, ordinarily speaking, are not blasphemed because of their own excellence but because of their close relationship to God (Theol. Moral., lib. IV, n. 132).

The Penalties Attached to Blasphemy.—In the Old Law the blasphemer was punished by death. So God appointed on the occasion of the blasphemy of Salumith's son: "The man that curseth His God, shall bear his sin: And he that blasphemeth the name of the Lord, dying let him die: all the multitude shall stone him, whether he be a native or a stranger. He that blasphemeth the name of the Lord, dying let him die" (Lev., xxiv, 15–16). Upon hearing blasphemy the Jews were wont in detestation of the crime to rend their clothes (IV Kings, xviii, 37, xix, 1; Matt., xxvi, 65).

Among the Athenians blasphemy was actionable and according to Plutarch, Alcibiades was made to suffer the confiscation of his goods for ridiculing the rites of Ceres and Proserpine (Plutarch, Alcibiades). Among the ancient Romans blasphemy was punishable, though not by death (Manutius, "De Legibus Romanis", quoted by Disney, "A view of Ancient Laws against Immorality and Profaneness", p. 826). In the time of Justinian we find most severe enactments against this sin. In a constitution of A. D. 538 the people are called upon to abstain from blasphemy, which provokes God to anger. The prefect of the city is commanded to apprehend all such as shall persist in their offence after this admonition and put them to death, that so the city and the empire may not suffer because of their impiety (Auth. Col., Tit. vii, 7 November). Among the Visigoths, anyone blaspheming the name of Christ or expressing contempt of the Trinity had his head shorn, was subjected to a hundred stripes, and suffered perpetual imprisonment in chains (Ll. Wisigoth., lib. XII, tit. iii, l. 2). Among the Franks, according to a law enacted at the Diet of Aachen, A. D. 818, this sin was a capital offence. In the Gospels blasphemy is described as one of "the things that defile a man" (Matt., xv, 20; Mark, vii, 21–23).

Medieval canon law punished the blasphemer most severely. By a decree of the thirteenth century one convicted of blasphemy was compelled to stand at the door of the church during the solemnities of the Mass for seven Sundays, and on the last of these days, divested of cloak and shoes, he was to appear with a rope about his neck. Obligations of fasting and almsgiving were likewise imposed under heaviest penalties (Decret., lib. V, tit. xxvi). The rigours of the ancient discipline were insisted upon by Pius V in his Constitution "Cum primum apostolatus" (§ 10). According to the law herein laid down, the layman found guilty of blasphemy was fined. The fine was increased upon his second offence, and upon his third he was sent into exile. If unable to pay the fine, he was upon the first conviction condemned to stand before the door of the church, his hands tied behind him. For the second offence he was flogged, and for the third his tongue was pierced, and he was sentenced to the galleys. The blasphemous cleric, if possessed of a benefice, lost upon his first offence a year's income; upon his second he was deprived of his benefice and exiled. If enjoying no benefice, he was first subjected to a fine and bodily punishment; on repeating the offence he was imprisoned, and still persisting, he was degraded and condemned to the galleys.

BLASPHEMY IN CIVIL LAW.—Blasphemy cognizable by common law is defined by Blackstone to be "denying the being or providence of God, contumelious reproaches of our Saviour Jesus Christ, profane scoffing at the Holy Scripture, or exposing it to contempt or ridicule". In the United States we find many penal statutes against blasphemy, which have been declared constitutional as not subversive of the freedom of speech or liberty of the press (Am. and Eng. Ency. of Law, Vol. IV, 582). In the American Decisions (Vol. V, 335) we read that "Christianity being recognized by law therefore blasphemy against God and profane ridicule of Christ or the Holy Scriptures are punishable at common law". Accordingly where one uttered the following words "Jesus Christ was a bastard and his mother was a whore", it was held to be a public offence, punishable by the common law. The defendant found guilty by the court of common pleas of the blasphemy above quoted was sentenced to imprisonment for three months and to pay a fine of five hundred dollars.

ST. THOMAS AQUINAS, *Sum. Theol.*, II–II, Q. xiii, a. 3; Q. cv. a. 2nd, 3am; Q. lxxx, a. 3; I–II, Q. x, a. 2; ST. LIGUORI, *Theol. moral.*, lib. IV, tract. ii, c. i; BALLERINI, *Opus. theol. moral.*, II, 366 sqq.; NOLDIN, *Theol. moral.*, II, 195; DISNEY, *A View of Ancient Laws against Immorality and Profaneness;* OBLET in *Dict. de théol. cath.*, s. v. *Blasphème.*

JOHN WEBSTER MELODY.

Blasphemy against the Holy Spirit. See HOLY GHOST.

Blastares, MATTHEW, a monk of the Order of St. Basil, living in the fourteenth century, who applied himself to the study of theology and canon law. Through the labours of John the Scholastic, Photius, Zonaras, Balsamon, and others the Greek Church possessed some collections of laws and commentaries. There was, however, need of a more comprehensive work, and one better adapted to the needs of the time. It appeared about 1335, in the "Syntagma" of Blastares, a collection of ecclesiastical constitutions in alphabetical order, written in Greek. The full title might be translated into Latin thus: "Syntagma alphabeticum rerum omium, quæ in sacris divinisque canonibus comprehenduntur, elaboratum pariter et compositum per minimum ex hieromonachis Matthæum Blastarem". The collection, which contains a long preface, is arranged alphabetically by means of the initial letters of the words which indicate the subject-matter of each chapter; several chapters are thus found under one letter. For example under the Greek Γ: Thoughts concerning the degrees of relationship in reference to matrimony, concerning marriages permitted and prohibited. Under Δ: Thoughts on last testaments, deacons, justice, ecclesiastical trials, etc.

In each chapter the author first gives the law of the Church on the subject and then, if there be any, the civil law also, setting forth the sense rather than the exact wording of either, and contenting himself with noting where the constitutions referred to may be found. The "Syntagma", commonly called "Nomocanon" or, by metaphor,

πηδάλιον (rudder), soon became extensively employed, and is still used in the Greek Church, as is evidenced by the fact that an edition of the work in six volumes was published in Athens from 1852 to 1860, under the auspices of the Holy Synod. This edition bears the title: Σύνταγμα τῶν Θείων καὶ ἱερῶν κανόνων. This work is also found in the Synodicon of Beveridge (P. G., CXLIV, CXLV) published at Oxford in 1672. There are also attributed to Blastares a tract on matrimonial cases, and two poems published by Goar in Greek and Latin, one on the offices of the Church of Constantinople, the other on the court. His "Syntagma", like other medieval law-books of the Greeks, breathes a spirit inimical to the Roman Church.

MÖHLER in *Kirchenlex.;* VERING, *Lehrbuch des Kirchenr.*, 17; WALTER, *Lehrbuch des Kirchenr.*, xiv, 79, 80; BEVERIDGE, *Prolegom.* in *Pandecta Canonum*, I, 21 sqq.; KRUMBACHER, *Gesch. der byzant. Litt.* (Munich, 1897), 607.

A. B. MEEHAN.

Blathmac, SAINT, a distinguished Irish monk, b. in Ireland about 750. He suffered martyrdom in Iona, about 835. He is fortunate in having had his biography written by Strabo, Benedictine Abbot of Reichenau (824–849), and thus the story of his martyrdom has been handed down through the ages. Strabo's life of this saint is in Latin hexameters, and is to be found in Messingham's "Florilegium Insulæ Sanctorum" (Paris, 1624). A scion of a noble family he early showed a religious turn of mind, and longed to be enrolled in the noble army of martyrs, a wish which was afterwards fulfilled. His name was latinized *Florentius* (from the fact of the Irish word *Blath* meaning a flower), and as a religious, he was most exemplary, finally becoming abbot. In 824 he joined the community of Columban monks at Iona, and not long afterwards the Danes ravaged the island. One morning, as he was celebrating Mass, the Scandinavian rovers entered the monastic church and put the monks to death. St. Blathmac refused to point out the shrine of St. Columba, which was really the object of plunder, and he was hacked to pieces on the altar step. His body was afterwards reverently interred where the scene of martyrdom took place, and numerous miracles are claimed to have been wrought through his intercession. The date of his death is given by the "Annals of Ulster" as 825, although Mabillon places it thirty-six years earlier.

REEVES, *Adamman* (Dublin, 1857); O'DONOVAN, *Four Masters* (Dublin, 1856); MESSINGHAM, *Florilegium Insulæ Sanctorum* (Paris, 1624); MABILLON, *Annales Ordinis S. Benedicti*, III; *P. G.*, CXIII; *Annals of Ulster* (Rolls Series); HEALY, *Insula Sanctorum et Doctorum* (Dublin, 1902), 4th ed.; MORAN, *Irish Saints in Great Britain* (Callan, 1903).

W. H. GRATTAN FLOOD.

Blemmida (BLEMMYDES) NICEPHORUS, a learned monk and writer of the Greek Church, b. about 1198, at Constantinople; d. 1272. After the establishment of the Latin Empire (1204) his family emigrated to Asia Minor. Blemmida there received a careful training and was soon reputed one of the most learned men of his time. About 1223 he became one of the Byzantine clergy, at that time established in Nicæa. But owing to difficulties and jealousies he renounced all worldly prospects, became a monk, and built a monastery-near Ephesus, over which he presided until his death. In this condition he felt free from all entanglements and on various occasions exhibited independence and courage. At one time he dismissed from the church of his monastery the Princess Marcesina, a mistress of the Emperor John Ducas Batatzes (1222–54), and in justification of his conduct wrote an encyclical letter. Again, when the Patriarch Joseph of Constantinople (1268–75) sought to obtain recognition against the former Patriarch Arsenius (1255–66), he met with a straight refusal from Blemmida. Nevertheless Blemmida was held in high esteem by the contemporary Greek Emperors. The aforementioned John Ducas, far from venting his wrath on him, accepted the rebuke as well merited. When the Patriarchal See of Constantinople fell vacant, in 1255, it was offered to Blemmida by Emperor Theodore II, Lascaris (1254–58); but he preferred his quiet monastic life.

The reputation of Blemmida was really due to his vast learning. Many a Greek youth of high estate learned from him the beauty of letters, or the secrets of philosophy and theology. Among his pupils were the learned Georgius Acropolites and the royal prince, afterwards emperor, Theodore II, Lascaris. Blemmida was the author of several poems, of letters, of a work on the duties of an emperor, of two autobiographies, of two geographical works, of philosophical writings on logic and physics, and of a rule of life for his monks. Among his theological works may be mentioned a commentary on the Psalms, a discourse on the Trinity and Christology, and two orations on the Holy Ghost. One of these orations was addressed to Jacob, Archbishop of Bulgaria; the other to Theodore Lascaris. In both he proved, from passages of Athanasius, Basil, Gregory Nazianzen, Gregory of Nyssa, Cyril of Alexandria and other Fathers, that the procession of the Holy Ghost from Father and Son, or from the Father through the Son, was genuine Catholic doctrine. In this precisely consists his importance. He was among the few Greek writers who recognized that the Latin Church was correct in its belief. This is evident not only from his own writings, but also from the explicit contemporary evidence of such men as Beccus, Pachymeres, and Nicephorus Gregoras. It was through the reading of the works of Blemmida that Beccus was converted to the teaching held by the Latin Church, and induced to write in its defence. Most of the works of Blemmida so far published are found in Migne's "Patrologia Græca", CXLII (Paris, 1855), or in the "Bibliotheca Teubneriana" (Leipzig, 1896).

Georgius Acropolites, *Annales* in *P. G.*, CXL (Paris, 1857); see also CXLIII, CXLIV, CXLVIII; Raynaldus, *Annales Eccl.* (Lucca, 1747, 1748), II, III; Krumbacher, *Gesch. der byzant. Literatur* (Munich, 1897).

Francis J. Schaefer.

Blenk, James Hubert. See New Orleans, Archdiocese of.

Blenkinsop, Peter, Catholic publisher, b. in Ireland; married a sister of Archbishop Oliver Kelly of Tuam and emigrated with his family from Dublin to Baltimore, Maryland, U. S. A., in 1826, where he established a printing and publishing house for Catholic books; he issued (1827) Pise's "History of the Church", 5 vols., and began the "Metropolitan", a monthly magazine (1830). Blenkinsop had three children: William A., Peter J., and Catherine.

William A. Blenkinsop was b. in Dublin, 1819; d. 8 January, 1892, in Boston, Massachusetts, U. S. A. He studied at St. Mary's College, Baltimore, from 1833–39, taught there (1839–44) taking the degree of A. M., and was ordained by Archbishop Eccleston in 1843. He went with Bishop Chanche to Natchez and laboured on the Mississippi mission for seven years; in 1850 he became affiliated to the Diocese of Boston and was appointed pastor of Cabotsville (now Chicopee), where he built a church, one of the finest in the State; his pastoral charge included a large part of the Connecticut Valley in Massachusetts. When offered the position of Vicar-General of Natchez, he responded that he had more people in his parish than were in the whole Diocese of Natchez. In 1864, he became pastor of the Church of Sts. Peter and Paul, Boston, where he remained for twenty-eight years. He was a model of priestly virtue, courtly in manners, simple as a child, and

generous to the poor. He was buried in St. Augustine's Cemetery, S. Boston.

Peter J. Blenkinsop was b. in Dublin, 19 April, 1818; d. in Philadelphia, Pennsylvania, 5 November, 1896. He studied at Georgetown College, Washington, D. C., entered the Society of Jesus in 1834, and was ordained by Archbishop Eccleston 26 July, 1846. He was President of Holy Cross College, Worcester, Massachusetts, from 1854–57, which he rebuilt after its destruction by fire. He was also pastor at Frederick, Maryland, St. Joseph's Church, Philadelphia, and was stationed at various times in the Jesuit colleges at Worcester, Georgetown, and Philadelphia.

Catherine Blenkinsop, b. in Dublin, 18 April, 1816; d. at Emmitsburg, Maryland. She entered the Sisters of Charity at the latter place in May, 1831, at the age of fifteen. She took the name of Euphemia with the religious habit and was stationed successively at St. Joseph's School, New York, St. Peter's School, Baltimore, St. Mary's Asylum in the same city, and in 1855, at the mother-house, as assistant. During the Civil War she was entrusted with the delicate mission of directing the institutions of the Sisters of Charity in the South, and was the mainstay of the Sisters in their arduous labours; in 1866 she was appointed visitatrix of the community, which she continued to direct until her death.

McCoy, *History of Springfield Diocese* (Boston, 1900); Healy, *Sermon Preached on Death of Mother Euphemia* (Boston, 1887).

E. I. Devitt.

Blessed. See Heaven.

Blessed, The.—There are at present two ways in which the Church allows public worship to be paid those who have lived in the fame of sanctity or died as martyrs. Of these some are beatified, others are canonized. (See Beatification and Canonization.) Beatification is a permission for public worship restricted to certain places and to certain acts. In the more recent discipline of the Church, the pope alone can beatify, though formerly bishops could grant the honour of beatification to those of the faithful who had shed their blood for Christ or lived lives of heroic virtue. All those permissions for public worship which in the early ages of the Church were granted to particular churches and spread thence with the sanction of other bishops to other congregations, to be finally made a matter of precept for the universal Church by the Roman pontiff, constituted beatification and canonization in the exact sense of the word. It was only beatification while the cult, of the martyr for instance, was restricted to the place where he had suffered, but became canonization when it was received in the entire Church. The difference between canonization and beatification lies in the presence or absence of two elements which are found united in canonization and either separate or entirely absent from beatification, though generally only one is lacking. These elements are: (1) the precept regarding public worship, and (2) its extension to the whole Church. In exceptional cases one or other of these is wanting; sometimes the cult of the beatified is not only permitted but enjoined, though not for the universal Church, and in other instances it is permitted for the whole Church but not enjoined. The case of St. Rose of Lima is an instance of the occurrence of both elements, though that did not of itself suffice for her canonization, as one of the elements was not really complete. When Clement X chose her as patron of all America, the Philippines, and the Indies, and by the same act allowed her cultus in the entire Church, it was clearly a case where a cultus was enjoined in America and merely allowed for the remainder of the Church.

The nature of beatification makes it evident that the worship of the blessed is restricted to certain places and persons, and may be given only after permission. Such permission is usually granted to those persons or places which have in some way been connected with the blessed. In the case of a religious, it is granted to the members of the order or congregation to which he belonged; if a canon of a church, that church or chapter receives the permission; if a martyr, a bishop, or resident of some place for a long period, the concession is made to the place of his martyrdom or to his see or to the place that he adorned with his virtues. In some cases the place of his birth or burial is included. And in all these instances it may be that the concession is made only to the mother church, or to the church in which his body lies, or it may be extended to the whole city or diocese. With Benedict XIV (De canonizatione de SS., Lib. IV, part. II, cap. i, n. 12) we may add that such grants are affixed to the day on which the blessed died or to some other determined day. When this cultus is allowed to certain persons or places it is still further restricted with respect to the manner in which it is to be given, and not all acts of worship which the customs and discipline of the Church allow to be paid canonized saints may be used in the worship of the beatified. Benedict XIV (loc. cit., c. ii) treats the question at length and with regard to the inquiry as to whether a votive Mass may be said in honour of the blessed in places where the cultus has been granted decides in the negative against Castropalao and Del Bene. His opinion has since been confirmed by the decree of Alexander VII of 27 September, 1659, in which decree the pope settled many questions regarding the worship of the blessed. It may be remarked that ordinarily votive Masses cannot be said in honour of the blessed, though for several centuries they have been said in virtue of special indults. The oldest indult which Benedict XIV quotes in this connexion is that granted by Clement VII to the Dominicans of the Convent of Forlì, 25 January, 1526, to celebrate the Mass of Blessed James Salomonio "as often during the year as their devotion may move them to do so". Besides this indult there is another granted by Alexander VII at the request of Ferdinand Gonzaga, Prince of Castiglione, on 22 May, 1662, "to celebrate votive Masses in honour of Blessed Aloysius (Gonzaga) in the collegiate mother church of the town of Castiglione during the year". And this indult, a few months afterwards, was extended so as to allow "votive Masses of the same Blessed Aloysius to be celebrated in the church of the Regular Clerics of the Society of Jesus during the year on days not impeded by the rubrics".

Alexander VII further ordered that images of the blessed should not be exposed in any church, sanctuary, or oratory whatever, and especially in those in which Mass or other Divine services are held, without previous consultation with the Holy See. This rule is of such strict interpretation that in virtue of the granting of this indult it cannot be presumed that permission is had to place the images of the blessed upon the altars. They may be placed upon the walls of the church only. However, an indult permitting a contrary use is not of altogether rare occurrence in the recent discipline of the Church, and it is to be remarked that even in the time of Alexander VII a decree of the Congregation of Rites of 17 April, 1660, declared that the concession of an indult to say the Mass and Office of a blessed implied permission to place his picture or statue upon the altar, though the opposite does not hold. The same pope also decided that the names of the blessed should be entered in no catalogue except those proper to the persons who had received permission to honour them with cultus and a Mass and Office. He ruled too that no prayers should be addressed the blessed in public services except those granted and approved

by the Holy See and that their relics should not be carried in procession. It must, however, be observed here in passing that Alexander VII, as he especially declares in his decree, did not intend to do away with any cultus that had been rendered to the blessed with the common consent of the Church, or from time immemorial, or approved by the writings of the Fathers and the saints, or even one which had been tolerated by the Holy See and the different ordinaries for more than a hundred years. In addition to all this, we have other decrees of the Congregations of Rites, such as: that the names of the blessed are not to be enrolled in the martyrology; that neither altars nor churches may be dedicated to them; that they may not be chosen as local patrons. It must not be forgotten that exceptions may be made by indult even in these cases. Recently, to quote an instance, Pius X at the request of the English bishops, in the matter of the English martyrs whom Leo XIII had beatified, granted that in each diocese an altar might be erected to each of the nine principal martyrs whose names are mentioned in the decree, the churches in which they were to be erected being designated by the bishops. Beatification is an entirely different matter from canonization, and is but a step to it, being in no wise an irreformable decision of ecclesiastical authority. The observation of Benedict XIV then goes without saying, that the blessed are not to be given the title of saint; further that the distinctive signs which ecclesiastical use has made customary in regard to statues and pictures of saints cannot be used in the case of blessed, who are not to be represented with the aureola, but with rays above (op. cit., Lib. I, c. xxxvii).

To conclude, we may observe that in the cultus of the blessed great attention must be given to the indult which in each specific instance determines, according to the wishes of the sovereign pontiff, the restrictions with regard to persons, places, and acts of worship. This matter, and very justly so, has been made the subject of special legislation on the part of the Congregation of Rites which decreed on 5 October, 1652, that no one could go beyond the limits set by the words of the indults of the Holy See in regard to beatification. The solemnities of beatification cannot be compared with those of canonization. They are briefly as follows: On the day on which beatification takes place Mass is said in St. Peter's in presence of the entire Congregation of Rites. After the Gospel, instead of a homily, the secretary of the Congregation reads the pope's decree, on the conclusion of which the painting of the newly beatified, which stands over the altar, is uncovered and the Mass is finished. About the hour of Vespers the Holy Father comes down to the basilica to venerate the new blessed. After the beatification permission is granted to celebrate solemn triduums, and by a special decree Mass and Office are allowed to be said yearly on a fixed day, but with restrictions as to place, and it is permitted to insert the name in the special martyrologies. The expenses of a beatification from the first steps to its conclusion approximate 100,000 lire ($20,000). (See BEATIFICATION AND CANONIZATION.)

For bibliography see BEATIFICATION AND CANONIZATION.

CAMILLUS BECCARI.

Blessed Sacrament, CONGREGATION OF THE, an enclosed congregation and a reform of the Dominican Order devoted to the perpetual adoration of the Blessed Sacrament. It was founded in the face of great opposition by Father Anthony Le Quieu, a French Dominican, whose canonization was stopped by the French Revolution. Born in 1601 at Paris, he entered the Order of Friars Preachers in the Rue St. Honoré, in 1622, and was in due time made master of novices first in his own monastery, and afterwards at Avignon (1634). While at the latter place (1639) he began to lay the foundation of the institute he desired to establish, but it was not till twenty years later (1659) that, after great difficulty, the first house was opened at Marseilles for the three ladies whom the saintly founder had begun to train at Avignon. The Bishop of Marseilles gave them the habit the following year, approved the rule and constitutions Father Le Quieu had drawn up, and erected them into a simple congregation. It was not till after the death of the founder, who lived to see another foundation made at Bollène, that the constitutions were approved by Pope Innocent XII (1693), who authorized the nuns to take solemn vows and bound them to enclosure. This was the first congregation instituted for the perpetual adoration of the Blessed Sacrament; it is not an austere one, but the degree of perfection put before the members by the founder is very high. The original mother-house at Marseilles was suppressed at the French Revolution, when the nuns were dispersed, but it was reopened in 1816; the Bollène house suffered more severely. Thirteen of the nuns endured martyrdom under the Commune; their cause of beatification is now before the Holy See; the remainder of the Bollène community returned to their convent and resumed their work of perpetual adoration in 1802. The Bollène nuns sent three of their number with one lay sister, under the Reverend Mother Emilie Pellier to England, to found a house at Cannington (1863), a community which was afterwards moved to Taunton in Somersetshire, where it has since remained. There is also a house at Oxford, and another near Newport. After Father Le Quieu's death foundations were made in the south of France, and after the French Revolution other houses were founded in the same locality. Since then a house has been established in Normandy, from which another convent has been opened at Hal in Belgium. There are no houses of this congregation in America.

PALLOT, *Vie du Père Antoine Le Quieu* (1847); STEELE, *Convents of Great Britain* (St. Louis, 1902), 117.

FRANCESCA M. STEELE.

Blessed Sacrament, SISTERS OF THE, one of the most recent congregations of religious women in the Catholic Church and one of entirely American origin, founded by Miss Katharine Drexel at Philadelphia, Pa., in 1889, for missionary work among the Indians and coloured people of the United States. The formal approbation of the Holy See was given to the congregation in July, 1907.

The Third Plenary Council of Baltimore gave a new impetus to missionary work among the coloured and Indian races and as one of the results of its recommendations, Right Reverend James O'Connor, Bishop of Omaha, acting in conjunction with Miss Katharine Drexel, daughter of the late Francis A. Drexel of Philadelphia, decided with the approval of the Most Reverend P. J. Ryan, Archbishop of Philadelphia, to form a new congregation of religious women devoted exclusively to missionary work among these two races. For some years previous to this step, Miss Drexel had been very active in re-establishing and supporting schools in many of the Indian reservations. The greater portion of the income which she derived from her father's estate was used in maintaining and furthering these missionary projects. At this period a survey of the field of work revealed about 250,000 Indians neglected, if not practically abandoned, and over nine millions of negroes still struggling through the aftermath of slavery.

The piteous condition of these two races decided Miss Drexel to devote both her fortune and her life to them. With the approval of high church authorities in the United States she gathered around her young women imbued with the same ideas, and

thus founded, towards the close of 1899, the nucleus of the new community. In order to be well grounded in the principles of the religious life, the first members made a two years' novitiate with the Sisters of Mercy. After this, they continued their period of preparation in the old Drexel homestead, Torresdale, near Philadelphia. Early in 1892 a mother-house and novitiate

ST. ELIZABETH'S CONVENT, SISTERS OF THE BLESSED SACRAMENT, CORNWELLS, PENN.

were opened at Maud, Pennsylvania, adjoining which was erected a manual training and boarding school for coloured boys and girls.

The distinctive spirit of this institute is the consecration of its members, body and soul, to the service of Jesus Christ ever present in the Holy Eucharist. His Eucharistic life is to be the inspiration of the entire varied activity of the sisters. Besides the vows usual in all religious communities, the sisters pledge themselves to work exclusively for the spiritual and temporal welfare of the Indian and coloured races. By their rule, the Sisters of the Blessed Sacrament may (1) undertake all kinds of educational works; (2) they may care for orphans or spiritually or corporally destitute children; (3) they may attend the sick by visiting them in their homes or by conducting hospitals; (4) they may shelter destitute and deserving women; (5) they may visit and instruct inmates of prisons and reformatories; (6) they may establish and conduct homes for the aged; (7) they may establish schools and classes outside their own houses, visit the poor in order to look after their religious welfare and also to teach them habits of good living, neatness, and thrift—in short, to make them self-sustaining men and women.

The sisterhood now numbers one hundred and twelve members. In 1894, St. Catharine's boarding and industrial school for Pueblo Indians was opened at Santa Fé, New Mexico; in 1899, the Institute of St. Francis de Sales, Rock Castle, Va., a boarding academy and industrial school was opened for the training of Southern coloured girls; in 1902, St. Michael's Mission, Arizona, for the education of Navajo Indians, a boarding and industrial school, was completed and opened. The Academy of the Immaculate Mother, Nashville, Tenn., was opened in 1905. In this school girls are also trained to become teachers, while others not desiring to teach may take a full course of domestic science and dressmaking. In 1906, the sisters commenced work at Carlisle, Pa., by instructing the Indian pupils of the Government School, and conducting a day school for coloured children.

M. M.

Blessing.—In its widest acceptation this word has a variety of meanings in the sacred writings: (1) It is taken in a sense that is synonymous with praise; thus the Psalmist, "I will bless the Lord at all times, his praise shall be always in my mouth"

(Ps. xxxiii, 1). (2) It is used to express a wish or desire that all good fortune, especially of a spiritual or supernatural kind, may go with the person or thing, as when David says: "Blessed art thou, and it shall be well with thee" (Ps. cxxvii, 2). (3) It signifies the sanctification or dedication of a person or thing to some sacred purpose; "Christ took bread, and blessed, and broke" (Matt., xxvi, 26). (4) Finally, it is employed to designate a gift; so Naaman addresses Eliseus: "I beseech thee therefore take a blessing of thy servant" (IV Kings, vi, 15). With these various significations it is not the present purpose to deal. Coming, then, to its strictly liturgical and restricted sense, blessing may be described as a rite, consisting of a ceremony and prayers performed in the name and with the authority of the Church by a duly qualified minister, by which persons or things are sanctified or dedicated to Divine service, or by which certain marks of Divine favour are invoked upon them. The following aspects of the subject will be discussed: (I) Antiquity; (II) Minister; (III) Objects; (IV) Efficacy; and (V) Rite employed in administering.

I. ANTIQUITY.—The custom of giving blessings goes back to the very earliest times. In the morning of Creation, on the completion of each day's work, God blessed the living creatures that came from His hands, bidding them increase and multiply and fill the earth (Gen., i–ii). When Noe emerged from the Ark, he received God's benediction (Gen., ix, 1), and this heritage he transmitted through his sons, Sem and Japheth, to posterity. The pages of the Old Testament testify abundantly to the great extent to which the practice of blessing prevailed in the patriarchal ages. The head of each tribe and family seemed to be privileged to bestow it with a special unction and fruitfulness, and the priests at the express direction of God were wont to administer it to the people. "Thus shall you bless the children of Israel . . . and the Lord will turn His countenance and give them peace" (Num., vi, 23–26). That great value was attributed to blessings is seen from the stratagem adopted by Rebecca to secure Jacob's blessing for her favourite son. In general estimation it was regarded as a mark of Divine complacency and as a sure way to secure God's benevolence, peace, and protection. The New Dispensation saw the adoption of this rite by Our Divine Lord and His Apostles, and so, elevated, ennobled, and consecrated by such high and holy usage, it came at a very early stage in the Church's history to assume definite and concrete shape as the chief among her sacramentals.

II. MINISTER.—Since, then, blessings, in the sense in which they are being considered, are entirely of ecclesiastical institution, the Church has the power to determine who shall have the right and duty to confer them. This she has done by entrusting their administration to those who are in sacerdotal orders. The solitary case in which one inferior to a priest is empowered to bless, is where the deacon blesses the paschal candle in the ceremonies of Holy Saturday. This exception is more apparent than real. For in the instance referred to the deacon acts by way of a deputy, and, moreover, employs the grains of incense already blessed by the celebrant. Priests, then, are the ordinary ministers of blessings, and this is only in the fitness of things, since they are ordained, as the words of the Pontifical run; "ut quæcumque benedixerint benedicantur, et quæcumque consecraverint consecrentur" (That whatever they bless may be blessed, and whatever they consecrate shall be consecrated). When, therefore, laymen and women are represented as blessing others it is to be understood that this is an act of good will on their part, a wish or desire for another's spiritual or temporal prosperity, an appeal to God

which has nothing to recommend it but the merits of personal sanctity. The ordinary greetings and salutations that take place between Christians and Catholics, leavened by mutual wishes for a share of heavenly grace, must not be confounded with liturgical blessings. St. Gregory first definitely taught that the angels are divided into hierarchies or orders, each having its own rôle to play in the economy of creation. Similarly the Church recognizes different orders or grades among her ministers, assigning to some higher functions than to others. The working out of this idea is seen in the case of conferring blessings. For while it is true that a priest can ordinarily give them, some blessings are reserved to the Supreme Pontiff, some to bishops, and some to parish priests and religious. The first class is not large. The pope reserves to himself the right to bless the pallium for archbishops, Agnus-Deis, the Golden Rose, the Royal Sword, and also to give that benediction of persons to which an indulgence of some days is attached. He may, and in the case of the last mentioned often does, depute others to give these. To bishops belongs the privilege of blessing abbots at their installation, priests at their ordination, and virgins at their consecration; of blessing churches, cemeteries, oratories, and all articles for use in connexion with the altar, such as chalices, vestments, and cloths, military standards, soldiers, arms, and swords; and of imparting all blessings for which Holy Oils are required. Some of these may, on delegation, be performed by inferiors. Of the blessings which priests are generally empowered to grant, some are restricted to those who have external jurisdiction, like rectors or parish priests, and others are the exclusive prerogative of persons belonging to a religious order. There is a rule, too, by which an inferior cannot bless a superior or even exercise the ordinary powers in his presence. The priest, for instance, who says Mass at which a bishop presides is not to give the final blessing without permission from the prelate. For this curious custom authors cite a text from the Epistle to the Hebrews: "And without all contradiction that which is less is blessed by that which is greater" (vii, 7). It would seem an overstraining of the passage to say that it affords an argument for maintaining that an inferior minister cannot bless one who is his superior in rank or dignity, for the text either merely enunciates an incident of common usage, or means that the inferior by the fact that he blesses is the greater, since he acts as the representative of God.

III. OBJECTS.—The range of objects that come under the influence of the Church's blessing is as comprehensive as the spiritual and temporal interests of her children. All the lower creatures have been made to serve man and minister to his needs. As nothing, then, should be left undone to enhance their utility towards this end, they are placed in a special way under the direct providence of God. "Every creature of God is good . . .", as St. Paul says, "for it is sanctified by the word of God and prayer" (I Tim., iv, 4–5). There is also the reflection that the effects of the Fall extended to the inanimate objects of creation, marring in a manner the original aim of their existence and making them, in the hands of evil spirits, ready instruments for the perpetration of iniquity. In the Epistle to the Romans St. Paul describes inanimate nature, blighted by the primal curse, groaning in travail and anxiously awaiting its deliverance from bondage. "The expectation of the creature waiteth for the revelation of the Sons of God. For the creature was made subject to vanity, not willingly, but by reason of him that made it subject, in hope" (viii, 19–20). From this it will be easily seen how very reasonable is the anxiety of the Church that the things which we use in daily life and particularly in the service of religion, should be rescued from contaminating influences and endowed with a potency for good. The principal liturgical blessings recognized and sanctioned by the Church are contained in the Roman Ritual and the Pontifical. The Missal, besides the blessing given at the end of Mass, contains only those blessings associated with the great functions incidental to certain days of the year, such as the blessing of palms and ashes. In the Pontifical are found the blessings that are performed *de jure* by bishops, such as the solemn blessing of persons already referred to, the forms for blessing kings, emperors, and princes at their coronation, and those before mentioned as of episcopal prerogative.

The great treasury of ecclesiastical blessings is the Roman Ritual. (1) *Formulæ for blessing persons.* First comes a blessing for pilgrims to the Holy Land, on their departure and return, containing beautiful prayers and apt allusions to the Magi journeying through the Arabian desert under the guidance of the Star, to Abraham leaving his own country and setting his face towards the distant land of Canaan, to the Angel companion of the younger Tobias, and, finally, an appeal to God to prove to the wayfarers a solace on their journey, a shade from summer heats, a shelter in storm, and a haven of safety. Next follow blessings of persons with Holy Water before Mass, for an adult who is sick, for a number of sick people, one for a woman on the approach of confinement and another after childbirth, blessings for infants, for children come to the use of reason and for those arrived at years of discretion, for children on their presentation in Church, that they may lead good Christian lives, for boys and girls on the Feast of the Holy Infancy that they may grow up to imitate the virtues of the Saviour and reach salvation under His guidance.

(2) *Blessings for things.* (a) In addition to the blessings already mentioned for articles destined for altar purposes, the Roman Ritual has formulæ for blessing crosses, images of Our Lord, of the Blessed Virgin and saints, church organs, processional banners, new bells for church uses and for other purposes, dress and cinctures worn in honour of Our Lady and of other saints, monstrances, reliquaries, vessels for Holy Oils, church ornaments, clerical habits, medals, pictures, and crosses for the Stations, rosaries of all the recognized kinds, water, candles, the Trisagion of the Holy Trinity, the different scapulars of Our Lady, of Our Lord, of the Blessed Trinity, of St. Joseph, St. Michael the Archangel, and other saints. Most of the objects just enumerated, as, for instance, rosaries and scapulars, receive what is called an indulgenced blessing, that is to say, by the pious employment and use of them persons are enabled to gain an indulgence. (b) The following articles of food have benedictions assigned to them: paschal lamb, eggs, oil, wine, lard, cheese, butter, dripping, salt, and water which is used as an antidote to rabies. There is also a form for everything that may be eaten. The fruits of the earth, such as grapes, corn, and the garnered harvest, seeds that are put into the earth, wine and the vintage, herbs and grasses, may all in fitting and appropriate language be "sanctified by the word of God and prayer". (c) The lower animals which minister to the reasonable requirements of the human family may have blessings invoked upon them in order that the measure of their usefulness may be increased. Thus, birds of the air, beasts of the field, bees that afford such examples of industry to man, horses and oxen broken to the yoke, and other beasts of burden are included in the formularies of the Ritual. The Creator is invoked to grant to the brute strength and health to bear his burthen and, if attacked by sickness or plague, to obtain de-

liverance. (d) The Ritual has blessings for houses and schools and for the laying of their foundation stones; for stables for the lower animals and every other building of any description for which no special formula is at hand. There is also a special blessing for the bridal chamber. (e) Lastly, inanimate things that subserve the equitable needs and conveniences of society may receive from the Church the stamp of her benediction before they are sent on their way to do their appointed tasks. Such, for instance, are new ships, new railways with trains and carriages, new bridges, fountains, wells, cornmills, limekilns, smelting-furnaces, telegraphs, steam engines, machines for producing electricity. The many serious accidents that occur explain the concern of the Church for those whose lives are exposed to danger from these various sources.

IV. EFFICACY.—The inquiry will be confined to the blessings approved of by the Church. As has been said, the value of a blessing given by a private person in his own name will be commensurate with his acceptableness before God by reason of his individual merits and sanctity. A blessing, on the other hand, imparted with the sanction of the Church has all the weight of authority that attaches to the voice of her who is the well-beloved spouse of Christ, pleading on behalf of her children. The whole efficacy, therefore, of these benedictions, in so far as they are liturgical and ecclesiastical, is derived from the prayers and invocations of the Church made in her name by her ministers. Blessings may be divided into two classes, viz: invocative and constitutive. The former are those in which the Divine benignity is invoked on persons or things, to bring down upon them some temporal or spiritual good, without changing their former condition. Of this kind are the blessings given to children, and to articles of food. The latter class are so called because they permanently depute persons or things to Divine service by imparting to them some sacred character, by which they assume a new and distinct spiritual relationship. Such are the blessings given to religious at their profession, and to churches and chalices by their consecration. In this case a certain abiding quality of sacredness is conferred in virtue of which the persons or things blessed become inviolably sacred, so that they cannot be divested of their religious character or be turned to profane uses. Again, theologians distinguish blessings of an intermediate sort, by which things are rendered special instruments of salvation without at the same time becoming irrevocably sacred, such as blessed salt, candles, etc. Blessings are not sacraments; they are not of Divine institution; they do not confer sanctifying grace; and they do not produce their effects in virtue of the rite itself, or *ex opere operato*. They are sacramentals and, as such, produce the following specific effects: (1) Excitation of pious emotions and affections of the heart and, by means of these, remission of venial sin and of the temporal punishment due to it; (2) freedom from power of evil spirits; (3) preservation and restoration of bodily health; (4) various other benefits, temporal or spiritual. All these effects are not necessarily inherent in any one blessing; some are caused by one formula, and others by another, according to the intentions of the Church. Neither are these effects to be regarded as infallibly produced, except in so far as the impetration of the Church has this attribute. The religious veneration, therefore, in which the faithful regard blessings has no taint of superstition, since it depends altogether on the Church's suffrages offered to God that the persons using the things she blesses may derive from them certain supernatural advantages. Instances are alleged in the lives of the saints where miracles have been wrought by the blessings of holy men and women. There is no reason to limit the miraculous interference of God to the early ages of the Church's history, and the Church never accepts these wonderful occurrences unless the evidence in support of their authenticity is absolutely unimpeachable.

V. RITE EMPLOYED.—Before a minister proceeds to impart any blessing he should first satisfy himself that it is one which he is duly qualified to give, either by his ordinary or delegated powers. He should next use the prescribed rite. As a rule, for the simple blessings of the Ritual, a soutane, surplice, and stole of the requisite colour will be sufficient. A clerk should be at hand to carry the Holy Water or incense if required, or to prepare a lighted candle. The blessings are ordinarily given in a church; but, if necessary, they can be lawfully administered elsewhere according to the exigencies of place or other circumstances or privileges, and without any sacred vestment.

PATRICK MORRISROE.

Blessing, APOSTOLIC, the solemn blessing (*urbi et orbi*) which, before 1870, the Holy Father himself gave from the loggias of the following churches: of St. Peter's, on Maundy Thursday and Easter; of the Lateran, on Ascension Day; and of Santa Maria Maggiore, on the feast of the Assumption of the B. V. M. The popes very often delegated to others the power to give this blessing in answer to petitions from princes, at the close of missions, and on such occasions. This power was restricted by Clement XIII, 3 September, 1762, to patriarchs, primates, archbishops, and bishops, who petition the Apostolic See for it; they can give the Apostolic blessing on Easter Sunday and on some other feasts. Prelates who have the use of the *pontificalia* and jurisdiction over a certain territory can give it only once a year. A certain formula is prescribed. The superiors of certain religious orders, especially the Franciscans, can give it twice a year in the churches of their own order; they must use a formula and ask permission of the ordinary (30 August, 1763). The faculty is occasionally granted to particular priests, regular or secular, to give the Apostolic blessing upon return from Rome, at the close of missions or retreats; in this case no solemn rite is required. The Apostolic blessing is a sacramental with which is granted a plenary indulgence (under the usual conditions), but no absolution from ecclesiastical censures. During a jubilee this blessing cannot be given. A special feature of this blessing is the Apostolic benediction *in articulo mortis*. This blessing is given to those who are in danger of death by priests who possess the required faculty. A formula is prescribed by Benedict XIV; to gain the indulgence it is necessary to receive the sacraments, to invoke the name of Jesus, and to be resigned to the will of God. In missionary countries the bishops can subdelegate every priest to grant this indulgence (5 April, 1772). It is not suspended by a jubilee.

BERINGER, *Die Ablässe, ihr Wesen und Gebrauch* (Germ. tr., 13th ed., Paderborn, 1905).

FREDERICK G. HOLWECK.

Blessing of Abbots and Abbesses. See ABBOT; ABBESS.

Blind, EDUCATION OF THE. See EDUCATION OF THE BLIND; HAÜY.

Blois (BLESENSIS), DIOCESE OF, coextensive with the civil department of Loir-et-Cher and a suffragan of Paris. On 1 July, 1697, Innocent XII canonically erected the Bishopric of Blois, that territory having theretofore been dependent on the Diocese of Chartres. Prior to the Revolution, the Diocese of Blois was less extensive than at present, almost the entire arrondissement of Romorantin being subject to the Bishopric of Orléans, and the Bas-Vendômois to that of Mans. The Concordat of 1802 gave Loir-et-

Cher to the Diocese of Orléans, and in 1822 the Diocese of Blois was re-established. Monseigneur de Thémines, who was Bishop of Blois in 1776 and died in exile in 1829, was one of the most obstinate enemies of the Concordat. St. Solennius, Bishop of Chartres under Clovis, is a patron of Blois; his relics were preserved by a miracle.

Owing to the proximity of the monasteries of Micy and Marmoutier, Blois counts among its saints a number of monks; Lubinus, Bishop of Chartres in the sixth century; Laumerus, Abbot of Corbion in the Diocese of Chartres (d. about 590), whose body was transported to Blois, at the time of the Norman invasions, by fugitive monks, who founded in that city the Abbey of St. Laumer; St. Deodatus, the anchorite, also called St. Dié (sixth century), who assured Clovis of the victory at Vouillé (507); the solitaries Victor and Leonardus; and Aigulphus (seventh century), a native of Blois and Abbot of Lérins, who was assassinated. Peter of Blois, who came from the Abbey of St. Laumer, was conspicuous in the twelfth century for his defence of St. Thomas Becket and for encouraging devotion to the Blessed Virgin. The Venerable Charles of Blois, killed in 1364 at the Battle of Auray, was the son of Guy, Count of Blois. The Benedictines had several great abbeys in this diocese, one at Selles-sur-Cher, begun as early as the sixth century by the hermit, St. Eusinus, and another at Pontlevoy, now a college. The monastery of the Blessed Trinity at Vendôme, dedicated in 1040, was also quite celebrated. The Oratorians Jean Morin and Jerôme Viguier, learned ecclesiastics of the seventeenth century, were natives of Blois.

At the close of the year 1905, the Diocese of Blois had a population of 275,538; 28 pastorates, 266 mission churches, and 8 curacies with subventions from the State. According to the latest statistics, the following institutions are to be found in the diocese: 48 infant schools conducted by sisters; 2 orphanages where farming is taught, conducted by the Frères de St. François Régis and the Sœurs du Protectorat de St. Joseph; 7 girls' orphanages conducted by sisters; 1 house of refuge for young women, conducted by the Religieuses de Notre Dame de la Charité; 5 *patronages* at Blois; 1 *patronage* at Romorantin; 8 hospitals and hospices conducted by sisters; 5 houses of retreat conducted by sisters; 5 communities of sisters who care for the sick in their homes; and 9 homes for the aged conducted by sisters.

In 1900 the following congregations were represented in the diocese: the Capuchins at Blois and Premonstratensians at Authon. Among the local congregations are the Sisters of Our Lady of Providence, with mother-house at Blois, who have charge of orphan asylums. The most frequented place of pilgrimage is Notre Dame de Villethion at Saint Amand. Others are Notre Dame de Nanteuil at Montrichard, Notre Dame des Aydes at Blois, and Notre Dame des Blanches at Pontlevoy, a sanctuary built at the end of the tenth century by Gilduin, opponent of Foulques Nerra.

Gallia christiana (1744), VIII, 1343–1407; *Instrumenta*, 412–478; DUPRÉ, *Notice sur les saints de Blois* (Blois, 1860); CHEVALIER, *Topobibl.*, 421, 422.

GEORGES GOYAU.

Blois, FRANÇOIS-LOUIS DE. See BLOSIUS.

Blomevenna, PETER (PETER A LEYDIS), a Carthusian, b. at Leyden, in Holland, in 1466; d. 30 September, 1536. Owing to the avarice and cruelty of his parents and relatives, his early years were spent in poverty and hardship. But he led withal a singularly pure and devout life. Entering the Carthusian Order, he distinguished himself by his absorption in heavenly things and his zeal for the glory of God. In 1506 he was elected prior of the Carthusian monastery of Cologne, a post which he held until his death, twenty-nine years later. His long term of office enabled him to do much to promote strict religious observance both in his monastery and throughout the Rhenish province, of which he had been named visitor. Besides his active work among his brethren, he found time for the composition of several treatises which have a certain value as ascetic and controversial literature. In his "Enchiridion Sacerdotum" (1532) he enlarges upon the august mystery of the Holy Eucharist. His "De Bonitate Divinâ" is a valuable work for preachers of the word of God. In 1513 he translated into the Latin tongue the Franciscan De Herp's ascetic treatise "Directorium Aureum Contemplativorum", adding thereto explanatory notes. He also edited several volumes of Denis the Carthusian (Dionysius of Rickel) and wrote vigorously against the then nascent Protestant heresy. Among Blomevenna's controversial works are "Candela Evangelica" (1536); "Assertio Purgatorii" (1534); "De Auctoritate Ecclesiæ" (1535); "De Vario Modo adorandi Deum, Sanctos et eorum Imagines" (1535).

Hurter, *Nomenclator* (Innsbruck, 1899), IV, 1149.

E. J. Devine.

Blondus, Flavius. See Biondo, Flavio.

Blood Indians, a group of North American aborigines forming part of the Blackfeet Tribe, which, with the Arapahoes and Cheyennes, constitute the Western division of the great Algonquin family. (See Blackfoot Indians.) The Blood Indian (*Kœna*) group is now subdivided into several branches, or clans, the most important of which is (1) the Ini-poyex (Standing-buffaloes), which is sub-divided into (a) Keaý-etapix (Bear people), (b) Noto-spitax (All-tall-people), (c) Mami-ahoyin (Fish-eaters), (d) Ayom-okekax (Closely-camped), (e) Akæ-pokax (Many-children), (f) Apikax (Scabby). Other clans of the group are (2) the Six-immokax (Black-elks), (3) Akæ-namax (Many-scabbed-mouths), and (4) the Tsi-sokasimix (Buffalo-coats).

The language of the Blood Indians is like that of the other two groups of the Blackfeet, with but few and unimportant peculiarities. It is called Blackfoot, and is classed as one of the branches of the Algonquin, though it possesses only a very limited number of words in common with the other branches of the same family. The aboriginal name, *Kœna*, might, it seems, be translated "Already-chief"; but the true meaning is in fact altogether lost, and no one, even among these people themselves, could now give a satisfactory interpretation of it. In the sign language, the gesture for Kæna is made by rapidly passing the right hand, palm downward, in front of the mouth, of which gesture the exact signification is also lost.

In the year 1882 the Bloods were supposed to number about 1800 souls; they now number not more than 1200. The former of these estimates may have been exaggerated, as it was difficult at that time to obtain statistics of mortality, but it is undoubtedly true that the numbers of these people have considerably diminished in the last twenty-five years, and that they are still, slowly, but steadily, diminishing. They used to be, as a rule, well-developed and powerful physical specimens of humanity, some of the men being over 6 feet 6 inches in height, the women generally shorter, but strong and healthy-looking. Their present physical condition, however, shows the melancholy constitutional effects of consumption and scrofula. The country over which the Bloods, with the other Blackfeet tribes, formerly roamed extended from the basin of the Missouri, on the south, northwards to the Red Deer River in the Canadian Province of Alberta, with the Rocky Mountains as its western boundary. Since 1877,

when they entered into a treaty with the Canadian Government, they have been settled on the tract of land known as the Blood Reserve. This reserve, lying near the Belly Buttes, which had always been a favourite resort of the tribe, is bounded on the west by the Belly River, on the north by the Belly River and the Old Man River, on the east by the St. Mary River, and on the south by the Mormon settlement of Cardston.

Like most prairie Indians, the Bloods are very proud and superstitious. In their own way they are a very religious people, religion being a part of every important act of their lives. Their religious system closely resembles that of other Algonquins, but especially of the Crees. It centres in the worship of the sun (*Natos*), the moon (*Kokomi-kisum*), some constellations, and also some minor deities—genii of the mountains, forests, and streams. The most important of their religious practices is the sundance (*okan*), an elaborate ceremonial performance which needs months of preparation and ends with a week or so of festivities, in which fasting, self-torture, and self-mutilation are joined with rejoicings and frolics of every description. This practice, although dying out, is still revived from time to time. Other superstitious dances and performances are parts of the same curious and intricate system.

While the tribe was constantly roaming from place to place in the immense territory which now forms the States of Montana and the Dakotas, and the Province of Alberta, they were but rarely and irregularly visited by Catholic missionaries, among whom were Fathers de Smet and Imoda, S. J., and Father A. Lacombe, O. M. I. After the settlement of the tribe on their reserve, however, in 1877, it became possible to establish permanent missions among them. Of the three denominations—Catholic, Anglican, and Methodist—which had established missions among the Bloods in 1881, the first and second have remained in the field. They maintain industrial and boarding schools, and have educated a number of Indian children. The progress of Christianity has been slow. Unfortunately, the example of many of the whites has not been of a nature to attract the Indians to the white man's religion; yet there is a goodly number (about 35) of young Catholic families, mostly made up of the boys and girls educated in the Catholic schools. Besides, most of the children are baptized Catholics when young, and when these have been trained and educated the number of Catholic families will increase. There are also a few Protestant families. At the present time there are two Catholic priests on the Blood Reserve, with a neat little church, a residence, and a boarding school conducted by seven Sisters with some forty pupils. Children are also sent to the industrial school, which is established at a place about 100 miles distant from the Reserve, and is open to all the Blackfeet tribes. On the reserve there is a hospital conducted by Sisters of Charity for the exclusive benefit of the Indians, an institution which was probably unique of its kind at the time of its foundation, in 1893. Polygamy has been almost entirely eradicated, yet the bulk of the adult population—over thirty years of age, that is—are still pagans, and can be thoroughly habituated to Catholic practices only in a very limited number of cases. One most remarkable case of this kind was that of Chief Red-Crow (*Mik-ahestow*), who was converted and lived the life of a practical Catholic for several years preceding his death, which occurred in 1890.

The progress of civilization among the Bloods during the last twenty-five years may be regarded as marvellous in the extreme. At first they were trained to become farmers; but this occupation was not to their liking, and little progress was made.

For the last twelve years, therefore, a new policy has been adopted which has proved to be the right one. In pursuance of this later policy, the Indians have been set to ranching and cattle-raising—a congenial occupation. Many of them now have herds of their own, and are self-supporting. Noteworthy progress has also been achieved in their dress, housing, preparation of food, treatment of wives, and, generally, in their ideas of social relations; so much so that the Blood Indian of to-day may be considered an entirely different being from his predecessor of twenty-five years ago.   EMILE J. LEGAL.

Blood of St. Januarius. See JANUARIUS, ST.

Blood Relationship. See CONSANGUINITY.

Bloody Sweat. See AGONY OF CHRIST.

Blosius (or DE BLOIS), FRANÇOIS-LOUIS, a Benedictine abbot and spiritual writer, b. at Donstienne, near Liège, Flanders, 1506; d. at Liessies, 1566. His parents were nobles of Hainault, his father being Sieur of Jumigny. He became page to the Archduke

FRANÇOIS-LOUIS BLOSIUS

Charles (afterwards Emperor Charles V) but entered the Abbey of Liessies when only fourteen. Whilst still a novice he was sent to study at the University of Louvain, whence he was recalled in 1527 to become coadjutor to the Abbot, Gilles Gippus, his nomination as such being confirmed by a Bull of Pope Paul III. Three years later, in 1530, he succeeded Gippus as thirty-fourth Abbot of Liessies, and received ordination and the abbatial blessing in the same year. His first care was the cultivation in his abbey of a true monastic spirit and strict discipline, which had somewhat declined under his predecessors. He had hardly settled down to the work of reform before Flanders was immersed in war owing to its invasion by Francis I of France, which occurred in 1537. Liessies, being on the frontier, became in consequence an unsafe habitation and Blosius proposed a move to the priory of Ath, in the interior, but most of his monks, being opposed to his reform, either elected to remain at Liessies or else went to other laxer monasteries. The abbot, however, with three monks, retired to Ath and there he at once restored the primitive observance of the rule. In spite of opposition the reform gained ground and numbers increased rapidly. When a return to Liessies became possible, in 1545, the reform was accepted by those that had remained there and was confirmed by a Bull of Pope Paul III. Blosius next began a restoration and enlargement of the abbey buildings, which were only completed after his death. In 1556 Charles V offered him the Archbishopric of Cambrai and the abbacy of Tournai, both of which he refused in order that he might remain at Liessies. In personal character he was distinguished for his gentleness, his generosity to the poor, his love of chastity, and his devotion to the Mother of God. He was a diligent student, especially of the Scriptures, the works of the Fathers, and the mystical writers of the fourteenth century. His own writings were numerous, the chief being "Speculum Monachorum", written in Latin, translated into French 1726, and into English 1872

(Mirror for Monks, by Sir John Coleridge), "Entretiens spirituels", and "Instructions spirituelles et pensées consolantes". His complete works were first published at Louvain in 1568 and have been many times reprinted and translated. Of English editions, besides the "Mirror for Monks", there are "A Book of Spiritual Instruction" (London, 1900) and "Comfort for the Faint-hearted" (London, 1902), both translated by Father Bertrand Wilberforce, O.P.

Acta SS., I, 430; ZIEGELBAUER, *Hist. Lit. O. S. B.* (Augsburg, 1754), I, 100–482; HURTER, *Nomenclator* (Innsbruck, 1892), I, 43; *De Blois, A Benedictine of the Sixteenth Century,* tr. LOVAT (London, 1878).

G. CYPRIAN ALSTON.

Blyssen, HEINRICH, b. at Cologne or Bonn, Germany, in 1526; d. at Graz, 24 April, 1586. He entered the Society of Jesus, and St. Ignatius, appreciating his logic and his knowledge of theology, sent him with eleven other Jesuits to Bohemia to combat heresy there, and to sustain a public disputation with the disciples of Luther and Hus. Though only twenty-five years of age, he acquitted himself with honour, and in 1556 he became professor of theology and Hebrew at the Jesuit college at Prague. Still maintaining his controversies with the heretics of Bohemia, he published a collection of theses: "De ciborum delectu atque jejunio" (Prague, 1559). To continue the work of public lectures which he had begun, he gave a Sunday course of polemics to the clergy and laity. Appointed rector of the college at Prague in 1561, he was transferred in 1570 to the college at Graz where he vigorously continued his lectures on theology. Attacked by Jacob Heerbrand on his doctrine concerning the Church, he published a defence of his thesis: "Defensio assertionum theologicarum de verâ et sacrosanctâ Christi, quam habet in terris, Ecclesiâ militante" (Ingolstadt, 1577). His last and principal work "De uno geminoque sacræ eucharistiæ synaxeos salubriter percipiendæ ritu ac usu" was published (Ingolstadt, 1585) when he was provincial of Austria.

ORLANDINI, *Hist. Soc. Jesu* (Rome, 1614), XII, 283; XVI, 396; SOCHER, *Historia prov. Austr. Soc. Jesu* (Vienna), VIII, 320; SCHMIDT, *Historia Soc. Jesu prov. Bohemiæ* (Prague, 1747), I, 536; SOMMERVOGEL, *Bibl. de la c. de J.* (1550), I.

M. DE MOREIRA.

Blyth, FRANCIS, English Carmelite, reviser of the Douay Bible, born c. 1705; d. in London, 11 December, 1772. Though born of Protestant parents, he joined the Catholic Church while yet a youth, and entered the Carmelite novitiate at Modena in 1723, taking the name Simon Stock of the Blessed Trinity. Having obtained a dispensation from irregularity on account of a defect in vision, he proceeded to Malta for a course of studies, and after ordination returned to England, in November, 1730, where he first served a mission in Wiltshire. In 1741 he became assistant chaplain, and in 1756 chaplain-major to the Portuguese embassy in London, where he remained until his death. From 1742 till 1755, he also was Vicar Provincial of the English Carmelites. While in London, he assumed the name of Courtney. The chapels of the various embassies being recognized as places of worship for Catholics, the chaplains held a position not unlike that of parish priests, and Father Blyth distinguished himself by his eloquent and zealous preaching. The first ambassador under whom Father Blyth served was Dom Sebastião-José de Carvalho e Mello, afterwards Marquez de Pombal (1739–45), whom he was, at a later period, accused of having aided in high-handed proceedings against the Jesuits. He indignantly protested against the calumny. Blyth was buried in the cemetery of St. Pancras, London, and, being a man of great literary attainments and author of many works, a memorial was raised there in his honour. His chief labour was the revision, in conjunction with Bishop Challoner, of the so-called Douay Bible; while adhering closely to the text of the Vulgate, the revisers sacrificed the energetic language of the older translators for a much weaker one which frequently lacks dignity. His other works comprise expositions of the Penitential Psalms and other portions of Holy Scripture, sermons, and controversial writings.

The Rheims Testament, with Annotations (London, 1738); GILLOW, *Bibl. Dict. Eng. Cath.*, I, 252; ZIMMERMAN, *Carmel in England* (London, 1899), 373.

B. ZIMMERMAN.

Boast, JOHN. See TRITHEMIUS.

Bobadilla, NICOLAS, b. at Valencia, Spain, 1511; d. at Loretto, Italy, 23 September, 1590. After having taught philosophy in his native country, he went to Paris to acquire a more perfect knowledge of Greek and Latin. Here he met Ignatius of Loyola, joined him in his plans and was among the first seven followers of the saint to consecrate themselves to God in the Society of Jesus, at Montmartre, 15 August, 1534. Hereafter Bobadilla's career was a very active one, as a most zealous worker in the cause of the Catholic Faith. While serving the sick in the camp of the army of Charles V about Ratisbon, he himself caught the plague. Here too, about this time, 1546, as he was returning from the camp into the city he was waylaid by assassins and severely wounded. At another time he barely escaped with his life from an attempt to poison him.

By order of the Sovereign Pontiff Paul III, Bobadilla took a prominent part in the Diets of Nuremberg, 1543, and of Speyer, 1543, as well as in that of Ratisbon, 1546. Shortly after this an incident occurred which forced him to leave Germany. In 1548, the "Interim" of Augsburg was published by the Emperor, Charles V. It was a tentative document intended to suggest a basis of agreement between Catholics and Protestants until their religious differences could be definitely settled. But as it seemed in the eyes of many Catholics to go too far, and in the eyes of many Protestants not far enough, it satisfied neither party. Bobadilla opposed it in speech and in writing, and so vigorously, that although he was highly esteemed in the imperial court, he was obliged, by the Emperor's order, to retire from Germany. He was a most popular preacher, as is evidenced by the fact that he delivered sermons in seventy-seven archbishoprics and bishoprics in Italy, Germany, and Dalmatia.

The writings of Bobadilla cover a wide range of topics. Among them are commentaries on some chapters of Genesis and other portions of the Old and New Testaments; annotations on the Gospels; treatises on predestination, the sacraments and their use, against the Lutherans, cases of conscience; a defence of the Council of Trent against Melancthon and Calvin, etc. The last survivor of the seven first companions of Ignatius of Loyola, Bobadilla took part in the election of four generals of the Society of Jesus.

BOERO, *Vita del servo di Dio P. Nicola Bobadilla, della c. di. G.* (Florence, 1879); SOMMERVOGEL, *Bibl. de la c. de J.*, I, 1553; ORLANDINI, *Hist. Soc. Jesu*, I, 81, 135, 170.

JOSEPH M. WOODS.

Bobbio, ABBEY AND DIOCESE OF.—The diocese (*Ebovium*, or *Bobium; Diœcesis Eboviensis*, or *Bobiensis*), which is suffragan to the Archiepiscopal See of Genoa, is conterminous with the civil district of Bobbio. This district is situated in the Province of Pavia and contains, besides Bobbio, its chief town, only two small villages and eighteen communes. The diocese was suppressed from 1803 to 1817, during which time it was annexed to Alexandria, then to Casala. Pius VII re-established it in 1818. The population, entirely Catholic, is (1907) about 30,000. There are 52 parishes and 105 churches or chapels, served by 80 secular priests. The cathedral chapter consists of a provost, archpriest, and ten canons. In the diocesan seminary there are at present 40 students. Under Bishop Gianelli a congregation of priests was formed in 1839 under the title of Oblates of St. Alphonsus Liguori. They devote themselves especially to hearing confessions in prisons and hospitals, as well as to spreading good literature among the people. Bobbio also possesses a Congregation of Daughters of Mary, popularly known as *Gianelliane*.

HISTORY.—The origin of the See of Bobbio, indeed of the town itself, is due to the establishment of a monastery here by the Irish saint, Columban, in 614. The Lombards, with other savage tribes, had invaded northern Italy under their leader Alboin in 568. A half-Arian, half-heathen horde, wherever they passed all the horrors of wanton destruction and cruelty marked their track. But at length the new barbarian ruler, Agilulph, became less hostile and by degrees even not unfavourably disposed towards the Catholic Faith. Queen Theodelinda, whom he married in 590, was a fervent Catholic; she had wonderful influence over her consort, and at last he was converted by the preaching of Columban. From the day of his baptism, Agilulph displayed great zeal for the conversion of his subjects, and for this purpose gave St. Columban a ruined church and devastated district known as Ebovium, which, before the Lombards seized it, had formed part of the Patrimony of St. Peter. Columban had set his heart on this secluded place, for while intent on instructing the Lombards he chose solitude for his monks and himself. By the side of this little church, which was dedicated to St. Peter, soon arose the walls of an abbey. Here the nucleus of what was to be the most celebrated library in Italy was formed by the MSS. which Columban had brought from Ireland and the treatises of which he himself was the author.

The sainted founder of Bobbio was soon afterwards laid to rest (23 November, 615), but his crosier passed into worthy hands. The names of St. Attala (627) and St. Bertulf (640) will live forever in ecclesiastical history. Both were conspicuous for holiness and learning, and both inherited Columban's apostolic spirit. It was indeed sorely needed, for a reaction towards Arianism set in, which became formidable under the Arian king, Rotharis (636–652). Arioald, the immediate predecessor of Rotharis, who became a Catholic, had before his conversion caused St. Bladulf, a monk of Bobbio, to be assassinated, because Bladulf would not salute him, as being an Arian. It is said that Attala restored Bladulf to life and delivered Arioald from a diabolical possession, the punishment of his crime; and that this twofold miracle led to Arioald's conversion. In 628, when St. Bertulf made a pilgrimage to Rome, Honorius I exempted Bobbio from episcopal jurisdiction, thus making the abbey immediately subject to the Holy See. Under the next abbot, Bobolen, the rule of St. Benedict was introduced. At first its observance was optional, but in course of time it superseded the more austere rule hitherto in use, and Bobbio joined the Congregation of Monte Cassino. In 643, at the request of Rotharis and Queen Gundelberga, Pope Theodore I granted to the Abbot of Bobbio the use of the mitre and other pontificals. It has even been asserted that Bobbio had a bishop, named Peter Aldus, as early as the seventh century, but according to the best authorities (Ughelli, Gams, and others) the See of Bobbio was not founded till four centuries later, although recent investigation has shown that the name of its first bishop really was Peter Aldus (Savio, 158).

From the seventh century on, in the midst of widespread turmoil and ignorance, Bobbio remained a home of piety and culture. Through the efforts of St. Columban's disciples, increasing numbers of the Lombards were received into the Church. But during the first half of the seventh century, the large tract of country lying between Turin and Verona, Genoa and Milan, was in a very irreligious and disturbed state; and even idolatry was not unknown. In fact not until the reign of the usurper Grimoald (663–673), himself a convert, was the bulk of the nation brought into the Church. But from that time Arianism disappeared in the West. The historians of the abbey regard as one of its chief glories the prominent part which it took in the final contest with this heresy. Theodelinda's nephew, the pious Arribert (653–663), restored all the lands of Bobbio which belonged by right to the Prince of the Apostles. Arribert II also gladly confirmed this restitution to John VII in 707. The unruly Lombards soon dispossessed the pope, but in 756 Aistulf was compelled by Pepin to give up the lands. In 774 Charlemagne made liberal grants to the abbey. In 1153 Frederick Barbarossa confirmed by two charters various rights and possessions. Thus it came to pass that the abbots were for centuries entrusted with a large administration of temporals.

The fame of Bobbio reached the shores of Ireland, and the memory of Columban was dear to the hearts of his countrymen. Bobolen's successor was St. Comgall who had resigned his see in Ireland in order to become a monk of Bobbio; St. Cummian who did the same died in the abbey about 730 (Holder-Egger in "Mon. Germ. Hist."); and the learned St. Dungal (d. after 827) bequeathed to the abbey his valuable library, consisting of some seventy volumes, among which was the famous "Antiphonary of Bangor". A tenth-century catalogue, published by Muratori, shows that at that period every branch of knowledge, divine and human, was represented in this library. Many of the books have been lost, the rest have long since been dispersed and are still reckoned among the chief treasures of the later collections which possess them. In 1616 Cardinal Federigo Borromeo took for the Ambrosian Library of Milan eighty-six volumes, including the famous "Bobbio Missal", written about 911, the "Antiphonary of Bangor", and the palimpsests of Ulfilas's Gothic version of the Bible. Twenty-six volumes were given, in 1618, to Paul V for the Vatican Library. Many others were sent to Turin, where, besides those in the Royal Archives, there were seventy-one in the University Library until the disastrous fire of 26 January, 1904. As scholars of later ages have owed a great deal to the Bobbio MSS., so, too, did those of the tenth century. Gerard of Aurillac, for example, who was afterwards Pope Sylvester II, became Abbot of Bobbio in 982; and with the aid of the numerous ancient treatises which he found there he composed his celebrated work on geometry. And indeed it appears that at a time when Greek was almost unknown in western Europe, the Irish monks of Bobbio read Aristotle and Demosthenes in the original tongue.

In the year 1014, the Emperor Henry II, on the occasion of his own coronation in Rome, obtained from Benedict VIII the erection of Bobbio as a see. Peter Aldus, its first bishop, had been Abbot of Bobbio since 999, and his episcopal successors for a long time lived in the abbey, where many of them had been monks. According to Ughelli and others, Bobbio was made a suffragan see of Genoa in 1133; but Savio finds this subordination mentioned for the first time in a Bull of Alexander III, dated 19 April, 1161. From time to time disputes arose between the bishop and the monks, and in 1199 Innocent III issued two Bulls, restoring the abbey in spirituals and temporals, and empowering the bishop to depose an abbot if within a certain time he did not obey.

Bobbio's greatest bishops have been (1) Blessed Albert (1184), who was translated to the Patriarchal See of Jerusalem and died a martyr at Acre in 1214; (2) the learned canonist Giovanni de Mondani (1477–82), whose remains were found incorrupt in 1614; and (3) Venerable Antonio Gianelli (1838–46), whose cause has been introduced. St. Columban's abbey and church were taken from the Benedictines by the French soldiers in 1803; what remains of the abbey is now used as a municipal school, and the church, where the relics of Sts. Columban, Attala, Bertulf, Cummian, and others repose, is now a parish church, served by secular priests. The altars and the sarcophagi in the crypt present beautiful specimens of the interlaced ornamentation which is characteristic of Irish art. In the Cathedral of Bobbio there is a beautiful tabernacle in the Ravenna style.

WARNEFRIED, *De gestis Longobardorum* in *Mon. Germ. Hist.* (Hanover, 1878), III; MIGNE, *P. L.*, LXXVII, CLXXIX, CCXIV; JAFFÉ-EWALD, *Regesta Rom. Pont.* (Leipzig, 1885, 1886); POTTHAST, *Regesta Rom. Pont.* (Berlin, 1872); ID., *Bibliotheca Hist. medii ævii* (2d ed. Berlin, 1896); PRESSUTI, *Regesta Honorii III* (Rome, 1888–95); DUCHESNE, *Liber Pontificalis* (Paris, 1892), II; UGHELLI-COLETI, *Italia Sacra* (Venice), IV; MABILLON, *Acta Sanctorum Ord. S. Ben.* (2d ed., Venice, 1733), I; MURATORI, *Antiquitates Italiæ* (Milan, 1740), III; BELLESHEIM, *Geschichte der katholischen Kirche in Irland* (Mainz, 1890), I; GUÉRIN, *Les petits Bollandistes* (Paris, 1882——); MORAN, *Essays on the Early Irish Church* (Dublin, 1864); O'HANLON, *Lives of Irish Saints* (Dublin, 1875–1906); MARTIN, *Saint Columban* in *Les Saints* (Paris, 1905); ROSETTI (an Abbot of Bobbio), *Bobbio Illustrato* (1795); AMATI, *Dizionario Corografico d'Italia* (Milan, 1862); *Corografia d'Italia* (Milan, s. d.); HEALY, *Ireland's Ancient Schools and Scholars* (Dublin, 1890); STOKES, *Six Months in the Apennines* (Dublin, 1892); *Historiæ Patriæ Monumenta* (Turin, 1836–84); PEYRON, *Præfatio De Bibliothecâ Bobbiensi; M. T. Cic. Fragm.*, (Turin, 1824); VON GEBHARD, *Ein Bücherfund in Bobbio;* SEEBASS, *Handschriften von Bobbio* respectively in V and XIII of *Centralblatt f. Bibliothekenwesen* (Leipzig, 1888–96); OTTINO, *I codici Bobbiesi* (Turin, 1890; a facsimile edition from copies of the Turin MSS. is appearing at Milan since 1906); WERNER, *Gerbert von Aurillac* (Vienna, 1881); HEIMBUCHER, *Die Orden u. Kongregationen der kath. Kirche* (Paderborn, 1896, 1897); GAMS, *Series episcoporum Ecclesiæ catholicæ* (Ratisbon, 1873–88); EUBEL, *Hierarchia Catholica medii ævi* (Münster, 1898), I; SAVIO, *Gli antichi vescovi d'Italia; Piemonte* (Turin, 1899), I, 158–174.

REGINALD WALSH.

Boccaccino, BOCCACCIO, an eminent Italian painter, b. at Cremona, 1460, and d. probably in 1525 rather than in 1518, the date usually given. He studied, it is thought, with followers of Mantegna, at Ferrara, and was a pupil or fellow-student of Domenico Panetti. At Cremona he painted in Sant' Agostino a series of frescoes. He had as an assistant Benvenuto Garofalo, who left him and went to Rome. The master followed and painted a "Coronation of the Virgin" in Santa Maria in Trastevere. This, however, was so ridiculed by the public, which had expected much of one who had had the hardihood to criticize Michael Angelo, that the disappointed artist returned to Cremona where, among his most appreciated works, is a frieze in the cathedral, showing the "Birth of the Virgin" and other subjects from the life of Our Lady. Lanzi, who considered Boccaccino as the best modern among the ancients and the best ancient among the moderns, compares his work in these productions with that of Perugino, treating it as inferior in some qualities while superior in others.

The works of Boccaccino possess much charm, and a number of them greatly resemble those of Perugino. This is notably so in his "Marriage of the Virgin" and "The Madonna with St. Vincent and St. Anthony" in the church of San Vincenzo at Cremona, which have often been assumed to be the work of the greater painter. Among Boccaccino's works in the cathedral at Cremona, in addition to those already spoken of, are: "The Appearance of the Angel to Joachim"; "The Meeting of Joachim and Anna"; "The Circumcision"; "Christ Reasoning with the Doctors"; and "Christ with the four Patron Saints of Cremona". At the Academy in Venice is his much admired "Marriage of St. Catherine" and "Virgin and Child in a Landscape", and in the church of San Giuliano, in the same city, is his "Virgin and Child with four Saints". The Louvre possesses a "Holy Family"; the London National Gallery a "Procession to Calvary", formerly in a Cremona church; and the Ferrara Pinacoteca a "Death of the Virgin". Light grey eyes outlined with a dark rim are characteristic of the pictures of Boccaccino.

BOCCACCINO, CAMILLO, a short-lived but brilliant painter, b. at Cremona, 1511; d. 1546. He was the son and pupil of Boccaccio Boccaccino, whom he surpassed, taking care, it is pointed out, to avoid the errors into which his father's self-esteem had led him. He early showed both originality and strength, and his work has been considered to approach that of Correggio, notably his "Four Evangelists" in the niches of the cupola of San Sigismondo near Cremona, which are thoroughly in the Correggio style and were painted when the artist was only twenty-six. Camillo Boccaccino is thought by Lanzi to be the greatest artist of the Cremonese school. Two of his works at Cremona are "The Raising of Lazarus" and the "Adultress before Christ", surrounded by friezes showing many angels.

CHAMPLIN AND PERKINS, *Cyclopedia of Painters and Painting* (New York, 1886–88); BRYAN, *Dictionary of Painters and Engravers* (London and New York, 1903–05).

AUGUSTUS VAN CLEEF.

Boccaccio, GIOVANNI, Italian novelist, b. in Paris, 1313; d. in Certaldo, 21 December, 1375. His father, a merchant from Certaldo and a man of some prominence in Florence, had gone into business in Paris. Shortly afterwards the elder Boccaccio deserted Giannina, the mother of Giovanni, and brought the boy to Florence, where he put him to school until he was ten years old, when he took him into business. In 1327 Giovanni was sent to Naples to study law. But he gave himself up almost entirely to literature, and became intimately acquainted with some of the most prominent men and women of the court of Anjou. It is supposed that it was in 1334 that he saw for the first time Maria d'Aquino, a married woman and natural daughter of King Robert. She was the inspiration of his earlier works, and the heroine of whom he tells under the name of Fiammetta. In 1340 we find him back in Florence; on the death of his father in 1348, he became the guardian of a younger brother. He held certain public offices in Florence and was entrusted with diplomatic missions to Padua, the Romagna, Avignon, and elsewhere. After 1350 began his friendship with Petrarch, which lasted until the latter's death in 1374. In spite of his advanced age and the political dissensions in Florence which afflicted him sorely, he began, in 1373, his course of lectures in that city on the poems of Dante. He died two years later at his ancestral home in Certaldo.

The earliest, longest, and perhaps the weakest of Boccaccio's works is the "Filocolo", written between 1338 and 1340; it is a version of the story, widespread in the Middle Ages, of Floire and Blanchefleur, and contains a curious admixture of pagan myths and Christian legends. The "Ameto", written in the two following years, is an allegorical novel, telling, among other love-adventures, the sad story of the life of Boccaccio's mother. The "Amorosa Visione", in praise of love, dates from about the year 1342, and consists of fifty cantos in *terzine*, and the initial letters of the verses form an acrostic of two sonnets and one *ballata*. The "Teseide", probably of the year 1341, is the first artistic work in *ottava rima*. It contains many imitations of antiquity, and was widely read up to the sixteenth century. Tasso thought so highly of it that he annotated it. The subject is the story of Palemon

and Arcite which Chaucer used for his "Knight's Tale".

The "Filostrato", written in the same year and likewise in *ottava rima*, tells of the love of Troilus for Chryseis. The subject may have been suggested to Boccaccio by his adventure with Fiammetta. The "Ninfale Fiesolano", a short poem in *ottava rima*, is the best, in style and invention, of the minor works of Boccaccio. The "Fiammetta" is one of the best written of his works, the most original and the most personal. Panfilo, the hero and lover of Fiammetta, is supposed to represent Boccaccio himself. The "Corbaccio" (1354) has had its admirers, but it is one of the most bitter and indecent satires ever written against woman. The "Vita di Dante" (about 1364), based chiefly on information furnished by contemporaries of Dante, remains one of the best lives of the poet. The "Commento sopra la Commedia", the fruit of his public lectures on Dante, was planned to be a colossal work, but Boccaccio had commented only upon the first seventeen cantos when it was broken off by his death.

Boccaccio shares with Petrarch the honor of being the earliest humanist. In their time there were not a dozen men in Italy who could read the works of the Greek authors in the original. Boccaccio had to support at his house for three years a teacher of Greek, with whom he read the poems of Homer. Of Boccaccio's Latin works the following are to be mentioned: "De genealogiis deorum gentilium" (between 1350 and 1360), but published first in 1373. This dictionary of classical mythology shows remarkably wide reading and a very good understanding of the works of the ancients and, in spite of errors which it could not but contain, it continued for several hundred years to be an authority for the student of classical antiquity. Two biographical works: "De claris mulieribus" and "De casibus virorum illustrium" (between 1357 and 1363) are of little interest, since they tell of men and women of ancient times and but rarely of the author's contemporaries. There remain the Latin letters and eclogues, which are not of much worth, and eight or ten unimportant works which have been ascribed to Boccaccio.

The book with which Boccaccio's name is inseparably linked is the "Decameron", which was finished in 1353, but part of which had probably been written before the "Black Death" reached its height in 1348. The "Decameron" opens with a masterly description of the terrors of the pest, and we are then introduced to a gay company of seven ladies and three young men who have come together at a villa outside Naples to while away the time and to escape the epidemic. Each in turn presides for a day over the company and on each of the ten days each of the company tells a story, so that at the end one hundred stories have been told. It is difficult to say whether such a company as Boccaccio describes ever met. At all events, he says that he has taken pains to conceal the real names of the persons mentioned in the stories. There are reasons to believe, however, that Fiammetta is the same lady to whom Boccaccio has given that name in other works, while Dioneo may well represent Boccaccio himself.

The great charm of the "Decameron" lies in the wonderful richness and variety of the adventures which he relates, in the many types of character and the close analysis of all shades of feeling and passion, from the basest to the noblest. The style is now Ciceronian, now that of the everyday speech of Florence. The sentence-structure is, to be sure, often involved and inverted, and it often requires several readings to enjoy a full understanding of the phrase. Boccaccio found the germs of his *novelle* in other literatures, in historic events, and in tradition, but, like Shakespeare, whatever he borrowed he made his own and living, by placing the adventures in the lives of his contemporaries. The indecency which is the greatest blot on the "Decameron", but to which it undoubtedly owes not a little of its celebrity, is no greater than is to be found elsewhere in medieval literature, and is due as much to the time and the circle in which the work was written as to the temperament of the author. He himself in his later years expressed deep repentance for the too free works of his youth; moreover, his jibes and anecdotes at the expense of clerics did not impair his belief in the teachings of the Church. Boccaccio's character was by no means a despicable one. He was a steadfast friend, a son who felt tenderly for his mother and never forgave his father for having abandoned her. He speaks with affection of his daughters who had died in childhood; it is not known who their mother was. He was a scholar of the first rank for his time, a man of independent character, and a good patriot.

No autograph copy of the "Decameron" exists, but there are three manuscript copies dating from the fourteenth century. The first edition was not printed until 1470 in Venice, and since then numerous editions have appeared, but there is as yet no critical edition. Of the modern editions P. Fanfani's is convenient (2 vols., reprinted Florence, 1904). An excellent school edition of selected *novelle* with notes is that of R. Fornaciari (Florence, 1890). The "Decameron" has been translated into nearly every European tongue; the first complete English edition dates from 1620.

The best edition of the Italian works of BOCCACCIO is MOU-TIER, *Opere volgari di Giovanni Boccaccio corrette su i testi a penna* (Florence, 1827–34). For sources of the *Decameron*, LANDAU, *Die Quellen des Dekameron* (Stuttgart, 1884); for BOCCACCIO's life and works in general, LANDAU, *Giovanni Boccaccio, sein Leben u. seine Werke* (Stuttgart, 1877); CRE-SCINI, *Contributo agli studi sul Bocc.* (Turin, 1887); see also FERRARI, *Bibliografia Boccaccesca* (Florence, 1888).

JOSEPH DUNN.

Böcken (BÖCKHN), PLACIDUS, a German Bene-dictine, canonist, and Vice-Chancellor of the Uni-versity of Salzburg, b. at Munich, in Bavaria, 13 July, 1690; d. at Salzburg, 9 February, 1752. He entered the Order of St. Benedict at an early age, made his religious profession at the Abbey of St. Peter, Salz-burg, in 1706, and was ordained to the priesthood in 1713. Having been made a Doctor of Canon and Civil Law (1715), he was sent to Rome and on his re-turn was chosen, in 1721, to succeed the noted can-onist Benedict Schmier, as professor of canon law at the Benedictine University of Salzburg, where he re-mained for a period of twenty years. He proved himself a brilliant jurist, and an exceptionally gifted teacher. In 1729 he was appointed vice-chancellor of the university. He was also attached to the theological faculties of Salzburg and Fulda, was secre-tary of the university, and a valued ecclesiastical councillor of four successive archbishops in the See of Salzburg and of the Prince-Abbot of Fulda. Event-ually he appears to have incurred the displeasure of Archbishop Leopold of Salzburg, and in consequence of repeated friction resigned his position in 1741. He was then made pastor of Dornbach, a suburb of Vienna, and, two years later, superior of Maria-Plain near Salzburg, where he spent the last nine years of his life as confessor to the many pilgrims frequenting that famous shrine.

The "Commentarius in Jus Canonicum universum" which Böcken published at Salzburg (1735–39), and dedicated to his friend and patron the Prince-Abbot of Fulda, is his most important work. He had previously (1722–28) issued a number of separate treatises on the five books of the Decretals, all written with great learning and care; these, now thoroughly revised and supplemented, were incorporated in his

larger work, to the third volume of which, in an ap-pendix, he also added a lengthy disquisition "De præscriptionibus". A reprint of the "Commenta-rius" appeared at Paris in 1776. Böcken's work, like that of the Salzburg canonists generally, is one of definite value. Böcken held rather extreme views on the subject of the veneration due the saints. He maintained that the special veneration and invoca-tion of the saints, particularly of the Blessed Virgin Mary, is absolutely necessary for salvation. A ser-mon which he preached on this subject in 1740 pre-cipitated an acrid discussion at the university be-tween the members of the "Old School" and the "New School" of theology, between the *Sycophantæ* and the *Illuminati* as they were called. The ser-mon appeared also in print, with annotations wherein Böcken characterized as erroneous the contrary opin-ion of Muratori.

Chronicon noviss. monasterii S. Petri, 674–677; SATTLER, *Kollectaneenblätter* (1890), 337 sqq.; SEDELMAYER, *Hist. Univ. Salisburg.*, 405; ZIEGELBAUER, *Hist. rei lit. O. S. B.* (Augsburg, 1754), III, 484, 485.

THOMAS OESTREICH.

Bocking (or BOKKYNG), EDWARD, English Bene-dictine, b. of East Anglian parentage, end of fifteenth century; d. 20 April, 1534. He graduated B. D. at Oxford, in 1513, and D. D. in 1518, was for some time Warden of Canterbury College there, and be-came a monk at Canterbury 1526. When Elizabeth Barton, "The Holy Maid of Kent", commenced her alleged Divine revelations, Bocking, with another monk, was sent to examine and report upon their authenticity, and he is said to have induced her to declare herself an inspired emissary for the over-throw of Protestantism and the prevention of the divorce of Queen Catherine. To further this scheme he had her removed to the Convent of St. Sepulchre at Canterbury. There is little doubt that he was her chief instigator in the continuance of her career of deception. His share in the affair, though it cannot be excused, must be ascribed to a mistaken zeal for the preservation of the ancient Faith. After the divorce of Queen Catherine and Henry's marriage to Anne Boleyn in 1533, Cromwell had Elizabeth Barton arrested, together with Bocking and others. Bocking confessed the imposture and, with his accomplices, did public penance at Paul's Cross. He and six others were hanged at Tyburn.

Documents from Cottonian MSS. in WRIGHT, *Suppression of the Monasteries* (London, 1843), 13–34; GAIRDNER, *Letters and Papers of Henry VIII for 1533– 34*(London, 1882–83); SANDER, ed. LEWIS, *Rise and Growth of the Anglican Schism* (London, 1877), III; BURNET, ed. POCOCK, *Hist. of the Reformation* (Oxford, 1865), I; STRYPE, *Memorials* (Oxford, 1882), I, i, 271; GASQUET, *Henry VIII and the English Monasteries* (London, 1899), I, iv; STEPHENS AND HUNT, *History of the English Church* (London, 1902), IV, 144.

G. CYPRIAN ALSTON.

Bodenstein. See KARLSTADT, ANDREAS RUDOLF.

Bodey, JOHN, VENERABLE, martyr, b. at Wells, Somerset, 1549; d. at Andover, Wilts., 2 November, 1583. He studied at Winchester and New College, Oxford, of which he became a Fellow in 1568. In June, 1576, he was deprived, with seven other Fel-lows, by the Visitor, Horne, Protestant Bishop of Winchester. Next year he went to Douay College to study civil law, returned to England in February, 1578, and probably married. Arrested in 1580, he was kept in iron shackles in Winchester gaol, and was condemned in April, 1583, together with John Slade, a schoolmaster, for maintaining the old religion and denying the Royal Supremacy. There was appar-ently a feeling that this sentence was unjust and il-legal, and they were actually tried and condemned again at Andover, 19 August, 1583, on the same in-dictment. Bodey had a controversy with Humph-reys, Dean of Winchester, on the Nicene Council, and the martyr's notes from Eusebius still exist. After his second trial, he wrote from prison to Dr. Humphrey Ely, "We consider that iron for this cause borne on earth shall surmount gold and precious stones in Heaven. That is our mark, that is our desire. In the mean season we are threatened daily, and do look still when the hurdle shall be brought to the door. I beseech you, for God's sake, that we want not the good prayers of you all for our strength, our joy, and our perseverance unto the end. . . . From our school of patience the 16th September, 1583."

At his martyrdom, Bodey kissed the halter, saying, "O blessed chain, the sweetest chain and richest that ever came about any man's neck", and when told he died for treason, exclaimed, "You may make the hearing of a blessed Mass treason, or the saying of an *Ave Maria* treason . . . but I have committed no treason, although, indeed, I suffer the punishment due to treason". He exhorted the people to obey Queen Elizabeth and died saying, "*Jesu, Jesu, esto mihi Jesus*". His mother made a great feast upon the occasion of her son's happy death, to which she invited her neighbours, rejoicing at his death as his marriage by which his soul was happily and eternally espoused to the Lamb.

Account of the trial and execution of John Slade, schoolmaster, and John Body, M.A., by R. B. (London, 1583); CHALLONER, *Memoirs*; SANDERS, *Anglican Schism*, ed. LEWIS (London, 1877); POLLEN, *Acts of English Martyrs* (London, 1891); WAINEWRIGHT, *Two English Martyrs: Body and Munden* (London, Cath. Truth Soc.); KNOX, *Douay Diaries* (London, 1878); ALLEN, *A true, sincere, and modest defence of English Catholiques* (Reims, 1584).

BEDE CAMM.

Bodin, JEAN, b. at Angers, 1520, probably of Jewish origin; d. at Laon, 1596. He studied and taught law at Toulouse, where in 1559 he pronounced his "Oratio de instituendâ in republicâ juventute", on the public instruction of youth. At the age of forty, he went to Paris, his name being still obscure. By his "Methodus ad facilem historiarum cognitionem" (1566) he laid the foundation of the philosophy of history, and set forth his theory of the effect of climate on society and government, likewise his theory of progress, both of which were later expanded in "La République". In his "Réponse aux paradoxes de M. de Malestroit, touchant le fait des monnaies et l'enchérissement de toutes choses" (1568), he developed his thesis on the necessity of free trade. The "République" in six books (French, 1577; Latin, 1586) was written to defend the principle of authority and to describe the ideal commonwealth. Bodin represents a reaction against Machiavelli in the field of moral and political science. Unlike Cujas and the "Romanist" jurisconsults, who confined themselves to the observation of Greek and Roman antiquity, he drew upon the modern history of Germany, England, Spain, and Italy. His theory of the influence of climates foreshadows that of Montesquieu. Bodin collects carefully numerous small facts, definite and concrete information; daily experience and the observation of current events are the sources of his almost "scientific" researches concerning the laws of political life. It is somewhat surprising to note that as early as 1580 this thoughtful writer wrote a work (La Démonomanie des Sorciers) to demonstrate the existence of sorcerers and the legality of their condemnation, on the basis of "experience" and respect for *res judicatæ* or the reliability of the courts. This belief in witchcraft rests on the same arguments as his theory of civil government.

In 1576 this somewhat puzzling man was chosen a deputy of the Third Estate (*tiers état*) to the States-General of Blois where he championed the cause of the Reformers, thereby incurring the royal displeasure. Fourteen years later (1590) as Attorney-General at Laon, he sided with the "Ligue", persuaded the citizens to do likewise, and finally went over to Henry IV. This superstitious believer in sorcery left in manuscript a work known as "Colloquium Heptaplomeres" which propounds a certain rationalistic spiritualism. Though a civil magistrate and a partisan of the Ligue, his writings exhibit him as one of the earliest advocates of the theory of religious toleration. Brunetière assigns Bodin a place in French literature beside Henri Estienne and Amyot; at a time when men looked to antiquity for guidance only in the domain of good taste, all three showed that from the same source could be drawn lessons in history, politics, and morality.

Though Bodin never abandoned the Catholic religion, and was buried in the Franciscan Church at Laon, his writings often betray an un-Catholic temper, when they are not more or less openly hostile to the existing ecclesiastical order. In religion he inclines to an abstract theism. In keeping with the Gallican legists of France he champions the absolute supremacy of the State, though he bases it on the Divine will and the natural law; his ideal prince is not an impious and unjust ruler of the Machiavelli type. All the works of Bodin were placed on the Index in 1628; the edition of 1900 continues the prohibition of his "Universæ naturæ theatrum". Catholic theologians, like Possevin have noted and refuted in the "République" certain errors and anti-Christian subtleties. "To judge by his writings," says Toussaint (Dict. de théol. cath., II, 918), "he was a bizarre, inconstant, and superficial" man.

BAUDRILLART, *Jean Bodin et son temps* (Paris, 1853); FRANCK, *Réformateurs et publicistes de l'Europe* (Paris, 1864); JANET, *Histoire de la science politique* (Paris, 1887); BRUNETIÈRE, *Trois artisans de l'idéal classique* in *Revue des deux mondes* (1 March, 1907); GRAMICH-WEINAND in *Staatslexikon* (2d ed., Freiburg, 1901), I, 946–952.

GEORGES GOYAU.

Bodleian Codex. See MSS. OF THE BIBLE.

Bodone, a titular see of Albania. The name is a dialectic form of Dodone, in Epirus, near Janina at the foot of Mount Tomaros, or Tmaros, the present Olitsika (C. Carapanos, Dodone et ses ruines, Paris, 1878). At an early date a Christian church was built here on the site of the temple of Zeus. Theodorus, a Bishop of Dodona, was present at Ephesus, in 431; Philotheus appeared at Chalcedon in 451; Uranius, in 458, signed the letter of the bishops of Epirus Vetus to Emperor Leo; Philippus in 516 subscribed a synodal report of the bishops of Epirus to Pope Hormisdas concerning the election of John to the See of Nicopolis, the metropolis of the province (Hierocles, Synecdemos, 651, 5). When Naupactus was substituted for Nicopolis about the end of the tenth century, Dodona was the first suffragan see; the "Nova Tactica" (Georgius Cyprius, ed. Gelzer, 1661) has Μούνδιτξα, but this is an evident mistake for Βούνδιτξα, a form derived from Bodone (Parthey, Notit. episcop., App. 48). In fact the later "Notitiæ" wrote only Bounditza (ibid., III, 524), or Bonditza (ibid., X, 616; XIII, 467). John, Bishop of Bonditza, signed a synodal act in 1229 (P. G., CXIX, 797). The present name is Bonitza. When the Greek residential bishopric disappeared is unknown; the Roman curia used for a long time the forms Bodona and Bodonensis, and a decree of 1894 directed this see to be suppressed at the death of its titular.

LEQUIEN, *Or. Christ.*, I, 139; GAMS, *Series episcop.*, 429; ARABANTINOS, *Chronography of Epirus*, Gr. (Athens, 1857), II, 34.

L. PETIT.

Body, RESURRECTION OF THE. See RESURRECTION.

Body, SPIRITUAL. See RESURRECTION.

Boece (also BOYCE and BOETHIUS), HECTOR, chronicler and one of the founders of the University of Aberdeen, b. at Dundee c. 1465; d. 1536. At

Paris he was a student, then Bachelor of Divinity, and finally a professor at the College of Montaigu, whose course had been reorganized on the principles of monastic poverty and severe routine by James Standone of Brabant, at one time rector of the university. At the college, Boece formed a lasting friendship with Erasmus. From about 1495, Boece was zealously aiding Wm. Elphinstone, the learned Bishop of Aberdeen, to carry out the provisions of a Bull of Alexander VI, obtained at the request of James IV, chartering a university with all faculties in the city of Aberdeen. Finally, in 1505, having received help from various sources, they founded the collegiate church of St. Mary of the Nativity, later known as King's College, and regular teaching took the place of the occasional lectures of the canons. The organization was modelled upon that of the Universities of Paris and Orléans. The foundation was to support, on meagre stipends, four doctors in the respective faculties, two teaching masters, five student masters, thirteen poor scholars, eight chaplains, and four choristers. Boece was principal and read lectures on divinity and on medicine. History was not regularly taught, but both Elphinstone and Boece made collections of materials. In 1527, Boece received a pension of £50 Scots, and, from 1529 to 1534, a like amount, to be paid annually until he should obtain a benefice of 100 marks Scots. Besides his principalship, he held the offices of Canon of Aberdeen and Rector of Tyrie.

Boece published at Paris, 1522, "Lives of the Bishops of Murthlack and Aberdeen", about a third of which is devoted to Elphinstone (d. 1514). In 1527 appeared, also at Paris, his "Scotorum Historiæ" in seventeen books. Boece was preceded in the field of published Scottish history only by the learned work of Mair. The Scottish translation of this work by Bellenden, in 1536, was later used by Holinshed and thus indirectly by Shakespeare. As a historian, Boece has been praised for elegance, patriotism, and love of freedom; and most severely arraigned, even by contemporaries, for his credulity in the matter of historic origins. His literary honesty, attacked in his own day, has more recently been defended. The impetus which he gave to historical studies at Aberdeen has been of lasting effect.

MACKAY in *Dict. Nat. Biog.*; HENDERSON, *Scottish Vernacular Literature* (London, 1898); MORLEY, *English Writers*, VII; *Episcoporum Murthlacensium et Aberdonensium per Hectorem Boetium Vitæ* (reprinted by Bannatyne Club, Edinburgh, 1825, and by New Spalding Club, 1895, with tr.); *The History and Chronicle of Scotland*, tr. BELLENDEN (1821).

J. VINCENT CROWNE.

Boeri (BOHIER), PETRUS, a French Benedictine canonist and bishop, b. during the first quarter of the fourteenth century at Laredorte, department of Aude, canton of Peyriac Minervois; d. probably 1388. Of his early life nothing is known. In 1350, when he is first mentioned, Boeri was Abbot of St. Chinian (*St.-Anianus*, Hérault) in the small Diocese of Saint-Pons de Tomières (*Sancti Pontii Tomeriarum*) which at that time formed a part of the Metropolitan Province of Narbonne. By his virtue and learning he attracted the favourable notice of Urban V, who appointed him Bishop of Orvieto, 16 Nov., 1364. A few years later (7 Oct., 1370) he was transferred by the same pontiff to the See of Vaison, near Avignon in France. But in 1371, shortly after Urban's death, he returned to Orvieto and remained in possession of that see until 28 June, 1379, when he was deprived of his bishopric by Urban VI for having espoused the cause of the Antipope Robert of Geneva, then reigning at Avignon as Clement VII. Upon his subsequent withdrawal to France he served Charles V in the capacity of ambassador to the pontifical court at Avignon. (Duchesne, Liber Pontificalis, II, 27–28.) However, 31 August, 1387, Clement VII likewise deposed him from his episcopal

office and entrusted the temporal and spiritual administration of Orvieto to Thomas de Jarente, Bishop of Grasse. Boeri died shortly afterwards. He was the author of two commentaries on the Rule of St. Benedict; in one, written when he was Abbot of St. Chinian, he deals with the Rule from the point of view of the canonist; in the other, written in the *Sacro Speco* at Subiaco when he was Bishop of Orvieto, he deals with it more from the point of view of the ascetic. He dedicated the later commentary to Charles V, King of France. He also wrote a commentary on the Constitution "Pastor bonus" of Benedict XII; "Speculum Monachorum"; "De Signis locutionum"; "Notæ in Damasi Pontificale" (an annotated copy of the "Liber Pontificalis", likewise dedicated to Charles V); and began at Rouen in 1379 a treatise on the question of calling a general council with a view to ending the deplorable schism then distracting the Church. This treatise remained unfinished. With the exception of "In Regulam S. P. Benedicti Commentarium" (ed. Dom Leone Allodi, Subiaco, Rome), and "Notæ in Damasi Pontificale" Boeri's works have never been printed.

EUBEL, *Hierarchia cathol. med. ævi* (Münster, 1898–1901), I, 537; FABRICIUS, *Bibliotheca Lat. Mediæ et Infimæ Ætatis* (Hamburg, 1734), I, 686, 687; V, 737; SCHULTE, *Geschichte der Quell. u. Litt. des kanonischen Rechts* (1875–80), II, 256; VALOIS, *La France et le Grand Schisme* (Paris, 1896), I, 325, 326, 398; II, 129; ZIEGELBAUER, *Hist. rei literariæ Ord. S. Benedicti* (Augsburg, 1754), I, 77; III, 613; IV, 581, 702.

THOMAS OESTREICH.

Bœrnerian Codex. See MSS. OF THE BIBLE; LE LONG, JACQUES.

Boethius, ANICIUS MANLIUS SEVERINUS, Roman statesman and philosopher, often styled "the last of the Romans", regarded by tradition as a Christian martyr, b. at Rome in 480; d. at Pavia in 524 or 525. Descended from a consular family, he was left an orphan at an early age and was educated by the pious and noble-minded Symmachus, whose daughter, Rusticiana, he married. As early as 507 he was known as a learned man, and as such was entrusted by King Theodoric with several important missions. He enjoyed the confidence of the king, and as a patrician of Rome was looked up to by the representatives of the Roman nobility. When, however, his enemies accused him of disloyalty to the Ostrogothic king, alleging that he plotted to restore "Roman liberty", and added the accusation of "sacrilege" (the practice of astrology), neither his noble birth nor his great popularity availed him. He was cast into prison, condemned unheard, and executed by order of Theodoric. During his imprisonment, he reflected on the instability of the favour of princes and the inconstancy of the devotion of his friends. These reflections suggested to him the theme of his best-known philosophical work, the "De Consolatione Philosophiæ".

Tradition began very early to represent Boethius as a martyr for the Christian Faith. It was believed that among the accusations brought against him was devotion to the Catholic cause, which at that time was championed by the Emperor Justin against the Arian Theodoric. In the eighth century this tradition had assumed definite shape, and in many places Boethius was honoured as a martyr, and his feast observed on the twenty-third of October. In recent times, critical scholarship has gone to the opposite extreme, and there have not been wanting critics who asserted that Boethius was not a Christian at all, or that, if he was, he abjured the Faith before his death. The foundation for this opinion is the fact that in the "Consolations of Philosophy" no mention is made of Christ or of the Christian religion. A saner view, which seems at the present time to be prevalent among scholars, is that Boethius was a Christian and remained a Christian to the end.

That he was a Christian is proved by his theological

tracts, some of which, as we shall see, are undoubtedly genuine. That he remained a Christian is the obvious inference from the ascertained fact of his continued association with Symmachus; and if the "Consolations of Philosophy" bears no trace of Christian influence, the explanation is at hand in the fact that it is an entirely artificial exercise, a philosophical dialogue modelled on strictly pagan productions, a treatise in which, according to the ideas of method which prevailed at the time, Christian feeling and Christian thought had no proper place. Besides, even if we disregard certain allusions which some interpret in a Christian sense, there are passages in the treatise which seem plainly to hint that, after philosophy has poured out all her consolations for the benefit of the prisoner, there are more potent remedies (*validiora remedia*) to which he may have recourse. There can be no reasonable doubt, then, that Boethius died a Christian, though it is not easy to show from documentary sources that he died a martyr for the Catholic Faith. The absence of documentary evidence does not, however, prevent us from giving due value to the constant tradition on this point. The local cult of Boethius at Pavia was sanctioned when, in 1883, the Sacred Congregation of Rites confirmed the custom prevailing in that diocese of honouring St. Severinus Boethius, on the 23d of October.

To the science of mathematics and the theory of music Boethius contributed the "De Institutione Arithmeticâ Libri II", "De Institutione Musicâ Libri V", and "Geometria Euclidis a Boethio in Latinum translata". The last-mentioned work is found in various MSS. of the eleventh and twelfth centuries. There is also found among the MSS. a work "De Geometriâ", which, in its extant form, is considered to be a ninth- or tenth-century elaboration of a work of Boethius. How far the work is genuine, and to what extent interpolations have crept in, is a question of more than ordinary interest for the student of general history, for on the answer to this question depends the determination of the date of the first use of Arabic numerals in Western Europe. Boethius' philosophical works include: (a) translations from the Greek, e. g. of Aristotle's logical treatises (with commentaries) and of Porphyry's "Isagoge" (with commentaries); (b) commentaries on Porphyry's "Isagoge", translated by Marius Victorinus, and on Cicero's "Topica"; (c) original logical treatises, "De Categoricis Syllogismis", "Introductio ad Syllogismos Categoricos", "De Divisione" (of doubtful authenticity), and "De Differentiis Topicis". These exercised very great influence on the development of medieval terminology, method, and doctrine, especially in logic. In fact, the schoolmen, down to the beginning of the twelfth century, depended entirely on Boethius for their knowledge of Aristotle's doctrines. They adopted his definitions and made them current in the schools; for instance, the definitions of "person", "eternity", etc.

The theological works of Boethius include: "De Trinitate"; two short treatises (*opuscula*) addressed to John the Deacon (afterwards Pope John I); "Liber contra Eutychen et Nestorium"; and "De Fide Catholicâ" (generally regarded as spurious, although the only argument against its genuineness is the lack of manuscript authority). These were much studied in the early Middle Ages, as is testified by the number of glosses found in the MSS. as far back as the ninth century (e. g. glosses by John Scotus Erigena and Remi of Auxerre). To the theologians of the Middle Ages generally they appealed as the genuine works of the Christian martyr, Boethius. In modern times, those who denied that Boethius was a Christian were, of course, obliged to reject all the *opuscula* as spurious. However, the publica-

tion of the so-called "Anecdoton Holderi" (ed. by Usener, Leipzig, 1877) brought to light a new argument for their genuineness. For, as Cassiodorus ought certainly to have known which works of Boethius were genuine, when he wrote "[Boethius] scripsit librum de Sanctâ Trinitate et capita quædam dogmatica et librum contra Nestorium", he settled the question as far as four of the treatises are concerned.

Boethius' best-known work is the "Consolations of Philosophy" written during his imprisonment— "by far the most interesting example of prison literature the world has ever seen." It is a dialogue between Philosophy and Boethius, in which the Queen of Sciences strives to console the fallen statesman. The main argument of the discourse is the transitoriness and unreality of all earthly greatness and the superior desirability of the things of the mind. There are evident traces of the influence of the Neo-Platonists, especially of Proclus, and little, if anything, that can be said to reflect Christian influences. The recourse to Stoicism, especially to the doctrines of Seneca, was inevitable, considering the nature of the theme. It does astonish the modern reader, although, strange to say, it did not surprise the medieval student, that Boethius, a Christian, and, as everyone in the Middle Ages believed, a Christian martyr, should have failed, in his moment of trial and mental stress to refer to the obvious Christian sources of consolation. Perhaps the medieval student of Boethius understood better than we do that a strictly formal dialogue on the consolation of philosophy should adhere rigorously to the realm of "natural truth" and leave out of consideration the lesson to be derived from the moral maxims of Christianity—"supernatural truth".

The work takes up many problems of metaphysics as well as of ethics. It treats of the Being and Nature of God, of providence and fate, of the origin of the universe, and of the freedom of the will. In medieval times, it became one of the most popular and influential philosophical books, a favourite study of statesmen, poets, and historians, as well as of philosophers and theologians. It was translated into Anglo-Saxon by King Alfred the Great, and into Old German by Notker Teutonicus; its influence may be traced in Beowulf and in Chaucer, in Anglo-Norman and Provençal popular poetry, in the first specimens of Italian verse, as well as in the "Divina Commedia". The important part which it played in Dante's mental struggle after the death of Beatrice is described in the "Convitto", where, strange to say, it is referred to as "a book not known to many". Echoes of it and citations from it occur frequently in the "Divina Commedia". For instance, the lines which Tennyson paraphrases by "a sorrow's crown of sorrow" are themselves at least a haunting memory of Boethius' "In omni adversitate fortunæ infelicissimum genus est infortunii fuisse felicem" (De Consol. Phil., II, Pros. IV). That the "De Consolatione" was a favourite study of the theologians as well as of the poets is evidenced by the numerous imitations under the title "De Consolatione Theologiæ" which were widely read during the later Middle Ages. The complete works of Boethius were first published at Venice in 1497; the best edition is in *P. L.* LXIII, LXIV. A good edition of the *De Consolatione* is that of PEIPER in *Teubner Collection*, where are also to be found the commentaries on ARISTOTLE, ed. MEISER.

STEWART, *Boethius* (London, 1891); BOSISIO, *Sul cattolicismo di Boezio* (Pavia, 1867); SEMERIA, *Il cristianesimo di Boezio rivendicato* (Rome, 1900); PRIETZEL, *Boëthius u. seine Stellung zum Christenthum* (Löbau, 1879); *Acta Sæ. Sedis* (Rome, 1883), XVI, 302, 303.

WILLIAM TURNER.

Bogadines. See FRANCISCANS.

Bogomili, a Neo-Manichæan sect, found in the

later Middle Ages at Constantinople and in the Balkan States. *Doctrinal Principles.*—The admission of a twofold creative principle, one good, the other evil, formed the basis of the doctrinal system of the Bogomili, as of all Manichæan sects. Originally, they seem to have claimed eternity for these two principles, but their teaching in its fuller development was less dualistic. God the Father, according to them, had a human appearance but was incorporeal. He had two sons, the first-born, Satanael, and the younger, Jesus Christ or Michael. Satanael, though seated at the right hand of the Father and endowed with creative power, rebelled and was, with some of the angels, his followers, cast out of heaven. He created a second heaven and a second earth, and formed man out of earth and water. Being unable to give him a living spirit, he besought the Father to bestow life on this new creation, which would be their common property. God consented and thus man is the production of two creators. Eve, created in a similar manner, was seduced by Satanael. In punishment of this sin, Satanael lost his creative power, but retained sway over his own creation and strove successfully for the ruin of man. To save mankind, God sent His second son, Jesus, who penetrated the right ear of Mary and took from her the semblance of a human body; indeed, everything material in Him was merely appearance. Jesus vanquished Satanael, who lost his divine name *El*, and was henceforth called Satan. His place in heaven was now occupied by his conqueror. The Holy Ghost was sent forth, but dwells only in the Bogomili. Both He and Jesus will ultimately be absorbed by the Father, the only surviving person in God. The sect rejected the Old Testament, except the Psalter and the Prophetical books. Instead of baptism by water, it admitted only a spiritual baptism; it denied the Real Presence in the Eucharist, condemned marriage, rejected images, and prohibited the eating of meat.

History.—The name of the Bogomili has been traced by some to *Bog Milui* (God have mercy), a formula of prayer believed to have been in frequent use among them; others have sought its origin in *Bogomil* (beloved of God), which is also said to have been the name of a prominent representative of their doctrine in the tenth century. Other names were also applied to the members of the sect by its adversaries; but they called themselves Christians. The Bogomili probably developed from the Euchites and, although they existed previously, came into prominence in the twelfth century. They are first mentioned by name in 1115 at Philippopolis (European Turkey). More definite knowledge regarding them was obtained when their leader Basil, monk and physician, who had surrounded himself with twelve apostles, became known at Constantinople to the emperor Alexius I, Comnenus (1081–1118). The latter cleverly obtained from Basil a frank exposition of the doctrine of the sect. Having received this information, he demanded from the leader and those of his followers who could be seized a retractation of their errors. Some complied with this demand and were released; others remained obstinate and died in prison. Basil alone was condemned to death (1118) and burned. Vigorous as the repression was, it did not suppress the heresy. A synod of Constantinople (1140) ordered the destruction of writings propagating the errors of the sect; in 1143, two bishops of Cappadocia were deposed for embracing its tenets; and the favour extended to one of its adherents, the monk Niphon, caused the deposition of Cosmas, Patriarch of Constantinople (1147). The Patriarch Germanus (1221–39) continued to combat the pernicious doctrines; new condemnations were issued by the synods of Constantinople in 1316 and 1325. The Bogomili, however, remained until the conquest of the Balkan States by the Mussulmans in the fourteenth and fifteenth centuries.

EUTHYMIUS ZYGABENUS, *Panoplia Dogmatica* in P. G., CXXX, 1289–1332; ANNA COMNENA, *Alexias*, ed. *Reifferscheid* (Leipzig, 1884), II, 294 sqq.; DÖLLINGER, *Beiträge zur Sektengesch.* (Munich, 1890), I, 34–51; LÉGER, *L'hérésie des Bogomiles* in *Rev. des quest. hist.* (1870), VIII, 479–517; FUNK in *Kirchenlex.*, s. v.; VERNET in *Dict. de théol. cath.*, II, 926–930; 'HERGENRÖTHER-KIRSCH, *Kirchengesch.* (Freiburg, 1905), II, 549–552.

N. A. WEBER.

Bogotá (BOGOTENSIS), ARCHDIOCESE OF SANTA FÉ DE.—The city of Bogotá, capital of the republic of Colombia, is situated on a plateau 8700 feet above the sea level, at the western base of the Guadalupe and Monserrat mountains, in the eastern cordillera of the Andes. High mountains surround this plateau on all sides except to the southwest, where the River Funcha cuts its way to Magdalena, forming, a few miles from the city, the falls of Tequendana 475 feet in height. Two other rivers, the S. Francisco and the S. Augustino, divide the city. Bogotá was settled by the Spaniards in 1538 and became, in 1598, the capital of Nueva Grenada, which was then a viceregal province, and in 1819, when Colombia became independent of Spain, Bogotá was made the capital of the new republic. Bogotá is a quaint city, its lack of easy communication with other foreign cities having perpetuated its ancient Spanish character. Though the capital of the republic, it has a population of only 100,000 inhabitants.

The Archdiocese of Bogotá, the primatial see of Colombia, was created by Pope Pius IV in 1564. At first it had six suffragans, but, on account of the tremendous growth of the population of the diocese, Pope Leo XIII, in 1902, separated the Bishopric of Medellín from it, and erected it into a province. The actual suffragan sees of Bogotá are: Antioquia (Antioquiensis), which was erected a bishopric by Pius VII, 31 August, 1804, re-erected by Pope Leo XII, 19 January, 1829, suppressed in 1868, and re-established by Pius IX, 29 January, 1873. This bishopric contains 211,000 Catholics, 69 Protestants, 75 secular priests, and 80 churches and chapels. Ibagué (*Ibaguensis*), of which no accurate statistics can be given, as the diocese has only lately been created. It was formerly, with the bishopric of Gazan, suffragan to the see of Tolina, and at the extinction of this see was assigned to the Metropolitan of Bogotá. It has for its territory the two provinces of North and Central Colombia. Nueva Pamplona (*Neo-Pampilonensis*), erected into a bishopric by Gregory XVI, 25 September, 1835. It contains 250,000 Catholics, 8 secular priests, 7 regular priests, and 46 churches and chapels. Socorro (*de Succursu*), erected as a bishopric by Pope Leo XIII, 20 March, 1895, contains 230,000 Catholics. Tunja (*Tunquensis*), erected as a bishopric in July, 1880, by Pope Leo XIII, contains 350,000 Catholics, 10,000 pagans, 53 parishes, and 159 churches and chapels.

The religious orders of men represented in the Archdiocese of Bogotá are: Jesuits, Franciscans, Augustinians, Salesians, and the Brothers of the Christian Doctrine. Those for women are: Sisters of Charity, of the Visitation, of the Good Shepherd, Salesians, Dominicans, Carmelites, and the Little Sisters of the Poor. Most of these orders, especially those for men, have charge of the schools and colleges. There are in the archdiocese 1 seminary, 30 colleges and academies, 150 schools, and 14 hospitals.

Conversations-Lex. I, 1696; BATTANDIER, *Annuaire pont. Cath.*

M. DE MOREIRA.

Bohemia (Germ. *Böhmen*, or formerly *Böheim*; Lat. *Bohemia* or *Bojohemum*), a cisleithan (i. e. west of the River Leitha) crown province of the Austro-

Hungarian Monarchy, which until 1526 was an independent kingdom.

PHYSICAL CHARACTERISTICS.—Bohemia has an area of 20,058 square miles. It is bounded on the north-west by Saxony, on the north-east by Prussian Silesia, on the south-east by Moravia and the Grand duchy of Lower Austria, on the south by the Grand duchy of Upper Austria, and on the south-west by Bavaria. It is enclosed on three sides by mountain ranges, namely: the Bohemian Forest (Böhmerwald), the Ore mountains (Erzgebirge), and the Sudetic mountains. The highest peaks of these ranges seldom rise above 4,593 feet. On the fourth, or south-eastern, border Bohemia is separated from Moravia by a moderately high range called the Bohemian-Moravian highlands (about 1,968 feet high). The country resembles the flat bottom of a trough with a depression towards the north. The average height above sea-level is 1,460 feet. Bohemia is drained by the Elbe, which rises in the Isergebirge, a range of the Sudetic mountain system. After receiving the waters of the Moldau, a stream from the south, the Elbe, now greatly increased in size, passes out of Bohemia at Tetschen near the most northern point of the country. Besides the Moldau, which may be called the most important river of Bohemia, the chief tributaries of the Elbe are the Iser and the Eger.

Geologically the country forms the so-called Bohemian system of mountain ranges, the spurs of which run into Moravia and Silesia. The greater part consists of old crystalline rocks; in the south gneiss predominates, in the north the formation is chiefly cretaceous sandstone, with tertiary deposits due to the action of water from the south. This part of the country also shows volcanic action, as in the Bohemian mineral springs. The climate is moderate and, with the exception of the mountain districts, does not show great variations of temperature. The mean temperature of the year is about 46.4° Fahrenheit. Bohemia has much mineral wealth; it is especially rich in silver, tin, lead, semi-precious stones, such as Bohemian garnets, hard coal, and lignite.

POPULATION.—According to the last census (31 December, 1900), Bohemia has a population of 6,318,697. It is one of the most thickly settled provinces of the monarchy, having 315 inhabitants to the square mile. The Czechs form 63 per cent of the population, and the Germans 36 per cent. The Germans live chiefly near the boundaries of the country, especially near the northern and north-western boundaries.

NATIONAL HISTORY.—Bohemia (home of the Boii) owes its name to the Boii, a Celtic people which occupied the country in prehistoric times. About 78 B. C. the land was occupied by a Suevic people, the Marcomanni, while the related tribe of the Quadi settled in Moravia and that part of Hungary adjoining Moravia. Some years after the birth of Christ, Marbod, King of the Marcomanni, united the German tribes as far as the North Sea and the Baltic to form a great confederation which menaced the Roman Empire. When the Marcomanni and the Quadi left Bohemia and Moravia in the sixth century, there came in from the north-east a Slavonic people which was soon to appear in history under the general name of Cechen (Czechs). Before the close of the sixth century this Slavonic people came under the domination of the Avars of Hungary. But early in the seventh century they regained their freedom with the aid of the Frank, Samo, whom the Czechs elected as their king. In 796, Bohemia paid tribute to Charlemagne. Eighty years later Borziwoi, Grand Duke of the Cechen (Czechs), seems to have been tributary to Swatopluk, King of Great Moravia. In the confusion which followed the break-up of the Empire of Great Mo-

ravia Spitihnev I succeeded in uniting the various tribes of Czechs under his rule. From his time there is an unbroken succession of dukes of the Premysl line. One duke of this line, Wratislaw II, received the title of King for life from the German Emperor, Henry IV. After 1158 the title of King became hereditary. Ottokar I and Ottokar II were the most conspicuous rulers of the Premysl dynasty. After this line became extinct (1306) Bohemia came under the sway of John of Luxembourg (1310–46). The Bohemian rulers of the Luxembourg line, from Charles I, of Bohemia (the Emperor, Charles IV), until the extinction of the dynasty at the death of Sigismund (1437), were all German emperors. Bohemia reached the height of its prosperity under the Emperor Charles IV, who conquered Silesia and also occupied for a time the Mark of Brandenburg and the Upper Palatinate. In 1348, Charles founded the University of Prague, the first university on German soil. By his Golden Bull, Charles IV gave Bohemia the highest secular electoral dignity of the Holy Roman Empire. After 1437, Bohemia was ruled by kings of various lines until the death of Ludwig II, of the Jagellon dynasty, who was King of Bohemia and Hungary. He fell in the battle of Mohácz (1526). Both Bohemia and Hungary after this battle came into the possession of Ferdinand I of Hapsburg who had married the sister of Ludwig II. (For the further history of Bohemia see AUSTRO-HUNGARIAN MONARCHY.)

INTRODUCTION OF CHRISTIANITY.—Fritigil, Queen of the Marcomanni, in 396 applied to Ambrose of Milan for instruction in the doctrines of Christianity. In 846, fourteen princes of the Czechs were baptized at Ratisbon. Although the two brothers, Cyril and Methodius, the Apostles of the Slavs, never entered Bohemia, yet Methodius was able to win over the Bohemian Duke Borziwoi to Christianity when the latter was at the court of Swatopluk, Grand Duke of Moravia. In 878, Borziwoi was baptized by Methodius at Welehrad. Soon after this Borziwoi's wife, Ludmilla, and most of his relations were also baptized. The grandson of Borziwoi and Ludmilla, St. Wenzel I (Wenceslaus), was murdered in 935 at Alt-Bunzlau by his brother and successor Boleslaw I. Religious and national motives prompted this act. Christianity made such progress in Bohemia that in the latter part of the tenth century (973) the German Emperor Otto I gave the country a bishop of its own with his see at Prague, the capital of the country. Bohemia had until then formed a part of the Diocese of Ratisbon. In 1344, the Diocese of Leitomischl was founded, while Prague was made an archbishopric with the Diocese of Olmütz as suffragan. The thirteenth and fourteenth centuries may be called the golden age of Christianity in Bohemia. In 1384, 240 ecclesiastics were attached to the Cathedral of Prague. Bohemia contained at that time 1,914 parish priests with many assistants; there were one hundred monasteries, and almost a third of the land belonged to the Church. But when John Hus was condemned by the Council of Constance for spreading the errors of Wyclif, and was burned at the stake in 1415 by the secular authorities, the Hussite wars followed (1420–34), and the Church in Bohemia met with losses which it took centuries to repair.

The causes of this religious-national movement were the excessive numbers and wealth of the clergy, their moral decay, and, in addition, the national reaction against the disproportionate power of the Germans, and the weakness of the secular government. Notwithstanding the death of the leaders, Hus and Jerome of Prague, the fire of revolution broke out when the followers of Hus demanded the Lord's Supper under both kinds (Utraquists). Those in revolt encamped with their leaders, Ziska,

II.—39

Procopius the Great, and Procopius the Less, upon Mount Tabor, and from 1419 to 1434 they made marauding expeditions from that point in all directions. The army of Sigismund, in the Fifth Crusade, accomplished nothing. An agreement was finally made with the moderate Utraquists (called Calixtines) in 1433. By this agreement, which is called "the Compactata of Basle", or "of Prague", the cup was granted to the laity; at the same time the teaching of the Church as to the Real Presence of Christ under each form was insisted upon. From the descendants of the radical Taborites sprang later the Bohemian and Moravian Brethren.

A great number of parishes and other cures of souls had been obliterated during the Hussite wars; in those which still remained there was a woeful lack of priests, especially for the German population. It was, therefore, easy for Protestantism to make rapid advances, especially as it was looked on with favour by both the nobility and the people. Desertion of the Church was accompanied by treason against the hereditary dynasty. In 1547, a large part of the population took sides with the League of Smalkald, and in 1618 Bohemia was the starting point of the Thirty Years' War which brought such terrible disasters upon the whole of Germany. During this war the population of Bohemia fell from three millions to eight hundred thousand. The Hapsburg dynasty finally gained the victory. The nobility were punished for their treason, either by execution or by banishment, with confiscation of property; the rebellious cities lost their freedom; the common people either emigrated or returned to the Catholic Faith. In 1655, the See of Leitmeritz was founded; in 1644 the Emperor Ferdinand IV erected a new bishopric at Königgrätz, to take the place of Leitomischl, which had disappeared during the Hussite wars. Finally, in 1784, the Emperor Joseph II made the new Bishopric of Budweis out of the southern part of the Archdiocese of Prague.

STATISTICS OF BOHEMIAN CLERGY

Diocese	Year	Total Number	Employed in Diocese	Employed outside of Diocese	From Foreign Dioceses	Regular Clergy
			Secular Clergy			
Prague (Archd.)	1905	1,385	1,219	126	40	413
Leitmeritz	1906	955	890	38	27	131
Königgrätz	1906	993	932	46	15	88
Budweis	1905	858	822	36	?	133
		4,191	3,863	246	82	765

CHURCH LIVINGS IN BOHEMIA

Diocese	Year	Provost-ships	Archdeaconships	Deaneries	Parishes	Curacies, Chaplaincies, etc.
Prague	1905	3	3	45	539	334
Leitmeritz	1905	1	3	37	392	346
Budweis	1906	1	2	53	371	281
Königgrätz	1906	2	3	38	404	474
		7	11	173	1,706	1,435

POPULATION OF DIOCESES BY DENOMINATIONS

Diocese	Year	Catholics	Non-Catholics	Jews	Total
Prague	1905	2,062,683	54,235	50,493	2,167,411
Leitmeritz	1905	1,561,432	50,778	18,016	1,620,281
Budweis	1906	1,109,625	4,020	12,559	1,126,204
Königgrätz	1906	1,476,645	56,159	11,689	1,544,493
		6,210,385	165,192	92,757	6,458,389

PRESENT STATE OF DIOCESES.—Bohemia is divided ecclesiastically as follows: The Archdiocese of Prague includes the north-western and central parts of the country, the Diocese of Leitmeritz embraces the northern part, the Diocese of Königgrätz takes in the eastern part, and the Diocese of Budweis the southern part of the country. In addition to its share of the territory of Bohemia, the Archdiocese of Prague also includes the countship (*Grafschaft*) of Glatz in Prussian Silesia.

Religious Orders.—There are in the archdiocese 14 orders for men, having 35 houses; the total number of members of the orders is 704, of these 416 are priests, 135 are clerics preparing for the priesthood, and 153 are lay brothers. Special mention should be made of the Benedictines at Emaus, of the Jesuits at Prague, and of the Premonstratensians at Tepl. There are also 21 orders for women, with 1,517 members. The Diocese of Leitmeritz has 13 orders for men, with 31 houses. The members of these orders include 136 priests, 15 clerics preparing for the priesthood, and 49 lay brothers. The Cistercian Abbey of Osseg and the Jesuit college at Mariascheim are worthy of special mention. There are 10 orders for women, with 62 houses and 651 members. The Diocese of Königgrätz has 9 orders for men, with 88 priests; and 8 orders for women, with 442 members. The Diocese of Budweis has 13 orders for men, in 32 houses; these orders include 131 regular priests; the orders for women are 7, with 419 members. The Cistercian Monastery of Hohenfurt, founded in 1259, should be mentioned in connexion with this diocese.

Educational and Charitable Institutions.—In the Archdiocese of Prague there are: 1 seminary for priests, 1 private gymnasium, 3 homes for university students preparing for the priesthood, 52 hospitals, homes for the poor, orphan asylums, etc., over 200 endowments for the aid of the poor, and 34 associations of St. Vincent de Paul. In the Diocese of Leitmeritz there are: 1 theological school, 1 high school for boys, 5 homes for university students preparing for the priesthood, 11 Catholic primary schools, 2 grammar-schools, 8 boarding-schools, 18 industrial and advanced schools, 20 orphanages, 7 asylums for children, 14 kindergartens, 20 crèches, and over 130 homes for the poor, hospitals, etc., as well as 13 Conferences of St. Vincent de Paul. In the Diocese of Königgrätz there are: 1 theological school, 1 seminary for priests, 1 boys' seminary, 7 boarding-schools for girls, 2 training-schools for women teachers, 10 other schools for girls and young women, 21 institutions for the care of children, 67 orphanages, hospitals, etc., 8 conferences of St. Vincent de Paul, and numerous endowments for the aid of the poor. In the Diocese of Budweis, besides 1 theological school and 1 seminary for priests, there are under ecclesiastical control: 1 boys' seminary, 1 home for university students preparing for the priesthood, 12 public and industrial schools 23 kindergartens, 7 boarding-schools, about 140 stipends for students, 99 hospitals, homes for the aged and the poor, and 8 conferences of St. Vincent de Paul.

RELATIONS OF CHURCH AND STATE.—Since the last years of the reign of Maria Theresa, and especially since the time of Joseph II, the Catholic Church in Austria has suffered from state interference. According to existing laws, the State at present guarantees to the recognized denominations freedom from molestation in the management of their internal affairs. The State avoids every interference in matters of faith, of ritual, and of ecclesiastical discipline, but it also claims that the religious associations, like all other associations, are subject to the general state laws in their "outward legal relations". The sore point in this condition of affairs is this: that the State assumes for itself the right to define the boundary between internal and external legal relations. At present state control shows itself in the appointment of ecclesiastical officials, in the co-operation of the State in determining and collecting church dues and taxes, in measures for the protection of the property of the Church, and in a certain supervision of the church press, which is hardly perceptible. The legal position of the Catholic Church in Austria rests on the Imperial Patent of 8 April, 1861, and the Law of 7 May, 1874.

Incorporation of Churches.—In the Archdiocese of Prague there are 32 parishes incorporated with the Premonstratensian foundation at Tepl, the other orders in the diocese have 28 parishes incorporated with them; in the Diocese of Leitmeritz the Cistercians at Osseg control 11 parishes, the other orders for men, 12; in the Diocese of Königgrätz there are 10 parishes united with the Benedictine houses, and 6 with the Premonstratensian; in the Diocese of Budweis the Monastery of Hohenfurt controls 16 parishes, the other orders have 13 incorporated with their foundations.

Taxation of Churches.—Churches, public chapels, and cemeteries are exempt from the income-tax, ground- and dwelling-tax.

Privileges of the Clergy.—Theological students are exempt, both in war and in peace, from all forms of military service, from military training, exercise with weapons, and reserve service; but after they have been ordained they can be called upon to serve as army chaplains in case of the mobilization of the whole army. Parish priests are exempt from paying the direct and the local taxes, and from jury duty. Parish priests have the right to accept an election to community and district boards of commissioners. Regularly installed ecclesiastics have the right of legal residence in that community in which they live permanently. Without regard to the actual payment of taxes they are entitled to vote for the local boards, for the provincial diet and for the imperial parliament (Reichstag); as a rule they are included in the first class of the electoral body. Only one-third of the fees of a parish priest can be attached for debt; besides this, his income cannot be reduced below 1,600 kronen ($320), nor the income of a retired priest below 1,000 kronen ($200). According to the law of 1898, which was intended to equalize clerical salaries, the salary of a parish priest at Prague was set at 2,400 kronen ($480); in the suburbs, up to a distance of over nine miles from the capital, and in cities with over 5,000 inhabitants, at 1,800 kronen ($360); in other places at 1,600 kronen ($320) or 1,400 kronen ($280). In Prague the salary of an assistant priest was set at 800 kronen ($160) or 700 kronen ($140).

Marriage and Divorce.—Marriage, for Catholics, rests on the Law of 25 May, 1868, with which the second main section of the civil code, treating of the law of marriage, came again into force. According to this anyone can enter into a marriage contract when there is no legal impediment. Apart from the impediments arising from the duties of certain positions and those due to the army laws,

these impediments rest on: (1) lack of consent; (2) lack of ability for the married state, and (3) lack of the necessary formalities. Under the first head are (a) impediments from inability to give consent, as mental disease (violent mania, lunacy, imbecility); minority, and control of guardians, or lack of free choice; (b) impediments resting on lack of actual consent, as compulsion through well-grounded fear, seduction, mistake in the identity of the future consort, pregnancy of the woman before marriage by another person. Under (2) belong (a) the impediment of impotency and (b) impediment from the lack of moral ability, such as an unexpired sentence of imprisonment for felony; a still existing previous marriage; consecration to Holy orders, or a solemn vow of celibacy; difference in religion (e. g. the marriage of a Christian and a non-Christian); relationship in the ascending and descending line, or close family connexion (as brothers and sisters, cousins, uncle and niece, aunt and nephew); degrees of affinity parallel to the forbidden degrees of consanguinity; adultery proved before the contracting of the new marriage; and murder or attempted murder of a consort. In (3) are (a) the impediments arising from the lack of publication of the banns, and (b) those from lack of the prescribed formalities of a marriage contract. Lastly, there should also be mentioned the impediments, enacted by the Catholic Church (for Catholics), of participation in the cause of divorce, and the impediment caused by the lack of a certificate of birth. A temporary impediment exists for widows, who are not allowed, as a rule, to marry again before the expiration of six months after the death of the husband. Some of these ecclesiastical impediments to marriage can be set aside; others are irremovable. Among the latter are all those which would give an appearance of guilt to a marriage contracted under the existing circumstances. Dispensation from these impediments are granted by the civil authorities. Catholic married couples can be separated from bed and board. A dissolution of the bond of marriage does not take place; that is, no married Catholic, either husband or wife, can enter upon a new valid marriage before the death of the consort.

Testamentary Laws.—A secular cleric has the right to free disposal of his property both in life and at death. The bishop of a diocese has no testamentary control over those objects which belong to his office, and which by law descend to his successor, such as mitres, vestments intended to be worn during Mass, etc. In consequence of the vow of poverty, members of religious orders are incapable of inheriting or disposing of property. Large legacies to a church, a religious or charitable foundation, or a public institution must be announced at once by the court to the governor or president of the province. A half-yearly list of smaller legacies must be sent to these authorities. Legacies for the benefit of the poor, those intended for religious or charitable foundations, for churches, schools, parishes, public institutions, or other religious and benevolent purposes must be paid over or secured before the heirs can inherit the property.

Burial Laws.—Old graveyards are ordinarily regarded as dependencies of the parish church, and as such are considered, even by the Law of 30 April, 1870, as being ecclesiastical institutions. But in sanitary regards, as places of burial, they are controlled by the police regulations of the community. Denominational cemeteries can be enlarged or laid out anew. For this, however, the consent of the civil authorities and of the parties interested is necessary, although, if the parish community refuses to enlarge the cemetery, the responsibility for providing a proper burial-place falls on the civil community. But a parish community or a church vestry cannot be compelled by the authorities to enlarge or lay out a church cemetery. If in the same community both a town cemetery and a Catholic cemetery exist, the burial of the dead in the public cemetery is not obligatory, but every Catholic has the right to bury the members of his family in the Catholic cemetery. When a Catholic cemetery serves also for the burial of non-Catholics, a part of the cemetery is to be set apart for the exclusive use of the non-Catholic community. Where a part of a Catholic cemetery is used for non-Catholic burial without the formal separation of the parts, the non-Catholic clergyman must follow the regulations of the law; he may conduct the burial with prayer and benediction, but there can be no singing nor address.

SCHINDLER ed., *Das soziale Wirken der katholischen Kirche in Oesterreich* (9 vols.); LANDENBAUER, *Die Diözese Budweis* (Vienna, 1899); SCHINDLER, *Die Erzdiözese Prag* (Vienna, 1902); ENDLER, *Die Diözese Leitmeritz* (Vienna, 1903); BENES, *Die Diözese Königgrätz* (Vienna, 1897); KIRCHHOFF ed., *Schematismen der Diözesen Prag, Leitmeritz, Königgrätz, und Budweis* in *Länderkunde von Europa*, Pt. I, 2d half; SUPAN, *Oesterreich-Ungarn* (Vienna and Prague, 1889); *Die österreich.-ungarische Monarchie in Wort und Bild* (1894–96): *Böhmen* (1894–96) 2 vols.; *Mitteilungen des Vereines für Geschichte der Deutschen in Böhmen*, and the other publications of this society; FRIND, *Kirchengeschichte Böhmens* (Prague, 1866–78); ID., *Geschichte der Bischöfe und Erzbischöfe von Prag* (Prague, 1873); GINDELY, *Geschichte des 30 jährigen Krieges* (Prague, 1882); ID., *Geschichte der Gegenreformation.*

KARL KLAAR.

Bohemian Brethren (MORAVIAN BRETHREN, or UNITAS FRATRUM).—DEFINITION AND DOCTRINAL POSITION.—Bohemian Brethren, Moravian Brethren are the current popular designations of the *Unitas Fratrum* founded in Bohemia in 1457, renewed by Count Zinzendorf in 1722, and still active in our own day. Placing life before creeds, the Moravian Church seeks "to exemplify the living Church of Christ constituted of regenerated men and women, while it affords a common meeting-point for Christians who apprehend dogmas variously". Personal faith in the crucified Saviour constitutes the chief foundation for the fellowship thus established. Scripture is the only rule of faith, but "nothing is posited as to the mode of inspiration, for this partakes of the mysteries which it has not pleased God to reveal". The Trinity, the Fall, Original Sin, and "Total Depravity" are admitted, but "discussion about them is shunned". The Love of God manifested in Christ—without theories about the mode—is the centre of Moravian belief and practice. Justification by faith alone and the necessity of regeneration "are posited as facts of personal experience". Sanctifying grace, the need of prayer, and other public means of grace, a complete ritual, a strict discipline, "the orders of the ministry with no conception of the functions of the episcopate", i. e. bishops ordain, but the episcopal office implies no further ruling or administrative power (see *infra* in regard to Zinzendorf), Baptism and the Lord's Supper as the only sacraments, and the common Christian eschatology: Resurrection, Judgment, Heaven, Hell; such are the tenets from which Moravians are expected not to depart, whilst they are allowed to speculate about them on Scriptural lines with entire liberty.

HISTORY OF THE ANCIENT UNITAS FRATRUM (1457–1722).—The Bohemian Brethren are a link in a chain of sects beginning with Wyclif (1324–84) and coming down to the present day. The ideas of the Englishman found favour with Hus, and Bohemia proved a better soil for their growth than England. Both Wyclif and Hus were moved by a sincere desire to reform the Church of their times; both failed and, without intending it, became the fathers of new heretical bodies—the Lollards and the Hussites. The former were persecuted out of existence in Eng-

land by Catholic rulers; the latter prospered in Bohemia, thanks to royal and national support. The burning of John Hus at the stake for his stubborn adherence to the condemned doctrines of Wyclif (at Constance, 6 July, 1415) was considered an insult to the faith of the Bohemian nation, which, since its first conversion to Christianity, had never swerved from the truth. The University of Prague came boldly forward to vindicate the man and his doctrines; the party which hitherto had worked at reforming the Church from within now rejected the Church's authority and became the Hussite sect. Divisions at once arose amongst its members. Some completely set aside the authority of the Church and admitted no other rule than the Bible; others only demanded Communion under both kinds for the laity and free preaching of the Gospel, with some minor reforms. The former, who met for worship at "Mount Tabor", were called Taborites; the latter received the name of Calixtines, i. e. the party of the Chalice. As long as they had a common enemy to fight they fought together under the leadership of that extraordinary man, John Trocznowski, known as Zizka (the one-eyed), and for fully fifteen years proved more than a match for the imperial armies and papal crusaders sent to crush them. Peace was at length obtained, not by force of arms, but by skilful negotiations which resulted in the "Compactata of Basle" (30 November, 1433). The compact was chiefly due to the concessions made by the Calixtine party; it found little or no favour with the Taborites. The discontent led to a feud which terminated at the Battle of Lippau (30 May, 1434) with the death of Procopius, the Taborite leader, and the almost total extinction of his party. The small remnant, too insignificant to play a rôle in politics, withdrew into private life, devoting all their energies to religion. In 1457 one section formed itself into a separate body under the name of the "Brethren's Union" (*Unitas Fratrum*), which is now generally spoken of as the Bohemian Brethren. Their contemporaries coined for them several opprobrious designations, such as Jamnici (cave-dwellers) and Pivnicnici (beerhouse men), Bunzlau Brethren, Picards (corrupted to Pickarts), etc.

The originator of the new sect was a certain Gregory, a nephew of the leading Calixtine preacher, Rokyzana, whose mind was imbued with the conviction that the Roman Church was helplessly and hopelessly corrupt. Gregory therefore decided to found a new Church in accordance with his uncle's and his own ideas of what a perfect Church should be. Through Rokyzana's influence he obtained leave from the governor George von Podiebrad to organize a community in the village of Kunwald near Senftenberg. Michael, the parish priest of Senftenberg, and Matthias, a farmer of Kunwald, joined Gregory, and soon the community counted several thousand members. Their distinguishing tenets at this early period were rather vague: abolition of all distinctions of rank and fortune, the name of Christian being the one all-sufficient dignity; abolition of oaths, of military service, etc. Governor von Podiebrad kept a vigilant eye on the growing community. In 1461 he had Gregory and several other persons arrested on suspicion of reviving the heresies of the Taborites. The accused admitted that they did not believe in the real presence of Christ in the Holy Eucharist, but had partaken of the bread and wine at their nocturnal meetings as of common food. They were set free, but, to avoid further interference, Gregory and his companions fled into the Lordship of Reichenau, where they lived hidden in the mountains. There, in 1464, was held a secret assembly consisting of Brethren from Bohemia and Moravia, who accepted as basis of their creed the doctrine that justification is obtained through faith and charity and confers the hope of eternal salvation. The rich were requested to abandon their wealth and worldly pomp and to live in voluntary poverty. The Brethren were to give up private property for the benefit of the Brotherhood. Anyone not observing the brotherhood of faith and practice was to be separated from the community.

Meanwhile the persecution continued. The Utraquist (Calixtine) priests refused the Sacrament to the Brethren. These, therefore, were forced to constitute a priesthood of their own belief. A bishop and a number of priests were chosen by lot, and the separation from the Utraquists became an accomplished fact. The head of the Austrian Waldenses, who was believed to have received consecration from a real bishop, gave episcopal orders to the ex-parish priest, Michael, and Michael consecrated his friend, Matthias, bishop and ordained several priests. The new Bishop Matthias of Kunwald then reordained his consecrator, to make him a true priest of the Brotherhood. This happened in 1467 at the synod of Lhotka, near Reichenau, where also all those present were rebaptized. The breach with both Catholics and Utraquists was now completed, and the Brethren began to order their community on the model of "the primitive Church". The governing power centred in a council presided over by a judge. Four seniors, or elders, held the episcopal power. The priests had no property and were encouraged to celibacy. The strictest morality and modesty were exacted from the faithful. All acts subservient to luxury were forbidden; oaths and military service were only permited in very exceptional cases. Public sins had to be publicly confessed, and were punished with ecclesiastical penalties or expulsion. A committee of women watched with relentless severity over the behaviour of their sisters.

A new persecution quickly followed on the synod of Lhotka. The Brethren defended their cause in copious writings, but in 1468 many of them were imprisoned and tortured, one was burnt at the stake. The death of the governor George von Podiebrad in 1471 brought some relief. Brother Gregory died in 1473. From 1480 Lucas of Prague was the leading man. Thanks to him, and to toleration granted the Brethren by King Ladislaus II, the Brotherhood rapidly increased in numbers. By the end of the fifteenth century there were 400 communities. Pope Alexander VI's endeavour to reconvert the Brethren (in 1499) proved futile. About this time an internal feud in the "Unity of Brethren" led to a renewal of persecution. The Amosites, so called from their leader, Brother Amos, accused their more moderate Brethren of fomenting violent opposition to the Government in imitation of their spiritual ancestors, the Taborites. King Ladislaus II thereupon issued a decree prohibiting the meetings of the Brethren under heavy penalties. In many places, however, the decree was left unheeded, and powerful landowners continued to protect the Brotherhood. Once more the king resorted to milder measures. In 1507 he invited the chiefs of the Brethren to meet the Utraquists in conference at Prague. The Brethren sent a few rude, unlettered fellows unable to give answers to the questions of the professors. The king regarded this as an insult and ordered all the meetings of the "Pickarts" to be suppressed, all their books to be burnt, and the recalcitrants to be imprisoned (1508).

The Brethren now began to look for foreign sympathy. Erasmus complimented them on their knowledge of truth, but refused to commit himself further. Luther objected to their doctrine on the Eucharist, to the celibacy of their clergy, to the practice of rebaptizing, and to the belief in seven sacraments. Brother Lucas answered in a sharp pamphlet and, having ascertained the low standard of church discipline among the Lutherans of Witten-

berg, ceased all attempts at union. At the same time (1525) Lucas rejected the Zwinglian doctrines which some Brethren were trying to introduce. After the death of Lucas (1528) the government of the Brotherhood passed into the hands of men fond of innovations, among whom John Augusta is the most remarkable. Augusta reopened negotiations with Luther and so modified his creed that it gained the Reformer's approbation, but the union of the two sects was again prevented by the less rigid morals of the Lutherans in Bohemia and Moravia. Augusta pleaded for stricter church discipline, but Luther dismissed him, saying: "Be you the apostle of the Bohemians, I will be the apostle of the Germans. Do as circumstances direct, we will do the same here" (1542). Soon afterwards the Bohemian Estates were requested to join Charles V in his war against the Smalkaldic league. Catholics and old Utraquists obeyed, but the Bohemian Protestants, having met in the house of Brother Kostka, established a kind of provisional government composed of eight members, four of whom belonged to the Brotherhood, and appointed a general to lead the armed rebels into Saxony against the emperor. Charles's victory over the Smalkaldians at Mühlberg (1547) left the rebels no choice but to submit to their king, Ferdinand I. The Brethren, who had been the chief instigators of the rebellion, were now doomed to extinction. John Augusta and his associate, Jacob Bilek, were cast into prison; the Brethren's meetings were interdicted throughout the whole kingdom; those who refused to submit were exiled. Many took refuge in Poland and Prussia (1578); those who remained in the country joined, at least *pro formâ*, the Utraquist party. Owing to Maximilian II's leniency and Protestant propensities, the Bohemian diet of 1575 could draw up the "Bohemian Confession of Faith" in which the principles of the Brethren find expression along with those of the Lutherans. Under Rudolph II (1584) persecution was again resorted to, and lasted with more or less intensity down to 1609, when Rudolph's Charter granted the free exercise of their religion to all Protestants. No sooner, however, did external oppression relent than internal dissension broke out in the Protestant ranks. The Consistory, composed of Lutherans and Brethren, was unable to maintain peace and union between the two parties. Ferdinand II, after his victory over the rebellious Bohemians at the White Mountain near Prague (1620), offered them the choice between Catholicism and exile. Many Brethren emigrated to Hungary, but a greater number to northern Poland, where they settled in Lissa (now in Prussian Posen). Even to this day there are in that district seven communities calling themselves Brethren, although their confession of faith is the Helvetic. In Prussian Silesia there are also three communities of Brethren claiming descent from the Bohemian Brotherhood.

THE BOHEMIAN BRETHREN AND ENGLAND.—During the reign of Maximilian II and Rudolph II the Bohemian Brethren enjoyed a period of prosperity which allowed them to establish relations with younger Protestant churches. They sent students to Heidelberg and one at least to Oxford. In 1583 "Bernardus, John, a Moravian", was allowed to supply B. D. He had studied theology for ten years in German universities and was now going to the universities of Scotland. This Bernardus, however, has left no trace but the entry in the Register of Oxford just quoted. The man who brought the Brotherhood prominently before the Anglican Church was Johann Amos, of Comna, generally known as Comenius. As a scholar and educationist he was invited by his English friends to assist in improving the state and administration of the universities, then under consideration in Parliament. The outbreak of the Civil War brought all these plans to naught, and Comenius returned to Germany in 1642. His influence in England allowed him to set on foot several collections for his severely persecuted church in Poland: the first three were failures, but the fourth, authorized by Cromwell, produced £5,900, of which sum Cambridge University contributed £56. This was in 1658-59. Intercourse with the Anglican Church was kept up uninterruptedly until the remnants of the ancient Brotherhood had dwindled away and been swallowed up by other Evangelical confessions. When the renewed Brotherhood was established in England it benefited by the memory of former friendly relations.

History of the Renewed Brotherhood.—Persecution from without and dissension within well-nigh brought about the total extinction of the Bohemian Brethren. The small but faithful remnant was, however, destined to blossom into a new and vigorous religious body under the name of *Moravian Brethren*. The founder and moulder of this second *Unitas Fratrum* was the pious and practical Count Zinzendorf (b. 1700, d. 1760). In 1722 the Lutheran Pastor Rothe, of Berthelsdorf in Upper Lusatia, introduced to the Count, from whom he held his living, a Moravian carpenter named Christian David. This man had been deputed by his co-religionists to look out for a concession of land where they could freely practise their religion. Zinzendorf was so far unacquainted with the history and the tenets of the Bohemian Brethren, but in his charity, he granted them the desired land, on the slopes of the Hutberg in the parish of Berthelsdorf. In a short time emigrants from Moravia founded there a colony, called Herrnhut. The colonists worshipped at the Lutheran parish church. Two years later, there arrived from Zauchenthal in Moravia five young men fully conscious of being true members of the old "Bohemian Brotherhood". At once religious quarrels arose, to the annoyance of Count Zinzendorf and his friends. The count was not slow in perceiving that the colonists, all simple labourers and craftsmen, were more concerned with church discipline and Christian rules of life than with dogma. Accordingly he set about elaborating a constitution for a community of which religion should be the chief concern and bond of union. He left Dresden and, with the pastor's leave, began to work as a lay catechist among the Brethren at Herrnhut. The community met for their religious services in their own hall where one of the Brethren, either chosen by lot or elected by the assembly, acted as minister. In 1731 they seceded from the parish church and added to their usual services the celebration of the Lord's Supper. They were divided in "choirs" according to age, sex, and calling; each choir was ruled by elders (male and female), pastors, and administrators chosen among its members. The female choirs were distinguished by their dresses. Widows, unmarried young men, and young women formed separate choirs under the supervision of elders. Everything at Herrnhut was controlled by the College of Elders, even matrimony, subject to the sanction of the lot. Provision was made for the poor and the sick, for prayer meetings and so forth. Deacons, acting for the Elders, administered the property accruing to the community from donations. Great care was given to the education of the young, Zinzendorf being anxious to raise a generation that would perpetuate his work. The organization of the renewed Brotherhood was complete in 1731. It bore the stamp of the personality of its founder, a man deeply religious, nurtured in Spener's Pietism by the two noble ladies who brought him up, and well acquainted with Catholic life from his sojourn in Paris. As soon as the foundations were solidly laid at Herrnhut Zinzendorf began to think of missionary work. His personal connexion with the Danish Court led him to choose the Danish

possessions in the West Indies and in Greenland for the field of his labours. His first missionaries were sent out in 1732 and 1733. Feeling, however that as a simple layman he could not well confer missionary powers, he took orders at Tübingen in 1734 and, moreover, received episcopal consecration from the Reformed court-preacher Jablonsky of Berlin, in whose family the Moravian episcopacy, originated in 1467 by a validly ordained Waldensian bishop, had been—or was said to have been—preserved. Persecution was not long in coming. The orthodox Lutherans became the Brethren's bitterest enemies. The Imperial Government in Vienna strongly objected to their propaganda in Bohemia, which caused Austrian subjects to emigrate and sowed discontent in the country. Under imperial pressure the King of Saxony banished Zinzendorf "for ever". The zealous count put his exile to good use. During the ten years (1737-47) of his absence from Saxony he founded congregations in Holland, England, Ireland, America; new ones also arose in Germany at Herrenhag, Neuwied, Gnadenfrei, Gnadenberg, and Neusatz. Zinzendorf showed a special predilection for the London establishment. In 1750 he fixed his residence in the English capital and from there ruled the whole "Unity of Brethren". But in 1755 he returned to Herrnhut, which now became and remained the centre of the whole administration. To the present day the "Provincial Board of Elders for Germany" occupies Zinzendorf's own house at Berthelsdorf. The finishing touch of the new church system is the liberty enjoyed by those who join it to retain the Lutheran, the Reformed, or the Moravian Confession to which they belonged, and to be placed under the rule of Elders of the same belief. This peculiar feature shows the founder's disregard for dogma and the great value he attached to Christian practice and ecclesiastical discipline. He held that faith and justification could only be found by individuals who were, or became, members of a religious community. However much, in this and in other points, he copied the Catholic Church, yet he was to the end a faithful adherent of the Augsburg Confession and obtained from the Consistory in Dresden an official acknowledgment that the Moravian Brethren were followers of the same faith. He also succeeded after a long struggle in securing for the Brotherhood recognition by the Saxon government. When, regretted by all, he died in 1760, his work and his spirit lived on in the strongly organized body of the "Unity of Brethren". No material changes have taken place since. In 1775 the Brethren, assembled in a synod at Barby, adopted the following statement of principles:—

"The chief doctrine to which the Church of the Brethren adheres, and which we must preserve as an invaluable treasure committed unto us, is this: That by the sacrifice for sin made by Jesus Christ, and by that alone, grace and deliverance from sin are to be obtained for all mankind. We will, therefore, without lessening the importance of any other article of the Christian faith, steadfastly maintain the following five points: (1) The doctrine of the universal depravity of man: that there is no health in man, and that, since the Fall he has no power whatever left to help himself. (2) The doctrine of the Divinity of Christ: that God, the Creator of all things, was manifest in the flesh, and reconciled us to Himself; that He is before all things and that in Him all things exist. (3) The doctrine of the atonement and satisfaction made for us by Jesus Christ: that He was delivered for our offences and raised again for our justification and that by His merits *alone* we receive freely the forgiveness of sin, faith in Jesus and sanctification in soul and body. (4) The doctrine of the Holy Spirit and the operation of His grace: that it is He who worketh in us conviction of sin, faith in Jesus, and pureness in heart. (5) The doctrine of the fruits of faith: that faith must evidence itself by willing obedience to the commandments of God, from love and gratitude."

Faith in the Redemption and entire surrender of self to Christ (with Whom in 1741 a spiritual covenant was made) are held to be the very essence of religion. The will of Christ was ascertained by casting of lots as the final sanction in case of marriage (until 1820), in the election of superiors (until 1889), etc. Zinzendorf ruled as bishop over all the communities, both in Europe and America, but since his death the episcopal office has remained a mere title. In 1857 the British and American Unity became independent; the only bond of union being now the General Synod held once every ten years.

THE MORAVIANS IN ENGLAND.—The beginnings of the Brethren's Church in England are an interesting chapter in the commerce of thought between Germany and that country. The German dynasty on the English throne had attracted a strong colony of their countrymen; towards the middle of the eighteenth century London alone numbered from 4000 to 5000 Germans among its inhabitants. These would naturally be in sympathy with the Brethren. But the "Religious Societies" founded by Doctor Smithies, curate of St. Giles, and Dr. Horneck, of the Lower Palatinate, together with the writings of William Law—the father of the religious revival of the eighteenth century—had prepared the minds of many Englishmen for stronger spiritual food than that offered by the established religion. Horneck was a German Pietist, and William Law, in his "Serious Call", sets up a standard of perfection little short of Catholic monasticism. John Wesley, who confesses that he was stimulated into activity by William Law, at first sought satisfaction of his spiritual cravings in the Moravian Brotherhood. He, with three other Oxford Methodists, met the Moravian Bishop Nitschmann and twenty Brethren at Gravesend, where they were waiting for the vessel that was to carry them all to Georgia (1736). The Englishmen were favourably impressed with the religious fervour of the Germans, and a fruitful friendship sprang up between them. As early as 1728 Zinzendorf had sent to England a deputation headed by the Moravian Johannn Töltschig "to tell such as were not blinded by their lusts, but whose eyes God had opened, what God had wrought". Countess Sophia von Schaumburg-Lippe, Lady-in-Waiting at the English Court, used her influence in their behalf, but was unable to counteract the opposition of the Lutheran court-chaplain Ziegenhagen. The embassy had little or no result. Other visits followed at intervals, most of them by missionaries and emigrants on their way to America. On the occasion of such a visit Zinzendorf himself induced some young people to form a society for the reading of the Bible, mutual edification, abstention from theological controversy, brotherly love, etc. It was the first step towards realizing his ideals in England. The next step was Peter Boehler's zealous preaching to the "religious societies" and the working classes.

It was Boehler who founded the religious society in Fetter Lane of which John Wesley became a member, and for which he framed most of the rules; it seems also due to the influence of Boehler that John and Charles Wesley "found conversion" (June, 1738), yet not a conversion exactly of the Moravian type. A visit of John Wesley to the German centres made it clear that the Brotherhood had no room for two men like Zinzendorf and Wesley, both being born leaders of men, but having little else in common. Little by little Wesley became estranged from the Brethren, and his former friendship turned to open hostility (12 November, 1741, according to Wesley's journal). At a meeting in Fetter Lane Wesley ac-cused the Brethren of holding false doctrines and left the hall exclaiming: "Let those who agree with me follow me." Some eighteen or nineteen of the members went out after him, the rest called upon the Brethren to be their leaders. Thus a religious society of the Church of England became a society of the Brethren. After their rupture with Wesley the Brethren began to work on their own account in England. Professor Spangenberg organized the young church with rare talent, and its activity spread far and wide in the provinces, even to Scotland and Ireland, but their success was greatest in Yorkshire. They also came in for some persecution from people who still confused them with the Methodists. The legal status of the Brotherhood was now to be determined. They did not wish to be classed as Dissenters, which would at once have severed them from the Anglican Church, and, on the other hand, the Anglican Church disowned them because they neither had Anglican orders nor did they use the Book of Common Prayer. Archbishop Potter would grant them no more than the toleration accorded to foreign Protestants. To obtain a license from a Justice of the Peace they had to adopt a name, and Spangenberg decided on "Moravian Brethren, formerly of the Anglican Communion". This name implied a new denomination and led to the immediate formation of the first congregation of Brethren of English nationality (1742). Zinzendorf greatly objected to the name of Moravians being given to his Brethren whom he considered as an *ecclesiola in ecclesiâ*, a select small church within a greater one, which might exist in almost any denomination. The proposed designation, "Old Lutheran Protestants", was distasteful to English members. They resolutely clung to the names "United Brethren" and "Moravians" as their official and popular designations, and the "Bill for encouraging the people known by the name of Unitas Fratrum or United Brethren to settle in His Majesty's colonies", passed in 1749, gives official sanction to the old name, recognizes that the Brethren belonged to an "ancient protestant and episcopal Church", and maintains their connexion with Germany.

BEGINNINGS OF THE MORAVIAN CHURCH IN AMERICA.—In 1734 Zinzendorf obtained for thirty families of banished Schwenkfelders (adherents of Kaspar von Schwenkfeld) a home in Georgia which had just been carved out of the Carolina grant "to serve as an asylum for insolvent debtors and for persons fleeing from religious persecution". These exiles, however, found it preferable to join an older colony in Pennsylvania. The Brethren now conceived the plan of securing for themselves in Georgia a home of refuge in time of persecution. The governor general, Oglethorpe, granted them 500 acres, and Spangenberg, the negotiator, received a present of 50 acres for himself, a part of the site on which the city of Savannah now stands. The first eleven immigrants reached Savannah 17 April, 1734, led by Spangenberg. Bishop Nitschmann brought over another twenty, 7 February, 1736. The work of evangelizing and colonizing was at once vigorously taken in hand and carried on with more courage than success. The climate, wars, enmities from within and without, checked the growth and cramped the organization of the Brotherhood.

PRESENT CONDITION OF THE MORAVIAN BODY.— The outcome of their faithful struggles during 175 years is shown in the subjoined statistics, and may be read in detail in the "Transactions of the Moravian Historical Society," Vol VI:—

Statistics for America (from "The Moravian," 13 March, 1907).—On the 1st of January, 1907, there were in the five northern districts of America 96 congregations with 13,859 communicants, 1,194 noncommunicants, and 5,316 children; a total membership of 20,369; an increase of 228 over the previous year. In Sunday schools there were 9,666 pupils under 1,156 officers and teachers, a total membership of 10,822, against 11,012 in the preceding year, implying a loss of 187.—Receipts from all sources: 31 December, 1906, $145,517.67; a decrease of $8,006.19 on 1905. Expenses exactly balance receipts. In the Southern Province of America there were on the 1st of January, 1907, 3,703 communicants, 320 non-communicants, 1,819 children; total, 5,842. Sunday schools contained 3,883 pupils, 323 officers and teachers; total, 4,206.— Total membership in both provinces: 26,211 against 25,877 in 1906—an increase of 334.

In Great Britain and Ireland, the Moravian Church numbered on the 31st of December, 1906, 41 congregations, with a total membership of 6,343; an increase of 211 on 1905; 5,072 pupils attended Sunday schools, with 568 teachers; there were also 213 pupils, with 5 teachers, in 5 day schools, and 305 scholars, with 38 teachers, in 5 boarding schools.

The German Province, 31 December, 1905, had 25 congregations, with total membership of 7,958, of whom 5,795 were communicants; 50 missionary centres ministered to about 70,000 persons (the "Diaspora").

The Mission Fields of the Moravians: In North America, Labrador, begun 1771; Alaska, 1885; California, 1890.—In Central America, Mosquito Coast, 1849.—In South America, Surinam, 1735, Demerara, 1878.—In the West Indies, Jamaica, 1754; St. Thomas, 1732, St. Jan, 1754; St. Croix, 1740; Antigua, 1756; St. Kitts, 1777; Barbadoes, 1765; Tobago, 1790; Trinidad, 1890.—In Africa, Cape Colony, East and West, 1736; German East Africa, 1891.—In Asia, West Himalaya, 1853; Jerusalem, Leper House, 1867.—In Australia, Victoria, 1849; North Queensland, 1891. The work is carried on by 470 missionaries of whom 76 are natives. Bohemia and Moravia are also counted among the mission fields. The mission work there, like that of the foreign missions, is a joint undertaking of all the Provinces of the Church. In December, 1905, the total membership was 984; income (of which £111 was from the British Province), £1761, 16/4; outlay, £1,991, 10/9.

CAMERARIUS, *Historica narratio de Fratrum orthodoxorum ecclesiis in Bohemiâ, Moraviâ, et Poloniâ* (Frankfort, 1625); BOROWÝ, s. v. *Brüder, Böhmische* in *Kirchenlex.*, II; HAMILTON, *A History of the Moravian Church, or the Unitas Fratrum* (Bethlehem, Pa., 1900); WAUER, *The Beginnings of the Brethren's Church in England* (Baildon, near Shipley, Yorks, 1901); *The Moravian* (official organ of the N. Prov. of the Unitas Fratrum in America); *The Moravian Messenger.*—See also *Bibliography* prefixed to SCHWEINITZ, *History of the Unitas Fratrum.*

J. WILHELM.

Bohemians of the United States, The.—A traveller who has seen the natural beauties of Bohemia, its vast resources, and the thrift of its people, will, no doubt, be surprised at the comparatively great number of persons who have emigrated to the United States of America. The causes for this are political, religious, and economical. Religious dissensions at the beginning of the seventeenth century induced many to leave their native country and even to cross the ocean. The religious revolution stirred up by the preachings and teachings of John Hus gave birth to several religious sects in Bohemia, the suppression of which, after the battle of White Mountain near Prague (1620), caused many to emigrate to other countries and several even as far as America. Of the latter Augustýn Heřman (d. 1692) and Frederick Filip (d. 1702) are the most important from an historical standpoint. Heřman must have been a man of good education, for Governor Stuyvesant, of New Amsterdam, entrusted him with many important missions. He made the first map of the State of Maryland, of which one copy is still preserved in the British Museum and another at Richmond, in the archives of the State of Virginia. Heřman always publicly professed his nationality. The sec-

ond of these Bohemian emigrants, Filip, or Philipps as he is commonly known, was likewise a man of prominence and his descendants played no small part in the development of New Amsterdam. He was buried in the cemetery of Sleepy Hollow, near Tarrytown, New York. Though historical proof is lacking, without doubt many other Bohemians, of similar religious convictions, emigrated to this country at the same time. Their families either died out, or, as is more probable, were entirely assimilated by the American people so that they have left no trace. Of late years emigration from Bohemia has been chiefly caused by political conditions. Many Bohemian patriots, especially during the stormy year of 1848, sought refuge beyond the sea to evade the consequences of patriotic zeal, as the courts showed little mercy to those accused of political crimes. A similar state of affairs existed later on when the reins of the Austrian Government passed into the hands of the enemies of Bohemia, who punished every patriotic act as high treason to Austria. These political conditions, coupled with the Austro-Prussian war of 1866, in which Bohemia suffered great loss of life and property, forced many to seek their fortunes in the land of freedom. The greater number of emigrants, however, came to this country on account of poverty, brought on, for the most part, by the failure of the Government to interest itself in the welfare of certain parts of Bohemia, especially the southern and eastern parts, where, for lack of industry, the people were forced to depend for their livelihood, almost exclusively, on the fruits of the fields. This poverty was increased by overtaxation and frequent failures of crops. It was precisely these parts of Bohemia that sent thousands of their best citizens to America about 1870, and are sending a still greater number at the present time.

It will be impossible to give the exact number of Bohemian immigrants to the United States, as the Immigration Bureau up to the year 1881 enrolled all immigrants that came from any province of Austria as Austrians, and even after 1881, many Bohemians were listed as Austrians. As later immigration reports in which Bohemians were entered separately show that one-third of all immigrants from Austria come from Bohemia, the total number of Bohemians who came to this country before 1881 may be estimated approximately. It must be stated, however, that after 1881 many immigrants from Moravia and Silesia, Austrian provinces in which the Bohemian language is spoken, were enrolled as Bohemians. Taking all these facts into consideration, it is safe to give the number of foreign born Bohemians in the United States as 222,000. The number of American-born Bohemians is about 310,000, making the total Bohemian population of the United States about 522,000. It is worthy of note that these figures are almost equally divided between males and females, which shows that the Bohemian immigrants have come to this country to stay. Statistics prove that only a very small number of Bohemians return to their native country to live. In 1906, 12,958 Bohemian immigrants were received, eclipsing the record of all previous years. The latest report of the Commissioner of Immigration shows only two per cent of Bohemian immigrants illiterate, as compared with four per cent of Germans and still higher proportions for other nations. The following table gives the approximate Bohemian population according to states:—

	Number of Bohemians	Foreign born
Illinois	115,000	40,000
New York	45,000	17,700
Ohio	43,000	16,200
Maryland	11,000	
Nebraska	60,000	18,000

	Number of Bohemians	Foreign born
Wisconsin	43,000	14,900
Minnesota	36,000	12,500
Texas	40,000	12,000
Iowa	35,000	10,800
Kansas	17,000	
Missouri	15,000	
North and South Dakota	15,000	
Michigan	10,000	
Pennsylvania	7,000	
New Jersey	5,000	
Massachusetts	2,400	
Oklahoma	4,000	
California	2,100	
Colorado	1,300	
Indiana	1,800	
Connecticut	1,300	
Arkansas	1,000	
Other States	5,000	

Of the larger cities Chicago has a Bohemian population of about 100,000; New York, 40,000; Cleveland, 40,000; Baltimore, 8,500; Omaha, 8,000; Milwaukee, 5,500; St. Paul, 6,000; and St. Louis, 8,000.

It is in the farming districts that the Bohemian immigrants have attained the greatest degree of success. It is here that we can best see the great share they had in building up the United States. Coming for the most part from rural districts, accustomed to hard labour, and ever willing to undergo the hardships of pioneer life, the Bohemians have attained an honourable place amongst the Western farmers. There is a saying amongst the Western farmers that if anyone can wrest crops from the soil, it is the Bohemian farmer. About half of the Bohemian immigrants have cast their lot with farming communities.

SOCIETIES.—Amongst the great number of Bohemians in this country, there is no one organization uniting them into one national body. This may be explained by the fact that they are divided into two strongly antagonistic camps: Catholics and atheists or free-thinkers. The latter are chiefly those who have apostatized from the faith of their fathers. Only an insignificant percentage of Bohemians are adherents of Protestant sects, though Protestants have expended great labour and large sums in proselytizing amongst the Bohemians. The two camps are entirely separate, each with its own fraternal organizations. The Catholics have the following fraternal or benevolent organizations: The First Bohemian Roman Catholic Central Union (*První Římsko-Katolická Ústřední Jednota*), founded in 1877 at St. Louis, has a membership of 11,505; the Catholic Workman (*Katolický Dělník*), founded in 1891, 3,225; the Bohemian Roman Catholic Central Union of the State of Wisconsin (*Česká Římsko-Katolická Ústřední Jednota ve Státu Wisconsin*) founded in 1888, 1,380; the Bohemian Catholic Union of the State of Texas (*Katolická Jednota Texaská*), founded in 1889, 1,900; the Western Bohemian Catholic Union (*Západní Česko-Katolická Jednota*), founded in 1898, 3,000; the Bohemian Catholic Union of Cleveland (*Česko-Římsko-Katolická Jednota ve Cleveland, O.*), founded in 1899, 1,800; the Bohemian Catholic Central Union of American Women (*Ústřední Jednota Žen Amerických*) established in 1880, 14,100; the Bohemian Catholic Union of Women of The State of Texas (*Česká Římsko-Katolická Jednota Žen ve Státu Texas*) likewise a large membership. All these organizations are thoroughly Catholic in spirit, and not only practise benevolence and charity towards their members, but have been the right hand of the clergy in building Catholic churches and schools and in fostering the spirit of religion amongst their countrymen.

Opposed to these Catholic organizations are the fraternal organizations of the freethinking Bohemians. The strongest of these is the Bohemian Slavic Benevolent Society (*Česko-Slovanská Podporující Společnost*), established at St. Louis in 1854, which has a membership of about 15,000. This organization is chiefly responsible for the loss of faith amongst many Bohemians of this country, having enticed thousands of well-meaning people to join its ranks under the pretext of strict neutrality in religious matters. By association with freethinkers, and under other evil influences, thousands grew lukewarm in the performance of their religious duties and finally lost their faith entirely. This organization is atheistic in spirit and propagates atheism amongst its members. A similar tendency is exercised by the gymnastic or athletic societies commonly called the *Sokol* (turners); by the Western Benevolent Society (*Západní Česká Bratrská Jednota*), which has a membership of about 7,000; by the Society of Bohemian Ladies (*Jednota Českých Dam*), with a membership of about 15,000, as well as several minor organizations of the same type.

SCHOOLS.—Wherever it is possible Bohemian Catholics endeavour to build a school. Love of their faith as well as love of their native tongue impels them to send their children to these schools, it being the desire of Bohemian parents that their children learn at least to read and write the language of their parents. Experience shows that without such schools children are soon estranged to the language and lose many of the good characteristics of their parents. The number of Bohemian Catholic parochial schools in this country is seventy-five, with a total attendance of about 14,000. There is also an institution of higher education, St. Procopius College at Lisle, Illinois, founded and conducted by the Bohemian Benedictine Order. The object of this institution is not only to train candidates for the priesthood, but to give young men in general such an education as to enable them to become leaders of their people in the various walks of life.

PRESS.—The first, and for a long time the only, Bohemian Catholic newspaper published in the United States, was the "Hlas" (Voice) of St. Louis, published semi-weekly. After its establishment in 1873 it was edited and managed for many years by its venerable founder, Monsignor Joseph Hessoun, pastor of St. John's Church, St. Louis, who gave it a special prestige among the Bohemian Catholics of the United States. In the year 1890 the "Přítel Dítek" (Friend of Children) was established in Chicago, a weekly periodical, and, as its name implies, issued chiefly for children. In the year 1892 the "Katolík" (The Catholic) was founded, published twice a week, and by far the best periodical in the Bohemian language in this country. The "Katolík" was followed by the daily "Národ" (Nation) and the "Hospodářské Listy" (Agricultural News), established in 1898, which appears twice a month. All of these papers are published by the Bohemian Benedictine Order of Chicago. In addition, there are the following Bohemian Catholic papers: "Nový Domov" (The New Home), a weekly publication of Hallettsville, Texas; the "Vlastenec" (Patriot) published weekly at La Crosse, Wisconsin; the "Měsíční Věstník", published by the Redemptorist Fathers of New York once a month. All of these publications are doing inestimable service in the cause of religion.

The freethinking press is no less powerful. Four Bohemian dailies are *ex professo* hostile to religion, while two others, though posing as neutral and independent papers, are in reality anti-religious in their sympathies and tendencies. Three Bohemian dailies are published in Chicago, two in New York, and two in Cleveland. There are in addition four bi-weeklies, ten weeklies, and several smaller publications.

COMMUNITIES AND CHURCHES.—There are three Bohemian religious communities in the United States.

The first and oldest, the Bohemian Benedictine Order of Chicago was founded in 1887 by the Right Rev. Boniface Wimmer, O. S. B., first Abbot of St. Vincent's, Beatty, Pennsylvania. This apostolic man, perceiving the great dearth of priests among the Bohemians in the United States, invited Bohemian young men to his abbey, educated them free of charge, and fitted them for exercising the ministry amongst their own countrymen. At his request the pope granted permission for the establishment of an independent or canonical Bohemian priory, in St. Procopius Priory of Chicago, which in 1894 was raised by His Holiness Leo XIII to the dignity of an abbey; the Right Rev. John Nepomuk Jæger, O. S. B., was elected the first abbot. The Bohemian Benedictine Fathers have charge of three Bohemian and two Slovak congrega-

tions in the city of Chicago, amongst them the congregation of St. Procopius, the largest Bohemian parish in the United States, with a membership of about 10,000. They have likewise a large modern printing plant in which four leading Bohemian Catholic newspapers are printed. The order has 13 priests, 3 clerics, 3 novices, and 10 lay-brothers. The second purely Bohemian religious community is that of the Bohemian Benedictine Sisters of the Sacred Heart at Chicago, established in 1894. These sisters are also in charge of St. Joseph's Orphanage at Lisle, Illinois. A second Bohemian orphanage is to be established at St. Louis, in connexion with St. John's church, the oldest Bohemian parish in the United States. The Bohemian Benedictine Sisters have at present 27 sisters, 7 novices, and 1 candidate, and teach in several Bohemian schools. Besides these two exclusively Bohemian religious communities we have the Bohemian Redemptorist Fathers of New York and Baltimore, who do not, however, form independent communities, but are directly under the provincial who is at the head of all Redemptorist communities belonging to the Eastern province. They are in charge of the church of Mary Help, New York City, which has four Bohemian priests, and of St. Wenceslaus Church, Baltimore, which has three.

There are in the United States 138 Bohemian Catholic churches with resident pastors and about 129 missions; many of the missions, however, are attended from churches of different nationalities. The number of Bohemian priests in the United States is 208; 35 minister to non-Bohemian parishes, 30 of them to Slovak congregations.

DISTINGUISHED REPRESENTATIVES.—The name of the Very Rev. Monsignor Joseph Hessoun (b. 1830; d. 4 July, 1906), late pastor of the church of St. John Nepomuk, St. Louis, is held in grateful remembrance by the Bohemian Catholic people of the United States. Born at Vrcovic, Bohemia, he came to the United States in 1865, eleven years after his ordination, and up to his death worked with untiring zeal among his people. The fruits of his labours were felt by Bohemians throughout the country. He

not only encouraged them to perseverance by his editorials in the "Hlas", but he often sacrificed his last cent to assist in the building of Catholic churches. Furthermore, he did everything that lay in his power to procure priests for his people. Whenever necessity demanded he visited the Bohemian parishes without Bohemian priests. In his old age he was universally called *náš tatíček* (our little father). Among other Bohemian priests who have laboured with untiring zeal for the salvation of the Bohemians in this country must be mentioned the Very Rev. William Čoka, Vicar-General of Omaha, b. at Černovir, Moravia; d. 1902; the Rev. Father Sulák, S. J., of Chicago, the oldest Bohemian missionary; the Right Rev. John Nepomuk Jæger, Abbot of the Bohemian Benedictine Order of Chicago; the Rev. Wenceslaus Kočárník, O. S. B., of Chicago; the Rev. John Vránek of Omaha, a Bohemian poet of great ability and merit. Above all there is the noble pioneer of Bohemian priests on the soil of the new world, the saintly John Nepomuk Neuman, fourth Bishop of Philadelphia, b. at Prachatitz, Bohemia, 1811; d. 1860.

The Bohemians all over the world are renowned for their musical gifts. In Bohemian churches of this country church music has attained a high degree of excellence, especially noticeable by the congregational singing in the larger churches. Not a few Bohemian priests are finished musicians. The feasts of the national patrons, those of St. John Nepomuk and of St. Wenceslaus, the first Christian Prince of Bohemia, are celebrated with special pomp, according to the usages of Bohemia. Good Friday is likewise observed with a solemnity unusual in this country. The Resurrection of Our Lord is celebrated with great pomp in the evening of Holy Saturday, wherever possible in the open air.

Bureau of Statistics: Immigration into the U. S., 1820–1903 (Washington, 1903); *Annual Reports of the Commissioner-General of Immigration* (Washington); BALCH, *Slav Immigration at Its Source* in *Charities* (New York, 1906); HOUŠŤ, *Krátké dějiny česko-katol. osad ve Spoj. Státech* (St. Louis, 1890); WAGNER, *Čeští osadníci v Americe* (Prague, 1887); HABENICHT, *Dějiny Čechů Amerických* (St. Louis, 1906); ROSICKÝ, *Jak je v Americe?* (Omaha, 1906); CAPEK, *Památky českých emigrantů v Americe* (Omaha, 1907).

JOS. ŠINKMAJER.

Boiano, DIOCESE OF, in the province of Benevento, Italy, suffragan to the Archbishopric of Benevento. The city, situated at the foot of Monte Matese, occupies the site of the ancient Roman colony of Bovianum, or Bobianum. Cappelletti has demonstrated the error of Ughelli (Italia Sacra, VIII, 241) who thought he recognized a bishop of this see in a certain Laurentius at the beginning of the sixth century. The see, however, is decidedly ancient. Its first recorded bishop is Adalberto (1071). Others worthy of note are: Poliziano (1215) who consecrated the cathedral; Giovanni (1226), who decorated the façade at his own expense, as recorded in an inscription; Silvio Pandoni (1489), who restored the work of Giovanni; Cardinals Franciotto Orsini (1519) and Carlo Carafa (1572), who adorned the cathedral with costly furnishings; Celestino Bruni (1653), a distinguished theologian and preacher. After the death of Bishop Nicolò Rosetti (elected in 1774), differences between the Holy See and the court of Naples prevented the appointment of a successor until 1836, when Giuseppe Riccardi was appointed. The most notable sacred edifice is the cathedral, dedicated to St. Bartholomew the Apostle. The diocese has a population of 90,300, with 33 parishes, 134 churches and chapels, 173 secular priests, 19 regulars, and 62 seminarians.

CAPPELLETTI, *Le chiese d'Italia* (Venice, 1844), XIX, 191; BATTANDIER, *Ann. pont. cath.* (Paris, 1907).

U. BENIGNI.

Boiardo, MATTEO MARIA, an Italian poet, b. about 1434, at, or near, Scandiano (Reggio-Emilia); d. at Reggio, 20 December, 1494. The son of Giovanni di Feltrino and Lucia Strozzi, he was of noble lineage, ranking as Count of Scandiano, with seigniorial power over Arceto, Casalgrande, Gesso, and Torricella. Boiardo was an ideal type of the gifted and accomplished courtier possessing, at the same time, a manly heart and deep humanistic learning. Up to the year of his marriage to Taddea Gonzaga, the daughter of the Count of Novellara (1472), he had received many marks of favour from Borso d'Este, Duke of Ferrara, having been sent to meet Frederick III (1469), and afterwards visiting Pope Paul II (1471), in the train of Borso. In 1473 he joined the retinue which escorted Eleonora of Aragon, the daughter of Ferdinand I, to meet her spouse, Ercole, at Ferrara. Five years later he was invested with the governorship of Reggio, an office which he filled with signal success till his death, except for an interval (1481–86) during which he was governor of Modena.

His great poem of chivalry and romance "L'Orlando innamorato" (Scandiano, 1495), consisting of sixty-eight cantos and a half, was begun about his thirty-eighth year, interrupted for a time by the Venetian war, then resumed, to be left unfinished on account of the author's death. To material largely quarried from the Carlovingian and Arthurian cycles the Count of Scandiano added a gorgeous superstructure of his own. As the plot is not woven around a single pivotal action, the inextricable maze of most cunningly contrived episodes must be linked, first, with the quest of beautiful Angelica by love-smitten Orlando and the other enamoured knights, then with the defence of Albracca by Angelica's father, the King of Cathay, against the beleaguering Tartars, and, finally, with the Moors' siege of Paris and their struggle with Charlemagne's army. The whole, in spite of a lack of finish and sundry rhythmical deficiencies, formed a magnificent work of art, echoing from every *ottava* the poet's ardent devotion to Love and Loyalty, shedding warmth and sunshine wherever the lapse of ages had rendered the legends colourless and cold, and opening a path which Ariosto and Tasso were soon to tread. Still, the poem, after sixteen editions, was not to be republished for nearly three centuries. Francesco Berni's *rifacimento*, or re-casting of "L'Orlando" appeared in 1542, and from that date till 1830, when Panizzi revived it, Boiardo's name was well-nigh forgotten. A similar fate had befallen the count's "Rime" (Scandiano, 1499), which Panizzi's edition (London, 1835), snatched from oblivion. In his youth Boiardo had been a successful imitator of Petrarca's love strains. Evidence of his more severe attainments is furnished in an "Istoria Imperiale", some versions from Nepos, Apuleius, Herodotus, Xenophon, etc., and by his Latin Eclogues. A comedy, "Il Timone" (1487?), adds little to his credit. See BERNI.

SOLERTI, *Le Poesie volgari e latine di Matteo Maria Boiardo* (Bologna, 1894); SOLERTI, *Orlando Furioso di Ariosto*, ed. ANTONIO PANIZZI (London, 1830); FERRARI, CAMPANINI, AND OTHERS, *Studi su Matteo Maria Boiardo* (Bologna, 1894); TAPPERT, *Bilder und Vergleiche aus dem Orlando innamorato* (Marburg, 1886); NEPPI, *La pluralità degli amori cantati dal Boiardo nel canzoniere*, in *Giornale storico di lett. Ital.*, XLII, 360–373; RAZZOLI, *Per le fonti dell' Orlando innamorato* (Milan, 1901). UGO FOSCOLO's views on the poet are found in Q. Rev., n. 62, 527; and LEIGH HUNT's in *Stories from the Italian Poets* (London, 1846). ALSOP (New York, 1806) and ROSE (Edinburgh, 1823) have published fragmentary translations of Berni's recast.

EDOARDO SAN GIOVANNI.

Boil, BERNARDO. See BUIL, BERNARDO.

Boileau-Despréaux, NICHOLAS, French poet, b. at Paris, 1 November, 1636; d. there, 13 March, 1711. He was educated at the college of Beauvais and was at first destined to enter the Church, but soon abandoned the study of theology and, to please his father, prepared himself for the Bar. Though admitted as counsellor-at-law (December, 1656), he never practised and his father having died leaving him enough to satisfy his wants, he devoted himself entirely to poetry. He was then twenty-one years old. Four years later he published his first satirical poem: "Adieux d'un poète à la ville de Paris"; immediately after this he published six others: "Les embarras de Paris", "La satire à Molière", "Le repas ridicule", "La noblesse", and two others of minor importance. In these satires not only did Boileau parody and attack such writers as Cotin, Chapelain, and Le Voyer, but he also developed the practical capabilities of the French language. Prose, in the hands of such writers as Descartes and Pascal, had proved itself a flexible instrument of expression, while with the exception of Malherbe, there had been no system in French versification.

Enfin Malherbe vint et, le premier en France, Fit sentir dans les vers une juste cadence.

Above all, these satires inaugurated in France a systematic literary criticism for art's sake, where previously criticism had been nothing but the expression of envy or anger. Indeed, in these imitations of Juvenal and Horace, one recognizes a judge of his own masters, who judged them by a higher standard than his personal tastes. In 1660 Boileau published the "Epistles", more serious in tone and also more polished in style. In 1674 appeared "Le lutrin" which, lighter in tone, still deserves a certain degree of admiration. It furnished the model for the "Rape of the Lock", but the English poem is superior in richness and imagination. His masterpiece, however, and that of the didactic school in French, was without doubt, "L'art poétique". This was also the first code of French versification. It comprises four books, the first and the last containing general precepts; the second treating of the pastoral, the elegy, the ode, the epigram, and the satire; and the third of tragic and epic poetry. His later publications were chiefly poems which he composed to defend himself against the numerous enemies his satires had raised up against him.

The end of Boileau's life was sad. He suffered a great deal from an operation which he underwent while young, and which, together with deafness, obliged him to retire from public life and even from the society of his friends. The death of Racine, his very best friend (1699), affected him deeply and his thoughts turned strongly towards religion. He was preparing a new edition of his works when death called him away. He holds a well-defined place in French literature as the first to introduce a regular system into its method of versification.

DESMAISEAUX, *La vie de Boileau-Despréaux* (1712); ALEMBERT, *Eloge de Despréaux* (1779); CHAUFÉPIÉ, *Dictionnaire*, s. v. *Boileau*; GARNIER, *Œuvres complètes* (1860); FABRE, *Eloges de Boileau Despréaux* (1805); PORTIEN, *Essai sur Boileau Despréaux* (1805)

M. DE MOREIRA.

Boise, DIOCESE OF (*Xylopolitana*), created by Leo XIII, 25 August, 1893, embraces the whole State of Idaho, U. S. A., an area of 84,290 square miles. In 1842 a mission was started among the Cœur d'Alène Indians (whom Father De Smet, S.J., had recently visited) by Father Nicholas Point, S.J., and Brother Charles Huet, S.J. Father Joset followed next. The first Catholic church in Idaho was built sixteen miles from Cœur d'Alène Lake by the Jesuit Fathers Gazzoli and Ravalli, aided by the red men. In its construction wooden pegs were used instead of nails. In 1863, the pioneer secular priests, the Rev. Toussaint Mesplié, a Frenchman, and the Rev. A. Z. Poulin, a Canadian, were successively sent to the placer miners of Boisé Basin by Archbishop F. N. Blanchet, first administrator of Idaho Territory. Within six months they built the first churches erected for white people in Idaho City, Placerville, Centerville, and Pioneer; and later, a school at Idaho City, of which Sisters of the Holy Names, from Portland, Oregon, took charge. Father J. M. Cataldo, S.J., made unsuccessful advances to the Nez Percés in 1867. Recalled by them in 1872, he soon baptized three hundred of these fierce warriors. In 1876, Father Gazzoli drew many to the Faith by his remarkable medical skill. Interrupted by the Nez Percés war (1877), the work has since been successfully carried on, Archbishop Seghers' visits in 1879–83 having given it a new impetus. The Holy See, 3 March, 1868, established Idaho as a vicariate Apostolic and placed it in charge of the Right Rev. Louis Lootens who was consecrated Titular Bishop of Castabala, at San Francisco, 9 August, 1868. Born in Bruges, Belgium, 17 March, 1827, he emigrated to Victoria in 1852, and spent nine years as a missionary in Vancouver Island and six in California. The new vicar Apostolic reached Idaho in January, 1869, and took up his abode at Granite Creek. In 1870 the first Catholic church was erected in the capital by Fathers Mesplié and Poulin, on a site donated by John A. O'Farrell, Col. A. St. Clair, commander of Fort Boisé, being the priests' main helper in this laborious work. It was scarcely dedicated, however, when it was burned down. Bishop Lootens resigned 16 July, 1875, and died 13 January, 1898. He was succeeded by the second vicar Apostolic, the Right Rev. Alphonsus Joseph Glorieux, consecrated at Baltimore, Maryland, titular Bishop of Apollonia, 19 April, 1885. He found in his territory about 2,500 Catholics with ten churches attended by two secular and several Jesuit priests. When Boise was made an episcopal see he was transferred thither as its first bishop, 26 August, 1893.

The diocese has fifty-four churches and chapels, 34 priests, 7 academies, and 5 parochial schools, with 950 pupils; 2 industrial and reform schools with 150 inmates; 3 hospitals and a Catholic population of about 15,000, mostly of Irish and German racial affiliations, a sprinkling of Canadians, and 4,000 Indians. On 11 November, 1906, the corner-stone of a fine cathedral was laid near the new episcopal residence. Among the pioneer priests who did splendid missionary work here were Fathers L. Verhaag, E. Nattini, F. Hartleib, W. Hendrickx, and C. Van der Donckt, the last being the first priest ordained for Idaho in 1887, and stationed at Pocatello since June, 1888. The academies and parochial schools are conducted respectively by the Sisters of the Holy Cross, of St. Joseph, of the Visitation, of Charity, of Providence, of St. Benedict, and of the Immaculate Heart of Mary.

VAN DER DONCKT, *The Founders of the Church in Idaho* in the *Eccles. Review*, XXXII, Nos. 1, 2, 3; SHEA, *Hist. Cath. Ch. in U. S.* (New York, 1894); REUSS, *Biographical Encycl. of the Cath. Hierarchy* (Milwaukee, Wisconsin).

C. VAN DER DONCKT.

Boisgelin, JEAN DE DIEU-RAYMOND DE CUCÉ DE, French prelate and cardinal, b. of an ancient family at Rennes in Brittany, 27 February, 1732; d. 22 August, 1804. Destined from his early youth to the ecclesiastical state, he achieved remarkable success in his studies. The death of his elder brother made him the head of his family, but, giving up his birthright, he consecrated his life to the Church. First made Vicar-General of Pontoise, he was in 1765 raised to the Bishopric of Lavaur, and in 1770 to the archiepiscopal See of Aix in Provence. In this last position he won for himself the name of skilful administrator and princely benefactor. Provence owes to him the digging of a canal bearing his name, several works of public utility, such as a bridge at Lavaur and educational institutions for poor children. When in a time of scarcity and of political ferment, at the outset of the French Revolution, Aix was threatened with violence and famine, the archbishop by his

firmness, great ascendancy, wisdom, and generosity, proved its saviour. The mob had pillaged the public granaries, and had answered by insults the summons of authority; Boisgelin assembled the magistrates, chief citizens, and merchants, dispelled their fears, and prevailed upon these men to procure for Aix an abundant supply of grain, towards the payment of which he contributed one hundred thousand livres. He issued a pastoral letter to his clergy, asking them to urge the people to restore to the granaries the grain they had carried away. Where law had failed, religion and piety triumphed. The people obeyed and, flocking to the cathedral, expressed in touching terms their gratitude to the archbishop who was so absolutely devoted to their welfare.

Boisgelin was elected to represent the higher clergy of his province at the States-General, 1789. In that famous assembly his practical political wisdom and moderation appeared on many occasions; he voted, in the name of the clergy, for the union of the three orders, the abolition of feudal rights, and offered 400,000 livres to the public treasury; but he opposed the abolition of tithes and the confiscation of church property. His political sagacity and eloquence made him the recognized leader and spokesman of thirty bishops, his colleagues in the assembly. He spoke the language of liberty and that of religion with equal eloquence; he would have every citizen share in the establishment and maintenance of the government, with his political rights as indestructible as his natural and civic rights. The majority of the assembly voted for the civil constitution, a constitution subversive of the government of the Church, and of its discipline, a constitution that denied the supreme jurisdiction of the pope, subjected ecclesiastics to the civil power, and decreed that all the members of the clergy, beginning with those in the assembly, should take the oath of allegiance to the constitution, under penalty of exile and the forfeiture of their salaries. This legislation placed the clergy between two evils, schism and dishonour on one side, dire poverty, exile, if not death, on the other. Boldly and firmly Boisgelin rose to champion the cause of the Church: "Let the law", he exclaimed in the assembly, "leave us our honour and liberty; take back your salaries." It was he who wrote the famous "Exposition of Principles", signed by all except four of the bishops of France, condemning the Civil Constitution of the Clergy; it was he who in the name of his colleagues corresponded during two years with Rome, he who in a letter, dated 3 May, 1791, proposed to the bishops to lay their resignations at the feet of Pius VI; in 1801 he effectively made to Pius VII the sacrifice not accepted by Pius VI. When persecutions drove him out of France he went to England. In his answer to a letter from Edmund Burke in which the orator expressed his admiration for the spirit of disinterestedness and dignity of character of the French episcopacy, he complains that he is expelled from France in the name of that liberty he had in perfect faith contributed to establish, and under whose protection he hoped to end his days.

Boisgelin returned to France when Napoleon restored peace to the Church and to France by his Concordat, 15 July, 1801. In 1802, he was raised to the archiepiscopal See of Tours and soon after created cardinal. Boisgelin who had displayed administrative qualities of a high order at Aix, was no less remarkable for his literary and oratorical talents. Simplicity, grace, and pathos characterize his eloquence. In 1776 he was chosen member of the French Academy. His works include: "Collection de diverses pièces en vers" (1783); "L'art de juger d'après l'analogie des idées" (1789); "Considérations sur la paix publique adressées aux chefs de la Révolution" (1791); "Exposition des principes sur la constitution du clergé" (1791); "Le Psalmiste, traduction des Psaumes en vers" (1799); "Traduction des Héroïdes d'Ovide" (1784). His complete works appeared in Paris, 1818.

De Bausset, *Notice historique sur Boisgelin* in *Biographie universelle* (Paris, 1812); Rohrbacher, *Histoire universelle de l'église catholique* (Paris, 1874); Sicard. *L'ancien clergé de France, avant et pendant la Révolution* (Paris, 1902); De Feller, *Biographie universelle* (Paris, 1847); Guérin, *Dictionnaire des dictionnaires* (Paris, 1892).

L. F. M. Dumont.

Boisil, Saint, superior of Melrose Abbey, d. 664. Almost all that is known of St. Boisil is learnt from Bede (Eccles. Hist., IV, xxvii, and Vita Cuthberti). He derived his information from Sigfrid, a monk of Jarrow, who had previously been trained by Boisil at Melrose. St. Boisil's fame is mainly due to his connexion with his great pupil, St. Cuthbert, but it is plain that the master was worthy of the disciple. Contemporaries were deeply impressed with Boisil's supernatural intuitions. When Cuthbert presented himself at Melrose, Boisil exclaimed "Behold a servant of the Lord", and he obtained leave from Abbot Eata to receive him into the community at once. When in the great pestilence of 664 Cuthbert was stricken down, Boisil declared he would certainly recover. Somewhat later Boisil himself, as he had foretold three years before, fell a victim to this terrible epidemic, but before the end came he predicted that Cuthbert would become a bishop and would effect great things for the Church. After his death Boisil appeared twice in a vision to his former disciple, Bishop Ecgberht. He is believed, on somewhat dubious authority, to have written certain theological works, but they have not been preserved. St. Boswell's, Roxburghshire, commemorates his name. His relics, like those of St. Bede, were carried off to Durham in the eleventh century by the priest Ælfred. In the early Calendars his day is assigned to 23 February, but the Bollandists treat of him on 9 September.

Acta SS., January, II and March, III; *Acta SS. Ben., Sæc,* II, p. 850; Stubbs in *Dict. Christ. Biog.*; Hunt in *Dict. Nat. Biog.*; Plummer in *Bede's Eccles. Hist.* (Oxford, 1896); Stanton, *Menology* (London, 1892), 318.

Herbert Thurston.

Bois-le-Duc, The Diocese of (Buscoducensis) lies within the Dutch province of Brabant, and is suffragan of Utrecht. The city of Bois-le-Duc (s'Hertogenbosch, or Hertzogenbusch—*Sylva Ducis*) was founded in 1184, but, with the surrounding territory, was included in the Diocese of Liège until 12 March, 1561. At that time, and in order to check the spread of Protestantism, Pius IV raised it to the dignity of a see, and made it suffragan to Mechlin. The first bishop was the illustrious theologian Francis Sonnius (1562–69), afterwards transferred to the See of Antwerp. His successors suffered not a little amid the political disorders and the disastrous wars of the last quarter of the sixteenth century. When after a long siege the city was captured by Prince Frederic Henry (14 Sept., 1629) and held in the name of the States-General, the sixth bishop, Michael Ophorius, was obliged to abandon his see, which he did in a solemn procession, surrounded by his clergy, and bearing with him a famous miraculous statue of the Blessed Virgin which he placed in safety at Brussels.

Joseph de Bergaigne (1638–47) was really little more than bishop in name. He was unable to assert his right to the office, and lived an exile from the see to which he was deeply attached, but which he beheld in the power of Dutch Calvinists. By the Treaty of Westphalia (1648) the entire territory of Bois-le-Duc was recognized as a permanent conquest of the seventeen united provinces, and made directly subject to their jurisdiction, i. e. to the States-General. The exercise of the Catholic religion was forbidden by law, and the pertinent decrees were applied with all possible rigour in the hope of extirpating the ancient Faith. Catholic priests, however, continued secretly their ministry of preaching and their administration of the sacraments, while their flocks met with invincible patience the storm of persecution. The diocese became a simple mission, governed by a vicar-Apostolic, nearly always, however, a titular bishop.

Bois-le-Duc was administered in this fashion until 1853. Napoleon had tried (1810) to create another diocese under that name, inclusive of the territory known as Bouches du Rhin, and had even obtained a titular for the new see in the person of the imperial courtier, Monsignor Van Camp, but the latter was despised by all good Catholics, and the arbitrary act of the emperor was doomed to failure. A similar failure awaited the attempt, authorized by the Concordat of 27 August, 1827, to divide all Holland into two large dioceses, Amsterdam and Bois-le-Duc. The ancient see was finally revived by Pius IX on the occasion of the restoration of the hierarchy in Holland, where, since 1848, the revised constitution has assured to Catholics full political and religious liberty. Together with three other Dutch sees, Bois-le-Duc was re-established by the pontifical Brief of 4 March, 1853, and with its former limits; all four sees were made suffragan to Utrecht. The Right Rev. Jan Zwÿsen, a native of the diocese and its most illustrious son, hitherto vicar-Apostolic, was the first bishop of the re-established see, though temporarily he was known as administrator-Apostolic, since he was already Archbishop of Utrecht, with which office he was to unite the government of Bois-le-Duc.

In 1865 the first provincial synod was held there, the decrees of which form the actual ecclesiastical discipline in all the dioceses of Holland, and exhibit Archbishop Zwÿsen as the true organizer of the ecclesiastical order in that country. In 1868 he was allowed to resign the archiepiscopal See of Utrecht. Thenceforth, until his death in 1877, he devoted himself to the administration of his beloved See of Bois-le-Duc. He was succeeded by the Right Rev. Adrian Godschalk, who died in 1892, leaving the see to be filled by Bishop William van den Ven. The cathedral of Bois-le-Duc, dedicated to St. John the Evangelist, is the finest monument of medieval Gothic in the possession of the Catholics of Holland. Though it was almost entirely rebuilt after the conflagration of 1419, it had again suffered notable decay in succeeding centuries. A thorough restoration of the edifice, however, was later begun. Bois-le-Duc had a collegiate chapter as early as 1360, which was made a cathedral chapter in 1561. The above-mentioned miraculous statue of the Blessed Virgin has been restored to the cathedral and is once more the object of general devotion. There are two diocesan seminaries, one at St. Michiels-Gestel for preparatory studies and the other at Haaren for philosophy and theology. The diocese includes 451,670 Catholics, 260 parishes, 625 priests, 143 charitable institutions, and 476 free (Catholic) schools.

Foppens, *Historia episcopatus Sylvæducensis* (Brussels, 1721); Coppens, *Nieuwe beschryving van het bisdom s'Hertogenbosch* (Bois-le-Duc, 1840–44), i–iv; Hezenmans, *De St. Janskerk te s'Hertogenbosch en hare geschiedenis* (Bois-le-Duc, 1866); Albers, *Geschiedenis van het herstel der hierarchie in de Nederlanden* (Nymegen, 1903–1904), i–ii; *Neerlandia catholica* (Utrecht, 1888).

Gisbert Brom.

Boismenu, Alan de. See New Guinea, Archdiocese of.

Bokenham (or Bokenam), Osbern, English Augustinian friar and poet, b. 1393 (the year in which the most famous of English Augustinians, John Capgrave, was also born); d. probably, in 1447. The assertion of Horstmann, his German editor, that Bokenham was born at Bookham, Surrey, appears to be contradicted by the friar's own statement that his birthplace was in the vicinity of a "pryory of blake [black] canons" which Mr. Sydney Lee (Dict. Nat. Biogr., V, 314) identifies with a famous house of Augustinian canons at Bokenham, now Old Buckenham, Norfolk. Bokenham may or may not have got some early schooling from these "blake canons", but he certainly spent five years as a young man in Italy, chiefly at Venice, making frequent pilgrimages to the great Italian centres of devotional life, Rome, of course, among them. His long residence in Italy, in a generation to which the memory of Petrarch (d. 1374) was still recent, must have been in itself something of a liberal education. Bokenham is known to have read both Cicero and Ovid—classical accomplishments not by any means a matter-of-course with young Englishmen destined to the ecclesiastical state in those days. Lydgate (d. 1451?) was among his contemporaries; Gower (d. 1402) and Chaucer (d. 1400) had been living in England in his boyhood, and had demonstrated the splendid possibilities of a language which for more than three centuries had been a mere rustic vernacular. His admission to the Order of Hermit-Friars of St. Augustine, whatever the exact date, certainly fell within the period of that order's greatest intellectual activity in England, when Dr. John Lowe (d., Bishop of Rochester, 1436) was making such valuable additions to the great Austin-Friars library in London. Bockenham finally became a professed religious in the Augustinian convent at Stoke Clare, Suffolk.

His writings were chiefly religious in theme and feeling. A "Dialogue" (printed in vol. VI of Dugdale's "Monasticon"), on the genealogy of a great Suffolk family, is attributed to Bokenham on internal evidence. The "Lyvys of Seyntys" he compiled chiefly from the "Legenda Aurea" of Jacobus à Voragine. These are the lives of twelve female saints, with an account of the legendary "11,000 virgins". Though valuable in a legendary sense, the "Lyvys of Seyntys" cannot be very seriously considered by modern hagiologists; but as illustrating the evolution of English literature, their historical value is inestimable. The language, described by its author as "of Suthfolke speche", is forced into the exotic form of *ottava rima*. This work, preserved among the Arundel MSS. in the British Museum, was printed for the Roxburghe Club in 1835; but Horstmann's edition (vol. I of Kölbing's "Altenglische Bibliothek") had appeared at Heilbronn two years earlier. Bokenham's ideas of religious humility are curiously illustrated by his using the names of several contemporary ladies of high rank as *noms de plume* to cover his own authorship.

Dict. of Nat. Biogr. (London and New York, 1886), V, s. v.; STEELE, *Monasteries and Religious Houses* (London, New York, etc., 1903). The two printed editions of Bokenham's poem furnish material for critical study of the author.

E. MACPHERSON.

Bolanden, CONRAD VON (JOSEPH BISCHOFF), a German novelist, son of a rich merchant, b. 9 August, 1828, at Niedergeilbach, a village of the Palatinate. He attended the Latin school at Blieskastel, the seminary at Speyer, and in 1849 entered the University of Munich to study theology. Ordained priest in 1852 he was appointed assistant pastor at the cathedral. Two years later he became pastor at Kirchheim Bolanden whence his pen name "Conrad von Bolanden". The following year he was transferred to Börrstadt and three years later to Berghausen. During this time he wrote his first four works: "A Wedding Trip", "Queen Bertha", "Historical Tales of Frederick II", and "Gustav Adolf". In 1870 he resigned his parish to devote himself exclusively to literary work, and lived in strict retirement at Speyer. He published numerous novels of which the most noteworthy are: "Canossa", "Trowel

or Cross", "Night of St. Bartholomew", "Savonarola", "Crusades", "Wambold", "Charlemagne", "Otto the Great", "Pillar of Truth".

His novels and romances, though not all of equal worth, are written for the people, brilliant in conception, simple in style. He fearlessly defends the Catholic standpoint and supports his position by frequent quotations from original sources. But in discussing questions of the day his criticisms are often severe and unjust. His works are widely read and have been translated into English and other European languages.

The Catholic World, XVII, 308; KEITER, *Katholische Erzähler*, 131.

B. DIERINGER.

Boleslaw. See POLAND.

Bolgeni, GIOVANNI VINCENZO, theologian and controversialist, b. at Bergamo, Italy, 22 January, 1733; d. at Rome, 3 May, 1811. He entered the Society of Jesus, 31 October, 1747, taught philosophy and theology with marked success at Macerata and was a member of the Society when it was suppressed by Clement XIV. Henceforth he devoted himself to controversy and in recognition of his signal services against Jansenism and Josephinism, Pius VI appointed him Theologian-Penitentiary, an office of which he was deprived by Pius VII on account of the Jacobin principles he tolerated and advocated during the occupation of Rome by Napoleon I.

Of Bolgeni's theological writings, the best known and at the same time the least fortunate was his "Della carità o amor di Dio" (Rome, 1788). In it he endeavoured to refute the Dominican, de Rubeis, by demonstrating that the theological virtue of charity essentially consists in loving God as He is good to us and not as He is absolute goodness. This position won for him misrepresentation at the hands of Teofilo Cristiani, fictitious author of "Lettera teologico-critica sull' amore di Dio" (1791) and opposition from his former Jesuit comrades, Mazzarelli (1790–91), Regono (1791), Cortes (1790–93), Chantre y Herrera (1790–92) and Gentilini (1803). Against Cristiani he successfully disposed of the charge that he held purely servile fear a sufficient motive for attrition, but the arguments of his other adversaries he met at first with more subtlety than precision, and later with silence. He did not attempt to answer the searching criticism of his doctrine contained in Palestrina's "Idea genuina della carità o amor di Dio" (1800). In addition to his original work he contributed to the controversy, "Schiarimenti in confermazione e difesa della sua dissertazione" (Rome, 1788; Foligno, 1790), and "Apologia dell' amor di Dio detto di concupiscenza" (Foligno, 1792). Though practically defeated in this dispute Bolgeni's presentation of his case proved that he was endowed with controversial talents of no mean order, and these he used with telling effect in his writings on moral subjects and on matters which may be classed as politico-theological. As Theologian-Penitentiary he edited a novel defence of probabilism under the caption, "Il posesso, principio fondamentale per decidere i casi morali". The second part of this work, "Dissertazione seconda fra le morali sopra gli atti umani" (Cremona, 1816; Orvieto, 1853), together with a treatise on usury, published under his name but probably not written by him, appeared after his death. The defence of probabilism aroused a storm of controversy, and among the noted anti-probabilists who engaged in the discussion may be mentioned the Bishop of Asissi (1798) Agapitus de Palestrina, O. Min. Ref. (1799), Cajetan Maria de Fulgore (1798), Canon John Trinch of the Cathedral of Tivoli (1850), and Montbach (1857). Of these Trinch added to his "Il Bolgenismo Confutato" a "digression on the necessity of confessing all mortal sins, whether certain or doubtful, just as they are in conscience."

The remaining productions of Bolgeni are chiefly devoted to attacks on Jansenism, Josephinism, and Jacobinism. Not long after the suppression of the Society of Jesus he entered the lists with the Society's traditional enemy, Jansenism, by publishing "Esame della vera idea della Santa Sede" (Macerata, 1785; Foligno, 1791), a work undertaken in refutation of the Jansenistic doctrines contained in "La Vera Idea della Santa Sede" by Pietro Tamburini, a celebrated professor of the University of Pavia. Several replies to the criticisms of Tamburini and to the censures of the Archpriest Guadagnini were published in rapid succession. In 1787, he wrote "Stato de' bambini morti senza battesimo", and in it scored the rigid doctrine of Guadagnini that infants dying without baptism are doomed to the torments of Hell. This controversy over, he devoted his pen to defending the juridical powers of the hierarchy, cataloguing the errors of the day, and combating the principles of Josephinism in Austria and of the Revolution in France. His publications at this period were: "Fatti dommatici ossia dell'infallibilità della Chiesa nel decidere sulla dottrina buona, o cattiva de' libri" (Brescia, 1788); "Specchio istorico da servire di preservativo contra gli errori correnti" (1789); "L'episcopato ossia della potestà di governare la Chiesa" (1789). These literary labours led to his appointment by Pius VI as Theologian-Penitentiary and in this capacity he issued a defence of "L'episcopato" (Rome, 1791), and "Dissertazione sulla giurisdizione ecclesiastica" (Rome, 1791), a refutation of George Sicard's contention that the powers of orders and jurisdiction were identical. About the same time he renewed his attacks on Guadagnini and Tamburini, refuting the former's state-deifying proclivities in "L'Economia della Fede Cristiana" (Brescia, 1790), and the latter's anti-ecclesiasticism in "Problema se i Giansenisti siano Giacobini" (Rome, 1794). "L'Economia della Fede Cristiana" was of such merit that it was incorporated by Migne in his "Démonstrations Evangéliques", vol. XVIII.

The last phase of Bolgeni's life is to say the least a strange one. After Napoleon I had seized Rome, Bolgeni, with wellnigh unintelligible inconsistency, favoured the anti-regal oath of allegiance imposed by the conqueror. This change of front he defended vigorously and subtly, but vainly. He was obliged to make a retractation in the presence of the cardinals assembled at Vienna for the election of a pope; "Ritrattazione di Gio. Vincenzo Bolgeni diretta a Monsignor Illmo. e Rmo. Vicegerente di Roma". His writings during this unfortunate stage of his career were: "Parere sul giuramento civico" (Rome, 1798); "Sentimenti de' professori della università del Collegio Romano sopra il giuramento prescritto dalla Republica Romana" (Rome, an. VII); "Sentimenti sul giuramento civico" (Rome, an. VII); "Metamorfosi del dott. Gio. Marchetti, da penitenziere mutato in penitente" (1800); "Parere . . . sull'alienazione de' beni ecclesiastici"; "Schiarimenti" to confirm the preceding. After his death a work was edited, believed by some to be from his pen, "Dei limiti delle due potestà ecclesiastica e secolare" (Florence, 1849), and it was put on the Index *donec corrigatur*. It is most probably unauthentic.

HURTER, *Nomenclator*, III, 530; DE BACKER, *Bibl. des écriv. de la c. de J.*, II, 70; BERNARD in *Dict. de théol. cath.*, s. v.; SOMMERVOGEL, *Bibl. de la c. de J.*, I, 1161; *Civiltà cattolica* (1850), II, 451; PALMIERI, *De pœnitentiâ*, 234.

J. T. LANGAN.

Bolivia, a South American republic which lies between longitudes west of Greenwich 57° 30' and 74°, and latitudes 8° and 22° 50' south. These figures are, however, still subject to treaty changes.

AREA, POPULATION, ETC.—The republic covers an area of 702,767 sq. miles (1,822,334 sq. kilometers) and ranks as third in size among the South American countries. In 1905 its population was estimated at 1,816,271, or a little more than five persons to every two square miles. Of these, 231,088 are reported as whites; 484,611 as mestizos, and 792,850 as Indians. Besides these, there were about 4,000 negroes, and the residue are of unascertained origin. The proportion of Catholics to non-Catholics is approximately as seventy-two to one. All these figures are to be taken with reserve, since the efforts at serious statistics are but very recent.

Since the close of the war with Chile in 1881, Bolivia has had no sea-coast. It is bounded on the west, north-west, and north by Peru; on the north-east and east by Brazil; on the south-east by Paraguay; on the south by the Argentine Republic, and on the south-west by Chile. Its communications with the outer world were still defective in 1905. A line of steamers on Lake Titicaca then plied between the Peruvian port of Puno and the Bolivian of Huaqui, and stage lines, between La Paz and the Chilian frontier. On the east side of the Andes, in the Basin of the Amazon, rivers, which are often interrupted in their upper course by rapids (*cachuelas*), afford the only means of transit. Bolivia had two short railroad lines of its own, besides the Chilian line to Oruro, of which the terminus is upon

A STREET IN LA PAZ

Bolivian soil. The two Bolivian railroads were trunk-lines, with an aggregate length of sixty-five miles. Work was, however, progressing on several other newly begun lines.

Bolivia is divided into nine departments and a "National Territory of Colonies", the area of which covers somewhat less than one-third of the whole surface of the republic, while its population is only one-sixtieth of the whole. Of the nine departments, La Paz is the most populous. Since 1899 the national capital has been La Paz de Ayacucho, with a population of 59,014 souls, situated in this department. Next to La Paz in importance is Cochabamba with 21,886 inhabitants. Sucre and Potosí are reported with 20,900 each, and Santa Cruz de la Sierra with 18,000, while the important mining centre of Oruro has a little over 15,000 inhabitants.

NATURAL FEATURES AND RESOURCES.—The southwestern third of the country lies at a great altitude above the Pacific Ocean. The Puna, or table-land comprised within the Departments of La Paz, Oruro, and Potosí, has an average elevation of nearly 13,000 feet. Two lofty mountain ranges form natural breastworks to Bolivia: in the West, the Coast Cordillera (Chilian frontier) and, in the East, the Bolivian chain, consisting of the Andes of Carabaya and Apolobamba towards the North, and the Royal Cordillera or central Bolivian range, with its southern ramifications and prolongations to the Argentine lines. The mountainous section of Bolivia has no important rivers. Its drainage is in the North to Lake Titicaca, which itself empties to the South into the Lago (Lake) Poópó, which has no visible outlet. Towards the East mountain streams descend abruptly into the Basin of the Amazon. But the mountainous section has the two largest, and also most elevated lakes of South America: Titicaca,

able ores. Gold is not generally distributed, and is extracted mainly by "placer" mining, as for instance at Chuquiaguillo, near La Paz. In the first half of the nineteenth century the Tipuani district, so difficult of access, was productive of gold of great fineness, and in quantities very considerable for that time, and the Tipuani mines are even now far from exhausted. Quartz gold is worked at Araca. Silver is very plentiful, and is extensively extracted in places. Native copper is mined at Corocoro, where it crops out in veins of unusual richness and width, but other copper ores are found in abundance also. Of late it has been established that Bolivia is probably one of the countries in the world, where tin (cassiterite) is most abundant, and the same may be said of bismuth. While on the eastern slope of the Andes the existence of gold and other mineral wealth has been proved, the attention of prospectors and miners has been turned chiefly towards the mountains themselves. The processes of mining and treatment of the ores are still, in many places, rudimentary and primitive, but with the influx of

MISSION CONVENT ON THE RIVER BENI

12,500 feet above sea-level, 138 miles long from northwest to south-east, and of varying width, and Poópó, farther south. The eastern two-thirds of Bolivia, that section lying towards the Atlantic, is traversed by mighty streams (e. g. the Beni and Mamoré) and their affluents, all of which rise in the central Bolivian chain. Bolivia has properly but two seasons: winter, corresponding in time to summer and part of fall and spring in the Northern Hemisphere, and summer embracing the rest of the year.

The mineral resources of this republic are known to be very important, but as yet they have been only superficially prospected. Difficulty of access to the country, unsettled political conditions in former times, and cumbersome, primitive transportation have been the main cause of this backwardness. The upper regions of the Amazonian Basin are known to contain coal, but there attention has been given chiefly to the vegetable resources, the India rubber tree having rendered possible the establishment of a highly important and growing industry. The same section, also, produces both coffee and sugar, and to-day the coca shrub is a staple, while calisaya bark is returning into favour. The highlands in the departments of La Paz, Oruro, Potosí, parts of Cochabamba and Tarija abound in a variety of valu-

foreign capital and the introduction of machinery, conditions are rapidly improving. On the shores of Lake Titicaca bituminous coal is found both east and west of that lake. Besides mining, the chief industry of the mountain region is agriculture. As this branch is almost entirely in the hands of the Indians, it will be treated in connexion with the ethnography of Bolivia.

The Amazon Basin and its forests, as well as open spaces with high grass, are full of animal life. The large rivers, as everywhere in tropical South America, teem with fish, crocodiles, snakes, and other amphibia, and the manatee also occurs. Aquatic birds, parrots, etc., are abundant. The fauna of the mountain districts is more in evidence, but much poorer in species and individuals, than in the adjacent countries. The llama and its congeners, the alpaca, vicuña, and guanaco, belong to the Bolivian fauna. The llama and alpaca are domesticated by the Indian. Beasts of prey are not numerous and are found only within the limits of arboreal vegetation. Lower down the great ant-eater is occasionally seen, the puma and the bear (*Ursus ornatus*). In southern Bolivia, as well as in the eastern sections, the American ostrich occurs, and a tiny armadillo has its home in the cold, arid Puna.

south of Lake Titicaca. Over the highest peaks soars the condor.

GOVERNMENT, THE CHURCH, AND EDUCATION.— Bolivia, then the Spanish colony of *Alto Peru*, or Upper Peru, declared its intention to achieve political independence 16 July, 1809, and actually became an autonomous republic 6 August, 1825, taking its name in honour of Simon Bolivar, its founder. The Constitution under which the republic is now governed dates from 28 October, 1880, and aims at a "unitarian republican" polity. Under this Constitution the legislative power is vested in a Congress which comprises a Chamber of Deputies and a Senate, the former body consisting of 72 members elected by direct popular vote for terms of four years, the latter of 16 members also elected by direct popular vote, but for terms of six years. The executive power is vested in a president, elected by direct popular vote for a term of four years. The president, however, can exercise his authority only through his Cabinet, which consists of five *Ministros de Estado*, jointly responsible with him for all his official acts. Under this chief executive the civil government of the country is carried on by prefects of Departments, appointed by it and directly responsible to it, and they in turn have under their jurisdiction sub-prefects and *Corregidores* for the subdivisions of Departments. The revenue of the republic for 1905 was stated at 7,928,730 bolivianos (1 boliviano = $0.422 in United States currency).

By Article 2 of the Constitution of Bolivia, "The State recognizes and supports the Roman Apostolic Catholic religion, the public exercise of any other worship being prohibited, except in the colonies, where it is tolerated". For the support of Catholic worship in general the State pays the sum of 182,027 bolivianos ($76,815 U. S. currency), besides 14,000 bolivianos ($5,908) for missions to the aboriginal tribes. There is one archbishopric, Sucre, or Charcas, formerly La Plata, with 146 parishes, three colleges of the Propagation of the Faith, and five monasteries. The suffragan bishoprics are: La Paz, with 102 parishes, and 5 monasteries; Cochabamba, with 69 parishes and 4 convents, and Santa Cruz, divided into 73 parishes. Both La Paz and Santa Cruz were erected into bishoprics in 1605, the Archbishopric of Charcas was founded 1609, and the Diocese of Cochabamba in 1847. Efforts are kept up to gather the unsettled tribes of the Amazon Basin into permanent settlements (reductions), a very slow and difficult task.

The legal status of marriage is thus summed up in Art. 99 of the Civil Code of Bolivia: "Matrimony being in the Republic elevated to the dignity of a sacrament, the formalities necessary for its celebration will be the same as those which the Council of Trent and the Church have designated." Bolivian law recognizes no divorce permitting re-marriage, and all questions arising between husband and wife can be decided only by the ecclesiastical tribunals.

ETHNOGRAPHY.—The comparatively small proportion of whites among the Bolivian population makes of the Indian the numerically preponderant stock. The mestizos, while not disclaiming their partly white origin, sometimes stand, in the country and among the lower classes in towns and cities, but slightly higher than the aborigines, being distinguished from the latter mostly by the fact that they wear European costume. Of the Indians several linguistic stocks inhabit the country. The roaming tribes of the Amazon lowlands are neither numerous nor important enough to deserve mention here. But in the mountains two powerful stocks, sedentary, agricultural, and pastoral ever since they have been known to the whites, form the working lower class of the people of Bolivia. These stocks are the Quichua and the Aymará. These two large tribes

II.—40

may, perhaps be about equally numerous. The Quichua occupy southern Bolivia and the Andean districts adjacent to Lake Titicaca on the East; the Aymará hold the upper valleys of the Andes, the West, and the centre. Physiologically, no great difference in type exists. They are, first of all, husbandmen, in fact they control agriculture. Nearly all agricultural lands being held by whites or mestizos, who do not themselves cultivate, but prefer to live in settlements following some trade or commerce, the Indians, who are settled everywhere, take care of the fields. This they do, either in a kind of serfdom, living on the property and performing, also, some personal services for the proprietors, or, as Indian communities settled near the land, they have a tacit lease of it. The Indians organized in communities according to their primitive customs control the land, through their labour, virtually more than the owners, and thus remain a power in the republic, since they are the feeders of the people. Their serfdom is much more apparent than real, for the masters depend upon them for subsistence. Some alimentary plants in the high regions are potatoes, quinua, oca, etc., as well as maize in districts suitable for its growth, with coarse beans (*habas*) and barley, the last two being of European origin. The Indians raise cattle for themselves and sometimes for the landowners. All their farming is done in a primitive and very slovenly way. Next to agriculture, transportation and

CATHEDRAL AT COPACABANA

personal service in housework are also in the hands of the Indians. In fact their silent influence pervades the whole of public and private life; their industrial methods are obsolete, and they resist improvement with the greatest tenacity.

As the Indian has maintained his primitive organization with few changes, he might form a State within the State, and thus become a grave danger to the whites. But as he never had any conception of a State, being, moreover, divided into autonomous or independent tribes, that danger is much diminished. Neither the Aymará nor the Quichua could coalesce to form a homogeneous body. This they have shown ever since the Spanish occupation, and during the most alarming of their attempted uprisings, such as that of 1781. They would like to return to their primitive condition of barbarism, but feel that, despite their vast superiority of numbers, they are virtually powerless. In addition to these two principal Indian groups, the mountain districts still shelter the Uros, feeble remnants of a tribe dwelling among rushes and reeds, and comparatively little known. Of the white population of Bolivia little need be said that is not applicable generally to the whites in other South American countries. They differ of course from the inhabitants of less mountainous countries in that they have the general characteristics common to all mountaineers.

(For special information on the individual dioceses, aboriginal tribes, languages, etc., of Bolivia, see articles under separate headings.)

INTERNATIONAL BUREAU OF THE AMERICAN REPUBLICS, *Bolivia* (Washington, D. C., 1904); RENÉ MORENO, *Biblioteca Boliviana* (Santiago, Chile, 1879). Of the latter very full and very reliable book a supplement was issued by the author in 1899, and VALENTÍN ABEICIA published *Adiciones*, in 1902. These Chilian publications are not very easy to obtain; easier of access is *Geografía de la República de Bolivia* (La Paz, 1905). The colonial history of Bolivia is so intimately connected with that of Peru that the early sources touching the former are also those for the latter. Of general works from the sixteenth and seventeenth century, GOMARA, ACOSTA, HERRERA, GARCÍA are of course indispensable for consultation.

AD. F. BANDELIER.

Bollandists, THE, an association of ecclesiastical scholars engaged in editing the Acta Sanctorum. This work is a great hagiographical collection begun during the first years of the seventeenth century, and continued to our own day. The collaborators are called Bollandists, as being successors of Bolland, the editor of the first volume. The collection now numbers sixty-three volumes in folio, to which must be added a supplementary volume, published in 1875 by a French priest, and containing chiefly certain tables and directions facilitating research in the volumes which had appeared at that time. Although Bolland has given his name to the work, he is not to be regarded as its founder. The idea was first conceived by Heribert Rosweyde (b. at Utrecht, 1569; d. at Antwerp, 1629). He entered the Society of Jesus in 1588. An indefatigable worker and a fearless but judicious investigator, notwithstanding his duties as professor of philosophy in the Jesuit college at Douai during the last years of the sixteenth century, Rosweyde devoted the leisure of his vacations and holidays to exploring the libraries of the numerous monasteries scattered through Hainault and French Flanders. He copied with his own hand a vast number of documents relating to church history in general, and to hagiography in particular, and found in the old texts contained in the manuscripts coming under his observation quite a different flavour from that of the revisions to which many editors, notably Lippomano and Surius, then the latest and most celebrated, had believed it necessary to subject them. Rosweyde thought it would be a useful work to publish the texts in their original form. His superiors, to whom he submitted his plan in 1603, gave it their hearty approval, and allowed him to prepare the projected edition, without, however, relieving him of any of the occupations on which he was expending his prodigious activity. So, for the time being, he was allowed merely the privilege of devoting his spare moments to the preparation of the work. Rosweyde did not cease to pursue his project, which he announced publicly in 1607, as well as the plan he proposed to follow. Under the title: "Fasti sanctorum quorum vitæ in belgicis bibliothecis manuscriptæ", he gave in a little volume in 16mo., published by the Plantin press at Antwerp, an alphabetical list of the names of the saints whose acts had been either found by him or called to his attention in old manuscript collections. This list filled fifty pages; the prefatory notice in which he indicates the character and arrangement of his work, as he had conceived it, takes up fourteen. Finally, the work contains an appendix of twenty-six pages containing the unpublished acts of the passion of the holy Cilician martyrs, Tharsacus, Probus, and Andronicus, which Rosweyde regarded—wrongly—as the authentic official report from the pen of a clerk of the court of the Roman tribunal. According to this programme the collection was to comprise sixteen volumes, besides two volumes of explanations and tables. The first volume was to present documents concerning the life of Jesus Christ and the feasts established in honour of the special events of His life; the second volume would be devoted to the life and the feasts of the Blessed Virgin, and the third to the feasts of the saints honoured with a more special cult. The twelve succeeding volumes were to give the lives of the saints whose feasts are celebrated respectively in the twelve months of the year, one volume for each month. This calendar arrangement had been prescribed by his superiors, in preference to the chronological order Rosweyde himself favoured. But this presented, especially at that time, formidable difficulties. Lastly, the sixteenth volume was to set forth the succession of martyrologies which had been in use at different periods and in the various Churches of Christendom. The first of the two supplementary volumes was to contain notes and commentaries bearing on the lives already published. It was to be divided into eight books treating respectively of the following subjects: (1) The authors of the lives; (2) the sufferings of the martyrs; (3) the images of the saints; (4) liturgical rites and customs mentioned in hagiographical documents; (5) profane customs to which allusions had been made; (6) questions of chronology; (7) names of places encountered in these same documents; (8) barbarous or obscure terms which might puzzle the readers. The other supplementary volume was to present a series of copious tables giving: (1) the names of the saints whose lives had been published in the preceding volumes; (2) the same names followed by notes indicating the place of the saint's birth, his station in life, his title to sanctity, the time and place in which he had lived, and the author of his life; (3) the state of life of the various saints (religious, priest, virgin, widow, etc.); (4) their position in the Church (apostle, bishop, abbot, etc.); (5) the nomenclature of the saints according to the countries made illustrious by their birth, apostolate, sojourn, burial; (6) nomenclature of the places in which they are honoured with a special cult; (7) enumeration of the maladies for the cure of which they are especially invoked; (8) the professions placed under their patronage; (9) the proper names of persons and places encountered in the published lives; (10) the passages of Holy Scripture there explained; (11) points which may be of use in religious controversies; (12) those applicable in the teaching of Christian doctrine; (13) a general table of words and things in alphabetical order. "And others still" adds the author, "if anything of importance presents itself, of which our readers may give us an idea."

Cardinal Bellarmine, to whom Rosweyde sent a copy of his little volume, could not forbear exclaiming after he had read this programme: "This man counts, then, on living two hundred years longer!" He addressed to the author a letter, the original of which is preserved in the present library of the Bollandists, signed, but not written, by the hand of Bellarmine, in which he intimates in polished but perfectly plain language that he regarded the plan as chimerical. Rosweyde was nowise disconcerted by this. From various other sources he received encouragement, enthusiastic praise, and valuable assistance. The new enterprise found an especial protector, as generous as he was zealous and enlightened, in Antoine de Wynghe, abbot of the celebrated monastery of Liessies in Hainault. Venerable Louis of Blois, whose third successor de Wynghe was, seemed to have bequeathed to him his affectionate devotion to the sons of St. Ignatius of Loyola. The large sympathy of this religious Mæcenas manifested itself in every way; in letters of recommendation to the heads of the various houses of the great Benedictine Order, which opened to Rosweyde and his associates monastic libraries; in loans and gifts of books, of manuscripts, and of copies of manuscripts; and in pecuniary assistance. Rosweyde quite counted on completing by his own efforts the monument of which he had dreamed, and on bringing it to a worthy end. As a matter of fact, he did not get beyond the first stages of the structure. His literary activity was expended on a multitude of historical works, both religious and polemical, some of which, it is true, would have later formed a part of the great hagiographical compilation. The majority, however, bear no relation whatever to the work. The writings which would have been available are: the edition of the Little Roman Martyrology, in which Rosweyde believed he recognized the collection mentioned by St. Gregory the Great in his letter to Eulogius of Alexandria; the edition of the martyrology of Ado of Vienne (1613); the ten books of the Lives of the Fathers of the Desert, which he first published in Latin (1615 in fol.), dedicating the work to the Abbot of Liessies, and later in Flemish (1617 in fol.), with an inscription to Jeanne de Bailliencourt, Abbess of Messines. The rest, however, as for instance the Flemish edition of Ribadeneira's "Flowers of the Saints" (1619, two folio volumes), the "General History of the Church" (1623), to which he added as an appendix the detailed history of the Church in the Netherlands, both in Flemish; the Flemish lives of St. Ignatius and St. Philip Neri; the Flemish translation of the first part of the "Treatise on Perfection", drew his attention completely from what he should have regarded as his principal task. It is due to him, however, to say that for several years his superiors, without ceasing to encourage him in the pursuit of his project, were forced through the necessity of filling vacant offices, to lay upon him duties which did not leave him the absolutely indispensable leisure. He set this forth clearly himself in the memorandum addressed to them in 1611, in response to their inquiry as to how he was progressing with the preparation of his volumes. But it is not less true that nearly all his publications, the most important of which have been mentioned above, are of a later date than this, and undoubtedly Rosweyde himself was chiefly to blame for the delay, which, however, may be called a fortunate one, since it resulted in advantageous modifications of the plan of the work. At the time of Rosweyde's death, then, which took place in Antwerp in 1629, not a page was ready for the printer. Moreover, the superiors of the order, on their part, hesitated to have the work carried on by another. For more than twenty years, however, Rosweyde had been extremely active; he had secured access to a quantity of manuscripts and had enlisted the co-operation of many learned men who had manifested the keenest interest in his undertaking; thanks to their assistance, he had collected many manuscripts and books relating to the lives of the saints; in a word, he had aroused an eager interest in his compilation, so great and so universal that it was necessary to satisfy it.

Father John van Bolland (b. at Julemont, in Limburg, 1596; d. at Antwerp, 12 September, 1665) was at this time prefect of studies in the college of Mechlin, and had charge of a congregation composed of the principal people of the city. It was called the "Latin Congregation", because all the exercises, sermons included, were conducted in that language. His family either took their name from, or gave it to, the village of Bolland, near Julemont. Before making his theological studies he had taught belles-lettres with distinction in the three higher classes of the humanities at Ruremonde, Mechlin, Brussels, and Antwerp. The superior of the Belgian province of the Society of Jesus bade him examine the papers left by Rosweyde, and report to him his opinion as to what it was advisable to do with them. Bolland

went to Antwerp, familiarized himself with the manuscripts, and, while admitting that the work was still merely a rough and faulty draft, gave reasons for believing that without an undue expenditure of labour it might be brought to a successful completion. He even showed himself disposed to take charge of the work, but only under two conditions: first, that he should be left free to modify the plan of Rosweyde as he understood it; second, that the copies, notes, and books which had been collected by Rosweyde should be removed from the library of the Professed House, where they were interspersed among the books in common use, and set apart in a place of their own for the exclusive use of the new director of the undertaking. The provincial,

JOHN VAN BOLLAND, S. J.

Jacques van Straten, accepted with alacrity both offer and conditions. Bolland was removed from the college of Mechlin and attached to the Professed House at Antwerp, to be director of the Latin Congregation and confessor in the church, and with the charge of preparing, in his leisure hours (*horis subsecivis*) the Acta Sanctorum for publication. Happily, he had not the least idea, any more than had the provincial, of all the undertaking involved. He fancied that he could finish it by his own unaided efforts, and that after the completion of the work proper and the preparation of historical, chronological, geographical, and other tables, as announced by Rosweyde, he could complete the publication by adding to it a comprehensive collection of notices of holy persons who flourished in the Church subsequent to the fifteenth century, but have not been honoured with a public cult. "And after all that is done", he wrote in his general preface, at the beginning of the first volume of January, "if I still have any time to live, I shall lend a charm to the leisure hours of my old age by gathering the ascetical doctrine found in the teachings of the saints recorded in this work." And nevertheless, he began by outlining a plan of quite another vastness from that of Rosweyde, whose programme had already appalled Bellarmine. Rosweyde had confined his quest of original texts to the libraries of Belgium and the neighbouring regions. He had not gone beyond Paris to the south, or Cologne and Trier to the east. Bolland made appeal to collaborators, either Jesuits or others, residing in all the different countries of Europe. Then Rosweyde had proposed to publish at first only the original texts, without commentaries or annotations, relegating to the last volumes the studies intended to enable one to appreciate their value and to throw light on their difficulties. Bolland recognized at once how defective this plan was. So he decided to give in connexion with each saint and his cult all the information he had been able to find, from whatever sources; to preface each text with a preliminary study destined to determine its author and its historical value, and to append to each notes of explanation for the purpose of clearing away difficulties. The duties of the various offices filled by Bolland, added to the formidable correspondence imposed on him by his research into documents and other sources of information concerning the life and cult of the saints to be treated in the work, together with the answers to the numerous letters of consultation addressed to him from all parts, concerning matters of ecclesiastical learning, left him no leisure for the discharge of his duties as hagiographer. Thus, after five years at Antwerp, he was forced to admit that the work was almost where Rosweyde had left it, except that the mass of material which the latter had begun to classify was notably augmented; as a matter of fact it was more than quadrupled. Meanwhile, eager desire for the appearance of the hagiographical monument announced by Rosweyde almost thirty years previously grew apace in the learned and the religious world. There was nothing left for Bolland but to admit that the undertaking was beyond his individual strength and to ask for an assistant. The generous Abbot of Liessies, Antoine de Wynghe, effectually supported his demand by volunteering to defray the living expenses of the associate who should be assigned to Bolland, as the Professed House at Antwerp, which depended on the alms of the faithful for its support, could not pay a man to do work which was not strictly in the field of its ministrations.

The assistant chosen, doubtless at Bolland's suggestion, for he had been one of his most brilliant pupils in the humanities, was Godfrey Henschen (b. at Venray in Limburg, 1601; d. 1681), who had entered the Society of Jesus in 1619. He was assigned to his former master in 1635 and laboured at the publication of the Acta Sanctorum up to the time of his death in 1681, forty-six years later. Twenty-four volumes had then appeared, of which the last was the seventh volume of May. He had, moreover, prepared a great amount of material and many commentaries for June. It may be safely said that the Bollandist work owes its final form to Henschen. When he arrived at Antwerp, Bolland had succeeded in putting into good order the documents relating to the saints of January, and had found a publisher in the person of John van Meurs. Doubtless for the purpose of trying Henschen, he bade him study the acts of the February saints, leaving him every latitude as to the choice of his first subjects and the manner of treating them. Bolland then gave himself entirely to the printing of the volumes for January. It was well under way when Henschen brought to Bolland the first fruits of his activity in the field of hagiography. They were studies for the history of St. Vaast and that of St. Amand, printed later in the first volume of February under date of February sixth. Bolland was absolutely astonished, and possibly somewhat abashed, by the great scope and solidity of the work which his disciple had to show him. He himself had not dared to dream of anything like it. His preliminary commentaries on the acts of the various saints of January were practically confined to designating the manuscripts where the texts he was publishing had been found, to annotations, and a list of the variants in the various copies and the previous editions. The commentaries and annotations of Henschen solved, or at least tried to solve, every problem to which the text of the Acts could give rise, in the matter of chronology, geography, history, or philological interpretation, and all these questions were treated with an erudition and a method which could be called absolutely unknown hitherto. Modest and judicious savant that he was, Bolland at once admitted the superiority of the new method and desired Henschen, despite the

reluctance occasioned by his humility and the profound respect in which he held his master, to review the copy already in press. He held it back for a considerable time to enable his colleague to make the additions and corrections he judged necessary or advantageous. The pages containing the material for the first six days of January had already come from the press; the pages which seemed most defective to Henschen were replaced by revises. His hand is more clearly apparent in the following pages, although he persisted in employing a reserve and watchfulness which sometimes seems to have cost him an effort, in order to avoid too marked a difference between Bolland's commentaries and his own. Papebroch, in his notice on Henschen printed at the beginning of the seventh volume of May, points out as particularly his the toil expended on the acts of St. Wittikind, St. Canute, and St. Raymond of Pennafort on the seventh of January; of St. Atticus of Constantinople and Blessed Laurence Justinian on the eighth; of Sts. Julian and Basilissa on the ninth. "But from this day on", he adds, "Bolland left to Henschen the Greek and Oriental saints, as well as the majority of those of France and of Italy, reserving for himself only those of Germany, Spain, Brittany, and Ireland". He still desired to associate the name of Henschen with his own on the title-page of the various volumes, but the humble religious would not allow it to appear except as his assistant and subordinate. Meanwhile Bolland, in his general preface to the first volume of January, did not fail to tell what he owed to his excellent collaborator. He then insisted that in the volumes of February and the following ones, Henschen's name should figure on the title-page as prominently as his own and, moreover, that in the course of these volumes all commentaries from the pen of Henschen should be signed with his initials, claiming, doubtless not without some foundation, that he received a great number of letters relating to articles written by his colleague, which caused him difficulty. The two volumes of January, containing respectively, if we take into account the various tables and preliminary articles, the first, 1,300 pages, the second, more than 1,250, appeared in the course of the same year, 1643. They aroused in the learned world positive enthusiasm, which is easily understood when we consider how far the new publication surpassed anything of the kind known up to that time—the Golden Legend, Guido Bernardus, Vincent of Beauvais, St. Antoninus of Florence, Peter de Natali, Mombritius, Lippomano, and Surius. There was another marked difference when, fifteen years later, in 1658, the three volumes for February were published, showing a notable improvement over those for January. Congratulations and warm encomiums came from every side to testify to Bolland and his companion the admiration aroused by their work. The encouragement was not only from Catholics. Learned Protestants of the foremost rank did not hesitate to praise highly the truly scientific spirit which marked the new collection. Among others who had been heard from even before the publication of the February volumes, was the celebrated Gerard Vossius. The editors had the satisfaction of seeing added to all these approbations that of Alexander VII, who publicly testified that there had never been undertaken a work more useful and glorious to the Church. The same pontiff and, at his suggestion, the General of the Society of Jesus, Goswin Nickel, immediately invited Bolland to Rome, promising him a rich harvest of materials. The invitation was equivalent to a command, though for that matter this literary journey was of too great advantage to the work in hand for Bolland to do anything but gladly accept it. Finding, however, that he was too much enfeebled by recent illness to stand the fatigues of the journey, and that, moreover, it was necessary for one of the editors to remain in Antwerp, the centre of correspondence, he easily obtained permission from the Father General to send in his place Henschen, who was already so favourably known through his collaboration in the volumes published.

At this time, the hagiographers were joined by a new companion, who was to accompany Henschen on his journey, and who later was to shed as great glory on the work as had his two predecessors. This was Father Daniel von Papenbroeck, better known under the slightly altered form of Papebroch (b. at Antwerp, 1628; d. 28 June, 1714). He entered the Society in 1646, after having been, like Henschen, a brilliant pupil of Bolland's in the course of the humanities. He had just completed his thirty-first year when he was called on, in 1659, to give himself entirely to the work of hagiography, in which he was to have a remarkably long and fruitful career, for it lasted till his death, which occurred in the eighty-seventh year of his age, and the fifty-fifth of his work in this field. At the same time that they appointed Papebroch a collaborator to Bolland and Henschen, the superiors of the order, at the instance of important persons who wished the publication of the "Acta Sanctorum" hastened as much as possible, relieved the Fathers in charge of the work of every other regular occupation, in order that they might thenceforth devote their entire time to the hagiographical work. They were not obliged to fulfil any duties of the sacred ministry except for the distraction and rest that men of such great intellectual activity might find in a change of occupation. About the same time they were granted another favour. We have seen that Bolland, in accepting the succession to Rosweyde's post, had obtained that a special place should be set apart for the manuscript copies and books collected by Rosweyde, which had hitherto been scattered among the books belonging to the general library of the Professed House. This embryo of the Bollandist Museum consisted of two small mansard rooms, lighted by dormer windows so narrow that in the corners it was impossible to see clearly enough to read the titles of the books, even at noonday. Moreover, the walls were not fitted with shelves where the books could be arranged. They were merely piled one above the other without any attempt at order. It required Bolland's wonderful local memory to find anything in this chaos. About 1660, he had the satisfaction of having a spacious hall on the first floor placed at his disposal, where books and manuscripts could be placed on shelves in methodical order. The library, or the "Hagiographical Museum", as it became customary to call it, had already received, and continued to receive daily, thanks to the gifts of generous benefactors and judicious purchases, many acquisitions, so that Henschen during the course of his literary journey was able to say that he found very few historical libraries, public or private, that could compare with the "Hagiographical Museum" of Antwerp. This library was greatly enriched some years later when Papebroch, through the death of his father, a rich merchant of Antwerp, was enabled to apply to the work on which he was engaged his large inheritance.

Bolland's two companions began their journey on the feast of St. Mary Magdalen, 22 July, 1660. Their old master accompanied them as far as Cologne, where they left him after a week's stay. An almost daily correspondence kept up with him, and preserved nearly entire at Brussels, partly at the Royal Library and partly at the Library of the Bollandists, allows us to follow each step of their learned pilgrimage through Germany, Italy, and France. In Germany, they visited successively Coblenz, Mainz, Worms, Speyer, Frankfort, Aschaffenburg, Würzburg, Bamberg, Nuremberg, Eichstädt, Ingolstadt, Augsburg, Munich, and Innsbruck. Everywhere the name of Bolland ensured them an enthusiastic welcome and opened every library to them; everywhere they found precious material to take with them for use in the succeeding volumes of the "Acta". A reception no less friendly and a harvest even more abundant awaited the travellers in Italy, at Verona, Vicenza, Padua, Venice, Ferrara, Imola, Florence, Ravenna, Forlì, Rimini, Pesaro, Fano, Sinigaglia, Ancona, Osimo, Loreto, Assisi, Perugia, Foligno, and Spoleto. They arrived in Rome the day before the Vigil of Christmas, and remained there until 3 October of the following year, 1661. During all this time they were overwhelmed with attentions and favours by Alexander VII, who in person did the honours of his rich Chigi library and commanded by special Briefs that all libraries should be opened to them, and especially that they should be allowed access to the manuscripts of the Vatican. They were received with no less courtesy by the cardinals, the heads of the various orders, the savants Allatius, Aringhi, Ughelli, Ciampini, and others, then shining lights in the capital of the Christian world. The five or six copyists placed at their disposal were kept constantly busy during the nine months they were in Rome in transcribing manuscripts according to their directions, and this occupation was continued by them a long time after the Bollandists' departure. As for the Bollandists themselves, their time was principally employed in collecting Greek manuscripts, in which they were diligently assisted by the celebrated Hellenist, Laurentius Porcius, and the abbot Francesco Albani, later cardinal, and pope under the name of Clement XI. The learned Maronite, Abraham of Eckel, who had just brought to Rome a great number of Syriac manuscripts, was willing to make extracts and translate for them the Acts of the Saints found therein. Ughelli gave them two volumes in folio of notes which he had collected for the completion of his "Italia Sacra". The Oratorians put them in touch with the manuscripts of Baronius, and a large collection of lives of the saints which they had intended to publish themselves. On leaving Rome they visited Naples, Grotta-Ferrata, and Monte Cassino, then Florence, where they remained for four months, and lastly Milan. Everywhere, as at Rome, they left behind them copyists who continued for years the work of transcribing which had been marked out for them. They then spent more than six months in travelling through France, where they halted successively at the Grande Chartreuse of Grenoble, at Lyons, at the monasteries of Cluny and Cîteaux, at Dijon, Auxerre, Sens, and lastly at Paris. They arrived in the great capital, 11 August, 1662, and were immediately put in touch with whatever distinguished savants Paris could then boast of. They found at their command, with unrestricted leave to copy whatever served their purpose, the wealth of hagiographical matter contained in the rich libraries of Saint-Germain-des-Prés and St. Victor, as well as those of the Celestines and Feuillants, of Wion d'Hérouval, de Thou, de Séguier, and lastly the Mazarine an the Royal Library. Their stay at Paris extended over three months, every moment of which time they spent in transcribing and collating, besides enlisting the services of several copyists during the entire time.

They left Paris 9 November and turned their steps toward Rouen, then went through Eu, Abbeville, and Arras, omitting, to their great regret, the city of Amiens, because of the impassable roads, washed out by rains, and the impossibility of securing means of transportation. They reached Antwerp 21 December, 1662, after an absence of twenty-nine months. They not only brought back with them an enormous mass of documents transcribed by themselves and by the copyists they had been obliged to engage, but they found awaiting them at Antwerp a like number from the copyists whom they had employed in the principal cities they had visited (notably, Rome, Florence, Milan, and Paris) and who were still carrying on the labour with which they had been charged. This long journey caused little delay in the progress of the work, for which, on the other hand, it was so productive of good results. Thanks to the incredible activity of the three eminent hagiographers, the three volumes for March were given to the public in 1668. They bore only the names of Henschen and Papebroch, as Bolland had passed to a better life, 12 September, 1665, thirty-six years after succeeding Rosweyde in the preparation of the "Acta Sanctorum". Seven years later, in 1675, the three volumes for April appeared, preceded by preliminary treatises, the subjects of which were respectively: in the first volume, the two most ancient collections of notices on the popes (catalogues of Liberius, and Felix) and the date of St. Ambrose's death, both by Henschen; in the second, the attempt at a diplomatical treatise by Papebroch, "whose chief merit", as the author himself was fond of saying with as much sincerity as modesty, "was that it inspired Mabillon to write his excellent work: 'De re diplomaticâ'"; in the third, a new revised edition of the "Diatriba de tribus Dagobertis", which had made the name of Henschen celebrated twenty years previously. The custom of having these "Parerga" was kept up in the succeeding volumes; there was even an entire volume, the "Propylæum ad tomos Maii", filled with notes of Papebroch on the chronology and history of the popes from St. Peter to Innocent XI. Another happy thought first carried out at that time was the publication of the Greek acts in their original text; previously, only Latin versions had been given. The Greek texts were still relegated to the end of the volumes in the form of appendices; it was only in the fourth volume of May that they were first printed in the body of the work. The first three volumes of May were published in 1688. Besides the names of Henschen and Papebroch, the title-page bore those of Conrad Janninck and François Baert, who had been appointed to the work, the former in 1679; the latter in 1681, at the same time as Father Daniel Cardon, who was carried off by a premature death the second year after his appointment.

Up to this time Bolland and his first two companions had met with nothing but encouragement. A severe storm was soon to burst on the one who was now head of the undertaking and on the work itself. In the first volume of April Papebroch had occasion to treat, under date of the eighth, the Acts of St. Albert Patriarch of Jerusalem, and author of the Carmelite rule. In his preliminary commentary he had combated, as insufficiently grounded, the tradition universally received by the Carmelites, that the origin of the order dated back to the prophet Elias, who was regarded as its founder. This was the signal for an outburst of wrath on the part of these religious. From 1681 to 1693 there appeared no less than twenty to thirty pamphlets filled with abusive language against the unfortunate critic, and adorned with titles often ludicrous through their very efforts at violence: "Novus Ismaël, cuius manus contra omnes et manus omnium contra eum, sive P. Daniel Papebrochius . . . "; "Amyclæ Jesuiticæ, sive Papebrochius scriptis Carmeliticis convictus . . . . . "; "Jesuiticum Nihil . . . "; "Hercules Commodianus Joannes Launoyus . . . redivivus in P Daniele Papebrochio . . . "; "R. P. Papebrochius Historicus Conjecturalis Bombardizans S. Lucam et Sanctos Patres", etc. The series culminated in the large quarto volume signed with the name of Father Sebastian of St. Paul, provincial of the Flemish-Belgian province of the Carmelite Order, and entitled: "Exhibitio errorum quos P. Daniel Papebrochius Societatis Jesu suis in notis ad Acta Sanctorum commisit contra Christi Domini Paupertatem, Ætatem, etc. Summorum Pontificum Acta et Gesta, Bullas, Brevia et Decreta; Concilia; S. Scripturam; Ecclesiæ Capitis Primatum et Unitatem; S. R. E. Cardinalium Dignitatem et authoritatem; Sanctos ipsos, eorum cultum, Reliquias, Acta et Scripta; Indulgentiarum Antiquitatem; Historias Sacras; Breviaria, Missalia, Martyrologia, Kalendaria, receptasque in Ecclesia traditiones ac revelationes, nec non alia quævis antiqua Monumenta Regnorum, Regionum, Civitatum, ac omnium fere Ordinum; idque nonnisi ex meris conjecturis, argutiis negativis, insolentibus censuris, satyris ac sarcasmis, cum Æthnicis, Hæresiarchis, Hæreticis aliisque Authoribus ab Ecclesia damnatis. —Oblata Sanctissimo Domino Nostro Innocentio XII . . . Coloniæ Agrippinæ, 1693." Papebroch, who was receiving at the same time from the most distinguished scholars lively protests against the attacks of which he was made the object, met them at first merely with a silence which perhaps seemed disdainful. But learning that active steps were being taken at Rome to obtain a condemnation of the collection of the Acta Sanctorum or of some of its volumes, he and his companions decided that the time for silence had passed. It was Father Janninck who entered the lists in an open letter to the author of the "Exhibitio Errorum", followed soon afterwards by another in which he replied to a new little book published in support of the work of Father Sebastian of St. Paul. The two letters were printed in 1693. They were followed by a more extended apology for the "Acta", published by the same Janninck in 1695; and lastly there appeared in 1696, 1697, and 1698 the three volumes of the "Responsio Danielis Papebrochii ad Exhibitionem Errorum", in which the valiant hagiographer takes up one by one the charges hurled against him by Father Sebastian and confutes each with an answer as solid in argument as it was temperate in tone. The adversaries of Papebroch, fearing lest they should not be able to obtain from the Court of Rome the condemnation for which they were begging, addressed themselves, with the utmost secrecy, to the tribunal of the Spanish Inquisition, where they won over to their side the most powerful influences. Before the writers of Antwerp had any suspicion of what was being plotted against them, there was issued, in November, 1695, a decree of this tribunal condemning the fourteen volumes of the "Acta Sanctorum" published up to that time, under the most rigorous qualifications, even going so far as to brand the work with the mark of heresy. Papebroch was painfully and deeply moved by the blow. He could submit to all the other insults heaped upon him, but he was obliged to refute the charge of heresy. He made the most vehement entreaties and had all his friends in Spain on the alert to let him know which propositions the Holy Office of Spain had regarded as heretical, in order that he might retract them, if he was unable to furnish satisfactory explanations, or secure the correction of the sentence, if his explanations were acceptable. His efforts proved fruitless. Having fallen seriously ill in 1701, and believing himself at the point of death, immediately after receiving the last sacraments he had a notary-public draw up in his presence and before witnesses a solemn protest which shows how greatly he was affected by the condemnation levelled at his head by the Spanish Inquisition. "After forty-two years of assiduous toil, devoted to the elucidation of the Acts of the Saints, hoping to go to the enjoyment of their society, I ask only one thing on earth, and it is that His Holiness Clement XI be immediately implored to grant me after death what in life I have sought in vain from Innocent XII. I have lived a Catholic, and I die a Catholic, by the grace of God. I have also the right of dying a Catholic in the eyes of men, which is not possible so long as the decree of the Spanish Inquisition shall appear justly issued and published, and so long as people read that I have taught in my books heretical propositions for which I have been condemned." Papebroch had accepted without appeal or murmur the decision of the Roman Congregation of 22 December, 1700, placing on the Index his chronological and historical Essay on the Popes, published in the "Propylæum Maii", a decree issued, as was expressly stated, on account of the sections bearing on certain conclaves and requiring merely the correction of the passages in question. But he did not cease working during the twelve years and a half that he still lived, both by his own efforts and those of his friends, not only to prevent the confirmation by Rome of the decree of the Spanish Inquisition, but also to secure the retraction of the decree. Father Janninck was even sent to Rome with this end in view and remained there for over two years and a half, from the end of October, 1697, till June, 1700. He was completely successful with respect to the first object of his mission, as in December, 1697, he received the assurance that no censure would be passed against the volumes condemned in Spain. The persecutors of Papebroch were compelled to sue for an injunction to silence for both parties, which was accorded them by a Brief of 25 November, 1698, gratefully accepted by Papebroch. More time was necessary, however, to bring about a final decision in the second matter. Whether it was judged prudent in Rome not to enter into conflict with the Spanish tribunal, or whether the latter prolonged the affair by passive resistance, the decree of condemnation made in 1695 was not revoked until 1715, the year following the death of Papebroch. As for the "Propylæum Maii", it was not withdrawn from the Index of Forbidden Books until the last edition (1900); but this did not prevent the French editor, Victor Palmé, from publishing it in his reprint of the Acta Sanctorum, which he undertook about 1860.

A grievous trial of another sort was visited on Papebroch during the last years of the seventeenth century. A cataract affecting both eyes reduced him for about five years to a state of total blindness, which compelled him to give up all literary composition. The sight of his left eye was restored in 1702 by a successful operation. He immediately took up his work again and continued the Acta Sanctorum as far as the fifth volume of June, the twenty-fourth of the whole collection, which appeared in 1709. The weight of age—he was then eighty-one—and his infirmities compelled him to abandon the more arduous work of the Bollandist museum. He lived for almost five years, which he devoted to editing the "Annales Antverpienses" from the foundation of Antwerp down to the year 1700. The manuscript of this work comprised eleven volumes in folio, seven of which are at the Royal Library of Brussels, the others probably having been lost. An edition of the volumes which have been preserved to us was published at Antwerp, 1845–48, in five volumes in octavo.

We shall not pursue further the history of the Bollandist work during the eighteenth century up to the suppression of the Society of Jesus, in 1773. The publication continued regularly, though with more or less unevenness as to the value of the commentaries, up to the third volume of October, which appeared in 1770. The suppression of the Society brought about a crisis in which the work nearly foundered. The Bollandists then in office were Cornelius De Bye, James De Bue, and Ignatius Hubens. The Fathers Jean Clé and Joseph Ghes-

quière had but recently been transferred from the work. The former, at the time of the suppression of the Society, was superior of the Flemish-Belgian province; the latter was in charge of the projected publication of the "Analecta Belgica", a collection of documents relating to the history of Belgium, a work for which the funds of the Musée Bellarmin were appropriated. This Museum was established at Mechlin at the beginning of the eighteenth century, for the purpose of opposing the Jansenists, but was afterwards transferred to the Professed House at Antwerp. On 20 September, 1773, commissaries of the Government presented themselves at the residence of the professed Jesuit Fathers at Antwerp, and before the assembled community read the Bull of suppression of Clement XIV and the imperial letters patent empowering them to execute it. They then affixed seals to the entrances of the archives, libraries, and any rooms of the Fathers which contained money or objects of value. A like proceeding took place on the same day in all the houses of the Society then existing in Belgium. Nevertheless a special order was issued enjoining the members of the commission charged with executing the decree on the Professed House at Antwerp "to summon the ci-devant Jesuits employed in the publication of the 'Acta Sanctorum' and to announce to them that the government, satisfied with their labours, was disposed to exercise special consideration in their regard". Father Ghesquière and his collaborators in the "Analecta Belgica" were included in this indulgence granted to the Bollandists. This favourable attitude of the Government resulted, after various tiresome conferences, in the removal, in 1778, of the Bollandists and the historiographers of Belgium, together with their libraries, to the abbey of Caudenberg, at Brussels. Each of the Bollandists was to receive an annual pension of 800 florins, besides 500 florins to be given to the community of Caudenberg in payment for their board and lodging. The same indulgence was accorded to Ghesquière in consideration of his office of historian. The results of the sale of the volumes were to be divided between the abbey and the editors on condition that the abbey should take charge of the matter on hand, and provide a copyist to make fair copies of manuscripts for the printers, as well as religious who should be trained under the direction of the elder Bollandists for the continuation of the work. The other half of the profits was to be divided in equal portions among the writers. The four hagiographers took up their residence at the Abbey of Caudenberg, and with the consent of the abbot adopted two young religious as assistants. One of these soon left them to pursue his scientific studies, feeling that he had not the vocation for this work; the other was John-Baptist Fonson, at that time (1788) twenty-two years of age, whose name soon afterwards appeared on the title page as editor. Under this new condition of things there appeared in 1780 Volume IV of October under the names of Constantine Suyskens (d. 1771), Cornelius De Bye, John De Bue, Joseph Ghesquière, and Ignatius Hubens, all former Jesuits. In 1786, Volume V appeared, signed with the names of De Bye, De Bue, and Fonson. In the interval between these two volumes the corps of hagiographers had lost, in 1782, the youngest of the Antwerp members, Ignatius Hubens. He was replaced in October, 1784, by a French Benedictine, Dom Anselm Berthod, who voluntarily resigned the high positions he held in his order and those for which he was intended, so that he might devote himself to the learned work which the Imperial Government of Vienna requested him to take up. He was to be engaged upon it only a little more than three years, for he died at Brussels, in March, 1788.

Two new volumes were issued from the royal press

of Brussels, to which had been sent all the equipments of the printing establishment which the Bollandists had founded at Antwerp exclusively for their work. The printing expenses as well as those of pensions and indemnities were largely made up to the public treasury by the confiscation of the capital amassed by the older Bollandists through the sale of their volumes, the collective pension of 2,000 Brabant florins received from the government all through the eighteenth century up to the suppression of the Society, and the liberality of certain benefactors. This capital had grown by 1773 to the sum of 130,000 Brabant florins, ($47,166) yielding an annual revenue of 9,133 florins and 18 sous to which were added the results of the sale of the Acta Sanctorum which averaged 2,400 florins yearly. The Empress Maria Theresa to the very last showed favour to the work of the Bollandists. The same benevolence was not experienced from her successor, Joseph II. The Bollandists now felt the consequences of one of the so-called reforms introduced into the ecclesiastical domain by this imperial philosopher. Among the religious houses suppressed as useless was the Abbey of Caudenberg. The decree of suppression was enforced in May, 1786. The Bollandists were not at first involved in the catastrophe, as they were assigned a dwelling-place and library in a part of the buildings formerly occupied by the college of the Society of Jesus, and were allowed to retain the pensions and privileges granted them in 1778. This was only a short postponement, however, of the complete destruction of the work. Already, in 1784, the Prince von Kaunitz, minister of Joseph II and his chief counsellor in the matter of religious reform, had intimated that the Emperor was not content with the slow progress of the undertaking, and that for the future he would expect to see the publication of at least a volume a year, so that the work might be entirely finished in ten years. The minister even went so far as to send word to the municipality of Brussels that "he attributed the lack of activity on the part of the Bollandists to their desire to keep up forever [*éterniser*] the profits accruing from the work, and that if they did not give satisfaction there was nothing to do but suppress the establishment." The accused had no difficulty in justifying themselves. But the Court of Vienna had fully decided to hear no explanation, and in 1788 asked for a report from the Court of Accounts concerning the expenses entailed by the work of the Bollandists. The conclusion deduced from this report was that the suppression of this work and that of the historiographers would result in an annual gain to the treasury of two to three thousand florins. The Chamber, moreover, took it on itself to say that there was no advantage to be gained by continuing it. The ecclesiastical commission and commission of studies (one and the same), consulted in its turn, gave a decision to the same effect (11 October, 1788). "The work of the Bollandists", it said, "is far from completion, and we cannot flatter ourselves that the end is yet in sight. This work has no merit but that of being an historical repertory, filled with an enormous quantity of details, which will always have but slight attraction for real savants. It is astonishing that at the time of the suppression of the Jesuit Order, they should have been successful in interesting the Government in such trash, and that it is such is proved by the scanty profit the Bollandists have derived from their labours. In business parlance, it is a very poor investment, and as it is not better, regarded from a scientific standpoint, it is quite time to put an end to it." Strengthened by this advice, the "Government Council" notified the Court of Accounts by a despatch dated 16 October, 1788, that it had been decided to put a stop to the work of the Acta Sanctorum, and that in consequence, beginning from

that date, no more payments should be made to the Fathers De Bye, De Bue, Fonson, Ghesquière, and Cornelius Smet (a former Jesuit, associated first with Ghesquière in the publication of the "Analecta Belgica" and later enrolled among the Bollandists) of the annual pension of 800 florins which had been assured them. It was to be decided later what should be done with the printing outfit and the other effects of the suppressed establishment. These spoils comprised the library of the Bollandists and the copies of the volumes already published which they had in stock. This involved no slight annoyance. Once the series was abandoned, it would be difficult to find a purchaser for these works, and they wished to realize as much money as possible from them. It was decided to ask the Bollandists themselves to undertake the sale of these effects for the benefit of the public treasury. The Bollandists willingly accepted the charge, hoping to keep intact the treasures of their library and thus to ensure, in a certain measure, the resumption of the work, if not at once, at least in the near future.

Cornelius De Bye, who had been especially commissioned to conduct the sale, turned first to Martin Gerbert, the learned abbot of the monastery of St. Blasius in the Black Forest. On behalf of the Government commissioners he named a purchase price for the library and such of the published volumes as remained unsold, and offered to come to St. Blasius for some months in order to train some of the young religious of the abbey for the work of publishing the Acta Sanctorum. His letter, dated 11 November, 1788, remained unanswered, whether as a result of dispositions little favourable to the Society of Jesus, such as had been more than once manifested by this famous abbot, or whether, already absorbed by many important works, he felt he could not think of undertaking yet another entirely new. About the same time, i. e. in November and December, 1788, the Congregation of Benedictines of Saint-Maur, in France, of its own accord made advances to the officials of the Imperial Government of Vienna for the acquisition of the Bollandist library, with a view to continuing the publication. This attempt was equally void of result. It was with the abbey of the Premonstratensians of Tongerloo that arrangements were finally concluded. By a contract signed 11 May, 1789, the Government transferred to this abbey the Bollandist library and the Bellarmine Museum, together with the furnishings appertaining to them, and the volumes already printed and the printing equipment. In return, the abbey was to pay the government for the libraries 12,000 Brabant florins ($4,353.84) and for the other things 18,000 florins. Half of the latter sum was turned over to the three hagiographers, De Bye, De Bue, and Fonson. Moreover, the abbey agreed to pay a yearly salary to these three as well as to Ghesquière and Smet. The Bollandists were scarcely established in their new home when the Brabantine Revolution broke out. Nevertheless, they continued their labours and in 1794 published the sixth volume of October, signed with the names of Cornelius De Bye and James De Bue, former Jesuits, John Baptist Fonson, ex-Canon of Caudenberg, Anselm Berthod the Benedictine, and Siard van Dyck, Cyprian van de Goor, and Matthias Stalz, Premonstratensian canons. The same year Belgium was invaded by French troops and reunited to the great Republic. Ecclesiastical goods were confiscated, priests and religious hunted like criminals, the Premonstratensians of Tongerloo and the Bollandists whom they harboured forced to disperse, and the work of the Bollandists actually suppressed. Part of the treasures of the library were concealed in the homes of neighbouring peasants, and the rest, hastily piled into wagons, were taken to Westphalia. When the storm of persecution had somewhat abated, an attempt was made to collect these scattered effects. Naturally, many of them were lost or destroyed. The remainder were restored to the abbey of Tongerloo, where they were undisturbed until 1825. Then, as all hope of resuming the Bollandist work seemed lost, the canons of Tongerloo disposed of a great number of the books and manuscripts by public sale. Such as remained were given to the Government of the Netherlands, which hastened to incorporate the volumes into the Royal Library of The Hague. The manuscripts seemed destined to a like fate, but as a result of earnest solicitations they were deposited in the Library of Bourgogne, Brussels, where they still remain. Nevertheless, the idea of resuming the publication of the Acta Sanctorum had never been entirely abandoned in Belgium. The prefect of the department of the Deux Nèthes (province of Antwerp), in 1801; the Institute of France, with the Minister of the Interior of the French Republic as mediator, in 1802; and lastly, in 1810, the Baron de Tour du Pin, Prefect of the Department of the Dyle (Brussels), at the request of the incumbent of the same important office, then the Count de Montalivet, applied to such of the former

that by 29 January, 1837, he received from Father van Lil, Provincial of the Society in Belgium, assurance of the appointment by the Society of new Bollandists, with their residence at the College of Saint-Michel at Brussels. These were Fathers Jean-Baptiste Boone, Joseph Van der Moere, and Prosper Coppens, to whom was added, in the course of the same year, Father Joseph Van Hecke. The provincial, in behalf of these Fathers, asked free access to public libraries and archives, and the privilege of taking home with them from the Library of Bourgogne and the Royal Library, such manuscripts and books as they would need for reference in the course of their work. Both requests were immediately granted. Moreover, an annual subsidy was promised, which was fixed in May, 1837, at 6,000 francs. This subsidy was continued from year to year under the different governments, both Catholic and Liberal, which succeeded to power, until the parliamentary session of 1868, in the course of which the Liberal majority of the Chamber of Deputies cut it out of the budget. It has never been re-established.

The new hagiographers began by drawing up a list of the saints whose acts or notices remained to be published, that is to say, those who are hon-

COLLEGE OF SAINT-MICHEL, BRUSSELS

Bollandists as were still living, to induce them to resume their task once more. But the attempts were futile.

Matters rested here until 1836. It was then learned that a hagiographical society had been formed in France under the patronage of several bishops and of M. Guizot, Minister of Public Instruction, and that it especially proposed to itself the resumption of the work of the Bollandists. The chief promoter of the enterprise, Abbé Théodore Perrin, of Laval, came to Belgium that same year, 1836, to solicit the support of the Government and the collaboration of Belgian savants. He did not meet with the reception he had hoped for. On the contrary, it aroused indignation in Belgium that a work which had come to be regarded as a national glory should pass into the hands of the French. The Abbé de Ram, *Rector Magnificus* of the University of Louvain and member of the Royal Commission of History, expressed this feeling in a letter addressed under date of 17 October to the Count de Theux, Minister of the Interior, urgently imploring him to lose no time in securing for their native land of Belgium the honour of completing the great hagiographical collection, and engaged him to entrust the work to the Fathers of the Society of Jesus, by whom it had been begun and carried so far in the preceding centuries. The Minister immediately took the field and conducted negotiations with such energy

oured in the Catholic Church on the various days of October, November, and December, beginning from 15 October, the day at which the work of their predecessors had been brought to a halt. This list was published in the month of March, 1838, with an introduction containing a summary of the history of the Bollandist movement, the announcement of the resumption of the work, and an earnest appeal to all friends of religious learning, imploring their assistance in securing what was felt by the new workers as the most necessary thing for their success, namely, a hagiographical library. This was published under the title of "De prosecutione operis Bollandiani" (in octavo, 60 pp.). The appeal was heard. Most of the European governments, many societies of learned men, and several great publishers sent copies of the historical works undertaken by them or under their patronage; private individuals made generous donations of books, often precious and rare volumes that had adorned their libraries. Everywhere, also, on their literary journeys, the Bollandists were accorded the most enthusiastic and flattering receptions.

The first volume published after the resurrection of Bollandism, Volume VII of October, appeared in 1845, containing over 2,000 pages in folio. There followed successively Volumes VIII to XIII of October, and I and II of November, besides the "Propylæum Novembris", an edition of the Greek Synaxarion called "de Sirmond", with the variants of sixty manuscripts scattered through the various public libraries of Europe.

The author of this article does not consider himself qualified to give an estimate of the work of these later Bollandists, having himself been a member of the body for too long a time. He is able, however, to cite the appreciations of the most distinguished and capable scholars in this field, who testify that the volumes published by the later Bollandists are in no wise inferior to those of their predecessors of the seventeenth and eighteenth centuries. The reservations made by certain eminent critics in their commendation are generally due to the prolixity of the commentaries, which they think is often excessive, and to the timidity of certain conclusions, which do not seem to them to correspond with what the discussions had led them to expect. Another class of censors reproach the Bollandists for quite the reverse, accusing them of not showing sufficient respect towards what they call tradition, and of being too often hypercritical. The present members of the body are firmly resolved to be on their guard against these contrary excesses, something, indeed, which becomes easier for them as time passes, owing to the constant progress of good scientific methods. We may be permitted one word, in conclusion, as to what has been done during these latter years towards keeping the work up to the high level of contemporary historical erudition. It has been judged opportune, in the first place, to publish, besides the great volumes of the principal collection itself, which appear at undetermined intervals, a periodical review intended chiefly to make known to the learned public materials recently discovered by the Bollandists or their friends, which go towards completing either the Acts published in the volumes already printed or the entire mass of material to be employed in the future volumes of the work. This review was begun under the title of "Analecta Bollandiana" in the early part of 1882. At the rate of one volume in octavo a year, it has reached in the present year (1907) the twenty-sixth volume. In volumes subsequent to the sixth there have been inserted, besides unedited documents, various notes bearing on hagiographical matters. Since the publication of the tenth volume, each quarterly issue has contained a "Bulletin des publications hagiographiques" in which are announcements and summary appreciations of recent works and articles in reviews which concern matters of hagiography. Other auxiliary works have exacted long years of laborious preparation. They are the "Bibliotheca Hagiographica Græca" and the "Bibliotheca Hagiographica Latina", in which are enumerated under the name of each saint, following the alphabetical order of their names, all documents relating to his or her life and cult written in Greek or in Latin before the beginning of the sixteenth century, together with the indication of all collections and books where they can be found. The first of these collections, which appeared in 1895, numbers 143 pages. (There is now in preparation a new edition notably enlarged.) The second, issued 1898–99, has 1,387 pages. It is hoped that a "Bibliotheca Hagiographica Orientalis" will soon be printed. Moreover, there is a third class of auxiliary works to which the Bollandists of the present generation are directing their activity, and that is the careful preparation of catalogues containing a systematic detailed description of the Greek and Latin hagiographical manuscripts of various great libraries. A great many of these catalogues have been incorporated in the "Analecta". Such are the catalogues of the Greek manuscripts in the Roman libraries of the Barberini, the Chigi, and the Vatican; the National Library of Naples; the library of the University of Messina, and that of St. Mark's, in Venice; catalogues of the Latin manuscripts in the

Royal Library of Brussels (2 vols. in octavo), in the libraries of the cities, or of the universities, of Bruges, Ghent, Liège, and Namur, in Belgium; of the municipal libraries of Chartres, Le Mans, Douai, and Rouen, in France; those of The Hague in Holland, and, in Italy, of Milan (the Ambrosian), as well as the various libraries of Rome; also in the private library of His Majesty the Emperor of Austria, at Vienna, and that of Alphonsus Wins at Nivelles; and lastly, of

LIBRARY, COLLEGE OF SAINT-MICHEL, BRUSSELS

the Bollandist Library. Besides the "Analecta", there have appeared the catalogue of the old (before 1500) Latin manuscripts in the National Library of Paris (three octavo volumes, also the tables) and a list of the Greek manuscripts in the same library (compiled in collaboration with M. H. Omont). All these publications, although certainly delaying somewhat the appearance of succeeding volumes of the Acta Sanctorum, have gained for the Bollandists warm words of encouragement and commendation from the greatest scholars. In view of the impossibility of quoting at length these flattering testimonies, we shall confine ourselves to mentioning, as they come to mind, the articles of Mgr. Duchesne (Bulletin critique, 1 April, 1890); Léopold Delisle (Bibliothèque de l'école des Chartres, LI, 1890, 532); M. Solomon Reinach (Revue Archéologique, 1895, II, 228); Krieg (Litterarische Rundschau, 1 December, 1900); a passage in the Belgian Archives (1901), III, 31. There is a final detail which may not be without interest. The Bollandists had found themselves greatly hampered in the arrangement of their library at their residence in the Rue des Ursulines at Brussels which they had occupied since the resumption of the work in 1837. During the latter part of 1905 they were transferred to the new College of Saint-Michel on the Boulevard Militaire, where ample and convenient quarters for the library were assigned in the lofty buildings of the vast establishment. The 150,000 volumes contained in their literary museum are most suitably arranged here. A large space was also set apart for historical and philological reviews (about 600), nearly all of which are sent regularly by learned societies, either gratuitously or in exchange for the "Analecta Bollandiana". To class these according to the place of publication and the language chiefly employed in their preparation: 228

are French (a certain number of which are published in Belgium, Switzerland, and other countries than France); 135, German; 88, Italian; 55, English (of which ten are American); 13, Russian; 11, Dutch; 7, Flemish; 7, Spanish; 7, Croatian; 4, Swedish; 3, Portuguese; 2, Irish; 2, Hungarian; 1, Czech; 1, Polish; 1, Rumanian; 1, Dalmatian; and 1, Norwegian. Moreover, there are 9 printed in Greek, 6 in Latin, 4 in Armenian and 1 in Arabic. Finally, a large hall near the library has been set apart, and after October, 1907, it will be thrown open to foreign students who may wish to consult original sources of information likely to assist them in their researches.

The quotations of the Acta Sanctorum refer to three different editions. The first, the original one, commonly called the Antwerp edition, has been sufficiently described in the above article. The volumes of the Antwerp collection were first reprinted at Venice from 1764 to 1770. They reached then to volume VI of September. The main difference between this reimpression and the Antwerp edition lies in the fact that the supplementary additions to sundry commentaries printed by the Bollandists at the end of the single volumes, or of a set of volumes are transposed in the Venetian edition and joined to the commentary to which they refer; hence the contents of each volume are not in close correspondence in the volumes similarly marked in both editions. Moreover, many of the *parerga* or preliminary treatises scattered through the Antwerp collection have been brought together in three separate volumes. But the whole printing teems with typographical blunders. Lastly another reprinting of the Antwerp publication was undertaken by the Parisian editor, Victor Palmé, from 1863 to 1869, and carried on to the tenth volume of October. This edition reproduces exactly, volume by volume, the original one, except for the months of January and June. The two big volumes of January have been divided into three, and in the volumes of June also some changes have been made in the disposition of matter, in order to render the use of them easier to readers. Besides, to each of the volumes of the first four months were added a few unpublished short notes (filling from one to six pages) of Daniel Papebroch, found in his papers and relating to the commentaries printed in the volume.

BOLLAND, *Præfatio generalis in Acta Sanctorum* (at the beginning of vol. I for January); PAPEBROCH, *De vitâ, virtutibus et operibus Joannis Bollandi* (at the beginning of vol. I for March); PAPEBROCH, *De vitâ . . . Godefridi Henschenii* (at the beginning of vol. VII for May); J. PIEN, *De Vitâ Danielis Papebrochii* (at the beginning of vol. VI for June); J. VAN HECKE, *De ratione universi operis [Bollandiani]* (beginning of vol. VII for October).

CH. DE SMEDT.

Bollandus (BOLLAND). See BOLLANDISTS.

Bollig, JOHANN, distinguished Orientalist, b. near Düren in Rhenish Prussia, 23 August, 1821; d. at Rome in 1895. He studied theology and Semitic languages at Rome, where he entered the Society of Jesus in 1853. In 1862–63 he sojourned in Syria as professor of theology for the native seminaries, at the same time pursuing his researches in Oriental literature. After his return to Rome, he was appointed professor of Arabic and Sanskrit at the Roman College (afterwards the Gregorian University) and at the Sapienza. He was a member of the commission appointed by Pius IX to arrange the details of the Vatican Council and acted as pontifical theologian during the Council. For many years he was Consultor of the Congregation of the Propaganda for Oriental affairs. In 1880 he was appointed Prefect of the Vatican Library, which office he held till his death. Among his published works are: "Brevis Chrestomathia arabica" (Rome, 1882); "Sti. Gregorii lib. carm. iambic.", an ancient

Syriac translation (Beirut, 1895). He left many unpublished writings on Oriental philology.

Catalogues of the Rom. Prov. S.J.; HERDER, *Konversationslex.,* I, s. v.

B. GULDNER.

Bologna, ARCHDIOCESE OF.—*History.*—Bologna is the principal city in the province of the same name, Italy, and contains about 150,000 inhabitants. It was founded by the Etruscans, who called it Felsina. Later it fell into the hands of the Boii, a Gallic tribe, and from that time took the name of Bononia, whence the present form. The regions round about having been laid waste by the continual wars, in 189 B. C. the Romans established a colony there, which was enlarged and beautified by Augustus. After Byzantium had broken the power of the Goths in Italy, Bologna belonged to the Exarchate of Ravenna (536). By the donation of Pepin Bologna was made part of the patrimony of the Holy See, but during the disturbances of the ninth century was wrested from the popes. At the beginning of the ninth century it was laid waste during the incursions of the Hungarians. Otto I did much to restore the city to its former condition, giving it the privilege of enacting its own laws, and making it directly dependent on the imperial authority. Bologna was then governed by consuls. During the struggles between the empire and the popes, the city took the part of the latter and was enabled to assert its independence, which was definitely recognized by Henry V in 1122. Bologna was among the first to join the Lombard League. From 1153 it was ruled by podestas, who were for the most part foreigners. From the accession of Frederick II, Bologna was rent into the two factions of Guelphs and Ghibellines, the former being in the majority. On 26 May, 1249, the inhabitants of Bologna in the battle of Fossalto conquered the troops of Frederick II under the leadership of King Enzo (Ezzelino); Enzo himself was taken prisoner, and neither the threats nor the promises of Frederick availed to secure his liberty. He remained in captivity until his death, eleven years later, although for the rest he was always treated with the greatest consideration.

In 1276, in order more thoroughly to safeguard their communal liberty, the inhabitants of Bologna placed themselves under the protection of the Holy See, and Pope Nicholas III sent them as legate his nephew, Bertoldo Orsini, whom he also commissioned to reconcile the opposing factions. In the fourteenth century the preponderance of power was in the hands of the Pepoli family, but later passed to the Visconti of Milan, who alternated with the Bentivoglio family in holding the reins of power. At intervals the popes attempted to make their authority recognized, or else the city spontaneously recognized their sovereignty (1327–34; 1340–47; 1360–76, through the efforts of Cardinal Albornoz; 1377–1401; 1403–11, during the pontificate of John XXIII; 1412–16; 1420–28, under Cardinal Condulmer). In the beginning of the fifteenth century there were frequent popular uprisings against the nobility. From 1443 to 1506 three of the Bentivoglio family succeeded each other as masters of Bologna. In 1506 Julius II incorporated Romagna into the Papal States, Bologna included; the city, however, retained a great degree of communal autonomy. The papal authority was vested in a legate, who in the beginning was generally a cardinal, later, however, only a titular bishop. In 1796 Bologna was occupied by the French and made a part of the Cisalpine Republic, and afterwards of the Italian Kingdom. In 1814 it was seized by the Austrians, who in 1815 restored it to the pope. From the time of its restoration, Bologna was the scene of a series of deep-seated agitations and revolts against the papal rule. These uprisings were repressed by Austrian troops. Finally, in 1859 Romagna, together with the Marches and Umbria, was annexed to the Kingdom of Italy.

Christianity in Bologna.—The only sources for the history of the beginnings of Christianity in Bologna are legendary accounts, according to which St. Apollinaris, disciple of St. Peter and first Bishop of Ravenna, was the first to preach the Gospel in Bologna. The first bishop is said to have been St. Zama, who is supposed to have been ordained by Pope St. Dionysius (270). However, it may be maintained with certainty that Christianity, and likewise the episcopate, in Bologna dates back to a more remote period. During the persecution of Diocletian, Bologna was the scene of the martyrdoms of Sts. Vitalis and Agricola, whose bodies were interred in a Jewish cemetery and only discovered in the time of St. Ambrose, in 392, as related by him in a letter (Ep. lv), the authenticity of which, however, is questioned. The fact is referred to, perhaps, by Paulinus in his life of the saint, when he speaks of Ambrose taking to Florence some relics of these martyrs. It was possibly in the same persecution that the martyrdom of St. Proculus occurred. The episcopal See of Bologna was first subject to the Metropolitan of Milan, and later, probably after Milan had fallen into the hands of the Lombards, it recognized the authority of the Metropolitan of Ravenna. In 1106 it was placed immediately under the Holy See. Finally, in 1582 Gregory XIII raised the Bishop of Bologna to the dignity of a metropolitan, assigning him as suffragans the Sees of Imola, Cervia, Modena, Reggio, Parma, Piacenza, and Crema; to-day, however, only Imola and Faenza are suffragan to Bologna.

Among the Bishops of Bologna worthy of note are Sts. Faustinianus, Basil, and Eusebius, in the fourth century. About 400 there is record of St. Felix, succeeded about 430 by St. Petronius, who is extolled for having restored the church of Bologna, and who later became patron of the city. His relics are preserved in the church of San Stefano. A number of the Bishops of Bologna were later raised to the papal chair, as, for instance, John X; Cosimo Migliorati, who assumed the name of Innocent VII; Tomaso Parentuccelli, later Nicholas V; Giuliano della Rovere, who became Julius II; Alessandro Ludovisi, or Gregory XV; and Prospero Lambertini, or Benedict XIV. The last two mentioned were born in Bologna. Other celebrated bishops were: Cardinal Filippo Caraffa (1378–89); Cardinal Antonio Correr (1407–12); Blessed Nicolò, Cardinal Albergati (1417–34); Cardinal Lorenzo Campeggi, known for the many embassies on which he was sent to Germany and England, in connexion with the Reformation and the marriage of Henry VIII (1523–25). After Bologna became an archiepiscopal see, almost all the metropolitans were cardinals, among whom may be mentioned: Gabriele Paleoti (1591–97), who left the cathedral as it exists to-day, built the episcopal palace, and endeavoured to put the Tridentine reforms into execution in Bologna; Vincenzo Malvezzi (1754–75), to whom the cathedral and the seminary owed much; Carlo Opizzoni (1802–55); Michele Viale Prelà (1855–60); Lucido Maria Parocchi (1877–82). Bologna was also the birthplace of the following popes, in addition to the two already mentioned: Honorius II (Lamberto Scannabecchi), Lucius II (Gherardo Caccianemici dell' Orso), Alexander V (Pietro Filargo), Gregory XIII (Ugo Buoncompagni), and Innocent IX (Giannantonio Facchinetti).

Churches.—Chief among the sacred edifices of Bologna is the cathedral, dedicated to St. Peter and erected by the commune in 910 to replace the ancient cathedral which stood outside the city walls. Destroyed by fire in 1130, it was but rebuilt in 1165;

in its present form it dates from 1605, according to plans drawn up by Magenta, a Barnabite. The façade, however, was designed by Alf. Torreggiani, who also added the first two chapels to the church. The majority of the paintings are by famous masters, as, for instance, Ventura da Bologna, Ercole Graziani, Francesco Tadolini, Onofrio Zanotti, del Bagnacavallo (Bartolommeo Ramenghi), Ludovico Caracci, and others. There is also a lower church with five altars. Worthy of note is a crucifix of cedar wood dating from the time of the old cathedral. The church of San Petronio, dedicated to the patron of the city, was built by order of the Secento, at public expense, in 1390. A competition was announced for the plans, and among all the designs the preference was given those of Antonio Vincenzi,

BASILICA OF ST. PETRONIUS

while the supervision of the work of erection was entrusted to Andrea Manfredi da Faenza. However, the original drawings, providing for an octagonal dome 500 feet high, were not adhered to. The façade still remains incomplete, only the lower part being covered with sculptures in marble. The ornamentation of the larger door is the work of Pietro della Fonte; many of the figures compare favourably with the works of an age in which the art was more highly developed. In the architrave is the Madonna and Child. The two naves are adorned with statues of Sts. Petronius and Ambrose. The carving of the doors was done by Sigismondo Bargelloso, aided by Andrea Magnani and Gabriele di Zaccaria. The two side doors are also adorned with magnificent carvings, the work of other artists. It is a three-naved church, the twenty-three chapels being adorned with the masterpieces of distinguished artists of different ages. Worthy of note is the statue of St. Anthony of Padua by Sansovino. A sun-dial is to be found there, likewise two clocks, among the first to be made in Italy with pendulums. In Bologna is also the church of Corpus Domini, founded by St. Catherine de' Vigri, commonly known as St. Catherine of Bologna, and adjoining it the monastery of the Poor Clares. In one of the chapels is preserved the mummified body of the saint, together with many objects used by her during life. There is also a beautiful church of St. Dominic, close by the Dominican convent in which the death of St. Dominic occurred. The tomb of the saint is in itself a veritable museum of works of art by the great masters. The casket was carved by Nicolò Pisano, and one of the angels was done by Michelangelo in his youth. The choir is beautifully inlaid with tinted wood, the work of Fra Damiano da Bergamo, a Dominican lay brother. The church is cruciform, and in one chapel of the cross is the tomb of King Ezzelino; in another that of Guido Reni.

Among the many other churches, all rich in monuments, mention will be made only of San Stefano, made up of a group of chapels once used by ancient monks from Egypt, who dwelt there before the time of St. Benedict. The site later passed into the hands of the Benedictines who erected there a monastery, which in 1447 was reduced to the rank of an abbey to be held *in commendam*. In 1493 the Celestines took possession, and remained there until 1797. A tablet found there proves that this was once the site of a temple of Isis. Among the different chapels should be mentioned Calvary, or of the Holy Sepulchre; it is octagonal in form, and contains a replica in marble of the Holy Sepulchre in Jerusalem; here was probably situated the baptistery of the ancient cathedral, which was not far distant. The chapels of San Giacomo Maggiore, built in 1267; San Giovanni in Monte, said to have been erected by St. Petronius and renovated in 1221 and 1824; San Isaia the most ancient; Santa Maria di Galliera; Santa Maria dei Servi; San Martino; San Paolo; and San Francesco, still incomplete—all rich in monuments of artistic and historic interest. Outside Bologna is situated the celebrated Certosa, built in 1334 and in 1802 converted into a community burying-ground. The church attached to the convent is dedicated to St. Jerome. On the Monte della Guardia is the shrine of the Madonna di San Luca, which is connected with the Saragossa Gate by a portico with 635 arches 11,483 feet (2.17 miles), in length, constructed between 1661 and 1739. The shrine takes its name from a painting of the Madonna attributed to St. Luke, which was brought here in 1160 by Euthymius, a monk of Constantinople. The present church dates from 1731.

With respect to profane architecture, the first thing to be remarked are the porticoes in which nearly all the roads terminate. Noteworthy also are the towers, particularly that of the Asinelli, 320 feet in height, erected between 1105 and 1109, and, nearby, that of the Garisendi, built in 1110, the inclination of which, it seems, was due to a subsidence of the earth, in the fourteenth century, which carried away the uppermost part of the tower; it is 154 feet in height, and has an inclination of 7.77 feet. First among the palaces is that of the Podestà, a structure dating back to 1801, where the conclave for the nomination of John XXIII was held in 1410; next in importance are the communal palace, the civic museum, and the Archiginnasio, or ancient university.

The Archdiocese of Bologna contains 389 parishes, 1172 churches, chapels, and oratories, 837 secular priests, 119 regular, 311 seminarians, 48 lay brothers, 521 sisters, 10 schools for boys, 21 for girls, and a population of 565,489.

CAPPELLETTI, *Le chiese d'Italia* (Venice, 1844), III; SIGONII CAROLI, *De episcopis Bononiensibus libri V* (Bologna, 1586), continued by RUBBI up to 1731; SAVIOLI, *Annali Bolognesi* (Bassano, 1784); TROMBA, *Serie cronologica dei vescovi*, etc. (Bologna, 1787).

U. BENIGNI.

Bologna, GIOVANNI DA, Flemish Renaissance sculptor, b. at Douai, in Flanders, about 1524; d. at Florence in 1608. Vasari gives little information about this eminent sculptor. He calls him "a youth of great talent and of spirit" and says he was one of the competitors with Cellini for the colossal figure of Neptune in his chariot drawn by sea horses. The duke, who was to decide the competition, although assured that Giovanni's model was superior to the others, did not confide the undertaking to him. We can judge of what he would have made of that commission from the bronze Neptune prepared for the fountain at Bologna.

Giovanni was called Il Fiammingo from the place of his birth. He studied in Rome and settled in Florence, having been adopted by the wealthy

Bernardo Vecchietti, who treated him as his son. He was thoroughly Florentine in sentiment, and in Florence are preserved his two masterpieces, "Mercury" and the "Rape of the Sabines". In the former, in the Bargello, he has come nearer to expressing swift, flashing motion and airy lightness than has any other artist of that or a later period. The figure of the youth with winged feet, holding the caduceus, and borne aloft upon a head of Æolus, is masterly in its expression of earnest purpose and light, easy movement. Hardly less important is the "Rape of the Sabines" in marble, under the Loggia dei Lanzi, in which Count Ginori posed for the figure of the triumphant youth who carries away a struggling woman in his embrace. Other works are the group of "Hercules and Nessus", the equestrian bronze figure of "Duke Cosimo I" in the Piazza Signoria and the bas-relief of the doorway of the Cathedral of Pisa. Besides these, he executed more than one crucifix, a figure of "Diana", another of "Venus", and four syrens similar to the larger ones on the Bologna fountain. Vasari mentions a bronze figure of "Bacchus", and a "Samson" in combat with two Philistines, both larger than life size. Giovanni's work is marked by freedom and grace, while free from the fault of exaggeration which so injures much of the sculpture of the very late Renaissance.

DESJARDINS, *La vie de Jean Boulogne* (1883).

GEORGE CHARLES WILLIAMSON.

Bologna, THE UNIVERSITY OF.—A tradition of the thirteenth century attributed the foundation of this university to Theodosius II (433); but this legend is now generally rejected. The authentic "Habita", issued by Frederick Barbarossa in 1158, was at best only an implicit recognition of the existence of the school at Bologna, and the bull of Clement III (1189), though it speaks of "masters and scholars", has no reference to a university organization. The university, in fact, developed out

THE UNIVERSITY OF BOLOGNA

of the "Schools of the Liberal Arts" which flourished at Bologna early in the eleventh century. An important feature of the general education given in these schools was the *Dictamen*, or Art of Composition which included rules for drawing up briefs and other legal documents. The study of grammar and rhetoric was closely connected with the study of law. At the same time, the political, commercial and intellectual growth of the Lombard cities created a demand for legal instruction. Ravenna, long the home of jurisprudence, lost its prestige through its conflict with the papacy, and Bologna was its successor. Towards the close of the eleventh century Pepo is mentioned in connexion with the revived study of the "Digest"; but it was Irnerius who began the study of the entire "Corpus Juris Civilis" and organized the school of law as distinct from the arts school (1100–30). Along with this revival of the Civil Law came the epoch-making compilation of the Camaldolese (or Benedictine) monk, Gratian. The "Decretum Gratiani" (q. v.), published about 1140, became at once the recognized textbook of canon law. Bologna was thus, in its origin, a "jurist" university. The work of Irnerius and Gratian was continued by such men as Odopedus (d. 1300), Joannes Andrea (1270–1348), St. Raymond of Pennafort (1175–1275), and Ricardus Anglicus, who later became Bishop of Chichester (about middle of thirteenth century).

The fame of its professors drew to Bologna students from all parts of Italy and from nearly every country of Europe. It is said that their number at the beginning of the thirteenth century was 10,000. Bologna was known as the "Mater studiorum", and its motto, "Bononia docet", was literally true. The foreign (non-Bolognese) students formed two "universities"; that of the Cismontanes and that of the Ultramontanes. The former comprised seventeen "Nations", the latter, eighteen, including the English. The nations were organized on a plan similar to that of the guilds. Each framed its own statutes, elected its own "Consiliarii," and held its own meetings. The rector was elected by the students. The masters, also, were grouped in guilds or colleges. In the examination of candidates for degrees, the authority of the masters was supreme; in other matters the students had full control. In the conflicts that often arose between them and the city, the students enforced their claims by emigrating to other towns—Vicenza (1204), Arezzo (1215), Padua (1222), Sienna (1321). Appeal was sometimes taken to the pope, who as a rule decided in favour of the university. Notable among these papal interventions was the Bull of Honorius III (1217).

Bologna in its earliest organization was a "student" university: professors were hired by the students to give instruction. The lectures were either "ordinary" or "extraordinary", a distinction which corresponded with that between the more essential and the less essential of the law-texts (Rashdall). Ordinary lectures were reserved for the doctors; the extraordinary might be given by a student as part of his preparation for the baccalaureate. (See ARTS, BACHELOR OF.) This classification of teachers survives in the modern German university. At Bologna, no examination was required for the Bachelor's degree; permission to lecture was granted the student after a five years' course in law. For the Licentiate, the candidate was obliged to pass a private, and for the Doctorate a public, examination (*Conventus, Inceptio*). The examinations and the conferring of degrees belonged originally to the masters; but in 1219 Honorius III prescribed that no one should receive the Doctorate without the consent of the Archdeacon of Bologna. In 1292 Nicholas IV decreed that all who were licensed doctors by the Archdeacon of Bologna should have the right, without further examination or approbation, to teach everywhere. These enactments not only enhanced the value of the degree, but also affected the organization of the university. Functions hitherto exercised by private corporations passed into the hands of an official commissioned by public authority, and that authority was ecclesiastical. The degree system of Bologna was henceforth the same as that which had already been established at Paris; and these two schools became the models upon which the later universities were organized.

The development of the law schools at Bologna had as one result the reduction of the Liberal Arts to a position of secondary importance. On the other hand, two factors in the situation favoured the Arts and made possible a new growth in the university, namely, the restoration of the Aristotelean philosophy and the introduction of mathematics from the Arabian schools. The physics and physiology of Aristotle formed the basis of the study of medicine, while mathematics opened the way to astrology, and eventually to astronomy. Among the physicians of note in Bologna were a number of ecclesiastics, one of whom, Nicolaus de Farnham, became (1241) Bishop of Durham. Churchmen were forbidden to study medicine by Honorius III (1219). But there was no regularly organized school of medicine until Thaddeus of Florence began his teaching, about 1260. From that time onward the medical faculty grew in importance. Surgery received special attention; dissection was practised, and the foundations of modern anatomy were laid by Mundinus (1275–1326). Closely allied with the work in medicine was the study of astrology. A famous astrologist, Cecco d'Ascoli (d. 1327), declared that a physician without astrology would be like an eye without the power of vision. The scientific study of astronomy was founded by the investigations of Novara and his disciple Copernicus (1473–1543). Both medical and mathematical studies were influenced by Arabian scholarship, in particular by that of Avicenna and Averroes. As these were also philosophers, their theories came to be part of the Scholasticism of Bologna, and their authority was scarcely inferior to that of Aristotle.

Theology had long been taught in the monastic schools; but the faculty of theology in the university was established by Innocent VI in 1360. Its chancellor was the Bishop of Bologna, and its doctors depended upon him rather than upon the student-body. The faculty received many privileges from Urban V, Boniface IX, and their successors. The popes, in fact, favoured the university in every possible way. Gregory IX and Boniface VIII sent it the Decretals (q. v.); Benedict XIV, various bulls and encyclicals. Among its benefactors were Martin V, Eugene IV, Nicholas V, Paul II, Innocent VIII, Paul III, Pius IV, Clement VIII, Urban VIII, Innocent X, and Clement XII. Gregory XI founded (1372), in connexion with the university, the *Collegium Gregorianum* for poor students of medicine and philosophy. Other colleges with similar scope were established by laymen and ecclesiastics (see list in Moroni). One of the most important was the College of Spain (*Casa Spagnuola*, or *Collegio Maggiore*), which owed its existence and endowment to Cardinal Albornoz (1364). The papal legates at Bologna took an active part in the direction of the university and eventually became the supreme authority. In the course of time, also, the student-body lost its control, and the various schools were consolidated in one university organization.

In the development of modern literature and science Bologna took an important part. The famous Cardinal Bessarion, a leader in the Renaissance movement, was legate from 1451 to 1455. Under his influence classical studies flourished in the university, and Humanists like Filelfo (1398–1481) and Guarino were among its professors. To these should be added, in more recent times, the great Mezzofanti (1774–1849). In the natural sciences, especially, Bologna points to a long list of distinguished men: the anatomists Achillini (1463–1512), Vesalius (1514–64), Varoli (1542–75), and Malpighi (1628–94), the botanist Aldrovandi (1522–1607), and the physicist Galvani (1737–98) are among the most illustrious. The number of women who taught at Bologna is also remarkable, including Novella, daughter of Joannes Andrea the jurist, Laura Bassi (1711–78), and Maria Agnesi (1718–99), mathematicians, and Clotilda Tambroni (1758–1817), professor of Greek.

During the Napoleonic wars, the university suffered considerably: chairs were suppressed, and the existence of the entire university was often endangered. The popes, in particular Leo XII, came to its assistance, reorganized the faculties, and provided generously for the continuation of scientific work. Their control, however, ceased when the Papal States were merged in the present Kingdom of Italy.

The university now comprises the faculties of philosophy and letters, mathematics and science, law, and medicine, with schools of pharmacy, agriculture, and engineering. The professors and instructors number 190; the students, 1800. The library, founded in 1605 by Aldrovandi, contains 250,000 volumes. One of the most important institutes connected with the university is the Academy of Science, established in 1690 by the generous Count Marsigli, and reorganized by Pius VIII in 1829.

RASHDALL, *The Universities of Europe in the Middle Ages* (Oxford, 1895), I; KIRKPATRICK, *The Octocentenary Festival of the University of Bologna* (Edinburgh, 1899); SAVIGNY, *The University of Bologna in the Middle Ages in Amer. Jour. of Education* (1871); SARTI, *De claris archigymnasii Bononiensis professoribus* (Bologna, 1769); ID., new ed. by ALBICINIUS (ibid., 1888); CASSANI, *Dell' Antico Studio di Bologna e sua origine* (ibid., 1888); MALAGOLA, *Monografie Storiche sullo Studio Bolognese* (ibid., 1888); FITTING, *Die Anfänge der Rechtsschule zu Bologna* (Berlin and Leipzig, 1888); MORONI, *Dizionario*, LXXXIV; CHEVALIER, *Topo-Bibliographie*, s. v.

E. A. PACE.

Bolsec, JÉRÔME-HERMÈS, a theologian and physician, b. probably at Paris, date unknown; d. at Lyons c. 1584. He became a Carmelite monk at Paris. A sermon which he preached there aroused misgivings in ecclesiastical circles regarding the soundness of his ideas, and Bolsec left Paris. Having separated from the Catholic Church about 1545 he took refuge at the Court of Renée, Duchess of Ferrara, who was favourably disposed towards persons holding Protestant views. Here he married, and began the study of medicine, about 1550 settling as a physician at Veigy, near Geneva. A theological controversy with Calvin, whose doctrine of predestination he deemed an absurdity, soon ensued. In 1551, at one of the religious conferences or public discussions, then held at Geneva every Friday, he interrupted the orator of the day, Jean de Saint André, who was speaking on predestination, and argued against him. As the triumph of his ideas would have meant the ruin of Calvin's influence in the Swiss city, Bolsec was arrested, and through the influence of the reformer banished forever from Geneva (1551). In 1555 he was also driven from Thonon, in the Bernese territory, whither he had retired. He went to Paris and sought admission into the ministry of the Reformed Church. But his opinions were not found sufficiently orthodox, from a Reformed point of view, for one wishing to hold such a position. He was asked for a declaration of faith, but refused. He went to Lausanne (c. 1563), but as the signing of the Confession of Bern was made a condition of his residence here, he preferred to return to France. Shortly after this, he recanted his errors, was reconciled with the Catholic Church, and published biographies of the two Genevan reformers, Calvin and Beza (1519–1605). These works are violent in tone, and find little favour with Protestant writers. Their historical statements cannot always be relied on. They are "Histoire de la vie, des mœurs . . . de Jean Calvin" (Lyons and Paris, 1577; published in Latin at Cologne in 1580; German tr. 1581); "Histoire de la vie et des mœurs de Th. de Bèze" (Paris, 1582). The life of Calvin was edited by L. F. Chastel in 1875 with extracts from the life of Beza.

FRITZ in *Kirchenlex.*; SCHAFF, *History of the Christian Church* (New York, 1903), VII, 614–621; WALKER, *John Calvin* (New York, 1906), 116–119, 315–320. N. A. WEBER.

Bolsena. See ORVIETO.

Bolsena, MIRACLE OF. See ORVIETO.

Bolton, EDMUND, historian, antiquary, and poet, born c. 1575; died c. 1633. The genuine loyalty to the Catholic Faith which seems to have marked the career of this eccentric and unfortunate genius is indicated by the second name which appears in a signature of his preserved in Harleian MS. 6521 at the British Museum—"Edmundus Maria Boltonus".

The same MS. furnishes us with a clue to sundry details of his life. He seems to have been born of Catholic parents in Leicestershire, and must have been of good family and position, for he claims to have continued "many years on his own charge a free commoner at Trinity Hall, Cambridge", and after going to London to study law to have lived there "in the best and choicest company of gentlemen". There can be no doubt that there was a strong Catholic element among the lawyers of the Inner Temple (Richard Southwell, the father of the martyr, might be named as one example among many), and the tone of the drama and much of the lighter literature of the late Elizabethan and early Jacobean period shows that the Bohemian society into which Bolton and his fellows were thrown was often pronouncedly papist. But while many who for a while were Romanizers, like his friend Ben Jonson, ultimately fell away, Bolton, much to his credit, remained stanch to his principles. Of his ability and zeal in the pursuit of knowledge there can be no question. He was the friend of Cotton and Camden, whose antiquarian researches he shared, and as a writer of verses he was associated with Sidney, Spenser, Raleigh, and others in the publication of "England's Helicon". Many influential friends, including for example the Duke, then Marquess, of Buckingham, tried to help him in his pecuniary embarrassments, but there seems no doubt that his Catholicism stood in the way of his making a living by literature. For instance, a life of King Henry II which he had prepared for an edition of Speed's "Chronicle", then in course of publication, was rejected on account of the too favourable aspect in which he had depicted St. Thomas of Canterbury. It seems, however, that through Buckingham's influence he obtained some small post about the court of James I, and in 1617 he proposed to the king some scheme for a royal academy or college of letters which was to be associated with the Order of the Garter, and which was destined in the mind of its designer to convert Windsor Castle into a sort of English Olympus. James I gave some encouragement to the scheme, but died before it was carried into execution. With the accession of Charles I, Bolton seems to have fallen on evil days. The last years of his life were mostly spent either in the Fleet or in the Marshalsea as a prisoner for debt, to which no doubt the fines he incurred as a "recusant convict" largely contributed. The exact date of his death is unknown. Besides his contributions in English verse to "England's Helicon" Bolton wrote a certain amount of Latin poetry. He is best remembered, however, as the author of "The Elements of Armories", a curious heraldic dialogue published anonymously in 1610, and of "Nero Cæsar, or Monarchie depraved", a book of Roman history dealing in part with the earliest notices of Britain. A translation of the "Histories" of Florus which he also published is signed "Philanactophil" (i. e. friend of the king's friend). Bolton's "Hypercritica", a useful work of literary criticism, was published long after his death.

COOPER in *Dict. Nat. Biog.*, V, 325; GILLOW, *Bibl. Dict. Eng. Catholics*, I, 257–259; *Archæologia*, xxxii, 132–149.

HERBERT THURSTON.

Bolzano, BERNHARD, Austrian mathematician

and philosopher, b. at Prague, 5 October, 1781; d. 18 December, 1848. As a student he devoted himself chiefly to mathematics with marked success. Against the wish of his father, he entered the ecclesiastical state and was ordained in 1805. In the same year he was appointed professor of the philosophy of religion in the University of Prague. His lectures and discourses were strongly tinged with rationalism, and it was not long before he was denounced to the ecclesiastical authorities. Through the personal intervention of the Prince-Archbishop Salm-Salm of Prague, he retained his professorship until 1820, when the long-threatened dismissal was suddenly put into effect in consequence of disorders that occurred in the seminary of Leitmeritz then under the direction of Dr. Fessl, who, as a disciple and friend of Bolzano, was strongly imbued with the latter's rationalizing spirit. Bolzano spent the remainder of his life in studious retirement, first on the estate of his friend Johann Hoffmann, at Techobuz, near Prague, and later in the house of his brother at Prague. A small pension, and the generosity of Count Leo Thun, relieved him of all monetary care.

Bolzano was always a loyal son of the Catholic Church. There is, however, a strong rationalizing tendency in his writings on doctrinal subjects, and his refusal to retract several propositions taken from his printed works justified his dismissal from the University of Prague. Bolzano's contributions to the science of mathematics are of the highest order. In 1804 he published a theory of parallel lines which anticipated Legendre's well-known theory. He shares with Cauchy the honour of having developed the theory of functions of one real variable. He made notable additions to the theory of differentiation, to the concept of infinity, and to the binomial theorem. As a philosopher, Bolzano had no sympathy for speculation as such. His mathematical bent made him a partisan of strict, methodic inquiry. His contributions to philosophy comprise a textbook on the "Science of Religion" (4 vols., Sulzbach, 1834), and one on the "Science of Knowledge" (4 vols., Sulzbach, 1837). Bolzano's complete writings fill twenty-five volumes. The full list is found in the "Sitzungsberichte" of the Vienna Academy (1849).

FESSL, *Bolzanos Autobiographie* (Vienna, 1875); WISSHAUPT, *Skizzen aus dem Leben Bolzanos* (Leipzig, 1849); ERDMANN, *History of Philosophy*, tr. (London, 1890), II, 463–471.

MATTHIAS LEIMKUHLER.

Bombay (BOMBAYENSIS), ARCHDIOCESE OF, comprises the Island of Bombay with several outlying churches in the neighbouring Island of Salsette, and a large portion of the Bombay Presidency stretching northwards from the river Nerbudda as far as Quetta, including the districts of Gujerat (Broach, Baroda, Ahmedabad), Kathiawar, Cutch, Sind and a portion of Beluchistan. Most of the archdiocese is thus separated from its centre in Bombay Island by a distance of about 200 miles, the intervening country being assigned to the Diocese of Damaun. The Catholic population under the archbishop is reckoned at about 18,000, of which about 8,000 are in Bombay Island; 3,500 in Salsette; 2,000 in Gujerat, Kathiawar, and Cutch, and 4,500 in Sind and Beluchistan. The archdiocese is served by 50 fathers, 19 scholastics, and 16 lay brothers of the German province of the Society of Jesus, and 19 native secular priests, attending 24 churches and 25 chapels, besides Sisters of the Orders of Jesus and Mary and the Daughters of the Cross engaged in education and charitable work.

HISTORY.—In 1534 the Portuguese began to settle in Bombay. They were accompanied by the Franciscans, who gradually covered the island with churches, monasteries, and communities of converts. When in 1665 the island was ceded to the English, the work was continued by the same order and by secular clergy from Goa. In 1720, on political grounds, the Goanese clergy were expelled by the Government, and the Vicar of the Great Mogul (formerly the Vicar of the Deccan) was invited to take charge of the Catholics. Although

CHURCH OF THE HOLY NAME, BOMBAY

this was done with the approval of Rome, the Goanese clergy from time to time tried with the Government to recover their position, and in 1764 established a "double jurisdiction". At first the vicariate extended indefinitely over the north of India; but in 1784 the northern portion was separated and given over to the Mission of Tibet. The vicariate then gradually began to be called the Vicariate of Bombay. It was under the care of the Carmelite fathers from 1720 to 1854. When they resigned their charge the vicariate was divided, the northern, or Bombay portion, being taken over by the Capuchins, while the southern, or Poona portion, was given to the German Jesuits. A few years later the Capuchins also resigned, and hence in 1858 the whole of the Bombay-Poona Mission came into the hands of the German Jesuits. Meantime a distressing conflict over the rights of jurisdiction (often referred to in literature as the Goan or Indo-Portuguese schism) was raging between the Goanese clergy of the Portuguese "padroado" and the vicars Apostolic under Propaganda, which, in spite of certain ineffectual negotiations, continued till 1886. In that year a concordat with Portugal was entered into by the Holy See, which brought the quarrel to a close, and at the same time the whole of India was placed under a fully constituted hierarchy. The Archbishop of Bombay received territorial jurisdiction over Bombay Island and over the northern districts already described, with Poona as a suffragan diocese. Mangalore and Trichinopoly were added as suffragan sees in 1893, in which year the First Provincial Council was held (Acta et Decreta, Bombay, 1898). The Island of Salsette and the coast country as far as the Nerbudda were placed under the jurisdiction of the Bishop of Damaun who also received personal jurisdiction in Bombay Island over all who came from Goa, or from any other district under the Portuguese ecclesiastical regime. This arrangement is popularly known as the "double jurisdiction".

SUCCESSION OF PRELATES.—*Vicars-Apostolic of the Carmelite order:* Maurice of St. Teresa, 1718–26; Peter D'Alcantara of the Most Holy Trinity, 1728–45; Innocent of the Presentation, 1746–53; John Dominic of St. Clara, 1755–72; Charles of St. Conrad, 1775–85; Victor of St. Mary, 1787–93; Peter D'Alcantara of St. Antony, 1794–1840; Aloysius Mary Fortini, 1840–48; John F. Whelan, 1848–

50. *Capuchin*, Anastasius Hartmann, 1850–58.
Jesuits: Alexis Canoz (administrator), 1858–61;
Walter Steins, 1861–1867; Leo Meurin (a writer and
lecturer of considerable merit), 1867–87; George
Porter (first archbishop), 1886–89; Theodore Dalhoff,
1891–1906; Hermann Jurgens, appointed 28 May,
consecrated, 14 July, 1907.

INSTITUTIONS.—*In Bombay Island.*—The High
School of St. Xavier with 1,400 pupils; the College
of St. Xavier with about 350 students preparing
for Bombay University degrees. The majority of
these pupils are non-Christians, whose admission,
however, brings prestige, personal respect and esteem
to the Catholic body, and enables the College to work
on a financial basis, making it possible to provide a
good education for Catholics. Further, St. Mary's
High School with 190 boarders and 310 day-scholars,
mostly Europeans or Eurasians. The teaching staff of

ST. XAVIER'S HIGH SCHOOL

these three institutions consists of Jesuit fathers and
scholastics, assisted by lay masters. For girls, High
Schools at Clare Road, Parel, and the Fort, and a
native school at Cavel, under the Nuns of Jesus and
Mary. Other charitable institutions: St. Joseph's
Foundling Home and St. Vincent's Home for poor
women and girls, under the Daughters of the Cross;
St. Elizabeth's Widows' Home, under the Nuns of
Jesus and Mary; the Allbless Leper Home, Trombay,
and the Deaf and Dumb Institute under a European
secular priest. *In Salsette:* St. Stanislaus's Institution, Bandra, under the Jesuit fathers, with 240
native boarders and 450 day-scholars; St. Joseph's
Convent, Bandra, under the Daughters of the Cross,
for native girls, with 330 boarders and 220 day-
scholars. *In the Northern Districts:* St. Patrick's High
School, at Karachi, with 306 pupils; St. Joseph's
Convent School, Karachi, with 70 boarders and 300
day-scholars; St. Paul's Orphanage belonging to the
pagan mission at Anand in Gujerat with 100 orphans;
St. Joseph's Convent, Ahmedabad, with 100 pupils;
besides smaller establishments of all kinds scattered
over the archdiocese. There is no diocesan seminary,
the native secular clergy being trained at the Papal
Seminary at Kandy in Ceylon. The finest buildings
in the archdiocese are the Church of the Holy Name
with the archbishop's residence and Convent School,
Bombay; the Bombay Cathedral, a large structure in
the Portuguese style; St. Patrick's Church, Karachi;
the collegiate buildings of St. Xavier's and St. Mary's,
Bombay, to which latter St. Anne's Church is attached. Local publications include "The Examiner"
(formerly called the " Bombay Catholic Examiner ")
edited by a Jesuit father; established in 1849 it is

II.—41

published weekly at the Examiner Press which is the
property of the archbishop; "The Bombay East
Indian", the weekly organ of the Native Christians
of Bombay; a local "Supplement" to the English
"Messenger"; a "Messenger of the Sacred Heart"
in Marathi, besides a number of vernacular books in
Marathi, Gujerati, etc., published according to need.

The Catholic Directory (Madras, 1907); Catalogues of the
Bombay Mission; Diocesan Archives and Records (unpublished);
The Examiner and The Pastoral Gazette (the latter ceased
publication in 1904) files; Life of Dr. Hartmann (Calcutta,
1868); Monseigneur Alexis Canoz (Paris, 1891). No proper
history of the Mission has yet been written, though materials
are being collected for that purpose.

ERNEST R. HULL.

Bommel, CORNELIUS RICHARD ANTON VAN, Bishop of Liège, was b. at Leyden, in Holland, on
5 April, 1790; d. 7 April, 1852. He was educated at
the college of Willingshegge near Münster, and later
at the advanced school of Borght. Against strong
opposition he entered the seminary of Münster and
was ordained priest in 1816 by Bishop Gaspard
Droste de Vischering. On his return to Holland he
founded a college for young men at Hageveld, near
Haarlem. This college was closed in 1825 in consequence of the royal decree that subjected all the
educational institutions to State control. King William offered van Bommel the presidency of another
college, but met with a firm refusal. The Catholics
and Liberals joined forces in opposing the arbitrary
policy of the Government, and van Bommel took a
prominent part in the agitation that forced the king
to promulgate the Concordat concluded with Leo XII.
Under the provisions of the Concordat, van Bommel
was nominated to the See of Liège and consecrated
on 15 November, 1829. He took no active part in
the revolution of 1830, but as Bishop of Liège he was
forced to sever his connexion with Holland. In a
few years he remedied the evils which a vacancy of
more than twenty years had occasioned in his diocese. He reorganized the seminary, revived Catholic
elementary education, and gave the first impetus to
the foundation of a Catholic university.

Bishop van Bommel was a zealous defender of the
primacy of the Holy See, an aggressive opponent of
Freemasonry, and an ardent advocate of religious
education. At the reorganization of public instruction in 1842, his educational views were put in force
in those gymnasia and technical schools which the
State maintained wholly or in part. His writings
comprise three volumes of "Pastoral Letters", and
a number of pamphlets on ecclesiastical and educational questions.

SMET in Biographie Nationale (Brussels, 1868), II; CAPI-
TAINE, Nécrologie liégeoise pour 1853; JACQUEMOTTE, Eloge
funèbre.

MATTHIAS LEIMKUHLER.

Bona, GIOVANNI, a distinguished cardinal and
author, b. of an old French family at Mondovi in
Piedmont, 19 October, according to some 10 October,
1609; d. at Rome, 28 October, 1674. Although his
father favoured a military career for him, after passing some years at a nearby Jesuit college he entered
the Cistercian monastery at Pignerola, where, as also
later at Rome, he pursued his studies with exceptional
success. He laboured for fifteen years at Turin,
then as prior at Asti and as abbot at Mondovi, and
in 1651 was called to preside over the whole congregation. During his seven years of official life in Rome
he modestly declined all further honours, at one time
even refusing the Bishopric of Asti. He welcomed
the expiration of his third term in the scholar's hope
that he would be allowed to enjoy a life of retirement
and study, but his intimate friend, Pope Alexander
VII, wishing to honour his learning and piety, made
him Consultor to the Congregation of the Index and
to the Holy Office. In 1669 he was created cardinal,
and then the beauty of his character was fully re-

vealed; there was no change in his extremely simple manner of life, and every year he donated his surplus revenue to the needy priests of the Missionary College at Rome.

His best known ascetical works are: "Via Compendii ad Deum" (1657); "Principia et documenta vitæ Christianæ" (1673); "Manuductio ad cœlum" (1658); and "Horologium Asceticum" (Paris, 1676). The "Manuductio" is often compared to the "Imitation of Christ" on account of the simplicity of the style in which the solid doctrine is taught. It has always been extremely popular. Besides passing through fourteen Latin editions in four decades, it has been translated into Italian, French, German, Armenian, and Spanish. The latest translation is in English by Sir Robert L'Estrange (A Guide to Eternity, London, 1900). Shortly after his ordination he collected together some of the most beautiful passages in the Fathers on the august Sacrifice of the Mass, and later published them in a booklet, which with certain additions grew into his "De Sacrificio Missæ", a useful Mass book. In addition he composed several unpublished works, known as "Ascetici", for the instruction of members of his own order.

But his fame does not rest solely on his devotional writings. He was a deep student of antiquity, and so successful in treating of the use of the Psalter in the Christian Church (De Divinâ Psalmodiâ, Paris, 1663) that Cardinal Pallavicini urged him to undertake the history of the Sacrifice of the Mass. Realizing the magnitude of the task he at first declined, but finally set to work and after more than seven years' labour brought out his famous work familiar to all students of liturgy: "De Rebus Liturgicis" (Rome, 1671). It is a veritable encyclopedia of historic information on all subjects bearing on the Mass, such as rites, churches, vestments, etc. Not least remarkable about these volumes, besides the wealth of material gathered together, are the classic purity, the manly vigour, and the charming simplicity of the Latin style. The best edition of this work is by Robert Sala (Turin, 1747–53), who also in 1755 brought out a very interesting volume of Bona's letters. The first of the many editions of his complete works was published at Antwerp in 1677.

Fabroni, Vitæ Italorum doctrinâ excellentium, etc. (Pisa, 1778–1805), XIII, 7; Mazzuchelli, Gli scrittori d'Italia (Brescia, 1753–63, II; Part III, 1515); Bertolotti, Vita Joannis Bona (Asti, 1677); Goujet, Vie du cardinal Bona in the French translation of De principiis vitæ Christianæ (Paris, 1728); Dupin, Bibliothèque des auteurs ecclés. du XVIIᵉ siècle (Paris, 1708), III, 56.

Leo F. O'Neil.

Bonacum, Thomas. See Lincoln, Diocese of.

Bona Fides. See Faith.

Bonagratia of Bergamo (or Pergamo), Friar Minor, theologian, and canonist, date of birth unknown; d. at Munich, 1343. Before his entrance into religion, he was known as Boncortese, a name which was adopted at times by Clement V who used to call him dilectus filius Frater Boncortese, dictus Bonagratia de Pergamo. Though Bonagratia took an active and important part in the controversy with the so-called Spiritual Friars, especially with Ubertino of Casale, one of their leaders, his biography is interesting principally because of his connexion with the famous dispute concerning the poverty of Christ. The contest began at Narbonne in 1321 between the Dominicans and Franciscans, and the main question at issue seems to have been whether it is heretical to assert that Christ and His Apostles possessed no property either in particular or in common. On account of the important bearing of the controversy on the rule of the Friars Minor, a general chapter of the order was convoked at Perugia, in June of the year 1322, and the minister general, together with the other members of the chapter, caused two letters or communications to be published in which the mind of the chapter regarding the controversy is set forth at considerable length, and with unmistakable distinctness; while Bonagratia was chosen to be the representative of the chapter before the papal Curia at Avignon. Displeased at the action of the chapter at Perugia, Pope John XXII published the Bull "Ad conditorem canonum" in which he renounces the dominion of all the goods of the Friars Minor hitherto assumed by the Roman pontiffs, and declares that the ownership of a thing cannot be separated from its actual use or consumption. At the public consistory held in January, 1323, Bonagratia appeared in the presence of the pope and cardinals, and with more zeal perhaps than discretion openly opposed the papal constitution. His boldness, however, was of little avail, for the Bull "Ad conditorem" was again promulgated in lengthier form, but bearing its previous date of 8 December, 1322, and the audacious Bonagratia himself was cast into prison. He was released after a year's confinement, and in 1330 followed the Emperor Louis of Bavaria to Munich, together with the Ex-Minister General Michael of Cesena and William of Occam. Still under sentence of excommunication, Bonagratia died there and was buried in the Barfüsserkirche, where Michael of Cesena and William of Occam also found their last resting-place. Among the writings of Bonagratia may be mentioned his "Articuli probationum", composed in confutation of the errors of Ubertino of Casale above mentioned.

Wadding, Annales Minorum, VI, 401–405; VII, 1–7; Bullarium Franciscanum, V, 233–246; Hurter, Nomenclator, IV, 483; Analecta Franciscana (Quaracchi, 1887), II, 81, 89, passim; Othon de Pavie, L'Aquitaine Séraphique (Auch, 1900), XIX, 188, 190.

Stephen M. Donovan.

Bonal, François de, Bishop of Clermont, b. 1734 at the castle of Bonal, near Agen; d. at Munich, 1800. He had been Vicar-General of Agen and Director of the Carmelite Nuns in France when he was made Bishop of Clermont, 1776. On the eve of the Revolution, as he was warning his diocesans against the license of the press, he foretold the visitations of God that were coming. He went as one of the deputies of the clergy to the Etats-Généraux of 1789, where he distinguished himself by his moderation and firmness. To Target who spoke of the "God of peace" he replied that the God of peace was also the God of order and justice. From his prison Louis XVI sent for his opinion as to whether he should receive Paschal Communion. The answer was full of sympathy, yet the unfortunate monarch was advised to abstain "for having sanctioned decrees destructive of religion". Bonal was alluding chiefly to the civil constitution of the clergy. Having declined to take the constitutional oath, he was compelled to leave his diocese and country. He passed to Flanders and later to Holland, was captured and sentenced to deportation by the French, but succeeded in making his escape and spent the last years of his life in various cities of Germany. He is the author of a "Testament spirituel".

Feller, Biographie Universelle (Paris, 1866); de Crèvecœur, Journal d'Andrien Duquesnoy (Paris, 1894).

J. F. Sollier.

Bonal, Raymond, French theologian and founder of the Congregation of the Priests of St. Mary (Bonalists), b. at Villefranche in Rouergue, 15 August, 1600; d. at Agde, Hérault, France, c. 1653. He studied classics and philosophy with the Jesuits at Cahors; theology and canon and civil law at the University of Toulouse, where he received the degree of Doctor in Theology in 1628. In 1632, he conceived the idea of organizing a community of priests in whose life and labours should be exemplified the spirit of St. Francis de Sales. With two other ecclesiastics, he began to lead a community life in a house near the church of Our Lady of Pity, Villefranche. He was soon joined by others, and in 1639 the parish of Foix in the Diocese of Pamiers was entrusted to his community, which a few years later opened a seminary at Villefranche with Bonal as its director. In 1650 he organized a seminary and college at Toulouse and, having gone to Agde with a similar purpose, in 1653, fell a victim to an epidemic. The congregation founded by Bonal was approved in 1665 by Pope Alexander VII, and in 1678 by King Louis XIV. For lack of subjects, however, the seminaries confided to the Bonalists languished and were successively handed over to the Congregation of the Mission. After a little more than a hundred years of existence, the congregation itself was absorbed by the Lazarists.

Raymond Bonal published a "Cours de théologie morale" the 8th edition of which is dated, Paris, 1685. This course, which was followed in the Sulpician seminaries at Toulouse, Valence, Thiers, and elsewhere, was translated into Latin by Pierre Laur (Toulouse, 1674), under the title "Theologia Moralis R. Bonalis". Another work of Raymond Bonal, "Explication littérale et mystique des rubriques" was published at Lyons in 1679.

MANGENOT in *Dict. de théol. cath.*; FAILLON, *Vie de M. Olier* (Paris, 1873), X; MERCADIER, *Les constitutions, règlements et directoires de la congrégation des Prêtres de Sainte Marie* (Mende, 1689); BERTRAND, *Bibliothèque Sulpicienne* (Paris, 1900),I; *Recueil des principales circulaires des supérieurs généraux de la congrégation de la mission* (Paris, 1877), I; *Archives nationales* (Paris), S. 6705, 6715, 6716; *Archives of the Congregation of the Mission* (Paris), MS. 1101.

F. V. NUGENT.

Bonald, LOUIS-GABRIEL-AMBROISE, VICOMTE DE, French statesman, writer, and philosopher, b. at Monna, near Millau, in Rouergue (Aveyron) 2 October, 1754; d. at Paris, 23 November, 1840. He was educated by the Oratorians at the College of Juilly; joined the king's musketeers, returned to his own province in 1776, was elected mayor of Millau in 1785, and in 1790 was chosen member of the departmental Assembly for Aveyron. He resigned in 1791, emigrated, became a soldier in the army of Condé, and, when the army was disbanded, retired to Heidelberg, where he took charge of the education of his two elder sons.

Bonald published at Constance, in 1797, his first work: "Théorie du pouvoir politique et religieux", which was suppressed in France by order of the Directory. In 1797 Bonald returned to France under the name of Saint-Séverin, and published "Essai analytique sur les lois naturelles de l'ordre social" (1800); "Du divorce" (1801); and "La législation primitive" (1802). He also collaborated with Chateaubriand and others in the "Mercure de France", contributing several articles which were published in book form with other studies in 1819 under the title "Mélanges littéraires, politiques, et philosophiques". In 1808 he declined to be a member of the Council of the University, but finally accepted in 1810. He refused to take charge of the education of the son of Louis Bonaparte, King of Holland, and of the King of Rome, the son of Napoleon I.

A monarchist and royalist by nature and by principles, Bonald welcomed the restoration of the Bourbons. He was appointed a member of the Academy by royal decree in 1816. From 1815 to 1822 he served as deputy from Aveyron, and in 1823 became a peer of France. He then directed his efforts against all attempts at liberalism in religion and politics. The law against divorce was proposed by him in 1815 and passed in 1816. He took a prominent part in the law of 1822 which did away with the liberty of the press and established a committee of censure of which he was the president. In 1815 he published his "Réflexions sur l'intérêt général de l'Europe"; in 1817, "Pensées sur divers sujets" in 2 vols. 8vo. (2d ed., Paris, 1887); in 1818 "Recherches philosophiques sur les premiers objets des connaissances morales"; in 1827, "Démonstration philosophique du principe constitutif des sociétés". Meanwhile he collaborated with Chateaubriand, Lamennais, and Berryer, in the "Conservateur", and later in the "Défenseur" founded by Lamennais. In 1830 he gave up his peerage and led a life of retirement in his native city.—"There is not to be found in this long career", says Jules Simon, "one action which is not consistent with his principles, one expression which belies them."

G. M. SAUVAGE.

Bonald, LOUIS-JACQUES-MAURICE DE, Cardinal, b. at Millau, in Rouergue (now Aveyron), 30 October, 1787; d. at Lyons, 25 Feb., 1870. He was the fourth son of the Vicomte de Bonald, the celebrated statesman and philosopher. Destined for the Church, he studied at Saint-Sulpice and was ordained priest in 1811. He was first attached to the imperial chapel and after the Restoration went to Rome as secretary to Archbishop de Pressigny, who was entrusted by Louis XVIII with the task of arranging for a new Concordat. Three years later Bishop Latil of Chartres made him his vicar-general. When the Diocese of Puy was re-established (1823) Bonald became its first bishop and remained there for six-

LOUIS CARDINAL DE BONALD

teen years, until his promotion to the primatial See of Lyons (1839), and in 1841 Gregory XVI made him cardinal. Cardinal de Bonald is one of the glories of the French episcopate. His personal qualities, as well as the salient features of his episcopal career, are most easily found in the only work we have from his pen, that long series of "Mandements et lettres pastorales", which show him to have been pious, sympathetic, eloquent, and full of zeal. His zeal seems to have embraced all vital interests. In point of doctrine, Bonald contributed a large share towards destroying all remnants of Gallicanism and Jansenism. The Jansenistic interpolations made by Montazet in the liturgical books of Lyons were, after a long struggle, finally suppressed. Dupin's Gallican book, "Manuel de droit ecclésiastique", was severely condemned by the primate, and when the Council of State declared him guilty of abuse (1845), Bonald replied that the censure had not even touched him because "when the Council of State has pronounced on questions of doctrine, the cause is not finished". In matters of discipline Cardinal de Bonald corrected many abuses, and he crowned his work by convening a provincial synod (1850), whose statutes touched all the main points of church government. He always took great interest in social questions, and never was more eloquent than when appealing for help in behalf of misery, as for instance during the floods of 1840 and 1846 and the destitution of the Spanish refugees (1842). The closing of silk factories in Lyons gave him an opportunity of showing not only his liberality towards the needy, but also his broad sympathy for the toiling class in general.

The mainspring of Cardinal de Bonald's life, however, was his love of the Church, which he desired first of all to have respected. In 1825 the royal court of Paris, in rendering a verdict, implied that the whole body of clergy was disloyal to the Crown; Bonald in a dignified letter of protest to the king replied: "Were the clergy less loyal, they would not be the object of such hatred". He also desired the freedom of the Church, and his pastoral letter of 1846, "La liberté de l'Eglise", remains one of his best efforts. Of all the privileges essential to the Church, that of teaching seemed to him first and foremost. On several occasions he wrote either to approve or to condemn the legislation concerning schools. The royal ordinance of 1824 placing the schools under the surveillance of the bishops met with his entire approval; but the ordinances of 1828 establishing a new mode of 'direction for primary schools and even interfering with ecclesiastical schools for secondary education, as well as the Villemain educational bill of 1844 and Salvandy's project of 1847, he strongly opposed, thus preparing the way for the law of 1850. Having become, by the constitution of 1852, and by virtue of his dignity as cardinal, a member of the French Senate, Bonald showed once more his love of the Church by throwing the whole weight of his influence on the side of the Roman pontiff and the independence of the Holy See.

The long episcopal career of Bonald covers many successive political regimes. Although by birth and education a stanch legitimist, yet, as a bishop, he looked above the changes of human government to the Church and her welfare. Because the Revolution of February, 1848, with its motto "Liberty, Equality, Fraternity", seemed to him favourable to the best interests of the Church, he was one of the first bishops to welcome it. He wrote to his priests: "Give to the faithful the example of submission and obedience to the Republic. You have long cherished the hope of enjoying the liberty which makes our brethren of the United States so happy; that liberty you shall have." The same broadness of view he evinced when he refused to side with the Abbé Gaume on the question of the classics: "We decline to believe that the study of pagan authors has for three centuries instilled paganism into the social body."

FISQUET, La France pontificale, Métropole de Lyons (Paris); MIGNE, Orateurs sacrés (Paris) XIV; BEAUMONT, Vie du Cardinal de Bonald (Paris, 1870); L'épiscopat français depuis le Concordat jusqu'à la Séparation (Paris, 1907).

J. F. SOLLIER.

Bona Mors Confraternity, THE (HAPPY DEATH), was founded 2 October, 1648, in the Church of the Gesù, Rome, by Father Vincent Caraffa, seventh General of the Society of Jesus, and approved by the Sovereign Pontiffs Innocent X and Alexander VII. In 1729 it was raised to an archconfraternity and enriched with numerous indulgences by Benedict XIII. He authorized the Father General of the Society of Jesus, who, in virtue of his office, was the director, to erect Bona Mors confraternities in all churches of his order. In 1827 Leo XII gave to the director general the power to erect and affiliate branch confraternities in churches not belonging to the Society of Jesus, and to give them a share in all the privileges and indulgences of the archconfraternity. The object of the association is to prepare its members by a well regulated life to die in peace with God. The longer title: "Confraternity of Our Lord Jesus Christ dying on the Cross, and of the most Blessed Virgin Mary, His sorrowful Mother", expresses the chief means to attain that end, devotion to the Passion of Christ and to the sorrows of Mary. Besides this the union of prayers and good works of the associates and the

special instructions at the public meetings help powerfully to prepare for a happy death. The conditions for membership are to present oneself to the director; to express to him one's desire to become a member; to receive from him an outward sign of acceptance, usually in the form of a certificate of admission; and to have one's name registered in the local Bona Mors Register. Only "by an unusual and extraordinary exception", says a decree of the Sacred Congregation of Indulgences, "is it allowed to enroll those absent". The director is authorized to decide what constitutes such an exceptional case. The practices of the association and the indulgences granted to the members are specified in the manual of the confraternity (New York, 1896).

JOHN J. WYNNE.

Bonaparte, CHARLES-LUCIEN-JULES-LAURENT, PRINCE OF CANINO AND MUSIGNANO, ornithologist, b. in Paris, 24 May, 1803; d. in the same city 29 July, 1857. He was the eldest son of Lucien Bonaparte, the brother of Napoleon, and was educated in the universities of Italy. After his marriage to his cousin Zenaïde, daughter of Joseph Bonaparte, on 29 June, 1822, he came to the United States where his father-in-law was residing. While here he devoted himself to the study of natural science and particularly of ornithology. He undertook the completion of Wilson's "Ornithology or History of the Birds of the United States" in four volumes (Philadelphia, 1825–33). In this work he describes more than one hundred new species discovered by himself. He also published "Observations on the Nomenclature of Wilson's Ornithology" (in the Journal of the Philadelphia Academy); "Synopsis of the Birds of the United States" (in the Annals of the Lyceum of New York), etc. He returned to Europe in 1828 and took up his residence in Rome where he continued his scientific work. Upon the death of his father, Lucien, in 1840, he became Prince of Canino and Musignano and afterwards entered the political arena, associating himself with the anti-Austrian party. He did not, however, lose interest in his favourite studies for he organized and presided over several scientific congresses in Italy. He had been attached to Pius IX, but in 1848 he joined the radical party and in the following year was elected deputy of Viterbo and Vice-President of the Assembly. After the fall of the Republic he was obliged to leave Italy (July, 1849), but his cousin, Louis-Napoleon, refused to permit him to enter France until the following year when he settled in Paris. In 1854 he became director of the Jardin des Plantes. Bonaparte had twelve children of whom eight survived him. Among them was Lucien-Louis-Joseph-Napoleon, who was ordained priest in 1853 and was made cardinal in 1868. Bonaparte became an honorary member of the Academy of Upsala in 1833, and of the Academy of Sciences of Berlin in 1843, and corresponding member of the "Institut" in 1844. Besides his published works already referred to may be mentioned: "Specchio comparativo delle ornitologie di Roma e di Filadelfia" (Paris, 1827); "Iconografia della Fauna Italica" (Rome, 1834–41). This is his principal work and is illustrated with fine coloured plates. "Geographical and Comparative List of Birds of Europe and North America" (London, 1838); "Catalogo metodico degli uccelli Europei" (Bologna, 1842); "Conspectus systematis ornithologiæ" (Leyden, 1850); "Conspectus systematis ichthyologiæ" (Leyden, 1850); "Ornithologie fossile" (Paris, 1858).

DEBIDOUR in La grande encyc.; WOUTERS, Les Bonaparte depuis 1815; CANTÙ, Hist. de l'indépendance italienne, III; BALLYDIER, Hist. de la révolution de Rome de 1846–1850.

H. M. BROCK.

Bonaventure, SAINT, Doctor of the Church, Cardinal-Bishop of Albano, Minister General of the

Friars Minor, b. at Bagnorea in the vicinity of Viterbo in 1221; d. at Lyons, 15 July, 1274.

Nothing is known of Bonaventure's parents save their names: Giovanni di Fidanza and Maria Ritella. How his baptismal name of John came to be changed to that of Bonaventure is not clear. An attempt has been made to trace the latter name to the exclamation of St. Francis, *O buona ventura*, when Bonaventure was brought as an infant to him to be cured of a dangerous illness. This derivation is highly improbable; it seems based on a late fifteenth-century legend. Bonaventure himself tells us (Legenda S. Francisci Prolog.) that while yet a child he was preserved from death through the intercession of St. Francis, but there is no evidence that this cure took place during the lifetime of St. Francis or that the name Bonaventure originated in any prophetical words of St. Francis. It was certainly borne by others before the Seraphic Doctor. No details of Bonaventure's youth have been preserved. He entered the Order of Friars Minor in 1238 or 1243; the exact year is uncertain. Wadding and the Bollandists hold for the later date, but the earlier one is supported by Sbaralea, Bonelli, Panfilo da Magliano, and Jeiler, and appears more probable. It is certain that Bonaventure was sent from the Roman Province, to which he belonged, to complete his studies at the University of Paris under Alexander of Hales, the great founder of the Franciscan School. The latter died in 1245, according to the opinion generally received, though not yet definitely established, and Bonaventure seems to have become his pupil about 1242. Be this as it may, Bonaventure received in 1248 the "licentiate" which gave him the right to

teach publicly as *Magister regens*, and he continued to lecture at the university with great success until 1255, when he was compelled to discontinue, owing to the then violent outburst of opposition to the Mendicant orders on the part of the secular professors at the university. The latter, jealous, as it seems, of the academic successes of the Dominicans and Franciscans, sought to exclude them from teaching publicly. The smouldering elements of discord had been fanned into a flame in 1255, when Guillaume de Saint-Amour published a work entitled "The Perils of the Last Times", in which he attacked the Friars with great bitterness. It was in connexion with this dispute that Bonaventure wrote his treatise, "De paupertate Christi". It was not, however, Bonaventure, as some have erroneously stated, but Blessed John of Parma, who appeared before Alexander IV at Anagni to defend the Franciscans against their adversary. The Holy See having, as

is well known, re-established the Mendicants in all their privileges, and Saint-Amour's book having been formally condemned, the degree of Doctor was solemnly bestowed on St. Bonaventure and St. Thomas Aquinas at the university, 23 October, 1257.

In the meantime Bonaventure, though not yet thirty-six years old, had on 2 February, 1257, been elected Minister General of the Friars Minor—an office of peculiar difficulty, owing to the fact that the order was distracted by internal dissensions between the two factions among the Friars designated respectively the *Spirituales* and the *Relaxti*. The former insisted upon the literal observance of the original Rule, especially in regard to poverty, while the latter wished to introduce innovations and mitigations. This lamentable controversy had moreover been aggravated by the enthusiasm with which many of the "Spiritual" Friars had adopted the doctrines connected with the name of Abbot Joachim of Floris and set forth in the so-called "Evangelium æternum". The introduction to this pernicious book, which proclaimed the approaching dispensation of the Spirit that was to replace the Law of Christ, was falsely attributed to Bl. John of Parma, who in 1257 had retired from the government of the order in favour of Bonaventure. The new general lost no time in striking vigorously at both extremes within the order. On the one hand, he proceeded against several of the Joachimite "Spirituals" as heretics before an ecclesiastical tribunal at Città-della-Pieve; two of their leaders were condemned to perpetual imprisonment, and John of Parma was only saved from a like fate through the personal intervention of Cardinal Ottoboni, afterwards Adrian V.

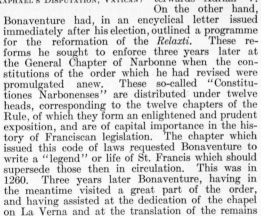

St. Bonaventure (Detail from Raphael's Disputation, Vatican)

On the other hand, Bonaventure had, in an encyclical letter issued immediately after his election, outlined a programme for the reformation of the *Relaxti*. These reforms he sought to enforce three years later at the General Chapter of Narbonne when the constitutions of the order which he had revised were promulgated anew. These so-called "Constitutiones Narbonenses" are distributed under twelve heads, corresponding to the twelve chapters of the Rule, of which they form an enlightened and prudent exposition, and are of capital importance in the history of Franciscan legislation. The chapter which issued this code of laws requested Bonaventure to write a "legend" or life of St. Francis which should supersede those then in circulation. This was in 1260. Three years later Bonaventure, having in the meantime visited a great part of the order, and having assisted at the dedication of the chapel on La Verna and at the translation of the remains of St. Clare and of St. Anthony, convoked a general chapter of the order of Pisa at which his newly composed life of St. Francis was officially approved as the standard biography of the saint to the exclusion of all others. At this chapter of 1263, Bonaventure fixed the limits of the different provinces of the order and, among other ordinances, prescribed that at nightfall a bell should be rung in honour of the Annunciation, a pious practice from which the Angelus seems to have originated. There are no grounds, however, for the assertion that Bonaventure in this chapter prescribed the celebration of the feast of the Immaculate Conception in the order. In 1264, at the earnest request of Cardinal Cajetan, Bonaventure consented to resume the direction of the Poor Clares which the Chapter of Pisa had entirely renounced the year before. He required the Clares, however, to acknowledge occasionally in writing that the favours tendered them by the Friars were voluntary acts of charity not arising from any obligation whatsoever. It is said that Pope Urban IV acted at Bonaventure's suggestion in attempting to establish uniformity of observance throughout all the monasteries of Clares. About this time (1264) Bonaventure founded at Rome the Society of the Gonfalone in honour of the Blessed Virgin which, if not the first confraternity instituted in the Church, as some have claimed, was certainly one of the earliest. In 1265 Clement IV, by a Bull dated 23 November, nominated Bonaventure to the vacant Archbishopric of York, but the saint, in keeping with his singular humility, steadfastly refused this honour and the pope yielded.

In 1266 Bonaventure convened a general chapter in Paris at which, besides other enactments, it was decreed that all the "legends" of St. Francis written before that of Bonaventure should be forthwith destroyed, just as the Chapter of Narbonne had in 1260 ordered the destruction of all constitutions before those then enacted. This decree has excited much hostile criticism. Some would fain see in it a deliberate attempt on Bonaventure's part to close the primitive sources of Franciscan history, to suppress the real Francis, and substitute a counterfeit in his stead. Others, however, regard the decree in question as a purely liturgical ordinance intended to secure uniformity in the choir "legends". Between these two conflicting opinions the truth seems to be that this edict was nothing more than another heroic attempt to wipe out the old quarrels and start afresh. One cannot but regret the circumstances of this decree, but when it is recalled that the appeal of the contending parties was ever to the words and actions of St. Francis as recorded in the earlier "legends", it would be unjust to accuse the chapter of "literary vandalism" in seeking to proscribe the latter. We have no details of Bonaventure's life between 1266 and 1269. In the latter year he convoked his fourth general chapter at Assisi, in which it was enacted that a Mass be sung every Saturday throughout the order in honour of the Blessed Virgin, not, however, in honour of her Immaculate Conception as Wadding among others has erroneously stated. It was probably soon after this chapter that Bonaventure composed his "Apologia pauperum", in which he silences Gerard of Abbeville who by means of an anonymous libel had revived the old university feud against the Friars. Two years later, Bonaventure was mainly instrumental in reconciling the differences among the cardinals assembled at Viterbo to elect a successor to Clement IV, who had died nearly three years before; it was on Bonaventure's advice that, 1 September, 1271, they unanimously chose Theobald Visconti of Piacenza who took the title of Gregory X. That the cardinals seriously authorized Bonaventure to nominate himself, as some writers aver, is most improbable. Nor is there

any truth in the popular story that Bonaventure on arriving at Viterbo advised the citizens to lock up the cardinals with a view to hastening the election. In 1272 Bonaventure for the second time convened a general chapter at Pisa in which, apart from general enactments to further regular observances, new decrees were issued respecting the direction of the Poor Clares, and a solemn anniversary was instituted on 25 August in memory of St. Louis. This was the first step towards the canonization of the holy king, who had been a special friend of Bonaventure, and at whose request Bonaventure composed his "Office of the Passion". On 23 June, 1273, Bonaventure, much against his will, was created Cardinal-Bishop of Albano, by Gregory X. It is said that the pope's envoys who brought him the cardinal's hat found the saint washing dishes outside a convent near Florence and were requested by him to hang it on a tree nearby until his hands were free to take it. Bonaventure continued to govern the Order of Friars Minor until 20 May, 1274, when at the General Chapter of Lyons, Jerome of Ascoli, afterwards Nicholas IV, was elected to succeed him. Meanwhile Bonaventure had been charged by Gregory X to prepare the questions to be discussed at the Fourteenth Œcumenical Council, which opened at Lyons 7 May, 1274.

The pope himself presided at the council, but he confided the direction of its deliberations to Bonaventure, especially charging him to confer with the Greeks on the points relating to the abjuration of their schism. It was largely due to Bonaventure's efforts and to those of the Friars whom he had sent to Constantinople, that the Greeks accepted the union effected 6 July, 1274. Bonaventure twice addressed the assembled Fathers, on 18 May, during a session of the Council, when he preached on Baruch, v, 5, and on 29 June, during pontifical Mass celebrated by the pope. While the council was still in session, Bonaventure died, Sunday, 15 July, 1274. The exact cause of his death is unknown, but if we may credit the chronicle of Peregrinus of Bologna, Bonaventure's secretary, which has recently (1905) been recovered and edited, the saint was poisoned. He was buried on the evening following his death in the church of the Friars Minor at Lyons, being honoured with a splendid funeral which was attended by the pope, the King of Aragon, the cardinals, and the other members of the council. The funeral oration was delivered by Pietro di Tarantasia, O.P., Cardinal-Bishop of Ostia, afterwards Innocent V, and on the following day during the fifth session of the council, Gregory X spoke of the irreparable loss the Church had sustained by the death of Bonaventure, and commanded all prelates and priests throughout the whole world to celebrate Mass for the repose of his soul.

Bonaventure enjoyed especial veneration even during his lifetime because of his stainless character and of the miracles attributed to him. It was Alexander of Hales who said that Bonaventure seemed to have escaped the curse of Adam's sin. And the story of St. Thomas visiting Bonaventure's cell while the latter was writing the life of St. Francis, and finding him in an ecstasy is well known. "Let us leave a saint to work for a saint", said the Angelic Doctor as he withdrew. When, in 1434, Bonaventure's remains were translated to the new church erected at Lyons in honour of St. Francis, his head was found in a perfect state of preservation, the tongue being as red as in life. This miracle not only moved the people of Lyons to choose Bonaventure as their special patron, but also gave a great impetus to the process of his canonization. Dante, writing long before, had given expression to the popular mind by placing Bonaventure among the saints in his "Paradiso", and no canonization was ever more ardently or universally desired than that of Bonaventure. That its inception was so long delayed was mainly due to the deplorable dissensions within the order after Bonaventure's death. Finally on 14 April, 1482, Bonaventure was enrolled in the catalogue of the saints by Sixtus IV. In 1562 Bonaventure's shrine was plundered by the Huguenots and the urn containing his body was burned in the public square. His head was preserved through the heroism of the superior, who hid it at the cost of his life, but it disappeared during the French Revolution and every effort to discover it has been in vain. Bonaventure was inscribed among the principal Doctors of the Church by Sixtus V, 14 March, 1587. His feast is celebrated 14 July.

Bonaventure, as Hefele remarks, united in himself the two elements whence proceed whatever was noble and sublime, great and beautiful, in the Middle Ages, viz., tender piety and profound learning. These two qualities shine forth conspicuously in his writings. Bonaventure wrote on almost every subject treated by the Schoolmen, and his writings are very numerous. The greater number of them deal with philosophy and theology. No work of Bonaventure's is exclusively philosophical, but in his "Commentary on the Sentences", his "Breviloquium", his "Itinerarium Mentis in Deum" and his "De reductione Artium ad Theologiam", he deals with the most important and difficult questions of philosophy in such a way that these four works taken together contain the elements of a complete system of philosophy, and at the same time bear striking witness to the mutual interpenetration of philosophy and theology which is a distinguishing mark of the Scholastic period. The "Commentary on the Sentences" remains without doubt Bonaventure's greatest work; all his other writings are in some way subservient to it. It was written, *superiorum præcepto* (at the command of his superiors) when he was only twenty-seven and is a theological achievement of the first rank. It comprises more than four thousand pages in folio and treats extensively and profoundly of God and the Trinity, the Creation and Fall of Man, the Incarnation and Redemption, Grace, the Sacraments, and the Last Judgment, that is to say, traverses the entire field of Scholastic theology. Like the other medieval Summas, Bonaventure's "Commentary" is divided into four books. In the first, second, and fourth Bonaventure can compete favourably with the best commentaries on the Sentences, but it is admitted that in the third book he surpasses all others. The "Breviloquium", written before 1257, is, as its name implies, a shorter work. It is to some extent a summary of the "Commentary" containing as Scheeben says, the quintessence of the theology of the time, and is the most sublime compendium of dogma in our possession. It is perhaps the work which will best give a popular notion of Bonaventure's theology; in it his powers are seen at their best. Whilst the "Breviloquium" derives all things from God, the "Itinerarium Mentis in Deum" proceeds in the opposite direction, bringing all things back to their Supreme End. The latter work, which formed the delight of Gerson for more than thirty years, and from which Bl. Henry Suso drew so largely, was written on Mount la Verna in 1259. The relation of the finite and infinite, the natural and supernatural, is again dealt with by Bonaventure, in his "De reductione Artium ad Theologiam", a little work written to demonstrate the relation which philosophy and the arts bear to theology, and to prove that they are all absorbed in it as into a natural centre. It must not be inferred, however, that philosophy in Bonaventure's view does not possess an existence of its own. The passages in Bonaventure's works on which such an opinion

might be founded only go to prove that he did not regard philosophy as the chief or last end of scientific research and speculation. Moreover, it is only when compared with theology that he considers philosophy of an inferior order. Considered in itself, philosophy is, according to Bonaventure, a true science, prior in point of time to theology. Again, Bonaventure's pre-eminence as a mystic must not be suffered to overshadow his labours in the domain of philosophy, for he was undoubtedly one of the greatest philosophers of the Middle Ages.

Bonaventure's philosophy, no less than his theology, manifests his profound respect for tradition. He regarded new opinions with disfavour and ever strove to follow those generally received in his time. Thus, between the two great influences which determined the trend of Scholasticism about the middle of the thirteenth century, there can be no doubt that Bonaventure ever remained a faithful disciple of Augustine and always defended the teaching of that Doctor; yet he by no means repudiated the teaching of Aristotle. While basing his doctrine on that of the old school, Bonaventure borrowed not a little from the new. Though he severely criticized the defects of Aristotle, he is said to have quoted more frequently from the latter than any former Scholastic had done. Perhaps he inclined more, on the whole, to some general views of Plato than to those of Aristotle, but he cannot therefore be called a Platonist. Although he adopted the hylomorphic theory of matter and form, Bonaventure, following Alexander of Hales, whose Summa he appears to have had before him in composing his own works, does not limit matter to corporeal beings, but holds that one and the same kind of matter is the substratum of spiritual and corporeal beings alike. According to Bonaventure, *materia prima* is not a mere *indeterminatum quid*, but contains the *rationes seminales* infused by the Creator at the beginning, and tends towards the acquisition of those special forms which it ultimately assumes. The substantial form is not in Bonaventure's opinion, essentially, one, as St. Thomas taught. Another point in which Bonaventure, as representing the Franciscan school, is at variance with St. Thomas is that which concerns the possibility of creation from eternity. He declares that reason can demonstrate that the world was not created *ab æterno*. In his system of ideology Bonaventure does not favour either the doctrine of Plato or that of the Ontologists. It is only by completely misunderstanding Bonaventure's teaching that any ontologistic interpretation can be read into it. For he is most emphatic in rejecting any direct or immediate vision of God or of His Divine attributes in this life. For the rest, the psychology of Bonaventure differs in no essential point from the common teaching of the Schoolmen. The same is true, as a whole, of his theology.

Bonaventure's theological writings may be classed under four heads: dogmatic, mystic, exegetical, and homiletic. His dogmatic teaching is found chiefly in his "Commentary on the Sentences" and in his "Breviloquium". Treating of the Incarnation, Bonaventure does not differ substantially from St. Thomas. In answer to the question: "Would the Incarnation have taken place if Adam had not sinned?", he answers in the negative. Again, notwithstanding his deep devotion to the Blessed Virgin, he favours the opinion which does not exempt her from original sin, *quia magis consonat fidei pietati et sanctorum auctoritati*. But Bonaventure's treatment of this question marked a distinct advance, and he did more perhaps than anyone before Scotus to clear the ground for its correct presentation. His treatise on the sacraments is largely practical and is characterized by a distinctly devotional element. This appears especially in his treatment of the Holy Eucharist. He rejects the doctrine of physical, and admits only a moral, efficacy in the sacraments. It is much to be regretted that Bonaventure's views on this and other controverted questions should be so often misrepresented, even by recent writers. For example, at least three of the latest and best known manuals of dogma in treating of such questions as "De angelorum naturâ", "De scientiâ Christi", "De naturâ distinctionis inter caritatem et gratiam sanctificantem", "De causalitate sacramentorum", and "De statu parvulorum sine baptismo morientium", gratuitously attribute opinions to Bonaventure which are entirely at variance with his real teaching. To be sure Bonaventure, like all the Scholastics, occasionally put forward opinions not strictly correct in regard to questions not yet defined or clearly settled, but even here his teaching represents the most profound and acceptable ideas of his age and marks a notable stage in the evolution of knowledge. Bonaventure's authority has always been very great in the Church. Apart from his personal influence at Lyons (1274), his writings carried great weight at the subsequent councils at Vienne (1311), Constance (1417), Basle (1431), and Florence (1438). At Trent (1546) his writings, as Newman remarks (Apologia, ch. v) had a critical effect on some of the definitions of dogma, and at the Vatican Council (1870), sentences from them were embodied in the decrees concerning papal supremacy and infallibility.

Only a small part of Bonaventure's writings is properly mystical. These are characterized by brevity and by a faithful adherence to the teaching of the Gospel. The perfecting of the soul by the uprooting of vice and the implanting of virtue is his chief concern. There is a degree of prayer in which ecstasy occurs. When it is attained, God is sincerely to be thanked. It must, however, be regarded only as incidental. It is by no means essential to the possession of perfection in the highest degree. Such is the general outline of Bonaventure's mysticism which is largely a continuation and development of what the St. Victors had already laid down. The shortest and most complete summary of it is found in his "De Triplici Via", often erroneously entitled the "Incendium Amoris", in which he distinguishes the different stages or degrees of perfect charity. What the "Breviloquium" is to Scholasticism, the "De Triplici Via" is to mysticism—a perfect compendium of all that is best in it. Savonarola made a pious and learned commentary upon it. Perhaps the best known of Bonaventure's other mystical and ascetical writings are the "Soliloquium", a sort of dialogue containing a rich collection of passages from the Fathers on spiritual questions; the "Lignum vitæ", a series of forty-eight devout meditations on the life of Christ, the "De sex alis seraphim", a precious opuscule on the virtues of superiors, which Father Claudius Acquaviva caused to be printed separately and circulated throughout the Society of Jesus; the "Vitis mystica", a work on the Passion, which was for a long time erroneously ascribed to St. Bernard, and "De Perfectione vitæ", a treatise which depicts the virtues that make for religious perfection, and which appears to have been written for the use of Blessed Isabella of France, who had founded a monastery of Poor Clares at Longchamps.

Bonaventure's exegetical works were highly esteemed in the Middle Ages and still remain a treasure house of thoughts and treatises. They include commentaries on the Books of Ecclesiastes and Wisdom and on the Gospels of St. Luke and St. John. In addition to his commentary on the Fourth Gospel, Bonaventure composed "Collationes in Joannem", ninety-one conferences on subjects relating to it. His "Collationes in Hexameron" is a work of the

same kind, but its title, which did not originate with Bonaventure, is somewhat misleading. It consists of an unfinished course of instructions delivered at Paris in 1273. Bonaventure did not intend in these twenty-one discourses to explain the work of the six days, but rather to draw some analogous instructions from the first chapter of Genesis, as a warning to his auditors against some errors of the day. It is an exaggeration to say that Bonaventure had regard only to the mystical sense of Scripture. In such of his writings as are properly exegetical he follows the text, though he also develops the practical conclusions deduced from it, for in the composition of these works he had the advantage of the preacher mainly in view. Bonaventure had conceived the most sublime idea of the ministry of preaching, and notwithstanding his manifold labours in other fields, this ministry ever held an especial place among his labours. He neglected no opportunity of preaching, whether to the clergy, the people, or his own Friars, and Bl. Francis of Fabriano (d. 1322), his contemporary and auditor, bears witness that Bonaventure's renown as a preacher almost surpassed his fame as a teacher. He preached before popes and kings, in Spain and Germany, as well as in France and Italy. Nearly five hundred authentic sermons of Bonaventure have come down to us; the greater part of them were delivered in Paris before the university while Bonaventure was professor there, or after he had become minister general. Most of them were taken down by some of his auditors and thus preserved to posterity. In his sermons he follows the Scholastic method of putting forth the divisions of his subject and then expounding each division according to the different senses.

Besides his philosophical and theological writings, Bonaventure left a number of works referring to the religious life, but more especially to the Franciscan Order. Among the latter is his well-known explanation of the Rule of the Friars Minor; in this work, written at a time when the dissensions within the order as to the observance of the Rule were so painfully marked, he adopted a conciliatory attitude, approving neither the interpretation of the *Zelanti* nor that of the *Relaxti*. His aim was to promote harmony in essentials. With this end in view, he had chosen a middle course at the outset and firmly adhered to it during the seventeen years of his generalship. If anyone could have succeeded in uniting the order, it would have been Bonaventure; but the *via media* proved impracticable, and Bonaventure's personality only served to hold in check the elements of discord, subsequently represented by the Conventuals and the Fraticelli. Following upon his explanation of the Rule comes Bonaventure's important treatise embodying the Constitutions of Narbonne already referred to. There is also an answer by Bonaventure to some questions concerning the Rule, a treatise on the guidance of novices, and an opuscule in which Bonaventure states why the Friars Minor preach and hear confessions, besides a number of letters which give us a special insight into the saint's character. These include official letters written by Bonaventure as general to the superiors of the order, as well as personal letters addressed like that "Ad innominatum magistrum" to private individuals. Bonaventure's beautiful "Legend" or life of St. Francis completes the writings in which he strove to promote the spiritual welfare of his brethren. This well-known work is composed of two parts of very unequal value. In the first Bonaventure publishes the unedited facts that he had been able to gather at Assisi and elsewhere; in the other he merely abridges and repeats what others, and especially Celano, had already recorded. As a whole, it is essentially a *legenda pacis*, compiled mainly with a view to pacifying the unhappy discord still ravaging the order. St. Bonaventure's aim was to present a general portrait of the holy founder which, by the omission of certain points that had given rise to controversy, should be acceptable to all parties. This aim was surely legitimate even though from a critical standpoint the work may not be a perfect biography. Of this "Legenda Major", as it came to be called, Bonaventure made an abridgment arranged for use in choir and known as the "Legenda Minor".

Bonaventure was the true heir and follower of Alexander of Hales and the continuator of the old Franciscan school founded by the *Doctor Irrefragabilis*, but he surpassed the latter in acumen, fertility of imagination, and originality of expression. His proper place is beside his friend St. Thomas, as they are the two greatest theologians of Scholasticism. If it be true that the system of St. Thomas is more finished than that of Bonaventure, it should be borne in mind that, whereas Thomas was free to give himself to study to the end of his days, Bonaventure had not yet received the Doctor's degree when he was called to govern his order and overwhelmed with multifarious cares in consequence. The heavy responsibilities which he bore till within a few weeks of his death were almost incompatible with further study and even precluded his completing what he had begun before his thirty-sixth year. Again, in attempting to make a comparison between Bonaventure and St. Thomas, we should remember that the two saints were of a different bent of mind; each had qualities in which he excelled; one was in a sense the complement of the other; one supplied what the other lacked. Thus Thomas was analytical, Bonaventure synthetical; Thomas was the Christian Aristotle, Bonaventure the true disciple of Augustine; Thomas was the teacher of the schools, Bonaventure of practical life; Thomas enlightened the mind, Bonaventure inflamed the heart; Thomas extended the Kingdom of God by the love of theology, Bonaventure by the theology of love. Even those who hold that Bonaventure does not reach the level of St. Thomas in the sphere of Scholastic speculation concede that as a mystic he far surpasses the Angelic Doctor. In this particular realm of theology, Bonaventure equals, if he does not excel, St. Bernard himself. Leo XIII rightly calls Bonaventure the Prince of Mystics: "Having scaled the difficult heights of speculation in a most notable manner, he treated of mystical theology with such perfection that in the common opinion of the learned he is *facile princeps* in that field." (Allocutio of 11 October, 1890.) It must not be concluded, however, that Bonaventure's mystical writings constitute his chief title to fame. This conclusion, in so far as it seems to imply a deprecation of his labours in the field of Scholasticism, is opposed to the explicit utterances of several pontiffs and eminent scholars, is incompatible with Bonaventure's acknowledged reputation in the Schools, and is excluded by an intelligent perusal of his works. As a matter of fact, the half of one volume of the ten comprising the Quaracchi edition suffices to contain Bonaventure's ascetic and mystic writings. Although Bonaventure's mystical works alone would suffice to place him in the foremost rank, yet he may justly be called a mystic rather than a Scholastic only in so far as every subject he treats of is made ultimately to converge upon God. This abiding sense of God's presence which pervades all the writings of Bonaventure is perhaps their fundamental attribute. To it we may trace that all-pervading unction which is their peculiar characteristic. As Sixtus V aptly expresses it: "In writing he united to the highest erudition an equal amount of the most ardent piety; so that whilst enlightening his readers he also touched their hearts penetrating to the inmost recesses of their souls" (Bull, Triumphantis Jerusalem). St.

Antoninus, Denis the Carthusian, Louis of Granada, and Father Claude de la Colombière, among others, have also noted this feature of Bonaventure's writings. Invariably he aims at arousing devotion as well as imparting knowledge. He never divorces the one from the other, but treats learned subjects devoutly and devout subjects learnedly. Bonaventure, however, never sacrifices truth to devotion, but his tendency to prefer an opinion which arouses devotion to a dry and uncertain speculation may go far towards explaining not a little of the widespread popularity his writings enjoyed among his contemporaries and in all succeeding ages. Again Bonaventure is distinguished from the other Scholastics not only by the greater warmth of his religious teaching, but also by its practical tendency as Trithemius notes (Scriptores Eccles.). Many purely speculative questions are passed over by Bonaventure; there is a directness about all he has written. No useful purpose, he declares, is achieved by mere controversy. He is ever tolerant and modest. Thus while he himself accepts the literal interpretations of the first chapter of Genesis, Bonaventure acknowledges the admissibility of a different one and refers with admiration to the figurative explanation propounded by St. Augustine. He never condemns the opinions of others and emphatically disclaims anything like finality for his own views. Indeed he asserts the littleness of his authority, renounces all claims to originality and calls himself a "poor compiler". No doubt Bonaventure's works betray some of the defects of the learning of his day, but there is nothing in them that savours of useless subtlety. "One does not find in his pages", writes Gerson (De Examin. Doctrin.) "vain trifles or useless cavils, nor does he mix as do so many others, worldly digressions with serious theological discussions". "This", he adds, "is the reason why St. Bonaventure has been abandoned by those Scholastics who are devoid of piety of whom the number is alas! but too large". It has been said that Bonaventure's mystical spirit unfitted him for subtle analysis. Be this as it may, one of the greatest charms of Bonaventure's writings is their simple clearness. Though he had necessarily to make use of the Scholastic method, he rose above dialectics, and though his argumentation may at times seem too cumbersome to find approval in our time, yet he writes with an ease and grace of style which one seeks in vain among the other Schoolmen. To the minds of his contemporaries impregnated with the mysticism of the Middle Ages, the spirit that breathed in Bonaventure's writings seemed to find its parallel only in the lives of those that stand nearest to the Throne, and the title of "Seraphic Doctor" bestowed upon Bonaventure is an undeniable tribute to his all-absorbing love for God. This title seems to have been first given to him in 1333 in the Prologue of the "Pantheologia" by Rayner of Pisa, O.P. He had already received while teaching in Paris the name of *Doctor Devotus*.

The Franciscan Order has ever regarded Bonaventure as one of the greatest Doctors and from the beginning his teaching found many distinguished expositors within the order, among the earliest being his own pupils, John Peckham later Archbishop of Canterbury, Matthew of Aquasparta, and Alexander of Alexandria (d. 1314), both of whom became ministers general of the order. The last named wrote a "Summa quæstionum S. Bonaventuræ". Other well-known commentaries are by John of Erfurt (d. 1317), Vorilongus (d. 1464), Brulifer (d. c. 1497), de Combes (d. 1570), Trigosus (d. 1616), Coriolano (d. 1625), Zamora (d. 1649), Bontemps (d. 1672), Hauzeur (d. 1676), Bonelli (d. 1773), etc. From the fourteenth to the sixteenth century the influence of Bonaventure was undoubtedly somewhat overshadowed by that of

Duns Scotus, owing largely to the prominence of the latter as champion of the Immaculate Conception in the disputes between the Franciscans and Dominicans. Sixtus V, however, founded a special chair at Rome for the study of St. Bonaventure; such chairs also existed in several universities, notably at Ingolstadt, Salzburg, Valencia, and Osuna. It is worthy of note that the Capuchins forbade their Friars to follow Scotus and ordered them to return to the study of Bonaventure. The centenary celebrations of 1874 appear to have revived interest in the life and work of St. Bonaventure. Certain it is that since then the study of his writings has steadily increased.

Unfortunately not all of Bonaventure's writings have come down to us. Some were lost before the invention of printing. On the other hand, several works have in the course of time been attributed to him which are not his. Such are the "Centiloquium", the "Speculum Disciplinæ", which is probably the work of Bernard of Besse, Bonaventure's secretary; the rhythmical "Philomela", which seems to be from the pen of John Peckham; the "Stimulus Amoris" and the "Speculum B. M. V.", written respectively by James of Milan and Conrad of Saxony; "The Legend of St. Clare", which is by Thomas of Celano; the "Meditationes vitæ Christi" composed by a Friar Minor for a Poor Clare, and the "Biblia pauperum" of the Dominican Nicholas of Hanapis. Those familiar with the catalogues of European libraries are aware that no writer since the Middle Ages had been more widely read or copied than Bonaventure. The earliest catalogues of his works are those given by Salimbene (1282), Henry of Ghent (d. 1293), Ubertino of Casale (1305), Ptolemy of Lucca (1327) and the "Chronicle of the XXIV Generals" (1368). The fifteenth century saw no less than fifty editions of Bonaventure's works. More celebrated than any preceding edition was that published at Rome (1588–96) by order of Sixtus V (7 vols. in fol.). It was reprinted with but slight emendations at Metz in 1609 and at Lyons in 1678. A fourth edition appeared at Venice (13 vols. in 4to) 1751, and was reprinted at Paris in 1864. All these editions were very imperfect in so far as they include spurious works and omit genuine ones. They have been completely superseded by the celebrated critical edition published by the Friars Minor at Quaracchi, near Florence. Any scientific study of Bonaventure must be based upon this edition, upon which not only Leo XIII (13 December, 1885) and Pius X (11 April, 1904), but scholars of all creeds have lavished the highest encomiums. Nothing seems to have been omitted which could make this edition perfect and complete. In its preparation the editors visited over 400 libraries and examined nearly 52,000 MSS. while the first volume alone contains 20,000 variant readings. It was commenced by Father Fidelis a Fanna (d. 1881) and completed by Father Ignatius Jeiler (d. 1904): "Doctoris Seraphici S. Bonaventuræ S. R. E. Episcopi Cardinalis Opera Omnia, edita studio et curâ P. P. Collegii S. Bonaventuræ in fol. ad Claras Aquas [Quaracchi] 1882–1902". In this edition the works of the saint are distributed through the ten volumes as follows: the first four contain his great "Commentaries on the Book of Sentences"; the fifth comprises eight smaller scholastic works such as the "Breviloquium" and "Itinerarium"; the sixth and seventh are devoted to his commentaries on Scripture; the eighth contains his mystical and ascetic writings and works having special reference to the order; the ninth his sermons; whilst the tenth is taken up with the index and a short sketch of the saint's life and writings by Father Ignatius Jeiler.

We do not possess any formal, contemporary biography of St. Bonaventure. That written by

the Spanish Franciscan, Zamorra, who flourished before 1300, has not been preserved. The references to Bonaventure's life contained in the works of Salimbene (1282), Bernard of Besse (c. 1380) Bl. Francis of Fabriano (d. 1322), Angelo Clareno (d. 1337), Ubertino of Casale (d. 1338), Bartholomew of Pisa (d. 1399) and the "Chronicle of the XXIV Generals" (c. 1368), are given in vol. X of the Quaracchi Edition (pp. 39–72).

Acta SS., 3d ed., July, III, 776–822; WADDING, *Annales Min.* (Rome, 1732), IV, *passim;* IDEM, *Script. Ord. Min.* (1650), 61–81; SBARALEA, *Supplementum* (1806), 142–172, 726; GASPARE DA MONTE SANTO, *Gesta e dottrina del seraf. dott. S. Bonaventura* (2d ed., Florence, 1874); BERTHAUMIER, *Histoire de S. Bonaventure* (Paris, 1858); MARIANI, *S. Bonaventura* (Florence, 1874); MARANGONI, *Vita di S. Bonaventura* (Padua, 1874); ISIDORUS A BUSCOMARI, *S. Bonaventura, O. F. M. minister generalis* (Rome, 1874); ANTON. MARIA DA VICENZA, *Vita di S. Bonaventura* (Rome, 1874), German tr. JEILER (Paderborn, 1874); PANFILO DA MAGLIANO, *Storia compendiosa di S. Francesco e dei francescani* (Rome, 1874), I, 619 and *passim;* SKEY, *Life of St. Bonaventure* (London, 1889); LEO DE CLARY, *Lives of the Saints and Blessed of the Three Orders of St. Francis* (Taunton, 1886), II, 466–490; PROSPER DE MARTIGNÉ, *La scholastique et les traditions franciscaines* (Paris, 1888), 77–153; CHÉRANCÉ, *S. Bonaventure* (Paris, 1899); and SMEETS in *Dict. de théol. cath.* (Paris, 1904), II, 962–986.

Among those who of recent years have written on Bonaventure's doctrine or special points of it are MARGERIE, *Essai sur la philosophie de S. Bonaventure* (Paris, 1855); VAN LOO, *Specimen doctrinæ . . . . ad mentem S. Bonaventuræ* (Louvain, 1856); HOLLENBERG, *Studien zu Bonaventura* (Berlin, 1862); FIDELIS A FANNA, *Seraphici Doctoris, Bonaventuræ, doctrina de Romani Pontificis primatu et infallibilitate* (Turin, 1870); IDEM, *Ratio novæ collectionis operum S. Bonaventuræ* (Turin, 1874); MARCELLINO DA CIVEZZA, *Della vera filosofia e delle dottrine del serafico dottore S. Bonaventura* (Genoa, 1874); LUDOVICUS A CASTROPLANIO, *Seraphicus Doctor S. Bonaventura in Œcumenicis cath. eccl. conciliis* (Rome, 1874); FRANCISCUS MARIA A SALERNO, *Della poesia nel serafico dottore S. Bonaventura* (Genoa, 1874); WERNER, *Die Psychologie und Erkenntnisslehre des hl. Bonaventura* (Vienna, 1876); ANT. M. A VINCENTIA ET JO. A RUBINO, *Lexicon Bonaventurianum philosophico-theologicum* (Vienna, 1880); *De humanæ cognitionis ratione; anecdota quædam S. Bonaventuræ et nonnullorum ipsius discipulorum* (Quaracchi, 1883); BARONI, *La scuola francescana guidata dal suo serafico dottore S. Bonaventura* (Florence, 1886); CANALI, *Oratio super characteribus doctrinæ Bonaventurianæ* (Piacenza, 1887); JEILER, *S. Bonaventuræ principia de concursu Dei generali ad actiones causarum secundarum* (Quaracchi, 1887); STATECZNY, *Compendium historiæ philosophiæ* (Rome, 1898), 312, *passim;* BISOGNO, *S. Bonaventura e Dante* (Milan, 1899); ÉVANGÉLISTE DE SAINT-BÉAT, *Le séraphin de l'école, études sur S. Bonaventure* (Paris, 1900); ZORZOLI, *La questione di S. Bonaventura, De cognitionis humanæ supremæ ratione, commentata e difesa* (Turin, 1900); VILLANOVA, *S. Bonaventura und das Papstthum* (Bregenz, 1902); ROSATI, *L'eloquenza cristiana in S. Bonaventura* (Florence, 1903); FACIN, *Dissertatio de studio bonaventuriano* (Quaracchi, 1902); *S. Bonaventura, Doctor Seraphicus, discipulorum S. Augustini alter princeps* (Venice, 1904); STÖCKL, *Handbook of the History of Philosophy,* tr. FINLAY (Dublin, 1903), I, 402–406; TURNER, *History of Philosophy* (Boston, 1903), 329–335; FELDER, *Geschichte der wissenschaftlichen Studien im Franziskanerorden bis um die Mitte des 13. Jahrhunderts* (Freiburg, 1904), 215–227, *passim;* VIVES, *Summula Commentariorum Seraphici Doctoris, Bonaventuræ* (Rome, 1905); DE WULF, *Histoire de la philosophie médiévale* (2d ed., Louvain and Paris, 1905), 299–308; UEBERWEG-HEINZE, *Grundriss der Geschichte der Philosophie* (Berlin, 1905, 9th ed.), II, 279–286; UBALD D'ALENÇON in *Etudes Franciscaines* (July, 1905), 91–102; LAURENCE, *The Life and Writings of St. Bonaventure in The Franciscan Monthly* (London, 1904–06).

PASCHAL ROBINSON.

Bonaventure, MARY STEPHEN. See NAGPUR, DIOCESE OF.

Boncompagni, BALTHASAR, an Italian mathematician, b. at Rome, 10 May, 1821; d. 13 April, 1894. He was a member of the illustrious family to which had belonged Gregory XIII, the reformer of the calendar. He studied mathematics and physics under Santucci and became known as a prolific writer on mathematical and historical subjects. At an early age (1840) he contributed to the "Giornale Arcadico" biographical sketches of Father Joseph Calandrelli, director of the observatory of the Roman College after the suppression of the Society of Jesus, and his assistant Conti. These were followed by his "Recherches sur les intégrales définies", which appeared in "Crelle's Journal" (Berlin). In 1846 the "Giornale Arcadico" published his "Studi intorno ad alcuni avanzamenti della fisica in Italia nei secoli

XVI e XVIII". In 1847 he became a member of the Accademia dei Lincei and shortly after its librarian.

Boncompagni contributed much to the study of the history of mathematics by his "Bolletino", which he founded in 1868 and conducted until 1887. To it he contributed numerous essays, biographies, reviews, etc. Among his essays published before the founding of the "Bolletino" may be mentioned, "Della vita e delle opere di Gherardo Cremonese traduttore del secolo XII" (1850); "Gherardo da Sabionetta, astronomo del secolo XIII" (1851); "Della vita e delle opere di Guido Bonatti" (1851); "Memoria sopra Leonardo" (1854); "Saggio intorno ad alcune opere di Leonardo" (1854); "Tre scritti inediti di Leonardo da un manoscritto dell' Ambrosiana di Milano" (Florence, 1854); "Intorno ad una proprietà dei numeri" (in the "Annali delle scienze matematiche e fisiche" 1855); "Scritti inediti del P. D. Pietro Cossali" (1857); "Dissertazione intorno ad un trattato di aritmetica stampato nel 1478" (in the "Atti dei Nuovi Lincei" 1862–63). In 1857 Boncompagni also published the "Algoritmi de numero Indorum" which he had found in the Library of Cambridge University. It is supposed to be a translation of the famous treatise on arithmetic of Al-khwarizmi, the most illustrious of the Arabian mathematicians.

Nuova Enciclopedia Italiana, Suppl., 6th ed., Turin; BALL, *Hist. of Mathematics* (New York, 1888).

H. M. BROCK.

Bonet, JUAN PABLO, a Spanish priest and one of the first to give attention to the education of the deaf and dumb, b. towards the end of the sixteenth century. He became secretary of the High Constable of Castile. The latter's brother being a deaf-mute, Bonet took his education in hand. To make his pupil understand words and speak them he invented a system of visible signs and of gymnastics for pronunciation. This consisted in certain signs representing to the sense of sight the sounds of words, in exercises of breathing in the formation of sounds and to adapt the different organs of articulation, the lips, tongue, and teeth, to the proper pronunciation of each sound. He reduced his system to practice by means of a manual alphabet—a combination of signs made with the hands representing the various letters—and a description of the dispositions of the vocal organ necessary to the pronunciation of each letter. He succeeded fairly well with his pupil and explained the principles of his system in a book, "Reducción de las letras y arte para enseñar á hablar los mudos" (Madrid, 1620).

KENELM DIGBY, *Of Bodies and of Man's Soul* (London, 1669); DE L'EPÉE, *Instruction des sourds-muets* (Paris, 1776); DE GERANDO, *De l'Education des sourds-muets* (Paris, 1827).

G. M. SAUVAGE.

Bonet, NICHOLAS, Friar Minor, theologian, and missionary, date of birth uncertain; d. 1360. Probably a Frenchman by birth, he taught theology with great success at Paris, where he received the title of "Doctor Pacificus" (The Peaceful Doctor) on account of his suave and tranquil mode of lecturing. Bonet took an important part in the dispute concerning the beatific vision which was warmly discussed during the pontificate of John XXII and finally settled by the decree of his successor, Benedict XII, "Benedictus Deus". As a member of the papal embassy sent by Benedict XII to Kublai Khan, grandson of the famous conqueror Genghis Khan, Bonet exchanged the comparative ease and comfort of the professor of theology for the arduous and perilous labours of the missionary. The Franciscan missions in Tatary were founded as early as the year 1245 by the zealous apostles of the Faith, Lorenzo da Portogallo and Giovanni da Pian Carpino; and in his desire to see the great work which was inaugurated by them and continued by the saintly Archbishop

John of Monte Corvino kept up and extended, the great khan was induced to send an embassy to Benedict XII to petition for new labourers in the missions of Asia. The pope received the legates with every mark of honour and, acceding to the wish of the Mongolian monarch, commissioned four religious of the order of Friars Minor as his legates, on whom he conferred all the Apostolic faculties and privileges necessary for their missionary labours. These were John of Florence, afterwards Bishop of Bisignano in Calabria, Nicholas Bonet, Nicolas da Molano, and Gregory of Hungary. The embassy bearing letters from the pope to the khan left Avignon towards the end of the year 1338, and after a long and arduous journey arrived at Peking in China, the residence of the Tatar emperor at the beginning of 1342. The missionaries were encouraged in their apostolic labours by the kindly attitude of Kublai Khan and succeeded in founding numerous Christian settlements throughout the vast Mongolian empire. About the year 1346 they set out again for Italy. Part of the homeward journey they made by sea and the remainder, from the Kingdom of Persia, by land, arriving in Avignon at the beginning of the year 1354. Shortly after the return of the missionaries, Bonet was consecrated titular Bishop of Mileve in Africa in recognition of his devoted services while on the mission of Mongolia. Among the writings of Nicholas Bonet, the "Tractatus de conceptione B. Mariæ jussu Clementis V scriptus", the "Formalitates e Doctrinâ Scoti" and his "Commentarius in IV libros sententiarum" deserve special mention.

CUSACK, *St. Francis and the Franciscans* (New York, 1867), XIV, 470–472; SBARALEA, *Suppl. et castig. ad script. ord. min.*, 552; DA CIVEZZA, *Storia delle missioni Francescane* (Rome, 1859), III, xv, 599–617; WADDING, *Annales Minorum*, VII, 213–219; DE GUBERNATIS, *De missionibus antiquis* (Rome, 1689), I, 399; *Analecta Franciscana* (Quaracchi, 1887), II, 178.

STEPHEN M. DONOVAN.

Bonfrère, JACQUES, Biblical scholar, b. at Dinant, Belgium, 12 April, 1573; d. at Tournai, 9 May, 1642. He entered the Society of Jesus in 1592. After having taught rhetoric, philosophy, and theology, he devoted himself to the Sacred Scriptures. He was long a professor of Scripture and Hebrew at Douai, where he was superior of the Scots College. Sweert, in his "Athenæ Belgicæ", speaks of him as a man of rare virtue; he praises his industry and prudence, as well as the penetration of his mind and the solidity of his judgment. His work in the department of Sacred Scriptures, into which, he tells us, he had been initiated by Cornelius à Lapide, has always been highly appreciated. His "Præloquia" was, in 1839, selected by Migne as the most suitable treatise or general introduction with which to begin his "Sacræ Scripturæ Cursus Completus" (I, cols. 5–242). In this work Bonfrère deals with subjects pertaining to the Bible as a whole. His selection and treatment of topics was determined largely by the controversies of the time regarding the value of the Vulgate, the obscurity of Scripture, etc. But many of them still retain their interest; and they are all handled in a clear and interesting way. The historical methods now applied to the canon, text, and hermeneutics of Sacred Scripture were not known in his time. He deals with inspiration in one chapter (ch. viii: *De modo quo Deus cum hisce Scriptoribus hagiographis habuit*). The views he sets forth here do not in all respects agree with the teaching of modern theologians. He holds, for instance, that approval of a writing by God, subsequent to its composition, would suffice to make it canonical. In point of fact, though, he assures us, no book of the Bible was so composed. Then he expresses the opinion that when writing on what they knew without revelation, the sacred authors only had the assistance necessary to preserve them from error. He does not make a clear distinction between inspiration and revelation. (See Pesch, "De Inspiratione," Nos. 323 and 324.)

The "Præloquia" were published along with a commentary on the Pentateuch in a volume entitled: "Pentateuchus Mosis commentario illustratus, præmissis præloquiis perutilibus" (fol., Antwerp, 1625). This was followed by his commentary on Josue, Judges, and Ruth, to which he added a treatise on sacred geography, composed by Eusebius and translated by St. Jerome: "Josue, Judices et Ruth commentario illustrati. Accessit Onomasticon" (fol., Paris, 1631). Bonfrère had undertaken to explain the Books of Kings before his work on the Pentateuch, he tells us in his preface to the latter; but he had felt the need of going back to the beginning of things. His "Libri Regum et Paralipomenon commentariis illustrati", was given to the press at Tournai, in 1643, after his death. But the printing-house was burned, and the work did not appear. Bibliographers have no reference even to the MSS. The learned professor is said to have left commentaries on nearly all the other books of the Bible. Bonfrère's explanation of the text of Scripture shows a very good knowledge of Hebrew, and he pays special attention to the places mentioned. His erudition was extensive for his time. The soberness and judiciousness of his comments are generally admired.

ALEGAMBE, *Bibl. Script. S.J.*, ANDRÉ, *Bib. Belgica;* SWEERT, *Athenæ Belgicæ.*

W. S. REILLY.

Boniface (WINFRID, WYNFRITH), SAINT, Apostle of Germany, date of birth unknown; martyred 5 June, 755 (754); emblems: the oak, axe, book, fox, scourge, fountain, raven, sword. He was a native of England, though some authorities have claimed him for Ireland or Scotland. The place of his birth is not known, though it was probably in the south-western part of Wessex. Crediton (Kirton) in Devonshire is given by more modern authors. The same uncertainty exists in regard to the year of his birth. It seems, however, safe to state that he was not born before 672 or 675, or as late as 680. Descended from a noble family, from his earliest years he showed great ability, and received a religious education. His parents intended him for secular pursuits, but, inspired with higher ideals by missionary monks who visited his home, Winfrid felt himself called to a religious state. After much difficulty he obtained his father's permission and went to the monastery of Adescancastre on the site of the present city of Exeter, where, under the direction of Abbot Wolfhard, he was trained in piety and learning. About seven years later he went to the Abbey of Nhutscelle (Nutshalling) between Winchester and Southampton. Here, leading an austere and studious life under Abbot Winbert, he rapidly advanced in sanctity and knowledge, excelling especially in the profound understanding of the Sacred Scriptures, of which he gives evidence in his letters. He was also well educated in history, grammar, rhetoric, and poetry. He made his profession as a member of the Benedictine Order and was placed in charge of the monastic school. At the age of thirty he was ordained priest. Through his abbot the fame of Winfrid's learning soon reached high civil and ecclesiastical circles. He also had great success as a preacher. With every prospect of a great career and the highest dignities in his own country, he had no desire for human glory, for the thought of bringing the light of the Gospel to his kindred, the Old Saxons, in Germany, had taken possession of his mind. After many requests Winfrid at last obtained the permission of his abbot.

In 716 he set out for the mission in Friesland. Since the Faith had already been preached there by Wigbert, Willibrord, and others, Winfrid expected to find a good soil for his missionary work, but po-

litical disturbances caused him to return temporarily to England. Towards the end of 717 Abbot Winbert died, and Winfrid was elected to succeed him, but declined and induced Daniel, Bishop of Winchester, to influence the monks to elect another. Winfrid was left free to follow out his intentions, but before going back to his apostolic work he wished to visit Rome and to obtain from the pope the apostolic mission and the necessary faculties. Bishop Daniel gave him an open letter of recommendation to kings, princes, bishops, abbots, and priests, and a private letter to the pope. On Winfrid's arrival in Rome, in the fall of 718, Pope Gregory II received him kindly, praised his resolution, and, having satisfied himself in various conferences as to the orthodoxy of Winfrid, his morals, and the purity of his motives, on 15 May, 719, he gave him full authority to preach the Gospel to the heathens in Germany to the right of the Rhine, ordering him at the same time to adhere to the Roman practice in the administration of the Sacrament of Baptism, and to consult with the Holy See in case of difficulties.

Having received instructions to make his first journey through the country, only a tour of inspection, he travelled through Bavaria and found the Church flourishing, with a number of churches and monasteries. In Alamannia, which he crossed on his way to Thuringia, he found similar conditions. Thuringia was considered by Rome as Christian, and the mission of Winfrid was supposed to be that of an authorized reformer. He found the country, however, in a sad condition. St. Kilian had laboured with energy, but without success. Duke Gotzbert and some years later his son, Hethan II, both converts of St. Kilian had been murdered, perhaps on account of their injudicious zeal in trying to spread Christianity. Great numbers of their rebellious subjects had lapsed into heathenism, or a mixture of Christianity and idolatry. Winfrid tried to enkindle a missionary spirit in the priests and to make the people live up to the pure precepts of the Christian religion. Though he converted some of the heathens, he did not meet with the success which he had anticipated. On his way to the court of Charles Martel, possibly to interest that prince in the matter, he received news of the death of the Frisian King Radbod, and went to Friesland. Here he spent three years under the aged St. Willibrord, travelling about with tireless energy, and preaching fearlessly as he went. Multitudes of Christians who had fallen away during the persecution of Radbod were brought to repentance and thousands of pagans accepted the Faith. Many of the converts were brought together to lead a religious life under the Rule of St. Benedict. St. Willibrord, feeling the weight of his years, wished to make Winfrid his assistant and successor in the See of Utrecht. Winfrid refused, giving as his main reason that the pope had sent him for missionary work. He therefore left and followed in the wake of the army of Charles Martel as far as Trier. Near this city was the Abbey of Pfalzel (*Palatiolum*). From there he took with him as a disciple and companion Gregory, a boy of about fourteen or fifteen, afterwards abbot in Utrecht, and continued his journey to Thuringia, where he converted many. He then went into Hessia, where many more were brought into the fold of Christ. With the assistance of two chiefs whom he had converted he established a monastic cell at Amöneburg at the River Ohm (then called Amana) in Upper Hessia, as a kind of missionary centre in which native clergy were to be educated.

While Winfrid was under the jurisdiction of St. Willibrord he had no special reason for reporting to the Holy See, but, now working independently, he considered it his duty to do so. He therefore sent Bynnan, one of his disciples, with a letter to Gregory II, recounting his labours of the past years and asking for further directions. Bynnan promptly executed his commission and soon returned with the pope's answer, expressing satisfaction with what had been done and a desire to confer with Winfrid personally. Winfrid accordingly set out for Rome, taking his course through France and Burgundy. He was warmly welcomed by the pope, who questioned him carefully, made him take the usual oath of allegiance, received from him a profession of faith, and on 30 November, 722 (723), consecrated him a regional bishop, with the name Boniface. Some say that Winfrid had taken this name at the time of his religious profession; others, that he received it on his first visit to Rome. The same discrepancy of opinion exists in regard to its derivation from *bonum facere* or *bonum fatum;* perhaps it is only an approximate Latinization of Wyn-frith. Pope Gregory then sent Boniface back with letters to his diocesans in Thuringia and Hessia demanding obedience for their new bishop. A letter was also addressed to Charles Martel asking his protection. Boniface himself had received a set of ecclesiastical canons for his guidance.

Boniface returned to Upper Hessia and repaired the losses which occurred during his absence, many having drifted back into paganism; he also administered everywhere the Sacrament of Confirmation. He continued his work in Lower Hessia. To show the heathens how utterly powerless were the gods in whom they placed their confidence, Boniface felled the oak sacred to the thunder-god Thor, at Geismar, near Fritzlar. He had a chapel built out of the wood and dedicated it to the prince of the Apostles. The heathens were astonished that no thunderbolt from the hand of Thor destroyed the offender, and many were converted. The fall of this oak marked the fall of heathenism. Tradition tells us that Boniface now passed on to the River Werra and there erected a church of St. Vitus, around which sprang up a town which to the present day bears the name of Wannfried. At Eschwege he is said to have destroyed the statue of the idol Stuffo. Thence he went into Thuringia.

The difficulties that confronted him here were very great. Christianity had indeed made great progress, but it had become mixed up with heretical tenets and pagan customs. This was due to a great extent to some Celtic missionaries, several of whom had never been ordained, while others had been raised to the priesthood by non-Catholic bishops, though all performed priestly functions. These taught doctrines and made use of ceremonies at variance with the teaching and use of the Roman Church, especially in regard to the celebration of Easter, the conferring of baptism, celibacy, the papal and episcopal authority. Besides, many were wanting in education, some scarcely able to read or write, and equally ready to hold services for the Christians and to offer sacrifices to the idols for the heathens. A neighbouring bishop (probably of Cologne) also gave trouble, by laying claim to a part of the district under Boniface's jurisdiction and treating his authority as an intrusion, thereby indirectly strengthening the party of the heretics. All this caused him great anxiety and suffering, as may be seen from his letters to England. He overcame all, thanks to his episcopal dignity and to his own personality, full of courage and zeal in the cause which he defended, and supported by the authority of the pope and of Charles Martel. His friends helped him not only by their prayers, but also by material aid. Many valuable books, ecclesiastical articles, and the like were sent to him with words of encouragement. Numbers of men and women went to Germany at different times to be his helpers. Among them were Lullus, Denehard, Burchard, Wigbert, Sola, Witta (called also Wizo and Albinus) Wunibald, Willibald and the pious women Lioba, Chunihild, Chunitrude, Berthgit, Walburga, and Thecla. With these, and others re-

cruited in Thuringia and elsewhere in Germany, he continued his labours. The number of the faithful increased wonderfully, including many of the nobility and the educated of the country. These assisted him in the building of churches and chapels. Boniface took care to have institutions in which religious life would be fostered. In Thuringia he built the first monastery Ohrdruf on the River Ohrn near Altenberga. He appointed Thecla Abbess of Kitzingen, Lioba of Bischofsheim, and Walburga of Heidenheim.

Pope Gregory II died 11 February, 731, and was succeeded on 18 March by Gregory III. Boniface hastened to send a delegation to the new pontiff, to pay his respects and to assure him of his fidelity. The answer to this seems to be lost. In 732 Boniface wrote again and stated among other things that the work was becoming too much for one man. In answer Gregory III congratulated him on his success and praised his zeal, in recognition sending him the pallium, and making him an archbishop, but still without a fixed see. He gave him instructions to appoint bishops wherever he thought it necessary. Boniface now enlarged the monastery of Amöneburg and built a church, dedicating it to St. Michael. Another monastery he founded at Fritzlar near the River Eder, which was completed in 734. The church, a more magnificent structure, was not finished before 740. In 738 Boniface made his third journey to Rome, intending to resign his office and devote himself exclusively to the mission among the Saxons. He was accompanied by a number of his disciples, who were to see true Christian life in the centre of Christianity. Gregory III received him graciously and was rejoiced at the result of Boniface's labour, but would not allow him to resign. Boniface remained in Rome for about a year and then returned to his mission invested with the authority of a legate of the Holy See. His first care on his return was the Church in Bavaria.

In 715 (716) Duke Theodo had come to Rome out of devotion, but probably also to secure ecclesiastical order in his provinces. Gregory II sent three ecclesiastics with instructions to do away with abuses. Their work, however, was rendered futile by the death of Theodo in 717 and the subsequent political quarrels. Boniface had twice passed through the country. Now with the help of Duke Odilo and of the nobles, he began the work of reorganization acting entirely according to the instructions of Gregory II. He examined the orders of the clergy, deposed the obstinate, reordained those whose ordination he found invalid, provided they had erred through ignorance and were willing to submit to authority. He made a new circumscription of the dioceses and appointed bishops for the vacant sees, viz., the Abbot John to the See of Salzburg, vacant since the death of St. Rupert in 718; Erembert to Freising, vacant since the death of his brother, St. Corbinian, in 730; Gaubald for Ratisbon. Passau had been established and provided for by the pope himself through the nomination of Vivilo. About this time Boniface founded the new Diocese of Buraburg, and named Witta as its bishop. This diocese existed only for a short time, during the administration of two bishops, and was then joined to Augsburg. Somewhat later the dioceses of Eichstätt and Erfurt (Erphesfurt) were formed, and Willibald was consecrated bishop for the former about October, 741; for the latter Boniface appointed as first (and last) bishop Adalar, who, it seems, never received episcopal consecration, as he is continually spoken of as a priest. Burchard was chosen for Würzburg.

Charles Martel had died 22 October, 741, at Quiercy on the Oise and was succeeded by his sons Carloman and Pepin. In Rome Pope Gregory III died 28 November, 741, and was followed by Zachary. Carloman asked Boniface, his former preceptor, to a consultation. The result of this was a letter to the pope in which Boniface reported his actions in Bavaria and asked advice in various matters. He also stated the wish of Carloman that a synod be held. In answer Pope Zachary, 1 April, 742, confirmed the erection of the dioceses, sanctioned the holding of the synod, and gave the requested information. The synod, partly ecclesiastical and partly secular, was held 21 April, 742, but the place cannot be ascertained. The bishops appointed by Boniface were present and several others, but it was mainly the authority of Boniface and the power of Carloman that gave weight to the first German synod. Among its decrees the most noteworthy are those ordaining the subjection of the clergy to the bishop of the diocese, and forbidding them to take any active part in wars, to carry arms, or to hunt. Very strict regulations were made against carnal sins on the part of priests and religious. The Rule of St. Benedict was made a norm for religious. Laws were also enacted concerning marriage within the forbidden degrees of kindred. A second national synod was held 1 March, 743, at Liptina in Hainault, and another at Soissons, 2 March, 744. In this synod a sentence of condemnation was passed against two heretics, Adalbert and Clement, the former a native of Gaul, the latter of Ireland. They were again condemned in 745 and also at a synod held in Rome. Several other synods were held in Germany to strengthen faith and discipline. At the request of Carloman and Pepin the authority of Boniface over Bavaria was confirmed and extended over Gaul.

In 744 St. Willibrord, Bishop of Utrecht, died, and Boniface took the diocese under his charge, appointing an assistant or *chor-episcopus*. About the same time the See of Cologne became vacant through the death of Ragenfried, and it was the intention of Boniface as well as the wish of Pope Zachary to make this his archiepiscopal see, but the clergy opposed. Before the project could be carried out the Diocese of Mainz lost its bishop through the deposition of Gewilieb who led a very irregular life and had killed the slayer of his father, who was his predecessor in the episcopal office. Pope Zachary, 1 May, 748 (747), appointed Boniface Archbishop of Mainz and Primate of Germany. The new archdiocese comprised the dioceses of Tongem, Cologne, Worms, Speyer, Utrecht, and the dioceses erected by Boniface himself: Buraburg, Eichstätt, Erfurt, and Würzburg. Of Augsburg, Coire, and Constance the decree does not speak, but they are shortly afterwards mentioned as belonging to the province. After a few years Boniface was able to reconcile his enemies with the Holy See, so that the supremacy of the pope was acknowledged in Great Britain, Germany, and Gaul, as well as in Italy.

In 747 Carloman resigned his share of the government to his brother Pepin and left to spend the remainder of his days as a monk. He built a monastery in honour of St. Silvester at Soracte near Rome, and later retired to Monte Cassino. His motives for this are not known, but perhaps he was frightened at the severity of the measures he had felt himself obliged to use in order to obtain a union among the German tribes. Pepin, now the sole ruler, became the founder of the Carlovingian dynasty. That Boniface had anything to do with the disestablishment of the old royal family and the introduction of a new one cannot be proved. He did not mingle in the politics of the country, except in this, that he did all in his power to convert the people to the true Faith, and to bring them into spiritual subjection to the Roman pontiff. It is generally stated that Boniface anointed and crowned Pepin by order of the pope, though this is denied by some.

The rest of his life Boniface spent in confirming what he had achieved in Germany. This he did by frequently holding synods and by enforcing the sacred canons. He did much for true religious life in the monasteries, especially at Fulda, which had been established under his supervision by St. Sturm, and into which Boniface retired yearly to train the monks and to spend some days in prayer and meditation. At his request Pope Zachary exempted the abbey from all episcopal jurisdiction and placed it under the immediate care of the Holy See. This was something new for Germany, though already known and practised in Italy and England. It seems that Boniface's last act as Archbishop of Mainz was the repudiation of the claim of the Archbishop of Cologne to the Diocese of Utrecht. The matter was laid before Pepin, who decided against Cologne. The same decision must have been given by Pope Stephen II (III) who had become the succesor of Zachary, 26 March, 752, for after that time no further claim was made by Cologne. No change was made until the ninth century, when Cologne was made an archdiocese and Utrecht one of its suffragan sees. Boniface appointed Abbot Gregory as administrator of Utrecht, and Eoban, who had been assistant, he took as his companion.

When Boniface saw that all things had been properly taken care of, he took up the work he had dreamed of in early manhood, the conversion of the Frisians. With royal consent, and with that of the pope previously given, he in 754 resigned the Archdiocese of Mainz to his disciple Lullus, whom in 752 he had consecrated bishop, again commenced a missionary tour, and laboured with success to the East of the Zuider Zee. Returning in the following year, he ordered the new converts to assemble for confirmation at Dokkum on the River Borne. The heathens fell upon them and murdered Boniface and fifty-two companions (according to some, thirty-seven). Soon afterwards, the Christians, who had scattered at the approach of the heathens, returned and found the body of the martyr and beside him the blood-stained copy of St. Ambrose on the "Advantage of Death". The body was taken to Utrecht, afterwards through the influence of Lullus removed to Mainz, and later, according to a wish expressed by the saint himself during his lifetime, to the Abbey of Fulda. Portions of his relics are at Louvain, Mechlin, Prague, Bruges, and Erfurt. A considerable portion of an arm is at Eichfeld. His grave soon became a sanctuary, to which the faithful came in crowds especially on his feast and during the Octave. England is supposed to have been the first place where his martyrdom was celebrated on a fixed day. Other countries followed. On 11 June, 1874, Pope Pius IX extended the celebration to the entire world. Brewers, tailors, and file-cutters have chosen St. Boniface as their patron, also various cities in Germany. The writings of St. Boniface which have been preserved are: "Collection of Letters"; "Poems and Riddles"; "Pœnitentiale"; "Compendium of the Latin Language"; "Compendium of Latin Prosody"; "Sermons" (doubtful).

JAFFÉ, *Bibl. Rer. Germanic.*, III, 24–315; *P. L.*, LXXXIX, 687–892; HAUCK, *Kirchengesch. Deutschlands*; *Historisches Jahrbuch der Görres Gesellschaft*, I, 252 sqq.; *Historisch-politische Blätter*, 88, 721 sqq.; HOPE, *Conversion of the Teutonic Races*, II; SMITH in *Dict. Christ. Biog.*, s. v.; THOMPSON in *Dict. Nat. Biog.*, s. v.

FRANCIS MERSHMAN.

Boniface I, SAINT, Pope; elected 28 December, 418; d. at Rome, 4 September, 422. Little is known of his life antecedent to his election. The "Liber Pontificalis" calls him a Roman, and the son of the presbyter Jocundus. He is believed to have been ordained by Pope Damasus I (366–384) and to have served as representative of Innocent I at Constantinople (c. 405).

At the death of Pope Zosimus, the Roman Church entered into the fifth of the schisms, resulting from double papal elections, which so disturbed her peace during the early centuries. Just after Zosimus's obsequies, 27 December, 418, a faction of the Roman clergy consisting principally of deacons seized the Lateran basilica and elected as pope the Archdeacon Eulalius. The higher clergy tried to enter, but were violently repulsed by a mob of adherents of the Eulalian party. On the following day they met in the church of Theodora and elected as pope, much against his will, the aged Boniface, a priest highly esteemed for his charity, learning, and good character. On Sunday, 29 December, both were consecrated, Boniface in the Basilica of St. Marcellus, supported by nine provincial bishops and some seventy priests; Eulalius in the Lateran basilica in the presence of the deacons, a few priests and the Bishop of Ostia, who was summoned from his sickbed to assist at the ordination. Each claimant proceeded to act as pope, and Rome was thrown into tumultuous confusion by the clash of the rival factions. The Prefect of Rome, Symmachus, hostile to Boniface, reported the trouble to the Emperor Honorius at Ravenna, and secured the imperial confirmation of Eulalius's election. Boniface was expelled from the city. His adherents, however, secured a hearing from the emperor who called a synod of Italian Bishops at Ravenna to meet the rival popes and discuss the situation (February, March, 419). Unable to reach a decision, the synod made a few practical provisions pending a general council of Italian, Gaulish, and African bishops to be convened in May to settle the difficulty. It ordered both claimants to leave Rome until a decision was reached and forbade return under penalty of condemnation. As Easter, 30 March, was approaching, Achilleus, Bishop of Spoleto, was deputed to conduct the paschal services in the vacant Roman See. Boniface was sent, it seems, to the cemetery of St. Felicitas on the Via Salaria, and Eulalius to Antium. On 18 March, Eulalius boldly returned to Rome, gathered his partisans, stirred up strife anew, and spurning the prefect's orders to leave the city, seized the Lateran basilica on Holy Saturday (29 March), determined to preside at the paschal ceremonies. The imperial troops were required to dispossess him and make it possible for Achilleus to conduct the services. The emperor was deeply indignant at these proceedings and refusing to consider again the claims of Eulalius, recognized Boniface as legitimate pope (3 April, 418). The latter re-entered Rome 10 April and was acclaimed by the people. Eulalius was made Bishop either of Nepi in Tuscany or of some Campanian see, according to the conflicting data of the sources of the "Liber Pontificalis". The schism had lasted fifteen weeks. Early in 420, the pope's critical illness encouraged the partisans of Eulalius to make another effort. On his recovery Boniface requested the emperor (1 July, 420) to make some provision against possible renewal of the schism in the event of his death. Honorius enacted a law providing that, in contested papal elections, neither claimant should be recognized and a new election should be held.

Boniface's reign was marked by great zeal and activity in disciplinary organization and control. He reversed his predecessor's policy of endowing certain Western bishops with extraordinary papal vicariate powers. Zosimus had given to Patroclus, Bishop of Arles, extensive jurisdiction in the provinces of Vienna, and Narbonne, and had made him an intermediary between these provinces and the Apostolic See. Boniface diminished these primatial rights and restored the metropolitan powers of the chief bishops of provinces. Thus he sustained Hilary, Archbishop of Narbonne in his choice of a bishop of the vacant See of Lodeve, against Patroclus, who tried to intrude another (422). So, too, he insisted that Maximus, Bishop of Valence, should

be tried for his alleged crimes, not by a primate, but by a synod of the bishops of Gaul, and promised to sustain their decision (419). Boniface succeeded to Zosimus's difficulties with the African Church regarding appeals to Rome and, in particular, the case of Apiarius. The Council of Carthage, having heard the representations of Zosimus's legates, sent to Boniface on 31 May, 419, a letter in reply to the *commonitorium* of his predecessor. It stated that the council had been unable to verify the canons which the legates had quoted as Nicene, but which were later found to be Sardican. It agreed, however, to observe them until verification could be established. This letter is often cited in illustration of the defiant attitude of the African Church to the Roman See. An unbiased study of it, however, must lead to no more extreme conclusion than that of Dom Chapman: "it was written in considerable irritation, yet in a studiously moderate tone" (Dublin Review, July, 1901, 109–119). The Africans were irritated at the insolence of Boniface's legates and incensed at being urged to obey laws which they thought were not consistently enforced at Rome. This they told Boniface in no uncertain language; yet, far from repudiating his authority, they promised to obey the suspected laws, thus recognizing the pope's office as guardian of the Church's discipline. In 422 Boniface received the appeal of Anthony of Fussula who, through the efforts of St. Augustine, had been deposed by a provincial synod of Numidia, and decided that he should be restored if his innocence be established. Boniface ardently supported St. Augustine in combating Pelagianism. Having received two Pelagian letters calumniating Augustine, he sent them to him. In recognition of this solicitude Augustine dedicated to Boniface his rejoinder contained in "Contra duas Epistolas Pelagianorum Libri quatuor".

In the East he zealously maintained his jurisdiction over the ecclesiastical provinces of Illyricum, of which the Patriarch of Constantinople was trying to secure control on account of their becoming a part of the Eastern empire. The Bishop of Thessalonica had been constituted papal vicar in this territory, exercising jurisdiction over the metropolitans and bishops. By letters to Rufus, the contemporary incumbent of the see, Boniface watched closely over the interests of the Illyrian church and insisted on obedience to Rome. In 421 dissatisfaction expressed by certain malcontents among the bishops, on account of the pope's refusal to confirm the election of Perigines as Bishop of Corinth unless the candidate was recognized by Rufus, served as a pretext for the young emperor Theodosius II to grant the ecclesiastical dominion of Illyricum to the Patriarch of Constantinople (14 July, 421). Boniface remonstrated with Honorius against the violation of the rights of his see, and prevailed upon him to urge Theodosius to rescind his enactment. The law was not enforced, but it remained in the Theodosian (439) and Justinian (534) codes and caused much trouble for succeeding popes. By a letter of 11 March, 422, Boniface forbade the consecration in Illyricum of any bishop whom Rufus would not recognize. Boniface renewed the legislation of Pope Soter, prohibiting women to touch the sacred linens or to minister at the burning of incense. He enforced the laws forbidding slaves to become clerics. He was buried in the cemetery of Maximus on the Via Salaria, near the tomb of his favourite, St. Felicitas, in whose honour and in gratitude for whose aid he had erected an oratory over the cemetery bearing her name. The Church keeps his feast on 25 October.

Liber Pontificalis, ed. DUCHESNE (Paris, 1886), I, pp. lxii, 227–229; JAFFÉ, *Regesta Romanorum Pontificum* (Leipzig, 1885), I, 51–54; *Acta SS.*, XIII, 62*; LIX, 605–616; BARONIUS, *Annales* (Bar-le-Duc, 1866), VII, 152–231; TILLEMONT, *Mémoires* (Venice, 1732), XII, 385–407; 666–670; *P. L.*, XVIII, 397–406; XX, 745–792; HEFELE, *Conciliengeschichte* and translation, §§ 120, 122; DUCHESNE, *Fastes Episcopaux de l'Ancienne Gaul* (Paris, 1894), I, 84–109; *Les Eglises Séparées* (Paris, 1905), 229–279; BUCHANAN in *Dict. Christ. Biog.*, s. v.; GREGOROVIUS-HAMILTON, *Hist. o*' *Rome in the Middle Ages* (London, 1894), I, 180–181.

JOHN B. PETERSON.

Boniface II, POPE, elected 17 September, 530; d. October, 532. In calling him the son of Sigisbald, the "Liber Pontificalis" makes first mention of a pope's Germanic ancestry. Boniface served the Roman Church from early youth. During the reign of Pope Felix IV, he was archdeacon and a personage of considerable influence with the ecclesiastical and civil authorities. His elevation to the papacy is remarkable as offering an unquestionable example of the nomination of a pope by his predecessor, without even the formality of an election. Felix IV apprehending death and fearing a contest for the papacy between Roman and Gothic factions, gathered about him several of his clergy and a number of Roman Senators and patricians who happened to be near. In their presence, he solemnly conferred on his aged archdeacon the pallium of papal sovereignty, proclaiming him his successor and menacing with excommunication those refusing to recognize and obey Boniface as validly chosen pope. On Felix's death Boniface assumed succession, but nearly all of the Roman priests, sixty out of perhaps about seventy, refused to accept him and elected Dioscorus. They feared the undue influence in papal affairs of the Ostrogothic King Athalaric, whose grandfather, Theodoric I, had helped to elect Pope Felix IV, a circumstance rendering more odious the latter's nomination of Boniface. Both popes were consecrated 22 September, 530, Boniface in the basilica of Julius, and Dioscorus in the Lateran. The Roman Church was thus involved in the seventh anti-papal schism. Fortunately it endured but twenty-two days, for Dioscorus died 14 October, leaving Boniface in possession. He soon convened a Roman synod and presented a decree anathematizing his late rival to which he secured the signatures of the priests who had been Dioscorus's partisans (December, 530). Each of these expressed regret for their participation in the irregular election and pledged future obedience. Boniface reconciled many by his mild, conciliatory administration, but some resentment remained, for he seems not to have been tendered a formal election by those who, despite their submission, had impugned the validity of his nomination; and five years later a pope of their own choice solemnly burned the anathema against Dioscorus. (See AGAPETUS I.) In a second synod, held (531) in St. Peter's, Boniface presented a constitution attributing to himself the right to appoint his successor. The Roman clergy subscribed to it and promised obedience. Boniface proposed as his choice the deacon Vigilius and it was ratified by priests and people. This enactment provoked bitter resentment and even imperial disfavour, for in a third synod (531) it was rescinded. Boniface burned the constitution before the clergy and senate and nullified the appointment of Vigilius.

The reign of Boniface was marked by his active interest in diverse affairs of the Western and Eastern churches. Early in his pontificate he confirmed the acts of the Second Council of Orange, one of the most important of the sixth century, which effectually terminated the Semipelagian controversies. Its presiding officer, Cæsarius, Archbishop of Arles, an intimate friend of Boniface, had, previous to the latter's succession, sent the priest Armenius to Rome to ask Boniface to secure the pope's confirmation of the council. Being himself pope when the messenger came, Boniface sent a letter of confirmation to Cæsarius (25 January, 531) in which he condemned certain Semipelagian doctrines. He received an appeal from the African bishops, who were labouring

at the reorganization of their church after the Vandal devastation, requesting him to confirm in primatial rights the Archbishop of Carthage, that the latter might be better able to profit by the help of the Roman See. In the east he asserted the rights of the pope to jurisdiction in Illyricum. (See BONIFACE I.) In 531, Epiphanius, Patriarch of Constantinople, declared irregular the election of Stephen to the Archbishopric of Larissa in Thessaly. Despite the severe measures taken in Constantinople to thwart his purpose, Stephen appealed to Rome on the ground that Epiphanius was not competent to decide the case, maintaining his point in terms which reveal a clear conception of Roman primacy. Boniface convened a fourth Roman synod 7–9 December, 531, in which some twenty-five documents were adduced in support of Rome's claim to jurisdiction in Illyricum. The outcome of the synod is not known. Boniface was esteemed for his charity, particularly towards the suffering poor of Rome during a year of famine. He was buried in St. Peter's, 17 October, 532, where a fragment of his epitaph may yet be seen (Dufresne, Les Cryptes Vaticanes, Rome, 1902).

Liber Pontificalis, ed. DUCHESNE (Paris, 1886), pp. xl–xli, 281–284; JAFFÉ, *Regesta Romanorum Pontificum* (Leipzig, 1885), I, 111–112; *Acta SS.*, XIII, 78–79; BARONIUS, *Annales Eccl.* (Bar-le-Duc, 1867), IX, 389–405; HEFELE, *Conciliengeschichte*, and translations §§ 242, 244; *P. L.*, LXV, 29–48; LXXXIV, 675–680.
On the election of Boniface no literature is reliable which antedates 1883, when AMELLI published the documents on which he comments in *Scuola Cattolica* (Milan), XXI, fascic. 123; DUCHESNE, *La succession du Pape Félix IV* in *Mélanges de l'Ecole de Rome* (1883), III, 238, 266; CREAGH in *Ecclesiastical Review* (January, 1903), XXVIII, 41–50; EWALD, *Akten zum Schisma des Jahres 530* in *Neues Archiv.* (1885–86); GREGOROVIUS-HAMILTON, *Hist. of the City of Rome in the Middle Ages* (London, 1894), I, 346–348; HUTTON, *The Church of the Sixth Century* (London, 1897).

JOHN B. PETERSON.

Boniface III–VII, POPES.—BONIFACE III, POPE, of Roman extraction and the son of John Cataadioce, was elected to succeed Sabinian after an interregnum of nearly a year; he was consecrated 19 February, 607; d. 12 November of the same year. He had been ordained a deacon of the Roman Church, and in 603 sent by Gregory the Great as *apocrisiarius*, or legate, to the court of Constantinople, where, by his tact and prudence, he appears to have gained the favourable regard of the Emperor Phocas. After his elevation to the See of Rome, Boniface obtained a decree from Phocas, against Cyriacus, Bishop of Constantinople, by which it was ordained, that "the See of Blessed Peter the Apostle should be the head of all the Churches", and that the title of "Universal Bishop" belonged exclusively to the Bishop of Rome—an acknowledgment somewhat similar to that made by Justinian eighty years before (Novell., 131, c. ii, tit. xiv). At Rome Boniface held a council, attended by seventy-two bishops and all the Roman clergy, wherein he enacted a decree forbidding anyone under pain of excommunication, during the lifetime of a pope or of a bishop, to treat of or to discuss the appointment of his successor, and setting forth that no steps were to be taken to provide for a successor until three days after the burial of the deceased. The acts of the council are lost, and it is not known what may have been the occasion for the decree. Pope Boniface was a man "of tried faith and character" (St. Greg., ep. xiii, 41). He died within a year of his elevation and was buried in St. Peter's. His epitaph is found in the works of Duchesne and Mann.

Liber Pontificalis (ed. DUCHESNE), I, 316; JAFFÉ, *Regesta RR. PP.* (2nd ed.), I, 220; MANN, *The Lives of the Popes in the Early Middle Ages* (London, 1902), I, 259–267; GREGOROVIUS, *Gesch. der Stadt Rom im M. A.* (4th ed., Stuttgart, 1889), II, 104, also in Eng. trans.; GRISAR, *Gesch. Roms und der Päpste in M. A.* (Freiburg im Br., 1901), I, 273; HEFELE, *Conciliengesch.*, 2nd ed., II, 737; HERGENRÖTHER, *Photius* (Ratisbon, 1867), I, 195; LANGEN, *Gesch. der römischen Kirche von Leo I. bis Nikolaus I.* (Bonn, 1885); JUNGMANN, *Dissertationes*, II, 388.

BONIFACE IV, SAINT, POPE, son of John, a physician

a Marsian from the province and town of Valeria; he succeeded Boniface III after a vacancy of over nine months; consecrated 25 August, 608; d. 8 May, 615 (Duchesne); or, 15 September, 608—25 May, 615 (Jaffé). In the time of Pope St. Gregory the Great he was a deacon of the Roman Church and held the position of *dispensator*, i. e. the first official in connexion with the administration of the patrimonies. Boniface obtained leave from the Emperor Phocas to convert the Pantheon into a Christian Church, and on 13 May, 609 (?) the temple erected by Agrippa to Jupiter the Avenger, to Venus, and to Mars was consecrated by the pope to the Virgin Mary and all the Martyrs. (Hence the title S. Maria ad Martyres; from its shape also called S. Maria Rotunda.) It was the first instance at Rome of the transformation of a pagan temple into a place of Christian worship. Twenty-eight cartloads of sacred bones were said to have been removed from the Catacombs and placed in a porphyry basin beneath the high altar. During the pontificate of Boniface, Mellitus, the first Bishop of London, went to Rome "to consult the pope on important matters relative to the newly established English Church" (Bede, H. E., II, iv). Whilst in Rome he assisted at a council then being held concerning certain questions on "the life and monastic peace of monks", and, on his departure, took with him to England the decrees of the council together with letters from the pope to Lawrence, Archbishop of Canterbury, and to all the clergy, to King Ethelbert, and to all the English people "concerning what was to be observed by the Church of England". The decrees of the council now extant are spurious. The letter to Ethelbert (in William of Malmesbury, De Gest. Pont., I, 1464, ed. Migne) is considered spurious by Hefele (Conciliengeschichte, III, 66), questionable by Haddan and Stubbs (Councils, III, 65), and genuine by Jaffé [Regest. RR. PP., 1998 (1548)].

Between 612–615, St. Columban, then living at Bobbio in Italy, was persuaded by Agilulf, King of the Lombards, to address a letter on the condemnation of the "Three Chapters" to Boniface IV, which is remarkable at once for its expressions of exaggerated deference and its tone of excessive sharpness. In it he tells the pope that he is charged with heresy (for accepting the Fifth Council, i. e. Constantinople, 553), and exhorts him to summon a council and prove his orthodoxy. But the letter of the impetuous Celt, who failed to grasp the import of the theological problem involved in the "Three Chapters", seems not to have disturbed in the least his relation with the Holy See, and it would be wrong to suppose that Columban regarded himself as independent of the pope's authority. During the pontificate of Boniface there was much distress in Rome owing to famine, pestilence, and inundations. The pontiff died in monastic retirement (he had converted his own house into a monastery) and was buried in the portico of St. Peter's. His remains were three times removed— in the tenth or eleventh century, at the close of the thirteenth under Boniface VIII, and to the new St. Peter's on 21 October, 1603. For the earlier inscription on his tomb see Duchesne; for the later, Grisar, "Analecta Romana", I, 193. Boniface IV is commemorated as a saint in the Roman Martyrology on 25 May.

Liber Pontificalis (ed. DUCHESNE), I, 317; JAFFÉ, *Regesta RR. PP.* (2nd ed.), I, 220; *Acta et Epistolæ* in MANSI, X, 501; PAUL THE DEACON, *Hist. Longobard.*, IV, 36 (37); GASQUET, *A Short History of the Catholic Church in England* (London, 1903), 19; HUNT, *A History of the English Church from its Foundation to the Norman Conquest* (London, 1901), 42; MANN, *Lives of the Popes*, I, 268–279; VON REUMONT, *Gesch. der Stadt Rom* (Berlin, 1867), II, 156, 165; GREGOROVIUS, II, 104; LANGEN, 501.

BONIFACE V, POPE, a Neapolitan who succeeded Deusdedit after a vacancy of more than a year; consecrated 23 December, 619; d. 25 October, 625. Be-

II.—42

fore his consecration Italy was disturbed by the rebellion of the eunuch Eleutherius, Exarch of Ravenna. The patrician pretender advanced towards Rome, but before he could reach the city, he was slain by his own troops. The "Liber Pontificalis" records that Boniface made certain enactments relative to the rights of sanctuary, and that he ordered the ecclesiastical notaries to obey the laws of the empire on the subject of wills. He also prescribed that acolytes should not presume to translate the relics of martyrs, and that, in the Lateran Basilica, they should not take the place of deacons in administering baptism. Boniface completed and consecrated the cemetery of St. Nicomedes on the Via Nomentana. From the Venerable Bede we learn of the pope's affectionate concern for the English Church. The "letters of exhortation" which he is said to have addressed to Mellitus, Archbishop of Canterbury, and to Justus, Bishop of Rochester, are no longer extant, but certain other letters of his have been preserved. One is written to Justus, after he had succeeded Mellitus as Archbishop of Canterbury (624), conferring the pallium upon him and directing him to "ordain bishops as occasion should require". According to Bede, Pope Boniface also sent letters to Edwin, King of Northumbria (625), urging him to embrace the Christian Faith, and to the Christian Princess Ethelberga, Edwin's spouse, exhorting her to use her best endeavours for the conversion of her consort (Bede, H. E., II, vii, viii, x, xi). In the "Liber Pontificalis" Boniface is described as "the mildest of men", whose chief distinction was his great love for the clergy. He was buried in St. Peter's, 25 October, 625. His epitaph is found in Duchesne.

Liber Pontificalis (ed. DUCHESNE), I, 321–322; JAFFÉ, *Regesta RR. PP.* (2nd ed.), I, 222; *Letters* in MANSI, X, 547–554, and in BEDE, *Hist. Eccles. Gent. Angl.*; MANN, *Lives of the Popes*, etc., I, 294–303; GASQUET, *A Short History of the Catholic Church in England*, 19; HUNT, *A History of the English Church*, etc., 49, 56, 58; GREGOROVIUS, II, 113; LANGEN, 506; JUNGMANN, *Dissertationes*, II, 389.

BONIFACE VI, POPE, a Roman, elected in 896 by the Roman faction in a popular tumult, to succeed Formosus. He had twice incurred a sentence of deprivation of orders, as a subdeacon and as a priest. At the Council of Rome, held by John IX in 898, his election was pronounced null. After a pontificate of fifteen days, he is said by some to have died of the gout, by others to have been forcibly ejected to make way for Stephen VI, the candidate of the Spoletan party.

Liber Pontificalis (ed. DUCHESNE), II, 228; IDEM, *Les premiers temps de l'état pontifical* (2nd ed., Paris, 1904), 299; JAFFÉ, *Regesta RR. PP.*, I, 439; JUNGMANN, *Dissertationes*, IV, 22.

BONIFACE VII, ANTIPOPE (previously BONIFACE FRANCO), a Roman and son of Ferrucius, was intruded into the Chair of St. Peter in 974; reinstalled, 984; d. July, 985. In June, 974, one year after the death of Emperor Otto I, Crescentius the son of Theodora and brother of John XIII, stirred up an insurrection at Rome, during which the Romans threw Benedict VI into the Castle of Sant' Angelo, and elevated as his successor the Cardinal-Deacon Franco, who took the name of Boniface VII. The imprisoned pontiff was speedily put to death by the intruder. But in little more than a month the imperial representative, Count Sicco, had taken possession of the city, and Boniface, not being able to maintain himself, robbed the treasury of the Vatican Basilica and fled to Constantinople. After an exile of nine years at Byzantium, Franco, on the death of Otto II, 7 December, 983, quickly returned to Rome, overpowered John XIV (April, 984), thrust him into the dungeons of Sant' Angelo, where the wretched man died four months later, and again assumed the government of the Church. The usurper had never ceased to look upon himself as the lawful pontiff, and reckoned the years of his reign from the deposition of Benedict VI in 974. For more than a year Rome endured this monster steeped in the blood of his predecessors. But the vengeance was terrible. After his sudden death in July, 985, due in all probability to violence, the body of Boniface was exposed to the insults of the populace, dragged through the streets of the city, and finally, naked and covered with wounds, flung under the statue of Marcus Aurelius, which at that time stood in the Lateran Place. The following morning compassionate clerics removed the corpse and gave it Christian burial.

Liber Pontificalis (ed. DUCHESNE), II, 257; IDEM, *Les premiers temps de l'état pontifical* (2nd ed., Paris, 1904), 357, 358; JAFFÉ, *Regest. RR. PP.*, I, 485; WATTERICH, *Vitæ Rom. Pont.*, I, 66; FERRUCCI, *Investigazioni storico-critiche su la persona ed il pontificato di Bonifazio VII* (Lugo, 1856); HEFELE, *Conciliengesch.*, IV, 632, 634; JUNGMANN, *Dissertationes*, IV, 88–91; FLOSS, *Die Papstwahl unter den Ottonen* (Freiburg, 1858), 42; GREGOROVIUS, III, 363, 369, 381–383; VON REUMONT, *Gesch. der Stadt Rom*, II, 293, 296.

THOMAS OESTREICH.

Boniface VIII, POPE (BENEDETTO GAETANI), b. at Anagni about 1235; d. at Rome, 11 October, 1303. He was the son of Loffred, a descendant of a noble family originally Spanish, but long established in Italy—first at Gaeta and later at Anagni. Through his mother he was connected with the house of Segni, which had already given three illustrious sons to the Church, Innocent III, Gregory IX, and Alexander IV. Benedetto had studied at Todi and at Spoleto in Italy, perhaps also at Paris, had obtained the doctorate in canon and civil law, and been made a canon successively at Anagni, Todi, Paris, Lyons, and Rome. In 1265 he accompanied Cardinal Ottobuono Fieschi to England, whither that prelate had been sent to restore harmony between Henry III and the rebellious barons. It was not until about 1276 that Gaetani entered upon his career in the Curia, where he was, for some years, actively engaged as consistorial advocate and notary Apostolic, and soon acquired considerable influence. Under Martin IV, in 1281, he was created Cardinal-Deacon of the title of S. Nicolò *in carcere Tulliano*, and ten years later, under Nicholas IV, Cardinal-Priest of the title of SS. Silvestro e Martino ai Monti. As papal legate he served with conspicuous ability in France and in Sicily (H. Finke, Aus den Tagen Bonifaz VIII, Münster, 1902, 1 sqq., 9 sqq.).

On the 13th of December, 1294, the saintly but wholly incompetent hermit-pope Celestine V, who five months previously, as Pietro di Murrhone, had been taken from his obscure mountain cave in the wilds of the Abruzzi and raised to the highest dignity in Christendom, resigned the intolerable burden of the papacy. The act was unprecedented and has been frequently ascribed to the undue influence and pressure of the designing Cardinal Gaetani. That the elevation of the inexperienced and simple-minded recluse did not commend itself to a man of the stamp of Gaetani, reputed the greatest jurist of his age and well-skilled in all the arts of curial diplomacy, is highly probable. But Boniface himself declared, through Ægidius Colonna, that he had at first dissuaded Celestine from taking the step. And it has now been almost certainly established that the idea of resigning the papacy first originated in the mind of the sorely perplexed Celestine himself, and that the part played by Gaetani was at most that of a counsellor, strongly advising the pontiff to issue a constitution, either before or simultaneously with his abdication, declaring the legality of a papal resignation and the competency of the College of Cardinals to accept it. [See especially H. Schulz, Peter von Murrhone—Papst Cœlestin V—in Zeitschrift für Kirchengeschichte, xvii (1897), 481 sqq.; also Finke, op. cit., 39 sqq.; and R. Scholz, Die Publizistik zur Zeit Philipps des Schönen und Bonifaz VIII, Stuttgart, 1903, 3.] Ten days after Celes-

tine the Fifth's *gran rifiuto* the cardinals went into conclave in the Castel Nuovo at Naples, and on the 24th of December, 1294, by a majority of votes elected Cardinal Benedetto Gaetani, who took the name of Boniface VIII. (For details of the election see Finke, op. cit., 44–54.) With the approval of the cardinals, the new pope immediately revoked (27 December, 1294) all the extraordinary favours and privileges which "in the fullness of his simplicity" Celestine V had distributed with such reckless prodigality. Then, early in January of the following year, in spite of the rigour of the season, Boniface set out for Rome, determined to remove the papacy as soon as possible from the influence of the Neapolitan court. The ceremony of his consecration and coronation was performed at Rome, 23 January, 1295, amid scenes of unparalleled splendour and magnificence. King Charles II of Naples and his son Charles Martel, titular king and claimant of Hungary, held the reins of his gorgeously accoutred snow-white palfrey as he proceeded on his way to St. John Lateran, and later, with their crowns upon their heads, served the pope with the first few dishes at table before taking their places amongst the cardinals. On the following day the pontiff issued his first encyclical letter, in which, after announcing Celestine's abdication and his own accession, he depicted in the most glowing terms the sublime and indefectible nature of the Church.

The unusual step taken by Celestine V had aroused much opposition, especially among the religious parties in Italy. In the hands of the Spirituals, or Fraticelli, and the Celestines—many of whom were not as guileless as their saintly founder—the former pontiff, if allowed to go free, might prove to be a dangerous instrument for the promotion of a schism in the Church. Boniface VIII, therefore, before leaving Naples, ordered Celestine V to be taken to Rome in the custody of the Abbot of Monte Cassino. On the way thither the saint escaped and returned to his hermitage near Sulmona. Apprehended again, he fled a second time, and after weary weeks of roaming through the woods of Apulia reached the sea and embarked on board a vessel about to sail for Dalmatia. But a storm cast the luckless fugitive ashore at Vieste in the Capitanata, where the authorities recognized and detained him. He was brought before Boniface in his palace at Anagni, kept in custody there for some time, and finally transferred to the strong Castle of Fumone at Ferentino. Here he remained until his death ten months later, 19 May, 1296. The detention of Celestine was a simple measure of prudence for which Boniface VIII deserves no censure; but the rigorous treatment to which the old man of over eighty years was subjected—whoever may have been responsible for it—will not be easily condoned. Of this treatment there can now no longer be any question. The place wherein Celestine was confined was so narrow "that the spot whereon the saint stood when saying Mass was the same as that whereon his head lay when he reclined" (quod, ubi tenebat pedes ille sanctus, dum missam diceret, ibi tenebat caput, quando quiescebat), and his two companions were frequently obliged to change places because the constraint and narrowness made them ill. (In this connexion see the very important and valuable paper "S. Pierre Célestin et ses premiers Biographes" in "Analecta Bolland.", XVI, 365–487; cf. Finke, op. cit., 267.)

Thoroughly imbued with the principles of his great and heroic predecessors, Gregory VII and Innocent III, the successor of Celestine V entertained most exalted notions on the subject of papal supremacy in ecclesiastical as well as in civil matters, and was ever most pronounced in the assertion of his claims. By his profound knowledge of the canons of the Church, his keen political instincts, great practical experience of life, and high talent for the conduct of affairs, Boniface VIII seemed exceptionally well qualified to maintain inviolate the rights and privileges of the papacy as they had been handed down to him. But he failed either to recognize the altered temper of the times, or to gauge accurately the strength of the forces arrayed against him; and when he attempted to exercise his supreme authority in temporal affairs as in spiritual, over princes and people, he met almost everywhere with a determined resistance. His aims of universal peace and Christian coalition against the Turks were not realized; and during the nine years of his troubled reign he scarcely ever achieved a decisive triumph. Though certainly one of the most remarkable pontiffs that have ever occupied the papal throne, Boniface VIII was also one of the most unfortunate. His pontificate marks in history the decline of the medieval power and glory of the papacy.

Boniface first endeavoured to settle the affairs of Sicily, which had been in a very distracted condition since the time of the Sicilian Vespers (1282). Two rivals claimed the island, Charles II, King of Naples, in right of his father Charles of Anjou, who had received it from Clement IV, and James II, King of Aragon, who derived his claims from the Hohenstaufen, through his mother Constance, the daughter of Manfred. James II had been crowned King of Sicily at Palermo in 1286, and had thereby incurred the sentence of excommunication for daring to usurp a fief of the Holy See. On his succession to the throne of Aragon, after the death of his brother Alfonso III, in 1291, James agreed to surrender Sicily to Charles II on condition that he should receive the latter's daughter, Blanche of Naples, in marriage, together with a dowry of 70,000 pounds of silver. Boniface VIII, as liege lord of the island, ratified this agreement 21 June, 1295, and further sought to reconcile the conflicting elements by restoring James II to peace with the Church, confirming him in his possession of Aragon, and granting him the islands of Sardinia and Corsica, which were fiefs of the Holy See, in compensation for the loss of Sicily. By these measures Boniface VIII merely adhered to the traditional policy of the papacy in dealing with Sicilian affairs; there is no evidence to show that, either before or shortly after his election, he had pledged himself in any way to recover Sicily for the House of Anjou. Sicily was not, however, pacified by this agreement between the pope and the kings of Aragon and Naples. Threatened with a renewal of the detested rule of the French, the inhabitants of that island asserted their independence, and offered the crown to Frederick, the younger brother of James II. In an interview with Frederick at Velletri, the pope sought to dissuade him from accepting the offer by holding out prospects of a succession to the throne of Constantinople and a marriage with Princess Catherine of Courtenay, granddaughter and heir of Baldwin II, the last Latin Emperor of the East. But the young prince would not be dissuaded. The papal legate was expelled from the island, and, against the protests of Boniface VIII, Frederick was crowned King of Sicily at Palermo, 25 March, 1296. He was at once excommunicated and the island placed under interdict. Neither the king nor his people paid any heed to the censures. At the instigation of the pope a war ensued, in which James of Aragon, as Captain-General of the Church, was compelled to take part against his own brother. The contest was brought to a close (1302) through the efforts of Prince Charles of Valois, whom the pope had called to his assistance in 1301. Frederick was to be absolved from the censures he had incurred, to marry Eleanora, younger daughter of Charles II, and to retain Sicily during his lifetime. After his death the island

should revert to the King of Naples. Though frustrated in his hopes, Boniface VIII ratified the treaty 12 June, 1303, and agreed to recognize Frederick as vassal of the Holy See.

In the meantime Boniface VIII had directed his attention also to the north of Italy, where, during a period of forty years, the two rival republics of Venice and Genoa had been carrying on a bitter contest for commercial supremacy in the Levant. A crusade was wellnigh impossible without the active co-operation of these two powers. The pope, therefore, commanded a truce until 24 June, 1296, and ordered both the contestants to send ambassadors to Rome with a view to arranging terms of peace. The Venetians were inclined to accept his mediation; not so the Genoese, who were elated by their success. The war continued till 1299, when the two republics were obliged finally to conclude peace from sheer exhaustion, but even then the intervention of the pope was rejected.

The efforts made by Boniface VIII to restore order in Florence and Tuscany proved equally futile. During the closing years of the thirteenth century the great Guelph city was torn asunder by the violent dissensions of the Bianchi and the Neri. The Bianchi or Whites, of Ghibelline tendencies, represented the popular party and contained some of the most distinguished men in Florence—Dante Alighieri, Guido Cavalcanti, and Dino Compagni. The Neri or Blacks, professing the old Guelph principles, represented the nobles or aristocracy of the city. Each party as it gained the ascendancy sent its opponents into exile. After a vain attempt to reconcile the leaders of the two parties, Vieri dei Cerchi and Corso Donati, the pope sent Cardinal Matteo d'Acquasparta as papal legate to mediate and establish peace at Florence. The legate met with no success and soon returned to Rome leaving the city under an interdict. Towards the end of 1300, Boniface VIII summoned to his aid Charles of Valois, brother of Philip the Fair. Appointed Captain-General of Church and invested with the governorship of Tuscany (in consequence of the vacancy of the empire), the French prince was given full powers to effect the pacification of the city. Valois arrived at Florence on 1 November, 1301. But instead of acting as the official peacemaker of the pope, he conducted himself as a ruthless destroyer. After five months of his partisan administration, the Neri were supreme and many of the Bianchi exiled and ruined—among them Dante Alighieri. Beyond drawing on himself and the pope the bitter hatred of the Florentine people, Charles had accomplished nothing. (Levi, Bonifazio VIII e le sue relazioni col commune di Firenze, in Archiv. Soc. Rom. di Storia Patria, 1882, V, 365-474. Cf. Franchetti, Nuova Antologia, 1883, 23-38.) It may be noted here that many scholars of repute seriously question Dante's famous embassy to Boniface VIII in the latter part of 1301. The only contemporary evidence to support the poet's mission is a passage in Dino Compagni, and even that is looked upon by some as a later interpolation.

While thus endeavouring to promote peaceful relations between various states in Northern and Southern Italy, Boniface had himself become engaged in a desperate struggle at Rome with two rebellious members of the Sacred College, Jacopo Colonna and his nephew Pietro Colonna. The Colonna cardinals were Roman princes of the highest nobility and belonged to a powerful Italian family that had numerous palaces and strongholds in Rome and in the Campagna. The estrangement which took place between them and Boniface, early in 1297, was owing chiefly to two causes. Jacopo Colonna, upon whom the administration of the vast Colonna family possessions had been conferred, violated the rights of his brothers,

Matteo, Ottone, and Landolfo, by appropriating the property rightfully belonging to them, and bestowing it on his nephews. To obtain redress they appealed to the pope, who decided in their favour, and repeatedly admonished the cardinal to deal justly with his brothers. But the cardinal and his nephews bitterly resented the pope's intervention and obstinately refused to abide by his decision. Moreover, the Colonna cardinals had seriously compromised themselves by maintaining highly treasonable relations with the political enemies of the pope—first with James II of Aragon, and later with Frederick III of Sicily. Repeated warnings against this alliance having availed nothing, Boniface, in the interests of his own security, ordered the Colonna to receive papal garrisons in Palestrina—the ancestral home of the family—and in their fortresses Zagarolo and Colonna. This they declined to do and forthwith broke off all relations with the pope. On the 4th of May, 1297, Boniface summoned the cardinals to his presence, and when, two days later (6 May), they appeared, he commanded them to do three things: to restore the consignment of gold and silver which their relative Stefano Colonna had seized and robbed from the pope's nephew, Pietro Gaetani, as he was bringing it from Anagni to Rome; to deliver up Stefano as a prisoner to the pope; and to surrender Palestrina together with the fortresses Zagarolo and Colonna. They complied with the first of these demands, but rejected the other two. Thereupon Boniface on the 10th of May, 1297, issued a Bull, "In excelso throno", depriving the rebellious cardinals of their dignities, pronouncing sentence of excommunication against them, and ordering them, within a space of ten days, to make their submission under penalty of forfeiting their property. On the morning of the same day (10 May) the Colonna had attached to the doors of several Roman churches, and even laid upon the high altar of St. Peter's, a manifesto, in which they declared the election of Boniface VIII invalid on the ground that the abdication of Celestine V was uncanonical, accused Boniface of circumventing his saintly predecessor, and appealed to a general council from whatever steps might be taken against them by the pope. This protest, compiled at Longhezza, with the assistance of Fra Jacopone da Todi and of two other Spirituals, had somewhat anticipated the papal Bull, in answer to which, however, the Colonna issued the second manifesto (16 May) containing numerous charges against Boniface and appealing anew to a general council. The pope met this bold proceeding with increased severity. On the 23rd of May, 1297, a second Bull, "Lapis abscissus", confirmed the previous excommunication, and extended it to the five nephews of Jacopo with their heirs, declared them schismatics, disgraced, their property forfeited, and threatened with the interdict all such places as received them. Boniface at the same time pointed out how the Colonna cardinals had themselves favoured his election (in the conclave they had voted for Gaetani from the first, as they had been among those who counselled Celestine's abdication), had publicly acknowledged him as pope, attended his coronation, entertained him as their guest at Zagarolo, taken part in his consistories, signed all state documents with him, and had for nearly three years been his faithful ministers at the altar. The rebels replied with a third manifesto (15 June), and immediately set about preparing their fortresses for defense.

Boniface now withdrew from Rome to Orvieto, where, on the 4th of September, 1297, he declared war and entrusted the command of the pontifical troops to Landolfo Colonna, a brother of Jacopo. In December of the same year he even proclaimed a crusade against his enemies. The fortresses and castles of the Colonna were taken without much

difficulty. Palestrina (Præneste), the best of their strongholds, alone held out for some time, but in September, 1298, it too was forced to surrender. Dante says it was got by treachery by "long promises and short performances" as Guido of Montefeltro counselled, but the tale of the implacable Ghibelline has long since been discredited. Clad in mourning, a cord around their necks, the two cardinals, with other members of the rebellious family, came to Rieti to cast themselves at the feet of the pontiff and implore his forgiveness. Boniface received the captives amid all the splendours of the papal court, granted them pardon and absolution, but refused to restore them to their dignities. Palestrina was razed to the ground, the plough driven through and salt strewn over its ruins. A new city—the Città Papale —later replaced it. When shortly afterwards the Colonna organized another revolt (which was however speedily suppressed), Boniface once more proscribed and excommunicated the turbulent clan. Their property was confiscated, and the greater part of it bestowed on Roman nobles, more especially on Landolfo Colonna, the Orsini, and on the relatives of the pope. The Colonna cardinals and the leading members of the family now withdrew from the States of the Church—some seeking shelter in France, others in Sicily. (Denifle, see below, and Petrine, Memorie Præenestine, Rome, 1795.)

Early in the reign of Boniface, Eric VIII of Denmark had unjustly imprisoned Jens Grand, Archbishop of Lund. Isarnus, Archpriest of Carcassonne, was commissioned (1295) by Boniface to threaten the king with spiritual penalties, unless the archbishop were freed, pending the investigation of the matter at Rome, whither the king was invited to send representatives. The latter were actually sent, but were met at Rome by Archbishop Grand, who had in the meanwhile escaped. Boniface decided for the archbishop, and, when the king refused to yield, excommunicated him and laid the kingdom under interdict (1298). In 1303 Eric yielded, though his adversary was transferred to Riga and his see given (1304) to the legate Isarnus. In Hungary Charobert or Canrobert of Naples claimed the vacant crown as descendant of St. Stephen on the distaff side, and was supported by the pope in his quality of traditional overlord and protector of Hungary. The nobles, however, elected Andrew III, and on his early demise (1301) chose Ladislaus, son of Wenceslaus II of Bohemia. They paid no heed to the interdict of the papal legate, and the arbitration of Boniface was finally declined by the envoys of Wenceslaus. The latter had accepted from the Polish nobles the Crown of Poland, vacant owing to the banishment (1300) of Ladislaus I. The solemn warning of the pope and his protest against this violation of his right as overlord of Poland were unheeded by Wenceslaus, who soon, moreover, allied himself with Philip the Fair.

In Germany, on the death of Rudolph of Hapsburg (1291), his son Albert, Duke of Austria, declared himself king. The electors, however, chose (1292) Count Adolph of Nassau, whereupon Albert submitted. Adolph's government proving unsatisfactory, three of the electors deposed him at Mainz (23 June, 1298) and enthroned Albert. The rival kings appealed to arms; at Göllheim, near Worms, Adolph lost (2 July, 1298) both life and crown. Albert was re-elected king by the Diet of Frankfort and crowned at Aachen (24 August, 1298). The electors had sought regularly from Boniface recognition of their choice and imperial consecration. He refused both on the plea that Albert was the murderer of his liege lord. Very soon Albert was at war with the three Rhenish archbishop-electors, and in 1301 the pope summoned him to Rome to answer various charges. Victorious in battle (1302), Albert sent agents to Boniface with letters in which he denied having slain King Adolph, nor had he sought the battle voluntarily, nor borne the royal title while Adolph lived, etc. Boniface eventually recognized his election (30 Apr., 1303). A little later (17 July) Albert renewed his father's oath of fidelity to the Roman Church, recognized the papal authority in Germany as laid down by Boniface (May, 1300), and promised to send no imperial vicar to Tuscany or Lombardy within the next five years without the pope's consent, and to defend the Roman Church against its enemies. In his attempt to preserve the independence of Scotland, Boniface was not successful. After the overthrow and imprisonment of John Baliol, and the defeat of Wallace (1298), the Scots Council of Regency sent envoys to the pope to protest against the feudal superiority of England. Boniface, they said, was the only judge whose jurisdiction extended over both kingdoms. Their realm belonged of right to the Roman See, and to none other. Boniface wrote to Edward I (27 June, 1299) reminding him, says Lingard, "almost in the very words of the Scottish memorial", that Scotland had belonged from ancient times and did still belong to the Roman See; the king was to cease all unjust aggression, free his captives, and pursue at the court of Rome within six months any rights that he claimed to the whole or part of Scotland. This letter reached the king after much delay, through the hands of Robert of Winchelsea, Archbishop of Canterbury, and was laid by Edward before a parliament summoned to meet at Lincoln. In its reply (27 Sept., 1300) the latter denied, over the names of 104 lay lords, the papal claim of suzerainty over Scotland, and asserted that a king of England had never pleaded before any judge, ecclesiastical or secular, respecting his rights in Scotland or any other temporal rights, nor would they permit him to do so, were he thus inclined (Lingard, II, ch. vii). The king, however (7 May, 1301), supplemented this act by a memoir in which he set forth his royal view of the historical relations of Scotland and England. In their reply to this plea the representatives of Scotland re-assert the immemorial suzerainty of the Roman Church over Scotland "the property, the peculiar allodium of the Holy See"; in all controversies, they said, between these equal and independent kingdoms it is to their equal superior, the Church of Rome, that recourse should be had. This somewhat academic conflict soon seemed hopeless at Rome, owing to the mutual violence and quarrels of the weaker party (Bellesheim, "Hist. of the Cath. Church of Scotland", London, 1887, II, 9–11), and is of less importance than the strained relations between Boniface and Edward, apropos of the unjust taxation of the clergy.

In 1294, of his own authority, Edward I sequestered all moneys found in the treasuries of all churches and monasteries. Soon he demanded and obtained from the clergy one half their incomes, both from lay fees and benefices. In the following year he called for a third or a fourth, but they refused to pay more than a tenth. When, at the Convocation of Canterbury (November, 1296), the king demanded a fifth of their income, the archbishop, Robert of Winchelsea, in keeping with the new legislation of Boniface, offered to consult the pope, whereupon the king outlawed the clergy, secular and regular, and seized all their lay fees, goods, and chattels. The northern Province of York yielded; in the Province of Canterbury many resisted for a time, among them the courageous archbishop, who retired to a rural parish. Eventually he was reconciled with the king, and his goods were restored, but as Edward soon after demanded in his own right a third of all ecclesiastical revenues, his recognition of the Bull "Clericis laicos" was evanescent.

The memorable conflict with Philip the Fair of France began early in the pope's reign and did not end even with the tragic close of his pontificate. The pope's chief aim was a general European peace, in the interest of a crusade that would break forever, at what seemed a favourable moment, the power of Islam. The main immediate obstacle to such a peace lay in the war between France and England, caused by Philip's unjust seizure of Gascony (1294). The chief combatants carried on the war at the expense of the Church, whose representatives they sorely taxed. Such taxation had often been permitted in the past by the popes, but only for the purpose (real or alleged) of a crusade; now it was applied in order to raise revenue from ecclesiastics for purely secular warfare. The legates sent by Boniface to both kings a few weeks after his elevation accomplished little; later efforts were rendered useless by the stubborn attitude of Philip. In the meantime numerous protests from the French clergy moved the pope to action, and with the approval of his cardinals he published (24 Feb., 1296) the Bull "Clericis laicos", in which he forbade the laity to exact or receive, and the clergy to give up, ecclesiastical revenues or property, without permission of the Apostolic See; princes imposing such exactions and ecclesiastics submitting to them were declared excommunicated. Other popes of the thirteenth century, and the Third and Fourth Lateran Councils (1179, 1215), had legislated similarly against the oppressors of the clergy; apart, therefore, from the opening line of the Bull, that seemed offensive as reflecting on the laity in general (*Clericis laicos infensos esse oppido tradit antiquitas,* i. e., "All history shows clearly the enmity of the laity towards the clergy,"—in reality a byword in the schools and taken from earlier sources), there was nothing in its very general terms to rouse particularly the royal anger. Philip, however, was indignant, and soon retaliated by a royal ordinance (17 Aug.) forbidding the export of gold or silver, precious stones, weapons, and food from his kingdom. He also forbade foreign merchants to remain longer within its bounds. These measures affected immediately the Roman Church, for it drew much of its revenue from France, inclusive of crusade moneys, whence the numerous papal collectors were henceforth banished. The king also caused to be prepared a proclamation (never promulgated) concerning the obligation of ecclesiastics to bear the public burden and the revocable character of ecclesiastical immunities. (For the generous contributions of the French clergy to the national burdens, see the exhaustive statistics of Bourgain in "Rev. des quest. hist.", 1890, XLVIII, 62.) In the Bull "Ineffabilis Amor" (20 Sept.) Boniface protested vigorously against these royal acts, and explained that he had never meant to forbid voluntary gifts from the clergy or contributions necessary for the defence of the kingdom, of which necessity the king and his council were the judges. During 1297 the pope sought in various ways to appease the royal embitterment, notably by the Bull "Etsi de Statu" (31 July), above all by the canonization (11 Aug., 1297) of the king's grandfather, Louis IX. The royal ordinance was withdrawn, and the painful incident seemed closed. In the meantime the truce which in 1296 Boniface had tried to impose on Philip and Edward was finally accepted by both kings early in 1298, for a space of two years. The disputed matters were referred to Boniface as arbiter, though Philip accepted him not as pope, but as a private person, as Benedetto Gaetano. The award, favourable to Philip, was issued (27 June) by Boniface in a public consistory.

In the Jubilee of 1300 the high spirit of Boniface might well recognize a compensation and a consolation for previous humiliations. This unique celebration, the apogee of the temporal splendour of the papacy (Zaccaria, De anno Jubilæi, Rome, 1775), was formally inaugurated by the pope on the feast of Sts. Peter and Paul (29 June). Giovanni Villani, an eyewitness, relates in his Florentine chronicle that about 200,000 pilgrims were constantly in the City. It was necessary to make an opening in the wall of the Leonine City, near the Tiber, so that the multitude might have a larger freedom of movement. Pilgrims came from every country in Europe and even from distant Asia. Ominously enough, if we except the elder son of the King of Naples, none of the kings or princes of Europe came to pay their respects to the Vicar of Christ. The second crown in the papal tiara, indicative of the temporal power, is said to date from the reign of Boniface, and may have been added at this time.

In the meantime Philip continued in a merciless way his fiscal oppression of the Church, and abused more than ever the so-called *regalia*, or royal privilege of collecting the revenues of a diocese during its vacancy. Since the middle of 1297 the exiled Colonna had found refuge and sympathy at the court of Philip, whence they spread calumnious charges against Boniface, and urged the calling of a general council for his deposition. The royal absolutism was now further incited by suggestions of a universal Christian dominion under the hegemony of France. The new state was to secure, besides the Holy Land, a universal peace. Both empires, the Byzantine and the German, were to be incorporated in it, and the papacy was to become a purely spiritual patriarchate, its temporalities administered by the French king, who would pay the pope an annual salary corresponding to his office. Such was the new Byzantinism outlined in a work on the recovery of the Holy Land ("De recuperatione terræ sanctæ", in Bongars, "Gesta Dei per Francos", II, 316–61, ed. Langlois, Paris, 1891), and though only the private work of Pierre Dubois, a civil servant of Philip, it probably reflected some fantastic plan of the king (Finke, Zur Charakteristik, 217–18).

In the first half of 1301 Boniface commissioned Bernard de Saisset, Bishop of Pamiers (Languedoc), as legate to Philip. He was to protest against the continued oppression of the clergy, and to urge the king to apply conscientiously to a crusade the ecclesiastical tithes collected by papal indults. For various reasons De Saisset was not a welcome envoy (Langlois, Hist. de France, ed. Lavisse, III, 2, 143). On his return to Pamiers he was accused of treasonable speech and incitement to insurrection, was brought to Paris (12 July, 1301), thence to Senlis, where he was found guilty in a trial directed by Pierre Flote, and known to modern historians (Von Reumont) as "a model of injustice and violence". De Saisset in vain protested his innocence and denied the competency of the civil court; he was committed temporarily to the care of the Archbishop of Narbonne, while Pierre Flote and Guillaume de Nogaret went to Rome to secure from Boniface the degradation of his legate and his delivery to the secular authority. Boniface acted with decision. He demanded from the king the immediate liberation of De Saisset and wrote to the Archbishop of Narbonne to detain the latter no longer. By the Bull "Salvator Mundi" he withdrew the indults by which the French king collected canonically ecclesiastical revenue for the defence of the kingdom, i. e., he re-established in vigour the "Clericis laicos", and in the famous Bull "Ausculta Fili" (Listen, O Son) of 5 Dec., 1301, he stood forth as the mouthpiece of the medieval papacy, and as the genuine successor of the Gregories and the Innocents. In it he appeals to the king to listen to the Vicar of Christ, who is placed over kings and kingdoms (cf. Jer., i, 10). He is the keeper of the keys, the judge of the living and the dead, and sits on the throne of justice, with power to extirpate all iniquity. He is the head of the Church, which is one and stainless, and not a many-headed monster, and has full Divine authority to pluck out and tear down, to build up and plant. Let not the king imagine that he has no superior, is not subject to the highest authority in the Church. The pope is concerned for the welfare of all kings and princes, but particularly for the house of France. He then goes on to relate his many grievances against the king, the application of ecclesiastical goods to secular uses, despotic procedure in dragging ecclesiastics before civil courts, hindrance of episcopal authority, disrespect for papal provisions of benefices, and oppression of the clergy. He will no longer be responsible for the protection (*custodia*) of the monarch's soul, but has decided, after consulting his cardinals, to call to Rome for 4 Nov., 1302, the French bishops and doctors of theology, principal abbots, etc., to "dispose what is suitable for the correction of abuses, and for the reformation of the king and the kingdom". He invites the king to be present personally or through representatives, warns him against his evil counsellors, and finally reminds him eloquently of the royal neglect of a crusade. An impartial reader, says Von Reumont, will see that the document is only a repetition of previous papal utterances and resumes the teaching of the most esteemed medieval theologians on the nature and extension of papal authority. It was presented to the king (10 Feb., 1302) by Jacques de Normans, Archdeacon of Narbonne. The Comte d'Artois tore it from the archdeacon's hands and cast it into the fire; another copy destined for the French clergy was suppressed (Hefele, 2d ed., VI, 329). In the place of the "Ausculta Fili", there was at once circulated a forged Bull, "Deum time" (Fear God), very probably the work of Pierre Flote, and with equal probability approved by the king. Its five or six brief haughty lines were really drawn up to include the fateful phrase, *Scire te volumus quod in spiritualibus et temporalibus nobis subes* (i. e., We wish thee to know that thou art our subject both in spiritual and in temporal matters). It was also added (an odious thing for the grandson of St. Louis) that whoever denied this was a heretic.

In vain did the pope and the cardinals protest against the forgery; in vain did the pope explain, a little later, that the subjection spoken of in his Bull was only *ratione peccati*, i. e., that the morality of every royal act, private or public, fell within the papal prerogative. The general tone of the "Ausculta Fili", its personal admonitions couched in severe Scriptural language, its proposal to provide from Rome a good and prosperous administration of the French Kingdom, were not calculated to soothe at this juncture the minds of Frenchmen already agitated by the events of the preceding years. It is also improbable that Boniface was personally very popular with the French secular clergy, whose petition (1290) against the encroachments of the regular orders he had rejected in his rough sarcastic manner, when legate at Paris (Finke in "Römische Quartalschrift", 1895, IX, 171; "Journal des Savants", 1895, 240). The national concern for the independence and honour of the French king was further heightened by a forged reply of the king to Boniface, known as "Sciat maxima tua fatuitas". It begins: "Philip, by the grace of God King of the Franks, to Boniface who acts as Supreme Pontiff. Let thy very great fatuity know that in temporal things we are subject to no one, ..." Such a document, though probably never officially presented at Rome (Hefele), certainly made its way thither. After forbidding the French clergy to go to Rome or to send thither any moneys, and setting a watch on all roads, ports, and passes leading to Italy, Philip forestalled the pope's November council by a national assembly at

Paris (10 April, 1301) in the Cathedral of Notre Dame. The forged Bull was read before the representatives of the three estates; the pope was violently denounced by Pierre Flote as aiming at temporal sovereignty in France; the king besought as their friend, and as their ruler commanded all present to aid him with their counsel. Nobles and burghers offered to shed their blood for the king; the clergy, confused and hesitating, sought delay, but finally yielded so far as to write to the pope quite in the sense of the king. The lay estates directed to the cardinals a defiant protest, in which they withheld the papal title from Boniface, recounted the services of France to the Roman Church, and re-echoed the usual royal complaints, above all the calling to Rome of the principal ecclesiastics of the nation. The letter of the bishops was directed to Boniface and begged him to maintain the former concord, to withdraw the call for the council, and suggested prudence and moderation, since the laity were prepared to defy all papal censures. In the reply of the cardinals to the lay estates, they assert their complete harmony with the pope, denounce the aforesaid forgeries, and maintain that the pope never asserted a right of temporal sovereignty in France.

In his reply Boniface roundly scourged the bishops for their cowardice, human respect, and selfishness; at the same time he made use, after his fashion, of not a few expressions offensive to the pride of French ecclesiastics and poured sarcasm over the person of the powerful Pierre Flote (Hefele). Finally, in a public consistory (August, 1302) at which the envoys of the king were present, the Cardinal-Bishop of Porto formally denied that the pope had ever claimed any temporal sovereignty over France and asserted that the genuine Bull (Ausculta Fili) had been well weighed and was an act of love, despite the fatherly severity of certain expressions. He insisted that the king was no more free than any other Christian from the supreme ecclesiastical jurisdiction of the pope, and maintained the unity of ecclesiastical authority. The Apostolic See, he said, was not foreign territory, nor could its nominees be rightly called foreigners. For the rest, the pope had full authority in temporal matters *ratione peccati*, i. e., in as far as the morality of human acts was concerned. He went on, however, to say that in temporal jurisdiction one must distinguish the right (*de jure*) and its use and execution (*usus et exsecutio*). The former belonged to the pope as Vicar of Christ and of Peter; to deny it was to deny an article of faith, i. e., that Christ judges the living and the dead. This claim, says Hefele (2d ed., VI, 346), "must have appeared to the French as quite destructive of the aforesaid limitation *ratione peccati*. Gregory IX had maintained (1232, 1236), in his conflict with the Greeks and with Frederick II, that Constantine the Great had given temporal power to the popes, and that emperors and kings were only his auxiliaries, bound to use the material sword at his direction (Conciliengesch., 2d ed., V, 102, 1044). This theory, however, had never yet been officially put forth against France, and was all the more likely to rouse opposition in that nation, since it was now a question not of a theory, but of a practical situation, i. e., of the investigation of Philip's government and the menace of his deposition." He refers to the closing words of the discourse with which Boniface supplemented that of the Cardinal-Bishop of Porto, viz., that his predecessors had deposed three French kings, and, though unequal to such popes, he would, however sorrowfully, depose King Philip, *sicut unum garcionem* (like a servant); he thinks it not impossible (Hergenröther, Kirche und Staat, 229; Hefele, IV, 344) that the present harsh conclusion of the discourse of Boniface is one of the numerous forgeries of Pierre Flote and Nogaret. In the first half of this discourse the pope

insists on the great development of France under papal protection, the shameless forgeries of Pierre Flote, the exclusive ecclesiastical nature of the grant (*collatio*) of benefices, and the papal preference for doctors of theology as against lay nepotism in matter of benefices. He is wroth over the assertion that he claimed France as a papal fief. "We have been a doctor of both laws (civil and canon) these forty years, and who can believe that such folly [*fatuitas*] ever entered Our head?" Boniface also expressed his willingness to accept the mediation of the Duke of Burgundy or the Duke of Brittany; the efforts of the former, however, availed not, as the cardinals insisted on satisfaction for the burning of the papal Bull and the calumnious attacks on Boniface. The king replied by confiscating the goods of the ecclesiastics who had set out for the Roman Council, which met 30 Oct., 1302.

There were present four archbishops, thirty-five bishops, six abbots, and several doctors. Its acts have disappeared, probably during the process against the memory of Boniface (1309–11). Two Bulls, however, were issued as a result of its deliberations. One excommunicated whoever hindered, imprisoned, or otherwise ill-treated persons journeying to, or returning from, Rome. The other (18 Nov., 1302) is the famous "Unam Sanctam", probably the composition of Ægidius Colonna, Archbishop of Bourges and a member of the council, and largely made up of passages from such famous theologians as St. Bernard, Hugo of St. Victor, St. Thomas Aquinas, and others. Its chief concepts are as follows (Hergenröther-Kirsch, 4th ed., II, 593): (1) There is but one true Church, outside of which there is no salvation; but one body of Christ with one head and not two. (2) That head is Christ and His representative, the Roman pope; whoever refuses the pastoral care of Peter belongs not to the flock of Christ. (3) There are two swords (i. e., powers), the spiritual and the temporal; the first borne by the Church, the second for the Church; the first by the hand of the priest, the second by that of the king, but under the direction of the priest (*ad nutum et patientiam sacerdotis*). (4) Since there must be a co-ordination of members from the lowest to the highest, it follows that the spiritual power is above the temporal and has the right to instruct (or establish—*instituere*) the latter regarding its highest end and to judge it when it does evil; whoever resists the highest power ordained of God resists God Himself. (5) It is necessary for salvation that all men should be subject to the Roman Pontiff—"Porro subesse Romano Pontifici omni humanæ creaturæ declaramus, dicimus, definimus et pronunciamus omnino esse de necessitate salutis". (For a more detailed account of the Bull and several controversies concerning it see UNAM SANCTAM.)

Philip had a refutation of the Bull prepared by the Dominican Jean Quidort (Joannes Parisiensis) in his "Tractatus de potestate regiâ et papali" (Goldast, Monarchia, II, 108 sq.), and the conflict passed at once from the domain of principle to the person of Boniface. The king now rejected the pope as arbiter in his disputes with England and Flanders, and gave a courteous but evasive answer to the Legate, Jean Lemoine, whom the pope sent (February, 1303) on a mission of peace, but with insistence, among other conditions, on recognition of the aforesaid rights of the papacy. Lemoine was further commissioned to declare to Philip that, in default of a more satisfactory reply to the twelve points of the papal letter, the pope would proceed *spiritualiter et temporaliter* against him, i. e., would excommunicate and depose him. Boniface also sent to Lemoine (13 Apr., 1303) two Briefs, in one of which he declared the king already excommunicated, and in the other ordered all French prelates to come to Rome within three months.

In the meantime there was brewing at Paris the storm in which the pontificate of Boniface was so disastrously to close. Philip concluded peace with England, temporized with the Flemings, and made concessions to his subjects. Boniface on his side acknowledged, as aforesaid, the election of Albert of Austria, and brought to an end his hopeless conflict with the Aragonese King of Sicily. Otherwise he seemed politically helpless, and could only trust, as he publicly stated, in his sense of right and duty. Later events showed that in his own household he could not count on loyalty. In an extraordinary session of the French Council of State (12 March, 1303) Guillaume de Nogaret appealed to Philip to protect Holy Church against the intruder and false pope, Boniface, a simonist, robber, and heretic, maintaining that the king, moreover, ought to call an assembly of the prelates and peers of France, through whose efforts a general council might be convoked, before which he would prove his charges. Such an assembly was called for 13 June, and met at the Louvre in Paris. The papal messenger with the aforesaid Briefs for the legate was seized at Troyes and imprisoned; Lemoine himself, after protesting against such violence, fled. At this assembly, packed with friends or creatures of Philip, the knight Guillaume de Plaisians (Du Plessis) submitted a solemn accusation against the pope in twenty-nine points, offered to prove the same, and begged the king to provide for a general council. The Colonna furnished the material for these infamous charges, long since adjudged calumnious by grave historians (Hefele, Conciliengesch., 2nd ed., VI, 460–63; Giovanni Villani, a contemporary, says that the Council of Vienne, in 1312, formally absolved him from the charge of heresy. Cf. Muratori, "SS. Rer. Ital.", XIV, 454; Raynaldus, *ad an.* 1312, 15–16). Scarcely any possible crime was omitted—infidelity, heresy, simony, gross and unnatural immorality, idolatry, magic, loss of the Holy Land, death of Celestine V, etc. The king asserted that it was only to satisfy his conscience and to protect the honour of the Holy See that he would co-operate in the calling of a general council, asked the help of the prelates, and appealed (against any possible action of Boniface) to the future council, the future pope, and to all to whom appeal could be made. Five archbishops, twenty-one bishops, and some abbots sided with the king. The resolutions of the assembly were read to the people, and several hundred adhesions were secured from chapters, monasteries, and provincial cities, mostly through violence and intimidation. The Abbot of Cîteaux, Jean de Pontoise, protested, but was imprisoned. Royal letters were sent to the princes of Europe, also to the cardinals and bishops, setting forth the king's new-found zeal for the welfare of Holy Church.

In a public consistory at Anagni (August, 1303) Boniface cleared himself on his solemn oath of the charges brought against him at Paris and proceeded at once to protect the Apostolic authority. Citations before the Holy See were declared valid by the mere fact of being affixed to the church doors at the seat of the Roman Curia, and he excommunicated all who hindered such citations. He suspended Archbishop Gerhard of Nicosia (Cyprus), the first signatory of the schismatical resolutions. Pending satisfaction to the pope, the University of Paris lost the right to confer degrees in theology and in canon and civil law. He suspended temporarily for France the right of election in all ecclesiastical bodies, reserved to the Holy See all vacant French benefices, repelled as blasphemies the calumnious charges of de Plaisians, saying, "Who ever heard that We were a heretic?" (Raynaldus, *ad an.* 1311, 40), and denounced the appeal to a future general council which could be convoked by none other than himself, the

legitimate pope. He declared that unless the king repented he would inflict on him the severest punishments of the Church. The Bull "Super Petri solio" was ready for promulgation on 8 September. It contained in traditional form the solemn excommunication of the king and the liberation of his subjects from their oath of fidelity. Philip, however, and his counsellors had taken measures to rob this step of all force, or rather to prevent it at a decisive moment. It had long been their plan to seize the person of Boniface and compel him to abdicate, or, in case of his refusal, to bring him before a general council in France for condemnation and deposition. Since April, Nogaret and Sciarra Colonna had been active in Tuscany for the formation, at Philip's expense, of a band of mercenaries, some 2,000 strong, horse and foot. Very early on the morning of 7 September the band appeared suddenly before Anagni, under the lilies of France, shouting, "Long live the King of France and Colonna!" Fellow-conspirators in the town admitted them, and they at once attacked the palaces of the pope and his nephew. The ungrateful citizens fraternized with the besiegers of the pope, who in the meanwhile obtained a truce until three in the afternoon, when he rejected the conditions of Sciarra, viz., restoration of the Colonna, abdication, and delivery to Sciarra of the pope's person. About six o'clock, however, the papal stronghold was penetrated through the adjoining cathedral. The soldiers, Sciarra at their head, sword in hand (for he had sworn to slay Boniface), at once filled the hall in which the pope awaited them with five of his cardinals, among them his beloved nephew Francesco, all of whom soon fled; only a Spaniard, the Cardinal of Santa Sabina, remained at his side to the end.

In the meantime the papal palace was thoroughly plundered; even the archives were destroyed. Dino Compagni, the Florentine chronicler, relates that when Boniface saw that further resistance was useless he exclaimed, "Since I am betrayed like the Saviour, and my end is nigh, at least I shall die as Pope." Thereupon he ascended his throne, clad in the pontifical ornaments, the tiara on his head, the keys in one hand, a cross in the other, held close to his breast. Thus he confronted the angry men-at-arms. It is said that Nogaret prevented Sciarra Colonna from killing the pope. Nogaret himself made known to Boniface the Paris resolutions and threatened to take him in chains to Lyons, where he should be deposed. Boniface looked down at him, some say without a word, others that he replied: "Here is my head, here is my neck; I will patiently bear that I, a Catholic and lawful pontiff and vicar of Christ, be condemned and deposed by the Paterini [heretics, in reference to the parents of the Tolosan Nogaret]; I desire to die for Christ's faith and His Church." Von Reumont asserts that there is no evidence for the physical maltreatment of the pope by Sciarra or Nogaret. Dante (Purgatorio, XX, 86) lays more stress on the moral violence, though his words easily convey the notion of physical wrong: "I see the flower-de-luce Anagni enter, and Christ in his own Vicar captive made; I see him yet another time derided; I see renewed the vinegar and gall, and between living thieves I see him slain." Boniface was held three days a close prisoner in the plundered papal palace. No one cared to bring him food or drink, while the banditti quarrelled over his person, as over a valuable asset. By early morning of 9 September the burghers of Anagni had changed their minds, wearied perhaps of the presence of the soldiers, and ashamed that a pope, their townsman, should perish within their walls at the hands of the hated *Francesi*. They expelled Nogaret and his band, and confided Boniface to the care of the two Orsini cardinals, who had come from Rome with four hundred horsemen; with them he returned to Rome. Before leaving Anagni he pardoned several of the marauders captured by the townsmen, excepting the plunderers of Church property, unless they returned it within three days. He reached Rome, 13 Sept., but only to fall under the close surveillance of the Orsini. No one will wonder that his bold spirit now gave way beneath the weight of grief and melancholy. He died of a violent fever, 11 October, in full possession of his senses and in the presence of eight cardinals and the chief members of the papal household, after receiving the sacraments and making the usual profession of faith. His life seemed destined to close in gloom, for, on account of an unusually violent storm, he was buried, says an old chronicler, with less decency than became a pope. His body lies in the crypt of St. Peter's in a large marble sarcophagus, laconically inscribed BONIFACIUS PAPA VIII. When his tomb was opened (9 Oct., 1605) the body was found quite intact, especially the shapely hands, thus disproving another calumny, viz., that he had died in a frenzy, gnawing his hands, beating his brains out against the wall, and the like (Wiseman).

Boniface was a patron of the fine arts such as Rome had never yet seen among its popes, though, as Guiraud warns us (p. 6), it is not easy to separate what is owing to the pope's own initiative from what we owe to his nephew and biographer, the art-loving Cardinal Stefaneschi. Modern historians of Renaissance art (Müntz, Guiraud) date its first efficient progress from him. The "idolatry" accusation of the Colonna comes from the marble statues that grateful towns, like Anagni and Perugia, raised to him on public sites, "where there once were idols", says a contemporary, an anti-Bonifacian libel (Guiraud, 4). The Anagni statue stands yet in the cathedral of that town, repaired by him. He also repaired and fortified the Gaetani palace in Anagni, and improved in a similar way neighbouring towns. At Rome the Palace of the Senator was enlarged, Castel Sant' Angelo fortified, and the Church of San Lorenzo in Panisperna built anew. He encouraged the work on the cathedral of Perugia, while that gem of ornamental Gothic, the cathedral of Orvieto (1290–1309), was largely finished during his pontificate. For the great Jubilee of 1300 he had the churches of Rome restored and decorated, notably St. John Lateran, St. Peter's, and St. Mary Major. He called Giotto to Rome and gave him constant occupation. A portrait of Boniface by Giotto is still to be seen in St. John Lateran; in our own day M. Müntz has restored the original concept, and in it is seen the noble balcony of Cassetta, whence, during the jubilee, the pontiff was wont to bestow upon the vast multitude the blessing of Christ's vicar. In the time of Boniface the Cosimati continued and improved their work and under the influence of Giotto rose, like Cavallini, to higher concepts of art. The delicate French miniaturists were soon equalled by the pope's Vatican scribes; two glorious missals of Oderisio da Gubbio, "Agubbio's honour", may yet be seen at the Vatican, where lived and worked his disciple, likewise immortalized by Dante (Purg., XI, 79), who speaks of "the laughing leaves touched by the brush of Franco Bolognese". Finally, sculpture was honoured by Boniface in the person of Arnolfo di Cambio, who built for him the "Chapel of the Crib" in St. Mary Major, and executed (Müntz) the sarcophagus in which he was buried. Boniface was also a friend of the sciences. He founded (6 June, 1303) the University of Rome, known as the Sapienza, and in the same year the University of Fermo. Finally, it was Boniface who began anew the Vatican Library, whose treasures had been scattered, together with the papal archives, in 1227, when the Roman Frangipani passed over to the side of Frederick II

and took with them the *turris chartularia*, i. e. the ancient repository of the documents of the Holy See. The thirty-three Greek manuscripts the Vatican Library contained in 1311 are pronounced by Fr. Ehrle the earliest known, and long the most important, medieval collection of Greek works in the West. Boniface honoured with increased solemnity (1298) the feasts of the four evangelists, twelve Apostles, and four Doctors of the Church (Ambrose, Augustine, Jerome, Gregory the Great, *egregios ipsius doctores Ecclesiæ*) by raising them to the rank of "double feasts". He was one of the most distinguished canonists of his age, and as pope enriched the general ecclesiastical legislation by the promulgation ("Sacrosanctæ", 1298) of a large number of his own constitutions and of those of his predecessors, since 1234, when Gregory IX promulgated his five books of Decretals. In reference to this the collection of Boniface was entitled "Liber Sextus", i. e., Sixth Book of Pontifical Constitutions (Laurin, Introd. in Corp. Juris can., Freiburg, 1889), being constructed on the same lines. Few popes have aroused more diverse and contradictory appreciations. Protestant historians, generally, and even modern Catholic writers, wrote Cardinal Wiseman in 1844, class him among the wicked popes, as an ambitious, haughty, and unrelenting man, deceitful also and treacherous, his whole pontificate one record of evil. To dissipate this grossly exaggerated and even calumnious view, it is well to distinguish his utterances and deeds as pope from his personal character, that even in his lifetime seemed to many unsympathetic. Careful examination of the sources of his most famous public pronouncements has shown that they are largely a mosaic of teachings of earlier theologians, or solemn re-enforcements of the canons of the Church and well-known Bulls of his predecessors. His chief aims, the peace of Europe and the recovery of the Holy Land, were those of all preceding popes. He did no more than his duty in defending the unity of the Church and the supremacy of ecclesiastical authority when threatened by Philip the Fair. His politico-ecclesiastical dealings with the kings of Europe will naturally be blamed by Erastians and by those who ignore, on the one hand, the rapacity of an Edward and the wily vindictiveness and obtuse selfishness of a Philip, and on the other, the supreme fatherly office of the medieval pope as the respected head of one mighty family of peoples, whose civil institutions were only slowly coalescing amid the decay of feudalism and ancient barbarism (Gosselin, Von Reumont), and who were long conscious that in the past they owed to the Church alone (i. e., to the pope) sure and swift justice, equitable courts and procedure, and relief from a feudal absolutism justified as yet by no commensurate public service. "The loftiest, truest view of the character and conduct of the popes has often been overlooked", says Cardinal Wiseman (op. cit.); "the divine instinct which animated them, the immortal destiny allotted to them, the heavenly cause confided to them, the superhuman aid which strengthened them could not be appreciated but by a Catholic mind, and are too generally excluded from Protestant historians, or are transformed into corresponding human capacities, or policies, or energies, or virtues." He goes on to say that, after examination of several popular assertions affecting the moral and ecclesiastical conduct of Boniface, this pope appeared to him in a new light, "as a pontiff who began his reign with most glorious promise and closed it amid sad calamities; who devoted, through it all, the energies of a great mind, cultivated by profound learning and matured by long experience in the most delicate ecclesiastical affairs, to the attainment of a truly noble end; and who, throughout his career, displayed many great virtues, and could plead in extenuation of his faults the convulsed state of public affairs, the rudeness of his times, and the faithless, violent character of many among those with whom he had to deal These circumstances, working upon a mind naturally upright and inflexible, led to a sternness of manner and a severity of conduct, which, when viewed through the feelings of modern times, may appear extreme, and almost unjustifiable. But after searching through the pages of his most hostile historians, we are satisfied that this is the only point on which even a plausible charge can be brought against him."

The memory of Boniface, curiously enough, has suffered most from two great poets, mouthpieces of an ultra-spiritual and impossible Catholicism, Fra Jacopone da Todi and Dante. The former was the "sublime fool" of spiritual love, author of the 'Stabat Mater", and chief singer of the "Spirituals", or extreme Franciscans, kept in prison by Boniface, whom he therefore satirized in the popular and musical vernacular of the peninsula. The latter was a Ghibelline, i. e., a political antagonist of the Guelph pope, to whom, moreover, he attributed all his personal misfortunes, and whom he therefore pilloried before the bar of his own justice, but in quivering lines of immortal invective whose malignant beauty will always trouble the reader's judgment. Catholic historians like Hergenröther-Kirsch (4th ed., II, 597–98) praise the uprightness of the pope's motives and that courage of his convictions which almost on the eve of his death made him count as straws all earthly rulers, if only he had truth and justice on his side (op. cit., II, 597, note 4). They admit, however, the explosive violence and offensive phraseology of some of his public documents, and the occasional imprudence of his political measures; he walked in the footsteps of his immediate predecessors, but the new enemies were more fierce and logical than the extirpated Hohenstaufen, and were quicker to pervert and utilize the public opinion of young and proud nationalities. A contemporary and eyewitness, Giovanni Villani, has left in his Florentine chronicle (Muratori, XIII, 348 sqq.) a portrait of Boniface which the judicious Von Reumont seems to consider quite reliable. According to it Boniface, the most clever canonist of his time, was a great-hearted and generous man and a lover of magnificence, but also arrogant, proud, and stern in manner, more feared than loved, too worldly-minded for his high office and too fond of money, both for the Church and for his family. His nepotism was open. He founded the Roman house of the Gaetani, and in the process of exalting his family drew down upon himself the effective hatred of the Colonna and their strong clansmen. Gröne, a German Catholic historian of the popes, says of Boniface (II, 164) that while his utterances equal in importance those of Gregory VII and Innocent III, the latter were always more ready to act, Boniface to discourse; they relied on the Divine strength of their office, Boniface on the cleverness of his canonical deductions. For the process against his memory see CLEMENT V.

Original Materials.—The history of Boniface is best found in DIGARD, FAUCON, AND THOMAS, *Les registres de Boniface VIII.* (Paris, 1884, sqq.); Du PUY (Gallican), *Hist. du différend du pape Boniface VIII. avec Philippe le Bel* (Paris, 1655), with a very partial selection and arrangement of valuable, but badly edited, materials; BAILLET (violent Jansenist), *Hist. des désmelez du pape Boniface VIII. avec Philippe le Bel* (Paris, 1718). On the Roman side see: VIGOR, *Historia eorum quæ acta sunt inter Philipp. Pulcher. et Bonif. VIII.* (Rome, 1639); RUBEUS, *Bonifatius VIII et Familia Caietanorum* (Rome, 1651). The earlier career and coronation of the pope are related (in verse) by CARDINAL STEFANESCHI (STEPHANESIUS) in *Acta SS.* (May, IV, 461). RAYNALDUS, *Ann. Eccl.* (1294–1303), where many of the most important documents are given in full.
Contemporary Chroniclers.—VILLANI, *Hist. Fiorentine*, in *Muratori SS. Rer. Ital.*, XIII, 348; DINO COMPAGNI, *Chronica*, ed. DE LUNGO (Florence, 1879–87); the Italian chroniclers quoted in HERGENRÖTHER-KIRSCH (4th ed.) are in MURATORI, *Scriptores*. For the election of Boniface see HEFELE, *Conciliengesch.*; SOUCHON, *Die Papstwahlen von Bonifaz VIII.*

bis Urban VI., etc. (Brunswick, 1888); FINKE, *Aus den Tagen* etc., 44–76; DENIFLE, *Die Denkschrift der Colonna gegen Bonifaz VIII., u. der Kardinäle gegen die Colonna*, in *Archiv für Litt. u. Kircheng. des M. A.* (1892), V, 493. For the Anagni incident see: KERVYN DE LETTENHOVE, in *Rev. des quest. hist.* (1872), XI., 511; DIGARD, ibid. (1888), XXXII, 557.

Catholic Biography.—Besides the general historians, FLEURY (Gallican), ROHRBACHER, CHRISTOPHE, see CHANTREL, *Boniface VIII.* (Paris, 1862), and the excellent work of TOSTI, *Storia di Bonifazio VIII e de' suoi tempi* (Monte Cassino, 1846). The most important modern critical contributions to the life of Boniface are those of FINKE, op. cit. (Munich, 1902), the result of new discoveries in medieval archives, especially at Barcelona, among the papers of the reign of James II, King of Aragon and contemporary of Boniface (reports of the royal agents at Rome, etc.). Cf. *Anal. Bolland.* (1904), XXIII, 339; *Rev. des quest. hist.* (1903), XXVI, 122; *Lit. Rundschau* (1902), XXVIII, 315; and *Canoniste Contemporain* (1903), XXVI, 122. See also FINKE, *Bonifaz VIII.*, in *Hochland* (1904), I; IDEM, *Zur Charakteristik Philipps des Schönen* in *Mittheil. des Inst. f. œst. Geschichtsforschung* (1905), XXIV, 201–14. An excellent apology is that of (CARDINAL) WISEMAN, *Pope Boniface VIII*, in *Dublin Review* (1844), reprinted in *Historical Essays*; HEMMER, in *Dict. de théol. cath.*, II, i, 992–1003 (good bibliography); and the thorough study of HEFELE, op. cit. (2nd ed. Freiburg, 1890), VI, 281 passim; JUNGMANN, *Diss. selectæ in hist. eccl.* (Ratisbon, 1886), VI. The (non-Catholic) work of DRUMANN, *Geschichte Bonifaz VIII.* (Königsberg, 1852), is learned but partisan.

Political Situation and Attitude of Medieval Popes.—See the solid work of GOSSELIN, *The Power of the Pope in the Middle Ages*, tr. KELLY (London, 1883); the erudite work of HERGENRÖTHER, *Kath. Kirche und christ. Staat* (Freiburg, 1873; Eng. tr. London, 1876); BAUDRILLARD, *Des idées qu'on se faisait au XIVe siècle sur le droit d'interven. du Souv. Pont. dans les affaires polit.*, in *Revue d'hist. et de litt. relig.* (1898); PLANCK, *Hist. de la const. de la soc. eccl. chrét.* (1809), V, 12–154 (favourable).

The most notable of the modern French writers favourable to Philip are: LECLERC and RENAN, in *Hist. Litt. de la France au XIVe siècle* (Paris, 1865); [see RENAN, *Etudes sur la polit. relig. du règne de Philippe le Bel* (Paris, 1889)]; and LANGLOIS, *Hist. de France*, ed. LAVISSE (Paris, 1901), III, II, 127–73; cf. the equitable study of BOUTARIC, *La France sous Philippe le Bel* (Paris, 1861); also the fair narrative of VON REUMONT, *Gesch. der Stadt Rom* (Berlin, 1867), II, i, 614–71; GREGOROVIUS (non-Catholic), *Gesch. d. Stadt Rom* (3d. ed., Stuttgart, 1878), V, 502, tr. by Hamilton; HÖFLER, *Rückblick auf Papst Bonifaz VIII.*, in *Abhandl. d. bayrisch. Akad. d. Wiss. hist. Kl.* (Munich, 1843), III, iii, 32 sqq.; ROCQUAIN, *La Cour de Rome et l'esprit de réforme avant Luther* (Paris, 1895), II, 258–312; LAURENT, *L'Eglise et l'Etat, moyen âge et réforme* (Paris, 1866), violent and unjust.

Pamphlet Literature.—For both sides, see: SCHOLZ, *Die Publizistik zur Zeit Ph. des Schönen und Bonif. VIII.* (Stuttgart, 1903); also SCADUTO, *Stato e Chiesa negli scritti politici*, 1112–1347 (Florence, 1847); and RIEZLER, *Die literarischen Widersacher der Päpste zur Zeit Ludwigs des Bayern* (Munich, 1874). Important new monographs concerning chief figures in the conflict are those of HOLTZMANN, *Wilhelm von Nogaret* (Freiburg, 1898); and HUYSKENS, *Kardinal Napoleon Orsini, ein Lebensbild*, etc. (Marburg, 1902). Among the latest studies, based on the above-described researches of Dr. Finke, are: SCHOLZ, *Zur Beurteilung Bonifaz VIII. und seines sittlich-religiösen Charakters*, in *Hist. Vierteljahrschrift* (1906), IX, 470–506; WENCK, *War Bonifaz VIII. ein Ketzer?* in *Hist. Zeitschrift* (1905), 1–66 (maintaining that Boniface was an Averroist), and the good refutation by HOLTZMANN, *Papst Bonifaz VIII., ein Ketzer?* in *Mittheil. d. Inst. f. œst. Gesch.* (1905), 488–98; cf. WENCK's reply, ibid. (1906), 185–95.

The Bull "Unam Sanctam": BERCHTOLD, *Die Bulle Unam Sanctam*, etc., *und ihre wahre Bedeutung für Kirche und Staat* (1887); cf. GRAUERT in *Hist. Jahrbuch* (1887). MUMRY, in *Rev. des quest. hist.* (July, 1887), abandoned his (andDANBERGER's) thesis that this Bull was a forgery (ibid., 1879), 91–130. On the exact sense of the much-disputed *instituere* (instruct or establish?) in "Unam Sanctam", see FUNK, *Kirchengesch. Abhandlungen* (Paderborn, 1897), I, 483–89.

For the services of Boniface to the sciences and the fine arts, see EHRLE, *Zur Gesch. des Schatzes, der Bibl. und des Archivs der Päpste im 14. Jahrh.*, in *Archiv für Litt. u. Kircheng. des M. A.* (1885), I, i, 228; IDEM, *Hist. Biblioth. Avenionen.* (Rome, ——); MOLINIER, *Inventaire du trésor du Saint-Siège sous Boniface VIII.*, in *Bibl. de l'Ecole des Chartes* (1882–85); the writings of the art-historian, MÜNTZ, and GUIRAUD, *L'Eglise et les Origines de la Renaissance* (Paris, 1904).

THOMAS OESTREICH.

Boniface IX, POPE, elected at Rome, 2 November, 1389, as successor of the Roman Pope, Urban VI; d. there, 1 October, 1404. Piero (Perino, Pietro) Tomacelli came of an ancient but impoverished baronial family of Naples. He lacked good theological training and skill in the conduct of curial business, but was by nature tactful and prudent. His firm character and mild manner did much to restore respect for the papacy in the countries of his own obedience (Germany, England, Hungary, Poland, and the greater part of Italy). The Avignon Pope,

Clement VII, had just crowned (1 November, 1389) as King of Naples the French prince, Louis of Anjou. Boniface took up the cause of the youthful Ladislaus, heir of Charles III of Naples and Margaret of Durazzo, had him crowned King of Naples at Gaeta (29 May, 1390), and for the next decade aided him efficiently to expel the Angevin forces from Italy. In the course of his reign Boniface extinguished the municipal independence of Rome and established the supremacy of the pope. He secured the final adhesion of the Romans (1398) by fortifying anew the Castle of Sant'Angelo, the bridges, and other points of vantage. He also took over the port of Ostia from its cardinal-bishop. In the Papal States Boniface gradually regained control of the chief strongholds and cities, and is the true founder of these States as they appear in the fifteenth century. Owing to the faithlessness and violence of the Romans he resided frequently at Perugia, Assisi, and elsewhere. Clement VII, the Avignon pope, died 16 September, 1394. Boniface had excommunicated him shortly after his own election, and in turn had been excommunicated by Clement. In 1392 Boniface attempted, but in vain, to enter into closer relations with Clement for the re-establishment of ecclesiastical unity, whereupon Boniface reasserted with vigour his own legitimacy. Clement was succeeded at Avignon, 28 September, 1394, by Cardinal Pedro de Luna, as Benedict XIII. Suffice it to say here that Boniface always claimed to be the true pope, and at all times rejected the proposal to abdicate even when it was supported by the principal members of his own obedience, e. g. Richard II of England (1396), the Diet of Frankfort (1397), and King Wenceslaus of Germany (Reims, 1398).

During the reign of Boniface two jubilees were celebrated at Rome. The first took place in 1390, in compliance with an ordinance of his predecessor Urban VI, and was largely frequented from Germany, Hungary, Poland, Bohemia, and England. Several cities of Germany obtained the privileges of the jubilee, but the preaching of the indulgences gave rise to abuses and to impositions on the part of unaccredited agents of the pope, so that he was obliged to proceed against them with severity. The jubilee of 1400 drew to Rome great crowds of pilgrims, particularly from France. In spite of a disastrous plague Boniface remained at his post. In the latter part of 1399 bands of penitents, known as the *Bianchi*, or *Albati* (White Penitents), arose, especially in Provence and Italy. They went in procession from city to city, clad in white garments, with faces hooded, only the eyes being left uncovered, and wearing on their backs a red cross. For a while their penitential enthusiasm had some good results. After they had satisfied their spiritual ardour at Rome, Boniface gradually discountenanced these wandering crowds, an easy prey of agitators and conspirators, and finally dissolved them. In England the anti-papal virulence of Wyclif increased the opposition of both Crown and clergy to the methods of Boniface in the granting of such English benefices as fell vacant in the Roman Curia through the death or promotion of the incumbent. The Parliament confirmed and extended more than once the statutes of Provisors and Præmunire, of Edward III. Boniface protested vigorously, particularly in 1391, but in the end found himself unable to execute his grants without the king's consent and sanction. "Thus ended", says Lingard (*ad. an.* 1393), "this long and angry controversy entirely to the advantage of the Crown." Nevertheless, at the Synod of London (1396), the English Church condemned the anti-papal teachings of Wyclif, and in 1398 the University of Oxford, consulted by Richard II, issued in favour of Boniface an influential document, while in 1390 and again in 1393 the spiritual peers upheld the right of the pope to excommunicate even those who obeyed the statutes

of Provisors. In Germany the electors had deposed at Rhense (20 August, 1400) the unworthy Wenceslaus, King of the Romans, and had chosen in his place Rupert, Duke of Bavaria and Rhenish Count Palatine. In 1403 Boniface abandoned his uncertain attitude towards both, approved the deposition of Wenceslaus as done by papal authority, and recognized the election of Rupert. In 1398 and 1399 Boniface appealed to Christian Europe in favour of Emperor Emmanuel, threatened at Constantinople by Sultan Bajazet. St. Bridget of Sweden was canonized by Boniface, 7 October, 1391. The universities of Ferrara (1391) and Fermo (1398) owe him their origin, and that of Erfurt its confirmation (1392). In 1404 Benedict XIII sent the last of his embassies to Boniface, who received the agents of Benedict 29 September, but the interview ended unfavourably. The pope, highly irritated, took to his bed with an attack of gravel, and died after an illness of two days.

Contemporary and later chroniclers praise the political virtues of Boniface, also the purity of his life, and the grandeur of his spirit. Some, like Dietrich of Niem, charge him with an inordinate love of money, dishonest traffic in benefices, the sale of dispensations, etc. But Dietrich is no impartial writer and is blamed by Raynaldus for being bitter and unjust (*acerbus et iniquus*). In his gossipy pages one misses a proper appreciation of the difficulties that surrounded Boniface—local sources of revenue lost in the long absence of the papacy from Rome, foreign revenue diminished by the schism, extraordinary expenses for the restoration of papal Rome and the reconquest of the Papal States, the constant wars necessitated by French ambition, the inheritance of the financial methods of Avignon, and the obligation of conciliating supporters in and out of Italy. Boniface sought nothing for himself and died poor. He is also charged with nepotism and he certainly provided generously for his mother, brothers, and nephews. It may be said, however, that in the semi-anarchic conditions of the time good government depended upon such personal support as a temporal ruler could gather and retain, i. e. could reward, while fidelity was best secured by close domestic ties. Boniface was the first pope to introduce the form of revenue known as *annates perpetuæ*, or reservation of one-half the first year's fruits of every benefice granted in the Roman Court, this in addition to other traditional expenses. It must be remembered that at this time the cardinals claimed a large part of these revenues, so that the Curia was perhaps more responsible than the pope for new financial methods destined in the next century to arouse bitter feelings against Rome, particularly in Germany.

DIETRICH (THEODERICUS) VON NIEM, *De Scismate libri III*, ed. ERLER (Leipzig, 1890); GOBELINUS PERSONA, *Cosmidromius (Cosmodromium)*, ed. JANSEN (1904); RAYNALDUS, *Ann. eccl. ad. ann. 1389–1404*, containing many important documents; others are found in D'ACHÉRY, *Spicilegium* (Paris, 1655), MARTÈNE AND DURAND, *Thesaur. nov. anecdotorum* (Paris, 1717); *Vet. Script. coll. ampliss.* (Paris, 1724); *Vita Bonifatii IX*, in MURATORI, *Rer. Ital. Script.*, III, ii, 830 sqq.; *Liber Pontificalis*, ed. DUCHESNE, II, 507, 530, 549; the histories of the city of Rome by GREGOROVIUS and by VON REUMONT; JUNGMANN, *Dissert. Selectæ* (1886) VI, 272; CREIGHTON, *A History of the Papacy during the Period of the Reformation* (London, 1892) I, 98–161; PASTOR, *History of the Papacy*; LINGARD, *History of England*, III, c. iv; ERLER, *Die historischen Schriften Dietrichs von Nieheim* (Leipzig, 1887); HEFELE, *Conciliengesch.*, VI, 812 sqq.; N. VALOIS, *La France et le grand schisme d'Occident* (Paris, 1896–1902); ROCQUAIN, *La Cour de Rome et l'esprit de réforme avant Luther* (Paris, 1897); M. JANSEN, *Papst Bonifatius IX, und seine Beziehungen zur deutschen Kirche* (Freiburg, 1904). For the Bulls of Boniface concerning Hungary see *Mon. Vaticana hist. regni Hung. illustr.* (Budapest, 1888), Ser. I, III, 1389–96; for Bohemia, KROFTA, *Acta Urb. VI. et Bonif. IX*, p. I, in *Mon. Vaticana res gestas Bohemiæ illustrantia* (Prague, 1903), V.

THOMAS OESTREICH.

Boniface Association (BONIFATIUSVEREIN), one of the most successful Catholic societies of Germany, owes its origin to a suggestion made by Döllinger at the Third Catholic Congress of Germany, held at Ratisbon in 1849. The object of the association is to maintain what the Catholic Church possesses in those regions where Catholics are few in number, to found and support missions and schools, and to erect churches, parish-houses, and schools for Catholics in the Protestant parts of Germany. The territories which the association takes under its especial care are: the Diocese of Kulm; the Delegature of Brandenburg and Pomerania, belonging to the Prince-Bishopric of Breslau; the Vicariate Apostolic of Saxony; the Dioceses of Paderborn, Hildesheim, Osnabrück, and Fulda; the Northern Missions, etc. The association is managed by a general committee at Paderborn; the diocesan committees have entire control of the contributions they receive; after consultation with their respective diocesan councils, and under the approval of the general committee, the diocesan committees designate the objects to which the money shall be given. Since the association was founded about $9,250,000 has been collected and some 2,600 churches have been erected or aided.

Besides the diocesan committees another important branch is formed by the Boniface collecting societies. The first of these was founded in 1885 among the merchants of Paderborn by the Marist congregation; the aim of this branch of the association is, by the founding of orphan asylums and institutions where children are prepared for their first communion, to care for the religious training of Catholic children in non-Catholic communities. The funds are obtained by the collection and sale of objects of little value in themselves, such as, tin-foil, old postage stamps, clothing, leaden seals, old coins, books, cigar bands, cigar tips, and such trifles. More than $625,-000 has been raised by this branch association since its foundation; it aids more than 120 institutions for first communicants and orphan asylums, besides contributing considerable sums to children in non-Catholic communities for railway tickets, school and living expenses.

Another branch is the Academic Boniface Association which has existed for forty years at the German universities, the first one of these societies being founded at Münster in 1867. In 1888 the various university branches met at Freiburg and united into a common organization; in 1907 they included thirty-six branches with a membership of 750. Their organ is the "Akademische Bonifatius-Korrespondenz". Since 1860 the general association has had a printing office and since 1888 a bookstore for old and new publications, both at Paderborn. The popes have granted indulgences and privileges to priests connected with the association. The association issues the "Bonifatiusblatt", founded in 1850; the "Schlesisches Bonifatiusblatt", 1860; and the "St. Bonifatiusblatt" at Prague, founded in 1904.

KLEFFNER AND WOKER, Festschrift (Paderborn, 1899); ARNDT, Die dem Bonifatiusverein vom heiligen Stuhl verliehenen Gnaden (Paderborn, 1902); Der Bonifatius-Sammelverein (Paderborn, 1907); Financial statements of the managing committee, annual reports of the combined Boniface collecting societies, etc.

JOSEPH LINS.

Boniface of Savoy, forty-sixth Archbishop of Canterbury and son of Thomas, Count of Savoy, date of birth uncertain; d. in Savoy, 14 July, 1270. While yet a child he became a Carthusian. In 1234, as sub-deacon, he was elected Bishop of Belley in Burgundy: and, in 1241, administered the Diocese of Valence. His connexion with the royal house of England secured his promotion to the primacy. The Queen of Henry III was Eleanor, daughter of Berengar, Count of Provence, and Beatrice of Savoy. This Beatrice was the sister of the future archbishop. When St. Edmund died, in 1241, the Queen's uncle was elected. But Gregory IX and Celestine IV dying unexpectedly, it was not until the end of 1243

that the new Pope, Innocent IV, was able to confirm his election. In the following year Boniface went to England for the first time. He found his see in debt. The heavy taxation during the sequestration in St. Edmund's primacy had severely burdened its already slender resources. Therefore his first act was to make every economy, abolishing all sinecures and unnecessary offices connected with the archbishopric. He ordered the tenants and clergy to contribute towards the liquidation of the debt.

In 1244 he set out for the Council of Lyons, where he was consecrated (15 January, 1245) by the pope. His brother Philip, afterwards Count of Savoy, although not consecrated, held the archbishopric of Lyons and was in command of the papal troops. During the sitting of the council Boniface held a commission under him. He obtained from the pope the grant of the first-fruits of all vacant benefices in the Province of Canterbury during seven years, and his claim to levy a contribution from the whole province to meet the debt of the metropolitan see was allowed. In 1249 he returned to England and was enthroned with great pomp at Canterbury on All Saints' Day. The archbishop then began a personal visitation of his diocese, correcting abuses and levying fines. But, on extending his visitation to the dioceses of his suffragans, resistance was offered to him. In London the Dean and Canons of St. Paul's protested that the Bishop of London was their visitor and appealed. They were promptly excommunicated. On the following day the archbishop visited the Priory of St. Bartholomew. He was met by the sub-prior and brethren, who welcomed him as a prelate but not as a visitor. Like the clergy of St. Paul's they represented that they had their own bishop and would not submit to other jurisdiction without permission from him. The archbishop was so incensed that he felled the venerable sub-prior to the earth. This was more than the Londoners could stand from a foreigner, even were he their archbishop. They fell upon him, his vestments were torn in the struggle, and the coat of mail worn beneath them disclosed. He was rescued by his bodyguard and escaped by barge to Lambeth, where he proceeded to excommunicate the clergy of St. Bartholomew's and the Bishop of London.

He then announced his intention of holding a visitation at St. Albans. The suffragans met and resolved to resist him. The clergy of the province levied a tax upon themselves in order to proceed against him at Rome. Learning of these things he promptly set out for the Roman court. The result was a compromise, the pope confirming the right of visitation, but restricting its use. Godwin says of him that Boniface did three worthy things: he paid off a debt of 22,000 marks; he built and endowed the hospital at Maidstone; and he finished the great hall of the archbishop's palace.

Pope Gregory XVI, at the suit of Charles Albert of Savoy, King of Sardinia (1831–49), approved the cult of Boniface, Archbishop of Canterbury, as *ab immemorabili*.

STRICKLAND, Ricerche storiche sopra il b. Bonifacio di Savoia in Miscell. stor. Ital. (1895), I, 349–432; GODWIN, De Præsulibus Angliæ; GUICHERON, Histoire généalogique de la royale maison de Savoie; HOOK, Lives of the Archbishops of Canterbury; LUARD, Annales; RYMER, Fœdera; MATTHEW PARIS, Letters of Grosseteste; Letters of Adam de Marisco.

FRANCIS AVELING.

Bonifacius de Vitalinis. See VITALINI, BONIFACIO DE.

Boni Homines (or BONSHOMMES).—This name was popularly given to at least three religious orders in the Church:

I.—THE ORDER OF GRANDMONT, founded by St. Stephen of Muret (b. 1046, d. 1124) for an austere order of eremitical friars professing the rule of St. Augustine (though they have sometimes been claimed also by the Benedictines). Towards the end of the twelfth century they possessed more than sixty houses, principally in Aquitaine, Anjou, and Normandy. The kings of England (then rulers of Normandy) were great benefactors of these friars, who were known as the Bonshommes of Grandmont from the earliest times. The oldest house of the order was at Vincennes (founded by Louis VII, in 1164); and this more than four centuries later came into the possession of the Minims, who were hence known afterwards as Bonshommes. The observance of the order had become greatly relaxed when a general chapter was held at Grandmont (after an interval of more than a century) in 1643, with the object of re-establishing regular discipline. New statutes, modifying the original rigour of the rule, were drawn up and approved. The habit of the order was black, with a hood and a broad scapular. At the time when Hélyot wrote his great work on the religious orders (1714–21) there were in France also three houses of nuns of the Order of Grandmont; but both monasteries and convents were suppressed at the Revolution sixty years later. A reformed branch of the order was established in 1642 by Père Frémont, but the members of this institution do not seem to have been known by the old name of Bonshommes.

II.—The FRATRES SACCATI, or BROTHERS OF PENITENCE, were also known as Boni Homines, Bonshommes, or, as Leland calls them, Bones-homes. Their origin, as well as the date of their foundation, is obscure, but they had a house at Saragossa in the time of Pope Innocent III (d. 1216) and one about the same time at Valenciennes. Their rule was founded on that of St. Augustine. They had one house in Paris, in a street called after them the *rue des Sachettes*, and in 1257 they were introduced into England. Matthew Paris records under this year that "a certain new and unknown order of friars appeared in London", duly furnished with credentials from the pope; and he mentions later that they were called from the style of their habit *Fratres Saccati*. We learn from Polydore Vergil that Edmund (son of Richard, Earl of Cornwall) founded a little later (according to Tanner, in 1283) a monastery at Ashridge, Herts, for a rector and twenty canons of "a new order not before seen in England, and called the Boni homines". It was finished in 1285. The first rector was Richard, and the last Thomas Waterhouse (1529), who surrendered the house to Henry VIII. The suppressed college was granted first to the king's sister Elizabeth, and afterwards to the Egertons, later created Earls and Dukes of Bridgewater. The church was destroyed under Elizabeth; but in 1800 the last duke was living in a portion of the old college. He sold the great hall piecemeal, and pulled down the cloisters. The estate and (modern) mansion now belong to Earl Brownlow. The only other English house of the Boni Homines was at Edington in Wilts. The former college there (consisting of a dean and prebendaries) was granted to them by desire of Edward the Black Prince, who (says Leland) "had a great favour to the Bones-homes beyond the Se". The first rector (brought from Ashridge) was John de Aylesbury, the last John Ryve. Edward VI granted the property to Lord St. John; it now belongs to the Watson-Taylor family. The splendid church, one of the finest of its period, still remains. (Little, The Friars of the Sack, in Eng. Hist. Review, 1894, 33, 121.)

III. The PORTUGUESE BONI HOMINES.—The identity of the *Fratres Saccati* mentioned by Matthew Paris as, in 1257, a "new order in England", with the "new order" (the Bonshommes) established a little later at Ashridge and Edington, seems to be generally admitted. An entirely separate institute, however, was that of the Portuguese Boni Homines, or Secular Canons of St. John the Evangelist, founded

by John de Vicenza, afterwards Bishop of Lamego, in the fifteenth century. Living at first independently in a monastery granted to them by the Archbishop of Braga at Villar de Frades, they afterwards embraced the institute of Secular Canons of St. George in Alga (in Venice), and the Portuguese order was confirmed by Pope Martin V under the title of "Boni Homines of Villar de Frades". They had fourteen houses in Portugal, and King John III gave them charge of all the royal hospitals in the kingdom, while many of the canons went out as missionaries to India and Ethiopia. Several members of the order have won a high reputation as scholars and theologians

LÉVÊQUE, *Annal. Ord. Grandmont* (1663); HÉLYOT, ed. MIGNE, *Histoire des ordres monastiques religieuses et militaires*, II, 412–424, 563–566; III, 421–425; POLYDORE VERGIL, *Angl. Histor.*, lib. XVI (in ed. 1649, p. 402); DUGDALE, *Monast. Angl.*, VI, 514, 535; GASQUET, *English Monastic Life* (1904), 249; FRANCISCO DE S. MARIA, *Hist. das sagradas Congregações dos conegos seculares de S. João Evang. em Portugal*.

D. O. HUNTER-BLAIR.

Bonizo of Sutri (or BONITHO), Bishop of Sutri in Central Italy, in the eleventh century, an adherent of Gregory VII and advocate of the ideals of that pope; b. about 1045, probably in Cremona, Northern Italy; put to death 14 July, 1090. Early in his life he joined the party known as the Pataria, and when a subdeacon in Piacenza he came into conflict with Dionysius, bishop of that city. In 1074 he went to Rome, and won the favour of Pope Gregory, by whom he was soon appointed to the episcopal See of Sutri. Bonizo took part in several councils held in Rome; in 1078 he went to Cremona as papal legate and consecrated there the church of St. Thomas. In the struggle between Gregory VII and Henry IV he was ever on the side of the pope. He was seized by Henry in 1082 and entrusted to the custody of the antipope Clement III. About a year afterwards Bonizo made his escape, and lived for several years under the protection of Countess Mathilda of Tuscany. In 1086 he was present at the funeral of his friend, Anselm, Bishop of Lucca. He was, soon after, elected to the See of Piacenza by the Pataria, but owing to strong opposition was unable to take possession of it until the year 1088, when he was strongly supported by Pope Urban II. His enemies, however, contrived to bring about his death.

Bonizo wrote: (1) the "Paradisus", or extracts from the writings of St. Augustine (still unpublished); (2) a short treatise on the sacraments (Muratori, "Antiquitates Italicæ Med. Ævi", III, in Migne, P. L., CL); (3) the "Decretum" or "De vitâ Christianâ", a work in ten books on ecclesiastical law and moral theology written at the request of a certain priest Gregory [fragments of this work are in Mai's Nova Bibliotheca, VII, iii, 1–76 (Rome, 1854)]; (4) "In Hugonem schismaticum", now lost, probably against the schismatic Cardinal Hugo Candidus; (5) a description of the various classes of judges in the Roman Empire and in the Roman Church (ed. Blühme, in Mon. Ger. Hist. Leges, IV); (6) his most important work the "Liber ad amicum", a history of the Church, in which the author relates events of his own times.

SAUR, *Studien über Bonizo* in Forsch. zur deutsch. Gesch. (Göttingen, 1868), VIII, 397–464; MIRBT, *Die Publizistik im Zeitalter Gregors VII* (Leipzig, 1894); DÜMMLER in preface to his edition of *Liber ad amicum* in Mon. Germ. Hist., *Libelli de lite Imp. et Pont.*, I, 568 sqq.; MARTENS in *Tübing. Theol. Quartalschrift* (1883), 457 sqq.; GIESEBRECHT, *Gesch. der deutsch. Kaiserzeit* (Leipzig, 1885, 1890), II, III; WATTENBACH, *Deutschlands Geschichtsquellen* (6th ed., 1893), II, 223, 224; DALLER in *Kirchenlex.*, II, 1087 sqq.; HERZOG, *Realencyk.* (Leipzig, 1897), III; DELARC, *St. Grégoire VII et la réforme de l'église* (Paris, 1889–90).

FRANCIS J. SCHAEFER.

Bonn, UNIVERSITY OF (RHEINISCHE FRIEDRICH-WILHELMS-UNIVERSITÄT). An academy was founded at Bonn in 1777 by Max Friedrich, Prince-Archbishop of Cologne. To secure its support he ordered that every monastery and convent within the archdiocese should either provide two professors or contribute a certain sum of money. He also endeavoured to obtain the papal sanction, but failed. In 1784 Kaiser Joseph II raised the academy to the rank of a university, and the inauguration took place 20 November, 1786. In this first period the university suffered from Febronianism and Rationalism. The leaders were Hedderich (1744–1808), Dereser (1757–1827), and Schneider (1756–94). Pius VI in a Brief of 24 March, 1790, called the archbishop's attention to the deplorable condition of the university, but without result. In 1794 the French invasion obliged the professors to suspend their courses, and in 1797 the university was closed. It was restored in 1818 by King Friedrich Wilhelm III. Among its professors of theology were George Hermes (1775–1831), Achterfeldt (1788–1879), and Braun (1801–63), originators of the movement known as Hermesianism. Some of their followers, e. g. Elverich (1796–1886), joined the "Old Catholics", a party which also had as adherents Reusch (1825–1900) and several other members of the faculty. Their action led finally to their suspension and excommunication after having created a division among both professors and students of theology. The other departments of the university developed rapidly under the direction of Niebuhr (1776–1831) and Arndt (1769–1860) in history, A. W. Schlegel (1767–1845) in literature, Nasse (1778–1851) in medicine, Kekule (1829–96) and Mohr (1806–79) in chemistry, Clausius (1822–88) in physics, Von Rath (1830–88) in mineralogy, Preyer (1841–97) and Pfluger (1829–—) in physiology. Since 1868 new buildings have been provided for the scientific departments either in Bonn or in Pappelsdorf. The university comprises at present the Catholic faculty of theology, the Protestant faculty of theology, and the faculties of law, medicine, and philosophy. There are 284 instructors and 3488 students. In 1905–06, the Catholic faculty of theology had 309 students, the Protestant 80. The library contains 350,000 volumes.

E. A. PACE.

Bonnard, JEAN LOUIS, VENERABLE, a French missionary and martyr, b. 1 March, 1824 at Saint-Christôt-en-Jarret (Diocese of Lyons); beheaded 30 April, 1852. After a collegiate course at Saint-Jodard, he entered the seminary of Lyons, which he left at the age of twenty-two, to complete his theological studies at the Seminary of the Foreign Missions in Paris. From Nantes, where he was ordained, he sailed for the missions of Western Tongking and reached there in May, 1850. In 1851, he was put in charge of two parishes there; but as early as 21 March, 1852, he was arrested and cast into prison. Sentence of death was pronounced against him and was executed immediately upon receipt of its confirmation by the king (30 April, 1852). His remains were thrown into the river, but recovered by Christians and sent by them to the Seminary of Foreign Missions. Bonnard has been declared Venerable by the Church.

LAUNAY, Les cinquante-deux serviteurs de Dieu (Paris, 1895), 355–373.

N. A. WEBER.

Bonnechose, HENRI-MARIE-GASTON BOISNORMAND DE, cardinal and senator, b. at Paris, 1800; d. 1883. Entering the magistracy, he became attorney-general for the district of Besançon in 1830, but having received sacred orders at Strasburg, under the episcopate of de Trevern, he was made professor of sacred eloquence in the school of higher studies founded at Besançon by Cardinal de Rohan. After the death of de Rohan, he went to Rome to settle the differences between Bishop de Trevern and himself, due to phil-

osophical opinions found in his work, "Philosophy of Christianity", for which Bonnechose had written an introduction. In 1844, he was named by Rome superior of the community of St. Louis; in 1847 he became Bishop of Carcassonne, was transferred, 4 November, 1854, to Evreux, and in 1854 raised to the archiepiscopal See of Rouen. Created cardinal in 1863, he became ex-officio senator of the empire. The cardinal showed himself a warm advocate of the temporal power of the popes, and firmly protested against the withdrawal of the French army from the Pontifical States. In 1870, at the urgent prayers of the citizens of Rouen, notwithstanding his advanced years, he went in the rigour of the season to Versailles, the headquarters of the German armies, to entreat King William of Prussia to reduce the war contribution imposed on the city of Rouen. Under the republican government he uniformly opposed the laws and measures passed against religious congregations and their schools, but endeavoured to inspire his clergy with sentiments of deference and conciliation in their relations with the civil authorities. His best known work is "Introduction à la philosophie du Christianisme" (1835), two octavo volumes.

GUÉRIN, Dict. des dict. (Paris, 1892); LAROUSSE, Dict. univ. du XIXᵉ siècle (Paris, 1867).

F. M. L. DUMONT.

Bonne-Espérance, THE ABBEY OF, situated near Binche, province of Hainault, Diocese of Tournai, Belgium. It owes its foundation to the conversion of William, the only son and heir of Rainard, the Knight of Croix. William had been seduced by the heresies of Tanchelm, but through the persuasive exhortations of St. Norbert he had been brought back to the true Church, and his grateful parents, Rainard and Beatrix, had given land to St. Norbert for the foundation of an abbey at Ramignies, while William followed St. Norbert to Prémontré. Ramignies having been found unsuitable, Odo, the first abbot, led his young colony to another locality in the neighbourhood. The legend says that when Odo saw the spot he exclaimed: "Bonæ spei fecisti filios tuos" (Wis., xii, 19—O God, Thou hast made Thy children to be of good hope). Others say that the statue of Our Lady of Good Hope was venerated there. Whatever may have been the cause, Blessed Odo's confidence was not misplaced. The abbey grew and prospered and has ever sent forth numbers of holy and learned priests. Blessed Odo was succeeded by Blessed Philip, surnamed the Almoner. Abbot Philip is the author of several books which have been published in Migne, P. L., CCIII. Blessed Oda, whose heroic act in defence of her virginity has been described by Abbot Philip, was a Norbertine nun in the convent of Rivreulle under the direction of the Abbot of Bonne-Espérance. The forty-sixth and last Abbot of Bonne-Espérance, Bonaventure Daublain, saw in 1792 and again in 1794 the abbey taken and pillaged and his religious dispersed by the French Republican army. At the time of its suppression the abbey counted sixty-seven inmates. Greatly though they wished to live in community, they were not allowed to do so during the French Republic, nor after 1815 under William I, King of the Netherlands. The last surviving religious gave the abbey to the Bishop of Tournai for a diocesan seminary. The church is still Norbertine in its appearance, possessing as it does the body of St. Frédéric, which had been saved from the Protestants and brought from the Norbertine Abbey in Holland to the Abbey of Bonne-Espérance in Belgium. The church is still adorned with the statues of St. Norbert, of St. Frédéric, and of two Norbertine bishops, St. Evremonde and St. Isfrid. At the time of the suppression the miraculous statue of Our Lady of Good Hope was hidden; and when peace was restored, it was brought to the church of Vellereille of which one of the canons of Bonne-Espérance was the parish priest. In 1833 it was solemnly brought back to the abbey church, or, as it is now, the seminary church.

Annales Premonst., The Life of St. Frederic; DECLÈVES, Notre Dame de Bonne-Espérance.

MARTIN GEUDENS.

Bonner, EDMUND, Bishop of London, b. about 1500; d. 1569. He was the son of Edmund Bonner, a sawyer of Potter's Henley in Worcestershire, England, and Elizabeth Frodsham. Doubt was cast on his legitimacy by Bale and other opponents, who asserted that he was the natural son of a priest named Savage, but Strype and other Anglican writers, including the historian S. R. Maitland, have shown the groundless nature of these assertions. He was educated at Pembroke College, Oxford, then Broadgate Hall, where he took his degree as Bachelor both of canon and of civil law in 1519, and was ordained priest about the same time. In 1525 he became doctor of civil law and soon after entered the service of Cardinal Wolsey, which brought him to the notice of the king and Cromwell, and thus led to a diplomatic career. After the fall of Wolsey, he remained faithful to him and was with him at the time of his arrest and death. When the question of the king's divorce was raised, he was employed by the king as his agent at Rome, where he remained a whole year, 1532–33. During the following years he was much employed on important embassies in the king's interests, first to the pope to appeal against the excommunication pronounced in July, 1533, afterwards to the emperor to dissuade him from attending the general council which the pope wished to summon at Vicenza, and again to the French Court to succeed Gardiner there as ambassador. In this capacity he proved capable and successful, though irritation was frequently caused by his overbearing and dictatorial manner. Meanwhile his services were rewarded by successive grants of the livings of Cherry Burton (Yorks), Ripple (Worcester), Blaydon (Durham), and East Dereham (Norfolk), and he was made Archdeacon of Leicester in 1535. Finally, while ambassador in France, he was elected Bishop of Hereford (27th November, 1538) but owing to his absence he could neither be consecrated nor take possession of his see, and he was still abroad when he was translated to the Bishopric of London. Elected in November, 1539, he returned, and was consecrated 4th April, 1540. Almost his first duty was to try heretics under Henry's Act of the Six Articles, and though his action seems to have been only official, accusations of excessive cruelty and bias against the accused were spread broadcast by his enemies, and from the first he seems to have been unpopular in London. During the years 1542–43 he was again abroad in Spain and Germany as ambassador to the emperor, at the end of which time he returned to London. The death of the king on 28th January, 1547, proved the turning point in his career. Hitherto he had shown himself entirely subservient to the sovereign, supporting him in the matter of the divorce, approving of the suppression of the religious houses, taking the oath of supremacy which Fisher and More refused at the cost of life itself, and accepting schismatical consecration and institution. But while acting in this way, he had always resisted the innovations of the Reformers, and held to the doctrines of the old religion. Therefore from the first he put himself in opposition to the religious changes introduced by Protector Somerset and Archbishop Cranmer.

He opposed the "Visitors" appointed by the Council, and was committed to prison for so doing. Though not long a prisoner, after two years of unsatisfactory struggle he came again into conflict with the Protector owing to his omission to enforce the use of the new Prayer Book. When ordered to preach at St. Paul's Cross he did so, but with such significant omissions in the matter which had been prescribed touching the king's authority, that he was finally deprived of his see and sent as a prisoner to the Marshalsea. Here he remained till the accession of Mary in 1553. On 5th of August in that year he took possession of his diocese once more. In estimating Bishop Bonner's conduct on his restoration to his see the difficulties of the position must be recalled. There was in London an extremely violent reforming element which opposed in every way the restoration of Catholic worship. For twenty years the authority of the Holy See had been set at naught and ridiculed in unsparing terms, and though the Parliament in 1554 welcomed Pole as Papal Legate and sought absolution and reconciliation from him with apparent unanimity, there was a real hostility to the whole proceeding among a considerable section of the populace. During 1554 Bonner carried out a visitation of his diocese, restoring the Mass and the manifold practices and emblems of Catholic life, but the work was carried out slowly and with difficulty. To help in the work, Bonner published a list of thirty-seven "Articles to be enquired of", but these led to such disturbances that they were temporarily withdrawn. While many rejoiced to have the old worship restored, others exhibited the most implacable hostility. As Bonner sat at St. Paul's Cross to hear Gilbert Bourne preach, when reference was made to the bishop's sufferings under Edward VI a dagger was thrown at the preacher. At St. Margaret's, Westminster, a murderous assault was made on the priest giving Holy Communion, the Blessed Sacrament itself was the object of profane outrages, and street brawls arising out of religious disputes were frequent. Meanwhile many of the Reformers attacked the Queen herself in terms that were clearly treasonable. Had these been proceeded against by the civil power much evil might have been averted, but unfortunately it was thought at the time that, as the root of the evil lay in the religious question, the offenders would best be dealt with by the ecclesiastical tribunals, and on Bonner, as Bishop of London, fell the chief burden. Besides his judicial work in his own diocese, Bonner was appointed to carry out the painful task of degrading Cranmer at Oxford in February, 1556. The part he took in these affairs gave rise to intense hatred on the part of the Reformers, and by them he was represented as hounding men and women to death with merciless vindictiveness. Foxe in his "Book of Martyrs" summed up this view in two doggerel lines:
"This cannibal in three years space three hundred martyrs slew
They were his food, he loved so blood, he spared none he knew."

That this was an absolutely ungrounded charge is shown by the letter from the king and queen in Council, addressed to Bonner on the express ground that he was not proceeding with sufficient energy. As to the number of his "victims" Foxe, whose untrustworthiness now needs no demonstration, has exaggerated according to his wont. The number of persons who were executed under the laws against heresy in his jurisdiction seems to have been about 120. As to these persons Mr. Gairdner writes "Over their ultimate fate it must be remembered he had no control, when once they were declared to be irreclaimable heretics and handed over to the secular power; but he always strove by gentle suasion first to reconcile them to the Church". Throughout the "Book of Martyrs" Foxe is unsparing in his accusations of cruelty against the bishop; but his charges have been impartially examined at great length by Dr. Maitland, who comes to the same decision as the Catholic writers against Foxe, and sums it up by remarking that when anyone "calmly inquires what these tales so full of rage and fury really mean, when they mean anything, he finds the bloody wolf transformed . . . into something much more like a good-tempered mastiff, who might safely be played with, and who, though he might be teased into barking and growling, had no disposition to bite and would not do it without orders". (Essays, 422–424.)

Another virulent opponent of Bonner was John Bale, formerly a friar and ex-Bishop of Ossory, who in 1554 published from his place of exile at Basle, an attack on the bishop, in which he speaks of him as "the bloody sheep-bite of London", "bloody Bonner", and still coarser epithets. Concerning this outburst Dr. Maitland quietly remarks, "when Bale wrote this book, little that could be called persecution had taken place. Not one martyr had suffered." These attacks of Foxe and Bale are noteworthy as being the foundation on which the current traditional view of Bonner's work and character has been based, a tradition that has only been broken down by the research of the past century. A man so regarded could expect small consideration when the death of Mary (17th November, 1558) placed Elizabeth on the throne, and the new queen's attitude to the bishop was marked at their first interview, when she refused him her hand to kiss. From 24th June, 1559, the Mass was forbidden as well as all other services not in the Book of Common Prayer, but long before that date the Mass ceased in most London churches, though Bonner took care that in his cathedral at least it should still be celebrated. On 30th May, Il Schifanoya, envoy from the Court of Mantua, wrote: "The Council sent twice or thrice to summon the Bishop of London to give him orders to remove the service of the Mass and of the Divine Office in that Church; but he answered them intrepidly 'I possess three things—soul, body, and property. Of the two latter, you can dispose at your pleasure, but as to the soul, God alone can command me.' He remained constant about body and property, and again to-day he has been called to the Council, but I do not yet know what they said to him." (Phillips, op. cit. *infra*, 103.) As a matter of fact, they had ordered him to resign the bishopric, which he refused to do, adding that he preferred death. He was then deprived of the office and went for a time to Westminster Abbey. On 20th April, 1560, he was sent as a prisoner to the Marshalsea. During the next two years representatives of the reforming party frequently clamoured for the execution of Bonner and the other imprisoned bishops. When the Parliament of 1563 met, a new Act was passed by which the first refusal of the oath of royal supremacy was *præmunire*, the second, high treason. The bishops had refused the oath once, so that by this Act, which became law on 10th April, their next refusal of the oath might be followed by their death. On 24th April, the Spanish Ambassador writes that Bonner and some others had been already called on to take the oath. Partly owing to the intervention of the emperor and partly to an outbreak of the plague, no further steps seem to have been taken at the time. A year later, on 29th April, 1564, the oath was again tendered to Bonner by Horne, the Anglican Bishop of Winchester. This he firmly refused, but the interference of the Spanish ambassador and his own readiness of resource saved immediate consequences. Being well skilled both in civil and canon law, he raised the point that Horne, who offered him the oath, was not qualified to do so, as he had not been validly consecrated bishop. This challenged the new hierarchy as to the validity of their orders, and so strong was Bonner's case that the Government evaded meeting it, and the proceedings commenced against him were adjourned time after time. Four times a year for three years he was forced to appear in the courts at Westminster only to be further remanded. The last of these appearances took place in the Michaelmas term of 1568, so that the last year of the bishop's life was spent in the peace of his prison. His demeanour during his long imprisonment was remarkable for unfailing cheerfulness, and even Jewel describes him in a letter as "a most courteous man and gentlemanly both in his manners and appearance" (Zurich Letters, I, 34). The end came on 5th September, 1569, when he died in the Marshalsea. The Anglican Bishop of London wrote to Cecil to say that he had been buried in St. George's churchyard, Southwark, but if this was so the coffin was soon secretly removed to Copford, near Colchester, where it was buried under the north side of the altar. Sander, Bridgewater, and other contemporary writers attributed to Bonner and the other bishops who died in prison the honour of martyrdom: *in vinculis obierunt martyres*. On the walls of the English College, Rome, an inscription recording the death of the eleven bishops, but without naming them, found a place among the paintings of the martyrs. In a work quoted below the Catholic tradition with regard to these bishops has been ably set forth by Rev. George Phillips, avowedly for the purpose of promoting their beatification. Bishop Bonner differs from the others in this respect, that owing to the prominent part circumstances compelled him to play in the persecution, he was attacked during life with a hatred which has followed him even after death, so that in English history few names have been so execrated and vilified as his. Tardy justice is now being done to his memory by historians, Catholic and Protestant alike, yet there remains immense prejudice against his memory in the popular mind. Nor could this be otherwise in face of the calumnies that have been repeated by tradition. The reckless charges of Bale and Foxe were repeated by Burnet Hume, and others, who join in representing him as an inhuman persecutor, "a man of profligate manners and of a brutal character, who seemed to rejoice in the torments of the unhappy sufferers" (Hume c. xxxvii). The first historian of note to challenge this verdict was the Catholic, Lingard, though even he wrote in a very tentative way and it was by an Anglican historian, S. R. Maitland, that anything like justice was first done to Bonner. This writer's analysis remains the most discriminating summary of the bishop's character. "Setting aside declamation and looking at the details of facts left by those who may be called, if people please, Bonner's victims, and their friends, we find, very consistently maintained, the character of a man, straightforward and hearty, familiar and humorous, sometimes rough, perhaps coarse, naturally hot tempered, but obviously (by the testimony of his enemies) placable and easily intreated, capable of bearing most patiently much intemperate and insolent language, much reviling and low abuse directed against himself personally, against his order, and against those peculiar doctrines and practices of his church for maintaining which he had himself suffered the loss of all things, and borne long imprisonment. At the same time not incapable of being provoked into saying harsh and passionate things, but much more frequently meaning nothing by the threatenings and slaughter which he breathed out, than to intimidate those on whose ignorance and simplicity argument seemed to be thrown away—in short, we can scarcely read with attention any one of the cases detailed by those who were no friends of Bonner, without seeing in him a judge who (even if we grant that he was dispensing bad laws badly) was obviously desirous to save the prisoner's life." This verdict has been generally followed by later historians, and the last word has been added, for the present, in the recently published volume on the Reformation, in the "Cambridge Modern History" planned by Lord Acton (1903) where the statement is expressly made: "It is now generally admitted that the part played by Bonner was not that attributed to him by Foxe, of a cruel bigot who exulted in sending his victims to the stake. The number of those put to death in his diocese of London was undoubtedly disproportionately large, but this would seem to have been more the result of the strength of the reforming element in the capital and in Essex, than of the employment of exceptional rigour; while the evidence also shows that he himself patiently dealt with many of the Protestants, and did his best to induce them to renounce what he conscientiously believed to be their errors."

Bonner's writings include "Responsum et Exhortatio in laudem Sacerdotii" (1553); "Articles to be enquired of in the General Visitation of Edmund Bishop of London" (1554); "Homelies sette forth by Eddmune Byshop of London, . . . to be read within his diocese of London of all Parsons, vycars and curates, unto their parishioners upon Sondayes and holy days" (1555). There was also published under his name a catechism, probably written by his chaplains, Harpsfield and Pendleton, entitled "A profitable and necessary doctrine" (1554; 2d ed. 1555). He also wrote the preface to Bishop Gardiner's "Book of Obedience" (1534).

State Papers of Henry VIII; DODD, *Church History* (London, 1737), Part III, Bk. II, art. 3; MAITLAND, *Essays on the Reformation in England* (London, 1849), Essays III, XVII, XVIII, XX; GILLOW, *Bib. Dict. Eng. Cath.* (London, 1885), I, 260–265; GAIRDNER in *Dict. Nat. Biog.* (London, 1886), V, 356–360; BRIDGETT AND KNOX, *Queen Eliz. and the Cath. Hierarchy* (London, 1889); STONE, *History of Mary I* (London, 1901); PHILLIPS, *Extinction of the Ancient Hierarchy* London, 1905).

EDWIN BURTON.

Bonnetty, AUGUSTIN, a French writer, b. at Entrevaux (dept. of Basses-Alpes) 9 May, 1798; d. at Paris, 26 March, 1879. In 1815 he entered the seminary at Digne and studied for the priesthood. After completing his philosophical and theological studies, as he was too young to be ordained, he went to Marseilles as private tutor in an excellent family. He soon felt that his mission was to use science and philosophy in the defence of the Church and to remain a layman. In 1825 he went to Paris, and five years later founded the "Annales de philosophie chrétienne" (first number 31 July, 1830) which he edited until his death. His main object was to show the agreement of science and religion, and to point out how the various sciences contributed to the demonstration of Christianity. In 1838 he also took up the direction of the "Université catholique" founded two years before by Gerbet, de Salinis, de Scorbiac, and de Montalembert. Having become the sole owner of this review in 1846, he suspended its publication, in 1855, in order to devote himself exclusively to the "Annales". Among the main features of the "Annales" was the attempt to show the universality of a primitive revelation which is recognizable even in the myths and fables of all nations. But Bonnetty went farther, exaggerating the necessity of this primitive revelation, and minimizing the value of reason in attaining truth. This tendency to the system known as "traditionalism" soon drew the attention of the ecclesiastical authorities. A report was sent to the Congregation of the Index by Archbishop Sibour of Paris, and two years later (1855) Bonnetty was asked to sign the following four propositions: " (1) Although faith is superior to reason, yet no discord or disagreement can ever be found between them, since both proceed from one and the same unchangeable source of truth, God infinite in perfection, and thus are of mutual assistance. (Encyclical of Pius IX, 9 November, 1846.) (2) Reasoning can demonstrate with certainty the existence of God, the spirituality of the soul, and the freedom of man. Faith is posterior to revelation, and in consequence cannot consistently

be adduced to prove the existence of God against an atheist, or the spirituality and freedom of the rational soul against an adherent of naturalism and fatalism. (Proposition subscribed to by Bautain, 8 September, 1840.) (3) The use of reason precedes faith, and, with the help of revelation and grace, leads man to faith. (Prop. subscribed to by Bautain, 8 September, 1840.) (4) The method used by St. Thomas, by St. Bonaventure, and, after them, by other scholastics, does not lead to rationalism, nor does it explain why, in modern schools, philosophy should fall into naturalism and pantheism. Hence these doctors and masters cannot be reproached for using that method, especially with the approval, at least tacit of the Church. (Prop. contradictory to propositions, extracted from different passages of Bonnetty.) "

It must be noted that in the letter sent at the same time as these propositions by Father Modena, the secretary of the Congregation of the Index, to Monsignor Sacconi, the papal nuncio in Paris, it was stated that Bonnetty's attachment to the Holy See and to Catholic doctrines was never suspected. The intention was not to pronounce any judgment declaring his opinions "erroneous, suspicious, or dangerous", but only "to prevent the possible consequences, proximate or remote, which others might deduce from them, especially in matters of faith". Bonnetty, without any hesitation, gave his full assent to the above propositions. He declared that he had meant all along to defend these doctrines, and that he would hereafter endeavour to do so with greater accuracy.

Bonnetty was a member of the "Société des études littéraires", the "Association pour la défense de la religion catholique", the "Société asiatique", and the "Roman Academy of the Catholic Religion". He was also a knight of the Order of St. Gregory the Great and of the Order of Pius IX. In addition to his numerous articles in the "Annales de philosophie chrétienne" and the "Université catholique", he wrote the following works most of which, however, were first published as articles in the Annales: "Beautés de l'histoire de l'Eglise" (Paris, 1841); "Le christianisme et la philosophie" (Paris, 1845); "Table de tous les auteurs édités par le cardinal Mai" (Paris, 1850); "Documents historiques sur la religion des Romains" (Paris, 1867–78); "Dictionnaire raisonné de diplomatique", based on that of Dom de Vaines (Paris, 1863–65); a translation of the Latin work by Father de Prémare, a Jesuit missionary in China (1666–1734), "Vestiges des principaux dogmes chrétiens tirés des anciens livres chinois" (1879).

Annales de philosophie chrétienne, passim; DEDOUE, *Augustin Bonnetty,* ibidem (1879, I), XCVI, 348–441; *Polybiblion* (1879), I, 454; DUBLANCHY in *Dict. de théol. cath.,* II, 1019.

C. A. DUBRAY.

Bonosus, Bishop of Sardica, a heretic in the latter part of the fourth century. Against the common teaching of the Church he held that, after Jesus, Mary had several other children. The Council of Capua (391), before which the matter was brought, did not pass any judgment on it, but referred it to the Metropolitan Anysius of Thessalonica and the other bishops of Illyria. They condemned Bonosus and tried to exclude him from his church. In a letter to the same bishops Pope Siricius approves the sentence and also condemns the opinion that Mary did not always preserve her virginity. Notwithstanding his condemnation, and the prudent advice of St. Ambrose to submit, Bonosus continued to exercise the episcopal functions, to consecrate bishops and ordain priests. According to two letters of Pope Innocent I, one to Martian of Naïssa (409), and the other to the bishops of Macedonia (414), those ordained by Bonosus before his condemnation were to be received in the Church without a new ordination; those ordained since Bonosus's condemnation, especially if they had themselves sought to be ordained by him, were to be deprived of their dignity. As Innocent speaks of Bonosus as no longer living, we may infer that he died at the end of the fourth, or the beginning of the fifth century.

Whether, besides denying Mary's perpetual virginity, Bonosus also denied Christ's divinity cannot be determined with certainty. But it is certain that his followers, the Bonosians, to whom we find references in the councils and in ecclesiastical writers up to the seventh century, denied this dogma. On this point they were at one with the Photinians. As a consequence, they affirmed the purely adoptive divine filiation of Our Lord. However, they differed from the Adoptionists in rejecting all natural sonship, whereas the Adoptionists, distinguishing in Christ the God and the man, attributed to the former a natural, and to the latter an adoptive sonship. The baptism conferred by the Bonosians was by some declared valid and by others invalid.

Besides the collections of JAFFÉ, MANSI, MIGNE, CONSTANT, etc., see HEFELE, *Conciliengeschichte* (2 ed., Freiburg, 1873), II, III, V; WALCH, *Dissertatio de Bonosio hæretico* (Göttingen, 1754); ID., *Entwurf einer vollständigen Historie der Ketzereien, Spaltungen und Religionsstreitigkeiten* (Leipzig, 1762–85), III, 598; TILLEMONT, *Mémoires pour servir à l'histoire ecclésiastique* (Paris, 1701–12), X, 239–243; CEILLER, *Histoire générale des auteurs sacrés* (2 ed. Paris, 1860–1868), IV, 652; VI, 107; VII, 514; LE BACHELET in *Dict. de théol. cath.* II, 1027; VENABLES in *Dict. Christ. Biog.* I, 330.

C. A. DUBRAY.

Bon Secours (DE PARIS), INSTITUTE OF, the first of the congregations of nursing sisters, *gardes malades*, founded in France during the nineteenth century, whose object is to take care of both rich and poor patients in their own homes. This congregation was begun by Archbishop de Quélen of Paris in 1822 and was formally approved by Pope Pius IX in June, 1875. Its members nurse the poor gratuitously. Patients who can afford it pay for such service. The habit of the sisters is black; they wear a white cap with frilled border and a black veil. Besides the sixteen houses of the congregation in France, there are four in Ireland, one in England, two in the United States, and one in Belgium. The mother-house is in Paris. The scope of the institute is expressed in the constitutions: "After the personal sanctification of its members, the principal aim of this pious society is the care of the sick in their own homes". Although these sisters had governmental approbation and complied with the fiscal laws in France they have suffered heavily by the recent religious persecution. Four large schools which had been started in behalf of miners' children and at the urgent request of the mining population of Northern France (Lille, Lens, etc.) were closed on the plea that they formed no part of the institute's approved charter. And with the schools were also suppressed attendance by the sisters on sick or wounded miners and a very interesting work called "*la goutte de lait*", or "the drop of milk," a sort of dispensary wherein the sisters superintended the food of miners' infants.

II. BON SECOURS (DE TROYES), INSTITUTE OF, a congregation founded at Arcis-sur-Aube, France, in 1840, by the Very Reverend Paul-Sébastien Millet, canon of the Cathedral of Troyes. The mother-house was moved to Troyes in 1843 and the name of that place was added to the title of the congregation in order to distinguish it from other sisterhoods whose object is also to nurse the sick in their own homes. The members of this congregation make no distinction because of the creed or financial condition of their patients. The poor are nursed free, those who can afford to make some recompense do so, and the sisters accept what is given them, but are not allowed to beg. The approbation of the constitutions of the congregation was not given by the Holy See until 21 March, 1899. The novices go to the mother-house

in France for three years. Vows are renewed annually for five years, then made for five years, and finally perpetual vows are taken. The habit is black with a small black cape, a black veil, and white guimpe. A crucifix suspended by a purple ribbon is worn round the neck. There are 120 houses of these sisters in various countries, most of them in France, outside of which territory there are 3 in Belgium, 4 in Italy, 1 in Spain, 3 in England, 1 in the United States, and 6 in Africa. The sisters number about 1,000.

STEELE, *The Convents of Great Britain* (St. Louis, 1902); *The Catholic Directory* (Milwaukee, 1907); *Constitutions des Sœurs de Bon Secours* (Paris, 1877); *Coutumier à l'usage des Sœurs de Bon Secours* (Paris, 1881).

THOMAS F. MEEHAN.

Bonvicino, ALESSANDRO (called IL MORETTO, or MORETTO DA BRESCIA), one of the finest North Italian painters of the sixteenth century, b. at Brescia about 1498; d. at the same place, 1555. It is said that he was a pupil of Titian, but it is considered more likely that he was but an earnest student of the works of this great master whose style he imitated so closely that many of his portraits bear well a comparison with those of the noted Venetian. It is known that he studied under his father, also a painter, and under Floriano Ferramola, and that G. Romanino had much influence over him. He himself had as a pupil that superb portrait painter, Giambattista Moroni. Bonvicino's manner is most natural and attractive; his feeling, where necessary, most devotional, his colour remarkable for its freshness and opulence, and his figures sympathetic and graceful. He was in his later life greatly influenced by Raphael. He assisted Ferramola in painting an altar screen for the old cathedral at Brescia and did similar work for Romanino in the church of San Giovanni Evangelista in that city. It was here, also, that he produced his notable painting, the "Massacre of the Innocents".

Among his other church works at Brescia are the "Coronation of the Virgin", and "Christ in Glory", at Santi Nazzaro e Celso; "The Ascension of the Virgin", "Five Virgin Martyrs", and "St. Ursula", in San Clemente; "The Majesty of St. Margaret", in San Francesco; "The Enthronement of St. Anthony of Padua", in Santa Maria delle Grazie; "The Virgin and St. Nicholas", in Santa Maria de Miracoli; and "Christ in the House of Simon", in Santa Maria Calchera. In the Brescia Gallery, among other works, is a "St. Nicholas of Bari"; in Venice at Santa Maria della Pietà is his "Feast in the House of Simon"; in the Uffizi, at Florence, are "The Descent of Christ into Hades", "The Death of Adonis", and a male portrait; at the Brera in Milan, "The Assumption", "Virgin in Glory", "Sts. Clara and Catherine", and "St. Jerome and an Apostle"; at the Ambrosiana in the same city the "Death of Peter Martyr". At the Louvre are "St. Bernardine and St. Louis of Toulouse" and "Sts. Bonaventure and Anthony"; at the National Gallery in London a "Virgin and Child with two Saints", "St. Bernardine of Sienna", and two portraits of Italian noblemen. In the Städel Institute at Frankfort is the "Enthroned Madonna" with four doctors of the Church below, and there are examples in many other European galleries.

FENAROLI, *Alessandro Bonvicino, etc.* (Brescia, 1875); BRYAN, *Dictionary of Painters and Engravers* (London and New York, 1903–05).

AUGUSTUS VAN CLEEF.

Bonze. See BUDDHISM.

Book of Common Discipline. See PURITANS.

Book of Common Prayer.—I. HISTORY.—On 21 January, 1549, the first Act of Uniformity was passed, imposing upon the whole realm of England

"The Book of the Common Prayer and Administration of the Sacraments and other Rites and Ceremonies of the Church after the Use of the Church of England". Before this date (with some recent exceptions) the services had always been conducted in Latin; and though there were various "uses", e. g. Salisbury, Hereford, Bangor, York, and Lincoln, these were all derived from, and for the most part identical with, the Roman liturgy. "Altogether, some eighteen English uses are known. . . . Without exception these English Missals are Roman— they have the Roman Canon to begin with; they have the Roman variables; in short, their structure is identical with that of the Roman Missal" (J. Wickham Legg, 27 February, from a correspondence in "The Guardian", February and March, 1907). Though the motive for the introduction of the new liturgy is stated to be the desire for uniformity, simplicity, and the edification of the people, it is clear that this was merely a pretext. The real motive was the removal from the service books of the doctrines rejected by the Protestant Reformers. *Lex orandi, lex credendi.* The old books clearly contained the Real Presence, the Sacrifice of the Mass, Invocation of the Blessed Virgin and the Saints, Prayer for the Dead, the Seven Sacraments, with Auricular Confession, and a Sacrificing Priesthood. The Act of Uniformity states that the king by the advice of Somerset and the rest of the Council, "appointed the archbishop of Canterbury and certain of the most learned and discreet bishops and other learned men of this realm" to draw up the new book. Who these were, besides Cranmer, cannot now be determined. No list is known earlier than that given in Fuller's "Church History", published in 1657. However, "the history of the Prayerbook down to the end of Edward's reign is the biography of Cranmer, for there can be no doubt that almost every line of it is his composition" (Mason, Thomas Cranmer, 139). With regard to the authority by which it was composed and issued, Abbot Gasquet and Mr. Bishop have carefully gone over the evidence (Edward VI and the Book of Common Prayer, ch. x), and they have come to the same conclusion as the Anglican Canon Dixon, who affirms that "the Convocation of the clergy had nothing to do with the first Act of Uniformity of religion. Laymen made the first English Book of Common Prayer into a schedule of a penal statute. As little in the work itself, which was then imposed upon the realm, had the clergy originally any share" (Hist. of the Ch. of England, III, 5). The instruction given by royal authority was that the framers of the book should "have as well eye and respect to the most sincere and pure Christian religion taught by scripture as to the usages in the primitive Church". How this was carried out will appear when we come to examine the contents of the book. Meantime we may observe that the Communion Service cannot be classed with any of the old liturgies, but rather resembles the form drawn up by Luther in 1523 and 1526. Both agree in the elimination of anything denoting offertory or sacrifice in the true sense of the words. "Even if it were not an ascertained fact that during the year when it was in preparation, Cranmer was under the influence of his Lutheran friends, the testimony of the book itself would be sufficient to prove beyond doubt that it was conceived and drawn up after the Lutheran pattern" (Gasquet and Bishop, op. cit., 228; cf. ch. xiii). Though there were of course some who welcomed the new service, the imposition of it gave rise to strenuous opposition in most parts of the country. By the time, however, that the Book of 1549 appeared, Cranmer had already adopted views more advanced than those contained in it, and was preparing for a further revision. Early in 1550 an act was passed approving of a new ordinal

(see ANGLICAN ORDERS) and the altars were removed and tables substituted for them in many places. In this same year Gardiner, while still a prisoner in the Tower, made use of the words of the Prayer Book to refute Cranmer's own work on the Sacrament of the Body and Blood of our Saviour. About the same time Bucer completed his elaborate "Censura" of the Prayer Book. Accordingly in 1552 a second Book of Common Prayer was published, in which everything in the First Book which had been fixed upon by Gardiner as evidence that the new liturgy did not reject the old beliefs, and everything which Bucer had objected to was in the revision carefully swept away and altered. Before this book could come into general use the old Catholic services were restored by Mary. After her death the Second Book was imposed by Elizabeth in 1559 with some few, though important, changes. Further changes were made in 1604 and again in 1662, but the Prayer Book as a whole practically remains what it was in 1552. "The position which was deliberately abandoned in 1549 and still further departed from in 1552 has never been recovered. The measure of the distance traversed in these new liturgies by those who controlled the English reformation can only be duly estimated on an historical survey of the period in which the ground was lost" (Gasquet and Bishop, op. cit., 307).

II. CONTENTS.—The Book of Common Prayer is really a combination of four of our liturgical books viz., the Breviary, Missal, Pontifical, and Ritual.

(1) *The New Calendar.*—The old Sarum and other calendars in use before the Reformation contained the fast days and the feasts for most of the days in the year. Among these were the Purification, Annunciation, Visitation, Assumption, Nativity, and Conception of "the Blessed Mary"; a large number of purely Roman saints; and All Souls' Day. Corpus Christi was kept on the Thursday after Trinity Sunday. The Calendar of the First Prayer Book omitted the fast days altogether and gave only twenty-two saints' days, all being New Testament saints; the only feasts of the Blessed Virgin retained are the Purification and the Annunciation; All Souls' Day is omitted, and there is no office for Corpus Christi. Hardly any change was made in this part in the Second Prayer Book, though the "dog Daies" are characteristically noted. The Calendar of the Third Prayer Book (1559–61) reintroduced the mention of the fast days and a goodly number of feasts; among the latter, the Visitation of the "Blessed Virgin Mary", the Conception and the Nativity of "the Virgin Mary"; but no special offices were appointed for any of these feasts. "The reason why the names of these Saints-days and Holy-days were resumed into the calendar are various", says Wheatly in "A Rational Illustration of the Book of Comm. Prayer" (Pt. II, Introd.), "some of them being retained upon account of our Courts of Justice. . . . Others are probably kept for the sake of such tradesmen as are wont to celebrate the memory of their tutelar Saints. . . . And again, it has been the custom to have Wakes or Fairs kept upon these days; so that the people would be displeased if their favourite Saint's name should be left out. . . . For these reasons our second reformers under Queen Elizabeth . . . thought convenient to restore the names of them to the Calendar, though not with any regard of being kept holy by the Church".

(2) *The Breviary.*—The Sarum Breviary contained the canonical Hours, the Psalms distributed through the week, antiphons, versicles and responses, and Little Chapters much the same as the modern breviary—of course without the modifications since introduced by St. Pius V and later pontiffs. But

in 1535 there appeared a new breviary drawn up by Cardinal Quignonez, in which a complete break had been made with the old order of the Office. The canonical Hours had indeed been retained, but the antiphons, versicles, responses, and Little Chapters had been omitted, the Psalms were distributed in such a way that three were said at each hour, and the same Psalms said every day of the week in the same order. A striking feature of this breviary was the great length of the Scripture lessons which enabled the priest to read through in the course of the year almost the whole of the Old Testament and the whole of the New Testament, with the Epistles of St. Paul twice over. It was this book which Cranmer had before him when framing the office portion of the First Prayer Book. Indeed he copied word for word in his preface a considerable portion of Quignonez's preface. (See Gasquet and Bishop, op. cit., App. III.) He reduced, however, the Hours to two—Matins and Evensong (called Morning and Evening Prayer in the Second Book)—and arranged the Psalms for recital once a month instead of once a week. He also introduced two Scripture lessons, one from the Old Testament and one from the New Testament at both hours of prayer, and entirely omitted the lessons of the saints. In the Second Book he introduced "When the wicked man", "Dearly beloved brethren, the Scripture moveth us", the general confession ("Almighty and most merciful Father"), and the Absolution ("Almighty God, the Father of our Lord Jesus Christ"), which have remained to the present day. When we remember that more than a hundred editions of Quignonez's breviary were printed during the short space of twenty years, and that it was on the point of being adopted universally, we can see that this portion of the Book of Common Prayer has some justification. No doctrinal questions were at stake—unless it might be the omission of the intercession of the saints.

(3) *The Missal.*—The Canon of the Mass in the Sarum Missal is taken almost word for word from the Roman Missal. In the First Prayer Book the Communion service is styled "The Supper of the Lord and the Holy Communion, commonly called the Mass"; in the Second, and also in the present book, "The Order for the Administration of the Lord's Supper, or the Holy Communion". It is not possible within the limits of the present article to compare in detail the First Book with the Sarum on the one hand, and with the subsequent books on the other. (See Gasquet and Bishop, ch. xii and xvi). The word *altar* is used in the First Book, though with the alternative of "God's board"; in the Second Book and subsequent Books "table" and "board" alone occur. As regards vestments the First Book directs that the priest shall wear "a white alb plain, with a vestment (chasuble?) or cope", and the assisting clergy "albs with tunacles"; the Second Book "the minister at the time of the Communion and all other times in his ministration, shall use neither alb, vestment, nor cope; but being archbishop or bishop, he shall have and wear a rochet, and being a priest or deacon, he shall have and wear a surplice only". In the Third Book (1559) "it is to be noted that such ornaments of the church and of the ministers thereof, at all times of their ministration, shall be retained, and be in use, as were in the Church of England by the authority of Parliament in the second year of the reign of King Edward the Sixth". As is well known, the meaning of this rubric has long been a matter of dispute. The First Book directs the priest to stand "humbly before the midst of the altar"; the Second, to stand "at the north side of the table", as is still the rule. No mention is made of incense, or lights, or holy water in any of the books. As to the service itself,

the changes may be briefly summed up as follows: The First Book omitted all mention of any true sacrifice, but retained expressions capable of referring to the Real Presence; the Second Book excluded these; the Third and subsequent Books re-admitted and combined expressions which might be taken in either sense. "On comparing the first with the second Communion office what is obvious at first sight is, that whilst the former, in spite of the substantial change made in the ancient mass, manifested a general order and disposition of parts similar to the mass itself, the latter was changed beyond recognition" (Gasquet and Bishop, 288). It will be sufficient to note here that while the First retained something like the preparatory prayer of Consecration ("Vouchsafe to bl+ess and sanc+tify these thy gifts, and creatures of bread and wine that they may be unto us the body and blood of thy most dearly beloved Son Jesus Christ"), the Second and subsequent Books omitted this altogether; in the Second Book no directions were given as to the acts of the minister—he might recite the words of Consecration as a mere lesson; but in the later Books he was directed to take the paten and cup into his hands. Most significant, too, are the changes made in the form of administering the Holy Communion. In 1549: "When he delivereth the Sacrament of the Body of Christ, he shall say unto every one these words: 'The body of our Lord Jesus Christ which was given for thee, preserve thy body and soul unto everlasting life'. And the Minister delivering the Sacrament of the Blood . . . shall say 'The blood of our Lord Jesus Christ which was shed for thee, preserve thy body and soul unto everlasting life'". In 1552: "And when he delivereth the bread, he shall say: 'Take and eat this, in remembrance that Christ died for thee, and feed on him in thy heart by faith, with thanksgiving'. And the Minister that delivereth the cup shall say: 'Drink this in remembrance that Christ's blood was shed for thee, and be thankful'". In 1559 and the present Book: "And when he delivereth the Bread to any one he shall say, 'The Body of our Lord Jesus Christ which was given for thee, preserve thy body and soul unto everlasting life. Take and eat this in remembrance that Christ died for thee, and feed on him in thy heart by faith with thanksgiving'. And the Minister that delivereth the cup shall say: 'The Blood of our Lord Jesus Christ, which was shed for thee, preserve thy body and soul unto everlasting life. Drink this in remembrance that Christ's Blood was shed for thee, and be thankful'". The First Book forbade "any elevation or showing the Sacrament to the people"; the Second Book added the so-called "Black Rubric" denying any "real and essential presence of Christ's natural flesh and blood". This was omitted in 1559, but was reintroduced in 1662, shortened and slightly altered, "corporal presence" being substituted for "real and essential".

(4) *The Ritual.*—The order of the administration of Baptism in the old Sarum Manuale (Ritual) was almost identical in words and ceremonies with that now in use among us. (For the differences see SARUM.) The principal changes in 1549 were the omission of the blessing of the font, of the giving of the blessed salt, and of the first anointing. New prayers were also introduced, but the general character of the old service was preserved, including the exorcisms, the giving of the white garment, and the second anointing. All of these met with Bucer's disapproval, and were accordingly removed in 1552, and have never been restored. The present rite is exactly the same as that of 1552, with a few verbal alterations.

As the Reformers did not recognize Confirmation as a sacrament, we are not surprised to find that the rite of administering it has undergone great changes. In 1549 the anointing with chrism was omitted, but the prayer that the Holy Ghost might come down upon those about to be confirmed was retained, and they were signed with the sign of the cross on their forehead. In 1552, owing again to Bucer's influence, the first prayer was altered ("strengthen them . . . with the Holy Ghost"); the signing with the cross was omitted; and a colourless form of words used. This latter rite is still in use; but in 1662 the renewal of baptismal vows was prefixed to it.

The "Form of Solemnization of Matrimony" comes next. As the essential part of the ceremony is the contracting of the parties, considerable latitude has existed in the Church with regard to the rest of the service. The First Book followed the old rite rather closely, but the blessing of the ring and the nuptial Mass were omitted. Of course the Reformers looked upon matrimony merely as a "state of life allowed in the Scriptures", and not as a sacrament.

"The Order of the Visitation of the Sick" contains matters of grave importance. In the First Book and in all subsequent Books, the "sick person shall make a special confession, if he feels his conscience troubled with any weighty matter; after which the priest shall absolve him after this form [sort]. . . . 'I absolve thee from thy sins'". The First Book alone adds: "and the same form of absolution shall be used in all private confessions. Moreover the First Book alone contains the anointing of the sick: "If the sick person desire to be anointed, then shall the priest anoint him upon the forehead or breast only, making the sign of the cross", and afterwards reciting a long prayer entirely different from the old forms, which were the same as the present Catholic ones. This ceremony was removed at Bucer's suggestion. The First Book also has a rubric about reservation of the Blessed Sacrament: "If there be more sick persons to be visited the same day . . . then shall the curate reserve so much of the sacrament of the body and blood as shall serve the other sick persons, and such as be appointed to communicate with them if there be any; and shall immediately carry it and minister it unto them." Bucer does not seem to have objected to this; nevertheless no mention of reservation is made in any of the later Books.

The Sarum Office of the Dead included Vespers (*Placebo*), Matins (*Dirige*), Lauds, Mass (*Requiem*), the Absolution, and the Burial. As might be expected from the views of the Reformers on prayer for the dead, nothing was preserved in the new Books but the "Order for the Burial of the Dead". The First Book, indeed, contains distinct prayers for the soul of the departed, but these were removed in 1552, and have never been restored. For the Catechism and the Thirty-nine Articles see the respective articles.

In recent years attempts have been made to reform the Prayer Book in two opposite directions. The Evangelicals have considered it as still containing too much of the old "popery"; while the High Church party have endeavoured to get back the portions omitted or altered since 1549. Various changes have actually been made in the Prayer Book as used by the Protestant Churches of Scotland, Ireland, and America.

It is only fair, in concluding, to note Cranmer's "splendid command of the English language and his instinctive sense of what would suit average English minds. His genius for devotional composition in English is universally recognized, even by those who have least sympathy with his character and career" (Mason, Thomas Cranmer, 140). "I value the Prayer Book, as you cannot do", says one of the Anglican characters in Newman's "Loss and Gain" (ch. viii), "for I have known what it is to one in affliction. May it be long before you know it in a similar way; but if affliction comes on you, depend on it all these new fancies and fashions will vanish from you like the wind, and the good old Prayer Book alone will stand you in any stead."

The best work on the subject is GASQUET AND BISHOP, *Edward VI and the Book of Common Prayer;* FRERE, *Revision of Procter's Book of Common Prayer;* WESTON, *The Prayer Book in the Making* (1907), a poor and prejudiced work; WHEATLY, *A Rational Illustration of the Book of Comm. Pr.*, being the substance of everything liturgical in Bishop Sparrow, MR. L'ESTRANGE, DR. COMBER DR. NICHOLS, and all former ritualists, commentators, and others upon the same subject; MASON, *Thomas Cranmer;* and various other works treating of the Reformation in England, especially in the reign of Edward VI.   T. B. SCANNELL.

Book of Enoch. See APOCRYPHA.

Book of Jubilees. See APOCRYPHA.

Book of Life. See PREDESTINATION.

Book of Martyrs, FOXE'S.—John Foxe was born at Boston in Lincolnshire, England, in 1516, and was educated at Magdalen School and College, Oxford. He joined the more extreme Reformers early in life and under Edward VI acted as tutor to the children of the recently beheaded Earl of Surrey. In Mary's reign he fled to Germany and joined the exiles at Frankfort. In the controversy which arose there he took sides with Knox and the extremists and after the break up of the Frankfort colony he went to Basle where poverty compelled him to take service with the Protestant printer Oporinus. In 1559 he returned to England and entered the ministry; he was helped by his old pupil the Duke of Norfolk and was mainly occupied with his martyrology. He still belonged to the extremists and objected to the surplice. His opinions interfered with his prospects, but he was not an ambitious man. Though violent and dishonest in controversy, he was personally of a kind and charitable temper. Besides his "Acts and Monuments" he published a number of sermons, translations, and controversial attacks on Catholicism. He died in 1587.

Even before leaving England in 1554 Foxe had begun the story of the persecutions of the Reformers. The result was the publication of a little Latin work dealing mainly with Wyclifism. While at Basle he was supplied by Grindal with reports of the persecution in England and in 1559 he published a large Latin folio of 740 pages which began with Wyclif and ended with Cranmer. After his return to England he began to translate this book and to add to it the results of fresh information. The "Acts and Monuments" were finally published in 1563 but came almost immediately to be known as the "Book of Martyrs". The criticism which the work called forth led to the publication of a "corrected" edition in 1570. Two more (1576 and 1583) came out during his life and five (1596, 1610, 1632, 1641, 1684) within the next hundred years. There have been two modern editions, both unsatisfactory; they are in eight volumes and were published in 1837–41 and 1877. The size of the work may be gathered from the fact that in the edition of 1684 it consists of three folio volumes of 895, 682, and 863 pages respectively. Each page has two columns and over eighty lines. The first volume besides introductory matter contains the story of early Christian persecutions, a sketch of medieval church history and an account of the Wyclifite movement in England and on the continent. The second volume deals with the reigns of Henry VIII and Edward VI and the third with that of Mary. A large number of official documents such as injunctions, articles of accusation, letters, etc., have been included. The book is illustrated throughout by woodcuts, some of them symbolizing the triumph of the Reformation, most of them depicting the sufferings of the martyrs.

The convocation of the English Church ordered in 1571 that copies of the "Book of Martyrs" should be kept for public inspection in all cathedrals and in the houses of church dignitaries. The book was also exposed in many parish churches. The passionate intensity of the style, the vivid and picturesque dialogues made it very popular among Puritan and Low Church families down to the nineteenth century. Even the fantastically partisan church history of the earlier portion of the book, with its grotesque stories of popes and monks and its motley succession of witnesses to the truth (including the Albigenses, Grosseteste, Dante, and Savonarola) was accepted amongst simple folk and must have contributed much to anti-Catholic prejudices in England. When Foxe treats of his own times his work is of greater value as it contains many documents and is largely based on the reports of eyewitnesses; but he sometimes dishonestly mutilates his documents and is quite untrustworthy in his treatment of evidence. He was criticized in his own day by Catholics such as Harpsfield and Father Parsons and by practically all serious ecclesiastical historians.

The most careful examination of his methods is to be found in MAITLAND, *Essays on the Reformation in England* (1849), and in GAIRDNER, *History of the English Church from the ascension of Henry VIII to the Death of Mary* (1903); LEE in *Dict. of Nat. Biog.* GERARD, *John Foxe and His Book of Martyrs* (Catholic Truth Society, London), includes the opinions of a number of Foxe's critics.

F. F. URQUHART.

Book of Middle Ages. See EDUCATION IN THE MIDDLE AGES.

Book of Sentences. See LOMBARD, PETER.

Book of the Dead. See IMMORTALITY; EGYPT.

Books, CARLOVINGIAN. See CARLOVINGIAN BOOKS.

Books, LITURGICAL. See LITURGICAL BOOKS.

Books, SIBYLLINE. See SIBYLLINE BOOKS.

Bordeaux (BURDIGALA), ARCHDIOCESE OF, comprises the entire department of the Gironde and was established conformably to the Concordat of 1802 by combining the ancient Diocese of Bordeaux (diminished by the cession of Born to the Bishopric of Aire) with the greater part of the suppressed Diocese of Bazas. Constituted by the same Concordat metropolitan to the Bishoprics of Angoulême, Poitiers, and La Rochelle, the See of Bordeaux received in 1822, as additional suffragans, those of Agen, withdrawn from the metropolitan jurisdiction of Toulouse, and the newly re-established Périgueux and Luçon; and still later, in 1850, the three colonial Bishoprics of Fort-de-France (Martinique), Basse-Terre (Guadeloupe), and Saint-Denis (Réunion).

The Old Diocese of Bordeaux.—According to old Limousin legends which date back to the beginning of the eleventh century, Bordeaux was evangelized in the first century by St. Martial (Martialis), who replaced a temple to the unknown god, which he destroyed, with one dedicated to St. Stephen. The same legends represent St. Martial as having brought to the Soulac coast St. Veronica, who is still especially venerated in the church of Notre-Dame de Fin des Terres at Soulac; as having cured Sigebert, the paralytic husband of the pious Benedicta, and made him Bishop of Bordeaux; as addressing beautiful Latin letters to the people of Bordeaux, to which city he is said to have left the pastoral staff which has been treasured as a relic by the Chapter of Saint-Seurin (For this cycle of legends see LIMOGES).

The first Bishop of Bordeaux known to history, Orientalis, is mentioned at the Council of Arles, in 314. By the close of the fourth century Christianity had made such progress in Bordeaux that a synod was held there (385–386) for the purpose of adopting measures against the Priscillianists, whose heresy had

caused popular disturbances. This was during the episcopate of Delphinus (380–404), who attended the Council of Saragossa in 380 and maintained correspondence with St. Ambrose and with St. Paulinus of Nola. At the beginning of the fifth century a mysterious personage who, according to St. Gregory of Tours, came from the East, appeared at Bordeaux. This was St. Seurin (or Severinus), in whose favour Bishop Amand abdicated the see from 410 to 420, resuming it after Seurin's death and occupying it until 432. In the sixth century Bordeaux had an illustrious bishop in the person of Leontius II (542–564), a man of great influence who used his wealth in building churches and clearing lands and whom the poet Fortunatus calls *patriæ caput*. During this Merovingian period the cathedral church, founded in the fourth century, occupied the same site that it does to-day, back to back against the ramparts of the ancient city. The Faubourg Saint-Seurin outside the city was a great centre of popular devotion, with its three large basilicas of St. Stephen, St. Seurin, and St. Martin surrounding a large necropolis from which a certain number of sarcophagi are still preserved. This faubourg was like a holy city; and the cemetery of St. Seurin was full of tombs of the Merovingian period around which the popular imagination of later ages was to create legends. In the high noon of the Middle Ages it used to be told how Christ Himself had consecrated this cemetery and that Charlemagne, having fought the Saracens near Bordeaux, had visited it and laid Roland's wonderful horn Olivant on the altar of Saint-Seurin.

Dessus l'autel de Saint Seurin le baron,
Il met l'oliphant plein d'or et de mangons

—says the "Chanson de Roland". Many tombs passed for those of Charlemagne's gallant knights, and others were honoured as the resting-places of Veronica and Benedicta. At the other extremity of the city, the Benedictines filled in the marshes of l'Eau-Bourde and founded there the monastery of Sainte-Croix. While thus surrounded by evidences of Christian conquest, the academic Bordeaux of the Merovingian period continued to cherish the memory of its former school of eloquence, whose chief glories had been the poet Ausonius (310–395) and St. Paulinus (353–431), who had been a rhetorician at Bordeaux and died Bishop of Nola. The reigns of William VIII and William IX, Dukes of Aquitaine (1052–1127), were noted for the splendid development of Romanesque architecture in Bordeaux. Parts of the churches of Sainte-Croix and Saint-Seurin belong to that time, and the Cathedral of Saint-André was begun in 1096.

In the Middle Ages, a struggle between the Sees of Bordeaux and Bourges was brought about by the claims of the latter to the primacy of Aquitaine. This question has been closely investigated by modern scholars, and it has been ascertained that a certain letter from Nicholas I to Rodolfus, which would date the existence of the primacy of Bourges from the ninth century, is not authentic. As the capital of *Aquitania prima*, Bourges at an early date vaguely aspired to pre-eminence over the provinces of *Aquitania secunda* and *tertia*, and thence over Bordeaux. It was about 1073 that these aspirations were more formally asserted; between 1112 and 1126 the papacy acknowledged them, and in 1146 Eugenius III confirmed the primacy of Pierre de la Châtre, Archbishop of Bourges, over Bordeaux. In 1232, Gregory IX gave the Archbishop of Bourges, as patriarch, the right to visit the province of Aquitaine, imposed upon the Archbishop of Bordeaux the duty of assisting, at least once, at the councils held by his "brother" of Bourges, and decided that appeals might be made from the former to the latter. Occasionally, however, as in 1240 and 1284, the

Archbishops of Bourges, coming to Bordeaux, found the doors of the churches closed against them, and answered with excommunication the solemn protests which the Bordeaux clergy made against their visits. Aquitaine was lost to France by the annulment of that marriage between Louis VII and Eleanor of Aquitaine which was celebrated in the Cathedral of Bordeaux in the year 1137, and Bordeaux became the capital of the English possessions in France. Thereupon the struggle between the Sees of Bordeaux and Bourges assumed a political character, the King of France necessarily upholding the claims of Bourges. Most of the archbishops were conspicuous as agents of English policy in Aquitaine, notable amongst them being Guillaume Amanieu (1207–26), on whom King Henry III of England conferred the title of seneschal and guardian of all his lands beyond the sea, and who took part in Spain in the wars against the Saracens; Gérard de Mallemort (1227–60), a generous founder of monasteries, who acted as mediator between St. Louis and Henry III, and defended Gascony against the tyranny of Simon de Montfort, Earl of Leicester. During the episcopate of Gérard de Mallemort the old Romanesque church of Saint-André was transformed into a Gothic cathedral. Pope Clement V (1305–14) was unfavourable to the claims of Bourges. He was a native of Villandraut near Bazas, where he had built a beautiful collegiate church, was Archbishop of Bordeaux from 1300 to 1305, and political adviser to Philip the Fair. When he became pope, in spite of his French sympathies, his heart was set upon the formal emancipation of Bordeaux from Bourges. Blessed Pierre Berland, or Peyberland as tradition calls him (1430–57), was an Archbishop of Bordeaux, illustrious for his intelligence and holiness, founder of the University of Bordeaux and of the College of St. Raphael for poor students, who, after helping the English to defend Bordeaux against the troops of Charles VII, received Dunois into his episcopal city and surrendered it to France. It was during his episcopate that the beautiful campanile known as the Pey Berland Tower was added to the cathedral.

The rich and powerful chapters of Saint-André and Saint-Seurin subsisted in the Middle Ages as a vestige of that duality which was already noticeable in Merovingian Bordeaux. Between the two there were frequent and very animated conflicts. The artistic feeling of the canons in the thirteenth century is attested by the Gothic portal of Saint-Seurin which is still extant. At the end of the fourteenth century Canon Vital de Carle established the great Hospital of Saint-André, which he placed under the protection of the municipality; and it was through the exertions of the chapter of Saint-André that the first city library of Bordeaux was founded, towards the year 1402. During the Middle Ages Bordeaux was a great monastic city, with its Carmelite, Franciscan, and Dominican convents, founded respectively in 1217, 1227, and 1230. In 1214 an important council was held in Bordeaux against usurers, highwaymen, and heretics. When, after the Hundred Years' War, Bordeaux again became French, Louis XI flattered its citizens by joining the confraternity of Notre-Dame de Montuzet, a religious association formed of all the mariners of the Gironde, by heaping favours on the church of Saint-Michel, the tower of which, built in the period between 1473 and 1492, was higher than the Pey Berland, and by furthering the canonization of its former archbishop, Pierre Berland.

Among the Archbishops of Bordeaux, in the modern epoch, may be mentioned: Charles de Gramont (1530–44), who during its earliest years helped the College of Guyenne (founded in 1533) and introduced into Bordeaux the art of the Renaissance; François de Sourdis (1599–1628), who had great political influence during the minority of Louis XIII, caused the marshes in the neighbourhood of Bordeaux to be filled in, erected there a magnificent Carthusian monastery, welcomed to Bordeaux many congregations devoted to ecclesiastical reform, approved (1606) the teaching order of the Filles de Notre-Dame, founded by Blessed Jeanne de Lestonnac, and befriended the College of the Madeleine founded by the Jesuits in opposition to the College of Guyenne which, during the sixteenth century, was open to Protestant influences; Cardinal de Cheverus (1826–36), who during the cholera epidemic had the sign *Maison de Secours* (House of Refuge) put over his palace, of whom M. Jullian said that no prelate in the history of the diocese had come nearer the ideal of sanctity, and during whose episcopate Thérèse de Lamourus, the "Good Mother", considered by Cardinal Cheverus a saint worthy of the early days of the Church, opened for repentant women the Maison de la Miséricorde; Cardinal Donnet (1837–82), who re-established the old provincial councils interrupted for 224 years.

The Old Bishopric of Bazas.—According to Gregory of Tours, Bazas had a bishop at the time of the Vandal invasion in the fifth century. The dedication of the cathedral to St. John the Baptist is explained in an account given by the same historian, that a lady of Bazas, whom certain hagiographers of the nineteenth century believe to have been St. Veronica, brought from Palestine a relic of St. John the Baptist at the time of that saint's death. For two hundred and fifty years prior to 1057, the Bishop of Bazas bore the title of Bishop of Aire, Dax, Bayonne, Oloron, and Lescar. Urban II (1088–99) preached the crusade at Bazas.

Places of Ecclesiastical Interest in the Archdiocese.— The town of La Réole (from *Regula*, rule) owes its origin, and even its name, to a Benedictine monastery founded in 777, destroyed by the Northmen, and rebuilt in 977 by Sancho of Gascony and his brother, Bishop Gombald. It was there that Abbo, Abbot of Fleury, who came to reform the monastery in 1004, was assassinated. The town of Saint-Émilion is likewise indebted for its origin to the hermit of that name, a native of Vannes, who died in 767 after having founded in these parts an abbey which the Augustinians occupied after the year 1110. The Abbey of Saint-Romain at Blaye in which, it is said, the remains of Roland, nephew of Charlemagne, were once preserved, was founded on the spot where, in the fourth century, St. Romanus, the recluse, died in the arms of St. Martin. The Benedictine monastery of the Grande Sauve entre Deux Mers was founded in 1080 by St. Gerard of Corbie. The Abbey of Notre Dame at Guitres had for abbot, between 1624 and 1637, Peiresc the celebrated numismatist, one of the greatest scholars of the seventeenth century (1580–1637).

The most important pilgrimage is that of Notre Dame of Verdelais, founded in 1390 by Isabella, Countess of Foix, when her mule stumbled over a buried statue of the Blessed Virgin.

Statistics.—In 1900 the religious orders for men were represented in the Archdiocese of Bordeaux as follows: Augustinians, Jesuits, Franciscans, Lazarists, Carmelites, and Fathers of the Holy Ghost at Bordeaux; Olivetans at Soulac; Dominicans at Arcachon; Redemptorists at Coutras; Marists at Notre Dame de Verdelais and several houses of Marianists. In 1900 the congregations for women peculiar to the diocese were, in addition to those mentioned above: Sisters of Charity of the Holy Agony, a teaching and nursing order founded in 1849, with the mother-house at Bordeaux; Sisters of the Christian Doctrine, founded in 1814, with the mother-house at Bordeaux; Sisters of the Holy Family, founded in 1820 by the Abbé Noailles. The last-named congregation has 200 houses, in different parts of the world. It includes the: Sisters of St. Joseph, who have charge of asylums for orphans and working women; Sisters of the Immaculate Conception and Ladies of the Immaculate Conception, who conduct boarding-schools; Agricultural Sisters (Sœurs Agricoles); Sisters of Hope, attendants on the sick; Contemplative Sisters (Sœurs Solitaires); Sisters of St. Martha, for domestic service. In 1899, the following charitable and educational institutions were to be found in the Archdiocese of Bordeaux: 1 foundling hospital, 11 infant asylums, 66 infant schools, 2 children's infirmaries, 2 deaf-mute institutes for girls, 2 orphanages where farming is taught, 1 boys' and girls' orphanage, 34 girls' orphanages, 1 servants' guild, 2 guilds for penitent women, 10 charity kitchens, 12 hospitals or hospices, 8 communities for the care of the sick in their homes, 8 houses of retreat, 3 homes for incurables, 2 insane asylums, and 7 homes for the aged, all conducted by sisters; and 1 institute for deaf, dumb, and blind boys, and 1 orphanage where farming is taught, both conducted by brothers. At the close of the year 1905 the archdiocese contained 823,131 inhabitants, 79 parishes, 431 mission churches, and 70 curacies.

Gallia Christiana (nova), (1715) I, 1189–1222, *instrumenta*, 188–190; *nova* (1720), II, 785–858; *instrumenta*, 261–326; Fisquet, *France pontificale* (Bordeaux, 1868); Cirot de la Ville, *Origines chrétiennes de Bordeaux, ou histoire et description de l'église de Saint-Seurin* (Bordeaux, 1867); Jullian, *Histoire de Bordeaux depuis les origines jusqu'en 1895* (Bordeaux, 1895); Leroux, *La primatie de Bourges* in *Annales du Midi*, VII, 1895; Pariset, *L'établissement de la primatie de Bourges* in *Annales du Midi*, XIV, 1902; Duchesne, *Fastes Épiscopaux*, II, 9–20. 58–62 and 101; Chevalier, *Rép. des sources hist.-topobibl.*, 332 and 448–450.

GEORGES GOYAU.

Bordeaux, University of, was founded during the English domination, under King Henry VI, in 1441, by a Bull of Pope Eugenius IV, at the demand of the archbishop's officials, Pierre Berland being at the time archbishop, and of the Aquitanian councillors. It did not, however, receive official recognition from the king until the reign of Louis XI. According to the terms of the Bull, it was to be organized on the model of the *studium* of the University of Toulouse. The Archbishop of Bordeaux was the chancellor for life. It included all the different faculties: theology, canon law, civil law, arts, etc. On account of the constant lack of endowment, the University of Bordeaux, from the time of its foundation until the French Revolution, never had any remarkable standing. After the Revolution, when the universities were reorganized in France by the Government, Bordeaux was one of the cities chosen to be the seat of a university. During the nineteenth century it had a brilliant career, especially in the field of medicine, among its professors being such men as Azam, Pitres, and others who were famous on account of their pathological researches.

Barckhausen, *Statuts et règlements de l'ancienne université de Bordeaux* (Libourne and Bordeaux, 1886); Gaullieur, *Histoire du collège de Guyenne* (Paris, 1874); Denifle, *Universit. des Mittelalters* (1885); Fournier, *Les statuts et privilèges des universités françaises depuis leur fondation jusqu'en 1789* (Paris, 1890–92); *Histoire de la science du droit en France* (Paris, 1892); Rashdall, *Universities of Europe in the Middle Ages* (Oxford, 1895), II, pt. I.

G. M. SAUVAGE.

Bordone, Cavaliere Paris, an eminent painter of the Venetian school, b. at Treviso, 1500; d. at Venice, 1570. A member of a noble family, he early showed an inclination for art and, after being given a good general education, was placed in the school of Titian with whom he studied for several years. He afterwards had Giorgione for his master. While feeling strongly the influence of both great painters, Bordone finally settled down to the style of Titian, whose manner he so successfully imitated

that his works have sometimes been mistaken for Titian's. In portraiture he was most successful, ceding to none but to Titian in excellence. In his early career he painted at Venice, Vicenza, and Treviso. At the last place his most important work was in the church of San Vicenzo, where he painted in the six compartments of the dome "The Annunciation", "The Nativity", "The Adoration of the Shepherds", "The Crucifixion", "The Ascension", and "The Assumption of the Virgin". Bordone was invited to visit France, some say by Francis I, and others by Francis II, by whom he was knighted. He remained, according to the latter authority, after the death of that king, for several years at the court of Charles IX, before returning to Italy. He painted the portraits of the royal family and the principal figures of their courts, working notably for the Duke of Guise and the Cardinal de Lorraine.

The most famous work of Bordone is the large painting in the Academy at Venice, representing with great brilliancy of colour and effect "The Fisherman Presenting the Ring of St. Mark to the Doge". On his return to Venice from France, Bordone stopped at Augsburg, where he did some work in the Fugger Palace, and at Milan, where he painted in the chapel of St. Jerome. Among the principal works of Bordone in European galleries are: Louvre, "Vertumna and Pomona", "Portrait of a Man", and "Portraits (presumed) of Philip II, King of Spain, and his Preceptor"; National Gallery, London, "Daphnis and Chloe", and "Portrait of a Genoese Lady"; Berlin Museum, "Madonna and Saints", "The Chess Players", and "Man in Black"; Dresden Gallery, "Holy Family with St. Jerome and St. Elizabeth", and "Diana, Apollo and Marsyas"; Munich, Old Pinakotek, "Portrait of a Man", and "Man Counting Jewels"; Vienna Gallery, seven works including "Venus and Adonis in an Arbour", and "A Young Lady at her Toilet"; St. Petersburg Hermitage, "Madonna and Saints"; Brera, Milan, "Baptism of Christ"; Venice, Academy, "Presenting the Ring", and "The Tiburtine Sibyl"; Rome, Colonna Palace, "Holy Family"; Doria Palace, "Mars and Venus"; Padua Gallery, "Christ Taking Leave of His Mother"; Lovere, Tadini Collection, "Madonna and Two Saints"; Genoa, Brignole Palace, two portraits.

Bryan, *Dictionary of Painters and Engravers* (London, and New York, 1903–05).

AUGUSTUS VAN CLEEF.

Borgess, Caspar Henry, third Bishop of Detroit, Michigan, U. S. A., b. at Kloppenburg, Hanover, Germany, 1 August, 1824; d. at Kalamazoo, Michigan, 3 May, 1890. He emigrated to the United States in boyhood and made his classical and theological studies at St. Xavier's College, Cincinnati, and at St. Charles's Seminary, Philadelphia. He was ordained priest at Cincinnati, 8 December, 1847, after which he was stationed for ten years at Columbus.

In 1859 he was made rector of St. Peter's Cathedral, Cincinnati, and remained there until he was consecrated titular Bishop of Calydon and administrator of Detroit, 24 April, 1870. The first Bishop of Detroit, the Right Rev. Frederick Rese, consecrated 6 October, 1833, the first German in the United States to be raised to the episcopal dignity, became demented four years after his consecration and was called to Rome. He never resigned his charge and lived until 30 December, 1871, when he died in an institution at Hildesheim, Germany. As a consequence, Detroit was ruled by an administrator for thirty years, Bishop Borgess assuming the title only in 1871. The see up to his appointment had been dominated by Belgian and French influences, and he gradually made the changes to the English speaking regime that the growth of the new population

THE FISHERMEN PRESENTING THE RING OF ST. MARK TO THE DOGE BARTOLOMMEO
GRADENIGO. (BORDONE'S MASTERPIECE—ACADEMY, VENICE)

demanded. The Jesuits were introduced into the diocese by him. He resigned the see 16 April, 1888, and spent his last days in retirement, having received the titular see of Phacusites.

REUSS, *Biog. Encycl. of the Cath. Hierarchy of the U. S.* (Milwaukee, 1898); *The Michigan Catholic* (Detroit) contemporaneous files.

THOMAS F. MEEHAN.

Borgia, SAINT FRANCIS. See FRANCIS BORGIA, ST.

Borgia, CÆSAR. See ALEXANDER VI.

Borgia, LUCREZIA. See ALEXANDER VI.

Borgia, STEFANO, Cardinal, b. at Velletri, 3 December, 1731; d. at Lyons, 1804; Italian theologian, antiquarian, and historian. He belonged to a well-known family of Velletri, not to be confounded with the Spanish Borgias or Borjas. His early education was controlled by his uncle Alessandro (1682–1764), Archbishop of Fermo. From his youth, Stefano Borgia manifested a great aptitude for historical research, but his dominant trait was his extraordinary taste for relics of ancient civilizations, a line in which he succeeded so well that, at the age of nineteen, he was received into the Academy of Cortona. He founded a museum at Velletri, in which, during his whole life, he gathered coins and manuscripts, especially Coptic, and which may be considered as his greatest undertaking and achievement. Such was his passion for antiquities that he is known to have sold his jewels and precious earthenware in order to secure the coveted treasures and have the description of them printed. In his scientific career Borgia showed great disinterestedness, placing his collection at the disposal of learned men, regardless of creed and country, and giving them all possible encouragement and support. His amiable temperament and broad-minded character attracted to him all those with whom he came in contact; Paolino da S. Bartolomeo, Adler, Zoega, Heeren, and many others were among his enthusiastic friends.

Borgia was not left, however, entirely to his chosen field of activity, but was called to fill several important political positions. Benedict XIV appointed him Governor of Benevento, and Borgia showed there great administrative talent. In 1770 he was made secretary of the Congregation de Propaganda Fide, an office of which he naturally took advantage to acquire antiquities by the help of the missionaries, a help, be it said to their credit, which proved always forthcoming. He was made a cardinal in 1789. In the troubled period of the French invasion Borgia was given charge of Rome by Pius VI (1797–98). After the proclamation of the Republic, he was arrested (1798), but quickly released, whereupon he immediately resumed his studies and work of collecting; soon afterwards he joined Pius VI at Valencia, and endeavoured to have this pontiff send to Asia and Africa a body of missionaries who would preach the Gospel and gather various monuments.

Cardinal Borgia was of the greatest service to Pope Pius VII in the reorganization of the Pontifical States. In 1801 he was made Rector of the Collegium Romanum, and he was in the retinue of Pius VII when this pontiff went to France to crown the new emperor, Napoleon. Having arrived at Lyons, Cardinal Borgia was taken ill and died. After his death his collection of Coptic MSS. was divided: the non-Biblical MSS. were taken to Naples and placed in the Biblioteca Borbonica, now the Biblioteca Nazionale; and the Biblical MSS., excepting a few which were taken to Naples by mistake, given to the Propaganda, together with the collection of coins and monuments, forming the Museo Borgiano. (Cf. Ciasca, Fragmenta Copto-Sahidica, I, p. xvii.) Only a few years ago the MSS. of the Museo Borgiano were transferred to the Vatican library, where they are to be found to-day. Before the partition of the MSS. was made the eminent scholar and convert, Zoega, wrote a complete and accurate description of them in his posthumous work "Catalogus Codicum Copticorum manu scriptorum qui in Museo Borgiano Velitris adservantur" (Rome, 1810). Besides the many services which Cardinal Borgia rendered to science and scientists, he published several works bearing especially on historical topics: "Monumento di papa Giovanni XVI" (Rome, 1750); "Breve istoria dell' antica città di Tadino" (ibid., 1751); "Memorie storiche della città di Benevento" (ibid., 1763–69); "Vaticana confessio B. Petri chronologicis testimoniis illustrata" (ibid., 1776); "De Cruce Vaticanâ" (ibid., 1779); "De Cruce Veliternâ" (ibid., 1780); "Istoria del dominio temporale della Sede Apostolica nelle Due-Sicilie" (ibid., 1788).

PAOLINO DA S. BARTOLOMEO, *Vitæ Synopsis Steph. Borgiæ* (Rome, 1805); CANCELLIERI, *Elogio del Card. Stefano Borgia* (Rome, 1806).

R. BUTIN.

Borgianus Codex. See MSS. OF THE BIBLE.

Borgognone, AMBROGIO, real name AMBROGIO STEFANI DA FOSSANO, a distinguished Italian painter and architect, b. Milan, c. 1455; d. at Milan, 1523. The name Borgognone is variously accounted for. By some authorities it is attributed to some Flemish characteristics in his art, and by others to the fact that some of his ancestors had lived in Flanders, then known to the Italians as Borgogna. It is supposed that he studied with Vincenzo Foppa, with Zenale, and with Buttinone, but there is little known of the details of his career. The earliest work credited to him is the façade of the Carthusian convent or Certosa near Pavia. The stalls and other woodwork in the choir were carved from the designs of Borgognone, who painted there, among other works, an altar piece of the Crucifixion. Great refinement and deep religious feeling mark his work, which is likewise

THE MADONNA ENTHRONED

notable for its beautiful celestial and mundane types. On his return to Milan he went to work in the church of San Satiro, and his productions appeared, among other churches, at Sant' Ambrogio, San Simpliciano, and Sant' Agostino. At San Simpliciano he painted scenes, since lost, from the story of St. Sisinius. He worked also at Lodi in the church of the Incoronata and did an altar piece for San Satiro at Bergamo.

Borgognone painted in tempera and also in oil in the style of tempera and in fresco. His early work lacked freedom, but later he fell under the beneficent influence of Leonardo da Vinci. Among his works in public galleries are: National Gallery, London, "Marriage of St. Catherine of Alexandria"; a triptych with a "Virgin and Child Enthroned", having at one side the "Agony in the Garden", and on the other "Christ Bearing His Cross", and two groups of family portraits; Louvre, "Presentation in the Temple", and "St. Peter of Verona", with a kneeling woman; Berlin Museum, "Madonna Enthroned", and "Madonna with Saints"; Munich, Old Pinakotek, "Madonna in Adoration"; Dresden Gallery, "Madonna in Adoration"; Brera Gallery, Milan, "The Assumption of the Virgin"; and Pavia Academy, "Christ Bearing His Cross, followed by Carthusians". In the Casa Borromeo at Milan is a portrait of Bishop Andrea Novelli. The Pavia picture is considered without an equal in art in simple pathos and deep religious meaning. Lanzi and other authors have treated Ambrogio da Fossano, the architect, and Ambrogio Borgognone, the painter, as two different persons, but the signatures he left show that this was not the case.

BRYAN, *Dictionary of Painters and Engravers* (London, and New York, 1903–05).

AUGUSTUS VAN CLEEF.

Borgo San-Donnino, DIOCESE OF, in the province of Parma, Italy. The city takes its name from St. Domninus, who fled to that place during the persecution of Maximian (286–305) and suffered martyrdom. It did not become an episcopal see until 1601, under Clement VIII, having until then been governed ecclesiastically by a provost with full faculties, subject directly to the Holy See. The last provost, Papiro Picedi da Castel Vezzano, was the first Bishop of Borgo San-Donnino. The cathedral, dating from the twelfth century, is a beautiful monument of Romanesque architecture; its façade, however, is still unfinished. Among the notable occupants of this see have been: Alfonso Pozzi (1620), a learned and zealous man; Ranuccio Scoti (1626), several times papal nuncio under Urban VIII, particularly to Switzerland; Filippo Casoni (1650), who urged Ughelli to write his "Italia Sacra"; Alessandro Parravicini, a Benedictine (1660); Gaetano Garimberti (1675), who enlarged the episcopal residence and enriched the cathedral with gifts of sacred vessels and furnishings; Alessandro Roncovieri (1700), distinguished for his zeal and charity; Gerardo Giandemaria (1719), who held a diocesan synod the wise decrees of which are still in force; Girolamo Baiardi (1753), who restored the episcopal residence and founded a hospital; Alessandro Garimberti (1776) who was distinguished for his prudent conduct during the French invasion, and who left his library to the seminary. This diocese has a population of 60,400, with 54 parishes, 76 churches and chapels, 100 secular priests, 10 regulars, and 70 seminarians.

BATTANDIER, *Ann. pont. cath.* (Paris, 1907).

U. BENIGNI.

Borgo San-Sepolcro, DIOCESE OF, situated in the province of Arezzo, Tuscany, Italy. The city is believed by some to be the ancient Biturgia mentioned by Ptolemy, and is so designated in the usage of the Roman Curia. The foundation of the present city is attributed to two pilgrims of the tenth century, who halted in this neighbourhood on their return from Palestine, and built an oratory in which they placed the relics they had brought from the holy places. This oratory attracted many pilgrimages; gradually there grew up about it a settlement of considerable size known as Borgo San-Sepolcro. Later on, Camaldoli monks erected a monastery there, the abbot of which had temporal jurisdiction over the town. Guido Petramala, Bishop of Arezzo, fortified Borgo San-Sepolcro, and made it a Ghibelline stronghold. At first subject to the Diocese of Castello, it was made an episcopal see by Leo X in 1515, the first bishop being Giovanni Ev. Galeotto Graziani. Among

the bishops worthy of record are Nicolò Tornabuoni (1560), a learned theologian, author of a treatise on the controversies between Catholics and Calvinists; Dionisio Bussotti (1638), likewise a skilled theologian; Gian Lorenzo Tilli (1704), founder of the seminary. The cathedral is a splendid three-nave Romanesque edifice, showing, however, a marked tendency towards the Gothic. A famous image of the Holy Face (*Volto Santo*) is venerated in the cathedral. It is a wooden crucifix of heroic size; the sacred Body is covered with a long tunic, and a crown rests on the head. It resembles the *Volto Santo* of Lucca, and has been in this cathedral since the tenth century; previously it was kept in the neighbouring castle of Bibbiona. Nothing certain is known as to its origin. However, the crucified Christ dressed in a long garment (*colobium*) indicates a great antiquity, perhaps the eighth or ninth century. Other beautiful churches are those of San Agostino and Santa Maria; the latter has a beautiful baptistery, brought thither from the ancient church of San Agostino. Noteworthy also is the church of San Nicola, built in 1258 by the Franciscan, Fra Tommaso da Spello, and restored in the eighteenth century. This diocese has a population of 60,500 Catholics, with 135 parishes, 250 churches and chapels, 190 secular priests, 26 regulars, and 60 seminarists, There are 3 academies, one for girls, and 2 for boys. The male religious orders represented are: Minors Conventual, Servites, Capuchins; the female congregations are: Franciscans, Capuchins, Benedictines, Sisters of St. Anne, Sisters of Charity, Sisters of the Sacred Heart, Salesian Sisters, about 70 in all.

CAPPELLETTI, *Le chiese d'Italia* (Venice, 1844), XVII; *Annuario Eccl.* (Rome, 1907), 331–334.

U. BENIGNI.

Borie, PIERRE-ROSE-URSULE-DUMOULIN, Bishop-elect of Acanthus, Vicar Apostolic of Western Tongking and Martyr; b. 20 February, 1808, at Beynat, Diocese of Tulle, France; beheaded 24 November, 1838. He studied successively at the colleges of Beaulieu and Servières, and in 1826 entered the seminary of Tulle. Meanwhile the desire to devote his life to the evangelization of distant lands matured, and in 1829 he proceeded to Paris and spent thirteen months at the Seminary of the Foreign Missions. Too young for the priesthood, he was to have been ordained at Pondicherry, on his way to his missionary post. However, a dispensation from Rome permitted his immediate ordination, which took place at Bayeux (1830). He sailed from Havre, 1 December, 1830, and, after spending some time at Macao, in China, arrived in Tongking in the year 1832. His progress in the language of the country was rapid, but eight months after his installation an edict of persecution was issued (January, 1833). Borie had to remain almost continually concealed and to endure great privations. In 1834, failing health increased the acuteness of the sufferings of persecution. He regained his strength the following year and was enabled to visit even the least accessible Christian communities of the vast district of which he was in charge. He fell into the hands of the persecutors in 1838. During his captivity he received the news of his nomination to the Vicariate Apostolic of Western Tongking, with Acanthus as titular see. Shortly after this, on the 24th of November, 1838, the death-sentence was pronounced on him and two native priests; the execution took place that same day. His remains were brought to France in 1843, and are religiously kept at the Seminary of the Foreign Missions, in Paris. The cause of his beatification has been introduced at Rome.

P. D. H. BORIE (brother of Monseigneur Borie, writing anonymously), *Vie de Mgr. Borie, par un prêtre du diocèse de Tulle* (Paris, 1844; 2d ed., 1846); LAUNAY, *Les cinquante-deux serviteurs de Dieu* (Paris, 1895), 133–162.

N. A. WEBER.

Borneo, Prefectures Apostolic of.—
I. Dutch Borneo.—The former Vicariate of Batavia was composed of Sumatra, Java, and the other Sunda Islands, including Borneo, under the control of Holland. The northern part of Borneo, now under British suzerainty, was separated from this immense vicariate, 27 August, 1855; that part of Borneo which is under Dutch rule was taken from the Vicariate Apostolic of Batavia, 11 February, 1905, and made into a separate prefecture under the care of the Capuchins. The missionaries for the new prefecture were selected from the Dutch province of this order, and the first prefect Apostolic was appointed 10 April, 1905. Up to the time of the separation what is now the Prefecture of Dutch Borneo was administered by the Jesuits who had charge of the Vicariate of Batavia, and who visited the Catholics of Dutch Borneo twice a year. In 1875 the Jesuit Father de Vriez built a little church at Singkawang, a small town situated on the west coast of the island. In the neighbourhood of Singkawang there were nearly 200 Chinese Catholics and 118 soldiers. In 1890 Father Staal, afterwards Vicar Apostolic of Batavia, founded a station in the interior at Smitau. The station was afterwards transferred to Sedjiram on the Penboeang in the region inhabited by the Dyaks. The mission at Sedjiram gave good promise of success and in 1897 included 400 baptized persons, but the missionaries were too few in number to give the station constant supervision, and it was consequently abandoned. Later the Holy See decided to erect a separate prefecture covering an area of 204,633 square miles. According to the "Statistics of the Capuchin Missions" for 1906, there were in Dutch Borneo at that date 8 Capuchin priests; 4 brothers; 396 Catholics, consisting of 210 Chinese, 100 Dyaks, and 86 Europeans; 2 stations, Singkawang and Sedjiram; 3 chapels; 20 conversions were claimed. There had been 56 baptisms and 156 communions, the latter number referring to the Catholic laity as, outside of the Capuchins, there are no religious in the prefecture. The population included in the prefecture is 2,000,000. A report of 26 November, 1906, gave the founding of a third station at Samarinda on the east coast of Borneo, some two weeks' sail from Singkawang, and of a fourth station at Pamangkat, which is seven hours from Singkawang.

Analecta Ord. Min. Cap. (September, 1805; April, 1907); Streit, Atlas des missions cath.; Bemmelen and Hooper, Guide to the Dutch East Indies (London, 1897); Statesman's Year Book (1907), 1251.

II. British Borneo, or The Prefecture of North Borneo and Labuan.—In 1687 Father Ventimiglia, a Theatine, was commissioned by Pope Innocent XI to preach Christianity in Borneo. There are no memorials of this mission, which has left no traces in the island although the missionary declared that God had blessed his labours. The Propaganda, 27 August, 1855, decreed the erection of the northern part of the island of Borneo into an independent prefecture and entrusted it to the Rev. Charles Cuarteron, a Spaniard. Father Cuarteron was originally a sea-captain and had vowed, after escaping great peril, to devote himself to the evangelization of Borneo. He landed at Labuan in 1857, in company with several missionaries who deserted him in 1860. Although alone in the island of Labuan, Father Cuarteron courageously continued his labours. At length, seeing that isolation made him powerless, he went to Rome in 1879 to request that the Propaganda place the mission in charge of an institute. From Rome Father Cuarteron went to Spain, where he soon died. The British had obtained the island of Labuan in 1846; they gradually extended their power over the petty rulers of the northern part of Borneo until, in 1888, the British Protectorate of North Borneo was formally acknowledged. English-speaking missionaries being desired in the British part of Borneo, the Propaganda (19 March, 1881) confided the mission of North Borneo and Labuan to the Society for Foreign Missions of Mill-hill, England. The first prefect Apostolic appointed under the new administration was the Rev. Thomas Jackson. The society has since continued in charge of the mission.

The island of Labuan has an area of 30 square miles and contains 6,800 inhabitants; it is an important shipping station between Singapore and Hong-Kong. The prefect Apostolic lives at Labuan. The stations served are Labuan and Sarawak (Kuching), the two most important towns. Outside of these two places where the missionaries live there are ten stations which are visited: Sibu, Kanowit, Egan, Oya, Mukah, Baram, Papar, Jesselton, Patatan, and Sandakan. According to the "Missions-Atlas" of P. Streit, the statistics of the mission are: 19 regular priests; 2 lay brothers; 15 sisters; 8 churches; 20 chapels; 16 catechists; 14 schools with 740 pupils; 2,600 baptisms; about 1,000 catechumens.

Werner, Orbis terr. Cath. (Freiburg, 1890); Battandier, Ann. Pont. Cath. (1907); Missiones Catholicæ (Rome, 1901); Guillemard, Australasia (London, 1894), II; Beccari, In the Great Forests of Borneo (London, 1904); Nyoak, The Religious Rites and Customs of the Ibau or Dyaks of Sarawak in Anthropos (Salzburg, 1906), I, 11 sqq.; British North Borneo Herald (Sandakan), files. Albert Battandier.

Borras, Francisco Nicolás, a distinguished Spanish painter, b. at Cocentaina, 1530; d. at Gandia, 1610. Going to Valencia at an early age to study under Vicente Joanes, he became that master's most noteworthy pupil. His works in general resemble those of Joanes and some of them are good enough to have been taken for the master's. Entering the priesthood, he was assigned to his native place, where he devoted all his spare moments to painting and acquired such skill that the authorities of the monastery of St. Jerome, at Gandia, employed him to paint the picture for the high altar of their church. He enjoyed his stay at the monastery so much, that taking a great liking to the brothers and their life he determined to ask for no other payment for his work than membership in the order. He received the habit in 1575, and took the final vows the following year. Three years thereafter, Fra Nicolás, in search, perhaps, of an even more austere life, spent some little time with the Capuchins at the Franciscan monastery of San Juan de la Riviera near Valencia. He was soon back, however, at Gandia where he passed the rest of his life painting in every part of the monastery, in the church, chief chapel, chapter house, oratories, refectories, and cloisters, leaving twelve altar pieces in the church alone. He also spent his own money in the employment of sculptors and builders for the embellishment of his beloved monastery.

Besides his great labours at Gandia, Borras also did much work for churches and religious houses in Valencia, at the capital, and elsewhere. His paintings appeared at the cathedral at Valencia and at the Hieronymite monastery in the city of San Miguel de los Reyes, where there was a "Christ at the Column", and a picture of the painter in adoration of "The Holy Virgin". Others were at his native place in the church of St. Stephen, in the Escorial at Aldaya, and at Ontiniente. In the Museum at Valencia there are some fifty paintings by Borras chiefly from Gandia and San Miguel. Among them are "The Last Supper", "Christ Bearing His Cross", "The Dead Saviour in the Arms of the Eternal Father", and "The Archangel Michael Driving Souls into Purgatory and Hell". In the last Borras is supposed to have pictured himself as a white robed monk kneeling on the brink.

Stirling-Maxwell, Annals of the Artists of Spain (London, 1891). Augustus van Cleef.

Borromeans. See SISTERS OF MERCY OF ST. CHARLES BORROMEO.

Borromeo, ANDREA, an Italian missionary, b. in the first half of the seventeenth century, at or near Milan; d. in 1683. He was the son of Count Giulio Cesare Borromeo, and was received into the religious order of the Theatines in 1637. In 1652 he visited Mingrelia and Georgia (Russian Transcaucasia) as a missionary, and laboured with success for eleven years, to convert the inhabitants. On his return to Rome he was elected procurator for these missions. He declined the offer of a bishopric. He left an account of the above mentioned missions of his order entitled: "Relazione della Georgia, Mingrelia, e Missioni de' Padri Teatini in quelle parti" (Rome, 1704).

MAZZUCHELLI, *Scrittori d'Italia* (Brescia, 1762), II, iii, 1793.
N. A. WEBER.

Borromeo, SAINT CHARLES. See CHARLES BORROMEO, ST.

Borromeo, FEDERICO, Cardinal and Archbishop of Milan, cousin and successor of St. Charles Borromeo, b. at Milan 18 August, 1564; d. there, 22 September, 1631. He was the son of Giulio Cesare Borromeo and Margherita Trivulzio, members of the Milanese aristocracy. He studied successively at Bologna and Pavia, in which latter city he was the first pupil of the Borromeo College. Later he went to Rome for higher studies and was there strongly influenced by St. Philip Neri, Cardinal Baronius, and Cardinal Bellarmine. In 1580 he began his ecclesiastical career under the guidance of St. Charles Borromeo. He was made cardinal at the age of twenty-three, in 1587, by Sixtus V; and, in 1595, Archbishop of Milan by Clement VII, who personally consecrated him to this high office. During thirty-six years he gave the world an example of episcopal virtue, zeal, and dignity. He was tireless in preaching and in instructing both clergy and people, was an apostle of religious education and a persistent reformer of all abuses, both lay and ecclesiastical. An almost constant conflict with the local Spanish authorities, suspicious and haughty by nature, did not diminish his sweetness of temper nor his patience; the traditional immunities and authority of the ecclesiastical order were defended as an inheritance of his see that he dared not abandon. Von Reumont thinks that, though often right, he went at times too far, e. g. in the assertion of minute ceremonial rights; it may be said, however, that in all probability it was the principle and substance of customary ecclesiastical rights that the fearless pastor ever intended to preserve and hand down. His affection for the people of Milan was made evident during the great famine and pest of 1627–28, when he fed daily 2,000 poor at the gates of his residence, and was personally an example of such absolute heroism that nearly one hundred of his clergy (sixty-two parish priests and thirty-three vicars) gave up their lives in attendance on the perishing multitudes. Alessandro Manzoni has immortalized this extraordinary devotion in his "I Promessi Sposi" (The Betrothed). If Cardinal Borromeo shared the current excessive credulity in witchcraft and magic, he was in every other way far in advance of his time as a friend of the people and a promoter of intellectual culture and social refinement based on a practical religious life. He is the founder of the famous Ambrosian Library (q. v.) opened by him in 1609, as a college of writers, a seminary of savants, a school of fine arts, and after the Bodleian at Oxford the first genuinely public library in Europe. The cares of a thickly populated diocese did not prevent him from acquiring great ecclesiastical erudition or from composing some seventy-one printed and forty-six manuscript books written mostly in Latin that treat of various ecclesiastical sciences. The universal approbation of his own and later times is echoed in the following words from the above-mentioned work of Manzoni, engraved on the pedestal of the marble statue that the citizens of Milan erected in 1865 before the gates of the Ambrosiana Library: "He was one of those men rare in every age, who employed extraordinary intelligence, the resources of an opulent condition, the advantages of privileged station, and an unflinching will, in the search and practice of higher and better things."

His life was first written by FRANCESCO RIVOLA (Milan, 1656), later by G. RIPAMONTI. CANTÙ, *La Lombardia nel secolo XVII* (Milan, 1832), which includes a catalogue of his works; ROBERTI, *Apologia del Card. Federigo Borromeo* (Milan, 1870); VON REUMONT in *Kirchenlex.*, II, 1125 sqq.; BOUQUILLON in *Catholic University Bulletin* (Washington, 1895), I, 566–572.

THOMAS J. SHAHAN.

Borromeo, THE SOCIETY OF ST. CHARLES (BORROMÄUSVEREIN), a German Catholic association for the encouragement and diffusion of edifying, instructive, and entertaining literature. It was founded at Bonn, in 1845, by Franz Xavier Dieringer, one of the professors of the Catholic theological faculty at Bonn, August Reichensperger, and Freiherr Max von Loë. From the first the society placed itself under the protection of the episcopate. Cardinal Johannes von Geissel, Cardinal Krementz, and Archbishop Simar did much to further its aims, and it gradually spread over the whole of Germany, so that by the middle of 1907 it had 145,250 members, who were grouped in 258 main societies and 3,247 branches. The administrative department and chief office are at Bonn. The society has 73 branches outside of Germany: in Belgium, 6; France, 2; Holland, 4; Italy, 1; Luxemburg, 36; Austria, 6; Switzerland, 18. In 1906 its total income was $124,743, and its expenses, $123,174. In accordance with its by-laws the society seeks: (1) to send every year one book or several books as a gift to each of its members, the quantity of reading matter thus bestowed being dependent on the ability of the society and the amount of the annual subscription, as the dues vary from $1.50 to 75 or 38 cents a year; (2) to use the annual surplus in founding libraries (those thus founded numbered over 3,000 in 1907) and in the support of libraries; (3) to aid workingmen's and people's libraries and those of asylums, hospitals, and other charitable or social institutions. Formerly the society was able to supply its members with a large number of books at a reduced price, which was often not more than two-thirds of the ordinary cost of the volumes. The society's catalogue for 1906 contained over 10,000 titles of works which could be thus purchased. But since 1907 it has been obliged to abandon this branch of its activity, on account of the position taken by the business union of the German book-sellers. In the larger cities the society has opened free reading-rooms for the use of the public in connexion with its libraries. Since 1902 the society has issued a periodical; originally this publication was called "Borromäusblätter"; it now bears the name of "Die Bücherwelt".

Die Gründung und Thätigkeit des Vereins vom hl. Karl Borromäus—Festschrift zum fünfzigjährigen Jubelfest des Vereins (Cologne, 1895); *Jahresberichte der Zentralstella.*

JOSEPH LINS.

Borromini, FRANCESCO, architect and sculptor; b. 25 September, 1599, at Bissone; d. (by his own hand) 1 August, 1667, at Rome. He studied architecture under Carlo Maderna, a relative. On the death of Maderna, he was nominated as architect of St. Peter's, under the direction of Bernini. His most extravagant effort was the church of San Carlo alle Quattro Fontane (1640–67), a good example of the fully developed baroque style in Rome. In the church and part of the College of Propaganda Borromini's fancies are wildest; the cupola and campanile of Sant' Andrea delle Fratte are in better taste. The great nave of Saint John Lateran was modernized, as it now stands, by Borromini. His best work is the façade of Santa Agnese in the Piazza Navona. Borromini is generally considered the father of all modern abuses in architecture. He inverted the whole system of Greek and Roman architecture, without offering a substitute.

THOMAS H. POOLE.

Borrus (BORRI, BURRUS), CHRISTOPHER, missionary, mathematician, and astronomer, b. at Milan in 1583; d. at Rome, 24 May, 1632. His family was one of good standing in Milan. He became a member of the Society of Jesus, 16 September, 1601; in 1618 he was sent from Macao with Father Petrus Marquez, S.J., as one of the first missionaries to Cochin-China. Here he stayed until 1622, being known under the name of Bruno. After his return he taught mathematics at Coimbra; in 1632 he entered the Cistercian Order, taking the name of Father Onofrio, and died the same year. His most important work "Relatione della nuova missione delli P. P. della Compagnia di Gesù al Regno della Cocincina" appeared at Rome in 1631 and was translated into French (Rennes, 1631), Dutch (Louvain, 1632), Latin and German (Vienna, 1633), and English (London, 1633). It was also inserted in Churchill's "Collection of Voyages" (1704), II, 787–838, and in Sprengel and Forster's "Neue Beiträge zur Völker- und Länderkunde" (Leipzig, 1793), II, 27–110. The work was considered one of the best sources of information concerning Cochin-China on account of its excellent description of the physical, political, and ecclesiastical conditions of the country. The observations of Borrus on the magnetic variation of the compass appear to be of more importance, but unfortunately they have not yet been published. According to Kircher he drew up the first chart for the Atlantic and Indian Oceans showing the spots where the magnetic needle makes the same angles with the meridian; in this he is to be regarded as the forerunner of Halley. Borrus gives the explanation to the chart in a manuscript that belongs to the Royal Academy at Lisbon. In another manuscript, now at Evora, "Tratada da arte de navegar pelo Cristovão Bruno", which bears on the same subject, he makes excellent suggestions, according to Albertius, as to a new method for determining the longitude at sea and also concerning improvements in sea-charts. Father Le Jeunehomme undertook a translation of the treatise into Latin. Philip of Spain, desiring to understand the nautical studies and inventions of Borrus, once summoned the latter from Coimbra to Madrid. Besides what has been already mentioned Borrus wrote, "Doctrina de Tribus Cœlis, Aereo, Sydereo et Empeireo" (Lisbon, s. d.), which Pietro de Valle translated into Persian (Maius, Scriptor. vet. nova collect., IV, n. ix), and also some accounts of his travels for the Propaganda.

ALLATIUS, *Apes Urbanæ* (Rome, 1633), 66; KIRCHER, *Magnes sive de arte magneticâ* (Rome, 1641), 502; DE VISCH, *Bibliotheca scriptorum Sacr. Ord. Cisterciensis* (Cologne, 1656), 71; ARGELATI, *Biblioth. Scriptor. Mediolanensium* (Milan, 1745), I, ii, 238; D'AVEZAC, *Aperçus historiques sur la boussole* in *Bullet. de la Soc. de Géogr.* (Paris, 1860), XIX, 358; CARAYON, *Docum. inédits* (Poitiers, 1864), IV, 39; VON HUMBOLDT, *Kosmos* (Stuttgart, 1869), IV, 171; PESCHEL-RUGE, *Geschichte der Erdkunde* (2d ed., Munich, 1877), 726; AMAT DI' S. FILIPPO, *Biografia dei viaggiatori italiani* (2d ed., Rome, 1882), 375–377; CORVO, *Roteiro de Lisboa a Goa por D. João de Castro* (Lisbon, 1882), 393 sqq.; BACKER-SOMMERVOGEL, *Bibl. de la c. de J.* (1890), I, 1821–22; VIII, 1878; HELLMANN, ed., *Neudrucke von Schriften und Karten über Meteorologie und Erdmagnetismus* (Berlin, 1895), No. IV, 18.

OTTO HARTIG.

Bosa, DIOCESE OF, in the province of Cagliari, Sardinia, and suffragan to the Archdiocese of Sassari. The city numbers about 35,000 inhabitants. St.

Gregory the Great, in one of his letters, speaks of a Bishop of Bosa, without, however, mentioning the bishop's name. In 1073 Costantino de Castro, Bishop of Bosa, who, according to an inscription, had built the cathedral dedicated to St. Peter, was appointed Metropolitan of Torres by St. Gregory VII. Among the most illustrious bishops of this see are numbered: the learned Cardinal Giovanni Casanova (1424); G. Francesco Fara (1591), author of the first (but very inaccurate) history of Sardinia; Serafino Esquirro, a learned theologian, who had been General of the Servites (1677). It is asserted by some that the see was originally at Calmedia, but was transferred to Bosa after the destruction of the former town; also, that the first bishop was St. Emilius, sent thither by St. Peter and martyred in 70—for this, however, there is no historical evidence. The diocese has a population of 40,200, with 21 parishes, 104 churches and chapels, 100 secular priests, and 40 seminarians.

CAPPELLETTI, *Le chiese d'Italia* (Venice, 1844), XIII; BATTANDIER, *Ann. pont. cath.* (Paris, 1907).

U. BENIGNI.

Bosch, PETER VAN DER, Bollandist, b. at Brussels, 19 October, 1686; d. 14 November, 1736. After studying the humanities at the College of Brussels, 1698–1705, he entered the novitiate of the Society of Jesus at Mechlin, 25 September, 1705. At the close of his novitiate he studied philosophy at Antwerp, 1707–09, and then spent a year in Italy to complete his literary training. Recalled to Antwerp in 1710, he spent six years in teaching and then went to Louvain, where he took a theological course, 1716–20. He was ordained priest at Louvain in 1719 and distinguished himself by the public defence of theses in March and September, 1719, and by his defence "De Universâ Theologiâ" in 1720. In 1721, at the end of his third year of probation, he was made an assistant to the Bollandists and remained a member of this body during the rest of his life. His hagiographical writings are found in July, IV–VI, and August, I–III.

DOLMAUS, *Elogium R. P. Petri Boschi hagiographi* in *Acta SS.*, III.

CH. DE SMEDT.

Bosco, GIOVANNI MELCHIOR, VENERABLE (DON BOSCO), founder of the Salesian Society, b. of poor parents in a little cabin at Becchi, a hill-side hamlet near Castelnuovo, Piedmont, Italy, 16 August, 1815; d. 31 January, 1888; declared Venerable by Pius X, 24 July, 1907. When he was little more than two years old his father died, leaving the support of three boys to the mother, Margaret Bosco. John's early years were spent as a shepherd and he received his first instruction at the hands of the parish priest. He possessed a ready wit, a retentive memory, and as years passed his appetite for study grew stronger. Owing to the poverty of the home, however, he was often obliged to turn from his books to the field, but the desire of what he had to give up never left him. In 1835 he entered the seminary at Chieri and after six years of study was ordained priest on the eve of Trinity Sunday by Archbishop Franzoni of Turin.

Leaving the seminary, Don Bosco went to Turin where he entered zealously upon his priestly labours. It was here that an incident occurred which opened up to him the real field of effort of his afterlife. One of his duties was to accompany Don Cafasso upon his visits to the prisons of the city, and the condition of the children confined in these places, abandoned to the most evil influences, and with little before them but the gallows, made such an indelible impression upon his mind that he resolved to devote his life to the rescue of these unfortunate outcasts. On the eighth of December, 1841, the feast of the Immaculate Conception, while Don Bosco was vesting for Mass, the sacristan drove from the church a ragged urchin because he refused to serve Mass. Don Bosco heard his cries and recalled him, and in the friendship which sprang up between the priest and Bartholomeo Garelli was sown the first seed of the "Oratory", so called, no doubt, after the example of St. Philip Neri and because prayer was its prominent feature. Don Bosco entered eagerly upon the task of instructing this first pupil of the streets; companions soon joined Bartholomeo, all drawn by a kindness they had never known, and in February, 1842, the Oratory numbered twenty boys, in March of the same year, thirty, and in March, 1846, four hundred.

As the number of boys increased, the question of a suitable meeting-place presented itself. In good weather walks were taken on Sundays and holidays to spots in the country about Turin where lunch was eaten, and realizing the charm which music held for the untamed spirits of his disciples Don Bosco organized a band for which some old brass instruments were procured. In the autumn of 1844 he was appointed assistant chaplain to the *Rifugio*, where Don Borel entered enthusiastically into his work. With the approval of Archbishop Franzoni, two rooms were secured adjoining the *Rifugio* and converted into a chapel, which was dedicated to St. Francis de Sales. The members of the Oratory now gathered at the *Rifugio*, and numbers of boys from the surrounding district applied for admission. It was about this time (1845) that Don Bosco began his night schools and with the closing of the factories the boys flocked to his rooms where he and Don Borel instructed them in rudimentary branches.

The success of the Oratory at the *Rifugio* was not of long duration. To his great distress Don Bosco was obliged to give up his rooms and from this on he was subjected to petty annoyances and obstacles which, at times, seemed to spell the ruin of his undertaking. His perseverance in the face of all difficulties led many to the conclusion that he was insane, and an attempt was even made to confine him in an asylum. Complaints were lodged against him, declaring his community to be a nuisance, owing to the character of the boys he befriended. From the *Rifugio* the Oratory was moved to St. Martin's, to St. Peter's Churchyard, to three rooms in Via Cottolengo, where the night schools were resumed, to an open field, and finally to a rough shed upon the site of which grew up an Oratory that counted seven hundred members. Don Bosco took lodgings nearby, where he was joined by his mother. "Mama Margaret", as Don Bosco's mother came to be known, gave the last ten years of her life in devoted service to the little inmates of this first Salesian home. When she joined her son at the Oratory the outlook was not bright. But sacrificing what small means she had, even to parting with her home, its furnishings, and her jewelry, she brought all the solicitude and love of a mother to these children of the streets. The evening classes increased and gradually dormitories were provided for many who desired to live at the Oratory. Thus was founded the first Salesian Home which now houses about one thousand boys.

The municipal authorities by this time had come to recognize the importance of the work which Don Bosco was doing, and he began with much success a fund for the erection of technical schools and workshops. These were all completed without serious difficulty. In 1868, to meet the needs of the Valdocco quarter of Turin, Don Bosco resolved to build a church. Accordingly a plan was drawn in the form of a cross covering an area of 1,500 sq. yards. He experienced considerable difficulty in raising the necessary money, but the charity of some friends finally enabled him to complete it at a cost of more than a million francs (about $200,000). The church was consecrated 9 June, 1868, and placed under the patronage of Our Lady, Help of Christians. In the same year in which Don Bosco began the erection of the church fifty priests and teachers who had been assisting him formed a society under a common rule which Pius IX, provisionally in 1869, and finally in 1874, approved.

Character and Growth of the Oratory.—Any attempt to explain the popularity of the Oratory among the classes to which Don Bosco devoted his life would fail without an appreciation of his spirit which was its life. From his earliest intercourse with poor boys he had never failed to see under the dirt, the rags, and the uncouthness the spark which a little kindness and encouragement would fan into a flame. In a vision or dream which he is said to have had in his early boyhood, wherein it was disclosed to him what his lifework would be, a voice said to him: "Not with blows, but with charity and gentleness must you draw these friends to the path of virtue." And whether this be accounted as nothing more than a dream, that was in reality the spirit with which he animated his Oratory. In the earlier days when the number of his little disciples was slender he drew them about him by means of small presents and attractions, and by pleasant walks to favourite spots in the environs of Turin. These excursions occurring on Sunday, Don Bosco would say Mass in the village church and give a short instruction on the Gospel; breakfast would then be eaten, followed by games; and in the afternoon Vespers would be chanted, a lesson in Catechism given, and the Rosary recited. It was a familiar sight to see him in the field surrounded by kneeling boys preparing for confession.

Don Bosco's method of study knew nothing of punishment. Observance of rules was obtained by instilling a true sense of duty, by removing assiduously all occasions for disobedience, and by allowing no effort towards virtue, how trivial soever it might be, to pass unappreciated. He held that the teacher should be father, adviser, and friend, and he was the first to adopt the preventive method. Of punishment he said: "As far as possible avoid punishing . . . try to gain love before inspiring fear." And in 1877 he wrote: "I do not remember to have used formal punishment; and with God's grace I have always obtained, and from apparently hopeless children, not alone what duty exacted, but what my wish simply expressed." In one of his books he has discussed the causes of weakness of character, and derives them largely from a misdirected kindness in the rearing of children. Parents make a parade of precocious talents; the child understands quickly, and his sensitiveness enraptures all who meet him, but the parents have only succeeded in producing an affectionate, perfected, intelligent animal. The chief object should be to form the will and to temper the character. In all his pupils Don Bosco tried to cultivate a taste for music, believing it to be a powerful and refining influence. "Instruction", he said, "is but an accessory, like a game; knowledge never makes a man because it does not directly touch the heart. It gives more power in the exercise of good or evil; but alone it is an indifferent weapon, wanting guidance." He always studied, too, the aptitudes and vocations of his pupils, and to an almost supernatural quickness and clearness of insight into the hearts of children must be ascribed no small part of his success. In his rules he wrote: "Frequent Confession, frequent Communion, daily Mass: these are the pillars which should sustain the whole edifice of education." Don Bosco was an indefatigable confessor, devoting days to this work among his children. He recognized that gentleness and patience alone were not enough to bring to the task of education. He thoroughly believed in play as a means of arousing childish curiosity—more than this, he places it among his first recommendations, and for the rest he adopted St. Philip Neri's words: "Do as you wish, I do not care so long as you do not sin."

Statistics.—At the time of Don Bosco's death in 1888 there were 250 houses of the Salesian Society in all parts of the world, containing 130,000 children, and from which there annually went out 18,000 finished apprentices. In the mother-house Don Bosco had selected the brightest of his pupils, taught them Italian, Latin, French, and mathematics, and this band formed a teaching corps for the new homes which quickly grew up in other places. Up to 1888 over six thousand priests had gone forth from Don Bosco's institutions, 1,200 of whom had remained in the society. The schools begin with the child in his first instruction and lead, for those who choose it, to seminaries for the priesthood. The society also conducts Sunday schools, evening schools for adult workmen, schools for those who enter the priesthood late in life, technical schools, and printing establishments for the diffusion of good reading in different languages. Its members also have charge of hospitals and asylums, nurse the sick, and do pastoral work, especially in rural districts. The society has houses in the following countries: Italy, Spain, Portugal, France, England, Belgium, Switzerland, Austria, Palestine, and Algiers; in North America, Mexico, in South America, Patagonia, Terra del Fuego, Ecuador, Brazil, Paraguay, the Argentine Republic, Bolivia, Uruguay, Chile, Peru, Venezuela, and Colombia. In the United States the Salesians have four churches: Sts. Peter and Paul and Corpus Christi in San Francisco, California; St. Joseph's in Oakland, California; and the Transfiguration in New York City. Very Rev. Michael Borghino, Provincial for America, resides in San Francisco.

Don Bosco's Apostolate and Other Sketches (Salesian Press, Turin, 1901); WEBER in *Kirchenlex.*, X, 1558 sqq.; VILLEFRANCHE, *Don Bosco*, tr. MARTIN (London).

E. F. SAXTON.

Boscovich, RUGGIERO GIUSEPPE, a Dalmatian Jesuit and well-known mathematician, astronomer, and natural philosopher, b. at Ragusa, 18 May, 1711; d. at Milan, 13 February, 1787. He was the youngest of six brothers and his education was begun at the Jesuit college of his native city. Being early impressed by the success achieved by his masters he resolved to seek admission in their ranks and on 31 October, 1725, at the youthful age of fourteen, he entered the noviti-ate of the Society of Jesus in Rome. His unusual talents manifested themselves par-ticularly during the years devot-ed to literary and philosophical studies at the Collegio Romano, the most cele-brated of the colleges of the Society of Jesus. Thus, for example, young Boscovich discovered for himself the proof of the theorem of Pythagoras. His professors, especially Father Horatius Borgondi, professor of mathematics, knew how to cultivate his

RUGGIERO GIUSEPPE BOSCOVICH

talents, and he made such progress, especially in mathematics, that he was able to take the place of his former professor at the Roman College even before the completion of his theological studies. As soon as he had completed the ordinary studies of a young Jesuit, he was appointed regular professor of mathematical science in the same college. He performed the duties of this office with much distinction for a whole generation, as is evidenced by the numerous Latin dissertations which he published nearly every year, according to the custom of the time. These show Boscovich's preference for astronomical problems. Among them may be mentioned: "The Sunspots" (1736); "The Transit of Mercury" (1737); "The Aurora Borealis" (1738); "The Applications of the Telescope in Astronomical Studies" (1739); "The Figure of the Earth" (1739); "The Motion of the heavenly Bodies in an unresisting Medium" (1740); "The various Effects of Gravity" (1741); "The Aberration of the Fixed Stars" (1742). Problems in pure mathematics as well as philosophical speculations regarding the various theories on the constitution of matter also engaged his attention and he took an active part in all scientific discussions which agitated the learned world of his time. To these belong his "The Deviation of the Earth from the probable Spherical Shape"; "Researches on Universal Gravitation"; "The Computation of a Comet's Orbit from a Few Observations", etc. His able treatment of these and similar problems attracted the attention of foreign, as well as of Italian, Academies, several of which—among them Bologna, Paris, and London —admitted him to membership. At Paris he shared with the famous mathematician Euler the honour of having submitted the correct solution of a prize problem.

Boscovich also showed much ability in dealing with practical problems. To him was due the project of the Observatory of the Collegio Romano, which afterwards became so well known. He first suggested using the massive dome-pillars of the college church of St. Ignatius as a foundation, on account of their great stability. (The church dome has not yet been completed, so the pillars still await the superstructure planned by the architect.) The un-favourable circumstances of the time and the storms brewing against the Jesuits, which ended, as is well known, in the suppression of the Society, prevented Boscovich's plan from being carried out until 1850, when Father Secchi, his worthy successor, was able to bring it to completion. There is a close parallel, it may be observed, between these two *coryphæi* of the Roman College, and Boscovich may, without hesitation, be considered the intellectual forerunner of Secchi. Like Secchi, too, he was the adviser of the papal Government in all important technical questions. Thus, when in the middle of the eighteenth century the great dome of St. Peter's began to show cracks and other signs of damage, causing consternation to the pope and to the Eternal City, Boscovich was consulted, and the excitement was not allayed until his plan to place large iron bands about the dome was carried out. His advice was sought when there was question of rendering innocuous the Pontine marshes and he was also entrusted with the survey of the Papal States. Pope Benedict XIV commissioned him and his fellow-Jesuit, Le Maire, to carry out several precise meridian arc measurements, and it seems to have been due chiefly to his influence that the same pope, in 1757, abrogated the obsolete decree of the Index against the Copernican system.

Many universities outside of Italy sought to number Boscovich among their professors. He himself was full of the spirit of enterprise, as was shown when King John V of Portugal petitioned the general of the Jesuits for ten Fathers to make an elaborate survey in Brazil. He voluntarily offered his services for the arduous task, hoping thus to be able to carry out an independent survey in Ecuador, and so obtain data of value for the final solution of the problem of the figure of the earth, which was then exciting much attention in England and France. His proposal led to the institution of similar surveys in the Papal States, the pope taking this means of retaining him in his own domain. A detailed account of the results of the work appeared in a large quarto volume (Rome, 1755) entitled: "De litterariâ expeditione per Pontificiam ditionem ad dimetiendos duos meridiani gradus et corrigendam mappam geographicam". A map of the Papal States made at the same time, which corrected many previous errors, proved to be likewise a welcome contribution to the discussion regarding the more or less spherical form of the earth. Many of the triangulations were accompanied by no slight difficulties. The two base-lines employed in the survey—one on the Via Appia, the other in the neighbourhood of Rimini—were measured with great care. The first was redetermined in 1854–55 by Father Secchi, as the mark indicating one end of the line measured by Boscovich and Le Maire had been lost. (Cf. Secchi's work: Misura della Base trigonometrica esequita sulla via Appia per ordine del governo pontificio, Roma, 1858.) Besides his work in mathematical astronomy we also find Boscovich speculating, upon scientific grounds, on the essence of matter and endeavouring to establish more widely Newton's law of universal gravitation. As early as 1748 we meet essays from his pen in this field of thought, e. g. "De materiæ divisibilitate et de principiis corporum dissertatio" (1748); "De continuitatis lege et ejus consectariis pertinentibus ad prima materiæ elementa eorumque vires" (1754); "De lege virium in naturâ existentium" (1755); "Philosophiæ naturalis theoria redacta ad unicam legem virium in naturâ existentium" (1758). Boscovich, according to the views expressed in these essays, held that bodies could not be composed of a continuous material substance, nor even of contiguous material particles, but of innumerable, point-like structures whose individual components lack all extension and divisibility. A repulsion exists between them which is indeed infinitesimal but cannot vanish without compenetration taking place. This repulsion is due to certain forces with which these elements are endowed. It tends to become infinite when they are in very close proximity, whereas within certain limits it diminishes as the distance is increased and finally becomes an attractive force. This change is brought about by the diverse directions of the various forces. Boscovich divided his last-mentioned exhaustive work into three parts, first explaining and establishing his theory, then pointing out its applications to mechanical problems, and finally showing how it may be employed in physics. His attempt to reduce the most complicated laws of nature to a simple fundamental law aroused so much interest that in 1763 a third, and enlarged, edition of his "Theoria philosophiæ naturalis" (Venice, 1763) had become necessary. The publisher added as an appendix a catalogue of Boscovich's previous works. There are no less than sixty-six treatises dating from 1736—a proof of his literary activity. Some have already been mentioned and to these may be added his "Elementorum matheseos tomi tres", in quarto (1752).

Boscovich attracted attention by his political writings as well as by his scientific achievements. His Latin verses in which he eulogized the Polish king, Stanislaus, Pope Benedict XIV, and various Venetian noblemen, were read before the Arcadian Academy of Rome. His "Carmen de Solis ac Lunæ defectibus" (5 vols., London, 1760) was much admired. His services were also in demand in several cities and provinces. Thus, in 1757, he was sent by the city of Lucca to the Court of Vienna, to urge the damming of the lakes which were threatening the city. He acquitted himself of this task with such skill that the Luccans made him an honorary citizen and rendered him generous assistance on his scientific journeys, both in Italy, France, and England. While in England he gave the impulse to the observations of the approaching transit of Venus, on 6 June, 1761, and it is not unlikely that his proposal to employ lenses composed of liquids, to avoid chromatic aberration, may have contributed to Dollond's success in constructing achromatic telescopes. The citizens of Ragusa, his native town, besought him to settle a dispute in which they had become involved with the King of France—an affair which the pope himself deigned to adjust. Boscovich returned from England in company with the Venetian ambassador who took him by way of Poland as far as Constantinople. He availed himself of this opportunity to extend and complete his archæological studies in these countries, as may be gathered from his journal published at Bassano in 1784: "Giornale d'un viaggio da Constantinopoli in Polonia con una relazione delle rovine di Troja". The hardships of this journey shattered his health, yet we find him shortly after (1762) employed at Rome in various practical works, such as the draining of the Pontine marshes. In 1764 he accepted the appointment of professor of mathematics at the University of Pavia (Ticinum). At the same time Father La Grange, the former assistant of Father Pezenas of the Observatory of Marseilles, was invited by the Jesuits of Milan to erect an observatory at the large college of Brera. He was able to avail himself of the technical skill of Boscovich in carrying out his commission and it may be questioned to which of the two belongs the greater credit in the founding of this observatory which, even in our own time, with that of the Collegio Romano, is among the most prominent of Italy. It was Boscovich who selected the south-east corner of the college as a site for the observatory and worked out the complete plans, including the reinforcements and the necessary remodelling for the structure. Building operations were immediately begun and in the following year, 1765, a large room for the mural quadrants and meridian instruments, another for the smaller instruments, and a broad terrace, with several revolving domes to contain the sextants and equatorials, were completed. Such was the stability of the observatory that the new 18-inch glass of Schiaparelli could be mounted in it although a cylindrical dome with a diameter of 13 yards, 4 inches now takes the place of the octagonal hall of Boscovich.

The London Academy proposed to send Boscovich in charge of a scientific expedition to California to observe the transit of Venus in 1769 but, unfortunately, the opposition manifested everywhere to the Society of Jesus and leading finally to its suppression, made this impossible. He continued, however, to give his services to the Milan Observatory for whose further development he was able to obtain no inconsiderable sums of money. In particular the adjustment of the instruments engaged his attention, a subject about which he has left several papers. But as his elaborate plans received only partial support from his superiors and patrons, he thought seriously in 1772 of severing his connexion with the observatory and, in fact, in the same year, Father La Grange was placed in complete charge of the new institution. Boscovich was to become professor at the University of Pisa, but Louis XV gained his services and invited him to Paris where a new office, Director of Optics for the Marine—d'optique au service de la Marine—with a salary of 8,000 francs, was created for him. He retained this position until 1783 when he returned to Italy to supervise the printing of his as yet unpublished works in five volumes, for it was not easy to find a suitable publisher in France for books written in Latin. In 1785 there appeared at Bassano, "Rogerii Josephi Boscovich opera pertinentia ad opticam et astronomiam . . . in quinque tomos distributa", the last important work from the pen of this active man, who, after its completion, retired for a time to the monastery of the monks of Vallombrosa. He returned to Milan with new plans, but death shortly overtook him at the age of seventy-six, delivering him from a severe malady which was accompanied by temporary mental derangement. He was buried in the church of Santa Maria Podone.

Boscovich, by his rare endowments of mind and the active use which he made of his talents, was preeminent among the scholars of his time. His merits were recognized by learned societies and universities, and by popes and princes who honoured him and bestowed favours upon him. He was recognized as a gifted teacher, an accomplished leader in scientific enterprises, an inventor of important instruments which are still employed (such as the ring-micrometer, etc.), and as a pioneer in developing new theories. All this, however, did not fail to excite envy against him, particularly during the later years of his life in France, where men like d'Alembert and Condorcet reluctantly saw the homage paid to the former Jesuit, and that, too, at a time when so many frivolous charges were being made against his lately suppressed order. This hostility was further increased by various controversies which resulted in differences of opinion, such as the contention between Boscovich and Rochon regarding priority in the invention of the rock crystal prismatic micrometer. (Cf. Delambre, Histoire de l'Astronomie du XVIIIe siècle, p. 645.) The invention of the ring-micrometer just mentioned, which Boscovich describes in his memoir "De novo telescopii usu ad objecta cœlestia determinanda" (Rome, 1739), has been ascribed without reason by some to the Dutch natural philosopher Huygens. The chief advantage of the simple measuring instrument devised by Boscovich consists in its not requiring any artificial illumination of the field of the telescope. This makes it useful in observing faint objects, as its inventor expressly points out in connexion with the comet of 1739. The novel views of Boscovich in the domain of natural philosophy have not, up to the present time, passed unchallenged, even on the part of Catholic scholars. Against his theory of the constitution of matter the objection has been raised that an inadmissible *actio in distans* is inevitable in the mutual actions of the elementary points of which material bodies are supposed to be composed. The theory therefore leads to Occasionalism. Acknowledgment must, however, be made of the suggestiveness of Boscovich's work in our own day, and the germs of many of the conclusions of modern physics may be found in it. His illustrious successor at the Observatory of the Collegio Romano, Father Angelo Secchi, in his "Unità delle forze fisiche", has in many respects followed in his footsteps, and in fact the cosmological views held by many later natural philosophers furnish unequivocal proof of the influence of the theories maintained by Boscovich.

Among his many smaller works (for full list cf. Sommervogel, cited below) the following deserve special attention: "De annuis stellarum fixarum aberrationibus" (Rome, 1742); "De orbitis cometarum determinandis ope trium observationum parum a se invicem remotarum" (Paris, 1774); "De recentibus compertis pertinentibus ad perficiendam dioptricam" (1767). His chief works, however, are: (1) "De litterariâ expeditione per Pontificiam ditionem" (1755); (2) "Theoria philosophiæ naturalis" (1758); (3) "Opera pertinentia ad opticam et As-

II.—44

tronomiam maxima ex parte nova et omnia hucusque inedita" (1785). The second was published in Vienna 1758–59, in Venice, 1763, and again in Vienna in 1764. The last-named work was subjected to an exhaustive criticism by Delambre, by no means a friend of the Jesuits. He closes with these words: "Boscovich in general manifests a preference for graphical methods in the use of which he gives evidence of great skill. In his whole work he shows himself a teacher who prefers to lecture rather than to lose himself in speculations".

The most extended biographical account of Boscovich may be found in *Vitæ Italorum, Auctore Angelo Fabronio, Academiæ Pisanæ curatore* (Pisa, 1789), XIV; cf. also SOMMERVOGEL, *Bibl. de la c. de J.* (Brussels, 1890), I, col. 1828–50. For shorter accounts cf. ZAMAGNA (Ragusa, 1787); LALANDE (Paris, 1792); RICCA (Milan, 1789); BAGAMONTI (Ragusa, 1789); BIZZARRO (Venice, 1817); *Galleria di Ragusani illustri* (Ragusa, 1841); VACCOLINI in *Giornale arcadico* (1842), XCII, 174.

ADOLF MÜLLER.

Bosio, ANTONIO, known as "The Columbus of the Catacombs", b. in the island of Malta about the year 1576; d. 1629. While still a boy he was sent to Rome and placed in charge of an uncle who represented the Knights of Malta in the Eternal City. In the Roman schools he studied literature, philosophy, and jurisprudence, but at the age of eighteen he gave up his legal studies and for the remaining thirty-six years of his life all his time was devoted to archæological work in the Roman catacombs. The accidental discovery, in 1578, of an ancient subterranean cemetery on the Via Salaria had for the moment attracted general attention in Rome. Few, however, realized the importance of the discovery, and, with the exception of three foreign scholars, Ciacconio, De Winghe, and L'Heureux, no one seriously thought of pursuing further investigations. It was reserved for Bosio to begin the systematic exploration of subterranean Rome and thus to become the founder of the science of Christian archæology. The young explorer from the beginning realized that in early Christian literature he would find an indispensable ally, and accordingly he began to study the Acts of the Martyrs and of the Councils, the writings of the Greek and the Latin Fathers, and in fact every species of document that might help to throw light on the obscurities of his subject. An idea of the vast scope of his reading may be obtained from the two great tomes of his manuscript notes in the Vallicelliana library at Rome, each of which contains about a thousand pages in folio.

The literary labours of Bosio account for only half of his time; the other half was consumed in systematic efforts to utilize the information derived from his reading for his particular object. Thus, for example, after he had collected all the data possible relative to the location of a catacomb on one of the great roads leading from Rome, Bosio would betake himself to the place indicated, and go over every inch of ground carefully in the hope of discovering a forgotten stairway, or *luminarium*, of a cemetery. If fortune crowned his investigations with success, he would then descend to the subterranean abode of the long-forgotten dead, and, sometimes at the imminent danger of being lost in the labyrinth of galleries, commence his explorations. The great work achieved by Bosio was almost unknown till the publication three years after his death of his "Roma Sotterranea". The folio volume was brought out under the patronage of the Knights of Malta, by the Oratorian Severano, who had been entrusted with its editorship by Cardinal Francesco Barberini. Its full title is "Roma Sotterranea, opera postuma di Antonio Bosio Romano, antiquario ecclesiastico singolare de' suoi tempi. Compita, disposta, et accresciuta dal M. R. P. Giovanni Severani da S. Severino" (Rome, 1632). The great merit of the new publication was at once recognized. A Latin translation was undertaken by Severano, but never published. Aringhi's Latin translation appeared in 1651, but the liberties which this writer took with the original text were far from being improvements. Bosio's "Roma Sotterranea" is entirely devoted to a description of the cemeteries explored by the great archæologist. His leading thought was to ascertain all that was possible regarding the history of each cemetery, by what name it was known in antiquity, who were its founders, what martyrs and illustrious Christians were interred there. Many of his conclusions have in modern times been found to be erroneous, but on the other hand, recent research has shown, in one important instance, that a conjecture of Bosio's, which de Rossi thought without foundation, was wholly correct. (See CHRISTIAN ARCHÆOLOGY.) Bosio's method is acknowledged by all to have been scientific; his shortcomings were those of the age in which he lived. In view of the fact that numerous frescoes which existed in the early seventeenth century have since been destroyed, it is unfortunate that the copyists employed by Bosio were not equal to the task assigned to them. Wilpert states that the illustrations of "Roma Sotteranea" are of little use to the modern archæologist.

NORTHCOTE AND BROWNLOW, *Roma Sotterranea* (London, 1878); WILPERT, *Pitture delle Catacombe Romane* (Rome, 1903); MÜLLER in *Realencyklopädie für prot. Theol.*, s. v. *Koimeterien* (Leipzig, 1901).

MAURICE M. HASSETT.

Bosnia, DIOCESE OF. SEE SZEREM.

Bosnia and Herzegovina.—Bosnia and Herzegovina form the north-western corner of the Balkan Peninsula. Taking the two together as one territory, Bosnia-Herzegovina is bounded on the north by the Austrian provinces and titular kingdoms of Croatia and Slavonia, on the east by the Kingdom of Servia, on the south by one of the nominal provinces of Turkey, the principality of Montenegro, and the titular kingdom and Austrian province of Dalmatia, and on the west by Dalmatia and Croatia. The Dinaric Alps and the Save and Drina Rivers form a large part of the boundary line of the country which in shape closely resembles an equilateral triangle. The joint territory has an area of about 19,702 square miles and belongs nominally to the Turkish Empire. Article 25 of the Treaty of Berlin, 13 July, 1878, granted Austria-Hungary the right to occupy and administer the two provinces. Since then they have been under the control of the Minister of Finance of the Austro-Hungarian monarchy as crown provinces. Bosnia and Herzegovina belong, with their alternating highlands and mountain chains, to the region of the Karst mountains. The Karst region forms a part of the spurs of the southern Alps. It is a mountainous limestone district of the mesozoic period with valleys of incomplete formation. The rocky, unfruitful character of the Karst region is more evident in the southern part of the territory than in the northern, for in the north the forest-covered ranges, running chiefly from south-east to north-west, enclose fertile valleys. The only flat country is the district called Posavina, lying on the Save. There is in general a terrace-like descent from the mountainous region towards the Adriatic and the Hungarian depression.

Bosnia may be regarded as a succession of great terraces, but Herzegovina, in which the mountain sides slope down towards the Narenta River, has more the shape of a basin. The former belongs to the region of the Black Sea, the latter to that of the Adriatic. The highest peaks, the Ločike (6,913 feet), the Treskavica-Planina (6,851 feet), and the Bjelasnica-Planina (6,782 feet) lie near the border of Herzegovina, respectively west and south-west of Serajevo. The Save is the chief river of Bosnia and its tributaries are the Una, the Vrbas, the Ukina, the Bosna,

and the Drina. Herzegovina is drained by the Narenta (Neretva) River. As Bosnia falls away towards the north until it descends into the low-lying region of the Save, it is easy of access from central Europe and was, consequently, exposed to incursions by the kings of Hungary. After crossing the Saxe the Hungarian armies could penetrate into the heart of the country without encountering any natural obstacles. Bosnia was also, in consequence of the physical formation of the land, frequently divided politically into two parts, the upper or mountainous Bosnia, which extended to where the rivers pass into the flat country of the Save, and the Bosnian plain along the Save. The Romans observed this natural line of division and made it the boundary between the provinces of Dalmatia and Pannonia. Just as the political unity of Bosnia was made more difficult by its natural configuration, so on the other hand, the development of a compact principality was favoured in Herzegovina (called also Hum, Chulm, and Chulmo) by its basin-like shape.

Physical Formation.—Mesozoic formations appear throughout this territory especially in the shape of Triassic rocks; where there are dislocations the underlying palæozoic rocks frequently project. These latter are made of slate, sandstone, and limestone, as for example, the famous mountain range of slate rock called Kreševo, in the western part of the Serajevo district, and the range called Posara on the Save. Jurassic rock and chalk formations appear chiefly in Herzegovina and western Bosnia. Of far greater extent are the neogenic fresh water formations containing the great coal deposits of the two territories. There is also much volcanic rock of various ages. The climate of Bosnia is in general the usual continental one of cold winters and hot summers, while in Herzegovina the nearness of the sea makes the climate almost semi-tropical. The average yearly temperature is from 48.2° to 50° Fahr. The average temperature of Travnik, situated at a height of 1,640 feet in about the centre of the country, is in January 28.4° Fahr., in April 50.5°, in July, 68.3°, and in October 50.3°. Since the time of the Romans Bosnia has yielded a large amount of iron; lignite or brown coal and salt are also obtained in a number of places. Mineral and hot springs abound; among these are the hot spring at Ilidže near Serajevo, the chalybeate spring at Kiseljak, and a spring impregnated with arsenic at Srebrenica. Bosnia contains a large amount of timber; 50 per cent of its area is covered with forests; 34 per cent is productive farming-land, and the remaining 16 per cent is in the rocky Karst region. The Bosnian forests are full of boars, bears, wolves, foxes, lynxes, and deer. Agriculture is of a very primitive character and could be made far more productive. The chief agricultural products of the country are maize and wheat; oats, rye, barley, hemp, and buckwheat are also raised. In Herzegovina in addition to these staples wine and oil are produced and figs are cultivated.

Population.—According to the census of 22 April, 1895, Bosnia has 1,361,868 inhabitants and Herzegovina 229,168, giving a total population of 1,591,036. The number of persons to the square mile is small (about 80), less than that in any of the other Austrian crown provinces excepting Salzburg (about 70). This average does not vary much in the six districts (five in Bosnia, one in Herzegovina). The number of persons to the square mile in these districts is as follows: Doljna Tuzla, 106; Banjaluka, 96; Bihač, 91; Serajevo, 73; Mostar (Herzegovina), 65; Travnik, 62. There are 5,388 settlements, of which only 11 have more than 5,000 inhabitants, while 4,689 contain less than 500 persons. Excluding some 30,000 Albanians, living in the south-east, the Jews who emigrated in earlier times from Spain, a few Osmanli Turks, the merchants, officials, and Austrian troops, the rest of the population (about 98 per cent) belong to the southern Slavonic people, the Serbs. Although one in race, the people form in religious beliefs three sharply separated divisions: the Mohammedans, about 550,000 persons (35 per cent), Greek Schismatics, about 674,000 persons (43 per cent), and Catholics, about 334,000 persons (21.3 per cent). The last mentioned are chiefly peasants. The Mohammedans form the mass of the population in the region called the Krajina in the north-west, in the district of Serajevo and in the south-eastern part of the territory; the Greek Schismatics preponderate in the district of Banjaluka. The Catholics of the Latin Rite exceed the other two denominations only in the district of Travnik and in northern Herzegovina. There are in addition 8,000 Jews and 4,000 Protestants. Divided according to occupation 85 per cent of the population are farmers or wine-cultivators (1,385,291). There are 5,833 large estates, the owners of which are chiefly Mohammedans, 88,970 cultivators of land not their own (*kmeten*), 88,867 free peasants who own the land they till, and 22,625 peasants who own farming-land and also cultivate the land of others. The population of the towns is small.

History.—There are traces of human settlements in Bosnia dating from the Stone Age. The earliest inhabitants of Bosnia and Herzegovina of whom there is any certainty are the Illyrians, an exceedingly rapacious pastoral people who were divided into various tribes. The best known of these are: a small tribe called the Liburnians living in the north-west, who were notorious pirates; the Ardiæans living south of the Liburnians, and the Antiariats, who were neighbours of the Ardiæans living still farther to the south. The migrations of the Celts in the third and fourth centuries before Christ drove various Illyrian tribes out of their former possessions. From the third century until 167 B. C., a powerful Illyrian kingdom existed, under rulers called Agron, Teuta, and Gentius, in southern Dalmatia, and the adjoining Herzegovina and Montenegro. The Romans had a hard struggle before they succeeded finally in breaking the power of the Illyrians and in getting control of Bosnia and Herzegovina (6 B. C.–A. D. 9). The sagacious Romans saw that in order to control the line of the Danube and the east coast of Italy it was necessary to absorb the triangular shaped country of the Illyrians. No part of the peninsula contains so many traces of Roman civilization as Dalmatia and the adjoining Bosnia. The Romans built a road from Mitrovič or Mitrovitza (Sirmium) near the Save to Gradisca and continued it from Gradisca through what is now western Bosnia or Turkish Croatia as far as Salona; they constructed a second road through upper Bosnia across the present district of Serajevo to Domavia on the Drina, and from here to Mitrovič; a third road went from Salona to Narona (near Dubrawa) and to Scodra (Scutari). The Romans named the province Dalmatia after the largest and bravest of the tribes living on the coast. They divided it into three administrative dioceses, the chief cities being, respectively, Salona, the capital of the whole province, Scardona, and Narenta. The northernmost part of Bosnia, extending for some distance from the Save, was included in the province of Pannonia. The Illyrians who had been familiar only with war and cattle-raising now turned their attention, under the guidance of the Romans, to mining, placer-mining for gold, and agriculture. They became largely Romanized and for hundreds of years their legions bravely defended the empire.

After the fall of the Western Roman Empire Dalmatia and Pannonia came into the possession of the Ostrogoths under King Theodoric. During the war that followed (535–554) between Justinian and the Ostrogoths, the Slavs made repeated incursions into the provinces. It may be that they were called in by the Ostrogoths. After the Slavs the Avars raided the territory and in 598 turned Dalmatia almost into a wilderness. After this the Slavs greatly desired the country and succeeded in taking possession during the first half of the seventh century. Among the tribes which now owned the land, the Hroati (later called Croats) lived on the Dalmatic coast and the Serbi in the interior. Up to the eighth century the influence of the Byzantine Empire was paramount. At the end of the ninth century when the power of the Carlovingian dynasty extended as far as the south-eastern Alpine provinces, the Croats came under the influence of Western civilization and embraced Latin Christianity. The tribes of the interior retained the patriarchal form of government and the old pagan worship much longer than the dwellers on the coast, notwithstanding the connexion which they had had for centuries with Constantinople. Bosnia seems to have belonged to Croatia as late as the beginning of the tenth century. A little later the Servian prince Ceslav (931–960) succeeded in freeing Servia from the suzerainty of Bulgaria and built up a confederation of which Bosnia formed a part. About 955 Ceslav was obliged to defend the dependent *banat*, or district, of Bosnia (originally merely the valley of the upper Bosna) from an incursion of the Magyars. After the death of Ceslav and the dissolution of his kingdom, Bosnia was ruled by native *bans* or chiefs. In 968 however, Bosnia was conquered by the Croatian king Kresimir and in 1019 the whole north-western part of the Balkan Peninsula came under the sway of the Eastern Roman Emperor, Basil II. After Basil's death Bosnia regained its independence and was ruled by native bans until it was united with the domain of Béla II, King of Hungary. In 1135 this ruler called himself for the first time King of Rama (Bosnia).

During the entire reign of the Emperor Manuel I, Comnenus, (1143–80) a long and fierce struggle went on between the Byzantine Empire on the one side and Hungary and the southern Slavs on the other; in this Ban Boris, the first ruler of Bosnia known by name, remained faithful to Hungary. In 1163, however, Boris took sides against Stephen III in the quarrel over the succession to the Hungarian throne. He was defeated by Gottfried of Meissen who was sent with an army against him, and his family lost their power in Bosnia. The Banat of Boris extended from Livno and the valley of the Rama in the west to the Drina River in the east. Three years later Bosnia, Syrmia, Croatia, and Dalmatia became subject to the Byzantine Empire. After the death of Manuel I, Comnenus (1180) the new Ban, Kulin, was able to shake off the foreign yoke. But Béla III of Hungary, desiring to make Bosnia a dependency of his own kingdom, persuaded the pope to place the Bishopric of Bosnia and the Diocese of Ston in Herzegovina under the Archdiocese of Spalato, the territory of which belonged to Hungary. Before this Bosnia had been suffragan to Ragusa. In order to counteract this indirect Hungarian control Kulin, his family, and 10,000 Bosnians, between the years 1190–99, became adherents of the Paterine heresy. When Pope Innocent III and King Emmerich of Hungary joined forces to exterminate the Paterines and to conquer Bosnia, Kulin preserved Bosnia's independence of Hungarian control by returning in 1203 to the Catholic religion in the presence of the papal legate, Johannes de Casamaris. During the reign of his successor, Ban Stephen, the Paterines grew so powerful that they deposed Stephen and substituted one of their own adherents, the able Matthias Ninoslav (1232–50), who was probably related to Kulin. In 1233 Ninoslav returned to the Catholic Faith, but notwithstanding this the land was filled with the adherents of the Paterine belief, and in 1234–39 a crusade was preached against Bosnia but was not, however, carried out. Although Ninoslav maintained his position as Ban of Bosnia, he was not able to found a dynasty and after his death his principality gradually fell to pieces. The districts of Herzegovina near Ragusa aimed at individual independence, while the rest of the territory now included in Bosnia and Herzegovina gradually came into a more complete dependence on Hungary.

During the reign of Béla IV of Hungary (1235–70) upper Bosnia and the district of Posavina were formed into the Banat of Bosnia, the region in the west on the Usora into the Banat of Usora, and the region in the east on the Drina into the Banat of Soli or Tuzla, while the western part of the present territory of Herzegovina, the region of the Rama, and southern Bosnia were ruled by various powerful Croatian families. At this time a relative of Ninoslav named Prÿezda lived on the upper part of the Bosna River. Prÿezda's son, Stephen Katroman (1322–53), was the first of the Katroman family from which for a century and a half came the bans and kings of Bosnia. Stephen was a vassal of the kings of Hungary, who were his relatives and members of the house of Anjou. Through this connexion Stephen was able, after defeating the rulers of the present Herzegovina, to unite this territory to his domains. From the tenth century Herzegovina had formed a so-called buffer district between the Dalmatic coast and Bosnia on the one side and Servia on the other. On the dismemberment of the great Servian empire of Dusan the Strong, Tvrtko, Stephen Katroman's nephew and successor, with the help of King Louis I (the Great) of Hungary, became master of the district of the upper Drina, Trebinje, and Cánale. Tvrtko now, with the consent of Louis, took the title of King of Bosnia. A few years later (1384) Bosnia and Herzegovina were laid waste for the first time by the Turks. After the death of Louis the Great (1382) Tvrtko threw off the suzerainty of Hungary and conquered the cities on the Dalmatic coast. During the reigns of his successors Stephen Dabischa (1391–95), Queen Helena (1395–98), Stephen Osoja (1398–1418), Stephen Ostojitsch (1418–21), Stephen Tvrtko II (1404–31) (the rival of the two last-named kings), Stephen Thomas (1443–61), and Stephen Thomaschewitz (1461–63) the kingdom rapidly declined in power so that these rulers were not able to maintain their authority over the conquered districts or to keep the insubordinate vassals and nobles in check. The nobles ruled their territories with little regard for the king; they had their own courts with state officials, granted pardons, had relations with foreign powers, and carried on bloody wars with one another.

The last king, who possessed only the land on the right bank of the Bosna, sought to strengthen his position by becoming a vassal of the pope. He hoped by this means to obtain the aid of the Christian countries of Western Europe in defending himself against the threatening power of the Turks. In 1462 he refused to pay tribute to the Sultan Mohammed II; but when in the following spring Mohammed invaded Bosnia with a powerful army, the young king found himself deserted. Deceit and treason, especially on the part of the Bogomili, completed his ruin. He was taken prisoner by the Turks and beheaded, by the order of the sultan, July, 1463, probably near Jajce (Jaitza). The campaign of the Turks ended in the overthrow of the Bosnian kingdom; only Herzegovina maintained its independence. One hundred thousand prisoners of both sexes were taken; 30,000 Bosnian youths were compelled to join the janizaries. The nobility, especially the Bogomili, became Mohammedans. A large part of the remaining population left the country. The following year King Matthias Corvinus of Hungary freed from the Turkish yoke a part of Bosnia, the Banats of Jajce and Srebrenica (Srebrenitza) which belonged to Hungary until the battle of Mohács (1526). Herzegovina came under the do-

minion of the Turks twenty years after the fall of Bosnia (1483). The long period of Turkish oppression is lightened by the daring feat of Prince Eugene, who in the autumn of 1697 after the battle of Zenta, with 4,000 cavalry and 2,000 infantry advanced towards the capital of Bosnia; as the expected rising of the Christian population failed to take place, he retreated, carrying with him 40,000 liberated Christians. By the Treaty of Passarowitz (1718) the northern part of Bosnia and Servia was given to Austria, but the Treaty of Belgrade restored this district to the Turks.

Among the many revolts in Bosnia against the bureaucratic rule of the Osmanli Turks that of 1830–31 under Hussein Aga deserves mention; of the revolts in Herzegovina that of 1875. Article 25 of the Treaty of Berlin, 13 July, 1878, granted Austria the right to occupy and govern Bosnia and Herzegovina. The main column of the Austrian troops (thirteenth army corps), under the command of General of the Ordnance Joseph Freiherr von Philoppovich crossed the Save into Bosnia near Brod 29 July; two days later Major-General Jovanovic entered Herzegovina with a division. As the occupation took place with the consent of the *Porte*, it was thought that there would be no fighting. But the Mohammedan population, secretly incited by Servia, rose under the leadership of the adventurer, Hadschi Loja, against the "foreign conquerors". They were joined by large bands of Arnauts from Albania and by the Turkish troops who had received no instructions. The insurgents were defeated in bloody battles at Maglaj, Zepce, Jajce, Tuzla, and other places. On the evening of 18 August the Austrian troops stood before Serajevo which was taken by storm the next day. In order to hasten the end of the revolt three other Austrian army corps entered the contested district; by the end of September, 1878, both territories were subdued with the exception of a few points in the north-western part. In the *sanjak* (subdivision of a Turkish province) of Novibazar Austria holds some important military positions and controls the commercial routes; the Turks still retain the civil administration.

Introduction of Christianity.—Christianity was introduced into both Bosnia and Herzegovina from Salona at a very early date. Many of the dioceses which were suffragans of the Archdiocese of Salona in the sixth century must be sought within the present limits of Bosnia and Herzegovina. This is especially true of the Bishopric of Bistue (*Bestœensis ecclesia*) which was situated in the heart of the upper part of the present Bosnia. When the Arian Ostrogoths came into possession of these districts they did not interfere with the organization of the Church nor did they persecute the Catholics. The acts of the two provincial synods of Dalmatia which were held at Salona in 530 and 532 have been preserved and these show that in the year 530 four dioceses existed in Bosnia-Herzegovina. At the second synod two new dioceses were founded, Ludricensis (Livno), and Sarsenterensis (Sarsitero), the last named lying north of Mostar. During the war that lasted twenty years between Justinian and the Ostrogoths, the latter changed their policy towards the Catholics and persecuted them. Only one of the dioceses just mentioned, Bistue, survived the Slavonic invasion. Until the middle of the eleventh century Bistue was suffragan to the Archdiocese of Spalato; in 1067 it was transferred to the Archdiocese of Dioclea-Antivari, and shortly after it was made suffragan to the Archdiocese of Ragusa. Disputes now arose between the two last mentioned archdioceses as to the administration of the Bosnian bishopric; the strife was unfortunate for it allowed the sect of the Bogomili to gain a firm footing in Bosnia.

The heresy of the Bogomili was started in the tenth century by Jeremiah, also called Bogomil, a Bulgarian priest. His followers called themselves Christians and considered their faith the only true one. In Bosnia they were named Paterines. The Paterines, or Bogomili, rejected marriage, forbade intercourse with those of other faiths, disbelieved in war, in any execution of human beings, in oaths, in seeking for wealth, and in subjection to secular authority. The Paterines greatly increased in number and influence in Bosnia after the accession to their faith of Ban Kulin, and gained numerous adherents in the neighbouring districts of Croatia and Slavonia and in the cities of the Dalmatic coast. A similar sect, the Albigenses, appeared at the same time. At the beginning of the thirteenth century even the Bosnian bishop was an adherent of the Paterines; Pope Gregory IX, therefore, deposed him in 1233 and raised to the see Johannes, a German Dominican from Wildhausen in Westphalia. It is to the great credit of the Dominicans that they entered upon a successful spiritual campaign against the Paterines in Bosnia and Dalmatia. The Franciscans who had an intimate knowledge of the common people had even greater success. They not only brought back the population of the Dalmatic coast to the Church, but they also extended their spiritual activity to the interior of the country. Yet notwithstanding these efforts and those of the popes, in spite of two Bosnian crusades, and of the transfer of the Diocese of Bosnia to the Archdiocese of Kalocsa in Hungary, the sect was not suppressed. The formal return of the Bosnian nobles and monarchy to Catholicism was merely superficial.

The Turkish conquest of 1463 drove a large part of the Catholic population out of Bosnia. This led the courageous Franciscan monk, Angelus Zojezdovic, to go before the Sultan Mohammed II to call his attention to the fact that the Christian inhabitants were going out of Bosnia in all directions. The sultan, not wishing to have the newly conquered province depopulated, granted as a favour to the Franciscans that Christians should be allowed the free exercise of their religion. From that time until the present the Franciscan Order has been the only shield of the Christians in these two territories.

Church Statistics.—After the Turkish conquest the Bishopric of Bosnia had only a nominal existence. In 1735 the diocese was reorganized as the Vicariate Apostolic of Bosnia and Herzegovina and its administration confided to the Franciscans. Since 1846 the country has been divided into two vicariates. Three years after the Austrian occupation Pope Leo XIII erected the Archdiocese of Serajevo with the suffragan dioceses of Banjaluka in the north-western part of Bosnia, Mostar-Duvno in the northern part of Herzegovina, and Markana-Trebinje in the southern part of the same province. The Diocese of Markana-Trebinje which was founded in 870 has no bishop of its own but is administered by the Bishop of Mostar-Duvno. The training of the secular priests in all four dioceses is in the hands of the Jesuits. The other male religious orders represented are: the Franciscans who possess 17 monasteries, and have almost entire charge of the work of the sacred ministry in the Archdiocese of Serajevo and the Diocese of Mostar-Duvno; and the Trappists, with 3 monasteries and 182 members. The female congregations are: the Sisters of Mercy, with 12 convents; the Daughters of Divine Love, 5 convents; the Sisters of the Precious Blood, 9 convents; the School Sisters, 1 convent.

The Austrian occupation of Bosnia and Herzegovina since 1878 has not only done much for the material prosperity of these provinces, but has also been of great assistance to the Catholic religion. This is shown by a comparison with earlier years. In 1850 the two territories contained 150,000 Catholic inhabitants; in 1874, 185,503; in 1897, 334,142, or one-fourth of the whole population, and in 1907, 334,000. About 1880 there were no Catholic families in the district between Gradisca and Banjaluka, now there are 10 monasteries in this region. Before the Austrian occupation there were only 7 Catholic families in Trebinje; Trebinje has now several parishes and churches. In Herzegovina 8 parishes, 25 priests, and 36,000 Catholics have increased to 45 parishes, 100 priests, and 110,000 Catholics. The many churches, monasteries, school-houses, etc., which have come into existence since 1878 are proofs of the advance in intelligence and religion. Both territories show how beneficent has been the action of Austria in the Balkan Peninsula. In the agreement made between Austria-Hungary and Turkey of 21 April, 1879, the former country bound itself to protect in Bosnia and Herzegovina the religious liberty of the inhabitants as well as of temporary residents. This agreement includes Catholics. The regulations in regard to marriage and divorce, as well as the exemption of the clergy from public services and military duty, are about the same as those in Austria. The cemeteries are still denominational institutions and are reserved even more exclusively than in Austria for the adherents of each faith.

VJEKOSLAV, *Gesch. Bosniens von den ältesten Zeiten bis zum Verfalle des Königreiches*, Germ. tr. from the Croatian by VON BOJNIČIĆ (Leipzig, 1885); SUPAN, *Oesterreich-Ungarn in Länderkunde von Europa* (Vienna, Prague, and Leipzig, 1889), pt. 1, Div. II; *Bosnia und Herzegovina* in *Die österreich.-ungar. Monarchie in Wort und Bild* (Vienna, 1901); SCHWEIGER-LERCHENFELD, *Bosnien, das Land und seine Bewohner* (Vienna, 1879); *Die Occupation Bosniens und der Herzegovina durch k. k. Truppen*, from the royal and imperial war-archives (6 pts., Vienna, 1879, 1880); T. VON ASBOTH, *Bosnien und Herzegovina* (4 pts., Vienna, 1888); *Wissenschaftl. Mitteilungen aus Bosnien und der Herzegovina*, publication of the National Museum at Serajevo (13 vols., Vienna, 1893–1905); HÖRNES, *Altertümer der Herzegovina und der südl. Teile Bosniens* (Vienna, 1882); SCHNELLER, *Die staatsrechtl. Stellung von Bosnien und der Herzegovina* (Leipzig, 1892); *Correspondence Respecting Affairs in Bosnia and Herzegovina* (Eng. Foreign Office, 1876—); MILLER, *Travels and Politics in the Near East* (London, 1899); *Statesman's Year Book*, (London, 1907).

KARL KLAAR.

Boso, first Bishop of Merseburg, in the present Prussian Province of Saxony, and Apostle of the Wends, d. November, 970. He was a Benedictine monk of St. Emmeram in Ratisbon whence he was summoned to the court of Otto I. The emperor, considering the conversion of the lately subjugated Wends indispensable to the security of the German Empire, sent Boso to Christianize them. In the beginning Boso's mission appeared useless, owing to the hate of the Wends for the Germans who had deprived them of their liberty. Boso, however, being a true apostle, did not despair, but studied the language of the Wends in order to preach to them in their own tongue. They appreciated the unselfish devotion with which Boso worked for their temporal and spiritual welfare, and their hatred soon turned into love. In 968 Boso was able to provide for the creation of three new sees, Merseburg, Meissen, and Zeitz. Being given his choice he selected Merseburg as his bishopric; Hugo, another Benedictine monk, became Bishop of Zeitz, and Burchard, of Meissen. All three were consecrated on Christmas Day, 968, by their metropolitan, Adalbert of Magdeburg. Boso continued his missionary labours, but died on a visit to his native Bavaria.

THIETMAR, *Chronicon Merseburgense*, ed. LAPPENBERG, in *Mon. Germ. Hist.: Script.*, III, 750; HAUCK, *Kirchengesch. Deutschlands* (Leipzig, 1906), III, 95 sqq.

MICHAEL OTT.

Boso (BREAKSPEAR), third English Cardinal, date of birth uncertain; d. at Rome, about 1181. He was a Benedictine monk of St. Albans Abbey and the nephew of Adrian IV. Though this relationship was on the maternal side, Cardella states that Boso as well as Adrian IV bore the surname of Breakspear. He had a reputation not only for piety, but also for learning, and was esteemed by contemporary writers as among the most eminent theologians of his age. He compiled or wrote the lives of several eleventh and twelfth century popes, among them the life of his uncle, and indulged in the lighter accomplishment of versifying, examples of his poetic powers still existing in the Cotton MSS. in the British Museum, in the form of metrical lives of saints. He followed his uncle to Rome; and on the latter's elevation to the Papal Chair, was created by him Cardinal-Deacon of the title of Sts. Cosmas and Damian, in December, 1155, and was also appointed Camerlengo of the Holy See. Adrian sent Boso on a mission to Portugal; for what precise purpose does not transpire, but the fact is attested by the registers of Pope Innocent III. He also confided to him the governorship of the Castle of Sant' Angelo, being somewhat suspicious of the fidelity of the Roman populace. When Adrian IV died in 1159, dissensions arose in the conclave as to the choice of his successor, the result of which was the creation of a schism lasting seventeen years. Four cardinals in the imperial interest voted for Cardinal Octavian, who assumed the name of Victor IV, but he was acknowledged only by the Germans. On the very day of Adrian's burial in the Vatican basilica, 5 September, Cardinal Boso, who appears to have taken the lead, withdrew with the majority, twenty-three, of the cardinals within the fortress of Sant' Angelo to escape the vengeance of the anti-pope, and straightway elected as pope, Cardinal Rolando (Bandinelli) of Siena, who was consecrated under the name of Alexander III. The new pope was not unmindful of his obligations to Boso, and soon (1163) promoted him Cardinal-Priest of the title of St. Pudentiana. When Alexander made his memorable journey to Venice to receive the submission and allegiance of the Emperor Frederick, and to ratify the "Peace of Venice" (24 June, 1177) which closed the schism, he was accompanied by Boso. Alexander also entrusted Boso with a mission to Tuscany, an event attested by the registers of Alexander IV. Boso's name appears attached to many Bulls, both of Adrian IV and of Alexander III.

Dict. Nat. Biogr., V, 421; CARDELLA, Memorie Storiche de' Cardinali; EGGS, Purpura docta (Munich, 1714–29); DUCHESNE, Liber Pontif., II, xxxix–xliii, 351–446; WATTENBACH, Deutschlands Geschichtsquellen, 6th ed., II, 331; REUTER, Alexander III (1860–64); JAFFÉ, Regesta RR. PP., II, s. vv., Adrian IV, Alexander III.

HENRY NORBERT BIRT.

Bossu, JACQUES LE, French theologian and Doctor of the Sorbonne, b. at Paris 1546; d. at Rome 1626. He entered the Benedictine Order at the Royal Abbey of St. Denis, of which he became claustral prior. He was preceptor to the Cardinal de Guise and took a prominent part in the Catholic League and the disputes concerning the successor to Henry III, whose death he considered to be a just punishment. The accession of Henry IV, against whom he had written, and the execution of de Guise in 1587 necessitated his leaving France in 1591, and he went to Rome, where he entered the service of the Curia. He was made a consultor of the Congregation de Auxiliis, established in 1599 to settle the controversy on grace between the Dominicans and the Jesuits. On its dissolution, in 1607, he desired to return to France, but the pope, Paul V, kept him in Rome. His chief work consisted of "Animadversiones" against twenty-five propositions of Molina, a Spanish Jesuit who had written a book on grace, defending the doctrines of Scotus against those of the Dominicans. The "Animadversiones" were published by Antonio Raynaldo, the Dominican, in 1644. Le Bossu's "Diarium Congregationis de Auxiliis" has unfortunately perished.

ZIEGELBAUER, Hist. Lit. O.S.B. (Augsburg, 1754), III, 371; HURTER, Nomenclator (Innsbruck, 1892), I, 270.

G. CYPRIAN ALSTON.

Bossuet, JACQUES-BÉNIGNE, a celebrated French bishop and pulpit orator, b. at Dijon, 27 September, 1627; d. at Paris, 12 April, 1704. For more than a century his ancestors, both paternal and maternal, had occupied judicial functions. He was the fifth son of Bénigne Bossuet, a judge in the Parliament of Dijon, and Madeleine Mochet. He began his classical studies at the Collège des Godrans, conducted by the Jesuits, in Dijon, and, on his father's appointment to a seat in the Parliament of Metz, he was left in his native town, under the care of his uncle, Claude Bossuet d'Aiseray, a renowned scholar. His extraordinary ardour for study gave occasion to the schoolboy joke, deriving his name from Bos suetus aratro. In a very short time, he mastered the Greek and Latin classics. Homer and Virgil were his favourite authors, while the Bible soon became his livre de chevet. Speaking of the Scriptures, he used to say: "Certe, in his consenescere, in his immori, summa votorum est." Early destined to the Church, he received the tonsure when he was only eight years old, and at the age of thirteen he obtained a canonicate in the cathedral of Metz. In 1642, he left Dijon and went to Paris to finish his classical studies and to take up philosophy and theology in the Collège de Navarre. A year later he was introduced by Arnauld at the Hotel de Rambouillet, where, one evening at eleven o'clock, he delivered an extempore sermon, which caused Voiture's remark: "I never heard anybody preach so early nor so late." A Master of Arts in 1644, he held his first thesis (tentativa) in theology, 25 January, 1648, in the presence of the Prince de Condé. He was ordained sub-deacon the same year, and deacon the following year, and preached his first sermons at Metz. He held his second thesis (sorbonica) 9 November, 1650. For two years, he lived in retirement, preparing himself for the priesthood under the direction of St. Vincent de Paul, and was ordained 18 March, 1852. A few weeks later, the degree of Doctor of Divinity was conferred upon him. Appointed Archdeacon of Sarrebourg (January, 1652), he resided for seven years at Metz, devoting himself to the study of the Bible and the Fathers, preaching sermons, holding controversies with Protestants, and yet, finding time for the secular affairs for which he was responsible, as a member of the Assembly of the Three Orders. In 1657 he was induced by St. Vincent de Paul to come to Paris and give himself entirely to preaching.

Though living in Paris, Bossuet did not sever his connexion with the cathedral of Metz; he continued to hold his benefice, and was even appointed dean in 1664, when his father, a widower, had just received the priesthood and become a canon of the same cathedral. There are extant one hundred and thirty-seven sermons which were delivered by Bossuet between 1659 and 1669, and it is estimated that more than one hundred have been lost. In 1669 he was appointed Bishop of Condom, without being obliged to reside in his diocese, was consecrated 21 September, 1670, but, obeying scruples of conscience, resigned his bishopric a year later, in which year, also, he was elected to the French Academy. Appointed preceptor to the Dauphin, 13 September, 1670, he threw himself with indefatigable energy into his tutorial functions, composing all the books deemed necessary for his pupil's instruction, models of handwriting as well as manuals of philosophy, and himself giving all the lessons, three times a day. When his functions as preceptor ended (1681), he was appointed to the bishopric of Meaux. He took a prominent part in the Assembly of the French Clergy in 1682. Unlike the court bishops, Bossuet constantly resided in his diocese and busied himself with the details of its administration. In that period he completed his long-interrupted works of historical controversy,

BOSSUET

FROM THE PAINTING BY RIGAUD

wrote innumerable spiritual letters, took care of his religious communities (for whom he composed "Meditations on the Gospel" and "Uplifting of the Soul on the Mysteries"), and entered on endless polemics with Ellies du Pin, Caffaro, Fénelon, the Probabilists, Richard Simon and the Jansenists. From 1700, his health began to fail, which, however, did not prevent him from wrestling in defence of the Faith. Confined to his bed by illness, he dictated letters and polemical essays to his secretary. As Saint-Simon says, "he died fighting".

A list and criticism of Bossuet's chief works will be found in the following appreciation, by the late Ferdinand Brunetière. Out of one hundred and thirty works composed by Bossuet from 1653 to 1704, eighty were edited by himself, seven or eight by his nephew, the Abbé Bossuet, afterwards Bishop of Troyes; the remainder, about forty-two, not including the "Letters" and "Sermons", appeared from 1741 to 1789. The principal complete editions are: the Versailles edition 1815-19, 47 vols. in-8; Lachat (Vivès), Paris, 1862-64, 31 vols. in-8; Guillaume, Paris, 10 vols. in-4. No critical and chronological edition of Bossuet's complete works has been made as yet, only the sermons having been edited (in a most scientific manner) by the Abbé Lebarcq: "Œuvres oratoires; édition critique complète, avec introduction grammaticale, préface, notes, et choix de variantes", Paris, 1890, 6 vols. in-8.

LOUIS N. DELAMARRE.

BOSSUET, LITERARY AND THEOLOGICAL APPRECIATION OF.—The life of this great man, perfectly simple as it was, and all of one piece with itself, may be divided into three epochs, to each of which as a matter of fact there are found to correspond, if not a new aspect of his genius, at least occupations or labours which are not altogether of the same nature, and which consequently show him to us in a somewhat different light. At first, one perceives in him only the orator, the greatest, perhaps, who has ever appeared in the Christian pulpit—greater than Chrysostom and greater than Augustine; the only man whose name can be compared in eloquence with those of Cicero and of Demosthenes (1617-70).

Appointed preceptor to the Dauphin, son of Louis XIV, he devoted himself for more than ten years entirely to this onerous task (1670-81), appeared in the pulpit only at rare intervals, returned to the studies which he had somewhat neglected, and composed for his pupil works of which the "Discourse on Universal History" is still the most celebrated. Finally, in the last period of his life (1681-1704), having become Bishop of Meaux, though he still preaches regularly to his own flock, and raises his eloquent voice on solemn occasions—to open the Assembly of the Clergy of France, in 1681, or to pronounce the funeral oration of the Prince de Condé, in 1687—yet it is above all the great controversialist that his contemporaries admire in him, the defender of tradition against all the novelties which sought to weaken it, the unwearying opponent of Jurieu, of Richard Simon, of Madame Guyon, and, incidentally, of Fénelon himself; he is the theologian of Providence, and—startling contrast—on the eve of the Regency, he is "the last of the Fathers of the Church".

FIRST PERIOD (1627-70).—He made his first studies with the Jesuits of his native city, completed them in Paris at the College of Navarre, and, ordained priest, entered into possession of the archdeaconry of Sarrebourg, in the Diocese of Metz, in 1652. Anywhere else than at Metz, no matter in what part of the world, he would without doubt have been himself. In literary history, environment commonly shows its effects only in the formation of mediocrities. But, as there existed at Metz a large

Jewish community (and in some respects, the only one in France that was recognized by the State), and as the Protestants were numerous, and still fervent, in the neighbouring province of Alsace, one may believe that Bossuet's natural tendency to take religion on its controversial side was encouraged or strengthened by these circumstances. Proof of this, if desired, may be found in the fact that the manuscript of one of his first sermons, "On the Law of God", 1653, still bears this statement in his own handwriting: "Preached at Metz against the Jews"; and in this other fact, that the first work he had printed was a "Refutation", in 1655, of the catechism of Paul Ferry, a renowned Protestant pastor of Metz. Be that as it may, as soon as the young archdeacon began to preach his reputation quickly spread, and very soon the pulpits of Paris were vying with one another to secure him. It may therefore be said that from 1656 to 1670 he gave himself entirely to the ministry of preaching, and as a matter of fact, three-fourths of the two hundred, or more, "Sermons" which have reached us, either complete or in fragments, date from this period. They may be distinguished as "Sermons", properly so called; "Panegyrics of Saints"; and "Funeral Orations". These last number ten in all. In some editions the "Sermons on Religious Professions" (*Sermons de Vêture*), of which the most celebrated is that for the profession of Madame de la Vallière, preached in 1674, and the "Sermons for the Feasts of the Virgin", are classed by themselves.

What are the essential characteristics of Bossuet's eloquence? In the first place, the force, or, to put it, perhaps, better, the energy, of speech, or of the word, and by this I mean, inclusively, exactitude and precision, the fitness of phrase, the neatness of turn, the impressiveness of the gesture implied in his words, and, generally, all the qualities of that French writer who, entertaining, with Pascal, a great horror of the artifices of rhetoric, for that very reason best understood the resources of French prose. There is nothing, in French, which surpasses a fine page of Bossuet.

The second characteristic of his eloquence is what Alexandre Vinet, though a Protestant, has not feared to call, in an essay on Bourdaloue, the depth and reach of its philosophy. He meant that while the illustrious Jesuit in his "Sermons" is always strictly and evidently Catholic, Bossuet, surely no less so, excels, besides, in demonstrating, even apart from Catholicism, the peremptory reasons in the depths of our nature and in the sequence of history why one should feel and think like a Catholic even if one were not a Catholic. Those who care to verify this opinion of Vinet may read Bossuet's sermons on "Death", "Ambition", "Providence", "The Honour of the World", "Our Dispositions in Regard to the Necessities of Life", "The Eminent Dignity of the Poor", "Submission to the Law of God", and also the sermons for the Feasts of the Blessed Virgin. The "Sermon for the Profession of Madame de la Vallière" is another beautiful example of this philosophic character of Bossuet's eloquence.

Lastly, its third characteristic is its movement and lyric power. Bossuet—the Bossuet of the "Sermons" and of the "Funeral Orations"—is a poet, a great poet; and he is lyrical in his blending of personal and interior emotions with the expression of truths which he unfolds. "The Uplifting of the Soul by the Divine Mysteries" and "Meditations on the Gospel" are titles of two of his most beautiful works, in which in his old age he, as it were, condensed the substance of his "Sermons". But it may be truly said that there is no sermon of his which is not either a "Meditation" or an "Uplifting of the Soul". And is it not strange that at the beginning of the nineteenth century these titles, "Uplifting of the Soul" and "Meditations", were applied by Lamartine and Vigny to their own first poetic works? Such are the essential characteristics of Bossuet's eloquence, to which might easily be added a great many others, perhaps more showy, but which may be found in other preachers, while those we have mentioned belong to him alone.

Meanwhile, the reputation of the preacher was growing every day. Above all, his Lenten conferences before the Court in 1662 and in 1666 had brought him into prominence, particularly the second series, which included some of his finest "Sermons". The Protestants, on the other hand, although they had no adversary more moderate than he, had none more formidable; and when some startling conversion, like that of Turenne, took place, the honour or the blame of it was laid upon the Abbé Bossuet. His little book, circulated in manuscript under the title of "Exposition of the Doctrine of the Catholic Church on Subjects of Controversy", worried the Protestant divines more than had any folio in fifty years. The public voice marked him out for a bishopric. We know, too, that, though doubtless without his being aware of it, his name figured, after 1667, among the candidates for the office of preceptor to the Dauphin, those names having been selected, by the king's command, under the direction of Colbert. It is true that Louis XIV did not favour Bossuet's appointment; he preferred the President De Périgny. In 1669, however, Bossuet was appointed Bishop of Condom. It was as Bishop of Condom that in September of that same year he pronounced the "Funeral Oration on Henrietta of France", and was summoned to preach the Advent of 1669 at Court. When, soon after this, the daughter followed her mother to the grave, he was again summoned, in 1670, to pronounce the "Funeral Oration of the Duchess of Orleans". In the meanwhile, the President De Périgny died unexpectedly, and this time the choice of Louis XIV went straight to Bossuet. He was named preceptor to the Dauphin, 5 September, 1670, and a new period began in the history of his life.

SECOND PERIOD (1670–81).—In order to devote himself solely to his task, he gave up his Bishopric of Condom, which he never saw, and returned to the profane studies which he had been obliged to abandon. He himself laid down in his letter to Pope Innocent XI, the programme he made his royal pupil follow, a programme the intelligent liberality of which it is impossible not to admire. But, while giving the closest personal attention to the Dauphin's education, his own genius completed, in a way, its process of ripening by contact with antiquity; his ideas collected themselves and gained in precision; he took conscious possession of what may be called his originality as a thinker, and made for himself his private domain, as it were, in the vast field of apologetics. And, as the other Fathers of the Church have been, in the history of Christian thought, one the theologian of the Incarnation, another, the theologian of Grace, so did Bossuet then become the theologian of Providence.

Here we may take an excellent example of what is to-day called the development, or evolution, of a dogmatic truth. The idea of Providence surely constitutes the basis of Christian belief in all that touches the relations of man with God, and in this respect it may be said that the "Discourse on Universal History" is completely anticipated in the "City of God" of St. Augustine, or in the "De Gubernatione Dei" of Salvianus. We are perfectly willing to add that in this wide, and even slightly vague, sense it is found also in the Old Testament, and notably in the Book of Daniel. But that does not alter the fact that Bossuet in his turn appropriated this idea of Providence to himself, made it profoundly his own,

and without any innovation—for every innovation in this field inspired him with horror—formed from it deductions which up to his time had never been perceived.

The idea of Providence, in Bossuet's theology, appears to us as at once (a) the sanction of the moral law, (b) the very law of history, and (c) the foundation of apologetics.

(a) It is the sanction of the moral law, in the first place, inasmuch as, being able to act only under the eyes of God, no act of ours is indifferent, since there is not one but is for us an occasion of, or, to put it better, a manner of acquiring, merit or demerit. It is under this aspect that the idea of Providence seems to have presented itself primarily to Bossuet, and that it is found in some sort scattered or diffused in his earliest "Sermons". But, since, moreover, nothing happens to us which is not an effect of God's Will, therefore we ought always to see in whatever happiness or unhappiness—according to the world's judgment—may befall us only a chastisement, a trial, or a temptation, which it is for us to make a means either of salvation or of damnation. Here is the mystery of pain and the solution of the problem of evil. If we did not place entire confidence in Providence, the existence of evil and the prosperity of the wicked would be for the human mind nothing but an occasion of scandal; and if we did not accept our sufferings as a design of God in our regard, we should fall into despair. A source of resignation, our trust in Providence is also a source of strength, and it governs, so to speak, the entire domain of moral action. If our actions are moral, it is by reason of their conformity with, or at least of their analogy to, the views of Providence, and thus the life of the Christian is only a perpetual realization of the Will of God. We merit according to our endeavours to know it in order to carry it into effect; and, on the contrary, to demerit consists exactly in not taking account of God's Will or warnings, whether the omission be through negligence, pride, or stubbornness.

(b) This is why the idea of Providence is at the same time the law of history. If the crash of empires "falling one upon another" does not in truth express some purpose of God regarding humanity, then history, or what is called by that name, is indeed no longer anything but a chaotic chronology, the meaning of which we should strive in vain to disentangle. In that case, Fortune, or rather Chance, would be the mistress of human affairs; the existence of humanity would be only a bad dream, or phantasmagoria, whose changing face would be inadequate to mask a void of nothingness. We should be fretting ourselves in that void without reason and almost without cause, our very actions would be but phantoms, and the only result of so many efforts accumulated through so many thousands of years would be the conviction, every day more clear, of their uselessness, which would be another void of nothingness. And why, after all, were there Greeks and Romans? Of what use was Salamis?—Actium?—Poitiers?— Lepanto? Why was there a Cæsar, and a Charlemagne? Let us frankly own, then, that unless something Divine circulates in history, there is no history. Nations, like individuals, live only by maintaining uninterrupted communication with God, and it is precisely this condition of their existence which is called by the name of Providence. The hypothesis of Providence is the condition of the possibility of history, as the hypothesis of the stability of the laws of nature is the condition of the possibility of science.

(c) Having made Providence the sanction of morality, we are now led to make it the basis of apologetics. For if there be indeed more than one way which leads to God, or, in other words, many means of establishing the truth of the Christian religion, there is, in Bossuet's view, none more convincing than that which is at once the highest expression and the summing-up of the history of humanity, that is to say, "the very sequence of religion", or "the relation of the two Testaments", and, in a more objective manner, the visible manifestation of Providence in the establishment of Christianity. It was Providence that made of the Jewish people a people apart, a unique people, the chosen people, charged with maintaining and defending the worship of the true God throughout the pagan centuries, against the prestige of an idolatry which essentially consisted in the deification of the energies of nature. It was Providence that, by means of Roman unity and of its extension throughout the known universe, rendered not only possible, but easy and almost necessary, the conversion of the world to Christianity. It was Providence, again, that developed the features of the modern world out of the disorder of barbarous invasions and reconciled the two antiquities under the law of Christ. The full importance of these views of Bossuet—for we are only summarizing here the "Discourse on Universal History"—will be understood if we observe that, in our day, when the Strausses and Renans have sought to give us their own version of the origins of Christianity, they have found nothing more than this and nothing else; and all their ingenuity has issued in the conclusion that things have happened in the reality of history *as if* some mysterious will had from all eternity proportioned effects and causes. But the real truth is that Christianity, in propagating itself, has proved itself. If the action of Providence is manifest anywhere, it is in the sequence of the history of Christianity. And what is more natural under the circumstances than to make of its history the demonstration of its truth?

It was appropriate to insist here upon this idea of Providence, which is, in a manner, the masterpiece of Bossuet's theology. Besides the "Discourse on Universal History", he wrote other works for the education of the Dauphin; notably the "Treatise on the Knowledge of God and of Oneself" and the "Art of Governing, Drawn from the Words of Holy Scripture", which appeared only after his death; the "Art of Governing", in 1709, and the "Treatise on the Knowledge of God", in 1722. To the "Treatise on Free Will" and the "Treatise on Concupiscence", also posthumous, a like origin has been assigned; but this is certainly a mistake; these two works, which contain some of Bossuet's most beautiful pages, were not written for his royal pupil, who certainly would not have understood them at all. Did he even understand the "Discourse on Universal History"? In this connexion it has been questioned whether Bossuet, in his quality of preceptor, did not fail in his first obligation, which was, as his critics assert, to adapt himself to his pupil's intelligence. Here we can only reply, without going to the bottom of the question, that the end which Bossuet intended was no ordinary education, but the education of a future King of France, the first obligation incumbent upon whose preceptor was to treat him as a King. Thus, for that matter, professors in our universities never seem to subordinate their teaching to the capacity of their pupils, but only to the exigencies of the science taught. And we will add, moreover, that as the Dauphin never reigned, no one can really say how much he did, or did not, profit by a preceptor such as Bossuet was.

The education of a prince ordinarily, and naturally, ended with his marriage. The functions of Bossuet as preceptor ceased, therefore, in 1681. He had been appointed Bishop of Meaux; he was made Almoner to the Dauphin, quite in accordance with usage, and the King honoured him with the title of General Councillor (*Conseiller en tous les conseils*). We may be

permitted to call attention to the fact that this was only an honorary title, and one need not therefore conclude, as seems to have been done sometimes, that Bossuet took his seat, or voted, in, for instance, the *Conseil des dépêches*, which was the Council of Foreign Affairs, or in the *Conseil du Roi*, which busied itself with the internal affairs of the kingdom. But during his preceptorship, and independently of any participation in the councils, his authority had nevertheless become of considerable importance at Court, with Louis XIV personally. No member of the French clergy was thenceforth more in evidence than he; no preacher, no bishop. He had no reason, then, to fear that, having accomplished the education of the Dauphin, his activity would fail to find employment. In truth, the last epoch of his life was to be its fullest.

THIRD PERIOD (1681–1704).—This period was the most laborious, indeed the most painful; and the impassioned struggles in which he becomes engaged will now end only with his life. But why so many struggles at the time of life when most men seek for rest? What circumstances occasioned them? And if we recall that up to this time his existence had not been disturbed by any agitation that could be called deep, whence this sudden combative ardour? It cannot be explained without a preliminary remark. The reconciliation of Protestantism and Catholicism had been an early dream of Bossuet; and, on the other hand, France in the seventeenth century had, in general, ill chosen her side in a division which she regarded as not only regrettable from the standpoint of religion, but destructive, and even dangerous to her political unity. This is why Bossuet was to work all his life and with all his strength for the reunion of the Churches, and to force himself to exert every effort for the attainment of those conditions which he believed necessary to that end. Abundant and instructive details on this point are to be found in M. A. Rébelliau's charming work, "Bossuet, historien du Protestantisme". Being, moreover, too reasonable and too well-informed not to recognize the legitimate element which the Reformation movement had had in its time, Bossuet was convinced that it was of the greatest moment not indeed to—in the phrase of our own day—"minimize" the demands of the Catholic verity, but at all events not to exaggerate those demands; and, therefore, (1) to make to Protestant opinion every concession which a rigorous orthodoxy would permit; and (2) not to add anything, on the other hand, to a creed more than one difficulty of which was already repelling the Protestants.

Thus may we explain his part in the Assembly of the French Clergy in 1682; the plan of his "History of the Variations of the Protestant Churches", as well as the character of his polemics against the Protestants; his fundamental motive in the matter of Quietism and the true reason for his fierce animosity against Fénelon; his writings against Richard Simon, such as his "Defence of Tradition and of the Holy Fathers"; such steps as those which he took against the mystic reveries of Maria d'Agreda; and, lastly, the approbation which, in 1682 and 1702, he so loudly expressed for the renewed censures of the Assemblies of the Clergy upon the relaxed morals of the day. However, it is little to our purpose to ascertain whether Bossuet, in the course of all these controversies, more than once allowed himself to be drawn on beyond the point which he intended, especially, as he has been reproached, in the questions of Gallicanism and of Quietism. The celebrated Declaration of 1682 seems to have altogether exceeded the measure of what it was useful or necessary to say in order to defend the temporal power of the prince or the independence of nations against the Roman Curia. Quietism, too, was perhaps not so great a danger as he believed it to be; nor, above all, a danger of the kind to repel Protestants from Catholicism, since, after all, it is in a Protestant country that the works of Madame Guyon are still read in our day. But to properly explain these points we should have to write volumes; it suffices here to throw some light on Bossuet's controversial work with this general remark: his essential purpose was to get rid of the reasons for resistance which Protestants drew from the substance or the form of Catholicism, in opposition to the reasons for reunion.

In this remark, also, is to be found the decisive answer to the question, often raised, and amply discussed for some years, of the Jansenism of Bossuet. Jansenism, indeed, involves two things: the "Five Propositions"—a doctrine, or a heresy, formally and solemnly condemned; and a general tendency, very much like that of Calvin, to rationalize Christian morality and even dogma. So far as Jansenism is a heresy, Bossuet was never a Jansenist; but so far as it is a mere tendency, an intellectual disposition and a tendency to effect a mutual drawing together of reason and faith, it is scarcely possible to deny that he leaned towards Jansenism. Quite apart from the satisfaction which his own genius, naturally attracted to order and to clarity, found in this conciliation of reason and faith, he judged this the most propitious ground of all for the reconciliation of Protestantism with Catholicism. But to this it should be added at once that Bossuet, while not adding to the difficulties of faith, made it a condition that care must be taken not to trench upon faith, and this trait it is which completes the picture of Bossuet's character. Tradition has never had a more eloquent or a more vigorous defender. *Quod ubique, quod semper, quod ab omnibus creditum est;* this was for Bossuet, in a manner, the absolute criterion of Catholic truth. He had no difficulty in deducing from it "the immutability of morality or of dogma"; and in this precisely, as is well known, consists his great argument against the Protestants. The "History of the Variations of the Protestant churches" is nothing more than a history of the alterations, if one may say so, to which the Protestant Churches have subjected dogma, and the adjustments or adaptations of dogma which they have pretended to make to circumstances that had nothing but what was transitory and contingent. But "the truth which comes from God possesses from the first its complete perfection", and from that it follows that as many "variations" as there are, so many "errors" are there in faith, since they are so many contradictions or omissions of tradition.

This point has been reserved for the last in the present article, because no other trait of Bossuet's genius seems to have gone further towards establishing the common conception of it. It is easy to see that that conception is not altogether false; but neither is it altogether true, nor, above all, fair when, as is often done, it is extended from the genius of the controversialist or theologian to the character of the man himself. Tradition, we repeat, has had no more eloquent or more implacable champion; it has had none more sincere; but tradition such as he comprehended it is not all of the past, for so understood it would include even heresy and schism. Tradition, for Bossuet as for the Catholic Church, is only what has survived of the past. If Nestorian Christianities still exist to-day—and some do exist—they are as if they were not, and Nestorianism does not on that account constitute a part of tradition. It would, and does, constitute a part of the tradition of Free Thought. But for the Church, tradition is only what she has thought herself obliged to preserve out of those doctrines which have succeeded one another in the course of her development, among which she has made her choice in virtue of her

magisterium, retaining some, rejecting others, without even being always obliged to condemn the latter. It can be proved, on the other hand, that, thus understood, tradition in the writings of Bossuet, and on his lips when he invokes it, does not exclude religious progress, even if, perhaps, the former does not postulate the latter as a condition. And already, doubtless, it is beginning to be half seen that the true Bossuet, even in theology, even in his long combats with the heretics, was not the unbending, irreconcilable man he is commonly painted.

This will be still better seen if we reflect that a great writer is not always the man of his style. In his sermons as in his writings, it would be impossible to deny that Bossuet has an imperious and authoritative style. He counsels nothing which he does not command, or which he does not impose; and to everything which he advances he communicates the character and force of a demonstration by his manner of expressing it. Not that many pages of a different tenor might not be cited from him, and some such will be found notably in his "Uplifting of the Soul", his "Meditations", or his "Sermons for Festivals of the Virgin". But the habitual quality of his style, for all that, remains, as we have said, imperious and authoritative, because it is in harmony with the nature of his mind, which demands first and foremost clearness, certainty, and order. It may be said of him that, seeing all things in their relation to Providence, he expresses nothing except under the aspect of eternity. A great poet in later times has said: "Qu'est-ce que tout cela qui n'est pas éternel", and, looked at in this light, there is a perfect agreement between the style and the thought of Bossuet. But as to his character the same thing cannot be said; here every testimony alike shows us in this writer, whose accent seems to brook no contradiction, the most gentle, the most affable, and sometimes the most hesitating of men.

Such was the true Bossuet. In his life we cannot always find the daring of his eloquence, nor in his conduct the audacity of his reasoning. This great dominator of the ideas—one might even say of the intelligences—of his time suffered himself to be dominated more than once by the thoroughly human dread of being disagreeable and, above all, of giving offence. "He has no joints", he himself said of one of the gentlemen of Port Royal who was somewhat lacking in flexibility; to which the individual in question retorted: "And as for him, you may tell him that he has no bones!" The strong, concise *mot* sums up all the reproaches that can be made against this great memory. Had his strength of character and his apostolic vigour equalled the force of his genius, he would have been a St. Augustine. Falling short of St. Augustine, a Catholic and a Frenchman may be permitted to believe that it is still something rare, something exalted among men to have been merely Jacques Bénigne Bossuet.

DE BURIGNY, *Vie de Bossuet* (1731); DE BAUSSET, *Histoire de Bossuet* (4 vols., 1814); FLOQUET, *Etudes sur la vie de Bossuet* (4 vols., 1855–70—these four volumes, unfortunately, do not go beyond 1681); RÉAUME, *Histoire de Bossuet* (3 vols., 1869); LANSON, *Bossuet* (1890); RÉBELLIAU in *Grands écrivains français; Bossuet; Journal de l'abbé* LE DIEU (4 vols., 1856–57); DELMONT, *Autour de Bossuet;* LEBARCQ, *Histoire de la prédication de Bossuet* (1888).

For an almost complete list of historical works and literary criticism which deal with Bossuet, cf. BOURSEAUD, *Histoire et déscription des manuscrits et des éditions originales des ouvrages de Bossuet*, with an indication of the translations of them, and of the writings which they occasioned at the time of their publication (Paris, 1897); URBAIN in *Bibliothèque de bibliographies critiques* (Paris, Société des Etudes historiques).

F. BRUNETIÈRE.

Bost, ARNOLD. See TRITHEMIUS.

Boste (or BOAST), JOHN, VENERABLE, priest and martyr, b. of good Catholic family at Dufton, in Westmoreland, about 1544; d. at Durham, 24 July, 1594. He studied at Queen's College, Oxford, 1569–

72, became a Fellow, and was received into the Church at Brome, in Suffolk, in 1576. Resigning his Fellowship in 1580, he went to Reims, where he was ordained priest, 4 March, 1581, and in April was sent to England. He landed at Hartlepool and became a most zealous missioner, so that the persecutors made extraordinary efforts to capture him. At last, after many narrow escapes, he was taken at Waterhouses, the house of William Claxton, near Durham, betrayed by one Eglesfield, 5 July, 1593. The place is still visited by Catholics. From Durham he was conveyed to London, showing himself throughout "resolute, bold, joyful, and pleasant", although terribly racked in the Tower. Sent back to Durham for the July Assizes, 1594, he behaved with undaunted courage and resolution, and induced his fellow-martyr, George Swalwell, a convert minister, who had recanted through fear, to repent of his cowardice, absolving him publicly in court. He suffered at Dryburn, outside Durham. He recited the Angelus while mounting the ladder, and was executed with extraordinary brutality; for he was scarcely turned off the ladder when he was cut down, so that he stood on his feet, and in that posture was cruelly butchered alive. An account of his trial and execution was written by an eye-witness, Venerable Christopher Robinson, who suffered martyrdom shortly afterwards at Carlisle.

British Museum MS. Lansdowne, 75, f. 44; CHALLONER, *Memoirs*; SHARPE, *Memorials of the Rebellion of 1569*; FOLEY, *Records*, III; *Catholic Record Society, Miscellanea* (Christopher Robinson's account), I; COOPER in *Dict. Nat. Biog.* WAINEWRIGHT, *Venerable John Boste* (London, Cath. Truth Soc., 1907); GOLDIE, *The Martyr of Waterhouses* in *Ushaw Magazine*, 1902, 1903.

BEDE CAMM.

Boston, ARCHDIOCESE OF, comprises Essex, Middlesex, Suffolk, Norfolk, and Plymouth counties in the State of Massachusetts, U. S. A., the towns of Mattapoisett, Marion, and Wareham excepted, embracing an area of 2,465 square miles. The see was erected 8 April, 1808, and created an archbishopric in 1875. When the first Bishop of Boston was consecrated his jurisdiction extended over all New England and a mere handful of Catholics. There are now eight dioceses in the same territory with about 2,100,000 Catholics of whom 850,000 are within the limits of the Archdiocese of Boston where the first bishop found a scant hundred. The growth of the Church has been due mainly to the immigrants attracted by the advantages offered by the great and varied manufacturing interests of New England. The Irish came first, after them the French Canadians, the Italians, the Poles, the Portuguese, and representatives of nearly all the peoples of the globe.

EARLY HISTORY.—Early Irish emigration to America took place in three distinct periods, from 1621 to 1653; from 1653 to 1718, and from 1718 to 1775. But the mistake must not be made, as it often is, that these immigrants were all Catholics. Many of them were not, and those who were had few inducements to settle in the Puritan colony where their Faith was held in detestation. Some who were sold to the Barbadoes in the time of Cromwell were afterwards found in the Massachusetts settlements. One of these, Ann Glover, and her daughter had lived in Boston before she fell a victim, in 1688, to Cotton Mather's witchcraft mania. In his "Magnalia" he calls her "a scandalous old Irishwoman, very poor, a Roman Catholic and obstinate in idolatry". Robert Calef, a Boston merchant who knew her, says "Goody Glover was a despised, crazy, poor old woman, an Irish Catholic who was tried for afflicting the Goodwin children. Her behaviour at her trial was like that of one distracted. They did her cruel. The proof against her was wholly deficient. The jury brought her guilty. She was hung. She died a Catholic" (More Wonders of the Invisible World, London, 1700). Other immigrants came as bond slaves or "redemptioners" and were not so steadfast in the Faith as Goody Glover. Their environment precluded any open manifestation of their religion or the training of their children in its precepts. As an instance of many such may be cited the famous Governors Sullivan of Massachusetts and New Hampshire. Their grandfather was one of the "Wild Geese" who fled with Sarsfield from Limerick to France. His son married Margaret Brown, a fellow "redemptioner", and with their six children all drifted into Protestantism. One of their sons, General John Sullivan, of Revolutionary fame, writing on 5 September, 1774, of the "Quebec Act" that gave religious freedom to the Catholics of Canada under British rule, denounced these co-religionists of his grandfather as "determined to extirpate the race of Protestants from America to make way for their own cursed religion".

Traces of the Church in New England begin with the arrival of the Jesuit missioner, Peter Biard, among the Abenaki Indians of Maine in June, 1611. Others, notably Father Gabriel Druilletes (15 August, 1643), followed. About the same date, the ship of La Tour, the French commander of Canada, which visited Boston harbour had "two friars" on board, but they did not land. In September, 1646, another French ship, commanded by D'Aulnay, also having two priests on board, was in port. The priests visited the governor, who entertained them at his residence. Four years later Father Druilletes visited Boston to confer with General Gibbons as to the details of a trading pact and alliance with the Canadian French against the Iroquois. The governor entertained him for two weeks at his home, which was on what is now Washington Street, near Adams Square (Memorial Hist. of Boston, II, p. xiv), and it is surmised that he said Mass in private there during that time. John Eliot, John Endicott, and other noted men of the time were among those he met there and who united in urging him to prolong his visit, though their efforts were unsuccessful. The "Andros Papers" (quoted in Memorial Hist. of Boston) declare that in 1689 there was not a single "Papist" in all New England. They began to drift in soon, however, for in the Boston "Weekly Rehearsal" of 20 March, 1732, is this statement: "We hear that Mass has been performed in town this winter by an Irish priest among some Catholics of his own nation of whom it is not doubted we have a considerable number among us." During the war with France one hundred French Catholics were arrested in Boston in 1746 "to prevent any danger the town may be in", but the sheriff much to the disgust of their captors, refused to hold them. In 1756 the exiled Acadians, of whom nearly 2000 had landed in Massachusetts, were denied the services of a priest because, as Governor Hutchinson declared, "the people would upon no terms have consented to the public exercise of religious worship by Roman Catholick priests". The Boston "Town Records" (1772, pp. 95–96) while admitting that toleration in religion was "what all good and candid minds in all ages have ever practiced" excluded "Roman Catholicks" because their belief was "subversive of society".

With the Revolution, however, came the dawn of a better era, the upsetting of religious as well as political barriers, and the beginning of the slow but sure growth of the Church which has resulted in the wonderful change of the present. A favourite New England diversion was an annual procession, on 5 November, of the Pope and the Devil in celebration of the famous "Gunpowder Plot". In Boston it was usually attended by riot and violence. In 1775 Washington, while at Boston, issued an order in which he could not "help expressing his surprise that there should be officers and soldiers in this army so void of common sense" as to thus insult the religious feelings of the Canadians with whom friendship and an alliance was then being sought. The stay of the French fleet in New England waters and the settling of some of the allies there after the war had ended laid the foundations of the first Catholic parish in the heart of New England. There appeared in Boston, in 1788, a French priest who called himself Claudius Florent Bouchard de la Poterie, "Priest, Doctor of Divinity, Clerk, and Apostolic Missionary". He had faculties from the prefect Apostolic, Dr. Carroll, and announced his advent in a pompous "pastoral letter". He secured the old French Huguenot church at what is now No. 18 School Street and opened there on All Saints' Day, 1788, under the patronage of the Holy Cross, the first Catholic church in New England. The report of the celebration of the first Mass on that date can be read in the Boston "Independent Chronicle", 6 November, 1788. To the aid of this church subscriptions were received from Canada, and the Archbishop of Paris, in answer to an appeal from the little French colony in Boston, sent a needed outfit of vestments and vessels for the altar. He also notified them that the Abbé de la Poterie was an unworthy priest (Campbell in U. S. Cath. Magazine, VIII, 102). His conduct in Boston proved this, and the prefect Apostolic, finding he had been imposed on, sent the Rev. William O'Brien, O. P., of New York to Boston to depose de la Poterie. A violent pamphlet printed in Philadelphia (1789) followed. It was dedicated "To the new Laurent Ricci in America the Rev. Fr. John Carroll, Superior of the Jesuits in the United States also to the friar-monk-inquisitor William O'Brien", and represented de la Poterie as a victim to their wiles.

After his suspension de la Poterie went to Canada and was succeeded in Boston by the Rev. Louis Rousselet, who was in turn suspended and went to Guadeloupe, where he was killed in a revolution. In 1790 the Catholic colony numbered less than two hundred, and the Rev. John Thayer, a convert, was sent to take charge of the church which he found "dilapidated and deserted" after his predecessor's departure. Thayer had been a Congregationalist minister, and chaplain to Governor Hancock. At the close of the Revolution, being in his twenty-sixth year, he went abroad, and became a convert in Rome 25 May, 1783. He determined to become a priest in order to labour for the conversion of New England to the Catholic Faith and was ordained at St. Sulpice in Paris, in 1787. He returned to Boston 4 January, 1790. The first of a genuine New England family to enter the priesthood, he retained much of his inherited Puritanical oppressiveness, and, as Bishop Carroll said of him, he lacked "amiable and conciliatory manners" and was not a success as an administrator. Rousselet, who did not leave Boston immediately, set up a rival church and divided the little congregation, the French element siding with him and the Irish with Thayer. In the spring of 1791 Bishop Carroll had to visit the parish to restore unity. He was received with courtesy by all citizens and was made the guest of honour at the annual dinner of the most important social and military organization there, the Ancient and Honorable Artillery Company. Governor John Hancock attended Mass as a mark of respect for him. "It is wonderful", the bishop wrote, "to tell what great civilities have been done to me in this town, where a few years ago a Popish priest was thought to be the greatest monster in the creation. . . . If all the Catholics here were united their number would be about one hundred and twenty" (U. S. Cath. Magazine, Baltimore, VIII, 149).

Father Thayer having failed as a pastor he was relieved by the Rev. Francis A. Matignon, one of the many French priests exiled by the Revolution, and to whom the Church in the United States owes so

much. Born in Paris, in 1753, he was ordained priest in 1773 and taught theology in the College of Navarre. Having arrived in Boston, 20 August, 1792, he soon healed all the local dissensions and by his zeal, eloquence, piety, and winning courtesy made an immediate success of his pastorship. In 1796 he invited his old friend and associate, the Rev. John Louis de Cheverus, then an exile in England, to Boston to help him, and to his great joy the call was heeded. The Abbé de Cheverus arrived on the third of October of that year. He remained in Boston with Father Matignon until July, 1797, when he went at Bishop Carroll's request to visit the Indian missions in Maine. On his way, he looked after the scattered Catholics between Boston and the Penobscot. According to a report then made to Bishop Carroll of the Easter Communions of 1798 there were 210 Catholics in Boston; 15 in Plymouth; 21 in Newburyport, and 3 in Salem. Outside Boston the only important Catholic colony was at Damariscotta, Lincoln County, Maine, where Roger and Patrick Hanly, two Irishmen, had settled some time before, and their descendants and friends made up the community. The leading merchants and shipbuilders of Newcastle, James Kavanagh (father of Edward Kavanagh, later Governor of Maine, the hero of Longfellow's novel "Kavanagh", and the first Catholic governor of a New England State) and Matthew Cottrill, built a chapel and later, in 1808, a brick structure, St. Patrick's church, for the use of their fellow Catholics. This was the only church in New England outside Boston. Having put these missions in order Father Cheverus returned to Boston and with Father Matignon exhibited heroic courage and charity during the yellow fever epidemic of 1798. By this time the old church in School Street was no longer fit for Divine service and another site on Franklin Street near Devonshire Street, was secured for $2,500. Speaking at the centennial observance (29 September, 1903) of the dedication of this church, Archbishop Williams said: "We bought that land from the Boston Theatre. Remember the site of the old cathedral was in the most beautiful part of the town—at the end of Franklin Square—and the theatre owned both sides of the lower part of the street. The theatre people agreed to sell us that lot at one-half what they could get for it when we bought it. And remember in that street in those days were some of the principal families of the city. I remember the Bradleys, the Wigglesworths, the Amorys, and others who lived each side of the street, showing what a choice spot it was and one of the select streets of the city." The Spanish consul-general, Don Juan Stoughton, brother of •the Don Tomas Stoughton who had so much to do with the building of St. Peter's, the first church in New York, lived opposite the site selected. At a meeting held 31 March, 1799, he and John Magner, Patrick Campbell, Michael Burns, Owen Callahan, John Duggan, and Edmund Connor were named the committee to take charge of the new project. From the congregation they collected $16,000. Members of the leading Protestant families headed by President John Adams added $11,000 to this, and from Catholics in other places and other sources $5,500 more was received. The famous architect Charles Bulfinch, also a Protestant, who designed the capitol at Washington and the State House in Boston, supplied the plans without charge for a brick building 80 feet long and 60 wide of Ionic style, severely simple but impressive. Ground was broken for it on St. Patrick's Day 1800 and it was ready for dedication 29 September, 1803, having cost $20,000. Prominent among this first congregation, besides those already mentioned, were James Kavanagh, John Ward, David Fitzgerald, Stephen Roberts, John Driscoll, William Daly, Daniel English, Thomas Murphy, John Hanly, Abraham Fitton,

BOSTON

1. CATHEDRAL OF THE HOLY CROSS   2. THEOLOGY HOUSE, BRIGHTON SEMINARY

3. OLD CHURCH OF THE HOLY CROSS, FRANKLIN STREET (FIRST CATHEDRAL)

Mary Lob, and representatives of the Duport, Dusseaucoir, Dumesnil, Lepouse, and Julien families. Bishop Carroll went on from Baltimore to perform the ceremony of dedication. This visit of the bishop occasioned the greatest local satisfaction, and the two priests continued their zealous ministrations with such success that in 1805 their flock had increased to about 500. Soon Bishop Carroll saw the necessity of having a bishop in Boston and desired to nominate Father Matignon for the see, but the latter refused to allow his name to be considered. "The good accomplished here", he wrote, "is almost exclusively the work of Mr. Cheverus; he it is who fills the pulpit, who is most frequent in the confessional." Bishop Carroll therefore sent the name of the Rev. John Louis Cheverus to Rome declaring him to be "in the prime of life, with health to undergo any necessary exertion, universally esteemed for his unwearied zeal and his remarkable facility and eloquence in announcing the word of God, virtuous, and with a charm of manner that recalled Catholics to their duties and disarmed Protestants of their prejudices". Bishop Cheverus was appointed 8 April, 1808, but owing to the difficulties of communication the Bull did not reach him for nearly two years afterwards, when he was consecrated the first Bishop of Boston, in Baltimore, 1 November, 1810. He then went back to Boston to continue his simple, modest way of life. His old friend, Father Matignon, enjoyed honour and the esteem of all to the end of his long and useful career which came on the 18th of September, 1818.

BISHOPS.—(1) His many years of hard work at length began to tell on Bishop Cheverus and his physicians advised a return to his native land to escape repeated attacks of asthma. In 1823 King Louis XVIII of France nominated him to the vacant See of Montauban, and to the regret of all in the United States he embarked for Europe, 1 October, 1823. He remained in charge at Montauban until 30 July, 1826, when he was promoted to the Archbishopric of Bordeaux. On 1 February he was created cardinal. He died at Bordeaux, 19 July, 1836, in his sixty-ninth year. (See CHEVERUS, JOHN LOUIS DE.) During the administration of Bishop Cheverus the Ursuline nuns were introduced into the Diocese of Boston through the zeal of the Rev. John Thayer, who, when on a visit to Limerick, Ireland, where he died in 1815, enlisted the sympathy of Mary and Catharine, daughters of James Ryan of that city, in the project of founding a convent in Boston. They emigrated to Boston in 1817 and by direction of the bishop went to the Ursuline Convent at Three Rivers, Canada. They made their profession, 4 October, 1819. They returned to Boston, and a convent was secured for them on Federal Street near the cathedral. Here they remained until 17 July, 1826, when their new convent, Mount Benedict, Charlestown, was opened. This was the institution sacked and burned by an anti-Catholic mob on the 11th of August, 1834. Assisting in the work at the old School Street and Franklin Street churches at various times were the Rev. James Romagne, a West Indian priest, who also looked after the Indian missions in Maine, the Rev. J. S. Tisseraud, Fathers Matthew O'Brien and F. X. Brosius, an Alsatian, who opened a school near Harvard University and was the only teacher of German then in Boston, also the Revs. Gabriel Richard, John Grassi, S.J., Philip Lariscy, the Augustinian, and Paul McQuade. In twenty years the bishop had no regular assistant. In 1817 he ordained his first ecclesiastical student, Denis Ryan, a native of Kilkenny, Ireland. In 1820 he ordained the second of his pupils Patrick Byrne, also from Kilkenny. In December, 1822, Virgil Barber (see BARBER FAMILY) was raised to the priesthood, and to the school he opened at Claremont, New Hampshire, were sent as further recruits

for the work of the diocese James Fitton, William Wiley, who later became successful and long-lived pastors, and William Tyler, first Bishop of Hartford. Churches were built in Salem, South Boston, and other places. A cemetery was purchased near Dorchester Heights, South Boston, and a memorial erected there to Father Matignon. The chapel was dedicated to St. Augustine in compliment to Father Lariscy who collected most of the funds for the purchase of the ground. There were a number of converts through the zeal and instruction of Bishop Cheverus, notable among them being Thomas Walley, who had a private chapel at his residence in Brookline; Dr. Henry B. C. Greene, who was elected to the State legislature in 1841 and served for four terms, being the first Catholic office-holder in the State; Stephen Cleveland Blythe, the Rev. Calvin White, William Wiley, afterwards a priest, Mrs. John C. Sefton, Samuel Bishop, Captain Bela Chase, Nicholas Hazelborn, the Barber family, and General Ethan Allen's daughter Frances, who was the first nun from New England.

(2) BENEDICT JOSEPH FENWICK, second bishop, appointed 10 May, 1825. He was born 3 September, 1782, near Leonardstown, Maryland, Cuthbert Fenwick, the founder of the family in America, being one of the original Catholic settlers of Lord Baltimore's colony in Maryland. He was sent with his brother Enoch to Georgetown College in 1793, and in 1805 entered the Sulpician Seminary at Baltimore to study for the priesthood. When the Society of Jesus was restored in the United States in 1806 he and his brother were among the first scholastics received. He was ordained priest 12 March, 1808. In the succeeding years he was pastor in New York, director of its first Catholic Collegiate school, administrator and vicar-general of the diocese, missionary in South Carolina, and twice president of Georgetown College. He was then named Bishop of Boston, was consecrated in Baltimore on 1 November, 1825, and took possession of his see, 3 December. There were then only two priests in the diocese, the Revs. P. Byrne in Boston and D. Ryan at New Castle, Maine; and besides the cathedral only three churches. The bishop at once started a seminary in his own house and, having prepared Fathers Fitton, Wiley, Smith, Tyler, and Thomas J. O'Flaherty, ordained them. Other students were sent to study at Rome, Paris, Baltimore, and Montreal. The Rev. John Mahony was sent to take charge at Salem; C. D. Ffrench, a Dominican, to Maine in 1826, and Robert D. Woodley to look after the scattered congregations in Rhode Island and Connecticut. In 1828 Bishop Fenwick enlarged the cathedral and began a school in the basement, which was taught by his theological students, assisted by Patrick Haney, a mulatto from the West Indies. The erection of new churches, the providing of more priests for the increasing number of Catholics, the promotion of Catholic education, and the regulation of the general discipline of the Church took up the remaining years of his life, which ended on the eleventh of August, 1846. In 1844 he was given a coadjutor, the Right Rev. John Bernard Fitzpatrick. Bishop Fenwick began, on 8 September, 1829, for the defence of the Faith, the publication of "The Jesuit, or Catholic Sentinel", one of the first Catholic papers printed in the United States. In 1843 he founded the College of the Holy Cross at Worcester and entrusted it to the Jesuits. In 1829 he attended the First Provincial Council of Baltimore. At his death Boston had about fifty churches with attendant priests, a college, an orphan asylum, and numerous schools, and a portion of its original territory—the States of Connecticut and Rhode Island—had been erected into the new Diocese of Hartford (28 November, 1843). Three Sisters of Charity from Emmitsburg, Maryland, opened the first orphan

asylum in 1831. The first diocesan synod was held in 1842 and was attended by thirty priests. The clergy of this period were all men of broad, solid culture and knowledge. Among others not named above may be mentioned the Rev. Jeremiah O'Callaghan, a native of Cork, Ireland, whose strict views on the doctrine of usury brought him into conflict with the bishop of that place. He later became a tutor in the family of William Cobbet and came to New York in 1830. The mission of Burlington, Vermont, was given to his care, and there in 1834 he published a book under the title "Usury, Funds and Banking". Dr. Thomas J. O'Flaherty, a physician from Kerry, Ireland, was ordained priest in 1829. He edited "The Jesuit" for the bishop and made a translation of Joseph de Maistre's "Spanish Inquisition". The Rev. C. E. Brasseur de Bourbourg was for a time in the diocese and two years after the bishop's death went to Mexico, where he devoted much time to decyphering the native picture writings. In 1845 it was estimated there were 53,000 Catholics in the State, an increase of more than 20,000 in ten years. (See FENWICK, BENEDICT JOSEPH.)

(3) JOHN BERNARD FITZPATRICK, third bishop, was consecrated titular Bishop of Callipolis and coadjutor of Boston, 24 March, 1844. He was born in Boston, 1 November, 1812, his parents having emigrated from Ireland in 1805. His early education was received in the local grammar and Latin schools, and in 1829 he went to the Sulpician college at Montreal. After eight years spent there as student and professor he entered the Seminary of St. Sulpice, Paris, to complete his ecclesiastical course and was ordained priest there 13 June, 1840. He then returned to Boston and after a year as assistant at the cathedral was made pastor of the church at East Cambridge. In 1844 he was appointed coadjutor to Bishop Fenwick. He took part in the Sixth Provincial Council of Baltimore in 1846 and attended the subsequent provincial councils and the first plenary council (1853), which further reduced the original limits of his jurisdiction by creating the dioceses of Burlington and Portland. During 1854 he paid his official visit to Rome after having suffered, together with his people, the utmost indignities and persecution at the hands of bigots. In July of that year the churches at Dorchester, at Bath, and at Manchester, New Hampshire, were destroyed by mobs. In October, at Ellsworth, Maine, the Rev. John Bapst, S.J., was taken by a band of masked men, stripped, smeared with tar and feathers, and forced out of the place. The legislature of Massachusetts also appointed a special committee to investigate convents, and the members forced their way into several institutions. From the pope Bishop Fitzpatrick received consolation and encouragement and the message to his people to "persevere under afflictions". The anti-Catholic sentiment in the community continued. On 14 March, 1859, a Catholic boy named Thomas J. Wall was whipped for refusing to read the Protestant Bible and recite Protestant prayers in one of the Boston public schools. Thereupon so strong a protest was made by the bishop against the injustice done to the Catholics of the community by the system and regulations then in operation that for the first time in the history of the city a priest and several Catholic laymen were named on the school committee. For many years the bishop was an invalid and a great sufferer, but he kept up his activities to the end and before his death on 13 February, 1866, saw the prosperity of the diocese increased nearly threefold. In 1860 Bishop Fitzpatrick, intending to build a new cathedral, sold the old church in Franklin Street for $115,000, the neighbourhood having changed into a business centre. Among his prominent converts may be noted Josue Moody, afterwards Bishop of Erie, Fathers George J. Goodwin, H. Tucker,

J. Coolidge Shaw, S.J., Edward H. Welch, S.J., Orestes A. Brownson, the philosopher, Buckley Hastings, General Joseph W. Revere (Paul Revere's grandson), and other members of old New England families. Chaplains in the regiments who volunteered in the Civil War were Fathers Thomas Scully, Charles L. Egan, Nicholas O'Brien, and Lawrence S. McMahon (afterwards Bishop of Hartford). Editors and writers were Fathers Joseph M. Finotti, John P. Roddan, and John Boyce.

(4) JOHN JOSEPH WILLIAMS, fourth bishop, consecrated 11 March, 1866; created first archbishop, 12 February, 1875. He was born in Boston of Irish parents 27 April, 1822, and died in Boston, 30 August, 1907. His boyhood and early manhood were spent under the spiritual direction of Bishop Fenwick. He attended the cathedral school and thence passed to the Sulpician college in Montreal and their seminary at Paris, where he was ordained priest in 1845. He was the special friend of Bishop Fitzpatrick, who made him his vicar-general at an early age and rector of St. James's church, where in 1842 he established the first Conference of the Society of St. Vincent de Paul in New England. Two other rectors of this church became bishops: the Rev. James A. Healy, appointed Bishop of Portland in 1875, and M. A. Harkins Bishop of Providence in 1887. Shortly before his death Bishop Fitzpatrick sought to have Father Williams made his coadjutor, but he did not live to see him consecrated. Boston was made an archdiocese in 1875, and Bishop Williams was promoted to be its metropolitan. He received as an auxilliary the Right Rev. John Brady, consecrated Titular Bishop of Alabanda, 5 August, 1891, and a coadjutor with the right of succession in the Right Rev. William H. O'Connell of Portland, who was promoted to be Titular Archbishop of Tomi and coadjutor of Boston, 8 February, 1906. Archbishop Williams also saw organized, within the limits of the Diocese of Boston as it was when he was born, the Dioceses of Springfield, 1870; Providence, 1872; Manchester, 1884; and Fall River, 1905, and among those immediately under his jurisdiction representatives of nearly every country and language of Europe. Prominent among the memorials of his long episcopate and priesthood were the new Cathedral of the Holy Cross, dedicated 8 December, 1875, and St. John's Ecclesiastical Seminary at Brighton, erected in 1884, which is in charge of the Sulpicians. Boston College was opened by the Jesuits in 1863. In the same year the Carney Hospital was established through the generosity of Andrew Carney, who with his family has given it $75,000. The House of the Angel Guardian for boys, founded in 1849 by the Rev. G. F. Haskins, in 1876 was entrusted to the care of the Brothers of Charity from Montreal. St. Mary's Infant Asylum was opened in 1872; the Home for the Aged by the Little Sisters of the Poor, in 1870; the House of the Good Shepherd in 1867, and the Daly Industrial School was made possible by the gift in 1899 of $50,000 from the Rev. Patrick J. Daly. The Home for Destitute children was opened in 1864; the Working Boys Home in 1883, and the Home for Girls in 1884. St. Elizabeth's Hospital dates from 1868, the Free Home for Consumptives from 1891, the Holy Ghost Hospital for Incurables from 1893. The Sisters of St. Joseph made their first foundation in the diocese in 1873; the Franciscan Sisters, in 1884; the Ladies of the Sacred Heart, in 1880; and the Carmelites from Baltimore, in 1890. The Redemptorists began a mission in the late sixties, and built their first church in the Roxbury District, in 1871. In 1883 the Marist Fathers began their local work, and the Augustinians established themselves in Lawrence in 1861. French immigration from Canada, which had been going on since 1815, began to attract special attention about 1870. In

1868 the first distinctively French parish was organized in Lowell. Italian and Portuguese congregations date from 1872, the former in Boston and the latter in Gloucester. One congregation in Gloucester has a respectable section made up of Gaelic speaking Scotch from Cape Breton and Antigonish. There is one German Congregation in Boston, and one in Lawrence; that in Boston, the church of Holy Trinity, dates from 1836 and has the distinction of starting in 1844 one of the first parish schools in New England. There are also Polish, Lithuanian, and Syrian congregations in Boston. Archbishop Williams was a quiet, conservative prelate, known best as an administrator. He was one of the bishops who attended the Vatican Council and helped largely to establish the American College at Rome.

THE MOST REV. WILLIAM HENRY O'CONNELL, second archbishop, was born 8 December, 1859, at Lowell, Massachusetts, and received his early education in its local schools and at St. Charles's College, Ellicott City, Maryland. He then graduated in 1881 at the Jesuit College in Boston and was sent to the American College, Rome, to make his studies for the priesthood. He was ordained there 8 January, 1884, and returned to Boston in 1886. The following years he was stationed as an assistant at Medford, and at Boston until 1895 when he was appointed rector of the American College, Rome. He held this office five years, and was then appointed Bishop of Portland, Maine, being consecrated 19 May, 1901. In the fall of 1905 the pope sent him as a special envoy to Japan in the interests of the Church. He was decorated by the Mikado and on his return to Rome was warmly commended for the success of his efforts by the pope, who on 26 January, 1906, named him titular Archbishop of Tomi, and coadjutor of Boston. On the death of Archbishop Williams, he immediately took possession of the See of Boston.

The Right Rev. John Brady, auxiliary bishop, was born at Crosserlough, County Cavan, Ireland, 11 April, 1842. He made his first studies in the local diocesan schools and then completed his theological course at the Missionary College of All Hallows, where he was ordained priest for the Diocese of Boston, 4 December, 1864. He served as a curate in Boston and at Newburyport until 1868, when he was made pastor at Amesbury. He continued in this charge until he was nominated Titular Bishop of Alabanda and Auxiliary Bishop of Boston for which see he was consecrated 5 August, 1891.

SOCIAL PROGRESS.—"The foundation of a Catholic Church in Boston could only be surpassed by devoting a chamber in the Vatican to a Protestant Chapel" said William Tudor, writing in his "Letters on the Eastern States" (Boston, 1819). The records show that the notable constructive Catholic social period of the diocese did not begin until after the Civil War. Though the Catholics formed a quarter of the population of Boston in 1844 and two-fifths in 1853, not a single one of that faith ever held an elective or appointive public office in the city of Boston. There were only three Catholic teachers in the public schools until 1860. The first Catholic Member of the Common Council, John H. Barry, was elected in 1857, the first alderman, Christopher A. Connor, in 1870, and the first Member of Congress, Patrick A. Collins, in 1882. The changed conditions are shown by the fact that for ten of the past twenty-three years Boston has been ruled by Catholic Mayors, and public memorials have been set up amid general approval to the soldier, Colonel Thomas Cass; the poet journalist, John Boyle O'Reilly; and the statesman, Patrick Andrew Collins. In justice it must be said that much of the progress thus made was owing to Patrick Donahoe, who after the failure of "The Jesuit" continued in "The Pilot" (begun 2 January, 1836) the illustrations of Catholic truth and the defence of Catholic rights. From his publication house issued for more than half a century a steady output of Catholic literature that aided materially the education of his fellow Catholics and won for the Faith a general popular appreciation. Other periodicals and publications in the archdiocese are the weeklies "The Republic" and the "Sacred Heart Review" (Boston); "The Catholic Citizen" (Chelsea); "The Sunday Register" (Lawrence); the monthlies "Donahoe's Magazine" (Boston); "The Index" (Haverhill); the French weeklies "Le Défenseur", "La Justice" (Holyoke); "L'Etoile", daily and weekly (Lowell).

STATISTICS.— Records of the Archdiocese of Boston for 1907 give these figures: 1 archbishop, 1 bishop, 598 priests (488 secular and 110 regular), 194 churches with resident priests, 54 missions with churches, 1 theological seminary with 86 students, 3 colleges for boys, 8 academies for girls, 76 parishes with schools and an attendance of 48,192 children; 6 orphan asylums with 650 inmates; 24 charitable institutions; the total number of children in Catholic institutions 48,740; 1 infant asylum, 538 inmates; industrial and reform schools 4, inmates 915; homes 7, inmates 826; brothers 140; religious women 1567; seminary for diocesan clergy 1, students 86; estimated Catholic population 850,000.

The following religious orders and congregations have foundations in the archdiocese: *Communities of Men*, Augustinians, 16; Franciscans (O. M. C.), 5; Jesuits, 32; Marists, 15; Oblates, 22; Congregation of St. Charles Borromeo, 4; Redemptorists, 16; Brothers of Charity of St. Vincent de Paul, 25; Brothers of the Christian Schools, 11; Little Brothers of Mary, 19; Xaverian Brothers, 58. *Communities of Women*, Sisters of St. Ann, Sisters of the Assumption, Sisters of Charity (Madison, New Jersey), Sisters of Charity (Grey Nuns, Montreal), Sisters of Charity of Nazareth, Sisters of Charity (Emmitsburg), Sisters of Charity (Halifax, N. S.), Sisters of the Holy Union of the Sacred Hearts, Sisters of St. Dominic (Jersey City, N. J.), Sisters of the Third Order of St. Francis, Sisters of St. Dominic (Springfield, Kentucky), Sisters of St. Francis (Allegany, N. Y.), Sisters of St. Francis (Rome), Sisters of the Good Shepherd, Sisters Servants of the Immaculate Heart of Mary, Grey Nuns of the Cross (Ottawa, Ontario), Ladies of the Sacred Heart, Missionary Sisters of the Sacred Heart (Rome), Sisters of St. Joseph, Sisters of Mary, Sisters of Mercy (Manchester, New Hampshire), Sisters of Notre Dame, of Namur, since 1849, School Sisters of Notre Dame (Baltimore, Maryland), Little Sisters of the Poor, Sisters of Providence, Sisters of the Holy Union of the Sacred Hearts, Filles de Jésus, Franciscan Poor Clare nuns, Sisters of the Holy Childhood.

SHEA, *History of the Cath. Ch. in U. S.* (New York, 1886); IDEM, *Life and Times of the Most Rev. John Carroll* (Ib., 1888); HAMON, *Vie du Cardinal de Cheverus* (Paris, 1858, tr. WALSH, Philadelphia, 1839; tr. STEWART, Boston, 1839); FITTON, *Sketches of the Establishment of the Church in New England* (Boston, 1872); CREAGH, *Laity's Directory* (New York, 1822); *Catholic Observer* (Boston, 1847), files; *Mémoires de P. De Sales Laternere* (Quebec, 1813); *Gazette de Québec* (22 October, 1784 supplement); *American Cath. Hist. Researches* (January, 1889, July, 1902); FINOTTI, *Bibliographia Cath. Americana* (New York, 1872); CLARKE, *Lives of the Deceased Bishops* (New York, 1872); *The Pilot* (Boston, 2 January, 1836–1907), files; REUSS, *Biog. Cycl. of the Hierarchy of the U. S.* (Milwaukee, 1879); *U. S. Cath. Magazine* (Baltimore), VIII, 102 sqq.; U. S. CATH. HIST. SOC., *Hist. Records and Studies* (New York, October, 1906), IV, parts I and II; SULLIVAN, *Catholic Church of New England, Archdiocese of Boston* (Boston and Portland, 1895); LEAHY in *History of Catholic Church in the New England States* (Boston, 1899), I; *Memorial Volume, One Hundredth Anniversary Celebration of the Dedication of the Church of the Holy Cross, Boston* (Boston, 1904); H. F. BROWNSON, *Orestes A. Brownson's Early Life*; IDEM, *Middle Life* (Detroit, 1898–99).

THOMAS F. MEEHAN.

Bostra, a titular see of Syria. Bostra, "The fortress", is neither Bosor of Reuben and Moab (Deut., iv, 24; Jos., xx, 8), nor Bosrah of Edom

(Gen., xxxvi, 33; Jer., xlix, 13, etc.), now Bouseira between Tafilé and Shobaq. Perhaps it is the same as Bosor, or Bosora, taken by the Machabees (1 Mach., v, 26, 28, 36), an independent town in Peræa. It was included in the Nabatean Kingdom (M. de Vogüé, La Syrie centrale, Inscriptions, 103) and last held by the Romans. When the kingdom was destroyed by Cornelius Palma (105 or 106), a general of Trajan, Bostra became the metropolis of Arabia and was known as Nova Trajana Bostra. There the Third *Legio Cyrenaica* held its garrison. In the same year began the era of Bostra, after which the numerous inscriptions in trans-Jordanic Palestine are reckoned. The city was already a very important one; it was there that the great Roman road began which ran to the Red Sea, as well as most of the other roads that crossed the country in every direction; the governor of the province had his residence there.

Under Alexander Severus (222–235) Bostra became a Roman colony. In the fourth century it is called "a great city", by Ammianus Marcellinus (Res gestæ, XIV, 8, 3), and from the extent of its ruins G. Rindfleisch has calculated that it must have had about 80,000 inhabitants (Zeitschrift des deutschen Palästinavereins, xxi, 32). Remains of splendid monuments are yet visible, colonnades, triumphal arches, baths, a theatre, temples, churches, etc. Bostra, being an important trade centre for caravans, was visited by Mahomet; it was there that Bahira, a Nestorian monk, acknowledged him as a prophet. The Crusaders tried vainly to take it. Its decline was the result of earthquakes, chiefly that of 1151, when the city was left in ruins. Under its present name of Bosra Eski-Sham (Bostra Old Damascus), it has hardly 1000 wretched inhabitants and a little Turkish garrison.

The Christian religion, which soon penetrated the neighbouring Arabia, was not long in reaching Bostra. As metropolis of the province of Arabia it had nineteen or twenty suffragan sees. Lequien (Or. Chr., II, 853–860) enumerates a list of sixteen bishops at Bostra; among the most celebrated are Beryllus, who fell into a Christologic heresy and was reclaimed by Origen at a council held between A. D. 218 and 244 (Euseb., H. E., vi, 33); Titus, who suffered much under Julian the Apostate, and who was an important writer, J. Sickenberger devoting a long essay to him (Titus von Bostra, Leipzig, 1901); St. Antipater, about 458; Stephen, at the beginning of the eighth century; and Arsenius, who lived in 1365 (Miklosich and Müller, Acta patriarch. C. P., I, 465). The diocese existed till 1715 (Chrysanthus, Synodicon, 70). Subsequent to that it was suppressed by the Greeks, and its 6000 faithful are subjects of the Diocese of Damascus. The Catholic Greeks, or Melchites, however, have always maintained this see, under the title of Bostra and Hauran. Their metropolitan resides usually at Damascus and goes to Bostra only two or three times a year; his diocese contains about 8000 Catholics, 12 priests, and 12 parishes. The Crusaders by a mistake ranked Bostra under the authority of the Patriarchate of Jerusalem, instead of under that of Antioch.

PORTER, *Five Years in Damascus* (London, 1855), II, 142–169; *The Giant Cities of Bashan* (London, 1872), 64–73; REY, *Voyage dans le Haouran* (Paris, 1860), 179–199; WADDINGTON, *Explication des inscriptions recueillies . . . en Syrie*, 454–469; VAILHÉ, *La province ecclésiastique d'Arabie* in *Echos d'Orient*, II, 166–179.

S. VAILHÉ.

Bothrys, a titular see situated in Phœnicia. Bothrys is the Greek name of a city founded by Ithobaal, King of Tyre and father of Jezabel (897–866 B. C.), on the seashore near Cape Lithoprosopon (Menander, in Josephus, "Ant. Jud.", VIII, 13, 2). It is mentioned by all the ancient geographers, Strabo, Pliny, Ptolemy, Stephanus Byzantius, Hierocles, etc. The city belonged to Phœnicia

Prima, and became a suffragan of Tyre in the Patriarchate of Antioch. In 551 it was destroyed by an earthquake, on which occasion the cape cracked in the very middle so that quite a large harbour was opened (Malalas, Chronogr., XVIII, in P. G., XCVII, 704). Theophanes, relating the same event (ad an. 543), calls the city Bostrys, which form is also found elsewhere. Three Greek bishops are known: Porphyrius in 451; Elias about 512; and Stephen in 553 (Lequien, II, 827). According to a Greek "Notitia episcopatuum", the see still existed in the tenth century and was then called Petrounion. Its present Arabic name is Batroun. There are 2,500 inhabitants (1,200 Maronites, 1,200 Greeks). It is the centre of a *caza* in the *mutessariflik* of Lebanon and the seat of a Maronite diocese suffragan to the Maronite patriarchate. There are 60,000 Catholics, 50 churches or chapels, 30 priests, 1 seminary, 64 elementary schools, and 12 monasteries of Baladites, Aleppines, and monks of St. Isaiah in this Diocese.

S. VAILHÉ.

Bothwell, JAMES, EARL OF. See MARY QUEEN OF SCOTS.

Botri, DIOCESE OF See GIBAIL AND BOTRI.

Bottero, H. M. See KUMBAKONAM, DIOCESE OF.

Botticelli, SANDRO, a famous Florentine painter, b. at Florence about 1447; d. in the same city, 1510. Botticelli's name is properly Alessandro di Mariano Filipepi, Mariano Filipepi being his father, but he is called after the Florentine painter and goldsmith, Botticelli, to whom he was first apprenticed. Later on he was a pupil of Fra Filippo Lippi and learned from this master to paint in the ideal manner of Fra Angelico. Through the influence of Verrocchio and the brothers Pollajuoli this idealism was combined with the naturalness of Masaccio. These qualities explain Botticelli's great influence over later painters. Botticelli's life was a retired one passed largely in very modest circumstances. We know, however, that he was in the employ of the Medici and other prominent Florentine families from about 1483 to 1500. Although never inclined to frivolity he was yet influenced by the worldly spirit of the age until Savonarola's powerful call to repentance aroused his moral nature and guided his powers, as it seems, into entirely new paths. He never knew how to take care of money and he died at last in need. Botticelli was too unassuming to sign and date his works in most instances, so that the order in time of his paintings has to be judged from the canvases themselves.

I. *Madonnas.*—Botticelli enjoys, above all, a well-earned fame as a painter of the Madonna. In these pictures the fascination lies more in the expression of the Mother and Child and in the look on the faces of the half-grown boy-angels than in the unaffected simplicity of the pose and composition. Two of these pictures, circular in form (called *tondo*, round) have become very famous. Both are in Florence: one is the "Magnificat", and in the other the Child is holding a pomegranate. A circular canvas at Berlin which depicts the Madonna enthroned and surrounded by angels carrying candles is characterized by deep religious feeling. A number of small pictures of the Madonna recall Fra Filippo; others more severe in tone seem to show the influence of Verrocchio. The Child's expression is always sweet and winning, yet thoughtful as well, and at times the look is one of intense earnestness. The Mother in holy awe restrains her tenderness and seems to have a presentiment of future sorrow. This feeling of melancholy foreboding is also expressed in the attendant angels and saints. A painting of this enthroned Madonna with the two Johns is at Berlin; two canvases at Florence depict the same Madonna surrounded by numerous saints. It is plain that the

THE MADONNA OF THE MAGNIFICAT

SANDRO BOTTICELLI, UFFIZI GALLERY, FLORENCE

look of melancholy on the face of the Mother of God had a strange attraction for the painter. His portrait of himself in the "Destruction of Core, Dathan, and Abiron" shows his natural inclination to intense earnestness, and in the "Outcasts" he has depicted the profoundest depths of grief.

II. *Biblical Subjects.*—In 1481 Sixtus IV summoned Botticelli, along with other painters, to Rome to decorate the new Sistine Chapel. According to the biographer, Vasari, he was even to superintend the entire work. In the chapel Botticelli painted three frescoes which represent events in the lives of Moses and Christ. No less than seven scenes are united in the "Life of the Youthful Moses", so that the composition lacks unity. Without doubt the artist laboured under a feeling of restraint. The composition is animated in parts and is intended to arouse the feelings. The "Destruction of Core, Dathan, and Abiron" is represented in three scenes. The figure of Moses appears here in all the majesty which God had granted him for the punishment of the rebels. There is an interesting connexion between this picture and Perugino's "Granting of the Keys to Peter" on the opposite wall. Moses in the fullness of his might is the counterpart of Peter to whom the Keys of Heaven are entrusted. Over against the fresco of the proving of the youthful Moses, Botticelli painted from the New Testament the "Temptation of Christ". The pope has this picture before him when, seated upon his throne, he is present at the celebration of the Mass. Strange to say, the foreground of the painting represents the purification of a leper before a company of ecclesiastics and secular dignitaries and contains besides an allusion to the pope. The explanation of the scene is as follows: Moses had to undergo trials before he could become the leader of his people, so also the Saviour had to suffer in order to heal mankind from the leprosy of sin, and so also the pope in order to carry out Christ's missions. As an allegorical indication of this a hospital built by Sixtus IV is shown in the picture. It must be acknowledged that the painter executed the difficult task assigned to him in the chapel with striking skill. Feeling the importance of this work Botticelli carried out his designs almost entirely himself; the smallest details show the infinite pains he took. In these frescoes he has given a large amount of space to Roman architecture, thereby setting a good working example to the painters coming after him. Of Botticelli's other Biblical pictures mention may be made of the "Birth of Christ", which was intended to be a memorial of Savonarola. While a chorus of angels sing the praises of God above the manger, in this picture, three angels below lead Dominican monks towards the Saviour, Christ, who had been proclaimed by Savonarola to be king of the city of Florence. We have also an "Adoration of the Magi" in four examples (Florence, London, and St. Petersburg). This canvas is full of figures and has a background composed of stately architecture and landscape. The copy at Florence is famous on account of the portraits of the Medici it contains, which were introduced in accordance with the custom of the time. About 1500 Botticelli produced the two examples of the "Lamentation of Christ" which are now at Munich and Milan. In this composition the expression of grief is deep but subdued.

III. *Portraits.*—Among the twenty-four portraits of popes in the Sistine chapel five are by Botticelli. In the church of the Ognissanti at Florence there is a celebrated picture of St. Augustine by Botticelli opposite to a St. Jerome by Ghirlandajo. There are two portraits of Giuliano de' Medici in existence and an excellent portrait of a woman at Frankfort.

IV. *Other Subjects.*—In celebration of a wedding Botticelli painted in the villa of the Tornabuoni near Fiesole an allegorical scene representing the Seven Arts and the Virtues paying their homage to the newly married pair. Among his mythological pictures may be mentioned the "Venus" who sails upon a shell towards the island which she has chosen for her habitation. Another mythological subject is "Venus and Mars". Botticelli contributed the enthroned "Fortitude" and "Spring" to the allegorical style of painting so popular in his day. The "Calumny of Apelles", which is realistic in execution, is essentially allegorical. Closely related to these works are the more than ninety illustrations to Dante's "Divine Comedy", that poem which, from Giotto to Michelangelo, has stimulated the imagination of so many painters. Four sheets executed in colour seem to indicate an intention to carry out the whole work in the same manner after the designs had once been made with pen and pencil. Many of the pictures are not more than outlined or sketched. There is, however, much that is admirable in these designs, which formed one of the chief occupations of the last years of the painter. The fidelity to nature in the drawing of the human figure, the contemplative expression of the faces, the dramatic animation of the action, and the skilful arrangement of the perspective make these designs a last triumph for Botticelli.

Monographs by SUPINO (Florence, 1900); STEINMANN (Leipzig, 1897); DODSON, tr. (New York, 1901); BERENSON, *The Florentine Painters of the Renaissance* (New York and London, 1898); PLUNKETT, *Sandro Botticelli* (London, 1900).

G. GIETMANN.

Botulph (or BOTOLF), SAINT, Abbot, date of birth unknown; died c. 680. St. Botulph, the saint whose name is perpetuated in that of the American city of Boston, Massachusetts, was certainly an historical personage, though the story of his life is very confused and unsatisfactory. What information we possess about him is mainly derived from a short biography by Folcard, monk of St. Bertin and Abbot of Thorney, who wrote in the eleventh century (Hardy, Catalogue of Brit. Hist., I, 373). According to him Botulph was born of noble Saxon parents who were Christians, and was sent with his brother Adulph to the Continent for the purpose of study. Adulph remained abroad, where he is stated to have become Bishop of Utrecht, though his name does not occur in any of the ancient lists. Botulph, returning to England, found favour with a certain Ethelmund, "King of the southern Angles", whose sisters he had known in Germany, and was by him permitted to choose a tract of desolate land upon which to build a monastery. This place, surrounded by water and called Icanhoe (Ox-island), is commonly identified with the town of Boston in Lincolnshire, mainly on account of its name (Boston = Botulph's town). There is, however, something to suggest that the true spot may be the village of Iken in Suffolk which of old was almost encircled by the little river Alde, and in which the church is also dedicated to St. Botulph. In favour of Lincolnshire must be reckoned the fact that St. Botulph was much honoured in the North and in Scotland. Thus his feast was entered in the York calendar but not in that of Sarum. Moreover, even Folcard speaks of the Scots as Botulph's neighbours (*vicini*). In favour of Suffolk, on the other hand, may be quoted the tradition that St. Botulph, who is also called "bishop", was first buried at Grundisburgh, a village near Woodbridge, and afterwards translated to Bury St. Edmunds. This, however, may be another person, since he is always closely associated with a certain St. Jurmin (Arnold, Memorials of Bury, I, 352). That Botulph really did build a monastery at Icanhoe is attested by an entry in the Anglo-Saxon Chronicle under the year 654: *Botulf ongan thæt mynster timbrian æt Yceanho*, i. e. Botulph began

II.—45

to build the minster at Icanhoe. That the saint must have lived somewhere in the Eastern counties is proved by the indisputable evidence of the "Historia Abbatum" (Plummer's Bede, I, 389), where we learn that Ceolfrid, Bede's beloved master at Wearmouth, "journied to the East Angles in order that he might see the foundation of Abbot Botulphus, whom fame had proclaimed far and wide to be a man of remarkable life and learning, full of the grace of the Holy Spirit", and the account goes on to say that Ceolfrid "having been abundantly instructed, so far as was possible in a short time, returned home so well equipped that no one could be found more learned than he either in ecclesiastical or monastic traditions". Folcard represents St. Botulph as living and dying at Icanhoe in spite of the molestations of the evil spirits to which he was exposed at his first coming. Later accounts, e. g. the lessons of the Schleswig Breviary, suppose him to have changed his habitation more than once and to have built at one time a monastery upon the bank of the Thames in honour of St. Martin. His relics are said after the incursions of the Danes to have been recovered and divided by St. Æthewold between Ely, Thorney Abbey, and King Edgar's private chapel. What is more certain is that St. Botulph was honoured by many dedications of churches, over fifty in all, especially in East Anglia and in the North. His name is perpetuated not only by the little town of Boston in Lincolnshire with its American homonym, but also by Bossal in Yorkshire, Botesdale in Suffolk, Botolph Bridge in Huntingdonshire, and Botolph in Sussex. In England his feast was kept on 17 June, in Scotland on 25 June.

STANTON, *Menology*, 271; *Acta SS.*, June, III, 402; MABILLON, *Acta SS. Benedict.*, III, 1; STUBBS in *Dict. Christ. Biog.*; GRANT in *Dict. Nat. Biog.*; FORBES, *Calendars of Scottish Saints* (Edinburgh, 1872), 283; and especially ARNOLD-FORSTER, *Church Dedications* (London, 1899), II, 52–56.

HERBERT THURSTON.

Boturini Benaducci, LORENZO, a native of Milan in Lombardy who went to Mexico in 1736 by permission of the Spanish government and remained there eight years, familiarizing himself with the Nahuatl or Mexican language. He gathered a number of Indian pictographs on tissue paper, etc., the first collection of the kind of importance. His frequent intercourse with the aborigines excited suspicion, as he was a foreigner, and the authorities, ever on the watch for intrigues against Spanish rule by strangers, deprived him of all his material, including prints, while he himself was sent to Spain under surveillance. There he succeeded in clearing himself of the accusations, but never obtained restitution of the precious collection, which afterwards was neglected and partly lost. Notwithstanding these drawbacks, Boturini, from such notes as he had saved, composed a treatise with the title of: "Idéa y ensayo de una historia general de la América setentrional" (Madrid, 1746). The most valuable part of this book relates to his former library and to other literary material. His text, especially concerning migrations of Indian tribes, is of less importance. Besides the "Idéa", he is credited with the authorship of the following writings: "Oratio ad Divinam Sapientiam" (Valencia, 1750), and "Oratio de iure naturali septentrionalium Indorum" (Valencia, 1751). The date and place of his death are unknown.

CLAVIGERO, *Storia antica dell' Messico* (Cesena, 1780); BÉRISTAIN DE SOUZA, *Biblioteca hispano-americana setentrional* (Mexico, 1816).

AD. F. BANDELIER.

Boucher, PIERRE, b. at Lagny, a village near Mortagne in the Perche, France, 1622; d. at Boucherville, 1717. In 1634 he went to Canada with his father, Gaspard Boucher, a simple joiner. At the age of eighteen he entered the service of the Jesuit Fathers and went to their Huron missions at Georgian Bay. On his return to Quebec in 1641 he served as a soldier in the garrison of that city. In 1645 he was interpreter of Indian languages at Three Rivers and in 1648 commissary-general of the trading station at that place. Elected captain of the militia in 1651, while in command of the place during an interim in 1653 he repelled an Iroquois attack. Owing to his efficient defence he was placed in charge of the city, and retained the position until 1658. In 1661 he was sent to France to represent the needs of the colonies and plead the cause of the inhabitants. On his return to Canada, in 1662, he was reappointed Governor of Three Rivers, an office which he only resigned in 1667 when he withdrew from public affairs to found the seigniorial parish called after his name Boucherville, situated opposite Montreal. He was succeeded in the governorship of Three Rivers by his son-in-law, René Gauthier de Varennes, forbear of the discoverer of Western Canada.

In 1664 Pierre Boucher had printed at Paris by the press of Florentin Lambert "L'histoire véritable et naturelle des mœurs et productions du pays de la Nouvelle-France, vulgairement dite le Canada". This work was published in 1849 in "L'Album Canadien", in 1882 at Montreal, and in 1896 in the "Mémoires de la Société Royale du Canada". An English translation appeared in 1883. Pierre Boucher is considered the best type of a Canadian landed proprietor, filled with piety, rectitude, and honour. At his death he left a numerous posterity. The family is still in existence, and the highest stations are filled by members bearing the names Boucherville, Bruère, Niverville, Grosbois, and Montizambert. Pierre Boucher was the first Canadian colonist to be ennobled by King Louis XIV. His letters of nobility, dated 1661, were renewed in 1707.

Registres des insinuations du Conseil supérieur de la Nouvelle-France, III, D, 46; DANIEL, *Grandes familles canadiennes*; SULTE, *Pierre Boucher et son livre* in *Royal Society of Canada, Transactions*, new series, II, 99–148; LALANDE, *La paroisse de Boucherville* (1890); ROY, *Histoire de la seigneurie de Louzon*, I, II.

J. EDMOND ROY.

Bougaud, LOUIS-VICTOR-EMILE, Bishop of Laval in France, b. at Dijon, 28 February, 1823; d. at Laval, 7 November, 1888. He received his classical education at Autun, where his professor of rhetoric was the Abbé, afterwards Cardinal, Pitra. He studied theology at Dijon and Paris, was ordained priest by Monseigneur Affre in 1846, was professor of church history at the Seminary of Dijon (1846–51), and then chaplain of the Convent of the Visitation in the same city (1851–61). In 1861 he accepted the position of Vicar-General to Bishop Dupanloup at Orleans. In 1886 he was appointed Bishop of Laval.

Besides the sermons which he delivered in Paris and other cities, Bishop Bougaud wrote numerous works. While chaplain of the Visitation Convent, he wrote "Histoire de Saint Bénigne, premier évêque de Dijon" and "Histoire de Sainte Chantal". While Vicar-General of Orléans, he wrote "Histoire de Sainte Monique", "Histoire de la bienheureuse Marguerite-Marie", "Le Christianisme et les temps présents" (his great apologetical work, in 5 vols.); "Le grand péril de l'Eglise de France au XIXᵉ siècle", and "Histoire de Saint Vincent de Paul" (2 vols.). A volume of his discourses was published by his brother.

He was a preacher and writer of great influence, in consequence of his appreciation of all noble thoughts and deeds, his deep compassion for human suffering, his great power of reflection, and his refined artistic taste. In his apologetics he evinces thorough sympathy with his own time and an unwavering hope for the triumph of the Church. His purpose was to adapt the explanations of the dogmas, precepts, and organization of the Church to the moral and intellectual aspirations of his contemporaries without any sacrifice of Catholic doctrine.

LAGRANGE, *Notice historique sur Mgr. Bougaud* in *Discours de Mgr. Bougaud* (Paris, 1891); *Semaine Religieuse de Laval* (1888).

G. M. SAUVAGE.

Bougeant, GUILLAUME-HYACINTHE, b. at Quimper in Brittany, in 1690; d. at Paris, 1743. He entered the Society of Jesus in 1706, taught the classics in the College of Caen and Nevers and lived for a number of years in Paris until his death. His "Amusement philosophique sur le langage des bêtes", published in 1737, became a cause of considerable annoyance to him and of a short exile from Paris. It was translated into English, Italian, and German. His historical works, on the Thirty Years' War, and on the Treaty of Westphalia have been highly praised and are regarded as among the best historical books written by Jesuits. They were translated into German. He is also the author of a theological treatise on the form of consecration of the Eucharist, and of a Catechism divided into three parts, historical, dogmatic, and practical. This catechism, translated into Italian and German, went through many editions and is still in use. In his three celebrated Comedies, "La Femme Docteur", "Le Saint déniché", and "Les Quakres français" he satirizes the Jansenists. The first of the three went through twenty-five editions in a few months and was translated into Italian, Spanish, Polish, and Dutch. Between 1725 and 1737 he contributed many articles to the Mémoires de Trévoux.

SOMMERVOGEL, *Bibliothèque de la c. de J.*, I, 1873–85.

B. GULDNER.

Bouhours, DOMINIQUE, French Jesuit author, b. at Paris, 15 May, 1632; d. 27 May, 1702. Entering the Society of Jesus at sixteen, he taught grammar and rhetoric at Paris, Tours, and Rouen. A number of works which he composed against the Jansenists, notably "Lettre à un Seigneur de la cour" and "Lettre à Messieurs de Port-Royal", had a large circulation, and gained him a prominent place among the critics and *littérateurs* of the seventeenth century. He also translated the New Testament into French, and his translation has often been reprinted. He is best known to English readers, however, by his "Vie de S. Ignace" (Paris, 1679) and "Vie de S. François-Xavier" (Paris, 1682). These two biographies were translated into English and published at London in 1686 and 1688 respectively. A new translation, by a clergyman of the Diocese of Philadelphia, was published at Philadelphia by E. Cummiskey in 1840, and for a number of years these two works of Bouhours' were the most widely circulated biographies of the two saints. The only other of the author's works done into English is "La manière de bien penser dans les œuvres d'esprit", which appeared in London in 1705 under the title, "The Art of Criticism".

DONCIEUX, *Un jésuite homme de lettres au xviie siècle* (Paris, 1886); *Bibliothèque de la c. de J.*, VII, 1886; DUTOUQUET in *Dict. de théol. cath.*, II, 1091.

S. H. FRISBEE.

Bouillart, JACQUES, a Benedictine monk of the Congregation of St.-Maur, b. in the Diocese of Chartres, 1669; professed at the Monastery of St. Faron de Meaux 1687, d. 11 December, 1726. He was the author of "Histoire de l'abbaye royale de Saint-Germain-des-Prés" (Paris, 1724). This valuable history of the celebrated Benedictine monastery contains biographies of the abbots that ruled over it since its foundation by Childeric I in 543 and many important historical events relative to the famous abbey. Bouillart also edited a martyrology of Usuard. In this publication he attempts to establish the genuineness and authenticity of the manuscript preserved

at Saint-Germain-des-Prés, against the Jesuit hagiographer Du Sollier, who in his revised edition of Usuard's martyrology had paid no attention to this manuscript.

DE LAMA, *Bibliothèque des écrivains de la congrégation de Saint-Maur* (Munich and Paris, 1882), 128; ZIEGELBAUER, *Hist. rei lit. O. S. B.* (Augsburg and Würzburg, 1754), IV, 558; HURTER, *Nomenclator* (Innsbruck, 1893), II, 1201; LE CERF, *Bibl. hist. et crit. des auteurs de la c. de St. Maur* (The Hague 1726).

MICHAEL OTT.

Bouillon, EMMANUEL THÉODORE DE LA TOUR D'AUVERGNE, CARDINAL DE, French prelate and diplomat, b. 24 August, 1643, at Turenne; d. 2 March, 1715, at Rome. The son of Frederick Maurice, Prince of Sedan, he was of the family of the great Marshal Turenne. In 1658, he was appointed a canon of Liège; doctor of the Sorbonne in 1667; created a cardinal in 1669, at the early age of twenty-four, and, finally, provided with several rich benefices and made chief almoner to Louis XIV. But Louvois, the powerful minister of Louis XIV, inspired by enmity to the house of Turenne, successfully opposed certain of his demands on the king for the benefit of members of his family, and the cardinal's disappointment vented itself in a bitter satire on his royal master. This was used to effect Bouillon's downfall at court. The cardinal then put forth great efforts to obtain the vacant Prince-Bishopric of Liège, but could not overcome the opposition of Louvois, who secured the dignity for Clement Joseph of Bavaria. Bouillon eventually regained the royal favour and was sent as ambassador to Rome. There, contrary to the wishes of his king, he championed the cause of Fénelon against that of Bossuet and did all he could to prevent the condemnation of Fénelon's "Explication des maximes des Saints". He was recalled to France, but alleging as a reason his duties as Dean of the Sacred College, he refused to obey the royal order. His property in France was then seized, whereupon he submitted and returned, but, on his arrival in France, was exiled to his Abbey of Tournus. While in this retirement, and under the influence of bitter ennui, the cardinal caused to be composed by Baluze his "Histoire généalogique de la maison d'Auvergne" (1708, 2 vols. in fol.). From his place of retreat, also, on the breaking out of the War of the Spanish Succession, he entered into correspondence with the English Duke of Marlborough, the Earls of Orrery and Galway, and others; and in 1710, after long and vainly soliciting his recall to court, he fled to the Low Countries. A warrant for his arrest was issued by the Royal Parliament, and his possessions again confiscated. But after some years spent abroad, during which the cardinal sent to the king numerous memoirs, endeavouring to justify his conduct, he at last succeeded in obtaining the restitution of his revenues and permission to take up his residence at Rome, where he spent in peace his last days.

DE FELLER-PÉRENNÈS, *Biogr. Gener.* (Paris, 1834), II, 470.

EDWARD A. GILLIGAN.

Bouix, MARIE DOMINIQUE, one of the best known and most distinguished of modern French canonists, b. 15 May, 1808, at Bagnères-de-Bigorre, in the diocese of Tarbes; d. at Montech, France, 26 December, 1870. In 1825, on the completion of his college course in an institution of his native town, he entered the Society of Jesus at Avignon, with his brother Marcel, and later taught the classics and occupied chairs of philosophy and theology in houses of the order. In 1842, when he was on the eve of his solemn profession, the precarious condition of his health rendered a continuance of the religious life impossible, and he obtained permission to retire from the Society. This necessary withdrawal was a great disappointment to Bouix, who to the end of his life maintained the most cordial relations with his former brethren in religion, and received from them many evidences of a reciprocal regard. Father Roothan, General of the Jesuits, created him Doctor of Theology in 1851, in virtue of a power delegated by the Holy See to Jesuit generals; and Bouix's work, "Du Concile Provincial", published in 1850, was dedicated to members of the order with whom he had previously been associated in scholastic work. The first two years of his life as a secular priest were spent in a curacy at the church of Saint Vincent de Paul, in Paris. Here he interested himself especially in the soldiers garrisoned at the capital, and founded in their behalf the Society of Saint Maurice, which later spread throughout France. In 1847 he was named to a chaplaincy, and became editor of the "Voix de la Verité", to which he had already been a frequent contributor. In spite of the fact that all self-seeking was entirely foreign to his character, he now became a prominent figure in the political and ecclesiastical life of Paris and was a member of the educational commission with Montalembert and Monsignor Parisis. General Cavaignac, who aspired to the presidency of the republic, thought it wise to endeavour to enlist the sympathies of Bouix. It was at this time, in 1848, that his first book appeared, combating an heretical organization known as the Œuvre de la Miséricorde. In 1849 his zeal impelled him to abandon for a time all other pursuits to minister to the victims of the cholera, which was then epidemic in Paris. Up to this time he had stood high in the favour of the ecclesiastical authorities of the diocese, but now an event occurred which was destined to affect seriously his ecclesiastical status and to give a new direction to his life work. Monsignor Fornari, the Nuncio at Paris, desiring to further the restoration of provincial councils, held a conference with Bouix and the Bollandist Van Hecke, at which it was decided that the best means of influencing public opinion aright would be the preparation of a book explaining the law of the Church on provincial councils. Bouix was charged with this important work, and first published in the "Univers" four articles, setting forth the salient features of the question and preparing the public for the complete treatise, "Du Concile Provincial", which appeared in 1850. A fifth article in the "Univers", simply reaffirming the canon law on synods and combating therefore, in the judgment of some, the tendencies of Gallicanism, was followed immediately by the loss of his chaplaincy. This event determined him to devote his life to dispelling the prejudices and errors which he believed had largely infected the clergy of France in regard to matters of law and discipline. To equip himself for this work he turned his steps towards Rome, where, with no other means of support than the stipend of his daily Mass, he passed the next four years (1851–55) in study and in the preparation of the several works on canonical topics. In 1854, the degree of Doctor of Both Laws was conferred upon him by order of Pius IX. Returning to Paris in 1855, he continued his studies, and added to the series of treatises which established his fame as a canonist. To further the great purpose to which he had consecrated his life, he founded at Arras, in 1860, the "Revue des sciences ecclésiastiques", of which he was for one year the editor, and in which during the next nine years many important articles appeared from his pen. In 1864, just as his anti-Gallican opinions were about to subject him to new rigours at the hands of Monseigneur Darboy, Bouix was named Vicar-General of the Diocese of Versailles, a sufficient commentary on the division of opinion in the French episcopate as to the character of his

teaching. The next year, when the royal exequatur came up for discussion in the French Senate, and Archbishop Darboy advocated there the Gallican view, Bouix answered with a publication which contested the correctness of the archbishop's contentions. The wonderful activity of his pen continued until 1870. Then, when he was broken by labour and disease and was really too weak to undertake a long journey, he went to the Vatican Council as theologian of the Bishop of Montauban, and was able to witness what appeared to him a signal triumph of the principles to which his life had been devoted. He returned with difficulty to France, where with undaunted spirit he endeavoured to complete a work on the Church, which he had already planned. It was while engaged on this work that death overtook him at Montech, in a religious house of which his sister was superior. His life was a long battle with Gallicanism, but always remained singularly free from bitterness and discontent, in spite of the difficulties by which he was beset and the atmosphere of combat which his zeal forced him to breathe. As to his reputation as a canonist, while all must acknowledge his wonderful productivity and his high purpose, and while he has been justly called the restorer of the science of canon law in France, it must nevertheless be said that he falls short of being a great canonist; he is too often a compiler rather than a genuine author, and he too frequently betrays a lack of that juridical sense which comes more from practice than from theory, and which begets the ability to pronounce justly on the lawfulness and unlawfulness of existing practices. However, the value of his works cannot be questioned, and is proved by the general favour which they still enjoy. Besides many articles, contributed to newspapers and reviews, especially to the "Revue des sciences ecclésiastiques", we owe to the pen of Bouix the following works: "Du concile provincial" (published also in Latin translation, De Concilio Provinciali); "Tractatus de Principiis Juris Canonici"; "Tractatus de Capitulis"; "Tractatus de Jure Liturgico"; "Tractatus de Judiciis Ecclesiasticis", 2 vols.; "Tractatus de Parocho"; "Tractatus de Jure Regularium", 2 vols. (an abridged translation of which appeared in German); "Tractatus de Episcopo", 2 vols.; "Tractatus de Curiâ Romanâ"; "Tractatus de Papa", 3 vols.; "La vérité sur l'assemblée de 1682"; "Le prétendu droit d'exequatur"; "La vérité sur la faculté de théologie de Paris, de 1663 à 1682" ; "L'Œuvre de la miséricorde"; "Méditations pour tous les jours de l'année", 4 vols.; "Le solitaire des rochers"; "Histoire des vingt-six martyrs de Japon," 2 vols. Several of his works were honoured with pontifical letters of commendation, and most of his canonical treatises have gone through three editions.

HURTER, *Nomenclator Literarius*, III, 1424; SCHULTE, *Geschichte der Quellen*, III, 669; WERNZ, *Jus Decretalium*, I, 454; *Revue des Sciences Ecclésiastiques*, XXII, 193, XXIII, 129.

JOHN T. CREAGH.

MARCEL, author, editor, and translator, brother of Marie Dominique Bouix, was born at Bagnères-de-Bigorre, France, 25 June, 1806; d. at Paris, 28 December, 1889. He entered the Society of Jesus at the age of nineteen and taught in the colleges of the Society in Spain and Switzerland. He spent some years of his life in the exercise of the sacred ministry, but the work to which he devoted himself for nearly forty years was the translation, revision, and publication of new editions of the great spiritual writers. These he enriched with introductions, commentaries, and historical notes of great value. His various editions of the life and works of St. Teresa, to the study and translation of which he gave sixteen years of his life, from 1848 to 1864, caused a remarkable revival of interest in the great Carmelite reformer. His "Vie de Sainte Thérèse, écrite par elle-même" (Paris, 1852), passed through twelve editions, and was translated into German and Dutch. His "Œuvres de Sainte Thérèse", in three volumes (Paris, 1852–54–56), reached a third edition in 1860. "Œuvres spirituelles du Saint Pierre d'Alcantara" (Paris, 1862), Father Caraffa's "School of Divine Love" (Lyons, 1863), and a new translation of "The Following of Christ" (Poitiers, 1864) are three of the eight works issued in two plays. Revised editions of Father Mumford's "Purgatory" (Paris, 1863), of St. Francis de Sales' "Treatise on the Love of God" (Paris, 1864), and of "The Spiritual Works of St. Francis Borgia" (Paris, 1869) are valuable contributions to ascetic theology. "Saint Joseph d'après les saints et les maîtres de la vie spirituelle" (Paris, 1863) is Father Bouix's own original contribution to religious literature. One of his most valuable services was the publication, for the first time, of the "Memoriale" of Pierre Lefèvre, (Bl. Peter Faber) one of the first companions of St. Ignatius Loyola, in the original Latin and in a French translation (Paris, 1873). This work was translated into English by Father H. J. Coleridge, S.J. (London, 1873). Father Bouix translated into French the letters of St. Ignatius (Paris, 1870) and Father du Pont's "Life of Father Alvarez" (Paris, 1873). He published the "Œuvres spirituelles" of Father Jean-Joseph Surin in three volumes (Paris, 1879–82). The translation of Leonard Lessius's "Les noms divins" (Paris, 1882) was one of the last works from the pen of this indefatigable writer, whose many years of labour enriched the literature of France with popular spiritual books of sound Catholic theology.

DUTOUQUET in *Dict. de théol. cath.*, II, 1091–92; SOMMERVOGEL, *Bibl.*, I, 1922–28.

PATRICK H. KELLY.

Boulainvilliers, HENRI, COUNT OF, b. at Saint-Saire (Seine-Inférieure) France, 11 October, 1658; d. at Paris, 23 January, 1722. He was one of the first French historians to write the history of the institutions or fundamental laws of the nation and, although systematic and decidedly partial, was none the less a pioneer in this particular line of work. Until the death of his father in 1697, he followed a military career, but some complications concerning an estate obliged him to make a close investigation of his family, titles and this it was that led to his becoming an historian. Like Saint-Simon, Boulainvilliers was saturated with ultra-aristocratic notions and was also an ardent adherent of the old feudal system, his books being a long, violent tirade against the French monarchy which, according to him, was responsible for the gradual ruin of the privileges of the nobility and the annihilation of feudalism.

The Franks, according to his doctrine, established themselves in Gaul by right of conquest; they divided its land among themselves and they exercise public authority. They constitute the French nation; they are Frenchmen. Every Frenchman is free and independent, is supreme in his domain, in his fee, where he administers justice to his subjects. The king is merely a civil magistrate chosen to settle the disputes of private individuals; he has no special power over the life, property, or liberty of other Frenchmen who are in no wise his subordinates. Frenchmen who belong to the nobility are all on an equality: they are the peers of the king and of his relatives. Relationship with kings confers no rank even upon descendants in the male line. Such is the feudal system as claimed by Boulainvilliers to be the only one that is just, legitimate, and conformable to the reality of history.

Now, what caused Frenchmen or nobles to be dispossessed of their rights? First, the Crusades. To defray the expenses of these expeditions many noblemen either mortgaged or sold their fees and

wealthy plebeians, who were not noble, but, according to Boulainvilliers, "ignoble", thus became the owners of fees and, by introducing themselves into the nobility, corrupted it. Next came the ignorance of the lords or owners. The ignorance and negligence of the lords rendering them generally incompetent to discharge the functions that rightfully belonged to them, the principal of which was to dispense justice in their fees, they soon transferred all their judicial authority to clerks or jurists. Thanks to the dignity of their rôle, these clerks or jurists soon became as important as the lords and thus originated the *noblesse de la robe* (nobility of the long robe) which Boulainvilliers considers a monstrosity.

Finally came the policy of the Capetian Kings which Boulainvilliers regards as chiefly instrumental in ruining feudalism and therefore the French nation. This policy consisted in adding the great fees to the royal domain by reason of conquest, purchase, or marriage, with the result that the Kings of France assumed an importance theretofore unknown to them, and which soon became entirely disproportionate; while the lords, fascinated by the brilliancy of the royal courts, instead of remaining the peers of these kings, became their servants. The kings diminished the power of the French nobles still more by favouring the emancipation of the communes and raising to the ranks of the nobility plebeians whom they entrusted with high offices to which they had no right. Moreover, they admitted to seats in the States General, which should have been composed exclusively of representatives of the French, delegates from among the lower clergy and liberated serfs, and of course this arbitrary measure completed the overthrow of the nobility. Such then, is the teaching set forth in Boulainvilliers's three most important works: "Histoire de l'ancien gouvernement de France", "Lettres sur les Parlements ou Etats-Généraux", and "Essais sur la noblesse" which, taken as a whole, constitute an earnest plea for feudalism against monarchism. These works, written by Boulainvilliers for his grandchildren, did not appear until after his death. The "Histoire de l'ancien gouvernement de la France" with fourteen historical "Lettres sur les Parlements ou Etats-Généraux" were published in Amsterdam and the Hague in 1727, the "Essais sur la noblesse" (containing a dissertation by the late Count of Boulainvilliers on the origin and decline of the nobility) coming out in Amsterdam, 1732. It is only within the last twenty-five years that Boulainvilliers' works have been duly appreciated and their conclusions taken up by the historic school of which Fustel de Coulanges was the chief representative.

RENÉ DOUMIC.

Boulanger, ANDRÉ DE (PETIT-PÈRE ANDRÉ), a French monk and preacher, b. at Paris in 1578; d. 27 September, 1657. He was the son of a President of the Parlement (High Court) of Paris. At an early age he entered the Augustinian Order and became a well-known preacher, being heard for over half a century in most of the great pulpits of France. Boulanger lived at a period when the jocose style of preaching, introduced by such men as Menot and Maillard, still lingered, and he made large use of the burlesque, notwithstanding its bad taste, in his own preaching. It is indeed this habit of jesting that has preserved his name. Boileau refers to Boulanger when, speaking of trivial plays on words and witticisms, he writes:

L'avocat au palais en hérissa son style,
Et le docteur en chaire en sema l'Evangile.

—"The style of the advocate in court bristles with them and the doctor in the pulpit scatters them through the Gospel." Father André's style of preaching may be judged from the following example. In one of his passages he thus compared the four great

Doctors of the Latin Church to the kings of the four suits of cards: St. Augustine to the King of Hearts, because of his large-heartedness; St. Ambrose to the King of Clubs (*trèfle*, clover), on account of his flowery eloquence; St. Jerome to the King of Spades (*pique*, lance), because of his biting style; St. Gregory the Great to the King of Diamonds (*carreau*, in the sense of "foot-stool") on account of his lowliness of thought. However, this exaggeration of speech was but one side, and that the least important one, of Father André's eloquence. Tallemant des Réaux said: "He was a good member of his order and had a large following of all sorts of people; some came to laugh, others came because he moved them." The critic Guéret, who had heard the facetious monk, represents him, in a dialogue of the dead, as saying in his own defence against his accuser Cardinal du Perron: "Joker as you take him to be, he has not always made those laugh who heard him; he has said truths which have sent bishops back into their dioceses. He has found the art of stinging while laughing." The Regent Anne of Austria and the Prince of Condé enjoyed his sermons. Boulanger was several times provincial of his order and much occupied in other ways; consequently he was not able to attend to the printing of his works. The only one of his writings which has been published, "L'Oraison de Marie de Lorraine, abbesse de Chelles", is mediocre.

GUÉRET, *La guerre des auteurs anciens et modernes* (Paris, 1671), 152; JACQUINET, *Les prédicateurs du xviie siècle avant Bossuet* (Paris, 1885).

A. FOURNET.

Boulay (BULÆUS), CÉSAR-EGASSE DU, a French historian, b. in the beginning of the seventeenth century at Saint-Ellier (department of Mayenne); d. 16 October, 1678. After teaching humanities in the College of Navarre he occupied important positions in the University of Paris, especially those of rector and historian of the university. His main work is the "Historia Universitatis Parisiensis" covering the period from the supposed foundation of the university by Charlemagne (800) to 1600. The first three volumes published in 1665 were censured by the university. To justify himself the author wrote the "Notæ ad censuram . . ." (Paris, 1667). The censors appointed by the king found nothing blameworthy in the work, and the last three volumes were published in 1673. Du Boulay's history is very important on account of the many original documents which it reproduces, but its value is lessened by the insufficient judgment and criticism of the author. Other writings of Du Boulay refer to the same topic of the university, its foundation, patrons, administration, and privileges: "De patronis quatuor nationum universitatis" (1662); "Carlomagnolia . . ." (1662); "De decanatu nationis Gallicanæ . . ." (1662); "Remarques sur la dignité, rang . . . du recteur" (1668); "Remarques sur l'élection des officiers de l'Université" (1668); "Recueil des privilèges de l'Université . . ." (1674); "Fondation de l'Université par l'empereur Charlemagne . . ." (1675). In addition to these Du Boulay wrote "Speculum eloquentiæ" (1658) and "Trésor des antiquités romaines" (1651).

FÉRET, *La faculté de théologie de Paris et ses docteurs les plus célèbres, Epoque moderne* (Paris, 1904), III, 435; HURTER, *Nomenclator* (2d ed., Innsbruck, 1893), II, 241; *Biographie universelle* (Paris, 1811–28), V, 326; DENIFLE, *Die Entstehung der Universitäten des Mittelalters bis 1400* (Berlin, 1885).

C. A. DUBRAY.

Boulogne, ETIENNE-ANTOINE, French bishop, b. at Avignon, 26 December, 1747; d. at Troyes, 13 March, 1825. He was the son of poor parents and obtained an education from the Christian Brothers of his native city. He exhibited talent and industry and was ordained in 1771. His oratorical gifts attracted general attention, and he soon became one of the most admired preachers in Paris. For a while the Archbishop of Paris interdicted him from preaching; but was eventually induced to withdraw his opposition when a eulogy composed by the Abbé Boulogne on the late Dauphin, the father of Louis XVI, obtained a prize. The Abbé's reputation as a preacher now grew steadily. He preached the Lenten sermons *aux Quinze-Vingts* in 1786, and at the court of Versailles in 1787. In one of his sermons at court he clearly pointed out the fearful storm which was threatening society, brought on by the false philosophy and irreligion of the day. The storm advanced unchecked and broke over France sooner and with greater violence than had been foreseen, except by the keenest observers. Boulogne refused to take the oath of the civil constitution of the clergy demanded by the laws and was in consequence stripped of his titles and benefices. He also refused to leave his country in her need. He was arrested three times, but each time succeeded in recovering his liberty; condemned to deportation on another occasion for having defended Christianity against the attacks of Larevellière Lépeaux, he again evaded the unjust decree. The worst of the revolutionary storm had scarcely blown over when he reappeared, contending in the "Annales Catholiques", of which he had become the sole editor, with unbelievers and those of the clergy who had taken the oath of the civil constitution. In spite of incessant and fierce opposition he published this magazine under one title or another until the year 1807. He also resumed his labours as preacher with greater authority and success than ever. Napoleon, always in search of men of talent who were capable of furthering his ambitious designs, first appointed the Abbé Boulogne his chaplain, then Bishop of Troyes. The Abbé foresaw clearly that his position would be one of great difficulty; but already schooled to adversity, he did not shrink from the new trials which awaited him.

In 1811 Napoleon had the bishops of France and Northern Italy summoned to a council to be held at Paris. Bishop Boulogne preached the opening sermon in the church of Notre Dame. "Whatever vicissitudes", he said in conclusion, "the See of Peter may experience, whatever be the state and condition of his august successor, we shall firmly cling to him with bonds of filial respect and reverence; the See may be displaced, it cannot be destroyed; wherever that See may be, the others will take their stand around it; whithersoever that See moves, thither all Catholics will follow; for there alone is the last link of true succession; there the centre of the Church's government; there, the deposit of Apostolic tradition." It is easy to see how distasteful these courageous words, which produced a profound impression on the assembly, must have been to Napoleon who, at this very time, was holding Pius VII in captivity away from Rome and was using his wonted violence and deception to extort from the assembled prelates a decision that would enable him to do without ecclesiastical investiture for the bishops of his choice. Yet this displeasure did not prevent the assembled bishops from choosing the preacher as secretary of the council and member of the committee on the reply to the imperial message. When this committee reported that there was no authority in France that could supply, even provisionally and for a case of necessity, the absence of the pope's Bulls of episcopal investiture, Napoleon dissolved the council and that very night Bishop Boulogne was arrested and imprisoned. He was not restored to his flock before the events of 1814. During the first Bourbon Restoration, he was chosen to preach the funeral oration of Louis XVI, and, at the second, he preached, 6 January, 1816, his well-known sermon "La France veut son Dieu, la France veut son roi". Louis XVIII made him peer of France and Leo XII granted him the title of archbishop bestowing on him the pallium. Up to the last he exercised the ministry of the word of God with remarkable zeal and talent. His writings, literary, historical, and apologetic, disclose unusual soundness and strength of mind.

Œuvres de Mgr. Boulogne (Paris, 1826); ROHRBACHER, *Histoire de l'église* (Paris, 1825), XXVIII, 130–132.

CHARLES B. SCHRANTZ.

Boulogne, DIOCESE OF. See ARRAS, THE DIOCESE OF.

Bouquet, MARTIN, a learned Benedictine of the Congregation of St.-Maur, b. at Amiens, France, 6 August, 1685; d. at the monastery of Blancs-Manteaux, in Paris, 6 April, 1754. When a boy he resolved to enter the secular priesthood. Subsequently, however, not wishing to expose his soul to the dangers of the world, he determined to become a Benedictine. The Congregation of St.-Maur was then in its most flourishing condition. Bouquet joined this congregation and took vows at the monastery of St.-Faron, at Meaux, 16 August, 1706.

Shortly after his elevation to the priesthood his superiors appointed him librarian at the monastery of St.-Germain-des-Prés which at that time possessed a library of 60,000 books and 8,000 manuscripts. Being well versed in the Greek language, Bouquet was of great assistance to his confrère, Bernard de Montfaucon, in his edition of the works of St. Chrysostom. He himself was preparing a new edition of the Jewish historian, Flavius Josephus, and had already progressed far in his work when he heard that the Dutch writer, Sigebert Haverkamp, was engaged on a new edition of the same author. He at once sent all the material he had collected to Haverkamp, who embodied it in his edition. Bouquet's greatest work, however, is his collection of the historians of Gaul and France, entitled: "Rerum Gallicarum et Francicarum Scriptores".

Attempts to collect the sources of French history had been made at various times. Thus Pierre Pithou (d. 1596) had collected some material, and André Duchesne (d. 1640) had begun a work entitled "Historiæ Francorum Scriptores", to be published in twenty-four volumes, but died before finishing the fifth volume. Colbert, the great French minister of finance, desired to have Duchesne's work continued at the expense of the State, but he died in 1683 without finding a suitable historian to complete what Duchesne had begun. In 1717, D'Aguesseau, who was then chancellor, entrusted to the Benedictine, Edmond Martène, the drawing up of a new plan for the work. The design was accepted and the Oratorian LeLong who had just finished his "Bibliothèque historique de la France" was entrusted with the task. He had scarcely begun when death put an end to his labours in 1721.

The Congregation of St.-Maur now undertook the publication of the work and Dionysius de Sainte-Marthe, who was then superior-general of the congregation, placed Bouquet in charge of the undertaking. Because Duchesne's five volumes had become rare, Bouquet began an entirely new work and had the first two volumes ready for print in 1729, but their publication was delayed. Some monks of the Congregation of St.-Maur refused to submit to the Bull "Unigenitus" which was directed against Quesnel. Bouquet submitted after some hesitation. When, however, Cardinal De Bissy required the monks of St.-Germain-des-Prés to sign a formula of submission drawn up by himself, Bouquet and seven others refused their signature because De Bissy, being merely Abbot *in commendam* of St.-Germain-des-Prés, had no spiritual jurisdiction over the monks. Bouquet was banished to the monastery of St.-Jean, at Laon, but in 1735, D'Aguesseau and a few other influential persons succeeded in having him recalled to Argenteuil, and afterwards to Blancs-Manteaux,

where he could more easily supervise the publication of his work. He brought out eight volumes between 1738 and 1752. The greater part of the material for the ninth volume was ready when Bouquet died (1754), after receiving the last rites of the Church.

The eight volumes published comprise the sources of the history of France from the earliest days of its existence to the year 987. The work was continued by other members of the Congregation of St.-Maur in the following order: vols. IX–X were published by the two brothers, John and Charles Haudiquier; vol. XI, by Housseau, Précieux, and Poirier; vols. XII–XIII, by Clément and Brial; vols. XIV–XVIII, by Brial. The remaining five volumes were published by the Académie des Inscriptions which completed the work in 1876. A new edition in twenty-five volumes, undertaken by Leopold Delisle, a member of the Académie des Inscriptions, has reached the twenty-fourth volume.

TASSIN, *Histoire littéraire de la congr. de St. Maur* (Brussels, 1770), s. v.; the same work in German, *Gelehrtengeschichte der Congregation von St. Maurus* (Frankfort and Leipzig, 1774); DE LAMA, *Bibliothèque des écrivains de la congr. de St. Maur* (Munich and Paris, 1882), s. v.; FRANÇOIS, *Bibliothèque générale des écrivains de l'ordre de St. Benoît* (Bouillon, 1777), I, 143; MEUSEL, *Bibliotheca Historica* (Leipzig, 1793), VI, Part II, 270 sqq.; ZIEGELBAUER, *Historia Rei Literariæ O. S. B.* (Augsburg and Würzburg, 1754), IV, 348; WEISS, *Weltgeschichte* (4th ed. Graz and Leipzig, 1898,), XI, 396 sqq.

MICHAEL OTT.

Bouquillon, THOMAS, b. at Warneton, Belgium, 16 May, 1840; d. at Brussels, 5 November, 1902; a Belgian theologian, and at the time of his death professor of moral theology in the Catholic University of America. The second son among five children in a family of small landholders long established at Warneton near Ypres, he received his early education in local schools and in the College of St. Louis at Menin. His course in philosophy was made at Roulers; in theology, at the seminary of Bruges. Having entered the Gregorian University in Rome, in 1863, he was ordained priest in 1865 and made doctor of theology in 1867. After ten years in the Bruges seminary (1867–77) and eight years in the Catholic University of Lille, France, as professor of moral theology, Dr. Bouquillon retired to the Benedictine monastery at Maredsous and devoted his energies to the preparation of the second edition of his treatise on fundamental moral theology, a work which fixes him permanently among the great men in the history of that science. He accepted the chair of moral theology in the Catholic University at Washington in 1889, where he remained until his death in 1902. He was one of the most eminent theologians of his time, a man of prodigious erudition in theology, history of theology, church history, canon law, and bibliography. Though never in robust health, he was a tireless student, marked by quiet, simple habits, deep faith, broad sympathies, and great concentration. When he entered the field of moral theology he found the science enjoying no prestige, dwindled to mere compilations of conclusions to the neglect of principles. It was out of touch, consequently, with the closely related dogmatic and advancing social sciences, and the methods employed in teaching it were far from perfect. In his whole career as professor and author he aimed to rescue moral theology from that condition and to restore to it its proper scientific method and dogmatic dignity. He emphasized strongly the historical and sociological aspects of principles and problems in the science, neglecting no results of modern research which contributed to clearness and solidity in his exposition of them. To him is due much credit for the improved methods seen in the recent history of moral theology. Possibly few theologians of his day were more widely consulted in Europe and America than Dr. Bouquillon. He enjoyed and retained the intimate confidence of Leo XIII and of many eminent churchmen, and showed throughout his life unyielding devotion to the ideals, teaching, and administration of the Church. His extraordinary grasp of current thought developed in him an openmindedness and a sympathy with real progress which, combining with his other traits, gave a peculiar fascination to his character. In 1891 he was induced to publish a pamphlet on education setting forth the abstract principles involved. His views met with considerable opposition. In all his published replies to critics he maintained his original positions without any modification whatever and ascribed the opposition to misunderstanding of his point of view and of his statement of principles Dr. Bouquillon was active and influential in the organization of the Catholic Universities of Lille and Washington. In both he gained a name for great practical wisdom in questions of organization and law and for extraordinary power as a teacher.

He published: "Theologia Moralis Fundamentalis" (3d ed., Bruges, 1903), a masterpiece of erudition, analysis, and exposition; "De Virtutibus Theologicis" (2d ed., Bruges, 1890); "De Virtute Religionis" (2 vols., Bruges, 1880); "Education" (Baltimore, 1891); "Education, a Rejoinder to Critics" (Baltimore, 1892); "Education, a Rejoinder to the 'Civiltà Cattolica'" (Baltimore, 1892); the last three of which were translated into French. He published many critical studies in the "Revue des sciences ecclésiastiques", of which he was at one time editor, in the "Nouvelle revue théologique", the "Revue Bénédictine", "The American Catholic Quarterly", and "The Catholic University Bulletin". He edited, with notes and comments, Stapleton, "De Magnitudine Ecclesiæ Romanæ" (Bruges, 1881); "Leonis XIII Allocutiones, Epistolæ aliaque acta" (2 vols., Bruges, 1887); Platelii, "Synopsis cursus Theologiæ" (Bruges); "Catechismus ex decreto Concilii Tridentini" (Tournai, 1890); "Dies Sacerdotalis" of Dirckinck (Tournai, 1888); Louis de Grenade, "L'Excellence de la très sainte Eucharistie" (Lille); Coret, "L'Année sainte" (1676) (Bruges, 1889).

ROMMEL, *Thomas Bouquillon, Notice bio-bibliographique* (Brussels, 1903); *The Catholic University Bulletin* (1903), IX, 152–163.

WILLIAM J. KERBY.

Bourassé, JEAN-JACQUES, archæologist and historian, b. at Ste.-Maure (Indre-et-Loire), France, 22 December, 1813; d. at Tours, 4 October, 1872. He made his preparatory studies for the priesthood in Paris. In 1835, he taught the natural sciences at the preparatory seminary of Tours, where he began a course of archæology that soon attracted attention. The results achieved by him in a field of research, then comparatively new, were such as to entitle him to be considered a veritable pioneer in France, of the science of Christian archæology. In 1884 he became professor at the *grand séminaire* and held the chair of dogmatic theology there for six years. He then discontinued teaching in order to devote himself entirely to the preparation of his various archæological works. Among the productions published by him the best known are: "Archéologie Chrétienne" (1841); "Les Cathédrales de France" (1843); "Les plus belles églises du monde" (1857); "Recherches hist. et archéol. sur les églises romaines en Touraine" (1869).

BUCHBERGER, *Kirchliches-Handlexicon*, I, 116; VIGOUROUX in *Dict. de la Bible*, I, 1894; CHEVALIER, *L'abbé Bourassé* in *Bulletin de la Société archéologique de Touraine* (1873), II 377–423.

M. J. WALDRON.

Bourbon, DIOCESE OF. See SAINT-DENIS, DIOCESE OF.

Bourchier, THOMAS, b. 1406; d. 1486, Cardinal, was the third son of William Bourchier, Earl of Eu, and of Lady Anne Plantagenet, a daughter of Thomas of Woodstock, Duke of Gloucester, youngest son of Edward III. At an early age he entered the University of Oxford, and in due course, embracing a clerical career, was collated to the living of Colwich, Staffordshire, in the Diocese of Coventry and Lichfield, on 24 May, 1424. His next promotion was to the Deanery of St. Martin-le-Grand in London, 1 December, 1427, and he was likewise inducted to the prebend of West Thurrock; it was not till 24 September, 1429, that he was ordained acolyte and subdeacon. This rapid promotion was doubtless due to his high birth, and though no evidence exists of any special attainments as a scholar, he was further appointed Chancellor of the University of Oxford in 1434, a post which he held for three years; in 1433, notwithstanding his youth, he was recommended for the then vacant See of Worcester. The pope had, however, already made another choice, but interest was exerted with the result that the previous nomination was cancelled, and Eugenius IV by a Bull dated 9 March, 1434 appointed Bourchier Bishop of Worcester, the temporalities of the see being restored to him on 15 April, and on 15 May he received episcopal consecration. Not long after, the Bishop of Ely died, and the Benedictine Cathedral Chapter desiring Bourchier for their pastor, sent to Rome to procure Bulls for his translation. These were expedited; but the King of England steadily refused to restore the temporalities to him, so Bourchier renounced the election. Ely was kept vacant till 1443, under the administration of Louis de Luxembourg, Archbishop of Rouen. This arrangement, sanctioned by the pope, had been made in order that Louis de Luxembourg might enjoy the revenues, a convenient form of reward employed by the English sovereigns at that time, since it proved no burden to the royal exchequer. On the death of the Archbishop of Rouen, Bourchier, this time nominated by the king, was at once elected by the Chapter of Ely, the Bulls for the translation, dated 20 December, 1443, procured, and after the usual confirmation he received the temporalities on 27 February, 1443–44, but it seems that he was not enthroned till another two years had elapsed. Both as Bishop of Worcester and of Ely he was frequently called to the royal councils. The Archbishopric of Canterbury fell vacant early in 1454, and Bourchier was recommended for the primatial see. To this he was translated on 22 April, and was enthroned in February, 1454–55. On 5 March following he was appointed Lord Chancellor and received the Seals from Henry VI during that monarch's temporary recovery from the insanity that was settling on him. The troubles between the rival factions of the Yorkists and Lancastrians were then fomenting, and it was hoped that Bourchier might possibly keep the balance even between them. When the Yorkists marched south, their leaders informed the chancellor that their objects were peaceable; but though Bourchier endeavoured to inform the king of their assurances, his communication never reached the sovereign, and the hostile forces met in battle at St. Albans, 22 May, 1455, when Henry VI was defeated and taken prisoner. This action marks the commencement of the Wars of the Roses. A Parliament was summoned for July, when the Duke of York received pardon. The meeting was then prorogued till November, but in the meanwhile Henry relapsed into imbecility, and the Duke of York was named Protector. Bourchier resigned the Great Seal in October, 1456, when Queen Margaret obtained possession of the king, and with him the chief power fell into her hands. Although the archbishop and Waynflete, as peacemakers, drew up terms of agreement between the parties, dissensions soon broke out again, and after hearing the Yorkists' grievances, Bourchier undertook to accompany them to the king, then at Northampton, with a view to securing a settlement.

The king refused them audience, and a battle was then fought at Northampton (July, 1460), when Henry found himself once more a prisoner. The Duke of York now claimed the throne, but a compromise was effected whereby he was to succeed Henry to the exclusion of the latter's son, Edward. Bourchier seems to have accepted this solution; and when Queen Margaret again opened hostilities, he threw in his lot definitely with the Yorkists, and was one of the lords who agreed to accept Edward (IV) as rightful king. As archbishop, he crowned Edward on 28 June, 1461, after Edward's marriage with Elizabeth Woodville, also crowned his consort (May, 1465). Edward besought Pope Paul II to bestow a cardinal's hat on Bourchier in 1465; but delays occurred, and it was not till 1473 that Sixtus IV finally conferred that honour upon him. In 1475 Bourchier was employed as one of the arbitrators on the differences pending between England and France. Growing feeble, in 1480 he appointed as his coadjutor William Westkarre who had been consecrated in 1458 Bishop of Sidon. In 1483, on the death of Edward IV, he formed one of the deputation who persuaded the queen-dowager, then in sanctuary with her family at Westminster, to deliver her second son Richard to his uncle Richard, Duke of Gloucester, to be with his brother the boy-king Edward V. Bourchier had pledged his honour to the distrustful queen for the lad's security; yet, three weeks later he was officiating at the coronation of the usurper, Richard III. He performed the like solemn office for Henry VII in 1485 after the death of Richard on the field of Bosworth; and, as a fitting close to the career of a man who was above all a peacemaker, he married Henry VII to Elizabeth of York on 18 January, 1485–86, thus uniting the factions of the Red and White Roses. He died on 6 April, 1486, at Knowle, a mansion he had purchased for his see, and was buried in Canterbury cathedral. It fell to his lot as archbishop to preside in 1457 at the trial of Reginald Peacock, Bishop of Chichester, charged with unorthodoxy. Though the incriminated bishop withdrew his works condemned as unsound, he was kept in custody by Bourchier till his death two years later, although he had been compelled to resign his see.

GAIRDNER in *Dict. Nat. Biogr.*; DOYLE, *Official Baronage;* GODWIN, *De Præsulibus;* WHARTON, *Anglia Sacra;* HOOK, *Lives of the Abps. of Cant.*; RYMER, *Fædera;* MORERI, *Dictionnaire;* STUBBS, *Episc. Succession;* LINGARD, *Hist. of England* (London, 1878), *passim.*

HENRY NORBERT BIRT.

Bourdaloue, LOUIS, b. at Bourges, 20 August, 1632; d. at Paris, 13 May, 1704, is often described as the "king of preachers and the preacher of kings". He entered the Society of Jesus at the age of fifteen years. His father, Étienne Bourdaloue, a distinguished legal official of Bourges, though opposing his choice for a time, in order to test its sincerity, willingly consented, having had similar aspirations himself in his youth. A genealogist of the seventeenth century named Hodeau has attempted to trace back the family to the time of the Crusades, but the learned and laborious Tausserat informs us that the first of the race was Macé Bourdaloue, an humble tanner of Vierzon, about 1450. During Bourdaloue's lifetime there were some titles of nobility in the family for military prowess, and although his father was conspicuous in his profession, yet they were by no means wealthy. One of his relatives married a shoemaker, and considerable difficulty was experienced in providing her with a modest dower. Attempts have been made to discover some descendants of the Bourdaloues in our own times, but though the name is common enough, the family is extinct.

When young Bourdaloue entered the Society he immediately attracted attention by his quick and penetrating intelligence, his tireless industry, and his strict observance of religious discipline. He was subsequently made professor of philosophy and moral theology, but certain sermons which he was called on to preach unexpectedly brought him into notice as an orator, and it was determined to devote him altogether to the work of preaching. He began in the Provinces in 1665, was transferred to Paris in 1669, and for thirty-four consecutive years preached with a success that reached its climax only at the end of his career. He was the contemporary and friend of Bossuet, and though quite unlike each other in their methods, their eloquence gave to the French pulpit a glory which has

LOUIS BOURDALOUE

perhaps never been equalled in modern times. They died within two months of each other, though Bossuet was famous long before Bourdaloue appeared. They followed different lines: Bossuet was distinguished for the sublimity and vast sweep of his conceptions, the marvellous conciseness, splendour, and grandeur of his language, as well as the magisterial and almost royal manner in which he grasped his subject and dominated his hearers. He often spoke with scant preparation, so that very few of his wonderful discourses were put on paper before being delivered. His glory as an orator is based mainly on his wonderful "Oraisons Funèbres". Bourdaloue, on the contrary, was essentially a preacher. He wrote his discourses with extreme care, and although they are numerous enough to form editions of twelve and sixteen volumes, there is only one sermon that is incomplete. He had a pronounced dislike of the *Oraisons Funèbres;* he even objected to the name, and called them *éloges.* In the entire collection of his discourses, we find but two of that character, both of them panegyrics of the Condés, Henri and Louis, and both undertaken to pay a debt of gratitude which the Jesuits owed to that family. The first was prompted also by the purpose of gaining an influence over the Great Condé, in order to lead him to a better life. This was realized, for when, only four years after the first discourse Condé's corpse was borne to the same church where he had listened to the panegyric of his father, Bourdaloue was again the orator, and startled his audience by saying: "God gave me a presentiment of the Prince's conversion. I had not only formed the wish, but, as it were, anticipated it by a prayer which seemed then to contain something of a prediction. Whether it was an inspiration or a feeling of zeal, I was transported beyond myself, O Lord, and I was assured by Thee, that Thou wouldst not leave this great man, whose heart was so true as I knew it to be, in the way of perdition and the corruption of the world. He heard my voice; he has heard Thine."

This apostolic motive never failed to reveal itself in all his utterances. Nevertheless, his funeral oration on Henri de Bourbon was considered at the time equal oratorically to any of Bossuet's. Mme. de Sévigné describes it as "the most beautiful that could be imagined. It is the finest and most Christian panegyric that has ever been pronounced."

Such indeed was the universal verdict at the time. Condé himself according to Chérot, let it be known that he considered "the oration to be so noble, so eloquent, and so solid, that it would be difficult enough to surpass it, or perhaps even to imitate it". He had Jouvency translate it immediately into Latin, and he himself supervised the work. Boileau, though somewhat of a Jansenist, says that Bourdaloue was *le plus grand orateur dont le siècle se vante*. This appreciation, however, does not agree with that of some later critics, and Villemain, while acknowledging "numerous beauties of a superior order", declared that Bourdaloue was not well fitted for funeral orations, "on account of the richness and fecundity of imagination which they require". On the other hand, Lord Brougham, himself an orator, says that "Bourdaloue displays a fertility of resources and an exuberance of topics whether for observation or argument, not equalled by any other orator, sacred or profane". He ranks him far beyond Bossuet, but for other reasons inferior to Massillon, about whom another writer remarks that whereas "Bourdaloue preached to the men of a vigorous age, Massillon addressed those of a period remarkable for its effeminacy. Bourdaloue raised himself to the level of the great truths of religion; Massillon conformed himself to the weakness of the men with whom he lived." Nisard, in his "Histoire de la littérature française", says that "Bourdaloue's success was the most brilliant and sustained that human speech has ever obtained". Taine ranks him with Cicero, Livy, Bossuet, Burke, and Fox; Fénelon, however, is said to have depreciated him in the "Dialogues sur l'éloquence", but according to the "Revue Bourdaloue", the authenticity of the "Dialogues" is doubtful, and besides Bourdaloue is not named; the description is assigned to him only by conjecture.

As his object was exclusively the salvation of souls, Bourdaloue adapted himself to the audience which, in spite of its worldliness, frivolity, and vice, prided itself, and with reason, on its power of appreciating what was intellectual and scholarly, and although scandalously irreverential in the very temple of God, had an insatiable craving for religious discourses. To influence them, the preacher had to resort to reason; and consequently his discourses were constructed after a clearly defined and frankly enunciated plan, each part closely knit with, and evolved from, the preceding. The proposition is always distinctly stated; argument after argument is elaborated with irresistible logic; doctrines whose orthodoxy is without reproach are carefully and minutely explained, and moral principles are expounded, but never exaggerated or strained in the practical application which he never fails to make; sophistries are dispelled, objections answered, and errors refuted, the orator not fearing to return to a point for a greater clearness; mysteries are discussed, though he purposely avoided what is too profound, even if by doing so he incurred the reproach of avoiding the sublime, for he is aiming at a moral deduction; the whole delivered in a style which Fénelon says, "had, perhaps, arrived at the perfection of which our language is capable in that kind of eloquence", and with a lucidity and clearness that amazed and captivated his hearers, and evoked applause which he was powerless to prevent. There is never a diversion made merely to dazzle or delight, there is rarely an appeal to the emotions; but the vividness and splendour of the doctrine he was propounding, the startling truthfulness of the psychological picture he was placing before their eyes— even La Bruyère professed to be his disciple in this respect—entreated, or induced, or compelled his hearers to a reformation of life. He hurried on with an extraordinary rapidity of utterance, but with a

distinctness of enunciation and a marvellous sweetness and power of voice that filled every part of the edifice in which he was speaking, and kept his audience spellbound to the end of his discourse. Places were secured at daybreak; princes and prelates crowded to hear him, and on one memorable occasion, several of the most distinguished members of the hierarchy, among them Bossuet himself, withdrew in anger because the seats they claimed were not granted. Bossuet it is said, however, remained in a gallery apart to listen to the discourse.

Although covering such a vast field in every one of his sermons, Bourdaloue never exhausted his subject, and we find two and even three on the same theme, not only without any repetition, but each one improving on what preceded, so that Louis XIV said he would rather "hear Bourdaloue's repetitions than what was novel from any one else". He appeared at the court on ten different occasions for courses of sermons and each time his welcome was more enthusiastic than before. He was a court preacher but did not flatter, and one of his sermons is made use of by modern Socialists in support of their teaching. A few years ago considerable controversy was evoked by it, and Jules Lemaître finds in it a condemnation of contemporary egoism. He was preaching on "Riches" and used the phrase of St. Jerome: "Every rich man is an unjust man or the heir of one." "If you go to the source of riches", he said, "even in houses and families who are proud of their origin, nay even those who are distinguished for their probity and religion, you will discover things which will make you tremble." In the twelve-volume edition there is one number containing sermons for Advent, three others of Lenten discourses, three more for Sundays of the year, two on the Mysteries, while the last two books contain sixteen panegyrics, six sermons for religious investitures, and the two funeral orations. Considerable ingenuity has been exercised by his editors in fixing the time when the various discourses were pronounced; they are all undated. When they were given is largely a matter of conjecture. The sermons of least merit are those on the Mysteries, but it is explained that he purposely avoided any sublime or profound considerations on those topics and restricted himself to what could be easily stated, so as to have the opportunity of deducing a moral lesson. "Everything was practical", says Joubert, "in the judicious Bourdaloue." Some one has said that "the Jesuits answered Pascal's attacks about their moral teaching by making Bourdaloue preach." As regards his literary style, Sainte-Beuve says: "He *was* a good orator, he *is* a good writer." He is free from the turgid, pedantic, and ridiculous phraseology which was rampant at that time in forensic as well as sacred eloquence—though there are some examples of it. His compliments to the exalted personages in the audience are not so much an evidence of bad literary taste as a mark of the servitude to which the court preachers of that day had to submit. About his correctness of language, however, the "Revue Bourdaloue" (1 April, 1904) admits that authentic manuscripts no longer exist, and that it is impossible to make out how much his editor, Bretonneau, has tampered with the text.

If not the originator, Bourdaloue is largely the model, of French pulpit oratory in the arrangement of sermons. The method he adopted is condemned by Fénelon as never having been used before, and as being poorly adapted to arouse the feelings of the audience. Its use by Bourdaloue is explained by the fact that he was combating Protestant Rationalism which was at that time making inroads upon Catholic thought, and also because the use of clever and convincing reasoning was the vogue of the day. A reaction had set in from the silly idealism of a short time before. Bourdaloue took his hearers as he found them, and Voltaire, referring to this form of his discourses, says "he was the first one to make reason speak, and always eloquently". Possibly the inaptness of the instrument he employed only shows more clearly his greatness as an orator. Only such a man as he could use it. For most readers the printed text of his discourses is wearisome in spite of the wealth of instruction it contains. It needs the voice and action of the orator to give it power. The vogue which his method has obtained is sometimes considered a mistake, if not a misfortune, for French pulpit eloquence. It supposes a Bourdaloue, as well as conditions which have long since ceased. Chérot who has made an exhaustive study of Bourdaloue dismisses with contempt the story that the orator spoke with his eyes shut. For a court preacher who had to distribute compliments to the dignitaries present, and who angered them if he did not do it skilfully, or omitted anyone who expected it (as happened in the case of Mme. de Guise), it would have been a difficult or rather impossible task to perform that duty if he did not use his eyes. The picture that so represents him was taken after his death. Similarly, to suppose that he would dare to say to Louis XIV in the sermon on "Adultery": *tu es ille vir*, like Nathan to David, is to be ignorant of conditions that prevailed in that servile court. The alleged sermon, moreover, is nowhere to be found. It is said to have been burnt. More likely it was never written. Mme. de Sévigné speaks of a sermon on "Impurity" in which Bourdaloue was merciless, but had that reproach been addressed to the king, she, above all writers, would have told it. Besides, that sermon was preached in the Jesuit church, and there is no assurance that it was repeated at Versailles. Again, some of his biographers in speaking of his sermon on "The Magdalene", insinuate that it was directed at Mmes. de Montespan and de Fontanges, the king's mistresses who sat before him. It is not certain that "The Magdalene" sermon was ever preached before the court. Moreover, Bourdaloue was too prudent to irritate uselessly.

Considerable discussion has been raised with regard to his attitude in the quarrel between the pope and the king about the Four Gallican Articles. It is admitted that in the Panegyric of St. Louis, pronounced in presence of Louis XIV, the preacher referred to "the rights of the Crown" and "the new attempts of the Court of Rome", and also the manner in which St. Louis defended those rights. He added, however, that "while Louis in his quality of king recognized no superior on earth" (all of which has a Gallican tinge), yet the monarch should remember that he was, at the same time, the eldest son of the Church. His defenders maintain that we have no right to infer from this phrase that he was a Gallican or stood side by side with Bossuet. Another point which has called for inquiry is his "abstention" from the subject of the infallibility of the pope; he never spoke of it. Not only that, but when asked about it by Father Alleaume, he said that he had a sermon on the "Infallibility of the Church" which he had never preached. Beyond that, we have no means of knowing his theological view on the question of the pope. However, papal infallibility was not then a matter of discussion. His sermon on the "Infallibility of the Church" is not to be found, under that heading at least; but in the second sermon on the Feast of St. Peter, on "Obedience to the Church", he speaks explicitly of the Church's infallibility.

Bourdaloue seems to have written but very few letters. The collator, Monseigneur Blampignon, found only eighteen; five more have been discovered since—none of them letters of friendship. Some of them are requests for interviews, which would suggest a preference for information by the medium of conversation. One of these letters is noteworthy as it is a congratulation to his intimate friend, the Duc de Noailles, on the appointment to the See of Paris of the duke's brother. Bourdaloue "thanks God for having inspired the king to appoint such a worthy and holy bishop". The prelate became afterwards very unfriendly to the Jesuits. In this communication he speaks of himself as one of the ancient servitors of the house of Noailles, a phrase which intimates who was at the back of Bourdaloue's mission to the Protestants of Languedoc after the Revocation of the Edict of Nantes. In the fulfilment of that mission Protestants and Catholics came in throngs to hear him, and his gentleness and prudence won all hearts. There is a very elaborate letter, or rather disquisition, in the collection, addressed to Mme. de Maintenon who was being alienated from the Jesuits. Bourdaloue was remarkable as a director of souls. While paying proper respect to the great, he was the devoted friend of the poor, and assiduous in the confessional. He was of a gentle and amiable disposition and exerted a wonderful power at the death-bed, especially of hardened sinners. Towards the end of his life he desired to quit Paris, and live in seclusion at La Flèche, and though he had received the permission of the general, the provincial thwarted the plan. It only increased his zeal and he continued to preach, hear confessions, and visit the poor till the end of his life. After a sickness of two days he died at the age of seventy-two.

GRISELLE, *Bourdaloue* (Paris, 1901); CASTETS, *Bourdaloue* (Paris, 1901); *Etudes*, LXXV, 83-84; SOMMERVOGEL, *Bibl. de la c. de J.* (Brussels, 1892); BRETONNEAU, *Pref. des serm. de Bourdaloue* (Paris, 1723); BROUGHAM, *Edinb. Review* (December, 1826); *Revue Bourdaloue;* LAURAS, *Bourdaloue* (Paris, 1880), 2 vols.

T. J. CAMPBELL.

Bourdeilles, HÉLIE DE, Archbishop of Tours and Cardinal, b., probably, towards 1423, at the castle of Bourdeilles (Périgord); d. 5 July, 1484, at Artannes near Tours. He was the son of the Viscount Arnaud de Bourdeilles. Having entered the Franciscan Order at an early age, he was only twenty-four when, at the request of Charles VII, he was appointed to the See of Périgueux (1447). During the wars between France and England he was held prisoner for several years by the English, in consequence of his defence of ecclesiastical immunity. In 1468 he was appointed to the Archiepiscopal See of Tours, and in 1483 was raised to the cardinalate by Sixtus IV. Bourdeilles continued, during his episcopate, to practise religious poverty and was an intimate friend of St. Francis of Paula. He is mentioned among the Blessed in the Franciscan Martyrology for the 5th day of July. A stanch defender of the rights of the Church against the encroachments of the State, Bourdeilles advocated the abolition of the Pragmatic Sanction of Bourges, as may be seen from his treatise, "Pro Pragmaticæ Sanctionis Abrogatione" (Rome, 1486). He also wrote "Libellus in Pragmaticam Sanctionem Gallorum" (Rome 1484); and a Latin defence of Jeanne d'Arc which is attached in manuscript to the process of her rehabilitation.

HURTER, *Nomenclator* (3d ed., Innsbruck, 1906), II, 1067-69. For full text of his treatise on Jeanne d'Arc see LANERY DE L'ARC in his documentary *Livre d'or de Jeanne d'Arc* (Paris, 1894).

N. A. WEBER.

Bourdeilles, PIERRE DE. See BRANTÔME.

Bourdon, JEAN, b. at Rouen, France, 1612; d. at Quebec, 1668. In 1634 he went to Canada and became the first engineer-in-chief and land-surveyor in the colony of New France, and the first attorney-general of the Conseil Superieur, established in 1663.

It was Bourdon who surveyed and laid out all the domains and land grants assigned in this territory under the supervision of land companies. He laid out the first streets of Quebec, and drew up the plans and supervised the construction of the first château, Saint-Louis, at the order of Montmagny. He left a chart of the Beaupré shore and vicinity (1641) and two plans of Quebec (1660–64). He also traced a map of the territory through which he travelled in 1646 when he was dispatched with Father Isaac Jogues, S.J., to Albany, to make a treaty of peace with the Iroquois; this, however has been lost. Well-informed, reliable, and conscientious, Bourdon was the confidential agent of the governors, who employed him on several missions with success. In 1657 he embarked for Hudson's Bay, but driven back by the savages, and his way blocked by ice, he was forced to return to Quebec, after having reached 55 degrees N. lat. Jean Bourdon colonized the manorial estate of Pointe-aux-Trembles at a distance of twenty miles from the capital, and at a later date a fief, called after him Saint-Jean, still preserved in one of the principal suburbs of Quebec.

MARCEL, *Cartographie de la Nouvelle-France* (Paris, 1885); ROY, *Bourdon et la Baie d'Hudson* (Quebec, 1896); GOSSELIN, *Jean Bourdon et son ami l'abbé de Saint-Sauveur* (1904); *The Jesuit Relations and Allied Documents*, XI, 277.

J. EDMOND ROY.

Bourgade, FRANÇOIS, a French missionary and philosopher, b. 7 July, 1806, at Gaujan, department of Gers; d. 21 May, 1866, at Paris. He pursued his theological studies at the seminary of Auch and was ordained priest in 1832. His immediate request to be authorized to work among the infidels of Africa was granted only in 1838. He proceeded to Algeria and, after ministering for some time in the hospitals of this colony, passed over to the regency of Tunis, where he founded a hospital and several schools. He was put in charge of the chapel which Louis Philippe (1830–48) had erected on the spot where St. Louis died, and he received several decorations, among them the Legion of Honour. The chief object of his literary productions was to spread the knowledge of Christianity among the Mohammedans. He published "Soirées de Carthage" (1847); "La clef du Coran" (1852); "Passage du Coran à l'Evangile" (1855); the important philological work, "La toison d'or de la langue phénicienne" (1852, 1856); a refutation of Renan's "Life of Jesus", under the title, "Lettre à M. E. Renan" (1864).

VAPEREAU, *Dict. univer. des contemporains*, s. v. in the first four editions; HURTER, *Nomenclator* (Innsbruck, 1895), III, 989, 990.

N. A. WEBER.

Bourgade, PETER. See SANTA FÉ, ARCHDIOCESE OF.

Bourgeoys, MARGUERITE. See NOTRE DAME, CONGREGATION OF.

Bourges (BITURICÆ), ARCHDIOCESE OF, coextensive with the departments of Cher and Indre. After the Concordat of 1802 it became the metropolitan of the Sees of Clermont, Saint-Flour, and Limoges, and in 1822 received as new suffragans the Sees of Tulle and Le Puy. As Gregory of Tours assigns a date subsequent to the "mission of the twelve bishops", that is, to the year 250, for the foundation of the Church at Bourges; and as Leo, who occupied the See of Bourges in 453, was its twelfth bishop; Duchesne, after most careful calculation, places the episcopate of St. Ursinus, founder of the see, near the close of the third century. He explains that the legend which makes Ursinus one of the seventy-two disciples seems to be of later origin than that of St. Martial, being met with for the first time in an eleventh-century manuscript. Fifteen saints figured among Leo's successors up to the end of the ninth century: Sevitianus, Ætherius, Thecretus, Mar-

cellus (all prior to 337); Palladius (377–384); Simplicius (472–480); Desideratus (549–550); Probianus, Felix, Remedius, and the first Sulpicius (all in the second half of the sixth century); Austregisilus (612–624); the second Sulpicius (624–644), after whom the celebrated church of St.-Sulpice in Paris was named; David (793–802); and Agilulfus (c. 820–840). Among later bishops are: St. Guillaume de Donjeon (1200–09); the celebrated theologian, Ægidius a Columnis (1298–1316); and Jean Cœur (1447–83), son of the treasurer Jacques Cœur and during whose episcopate the University of Bourges was founded.

The claims of the See of Bourges to the primacy in Aquitaine are treated at length in the article on Bordeaux. Pope Clement V (1305–14) opposed these claims; nevertheless the See of Bourges always prided itself upon a sort of platonic supremacy, and when, in 1678, the Bishop of Albi became Archbishop, he recognized explicitly the claims of Bourges. Even to-day the Archbishop of Bourges retains the title of Primate of Aquitaine; in this way, the name of Aquitaine which, after the thirteenth century, disappeared from political geography (being replaced by that of Guyenne) has been perpetuated in the terminology of the Church. In 1107 Pascal II, and in 1163 Alexander III, visited the Diocese of Bourges. Many councils were held at Bourges, the principal among them being those of 1225 and 1226 which dealt with the Albigenses; that of 1438, after which Charles VII promulgated the Pragmatic Sanction whereby the decrees of Basle were ratified in France, and the organization of a Gallican Church was attempted; and the council of 1528 which combated the Protestant encroachments favoured at Bourges on the one side by the university in which Calvin and Theodore Beza studied, and on the other by the court of Margaret of Valois.

The following great abbeys were located within the diocese: the Benedictine Abbey of Déols near Châteauroux, founded in the tenth century, where St. Lusorius, son of the senator Leocadius, was interred; the Abbey of St.-Satur near Sancerre, founded in 463; and that of Chezal-Benoît founded in 1098 by Blessed André of Vallombrosa, and mother-house of the great Benedictine congregation which included the Parisian Abbey of St.-Germain-des-Prés and was later merged into the Congregation of St.-Maur. St. Leman, Archbishop of Seville, who fled the persecutions of Totila, suffered martyrdom at Vatan in the middle of the sixth century. Louis VII (1120–80) was crowned in the Cathedral of Bourges, and Louis XI (1423–83) and the great Condé (1621–86) were baptized at Bourges. Labbe, author of the "Collection of Councils" (1607–67) and Bourdaloue, the illustrious preacher (1632–1704), both Jesuits, were born at Bourges. The Cathedral of Bourges (thirteenth century) has beautiful windows and its sacristy (fifteenth century) was built at the expense of Jacques Cœur.

The places of pilgrimages in the diocese are: (1) Notre Dame of Déols near Châteauroux, a pilgrimage begun in the tenth century by Ebbo. The church was consecrated by Pascal II. Pope Alexander III when in exile lived there and received Henry II of England; Pope Honorius III visited it. (2) Notre Dame du Bien Mourir at Fontgombault. (3) The pilgrimage of Ste.-Solange, patron saint of the County of Berry. Ste.-Solange was born at Villemont, three leagues from Bourges, and suffered death to preserve her virginity. (4) Notre Dame du Sacré Cœur at Issoudun. (5) Notre Dame de Pellevoisin, famous for the visions that date back to 1876 and concerning which ecclesiastical authority is still silent.

In 1899, the following institutions were found in the archdiocese: 36 infant schools in Cher and 29 in Indre, conducted by sisters, 3 girls' orphanages in

WINDOW IN THE CATHEDRAL OF ST. ETIENNE, BOURGES
THE WINDOW IS TO THE LEFT FACING THE CENTRAL ALTAR

Cher and 2 in Indre, 1 house of refuge for young women in Cher, 2 *patronages* for girls in Cher, 20 hospitals or hospices in Cher and 14 in Indre, 5 communities for the care of the sick in their homes in Cher and 4 in Indre, 1 insane asylum in Cher, 6 homes for the aged in Cher and 2 in Indre, 1 orphanage for deaf-mute and blind girls in Indre, and 1 home for incurables in Indre, all conducted by nuns.

In 1900 the religious orders of men in the diocese were: Jesuits and Franciscans at Bourges; Trappists at Fontgombault. The societies peculiar to the diocese were: Men: Missionaries of the Sacred Heart, founded in 1854 with the mother-house at Issoudun. This house is the centre of the universal Archconfraternity of Our Lady of the Sacred Heart which has vicariates Apostolic in Oceanica. Women: (1) Benedictines of the Holy Sacrament or of St. Laurence, a congregation said to date back to the time of Charlemagne. They are Sisters of the Perpetual Adoration and teachers. (2) Sisters of Charity and of the Holy Sacrament, called de Montoire, with the mother-house at Bourges. This congregation, founded in 1662 by Antoine Moreau, devotes itself to teaching and hospital nursing. It has 150 houses of which 106 are in the Diocese of Bourges. (3) Religious of the Immaculate Mary, hospital nurses and teachers, with the mother-house at Bourges. After the Revolution, the congregation took the place of the lay confraternity of the Immaculate Mary, and, subsequent to 1857 had charge of the general hospital. (4) Daughters of the Sacred Heart of Issoudun with houses in Belgium and Australia. At the close of 1905 the Archdiocese of Bourges had 652,681 inhabitants, 65 pastorates 430 succursal parishes (mission churches), and 28 curacies.

Gallia christiana (1720), II, 1–115; *instrumenta*, 1–72; LEROUX, *La primatie de Bourges* (*Annales du Midi*) (1895), VII; PARISET, *L'établissement de la primatie de Bourges* in *Annales du Midi* (1902), XIV; DE GIRARDOT AND DURANT, *La Cathédrale de Bourges* (Moulins, 1849); DUCHESNE, *Fastes épiscopaux*, II; VALOIS, *Hist. de la pragmatique Sanction de Bourges sous Charles VII* (Paris, 1906); CHEVALIER, *Topobibl.*, 465–466.

GEORGES GOYAU.

Bourget, IGNACE, first Bishop of Montreal, P. Q., Canada, and titular Archbishop of Martianopolis, b. at Point Lévis, Province of Quebec, 30 October, 1799; d. at Sault-au-Recollet, near Montreal, 8 June, 1885. Remarkable for his piety and learning, he played throughout sixty years a potent part in the religious, and even in the civil, life of Canada. Monseigneur Bourget was the eleventh of thirteen children born to Pierre Bourget and Thérèse Paradis. Sixty-two years of his life were spent in the priesthood, almost fifty in the episcopate, and for nearly thirty-six years he administered the then extensive Diocese of Montreal. He received his elementary instruction at home and at the Point Lévis school and afterwards took the regular course of studies at the Seminary of Quebec, where he was distinguished for his strength of character and brilliant intellect. Here, also, he studied theology for two years, subsequently entering Nicollet College, where he received the sub-diaconate, 21 May, 1821, being chosen that same year by Archbishop Plessis of Quebec to act as

IGNACE BOURGET

secretary to Bishop Lartigue of Montreal. Thus, even before receiving Holy orders, Ignace Bourget was launched upon an active life. On 23 November, 1821, he was made deacon and on 30 November, 1822, was ordained priest in the chapel of the Hôtel-Dieu where he said his first Mass. The young priest soon won the entire confidence of his bishop, who, in 1836, named him vicar-general of the diocese. On 10 March, 1837, Pope Gregory XVI appointed him coadjutor to Bishop Lartigue, and on 25 July of the same year he was consecrated titular Bishop of Telemessa in Lycia. He took possession, on 23 April, 1840, of the See of Montreal, made vacant some two weeks previously by the death of Bishop Lartigue.

Bishop Bourget inaugurated a retreat for the clergy of his diocese, 4 August, 1840; in the same year he carried out the desire of his predecessor by creating a chapter of canons, the installation taking place 31 January, 1841. In December, 1841, after his return from France and Rome, where he had visited many religious communities, he brought the Oblate Fathers to Montreal and in January, 1842, founded the Petit Séminaire de Sainte-Thérèse and canonically established the Temperance Society. The community of the Sisters of the Holy Names of Jesus and Mary, now flourishing in Canada and the United States, was founded under his patronage in 1843, and about the same time the Sisters of Providence. The Providence Asylum was established 29 March, 1844. On 11 July, 1844, Bishop Bourget installed the Sisters of the Good Shepherd from Angers. In a pastoral letter, June, 1845, he commended the work of the Jesuit Fathers whose first establishment he blessed 31 July, 1851. On his return from Rome in 1847, he introduced the Fathers of the Congregation of the Holy Cross, the Clerics of St. Viator, and the Sisters of the Holy Cross, and, a little later, placed the orphans under the care of the Dames de Charité. In 1848 he installed the Sisters of Miséricorde; and on 30 August, 1850, was begun an institute for deaf-mutes known as the Hospice of the Holy Child Jesus. In the same year he founded the teaching order of the Sisters of Sainte Anne who have now several missions in the United States, one even in Alaska. All these religious orders have since attained notable proportions.

After the fire of 1852 which destroyed the cathedral, the episcopal palace, and one of the most beautiful sections of Montreal, Bishop Bourget made his home in the Hospice Saint-Joseph until 31 August, 1855, when he removed to Mont Saint-Joseph, the episcopal residence. In 1854 he went to Rome on the invitation of the Holy Father to assist at the proclamation of the Dogma of the Immaculate Conception, and in 1857 he instituted the Forty Hours' Devotion in his diocese, and organized the Conférences Ecclésiastiques. He returned to Rome in 1862 to represent the Province of Quebec at the canonization of the Japanese martyrs and was made a Roman Count and Assistant at the Papal Throne. During the same year he established the Third Order of St. Francis, and on 15 October organized the confraternity for perpetual devotion to St. Joseph. In 1864 he entrusted the deaf-mutes to the care of the Sisters of Providence. Believing that the people would benefit by the division of the parish of Montreal, he began the change in 1866–67, and after a lapse of forty years the increase to more than forty new parishes shows the wisdom of the step. In 1869 Bishop Bourget went to Rome to attend the Vatican Council. In 1870 he laid the foundation-stone of the Montreal Cathedral and in 1872 celebrated his golden jubilee. He tendered his resignation as Bishop of Montreal in 1876, was named titular Archbishop of Martianopolis, and withdrew to the St. Janvier residence at Sault-au-Recollet. In

1879, at the age of eighty, he made his last journey to Rome; five years later he heroically set out upon a tour of his former diocese with a view to re-establishing its badly compromised finances.

The remains of Bishop Lartigue and those of Archbishop Bourget were interred together in a vault under one of the pillars (the south-west) that support the dome of the cathedral. After the services held at Notre Dame at which the Very Rev. Father Collin, Superior of St. Sulpice, delivered the funeral oration over the body of Archbishop Bourget, another service was conducted at the pro-cathedral for the two deceased prelates whose eulogy was pronounced by Archbishop Taché of St. Boniface. In June, 1903, a handsome monument was dedicated to the memory of Archbishop Bourget. This work of art, by the sculptor Hébert, stands in front of the cathedral. It was erected by both clergy and faithful, who contributed $25,000, and is a testimony of affection to a great bishop who was at the same time a great citizen. The published works of Archbishop Bourget comprise eight volumes of pastoral letters.

De Brumath, *Mgr. Bourget, archevêque de Martianopolis, ancien évêque de Montréal; Archives of the Archdiocese of Montreal; Semaine Religieuse* files (Montreal), V, XLI.

PAUL BRUCHÉSI.

Bourgoing, FRANÇOIS, third Superior General of the Congregation of the Oratory in France and one of the ten early companions of Cardinal de Bérulle, the founder of the French Oratorians, b. at Paris, 1585; d. in 1662. Bourgoing came from a family of which many members had been magistrates. Before joining the Oratorians he was curé of Clichy and resigned this position in favour of St. Vincent de Paul, who was also a disciple and friend of de Bérulle. After entering the congregation he was soon occupied in founding and directing new houses of the Oratorians, being called in all directions by the bishops of France and Flanders. In 1631 he was made assistant to the Superior General, Père de Condren, and in 1641, upon the death of the latter, he was appointed to the vacant office. As superior general he toiled with unceasing zeal in organizing and developing the congregation. He was also an energetic opponent of the Jansenist heresy. After his death Bossuet delivered the funeral oration. Father Bourgoing was a writer of the first rank on asceticism, as Bossuet testifies. His principal work, "Vérités et excellences de Jésus Christ notre Sauveur", has been issued more than thirty times, including an edition in 1906, and has been translated into several languages. Equally remarkable is his work, "Exercices de retraites", of which he published four series.

Cloyseault, *Recueil de vies de quelques prêtres de l'Oratoire* (Paris, 1882), II, 1; Ingold, *Essai de bibliographie oratorienne* (Paris, 1880), 21; Batterel, *Mémoires*, II, 285.

A. M. P. INGOLD.

Bourne, FRANCIS. See WESTMINSTER, ARCHDIOCESE OF.

Bourne, GILBERT, last Catholic Bishop of Bath and Wells, England, son of Philip Bourne of Worcestershire, date of birth unknown; d. 10 Sept., 1569, at Silverton in Devonshire. Entering Oxford University in 1524, he became Fellow of All Souls College in 1531, proceeded in Arts in 1532, and was admitted B. D. in 1543, having in 1543 been named prebendary of Worcester on the suppression of the old monastic chapter. Removing to London in 1545 he became a prebendary of St. Paul's, and in 1549 Archdeacon of Bedford with the living of High Ongar in Essex. At the time in question the holding of such preferments involved at least some acceptance of the religious changes effected under Henry VIII and his successor. However, like many others who then externally submitted, Bourne seems to

have always been a Catholic at heart, and the sincerity of his return to the old religion under Mary was proved later by his unalterable firmness under persecution. Soon after her accession, whilst preaching at St. Paul's Cross, he narrowly escaped a dagger which a fanatic hurled on hearing him allude to Bishop Bonner's recent sufferings under the late regime. On being appointed to the Bishopric of Bath and Wells, Bourne received absolution from Cardinal Pole, the papal legate, by letters dated Paris, 17 March, 1554, from all censures incurred in the time of schism, and on 1 April was consecrated with five others by Bishop Bonner, assisted by Bishops Gardiner and Tunstall. During his brief episcopate he laboured zealously for the restoration of the Catholic religion, although towards heretics, as even Godwin, a Protestant, admits, he always used kindness rather than severity, nor do any seem to have been executed in his diocese. Queen Mary showed her high esteem for him by naming him Lord President of the Council of Wales. Elizabeth, however, whilst expressing herself contented with his service, relieved him quickly of that office in pursuance of her policy to remove Catholics from such posts of trust.

At the beginning of Elizabeth's reign Bourne was kept away from London by illness and official duties, and he is only mentioned once as present in the Parliament. For this reason he was one of the last bishops to be deposed, and he was even named amongst those first commissioned to consecrate Parker, appointed primate of the queen's new hierarchy. On his refusal, and on his rejection of the Supremacy Oath, which four Somersetshire justices were commissioned on 18 October, 1559, to administer, his deprivation followed. For a little time he still was left in Somerset, apparently a prisoner on parole; but on 31 May, 1560, he received a summons to appear within twelve days before Parker and the Commissioners in London. He set out, as his reply to Parker shows, well knowing what to expect, and was committed on 18 June a close prisoner to the Tower, where already five of his brother prelates were immured. There in solitary confinement, for the most part, he remained three years, when an outbreak of the plague in September, 1563, caused him and his companions to be for a time transferred into the perhaps equally objectionable keeping of certain of their Protestant successors; Bourne himself being committed to that apparently of Bullingham of Lincoln.

Thus began that continual "tossing and shifting" of the deposed prelates "from one keeper to another, from one prison to another", which Cardinal Allen, who had every means of knowing, describes as one part of their "martyrdom". Accordingly we find the Council, in June, 1565, sending them all back to the Tower, although a little later, in a letter of Parker (January, 1566), Bullingham is mentioned as though again for a time Bishop Bourne's actual or intended keeper, whilst all the captive prelates continue during the next two years to be referred to as then in the public prisons. After nearly ten years of this suffering existence Bishop Bourne expired 10 September, 1569, at Silverton in Devonshire, having been there committed (apparently not long) to the custody of Carew, Archdeacon of Exeter and Dean of Windsor, There he was buried in the church, though no monument marks the spot.

The oft repeated story of the kindly treatment shown by Elizabeth to the prelates she deposed proves to rest solely on Lord Burghley's interested statement (Execution of Justice, 1583) which his own acts and papers contradict, but which was eagerly adopted and enlarged by the prejudiced defenders of Elizabeth, Andrewes (Tortura Torti, 1609), Camden (Annales, 1615),

Strype, and others. On the other hand, Cardinal Allen describes the bishops, in his reply to Burghley, as having been "vexed, spoiled, tormented, and slain; . . . whose martyrdom", he says, "is before God as glorious, as if they had by a speedy violent death been despatched". The same in fact is affirmed by the other Catholic writers of the time. In all the lists of sufferers, drawn up by these, Bishop Bourne is named amongst those dead for the Faith in prison, whilst Bridgewater says expressly that "he died in chains a martyr". Moreover, he is one of those "Eleven Bishops", a picture of whose prison was allowed by Gregory XIII to be erected in the English College church at Rome, amongst pictures of the English Saints and Martyrs, with an inscription declaring that they "died for their confession of the Roman See and Catholic faith, worn out by the miseries of their long imprisonment".

BRIDGETT, *Queen Elizabeth and the Catholic Hierarchy* (London, 1889); PHILLIPS, *Extinction of the Ancient Hierarchy* (London, 1905); GAIRDNER, *English Historical Review* (April, 1906) 377; ALLEN, *Defence of Catholics* (Ingolstadt, 1584); SANDERS, *Report to Card. Morone*, 1561 (Cath. Record Society, 1905), I; SANDERS, *De Visibili Monarchia* (Louvain, 1571); RISHTON-SANDERS, *Rise of Anglican Schism Continued*, tr. LEWIS (London, 1877); BRIDGEWATER, *Concertatio* (August. Trev. 1588); GODWIN, *Catalogus Episcoporum Bathon. et Wellen.* (1594), in MS. Trin. Coll. Camb.

G. E. PHILLIPS.

Bouvens, CHARLES DE, French pulpit orator, b. at Bourg in 1750; d. in 1830. At an early age he embraced the ecclesiastical state and became vicar-general to his fellow-townsman, Monseigneur de Conzié, Archbishop of Tours. When the Revolution broke out, he refused to take the required oaths, and followed his archbishop to Germany. The latter having died in the vicinity of Frankfort, de Bouvens went to London, where the Bishop of Arras, brother of Archbishop Conzié was minister to the Comte d'Artois, later Charles X. Here he delivered, either in the church of St. Patrick or in the chapel built by the Sulpician Bourret in King Street, several funeral orations in the presence of Louis XVIII and the Comte d'Artois. The best known of these orations are: the one on Marie-Josephine-Louise of Savoy, wife of Louis XVIII; that on the Duc d'Enghien (1804), and the one on the Abbé Henry Allen Edgeworth de Firmont, confessor of Louis XVI. These eulogies were printed at Paris for the first time in 1814, being issued separately. A complete edition in one volume appeared at Paris in 1824 under the title: "Oraisons funèbres". The volume contains, besides the addresses mentioned above, a funeral oration on Louis XVIII. At the time of the Restoration (1815), he returned to France and was named chaplain to Louis XVIII. In 1828 the infirmities of age forced him to resign, but he retained the title of Honorary Chaplain. The Revolution of 1830 drove him from Paris, and he died shortly afterwards.

QUÉRARD, *La France littéraire* (Paris, 1827), I; MICHAUD, *Biog. univ.*, s. v.

A. FOURNET.

Bouvet, JOACHIM, Jesuit missionary, b. at Le Mans, France (date unknown); d. at Peking, China, 28 June, 1732. He was one of the first six Jesuits selected by Louis XIV for the mission in China. Before setting out for their destination, he and his associates were admitted to the Académie des Sciences and were commissioned by that learned body to carry on astronomical observations, to determine the geographical positions of the various places they were to visit, and to collect various scientific data. The little band, after being provided by order of the King with all necessary scientific instruments, sailed from Brest, 3 March, 1685, with Father Fontaney as Superior. After spending some time in Siam, they finally arrived in Peking, 7 February, 1688. They were favourably received by the

emperor the famous Khang-hi, who retained Father Bouvet, together with Father Gerbillon, near his person and made them his instructors in mathematics. While engaged in this work, the two fathers wrote several mathematical treatises in the Tartar language, which the emperor caused to be translated into Chinese, adding the prefaces himself. So far did they win his esteem and confidence that he gave them a site within the palace enclosure for a church and residence which were finally completed in 1702. In 1679 he sent Father Bouvet back to France to obtain new missionaries and made him the bearer of a gift of forty-nine volumes in Chinese for the king. These were deposited in the Royal Library, and Louis XIV, in turn, commissioned Father Bouvet to present to the emperor a magnificently bound collection of engravings.

In 1699 Father Bouvet arrived a second time in China, accompanied by ten missionaries, among them men of great ability, such as Fathers de Prémare, Régis, and Parrenin. Khang-hi honoured him further with the title of interpreter to his son, the heir-apparent. In 1700, with four of his fellow missionaries, he presented a memorial to the emperor, asking for a decision as to the meaning attached to the various ceremonies of the Chinese in honour of Confucius and their ancestors. The emperor, who had taken a keen interest in the controversy regarding the ceremonies, replied that they were simply civil usages, having no religious significance whatever. The memorial, together with the emperor's reply, was published in the "Gazette de Pekin", but failed to allay the excitement then raging in Europe over the question. From 1708 to 1715 Father Bouvet was engaged in a survey of the empire and the preparation of maps of the various provinces. He was a man of great energy and ability, and of simple, unselfish piety. For nearly fifty years he shared all the labours of the missionaries and was engaged from time to time in various scientific works. During this long period, chiefly on account of his services to the emperor and the favour he enjoyed with him, he did much to advance the interests of Christianity and to facilitate the entrance and the labours of his fellow-missionaries. His Chinese name was Petsin. Besides his works on mathematics, Father Bouvet was the author of "Etat présent de la Chine, en figures gravées par P. Giffart sur les dessins apportés au roi par le P. J. Bouvet" (Paris, 1697); "Portrait historique de l'empereur de la Chine" (Paris, 1697). The library at Le Mans contains a collection of his manuscripts including a Chinese dictionary.

DE BACKER, *Bibliothèque des écrivains de la c. de Jésus* (Paris, 1869), I; MICHAUD, *Biographie Universelle*, V.

HENRY M. BROCK.

Bouvier, JEAN-BAPTISTE, Bishop of Le Mans, theologian, b. at St. Charles-la-Forêt, Mayenne, 16 January, 1783; d. at Rome, 28 December, 1854. Having received merely an elementary education, he learned his father's trade of carpentry, but he gave his spare time to the study of the classics under the direction of the parish priest. In 1805 he entered the seminary of Angers, where he made rapid progress. He was ordained priest in 1808 and appointed professor of philosophy at the College of Château Gonthier. In 1811 he was transferred to the seminary of Le Mans, where he taught philosophy and moral theology. In 1819 he was made superior of that institution and vicar-general of the diocese, a position which he held until 1834, when he was raised to the episcopal see of Le Mans. The influence exerted by his "Institutiones Theologicæ" (in fifteen editions), which was in use in almost all the seminaries of France, as well as in the United States and Canada, gives Bishop Bouvier a unique and honourable position in the history of theology during the nineteenth century. His compendium had the distinction of being the first manual, and for many years the only one well adapted to that period of transition (1830–70), marked on the one hand by the death struggles of Gallicanism and Jansenism, and on the other by the work of reform undertaken in all departments of ecclesiastical learning.

At first, Bishop Bouvier published separate theological treatises, which formed a collection of thirteen volumes (1818–33), reduced in 1834 to six, and published in that form until 1852. The author endeavoured to improve his work in the successive editions, but his failure to remove from it all traces of Gallicanism provoked criticism. A Gallican, through prejudices derived from his early training rather than from personal conviction, Bouvier readily consented to submit his work to the corrections of the theologians appointed by Pius IX. Their revision resulted in the eighth edition (1853). After the death of Bouvier, the professors of the seminary of Le Mans eliminated many imperfections which had been overlooked by the revisers of 1853. The manual was shortly afterwards adopted in more than sixty seminaries. Bouvier's treatment of moral theology is remarkable; he took a decided stand against Jansenism and adopted the doctrines of St. Alphonsus; though even this reaction against rigorism did not bring his work up to the standard of the manuals of theology of the present time.

Some critics condemned much of the information in the "Institutiones" as a crude and confused mass, irrelevant, and only indirectly connected with moral theology. It must be recalled, however, that Bishop Bouvier did not enjoy the advantages of the present day, when the various branches of clerical study are classified, and each given its proper place. Notwithstanding the incompleteness of preparatory studies eighty years ago, the scarcity of vocations, the urgent need of priests, and limited pecuniary resources made it necessary to limit the clerical course to three years and, at the same time, to include in the curriculum all the studies necessary for the exercise of the sacred ministry in parishes. Under such circumstances it was impossible to observe nice distinctions in the classification of ecclesiastical sciences. However, in spite of defects, the "Institutiones Theologicæ" will stand as a signal achievement on the morrow of the Revolution. The bishop gradually brought the education of the clergy out of the errors and lethargy of the preceding chaotic age, and prepared for the reforms of the latter part of the nineteenth century. Like Cardinal Gousset he must be regarded as one of the foremost reformers of moral theology. Pius IX conceived the highest esteem for him and invited him to be present at the definition of the dogma of the Immaculate Conception.

GUÉRIN, Dict. des dict. (Paris, 1886), II, 302; DESHAYES in Dict. de théol. cath., XIII, 1118; HURTER, Nomenclator (Innsbruck, 1886); BALLERINI, Opus Theologicum (2d ed., Prato, 1891), VII, 421; LEHMKUHL, Theologia Moralis (Freiburg, 1886), II, 796.

P. DISSER.

Bova, DIOCESE OF, situated in the civil province of Reggio, in Calabria, Italy, suffragan to the Archdiocese of Reggio. Luminosus, who attended the Lateran Council (649), under Pope Martin I, is believed by some to have been the first Bishop of Bova; in reality he was Bishop of Bologna. The city of Bova (and consequently the see) is of much later origin than the pontificate of Martin I; it was peopled about 1477 by Albanian refugees fleeing from the Turkish invasions that followed upon the death of Scanderbeg. In their new home these Albanians retained the Greek Rite, which remained in use until the reign of Pope Gregory XIII. One of the most distinguished Bishops of Bova was Achille Brancia (1549), a member of the Council of Trent. The diocese contains about 20,000 souls, 14 parishes, 34 churches and chapels, 34 secular priests, and 25 seminarians.

CAPPELLETTI, Le chiese d'Italia (Venice, 1844), XXI; BATTANDIER, Ann. pont. cath. (Paris, 1907).

U. BENIGNI.

Bovino, DIOCESE OF, in the province of Foggia, Italy, suffragan to the Archdiocese of Benevento. The city, built on a gentle slope, has a population of over 30,000. The first Bishop of Bovino known to history is a certain Joannes mentioned in a deed of Landulphus I, Archbishop of Beneventum, dated 971. Among other bishops are Ugo (1099), whose services and bounty to the Church are eulogized on two tablets, one preserved in the episcopal residence, the other in the cathedral; Giso (1100), commemorated on the façade of the church of San Pietro; Roberto (1190), who built the shrine of San Michele; Pietro, who erected a new cathedral to replace the ruinous old one; Bartolomeo della Porta (1404), a distinguished jurisconsult; Cardinals Benedetto Accolti (1530) and Gabriele Marini (1535); Gian Domenico Annio, successor to his brother, Gian Ferdinando (1565), and the greatest canonist of his time; Paolo Tolosa (1601), founder of the seminary and later Archbishop of Chieti; Angelo Ceraso (1685), a man of great sanctity, who always made the visitation of his diocese on foot.

On account of political entanglements consequent upon difficulties which had arisen between the pope and the court of Naples, this see remained vacant from the death of Bishop Nicolò Molinari, in 1792, until 1818. There exists to the present day in this diocese a famous shrine of Our Lady (Santa Maria in Valverde) erected in 1244 by Bishop Giambattista. The little town of Castelluccio in this diocese is inhabited almost entirely by descendants of Greeks who took refuge in Italy in the fifteenth century. They have a clergy and a liturgy of their own rite. The diocese contains 32,710 Catholics, 10 parishes, 76 churches and chapels, 80 secular priests, and 13 seminarians.

CAPPELLETTI, Le chiese d'Italia (Venice, 1844); BATTANDIER, Ann. pont. cath. (Paris, 1907).

U. BENIGNI.

Bowyer, SIR GEORGE, Baronet, an eminent English writer on jurisprudence, as well as a prominent defender of the Holy See and of Catholic interests in general, both by voice and pen, was born at Radley House, in Berkshire, 8 October, 1811; d. in London, 7 June, 1883. His family, traceable much farther back, settled, early in the seventeenth century, at Denham Court, Buckinghamshire, and in 1660 the head of the house was made a baronet. His grandfather was a naval officer of high distinction, who took part in Howe's famous victory off Ushant, 1 June, 1794. George Bowyer was at first intended for the army, and so for a while he was a cadet at Woolwich. His bent, however, was towards the law; accordingly, in 1836, he was admitted a student at the Middle Temple, his call to the English Bar regularly ensuing in 1839. Five days after his call to the Bar, partly, perhaps, because of two learned works published by him in the foregoing year, and partly, perhaps, by reason of his family's neighbourhood at Radley, the University of Oxford created him an honorary M. A., Mr. Bowyer forthwith began practice as an equity draughtsman and conveyancer, without ceasing to devote himself to congenial literary work. In 1841 he published "The English Constitution, a Popular Commentary on the Constitutional Laws of England", which in 1844 was followed by "Commentaries on the Civil Law". So valuable were these works that at midsummer of the latter year the University of Oxford bestowed on him the highest honour in its gift by creating him a D.C.L. In 1849 he endeavoured to get into Parliament as a representative of Reading Borough in his native Berkshire, but his hour for parliamentary life was not yet.

Next year, 1850, there happened the gravest and most far-reaching event of Bowyer's career: his conversion from Anglican Protestantism to the Catholic religion. That same year Pope Pius IX set up in England a new Catholic episcopal hierarchy. At this proceeding, vulgarly styled "the Papal Aggression", English Protestantism went wild with rage and resentment for the space of several months. To Bowyer this popular mania offered a golden opportunity to stand forth boldly in the Holy Father's defence. His pamphlet, "The Cardinal Archbishop of Westminster and the New Hierarchy", ran through four editions, and was followed at intervals by several more publications on the same theme. From this beginning to the end of his days he was the foremost lay champion in England of the Catholic Church and her earthly head. His letters addressed to the newspapers, principally to the "Times", were many, vigorous, and unanswerable; and in those days he was practically the only competent Catholic whose controversial letters were admitted into the English Protestant press. At the same time he zealously prosecuted his legal studies and writings. His "Commentaries on Universal Public Law" came out in 1854 and is commonly considered his greatest literary achievement; "Introduction to the Study and Use of the Civil Law", his last publication, appeared in 1874.

To go back to 1850, the period of his conversion, Mr. Bowyer was that year appointed Reader in Law at the Middle Temple. In 1852 he at last found his desired seat in Parliament, as member for the Irish borough of Dundalk, whose representative he continued to be for the next sixteen years. During that stirring period there came the Italian Unity movement, and the despoiling of the Roman Pontiff of the greater part of his temporal dominions, to be followed some years later by the seizure of the remainder. Then it was that Sir George Bowyer (who, on the death of his father, in 1860 had succeeded to the baronetcy), in company with John Pope Hennessy, John Francis Maguire, and others, took every occasion to denounce in Parliament the Italian revolutionaries, especially for the robbery and virtual captivity of the Roman Pontiff, and the atrocities committed by King Victor Emmanuel's soldiery in the lately annexed Neapolitan realm. For all these misdeeds the Member for Dundalk continually called to account Lord Palmerston, Lord John (afterwards Earl) Russell, Mr. Gladstone, and other English governmental abettors of the Italian Revolution, who could answer only by parading principles at once subversive and immoral. In 1868 he lost his seat for Dundalk, and for the next six years remained out of Parliament, until 1874, when, as a Home Ruler, he was chosen a representative of the Irish County of Wexford, retaining that seat until 1880. Meanwhile, as his principles and attitude with regard to the Italian question, to say nothing of other matters, were in nowise to the taste of the British Liberal party, he was, in 1876, turned out of the London Reform Club.

On the 7th of June, 1883, Sir George Bowyer was found dead in bed at his London chambers, No. 13, King's Bench Walk, in the Temple. His obsequies took place in the Catholic church of St. John of Jerusalem, which, alongside of the Hospital of Sts. John and Elizabeth, in Great Ormond Street, he had built at his own cost. And here it may be remarked that in architecture Sir George Bowyer had a strong leaning for the Palladian, or Italian, style, as against the Gothic, especially for public buildings, and his principles he put into practice in the aforesaid church, which is a little Palladian gem. The church has now been removed bodily to St. John's

II.—46

Wood, there to serve the transferred and new-built hospital. Sir George Bowyer was a Knight Commander of the Order of Pius IX, and a Papal Chamberlain; Knight Grand Cross of the Order of St. Gregory the Great, Knight of Justice of the Sovereign Order of St. John of Jerusalem (or of Malta), etc. At home he was a Justice of the Peace and Deputy Lieutenant of Berkshire. He never married, and was succeeded in the baronetcy by his younger brother.

Dict. Nat. Biog. (London, 1886); Annual Register, 1883, 152, 153; GILLOW, Bibl. Dict. of Eng. Cath., I, 282–284; Times, Tablet, and other London newspapers for June, 1883.

C. T. BOOTHMAN.

Boy-Bishop.—The custom of electing a boy-bishop on the feast of St. Nicholas dates from very early times, and was in vogue in most Catholic countries, but chiefly in England, where it prevailed certainly in all the larger monastic and scholastic establishments, and also in many country parishes besides, with the full approbation of authority, ecclesiastical and civil. The boy-bishop was chosen from among the children of the monastery school, the cathedral choir, or the pupils of the grammar-school. Elected on St. Nicholas's day (6 December), he was dressed in pontifical vestments and, followed by his companions in priest's robes, went in procession round the parish, blessing the people. He then took possession of the church, where he presided at all the ceremonies and offices until Holy Innocents' day (28 December). At Salisbury he is said to have had the power of disposing of any benefices that fell vacant during his reign, and if he died in office the funeral honours of a bishop were granted him. A monument to such a boy-prelate still exists there, though its genuineness has been questioned, and at Lulworth Castle another is preserved, which came from Bindon Abbey. The custom was abolished by Henry VIII in 1542, restored by Queen Mary, and again abolished by Elizabeth, though here and there it lingered on for some time longer. On the Continent it was suppressed by the Council of Basle in 1431, but was revived in some places from time to time, even as late as the eighteenth century.

ROCK, Church of our Fathers (London, 1853), III, xii; LEE, Glossary of Liturgical and Ecclesiastical Terms (London, 1877); GASQUET, Parish Life in Medieval England (London, 1906); Camden Society, Machyn's Dairy (London, 1848); DU CANGE, Glossarium, ed HENSCHEL (London, 1884), s. vv. Episcopus Innocentium and Episcopus Puerorum; HAMSON, Medii Ævi Kalendarium, Dates, Charters and Customs of the Middle Ages (London, 1841), 61, 78, 82.

G. CYPRIAN ALSTON.

Boyce, JOHN, novelist, lecturer, and priest, well known under the assumed name of "Paul Peppergrass", b. in Donegal, Ireland, in 1810; d. in Worcester, Mass., 2 January, 1864. His father was a respectable and wealthy citizen, proprietor of the principal hotel in the town and a magistrate of the county. John early manifested a taste for literary pursuits, and with the desire of studying for the priesthood, entered the preparatory seminary at Navan, County Meath, and was graduated with the highest honours in rhetoric and philosophy. He completed his studies at the Royal College of Maynooth and was ordained priest in 1837. For eight years he laboured on the Irish mission, but in 1845 he resolved to share the lot of his countrymen in America. From Eastport, Maine, the scene of his first missionary labours, he was transferred, 14 November, 1847, to St. John's Church, Worcester, where he remained until his death. Father Boyce was an eloquent lecturer and gifted writer. His published works are: "Shandy Maguire, or Tricks upon Travellers" (New York, 1848), which was dramatized by "J. Pilgrim"; "The Spæwife, or the Queen's Secret" (Baltimore, 1853); "Mary Lee, or the Yankee in Ireland" (1859), first published serially in the "Metropolitan Magazine" of Baltimore. These novels do not reveal the varied gifts and ripe scholarship of the man, though they illustrate the strong powers of a keen observer, and the humour and pathos of a graceful and instructive writer. Besides these books he contributed to the editorial columns of the Boston "Pilot", wrote many sketches and criticisms which appeared in print, and a lecture on "The Satisfying Influence of Catholicity on the Intellect and Senses", delivered before the Catholic Institute in New York in 1851.

Biographical sketch by J. FAIRFAX MCLAUGHLIN in later editions of *The Spœwife; Golden Jubilee Souvenir of St. John's Parish* (Worcester); *Messenger* (Worcester, Mass.), 3 December, 1898; *Pilot* (Boston, Mass.) files 16 January, 1864.

EDWARD P. SPILLANE.

Boyle Abbey, a celebrated Cistercian house situated on the River Boyle, nine miles northwest of Elphin, in the present County of Roscommon, Ireland. It was founded by Maurice O'Duffy in the year 1161, and was in close connexion with Mellifont, the parent house of the Cistercian Order in Ireland. In the year 1218 (Annals of Ireland) the church of Boyle Abbey was solemnly consecrated. A great number of the Abbots of Boyle were appointed bishops in the Province of Connaught during the thirteenth and fourteenth centuries, and more especially in the Dioceses of Elphin and Achonry. In 1235 the English forces under the joint command of Maurice Fitzgerald and McWilliam forcibly took possession of the abbey, seized all the goods, vestments, and chalices belonging to the monastery and stripped the monks of their habits in their cloister. During the reign of Queen Elizabeth the abbey was suppressed and its lands and possessions handed over (1569) to Patrick Cusack of Gerrardston, County Meath. From the list of its lands then made it is clear that Boyle must have been one of the most richly endowed religious houses in Ireland. In 1589 a lease of the abbey was granted to William Ussher. During the reign of King James I several inquisitions were held in connexion with the lands of Boyle Abbey, and in 1603 a lease of it was granted to Sir John King.

Perhaps the most eminent of the Abbots of Boyle was Donchad O'Daly who died in 1250, and who was recognized as a poet of very special merit. He is spoken of as the Ovid of Ireland. Many of the princes of Connaught retired to Boyle before their death and more especially the princes of the family of McDermot of Moylurg. The Abbey of Boyle is now in ruins, but from the remains still to be seen near the present town of Boyle it was evidently a place of great importance and of some architectural pretensions.

ARCHDALL, *Monasticon Hibernicon* (601–606); ALEMAND, *Histoire Monastique de l'Irlande* (Paris, 1690), 191; MURPHY, *Our Martyrs*, 115; RUSHE, *A Second Thebaid* (Dublin, 1905), 130; O'FLAHERTY, *West Connaught*, 355–379.

JAMES MACCAFFREY.

Bracara. See BRAGA, ARCHDIOCESE OF.

Bracciolini. See POGGIO BRACCIOLINI, GIOVANNI FRANCESCO.

Bracken, THOMAS, poet, journalist, politician, b. in Ireland 21 December, 1843; d. at Dunedin, New Zealand, 16 February, 1898. Having lost his parents he emigrated in his twelfth year to Victoria, Australia. He went to Otago, New Zealand, as a shearer in 1869, and published there a small volume of verse, "Flights among the Flax", which brought him into some notice. In Dunedin he was associated with the commercial staffs of "The New Zealand Tablet", "The Otago Guardian", and the "Morning Herald", and was founder and part proprietor of the "Saturday Advertiser", which was a literary and commercial success only so long as he directly controlled it. He was twice returned to Parliament

(in 1884 and 1886) for Dunedin in the Liberal interest. He died in the Dunedin hospital. He is best known in New Zealand and Australia for his verse. His poetic publications in book form, in addition to the one already mentioned, are: "Flowers of the Freeland"; "Behind the Tomb and Other Poems"; "The Land of the Maori and the Moa"; and "Musings in Maoriland" (Dunedin, 1890), his last and fullest collection. Bracken's themes are mostly local and colonial. He is not a world-poet, but takes honourable rank among the pioneers of Australian poetry. In his best verse, much true and tender poetic feeling finds skilled and picturesque expression.

MENNELL, *Australasian Biography* (London, 1892); *The Otago Daily Times*, files (17 February, 1898); *The Evening Star* (Dunedin), files (17 February, 1898); *The New Zealand Tablet*, files (25 February, 1898).

HENRY W. CLEARY.

Bracton, HENRY DE, also called HENRY of BRACTON, a famous English juridical writer, the Blackstone of the thirteenth century, b. probably in King John's reign and died about four years before the close of that of Henry III. His lifetime therefore comprised and almost coincided with the momentous period between the grant of Magna Charta and the defeat and death of Simon of Montfort, Earl of Leicester, at the battle of Evesham. By birth, property, and ecclesiastical preferment he appears to have been a man of Devon, in which shire there are two parishes of the name of Bratton, viz., Bratton-Clovelly and Bratton-Fleming, one or the other of these parishes being almost certainly his birthplace, for the claim of Minehead parish in Somerset, may be dismissed as untenable. Hence it may be gathered that the correct form of this great jurist's name is hardly Bracton, but rather Bratton, by which appellation, as well as by the occasional variant of Bretton (most likely then sounded much like Bratton) he was almost invariably described in his own day, not to add that, in point of etymology, "Bradtone" (broad town) seems likelier than "Bractone" to have been the earlier form of the name. To come to his laborious and distinguished career, it is said that Bratton in his youth was a student at the University of Oxford, where he is further alleged to have taken the degree of doctor of civil and of canon law but this, though indeed possible, is altogether lacking of proof. Certain it is that he was taken into the service of King Henry III. By this time the king's curia had grown distinct from King's Council and a race of professional judges had sprung into existence. Of these professional judges Henry Bratton became one. It is in 1245 that we first find him acting in a judicial capacity, and from that year onward we continually meet with him either as a justice in Eyre (especially in his native Devon and other neighbouring counties) or as holding pleas before the king himself, until the end of the year 1267. Thus he was undoubtedly a regular permanent judge, though he never appears as sitting *placito de banco*, in other words, as sitting on the Bench at Westminster. Meanwhile more than one special mark of royal favour towards him is upon record. Yet in the civil broils of his time he was neither side's partisan and was respected and trusted alike by king and barons. Of his great and epoch-making literary work, "De Legibus et Consuetudinibus Angliæ", Professor Paul Vinogradoff (the Athenæum, 19 July, 1884) writes that it is a treatise which "testifies to the influence of Roman jurisprudence and of its medieval exponents, but at the same time remains a statement of genuine English law, a statement so detailed and accurate that there is nothing to match it in the whole legal literature of the Middle Ages." The number of decided cases therein referred to (for Bratton's law is naturally case-law) amounts to four hundred and fifty. Like all or almost all of the professional judges of his time, Bratton was an ecclesiastic. His known church preferments are Barnstaple archdeaconry, conferred upon him in 1264, but which the same year he quitted for the chancellorship of Exeter cathedral, retaining this latter dignity until his death in 1268. At his decease he enjoyed likewise a canonry, and prebend as well, in Exeter cathedral church, as in the collegiate church of Bosham. All these benefices were of the Bishop of Exeter's gift. At the same time as the king's clerk engaged in the king's business, Bracton could seldom or never have kept residence. His body was buried in Exeter cathedral, before an altar at which he had founded a perpetual chantry for his soul. Of Bratton's great and comprehensive treatise "De Legibus", etc., written before 1259, the first printed edition was published in 1569 in folio, and reprinted in quarto in 1640. A recension and translation of the whole work in six volumes, by Sir Travers Twiss, was issued in London (Rolls publications) from 1878 to 1883.

Foss, *Biographical Dictionary of the Judges of England* (London, 1870); *Dict. of Nat. Biog.* (London, 1886), VI; MAITLAND, *Bracton's Note Book* (London, 1887), for biography see introd. pp. 13–25.

C. T. BOOTHMAN.

Bradley, DENIS MARY, first Bishop of Manchester, New Hampshire, U. S. A., b. 25 February, 1846, at Castle-island, County Kerry, Ireland; d. at Manchester, 13 December, 1903. Shortly after his father's death his mother, with a family of five, emigrated to the United States and settled at Manchester. He was then eight years old. After attending the local schools, he was sent to Holy Cross College, Worcester, Massachusetts, in 1863, and closed his academic career there in June, 1867. He was then enrolled as an ecclesiastical student at St. Joseph's Seminary, Troy, New York, where he was ordained priest 3 June, 1871. Shortly after this he was located at Portland, Maine, under Bishop Bacon, and subsequently under Bishop Healy, by whom he was appointed rector of the cathedral and chancellor of the diocese. In June, 1881, he was made pastor of St. Joseph's, Manchester, which became his cathedral when he was consecrated first Bishop of the new See of Manchester, 11 June, 1884. He had the honour of being the first alumnus of St. Joseph's Seminary of Troy, New York, to be raised to the episcopacy.

In the rural sections of New Hampshire there were many scattered Catholics who up to that time had had few facilities for practising their faith, and his first and earnest efforts were directed towards providing for them, and with the most gratifying results. He held the first synod of the diocese 24 October, 1886, and under the energizing influence of his zeal and enthusiasm there was a general upbuilding of Catholicism throughout the State. The silver jubilee of his ordination was made the occasion of a striking demonstration of his great personal popularity, and this had another manifestation when every non-Catholic pulpit in Manchester bore sincere testimony to the loss his death had occasioned to the city and to the State.

Catholic News files (New York, December, 1903); *Catholic Directory* (Milwaukee, 1904); REUSS, *Biog. Encycl. of the Cath. Hierarchy* (Milwaukee, 1898); GABRIELS, *History of St. Joseph's Seminary, Troy* (New York, 1906).

THOMAS F. MEEHAN.

Bradshaigh, EDWARD, an English Carmelite friar known in religion as Elias à Jesu; b. in Lancashire, England, early in the seventeenth century; d. at Benfold, 25 September, 1652. He was the fourth son of Roger Bradshaigh, of Haigh Hall, near Wigan, England, a member of one of the oldest families in Lancashire; of his immediate family three of the brothers were Jesuits, and one brother was a secular priest. While yet young he was sent to the Cassinese Bene-

dictines to be educated. In 1619 he joined the Discalced Carmelites in Belgium. In 1626 he was sent to England, where he laboured zealously until he was arrested and brought before the Archbishop of Canterbury, charged with being a Catholic priest. He was thrown into prison and suffered great hardships, but at length, at the intercession of powerful friends, including the King of Spain, he was liberated, and banished to France. In Paris he filled the office of reader in the Carmelite monastery until 1632, when by order of his superior he returned to England and took up his residence with his family at Haigh Hall. There he visited the poor, performed his priestly duties, and made many converts. Towards the close of his life he devoted his time chiefly to the study of English antiquities. Bradshaigh was the author of two works on British antiquities, "De antiquis Monachis Insularum Britanniæ, sub primitiva Ecclesiâ viventibus", and "Angliæ Sanctæ et Catholicæ", both of which were lost in MS. A volume of poems, entitled "Virginialia, or Spiritual Sonnets in praise of the most glorious Virgin Marie", published in 1632, is attributed to him.

GILLOW, *Bibl. Dict. Eng. Cath.*, I, 286.

THOMAS GAFFNEY TAAFFE.

Bradshaw, HENRY, English Benedictine and poet, b. in the City of Chester, England, date unknown; d. 1513. From very early years his life was spent at St. Werburgh's monastery, with the exception of a period during which he was pursuing a course in theology at Gloucester College, Oxford. His writings are "De Antiquitate et magnificentiâ Urbis Cestriæ", and "Chronicon and a Life of St. Werburgh". This second work, in English verse, includes the "Foundation of the City of Chester" and the "Chronicle of the Kings"; it fixes the year of Bradshaw's death by a poem addressed to him, was printed by Pinson in 1521, and re-edited by E. Hawkins for the Chetham Society, 1848. The poet followed mainly a Latin work then in the library of St. Werburgh, called "The True or Third Passionary", by an author whose name was unknown to Bradshaw. His work, written not for the learned, but for the ruder classes, has been variously appraised by critics.

HUNT in *Dict. Nat. Biog.*; WARTON, *History of English Poetry*.

J. VINCENT CROWNE.

Bradwardine, THOMAS. See THOMAS OF BRADWARDINE.

Brady, JOHN. See BOSTON, ARCHDIOCESE OF.

Brady, WILLIAM MAZIERE, ecclesiastical writer, b. in Dublin, 8 January, 1825; d. in Rome, 19 March, 1894. He was nephew of Sir Maziere Brady, Bart., Lord Chancellor of Ireland, and youngest son of Sir Nicholas W. Brady who, whilst Lord Mayor of Dublin, was knighted by George IV during his visit to that city. William Maziere Brady entered Trinity College, Dublin, in 1842, received the Degree of B.A. in 1848, B.D. in 1858, and D.D. in 1863. In 1848 he was appointed Anglican curate of Maynooth and in 1849, curate of Kilkeedy, Limerick. In 1851 he became curate of St. Dolough's, Dublin, and in the same year Rector of Farrahy, County Cork. In this year, also, he married a lineal descendant, on the maternal side, of the famous Protestant divine, Jeremy Taylor, Bishop of Down and Connor. Dr. Brady acted as chaplain to several successive viceroys, and in 1681 became Vicar of Clonfert, County Cork. While here he published in three volumes the "Clerical and Parochial Records of Cork, Cloyne and Ross" (Dublin, 1863), which he compiled from diocesan and parish registries and manuscripts in the principal libraries and public offices of Oxford, Dublin, and London, and from private and family papers. These "Records" are mainly those of the Protestant Dioceses of Cork, Cloyne, and Ross, but will no doubt be of great service to the future Catholic historians of these dioceses.

Dr. Brady published several works in favour of the disestablishment of the Irish Protestant Church, such as: "Remarks on the Irish Church Temporalities" (1865); "Facts or Fiction; The alleged Conversion of the Irish Bishops to the Reformed Religion at the Accession of Queen Elizabeth and the Assumed Descent of the Present Established Hierarchy from the Ancient Irish Church Disproved" (1866), which went through five editions; "State Papers concerning the Irish Church in the time of Queen Elizabeth" (1868); "Some Remarks on the Irish Church Bill" (1869); and "Essays on the English State Church in Ireland" (1869). On the Irish Church question he also contributed numerous letters to the newspaper press, and articles to "Fraser's" and "The Contemporary", many of which were subsequently reprinted in pamphlet or book form. Some interesting articles from his pen appeared in the "Catholic World" on "Ireland's Mission" (May, 1870); "The Ancient Irish Churches" (July, 1870), written while yet a Protestant, and "Pius IX and Mr. Gladstone's Misrepresentations" (May, 1875). His only work of a purely secular character is "The McGillicuddy Papers; a Selection from the Family Archives of the McGillicuddy of the Reeks, with an Introductory Memoir" (1867).

When the Church Disestablishment act was passed. Dr. Brady went to Rome, where he examined the Vatican archives for information touching the ecclesiastical affairs of England, Ireland, and Scotland. He shortly resigned his benefices as Vicar of Donoughpatrick, and Rector of Kilbery, Meath, to which he had been promoted from Cork, and in May, 1873, was received into the Catholic Church by Monsignor, afterwards Archbishop, Kirby, Rector of the Irish College at Rome. His Vatican researches led to the publication of two volumes on "Episcopal Succession in England, Scotland, and Ireland, A. D. 1400 to 1875, with Appointments to Monasteries, and Extracts from Manuscripts in Public and Private Libraries in Rome, Florence, Bologna, Vienna, and Paris" (Rome, 1876-77). He also brought out, "Annals of the Catholic Hierarchy in England and Scotland, A. D. 1585-1876, with a Dissertation on Anglican Orders" (Rome, 1877; London, 1883). During his stay in Rome, Dr. Brady acted for a long time as correspondent of the London "Tablet", and issued a pamphlet on "The Pope's Anti-Parnellite Circular" (London, 1883). The last of his works was the "Anglo-Roman Papers", published in 1890. He had a large share in the political controversies of the day and corresponded much with Gladstone and other eminent statesmen. He died of apoplexy and was buried in the Campo Verrano Cemetery in Rome. His grave is marked with an Irish Cross on white marble, bearing the inscription, "In memory of William Maziere Brady, Cavalier of the Order of Pius IX, and Private Chamberlain to his Holiness Pius IX and his Holiness Leo XIII. Born in Dublin, January 8, 1825, died in Rome, March 19, 1894".

Irish Celts (Detroit, 1884); *Journal of the Cork Archæological Society,* 2nd series, vol. IX, No. 59 (July–September, 1903), s. v. *Seven Clerical Worthies;* ALLIBONE, *Dict. of Authors,* Suppl., I.

EDWARD P. SPILLANE.

Braga, ARCHDIOCESE OF (BRACARA AUGUSTA, CIVITAS BRACARENSIS), is situated in a flat fertile tract of land between the rivers Este and Cavado, in the province of Minho, in the Kingdom of Portugal. The name was derived from the costume worn by the ancient native inhabitants, which reached from the waist to the knee, unlike the tunics worn by the Romans; for this reason the latter called these *bragas* (*bracas*) a barbarous costume, and those who wore them—Persians, Scythians, and the Celtic inhabitants of Gaul—barbarians. The city of Braga is very ancient as the etymology of the name implies. Some, like St. Isidore, believe it is derived from the Greek Βραχύς, short, others from ῥάχος, thorn-bush; others again, like Diodorus Siculus, say that it is of Celtic origin. In the fifth book of his "Historical Library", speaking of the Gauls he says, *quas bracas illi nominant.* Braga, the metropolis of Galicia, was one of the principal cities of Lusitania (Portugal), until the Emperor Augustus, having brought his wars to a close, made a new division of the provinces and united it to Hispania Tarraconensis, giving it the name of Augusta, and making it one of the three judicial divisions into which the province of Galicia was divided. It was one of the first cities of Spain to receive the light of the Gospel. The tradition that St. Peter de Rates, a disciple of St. James, preached here, is handed down in the ancient Breviary of Braga (Breviarium Bracarense) and in that of Evora; but this, as the Bollandists tell us, is purely traditional. Paternus was certainly bishop of the see about 390.

Some have denied that Braga was a metropolitan see; others have attempted without sufficient evidence, however, to claim two metropolitan sees for Galicia before the sixth century. The real facts in the case are that after the destruction of Astorga (433) by the Visigoths Braga was elevated to the dignity of a metropolitan see in the time of St. Leo I (440-461). Balconius was then its bishop and Agrestius, Bishop of Lugo, was the metropolitan. At the latter's death the right of metropolitan rank was restored to the oldest bishop of the province, who was the Bishop of Braga. From this time, until the Mohammedans invaded Spain (711) he retained the supremacy over all the sees of the province. In 1110 Pope Paschal II restored Braga to its former metropolitan rank. When Portugal separated from Spain, Braga assumed even greater importance. It contested with Toledo the primacy over all the Spanish sees, but the popes decided in favour of the latter city. At present it has for suffragans the dioceses of Porto, Coimbra, Visco, Bragança-Miranda, Aveiro, and Pinhel. There have been many very famous bishops and writers in this diocese. Among its earlier bishops, besides the traditional St. Peter already mentioned, the most famous is St. Martin of Braga who died in 580, noted for his wisdom and holiness. St. Gregory of Tours says of him (Hist. France, V, xxxvii) that he was born in Pannonia, visited the Holy Land, and became the foremost scholar of his time. St. Isidore of Seville ("De Viris illustribus", c. xxxv) tells us that he "was abbot of the monastery of Dumio near Braga, came to Galicia from the East, converted the Suevic inhabitants from the errors of Arianism, taught them Catholic doctrine and discipline, strengthened their ecclesiastical organization, and founded monasteries. He also left a number of letters in which he recommended a reform of manners, a life of faith and prayer, and giving of alms, the constant practice of all virtues and the love of God." For his writings see Bardenhewer, "Patrologie" (2nd ed., 1901), 579-581. Braga having been destroyed by the Saracens, and restored in 1071, a succession of illustrious bishops occupied the see. Among these were Mauricio Burdinho (1111-14), sent as legate to the Emperor Henry V (1118), and by him created antipope with the title of Gregory VIII; Pedro Juliano, Archdeacon of Lisbon, elected Bishop of Braga in 1274, created cardinal by Gregory X in 1276, and finally elected pope under the name of John XXI; Blessed Bartholomew a Martyribus (1559-67), a Dominican, who in 1566, together with Father Luis de Sotomayor, Francisco Foreiro, and others, assisted at the Council of Trent; the Agustín de Castro, an Augustinian (1589–1609), who consecrated the cathedral, 28 July, 1592. Alejo de Meneses, also an Augustinian, was transferred to Braga from the archiepiscopal see of Goa. He had been an apostle to the Nestorians of the Malabar Coast in Farther India and had converted them to Catholicism with the help of missionaries of the various religious orders. Under him was held the Council of Diamper (1599), for the establishment of the Church on the Malabar Coast. He died at Madrid in 1617 in his fifty-eighth year in the odour of sanctity, being then President of the Council of Castile. Three other bishops of note were Roderico de Cunha (1627–35), historian of the Church in Portugal; Roderico de Moura (1704–28), who restored the cathedral, and Cayetano Brandão, who was reputed a saint among the faithful.

In its early period the Diocese of Braga produced the famous writer Paulus Orosius (fl.418) also Avitus of Braga. At the beginning of the eighteenth century a contest was waged over the birthplace of Orosius, some claiming him for Braga and others for Tarragona. The Marquis of Mondejar, with all the evidence in his favour, supported the claim of Braga; Dalmas, the chronicler of Catalonia, that of Tarragona. Avitus of Braga, another writer of some importance, was a priest who went to the East to consult with St. Augustine at the same time that Orosius, who had been sent by St. Augustine, returned from consulting St. Jerome. It was through him that the priest, Lucian of Caphar Gamala near Jerusalem, made known to the West the discovery of the body of St. Stephen (December, 415). The Greek encyclical letter of Lucian was translated into Latin by Avitus and sent to Braga with another for the bishop, Balconius, his clergy, and people, together with a relic of St. Stephen. Avitus also attended the Council of Jerusalem against Pelagius (415). There were two others of the same name, men of note, who, however, wrought incalculable harm by introducing into these provinces the doctrines of Origen and Victorinus.

In 1390 Braga was divided to make the Archdiocese of Lisbon, and in 1540 its territory was again divided to create the Archdiocese of Evora. There are some fine edifices in the diocese, among them the Cathedral of the Assumption, very large and architecturally perfect; the archbishop's palace; the seminary, and the Institute of Charity. The sanctuary of *do Senhor Jesus do Monte* is the object of great devotion to which many pilgrimages are made every year.

FLÓREZ, *España Sagrada* (Madrid, 1754–), IV, 234–240; XV, 82–364, and *passim*; AGUIRRE, *Collectio maxima conciliorum Hispaniæ* (Rome, 1693); THOMAS AB INCARNATIONE, *Hist. Eccl. Lusitanæ* (Coimbra, 1759–63); TEJADA Y RAMIRO, *Canones de la Iglesia de España* (Madrid, 1859); GAMS, *Kircheng. Spaniens* (1862–79). For the local historians: ARGOTE, CUNHA, CORRÉA, et al., see CHEVALIER, *Topo-bib.* (Paris, 1894–99), 479; *ibid.*, Lisbon and Evora.

Councils of Braga.—Many councils were held in this diocese, some of them important. The authenticity of the so-called council of 411 is very doubtful. It was probably invented by Father Bernardo Brito. In the council of 563 eight bishops took part, and twenty-two decrees were promulgated, among others the following: that in the services of the church the same rite should be followed by all, and that on vigils and in solemn Masses the same lessons should be said by all; that bishops and priests should salute the people with *Dominus vobiscum*, as in the Book of Ruth, the response being *Et cum spiritu tuo*, as was the custom in the East, without the alterations introduced by the Priscillianists; that Mass should be said according to the *ordo* sent from Rome to Profuturus; that the form used for baptism in the Metropolitan See of Braga should not be altered; that bishops should take rank after the metropolitan according to the date of their conse-

cration; that bishops should not ordain candidates from other dioceses without dimissorial letters from their bishop; that nothing should be sung in the church but the Psalms and parts of the Old and New Testament; that all priests who abstained from eating meat should be obliged to eat vegetables cooked in meat, to avoid all suspicion of the taint of Priscillianism, and that if they refused they should be excommunicated; that suicides and catechumens should not be buried with great ceremony, nor should anyone be buried inside the church; that priests should be appointed for the blessing of the chrism.

The second council held in 572, presided over by the aforesaid St. Martin, was held to increase the number of bishops in Galicia. Twelve bishops assisted at this council, and ten decrees were promulgated: (1) that the bishops should in their visitations see in what manner the priests celebrated the Holy Sacrifice and administered baptism and the other sacraments, thanking God if they found everything as it should be, and instructing the priests if they were found wanting in knowledge, and obliging all catechumens to attend instructions for twenty days before baptism and to learn the creed; (2) that the bishop must not be tyrannical towards his priests; (3–4) that no fee must be accepted for Holy orders, and the holy chrism must be distributed free; (5–6) that the bishop must not ask a fee for consecrating a church, that no church should be consecrated without the bishop being sure of the endowment and the ministers, and that no church built on private property for the purpose of emolument should receive consecration; (8) that if a cleric should accuse any one of unchastity without the evidence of two or three witnesses he should be excommunicated; (9) that the metropolitan should announce the date of Easter, and have it made known to the people after Christmas, so that they might be prepared for the beginning of Lent, when litanies were to be recited for three days; on the third day the Lenten fast should be announced after the Mass; (10) that any one saying Mass without fasting, as many did, as a result of Priscillianist tendencies, should be deprived of his office. This council was attended by the bishops of the suffragan sees of Braga, and by those of the Diocese of Lugo, and Pope Innocent III removed all doubt as to its authenticity.

The Third Council of Braga was held in 675, during the primacy of Leodegisius, and in the reign of King Wamba. Eight decrees were promulgated at this council; (1) that no one should dare to offer in sacrifice milk and grapes, but bread and wine mixed with a drop of water in a chalice, nor should bread soaked in wine be used; (2) that laymen should be excommunicated, and ecclesiastics deprived of their office, if either put the sacred vessels to profane uses; (4) that no priest should have any woman but his mother in his house; (5–6) that bishops, when carrying the relics of martyrs in procession, must walk to the church, and not be carried in a chair, or litter, by deacons clothed in white; that corporal punishment was not to be inflicted on youthful ecclesiastics, abbots, or priests, except for grievous faults; (7–8) that no fee must be accepted for Holy orders, and that the rectors of the churches must not require the members of their ecclesiastical households to do work on their private farms; if they did so they must recompense the church for the injury done thereby. There were other councils in 1278–80, 1301, 1328, 1436, 1488, 1537, besides various diocesan and provincial synods of lesser importance.

HEFELE, *Concilieng.* (2d ed.), II, 104, and *passim*.

TIRSO LÓPEZ.

Bragança-Miranda, DIOCESE OF (Brigantiensis), is situated in the north-eastern part of the Kingdom of

Portugal, in the civil province of Tras-os-Montes, and lies between 2° and 3° 3′ of longitude west of the meridian of Madrid, 41° 20′ and 42° of north latitude. It is bounded on the north by the Dioceses of Astorga and Orense, on the east by those of Salamanca and Zamora, on the south by that of Lamego, and on the west by the Archdiocese of Braga. The civil province is bounded on the north and east by the frontier of Spain comprising portions of the Provinces of Salamanca, Zamora, Leon, and Orense. The greater part of the territory of this diocese is undulating and mountainous and is traversed by several rivers, which, rising in the Sierras de Sanabria and the Sierra Seca y Segundera, flow from north to south, emptying finally into the river Duero. The climate in general is cold especially in the mountainous region. The southern part and the banks of some rivers and the level tracts of land, such as the one in which Bragança is situated, are fertile, but the rest is unproductive of cereals, although there are broad tracts of land that pasture large herds of cattle which supply a great part of Portugal and Spain with meat.

This see is comparatively modern. It was erected by Pope Paul III in the town of Miranda bordering on Spain, its territory being taken from the Archdiocese of Braga, but Clement XIV in 1770 transferred it to Bragança, from which the name Bragança-Miranda is derived. The diocese is a suffragan of Braga. The city of Bragança, which is the capital of the province of Tras-os-Montes, is situated in a delightful valley near the confluence of the rivers Pervenza and Sabor. The cathedral, dedicated to the Annunciation, is one of the prominent buildings of the city. It has a very large chapter composed of the dean, nine canons, including the theologian, six beneficed clergy, eight chaplains, and six clerics. The episcopal household receives 1,166 florins from the Government for its support. The episcopal palace and the diocesan seminary for the education of students for the priesthood are large and spacious. Besides the cathedral there is another church which has collegiate rank, and throughout the diocese there are schools and classes for instruction in Christian doctrine. There is a hospital and a *Monte de piedad*, and before the secularization there were three religious communities, one of men and two of women. The city of Bragança is fortified, having a citadel or small fortress for its defence. The reigning house of Portugal is descended from the Dukes of Bragança and has occupied the throne of Portugal since the separation of Spain and Portugal in the time of Philip IV.

MORERI, *Le grand dict. hist.*

TIRSO LÓPEZ.

Brahmin. See BRAHMINISM.

Brahminism.—By Brahminism is meant the complex religious and social system which grew out of the polytheistic nature-worship of the ancient Aryan conquerors of Northern India, and came, with the spread of their dominion, to be extended over the whole country, maintaining itself, not without profound modifications, down to the present day. In its intricate modern phases it is generally known as Hinduism.

I. BRAHMIN TEXTS.—Our knowledge of Brahminism in its earlier stages is derived from its primitive sacred books, originally oral compositions, belonging to the period between 1500–400 B. C. First of all, there are the four Vedas (*veda* means wisdom) dating from 1500 to 800 B. C., and consisting (1) of a collection of ancient hymns (*riks*), the so-called Rig-Veda, in praise of the many gods; (2) of the Sama-Veda, compiled from parts of the Rig-Veda as a song service for the soma-sacrifice; (3) of the Yajur-Veda, a liturgy composed partly of ancient hymns and

partly of other prayers and benedictions for use in the various forms of sacrifice; and (4) of the Atharva-Veda, a collection of popular exorcisms and magical incantations largely inherited from primitive Aryan days.

Next in order are the Brahmanas (about 1000–600 B. C.). They are a series of verbose and miscellaneous explanations of the texts, rites, and customs found in each of the four Vedas, composed expressly for the use of the Brahmins, or priests. These are followed (800–500 B. C.) by the so-called Upanishads, concerned chiefly with pantheistic speculations on the nature of deity and the end of man; and lastly, by the Sutras (600–400 B. C.), which are compendious guides to the proper observance of rites and customs. The most important are the Grhya-Sutras, or house-guides, treating of domestic rites, and the Dharma-Sutras, or law-guides, which were manuals of religious and social customs. Being meant for layman as well as priest, they reflect the popular, practical side of Brahminism, whereas the Brahmanas and Upanishads show us the religion on its priestly, speculative side. Closely related to the law-guides is the justly famed metrical treatise, Manava-Dharma-Sastra, known in English as the Laws of Manu. It belongs probably to the fifth century B. C. These, together with the two sacred epics of a later age, the " Ramayana " and the " Mahabharata," embrace what is most important in sacred Brahmin literature.

II. EARLY BRAHMINISM OR VEDISM.—The religion of the Vedic period proper was comparatively simple. It consisted in the worship of many deities, great and small, the personified forces of nature. Prominent among these were Varuna, the all-embracing heaven, maker and lord of all things and upholder of the moral law; the sun-god, variously known as Surya, the enemy of darkness and bringer of blessings, as Pushan the nourisher, as Mitra the omniscient friend of the good, and the avenger of deceit, as Savitar the enlivener, arousing men to daily activity, and as Vishnu, said to have measured the earth in three strides and to have given the rich pastures to mortals; the god of the air, Indra, like Mars, also, the mighty god of war, who set free from the cloud-serpent Ahi (or Vritra), the quickening rain; Rudra, later known as Siva, the blessed one, the god of the destructive thunderstorm, an object of dread to evil-doers, but a friend to the good; Agni, the fire-god, the friend and benefactor of men, dwelling on their hearths and bearing to the gods their prayers and sacrificial offerings; Soma, the god of that mysterious plant whose inebriating juice was so dear to the gods and to man, warding off disease, imparting strength, and securing immortality.

There were no temples at this early period. On a small mound of earth or of stones the offering was made to the gods, often by the head of the family, but in the more important and complicated sacrifices by the priest, or Brahmin, in union with the householder. The object of every sacrifice was to supply strengthening food to the gods and to secure blessings in return. Human victims, though rare, were not wholly unknown, but animal victims were at this period in daily use. First in importance was the horse, then the ox or cow, the sheep, and the goat. Offerings of clarified butter, rice, wheat, and other kinds of grain were also very common. But dearer to the gods than any of these gifts, and rivalling the horse-sacrifice in solemnity, was the offering of the inebriating juice of the Soma-plant, the so-called Soma-sacrifice. Hymns of praise and petitions, chiefly for the good things of life, children, health, wealth, and success in undertakings, accompanied these sacrificial offerings. But the higher needs of the soul were not forgotten. In the hymns to Varuna, Mitra, and other gods there are striking texts expressing a sense of guilt and asking for forgiveness. At a time when the early Hebrew Scriptures were silent as to the rewards and punishments awaiting man in the future life, we find the ancient Rik-bards giving repeated expression to their belief in a heaven of endless bliss for the just, and in an abyss of darkness for the wicked.

Devotion to the *Pitris* (Fathers), or dead relatives, was also a prominent element in their religion. Though the *Pitris* mounted to the heavenly abode of bliss, their happiness was not altogether independent of the acts of devotion shown them by the living. It could be greatly increased by offerings of Soma, rice, and water; for like the gods they were thought to have bodies of air-like texture and to enjoy the subtile essence of food. Hence the surviving children felt it a sacred duty to make feast-offerings, called Śraddhas, at stated times to their departed *Pitris*. In return for these acts of filial piety, the grateful *Pitris* protected them from harm and promoted their welfare. Lower forms of nature-worship also obtained. The cow was held in reverence. Worship was given to trees and serpents. Formulæ abounded for healing the diseased, driving off demons, and averting evil omens. Witchcraft was dreaded, and recourse to ordeals was common for the detection of guilt.

III. POPULAR BRAHMINISM.—In the period that saw the production of the Brahmanas and Upanishads, the Vedic religion underwent a twofold change. On its practical side there was an exuberant growth of religious rites and of social restrictions and duties, while on the theoretical side Vedic belief in the efficacy of personal deities was subordinated to a pantheistic scheme of salvation. Thus the earlier religion developed on the one hand into popular, exoteric Brahminism, and on the other into priestly, esoteric Brahminism. The former is reflected in the Brahmanas and Sutras; the latter in the Upanishads.

The transformation to popular Brahminism was largely due to the influence of the Brahmins, or priests. Owing to their excessive fondness for symbolic words and forms, the details of ritual became more and more intricate, some assuming so elaborate a character as to require the service of sixteen priests. The sacrifice partook of the nature of a sacramental rite, the due performance of which was sure to produce the desired end, and thus became the all-important centre around which the visible and invisible world revolved. Hence it merited liberal fees to the officiating priests. Still it was not a mere perfunctory rite, for if performed by an unworthy priest it was accounted as both useless and sacrilegious. In keeping with this complicated liturgy was the multiplicity of prayers and rites which entered into the daily life of both priest and layman. The daily recitation of parts of the Vedas, now venerated as Divine revelation, was of first importance, especially for the Brahmins. It was a sacred duty for every individual to recite, morning and evening, the Savitri, a short prayer in honour of the vivifying sun. A scrupulous regard for ceremonial purity, surpassing even that of the Jewish Pharisee, gave rise to an endless succession of purificatory rites, such as baths, sprinkling with water, smearing with ashes or cow-dung, sippings of water, suppressions of breath—all sacramental in character and efficacious for the remission of sin. There is reason to believe that the consciousness of guilt for sin committed was keen and vivid, and that in the performance of these rites, so liable to abuse, a penitential disposition of soul was largely cultivated.

In popular Brahminism of this period the idea of retribution for sin was made to embrace the most rigorous and far-reaching consequences, from which, save by timely penance, there was no escape. As every good action was certain of future recompense, so every evil one was destined to bear its fruit of misery in time to come. This was the doctrine of *karma* (action), with which the new idea of rebirth was closely connected. While the lasting bliss of heaven was still held out to the just, different fates after death were reserved for the wicked, varying, according to the nature and amount of guilt, from long periods of torture in a graded series of hells, to a more or less extensive series of rebirths in the forms of plants, animals, and men. From the grade to which the culprit was condemned he had to pass by slow transition through the rest of the ascending scale till his rebirth as a man of honourable estate was attained.

This doctrine gave rise to restrictive rules of conduct that bordered on the absurd. Insects, however repulsive and noxious, might not be killed; water might not be drunk till it was first strained, lest minute forms of life be destroyed; carpentry, basket-making, working in leather, and other similar occupations were held in disrepute, because they could not be carried on without a certain loss of animal and plant life. Some zealots went so far as to question the blamelessness of tilling the ground on account of the unavoidable injury done to worms and insects. But on the other hand, the Brahmin ethical teaching in the legitimate sphere of right conduct is remarkably high. Truthfulness, obedience to parents and superiors, temperance, chastity, and almsgiving were strongly inculcated. Though allowing, like other religions of antiquity, polygamy, and divorce, it strongly forbade adultery and all forms of unchastity. It also reprobated suicide, abortion, perjury, slander, drunkenness, gambling, oppressive usury, and wanton cruelty to animals. Its Christianlike aim to soften the hard side of human nature is seen in its many lessons of mildness, charity towards the sick, feeble, and aged, and in its insistence on the duty of forgiving injuries and returning good for evil. Nor did this high standard of right conduct apply simply to external acts. The threefold division of good and bad acts into thoughts, words, and deeds finds frequent expression in Brahminic teaching.

Intimately bound up with the religious teaching of Brahminism was the division of society into rigidly defined castes. In the earlier, Vedic, period there had been class distinctions, according to which the warrior class (Kshatriyas, or Rajanas) stood first in dignity and importance, next the priestly class (Brahmins), then the farmer class (Vaisyas), and last of all, the servile class of conquered natives (Śudras). With the development of Brahminism, these four ancient divisions of society became stereotyped into exclusive castes, the highest place of dignity being usurped by the Brahmins. As teachers of the sacred Vedas and as priests of the all-important sacrifices, they professed to be the very representatives of the gods and the peerage of the human race. No honours were too great for them, and to lay hands on them was a sacrilege. One of the chief sources of their power and influence lay in their exclusive privilege to teach the youth of the three upper castes, for education then consisted largely in the acquisition of Vedic lore, which only priests could teach. Thus the three upper castes alone had the right to know the Vedas and to take part in the sacrifices, and Brahminism, far from being a religion open to all, was exclusively a privilege of birth, from which the despised caste of Śudras was excluded.

The rite of initiation into Brahminism was conferred on the male children only, when they began their studies under a Brahmin teacher, which took place generally in the eighth year for the Brahmin, and in the eleventh and twelfth for the Kshatriya and Vaisya respectively. It consisted in the investiture of the sacred cord, a string of white cotton-yarn, tied together at the ends, and worn like a deacon's stole suspended on the left shoulder. This investiture was a sort of sacrament in virtue of which the youth was freed from guilt contracted from his parents, and became *Dvi-ja*, twice-born, with the right to learn the sacred Vedic texts and to take part in the sacrifices. The period of studentship was not long for the members of the warrior and farmer castes, but for the young Brahmin, who had to learn all the Vedas by heart, it consumed nine years or more. During this period, the student was subjected to severe moral discipline. He had to rise before the sun, and was not allowed to recline till after sunset. He was denied rich and dainty foods, and what he ate at his two daily meals he had to beg. He was expected to observe the strictest chastity. He was bound to avoid music, dancing, gambling, falsehood, disrespect to superiors and to the aged, covetousness, anger, and injury to animals.

Marriage was held to be a religious duty for every twice-born. It was generally entered upon early in life, not long after the completion of the time of studentship. Like the initiation-rite, it was a solemn sacramental ceremony. It was an imperative law that the bride and groom should be of the same caste in the principal marriage; for, as polygamy was tolerated, a man might take one or more secondary wives from the lower castes. For certain grave reasons, the householder might repudiate his wife and marry another, but a wife on her part had no corresponding right of divorce. If her husband died, she was expected to remain for the rest of her life in chaste widowhood, if she would be honoured on earth and be happy with him in heaven. The later Hindu practice known as the Suttee, in which the bereaved wife threw herself on the funeral pyre of her husband, seems at this period to have been unknown. All knowledge of the Vedic texts was withheld from woman, but she had the right to participate with her husband in the sacrifices performed for him by some officiating priest. One important sacrifice remained in his own hands—the morning and evening offering of hot milk, butter, and grain to the fire on the hearth, which was sacred to Agni and was kept always burning.

A strong tendency to asceticism asserted itself in the Brahminism of this period. It found expression in the fasts preceding the great sacrifices, in the severe penances prescribed for various kinds of sin, in the austere life exacted of the student, in the conjugal abstinence to be observed for the first three days following marriage and on certain specified days of the month, but, above all, in the rigorous life of retirement and privation to which not a few devoted their declining years. An ever increasing number of householders, chiefly Brahmins, when their sons had grown to man's estate, abandoned their homes and spent the rest of their lives as ascetics, living apart from the villages in rude huts or under the shelter of trees, eating only the simplest kinds of food, which they obtained by begging, and subjecting themselves to extraordinary fasts and mortifications. They were known as *Sannyasis*, or *Yogis*, and their severity of life was not so much a penitential discipline for past offences as a means of acquiring abundant religious merits and superhuman powers. Coupled with these mortifications was the practice of *Yogi* (union). They would sit motionless with legs crossed and, fixing their gaze intently on an object before them, would concentrate their thought on some abstract subject till they lapsed into a trance. In this state they fancied they were united with the deity, and the fruit of these contemplations was the pantheistic view of religion which found expression in the Upanishads, and left a permanent impress on the Brahmin mind.

IV. PANTHEISTIC BRAHMINISM.—The marked monotheistic tendency discernible in the later Vedic hymns had made itself more and more keenly felt in the higher Brahmin circles till it gave rise to a new deity, a creation of Brahmin priests. This was Prajapati, lord of creatures, omnipotent and supreme, later known as Brahmā, the personal creator of all things. But in thus looking up to a supreme lord and creator they were far removed from Christian monotheism. The gods of the ancient pantheon were not repudiated, but were worshipped still as the various manifestations of Brahmā. It was an axiom then, as it has been ever since with the Hindu mind, that creation out of nothing is impossible. Another fundamental Brahmin principle is that every form of conscious individuality, whether human or Divine, implies a union of spirit and matter. And so, outside the smaller school of thinkers who held matter to be eternal, those who stood for the supreme personal god explained the world of visible things and invisible gods as the emanations of Brahmā. They arrived at a personal pantheism. But speculation did not end here. To the prevailing school of dreamy Brahmin ascetics, whose teachings are found in the Upanishads, the ultimate source of all things was not the personal Brahmā, but the formless, characterless, unconscious spirit known as Atman (self), or more commonly, Brahmă. (Brahmă is neuter, whereas Brahmā, personal god, is masculine.) The heavens and the earth, men and gods, even the personal deity, Brahmā, were but transitory emanations of Brahmă, destined in time to lose their individuality and be absorbed into the great, all-pervading, impersonal spirit. The manifold external world thus had no real existence. It was Maya, illusion. Brahmă alone existed. He alone was eternal, imperishable.

This impersonal pantheism of the Brahmin ascetics led to a new conception of the end of man and of the way of salvation. The old way was to escape rebirths and their attendant misery by storing up merits of good deeds so as to obtain an eternal life of conscious bliss in heaven. This was a mistake. For so long as man was ignorant of his identity with Brahmă and did not see that his true end consisted in being absorbed into the impersonal all-god from which he sprang; so long as he set his heart on a merely personal existence, no amount of good works would secure his freedom from rebirth. By virtue of his good deeds, he would, indeed, mount to heaven, perhaps win a place among the gods. But after a while his store of merits would give out like oil in a lamp, and he would have to return once more to life to taste in a new birth the bitterness of earthly existence. The only way to escape this misery was through the saving recognition of one's identity with Brahmă. As soon as one could say from conviction, "I am Brahmă", the bonds were broken that held him fast to the illusion of personal immortality and consequently to rebirth. Thus, cultivating, by a mortified life, freedom from all desires, man spent his years in peaceful contemplation till death put an end to the seeming duality and he was absorbed in Brahmă like a raindrop in the ocean.

V. EARLY HINDUISM.—The pantheistic scheme of salvation just described, generally known as the Vedanta teaching, found great favour with the Brahmins and has been maintained as orthodox Brahmin doctrine down to the present day. But it made little progress outside the Brahmin caste. The mass of the people had little interest in an impersonal Brahmă who was incapable of hearing their prayers, nor had they any relish for a final end which meant the loss forever of conscious existence. And so, while the priestly ascetic was chiefly concerned with meditation on his identity with Brahmă, and with the practice of mortification to secure freedom from all desires, the popular mind was still bent on prayer, sacrifices, and other good works in honour of the Vedic deities. But at the same time their faith in the efficacy of these traditional gods could not but be weakened by the Brahmin teaching that freedom from rebirth was not to be obtained by acts of worship to personal deities who were powerless to secure even for themselves eternal conscious bliss. The result was the popular development of special cults to two of the old gods, now raised to the position of supreme deity, and credited with the power to secure a lasting life of happiness in heaven.

It was in the priestly conception of the supreme personal Brahmā that the popular mind found the model for its new deities. Brahmā was not a traditional god, and seems never to have been a favourite object of cult with the people. Even to-day, there are but two temples to Brahmā in all India. His subordination to the great impersonal all-god did not help to recommend him to the popular mind. Instead, we find two of the traditional gods honoured with special cults, which seem to have taken rise independently in two different parts of the country and, after acquiring a local celebrity, to have spread in rivalry over the whole land. One of these gods was the ancient storm-god, Rudra, destructive in tempest and lightning, renewing life in the showers of rain, sweeping in lonely solitude over mountain and barren waste. As the destroyer, the reproducer, and the type of the lonely ascetic, this deity rapidly rose in popular esteem under the name of Śiva, the blessed. The other was Vishnu, originally one of the forms of the sun-god, a mild beneficent deity, whose genial rays brought gladness and growth to living creatures. His solar origin was lost sight of as he was raised to the position of supreme deity, but one of his symbols, the discus, points to his earlier character.

These two rival cults seem to have arisen in the fifth or fourth century B. C. As in the case of the personal god, Brahmā, neither the worship of Śiva nor of Vishnu did away with the honouring of the traditional gods and goddesses, spirits, heroes, sacred rivers and mountains and trees, serpents, earth, heaven, sun, moon, and stars. The pantheism in which the Hindu mind is inevitably cast saw in all these things emanations of the supreme deity, Śiva or Vishnu. In worshipping any or all, he was but honouring his supreme god. Each deity was credited with a special heaven, where his devotees would find after death an unending life of conscious happiness. The rapid rise in popular esteem of these cults, tending more and more to thrust Brahminism proper into the background, was viewed by the priestly caste with no little concern. To quench these cults was out of the question; and so, in order to hold them in at least nominal allegiance to Brahminism, the supreme god Brahmā was associated with Vishnu and Śiva as a triad of equal and more or less interchangeable deities, in which Brahmā held the office of creator, or rather evolver, Vishnu of preserver, and Śiva of dissolver. This is the so-called Trimurti (tri-form), or trinity, altogether different from the Christian conception of three eternally distinct persons in one Godhead, and hence offering no legitimate ground for suggesting a Hindu origin for the Christian doctrine.

More remarkable was the intimate association of other new deities—the creations of the religious fancy of the common people—with the gods Śiva and Vishnu. With Śiva two popular gods came to be associated as sons. One was Ganeśa, lord of troops and of mischievous imps, who has remained ever since a favourite object of worship and is invoked at the beginning of every undertaking to ensure success. The other was Scanda, who seems in great measure to have replaced Indra as the god of battle.

Beyond the doubtful derivation of the name Scanda from Alexander, there is nothing to indicate that either of these reputed sons of Śiva had ever lived the life of men. Not so the gods that enlarged the sphere of Vishnu's influence. In keeping with Vishnu's position as god of the people, two of the legendary heroes of the remote past, Rama and Krishna, whom popular enthusiasm had raised to the rank of gods, came to be associated with him not as sons, but as his very incarnations. The incarnation of a god descending from heaven to assume a human or animal form as a sort of saviour, and to achieve some signal benefit for mankind, is known as an avatar. The idea antedates Buddhism and, while applied to Brahmā and other gods, became above all a characteristic of Vishnu. Popular fancy loved to dwell on his avatar as a fish to save Manu from the devastating flood, as a tortoise to recover from the depths of the sea precious possessions for gods and men, as a boar to raise the submerged earth above the surface of the waters, but most of all, as the god-men Rama and Krishna, each of whom delivered the people from the yoke of a tyrant. So popular became the cults to Rama and Krishna that Vishnu himself was largely lost sight of. In time the Vishnuites became divided into two rival schisms: the Ramaites, who worshipped Rama as supreme deity, and the Krishnaites, who gave this honour rather to Krishna, a division that has persisted down to the present day.

The evidence of the early existence of these innovations on Brahmin belief is to be found in the two great epics known as the "Ramayana" and the "Mahabharata." Both are revered by Brahmins, Śivaites, and Vishnuites alike, particularly the latter poem, which is held to be directly revealed. In the "Ramayana," which belongs to the period 400–300 B. C., the legendary tales of the trials and triumphs of the hero Rama and his faithful wife Sita were worked into a highly artificial romantic poem, largely in the interests of Vishnu worship. The "Mahabharata," the work of many hands, was begun about the fifth century B. C. under Brahmin influence, and in the following centuries received additions and modifications, in the interests now of Vishnuism now of Śivaism, till it assumed its final shape in the sixth century of the Christian Era. It is a huge conglomeration of stirring adventure, popular legend, myth, and religious speculation. The narrative centres chiefly around the many-sided struggle for supremacy between the evil tyrant of the land and the hero Arjuna, aided by his four brothers. The rôle that Krishna plays is not an integral part of the story and seems to have been interpolated after the substance of the epic had been written. He is the charioteer of Arjuna and at the same time acts as his religious adviser. Of his numerous religious instructions, the most important is the metrical treatise known as the "Bhagavadgita," the Song of the Blessed One, a writing that has exercised a profound influence on religious thought in India. It dates from the second or third century of the Christian Era, being a poetic version of a late Upanishad with its pantheistic doctrine so modified as to pass for a personal revelation of Krishna. While embodying the noblest features of Brahmin ethics, and insisting on the faithful performance of caste-duties, it proclaims Krishna to be the supreme personal all-god, who, by the bestowal of special grace, helps on his votaries to the attainment of eternal bliss. As an important means to this end, it inculcates the virtue of *Bhakti*, that is a loving devotion to the deity, analogous to the Christian virtue of charity.

Unhappily for the later development of Vishnuism, the Krishna of the "Bhagavad-gita" was not the popular conception. Like most legendary heroes of folk-lore, his character was in keeping with the crude morals of the primitive age that first sounded his praises. The narrative portions of the epic show him to have been sly and unscrupulous, guilty in word and deed of acts which the higher Brahmin conscience would reprove. But it is in the fuller legendary story of his life as given in the so-called "Hari-vansa", a later supplement to the epic, and also in some of the Puranas of the ninth and tenth centuries of our era, that the character of the popular Krishna appears in its true light. Here we learn that Krishna was one of eight sons of noble birth, whom a Herod-like tyrant was bent on destroying. The infant god was saved from the wicked designs of the king by being secretly substituted for a herdsman's babe. Krishna grew up among the simple country-people, performing prodigies of valour, and engaging in many amorous adventures with the Gopis, the wives and daughters of the herdsmen. Eight of these were his favourites, but one he loved best of all, Radha. Krishna finally succeeded in killing the king, and brought peace to the kingdom.

Between this deified Hindu Hercules and Our Divine Lord, there is no ground for comparison, one only for contrast. That the idea of incarnate deity should be found in pre-Christian Hindu thought is not so remarkable when we consider that it answers to the yearning of the human heart for union with God. But what is at first sight astonishing is to find in the religious writings subsequent to the "Mahabharata" legendary tales of Krishna that are almost identical with the stories of Christ in the canonical and apocryphal Gospels. From the birth of Krishna in a stable, and his adoration by shepherds and magi, the reader is led on through a series of events the exact counterparts of those related of Our Divine Lord. Writers hostile to Christianity seized on this chain of resemblances, too close to be mere coincidence, in order to convict the Gospel writers of plagiarism from Hindu originals. But the very opposite resulted. All Indianists of authority are agreed that these Krishna legends are not earlier that the seventh century of the Christian Era and must have been borrowed from Christian sources.

VI. LATER, OR SECTARIAN, HINDUISM.—The steady weakening of Brahmin influence, in consequence of the successive waves of foreign conquest, made it possible for the religious preferences of the huge, heterogeneous population of India to assert themselves more strongly. Both Sivaism and Vishnuism departed more and more from traditional Brahminism, and assumed a decidedly sectarian character towards the older religion and also towards each other. With this weakening of Brahmin influence they absorbed the grosser elements of low-grade popular worship, and became debased by the accretion of immoral rites and grovelling superstitions. While, on the one hand, the practice of asceticism was pushed to the utmost extremes of fanaticism, on the other, the doctrine of Bhakti was perverted into a system of gross sexual indulgence, for which the amours of Krishna and the Gopis served as the model and sanction. The Brahmin caste-distinctions were broken down, and an equality of all men and women was asserted, at least during the ceremonies of public worship. The Brahmin rites were in great measure replaced by others peculiar to each cult and held to be all-sufficient for salvation. Everywhere splendid temples arose to Siva, Vishnu, and his two human avatars; idols and phallic symbols innumerable filled the land; and each rival cult lauded its own special deity as supreme, subordinating all others to it, and looking down with more or less contempt on forms of worship other than its own. One factor which contributed strongly to the degradation of these sectarian forms of religion was the veneration of the *Sakti*, or female side, of these deities. Popular

theology would not rest till each deity was supplemented with a wife, in whom the active nature of the god was personified. With Brahmā was associated an ancient river-goddess, Sarasvati, honoured as the patroness of letters. Vishnu's Sakti was Sri, or Lakshmi, patroness of good fortune. With Siva the destroyer, was associated the terrible, bloodthirsty, magical goddess, Durga, or Kali, formerly delighting in human victims, now appeased with sacrifices of goats and buffaloes. Rama had his consort, Sita, and Krishna his favourite Gopi, Radha. The worship of these Saktis, particularly Siva's consort, Durga-Kali, degenerated into shocking orgies of drunkenness and sexual immorality, which even to-day are the crying scandal of Hinduism.

Such were the sectarian developments of post-epic times. They found expression in the inferior, quasi-historical Puranas, of the seventh and following centuries, and in the Tantras, which are more modern still and teach the symbolic magic of Sakti-worship. Neither of these classes of writings is regarded by the orthodox Brahmin as canonical.

Of the two hundred million adherents of Hinduism to-day, only a few hundred thousand can be called orthodox Brahmin worshippers. Sivaism and Vishnuism have overshadowed the older religion like a rank growth of poisonous weeds. In their main outlines, these two great sects have retained the characteristics of the Purana period, but differences of view on minor points have led to a multiplication of schismatic divisions, especially among Vishnu-worshippers. Both sects, which to-day are fairly tolerant of each other, have a number of devotional and liturgical practices that are alike in kind, though marked by differences of sectarian belief. Both Sivaite and Vishnuite lay great stress on the frequent recital of the numerous names of their respective supreme gods, and, to facilitate this work of piety, each carries with him, often about his neck, a rosary, varying in material and the number of beads according as it is dedicated to Siva or to Vishnu. Each sect has an initiation-rite, which is conferred on the young at the age of reason and in which the officiating guru puts a rosary around the neck of the applicant and whispers into his ear the *mantra*, or sacred motto, the recital of which serves as a profession of faith and is of daily obligation. Another rite common to both is that in which the presiding officer brands on the body of the worshipper with hot metal stamps, the sacred symbols of his sect, the trident and linga of Siva, or the discus and conch-shell (or lotus) of Vishnu.

But in their highest act of ceremonial worship the two sects differ radically. The Sivaite takes his white stone pebble, the conventional phallic emblem which he always carries with him, and while muttering his *mantra*, sprinkles it with water and applies to it cooling Bilva leaves. Owing to its simplicity and cheapness, this rite is much in vogue with the ignorant lower classes. The Vishnuite rite is less degrading but more childish. It consists in an elaborate and costly worship of the temple image of Vishnu, or more often, of Rama, or Krishna. The image is daily awakened, undressed, bathed, decked with rich robes, and adorned with necklaces, bracelets, crowns of gold and precious stones, fed with choice kinds of food, honoured with flowers, lights, and incense, and then entertained with vocal and instrumental music, and with dancing by the temple-girls of doubtful virtue, consecrated to this service. As Krishna is generally worshipped in the form of a child-image, his diversion consists largely in the swinging of his image, the spinning of tops, and other games dear to the heart of the child.

Siva, too, has his temples, vying in magnificence with those of Vishnu, but in all these the holy place is the linga-shrine, and the temple worship consists in the application of water and Bilva leaves to the stone symbol. The interior walls of these, and of Vishnu temples as well, are covered with shocking representations of sexual passion. And yet, strange to say, these forms of religion, while giving a sanction to the indulgence of the lowest passions, at the same time inspire other devotees to the practice of the severest asceticism. They wander about in lonely silence, naked and filthy, their hair matted from long neglect, their bodies reduced to mere skin and bones by dint of incredible fasts. They will stand motionless for hours under the blazing sun, with their emaciated arms uplifted towards heaven. Some go about with face ever turned upwards. Some are known to have kept their fists tightly clenched until their growing nails protruded through the backs of their hands.

VII. REFORM MOVEMENTS.—Enlightened Hindus of modern times have made attempts to institute a reform in Hinduism by rejecting all idolatrous and immoral rites, and by setting up a purely monotheistic form of worship. Of these the earliest and the most noted was the so-called Brahmā Samaj (Congregation of Brahmā), founded in Calcutta in 1828, by the learned Rammohun Roy. He tried to combine a Unitarian form of Christianity with the Brahmin conception of the supreme personal God. After his death, in 1833, differences of view as to the nature of God, the authority of the Vedas, and the obligation of caste-customs caused the society to split up into a number of small congregations. At present there are more than a hundred independent theistic congregations in India. Some, like the Arya Samaj, rest on the sole authority of the Vedas. Others are eclectic, even to the extent of choosing for devotional reading in their public services passages from the Avesta, Koran, and Bible. Few of them are altogether free from the taint of pantheism, and, being more like clubs for intellectual and moral improvement than for ritualistic forms of worship, they make but little progress in the way of conversion.

In short, Brahminism cannot succeed in reforming itself. Its earlier sacred books are steeped in the polytheism out of which it grew. And the pantheistic view of the world, to which it was afterwards committed, has been like a dead weight dragging it hopelessly into the stagnant pool of superstition, pessimism, and immorality. In virtue of its pantheistic attitude, there is no form of religion, high or low, that cannot be tolerated and incorporated into its capacious system. The indifference of Brahminism to the gross abuses of Hinduism is, after all, but a reflex of the indifference of its supreme god. Sin loses most of its hideousness when it can be traced ultimately to the great impersonal Brahmă. There is but one form of religion which has any prospect of reforming the religious life of India, and that is the Roman Catholic. For the shadowy pantheistic deity it can set forth the One, Eternal, Personal Spirit and Creator; for the crude Tri-murti, the sublime Trinity; and for the coarse and degrading avatars of Vishnu, the Incarnation of the Son of God. It can replace the idolatrous and immoral Hindu rites with its own imposing liturgy, and substitute the Cross for the abominable linga.

Brahminism, being a national religion and a privilege of Hindu birth, has never made any concerted attempt at proselytizing in foreign lands. But some years ago steps were taken by a few individuals of England to foist upon English-speaking people a new religious system embodying the pantheistic belief and magical superstition of the Vedanta school of Brahminism. This new system, known as Theosophy, was to embrace within its fold members of every form of religion, reconciling all differences of creed in the pantheistic view that all deities, high and low, are but transitory emanations of the su-

preme, incomprehensible Reality, devotion to which was the highest religion. This quasi-cult, which also made pretensions to the exercise of magical powers, soon met the ridicule and obloquy it deserved. It is practically obsolete at the present day.

TEXTS.—MUIR, *Original Sanskrit Texts*, 5 vols. (London, 1868–70); MÜLLER, *Vedic Hymns* in *Sacred Books of the East*, XXXII; OLDENBERG, *Vedic Hymns*, op. cit., XLVI; BLOOMFIELD, *The Atharva Veda*, op. cit., XLII; EGGELING, *The Satapatha Brahmana*, op. cit., XII, XXVI, XLI; MÜLLER, *The Upanishads*, op. cit., XV; OLDENBERG and MÜLLER, *The Grihya-Sutras*, op. cit., XXIX, XXX; BÜHLER, *The Sacred Laws of the Aryas*, op. cit., II, XIV; IDEM, *The Laws of Manu*, op. cit., XXV; THIBAUT, *The Vedanta-Sutras*, op. cit., XXXIV, XXXVIII; TELANG, *The Bhagavad-gita*, op. cit., VIII; BURNOUF-ROUSSEL, *Le Bhagavata Purana*, 5 vols. (Paris, 1898).

GENERAL TREATISES.—BARTH, *The Religions of India* (London, 1882); MONIER-WILLIAMS, *Brahmanism and Hinduism, or Religious Thought and Life in India* (London, 1891); IDEM, *Hinduism* (London, 1897); IDEM, *Indian Wisdom* (London, 1876); HOPKINS, *The Religions of India* (Boston, 1895); DUBOIS, *Hindu Manners, Customs and Ceremonies* (Oxford, 1897); GOUGH, *The Philosophy of the Upanishads and Ancient Indian Metaphysics* (London, 1882); DEUSSEN, *Das System des Vedanta* (Leipzig, 1883); IDEM, *Die Philosophie der Upanishads* (Leipzig, 1899); KÆGI, *The Rig-Veda* (Boston, 1886); OLDENBERG, *Die Religion des Veda* (Berlin, 1894); COLEBROOKE, *Miscellaneous Essays*, (2 vols., London, 1873); WEBER, *The History of Indian Literature* (London, 1892); DAHLMANN, *Das Mahabharata* (Berlin, 1895); SCHŒBEL, *La Ramayana* in *Annales du musée Guimet* (Paris, 1888), XIII; DE LA SAUSSAYE, *Lehrb. der Religionsgesch.* (Freiburg, 1905), II.

CHARLES F. AIKEN.

Braille, LOUIS, a French educator and inventor, b. 4 January, 1809, at Coupvray, Seine-et-Marne, France; d. 6 January, 1852. He became blind when three years of age, and at the age of thirteen was sent to the Institution for the Blind at Paris. There he showed a talent for intellectual studies and for music; and when his instruction had been completed he was appointed professor in that institution. It was then that he invented his system of writing in raised or relief points for the blind. Before him, Valentin Haüy, the founder of the Institution for the Blind, had invented the method of printing in raised letters which allowed the blind to read by touch; Charles Barbier had invented a sonographic point system as distinguished from Haüy's line or letter system, and had devised a simple instrument by which the blind could emboss the words or print them in relief. But this system of writing, based on the sounds of the French language, was too conventional and did not furnish the signs necessary for punctuation and ciphers. Braille, keeping to Barbier's point system and the principle of relief writing, found the means of representing, by the various combinations of six dots, not the sounds, but the alphabetical letters and all the signs of punctuation, and even of music. This invention, being alphabetic instead of sonographic, was a great advance in the education of the blind, and though it has been modified, at times, as to the combinations of dots (American, English, and English revised systems), the system is still, in most countries, the basis of methods for the education of the blind. The inventor set forth the principles of his system in his work: "Procédé pour écrire les paroles, la musique, et la plein-chant, à l'usage des aveugles", printed in raised letters in 1829. Though this system cannot be said to be the definitive method of education and writing for the blind, the name of Braille will always remain associated with one of the greatest and most beneficent devices ever invented.

GAUDET, *L'institut des jeunes aveugles de Paris, son histoire et ses procédés d'enseignement;* BUISSON in *Dictionnaire de pédagogie*, s. v. *Aveugles;* MELL, *Wandbuch des Blindenwesens.*

G. M. SAUVAGE.

Bralion, NICOLAS DE, a French Oratorian and ecclesiastical writer, b. at Chars-en-Vexin, France, c. 1600; d. at Paris, 11 May, 1672. He joined the Paris Oratory in 1619, and, in 1625, went to Rome, where he remained fifteen years at San Luigi dei Francesi, then an Oratorian establishment, devoting his time to research and literary work. There he published an Italian translation of Cardinal de Bérulle's "Elévation" (1640) and of a portion of Ribadeniera's "Saintly Lives". He returned to Paris about 1640 and spent the rest of his life at the Church of St. Honoré. Among other works he published "Vie de St. Nicholas, archevêque de Myre" (1646); "Pallium Archiepiscopale" (1648—the first serious study published in France on the significance, tradition, and use of that vestment); "Histoire chrétienne" (1656); "La curiosité de l'une et l'autre Rome" (1655–59); "Cæremoniale Canonicorum" (1657—a practical guide on Roman lines); "Histoire de la sainte chapelle de Lorette" (1665).

INGOLD, *Essai de bibliogr. oratorienne* (Paris, 1882), 27; MICHAUD, *Biog. univ.* (Paris, 1811), V, 477.

JOHN B. PETERSON.

Bramante, DONATO (also called D'ANGNOLO after his father Angelo), Italian architect and painter, b. about 1444 at Monte Asdrualdo (hence, sometimes ASDRUALDINO); d. in Rome, 11 March, 1514. Nothing is known of his early youth. His early artistic development also, about which Vasari has made so many erroneous statements, is mostly a matter of conjecture. To-day, however, it seems fairly certain that Laurana, the architect of the ducal palace at Urbino, showed him the way to the impressive style of the High Renaissance. Bramante's artistic activity is divided into two periods of which the first was spent in Milan and the other in Rome. His work in Milan is characterized by a pronounced picturesque, decorative style. In Rome, on the other hand, we find a style which is more proper to the High Renaissance, exemplified in works that are, as far as possible, free from all external decoration, impressive by reason of their proportions, and recalling the antique by their grandeur and power. In 1476 Bramante became the court architect of Lodovico Sforza (Il Moro), having been in Milan, as has been abundantly shown, from 1474. At first he seems to have been engaged principally as a painter, following the vigorous manner of Mantegna and Melozzo da Forlì. It is true that only scanty remains of his work at this time have been found. Such are the recently discovered fresco fragments, transported from the Casa Prinetti to the Brera (single figures of warriors, philosophers, poets, and singers); the more poorly preserved decorative paintings of the Casa Fontana, and among panel pictures, undoubtedly the Scourging of Christ (Badia Chiaravalle near Milan). Bartolomeo Suardi, called Bramantino [cf. Suida in Jahrbuch der Kunstsammlungen des allerhöchsten Kaiserhauses (1905), 1 sqq.], was his assistant and rather weak imitator in the field of painting, but not his teacher as was thought by Vasari (ed. Milanesi-Sansoni, IV, 175). If Bramante occasionally devoted himself to Gothic, as he unquestionably did in some designs for the Milan cathedral, he exhibits from the start an excellent style, which, as *Stile Bramantesco*, became typical for the Renaissance architecture of Lombardy. It is characterized by ambitious proportions, internal concentration, a greater organic relation of parts, and by rich and fresh decorative forms.

His first great achievement in this line is the choir of the church of Santa Maria presso S. Satiro, begun in 1476. The choir has a flat end and a false apse, rendered in relieved perspective. The adjoining sacristy, octagonal in plan and surmounted by a dome, is charming on account of the richness of the interior articulation and most effective space-development. Its two interior stories are separated by a splendid terra-cotta frieze overlaid with bronze. The church came to have the same significance in Northern Italy as the Pazzi Chapel or the Sacristy of Santo Spirito in Florence. Still richer in ornament are the transept and choir of Santa Maria

delle Grazie (1492–99), by which the superiority of the imposing new style over the Gothic can best be shown. In addition to these great churches, the Canonica, or canons' residence, of San Ambrogio (1492, only half completed) and the remodelled court of the Ospedale Maggiore are the only examples of Bramante's genius in Milan. A further development of this somewhat more decorative style to the larger, simpler proportions of the Roman period is suggested by the church of the Barnabites, Santa Maria di Capenuova in Pavia (1492), and also by the churches of Busto Arsizio and Santa Maria in Legnano. The magnificent articulation of the façade of Abbiategrasso shows in full development the powerful boldness of the Roman style whose growth, in Rome, was influenced not only by the antique, but also by the use of a more intractable material (travertine) which made small, detail treatment an impossibility. The date of this church is probably 1497 instead of 1477, as Geymüller read it. Other ecclesiastical structures of Lombardy upon which the influence or imitation of Bramante is perceptible, are the Cathedral of Como (south portal), the Pilgrimage Church at Crema, and the Incoronata at Lodi.

Even greater is the number of structures indirectly influenced by Bramante in Northern and Middle Italy after the downfall of the Sforzas in Milan (1499). Bramante at the end of the same year moved to Rome where he found in Alexander VI and still more in Julius II magnanimous patrons. Here, too, very little is known of his early work. It is still disputed whether or not the cloister of Santa Maria della Pace and the façade of the Church of the Anima can be ascribed to him. This is also true of the immense palace of Cardinal Raffaello Riario (the present Cancelleria) with the adjoining church of San Lorenzo in Damaso. On account of the inscribed dates (1489 and 1495) Gnoli ascribes them not to Bramante but to a Tuscan master, whereas Geymüller more collectly persists in ascribing them to Bramante, basing his view on considerations of style and on Bramante's relations with the Sforzas and the Riarios; this would also explain Bramante's working in Rome prior to 1492 [cf. Gnoli in Arch. stor. dell' arte (1892), IV, 176 sqq.; Riv. d'Italia (1898); and Geymüller in Rassegna d'arte (October and December, 1901), I]. The Palace Giraud Torlonia is a structure similar to the Cancelleria in its beautiful rhythmic articulation, its simplicity, and its monumental character. Undoubtedly Bramante is the designer of the pretty little circular temple in the court of San Pietro in Montorio (completed in 1502). It is planned quite after the manner of an antique temple and is the first structure consciously designed and executed in the classic spirit, embodying the purest and simplest forms and the most agreeable proportions. A peristyle, never carried out, was intended to complete the building. Other works of Bramante's first Roman period are the choir of Santa Maria del Popolo, the plan for the reconstruction of the Vatican, the extension of the Belvedere court, etc. The most majestic creation, not only of Bramante and of the High Renaissance, but in fact of Christian art, is the new St. Peter's. According to Vasari, this was intended originally to enclose the magnificent tomb of Julius II, begun by Michaelangelo. But on account of the hopelessly ruinous condition of the old St. Peter's, its rebuilding became an immediate necessity and, indeed, was determined upon shortly after the accession of Julius II, probably in connexion with the reconstruction of the Vatican. As early as 18 April, 1506, the cornerstone of the pier of St. Helena was laid, and a year later those of the other three piers at the transept were in position. The ways and means employed by Bramante in dealing with the old building brought him many

BRAMANTE'S CIRCULAR TEMPLE

IN THE COURTYARD OF S. PIETRO IN MONTORIO — ON THIS SPOT, TRADITION SAYS, ST. PETER WAS CRUCIFIED

severe reproaches for his lack of sentiment and earned for him the nickname of *Ruinante*. Nevertheless, the incomparable significance of this creation must not be overlooked because of such romantic sentiments, nor must it be forgotten that the pope had Bramante's plan carried out in spite of all remonstrances and of the enormous cost.

The artistic aims of the structure, or more especially of the original plans, are revealed by the numerous drawings, executed partly by the master himself, and partly by his assistants. Their critical examination and æsthetic appreciation are among Geymüller's chief achievements. According to him this brilliant plan passed through three stages: in the first, only a small chapel for the tomb of Julius II was contemplated; in the second, the continuation of the erection of the new buildings undertaken during the reigns of Nicholas V and Paul II; only in the third stage was an entirely independent new building decided upon. For it Bramante had in view, from the first, a building of centralized plan, more particularly the plan of a Greek cross. In this he saw the architectonic ideal which combined the greatest harmony, the most serviceable space-relations, as well as a tendency to the monumentally sublime. It was only as an alternative, so far as can be judged from extant sketches, that the master seems to have reserved for himself the possibility of using the Latin cross, being evidently compelled to make concessions to the liturgical needs of the Church. According to the oldest drawings and a memorial medal of Caradosos, dated 1506, the original ground plan was a pure Greek cross, the termination of whose arms was apsidal on the interior, rectangular on the exterior. An immense dome was carried over the crossing. The predominant form of the interior was rotunda-like. For the four corners immense chapels were planned, which again repeated the Greek cross; they were crowned by smaller domes, and each was flanked on the exterior by a tower. Between the apses of the cross-arms and these corner-towers lay large vestibules for the chapels of the flanking domes. In a second design the cross-arms are rounded and enclosed by immense ambulatory halls. The main dome is encircled by an arcaded colonnade. The piers of the domes were enriched by niches emphasizing the dominant idea of the interior. In Milan, San Lorenzo, a church of centralized plan (see BYZANTINE ARCHITECTURE), evidently served as a model for this design. The principal ideas, however, were taken from the Pantheon and the Temple of Peace, which was the origin of the saying attributed to Bramante, that he would set the Pantheon on the Temple of Peace. The master was permitted to see only the initial steps towards the execution of his plan. He was able, nevertheless, to establish firmly its main lines for the architects who followed, inasmuch as the dome-supports with their arches, the southern transept, and the side domes were carried out under his direction. After his death in 1514 the continuation of the work was entrusted to the aged Fra Giocondo, and soon after (on a recommendation made by Bramante during his lifetime) to Raphael. Later on, San Gallo and Peruzzi were placed in charge. Bramante's plans suffered many changes and encroachments under the various directors until Michaelangelo returned to the fundamental ideas of the brilliant creator, and by the completion of the dome substantially carried the work to a conclusion. The curvature of the dome is not quite as bold and effective as that planned by Bramante; on the other hand it offers in its greater rise, a much more elegant and vigorous silhouette.

Under Julius II the influence of Bramante was predominant. Not only were the most daring works of architecture entrusted to him, but all other impor-

tant building operations, and, in general, all artistic undertakings depended on his initiative and approbation, as the painting of the ceiling of the Sistine Chapel and of the *loggie* and the *stanze*, or halls, of the Vatican. In this way, Raphael, his younger townsman, received the greatest possible aid and favour, whilst Bramante's intrigues against Michaelangelo were positively spiteful, according to Vasari. Through envy of Michaelangelo's mighty genius, he assigned to this great master only unsuitable and unpleasant commissions. Though these tragically strained relations between the two great artists at the court of the Rovere pope seem to be a psychological puzzle, the key is to be found in the hard and self-torturing character of the Florentine. Bramante on the contrary, was a man who enjoyed life in a happy and liberal way, and who knew how to live up to the dignity of his prominent position. The manifold character of his interests and activities is yet visible in his poems which have come down to us. With Michaelangelo, Raphael, and Leonardo, he is one of the great intellects of the High Rennaissance; he resembles them also in the fact that only a small part of his plans was completed.

PUNGILEONI, *Memorie interno alla vita di Bramante* (Rome, 1836); VON GEYMÜLLER, *Les projets primitifs de la basilique de S. Pierre* (Paris, 1875); SEMPER in DOHME, *Kunst u. Künstler* (Leipzig, 1879), III, nos. 56–57; RICCI, *Gli affreschi di Bramante* (Milan, 1902); CAROTTI, *Leonardo, Bramante, e Raffaello* (Milan, 1905.)

JOSEPH SAUER.

Brancaccio, an ancient and illustrious Neapolitan family, from which the "Brancas" of France were descended. The family founded the celebrated Brancacciana Library at Naples, gave prominent officials to the State and from the fourteenth to the seventeenth century, seven cardinals to the Church. It is represented to-day by two branches, the "Principi di Ruffano" and the "Principi Brancaccio". The seven cardinals were as follows: (1) LANDOLFO, b. at Naples; d. at Avignon, 1312. He was created cardinal in 1294 by Celestine V, entrusted with difficult negotiations under Boniface VIII and Clement V, and attended the General Council of Vienne (1311–12). (2) LUIGI, a learned canonist, d. 1411. He was appointed by Innocent VII Nuncio to Naples, and made Archbishop of Taranto and cardinal (1408) by Gregory XII. (3) NICOLÒ, d. at Florence, 1412. He was made Archbishop of Cosenza in 1376; he sided with the antipopes Clement VII and Benedict XIII, and was created cardinal by the former in 1378. (4) RINALDO, d. at Rome, 1427. He was raised to the cardinalate by Urban VI in 1384, was present at the Council of Constance (1414–18), and filled several important missions. (5) TOMMASO, d. in Rome, 1427. He was created cardinal in 1411 by his uncle, John XXIII, and was present at the Council of Constance. His private life is said to have been far from exemplary. (6) FRANCESCO MARIA, b. about 1591; d. 1675. He became Bishop of Capacio, Viterbo, and Porto, and was created cardinal in 1634 by Urban VIII. Among other writings, he has left a dissertation on the question whether chocolate breaks the fast or not. (7) STEFANO, nephew of Francesco Maria, b. at Naples, 1618; d. 1682. He was nuncio at Florence and Venice, Bishop of Viterbo in 1670, and cardinal in 1681.

VAST in *La grande encyc.*, VII, 985.

N. A. WEBER.

Brancati, FRANCESCO, b. in Sicily in 1607; he entered the Society of Jesus in 1624 and went to the Chinese Missions in 1637. For nearly thirty years he laboured with admirable zeal and success in the Province of Kiang-nan, building, it is said, more than ninety churches and forty-five chapels. In 1665 he was exiled from Peking to Canton, where he died in 1671 (according to Sommervogel, at Shanghai). He wrote and published numerous books in Chinese, most of which, being of great merit, were reprinted by the Jesuit missionaries in the nineteenth century. Among these are a treatise on the Eucharist, instructions on the Decalogue and on the Commandments of the Church, a refutation of divinations, and particularly a Catechism, entitled in Chinese, "Conversations of the Angels". The Russian Archimandrite, who was at the head of the Orthodox mission at Peking, published in the second decade of the nineteenth century an extract from this Catechism, adapted to the Greek Rite, in which he omitted everything that disagreed with the Russian schismatic teaching. Brancati also composed in Chinese several volumes of sermons and homilies for the Sundays and feast-days of the ecclesiastical year. His work on the Chinese rites was published in two volumes at Paris in 1700. It bears the title "De Sinensium Ritibus politicis Acta", etc.

SOMMERVOGEL, *Bibl. de la c. de J.*, II, 81–83; MICHAUD, *Biog. univ.*, s. v.

B. GULDNER.

Brancati di Lauria, FRANCESCO LORENZO, Cardinal, Minor Conventual, and theologian, b. at Lauria in the then Kingdom of Naples, 10 April, 1612; d. in Rome, 30 November, 1693. Stricken at the age of seventeen with a dangerous illness, he made a vow that in the event of his recovery he would enter the order of Minor Conventuals. In July, 1630, he received the religious habit at Lecce in Apulia, and shortly after the completion of his novitiate was called to Rome. He subsequently visited several of the most noted convents of his order in Italy, in which he taught philosophy and theology with marked success. In 1647, he was again recalled to Rome and was shortly afterwards made guardian of the convent attached to the Conventual Church of the Twelve Apostles, where the minister general of the order resides. In 1653, he was appointed to the chair of dogmatic theology in the Roman University, and was later made Consultor of the Congregation of the Holy Office by Alexander VII who used to call him "The right arm of the Apostolic See". He was made chief librarian of the Vatican library by Clement X, and in recognition of his devoted services to the Church was raised to the cardinalatial dignity by Innocent XI in 1681. As cardinal he was actively connected with at least ten of the Roman Congregations. Brancati would in all probability have succeeded Innocent XI in the chair of St. Peter, had not the Spanish Government used its right of veto. As it was he received fifteen votes, the successful candidate being Cardinal Pietro Ottoboni who took the name of Alexander VIII. Brancati was a man of vast learning, singular piety, and unbounded liberality towards the poor. During the twelve years he was cardinal, he continued to keep faithfully to the observance of his obligations as a religious, remaining with his brethren in the Convent of the Twelve Apostles, the church of which he caused to be completed and adorned. He prepared himself for death in a most edifying manner, and had his tomb constructed with the inscription over it: "Ossa Fratris Laurentii Brancati de Lauria". He died in the eighty-first year of his age.

Brancati is the author of several important works on theology and asceticism. Perhaps the most noted of these is the commentary on the third and fourth books of the "Sentences" of Duns Scotus which appeared at Rome in eight folio volumes between the years 1653 and 1682. In this work he treats exhaustively wellnigh all the subjects that pertain to special dogmatic theology. In his "Opuscula tria de Deo", published at Rome in 1687, and at Rouen in 1705, he defends the gratuitousness of predestination which he endeavours

to show was taught by St. Augustine, though reliable authorities are not agreed as to whether St. Augustine was explicit on this point. Brancati's "Epitome Canonum", which went through two editions at Rome, four at Venice, and two at Cologne, contains a complete list of all the canons to be found in the general and provincial councils, in the Decretals of Gratian and of Gregory IX, and in the encyclical letters and constitutions of the Roman Pontiffs up to the time of Alexander VII. Among his ascetical works may be mentioned the "Opuscula octo de oratione Christiana", published at Rome in 1685, a work in which the author exhibits his profound knowledge of the spiritual life of which he became a master more perhaps by his own holy living than by the abstract study of asceticism. The life of Brancati, written in Italian by Gabriele Baba, was published in Rome in 1699.

HURTER, *Nomenclator* (Innsbruck, 1893), II, 346; GRAMMER in *Kirchenlex.*, II, 1192.

STEPHEN DONOVAN.

Branch Churches, THEORY OF. See CHURCH.

Branch Sunday, one of the medieval English names for Palm Sunday. The difficulty of procuring palms for that day's ceremonies led to the substitution of boughs of yew, willow, or other native trees. The Sunday was often designated by the names of these trees, as "Yew Sunday" or by the general term "Branch Sunday". (See PALM SUNDAY.)

FEASY, *Ancient English Holy Week Ceremonial* (London, 1897), 53 sqq.; THURSTON, *Holy Week* (London, 1904), 225–229.

JOHN B. PETERSON.

Brandenburg, formerly an electoral principality (the Mark of Brandenburg), and a diocese in the heart of the present Kingdom of Prussia, now a Province of Prussia and in ecclesiastical order an Apostolic Delegature.

I. HISTORY.—The lands extending eastward from the Elbe to the Vistula, once inhabited by Germans, were invaded by Slavic tribes who, during the sixth century of the Christian era, pushed their way as far as the Elbe and the Saale in Thuringia. Charlemagne was the first to check their advance; later, Henry I attacked them, captured Brennabor, the stronghold of the Lusatians, and to safeguard his conquests established the North Mark. In 939 Otto I brought the country of the Hevelli under his power, placed the Slavic races as far as the Oder under tribute, and to further the work of their conversion founded the dioceses of Havelberg and Brandenburg (948), which in 968 were placed under the recently founded Archdiocese of Magdeburg. Nevertheless, Christianity made slow progress. The hate of the subdued for their German conquerors, far from abating, burst forth in a great uprising (983). The Slavs pressed on as far as the Elbe, conquered Brandenburg and Havelberg, and destroyed the seeds of Christian civilization that had been planted there. Emperors Henry II and Conrad II, it is true, again brought the Lusatians under the power of the German Empire, but the real evangelization of the country was not resumed until the time of Count Albert of Ballenstädt, founder of the Ascanian line, who had been made Margrave of the North Mark by Emperor Lothair II (1134). Albert entered into friendly relations with the Wendish prince, Pribislav, at that time the ruler of Brandenburg, was chosen by him as his heir, and in 1150 took possession of the land, assuming at the same time the title of Margrave of Brandenburg. He brought colonists from the Lower Rhine and Utrecht, who by the methods learned in their old homes reclaimed the swamp lands of the Mark for agricultural purposes; the cities were peopled anew; the Dioceses of Brandenburg and Havelberg re-established; churches and monasteries erected; and the Wendish population soon won over to Christianity and the German Empire. The most active part in the conversion of the country was taken by the Premonstratensians and Cistercians. Even before the death of their founder, St. Norbert, Bishop of Magdeburg (1126-34), the Premonstratensians founded the monastery of Gottesgnaden (1131) and later that of Leitzkau, near Magdeburg (1149), as well as monasteries at Jerichow (1144), the city of Brandenburg (1165), Gramzow in the Uckermark (c. 1180), and elsewhere. The bishoprics of Brandenburg and Havelberg and the seats in their respective cathedral chapters were held by members of this order. The Premonstratensians were equalled in zeal, particularly during the thirteenth century, by the Cistercians, who had been introduced into the country by Albert's son and successor. Their foundations at Zinna (1170), Lehnin (1183), Chorin (1272), Jüterbog (1282), Himmelpforte (c. 1290), etc., were centres for the work of colonization, which was conducted on a large scale.

When the Ascanian line had become extinct, Emperor Louis the Bavarian annexed the Mark to his own territories (1320), but as early as 1373 the House of Wittelsbach was forced to relinquish Brandenburg, which in 1356 had been raised to the rank of an electorate, to Emperor Charles IV, who made it a dependency of the Bohemian Crown. Charles restored discipline, put an end to the extortion of the nobles, established the cathedral chapter of Tangermünde, and raised the Mark to renewed prosperity. The Dioceses of Brandenburg and Havelberg, however, ceased to be direct fiefs of the empire. Charles's son, Sigismund, mortgaged the Mark (1388-1411) and in 1411 appointed as *Statthalter* (Governor) Burgrave Frederick of Nuremberg, who took possession in 1412, and, having overcome the opposition of the nobles, was solemnly invested with the Mark of Brandenburg as an elector of the German Empire (1417). In this way Brandenburg passed into the possession of the Hohenzollerns, who have since held it without interruption. While Frederick I occupied himself almost exclusively with matters connected with the empire, his son, Frederick II (1440-70), concentrated his attention on the government of his territory. Distinguished from his youth for great piety, he promoted the religious life of his subjects, worked for the reform of the clergy and monasteries, made the cathedral chapters of Brandenburg and Havelberg centres of religious and secular culture, founded the Order of the Swan for nobles, and received from Pope Nicholas V (1447) the right of appointment for the dioceses of the Mark. His grandson John, surnamed Cicero (1486-99), took the initiative in the establishment of the University of Frankfort on the Oder, opened in 1506, and destined to be for a time a stronghold of Catholicism in the religious wars stirred up by Luther.

Dissensions between bishops and people had co-operated with other unfortunate circumstances in the Mark of Brandenburg, to create conditions amid which the new teachings took rapid root. Elector Joachim I (1499-1535), whose younger brother, Albert, was made Archbishop of Magdeburg and Bishop of Halberstadt in 1513, and in 1514 Archbishop and Elector of Mainz and Archchancellor of the German Empire, was extremely hostile towards the religious innovations, and endeavoured to have the edict formally condemning Luther passed by the Reichstag, at Worms. He forbade the circulation of Luther's translation of the Bible and the preaching of the new doctrines within his territory, and he prohibited his subjects from attending the University of Wittenberg.

Through the efforts of wandering preachers, nevertheless, Luther's teachings soon gained a large following, not only in various parts of the Mark,

but in the very family of the elector, counting among its adherents his cousin Albert, Grand Master of the German Order, his son-in-law, John of Anhalt, and even his wife, Elizabeth. Before his death, Joachim made his two sons, coheirs of his lands, solemnly promise fidelity to the Catholic Church. In spite of this, the younger, John of Küstrin, as early as 1538, became a Protestant and was followed by his subjects. The elder, Elector Joachim II (1535-70), influenced by his wife, daughter of the Polish king, Sigismund, at first held fast to the old Faith, though allowing Protestant clergymen to minister to several parishes in his territory; finally, at Spandau in 1539, he received the sacrament under both forms at the hands of Matthias von Jagow, Bishop of Brandenburg, likewise a partisan of the new doctrines. His defection was imitated by the majority of the cities in the Mark, Berlin at their head, and by the nobles almost as a body. The Bishops of Havelberg and Lebus alone offered steady resistance. In 1540 the electoral prince, by virtue of his authority as national bishop, issued a new church ordinance which was based on Luther's doctrine of justification, though preserving many Catholic institutions, such as the episcopal system of organization, and many Catholic ceremonies and customs, even to the Latin Mass, feasts of the Blessed Virgin, processions, etc., that the common people might not realize how the Catholic Faith was being gradually withdrawn from them. Between 1540 and 1542 an ecclesiastical visitation of the whole Mark was undertaken; the secular and regular clergy who had withstood the innovations of the elector were mercilessly expelled; the foundations of religious orders of men were suppressed; convents were converted into asylums for noble maidens; much church property and many endowment funds were confiscated and mortgaged to nobles or cities; and church plate and valuables were melted down. In 1543, the Consistory was constituted the highest spiritual authority. The elector took advantage of the rights obtained through the Religious Peace of Augsburg (1555) to complete the work of the Reformation in his principality. After the death of the last bishops who held fast to the Church—those of Lebus (1555) and Havelberg (1561) —he succeeded in having his eldest grandson, later Prince Elector Joachim Frederick, appointed bishop, thus preparing for the future secularization of the bishoprics. The administration of the Diocese of Brandenburg he confided to his son, John George. This gave the Reformation a complete victory; whatever savoured of Catholic teaching was gradually eliminated, and by the beginning of the seventeenth century, Catholic services were absolutely prohibited. Not until the establishment of the Kingdom of Prussia were Catholics again allowed to hold public worship. (For the later history of the Mark of Brandenburg, see PRUSSIA.)

The Diocese of Brandenburg, founded 1 October, 948, by Otto the Great, was bounded on the east by the Oder, on the west and south by the Elbe and the Black Elster, and on the north by the Uckermark. The first bishop was Thietmar or Ditmar (d. before 980); his successor, Dodilo, was murdered in 980. The succeeding bishops, after the heathen Wends again conquered Brandenburg (983), lived for the most part as coadjutors to other prelates in various places in Germany. Bishop Wigger, the fifteenth in line of succession (1138-60), was the first who was able to return to his diocese. Like his successors, as late as the middle of the fifteenth century, Bishop Wigger belonged to the Order of Premonstratensians, and formed his cathedral chapter from members of his order. Among the bishops of the fifteenth century, Stephan Bodeker (1421-59) distinguished himself by unusual activity along the lines of education and reform. Matthias von Jagow

(1527–44), the forty-fourth bishop, was one of the most zealous promoters of the so-called Reformation; although in 1528 he bound himself by oath to the pope and to Elector Joachim I to withstand the Lutheran innovations, he installed a Lutheran preacher in the city of Brandenburg in the same year, released his priests from their vow of celibacy (1535), and introduced the administration of Communion under both forms. After the resignation of his successor, Joachim, Duke of Münsterberg Prince Elector John George was appointed administrator of the diocese, which by that very act was secularized. The cathedral chapter was preserved in name, and consists to the present day of one cathedral dean, one senior and seven cathedral capitulars; these positions are bestowed as sinecures on Prussian statesmen, generals, theologians, etc.

II. Statistics.—Ecclesiastically, the former Mark of Brandenburg, with the city of Berlin and the greater part of the province of Pomerania, forms the "Apostolic Delegature for the Mark Brandenburg and Pomerania", which is administered by the Prince-Bishop of Breslau as Apostolic Delegate, indirectly through the Dean of St. Hedwig's in Berlin as delegate of the prince-bishop. According to the census of 1 December, 1900, the number of Catholics was 314,287; in 1907 it had reached 443,100. For the work of the ministry, the delegature is divided into 7 archipresbyterates with 82 spiritual charges, 6 curateships, etc. Catholic churches and chapels number 128. The clergy of the delegature include (in addition to the delegate of the prince-bishop, the army bishop for the Prussian troops, and the secretary of the delegation) 160 priests, viz.: 72 priests having charges, 54 chaplains and curates, 19 priests having other appointments, 15 living in community. The following orders of men have foundations (1907): Dominicans 1, with 10 priests and 7 lay brothers; Alexians 1, with 22 brothers; Poor Brothers of St. Francis 1, with 17 brothers. Orders and congregations of women have 42 foundations, with 733 sisters: Ursulines 1, with 24 choir sisters, 1 choir novice, and 12 lay sisters; the Sisters of the Good Shepherd 2, with 135 sisters; Sisters of St. Charles Borromeo 6, with 132 sisters; Dominicans of St. Catherine of Sienna 11, with 152 sisters; the Grey Nuns of St. Elizabeth 17, with 219 sisters; the Sisters of Mary 4, with 58 sisters; the Sisters of St. Joseph 1, with 13 sisters. The orders of women devote themselves almost exclusively to the care of the sick and the poor, and the education of young girls.

The Catholics of the delegature have but one private high school for boys; there are 4 Catholic high schools for girls, one of which is conducted by the Ursulines. There are 30 Catholic primary schools in Berlin and outside of Berlin 52; elsewhere Catholic children are given religious instruction by clergy and secular teachers, in some places in non-Catholic schools (140), elsewhere in churches and chapels, or in private houses. Religious orders of women conduct 15 protectorates for small children, and 9 schools of domestic economy and manual training.

The Catholic charitable institutions of the delegature are almost exclusively under the control of religious congregations of women. There are 10 hospitals and sanatoria, 5 homes for convalescents and those in need of rest, 1 institution for the mentally deranged, 1 maternity home, 29 institutions for visiting nurses, 7 homes for invalids, 6 for the care of small children, 8 crèches and homes for children, 3 hospices for men, 9 refuges and boarding-houses for women, 8 homes for girls out of work, 15 institutions for the care of orphans and the instruction of first-communicants, and 4 homes for the shelter and reclamation of girls. It should be noted that in many cases several of these institutions form one establishment and are under the same management.

The organization of Catholics in the delegature has reached a high stage of development. There are about 300 religious associations. Among the confraternities and rosary unions are: 30 societies of the Holy Family, 50 societies of St. Charles Borromeo, 35 associations of young men and societies of St. Aloysius, 25 congregations of Mary and societies of young women. Among charitable associations, mention may be made of the Society of St. Vincent de Paul, with about 40 conferences of men and women, and the Charitable Association (*Charitasverband*) for Berlin and other centres of charitable work. Among Catholic trade unions are Catholic labour unions, about 60; local societies of Christian workmen, 32; Catholic *Gesellenvereine*, 8; masters' unions, 3; apprentices' unions, 4; mercantile unions, 5; associations of teachers, 5; corporations of students, 10; national bureaus (*Volksbureaus*), 2, etc. Among political organizations are the National Union for Catholic Germany (*Volksverein für das katholische Deutschland*) and the Windthorst leagues. Catholic social organizations are numerous: societies of men, civic associations, choral unions and the like. (For politico-ecclesiastical relations see Prussia.)

Gercken, *Ausführliche Stiftshistorie von Brandenburg* (Wolfenbüttel, 1766); Raumer, *Ueber die älteste Geschichte und Verfassung der Churmark Brandenburg* (Zerbst, 1830); Riedel, *Die Mark Brandenburg im Jahre 1250* (Berlin, 1831–32); Raumer, *Regesta historiæ Brandenburgensis* (Berlin, 1836); Riedel, *Codex diplomaticus Brandenburgensis* (Berlin, 1838–69); Spieker, *Kirchen- und Reformationsgeschichte der Mark Brandenburg* (Berlin, 1839); Bassewitz, *Die Kurmark Brandenburg* (Leipzig, 1847–61); Winter, *Die Prämonstratenser des 12. Jahrhunderts* (Gotha, 1865); Idem, *Die Cisterstienser des nordöstlichen Deutschlands* (Gotha, 1867); Brosien, *Brandenburg im Mittelalter* (Leipzig, 1887); Heidemann, *Geschichte der Reformation in der Mark Brandenburg* (Berlin, 1889); Steinmüller, *Die Reformation in der Kurmark Brandenburg* (Halle, 1903); Curschmann, *Die Diözese Brandenburg* (Leipzig, 1906); *Amtlicher Führer durch die fürstbischöfliche Delegatur* (Berlin, 1906); *Märkische Forschungen* (Berlin, 1841–87); *Forschungen zur brandenburgischen und preussischen Geschichte* (Berlin, 1888——); *Märkisches Kirchenblatt* (Berlin, 1857——).

Joseph Lins.

Branly, Edouard, a French physicist and inventor of the coherer employed in wireless telegraphy, b. at Amiens, 23 October, 1846. After receiving his early education at the Lycée of St.-Quentin, his scientific studies were begun at the Lycée Henri IV at Paris, and in 1865 he entered the Ecole Normale Supérieure. In 1868 he became Licentiate in mathematics and physical science, and also *agrégé* in physical and natural science. After occupying a professor's chair at the Lycée of Bourges, he was appointed *chef des travaux* in 1869, and four years later he was made director of the Laboratory of Instruction in the department of physics at the Sorbonne. In the same year (1873) he won the doctorate in science with a thesis entitled "Electrostatic Phenomena in Voltaic Cells". In 1876 he resigned his post at the Sorbonne to become professor of physics at the Catholic University in Paris. He then took up the study of medicine, obtaining his degree in 1882, and thereafter divided his time between the practice of medicine, especially of physiotherapy and electrotherapy, and his researches in physics at the Catholic University.

Dr. Branly is best known by his researches concerning radio-conductors, and particularly by his so-called coherer. He began his studies in this field in 1890, being led to undertake them by observing the anomalous change in the resistance of thin metallic films when exposed to electric sparks. Platinum deposited upon glass was first employed. The effect was at first attributed to the influence of the ultra violet light of the spark. The variations in the resistance of metals in a finely divided state were even more striking, and they were shown by Dr. Branly to be due to the action of the electrical, or Hertzian, waves of which the spark was the source. The phenomenon was investigated at great length, and further experiment led to the coherer, which is simply a glass or ebonite tube containing metallic filings which connect the two ends of a wire conductor entering the tube. When the tube is made part of a battery circuit, the filings ordinarily offer a very great resistance to the passage of a current. But if a spark be produced in the neighbourhood between the terminals of an induction coil, or by the discharge of a Leyden Jar, the resistance of the filings is diminished, being no longer measured in millions but in hundreds of ohms. Upon tapping the tube the filings regain their normal resistance. This simple device was employed by Lodge in his researches and formed an important part of Marconi's successful system of wireless telegraphy. In fact the coherer first made wireless telegraphy possible. It serves as a receiver, being placed in series with a relay actuating a Morse sounder.

When electrical waves, sent out at a distant station according to an established code, impinge upon it, its resistance diminishes sufficiently to enable the relay to act and this in turn reproduces the signals in the sounder. A tapper automatically restores the resistance of the filings. Dr. Branly has given the name of radio-conductors to bodies which, like filings, can be made conductors or non-conductors at will. A number of other forms have since been devised, and he himself has found that the tripod coherer, composed of a metal disk making contact with a polished steel plate by means of three steel legs, is more sensitive and uniform in its action than the tube coherer. He has also applied his radio-conductors to "telemechanics without wires", i. e. to the production of divers mechanical effects at a distance by means of electrical waves. Among Dr. Branly's other researches have been those relating to the effect of ultra violet light upon positively and negatively charged bodies (1890–93), electrical conductivity of gases (1894), etc. It may be noted that the germ of the "antennæ", employed particularly in long distance telegraphy, may be found in his papers published in 1891.

Dr. Branly became Commander of the Order of St. Gregory the Great in 1899 and was nominated Chevalier of the Legion of Honour in 1900 for "having discovered the principle of wireless telegraphy". He received the *grand prix* at the Paris Exposition, 1900, for his radio-conductors, and the *prix Osiris*, in 1903, from the Syndicate of the Press. He was also made a titular member of the Pontifical Academy *dei Nuovi Lincei*. Besides his papers published chiefly in the "Comptes Rendus", Dr. Branly is the author of a "Cours élémentaire de physique" (5th ed., 1905); and "Traité élémentaire de physique" (3d ed., 1906). For various types of coherer and other apparatus employed in wireless telegraphy, cf. Collins, "Wireless Telegraphy" (New York, 1905).

H. M. BROCK.

Brant, SEBASTIAN, a German humanist and poet, b. at Strasburg in 1457 or 1458; d. at the same place, 1521. He attended the University of Basle where he at first studied philosophy, but soon after abandoned this for law, obtaining in 1489 the degree of Doctor of Canon and Civil Law. Prior to this, from 1484, Brant had begun to lecture at the university, practising his profession at the same time. He wrote a number of poems in Latin and German in which he set forth his religious and political ideals. The election of Maximilian as emperor had filled him and many other patriots with high hope. To see the emperor the supreme temporal ruler of Christian nations, and the Church the supreme spiritual ruler

on earth was his one great desire and henceforth coloured all his poems. Especially did he hope for the restoration of imperial power in Germany and the strengthening of the realm. But he was doomed to disappointment. In 1499 Basle was separated from the empire and became a member of the Swiss confederacy. Brant's position here now became untenable, and he decided to change his residence. In 1494 he had published his poem "The Ship of Fools", which had won him great popularity. Geiler von Kaisersberg, the famous Strasburg preacher, had made it the basis of a series of sermons, and he now recommended the appointment of Brant to the vacant position of city-syndic in Strasburg. The poet accepted the offer, and in 1501 he returned to his native city, where two years later he was appointed town-clerk and soon rose to considerable prominence. The remainder of his life was uneventful. Towards the great religious movement of his time, the Reformation, he maintained an attitude of passive indifference. Repeatedly he served his city in an official capacity, the last time in 1520, as spokesman of an embassy sent to the newly elected Emperor, Charles V, to obtain for Strasburg the usual confirmation of its ancient privileges.

The work to which Brant owes his fame is the "Narrenschiff" (Ship of Fools), a long didactic, allegorical poem, in which the follies and vices of the time are satirized. All the fools are loaded in a ship bound for Narragonia, the land of fools. But this plan is by no means carried out systematically, many descriptions being introduced which have no connexion with the main idea. The resulting lack of unity, however, has its advantage; for it enables the poet to discuss all kinds of social, political, and religious conditions. Not only follies in the usual sense of the word are satirized, but also crimes and vices, which are conceived of as follies in accordance with the medieval way of thinking. Hence among the fools appear such people as usurers, gamblers, and adulterers. A chapter is devoted to each kind of folly, and there are one hundred and twelve chapters in which one hundred and ten kinds of fools pass muster. As a work of art the poem does not rank high, though its tone is serious and earnest, especially where the poet pleads for his ideals, as in chapter xcix, entitled "Von abgang des glouben" (on the decline of faith). Knowledge of self is praised as the height of wisdom. The "Narrenschiff" enjoyed a tremendous popularity in Germany, which is attested by the numerous editions that appeared in rapid succession. But its fame was not confined to Germany. It was translated into Latin by Jacob Locher in 1497 (Stultifera Navis), into French by Paul Rivière in 1497, and by Jehan Droyn in 1498. An English verse translation by Alexander Barclay appeared in London in 1509, and again in 1570; one in prose by Henry Watson in London, 1509, and again in 1517. It was also rendered into Dutch and Low German.

Besides the "Narrenschiff" Brant wrote religious and political poems in Latin and German. He also edited and translated a number of legal and theological treatises. The most complete edition of the "Narrenschiff" is that of Father Zarncke (Leipzig, 1854), which contains also selections from Brant's other works. Other editions are by Karl Gœdeke (Leipzig, 1872) and F. Bobertag (in Kürschner's Deutsche National Litteratur, XVI). A modern German translation was made by Karl Simrock (Berlin, 1872). A new edition of the English translation of Barclay, by T. H. Jamieson, appeared at Edinburgh in 1874 in 2 vols.

For an essay on *Brant* see SCHMIDT, *Histoire littéraire de l'Alsace* (Paris, 1879), I, 189–333, and the introductions to the above-mentioned editions; see also JANSSEN, *History of the German People* (tr. London, 1896) I, 125.

ARTHUR F. J. REMY.

Brantôme, PIERRE DE BOURDEILLE, SEIGNEUR DE, one of the most famous of French writers of memoirs, b. in 1539, or a little later; d. 15 July, 1614. He was the son of a nobleman of Périgord and spent his childhood at the court of the Queen of Navarre. He studied at the College of France, at Paris, and at the University of Poitiers. When his education was completed he returned to court at a date not later than 1556, for he saw Mary Stuart "at the age of thirteen or fourteen, in the presence-chamber of the Louvre, publicly recite a Latin oration which she had composed, before King Henry, the queen, and all the court". In 1557 Bourdeille was granted the Abbey of Brantôme, the name of which he took.

Brantôme's life explains his writings, for it is the life of a traveller, a soldier, and a courtier. He himself in a few lines thus sums up its characteristics: "From the time when I began to outgrow subjection to father, and mother, and school, besides the journeys I made to the wars and the courts in France, I have made seven, when there was peace, outside of France to find adventure by war, or by seeing the world; I was in Italy, Scotland, England, Spain, Portugal—then in Italy again, at Malta for the siege, at La Goulette in Africa, in Greece, and other foreign places, which I have liked a hundred times better for sojourn than my own country, having the disposition of wandering musicians who love the houses of others better than their own." In 1558 he went for the first time to Italy. He returned to France only to leave it again in the suite of Mary Stuart who went to Scotland to take possession of her kingdom. Brantôme has left a touching account of this journey of the unfortunate queen. In 1562 he took part in the first civil war between the Catholics and Protestants of France and was present at the battle of Dreux, his first engagement. Then he began again to travel, going to Portugal, Spain, and to Malta; at this last place he spent three months and a half, the active and adventurous life of the Knights pleasing him so greatly that he thought for a moment of entering the order. On his return to France he took part in the second and third civil wars, was present at the battles of Meaux and St.-Denis, at the engagement at Jarnac, and the siege of La Rochelle. His military career came to an end in 1574 after the campaign in Périgord. The office of gentleman of the bed-chamber kept him near King Henry III, and his journeys now were merely to follow the court, where all that interested him seems to have been the love intrigues, the duels, the rivalries, and the assassinations.

Notwithstanding the services he had rendered, his bravery, and the amusement which his Gascon animation afforded the king, Brantôme never obtained an important post, but remained among "the minor attendants". This made him indignant and he contemplated going into the Spanish service when an accident—a fall from his horse—put an end to his active life. An invalid for four years, he retired to his château Richemond and resolved, in order to pass the time, to take up his pen and recount his past life. This was the occasion and the beginning of his career as a writer. But for this fortunate accident posterity would not have had the precious "Mémoirs" of Brantôme and would have lost in them an unequalled source of instruction concerning the men and affairs of the sixteenth century. The works of Brantôme include: "Vies des capitaines étrangers et français"; "Vies des dames illustres"; "Vies des dames galantes". His manner of writing is between the style of a biography and that of a personal memoir. At times he himself appears in his recital and most often he relates what he has personally seen. He says: "I have seen", "I have known". He has the most important qualification for a writer of memoirs:

curiosity. Wherever he went, and he travelled in countries of all kinds, he observed, he listened, he asked questions, he informed himself. But he has no power of criticism; he is a doubtful witness. He has, moreover, no sense of morality, in the modern meaning of the word. He admires but one thing in men and that is bravery; that this courage may be of a criminal character is of little consequence to him. He is not the man to bear malice towards others under pretext that they have "some little trifle of murder" on their conscience. In like manner he has few scruples either as to a choice of means or as to the sources of profit and ways of making gain. He writes in one place: "Nothing is so delightful, so sweet and attractive as spoils of any kind, whether gained by land or by sea." And he is strongly suspected of having plundered his benefice. In truth, when he talks of "honesty" and "virtue" he means what the Italians of that age called *virtù*, that is, personal courage, force, and elegance. Above all other spots Brantôme enjoyed the chamber and antechamber of the queen. He was never perfectly happy except when surrounded by the ladies who formed the real ornament of the court. This court of Catherine de Medici and its "flying squadron" of three hundred ladies made his paradise on earth. "Never since the world was made has its equal been seen." He made himself the historiographer of these dames of the Renaissance, both of the famous and of the notorious. Among his numerous portraits mention should be made of those of his favourites, Marguerite of Navarre and Mary Stuart. Light and frivolous, Brantôme passes over without mention some of the occurrences of his time of the greatest importance and most fraught with consequences. But we owe to him all sorts of small details, fingerposts to uses of the times. This brilliant and corrupt society, stamped with the characteristics of the sixteenth century, lives again in his "Mémoirs".

Brantôme is an uneven, incorrect, and rambling writer, but his works contain clever witticisms, imagination, and unexpected turns. He took more pains with his style than one would be apt to think, and sought renown as a man of letters. He directed his heirs to have the writings printed which he had made and composed "by his understanding and imagination, all very carefully corrected with much pains and time . . . I wish that the said impression be in beautiful and large type and in a stately volume in order to appear better. Otherwise I should lose my trouble and the glory that is due me." His desires, however, were not granted at once. His works did not appear for the first time until 1655 and then in a very imperfect and incorrect edition. It was not until the eighteenth century that his reputation, one of not very high order, was established. His writings are regarded, above all, as a collection of dubious anecdotes. From him the chroniclers of scandalous stories, the Tallemants des Réaux and the Bussy-Rabutins, are descended.

BRANTÔME, *Œuvres*, ed. by LALANNE in publications of the *Société de l'Histoire de France* (11 vols., 8vo); LALANNE, *Brantôme, sa vie et ses écrits*; DOUMIC, *Brantôme* in *Études sur la littérature française*, II.

RENÉ DOUMIC.

Brasses, MEMORIAL.—Just when memorial brasses first came into use is not known; the earliest existing dated examples are of the thirteenth century. They apparently originated from a desire to produce memorials of greater durability than the incised stone and marble slabs then in use, and their lasting value has been proved by the fact that they are incomparably in better condition than contemporary incised slabs of the hardest stone. The material of which they were made was principally manufactured at Cologne, and thence exported to all parts of Christendom; it is called *laton*, an alloy of copper, zinc, lead, and tin, beaten into thick plates of various sizes. England was the largest consumer, and in spite of the rapacious plunderers of the Reformation,

SYMBOL OF ST. JOHN (Donatello) BASILICA OF ST. ANTHONY, PADUA

Puritanic violence, and neglect, between three and four thousand brasses of the thirteenth, fourteenth, fifteenth, and sixteenth centuries have survived. The persons commemorated were as a rule represented upon the plates, usually life size, by deeply incised lines with very little attempt at shading, surrounded by architectural and heraldic accessories and inscriptions. In some cases the incisions were emphasized by black and red enamels, while in others the brasses were further embellished by the introduction of many-coloured Limoges enamels. These memorials attained their greatest artistic excellency in the fourteenth century, and then slowly deteriorated, becoming very much debased during the reigns of Elizabeth and James I, reaching their lowest type in the eighteenth century, when they ceased to be employed, until the Gothic revival brought them again into use. A great deal of time has been given by archæological investigators to the study of monumental brasses, and many finely illustrated works on the subject have been published; almost every county in England has one or more books upon those within its borders. Haines's "Manual of Monumental Brasses", with its 200 illustrations, is invaluable to the student; while the magnificent folio volume of coloured plates issued in 1864 by J. G. and L.

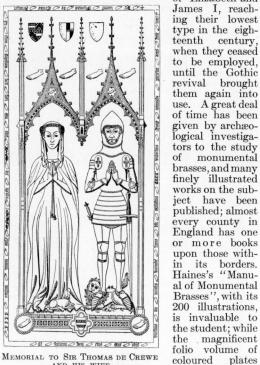

MEMORIAL TO SIR THOMAS DE CREWE AND HIS WIFE (Time of Henry IV)

A. B. Waller covers the ground of English brasses, and that of W. F. Creeny (London, 1884), fully describes those on the Continent. Military brasses can be studied in the transactions of the Yorkshire Architectural Society for 1885, and a history of the destruction of all kinds of brasses during the

progress of the Reformation in Weever's "Ancient Funeral Monuments" (London, 1731).

CARYL COLEMAN.

Brasseur de Bourbourg, CHARLES ETIENNE, ABBÉ, b. at Bourbourg (Département du Nord), France, 1814; d. at Nice in January, 1874. He left France for Canada in 1845 and was for a short time professor of ecclesiastical history at Quebec. In 1846 he was at Boston as vicar-general of that diocese, and then returned to Europe where he spent two winters at Rome, searching archives for documents relative to Spanish America. In 1848 he went to Mexico and became chaplain of the French Legation at that city. In 1851 he returned to Paris until 1854, when he sailed for New York and from there to the Isthmus and Central America, visiting Nicaragua, San Salvador, and Guatemala. He arrived in the latter city 1 February, 1855, and was made ecclesiastical administrator of the district of Rabinal in Vera Paz which position he occupied for a year. In 1857 he was again in France. In the years 1859 and 1860 he visited the Isthmus of Tehuantepec and Chiapas, also parts of Guatemala. In 1864 he became attached to the French scientific mission to Mexico, but political events in that republic drove him back to Guatemala in 1865, whence he returned to Europe. Exhausted by his long, arduous, and often dangerous labours, he died at Nice at the age of sixty. While an ecclesiastic worthy of high respect, and a teacher who has left a good record in the short period he devoted himself to instruction, Brasseur de Bourbourg was, above all, an indefatigable student of the American Indian, of his past and present. Hence the many and protracted journeys in Mexico and Central America, his permanent stay among aboriginal tribes, and his frequent visits to Europe were often made for the purpose of delving into archives for ethnographic, linguistic, and historic material from the past. He collected a large number of manuscripts and prints dating from early times in Central America, and improved his apostolic labours among the Indians for ethnographic purposes. His publications embrace the period from 1857 to 1871, and the value of these publications, if not unimpeachable, is still great. His defects were, at the outset, too great an enthusiasm and too vivid a fancy, and his intercourse with Prescott, whom he personally knew, was not calculated to lessen these failings. Later on, he was led to tread a very dangerous field, that of tracing relationships between American peoples and Eastern civilization and, as he advanced in years, the connection between the Old World and the New in pre-Columbian times, while not impossible, assumed in his mind the form of a fact absolutely certain. His main works are: " Histoire des Nations civilisées du Mexique et de l'Amérique centrale " (Paris, 1857–59, 4 vols.); " Voyage sur l'Isthme de Tehuantepec dans l'état de Chiapas et la République de Guatémala, 1859 et 1860 " (Paris, 1861); " Popol Vuh, le Livre sacré des Quichés, &c." (Paris, 1861); " Grammaire Quichée et le drame de Rabinal Achí " (Paris, 1862); " Quatre Lettres sur le Mexique " (Paris, 1868); " Cartas para servir de Introducción á la Historia primitiva de las Naciones civilizadas de la América setentrional " (Mexico, 1851); " Relation des choses du Yucatan " (Paris, 1864). In this work, which is a translation of the manuscript by Bishop Landa, the so-called Maya characters are given. Their value and significance are not yet fully established; " Monuments anciens du Mexique " (Palenque, etc., Paris, 1866); " Manuscrit Troano " (Paris, 1869–70); " Bibliothèque mexico-guatémalienne " (Paris, 1871).

With exception of short notices in some encyclopedias, there exists, apparently, no printed record of the life of Brasseur de Bourbourg. His own works, chiefly the Introduction to the *Histoire des nations civilisées etc. de Mexique etc.*, furnished the chief data for the above sketch.

AD. F. BANDELIER.

Brassicanus, JOHANN ALEXANDER, a German humanist, b. probably at Cannstatt, 1500; d. at Vienna, 25 November, 1539. He was a member of an ancient family of Constance, named Köl or Köll, latinized, *Brassicanus*, his father being Johannes Brassicanus, the Würtemberg humanist who taught in the Latin school at Urach up to 1508, and later in the pædagogium at Tübingen, but was chiefly known as a leader in the movement for the promotion of the humanities and as the author of a grammar then widely used, "Institutiones grammaticæ", thirteen editions of which were issued between 1508 and 1519. From his father, who died at Wildaad in 1514, Johann Alexander received an excellent education, which brought his intellectual powers to an early maturity, enabling him to matriculate at the University of Tübingen 13 January, 1514, and take his degree as Master of Arts in 1517. About this time he first gave evidence of his fertile poetic powers, and in 1518 he received the title of *Poeta et orator laureatus*. His coronation as poet must have taken place early in 1518, Emperor Maximilian at the same time granting him a coat of arms. The greatest humanists of the time kept in correspondence with Brassicanus, and are loud in praise of his intellectual powers. He lectured for a short time before the Faculty of Arts on the Latin poets; he also edited the eclogues of Calpurnius and Nemesianus which he had discovered. When, after Bebel's death (1516), a reaction once more set in against humanism, he availed himself of the first opportunity to absent himself temporarily from the scene of his former labours. In 1519 he attached himself to the suite of the royal orator Maximilian von Bergen, who was sent on various diplomatic missions by the king. After a sojourn in the Netherlands (1520) Brassicanus returned to Tübingen (1521) to pursue his study of law in connexion with his work as a teacher. In this way he was brought into intimate relations with Cantiuncula, the jurist of Basle. Removing to Ingolstadt, he received there the degree of Doctor of Laws, also succeeding Reuchlin in the important chair of philology (1522). His position in this stronghold of Catholicity, however, soon became untenable, as he, like so many orthodox minds of the time who openly sympathized with the reforming activities of Luther, was suspected of being a confirmed Lutheran. At this juncture he found friends ready to assist him, in Johann Faber and Johann Camers, who worked zealously for his appointment to the University of Vienna, and whose influence helped to give a more orthodox tone to his opinions on religious questions. In 1524 he was called to the University of Vienna as professor of rhetoric, next receiving the professorship of the laws of the Empire, and not till 1528 the coveted chair of Greek literature, in addition to which he still retained that of jurisprudence. His disapproval of the Lutheran movement was now most pronounced, partially as a result of a more profound study of the Church Fathers; he was particularly exercised over the disastrous influence of Lutheranism on educational activities. On the appearance of the Turks before Vienna (1529) he fled to his native city, where he remained for a considerable period of time. The succeeding years are marked by his editions of the Fathers and the classics. Often in poor health, he died at the prime of life, leaving only a very extensive library, as his material resources had at all times been meagre. His writings give no clear conception of his intellectual importance which his contemporaries found so noteworthy. Among his works of independent authorship are: "Oratio ad principes post obitum Maximiliani"

(1519); "Cæsar" (1519); "In divum Carolum electum Romanorum regem" (1519); and other occasional poems and addresses. These do not rise above the average level of the occasional literature of humanism. No subtler meaning and no original or striking thoughts are concealed under the mediocre forms of expression. For the history of the University of Vienna, on the contrary, Brassicanus is of great importance, being numbered among the most vigorous representatives of the humanist movement.

Among the editions issued by Brassicanus, the following are particularly well known: "Luciani Samosatensis Tragœdiæ" (1527); Salviani, "De vero judicio et providentiâ" (Basle, 1530); Gennadius, "De sinceritate christianæ fidei dialogus seu de viâ salutis humanæ" (Vienna, 1530); "Enchiridion de christianarum rerum memoriâ sive epitome historiæ ecclesiasticæ per Eusebium descriptæ auctore Haymone" (Hagenau, 1531); "Salonii Dialogi duo" (ibid., 1532); Pothonis, "De statu domus Dei" and "De magnâ domo sapientiæ" (ibid., 1532).

JOHANN LUDWIG BRASSICANUS, younger brother of Johann Alexander (b. at Tübingen, 1509; d. at Vienna, 3 June, 1549) went to Vienna with his brother in 1524 and likewise won distinction both as a philologist and jurist. He spent some time in the service of Sigmund von Herberstein and Nicolaus Olah, and obtained the title of court historiographer of the Roman King, after which he studied law at Heidelberg (after 1532). Having been professor of Greek in Vienna for a short time (1534) and likewise in Padua, where in 1536 he was made *doctor iuris*, he was appointed professor of the Institutes at Vienna in 1537, and later professor of canon law. King Ferdinand summoned him to his council, at the same time granting him letters patent of nobility and a coat of arms. He was twice rector of the university and four times dean. In 1544 he was made provincial superintendent, achieving considerable reputation as a public official. He seldom wrote anything for publication, and left only a few addresses and treatises on legal subjects.

The best source of information for Johann Alexander Brassicanus is his letters, most of which are still unpublished (Imperial Library of Vienna, cod. 9705 and 9737), likewise a volume of collected letters in the Munich Library; extracts from both by HORAWITZ in *Sitzungsberichte der Wiener Akademie, phil.-hist. Klasse*, LXXXVI, 274 sqq., LXXXIX, 188 sqq., XCIII, 425 sqq. Cf. ASCHBACH, *Gesch. der Wiener Univ.*, III, 126–135; KINK, *Gesch. der kaiserlichen Univ. Wien* (Vienna, 1854), I, Pt. II, 139; DÖLLINGER, *Die Reformation*, I, 525; HEFELE in *Kirchenlex.*, II, 1206 sqq.; HURTER, *Nomenclator* (3d ed., Innsbruck, 1906), II, 1275 sqq.; HARTL AND SCHRAUF, *Nachträge* [supplements] *zum 3. Band von J. Aschbachs Gesch. der Univ. Wien* (Vienna, 1898), 43–128; HERMELINK, *Die theolog. Facultät der Tübingen vor der Reformation* (Tübingen, 1906), 175.

JOSEPH SAUER.

Braulio, SAINT, Bishop of Saragossa, date of birth unknown; d. at Saragossa c. 651. In 631 he succeeded his brother John, whose archdeacon he had been, in the episcopal See of Saragossa. His influence extended not only to the bishops, but also to the Kings of Spain. In one of his letters (no. xxxvii) he urged King Chindaswinth to appoint a co-regent in the person of his son Recceswinth. To his insistence with his friend Isidore of Seville, is due the inception and completion of the latter's "Libri Etymologiarum". Braulio was present at the synods held in Toledo in 633, 636, and 638. The members of the last-mentioned council selected him to write an answer to Pope Honorius I, who had reproached the Spanish bishops with negligence in the performance of their pastoral duties. Braulio in his letter (no. xxi) cleverly and fearlessly defended the conduct of the Spanish episcopate. Towards the end of his life, he complained bitterly of the loss of his eyesight. He was buried in the church of Nuestra Señora Merced del Pilar, where his tomb was discovered in 1290. His feast is celebrated in Spain on 18 March, while the Roman Martyrology has it on the 26th.

Braulio is the author (1) of a life of St. Emilian (Æmilianus Cucullatus, or San Millan de la Cogolla), a priest of the Diocese of Turiasso, now Tarazona, and the writer of a hymn in honour of the same saint. (2) A collection of forty-four letters, of which there is no mention in antiquity, was discovered in the eighteenth century in the Spanish city of Leon. They form a valuable addition to our knowledge of the history of Spain under the Visigoths and were first published in the "España Sagrada" of Florez (XXX, 1775). (3) The division and titles of the "Etymologiarum Libri 20" of St. Isidore and a eulogistic notice of the latter's life, together with an enumeration of his writings, are also Braulio's work. This notice and catalogue he added to the "De Viris Illustribus" of Isidore. It is found printed in Migne, P. L. (LXXXI, 15–17). (4) Braulio's authorship of the "Acts of the Martyrs of Saragossa" is usually admitted. He may also have written the "Passio S. Leocadiæ". His works are accessible in P. L., LXXX, 639–720.

GAMS, *Kirchengesch. von Span* (Ratisbon, 1862–79), I, 320–329, 344; II, ii, 145–149, 224–227; VENABLES in *Dict. Christ. Biog.*, s. v.; CHEVALIER, *Rép. bio-bib.* (Paris, 1905), I, 692; *Anal. Boll.* (1905), XXIV, 153.

N. A. WEBER.

Braun, PLACIDUS, a Bavarian historian, b. at Peiting near Schongau in Upper Bavaria, 11 February, 1756; d. at Augsburg, 23 October, 1829. At thirteen he went as a choir-boy of the Benedictine Abbey of Saints Ulrich and Afra in Augsburg, and was a pupil for six years in the Jesuit gymnasium of the same city. He entered the Abbey of Saints Ulrich and Afra as a novice, 13 May, 1775, and was ordained priest, 18 September, 1779. In 1785 he was made head librarian of the abbey. He arranged and catalogued the library and made known to scholars the rarities it contained through the fine descriptions he gave of its early printed books and manuscripts in two works which he published while librarian. These publications were: "Notitia historico-litteraria de libris ab artis typographicæ inventione usque ad annum 1479 impressis, in bibliothecâ monasterii ad SS. Udalricum et Afram Augustæ extantibus. Pars I: Augs. Vindel. 1788. Pars II: Notitia . . . libros complectens ab anno 1480 usque ad annum 1500 inclusive impressos. Ibidem, 1789" and "Notitia Historico-litteraria de codicibus manuscriptis in bibliothecâ liberi ac imperialis monasterii O. S. Benedicti ad SS. Udalricum et Afram extantibus. Aug. Vindel., 6 partes, 1791–1796". After the abbey was dissolved, and its building converted into a barrack in 1806, Braun lived with a number of fellow-members of the order in a house near the church of St. Ulrich.

In these new surroundings he endeavoured to observe the rules of the order as far as possible, gave assistance in pastoral work, and devoted himself to the study of the history of the Diocese of Augsburg and its suppressed monastic foundations. He was made a foreign member of the Academy of Sciences of Munich, 3 August, 1808, which honour he accepted, but he declined to settle in Munich. Among his historical writings the following are still valuable: "Geschichte der Bischöfe von Augsburg, chronologisch und diplomatisch verfasst" (4 vols., Augsburg, 1813–15); "Codex diplomaticus monasterii S. Udalrici et Afræ notis illustratus", issued as volumes XXII and XXIII of the "Monumenta Boica", (Munich 1814–15); "Geschichte der Kirche und des Stiftes der hll. Ulrich und Afra in Augsburg" (Augsburg, 1817); "Historisch-topographische Beschreibung der Diöcese Augsburg", 2 vols. (Augsburg, 1823); "Die Domkirche zu Augsburg und der höhere und niedere Klerus an derselben" (Augsburg, 1829). Braun bequeathed his manuscripts, which were concerned chiefly with the history of the re-ligious foundations and monastic houses of the Diocese of Augsburg, to the diocesan archives.

LINDNER, *Die Schriftsteller u.s.w. des Benediktiner-Ordens im heutigen Königreich Bayern.*, II, 124–131 (Ratisbon, 1880); BERLIÈRE in the *Revue Bénédictine* (1899).

JOSEPH LINS.

Bravo, FRANCISCO, as far as known, author of the first book on medicine printed in America. His "Opera Medicinalia etc. (Authore Francisco Brauo Orsunensi doctore Mexicano medico)" was published at Mexico, 1570. Three years before, Dr. Pedrarias de Benavides had published his "Secretos de Chirurgía", at Valladolid in Spain, and while the latter work is invaluable for the knowledge of Indian medicinal practices, and is the earliest book on these topics known to have been published, the work of Dr. Bravo has the merit of being the first medical treatise printed in America. The first regular physician who came to Mexico appears to have been a Dr. Olivarez, although surgeon-barbers and other "healers and curers" are mentioned as having already practised with Cortez. Strict medical regulations were established by the municipal council of the city of Mexico in 1527, and extended to the apothecaries in 1529. Although the faculty of medicine at the University of Mexico was not founded until 1578, two "Doctors in Medicine" were received at that institution as early as 1553. Dr. Benavides was a native of Toro in Spain and came to Honduras about the year 1550. Thence he went to Mexico and returned to Spain, after having directed for eight years the hospital "del Amor de Dios" in the city of Mexico. Of Dr. Bravo it is only known that he was a native of Ossuna, and began to practice at Sevilla in 1553. He came to Mexico between that year and 1570. The date and place of his death are not known.

MENDOZA, *Historia del gran Reyno de China* (Antwerp, 1596), *Itinerario del Nuevo Mundo* in; GONZÁLEZ DÁVILA, *Teatro eclesiástico, etc.* (Mexico, 1649); YCAZBALCETA, *Bibliografía mexicana* (Mexico, 1886); MENDIETA, *Historia eclesiástica Indiana*, (1599, and published at Mexico, 1870); TORQUEMADA, *Monarquía Indiana* (2d. ed., Madrid, 1723). The latter contains incidental references to the early physicians of Mexico.

AD. F. BANDELIER.

Brazil, THE UNITED STATES OF.—A vast republic of central South America covering an area larger than that of the United States of America (if Alaska and the Philippines are not included). It extends from 5° N. to 33° 41′ S. latitude, and from 35° to 73° W. longitude. Its greatest length is 2,500 miles, its greatest breadth 2,600 miles, and it has an area of 3,218,130 square miles. It borders every other country on the continent of South America except Chile, being bounded on the north by Venezuela, British, Dutch, and French Guiana, and the Atlantic Ocean, on the east by the Atlantic Ocean, on the south by Uruguay and the Argentine Republic, and on the west by Paraguay, Bolivia, Peru, and Ecuador.

Brazil lies entirely east of the Andean mountain system. The basin of the Amazon occupies the northern and western portion of the country, and nearly the whole of this section is a vast plain, called the *Selvas*, which is, for the most part, less than 500 feet above sea level, and never exceeds 1,000 feet. The southern and eastern parts are plateaux, rising to heights of from 2,000 to 4,000 feet. Upon these plateaux are situated many mountain ranges. (This is said to be geologically the oldest part of the continent.) The mountain ranges of Brazil may be grouped into three systems, the most important of which is the Serra do Mar, which begins immediately north of the bay of Rio Janeiro, where the Organ mountains rise to 7,500 feet. This forms the southeastern slope of the plateau to the narrow strip of coast along the Atlantic. In this system, to the west of Rio de Janeiro, is the highest peak in Brazil, Itatiaia, which has a height of nearly 10,000 feet.

Connecting with this range near Rio de Janeiro, and stretching northward, is the Serra Central, while a third system stretches northwestwards, separating the headwaters of the São Francisco and Tocantins Rivers from those of the Paraná.

The Atlantic coast line of the republic is about 4,000 miles long. North of Cape St. Roque it is low, and the slope towards the sea is gradual, but to the south of this cape the coast line is more elevated, the slope to the sea is steeper, and in the extreme south it becomes abrupt. The northern coast is but little broken, thus having few good harbours and not many islands, but along the southern coast there are many fine harbours. The system of rivers is perhaps unequalled for their number and the length of their courses in any part of the world. They are especially important in the north of Brazil, where they constitute the chief means of travel through a region rich in natural resources. Owing to the copious rainfall, most Brazilian rivers are navigable throughout the year. The principal ones are the Amazon, which is 2500 miles long and is navigable throughout almost its whole length, the Tocantins, and the São Francisco.

CLIMATE.—Covering so large an extent of territory, Brazil naturally has variations of climate. In the lowlands of the north, which are within the tropics, there is great heat, and the year is divided between the rainy and dry seasons of tropical regions. The rainy season begins in December or January and lasts until May or June. The rest of the year is generally dry. However, dry periods frequently occur during the rainy season, and rainy periods during the dry season. In the highlands of the central and southern portions there are four fairly well marked seasons. The vast Amazon basin is remarkable for its small seasonal variation of temperature; the thermometer rarely rises above 90° or falls below 75°. In the two southernmost States, Rio Grande do Sul and São Paulo, the temperature at times goes to the freezing point, especially in the highlands. The prevailing winds are the trade winds from the east. These are the strongest in the valley of the Amazon from July to November, and thus the heat of the dry season is somewhat mitigated. The country is generally healthful, with the exception of the marshy banks of some of the rivers, the swamps, and regions where drainage is poor; in these places intermittent fevers are very common. Yellow fever has appeared at times, but has always been confined to the coast.

AGRICULTURE.—Brazil has extensive tracts of fertile land, especially along the Amazon and in the south-eastern portion; but the greater part of the plateaux is fit only for grazing. By far the most important product is coffee, of which Brazil produces more than any other country in the world. The principal coffee regions are São Paulo, Minas Geraes, Espirito Santo, and Rio de Janeiro. Sugar, the next product in importance, is extensively produced in Pernambuco, Bahia, and Ceara, tobacco in Bahia, and cocoa in the lower Amazon. Maize, beans, rice, and tropical fruits and vegetables are grown, but more for home consumption than for export.

MINERAL RESOURCES.—In mineral resources Brazil is probably the richest country in the world, but scarcity of population and capital have retarded its progress. It is rich in gold and diamonds, especially the State of Minas Geraes, which is to Brazil more than California and Pennsylvania together are to the United States. Gold-mining is carried on to a limited extent in Minas Geraes and Bahia, chiefly with British capital. These same two states were at one time the world's chief producers of diamonds, but the discovery of the South African mines has greatly depreciated the Brazilian product, which amounts to about 40,000 carats per year, and it is estimated that since the discovery of diamonds in

Brazil (1723) the total yield has been 12,000,000 carats, valued at $100,000,000. Besides gold and diamonds, Brazil is rich in iron, lead, copper, zinc, manganese, and quicksilver, but the mining of these is impeded by the lack of cheap fuel and labour.

MANUFACTURES.—These are generally on a comparatively small scale. The most important is the production of cotton goods, especially in the northern cities. In 1899 there were 134 cotton factories within the republic. Boots, shoes, cord, twine, hempen cloths for coffee sacks, furniture, saddles, and hats are also manufactured.

RAILROADS AND TRANSPORTATION.—Railway enterprise has made some little progress. In 1899 there were 8723 miles of railroad in operation, 4992 miles in course of construction, and 8440 miles projected. The most complete railroad systems are in the coffee regions of São Paulo, Minas Geraes, and Rio de Janeiro. A considerable proportion of these roads was built with a government guarantee of interest on the outlay. The rivers have steam navigation through many miles of their courses, and there are several Brazilian lines of coasting steamers.

COMMERCE.—The foreign commerce of Brazil is quite large and is increasing yearly. Coffee is the staple article of commerce, constituting about sixty per cent of the total exports. Most of it finds a market in the United States. Sugar is second in importance, and then come rubber, cotton, hides, tobacco, dye and cabinet woods, gold, and diamonds. The imports consist of all kinds of manufactured goods, cotton and woollen clothing, machinery, ironware, coal, petroleum, and foodstuffs. Great Britain controls about forty per cent of the import trade, Germany and France are next in importance, and the United States next.

POPULATION.—The population of Brazil, according to the official returns of 1890, was 14,333,915. A later census, taken in 1900, was rejected by the legislature as inaccurate. The population in 1903 according to an unofficial estimate was 19,500,000. According to the official figures of 1890, there were 14,179,615 Catholics; 143,743 Protestants; 3300 of other creeds; and 7257 who professed no religion. It will thus be seen that the country is overwhelmingly Catholic. The population is composed of: (1) people of pure Portuguese blood, who form a large percentage of the total; (2) full negroes; (3) native Indians; (4) people of mixed race (the most numerous of all); and (5) a few European immigrants. The Portuguese portion of the population, as they constitute the wealthy and educated class, have made Portuguese the national language. Most of the semi-civilized Indians, particularly in the eastern States, speak the *lingua geral*, a language adapted by the Jesuit missionaries from the original language of the Tupinambaras, one of the largest of the eastern tribes. There are many different tribes, among which the chief are the Tupi, the Guarany, and the Amagua.

GOVERNMENT.—Brazil is a federal republic of twenty States, with a Federal District. The constitution is modelled upon that of the United States. The legislative power is vested in the president of the republic and a national congress consisting of a Senate and a House of Representatives. The Senate consists of 63 members, three from each State and the Federal District, elected directly by the people for a period of nine years. The House of Representatives consists of a number of members elected by the people for a term of three years, one representative for each 70,000 inhabitants, but with a minimum membership of four for any State. All who are legally citizens of the republic exercise the right to vote, except beggars, illiterates, soldiers receiving pay, and those who for any reason may have lost their rights as citizens. The executive authority is exercised by the president, or in his absence or

JESUIT COLLEGE, ITÚ
BAY OF BOTAFOGO, RIO DE JANEIRO

BRAZIL

LAW SCHOOL, SÃO PAULO
HOSPITAL OF MERCY, RIO DE JANEIRO

disability, a vice-president. The president is elected by popular vote for a term of four years, and he cannot serve for two successive terms. He is assisted by a cabinet, the members of which he appoints or removes at will. The cabinet ministers preside over the following six departments: (1) finance; (2) war; (3) industry, railways, and public works; (4) interior and justice; (5) Navy; (6) foreign affairs. The president, by virtue of his office, is in supreme command of the Army and Navy. He possesses the veto power over legislation, but his veto may be overruled by a two-thirds vote of both Houses. The judicial power is vested in a federal supreme court consisting of fifteen members who are appointed for life by the president with the approval of the Senate. The States enjoy a greater measure of autonomy than those of the United States of North America. They are governed by their own legislatures and governors and have their own judicial systems. Each State is divided into municipalities; each municipality controlled by a council and a prefect.

RELIGION.—Under the Empire the Catholic was the only recognized Church, and it was supported by the States. Other religions were tolerated, but the Catholic was the official church. After the revolution of 1889, however, the separation of Church and State was decreed. The Provisional Government issued, 7 January, 1890, a decree proclaiming the separation of Church and State, guaranteeing freedom of worship, and declaring that no church thereafter should be subsidized by the government, nor in any way receive support either from the federal government or from those of the individual States. By the terms of this decree public officers were forbidden to interfere in any way with the formation of religious societies, and it was declared to be unlawful to stir up religious dissension among the people. Every religious body was at liberty to worship according to its own rites, while each individual could live according to his belief, and unite in societies with others, and build churches if he chose. The salaries of those in the service of the Church were ordered to be discontinued at the expiration of a year. The existing churchyards were secularized, and the question of the establishment of new cemeteries was left in the hands of individual communities. Religious bodies, however, could choose separate burial places, though always subject to the laws. The existing religious holidays, except Sunday, were abolished by another decree, and nine new ones established commemorating secular events. Later, a civil marriage law was passed, somewhat resembling those of the United States and France, and also a divorce law. This latter, however, bore the stamp of the religious

CHURCH OF THE CANDELARIA (PURIFICATION), RIO DE JANEIRO

training of the people, for by its terms, neither party was permitted to marry again during the life of the other.

The conversion of Brazil, beginning about the middle of the sixteenth century, was brought about by the Jesuits, after whom came the Franciscans, and these were followed by the Benedictines. The country to-day is almost entirely Catholic. Of the nineteen and a half millions, over eighteen millions are of the Catholic faith. There are 5127 churches and chapels, 2067 secular and 559 regular clergy; 2083 nuns engaged in hospitals and educational institutions; 524 schools, 12 large and 17 small seminaries.

ECCLESIASTICAL ORGANIZATION.—The entire republic is divided into the two ecclesiastical provinces of São Salvador da Bahia and São Sabastião (Rio de Janeiro). Each province containing nine suffragan dioceses, as follows: *Province of São Salvador da*

CHURCH OF BONFIN, BAHIA

Bahia (diocese created 1552, archidocese 1676); suffragan dioceses of Olinda (1676); São Luis do Maranhão (1676); Belem do Pará (1719); Goyaz (1826); Fortaleza, or Ceará (1854); Manaos (1893); Parahyba, (1893); Alagoas (1901); Piauhy (1902). *Province of São Sebastião* (diocese created 1675, archdiocese 1893); suffragan dioceses of Cuyabá (1745); Marianna (1745); São Paulo (1745); São Pedro do Rio Grande do Sul (1848); Diamantina (1854); Curityba do Paraná (1893); Petropolis (1893); Espirito Santo (1896); Porto Alegre (1900). Brazil has received a great honour at the hands of the present pope, that of having the first South American cardinal ever nominated chosen among its clergy.

EDUCATION.—During the three centuries of colonial rule, Brazil made very little progress in the education of its people. There were few schools except the Jesuit colleges, and whatever libraries there were belonged to private individuals. The wealthy classes sent their children to Portugal to study, while those who could not bear this expense remained ignorant. After the declaration of independence, in 1822, conditions were somewhat improved, but the educational system was so crude that little progress was made until 1854, when the whole school system was reorganized. Since then there has been good progress in education, literature, and science, especially in the large cities. In the interior education is in a backward state, owing to the isolation of the inhabitants, and to lack of facilities of communication. For this reason the percentage of illiteracy for the entire country remains high (above 84%). At the present time Brazil has a system of elementary, secondary, and higher education. Congress has the sole power to create institutions of higher instruction and secondary, or high-school, education throughout the country, as well as of primary education in the Federal District. The Constitution provides that instruction given in public institutions shall be secular, and that primary education be free and at the expense of the States and municipalities. In most of the States primary education is compulsory. The schools are generally well equipped with libraries, laboratories, and appliances and furniture of different kinds. The primary schools are divided into first- and second-grade schools. Secondary education is also organized on a good basis. At the head of these secondary schools stands the *Gymnasio Nacional* at Rio de Janeiro, which was formerly Pedro II College. The national institutions devoted to the higher, or university, education are: two law schools at Pernambuco and São Paulo; two medical schools at Rio de Janeiro and Bahia; a polytechnic school at Rio de Janeiro; a mining school at Ouro Preto, in the State of Minas Geraes; a school of fine arts at Rio de Janeiro. There are some excellent public libraries throughout the country, the largest being the National Library at Rio de Janeiro, which contains 235,000 printed volumes, 182,000 manuscripts, and 100,000 iconographical pieces. This institution was begun with the historical library which King John VI brought from Portugal and presented to Brazil, and it was greatly augmented by the collection of the great Portuguese writer Barbosa Machado.

HISTORY.— Brazil was discovered on the 26th of January, 1500, by Vicente Yanez Pinzón, a Spaniard who had been a companion of Columbus. Two months later Dom Manoel, King of Portugal, fitted out a squadron for a voyage around the southern end of Africa to the East Indies under command of Pedro Alvares de Cabral. Contrary winds, however, drove him far out of his course, and after drifting about for some time he came upon an unknown land. He cast anchor in a haven which he called Porto Seguro, on Good Friday, 24 April, 1500. On Easter Sunday an altar was erected, Mass was celebrated, and Cabral formally took possession of the country in the name of Portugal. He then continued on his way to India, but first dispatching one of his ships to Portugal to report his discovery. Cabral named the newly discovered land *Vera Cruz* (the land of the True Cross), but the king in notifying the sovereigns called it *Santa Cruz* (Holy Cross). Very shortly thereafter it began to be called *Brazil*, from the name of a wood which grew in that region, and the name has been retained ever since.

Although the country had been discovered by a Spaniard, Spain could make no claim. According to the Bull of Alexander VI (4 May, 1493) the dividing line between Spanish and Portuguese possessions had been fixed at a meridian 100 leagues west of Cape Verde. All discoveries east of this line were to belong to Portugal; those west of it to Spain. But

PUBLIC BUILDINGS, SÃO PAULO

in the year following, by the Treaty of Tordesillas, the dividing line was extended to 370 leagues west of the Cape Verde Islands, and Spain was thus barred from the eastern portion of South America. In order to encourage colonization, grants, or "captaincies", were given to prominent Portuguese who were willing to settle in the country. The grants comprised not less than fifty leagues of sea coast, with feudal powers and the privilege of extending their possessions as far inland as the grantees desired. Thus nearly the entire Brazilian coast was before long dotted with Portuguese settlements more or less skilfully administered. The first of these was established in 1532, at S. Vicente, within the present State of S. Paulo, by Martinho Affonso de Souza, and the others at intervals thereafter. Cattle and sugarcane were imported from Madeira, and the systematic cultivation of the latter began.

But these early settlers had great troubles—with the Spaniards, who sought to gain a foothold east of the line of demarcation; with the French, who were trying to establish themselves on the coast; with the natives who were antagonistic to all Europeans. So that, for their common protection, it was deemed expedient that the "captains" should forego some of their prerogatives, and concentrate all the Portuguese power into the hands of a Governor General appointed by the Crown. The first Governor General was Thomé de Sousa, who came over in 1547 and placed his capital at Bahia. The College of São Paulo was established in Piratininga soon after the arrival of the first Bishop of Brazil, in 1552, and of a number of the Jesuits in 1553. These first missionaries became friendly with the natives, and their college soon became a centre of influence. In 1555 Nicolas Durand de Villegaignon, aided by Coligny, the French Huguenot leader, settled with a few Frenchmen on a little island in the bay of Rio de Janeiro. But these French settlers were driven away by the Portuguese in 1560, and France was ever after unable to gain a foothold in Brazil. The settlement, however, was made permanent by the Portuguese who gave it the name of São Sebastião, and to this day Rio de Janeiro is officially called São Sebastião do Rio de Janeiro.

From 1580 to 1640, Brazil, as a dependency of Portugal, was in the hands of Spain, and during the latter part of this period Holland, being at war with Spain, seized a good portion of the country. A long struggle between Portugal and Holland for the possession of the country followed later, lasting until 1654, when the Dutch surrendered the places they held, and the Portuguese were rid of all European rivals. In 1763 the capital was changed to Rio de Janeiro, and the Governor was given the title of Viceroy of Portugal.

In 1807 Napoleon's troops invaded Portugal, with the intention of seizing the royal family. The prince regent, Dom João, fled, with the royal family, and under an English escort set sail for Brazil, where he was enthusiastically received. Here Dom João instituted several reforms, notable among which were the opening of all Brazilian ports to the commerce of the world and the decree of 16 January, 1815, declaring Brazil to be no longer a colony, but an integral part of the Kingdom of Portugal. Soon after this, the prince regent succeeded to the throne as Dom João VI. Revolutionary troubles in Portugal, in 1820, making it necessary for Dom João to return thither, he appointed his son Dom Pedro, a young man of twenty-three, "Lieutenant to the King" and set sail for Portugal in 1821. From that time the Portuguese Cortes began to regard Brazil with anxiety; Dom Pedro was considered as more Brazilian than Portuguese. Revolutionary disturbances, moreover, had broken out in several of the provinces, notably in Pernambuco and Bahia. To check the growing power of Brazil, measures were passed detrimental to her interests, and tending to a revival of colonial conditions. As the Brazilian members of the Cortes were greatly in the minority, their resistance could not be effective. Matters came to a crisis when the Cortes finally ordered Dom Pedro to return to Portugal. The Brazilians rallied and besought him to ignore the order. Realizing his opportunity, Dom Pedro struck the first blow for independence, his decision being received with the greatest enthusiasm. The few Portuguese troops stationed in the country made but a half-hearted resistance, and on the 12th of October, 1822, Dom Pedro was proclaimed Emperor and Perpetual Defender of Brazil.

A popular assembly was convened in May, 1823, and a message from the emperor was read proposing many liberal ideas to be embodied in the forthcoming constitution. But discontented spirits raised such bitter opposition in the assembly that the emperor dissolved it. He later appointed a committee of ten to draft the constitution, and it was finally adopted 24 March, 1825. Dom Pedro's popularity, however, soon began to wane. He produced the impression of not being truly Brazilian at heart, by his employment of a foreign force, by his continual interference in the affairs of Portugal, and especially by his appointment of Portuguese to the highest offices, to the exclusion of natives. The Brazilians became disgusted at seeing their government conducted by foreigners, and soon they were in open rebellion. After vain attempts to suppress the revolution, the emperor abdicated (7 April, 1831) in favour of his six-year-old son, Dom Pedro de Alcantara, and sailed away to Portugal.

The government was now placed in the hands of a regency, consisting at first of three members and later of a single individual. In 1840, when the young emperor had reached the age of fifteen, it was proposed by those who had become disgusted at the abuses of the regency, that the minority of Dom Pedro II be declared expired, in spite of the fact that the constitution had fixed the minority of the emperor at eighteen years. After a heated and acrimonious debate, the regency was abolished, and the young emperor placed in full possession of the throne (23 July, 1840). The new government had trouble at intervals with the Republican party, notably in 1848; but these risings were easily suppressed. In 1851 Brazil took an active part in thwarting the designs of the Argentine dictator, Rosas, who sought to seize Uruguay and Paraguay. Rosas was driven from the country and had to take refuge in England. In 1853 a decree was issued forbidding the importation of slaves. Yellow fever, until then unknown in Brazil, had made its appearance a short time before, and it was thought that the disease had been brought into the country by the slaves. In 1855 a fleet was sent to settle a dispute with Paraguay, concerning Brazil's right of way upon the Paraná River, the claim of Brazil being based upon the fact that the river has its origin within her

boundaries. The expedition was unsuccessful, and for ten years thereafter Brazil was hampered by many restrictions. In 1864 an outrage against Brazil on the part of Señor Lopez, the dictator of Paraguay, precipitated a conflict between Brazil, Argentina, and Uruguay on one side and Paraguay on the other. A bitter struggle now ensued, Paraguay offering a stubborn resistance which ended only with the death of Lopez in battle in 1870. Brazil, bearing the brunt of the war on her side, lost many thousands of men and a vast amount of money.

In 1871 the death-blow was given to slavery in Brazil by a decree providing that every child thereafter born of slave parents should be free. Slavery had been greatly checked since the decree of 1853 prohibiting the importation of slaves, so that, with this new law in force, it was not long before slavery came to an end in the country. On 1 May, 1886, the Princess Isabelle, regent of Brazil while the emperor was in Europe, proclaimed the abolition of slavery.

The fact that Dom Pedro reigned for nearly fifty years would indicate that he was liberal-minded, progressive, and enlightened, and that he was well liked by the people. But the work of freemasonry and the loss the planters suffered by the emancipation of their slaves created a spirit of disaffection. The outcome was that, after a bloodless revolution (15 November, 1889), Dom Pedro was deposed, and a Republic was proclaimed, with General Deodoro da Fonseca as head of the provisional government. A decree was issued continuing the imperial civil list and granting Dom Pedro a subsidy of $2,500,000, both of which offers were refused by him. On the following day (16 November) Dom Pedro and his family set sail for Portugal. The new Constitution, modelled upon that of the United States, was promulgated 23 June, 1890, and in February of the following year General Fonseca was elected president of the new republic. But before the end of that year his arbitrary methods precipitated a revolutionary movement in Rio de Janeiro, and he was compelled to resign. He was succeeded by the vice-president, General Peixoto. In 1893, a revolt, headed by Admirals Da Gama and Mello, was started; but it was of short duration. Rio de Janeiro was blockaded by the rebels, but the revolution collapsed soon after. In 1894 Peixoto was succeeded by Dr. Prudente de Moraes, who was called upon to face still another uprising, in 1897, under the leadership of Antonio Conseilheiro. After a few months this trouble also was crushed. In 1898 Dr. Campos Salles, who had been active in republican politics, succeeded to the presidential chair; Dr. Francisco Rodrigues Alves succeeded him 15 November, 1902, and Affonso Penna assumed office 15 November, 1906.

KIDDER AND FLETCHER, *Brazil and the Brazilians* (1857); AGASSIZ, *Journey in Brazil* (1868); LEVASSEUR, *Le Brésil* (1889); KOSTER, *Travels in Brazil* (1817); HARTT, *Geology and Physical Geography of Brazil* (1870); *United States Bureau of American Republics, Bulletin No. 7* (1901); SOUTHEY, *History of Brazil* (1810–19); VARNHAGEN, *Historia Geral do Brazil* (1855); DA SILVA, *Historia do fundação do imperio brazileiro* (5 vols., 1864–82); GALANTI, *Compendio de Historia do Brazil* (4 vols., 1896); GIRON Y ARCAS, *La Situación Jurídica de la Iglesia Católica en los Diversos Estados de Europa y América* (1905); WIDDER in BUCHBERGER, *Kirchliches Handlexikon* (1907); *Konversations Lexikon* (1903); SCHLITZ in *Stimmen aus Maria-Laach* (Freiburg im Br., 1906), LXX, No. 5.

VENTURA FUENTES.

Bread, LITURGICAL USE OF.—In the Christian liturgy bread is used principally as one of the elements of the Eucharistic sacrifice. Our Divine Lord consecrated bread and wine at the Last Supper, and commanded His disciples to do the same in commemoration of Him, and thus ever since bread made of wheaten flour has been offered at the altar for the officiating priest to consecrate into the Body of the Lord. It is a debated question whether Christ used leavened or unleavened bread at the institution of the Holy Eucharist, since different conclusions may be drawn, on the one hand, from the Gospel of St. John and from the synoptic Gospels on the other. History does not establish conclusively what the practice of the Apostles and their early successors was, but it may be asserted with some probability that they made use of whatever bread was at hand, whether azymous or fermented. Different customs gradually began to grow up in different localities, and then became traditional and fixed. The Eastern Churches for the most part made use of leavened bread, as they still do, while the Western Churches declared their preference for unleavened bread. At the time of the schism this difference of practice gave rise to much discussion of the value of their respective claims in following the example of Christ, and fomented bitter controversy even in recent years. Either kind of bread is, of course, valid matter for the sacrifice, so the difference of usage should be of little dogmatic importance. (See AZYMES).

In the primitive Church the bread and wine for the sacrifice were brought to the altar by the faithful, each contributing his share. A relic of this practice may now be seen in the rite of consecration of a bishop, for at the Offertory the newly consecrated bishop presents to the consecrator, among other gifts, two loaves of bread, one of which is gilded, the other silvered, and both ornamented with the coat of arms of the consecrator and of the bishop elect. A similar usage is found in the ceremony of the solemn canonization of saints, where at the Offertory, one of the cardinal-priests makes an offering to the pope of two loaves of bread, one gilded and the other silvered. Although in the beginning bread which served for common use was offered at the altar, still, growing reverence for the Holy Eucharist soon effected a change, so that the altar-breads were specially prepared, assuming a round form of moderate thickness, and were stamped with a cross or some other significant religious emblem having special reference to Our Lord in the Eucharist. These hosts became smaller and thinner in the Western Church until they assumed the light, wafer-like form now so common.

In the Holy Eucharist, bread thus serves for the offering of the sacrifice, and after the Consecration for the Communion of the celebrant, the clergy, and the laity, as well as for reservation in order that Communion may be brought to the absent, or that the Blessed Sacrament may be adored in the tabernacle or in the monstrance. In Rome at one time it was the custom of the pope to send a part of the consecrated bread to the priests in the titular churches that all might be united in offering the same sacrifice, so that this *fermentum*, as it was called, might in a spiritual sense leaven the whole mass of the faithful, and make them one with the pope in faith and worship. Bishops also were once accustomed to send the Eucharistic Bread to their priests for the same purpose, and also to each other to signify that they admitted one another into ecclesiastical communion. To prevent abuses and profanation to the Sacrament, this custom was early prohibited and soon disappeared. The usage then began of sending blessed bread instead of the Holy Eucharist to those who did not communicate at the Mass, and to those who might wish to receive this gift as a pledge of communion of faith. Those who did not communicate received bread offered at the Offertory of the Mass but not consecrated. It appears to have received no other blessing than that of the Offertory prayer, and was considered blessed because it formed part of the oblation. This bread is called *eulogia*, because it is blessed and because a blessing accompanies its use; it is also called *antidoron*, because it is a substitute for the *doron*, the real gift, which is the Holy Eucharist. The *eulogia* is prescribed in the liturgies of St. Basil and St. John Chrysostom, but now it is distributed to all,

both communicants and non-communicants. It existed also in the West, and is mentioned by St. Gregory of Tours, the Council of Nantes, and Leo IV, in terms which would make it appear a somewhat universal custom.

The little loaves or cakes of bread which received a special benediction and were then sent by bishops and priests to others, as gifts in sign of fraternal affection and ecclesiastical communion, were also called *eulogiæ*. Persons to whom the *eulogia* was refused were considered outside the communion of the faithful, and thus bishops sometimes sent it to an excommunicated person to indicate that the censure had been removed. Later, when the faithful no longer furnished the altar-bread, a custom arose of bringing bread to the church for the special purpose of having it blessed and distributed among those present as a token of mutual love and union, and this custom still exists in the Western Church, especially in France. This blessed bread was called *panis benedictus*, *panis lustratus*, *panis lustralis*, and is now known in France as *pain bénit*. It differs from the *eulogia* mentioned above, because it is not a part of the oblation from which the particle to be consecrated in the Mass is selected, but rather is common bread which receives a special benediction. In many places it is the custom for each family in turn to present the bread on Sundays and feast days, while in other places only the wealthier families furnish it. Generally the bread is presented with some solemnity at the Offertory of the parochial Mass, and the priest blesses it before the Oblation of the Host and Chalice, but different customs exist in different dioceses. The prayer ordinarily used for the blessing is the first or second *benedictio panis* printed in the Roman missal and ritual. The faithful were exhorted to partake of it in the church, but frequently it was carried home. This blessed bread is a sacramental, which should excite Christians to practise especially the virtues of charity and unity of spirit, and which brings blessings to those who partake of it with due devotion. The Church, when blessing it, prays that those who eat it may receive health both of soul and body: "ut omnes ex eo gustantes inde corporis et animæ percipiant sanitatem"; "ut sit omnibus sumentibus salus mentis et corporis". In some instances the *pain bénit* was used not only with superstitious intent, and its virtues exaggerated beyond measure, but also for profane purposes. This usage was brought from France to Canada, and was practised chiefly in the province of Quebec. There the *pain bénit* was blessed immediately after the Asperges, and then distributed to those who assisted at high Mass. The parishioners furnished it in turn, and vied with one another in presenting as rich and fine a *pain bénit* as possible, until finally the bishops, seeing that it entailed too much expense upon those in poorer circumstances, prohibited it. Within the last twenty-five or thirty years the custom has almost entirely disappeared.

In the present Roman ritual there are six blessings for bread. Two of these are entitled simply *benedictio panis*, and, as mentioned above, are often used for blessing the *pain bénit*. The third, entitled *benedictio panis et placentarum* (blessing of bread and cakes), is found in the appendix among the blessings which are not reserved. The other three are approved for particular localities, and are special blessings given under the invocation of certain saints, usually on their feast days, in order to gain special favours through their intercession. The first, approved for the Archdiocese of Cologne, is a blessing of bread, water, and salt given under the invocation of St. Hubert; the second, approved for the Diocese of Bois-le-Duc, is a blessing of bread and water under the invocation of St. Machutus; and the third, for the Diocese of Urgel, is a blessing of bread, wine, water, and fruit to be used on the feast of St. Blasius. Some other places have local customs of blessing bread on certain feast days, as for instance on the feasts of St. Genevieve, of St. Nicholas of Tolentino, and others.

Bread is also used in the rite of ordination of priests, as a Host is placed upon the paten which the candidates touch, in order to signify that power is given to them to consecrate bread into the Body of Christ. It is also sometimes prescribed in the rubrics that the bishop, after using the Holy Oils, as for example at confirmation and ordination, shall cleanse his fingers with crumbs of bread. Such, in the Christian liturgy, are the more important and general uses of bread, which, it will be seen, are confined principally to the Holy Eucharist. With the exception of some few blessings of bread for special purposes, most of these customs are closely connected with the Eucharistic sacrifice, and generally derive their origin from ceremonies practised with the Eucharistic bread. (See Antidoron, Azymes, Eucharist, Eulogia.)

Missale Romanum, Rituale, Pontificale; Migne, Encyc. Théol. (Paris, 1847), XVI, c. 1119; Du Cange, Glossarium mediæ et infimæ latinitatis (Niort, 1886), VI; Kraus, Real-Encyk. (Freiburg, 1880), I, 172, 451; Scudamore in Dict. of Christ. Antiq. (London, 1903), I, 600, 628; Neale, History of the Holy Eastern Church (London, 1850); Le Vavasseur, Cérémonial selon le rit romain (Paris, 1902), I, 460.

J. F. GOGGIN.

Breast, Striking of the, as a liturgical act is prescribed in the Holy Sacrifice of the Mass during the Confiteor at the phrase "Through my fault" (three times), at the Nobis Quoque Peccatoribus (once), at the Agnus Dei (three times), and at the Domine, Non Sum Dignus (three times). With bowed head, except at the Nobis Quoque Peccatoribus, moderately and without noise, the celebrant strikes his breast with the right hand, the fingers being held closely together and curved or fully extended, as the rubrics are silent on this point; after the consecration, however, with the last three fingers only, since the thumb and index finger, which are joined, must not come in contact with the chasuble. At the Agnus Dei in requiem Masses the striking of the breast is omitted, to show that the celebrant is thinking of the departed more than of himself. The faithful are accustomed to this practice as well as the priest.

The early Christians were familiar with the practice, as St. Augustine and St. Jerome testify. "No sooner have you heard the word 'Confiteor'", says the former, "than you strike your breast. What does this mean except that you wish to bring to light what is concealed in the breast, and by this act to cleanse your hidden sins?" (Sermo de verbis Domini, 13). "We strike our breasts", declares St. Jerome, "because the breast is the seat of evil thoughts: we wish to dispel these thoughts, we wish to purify our hearts" (In Ezechiel, c. xviii). A warrant for these statements is found in the Psalmist: A contrite and humbled heart, O God, Thou wilt not despise (Ps., l, 19). The petitioner at the Throne of Mercy would chasten his heart and offer it as a sacrifice to God, who healeth the broken of heart and bindeth up their wounds (Ps. cxlvi, 3). The ancient Christians were accustomed to strike the breast when they heard mention made of sensual sins; at the "Forgive us our trespasses" of the Pater Noster; and in detestation of the crime of the Jews, at the words of the Gospel, "Thou hast a devil", applied to Christ.

Seisenberger in Kirchenlex.; A. Carpo, Compendiosa Bibliotheca Liturgica (Bologna, 1885), s. vv. Confiteor, Nobis quoque peccatoribus, Agnus Dei, Domine non sum dignus.

ANDREW B. MEEHAN.

Brébeuf, Jean de, Jesuit missionary, b. at Condé-sur-Vire in Normandy, 25 March, 1593; d. in Canada, near Georgian Bay, 16 March, 1649. His desire was to become a lay brother, but he finally entered the Society of Jesus as a scholastic, 8 November, 1617. According to Ragueneau it was 5 October.

Though of unusual physical strength, his health gave way completely when he was twenty-eight, which interfered with his studies and permitted only what was strictly necessary, so that he never acquired any extensive theological knowledge. On 19 June, 1625, he arrived in Quebec, with the Recollect, Joseph de la Roche d'Aillon, and in spite of the threat which the Calvinist captain of the ship made to carry him back to France, he remained in the colony. He overcame the dislike of the colonists for Jesuits and secured a site for a residence on the St. Charles, the exact location of a former landing of Jacques Cartier. He immediately took up his abode in the Indian wigwams, and has left us an account of his five months' experience there in the dead of winter. In the spring he set out with the Indians on a journey to Lake Huron in a canoe, during the course of which his life was in constant danger. With him was Father de Noüe, and they established their first mission near Georgian Bay, at Ihonatiria, but after a short time his companion was recalled, and he was left alone.

JEAN DE BRÉBEUF, S.J.

Brébeuf met with no success. He was summoned to Quebec because of the danger of extinction to which the entire colony was then exposed, and arrived there after an absence of two years, 17 July, 1628. On 19 July, 1629, Champlain surrendered to the English, and the missionaries returned to France. Four years afterwards the colony was restored to France, and on 23 March, 1633, Brébeuf again set out for Canada. While in France he had pronounced his solemn vows as spiritual coadjutor. As soon as he arrived, viz., May, 1633, he attempted to return to Lake Huron. The Indians refused to take him, but during the following year he succeeded in reaching his old mission along with Father Daniel. It meant a journey of thirty days and constant danger of death. The next sixteen years of uninterrupted labours among these savages were a continual series of privations and sufferings which he used to say were only roses in comparison with what the end was to be. The details may be found in the "Jesuit Relations".

In 1640 he set out with Father Chaumonot to evangelize the Neutres, a tribe that lived north of Lake Erie, but after a winter of incredible hardship the missionaries returned unsuccessful. In 1642 he was sent down to Quebec, where he was given the care of the Indians in the Reservation at Sillery. About the time the war was at its height between the Hurons and the Iroquois, Jogues and Bressani had been captured in an effort to reach the Huron country, and Brébeuf was appointed to make a third attempt. He succeeded. With him on this journey were Chabanel and Garreau, both of whom were afterwards murdered. They reached St. Mary's on the Wye, which was the central station of the Huron Mission. By 1647 the Iroquois had made peace with the French, but kept up their war with the Hurons, and in 1648 fresh disasters befell the work of the missionaries—their establishments were burned and the missionaries slaughtered. On 16 March, 1649, the enemy attacked St. Louis and seized Brébeuf and Lallemant, who could have escaped but rejected the offer made to them and remained with their flock. The two priests were dragged to St. Ignace, which the Iroquois had already captured.

On entering the village, they were met with a shower of stones, cruelly beaten with clubs, and then tied to posts to be burned to death. Brébeuf is said to have kissed the stake to which he was bound. The fire was lighted under them, and their bodies slashed with knives. Brébeuf had scalding water poured on his head in mockery of baptism, a collar of red-hot tomahawk-heads placed around his neck, a red-hot iron thrust down his throat, and when he expired his heart was cut out and eaten. Through all the torture he never uttered a groan. The Iroquois withdrew when they had finished their work. The remains of the victims were gathered up subsequently, and the head of Brébeuf is still kept as a relic at the Hôtel-Dieu, Quebec. His memory is cherished in Canada more than that of all the other early missionaries. Although their names appear with his in letters of gold on the grand staircase of the public buildings, there is a vacant niche on the façade, with his name under it, awaiting his statue. His heroic virtues, manifested in such a remarkable degree at every stage of his missionary career, his almost incomprehensible endurance of privations and suffering, and the conviction that the reason of his death was not his association with the Hurons, but hatred of Christianity, has set on foot a movement for his canonization as a saint and martyr. An ecclesiastical court sat in 1904 for an entire year to examine his life and virtues and the cause of his death, and the result of the inquiry was forwarded to Rome.

ROCHEMONTEIX, *Les Jésuites et la nouvelle France* (Paris, 1896), II; SHEA, *The Catholic Church in Colonial Days* (New York, 1888); CHARLEVOIX, *Histoire de la nouvelle France*, tr. SHEA (New York, 1871); PARKMAN, *Jesuits in North America* (Boston, 1885); BANCROFT, *History of the U. S.* (Boston, 1853).

T. J. CAMPBELL.

Breda (BREDANA), DIOCESE OF, situated in the Dutch province of Brabant and suffragan of Utrecht. The city was founded in the twelfth century and with the surrounding territory formed the Barony of Breda, an imperial fief hereditary in the house of Nassau to which Queen Wilhelmina belongs. This barony was formerly within the ecclesiastical jurisdiction of the See of Liège, but became subject to Antwerp when Pius IV made that city (1561) the seat of a new diocese. Breda suffered much during the political disorders of the sixteenth and seventeenth centuries, in consequence of which the free exercise of the Catholic religion was more or less restricted. The iconoclasts in their outbreak of 22 August, 1566, left some sad traces yet visible at Breda. In the years immediately following, the city and its district were alternately held by Spanish troops and by those of the States-General, though the latter were destined to be its eventual masters. It passed finally into their hands 10 October, 1637, when it surrendered to the *Stadtholder*, Prince Frederick Henry.

Thenceforth, as was their custom, the Dutch Protestants prohibited strictly the exercise of the Catholic religion. At the Peace of Westphalia in 1648 the Barony of Breda was made directly subject to the States-General and lost thereby the last remnants of its ancient liberty. The " reformed " religion was alone allowed, and rigorous measures were used to prevent the exercise of the Catholic religion. However, as elsewhere in the Dutch provinces it was kept alive secretly by good priests whose exemplary zeal was imitated by their flocks, in whom the love of the ancient Faith was purified and intensified by persecution. This unhappy situation lasted until the beginning of the nineteenth century. A

little earlier the Batavian Republic had proclaimed (1796) liberty of religious worship, and in this Catholics saw a presage of better days. The constitution of the new Kingdom of the Netherlands (1815) guaranteed this boon more effectively.

When the Diocese of Antwerp was abolished by the Concordat of 15 July, 1801, Pius VII created by his Brief of 22 March, 1803, the Vicariate Apostolic of Breda and allotted to it the northern part of the former Diocese of Antwerp, then within the limits of the Batavian Republic. He also added thereto a part of the former Diocese of Ghent, situated in the province of Zeeland and known as Staats Vlaanderen. The Right Rev. Adriaan van Dongen (1803–26) was the first vicar Apostolic, and he established the diocesan (theological) seminary at Hoeven. By the terms of the Concordat, signed 17 August, 1827, between the Holy See and King William I, the Vicariate Apostolic of Breda was incorporated with the new See of Bois-le-Duc, whereby the ecclesiastical independence of the former was seriously threatened. Indeed, this arrangement was already becoming effective when the Belgian Revolution of 1830 broke out. The final separation of Belgium from Holland (1831) now made it impossible to execute the Concordat of 1827. The ecclesiastical situation, therefore, remained unchanged, except that the vicar Apostolic of Breda was made temporarily administrator Apostolic. When Pius IX re-established the hierarchy in Holland by his Brief, " Ex quâ die " (4 March, 1853), the Vicariate Apostolic of Breda was made one of the four suffragans of the new Archdiocese of Utrecht.

The first bishop of the new See of Breda was its vicar Apostolic, the Right Rev. Jan van Hooydonk, Apostolic administrator since 1826, and titular Bishop of Dardania since 1842. He died in 1867 and was succeeded first by the Right Rev. Jan van Genk who held two diocesan synods (1868, 1869) and died in 1874; later by the Right Rev. Hendrik van Beek, a celebrated Hellenist, who died in 1884; and then by the Right Rev. Peter Leyten. Besides the above-mentioned theological seminary at Hoeven there is a preparatory ecclesiastical seminary at Oudenbosch, known as De Ypelaar and founded in 1839. The new cathedral (1875) is dedicated to St. Barbara and is a masterpiece of the famous Dutch architect Cuypers. The finest of the churches of Breda is the superb Gothic edifice of Notre Dame, built in the fifteenth century. It has long been held by the Protestant community. In it may still be seen several sepulchral monuments of the house of Orange-Nassau. According to the most recent statistics there are in the Diocese of Breda 198,000 Catholics, 100 parishes, 245 priests in actual service, 23 charitable institutions, and 59 free (Catholic) schools.

KRUGER, *Kerkelijke geschiedenis van het bisdom van Breda* (Bergen-op-Zoom, 1875), i–iv; ALBERS, *Geschiedenis van het herstel der hierarchie in de Nederlanden* (Nimwegen, 1903–1904), i–ii; *Neerlandia catholica* (Utrecht, 1888).

GISBERT BROM.

Breeches Bible. See EDITIONS OF THE BIBLE.

Bréhal, JEAN, a French Dominican theologian of the convent of Evreux; died c. 1479. He was made Doctor of Theology at the University of Caen, 1443; Prior of St.-Jacques, Paris, 1455; and Inquisitor General of France, 1452, which office he held until 1474. At the instance of Charles VII, he was delegated to revise the acts and proceedings of the trial of Joan of Arc, and on 7 July, 1466, he solemnly declared her condemnation to have been iniquitous and unjust. His review of the case and his investigations, which are exhaustive, are given at length by the Dominican Fathers Belon and Balme in "Jean Bréhal, Grand Inquisiteur de France et la réhabilitation de Jeanne d'Arc " (Paris, 1893), and by the Jesuit Father Ayroles in "La vraie Jeanne d'Arc" (1790). Bréhal resigned his office in 1474 and retired to his convent of Evreux, where he spent the rest of his days in study, a model of conventual observance and discipline. He wrote: "De liberâ auctoritate audiendi confessiones religiosis mendicantibus concessâ", first edition, date and place of publication not given; later, 1479; and Paris, 1507.

QUÉTIF-ECHARD, Scriptores Ord. Præd. (Paris, 1719), I, 815; MANDONNET in Dict. de théol. cath. (Paris, 1903), 1127; HURTER, Nomenclator, II, 1059; Civiltà Cattol. (1894), IX, 463–467; MICHAEL in Zeitschrift f. kath. Theol. (1895), XIX, 136–140.

JOHN R. VOLZ.

Brehon Laws, THE.—Brehon law is the usual term for Irish native law, as administered in Ireland down to almost the middle of the seventeenth century, and in fact amongst the native Irish until the final consummation of the English conquest. It derives its name from the Irish word *Breitheamh* (genitive *Breitheamhan*, pronounced Brehoon or Brehon) which means a judge. That we have ample means for becoming acquainted with some of the principal provisions of the Brehon code is entirely owing to the labours of two men, O'Curry and O'Donovan, who were the first Irish scholars since the death of the great hereditary Irish antiquarian, Duald Mac Firbis (murdered by an English settler in 1670), to penetrate and understand the difficult and highly technical language of the ancient law tracts. After much laborious work in the libraries of Trinity College Dublin, in the Royal Irish Academy, in the British Museum, and in the Bodleian Library at Oxford, O'Curry transcribed eight volumes full of the so-called Brehon Laws containing 2,906 pages, and O'Donovan nine more volumes containing 2,491 pages. Nor was their labour by any means exhaustive. There are many more valuable Brehon documents still untranscribed in the library of Trinity College, in the British Museum, and in the Bodleian, and possibly some fragments in the Royal Irish Academy and other repositories. From the labours of O'Donovan and O'Curry the Government published in the Master of the Rolls series five great tomes and a sixth containing a glossary. But these five large volumes do not by any means contain the whole of Irish law literature, which, in its widest sense, that is, including such pieces as the "Book of Rights", would probably fill at least ten such volumes.

CONTENTS OF THE BREHON LAW BOOKS.—The first two volumes of the Brehon Law, as published, contain the *Seanchus Mór* (Shanahus More) or "Great Immemorial Custom" which includes a preface to the text, in which we are told the occasion of its being first put together and "purified", and the Law of Distress, a process which always had much influence in Irish legislation. The second volume contains the Law of Hostage Sureties, also a very important item in ancient Irish life, the law of fosterage, of tenure of stock, and of social connexions. The third volume contains the important document known as the "Book of Acaill", which is chiefly taken up with the law of torts and injuries. This book professes to be a compilation of the various dicta and judgments of King Cormac Mac Airt who lived in the third century, and of Cennfaeladh, a famous warrior who fought in the Battle of Moyrath (c. 634), and afterwards became a renowned jurist, who lived in the seventh. The fourth and fifth volumes consist of isolated law tracts, on taking possession, on tenancy, right of water, divisions of land, social ranks, the laws relating to poets and their verse, the laws relating to the Church, chiefs, husbandmen, pledges, renewals of covenants, etc. Although all these tracts go commonly under the generic name of the Brehon Laws, they are not really codes of law at all, or at least not essentially so. They are rather the digests or compilations of generations

of learned lawyers. The text of the *Seanchus Mór*, for instance, which is contained in the first two volumes, is comparatively brief. That part of it relating to the law of immediate seizure must, according to M. d'Arbois de Jubainville, have been written before the year 600, but not before the introduction of Christianity into Ireland, which probably took place in the third century. The rest of the *Seanchus* is not so old. The year 438 is that given by the Irish annalists themselves for the redaction of the *Seanchus Mór* which according to its own commentary was the joint effort of three kings, of two clerics, of Ross a doctor of the *Bérla Féine* or legal dialect, of Dubhthach a doctor of literature, of Fergus a doctor of poetry, and of St. Patrick himself, who struck out of it all that "clashed with the law of God". It is impossible to say how far certain parts of the law may have reached back into antiquity and become stereotyped by usage before they became stereotyped in writing. The text of the *Seanchus Mór* itself is not extensive. It is the great amount of commentaries written by generations of lawyers upon the text, and then the additional annotations written upon these commentaries by other lawyers, which swells the whole to such a size.

IRISH SOCIAL ORGANIZATION.—We are able to gather fairly well from these books the remains only of what must once have been an immense law literature, the social organization of a pure Aryan people, closely cognate with the ancestors of the modern Gauls, Spaniards, and Britons; and from what we learn of the ancestors of the present Irish people we may deduce a good deal that is probably no less applicable to the other Aryan Celts. Broadly speaking, the country was governed by a ruling class called "Kings", of different grades, the highest being the King of Ireland, and next to these were the nobles or princes called in Irish *Flaith* (pronounced flah or floih). In all there were, including kings and *flaiths*, nominally at least, seven different kinds of *aires* (arras), or nobles, and provision was carefully made that a wealthy farmer, or peasant grown rich through cattle, could, if he possessed twice the wealth of the lowest of the seven, and had held it for certain generations, become an *aire*, or noble, of the seventh, or lowest degree. Thus wealth and descent were carefully balanced over against each other. "He is an inferior chief whose father is not a chief", says the law. But it took care at the same time not to close to anyone the avenues to chieftainship. Under ancient Irish law the land did not belong to the king or the chief or the landlord, but to the tribe, and the lowest of the free-tribesmen had as much an inalienable right to his share as had the chief himself. In process of time parts of the tribal territory appear to have become alienated to sub-tribes or families, and the chief, who always exercised certain administrative duties with respect to the land, appears to have had certain specific portions of the tribal land allotted to himself for his own use, and for the maintenance of his household and relatives. He was in no sense, however, what is now known as a landlord, although the whole tendency of later times was to increase his power at the expense of his tribe and vassals.

FREE-TRIBESMEN.—The great bulk of the ancient Irish cultivators were the *Féine* (Faina) or free-tribesmen from whom the Brehon law is called in Irish *Féineachas*, or the "Law of the Free-tribesmen". In process of time many of these in hours of distress naturally found themselves involved in something like pecuniary transactions with their head-chiefs, and, owing to poverty, or for some other reason, were driven to borrow or accept cattle from them, either for milk or tillage. These tribesmen then became the chieftain's *céiles* (kailas) or vassals. They were known as *Saer-stock* and *Daer-stock Céiles*. The *saer-*

stock tenant—*saer* means free in the Irish language—accepted only a limited amount of stock; and retained his tribal rights, always most carefully guarded by the Brehon law, in their integrity. But the *Daer-stock*—*daer* means unfree—tenant, who took stock from his chief, became liable for heavier but still carefully defined duties. For instance for every three heifers deposited with him by his chief, he became liable to pay his chief the "proportionate stock of a calf of the value of a sack with its accompaniments", and refections for three persons in the summer, and work for three days. The tribesman, it will be observed, by accepting stock from his chief parted to some extent with his freedom, but his interests were carefully looked after by law, and it was provided that after food-rent and service had been rendered for seven years, if the chief should die, the tenant should become entitled to the stock deposited with him. If, on the other hand, the tenant died, his heirs were partly relieved from their obligation. It will be observed that while this to some extent resembles the well-known Metayer system, so common on the continent of Europe, where the landlord supplies the stock and the land, and the tenant the labour and the skill, it differs from it in this, namely that in Ireland the *saer-* and *daer-stock* farmer did not supply the land, which was theirs by right of their free tribesmanship. In this way, namely, by accepting stock from their over-lords, a rent-paying class grew up in Ireland, to which undoubtedly in time a large proportion of the ancient Irish came to belong, but the rent was paid not for the land but for the chief's property deposited with the tenant.

But outside of the Free-tribesman (the *Féine* and *Céile*) there grew up gradually a class of tenants who were not free, who in fact must have been in something very like a state of servitude. These were known by the name of *fuidirs* or *bothachs*, i. e. cottiers. They appear to have been principally composed of broken men, outcasts from foreign tribes, fugitives from justice, and the like, who, driven out of or forsaking their own tribes, sought refuge under some other chief. These men must have been natural objects of suspicion if not of detestation to the free tribesmen, and, being themselves absolutely helpless, and having no tribal rights of their own, they became entirely dependent upon their chief, who settled them down upon the outlying or waste lands of the tribe, or possibly at times upon his own separate land which as chief he held in severalty, and imposed upon them far heavier tolls or rents than the law permitted to be exacted from any other members of the tribe. As Ireland became more troubled by Northmen, Normans, and English, this class of tenant increased in numbers, so many tribes were broken or destroyed, and the survivors dispersed to find refuge in other tribes and under other chiefs. In this way there grew up gradually, even under Irish law, a body of tenants to whom their chiefs must have stood in the light of something like English landlords.

THE IRISH FAMILY OR FINE.—A curious Irish social unit was the *fine* (finna), consisting of one group of five persons and three groups of four, all males. The head of the family, called the *ceann-fine* (Kan-finna), and four members made up the first group, called *geil-fine*, the other three groups of four each were called *deirbh-fine*, or true family, *iar-fine*, or after family, and *inn-fine*, or end family. On the birth of a new male member in the *geil-fine* the eldest member of the group was moved up into the next four (the *deirbh-fine*), and one out of that four into the next four, and one out of the last four was moved out of the *fine* altogether, into the clan, or sept, this last male thereby ceasing to be a member of the family, or fine. The sept, to use the English term, sprang from the family, or the family after some generations grew into the sept and then into the clan, contracting a greater share of artificiality in proportion to its enlargement. Because, while all the members of the sept could actually point to a common descent, the descent from a single ancestor in the case of the whole tribe was more or less founded upon fiction. The portion of territory ruled over by a sub-king was called *tuath* (too-a) and contained within it, at all events in later times, members of different descents. The chief, both of the *tuath* and the sept, was elected by the tribe or clansmen. The law of primogeniture did not obtain in Ireland, and the selection was made of the man who being of the chieftain's near blood could best defend the tribe and lead it in both war and peace. "The head of every tribe", says the Brehon Law tract the *Cain Aigillne*, "should be the man of the tribe who is the most experienced, the most notable, the most wealthy, the most learned, the most truly popular, the most powerful to oppose, the most steadfast to sue for profits and to be sued for losses." As early as the third century, in a well-known piece of Irish literature, Cairbre, afterwards King of Ireland, is depicted as asking his father Cormac Mac Airt the question: "For what qualifications is a king elected over countries and tribes of people?" And Cormac in his answer embodied the views of practically every clan in Ireland down to the beginning of the seventeenth century. "He is chosen", said the king, "from the goodness of his shape and family, from his experience and wisdom, from his prudence and magnanimity, from his eloquence and bravery in battle, and from the number of his friends." He was, however, always chosen from the near kindred of the reigning chieftain.

IRISH CRIMINAL LAW.—There seems to have been no hard and fast line drawn between civil and criminal offences in the Brehon law. They were both sued for in the same way before a Brehon, who heard the case argued, and either acquitted or else found guilty and assessed the fine. In the case of a crime committed by an individual all the sept were liable. If the offence were one against the person, and the criminal happened to die, then the liability of the sept was wiped out, for, according to the maxim, "the crime dies with the criminal". If, however, the offence had been one causing damage to property or causing material loss, then the sept remained still liable for it, even after the death of the criminal. This regulation resulted in every member of the sept having a direct interest in suppressing crime. There was always a fine inflicted for manslaughter, even unpremeditated, which was called an *eric*. If the manslaughter was premeditated, or what we would call murder, the *eric* was doubled, and it was distributed to the relatives of the slain in the proportion to which they were entitled to inherit his property. If the *eric* were not paid, then the injured person or family had a right to put the criminal to death. This acceptance of a blood-fine or *eric* for murder was a great source of scandal to the English, but, as Keating points out in the preface to his history of Ireland written in Irish, it was really a beneficent and logical institution, made necessary by the number of tribes into which Ireland was divided. Nor was the punishment, though short of the capital one, by any means light, and it at least insured compensation to the murdered man's relatives, a compensation amounting to the entire "honour-price" of the murderer. For every man, from king to *fuidir* (the lowest class of tenant), had what was in Irish law termed his *eineachlan*, or honour-price, and this was forfeited in part or in whole, according to well-defined rules, for various crimes. It was always forfeited for taking human life. Clergy we find more heavily punished than laymen. A man of high rank was always fined more than one of low rank for the same misdemeanour. An assault on a person of rank was more severely punished than one on an ordinary man. Fines for crimes against the person were particularly heavy; two cows, for instance, was the fine for a blow which raised a lump but did not draw the blood. The punishments awarded by the Brehons were of a most humane character. There is no trace of torture or of ordeal in ancient Irish law.

From the earliest times in which the English invaders made the acquaintance of the Brehon law system they denounced it with the most unsparing invective. But all the Norman chiefs who ruled over Irish tribal lands governed their territories by it in preference to English law, and in Elizabeth's reign the great Shane O'Neill pointed out with bitter irony that if his Irish laws were so barbarous as the queen's ministers alleged, it was passing strange that three hundred families had migrated from the English pale and the beneficent operations of English law to take refuge in his dominions. As early as 1367 an English Statute of Kilkenny denounced Brehon law as "wicked and damnable". "Lewd" and "unreasonable" are the epithets applied to it by Sir John Davies. "In many things repugning quite both to God's law and man's" is how the poet Edmund Spenser characterized it.

The student, however, who views these laws dispassionately to-day, and merely from a juridical point of view, will find in them, to use the words of the great English jurist Sir Henry Maine, "a very remarkable body of archaic law unusually pure from its origin". It is, in fact, a body of law that reflects for us early Aryan custom in its purity, almost perfectly untainted or uninfluenced by that Roman law which overran so much of the rest of Europe. It is true that Brehon law does bear certain resemblances to Roman law, but they are of the slightest, and not even so strong as its resemblance to the Hindoo codes. It has in truth certain relations to all known bodies of Aryan law from the Tiber to the Ganges, some to the Roman laws of earliest times, some to the Scandinavian, some to the Slavonic, and some particularly strong ones to the Hindoo laws, and quite enough to old Germanic law of all kinds "to render valueless", to use the words of Sir Henry Maine, "the comparison which the English observers so constantly institute with the laws of England". "Much of it", says Maine, "is (now) worthless save for historical purposes, but on some points it really does come close to the most advanced legal doctrines of our day". "There is a singularly close approach", he remarks in another place, "to modern doctrines on the subject of contributory negligence, and I have found it possible to extract from the quaint texts of the 'Book of Acaill' some extremely sensible rulings on the difficult subject of the measure of damages, for which it would be in vain to study the writings of Lord Coke though these last are relatively of much later date". But he points out how heavily the Brehon Law pays in other respects for this striking anticipation of the modern legal spirit by its too frequent air of fancifulness and unreality and indulgence of imagination. In the "Book of Acaill", for instance, which, as mentioned before, is chiefly concerned with the law of torts, we find four long pages concerned solely with the injuries received from dogs in dog-fights—Ireland was famous for its hounds, and dog-fights figure more than once in old Irish literature—setting forth in the most elaborate way all the qualifications of the governing rule required in the case of owners, in the case of spectators, in the case of the "impartial interposer", in the case of the "half-interposer", that is the man who tries to separate the dogs with a bias in favour of one of them, in the case of an accidental onlooker, in the case of a youth under age, and in the case of an idiot. The Brehons, in fact, appear to have never hesitated about inventing or imagining facts upon which to base their theoretical judgments. They endeavour

to deal with all cases and all varieties of circumstances, and they have special rules for almost every relation of life and every detail of the social economy. A great number of the cases which come under discussion in the law books appear to be rather problematical than real, cases propounded by a teacher to his pupils to be argued on according to general principles, rather than actual subject for legal discussion.

ORIGIN AND GRADUAL GROWTH.—Ancient Irish law was not produced by a process resembling legislation, but grew up gradually round the dicta and judgments of the most famous Brehons. These Brehons may very well have been in old times the Irish equivalents of the Gaulish Druids. There were only four periods in the entire history of Ireland when special laws were said to have been enacted by legislative authority: first during the reign of that Cormac Mac Airt already mentioned, in the third century; second, when St. Patrick came; third, by Cormac mac Culinan, the King-Bishop of Cashel, who died in 908; and lastly by Brian Boru, about a century later. But the great mass of the Brehon code appears to have been traditional or to have grown with the slow growth of custom. The very first paragraph of the Law of Distress takes us back to a case which happened in the reign of Conn of the Hundred Battles in the second century, and this passage was already so antique at the close of the ninth century that it required a gloss, for Cormac mac Culinan (who died in 908) alludes in his glossary to the gloss upon this passage. There are many allusions in this glossary to the *Seanchus Mór*, always referring to the glossed text, which must consequently have been in existence before the year 900. The text of the *Seanchus Mór* relies upon the judgments of famous Brehons such as Sencha in the first century, but there is no allusion in its text to any books or treatises. The gloss, however, is full of such allusions. Fourteen different books of civil law are alluded to in it. Cormac in his glossary alludes to five. Only one of the five alluded to by Cormac is among the fourteen mentioned in the *Seanchus Mór*. This shows that the number of books upon law must in old times have been legion. They perished, with so much of the rest of Irish literature, under the horrors of the English invasion and the penal laws, when an Irish MS. was a source of danger to the possessor.

The essential idea of modern law is entirely absent from the Brehons, if by law is meant a command, given by some one possessing authority, to do or to forbear doing a certain thing under pains and penalties. There is no sanction laid down in the Brehon laws against those who violated them, nor did the State provide any such sanction. This was the great inherent weakness of Irish jurisprudence, that it lacked the controlling hand of a strong central government to enforce its decisions. It is a weakness inseparable from a tribal organization in which the idea of the State, which had begun to emerge under the early Irish kings, had beeen repressed. When a Brehon had heard a case and delivered his judgment, there was no machinery of law set in motion to force the litigant to accept it. The only executive authority in ancient Ireland which lay behind the decision of the judge was the traditional obedience and good sense of the people, and it does not appear that this was ever found wanting. The Brehons never appear to have had any trouble in getting their decisions accepted by the common people. The public appear to have seen to it that the Brehon's decision was always carried out. This was indeed the very essence of democratic government, with no executive authority behind it but the will of the people. There can be no doubt whatever that the system trained an intelligent and law-abiding public. Even Sir John Davies, the Elizabethan jurist, confesses "there is no nation or people under the Sunne that doth love equall and indifferent justice better than the Irish; or will rest better satisfied with the execution thereof although it be against themselves, so that they may have the protection and benefit of the law when upon just cause they do desire it".

INFLUENCE OF THE CATHOLIC CHURCH UPON BREHON LAW.—With regard to the influence of the Catholic Church upon Irish law as administered by the Brehons it is difficult to say much that is positive. Its influence was probably greatest in a negative direction. We have seen that the Brehons claimed the sanction of St. Patrick for the laws contained in the *Seanchus Mór*. We may also take it for granted that it was owing to the introduction of Christianity that Irish law began to be written down. The Gauls, as Cæsar tells us, had a superstition about committing their sacred things, which of course included their law, to writing, and if the Irish had the same, as is very probable, it did not survive the introduction of the Christian religion. Then the eric-fine for homicide, although it probably did not owe its origin to Christianity, yet supported itself "as a middle course between forgiveness and retaliation" by the case of one Nuada who had murdered St. Patrick's charioteer, being put to death for his crime and Patrick obtaining heaven for him. "At this day", says the text, "we keep between forgiveness and retaliation, for as at present no one has the power of bestowing heaven, as Patrick had at that day, so no one is put to death for his intentional crimes so long as eric-fine is obtained, and whenever eric-fine is not obtained he is put to death for his intentional crimes, and exposed on the sea for his unintentional crimes." Sir Henry Maine seems to think that the conception of a Will was grafted upon the Brehon Law by the Church, but if this were so, one would have expected that the law terms relating to it would have been derived from Latin sources; this, however, is not so, the terms being of purely native origin. In another most important matter, however, the Law of Contract, the Church may have exercised a greater influence; the sacredness of bequests and of promises being equally important to it as the donee of pious gifts. It is also likely that much of the law relating to the alienation of land, all the land belonging originally to the tribe, was influenced by the Church, and indeed the Church seems to have been the grantee primarily contemplated in these regulations. There is a great mass of jurisdiction relating to its territorial rights, and no doubt this must have affected the outside body of law as well. But all bodies of law are exceedingly unmalleable, and tend to resist the absorption of foreign elements; and Sir Henry Maine's conclusion is that "there has certainly been nothing like an intimate interpenetration of ancient Irish law by Christian principle". Still the effect of Christian principles must certainly have been great, but they were probably powerful as a negative rather than as a positive factor.

EXTINGUISHED BY THE ENGLISH.—The Brehon law code was ultimately extinguished by the English in every part of Ireland. So soon as they conquered a territory they stamped it out, banished or slew the Brehons, and governed the land by English law. It would have been a very inconvenient doctrine for them that the tribe owned the land or that the people had rights as apart from the chief. Whenever a chief made his submission he was recognized as owner and landlord of the territory of the tribe, and the territory was adjudged to descend by primogeniture to his eldest son. In this way the hereditary rights of the mass of the people of Ireland were taken from them, and they were reduced to the rank of ordinary tenants, and, the native nobility being soon exterminated, they mostly fell into the hands of English landlords, and were finally subjected to those rack rents which

have made the name of Irish tenant an object of commiseration for so many generations. The Brehon laws remained in force in every part of Ireland where the Irish held sway until the final conquest of the country. It has been shown that the system of land-tenure which the Fitzgeralds found obtaining in Munster in 1170 was left unchanged by them, and the land burdened with no additional charges until their subjugation in 1586. Duald Mac Firbis, the celebrated antiquary, who died in 1670, mentions that even in his own day he had known Irish chieftains who governed their clans according to "the words of Fithal and the Royal Precepts", that is according to the books of the Brehon Law. Amongst the many bitter injustices inflicted upon Ireland and the Irish by the English conquest none has had more cruel or more far-reaching effects than the abrogation of the Brehon law relating to land-tenure and division of property.

Brehon Laws (Master of the Rolls Series) I, (1865); II (1869); III (1873); IV (1879); V and VI (1901); D'ARBOIS DE JUBAINVILLE, *Études sur le droit Celtique, avec la collaboration de Paul Collinet* (2 vols. Paris, 1893); vol. I forms tome VII of M. D'ARBOIS' *Cours de littérature celtique*; MAINE, *Early History of Institutions* (London, 1875); GINNELL, *The Brehon Laws, a legal handbook* (London, 1894); HYDE, *A Literary History of Ireland* (London, 1903), xlii; *Memorandum on Land tenure*, appended to *Third Report of the Commission on Congestion in Ireland*, Government Blue Book (1907), 358, containing a brief but valuable summary of the secure and comfortable position of the masses in Ireland under the Brehon law system at the time of the confiscation of Munster, towards the close of the sixteenth century, and of the rack rents which followed the substitution of English law, by MRS. STOPFORD GREEN; JOYCE, *A Social History of Ancient Ireland* (Dublin, 1903); MEYER, *Kultur der Gegenwart* (Berlin, 1907), s. v. *Keltische Literaturen*.

DOUGLAS HYDE.

Bremen, formerly the seat of an archdiocese situated in the north-western part of the present German Empire. After Charlemagne's conquest of the Saxons, Christianity was preached in the region about the lower Elbe and the lower Weser by St. Willehad; in 787 Willehad was consecrated bishop, and that part of Saxony and Friesland about the mouth of the Weser assigned him for his diocese. He chose as his see the city of Bremen, which is mentioned for the first time in documents of 782, and built there a cathedral, praised for its beauty by St. Anschar; it was dedicated in 789. The Diocese of Bremen, however, was erected only under St. Willehad's successor, St. Willerich (804 or 805–838). After the death of the third bishop, Leuderich (d. 845), by an act of a synod of Mainz (848), Bremen was united with the Archdiocese of Hamburg, which, since its foundation, in 831, had been under St. Anschar, who was appointed first archbishop of the new archdiocese (848–865). Hamburg had been destroyed by the Vikings in 845, and in 1072, after a second destruction of the city, the archiepiscopal see was definitely transferred to Bremen, though the title was not formally transferred until 1223. Until the secularization of 1803 Hamburg had its own cathedral chapter. Before it was united with Hamburg, the Diocese of Bremen had belonged to the Province of Cologne. Despite the protests of the Archbishop of Cologne against the separation of Bremen, Pope Nicholas I, in 864, confirmed the new foundation, which fell heir to the task of evangelizing the pagan North.

Rembert (865–888), the successor of St. Anschar, summoned the Benedictines from Corvei and became a member of the order; his companion and successor, St. Adalgar (888–909), was likewise a Benedictine. Both performed great services in the conversion of the North to Christianity. When the Archbishop of Cologne renewed his claims to Bremen, Pope Formosus, in 892, gave the decision that the Archbishop of Bremen was to be independent of the Metropolitan of Cologne, but should take part in the diocesan synods of Cologne. Under St. Hoger (909–916), a Benedictine of Corvei, and Reginward (917–

918), the Hungarians laid waste the diocese and even burned the city of Bremen. The ninth bishop, St. Unni, died at Birka (936), while on a missionary journey to Scandinavia. Through the efforts of Archbishop Adaldag (937–988) Bremen received the privileges of a market town, and in 967 the same archbishop obtained the jurisdiction of a count over the city, as well as various crown-lands from Otto I, thus laying the foundation for the temporal possessions of the archbishops of Bremen. At the instance of Adaldag three dioceses were erected in Danish territory and in Schleswig, and made suffragans of Bremen. There was a considerable accession of territory to the archdiocese under Archbishop Unwan (1013–29). The foundation, however, of the later highly developed temporal power of Bremen was laid by Adalbert, the guardian and influential counsellor of Henry IV; during his long episcopate (1043–72) he brought nearly all the countships (*Grafschaften*) within the limits of the archdiocese under the jurisdiction of the Church of Bremen. His dream of raising the archdiocese to the dignity of a northern patriarchate, however, was never realized. During his episcopate the Obotrites were converted to Christianity, and three dioceses, Oldenburg, Mecklenburg, and Ratzeburg, were erected as suffragans of Bremen. The Northern churches, however, were separated from Bremen, and later placed under the Bishop of Lund, who was raised to the rank of a metropolitan in 1103. Like Adalbert, his immediate successors took the side of the emperors against the popes. At the Council of the Lateran the nominal metropolitan jurisdiction over the churches of Scandinavia was restored to Adalbert II (1123–48), but in reality they remained independent of Bremen. During the episcopate of Adalbert Vizelin succeeded in his task of evangelizing the Slavs of Holstein and Mecklenburg. Hartwich I (1148–68), Count of Stade, brought the countship of Stade under the jurisdiction of the Church of Bremen. His struggle with Henry the Lion, Duke of Saxony, entailed great suffering to the archdiocese; in 1155 the city of Bremen was captured and plundered, and the countship of Stade seized and held by Henry. After the fall of Henry, Archbishop Siegfried (1178–84) was the first to regain possession of the countship. Hartwich II (1184–1207) founded several monasteries and promoted the civilization of his people; his administration of temporal affairs, however, was unfortunate and involved the archdiocese in serious difficulties with Emperor Henry VI, resulting in revolt on the part of the bishop's subjects.

Dissensions over the choice of an archbishop and the claims of Palatine Count Henry, son-in-law of Henry the Lion, to the countship of Stade, left the Church of Bremen in sore straits at the beginning of the thirteenth century. After lengthy struggles, Archbishop Gerhard II (1219–57) finally received the undisputed possession of the countship, by which the territorial extent of the archdiocese was substantially fixed, covering, at that time, the land between the lower Weser and the lower Elbe, including also a part of the territory to the right of the mouth of the Elbe. Repeated difficulties over the choice of an archbishop, the growth of the city of Bremen, the continual disposal of diocesan privileges by archbishops under stress of financial embarrassment, misrule on the part of some archbishops, and other circumstances as well, contributed towards the decline of the power and splendour of the archdiocese which took place in the course of the fourteenth century. Among the more capable bishops of this period were: Johann Grant (1307–27), previously Archbishop of Lund, Burchard Grelle (1327–44), who held a synod in 1328 and redeemed several castles of the archdiocese, which had been given as security; Johann II Slamstorff (1406–21); Boldewin von

II.—48

Wenden (1435–41), who was also Abbot of St. Michael in Lüneburg; Gerhard III (1441–63), and others. Less fortunate was the episcopate of Heinrich von Schwarzburg (1463–96), who also became Bishop of Münster in 1466; the city of Bremen took advantage of the almost uninterrupted absence of the last-named archbishop to shake off the episcopal authority almost entirely. Several estates or castles were given in pledge or fell in ruins, and the dissatisfaction of the people under the ecclesiastical rule increased, preparing the soil for the Reformation.

The successor of Heinrich von Schwarzburg, Johann III Rohde (1497–1511), cleared the archdiocese of debt, and introduced many reforms. In spite of the fact that he came of the middle class, he sought to increase his prestige in the diocese by taking as coadjutor Prince Christopher of Brunswick (1500). The latter succeeded in 1511, but being at the same time Bishop of Verden, resided chiefly in Verden, and so was unable to devote the necessary attention to his Diocese of Bremen. The Reformation won its first victory in the city of Bremen; the Catholic clergy who opposed the new teaching were expelled, monasteries suppressed, the cathedral chapter banished from the city in 1533, and allowed to return only under the condition that no Mass be said or choir service held. From the city as a centre the new teaching spread through the surrounding territory and though the archbishop himself and some monasteries for a long time offered vigorous opposition, by the help of the Smalkaldic League, which Bremen had joined, the Reformation was introduced throughout the archdiocese, in some cases by force. After the death of Christopher (1558), the cathedral chapter, which was almost entirely Protestant by this time, chose as his successor his brother George (1558–66), who was already Bishop of Verden and Minden; during his episcopate, the archdiocese, with the exception of the cathedral and some country parishes, accepted the teaching of Calvin. George was succeeded by four Protestant archbishops, the last (1634) being Frederick, Prince of Denmark, later King of Denmark under the name of Frederick III. During the Thirty Years War, by the edict of restitution of Emperor Ferdinand II (1625), the archdiocese was restored to the Catholics, Catholic worship re-established, monasteries given back to the monks, and a college at Stade placed in charge of the Jesuits (1629–32). When, however, in 1632, the imperial troops were forced to evacuate the territory before the Swedes, Catholicism was once more rooted out. In 1644 the archdiocese was captured by the Swedes, and in 1648 secularized by the Peace of Westphalia, and ceded as a duchy to Sweden, and the cathedral chapter at Bremen suppressed. In 1712 the territory became a possession of Denmark, and in 1715 was purchased by the electoral Prince George of Hanover. The city of Bremen with the surrounding territory was in 1731 recognized as a free city of the empire, and in 1803 received an increase of territory; in 1815 it entered the German Confederation, in 1866 the North German Confederation, and in 1871 the German Empire. The greater part of the present duchy was ceded to Prussia with the Kingdom of Hanover (1866). Ecclesiastically, the territory of the former Archdiocese of Bremen is divided among several dioceses: the city of Bremen and the vicinity, with about 13,000 Catholics, is subject to the Vicariate Apostolic of the Northern Missions, the remaining territory to the Dioceses of Hildesheim, Osnabrück, and Münster.

A complete bibliography of the older literature on Bremen in DEHIO, *Gesch. des Erzbistums Bremen-Hamburg bis zum Ausgang der Mission* (2 vols., Berlin, 1877). Cf. also ADAMUS BREMENSIS, *Gesta Hamenburgensis ecclesiæ pontificum* (Hanover, 1846; 2nd ed., 1876), German tr. LAURENT, *Adams von Bremen Hamburgische Kirchengesch.* (Berlin, 1850), 2nd ed.

WATTENBACH (Leipzig, 1888); LAPPENBERG, *Geschichtsquellen des Erzstifts Bremen* (Bremen, 1841); WIEDEMANN, *Das Herzogtum Bremen* (2 vols., 1866); VON HODENBERG, *Bremer Geschichtsquellen* (3 parts, Celle, 1856–58); *Bremer, Ur-kundenbuch*, ed. EHMCK AND BIPPEN (5 vols., Bremen, 1873–1902); *Bremischen Jahrbücher* (21 vols., Bremen, 1684–1906); VON BIPPEN, *Geschichte der Stadt Bremen* (3 vols., Bremen and Halle, 1894–1904); BUCHENAU, *Die freie Hansestadt Bremen und ihr Gebiet* (3d ed., Bremen, 1900); VON SCHUBERT, *Hamburg, die Missionsmetropole des Nordens* (Bremen, 1904).
JOSEPH LINS.

Brenach, SAINT, an Irish missionary in Wales, a contemporary of St. Patrick, and among the earliest of the Irish saints who laboured among the Celts of that country. About the year 418 he travelled to Rome and Brittany, and thence to Milford Haven. He erected various oratories near the rivers Cleddau, Gwain, and Caman, and at the foot of Carn Engyli, or "Mountain of the Angels", which was his most famous foundation. Among his converts was Brecan (an Irish chief), the ruler of South Wales, about the year 425, and this Brecan is reckoned by the "Triads" as a saint, who founded numerous churches in Breck-nockshire, Carmarthenshire, Pembrokeshire, Den-bighshire, and Anglesey. From the Welsh "Lives" we learn that St. Brenach died 7 April, on which day his feast is celebrated. His church, overhanging the Severn, is a lasting memorial of the Irish pilgrim who was the instrument under God for the conversion of a great part of Wales.

REES, *Lives of the Cambro-British Saints* (Llandovery, 1853); ID., *Essay on the Welsh Saints* (1836); WILLIAMS, *Ecclesiastical Antiquities of the Cymry;* ID., *The Welsh Triads;* MORAN, *Irish Saints in Great Britain* (1903), new edition; FENTON, *Pembrokeshire; Acta SS.*, I, April; *Martyrologium Anglicanum;* O'HANLON, *Lives of the Irish Saints*, IV, 7 April.
W. H. GRATTAN FLOOD.

Brenan, MICHAEL JOHN, ecclesiastical historian, b. in Kilkenny, Ireland, in 1780; d. at Dublin, February, 1847. He was the son of a stonemason and after his ordination to the priesthood, speedily obtained reputation as a preacher, but, owing to his vanity and pride, came into collision with his bishop, and was suspended. He then left the Church, became a Protestant, and was taken up by the Priests' Protection Society under whose auspices he was announced to preach in St. George's Church, Dublin. In the meantime he reconsidered his position and repented of his folly. He resolved to make public reparation for his fault, and on the Sunday in 1809, when he was announced to commence his campaign against the Church, he ascended the pulpit of St. George's, began by blessing himself most reverently, and then to the relief of his audience took up the Bible, and said "This is the Word of God". After a brief pause, he added deliberately and earnestly, "And I swear by its contents that every word I have uttered against the Catholic Church is a lie", and at once left the building. He went to a neighbouring Capuchin friary, explained what had happened, and begged to be admitted into the order. After some time, his prayers were granted, and he became a Franciscan at Wexford where in later years he wrote (as a penance, it is said) his valuable "Ecclesiastical History of Ireland" (2 vols., Dublin, 1840, revised ed., 1864).

HOGAN, *History of Kilkenny* (pulpit incident reproduced in *Ossory Archæological Society Journal*, 1879), 423–425; *Mirror* files (Waterford, 7 November, 1809).
D. J. O'DONOGHUE.

Brendan, SAINT, of Ardfert and Clonfert, known also as Brendan the Voyager, b. in Ciarraighe Lu-achra, near the present city of Tralee, County Kerry, Ireland, in 484; d. at Enachduin, now Annaghdown, in 577. He was baptized at Tubrid, near Ardfert, by Bishop Erc. For five years he was educated under St. Ita, "the Brigid of Munster", and he completed his studies under St. Erc, who ordained him priest in 512. Between the years 512 and 530 St. Brendan built monastic cells at Ardfert, and at Shan-akeel or Ballynevinoorach, at the foot of Brandon Hill. It was from here that he set out on his famous voyage for the Land of Delight. The old Irish Calendars assigned a special feast for the "Egressio familiæ S. Brendani", on 22 March; and St. Aengus the Culdee, in his Litany, at the close of the eighth century, invokes "the sixty who accompanied St. Brendan in his quest of the Land of Promise". Naturally, the story of the seven years' voyage was carried about, and, soon, crowds of pilgrims and students flocked to Ardfert. Thus, in a few years, many religious houses were formed at Gallerus, Kilmalchedor, Brandon Hill, and the Blasquet Islands, in order to meet the wants of those who came for spiritual guidance to St. Brendan.

Having established the See of Ardfert, St. Brendan proceeded to Thomond, and founded a monastery at Inis-da-druim (now Coney Island, County Clare), in the present parish of Killadysert, about the year 550. He then journeyed to Wales, and thence to Iona, and left traces of his apostolic zeal at Kilbran-don (near Oban) and Kilbrennan Sound. After a three years' mission in Britain he returned to Ireland, and did much good work in various parts of Leinster, especially at Dysart (Co. Kilkenny), Killiney (Tub-berboe), and Brandon Hill. He founded the Sees of Ardfert, and of Annaghdown, and established churches at Inchiquin, County Galway, and at Inishglora, County Mayo. His most celebrated foundation was Clonfert, in 557, over which he appointed St. Moinenn as Prior and Head Master. St. Brendan was interred in Clonfert, and his feast is kept on 16 May.
W. H. GRATTAN FLOOD.

VOYAGE OF SAINT BRENDAN.—Saint Brendan belongs to that glorious period in the history of Ireland when the island in the first glow of its conversion to Christianity sent forth its earliest messengers of the Faith to the continent and to the regions of the sea. It is, therefore, perhaps possible that the legends, current in the ninth and committed to writing in the eleventh century, have for foundation an actual sea-voyage the destination of which cannot however be determined. These adventures were called the "Navigatio Brendani", the Voyage or Wandering of St. Brendan, but there is no historical proof of this journey. Brendan is said to have sailed in search of a fabled Paradise with a company of monks, the number of which is variously stated as from 18 to 150. After a long voyage of seven years they reached the "Terra Repromissionis", or Paradise, a most beautiful land with luxuriant vegetation. The narrative offers a wide range for the interpretation of the geographical position of this land and with it of the scene of the legend of St. Brendan. On the Catalonian chart (1375) it is placed not very far west of the southern part of Ireland. On other charts, however, it is identified with the "Fortunate Isles" of the ancients and is placed towards the south. Thus it is put among the Canary Islands on the Herford chart of the world (beginning of the fourteenth century); it is substituted for the island of Madeira on the chart of the Pizzigani (1367), on the Weimar chart (1424), and on the chart of Beccario (1435). As the increase in knowledge of this region proved the former belief to be false the island was pushed further out into the ocean. It is found 60° west of the first meridian and very near the equator on Martin Behaim's globe. The inhabitants of Ferro, Gomera, Madeira, and the Azores positively declared to Columbus that they had often seen the island and continued to make the assertion up to a far later period. At the end of the sixteenth century the failure to find the island led the cartographers Apianus and Ortelius to place it once more in the ocean west of Ireland; finally, in the early part of the nineteenth century belief in the existence of the island was completely abandoned. But soon a new theory arose, maintained by those scholars who claim for the Irish the glory of discovering America, namely, Mac-Carthy, Rafn, Beamish, O'Hanlon, Beauvois, Gaffarel, etc. They rest this claim on the account of the Northmen who found a region south of Vinland and the Chesapeake Bay called "Hvitramamaland" (Land of the White Men) or "Irland ed mikla" (Greater Ireland), and on the tradition of the Shawano (Shawnee) Indians that in earlier times Florida was inhabited by a white tribe which had iron implements. In regard to Brendan himself the point is made that he could only have gained a knowledge of foreign animals and plants, such as are described in the legend, by visiting the western continent. On the other hand, doubt was very early expressed as to the value of the narrative for the history of discovery. Honorius of Augsburg declared that the island had vanished; Vincent of Beauvais denied the authenticity of the entire pilgrimage, and the Bollandists do not recognize it. Among the geographers, Alexander von Humboldt, Peschel, Ruge, and Kretschmer, place the story among geographical legends, which are of interest for the history of civilization but which can lay no claim to serious consideration from the point of view of geography. The oldest account of the legend is in Latin, "Navigatio Sancti Brendani", and belongs to the tenth or eleventh century; the first French translation dates from 1125; since the thirteenth century the legend has appeared in the literatures of the Netherlands, Germany, and England. A list of the numerous manuscripts is given by Hardy, "Descriptive Catalogue of Materials Relating to the History of Great Britain and Ireland" (London, 1862), I, 159 sqq. Editions have been issued by: Jubinal, "La Légende latine de S. Brandaines avec une traduction inédite en prose et en poésie romanes" (Paris, 1836); Wright, "St. Brandan, a Medieval Legend of the Sea, in English Verse, and Prose" (London, 1844); C. Schröder, "Sanct Brandan, ein latinischer und drei deutsche Texte" (Erlangen, 1871); Brill, "Van Sinte Brandane" (Gronningen, 1871); Francisque Michel, "Les Voyages merveilleux de Saint Brandan à la recherche du paradis terrestre" (Paris, 1878); Fr. Novati, "La Navigatio Sancti Brandani in antico Veneziano" (Bergamo, 1892); E. Bonebakker, "Van Sente Brandane" (Amsterdam, 1894); Carl Wahland gives a list of the rich literature on the subject and the old French prose translation of Brendan's voyage (Upsala, 1900), XXXVI–XC.

Beamish, *The Discovery of America* (1881), 210–211; O'Hanlon, *Lives of the Irish Saints* (Dublin, 1875), V, 389; Peschel, *Abhandlungen zur Erd- und Volkerkunde* (Leipzig, 1877), I, 20–28; Gaffarel, *Les Voyages de Saint Brandan et des Papæ dans l'Atlantique au moyen âge* in *Bulletin de la Société de Géographie de Rochefort* (1880–81), II, 5; Ruge, *Geschichte des Zeitalters der Entdeckungen* (Leipzig, 1881); Schirmer, *Zur Brendanus Legende* (Leipzig, 1888); Zimmer, *Keltische Beiträge* in *Zeitschrift für deutsches Altertum und deutsche Litteratur* (1888–89), 33; Idem, *Die frühesten Berührungen der Iren mit den Nordgermanen* in *Report of the Royal Prussian Academy of Sciences* (Berlin, 1891); Kretschmer, *Die Entdeckung Amerikas* (Berlin, 1892, Calmund, 1902), 186–195; Brittain, *The History of North America* (Philadelphia, 1907), I, 10; *Rafn, Ant. Amer.*. XXXVII, and 447–450; Avezac, *Les Iles fantastiques de l'océan occidental* in *Nouv. An. des voyages et de science geogr.* (1845). I, 293; MacCarthy, *The voyage of St. Brendan*, in *Dublin University Magazine* (Jan., 1848), 89 sqq.

Otto Hartig.

Brentano, Klemens Maria, a German poet, one of the most prominent members of the Romantic School. He was born at Thal-Ehrenbreitstein 8 September, 1778; d. 28 July, 1842. After a futile attempt to become a merchant, he entered the University of Jena in 1797, where he remained with occasional interruptions until 1803. Here he made the acquaintance of the brothers August Wilhelm and Friedrich Schlegel and of Ludwig Tieck, the

founders and leaders of the Romantic School, to which Brentano also attached himself. In 1803 he married Sophie Mereau, the divorced wife of Professor Mereau, and the following year moved to Heidelberg, where with Achim von Arnim, who later became his brother-in-law, and Joseph Görres he was soon the leading spirit of the so-called younger Romantic School. It was during this period that he published jointly with Arnim the famous collection of old folksongs known as "Des Knaben Wunderhorn", which appeared in three volumes between the years 1805 and 1808. This collection established once for all the position of the *Volkslied* in German literature and had a powerful

Klemens Maria Brentano

effect on the lyric poetry not only of Germany, but also of other nations. Longfellow testifies that it had "the most wild and magic influence" on his imagination. It was of course not to be expected that the text of these poems should be philologically accurate, but this in no way diminishes the importance of the service which the editors rendered to German literature. In 1806 Brentano's wife died and he then led a wild, unsettled life, drifting to various places, Halle, Weimar, Kassel, Vienna, and Berlin. A second matrimonial venture proved disastrous; his wife was a woman of unbridled temper and habits, and he soon separated from her. Finally he drifted to Berlin restless and discontented. There he met the accomplished Luise Hensel, who later on achieved fame as a poetess. His ardent love for her was unrequited. Luise Hensel declined all offers of marriage. A great change now came over the poet. His previous indifference to the Catholic Faith, in which he had been born, was changed to the most fervid devotion. He left Berlin and in 1818 went to the secluded Westphalian town of Dülmen, attracted by the fame of the stigmatic nun, Katharina Emmerich. For six years he remained near her, making a record of her visions and revelations. The publication of this record occupied the greater part of the remaining years of his life. After her death in 1824 he again wandered, settling at last in 1833 in Munich, where with Görres he was the centre of a circle of distinguished Catholic scholars and men of letters. He died in 1842 while visiting his brother Christian in Aschaffenburg.

Brentano is chiefly known as the editor of "Des Knaben Wunderhorn", but he also has written a great deal of original matter. Among his earlier writings "Godwi" deserves notice, as a wild, formless romance in which some fine lyrics are interspersed, including the song of the "Lore Lay", later incorporated in the "Wunderhorn". This song inspired Heine's famous ballad on the same subject. "Die Romanzen vom Rosenkranz" (Romances of the Rosary) is an unfinished narrative allegorical poem containing a fanciful mixture of biographical, historical, and legendary traits, which was published in 1852 after the author's death. Especially noteworthy are the stories, or *Märchen*, such as the "Geschichte vom braven Kasperl und dem schönen Annerl" (1817), a tragic story of village life; and "Gockel, Hinkel und Gackeleia" (1838). A fantastic, whimsical humour pervades nearly all of Brentano's work; his style is marred by frequent and disagreeable eccentricities. When he wishes to be naïve, he often becomes merely childish. His poetic gifts, however, are undeniably of a high order; some of his lyric poems (e. g. "Lied der Spinnerin", "An eine Kranke") are among the best of their kind. But he lacked self-control and dissipated his great literary talents. His collected writings, edited by his brother Christian, appeared at Frankfort in nine volumes (1851–55).

Selections with biographical and critical introduction edited by Max Koch in Kürschner, *Deutsche National Litteratur,* vol. CXLVI, and by Diel (Freiburg im Br., 1873, 2 vols.); Guido Görres (ed.), *Märchen* (2 vols., Stuttgart and Tübingen, 1846); Diel, *Clemens Brentano, Ein Lebensbild,* suppl. and ed. by Kreiten (2 vols. Freiburg im Br., 1877); Johnson in *The Catholic World Magazine* (New York, 1899) L, 61–71.

Arthur F. J. Remy.

Brescia, Diocese of, takes its name from the principal city in the province of the same name in Lombardy, between the Mella and the Naviglio. The city of Brescia contains 60,000 inhabitants and is of great commercial importance. It was founded by the Gauls, and in 197 B. C. was captured by the Romans, who called it Brixia. When, in 312, Constantine advanced against Maxentius, an engagement took place at Brescia in which the enemy was forced to retreat as far as Verona. During the invasion of the Huns under Attila, the city was besieged. In 774 Charlemagne captured it from the Lombards.

The Bishops of Brescia received the title of Count from Louis II, and in consequence became civil rulers of the city and the countship. Many struggles followed, however, in particular after Arduin Lord Marcher of Ivrea, who had proclaimed himself King of Italy (1002), had slain the bishop of this city for holding allegiance to Emperor Henry II. Henry, to ensure the fidelity of the citizens of Brescia, was obliged to confirm the civil liberty granted them by Arduin, which is the origin of the commune of Brescia. In the successive struggles between the Lombard cities and the emperors, Brescia was implicated in some of the leagues and in all of the uprisings against them. Memorable in the history of these conflicts is the siege laid to Brescia by Frederick II in 1238 on account of the part taken by this city in the battle of Cortenova (27 November, 1237). Brescia came through this assault victorious. After the fall of the imperial house of Swabia republican institutions declined at Brescia, as well as in the other free cities and the leadership was contested between several powerful families, chief among them the Maggi and the Brusati, the latter of the Ghibelline party. In 1311 Henry VII laid siege to Brescia for six months, losing three-fourths of his army. Later the Scaligeri of Verona, aided by the exiled Ghibellines, sought to place Brescia under subjection. The citizens of Brescia then had recourse to John of Luxemburg; Mastino II della Scala, however, expelled the governor appointed by him. His mastery, in turn, was soon contested by the Visconti of Milan, but not even their rule was undisputed, as Pandolfo Malatesta in 1406 took possession of the city, but in 1416 bartered it to Filippo Visconti, who in 1426 sold it to the Venetians. The Milanese nobles, however, forced Filippo to resume hostilities against the Venetians, and thus to attempt the recovery of this city, but he was defeated in the battle of Maclodio (1427), near Brescia. In 1439 Brescia was once more besieged by Francesco Sforza, captain of the Venetians, who conquered Piccinino, Filippo's *condottiere.* Thenceforward Brescia acknowledged the authority of Venice, with the exception of the years between 1512 and 1520, when it was occupied by the French armies. From 1796 it shared the fortunes of the republic.

The Bishop of Brescia is suffragan to the Archbishop of Milan. Legend traces the beginnings of Christianity in Brescia to St. Barnabas, who is said to have made St. Anatolus bishop. However, Milan also claims Anatolus as its first bishop, consecrated by St. Barnabas. In any case, the Faith was probably brought to Brescia by way of Milan. During the reign of Hadrian, Brescia was the scene of the martyrdom of Sts. Faustinus and Jovita (cf. Acta SS., 15 February). From the time of the persecutions tradition mentions the names of several bishops, but nothing authentic is known concerning them. In the fourth century there was the celebrated St. Philastrius, a most zealous champion of orthodoxy against heresy, of whom it is related that he converted many pagans. He was succeeded by St. Gaudentius, consecrated by St. Ambrose (c. 387), who erected outside the city walls the church *Ad Concilia Sanctorum,* in which the holy matron Silvia was buried later. A great number of the bishops who ruled this diocese from the fourth to the seventh centuries are inscribed on the rolls of the saints, e. g. St. Paul, St. Theophilus, St. Silvinus, St. Gaudiosus, St. Ottapianus, St. Vigilius, St. Hercalanus, St. Poterius, St. Anastasius (610), who built the church of San Pietro, and made it the cathedral, and St. Dominic (613), who with the many gifts he received from Queen Theodolinda, erected the church called the Rotonda. Bishop Ramperto brought to Brescia the Benedictines, who constructed a church to which they transferred the relics of Sts. Faustinus and Jovita; he also took part in the Council of Mantua of 827. Notingus (844) was the first bishop who bore the title of Count. Landolfo II (1007) built the church of Santa Eufemia outside the walls.

During the episcopate of Manfredo Lucciaga (1133), Arnold of Brescia disseminated his teachings, with the result that the governors of the city all but confiscated the property of the churches of Brescia. Alberto Rezzato (1213) had the Paterines to contend against; he also brought many relics from the Holy Land. Blessed Gualla Ronio (1229), of the Friars Preachers, was distinguished for his virtue. Berardo Maggi (1275), a Guelph, was made Duke and Count of the city, and constructed among other works two canals diverting the waters of the Rivers Chiese and Mella, in order to furnish the motive force for many factories. Tommaso Visconti (1388) did much for the maintenance of discipline among the clergy. Under Bishop Francesco de' Mareri (1418), the preaching of St. Bernardine of Siena wrought a great moral reform in the city of Brescia. Pietro dal Monte (1442) adorned the episcopal palace, erected a hospital, and wrote various works. Paolo Zane (1481) built the shrine of Santa Maria delle Grazie and established the hospital for incurables. In the sixteenth century three cardinals succeeded each other: Francesco Cornaro (1532), Andrea Cornaro (1543), and Durante de' Duranti (1551). Domenico Bollani (1559) convened a diocesan synod (1574) in conformity with the decree of the Council of Trent, and founded the seminary. Giovanni Dolfin (1579) seconded St. Charles Borromeo in his work of reform, and that saint by his own desire celebrated the obsequies of Bishop Dolfin. Bishop Pietro Ottoboni (1654) was later elevated to the chair of St. Peter under the name of Alexander VIII. Cardinal Alb. Badoaro (1706) was a very zealous pastor, combating in an especial manner the Quietism which had infected his diocese. Cardinal Angelo M. Quirini (1727) was a man of great learning; he founded the library of the commune, which took its name from him, and did much towards the restoration of the cathedral. During the episcopate of Giovanni Nani (1773) the French invasion took place, with the attendant pillaging of churches and convents.

The most important churches of the city have

been mentioned in connexion with the bishops. There is still to be noted that of San Francesco, Romanesque in style, with a beautiful façade. Noteworthy, also, is the cemetery of Brescia, dating from the beginning of the nineteenth century, containing a large watch tower.

The diocese contains 79 rural deaneries, 389 parishes, 774 churches, chapels, and oratories, 997 secular priests, 77 regular clergy, 398 seminarists, 283 members of female religious orders, 4 schools for boys, and 8 for girls, and a population of 527,475.

CAPPELLETTI, *Le chiese d'Italia* (Venice, 1844), XI; *Annuario eccl.* (1907).

U. BENIGNI.

Breslau, THE PRINCE-BISHOPRIC OF, is seated at Breslau, on the River Oder in the Prussian Province of Silesia.

HISTORY.—Christianity was first introduced into Silesia by missionaries from Moravia and Bohemia. After the conversion of the Polish Duke Misiko (later Mieczyslaus) the work of bringing the people to the new faith went on more rapidly. Up to about the year 1000 Silesia had no bishop of its own, but was united to neighbouring dioceses. In this way arose the first connexion of Silesia with Germany. The upper part of the River Oder formed the boundary of the Kingdom of Poland; all the territory which is now Silesia lying on the right-hand bank of the Oder belonged, therefore, to the Diocese of Posen, which was suffragan to the Metropolitan See of Magdeburg. This part of Silesia was thus under the jurisdiction of that Jordan who was, in 968, appointed first Bishop of Posen. The part of Silesia lying on the left bank of the Oder belonged to the territory then included in Bohemia, and was consequently within the diocesan jurisdiction of Prague. The See of Prague, founded probably in 973, was suffragan to the Archdiocese of Mainz. The Polish ruler, Boleslaw Chrobry, the son of Misiko, obtained the Bohemian part of Silesia during his wars of conquest, and a change in the ecclesiastical dependence of the province followed. By a patent of Otto III, in 995, Silesia was attached to the See of Meissen, which, like Posen, was suffragan to the Archdiocese of Magdeburg. Soon after this the Emperor Otto III and Duke Boleslaw Chrobry, who was then the ruler of the whole of Silesia, founded the Diocese of Breslau, and together with the Dioceses of Cracow and Colberg, was placed under the Archdiocese of Gnesen, which was founded by Otto in the year 1000. The first Bishop of Breslau is said to have been named Johannes, but nothing more than this is known of him, nor is there extant any official document giving the boundaries of the diocese at the time of its erection. However, they are defined in the Bulls of approval and protection issued by Pope Adrian IV, 23 April, 1155, and by Pope Innocent IV, 9 August, 1245.

The powerful Polish ruler, Boleslaw Chrobry, was succeeded by his son Misiko II, who had but a short reign. After his death a revolt against Christianity and the reigning family broke out, the new Church organization of Poland disappeared from view, and the names of the Bishops of Breslau for the next half century are unknown. Casimir, the son of Misiko, and his mother were driven out of the country, but through German aid they returned, and the affairs of the Church were brought into better order. A Bishop of Breslau from probably 1051 to 1062 was Hieronymus, said by later tradition to have been a Roman nobleman. He was followed by Johannes I (1062–72), who was succeeded by Petrus I (1071–1111). During the episcopate of Petrus, Count Peter Wlast entered upon that work of founding churches and monasteries which has preserved his name. Petrus was followed by: Zyroslaus I (1112–20); Heimo (1120–26), who welcomed St. Otto of Bam-

berg to Breslau in May, 1124, when the saint was on his missionary journey to Pomerania; Robert I (1127–42), who was Bishop of Cracow; Robert II (1142–46); and Johannes II (1146–49), who became Archbishop of Gnesen. With the episcopate of Bishop Walter (1149–69) the history of the Diocese of Breslau begins to grow clearer. At Walter's request Pope Adrian IV, in 1155, took the bishopric under his protection and confirmed to it the territorial possessions of which a list had been submitted to him. Among the rights which the pope then confirmed was that of jurisdiction over the lands belonging to the castle of Ottmachau which had been regarded as the patrimony of the diocese from its foundation. During Walter's episcopate the Polish Duke Ladislaus and his family were driven from home and took refuge in Germany; in 1163 the sons of Ladislaus returned and, through the intervention of Frederick

THE CATHEDRAL OF BRESLAU

Barbarossa, received as an independent duchy the part of Silesia which was included at that date in the See of Breslau. Bishop Walter built a new, massively constructed cathedral, in which he was buried. Zyroslaus II (1170–98) encouraged the founding of the Cistercian monastery of Leubus by Duke Boleslaw the Long. In 1180 Zyroslaus took part in the national assembly at Lenczyc at which laws for the protection of the Church and its property were promulgated. Jaroslaus (1198–1201), the oldest son of Duke Boleslaw, and Duke of Oppeln, was the first prince to become Bishop of Breslau. Cyprian (1201–7) was originally Abbot of the Premonstratensian monastery of St. Vincent near Breslau, then Bishop of Lebus, and afterwards Bishop of Breslau. During Cyprian's episcopate Duke Heinrich I and his wife, St. Hedwig, founded the Cistercian convent at Trebnitz. The episcopate of Bishop Lorenz (1207–32) was marked by his efforts to bring colonies of Germans into the church territories, to effect the cultivation of waste lands. This introduction of German settlers by the bishop was in accordance with the example set by Heinrich I and St. Hedwig. The monasteries of the Augustinian Canons, Premonstratensians, and Cistercians took an active part in carrying out the schemes of the rulers by placing great numbers of Germans, especially Thuringians and Franconians, on the large estates that had been granted them.

One of the most noted bishops of the diocese was Thomas I (1232–68); he continued the work of German colonization with so much energy that even the marauding incursions of the Mongols (1241) made but a temporary break in the process. His defence of the rights of the Church involved him in bitter conflicts with Duke Boleslaw of Liegnitz. Thomas began the construction of the present cathedral, the chancel being the first part erected. St. Hedwig died during his episcopate; and he lived until the process of her canonization was completed, but died before the final solemnity of her elevation to the altars of the Catholic Church. After Thomas I,

Ladislaus, a grandson of St. Hedwig, and Archbishop of Salzburg, was Administrator of the Diocese of Breslau until his death in 1270. He was followed by Thomas II (1270–92), who was involved for years in a violent dispute with Duke Henry IV as to the prerogatives of the Church in Silesia. In 1287 a reconciliation was effected between them at Ratisbon, and in 1288 the duke founded the collegiate church of the Holy Cross at Breslau. Before his death, on the Eve of St. John in 1290, the duke confirmed the rights of the Church to sovereignty over the territories of Neisse and Ottmachau. Thomas II consecrated the high altar of the cathedral; he was present at the Œcumenical Council of Lyons (1274) and in 1279 held a diocesan synod. Johann III, Romka (1292–1301), belonged to the Polish party in the cathedral chapter. His maintenance of the prerogatives of the Church brought him, also, into conflict with the temporal rulers of Silesia; in 1296 he called a synod for the defence of these rights. In the election of Heinrich I, of Würben (1302–19), the German party in the cathedral chapter won, but this victory cost the new bishop the enmity of the opposing faction. He was made guardian of the youthful Dukes of Breslau, and this appointment, together with the factional disputes, led to the bringing of grave accusations against him. The researches of more recent times have proved the groundlessness of these attacks. He was kept in Avignon a number of years by a suit before the Curia which was finally settled in his favour. Notwithstanding the troubles of his life he was energetic in the performance of his duties. He carried on the construction of the cathedral, and in 1305 and 1316 held diocesan synods. The office of Auxiliary Bishop of Breslau dates from his episcopate. After his death a divided vote led to a vacancy of the see. The two candidates, Weit and Lutold, elected by the opposing factions, finally resigned, and Pope John XXII transferred Nanker, Bishop of Cracow, to Breslau (1326–41).

The constant division and subdivision of Silesian territory into small principalities for the members of the ruling families resulted in a condition of weakness that necessitated dependence on a stronger neighbour, and Silesia thus came, from the year 1327, under the control of Bohemia. A quarrel broke out between Bishop Nanker and the suzerain of Silesia, King John of Bohemia, when the king seized the castle of Militsch which belonged to the cathedral chapter. The bishop excommunicated the king and those members of the Council of Breslau who sided with him. On account of this he was obliged to flee from Breslau and take refuge in Neisse, where he died. Preczlaus of Pogarell (1341–1376) was elected bishop while pursuing his studies at Bologna, and was consecrated bishop at Avignon. Through his friendship with Carl, the son of King John, he was soon able to settle the discord that had arisen under his predecessor. The diocese prospered greatly under his rule. He bought the Duchy of Grottkau from Duke Boleslaw of Brieg and added it to the episcopal territory of Neisse. The Bishops of Breslau had, therefore, after this the titles of Prince of Neisse and Duke of Grottkau, and took precedence of the other Silesian rulers who held principalities in fief. Carl IV, the emperor at this date, wished to separate Breslau from the Archdiocese of Gnesen and to make it a suffragan of the newly erected Archbishopric of Prague, but the plan failed, owing to the opposition of the Archbishop of Gnesen. Preczlaus added to the cathedral the beautiful Lady Chapel, in which he was buried and where his tomb still exists. Dietrich, dean of the cathedral, who was elected as successor to Preczlaus, could not obtain the papal confirmation, and the Bishop of Olmütz, who was chosen in his place, soon died. After a long contest with the Bohemian King and German Emperor Wenzel,

Bishop Wenzel of Lebus, Duke of Liegnitz, was transferred to Breslau (1382–1417). The new bishop devoted himself to repairing the damage inflicted on the Church in Silesia by the despotic procedure of the Emperor Wenzel. He held two synods, in 1410 and 1415, with the object of securing a higher standard of ecclesiastical discipline; and he settled the right of inheritance in the territory under his dominion by promulgating the church decree called "Wenzel's law". Resigning his bishopric in 1417, Wenzel died in 1419. The episcopate of Conrad, Duke of Oels, the next bishop (1417–47), fell in the trying time for Silesia of the Hussite wars. Conrad was placed at the head of the Silesian confederation which was formed to defend the country against hostile incursions. In 1435 the bishop issued a decree of which the chief intent was to close the prebends in the Diocese of Breslau to foreigners, and thus prevent the Poles from obtaining these offices. The effort to shut out the Polish element and to loosen the connexion with Gnesen was not a momentary one; it continued, and led gradually to a virtual separation from the Polish archdiocese some time before the formal separation took place. The troubles of the times brought the bishop and the diocese into serious pecuniary difficulties, and in 1444 Conrad resigned, but his resignation was not accepted, and he resumed his office. In 1446 he held a diocesan synod and died in the following year. Conrad's successor was the provost of the cathedral of Breslau, Peter Novak (1447–56). By wise economy Bishop Peter succeeded in bringing the diocesan finances into a better condition and was able to redeem the greater part of the church lands which his predecessor had been obliged to mortgage. At the diocesan synod of 1454 he endeavoured to suppress the abuses that had arisen in the diocese.

Jodokus of Rosenberg (1456–67) was a Bohemian nobleman and Grand Prior of the Knights of St. John. His love of peace made his position a very difficult one during the fierce ecclesiastico-political contention that raged between the Hussite King of Bohemia, George of Podiebrad, and the people of Breslau, who had taken sides with the German party. Jodokus was followed by a bishop from the region of the Rhine, Rudolf von Rüdesheim (1468–82). As papal legate, Rudolf had become popular in Breslau through his energetic opposition to George of Podiebrad; for this reason the cathedral chapter requested his transfer from the small Diocese of Lavant in Carinthia, after he had confirmed their privileges. From this time these privileges were called "the Rudolfian statutes". Under his leadership the party opposed to Podiebrad obtained the victory, and Rudolf proceeded at once to repair the damage which had been occasioned to the Church during this strife; mortgaged church lands were redeemed; in 1473 and 1475 diocesan synods were held, at which the bishop took active measures in regard to church discipline. As coadjutor, he had selected a Swabian, Johann IV, Roth, Bishop of Lavant, a man of humanistic training. Urged by King Matthias of Hungary, to whom Silesia was then subject, the cathedral chapter, somewhat unwillingly, chose the coadjutor as bishop (1482–1506). His episcopate was marked by violent quarrels with the cathedral chapter. But at the same time he was a promoter of art and learning, and strict in his conception of church rights and duties. He endeavoured to improve the spiritual life of the diocese by holding a number of synods. Before he died the famous worker in bronze, Peter Vischer of Nuremberg, cast his monument, the most beautiful bishop's tomb in Silesia. His coadjutor with right of succession was Johann V (1506–20), a member of the noble Hungarian family of Turzo. Johann V took an active part in the intellectual life of the time and sought at the diocesan synods to promote learning and church discipline, and to improve the schools. On the ruins of the old stronghold of Fauernig he built the castle called Johannisberg, now the summer residence of the Prince-Bishop of Breslau.

The religious disturbances of the sixteenth century began to be conspicuously apparent during this episcopate, and soon after Johann's death Protestantism began to spread in Silesia, which country had, since 1526, belonged to Austria. Princes, nobles, and town councils were zealous promoters of the new belief; even in the episcopal principality of Neisse-Grottkau Protestant doctrines found approval and acceptance. The successors of Johann V were partly responsible for this condition of affairs. Jacob von Salza (1520–39) was personally a stanch adherent of the Church, yet the gentleness of his disposition caused him to shrink from carrying on a war against the powerful religious movement that had arisen. To an even greater degree than Jacob von Salza his successor, Balthasar von Promnitz (1539–63), avoided coming into conflict with Protestantism. He was more friendly in his attitude to the new doctrine than any other Bishop of Breslau. Caspar von Logau (1562–74) showed at first greater energy than his predecessor in endeavouring to compose the troubles of his distracted diocese, but later in his episcopate his attitude towards Lutheranism and his slackness in defending church rights gave great offence to those who had remained true to the Faith. These circumstances make the advance of Protestantism easy to understand. At the same time it must be remembered that the bishops, although also secular rulers, had a difficult position in regard to spiritual matters. At the assemblies of the nobles, and at the meetings of the diet, the bishops and the deputies of the cathedral chapter were, as a rule, the only Catholics against a large and powerful majority on the side of Protestantism. The Austrian suzerains, who lived far from Silesia, and who were constantly preoccupied by the danger of a Turkish invasion, were not in a position to enforce the edicts which they issued for the protection of the Church.

The Silesian clergy had in great measure lost their high concept of the priestly office, although there were honourable exceptions. Among those faithful were the majority of the canons of the cathedral of Breslau; they distinguished themselves not only by their learning, but also by their religious zeal. It was in the main due to them that the diocese did not fall into spiritual ruin. The chapter was the willing assistant of the bishops in the reform of the diocese. Martin von Gerstmann (1574–85) began the renovation of the diocese, and the special means by which he hoped to attain the desired end were: the founding of a seminary for clerics, visitations of the diocese, diocesan synods, and the introduction of the Jesuits. His successor, Andreas von Jerin (1585–96), a Swabian who had been educated at the German College at Rome, followed in his footsteps. At the diocesan synod of 1592 he endeavoured to improve church discipline. Besides his zeal in elevating the life of the Church, he was also a promoter of the arts and learning. The silver altar with which he adorned his cathedral still exists, and he brought the schools in the principality of Neisse into a flourishing condition. The bishop also rendered important services to the emperor, as legate, at various times. Bonaventura Hahn, elected in 1596, as the successor of Andreas von Jerin, was not recognized by the emperor and was obliged to resign his position. The candidate of the emperor, Paul Albert (1599–1600), occupied the see only one year. Johann VI (1600–8), a member of a noble family of Silesia named von Sitsch, took more severe measures than his predecessors against Protestantism, in the hope of checking it, especially in the episcopal principality of Neisse-Grottkau.

Bishop Carl (1608–24), Archduke of Austria, had greater success than his predecessor after the first period of the Thirty Years War had taken a turn favourable to Austria and the Catholic party. The battle of the White Mountain (1620) broke not only the revolt in Bohemia, but also the opposition of the allied Protestants of Silesia. Bishop Carl began the restoration of the principality of Neisse to the Catholic Faith. The work was completed by his successor, Carl Ferdinand, Prince of Poland (1625–55). Carl Ferdinand spent most of his time in his own country, but appointed excellent administrators for the diocese, such as the Coadjutor-Bishop Liesch von Hornau, and Archdeacon Gebauer. Imperial commissioners gave back to the Catholic Church those church buildings in the chief places of the principalities which had become the property of the sovereign through the extinction of fiefs. According to the terms of the Treaty of Westphalia, the remaining churches, 693 in number, of such territories were secularized in the years 1653, 1654, and 1668. This led to a complete reorganization of the diocese. The person who effected it was Sebastian of Rostock, a man of humble birth who was vicar-general and administrator of the diocese under the bishops Archduke Leopold Wilhelm (1656–62) and Archduke Carl Joseph (1663–64), neither of whom lived in the territory of Breslau. After Sebastian of Rostock became bishop (1664–71) he carried on the work of reorganization with still greater success than before. Friedrich, Landgrave of Hesse, Cardinal, and Grand Prior of the Order of St. John, was the next Bishop of Breslau (1671–82). The new bishop was of Protestant origin and had become a Catholic at Rome. Under his administration the rehabilitation of the diocese went on. He beautified the cathedral and elaborated its services. For the red cap and violet almutium of the canons he substituted the red mozetta. He was buried in a beautiful chapel which he had added to the cathedral in honour of his ancestress, St. Elizabeth of Thuringia. After his death the chapter presented Carl von Liechtenstein, Bishop of Olmütz, for confirmation. Their choice was opposed by the emperor, whose candidate was the Count Palatine Wolfgang of the ruling family of Pfalz-Neuburg. Count Wolfgang died, and his brother Franz Ludwig (1683–1732) was made bishop. The new ruler of the diocese was at the same time Bishop of Worms, Grand Master of the German Knights, Provost of Ellwangen, and Elector of Trier, and later, he was made Elector of Mainz. He separated the ecclesiastical administration and that of the civil tribunals, and obtained the definition, in the Pragmatic Sanction of 1699, of the extent of the jurisdiction of the vicariate-general and the consistory. In 1675, upon the death of the last reigning duke, the Silesian Duchy of Liegnitz-Brieg-Wohlau lapsed to the emperor, and a new secularization of the churches was begun. But when Charles XII of Sweden secured for the Protestants the right to their former possessions in these territories, by the treaty of Altranstädt, in 1707, the secularization came to an end, and the churches had to be returned. The Emperor Joseph I endeavoured to repair the loss of these buildings to the Catholic Faith by founding the so-called Josephine vicarships.

The next bishop, Philip, Count von Sinzendorf, Cardinal and Bishop of Raab (1732–47), owed his elevation to the favour of the emperor. During his episcopate the greater part of the diocese was added to the territory of Prussia. King Frederick II of Prussia (Frederick the Great) desired to erect a "Catholic Vicariate" at Berlin, which should be the highest spiritual authority for the Catholics of Prussia. This would have been in reality a separation from Rome, and the project failed through the opposition of the Holy See. Bishop Sinzendorf had neither the acuteness to perceive the inimical intent of the king's scheme, nor sufficient decision of character to withstand it. The king desired to secure a successor to Sinzendorf who would be under royal influence. In utter disregard of the principles of the Church, and heedless of the protests of the cathedral chapter, he presented Count Philip Gotthard von Schaffgotsch as coadjutor-bishop. After the death of Cardinal Sinzendorf the king succeeded in overcoming the scruples of the Holy Father, and Schaffgotsch became Bishop of Breslau (1748–95). Although the method of his elevation caused the new bishop to be regarded with suspicion by many strict Catholics, yet he was zealous in the fulfilment of his duties. During the Seven Years War he fell into discredit with Frederick on account of his firm maintenance of the rights of the Church, and the return of peace did not fully restore him to favour. In 1766 he fled to the Austrian part of his diocese in order to avoid the confinement in Oppeln which the king had decreed against him. After this Frederick made it impossible for him to rule the Prussian part of his diocese, and until the death of the bishop this territory was ruled by vicars Apostolic.

The former coadjutor of von Schaffgotsch, Joseph Christian, Prince von Hohenlohe-Waldenburg-Bartenstein (1795–1817), succeeded him as bishop. During this episcopate the temporal power of the Bishops of Breslau came to an end through the secularization, in 1810, of the church estates in Silesia. Only the estates in Austria remained to the see. The cathedral foundation, eight collegiate foundations, and over eighty monasteries were suppressed, and their property confiscated. Only those monastic institutions which were occupied with teaching or nursing were allowed to exist. Bishop Joseph Christian was succeeded by his coadjutor, Emmanuel von Schimonsky. The affairs of the Church in Prussia had been brought into order by the Bull "De salute animarum", issued in 1821. Under its provisions the cathedral chapter elected Schimonsky, who had been administrator of the diocese, as the first Exempt Bishop of Breslau (1824–32). The bishop received for himself and his successors the title of prince as partial compensation for the loss of the secularized principality of Neisse. He combated the rationalistic tendencies which were rife among his clergy in regard to celibacy and the use of Latin in the church services and ceremonies. During the episcopate of his predecessor the Government had promulgated a law which was a source of much trouble to Schimonsky and his immediate successors; this was that in those places where Catholics were few in number, the parish should be declared extinct, and the church buildings given to the Protestants. In spite of the protests of the episcopal authorities, over one hundred church buildings were lost in this way. King Frederick William put an end to this injustice, and sought to make good the injuries inflicted. For several years after Schimonsky's death the see remained vacant. It was eventually filled by the election, through Government influence, of Count Leopold von Sedlnitzki (1836–40). Bishop von Sedlnitzki was neither clear nor firm in his maintenance of the doctrines of the Church; on the question of mixed marriages, which had become one of great importance, he took an undecided position. At last, upon the demand of Pope Gregory XVI, he resigned his see. He went afterwards to Berlin, where he was made a privy-councillor, and where he later became a Protestant. The dean of the cathedral, Dr. Ritter, administered the diocese for several years until the election of the Grand Dean of the countship of Glatz, Joseph Knauer (1843–44). The new bishop, who was seventy-nine years old, lived only a year after his appointment.

His successor was Melchior, Freiherr von Diepenbrock (1845–53). This episcopate was the beginning of a new religious and ecclesiastical life in the diocese. During the revolutionary period the bishop not only maintained order in his see, which was in a state of ferment, but was also a supporter of the Government. He received unusual honours from the king and was made a cardinal by the pope. He died 20 January, 1853, at the castle of Johannisberg and was buried in the cathedral. His successor, Heinrich Förster (1853–81) carried on his work and completed it. Bishop Förster gave generous aid to the founding of churches, monastic institutions, and schools. The strife that arose between the Church and the State brought his labours in the Prussian part of his diocese to an end. He was deposed by the State and was obliged to leave Breslau and retire to the castle of Johannisberg. Here he died, 20 October, 1881. He was buried in the cathedral at Breslau. Leo XIII appointed as his successor in the disordered diocese Robert Herzog (1882–86), who had been delegate of the prince-bishop and provost of St. Hedwig's at Berlin. Bishop Herzog made every endeavour to bring order out of the confusion into which the quarrel with the State during the immediately preceding years had thrown the affairs of the diocese. Unfortunately, his episcopate was of but short duration; he died after a long illness, 26 December, 1886. The Holy See appointed as his successor a man who had done much to allay the strife between Church and State, the Bishop of Fulda, Georg Kopp. Bishop Kopp was born, 25 July, 1837, at Duderstadt in the Diocese of Hildesheim; he was ordained to the priesthood, 29 August, 1862; consecrated and installed Bishop of Fulda, 27 December, 1881; transferred to Breslau, 9 August, 1887, installed 20 October, 1887; created a cardinal, 16 January, 1893.

EXTENT AND STATISTICS OF THE DIOCESE.—The Diocese of Breslau includes the whole Prussian Province of Silesia with the exception of a part of the districts of Ratibor and Leobschütz, which belong to the Archdiocese of Olmütz, and the Countship (*Grafschaft*) of Glatz, also in Prussian Silesia, which is subject to the Archbishop of Prague. In Austrian Silesia the Diocese of Breslau includes the Principality of Teschen and the Austrian part of the Principality of Neisse. In the Province of Brandenburg the diocese still includes the districts of Schwiebus-Züllichau and Krossen, as well as the part formerly called Nieder-Lausitz. With the exception of the districts of Bütow and Lauenburg, the rest of Brandenburg and the Province of Pomerania have, since 1821, been supervised by delegation from the Prince-Bishop of Breslau. (See BERLIN, BRANDENBURG.)

Including the district governed by delegation the diocese contains, according to the last census (1 December, 1905), 3,342,221 Catholics; 8,737,746 Protestants; and 204,749 Jews. There are actively employed in the diocese 1,632 secular, and 121 regular, priests. The cathedral chapter includes the two offices of provost and dean, and has 10 regular, and 6 honorary, canons. The prince-bishopric is divided into 11 commissariates and 99 archpresbyterates, in which there are 992 cures of various kinds (parishes, curacies, and stations), with 935 parish churches and 633 dependent and mother-churches. Besides the theological faculty of the University of Breslau, the diocese possesses, as episcopal institutions for the training of the clergy, 5 preparatory seminaries for boys, 1 home (recently much enlarged) for theological students attending the university, and 1 seminary for priests. The statistics of the houses of the religious orders in the dioceses are as follows: Benedictines, 1 house; Dominicans, 1; Franciscans, 8; Jesuits, 3; Piarists, 1; Brothers of

Mercy, 8; Order of St. Camillus of Lellis, 1; Redemptorists, 1; Congregation of the Society of the Divine Word, 1; Alexian Brothers, 1; Poor Brothers of St. Francis, 2; Sisters of St. Elizabeth, 6; Magdalen Sisters, 1; Ursulines, 6; Sisters of the Good Shepherd, 4; Sisters of St. Charles Borromeo, (a) from the mother-house at Trebnitz, 181, (b) from the mother-house at Trier, 5; Servants of the Sacred Heart of Jesus, 2; Sisters of Poor Handmaids of Christ, 3; Sister-Servants of Mary, 27; German Dominican Sisters of St. Catharine of Siena, 11; Sisters of St. Francis, 9; Grey Sisters of St. Elizabeth, 169; Sisters of St. Hedwig, 9; Sisters of Mary, 27; Poor School-Sisters of Notre Dame, 15; Vincentian Sisters, 7; Sisters of the Holy Cross, 1; Sisters of St. Joseph, 1. In the above-mentioned monastic houses for men there are 512 religious; in those for women, 5,208 religious.

STENZEL, *Urkunden zur Geschichte des Bistums Breslau im Mittelalter* (Breslau, 1845); KASTNER, *Archiv für die Geschichte*

by King Ladislaus of Hungary, to which Silesia then belonged, when the University of Cracow, fearing competition, succeeded in bringing the scheme to naught. The efforts made in 1527 by the Protestants to found a Silesian University at Liegnitz and in 1616 at Beuthen also failed. The Catholics sought to establish a theological school for the education of the diocesan clergy, and the endeavour led to the founding at Breslau, in 1565, of a theological seminary which was transferred in 1575 to Neisse. In 1623 the Bishop of Breslau, Archduke Carl of Austria, founded at Neisse a Jesuit college to which he gave a large endowment. The bishop intended to unite with this college a university having departments of jurisprudence and medicine, but his death soon after the founding of the school prevented the carrying out of these plans.

A school founded by the Jesuits at Breslau in 1659 was more fortunate in its development. The Society conducted in the imperial citadel a gym-

THE UNIVERSITY OF BRESLAU

des Bistums Breslau (3 vols., Neisse, 1858); JUNGNITZ, *Veröffentlichungen aus dem fürstbischöflichen Diöcezesenarchive zu Breslau* (3 vols., Breslau, 1903); HEYNE, *Dokumentierte Geschichte des Bistums Breslau* (3 vols, Breslau, 1860); SOFFNER, *Geschichte der Reformation in Schlesien* (Breslau, 1887); *Scriptores rerum Silesiacarum* (17 vols., Breslau, 1835); *Codex diplomaticus Silesiæ* (23 vols., Breslau, 1857); *Acta publica* (8 vols., Breslau, 1865); *Zeitschrift für Geschichte Schlesiens* (40 vols., Breslau, 1855); GRÜNHAGEN, *Geschichte Schlesiens* (2 vols., Gotha, 1884); IDEM, *Schlesien unter Friedrich dem Grossen* (2 vols., Breslau, 1890).

UNIVERSITY OF BRESLAU.—The founding of a university at Breslau was first debated in 1409, when the Czechs made it impossible for the Germans to continue their studies at the University of Prague and virtually drove them from it. But Leipzig and not Breslau obtained the new seat of learning. About a century later, under the quickening impulse of Humanism, the project was again taken up by the city of Breslau in conjunction with the bishop, Johann Roth, and his coadjutor, Johann Turzo, and a "generale literarum gymnasium" to contain all four faculties was planned. The charter of this institution had been signed at Ofen, 20 July, 1505,

nasium, the higher classes of which corresponded to those in the philosophical department of a university. Theological studies were introduced in 1666. These two courses were carried on as in a university, but the school had no power to confer degrees. In order to obtain the charter necessary for the conferring of degrees and for the development of the institution, the Jesuit Father Wolf sought, from 1694 on, to obtain the consent of Emperor Leopold I to the erection of the school into a university. Father Wolf was also active in the negotiations between the courts of Berlin and Vienna concerning the concession of the title of King to the Elector Frederick III of Brandenburg. The plans Father Wolf sought to carry out were far-reaching. He held it a misfortune that Silesians were obliged to go to universities outside of Silesia, where Catholics often had no opportunity for the exercise of their religion. His scheme was a national Silesian university, endowed with all the academic privileges, which should be open to students irrespective of their religious beliefs. This project encountered the opposition of

Protestant prejudice against the Jesuits, and the town council of Breslau prevented the imperial confirmation of the plan for eight years. However, Leopold I signed at Vienna, 21 October, 1702, the charter raising the school to the rank of a university and obtained the papal confirmation for the decree.

The new university, called after the emperor, Leopoldina, was opened 15 November, 1702, but the change in status did not alter the internal organization. The buildings of the old citadel had long been too cramped for the needs of the institution, and it was resolved to erect a large new edifice, the cornerstone of which was laid 6 April, 1728. On account of the war with Frederick the Great of Prussia, and his conquest of Silesia, the plans for the new structure could not be carried out in their entirety. Although efforts were made to open departments of law and medicine, nothing more was attained than unofficial lectures by instructors in these branches. The number of scholars during the first decade of the life of the university continually increased. In 1740, 1,300 students attended the university and gymnasium; the number declined during the first Silesian war then rose again, until the Seven Years War once more reduced the attendance at lectures. During this latter conflict the building was used as a hospital and prison, and professors and students were obliged to go elsewhere. Only after the Peace of 1763 was the building restored to its original use The attendance increased rapidly during the next ten years, but fell off greatly after the suppression of the Society of Jesus. In 1803, when the Leopoldina was made a secular institution, the number of students was about 500.

After the suppression of the Jesuits the king established a Catholic-Schools Institute which included the Jesuits living in Silesia, and in which the candidates for the secular priesthood were to receive their training. The former independence disappeared and the institute and university were made dependent on the Silesian minister. The new institution maintained with difficulty what was already in existence; it was ruled by a spirit of narrow conservatism, and made no attempt to develop its courses or to enter new fields. Besides this, the teaching force was not well kept up even in the usual branches of learning. During the last decade of its existence the Leopoldina was carried on under the royal ordinance issued 26 July, 1800, in regard to the University of Breslau and the gymnasia connected with it. The Catholic school system, especially the gymnasia, underwent a reform at this epoch which led to the separation of the gymnasium from the university and the reorganization of the philosophical faculty. These two changes were carried out in 1811.

The founding of the University of Berlin in 1810 made uncertain the future existence of the Protestant university at Frankfort on the Oder, not far from Berlin. There was also a strong desire in Silesia for a university embracing all faculties, and King Frederick William III gave his consent, 3 August, 1811, to a "plan for uniting the University of Frankfort with the University of Breslau". The two universities were to be made one institution in regard to constitution, teaching staff, endowments, property, and income; the philosophical faculties were to form one body. "To satisfy the wishes of Catholic subjects" two professors of philosophy proper were appointed, one Protestant and one Catholic. The promise of the erection of a Catholic professorship of history was not carried out until 1855, in the reign of Frederick William IV. Outside of these positions religious belief was not to be taken into consideration in appointments to the faculties of philosophy, law, and medicine. Instruction from both Catholic and Protestant professors of theology in the same university was until then unheard of. The plan of union ordained by the king decreed "that the theological department of the combined university should be divided into two faculties, a Protestant theological faculty and a Catholic theological one. These two faculties, of equal rank in other respects, were to alternate in precedence from year to year in the matter of lecture-announcements, on academic occasions, and in affixing signatures. The public opening of the new university took place 19 October, 1811, the lectures began 21 October. In the second year of the new school patriotism led the great majority of the students to take part in the war against Napoleon called "the War of Liberation", and many of them died for their country. After peace was concluded the usual life of the university was resumed. In August, 1861, the semi-centennial of the university was celebrated with much pomp. The schools of learning shared in the great development of Germany after the wars of 1866 and 1870, 1871, and the University of Breslau received, through the increase of prosperity, many improvements in equipment. The departments of medicine and natural science deserve special mention.

The increase in the number of students has kept pace with the increase in the number of instructors. When the university was opened, in 1811, there were 35 regular professors, 4 assistant professors, 4 *docents*, and 8 lecturers and technical teachers; in 1861, at the time of the semi-centennial celebration, there were 41 regular professors, 11 assistant professors, 33 *docents*, and 12 lecturers and technical teachers; in 1906 there were 73 regular professors, 31 assistant professors, 66 *docents*, and 15 lecturers and technical teachers. In the first year of the institution there were 298 students; in the fiftieth, 775; and in 1906 the number reached 1,961. Of this last number, 241 attended the lectures of the Catholic theological faculty; 61 the lectures of the Protestant theological faculty; 565 attended the law course; 271, the medical course; 807, the philosophical course. The German students numbered 1,884; foreign students, 77. Besides matriculated students, permission to attend the lectures was granted to 285 other persons of whom 179 were women.

NÜRNBERGER, *Zum zweihundertjährigen Bestehen der katholischen Theologen-Fakultät an der Universität Breslau* (Breslau, 1903); ROPELL, *Die Geschichte der Stiftung der königlichen Universität Breslau* (Breslau, 1861); REINKENS, *Die Universität zu Breslau vor der Vereinigung der Frankfurter Viadrina mit der Leopoldina* (Breslau, 1861).

JOSEPH JUNGNITZ.

Bressani, FRANCESCO GIUSEPPE, an Indian missionary, b. in Rome, 6 May, 1612; d. at Florence, 9 September, 1672. He entered the novitiate of the Society of Jesus, 15 August, 1626 and studied at Rome and Clermont, teaching before his ordination at Sezza, Tivoli, and Paris. On his arrival in America he was assigned to the spiritual care of the French at Quebec, but in the following year was sent to the Algonquins at Three Rivers. In April, 1644, on the way to the Huron Mission he was captured by the Iroquois and cruelly tortured by them, at intervals, for over two months. He was at length ransomed by the Dutch at Fort Orange, and sent to France, where he arrived in November, 1644. In the following year he was again in Canada and laboured zealously on the Huron Mission until its destruction by the Iroquois four years later. He continued, however, to minister to the scattered and fugitive Hurons. He was also stationed for a time at Quebec, where he occasionally officiated at the church. In November, 1650, Bressani's failing health and the meagre resources of the mission obliged him to return to Italy, where he spent many years as a preacher and missionary, dying at Florence. Bressani wrote the "Breve Relatione d'alcune Missioni . . . nella Nuoua

Francia" (Macerata, 1653), which was translated into French by Father Martin, S. J. (Montreal, 1852).

Thwaites, *Jesuit Relations* (Cleveland, 1897), XXIII, 326, 327; Michaud, *Biog. Univ.*, V; Sommervogel, II.

EDWARD P. SPILLANE.

Bressano. See BRIXEN.

Brest, UNION OF. See UNION OF BREST.

Brethren, PLYMOUTH. See PLYMOUTH.

Brethren, UNITED. See HOLZHAUSER, BARTHOLOMÄUS.

Brethren of the Christian Doctrine. See CHRISTIAN DOCTRINE, RELIGIOUS CONGREGATIONS OF THE.

Brethren of the Common Life. See COMMON LIFE, BRETHREN OF THE.

Brethren of the Community. See FRANCISCANS.

Brethren of the Free Spirit. See ADAMITES.

Brethren of the Hospital. See BROTHERS HOSPITALLERS OF ST. JOHN OF GOD.

Brethren of the Lord, THE.—A group of persons closely connected with the Saviour appears repeatedly in the New Testament under the designation "his brethren", or "the brethren of the Lord" (Matt., xii, 46; xiii, 55; Mark, iii, 31, 32; vi, 3; Luke, viii, 19, 20; John, ii, 12; vii, 3, 5; Acts, i, 14; I Cor., ix, 5). Four such "brethren" are mentioned by name in the parallel texts of Matt., xiii, 55, and Mark, vi, 3 (where "sisters" are also referred to), namely, James (also mentioned Gal., i, 19), Joseph, or Joses, Simon, and Jude; the incidental manner in which these names are given, shows, however, that the list lays no claim to completeness. Two questions in connexion with these "brethren" of the Lord have long been, and are now more than ever, the subject of controversy: (1) The identity of James, Jude, and Simon; (2) The exact nature of the relationship between the Saviour and his "brethren".

(1) James is without doubt the Bishop of Jerusalem (Acts, xii, 17; xv, 13; xxi, 18; Gal., i, 19; ii, 9, 12) and the author of the first Catholic Epistle. His identity with James the Less (Mark, xv, 40) and the Apostle James, the son of Alpheus (Matt., x, 3; Mark, iii, 18), although contested by many Protestant critics, may also be considered as certain. There is no reasonable doubt that in Gal., i, 19: "But other of the apostles [besides Cephas] I saw none, saving James the brother of the Lord", St. Paul represents James as a member of the Apostolic college. The purpose for which the statement is made, makes it clear that "apostles" is to be taken strictly to designate the Twelve, and its truthfulness demands that the clause "saving James" be understood to mean, that in addition to Cephas, St. Paul saw another Apostle, "James the brother of the Lord" (cf. Acts, ix, 27). Besides, the prominence and authority of James among the Apostles (Acts, xv, 13; Gal., ii, 9; in the latter text he is even named before Cephas) could have belonged only to one of their number. Now there were only two Apostles named James: James the son of Zebedee, and James the son of Alpheus (Matt., x, 3; Mark, iii, 18; Luke, vi, 16; Acts, i, 13). The former is out of the question, since he was dead at the time of the events to which Acts, xv, 6 sqq., and Gal., ii, 9, 12, refer (cf. Acts, xii, 2). James "the brother of the Lord" is therefore one with James the son of Alpheus, and consequently with James the Less, the identity of these two being generally conceded. Again, on comparing John, xix, 25, with Matt., xxvii, 56, and Mark, xv, 40 (cf. Mark, xv, 47; xvi, 1), we find that Mary of Cleophas, or more correctly Clopas (Κλωπᾶς), the sister of Mary the Mother of Christ, is the same as Mary the mother of James the Less and of Joseph, or Joses. As married women are not distinguished by the addition of their father's name, Mary of Clopas must be the wife of Clopas, and not his daughter, as has been main-

tained. Moreover, the names of her sons and the order in which they are given, no doubt the order of seniority, warrant us in identifying these sons with James and Joseph, or Joses, the "brethren" of the Lord. The existence among the early followers of Christ of two sets of brothers having the same names in the order of age, is not likely, and cannot be assumed without proof. Once this identity is conceded, the conclusion cannot well be avoided that Clopas and Alpheus are one person, even if the two names are quite distinct. It is, however, highly probable, and commonly admitted, that Clopas and Alpheus are merely different transcriptions of the same Aramaic word Halphai. James and Joseph the "brethren" of the Lord are thus the sons of Alpheus.

Of Joseph nothing further is known. Jude is the writer of the last of the Catholic Epistles (Jude, i). He is with good reason identified by Catholic commentators with the "Judas Jacobi" ("Jude the brother of James" in the D. V.) of Luke, vi, 16, and Acts, i, 13, otherwise known as Thaddeus (Matt., x, 3; Mark, iii, 18). It is quite in accordance with Greek custom for a man to be distinguished by the addition of his brother's name instead of his father's, when the brother was better known. That such was the case with Jude is inferred from the title "the brother of James", by which he designates himself in his Epistle. About Simon nothing certain can be stated. He is identified by most commentators with the Symeon, or Simon, who, according to Hegesippus, was a son of Clopas, and succeeded James as Bishop of Jerusalem. Some identify him with the Apostle Simon the Cananean (Matt., x, 4; Mark, iii, 18), or the Zealot (Luke, vi, 15; Acts, i, 13). The grouping together of James, Jude or Thaddeus, and Simon, after the other Apostles, Judas Iscariot excepted, in the lists of the Apostles (Matt., x, 4, 5; Mark, iii, 18; Luke, vi, 16; Acts, i, 13) lends some probability to this view, as it seems to indicate some sort of connexion between the three. Be this as it may, it is certain that at least two of the "brethren" of Christ were among the Apostles. This is clearly implied in I Cor., ix, 5: "Have we not the power to carry about a woman, a sister, as well as the rest of the apostles, and the brethren of the Lord, and Cephas?" The mention of Cephas at the end indicates that St. Paul, after speaking of the Apostles in general, calls special attention to the more prominent ones, the "brethren" of the Lord and Cephas. The objection that no "brethren" of the Lord could have been members of the Apostolic college, because six months before Christ's death they did not believe in Him (John, vii, 3, 5), rests on a misunderstanding of the text. His "brethren" believed in his miraculous power, and urged him to manifest it to the world. Their unbelief was therefore relative. It was not a want of belief in His Messiahship, but a false conception of it. They had not yet rid themselves of the Jewish idea of a Messiah who would be a temporal ruler. We meet with this idea among the Apostles as late as the day of the Ascension (Acts, i, 6). In any case the expression "his brethren" does not necessarily include each and every "brother", wherever it occurs. This last remark also sufficiently answers the difficulty in Acts, i, 13, 14, where, it is said, a clear distinction is made between the Apostles and the "brethren" of the Lord.

(2) The texts cited at the beginning of this article show beyond a doubt that there existed a real and near kinship between Jesus and His "brethren". But as "brethren" (or "brother") is applied to stepbrothers as well as to brothers by blood, and in Scriptural, and Semitic use generally, is often loosely extended to all near, or even distant, relatives (Gen., xiii, 8; xiv, 14, 16; Lev., x, 4; I Par., xv, 5–10; xxiii, 21, 22), the word furnishes no certain indication of the exact nature of the relationship. Some ancient

heretics, like Helvidius and the Antidicomarianites, maintained that the "brethren" of Jesus were His uterine brothers the sons of Joseph and Mary. This opinion has been revived in modern times, and is now adopted by most of the Protestant exegetes. On the orthodox side two views have long been current. The majority of the Greek Fathers and Greek writers, influenced, it seems, by the legendary tales of apocryphal gospels, considered the "brethren" of the Lord as sons of St. Joseph by a first marriage. The Latins, on the contrary, with few exceptions (St. Ambrose, St. Hilary, and St. Gregory of Tours among the Fathers), hold that they were the Lord's cousins. That they were not the sons of Joseph and Mary is proved by the following reasons, leaving out of consideration the great antiquity of the belief in the perpetual virginity of Mary. It is highly significant that throughout the New Testament Mary appears as the Mother of Jesus and of Jesus alone. This is the more remarkable as she is repeatedly mentioned in connexion with her supposed sons, and, in some cases at least, it would have been quite natural to call them her sons (cf. Matt., xii, 46; Mark, iii, 31; Luke, viii, 19; Acts, i, 14). Again, Mary's annual pilgrimage to Jerusalem (Luke, ii, 41) is quite incredible, except on the supposition that she bore no other children besides Jesus. Is it likely that she could have made the journey regularly, at a time when the burden of child-bearing and the care of an increasing number of small children (she would be the mother of at least four other sons and of several daughters, cf. Matt., xiii, 56) would be pressing heavily upon her? A further proof is the fact that at His death Jesus recommended His mother to St. John. Is not His solicitude for her in His dying hour a sign that she would be left with no one whose duty it would be to care for her? And why recommend her to an outsider if she had other sons? Since there was no estrangement between Him and His "brethren", or between them and Mary, no plausible motive for such an action can be imagined. This argument is confirmed by the words with which He recommends her: ἴδε ὁ υἱός σου, with the article before υἱός (son); had there been other sons, ἴδε υἱός σου, without the article, would have been the proper expression.

The decisive proof, however, is that the father and mother of at least two of these "brethren" are known to us. James and Joseph, or Joses, are, as we have seen, the sons of Alpheus, or Clopas, and of Mary, the sister of Mary the Mother of Jesus, and all agree that if these are not brothers of the Saviour, the others are not. This last argument disposes also of the theory that the "brethren" of the Lord were the sons of St. Joseph by a former marriage. They are then neither the brothers nor the step-brothers of the Lord. James, Joseph, and Jude are undoubtedly His cousins. If Simon is the same as the Symeon of Hegesippus, he also is a cousin, since this writer expressly states that he was the son of Clopas the uncle of the Lord, and the latter's cousin. But whether they were cousins on their father's or mother's side, whether cousins by blood or merely by marriage, cannot be determined with certainty. Mary of Clopas is indeed called the "sister" of the Blessed Virgin, (John, xix, 25), but it is uncertain whether "sister" here means a true sister or a sister-in-law. Hegesippus calls Clopas the brother of St. Joseph. This would favour the view that Mary of Clopas was only the sister-in-law of the Blessed Virgin, unless it be true, as stated in MSS. of the Peshîttâ version, that Joseph and Clopas married sisters. The relationship of the other "brethren" may have been more distant than that of the above named four.

The chief objection against the Catholic position is taken from Matt., i, 25: "He [Joseph] knew her not till she brought forth her firstborn son"; and from Luke,

ii, 7: "And she brought forth her firstborn son". Hence, it is argued, Mary must have borne other children. "Firstborn" (πρωτότοκος), however, does not necessarily connote that other children were born afterwards. This is evident from Luke, ii, 23, and Ex., xiii, 2, 12 (cf. Greek text) to which Luke refers. "Opening the womb" is there given as the equivalent of "firstborn" (πρωτότοκος). An only child was thus no less "firstborn" than the first of many. Neither do the words "he knew her not till she brought forth" imply, as St. Jerome proves conclusively against Helvidius from parallel examples, that he knew her afterwards. The meaning of both expressions becomes clear, if they are considered in connexion with the virginal birth related by the two Evangelists.

For the Cousin Theory: St. Jerome, *Adv. Helvid.* in P. L., XXIII; Mill, *Pantheistic Principles*, 220–316; Vigouroux, *Les Livres saints et la critique*, V, 397–420; Corluy, *Les frères de N. S. J. C.* in *Etudes* (1878), I, 5, 145; Meinertz, *Der Jacobusbrief und sein Verfasser* (Freiburg im Br., 1905), 6–54; Cornely, *Introductio* (Paris, 1897), III, 592 sqq.; Schegg, *Jacobus der Bruder des Herrn* (Munich, 1883); Lagrange in *Rev. Bibl.* (1906), 504, 505.
For the Step-Brother Theory: Lightfoot, *Comm. on Gal.*, 252–291.
For the Helvidian View: Hastings, *Dict. Bib.*, I, 320; Zahn, *Forschungen*, VI, *Brüder und Vettern Jesu* (Leipzig, 1900). F. Bechtel.

Brethren of the Poor Life. See Apostolici.

Brethren of the Redemption. See Trinitarian Brothers.

Brethren of the Strict Observance. See Observants.

Brethren of the Twelve. See Narrow Controversy.

Breton, Raymond, a noted French missionary among the Caribbean Indians, b. at Baune, 3 September, 1609; d. at Caen, 8 January, 1679. He entered the Order of St. Dominic at the age of seventeen and was sent (1627) to the famous priory of St. Jacques, at Paris, to finish his classical education and make his course of philosophy and theology. Having obtained his degree in theology, he sailed with three other Dominicans for the French West Indies (1635). Nearly twenty years were devoted to the Antilles missions. During twelve of these he was on the Island of San Domingo, practically alone with the Indians. The other eight years he spent going from island to island, teaching and evangelizing the natives in their own tongue, becoming an adept in the various Carib languages. Returning to France in 1654, he devoted much of his time to preparing young priests for the West Indian missions. To this end he wrote: A Catechism of the Christian Doctrine in Carib (Auxerre, 1664); a French-Carib and Carib-French Dictionary, with copious notes, historical and explanatory, on the Carib language (ibid., 1665); a Carib grammar (ibid., 1667). At the request of the general of the order, he also wrote a valued history of the first years of the French Dominicans' missionary labours among the Caribbean Indians: "Relatio Gestorum a primis Prædicatorum missionariis in insulis Americanis ditionis gallicæ præsertim apud Indos indigenas quos Caribes vulgo dicunt ab anno 1634 ad annum 1643" (MSS). This is considered of great historical importance, and has been used by several writers.

Quétif and Echard, *Script. Ord. Præd.*, II.

Victor F. O'Daniel.

Breton Version. See Versions of the Bible.

Breviarium Alaricianum. See Roman Law.

Breviary.—This subject may be divided, for convenience of treatment, as follows: I. Definition; II. Contents; III. The Hours; IV. Component Parts of the Office; V. History of the Breviary; VI. Reforms.

I. Definition.—The word *breviary* (Lat. *brev-*

iarium), signifies in its primary acceptation an abridgment, or a compendium. It is often employed in this sense by Christian authors, e. g. *Breviarium fidei, Breviarium in psalmos, Breviarium canonum, Breviarium regularum*. In liturgical language *Breviary* has a special meaning, indicating a book furnishing the regulations for the celebration of Mass or the canonical Office, and may be met with under the titles *Breviarium Ecclesiastici Ordinis*, or *Breviarium Ecclesiæ Rominsæ* (*Romanæ*). In the ninth century Alcuin uses the word to designate an office abridged or simplified for the use of the laity. Prudentius of Troyes, about the same period, composed a *Breviarium Psalterii* (v. inf. V. HISTORY). In an ancient inventory occurs *Breviarium Antiphonarii*, meaning "Extracts from the Antiphonary". In the " Vita Aldrici " occurs "sicut in plenariis et breviariis Ecclesiæ ejusdem continentur". Again, in the inventories in the catalogues, such notes as these may be met with: "Sunt et duo cursinarii et tres benedictionales Libri; ex his unus habet obsequium mortuorum et unus Breviarius", or, "Præter Breviarium quoddam quod usque ad festivitatem S. Joannis Baptistæ retinebunt", etc. Monte Cassino about A. D. 1100 obtained a book entitled "Incipit Breviarium sive Ordo Officiorum per totam anni decursionem".

From such references, and from others of a like nature, Quesnel gathers that by the word *Breviarium* was at first designated a book furnishing the rubrics, a sort of *Ordo*. The title *Breviary*, as we employ it—that is, a book containing the entire canonical Office—appears to date from the eleventh century.

St. Gregory VII having, indeed, abridged the order of prayers, and having simplified the Liturgy as performed at the Roman Court, this abridgment received the name of *Breviary*, which was suitable, since, according to the etymology of the word, it was an abridgment. The name has been extended to books which contain in one volume, or at least in one work, liturgical books of different kinds, such as the Psalter, the Antiphonary, the Responsoriary, the Lectionary, etc. In this connexion it may be pointed out that in this sense the word, as it is used nowadays, is illogical; it should be named a *Plenarium* rather than a *Breviarium*, since, liturgically speaking, the word *Plenarium* exactly designates such books as contain several different compilations united under one cover. This is pointed out, however, simply to make still clearer the meaning and origin of the word; and section V will furnish a more detailed explanation of the formation of the Breviary.

II. CONTENTS.—The Roman Breviary, which with rare exceptions (certain religious orders, the Ambrosian and Mozarabic Rites, etc.) is used at this day throughout the Latin Church, is divided into four parts according to the seasons of the year: Winter, Spring, Summer, and Autumn. It is constructed of the following elements: (a) the Psalter; (b) the Proper of the Season; (c) Proper of the Saints; (d) the Common; (e) certain special Offices.

(a) *The Psalter.*—The Psalter is the most ancient and the most venerable portion of the Breviary. It consists of 150 psalms, divided in a particular way, to be described later. These psalms formed the groundwork of the Liturgy of the Jews for twelve centuries before Christ, and He certainly made use of these formularies for His prayers, and quoted them on several occasions. The Apostles followed His example, and handed down to the Christian Churches the inheritance of the Psalter as the chief form of Christian prayer. The Church has carefully preserved them during the lapse of centuries and has never sought to replace them by any other formularies. Attempts have been made from time to time to compose Christian psalms, such as the *Gloria in*

excelsis, the *Te Deum*, the *Lumen Hilare*, the *Te Decet Laus*, and a few others; but those which the Church has retained and adopted are singularly few in number. The rhythmic hymns date from a period later than the fourth and fifth centuries, and at best hold a purely secondary place in the scheme of the Office. Thus the Book of Psalms forms the groundwork of Catholic prayer; the lessons which fill so important a place in this prayer are not, after all, prayer properly so called; and the antiphons, responsories, versicles, etc., are but psalms utilized in a particular manner.

In the Breviary, however, the Psalter is divided according to a special plan. In the earliest period the use of the Book of Psalms in the Office was doubtless exactly similar to that which prevailed amongst the Jews. The president of the choir chose a particular psalm at his own will. Some psalms, such as xxi, seem specially appropriate to the Passion. Another was adapted to the Resurrection, a third suited the Ascension, while others again are specially referable to the Office of the Dead. Some psalms provide morning prayers, others those for night. But the choice was left in the hands of the bishop or president of the choir. Later, probably from the fourth century, certain psalms began to be grouped together, to respond to the divers requirements of the Liturgy.

Another cause led to these groupings and arrangements of the Psalter. Some monks were in the habit of reciting daily the whole of the 150 psalms. But this form of devotion, apart from lessons and other formularies, occupied so much time that they began to spread the recitation of the entire Psalter over a whole week. By this method each day was divided into hours, and each hour had its own portion of the Psalter. From this arrangement arose the idea of dividing the Psalter according to specially devised rules. St. Benedict was one of the earliest to set himself to this task, in the sixth century. In his Rule he gives minute directions how, at that period, the psalms were to be distributed at the disposition of the abbot; and he himself drew up such an arrangement. Certain psalms were set apart for the night offices, others for Lauds, others for Prime, Terce, Sext, and None, others for Vespers and Compline.

It is a subject of discussion amongst liturgists whether this Benedictine division of the psalms is anterior or posterior to the Roman Psalter. Although it may not be possible to prove the point definitely, still it would seem that the Roman arrangement is the older of the two, because that drawn up by St. Benedict shows more skill, and would thus seem to be in the nature of a reform of the Roman division. In any case, the Roman arrangement of the Psalter reaches back to a hoary antiquity, at least to the seventh or eighth century, since when it has not undergone any alteration. The following is its disposition. Psalms i–cviii are recited at Matins, twelve a day; but Sunday Matins have six more psalms divided between the three nocturns. Thus:—

Sunday—Psalms i, ii, iii, vi–xiv; xv, xvi, xvii; xviii, xix, xx.

Monday—Psalms xxvi–xxxvii.

Tuesday—Psalms xxxviii–xli, xliii–xlix, li.

Wednesday—Psalms lii, liv–lxi, lxiii, lxv, lxvii.

Thursday—Psalms lxviii–lxxix.

Friday—Psalms lxxx–lxxxviii, xciii, xcv, xcvi.

Saturday—Psalms xcvii–cviii.

The psalms omitted in this series, namely, iv, v, xxi–xxv, xlii, l, liii, lxii, lxiv, lxvi, lxxxix–xcii, and xciv, are, on account of their special aptitude, reserved for Lauds, Prime, and Compline.

The series, from Ps. cix to Ps. cxlvii inclusively, are used at Vespers, five each day, except Psalms cxvii, cxviii, and cxlii, reserved for other hours.

The last three, cxlviii, cxlix, and cl, which are specially called the psalms of praise (*Laudes*), because of the word *Laudate* which forms their leitmotiv, are always used in the morning Office, which thus gets its name of Lauds.

A glance at the above tables will show that, broadly speaking, the Roman Church did not attempt to make any skilful selection of the psalms for daily recitation. She took them in order as they came, except a very few set apart for Lauds, Prime, and Compline, and selected Ps. cxviii for the day hours. Other Liturgies, as the Ambrosian, the Mozarabic, and the Benedictine, or monastic, have Psalters drawn up on wholly different lines; but the respective merits of these systems need not be here discussed. The order of the ferial Psalter is not followed for the festivals of the year or for the feasts of saints; but the psalms are selected according to their suitableness to the various occasions.

The history of the text of this Psalter is interesting. The most ancient Psalter used in Rome and in Italy was the "Psalterium Vetus", of the Itala version, which seems to have been introduced into the Liturgy by Pope St. Damasus (d. 384). He it was who first ordered the revision of the Itala by St. Jerome, in A. D. 383. On this account it has been called the "Psalterium Romanum", and it was used in Italy and elsewhere till the ninth century and later. It is still in use in St. Peter's at Rome, and many of the texts of our Breviary and Missal still show some variants (Invitatory and Ps. xciv, the antiphons of the Psalter and the responsories of the Proper of the Season, Introits, Graduals, Offertories, and Communions). The Roman Psalter also influences the Mozarabic Liturgy, and was used in England in the eighth century. But in Gaul and in other countries north of the Alps, another recension entered into competition with the "Psalterium Romanum" under the somewhat misleading title of the "Psalterium Gallicanum"; for this text contained nothing distinctively Gallican, being simply a later correction of the Psalter made by St. Jerome in Palestine, in A. D. 392. This recension diverged more completely than the earlier one from the Itala; and in preparing it St. Jerome had laid Origen's Hexapla under contribution. It would seem that St. Gregory of Tours, in the sixth century, introduced this translation into Gaul, or at any rate he was specially instrumental in spreading its use; for it was this Psalter that was employed in the Divine psalmody celebrated at the much honoured and frequented tomb of St. Martin of Tours. From that time this text commenced its "triumphal march across Europe". Walafrid Strabo states that the churches of Germany were using it in the eighth century:—"Galli et Germanorum aliqui secundum quam emendationem Hieronymus pater de LXX composuit Psalterium cantant". About the same time England gave up the "Psalterium Romanum" for the "Gallicanum". The Anglo-Saxon Psalter already referred to was corrected and altered in the ninth and tenth century, to make it accord with the "Gallicanum". Ireland seems to have followed the Gallican version since the seventh century, as may be gathered from the famous Antiphonary of Bangor. It even penetrated into Italy after the ninth century, thanks to the Frankish influence, and there enjoyed a considerable vogue. After the Council of Trent, St. Pius V extended the use of the "Psalterium Gallicanum" to the whole Church, St. Peter's in Rome alone still keeping to the ancient Roman Psalter. The Ambrosian Church of Milan has also its own recension of the Psalter, a version founded, in the middle of the fourth century, on the Greek.

(b) *The Proper of the Season.*—This portion of the Breviary contains the Office of the different liturgical seasons. As is well known, these periods are now thus arranged: Advent, Christmastide, Septuagesima, Lent, Holy Week, paschal time, and the time after Pentecost. But only by slow degrees did this division of the liturgical year develop its present form. It must be traced through its various stages. It may indeed be said that originally there was no such thing as a liturgical year. Sunday, the day above all of the Eucharistic celebration, is at once the commemoration of the Passion, Death, and Resurrection of Jesus Christ; men spoke of the "Pasch of the Crucifixion", of the "Pasch of the Resurrection"—πάσχα σταυρώσιμον; πάσχα ἀναστάσιμον; every Sunday was a renewal of the paschal festival. It was only natural that on the actual anniversary the feast should be kept with peculiar solemnity, for it was the foremost Christian feast, and the centre of the liturgical year. Easter drew in its train Pentecost, which was fixed as the fiftieth day after the Resurrection; it was the festival commemorating the Descent of the Holy Ghost on the Apostles. These fifty days made up an unbroken festival, a Jubilee, a time of joy during which there was no fasting and when penitential exercises were suspended. These two feasts thus linked together are mentioned by ecclesiastical writers from the second century onwards.

Just as Easter was followed by fifty days of rejoicing, so it had its period of preparation by prayer and fasting, from which arose the season of Lent, which, after various changes, commenced finally forty days before Easter, whence its name of *Quadragesima*. The other rallying-point of the liturgical year is the feast of Christmas, the earliest observance of which is of very remote antiquity (the third century at least). Like Easter, Christmas had its time of preparation, called Advent, lasting nowadays four weeks. The remainder of the year had to fit in between these two feasts. From Christmas to Lent two currents may be observed: into one fell the feasts of the Epiphany and the Purification, and six Sundays after the Epiphany, constituting Christmastide. The remaining weeks after these Sundays fall under the influence of Lent and, under the name of *Septuagesima*, create a sort of introduction to it, since these three weeks, Septuagesima, Sexagesima, and Quinquagesima, really belong to Lent by reason of their character of preparation and penance.

The long period between Pentecost and Advent, from May to December, still remains to be dealt with. A certain number of Sundays cluster round special great festivals, as those of St. John the Baptist (24 June), the Holy Apostles Peter and Paul (29 June), St. Lawrence (10 August), and St. Michael (29 September). At a later date these days, which did not fit very conveniently into the general scheme, tended to disappear, and were absorbed into the common time after Pentecost, made up of twenty-four Sundays, thereby uniting Pentecost with Advent; and thus the cycle of the liturgical year is completed.

The Proper of the Season contains, therefore, the Office of all the Sundays and festivals belonging to it, with special lessons, extracts from the Gospels, and frequently also proper antiphons, responsories, and psalms, adapted to the peculiar character of these different periods. It is in the composition of this Liturgy that the Roman Church has displayed her gifts of critical judgment, liturgical taste, and theological acumen. The difference in the character of these periods may be studied in such works as Dom Guéranger's "Liturgical Year".

(c) *Proper of the Saints.*—Following on the Proper of the Season comes in the Breviary the Proper of the Saints, that is to say, that part which contains the lessons, psalms, antiphons, and other liturgical formularies for the feasts of the saints. In reality this Proper commemorates a very large number of saints who find mention in the ecclesiastical Calendar; this, however, need not be given here, as it can easily be consulted. But it may be noted that the greater number of the days of the year—at least nine-tenths —are appropriated to special feasts; and the question has therefore been seriously debated, every time a movement for the reform of the Breviary has arisen, as to how to save the Divine Office from being overwhelmed by these feasts, and as to how to restore to the ferial Office its rightful ascendancy. This is not the place for the discussion of such a problem; but it may be said that this invasion of the Proper of the Season has reached such proportions imperceptibly. It was not always thus; in the beginning, up to the seventh, and even up to the ninth, century, the feasts of saints observed in the Breviary were not numerous, as may be proved by comparing modern Calendars with such ancient ones as may be seen in "An Ancient Syrian Martyrology", "Le calendrier de Philocalus", "Martyrologium Hieronymianum", "Kalendarium Carthaginense". These Calendars contain little more than the following list, beyond the great festivals of the Church:—

Exaltation of Holy Cross—14 September.
Presentation of Jesus, or Purification of B. V. M.— 2 or 15 February.
Dormitio, or Assumption, B. V. M.—15 August.
St. Michael, Archangel—29 September.
Sts. Macchabees—1 August.
St. John Baptist—24 June.
St. Stephen, Protomartyr—26 December.
Sts. Peter and Paul—29 June.
Chair of St. Peter (at Antioch)—22 February.
St. Andrew, Ap.—30 November.
Sts. James the Greater and John, App.—27 or 28 December.
Sts. Philip and James the Less, App.—1 May.
Holy Innocents—23 or 28 December.
St. Sixtus II, Pope—1 or 16 August.
Sts. Perpetua and Felicitas, MM.—7 March.
St. Flavian or Fabian—15 May.
St. Lawrence, M.—10 August.
St. Hippolytus, M.—13 August.
St. Cyprian, M.—14 September.
St. Sebastian, M.—20 January.
St. Agnes, V. & M.—23 January.
St. Timothy, M.—22 August.
St. Vincent, M.—22 February.
St. Felicitas, M.—23 November.
St. Ignatius, M.—17 October, **or 20 December,** or 29 January, or 1 February.
St. Polycarp, M.—26 February.
Seven Holy Sleepers—variable.
St. Pantaleon—variable.

(d) *The Common.*—Under this designation come all the lessons, Gospels, antiphons, responsories, and versicles which are not reserved to a special occasion, but may be employed for a whole group of saints. These Commons are those of Apostles, Evangelists, Martyrs, Confessors Pontiffs, Confessors non-Pontiffs, Abbots, Virgins, and Holy Women. To these may be added the Offices of the Dedication of Churches, and of the Blessed Virgin. The Office of the Dead occupies a place apart. It is most difficult to fix the origin of these Offices. The most ancient seem to belong to the ninth, the eighth, and even the seventh century, and through special formularies may even date still further back. To give one example, the antiphons of the Common of Martyrs in paschal time, "Sancti tui, Domine, florebunt sicut lilium, et sicut odor balsami erunt ante te", "Lux perpetua lucebit sanctis tuis, Domine, et æternitas temporum", are taken from the Fourth Book of Esdras (apocryphal), which was rejected almost everywhere about the end of the fourth century; these verses, therefore, must probably have been borrowed at a period anterior to that date. Probably, also, in the very beginning, the most ancient of these Common Offices were Proper Offices,

and in some of them special features supporting this supposition may be noticed. Thus, the Common of Apostles is apparently referable to the Office of Sts. Peter and Paul and must have been adapted later for all the Apostles. Such versicles as the following in the Common of Martyrs: "Volo, Pater, ut ubi ego sum, illic sit et minister meus", "Si quis mihi ministraverit, honorificabit illum Pater meus", seem to point to a martyr-deacon (διάκονος, minister), and may perhaps specially refer to St. Lawrence, on account of the allusion to the words of his Acts: "Quo, sacerdos sancte, sine ministro properas?" Also, the numerous allusions to a crown or a palm in these same antiphons refer without doubt to the holy martyrs, Stephen, Lawrence, and Vincent, whose names are synonyms for the crown and laurel of victory. The details necessary for the proof of this hypothesis could only be given in a fuller treatise than this; suffice it to say that from the literary standpoint, as from that of archæology or liturgy, these Offices of the Common contain gems of great artistic beauty, and are of very great interest.

(e) *Special Offices.*—The Office of the Blessed Virgin, also very ancient in some of its parts, is of great dogmatic importance; but students of this subject are referred to the Rev. E. L. Taunton's "The Little Office of Our Lady".

The Office of the Dead is, without a shadow of doubt, one of the most venerable and ancient portions of the Breviary, and deserves a lengthy study to itself. The Breviaries also contain Offices proper to each diocese, and certain special Offices of modern origin, which, consequently, need not here detain us.

III. THE HOURS.—The prayer of the Breviary is meant to be used daily; each day has its own Office; in fact it would be correct to say that each hour of the day has its own office, for, liturgically, the day is divided into hours founded on the ancient Roman divisions of the day, of three hours apiece—Prime, Terce, Sext, None, and Vespers, and the night Vigils. In conformity with this arrangement, the Office is portioned out into the prayers of the night vigils, that is to say Matins and Lauds. Matins itself is subdivided into three nocturns, to correspond with the three watches of the night: nine o'clock at night, midnight, and three o'clock in the morning. The office of Lauds was supposed to be recited at dawn. The day offices corresponded more or less to the following hours: Prime to 6 A. M., Terce to 9 A. M., Sext to midday, None to 3 P. M., Vespers to 6 P. M.— It is necessary to note the words *more or less*, for these hours were regulated by the solar system, and therefore the length of the periods varied with the seasons.—The office of Compline, which falls somewhat outside the above division, and whose origin dates later than the general arrangement, was recited at nightfall. Nor does this division of the hours go back to the first Christian period. So far as can be ascertained, there was no other public or official prayer in the earliest days, outside the Eucharistic service, except the night watches, or vigils, which consisted of the chanting of psalms and of readings from Holy Scripture, the Law, and the Prophets, the Gospels and Epistles, and a homily. The offices of Matins and Lauds thus represent, most probably, these watches. It would seem that beyond this there was nothing but private prayer; and at the dawn of Christianity the prayers were said in the Temple, as we read in the Acts of the Apostles. The hours equivalent to Terce, Sext, None, and Vespers were already known to the Jews as times of prayer and were merely adopted by the Christians. At first meant for private prayer, they became in time the hours of public prayer, especially when the Church was enriched with ascetics, virgins, and monks, by their vocation consecrated to prayer. From that time, i. e. from the end of the third century, the monastic idea exercised a preponderant influence on the arrangement and formation of the canonical Office. It is possible to give a fairly exact account of the establishment of these Offices in the second half of the fourth century by means of a document of surpassing importance for the history we are now considering: the "Peregrinatio ad Loca Sancta", written about A. D. 388, by Etheria, a Spanish abbess. This narrative is specifically a description of the Liturgy followed in the Church of Jerusalem at that date.

The Offices of Prime and Compline were devised later, Prime at the end of the fourth century, while Compline is usually attributed to St. Benedict in the sixth century; but it must be acknowledged that, although he may have given it its special form for the West, there existed before his time a prayer for the close of the day corresponding to it.

IV. COMPONENT PARTS OF THE OFFICE.—Each of the hours of the Office in the Roman Liturgy is composed of the same elements: psalms (and now and then canticles), antiphons, responsories, hymns, lessons, versicles, little chapters, and collects (prayers). A few words must be said about each of these elements from the particular point of view of the Breviary.

(a) *Psalms and Canticles.*—Nothing need here be added to what has already been said in section II concerning the psalms, except that they are used in the Breviary sometimes in order of sequence, as in the ferial Offices of Matins and Vespers, sometimes by special selection, independently of the order of the Psalter, as in Lauds, Prime, Compline, and, in general, in the Offices of the Saints and other feasts. Another point to notice in the composition of the Roman Office is that it allows of the inclusion of a certain number of canticles, or songs, drawn from other portions of Holy Writ than the Psalter, but put on the same footing as the psalms. These are: the Canticle of Moses after the passage of the Red Sea (Exodus, xv); the Canticle of Moses before his death (Deut., xxxii); the Prayer of Anne the mother of Samuel (I Kings, ii); the Prayer of Jonas (Jon., ii); the Canticle of Habacuc (Habacuc, iii); the Canticle of Ezechias (Is., xxxviii); the Canticle of the Three Children (Dan., iii, 26); The Benedicite (Dan., iii, lii); lastly, the three canticles drawn from the New Testament: the Magnificat, the Benedictus, and the Nunc dimittis.

This list of canticles coincides more or less with those used in the Greek Church. St. Benedict admits these canticles into his Psalter, specifically stating that he borrows them from the Church of Rome, and thus providing a further argument for the priority of the Roman Office over the monastic.

(b) *Antiphons.*—The antiphons which are read nowadays in the Breviary are abridged formularies which almost always serve to introduce a psalm or canticle. They consist sometimes of a verse taken from a psalm, sometimes of a sentence selected from the Gospels or Holy Scripture, e. g. "Euge, serve bone, in modico fidelis, intra in gaudium Domini tui"; occasionally they consist of phrases not culled from the Bible, but modelled on its style, i. e. they are the invention of a liturgical author, for example: "Veni, Sponsa Christi, accipe coronam, quam tibi Dominus præparavit in æternum". Originally, the meaning of the word, and the function fulfilled by the antiphon, was not what it is now. Although it is difficult to determine precisely the origin and purport of the term, it seems that it is derived from *antiphona* (ἀντιφώνη) or from the adjective ἀντίφωνος, and that it signified a chant by alternate choirs. The singers or the faithful were divided into two choirs; the first choir intoned the first verse of a psalm, the second continued with the second verse, the first followed with the third verse, and so on to the end of the

psalm. The *antiphoned* chant is thus recitation by two choirs alternately. This term has given rise to technical discussions which cannot here be entered into.

(c) *Responsory*, whose composition is almost the same as that of the antiphon—verse of a psalm, sentence out of Holy Scripture or of ecclesiastical authorship—nevertheless differs from it entirely as to the nature of its use in recitation or chant. The precentor sang or recited a psalm; the choir or the faithful replied, or repeated either one of the verses or simply the last words of the precentor. This form, like the antiphon, had already been in use amongst the Jews, and appears even in the construction of certain psalms, as in cxxxv, "Laudate Dominum quoniam bonus", where the refrain, "Quoniam in æternum misericordia ejus", which recurs in each verse, certainly corresponds to a responsory.

(d) *Hymns.*—The term *hymn* has a less definite meaning than those of *antiphon* or *responsory*, and in the primitive liturgies its use is somewhat uncertain. In the Roman Breviary, at each hour either of the day or of the night there is a little poem in verses of different measures, usually very short. This is the hymn. These compositions were originally very numerous. Traces of hymns may be discerned in St. Paul's Epistles, and in the New Testament. In the fourth and fifth centuries hymnology received a great impetus. Prudentius, Synesius, St. Gregory of Nazianzus, St. Hilary, and St. Ambrose composed a great many. But it was above all in the Middle Ages that this style of composition most developed, and collections of them were made, filling several volumes. The Roman Breviary contains but a moderate number of hymns, forming a real anthology. Some of them are masterpieces of art. It was at a comparatively late date (about the twelfth century) that the Roman Liturgy admitted hymns into its Breviary. In its primitive austerity it had hitherto rejected them, without, however, condemning their employment in other liturgies.

(e) *Lessons.*—By this term is meant the choice of readings or of extracts in the Breviary, taken either from Holy Writ or from the Acts of the Saints, or from the Fathers of the Church. Their use is in accordance with the ancient Jewish custom, which, in the services of the Synagogues, enjoined that after the chanting of psalms, the Law and the Prophets should be read. The primitive Church partly adopted this service of the Synagogue, and thus brought into being the service of the night watches. But the course of readings was altered; after a lesson from the Old Testament, the Epistles of the Apostles or their Acts or the Gospels were read. Some Churches somewhat extended this usage; for it is certain that the letters of St. Clement of Rome, of St. Ignatius, and of Barnabas, and the "Pastor" of Hermas were read. Some Churches, indeed, less well instructed, allowed books not wholly orthodox, like the Gospel of Peter, to be read. In time lists were made out to fix what books might be read. Muratori's "Canon" and, still better, the "Decrees of Gelasius" may be studied from this point of view with profit. Later on men were not content to confine themselves to the reading of the holy books; certain Churches wished to read the Acts of the Martyrs. The Church of Africa, which possessed Acts of great value, signalized itself in this respect. Others followed its example. When the Divine Office was more developed, probably under monastic influence, it became customary to read, after Holy Writ, the commentaries of the Fathers and of other ecclesiastical writers on the passage of the Bible just previously heard. This innovation, which probably began in the sixth, or even in the fifth, century, brought into the Divine Office the works of St. Augustine, St. Hilary, St. Athanasius, Origen, and others. To these, later, were added those of St. Isidore, St. Gregory the Great, the Venerable Bede, and so on. This new development of the Office gave rise to the compilation of special books. In primitive times the Book of Psalms and the books of the Old Testament sufficed for the Office. Later, books were compiled giving extracts from the Old and New Testaments (Lectionary, Gospel, and Epistle Books) for each day and each feast. Then followed books of homilies (Homiliaries)—collections of sermons or of commentaries of the Fathers for use in the Office. All these books should be studied, for they form the constituent elements which later combined into the Breviary.

Further, as regards these lessons, it is well to notice that, as in the case of the psalmody, two lines of selection were followed. The first, that of the order of ferial Offices, ensures the reading of the Scripture, from Genesis to the Apocalypse, in sequence; the second, that of the order for feasts of the saints and festivals, breaks in upon this orderly series of readings and substitutes for them a chapter or a portion of a chapter specially applicable to the feast which is being celebrated.

The following is the table of lessons from the Bible. In its essential features, it goes back to a very venerable antiquity:—

Advent—Isaias, and St. Paul's Epistles.

Christmas, Epiphany—St. Paul, following this very ancient order:—Epp. to Romans, Corinthians, Galatians, Ephesians, Philippians, Colossians, Thessalonians, Timothy, Titus, Philemon, Hebrews.

Septuagesima and Lent—Genesis and the other books of the Pentateuch.

Passiontide—Jeremias.

Easter and Paschal Time—Acts of the App., Apocalypse, Epp. of St. James, St. Peter, St. John.

Time after Pentecost—Books of Kings.

Month of August—Proverbs, Ecclesiastes, Book of Wisdom, Ecclesiasticus.

Month of September—Job, Tobias, Judith, Esther.

Month of October—Machabees.

Month of November—Ezechiel, Daniel, the twelve minor Prophets.

(f) *Versicles and Little Chapters.*—The *Capitulum*, or Little Chapter, is really a very short lesson which takes the place of lessons in those hours which have no special ones assigned to them. These are: Lauds, Prime, Terce, Sext, None, Vespers, and Compline. By reason of their brevity and of their unimportance, they are much less complicated than the longer ones, and no more need here be said about them. The Versicles belong to the psalmody, like responsories and antiphons; usually they are taken from a psalm, and belong to the category of liturgical acclamations or shouts of joy. They are usually employed after lessons and little chapters, and often take the place of responsories; they are, in fact, brief responsories. The ferial *Preces* and the Litanies probably belong to the category of versicles.

(g) *Collects.*—Collects, also called prayers, are not psalmodic prayers; they are of a completely different character. Their place in the Breviary changes little; they come towards the end of the Office, after the psalmody, the lessons, little chapters, and versicles, but preceded by the *Dominus vobiscum*, and they gather up in a compendious form the supplications of the faithful. Their historical origin is as follows: During the earliest period, the president of the assembly, usually the bishop, was entrusted with the task of pronouncing, after the psalmody, chants, and litanies, a prayer in the name of all the faithful; he therefore addressed himself directly to God. At first this prayer was an improvisation. The oldest examples are to be found in the Διδαχὴ τῶν Ἀποστόλων, and in the Epistle of St. Clement of

Rome, and in certain Epistles of St. Cyprian. In time, towards the fourth century, collections of prayers were made for those who were not adepts in the art of improvisation; these were the earliest forerunners of Sacramentaries and Orationals, which later occupied so important a place in the history of the Liturgy. The Leonine, Gelasian, and Gregorian Sacramentaries form the chief sources whence are drawn the collects of our Breviary. It may be observed that they are of great theological importance, and usually sum up the main idea dominating a feast; hence, in them the significance of a festival is to be sought.

V. HISTORY OF THE BREVIARY.—In the preceding paragraphs, a certain portion of the history of the Breviary, as a choir book at least, has been given. At first, there was no choir book, properly so called; the Bible alone sufficed for all needs, for therein were the psalms for recitation and the books which furnished the various lessons. It is of course most probable that the Psalter is the most ancient choir book; it was published apart to fulfil this special function, but with divisions—marks to indicate the portions to be read; and at the end were copied out the canticles recited in the Office like the psalms, and sometimes, following each psalm, came one or more prayers. A study of manuscript Psalters, which has not as yet been methodically undertaken, would be extremely useful for the Liturgy. Then, little by little, as the canonical Office was evolved, books were drawn up to meet the wants of the day—Antiphonaries, Collectaria, etc. In the twelfth century John Beleth, a liturgical author, enumerates the books needed for the due performance of the canonical Office, namely:—the Antiphonary, the Old and New Testaments, the Passionary (Acts of the Martyrs), the Legendary (Legends of the Saints), the Homiliary, or collection of homilies on the Gospels, the *Sermologus*, or collection of sermons, and the treatises of the Fathers. In addition to these should be mentioned the Psalterium, Collectarium for the prayers, the Martyrology, etc. Thus, for the recitation of the canonical Office, quite a library was required. Some simplification became imperative, and the pressure of circumstances brought about a condensation of these various books into one. This is the origin of the Breviary. The word and the thing it represents appeared—confusedly, it might be—at the end of the eighth century. Alcuin is the author of an abridgment of the Office for the laity—a few psalms for each day with a prayer after each psalm, on an ancient plan, and some other prayers; but without including lessons or homilies. It might rather be called a Euchology than a Breviary. About the same time Prudentius, Bishop of Troyes, inspired by a similar motive, drew up a *Breviarium Psalterii*. But we must come down to the eleventh century to meet with a Breviary properly so called. The most ancient manuscript known as containing within one volume the whole of the canonical Office dates from the year 1099; it comes from Monte Cassino, and at the present time belongs to the Mazarin Library. It contains, in addition to other matter which does not concern the present inquiry, the Psalter, canticles, litanies, hymnary, collects, blessings for the lessons, little chapters, antiphons, responsories, and lessons for certain Offices. Another manuscript, contemporary with the preceding, and also coming from Monte Cassino, contains Propers of the Season and of the Saints, thus serving to complete the first-mentioned one. Other examples of the Breviary exist dating from the twelfth century, still rare and all Benedictine. The history of these origins of the Breviary is still somewhat obscure; and the efforts at research must continue tentatively till a critical study of these manuscript Breviaries has been made on the lines of such workers as Delisle, Ebner, or Ehrensperger, on the Sacramentaries and Missals.

It was under Innocent III (1198–1216) that the use of Breviaries began to spread outside Benedictine circles. At Rome, no longer solely for the Roman Basilicas, but still for the Roman Court alone, *Breviaria* were drawn up, which, from their source, are called *Breviaria de Camerâ*, or *Breviaria secundum usum Romanæ Curiæ*. Texts of this period (beginning of thirteenth century) speak of "Missalia, Breviaria, cæterosque libros in quibus Officium Ecclesiasticum continetur", and Raoul de Tongres specifically refers to this Roman Breviary. But this use of the Breviary was still limited, and was a kind of privilege reserved for the Roman Court. A special cause was needed to give the use of this Breviary a greater extension. The Order of Friars Minor, or Franciscans, lately founded, undertook the task of popularizing it. It was not a sedentary order vowed to stability, like those of the Benedictines or Cistercians, or like the Regular Canons, but was an active, missionary, preaching order. It therefore needed an abridged Office, convenient to handle and contained in a single volume small enough to be carried about by the Friars on their journeys. This order adopted the Breviarium Curiæ with certain modifications which really constitute, as it were, a second edition of this Breviary. It is sometimes called the Breviary of Gregory IX because it was authorized by that pontiff. One of the chief modifications effected by the Friars Minor was the substitution of the Gallican version of the Psalter for the Roman. The cause was won; this eminently popular and active order spread the use of this Breviary everywhere. Antiphonaries, Psalters, Legendaries, and Responsoraries disappeared by degrees before the advance of the single book which replaced them all. Still more, by a kind of *jus postliminii*— a right of resumption—the Church of Rome, under Nicholas III (1277–80), adopted the Breviary of the Friars not merely for the Curia, but also for the Basilicas; and, as an inevitable consequence, this Breviary was bound, sooner or later, to become that of the Universal Church.

VI. REFORMS OF THE BREVIARY.—In the preceding sections, the history of the ecclesiastical Office has been unfolded from its inception. If this history could be put into few words, though necessarily forming an incomplete statement, it might be said that from the first to the fifth century it was in formation; from the fifth to the eleventh century it was in process of development and expansion; and during the twelfth and thirteenth centuries the Breviary properly so called was emerging into being. From then till now (that is, from the fourteenth century onwards) might be termed the period of reform. The fourteenth and fifteenth centuries represent for the Liturgy, as for the greater number of other ecclesiastical institutions, a period of decline, for it is the time of schisms, and in that one word everything harmful is summed up. The few documents that are available for the liturgical history of that time attest this, as, for example, the "Gesta Benedicti XIII" and the "XV Ordo Romanus". Disorder and abuses crept into the Liturgy as into everything else.

Dom Bäumer, in his "Histoire du bréviaire", repeatedly points out that it is impossible to separate the history of the Liturgy from the occurrences that make up the general history of the Church, and that the phases through which the general history takes us are reflected in the evolution of the Liturgy. It is not surprising, therefore, that the sojourn of the popes at Avignon and the Great Schism have exerted their baneful influence on the history of the Liturgy. And the reaction is still being felt. Raoul de Tongres, who died early in the fifteenth

century, was even at that early period a critic and a reformer; in his famous work "De observantiâ Canonum" he agitated for some settlement of liturgical rules. The "XV Ordo Romanus" already referred to, the work of Amelius, sacristan to Urban V and librarian to Gregory XI, breathes the same idea. The abuses pointed out by the different authors of the time may be reduced to the following: (a) The almost complete suppression of the Offices of Sundays and ferias, so that it became impossible that the whole Psalter should be recited every week, and certain psalms were never recited at all. (b) An accumulation of Offices on the same day, tending to the destruction of their solemnity and also to the elimination of the Offices of the Season. (c) Substitution for the lessons from Holy Scripture of legends and apocryphal histories and of texts of doubtful value for antiphons, hymns, and responsories. On this subject the "Consultatio" presented by John de Arzo to the Council of Trent should be studied. (d) The introduction of superstitious usages, strange formularies of prayer, and feasts bordering in character on the grotesque.

The Humanism of the Renaissance, which had its ardent champions even in the Church, as Bembo, Sadoletus, etc., to say nothing of certain popes, caused the idea of a special reform of the Breviary, in the direction of greater literary purity and perfection, to be entertained in certain quarters. Strange schemes were propounded, little in consonance with the spirit of the Church. A Florentine canon, Marsiglio Ficino, and Peter Pomponatius, for instance, suggested that the clergy should read the classical authors instead of the Breviary. Others, though not going so far as this, thought the diction of the Breviary barbaric, and wanted to translate it into Ciceronian Latin. The corrections suggested included such astounding phrases as the following: the forgiveness of sins becomes "superosque manesque placare"; the Begetting of the Word was to be "Minerva Jovis capite orta"; the Holy Ghost was "Aura Zephyri cœlestis", etc. These attempts failed; nevertheless, at a later date, under Urban VIII, similar Humanist tendencies came again to the surface and this time asserted their power by an emendation of the hymns. Amongst such attempts may be mentioned that of Ferreri. He was the Bishop of Guarda Alfieri in the Kingdom of Naples, a Humanist, and wrote under the auspices and patronage of Leo X. He began with the hymns. His work, which has been preserved, is interesting and contains some very beautiful pieces, polished in style. A good number of them have, unfortunately, nothing more of the spirit of poetry in them than harmony and rhythm; they are wanting in inspiration and above all in the warmth of piety; nearly all are strewn with Pagan names and allusions, representing Christian verities, as "Triforme Numen Olympi" for the Trinity, "Natus Eumolpho Lyricenque Sappho . . . Thracius Orpheus", referring to the Blessed Virgin, etc. Ferreri also busied himself with a revision of the Breviary, but nothing was published, and now no trace of the materials he collected is forthcoming.

Another attempt at reform, much better known, and having results of far-reaching importance, was that of Quignonez, Cardinal of Santa Croce in Gerusalemme, who was entrusted by Clement VII with the task of completing the work begun by Ferreri. He was a Franciscan, and had been successfully employed on various commissions. His revision was the most original that has ever been attempted, and liturgical experts, like Guéranger, Edmund Bishop, and Bäumer, have studied his labours in detail. Only the principal points of his scheme can be mentioned here. Considered theoretically, it cannot be denied that his Breviary is drawn up on easy, convenient, and logical lines, and, on the whole, is felicitously arranged. But in the light of tradition and of liturgical principles the only possible verdict is that Quignonez' Breviary, being constructed on a priori principles, violating most of the liturgical rules, must be condemned. The author starts with the theory, contrary to all tradition, that an essential difference exists between the public celebration of the Office and its private recitation. For private recitation, therefore, all such portions as antiphons, responsories, versicles, little chapters, even hymns may be eliminated, as, according to Quignonez, these are meant solely for choir use. According to his arrangement, the entire Psalter was to be recited once a week—an excellent idea, in consonance with primitive practice; but it was applied too rigidly and narrowly, for no attention was paid to the suitability of certain psalms to special feasts. Feasts were never to change the order of the psalms, which were to be recited successively from i to cl.

Every hour had three psalms; and in consequence of this severe regularity, there disappeared the deep and historical motive which gave to each hour its own characteristics. The legends of the saints and the hymns underwent drastic, but designed, revision. Another principle, which would be deserving of all praise had it not been applied too rigorously, was that the entire Scriptures should be read through every year. Quignonez' Breviary, as might be expected, met both with enthusiastic approval and with determined opposition. Its success may be judged from the number of editions through which it passed. The Sorbonne criticized it severely, and other experts declared against Quignonez and attacked his work mercilessly. In the end, opposition proved the stronger, and even popes rejected it. Moreover, it was supplanted by other revisions made on more orthodox liturgical lines, less ambitious in scope, and more in accordance with tradition. The newly founded Congregation of Theatines applied itself to this task with energy and enthusiasm. Caraffa, one of its founders, took a share in the work, and when he became pope under the name of Paul IV (1555-59), he continued his labours, but died before seeing their completion, and it was thus reserved to others to bring them to a successful issue.

The Council of Trent, which effected reforms in so many directions, also took up the idea of revising the Breviary; a commission was appointed concerning whose deliberations we have not much information, but it began to make definite inquiries about the subject entrusted to it. The council separated before these preliminaries could be concluded; so it was decided to leave the task of editing a new Breviary in the pope's own hands. The commission appointed by the council was not dissolved, and continued its investigations. St. Pius V, at the beginning of his pontificate (1566), appointed new members to it and otherwise stimulated its activity, with the result that a Breviary appeared in 1568, prefaced by the famous Bull, "Quod a nobis". The commission had adopted wise and reasonable principles: not to invent a new Breviary and a new Liturgy; to stand by tradition; to keep all that was worth keeping, but at the same time to correct the multitude of errors which had crept into the Breviaries and to weigh just demands and complaints. Following these lines, they corrected the lessons, or legends, of the saints and revised the Calendar; and while respecting ancient liturgical formularies such as the collects, they introduced needful changes in certain details. More intimate accounts of this revision should be studied at length in the approved authorities on the history of the Breviary. Here it will be enough to give a short sketch of the chief points affecting this Breviary, as it is substantially the same as that used at this date. The celebrated Bull of approval, "Quod a nobis" (9 July, 1568), which prefaced it, explains the reasons which had weighed with Rome in putting forth an official text of public prayer, and gives an account of the labours which had been undertaken to ensure its correction; it withdrew the papal approbation from all Breviaries which could not show a prescriptive right of at least two centuries of existence. Any Church which had not such an ancient Breviary was bound to adopt that of Rome. The new Calendar was freed from a large number of feasts, so that the ferial Office was once more accorded a chance of occupying a less obscure position than of late it had. At the same time the real foundation of the Breviary—the Psalter—was respected, the principal alterations made being in the lessons. The legends of the saints were carefully revised, as also the homilies. The work was one not only of critical revision, but also of discriminating conservatism, and was received with general approval. The greater number of the Churches of Italy, France, Spain, Germany, England, and, generally, all the Catholic States, accepted this Breviary, saving only certain districts, as Milan and Toledo, where ancient Rites were retained.

This Pian Breviary (Breviarium Pianum), while still remaining the official prayer book of the Universal Church, has undergone certain slight alterations in the course of time, and these must here be noted, but without reference to the new feasts of saints which have been added to the Calendar century by century, even though they occupy a not inconsiderable space in the ecclesiastical disposition of the year. The chiefest and most important changes were made under Sixtus V. At first the text of the versions of the Bible used in the Liturgy was altered. As soon as the revision of the Vulgate undertaken during this pontificate was completed, the new text replaced the old one in all official books, particularly in the Breviary and the Missal. Sixtus V instituted a new Congregation—that of Rites—in 1588, charging it with a study of the reforms contemplated in the Pian Breviary, which had then been in use more than twenty years. To him is due the honour of this revision of the Breviary, although till lately it had been ascribed to Clement VII (1592-1605). Although the first suggestion came from Sixtus V, nevertheless it was only under Clement VII that the work was really vigorously pushed forward and brought to a conclusion. The revising committee had as its members such men as Baronius, Bellarmine, and Gavanti. The first-named especially played a most important part in this revision, and the report which he drew up has recently been published. The emendations bore especially on the rubrics: to the Common of Saints was added that of Holy Women not Virgins; the rite of certain feasts was altered; and some new feasts were added. The Bull of Clement VII, "Cum in Ecclesiâ", enjoining the observance of these alterations, is dated 10 May, 1602.

Further changes were made by Urban VIII (1623-44). The commission appointed by him was content to correct the lessons and some of the homilies, in the sense of making the text correspond more closely with the oldest manuscripts. There would therefore be no call to treat of this revision under Urban VIII at greater length but for the fact that, outside the work of this commission, he effected a still more important reform, over which even now discussion has not ceased to make itself heard. It affected the hymns. Urban VIII, being himself a Humanist, and no mean poet, as witness the hymns of St. Martin and of St. Elizabeth of Portugal, which are of his own composition, desired that the Breviary hymns which it must be admitted are sometimes trivial in style and irregular in their prosody, should be corrected according to grammatical rules and put into true metre. To this end he called in the aid of certain Jesuits of distinguished literary attainments. The corrections made by these purists were so numerous—952 in all—as to make a profound alteration in the character of some of the hymns. Although some of them without doubt gained in literary style, nevertheless, to the regret of many, they also lost something of their old charm of simplicity and fervour. At the present date, this revision is condemned, out of respect for ancient texts; and surprise may be expressed at the temerity that dared to meddle with the Latinity of a Prudentius, a Sedulius, a Sidonius Apollinaris, a Venantius Fortunatus, an Ambrose, a Paulinus of Aquileia, which, though perhaps lacking the purity of the Golden Age, has, nevertheless, its own peculiar charm. Even the more barbarous Latinity of a Rhabanus Maurus is not without its archaic interest and value. Moreover, the revisers were ill-advised inasmuch as they adopted a *via media;* they stopped half-way. If, as it is freely admitted, the Roman Breviary contains many hymns of inferior poetic worth, and whose sentiment is perhaps commonplace, then there is no reason why they should not be eliminated altogether, and replaced by new ones. Many of the older ones, however, were worthy of being preserved just as they stood; and, in the light of the progress made in philology, it is certain that some of the corrections in prosody made under Urban VIII convict their authors of ignorance of certain rhythmic rules, whose existence, it is only right to say, came to be known later. However it may be, these corrections have been retained till the present time. A comparison of the older with the modern text of the hymns may be consulted in Daniel, "Thesaurus Hymnologicus", (Halle, 1841).

Nothing further was done under the successors of Urban VIII, except that new Offices were added from time to time, and that thus the ferial Office began again to lose ground. We must come down to the pontificate of Benedict XIV, in the second half of the eighteenth century, to meet with another attempt at reform; but before doing so, reference must be made to efforts inaugurated in France during the seventeenth and eighteenth centuries, whose history has been learnedly elucidated in detail by Dom Guéranger in vol. II of his "Institutions liturgiques", devoted in great part to an account of this struggle. The Roman Breviary, revised by Pius IV, had been received in France without opposition. Under Louis XIV, however, attempts at revision were made, inspired by a spirit of resistance and antagonism to the Roman Court. They took form amongst the two parties which made open profession of Gallicanism and Jansenism. The supporters of this reform, several of whom were men of learning and culture, were aided by the historical and critical works which at that time were being poured forth in France, so that in these projects for the reform of the Breviary, side by side with rash suggestions, there were many which were both useful and well judged. One of the first schemes was that of the Paris Breviary, mooted in 1670 and pursued under the patronage of Archbishops Hardouin de Péréfixe and de Harlay. The Breviary called after de Harlay appeared in 1680. The corrections it embodied affected in particular the legends of the saints and the homilies, but numerous other parts were also touched. The details and the examination of them may best be studied in Dom Guéranger's pages. Although it might have seemed that the Breviary had by then been sufficiently emended, in the following century another Archbishop of Paris, Monseigneur de Vintimille, had another Breviary drawn up, which was published in 1736, and remained in use till the middle of last century. It partly embodied what is called the "liturgical Utopia of Quignonez". Its source, however, was not above suspicion, for some of those who had laboured at its production were Jansenists.

This reform, while not wanting in sound ideals, was carried out, however, regardless of liturgical traditions.

What had been going on in Paris had its counterpart in other dioceses of France, where new Breviaries were introduced, for the most part inspired by the ideas which had dominated those of de Harlay and of Vintimille. A reaction against these broke out in France between 1830 and 1840, having for its leader a Benedictine monk, Dom Guéranger, Abbot of Solesmes and an eminent liturgist, who, in his "Institutions liturgiques", arraigned the new Breviaries, exposed the mistakes underlying their construction, and proved that their authors had acted without warrant. His onslaught met with immediate success for in twenty years the greater number of the dioceses gave up their Gallican Breviaries and adopted once more the Roman Liturgy. The exact figures are as follows: in 1791 eighty dioceses had rejected the Roman Liturgy and had fashioned special liturgies for themselves; in 1875 Orléans, the last French diocese which had retained its own liturgy, re-entered Roman liturgical unity.

While France, during the seventeenth and eighteenth centuries, was letting herself be carried away in the reform of her Breviaries by Gallican and Jansenist leanings, other countries were following in her wake. In Italy, Scipio Ricci, Bishop of Pistoia, an ardent Jansenist, drew up a new Breviary, and certain districts of Germany adopted the same course, with the result that Breviaries modelled on those of France appeared at Trier, Cologne, Aachen, Münster, and Mainz; and it was long before Germany returned to liturgical unity.

While the Jansenists and Gallicans were creating a new Liturgy, Prosper Lambertini, one of the most learned men in Rome, who became pope under the name of Benedict XIV, determined to copy the example of some of his predecessors, and to carry out a further reform of the Breviary. A congregation was instituted for the special purpose; its papers, for long unedited, have of late years been gone through by MM. Roskovány and Chaillot, each of whom has published considerable portions of them. The first meeting of the congregation was in 1741, and the discussions which took place then and later are of interest from the liturgist's point of view, but need not detain us. Although this project of reform came to nothing, nevertheless the work accomplished by the congregation was of real value and reflects credit on its members, some of whom, like Giorgi, were eminent liturgists. Future workers in this department of learning will have to take account of their collections. After the death of Benedict XIV (4 May, 1758) the labours of this congregation were suspended and were never again seriously resumed. Since Benedict XIV's time changes in the Breviary have been very few, and of minor importance, and can be outlined in a few words. Under Pius VI the question of a reform of the Breviary was brought up once more. By that pontiff's orders a scheme was drawn up and presented to the Congregation of Rites, but it was found impossible to overcome the difficulties which surrounded an undertaking of this kind. In 1856 Pius IX appointed a commission to examine the question: Is the reform of the Breviary opportune? But again only preliminary matters engaged their attention. Amongst the Acts of the Vatican Council a series of propositions are to be found, whose object was the simplification or correction of the Breviary, but the inquiry never got beyond that stage. Finally, under Leo XIII, a commission was appointed, at the close of 1902, whose duties were a study of historico-liturgical questions. Its province is a wider one, comprising not only the Breviary, but also the Missal, the Pontifical, and the Ritual. It has, further, to supervise future liturgical editions, and thus to see that they conform as closely as possible with historical data. This commission, though attached to the Congregation of Rites, is nevertheless autonomous. It consisted at first of five members under the presidency of Monsignor Duchesne, namely: Mgr. Wilpert, Father Ehrle, S. J., Father Roberti, Mgr. Umberto Benigni, Mgr. Mercati, and a few consultors. What the results of their labours may be is not yet known.

This sketch of the reforms of the Breviary proves, however, the desire of the Church to eliminate the blemishes which disfigure this book. All these efforts have not been sterile; some of these revisions mark real progress; and it may be hoped that the present commission will effect certain improvements which the progress of historical studies and criticism have made the more needful.

On the different Breviaries: Breviary of Cluny; Brigittine Breviary; Breviary of St. Bernard; Durham Breviary; Hereford Breviary; Mozarabic Breviary; Breviary of Rouen; Sarum Breviary; etc., CABROL, *Introduction aux études liturgiques*, s. v. *Bréviaire, Breviarium, Breviary*. On the Milan Breviary, Mozarabic Breviary, and Eastern Breviaries, PROBST, in *Kirchenlex.* (1883), II, s. v. *Brevier;* BÄUMER, *Geschichte des Breviers* (Freiburg, 1895), the most important and most complete work on the subject, Fr. tr., with additions and corrections by BIRON, as *Histoire du bréviaire* (Paris, 1905). ID., *Breviarii Romani editio nova Tornacensis, 1882, collata Vaticanæ Urbano Papâ VIII evulgatæ, 1632* (1882); BATIFFOL, *L'Histoire du bréviaire Romain* (Paris, 1893; tr. London); BAUDOT, *Le bréviaire romain* (1907); GRANCOLAS, *Commentaire historique sur le bréviaire romain* (Paris, 1727; Lat. tr., Venice, 1734); ROSKOVÁNY, *De Cœlibatu et Breviario* (1861, 1877, 1881, 1888); PROBST, *Brevier und Breviergebet* (Tübingen, 1868); PIMONT, *Les hymnes du bréviaire romain* (Paris, 1874–84); PLEITHNER, *Ælteste Geschichte des Breviergebetes* (Kempten, 1887); NILLES, *Kalendarium Manuale utriusque Ecclesiæ Orientalis et Occidentalis* (Innsbruck, 1896); Article *Brevier, Realencyklopädie, IV;* GUÉRARD, *Polyptique de l'abbaye de St. Rémy de Reims* (Paris, 1853); BECKER, *Catalogi Bibliothecarum antiqui* (Rome, 1885); DUCANGE, *Glossarium; MICROLOGUS, de ecclesiasticis observationibus* in *Bibl. Vet. Patr.* (Lyons), XVIII; GUÉRANGER, *Instit. liturg.* (2nd ed.), I; GERBERT, *Vet. Liturg.,* II; *Katholik.* (1890), II, 511; KAULEN, *Einleitung in die Heilige Schrift; Geschichte der Vulgata* (Mainz, 1868); THOMASI, *Opera,* ed., VEZZOSI (Rome, 1747), II; BERGER, *Histoire de la Vulgate pendant les premiers siècles du Moyen Age* (Paris, 1893); *Anglo-Saxon Psalter* (1843); WALAFRID STRABO, *De rebus ecclesiasticis* in *P. L.,* CXIV, 957; MURATORI, *Anecdota Ambrosiana,* IV, *P. L.,* LXXII, 580 sqq.; WARREN, *The Antiphonary of Bangor* (London, 1893); CABROL, *Le Livre de la Prière Antique* (Paris, 1900); CABROL, *Dict. d'archéologie et de liturgie;* TAUNTON, *The Little Office of Our Lady* (London, 1903); *Peregrinatio Etheriæ,* tr., *Holy Week in Jerusalem in the Fourth Century,* reprinted from DUCHESNE, *Christian Worship* (London, 1905); *Rev. d'histoire et de littérature religieuses* (Paris, 1898); PROBST, *Lehre und Gebet in den drei ersten Jahrh.;* PITRA, *Hymnographie de l'Eglise Grecque* (Paris, 1867); MONE, *Lateinische Hymnen des Mittelalters* (Freiburg im Br., 1853–55); DANIEL, *Thesaurus Hymnologicus* (Halle, 1841); CHEVALIER, *Topo-bibliographie,* s. v. *Hymnes;* LECLERCQ, *Actes des Martyrs in Dict. d'archéol.,* I, 379; BRAMBACH, *Psalterium. Bibliographischer versuch über die liturgischen Bücher des christl. Abendlandes* (Berlin, 1887); BELETH, *Rationale Divinorum Officiorum;* MOLINIER, *Catalogue des mss. de la biblioth. Mazarine;* RADULPHUS TONGRENSIS, *De Canonum observantiâ* in *Max, Biblioth. Vet. Patrum.,* XXVI; *Rassegna Gregor.,* September-October, 1903, 397 sqq.; WICKHAM LEGG, *Some Local Reforms* (London, 1901); SCHMID, *Studien über die Reform des Römischen Breviers* in *Theol. Quartalsch.* (Tübingen, 1884); BERGEL, *Die Emendation des Römischen Breviers in Zeitsch. f. kathol. Theol.* (Innsbruck, 1884); KIRCH, *Die Liturgie der Erzdiöcese Köln* (Cologne, 1868); ROSKOVÁNY, *Breviarium, V;* CHAILLOT, *Analecta Juris Pont.* (1885), XXIV; MARTIN, *Omn. Conc. Vatic. Documentorum Collecto* (2nd ed., Paderborn, 1873); *Acta et Decreta in Collectio Lacensis* (Freiburg im Br., 1890), VII; LECLERCQ, *Les Martyrs* (Paris, 1905), IV.

FERNAND CABROL.

Breviary, ABERDEEN, THE.—This breviary may be described as the Sarum Office in a Scottish form. The use of the ancient Church of Salisbury was generally adopted in Scotland and Ireland during the Middle Ages, both for the Liturgy (or Mass) and for the canonical hours. Its introduction into Scotland has been sometimes incorrectly attributed to Edward I, King of England, and assigned to the year 1292; but there is evidence to show that the date of its introduction was considerably earlier. For example, Herbert, Bishop of Glasgow from 1147 to 1164, certainly adopted the Sarum Use for his church, and received the papal sanction for so doing. Father Innes, who died in Paris in 1744, asserts that "all the Scots missals or breviaries I ever saw are *secundum usum Sarum*, local saints being written in". According to the "Registrum Moraviense", the bishop, dean, and chapter of Moray received and duly approved the *Ordo* of the Church of Salisbury in the year 1242. The Diocese of Moray was contiguous with that of Aberdeen. The preference shown by the Scots for the Sarum Rite was evidently the outcome of the strong feeling, of which we find constant evidence in the history of the Scottish Church, against anything which seemed like admitting the claim to jurisdiction over her so often put forward by the Church of York. There might, it was no doubt thought, have been some apparent justification for this claim, had the Scottish Church adopted and maintained the Use of York in her liturgy and office.

The Breviary of Aberdeen was mainly the work of the learned and pious William Elphinstone, Bishop of Aberdeen from 1483 to his death in 1514. Not only did he bring together the materials, but in some instances, notably in that of the Scottish saints, he himself composed the lessons. A peculiar feature of this breviary, and one in which it differs from nearly every other, is that in some of the festivals of saints the whole of the nine lessons at Matins are concerned with their lives. These legends of the saints of Scotland are of singular interest and considerable historical value, and they have been extensively drawn upon by the Bollandists and the later Scottish martyrologists. The accuracy of the quotations and references occurring in the book have been tested and admitted by many modern historians. Although the breviary is in its structure and essentials entirely in uniformity with that of Sarum, it is nevertheless exclusively proper to Scotland, and it was, as we know, intended to supersede all service-books issued in connexion with the famous Church of Salisbury. This fact is quite clear from the royal mandate dated 15 September, 1501, wherein the Aberdeen book is set forth as the "Breviary for general use within the realm of Scotland".

The work was produced from the printing-press which Walter Chapman and Andrew Myllar had set up in Edinburgh, in the year 1507. Four copies of the original breviary (in black-letter) are known to exist; one in Edinburgh University library; a second in the Library of the Faculty of Advocates, Edinburgh; a third in the private library of the Earl of Strathmore; and a fourth (an imperfect copy) in the library of King's College, Aberdeen. The reprinting of the volume was undertaken in 1854, under the supervision of the Rev. William Blew, M.A., and it was subsequently published by Mr. G. J. Toovey, for private circulation among the members of the Bannatyne Club. The originally printed copies are of small octavo size, and bear the dates of 1509 and 1510. As a printed Office-book its actual use was but of short duration, only about half a century elapsing between its issue and the overthrow of the ancient Church of Scotland (1560). There is no positive proof that it was ever generally adopted throughout the dioceses of Scotland; indeed the probabilities are against its ever having become anything like universal at the time of the Reformation. It must be remembered, in connexion with this, that the injunction for its adoption was civil rather than ecclesiastical, and there is some reason to suppose that on this account it was not considered strictly binding by the church authorities of the kingdom. It is interesting to note that in the new Scottish *Proprium*, which in 1903 was formally sanctioned and adopted for use in the Scottish dioceses forming the Province of St. Andrews (the *cultus* of the ancient Scottish saints having been approved by the Holy See several years previously), many collects, antiphons, etc.

are found which have been borrowed from the offices in the Aberdeen Breviary.

Miscellany of the Spalding Club, II, 364–366, and Preface, p. cxx (Aberdeen, 1842); *Kalendars of Scottish Saints* (ed. FORBES, Edinburgh, 1862); *Registrum Episcopatus Moraviensis* (ed. Bannatyne Club, Edinburgh, 1837); *Breviarium Aberdonense* (London, 1854), Pref. by LAING; VIAN in *Dict. Nat. Biog.*, s. v. *Elphinstone, William.*

D. O. HUNTER-BLAIR.

Brewer, HEINRICH, a German historian, b. at Puffendorf in Germany, 6 September, 1640; d. at the same place about 1713. He was educated at the *Gymnasium Tricoronatum* in Cologne and was ordained priest in 1664. After this he was for a time a private tutor at Cologne, then curate of the cathedral at Bonn. He continued his studies while filling these positions and in 1667 was made lecturer on theology at the University of Cologne. From 1669 to 1682 he was rector of a convent of nuns at Cologne, a position which gave him the leisure to carry on his historical studies. In 1682 he became parish priest of the church of St. Jacob at Aachen. After twenty-nine years of fruitful labour he resigned his pastorate in 1712 and returned to his quiet native town. During his residence at Bonn he published, in 1668, a poem of slight poetic value entitled: "Crinitum poli Sidus". His most important work is: "Historica rerum notabiliorum ubique pæne terrarum gestarum enarratio; breviter et succincte pro historiæ universalis Brachelio-Thuldenanæ continuatione adornata", (Cologne, 1672–75, two volumes). Shortly after this he published a revised edition of the "Historia Universalis Brachelio-Thuldenana" in eight volumes. Brewer now received the title of Imperial Historiographer. The honour was fitly bestowed, for Brewer was one of the few historians who seek out original sources and make full use of them. He added to each volume copies of important official documents, besides making skilful use of pictures and maps. A much discussed question of the time was the identity of the author of the "Imitation of Christ". Brewer made an independent investigation and tried to prove that Thomas à Kempis was the author in a work entitled: "Thomæ à Kempis biographia" (Cologne, 1681). Even from the modern point of view this work is a very creditable one. A publication of less importance and one which is at times strongly marked by local feeling is that entitled: "Der in der Reliquienverehrung rechtschaffen catholisch und wahrhaftig grosser Kayser Karl bey gewöhnlicher Eröffnung der Aachischen Schatzkammer Heyligthumbs" (Aachen, 1685).

HARTZHEIM, *Bibliotheca Coloniensis*, 114.

PATRICIUS SCHLAGER.

Breynat, GABRIEL. See MACKENZIE, DIOCESE OF.

Brian Boroimhe (BORU). See IRELAND.

Briand, JOSEPH OLIVIER, seventh Bishop of Quebec, b. in 1715 at Plérin, Brittany; d. 25 June, 1794. He studied at the Seminary of St. Brieuc, and was ordained in 1739, but left home secretly to follow Bishop Pontbriand to Canada. Briand was a strenuous worker, self-possessed, tactful, and devoted. During the siege of Quebec (1759), he, as vicar-general, directed the diocesan affairs in the absence of the bishop. He ministered to the dying at the battle of St. Foy (1760), and after the bishop's death was appointed administrator of the diocese which then included Acadia, Louisiana, and Illinois. During the crisis in New France, when many colonists abandoned the country, Briand foresaw that a change of allegiance was inevitable, and realized the benefit which would accrue to the people of Canada.

When the Treaty of Paris (1763) was signed he ordered a Te Deum for the cessation of the Seven Years' War and praised General Murray for his humanity towards the conquered. In the midst of the fanaticism which attempted to violate the treaty

and hamper religious freedom, Briand appealed to London to maintain the rights of the Church. The British Crown finally gave ear to his demand, and he was consecrated in Paris (1766).

Hailed as the second founder of the Church in Canada, Briand was joyfully received by the people and the British governor. The pope also expressed his pleasure and approved Bishop Briand's past attitude, thereby removing the charges that he had acted with timidity towards Murray and Dorchester (see Brasseur and Faillon). Despite his poverty, he declined a gift of the clergy and a plan for his support, and took up his residence at the Seminary of Quebec. Briand's purpose in reconciling the claims of Rome and London was to insure the permanence of the episcopacy. He demanded two bishops simultaneously, so that the survivor, Rome permitting, might consecrate his successor. This request was finally granted. Through his influence and tact, further plans for perverting the faithful were thwarted. The Test Oath was modified so as to be acceptable to the Holy See, and the passage of the Quebec Act (1774), admitting Catholics to public functions and confirming religious freedom, and of the Habeas Corpus Act, granting Catholics the rights and privileges of British subjects, was also partly due to Briand's efforts.

After the expulsion of the Jesuits from Louisiana and Illinois, Bishop Briand appointed Father Meurin vicar-general in the latter section of the country. When the forces of the Continental army invaded Canada in 1775, he issued a pastoral letter in which he enjoined fidelity to the king. The Continental Congress in an address to the king and people of England had protested against the Quebec Act, while in its appeal to the Canadians there were no features which were objectionable to Catholics. Briand denounced this duplicity and drew attention to the actions of the Colonists twenty years previous both in their cruelty towards the Acadians and their laws against missionaries. Upon Montgomery's defeat he ordered a Te Deum, and in 1776 he isssued another energetic letter in which he urged to repentance those Canadians who had aided the invading troops, whom he characterized as enemies of the Faith. This, together with the drastic measure of refusing the sacraments to all Canadian sympathizers with the Colonial cause, preserved Canada to the British Crown. Later, Briand, who was invited by Cardinal Castelli, the Prefect of the Propaganda, to administer confirmation in Pennsylvania and Maryland, abandoned the plan upon the protest of Father Ferdinand Steinmeyer, S. J. (popularly known as Father Farmer), who drew attention to the anti-Catholic feeling which was then prevalent in the Colonies.

In 1765 Briand published a "Catechism", the first book printed in Canada. He resigned his see in 1784 and was the consecrator of his two successors: the Rt. Rev. Louis Philippe Marianchau d'Esglis, 29 Nov. 1784, who died 4 June, 1788; and the Rt. Rev. Jean François Hubert, 19 Nov., 1786. Briand died after fifty-five years in the priesthood and twenty-eight in the episcopate.

TÊTU, *Les évêques de Québec* (Quebec, 1889); BRASSEUR DE BOURBOURG, *Histoire du Canada* (Paris, 1852); FAILLON, *Hist. de la colonie française en Canada* (Villemarie, 1865).

LIONEL LINDSAY.

Bribery, the payment or the promise of money or other lucrative consideration to induce another, while under the obligation of acting without any view to private emolument, to act as the briber shall prescribe. Only the moral aspect of bribery will be touched upon here; the historical aspect of the question will be dealt with in the articles on the nations and countries.

The word is ordinarily used with reference to payments or other lucrative consideration illicitly made in favour of persons whose duty to the commonwealth binds them to act for the common good. Thus judges are bound, as servants of the commonwealth, to administer justice without fear or favour, and they are forbidden to take bribes from litigants or others. Similarly, regard for the public good should be the motive which influences those who appoint to public offices, or who have the placing of contracts for public works or institutions, or who are entrusted with the execution of the laws, or who elect representatives to seats in the legislature. They should appoint only worthy candidates who will serve the public well. If they neglect the common good, and seek private advantage from the exercise of the trust committed to them, they violate their duty to the commonwealth, and they make themselves accomplices in all the evil which results from the incompetence or the roguery of those whom they elect. The general principle is obvious enough, but in the matter of details difficulties are encountered which cannot all be solved in the same way. An elector may say that as a rule there is very little to choose between the candidates for some public position or office, and that even if there were a difference in their moral character and capacity to serve the public, it is difficult for the ordinary voter to detect it. Why should he not make a little money by promising to vote for the candidate who is ready to pay the highest price?

It may be that in this hypothesis no injustice is done by taking a bribe and that there is no obligation incurred of making restitution. Still the action is immoral, and rightly forbidden by law. A person who has a vote in the appointment to offices or in the election of representatives is under a serious responsibility to use his power to the best of his ability. If he takes a bribe he renders himself practically incapable of exercising a discriminating judgment. He is bound to do what he can to make sure that the person for whom he votes is worthy of the post; but if he takes a bribe this blinds him, blunts his judgment, and makes him incapable of doing his duty. Besides, in questions of this kind, we must look at the general result of the action whose moral quality we are studying; the general result of the willingness of voters to sell their vote for money is that power and office are put in the hands of that portion of the moneyed class which is least worthy and most selfish.

Those who hold public offices to which patronage or power of any sort is attached are specially bound to use their power for the common good. They accepted office under the express or tacit condition that they would use their influence for the public benefit, not merely for their private emolument. If they sell the posts, offices, or favours of any kind, in their gift, for money or any lucrative consideration, they violate the express or tacit pledge which they gave on their assumption of office. There is more malice in such actions than in that of the venal elector who sells his vote for money. They also produce more direct and more immediate evils in the commonwealth. A man who has bought an office, or a post, or a contract for money will as a rule try to recoup himself at the expense of the public. It is not likely that he will be an honourable or even an honest servant, and the disastrous consequences of his appointment begin to show themselves at once. The evils are perhaps less, but they do not cease, if offices or favours are bestowed in consideration of money contributed to the funds of the political party. Power, influence, and even an external respectability are sometimes given to unscrupulous men whose only recommendation is the possession of wealth.

Moralists have devoted special attention to the question of bribery in connexion with the administration of justice. The judge on his assumption of office undertakes to administer justice to all who come before him, and in most countries binds himself by a special oath to do his duty. He receives a salary for his services. If he accepts bribes from suitors or criminals he makes himself practically incapable of exercising an unbiased judgment, fails in the execution of his duty, and violates his oath. If he takes money for giving a sentence which is just, he commits a sin against justice and is bound to restore the bribe to him who gave it. For the judge is bound in justice to pronounce a just sentence apart from the bribe, and his action affords him no title to take payment for what is due in justice without payment. If he takes a bribe for giving a sentence which is unjust, he will of course sin against justice on account of the sentence, and will be bound to make reparation to the injured party for the wrong that he has suffered. Some moralists, however, refuse to impose on him the obligation of restoring the bribe, on the ground that something was given for it which indeed the judge had no right to give, but which, for all that, was worth the money to him who paid the bribe. The same principles are applicable to jurymen, arbitrators, and referees, who have obligations similar to those of judges. Bribery under all the above aspects is in most countries forbidden by positive law and punished by severe penalties.

Lugo, *De justitiâ et jure* (Paris, 1869), disp. xxxiv, disp. xxxvii, n. 123 sqq.; Lehmkuhl, *Theologia Moralis* (Freiburg, 1898), I, 809, 810.

T. Slater.

Briçonnet, (1) Guillaume, a French Cardinal, b. at Tours, date of birth unknown; d. at Narbonne, 14 December, 1514. He was a younger son of Jean Briçonnet, Lord of Varennes, in Touraine, Secretary to the king and Collector-general of Customs. Appointed Superintendent of Finances for the Province of Languedoc under Louis XI, Guillaume Briçonnet discharged the duties of his office with such integrity and efficiency, and showed himself so devoted to the interests of Louis that that monarch recommended him to his successor. Charles VIII made him Secretary of the Treasury, raised him to the first place in the Council of State, and, according to the historian Guicciardini, would undertake nothing in the government of his kingdom without the advice of Briçonnet. Ludovico Sforza, called the Moor, wishing to dispossess his nephew of the Duchy of Milan, and finding himself opposed by Ferdinand, King of Naples, sent an embassy under the Count of Belgiojoso to Charles to induce the French king to assert his claims to the Kingdom of Naples as heir to the house of Anjou. Sforza promised to place all his troops at the king's service. Briçonnet having shortly before this lost his wife, Raoulette de Beaune, by whom he had three sons, had entered the ecclesiastical state and been named Bishop of St.-Malo. To flatter his ambition the Milanese ambassadors assured him that the king's influence would raise him to the cardinalate. Briçonnet, thus won over to the Sforza interest, adroitly encouraged the warlike dispositions of his sovereign, triumphed over the opposition of the royal council, of the Duke of Bourbon, and of Anne of France, the Duke's wife, influenced Charles to sign a secret treaty with Sforza, and assured the king of his ability to raise the funds necessary to carry on the war both on land and sea.

Pope Alexander VI, alarmed at the apparent danger threatening Italy, promised the cardinal's hat to Briçonnet if he could prevail upon Charles to abandon his enterprise; but Briçonnet, realizing that he could not govern without flattering the king's passion for conquest, urged him on, and, notwithstanding the dilapidated state of the treasury, succeeded in meeting the expenses of the war. Accompanying Charles on his expedition, he provoked a mutiny in the French army, by his treachery in sacrificing the Pisans, allies of France, to their enemies, the Florentines, and had he not hidden himself from the fury of the soldiers they would have taken his life. Upon this occasion, as upon others, Briçonnet's ambition led him into conduct at variance with his motto: *Ditat servata fides*. Charles had entered Rome as a conqueror, greatly irritated against Alexander VI who had stirred up opposition against him; but the adroit Briçonnet reconciled his royal master with the pope, and for reward received the cardinal's hat. This honour was conferred in a special consistory held in the king's presence, 16 January, 1495, the new cardinal taking the title of Cardinal of St.-Malo, from his episcopal see.

Briçonnet soon had cause to repent the advice he had given to invade Italy. A formidable league was formed for the purpose of cutting off the French retreat, and neither the diplomacy nor the entreaties of the French cardinal had any effect on the hostile generals. The prowess of Charles and the invincible valour of his troops alone saved the French from a humiliating defeat. With 8,000 men the king defeated, at Tornovo, an army of 40,000, and opened a road to France. Soon after this Briçonnet, induced by a tempting promise of preferment for one of his sons, tried to persuade Charles to break off the peace negotiations and support with an army the Duke of Orléans' claims to the Duchy of Milan. Charles, however, preferred the counsels of Philippe de Comines and sacrificed the interests of the duke, and the king's premature death put an end to the influence of Briçonnet, Louis XII giving his confidence to the Cardinal d'Amboise. But whilst serving his king and the State, the Cardinal of St.-Malo had not overlooked his own interests; he had obtained from Alexander VI the Bishopric of Nîmes. His title being disputed by the nominee of the chapter, there arose a litigation which lasted until the year 1507, when Briçonnet was awarded the title, In 1497 he had received *in commendam* the Bishopric of Toulon, and in the same year succeeded his brother in the archiepiscopal See of Reims. On the 27th of May, 1498, he crowned Louis XII in his cathedral and followed the king to Paris. As a peer of France, he assisted at the session of the Council of State at which the marriage of Louis with Jeanne, the daughter of Louis XI, was annulled.

When he had ceased to be a minister of State, Briçonnet retired to Rome for two years. Louis then made use of his talents to check what he called the arrogance of the warrior pope, Julius II. By his king's direction Briçonnet took steps to assemble at Pisa a council of cardinals opposed to the policy of Julius, and bent on the reformation of the head and hierarchy of the Church. He left Rome suddenly and secretly with a group of cardinals whom he had won over, and opened his council at Pisa, but soon transferred it to Milan, and thence to Lyons. He was, however, summoned to appear before the pope, was deprived of the Roman purple and excommunicated. Louis, on his side, bestowed upon him *in commendam* the rich Abbey of St.-Germain-des-Prés and the government of Languedoc. At the death of Julius II Briçonnet was absolved from all censures and excommunication, and restored by Leo X to the Sacred College. He then retired to end his days at Narbonne, for which see he had exchanged Reims. He was buried in a superb mausoleum which he had built for himself in the church of Our Lady.

Whilst in power, Briçonnet showed himself a patron of men of letters; they dedicated their works to him and became his panegyrists. He was called *oraculum regis* and *regni columna*. His life was in fact swayed by ambition and occupied by intrigues. He composed a manual of Latin prayers, dedicated to Charles VIII. At Saint-Malo he issued several synodal instructions.

(2) GUILLAUME, Bishop of Meaux, France, b. at Tours in 1472; d. at the château of Esmant near Montereau, 24 January, 1534. He was a son of Cardinal Briçonnet (see above), and before entering the ecclesiastical state was known as the Count de Montbrun. In 1489 he was named Bishop of Lodève. Distinguished by remarkable judgment, great learning, and a love of study, he received from Louis XII several preferments, and was named as chaplain to the Queen. In 1507 he succeeded his father as Abbot of St.-Germain-des-Prés. The king entrusted him with delicate and difficult missions, and sent him, in the same year that Guillaume became abbot, to Rome as extraordinary ambassador for the purpose of justifying the conduct of his prince against the accusations of the Emperor Maximilian. In an eloquent Latin speech pronounced in the presence of the pope and of the Sacred College, the bishop fully vindicated Louis. Guillaume enjoyed equally the confidence of Francis I, who transferred him to the See of Meaux, and sent him as ambassador to Leo X to Rome, where he resided for two years. As Abbot of St.-Germain, he displayed a great zeal for the reform of abuses, put an end to disorders, and revived monastic regularity, spirit, and fervour. As Bishop of Meaux, he held a number of synods, and made wise regulations against the depravity of morals and the relaxation of ecclesiastical discipline, and promoted among his clergy a taste for learning, to bring back to the Catholic Faith the disciples of the new doctrine, who were already numerous in his diocese. He was no less zealous in opposing the encroachments of the religious and in directing them back to the spirit of their state. The Cordeliers, a branch of the Franciscan Order, accused the bishop of heresy, basing their accusation on the protection given by him to the partisans of Humanism. The bishop defended himself and was declared innocent. His love of letters caused him to increase considerably the library of the Abbey of St.-Germain. He translated into French the "Contemplationes Idiotæ de amore divino".

(3) ROBERT, Archbishop of Reims, France, fifth son of Jean Briçonnet, an elder brother of the Cardinal [see (1)]. Date of birth uncertain; d. at Moulins, 3 June, 1497. He owed to the credit which Guillaume had with Charles VIII his rapid elevation to public offices and dignities. He was named Canon of St.-Aignan at Orléans, Abbot of the rich Abbey of St.-Vaast at Arras, and in 1493 he was raised to the archiepiscopal See of Reims, four years before the Cardinal was appointed to that see. Charles appointed him President of the Superior Tribunal of Finances, and Chancellor of France. He enjoyed this new dignity for only twenty-two months before his death. He showed himself, as did his brothers and nephews, a patron of men of letters.

FISQUET, *La France pontificale* (Paris); *Biographie universelle, ancienne et moderne* (Paris, 1812); FELLER, *Biographie universelle* (Paris, 1847); GUÉRIN, *Dictionnaire des dictionnaires* (Paris, 1892).

F. M. L. DUMONT.

Bridaine, JACQUES, preacher, b. at Chusclan, France, 21 March, 1701; d. at Roquemaure, 22 December, 1767. Having completed his studies at the Jesuit college of Avignon he entered the Seminary of the Royal Missions of St. Charles of the Cross. His oratorical ability announced itself before his ordination to the priesthood by the remarkable talent he brought into play in awakening interest and exciting emotion even in the catechetical instructions which he was deputed to give. When only in minor orders, he was assigned as Lenten preacher in the Church of Aigues-Mortes. It was there he first made use of his peculiar methods. His extreme youth provoked the derision of the people and when Ash Wednesday arrived, the church was empty.

Undismayed, he put on his surplice and went out in the principal streets, ringing a bell, and inviting the people to hear him. He succeeded in bringing an immense multitude to the church who came out of curiosity, but when he began in a most unusual fashion by singing a canticle about death the con-

JACQUES BRIDAINE

gregation burst out in loud laughter; whereupon he opened upon them with such fierceness of denunciation that silence and amazement took possession of all. He was characteristically sensational. He wrote little and gave way to the inspiration of the moment and as a consequence his utterances present at times an incoherent jumble of incongruous figures and ideas, which clash with each other and are often even grotesque. It was Cardinal Maury who called attention to his exordium in the sermon on Eternity which was said to be improvised. Father Cahour, S.J., inserts it in his "Chefs-d'Œuvre d'éloquence", and Maury who wrote it from memory declares that it was not unworthy of Bossuet or Demosthenes. It was pronounced at St.-Sulpice, before an audience in which there were many bishops, a vast crowd of ecclesiastics and men of distinction in civil and military life. Bridaine assures them that in spite of their worldly greatness he is not abashed by their presence, and in the most impassioned language denounces them as sinners, and bids them, haughty and disdainful as they are, to tremble before him. "To-day I hold your condemnation in my hand." Opinions are divided about its excellence as an example of oratory; some finding a self-consciousness in it which is unapostolic.

His voice was so sonorous and penetrating that he could easily be heard by an audience of ten thousand people. To his natural oratorical gifts he added, in order to produce the impression he was aiming at, all the effect that could be obtained by the most gorgeous and elaborate church ceremonial, as well as whatever excitement could be produced by singing, by splendid processions, by unusual prayers, and by novel situations which were all skilfully arranged so as to captivate the eye or ear, or to fix or startle the imagination. A supreme instance of these "methods" as he called them, and which he always insisted upon being carried out, is narrated by Madame Necker in the "Nouveaux Mélanges" (I, 138). He had just delivered a stirring discourse when addressing himself to the great procession which had followed him he said: "I am now going to bring you home" and he led them to the grave-yard. Sensational as he was he wrought many astounding conversions. In the course of his life he preached two hundred and fifty-six missions, travelling to almost every town of France in the performance of his work. Pope Benedict XIV gave him permission to preach anywhere in Christendom. Medals were struck in his honour, and the most distinguished prelates showed him the greatest reverence and affection. He was of a sweet, modest, simple disposition, of lively faith and deep piety. His "Cantiques Spirituels" passed through forty-seven editions. He has also left five volumes of sermons. The Protes-

tants of France are said to have been particularly friendly to him, because of the many good offices he performed in their regard. For fourteen years he followed the spiritual guidance of a missionary like himself named Mahistre. In 1742 Cardinal Fleury proposed to establish a missionary congregation for all France under the direction of Bridaine, but the death of the cardinal caused the project to fall through.

France was wild with excitement about him. His appeals were so powerful that in a mission which he preached at Chalon-sur-Saône in 1745 there were restitutions to the amount of 100,000 francs. His reputation as an orator was so great that even Massillon was unwilling to preach in his presence. In the course of his missions he established what he called "peace tribunals", courts composed of some of his associate missionaries, a number of irreproachable laymen, and the parish priest. To these courts all disputes were submitted and the decisions were accepted as final. His life was written by the Abbé Carron. The book was frequently translated into English, but the last edition was published as far back as 1831.

Cahour, Chefs-d'Œuvre d'Éloquence (Paris, 1854); Goschler, Dict. encyc. de théol. cath. (Paris, 1869).

T. J. Campbell.

Bridal Ring. See Ring.

Bridge-Building Brotherhood, The.—During the twelfth and thirteenth centuries, we hear of the existence of various religious associations founded for the purpose of building bridges. This work, which tended greatly to the relief of travellers and particularly of pilgrims, was regarded as a work of piety quite as much as of public utility. Even where no religious organization was formed it was customary for the bishops to grant indulgences to those who, by money or labour, contributed to the construction of a bridge. Of this the register of Archbishop Grey of York, for instance, in the thirteenth century, affords many examples. But in the South of France, regular associations were commonly formed for the purpose, and these it has been the custom to regard as religious orders living under vows. Upon more accurate investigation, however, this idea has proved to be erroneous. The brotherhoods in question seem rather to have been of the nature of guilds or confraternities, or, at most, to have been organized in something the same way as a "third Order", wearing a habit with a distinctive badge, but not being bound by perpetual vows.

In many cases, these associations were constituted of three branches: knights, who contributed most of the funds and were sometimes called *donati;* clergy who might be in the strict sense monks, and artisans who performed the actual work of building. We also hear sometimes of "sisters" belonging to the same association. Besides the construction of bridges, the lodging and entertainment of travellers, as well as the *quête,* or collection of alms commonly entered into the scope of the brotherhoods. The origin of these institutions is wrapped in much obscurity. The brotherhood known in particular as the *Fratres Pontifices* (*Ponti-fices*=bridge-builders) or *Frères Pontifes,* is commonly said to have been founded by St. Bénézet (a Provençal variant of the name Benedict), a youth who, according to the legend, was Divinely inspired to build the bridge across the Rhone at Avignon. Although the Bull supposed to have been addressed to the *Fratres Pontifices,* in 1191, by Clement III may not be authentic, it is certain that a number of bridges were built about this time in that part of France; also that the old bridge at Avignon, some arches of which still remain, dates from the end of the twelfth century, and it is certain that St. Bénézet was a historical personage. The *Fratres Pontifices* were certainly very active, and if they did not construct the Avignon bridge they built others at Bonpas, Lourmarin, Mallemort, Mirabeau, etc. On the other hand, the famous bridge over the Rhone at Saint-Esprit was certainly constructed by a separate association. Many of the official documents connected with it are still preserved.

FALK in *Historisch-Politische Blätter* (1881), LXXXVII; IDEM in *Kirchenlex.*, II, 1331. These contributions of Dr. Falk must be read with some caution. LENTHÉRIC in *Mémoires de l'Académie de Nîmes* (1889–90), 72–91; HÉLYOT-BADICHE, *Dictionnaire des ordres religieux*, III, 237–245; BRUGUIER-ROURE, *Les constructeurs de ponts au moyen âge* (Paris, 1875); GRÉGOIRE, *Recherches historiques sur les congrégations de frères pontifes* (Paris, 1806); LEFORT in *Travaux de l'Académie de Reims*, LXXI, 372–399 and LXXVI, 206–227; JUSSERAND, *English Wayfaring Life*, tr. (London, 1889), 33–89; ENLART, *Manuel d'archéologie française* (Paris, 1904), II, 264–272.

HERBERT THURSTON.

Bridget of Sweden (also BIRGITTA), SAINT, the most celebrated saint of the Northern kingdoms, born c. about 1303; d. 23 July, 1373. She was the daughter of Birger Persson, governor and provincial judge (*Lagman*) of Uppland, and of Ingeborg Bengtsdotter. Her father was one of the wealthiest landholders of the country, and, like her mother, distinguished by deep piety. St. Ingrid, whose death had occurred about twenty years before Bridget's birth, was a near relative of the family. Birger's daughter received a careful religious training, and from her seventh year showed signs of extraordinary religious impressions and illuminations. To her education, and particularly to the influence of an aunt who took the place of Bridget's mother after the latter's death (c. 1315), she owed that unswerving strength of will which later distinguished her. In 1316, at the age of thirteen, she was united in marriage to Ulf Gudmarsson, who was then eighteen. She acquired great influence over her noble and pious husband, and the happy marriage was blessed with eight children, among them St. Catherine of Sweden. The saintly life and the great charity of Bridget soon made her name known far and wide. She enjoyed intercourse with several learned and pious theologians, among them Nicolaus Hermanni, later Bishop of Linköping, Matthias, canon of Linköping, her confessor, Peter, Prior of Alvastrâ, and Peter Magister, her confessor after Matthias. She was later at the court of King Magnus Eriksson, over whom she gradually acquired great influence. Early in the forties (1341–43) in company with her husband she made a pilgrimage to Santiago de Compostella. On the return journey her husband was stricken with an attack of illness, but recovered sufficiently to finish the journey. Shortly afterwards, however, he died (1344) in the Cistercian monastery of Alvastrâ in East Gothland. Bridget now devoted herself entirely to practices of religion and asceticism, and to religious undertakings. The visions which she believed herself to have had from her early childhood now became more frequent and definite. She believed that Christ Himself appeared to her, and she wrote down the revelations she then received, which were in great repute during the Middle Ages. They were translated into Latin by Matthias Magister and Prior Peter. St. Bridget now founded a new religious congregation, the Brigittines, or Order of St. Saviour, whose chief monastery, at Vadstena, was richly endowed by King Magnus and his queen (1346). To obtain confirmation for her institute, and at the same time to seek a larger sphere of activity for her mission, which was the moral uplifting of the period, she journeyed to Rome in 1349, and remained there until her death, except while absent on several pilgrimages, among them one to the Holy Land in 1373. In August, 1370, Pope Urban V confirmed the Rule of her congregation. Bridget made earnest representations to Pope Urban, urging the removal of the Holy See from Avignon back to Rome. She accomplished the greatest good in Rome,

however, by her pious and charitable life, and her earnest admonitions to others to adopt a better life, following out the excellent precedents she had set in her native land. The year following her death her remains were conveyed to the monastery at Vadstena. She was canonized, 7 October, 1391, by Boniface IX.

Vita S. Birgittæ, compiled by her confessors PETER OF VADSTENA, and PETER OF ALVASTRÂ in 1373, ANNERSTEDT ed. in *Script. rerum Svecicarum medii ævi* (Upsala, 1871–76), III, Pt. II, 188 sqq.: *Vita S. Birgittæ auctore Birgero, archiep. Upsalensi* in *Acta SS.*, Oct., IV, 485 sqq.; *Vita auctore Bartholdo de Roma* (Rome) 495 sqq.; SCHÜCK, *Svensk Literaturhistoria* (Stockholm, 1890), 129 sqq.; HAMMERICH, *Den hellige Birgitta og Kirken i Norden* (Copenhagen, 1863), German tr. MICHELSEN (Gotha, 1872); BINDER, *Die hl. Birgitta von Schweden und ihr Klosterorden* (Munich, 1891); RINGSEIS, *Leben der hl. Birgitta* (Ratisbon, 1890); FLAVIGNY, *Ste. Birgitte de Suede* (Paris, 1892); JOANN. DE TURRECREMATA, *Liber revelationum celestium S. Birgitte de regno Swecie* (Rome, 1488, and often reprinted), with notes by GUNDISALVI DURANTI (Rome, 1606); HEUSER (ed.), *Revelationes selectæ* (Cologne, 1851); KLEMMING (ed.), *H. Birgittas uppenbarelser* (4 vols., Stockholm, 1857–62); *Certayne reuelacyons of St. Birgitte, with an epistle of St. Bernard* (London, s. d.); MEGERLE tr., *Birgittæ von Schweden himmlische Offenbarungen* (2 vols., Cologne, 1664).

J. P. KIRSCH.

Bridgett, THOMAS EDWARD, priest and author, b. at Derby, England, 20 January, 1829, of Protestant parents; d. at St. Mary's Clapham, 17 February, 1899. His father was a silk manufacturer, and sent his son first to Mill Hill, a Congregationalist College near London, then to Tonbridge, a Church of England public school, where he was baptized at the age of sixteen, and finally, in October, 1847, to St. John's College, Cambridge, the home of Blessed John Fisher whose life Father Bridgett afterwards wrote. In 1850, while an undergraduate, he left the university, being unable to accept the oath of Royal Supremacy which was then required before taking a degree

THOMAS EDWARD BRIDGETT

Shortly afterwards, having attended Dr. Newman's lectures on "Anglican Difficulties" at the London Oratory, he was received into the Catholic Church by the Oratorian, Father Stanton, 12 June, 1850, and on 15 October of the next year made his religious profession in the Redemptorist novitiate of St. Trond, Belgium. He pursued his theological studies at Wittem in Holland and was ordained priest in August, 1856. After being five years minister and consultor to the viceprovincial in Clapham, the London house of his Congregation, he went to Limerick for nine years, where as rector he founded, in 1868, the celebrated Confraternity of the Holy Family for men. This soon consisted of over 5,000 active members, the largest association of its kind in any one locality, in the Church. In 1871, he returned to Clapham as rector, where he spent the greater part of his remaining years.

Father Bridgett was a missionary like all the members of his Congregation, but with advancing years he devoted himself to giving retreats, particularly to the clergy. It was not till 1867 that he turned his thoughts to writing—a sermon on ritual developing into his first book, "In Spirit and in Truth". This work was called in later editions "The Ritual of the New Testament". It was followed in 1875 by "Our

Lady's Dowry", showing by many illustrations from history and literature the devotion of medieval England to the Mother of God. In this and in "The History of the Holy Eucharist in Great Britain", a work on the same plan published in 1881, the author shows a learning which is truly encyclopedic. The "Life of Blessed John Fisher", which led to a correspondence with Mr. Gladstone, followed in 1888; "The True Story of the Catholic Hierarchy deposed by Queen Elizabeth", a work written in conjunction with Father Knox of the Oratory, came out in 1889; "Blunders and Forgeries", a very fine piece of cross-examination, in 1890; and the "Life of Blessed Thomas More", his most popular work, in 1891. Father Bridgett also published devotional verse of considerable merit, both in a collection which he edited called "Lyra Hieratica", and in "Sonnets and Epigrams", an entirely original work. He died after a long and painful illness and was buried in the Catholic cemetery at Mortlake, near London.

RYDER, *Life of Thomas Edward Bridgett* (London, 1906); *The Messenger* (New York, June, 1907); *The Tablet*, files (London, Feb. 1899).

HAROLD CASTLE.

Bridgewater, JOHN, known also as AQUAPONTANUS, historian of the Catholic Confessors under Queen Elizabeth, b. in Yorkshire about 1532; d. probably at Trier, about 1596. He proceeded M. A. at Oxford in 1556, was ordained priest, and in 1563 became Rector of Lincoln College in that university. He also held several other important preferments, all of which he resigned in 1574, when with several of his students he crossed over to Douai, preferring "the old form of religion" to the novelties of those whom he styled "Calvinopapists and Puritans". He probably never returned to England, but lived at various places on the Continent (Reims, Paris, Rome, Trier); in 1588 and 1594 he resided at Trier. Ribadaneira, followed by Father Southwell and Brother Foley, account him a member of the Society of Jesus, though there is no proof of the fact (Records of English Catholics, I, 408). He refuted (Trier, 1589) a Protestant work on the pope as Antichrist and wrote also an "Account of the Six Articles usually Proposed to the Missioners that Suffered in England", and against which he voted in 1562.

Bridgewater is best known as the earliest martyrologist of Catholic England. His work, conceived in the spirit of Eusebius as a triumphant apology for Catholicism, is entitled "Concertatio Ecclesiæ Catholicæ in Angliâ adversus Calvinopapistas et Puritanos sub Elizabethâ Reginâ quorundam hominum doctrinâ et sanctitate illustrium renovata et recognita, etc.", i. e. The Battle of the Catholic Faith in England under Queen Elizabeth, renewed in the lives of certain men illustrious for learning and sanctity, among them more than one hundred martyrs, and a very great number of others distinguished for their (religious) deeds and sufferings; confirmed also by the retractations of apostates, by new edicts of the persecutors, and by the writings of very learned Catholics against the Anglican, or rather female, pontificate, and in defence of the authority of the Roman pontiff over Christian princes (Trier, 1588, about 850 pp. in 8vo). Another edition was brought out (ibid.) by Cardinal Allen in 1594; it served thenceforth as an original record of English Catholic sufferings for the Faith and Dodd, Challoner, and Lingard used extensively its reliable biographical and historical data. Its rather miscellaneous contents are described in the Chetham Society's Remains (XLVIII, 47–50).

GILLOW, *Bibl. Dict. of Eng. Cath.*, I, 294–295; COOPER in *Dict. of Nat. Biogr.*, s. v.; *Douay Diaries*, 99, 119, and *passim*; *Life and Letters of Cardinal Allen*, 77; DODD, *Ch. Hist. of Eng.*, I, 510; II, 60; WOOD, *Athenæ Oxon.*, ed. BLISS, I, 625; FOLEY, *Records*, IV, 481–482, 485; VII, 299.

THOMAS J. SHAHAN.

Bridgewater Treatises.—These publications derive their origin and their title from the Rev. Francis Henry Egerton, eighth and last Earl of Bridgewater who, dying in the year 1829, directed certain trustees named in his will to invest in the public funds the sum of £8,000, which sum with the accruing dividends was to be held at the disposal of the president, for the time being, of the Royal Society of London, to be paid to the person or persons nominated by him. It was further directed that those so selected should be appointed to write, print, and publish one thousand copies of a work: "On the Power, Wisdom, and Goodness of God as manifested in the Creation, illustrating such work by all reasonable arguments, as, for instance, the variety and formation of God's creatures, in the animal, vegetable and mineral kingdoms; the effect of digestion and thereby of conversion; the construction of the hand of man and an infinite variety of other arguments; as also by discoveries ancient and modern in arts, sciences, and the whole extent of modern literature".

The President of the Royal Society was then Davies Gilbert, who with the advice of the Archbishop of Canterbury, the Bishop of London, and a nobleman who had been intimate with the testator, determined that the money should be assigned to eight several persons for as many distinct treatises. The works produced in consequence were the following: (1) "The Adaptation of External Nature to the Moral and Intellectual Constitution of Man", by Thomas Chalmers (1833); (2) "Chemistry, Meteorology, and Digestion", by William Prout, M. D. (1834); (3) "History, Habits, and Instincts of Animals", by William Kirby (1835); (4) "The Hand, as Evincing Design", by Sir Charles Bell (1837); (5) "Geology and Mineralogy", by Dean Buckland, (1837); (6) "The Adaptation of External Nature to the Physical Condition of Man", by J. Kidd, M. D. (1837); (7) "Astronomy and General Physics", by Dr. William Whewell (1839); (8) "Animal and Vegetable Physiology", by P. M. Roget, M. D. (1840). The nature of the Treatises is clearly indicated by Lord Bridgewater's instructions, and by their several titles.

The selection of writers was somewhat severely criticized at the time, and the treatises are undoubtedly of unequal merit, but several of them took a high rank in apologetic literature, the best known being probably those by Buckland, Bell, and Whewell. At the present day, however, they are wellnigh forgotten and their value for the purpose they were designed to serve is very small. This is partly because the marvellous advances of recent years have made much of their science antiquated and out of date, but still more because of the almost total abandonment of the point of view on which their authors founded arguments to demonstrate the existence of design in nature. It is now generally felt to be an unsatisfactory, or, at least, less satisfactory, method, to argue from particular examples in which analogy can be traced between the mechanism found in nature and that contrived by man, as, for instance, to take one specially mentioned by Darwin, in the hinge of a bivalve shell, as though it were in such cases alone that the operation of Mind manifested itself. The best modern apologists insist rather on the note of law and order stamped everywhere upon the universe, inorganic no less than organic, upon the reality and ubiquity of which the validity of all scientific methods wholly depends, while the progress of scientific discovery does but immensely enhance the weight of the argument based upon it. At the same time, it cannot be admitted that the old-fashioned natural theology of the Treatises is so devoid of value as many modern critics pretend. The marvellous contrivances which we meet everywhere in organic nature remain wholly inexplicable by natural selection or other non-intelligent agents in which purpose is not included, and to the ordinary unsophisticated mind they bring home, as what may be deemed more philosophical arguments cannot, the truth that here we have direct evidence of a Supreme Artificer.

JOHN GERARD.

Brief. See BULLS AND BRIEFS.

Brieuc (BRIOCUS, BRIOC, or BRU), SAINT, a Celtic saint of Brittany who received his education in Ireland and then studied under St. Germanus, said to be the famous St. Germanus of Auxerre. Much of what we read concerning his early years must be received with caution; indeed, Ussher asserts that he was of Irish birth, but it is tolerably certain that he returned to France early in 431, bringing with him St. Iltud. Even before his ordination to the priesthood, St. Brieuc worked several miracles, duly chronicled in his "Acts" (edited by F. Godefrid Herschenn), and after a short period spent with his parents, he entered on his missionary career. In 480, he settled in Armorica, and founded a monastery at Landebaeron. Thence he proceeded to Upper Brittany where he established an oratory at a place ever since known as St. Brieuc-des-Vaux, between St. Malo and Land Triguier, and of which he was named first bishop. Numerous miracles are cited in the "Acts", especially his cure of Count Riguel, who gave the saint his own palace of Champ-du-Rouvre, as also the whole manorial estates. Authorities differ as to date of St. Brieuc's death, but it was probably in 502, or in the early years of the sixth century. He died in his own monastery at St. Brieuc-des-Vaux, and was interred in his cathedral church, dedicated to St. Stephen. Baring-Gould says that St. Brieuc is represented as "treading on a dragon", or else "with a column of fire" as seen at his ordination. His relics were translated to the Church of SS. Sergius and Bacchus of Angers, in 865, and again, in a more solemn manner, on 31 July, 1166. However, in 1210, a portion of the relics was restored to St. Brieuc Cathedral, where the saint's ring is also preserved. The festival of St. Brieuc is celebrated on 1st May, but, since 1804, the feast is transferred to the second Sunday after Easter. Churches in England, Ireland, and Scotland are dedicated to this early Celtic saint.

Acta SS. (1 May), I; BUTLER, *Lives of the Saints* (1 May); LOBINEAU, *Vies des Saints de Bretagne*, TRESVAUD ed. (1836); BARING-GOULD, *Lives of the Saints* (1 May), V; BAILLET, *Vies des Saints;* LE BARD, *Histoire de Bretagne;* CRESSY, *Church History of Brittany;* LE GRAND, *De Vitis Sanctorum Britanniæ Armoricæ;* O'HANLON, *Lives of the Irish Saints* (1 May), V; LELAND, *Itinerary,* III; GODESCARD, *Les Vies des Pères et des Martyrs* (1 May); *Tractarian Lives of the English Saints,* IX; LANIGAN, *Ecclesiastical History of Ireland,* I; PALLISER, *Brittany and its Byways* (1869).

W. H. GRATTAN FLOOD.

Brigid, SAINT, of Ireland (incorrectly known as BRIDGET), b. in 451 or 452 of princely ancestors at Faughart, near Dundalk, County Louth; d. 1 February, 525, at Kildare. Refusing many good offers of marriage, she became a nun and received the veil from St. Macaille. With seven other virgins she settled for a time at the foot of Croghan Hill, but removed thence to Druin Criadh, in the plains of Magh Life, where under a large oak tree she erected her subsequently famous Convent of *Cill-Dara* that is, "the church of the oak" (now Kildare), in the present county of that name. It is exceedingly difficult to reconcile the statements of St. Brigid's biographers, but the Third, Fourth, and Fifth Lives of the saint are at one in assigning her a slave mother in the court of her father Dubhthach, an Irish chieftain of Leinster. Probably the most ancient life of St. Brigid is that by St. Broccan Cloen, who is said to have died 17 September, 650. It is metrical, as may be seen from the following specimen:—

Ni bu Sanct Brigit suanach
Ni bu húarach im sheire Dé,
Sech ni chiuir ni cossena
Ind nóeb dibad bethath che.

Saint Brigid was not given to sleep,
Nor was she intermittent about God's love;
Not merely that she did not buy, she did not seek for
The wealth of this world below, the holy one.

Cogitosus, a monk of Kildare in the eighth century, expounded the metrical life of St. Brigid, and versified it in good Latin. This is what is known as the "Second Life", and is an excellent example of Irish scholarship in the mid-eighth century. Perhaps the most interesting feature of Cogitosus's work is the description of the Cathedral of Kildare in his day: "Solo spatioso et in altum minaci proceritate porruta ac decorata pictis tabulis, tria intrinsecus habens oratoria ampla, et divisa parietibus tabulatis". The rood-screen was formed of wooden boards, lavishly decorated, and with beautifully embroidered curtains. Probably the famous Round Tower of Kildare dates from the sixth century. Although St. Brigid was "veiled", or received, by St. Macaille, at Croghan, yet, it is tolerably certain

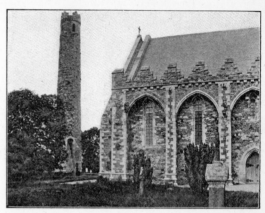

THE ROUND TOWER OF KILDARE

that she was professed by St. Mel of Ardagh, who also conferred on her abbatial powers. From Ardagh St. Macaille and St. Brigid followed St. Mel into the country of Teffia in Meath, including portions of Westmeath and Longford. This occurred about the year 468. St. Brigid's small oratory at *Cill-Dara* became the centre of religion and learning, and developed into a cathedral city. She founded two monastic institutions, one for men, and the other for women, and appointed St. Conleth as spiritual pastor of them. It has been frequently stated that she gave canonical jurisdiction to St. Conleth, Bishop of Kildare, but, as Archbishop Healy points out, she simply "selected the person to whom the Church gave this jurisdiction", and her biographer tells us distinctly that she chose St. Conleth "to govern the church along with herself". Thus, for centuries, Kildare was ruled by a double line of abbot-bishops and of abbesses, the Abbess of Kildare being regarded as superioress general of the convents in Ireland.

Not alone was St. Brigid a patroness of students, but she also founded a school of art, including metal work and illumination, over which St. Conleth presided. From the Kildare scriptorium came the wondrous book of the Gospels, which elicited tabunbounded praise from Giraldus Cambrensis, but which has disappeared since the Reformation. According to this twelfth-century Welsh ecclesiastic, nothing that he had ever seen was at all comparable to the "Book of Kildare", every page of which was gorgeously illuminated, and he concludes a most laudatory notice by saying that the interlaced work and the harmony of the colours left the impression that "all this is the work of angelic, and not human skill". Small wonder that Gerald Barry assumed the book to have been written night after night as St. Brigid prayed, "an angel furnishing the designs, the scribe copying". Even allowing for the exaggerated stories told of St. Brigid by her numerous biographers, it is certain that she ranks as one of the most remarkable Irishwomen of the fifth century and as the Patroness of Ireland. She is lovingly called the "Queen of the South: the Mary of the Gael" by a writer in the "Leabhar Breac". St. Brigid died leaving a cathedral city and school that became famous all over Europe. In her honour St. Ultan wrote a hymn commencing:—

> Christus in nostrâ insulâ
> Que vocatur Hibernia
> Ostensus est hominibus
> Maximis mirabilibus
> Que perfecit per felicem
> Celestis vite virginem
> Precellentem pro merito
> Magno in mundi circulo.

(In our island of Hibernia Christ was made known to man by the very great miracles which he performed through the happy virgin of celestial life, famous for her merits through the whole world.)

The sixth Life of the saint printed by Colgan is attributed to Coelan, an Irish monk of the eighth century, and it derives a peculiar importance from the fact that it is prefaced by a foreword from the pen of St. Donatus, also an Irish monk, who became Bishop of Fiesole in 824. St. Donatus refers to previous lives by St. Ultan and St. Aileran. When dying, St. Brigid was attended by St. Ninnidh, who was ever afterwards known as "Ninnidh of the Clean Hand" because he had his right hand encased with a metal covering to prevent its ever being defiled, after being the medium of administering the viaticum to Ireland's Patroness. She was interred at the right of the high altar of Kildare Cathedral, and a costly tomb was erected over her. In after years her shrine was an object of veneration for pilgrims, especially on her feast day, 1 February, as Cogitosus relates. About the year 878, owing to the Scandinavian raids, the relics of St. Brigid were taken to Downpatrick, where they were interred in the tomb of St. Patrick and St. Columba. The relics of the three saints were discovered in 1185, and on 9 June of the following year were solemnly translated to a suitable resting place in Downpatrick Cathedral, in presence of Cardinal Vivian, fifteen bishops, and numerous abbots and ecclesiastics. Various Continental breviaries of the pre-Reformation period commemorate St. Brigid, and her name is included in a litany in the Stowe Missal. In Ireland to-day, after 1500 years, the memory of "the Mary of the Gael" is as dear as ever to the Irish heart, and, as is well known, Brigid preponderates as a female Christian name. Moreover, hundreds of place-names in her honour are to be found all over the country, e. g. Kilbride, Brideswell, Tubberbride, Templebride, etc. The hand of St. Brigid is preserved at Lumiar near Lisbon, Portugal, since 1587, and another relic is at St. Martin's, Cologne.

Viewing the biography of St. Brigid from a critical standpoint we must allow a large margin for the vivid Celtic imagination and the glosses of medieval writers, but still the personality of the founder of Kildare stands out clearly, and we can with tolerable accuracy trace the leading events in her life, by a careful study of the old "Lives" as found in Colgan. It seems certain that Faughart, associated with memories of Queen Meave (Medhbh), was the scene of her birth; and Faughart Church was founded by St. Morienna in honour of St. Brigid. The old well of St. Brigid's

adjoining the ruined church is of the most venerable antiquity, and still attracts pilgrims; in the immediate vicinity is the ancient mote of Faughart. As to St. Brigid's stay in Connacht, especially in the County Roscommon, there is ample evidence in the "Trias Thaumaturga", as also in the many churches founded by her in the Diocese of Elphin. Her friend-

St. Brigid's Well

ship with St. Patrick is attested by the following paragraph from the "Book of Armagh", a precious manuscript of the eighth century, the authenticity of which is beyond question: "Inter sanctum Patricium Brigitamque Hibernensium columpnas amicitia caritatis inerat tanta, ut unum cor consiliumque haberent unum. Christus per illum illamque virtutes multas peregit". (Between St. Patrick and St. Brigid, the columns of the Irish, there was so great a friendship of charity that they had but one heart and one mind. Through him and through her Christ performed many miracles.) At Armagh there was a "Templum Brigidis"; namely, the little abbey church known as "Regles Brigid", which contained some relics of the saint, destroyed in 1179, by William Fitz Aldelm. It may be added that the original manuscript of Cogitosus's "Life of Brigid", or the "Second Life", dating from the closing years of the eighth century, is now in the Dominican friary at Eichstätt in Bavaria.

Acta SS.; Acta Sanct. Hib. ex Cod. Salmant.; COLGAN, Trias Thaumaturga (Louvain, 1647); STOKES, Lives of the Saints from the Book of Lismore; ID., Three Middle Irish Homilies; O'HANLON, Lives of the Irish Saints (1 February), II; TODD, Liber Hymnorum; Stowe Missal; Leabhar Breac; MESSINGHAM, Florilegium; ATKINSON, St. Brigid in Essays (Dublin, 1892); HEALY, Ireland's Ancient Schools and Scholars; STOKES, Early Christian Art in Ireland; HYDE, Literary History of Ireland (1900); KNOWLES, Life of St. Brigid (1907). Cf. CHEVALIER, Bio-bibliogr. (Paris, 1905, 2nd ed.), s. v.

W. H. GRATTAN FLOOD.

Brigittines.—The Brigittine Order (also, ORDER OF ST. SAVIOUR) was founded in 1346 by St. Brigit, or Bridget, of Sweden at Vadstena in the Diocese of Linköping. The saint, who was canonized twenty years after her death, was a Swedish princess renowned for her piety from her childhood; she was given in marriage to Ulf, Prince of Mercia, by whom she had a large family. Ulf died in 1344, and two years later tradition relates that St. Bridget had revealed to her the rule of the new order she was to found at Vadstena. Here with the help of King Magnus she established on her own estate the first monastery for men and women, of which Katharine, her daughter, became the first abbess soon after her death in 1375. At this time double monasteries were not unusual; the monks and nuns used the same chapel, but lived in separate wings of the monastery, the confessor alone having access to the nuns. In

Brigittine monasteries the nuns, who were strictly enclosed, attended to the cooking, washing, and making and mending of clothes for the monks as well as for themselves, but everything was passed through a turnstile from one wing to the other. This arrangement, unsuitable to modern times, has long ceased.

In the new order the abbess, who was called the "Sovereign", was supreme in all things temporal for both houses; all deeds were in her name, all charters were addressed to her; but in spiritual things the abbess was not allowed to interfere with the monks who were priests, and the nuns were under the direction of the superior of the monks who was appointed confessor-general. The order was founded principally for women, and for this reason the supreme government was vested in the abbess; the monks were founded to give the nuns the spiritual help they needed. The special interior devotion of the order is to the Passion of Our Lord and to His Blessed Mother.

RULE OF ST. BRIDGET.—The Rule enacts "that the number of choir nuns shall not exceed sixty, with four lay sisters; the priests shall be thirteen, according to the number of the thirteen Apostles, of whom Paul the thirteenth was not the least in toil; then there must be four deacons, who also may be priests if they will, and they are the figure of the four principal Doctors, Ambrose, Augustine, Gregory, and Jerome, then eight lay brothers, who with their labours shall minister necessaries to the clerics, therefore counting three-score sisters, thirteen priests, four deacons, and the eight servitors, the number of persons will be the same as the thirteen Apostles and the seventy-two disciples". (The Rule of St. Bridget.) The nuns were not to be professed before they were eighteen and the monks not before they were twenty-five years of age. The counsel of holy poverty is strictly enjoined by the Rule on all the members of the order, who are forbidden to possess anything, though at the same time they may expect the abbess to supply them with all necessaries; one luxury is allowed them, they may have as many books as they like for study. All the cast-off clothing and the surplus of their yearly income, after all has been provided for, are to be given to the poor, and the Rule strictly forbids the abbess to make larger buildings than are necessary.

The Constitutions were first approved by Pope Urban V, afterwards by Urban VI, and finally by Martin V. In 1603 Pope Clement VIII made certain changes for double monasteries in Flanders, and in 1622 Gregory XV changed certain articles in the Constitutions which refer only to double convents for the Monastery of Ste. Marie de Foi, in the Diocese of Ypres. These new Constitutions ordained that manual work should be done during certain hours of the day by the members of the order, that a red cross should be worn on the mantle, that the nuns might be professed at the age of sixteen, and that the monks should say the Divine Office according to the Roman Breviary. Those who followed these Constitutions took the name of Brigittines Novissimi of the Order of St. Saviour, to distinguish them from those who lived in double convents.

FOUNDATIONS.—The order spread into France, Italy, Germany, Bavaria, Poland, Norway, Denmark, Finland, Holland, Belgium, Spain, Portugal, and Russia. Four foundations were made in France, at Lille, Valenciennes, Arras, and Douai, but all were destroyed in the Revolution. In Belgium several houses were founded, but except that of Dendermonde they did not last very long, and all have now disappeared. The first Italian house was founded in 1394, when the Monastery of Paradiso was opened at the gates of Florence, and about this time some of the monks of the order took up their abode in Rome, in the house in which St. Bridget died. In 1426 a monastery was opened at Genoa, and that same year

the order was introduced into Bavaria, where several foundations were made, one of which still remains. This is the celebrated old Benedictine Monastery of Mary—Altomünster, between Munich and Augsburg, of which the Brigittines took possession in 1497 establishing a double convent there. This monastery was twice plundered and partially destroyed by fire, and the monks and nuns who were dispersed at the Reformation twice returned to it, In 1803 it was suppressed, and it is only since 1844 that a community of Brigittine nuns again lives there. The monastery of Revel in Russia was burnt by schismatics in 1575, but in Poland most of the monasteries were preserved till the middle of the sixteenth century, and three new foundations were made. Holland still possesses two Brigittine houses, both of which now take pupils.

At the Reformation most of the double monasteries had to be given up, and the rule as to numbers could no longer be observed, while many of the houses were suppressed altogether. The nuns at Vadstena endured much persecution at this time; the Protestants threatened to tear them to pieces and expelled them from their monastery, but in 1588, King John III became their protector, and restored their monastery to them. In England the Brigittine Order is the only pre-Reformation order in existence. The celebrated Brigittine Monastery of Syon House was founded in 1415, when Henry V himself laid the foundation-stone on part of the royal manor of Isleworth on the Thames. It is supposed that the cause of the extension of the order in England was due to the fact that Henry's sister Philippa was the wife of Eric XIII, King of Sweden. King Henry endowed the monastery richly and transferred the property of certain houses dependent on French monasteries to Syon. At the dissolution of monasteries under Henry VIII, who in the earlier years of his reign had himself been a benefactor of the abbey, the nuns were dispersed and took refuge in a convent of their order at Dendermonde in Flanders. Here they were visited by Cardinal Pole, and through his influence were re-established at Syon under Queen Mary, but they were driven into exile again when Elizabeth came to the throne, and returned to Dendermonde. After several attempts to settle in different parts of Belgium, they went to Rouen where they remained fourteen years, and finally in 1594, they moved to Lisbon where they remained for 267 years. In 1809 an attempt was made to return to England, but it was not till 1861 that the nuns found a home at Spettisbury in Dorsetshire, whence they moved to Chudleigh in Devonshire in 1887, where they are still living.

BRIGITTINES OF THE RECOLLECTION.—The Brigittines of the Recollection were founded at Valladolid in the seventeenth century by Venerable Marina de Escobar, formerly a Carmelite nun, who modified the Rule to suit the Spanish nation and the age in which she lived. The Constitutions were approved by Pope Urban VIII. Like St. Bridget she neither took the habit herself nor did she live to see the first monastery of the order erected. This congregation which has five houses was founded for nuns only; the habit and the office differ slightly from those of the Brigittines.

In all houses of the Brigittine Order prayers are constantly offered for the restoration of the Monastery of Vadstena. This was formerly the great centre and stronghold of Catholicism in Sweden, a place where kings and queens frequently visited, sometimes took refuge, and were occasionally imprisoned, but which was suppressed and the religious dispersed under Gustavus Vasa. Nine Brigittine monasteries are now in existence: Syon Abbey, Chudleigh in Devonshire, Altomünster in Bavaria, Uden and Weert in Holland; and the five Spanish houses of the Brigittines of the Recollection: Valladolid founded in 1651, Vittoria founded in 1653, Lasarte and Parades de Nava in 1671, and Ascoytia in 1690.

FLAVIGNY, *Ste. Brigitte de Suède;* BURNS, *Syon Abbey;* MS. copy of the *Rule of St. Bridget; History of the English Brigittine Nuns* (Plymouth, 1887); BILDT, *Swedish Memories and Traces in Rome;* HÉLYOT, *Histoire des ordres monastiques*, IV, 25–49; HEIMBUCHER, *Ord. u. Kongr. der kath. Kirche.*

FRANCESCA M. STEELE.

Brignon, JOHN, b. at Saint Malo in 1629; d. at Paris, 12 June, 1712. He was a member of the Society of Jesus and occupied during the sixty-five years of his religious life chiefly in the translation of works of piety into French. Among these are the works of De Ponte and Nieremberg, the "Spiritual Combat", the "Imitation of Christ", and the short treatises of Bellarmine. All these translations have passed through a number of editions. He also edited and revised "The Devout Life" of St. Francis De Sales and the "Fondements" of Père Surin, S.J. The only English works he translated into French are the "Decem Rationes" of Blessed Edmund Campion and the "Tractatus de Misericordiâ fidelibus defunctis exhibendâ" by Father Mumford, S.J.

Bibl. de la c. de Jésus, XI, col. 166; *Dict. de théol. cath.*, I, col. 1131.

S. H. FRISBEE.

Bril, PAULUS, a brilliant Flemish painter and engraver, b. at Antwerp, 1556; d. in Rome, 7 October, 1626. He first studied with Damiaen Oertelmans, a member of the guild of St. Luke in his native city. Fired by the news of the success of his brother Matthys, in Rome, he left his parents secretly and started for that city. He was detained at Lyons by lack of funds, and worked there in order to be able to continue his journey. At Rome he studied with his brother, but found his best inspiration later in the copies he made of the landscapes of Titian. With these as a basis he developed a vigorous and individual style of his own, the manifestations of which are said to have led greatly to the development of landscape art by their influence on Rubens, Annibale Carracci, and Claude Lorraine. He assisted his brother in his works at the Vatican, and on the death of the latter (b. about 1548, d. 1584) he continued his labours. Pope Gregory XIII gave him his brother's pension, and confided to him the work which they had jointly undertaken.

Bril's principal production in the Vatican is a landscape in fresco sixty-eight feet long, ordered by Pope Clement VIII for the Sala Clementina, in which appears St. Clement, with an anchor fastened to his neck, being cast into the sea. Bril worked in the Sistine Chapel, in Santa Maria Maggiore, and in the chapel of the Scala Santa in St. John Lateran. He introduced figures in his landscapes with much success, but in some of them appear compositions of Annibale Carracci. His "Duck Hunt", "Diana and Nymphs", "Fishermen", "Pan and Syrinx", "St. Jerome in Prayer", and three other landscapes are in the Louvre. His "Prodigal Son" is in the Antwerp Museum, and his "St. Paul in the Desert", "Boar Hunt", and "Triumph of Psyche" in the Uffizi at Florence. His works appear in number in all the principal European galleries.

LÜBKE, *History of Art* (tr. New York, 1881).

AUGUSTUS VAN CLEEF.

Brillmacher, PETER MICHAEL, b. at Cologne in 1542; d. at Mainz, 25 August, 1595. He entered the Society of Jesus in 1558, and studied under Maldonatus, in Paris. Later he returned to Cologne, where, by his diplomatic skill, he rendered invaluable aid to the German princes in affairs of state. His eloquence attracted multitudes, thwarted the efforts of the so-called reformers, and made such deep inroads in their ranks that they determined upon his death. Inviting him to a banquet on pretence of debating disputed doctrines, they mingled poison with his food thus accomplishing his end.

Brillmacher took an active part in the controversies so frequent in his day and was fearless in his attacks upon heresy. An instance of his alertness in the detection of heresy is that of the curé of Notre Dame of Cologne, Stephen Isaac, a converted Jew, who, in 1589, preaching on the Holy Eucharist, advanced arguments which tended to compromise rather than substantiate the doctrine. Brillmacher immediately published his "Controversiarum de Eucharistiâ Dialogi", in which he advanced all the arguments which had been brought for and against the Real Presence, Transubstantiation, etc. In the third of these dialogues he so clearly exposed the duplicity of Isaac that the latter was forced openly to avow his apostasy to Calvinism. In a public letter to John of Münster, Isaac vilified the Jesuit and called forth the latter's second work, "Detectio Erroris Joannis a Münster", followed shortly by another "Exceptio Prodromi Calviniana" (1592, in Latin and German) and still later (1593) by "Epistola ad Amicum". The widespread publication and popularity of these overwhelmed his adversaries and won back to the Faith many who had been deceived by the specious arguments of the heretics. Brillmacher's "Catechismus" first published in 1586, ran through various editions (Latin, German, and Flemish), and was the foundation of many similar works. He also wrote: "Serta Honoris" (various editions in Latin and German, 1565 to 1713) and two early publications "De Communione sub alterâ Specie" and "Commentarium in Aristotelis Logica".

DE BACKER, I, 886–888; SOMMERVOGEL, *Bibliothèque*, II, 182–186.

T. J. YOUNG.

Brindholm (or BRYNDEHOLME), EDMUND, VENERABLE, martyr and parish priest of Our Lady's Church at Calais, accused of being concerned in a plot to betray Calais to the French. It was said that Sir Gregory Botolf, chaplain to Lord Lisle, Governor of Calais, had been to Rome on this business, and had requested the pope to grant a living in the English Hospital of St. Thomas to Brindholm, who was about to go to Rome when he was arrested. There seems, however, no evidence that he was really concerned in any plot. He was examined 11 April, 1540, and was attainted in the Parliament of that year, together with "Clement Philpott late of Calais, gentleman, who have adhered to the King's enemy, the Bishop of Rome, and assisted Raynold Poole [Cardinal Pole], an abominable and arrogant traitor, compassing the surprise of the town of Calais". He suffered, together with Philpott, the Blessed William Horne, a Carthusian lay brother, and others, at Tyburn, 4 August, 1540.

Letters and Papers Henry VIII (1540), XV, No. 495, sqq.; HOLINSHED, *Chronicle*, III, 952.

BEDE CAMM.

Brindisi, DIOCESE OF.—Brindisi, called by the Romans *Brundusium* or *Brundisium*, by the Greeks Βρεντήσιον, is a city in the province of Lecce, in Apulia, on a rocky peninsula which extends into the Adriatic. In ancient times it was very important as a seaport, being accessible in all winds. In 245 B. C. the Romans captured Brindisi without striking a blow and established a Roman colony there. This city was one terminal of the Via Appia. In the civil wars between Cæsar and Pompey Brindisi was the base of naval operations. Brindisi was the birthplace of the poet Pacuvius; here also Virgil died in 19 B. C., on his return from Greece. During the invasions of the barbarians it was taken and destroyed several times, but was always rebuilt within a short space of time, so that as late as the twelfth century it had a population of 60,000, which has since dwindled to about 20,000. The harbour gradually filled up, which hindered navigation. The Italian Government made great attempts to remedy this, but on account of an error of judgment the beneficial results anticipated were not permanent.

According to a local legend, the first Bishop of Brindisi was St. Leucius, about 165, who later underwent martyrdom. However, taking into consideration the geographical position of this city, the beginnings of Christianity in Brindisi must date back to the first century. There is no historical proof for this except the account given by Arnobius of the fall of Simon Magus, who according to him withdrew to Brindisi and cast himself from a high rock into the sea. The Diocese of Brindisi at first embraced the territory comprised within the present Diocese of Oria. In the tenth century, after Brindisi had been destroyed by the Saracens, the bishops took up their abode at Oria, on account of its greater security. In 1591, after the death of Bishop Bernardino di Figueroa, Oria was made the seat of a new diocese. In the reorganization of the dioceses of the Kingdom of Naples in 1818 Brindisi was combined with the Diocese of Ostuni, formerly its suffragan. Brindisi has been an archiepiscopal see since the tenth century. The ancient cathedral was located outside the city, but in 1140 Roger II, King of Sicily and Naples, built the present cathedral in the centre of the city.

The bishops of Brindisi worthy of mention are: St. Aproculus (Proculus), who died in 352 at Ardea, when returning from Rome, and was buried at Anzio; St. Cyprian, who died in 364; Andrea, murdered by the Saracens in 979; Eustachio (1060), the first to bear the title of archbishop; Guglielmo (1173), author of a life of St. Leucius; Girolamo Aleandro (1524), a learned humanist, and papal nuncio in Germany in connexion with Luther's Reformation, and later Cardinal; Pietro Caraffa, Bishop of Chieti, and afterwards Pope Paul IV, for some time the Apostolic administrator of this diocese; Francesco Aleandro (1542); G. Bovio, from Bologna, who translated the works of St. Gregory of Nyssa, and was prominent in the Council of Trent; Paolo de Vilanaperlas (1716), founder of the seminary; Andrea Maddalena (1724), who restored the cathedral after it had been damaged by the earthquake of 1743.

In this diocese is the shrine of Mater Domini, near Mesagne. A beautiful church was erected there in 1605 to replace the ancient rustic chapel. The diocese has a population of 119,907, with 23 parishes, 89 churches and chapels, 181 secular and 15 regular clergy, and 64 seminarians.

CAPPELLETTI, *Le chiese d'Italia* (Venice, 1844), XXI, 113–122; GUERRIERI, *Sui vescovi della chiesa metropolitana di Brindisi* (Naples, 1846); *Annuario Eccl.* (Rome, 1907), 346–348.

U. BENIGNI.

Brindle, ROBERT. See NOTTINGHAM, DIOCESE OF.

Brinkley, STEPHEN, Confessor of the Faith, imprisoned and tortured as manager of a secret press for the publication of devotional and controversial works in the reign of Queen Elizabeth; b. about 1550, and lost to view after 1585. He was a member of a Catholic association of unmarried gentlemen of property, organized by George Gilbert, and solemnly blessed by Gregory XIII, 1580. Their purpose was to raise funds for the support of priests, to prepare Protestants for the Faith, and, at a time when priests travelled in disguise, without papers of identification, to arrange for introductions which would guard both priests and laity against betrayal. The members undertook to content themselves with the bare necessaries of their state of life, to spend the remainder of their goods in the cause of the Church, and to devote themselves wholly to the salvation of souls and the conversion of heretics. At this time the Jesuit Fathers Robert Parsons and (Blessed) Edmund Campion

were preparing for a vigorous propaganda through the press. With the assistance of several of the old Marian priests and of one Brooks, Parsons procured from the elder Brooks, owner of a large house called Greenstreet, at East Ham in Essex, five miles from London, permission for certain gentlemen to lodge there. To this house, chiefly with the assistance of Brinkley, Parsons conveyed a printing press and materials. Brinkley's seven workmen appeared in public with fine clothes and horses, to avert suspicion. The parson and churchwardens urged the newly arrived gentlemen to attend services; an incautious purchase of paper almost gave a clue to the discovery of the press, and a servant of Brinkley's was caught and racked.

Their first book, however, which was very probably a work of devotion or of encouragement to Catholics, was successfully issued. Brinkley then moved the press to Henley Park, to the house of Francis Browne, brother of Viscount Montague. Parsons issued, 1581, "A brief Censure upon two Books written in answer to M. Edmund Campion's Offer of Disputation." Campion's challenge was then circulating in manuscript. Extreme caution was required in the management of Brinkley's press. Government experts, like Norton, reported that the Brinkley books, in spite of the Douai imprint, had been produced in England; the landlord Brooks was suspicious; information as to the press was also asked of Father Briant upon the rack. After a second removal, Brinkley printed, at a lodge belonging to Dame Cecilia Stonor's house, near Henley, Campion's "Decem Rationes". At Oxford, on Commemoration Day, 27 June, 1581, the benches of St. Mary's Church were found strewn with copies of this ringing challenge to the universities. The capture of Campion near Oxford Sunday evening, 16 July, was followed in a few weeks by that of Brinkley and his printers. Brinkley, though tortured in the Tower, escaped the fate of his fellow prisoner, William Carter, a Catholic printer, who was executed at Tyburn. Brinkley was discharged in June, 1583. He accompanied Father Parsons first to Rome, where we find his name in the Pilgrim Book of the English College in the following September, and thence in the following year to Rouen. Here, with George Flinton, Brinkley printed a second edition of a work which Flinton had brought out in 1581, "The Christian Directory". After Flinton's death about 1585, Brinkley continued to issue Catholic books. The date of his death is unknown. Gillow mentions a work translated from the Italian (Paris, 1579), entitled "The Exercise of a Christian Life . . . newly perused and corrected by the translatour" (James Sancer). Sancer, or Sanker, is known to have been the pseudonym of Brinkley. This work, perhaps, is one of the early issues of Brinkley's own press.

GILLOW, *Bibl. Dict. of English Catholics*; MORRIS, *Troubles of Our Catholic Forefathers*, second series; SIMPSON, *Life of Edmund Campion* (London, 1867); LAW, *Historical Sketch of the Jesuits and Seculars in the Reign of Elizabeth* (London, 1900).

J. VINCENT CROWNE.

Brisacier, JACQUES-CHARLES DE, orator and ecclesiastical writer, b. at Bourges in 1641; d. at Paris, 23 March, 1736. At the age of twenty-five he entered the Society of the Foreign Missions at Paris, and devoted seventy years of his life to this great work. The scion of a rich and distinguished family, son of the collector-general for the Province of Berry, endowed with a remarkable talent for preaching, chaplain in ordinary to Queen Marie-Thérèse, wife of Louis XIV, he might have aspired to high ecclesiastical honours. Many bishoprics were offered to him. He refused them all, however, in order to remain in the Society of the Foreign Missions of which he was elected superior in 1681. He filled this office for eight terms, but as the rule of the Society is that no one shall be elected superior for more than three consecutive years, he filled this charge alternately with Louis Tiberge. He was also one of eight of its members who in 1698 composed the rules for its government which are still in force.

Madame de Maintenon asked him to become the associate of Bourdaloue and Fénelon, in compiling the regulations for the school of Saint Cyr, which she had just founded. So pleased was she with his wisdom and judgment that she asked him again, in connexion with Bourdeloue and M. Fronson, superior of Saint Sulpice, to give his opinion on the books of Madame Guyon and upon Quietism. On this point, however, the director of the Society of the Foreign Missions did not agree with the views of Fénelon. He took a very prominent part in the discussion on Chinese ceremonies. After having asked the advice of Fénelon and Bossuet on this question, Brisacier did not hesitate to declare himself of an opinion different from that of the Jesuits. The Bishop of Meaux wrote him three letters on this subject (30 August, 1701; 8 and 12 September, 1701). Brisacier, however, did not wait for these letters to declare himself. On 20 April, 1700, he published a pamphlet entitled "Lettre de MM. des Missions étrangères au Pape, sur les idolatries et les superstitions chinoises, avec une addition à la dite lettre, par MM. Louis Tiberge and Jacques Charles de Brisacier". Brisacier pronounced the funeral orations of the Duchesse d'Aiguillon and also of Mlle de Bouillon, both benefactresses of the Foreign Missions.

LAUNAY, *Histoire générale de la société des Missions étrangères* (Paris, 1894); *Histoire de Fénelon*, XI, 293.

A. FOURNET.

Brisacier, JEAN DE, controversialist, b. at Blois, France, 9 June, 1592; entered the Society of Jesus in 1619; d. at Blois, 10 September, 1668. On the completion of his studies, he gave himself to preaching for many years, with great zeal and success. Afterwards he was in turn Rector of the colleges of Aix, Blois, and Rouen, Visitor to the province of Portugal, Procurator of the Society for Foreign Missions and Superior of the Professed House in Paris. His love for missionary work was such that shortly before his death, he remarked that he counted as nothing all the years he had not spent in it. Brisacier was an ardent opponent of Jansenism, and never lost an opportunity of attacking it. In a sermon preached at Blois, in 1651, he denounced the deceit practised by the Jansenists, particularly in the district around his native town, where the curé of Cour-Cheverny, M. L'Abbé Callaghan, was very active in promoting the heresy. This gave rise to a spirited controversy, in which Brisacier displayed activity and courage. In reply to the Jansenists' answer to his sermon, he repeated his indictment, and offered proof of it, in a publication entitled "Le jansénisme confondu dans l'advocat du sieur Callaghan, par le P. Brisacier, avec la deffense de son sermon fait à Blois, le 29 Mars, 1651, contre la response du Port Royal". This work was quickly condemned by Jean François de Gondi, Archbishop of Paris, because of its personal attacks directed especially against the Jansenistic religious of Port Royal. After this censure the dispute continued for some time, and called forth a long series of pamphlets. As late as 1862, the controversy was kept up by Abbé Pletteau and G. Bordillon.

SOMMERVOGEL, *Bibl. de la c. de J.*, II, 186; BRUCKER in *Dict. de théol. cath.*, s. v.; HURTER, *Nomenclator*, II, 70.

R. H. TIERNEY.

Brisbane, ARCHDIOCESE OF, comprises that part of the State of Queensland, Australia, which lies south of the 24th parallel of south latitude. The area is about 200,000 square miles. Brisbane, the cathedral city, is the capital of Queensland. The population

II.—50

at the census of 1901 (metropolitan area) was 119,907.

HISTORY.—Queensland (known till 1859 as the Moreton Bay District of New South Wales) was first settled in 1825 as a convict station, was visited by Father Therry and abandoned after three years. Permanent colonization began when it was thrown open to free settlers in 1842. In 1843, four Passionist Fathers established a mission for aboriginals on Stradbroke Island, but abandoned it for lack of provisions and other causes in 1846. The work of evangelizing the Queensland blacks was afterwards carried on by other missionaries, the most successful of whom were Father Luckie and the later and still more noted apostle of the aboriginals, Father Duncan McNab. Missionary work among the blacks was, however, hampered to an almost hopeless degree by the bad example, the brutalities, and the communicated vices and diseases of degraded whites. In 1843, a rude shanty, hastily constructed during Dr. Polding's visit to Brisbane in that year, was the only building in the Moreton Bay District that stood for a church. There was no school, and the white population of the whole District was only 2,257 souls. Fathers McGinnety and Hanly arrived there in December, 1843. They were, says Cardinal Moran, "the first priests stationed for ordinary missionary work in the Moreton Bay territory". In 1859, the year in which the Moreton Bay District became a separate colony under the name of Queensland, it was erected into the Diocese of Brisbane. Its first bishop was the Right Rev. James O'Quinn, who was consecrated in Dublin on the 29th of June, 1859. In 1860 there were only two priests, two churches, two small schools, and 7,676 Catholics, out of a total population of 28,056, in his vast diocese of 668,497 square miles. He arrived in Brisbane, with five priests and six sisters, in 1861, and launched forthwith into the work of organization, carrying on for years long and exhausting visitations, in which the bare earth was often his only bed, and sardines and "damper" his principal food. With the sanction of the Government, he organized the Queensland Immigration Society, which brought settlers (chiefly Irish Catholics) to the colony. Considerable numbers of these were placed on land granted for the purpose by the Government. Racial and sectarian passions took alarm. A clamour arose that the colony was being inundated with Irish Catholics, and that it would soon deserve to be called, not "Queensland", but "Quinn's Land". The Immigration Society bent before the storm and dissolved in 1865, after having enriched Queensland with ten shiploads of picked colonists.

Dr. O'Quinn was a man of ripe intellectual culture and of much foresight and administrative wisdom. He established a Catholic paper, "The Australian", founded two orphanages and an industrial school, wrought strenuously in the matter of church- and

BRISBANE FROM THE OBSERVATORY GARDENS

school-extension, erected the handsome cathedral of St. Stephen, and created and conserved rich educational and other endowments. State aid was finally withdrawn from all denominational schools with the close of the year 1880; but at his death, 18th August, 1881, there were 52 Catholic primary schools in the diocese, attended by 6,510 children. The Provicariate of North Queensland was formed out of the Diocese of Brisbane in 1876, and that of Rockhampton in 1882. On the 18th of June, 1882, the Right Reverend Robert Dunne was consecrated Bishop of Brisbane in succession to Dr. O'Quinn. By his solid scholarship and his ability as a writer Dr. Dunne rendered important services as secretary to the Plenary Council of Australasia held in Sydney in 1885. At the request of that council, Queensland was in 1887 created a separate ecclesiastical province, with Brisbane as its metropolitan see; and the Provicariate of North Queensland was erected into the Vicariate-Apostolic of Cooktown. The present stately archiepiscopal residence in Brisbane was built during Dr. Dunne's visit *ad limina* in 1890, and presented to him on his return. His episcopate has been fruitful in church- and school-extension, and general progress.

ALL-HALLOWS'S CONVENT SCHOOL, BRISBANE

Religious Statistics (1907).—Parochial districts, 31; churches, 91; secular clergy, 56; religious brothers, 25; nuns, 186; lay teachers in Catholic schools, 126; seminary 1; boarding schools for girls, 12; for boys, 4; high schools, 6; primary schools, 41; children in Catholic schools, 6,713; industrial school for boys (with printing office), 1; for girls, 1; orphanage, 1; Magdalen asylum, 1; servants' home, 1; total population, about 240,000; Catholic population, about 60,000.

MORAN, *History of the Catholic Church in Australasia* (Sydney, s. d.); *The Australian Handbook* (Sydney, 1906); JOSÉ, *History of Australasia* (Sydney, 1901); *Australasian Catholic Directory for 1907* (Sydney, 1907).

HENRY W. CLEARY.

Brischar, JOHANN NEPOMUCENE, church historian, b. at Horb in Würtemberg in 1819, studied theology at the University of Tübingen, was appointed parish priest of Bühl near Rottenburg in 1853, where he died in 1897. His principal work is the continuation of Count Leopold Stolberg's "History of the Religion of Jesus Christ" of which he wrote volumes forty-five to fifty-four. His share of the work does not reach the high standard of his great predecessor. He is also the author of a work in two volumes on the controversies between Paolo Sarpi and Pallavicini, and of a monograph on Pope Innocent III. His "Catholic Pulpit Orators of Germany" in five volumes was published in Schaffhausen, in the years 1866–71. He contributed many articles to Herder's "Kirchenlexicon".

Kathol. Litteraturkalender (Ratisbon, 1897), s. v.; HERDER, *Conversationslex.*, II, s. v.

B. GULDNER.

Bristol (BRISTOLIA, BRISTOLIENSIS), ANCIENT DIOCESE OF.—This English diocese, which takes its very origin from measures directed against the Church, has a very brief Catholic history, for it only had one bishop acknowledged by the Holy See. It was one of the six bishoprics which Henry VIII, acting as head of the Church, attempted to found by Act of Parliament out of the spoils of the suppressed monasteries. This was in 1542, the bishoprics in question being those of Bristol, Oxford, Westminster, Gloucester, Peterborough, and Chester. The fact that the city was then one of the leading towns in England and the chief seaport, explains why it was selected as one of the new sees. Like the others, it possessed an important religious house, the buildings of which might serve the new purposes. As it was, the new diocese nearly lost its cathedral, for the abbey church of the Augustinian Canons, which had been plundered at the time of the suppression of that house in 1539, was already in process of demolition, when the king's order came arresting the devastation. This house of Augustinians had been founded four hundred years before its dissolution by one Robert Fitzharding, who began to build "the abbeye at Bristowe, that of Saint Austin is" in 1133. The abbey church, destined to serve hereafter as a cathedral, was of different dates: the old Norman nave built by Fitzharding seems to have stood till the suppression, but the chancel, which still exists, was early fourteenth century, and the transepts late fifteenth. The building as a whole was well worthy to serve as a cathedral. Yet at first Bristol does not seem to have been thought of as a bishopric, for it is not included in the list of projected sees now among the Cottonian MSS. in the British Museum.

It has been suggested that its ultimate selection for this honour was due to Cranmer, who visited Bristol shortly before his election as Archbishop of Canterbury, and busied himself in ecclesiastical affairs there. The first bishop to be appointed when the king's charter of 1542 founded the new see, was Paul Bush, formerly master of the Bonshommes at Edyngton in Wiltshire, who, it is needless to say, neither sought nor obtained recognition by the pope. Himself an Augustinian and a man of some repute both as scholar and poet, he held fast to many of the old doctrines, and opposed Cranmer with regard to transubstantiation and Masses for the dead. Yet he followed the new opinions so far as the marriage of the clergy was concerned, and took as a wife one Edith Ashley. This fact caused him to be proceeded against as a married cleric in Queen Mary's reign. In 1554 a commission passed sentence of deprivation against him, which he anticipated by a voluntary resignation. This was the opportunity for placing the irregularly constituted diocese on a proper canonical footing, and Pope Paul IV empowered Cardinal Pole to refound the See of Bristol. The first and, as it proved, the only Catholic bishop was John Holyman, a Benedictine monk of great reputation for learning and sanctity, who had been the friend and subject of the martyred Abbot of Reading, Blessed Hugh Cook.

As bishop, Dr. Holyman gave general satisfaction, and, though he took part in the trial of Hooper, and served on a commission to try Ridley and Latimer, he took no active part in the proceedings on the score of heresy. He died in the summer or autumn of 1558, and was thus spared the troublous times that began with the accession of Elizabeth in the following November. He was succeeded in the bishopric by the Anglican, Dr. Richard Cheney (1562–79), who, though a schismatic, was yet suspected of Catholic leanings, and was the early friend of Blessed Edmund Campion. But the history of Bristol as a Catholic see ends with the death of Bishop Holyman. The diocese was formed by taking the county and archdeaconry of Dorset from Salisbury, and several parishes from the Dioceses of Gloucester and Worcester, with three churches in Bristol, which had belonged to Bath and Wells. The arms of the see were sable, three ducal crowns in pale or. The dedication was changed at the dissolution from St. Augustine to the Holy Trinity.

HEYLYN, *Catalogue of the Bishops* (1709 ed.); HYETT AND BAZELEY, *Bibliographer's Manual of Gloucestershire Literature* (1895–97); MASSÉ, *The Cathedral Church of Bristol and a Brief History of the Episcopal See* (1901); PRYCE, *History of Bristol* (1861); NICHOLLS AND TAYLOR, *Bristol Past and Present* (1881–82); EVANS, *History of Bristol* (1824).

EDWIN BURTON.

Bristow, RICHARD, b. at Worcester, 1538, d. at Harrow-on-the-Hill, 1581. He went to the University of Oxford in 1555, probably as a member of Exeter College, though Wood doubts this. In 1559 he took his Bachelor's degree and proceeded to the degree of Master of Arts as a member of Christ Church, in 1562. He was exceptionally brilliant and eloquent and so esteemed as an orator that, with the celebrated Edmund Campion, he was chosen to hold a public disputation before Queen Elizabeth in 1566. Shortly afterwards, having applied himself to theology and acquired a wide reputation for his learning, he was made a Fellow of Exeter College (1567) by the interest of Sir William Petre, who had founded several fellowships there. His great ability would probably have won further promotion for him had not his religious opinions undergone a change, an indication of which was given in his argument with the Regius Professor of Divinity, whom he confuted. Two years after his appointment to the fellowship he left Oxford and proceeded to Louvain, where he met William (afterwards Cardinal) Allen. Recognizing his marked talent Allen secured him for his new college at Douai and appointed him its first prefect of studies. He was Allen's "right hand upon all occasions", acting as rector when he was absent and when the college was transferred (1578) to Reims.

Bristow is best known, however, as an earnest student, a powerful controversial writer, and, with Allen, as one of the revisers of the Douay Bible. His intense labours, while they earned for him the lasting gratitude of Catholics, told upon a constitution naturally weak, and he was obliged to relinquish his work in 1581. In May of the same year he went to Spa, but having obtained no advantage there he was advised, after two months, to return to England. This he did in September, staying until his death (18 October) with Mr. Jerome Bellamy, a Catholic of means, at Harrow-on-the-Hill. By his death the Catholic cause lost a zealous champion and a learned advocate. The Douai records speak of him in the highest terms as rivalling Allen in prudence, Stapleton in acumen, Campion in eloquence, Wright in theology, and Martin in languages. He wrote: (1) "A Briefe Treatise of diuerse and sure wayes to finde out the truthe in this doubtful and dangerous time of Heresie: conteyning sundry worthy Motives vnto the Catholic faith, or considerations to moue a man to beleue the Catholikes and not the Heretikes" (Third edition entitled "Motives inducing to the Catholike Faith"); (2) "Tabula in Summam Theologicam S. Thomæ Aquinatis"; (3) "A Reply to Will. Fulke"; (4) "Demandes to be proponed of Catholikes to the Heretikes"; (5) "A Defence of the Bull of Pope Pius V"; (6) "Annotations on the Rheims translation of the New Testament"; (7) "Carmina Diversa"; (8) "Motiva Omnibus Catholicæ Doctrinæ Orthodoxis Cultoribus pernecessaria", the last two being in manuscript.

WORTHINGTON, *Compendium Vitæ Auctoris* (prefixed to *Motiva*); *Records of the English Catholics*, I, II; DODD, *Church History of England*, ed. TIERNEY (London, 1843); GILLOW, *Bibl. Dict. Eng. Cath.*; WOOD, *Athenæ Oxonienses*; PITS, *De Angliæ Scriptoribus*.

FRANCIS AVELING.

British Columbia is the westernmost province of the Dominion of Canada. Territorially, it is also the largest, being 357,600 square miles in extent. It is composed of the mainland and islands. Prominent among the latter are Vancouver and Queen Charlotte Islands. The mainland is bounded on the south by the States of Washington and Idaho, on the east by the summits of the Rocky Mountain as far as a point where they meet the line of 120th degree of longitude, thence by that line to the 60th degree of latitude, the northern limit of the province. On the west it extends as far as the Pacific Ocean, except north of Portland Canal, where a narrow strip of coast land and a group of important islands form a part of Alaska.

PHYSICAL CHARACTERISTICS.—British Columbia has been called a sea of mountains, and this designation is fairly accurate, save perhaps for some forty miles on either side of the Chilcotin River, where are to be found rolling or tolerably level plateaux at least 3,000 feet above the sea and covered with excellent bunch grass. They are more or less open and the remainder of the province might be described as a continuous forest of conifers, interspersed here and there with deciduous trees and dotted at long intervals with natural prairies. The mountains are too numerous for enumeration. The principal ranges are the Lillooet mountains in the south-west, the Cariboo and the Babine mountains in the north-eastern and north-western interiors respectively, north of which numberless sierras connect the Rockies with the Cascade or Coast range, a chain of steep and rugged mounts that run parallel to the former. Between these many evidences of ancient physical upheavals lie either fertile valleys or deep, long, and narrow lakes. The latter are to be found especially in the northern interior. Prominent among them are lakes Babine, which covers an area of some 196,000 acres; Tatla, 152,000; Morice, 148,000; Stuart, 142,000; French, 140,000; Chilco, 109,760, and many others almost as large. In the south are lakes Kootenay, with an estimated area of 141,120 acres, Okanagan, 86,240, and Harrison, 78,400. Most of these sheets of water give rise to, or are drained by, rivers which in the spring assume generally the nature of torrents. The chief watercourses of the province are the Fraser River, with the Nechaco, the Quesnel, and the Thompson as tributaries; the Skeena, the Nass, and the Stickine in the north-west; the Finlay and its continuation, the Peace, with their tributary, the Parsnip, in the north-east, while the south-eastern corner is drained by the upper Columbia.

RESOURCES.—These streams, especially the Fraser and Skeena, are yearly ascended by immense shoals of salmon of the genus *oncorhynchus*, which are a great source of revenue, while the vast forests of the coast and southern interior, composed mostly of red cedar (*thuya gigantea*), fir (*pseudotsuga Douglassii*) and various species of spruce, are likewise the objects of remunerative industries. The country's most valuable treasures are, however, under ground, being found in the shape of minerals of which the following represents the production for 1906: copper, $8,288,565; gold, $5,579,039; lead, $2,667,578; silver, $1,897,320; other materials, $1,000,000. For the same period of time Vancouver Island and parts of the mainland yielded coal and coke to the value of $5,548,044, though it is well known that vast deposits of the same exist on the mainland, which only awaits capital to become productive. As to agriculture, it takes a rather secondary place in British Columbia; yet it is by no means neglected. In the valley of the lower Fraser and in the districts of Okanagan, Kamloops, Lillooet, etc., fruit-raising is considered more remunerative. Apples and pears of all kinds, peaches, tomatoes, and smaller fruit grow to perfection. From a climatological standpoint, extremes are to be found within the broad limits of the province. The coast enjoys an almost constantly mild, though wet, climate, and roses are grown in the open throughout the winter in Vancouver and Victoria. Beyond the Cascades is the dry belt, where irrigation becomes a necessity, while north of the 52d parallel the winters become more and more severe in proportion to the latitude and the altitude.

POPULATION.—The latest official census (1901) gave the population of the province as 178,657, of whom 33,081 were Catholic. The entire population cannot now be less than 260,000 with perhaps 48,000 Catholics. The capital is Victoria, in the southern extremity of Vancouver Island; population in 1901, 20,816, estimated now at 30,000 including 6,000 Orientals. The commercial metropolis is Vancouver, at the terminus of the Canadian Pacific Railway on Burrard Inlet. Founded, practically, in 1886, it had already 26,103 inhabitants in 1901. At the present time it claims a population of 71,150, some 4,500 of whom are Chinese and 1,800 Japanese. Next in importance are, on the mainland, New Westminster (about 10,000 inhabitants), Nelson (8,000), Rossland (7,150), and, on Vancouver Island, Nanaimo, a famous coal centre (6,230).

The figures for the total population of the province include 25,593 Indians divided into six very distinct stocks: (1) the Kootenays in the south-eastern corner; (2) the Salish, who are the aborigines of the southern portion of the mainland and the south-eastern coast of Vancouver Island; (3) the Kwakwiutl or Wakashans immediately north of the latter on the coast of the mainland and the northern and western parts of Vancouver Island; (4) the Haidas on Queen Charlotte Islands; (5) the Tsimpsians along the lower course of the Skeena and on the littoral of the mainland as far north as Alaska, and (6) the Dénés who range over the entire extent of the northern half of the province east of the Kwakwiutl and the Tsimpsians. The Kootenays number but 587, all Catholics, as well as the 2,500 Dénés of the north, but the Salish are fully 12,000, of whom about one-tenth are Protestants, the remainder Catholics. The Tsimpsians are partly heathen and partly Protestants, while the Wakashans and the Haidas, the former especially, have mostly retained their aboriginal faith in shamanistic practices, to the exclusion of any of the sects.

SECULAR HISTORY.—Navigators of various nationalities were the first representatives of our civilization to come in contact with these aborigines. In 1774 it was the Spanish Juan Perez; in 1778 the English Captain Cook; the French Lapérouse came in 1785; Captain Meares in 1787; Marchand, a Frenchman, in 1791; the American Gray in 1789, and the famous George Vancouver in 1792. But no settlement resulted from the visits of these mariners, who confined their operations to geographical work and fur trading with the natives. In 1793 Alexander Mackenzie crossed the Rocky Mountains from the east and reached the Pacific overland. The first white settlements were established in the northern interior by members of the Northwest Fur Trading Company: Fort McLeod in 1805; Forts St. James and Fraser in 1806, and Fort George, at the confluence of the Nechaco with the Great River the following year. The latter stream was explored to its mouth in 1808 by Simon Fraser, and is now known under his name. Shortly afterwards, other posts were founded and a brisk trade carried on in the northern interior, which was long called New Caledonia, and comprised at one time the basin of the Thompson, discovered in 1808 by the astronomer-geographer David Thompson.

The headquarters for the Pacific of the corporation (the Hudson's Bay Company since its absorption of the Northwest Company in 1821) which operated throughout the land were at Fort Vancouver, on the lower Columbia. When it became evident that this would be found to be in American territory, the authorities established (1843) another general dépôt at the southern end of Vancouver Island, which was at first called Fort Camosun, and then Victoria. Later on, the rich deposits of gold on the Fraser, and throughout the district of Cariboo, brought in large numbers of miners to the new post, round which a city of tents and shacks grew (1858) as if by magic. James Douglas (afterwards Sir), a prominent fur trader, was named governor of Vancouver Island as early as 1851. The gold mines and consequent influx of immigrants made it a necessity to erect the mainland into another colony, with him at its head (1858). A year later a capital for the new territory was chosen at a point on the mainland facing the apex of the Fraser delta, resulting in the founding of what is now New Westminster. Finally, after various vicissitudes, chief among which was the Chilcotin massacre of 1864, the colonies of British Columbia and Vancouver Island, already united in 1866 under one government at Victoria, were admitted into the Canadian Confederation on the 20th of July, 1871. Under the new regime, the province is governed by a lieutenant governor appointed and paid ($9,000 per annum) by Ottawa, with the help of responsible ministers and a Legislative Assembly composed of thirty-four members elected by the people.

RELIGIOUS HISTORY.—From a religious standpoint, the visits of the early navigators made little impression on the native mind. Some missionaries have wrongly supposed that the mantles worn on ceremonial occasions by the coast Indians originated in the copes of the priests that accompanied the Spanish and other ships. These are aboriginal with the natives. However, it is on record that, immediately prior to the advent of the white settlers, the old people among the Kwakwiutl tribe had a clear recollection of strangers "clad in black and having a crown of hair round the head, who had come to see the Indians" (Rapp, Sur les Missions de Québec, March, 1855, p. 113). The very first resident of what is now British Columbia (Lamalice, at Fort McLeod) was a Catholic, and so were the great explorer Simon Fraser, J. M. Quesnel, one of his two lieutenants, and all his French Canadian companions. These and the numerous servants of the trading posts, who were also Canadians, gave the aborigines their first ideas of Christianity. Later on, Father de Smet, S.J., visited the Kootenays, and in 1843 Father J. B. Z. Bolduc accompanied Douglas to Vancouver Island, where he ministered to crowds of wondering Indians. In 1842 Father M. Demers had made an extended trip through the inland tribes, visiting, in turn the Okanagans, the Shushwaps (both of the Salish stock) and the Carriers, a Déné tribe in the north. Four years later, a Jesuit priest, Father Nobili, walked in his footsteps and even went as far as Fort Babine, on the lake of the same name, instead of retracing his steps at Fort St. James, as his predecessors had done. The year thereafter (1847), Father Demers became the first bishop of the newly founded see of Vancouver Island, now the Archbishopric of Victoria. One of his first cares was to call for the help of the Oblates of Mary Immaculate already working in Oregon, one of whom, Father L. J. D'Herbomez, was consecrated Bishop of Miletopolis (9 October, 1864) and appointed to the Vicariate Apostolic of British Columbia, which on 2 September, 1890, became the Diocese of New Westminster, on the mainland.

CATHOLIC STATUS.—The chief Catholic institutions of Victoria are a hospital at the capital, together with an academy for girls, a college for boys, and a kindergarten, all, except the college, in charge of the Sisters of St. Ann. A protectory which was started at the same place is now at Quamichan; Nanaimo possesses, in addition to the Catholic school, an orphanage which originated in Victoria. There are schools for

Indian boys and girls at Kuper Island and among the Songhees of Victoria, and the Benedictine Fathers and Sisters conduct Indian schools on the west coast of the Island. On the mainland, identical institutions are to be found at St. Mary's Mission, North Vancouver, Sechelt, Kamloops, William's Lake, and Kootenay. These schools for the natives are supported, not always adequately, by the Federal Government of Canada. New Westminster, Vancouver, Cranbrook, and Greenwood each boast of a well-equipped hospital; New Westminster is the seat of St. Louis College, and Vancouver, in addition to a flourishing academy conducted by the Sisters of St. Ann, has a House of Refuge under the care of the Sisters of the Good Shepherd.

The public schools are on the American model and aiding religious institutions through grants or general exemption from taxes is prohibited. By virtue of an Act passed by Parliament after a signal public service rendered by the Sisters of St. Ann, the latter's Academy at Victoria enjoys freedom from such an encumbrance, and Church property may also be more or less favoured in this respect by special legislation on the part of the city councils. The clergy cannot be drafted into a jury or coerced into military service, though they may be allowed to serve if they so wish. Attending the provincial penitentiary and asylum for the insane, there are Catholic and Protestant chaplains paid by the federal authorities. Churches can be incorporated, and are then recognized as eligible for bequests and to acquire and possess property. While divorce in Canada is generally granted only by the Dominion Senate, the Supreme Court of British Columbia has jurisdiction over that issue, because at the time this province entered the Confederation, it was left free to enjoy the privileges it then possessed.

Hist. of B. C. (San Francisco, 1890); BEGG, *Hist. of B. C.* (Toronto, 1894); MORICE, *Au pays de l'ours noir* (Paris, 1897); *La Colombie brittannique* in *Les missions catholiques françaises au XIXe siècle* (Paris, 1903); *The Hist. of the Northern Interior of B. C.* (Toronto, 1904); GOSNELL, *The Year Book of B. C.* (Victoria, 1903); WADE, *The Thompson Country* (Kamloops, 1907).

A. G. MORICE.

British Guiana. See GUIANA, BRITISH.

Britius, FRANCIS, Orientalist, a monk of Rennes, in Brittany, date of birth and death unknown. He entered the Capuchin Order and spent the earlier years of his religious life in missionary work in the Levant, where he devoted himself with special zeal to the study of Oriental languages. His proficiency in these tongues soon came to the notice of his superiors, and, being summoned to Rome, he was employed by the Congregation of the Propaganda in the translation of several important works into Arabic. The first great fruit of his labours in this field was the translation of "L'Abrégé des annales ecclésiastiques de Baronius", continued by Sponde to the year 1646. The work was published at Rome in three volumes quarto, the first of which appeared in 1653, the second in 1655, and the third in 1671. Britius had also much to do with a translation of the Bible into Arabic, giving the Vulgate text in parallel columns, which was published by Mazari, at Rome, in 1671 (3 vols. fol.).

The works of Britius are now exceedingly rare, as practically the entire edition of both translations was sent to the East for use in the work of the missions.

Biogr. Univ., V, 629.

J. J. GEOGHAN.

Brittain, THOMAS LEWIS, b. near Chester, England, 1744; d. at Hartpury Court, 1827. His parents were Protestants, but at the age of sixteen Thomas became a Catholic. Shortly after his conversion he went to Picardy to pursue his studies, and later joined the Dominicans at Bornheim, where he made his profession 22 October, 1767. His studies were

continued at Louvain, and subsequently he taught with marked success at Bornheim, where he was made regent of studies. In 1790 the doctor's cap, with title of Master of Sacred Theology, was conferred on him. The same year he was transferred to Brussels, where he became director of the exiled English Dominican nuns, an office he held for thirty-seven years. In 1794, when the French army was expected at Brussels, Father Brittain conducted the sisters to Bornheim, whence, joined by eighteen Dominican fathers, they were conducted by an American captain to England. Father Brittain secured a foundation for the sisters at Hartpury Court near Gloucester. On 3 May, 1814, he was elected provincial of the Dominicans, and during his four years of office gained the respect and confidence of his brethren. He is the author of the following works: "Rudiments of English Grammar" (London, 1790), considered authoritative in its day, and highly commended by Walker, the lexicographer; "Principles of the Christian Religion and Catholic Faith Investigated" (London, 1790); "Collection of Poems Occasionally Written" (Cheltenham, 1822); "The Divinity of Jesus Christ and Beauties of His Gospels" (London, 1822); some unpublished MSS. are in the archives of the English province.

GILLOW, *Bibl. Dict. of Eng. Cath.*, s. v.; PALMER, *The Life of Cardinal Howard* (London, 1867).

JOHN T. MCNICHOLAS.

Britton (or BRETTON), JOHN, VENERABLE, layman and martyr, of an ancient family of Bretton near Barnsley in Yorkshire. An ardent Catholic, he was often separated from his wife and family, owing to constant persecution which he suffered for his faith. When advanced in years, he was maliciously and falsely accused of traitorous speeches against the queen and condemned to death. Refusing to renounce his faith he was executed at York, as in cases of high treason, 1 April, 1598. He was probably the father of Dr. Matthew Britton, prefect and professor at Douai in 1599.

CHALLONER, *Memoirs;* KNOX, *Douay Diaries;* PEACOCK, *List of Roman Catholics of Yorkshire* (London, 1872); FOLEY, *Records; Roman Diary* (London, 1880); GILLOW, *Bibl. Dict. Eng. Cath.* (London, 1885).

BEDE CAMM.

Brixen, DIOCESE OF, a Prince-Bishopric of Austria, suffragan of Salzburg, embracing the greater part of Northern Tyrol (with the exception of the part east of the Zillerbach, which belongs to Salzburg), as well as all Vorarlberg, and containing c. 6,705 square miles, and over 440,000 inhabitants.

I. HISTORY.—The Diocese of Brixen is the continuation of that of Säben (Sabiona), which, according to legend, was founded by St. Cassian. As early as the third century Christianity penetrated Sabiona, at that time a Roman custom station of considerable commercial importance. The first Bishop of Säben vouched for by history is Ingenuin, mentioned about 580, who appears as suffragan of the Patriarch of Aquileia. The tribes who pushed into the territory of the present Diocese of Brixen, during the great migratory movements, especially the Bajuvari and Langobardi, accepted Christianity at an early date; only the Slavs of the Puster valley (Pustertal) persisted in paganism until the eighth century. In the second half of the tenth century Bishop Rihpert (appointed 967) or Bishop Albuin I (967–1005) had the seat of the diocese, which since 798 has been under the Metropolitan of Salzburg, transferred to Brixen. Bishop Hartwig (1020–39) raised Brixen to the rank of a city, and surrounded it with fortifications. The diocese received many grants from the German emperors: thus from Conrad II in 1027 the Norital, from Henry IV in 1091 the Pustertal. In 1179 Frederick I conferred on the bishop the title and dignity of a prince of the German Empire. This accounts for the fact that during the difficulties between the papacy and the empire, the Bishops of Brixen generally took the part of the emperors; particularly notorious is the case of Altwin, during whose episcopate (1049–91) the ill-famed pseudo-synod of 1080 was held in Brixen, at which thirty bishops, partisans of the emperor, declared Pope Gregory VII deposed, and set up as antipope the Bishop of Ravenna.

The temporal power of the diocese soon suffered a marked diminution through the action of the bishops themselves who bestowed large sections of their territory in fief on temporal lords, as for example, in the eleventh century countships in the Inntal and the Eisacktal granted to the Counts of Tyrol, and in 1165 territory in the Inntal and the Pustertal to the Counts of Andechs-Meran. The Counts of Tyrol, in particular, who had fallen heir in large part to the territories of the Count of Meran, constantly grew in power; Bishop Bruno (1249–88) had difficulty in asserting his authority over a section of his territory against the claims of Count Meinhard of Tyrol. Likewise Duke Frederick IV, who was called the Penniless, compelled the Bishops of Brixen to acknowledge his authority. The dissensions between Cardinal Nicholas of Cusa (1450–64), appointed by Pope Nicholas V Bishop of Brixen, and Archduke Sigmund were also unfortunate; the cardinal was made a prisoner, and although the pope placed the diocese under an interdict, Sigmund came out victor in the struggle.

The Reformation was proclaimed in the Diocese of Brixen during the episcopate of Christoph I von Schrofenstein (1509–21) by German emissaries, like Strauss, Urban Regius, and others. In 1525, under Bishop Georg III of Austria (1525–39), a peasants' uprising broke out in the vicinity of Brixen, and several monasteries and strongholds were destroyed. The promise of King Ferdinand I, civil ruler of Tyrol, to redress the grievances of the peasants restored tranquillity, and at a diet held at Innsbruck, the most important demands of the peasants were acceded to. Although in 1532 these promises were withdrawn, peace remained undisturbed. Ferdinand I and his son Archduke Ferdinand II, in particular, as civil rulers took active measures against the adherents of the new teachings, chiefly the Anabaptists, who had been secretly propagating their sect; thus they preserved religious unity in the district of Tyrol and the Diocese of Brixen. At this time important services were rendered in safeguarding the Catholic Faith by the Jesuits, Capuchins, Franciscans, and Servites. Chief among the bishops of the period were: Cardinal Andreas of Austria (1591–1600), and Christoph IV von Spaur (1601–13), who in 1607 founded a seminary for theological students, enlarged the cathedral school, and distinguished himself as a great benefactor of the poor and sick. The seventeenth and eighteenth centuries saw a great reawakening of religious life in the Diocese of Brixen; many monasteries were founded, new missions for the cure of souls established, and the religious instruction of the people greatly promoted; in 1677 the University of Innsbruck was founded. The most prominent bishops of this period were: Kaspar Ignaz, Count von Künigl (1702–47), who founded many benefices for the care of souls, made diocesan visitations, kept a strict watch over the discipline and moral purity of his clergy, introduced missions under Jesuit Fathers, etc.: Leopold, Count von Spaur (1747–78), who rebuilt the seminary, completed and consecrated the cathedral, and enjoyed the high esteem of Empress Maria Theresa; Joseph Philipp, Count von Spaur (1780–91), a friend of learning, who, however, in his ecclesiastical policy, leaned towards Josephinism. The Government of Emperor Joseph dealt roughly with church interests; about twenty monas-

teries of the diocese were suppressed, a general seminary was opened at Innsbruck, and pilgrimages and processions were forbidden.

It was Bishop Franz Karl, Count von Lodron (1791–1828), who was to see the collapse of the temporal power of the diocese. In 1803 the principality was secularized, and annexed to Austria, and the cathedral chapter dissolved. During the brief rule of Bavaria the greatest despotism was exercised towards the Church; the restoration of Austrian supremacy (1814) improved conditions for the diocese. By the papal Bull "Ex imposito" (2 May, 1818) a new circumscription was given to the diocese which in this way received a considerable increase in territory; Vorarlberg, in particular, which had previously been divided among the three dioceses of Chur, Constance, and Augsburg, was added to the Diocese of Brixen. Vorarlberg was, as a matter of fact, to form a separate diocese, with Feldkirch as see, but this plan has never been put into execution; Vorarlberg is now administered by a vicar-general residing at Feldkirch, who, as a rule, is the auxiliary bishop of Brixen. In 1825 the cathedral chapter was re-established. All during the nineteenth century the episcopal see was occupied by distinguished men who safeguarded the unity of the Faith in the diocese, as is instanced in the enforced removal in 1830 of the Protestant families of the Zillertal, who actively championed the rights and privileges of the Church, and by missions and diocesan visitations, and by the introduction of religious orders endeavoured, with success, to raise the religious life of their diocese to a higher level. Karl Franz was succeeded by Bernhard Galura (1828–56), Vincenz Gasser (1856–79), Johann IX von Leiss, Laimburg (1879–84), Simon Aichner (1884–1904), who resigned 5 March, 1904, and Joseph Altenweisel (1904).

II. STATISTICS.—According to the figures for 1907 the Diocese of Brixen includes at the present time 438,448 Catholics in 501 spiritual charges. There are 28 deaneries, 6 in Vorarlberg, 380 parishes, 75 stations (*Exposituren*), 215 benefices and chaplaincies, and 725 primary schools with 1,333 classes. The cure of souls is exercised by 879 secular priests, and 580 regulars, 14 members of religious orders being at present outside the diocese. The cathedral chapter consists of 3 dignities (1 mitred provost, 1 dean, and 1 scholasticus), 4 capitular and 6 honorary canons. The prince-bishop as well as the members of the chapter, with the exception of the provost, are appointed by the emperor. In addition to the cathedral chapter there is a collegiate chapter of six canons at Innichen, a provost at Ehrenburg, and one at St. Gerold. Of the spiritual charges, 180 are subject to the free collation of the bishop, in 97 the municipality has the right of patronage, in 47 the right of patronage belongs to private individuals, in 87 to the Government or exchequer, in 15 to the religious fund, in 76 to religious corporations and monasteries. For the training of theologians there is a theological faculty at the University of Innsbruck with 17 professors, members of the Society of Jesus, and 352 theological students (many of them from the United States). There is a diocesan theological school in Brixen, with 8 professors; a seminary at Brixen, with 113 candidates for Holy orders (30 of them from other dioceses); the Seminarium Vincentinum (a diocesan preparatory seminary and gymnasium) with 21 professors; and the Cassianeum, with 3 professors and 51 students. Moreover, there are religious professors in the civil Higher Gymnasium at Brixen, and six other intermediate schools for boys conducted by the State.

Religious congregations of men possess 44 houses, and in 1907 numbered about 1,213 members, including 594 priests, 185 clerics, 348 lay brothers, 86 novices. There are two houses of Augustinian canons (at Neustift and Wilton), with 97 Fathers, 8 clerics, 3 lay brothers, and 4 novices; 2 Cistercian foundations (at Stams and Mehreran), with 84 Fathers, 9 clerics, 25 lay brothers, and 16 novices; 3 Benedictine foundations (at Fiecht, Marienberg, and Bregenz), with 48 Fathers, 5 clerics, 25 lay brothers, and 5 novices; 1 Benedictine priory (at Innsbruck), with 3 branch houses, 8 Fathers, 7 clerics, 61 lay brothers, and 19 novices; 3 Jesuit colleges (at Innsbruck, Feldkirch, and Tisis), with 100 priests, 59 clerics, 66 lay brothers, and 17 novices; 2 Redemptorist colleges, with 19 Fathers, 13 brothers, and 1 novice; 3 Servite monasteries, with 18 Fathers, 16 clerics, 10 brothers, and 4 novices; 8 Franciscan monasteries, with 100 Fathers, 23 clerics, 69 brothers, and 3 novices; 13 Capuchin monasteries with 100 Fathers and 59 brothers; 1 foundation of the Society of the Divine Word (Salvatorians), with 9 priests and 8 brothers; 1 mission house of St. Joseph at Brixen (with a branch at Mill Hill), with 6 priests and 11 clerics; 1 house of the Congregation of the Sons of the Most Holy Heart of Jesus, with 5 Fathers, 13 clerics, 9 lay brothers, and 17 novices; 1 foundation of the School Brothers, with 11 clerics. Besides the houses of theological studies for the members of the different orders, among the orders already mentioned, the Benedictines conduct in Fiecht a *Konvikt* (house of studies) for boys, and a school, the Cistercians in Mehreran a *Konvikt* for boys, the Jesuits a boarding school and gymnasium at Feldkirch (the celebrated institution known as the Stella Matutina), the School Brothers a seminary for teachers and a trade school, the Salvatorians a college, the Sons of the Most Holy Heart of Jesus an Apostolic school, and the Franciscans a Higher Gymnasium at Halle.

Religious congregations of women have established 234 religious houses with branches, about 2,644 sisters being within the limits of the diocese; these include 490 choir sisters, 1,884 lay sisters, and 270 novices. The various houses are divided as follows: the Poor Clares, 2 with 65 sisters; the Dominicans, 4 with 173 sisters; the Dominicans of the Third Order, 2 with 38 sisters; the Redemptorist sisters, 1 with 18 members; the Ursulines, 2 with 136 sisters; the Carmelites, 1 with 18 sisters; the Salesian Sisters, 1 with 54 members; the Cistercians, 1 with 39 members; the Sisters· of Divine Adoration, 1 with 51 members; the English Ladies, 1 institute with 79 members; the Tertiary Sisters, 6 houses and 13 branches, with 158 sisters; the Ladies of the Most Sacred Heart of Jesus, 1 with 99 sisters; the Poor-School Sisters of Notre Dame, 2 with 27 members; the Benedictines, 1 monastery with 5 sisters; the Sisters of the High German Order, 1 house with 3 sisters. The Sisters of Mercy have a mother-house in Innsbruck with 92 branch houses and 931 sisters, and one at Zams with 72 branches and 608 sisters. The Sisters of Mercy of the Holy Cross have 1 provincial house at Innsbruck with 26 branches and 131 sisters. The orders and congregations of women are engaged almost exclusively in the training of girls, and the care of the sick, children, and the aged, etc. The above-named congregations have charge of 8 educational institutions, 1 lyceum for girls, 12 industrial schools, 82 schools for girls, 41 schools for boys and girls, 46 crèches, 3 hospitals, 7 orphan asylums, 23 asylums, 3 sanatoria, 56 homes for the poor, 2 public insane asylums, 2 houses for lepers, 1 institution for the deaf and dumb, 4 homes for servants, 1 asylum for priests in ill health, and about 25 other charitable institutions.

The cathedral of the Diocese of Brixen dates, in its present form, from the eighteenth century, having been built between 1745 and 1758. The only remains of the earlier Gothic building is the cloister, which contains frescoes and monuments dating from the thirteenth to the fifteenth century. Other prominent ecclesiastical buildings of the diocese are: the Court or Franciscan church at Innsbruck, in which is the celebrated monument to Emperor Maximilian I; the Jesuit church at Innsbruck, built between 1620 and 1640 in barocco style; the Gothic cathedral at Feldkirch, built in 1478; the Cistercian church at Mehreran; the fifteenth-century parish church of Schwaz, built in Gothic style, and others. Among the places of pilgrimage are: Absam, St. Georgenberg near Feubach, Maria Waldrast near Deutsch-Matrei, the pilgrimage church on the Frauenberg near Rankweil, that on the Gebhardsberg near Bregenz, and others.

RESCH, *Annales ecclesiæ Sabionensis nunc Brixinensis* (3 vols., Augsburg, 1755–67); SINNACHER, *Biographien von Bischöfen im Bistum Brixen* (Brixen, 1814); IDEM, *Beiträge zur Geschichte der bischöflichen Kirchen Säben und Brixen in Tirol* (9 vols., Brixen, 1824–36); TINKHAUSER, *Topographisch-historisch-statistische Beschreibung der Diöcese Brixen* (2 vols., Brixen, 1854–79), continued by RAPP (3 vols., 1880–91); REDLICH, *Die Traditionsbücher des Hochstifts Brixen* (Innsbruck, 1886); RAPP, *Topographisch-historische Beschreibung des Generalvikariates Vorarlberg* (4 vols., Brixen, 1892–1902). Cf. also bibliography to TYROL.

JOSEPH LINS.

Broad Church Party. See ANGLICANISM.

Brogan, SAINT, flourished in the sixth or seventh century. Several persons in repute for holiness seem to have borne this name, which is variously written *Brogan, Broccan, Bracan,* and even *Bearchan* and *Bearchanus.* Of these, two are commemorated in the Irish Martyrologium of Aengus, the early date of which (c. 800) is now generally admitted. There, under 8 July, we read: "Brocan, the scribe, gained a noble triumph without any fall"; and under 17 September: "Broccan of Ross Tuirc thou shouldst declare". Colgan (*Trias Thaumat.*, p. 518) speaks as if he were inclined to identify both these persons with the author of an early Irish hymn upon St. Brigid. The glosses upon Aengus and the Martyrology of Gorman, while seemingly treating them as distinct, prove that the matter admits of no certainty. Some modern hagiographers incline to regard the St. Brogan of 8 July as the amanuensis and possibly the nephew of St. Patrick. They style him bishop and locate him at Maethail-Brogain, now Mothil in Waterford; but this is admittedly quite doubtful. St. Brogan of Rosstuirc, on the other hand, is identified with the author of the hymn to St. Brigid, and is believed to be the Abbot Brochanus referred to in the Life of St. Abban, preserved in the "Codex Salmanticensis". Rosstuirc is generally assigned to the Diocese of Ossory, and may be Rossmore in Queen's County.

Other Brochans are mentioned in the Martyrology of Gorman under 1 January, 9 April, 27 June, and 25 August.

O'HANLON, *Lives of the Irish Saints* (Dublin, 1892–1902), July Vol., 170; September Vol., 435–440; *Acta SS.* 17 September, Vol. V; CARRIGAN, *History of the Diocese of Ossory* (Dublin, 1905), II, 28 and 175; III, 334 and 441; IV, 174; ARCHDALL, *Monasticon Hibernicum;* FORBES in *Dict. Christ. Biog.,* I, 339; cf. 314; DE SMEDT, *Acta Sanctorum Hibern. ex Codice Salmanticensi,* 505–540.

HERBERT THURSTON.

Broglie, AUGUSTE-THÉODORE-PAUL DE, abbé, professor of apologetics at the Institut Catholique at Paris, and writer on apologetic subjects, b. at Auteuil, 18 May, 1834; d. 11 May, 1895. He was the son of Achille-Victor, Duc de Broglie, and his wife, Albertine de Staël, a Protestant and the daughter of Madame de Staël. After the death of the mother, who died young, he was brought up by the Baroness Auguste de Staël, *née* Vernet; this aunt, although also a Protestant, exerted herself "to make a large-minded Christian of him in the Church to which she did not belong" (Monseigneur d'Hulst in "Le Correspondant", 25 May, 1895). Entering the Navy young, Broglie was appointed Ensign in 1857 and soon after Lieutenant. While thus occupied he felt himself called to the ecclesiastical state. After taking the preparatory studies he was ordained priest, 18 October, 1870. In his numerous publications the Abbé de Broglie was always a faithful defender of Catholic dogma. At the time of his death, which resulted from the violence of an insane person, he was preparing a book on the agreement of reason and faith. His most important work is "L'histoire des religions". Of his other writings, some of which were pamphlets and some articles in reviews, the following may be mentioned: "Le positivisme et la science expérimentale"; "Religion de Zoroastre et religion védique"; "Le bouddhisme"; "Religions néo-brahmaniques de l'Inde"; "L'islamisme"; "La vraie définition de la religion"; "La transcendance du christianisme"; "L'histoire religieuse d'Israël"; "Les prophètes et les prophéties, d'après les travaux de Kuenen"; "L'idée de Dieu dans l'Ancien et le Nouveau Testament"; "Le présent et l'avenir du catholicisme en France". Two posthumous publications, "Questions bibliques" and "Religion et critique", were edited by the Abbé Piat.

PIAT, *L'apologétique de l'abbé de Broglie* (Paris, 1896).

CLODIUS PIAT.

Broglie, JACQUES-VICTOR-ALBERT, DUC DE, French statesman and historian, b. at Paris, 13 June, 1821; d. there 19 January, 1901. After a brief diplomatic career he resigned his post to devote himself to literature. His work, "L'Eglise et l'Empire romain au IVe siècle" (6 vols., 1856), won for him Lacordaire's seat in the French Academy (1862). In 1871 he was appointed ambassador to England, but was recalled in 1872 and, taking his seat in the Assembly, soon became the leading spirit of the opposition to the Republic and M. Thiers. Twice President of the Council (1873 and 1877), the Duke de Broglie was finally defeated in his own district and withdrew from public life.

Besides editing the "souvenirs" of his father (1886), the "Mémoires" of Talleyrand (1871), and the letters of the Duchesse Albertine de Broglie, he published a series of works on the diplomacy of Louis XV, which placed their author in the first rank of historians.

HANOTAUX, *Contemporary France*, tr. TARNER (New York, 1903–05); art. in *Dublin Review* (1874), Vol. XXIII; MEAUX, *Souvenirs politiques* in *Le Correspondant* (1903), 211; E. DAUDET, *Souvenirs de la présidence du Maréchal de MacMahon* (Paris, 1880).

JEAN LE BARS.

Broglie, MAURICE-JEAN DE, b. in Paris, 5 September, 1766; d. there, 20 June, 1821. He was the son of the Field-Marshal, Victor-François, Duc de Broglie, created, by Emperor Francis I, Prince of the Holy Roman Empire, a title which was to be hereditary in the family. Called to the ecclesiastical state, Maurice pursued his studies at St.-Sulpice. During the Reign of Terror, when persecution drove both his father and him out of France, they went to Berlin. King Frederick William received the duke with marked distinction and granted to the young prince a provostship in the cathedral chapter of Posen. Maurice returned to France in 1803, and the steps he took to recover some family property not yet sold, brought him to the attention of Napoleon, who invited him to his court and named him his almoner. Recognizing in the emperor the restorer and support of order and religion, de Broglie became a devoted follower of the monarch and eulogized him in a pastoral letter issued on the occasion of the victory of Austerlitz. In 1805 Napoleon nominated him to the See of Acqui, Italy, and in 1807 to Ghent, Belgium. When it became evident, however, to de Broglie that the pope and clergy were to be mere tools of the despot, and religion the instrument of his ambitious designs, he showed determined opposition to Napoleon. In 1809 the minister of worship wrote in a letter that the sovereign was highly displeased with the bishop because of his lack of devotion to the royal person; in

1810 the bishop refused the Cross of the Legion of Honour, sent to him by the emperor, judging that he could not accept such a distinction at the time when the Papal States had been seized, and he explained his refusal in a memoir, a model of moderation, sent to the minister.

By order of Napoleon, a council was assembled in Paris, 17 June, 1811, under the presidency of Cardinal Fesch, uncle of the emperor and Archbishop of Lyons. The object of Napoleon was to oblige the pope to grant the Bulls of institution to the priests nominated by him to bishoprics; this Pius VII had firmly refused. Napoleon wished, furthermore, to make an arrangement that would force the pope in the future to issue the Bulls within six months, and should His Holiness fail to do so in that time, the metropolitan or the oldest bishop of the ecclesiastical province would then confirm the nominee, the sovereign pontiff's silence being considered as assent. The fathers of the council solemnly assembled in the metropolitan church, there being present six cardinals, nine archbishops, and eighty bishops; this was the first and the last general session. After six preliminary particular sessions, a decree in compliance with the will of Napoleon was proposed to the bishops. At first only two, d'Aviau, Archbishop of Bordeaux, and de Broglie, Bishop of Ghent, rejected it; but subsequently, only four members were for the pure and simple acceptance of the decree. The pope had privately declared that such encroachments on his spiritual power were contrary to the laws of the Church and ecclesiastical discipline, destructive of the authority of the Holy See and of the principles on which depended the lawful mission of bishops.

The anger of Napoleon, provoked by such firm and general opposition, led him to prorogue the council and visit with severe punishments the bishops who had been most prominent in their opposition. Arrested on 12 July, 1811, de Broglie was cast into the dungeon at Vincennes and kept in close confinement for more than four months, without outside communication, and without books or writing materials. He was next sent as an exile to Beaune. On the mere suspicion that he had intercourse with his clergy, he was deported to the island of Ste.-Marguerite on the coast of Provence. De Broglie, while in prison signed, under compulsion, his resignation as Bishop of Ghent. Although it was not accepted by the pope and was consequently null, Napoleon named a successor to the see. As the great majority, however, of the clergy and people refused to acknowledge him, they were subjected to vexations and persecution. The fall of Napoleon restored peace, and de Broglie, returning to his diocese, was received amid the rejoicings of his clergy and flock.

The bishop was not to enjoy a long rest. The allied sovereigns of Europe after the overthrow of Napoleon had formed Holland and Belgium, or the Low Countries, into a kingdom and appointed William of Nassau to rule over them. The plenipotentiaries of the powers, assembled in London, 1814, made the Dutch Constitution the fundamental law of Belgium, with a proviso that it should be modified according to circumstances. The generality of Belgians are Catholics. On 18 July, 1815, William proposed the Dutch Constitution to the Belgians, and the representatives summoned to vòte upon it rejected it by 796 to 527. (See BELGIUM.) The king, disregarding the vote, imposed upon the Belgians a constitution that deprived the Catholics of all their rights. Joseph II by his petty persecutions had lost the Netherlands for Austria; Napoleon, following in the footsteps of the "emperor sexton", lost them for France; William, his imitator, brought about the secession of Belgium from Holland and its independence in 1830. De Broglie with the Bishops of Namur and Tournai, and the Vicars-General of Mechlin and Liège took up the defence of the Catholic cause, and issued a pastoral instruction and, later on, a doctrinal judgment on the required oath to the Constitution.

De Broglie also appealed to Pius VII, and the pontiff, on 16 May, 1816, sent an official note to the minister of the Low Countries residing in Rome, stating that the Belgian Constitution contained statements contrary to the Catholic Faith, that the opposition of the bishops could not in justice be reproved, and that no oath opposed to conscience should be imposed. New difficulties then arose, first when the bishop refused to offer public prayers for the king, and again when at the erection of new universities, de Broglie addressed a representation to the king in which he pointed out the introduction of dangerous books into public institutions, and strongly expressed his fears for the fate of the episcopal seminaries. Cited before the tribunal, he took refuge in France, and the court of Brussels by a judgment, 8 November, 1817, condemned him to deportation. The sentence was posted by the public executioner between the sentences of two public malefactors. The bishop's health broke down under the weight of so many severe trials; succumbing to a short illness, he died in Paris, venerated by all for his sterling qualities and austerity of life. In 1819, de Broglie printed a protest concerning the state of religious affairs in Belgium, which was addressed to the Emperors of Austria and Russia and to the King of Prussia.

ROHRBACHER, *Histoire universelle de l'église catholique* (Paris, 1874); LAROUSSE, *Dictionnaire universel du XIXe siècle* (Paris, 1867); DE FELLER, *Biographie universelle* (Paris, 1847).

F. M. L. DUMONT.

Brogny, JEAN-ALLARMET (or JEAN-ALOUZIER) DE, a French Cardinal, b. in 1342 at Brogny, in Savoy; d. at Rome, 1426. Biographers are not agreed as to his parentage and real name. According to some, he belonged to a peasant family of Brogny, called Allarmet; others say he was descended from the d'Alouzier, a noble house in Comtat-Venaissin. It is certain, however, that the future cardinal was a swineherd, when two monks, struck by his open disposition and thoughtful answers, took him with them to Geneva, and procured for him an education which was completed at the University of Avignon. Despite the friendship and the inducement of Marcossay, Bishop of Geneva, young Allarmet retired to the Chartreuse of Dijon, where his merits soon became widely known. When Robert of Geneva was elected pope by the faction hostile to Urban VI, Allarmet joined him at Avignon, either having been sent by the Duke of Burgundy or called by Robert himself.

At Avignon favours were bestowed upon him in quick succession by the so-called Clement VII; the Bishopric of Viviers, in 1380, the dignity of Cardinal, in 1385, and shortly after, the exalted office of Chancellor of the Holy See. Robert's successor, Peter of Luna, who called himself Benedict XIII, sanctioned all these preferments and even promoted Allarmet from Viviers to Ostia-Velletri, one of the suburbican dioceses. There is no doubt that at that time Cardinal de Brogny, like St. Peter of Luxemburg and St. Vincent Ferrer, considered the French obedience as legitimate. However, his thorough orthodoxy soon caused him to change his views. As early as 1398 he had left Avignon as a silent protest against the unapostolic spirit of that court. The elusive tactics of Gregory XII and Benedict XIII were met by him with more than a silent protest. He inaugurated the neutral party and brought about the Council of Pisa which resulted in the election of Alexander V (1409).

The new pope confirmed de Brogny in his double dignity of Bishop of Ostia and Chancellor of the Church. In the latter capacity he presided over Alexander's funeral and also over the conclave which elected John XXIII (1410). John held de Brogny in the highest esteem. The Metropolitan See of Arles having become vacant, he disregarded the candidate elected by the Arlesian chapter and appointed Cardinal de Brogny perpetual administrator of that see. This appointment was intended as a means of recovering the rights of the Church of Arles usurped by the Counts of Provence during the confusion consequent on the schism. The new metropolitan did not disappoint his patron. With the might of right he fought the usurpers till the last claim of the venerable see was secured. Cardinal de Brogny then left his diocese in care of the two Fabri and proceeded on a still more delicate mission. Owing to the obstinacy of the contestants, the Council of Pisa had really left the Church with three popes instead of one. Moreover, to the evils of schism John Hus was adding that of heresy. The Council of Constance was convened to meet this double difficulty, and after the withdrawal of John XXIII, de Brogny, in virtue of his title of Chancellor, presided over the sessions of the Council and evinced sterling qualities.

In behalf of unity, he did not hesitate to vote for the deposition of the three popes, two of whom had been his personal friends. No doubt he could have secured the election for himself, had he so desired; but he threw the weight of his influence in favour of Colonna, who took the name of Martin V. If John Hus remained contumacious and was condemned, it was not de Brogny's fault. The Protestant Senebier writes in his "Histoire littéraire de Genève":— "In the letters of John Hus we find a conversation with the prelate [de Brogny] who endeavoured to conquer him by such arguments as compassion, meekness, and Christian charity suggested".

In his old age de Brogny asked to be translated from Ostia to Geneva, but only his remains reached the beloved place of his youth; they were laid to rest in the chapel of the Machabees which had been added to the old cathedral by the cardinal himself. De Brogny is variously known in history as Cardinal of Viviers, Cardinal of Ostia, sometimes Cardinal of Arles, and Cardinal de Saluces. He founded the Dominican convents of Tivoli and Annecy; the *maladrerie* or lepers' hospital, of Brogny; part of the Celestines' monastery of Avignon; and, above all, the College of St. Nicholas, affiliated to the University of Avignon, and endowed with twenty scholarships for destitute students. Soulavie, president of St. Nicholas College, published (Paris, 1774) a "Histoire de Jean d'Alouzier de Brogny" of which only fifty copies were printed.

FISQUET, *La France pontificale, métropole d'Aix* (Paris, 1867); MIGNE, *Dict. des cardinaux* (Paris, 1857).

J. F. SOLLIER.

Bromyard, JOHN, theologian, d. about 1390. He takes his name from his birthplace in Herefordshire, England. He entered the Dominican order and was sent to Oxford where he distinguished himself in theology and jurisprudence. It is probable that he lectured on theology at Oxford while it is certain that he laboured in the same Faculty at Cambridge. He was one of the most pronounced opponents of the doctrines of Wyclif. Though his name is not mentioned in the acts of the London Synod of 1382 held by William de Courtenay, Archbishop of Canterbury, where the doctrines of Wyclif were condemned as heretical, it is admitted by all that he took a leading part in drawing up the decree of condemnation. He was also a much-prized writer as the many editions of his "Summa Prædicantium" attest. Excerpts were made from this work and published separately as brochures and widely circulated among the people. In his "Opus Trivium" he arranges for the convenience of preachers various topics drawn from theology, civil and canon laws. This work was later on edited by Philip Bromyard, and hence some maintain, but without reason, that he was the real author.

QUÉTIF AND ECHARD, SS. O.P., I, 700; LELAND, Commentarium de Scriptoribus Britannicis, 356; SCHULTE, Geschichte der Quellen und Litteratur des canonischen Rechts, II, 880, 561; MILLER in Dict. Nat. Biog., VI, 405.

THOS. M. SCHWERTNER.

Brondel, JOHN BAPTIST, first Bishop of Helena, Montana, U. S. A., b. at Bruges, Belgium, 23 February, 1842; d. at Helena, 3 November, 1903. He was educated at the American College of the University of Louvain and ordained priest at Mechlin, Belgium, by Cardinal Engelbert Stercks (17 December, 1864). Two years later he volunteered for the missions in the United States and was made rector of the church at Heilacoon, Washington Territory, early in 1867. Here he remained for nearly ten years and was then transferred to Walla Walla, but returned to his old charge the following year.

On 14 December, 1879, he was consecrated at Victoria, as third Bishop of Vancouver, British Columbia, in succession to Bishop Seghers, who had been made coadjutor to the Archbishop of Oregon City. Bishop Brondel retained this charge until by a Bull of 7 April, 1883, he was appointed Administrator of the Vicariate of Montana. When the Diocese of Helena was formed he was transferred to that see, 7 March, 1884, as its first bishop. During all his long and active career in this northwest section, he was particularly successful in his dealings with the many Indians under his charge. They looked up to him as a father and protector, and his great popularity among the various tribes was not only of benefit to the Church, but was utilized on numerous occasions by the United States Government to further the political, material, and moral welfare of the Indians. His death was regarded as a great loss to the work of the evangelization and civilization of the Indians. He was buried 7 November, 1903, in a vault under the cathedral in Helena.

Catholic News files (New York, Nov., 1903); REUSS, Biog. Encycl. Cath. Hierarchy (Milwaukee, 1898); Catholic Directory (Milwaukee, 1904).

THOMAS F. MEEHAN.

Brookby (or BRORBEY), ANTHONY, Friar Minor and English martyr; d. 19 July, 1537. Brookby was lecturer in divinity in Magdalen College, Oxford, was well versed in Greek and Hebrew, and enjoyed the reputation of being an eloquent preacher. At the command of King Henry VIII, who took offence at a sermon of Brookby's in which he attacked the king's actions and mode of living, he was apprehended, put to the rack, and tortured in the most cruel manner in order to make him retract what he had said; but all to no purpose. Having been rendered wellnigh helpless as a result of his tortures, Brookby was charitably cared for by a pious woman for a fortnight until, by the command of the king, an executioner strangled him to death with the Franciscan cord which he wore around his waist.

STONE, Faithful unto Death (London, 1892), iv, 76; PARKINSON, Coll. Anglo-Minor. (London, 1726), 239; THADDEUS, The Franciscans in England (London, 1898), III, 17; DANIELLE, Martirio e Morte d'alcuni Frati di San Francesco, III, 16.

STEPHEN M. DONOVAN.

Brookes, JAMES, last Catholic Bishop of Gloucester, England, b. May, 1512, in Hampshire; d. 1560. Proceeding to Oxford in 1528, he became Fellow of Corpus Christi in 1531, Doctor of Divinity, 1546, and Master of Balliol, 1547. Brookes was widely known as an eloquent preacher, and, on the deposition of Bishop Hooper, was elevated by Queen Mary to the See of Gloucester. He was consecrated 1 April, 1554. In 1555 he was one of the papal subdelegates in the royal commission for the trial of Cranmer, Latimer, and Ridley. He refused to degrade Ridley, probably on the ground that Ridley's consecration (1547) had been according to the invalid form which was established by law very soon after that date. If, as Foxe asserts, he refused to degrade Latimer, his position may have been based upon the fact that Latimer had lived for several years as a simple clergyman. It is hardly possible that Brookes, a man of learning and integrity, would have been actuated in this trial by the selfish considerations hinted at by some Protestant historians. After the accession of Elizabeth he refused to take the oath of supremacy, and died in prison. He was buried in Gloucester Cathedral. Two of his orations in the Cranmer case are given in Foxe, "Acts and Monuments". One of his sermons was printed by Robert Coly, or Caly, in 1553 and 1554.

GILLOW, Bibl. Dict. Eng. Cath.; DODD-TIERNEY, Church History of England (London, 1846); LINGARD, History of England; STONE, Reign of Queen Mary (London, 1901): POLLARD, Thomas Cranmer (1903); PHILLIPS, The Extinction of the Ancient Hierarchy (London, 1905).

J. VINCENT CROWNE.

Brooklyn, DIOCESE OF, comprises the counties of Kings, Queens, Nassau, and Suffolk, or all of Long Island, in the State of New York, U. S. A., an area of 1,007 square miles. The population of Long Island is about 2,000,000, according to the State census of 1905, and of this, 600,000 are Catholics. The Catholics are mostly of Irish, German, and Italian birth or race, but as a matter of fact, in this island see there is now every week a perpetual Pentecost, for the Gospel is preached to the faithful in twelve languages. Polish, French, Italian, German, Slav, Syrian, Greek, Hungarian, Lithuanian, Scandinavian, Bohemian, as well as English-speaking Catholics, have special ministrations for their respective nationalities.

Long Island was known to the early Spanish explorer Gomez and to Gordillo, a lieutenant of Vasquez de Ayllón, who in 1524-25 reached this latitude and on the 29th of June noted this island, which they named "Isla de los Apóstoles" (Island of the Apostles) in honour of the feast day of the Apostles Peter and Paul. It is so styled in the Spanish maps of Ribero, made in 1529. Settled later under the auspices of the Dutch West India Company (1636), there is scarcely a trace of Catholicism to be found during the period of the sway of that corporation. It would be strange indeed were Catholics attracted to a community that refused to enclose their cemeteries because such were "relics of superstitious observances", or to erect tombstones because in doing so they might give the "appearance of according to the ceremonies and requirements of

PETER TURNER, ORGANIZER OF THE FIRST CATHOLIC CONGREGATION IN BROOKLYN

BROOKLYN

1. ST. FRANCIS-IN-THE-FIELD (FIRST GERMAN CHURCH IN BROOKLYN)
2. ST. JAMES'S PRO-CATHEDRAL.   3. HOLY TRINITY CHURCH
4. OLD ST. JAMES'S (FIRST CATHOLIC CHURCH ERECTED ON LONG ISLAND)

Prelacy and Papacy". In April, 1657, there is record made of the fining of one "Nicholas the Frenchman" in the sum of twelve guilders, or $4.80, because, as the sheriff's report has it, on the "frivolous excuse" that he was a Catholic, Nicholas refused to pay his share of the tax levied for the salary of the Dutch Reformed minister who preached for the colony then located within the present limits of the Borough of Brooklyn. In addition to the Dutch there were a number of Walloons and Huguenots settled in this locality. Some of the unfortunate Acadian exiles were scattered through Long Island during 1756; and on the muster-rolls of the militia from the same section serving in the army of Sir William Johnson, in 1775, we find such names as Reilly, Shea, Burke, Power, Welsh, Doolly, Barry, Sullivan, Cassidy, Lynch, Ryan, Larkin, Mcloney, Fagan, Blake, Donnelly, Shields, Kinsella, and Downey. There are no records to show what became of them or their children. But an occasional curiously twisted patronymic among the old non-Catholic families of the interior districts of the island gives a clue to the reason of this. We have no positive evidence that any considerable body of Catholics became a component part of Brooklyn's local life till after the dawn of the nineteenth century and especially after the location there of the Navy Yard in 1801.

This government station at once gave employment to many mechanics in the various trades connected with the ship-building industry, and soon a number of Irish immigrants, mostly from the Catholic sections of the North, especially from Derry and Donegal, sturdy confessors of the Faith in their native land, settled in Brooklyn. Among these were the parents of the first American cardinal, John McCloskey, Archbishop of New York, and of his namesake, the first Rector of the American College at Rome, William George McCloskey, afterwards Bishop of Louisville, Kentucky. Until 1822 these Catholics had to cross the East River to New York to hear Mass and attend to their spiritual necessities, as the scarcity of priests and their own poverty brought about this inconvenient situation. Occasionally a priest would go over from New York to say Mass and preach in private houses, or wherever suitable accommodation could be obtained. The pioneer in this was the Augustinian missionary Father Philip Larissy, who said the first Mass in the house of William Purcell, at the north-east corner of York and Gold Streets, on a date now unknown. The little colony, constantly growing in numbers and influence, desired

a church of its own, and hence a meeting was held on the 7th of January, 1822, at the house of William Purcell, at which a committee of five was named to wait on Bishop Connolly of New York and ask his advice and consent for the organization of a congregation. It is notable that in the circular calling this meeting the reasons stated are: "In the first place we want our children instructed in the principles of our holy religion; we want more convenience of hearing the word of God ourselves. In fact, we want a church, a pastor, and a place for interment." Those prominent in the pioneer work of the congregation were Peter Turner, George S. Wise, then a purser in the United States navy, William Purcell, John Kenney, Nicholas Stafford, Denis Cosgrove, Jeremiah Mahoney, James Rose, George McCloskey, James and Patrick Freel, Dr. Andrew B. Cook, also of the United States navy, James Furey, Thomas Young, Hugh and James McLaughlin, Andrew Parmentier, James Harper, Quintin M. Sullivan, and Daniel Dempsey.

OLD CATHEDRAL RECTORY AND FIRST ORPHAN ASYLUM

As a result of this meeting eight lots were purchased on Jay Street, and St. James's, the first Catholic church on Long Island, was built and dedicated to Divine worship by Bishop Connolly, 28 August, 1823. The lots about the church were used as a graveyard until 1849, when Holy Cross Cemetery, Flatbush, was opened. The original church building stood until 1903, when its walls were enclosed in a new structure built on the same site for a pro-cathedral. The Reverend Dr. John Power of St. Peter's, New York, was the early and stanch friend of the new congregation. He used to cross the river frequently to minister to them. Other priests of the pioneer days were the Reverends Patrick Bulger, James McKenna, and James Doherty; the last two died in the service of the parish, and were buried in front of the church. The first regular pastor was the Reverend John Farnan, who was appointed in April, 1825. The second church in Brooklyn, St. Paul's, dedicated 21 January, 1838, was built on land given by Cornelius Heeney. He first offered the site for a seminary, but could not agree with Bishop Dubois as to the manner in which the title should be held, the old and troublesome idea of lay trusteeship proving an obstacle. It is notable that although the organization of the first congregation in Brooklyn was due mainly to lay effort there was never any of the subsequent difficulty over trustee authority and rights that made so much scandal elsewhere during this era. The Reverend Nicholas O'Donnell, O.S.A. (1840–47), was the second pastor of St. Paul's, and after him the Reverend Joseph Schneller, until his death in 1860, had charge there. Father Schneller was one of the most active priests in the New York controversies of the early years of the nineteenth century. His name, with those of the Reverend Dr. Power, Fathers Felix Varela and Thomas C. Levins, is to be found in most of the bitter public contests waged with non-Catholic assailants of the Church. He helped to found and edited for some time the "New York Weekly Register and Catholic Diary", established in 1833. Cornelius Heeney did not limit his generosity to the site for St. Paul's Church and the Girls' Industrial School that adjoins it. During his life his income was mainly devoted to charity, and 10 May, 1845, three years before his death, he had his estate legally incorporated as the Brooklyn Benevolent Society, and its officials directed to expend its yearly income for the benefit of the poor and orphans. This amounts now to about $25,000 annually, and the total expended by this charity since Mr. Heeney's death is more than a million dollars.

In 1841 another famous priest, the Very Reverend John Raffeiner, a native of the Austrian Tyrol, bought with his own money property on which was erected the church of the Most Holy Trinity and began there to minister to a colony of German Catholics. His efforts in this direction were extended to similar congregations in New York, Boston, and New Jersey. He laboured thus for more than twenty years and held the office of vicar-general when he died, in 1861. St. Charles Borromeo's parish was founded in 1849 by the Reverend Dr. Charles Constantine Pise, also one of the strong writers and publicists of that time. Before going to Brooklyn he had been stationed at St. Peter's, New York, and previous to that, in 1832, while officiating in Washington, he was, on motion of Senator Henry Clay, appointed Chaplain to the Congress of the United States and served during a session, the only instance on record of such an honour being given to a Catholic. Other priests whose earnest work in its formative period contributed to the building up of the Church in Long Island were the Reverends John Walsh, James McDonough, Richard Waters, James O'Donnell, David W. Bacon, afterwards the first Bishop of Portland, Maine, the Reverends Michael Curran, William Keegan, for many years Vicar-General of the diocese, and his associate in that office, the Right Reverend Mgr. Michael May, the Reverends Nicholas Balleis, O.S.B., Eugene Cassidy, Sylvester Malone, Peter McLoughlin, John Shanahan, Edward Corcoran, Hugh McGuire, Jeremiah Crowley, James McEnroe, Joseph Fransioli, Martin Carroll, T. O'Farrell, Anthony Arnold, John McCarthy, James O'Beirne, Joseph Brunneman, Anthony Farley, John McKenna, Patrick O'Neil, and James H. Mitchell. Father Mitchell was much interested in the work of societies for young men, and his administration as head of the national organization was specially successful.

When, in July, 1841, Father Raffeiner began the great German parish of the Most Holy Trinity on a part of the farm of the old Dutch Meserole family, this was known as the Bushwick section of the then town of Williamsburg, which was subsequently annexed to Brooklyn. The first German Catholic Church in the city of Brooklyn was the quaint little St. Francis'-in-the-Fields, which Father Raffeiner opened in 1850, at Putnam and Bedford avenues. Its title indicates its rural environment, and Father Maurus Ramsauer, a Benedictine just arrived from Germany, was made its first pastor. In 1855, under Father Bonaventure Keller, the original design of Father Raffeiner was carried out, and a sort of preparatory seminary for German ecclesiastical students was begun and lasted there for two years. When

Father Raffeiner died, in 1861, he left St. Francis', which was still surrounded by a garden, for the benefit of the orphans of the Holy Trinity parish. The little church was then closed, owing to changes in the neighbourhood, and was not reopened until 1866, when the Rev. Nicholas Balleis, a Benedictine, took charge and remained there until his death, 13 December, 1891. The old building was again closed and remained so until the property was purchased by the Sisters of the Precious Blood in 1892, when the structure was torn down, and the convent of that order built on the site.

Peter Turner (d. 31 December, 1863), who was the leader in organizing Brooklyn's pioneer parish, lived to see his son John ordained a priest, pastor of St. James's Church and first Vicar-General of the Diocese of Brooklyn. In 1895 the Brooklyn Catholic Historical Society, regarding Peter Turner as the typical layman of the pioneer period, erected a handsome bronze portrait bust as a memorial to him in St. James's churchyard. The inscription on the pedestal says: "To the memory of Peter Turner, who on January 1, 1822, organized his seventy fellow Catholics for the purchase of this ground on which the first Catholic Church of Long Island was erected. Thousands of Catholic children have helped to erect this monument as a grateful tribute to the man who made Catholic education the first reason for the establishment of a church in Brooklyn." Cardinal McCloskey's early years were spent in Brooklyn, where he attended his first school, which was taught by a retired English actress, Mrs. Charlotte Melmoth, a convert, who was a popular stage favourite in London and New York during the last years of the eighteenth century. Cornelius Heeney was also his patron and guardian after the family moved across the river to New York in 1820. Mr. Heeney's fortune was amassed as a fur-dealer, and for some time he was a partner in this business with John Jacob Astor.

BISHOPS OF THE SEE.—(1) The Right Reverend John Loughlin, consecrated 30 October, 1853. He was born in the County Down, Ireland, 20 December, 1817. As a boy of six he emigrated with his parents to the United States and settled in Albany, New York. His early school days were spent with the distinguished classical scholar, Dr. Peter Bullions, at the Albany Academy, and when fourteen he was sent to the college at Chambly, near Montreal, Canada, where he remained three years. He then entered Mount St. Mary's Seminary at Emmitsburg, Maryland, and after the usual theological course was ordained for the Diocese of New York, 18 October, 1840. His first assignment was on the mission at Utica and from there he was called to be an assistant to Bishop Hughes at St. Patrick's Cathedral, New York City. In 1850 the bishop made him his vicar-general and when the new Diocese of Brooklyn was formed he was consecrated its first bishop, 30 October, 1853, the officiating prelate being Archbishop Cajetan Bedini, a pro-nuncio on his way back to

RIGHT REV. JOHN LOUGHLIN

Rome from a diplomatic mission to Brazil. There were then but twelve churches on all Long Island and about 15,000 Catholics. During the thirty-eight years Bishop Loughlin ruled the see he built 125 churches and chapels, 93 schools, 2 colleges, 19 select schools and academies, 10 orphan asylums, 5 hospitals, 2 homes for the aged, a home for destitute boys, and the diocesan seminary. In the same time the Catholic population increased to nearly 400,000. Bishop Loughlin led a life of unostentatious routine, entirely devoted to his ecclesiastical duties. The only time he is recorded as having identified himself with any civic movement was in April, 1861, when he wrote a letter of sympathy and approval to the great mass-meeting of citizens that committed Brooklyn to the cause of the Union. In October, 1890, the golden jubilee of his ordination was celebrated by a three days' festival in which the whole city joined. He assisted at each of the Plenary Councils of Baltimore and visited Rome four times, once to be present at the Œcumenical Council of the Vatican. He was then made an assistant at the Papal throne. He died at his residence in Brooklyn, 29 December, 1891. That one man should have founded a diocese and in the course of his administration brought it to a position of such pronounced influence and efficiency, is one of the most remarkable facts in the history of the Church's progress in the United States.

The Sisters of Charity were the first religious to establish themselves in Brooklyn (1834), and they were followed by the Christian Brothers in 1851 and the Sisters of St. Dominic in 1852. To these Bishop Loughlin added the Sisters of the Visitation and the Sisters of Mercy in 1855; the Sisters of St. Joseph, 1856; the Franciscan Brothers, 1860; the Sisters of the Poor of St. Francis, 1866; the Congregation of the Mission, and the Sisters of the Good Shepherd, 1868; the Little Sisters of the Poor—their first foundation in the United States—1869; the Fathers of Mercy, 1871; the Sisters of the Sacred Heart of Mary, 1877; the Fathers of the Pious Society of Missions, 1884; and the Sisters of the Precious Blood, 1889.

Bishop Loughlin began the construction of a new cathedral of large dimensions in 1868, the work on which he carried on up to the first story and then stopped to give his attention to the promotion of the charitable institutions of the diocese. The chapel of St. John, at one end of the proposed Cathedral of the Immaculate Conception, was all that was ever finished and used; the extensive foundation walls of the main building remain in their incomplete state. The Catholic Benevolent Legion, a fraternal insurance association, was organized during Bishop Loughlin's life, September, 1881, and he was its first spiritual director. The St. Vincent de Paul Society received from him special encouragement (1855), and the formation of the third Particular Council in the United States was a result.

(2) The Right Reverend Charles Edward McDonnell, consecrated 25 April, 1892. Born in New York City, 1 February, 1854, his early education was received in the parochial schools and the De La Salle Academy. In 1868 he entered St. Francis Xavier's College, where he remained until he left, in 1872, to study for the priesthood at the American College, Rome. He was ordained in Rome, 19 May, 1878, and subsequently received the degree of Doctor of Divinity. Returning to New York, he was, after five years spent in parish work, made Secretary to Cardinal McCloskey. After the cardinal's death, Archbishop Corrigan left him in this position and appointed him chancellor as well. He was also made a private chamberlain by the pope, and was serving in these offices when Bishop Loughlin died. Named by the pope to succeed him, Mgr. McDonnell was consecrated the second Bishop of Brooklyn in St.

Patrick's Cathedral, New York, 25 April, 1892, and took possession of his see on the 2d of May. The new bishop, finding the material interests of the diocese so well administered by his predecessor, continued the good work thus begun and developed it also along its spiritual lines. The increase in population and the changes in the country districts necessitated the starting of many new parishes and the inception of new means and methods of meeting the polyglot needs of the representatives of the various nationalities that had settled in the diocese. For this Bishop McDonnell adopted the policy of securing members of some order for each of the races and languages in his jurisdiction. At his invitation foundations were made by the Redemptorists in 1892; the Benedictines, 1896; the Franciscans (Minor Conventuals), 1896; the Capuchins, 1897; the Fathers of the Congregation of Mary, 1903; the Franciscans (Italian), 1906; the Jesuits, 1907; the Sisters of the Holy Family of Nazareth, 1892; the Missionary Sisters of the Sacred Heart, 1892; the Daughters of Wisdom, 1904; the Sisters of the Infant Jesus (nursing Sisters of the Sick Poor), 1906. Up to 1907 Bishop McDonnell had started and dedicated fifty new parishes and churches. He presided over the Third Diocesan Synod in December, 1894, at which the full number of canonical diocesan officials were for the first time selected; and over the Fourth Synod, held in 1898. A unique spiritual event was a simultaneous mission under his inspiration held throughout the diocese to mark the close of the nineteenth century. He led three diocesan pilgrimages to Rome, the first for the General Jubilee of 1900; the second for the Silver Jubilee of Pope Leo XIII in 1902; and the third for the Jubilee of the Immaculate Conception in 1904. To the institutions of the diocese Bishop McDonnell added two hospitals and largely increased the capacity of one of those already established; the Ozanam Home for Friendless Women; the new St. Vincent's Home for Friendless Boys; two seaside recreation places for children and a trade school farm for orphans.

NOTABLE BENEFACTORS AND WORKERS.—Some of those distinguished for their zeal for religion and generosity to the Church in addition to those already mentioned have been: Judge Alexander McCue, Charles A. Hoyt, E. Louis Lowe (formerly Governor of Maryland), Hugh McLaughlin, Patrick C. Keeley (architect of many Catholic churches in various parts of the country, who began his career here), James A. McMaster, for many years editor of "The Freeman's Journal", Patrick Vincent Hickey, editor of the "Catholic Review", Laurence Kehoe, Manager of the Catholic Publication Society, John George Gottsberger, John Campbell, Andrew Dougherty, Kieran Egan, John O'Mahony, John D. Kieley, Jr., Jacob Zimmer, William W. Swayne, James Rorke, Edward Rorke, William H. Murtha, Anton Shimmel, Thomas Carroll, Joseph W. Carroll, John Loughran, Dr. Dominick G. Bodkin, John Good, Peter McGoldrick, M. F. McGoldrick, Thomas W. Hynes, William R. Grace, William Bourke Cockran, Morgan J. O'Brien, Mrs. Grace Masury, Mrs. A. E. Walsh, Charles O'Conor Sloane, James McMahon, Bernard Earl, Michael Hennessy, Joseph Eppig, Edward Feeney, and Dr. John Byrne.

STATISTICS.—Diocesan priests 308; priests of religious orders 54; total 362. Churches with resident priests 162, missions 10, stations 11, chapels 13; seminary 1, with 60 students; colleges 3, with 570 students; academies and select schools for young women 15, with 1017 pupils; parishes with schools 68, pupils enrolled 41,750; orphan asylums 11, inmates 3691; infant asylums 4, inmates 455; industrial school 1, pupils 143; young people under Catholic care 40,040; hospitals 6, treating more than 18,000 patients yearly; homes for aged 3, inmates 540. Catholic population estimated 600,000.

Mitchell, *Golden Jubilee of Bishop Loughlin* (Brooklyn, 1891); Stiles, *History of Brooklyn* (Brooklyn, 1867, 1870); *The Eagle and Brooklyn* (Brooklyn, 1893); *U. S. Catholic Hist. Magazine* (New York, 1890, 1891); *U. S. Cath. Hist. Soc. Hist. Records* (New York, 1900), II, pt. I; Shea, *Hist. Cath. Ch. in U. S.* (New York, 1894); Mulrenan, *A Brief Hist. Sketch of the Cath. Ch. on Long Island* (New York, 1871); O'Callaghan, *History of New Netherlands* (New York, 1846–48); *Long Island Star* files (Brooklyn, 1822, 1823, 1825).

Thomas F. Meehan.

Brooklyn Benevolent Society. See Heeney, Cornelius.

Brooks, Ferdinand. See Green, Hugh.

Brosse, Jean-Baptiste de la, a Jesuit missionary, b. 1724 at Magnac, Angoumois, France; d. 1782. He studied classics at the Jesuit College of St. Louis at Angoulême, and entered the novitiate of the society at Bordeaux, in 1740. After a full course of philosophy and theology in the latter city, he was ordained in 1753 and sent to Canada the following year. He first laboured on the Abenaki mission, held different positions in the College of Quebec, and finally succeeded, in the Montagnais mission, Father Coquart, who died in 1765 at Chicoutimi. De la Brosse was the twenty-first of his order to fill that post. Fixing his headquarters at Tadousac, at the mouth of the Saguenay, a rendezvous for the Montagnais and for the traders of the lower St. Lawrence, his apostolate radiated from that point along the Labrador coast, to the French settlements on the south shore of the great river, to the Micmacs of Restigouche, and as far east as Isle Saint-Jean (Prince Edward Island). Besides Christian doctrine, he taught the Montagnais reading, writing, and plainsong, creating and developing in their souls the taste for elementary instruction which is to be found to this day in each family of the tribe. The zealous and practical missionary had 3000 copies of the Montagnais alphabet, and 2000 copies of a catechism and prayer book in the same tongue printed at Quebec in 1767.

The latter is one of the first books issued from the press in Canada. It bears the author's name in Montagnais (Tshitstiisahigan), which signifies a broom or brush, in allusion to his family name. He also compiled a dictionary in the same language, being moreover familiar with the Abenaki and Micmac dialects. His inland mission-field embraced all the region watered by the Saguenay and Lake St. John. He braved the stubborn ferocity of the Naskapi Indians, who had so far resisted every attempt to convert them. A forest fire, whose ravages he is said to have miraculously stopped, was the occasion of their consenting to hear the Gospel. Father de la Brosse left a reputation of holiness which still endures. His remains lie in the old mission-chapel of Tadousac.

Roy, *Voyage au pays de Tadousac* (Quebec, 1889); Roche-monteix, *Les Jésuites et la Nouvelle-France au xviiie siècle* (Paris, 1906).

Lionel Lindsay.

Brosse, Joseph de la. See Ange de St. Joseph.

Brothers Hospitallers of St. John of God.— St. John of God, the founder of this religious institution, was born 8 March, 1495, at Montemór Novo, in Portugal. In his fortieth year he was drawn strongly to God's service and began a wonderful life of prayer, penance, and charity towards his neighbour. Pressed by the love of God, and of Christ's suffering members, he founded his first hospital at Granada in Spain, where he tenderly served the sick and afflicted. It is related in his life that one day the Lord appeared to him and told him that He was much pleased with his work, and for that reason He wished him to be called John of God. After ten years spent in the exercise of heroic charity, he died 8 March,

1550. He was canonized by Pope Alexander VIII, in 1690; and was declared heavenly patron of the dying and of all the hospitals by Pope Leo XIII, in 1898.

The charity of St. John of God was destined to be perpetuated among his brethren, whom he had formed by his lessons and example. His first companion Antoni Martin was chosen to succeed him as superior of the order. Thanks to the generosity of King Philip II, a hospital was founded at Madrid, another at Cordova, and several others in various Spanish towns. St. Pius V approved the Order of the Brothers Hospitallers in 1572 under the rule of St. Augustine. The order spread rapidly into the other countries of Europe, and even into the distant colonies. In 1584 Pope Gregory XIII called some of the Brothers to Rome and gave them the Hospital of St. John Calybita, which then became the mother-house of the whole order: Brother Pietro Soriano was appointed first superior. Brother Sebastiano Arias founded the hospital of Our Lady at Naples and the famous hospital of Milan. At that time a holy servant of God and of the poor joined the brotherhood and shed great lustre upon the order by his burning charity and profound humility: Blessed John Grande, who was beatified by Pius IX in 1852.

The first hospital of the order in France was founded in Paris, in 1601, by Queen Marie de' Medici. In the stormy days of the French Revolution the Brothers were expelled from the forty hospitals where they were caring for 4125 patients. But since then some large new hospitals have been established. The order is governed by a prior general, who resides in Rome; it is now divided into eleven provinces, with 102 hospitals, 1536 Brothers, and 12,978 beds, distributed as in the following table:—

Province	Number of Hospitals	Locations	Number of Beds	Number of Religious
Rome	13	Rome, Perugia, Velletri, Corneto, Florence, Rieti, Tivoli, Jesi, Narni, Amelia, Frascati.	1,100	132
Milan	8	Milan, Brescia, Venice, Padua, Marano.	996	60
Naples	3	Naples, Taranto, Foggia.	318	9
France	11	Paris, Lyons, Marseilles, Dinan, Lille, Cannes, Croisic.	3,540	250
Austria	15	Feldsberg, Vienna, Prague, Göritz, Texhen, Prossnitz, Kukus, Brünn, Lettowitz, Husseldorf, Lintz, Wisowitz, Zebrzidowitz, Cracow, Neustadt.	1,070	221
Styria	5	Graz, Algersdorf, St. Vitus, St. Remo.	458	81
Hungary	13	Pressburg, Erlau, Szepes, Temesvar, Papa, Einsenstadt, Grosswardein, Waes, Pécs, Szakolez, Agram, Buda, Szathmar.	1,152	197
Bavaria	13	Neuburg, Straubing, Kaisheim, Schweinspeint, Heilbronn, Algasing, Burglengensfeld, Attel.	1,645	213
Prussia	7	Breslau, Neustadt, Pilchowitz, Frankenstein, Stemen, Bugutschuetz.	699	125
Spain	14	Madrid, Seville, Manila, Barcelona, and other places.	2,000	248
	102		12,978	1536

In addition to these a hospice of the order has been established at Nazareth. In 1882 a home for demented patients (male) was founded at Stillorgan near Dublin, Ireland. The house at Scorton, near

Darlington, Yorkshire, was founded in 1880 for the reception of male patients suffering from chronic infirmities, paralysis, or old age. It is supported by charitable contributions and payments for inmates. It is pleasantly situated in a very healthy country district.

The Brothers undergo a special course of training in order to fit them for carrying out their various works of charity, to which they devote their life. In some provinces some of them are even graduates in medicine, surgery, and chemistry. The members are not in Holy orders, but priests wishing to devote their sacred ministry to the Brothers and patients are received. After the example of their founder, they seek their own sanctification and their patients' spiritual and corporal welfare. To the three solemn vows of religion they add a fourth, of serving the sick for life in their hospitals. They also perform the usual duties and pious exercises of the religious life. They assist daily at Holy Mass, meditation, the recital in choir of the office of Our Lady, and spiritual reading. Young men of good disposition, sound health and possessing aptitude for the order, and resolved to serve God generously in the religious life are received from the age of fifteen to thirty-five. The religious habit is usually given to postulants after three months. The time of novitiate is two years, after which the novice pronounces the vows which, although simple, are perpetual. Three years later, he can be admitted to solemn profession.

LOUIS GAUDET.

Brothers of Charity. See CHARITY, CONGREGATION OF THE BROTHERS OF.

Brothers of Mercy. See MERCY, BROTHERS OF.

Brothers of Our Lady of Lourdes. See OUR LADY OF LOURDES, BROTHERS OF.

Brothers of St. Gabriel. See ST. GABRIEL, BROTHERS OF.

Brothers of the Angels. See GICHTEL, JOHANN GEORG.

Brothers of the Christian Schools. See CHRISTIAN BROTHERS.

Brothers of the Cross. See CROSS, BROTHERS OF THE.

Brothers of the Holy Infancy. See HOLY INFANCY, BROTHERS OF THE.

Brothers of the Sacred Heart. See SACRED HEART, BROTHERS OF THE.

Broughton, RICHARD (*alias* ROUSE), b. about 1558 at Great Stukeley, Huntingdonshire; d. according to à Wood, 15 Kal. Feb. (i. e. 18 January, 1634); Catholic priest and antiquary, claiming descent from the Broughtons of Lancashire. He was ordained at Reims, 4 May, 1593, and soon after returned to England. John Pitts, a contemporary, says that he "gathered a most abundant harvest of souls into the granary of Christ" and eulogizes his attainments in being "no less familiar with literature than learned in Greek and Hebrew". Broughton became an assistant to the archpriest, a canon of the chapter, and vicar-general to Bishop Smith of Chalcedon. He also claims recognition for his influence on the study of antiquity; having earned, partly by his positive work and partly through controversy, the right to honourable mention with Spelman, Reyner, Dugdale, and other well-known antiquarians.

Broughton's chief works are: (1) "An Apologicall Epistle, serving as preface to . . . a Resolution of Religion", signed R. B. (Antwerp, 1601); (2) "The first part of the Resolution of Religion By R. B." (Antwerp, 1603), often mistaken for Persons' "Resolution"; (3) "A New Manuall of old Christian Catholick Meditations" (1617), dedicated to Anne of Denmark; (4) "The Judgment of the Apostles" (Douai, 1632), dedicated to Queen Henrietta Maria and directed against Rogers on the Thirty-nine Articles; (5) "Ecclesiasticall Historie of Great Britaine" (Douai, 1633), dedicated to the Duchess of Buckingham and the Countess of Rutland; (6) "A True Memorial" (London, 1650), published by G. S. P(riest) after Broughton's death. The 1654 edition is entitled "Monasticon Britannicum". (7) Broughton also wrote on the antiquity of the word Sterlingorum (Hearne, II, 318, 381); (8) on the alleged conversion (1621) of John King, Bishop of London; and (9) "A Relation of the Martyrdom of Nicholas Garlick".

WOOD, *Fasti*, ed. BLISS (London, 1815), I, 428; DODD, *Church History*, ed. TIERNEY (Brussels, 1742), III, 87; PITTS, *De Rebus Anglicis*, 815; FOLEY, *Records* (London, 1880), VI, 181; HURTER, *Nomenclator* (Innsbruck, 1871), I, 657; GILLOW, *Bibl. Dict. Eng. Cath.* (London, 1885), I, 318; GROVES in *Dict. Nat. Biog.*, VI, 462.

PATRICK RYAN.

Brouwer (BROWERUS), CHRISTOPH, a historian, b. 12 March, 1559, at Arnheim, Holland; d. in 1617, at Trier, Germany. In 1580 he entered the Society of Jesus, and after a thorough humanistic training, devoted himself especially to the study of church history. His attainments in other branches of learning are shown by his appointment as professor of philosophy at Trier; later he was appointed rector first at Fulda, and then at Trier. His chief work is entitled: "Antiquitates et annales Trevirenses et episcoporum Trevirensis ecclesiæ suffraganorum". The work extends to the year 1600 and was prepared at the request of two archbishops, Johann VII of Schönenberg and Lothar of Metternich, with the intent to disprove the partisan publication of Hermann (Kyriander), Syndic of Trier. Hermann's work was published in 1576 and was written to support the claims of the city against the rights of the archbishop. Brouwer devoted the greater part of his life to the preparation of his book and, according to the testimony of the historian, Hontheim, he is deserving of undying honour for his contributions to the history of the Archbishopric of Trier. Unfortunately, he did not live to complete his task. Brouwer's unflinching love of the truth and his true historical method were not agreeable to the councillors of the archbishop; so, although the publication of his work had been sanctioned by the authorities of his order, it could not be issued. It was not until 1626 that the work of printing his manuscript at Cologne could be undertaken, and then only after important alterations had been made in the text. New difficulties arose when the eighteenth book was in press. The completion of the printing was forbidden and all the sheets already struck off were suppressed as far as possible, so that only a few copies have come down to us.

Brouwer's labours were continued from 1600 to 1652 by Father Jacob Masenius, S.J., who issued the whole work in revised form in 1670 in two folio volumes at Liège. Brouwer was unable to complete his other great work, which was entitled: "Metropolis Ecclesiæ Trevericæ". It was intended to contain a description of all the cities, churches, and cloisters of the Archdiocese of Trier. This work did not appear until 1855-56 when it was issued at Coblenz in two volumes by Christian von Stramberg. The edition does not meet fully the demands of our time, nevertheless it contains much that is useful. Brouwer's history of the Diocese of Fulda is also worthy of praise. It is entitled: "Fuldensium antiquitatum libri 4" (Antwerp, 1612). Of less importance is the work issued at Mainz in 1616, entitled: "Sidera illustrium et sanctorum virorum, qui Germaniam ornarunt". Among the results of his humanistic studies is the edition of the works of Bishop Venantius Fortunatus, which was issued at Mainz in 1603, together with a life of St. Martin. A second edition appeared in 1617 augmented by the annotated poems of Archbishop Rhabanus Maurus.

REIFFENBERG, *Historia Societatis Jesu* (Cologne, 1764), 534; *Metropolis Ecclesiæ Trevericæ*, ed. VON STRAMBERG.

PATRICIUS SCHLAGER.

Brown, WILLIAM, a naval officer of the Republic of Buenos Aires, b. 1777, in the County Mayo, Ireland; d. 3 May, 1857, in Buenos Aires. His family emigrating to America in 1786, Brown shipped as a cabin boy on a vessel sailing from Philadelphia. During the war between France and England his ship, an English merchantman, was captured by a French privateer and he was made prisoner of war. He escaped to England, where, in 1809, he married a lady of good family and education. He re-entered the ocean trade with a ship of his own, which was wrecked on the coast of South America. Here he established the first regular packet service between Buenos Aires and Montevideo. In the revolt of Buenos Aires against Spain the insurgents appointed Brown, February, 1814, to the command of a squadron of seven ships. With these he achieved wonders. On St. Patrick's Day he captured the fort of Martin Garcia, called "The Gibraltar of the La Plata", compelling nine Spanish men-of-war under Admiral Romerate to retire. Later, at Montevideo, which capitulated 20 June, he captured several Spanish men-of-war. These he took to Buenos Aires, and received the rank of admiral. In 1816 Admiral Brown sailed round the Horn to succour the new republics on the western coast, but his expedition was only partly successful. Ten years later, when war ensued between the new republic and Brazil, Admiral Brown greatly distinguished himself against tremendous odds in the blockade of Buenos Aires, which he succeeded in breaking. Taking the offensive he scoured the coast as far as Rio de Janeiro. His most brilliant victory was the battle of Juncal, 24 February, 1827, when, with seven ships and eight one-gun launches, he destroyed a fleet of seventeen war-vessels under Admiral Pereira. He acted as Argentine Commissioner when, at the close of the war, the liberty of Buenos Aires was guaranteed by the treaty of Montevideo 4 October, 1827.

After a visit to his native land, Admiral Brown spent his last years in the republic in the founding of which he had been such a powerful factor. He died in Buenos Aires 3 May, 1857, and in the Recolta cemetery a lofty column marks his resting-place.

MULHALL, *The English in South America* (Buenos Aires, 1878).

P. G. SMYTH.

Browne, CHARLES FARRAR (ARTEMUS WARD), humorist, b. at Waterford, Oxford County, Maine, U. S. A., 26 April, 1834; d. in Southampton, England, 6 March, 1867. He went to school in his native town and at the age of fourteen was apprenticed in the printing office of "The Skowhegan Clarion". A year later he was employed in a like capacity on "The Carpet-Bag" of Boston, edited by B. P. Shillaber (Mrs. Partington), and to which Charles G. Halpine (Miles O'Reilly) and John G. Saxe were at that time contributors. In this journal appeared his first humorous article, a burlesque description of a Fourth of July celebration in Skowhegan. After his Boston experience, Browne travelled the Eastern States as a journeyman printer, sojourning for a while in the town of Tiffin, Ohio, where as reporter and compositor he received in wages four dollars a week. Going thence to Toledo, he contributed to the columns of "The Commercial" of that city. Already his reputation was gaining ground. Though vigorously assailed in a series of articles in "The Toledo Blade", he treated his opponents with unfailing courtesy and humour.

In 1858, at the age of twenty-four, his reputation first assumed a national character as a reporter of "The Cleveland Plaindealer" under the sobriquet of "Artemus Ward". His best work at this period consisted in burlesque descriptions of prize-fights, races, spiritualistic séances, and political meetings. Towards the close of 1860, he accepted an engagement in New York with "Vanity Fair", a comic paper edited after the manner of the London "Punch", and ere long succeeded the editor Charles G. Leland (Hans Breitmann) as editor. In this paper some of his best contributions were given to the public. It was, however, as a lecturer that "Artemus Ward" acquired both fame and fortune. His first appearance on the lecture platform in New York was in a travesty called "Babes in the Woods". His next hit was in a lecture on "Sixty Minutes in Africa", given in Music Fund Hall, Philadelphia. In 1866 he sailed for England where success far beyond his expectations awaited him. His stay in London is spoken of as "an ovation to the genius of American wit". He became at once a great favourite with the "Literary Club" of London and his letters in "Punch" recalled the days of "Yellowplush". But sickness brought his brilliant career to an unexpected close in the seventh week of his engagement at Egyptian Hall in London, and his death occurred a few months later. When he felt the end was near, he asked his friend Arthur Sketchly to procure him the ministrations of a priest. "So Sketchly", Clement Scott informs us, "took steps to carry out his friend's instructions." His remains were brought to his native land and laid to rest beside his father and brother in the little cemetery at Waterford, Maine.

Artemus Ward was a consummate humorist and represented a type distinctively American. His fun was a fountain that always bubbled, ministering naturally to the happiness of himself and others. In leading up to the joke whatever art was employed was carefully concealed, and the joke itself when it came was always a surprise but never an awkward or unwholesome one. The depth and strength of his character are revealed as well in the interest excited by his lectures and sayings as in the friendships he formed and retained to the end.

KNIGHT, *Artemus Ward and his Humor* with SWINBURNE's poem, *Putnam's Monthly*, February, 1907; LANDON (Eli Perkins), *The Complete Works of Artemus Ward*, with a *Biographical Sketch* (New York, 1898); CLEMENT SCOTT, *The Drama of Yesterday and To-day* (New York, 1899), I, 325.

EDWARD P. SPILLANE.

Browne, JAMES. See FERNS, DIOCESE OF.

Browne, ROBERT. See CLOYNE, DIOCESE OF.

Brownists. See CONGREGATIONALISTS.

Brownrigg, ABRAHAM. See OSSORY, DIOCESE OF.